PSYCHOLOGY

THEMES AND VARIATIONS
FOURTH EDITION

PSYCHOLOGY

THEMES AND VARIATIONS
FOURTH EDITION

WAYNE WEITEN
Santa Clara University

Brooks/Cole Publishing Company
I(T)P® An International Thomson Publishing Company

Pacific Grove • Albany • Belmont • Bonn • Boston • Cincinnati • Detroit • Johannesburg • London • Madrid
Melbourne • Mexico City • New York • Paris • Singapore • Tokyo • Toronto • Washington

Sponsoring Editor: Eileen Murphy
Marketing Team: Margaret Parks, Lauren Harp, Michael Campbell, and Alicia Barelli
Editorial Assistant: Susan Carlson
Production Coordinator: Marjorie Sanders
Production: Nancy Sjoberg, Del Mar Associates
Manuscript Editor: Jackie Estrada
Interior Design: John Odam
Cover Design: Vernon T. Boes
Cover Art: Victor Vasarely, *Gestalt-Zoeld, 1976.* Copyright ARS, NY. Private Collection, Paris, France
Interior Illustration: John Odam, Kim Fraley, Kristi Mendola
Permissions and Photo Research: Linda L. Rill
Digital Typography: John Odam Design Associates and Del Mar Associates
Color Separation: Thompson Type
Printing and Binding: Von Hoffman

Credits continue on page 803.

For more information, contact:

BROOKS/COLE PUBLISHING COMPANY
511 Forest Lodge Rd.
Pacific Grove, CA 93950
USA

International Thomson Publishing Europe
Berkshire House 168-173
High Holborn
London, WC1V 7AA
England

Thomas Nelson Australia
102 Dodds Street
South Melbourne, 3205
Victoria, Australia

Nelson Canada
1120 Birchmount Road
Scarborough, Ontario
Canada M1K 5G4

International Thomson Editores
Seneca 53
Col. Polanco
11560 México, D.F., México

International Thomson Publishing GmbH
Königswinterer Strasse 418
53227 Bonn
Germany

International Thomson Publishing Asia
221 Henderson Road
#05-10 Henderson Building
Singapore 0315

International Thomson Publishing Japan
Hirakawacho Kyowa Building, 3F
2-2-1 Hirakawacho
Chiyoda-ku, Tokyo 102
Japan

Printed in the United States of America

10 9 8 7 6 5 4 3 2 1

Library of Congress Cataloging-in-Publication Data
Weiten, Wayne, [date]
       Psychology: themes and variations / Wayne Weiten. — 4th ed.
          p.   cm.
       Includes bibliographical references and index.
       ISBN 0-534-34014-8
       1. Psychology. I. Title
       BF121.W38 1997b
       150—dc21   97-2684
                                                                          CIP

Beth, this one's for you

TO THE INSTRUCTOR

If I had to sum up in a single sentence what I hope will distinguish this text, the sentence would be this: I have set out to create a *paradox* instead of a *compromise*.

Let me elaborate. An introductory psychology text must satisfy two disparate audiences: professors and students. Because of the tension between the divergent needs and preferences of these audiences, textbook authors usually indicate that they have attempted to strike a compromise between being theoretical versus practical, comprehensive versus comprehensible, research oriented versus applied, rigorous versus accessible, and so forth. However, I believe that many of these dichotomies are false. As Kurt Lewin once remarked, "What could be more practical than a good theory?" Similarly, is rigorous really the opposite of accessible? Not in my dictionary. I maintain that many of the antagonistic goals that we strive for in our textbooks only seem incompatible, and that we may not need to make compromises as often as we assume.

In my estimation, a good introductory textbook is a paradox in that it integrates characteristics and goals that appear contradictory. With this in mind, I have endeavored to write a text that is paradoxical in three ways. First, in surveying psychology's broad range of content, I have tried to show that our interests are characterized by diversity *and* unity. Second, I have emphasized both research *and* application and how they work in harmony. Finally, I have aspired to write a book that is challenging to think about *and* easy to learn from. Let's take a closer look at these goals.

Goals

1. *To show both the unity and the diversity of psychology's subject matter.* Students entering an introductory psychology course are often unaware of the immense diversity of subjects studied by psychologists. I find this diversity to be part of psychology's charm, and throughout the book I highlight the enormous range of questions and issues addressed by psychology. Of course, our diversity proves disconcerting for some students who see little continuity between such disparate areas of research as physiology, motivation, cog-

nition, and abnormal behavior. Indeed, in this era of specialization, even some psychologists express concern about the fragmentation of the field.

However, I believe that there is considerable overlap among the subfields of psychology and that we should emphasize their common core by accenting the connections and similarities among them. Consequently, I portray psychology as an integrated whole rather than as a mosaic of loosely related parts. A principal goal of this text, then, is to highlight the unity in psychology's intellectual heritage (the themes), as well as the diversity of psychology's interests and uses (the variations).

2. *To illuminate the process of research and its intimate link to application.* For me, a research-oriented book is not one that bulges with summaries of many studies but one that enhances students' appreciation of the logic and excitement of empirical inquiry. I want students to appreciate the strengths of the empirical approach and to see scientific psychology as a creative effort to solve intriguing behavioral puzzles. For this reason, the text emphasizes not only *what* we know (and don't know) but *how* we attempt to find out. Methods are examined in some detail, and students are encouraged to adopt the skeptical attitude of a scientist and to think critically about claims regarding behavior.

Learning the virtues of research should not mean that students cannot also satisfy their desire for concrete, personally useful information about the challenges of everyday life. Most researchers believe that psychology has a great deal to offer those outside the field and that we should share the practical implications of our work. In this text, practical insights are carefully qualified and closely tied to data, so that students can see the interdependence of research and application. I find that students come to appreciate the science of psychology more when they see that worthwhile practical applications are derived from careful research and sound theory.

3. *To make the text challenging to think about and easy to learn from.* Perhaps most of all, I have sought to create a *book of ideas* rather than a compendium of studies. I consistently emphasize concepts and theories over facts, and I focus on major issues and tough questions that cut across

the subfields of psychology (for example, the extent to which behavior is governed by nature, nurture, and their interaction), as opposed to parochial debates (such as the merits of averaging versus adding in impression formation). Challenging students to think also means urging them to confront the complexity and ambiguity of our knowledge. Hence, the text doesn't skirt around gray areas, unresolved questions, and theoretical controversies. Instead, readers are encouraged to contemplate open-ended questions, to examine their assumptions about behavior, and to apply psychological concepts to their own lives. My goal is not simply to describe psychology but to stimulate students' intellectual growth.

However, students can grapple with "the big issues and tough questions" only if they first master the basic concepts and principles of psychology—ideally, with as little struggle as possible. I never let myself forget that a textbook is a teaching tool. Accordingly, great care has been taken to ensure that the book's content, organization, writing, illustrations, and pedagogical aids work in harmony to facilitate instruction and learning.

Admittedly, these goals are ambitious. If you're skeptical, you have every right to be. Let me explain how I have tried to realize the objectives I have outlined.

Special Features

This text has a variety of unusual features, each contributing in its own way to the book's paradoxical nature. These special features include unifying themes, featured studies, application sections, a didactic illustration program, an integrated running glossary, concept checks, recaps of key points, and practice tests.

Unifying Themes

Chapter 1 introduces seven key ideas that serve as unifying themes throughout the text. The themes serve several purposes. First, they provide threads of continuity across chapters that help students to see the connections among different areas of research in psychology. Second, as the themes evolve over the course of the book, they provide a forum for a relatively sophisticated discussion of enduring issues in psychology, thus helping to make this a "book of ideas." Third, the themes focus a spotlight on a number of basic insights about psychology and its subject matter that should leave lasting impressions on your students.

In selecting the themes, the question I asked myself (and other professors) was "What do I really want students to remember five years from now?" The resulting themes are grouped into two sets.

THEMES RELATED TO
PSYCHOLOGY AS A FIELD OF STUDY

Theme 1: Psychology is empirical. This theme is used to enhance the student's appreciation of psychology's scientific nature and to demonstrate the advantages of empiricism over uncritical common sense and speculation. I also use this theme to encourage the reader to adopt a scientist's skeptical attitude and to engage in more critical thinking about information of all kinds.

Theme 2: Psychology is theoretically diverse. Students are often confused by psychology's theoretical pluralism and view it as a weakness. I don't downplay or apologize for our theoretical diversity, because I honestly believe that it is one of our greatest strengths. Throughout the book, I provide concrete examples of how clashing theories have stimulated productive research, how converging on a question from several perspectives can yield increased understanding, and how competing theories are sometimes reconciled in the end.

Theme 3: Psychology evolves in a sociohistorical context. This theme emphasizes that psychology is embedded in the ebb and flow of everyday life. The text shows how the spirit of the times has often shaped psychology's evolution and how progress in psychology leaves its mark on our society.

THEMES RELATED TO
PSYCHOLOGY'S SUBJECT MATTER

Theme 4: Behavior is determined by multiple causes. Throughout the book, I emphasize, and repeatedly illustrate, that behavioral processes are complex and that multifactorial causation is the rule. This theme is used to discourage simplistic, single-cause thinking and to encourage more critical reasoning.

Theme 5: Our behavior is shaped by our cultural heritage. This theme is intended to enhance students' appreciation of how cultural factors moderate psychological processes and how the viewpoint of one's own culture can distort one's interpretation of the behavior of people from other cultures. The discussions that elaborate on this theme do not simply celebrate diversity. They strike a careful balance—that accurately reflect the research in this area—highlighting both cultural variations *and* similarities in behavior.

Theme 6: Heredity and environment jointly influence behavior. Repeatedly discussing this theme

Chapter	Theme						
	1 Empiricism	2 Theoretical Diversity	3 Sociohistorical Context	4 Multifactorial Causation	5 Cultural Heritage	6 Heredity and Environment	7 Subjectivity of Experience
1. The Evolution of Psychology	●	●	●	●	●	●	●
2. The Research Enterprise in Psychology	●						●
3. The Biological Bases of Behavior	●			●		●	
4. Sensation and Perception		●			●		●
5. Variations in Consciousness		●	●		●		●
6. Learning Through Conditioning			●			●	
7. Human Memory				●			●
8. Language and Thought	●				●	●	●
9. Intelligence and Psychological Testing			●		●	●	
10. Motivation and Emotion		●	●	●	●	●	
11. Development Across the Life Span		●	●	●	●	●	
12. Personality: Theory, Research, and Assessment		●	●		●		
13. Stress, Coping, and Health				●			●
14. Psychological Disorders			●	●	●	●	
15. Psychotherapy		●			●	●	
16. Social Behavior	●				●		●

permits me to air out the nature versus nurture issue in all its complexity. Over a series of chapters, students gradually learn how biology shapes behavior, how experience shapes behavior, and how scientists estimate the relative importance of each. Along the way, students will gain an in-depth appreciation of what we mean when we say that heredity and environment interact.

Theme 7: Our experience of the world is highly subjective. All of us tend to forget the extent to which we view the world through our own per-sonal lens. This theme is used to explain the principles that underlie the subjectivity of human experience, to clarify its implications, and to repeatedly remind the readers that their view of the world is not the only legitimate view.

After all seven themes have been introduced in Chapter 1, different sets of themes are discussed in each chapter, as they are relevant to the subject matter. The connections between a chapter's content and the unifying themes are highlighted in a standard section near the end of the chapter, in which I reflect on the "lessons to be learned" from the chapter. The discussions of the unifying themes are largely confined to these sections, titled "Putting It in Perspective." No effort was made to force every chapter to illustrate a certain number of themes. The themes were allowed to emerge naturally, and I found that two to five surfaced in any given chapter. The accompanying chart shows which themes are highlighted in each chapter.

Featured Studies

Each chapter except the first includes a Featured Study that provides a relatively detailed but clear summary of a particular piece of research. Each Featured Study is presented in the conventional purpose-method-results-discussion format seen in journal articles, followed by a comment in which I discuss why the study is featured (to illustrate a specific method, raise ethical issues, and so forth). By showing research methods in action, I hope to improve students' understanding of how research is done, while also giving them a painless introduction to the basic format of journal articles. Additionally, the Featured Studies show how complicated research can be, so students can better appreciate why scientists may disagree about the meaning of a study. The Featured Studies, incidentally, are fully incorporated into the flow of discourse in the text and are *not* presented as optional boxes.

In selecting the Featured Studies, I assembled a mixture of classic and recent studies that illustrate a wide variety of methods. To make them enticing, I tilted my selections in favor of studies that students find interesting. Thus, readers are given relatively detailed accounts of classics like Milgram's work on obedience, Rosenhan's study of pseudopatients, and Bandura's research on observational learning. They will also encounter more recent explorations of personality resemblance between twins, the media-violence question, the ape-language controversy, and the problem of homelessness among the mentally ill.

Application Sections

To reinforce the pragmatic implications of theory and research that are stressed throughout the text, each chapter closes with an Application section that highlights the personal, practical side of psychology. Each Application devotes three to six *pages* of text (rather than the usual box) to a single issue that should be of special interest to many of your students. Although most of the Application sections have a "how to" character, they continue to review studies and summarize data in much the same way as the main body of each chapter. Thus, they portray research and application not as incompatible polarities but as two sides of the same coin. Many of the Applications—such as those on finding and reading journal articles and understanding art and illusion—provide topical coverage unusual for an introductory text.

A Didactic Illustration Program

When I first outlined my plans for this text, I indicated that I wanted every aspect of the illustration program to have a genuine didactic purpose and that I wanted to be deeply involved in its development. In retrospect, I had no idea what I was getting myself into, but it has been a rewarding learning experience. In any event, I have been intimately involved in planning every detail of the illustration program. Collaborating with a superb art director (John Odam), I have endeavored to create a program of figures, diagrams, photos, and tables that work hand in hand with the prose to strengthen and clarify the main points in the text.

The most obvious results of our didactic approach to illustration are the five summary spreads that combine tabular information, photos, diagrams, and sketches to provide exciting overviews of key ideas related to the history of psychology, learning, development, personality theory, and psychological disorders. But I hope you will also notice the subtleties of the illustration program. For instance, diagrams of important concepts (conditioning, synaptic transmission, EEGs, experimental design, and so forth) are often repeated in several chapters (with variations) to highlight connections among research areas and to enhance students' mastery of key ideas. Numerous easy-to-understand graphs of research results underscore psychology's foundation in research, and we often use photos and diagrams to bolster each other (for example, see the treatment of classical conditioning in Chapter 6). Color is used carefully as an organizational device and visual schematics are used to simplify hard-to-visualize concepts (see the figure explaining reaction range for intelligence in Chapter 9). All of these efforts were made in the service of one master: the desire to make this an inviting book that is easy to learn from.

Integrated Running Glossary

An introductory text should place great emphasis on acquainting students with psychology's technical language—not for the sake of jargon, but because a great many of our key terms are also our cornerstone concepts (for example, independent variable, reliability, and cognitive dissonance). This text handles terminology with a running glossary embedded in the prose itself. The terms are set off in boldface italics, and the definitions follow in boldface roman type. This approach retains the two advantages of a conventional running glossary: vocabulary items are made salient, and their definitions are readily accessible. However, it does so without interrupting the flow of discourse, while eliminating redundancy between text matter and marginal entries.

Concept Checks

To help students assess their mastery of important ideas, Concept Checks are sprinkled throughout the book (two to four per chapter). In keeping with my goal of making this a book of ideas, the Concept Checks challenge students to apply ideas instead of testing rote memory. For example, in Chapter 6 the reader is asked to analyze realistic examples of conditioning and identify conditioned stimuli and responses, reinforcers, and schedules of reinforcement. Many of the Concept Checks require the reader to put together ideas introduced in different sections of the chapter. For instance, in Chapter 4 students are asked to identify parallels between vision and hearing and in Chapter 11 to analyze interactions between cognitive, moral, emotional, and social development. Some of the Concept Checks are quite challenging, but students find them engaging, and they report that the answers (available in the back of the book) are illuminating.

Recaps of Key Points

To help students organize and remember important ideas, each chapter includes five to eight Recaps of Key Points. These Recaps are generally found at the end of each major section in a chapter, just before the next level-one heading (some exceptions were made to this rule to accommodate very long or very brief sections). The Recaps appear in blue type (except in the Applications) so that it is readily apparent that they are pedagogical aids that represent optional reading. Taken together, the Recaps provide a more detailed summary of a chapter's main points than the Review of Key Ideas found at the end of the chapters. Interspersing them throughout the chapters permits students to check their understanding of each section's main ideas immediately after finishing

the section instead of waiting until the end of the chapter. This approach also allows students to work with more modest-sized chunks of information.

Practice Tests

Each chapter ends with a 15-item multiple-choice Practice Test that should give students a pretty realistic assessment of their mastery of that chapter and valuable practice taking the type of test that many of them will face in the classroom (if the instructor uses the Test Bank). This new feature grew out of some research that I conducted on students' use of textbook pedagogical devices (see Weiten, Guadagno, & Beck, 1996). This research indicated that students pay scant attention to some standard pedagogical devices. When I grilled my students to gain a better undertstanding of this finding, it quickly became apparent that students are very pragmatic about pedagogy. Essentially, their refrain was "We want study aids that will help us pass the next test." With this mandate in mind, I devised the Practice Tests. They should be very realistic, as I took all the items from the Test Bank for the third edition (these items do not appear in the main Test Bank for the fourth edition).

In addition to the special features just described, the text includes a variety of more conventional, "tried and true" features. The back of the book contains a standard *alphabetical glossary*. Opening *outlines* preview each chapter, and a thorough *review of key ideas* appears at the end of each chapter, along with lists of *key terms* and *key people* (important theorists and researchers). I make frequent use of *italics for emphasis*, and I depend on *frequent headings* to maximize organizational clarity. The preface for students describes these pedagogical devices in more detail.

Content

The text is divided into 16 chapters, which follow a traditional ordering. The chapters are not grouped into sections or parts, primarily because such groupings can limit your options if you want to reorganize the order of topics. The chapters are written in a way that facilitates organizational flexibility, as I always assumed that some chapters might be omitted or presented in a different order.

The topical coverage in the text is relatively conventional, but there are some subtle departures from the norm. For instance, Chapter 1 presents a relatively "meaty" discussion of the evolution of ideas in psychology. This coverage of history lays the foundation for many of the crucial ideas emphasized in subsequent chapters. The historical perspective is also my way of reaching out to the students who find that psychology just isn't what they expected it to be. If we want students to contemplate the mysteries of behavior, we must begin by clearing up the biggest mysteries of them all: "Where did these rats, statistics, synapses, and JNDs come from; what could they possibly have in common; and why doesn't this course bear any resemblance to what I anticipated?" I use history as a vehicle to explain how psychology evolved into its modern form and why misconceptions about its nature are so common.

I also devote an entire chapter (Chapter 2) to the scientific enterprise—not just the mechanics of research methods but the logic behind them. I believe that an appreciation of the nature of empirical evidence can contribute greatly to improving students' critical thinking skills. Ten years from now, many of the "facts" reported in this book will have changed, but an understanding of the methods of science will remain invaluable. An introductory psychology course, by itself, isn't going to make a student think like a scientist, but I can't think of a better place to start the process. Essential statistical concepts are introduced in Chapter 2, but no effort is made to teach actual calculations. For those who emphasize statistics, Appendix B in the back of the book expands on statistical concepts.

Overall, I trust you'll find the coverage up to date, although I do not believe in the common practice of piling up gratuitous references to recent studies to create an impression of currency. I think that an obsession with this year's references derogates our intellectual heritage and suggests to students that the studies we cite today will be written off tomorrow. I often chose to cite an older source over a newer one to give students an accurate feel for when an idea first surfaced or when an issue generated heated debate.

Writing Style

I strive for a down-to-earth, conversational writing style; effective communication is always the paramount goal. My intent is to talk *with* the reader rather than throw information *at* the reader. To clarify concepts and maintain students' interest, I frequently provide concrete examples that students can relate to. As much as possible, I avoid using technical jargon when ordinary language serves just as well.

Making learning easier depends, above all else, on clear, well-organized writing. For this reason, I've worked hard to ensure that chapters, sections, and paragraphs are organized in a logical manner, so that key ideas stand out in sharp relief against supportive information.

To keep myself on the path of clarity, I submit my chapters to the ultimate authority: my students, who take great delight in grading *me* for a change. They're given first drafts of chapters and are urged to slash away at pompous language and to flag sources of confusion. They are merciless—and enormously helpful.

Changes in the Fourth Edition

A good textbook must evolve with the field of inquiry it covers. Although the professors and students who used the first three editions of this book did not clamor for alterations, there are some changes. In addition to the two new pedagogical devices that I have already described (the Recaps and the Practice Tests), other changes include the following.

First, to help make room for the new pedagogical devices, I trimmed the length of the basic manuscript from 326,000 words to 318,000 words. The book remains intermediate in length when compared to the full range of other introductory psychology texts (see Weiten, 1988a).

Second, I have greatly increased my coverage of evolutionary psychology, which I have come to regard as a major new theoretical perspective in the field. In the last 4–5 years, evolutionary psychologists have published a great deal of thought-provoking research on an increasingly broad range of topics. I don't always agree with their conclusions, but I could make the same comment about all the major theoretical perspectives in psychology. In any event, the evolutionary perspective is discussed in 12 places in the current edition, with a heavy emphasis on recent research.

Third, you will find a lot of new graphics in this edition. My work on the new ancillary CD-ROM forced me to create many new graphical treatments for concepts that I had never seen illustrated before. Quite a few of these new diagrams and charts have made their way into the text. Overall, there are 78 entirely new or dramatically revised figures and tables, including a new two-page summary chart in the chapter on psychological disorders.

Fourth, the book has been thoroughly updated to reflect recent advances in the field. One of the exciting things about psychology is that it is not a stagnant discipline. It continues to move at what seems a faster and faster pace. This progress has necessitated a host of specific content changes that you'll find sprinkled throughout the chapters. Of the roughly 3400 references cited in the text, over 600 are new to this edition.

Finally, the biggest change by far is the addition of a completely new ancillary CD-ROM for your students, *Psyk.trek: A Multimedia Introduction to Psychology*, which I describe in the next section.

A New CD-ROM—*Psyk.trek: A Multimedia Introduction to Psychology*

I have spent much of the last three years working on a new multimedia supplement for students. *Psyk.trek* is a multifaceted teaching-learning tool that will provide students with new opportunities for active learning and reach out to "visual learners" with greatly increased efficacy. *Psyk.trek* is intended to give students a second pathway to learning much of the content of introductory psychology. Although it does not cover all of the content of the introductory course, I think you will see that a great many key concepts and principles can be explicated *more effectively* in an interactive audio-visual medium than in a textbook.

Psyk.trek consists of four components. The main component is a set of 59 *Interactive Learning Modules* that present the core content of psychology in a whole new way. These tutorials include thousands of graphics, hundred of photos, hundreds of animations, approximately four hours of narration, 36 carefully-selected videos, and about 150 uniquely visual concept checks and quizzes. The *Interactive Study Guide for Psychology: Themes & Variations* presents students with over 3000 review questions. Students can take randomly-generated multiple-choice tests on the chapters in the textbook until they achieve a prescribed level of mastery. A *Multimedia Glossary* allows students to look up over 800 psychological terms, access hundreds of pronunciations of obscure words, and pull up hundreds of related diagrams, photos, and videos. The *Simulations* allow students to explore complex psychological phenomena in-depth.

The key strength of *Psyk.trek* is its ability to give students new opportunities for active learning outside of the classroom. For example, students can run themselves through re-creations of classic experiments to see the complexities of data collection in action. Or they can play with visual illusions on screen in ways that will make them doubt their own eyes. Or they can stack color filters on screen to demonstrate the nature of subtractive color mixing. *Psyk.trek* is intended to supplement and complement *Psychology: Themes & Variations*. For instance, after reading about operant conditioning in the text, a student could review this material in the interactive study guide, work through three interactive tutorials on operant principles, watch three videos, including historic footage of B. F. Skinner shaping a rat, and then try to shape Morphy, the virtual rat, in one of the simulations.

Other Supplementary Materials

The teaching/learning package that has been developed to supplement *Psychology: Themes and Variations* also includes many other useful tools. The development of all its parts was carefully coordinated so that they are mutually supported.

Study Guide (by Richard Stalling and Ronald Wasden)

For your students, there is an exceptionally thorough *Study Guide* available to help them master the information in the text. It was written by two of my former professors, Richard Stalling and Ronald Wasden of Bradley University. They have over 20 years of experience as a team writing study guides for introductory psychology texts, and their experience is readily apparent in the high-quality materials that they have developed.

The review of key ideas for each chapter is made up of an engaging mixture of matching exercises, fill-in-the-blank items, free-response questions, and programmed learning. Each review is organized around learning objectives written by me. The *Study Guide* is closely coordinated with the *Test Bank,* as the same learning objectives guided the construction of the questions in the *Test Bank.* The *Study Guide* also includes a review of key terms, a review of key people, and a self-test for each chapter in the text.

Instructor's Resource Package (coordinated by Randolph Smith)

A talented roster of professors, whose efforts were coordinated by Randolph Smith, made contributions to the *Instructor's Resource Package (IRP)* in their respective areas of expertise. The *IRP* contains a diverse array of materials designed to facilitate efforts to teach the introductory course and includes the following sections.

• The *Instructor's Manual*, by Randolph Smith (Ouachita Baptist University), contains a wealth of detailed suggestions for lecture topics, class demonstrations, exercises, discussion questions, and suggested readings, organized around the content of each chapter in the text.

- *Strategies for Effective Teaching*, by Joseph Lowman (University of North Carolina), discusses practical issues such as what to put in a course syllabus, how to handle the first class meeting, how to cope with large classes, and how to train and organize teaching assistants.

- *Films and Videos for Introductory Psychology*, by Russ Watson (College of DuPage), provides a comprehensive, up-to-date critical overview of educational films relevant to the introductory course.

- *Computer Simulations for Introductory Psychology*, by Susan J. Shapiro and Michael Shapiro (Indiana University–East), offers a thorough listing of the computer simulations that are germane to the introductory course and analyzes their strengths and weaknesses.

- *Integrating Writing into Introductory Psychology*, by Jane Jegerski (Elmhurst College), examines the writing across the curriculum movement and provides suggestions and materials for specific writing assignments chapter by chapter.

- *Integrating Cross-Cultural Topics into Introductory Psychology*, by William Hill (Kennesaw State College), discusses the movement toward "internationalizing" the curriculum and provides suggestions for lectures, exercises, and assignments that can add a cross-cultural flavor to the introductory course.

- *Using the Internet in Teaching Introductory Psychology*, by Michael R. Snyder (University of Alberta), discusses how to work Internet assignments into the introductory course and provides a guide to many psychology-related sites on the World Wide Web.

Test Bank (by S. A. Hensch and William Addison)

Two outstanding professors have contributed to the development of the *Test Bank* that accompanies this text. Shirley Hensch (University of Wisconsin Center) and William Addison (Eastern Illinois University) did an excellent job revising all the test questions for the 16 chapters in the book.

The questions are closely tied to the chapter learning objectives and to the lists of key terms and key people found in both the text and the *Study Guide*. Most of the questions are categorized as either factual or conceptual. However, for each chapter there are also a few integrative questions that require students to link, synthesize, and interrelate information from different sections of the chapter. The test bank also includes a separate section that contains about 600 multiple-choice

questions based on the content of *Psyk.trek's Interactive Learning Modules*.

Computerized Test Items

Electronic versions of the *Test Bank* are available for a variety of computer configurations. The computerized test bank is sser-friendly and allows teachers to insert their own questions and to customize those provided.

Transparencies (by Susan Shapiro)

A collection of *text-specific transparencies* has been created to enhance visual presentations in the classroom. The development of the transparencies was supervised by Susan Shapiro, who has great expertise in the use of visual media in the classroom. Suzie has done a terrific job making the transparencies clear, readable, pedagogically sound, and technically accurate. A second set of transparencies from other Brooks/Cole texts is also available.

Challenging Your Preconceptions: Thinking Critically about Psychology (by Randolph Smith)

This brief paperback book is a wonderful introduction to critical thinking as it applies to psychological issues. Written by Randy Smith (Ouachita Baptist University), this book helps students apply their critical thinking skills to a variety of topics, including hypnosis, advertising, misleading statistics, IQ testing, gender differences, and memory bias. Each chapter ends with critical thinking challenges that give students opportunities to practice their critical thinking skills.

Culture and Modern Life (by David Matsumoto)

If you emphasize cultural diversity in your course, this is an ideal supplementary book. Written by David Matsumoto (San Francisco State University), a leading authority on cross-cultural psychology, this brief paperback will help students appreciate how cultural factors affect psychological processes. It includes chapters on self, social behavior, gender, work, and abnormal psychology.

Brooks/Cole Psychology Study Center on the World Wide Web

Students using *Psychology: Themes & Variations* can use the Brooks/Cole Psychology Study Center on the Web (http://psychstudy.brookscole.com). Through the Study Center, they can access updates on hot topics, demonstrations, tutorials, quizzes on the chapters in the text, links to additional psychology web sites.

ACKNOWLEDGMENTS

Creating an introductory psychology text is a complicated challenge, and a small army of people have contributed to the evolution of this book. Foremost among them are the psychology editors I have worked with at Brooks/Cole—Claire Verduin, C. Deborah Laughton, Phil Curson, and Eileen Murphy—and the developmental editor for this book, John Bergez. They have helped me immeasurably, and each has become a treasured friend along the way. I am especially indebted to Claire, who educated me in the intricacies of textbook publishing, and to John, who has left an enduring imprint on my writing.

I also want to thank Brooks/Cole's editor-in-chief, Craig Barth, and the president of Brooks/Cole, Bill Roberts, for giving me the freedom to pursue my personal vision of what an introductory text should be like. They have let me take some chances and have allowed me extensive input regarding every aspect of the book's production. I have never felt constrained by a conservative corporate mentality.

The challenge of meeting a difficult schedule in producing this book was undertaken by a talented team of people coordinated by Nancy Sjöberg at Del Mar Associates. Throughout all four editions of this text, the overall design and the illustration program have been developed by John Odam, who has shown remarkable ingenuity and creativity. Kristi Mendola and Chris Davis provided valuable assistance in designing this edition and Kim Fraley contributed excellent anatomical and vignette drawings. Linda Rill handled permissions and photo research with enthusiasm and extraordinary efficiency, and Jackie Estrada did an outstanding job once again in copy editing the manuscript. Finally, Nancy Sjöberg provided the organizational glue that held these efforts together.

A host of psychologists deserve thanks for the contributions they made to this book. I am grateful to Frank Landy for contributing an appendix on I/O psychology; to Rick Stalling and Ron Wasden for their work on the *Study Guide;* to Bill Addison and Shirley Hensch for their work on the *Test Bank;* to Randy Smith, Joseph Lowman, Russ Watson, Jane Jegerski, Bill Hill, Susan Shapiro, Michael Shapiro, and Michael Snyder for their contributions to the *Instructor's Resource Package;* to Susan Shapiro for her work on the transparencies, to Harry Upshaw, Larry Wrightsman, Shari Diamond, Rick Stalling, and Claire Etaugh for their help and guidance over the years; and to the chapter consultants listed on page xvii and the reviewers listed on page xviii, who provided insightful and constructive critiques of various portions of the manuscript.

Many other people have also contributed to this project, and I am grateful to all of them for their efforts. At Brooks/Cole, Marjorie Sanders monitored the production process and Vernon Boes designed a striking cover. Bill Bokermann, Margaret Parks, Michael Campbell, and Susan Carlson helped with varied aspects of the book's development, production, and marketing. At the College of DuPage, where I taught until 1991, all of my colleagues in psychology provided support and information at one time or another, but I am especially indebted to Barb Lemme and Don Green. I also want to thank my colleagues at Santa Clara University, who have been a fertile source of new ideas, the great many students from my classes who critiqued chapters, and Laura Abbey, who helped complete the reference entries.

I am also deeply indebted to the diverse array of people who contributed to the development of the *Psyk.trek* CD-ROM. At Brooks/Cole, Eileen Murphy, Marlene Thom, and May Clark worked above and beyond the call of duty. At Luminair Multimedia, George Elder, Kent Johnson, Laddie Odom, John Fuller, and Jocelyn Turpin worked with maniacal intensity to deliver *Psyk.trek* on time. Crucial contributions were also made by Alan Lanning, Roger Harnish, Linda Noble, Chris Evers, Linda Rill, and Jackie Estrada.

Last, but not least, I am grateful to many friends for their support over the years, especially Bruce Krattenmaker, Carol Ricks, Cheryl Kasel, Jerry Mueller, Sam Auster, Michael Block, and Tom Braden. My greatest debt is to my wife, Beth Traylor, who has been a steady source of emotional sustenance while enduring the grueling rigors of her medical career. Beth, thanks for the patience. This one's for you.

Wayne Weiten

INTRODUCTORY PSYCHOLOGY PACKAGE

Every Brooks/Cole introductory psychology text is accompanied by a wide variety of book-specific ancillaries, as well as the following teaching and learning tools:

Multimedia and Software Products

The Integrator for Introductory Psychology, 2.0
by Arthur J. Kohn and Wendy Kohn

This CD-ROM for Macintosh and Windows offers dramatic new ways for instructors to teach and students to learn! With a click of the mouse, students can reinforce their learning or explore independently by calling up interactive experiments, animations, homework assignments, video clips, transparencies, audio clips, dynamic images, demonstrations, study pages, and interactive surveys.

The CD-ROM includes the multimedia *LectureMaker,* a program that allows professors to prepare professional multimedia lectures quickly and easily. The *LectureMaker* tool enables professors to export multimedia elements to popular presentation packages, such as *PowerPoint, Persuasion, and ASTOUND.* All materials are directly keyed to Brooks/Cole introductory psychology textbooks. (ISBN: 0-534-34924-2)

PsychNow!: Interactive Experiences in Psychology
by Joel Margovsky, Brookdale Community College; Lonnie Yandell, Belmont University; Elizabeth Lynch, Glendale College; Tamara Ferguson, Utah State University; William McVaugh, Weber State University, and Dennis Coon, project consultant

This CD-ROM for Macintosh and Windows provides students with a dynamic, multimedia experience that goes beyond the boundaries of the classroom to let students explore the concepts of psychology like never before. Stunning graphics and animations, interesting video clips, and interactive exercises bring the theories of psychology to life. With *PsychNow!,* students can do more than just read about a topic—they can read, watch, listen, and react to it. (ISBN: 0-314-07220-9)

ASTOUND Presentation Software
This state-of-the-art multimedia presentation package provides you visual support in the classroom.

Custom presentations contain lecture material from the textbook, including text, art, photos, problems, and chapter outlines. You can use these presentations "as is," or customize the material to create your own unique presentations that include text, graphics, animations, and sound. (Windows ISBN: 0-314-09070-3; Macintosh ISBN: 0-314-09069-X)

MindScope Software
by Robert Hendersen

This software consists of 20 computerized exercises in perception, learning, memory, and cognition. The series helps students discover and analyze aspects of their own behavior that might otherwise be hidden from them. (ISBN: 0-314-06173-8)

Psych Lab I
by Roger Harnish of the Rochester Institute of Technology

Includes eight easy-to-use interactive demonstrations on the following topics: Hemispheric Specialization, Weber's Law, Optical Illusions, Classical Conditioning, Levels of Processing, Problem Solving, Emotional Expression, and Pressure and Performance. (DOS ISBN: 0-534-15344-5; Macintosh ISBN: 0-534-15349-6)

Psych Lab II
by Roger Harnish of the Rochester Institute of Technology

Includes six interactive demonstrations, experiments, and tutorials about the following subjects: Brain Anatomy, Memory, Classical Conditioning, Operant Conditioning, Shaping, and ESP. (DOS ISBN: 0-534-13618-4; Macintosh ISBN: 0-534-13619-2)

Videos and Videodiscs

Psychology/Careers for the Twenty-First Century Videotape
Brooks/Cole has an agreement to offer this dynamic, 13-minute video produced by the APA free to adopters of Brooks/Cole's introductory psychology texts. The video gives the viewer an overview of the emerging growth opportunities in psychology and advice about how to choose a career path.

Grade Improvement:
Taking Charge of Your Learning Videotape
This 20-minute video uses an upbeat and entertaining delivery to show first-year and reentry students different strategies they can use to enjoy greater success in college. Students will learn proven techniques for choosing an approach to learning, time management, class preparation, effective test taking, and more. Above all, it stresses that students must be actively involved in their learning. (ISBN: 0-314-05881-8)

Brooks/Cole Film and Video
Library for Introductory Psychology
Adopters can choose from the video options below. Please contact Brooks/Cole Marketing for information (800-354-0092).

The Pennsylvania State University's PCR—*Films and Videos in the Behavioral Sciences:* Adopters receive a set of three complimentary film/video rental vouchers and can choose from the world's largest collection of films and videos on human behavior.

The Brain videotapes: 30 video modules and a faculty guide, prepared by Frank Vattano of Colorado State University, in conjunction with the Annenberg/CPB Project Video Collection.

The Mind videotapes: 38 brief video modules offering examples of important concepts in introductory psychology and a faculty guide, prepared by Frank Vattano of Colorado State University, in cooperation with WNET, New York.

Seeing Beyond the Obvious: Understanding Perception in Everyday and Novel Environments: A videotape that provides an introduction to basic concepts of visual perception, created by the NASA Ames Research Center in conjunction with the University of Virginia.

Films for the Humanities and Sciences: Adopters can select one video from a collection that includes *Further Approaches to Learning, Memory Fabric of the Mind,* and *Dreams: Theater of the Night.*

Discovering Psychology videotapes: A series of 26 programs from the Annenberg/CPB Collection. This series encourages personal development while stimulating curiosity and critical thinking. The series integrates a historical and cutting-edge perspective of the field. Excellent computer animation and documentary footage of classic experiments help the viewer better understand psychological concepts and relate them to today's complex world.

Images of Psychology: Videodisc Library of Human Behavior
This two-disc set provides nearly two hours of video footage to help you prepare exciting classroom presentations. All of the videos have been carefully chosen to support major concepts in your introductory course. Several segments were designed and recorded specifically for this disc. Witnessing phenomena provides an instant spark that helps students understand textbook concepts. *Lecture Builder Software,* also available to qualified adopters, allows you to customize your lecture prior to class and program the disc, so you can present without the use of the hand-held remote control.

Books/Manuals, Testing, and Transparencies
College Survival Guide: Hints and References to Aid College Students, Fourth Edition
by Bruce M. Rowe, Los Angeles Pierce College
This new edition of Rowe's helpful guide for college students provides tips on managing time, studying, taking exams, and more. (ISBN: 0-534-35569-2)

Psychology/Careers for the Twenty-First Century Booklet
This is a 30-page pamphlet produced by the American Psychological Association. It describes the field of psychology, as well as the "how to" for career preparation in the many areas of psychology. Career options and resources are also discussed. This pamphlet can be shrink-wrapped with Brooks/Cole texts at no additional cost. (ISBN: 0-534-34293-0)

Complimentary Telephone Testing or Tele-Testing
ITP Technology Services will construct a test for instructors who have adopted a Brooks/Cole text. Technology Services requests a minimum of 48 hours' notice to construct these complimentary tests. For tele-testing call (800) 423-0563.

Introductory Psychology Transparencies
This set of 95 full-color transparencies illustrates a range of topics for the introductory course; it can be used to supplement the text-specific transparencies. (ISBN: 0-534-13013-5)

CONSULTANTS

Chapter 1

Charles L. Brewer
Furman University

David Hothersall
Ohio State University

E. R. Hilgard
Stanford University

Chapter 2

Larry Christensen
Texas A & M University

Francis Durso
University of Oklahoma

Donald H. McBurney
University of Pittsburg

Chapter 3

Nelson Freedman
Queen's University at Kingston

Michael W. Levine
University of Illinois at Chicago

James M. Murphy
Indiana University–Purdue University
Indianapolis

Chapter 4

Nelson Freedman
Queen's University at Kingston

Kevin Jordan
San Jose State University

Michael W. Levine
University of Illinois at Chicago

Lawrence Ward
University of British ColumbiaChapter 5

Chapter 5

Frank Etscorn
New Mexico Institute of Mining and Technology

Tracey L. Kahan
Santa Clara University

Wilse Webb
University of Florida

Chapter 6

A. Charles Catania
University of Maryland

Michael Domjan
University of Texas, Austin

William C. Gordon
University of New Mexico

Chapter 7

Tracey L. Kahan
Santa Clara University

Tom Pusateri
Loras College

Stephen K. Reed
San Diego State University

Patricia Tenpenny
Loyola University, Chicago

Chapter 8

John Best
Eastern Illinois University

David Carroll
University of Wisconsin-Superior

Tom Pusateri
Loras College

Stephen K. Reed
San Diego State University

Chapter 9

Charles Davidshofer
Colorado State University

Shalynn Ford
Teikyo Marycrest University

Timothy Rogers
University of Calgary

Chapter 10

Robert Franken
University of Calgary

Russell G. Geen
University of Missouri

Douglas Mook
University of Virginia

Chapter 11

Ruth L. Ault
Davidson College

John C. Cavanaugh
University of Deleware

Claire Etaugh
Bradley University

Chapter 12

Susan Cloniger
Russel Sage College

Caroline Collins
University of Victoria

Christopher F. Monte
Manhattanville College

Chapter 13

Robin M. DiMatteo
University of California, Riverside

Jess Feist
McNeese State University

Chris Kleinke
University of Alaska

Chapter 14

David A. F. Haaga
American University

Chris L. Kleinke
University of Alaska, Anchorage

Elliot A. Weiner
Pacific University

Chapter 15

Gerald Corey
California State University, Fullerton

Herbert Goldenberg
California State University, Los Angeles

Jane S. Halonen
Alverno College

Chapter 16

Jerry M. Burger
Santa Clara University

Donelson R. Forsyth
Virginia Commonwealth University

REVIEWERS

Lyn Y. Abramson
University of Wisconsin

Ruth L. Ault
Davidson College

Derryl K. Beale
Cerritos Community College

Daniel R. Bellack
Trident Technical College

Robert Bornstein
Miami University

Bette L. Bottoms
University of Illinois at Chicago

Allen Branum
South Dakota State University

Robert G. Bringle
Indiana University-Purdue University at
Indianapolis

Dan W. Brunworth
Kishwaukee College

James Butler
James Madison University

Mary M. Cail
University of Virginia

James F. Calhoun
University of Georgia

William Calhoun
University of Tennessee

Francis B. Colavita
University of Pittsburgh

Thomas B. Collins
Mankato State University

Stan Coren
University of British Columbia

Norman Culbertson
Yakima Valley College

Betty M. Davenport
Campbell University

Stephen F. Davis
Emporia State University

Kenneth Deffenbacher
University of Nebraska

Roger Dominowski
University of Illinois, Chicago

Robert J. Douglas
University of Washington

James Eison
Southeast Missouri State University

M. Jeffrey Farrar
University of Florida

Thomas P. Fitzpatrick
Rockland Community College

Karen E. Ford
Mesa State College

Donelson R. Forsyth
Virginia Commonwealth University

William J. Froming
University of Florida

Mary Ellen Fromuth
Middle Tennessee State University

Dean E. Frost
Portland State University

Richard Griggs
University of Florida

Arthur Gutman
Florida Institute of Technology

Jane S. Halonen
Alverno College

Roger Harnish
Rochester Institute of Technology

Philip L. Hartley
Chaffey College

Glenn R. Hawkes
Virginia Commonwealth University

Myra D. Heinrich
Mesa State College

Lyllian B. Hix
Houston Community College

John P. Hostetler
Albion College

Robert A. Johnston
College of William and Mary

Alan R. King
University of North Dakota

Melvyn B. King
State University of New York, Cortland

James Knight
Humboldt State University

Mike Knight
Central State University

Ronald Kopcho
Mercer Community College

Barry J. Krikstone
Saint Michael's College

Jerry N. Lackey
Stephen F. Austin State University

Robin L. Lashley
Kent State University, Tuscarawas

Peter Leppman
University of Guelph

Charles F. Levinthal
Hofstra University

Wolfgang Linden
University of British Columbia

Donald McBurney
University of Pittsburgh

Ronald K. McLaughlin
Juniata College

Sheryll Mennicke
University of Minnesota

James M. Murphy
Indiana University-Purdue University at
Indianapolis

Michael Murphy
Henderson State University

John Nezlek
College of William and Mary

David L. Novak
Lansing Community College

Richard Page
Wright State University

Joseph J. Palladino
University of Southern Indiana

John N. Park
Mankato State University

Bobby J. Poe
Belleville Area College

Gary Poole
Simon Fraser University

Maureen K. Powers
Vanderbilt University

Janet Proctor
Purdue University

Robin Raygor
Anoka-Ramsey Community College

Celia Reaves
Monroe Community College

Daniel W. Richards
Houston Community College

Fred Shima
California State University,
Dominguez Hills

Susan A. Shodahl
San Bernardino Valley College

Steven M. Smith
Texas A & M University

Marjorie Taylor
University of Oregon

Frank R. Terrant, Jr.
Appalachian State University

Donald Tyrrell
Franklin and Marshall College

Frank J. Vattano
Colorado State University

Wayne Viney
Colorado State University

Keith D. White
University of Florida

Randall D. Wight
Ouachita Baptist University

Cecilia Yoder
Oklahoma City Community College

BRIEF CONTENTS

CONTENTS

1

THE EVOLUTION OF PSYCHOLOGY

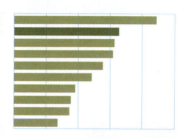

2

THE RESEARCH ENTERPRISE IN PSYCHOLOGY

3
THE BIOLOGICAL BASES OF BEHAVIOR

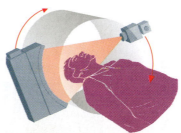

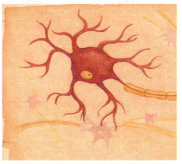

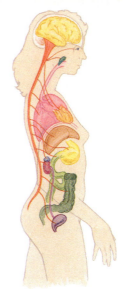

4
SENSATION AND PERCEPTION

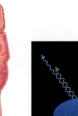
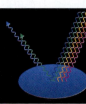

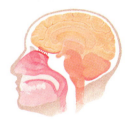

5
VARIATIONS IN CONSCIOUSNESS

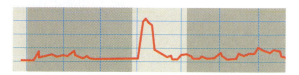

6

LEARNING THROUGH CONDITIONING

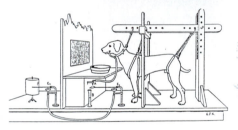

7

HUMAN MEMORY

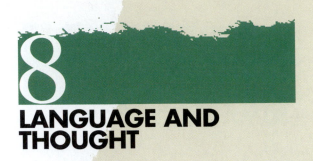

8
LANGUAGE AND THOUGHT

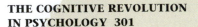

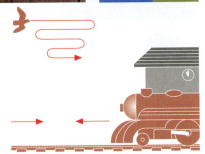

9

INTELLIGENCE AND PSYCHOLOGICAL TESTING

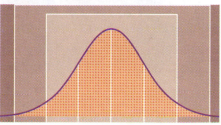

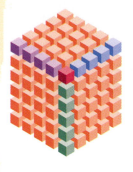

10
MOTIVATION AND EMOTION

11

HUMAN DEVELOPMENT ACROSS THE LIFE SPAN

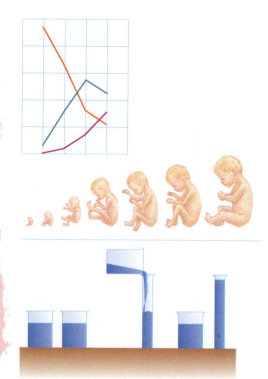

12

PERSONALITY: THEORY, RESEARCH, AND ASSESSMENT

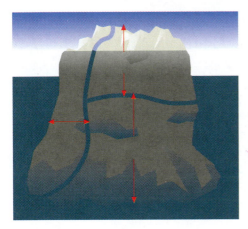

13
STRESS, COPING, AND HEALTH

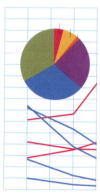

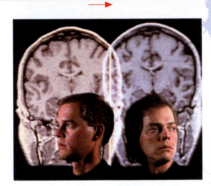

14
PSYCHOLOGICAL DISORDERS

15
PSYCHOTHERAPY

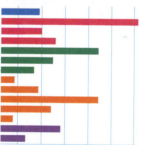

16
SOCIAL BEHAVIOR

TO THE STUDENT

Welcome to your introductory psychology textbook. In most college courses, students spend more time with their textbooks than with their professors, so it helps if students like their textbooks. Making textbooks likable, however, is a tricky proposition. By its very nature, a textbook must introduce students to many complicated concepts, ideas, and theories. If it doesn't, it isn't much of a textbook, and instructors won't choose to use it. Nevertheless, in writing this book I've tried to make it as likable as possible without compromising the academic content that your instructor demands. I've especially tried to keep in mind your need for a clear, well-organized presentation that makes the important material stand out and yet is interesting to read.

The Visual Guide

You're about to embark on a journey into a new domain of ideas. Your text includes many important features that are intended to highlight certain aspects of psychology's landscape. Before you plunge into your first chapter, I strongly recommend that you spend some time studying the Visual Guide to *Psychology: Themes & Variations* that appears on the pages that follow. The Visual Guide will give you a quick introduction to the book's key features, such as its unifying themes, featured studies, applications, and abundant learning aids. Taking a few minutes to become familiar with how the book works will help you to get more out of it.

Psyk.trek: A Multimedia Introduction to Psychology

Psyk.trek is a new multimedia CD-ROM I have developed to accompany this textbook. It is an enormously powerful learning tool that can enhance your understanding of many complex processes and theories, provide you with an alternative way to assimilate many crucial concepts, and add a little more fun to your journey through introductory psychology. *Psyk.trek* has been designed to supplement and complement your textbook. To help you use *Psyk.trek* effectively, a Visual Guide to *Psyk.trek* follows the Visual Guide to the text in the upcoming pages. I urge you to look through the guide and to take the much more detailed Guided Tour on the CD itself. If your professor has chosen not to order *Psyk.trek* in conjunction with the text, you can order a copy directly from the publisher by calling 1-800-354-9706.

Citations and References

Psychology textbooks customarily identify the studies, theoretical treatises, books, and articles that information comes from. These citations occur (1) when names are followed by a date in parentheses, as in "Smith (1982) found that . . ." or (2) when names and dates are provided together within parentheses, as in "In one study (Smith, Miller, & Jones, 1994), the researchers attempted to. . . ." All of the cited publications are listed by author in the alphabetized References section in the back of the book. The citations and references are a necessary part of a book's scholarly and scientific foundation. Practically speaking, however, you'll probably want to glide right over them as you read.

A Word About the Study Guide

A Study Guide is available to accompany this text. It was written by two of my former professors, who introduced me to psychology years ago. They have done a great job of organizing review materials to help you master the information in the book. I suggest that you seriously consider using it to help you study.

A Final Word

I'm very pleased to be a part of your first journey into the world of psychology, and I sincerely hope that you'll find the book as thought provoking and as easy to learn from as I've tried to make it. If you have any comments or advice on the book, please write to me in care of the publisher (Brooks/Cole Publishing Company, Pacific Grove, California, 93950). You can be sure I'll pay careful attention to your feedback. Finally, let me wish you good luck. I hope you enjoy your course and learn a great deal.

Wayne Weiten

8 LANGUAGE AND THOUGHT

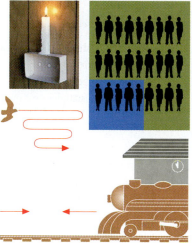

Visual Guide to *Psychology: Themes and Variations*

Chapter Outlines
An outline at the beginning of each chapter provides you with a detailed overview of the topics covered in the chapter. Think of the outlines as road maps, and bear in mind that it's easier to reach a destination if you know where you're going.

Narrative Chapter Openings
Each chapter begins with some type of anecdote or puzzle intended to put the chapter in context or engage your interest in the topics that follow.

Key Terms
Key terms are identified with italicized boldface type to alert you that these are important vocabulary items that are part of psychology's technical language.

Integrated Running Glossary
An integrated running glossary provides an on-the-spot definition of each key term as it's introduced in the text. These formal definitions are printed in boldface type. Most key terms are formally defined in the integrated running glossary only when they are first introduced. If you run into a technical term a second time and can't remember its meaning, it may be easier to look it up in the alphabetical glossary in the back of the book.

Theorist Photos
Photos of major theorists and researchers can be found in the page margins, accompanied by provocative quotes that typically highlight one of their key ideas.

"Dr. Watson—Mr. Sherlock Holmes," said Stamford, introducing us.

"How are you?" he said, cordially, gripping my hand with a strength for which I should hardly have given him credit. "You have been in Afghanistan, I perceive."

"How on earth did you know that?" I asked, in astonishment. (From A Study in Scarlet by Arthur Conan Doyle)

If you've ever read any Sherlock Holmes stories, you know that the great detective continually astonished his stalwart companion, Dr. Watson, with his extraordinary deductions. Obviously, Holmes could not arrive at his conclusions without a chain of reasoning. Yet to him even an elaborate reasoning process was a simple, everyday act. Consider his feat of knowing at once, upon first meeting Watson, that the doctor had been in Afghanistan. When asked, Holmes explained his reasoning as follows:

"I knew you came from Afghanistan. From long habit the train of thought ran so swiftly through my mind that I arrived at the conclusion without being conscious of the intermediate steps. There were such steps, however. The train of reasoning ran: "Here is a gentleman of a medical type, but with the air of a military man. Clearly an army doctor, then. He has just come from the tropics, for his face is dark, and that is not the natural tint of his skin, for his wrists are fair. He has undergone hardship and sickness, as his haggard face says clearly. His left arm has been injured. He holds it in a stiff and unnatural manner. Where in the tropics could an English army doctor have seen much hardship and got his arm wounded? Clearly in Afghanistan.' The whole train of thought did not occupy a second."

Admittedly, Sherlock Holmes's deductive feats are fictional. But even to read about them appreciatively—let alone imagine them, as Sir Arthur Conan Doyle did—is a remarkably complex mental act. Our everyday thought processes seem ordinary to us only because we take them for granted, just as Holmes saw nothing extraordinary in what to him was a simple deduction.

In reality, everyone is a Sherlock Holmes, continually performing magical feats of thought. Even elementary perception—for instance, watching a football game or a ballet—involves elaborate cognitive processes. People must sort through distorted, constantly shifting perceptual inputs and deduce what they see out there in the real world. Imagine, then, the complexity of thought required to read a book, fix an automobile, or balance a checkbook.

Of course, all this is not to say that human thought processes are flawless or unequaled. You probably own a $10 calculator that can run circles around you when it comes to computing square roots. As we'll see, some of the most interesting research in this chapter focuses on ways in which people's thinking can be limited, simplistic, or outright illogical.

THE COGNITIVE REVOLUTION IN PSYCHOLOGY

As we have noted before, **cognition refers to the mental processes involved in acquiring knowledge.** In other words, cognition involves thinking. When psychology first emerged as an independent science in the 19th century, it focused on the mind. Mental processes were explored through introspection—analysis of one's own conscious experience (see Chapter 1). Unfortunately, early psychologists' study of mental processes ran aground, as the method of introspection yielded unreliable results. Psychology's empirical approach depends on observation, and private mental events proved difficult to observe. Further-

more, during the first half of the 20th century, the study of cognition was actively discouraged by the theoretical dominance of behaviorism. Herbert Simon, a pioneer of cognitive psychology, recalls that "you couldn't use a word like *mind* in a psychology journal—you'd get your mouth washed out with soap" (Holden, 1986, p. 55).

Although it wasn't fully recognized until a decade later, the 1950s brought a "cognitive revolution" in psychology (Baars, 1986). Renegade theorists, such as Herbert Simon, began to argue that behaviorists' exclusive focus on overt responses was doomed to yield an incomplete understand-

"You couldn't use a word like mind in a psychology journal—you'd get your mouth washed out with soap."

HERBERT SIMON

Instead, experimenters concentrate on making sure that the experimental and control groups are alike on a limited number of variables that could have a bearing on the results of the study. These variables are called extraneous, secondary, or nuisance variables. *Extraneous variables* are any variables other than the independent variable that seem likely to influence the dependent variable in a specific study.

In Schachter's study, one extraneous variable would have been the subjects' tendency to be sociable. Why? Because subjects' sociability could affect their desire to be with others (the dependent variable). If the subjects in one group had happened to be more sociable (on the average) than those in the other group, the variables of anxiety and sociability would have been confounded. A *confounding of variables* occurs when two variables are linked together in a way that makes it difficult to sort out their specific effects. When an extraneous variable is confounded with an independent variable, a researcher cannot tell which is having what effect on the dependent variable.

Unanticipated confoundings of variables have wrecked innumerable experiments. That is why so much care, planning, and forethought must go into designing an experiment. One of the key qualities that separate a talented experimenter from a mediocre one is the ability to foresee troublesome extraneous variables and control them to avoid confoundings.

Experimenters use a variety of safeguards to control for extraneous variables. For instance, subjects are usually assigned to the experimental and control groups randomly. *Random assignment* of subjects occurs when all subjects have an equal chance of being assigned to any group or condition in the study. When experimenters distribute subjects into groups through some random procedure, they can be reasonably confident that the groups will be similar in most ways. To summarize the essentials of experimental design, Figure 2.6 provides an overview of the elements in an experiment, using Schachter's study as an example.

Variations in Designing Experiments 1b

We have discussed the experiment in only its simplest format, with just one independent variable and one dependent variable. Actually, many variations are possible in conducting experiments. Because you'll be reading about experiments with more complicated designs, these variations merit a brief mention.

First, it is sometimes advantageous to use only one group of subjects who serve as their own control group. The effects of the independent variable are evaluated by exposing this single group to two different conditions—an experimental condition and a control condition. For example, imagine that you wanted to study the effects of loud music on typing performance. You could have a group of subjects work on a typing task while loud music was played (experimental condition) and in the absence of music (control condition). This approach would ensure that the subjects in the experimental and control conditions would be alike on any extraneous variables involving their personal characteristics, such as motivation or typing skill. After all, the same people would be studied in both conditions.

Second, it is possible to manipulate more than one independent variable in a single experiment. Researchers often manipulate two or three independent variables to examine their joint effects on the dependent variable. For example, in a study of typing performance, you could vary room temperature and the presence of distracting noise (see Figure 2.7 on page 46). The main advantage of this approach is that it permits the experimenter to see whether two variables interact.

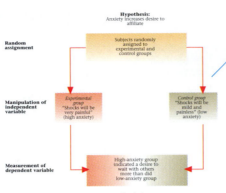

Figure 2.6
The basic elements of an experiment. As illustrated by the Schachter study, the logic of experimental design rests on treating the experimental and control groups exactly alike (to control for extraneous variables) except for the manipulation of the independent variable. In this way, the experimenter attempts to isolate the effects of the independent variable on the dependent variable.

Illustration Program

In this text, the illustrations, photos, diagrams, and charts are not decorative; they play a crucial role in the educational process. Careful attention to the figures, the photos, and their accompanying captions will greatly aid your understanding of the material discussed in the text.

Psyk.trek Icons

Icons highlighting the connections between the content of the text and the content of the *Psyk.trek* CD-ROM are sprinkled throughout the chapters. The icons are integrated into the level-two headings in the text. They look like tiny compact discs and have numbers and letters adjacent to them. The numbers and letters refer you to the specific Interactive Learning Modules on Psyk.trek that cover the same material. You can bolster your understanding of this material by working with the specified modules.

TABLE 2.2 COLLEGE MEN'S RESPONSES TO ITEMS ON COERCIVE SEXUALITY SCALE (%)

Coercive Act Engaged in "Against Her Will"	Never	Once or Twice	Several Times	Often
Held a woman's hand	57	34	7	1
Kissed a woman	47	41	10	2
Placed hand on a woman's knee	39	43	15	3
Placed hand on a woman's breast	39	37	18	5
Placed hand on a woman's thigh or crotch	42	40	16	2
Unfastened a woman's outer clothing	51	34	13	2
Removed or disarranged a woman's outer clothing	58	31	9	2
Removed or disarranged a woman's underclothing	68	27	3	2
Removed own underclothing	78	18	3	2
Touched a woman's genital area	63	30	6	1
Had intercourse with a woman	85	13	2	0

Note: Some rows do not total 100% because of rounding.
Source: Rapaport and Burkhart (1984)

pared to the strengths and weaknesses of experimental research in Figure 2.10 (on page 52). As a whole, the foremost advantage of these methods is that they give researchers a way to explore questions that could not be examined with experimental procedures. For example, after-the-fact analyses would be the only ethical way to investigate the possible link between poor maternal nutrition and birth defects in humans. In a similar vein, if researchers hope to learn how urban and rural upbringing relate to people's values, they have to depend on descriptive methods, since they can't control where subjects grow up. Thus, *descriptive/correlational research broadens the scope of phenomena that psychologists are able to study.*

Unfortunately, descriptive methods have one significant disadvantage: Investigators cannot control events to isolate cause and effect. *Consequently, correlational research cannot demonstrate conclusively that two variables are causally related.* As an example, consider the study of children's risk taking that we discussed earlier. Although Ginsburg and Miller (1982) found an association between sex and risk taking, their data do not permit us to conclude that a child's sex *causes* these differences. Too many factors were left uncontrolled in the study. For example, we do not know how similar the groups of boys and girls were. The groups could have differed in age distribution or other factors that might have led to the observed differences in risk taking.

Italics for Emphasis

Italics (without boldface) are used liberally throughout the text to emphasize crucial points, especially when important ideas fall in the middle or at the end of paragraphs.

Concept Checks

Concept Checks are sprinkled throughout the chapters to let you test your mastery of important ideas. Generally, they ask you to integrate or organize a number of key ideas or to apply ideas to real-world situations. Although they're meant to be engaging and fun, they do check conceptual understanding, and some are challenging. But if you get stuck, don't worry; the answers (and explanations, where they're needed) are in the back of the book in Appendix A.

CONCEPT CHECK 2.2
Matching Research Methods to Questions

Check your understanding of the uses and strengths of various research methods by figuring out which method would be optimal for investigating the following questions about behavioral processes. Choose from the following methods: (a) experiment, (b) naturalistic observation, (c) case study, and (d) survey. Indicate your choice (by letter) next to each question. You'll find the answers in Appendix A in the back of the book.

_____ 1. Are people's attitudes about nuclear disarmament related to their social class or education?

_____ 2. Do people who suffer from anxiety disorders share similar early childhood experiences?

_____ 3. Do troops of baboons display territoriality—that is, do they mark off an area as their own and defend it from intrusion by other baboons?

_____ 4. Can the presence of food-related cues (delicious-looking desserts in advertisements, for example) cause an increase in the amount of food that people eat?

Featured Studies

After Chapter 1, each chapter includes a clearly marked Featured Study, which is an in-depth look at an important, interesting, or provocative piece of research. Each is presented in a way that resembles a journal article, thereby acquainting you with the format of scientific reports. The Featured Studies are intended to enhance your understanding of how psychologists conduct research.

Data Graphs

Many graphs of research results are included throughout the book to underscore psychology's foundation in empirical research.

Evolution, Culture, and Mating Preferences — Featured Study

Investigator: David M. Buss (University of Michigan)

Source: Sex differences in human mate preferences: Evolutionary hypotheses tested in 37 cultures. *Behavioral and Brain Sciences,* 1989, *12,* 1–49.

According to evolutionary theories, human females enhance their chances of passing on their genes not by seeking larger or stronger partners (as in the animal kingdom), but by seeking male partners that possess or are likely to acquire more material resources that can be invested in children. Thus, evolutionary theorists assert that women emphasize education, income, status, ambition, and industriousness in potential partners. Men, on the other hand, are assumed to maximize their reproductive outlook by seeking female partners with good breeding potential. Thus, men are thought to look for youth, attractiveness, good health, and other characteristics presumed to be associated with higher fertility. If these evolutionary analyses of sexual motivation are on the mark, gender differences in mating preferences should transcend culture.

higher value than men on potential partners' status, ambition, and financial prospects (see Figure 10.10). These priorities were not limited to industrialized or capitalist countries; they were apparent in third-world cultures, socialist countries, and all varieties of economic systems. In contrast, men consistently showed more interest than women in potential partners' youthfulness and physical attractiveness (see Figure 10.11).

Cross-cultural variations in mate preferences were relatively modest. The most prominent variation was in the emphasis placed on chastity—a partner's lack of previous sexual intercourse. Chastity was highly valued in some societies but viewed with indifference in others. Some cross-cultural variability was also seen in the emphasis placed on partners' housekeeping skills and religious commitment.

Method
To test this hypothesis, David Buss coordinated the efforts of 50 scientists from around the world, who collected data on what people want in a mate. They surveyed more than 10,000 people from 37 cultures distributed across six continents and five islands. Subjects responded to two questionnaires, which asked them to rate the importance of 32 characteristics in potential mates.

Results
The findings revealed that males and females exhibit both similarities and differences in mating preferences. Many characteristics, such as kindness, emotional stability, dependability, and a pleasant disposition, were rated very highly by both sexes. However, a few crucial differences between males' and females' priorities were found, and these differences were universal across cultures. As a group, women placed a

Discussion
According to Buss, social scientists have traditionally assumed that mating preferences are shaped by learning and that they vary considerably from culture to culture. His findings suggest that culture matters, but only in a limited way. He also concludes that his data provide striking support for evolutionary theories of sexual motivation. As predicted, women emphasized males' prospects for acquisition of material resources, whereas men emphasized females' reproductive capacity.

Comment
Buss's fascinating data are consistent with evolutionary theories of sexual motivation, but, as is often the case with tests of evolutionary hypotheses, one can posit alternative explanations for the findings. For example, women's emphasis on males' material resources could be a by-product of economic forces

Figure 10.10 Gender and potential mates' financial prospects. Consistent with evolutionary theory, Buss (1989) found [that women] place more e[mphasis on] potential par[tners'] financial pro[spects than] do males. M[oreover, he] found that th[is trend] transcended [culture]. The specific resul[ts for six of] the 37 cul[tures studied by] Buss are sho[wn here.]

Mean ratings of importance
(3 = indispensable, 0 = unimportant)

- China
- Iran
- Zambia
- Bulgaria
- Venezuela
- USA

Females / Males

MOTIVATIO[N]

Unifying Themes

To help you make sense of a complex and diverse field of study, Chapter 1 introduces seven unifying themes that reappear in a number of variations as you move from chapter to chapter. These unifying themes are meant to provoke thought about important issues and to highlight the connections between chapters. They are discussed at the end of each chapter in a section called Putting It in Perspective, which reflects on the lessons to be learned from the chapter.

Recaps of Key Points

Each chapter includes five to eight Recaps of Key Points that are generally found at the end of major sections. The Recaps appear in blue type (except in the Applications), making it readily apparent that they represent optional reading. Interspersing them throughout the chapters permits you to check your understanding of each section's main ideas immediately after finishing the section instead of waiting until the end of the chapter.

PUTTING IT IN PERSPECTIVE

In this chapter, three of our unifying themes stand out in sharp relief. First, the way in which competing theories of color vision and hearing have been reconciled in recent decades shows how psychology's theoretical diversity can pay dividends. Second, the entire chapter relates to the idea that people's experience of the world is highly subjective. Third, we saw ample evidence of how our behavior is shaped by our cultural heritage. Let's discuss the value of theoretical diversity first.

Contradictory theories about behavior can be disconcerting and frustrating for theorists, researchers, teachers, and students alike. Most of us show a natural human tendency to want to tie things up in a neat, sensible package. As the Gestaltists would have put it, we prefer closure and simplicity.

Yet this chapter provides two dramatic demonstrations of how theoretical diversity can lead to progress in the long run. For decades, the trichromatic and opponent process theories of color vision and the place and frequency theories of pitch perception were viewed as fundamentally incompatible. These competing theories generated and guided the research that now provides a fairly solid understanding of how people perceive color and pitch. As you know, in each case the evidence eventually revealed that the opposing theories were not really incompatible. Both were needed to fully explain the sensory processes that each sought to explain individually. If it hadn't been for these theoretical debates, current understanding of color vision and pitch perception might be far more primitive, as the understanding of timbre still is.

Our coverage of sensation and perception should also have enhanced your appreciation of why human experience of the world is highly subjective. As ambiguous figures and optical illusions clearly show, there is no one-to-one correspondence between sensory input and perceived experience of the world. Perception is an active process in which people organize and interpret the information received by the senses. These interpretations are shaped by a host of factors, including the environmental context and perceptual sets. Small wonder, then, that people often perceive the same event in very different ways.

Finally, this chapter provided numerous examples of how cultural factors can shape behavior—in an area of research where one might expect to find little cultural influence. Most people are not surprised to learn that there are cultural differences in attitudes, values, social behavior, and development. But perception is widely viewed as a basic, universal process that should be invariant across cultures. In most respects it is, as the similarities among cultural groups in perception far outweigh the differences. Nonetheless, we saw cultural variations in depth perception, susceptibility to illusions, taste preferences, and pain tolerance. Thus, even a fundamental, heavily physiological process such as perception can be modified to some degree by one's cultural background.

The following Application demonstrates the subjectivity of perception once again. It focuses on how painters have learned to use the principles of visual perception to achieve a variety of artistic goals.

Recap of Key Points
- Sensory receptors in the skin respond to pressure, temperature, and pain. Tactile localization depends on receptive fields similar to those seen for vision. Some cells in the somatosensory cortex appear to function like feature detectors. There are nerve fibers that respond specifically to warmth and cold.
- Pain signals are sent to the brain along two pathways that are characterized as fast and slow. The perception of pain is highly subjective and may be influenced by mood, attention, and culture. Gate-control theory holds that incoming pain signals can be blocked in the spinal cord. Endorphins and a descending neural pathway appear responsible for the suppression of pain by the central nervous system.
- The kinesthetic system monitors the position of various body parts. Kinesthetic receptors, located in the joints and muscles, send signals to the brain along the same pathway as tactile stimulation. The sense of balance depends primarily on activity in the semicircular canals in the vestibular system.
- This chapter underscored three of our unifying themes: the value of theoretical diversity, the subjective nature of human experience, and the influence of culture on behavior.

APPLICATION: ACHIEVING SELF-CONTROL THROUGH BEHAVIOR MODIFICATION

Answer the following "yes" or "no."

1 Do you have a hard time passing up food, even when you're not hungry?

2 Do you wish you studied more often?

3 Would you like to cut down on your smoking or drinking?

4 Do you experience difficulty in getting yourself to exercise regularly?

5 Do you wish you had more will power?

If you answered "yes" to any of these questions, you have struggled with the challenge of self-control. This Application discusses how you can use the techniques of behavior modification to improve your self-control. If you stop to think about it, self-control—or rather a lack of it—underlies many of the personal problems that people struggle with in everyday life.

Behavior modification is a systematic approach to changing behavior through the application of the principles of conditioning. Advocates of behavior modification assume that behavior is a product of learning, conditioning, and environmental control. They further assume that *what is learned can be unlearned*. Thus, they set out to "recondition" people to produce more desirable patterns of behavior.

The technology of behavior modification has been applied with great success in schools, businesses, hospitals, factories, child-care facilities, prisons, and mental health centers (Goodall, 1972; Kazdin, 1982; Rachman, 1992). Moreover, behavior modification techniques have proven particularly valuable in efforts to improve self-control. Our discussion will borrow

Figure 6.29
Steps in a self-modification program. This flowchart provides an overview of the steps necessary to execute a self-modification program.

Step 1	Specify your target behavior
Step 2	Gather baseline data / Identify possible controlling antecedents / Determine initial level of response / Identify possible controlling consequences
Step 3	Design your program / Select strategies to increase response strength *or* Select strategies to decrease response strength
Step 4	Execute and evaluate your program
Step 5	Bring your program to an end

liberally from an excellent book on self-modification by David Watson and Roland Tharp (1993). We will discuss five steps in the process of self-modification, which are outlined in Figure 6.29.

Specifying Your Target Behavior

The first step in a self-modification program is to specify the target behavior(s) that you want to change. Behavior modification can only be applied to a clearly defined, overt response, yet many people have difficulty pinpointing the behavior they hope to alter. They tend to describe their problems in terms of unobservable personality *traits* rather than overt *behaviors*. For example, asked what behavior he would like to change, a man might say, "I'm too irritable." That may be true, but it is of little help in designing a self-modification program. To use a behavioral approach, vague statements about traits need to be translated into precise descriptions of specific target behaviors.

To identify target responses, you need to ponder past behavior or closely observe future behavior and list specific *examples* of responses that lead to the trait description. For instance, the man who regards himself as "too irritable" might identify two overly frequent responses, such as arguing with his wife and snapping at his children. These are specific behaviors for which he could design a self-modification program.

Gathering Baseline Data

The second step in behavior modification is to gather baseline data. You need to systematically observe your target behavior for a period of time (usually a week or two) before you work out the details of your program. In gathering your baseline data, you need to monitor three things.

First, you need to determine the initial response level of your target behavior. After all, you can't tell whether your program is working effectively unless you have a baseline for comparison. In most cases, you would simply keep track of how

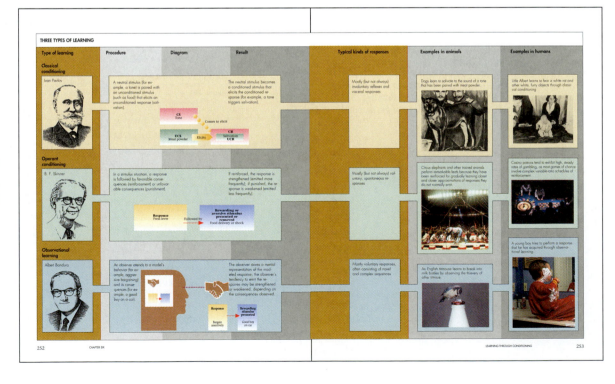

CHAPTER 4 REVIEW

Key Ideas

Psychophysics: Basic Concepts and Issues

◆ Absolute thresholds are not really absolute. Fechner's law asserts that larger and larger increases in stimulus intensity are required to produce just noticeable differences in the magnitude of sensation.

◆ According to signal-detection theory, the detection of sensory inputs is influenced by noise in the system and by decision-making strategies. In recent years, it has become apparent that perception can occur without awareness. Prolonged stimulation may lead to sensory adaptation, which involves a reduction in sensitivity.

Our Sense of Sight: The Visual System

◆ Light varies in terms of wavelength, amplitude, and purity. Light enters the eye through the cornea and pupil and is focused on the retina by the lens.

◆ Rods and cones are the visual receptors found in the retina. Cones play a key role in daylight vision and color perception, and rods are critical to night vision and peripheral vision. Dark adaptation and light adaptation both involve changes in the retina's sensitivity to light.

◆ The retina transforms light into neural impulses that are sent to the brain via the optic nerve. Receptive fields are areas in the retina that affect the firing of visual cells. Two visual pathways to the brain send signals through the thalamus to different areas of the visual cortex. The visual cortex contains cells that appear to function as feature detectors.

◆ Perceptions of color (hue) are primarily a function of light wavelength, while amplitude affects brightness and purity affects saturation. Perceptions of many varied colors depend on processes that resemble additive color mixing. The evidence now suggests that both the trichromatic and opponent process theories are necessary to account for color vision.

◆ According to feature analysis theories, people detect specific elements in stimuli and build them into recognizable forms through bottom-up processing. However, evidence suggests that form perception also involves top-down processing.

◆ Gestalt psychology emphasized that the whole may be greater than the sum of its parts (features), as illustrated by Gestalt principles of form perception. Other approaches to form perception emphasize that people develop perceptual hypotheses about the distal stimuli that could be responsible for the proximal stimuli that are sensed.

◆ Depth perception depends primarily on monocular cues. Binocular cues such as retinal disparity and convergence can also contribute to depth perception. Conscious perceptions of geographical slant tend to be greatly exaggerated, but haptic judgments seem largely immune to this perceptual bias.

◆ Perceptual constancies in vision help viewers deal with the ever-shifting nature of proximal stimuli. Optical illusions demonstrate that perceptual hypotheses can be inaccurate and that perceptions are not simple reflections of objective reality.

Our Sense of Hearing: The Auditory System

◆ Sound varies in terms of wavelength (frequency), amplitude, and purity. These properties affect mainly perceptions of pitch, loudness, and timbre, respectively. Auditory signals are transmitted through the brainstem and thalamus to the primary auditory cortex in the temporal lobe.

◆ Modern evidence suggests that place theory and frequency theory are complementary rather than incompatible explanations of pitch perception. People pinpoint the source of sounds by comparing interear differences in the intensity and timing of sounds.

Our Chemical Senses: Taste and Smell

◆ The taste buds are sensitive to four basic tastes: sweet, sour, bitter, and salty. Sensitivity to these tastes is distributed unevenly across the tongue. Taste preferences are largely learned and are heavily influenced by one's cultural background.

◆ Like taste, smell is a chemical sense. Chemical stimuli activate olfactory receptors lining the nasal passages. Most of these receptors respond to more than one odor.

Our Sense of Touch: Sensory Systems in the Skin

◆ Sensory receptors in the skin respond to pressure, temperature, and pain. There are nerve fibers that respond specifically to warmth and cold. Pain signals are sent to the brain along two pathways that are characterized as fast and slow.

◆ The perception of pain is highly subjective and may be influenced by mood, attention, personality, and culture. Gate-control theory holds that incoming pain signals can be blocked in the spinal cord. Endorphins and a descending neural pathway appear responsible for the suppression of pain by the central nervous system.

Our Other Senses

◆ The kinesthetic system monitors the position of various body parts. The sense of balance depends primarily on activity in the vestibular system.

Putting It in Perspective

◆ This chapter underscored three of our unifying themes: the value of theoretical diversity, the subjective nature of human experience, and the influence of culture on behavior.

Application: Thinking About Art and Illusion

◆ The principles of visual perception are often applied to artistic endeavors. Painters routinely use pictorial depth cues to make their scenes more lifelike. Color mixing, feature analysis, Gestalt principles, reversible figures, and impossible figures have also been used in influential paintings.

Key Terms

Absolute threshold
Additive color mixing
Afterimage
Auditory localization
Basilar membrane
Binocular depth cues
Bottom-up processing
Cochlea
Color blindness
Complementary colors
Cones
Convergence
Dark adaptation
Depth perception
Distal stimuli
Farsightedness
Feature analysis
Feature detectors
Fechner's law
Fovea
Frequency theory
Gate-control theory
Gustatory system
Impossible figures
Just noticeable difference (JND)
Kinesthetic system
Lateral antagonism
Lens
Light adaptation
Monocular depth cues
Motion
Nearsig
Olfacto
Oppon theor vision
Optic c
Optic d
Optical
Percept
Perceptual constancy
Perceptual hypothesis
Perceptual set
Phi phenomenon
Pictorial depth cues
Place theory
Proximal stimuli
Psychophysics
Pupil
Receptive field of a visual cell
Retina
Retinal disparity
Reversible figure
Rods
Sensation
Sensory adaptation
Signal-detection theory
Subjective contours
Subliminal perception
Subtractive color mixing
Threshold
Top-down processing
Trichromatic theory of color vision
Vestibular system
Volley principle
Weber's law

Key People

Linda Bartoshuk

174 CHAPTER FOUR

Chapter Reviews

A Chapter Review at the end of each chapter provides a concise summary of the chapter's key ideas, a list of key terms, and a list of key people (important theorists and researchers). It's wise to read over these review materials to make sure you've digested the information in the chapter.

Practice Tests

Each chapter ends with a 15-item multiple-choice Practice Test that should give you a realistic assessment of your mastery of the chapter and valuable test-taking practice. The answers to the questions can be found at the bottom of the page, along with the numbers of the pages on which the relevant information was covered.

Practice Test

1. In psychophysical research, the absolute threshold has been arbitrarily defined as:
   A. the stimulus intensity that can be detected 100% of the time.
   B. the stimulus intensity that can be detected 50% of the time.
   C. the minimum amount of difference in intensity needed to tell two stimuli apart.
   D. a constant proportion of the size of the initial stimulus.
2. A tone-deaf person would probably not be able to tell two musical notes apart unless they were very different. We could say that this person has a relatively large:
   A. just noticeable difference.
   B. relative threshold.
   C. absolute threshold.
   D. detection threshold.
3. In their study of the influence of subliminal perception on attitudes, Krosnick and his colleagues (1992) found:
   A. absolutely no evidence of such influence.
   B. overwhelming evidence that subliminal stimuli can and do influence subjects' attitudes.
   C. that subliminal stimuli may condition positive, but not negative, attitudes.
   D. small but measureable effects in both the positive and negative direction.
4. In farsightedness:
   A. close objects are seen clearly but distant objects appear blurry.
   B. the focus of light from close objects falls behind the retina.
   C. the focus of light from distant objects falls a little short of the retina.
   D. a and b.
   E. a and c.
5. The collection of rod and cone receptors that funnel signals to a particular visual cell in the retina make up that cell's:
   A. blind spot.
   B. optic disk.
   C. opponent process field.
   D. receptive field.
6. Lateral antagonism occurs when:
   A. you turn your head to one side to maximize visual acuity in the dark.
   B. the cones adapt to dark more quickly than the rods.
   C. the cones battle with nearby rods for control of vision.
   D. neural activity in a retinal cell inhibits activity in surrounding cells.
7. Which theory would predict that the American flag would have a green, black, and yellow afterimage?
   A. subtractive color mixing
   B. opponent process theory
   C. additive color mixing
   D. trichromatic theory
8. Treisman (1986) proposes that the preattentive stage of object perception involves ________ processing, and the subsequent focused-attention stage involves ________ processing.
   A. top-down; bottom-up
   B. top-down; top-down
   C. bottom-up; bottom-up
   D. bottom-up; top-down
9. In a painting, train tracks may look as if they go off into the distance because the artist draws the tracks as converging lines, a monocular cue to depth known as:
   A. interposition.
   B. texture gradient.
   C. relative size.
   D. linear perspective.
10. Which of the following statements is true?
    A. There is evidence of cultural variability in the perception of depth both in real, three-dimensional space and in two-dimensional pictures.
    B. There is no evidence of cultural variability in depth perception, either in real space or in two-dimensional pictures.
    C. While there is some evidence of cultural variability in perception of depth in two-dimensional pictures, there is little cultural variability in perception of depth in real space.
    D. While there is some evidence of cultural variability in perception of depth in three-dimensional space, there is little cultural variablity in perception of depth in two-dimensional pictures.
11. The facts that cultural groups with little exposure to roads are less susceptible to the Ponzo illusion and that those with less exposure to buildings are less susceptible to the Müller-Lyer illusion suggest that:
    A. not all cultures test perceptual hypotheses.
    B. people in technologically advanced cultures are more gullible.
    C. optical illusions can be experienced only by cultures that have been exposed to the concept of optical illusions.
    D. perceptual inferences can be shaped by experience.
12. Perception of pitch can best be explained by:
    A. place theory.
    B. frequency theory.
    C. both place theory and frequency theory.
    D. neither theory.
13. In what way(s) is the sense of taste like the sense of smell?
    A. There are four primary stimulus groups for both senses.
    B. Both systems are routed through the thalamus on the way to the cortex.
    C. The physical stimuli for both senses are chemical substances dissolved in fluid.
    D. All of the above.
    E. None of the above.
14. The fact that theories originally seen as being incompatible, such as the trichromatic and opponent process theories of color vision, are now seen as both being necessary to explain sensory processes illustrates:
    A. that psychology evolves in a sociohistorical context.
    B. the subjectivity of experience.
    C. the value of psychology's theoretical diversity.
    D. the nature-nurture controversy.
15. Which school of painting applied the theory of feature analysis to canvas by building figures out of simple features?
    A. Pointillism
    B. Impressionism
    C. Surrealism
    D. Cubism

Answers

1	B Page 124	6	D Page 134	11	D Page 154
2	A Page 125	7	B Pages 139–140	12	C Pages 158–159
3	D Page 128	8	D Page 143	13	C Page 162
4	B Pages 130–132	9	D Pages 148–149	14	C Page 167
5	D Page 134	10	C Pages 149–150	15	D Page 170

SENSATION AND PERCEPTION 175

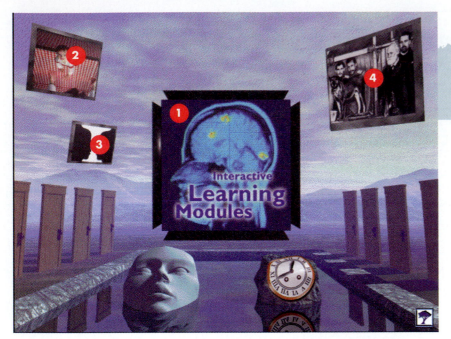

Visual Guide to *Psyk.trek*

This is the opening screen for *Psyk.trek.*

1 Rotate the navigation cube in the center of the screen to move among the major components of *Psyk.trek*, which are the Interactive Learning Modules, the Interactive Study Guide for *Psychology: Themes and Variations*, the Simulations, and the Multimedia Glossary. Clicking the face of the navigation cube takes you to the component shown.

2 Clicking this photo takes you to the Credits component of *Psyk.trek*.

3 If you click this photo, you will go to the Web Links component of *Psyk.trek*.

4 Clicking this photo takes you to the Main Menu for the Guided Tour.

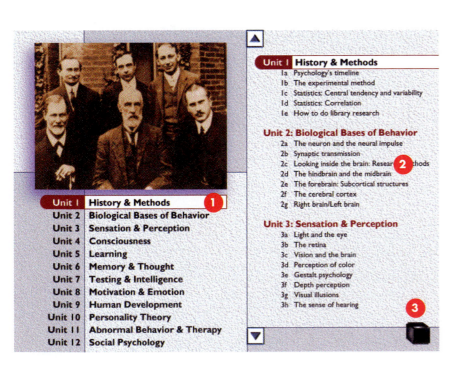

This is the Selector Menu for the Interactive Learning Modules, the chief teaching and learning component in *Psyk.trek*.

1 The modules are organized into the 12 topical units listed here. Click the items in this list to select a specific unit.

2 Clicking an item in this list takes you to a specific module.

3 Click the small cube to return to the opening screen and the navigation cube.

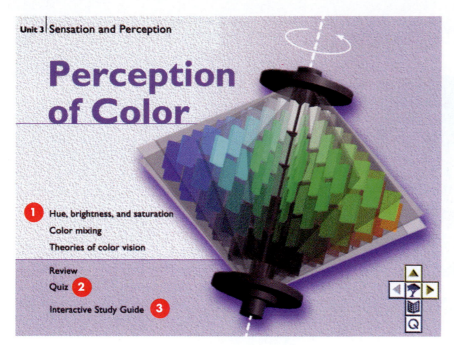

Unit 3 | Sensation and Perception

Perception of Color

1 Hue, brightness, and saturation

Color mixing

Theories of color vision

Review

Quiz **2**

Interactive Study Guide **3**

This is the Title Screen for Interactive Learning Module 3d.

1 Each module's Title Screen provides an outline of the module's contents. You can go directly to a specific part of the module by clicking that entry in the outline.

2 Each module ends with a thorough review of the concepts covered and an interactive quiz.

3 Each Title Screen also includes a button that will take you to the appropriate chapter in the Interactive Study Guide for *Psychology: Themes and Variations.*

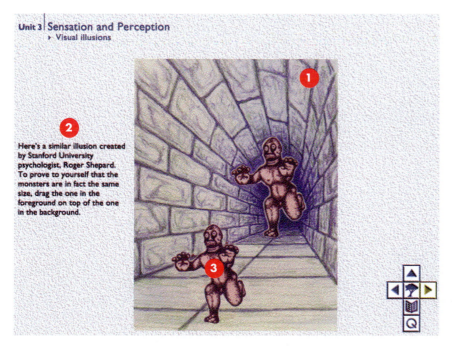

Unit 3 | Sensation and Perception
▸ Visual illusions

2 Here's a similar illusion created by Stanford University psychologist, Roger Shepard. To prove to yourself that the monsters are in fact the same size, drag the one in the foreground on top of the one in the background.

This is a screen from the interior of Module 3g.

1 Each module is fully narrated, so you can focus your attention on the photos, diagrams, figures, and animations that unfold onscreen.

2 You can also choose to have the text of the narration appear onscreen, so that you can take as much time as you like to review what was said.

3 The electronic environment of *Psyk.trek* provides many opportunities for interactivity and fun that cannot be found in any textbook. If you don't believe these monsters are the same size, try dropping one on the other in *Psyk.trek.*

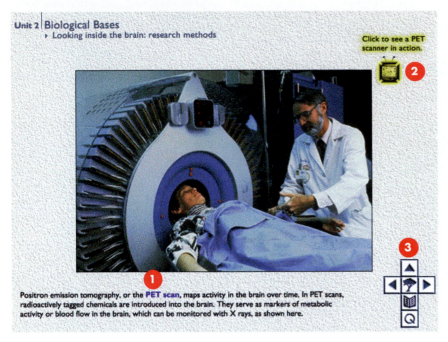

Click to see a PET scanner in action.

2

3

1

Positron emission tomography, or the **PET scan**, maps activity in the brain over time. In PET scans, radioactively tagged chemicals are introduced into the brain. They serve as markers of metabolic activity or blood flow in the brain, which can be monitored with X rays, as shown here.

This is a screen from the interior of Module 2c.

1 When glossary terms are first introduced in the text of the narration, they are shown in blue. If you click a blue glossary term, its definition will appear.

2 If there is a video relevant to a specific screen, a video icon will migrate onscreen. If you roll the cursor over the video icon, you will see a short description of the video. Clicking the icon brings up the video.

3 You move about in *Psyk.trek* by using the navigation buttons found in the lower-right corner of each screen. The Guided Tour in *Psyk.trek* explains exaxtly what each button does.

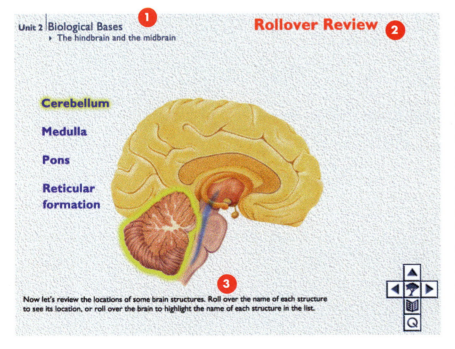

1

Rollover Review **2**

Cerebellum

Medulla

Pons

Reticular formation

3

Now let's review the locations of some brain structures. Roll over the name of each structure to see its location, or roll over the brain to highlight the name of each structure in the list.

This is a screen from the Review section of Module 2g.

1 Throughout each Interactive Learning Module, a header in the upper left corner indicates your current location. It shows the specific unit and module that you are working in.

2 Some modules include Rollover Reviews like this one, that allow you to explore important diagrams and figures in unique interactive ways.

3 Each module includes a Review section that provides a brief recap of the main ideas introduced in the module.

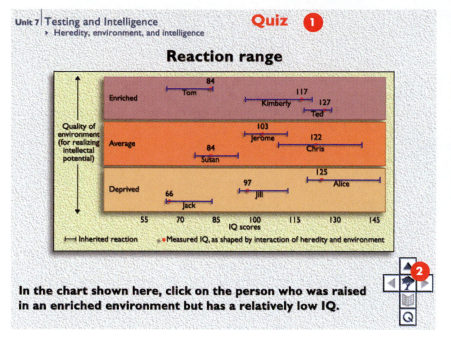

This is a screen from the Quiz at the end of Module 7d.

1 Each module ends with a highly visual Quiz that permits you to evaluate your understanding of *Psyk.trek's* rich teaching graphics.

2 *Psyk.trek* can provide you with a printed copy of your Quiz results, which will include your name if you have used the log in option on the Preferences Menu.

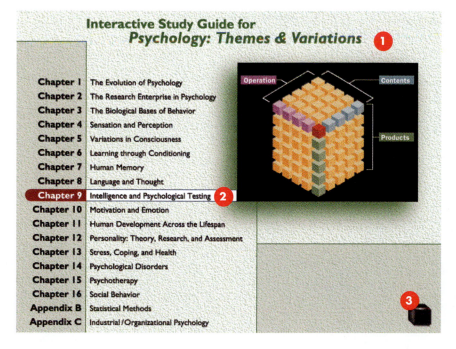

This is the Selector Menu for the Interactive Study Guide for *Psychology: Themes and Variations*.

1 The Interactive Study Guide is tied precisely to the 16 chapters of your text.

2 You can click an item in this list to review the material covered in a specific chapter or appendix in *Psychology: Themes and Variations*.

3 Click the small cube to return to *Psyk.trek's* opening screen and the navigation cube.

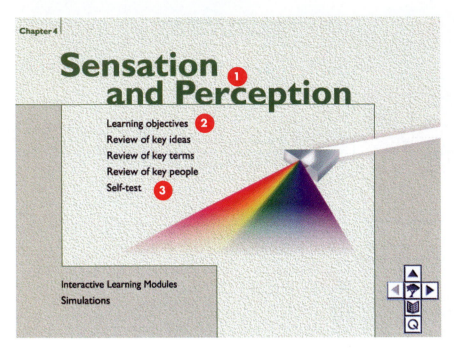

This is the Title Screen for Chapter 4 in the Interactive Study Guide for *Psychology: Themes and Variations.*

1 The Title Screen lists the various types of review exercises available. You can go directly to a specific type of review exercise by clicking that entry in the list.

2 Each chapter begins with a list of learning objectives. Clicking a specific learning objective will take you to that objective in the Review of Key Ideas.

3 The Self-Test for each chapter consists of 15 multiple-choice questions randomly drawn from a pool of 30 questions. Thus, you can retest yourself repeatedly on a chapter until you reach a certain level of mastery. You can also print your test results and a list of learning objectives for the items you missed.

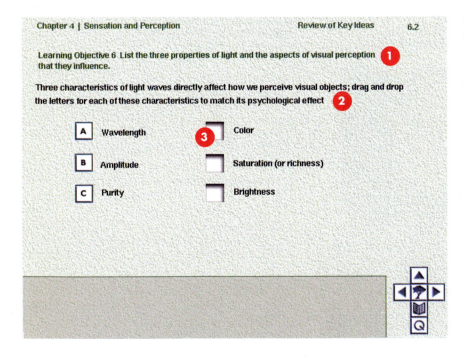

This screen is from the Chapter 4 Review of Key Ideas.

1 The Review of Key Ideas is organized around the learning objectives for the chapter.

2 Each Review of Key Ideas is a detailed, chronological, interactive review of the principal points made in that chapter.

3 Each response is followed by immediate auditory feedback that indicates whether it is correct or incorrect.

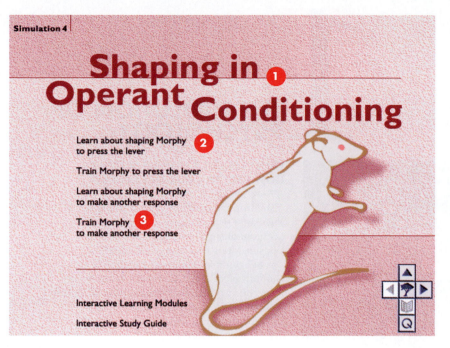

This is the Title Screen for one of the simulations in *Psyk.trek.*

1 The simulations in Psyk.trek are highly interactive demonstrations that allow you to experience psychological phenomena first-hand and to see research methods in action.

2 You can go directly to a particular part of a simulation by clicking that entry in the outline.

3 The simulations provide opportunities for active learning that cannot be matched by a textbook, and many of them are great fun.

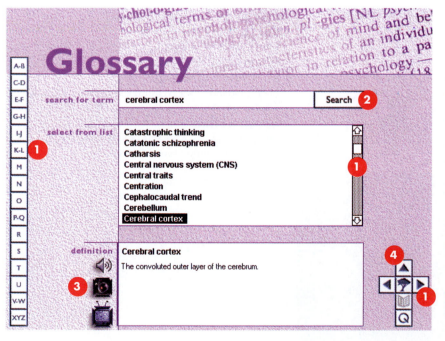

This is a screen from the Multimedia Glossary.

1 You can move through the alphabet by clicking the letters on the left, the scrollbar, or the navigation buttons.

2 You can also search for a specific term by typing in the term and clicking the Search button.

3 Many of the terms will bring up one or more of these three icons, which permit you to hear the pronunciation of the term, see a pertinent graphic, or view a pertinent video clip, respectively.

4 This button takes you back to your previous location before you entered the Multimedia Glossary.

What is psychology? Your initial answer to this question is likely to bear little resemblance to the picture of psychology that will emerge as you work your way through this book. I know that when I ambled into my introductory psychology course about 20 years ago, I had no idea what psychology involved. I was a pre-law/political science major fulfilling a general education requirement with what I thought would be my one and only psychology course. I encountered two things I didn't expect. The first was to learn that psychology is about a great many things besides abnormal behavior and ways to win friends and influence people. I was surprised to discover that psychology is also about how people are able to perceive color, how hunger is regulated by the brain, whether chimpanzees can use language to communicate, and a multitude of other topics I'd never thought to wonder about. The second thing I didn't expect was that I would be so completely seduced by the subject. Before long I changed majors and embarked on a career in psychology—a decision I have never regretted.

Why has psychology continued to fascinate me? One reason is that *psychology is practical*. It offers a vast store of information about issues that concern everyone. These issues range from broad social questions, such as how to reduce the incidence of mental illness, to highly personal questions, such as how to improve your self-control. In a sense, psychology is about you and me. It's about life in our modern world. The practical side of psychology will be apparent throughout this text, especially in the end-of-chapter Applications. The Applications focus on everyday problems, such as coping more effectively with stress, improving memory, enhancing performance in school, and dealing with sleep difficulties.

Another element of psychology's appeal for me is that it represents a *way of thinking*. We are all exposed to claims about psychological issues. For instance, we hear assertions that men and women have different abilities or that violence on television has a harmful effect on children. As a science, psychology demands that researchers ask precise questions about such issues and that they test their ideas through systematic observation. Psychology's commitment to testing ideas encourages a healthy brand of critical thinking. In the long run, this means that psychology provides a way of building knowledge that is relatively accurate and dependable.

Of course, psychological research cannot discover an answer for every interesting question about the mind and behavior. You won't find the meaning of life or the secret of happiness in this text. But you *will* find an approach to investigating questions that has proven to be fruitful. The more you learn about psychology as a way of thinking, the better able you will be to evaluate the psychological assertions you encounter in daily life.

There is still another reason for my fascination with psychology. As you proceed through this text, you will find that psychologists study an enormous diversity of subjects, from acrophobia (fear of heights) to zoophobia (fear of animals), from problem solving in apes to the symbolic language of dreams. Psychologists look at all the seasons of human life, from development in the womb to the emotional stages that people go through in the process of dying. Psychologists study observable behaviors such as eating, fighting, and mating. But they also dig beneath the surface to investigate how hormones affect emotions and how the brain registers pain. They probe the behavior of any number of species, from humans to house cats, from monkeys to moths. This rich diversity is, for me, perhaps psychology's most appealing aspect.

Mental illness, rats running in mazes, the physiology of hunger, the mysteries of love, creativity, and prejudice—what ties all these subjects together in a single discipline? How did psychology come to be such a diverse field of study? Why is it so different from what most people expect? If psychology is a social science, why do psychologists study subjects such as brain chemistry and the physiological basis of vision? To answer these questions, we begin our introduction to psychology by retracing its development. By seeing how psychology grew and changed, you will discover why it has the shape it does today.

After our journey into psychology's past, we will examine a formal definition of psychology. We'll also look at psychology as it is today—a sprawling, multifaceted science and profession. To help keep psychology's diversity in perspective, the chapter concludes with a discussion of seven unifying themes that will serve as connecting threads in

Modern psychology ranges widely in its investigations. It can, for example, focus on gender and sexual identity—as dramatized by this "Katoey," or transvestite carberet performer in Thailand. Or psychology can look at people in their work and play environments, such as these individuals at Snowbird Lodge in Utah.

the chapters to come. Finally, in the chapter's Application, we'll return to psychology's practical side, as we review research that gives insights on how to be an effective student.

FROM SPECULATION TO SCIENCE: HOW PSYCHOLOGY DEVELOPED

Psychology's story is one of people groping toward a better understanding of themselves. As psychology has evolved, its focus, methods, and explanatory models have changed. In this section we'll look at how psychology has developed from philosophical speculations about the mind into a modern behavioral science. A pictorial overview of the highlights of psychology's history can be found on pages 18–19.

The term *psychology* comes from two Greek words, *psyche,* meaning the soul, and *logos,* referring to the study of a subject. These two Greek roots were first put together to define a topic of study in the 16th century, when *psyche* was used to refer to the soul, spirit, or mind, as distinguished from the body (Boring, 1966). Not until the early 18th century did the term *psychology* gain more than rare usage among scholars. By that time it had acquired its literal meaning, "the study of the mind."

Of course, people have always wondered about the mysteries of the mind. In that sense, psychology is as old as the human race. But it was only a little over a hundred years ago that psychology emerged as a scientific discipline.

A New Science Is Born: The Contributions of Wundt and Hall 1a

Psychology's intellectual parents were the disciplines of *philosophy* and *physiology*. By the 1870s a small number of scholars in both fields were actively exploring questions about the mind. How are bodily sensations turned into a mental awareness of the outside world? Are people's perceptions of the world accurate reflections of reality? How do mind and body interact? The philosophers and physiologists who were interested in the mind viewed such questions as fascinating issues *within* their respective fields. It was a German professor, Wilhelm Wundt (1832–1920), who eventually changed this view. Wundt mounted a campaign to make psychology an independent discipline rather than a stepchild of philosophy or physiology.

The time and place were right for Wundt's appeal. German universities were in a healthy period of expansion, so resources were available for new disciplines. Furthermore, the intellectual climate favored the scientific approach that Wundt advocated. Hence, his proposals were well received by the academic community. In 1879 Wundt succeeded in establishing the first formal laboratory for research in psychology at the University of Leipzig. In deference to this landmark event, historians have christened 1879 psychology's "date of birth." Soon afterward, in 1881, Wundt established the first journal devoted to publishing research on psychology. All in all, Wundt's campaign was so successful that today he is widely characterized as the founder of psychology. As Thomas Leahey (1987) puts it, "Wundt is the founder because he wedded physiology to philosophy and made the resulting offspring independent. He brought the empirical methods of physiology to the questions of philosophy" (p. 182).

Wundt's conception of psychology dominated the field for two decades and was influential for several more. Borrowing from his training in physiology, Wundt (1874) declared that the new psychology should be a science modeled after fields such as physics and chemistry. What was the subject matter of the new science? According to Wundt, it was *consciousness*—the awareness of immediate experience. *Thus, psychology became the scientific study of conscious experience.* This orientation kept psychology focused squarely on the mind. But it demanded that the methods used to investigate the mind be as scientific as those of chemists or physicists.

Wundt was a tireless, dedicated scholar who generated an estimated 54,000 pages of books and articles in his career (Bringmann & Balk, 1992). His hard work and provocative ideas soon attracted attention. Outstanding young scholars, including many Americans, came to Leipzig to study under Wundt and do research on vision, hearing, touch, taste, attention, and emotion. As Benjamin and colleagues (1992) note, "Wundt imbued his students with a scientific attitude that allowed them to frame questions in ways that created the science of mind that most of his predecessors proclaimed would never be possible" (p. 130).

Many of Wundt's students then fanned out across Germany and America, establishing the research laboratories that formed the basis for the new, independent science of psychology. Indeed, it was in North America that Wundt's new science grew by leaps and bounds. Between 1883 and 1893, some 24 new psychological research laboratories sprang up in the United States and Canada, at the schools shown in Figure 1.1 (Garvey, 1929). Many of the laboratories were started by Wundt's students, or by his students' students.

One of Wundt's students, G. Stanley Hall (1846–1924), was a particularly important contributor to the rapid growth of psychology in America. Toward the end of the 19th century, Hall reeled off a series of "firsts" for American psychology. To begin with, he established America's first research laboratory in psychology at Johns Hopkins University in 1883. Four years later he launched America's first psychology journal. Furthermore,

Physiology informs us about those life phenomena that we perceive by our external senses. In psychology, the person looks upon himself as from within and tries to explain the interrelations of those processes that this internal observation discloses.

WILHELM WUNDT
1832–1920

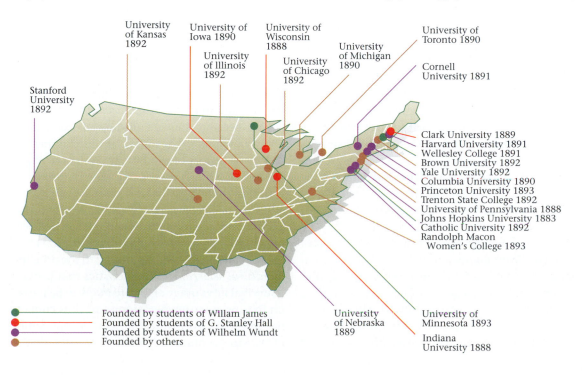

Figure 1.1
Early research laboratories in North America.
This map highlights the location and year of founding for the first 24 psychological research labs established in North American colleges and universities. As the color coding shows, a great many of these labs were founded by the students of Wilhelm Wundt, G. Stanley Hall (himself a student of Wundt), and William James. (Based on Garvey, 1929; Hilgard, 1987)

University of Kansas 1892
University of Iowa 1890
University of Wisconsin 1888
University of Illinois 1892
University of Chicago 1892
University of Michigan 1890
University of Toronto 1890
Cornell University 1891
Stanford University 1892

Clark University 1889
Harvard University 1891
Wellesley College 1891
Brown University 1892
Yale University 1892
Columbia University 1890
Princeton University 1893
Trenton State College 1892
University of Pennsylvania 1888
Johns Hopkins University 1883
Catholic University 1892
Randolph Macon Women's College 1893

Founded by students of William James
Founded by students of G. Stanley Hall
Founded by students of Wilhelm Wundt
Founded by others

University of Nebraska 1889
University of Minnesota 1893
Indiana University 1888

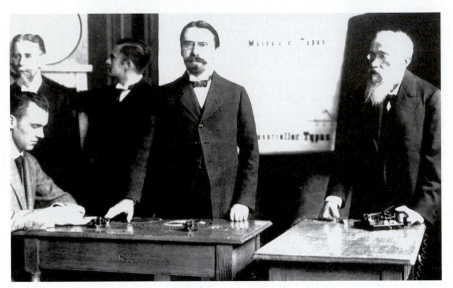

The establishment of the first research laboratory in psychology by Wilhelm Wundt (far right) marked the birth of psychology as a modern science.

in 1892 he was the driving force behind the establishment of the American Psychological Association (APA) and was elected its first president. Today the APA is the world's largest organization devoted to the advancement of psychology, with over 140,000 members and affiliates (Spielberger, 1990). Hall never envisioned such a vast membership when he and 26 others set up their new organization.

Exactly why Americans took to psychology so quickly is hard to say. Perhaps it was because America's relatively young universities were more open to new disciplines than were the older, more tradition-bound universities in Europe. In any case, although psychology was born in Germany, it blossomed into adolescence in America. Like many adolescents, however, the young science was about to enter a period of turbulence and turmoil.

The Battle of the "Schools" Begins: Structuralism Versus Functionalism 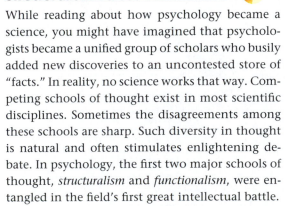 1a

While reading about how psychology became a science, you might have imagined that psychologists became a unified group of scholars who busily added new discoveries to an uncontested store of "facts." In reality, no science works that way. Competing schools of thought exist in most scientific disciplines. Sometimes the disagreements among these schools are sharp. Such diversity in thought is natural and often stimulates enlightening debate. In psychology, the first two major schools of thought, *structuralism* and *functionalism*, were entangled in the field's first great intellectual battle.

Structuralism emerged through the leadership of one of Wundt's students, Edward Titchener, an Englishman who emigrated to the United States in 1892. **Structuralism was based on the notion**

that the task of psychology is to analyze consciousness into its basic elements and investigate how these elements are related. Just as physicists were studying how matter is made up of basic particles, the structuralists wanted to identify and examine the fundamental components of conscious experience, such as sensations, feelings, and images.

Although the structuralists explored many questions, most of their work concerned sensation and perception in vision, hearing, and touch. To examine the contents of consciousness, the structuralists depended on the method of **introspection, or the careful, systematic self-observation of one's own conscious experience.** As practiced by the structuralists, introspection required training to make the subject—the person being studied—more objective and more aware. Once trained, subjects were typically exposed to auditory tones, optical illusions, and visual stimuli under carefully controlled and systematically varied conditions and were asked to analyze what they experienced.

The functionalists took a different view of psychology's task. **Functionalism was based on the belief that psychology should investigate the function or purpose of consciousness, rather than its structure.** The chief architect of functionalism was William James (1842–1910), a brilliant American scholar (and brother of novelist Henry James). James's formal training was in medicine. However, he did not find medicine to be very challenging intellectually, and he felt he was too sickly to pursue a medical practice (Ross, 1991). Hence, when an opportunity arose in 1872, he joined the faculty of Harvard University to pursue a less arduous career in academia. Medicine's loss proved to be a great boon for psychology, as James quickly became an intellectual giant in the field. James's landmark book, *Principles of Psychology* (1890), became standard reading for generations of psychologists and is perhaps the most influential text in the history of psychology (Weiten & Wight, 1992).

James's thinking illustrates how psychology, like any field, is deeply embedded in a network of cultural and intellectual influences. James had been impressed with Charles Darwin's (1859, 1871) concept of *natural selection*. According to the principle **of natural selection, characteristics that provide a survival advantage are more likely to be passed on to subsequent generations and thus come to be "selected" over time.** This cornerstone notion of Darwin's evolutionary theory suggested that all characteristics of a species must serve some purpose. Applying this idea to humans, James (1890) noted that consciousness obviously is an important characteristic of our species. Hence, he contended that psychology should investigate the *functions* rather than the *structure* of consciousness.

James also argued that the structuralists' approach missed the real nature of conscious experience. Consciousness, he argued, consists of a continuous *flow* of thoughts. In analyzing consciousness into its "elements," the structuralists were looking at static points in that flow. James wanted to understand the flow itself, which he called the "stream of consciousness."

Whereas structuralists naturally gravitated to the laboratory, functionalists were more interested in how people adapt their behavior to the demands of the real world around them. This practical slant led them to introduce new subjects into psychology. Instead of focusing on sensation and perception, functionalists such as James McKeen Cattell and John Dewey began to investigate mental testing, patterns of development in children, the effectiveness of educational practices, and behavioral differences between the sexes. These new topics may have played a role in attracting the first women into the field of psychology (see Figure 1.2).

The impassioned advocates of structuralism and functionalism saw themselves as fighting for high stakes: the definition and future direction of the new science of psychology. Their war of ideas continued energetically for many years. Who won? Neither camp scored a decisive victory, and in time the influence of both began to fade as new schools of thought entered the fray.

For their part, the structuralists eventually ran into difficulties with their method of introspection. They had hoped to discover the universal elements of conscious experience. However, because consciousness is highly personal and subjective, even well-trained introspectionists yielded inconsistent results when presented with the same experience. This inconsistency thwarted the structuralists' efforts to find the basic particles of consciousness (Hearst, 1979).

On balance, functionalism left a more enduring imprint on psychology. Indeed, Buxton (1985) has remarked that "nowadays no one is called a functionalist in psychology, and yet almost every psychologist is one" (p. 138). Although functionalism faded as a school of thought, its practical

It is just this free water of consciousness that psychologists resolutely overlook.

WILLIAM JAMES
1842–1910

Mary Whiton Calkins
(1863–1930)

Mary Calkins, who studied under William James, founded one of the first dozen psychology laboratories in America at Wellesley College in 1891, invented a widely used technique for studying memory, and became the first woman to serve as president of the American Psychological Association in 1905. Ironically, however, she never received her Ph.D. in psychology. Because she was a woman, Harvard University only reluctantly allowed her to take graduate classes as a "guest student." When she completed the requirements for her Ph.D., Harvard would only offer her a doctorate from its undergraduate sister school, Radcliffe. Calkins felt that this decision perpetuated unequal treatment of the sexes, so she refused the Radcliffe degree.

Margaret Floy Washburn
(1871–1939)

Margaret Washburn was the first woman to receive a Ph.D. in psychology. She wrote an influential book, *The Animal Mind* (1908), which served as an impetus to the subsequent emergence of behaviorism and was standard reading for several generations of psychologists. In 1921 she became the second woman to serve as president of the American Psychological Association. Washburn studied under James McKeen Cattell at Columbia University, but like Mary Calkins, she was only permitted to take graduate classes unofficially, as a "hearer." Hence, she transferred to Cornell University, which was more hospitable toward women, and completed her doctorate in 1894. Like Calkins, Washburn spent most of her career at a college for women (Vassar).

Leta Stetter Hollingworth
(1886–1939)

Leta Hollingworth did pioneering work on adolescent development, mental retardation, and gifted children. Indeed, she was the first person to use the term *gifted* to refer to youngsters who scored exceptionally high on intelligence tests. Hollingworth (1914, 1916) also played a major role in debunking popular theories of her era that purported to explain why women were "inferior" to men. For instance, she conducted a study refuting the myth that phases of the menstrual cycle are reliably associated with performance decrements in women. Her careful collection of objective data on gender differences forced other scientists to subject popular, untested beliefs about the sexes to skeptical, empirical inquiry.

Figure 1.2
Women pioneers in the history of psychology. Women have long made major contributions to the development of psychology (Russo & Denmark, 1987), and today roughly one-third of all psychologists are female. As in other fields, however, women have often been overlooked in histories of psychology (Furumoto & Scarborough, 1986). The three psychologists profiled here demonstrate that women have been making significant contributions to psychology almost from its beginning—despite formidable barriers to pursuing their academic careers.

orientation fostered the development of two descendants that have dominated modern psychology: applied psychology and behaviorism.

Watson Alters Psychology's Course as Behaviorism Makes Its Debut

 1a, 5b

The debate between structuralism and functionalism was only the prelude to other fundamental controversies in psychology. In the early 1900s, another major school of thought appeared that dramatically altered the course of psychology. Founded by John B. Watson (1878–1958), **behaviorism is a theoretical orientation based on the premise that scientific psychology should study only observable behavior.** It is important to understand what a radical change this definition represents. Watson (1913, 1919) was proposing that psychologists *abandon the study of consciousness altogether* and focus exclusively on behaviors that they could observe directly. In essence, he was redefining what scientific psychology should be about.

Why did Watson argue for such a fundamental shift in direction? Because to him, the power of the scientific method rested on the idea of *verifiability*. In principle, scientific claims can always be verified (or disproved) by anyone who is able and willing to make the required observations. However, this power depends on studying things that can be observed objectively. Otherwise, the advantage of using the scientific approach—replacing vague speculation and personal opinion with reliable, exact knowledge—is lost. For Watson, mental processes were not a proper subject for scientific study because they are ultimately private events. After all, no one can see or touch another's thoughts. Consequently, if psychology was to be a science, it would have to give up consciousness as its subject matter and become instead the *science of behavior*.

Behavior refers to any overt (observable) response or activity by an organism. Watson asserted that psychologists could study anything that people do or say—shopping, playing chess, eating, complimenting a friend—but they could *not* study scientifically the thoughts, wishes, and feelings that might accompany these observable behaviors.

Watson's radical reorientation of psychology did not end with his redefinition of its subject matter. He also staked out a rather extreme position on one of psychology's oldest and most fundamental questions: the issue of *nature versus nurture*. This age-old debate is concerned with whether behavior is determined mainly by genetic inheritance ("nature") or by environment and experience ("nurture"). To oversimplify, the question is this: Is a great concert pianist or a master criminal born, or made? Watson argued that each is made, not born. In other words, he downplayed the importance of heredity, maintaining that behavior is governed primarily by the environment. Indeed, he boldly claimed:

Give me a dozen healthy infants, well-formed, and my own special world to bring them up in and I'll guarantee to take any one at random and train him to become any type of specialist I might select—doctor, lawyer, artist, merchant-chief, and yes, even beggar-man and thief, regardless of his talents, penchants, tendencies, abilities, vocations and race of his ancestors. I am going beyond my facts and I admit it, but so have the advocates of the contrary and they have been doing it for many thousands of years. (1924, p. 82)

For obvious reasons, Watson's tongue-in-cheek challenge was never put to a test. Although this widely cited quote overstated and oversimplified Watson's views on the nature-nurture issue (Todd & Morris, 1992), his writings contributed to the strong environmental slant that became associated with behaviorism (Horowitz, 1992).

The behaviorists eventually came to view psychology's mission as an attempt to relate overt behaviors ("responses") to observable events in the environment ("stimuli"). A **stimulus** is any detectable input from the environment. Stimuli can range from light and sound waves to such complex inputs as the words on this page, advertisements on TV, or sarcastic remarks from a friend. Because the behaviorists investigated stimulus-response relationships, the behavioral approach is often referred to as *stimulus-response (S-R) psychology*.

Although it met resistance and skepticism in some quarters, Watson's behavioral point of view gradually took hold (Samelson, 1981). Actually, psychology had already been edging away imperceptibly from the study of consciousness toward the study of behavior for two decades before Watson's influential manifesto (Leahey, 1992). The gradual emergence of behaviorism was partly attributable to an important discovery made in 1904 by Ivan Pavlov, a Russian physiologist. As you'll learn in Chapter 6, Pavlov (1906) showed that dogs could be trained to salivate in response to the auditory stimulus such as a tone. This deceptively simple demonstration provided insight into how stimulus-response bonds are formed.

The time seems to have come when psychology must discard all references to consciousness.

JOHN B. WATSON
1878–1958

Such bonds were exactly what behaviorists wanted to investigate, so Pavlov's discovery paved the way for their work.

Behaviorism's stimulus-response approach contributed to the rise of animal research in psychology. Having deleted consciousness from their scope of concern, behaviorists no longer needed to study human subjects who could report on their mental processes. Many psychologists thought that animals would make better research subjects anyway. One key reason was that experimental research is often more productive if experimenters can exert considerable *control* over their subjects. Otherwise, too many complicating factors enter into the picture and contaminate the experiment. Obviously, a researcher can exert much more control over a laboratory rat or pigeon than over a human subject, who arrives at a lab with years of uncontrolled experience and who will probably insist on going home at night. Thus, the discipline that had begun its life a few decades earlier as the study of the mind now found itself heavily involved in the study of simple responses made by laboratory animals.

Ironically, although Watson's views shaped the evolution of psychology for many decades, he ended up watching the field's progress from the sidelines. After a heavily publicized divorce scandal in 1920, Watson was forced to resign from Johns Hopkins University. He left academia at the age of 42, never to return. Psychology's loss proved to be the business world's gain, as Watson went on to become an important pioneer in advertising (Brewer, 1991).

Although Watson's ideas proved very influential, they did not go unchallenged. One source of opposition was a school of thought called *Gestalt psychology,* which emerged at about the same time as Watson's behaviorism.

Recap of Key Points

- Psychology's intellectual parents were 19th-century philosophy and physiology, which shared an interest in the mysteries of the mind.
- Psychology became an independent discipline when Wilhelm Wundt established the first psychological research laboratory in 1879 at Leipzig, Germany. He defined psychology as the scientific study of consciousness.
- The new discipline grew rapidly in North America in the late 19th century, as illustrated by G. Stanley Hall's career. Hall established America's first research lab in psychology and founded the American Psychological Association.
- The structuralists, led by Edward Titchener, believed that psychology should use introspection to analyze consciousness into its basic elements.
- Functionalists, such as William James, believed that psychology should focus on the purpose and adaptive functions of consciousness. Functionalism paved the way for behaviorism and applied psychology.
- Behaviorists, led by John B. Watson, argued that psychology should study only observable behavior. Thus, they campaigned to redefine psychology as the science of behavior.
- Emphasizing the importance of the environment over heredity, the behaviorists began to explore stimulus-response relationships, often using laboratory animals as subjects.

CONCEPT CHECK 1.1

Understanding the Implications of Major Theories: Wundt, James, and Watson

Check your understanding of the implications of some of the major theories reviewed in this chapter by indicating who is likely to have made each of the statements quoted below. Choose from the following theorists: (a) Wilhelm Wundt, (b) William James, and (c) John B. Watson. You'll find the answers in Appendix A in the back of the book.

_____ 1. "Our conclusion is that we have no real evidence of the inheritance of traits. I would feel perfectly confident in the ultimately favorable outcome of careful upbringing of a healthy, well-formed baby born of a long line of crooks, murderers and thieves, and prostitutes."

_____ 2. "The book which I present to the public is an attempt to mark out a new domain of science. . . . The new discipline rests upon anatomical and physiological foundations. . . . The experimental treatment of psychological problems must be pronounced from every point of view to be in its first beginnings."

_____ 3. "Consciousness, then, does not appear to itself chopped up in bits. Such words as 'chain' or 'train' do not describe it fitly. . . . It is nothing jointed; it flows. A 'river' or 'stream' are the metaphors by which it is most naturally described."

Gestalt Psychology Challenges Behaviorism 1a, 3e

Founded by Max Wertheimer (1880–1943), Gestalt psychology surfaced as a theoretical school in Germany early in the 20th century. **Gestalt psychology was based on the belief that the whole is greater than the sum of its parts** (*Gestalt* is German for "form" or "shape"). An example of this fundamental principle is provided by the *phi phenomenon,* first described by Wertheimer (1912). **The *phi phenomenon* is the illusion of movement created by presenting visual stimuli in rapid succession.** For example, movies and TV consist of separate still pictures projected rapidly one after the other. Although we *see* smooth motion, in reality the "moving" objects merely take a slightly different position in successive frames. The same principle is illustrated by electric signs, such as those on movie marquees or at road construction sites (see the photo below). The bulbs' going on and off in turn, with the appropriate timing, gives the impression of motion. Of course, nothing in the sign really moves. The elements (the bulbs) are stationary. Working as a whole, however, they have a property (motion) that isn't evident in any of the parts. Some of the other perceptual phenomena identified by the Gestalt psychologists are described in Chapter 4.

Gestalt psychology's emergence in 1912 was in part a reaction against structuralism, an influential school of thought in Germany at the time. Obviously, the structuralists' interest in breaking conscious experience into its component parts seemed ill-advised in light of the Gestalt theorists' demonstration that the whole can be much greater than the sum of its parts. Nazi persecutions in Germany eventually forced the leading Gestalt theorists—

Wertheimer, Kurt Koffka, and Wolfgang Köhler—to move to the United States, where they attacked the theoretical edifice of behaviorism. They took issue with the behaviorists on two counts. First, they saw the behaviorists' attempt to analyze behavior into stimulus-response bonds as another ill-fated effort to carve the whole into its parts. Second, they felt that psychology should continue to study conscious experience rather than shift its focus to observable behavior.

Like structuralism and functionalism (to which it is compared in Table 1.1), Gestalt psychology had a limited life span. At its peak, it was an active combatant in psychology's theoretical wars and was responsible for some major advances in the study of perception, problem solving, and social behavior. However, after its relocation in North America, the Gestalt movement was unable to attract a large second generation of loyalists (Ash, 1985). Thus, it gradually faded as an important school of thought. However, the Gestalt school left its mark on the field, as it contributed to the eventual emergence of two contemporary theoretical perspectives in psychology: humanism and cognitive psychology. We'll discuss these perspectives later, after we look at the highly influential ideas of Sigmund Freud and B. F. Skinner.

Freud Brings the Unconscious into the Picture 1a, 10a

Sigmund Freud (1856–1939) was an Austrian physician who early in his career dreamed of achieving fame by making an important discovery. His determination was such that in medical school he dissected 400 male eels to prove for the first time that they had testes. His work with eels did not make him famous, but his subsequent work with people did. Indeed, his theories made him one of the most controversial intellectual figures of modern times.

Freud's (1900, 1933) approach to psychology grew out of his efforts to treat mental disorders. In his medical practice, Freud treated people troubled by psychological problems such as irrational fears, obsessions, and anxieties with an innovative procedure he called *psychoanalysis* (described in detail in Chapter 15). Decades of experience probing into his patients' lives provided much of the inspiration for Freud's theory. He also gathered material by looking inward and examining his own anxieties, conflicts, and desires.

His work with patients and his own self-exploration persuaded Freud of the existence of what he called the unconscious. According to Freud, **the**

The illusion of movement in a highway construction sign is an instance of the phi phenomenon, which is also at work in motion pictures and television. The phenomenon illustrates the Gestalt principle that the whole can have properties that are not found in any of its parts.

CHAPTER ONE

Perspective and Its Influential Period	Principal Contributors	Subject Matter	Basic Premise
Structuralism (1875–1930s)	Wilhelm Wundt Edward Titchener	Structure of consciousness	The content of conscious experience can be analyzed into its basic elements.
Functionalism (1890–1930s)	William James G. Stanley Hall James McKeen Cattell	Functions of consciousness	The adaptive purposes of conscious experience are more important than its structure.
Gestalt psychology (1912–1940s)	Max Wertheimer Kurt Koffka Wolfgang Köhler	Organization of consciousness	Conscious experiences and perceptions are more than the sum of their parts.

unconscious **contains thoughts, memories, and desires that are well below the surface of conscious awareness but that nonetheless exert great influence on behavior.** Freud based his concept of the unconscious on a variety of observations. For instance, he noticed that seemingly meaningless slips of the tongue (such as "I decided to take a summer school curse") often appeared to reveal a person's true feelings. He also noted that his patients' dreams often seemed to express important feelings that they were unaware of. Knitting these and other observations together, Freud eventually concluded that psychological disturbances are largely caused by personal conflicts existing at an unconscious level. More generally, his ***psychoanalytic theory* attempts to explain personality, motivation, and mental disorders by focusing on unconscious determinants of behavior.**

Freud's concept of the unconscious was not entirely new (it was anticipated by a few earlier theorists). However, it was a major departure from the prevailing belief that people are fully aware of the forces affecting their behavior. In arguing that behavior is governed by unconscious forces, Freud made the disconcerting suggestion that people are not masters of their own minds. Other aspects of Freud's theory also stirred up debate. For instance, he proposed that behavior is greatly influenced by how people cope with their sexual urges. At a time when people were far less comfortable discussing sexual issues than they are today, even scientists were offended and scandalized by Freud's emphasis on sex. Small wonder, then, that Freud was soon engulfed in controversy.

In part because of its controversial nature, Freud's theory gained influence only very slowly. However, he gradually won acceptance within medicine, attracting prominent followers such as Carl Jung and Alfred Adler. Important public recognition from psychology came in 1909, when G. Stanley Hall invited Freud to give a series of lectures at Clark University in Massachusetts (see the photo on page 10).

By 1920 psychoanalytic theory was widely known around the world, but it continued to meet with considerable resistance in psychology. Why? The main reason was that it conflicted with the spirit of the times in psychology. Many psychologists were becoming uncomfortable with their earlier focus on conscious experience and were turning to the less murky subject of observable behavior. If they felt that *conscious* experience was inaccessible to scientific observation, you can imagine how they felt about trying to study *unconscious* experience. Most psychologists contemptuously viewed psychoanalytic theory as unscientific speculation that would eventually fade away (Hornstein, 1992).

They turned out to be wrong. Psychoanalytic ideas steadily gained credence in the culture at large, influencing thought in medicine, the arts, and literature. According to Hornstein (1992), by the 1940s, "Psychoanalysis was becoming so popular that it threatened to eclipse psychology entirely" (p. 258). Thus, the widespread popular acceptance of psychoanalytic theory essentially forced psychologists to apply their scientific methods to the topics Freud had studied: personality, motivation, and abnormal behavior. As they turned to these topics, many of them saw merit in some of Freud's notions (Rosenzweig, 1985). Although psychoanalytic theory continued to generate heated debate, it survived to become an influential theoretical perspective. Today, many psychoanalytic concepts have filtered into the mainstream of psychology (Hillner, 1984).

The unconscious is the true psychical reality; in its innermost nature it is as much unknown to us as the reality of the external world.

SIGMUND FREUD
1856–1939

A portrait taken at the famous Clark University psychology conference, September 1909. Pictured are Freud, G. Stanley Hall, and four of Freud's students and associates. Seated, left to right: Freud, Hall, and Carl Jung; standing: Abraham Brill, Ernest Jones, and Sandor Ferenczi.

I submit that what we call the behavior of the human organisms is no more free than its digestion.

B. F. SKINNER
1904–1990

Skinner Questions Free Will as Behaviorism Flourishes 1a, 10b

While psychoanalytic thought was slowly gaining a foothold within psychology, the behaviorists were temporarily softening their stance on the acceptability of studying internal mental events. They were not about to go back to making conscious experience the focus of psychology. However, many did admit that stimulus-response connections are made by a living creature—an *organism*—that should not be ignored entirely. Under the leadership of Clark Hull, this modified behavioral approach still emphasized the study of observable behavior, but it permitted careful inferences to be drawn about an organism's internal states, such as drives, needs, and habits. For example, Hull (1943) argued that if an animal ate eagerly when offered food, it was not farfetched to infer the existence of an internal hunger drive.

This movement toward the consideration of internal states was dramatically reversed in the 1950s by the work of B. F. Skinner (1904–1990). Skinner set out to be a writer, but he gave up his dream after a few unproductive years. "I had," he wrote later, "nothing important to say" (1967, p. 395). However, he had many important things to say about psychology, and he went on to become one of the most influential of all American psychologists.

In response to the softening that had occurred in the behaviorist position, Skinner (1953) championed a return to Watson's strict focus on observable behavior. Skinner did not deny the existence of internal mental events. However, he insisted

that they could not be studied scientifically. Moreover, there was no need to study them. According to Skinner, if the stimulus of food is followed by the response of eating, we can fully describe what is happening without making any guesses about whether the animal is experiencing hunger. Like Watson, Skinner also emphasized how environmental factors mold behavior. Although he repeatedly acknowledged that an organism's behavior is influenced by its biological endowment, he argued that psychology could understand and predict behavior adequately without resorting to physiological explanations (Delprato & Midgley, 1992).

The fundamental principle of behavior documented by Skinner is deceptively simple: *Organisms tend to repeat responses that lead to positive outcomes, and they tend not to repeat responses that lead to neutral or negative outcomes.* Despite its simplicity, this principle turns out to be quite powerful. Working primarily with laboratory rats and pigeons, Skinner showed that he could exert remarkable control over the behavior of animals by manipulating the outcomes of their responses. He was even able to train animals to perform unnatural behaviors. For example, he once trained some pigeons to play Ping-Pong! Skinner's followers eventually showed that the principles uncovered in their animal research could be applied to complex human behaviors as well. Behavioral principles are now widely used in factories, schools, prisons, mental hospitals, and a variety of other settings.

Skinner's ideas had repercussions that went far beyond the debate among psychologists about what they should study. Skinner spelled out the full implications of his findings in his book *Beyond Freedom and Dignity* (1971). There he asserted that all behavior is fully governed by external stimuli. In other words, your behavior is determined in predictable ways by lawful principles, just as the flight of an arrow is governed by the laws of physics. Thus, if you believe that your actions are the result of conscious decisions, you're wrong. According to Skinner, we are all controlled by our environment, not by ourselves. In short, Skinner arrived at the conclusion that *free will is an illusion.*

As you can readily imagine, such a disconcerting view of human nature was not universally acclaimed. Like Freud, Skinner was the target of harsh criticism. Much of this criticism stemmed from misinterpretations of his ideas. For example, his analysis of free will was often misconstrued as an attack on the concept of a free society—which it was not—and he was often mistakenly condemned for advocating an undemocratic "scientific police state" (Dinsmoor, 1992). Despite all the controversy, however, behaviorism flourished as the dominant school of thought in psychology during the 1950s and 1960s (Gilgen, 1982).

The Humanists Revolt 1a, 10c

By the 1950s, behaviorism and psychoanalytic theory had become the most influential schools of thought in psychology. However, many psychologists found these theoretical orientations unappealing. The principal charge hurled at both schools was that they were "dehumanizing." Psychoanalytic theory was attacked for its belief that behavior is dominated by primitive, sexual urges. Behaviorism was criticized for its preoccupation with the study of simple animal behavior. Both theories were criticized because they suggested that people are not masters of their own destinies. Above all, many people argued, both schools of thought failed to recognize the unique qualities of *human* behavior.

Beginning in the 1950s, the diverse opposition to behaviorism and psychoanalytic theory blended into a loose alliance that eventually became a new school of thought called "humanism" (Bühler & Allen, 1972). In psychology, **humanism is a theoretical orientation that emphasizes the unique qualities of humans, especially their freedom and their potential for personal growth**. Some of the key differences between the humanistic, psychoanalytic, and behavioral viewpoints are summarized in Table 1.2, which compares six influential contemporary theoretical perspectives in psychology.

Humanists take an *optimistic* view of human nature. They maintain that people are not pawns of either their animal heritage or environmental circumstances. Furthermore, they say, because humans are fundamentally different from other animals, research on animals has little relevance to the understanding of human behavior. The most prominent architects of the humanistic movement have been Carl Rogers (1902–1987) and Abraham Maslow (1908–1970). Rogers (1951) argued that human behavior is governed primarily by each individual's sense of self, or "self-concept"—which animals presumably lack. Both he and Maslow (1954) maintained that to fully understand people's behavior, psychologists must take into account the fundamental human drive toward personal growth. They asserted that people have a basic need to continue to evolve as human beings and to fulfill their potentials. In fact, the humanists argued that many psychological

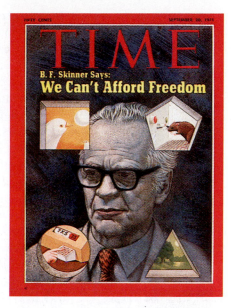

B. F. Skinner created considerable controversy when he asserted that free will is an illusion.

TABLE 1.2 OVERVIEW OF SIX CONTEMPORARY THEORETICAL PERSPECTIVES IN PSYCHOLOGY

Perspective and Its Influential Period	Principal Contributors	Subject Matter	Basic Premise
Behavioral (1913–present)	John B. Watson Ivan Pavlov B. F. Skinner	Effects of environment on the overt behavior of humans and animals	Only observable events (stimulus-response relations) can be studied scientifically.
Psychoanalytic (1900–present)	Sigmund Freud Carl Jung Alfred Adler	Unconscious determinants of behavior	Unconscious motives and experiences in early childhood govern personality and mental disorders.
Humanistic (1950s–present)	Carl Rogers Abraham Maslow	Unique aspects of human experience	Humans are free, rational beings with the potential for personal growth, and they are fundamentally different from animals.
Cognitive (1950s–present)	Jean Piaget Noam Chomsky Herbert Simon	Thoughts; mental processes	Human behavior cannot be fully understood without examining how people acquire, store, and process information.
Biological (1950s–present)	James Olds Roger Sperry	Physiological bases of behavior in humans and animals	An organism's functioning can be explained in terms of the bodily structures and biochemical processes that underlie behavior.
Evolutionary (1980s–present)	David Buss	Evolutionary bases of behavior in humans and animals	Behavior patterns have evolved to solve adaptive problems; natural selection favors behaviors that enhance reproductive success.

disturbances are the result of thwarting these uniquely human needs.

The humanists' greatest contribution to psychology has been their innovative treatments for psychological problems and disorders. The humanistic movement has provided a fertile breeding ground for the development of creative and successful approaches to psychotherapy. More generally, the humanists have argued eloquently for a different picture of human nature than those implied by psychoanalysis and behaviorism.

Recap of Key Points

- Gestalt psychology, founded by Max Wertheimer, was based on the belief that the whole is greater than the sum of its parts. The Gestalt school arose as a reaction to structuralism and challenged the behavioral view as well, but eventually it faded as a school of thought.
- Sigmund Freud was an Austrian physician who invented psychoanalysis. His psychoanalytic theory emphasized the unconscious determinants of behavior and the importance of sexuality.
- Freud's ideas were controversial, and they met with resistance in academic psychology. However, as more psychologists developed an interest in personality, motivation, and abnormal behavior, psychoanalytic concepts were incorporated into mainstream psychology.
- The influence of behaviorism was boosted greatly by B. F. Skinner's research. Like Watson before him, Skinner asserted that psychology should study only observable behavior.
- Working with laboratory rats and pigeons, Skinner demonstrated that organisms tend to repeat responses that lead to positive consequences and they tend not to repeat responses that lead to neutral or negative consequences.
- Based on the belief that all behavior is fully governed by external stimuli, Skinner argued in *Beyond Freedom and Dignity* that free will is an illusion. His ideas were controversial and often misunderstood.
- Finding both behaviorism and psychoanalysis unsatisfactory, advocates of a new theoretical orientation called humanism became influential in the 1950s. Humanism, led by Abraham Maslow and Carl Rogers, emphasized the unique qualities of human behavior and humans' freedom and potential for personal growth.

Psychology Comes of Age as a Profession

The 1950s also saw psychology come of age as a profession. As you know, psychology is not all pure science. It has a highly practical side. Many psychologists provide a variety of professional services to the public. Their work falls within the domain of *applied psychology*, **the branch of psychology concerned with everyday, practical problems.**

This branch of psychology, which is so prominent today, was actually slow to develop. Although the first psychological clinic was established as early as 1896, few psychologists were concerned with applications of their science until World War I (1914–1918), which created a huge demand for mental testing of military recruits. The first useful

*It seems to me that at bottom each person is asking, "Who am I, **really**? How can I get in touch with this real self, underlying all my surface behavior? How can I become myself?"*

CARL ROGERS
1905–1987

CONCEPT CHECK 1.2

Understanding the Implications of Major Theories: Freud, Skinner, and Rogers

Check your understanding of the implications of some of the major theories reviewed in this chapter by indicating who is likely to have made each of the statements quoted below. Choose from the following: (a) Sigmund Freud, (b) B. F. Skinner, and (c) Carl Rogers. You'll find the answers in Appendix A at the back of the book.

_____ 1. "In the traditional view, a person is free. . . . He can therefore be held responsible for what he does and justly punished if he offends. That view, together with its associated practices, must be reexamined when a scientific analysis reveals unsuspected controlling relations between behavior and environment."

_____ 2. "He that has eyes to see and ears to hear may convince himself that no mortal can keep a secret. If the lips are silent, he chatters with his fingertips; betrayal oozes out of him at every pore. And thus the task of making conscious the most hidden recesses of the mind is one which it is quite possible to accomplish."

_____ 3. "I do not have a Pollyanna view of human nature. . . . Yet one of the most refreshing and invigorating parts of my experience is to work with [my clients] and to discover the strongly positive directional tendencies which exist in them, as in all of us, at the deepest levels."

intelligence test had been devised only a few years before by French psychologist Alfred Binet and his colleagues (Binet & Simon, 1905). During the war, the military services experimented with intelligence testing as an aid in assigning recruits to jobs in accordance with their abilities. The war thus brought many psychologists into the applied arena for the first time and established mental testing as a routine professional activity conducted by psychologists.

After World War I, psychology continued to grow as a profession, but at a snail's pace. The principal professional arm of psychology was *clinical psychology*. As practiced today, **clinical psychology is the branch of psychology concerned with the diagnosis and treatment of psychological problems and disorders.** In the early days, however, the emphasis was almost exclusively on psychological testing, and few psychologists were involved in clinical work. As late as 1937 only about one in five members of the American Psychological Association reported an interest in clinical psychology (Goldenberg, 1983). Admittedly, that proportion was substantially higher than the 4% reported in 1918. However, clinicians were still a small minority in a field devoted primarily to research.

That picture was about to change with dramatic swiftness. Once again the impetus was a world war. During World War II (1941–1945), many academic psychologists were pressed into service as clinicians. They were needed to screen military recruits and to treat soldiers suffering from trauma. Many of these psychologists (often to their surprise) found the clinical work to be challenging and rewarding, and a substantial portion continued to do clinical work after the war. More significant, some 40,000 American veterans, many with severe psychological scars, returned to seek postwar treatment in Veterans Administration (VA) hospitals. With the demand for clinicians far greater than the supply, the VA stepped in to finance many new training programs in clinical psychology. These programs, emphasizing training in the treatment of psychological disorders as well as psychological testing, proved attractive. Within a few years, about half the new Ph.D.'s in psychology were specializing in clinical psychology (Goldenberg, 1983). Thus, during the 1950s the prewar orphan of applied/professional psychology rapidly matured into a robust, powerful adult.

In the halls of academia, many traditional research psychologists were alarmed by the pro-

fessionalization of the field. They argued that the energy and resources previously devoted to research would be diluted. Because of conflicting priorities, tensions between the research and professional arms of psychology have continued to grow. Although the American Psychological Association continues to work diligently to represent both the scientific and professional branches of psychology, recent years have brought complaints from many researchers that the APA has come to be dominated by clinicians. In 1988 this rift stimulated some research psychologists to form a new organization, the American Psychological Society (APS), to serve exclusively as an advocate for the science of psychology.

Despite the conflicts, the professionalization of psychology has continued at a steady pace. In fact, the trend has spread into additional areas of psychology. Today the broad umbrella of applied psychology covers a variety of professional specialties, including school psychology, industrial and organizational psychology, and counseling psychology. Whereas psychologists were once almost exclusively academics, the vast majority of today's psychologists devote some of their time to providing professional services.

Psychology Returns to Its Roots: Renewed Interest in Cognition and Physiology 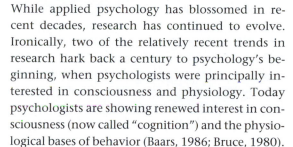 1a

While applied psychology has blossomed in recent decades, research has continued to evolve. Ironically, two of the relatively recent trends in research hark back a century to psychology's beginning, when psychologists were principally interested in consciousness and physiology. Today psychologists are showing renewed interest in consciousness (now called "cognition") and the physiological bases of behavior (Baars, 1986; Bruce, 1980).

World War I and World War II played a major role in the growth of applied psychology, as psychologists were forced to apply their expertise to practical problems, such as ability testing and training. The top photo shows military personnel working on one of a series of tests devised to aid in the selection of air crew trainees during World War II. The bottom photo shows a booklet sold to help recruits prepare for the Army General Classification Test and other related tests. Its popularity illustrates the importance attached to the military's mental testing program.

Cognition **refers to the mental processes involved in acquiring knowledge.** In other words, cognition involves thinking or conscious experience. For many decades, the dominance of behaviorism discouraged investigation of "unobservable" mental processes, and most psychologists showed little interest in cognition. During the 1950s and 1960s, however, this situation slowly began to change. Major progress in the study of children's cognitive development (Piaget, 1954), memory (Miller, 1956), language (Chomsky, 1957), and problem solving (Newell, Shaw, & Simon, 1958) sparked a surge of interest in cognitive psychology.

Since then, cognitive theorists have argued that psychology must study internal mental events to fully understand behavior (Gardner, 1985; Neisser, 1967). Advocates of the *cognitive perspective* point out that people's manipulations of mental images surely influence how they behave. Consequently, focusing exclusively on overt behavior yields an incomplete picture of why individuals behave as they do. Equally important, psychologists investigating decision making, reasoning, and problem solving have shown that methods *can* be devised to study cognitive processes scientifically. Although the methods are different from those used in psychology's early days, recent research on the inner workings of the mind has put the *psyche* back in contemporary psychology.

The 1950s and 1960s also saw many discoveries that highlighted the interrelations among mind, body, and behavior. For example, psychologists demonstrated that electrical stimulation of the brain could evoke emotional responses such as pleasure and rage in animals (Olds, 1956). Other work showed that the right and left halves of the brain are specialized to handle different types of mental tasks (Gazzaniga, Bogen, & Sperry, 1965). Excitement was also generated by the finding that people can exert some self-control over internal physiological processes, including electrical activity in the brain, through a strategy called biofeedback (Kamiya, 1969).

These and many other findings stimulated an increase in research on the biological bases of behavior. Advocates of the *biological perspective* maintain that much of human and animal behavior can be explained in terms of the bodily structures and biochemical processes that allow organisms to behave. As you know, in the 19th century the young science of psychology had a heavy physiological emphasis. Thus, the recent interest in the biological bases of behavior represents another return to psychology's heritage.

Although adherents of the cognitive and biological perspectives haven't done as much organized campaigning for their viewpoint as proponents of the older, traditional schools of thought have, these newer perspectives have become important theoretical orientations in modern psychology. They are increasingly influential regarding what psychology should study and how. The cognitive and biological perspectives are compared to other contemporary theoretical perspectives in Table 1.2.

Psychology Broadens Its Horizons: Increased Interest in Cultural Diversity

Throughout psychology's history, most researchers have worked under the assumption that they were seeking to identify general principles of behavior that would be applicable to all of humanity. In reality, however, psychology has largely been a Western (North American and European) enterprise with a remarkably provincial slant (Gergen et al., 1996). The vast preponderance of psychology's research has been conducted in the United States by middle- and upper-class white psychologists who have used mostly middle- and upper-class white males as subjects (Segall et al., 1990). Traditionally, Western psychologists have paid scant attention to how well their theories and research might apply to non-Western cultures, to ethnic minorities in Western societies, or even to women as opposed to men.

Why has the focus of Western psychology been so narrow? A host of factors have probably contributed (Albert, 1988). First and foremost, cross-cultural research is costly, difficult, and time-consuming. It has always been cheaper, easier, and more convenient for academic psychologists to study the white middle-class students enrolled in their schools. Second, psychology has traditionally been interested in the *individual* as its basic unit of analysis rather than the *group*. Hence, most psychologists have been content to let sociologists and anthropologists wrestle with analyses of cultural factors. Third, some psychologists worry that cultural comparisons may inadvertently foster stereotypes of various cultural groups, many of which already have a long history of being victimized by prejudice. Fourth, *ethnocentrism*—**the tendency to view one's own group as superior to others and as the standard for judging the worth of foreign ways**—may have contributed to Western psychologists' lack of interest in other cultures.

Despite these considerations, in recent years Western psychologists have begun to recognize that their neglect of cultural variables has diminished the value of their work, and they are devoting increased attention to culture as a determinant of behavior. What brought about this shift? Some of the impetus probably came from the sociopolitical upheavals of the 1960s and 1970s (Bronstein & Quina, 1988). The civil rights movement, the women's movement, and the gay rights movement all raised doubts about whether psychology had dealt adequately with human diversity. Above all else, however, the new interest in culture appears attributable to two recent trends: (1) advances in communication, travel, and international trade have "shrunk" the world and increased global interdependence, bringing more and more Americans and Europeans into contact with people from non-Western cultures, and (2) the ethnic makeup of the Western world has become an increasingly diverse multicultural mosaic, as the data in Figure 1.3 show for the United States (Brislin, 1993; Locke, 1992; Mays, et al., 1996).

These realities have prompted more and more Western psychologists to broaden their horizons and incorporate cultural factors into their theories and research (Shweder & Sullivan, 1993). These psychologists are striving to study previously underrepresented groups of subjects to test the generality of earlier findings and to catalog both the differences and similarities among cultural groups. They are working to increase knowledge of how culture is transmitted through socialization practices and how culture colors one's view of the world. They are seeking to learn how people cope with cultural change and to find ways to reduce misunderstandings and conflicts in intercultural interactions. In addition, they are trying to enhance understanding of how cultural groups are affected by prejudice, discrimination, and racism. In all these efforts, they are striving to understand the unique experiences of culturally diverse people *from the point of view of those people.* These efforts to ask new questions, study new groups, and apply new perspectives promise to enrich the discipline of psychology as it moves into the 21st century (Betancourt & Lopez, 1993).

Psychology Adapts: The Emergence of Evolutionary Psychology

The most recent major development in psychology has been the emergence of a new theoretical perspective that is likely to be influential in the years to come. Led most prominently by David Buss (1995, 1996) of the University of Michigan, evolutionary psychologists assert that the patterns of behavior seen in a species are products of evolu-

tion in the same way that anatomical characteristics are. *Evolutionary psychology* **examines behavioral processes in terms of their adaptive value for a species over the course of many generations.** The basic premise of evolutionary psychology is that natural selection favors behaviors that enhance organisms' reproductive success— that is, passing on genes to the next generation. Thus, if a species is highly aggressive, evolutionary psychologists argue that it's because aggressiveness conveys a survival advantage for that species, so genes that promote aggressiveness are more likely to be passed on to the next generation. Although evolutionary psychologists have a natural interest in animal behavior, they have not been bashful about analyzing the evolutionary bases of human behavior. As La Cerra and Kurzban (1995) put it, "The human mind was sculpted by natural selection, and it is this evolved organ that constitutes the subject matter of psychology" (p. 63).

Consider, for instance, evolutionary psychologists' analysis of differences between males and females in visual-spatial ability. On the average, males tend to perform slightly better than females on visual-spatial tasks involving mental rotation of images, map reading, and maze learning (see Chapter 11). Silverman and Eals (1992) assert that these aspects of spatial ability would have facilitated skill at *hunting,* a chore largely assigned to men over the course of human evolutionary history. In contrast, women have generally had responsibility for *gathering* food rather than hunting it. Hence, Silverman and Eals hypothesized that females ought to be superior to males on spatial skills that would have facilitated gathering, such as memory for locations, which is exactly what they found in a series of four studies. Thus,

Figure 1.3
Increased cultural diversity in the United States. The 1980s brought significant changes in the ethnic makeup of the United States. The nation's Hispanic population grew by 53% during the decade, and its Asian American population more than doubled (a 108% increase), while the white population increased by only 6%. Experts project that ethnic minorities will account for over one-third of the U.S. population early in the 21st century (Sue, 1991). These realities have contributed to psychologists' increased interest in cultural factors as determinants of behavior. (Data from U.S. Bureau of the Census)

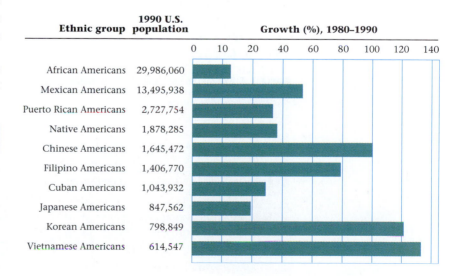

Ethnic group	1990 U.S. population	Growth (%), 1980–1990
African Americans	29,986,060	
Mexican Americans	13,495,938	
Puerto Rican Americans	2,727,754	
Native Americans	1,878,285	
Chinese Americans	1,645,472	
Filipino Americans	1,406,770	
Cuban Americans	1,043,932	
Japanese Americans	847,562	
Korean Americans	798,849	
Vietnamese Americans	614,547	

evolutionary psychologists explain gender differences in spatial ability—and many other aspects of human behavior (see Table 1.3 for more examples)—in terms of how they evolved to meet the adaptive pressures faced by our ancestors.

Looking at behavioral patterns in terms of their evolutionary significance is not an entirely new idea (Graziano, 1995). As noted earlier, William James and other functionalists were influenced by Darwin's concept of natural selection over a century ago. Until recently, however, applications of evolutionary concepts to psychological processes were piecemeal, half-hearted, and not particularly well-received. The situation began to change in the late 1980s. David Buss (1988, 1989) and a growing cadre of evolutionary psychologists published widely cited studies on a broad range of topics, including mating preferences, jealousy, aggression, sexual behavior, language, decision making, personality, and development (Kenrick & Keefe, 1992; Smuts, 1992; Tooby & Cosmides, 1989, 1990). By the mid-1990s, it became clear that psychology was witnessing the birth of its first major, new theoretical perspective since the cognitive revolution in the 1950s and 1960s.

As with all prominent theoretical perspectives in psychology, evolutionary theory has its critics (Caporael & Brewer, 1995; Gould, 1993). Among other things, they argue that evolutionary theory is untestable and that evolutionary explanations are post hoc accounts for obvious behavioral phenomena. However, evolutionary psychologists have articulated persuasive rebuttals to these and other criticisms, and the evolutionary perspective is rapidly gaining acceptance (Kenrick, 1995). Advocates of the evolutionary approach have heralded it as an "immense advance over traditional perspectives" (Masters, 1995, p. 65), a "revolutionary scientific paradigm" (Buss, 1995, p.85), and a "renaissance in the sciences of mind" (La Cerra & Kurzban, 1995, p. 62). These proclamations will probably prove to be overly enthusiastic, as is often the case when a new school of thought strives to establish its identity. Nonetheless, evolutionary psychology undeniably provides a thought-provoking, innovative perspective that promises to shake things up in the future.

Our review of psychology's past has shown the field's evolution. We have seen psychology develop from philosophical speculation into a rigorous science committed to research. We have seen how a highly visible professional arm involved in mental health services emerged from this science. We have seen how psychology's focus on physiology is rooted in its 19th-century origins. We have seen how and why psychologists began conducting research on lower animals. We have seen how psychology has evolved from the study of mind and body to the study of behavior. And we have seen how the investigation of mind and body has been welcomed back into the mainstream of modern psychology. We have seen how various theoretical schools have defined the scope and mission of psychology in different ways. We have seen how psychology's interests have expanded and become increasingly diverse. Above all else, we have seen that psychology is a growing, evolving intellectual enterprise.

Psychology's history is already rich, but its story has barely begun. The century or so that has elapsed since Wilhelm Wundt put psychology on a scientific footing is only an eyeblink of time in human history. What has been discovered during those years, and what remains unknown, is the subject of the rest of this book.

Recap of Key Points

• Only a handful of psychologists were involved with applied psychology before World War I created a huge demand for mental testing of military recruits.

• Stimulated by the demands of World War II, clinical

TABLE 1.3 EXAMPLES OF HUMAN BEHAVIORAL PHENOMENA EXPLAINED IN EVOLUTIONARY TERMS

Behavioral Phenomenon	Adaptive Value
Readily acquired fears of snakes and spiders	Avoids exposure to poisons
Greater sexual jealousy by males	Increases males' confidence about the paternity of their children
Preference for foods rich in fats and sugars	Increases acquisition of calories needed for energy, survival
Females' greater emphasis on potential mates' economic resources	Increases resources available for children

Source: Adapted from Buss (1995).

psychology grew rapidly in the 1950s. Thus, psychology became a profession as well as a science. This movement toward professionalization eventually spread to other areas in psychology.

• During the 1950s and 1960s advances in the study of cognition led to renewed interest in mental processes, as psychology returned to its roots. Advocates of the cognitive perspective argue that human behavior cannot be fully understood without considering how people think.

• The 1950s and 1960s also saw advances in research on the physiological bases of behavior. Advocates of the biological perspective assert that human and animal behavior can be explained in terms of the bodily structures and biochemical processes that allow organisms to behave.

• In the 1980s, Western psychologists, who had previously been rather provincial, developed a greater interest in how cultural factors influence behavior. This trend was sparked in large part by growing global interdependence and by increased cultural diversity in Western societies.

• The 1990s witnessed the emergence of a new theoretical perspective called evolutionary psychology. The central premises of this new school of thought are that patterns of behavior are the product of evolutionary forces and that natural selection favors behaviors that enhance reproductive success.

PSYCHOLOGY TODAY: VIGOROUS AND DIVERSIFIED

We began this chapter with an informal description of what psychology is about. Now that you have a feel for how psychology has developed, you can better appreciate a definition that does justice to the field's modern diversity: *Psychology* **is the science that studies behavior and the physiological and cognitive processes that underlie it, and it is the profession that applies the accumulated knowledge of this science to practical problems.**

Contemporary psychology is a thriving science and profession. Its growth has been remarkable. One simple index of this growth is the dramatic rise in membership in the American Psychological Association. Figure 1.4 shows that APA membership has increased eightfold since 1950. And this membership has continued to grow despite competition from the new APS, as many research psychologists are apparently joining both organizations (Fowler, 1990). In the United States, psychology is the second most popular undergraduate major (see Figure 1.5), and the field accounts for about 10% of all doctoral degrees awarded in the sciences and humanities. The comparable figure in 1945 was only 4% (Howard et al., 1986). Of course, psychology is an international enterprise. Today, over 1100 technical journals from all over the world publish research articles on psychology. Thus, by any standard of measurement—the number of people involved, the number of degrees granted, the number of studies conducted, the number of journals published—psychology is a healthy, growing field.

Psychology's vigorous presence in modern society is also demonstrated by the great variety of

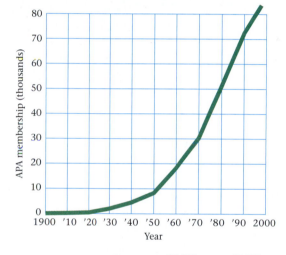

Figure 1.4
Membership in the American Psychological Association, 1900–1996. The steep rise in the number of psychologists in the APA since 1950 testifies to psychology's remarkable growth as a science and a profession. If graduate student members are also counted, the APA has over 140,000 members.

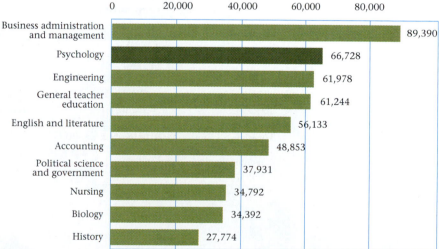

Figure 1.5
Leading college majors. This graphic lists the ten most popular undergraduate majors in the United States, based on the number of bachelor's degrees awarded in 1992–1993. As you can see, psychology ranked second only to business administration and management in the number of degrees awarded. (Data from U.S. Department of Education, National Center for Education Statistics, 1995)

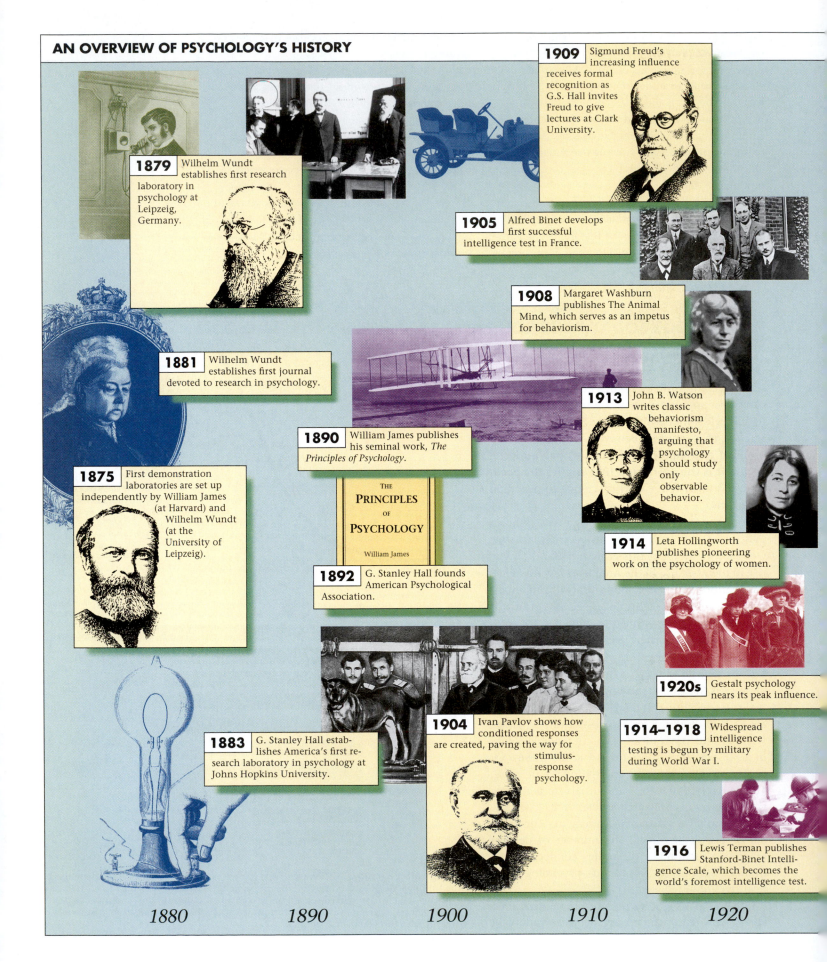

1909 Sigmund Freud's increasing influence receives formal recognition as G.S. Hall invites Freud to give lectures at Clark University.

1879 Wilhelm Wundt establishes first research laboratory in psychology at Leipzeig, Germany.

1905 Alfred Binet develops first successful intelligence test in France.

1908 Margaret Washburn publishes The Animal Mind, which serves as an impetus for behaviorism.

1881 Wilhelm Wundt establishes first journal devoted to research in psychology.

1890 William James publishes his seminal work, *The Principles of Psychology*.

1913 John B. Watson writes classic behaviorism manifesto, arguing that psychology should study only observable behavior.

THE
PRINCIPLES
OF
PSYCHOLOGY

William James

1875 First demonstration laboratories are set up independently by William James (at Harvard) and Wilhelm Wundt (at the University of Leipzig).

1892 G. Stanley Hall founds American Psychological Association.

1914 Leta Hollingworth publishes pioneering work on the psychology of women.

1920s Gestalt psychology nears its peak influence.

1904 Ivan Pavlov shows how conditioned responses are created, paving the way for stimulus-response psychology.

1914–1918 Widespread intelligence testing is begun by military during World War I.

1883 G. Stanley Hall establishes America's first research laboratory in psychology at Johns Hopkins University.

1916 Lewis Terman publishes Stanford-Binet Intelligence Scale, which becomes the world's foremost intelligence test.

1880   *1890*   *1900*   *1910*   *1920*

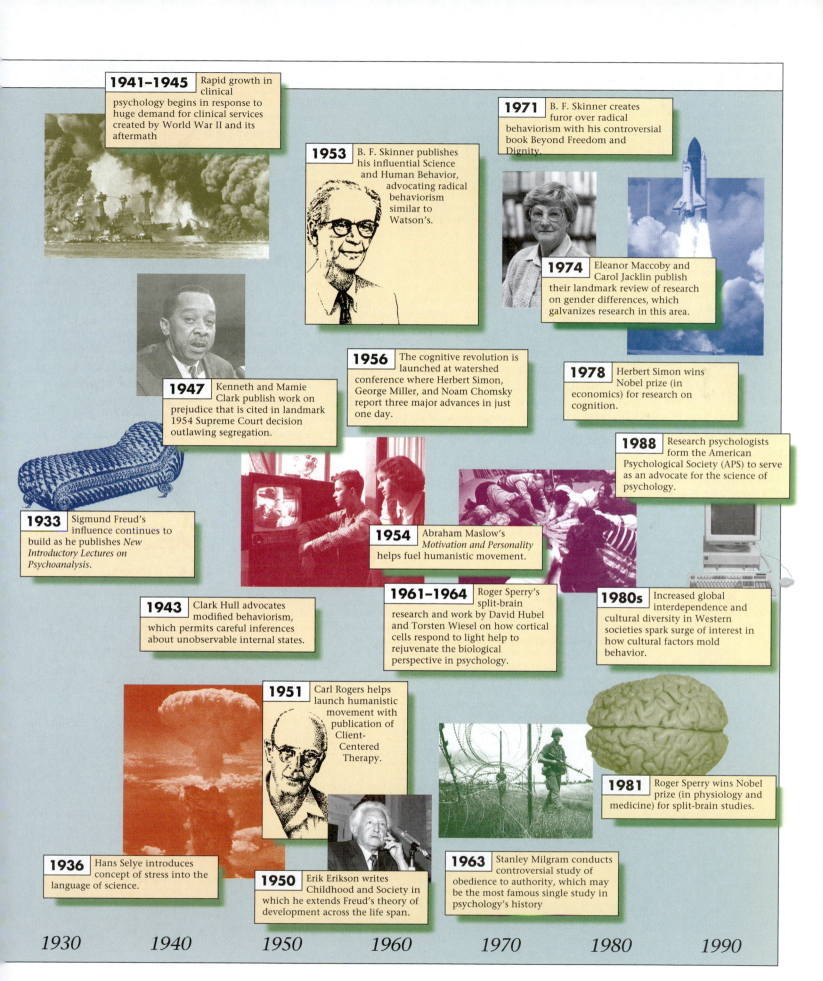

1941–1945 Rapid growth in clinical psychology begins in response to huge demand for clinical services created by World War II and its aftermath

1953 B. F. Skinner publishes his influential Science and Human Behavior, advocating radical behaviorism similar to Watson's.

1971 B. F. Skinner creates furor over radical behaviorism with his controversial book Beyond Freedom and Dignity.

1974 Eleanor Maccoby and Carol Jacklin publish their landmark review of research on gender differences, which galvanizes research in this area.

1947 Kenneth and Mamie Clark publish work on prejudice that is cited in landmark 1954 Supreme Court decision outlawing segregation.

1956 The cognitive revolution is launched at watershed conference where Herbert Simon, George Miller, and Noam Chomsky report three major advances in just one day.

1978 Herbert Simon wins Nobel prize (in economics) for research on cognition.

1988 Research psychologists form the American Psychological Society (APS) to serve as an advocate for the science of psychology.

1933 Sigmund Freud's influence continues to build as he publishes New Introductory Lectures on Psychoanalysis.

1954 Abraham Maslow's Motivation and Personality helps fuel humanistic movement.

1943 Clark Hull advocates modified behaviorism, which permits careful inferences about unobservable internal states.

1961–1964 Roger Sperry's split-brain research and work by David Hubel and Torsten Wiesel on how cortical cells respond to light help to rejuvenate the biological perspective in psychology.

1980s Increased global interdependence and cultural diversity in Western societies spark surge of interest in how cultural factors mold behavior.

1951 Carl Rogers helps launch humanistic movement with publication of Client-Centered Therapy.

1981 Roger Sperry wins Nobel prize (in physiology and medicine) for split-brain studies.

1936 Hans Selye introduces concept of stress into the language of science.

1950 Erik Erikson writes Childhood and Society in which he extends Freud's theory of development across the life span.

1963 Stanley Milgram conducts controversial study of obedience to authority, which may be the most famous single study in psychology's history

1930   *1940*   *1950*   *1960*   *1970*   *1980*   *1990*

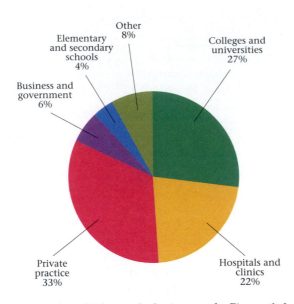

Figure 1.6
Employment of psychologists by setting. The work settings in which psychologists are employed have become very diverse. Recent survey data on the primary employment setting of APA members indicates that one-third are in private practice (compared to 12% in 1976) and only 27% work in colleges and universities (compared to 47% in 1976). These data may slightly underestimate the percentage of psychologists in academia, given the new competition between APA and APS to represent research psychologists. (Data based on *Profile of All APA Members: 1993*)

Other 8%
Elementary and secondary schools 4%
Business and government 6%
Colleges and universities 27%
Private practice 33%
Hospitals and clinics 22%

settings in which psychologists work. Figure 1.6 shows the distribution of psychologists employed in various categories of settings. Psychologists were once found almost exclusively in the halls of academia. However, today colleges and universities are the primary work setting for less than one-

third of American psychologists. The remaining two-thirds work in hospitals, clinics, police departments, research institutes, government agencies, business and industry, schools, nursing homes, counseling centers, and private practice.

Clearly, contemporary psychology is a multifaceted field, a fact that is especially apparent when we consider the many areas of specialization within psychology today. Let's look at the current areas of specialization in both the science and the profession of psychology.

Research Areas in Psychology

Although most psychologists receive broad training that provides them with knowledge about many areas of psychology, they usually specialize when it comes to doing research. Such specialization is necessary because the subject matter of psychology has become so vast over the years. Today it is virtually impossible for anyone to stay abreast of the new research in all specialties. Specialization is also necessary because specific skills and training are required to do research in some areas.

Figure 1.7
Major research areas in contemporary psychology. Most research psychologists specialize in one of the seven broad areas described here. The figures in the pie chart reflect the percentage of research psychologists belonging to APA who identify each area as their primary interest. (Data based on *Profile of All APA Members: 1993*)

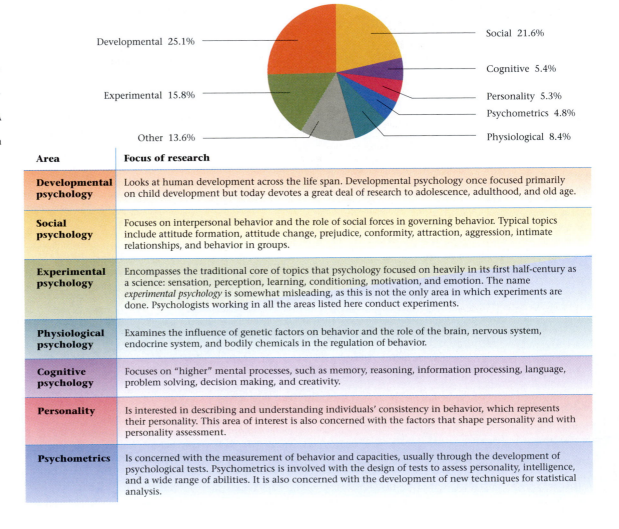

Developmental 25.1%
Experimental 15.8%
Other 13.6%
Social 21.6%
Cognitive 5.4%
Personality 5.3%
Psychometrics 4.8%
Physiological 8.4%

Area	Focus of research
Developmental psychology	Looks at human development across the life span. Developmental psychology once focused primarily on child development but today devotes a great deal of research to adolescence, adulthood, and old age.
Social psychology	Focuses on interpersonal behavior and the role of social forces in governing behavior. Typical topics include attitude formation, attitude change, prejudice, conformity, attraction, aggression, intimate relationships, and behavior in groups.
Experimental psychology	Encompasses the traditional core of topics that psychology focused on heavily in its first half-century as a science: sensation, perception, learning, conditioning, motivation, and emotion. The name *experimental psychology* is somewhat misleading, as this is not the only area in which experiments are done. Psychologists working in all the areas listed here conduct experiments.
Physiological psychology	Examines the influence of genetic factors on behavior and the role of the brain, nervous system, endocrine system, and bodily chemicals in the regulation of behavior.
Cognitive psychology	Focuses on "higher" mental processes, such as memory, reasoning, information processing, language, problem solving, decision making, and creativity.
Personality	Is interested in describing and understanding individuals' consistency in behavior, which represents their personality. This area of interest is also concerned with the factors that shape personality and with personality assessment.
Psychometrics	Is concerned with the measurement of behavior and capacities, usually through the development of psychological tests. Psychometrics is involved with the design of tests to assess personality, intelligence, and a wide range of abilities. It is also concerned with the development of new techniques for statistical analysis.

CHAPTER ONE

The seven major research areas in modern psychology are (1) developmental psychology, (2) social psychology, (3) experimental psychology, (4) physiological psychology, (5) cognitive psychology, (6) personality, and (7) psychometrics. Figure 1.7 describes these areas briefly and shows the percentage of research psychologists who identify each area as their primary interest (American Psychological Association, 1993). As you can see, social psychology and developmental psychology have become especially active areas of research.

Professional Specialties in Psychology

Within applied psychology there are four clearly identified areas of specialization: (1) clinical psychology, (2) counseling psychology, (3) educational and school psychology, and (4) industrial and organizational psychology. Descriptions of these specialties can be found in Figure 1.8, along with the percentage of professional psychologists working in each area (American Psychological Association, 1993). As the figure indicates, clinical psychology is currently the most prominent and widely practiced professional specialty in the field.

The data in Figures 1.7 and 1.8 are based on psychologists' reports of their single, principal area of specialization. However, many psychologists work on both research and application. Some academic psychologists work as consultants, therapists, and counselors on a part-time basis. Similarly, some applied psychologists conduct basic research on issues related to their specialty. For example, many clinical psychologists are involved in research on the nature and causes of abnormal behavior.

Many people are confused about the difference between clinical psychology and psychiatry. The confusion is understandable, as both clinical psychologists and psychiatrists are involved in analyzing and treating psychological disorders. Although there is some overlap between the two professions, the training and educational requirements for the two are quite different. Clinical psychologists go to graduate school to earn one of several doctoral degrees (Ph.D., Ed.D., or Psy.D.) in order to enjoy full status in their profession. Psychiatrists go to medical school for their postgraduate education, where they receive general training in medicine and earn an M.D. degree. They then specialize by completing residency training in psychiatry at a hospital. Clinical psychologists and psychiatrists also differ in the way they tend to approach the treatment of mental disorders, as we will see in Chapter 15. To summarize, *psychiatry* **is a branch of medicine concerned with the diagnosis and treatment of psychological problems and disorders.** In contrast,

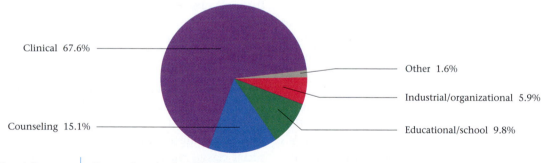

| Clinical 67.6% |
| Other 1.6% |
| Counseling 15.1% |
| Industrial/organizational 5.9% |
| Educational/school 9.8% |

Figure 1.8
Principal professional specialties in contemporary psychology. Most psychologists who deliver professional services to the public specialize in one of the four areas described here. The figures in the pie chart reflect the percentage of those psychologists belonging to APA who identify each area as their chief specialty. (Data based on *Profile of All APA Members: 1993*)

Specialty	Focus of professional practice
Clinical psychology	Clinical psychologists are concerned with the evaluation, diagnosis, and treatment of individuals with psychological disorders, as well as treatment of less severe behavioral and emotional problems. Principal activities include interviewing clients, psychological testing, and providing group or individual psychotherapy.
Counseling psychology	Counseling psychology overlaps with clinical psychology in that specialists in both areas engage in similar activities — interviewing, testing, and providing therapy. However, counseling psychologists usually work with a somewhat different clientele, providing assistance to people struggling with everyday problems of moderate severity. Thus, they often specialize in family, marital, or career counseling.
Educational and school psychology	Educational psychologists work to improve curriculum design, achievement testing, teacher training, and other aspects of the educational process. School psychologists usually work in elementary or secondary schools, where they test and counsel children having difficulties in school, and aid parents and teachers in solving school-related problems.
Industrial and organizational psychology	Psychologists in this area perform a wide variety of tasks in the world of business and industry. These tasks include running human resources departments, working to improve staff morale and attitudes, striving to increase job satisfaction and productivity, examining organizational structures and procedures, and making recommendations for improvements.

clinical psychology takes a nonmedical approach to such problems.

Recap of Key Points

• Contemporary psychology is a diversified science and profession that has grown rapidly in recent decades. The main work settings for contemporary psychologists are (1) private practice, (2) colleges and universities, and (3) hospitals and clinics.

• Major areas of research in modern psychology include experimental psychology, physiological psychology, cognitive psychology, developmental psychology, psychometrics, personality, and social psychology, which are described in Figure 1.7.

• Applied psychology encompasses four professional specialties: clinical psychology, counseling psychology, educational and school psychology, and industrial and organizational psychology, which are described in Figure 1.8.

• Although clinical psychology and psychiatry share some of the same interests, they are different professions with different types of training. Psychiatrists are physicians who specialize in the diagnosis and treatment of mental disorders.

PUTTING IT IN PERSPECTIVE: SEVEN KEY THEMES

The enormous breadth and diversity of psychology make it a challenging subject for the beginning student. In the pages ahead you will be introduced to many areas of research and a multitude of new ideas, concepts, and principles. Fortunately, all ideas are not created equal. Some are far more important than others. In this section, I will highlight seven fundamental themes that will reappear in a number of variations as we move from one area of psychology to another in this text. You have already met some of these key ideas in our review of psychology's past and present. Now we will isolate them and highlight their significance. In the remainder of the book these ideas serve as organizing themes to provide threads of continuity across chapters and to help you see the connections among the different areas of research in psychology.

In studying psychology, you are learning about both behavior and the scientific discipline that investigates it. Accordingly, our seven themes come in two sets. The first set consists of statements highlighting crucial aspects of psychology as a way of thinking and as a field of study. The second set consists of broad generalizations about psychology's subject matter: behavior and the cognitive and physiological processes that underlie it.

Themes Related to Psychology as a Field of Study

Looking at psychology as a field of study, we see three crucial ideas: (1) psychology is empirical; (2) psychology is theoretically diverse; (3) psychology evolves in a sociohistorical context. Let's look at each of these ideas in more detail.

Theme 1: Psychology Is Empirical

Everyone tries to understand behavior. Most of us have our own personal answers to questions such as why some people are hard workers, why some are overweight, and why others stay in demeaning relationships. If all of us are amateur psychologists, what makes scientific psychology different? The critical difference is that psychology is *empirical*. This aspect of psychology is fundamental, and virtually every page of this book reflects it.

What do we mean by empirical? **Empiricism is the premise that knowledge should be acquired through observation.** This premise is crucial to the scientific method that psychology embraced in the late 19th century. To say that psychology is empirical means that its conclusions are based on direct observation rather than on reasoning, speculation, traditional beliefs, or common sense. Psychologists are not content with having ideas that sound plausible. They conduct research to *test* their ideas. Is intelligence higher on the average in some social classes than in others? Are men more aggressive than women? Psychologists find a way to make direct, objective, and precise observations to answer such questions.

The empirical approach requires a certain attitude—a healthy brand of *skepticism*. Empiricism is a tough taskmaster. It demands data and documentation. Psychologists' commitment to empiricism means that they must learn to think critically about generalizations concerning behavior. If someone asserts that people tend to get depressed around Christmas, a psychologist is likely to ask, "How many people get depressed? In what population? In comparison to what baseline rate of depression? How is depression defined?" Their skeptical attitude means that psychologists are trained to ask, "Where's the evidence? How do you know?" If psychology's empirical orientation rubs off on you (and I hope it does), you will be asking similar questions by the time you finish this book.

Theme 2: Psychology Is Theoretically Diverse

Although psychology is based on observation, a string of unrelated observations would not be terribly enlightening. Psychologists do not set out to just collect isolated facts; they seek to explain and understand what they observe. To achieve these goals they must construct theories. **A *theory* is a system of interrelated ideas used to explain a set of observations.** In other words, a theory links apparently unrelated observations and tries to explain them. As an example, consider Sigmund Freud's observations about slips of the tongue, dreams, and psychological disturbances. On the surface, these observations appear unrelated. By devising the concept of the *unconscious*, Freud created a theory that links and explains these seemingly unrelated aspects of behavior.

Our review of psychology's past should have made one thing abundantly clear: psychology is marked by theoretical diversity. Why do we have so many competing points of view? One reason is that no single theory can adequately explain everything that is known about behavior. Sometimes different theories focus on different aspects of behavior—that is, different collections of observations. Sometimes there is simply more than one way to look at something. Is the glass half empty or half full? Obviously, it is both. To take an example from another science, physicists wrestled for years with the nature of light. Is it a wave, or is it a particle? In the end, it proved useful to think of light sometimes as a wave and sometimes as a particle. Similarly, if a business executive lashes out at her employees with stinging criticism, is she releasing pent-up aggressive urges (a psychoanalytic view)? Is she making a habitual response to the stimulus of incompetent work (a behavioral view)? Or is she scheming to motivate her employees by using "mind games" (a cognitive view)? In some cases, all three of these explanations might have some validity. In short, it is an oversimplification to expect that one view has to be right while all others are wrong. Life is rarely that simple.

Students are often troubled by psychology's many conflicting theories, which they view as a weakness. However, contemporary psychologists increasingly recognize that theoretical diversity is a strength rather than a weakness (Hilgard, 1987). As we proceed through this text, you will see how differing theoretical perspectives often provide a more complete understanding of behavior than could be achieved by any one perspective alone.

Theme 3: Psychology Evolves in a Sociohistorical Context

Science is often seen as an "ivory tower" undertaking, isolated from the ebb and flow of everyday life. In reality, however, psychology and other sciences do not exist in a cultural vacuum. Dense interconnections exist between what happens in psychology and what happens in society at large (Altman, 1990; Braginsky, 1985; Danziger, 1990). Trends, issues, and values in society influence psychology's evolution. Similarly, progress in psychology affects trends, issues, and values in society. To put it briefly, psychology develops in a *sociohistorical* (social and historical) context.

Our review of psychology's past is filled with examples of how social trends have left their imprint on psychology. In the late 19th century, psychology's rapid growth as a laboratory science was due, in part, to its fascination with physics as the model discipline. Thus, the spirit of the times fostered a scientific approach rather than a philosophical approach to the investigation of the mind. Similarly, Freud's groundbreaking ideas emerged out of a specific sociohistorical context. Cultural values in Freud's era encouraged the suppression of sexuality. Hence, people tended to feel guilty about their sexual urges to a much greater extent than is common today. This situation clearly contributed to Freud's emphasis on unconscious sexual conflicts. As another example, consider the impact of World War II on the development of psychology as a profession. The rapid growth of professional psychology was largely due to the war-related surge in the demand for clinical services. Hence, World War II reshaped the landscape of psychology in a remarkably short time. Finally, in recent years we have seen how growing global interdependence and increased cultural diversity in the United States have prompted psychologists to focus new attention on cultural factors as determinants of behavior.

If we reverse our viewpoint, we can see that psychology has in turn left its mark on society. Consider, for instance, the pervasive role of mental testing in modern society. Your own career success may depend in part on how well you weave your way through a complex maze of intelligence and achievement tests made possible (to the regret of some) by research in psychology. As another example of psychology's impact on society, consider the influence that various theorists have had on parenting styles. Trends in child-rearing practices have been shaped by the ideas of John B. Watson, Sigmund Freud, B. F. Skinner, and Carl Rogers—not to mention a host of additional psychologists yet to be discussed. In short, society and psychology influence each other in complex ways. In the chapters to come, we will frequently have occasion to notice this dynamic relationship.

Themes Related to Psychology's Subject Matter

Looking at psychology's subject matter, we see four additional crucial ideas: (4) behavior is determined by multiple causes; (5) our behavior is shaped by our cultural heritage; (6) heredity and environment jointly influence behavior; (7) our experience of the world is highly subjective.

Theme 4: Behavior Is Determined by Multiple Causes

As psychology has matured, it has provided more and more information about the forces that govern behavior. This growing knowledge has led to a deeper appreciation of a simple but important fact: Behavior is exceedingly complex, and most aspects of behavior are determined by multiple causes.

Although the complexity of behavior may seem self-evident, people usually think in terms of single causes. Thus, they offer explanations such as "Andrea flunked out of school because she is lazy." Or they assert that "teenage pregnancies are increasing because of all the sex in the media." Single-cause explanations are sometimes accurate insofar as they go, but they usually are incomplete. In general, psychologists find that behavior is governed by a complex network of interacting factors, an idea referred to as the *multifactorial causation of behavior.*

As a simple illustration, consider the multiple factors that might influence your performance in your introductory psychology course. Relevant personal factors might include your overall intelligence, your reading ability, your memory skills, your motivation, and your study skills. In addition, your grade could be affected by numerous situational factors, including whether you like your

psychology professor, whether you like your assigned text, whether the class meets at a good time for you, whether your work schedule is light or heavy, and whether you're having any personal problems.

As you proceed through this book, you will learn that complexity of causation is the rule rather than the exception. If we expect to understand behavior, we usually have to take into account multiple determinants.

Theme 5: Our Behavior Is Shaped by Our Cultural Heritage

Among the multiple determinants of human behavior, cultural factors are particularly prominent. Just as psychology evolves in a sociohistorical context, so, too, do individuals. Our cultural backgrounds exert considerable influence over our behavior. What is *culture*? It's the human-made part of our environment. More specifically, **culture refers to the widely shared customs, beliefs, values, norms, institutions, and other products of a community that are transmitted socially across generations.** Culture is a very broad construct, encompassing everything from a society's legal system to its assumptions about family roles, from its dietary habits to its political ideals, from its technology to its attitudes about time, from its modes of dress to its spiritual beliefs, and from its art and music to its unspoken rules about sexual liasions. We tend to think of culture as belonging to entire societies or broad ethnic groups within societies—which it does—but the concept can also be applied to small groups (a tiny Aboriginal tribe in Australia, for example) and to nonethnic groups (gay/homosexual culture, for instance). To further illustrate the nature of culture, Figure 1.9 highlights a few selected aspects of the cultural heritage of various ethnic groups in the United States, as described by Locke (1992).

Much of a person's cultural heritage is invisible (Brislin, 1993). Assumptions, ideals, attitudes, beliefs, and unspoken rules exist in people's minds and may not be readily apparent to outsiders. Moreover, because our cultural background is widely shared, we feel little need to discuss it with others, and we often take it for granted. For example, you probably don't spend much time thinking about the importance of living in rectangular rooms, trying to minimize body odor, limiting yourself to one spouse at a time, or using credit cards to obtain material goods and services. Although we generally fail to appreciate its influence,

Selected Aspects of United States Ethnic Groups' Cultural Heritage

African Americans
For most of the history of African Americans in the United States, there has been a tendency to omit the history of this group in Africa and to begin the history as of the time the first Africans arrived in the New World in 1619. . . . Many of the elements of African American culture are quite similar to elements found in West Africa, the location from which most of the slaves came. . . . These include dialect, adult-child relationships, family structure, music, generosity or hospitality, respect for the law, religion, sense of justice, and the work ethic. . . . African Americans were enslaved and subjected to a system of bondage with few parallels in human history. . . . Many of the differences between the primary social institutions in the African American community and in the dominant culture are a result of the long history of oppression. . . . Allen (1981) found that the child-rearing patterns of African American parents reflect the reality that their sons are being socialized to be confrontive. He concludes that African American parents recognize that future success for their sons hinges on an ability to be alternately and selectively assertive and acquiescent. (pp. 15–16, 18, 22, 25–26)

Native Americans
The holistic lifestyle of Native Americans is also reflected in their arts, in their traditions of music, dance, and crafts. Their art is woven throughout the fabric of everyday Native American life. . . . Native American children are reared by the extended family, clan, or tribe, with grandparents and other elders usually responsible for teaching the children. Children are given a great deal of freedom and are allowed to explore and be independent quite early in their lives. . . . Native American attitudes toward sex are likewise liberal; sex is treated as a part of the natural process of life. Sexual intercourse and facts surrounding it are understood at very early ages. . . . To Native Americans, religion is the universe. They believe that almost every act of life is regulated and determined by religion. . . . To Native Americans, time is not an entity, it just "is." Therefore they do not worry about or value time, and time is not structured in their everyday lives. (pp. 51, 53–54, 56)

Figure 1.9
Culture and behavior: some concrete examples. Culture is a terribly broad and difficult to define concept that is perhaps best explained with examples rather than definitions, which vary widely. The brief excerpts shown here, taken from Don Locke's (1992) book, *Increasing Multicultural Understanding,* describe selected aspects of the cultural heritage of six prominent ethnic groups in the United States. These examples should help to flesh out the complex, multifaceted concept of culture.

Chinese Americans
The religious roots of the Chinese are varied. The scholar gentry class practiced Confucianism, which is considered more a philosophy than a religion. . . . Unlike in Western religions, there is no sense of sin in Confucianism. Human nature is basically good and the evils of human society are due to the examples of immoral leaders. Morality does not rest on religious faith. . . . While the scholars embraced the intellectual aspects of Confucianism, the common people developed a folk religion that was supplemented over the centuries by the two other major Chinese religions, Buddhism and Taoism. . . . Selflessness is one of the oldest values in China. The selfless person is always willing to subordinate his or her interest or the interest of a small group to the interest of a larger social group. . . . Chinese Americans appear to be more acculturated than other groups. However, this may be because of their own cultural tendencies to conform, obey authority, and restrain strong feelings. (pp. 89–93)

Japanese Americans
Consistent with the value of respect for authority and elders, one finds among Japanese Americans values of allegiance to the family and dependency versus individualism and self-reliance. . . . There is very little eye contact among Japanese. Direct eye contact is considered impolite and even disrespectful toward seniors. . . . Japanese Americans value maintaining low visibility and conformity in order not to bring negative attention to themselves. A model Japanese leader is one who is informed, possesses thorough knowledge, and yet avoids the spotlight. . . . Another Japanese value is the concept of *enryo* (reserve, constraint), which helps to explain many differences in style of communication. . . . The interaction rules related to *enryo* are learned within the family, where a child is taught the importance of reticence, modesty, indirect communication, and humility. . . . Being future oriented and concerned about the welfare of their children, the Japanese value education. (pp. 68–69, 72, 74)

Figure 1.9 (continued)

Puerto Rican Americans
In many respects, Puerto Ricans share the heritage of the Spanish tradition in their interactions, retention of the language, fundamental Catholic theology, acceptance of class structure, hospitality, gregarious family patterns, machismo, and emphasis on the spiritual and human values of society. . . . One of the more obvious value shifts currently taking place among Puerto Rican Americans is the change in roles of males and females, with females becoming more independent. A shift is also occurring in the role of the child, with children beginning to behave according to dominant cultural standards of self-reliance, aggressiveness, competitiveness, inquisitiveness, and independence. . . . Many of the Puerto Rican values continue, such as personalism, which is a form of individualism that focuses on the inner importance of the person and role of the *padrino,* a person of influence who helps the Puerto Rican. (pp. 153–154)

Mexican Americans
Mexican Americans use an extended family structure that includes godparents (*compradazgo*) who ensure the welfare and religious education of the children. . . . Traditional godparents assume serious obligations toward their godchildren and take them into their own households whenever necessary. . . . Like the traditional family, the choosing of godparents has been declining, particularly in cities where pressures on Mexican Americans to acculturate are greater. . . . For the Mexican American, material objects are usually necessities and not ends in themselves. . . . The philosopher, poet, musician, and artist are more often revered in this culture than the businessman or financier. In the dominant culture of the United States, being responsible is equated with being punctual. The Mexican American concept of responsibility is based on other values, such as attending to the immediate needs of family and friends, and thus Mexican Americans do not place much value on, and may be casual about, punctuality. (pp. 139–140)

our cultural heritage has a pervasive impact on our thoughts, feelings, and behavior.

Let's look at a couple examples of this influence. In North America, when people are invited to dinner in someone's home they generally show their appreciation of their host's cooking efforts by eating all of the food they are served. In India, this behavior would be insulting to the host, as guests are expected to leave some food on their plates. The leftover food acknowledges the generosity of the host, implying that he or she provided so much food the guest could not eat it all (Moghaddam, Taylor, & Wright, 1993). Cultures also vary in their emphasis on punctuality. In North America, we expect people to show up for meetings on time, and if someone is more than 10 to 15 minutes late we begin to get upset. We generally strive to be on time, and many of us are quite proud of our precise and dependable punctuality. However, in many Asian and Latin American countries, social obligations that arise at the last minute are given just as much priority as scheduled commitments. Hence, people often show up for important meetings an hour or two late with little remorse, and they may be quite puzzled by the consternation of their Western visitors

(Brislin, 1993). These examples may seem trivial, but as you will see in upcoming chapters, culture can also influence crucial matters, such as educational success, mental health, and vulnerability to physical illnesses.

In discussing the importance of culture, Segall and his colleagues (1990) go so far as to assert that "it is rare (perhaps even impossible) for any human being ever to behave without responding to some aspect of culture" (p. 5). Although the influence of culture is everywhere, generalizations about cultural groups must always be tempered by the realization that there is great diversity within any society or ethnic group. Researchers may be able to pinpoint genuinely useful insights about Ethiopian, Korean American, or Ukrainian culture, for example, but it would be foolish to assume that all Ethiopians, Korean Americans, or Ukrainians exhibit identical behavior. It is also important to realize that there are both differences and similarities across cultures in behavior. As we will see repeatedly, psychological processes are characterized by both cultural variance and invariance.

Caveats aside, if we hope to achieve a sound understanding of human behavior, we need to consider cultural determinants. In upcoming chapters you'll see how cultural factors shape behavior and how the viewpoint of one's own culture can distort one's interpretation of the behavior of people from other cultures.

Theme 6: Heredity and Environment Jointly Influence Behavior

Are we who we are—athletic or artistic, quick-tempered or calm, shy or outgoing, energetic or laid back—because of our genetic inheritance or because of our upbringing? This question about the importance of nature versus nurture, or heredity versus environment, has been asked in one form or another since ancient times. Historically, the nature-versus-nurture question was framed as an all-or-none proposition. In other words, theorists argued that personal traits and abilities are governed entirely by heredity or entirely by environment. John B. Watson, for instance, asserted that personality and ability depend almost exclusively on an individual's environment. In contrast, Sir Francis Galton, a pioneer in mental testing, maintained that personality and ability depend almost entirely on genetic inheritance.

Today, most psychologists agree that heredity and environment are both important. A century of research has shown that genetics and experience jointly influence an individual's intelligence, temperament, personality, and susceptibility to many psychological disorders (Plomin & Rende, 1991; Rose, 1995). If we ask whether people are born or made, psychology's answer is "Both." This does not mean that nature versus nurture is a dead issue. Lively debate about the *relative influence of* genetics and experience continues unabated. Furthermore, psychologists are actively seeking to understand the complex ways in which genetic inheritance and experience interact to mold behavior.

Theme 7: Our Experience of the World Is Highly Subjective

People's experience of the world is highly subjective. Even elementary perception—for example, of sights and sounds—is not a passive process. We actively process incoming stimulation, selectively focusing on some aspects of that stimulation while ignoring others. Moreover, we impose organization on the stimuli that we pay attention to. These tendencies combine to make perception personalized and subjective.

The subjectivity of perception was demonstrated nicely in a study by Hastorf and Cantril (1954). They showed students at Princeton and Dartmouth universities a film of a recent football game between the two schools. The students were told to watch for rules infractions. Both groups saw the same film, but the Princeton students "saw" the Dartmouth players engage in twice as many infractions as the Dartmouth students "saw." The investigators concluded that the game "actually was many different games and that each version of the events that transpired was just as 'real' to a particular person as other versions were to other people" (Hastorf & Cantril, 1954). In this study, the subjects' perceptions were swayed by their motives. It shows how people sometimes see what they w*ant* to see.

Other studies reveal that people also tend to see what they *expect* to see. For example, Harold Kelley (1950) showed how perceptions of people are influenced by their reputation. Kelley told students that their class would be taken over by a new lecturer, whom they would be asked to evaluate later. Before the class, the students were given a short description of the incoming instructor, with one important variation. Half the students were led to expect a "warm" person, while the other half were led to expect a "cold" one (see Figure 1.10). All the subjects were exposed to the same 20 minutes of lecture and interaction with the new instructor. However, the group of subjects who *expected* a warm person rated the instructor as more considerate, sociable, humorous, good natured, informal, and humane than the subjects in the group who had expected a cold person.

Thus, it is clear that motives and expectations color our experiences. To some extent, we see what we want to see or what we expect to see. This subjectivity in perception turns out to explain a variety of behavioral tendencies that would otherwise be perplexing.

Human subjectivity is precisely what the scientific method is designed to counteract. In using the scientific approach, psychologists strive to make their observations as objective as possible. In some respects, overcoming subjectivity is what science is all about. Left to their own subjective experience, people might still believe that the earth is flat and that the sun revolves around it. Thus, psychologists are committed to the scientific approach because they believe it is the most reliable route to accurate knowledge.

Now that you have been introduced to the text's organizing themes, let's turn to an example of how psychological research can be applied to the challenges of everyday life. In our first Application, we'll focus on a subject that should be

Mr. Blank is a graduate student in the Department of Economics and Social Science here at M.I.T. He has had three semesters of teaching experience in psychology at another college. This is his first semester teaching Ec. 70. He is 26 years old, a veteran, and married. People who know him consider him to be a very warm person, industrious, critical, practical, and determined.

Figure 1.10
Manipulating person perception. Read the accompanying description of Mr. Blank carefully. If you were about to hear him give a lecture, would this description bias your perceptions of him? You probably think not, but when Kelley (1950) altered one adjective in this description (replacing the word *warm* with *cold*), the change had a dramatic impact on subjects' ratings of the guest lecturer.

Understanding the Seven Key Themes

Check your understanding of the seven key themes introduced in the chapter by matching the vignettes with the themes they exemplify. You'll find the answers in Appendix A.

Themes
1. Psychology is empirical.
2. Psychology is theoretically diverse.
3. Psychology evolves in a sociohistorical context.
4. Behavior is determined by multiple causes.
5. Our behavior is shaped by our cultural heritage.
6. Heredity and environment jointly influence behavior.
7. Our experience of the world is highly subjective.

Vignettes

_____ a. Several or more theoretical models of emotion have contributed to our overall understanding of the dynamics of emotion.

_____ b. According to the stress-vulnerability model, some people are at greater risk for developing certain psychological disorders for genetic reasons. Whether these people actually develop the disorders depends on how much stress they experience in their work, families, or other areas of their lives.

_____ c. Physical health and illness seem to be influenced by a complex constellation of psychological, biological, and social system variables.

_____ d. One of the difficulties in investigating the effects of drugs on consciousness is that individuals tend to have different experiences with a given drug because of their different expectations.

highly relevant to you: how to be a successful student.

Recap of Key Points

• As we examine psychology in all its many variations, we will emphasize seven key ideas as unifying themes. First, psychology is empirical because psychologists base their conclusions on observation through research rather than reasoning or common sense.

• Psychology is theoretically diverse, as there are many competing schools of thought in the field. This diversity has fueled progress and is a strength rather than a weakness. Psychology evolves in a socio-historical context, as trends, issues, and values in society influence what goes on in psychology, and vice versa.

• Behavior is determined by multiple causes, as most aspects of behavior are influenced by complex networks of interacting factors. Although cultural heritage is often taken for granted, it has a pervasive impact on people's thoughts, feelings, and behavior.

• Lively debate about the relative importance of nature versus nurture continues, but it is clear that heredity and environment jointly influence behavior. Our experience of the world is highly subjective, as we sometimes see what we want to see or what we expect to see.

APPLICATION:
IMPROVING ACADEMIC PERFORMANCE

Answer the following "true" or "false."

1 It's a good idea to study in as many different locations (your bedroom or kitchen, the library, lounges around school, and so forth) as possible.

2 If you have a professor who delivers chaotic, hard-to-follow lectures, there is little point in attending class.

3 Cramming the night before an exam is an efficient method of study.

4 In taking lecture notes, you should try to be a "human tape recorder" (that is, write down everything your professor says).

5 You should never change your answers to multiple-choice questions, because your first hunch is your best hunch.

All of the above statements are false. If you answered them all correctly, you may have already acquired the kinds of skills and habits that facilitate academic success. If so, however, you are *not* typical. Today, many students enter college with poor study skills and habits—and it's not entirely their fault. The American educational system generally provides minimal instruction on good study techniques. In this first Application, we will try to remedy this situation to some extent by reviewing some insights that psychology offers on how to improve academic performance. We will discuss how to promote better study habits, how to enhance reading efforts, how to get more out of lectures, and how to improve test-taking strategies. You may also want to jump ahead and read the Application for Chapter 7, which focuses on how to improve everyday memory.

Developing Sound Study Habits

Effective study is crucial to success in college. Although you may run into a few classmates who boast about getting good grades without studying, you can be sure that if they perform well on exams, they *do* study. Students who claim otherwise simply want to be viewed as extremely bright rather than studious.

Learning can be immensely gratifying, but studying usually involves hard work. The first step toward effective study habits is to face up to this reality. You don't have to feel guilty if you don't look forward to studying. Most students don't. Once you accept the premise that studying doesn't come naturally, it should be apparent that you need to set up an organized program to promote adequate study. According to Walter and Siebert (1990), such a program should include the following considerations:

1. *Set up a schedule for studying.* If you wait until the urge to study strikes you, you may still be waiting when the exam rolls around. Thus, it is important to allocate definite times to studying. Review your various time obligations (work, chores, and so on) and figure out in advance when you can study. When allotting certain times to studying, keep in mind that you need to be wide awake and alert. Be realistic about how long you can study at one time before you wear down from fatigue. Allow time for study breaks—they can revive sagging concentration.

It's important to write down your study schedule. A written schedule serves as a reminder and increases your commitment to following it. You should begin by setting up a general schedule for the quarter or semester, like the one in Figure 1.11 on page 30. Then, at the beginning of each week, plan the specific assignments that you intend to work on during each study session. This approach to scheduling should help you avoid cramming for exams at the last minute. Cramming is an ineffective study strategy for most students (Underwood, 1961; Zechmeister & Nyberg, 1982). It will strain your memorization capabilities, can tax your energy level, and may stoke the fires of test anxiety.

In planning your weekly schedule, try to avoid the tendency to put off working on major tasks such as term papers and reports. Time-management experts, such as Alan Lakein (1973), point out that many people tend to tackle simple, routine tasks first, saving larger tasks for later when they supposedly will have more time. This common tendency leads many individuals to repeatedly delay working on major assignments until it's too late to do a good job. A good way to avoid this trap is to break major assignments down into smaller component tasks that can be scheduled individually. You can assess other aspects of your time-management practices by responding to the questionnaire in Figure 1.12 (on page 31).

2. *Find a place to study where you can concentrate.* Where you study is also important. The key is to find a place where distractions are likely to be minimal. Most people cannot study effectively while the TV or stereo is on or while other people are talking. Don't depend on willpower to carry you through such distractions. It's much easier to plan ahead and avoid the distractions altogether. In fact, you would be wise to set up one or two specific places used solely for study (Hettich, 1992).

3. *Reward your studying.* One reason that it is so difficult to be motivated to study regularly is that the payoffs often lie in the

distant future. The ultimate reward, a degree, may be years away. Even more short-term rewards, such as an A in the course, may be weeks or months away. To combat this problem, it helps to give yourself immediate, tangible rewards for studying, such as a snack, TV show, or phone call to a friend. Thus, you should set realistic study goals for yourself and then reward yourself when you meet them. The systematic manipulation of rewards involves harnessing the principles of *behavior modification* described by B. F. Skinner and other behavioral psychologists. These principles are covered in the Chapter 6 Application.

Improving Your Reading

Much of your study time is spent reading and absorbing information. *These efforts must be active.* Many students deceive themselves into thinking that they are studying by running a marker through a few sentences here and there in their book. If they do so without thoughtful selectivity, they are simply turning a textbook into a coloring book.

You can use a number of methods to actively attack your reading assignments. One of the more worthwhile strategies is Robinson's (1970) SQ3R method. **SQ3R is a study system designed to promote effective reading, which includes five steps: survey, question, read, recite, and review.** Its name is an acronym for the five steps in the procedure.

Step 1: Survey. Before you plunge into the reading itself, glance over the topic headings in the chapter. Try to get a general overview of the material. If you know where the chapter is going, you can better appreciate and organize the information you are about to read.

Qtep 2: Question. Once you have an overview of your reading assignment, you should proceed through it one section at a time. Take a look at the heading of the first section and convert it into a question. This is usually quite simple. If the heading is

Weekly activity schedule

	Monday	Tuesday	Wednesday	Thursday	Friday	Saturday	Sunday
8 A.M.						Work	
9 A.M.	History	Study	History	Study	History	Work	
10 A.M.	Psychology	French	Psychology	French	Psychology	Work	
11 A.M.	Study	French	Study	French	Study	Work	
Noon	Math	Study	Math	Study	Math	Work	Study
1 P.M.							Study
2 P.M.	Study	English	Study	English	Study		Study
3 P.M.	Study	English	Study	English	Study		Study
4 P.M.							
5 P.M.							
6 P.M.	Work	Study	Study	Work			Study
7 P.M.	Work	Study	Study	Work			Study
8 P.M.	Work	Study	Study	Work			Study
9 P.M.	Work	Study	Study	Work			Study
10 P.M.	Work			Work			

Figure 1.11
One student's general activity schedule for a semester. Each week the student fills in the specific assignments to work on during each study period.

"Prenatal Risk Factors," your question should be "What are sources of risk during prenatal development?" If the heading is "Stereotyping," your question should be "What is stereotyping?" Asking these questions gets you actively involved in your reading and helps you identify the main ideas.

Rtep 3: Read. Only now, in the third step, are you ready to sink your teeth into the reading. Read only the specific section that you have decided to tackle. Read it with an eye toward answering the question you have just formulated. If necessary, reread the section until you can answer that question. Decide whether the segment addresses any

other important questions and answer them as well.

Rtep 4: Recite. Now that you can answer the key question for the section, recite the answer out loud to yourself in your own words. Don't move on to the next section until you understand the main ideas of the current section. You may want to write down these ideas for review later. When you have fully digested the first section, then you may go on to the next. Repeat steps 2 through 4 with the next section. Once you have mastered the crucial points there, you can go on again. Keep repeating steps 2 through 4, section by section, until you finish the chapter.

Step 5: Review. When you have read the entire chapter, refresh your memory by going back over the key points. Repeat your questions and try to answer them without consulting your book or notes. This review should fortify your retention of the main ideas. It should also help you see how the main ideas are related.

The SQ3R method should probably be applied to many texts on a paragraph-by-paragraph basis. Obviously, this will require you to formulate some questions without the benefit of topic headings. If you don't have enough headings, you can simply reverse the order of steps 2 and 3. Read the paragraph first and then formulate a question that addresses the basic idea of the paragraph. Then work at answering the question in your own words. The point is that you can be flexible in your use of the SQ3R technique. *What makes SQ3R effective is that it breaks a reading assignment into manageable parts and requires understanding before you move on.* Any method that accomplishes these goals should enhance your reading.

Besides topic headings, your textbooks may contain various other learning aids you can use to improve your reading. If a book provides a chapter outline, chapter summary, or learning objectives, don't ignore them. They can help you recognize the important points in the chapter. Good learning objectives practically create the questions for you in the SQ3R process. A lot of thought goes into formulating these and other learning aids. It is wise to take advantage of them.

Getting More out of Lectures

Although lectures are sometimes boring and tedious, it is a simple fact that poor class attendance is associated with poor grades. For example, in one study, Lindgren (1969) found that absences from class were much more common among "unsuccessful" students (grade average C– or below) than among "successful" students (grade average B or above), as shown in Figure 1.13. Even when you have an instructor who delivers hard-to-follow lec-

---

How Well Do You Manage Your Time?

Listed below are ten statements that reflect generally accepted principles of good time management. Answer these items by circling the response most charactistic of how you perform. Please be honest. No one will know your answers except you.

1 Each day I set aside a small amount of time for planning and thinking about my responsibilities.
0. Almost never 1. Sometimes 2. Often 3. Almost always

2 I set specific, written goals and put deadlines on them.
0. Almost never 1. Sometimes 2. Often 3. Almost always

3 I make a daily "to do" list, arrange items in order of importance, and try to get the important items done as soon as possible.
0. Almost never 1. Sometimes 2. Often 3. Almost always

4 I am aware of the 80/20 rule and use it. (The 80/20 rule states that 80% of your effectiveness will generally come from achieving only 20% of your goals.)
0. Almost never 1. Sometimes 2. Often 3. Almost always

5 I keep a loose schedule to allow for crises and the unexpected.
0. Almost never 1. Sometimes 2. Often 3. Almost always

6 I delegate everything I can to others.
0. Almost never 1. Sometimes 2. Often 3. Almost always

7 I try to handle each piece of paper only once.
0. Almost never 1. Sometimes 2. Often 3. Almost always

8 I eat a light lunch so I don't get sleepy in the afternoon.
0. Almost never 1. Sometimes 2. Often 3. Almost always

9 I make an active effort to keep common interruptions (visitors, meetings, telephone calls) from continually disrupting my work day.
0. Almost never 1. Sometimes 2. Often 3. Almost always

10 I am able to say no to others' requests for my time that would prevent my completing important tasks.
0. Almost never 1. Sometimes 2. Often 3. Almost always

To get your score, give yourself

3 points for each "almost always"
2 points for each "often"
1 point for each "sometimes"
0 points for each "almost never"
Add up your points to get your total score.

If you scored

0–15 Better give some thought to managing your time.
16–20 You're doing OK, but there's room for improvement.
21–25 Very good.
26–30 You cheated!

Figure 1.12
Assessing your time management. This brief questionnaire (from Le Boeuf, 1980) is designed to evaluate the quality of one's time management. It should allow you to get a rough handle on how well you manage your time.

---

tures, it is still important to go to class. If nothing else, you can get a feel for how the instructor thinks, which can help you anticipate the content of exams and respond in the manner expected by your professor.

Fortunately, most lectures are reasonably coherent. Research indicates that attentive note taking helps students identify and remember the most important points from a lecture, while weeding out ideas of lesser importance (Einstein, Morris, &

Smith, 1985). Books on study skills (Longman & Atkinson, 1991; Sotiriou, 1993) offer a number of suggestions on how to take good lecture notes, some of which are summarized here:

• Extracting information from lectures requires active listening. Focus full attention on the speaker. Try to anticipate what's coming and search for deeper meanings.
• When course material is especially com-

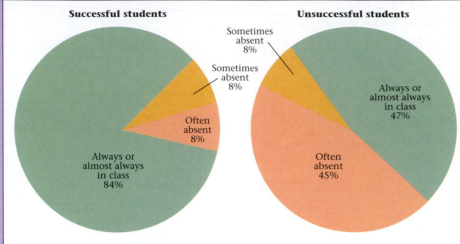

Figure 1.13
Attendance and grades. When Lindgren (1969) compared the class attendance of successful students (B average or above) and unsuccessful students (C– average or below), he found a clear association between poor attendance and poor grades.

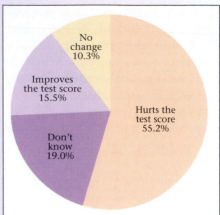

Figure 1.14
Beliefs about the effects of answer changing on tests. Benjamin et al. (1984) asked 58 college faculty whether changing answers on tests is a good idea. Like most students, the majority of the faculty felt that answer changing usually hurts a student's test score, even though the evidence contradicts this belief (see Figure 1.15).

plex, it is a good idea to prepare for the lecture by reading ahead on the scheduled subject in your text. Then you have less brand-new information to digest.

• You are not supposed to be a human tape recorder. Insofar as possible, try to write down the lecturer's thoughts in your own words. Doing so forces you to organize the ideas in a way that makes sense to you. In taking notes, pay attention to clues about what is most important. These clues may range from subtle hints, such as an instructor repeating a point, to not-so-subtle hints, such as an instructor saying "You'll run into this again."

• Asking questions during lectures can be helpful. Doing so keeps you actively involved in the lecture and allows you to clarify points that you may have misunderstood. Many students are more bashful about asking questions than they should be. They don't realize that most professors welcome questions.

Improving Test-Taking Strategies

Let's face it—some students are better than others at taking tests. *Testwiseness* is the ability to use the characteristics and format of a cognitive test to maximize one's score. Students clearly vary in testwiseness, and such variations are reflected in performance on exams (Fagley, 1987; Sarnacki, 1979). Testwiseness is *not* a substitute for knowledge of the subject matter. However,

skill in taking tests can help you show what you know when it is critical to do so.

A number of myths exist about the best way to take tests. For instance, it is widely believed that students shouldn't go back and change their answers to multiple-choice questions. Benjamin, Cavell, and Shallenberger (1984) found this to be the dominant belief among college *faculty* as well as students (see Figure 1.14). However, the old adage that "your first hunch is your best hunch on tests" has been shown to be wrong. Empirical studies clearly and consistently indicate that, over the long run, changing answers pays off. Benjamin and his colleagues reviewed 20 studies on this issue; their findings are presented in Figure 1.15. As you can see, answer changes that go from a wrong answer to a right answer outnumber changes that go from a right answer to a wrong one by a sizable margin. The popular belief that answer changing is harmful is probably attributable to painful memories of right-to-wrong changes. In any case, you can see how it pays to be familiar with sound test-taking strategies.

General Tips

The principles of testwiseness were first described by Millman, Bishop, and Ebel (1965). Let's look at some of their general ideas:

• If efficient time use appears crucial, set up

a mental schedule for progressing through the test. Make a mental note to check whether you're one-third finished when a third of your time is gone.

• Don't waste time pondering difficult-to-answer questions excessively. If you have no idea at all, just guess and go on. If you need to devote a good deal of time to the question, skip it and mark it so you can return to it later if time permits.

• Adopt the appropriate level of so-

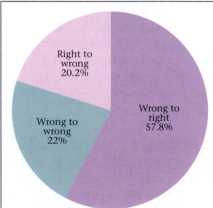

Figure 1.15
Actual effects of changing answers on multiple-choice tests. When the data from all the relevant studies are combined, they indicate that answer changing on tests generally does not reduce students' test scores (Benjamin et al., 1984). It is interesting to note the contrast between beliefs about answer changing (see Figure 1.14) and the actual results of this practice.

phistication for the test. Don't read things into questions. Sometimes students make things more complex than they were intended to be. Often, simple-looking questions are just what they appear to be.

• If you complete all of the questions and still have some time remaining, review the test. Make sure that you have recorded your answers correctly. If you were unsure of some answers, go back and reconsider them.

Tips for Multiple-Choice Exams

Sound test-taking strategies are especially important with multiple-choice (and true-false) questions. These types of questions often include clues that may help you converge on the correct answer (Mentzer, 1982; Weiten, 1984). You may be able to improve your performance on such tests by considering the following points:

• As you read the stem of each multiple-choice question, *anticipate* the answer if you can, before looking at the options. If the answer you anticipated is among the options, it is likely to be the correct one.

• Always read each question completely. Continue reading even if you find your anticipated answer among the options. There may be a more complete option farther down the list.

• Learn how to quickly eliminate options that are highly implausible. Many questions have only two plausible options, accompanied by "throwaway" options for filler. You should work at spotting these implausible options so that you can quickly discard them and narrow your task.

• Be alert to the fact that information relevant to one question is sometimes given away in another test item.

• On items that have "all of the above" as an option, if you know that just two of the options are correct, you should choose "all of the above." If you are confident that one of the options is incorrect, you should eliminate this option and "all of the above" and choose from the remaining options.

• Options that represent broad, sweeping generalizations tend to be incorrect. You should be vigilant for words such as *always, never, necessarily, only, must, completely, to-*

tally, and so forth that create these improbable assertions.

• In contrast, options that represent carefully qualified statements tend to be correct. Words such as *often, sometimes, perhaps, may,* and *generally* tend to show up in these well-qualified statements.

Tips for Essay Exams

There is little research on testwiseness as it applies to essay exams. This is because there are relatively few clues to take advantage of in the essay format. Nonetheless, various books (Pauk, 1990; Walter & Siebert, 1990) offer tips based on expert advice, including the following:

• Time is usually a crucial factor on essay tests. Therefore, you should begin by looking over the questions and making time allocations on the basis of (1) your knowledge, (2) the time required to answer each question, and (3) the points awarded for answering each question. Usually it's a good idea to answer the questions that you know best first.

• Many students fail to appreciate the importance of good organization in their essay responses. If your instructor can't follow where you are going with your answers, you won't get many points. Test essays are often poorly organized because students feel pressured for time and plunge into answering questions without any planning. It's a good idea to spend a minute getting organized first. Also, many examiners appreciate it if you make your organization quite explicit by using headings or by numbering the points you're making.

• In writing essays, the trick is to be concise while being complete. You should always try to get right to the point, and you should never pad your answer. Many examiners get cross when they have to wade through excess padding to track down the crucial ideas they're looking for. However, you should avoid writing in such a "shorthand" manner that you leave things ambiguous.

• In many courses you'll learn a great deal of jargon or technical terminology. Demonstrate your learning by using this technical vocabulary in your essay answers.

In summary, sound study skills and habits are crucial to academic success. Intelligence alone won't do the job (although it certainly helps). Good academic skills do not develop overnight. They are acquired gradually, so be patient with yourself. Fortunately, tasks such as reading textbooks, writing papers, and taking tests get easier with practice. Ultimately, I think you'll find that the rewards—knowledge, a sense of accomplishment, and progress toward a degree—are worth the effort.

Recap of Key Points

• To foster sound study habits, you should devise a written study schedule and reward yourself for following it. You should also try to find one or two specific places for studying that are relatively free of distractions.

• You should use active reading techniques to select the most important ideas from the material you read. SQ3R, one approach to active reading, breaks a reading assigment into manageable segments and requires that you understand each segment before you move on.

• Good note taking can help you get more out of lectures. It's important to use active listening techniques and to record lecturers' ideas in your own words. It also helps if you read ahead to prepare for lectures and ask questions as needed.

• Being an effective student requires sound test-taking skills. In general, it's a good idea to devise a schedule for progressing through an exam, to adopt the appropriate level of sophistication, to avoid wasting time on troublesome questions, and to review your answers whenever time permits.

• On multiple-choice tests it is wise to anticipate answers, to read questions completely, and to quickly eliminate implausible options. Options that represent carefully qualified assertions are more likely to be correct than options that create sweeping generalizations.

• On essay tests, it is wise to start with questions you know, to emphasize good organization, to be concise, and to use technical vocabulary when it is appropriate.

Key Ideas

From Speculation to Science: How Psychology Developed

◆ Psychology's intellectual parents were 19th-century philosophy and physiology, which shared an interest in the mysteries of the mind. Psychology was born as an independent discipline when Wilhelm Wundt established the first psychological research laboratory in 1879 at Leipzig, Germany. He argued that psychology should be the scientific study of consciousness.

◆ The structuralists believed that psychology should use introspection to analyze consciousness into its basic elements. Functionalists, such as William James, believed that psychology should focus on the purpose and adaptive functions of consciousness.

◆ Behaviorists, led by John B. Watson, argued that psychology should study only observable behavior. Thus, they campaigned to redefine psychology as the science of behavior. Emphasizing the importance of the environment over heredity, they began to explore stimulus-response relationships, often using laboratory animals as subjects.

◆ Gestalt psychology, founded by Max Wertheimer, was based on the belief that the whole is greater than the sum of its parts. The Gestalt school arose as a reaction to structuralism and challenged the behavioral view as well.

◆ Sigmund Freud's psychoanalytic theory emphasized the unconscious determinants of behavior and the importance of sexuality. Freud's ideas were controversial, and they met with resistance in academic psychology.

◆ Behaviorism continued as a powerful force in psychology, boosted greatly by B. F. Skinner's research. Like Watson before him, Skinner asserted that psychology should study only observable behavior, and he generated controversy by arguing that free will is an illusion.

◆ Finding both behaviorism and psychoanalysis unsatisfactory, advocates of a new theoretical orientation called humanism became influential in the 1950s. Humanism, led by Abraham Maslow and Carl Rogers, emphasized humans' freedom and potential for personal growth.

◆ Stimulated by the demands of World War II, clinical psychology grew rapidly in the 1950s. Thus, psychology became a profession as well as a science. This movement toward professionalization eventually spread to other areas in psychology.

◆ During the 1950s and 1960s advances in the study of cognitive processes and the physiological bases of behavior led to renewed interest in cognition and physiology, as psychology returned to its original roots.

◆ In the 1980s, Western psychologists, who had previously been rather provincial, developed a greater interest in how cultural factors influence thoughts, feelings, and behavior. This trend was sparked in large part by growing global interdependence and by increased cultural diversity in Western societies.

◆ The 1990s witnessed the emergence of a new theoretical perspective called evolutionary psychology. The central premise of this new school of thought is that patterns of behavior are the product of evolutionary forces, just as anatomical characteristics are shaped by natural selection.

Psychology Today: Vigorous and Diversified

◆ Contemporary psychology is a diversified science and profession that has grown rapidly in recent decades. Major areas of research in modern psychology include developmental psychology, social psychology, experimental psychology, physiological psychology, cognitive psychology, personality, and psychometrics.

◆ Applied psychology encompasses four professional specialties: clinical psychology, counseling psychology, educational and school psychology, and industrial and organizational psychology.

Putting It in Perspective: Seven Key Themes

◆ As we examine psychology in all its many variations, we will emphasize seven key ideas as unifying themes. Looking at psychology as a field of study, our three key themes are (1) psychology is empirical, (2) psychology is theoretically diverse, and (3) psychology evolves in a sociohistorical context.

◆ Looking at psychology's subject matter, the remaining four themes are (4) behavior is determined by multiple causes, (5) our behavior is shaped by our cultural heritage, (6) heredity and environment jointly influence behavior, and (7) our experience of the world is highly subjective.

Application: Improving Academic Performance

◆ To foster sound study habits, you should devise a written study schedule and reward yourself for following it. You should also try to find one or two specific places for studying that are relatively free of distractions.

◆ You should use active reading techniques to select the most important ideas from the material you read. SQ3R, one approach to active reading, breaks a reading assigment into manageable segments and requires that you understand each segment before you move on.

◆ Good note taking can help you get more out of lectures. It's important to use active listening techniques and to record lecturers' ideas in your own words.

◆ Being an effective student also requires sound test-taking skills. In general, it's a good idea to devise a schedule for progressing through an exam, to adopt the appropriate level of sophistication, to avoid wasting time on troublesome questions, and to review your answers whenever time permits.

Key Terms

Applied psychology
Behavior
Behaviorism
Clinical psychology
Cognition
Culture
Empiricism
Ethnocentrism
Evolutionary psychology
Functionalism
Gestalt psychology
Humanism
Introspection
Natural selection
Phi phenomenon
Psychiatry
Psychoanalytic theory

Psychology
SQ3R
Stimulus
Structuralism
Testwiseness
Theory
Unconscious

Key People

Sigmund Freud
G. Stanley Hall
William James
Carl Rogers
B. F. Skinner
John B. Watson
Wilhelm Wundt

Practice Test

1. For which of the following is Wilhelm Wundt primarily known?
    A. the establishment of the first formal laboratory for research in psychology
    B. the distinction between mind and body as two separate entities
    C. the discovery of how signals are conducted along nerves in the body
    D. the development of the first formal program for training in psychotherapy

2. G. Stanley Hall is noteworthy in the history of psychology because he:
    A. established the first American research laboratory in psychology.
    B. launched America's first psychological journal.
    C. was the driving force behind the establishment of the American Psychological Association.
    D. did all of the above.

3. Which of the following approaches might William James criticize for examining a movie frame by frame instead of seeing the motion in the motion picture?
    A. structuralism
    B. functionalism
    C. dualism
    D. humanism

4. Fred, a tennis coach, insists that he can make any reasonably healthy individual into an internationally competitive tennis player. Fred is echoing the thoughts of:
    A. Sigmund Freud.
    B. John B. Watson.
    C. Abraham Maslow.
    D. William James.

5. Which of the following approaches might suggest that forgetting to pick his mother up at the airport was Henry's unconscious way of saying that he did not welcome her visit?
    A. psychoanalytic
    B. behavioral
    C. humanistic
    D. cognitive

6. Which of the following is a statement with which Skinner's followers would agree?
    A. The whole is greater than the sum of its parts.
    B. The goal of behavior is self-actualization.
    C. Nature is more influential than nurture.
    D. Free will is an illusion.

7. Which of the following approaches has the most optimistic view of human nature?
    A. humanism
    B. behaviorism
    C. psychoanalysis
    D. structuralism

8. Which of the following historical events created a demand for clinicians that was far greater than the supply?
    A. World War I
    B. the Depression
    C. World War II
    D. the Korean War

9. The tendency to view one's own group as superior to others and as the standard for judging the worth of foreign ways is known as:
    A. behaviorism.
    B. ethnocentrism.
    C. humanism.
    D. functionalism.

10. The study of the endocrine system and genetic mechanisms would most likely be undertaken by a:
    A. clinical psychologist.
    B. physiological psychologist.
    C. social psychologist.
    D. educational psychologist.

11. The fact that psychologists do not all agree about the nature and development of personality demonstrates:
    A. that there are many ways of looking at the same phenomenon.
    B. the fundamental inability of psychologists to work together in developing a single theory.
    C. the failure of psychologists to communicate with one another.
    D. the possibility that personality may simply be incomprehensible.

12. A multifactorial causation approach to behavior suggests that:
    A. most behaviors can be explained best by single-cause explanations.
    B. most behavior is governed by a complex network of interrelated factors.
    C. data need to be analyzed by the statistical technique called factor analysis in order for the data to make sense.
    D. explanations of behavior tend to build up from the simple to the complex in a hierarchical manner.

13. Psychology's answer to the question of whether we are "born" or "made" tends to be:
    A. we are "born."
    B. we are "made."
    C. we are both "born" and "made."
    D. neither.

14. The reason the SQ3R method is effective is that:
    A. it breaks a reading assignment down into manageable segments and requires understanding before you move on.
    B. with this method, you only have to skim the reading assignment to pick out the main points.
    C. it allows you to memorize and recite great quantities of material even if you don't fully understand it.
    D. it requires you to read and re-read your text over and over.

15. Which of the following is not testwise?
    A. Set up a mental schedule for progress through the test if time is at a premium.
    B. If it is allowed, do not hesitate to ask the examiner to clarify a question when necessary.
    C. Do not take a question at face value—it may be more complex than it seems.
    D. If you complete the test and still have some time, review your answers.

Answers

1	A	Page 3	6	D	Page 10	11	A	Page 23
2	D	Pages 3–4	7	A	Page 11	12	B	Page 24
3	A	Page 5	8	C	Page 13	13	C	Page 27
4	B	Page 6	9	B	Page 14	14	A	Page 31
5	A	Page 9	10	B	Page 20	15	C	Page 32

2 THE RESEARCH ENTERPRISE IN PSYCHOLOGY

Can stress lead to physical disease? If so, what kinds of experiences make people more vulnerable to illness?
- How does anxiety affect people's desire to be with others? Does misery love company?
- Can hypnosis improve the accuracy of eyewitness testimony in court?
- Are there differences between young girls and young boys in their willingness to take risks?
- What are the psychological characteristics of people who receive the death penalty?
- How common is it for college men to force women into sexual acts against their will?

Questions, questions, questions—everyone has questions about behavior. The most basic question is, how should these questions be investigated? As noted in Chapter 1, *psychology is empirical*. Psychologists rely on formal, systematic observations to address their questions about behavior. This methodology is what makes psychology a scientific endeavor.

The scientific enterprise is an exercise in creative problem solving. Scientists have to figure out how to make observations that will shed light on the puzzles they want to solve. To make these observations, psychologists use a variety of research methods because different questions call for different strategies of study. In this chapter, you will see how researchers have used such methods as experiments, case studies, surveys, and naturalistic observation to investigate the questions listed at the beginning of this chapter.

Psychology's methods are worth a close look for at least two reasons. First, a better appreciation of the empirical approach will enhance your understanding of the research-based information that you will be reading about in the remainder of this book. Second, familiarity with the logic of the empirical approach should improve your ability to think critically about research. This skepticism is important because you hear about research findings nearly every day. The news media constantly report on studies that yield conclusions about how you should raise your children, improve your health, and enhance your interpersonal relationships. Learning how to evaluate these reports with more sophistication can help you use such information wisely.

In this chapter, we will examine the scientific approach to the study of behavior and then look at the specific research methods that psychologists use most frequently. We'll also see why psychologists use statistics in their research. After you learn how research is done, you'll also learn how *not* to do it. That is, we'll review some common flaws in doing research. Finally, we will take a look at ethical issues in behavioral research. In the Application, you'll learn how to find and read journal articles that report on research.

LOOKING FOR LAWS: THE SCIENTIFIC APPROACH TO BEHAVIOR

Whether the object of study is gravitational forces or people's behavior under stress, *the scientific approach assumes that events are governed by some lawful order*. As scientists, psychologists assume that behavior is governed by discernible laws or principles, just as the movement of the earth around the sun is governed by the laws of gravity. The behavior of living creatures may not seem as lawful and predictable as the "behavior" of planets. However, the scientific enterprise is based on the belief that there *are* consistencies or laws that can be uncovered. Fortunately, the plausibility of applying this fundamental assumption to psychology has been supported by the discovery of a great many such consistencies in behavior, some of which provide the subject matter for this text.

Goals of the Scientific Enterprise

Psychologists and other scientists share three sets of interrelated goals: measurement and description, understanding and prediction, and application and control.

1. *Measurement and description*. Science's commitment to observation requires that an investigator figure out a way to measure the phenomenon under study. For example, a psychologist could not investigate whether men are more or less sociable than women without first developing some

means of measuring sociability. Thus, the first goal of psychology is to develop measurement techniques that make it possible to describe behavior clearly and precisely.

2. *Understanding and prediction.* A higher-level goal of science is understanding. Scientists believe that they understand events when they can explain the reasons for their occurrence. To evaluate their understanding, scientists make and test predictions called hypotheses. A *hypothesis* is a **tentative statement about the relationship between two or more variables.** *Variables* **are any measurable conditions, events, characteristics, or behaviors that are controlled or observed in a study.** If we predicted that putting people under time pressure would lower the accuracy of their time perception, the variables in our study would be time pressure and accuracy of time perception.

3. *Application and control.* Ultimately, most scientists hope that the information they gather will be of some practical value in helping to solve everyday problems. Once people understand a phenomenon, they often can exert more control over it. Today, the profession of psychology attempts to apply research findings to practical problems in schools, businesses, factories, and mental hospitals. For example, a school psychologist might use findings about the causes of math anxiety to devise a program to help students control their math phobias.

How do theories help scientists to achieve their goals? As noted in Chapter 1, psychologists do not set out to just collect isolated facts about relationships between variables. To build toward a better understanding of behavior, they construct theories. A *theory* **is a system of interrelated ideas used to explain a set of observations.** For example, using a handful of concepts, such as natural selection and reproductive fitness, evolutionary theory (Buss, 1995, 1996) purports to explain a diverse array of known facts about mating preferences, jealousy, aggression, sexual behavior, and so forth (see Chapter 1). Thus, by integrating apparently unrelated facts and principles into a coherent whole, theories permit psychologists to make the leap from the *description* of behavior to the *understanding* of behavior. Moreover, the enhanced understanding afforded by theories guides future research by generating new predictions and suggesting new lines of inquiry.

A scientific theory must be testable, as the cornerstone of science is its commitment to putting ideas to an empirical test. Most theories are too complex to be tested all at once. For example, it would be impossible to devise a single study that could test all the many facets of evolutionary theory. Rather, in a typical study, investigators test one or two specific hypotheses derived from a theory. If their findings support the hypotheses, confidence in the theory that the hypotheses were derived from grows. If their findings fail to support the hypotheses, confidence in the theory diminishes, and the theory may be revised or discarded (see Figure 2.1). Thus, theory construction is a gradual, iterative process that is always subject to revision.

Figure 2.1
Theory construction. A good theory will generate a host of testable hypotheses. In a typical study, only one or a few of these hypotheses can be evaluated. If the evidence supports the hypotheses, our confidence in the theory they were derived from generally grows. If the hypotheses are not supported, confidence in the theory decreases and revisions to the theory may be made to accommodate the new findings. If the hypotheses generated by a theory consistently fail to garner empirical support, the theory may be discarded altogether. Thus, theory construction and testing is a gradual process.

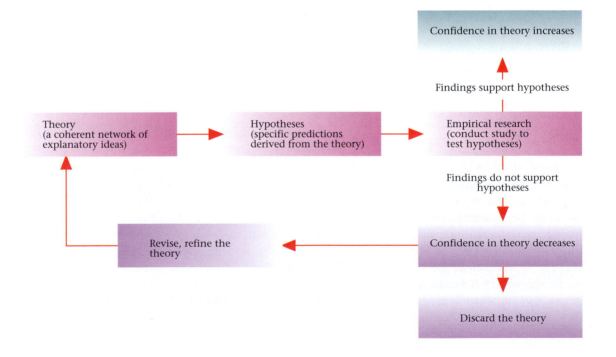

Psychology's Place in the Scientific Enterprise

Where does psychology fit into the scientific enterprise? The overriding purpose of all the sciences is to increase our knowledge of the world around us. In pursuing this end, the sciences are bound together by a common philosophy centering on the assumption that events are governed by laws or principles that can be discovered through empirical research. What distinguishes the scientific disciplines from one another is their subject matter. Each science focuses on a different set of phenomena. Physicists, for example, study the workings of matter and energy. Biologists examine the dynamics of life processes. Sociologists investigate human social systems, while psychologists try to unravel the mysteries of behavior. Ultimately, the individual disciplines represent convenient divisions of labor. These divisions are necessary because different areas of inquiry require specialized knowledge.

However, the world is not all that easy to carve up neatly, so some overlap occurs between disciplines in regard to their subject matter. For instance, psychology and biology share an interest in brain function, genetic inheritance, and a host of other topics. Psychology and sociology share an interest in prejudice and the link between social class and intelligence, to name but two examples. As an illustration of the flexible boundaries between disciplines, it is interesting to note that psychology professors have won Nobel prizes in economics (Herbert Simon in 1978) and physiology/medicine (Roger Sperry in 1981).

Although psychology is widely viewed by the public as a social science, it is really a hybrid with roots in both the natural sciences and the social sciences. The scientific disciplines that share the greatest kinship with psychology are biology, medicine, sociology, and anthropology, as demonstrated in Figure 2.2.

Steps in a Scientific Investigation

Curiosity about a question provides the point of departure for any kind of investigation, scientific or otherwise. Scientific investigations, however, are *systematic*. They follow an orderly pattern, which is outlined in Figure 2.3. Let's look at how this standard series of steps was followed in a study of stress by Thomas Holmes and his colleagues (Wyler, Masuda, & Holmes, 1971). Holmes wanted to know two things: Can stress lead to physical disease? Is stress due mostly to changes

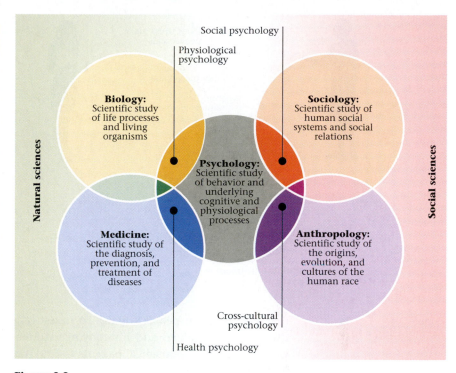

Figure 2.2
Psychology's relations to other sciences. Scientific disciplines are distinguished by their subject matter, but considerable overlap occurs among them. Psychology shares interests with a wide range of scholarly fields, but two social sciences (sociology and anthropology) and two natural sciences (biology and medicine) stand out as the scientific disciplines that overlap the most with psychology. The subfields within psychology most closely linked to each of these sciences are shown at the intersections in the diagram.

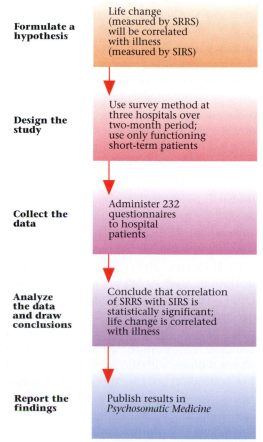

Figure 2.3
Flowchart of steps in a scientific investigation. As illustrated in a study by Wyler, Masuda, and Holmes (1971), a scientific investigation consists of a sequence of carefully planned steps, beginning with the formulation of a testable hypothesis and ending with the publication of the study, if its results are worthy of examination by other researchers.

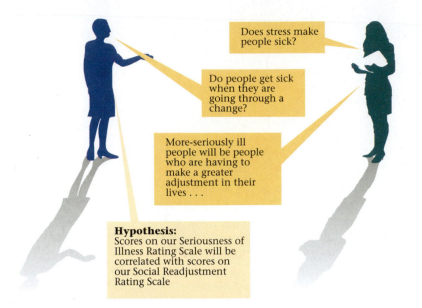

Does stress make people sick?

Do people get sick when they are going through a change?

More-seriously ill people will be people who are having to make a greater adjustment in their lives . . .

Hypothesis:
Scores on our Seriousness of Illness Rating Scale will be correlated with scores on our Social Readjustment Rating Scale

Figure 2.4
Formulating a hypothesis. Scientific hypotheses usually begin as intuitive ideas or educated guesses derived from psychological theories. To be scientifically testable, however, these preliminary notions must be refined into specific predictions in which each variable is carefully defined in measurable terms.

that take place in people's lives? To investigate these matters, Holmes and his co-workers interviewed thousands of medical patients to find out whether significant life changes had preceded the onset of their diseases.

Step 1: Formulate a Testable Hypothesis

The first step in a scientific investigation is to translate a theory or an intuitive idea into a testable hypothesis. Normally, hypotheses are expressed as predictions. They spell out how changes in one variable will be related to changes in another variable. Thus, Holmes hypothesized that an increase in life changes would be associated with increased physical illness (see Figure 2.4).

To be testable, scientific hypotheses must be formulated precisely, and the variables under study must be clearly defined. Researchers achieve these clear formulations by providing operational definitions of the relevant variables. **An *operational definition* describes the actions or operations that will be made to measure or control a variable.** Operational definitions establish precisely what is meant by each variable in the context of a study.

To illustrate, let's examine the operational definitions used by Wyler, Masuda, and Holmes (1971). They measured life change with the Social Readjustment Rating Scale (SRRS), a questionnaire that tabulates the occurrence of 43 major life changes. They measured the extent of participants' physical illness with the Seriousness of Illness Rating Scale (SIRS), a checklist of 126 common illnesses, with numerical values reflecting the severity of each illness. Thus, in this study the variable of life change was operationally defined as an

individual's score on the SRRS, while the variable of physical illness was operationally defined as his or her score on the SIRS.

Step 2: Select the Research Method and Design the Study

The second step in a scientific investigation is to figure out how to put the hypothesis to an empirical test. The research method chosen depends to a large degree on the nature of the question under study. The various methods—experiments, case studies, surveys, naturalistic observation, and so forth—each have advantages and disadvantages. The researcher has to ponder the pros and cons and then select the strategy that appears to be the most appropriate and practical. In this case, Wyler, Masuda, and Holmes decided that their question called for a *survey*. This method involves administering questionnaires to a large number of people.

Once researchers have chosen a general method, they must make detailed plans for executing their study. Thus, Wyler, Masuda, and Holmes had to decide when they would conduct their survey, how many people they needed to survey, and where they would get their subjects. **Subjects or participants are the persons or animals whose behavior is systematically observed in a study.** For example, Wyler, Masuda, and Holmes chose patients seen at three local hospitals during a specified two-month period.

Step 3: Collect the Data

The third step in the research enterprise is to collect the data. Thus, Wyler, Masuda, and Holmes spent two months administering their questionnaires to 232 patients who served as participants in their study. Psychologists use a variety of **data collection techniques, which are procedures for making empirical observations and measurements.** Commonly used techniques include direct observation, questionnaires, interviews, psychological tests, physiological recordings, and examination of archival records (see Table 2.1). The data collection techniques used in a study depend largely on what is being investigated. For example, questionnaires are well suited for studying attitudes, psychological tests for studying personality, and physiological recordings for studying brain function.

Step 4: Analyze the Data and Draw Conclusions

The observations made in a study are usually converted into numbers, which constitute the raw data of the study. In this instance, the subjects' responses to the two questionnaires were tabulated. This yielded two scores for each subject, one for the amount of life change the person had experienced and another for the amount of his or her physical illness.

Researchers use *statistics* to analyze their data and to decide whether their hypotheses have been supported. Thus, statistics play an essential role in the scientific enterprise. Based on their statistical analyses, Wyler, Masuda, and Holmes concluded that their data supported their hypothesis. As predicted, they found that high scores on the measure of life change were associated with high scores on the index of physical illness.

Step 5: Report the Findings

Scientific progress can be achieved only if researchers share their findings with one another and with the general public. Therefore, the final step in a scientific investigation is to write up a concise summary of the study and its findings. Typically, researchers prepare a report that is delivered at a scientific meeting and submitted to a journal for publication. A *journal* is a periodical that publishes technical and scholarly material, usually in a narrowly defined area of inquiry. The study by Wyler, Masuda, and Holmes (1971) was accepted for publication in a journal called *Psychosomatic Medicine*. It was one of several groundbreaking studies by Holmes and his colleagues linking life stress to physical illness that set a precedent for hundreds of follow-up studies by other researchers all over the world.

The process of publishing scientific studies allows other experts to evaluate and critique new research findings. Sometimes this process of critical evaluation discloses flaws in a study. If the flaws are serious enough, the results may be discounted or discarded. This evaluation process is a major strength of the scientific approach because it gradually weeds out erroneous findings. This self-correcting aspect of science emerged to some extent in the research that followed up on Holmes's original findings. His most basic conclusion—that there is a relationship between stress and vulnerability to physical illness—has been supported in hundreds of studies. However, subsequent research has revealed that (1) the association between stress and physical illness is not as strong as Holmes concluded, and (2) stress is not exclusively a function of change in a person's life (Smith, 1993; Turner & Wheaton, 1995). We'll discuss these issues in more detail in Chapter 13.

Advantages of the Scientific Approach

Science is certainly not the only method that can be used to draw conclusions about behavior. We all use logic, casual observation, and good old-fashioned common sense. Because the scientific method often requires painstaking effort, it seems reasonable to ask what advantages make it worth the trouble.

Basically, the scientific approach offers two major advantages. The first is its clarity and precision. Commonsense notions about behavior tend to be vague and ambiguous. Consider the old adage "Spare the rod and spoil the child." What exactly does this generalization about child rearing amount to? How severely should children be punished if

TABLE 2.1 KEY DATA COLLECTION TECHNIQUES IN PSYCHOLOGY

Technique	Description
Direct observation	Observers are trained to watch and record behavior as objectively and precisely as possible. They may use some instrumentation, such as a stopwatch or video recorder.
Questionnaire	Subjects are administered a series of written questions designed to obtain information about attitudes, opinions, and specific aspects of their behavior.
Interview	A face-to-face dialogue is conducted to obtain information about specific aspects of a subject's behavior.
Psychological test	Subjects are administered a standardized measure to obtain a sample of their behavior. Tests are usually used to assess mental abilities or personality traits.
Physiological recording	An instrument is used to monitor and record a specific physiological process in a subject. Examples include measures of blood pressure, heart rate, muscle tension, and brain activity.
Examination of archival records	The researcher analyzes existing institutional records (the archives) such as census, economic, medical, legal, educational, and business records.

parents are not to "spare the rod"? How do we assess whether a child qualifies as "spoiled"? A fundamental problem is that such statements have different meanings, depending on the person. When people disagree about this assertion, it may be because they are talking about entirely different things. In contrast, the scientific approach requires that people specify *exactly* what they are talking about when they formulate hypotheses. This clarity and precision enhance communication about important ideas.

The second and perhaps greatest advantage offered by the scientific approach is its relative intolerance of error. Scientists are trained to be skeptical. They subject their ideas to empirical tests. They also scrutinize one another's findings with a critical eye. They demand objective data and thorough documentation before they accept ideas. When the findings of two studies conflict, the scientist tries to figure out why, usually by conducting additional research. In contrast, common sense and casual observation often tolerate contradictory generalizations, such as "Opposites attract" and "Birds of a feather flock together." Furthermore, commonsense analyses involve little effort to verify ideas or detect errors. Thus, many "truisms" about behavior that come to be widely believed are simply myths.

All this is not to say that science has an exclusive copyright on truth. However, the scientific approach does tend to yield more accurate and dependable information than casual analyses and armchair speculation do. Knowledge of scientific data can thus provide a useful benchmark against which to judge claims and information from other kinds of sources.

Now that we have had an overview of how the scientific enterprise works, we can focus on how specific research methods are used. ***Research methods* consist of differing approaches to the observation, measurement, manipulation, and control of variables in empirical studies.** In other words, they are general strategies for conducting studies. No single research method is ideal for all purposes and situations. Much of the ingenuity in research involves selecting and tailoring the method to the question at hand. The next two sections of this chapter discuss the two basic types of methods used in psychology: *experimental research methods* and *descriptive/correlational research methods*.

Recap of Key Points

- The scientific approach assumes that there are laws of behavior that can be discovered through empirical research. The goals of the science of psychology include (1) the measurement and description of behavior, (2) the understanding and prediction of behavior, and (3) the application of this knowledge to the task of controlling behavior.
- By integrating apparently unrelated facts into a coherent whole, theories permit psychologists to make the leap from the description of behavior to the understanding of behavior. Confidence in a theory increases when hypotheses derived from it are supported by research.
- The various sciences share a common philosophy and methodology. They are distinguished by their focus on different subject matter. The sciences that overlap most with psychology in terms of interests are the social sciences of sociology and anthropology and the natural sciences of biology and medicine.
- A scientific investigation follows a systematic pattern that includes five steps: (1) formulate a testable hypothesis, (2) select the research method and design the study, (3) collect the data, (4) analyze the data and draw conclusions, and (5) report the findings.
- Scientists use operational definitions to clarify what their variables mean. They depend on statistics to analyze their data. The two major advantages of the scientific approach are its clarity in communication and its relative intolerance of error.

LOOKING FOR CAUSES: EXPERIMENTAL RESEARCH

Does misery love company? This question intrigued social psychologist Stanley Schachter. When people feel anxious, he wondered, do they want to be left alone, or do they prefer to have others around? Schachter's review of relevant theories suggested that in times of anxiety people would want others around to help them sort out their feelings. Thus, his hypothesis was that increases in anxiety would cause increases in the desire to be with others, which psychologists call the *need for affiliation*. To test this hypothesis, Schachter (1959) designed a clever experiment.

The *experiment* is a research method in which the investigator manipulates a variable under carefully controlled conditions and observes whether any changes occur in a second variable as a result. The experiment is a relatively powerful procedure that allows researchers to detect cause-and-effect relationships. Psychologists depend on this method more than any other.

Although its basic strategy is straightforward, in practice the experiment is a fairly complicated technique. A well-designed experiment must take into account a number of factors that could affect the clarity of the results. To see how an experiment is designed, let's use Schachter's study as an example.

Independent and Dependent Variables

The purpose of an experiment is to find out whether changes in one variable (let's call it X) cause changes in another variable (let's call it Y). To put it more concisely, we want to find out *how X affects Y*. In this formulation, we refer to X as the *independent variable* and to Y as the *dependent variable*.

An *independent variable* **is a condition or event that an experimenter varies in order to see its impact on another variable.** The independent variable is the variable that the experimenter controls or manipulates. It is hypothesized to have some effect on the dependent variable, and the experiment is conducted to verify this effect. **The *dependent variable* is the variable that is thought to be affected by manipulation of the independent variable.** In psychology studies, the dependent variable is usually a measurement of some aspect of the subjects' behavior. The independent variable is called *independent* because it is *free* to be varied by the experimenter. The dependent variable is called *dependent* because it is thought to *depend* (at least in part) on manipulations of the independent variable.

In Schachter's experiment, *the independent variable was the subjects' anxiety level*. He manipulated anxiety level in a clever way. Subjects assembled in his laboratory were told by a "Dr. Zilstein" that they would be participating in a study on the physiological effects of electric shock. They were further informed that during the experiment they would receive a series of electric shocks while their pulse and blood pressure were being monitored. Half of the subjects were warned that the shocks would be very painful. They made up the *high-anxiety* group. The other half of the subjects (the *low-anxiety* group) were told that the shocks would be mild and painless. In reality, there was no plan

to shock anyone at any time. These orientation procedures were simply intended to evoke different levels of anxiety. After the orientation, the experimenter indicated that there would be a delay while he prepared the shock apparatus for use. The subjects were asked whether they would prefer to wait alone or in the company of others. *The subjects' desire to affiliate with others was the dependent variable.*

Experimental and Control Groups

In an experiment the investigator typically assembles two groups of subjects who are treated differently with regard to the independent variable. These two groups are referred to as the experimental group and the control group. **The *experimental group* consists of the subjects who receive some special treatment in regard to the independent variable. The *control group* consists of similar subjects who do *not* receive the special treatment given to the experimental group.**

In the Schachter study, the subjects in the high-anxiety condition constituted the experimental group. They received a special treatment designed to create an unusually high level of anxiety. The subjects in the low-anxiety condition constituted the control group. They were not exposed to the special anxiety-arousing procedure.

It is crucial that the experimental and control groups in a study be very similar, except for the different treatment that they receive in regard to the independent variable. This stipulation brings us to the logic that underlies the experimental method. If the two groups are alike in all respects *except for the variation created by the manipulation of the independent variable*, then any differences between the two groups on the dependent variable *must be due to the manipulation of the independent variable*. In this way researchers isolate the effect of the independent variable on the dependent variable. Schachter, for example, isolated the impact of anxiety on the need for affiliation. As predicted, he found that increased anxiety led to increased affiliation. As Figure 2.5 indicates, the percentage of subjects in the high-anxiety group who wanted to wait with others was nearly twice that of the low-anxiety group.

Note that even when an independent variable has a clear impact on a dependent variable, not every subject in each group behaves exactly as predicted. In Schachter's study, for instance, only 63% of the high-anxiety subjects wanted to wait

Check your understanding of the experimental method by identifying the independent variable (IV) and dependent variable (DV) in the following investigations. Note that one study has two IVs and another has two DVs. You'll find the answers in Appendix A in the back of the book.

1. A researcher is interested in how heart rate and blood pressure are affected by viewing a violent film sequence as opposed to a nonviolent film sequence.

    IV _____

    DV _____

2. An organizational psychologist develops a new training program to improve clerks' courtesy to customers in a large chain of retail stores. She conducts an experiment to see whether the training program leads to a reduction in the number of customer complaints.

    IV _____

    DV _____

3. A researcher wants to find out how stimulus complexity and stimulus contrast (light/dark variation) affect infants' attention to stimuli. He manipulates stimulus complexity and stimulus contrast and measures how long infants stare at various stimuli.

    IV _____

    DV _____

4. A social psychologist investigates the impact of group size on subjects' conformity in response to group pressure.

    IV _____

    DV _____

Figure 2.5
Results of Schachter's study of affiliation. The percentage of people wanting to wait with others was higher in the high-anxiety (experimental) group than in the low-anxiety (control) group, consistent with Schachter's hypothesis that anxiety would increase the desire for affiliation. The graphic portrayal of these results allows us to see at a glance the effects of the experimental manipulation on the dependent variable.

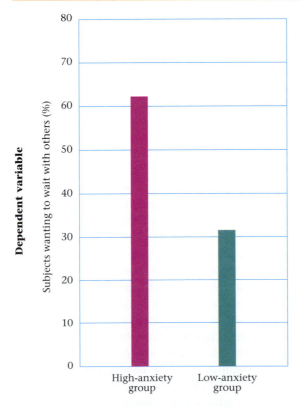

with others. People are not robots that respond identically. This lack of uniformity is quite normal and is one of the reasons that most scientific principles are expressed in terms of probabilities or tendencies.

Extraneous Variables **1b**

As we have seen, the logic of the experimental method rests on the assumption that the experimental and control groups are alike except for their treatment in regard to the independent variable. Any other differences between the two groups can cloud the situation and make it impossible to draw conclusions about how the independent variable affects the dependent variable.

In practical terms, of course, it is impossible to ensure that two groups of subjects are exactly alike in *every* respect. The experimental and control groups only have to be alike on dimensions that are relevant to the dependent variable. Thus, Schachter did not need to worry about whether his two groups were similar in hair color, height, or interest in ballet. Obviously, these variables weren't likely to influence the dependent variable of affiliation behavior.

Instead, experimenters concentrate on making sure that the experimental and control groups are alike on a limited number of variables that could have a bearing on the results of the study. These variables are called extraneous, secondary, or nuisance variables. **Extraneous variables are any variables other than the independent variable that seem likely to influence the dependent variable in a specific study.**

In Schachter's study, one extraneous variable would have been the subjects' tendency to be sociable. Why? Because subjects' sociability could affect their desire to be with others (the dependent variable). If the subjects in one group had happened to be more sociable (on the average) than those in the other group, the variables of anxiety and sociability would have been confounded. **A** *confounding of variables* **occurs when two variables are linked together in a way that makes it difficult to sort out their specific effects.** When an extraneous variable is confounded with an independent variable, a researcher cannot tell which is having what effect on the dependent variable.

Unanticipated confoundings of variables have wrecked innumerable experiments. That is why so much care, planning, and forethought must go into designing an experiment. One of the key qualities that separate a talented experimenter from a mediocre one is the ability to foresee troublesome extraneous variables and control them to avoid confoundings.

Experimenters use a variety of safeguards to control for extraneous variables. For instance, subjects are usually assigned to the experimental and control groups randomly. **Random assignment of subjects occurs when all subjects have an equal chance of being assigned to any group or condition in the study.** When experimenters distribute subjects into groups through some random procedure, they can be reasonably confident that the groups will be similar in most ways. To summarize the essentials of experimental design, Figure 2.6 provides an overview of the elements in an experiment, using Schachter's study as an example.

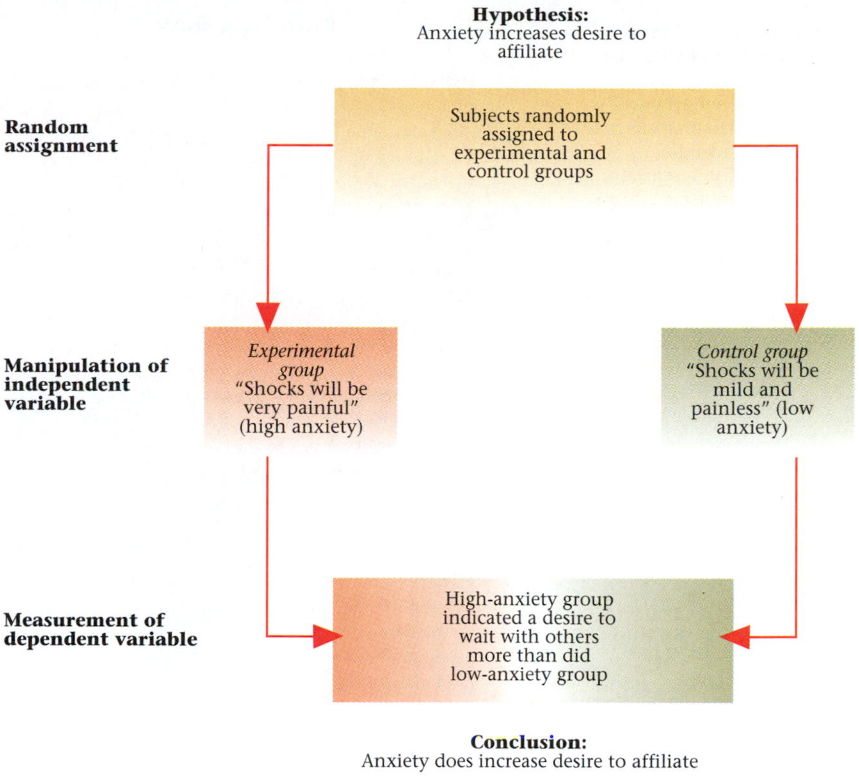

Variations in Designing Experiments 1b

We have discussed the experiment in only its simplest format, with just one independent variable and one dependent variable. Actually, many variations are possible in conducting experiments. Because you'll be reading about experiments with

more complicated designs, these variations merit a brief mention.

First, it is sometimes advantageous to use only one group of subjects who serve as their own control group. The effects of the independent variable are evaluated by exposing this single group to two different conditions—an experimental condition and a control condition. For example, imagine that you wanted to study the effects of loud music on typing performance. You could have a group of subjects work on a typing task while loud music was played (experimental condition) and in the absence of music (control conditon). This approach would ensure that the subjects in the experimental and control conditions would be alike on any extraneous variables involving their personal characteristics, such as motivation or typing skill. After all, the same people would be studied in both conditions.

Second, it is possible to manipulate more than one independent variable in a single experiment. Researchers often manipulate two or three independent variables to examine their joint effects on the dependent variable. For example, in another study of typing performance, you could vary both room temperature and the presence of distracting music (see Figure 2.7 on page 46). The main advantage of this approach is that it permits the experimenter to see whether two variables interact. An interac-

Hypothesis:
Anxiety increases desire to affiliate

Random assignment → Subjects randomly assigned to experimental and control groups

Manipulation of independent variable

Experimental group
"Shocks will be very painful" (high anxiety)

Control group
"Shocks will be mild and painless" (low anxiety)

Measurement of dependent variable

High-anxiety group indicated a desire to wait with others more than did low-anxiety group

Conclusion:
Anxiety does increase desire to affiliate

Figure 2.6
The basic elements of an experiment. As illustrated by the Schachter study, the logic of experimental design rests on treating the experimental and control groups exactly alike (to control for extraneous variables) except for the manipulation of the independent variable. In this way, the experimenter attempts to isolate the effects of the independent variable on the dependent variable.

Figure 2.7
Manipulation of two independent variables in an experiment. As this example shows, when two independent variables are manipulated in a single experiment, the researcher has to compare four groups of subjects (or conditions) instead of the usual two. The main advantage of this procedure is that it allows an experimenter to see whether two variables interact.

Distracting music

Present   Absent

Room temperature

High

Normal

tion means that the effect of one variable depends on the effect of another. For instance, if we found that distracting music impaired typing performance only when room temperature was high, we would be detecting an interaction.

Third, it is also possible to use more than one dependent variable in a single study. Researchers frequently use a number of dependent variables to get a more complete picture of how experimental manipulations affect subjects' behavior. For example, in your studies of typing performance, you would probably measure two dependent variables: speed (words per minute) and accuracy (number of errors).

Now that you're familiar with the logic of the experiment, let's turn to our Featured Study for Chapter 2. You will find a Featured Study in each chapter from this point onward. These studies are provided to give you in-depth examples of how psychologists conduct empirical research. Each is described in a way that resembles a journal article, thereby acquainting you with the format of scientific reports (see the Application at the end of the chapter for more information on this format). The Featured Study for this chapter gives you another example of an experiment in action.

Can Hypnosis Improve Eyewitness Memory?   Featured Study

Investigators: Glenn S. Sanders and William L. Simmons (State University of New York at Albany)

Source: Use of hypnosis to enhance eyewitness accuracy: Does it work? *Journal of Applied Psychology,* 1983, *68,* 70–77.

In criminal investigations, hypnosis has occasionally been used successfully to trigger witnesses' recall of information they were not originally able to remember. In light of this fact, Sanders and Simmons set out to discover whether hypnosis might also be used to improve the *accuracy* of eyewitness memory. They were intrigued by this possibility because eyewitness testimony is frequently riddled with inaccuracies. The hypothesis selected for the study was that hypnotized subjects would show better recall of a simulated crime than nonhypnotized subjects.

Method

Subjects. College students who volunteered to participate in a study that might involve hypnosis served as subjects. The 100 participants were assigned to small groups of one to eight people.

Procedure. In the initial session, participants were told to imagine that they were walking around campus one evening and happened to observe a scene that was about to be shown to them on videotape. They then watched a 20-second videotape that showed a pickpocket stealing someone's wallet (see the adjacent photo). The thief, wearing a distinctive black jacket, was on the screen for 8 seconds, and his face was shown clearly for 3 seconds. The participants were asked to return one week later to provide "testi-

mony" about the crime that they had witnessed on videotape. In the second session, the subjects were asked to identify the thief in a videotaped police lineup that included six possible suspects. On this second occasion, participants in the experimental group were hypnotized; participants in the control group were not.

One frame from the videotape used by Sanders and Simmons. Note the jacket worn by the "thief."

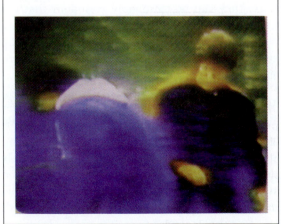

Design. The experimental design included two independent variables: (1) whether the subject (witness) was hypnotized, and (2) whether the thief was actually in the lineup. Two conditions were set up to manipulate the second independent variable. In one condition the thief occupied the fourth spot in the lineup. In the other condition the thief was absent from the lineup but another person wearing the same jacket was in the fourth spot. The dependent variables were the subjects' accuracy in identifying the thief, their confidence in their response, and their performance on a ten-item test that checked their recall of details in the incident.

Results

Figure 2.8 shows the percentage of correct responses (either identifying the thief or indicating that he was not in the lineup, depending on the condition) made by the hypnotized subjects and the control subjects. The control subjects were correct more often than the hypnotized subjects, both when the thief was present and when he was absent from the lineup. The control subjects also expressed confidence in their response more frequently than did the hypnotized subjects, although the difference was small. Data regarding participants' performance on the ten-item recall test also favored the control subjects.

Discussion

The findings indicate that hypnotizing eyewitnesses did *not* improve the accuracy of their testimony. In fact, the results show that hypnosis may actually make eyewitnesses more likely to make mistakes. Sanders and Simmons speculated that hypnosis may make witnesses more error prone by increasing their tendency to focus on prominent cues, such as the jacket worn by the thief. Thus, they concluded that the use of hypnosis in criminal investigations should probably be limited to helping witnesses overcome memory blocks.

Comment

This study was featured because it addresses an interesting question using a reasonably straightforward experimental design. It also illustrates the importance

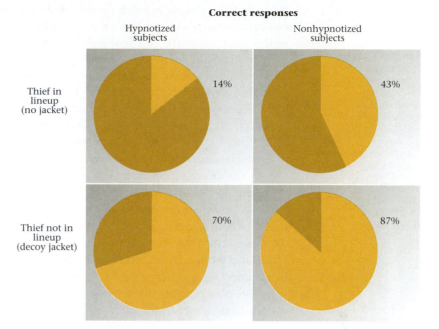

Correct responses

Hypnotized subjects | Nonhypnotized subjects

Thief in lineup (no jacket): 14% | 43%

Thief not in lineup (decoy jacket): 70% | 87%

Figure 2.8
Results of the Sanders and Simmons study. In both conditions (thief in the lineup and thief not in the lineup), the control subjects showed more accurate recall than the hypnotized subjects. Instead of improving recall, in this study hypnosis led to more mistakes by "eyewitnesses."

of collecting empirical data to answer psychological questions. If asked whether hypnosis would improve the accuracy of eyewitness testimony, many people (including some psychologists) would probably have answered "Yes." After all, there have been a number of highly publicized instances in which hypnosis has overcome memory blocks. However, the findings in this experiment suggest that hypnosis is unlikely to enhance the accuracy of eyewitness testimony. Without research data, we might be quite likely to assume otherwise.

Notice, too, that this study provides examples of some of the variations in experimental design discussed earlier. Specifically, Sanders and Simmons manipulated two independent variables and measured subjects' responses on three dependent variables. Of course, a single study on an issue does not settle the matter once and for all. Although similar results have been seen in other studies (Mingay, 1987), the effects of hypnosis on eyewitness testimony remain controversial, and more research is needed (Scheflin, 1994).

Advantages and Disadvantages of Experimental Research

The experiment is a powerful research method. Its principal advantage is that it permits conclusions about cause-and-effect relationships between variables. Researchers are able to draw these conclusions about causation because the precise control available in the experiment allows them to isolate the relationship between the independent variable and the dependent variable, while neutraliz-

ing the effects of extraneous variables. No other research method can duplicate this strength of the experiment. This advantage is why psychologists usually prefer to use the experimental method whenever possible.

For all its power, however, the experiment has limitations. One problem is that experiments are often artificial. Because experiments require great control over proceedings, researchers must often construct simple, contrived situations to test their hypotheses experimentally. For example, to investigate decision making in juries, psychologists have conducted many experiments in which subjects read a brief summary of a trial and then record their individual "verdicts" of innocence or guilt. This approach allows the experimenter to manipulate a variable, such as the race of the defendant, to see whether it affects the subjects' verdicts. However, critics have pointed out that having a subject read a short case summary and make an individual decision is terribly artificial in comparison to the complexities of real trials (Weiten & Diamond, 1979). In actual court cases, jurors may spend weeks listening to confusing testimony while making subtle judgments about the credibility of witnesses. They then retire for hours of debate to arrive at a group verdict, which is quite different from rendering an individual decision. Many researchers have failed to do justice to this complex process in their laboratory experiments. When experiments are highly artificial, doubts arise about the applicability of findings to everyday behavior outside the experimental laboratory.

Another disadvantage is that the experimental method can't be used to explore some research questions. Psychologists are frequently interested in the effects of factors that cannot be manipulated as independent variables because of ethical concerns or practical realities. For instance, you might be interested in whether a nutritionally poor diet during pregnancy increases the likelihood of birth defects. This clearly is a significant issue. However, you obviously cannot take 100 pregnant women and assign 50 of them to a condition in which they consume an inadequate diet. The potential risk to the health of the women and their unborn children would make this research strategy unethical.

In other cases, manipulations of variables are difficult or impossible. For example, you might want to know whether being brought up in an urban as opposed to a rural area affects people's values. An experiment would require you to assign similar families to live in urban and rural areas, which obviously is impossible to do. To explore this question, you would have to use descriptive/correlational research methods, which we turn to next.

Recap of Key Points

• Experimental research involves the manipulation of an independent variable to ascertain its effect on a dependent variable. This research is usually done by comparing experimental and control groups, which must be alike in regard to important extraneous variables.

• Any differences between the groups in the dependent variable ought to be due to manipulation of the independent variable, as long as there are no confounds. Variables are said to be confounded when they vary together so that researchers cannot isolate the effect of the independent variable on the dependent variable.

• Experimental designs may vary. For example, sometimes an experimental group serves as its own control group. And many experiments have more than one independent variable or more than one dependent variable.

• Some of these variations were seen in the Featured Study, which manipulated two independent variables and measured three dependent variables. This experiment suggested that hypnosis is unlikely to improve the accuracy of eyewitness testimony.

• An experiment is a powerful research method that permits conclusions about cause-and-effect relationships between variables. However, the experimental method is often not usable for a specific problem, and many experiments tend to be artificial.

LOOKING FOR LINKS: DESCRIPTIVE/CORRELATIONAL RESEARCH

As we just saw, in some situations psychologists cannot exert experimental control over the variables they want to study. Thomas Holmes's research on the relationship between life change and illness provides another example of this problem. Obviously, Holmes could not manipulate the amount of life change experienced by his subjects. Their divorces, retirements, pregnancies, promotions, mortgages, and such were far beyond his control.

In such situations, investigators must rely on *descriptive/correlational research methods*. These methods include naturalistic observation, case studies, and surveys. What distinguishes these methods is that the researcher cannot manipulate the variables under study. This lack of control means that these methods cannot be used to demonstrate cause-and-effect relationships between variables. *Descriptive/correlational methods permit investigators to only describe patterns of behavior and discover links or associations between variables. That is not to suggest that associations are unimpor-

As the name implies, naturalistic observation allows behavior to unfold naturally, without interference by the researcher. These photographs were taken in 1988 by Harvey Ginsburg during naturalistic observation of boys and girls in a "risky behavior" situation.

tant. You'll see in this section that information on associations between variables can be extremely valuable in our efforts to understand behavior.

Naturalistic Observation

Are males more likely to take risks than females? Harvey Ginsburg and Shirley Miller wanted to know whether young boys and young girls differ in their willingness to take risks. Popular belief suggests that males are bigger risk takers than females are. However, there was a notable lack of empirical evidence before Ginsburg and Miller (1982) conducted their study. They probably could have devised an experiment to examine this question. However, they wanted to focus on risk taking in the real world rather than in the laboratory.

The setting for their study was the San Antonio Zoo, where they used *naturalistic observation* to study children's risk taking. **In *naturalistic observation* a researcher engages in careful, usually prolonged, observation of behavior without intervening directly with the subjects.** Ginsburg and Miller identified four specific risky behaviors that children might engage in at this zoo: going for a ride on an elephant, petting a burro, feeding animals, and climbing a steep embankment. Without making their presence readily apparent, they

carefully recorded the number of boys and girls who engaged in each of these risky behaviors. Their observations revealed that an association did indeed exist between sex and risk taking, at least for these behaviors. They found that boys engaged in the risky behaviors more frequently than girls.

This type of research is called *naturalistic* because behavior is allowed to unfold naturally (without interference) in its natural environment—that is, the setting in which it would normally occur. The major strength of naturalistic observation is that it allows researchers to study behavior under conditions that are less artificial than in experiments. A major problem with this method is that researchers often have trouble making their observations unobtrusively so they don't affect their subjects' behavior. Moreover, the inability to intervene, ask questions, and probe more deeply means that naturalistic observation can't contribute much to understanding *why* certain patterns of behavior were observed.

Case Studies

Are death-row inmates the shrewd, coldly calculating individuals that many people believe them to be? A research team at New York University

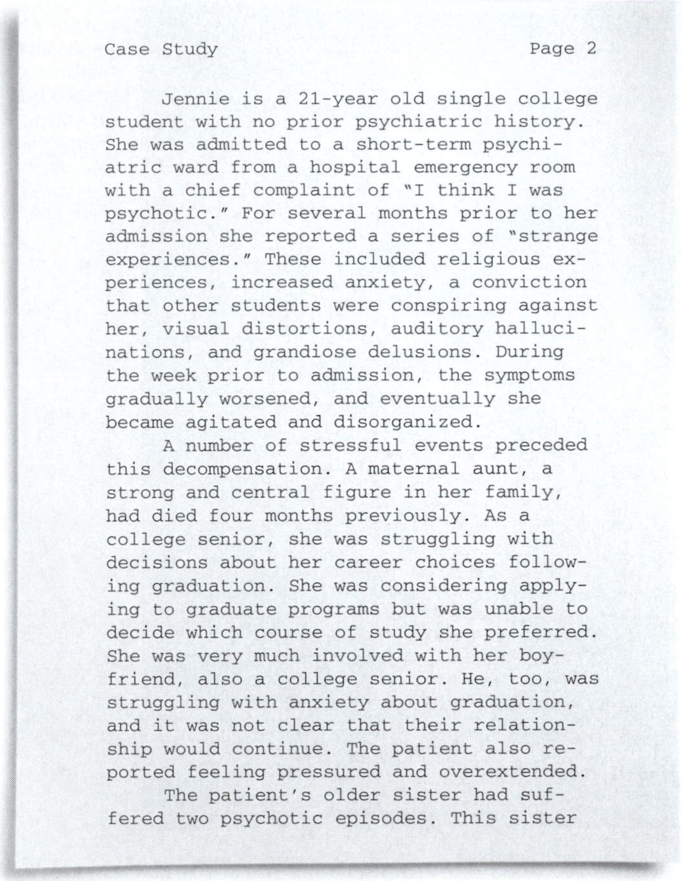

Jennie is a 21-year old single college student with no prior psychiatric history. She was admitted to a short-term psychiatric ward from a hospital emergency room with a chief complaint of "I think I was psychotic." For several months prior to her admission she reported a series of "strange experiences." These included religious experiences, increased anxiety, a conviction that other students were conspiring against her, visual distortions, auditory hallucinations, and grandiose delusions. During the week prior to admission, the symptoms gradually worsened, and eventually she became agitated and disorganized.

A number of stressful events preceded this decompensation. A maternal aunt, a strong and central figure in her family, had died four months previously. As a college senior, she was struggling with decisions about her career choices following graduation. She was considering applying to graduate programs but was unable to decide which course of study she preferred. She was very much involved with her boyfriend, also a college senior. He, too, was struggling with anxiety about graduation, and it was not clear that their relationship would continue. The patient also reported feeling pressured and overextended.

The patient's older sister had suffered two psychotic episodes. This sister

Figure 2.9
An example of a case study report. As this example illustrates, case studies are particularly appropriate to clinical situations in which efforts are made to diagnose and treat psychological problems. Usually, one case study does not provide much basis for deriving general laws of behavior. However, if you examine a series of case studies involving similar problems, you can look for threads of consistency that may yield general conclusions.

wanted to investigate the psychological characteristics of people given the death penalty (Lewis et al., 1986). Until this study, no one had done research either confirming or refuting the popular image of criminals sentenced to die.

The research team decided that their question called for a case study approach. **A case study is an in-depth investigation of an individual subject.** The researchers compiled case studies for 15 condemned individuals whose execution dates were close at hand. The findings were surprising. All 15 inmates had histories of severe head injuries. Twelve of them showed signs of brain damage, and most were well below average in intelligence. The investigators concluded that their data showed an unexpected link between neurological impairment and ending up on death row. Their findings suggest that our legal system doles out its harshest penalty to individuals who are anything but shrewd.

A variety of data collection techniques can be used in case studies. Typical techniques include interviewing the subject, direct observation of the subject, examination of records, and psychological testing. Clinical psychologists, who diagnose and treat psychological problems, routinely do case studies of their clients (see Figure 2.9). When

clinicians assemble a case study, they are *not* conducting empirical research. Case study *research* takes place only when investigators analyze a collection of case studies, looking for threads of consistency that permit general conclusions.

Case studies are particularly well suited for investigating certain phenomena, such as psychological disorders. They can also provide compelling, real-life illustrations that bolster a hypothesis or theory. However, the clinical samples typically seen in case study research may not be very representative of the general population. Moreover, the main problem with case studies is that they are highly subjective. Information from several sources must be knit together in an impressionistic way. In this process, clinicians often focus selectively on information that fits with their expectations, which usually reflect their theoretical slant. Thus, it is relatively easy for investigators to see what they expect to see in case study research.

Surveys

How common is it for college men to force women into sexual acts against their will? Karen Rapaport and Barry Burkhart (1984) set out to answer this question by conducting a survey. **In a *survey* researchers use questionnaires or interviews to gather information about specific aspects of subjects' behavior.** In their study, Rapaport and Burkhart defined coercive sexual behavior as any sexual act with a woman that is engaged in "against her will." They administered a questionnaire to 201 college men, inquiring whether they had ever engaged in any of 11 coercive sexual acts, such as placing a hand on a woman's breast or removing her underclothing, against her will. As you can see in Table 2.2, the survey revealed that a substantial proportion of the men had engaged in sexually coercive acts.

Surveys are often used to obtain information on aspects of behavior that are difficult to observe directly (such as sexual behavior). Surveys also make it relatively easy to collect data on attitudes and opinions from large samples of subjects. The major problem with surveys is that they depend on self-report data. As we'll discuss later, intentional deception, wishful thinking, memory lapses, and response sets can distort subjects' verbal reports about their behavior.

Advantages and Disadvantages of Descriptive/Correlational Research

Descriptive/correlational research methods have advantages and disadvantages, which are com-

TABLE 2.2 COLLEGE MEN'S RESPONSES TO ITEMS ON COERCIVE SEXUALITY SCALE (%)

Coercive Act Engaged in "Against Her Will"	Never	Once or Twice	Several Times	Often
Held a woman's hand	57	34	7	1
Kissed a woman	47	41	10	2
Placed hand on a woman's knee	39	43	15	3
Placed hand on a woman's breast	39	37	18	5
Placed hand on a woman's thigh or crotch	42	40	16	2
Unfastened a woman's outer clothing	51	34	13	2
Removed or disarranged a woman's outer clothing	58	31	9	2
Removed or disarranged a woman's underclothing	68	27	3	2
Removed own underclothing	78	18	3	2
Touched a woman's genital area	63	30	6	1
Had intercourse with a woman	85	13	2	0

Note: Some rows do not total 100% because of rounding.
Source: Rapaport and Burkhart (1984)

pared to the strengths and weaknesses of experimental research in Figure 2.10 (on page 52). As a whole, the foremost advantage of these methods is that they give researchers a way to explore questions that could not be examined with experimental procedures. For example, after-the-fact analyses would be the only ethical way to investigate the possible link between poor maternal nutrition and birth defects in humans. In a similar vein, if researchers hope to learn how urban and rural upbringing relate to people's values, they have to depend on descriptive methods, since they can't control where subjects grow up. Thus, *descriptive/correlational research broadens the scope of phenomena that psychologists are able to study.*

Unfortunately, descriptive methods have one significant disadvantage: Investigators cannot control events to isolate cause and effect. *Consequently, correlational research cannot demonstrate conclusively that two variables are causally related.* As an example, consider the study of children's risk taking that we discussed earlier. Although Ginsburg and Miller (1982) found an association between sex and risk taking, their data do not permit us to conclude that a child's sex *causes* these differences. Too many factors were left uncontrolled in the study. For example, we do not know how similar the groups of boys and girls were. The groups could have differed in age distribution or other factors that might have led to the observed differences in risk taking.

CONCEPT CHECK 2.2
Matching Research Methods to Questions

Check your understanding of the uses and strengths of various research methods by figuring out which method would be optimal for investigating the following questions about behavioral processes. Choose from the following methods: (a) experiment, (b) naturalistic observation, (c) case study, and (d) survey. Indicate your choice (by letter) next to each question. You'll find the answers in Appendix A in the back of the book.

_____ 1. Are people's attitudes about nuclear disarmament related to their social class or education?

_____ 2. Do people who suffer from anxiety disorders share similar early childhood experiences?

_____ 3. Do troops of baboons display territoriality—that is, do they mark off an area as their own and defend it from intrusion by other baboons?

_____ 4. Can the presence of food-related cues (delicious-looking desserts in advertisements, for example) cause an increase in the amount of food that people eat?

Research method		Description	Example	Advantages	Disadvantages
Experiment 		Manipulation of an independent variable under carefully controlled conditions to see whether any changes occur in a dependent variable	Youngsters are randomly assigned to watch a violent or nonviolent film, and their aggression is measured in a laboratory situation	Precise control over variables; ability to draw conclusions about cause-and-effect relationships	Contrived situations often artificial; ethical concerns and practical realities preclude experiments on many important questions
Naturalistic observation 		Careful, usually prolonged observation of behavior without direct intervention	Youngsters' spontaneous acts of aggression during recreational activities are observed unobtrusively and recorded	Minimizes artificiality; can be good place to start when little is known about phenomena under study	Often difficult to remain unobtrusive; can't explain why certain patterns of behavior were observed
Case studies 		In-depth investigation of a single subject using direct interview, direct observation, and other data collection techniques	Detailed case histories are worked up for youngsters referred to counseling because of excessive aggressive behavior	Well-suited for study of certain phenomena; can provide compelling illustrations to support a theory	Subjectivity makes it easy to see what one expects to see based on one's theoretical slant; clinical samples often unrepresentative
Surveys 		Use of questionnaires or interviews to gather information about specific aspects of subjects' behavior	Youngsters are given questionnaire that describes hypothetical scenarios and are asked about the likelihood of aggressive behavior.	Can gather data on difficult-to-observe aspects of behavior; relatively easy to collect data from large sample	Self-report data often unreliable, due to intentional deception, social desirability bias, response sets, memory lapses, and wishful thinking

Figure 2.10 Comparison of major research methods. This chart pulls together a great deal of information on key research methods in psychology and gives a simple example of how each method might be applied in research on aggression. As you can see, the various research methods each have their strengths and weaknesses.

Recap of Key Points
- Psychologists rely on descriptive/correlational research when they are unable to manipulate the variables they want to study. Naturalistic observation involves careful, prolonged observation of behavior in its natural setting without any intervention.
- Clinical research depends heavily on case studies, which involve in-depth investigations of individuals.

In a survey, researchers interview participants or administer questionnaires to gather information on specific aspects of behavior.
- Descriptive/correlational research methods allow psychologists to explore issues that might not be open to experimental investigation. They are also less artificial than experiments. However, these research methods cannot demonstrate cause-effect relationships.

LOOKING FOR CONCLUSIONS: STATISTICS AND RESEARCH

Whether researchers use experimental or correlational methods, they need some way to make sense out of their data. Consider, for instance, the situation encountered by Wyler, Masuda, and Holmes (1971) in their study of stress and illness. After collecting their data, they had a life change score and an illness severity score for each of their 238 subjects. How did they determine the meaning of these 476 numbers? How did they figure out whether these numbers showed an association between life change and illness? Did they scan the data and make a subjective judgment? Of course not. Science is more precise than that. They used *statistical analyses* to quantify the exact strength of the association between life change and illness.

Statistics is the use of mathematics to organize, summarize, and interpret numerical data. Statistical analyses permit researchers to draw conclusions based on their observations. Many students find statistics intimidating, but statistics are an integral part of modern life. Although you may not realize it, you are bombarded with statistics nearly every day. When you read about economists' projections for inflation, when you check a baseball player's batting average, when you see the popularity ratings of television shows, you are dealing with statistics. In this section, we will examine a few basic statistical concepts that will help you understand the research discussed throughout this book. For the most part, we won't concern ourselves with the details of statistical *computations*. These details and some additional statistical concepts are discussed in Appendix B at the back of the book. At this juncture, we will discuss only the purpose, logic, and value of the two basic types of statistics: descriptive statistics and inferential statistics.

Descriptive Statistics 1c, 1d

Descriptive statistics are used to organize and summarize data. They provide an overview of numerical data. Key descriptive statistics include measures of central tendency, measures of variability, and the coefficient of correlation.

Central Tendency

In summarizing numerical data, researchers often want to know what constitutes a typical or average score. To answer this question, they use three measures of central tendency: the median, the mean, and the mode. **The *median* is the score that falls exactly in the center of a distribution of scores.** Half of the scores fall above the median and half fall below it. **The *mean* is the arithmetic average of the scores in a distribution.** It is obtained by adding up all the scores and dividing by the total number of scores. Finally, **the *mode* is the most frequent score in a distribution.**

In general, the mean is the most useful measure

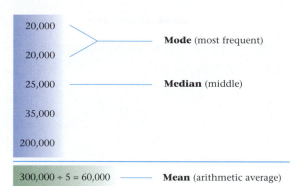

Figure 2.11
Measures of central tendency. The three measures usually converge, but some data produce quite different values for mean, median, and mode. Which measure is most useful depends on the purpose being served.

of central tendency because additional statistical manipulations can be performed on it that are not possible with the median or mode. However, the mean is sensitive to extreme scores in a distribution, which can sometimes make the mean misleading. To illustrate, imagine that you're interviewing for a sales position at a company. Unbeknownst to you, the company's five salespeople earned the following incomes in the previous year: $20,000, $20,000, $25,000, $35,000, and $200,000. You ask how much the typical salesperson earns in a year. The sales director proudly announces that her five salespeople earned a *mean* income of $60,000 last year (the calculations are shown in Figure 2.11). However, before you order that expensive, new sports car, you had better inquire about the *median* and *modal* income for the sales staff. In this case, one extreme score ($200,000) has inflated the mean, making it unrepresentative of the sales staff's earnings. In this instance, the median ($25,000) and the mode ($20,000) both provide better estimates of what you are likely to earn.

Variability

In describing a set of data it is often useful to have some estimate of the variability among the scores. **Variability refers to how much the scores in a data set vary from each other and from the mean. The *standard deviation* is an index of the amount of variability in a set of data.** This index has a simple relationship to the variability in a data set. When variability is great, the standard deviation will be relatively large. When variability is low, the standard deviation will be smaller.

This relationship is apparent if you examine the two sets of data in Figure 2.12 on page 54. The mean is the same for both sets of scores, but variability clearly is greater in set B than in set A. This greater variability yields a higher standard deviation for set B than for set A. Estimates of variability play a crucial role when researchers use statistics to

Figure 2.12
Variability and the standard deviation. Although these two sets of data produce the same mean, or average, an observer on Wild Street would see much more variability in the speeds of individual cars than an observer on Perfection Boulevard would. As you can see, the standard deviation for set B is higher than that for set A because of the greater variability in set B.

Speed (miles per hour)

A Perfection Boulevard		B Wild Street
35		21
34		37
33		50
37		28
38		42
40		37
36		39
33		25
34		23
30		48
35 ————	Mean	———— 35
2.87 ————	Standard deviation	———— 10.39

decide whether the results of their studies support their hypotheses.

Correlation

A *correlation* **exists when two variables are related to each other.** Investigators often want to quantify the strength of an association between two variables. In this effort, they depend extensively on a useful descriptive statistic: the correlation coefficient. **The *correlation coefficient* is a numerical index of the degree of relationship between two variables.** A correlation coefficient indicates (1) the direction (positive or negative) of the relationship and (2) how strongly the two variables are related.

POSITIVE VERSUS NEGATIVE CORRELATION. A *positive correlation* indicates that two variables covary in the *same* direction. This means that high scores on variable *X* are associated with high scores on variable *Y* and that low scores on variable *X* are associated with low scores on variable *Y*. For ex-

ample, there is a positive correlation between high school grade point average (GPA) and subsequent college GPA. That is, people who do well in high school tend to do well in college, and those who perform poorly in high school tend to perform poorly in college (see Figure 2.13).

In contrast, a *negative* correlation indicates that two variables covary in the *opposite* direction. This means that people who score high on variable *X* tend to score low on variable *Y*, whereas those who score low on *X* tend to score high on *Y*. For example, in most college courses there is a negative correlation between how frequently students are absent and how well they perform on exams. Students who have a high number of absences tend to get low exam scores, while students who have a low number of absences tend to earn higher exam scores (see Figure 2.13).

If a correlation is negative, a minus sign (–) is always placed in front of the coefficient. If a correlation is positive, a plus sign (+) may be placed in front of the coefficient, or the coefficient may be shown with no sign. Thus, if there's no sign, the correlation is positive.

STRENGTH OF THE CORRELATION. Whereas the positive or negative sign indicates the direction of an association, the *size of the coefficient* indicates the *strength* of an association between two variables. The coefficient can vary between 0 and +1.00 (if positive) or between 0 and –1.00 (if negative). A coefficient near zero indicates no relationship between the variables; that is, high or low scores on variable *X* show no consistent relationship to high or low scores on variable *Y*. A coefficient of +1.00 or –1.00 indicates a perfect, one-to-one correspon-

Figure 2.13
Positive and negative correlation. Notice that the terms *positive* and *negative* refer to the direction of the relationship between two variables, not to its strength. Variables are positively correlated if they tend to increase and decrease together and are negatively correlated if one tends to increase when the other decreases.

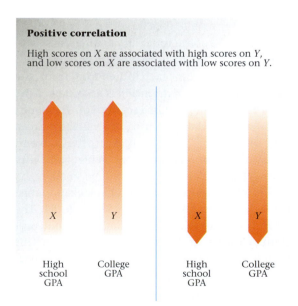

Positive correlation

High scores on *X* are associated with high scores on *Y*, and low scores on *X* are associated with low scores on *Y*.

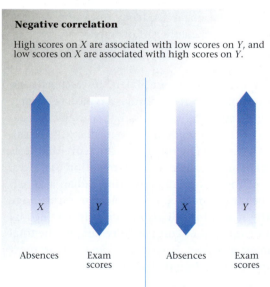

Negative correlation

High scores on *X* are associated with low scores on *Y*, and low scores on *X* are associated with high scores on *Y*.

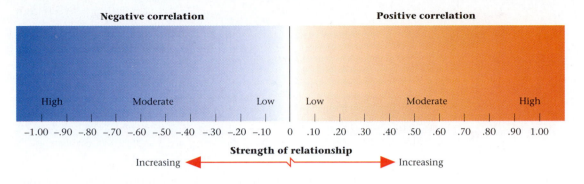

dence between the two variables. Most correlations fall between these extremes.

The closer the correlation to either −1.00 or +1.00, the stronger the relationship (see Figure 2.14). Thus, a correlation of .90 represents a stronger tendency for variables to be associated than does a correlation of .40. Likewise, a correlation of −.75 represents a stronger relationship than does a correlation of −.45. Keep in mind that the *strength* of a correlation depends only on the size of the coefficient. The positive or negative sign simply indicates the direction of the relationship. Therefore, a correlation of −.60 reflects a stronger relationship than a correlation of +.30.

Computation of correlation coefficients allowed Wyler, Masuda, and Holmes (1971) to determine whether their data showed an association between life change and illness. They found a correlation of +.32 between subjects' amount of life change in the year prior to their hospitalization and the severity of their illness. Thus, correlational analyses permitted Holmes and his colleagues to conclude that a moderate association existed between life change and illness in their sample of subjects.

CORRELATION AND PREDICTION. You may recall that one of the key goals of scientific research is accurate *prediction*. A close link exists between the magnitude of a correlation and the power it gives scientists to make predictions. *As a correlation increases in strength (gets closer to either −1.00 or +1.00), the ability to predict one variable based on knowledge of the other variable increases.*

To illustrate, consider how college admissions tests (such as the SAT or ACT) are used to predict college performance. When students' admissions test scores and college GPA are correlated, researchers generally find moderate positive correlations in the .40s and .50s (Donlon, 1984). Because of this relationship, college admissions committees can predict with modest accuracy how well prospective students will do in college. Admittedly, the predictive power of these admissions tests is far from perfect. But it's substantial enough to justify the use of the tests as one factor in making admissions decisions. However, if this correlation were much higher, say .90, admissions tests could predict with superb accuracy how students would perform. In contrast, if this correlation were much lower, say .20, the tests' prediction of college performance would be so poor that it would be unreasonable to consider the test scores in admissions decisions.

CORRELATION AND CAUSATION. Although a high correlation allows us to predict one variable from another, it does not tell us whether a cause-effect relationship exists between the two variables. The problem is that variables can be highly correlated even though they are not causally related. For example, there is a substantial positive correlation between the size of young children's feet and the size of their vocabulary. That is, larger feet are associated with a larger vocabulary. Obviously, increases in foot size do not *cause* increases in vocabulary size. Nor do increases in vocabulary size cause increases in foot size. Instead, both are caused by a third variable: an increase in the children's age.

When we find that variables *X* and *Y* are correlated, we can safely conclude only that *X* and *Y* are related. We do not know *how X* and *Y* are related. We do not know whether *X* causes *Y* or *Y* causes *X*, or whether both are caused by a third variable. For example, survey studies have found a positive correlation between smoking and the risk of experiencing a major depressive disorder (Breslau, Kilbey, & Andreski, 1991, 1993). Although it's clear that there is an association between smoking and depression, it's hard to tell what's causing what. The investigators acknowledge that they don't know whether smoking makes people more vulnerable to depression or whether depression increases the tendency to smoke. Moreover, they note that they can't rule out the possibility that both are caused by a third variable (*Z*). Perhaps anxiety and

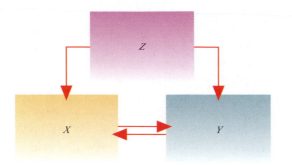

Figure 2.15
Three possible causal relations between correlated variables. If variables X and Y are correlated, does X cause Y, does Y cause X, or does some hidden third variable, Z, account for the changes in both X and Y? As the relationship between smoking and depression illustrates, a correlation alone does not provide the answer. We will encounter this problem of interpreting the meaning of correlations frequently in this text.

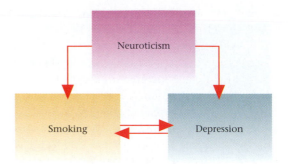

neuroticism increase the likelihood of both taking up smoking and becoming depressed. The plausible causal relationships in this case are diagrammed in Figure 2.15, which illustrates the "third variable problem" in interpreting correlations. This is a common problem in research, and you'll see this type of diagram again when we discuss other correlations. Thus, it is important to remember that *correlation is not equivalent to causation.*

Inferential Statistics

After researchers have summarized their data with descriptive statistics, they still need to decide whether their data support their hypotheses. ***Inferential statistics* are used to interpret data and draw conclusions.** Working with the laws of probability, researchers use inferential statistics to evaluate the possibility that their results might be due to the fluctuations of chance.

To illustrate this process, envision a hypothetical experiment. A computerized tutoring program (the independent variable) is designed to increase sixth-graders' reading achievement (the dependent variable). Our hypothesis is that program participants (the experimental group) will score higher than nonparticipants (the control group) on a standardized reading test given near the end of the school year. Let's assume that we compare 60 subjects in each group. We obtain the following results, reported in terms of subjects' grade-level scores for reading:

Control group		Experimental group
6.3	Mean	6.8
1.4	Standard deviation	2.4

We hypothesized that the training program would produce higher reading scores in the experimental group than in the control group. Sure

---

CONCEPT CHECK 2.3
Understanding Correlation

Check your understanding of correlation by interpreting the meaning of the correlation in item 1 and by guessing the direction (positive or negative) of the correlations in item 2. You'll find the answers in Appendix A.

1. Researchers have found a substantial positive correlation between youngsters' self-esteem and their academic achievement (measured by grades in school). Check any acceptable conclusions based on this correlation.

_____ a. Low grades cause low self-esteem.

_____ b. There is an association between self-esteem and academic achievement.

_____ c. High self-esteem causes high academic achievement.

_____ d. High ability causes both high self-esteem and high academic achievement.

_____ e. Youngsters who score low in self-esteem tend to get low grades, and those who score high in self-esteem tend to get high grades.

2. Indicate whether you would expect the following correlations to be positive or negative.

_____ a. The correlation between age and visual acuity (among adults).

_____ b. The correlation between years of education and income.

_____ c. The correlation between shyness and the number of friends one has.

enough, that is indeed the case. However, we have to ask ourselves a critical question: Is this observed difference between the two groups large enough to support our hypothesis? That is, do the higher scores in the experimental group reflect the effect of the training program? Or could a difference of this size have occurred by chance? If our results could easily have occurred by chance, they don't provide meaningful support for our hypothesis.

When statistical calculations indicate that research results are not likely to be due to chance, the results are said to be *statistically significant*. You will probably hear your psychology professor use this phrase quite frequently. In discussing research, it is routine to note that "statistically significant differences were found." In statistics, the word *significant* has a precise and special meaning. **Statistical significance is said to exist when the probability that the observed findings are due to chance is very low.** "Very low" is usually defined as less than 5 chances in 100, which is referred to as the .05 level of significance.

Notice that in this special usage, *significant* does not mean "important," or even "interesting." Statistically significant findings may or may not be theoretically significant or practically significant. They simply are research results that are unlikely to be due to chance.

You don't need to be concerned here with the details of how statistical significance is calculated. However, it is worth noting that a key consideration is the amount of variability in the data. That is why the standard deviation, which measures variability, is such an important statistic. When the nec-essary computations are made for our hypothetical experiment, the difference between the two groups does *not* turn out to be statistically significant. Thus, our results would not be adequate to demonstrate that our tutoring program leads to improved reading achievement. Psychologists have to do this kind of statistical analysis as part of virtually every study. Thus, inferential statistics are an integral element in the research enterprise.

Recap of Key Points

• Psychologists use descriptive statistics to organize and summarize their numerical data. The mean, median, and mode are widely used measures of central tendency. The mean tends to be the most useful of these indexes, but it can be distorted by extreme scores. Variability is usually measured with the standard deviation, which increases as the variability in a data set grows.

• Correlations may be either positive (when two variables covary in the same direction) or negative (when two variables covary in the opposite direction) The closer a correlation is to either +1.00 or –1.00, the stronger the association is.

• As a correlation increases in strength, the ability to predict one variable based on knowledge of the other variable increases. However, a correlation is no assurance of causation. When variables are correlated, we do not know whether X causes Y, or Y causes X, or a third variable causes both.

• Hypothesis testing involves deciding whether observed findings support the researcher's hypothesis. Findings are statistically significant only when they are unlikely to be due to chance.

LOOKING FOR FLAWS: EVALUATING RESEARCH

Scientific research is a more reliable source of information than casual observation or popular belief. However, it would be wrong to conclude that all published research is free of errors. As we just saw, when researchers report statistically significant differences at the .05 level, there are 5 chances in 100 that the results really are a misleading byproduct of chance fluctuation. This probability is pretty low, but it's not zero. Moreover, scientists' effort to minimize the probability of obtaining significant differences when none really exist increases the likelihood of the opposite mistake—failing to find significant differences when the groups really are different. Thus, even when research is conducted in a sound fashion, there's still a decent chance of erroneous findings. Above and beyond this problem, we need to recognize that scientists are fallible human beings who do not conduct flawless research. Their personal biases and innocent mistakes in designing studies can further contaminate research results.

For these reasons, researchers are reluctant to settle scientific questions on the basis of just one empirical study. Instead, important questions usually generate a flurry of studies to see whether key findings will stand the test of replication. **Replication is the repetition of a study to see whether the earlier results are duplicated.** The replication process helps science to identify and purge erroneous findings. Of course, the replication process

When University of Utah experimenters announced that they had successfully achieved "cold fusion," the world was astounded. If these chemists were right, it meant an inexhaustible supply of cheap energy for all. High hopes were dashed, though, when other laboratories across the globe tried to repeat the results but could not. Here, the test of replication fails at a laboratory in France. Replication is crucial to all sciences, including psychology.

sometimes leads to contradictory results. You'll see some examples in the upcoming chapters. Inconsistent findings on a research question can be frustrating and confusing for students. However, some inconsistency in results is to be expected, given science's commitment to replication.

Fortunately, one of the strengths of the empirical approach is that scientists work to reconcile or explain conflicting results. In their efforts to make sense of inconsistent research results, psychologists are increasingly depending on a technique called *meta-analysis,* which came into vogue in the 1980s (Cooper, 1990). *Meta-analysis* **combines the statistical results of many studies of the same question, yielding an estimate of the size and consistency of a variable's effects.** For example, when Hyde and Linn (1988) combined the results of 165 studies of gender differences in verbal skills, they concluded that females have a genuine, but terribly small, advantage over males in average verbal ability (see Chapter 11). Meta-analysis allows researchers to test the generalizability of findings across people, places, times, and variations in procedure in a relatively precise and objective way (Beaman, 1991; Cooper & Lemke, 1991). Indeed, Schmidt (1992) argues that "only meta-analytic integration of findings across studies can control chance and other statistical and measurement artifacts and provide a trustworthy foundation for conclusions" (pp. 1179–1180).

As you will see in upcoming chapters, scientific advances often emerge out of efforts to double-check perplexing findings or to explain contradictory research results. Thus, like all sources of information, scientific studies need to be examined with a critical eye. This section describes a number of common methodological problems that often spoil studies. Being aware of these pitfalls will make you more skilled in evaluating research.

Sampling Bias

A *sample* **is the collection of subjects selected for observation in an empirical study.** In contrast, **the** *population* **is the much larger collection of animals or people (from which the sample is drawn) that researchers want to generalize about** (see Figure 2.16). For example, when political pollsters attempt to predict elections, all of the voters in a jurisdiction represent the population, and the voters who are actually surveyed constitute the sample. If a researcher were interested in the ability of 6-year-old children to form concepts, those 6-year-olds actually studied would be the sample, and all similar 6-year-old children (perhaps those in modern, Western cultures) would be the population.

The strategy of observing a limited sample in order to generalize about a much larger population rests on the assumption that the sample is reasonably *representative* of the population. A sample is representative if its composition is similar to the composition of the population. *Sampling bias* **exists when a sample is not representative of the population from which it was drawn.** When a sample is not representative, generalizations about the population may be inaccurate. For instance, if a political pollster were to survey only people in posh shopping areas frequented by the wealthy, the pollster's generalizations about the voting public as a whole would be off the mark.

As we discussed in Chapter 1, historically, psychologists have tended to undersample women, ethnic minorities, and people from non-Western cultures. They have also tended to neglect older adults, while depending much too heavily on white, middle- and upper-class college students. This excessive reliance on college students may not be all that problematic for some research questions, but it certainly seems likely to distort results in many research areas (Sears, 1986). In general, then, when you have doubts about the results of a study, the first thing to examine is the composition of the sample.

Placebo Effects

In pharmacology, a *placebo* is a substance that resembles a drug but has no actual pharmacological effect. In studies that assess the effectiveness of medications, placebos are given to some subjects to control for the effects of a treacherous extraneous variable: subjects' expectations. Placebos are used because researchers know that subjects' expectations can influence their feelings, reactions, and behavior. **Thus, *placebo effects* occur when subjects' expectations lead them to experience some change even though they receive empty, fake, or ineffectual treatment.** In medicine, placebo effects are legendary. Many physicians tell of patients being "cured" by prescriptions of sugar pills. Similarly, psychologists have found that subjects' expectations can be powerful determinants of their perceptions and behavior when they are under the microscope in an empirical study.

For example, placebo effects have been seen in research on meditation. A number of studies have found that meditation can improve people's energy level, mental and physical health, and happiness (Alexander et al., 1990; Carrington, 1987). However, in many of the early studies of meditation, researchers assembled their experimental groups with volunteer subjects eager to

Before accepting the results of a survey poll, one should know something about how the poll was conducted. A polling could, for instance, contain *sampling bias*. Opinions collected solely from young, middle-class people but generalized to the voting public as a whole would be an example of such bias.

learn meditation. Most of these subjects *wanted* and *expected* meditation to have beneficial effects. Their positive expectations may have colored their subsequent ratings of their energy level, happiness, and so on. Better-designed studies have shown that meditation can be beneficial (see Chapter 5).

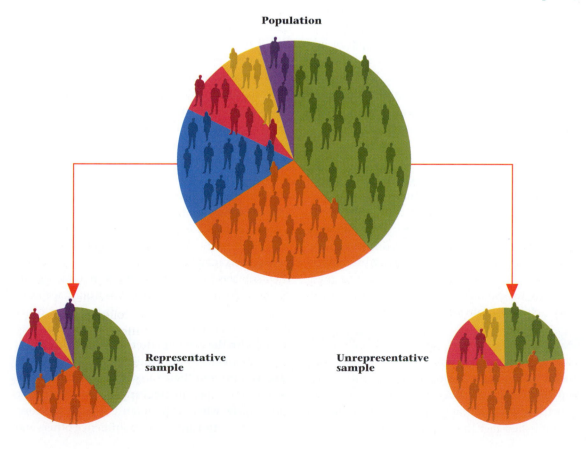

Population

Representative sample

Unrepresentative sample

Figure 2.16 The relationship between the population and the sample. The process of drawing inferences about a population based on a sample only works if the sample is reasonably representative of the population. A sample is representative if its demographic makeup is similar to that of the population, as shown on the left. If some groups in the population are overrepresented or underrepresented in the sample, as shown on the right, inferences about the population may be skewed or inaccurate.

However, placebo effects probably have exaggerated these benefits in some studies (Shapiro, 1987).

Researchers should guard against placebo effects whenever subjects are likely to have expectations that a treatment will affect them in a certain way. The possible role of placebo effects can be assessed by including a fake version of the experimental treatment (a placebo condition) in a study.

Distortions in Self-Report Data

Research psychologists often work with *self-report data,* made up of subjects' verbal accounts of their behavior. This is the case whenever questionnaires, interviews, or personality inventories are used to measure variables. Self-report methods can be quite useful, taking advantage of the fact that people have a unique opportunity to observe themselves full-time. However, self-reports can be plagued by several kinds of distortion.

One of the most problematic of these distortions is the *social desirability bias,* **which is a tendency to give socially approved answers to questions about oneself.** Subjects who are influenced by this bias work overtime trying to create a favorable impression (DeMaio, 1984). For example, many survey respondents will report that they voted in an election or gave to a charity when in fact it is possible to determine that they did not. Respondents influenced by social desirability bias also tend to report that they are healthier, happier, and less prejudiced than other types of evidence would suggest.

Other problems can also produce distortions in self-report data (Schuman & Kalton, 1985). Subjects misunderstand questionnaire items surprisingly often. Memory errors can undermine the accuracy of verbal reports. Response sets are yet another problem. **A *response set* is a tendency to respond to questions in a particular way that is unrelated to the content of the questions.** For example, some people tend to agree with nearly everything on a questionnaire, while others tend to disagree with nearly everything. Obviously, distortions like these can produce inaccurate results. Although researchers have devised ways to neutralize these problems, we should be especially cautious in drawing conclusions from self-report data.

Experimenter Bias

As scientists, psychologists try to conduct their studies in an objective, unbiased way so that their own views will not influence the results. However, objectivity is a *goal* that scientists strive for, not an accomplished fact that can be taken for granted.

In reality, most researchers have an emotional investment in the outcome of their research. Often they are testing hypotheses that they have developed themselves and that they would like to see supported by the data. It is understandable, then, that *experimenter bias* is a possible source of error in research.

***Experimenter bias* occurs when a researcher's expectations or preferences about the outcome of a study influence the results obtained.** Experimenter bias can slip through to influence studies in many subtle ways. One problem is that researchers, like others, sometimes *see what they want to see.* For instance, when experimenters make apparently honest mistakes in recording subjects' responses, the mistakes tend to be heavily slanted in favor of supporting the hypothesis (O'Leary, Kent, & Kanowitz, 1975).

Research by Robert Rosenthal (1976) suggests that experimenter bias may lead researchers to unintentionally influence the behavior of their subjects. In one study, Rosenthal and Fode (1963) recruited undergraduate psychology students to serve as the "experimenters." The students were told that they would be collecting data for a study of how subjects rated the success of people portrayed in photographs. In a pilot study, photos were selected that generated (on the average) neutral ratings on a scale extending from –10 (extreme failure) to +10 (extreme success). Rosenthal and Fode then manipulated the expectancies of their experimenters. Half of them were told that they would probably obtain average ratings of –5. The other half were led to expect average ratings of +5. The experimenters were forbidden from conversing with their subjects except for reading some standardized instructions. Even though the photographs were exactly the same for both groups, the experimenters who *expected* positive ratings *obtained* significantly higher ratings than those who expected negative ratings.

How could the experimenters have swayed the subjects' ratings? According to Rosenthal, the experimenters may have unintentionally influenced their subjects by sending subtle nonverbal signals as the experiment progressed. Without realizing it, they may have smiled, nodded, or sent other positive cues when subjects made ratings that were in line with the experimenters' expectations. Thus, experimenter bias may influence both researchers' observations and their subjects' behavior (Rosenthal, 1994). Experimenter bias effects appear to be most likely when experimenters have a strong desire for control and need to influence others and

"Quite unconsciously, a psychologist interacts in subtle ways with the people he is studying so that he may get the response he expects to get."

ROBERT ROSENTHAL

CHAPTER TWO

Check your understanding of how to conduct sound research by looking for methodological flaws in the following studies. You'll find the answers in Appendix A.

Study 1. A researcher announces that he will be conducting an experiment to investigate the detrimental effects of sensory deprivation on perceptual-motor coordination. The first 40 students who sign up for the study are assigned to the experimental group, and the next 40 who sign up serve in the control group. The researcher supervises all aspects of the study's execution. Experimental subjects spend two hours in a sensory deprivation chamber, where sensory stimulation is minimal. Control subjects spend two hours in a waiting room that contains magazines and a TV. All subjects then perform ten l-minute trials on a pursuit-rotor task that requires them to try to keep a stylus on a tiny rotating target. The dependent variable is their average score on the pursuit-rotor task.

Study 2. A researcher wants to know whether there is a relationship between age and racial prejudice. She designs a survey in which respondents are asked to rate their prejudice against six different ethnic groups. She distributes the survey to over 500 people of various ages who are approached at a shopping mall in a low-income, inner-city neighborhood.

Check the flaws that are apparent in each study.

Methodological flaw	Study 1	Study 2	Methodological flaw	Study 1	Study 2
Sampling bias	____	____	Confounding of variables	____	____
Placebo effects	____	____	Experimenter bias	____	____
Distortions in self-report	____	____			

when subjects have a strong need for social approval (Hazelrigg, Cooper, & Strathman, 1991).

The problems associated with experimenter bias can be neutralized by using a double-blind procedure. **The *double-blind procedure* is a research strategy in which neither subjects nor experimenters know which subjects are in the experimental or control groups.** It's not particularly unusual for subjects to be "blind" about their treatment condition. However, the double-blind procedure keeps the experimenter in the dark as well. Of course, a member of the research team who isn't directly involved with subjects keeps track of who is in which group.

Recap of Key Points

• Scientists often try to replicate research findings to double-check their validity. Although this process leads to some contradictory findings, science works toward reconciling and explaining inconsistent results.

• Meta-analysis, which involves combining the statistical results from many studies of the same question, can help psychologists evaluate findings and make sense of inconsistent research results.

• Sampling bias occurs when a sample is not representative of the population of interest. Placebo effects occur when subjects' expectations cause them to change their behavior in response to a fake treatment.

• Distortions in self-reports, such as response sets and the social desirability bias, are a source of concern whenever questionnaires and personality inventories are used to collect data. Experimenter bias occurs when researchers' expectations and desires distort their observations or unintentionally influence their subjects' behavior.

LOOKING AT ETHICS: DO THE ENDS JUSTIFY THE MEANS?

Think back to Stanley Schachter's (1959) study on anxiety and affiliation. Imagine how you would have felt if you had been one of the subjects in Schachter's high-anxiety group. You show up at a research laboratory, expecting to participate in a harmless experiment. The room you are sent to is full of unusual electronic equipment. An official-looking man in a lab coat announces that this equipment will be used to give you a series of painful electric shocks. His statement that the shocks will leave "no permanent tissue damage" is hardly reassuring. Surely, you think, there must be a mistake. All of a sudden, your venture into research has turned into a nightmare! Your stomach knots up in anxiety. The researcher explains that there will be a delay while he prepares his apparatus. He asks you to fill out a short questionnaire about whether you would prefer to wait alone or with others. Still reeling in dismay at the prospect of being shocked, you fill out the questionnaire. He takes it and then announces that you won't be shocked after all—it was all a hoax! Feelings of relief wash over you, but they're mixed with feelings of anger. You feel as though the experimenter has just made a fool out of you, and you're embarrassed and resentful.

Should researchers be allowed to play with your feelings in this way? Should they be permitted to deceive subjects in such a manner? Is this the cost that must be paid to advance scientific knowledge? As these questions indicate, the research enterprise sometimes presents scientists with difficult ethical dilemmas. *These dilemmas reflect concern about the possibility for inflicting harm on subjects.* In psychological research, the major ethical dilemmas center on the use of deception and the use of animals.

The Question of Deception

Elaborate deception, such as that seen in Schachter's study, has been fairly common in psychological research since the 1960s, especially in

The use of rats and other animals in scientific research is now a major ethical issue. Researchers claim that experiments on animals often yield results and knowledge beneficial to humankind. Opponents maintain that humans have no right to subject animals to harm for research purposes. What is your view?

the area of social psychology (Christensen, 1988). Over the years, psychologists have faked fights, thefts, muggings, faintings, epileptic seizures, rapes, and automobile breakdowns to explore a host of issues. They have led subjects to believe that they were hurting others with electrical shocks, that they had homosexual tendencies, and that they were overhearing negative comments about themselves. Why have psychologists used so much deception in their research? Quite simply, they are trying to deal with the methodological problems discussed in the last section. Deception is used to avoid or reduce problems due to placebo effects, the unreliability of self-reports, and the like.

Critics argue against the use of deception on several grounds (Baumrind, 1985; Kelman, 1982). First, they assert that deception is only a nice word for lying, which they see as inherently immoral. Second, they argue that by deceiving unsuspecting subjects, psychologists may undermine many individuals' trust in others. Third, they point out that many deceptive studies produce distress for subjects who were not forewarned about that possibility. Specifically, subjects may experience great stress during a study or be made to feel foolish when the true nature of a study is explained.

Those who defend the use of deception in research maintain that many important issues could not be investigated if experimenters were not permitted to mislead subjects (Aronson, Brewer, & Carlsmith, 1985). They argue that most research deceptions involve "white lies" that are not likely to harm participants. Moreover, they point out that critics have *assumed* that deception studies are harmful to subjects, without collecting empirical data to document these detrimental effects (C. P. Smith, 1983). In reality, a review of the relevant research by Larry Christensen (1988) suggests that deception studies are *not* harmful to subjects. Indeed, most subjects who participate in experiments involving deception report that they enjoyed the experience and that they didn't mind being misled. Moreover, a recent study found no support for the notion that deceptive research undermines subjects' trust in others (Sharpe, Adair, & Roese, 1992). Finally, researchers who defend deception argue that the benefits—advances in knowledge that often improve human welfare—are worth the costs. They assert that it would be unethical *not* to conduct effective research on conformity, obedience, aggression, and other important social issues.

The issue of deception creates a difficult dilemma for scientists, pitting honesty against the desire to advance knowledge. Today, institutions that con-

Some "animal rights" advocates are content with traditional means of protesting. Others have used terror tactics such as destroying research laboratories, trashing research records, and liberating experimental animals, all of which inhibit research.

duct research have committees that evaluate the ethics of research proposals before studies are allowed to proceed. These committees have often blocked studies requiring substantial deception. Many psychologists believe that this conservativism has obstructed important lines of research and slowed progress in the field. Although this may be true, it is not easy to write off the points made by the critics of deception. Warwick (1975) states the issue eloquently: "If it is all right to use deceit to advance knowledge, then why not for reasons of national security, for maintaining the Presidency, or to save one's own hide?" (p. 105). That's a tough question regarding a tough dilemma that will probably generate heated debate for a long time to come.

The Question of Animal Research

Psychology's other major ethics controversy concerns the use of animals in research. Psychologists use animals as research subjects for several reasons. Sometimes they simply want to know more about the behavior of a specific type of animal. In other instances, they want to see whether certain laws of behavior apply to both humans and animals. Finally, in some cases psychologists use animals because they can expose them to treatments that clearly would be unacceptable with human subjects. For example, most of the research on the

relationship between deficient maternal nutrition during pregnancy and the incidence of birth defects has been done with animals.

It's this third reason for using animals that has generated most of the controversy. Some people maintain that it is wrong to subject animals to harm or pain for research purposes. Essentially, they argue that animals are entitled to the same rights as humans (Regan, 1989). They accuse researchers of violating these rights by subjecting animals to unnecessary cruelty in many "trivial" studies (Hollands, 1989). They also assert that most animal studies are a waste of time because the results may not even apply to humans (Millstone, 1989). For example, Ulrich (1991) argues that "pigeons kept confined at 80% body weight in home cages that don't allow them ever to spread their wings, take a bath, or relate socially to other birds provide questionable models for humans" (pp. 200–201).

Although some animal rights activists simply advocate more humane treatment of research animals, a survey of 402 activists questioned at a Washington, D.C. rally found that 85% wanted to eliminate *all* research with animals (Plous, 1991). Some of the more militant animal rights activists have broken into laboratories, destroyed scientists' equipment and research records, and stolen experimental animals (Cunningham, 1985).

According to David Johnson (1990), the animal rights movement has enjoyed considerable success. He notes that "the single issue citizens write about most often to their congresspersons and the President is not homelessness, not the drug problem, not crime. It is animal welfare" (p. 214). More important, Johnson reports that concerns about harassment from activists and regulatory hassles have led many scientists to abandon potentially crucial lines of animal research.

In spite of the great furor, only 7%–8% of all psychological studies involve animals (mostly rodents and birds). Relatively few of these studies require subjecting the animals to painful or harmful manipulations (American Psychological Association, 1984). Psychologists who defend animal research point to the major advances attributable to psychological research on animals. Among them are advances in the treatment of mental disorders, neuromuscular disorders, strokes, brain injuries, visual defects, headaches, memory defects, high blood pressure, and problems with pain (Domjan & Purdy, 1995; Greenough, 1991; Miller, 1985). To put the problem in context, Neal Miller (1985), a prominent psychologist who has done pioneering work in several areas, notes the following:

At least 20 million dogs and cats are abandoned each year in the United States; half of them are killed in pounds and shelters, and the rest are hit by cars or die of neglect. Less than 1/10,000th as many dogs and cats were used in psychological laboratories. . . . Is it worth sacrificing the lives of our children in order to stop experiments, most of which involve no pain, on a vastly smaller number of mice, rats, dogs, and cats? (p. 427)

Far more compelling than Miller are the advocates for disabled people who have entered the fray to campaign against the animal rights movement in recent years. For example, Dennis Feeney (1987), a psychologist disabled by paraplegia, quotes a newsletter from an organization called The Incurably Ill for Animal Research:

No one has stopped to think about those of us who are incurably ill and are desperately waiting for new research results that can only be obtained through the use of animals. We have seen successful advances toward other diseases, such as polio, diphtheria, mumps, measles, and hepatitis. through animal research. We want the same chance for a cure, but animal rights groups would deny us this chance. (p. 595)

As you can see, the manner in which animals can ethically be used for research is a highly charged controversy. Psychologists are becoming increasingly sensitive to this issue. Although animals continue to be used in research, psychologists are taking greater pains to justify their use in relation to the potential benefits of the research. They are also striving to ensure that laboratory animals receive humane care.

The ethics issues that we have discussed in this section have led the APA to develop a set of ethical standards for researchers (American Psychological Association, 1992). Although most psychological studies are fairly benign, these ethical principles are intended to ensure that both human and animal subjects are treated with dignity. Some of the key guidelines in these ethical principles are summarized in Figure 2.17.

"Who are the cruel and inhumane ones, the behavioral scientists whose research on animals led to the cures of the anorexic girl and the vomiting child, or those leaders of the radical animal activists who are making an exciting career of trying to stop all such research and are misinforming people by repeatedly asserting that it is without any value?"

NEAL MILLER

PUTTING IT IN PERSPECTIVE

Two of our seven unifying themes have emerged strongly in this chapter. First, the entire chapter is a testimonial to the idea that psychology is empirical. Second, the discussion of methodological flaws in research provides numerous examples of how people's experience of the world can be highly subjective. Let's examine each of these points in more detail.

As explained in Chapter 1, the empirical approach entails testing ideas, basing conclusions on systematic observation, and relying on a healthy brand of skepticism. All of those features of the empirical approach have been apparent in our review of the research enterprise in psychology.

As you have seen, psychologists test their ideas by formulating clear hypotheses that involve predictions about relations between variables. They then use a variety of research methods to collect data, so they can see whether their predictions are supported. The data collection methods are designed to make researchers' observations systematic and precise. The entire venture is saturated with skepticism. Psychologists are impressed only by research results that are very unlikely to have occurred by chance. In planning and executing their research, they are constantly on the lookout for methodological flaws. They publish their findings so that other experts can subject their

APA Ethical Guidelines for Research

1 A subject's participation in research should be voluntary and based on informed consent. Subjects should never be coerced into participating in research. They should be informed in advance about any aspects of the study that might be expected to influence their willingness to cooperate. Furthermore, they should be permitted to withdraw from a study at any time if they so desire.

2 Subjects should not be exposed to harmful or dangerous research procedures. This guideline is intended to protect subjects from psychological as well as physical harm. Thus, even stressful procedures that might cause emotional discomfort are largely prohibited. However, procedures that carry a modest risk of moderate mental discomfort may be acceptable.

3 If an investigation requires some deception of subjects (about matters that do not involve risks), the researcher is required to explain and correct any misunderstandings as soon as possible. The deception must be disclosed to subjects in "debriefing" sessions as soon as it is practical to do so without compromising the goals of the study.

4 Subjects' rights to privacy should never be violated. Information about a subject that might be acquired during a study must be treated as highly confidential and should never be made available to others without the consent of the participant.

5 Harmful or painful procedures imposed upon animals must be thoroughly justified in terms of the knowledge to be gained from the study. Furthermore, laboratory animals are entitled to decent living conditions that are spelled out in detailed rules that relate to their housing, cleaning, feeding, and so forth.

6 Prior to conducting studies, approval should be obtained from host institutions and their research review committees. Research results should be reported fully and accurately, and raw data should be promptly shared with other professionals who seek to verify substantive claims. Retractions should be made if significant errors are found in a study subsequent to its publication.

---

methods and conclusions to critical scrutiny. Collectively, these procedures represent the essence of the empirical approach.

The subjectivity of personal experience became apparent in the discussion of methodological problems, especially placebo effects and experimenter bias. When subjects report beneficial effects from a fake treatment (the placebo), it's because they expected to see these effects. As pointed out in Chapter 1, psychologists and other scientists are not immune to the effects of subjective experience. Although they are trained to be objective, even scientists may see what they expect to see or what they want to see. This is one reason that the empirical approach emphasizes precise measurement and a skeptical attitude. The highly subjective nature of experience is exactly what the empirical approach attempts to neutralize.

The publication of empirical studies allows us to apply our skepticism to the research enterprise.

However, you cannot critically analyze studies unless you know where and how to find them. In the upcoming Application, we will discuss where studies are published, how to find studies on specific topics, and how to read research reports.

Recap of Key Points

• Research sometimes raises complex ethical issues. Critics argue that it is unethical to deceive subjects and to expose animals to harmful treatments. Those who defend deception in research argue that many important issues could not be investigated without misleading subjects.

• Psychologists who defend animal research argue that it has brought major advances that are worth the costs. The APA has formulated ethical principles to serve as guidelines for researchers.

• Two of the book's unifying themes are apparent in this chapter's discussion of the research enterprise in psychology: psychology is empirical, and people's experience of the world can be highly subjective.

Figure 2.17
Ethics in research. Key ethical principles in psychological research, as set forth by the American Psychological Association (1992), are summarized here. These principles are meant to ensure the welfare of both human and animal subjects.

APPLICATION: **FINDING AND READING JOURNAL ARTICLES**

Answer the following "yes" or "no."

1 I have read about scientific studies in newspapers and magazines and sometimes wondered, "How did they come to those conclusions?"

2 When I go to the library, I often have difficulty figuring out how to find information based on research.

3 I have tried to read scientific reports and found them to be technical and difficult to understand.

If you responded "yes" to any of the above statements, you have struggled with the information explosion in the sciences. We live in a research-oriented society. The number of studies conducted in most sciences is growing at a dizzying pace. This expansion has been particularly spectacular in psychology (see Figure 2.18). Moreover, psychological research increasingly commands attention from the popular press because it is often relevant to people's personal concerns.

This Application is intended to help you cope with the information explosion in psychology. It assumes that there may come a time when you need to examine original psychological research. Perhaps it will be in your role as a student (working on a term paper, for instance), in another role (parent, teacher, nurse, administrator), or merely out of curiosity. In any case, this Application explains the nature of technical journals and discusses how to find and read articles in them. You can learn more about how to use library resources in psychology from an excellent little handbook put out by the American Psychological Association titled *Library Use: A Handbook for Psychology* (Reed & Baxter, 1992).

The Nature of Technical Journals

As you will recall from earlier in the chapter, a *journal* is a periodical that publishes technical and scholarly material, usually in a narrowly defined area of inquiry. Scholars in most fields—whether economics, chemistry, education, or psychology—publish the bulk of their work in these journals. Journal articles represent the core of intellectual activity in any academic discipline.

In general, journal articles are written for other professionals in the field. Hence, authors assume that their readers are other interested economists, or chemists, or psychologists. Because journal articles are written in the special language unique to a particular discipline, they are often difficult for nonprofessionals to understand. You

will be learning a great deal of psychology's special language in this course, which will improve your ability to understand articles in psychology journals.

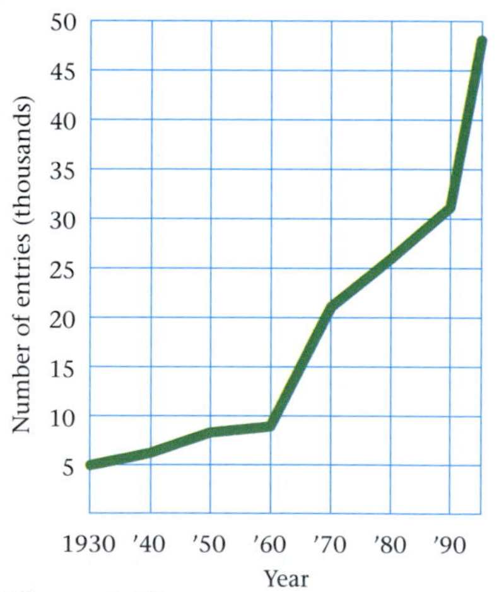

There are hundreds of journals devoted exclusively to the publication of psychological research, and hundreds more publish at least *some* research that has psychological elements. Many of these are interdisciplinary journals that bridge the gap between two or more fields. For instance, *Law and Human Behavior* is a psychology/law journal, while *Brain Research* is a psychology/biology journal.

Most journals are highly selective about what they publish. Experts carefully evaluate submissions, weighing their methodological soundness and their contribution to advancing knowledge. Some of the more prestigious psychology journals reject more than 90% of the articles submitted. Articles are usually rejected on the grounds that they are theoretically unimportant, methodologically unsound, or poorly written.

In psychology, most journal articles are reports that describe original empirical studies. These reports permit researchers to disseminate their findings to the scientific community. Another common type of article is the review article. *Review articles* summarize and reconcile the findings of a large number of studies on a specific issue. *Meta-analyses*, which we discussed in the main body of the chapter, are special types of review articles. Some psychology journals also publish comments or critiques of previously published research, book reviews, theoretical treatises, and descriptions of methodological innovations.

Finding Journal Articles

Reports of psychological research are commonly mentioned in newspapers and

Figure 2.18
Increase in psychological literature. The number of entries included in *Psychological Abstracts*, a journal that indexes and summarizes the research literature in psychology, has increased dramatically over the years. The sharp increase since 1990 occurred in part because *Psychological Abstracts* began indexing books and book chapters in addition to journal articles.

popular magazines. These summaries can be helpful to readers, but they often embrace the most sensational conclusions that might be drawn from the research. They also tend to include many oversimplifications and factual errors. Hence, if a study mentioned in the press is of interest to you, you may want to track down the original article to ensure that you get accurate information.

Most discussions of research in the popular press do not mention where you can find the original technical article. However, there is a way to find out. A journal devoted exclusively to summarizing and indexing the research literature in psychology, called *Psychological Abstracts,* makes it possible to locate specific articles and scholarly reports in books. It is also valuable for finding the research literature on general topics. For instance, you could locate articles on topics such as intelligence testing or the effects of day care.

Psychological Abstracts contains brief summaries, or abstracts, of journal articles, books, and chapters in edited books, reporting, reviewing, or theorizing about psychological research. This monthly publication also contains various kinds of indexes to help you find the material relevant to your interests. Over 1100 journals are scanned regularly in order to select items for inclusion. The summaries are grouped under general headings, such as educational psychology, social psychology, and developmental psychology. The abstracts are concise—about 75 to 175 words. In the case of original research, they briefly describe the hypotheses, methods, results, and implications of the studies. In the case of research reviews and theoretical treatises, they succinctly describe the main ideas and major conclusions. Each abstract should allow you to determine whether an item is relevant to your interest. If it is, you should be able to track it down in your library or order it from another library because a complete bibliographic reference is provided (see Figure 2.19).

Your search for a specific article or information on a broad topic can be greatly aided by judicious use of the subject and author indexes. These indexes list all the works on a particular topic or by a particular author. The relevant items are listed according to the index numbers they have been assigned. The subject and author indexes can be found in the back of each issue of *Psychological Abstracts.* Cumulative indexes are published annually.

Although news accounts of research rarely mention where a study was published, they often mention the name of the

---

Figure 2.19
Using *Psychological Abstracts.* The lower portion of the figure shows what a typical abstract in *Psychological Abstracts* looks like. Each abstract provides a summary of the article and complete bibliographical information. The upper portion of the figure shows an excerpt from the annual author index, which can be used to locate articles and books published by a particular person.

St. James, Paula J., 23S35
Stacy, Alan W., 23327, 23328
Stadier, Michael A. 23624
Stafford, Charles, 2i655
Stafford, Mark A., 24304
Stage, Christina, 24105
StaLans, Loretta J., 24746
Stall, Ron, 23558
Stamp, Glen H., 23362
Standing, Lionel, 22817
Stotsky, Sandra, 24362
Stott, Frances M., 24088
Stott, J. R. R., 22228
Stouthamer-Loeber, Magda, 23356
Stoycheva, Katya, 24419

Stravyoski, Ariel, 22982
Street, Sue, 22781 —— **Targeted author**
Strehlow, Ulrich, 23412
Streufert, Siegfried, 23330 —— **Index number of abstract listing this person as author**
Striegel-Moore, Ruth H., 23291
Stanford, Matthew S., 21660, 22912, 23433
Stanley, Eric Z., 22303
Stroebe, Margaret, 22936
Stanton, Mark E., 22020
Stroebe, Wolfgang, 22936

Talbott, John A., 23152
Talbott, Maria M., 24084
Taller, Alla M., 23112
Tamis-LeMonda, Catherine S.,

Index number   **Authors**   **Date, volume, and pages of the journal the article appeared in**   **First author's affiliation**

23330. **Streufert, Siegfried; Pogash, Rosanne; Braig, Daniela; Gingrich, Dennis et al.** (Pennsylvania State U, Coll of Medicine, Dept of Behavioral Science, Hershey) **Alcohol hangover and managerial effectiveness.**   —— **Title of journal article**
Alcoholism: Clinical & Experimental Research, 1995 (Oct), Vol 19(5), 1141-1146.—21 male managers who normally drank moderate amounts of alcohol participated in a placebo-controlled, double-blind, crossover experiment to determine whether alcohol-induced hangovers would influence managerial/professional task performance characteristics. Ss consumed either placebo or alcoholic drinks to attain a breath alcohol level of 0.10 during the evening before participation in Strategic Management Simulations. By the following morning, breath alcohol levels were measured at 0.00. Questionnaire responses indicated considerable hangover discomfort. Responses to semantic differential evaluative scales suggested that Ss evaluated their own managerial performance in the simulation setting as impaired. However, multiple measures of decision-making performance obtained in the simulation task did not show any deterioration of functioning.

Name of journal (pointing to *Alcoholism*)   **Summary of the article**

researcher. If you have this information, the easiest way to find a specific article is to look up the author in the author index of *Psychological Abstracts*. For example, let's say you read a news report that summarizes an interesting study by Siegfried Streufert on whether alcohol hangovers affect managerial effectiveness in the business world. To track down the original article, you would look up Streufert's name in the author index of recent issues of *Psychological Abstracts*. The upper portion of Figure 2.19 shows what you would find. The author index reveals that Streufert published one article during that period. The abstract for this article, found by its index number (23330), is shown at the bottom of Figure 2.19. As you can see, it shows that the original report was published in the October 1995 issue of *Alcoholism: Clinical and Experimental Research*. Armed with this information, you could obtain the article easily.

You can conduct a search for material on a particular topic by working through the subject index. It allows you to look up specific topics, such as achievement motivation, aggressive behavior, alcoholism, appetite disorders, or artistic ability. After each subject heading you will find a list of index numbers referring you to relevant abstracts. For instance, let's say that you wanted to find out whether there is any research on the effects of computer games. The place to start would be in the annual subject index of *Psychological Abstracts*, where you would find the term and a list of short descriptions with abstract numbers as seen in Figure 2.20. You could then examine the identified abstracts to decide which articles and books to obtain.

The widespread availability of computers has revolutionized the task of searching through mountains of technical literature in many disciplines, including psychology. The information contained in *Psychological Abstracts* from 1967 through the present is now stored in a computerized database called *PsycINFO*. Today, owners of personal computers equipped with a modem can access this database through phone lines (for a modest fee, of course) and conduct literature searches almost instantaneously. Another version of this database, called *PsycLIT*, is also available at some libraries in a CD-ROM format. *PsycLIT* works much the same as *PsycINFO*, except that the former is updated quarterly instead of continually.

Computerized literature searches can be much more powerful, precise, and thorough than traditional, manual searches. Computers can sift through a half-million abstracts in a matter of seconds. Then, they can print out abstracts of *all* the works on a subject, such as birth order. Obviously, there is no way you can match this efficiency stumbling around in the stacks at your library. Moreover, the computer allows you to pair up topics to swiftly narrow your search to exactly those issues that interest you. For example, Figure 2.21 shows a *PsycINFO* search that identified all the articles on marijuana *and* memory. If you were preparing a term paper on whether marijuana affects memory, this precision would be invaluable.

Reading Journal Articles

Once you find the journal articles you want to examine, you need to know how to decipher them. You can process the information in such articles more efficiently if you understand how they are organized. Depending on your needs and purpose, you may want to simply skim through some of the sections. Journal articles follow a fairly standard organization, which includes the following sections and features.

Abstract

Most journals print a concise summary at the beginning of each article. This abstract allows readers scanning the journal to quickly decide whether articles are relevant to their interests. The abstract also provides an overview that can guide you in reading the article.

Introduction

The introduction presents an overview of the problem studied in the research. It mentions relevant theories and quickly reviews previous research that bears on the problem, usually citing shortcomings in previous research that necessitate the current study. This review of the state of knowledge on the topic usually progresses to a specific and precise statement regarding the hypotheses under investigation.

Method

The next section provides a thorough description of the research methods used

trait & computer anxiety, performance on paper & pencil vs computer mode of
  administration for verbal section of GRE, college students, 42521
use of barcode technology for keyboard phobia & use of computers in large group
  testing. 35416
Computer Attitudes—Chapters
Children's apprehension and comprehension: Gender influences on computer literacy
  and attitude structures toward personal computers, 15323
Computer Games—Serials
aggression or violence in video game & personality traits feelings of aggressiveness,
  male vs female college students, 40446
application of public domain computer games to human services programs, 41650
BUSTED therapeutic simulation game, rehabilitation & reduction of antisocial
  behavior, youthful offenders, 38719
computer adventure game for exploration of choices in family situations, preparation
  for family placement, social workers & male 13 yr old in residential care following
  adoption breakdown, 38484
computer game as rehabilitation tool, control of right arm movement, male 13 yr old
  with Erb's palsy, 34578
computer games & simulations & interactive videodisc programs for human services
  education & training, 41899
computer games & simulations in health promotion activities, adolescents, 38344

Figure 2.20
Using the subject index of *Psychological Abstracts*. The subject index in *Psychological Abstracts* can be used to locate relevant abstracts by topic. This excerpt from the annual subject index for 1995 shows some of the listings under the topic of *computer games*. The term *serials* is another word for journals. Entries in *Psychological Abstracts* are grouped by type of publication into three categories: books, chapters in books, and journals (serials).

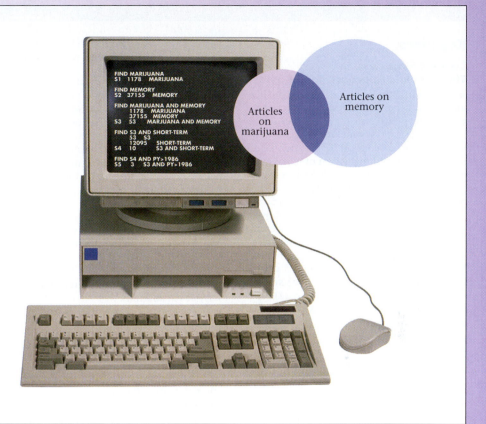

Figure 2.21
Using *PsycINFO* to locate journal articles. A computerized literature search can be a highly efficient way to locate relevant research. In this example, the first command (FIND MARIJUANA) asks the computer to find all the entries on marijuana in the database. The computer labels the 1178 articles it finds Set 1 (S1). The second command searches for all the articles on memory; the 37,155 such articles make up Set 2 (S2). To identify those articles that deal with both marijuana and memory, the third command searches S1 and S2 to find any articles that are listed in both sets (as depicted by the overlap in the circles). The resulting Set 3 (S3) consists of 53 articles on marijuana and memory. The fourth command directs the computer to scan these 53 articles and find any that are on short-term memory (it finds ten such articles). The last command asks the computer to narrow these articles to reasonably recent ones published after 1986 (PY = publication year). As you can see, only three articles meet this criterion. At any step along the way, the computer can print out the abstracts of the articles in a set.

in the study. Information is provided on the participants, the procedures, and the data collection techniques. This description is made detailed enough to permit another researcher to attempt to replicate the study.

Results

The data obtained in the study are reported in the results section. This section often creates problems for novice readers because it includes complex statistical analyses, figures, tables, and graphs. This section does not include any inferences based on the data, as such conclusions are supposed to follow in the next section. Instead, it simply contains a concise summary of the raw data and the statistical analyses.

Discussion

In the discussion section you will find the conclusions drawn by the author(s). In contrast to the results section, which is a straightforward summary of empirical observations, the discussion section allows for interpretation and evaluation of the data. Implications for theory and factual knowledge in the discipline are discussed.

Conclusions are usually qualified carefully, and any limitations in the study may be acknowledged. This section may also include suggestions for future research on the issue.

References

At the end of each article is a list of bibliographic references for any studies cited. This list permits the reader to examine firsthand other relevant studies mentioned in the article. The references list is often a rich source of leads about other articles that are germane to your topic.

As noted earlier in this chapter, the Featured Studies included in this text are summarized in a way that corresponds to the standard organization of a journal article. However, in our Featured Studies the abstract and references are omitted and explanatory comments are added. As with real articles, the introduction section does not have a section heading. Of course, real journal articles are much longer and more detailed than the Featured Studies. Nonetheless, these minisimulations of journal articles are intended to help you feel more

comfortable with the format used in research reports.

Recap of Key Points

• Journals publish technical and scholarly material. Usually they are written for other professionals in a narrow area of inquiry, and they may be highly selective about what they publish. In psychology, most journal articles are reports of original research.

• *Psychological Abstracts* contains brief summaries of newly published journal articles, books, and chapters in edited books. Works on specific topics can be found by using the author and subject indexes.

• The information contained in *Psychological Abstracts* is now stored in computerized databases called *PsycINFO* and *PsycLIT*. Computerized literature searches can be much more powerful and precise than manual searches.

• Journal articles are easier to understand if one is familiar with the standard format. Most articles include six elements: abstract, introduction, method, results, discussion, and references.

Key Ideas

Looking for Laws:
The Scientific Approach to Behavior

◆ The scientific approach assumes that there are laws of behavior that can be discovered through empirical research. The goals of the science of psychology include (1) the measurement and description of behavior, (2) the understanding and prediction of behavior, and (3) the application of this knowledge to the task of controlling behavior.

◆ By integrating apparently unrelated facts into a coherent whole, theories permit psychologists to make the leap from the description of behavior to understanding behavior. The various sciences share the same methods but are distinguished by their subject matter.

◆ A scientific investigation follows a systematic pattern that includes five steps: (1) formulate a testable hypothesis, (2) select the research method and design the study, (3) collect the data, (4) analyze the data and draw conclusions, and (5) report the findings. The two major advantages of the scientific approach are its clarity in communication and its relative intolerance of error.

Looking for Causes:
Experimental Research

◆ Experimental research involves the manipulation of an independent variable to ascertain its effect on a dependent variable. This research is usually done by comparing experimental and control groups, which must be alike in regard to important extraneous variables.

◆ Experimental designs may vary. For example, sometimes an experimental group serves as its own control group. And many experiments have more than one independent variable or more than one dependent variable. Some of these variations were seen in the Featured Study. This experiment suggested that hypnosis is unlikely to improve the accuracy of eyewitness testimony.

◆ An experiment is a powerful research method that permits conclusions about cause-and-effect relationships between variables. However, the experimental method is often not usable for a specific problem, and many experiments tend to be artificial.

Looking for Links:
Descriptive/Correlational Research

◆ Psychologists rely on descriptive/correlational research when they are unable to manipulate the variables they want to study. Key descriptive methods include naturalistic observation, case studies, and surveys.

◆ Descriptive/correlational research methods allow psychologists to explore issues that might not be open to experimental investigation. They are also less artificial than experi-

ments. However, these research methods cannot demonstrate cause-effect relationships.

Looking for Conclusions:
Statistics and Research

◆ Psychologists use descriptive statistics such as measures of central tendency and variability to organize and summarize their numerical data. The mean, median, and mode are widely used measures of central tendency. Variability is usually measured with the standard deviation.

◆ Correlations may be either positive (when two variables covary in the same direction) or negative (when two variables covary in the opposite direction). The closer a correlation is to either +1.00 or –1.00, the stronger the association is. Higher correlations yield greater predictability. However, a correlation is no assurance of causation.

◆ Hypothesis testing involves deciding whether observed findings support the researcher's hypothesis. Findings are statistically significant only when they are unlikely to be due to chance.

Looking for Flaws:
Evaluating Research

◆ Scientists often try to replicate research findings to double-check their validity. Meta-analysis, which involves combining the statistical results from many studies of the same question, can help psychologists evaluate findings and make sense of inconsistent research results.

◆ Sampling bias occurs when a sample is not representative of the population of interest. Placebo effects occur when subjects' expectations cause them to change their behavior in response to a fake treatment.

◆ Distortions in self-reports are a source of concern whenever questionnaires and personality inventories are used to collect data. Experimenter bias occurs when researchers' expectations and desires distort their observations or unintentionally influence their subjects' behavior.

Looking at Ethics:
Do the Ends Justify the Means?

◆ Research sometimes raises complex ethical issues. In psychology, the key questions concern the use of deception with human subjects and the use of harmful or painful manipulations with animal subjects. The APA has formulated ethical principles to serve as guidelines for researchers.

Putting It in Perspective

◆ Two of the book's unifying themes are apparent in this chapter's discussion of the research enterprise in psychology: psychology is empirical, and people's experience of the world can be highly subjective.

Application: Finding
and Reading Journal Articles

◆ Journals publish technical and scholarly material. Usually they are written for other professionals in a narrow area of inquiry.

◆ *Psychological Abstracts* contains brief summaries of newly published journal articles, books, and chapters in edited books. Works on specific topics can be found by using the author and subject indexes or by conducting a computerized literature search.

◆ Journal articles are easier to understand if one is familiar with the standard format. Most articles include six elements: abstract, introduction, method, results, discussion, and references.

Key Terms

Case study
Confounding of
  variables
Control group
Correlation
Correlation
  coefficient
Data collection
  techniques
Dependent variable
Descriptive statistics
Double-blind
  procedure
Experiment
Experimental group
Experimenter bias
Extraneous variables
Hypothesis
Independent variable
Inferential statistics
Journal
Mean
Median
Meta-analysis
Mode
Naturalistic
  observation
Operational
  definition

Participants
Placebo effects
Population
Random assignment
Replication
Research methods
Response set
Sample
Sampling bias
Social desirability
  bias
Standard deviation
Statistical
  significance
Statistics
Subjects
Survey
Theory
Variability
Variables

Key People

Thomas Holmes
Neal Miller
Robert Rosenthal
Stanley Schachter

Practice Test

1. The sciences are bound together by _____, and distinguished from each other by _____.
   A. their subject matter; their empirical research methodology
   B. the assumption that events are governed by general laws; their empirical research methodology
   C. their empirical research methodology; the assumption that events are governed by general laws
   D. their empirical research methodology; their subject matter

2. Researchers must describe the actions that will be taken to measure or control each variable in their studies. In other words, they must:
   A. provide operational definitions of their variables.
   B. decide if their studies will be experimental or correlational.
   C. use statistics to summarize their findings.
   D. decide how many subjects should participate in their studies.

3. A researcher found that clients who were randomly assigned to same-sex groups participated more in group therapy sessions than clients who were randomly assigned to coed groups. In this experiment, the independent variable was:
   A. the amount of participation in the group therapy sessions.
   B. whether or not the group was coed.
   C. the clients' attitudes toward group therapy.
   D. how much the clients' mental health improved.

4. A researcher wants to see whether a protein-enriched diet will enhance the maze-running performance of rats. One group of rats are fed the high-protein diet for the duration of the study; the other group continues to receive ordinary rat chow. In this experiment, the diet fed to the two groups of rats is the _____ variable.
   A. correlated
   B. control
   C. dependent
   D. independent

5. In a study of the effect of a new teaching technique on students' achievement test scores, an important extraneous variable would be the students':
   A. hair color.
   B. athletic skills.
   C. IQ scores.
   D. sociability.

6. Whenever you have a cold, you rest in bed, take aspirin, and drink plenty of fluids. You can't determine which remedy is most effective because of which of the following problems?
   A. sampling bias
   B. distorted self-report data
   C. confounding of variables
   D. experimenter bias

7. A psychologist monitors a group of nurseryschool children, recording each instance of altruistic behavior as it occurs. The psychologist is using:
   A. the experimental method.
   B. naturalistic observation.
   C. case studies.
   D. the survey method.

8. Among the advantages of descriptive/correlational research is (are):
   A. it can often be used in circumstances in which an experiment would be unethical.
   B. it permits researchers to examine subjects' behavior in natural, real-world circumstances.
   C. it can demonstrate conclusively that two variables are causally related.
   D. a and b.

9. Which of the following correlation coefficients would indicate the strongest relationship between two variables?
   A. .58
   B. .19
   C. –.97
   D. –.05

10. When psychologists say that their results are statistically significant, they mean that the results:
    A. have important practical applications.
    B. have important implications for scientific theory.
    C. are unlikely to be due to the fluctuations of chance.
    D. all of the above.

11. Sampling bias exists when:
    A. the sample is representative of the population.
    B. the sample is not representative of the population.
    C. two variables are confounded.
    D. the effect of the independent variable can't be isolated.

12. The problem of experimenter bias can be avoided by:
    A. not informing subjects of the hypothesis of the experiment.
    B. telling the subjects that there are no "right" or "wrong" answers.
    C. using a research strategy in which neither subjects nor experimenter know which subjects are in the experimental and control groups.
    D. having the experimenter use only nonverbal signals when communicating with the subjects.

13. Critics of deception in research have assumed that deceptive studies are harmful to subjects. The empirical data on this issue suggests that:
    A. many deceptive studies do produce significant distress for subjects who were not forewarned about the possibility of deception.
    B. most participants in deceptive studies report that they enjoyed the experience and didn't mind being misled.
    C. deceptive research seriously undermines subjects' trust in others.
    D. a and c.

14. *PsycINFO* is:
    A. a new journal that recently replaced *Psychological Abstracts*.
    B. a computerized database containing the information in *Psychological Abstracts* from 1967 on.
    C. a reference book that explains the format and techniques for writing journal articles.
    D. a computerized database containing information about studies that have not yet been published.

15. Which of the following would not be included in the results section of a journal article?
    A. descriptive statistics summarizing the data
    B. statistical analyses of the data
    C. graphs and/or tables presenting the data pictorially
    D. interpretation, evaluation, and implications of the data

Answers

1	D Page 39	6	C Page 45	11	B Page 58
2	A Page 40	7	B Page 49	12	C Page 61
3	B Page 43	8	D Page 51	13	B Page 62
4	D Page 43	9	C Pages 54–55	14	B Page 68
5	C Page 45	10	C Page 57	15	D Page 69

3

THE BIOLOGICAL BASES OF BEHAVIOR

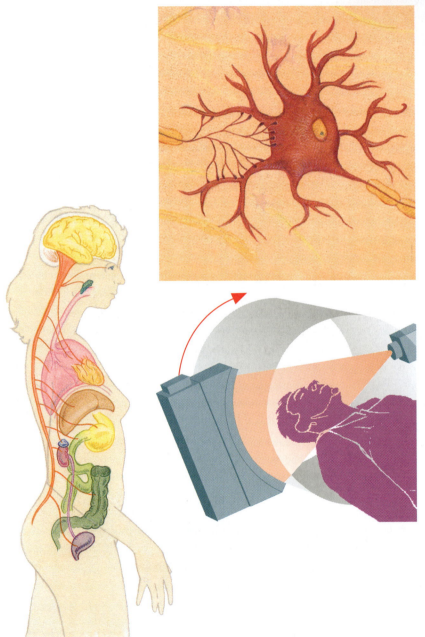

If you have ever visited an aquarium, you may have encountered one of nature's more captivating animals: the octopus. Although this jellylike mass of arms and head appears to be a relatively simple creature, it is capable of a number of interesting behaviors. The octopus has highly developed eyes that enable it to respond to stimuli in the darkness of the ocean. When threatened, it can release an inky cloud to befuddle enemies while it makes good its escape by a kind of jet propulsion. If that doesn't work, it can camouflage itself by changing color and texture to blend into its surroundings. Furthermore, the animal is surprisingly intelligent. In captivity, an octopus can learn, for example, to twist the lid off a jar with one of its tentacles to get at a treat that is inside.

Despite its talents, there are many things an octopus cannot do. An octopus cannot study psychology, plan a weekend, dream about its future, or discover the Pythagorean theorem. Yet the biological processes that underlie these uniquely human behaviors are much the same as the biological processes that enable an octopus to escape from a predator or forage for food. Indeed, some of science's most important insights about how the nervous system works came from studies of a relative of the octopus, the squid.

Organisms as diverse as humans and squid share many biological processes. However, their unique behavioral capacities depend on the differences in their physiological makeup. You and I have a larger repertoire of behaviors than the octopus in large part because we come equipped with a more complex brain and nervous system. The activity of the human brain is so complex that no computer has ever come close to duplicating it. Your nervous system contains as many cells busily integrating and relaying information as there are stars in our galaxy. Whether you are scratching your nose or composing an essay, the activity of those cells underlies what you do. It is little wonder, then, that many psychologists have dedicated themselves to exploring the biological bases of behavior.

How do mood-altering drugs work? Are the two halves of the brain specialized to perform different functions? What happens inside the body when you feel a strong emotion? Are some mental illnesses the result of chemical imbalances in the brain? To what extent is intelligence determined by biological inheritance? These questions only begin to suggest the countless ways in which biology is fundamental to the study of behavior.

In this chapter we will examine the principal biological structures and processes that make behavior possible. In the first two sections of the chapter, we'll discuss the workings of the nervous system. We'll then take an extended look at the most important behavioral organ of all, the brain. After completing our review of behavioral physiology with a brief discussion of the endocrine system, we will consider a key issue raised by the importance of biology: the impact of heredity on behavior. Finally, the chapter's Application examines the furor about the specialized abilities of the right and left halves of the brain.

COMMUNICATION IN THE NERVOUS SYSTEM

Imagine that you are watching a scary movie. As the tension mounts, your palms sweat and your heart beats faster. You begin shoveling popcorn into your mouth, carelessly spilling some in your lap. If someone were to ask you what you are doing at this moment, you would probably say, "Nothing—just watching the movie." Yet some very complicated processes are occurring without your thinking about them. A stimulus (the light from the screen) is striking your eye. Almost instantaneously, your brain is interpreting the light stimulus, and signals are flashing to other parts of your body, leading to a flurry of activity. Your sweat glands are releasing perspiration, your heartbeat is quickening, and muscular movements are enabling your hand to find the popcorn and, more or less successfully, lift it to your mouth.

Even in this simple example, you can see that behavior depends on rapid information processing. Information travels almost instantaneously from your eye to your brain, from your brain to the muscles of your arm and hand, and from your palms back to your brain. In essence, your nervous system is a complex communication network in which signals are constantly being received, integrated, and transmitted. The nervous system handles information, just as the circulatory system handles blood. In this section, we take a close look at communication in the nervous system.

Nervous Tissue: The Basic Hardware

 2a

Your nervous system is living tissue. It is composed entirely of cells, just like the rest of your body. The cells in the nervous system fall into two major categories: *glia* and *neurons*.

Glia: The Support System

Glia **are cells found throughout the nervous system that provide structural support and insulation for neurons.** Glia (literally "glue") hold the nervous system together and help maintain the chemical environment of the neurons. Among other things, glial cells may supply nutrients to neurons, remove their waste materials, repair damage, and provide insulation (Kandel, 1991). Although glia provide many important services, neurons perform the crucial functions of the nervous system.

Neurons: The Communication Links

Neurons **are individual cells in the nervous system that receive, integrate, and transmit information.** They are the basic links that permit communication within the nervous system. The vast majority of them are *interneurons*—**neurons that communicate only with other neurons.** However, a small minority, called *sensory neurons*, **receive signals from outside the nervous system.** The entire nervous system depends on

these specialized cells for its information about lights, sounds, and other stimuli outside the body and about interior stimuli (a stomachache, for instance). Of course, the plans of action formulated by the brain must get from your brain to the muscles of your body. This communication is handled by *motor neurons*, **which carry messages from the nervous system to the muscles that actually move the body.**

A highly simplified drawing of a few "typical" neurons is shown in Figure 3.1. Actually, neurons come in such a tremendous variety of types and shapes that no single drawing can adequately represent them. Trying to draw the "typical" neuron is like trying to draw the "typical" tree. In spite of this diversity, the drawing in Figure 3.1 highlights some common features of neurons.

The *soma,* **or cell body, contains the cell nucleus and much of the chemical machinery common to most cells** (*soma* is Greek for "body"). The rest of the neuron is devoted exclusively to handling information. We usually think of information as flowing from left to right, so the diagram in Figure 3.1 is set up for just such a flow. The neuron at the left has a number of branched, feelerlike structures called *dendritic trees* (*dendrite* is a Greek word for "tree"). Each individual branch is a *dendrite*. **Dendrites are the parts of a neuron that are specialized to receive information.** Most neurons receive information from many other cells—sometimes thousands of others—and so have extensive dendritic trees.

From the many dendrites, information flows into the cell body and then travels away from the soma along the *axon* (from the Greek for "axle"). **The** *axon* **is a long, thin fiber that transmits signals away from the soma to other neurons or to muscles or glands.** Axons may be quite long (sometimes several feet), and they may branch off to communicate with a number of other cells.

In humans, many axons are wrapped in a white, fatty substance called *myelin*. **The** *myelin sheath* **is insulating material, derived from glial cells, that encases some axons.** This coating is typically interrupted at intervals of about one millimeter by short unmyelinated sections of axon, called *nodes of Ranvier* (see Figure 3.1). The myelin sheath speeds up the transmission of signals that move along axons. The signals basically *jump* from one node of Ranvier to the next. If an axon's myelin sheath deteriorates, its signals may not be transmitted effectively. The loss of muscle control seen with the disease *multiple sclerosis* is due to a degeneration of myelin sheaths (Adams & Victor, 1993).

A light micrograph (a photograph taken through a light microscope) of neurons in the spinal cord. These cells have been stained and are magnified approximately 500 times.

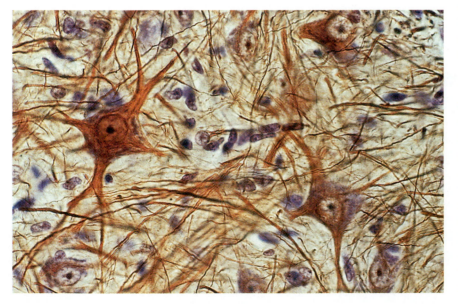

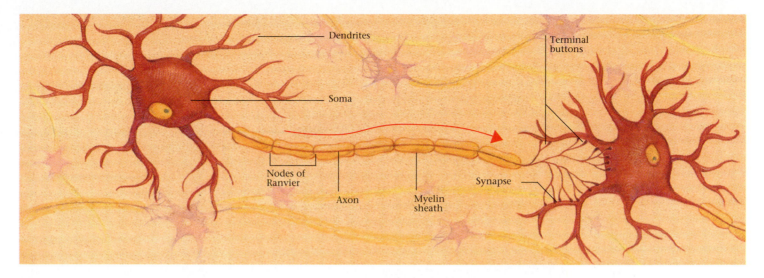

Dendrites

Terminal buttons

Soma

Nodes of Ranvier

Axon

Myelin sheath

Synapse

The axon ends in a cluster of **terminal buttons, which are small knobs that secrete chemicals called neurotransmitters.** These chemicals serve as messengers that may activate neighboring neurons. The points at which neurons interconnect are called *synapses*. **A *synapse* is a junction where information is transmitted from one neuron to another** (*synapse* is from the Greek for "junction").

To summarize, information is received at the dendrites, is passed through the soma and along the axon, and is transmitted to the dendrites of other cells at meeting points called synapses. Unfortunately, this nice, simple picture has more exceptions than the U.S. Tax Code. For example, some neurons do not have an axon, while others have multiple axons. Also, although neurons typically synapse on the dendrites of other cells, they may also synapse on a soma or an axon. Despite these and other complexities, however, the fundamental function of neurons is clear: they are the nervous system's input-output devices that receive, integrate, and transmit informational signals.

The Neural Impulse: Using Energy to Send Information

2a

What happens when a neuron is stimulated? What is the nature of the signal—the *neural impulse*—that moves through the neuron? These were the questions that Alan Hodgkin and Andrew Huxley set out to answer in their experiments with axons removed from squid. Why did they choose to work with squid axons? Because the squid has a pair of "giant" axons that are about a hundred times larger than those in humans (which still makes them only about as thick as a human hair). These giant axons serve the squid well. The thick size speeds up the transmission of messages to the squid's muscles, enabling it to make its remark-

able, jet-propelled escape from its enemies. The axons also serve physiologists well. Their large size permitted Hodgkin and Huxley to insert fine wires called *microelectrodes* into them. By using the microelectrodes to record the electrical activity in individual neurons, Hodgkin and Huxley unraveled the mystery of the neural impulse.

The Neuron at Rest: A Tiny Battery

Hodgkin and Huxley (1952) learned that the neural impulse is a complex electrochemical reaction. Both inside and outside the neuron are fluids containing electrically charged atoms and molecules called *ions*. Positively charged sodium and potassium ions and negatively charged chloride ions flow back and forth across the cell membrane, but they do not cross at the same rate. The difference in flow rates leads to a slightly higher concentration of negatively charged ions inside the cell. The net result is that the neuron membrane becomes *polarized*—negatively charged on the inside and positively charged on the outside.

The voltage difference that results from this polarization means that the neuron at rest is a tiny battery, a store of potential energy. **The *resting potential* of a neuron is its stable, negative charge when the cell is inactive.** As shown in Figure 3.2(a) on page 76, this charge is about –70 millivolts, roughly one-twentieth of the voltage of a flashlight battery.

The Action Potential

As long as the voltage of a typical neuron remains constant, the cell is quiet, and no messages are being sent. However, stimulation of sufficient intensity (signals from other neurons or from sensory stimuli) will disrupt this stability by momentarily altering the permeability of the cell

Figure 3.1
Structure of the neuron.
Neurons are the communication links of the nervous system. This diagram highlights the key parts of a neuron, including specialized receptor areas (dendrites), the cell body (soma), the fiber along which impulses are transmitted (axon), and the junctions across which chemical messengers carry signals to other neurons (synapses). Neurons vary considerably in size and shape and are usually densely interconnected.

Figure 3.2

The neural impulse. The electric charge of a neuron can be measured with a pair of electrodes connected to an oscilloscope. (**a**) At rest, the neuron is like a tiny wet battery with a resting potential of about –70 millivolts. (**b**) When a neuron is stimulated, a sharp jump in its electric potential occurs, resulting in a spike on the oscilloscope recording of the neuron's electrical activity. This change in voltage, called an action potential, travels along the axon. (**c**) Biochemical changes propel the action potential along the axon. An action potential begins when sodium gates in the membrane of an axon open, permitting positively charged sodium ions to flow into the axon. (**d**) By the peak of the action potential, the sodium gates have closed, but potassium gates have opened to let potassium ions flow outward. At the next point along the axon membrane, sodium gates open and the process is repeated, thus allowing the action potential to flow along the axon. (**e**) This blowup of the voltage spike associated with an action potential shows how these biochemical changes relate to the electrical activity of the cell.

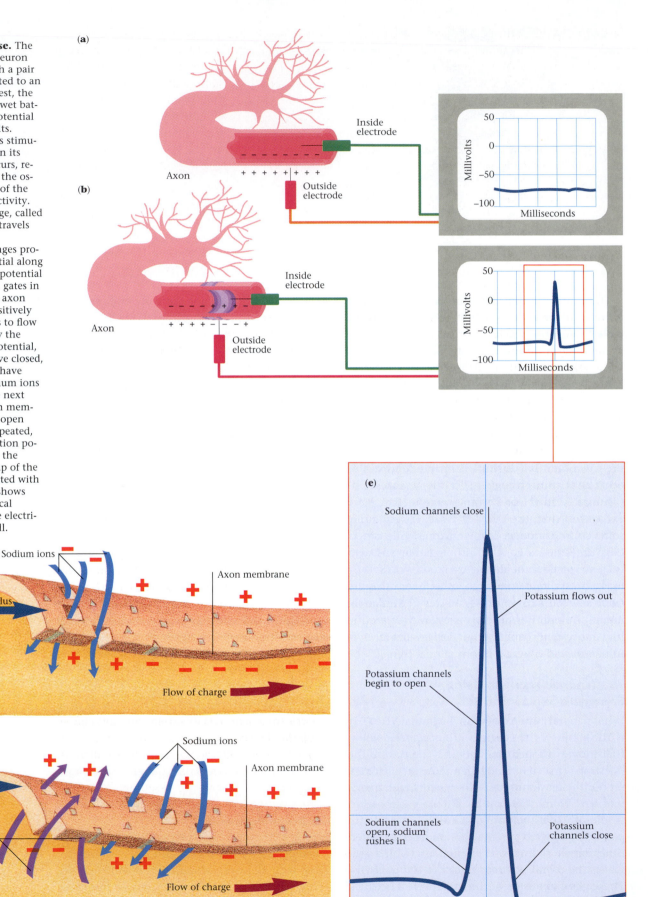

(a)

Axon

Inside electrode

Outside electrode

+ + + + + + + + +

Millivolts

50

0

–50

–100

Milliseconds

(b)

Axon

Inside electrode

Outside electrode

– – – – + + + –

+ + + – – – +

Millivolts

50

0

–50

–100

Milliseconds

(c)

Sodium ions

Stimulus

Axon membrane

Flow of charge

(d)

Stimulus

Sodium ions

Potassium ions

Axon membrane

Flow of charge

(e)

Sodium channels close

Potassium flows out

Potassium channels begin to open

Sodium channels open, sodium rushes in

Potassium channels close

membrane. When the neuron is stimulated, channels in its cell membrane open, briefly allowing positively charged sodium ions to rush in, as shown in Figure 3.2(c). For an instant, the neuron's charge is less negative, or even positive, creating an action potential (Koester, 1991). **An *action potential* is a very brief shift in a neuron's electrical charge that travels along an axon.** The firing of an action potential is reflected in the voltage spike shown in Figure 3.2(b). Like a spark traveling along a trail of gunpowder, the voltage change races down the axon. The firing of the action potential in one segment of the axon triggers the firing of the action potential in the next segment, and so on down the line. The size of the action potential (as measured by the voltage spike) remains constant as it travels down the axon.

Thus, a neural impulse is an electric current that flows along the axon as a result of an action potential. After the firing of an action potential, the channels in the cell membrane that opened to let in sodium close up, as shown in Figure 3.2 (d and e). Some time is needed before they are ready to open again. Until they are ready to reopen, the neuron cannot fire. **The *absolute refractory period* is the minimum length of time after an action potential during which another action potential cannot begin.** This "down time" isn't very long, only 1 or 2 milliseconds (msec). However, much longer periods of neural unresponsiveness can be produced by certain drugs, such as local anesthetics. For example, if your dentist gives you an injection of Novocaine before drilling, the drug exerts its painkilling effects by closing the sodium channels in neurons near the injection site. The result is that sensory neurons that would otherwise send pain signals to the brain are temporarily shut down.

The All-or-None Law

The neural impulse is an all-or-none proposition, like firing a gun. You can't half-fire a gun. The same is true of the neuron's firing of action potentials. Either the neuron fires or it doesn't and its action potentials are all the same size. Weaker stimuli do not produce smaller action potentials.

Even though the action potential is an all-or-nothing event, neurons *can* convey information about the strength of a stimulus. They do so by varying the *rate* at which they fire action potentials. In general, a stronger stimulus will cause a cell to fire a more rapid volley of neural impulses than a weaker stimulus will.

Various neurons transmit neural impulses at different speeds. Because thicker axons have less resistance to electrical current, they conduct action potentials more rapidly than thinner ones do, which is why the squid's thick axons serve their purpose so well. A neural impulse also travels faster on an axon insulated with myelin. Although neural impulses do not travel as fast as electricity along a wire, they *are* very fast, moving at up to 100 meters per second, which is equivalent to more than 200 miles per hour. The entire, complicated process of neural transmission takes only a few thousandths of a second. In the time it has taken you to read this description of the neural impulse, billions of such impulses have been transmitted in your nervous system!

The Synapse: Where Neurons Meet 2b

In the nervous system, the neural impulse functions as a signal. For that signal to have any meaning for the system as a whole, it must be transmitted from the neuron to other cells. As noted earlier, this transmission takes place at special junctions called *synapses*. In invertebrates and lower mammals, some synapses simply involve electrical currents that pass directly from cell to cell (Shepherd, 1988). In humans, however, it appears that all synapses depend on *chemical* messengers.

Sending Signals: Chemicals as Couriers

A "typical" synapse is shown in Figure 3.3 on page 78. The first thing that you should notice is that the two neurons don't actually touch. They are separated by the ***synaptic cleft, a microscopic gap between the terminal button of one neuron and the cell membrane of another neuron.*** Signals have to jump this gap to permit neurons to communicate. In this situation, the neuron that sends a signal across the gap is called the *presynaptic neuron,* and the neuron that receives the signal is called the *postsynaptic neuron.*

How do messages travel across the gaps between neurons? The arrival of an action potential at an axon's terminal buttons triggers the release of ***neurotransmitters—chemicals that transmit information from one neuron to another.*** Within the buttons, most of these chemicals are stored in small sacs, called *synaptic vesicles.* The neurotransmitters are released when a vesicle fuses with the membrane of the presynaptic cell and its contents spill into the synaptic cleft. After their release, neurotransmitters diffuse across the synaptic cleft to the membrane of the receiving cell. There they may bind with special molecules in the

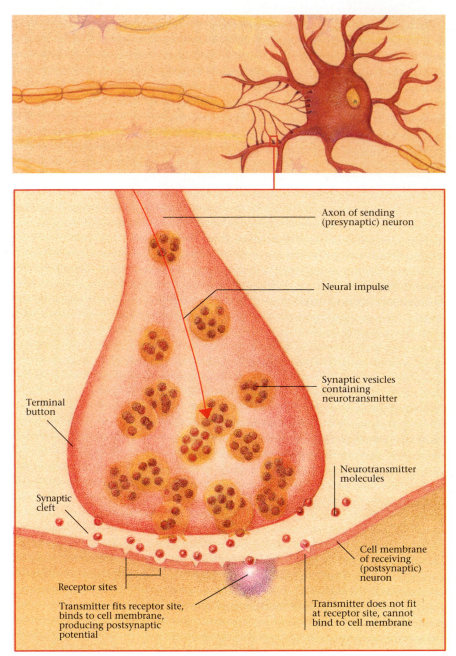

Axon of sending
(presynaptic) neuron

Neural impulse

Synaptic vesicles
containing
neurotransmitter

Terminal
button

Neurotransmitter
molecules

Synaptic
cleft

Cell membrane
of receiving
(postsynaptic)
neuron

Receptor sites

Transmitter fits receptor site,
binds to cell membrane,
producing postsynaptic
potential

Transmitter does not fit
at receptor site, cannot
bind to cell membrane

Figure 3.3
The synapse. When a neural impulse reaches an axon's terminal buttons, it triggers the release of chemical messengers called neurotransmitters. The neurotransmitter molecules diffuse across the synaptic cleft and bind to receptor sites on the postsynaptic neuron. A specific neurotransmitter can bind only to receptor sites that its molecular structure will fit into, much like a key must fit a lock.

postsynaptic cell membrane at various *receptor sites*. These sites are specifically "tuned" to recognize and respond to some neurotransmitters but not to others.

Receiving Signals: Postsynaptic Potentials

When a neurotransmitter and a receptor molecule combine, reactions in the cell membrane cause a *postsynaptic potential (PSP),* **a voltage change at a receptor site on a postsynaptic cell membrane.** When a PSP occurs, channels are opened in the cell membrane at the site, allowing specific ions to flood into or rush out of the cell. Postsynaptic potentials do *not* follow the all-or-none law as action potentials do. Instead, postsynaptic po-

tentials are *graded.* That is, they vary in size and they increase or decrease the *probability* of a neural impulse in the receiving cell in proportion to the amount of voltage change. Postsynaptic potentials last longer (10–100 msec) than action potentials (1–2 msec), but unlike action potentials, they diminish in size as they travel along a dendrite or across a soma.

If the voltage in the postsynaptic neuron shifts in a positive direction, the cell comes closer to its threshold for firing a neural impulse. **An *excitatory PSP* is a voltage shift that increases the likelihood that the postsynaptic neuron will fire action potentials.** If the voltage shifts in a negative direction, the postsynaptic neuron moves farther away from its threshold for firing a neural impulse. Thus, **an *inhibitory PSP* is a voltage shift that decreases the likelihood that the postsynaptic neuron will fire action potentials.** Both excitatory and inhibitory PSPs are depicted in Figure 3.4. The direction of the voltage shift, and thus the nature of the PSP (excitatory or inhibitory), depends on which receptor sites are activated in the postsynaptic neuron (Kandel & Schwartz, 1991).

Thus, there are two types of messages that can be sent from cell to cell: excitatory and inhibitory. Both types are essential to the functioning of the nervous system. If cells could only excite other cells, any excitation would grow and reverberate through the nervous system like a nuclear chain reaction. In fact, many kinds of seizures are due to insufficient inhibitory effects at synapses. Strychnine, perhaps the nastiest of poisons, works its deadly effects by disabling many inhibitory synapses. The resulting excitation causes uncontrollable convulsions that can be fatal.

The excitatory or inhibitory effects produced at a synapse last only a fraction of a second. If neurotransmitters remained bound to receptor sites forever, all such sites would soon be occupied and cells would remain permanently at a stable electric potential. Information processing in the nervous system would come to a halt. Why doesn't this happen? Because neurotransmitters drift away from receptor sites or are inactivated by enzymes that metabolize (convert) them into inactive forms. Most are reabsorbed into the presynaptic neuron through *reuptake,* a process in which neurotransmitters are sponged up from the synaptic cleft by the presynaptic membrane. This process allows synapses to recycle their materials.

The various processes in synaptic transmission are diagrammed in Figure 3.5. As you can see,

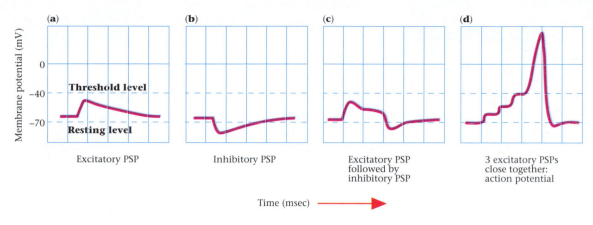

(a) Excitatory PSP

(b) Inhibitory PSP

(c) Excitatory PSP followed by inhibitory PSP

(d) 3 excitatory PSPs close together: action potential

Membrane potential (mV)

Threshold level

Resting level

0

−40

−70

Time (msec)

Figure 3.4
Postsynaptic potentials (PSPs). A postsynaptic potential is a change in the voltage of a neuron that occurs when a neurotransmitter binds with a receptor on the neuron. PSPs are either inhibitory or excitatory. **(a)** At some receptor sites, a PSP increases the postsynaptic neuron's voltage (an excitatory effect). **(b)** At other receptor sites, a PSP lowers the neuron's voltage (an inhibitory effect). **(c)** An excitatory PSP and an inhibitory PSP may balance each other out. **(d)** A series of excitatory PSPs may lead to an action potential.

communication at synapses involves five steps: (1) the synthesis and storage of transmitters, (2) the release of transmitters into the synaptic cleft, (3) the binding of transmitters at receptor sites on the postsynaptic membrane, (4) the inactivation (by enzymes) or removal (drifting away) of transmitters in the synapse, and (5) the reuptake of transmitters by the presynaptic neuron.

Integrating Signals: A Balancing Act

We have seen how neurons receive signals, transmit signals along axons, and send signals across synaptic clefts to other neurons. Keep in mind, however, that most neurons are interlinked in complex, dense networks. In fact, a neuron may have as many as 15,000 synapses receiving a sym-

phony of signals from thousands of other neurons. The same neuron may pass its messages along to thousands of other neurons as well.

Thus, a neuron must do a great deal more than simply relay messages it receives. It must integrate signals arriving at many synapses before it "decides" whether to fire a neural impulse. If enough excitatory PSPs occur in a neuron, the electrical currents can add up, causing the cell's voltage to reach the threshold at which an action potential will be fired (as shown in panel d of Figure 3.4). Excitatory PSPs can add up in a couple of ways. *Temporal summation* can occur when several or more PSPs follow one another in rapid succession at a receptor site. *Spatial summation* can take place when several or more PSPs occur

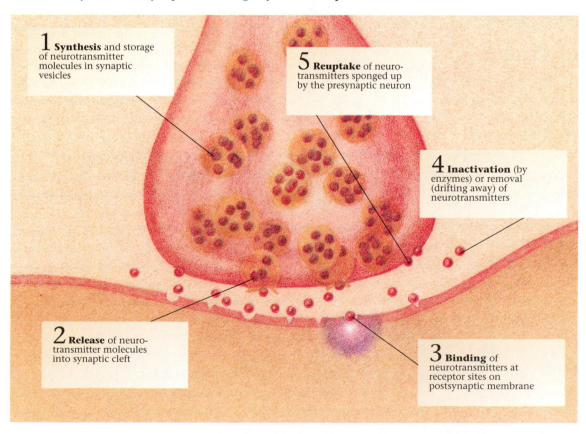

1 **Synthesis** and storage of neurotransmitter molecules in synaptic vesicles

5 **Reuptake** of neurotransmitters sponged up by the presynaptic neuron

4 **Inactivation** (by enzymes) or removal (drifting away) of neurotransmitters

2 **Release** of neurotransmitter molecules into synaptic cleft

3 **Binding** of neurotransmitters at receptor sites on postsynaptic membrane

Figure 3.5
Overview of synaptic transmission. The main elements in synaptic transmission are summarized here, superimposed on a blowup of the synapse seen in Figure 3.3. The five key processes involved in communication at synapses are (1) synthesis, (2) release, (3) binding, (4) inactivation, and (5) reuptake of neurotransmitters. As you'll see in this chapter and the remainder of the book, the effects of many phenomena—such as stress, drug use, and some diseases—can be explained in terms of how they alter one or more of these processes (usually at synapses releasing a specific neurotransmitter).

Figure 3.6
Temporal and spatial summation. Postsynaptic potentials can have cumulative effects through either temporal or spatial summation. In temporal summation PSPs are summed over time when they occur in rapid succession at a receptor site. Postsynaptic potentials can pile up at a receptor site because they last longer than action potentials. In spatial summation, PSPs at different receptor sites are summed when they occur at the same time.

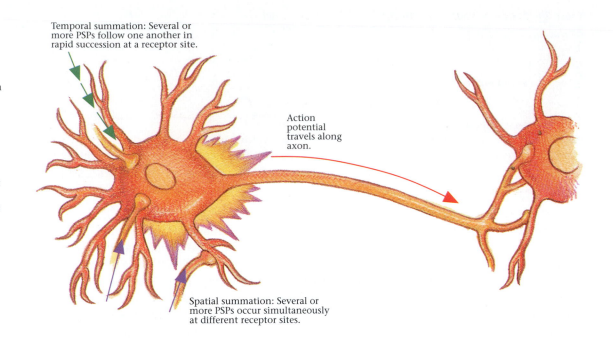

Temporal summation: Several or more PSPs follow one another in rapid succession at a receptor site.

Action potential travels along axon.

Spatial summation: Several or more PSPs occur simultaneously at different receptor sites.

simultaneously at different receptor sites (see Figure 3.6). Of course, inhibitory PSPs can add up in the same two ways. If many inhibitory PSPs occur, they will tend to cancel the effects of excitatory PSPs. Thus, the state of the neuron is a weighted balance between excitatory and inhibitory influences.

Neurotransmitters and Behavior

 2b, 4d

As we have seen, the nervous system relies on chemical couriers to communicate information between neurons. These *neurotransmitters* are fundamental to behavior, playing a key role in everything from muscle movements to moods and mental health.

You might guess that the nervous system would require only two neurotransmitters—one for excitatory potentials and one for inhibitory potentials. However, 15 to 20 chemical substances appear to qualify as neurotransmitters. In addition, scientists suspect that a number of other substances *may* function as transmitters, and new candidates are still being discovered. In general, a specific type of neuron contains the chemical factory for manufacturing only one of the transmitters. However, some neurons also release related chemicals called *neuromodulators*, which we'll discuss later.

Specific neurotransmitters work at specific kinds of synapses. You may recall that transmitter substances deliver their messages by binding to

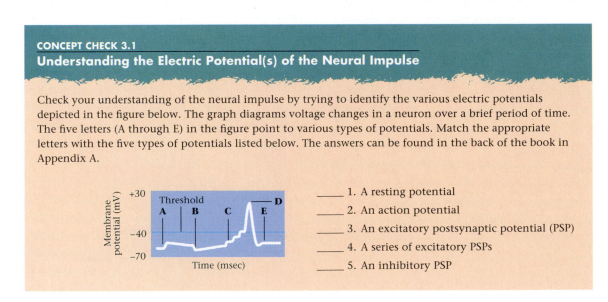

CONCEPT CHECK 3.1
Understanding the Electric Potential(s) of the Neural Impulse

Check your understanding of the neural impulse by trying to identify the various electric potentials depicted in the figure below. The graph diagrams voltage changes in a neuron over a brief period of time. The five letters (A through E) in the figure point to various types of potentials. Match the appropriate letters with the five types of potentials listed below. The answers can be found in the back of the book in Appendix A.

Membrane potential (mV)

+30

Threshold

A   B   C   D   E

−40

−70

Time (msec)

_____ 1. A resting potential

_____ 2. An action potential

_____ 3. An excitatory postsynaptic potential (PSP)

_____ 4. A series of excitatory PSPs

_____ 5. An inhibitory PSP

TABLE 3.1 COMMON NEUROTRANSMITTERS AND SOME OF THEIR FUNCTIONS

Neurotransmitter	Functions and Characteristics
Acetylcholine (ACh)	Activates motor neurons controlling skeletal muscles Contributes to the regulation of attention, arousal, and memory Decreased levels found in the brains of Alzheimer's patients Some ACh receptors stimulated by nicotine
Dopamine (DA)	Contributes to control of voluntary movement Decreased levels associated with Parkinson's disease Overactivity at DA synapses associated with schizophrenia Cocaine and amphetamines elevate activity at DA synapses
Norepinephrine (NE)	Contributes to modulation of mood and arousal Cocaine and amphetamines elevate activity at NE synapses
Serotonin	Involved in regulation of sleep and wakefulness Abnormal levels may contribute to depression and obsessive-compulsive disorder Prozac and similar antidepressant drugs affect serotonin circuits
GABA	Serves as widely distributed inhibitory transmitter Low levels associated with anxiety Valium and similar antianxiety drugs work at GABA synapses
Endorphins	Resemble opiate drugs in structure and effects Contribute to pain relief and perhaps to some pleasurable emotions "Runner's high" may be associated with high endorphin levels

receptor sites on the postsynaptic membrane. However, a transmitter cannot bind to just any site. The binding process operates much like a lock and key, as was shown in Figure 3.3. Just as a key has to fit a lock to work, a transmitter has to fit into a receptor site for binding to occur. Hence, specific transmitters can deliver signals only at certain locations on cell membranes.

Why are there many different neurotransmitters, each of which works only at certain synapses? This variety and specificity reduces crosstalk between densely packed neurons, making the nervous system's communication more precise. Let's briefly review some of the most interesting findings about how neurotransmitters regulate behavior, which are summarized in Table 3.1.

Acetylcholine

The discovery that cells communicate by releasing chemicals was first made in connection with the transmitter *acetylcholine* (ACh). ACh has been found throughout the nervous system. It is the only transmitter between motor neurons and voluntary muscles. Every move you make—typing, walking, talking, breathing—depends on ACh released to your muscles by motor neurons (Kandel & Schwartz, 1991).

ACh appears to contribute to attention, arousal, and memory. An inadequate supply of ACh in the brain has been implicated as a contributing factor

in the memory losses seen with *Alzheimer's disease*. This disease is endured by about 11% of people over the age of 65, as well as some younger people (Price et al., 1995). People with Alzheimer's disease gradually lose their ability to remember anything. Eventually, they don't recognize family members, can't find their way home, and can't finish their sentences because they don't remember what they were in the midst of saying. Examinations of the brains of people who have died from Alzheimer's disease reveal widespread atrophy (wasting away) of brain tissue and a variety of other abnormalities. Prominent among these is a severely depleted supply of ACh, which may decline by as much as 70% (Albert, 1992; Goldman & Coté, 1991). Researchers believe that cells responsible for the synthesis of ACh degenerate in victims of Alzheimer's, leaving the brain with an inadequate supply of this neurotransmitter, which appears to play an important role in memory processes.

The activity of ACh (and other neurotransmitters) may be influenced by other chemicals in the brain. Although synaptic receptor sites are sensitive to specific neurotransmitters, sometimes they can be "fooled" by other chemical substances. For example, if you smoke tobacco, some of your ACh synapses will be stimulated by the nicotine that arrives in your brain. At these synapses, the nicotine acts like ACh itself. It binds to receptor sites

"Brain research of the past decade, especially the study of neurotransmitters, has proceeded at a furious pace, achieving progress equal in scope to all the accomplishments of the preceding 50 years—and the pace of discovery continues to accelerate. The final years of the 20th century may witness unparalleled advances in our understanding of the brain and, even more exciting, in our ability to put this understanding to therapeutic use."

SOLOMON SNYDER

for ACh, causing postsynaptic potentials (PSPs). In technical language, nicotine is an ACh agonist. **An *agonist* is a chemical that mimics the action of a neurotransmitter.** In other words, an agonist functions as a substitute, producing some of the effects of the regular transmitter.

Not all chemicals that fool synaptic receptors are agonists. Some chemicals bind to receptors but fail to produce a PSP (the key slides into the lock, but it doesn't work). In effect, they temporarily *block* the action of the natural transmitter by occupying its receptor sites, rendering them unusable. Thus, they act as antagonists. **An *antagonist* is a chemical that opposes the action of a neurotransmitter.** For example, the drug *curare* is an ACh antagonist. It blocks action at the same ACh synapses that are fooled by nicotine. As a result, muscles are unable to move. Some South American natives use a form of curare on arrows. If they wound an animal, the curare blocks the synapses from nerve to muscle, paralyzing the animal.

Monoamines

The *monoamines* include three neurotransmitters: dopamine, norepinephrine, and serotonin. Neurons using these transmitters regulate many aspects of everyday behavior. Dopamine (DA), for example, is used by neurons that control voluntary movements. The degeneration of such neurons apparently causes *Parkinsonism,* a disease marked by tremors, muscular rigidity, and reduced control over voluntary movements (Coté & Crutcher, 1991).

Neural circuits using serotonin appear to play a prominent role in the regulation of sleep and wakefulness (McGinty & Szymusiak, 1988). The activity of serotonin-releasing neurons is highest when animals are awake and declines as they move into deeper stages of sleep. However, the modulation of physiological arousal is extremely complex. Arousal also appears to be mediated by another of the monoamines (norepinephrine), as well as quite a variety of other chemicals in the brain (D. Kelly, 1991; Panksepp, 1986).

Abnormal levels of monoamines in the brain have been related to the development of certain psychological disorders. For example, people who suffer from depression appear to have lowered levels of activation at norepinephrine (NE) and serotonin synapses (Delgado et al., 1992). Although a host of other biochemical changes may contribute to depression, abnormalities at NE and serotonin synapses appear to play a central role, as most antidepressant drugs exert their main effects at these synapses (Charney et al., 1995; Nathan et al., 1995).

In a similar fashion, alterations in activity at dopamine synapses have been implicated in the development of *schizophrenia*. This severe mental illness is marked by irrational thought, hallucinations, poor contact with reality, and deterioration of routine adaptive behavior. Afflicting roughly 1% of the population, schizophrenia requires hospitalization more often than any other psychological disorder. Many investigators believe that the main cause of schizophrenia is overactivity at DA synapses. Why? Primarily because the therapeutic drugs that tame schizophrenic symptoms are known to be DA antagonists that reduce the neurotransmitter's activity. Solomon Snyder (1986) has shown that most of these drugs work by binding to DA receptor sites and blocking normal DA activity at these sites (see Figure 3.7). Unfortunately, the antagonistic effects of these drugs at dopamine synapses often lead to Parkinsonism-like side effects (tremors and muscular rigidity) that make the drugs unpleasant for some patients.

Complexities in the biochemical explanations of depression and schizophrenia continue to be debated (see Chapter 14). Overactivity at dopamine synapses clearly is not the only factor at work in schizophrenia (Knable et al., 1995). Nonetheless, it's apparent that disturbances in the activity of monoamine neurotransmitters make a key contribution to some forms of mental illness.

Altered functioning at monoamine synapses also appears to account for the effects of several widely abused drugs, especially amphetamines, cocaine, and LSD (Cooper, Bloom, & Roth, 1996; Julien, 1995). The stimulant effects of amphetamines and cocaine and the hallucinogenic effects of LSD are described in detail in Chapter 5. At this point, we'll just discuss their mechanisms of action to further illustrate the enormous variety of phenomena that can be explained in terms of neurotransmitter activity. Amphetamines seem to exert most of their effects by increasing the release of dopamine and norepinephrine from presynaptic neurons and by slowing the reuptake of DA and NE. These actions leave an overabundance of DA and NE in synaptic clefts, thus causing a storm of increased activity at these synapses. Cocaine also elevates activity at DA and NE synapses, but it does so mainly by blocking the reuptake of dopamine and, to a lesser degree, norepinephrine. LSD is less well understood, but theorists believe that it

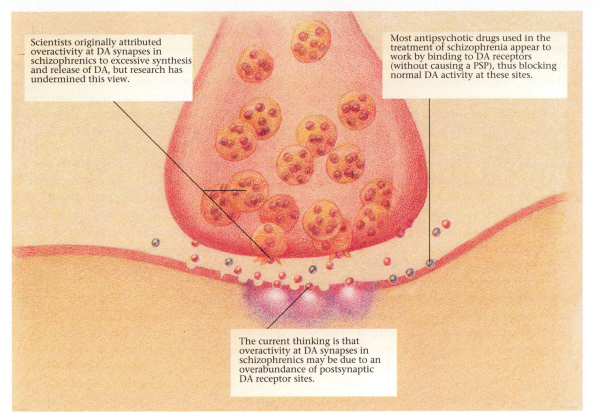

Scientists originally attributed overactivity at DA synapses in schizophrenics to excessive synthesis and release of DA, but research has undermined this view.

Most antipsychotic drugs used in the treatment of schizophrenia appear to work by binding to DA receptors (without causing a PSP), thus blocking normal DA activity at these sites.

The current thinking is that overactivity at DA synapses in schizophrenics may be due to an overabundance of postsynaptic DA receptor sites.

Figure 3.7
The dopamine hypothesis as an explanation for schizophrenia. Although other neurotransmitter systems may also be involved, overactivity at dopamine synapses has been implicated as a key cause of schizophrenic disorders. However, the exact mechanisms underlying this DA overactivity are still the subject of considerable debate.

alters serotonin activity by binding to a specific subtype of serotonin receptor. Thus, changes in neurotransmitter activity are the foundation for the dramatic, mysterious, and inexplicably powerful effects of amphetamines, cocaine, and LSD.

GABA

Another group of transmitters consists of small molecules called *amino acids*. Two of these, *gamma-aminobutyric acid* (GABA) and *glycine,* are notable in that they seem to produce only *inhibitory* postsynaptic potentials. Some transmitters, such as ACh and NE, are versatile. They can produce either excitatory or inhibitory PSPs, depending on the synaptic receptors they bind to. However, GABA and glycine appear to have inhibitory effects at virtually all synapses where either is present. GABA receptors are widely distributed in the brain and may be present at 40% of all synapses. GABA appears to be responsible for much of the inhibition in the central nervous system.

Studies also suggest that GABA contributes to the regulation of anxiety in humans (Paul, Crawley, & Skolnick, 1986). Generally, the inhibitory effects of GABA keep a lid on neural excitement. However, lowered levels of GABA activity may permit heightened neural excitement that translates into feelings of anxiety. Consistent with this theory, researchers have found that Valium and

other *benzodiazepine drugs* that are used to combat anxiety exert their effects at GABA synapses (Ballenger, 1995). These drugs bind to benzodiazepine receptor sites within GABA synapses, where they facilitate the binding of GABA to its receptors. The result is an increase in inhibitory activity in the GABA system that helps reduce anxiety. Ironically, millions of prescriptions were written for tranquilizers such as Valium before scientists discovered their mechanism of action in the late 1970s. Although the exact mechanisms remain elusive, abnormalities in the GABA neurotransmitter system probably play a role in the development of some types of anxiety disorders (Hollander, Simeon, & Gorman, 1994; Zorumski & Isenberg, 1991).

Endorphins

In 1970, after a horseback-riding accident, Candace Pert, a graduate student in neuroscience, lay in a hospital bed receiving frequent shots of *morphine,* a painkilling drug derived from the opium plant. This experience left her with a driving curiosity about how morphine works. A few years later, she and Solomon Snyder rocked the scientific world by showing that *morphine exerts its effects by binding to specialized receptors in the brain* (Pert & Snyder, 1973).

This discovery raised a perplexing question: Why

"When human beings engage in various activities, it seems that neurojuices are released that are associated with either pain or pleasure. And the endorphins are very pleasurable."

CANDACE PERT

would the brain be equipped with receptors for morphine, a powerful, addictive opiate drug not normally found in the body? It occurred to Pert and others that the nervous system must have its own, endogenous (internally produced) morphine-like substances. Investigators dubbed these as-yet undiscovered substances "endorphins" (endogenous morphines). A search for the body's natural opiate ensued. In short order, a number of endogenous, opiatelike substances were identified (Hughes et al., 1975). Subsequent studies revealed that endorphins and their receptors are widely distributed in the human body and that they clearly contribute to the modulation of pain, as well as a variety of other phenomena (E. Simon, 1992).

The term *endorphins* **refers to the entire family of internally produced chemicals that resemble opiates in structure and effects.** Given that opiate drugs are highly addicting, you may be wondering why people don't become addicted to their own endorphins. Apparently, the reason is that endorphins are quickly inactivated by enzymes. Unlike opiate drugs, they don't remain at receptor sites long enough to cause the tissue changes that probably underlie addiction (Snyder, 1986).

All of the endorphins are *neuropeptides,* which are strings of amino acids bound together. Some neuropeptides, such as *substance P,* appear to function as neurotransmitters. Many of the neural circuits that deliver pain signals to the spinal cord and brain seem to use substance P as a transmitter (Levine, Fields, & Basbaum, 1993). Although they may serve as transmitters at some synapses, *endor-*

phins often function as neuromodulators (E. Simon, 1992). *Neuromodulators* **are chemicals that increase or decrease (modulate) the activity of specific neurotransmitters.** Some endorphins, for instance, appear to reduce pain by preventing the release of substance P, so that fewer pain signals are sent to the brain (Jessell & Kelly, 1991).

The discovery of endorphins has led to revolutionary new theories and findings on the neurochemical bases of pain and pleasure. In addition to their painkilling effects, opiate drugs such as morphine and heroin produce highly pleasurable feelings of euphoria. This euphoric effect explains why heroin is so widely abused. Researchers suspect that the body's natural endorphins may also be capable of producing feelings of pleasure. This capacity might explain why joggers sometimes experience a "runner's high." The pain caused by a long run may trigger the release of endorphins, which neutralize some of the pain and create a feeling of exhilaration (Harte, Eifert, & Smith, 1995). Experts can't help but wonder whether endorphins might be the chemical basis for other pleasant emotions as well (Hawkes, 1992).

In this section we have highlighted just a few of the more interesting connections between neurotransmitters and behavior. These highlights barely begin to convey the rich complexity of biochemical processes in the nervous system. Most aspects of behavior are probably regulated by several types of transmitters, and most transmitters appear to be involved in many aspects of behavior. Although scientists have learned a great

---

CONCEPT CHECK 3.2
Linking Brain Chemistry to Behavior

Check your understanding of relations between brain chemistry and behavior by indicating which neurotransmitters (or neuromodulators) have been linked to the phenomena listed below. Choose your answers from the following list: (a) acetylcholine, (b) serotonin, (c) norepinephrine, (d) dopamine, (e) GABA, (f) endorphins. Indicate your choice (by letter) in the spaces on the left. You'll find the answers in Appendix A.

_____ 1. An inhibitory transmitter linked to anxiety; tranquilizers increase the activity of this transmitter.

_____ 2. A monoamine that plays a prominent role in the regulation of sleep and wakefulness.

_____ 3. A monoamine that has been linked to depression.

_____ 4. Chemicals that resemble opiate drugs in structure and that are involved in feelings of pain and pleasure.

_____ 5. A neurotransmitter for which abnormal levels have been implicated in Parkinsonism and schizophrenia.

_____ 6. The only neurotransmitter between motor neurons and voluntary muscles; it also plays a role in memory.

deal about neurotransmitters and behavior, much still remains to be discovered.

Recap of Key Points

• Behavior depends on complex information processing in the nervous system. Cells in the nervous system receive, integrate, and transmit information.

• Neurons are the basic communication links. They normally transmit a neural impulse along an axon to a synapse with another neuron. The neural impulse is a brief change in a neuron's electrical charge that moves along an axon.

• An action potential is an all-or-none event. Neurons convey information about the strength of a stimulus by variations in their rate of firing. The absolute refractory period is the minimum length of time after an action potential during which another action potential cannot begin.

• Action potentials trigger the release of chemicals called neurotransmitters that diffuse across a synapse to communicate with other neurons. Transmitters bind with receptors in the postsynaptic cell membrane, causing excitatory or inhibitory PSPs.

• Whether the postsynaptic neuron fires a neural impulse depends on the balance of excitatory and inhibitory PSPs. Postsynaptic potentials can have cumulative effects through either temporal or spatial summation. Neurotransmitters bind at specific sites according to a lock-and-key model.

• The transmitter ACh plays a key role in muscular movement, and a shortage of ACh has been implicated as a contributing factor in Alzheimer's disease. An agonist mimics the action of a neurotransmitter, whereas an antagonist blocks the action of a transmitter.

• Depression is associated with reduced activation at norepinephrine synapses. Schizophrenia has been linked to overactivity at dopamine synapses. Cocaine and amphetamines appear to exert their main effects by altering activity at monoamine synapses.

• GABA is a widely distributed inhibitory neurotransmitter that appears to be involved in the regulation of anxiety. Endorphins, which resemble opiates, contribute to pain relief and perhaps to the experience of pleasure.

ORGANIZATION OF THE NERVOUS SYSTEM

Clearly, communication in the nervous system is fundamental to behavior. So far we have looked at how individual cells communicate with one another. In this section, we examine the organization of the nervous system as a whole (see Figure 3.8).

Experts believe that there are *85 to 180 billion* neurons in the human brain (Kolb & Whishaw,

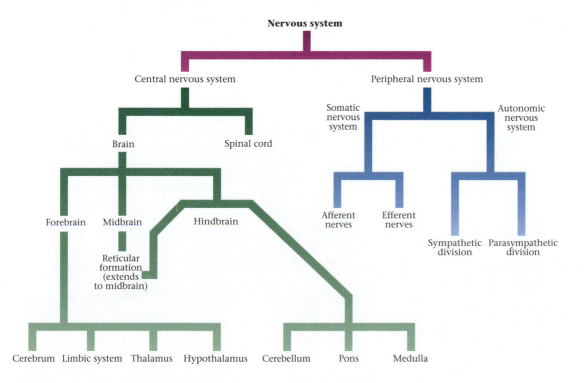

Figure 3.8
Organization of the human nervous system. The central nervous system is composed mostly of the brain, which is traditionally divided into three regions: the hindbrain, the midbrain, and the forebrain. All three areas control vital functions, but it's the highly developed forebrain that differentiates humans from lower animals. The reticular formation runs through both the midbrain and the hindbrain on its way up and down the brainstem. These and other parts of the brain are discussed in detail later in the chapter. The peripheral nervous system is made up of the somatic nervous system, which controls voluntary muscles and sensory receptors, and the autonomic nervous system, which controls smooth muscles, blood vessels, and glands.

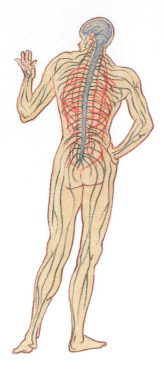

1990, Williams & Herrup, 1988). Obviously, this is only an *estimate*. If you counted them nonstop at the rate of one per second, you'd be counting for about 6000 years! The multitudes of neurons in your nervous system have to work together to keep information flowing effectively. To see how the nervous system is organized to accomplish this end, we will perform a series of "cuts" that will divide it into parts. In many instances, the parts will be cut once again. Figure 3.8 presents an organizational chart that shows the relationships of all the parts of the nervous system.

The Peripheral Nervous System 2a, 8c

The first and most important cut separates the *central nervous system* (the brain and spinal cord) from the *peripheral nervous system* (see Figure 3.9). **The *peripheral nervous system* is made up of all those nerves that lie outside the brain and spinal cord.** *Nerves* **are bundles of neuron fibers (axons) that are routed together in the peripheral nervous system.** This portion of the nervous system is just what it sounds like: the part that extends to the periphery (the outside) of the body. The peripheral nervous system can be subdivided into the *somatic nervous system* and the *autonomic nervous system*.

The Somatic Nervous System

The *somatic nervous system* is made up of nerves that connect to voluntary skeletal muscles and to sensory receptors. These nerves are the cables that carry information from receptors in the skin, muscles, and joints to the central nervous system and that carry commands from the CNS to the muscles. These functions require two kinds of nerve fibers. *Afferent nerve fibers* **are axons that carry information inward to the central nervous system from the periphery of the body.** *Efferent nerve fibers* **are axons that carry information outward from the central nervous system to the periphery of the body.** Each body nerve contains many axons of each type. Thus, somatic nerves are "two-way streets" with incoming (afferent) and outgoing (efferent) lanes. The somatic nervous system lets you feel the world and move around in it.

Figure 3.9
The central and peripheral nervous systems. The human nervous system is divided into the central nervous system, which consists of the brain and the spinal cord (shown in blue), and the peripheral nervous system, which consists of the remaining nerves that fan out throughout the body. The peripheral nervous system is divided into the somatic nervous system, which is shown in green, and the autonomic nervous system, which is shown in red.

Figure 3.10
The autonomic nervous system (ANS). The ANS is composed of the nerves that connect to the heart, blood vessels, smooth muscles, and glands. The ANS is divided into the sympathetic division, which mobilizes bodily resources in times of need, and the parasympathetic division, which conserves bodily resources. Some of the key functions controlled by each division of the ANS are summarized in the diagram.

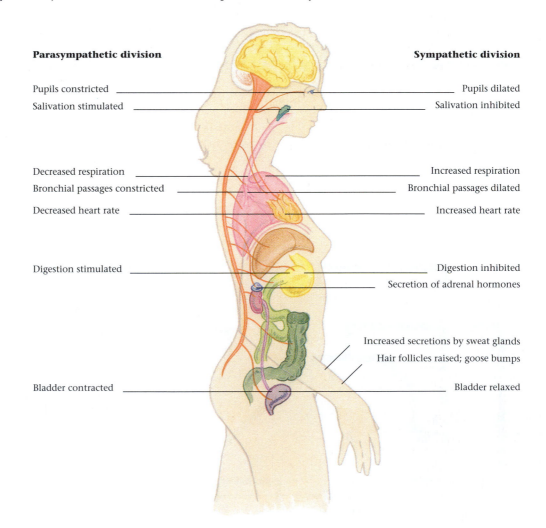

Parasympathetic division

Pupils constricted
Salivation stimulated
Decreased respiration
Bronchial passages constricted
Decreased heart rate
Digestion stimulated
Bladder contracted

Sympathetic division

Pupils dilated
Salivation inhibited
Increased respiration
Bronchial passages dilated
Increased heart rate
Digestion inhibited
Secretion of adrenal hormones
Increased secretions by sweat glands
Hair follicles raised; goose bumps
Bladder relaxed

The Autonomic Nervous System

The *autonomic nervous system (ANS)* is made up of nerves that connect to the heart, blood vessels, smooth muscles, and glands. As its name hints, the autonomic system is a separate (autonomous) system, although it is ultimately controlled by the central nervous system. The autonomic nervous system controls automatic, involuntary, visceral functions that people don't normally think about, such as heart rate, digestion, and perspiration.

The autonomic nervous system mediates much of the physiological arousal that occurs when people experience emotions. For example, imagine that you are walking home alone one night when a seedy-looking character falls in behind you and begins to follow you. If you feel threatened, your heart rate and breathing will speed up. Your blood pressure may surge, you may get goosebumps, and your palms may begin to sweat. These difficult-to-control reactions are aspects of autonomic arousal.

Walter Cannon (1932), one of the first psychologists to study this reaction, called it the *fight-or-flight response.* Cannon carefully monitored this response in cats—after confronting them with dogs. He concluded that organisms generally respond to threat by preparing physically for attacking (fight) or fleeing (flight) from the enemy. Unfortunately, as you will see in Chapter 13, this fight-or-flight response can backfire if stress leaves a person in a chronic state of autonomic arousal. Prolonged autonomic arousal can eventually contribute to the development of physical diseases (Selye, 1974).

The autonomic nervous system can be subdivided into two branches: the sympathetic division and the parasympathetic division (see Figure 3.10). **The *sympathetic division* is the branch of the autonomic nervous system that mobilizes the body's resources for emergencies.** It creates the fight-or-flight response. Activation of the sympathetic division slows digestive processes and drains blood from the periphery, lessening bleeding in the case of an injury. Key sympathetic nerves send signals to the adrenal glands, triggering the release of hormones that ready the body for exertion. In contrast, **the *parasympathetic division* is the branch of the autonomic nervous system that generally conserves bodily resources.** It activates processes that allow the body to save and store energy. For example, actions by parasympathetic nerves slow heart rate, reduce blood pressure, and promote digestion.

The Central Nervous System 2a

The central nervous system is the portion of the nervous system that lies within the skull and spinal column. Thus, **the *central nervous system (CNS)* consists of the brain and the spinal cord.** It is protected by enclosing sheaths called the *meninges* (hence *meningitis,* the name for the disease in which the meninges become inflamed).

In addition, the central nervous system is bathed in its own special nutritive "soup," the cerebrospinal fluid (see Figure 3.11). **The *cerebrospinal fluid* nourishes the brain and provides a protective cushion for it.** Although derived from the blood, the CSF is carefully filtered. To enter the CSF, substances in the blood have to cross **the *blood-brain barrier,* a semipermeable membrane-like mechanism that stops some chemicals from passing between the bloodstream and the brain.** This barrier prevents some drugs from entering the CSF and affecting the brain.

The Spinal Cord

The *spinal cord* connects the brain to the rest of the body through the peripheral nervous system. Although the spinal cord looks like a cable from which the somatic nerves branch, it is part of the central nervous system. Like the brain, it is enclosed

Figure 3.11
The ventricles of the brain. Cerebrospinal fluid (CSF) circulates around the brain and the spinal cord. The hollow cavities in the brain filled with CSF are called ventricles. The four ventricles in the human brain are depicted here.

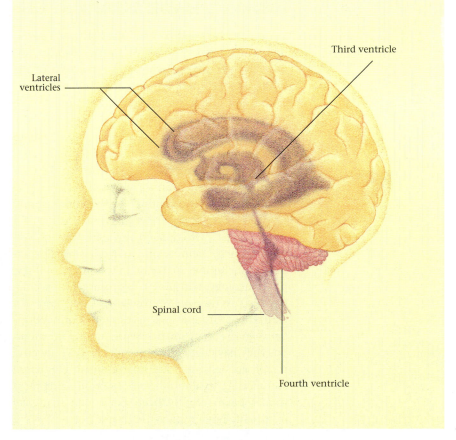

by the meninges and bathed in CSF. In short, the spinal cord is an extension of the brain.

The spinal cord runs from the base of the brain to just below the level of the waist. It houses bundles of axons that carry the brain's commands to peripheral nerves and that relay sensations from the periphery of the body to the brain. Many forms of paralysis result from spinal cord damage, a fact that underscores the critical role the spinal cord plays in transmitting signals from the brain to the motor neurons that move the body's muscles.

The Brain

The crowning glory of the central nervous system is, of course, the *brain*. Anatomically, the brain is the part of the central nervous system that fills the upper portion of the skull. Although it weighs only about three pounds and could be held in one hand, the brain contains billions of interacting cells that integrate information from inside and outside the body, coordinate the body's actions, and enable human beings to talk, think, remember, plan, create, and dream.

Because of its central importance for behavior, the brain is the subject of the next three sections of the chapter. We begin by looking at the remarkable methods that have enabled researchers to unlock some of the brain's secrets.

Recap of Key Points
• The nervous system can be divided into two main subdivisions, the central nervous system and the peripheral nervous system. The central nervous system consists of the brain and spinal cord.
• The peripheral nervous system consists of the nerves that lie outside the brain and spinal cord. It can be subdivided into the somatic nervous system, which connects to muscles and sensory receptors, and the autonomic nervous system, which connects to blood vessels, smooth muscles, and glands.
• The autonomic nervous system mediates the largely automatic arousal that accompanies emotion and the fight-or-flight response to stress. The ANS is divided into the sympathetic division, which mobilizes bodily resources, and the parasympathetic division, which conserves bodily resources.
• The spinal cord plays a critical role in distributing signals between the brain and the peripheral nervous system. The brain plays a crucial role in virtually all aspects of behavior.

LOOKING INSIDE THE BRAIN: RESEARCH METHODS

Scientists who want to find out how parts of the brain are related to behavior are faced with a formidable task. The geography, or *structure,* of the brain can be mapped out relatively easily by examining and dissecting brains removed from animals or from deceased humans who have donated their bodies to science. Mapping out brain *function,* however, requires a working brain. Thus, special research methods are needed to discover relations between brain activity and behavior.

Investigators who conduct research on the brain or other parts of the nervous system are called *neuroscientists.* Often, such research involves collaboration by neuroscientists from several disciplines, including anatomy, physiology, biology, pharmacology, neurology, neurosurgery, psychiatry, and psychology. Neuroscientists use many specialized techniques to investigate connections between the brain and behavior. Among the methods they have depended on most heavily are electrical recordings, lesioning, and electrical stimulation. In addition, new brain-imaging techniques have recently been developed that may eventually revolutionize brain research.

Electrical Recordings 2c

The electrical activity of the brain can be recorded, much as Hodgkin and Huxley recorded the electrical activity of individual neurons. Recordings of single cells in the brain have proven valuable, but scientists also need ways to record the simultaneous activity of many of the billions of neurons in the brain. Fortunately, in 1929 a German psychiatrist named Hans Berger invented a machine that could record broad patterns of brain electrical activity. **The *electroencephalograph (EEG)* is a device that monitors the electrical activity of the brain over time by means of recording electrodes attached to the surface of the scalp** (see Figure 3.12). An EEG electrode sums and amplifies electric potentials occurring in many thousands of brain cells.

Usually, six to ten recording electrodes are attached (with paste) at various places on the skull. The resulting EEG recordings are translated into line tracings, commonly called *brain waves*. These brain-wave recordings provide a useful overview of the electrical activity in the brain. Different brain-wave patterns are associated with different states of mental activity (Martin, 1991), as shown in Figure 3.12. The EEG is often used in the clinical diagnosis of brain damage and neurological disorders. In research applications, the EEG can be used to identify patterns of brain activity that occur when subjects engage in specific behaviors, ranging from daydreaming to working on math problems. One recent study even found a correlation between EEG patterns and personality (Jones & Fox, 1992). As you'll see in Chapter 5, the EEG has been invaluable to researchers exploring the physiology of sleep.

Lesioning 2c

Brain tumors, strokes, head injuries, and other misfortunes often produce brain damage in people. Many major insights about brain-behavior relations have resulted from observations of behavioral changes in people who have suffered damage in specific brain areas (H. Gardner, 1975). However, this type of research has its limitations. Subjects are not plentiful, and neuroscientists can't control the location or severity of their subjects' brain damage. Furthermore, variations in the subjects' histories create a host of extraneous variables that make it difficult to isolate cause-and-effect relationships between brain damage and behavior.

To study the relations between brain and behavior more precisely, scientists sometimes observe what happens when specific brain structures in animals are purposely disabled. *Lesioning* involves **destroying a piece of the brain.** This is typically done by inserting an electrode into a brain structure and passing a high-frequency electric current through it to burn the tissue and disable the structure.

Lesioning requires researchers to get an electrode to a particular place buried deep inside the brain. They do so with a *stereotaxic instrument,* **a device used to implant electrodes at precise locations in the brain.** The use of this surgical device is described in Figure 3.13. Of course, appropriate anesthetics are used to minimize pain and discomfort for the animals. The lesioning of brain structures in animals has proven invaluable in neuroscientists' research on brain functioning.

Electrical Stimulation of the Brain 2c

Electrical stimulation of the brain (ESB) **involves sending a weak electric current into a brain structure to stimulate (activate) it.** The current is delivered through an electrode, but the current is different from that used in lesioning. This sort of

Figure 3.12
The electroencephalograph (EEG). Recording electrodes attached to the surface of the scalp permit the EEG to record the brain's electrical activity over time. The EEG provides output in the form of line tracings called brain waves. Brain waves vary in frequency (cycles per second) and amplitude (measured in voltage). Various states of consciousness are associated with different brain waves. Characteristic EEG patterns for alert wakefulness, drowsiness, and deep, dreamless sleep are shown here. The use of the EEG in research is discussed in more detail in Chapter 5.

Awake
Low-voltage, high-frequency brain waves

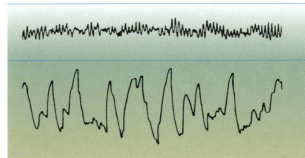

Drowsy
Higher-voltage, slower-frequency brain waves

Deep, dreamless sleep
High-voltage, low-frequency brain waves

electrical stimulation does not exactly duplicate normal electrical signals in the brain. However, it is usually a close enough approximation to activate the brain structures in which the electrodes are lodged. If areas deep within the brain are to be stimulated, the electrodes are implanted with the same stereotaxic techniques used in lesioning procedures.

Most ESB research is conducted with animals. However, ESB is occasionally used on humans in the context of brain surgery required for medical

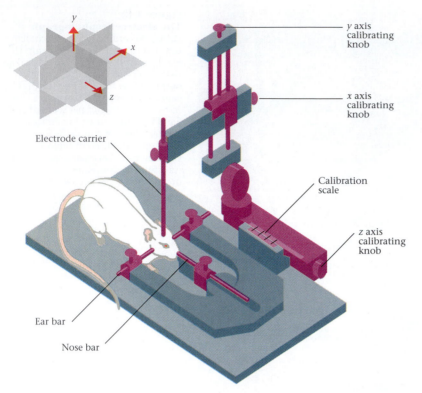

**y axis
calibrating
knob**

**x axis
calibrating
knob**

Electrode carrier

**Calibration
scale**

**z axis
calibrating
knob**

Ear bar

Nose bar

**Figure 3.13
An anesthetized rat in a
stereotaxic instrument.**
This rat is undergoing brain
surgery. After consulting a
detailed map of the rat brain,
researchers use the control
knobs on the apparatus to
position an electrode along
the three axes (*x*, *y*, and *z*)
shown in the upper left corner. This precise positioning
allows researchers to implant
the electrode in an exact location in the rat's brain.

purposes. After a patient's skull is opened, the surgeons may stimulate areas to map the individual patient's brain (to some extent, each of us is unique), so that they don't slice through critical areas. The patient is awake and describes the feelings produced by each stimulation. As various areas are stimulated, the patient reports visual sensations, muscular twitches, memories, and so forth.

What is the patient doing awake in the midst of major surgery? This procedure is not unusual. Neurosurgeons often prefer their patients to be awake to provide feedback, which can have enormous diagnostic value. Hence, they use only a local anesthetic to prevent pain as they open the patient's skull. The electrical stimulations of the brain are not painful, because brain tissue has no pain receptors.

Brain-Imaging Procedures **2c**

In recent years, the invention of new brain-imaging devices has led to spectacular advances in science's ability to look into the brain. Unfortunately, the use of most of these devices is prohibitively expensive, so their availability for research purposes is limited. Even medical use of these devices is judicious. However, this new technology is gradually opening new horizons in brain research.

The *CT (computerized tomography) scan* is a computer-enhanced X ray of brain structure. Multiple X rays are shot from many angles, and the com-

puter combines the readings to create a vivid image of a horizontal slice of the brain (see Figure 3.14). The entire brain can be visualized by assembling a series of images representing successive slices of the brain. Of the new brain-imaging techniques, the CT scan is the least expensive and thus the most widely used in research. For example, many researchers have used CT scans to look for abnormalities in brain structure among people suffering from specific types of mental illness (Andreasen, 1988).

In research on how brain and behavior are related, *PET (positron emission tomography) scans* may prove especially valuable. CT scans can portray only brain *structure*. PET scans can map actual *activity* in the brain over time. In PET scans, radioactively tagged chemicals are introduced into the brain. They serve as markers of blood flow or metabolic activity in the brain, which can be monitored with X rays. Thus, a PET scan can provide a color-coded map indicating which areas of the brain become active when subjects clench their fist, sing, or contemplate the mysteries of the universe (see Figure 3.15). In this way, neuroscientists are using PET scans to better pinpoint the brain areas that handle various types of mental activities (Raichle, 1994). PET scans are also being used to investigate which areas of the brain become active when people experience specific emotions, such as happiness or sadness (George et al., 1995). Because PET scans monitor chemical processes, they can also be used to study the activity of specific neurotransmitters (Martin, Brust, & Hilal, 1991). For example, PET scans have helped researchers map the locations of dopamine synapses in the human brain.

Research with PET scans has given neuroscientists a new appreciation of the complexity and interdependence of brain organization. The opportunity to look at ongoing brain function has revealed that even simple, routine mental operations depend on coordinated activation of several or more areas in the brain (Posner & Raichle, 1994).

The more recently developed *MRI (magnetic resonance imaging) scan* uses magnetic fields, radio waves, and computerized enhancement to map out brain structure and brain function (Martin et al., 1991). MRI scans provide much better images of brain structure than CT scans, producing three-dimensional pictures of the brain that have remarkably high resolution (see Figure 3.16). Unfortunately, this technology is very new and very expensive (the initial cost of an MRI scanner

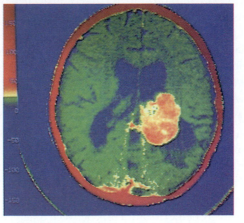

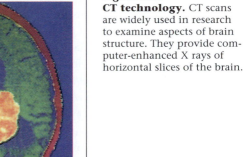

Figure 3.14
CT technology. CT scans are widely used in research to examine aspects of brain structure. They provide computer-enhanced X rays of horizontal slices of the brain.

(**a**) The patient's head is positioned in a large cylinder, as shown here.

(**c**) A computer combines X rays to create an image of a horizontal slice of the brain. This scan shows a tumor (in red) on the right.

(**b**) An X-ray beam and X-ray detector rotate around the patient's head, taking multiple X rays of a horizontal slice of the patient's brain.

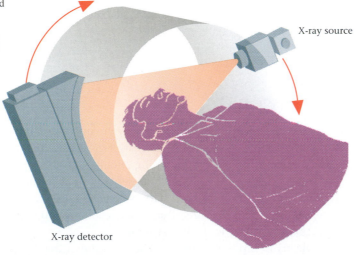

X-ray source

X-ray detector

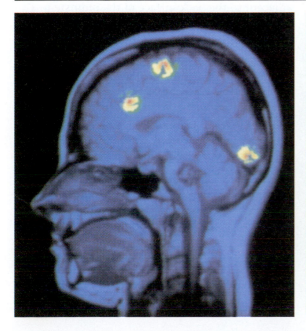

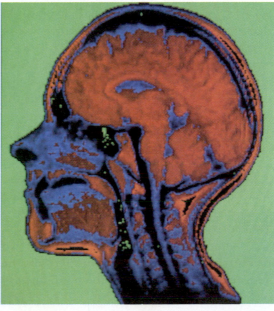

Figure 3.15 (left)
PET scans. PET scans are used to map brain activity rather than brain structure. They provide color-coded maps that show areas of high activity in the brain over time. The PET scan shown here pinpointed three areas of high activity (indicated by the color yellow) when a subject worked on a language task.

Figure 3.16 (right)
MRI scans. MRI scans can be used to produce remarkably high-resolution pictures of brain structure. A vertical view of the left side of a woman's brain is shown here.

is $1–$3 million), so relatively little behavioral research has been done.

However, MRI technology has enormous potential in behavioral research. For example, one study (Suddath et al., 1990) provided compelling new evidence that there may be an association between enlarged ventricles (the hollow, fluid-filled cavities) in the brain and schizophrenic disturbance. Previous studies relying on CT scans had found enlarged ventricles in about 20%–25% of the schizophrenic persons tested (Weinberger, Wagner, & Wyatt, 1983). Critics argued that these findings were too weak and inconsistent to conclusively demonstrate a link between enlarged ventricles and schizophrenia. However, working with far more precise images from MRI scans, Suddath and associates found a much higher prevalence of enlarged ventricles in their sample of schizophrenic patients. Their study highlights the exciting promise of the new brain-imaging technologies. Science depends on observation. Improvements in researchers' ability to observe the brain should result in increased knowledge of how the brain is related to behavior.

Recap of Key Points
• Neuroscientists use a variety of methods to investigate brain-behavior relations. The EEG can record broad patterns of electrical activity in the brain. Different EEG brain waves are associated with different states of consciousness.
• Lesioning involves destroying a piece of the brain. Another technique is electrical stimulation of areas in the brain in order to activate them. Both techniques depend on the use of stereotaxic instruments that permit researchers to implant electrodes at precise locations in animals' brains.
• In recent years, new brain-imaging procedures have been developed, including CT scans, PET scans, and MRI scans. These new techniques have enormous potential for exploring brain-behavior relations.

THE BRAIN AND BEHAVIOR

Now that we have examined the techniques of brain research, let's look at what researchers have discovered about the functions of different parts of the brain.

The brain can be divided into three major regions: the hindbrain, the midbrain, and the forebrain. The principal structures found in each of these regions are listed in the organizational chart of the nervous system in Figure 3.8. You can see where these regions are located in the brain by looking at Figure 3.17. They can be found easily in relation to the *brainstem*. The brainstem looks like its name—it appears to be a stem from which the rest of the brain "flowers," like a head of cauliflower. At its lower end it is contiguous with the spinal cord. At its higher end it lies deep within the brain.

We'll begin at the brain's lower end, where the spinal cord joins the brainstem. As we proceed upward, notice how the functions of brain structures go from the regulation of basic bodily processes to the control of "higher" mental processes.

The Hindbrain

The *hindbrain* includes the cerebellum and two structures found in the lower part of the brainstem: the medulla and the pons. The *medulla*, which attaches to the spinal cord, has charge of largely unconscious but essential functions, such as breathing, maintaining muscle tone, and regulating circulation. The *pons* (literally "bridge") includes a bridge of fibers that connects the brainstem with the cerebellum. The pons also contains several clusters of cell bodies involved with sleep and arousal.

The *cerebellum* (literally "little brain") is a relatively large and deeply folded structure located adjacent to the back surface of the brainstem. The cerebellum is critical to the coordination of movement and to the sense of equilibrium, or physical balance (Ghez, 1991). Although the actual commands for muscular movements come from higher brain centers, the cerebellum plays a key role in the execution of these commands. It is your cerebellum that allows you to hold your hand out to the side and then smoothly bring your finger to a stop on your nose. This is a useful roadside test for drunken driving because the cerebellum is one of the structures first depressed by alcohol. Damage to the cerebellum disrupts fine motor skills, such as those involved in writing, typing, or playing tennis.

The Midbrain

The *midbrain* is the segment of the brainstem that lies between the hindbrain and the

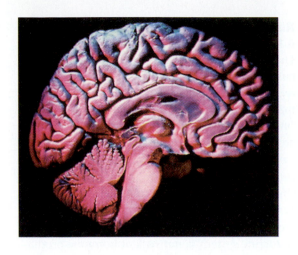

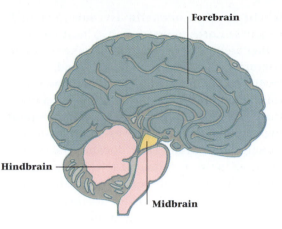

Forebrain

Hindbrain

Midbrain

Figure 3.17
Structures and areas in the human brain. (Top left) This photo of a human brain shows many of the structures discussed in this chapter. (Top right) The brain is divided into three major areas: the hindbrain, midbrain, and forebrain. These subdivisions actually make more sense for the brains of other animals than of humans. In humans, the forebrain has become so large it makes the other two divisions look trivial. However, the hindbrain and midbrain aren't trivial; they control such vital functions as breathing, waking, remembering, and maintaining balance. (Bottom) This cross section of the brain highlights key structures and some of their principal functions. As you read about the functions of a brain structure, such as the corpus callosum, you may find it helpful to visualize it.

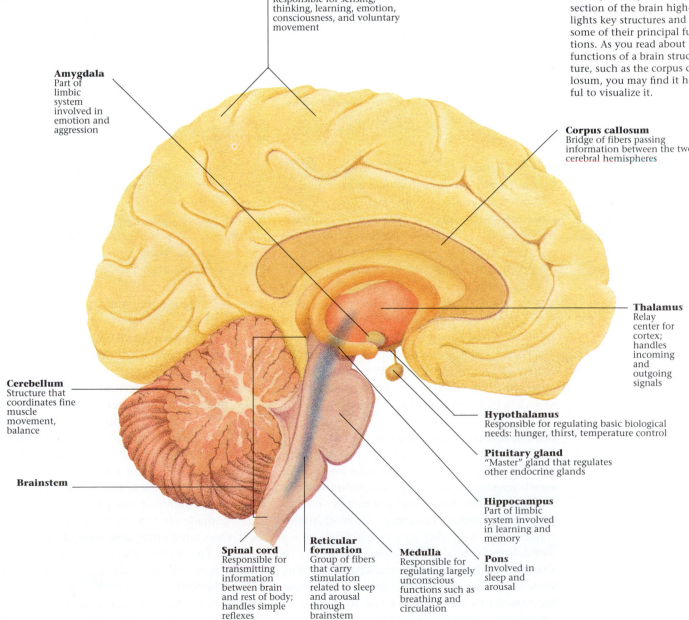

Cerebrum
Responsible for sensing, thinking, learning, emotion, consciousness, and voluntary movement

Amygdala
Part of limbic system involved in emotion and aggression

Corpus callosum
Bridge of fibers passing information between the two cerebral hemispheres

Thalamus
Relay center for cortex; handles incoming and outgoing signals

Cerebellum
Structure that coordinates fine muscle movement, balance

Hypothalamus
Responsible for regulating basic biological needs: hunger, thirst, temperature control

Pituitary gland
"Master" gland that regulates other endocrine glands

Brainstem

Hippocampus
Part of limbic system involved in learning and memory

Spinal cord
Responsible for transmitting information between brain and rest of body; handles simple reflexes

Reticular formation
Group of fibers that carry stimulation related to sleep and arousal through brainstem

Medulla
Responsible for regulating largely unconscious functions such as breathing and circulation

Pons
Involved in sleep and arousal

forebrain. The midbrain is concerned with certain sensory processes, such as locating where things are in space. For instance, when a sound triggers a reflexive turning of the head, an area in the midbrain is at work (Middlebrooks & Knudsen, 1984). An important system of dopamine-releasing neurons that projects into various higher brain centers originates in the midbrain. Among other things, this dopamine system is involved in the performance of voluntary movements. The decline in dopamine synthesis that causes Parkinsonism is due to degeneration of a structure located in the midbrain (Coté & Crutcher, 1991).

Running through both the hindbrain and the midbrain is the *reticular formation.* Lying at the central core of the brainstem, the reticular formation contributes to the modulation of muscle reflexes, breathing, and pain perception (Role & Kelly, 1991). It is best known, however, for its role in the regulation of sleep and wakefulness. Activity in the ascending fibers of the reticular formation is essential to maintaining an alert brain (Steriade et al., 1980). Indeed, damage to this area can cause a coma.

The Forebrain 2e, 2f

The *forebrain* **is the largest and most complex region of the brain, encompassing a variety of structures, including the thalamus, hypothalamus, limbic system, and cerebrum.** This list is not exhaustive, and some of these structures have their own subdivisions, as you can see in the organizational chart of the nervous system (Figure 3.8). The thalamus, hypothalamus, and limbic system form the core of the forebrain. All three structures are located near the top of the brainstem. Above them is the *cerebrum*—the seat of complex thought. The wrinkled surface of the cerebrum is the *cerebral cortex*—the outer layer of the brain, the part that looks like a cauliflower.

The Thalamus: A Way Station
The *thalamus* **is a structure in the forebrain through which all sensory information (except smell) must pass to get to the cerebral cortex.** This way station is made up of a number of clusters of cell bodies, or somas. Each cluster is concerned with relaying sensory information to a particular part of the cortex. However, it would be a mistake to characterize the thalamus as nothing more than a passive relay station. The thalamus also appears to play an active role in integrating information from various senses.

The Hypothalamus: A Regulator of Biological Needs
The *hypothalamus* **is a structure found near the base of the forebrain that is involved in the regulation of basic biological needs.** The hypothalamus lies beneath the thalamus (*hypo* means "under," making the hypothalamus the area under the thalamus). Although no larger than a kidney bean, the hypothalamus contains various clusters of cells that have many key functions. One such function is to control the autonomic nervous system. In addition, the hypothalamus serves as a vital link between the brain and the endocrine system (a network of hormone-producing glands, discussed later in this chapter).

The hypothalamus plays a major role in the regulation of basic biological drives related to survival, including the so-called "four F's": fighting, fleeing, feeding, and mating. For example, when researchers lesion the lateral areas (the sides) of the hypothalamus, animals lose interest in eating. The animals must be fed intravenously or they starve, even in the presence of abundant food. In contrast, when electrical stimulation (ESB) is used to *activate* the lateral hypothalamus, animals eat constantly and gain weight rapidly (Grossman et al., 1978; Keesey & Powley, 1975). Does this mean that the lateral hypothalamus is the "hunger center" in the brain? Not necessarily. The regulation of hunger turns out to be complex and multifaceted, as you'll see in Chapter 10. Nonetheless, the hypothalamus clearly contributes to the control of hunger and other basic biological processes, including thirst, sex drive, and temperature regulation (Kupfermann, 1991).

The Limbic System: The Seat of Emotion
The *limbic system* **is a loosely connected network of structures located roughly along the border between the cerebral cortex and deeper subcortical areas** (hence the term *limbic,* which means "edge"). First described by Paul MacLean (1954), the limbic system is *not* a well-defined anatomical system with clear boundaries. Indeed, scientists disagree about which structures should be included in the limbic system. Broadly defined, the limbic system includes parts of the thalamus and hypothalamus, the *hippocampus,* the *amygdala,* the *septum,* and other structures shown in Figure 3.18. The limbic system is involved in the regulation of emotion, memory, and motivation.

The hippocampus appears to play a role in the formation of memories (Zola-Morgan & Squire, 1990). Consistent with this notion is the fact that

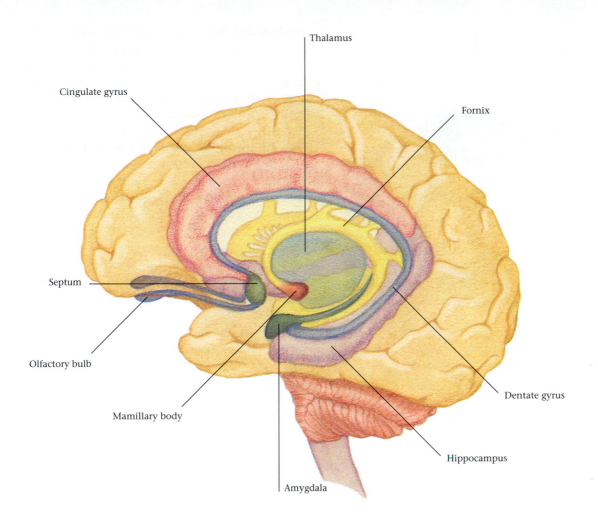

Thalamus

Cingulate gyrus

Fornix

Septum

Olfactory bulb

Mamillary body

Dentate gyrus

Hippocampus

Amygdala

Figure 3.18
The limbic system. The limbic system is a network of interconnected structures that play a role in emotion, motivation, memory, and many other aspects of behavior. These structures fall mostly along the border between the cortex and deeper, subcortical structures.

it is significantly damaged in patients suffering from Alzheimer's disease (Albert, 1992). However, many other brain structures contribute to memory processes, and the exact role of the hippocampus is not yet fully understood.

Similarly, there is ample evidence linking the limbic system to the experience of emotion, but the exact mechanisms of control are not yet well understood (Pribram, 1981). Recent evidence suggests that the amygdala may play a central role in the learning of fear responses (Phillips & LeDoux, 1992). The limbic system is also one of the areas in the brain that appears to be rich in emotion-tinged "pleasure centers." This intriguing possibility first surfaced, quite by chance, in brain stimulation research with rats. James Olds and Peter Milner (1954) accidentally discovered that a rat would press a lever repeatedly to send brief bursts of electrical stimulation to a specific spot in its brain where an electrode was implanted (see Figure 3.19 on page 96). They thought that they had inserted the electrode in the rat's reticular formation. However, they learned later that the electrode had been bent during implantation and

ended up elsewhere (probably in the hypothalamus). Much to their surprise, the rat kept coming back for more self-stimulation in this area. Subsequent studies showed that rats and monkeys would press a lever *thousands of times per hour,* until they sometimes collapsed from exhaustion, to stimulate certain brain sites. Although the experimenters obviously couldn't ask the animals about it, they *inferred* that the animals were experiencing some sort of pleasure.

Brain surgery cases have afforded neuroscientists a few opportunities to probe for similar pleasure centers in human subjects. Since they're often conscious during brain surgery, human subjects can be asked about their feelings, and electrically activated pleasure centers have indeed been found in humans (Delgado, 1969; Heath, 1964). However, the emotional reactions in humans have not been as strong as anticipated, given the ferocious way laboratory animals work to earn stimulation of pleasure centers (Valenstein, 1973).

Where are the self-stimulation centers located in the brain? Many self-stimulation sites have been found in the limbic system (Olds & Fobes, 1981).

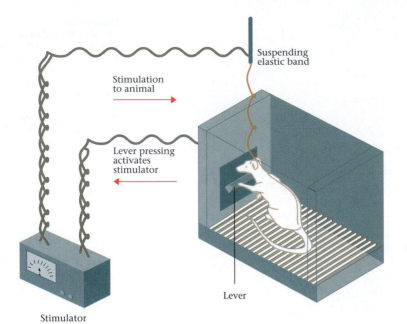

Suspending
elastic band

Stimulation
to animal

Lever pressing
activates
stimulator

Lever

Stimulator

**Figure 3.19
Electrical stimulation of the brain (ESB) in the rat.** Olds and Milner (1954) were using an apparatus like that depicted here when they discovered self-stimulation centers, or "pleasure centers," in the brain of a rat. In this setup, the rat's lever pressing earns brief electrical stimulation that is sent to a specific spot in the rat's brain where an electrode has been implanted.

The heaviest concentration appears to be where the *medial forebrain bundle* (a bundle of axons) passes through the hypothalamus. The medial forebrain bundle is rich in dopamine-releasing neurons. The rewarding effects of ESB at self-stimulation sites may be largely mediated by the activation of these dopamine circuits (Wise & Rompre, 1989). The rewarding, pleasurable effects of opiate and stimulant drugs (cocaine and amphetamines) may also depend on excitation of this dopamine system (Wise, 1995; Wise & Bozarth, 1987). Theorists

caution that this dopamine system is *not* the ultimate biological basis for *all* reward (the brain is never that simple). Nonetheless, recent evidence suggests that the brain's "pleasure centers" may not be anatomical centers so much as neural circuits releasing dopamine.

The Cerebrum: The Seat of Complex Thought

The *cerebrum* is the largest and most complex part of the human brain. It includes the brain areas that are responsible for the most complex mental activities, including learning, remembering, thinking, and consciousness itself. **The *cerebral cortex* is the convoluted outer layer of the cerebrum.** The cortex is folded and bent, so that its large surface area—about 1.5 square feet—can be packed into the limited volume of the skull (Hubel & Wiesel, 1979).

The cerebrum is divided into two halves called hemispheres. Hence, **the *cerebral hemispheres* are the right and left halves of the cerebrum** (see Figure 3.20). The hemispheres are separated in the center of the brain by a longitudinal fissure that runs from the front to the back of the brain. This fissure descends to a thick band of fibers called the *corpus callosum* (also shown in Figure 3.20). **The *corpus callosum* is the structure that connects the two cerebral hemispheres.** We'll discuss the functional specialization of the cerebral hemispheres in the next section of this chapter.

**Figure 3.20
The cerebral hemispheres and the corpus callosum.** (Left) As this photo shows, the longitudinal fissure running down the middle of the brain (viewed from above) separates the left and right halves of the cerebral cortex. (Right) In this drawing the cerebral hemispheres have been "pulled apart" to reveal the corpus callosum. This band of fibers is the communication bridge between the right and left halves of the human brain.

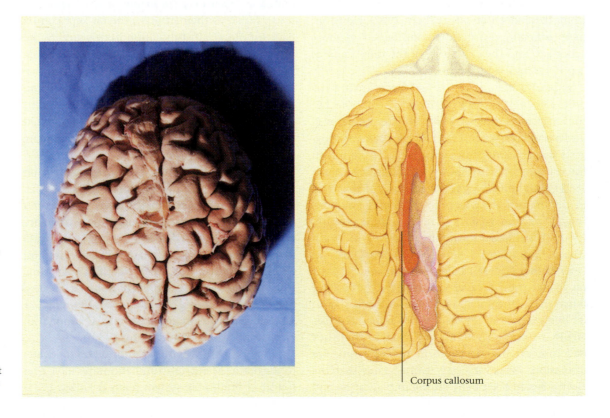

Corpus callosum

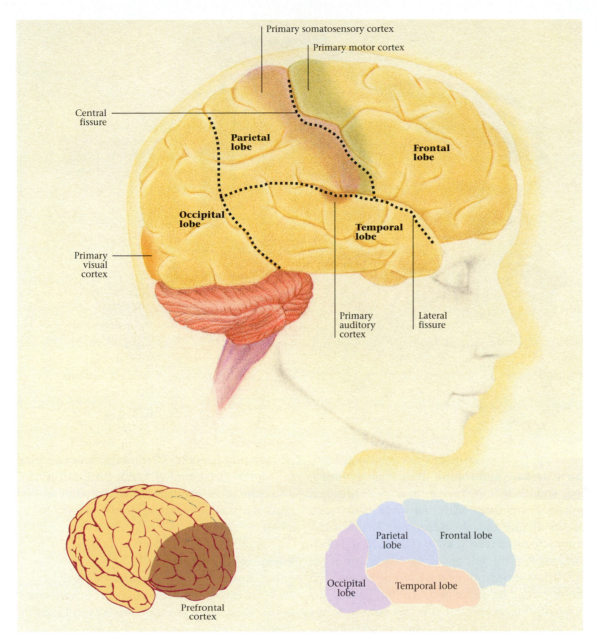

Primary somatosensory cortex

Primary motor cortex

Central fissure

Parietal lobe

Frontal lobe

Occipital lobe

Temporal lobe

Primary visual cortex

Primary auditory cortex

Lateral fissure

Prefrontal cortex

Parietal lobe

Frontal lobe

Occipital lobe

Temporal lobe

Figure 3.21
The cerebral cortex in humans. The cerebrum is divided into right and left halves, called cerebral hemispheres. This diagram provides a view of the right hemisphere. The cerebral cortex is the outer layer of the cerebrum. Each cerebral hemisphere can be divided into four lobes (which are highlighted in the bottom left inset): the occipital lobe, the parietal lobe, the temporal lobe, and the frontal lobe. Each lobe has areas that handle particular functions, such as visual processing or speech comprehension. The functions of the prefrontal cortex (highlighted in the bottom right inset), are something of a mystery, but may include representational memory.

Each cerebral hemisphere is divided into four parts called *lobes*. To some extent, each of these lobes is dedicated to specific purposes. The location of these lobes can be seen in Figure 3.21.

The *occipital lobe,* at the back of the head, includes the cortical area, where most visual signals are sent and visual processing is begun. This area is called the *primary visual cortex.* We will discuss how it is organized in Chapter 4.

The *parietal lobe* is forward of the occipital lobe. It includes the area that registers the sense of touch, called the *primary somatosensory cortex.* Various sections of this area receive signals from different regions of the body. When ESB is delivered in these parietal lobe areas, people report physical sensations—as if someone actually touched them on the arm or cheek, for example. The parietal lobe is also involved in integrating visual input and in monitoring the body's position in space.

The *temporal lobe* (meaning "near the temples") lies below the parietal lobe. Near its top, the temporal lobe contains an area devoted to auditory processing, called the *primary auditory cortex.* As we will see momentarily, damage to an area in the temporal lobe on the left side of the brain can impair the comprehension of speech and language.

Continuing forward, we find the *frontal lobe,* the largest lobe in the human brain. It contains the principal areas that control the movement of muscles, called the *primary motor cortex.* ESB applied in these areas can cause actual muscle contractions. The amount of motor cortex allocated to the control of a body part depends not on the part's size but on the diversity and precision of its

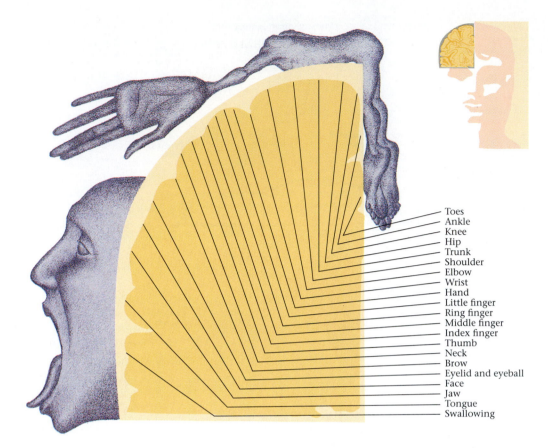

Figure 3.22
The primary motor cortex. If we were to remove the frontal lobe from the right hemisphere of the human brain and slice off the back portion of this section, we would cut out the right half of the primary motor cortex, the area in the brain that controls the movement of muscles. This diagram shows the amount of motor cortex devoted to the control of various muscles and limbs. The anatomical features in the drawing are distorted because their size is proportional to the amount of cortex devoted to their control. As you can see, more of the cortex is allocated to muscle groups that must make relatively precise movements.

Toes
Ankle
Knee
Hip
Trunk
Shoulder
Elbow
Wrist
Hand
Little finger
Ring finger
Middle finger
Index finger
Thumb
Neck
Brow
Eyelid and eyeball
Face
Jaw
Tongue
Swallowing

movements. Thus, more of the cortex is given to parts we have fine control over, such as fingers, lips, and the tongue. Less of the cortex is devoted to larger parts that make crude movements, such as the thighs and shoulders (see Figure 3.22). Interestingly, a recent study (Elbert et al., 1995) suggests that the amount of the motor cortex devoted to a specific appendage can be modified to some extent by experience. In this study, the amount of cortex allocated to the control of the fingers of the left hand was found to be "substantially enlarged" in a sample of violinists and other string players, whose musical work depends heavily on those fingers.

The large portion of the frontal lobe to the front of the motor cortex is something of a mystery. This area, which is called the *prefrontal cortex* (see Figure 3.21), was once assumed to house the highest, most abstract intellectual functions, but this view turned out to be an oversimplification. Recent studies suggest that the prefrontal cortex is crucial for responses that depend on briefly maintaining a mental representation of the world. For example, when monkeys are confronted with an experimental task in which they must hold a mental representation of where they saw a green light for 10 seconds in order to obtain food, they do just fine if their prefrontal cortex is intact. But their

performance crumbles after their prefrontal cortex is lesioned (Diamond & Goldman-Rakic, 1989). Thus, the prefrontal cortex may handle some aspects of representational memory (Goldman-Rakic, 1995).

Recap of Key Points
• The brain has three major regions: the hindbrain, midbrain, and forebrain. Structures in the hindbrain include the medulla, pons, and cerebellum. These structures handle essential functions such as breathing, circulation, coordination of movement, and the rhythm of sleep and arousal.
• The midbrain contributes to the coordination of sensory processes. Deterioration of an area in the midbrain has been implicated as a factor in Parkinson's disease.
• The forebrain includes many structures that handle higher functions. The thalamus is primarily a relay station. The hypothalamus is involved in the regulation of basic biological drives such as hunger and sex.
• The limbic system is a network of loosely connected structures located along the border between cortex and deeper subcortical areas. It includes the hippocampus, which appears to play a role in memory, the amygdala, which is involved in the regulation of emotion, and areas rich in self-stimulation sites.

• The cerebrum is the brain area implicated in most complex mental activities. The cortex is the cerebrum's convoluted outer layer, which is subdivided into four lobes.

• These lobes and their primary known functions are the occipital lobe (vision), the parietal lobe (touch), the temporal lobe (hearing), and the frontal lobe (movement of the body). Recent research suggests that the prefrontal cortex may contribute to representational memory.

RIGHT BRAIN/LEFT BRAIN: CEREBRAL LATERALITY

As we noted a moment ago, the cerebrum—the seat of complex thought—is divided into two separate hemispheres (see Figure 3.20). In recent decades, an exciting flurry of research has focused on *cerebral laterality*—**the degree to which the left or right hemisphere controls various cognitive and behavioral functions.** Research on laterality has revealed that the two hemispheres have very different abilities. Indeed, some theorists have gone so far as to suggest that we really have two brains in one!

Hints of this hemispheric specialization have been available for many years, from cases in which one side of a person's brain has been damaged. The left hemisphere was implicated in the control of language as early as 1861, by Paul Broca, a French surgeon. Broca was treating a patient who had been unable to speak for 30 years. After the patient died, Broca showed that the probable cause of his speech deficit was a localized lesion on the left side of the frontal lobe. Since then, many similar cases have shown that this area of the brain—known as *Broca's area*—plays an important role in the *production* of speech (see Figure 3.23). Another major language center—*Wernicke's area*—was identified in the temporal lobe of the left hemisphere in 1874. Damage in Wernicke's area (see Figure 3.23) usually leads to problems with the *comprehension* of language.

Evidence that the left hemisphere usually processes language led scientists to characterize it as the "dominant" hemisphere. Because thoughts are usually coded in terms of language, the left hemisphere was given the lion's share of credit for handling the "higher" mental processes, such as reasoning, remembering, planning, and problem solving. Meanwhile, the right hemisphere came to be viewed as the "nondominant," or "dumb" hemisphere, lacking any special functions or abilities.

This characterization of the left and right

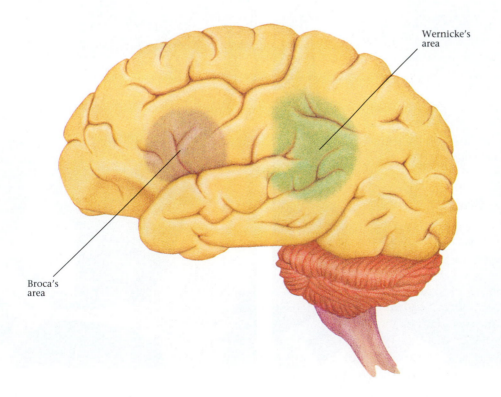

Wernicke's area

Broca's area

Figure 3.23
Language processing in the brain. This view of the left hemisphere highlights the location of two centers for language processing in the brain: Broca's area, which is involved in speech production, and Wernicke's area, which is involved in language comprehension.

Imagine that you are working as a neuropsychologist at a clinic. You are involved in the diagnosis of the cases described below. You are asked to identify the probable cause(s) of the disorders in terms of nervous system malfunctions. Based on the information in this chapter, indicate the probable location of any brain damage or the probable disturbance of neurotransmitter activity. The answers can be found in the back of the book in Appendix A.

Case 1. Miriam is exhibiting language deficits. In particular, she does not seem to comprehend the meaning of words.

Case 2. Camille displays spastic motor coordination and is diagnosed as having Parkinsonism.

Case 3. Neal, a 72-year-old retired dockworker, has gradually seen his everyday memory deteriorate badly. Sometimes he can't even find his way home from the grocery store a few blocks away. He is diagnosed as having Alzheimer's disease.

Case 4. Wendy is highly irrational, has poor contact with reality, and reports hallucinations. She is given a diagnosis of schizophrenic disorder.

hemispheres as major and minor partners in the brain's work began to change in the 1960s. It all started with landmark research by Roger Sperry, Michael Gazzaniga, and their colleagues who studied "split-brain" patients: individuals whose cerebral hemispheres had been surgically disconnected (Gazzaniga, 1970; Gazzaniga, Bogen, & Sperry, 1965; Levy, Trevarthen, & Sperry, 1972; Sperry, 1982). In 1981 Sperry received a Nobel prize in physiology/medicine for this work.

Architect Helmut Jahn and novelist Amy Tan exemplify the differing creative thinking popularly associated with the left brain and the right brain. Did the talents of each really arise from a different brain hemisphere? For more on this issue, see the Application on page 116.

Bisecting the Brain: Split-Brain Research

In *split-brain surgery* the bundle of fibers that connects the cerebral hemispheres (the corpus callosum) is cut to reduce the severity of epileptic seizures. It is a radical procedure that is chosen only in exceptional cases that have not responded to other forms of treatment. But the surgery provides scientists with an unusual opportunity to study people who have had their brain literally split in two.

To appreciate the logic of split-brain research, you need to understand how sensory and motor information is routed to and from the two hemispheres. *Each hemisphere's primary connections are to the opposite side of the body.* Thus, the left hemisphere controls, and communicates with, the right hand, right arm, right leg, right eyebrow, and so on. In contrast, the right hemisphere controls, and communicates with, the left side of the body.

Vision and hearing are more complex. Both eyes deliver information to both hemispheres, but there still is a separation of input. Stimuli in the right half of the *visual field* are registered by receptors on the left side of each eye, which send signals to the left hemisphere. Stimuli in the left half of the visual field are transmitted by both eyes to the right hemisphere (see Figure 3.24). Auditory inputs to each ear also go to both hemispheres. However, connections to the opposite hemisphere are stronger or more immediate. That is, sounds presented to the right ear are registered in the left hemisphere first, while sounds presented to the left ear are registered more quickly in the right hemisphere.

For the most part, people don't notice this asymmetric, "crisscrossed" organization because the two hemispheres are in close communication with each other. Information received by one hemisphere is readily shared with the other via the corpus callosum. However, when the two hemispheres are

"Both the left and right hemispheres of the brain have been found to have their own specialized forms of intellect."

ROGER SPERRY

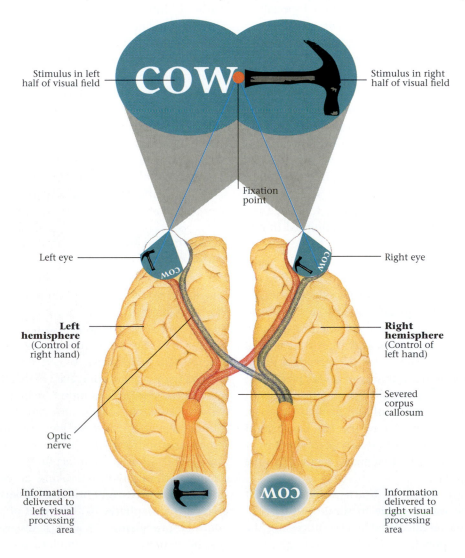

Figure 3.24
Visual input in the split brain. If a subject stares at a fixation point, the point divides the subject's visual field into right and left halves. Input from the right visual field strikes the left side of each eye and is transmitted to the left hemisphere. Input from the left visual field strikes the right side of each eye and is transmitted to the right hemisphere. Normally, the hemispheres share the information from the two halves of the visual field, but in split-brain patients, the corpus callosum is severed, and the two hemispheres cannot communicate. Hence, the experimenter can present a visual stimulus to just one hemisphere at a time.

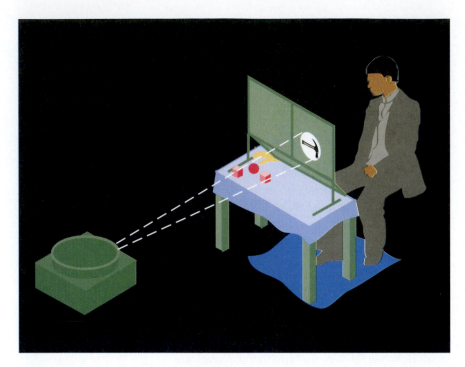

Figure 3.25
Experimental apparatus in split-brain research.
On the left is a special slide projector that can present images very briefly, before the subject's eyes can move and thus change the visual field. Images are projected on one side of the screen to present stimuli to just one hemisphere. The portion of the apparatus beneath the screen is constructed to prevent subjects from seeing objects that they may be asked to handle with their right or left hand, another procedure that can be used to send information to just one hemisphere.

surgically disconnected, the functional specialization of the brain becomes apparent.

In their classic study of split-brain patients, Gazzaniga, Bogen, and Sperry (1965) presented visual stimuli such as pictures, symbols, and words in a single visual field (the left or the right), so that the stimuli would be sent to only one hemisphere. The stimuli were projected onto a screen in front of the subjects, who stared at a fixation point (a spot) in the center of the screen (see Figure 3.25). The images were flashed to the right or the left of the fixation point for only a split second. Thus, the subjects did not have a chance to move their eyes, and the stimuli were only glimpsed in one visual field.

When pictures were flashed in the right visual field and thus sent to the left hemisphere, the split-brain subjects were able to name and describe the objects depicted (such as a cup or spoon). However, the subjects were *not* able to name and describe the same objects when they were flashed in the left visual field and sent to the right hemisphere. In a similar fashion, an object placed out of view in the right hand (communicating with the left hemisphere) could be named. However, the same object placed in the left hand (right hemisphere) could not be. These findings supported the notion that language is housed in the left hemisphere.

Although the split-brain subjects' right hemisphere was not able to speak up for itself, further tests revealed that it *was* processing the information presented. If subjects were given an

opportunity to *point out a picture* of an object they had held in their left hand, they were able to do so. They were also able to point out pictures that had been flashed to the left visual field. Furthermore, the right hemisphere (left hand) turned out to be *superior* to the left hemisphere (right hand) in assembling little puzzles and copying drawings, even though the subjects were right-handed. These findings provided the first compelling demonstration that the right hemisphere has its own special talents. Subsequent studies of additional split-brain patients showed the right hemisphere to be better than the left on a variety of visual-spatial tasks, including discriminating colors, arranging blocks, and recognizing faces.

In the split-brain studies, the other major finding was that subjects whose hemispheres were disconnected showed signs of having two minds in one brain (Bogen, 1969). Many split-brain patients reported that sometimes each hemisphere seemed to have a mind of its own. One patient reported that if he shifted a book from his right to his left hand, it would put the book down even though he was wrapped up in it. Apparently his right hemisphere just wasn't interested in reading. Another patient reported that when he angrily reached for his wife with his left hand, his right hand darted out to stop the left. A third patient found her right and left brains competing to dress her, as they chose different clothes to wear. Sometimes her left hand would unbutton a blouse nearly as fast as her right hand buttoned it. Thus, to some extent split-brain patients experience two independent streams of consciousness.

Hemispheric Specialization in the Intact Brain

The problem with the split-brain operation, of course, is that it creates an abnormal situation. The vast majority of us remain "neurologically intact." Moreover, the surgery is done only with people who suffer from prolonged, severe cases of epilepsy. These people may have had somewhat atypical brain organization even before the operation. Thus, theorists couldn't help wondering whether it was safe to generalize broadly from the split-brain studies. For this reason, researchers developed methods that allowed them to study cerebral specialization in the intact brain.

One method involves looking at *perceptual asymmetries—left-right imbalances between the cerebral hemispheres in the speed of visual or auditory processing.* As we just discussed, it is possible to present visual stimuli to just one visual field so they are sent to a particular hemisphere. It is also possible, as shown by Doreen Kimura (1967), to use a dichotic listening task to present auditory stimuli so that they arrive in a specific hemisphere first. In a *dichotic listening task,* different auditory inputs are simultaneously presented to each ear through headphones. In normal individuals with an intact corpus callosum, visual and auditory inputs sent to one hemisphere are quickly shared with the other. However, subtle differences in the "abilities" of the two hemispheres can be detected by precisely measuring how quickly and accurately subjects process different types of stimuli.

For instance, when verbal stimuli are presented to the right visual field or right ear (and thus sent to the *left hemisphere* first), they are identified more quickly and more accurately than when they are presented to the left visual field or left ear (right hemisphere). The faster reactions in the left hemisphere presumably occur because it can recognize verbal stimuli on its own, while the right hemisphere has to take extra time to "consult" the left hemisphere. In contrast, the *right hemisphere* is faster than the left on *visual-spatial* tasks, such as locating a dot or recognizing a face. The right hemisphere is also better at identifying environmental sounds (such as a bell, a cough, or a whistle) and melodies (Bradshaw, 1989; Bryden, 1982).

Researchers have also used a variety of other approaches to explore hemispheric specialization in normal people. Ultimately, they have concluded that the two hemispheres handle different cognitive tasks (Springer & Deutsch, 1993). *The left hemisphere usually handles verbal processing, such as language, speech, reading, and writing. The right hemisphere usually handles nonverbal processing, such as that required by spatial, musical, and visual recognition tasks.*

These findings on cognitive skills have led investigators to explore other aspects of behavior that may be related to hemispheric asymmetry. For example, studies suggest that the right hemisphere may be more involved than the left in the handling of emotions (Joseph, 1996). The right hemisphere has been implicated in both the production of facial expressions of emotion and the recognition of others' emotions from their facial expressions. Another line of research suggests that the right hemisphere may be more involved than the left in a crucial type of learning, called classical conditioning (Hugdahl, 1995), which we will discuss at length in Chapter 6. Yet another line of research has implicated right-hemisphere dysfunction in depressive disorders and left-hemisphere

dysfunction in schizophrenic disorders (Bruder, 1995). Obviously, cerebral lateralization is a burgeoning area of reseach that has broad implications, which we will discuss further in the Application.

Handedness and Laterality

Another aspect of human laterality that may be related to the hemispheric organization of the brain is *handedness*—**a preference for using one's right or left hand in most activities.** Although handedness is much easier to measure and observe than cerebral specialization, it may be just as complex. Contrary to popular belief, hand preference is not absolute. A person who writes with the right hand might use the left hand to throw a ball or wield scissors. To assess handedness effectively, researchers give people questionnaires that ask about their preferences in executing a variety of tasks. When researchers conduct a thorough assessment of handedness, they find that not everyone can be neatly categorized as right- or left-handed. In North America, typically, about 90% of subjects are found to be right-handed, about 7%–8% are left-handed, and the remainder display mixed-handedness (Iaccino, 1993). Across cultures, the prevalence of left-handedness varies moderately, but there are no cultures where left-handers even come close to being a majority. Moreover, the examination of people depicted in ancient works of art suggests that right-handedness has dominated for over 50 centuries (Coren & Porac, 1977).

Origins of Handedness

What determines a person's hand preference, and why are the vast majority of people right-handed? These questions have proven more perplexing than you might guess. Both environmental and genetic theories have failed to provide convincing explanations for observed patterns of handedness.

Environmental theories argue that people are born into a "right-handed world," where they are pressured into depending on their right hand. According to this view, most people become right-handed because tools, equipment, desks, pencil sharpeners, and so forth are designed for right-handers and because parents, teachers, and coaches push children to use their right hand in various activities—especially writing (Porac & Coren, 1981). Although environmental pressures can undoubtedly influence hand preference, environmental theories cannot account for the consistency in the prevalence of right- and left-handedness across

"Much of our work with visual perception has dealt with uncovering some of the specialized functions of the right hemisphere."

DOREEN KIMURA

These highly accomplished "lefties" from a variety of fields offer evidence against the many popular negative images frequently held about the small minority of the world's population who are left-handed. Clockwise from top left: rock star Jimi Hendrix, tennis champion Martina Navratilova, United States President Bill Clinton, American statesman Benjamin Franklin.

cultures. Some societies have systematically worked to stamp out left-handedness but have enjoyed only modest succcess. The most tenacious programs typically produce a moderate decline in the use of the left hand for socially monitored activities, such as writing in school, but have little impact on less obvious manifestations of left-handedness (Annett, 1985). In other societies that have been pretty open-minded about permitting left-handedness, it has increased only slightly (Harris, 1990). If handedness were simply a function of social pressures, there would be more cross-cultural variability in the prevalence of right- and left-handedness.

A number of genetic theories provide models of how handedness might be inherited (Annett, 1972; Levy & Nagylaki, 1972). The notion that hand preference is biologically built in fits nicely with the cross-cultural consistency seen in patterns of handedness. However, genetic models have difficulty accounting for a number of findings. For instance, left-handedness appears to be a recessive trait, which would mean that the children of two left-handed parents should all be left-handed. In reality, when both parents are left-handed, the probability of a left-handed child is only about 35% (Coren, 1992). Thus, genetic theories of handedness leave much to be explained.

The difficulties with environmental and genetic models of handedness have led theorists to look elsewhere for an explanation of hand preference. Many theorists suspect that handedness is somehow connected to the functional asymmetry of the human brain. Corballis (1991), for instance, asserts that "handedness is fundamentally a manifestation of cerebral rather than bodily asymmetry" (p. 105). However, the exact mechanisms that might link hand preference to lateralization in the brain remain a mystery (Peters, 1995).

Correlates of Handedness

Over the years, left-handedness has been linked to everything under the sun, from criminality to homosexuality. Many of these associations have not stood the test of time and replication, but some very interesting correlates of handedness have emerged. For example, there is an association between hand preference and patterns of cerebral specialization. In right-handers, language processing is almost always housed in the left hemisphere. However, atypical lateralization of language (in the right hemisphere or both hemispheres) is found in a significant minority of left handers (Bradshaw, 1989).

Investigators have also found associations between left-handedness and a surprising variety of pathological conditions. For example, left-handers are overrepresented in groups suffering from autism

(Bryson, 1990), schizophrenia (Flor-Henry, 1990), dyslexia (Porac & Coren, 1981), mental retardation (Pipe, 1990), alcoholism (London, 1990), and immune disorders (Searleman & Fugagli, 1987). These associations are weak, and it is important to emphasize that the vast majority of left-handers do not exhibit these disorders. Nonetheless, these correlations raise disturbing questions about the significance of left-handedness. Most disturbing of all, however, are the recent findings of Stanley Coren and Diane Halpern linking handedness to longevity, the subject of our Featured Study.

Do Left-Handers Die Younger? — Featured Study

Investigators: Stanley Coren (University of British Columbia) and Diane F. Halpern (California State University, San Bernardino)

Source: Left-handedness: A marker for decreased survival fitness. *Psychological Bulletin,* 1991, *109,* 90–106.

In an earlier study, Stanley Coren had unexpectedly discovered a correlation between age and the prevalence of left-handedness. In a diverse sample of over 5000 subjects, the percentage of left-handers dwindled from 13% at age 20 to 5% at age 50 and less than 1% at age 80 (see Figure 3.26). Although the idea seemed both macabre and implausible, Coren felt compelled to investigate the possibility that this age trend might be attributable to increased mortality among left-handers. In a preliminary effort to evaluate this possibility, Coren and Diane Halpern conducted archival research on over 2000 males who had played professional baseball (Halpern & Coren, 1988). This unusual sample was chosen because extensive data on their hand preference, age of birth, and age of death were readily available in *The Baseball Encyclopedia*. These data yielded a modest association between right-handedness and longer survival. However, Halpern and Coren wondered whether their findings might be peculiar to their unusual sample, so they set out to conduct a similar study with a more representative sample.

Method

Technically, the subjects were a random sample of recently deceased individuals, although the data were actually provided by their relatives. Inquiries were sent to the next of kin listed on 2875 death certificates posted in two counties in southern California. Given the sensitive nature of the situation, no effort was made to follow up on these inquiries, which yielded 987 usable responses. Information on the length of the subjects' life span was taken from their death certificates. Data on the subjects' hand preference were collected from their next of kin, who filled out a handedness questionnaire that was kept very short (three items) to make responding as brief and painless as possible.

Results

In the key analysis, subjects were classified as right-handers if their relatives indicated that they wrote, drew, and threw a ball with their right hand. The remaining subjects, who exhibited left-handedness or mixed-handedness, were lumped together and compared to the right-handers. The results of these comparisons are shown for males and females in Figure 3.27 on page 106. As you can see, left- and mixed-handedness was associated with reduced longevity of 5 years in females and 10 years in males.

Discussion

What could account for this peculiar link between left-handedness and reduced survival? Coren and Halpern review five considerations that might contribute to elevated mortality among left-handers. We'll discuss the two factors that appear most crucial. First, recent studies suggest that left-handers may be more accident-prone than right-handers, not because they're clumsy or spacey, but because they have to function in a right-handed world where safety levers, emergency brakes, and so forth are located poorly for them. Consistent with this view, Coren (1989b) found an 85% elevation in traffic accidents and 51% elevation in tool-related accidents among left-handers.

Second, left-handedness may be a marker associated with neurological damage due to birth stress, and this neurological damage may predispose left-handers to various disorders that affect their longevity. Some theorists believe that birth-related trauma (premature birth, prolonged labor, breech delivery, oxygen deprivation, and so on) may sometimes cause subtle, undetectable neurological damage that disrupts the development of normal hemispheric organization in the brain, resulting in left- or mixed-handedness (Bakan, 1990). Consistent with this view, quite a number of studies have found an elevated incidence of birth stress among left-handers. This theory could explain why atypical cerebral

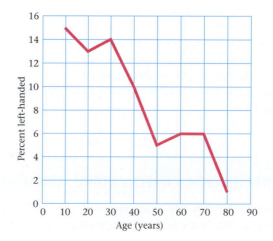

Figure 3.26
The prevalence of left-handedness as a function of age. Based on a sample of 5147 subjects, the percentage of the population that is left-handed is plotted as a function of age. As you can see, the percentage of left-handers declines precipitously in older age groups. (Adapted from Coren, 1992)

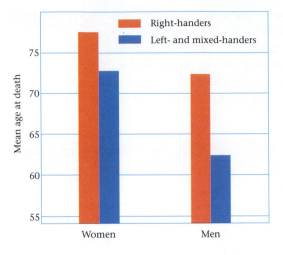

Figure 3.27
Average age of death as a function of handedness. Based on a sample of 987 death records, Coren and Halpern (1991) found that the mean age at death is noticeably younger in left-handers as opposed to right-handers for both females and males. The factors underlying left-handers' shorter life span are the subject of considerable speculation and debate.

"The composite picture that we have painted seems to indicate that left-handers may deviate from the physiological norm because of some developmental or pathological irregularity that may contribute to their reduced longevity. Furthermore, their interactions with the environment are apt to be more fraught with risk."

STANLEY COREN AND DIANE HALPERN

specialization is found in left-handers more than right-handers. Subtle neurological abnormalities resulting from birth stress might also contribute to the elevated incidence of autism, mental retardation, dyslexia, and schizophrenia observed in left-handers.

Comment

This study provides a nice example of how researchers often stumble onto perplexing findings, such as the age-related decrease in left-handedness, and then scramble to explain them by conducting more research. Many important lines of research have begun in this way. Coren and Halpern's work also illustrates the need for scientists to be open-minded, to entertain implausible or unpleasant possibilities, and to think the unthinkable.

Of course, thinking the unthinkable can cause consternation in some quarters, and this study gen-

erated considerable controversy when it was published. Left-handers have long complained about being stereotyped as clumsy and inept. Even our language subtly equates left-handedness with inferiority. For example, a *left-handed compliment* isn't much of a compliment, but a *right-hand man* is invaluable. Understandably, then, left-handers felt that this study poured salt into their wounds. Many were particularly offended by the theory linking left-handedness to brain damage, leading Stanley Coren (1992) to subsequently note, "I am not saying that every left-hander is some form of neurological cripple" (p. 151). Coren and Halpern have merely suggested—and many reputable laterality experts disagree (Bryden, 1993; Harris, 1993; Peters, 1995)—that there may be a modest statistical association between left-handedness and neurological anomalies.

Is the correlation between left-handedness and longevity cause for panic among left-handers? Concern, yes; panic, no. To put the findings in perspective, it may help to note that left-handers' decreased longevity is roughly similar to males' decreased longevity when compared to females, a well-known and better-documented phenomenon that has not led to panic in the streets. Moreover, awareness of their increased risk may motivate many left-handers—like many men—to alter their lifestyles in ways that may eventually narrow the longevity gap. In any case, it is apparent that human laterality has far-reaching and sometimes controversial implications, which we will return to in our upcoming Application. For now, however, let's turn our attention to the endocrine system.

Recap of Key Points

• The cerebrum is divided into right and left hemispheres connected by the corpus callosum. Evidence that the left cerebral hemisphere usually processes language led scientists to view it as the dominant hemisphere.

• However, studies of split-brain patients revealed that the right and left halves of the brain each have unique talents, with the right hemisphere being specialized to handle visual-spatial functions.

• Studies of perceptual asymmetries in normal subjects also showed that the left hemisphere is better equipped to handle verbal processing, whereas the right hemisphere is more adept at nonverbal processing.

• Handedness is an obvious but puzzling aspect of human laterality that may be related to the functional asymmetry of the human brain. Neither environmental nor genetic models can explain why about 90% of the population is right-handed and only 10% are left-handed.

• The Featured Study by Coren and Halpern (1991) tried to explain why there is a decline in the prevalence of left-handedness with increasing age. The investigators concluded that left-handedness is correlated with reduced longevity, probably because left-handedness increases one's accident risk and is a marker associated with neurological damage due to birth stress.

THE ENDOCRINE SYSTEM: ANOTHER WAY TO COMMUNICATE

The major way the brain communicates with the rest of the body is through the nervous system. However, the body has a second communication system that is also important to behavior. **The**

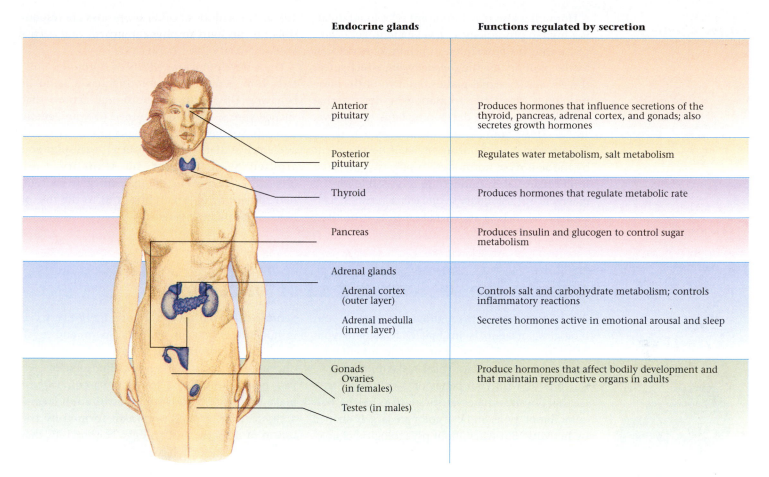

Endocrine glands	Functions regulated by secretion
Anterior pituitary	Produces hormones that influence secretions of the thyroid, pancreas, adrenal cortex, and gonads; also secretes growth hormones
Posterior pituitary	Regulates water metabolism, salt metabolism
Thyroid	Produces hormones that regulate metabolic rate
Pancreas	Produces insulin and glucogen to control sugar metabolism
Adrenal glands	
Adrenal cortex (outer layer)	Controls salt and carbohydrate metabolism; controls inflammatory reactions
Adrenal medulla (inner layer)	Secretes hormones active in emotional arousal and sleep
Gonads Ovaries (in females)	Produce hormones that affect bodily development and that maintain reproductive organs in adults
Testes (in males)	

endocrine system **consists of glands that secrete chemicals into the bloodstream that help control bodily functioning.** The messengers in this communication network are called hormones. *Hormones* **are the chemical substances released by the endocrine glands.** The endocrine system tends to be involved in the long-term regulation of basic bodily processes, as its action can't match the high speed of neural transmission. The major endocrine glands and their hormones are shown in Figure 3.28.

In a way, endocrine glands are like chemical synapses with distant receptors. Once released, the hormonal transmitters diffuse through the bloodstream and bind to special receptors on distant target cells. In fact, some chemical substances do double duty, functioning as hormones when they're released in the endocrine system and as neurotransmitters in the nervous system (norepinephrine, for example). There are some 30 different hormones in the human body. Some have specific target cells, while others affect a great many cells throughout the body.

Some hormones are released in response to changing conditions in the body and act to regulate those conditions. For example, hormones released by the stomach and intestines help control digestion. Kidney hormones play a part in regulating blood pressure. And pancreatic hormone (insulin) is essential for cells to use sugar from the blood.

Much of the endocrine system is controlled by the nervous system through the *hypothalamus*. This structure at the base of the forebrain has intimate connections with the pea-sized *pituitary gland,* to which it is adjacent. **The *pituitary gland* releases a great variety of hormones that fan out around the body, stimulating actions in the other endocrine glands.** In this sense, the pituitary is the "master gland" of the endocrine system, although the hypothalamus is the real power behind the throne.

The intermeshing of the nervous system and the endocrine system can be seen in the fight-or-flight response described earlier. In times of stress, the hypothalamus sends signals along two pathways—through the autonomic nervous system and through the pituitary gland—to the adrenal glands (Sapolsky, 1992). In response, the adrenal glands secrete hormones that radiate throughout the body, preparing it to cope with an emergency (see Chapter 13).

Figure 3.28
The endocrine system.
The endocrine glands secrete hormones into the bloodstream. As summarized here, these hormones regulate a variety of physical functions and may affect many aspects of behavior.

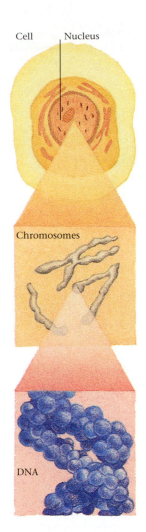

Cell   Nucleus

Chromosomes

DNA

Figure 3.29
Genetic material. This series of enlargements shows the main components of genetic material. (Top) In the nucleus of every cell are chromosomes, which carry the information needed to construct new human beings. (Center) Chromosomes are threadlike strands of DNA that carry thousands of genes, the functional units of hereditary transmission. (Bottom) DNA is a spiraled double chain of molecules that can copy itself to reproduce.

Hormones also play important roles in modulating human physiological development. For example, among the more interesting hormones released by the pituitary are the *gonadotropins,* which affect the *gonads,* or sexual glands. Prior to birth, these hormones direct the formation of the external sexual organs in the developing fetus (Breedlove, 1992). Thus, your sexual identity as a male or female was shaped during prenatal development by the actions of hormones. At puberty, increased levels of sexual hormones are responsible for the emergence of secondary sexual characteristics, such as male facial hair and female breasts (Chumlea,

1982). The actions of other hormones are responsible for the spurt in physical growth that occurs around puberty (see Chapter 11).

These developmental effects of hormones illustrate how genetic programming has a hand in behavior. Obviously, the hormonal actions that shaped your sex were determined by your genetic makeup. Similarly, the hormonal changes in early adolescence that launched your growth spurt and aroused your interest in sexuality were preprogrammed over a decade earlier by your genetic inheritance. Which brings us to the role of heredity in shaping behavior.

HEREDITY AND BEHAVIOR: IS IT ALL IN THE GENES?

As you have learned throughout this chapter, your biological makeup is intimately related to your behavior. That is why your genetic inheritance, which shapes your biological makeup, may have much to do with your behavior. Most people realize that physical characteristics such as height, hair color, blood type, and eye color are largely shaped by heredity. But what about psychological characteristics, such as intelligence, moodiness, impulsiveness, and shyness? To what extent are people's behavioral qualities molded by their genes? These questions are the central focus of ***behavioral genetics***—**an interdisciplinary field that studies the influence of genetic factors on behavioral traits.**

As we saw in Chapter 1, questions about the relative importance of heredity versus environment are very old ones in psychology. However, research in behavioral genetics has grown by leaps and bounds since the 1970s, and this research has shed new light on the age-old nature versus nurture debate. Ironically, although behavioral geneticists have mainly sought to demonstrate the influence of heredity on behavior, their recent work has also highlighted the importance of the environment (Plomin, 1993), as we shall see in this section.

Basic Principles of Genetics

Every cell in your body contains enduring messages from your mother and father. These messages are found on the *chromosomes* that lie within the nucleus of each cell.

Chromosomes and Genes

Chromosomes **are threadlike strands of DNA (deoxyribonucleic acid) molecules that carry**

genetic information (see Figure 3.29). Every cell in humans, except the sex cells (sperm and eggs), contains 46 chromosomes. These chromosomes operate in 23 pairs, with one chromosome of each pair being contributed by each parent. Parents make this contribution when fertilization creates a *zygote,* **a one-celled organism formed by the union of a sperm and an egg.** The sex cells that form a zygote each have 23 chromosomes; together they contribute the 46 chromosomes that appear in the zygote and in all the body cells that evolve from it. Each chromosome, in turn, contains thousands of biochemical messengers called genes. *Genes* **are DNA segments that serve as the key functional units in hereditary transmission.**

If all offspring are formed by a union of the parents' sex cells, why aren't family members identical clones? The reason is that a single pair of parents can produce an extraordinary variety of combinations of chromosomes. When sex cells form in each parent, it is a matter of chance as to which member of each chromosome pair ends up in the sperm or egg. Each parent's 23 chromosome pairs can be scrambled in over 8 million (2^{23}) different ways, yielding roughly 70 trillion possible configurations (2^{46}) when sperm and egg unite. Actually, this is a conservative estimate. It doesn't take into account complexities such as *mutations* (changes in the genetic code) or *crossing over* during sex-cell formation (an interchange of material between chromosomes). Thus, genetic transmission is a complicated process, and everything is a matter of probability. Except for identical twins, each person ends up with a unique genetic blueprint.

Like chromosomes, genes operate in pairs, with

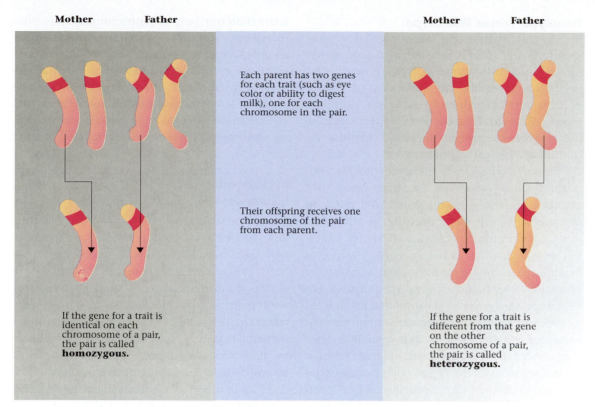

Each parent has two genes for each trait (such as eye color or ability to digest milk), one for each chromosome in the pair.

Their offspring receives one chromosome of the pair from each parent.

If the gene for a trait is identical on each chromosome of a pair, the pair is called **homozygous.**

If the gene for a trait is different from that gene on the other chromosome of a pair, the pair is called **heterozygous.**

Figure 3.30
Homozygous and heterozygous genotypes. Like chromosomes, genes operate in pairs, with one gene in each pair coming from each parent. When paired genes are the same, they are said to be homozygous. When paired genes are different, they are said to be heterozygous. (Adapted from Kalat, 1993)

one gene of each pair coming from each parent. **In the *homozygous condition,* the two genes in a specific pair are the same. In the *heterozygous condition,* the two genes in a specific pair are different** (see Figure 3.30). In the simplest scenario, a single pair of genes determines a trait. Eye color provides a nice example. When both parents contribute a gene for the same color (the *homozygous* condition), the child will have eyes of that color. When the parents contribute genes for different eye colors (the *heterozygous* condition), one gene in the pair—called the *dominant gene*—overrides or masks the other, called the *recessive gene.* Thus, **a *dominant gene* is one that is expressed when paired genes are different. A *recessive gene* is one that is masked when paired genes are different.**

Because genes operate in pairs, a child has a 50% probability of inheriting a specific gene in a specific gene pair from each parent. Hence, the *genetic relatedness* of parents and children is said to be 50%. The genetic relatedness of other types of relatives can be calculated in the same way; the results are shown in Figure 3.31. As you can see, genetic relatedness ranges from 100% for identical twins down to 6.25% for second cousins. The numbers in Figure 3.31 are purely theoretical, and for a variety of complicated reasons they underestimate the actual genetic overlap among people. But the key to the concept of genetic relatedness is

that members of a family share more of the same genes than nonmembers, and closer relatives share a larger proportion of genes than more distant relatives. These realities explain why family members tend to resemble one another and why this resemblance tends to be greater among closer relatives.

Figure 3.31
Genetic relatedness. Research on the genetic bases of behavior takes advantage of the different degrees of genetic relatedness between various types of relatives. If heredity influences a trait, relatives who share more genes should be more similar with regard to that trait than are more distant relatives, who share fewer genes. Comparisons involving various degrees of biological relationships will come up frequently in later chapters.

Relationship	Degree of relatedness	Genetic overlap	
Identical twins		100%	
Fraternal twins Brother or sister Parent or child	First degree relatives	50%	
Grandparent or grandchild Uncle, aunt, nephew, or niece Half-brother or half-sister	Second degree relatives	25%	
First cousin	Third degree relatives	12.5%	
Second cousin	Fourth degree relatives	6.25%	
Unrelated		0%	

Genotype Versus Phenotype

It might seem that two parents with the same manifest trait, such as brown eyes, should always produce offspring with that trait. However, that isn't always the case. For instance, two brown-eyed parents can produce a blue-eyed child (see Figure 3.32). This happens because there are unexpressed recessive genes in the family's gene pool—in this case, genes for blue eyes.

This point brings us to the distinction between genotype and phenotype. *Genotype* refers to a **person's genetic makeup.** *Phenotype* refers to **the ways in which a person's genotype is manifested in observable characteristics.** Different genotypes (such as two genes for brown eyes as opposed to one gene for brown and one for blue) can yield the same phenotype (brown eyes). Genotype is determined at conception and is fixed forever. In contrast, phenotypic characteristics (hair color, for instance) may change over time. They may also be modified by environmental factors.

Genotypes translate into phenotypic characteristics in a variety of ways. Not all gene pairs operate according to the principles of dominance. In some instances, when paired genes are different, they produce a blend, an "averaged out" phenotype. In other cases, paired genes that are different strike another type of compromise, and both characteristics show up phenotypically, as in the case of type AB blood.

Polygenic Inheritance

Most human characteristics appear to be *polygenic traits,* **or characteristics that are influenced by** more than one pair of genes. For example, three to five gene pairs are thought to interactively determine skin color. Complex physical abilities, such as motor coordination, may be influenced by tangled interactions among a great many pairs of genes. Most psychological characteristics that appear to be affected by heredity seem to involve complex polygenic inheritance (Plomin, 1990).

Investigating Hereditary Influence: Research Methods 7d

How do behavioral geneticists and other scientists disentangle the effects of genetics and experience to determine whether heredity affects behavioral traits? Researchers have designed special types of studies to assess the impact of heredity. Of course, with humans they are limited to correlational rather than experimental methods, as they cannot manipulate genetic variables by assigning subjects to mate with each other (this approach, called *selective breeding,* is used in animal studies). The three most important methods in human research are family studies, twin studies, and adoption studies. After examining these classic methods of research, we'll discuss the impact of new developments in genetic mapping.

Family Studies

In *family studies* researchers **assess hereditary influence by examining blood relatives to see how much they resemble one another on a specific trait.** If heredity affects the trait under scrutiny, researchers should find phenotypic similarity among relatives. Furthermore, they should find more similarity among relatives who share more genes. For instance, siblings should exhibit more similarity than cousins.

Illustrative of this method are the numerous family studies conducted to assess the contribution of heredity to the development of schizophrenic disorders. These disorders strike approximately 1% of the population, yet as Figure 3.33 reveals, 9% of the siblings of schizophrenic patients exhibit schizophrenia themselves (Gottesman, 1991). Thus, these first-degree relatives of schizophrenic patients show a risk for the disorder that is nine times higher than normal. This risk is greater than that observed for more distantly related, second-degree relatives, such as nieces and nephews (4%), who, in turn, are at greater risk than third-degree relatives, such as second cousins (2%). This pattern of results is consistent with the hypothesis that genetic inheri-

Figure 3.32
Dominant and recessive genes. This diagram shows how two brown-eyed parents with a heterozygous genotype (*Bb,* denoting brown-blue) have a 25% chance of producing brown-eyed offspring who are homozygous (*BB*), a 50% chance of producing brown-eyed offspring who are heterozygous (*Bb*), and a 25% chance of producing blue-eyed offspring, who must be homozygous (*bb*), since blue eye color is recessive. The genetic bases for behavioral traits appear to be much more complex than the simple rules that govern eye color.

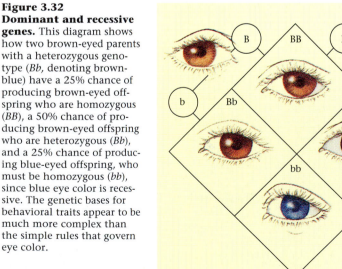

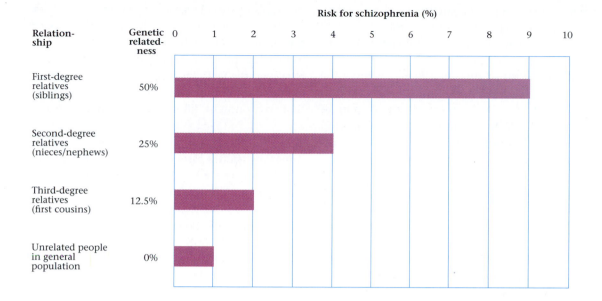

Risk for schizophrenia (%)

Relation-ship	Genetic related-ness	Risk for schizophrenia (%)
First-degree relatives (siblings)	50%	9
Second-degree relatives (nieces/nephews)	25%	4
Third-degree relatives (first cousins)	12.5%	2
Unrelated people in general population	0%	1

Figure 3.33
Family studies of risk for schizophrenic disorders. First-degree relatives of schizophrenic patients have an elevated risk of developing a schizophrenic disorder. For instance, the risk for siblings of schizophrenic patients is about 9% instead of the baseline 1% for unrelated people. Second- and third-degree relatives have progressively smaller elevations in risk for this disorder. Although these patterns of risk do not prove that schizophrenia is partly inherited, they are consistent with this hypothesis. (Adapted from data in Gottesman, 1991)

tance influences the development of schizophrenic disorders (Gottesman, 1993).

Family studies can indicate whether a trait runs in families. However, this correlation does not provide conclusive evidence that the trait is influenced by heredity. Why not? Because family members generally share not only genes but also similar environments. Furthermore, closer relatives are more likely to live together than more distant relatives. Thus, genetic similarity and environmental similarity *both* tend to be greater for closer relatives. Either of these confounded variables could be responsible when greater phenotypic similarity is found in closer relatives. Family studies can offer useful insights about the possible impact of heredity, but they cannot provide definitive evidence.

Twin Studies

Twin studies can yield better evidence about the possible role of genetic factors. **In *twin studies* researchers assess hereditary influence by comparing the resemblance of identical twins and fraternal twins with respect to a trait.** The logic of twin studies hinges on the genetic relatedness of identical and fraternal twins (see Figure 3.34 on page 112). ***Identical (monozygotic) twins* emerge from one zygote that splits for unknown reasons.** Thus, they have exactly the same genotype; their genetic relatedness is 100%. ***Fraternal (dizygotic) twins* result when two eggs are fertilized simultaneously by different sperm cells, forming two separate zygotes.** Fraternal twins are no more alike in genetic makeup than any two

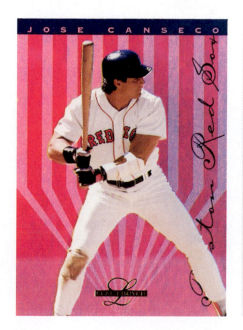

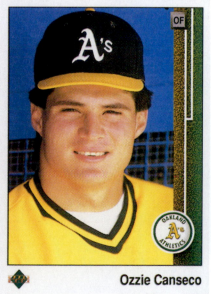

Ozzie Canseco

The Canseco twins appear to provide a dramatic illustration of how heredity and experience jointly influence many complex behavioral traits—in this case, baseball ability. Jose and Ozzie Canseco are identical twins, and the genetic inheritance that they share probably has much to do with the fact that both have demonstrated exceptional baseball ability by becoming professional baseball players. However, differences in their experiences probably explain why one brother (Jose) has become a superstar, whereas the other (Ozzie) has knocked around in the minor leagues for most of his career.

siblings born to a pair of parents at different times. Their genetic relatedness is only 50%.

Fraternal twins provide a useful comparison to identical twins because in both cases the twins usually grow up in the same home, at the same time, exposed to the same configuration of relatives, neighbors, peers, teachers, events, and so forth. Thus, both kinds of twins normally develop under equally similar environmental conditions. However, identical twins share more genetic kinship than fraternal twins. Consequently, if sets of identical twins tend to exhibit more similarity on a trait than sets of fraternal twins do, it is reasonable to infer that this greater similarity is probably due to heredity rather than environment.

Twin studies have been conducted to assess the impact of heredity on many different traits. Some representative results are summarized in Figure 3.35. The higher correlations found for identical twins indicate that they tend to be more similar to each other than fraternal twins on measures of general intelligence (McGue et al., 1993) and

measures of specific personality traits, such as extraversion (Loehlin, 1992). These results support the notion that intelligence and personality are influenced to some degree by genetic makeup. However, the fact that identical twins are far from identical in intelligence and personality also shows that environment influences these characteristics.

Adoption Studies

Adoption studies **assess hereditary influence by examining the resemblance between adopted children and both their biological and their adoptive parents.** Generally, adoptees are used as subjects in this type of study only if they were given up for adoption in early infancy and were raised without having contact with their biological parents. The logic underlying the adoption study approach is quite simple. If adopted children resemble their biological parents on a trait, even though they were not raised by them, genetic factors probably influence that trait. In contrast, if adopted children resemble their adoptive

Figure 3.34
Identical versus fraternal twins. Identical (monozygotic) twins emerge from one zygote that splits, so their genetic relatedness is 100%. Fraternal (dizygotic) twins emerge from two separate zygotes, so their genetic relatedness is only 50%. (Adapted from Kalat, 1996)

Identical (monozygotic) twins

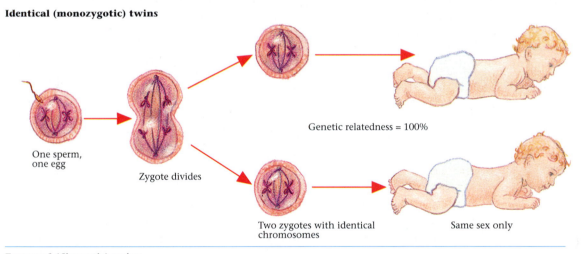

One sperm, one egg

Zygote divides

Two zygotes with identical chromosomes

Genetic relatedness = 100%

Same sex only

Fraternal (dizygotic) twins

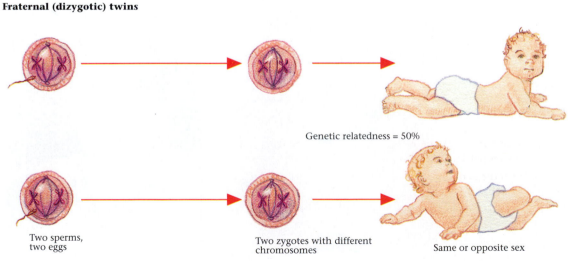

Two sperms, two eggs

Two zygotes with different chromosomes

Genetic relatedness = 50%

Same or opposite sex

parents, even though they inherited no genes from them, environmental factors probably influence the trait.

In recent years, adoption studies have contributed to science's understanding of how genetics and the environment influence intelligence. The research shows significant similarity between adopted children and their biological parents, as indicated by an average correlation of .36 (Vandenberg & Vogler, 1985). Interestingly, adopted children resemble their adoptive parents nearly as much (average correlation of .31). These findings indicate that both heredity and environment have an influence on intelligence.

The Cutting Edge: Genetic Mapping

While behavioral geneticists have recently made great progress in documenting the influence of heredity on behavior, *molecular geneticists,* who study the biochemical bases of genetic inheritance, have made even more spectacular advances in their efforts to unravel the genetic code. *Genetic mapping* **is the process of determining the location and chemical sequence of specific genes on specific chromosomes.** New methods of manipulating DNA are now allowing scientists to create detailed physical maps of the genetic material on chromosomes in plants, animals, and humans. A huge, 15-year international project intended to map out the estimated 100,000 genes found on the 23 pairs of human chromosomes is well under way. Gene maps, by themselves, do not reveal which genes govern which traits. However, the compilation of a precise genetic atlas will produce a quantum leap in the ability of scientists to pinpoint links between specific genes and specific traits and disorders. For example, medical research-

ers have already identified the genes responsible for cystic fibrosis, Huntington's chorea, and muscular dystrophy (Wingerson, 1990). These discoveries promise to yield dramatic advances in the diagnosis and treatment of these diseases.

Will genetic mapping permit researchers to discover the genetic basis for intelligence, extraversion, musical ability, and other *behavioral* traits? Perhaps eventually, but progress is likely to be gradual. Thus far, the major medical breakthroughs from genetic mapping have involved dichotomous traits (you either do or do not have the trait, such as muscular dystrophy) governed by a single gene pair. However, most behavioral traits do not involve a dichotomy, as everyone has varying amounts of intelligence, musical ability, and so forth. Moreover, virtually all behavioral traits appear to be *polygenic* traits that are shaped by many

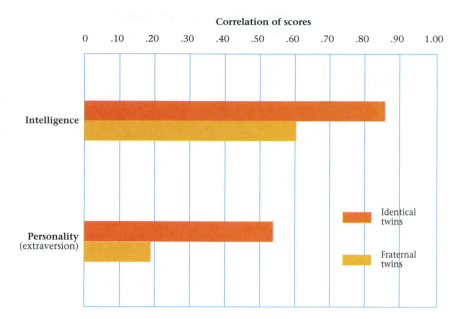

Figure 3.35
Twin studies of intelligence and personality. Identical twins tend to be more similar than fraternal twins (as reflected in higher correlations) with regard to general mental ability and specific personality traits, such as extraversion. These findings suggest that intelligence and personality are influenced by heredity. (Intelligence data from McGue et al., 1993; extraversion data based on Loehlin, 1992)

CONCEPT CHECK 3.4
Recognizing Hereditary Influence

Check your understanding of the methods scientists use to explore hereditary influences on specific behavioral traits by filling in the blanks in the descriptive statements below. The answers can be found in the back of the book in Appendix A.

1. The findings from *family studies* indicate that heredity may influence a trait if _____ show more trait similarity than _____.

2. The findings from *twin studies* suggest that heredity influences a trait if _____ show more trait similarity than _____.

3. The findings from *adoption studies* suggest that heredity influences a trait if children adopted at a young age share more trait similarity with their _____ than their _____.

4. The findings from *family studies, twin studies,* or *adoption studies* suggest that heredity does not influence a trait when _____ is not related to _____.

genes rather than a single gene. Because of these complexities, scientists are not likely to find the gene that controls intelligence, extraversion, or musical talent (Plomin, 1993). Instead, the challenge will be to identify specific constellations of genes that each exert modest influence over particular aspects of behavior (McClearn et al., 1991).

In spite of the daunting complexity of human behavior, genetic mapping holds great promise for behavioral genetics. According to Plomin and Rende (1991), by the year 2000 it is likely that "molecular-genetic techniques will have revolutionized human behavioral genetics" (p. 176). What's exciting is that until recently, behavioral geneticists were largely limited to investigating *how much* heredity influences various traits. Genetic mapping will allow them to begin investigating *how* heredity influences various traits.

The Interplay of Heredity and Environment

We began this section by asking, is it all in the genes? When it comes to behavioral traits, the answer clearly is no. According to Robert Plomin (1993), perhaps the leading behavioral genetics researcher in the last decade, what scientists find again and again is that heredity and experience jointly influence most aspects of behavior. Moreover, their effects are interactive—they play off each other.

For example, consider what researchers have learned about the development of schizophrenic disorders. Although the evidence indicates that genetic factors influence the development of schizophrenia, it does *not* appear that anyone directly inherits the disorder itself. Rather, what people appear to inherit is a certain degree of *vulnerability* to the disorder (Zubin, 1986). Whether this vulnerability is ever converted into an actual disorder depends on each person's experiences in life. As we will discuss in Chapter 14, certain types of stressful experience seem to evoke the disorder in people who are more vulnerable to it. Thus, as Richard Rose (1995) puts it in a major review of behavioral genetics research, "We inherit dispositions, not destinies."

"During the 1970s, I found I had to speak gingerly about genetic influence, gently suggesting that heredity might be important in behavior. Now, however, the transformation of the social and behavioral sciences from environmentalism to biological determinism is happening so fast that I find I more often have to say, 'Yes, genetic influences are substantial, but environmental influences are important, too.'"

ROBERT PLOMIN

PUTTING IT IN PERSPECTIVE

Three of our seven themes stood out in this chapter: (1) heredity and environment jointly influence behavior, (2) behavior is determined by multiple causes, and (3) psychology is empirical. Let's look at each of these points.

In Chapter 1, when it was first emphasized that heredity and environment jointly shape behavior, you may have been a little perplexed about how your genes could be responsible for your sarcastic wit or your interest in art. In fact, there are no genes for behavior per se. Experts do not expect to find genes for sarcasm or artistic interest, for example. Insofar as your hereditary endowment plays a role in your behavior, it does so *indirectly*, by molding the physiological machine that you work with. Thus, your genes influence your physiological makeup, which in turn influences your personality, temperament, intelligence, interests, and other traits. Bear in mind, however, that genetic factors do not operate in a vacuum. Genes exert their effects in an environmental context. The impact of genetic makeup depends on environment, and the impact of environment depends on genetic makeup.

It was evident throughout the chapter that behavior is determined by multiple causes, but this reality was particularly apparent in the discussions of schizophrenia. At different points in the chapter we saw that schizophrenia may be a function of (1) abnormalities in neurotransmitter activity (especially dopamine), (2) structural defects in the brain (enlarged ventricles), and (3) genetic vulnerability to the illness. These findings do not contradict one another. Rather, they demonstrate that a complex array of biological factors are involved in the development of schizophrenia. In Chapter 14, we'll see that a host of environmental factors also play a role in the multifactorial causation of schizophrenia.

The empirical nature of psychology was apparent in the numerous discussions of the specialized research methods used to study the physiological bases of behavior. As you know, the empirical approach depends on precise observation. Throughout this chapter, you've seen how investigators have come up with innovative methods to observe and measure elusive phenomena such as electrical activity in the brain, neural impulses, brain function, cerebral specialization, and the impact of heredity on behavior. The point is that empirical methods are the lifeblood of the scientific enterprise. When researchers figure out how to better observe something, their new methods usually facilitate major advances in our scientific knowledge. That is why brain-imaging techniques and genetic mapping hold such exciting promise.

The importance of empiricism will also be apparent in the upcoming Application, which looks at popular ideas about the specialized abilities of the right and left halves of the brain as they relate to cognitive processes. You'll see that it is important to learn to distinguish between scientific findings and conjecture based on those findings.

Recap of Key Points

• The endocrine system consists of the glands that secrete hormones, which are chemicals involved in the regulation of basic bodily processes. The control centers for the endocrine system are the hypothalamus and the pituitary gland.

• The basic units of genetic transmission are genes housed on chromosomes. Genes operate in pairs, and when heterozygous, one may be dominant and one recessive.

• Genotypes are translated into phenotypes in a variety of ways. Most behavioral qualities appear to involve polygenic inheritance.

• Researchers assess hereditary influence through a variety of methods, including family studies, twin studies, adoption studies, and genetic mapping. Family studies cannot provide conclusive evidence that a trait is influenced by heredity. Twin studies can provide much better evidence.

• Research indicates that most behavioral qualities are influenced jointly by heredity and environment, which play off of each other in complex interactions.

• Three of the book's unifying themes stand out in this chapter. First, we saw how heredity interacts with experience to govern behavior. Second, the discussions of biological factors underlying schizophrenia highlighted the multifactorial causation of behavior. Third, we saw how innovations in research methods often lead to advances in knowledge, underscoring the empirical nature of psychology.

APPLICATION: THINKING CRITICALLY ABOUT THE CONCEPT OF "TWO MINDS IN ONE"

Answer the following "true" or "false."

1 Our right and left brains give us two minds in one.

2 Each half of the brain has its own special mode of thinking.

3 Some people are left-brained while others are right-brained.

4 Our schools should devote more effort to teaching the overlooked right side of the brain.

Do we have two minds in one that think differently? Do some of us depend on one side of the brain more than the other? Is the right side of the brain neglected? These questions are too complex to resolve with a simple true or false, but in this Applica-tion we'll take a closer look at the issues involved in these proposed applications of the findings on cerebral specialization. You'll learn that some of these ideas are plausible, but in many cases the hype has outstripped the evidence.

Earlier, we described Roger Sperry's Nobel prize–winning research with split-brain patients, whose right and left hemi-spheres were disconnected (to reduce epileptic seizures). The split-brain studies showed that the previously underrated right hemisphere has some special talents of its own. This discovery detonated an explosion of research on cerebral laterality.

Cerebral Specialization and Cognitive Processes 2f

Using a variety of methods, scientists have compiled mountains of data on the spe-cialized abilities of the right and left hemi-spheres. These findings have led to exten-sive theorizing about how the right and left brains might be related to cognitive pro-cesses. Some of the more intriguing ideas include the following:

1. *The two hemispheres are specialized to process different types of cognitive tasks* (Cor-ballis, 1991; Ornstein, 1977). The findings of many researchers have been widely interpreted as showing that the left hemi-sphere handles verbal tasks, including lan-guage, speech, writing, math, and logic, while the right hemisphere handles nonver-bal tasks, including spatial problems, music, art, fantasy, and creativity. These conclusions have attracted a great deal of public interest and media attention. For example, Fig-ure 3.36 shows a *Newsweek* artist's depiction of how the brain divides its work.

2. *Each hemisphere has its own independent stream of consciousness* (Bogen, 1985; Pucetti, 1981). For instance, Joseph Bogen has asserted, "Pending further evidence, I believe that each of us has two minds in one person" (Hooper & Teresi, 1986, p. 221). Supposedly, this duality of con-sciousness goes largely unnoticed because of the considerable overlap between the experiences of each independent mind. Ultimately, though, the apparent unity of consciousness is but an illusion.

3. *The two hemispheres have different modes of thinking* (Galin, 1974; Joseph, 1992). According to this notion, the docu-mented differences between the hemi-spheres in dealing with verbal and nonverbal materials are due to more basic differences in *how* the hemispheres process information. This theory holds that the reason the left hemisphere handles verbal material well is that it is analytic, abstract, rational, logical, and linear. In contrast, the right hemisphere is thought to be bet-

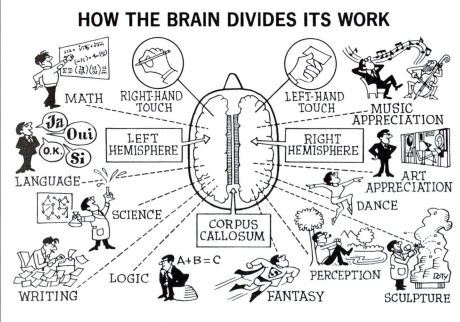

Figure 3.36
Popular conceptions of hemispheric specialization. As this *Newsweek* diagram illus-trates, depictions of hemispheric specialization in the popular press have often been oversimplified.

ter equipped to handle spatial and musical material because it is synthetic, concrete, nonrational, intuitive, and holistic. These proposed hemispheric differences in cognitive style are summarized in Figure 3.37.

4. *People vary in their reliance on one hemisphere as opposed to the other* (Bakan, 1971; Zenhausen, 1978). Allegedly, some people are "left-brained." Their greater dependence on their left hemisphere supposedly makes them analytic, rational, and logical. Other people are "right-brained." Their greater use of their right hemisphere supposedly makes them intuitive, holistic, and irrational. Being right-brained or left-brained is thought to explain many personal characteristics, such as whether an individual likes to read, is good with maps, or enjoys music. This notion of "brainedness" has even been used to ex-

plain occupational choice. Supposedly, right-brained people are more likely to become artists or musicians, while left-brained people are more likely to become writers or scientists.

5. *Schools should place more emphasis on teaching the right side of the brain* (Prince, 1978; Samples, 1975). "A real reform of the educational system will not occur until the individual teachers learn to understand the true duality of their students' minds," says Thomas Blakeslee (1980, p. 59). Those sympathetic to his view assert that American schools overemphasize logical, analytical left-hemisphere thinking (required by English, math, and science) while short-changing intuitive, holistic right-hemisphere thinking (required by art and music). These educators have concluded that modern schools turn out an excess of

left-brained graduates. They advocate curriculum reform to strengthen the right side of the brain in their students. This line of thinking has also spawned quite a collection of popular, self-help books, such as *Whole-Brain Thinking* (Wonder, 1992), *Unleashing the Right Side of the Brain* (Williams & Stockmyer, 1987), and *Teaching for the Two-Sided Mind* (Williams, 1986).

Complexities and Qualifications

The ideas just outlined are the source of considerable debate among psychologists and neuroscientists. These ideas are intriguing and have clearly captured the imagination of the general public. However, the research on cerebral specialization is complex, and doubts have been raised about many of these ideas (Corballis, 1980; Efron, 1990; Kinsbourne, 1982). Let's examine each point.

1. There *is* ample evidence that the right and left hemispheres are specialized to handle different types of cognitive tasks, *but only to a degree* (Gordon, 1990). Doreen Kimura (1973) compared the abilities of the right and left hemispheres to quickly recognize letters, words, faces, and melodies in a series of perceptual asymmetry studies, like those described earlier in the chapter. She found that the superiority of one hemisphere over the other was usually quite modest, as you can see in Figure 3.38 on page 118, which shows superiority ratios for four cognitive tasks.

Furthermore, in normal individuals, the hemispheres don't work alone. As Hellige (1993) notes, "In the intact brain, it is unlikely that either hemisphere is ever completely uninvolved in ongoing processing" (p. 23). For instance, the right hemisphere doesn't shut down entirely so the left hemisphere can read a book by itself. Most tasks probably engage *both* hemispheres, albeit to different degrees (Hellige, 1990). For instance, imagine that you are asked the following question: "In what direction are you headed if you start north and make two right turns and a left turn?" In answering this question, you're confronted with a *spatial* task that should engage the right hemisphere. However,

Left Hemisphere's Modes of Thinking	Right Hemisphere's Modes of Thinking
Verbal: Using words to name, describe, define	**Nonverbal:** Showing an awareness of things but minimal connection with words
Analytic: Figuring things out step by step and part by part	**Synthetic:** Putting things together to form wholes
Symbolic: Using a symbol to stand for something	**Analogic:** Seeing likenesses between things; understanding metaphoric relationships
Abstract: Taking out a small bit of information and using it to represent a whole thing	**Concrete:** Relating to things as they are at the present moment
Temporal: Keeping track of time; sequencing one thing after another, doing first things first, second things second, and so forth	**Nontemporal:** Being without a sense of time
Rational: Drawing conclusions based on reason and facts	**Nonrational:** Not requiring a basis of reason or facts; willing to suspend judgment
Digital: Using numbers as in counting	**Spatial:** Seeing where things are in relation to other things and how parts go together to form a whole
Logical: Drawing conclusions based on logic: one thing following another in logical order—for example, developing a mathematical theorem or a well-stated argument	**Intuitive:** Making leaps of insight, often based on incomplete patterns, hunches
Linear: Thinking in terms of linked ideas, one thought directly following another, often leading to a convergent conclusion	**Holistic:** Seeing whole things all at once; perceiving overall patterns and structures, which often leads to divergent conclusions

Figure 3.37
Proposed differences between the left and right hemispheres in cognitive style.
It is popular to suggest that the two hemispheres exhibit different modes of thinking. This summary, adapted from Edwards (1979, 1989), shows that theorists have tried to relate many polarities in cognitive style to the right and left brains. However, as the text explains, there is relatively little direct evidence to support these proposed dichotomies.

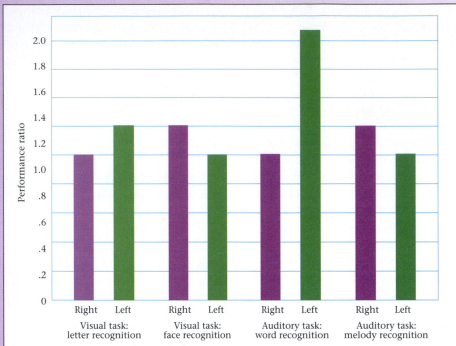

Figure 3.38
Relative superiority of one brain hemisphere over the other in studies of perceptual asymmetry. The performance ratios show the degree to which one hemisphere was "superior" to the other on each type of task in one study of normal subjects. For example, the right hemisphere was 20% better than the left hemisphere in quickly recognizing melodic patterns (ratio 1.2 to 1). Most differences in the performance of the two hemispheres are quite small. (Data from Kimura, 1973)

first you have to process the wording of the question, a *language* task that should engage the left hemisphere.

Furthermore, people differ in their patterns of cerebral specialization (Springer & Deutsch, 1993). Some people display little specialization—that is, their hemispheres seem to have equal abilities on various types of tasks. Others even reverse the usual specialization, so that verbal processing might be housed in the right hemisphere. These unusual patterns are especially common among left-handed people. For example, when Rasmussen and Milner (1977) tested subjects for the localization of speech, they found bilateral representation in 15% of the left-handers. A reversal of the usual specialization (speech handled by the right hemisphere) was found in another 15% of the left-handed subjects (see Figure 3.39). These variations in cerebral specialization are not well understood yet. However, they clearly indicate that the functional specialization of the cerebral hemispheres is not set in concrete.

2. The evidence for the idea that people have a separate stream of consciousness in each hemisphere is weak. There *are* clear signs of such duality among *split-brain patients* (Bogen, 1990; Mark, 1996). But this duality is probably a unique by-product of the radical procedure that they have undergone—the surgical disconnection of their hemispheres (Bradshaw, 1981). In fact, many theorists have been impressed by the degree to which even split-brain patients mostly experience *unity* of consciousness. There is little empirical basis for the idea that people have two independent streams of awareness neatly housed in the right and left halves of the brain.

3. Similarly, there is little direct evidence to support the notion that each hemisphere has its own mode of thinking, or *cognitive style* (Bradshaw, 1989). This notion is plausible, but far more evidence is needed (Gordon, 1990). One key problem with this idea is that aspects of cognitive style have proven difficult to define and measure (Brownell & Gardner, 1981). For instance, there is great debate about the

meaning of analytic versus synthetic thinking, or linear versus holistic thinking.

4. The evidence on the assertion that some people are left-brained while others are right-brained is inconclusive at best (Hellige, 1990). This notion has some plausibility—*if* it means only that some people consistently display more activation of one hemisphere than the other. However, more research is needed on these possible "preferences" in cerebral activation. The practical significance of any such preferences remains to be determined. At present, researchers do not have convincing data linking brainedness to musical ability, occupational choice, or the like (Springer & Deutsch, 1993).

5. The idea that schools should be reformed to better exercise the right side of the brain represents intriguing but wild speculation. In neurologically intact people it is impossible to teach just one hemisphere at a time, and there is no clear evidence that it is beneficial to "exercise" a hemisphere of the brain (Levy, 1985). Many sound arguments exist for reforming American schools to encourage more holistic, intuitive thinking, but these arguments have nothing to do with cerebral specialization.

In summary, the theories linking cerebral specialization to cognitive processes are highly speculative. There's nothing wrong with theoretical speculation. Unfortunately, the tentative, conjectural nature of these ideas about cerebral specialization has gotten lost in the popular book descriptions of research on the right and left hemispheres (Coren, 1992). Popular writers continue to churn out allegedly scientific books, applying brain lateralization concepts to a host of new topics on which there often is little or no real evidence. Thus, one can find books on how to have right-brain sex (Wells, 1991), develop right-brain social skills (Snyder, 1989), and lose weight with a right-brain diet (Sommer, 1987). Commenting on this popularization, Hooper and Teresi (1986) note, "A widespread cult of the right brain ensued, and the duplex house that Sperry built grew into the K mart of brain science.

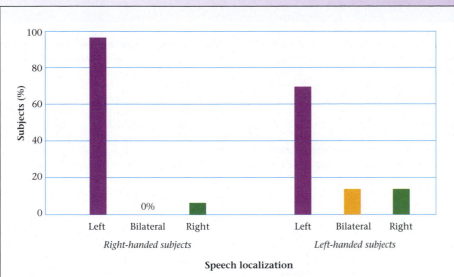

Figure 3.39
Handedness and patterns of speech localization. Left-handed people tend to show more variety in cerebral specialization and more bilateral representation than right-handers. For example, speech processing is almost always localized in the left hemisphere of right-handed subjects. However, Rasmussen and Milner (1977) found the usual pattern of speech localization in only 70% of their left-handed subjects.

Today our hairdresser lectures us about the "Two Hemispheres of the Brain" (p. 223). Cerebral specialization is an important and intriguing area of research. However, it is unrealistic to expect that the hemispheric divisions in the brain will provide a bio-logical explanation for every dichotomy or polarity in modes of thinking.

Recap of Key Points

• Split-brain research stimulated speculation about relations between cerebral spe-cialization and cognitive processes. Some theorists believe that each hemisphere has its own stream of consciousness and mode of thinking, which are applied to specific types of cognitive tasks.

• Some theorists also believe that people vary in their reliance on the right and left halves of the brain and that schools should work more to exercise the right half of the brain.

• The cerebral hemispheres *are* specialized for handling different cognitive tasks, but only to a degree, as most tasks engage both hemispheres. Moreover, people vary in their patterns of hemispheric specialization.

• Evidence for duality in consciousness divided along hemispheric lines is weak. Evidence on whether people vary in brainedness and whether the two hemi-spheres vary in cognitive style is inconclusive.

• There is no clear evidence that exercis-ing a hemisphere of the brain is useful, so a "right-brain curriculum" is pointless. Popular ideas about the right and left brain have gone far beyond the actual research findings.

Key Ideas

Communication in the Nervous System

◆ Neurons are the basic communication links in the nervous system. They normally transmit a neural impulse (an electric current) along an axon to a synapse with another neuron.

◆ The neural impulse is a brief change in a neuron's electrical charge that moves along an axon. It is an all-or-none event. Neurons convey information about the strength of a stimulus by variations in their rate of firing.

◆ Action potentials trigger the release of chemicals called neurotransmitters that diffuse across a synapse to communicate with other neurons. Transmitters bind with receptors in the postsynaptic cell membrane, causing excitatory or inhibitory PSPs. A variety of neurotransmitters bind at specific sites according to a lock-and-key model.

◆ ACh plays a key role in muscular movement. Disturbances in the activity of the monoamine transmitters have been related to the development of depression and schizophrenia. GABA appears to be involved in the regulation of anxiety. Endorphins contribute to the relief of pain and perhaps to the experience of pleasure.

Organization of the Nervous System

◆ The nervous system can be divided into the central nervous system and the peripheral nervous system. The central nervous system consists of the brain and spinal cord.

◆ The peripheral nervous system consists of the nerves that lie outside the brain and spinal cord. It can be subdivided into the somatic nervous system, which connects to muscles and sensory receptors, and the autonomic nervous system, which connects to blood vessels, smooth muscles, and glands.

Looking Inside the Brain: Research Methods

◆ The EEG can record broad patterns of electrical activity in the brain. Lesioning involves destroying a piece of the brain. Another technique is electrical stimulation of areas in the brain in order to activate them. In recent years, new brain-imaging procedures have been developed, including CT scans, PET scans, and MRI scans.

The Brain and Behavior

◆ The brain has three major regions: the hindbrain, midbrain, and forebrain. Structures in the hindbrain and midbrain handle essential functions such as breathing, circulation, coordination of movement, and the rhythm of sleep and arousal.

◆ The forebrain includes many structures that handle higher functions. The thalamus is primarily a relay station. The hypothalamus is involved in the regulation of basic biological drives such as hunger and sex. The limbic system is a network of loosely connected structures involved in emotion, motivation, and memory.

◆ The cerebrum is the brain area implicated in most complex mental activities. The cortex is the cerebrum's convoluted outer layer, which is subdivided into occipital, parietal, temporal, and frontal lobes.

Right Brain/Left Brain: Cerebral Laterality

◆ The cerebrum is divided into right and left hemispheres connected by the corpus callosum. Studies of split-brain patients and perceptual asymmetries have revealed that the right and left halves of the brain each have unique talents, with the right and left hemispheres specialized to handle visual-spatial and language functions, respectively.

◆ Handedness is an obvious but puzzling aspect of human laterality that may be related to the functional asymmetry of the human brain. Among the correlates of left-handedness, the most dramatic and controversial is the apparent reduction in longevity discovered in our Featured Study.

The Endocrine System: Another Way to Communicate

◆ The endocrine system consists of the glands that secrete hormones, which are chemicals involved in the regulation of basic bodily processes. The control centers for the endocrine system are the hypothalamus and the pituitary gland.

Heredity and Behavior: Is It All in the Genes?

◆ The basic units of genetic transmission are genes housed on chromosomes. Most behavioral qualities appear to involve polygenic inheritance.

◆ Researchers assess hereditary influence through a variety of methods, including family studies, twin studies, adoption studies, and genetic mapping. Research indicates that most behavioral qualities are influenced by a complex interaction between heredity and environment.

Putting It in Perspective

◆ Three of the book's unifying themes stand out in this chapter. First, we saw how heredity interacts with experience to govern behavior. Second, the discussions of biological factors underlying schizophrenia highlighted the multifactorial causation of behavior. Third, we saw how innovations in research methods often lead to advances in knowledge, underscoring the empirical nature of psychology.

Application: Thinking Critically About the Concept of "Two Minds in One"

◆ The cerebral hemispheres *are* specialized for handling different cognitive tasks, but only to a degree, and people vary in their patterns of hemispheric specialization. Evidence for duality in consciousness divided along hemispheric lines is weak.

◆ Evidence on whether people vary in brainedness and whether the two hemispheres vary in cognitive style is inconclusive. There is no clear evidence that exercising a hemisphere of the brain is useful, so a "right-brain curriculum" is pointless. Popular ideas about the right and left brain have gone far beyond the actual research findings.

Key Terms

Absolute refractory period
Action potential
Adoption studies
Afferent nerve fibers
Agonist
Antagonist
Autonomic nervous system (ANS)
Axon
Behavioral genetics
Blood-brain barrier
Central nervous system (CNS)
Cerebral cortex
Cerebral hemispheres
Cerebral laterality
Cerebrospinal fluid (CSF)
Chromosomes
Corpus callosum
Dendrites
Dominant gene
Efferent nerve fibers
Electrical stimulation of the brain (ESB)
Electroencephalograph (EEG)
Endocrine system
Endorphins
Excitatory PSP
Family studies
Forebrain
Fraternal (dizygotic) twins
Genes
Genetic mapping
Genotype
Glia
Handedness
Heterozygous condition
Hindbrain
Homozygous condition
Hormones
Hypothalamus
Identical (monozygotic) twins
Inhibitory PSP

Interneurons
Lesioning
Limbic system
Midbrain
Motor neurons
Myelin sheath
Nerves
Neuromodulators
Neurons
Neurotransmitters
Parasympathetic division
Perceptual asymmetries
Peripheral nervous system
Phenotype
Pituitary gland
Polygenic traits
Postsynaptic potential (PSP)
Recessive gene
Resting potential
Sensory neurons
Soma
Somatic nervous system
Spatial summation
Split-brain surgery
Stereotaxic instrument
Sympathetic division
Synapse
Synaptic cleft
Temporal summation
Terminal buttons
Thalamus
Twin studies
Zygote

Key People

Alan Hodgkin and Andrew Huxley
James Olds and Peter Milner
Candace Pert and Solomon Snyder
Robert Plomin
Roger Sperry and Michael Gazzaniga

Practice Test

1. A neural impulse is initiated when a neuron's charge momentarily becomes less negative, or even positive. This event is called:
   A. an action potential.
   B. a resting potential.
   C. impulse facilitation.
   D. neuromodulation.

2. An inadequate supply of_____ in the brain has been implicted as a factor in the memory loss seen with Alzheimer's disease.
   A. dopamine
   B. acetylcholine
   C. serotonin
   D. norepinephrine

3. Alterations in activity at dopamine synapses have been implicated in the development of:
   A. anxiety.
   B. schizophrenia.
   C. Alzheimer's disease.
   D. nicotine addiction.

4. Jim just barely avoided a head-on collision on a narrow road. With heart pounding, hands shaking, and body perspiring, Jim recognizes that these are signs of the body's fight-or-flight response, which is controlled by the:
   A. empathetic division of the peripheral nervous system.
   B. parasympathetic division of the autonomic nervous system.
   C. somatic division of the peripheral nervous system.
   D. sympathetic division of the autonomic nervous system.

5. The hindbrain consists of the:
   A. endocrine system and the limbic system.
   B. reticular formation.
   C. thalamus, the hypothalamus, and the cerebrum.
   D. cerebellum, the medulla, and the pons.

6. The thalamus can be characterized as:
   A. a regulatory mechanism.
   B. the consciousness switch of the brain.
   C. a relay system.
   D. a bridge between the two cerebral hemispheres.

7. The _____ lobe is to hearing as the occipital lobe is to vision.
   A. frontal
   B. temporal
   C. parietal
   D. cerebellar

8. The scientist who won a Nobel prize for his work with split-brain patients is:
   A. Walter Cannon.
   B. Paul Broca.
   C. Roger Sperry.
   D. James Olds.

9. Sounds presented to the right ear are registered:
   A. only in the right hemisphere.
   B. only in the left hemisphere.
   C. more quickly in the right hemisphere.
   D. more quickly in the left hemisphere.

10. In people whose corpus callosums have not been severed, verbal stimuli are identified more quickly and more accurately:
    A. when sent to the right hemisphere first.
    B. when sent to the left hemisphere first.
    C. when presented to the left visual field.
    D. when presented auditorally rather than visually.

11. Hormones are to the endocrine system as _____ are to the nervous system.
    A. nerves
    B. synapses
    C. neurotransmitters
    D. action potentials

12. Jenny has brown hair and blue eyes and is 5'8" tall. What is being described is Jenny's:
    A. genotype.
    B. phenotype.
    C. somatotype.
    D. physiognomy.

13. Adopted children's similarity to their biological parents is generally attributed to _____; adopted children's similarity to their adoptive parents is generally attributed to _____.
    A. heredity; the environment
    B. the environment; heredity
    C. the environment; the environment
    D. heredity; heredity

14. Which of the following statements represents the most logical resolution of the nature-nurture controversy?
    A. Environment is most important, at least for those individuals who have a normal genotype.
    B. Heredity and environment interact to affect an individual's development.
    C. Heredity is most important, but a high-quality environment can make up for genetic defects.
    D. The environment is like a rubber band that stretches to meet the needs of an individual's genotype.

15. For which of the following assertions is the empirical evidence strongest?
    A. The two cerebral hemispheres are specialized to handle different types of cognitive tasks.
    B. People have a separate stream of consciousness in each hemisphere.
    C. Each hemisphere has its own cognitive style.
    D. Some people are right-brained, while others are left-brained.

Answers

1	A Page 77	6	C Page 94	11	C Page 107
2	B Page 81	7	B Page 97	12	B Page 110
3	B Page 82	8	C Page 100	13	A Pages 112–113
4	D Page 87	9	D Page 101	14	B Page 114
5	D Page 92	10	B Page 103	15	A Pages 116–118

4 SENSATION AND PERCEPTION

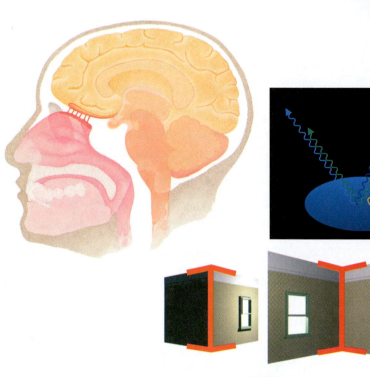

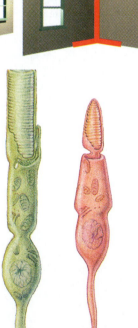

Take a look at the adjacent photo. What do you see?

You probably answered, "a rose" or "a flower." But is that what you really see? No, this isn't a trick question. Let's examine the odd case of "Dr. P." It shows that there's more to seeing than meets the eye.

Dr. P was an intelligent and distinguished music professor who began to exhibit some worrisome behaviors that seemed to be related to his vision. Sometimes he failed to recognize familiar students by sight, though he knew them instantly by the sound of their voices. Sometimes he acted as if he saw faces in inanimate objects, cordially greeting fire hydrants and parking meters as if they were children. On one occasion, reaching for what he thought was his hat, he took hold of his wife's head and tried to put it on! Except for these kinds of visual mistakes, Dr. P was a normal, talented man.

Ultimately Dr. P was referred to Oliver Sacks, a neurologist, for an examination. During one visit, Sacks handed Dr. P a fresh red rose to see whether he would recognize it. Dr. P took the rose as if he were being given a model of a geometric solid rather than a flower. "About six inches in length," Dr. P observed, "a convoluted red form with a linear green attachment."

"Yes," Sacks persisted, "and what do you think it is, Dr. P?"

"Not easy to say," the patient replied. "It lacks the simple symmetry of the Platonic solids . . ."

"Smell it," the neurologist suggested. Dr. P looked perplexed, as if being asked to smell symmetry, but he complied and brought the flower to his nose. Suddenly, his confusion cleared up. "Beautiful. An early rose. What a heavenly smell" (Sacks, 1987, pp. 13–14).

What accounted for Dr. P's strange inability to recognize faces and familiar objects by sight? There was nothing wrong with his eyes. He could readily spot a pin on the floor. If you're thinking that he must have had something wrong with his vision, look again at the photo of the rose. What you see *is* "a convoluted red form with a linear green attachment." It doesn't occur to you to describe it that way only because, without thinking about it, you instantly perceive that combination of form and color as a flower. This is precisely what Dr. P was unable to do. He could see perfectly well, but

he was losing the ability to assemble what he saw into a meaningful picture of the world. Technically, he suffered from a condition called *visual agnosia*, an inability to recognize objects through sight. As Sacks (1987) put it, "Visually, he was lost in a world of lifeless abstractions" (p. 15).

As Dr. P's case illustrates, without effective processing of sensory input, our familiar world can become a chaos of bewildering sensations. To acknowledge the need to both take in and process sensory information, psychologists distinguish between sensation and perception. ***Sensation*** **is the stimulation of sense organs.** ***Perception*** **is the selection, organization, and interpretation of sensory input.** Sensation involves the absorption of energy, such as light or sound waves, by sensory organs, such as the eyes and ears. Perception involves organizing and translating sensory input into something meaningful (see Figure 4.1). For example, when you look at the photo of the rose, your eyes are *sensing* the light reflected from the page, including areas of low reflectance where ink has been deposited in an irregular shape. What you *perceive,* however, is a picture of a rose.

The distinction between sensation and perception stands out in Dr. P's case of visual agnosia. His eyes were doing their job of registering sensory input and transmitting signals to the brain. However, damage in his brain interfered with his ability

Figure 4.1
The distinction between sensation and perception. Sensation involves the stimulation of sensory organs, whereas perception involves the processing and interpretation of sensory input. As this illustration shows, the two processes merge at the point where sensory receptors convert physical energy into neural impulses.

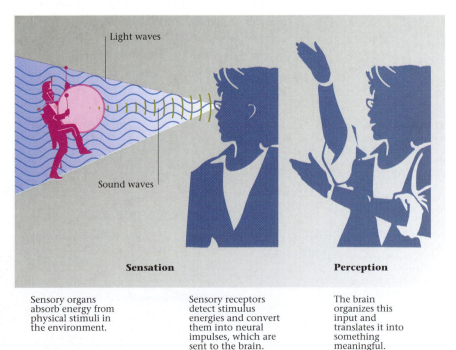

Sensation

Perception

Sensory organs absorb energy from physical stimuli in the environment.

Sensory receptors detect stimulus energies and convert them into neural impulses, which are sent to the brain.

The brain organizes this input and translates it into something meaningful.

to put these signals together into organized wholes. Thus, Dr. P's process of visual *sensation* was intact, but his process of visual *perception* was severely impaired.

Dr. P's case is unusual, of course. Normally, the processes of sensation and perception are difficult to separate because people automatically start organizing incoming sensory stimulation the moment it arrives. The distinction between sensation and perception has been useful in organizing theory and research, but in operation the two processes merge.

We'll begin our discussion of sensation and perception by examining some general concepts that are relevant to all the senses. Next, we'll examine individual senses, in each case beginning with the sensory aspects and working our way through to the perceptual aspects. The chapter's Application explores how principles of visual perception come into play in art and illusion.

"The method of just noticeable differences consists in determining how much the weights have to differ so that they can just be discriminated."

GUSTAV FECHNER

PSYCHOPHYSICS: BASIC CONCEPTS AND ISSUES

As you may recall from Chapter 1, the first experimental psychologists were interested mainly in sensation and perception. They called their area of interest *psychophysics*—**the study of how physical stimuli are translated into psychological experience**. A particularly important contributor to psychophysics was Gustav Fechner, who published a seminal work on the subject in 1860. Fechner was a German scientist working at the University of Leipzig, where Wilhelm Wundt later founded the first formal laboratory and journal devoted to psychological research. Unlike Wundt, Fechner was not a "campaigner" interested in establishing psychology as an independent discipline. However, his groundbreaking research laid the foundation that Wundt built upon.

Thresholds: Looking for Limits

Sensation begins with a *stimulus*, any detectable input from the environment. What counts as detectable, though, depends on who or what is doing the detecting. For instance, you might not be able to detect a weak odor that is readily apparent to your dog. Thus, Fechner wanted to know: For any given sense, what is the weakest detectable stimulus? For example, what is the minimum amount of light needed for a person to see that there is light?

Implicit in Fechner's question is a concept central to psychophysics: the threshold. **A *threshold* is a dividing point between energy levels that do and do not have a detectable effect.** For example, hardware stores sell a gadget with a photocell that automatically turns a lamp on when a room gets dark. The level of light intensity at which the gadget clicks on is its threshold.

An *absolute threshold* for a specific type of sensory input is the minimum amount of stimulation that an organism can detect. Absolute thresholds define the boundaries of an organism's sensory capabilities. Fechner and his contemporaries used a variety of methods to determine humans' absolute threshold for detecting light. They discovered that absolute thresholds are anything but absolute. When lights of varying intensity are flashed at a subject, there is no single stimulus intensity at which the subject jumps from no detection to completely accurate detection. Instead, as stimulus intensity increases, subjects' probability of responding to stimuli *gradually* increases, as shown in red in Figure 4.2. Thus, researchers had to arbitrarily define the absolute threshold as the stimulus intensity *detected 50% of the time*.

Using this definition, investigators found that under ideal conditions, human abilities to detect weak stimuli are greater than appreciated. Some concrete examples of the absolute thresholds for various senses can be seen in Table 4.1. For example, on a clear, dark night, in the absence of other distracting lights, you could see the light of a candle burning 30 miles in the distance! Of course, we're talking about ideal conditions—you would have to go out to the middle of nowhere to

Figure 4.2
The absolute threshold. If absolute thresholds were truly absolute, then at threshold intensity the probability of detecting a stimulus would jump from 0 to 100%, as graphed here in blue. In reality, the chances of detecting a stimulus increase gradually with stimulus intensity, as shown in red. Accordingly, an "absolute" threshold is defined as the intensity level at which the probability of detection is 50%.

find the darkness required to put this assertion to a suitable test.

Weighing the Differences: The JND

Fechner was also interested in how sensitive people are to differences between stimuli. **A *just noticeable difference (JND)* is the smallest difference in the amount of stimulation that a specific sense can detect.** JNDs are close cousins of absolute thresholds. In fact, an absolute threshold is simply the just noticeable difference from nothing (no stimulus input).

You might think that the JND would always have the same value for any given sense. For instance, what do you suppose is the smallest difference in weight that you can detect by lifting different objects? An ounce? Two ounces? Six ounces? As it turns out, the answer varies. The JND is greater for heavy objects than for light ones. However, the smallest detectable difference is a fairly stable *proportion* of the weight of the original object.

This principle was first demonstrated by Fechner's brother-in-law, Ernst Weber, and came to be known as Weber's law. **Weber's law states that the size of a just noticeable difference is a constant proportion of the size of the initial stimulus.** This constant proportion is called the *Weber fraction*. Weber's law applies not only to weight perception but to all the senses. However, different fractions apply to different types of sensory input, as you can see in Table 4.2. For example, the Weber fraction for lifting weights is approximately 1/30. That means that you should be just able to detect the difference between a 30-ounce weight and a 31-ounce weight (the JND for 30 ounces is 1 ounce). If you started with a 90-ounce weight, however, you would not be able to tell the difference between it and a 91-ounce weight. Why? Because the JND for 90 ounces is 3 ounces (1/30 of 90). In general, then, as stimuli increase in magnitude, the JND becomes larger. Weber's law does not apply with perfect precision, but it provides a good approximation of people's ability to detect differences between sensory stimuli (Engen, 1971).

Psychophysical Scaling

If one light has twice the energy of another, do you necessarily perceive it as twice as bright? When asked to make this kind of judgment, you are being asked to *scale* the magnitude of sensory experiences. Although it might seem that people's sensory experiences would correspond exactly to the differences in the stimuli that cause them, the truth turns out to be otherwise. In his work on the

TABLE 4.1 EXAMPLES OF ABSOLUTE THRESHOLDS

Sense	Absolute Threshold
Vision	A candle flame seen at 30 miles on a dark, clear night
Hearing	The tick of a watch under quiet conditions at 20 feet
Taste	One teaspoon of sugar in two gallons of water
Smell	One drop of perfume diffused into the entire volume of a six-room apartment
Touch	The wing of a fly falling on your cheek from a distance of 1 centimeter

Source: Galanter (1962)

TABLE 4.2 REPRESENTATIVE (MIDDLE-RANGE) VALUES FOR THE WEBER FRACTION FOR VARIOUS SENSES

Sense	Sensation Measured	Weber Fraction
Vision	Brightness, white light	1/60
Kinesthesis	Lifted weights	1/30
Pain	Thermally aroused on skin	1/30
Hearing	Tone of middle pitch and moderate loudness	1/10
Pressure	Cutaneous pressure "spot"	1/7
Smell	Odor of India rubber	1/4

Source: Data from Geldard (1962)

scaling of sensory experiences, Fechner used the JND as his unit of measurement. Reasoning that the JND is the smallest unit of sensation, he represented the perceived magnitude of a sensation by how many JNDs it was above absolute threshold.

Figure 4.3 (on page 126) shows what Fechner found when he related the strength of a stimulus (plotted on the horizontal axis) to the magnitude of sensation (plotted in JNDs on the vertical axis). His finding, known today as **Fechner's law, states that the magnitude of a sensory experience is proportional to the number of JNDs that the stimulus causing the experience is above absolute threshold.** In Figure 4.3, the size of the upward jumps stays the same, because each JND is assumed to have the same sensory effect, but the horizontal steps become wider because larger and larger increases in stimulus intensity are required to produce each JND.

An important ramification of Fechner's law is that constant increments in stimulus intensity produce smaller and smaller increases in the *perceived* magnitude of sensation. This principle is easy to illustrate. Imagine that you're in a dark room with

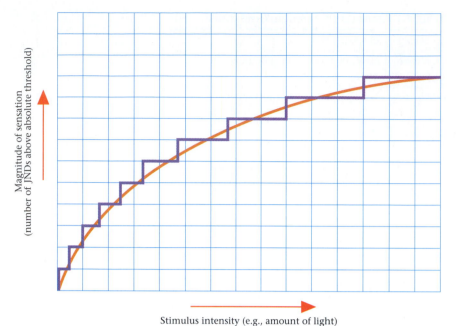

Stimulus intensity (e.g., amount of light)

Figure 4.3
Psychophysical scaling.
Fechner reasoned that a "just noticeable difference" could be considered a unit of sensation and mapped out the relationship between physical changes in stimulus intensity and measured changes in the magnitude of sensation. Each upward jump in the figure is the same because it represents one sensation unit. Wider and wider "steps" are associated with each jump because larger and larger increases in physical intensity are needed to produce them.

a single lamp that has three bulbs of the same wattage. You turn a switch, and one bulb lights. After a dark room, the difference is striking. Turn again, and a second bulb comes on. The amount of light is doubled, but the room does not seem twice as bright. When you turn the third bulb on, it adds just as much light as the second, but you barely notice the difference. Thus, three equal increases in stimulus intensity (the amount of light) produce progressively smaller differences in the magnitude of sensation (perceived brightness).

The merit of Fechner's approach to scaling sensation was eventually questioned by S. S. Stevens (1957, 1975). His approach to scaling, called *magnitude estimation*, simply involved asking subjects to assign numbers to stimuli on the basis of how intense they appeared to be. Using this approach,

he found that Fechner's law does not apply equally well to all sensory dimensions. Stevens showed that for some dimensions the shape of the curve relating stimulus intensity to perceived magnitude varies dramatically from Fechner's curve. Most modern psychophysicists believe that magnitude estimation is the best way to map the relations between stimulus intensity and sensory experience, but some of the details of this process continue to be debated (Krueger, 1989). It is clear, however, that people's inner "measurements" of sensory experiences are not a simple linear function of the physical intensity of the stimuli. What all this means is that perceptions can't be measured on absolute scales. In the domain of sensory experience virtually everything is relative.

Signal-Detection Theory

The idea that everything is relative applies not only to sensory scaling but to sensory thresholds as well. *Signal-detection theory* proposes that the **detection of stimuli involves decision processes as well as sensory processes, which are both influenced by a variety of factors besides stimulus intensity** (Egan, 1975; Swets, Tanner, & Birdsall, 1961).

Imagine that you are monitoring a radar screen, looking for signs of possible enemy aircraft. Your mission is to detect signals that represent approaching airplanes as quickly and as accurately as possible. In this situation, there are four possible outcomes, which are outlined in Figure 4.4: *hits* (detecting signals when they are present), *misses* (failing to detect signals when they are present), *false alarms* (detecting signals when they are not present), and *correct rejections* (not detecting signals when they are absent). Given these possibilities, signal-detection theory attempts to account for the influence of decision-making processes on stimulus detection. In detecting weak signals on the radar screen, you will often have to decide whether a faint signal represents an airplane or whether you're just imagining that it does. Your responses will depend in part on the *criterion* you set for how sure you must feel before you react. Setting this criterion involves higher mental processes rather than raw sensation and depends on your expectations and on the consequences of missing a signal or of reporting a false alarm.

According to signal-detection theory, your performance will also depend on the level of "noise" in the system. Noise comes from all the irrelevant stimuli in the environment and the neural activity they elicit. Noise is analogous to the background

Figure 4.4
Possible outcomes in signal detection theory.
Four outcomes are possible in attempting to detect the presence of weak signals. The criterion you set for how confident you want to feel before reporting a signal will affect your responding. For example, if you require high confidence before reporting a signal, you will minimize false alarms, but you'll be more likely to miss some signals.

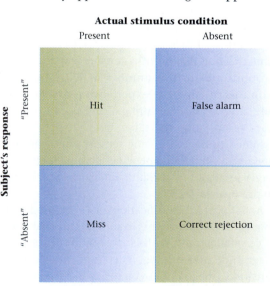

Actual stimulus condition

	Present	Absent
"Present"	Hit	False alarm
"Absent"	Miss	Correct rejection

Subject's response

static on a radio station. The more noise in the system, the harder it will be for you to pick up a weak signal. Variations in noise provide another reason why sensory thresholds depend on more than just the intensity of stimuli.

Signal-detection theory grew out of practical efforts to understand and improve the monitoring of complex, modern equipment, such as radar. However, the theory applies equally well to a broad range of everyday experiences involving the registration of sensory inputs. Suppose, for instance, you are eagerly awaiting the delivery of a pizza at a loud, raucous party. In this situation, you want to detect a signal (the doorbell) in the midst of background noise (music, people talking), and your criteria for "hearing" the doorbell will change as the expected time of delivery approaches.

The key point is that signal-detection theory replaces Fechner's sharp threshold with the concept of "detectability." Detectability is measured in terms of probability and depends on decision-making processes as well as sensory processes. In comparison to classical models of psychophysics, signal-detection theory is better equipped to explain some of the complexities of perceived experience in the real world.

Perception Without Awareness

The concepts of thresholds and detectability lie at the core of an interesting debate: Can sensory stimuli that fall beneath the threshold of awareness still influence behavior? This issue centers on the concept of *subliminal perception*—the **registration of sensory input without conscious awareness** (*limen* is another term for threshold, so *subliminal* means below threshold). This question might be just another technical issue in the normally staid world of psychophysics, except that subliminal perception has become tied up in highly charged controversies relating to money, sex, religion, and rock music.

The controversy began in 1957 when an executive named James Vicary placed hidden messages such as "Eat popcorn" in a film showing at a theater in New Jersey. The messages were superimposed on only a few frames of the film, so that they flashed by quickly and imperceptibly. Nonetheless, Vicary reported to the press that popcorn sales increased by 58%, and a public outcry ensued (McConnell, Cutler, & McNeil, 1958). Since then, Brian Wilson Key, a former advertising executive, has written several books claiming that sexual words and drawings are embedded subliminally in magazine advertisements to elicit favor-

Figure 4.5
Subliminal advertising: Is it all in the eye of the beholder? If you look closely at the ice cubes in this ad, you will see the word SEX spelled out. Former advertising executive Brian Wilson Key (1973) claims advertisers routinely place subliminal stimuli in their ads. Marketing companies maintain that people are merely reading things into their ads, much like you might see familiar forms in clouds. Although subliminal perception appears to be a genuine phenomenon, Thomas Creed (1987) has pinpointed a host of fallacies in Key's analysis, which he characterizes as pseudoscience.

able unconscious reactions from consumers (Key, 1973, 1976, 1980). One such advertisement discussed by Key is shown in Figure 4.5. If you look closely, you'll find the word SEX embedded in the ice cubes. Taking the sexual manipulation theme a step further, entrepreneurs are now marketing music audiotapes containing subliminal messages that are supposed to help people seduce unsuspecting listeners. Furthermore, according to *Time* magazine, subliminal self-help tapes intended to facilitate weight loss, better sleep, improved memory, and the like have become a $50 million industry. Religious overtones were added to this controversy in the 1980s when subliminal messages encouraging devil worship were allegedly found in rock music played *backward* (Vokey & Read, 1985).

Can listening to Led Zeppelin's "Stairway to Heaven" promote Satanic rituals? Can your sexual urges be manipulated by messages hidden under music? Can advertisers influence your product preferences with subliminal stimuli? Those who are concerned about subliminal messages assert that such messages are likely to be persuasive because people supposedly are defenseless against appeals operating below their threshold of awareness. How justified are these fears? Research on subliminal perception has been sporadic, because scientists initially dismissed the entire idea as preposterous. However, empirical studies have begun to accumulate in the last decade or so.

For example, Jon Krosnick and his colleages (1992) set out to determine whether subjects' attitudes toward a target person could be shaped without their awareness. Participants were asked to attentively view a series of slides showing a target person going about her daily activities. These slides were preceded by very brief (13/1000 of a second) subliminal presentations of photos expected to arouse positive emotions (a bridal couple, a pair of kittens, and so on) or negative emotions (a skull, a werewolf, and so on). After the slide presentations, subjects rated the target person on various dimensions. The researchers found statistically significant differences in participants' attitudes toward the target person that reflected the type of subliminal photos they had seen. Thus, subliminal inputs produced measurable, although small, effects in subjects who subsequently reported that they did not consciously register the stimuli.

Since the 1980s, a host of other studies have also found support for the existence of subliminal perception (Greenwald, 1992). Using diverse methodological and conceptual approaches, researchers examining a variety of phenomena, such as semantic priming (Marcel, 1983), implicit memory (Schacter, 1987), memory illusions (Jacoby & Whitehouse, 1989), subliminal affective conditioning (Niedenthal, 1990), subliminal mere exposure effects (R. Bornstein, 1992), nonconscious learning (Lewicki, Hill, & Czyzewska, 1992), and subliminal psychodynamic activation (Weinberger, 1992), have found evidence that perception without awareness *can* take place. Hence, the dominant view today is that subliminal perception is a genuine phenomenon, amenable to, and worthy of, experimental investigation (Loftus & Klinger, 1992).

So, should we be worried about the threat of subliminal persuasion? The research to date suggests that there is little reason for concern. The effects of subliminal stimuli turn out to be nearly as subliminal as the stimuli themselves. Subliminal stimulation generally produces weak effects (R. Bornstein, 1989; Greenwald, 1992; Kihlstrom, Barnhardt, & Tataryn, 1992). These effects can be detected only by very precise measurement, under carefully controlled laboratory conditions, in which subjects are asked to focus their undivided attention on visual or auditory materials that contain the subliminal stimuli. Although these effects are theoretically interesting, they appear unlikely to have much practical importance.

Indeed, when researchers have attempted to move beyond demonstrating the existence of subliminal perception to look at its practical effects in the real world, the results have not been impressive. For example, Greenwald and associates (1991) examined the efficacy of subliminal self-help tapes designed to improve memory or self-esteem. Over 200 subjects listened to the tapes regularly for a month. Their self-esteem and memory performance were measured at the beginning and again at the end of the study. No improvements in either self-esteem or memory were apparent on these measures. Curiously, though, when subjects were asked whether the tapes had produced any improvement in their self-esteem or memory, about half said yes. Thus, many people subjectively felt—presumably because of their positive expectations—that the tapes had helped them, when in reality, the tapes had no effects. This *placebo effect* probably explains why a great many people continue to tout the benefits of subliminal self-help tapes that have no real value.

In sum, there is no evidence that subliminal stimuli can lead people to buy specific products, abandon their sexual inhibitions, become Satan worshippers, or improve themselves. Research has not bolstered the idea that persuasive efforts operating beneath the surface of conscious awareness are especially powerful. More research on the manipulative potential of subliminal persuasion is needed, but so far there is no cause for alarm.

Sensory Adaptation

The process of sensory adaptation is yet another factor that influences registration of sensory input. **Sensory adaptation is a gradual decline in sensitivity to prolonged stimulation.** For example, let's say you find that the garbage in your kitchen has started to smell. If you stay in the kitchen without removing the garbage, the stench will soon start to fade. In reality, the stimulus intensity of the odor is stable, but with continued exposure, your *sensitivity* to it decreases. Sensory adaptation is a pervasive aspect of everyday life. When you put on your clothes in the morning, you feel them initially, but the sensation quickly fades. Similarly, if you jump reluctantly into a pool of cold water, you'll probably find that the water temperature feels fine in a few moments after you *adapt* to it.

Sensory adaptation is an automatic, built-in process that keeps people tuned in to the *changes* rather than the *constants* in their sensory input. It allows people to ignore the obvious. After all, you don't need constant confirmation that your clothes are still on. But, like most organisms, people are interested in changes in their environment that may signal threats to safety. Sensory adaptation shows again that there is no one-to-one correspondence between sensory input and sensory experience.

The general points we've reviewed so far begin to suggest how complex the relationships are between the world outside and people's perceived experience of it. As we review each of the principal sensory systems in detail, we'll see repeatedly that people's experience of the world depends on both the physical stimuli they encounter and their active processing of stimulus inputs. We begin our exploration of the senses with vision—the sense that most people think of as nearly synonymous with a direct perception of reality. The case is actually quite different, as you'll see.

Recap of Key Points

• Psychophysicists use a variety of methods to relate sensory inputs to subjective perception. They have found that absolute thresholds are not really absolute.

• Weber's law states that the size of a just noticeable difference is a constant proportion of the size of the initial stimulus. Fechner's law asserts that larger and larger increases in stimulus intensity are required to produce just noticeable differences in the magnitude of sensation.

• According to signal-detection theory, the detection of sensory inputs is influenced by noise in the system and by decision-making strategies. Signal-detection theory replaces Fechner's sharp threshold with the concept of detectability and emphasizes that factors besides stimulus intensity influence detectability.

• In recent years, a host of researchers, using very different conceptual approaches, have demonstrated that perception can occur without awareness. However, research indicates that the effects of subliminal perception are relatively weak and of little or no practical concern. Prolonged stimulation may lead to sensory adaptation, which involves a reduction in sensitivity to constant stimulation.

OUR SENSE OF SIGHT: THE VISUAL SYSTEM

"Seeing is believing." Good ideas are "bright," and a good explanation is "illuminating." This section is an "overview." Do you see the point? As these common expressions show, humans are visual animals. People rely heavily on their sense of sight, and they virtually equate it with what is trustworthy (seeing is believing). Although it is taken for granted, you'll see (there it is again) that the human visual system is amazingly complex. Furthermore, as in all sensory domains, what people "sense" and what they "perceive" may be quite different.

The Stimulus: Light 3a

For people to see, there must be light. *Light* is a form of electromagnetic radiation that travels as a wave, moving, naturally enough, at the speed of light. As Figure 4.6(a) on page 130 shows, light waves vary in *amplitude* (height) and in *wavelength* (the distance between peaks). Amplitude affects mainly the perception of brightness, while wavelength affects mainly the perception of color. The lights humans normally see are mixtures of different wavelengths. Hence, light can also vary in its *purity* (how varied the mix is). Purity influences perception of the saturation, or richness, of colors. Saturation is difficult to describe, but if you glance at Figure 4.7 (on page 130), you'll find it clearly illustrated. Of course, most objects do not emit light, they reflect it (the sun, lamps, and fireflies being some exceptions).

What most people call light includes only the wavelengths that humans can see. But as Figure 4.6(c) shows, the visible spectrum is only a slim portion of the total range of wavelengths. Vision is a filter that permits people to sense only a fraction of the real world. Other animals have different capabilities and so live in a quite different visual world. For example, many insects can see shorter wavelengths than humans can see, in the *ultraviolet* spectrum, whereas many fish and reptiles can see longer wavelengths, in the *infrared* spectrum. Although the sense of sight depends on light waves, for people to *see*, incoming visual input must be converted into neural impulses that are sent to the brain. Let's investigate how this transformation is accomplished.

The Eye: A Living Optical Instrument 3a

The eyes serve two main purposes: they channel light to the neural tissue that receives it, called the *retina*, and they house that tissue. The structure of the eye is shown in Figure 4.8 on page 131. Each eye is a living optical instrument that creates an image of the visual world on the light-sensitive retina lining its inside back surface.

Light enters the eye through a transparent

Figure 4.6
Light, the physical stimulus for vision. (**a**) Light waves vary in amplitude and wavelength. (**b**) Within the spectrum of visible light, amplitude (corresponding to physical intensity) affects mainly the experience of brightness. Wavelength affects mainly the experience of color, and purity is the key determinant of saturation. (**c**) If white light (such as sunlight) passes through a prism, the prism separates the light into its component wavelengths, creating a rainbow of colors. However, visible light is only the narrow band of wavelengths to which human eyes happen to be sensitive.

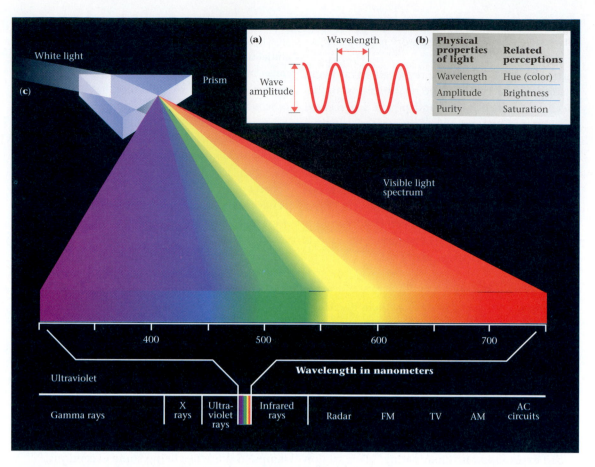

(b) Physical properties of light	Related perceptions
Wavelength	Hue (color)
Amplitude	Brightness
Purity	Saturation

"window" at the front, the *cornea*. The cornea and the crystalline *lens*, located behind it, form an upside-down image of objects on the retina. It might seem disturbing that the image is upside down, but the brain knows the rule for relating positions on the retina to the corresponding positions in the world.

The *lens* is the transparent eye structure that focuses the light rays falling on the retina. The lens is made up of relatively soft tissue, capable of adjustments that facilitate a process called accommodation. *Accommodation* occurs when the curvature of the lens adjusts to alter visual focus. When you focus on a close object, the lens of your eye gets fatter (rounder) to give you a clear image. When you focus on distant objects, the lens flattens out to give you a better image of them.

A number of common visual deficiencies are caused by focusing problems or by defects in the

lens (Guyton, 1991). For example, **in *nearsightedness*, close objects are seen clearly but distant objects appear blurry** because the focus of light from distant objects falls a little short of the retina (see Figure 4.9 on page 134). This focusing problem occurs when the cornea or lens bends light too much, or when the eyeball is too long. **In *farsightedness*, distant objects are seen clearly but close objects appear blurry** because the focus of light from close objects falls behind the retina. This focusing problem typically occurs when the eyeball is too short. A *cataract* is a lens that is clouded. This defect occurs mainly in older age groups, affecting three out of four people over the age of 65.

The eye can make adjustments to alter the amount of light reaching the retina. The *iris* is the colored ring of muscle surrounding the *pupil,* or black center of the eye. **The *pupil* is the opening in the center of the iris that helps regulate the amount of light passing into the rear chamber of the eye.** When the pupil constricts, it lets less light into the eye, but it sharpens the image falling on the retina. When the pupil dilates (opens), it lets more light in, but the image is less sharp. In bright light, the pupils constrict to take advantage of the sharpened image. But in dim light, the

Figure 4.7
Saturation. Variations in saturation are difficult to describe, but you can see examples for two colors here.

Saturation ➡

Figure 4.8

The human eye. Light passes through the cornea, pupil, and lens and falls on the light-sensitive surface of the retina, where images of objects are reflected upside down. The closeup shows the several layers of cells in the retina. The cells closest to the back of the eye (the rods and cones) are the receptor cells that actually detect light. The intervening layers of cells receive signals from the rods and cones and form circuits that begin the process of analyzing incoming information before it is sent to the brain. These cells feed into many optic fibers, all of which head toward the "hole" in the retina where the optic nerve leaves the eye—the point known as the optic disk (which corresponds to the blind spot).

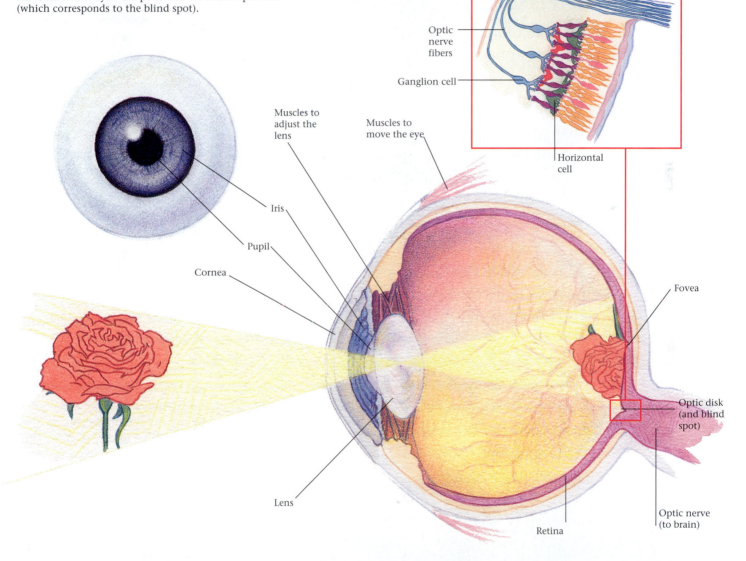

pupils dilate; image sharpness is sacrificed to allow more light to fall on the retina so that more remains visible.

The Retina: The Brain's Envoy in the Eye

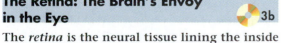 3b

The *retina* is the neural tissue lining the inside back surface of the eye; it absorbs light, processes images, and sends visual information to the brain. You may be surprised to learn that the retina *processes* images. But it's a piece of the central nervous system that happens to be located in the eyeball. Much as the spinal cord is a complicated extension of the brain (see Chapter 3), the retina is the brain's envoy in the eye. Although the retina is only a paper-thin sheet of neural tissue, it contains a complex network of specialized cells arranged in layers, as shown in the inset in Figure 4.8.

The axons that run from the retina to the brain converge at the *optic disk,* a hole in the retina where the optic nerve fibers exit the eye. Since

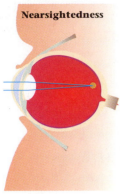

Nearsightedness

Farsightedness

Figure 4.9
Nearsightedness and farsightedness. The pictures on the left simulate how a scene might look to near-sighted and farsighted people. Nearsightedness occurs because light from distant objects focuses in front of the retina. Farsightedness is due to the opposite situation—light from close objects focuses behind the retina.

Figure 4.10
Demonstration of the blind spot. Close your right eye and stare steadily with your left eye at the approaching car. Vary the distance from the picture to your eye by moving the book slowly toward or away from you. If you're careful not to let your eye wander, at some point the stop sign will disappear. Its image will have fallen on your blind spot.

the optic disk is a *hole* in the retina, you cannot see the part of an image that falls on it. It is therefore known as the *blind spot.* You may not be aware that you have a blind spot in each eye (see Figure 4.10), as each normally compensates for the blind spot of the other.

Visual Receptors: Rods and Cones

The retina contains millions of receptor cells that are sensitive to light. Surprisingly, these receptors are located in the innermost layer of the retina. Hence, light must pass through several layers of cells before it gets to the receptors that actually detect it. Surprisingly, only about 10% of the light arriving at the cornea reaches these receptors (Leibovic, 1990). The retina contains two types of receptors, *rods* and *cones.* Their names are based on their shapes, as rods are elongated and cones are stubbier (see Figure 4.11a). Rods outnumber cones by a huge margin, about 125 million to 6.4 million (Pugh, 1988).

Cones **are specialized visual receptors that play a key role in daylight vision and color vision.** The cones handle most of our daytime vision, because bright lights dazzle the rods. The special sensitivities of cones also allow them to play a major role in the perception of color. However, cones do not respond well to dim light, which is why you don't see color very well in low illumination. Nonetheless, cones provide better *visual acuity*—that is, sharpness and precise detail—than rods. Cones are concentrated most heavily in the center of the retina and quickly fall off in density toward its periphery (see Figure 4.11b). **The *fovea* is a tiny spot in the center of the retina that contains only cones; visual acuity is greatest at this spot.** When you want to see something sharply, you usually move your eyes to center the object in the fovea.

Rods **are specialized visual receptors that play a key role in night vision and peripheral vision.** Rods handle night vision because they are more sensitive than cones to dim light. They handle the lion's share of peripheral vision because they greatly outnumber cones in the periphery of the retina. The density of the rods is greatest just outside the fovea and gradually decreases toward the periphery of the retina (see Figure 4.11b). Because of the distribution of rods, when you want to see a faintly illuminated object in the dark, it's best to look slightly above or below the place it should be. Averting your gaze this way moves the image from the cone-filled fovea, which requires more light, to the rod-dominated area just outside the fovea,

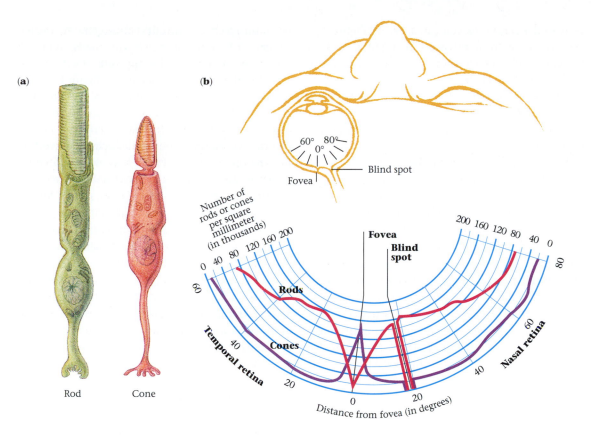

(a)

Rod Cone

(b)

60° 80°
0°

Blind spot

Fovea

Number of rods or cones per square millimeter (in thousands)

0 40 80 120 160 200

Fovea
Blind spot

200 160 120 80 40 0

Rods

Temporal retina

Cones

Nasal retina

0 20
Distance from fovea (in degrees)

Figure 4.11
The distribution of rods and cones. (a) The names for rods and cones are based on their shape. As you can see here, rods are a little more elongated and cones are stubbier. **(b)** This chart shows how rods and cones are distributed in the retina. The eye on top shows some of the locations (in degrees relative to the fovea) that are listed along the bottom of the chart. As the purple graph shows, most of the cones are concentrated in the fovea. The density of the rods, graphed in red, is greatest just outside each side of the fovea and then declines toward the periphery. There are no receptors of either type in the blind spot, which is why it is the blind spot. (Source: Adapted from Lindsay & Norman, 1977)

which requires less light. This trick of averted vision is well known to astronomers, who use it to study dim objects viewed through the eyepiece of a telescope.

Dark and Light Adaptation

You've probably noticed that when you enter a dark theater on a bright day, you stumble about almost blindly. But within minutes you can make your way about quite well in the dim light. This adjustment is called *dark adaptation*—**the process in which the eyes become more sensitive to light in low illumination.** Figure 4.12 maps out the course of this process. The declining absolute thresholds over time indicate that you require less and less light to see. Dark adaptation is virtually complete in about 30 minutes, with considerable progress occurring in the first 10 minutes. The curve (in Figure 4.12) that charts this progress consists of two segments because cones adapt more rapidly than rods (Walraven et al., 1990).

When you emerge from a dark theater on a sunny day, you need to squint to ward off the overwhelming brightness, and the reverse of dark adaptation occurs. *Light adaptation* is the process whereby the eyes become less sensitive to light in high illumination. As with dark adaptation, light adaptation improves your visual acuity under the prevailing circumstances. Both types of

adaptation are due in large part to chemical changes in the rods and cones, but neural changes in the receptors and elsewhere in the retina also contribute (Frumkes, 1990).

Information Processing in the Retina

In processing visual input, the retina transforms a pattern of light falling onto it into a very different representation of the visual scene. Light striking the retina's receptors (rods and cones) triggers neural signals that pass into the intricate network of

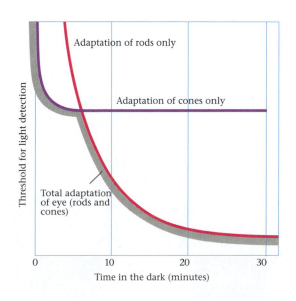

Adaptation of rods only

Adaptation of cones only

Total adaptation of eye (rods and cones)

Threshold for light detection

0   10   20   30
Time in the dark (minutes)

Figure 4.12
The process of dark adaptation. The declining thresholds over time indicate that your visual sensitivity is improving, as less and less light is required to see. Visual sensitivity improves markedly during the first 5 to 10 minutes after entering a dark room, as the eye's bright-light receptors (the cones) rapidly adapt to low light levels. However, the cones' adaptation, which is plotted in purple, soon reaches its limit, and further improvement comes from the rods' adaptation, which is plotted in red. The rods adapt more slowly than the cones, but they are capable of far greater visual sensitivity in low levels of light.

cells in the retina. As you can see from Figure 4.8, signals move from receptors to bipolar cells to ganglion cells, which in turn send impulses along the *optic nerve*—a collection of axons that connect the eye with the brain. These axons, which depart from the eye through the optic disk, carry visual information, encoded as a stream of neural impulses, to the brain.

A great deal of complex information processing goes on in the retina itself before visual signals are sent to the brain. Ultimately, the information from about 130 million rods and cones converges to travel along "only" 1 million axons in the optic nerve (Slaughter, 1990). This means that the bipolar and ganglion cells in the intermediate layers of the retina integrate and compress signals from many receptors. The collection of rod and cone receptors that funnel signals to a particular visual cell in the retina (or ultimately in the brain) make up that cell's *receptive field*. Thus, **the *receptive field of a visual cell is* the retinal area that, when stimulated, affects the firing of that cell.**

Receptive fields in the retina come in a variety of shapes and sizes. Particularly common are circular fields with a center-surround arrangement (Tessier-Lavigne, 1991). In these receptive fields, light falling in the center has the opposite effect of light falling in the surrounding area (see Figure 4.13). For example, the rate of firing of a visual cell might be *increased* by light in the *center* of its receptive field and *decreased* by light in the *surrounding area*, as Figure 4.13 shows. Other visual cells may work in just the opposite way. Either way, when receptive fields are stimulated, retinal cells send signals both toward the brain and *laterally* (sideways) toward nearby visual cells. These lateral signals, carried by the horizontal and amacrine cells (see Figure 4.8 inset), allow visual cells in the retina to have interactive effects on each other.

Lateral antagonism (also known as lateral inhibition) is the most basic of these interactive effects. ***Lateral antagonism* occurs when neural activity in a cell opposes activity in surrounding cells.** Lateral antagonism is responsible for the opposite effects that occur when light falls on the inner versus outer portions of center-surround receptive fields. It was first described for a simple eye, in the horseshoe crab, by H. K.

Figure 4.13
Receptive fields in the retina and lateral antagonism. Visual cells' receptive fields in the retina are often circular with a center-surround arrangement, so that light striking the center of the field produces the opposite result of light striking the surround. In the receptive field depicted here, light in the center produces excitatory effects (symbolized by blue at the synapse) and increased firing in the visual cell, whereas light in the surround produces inhibitory effects (symbolized by red at the synapse) and decreased firing. However, the arrangement in other receptive fields may be just the opposite. Note that no light (**a**) and light in both center and surround (**d**) produce similar baseline rates of firing; lateral antagonism makes this visual cell more sensitive to contrast than to absolute levels of light. In (**b**) and (**c**) there is a contrast between the light falling on the center versus the surround, producing increased or decreased activity in the visual cell.

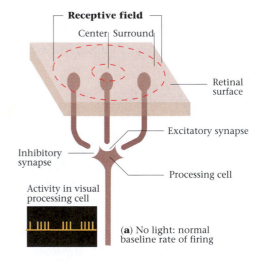

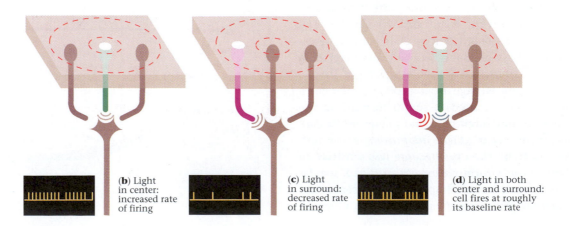

Hartline and Floyd Ratliff (1957). Lateral antagonism allows the retina to compare the light falling in a specific area (local lighting) with the general lighting. This means that the visual system can compute the *relative* amount of light at a point instead of reacting to *absolute* levels of light. This attention to *contrast* is exactly what is needed if a photograph, for instance, is to look the same regardless of the lighting conditions. Lateral antagonism can occur in various stages of visual processing: in two different layers of the retina, and again later, when signals reach the brain (Levine & Shefner, 1991). If you look at Figure 4.14, you will experience a perceptual effect attributable to lateral antagonism in the ganglion cells of the retina.

Vision and the Brain 3c

Light falls on the eye, but you see with your brain. Although the retina does an unusual amount of information processing for a sensory organ, visual input is meaningless until it is processed in the brain.

Visual Pathways to the Brain

How does visual information get to the brain? Axons leaving the back of each eye form the optic nerves, which travel to the **optic chiasm—the point at which the optic nerves from the inside half of each eye cross over and then project to the opposite half of the brain.** This arrangement ensures that signals from both eyes go to both hemispheres of the brain. Thus, as Figure 4.15 on page 136 shows, axons from the left half of each retina carry signals to the left side of the brain, and axons from the right half of each retina carry information to the right side of the brain.

After reaching the optic chiasm, the optic nerve fibers diverge along two pathways. The main pathway projects into the thalamus, the brain's major relay station. Here, the axons from the retinas finally synapse in the *lateral geniculate nucleus* (LGN). Visual signals are processed in the LGN and then distributed to areas in the occipital lobe that make up the *primary visual cortex* (see Figure 4.15). After the initial cortical processing of visual input takes place here, signals may be shuttled to the temporal and parietal lobes of the cortex for additional processing (Woolsey, 1981). The second visual pathway leaving the optic chiasm branches off to an area in the midbrain called the *superior colliculus* before traveling through the thalamus and on to the occipital lobe. However, the second pathway projects into different areas of

the thalamus and the occipital lobe than the main visual pathway does.

This segregation is necessary because the two

CONCEPT CHECK 4.1
Understanding Sensory Processes in the Retina

Check your understanding of sensory receptors in the retina and the concept of lateral antagonism by completing the following exercises. Consult Appendix A for the answers.

1. The receptors for vision are rods and cones in the retina. These two types of receptors have many important differences, which are compared systematically in the chart below. Fill in the missing information to finish the chart.

Dimension	Rods	Cones
Physical shape	Elongated	
Number in the retina		6.4 million
Area of the retina in which they are dominant receptor	Periphery	
Critical to color vision		
Critical to peripheral vision		No
Sensitivity to dim light	Strong	
Speed of dark adaptation		Rapid

2. The text notes that lateral antagonism in the retina is the probable cause of the illusory dark spots seen in the intersections of the Hermann grid (consult Figure 4.14). Try to construct an explanation of how lateral antagonism might account for this phenomenon. This is no small challenge, so don't feel bad if you have to consult Appendix A for the answer. Hint: The center-surround receptive fields shown in Figure 4.13 are crucial to the explanation. It will help if you draw a center-surround receptive field at one of the intersections in the grid and another adjacent to it.

Figure 4.14
The Hermann grid. If you look at this grid, you will see dark spots at the intersections of the white bars, except in the intersection you're staring at directly. This illusion is due to lateral antagonism (see Concept Check 4.1).

Figure 4.15
Visual pathways to the brain. (**a**) Input from the right half of the visual field strikes the left side of each retina and is transmitted to the left hemisphere (shown in red). Input from the left half of the visual field strikes the right side of each retina and is transmitted to the right hemisphere (shown in green). The nerve fibers from each eye meet at the optic chiasm, where fibers from the inside half of each retina cross over to the opposite side of the brain. After reaching the optic chiasm, the major visual pathway projects through the lateral geniculate nucleus in the thalamus and onto the visual cortex (shown with solid lines). A second pathway detours through the superior colliculus and then projects through another area of the thalamus (the pulvinar nucleus) and onto slightly different areas of the visual cortex (shown with dotted lines). (**b**) This inset shows a vertical view of how the optic pathways project through the thalamus and onto the visual cortex in the back of the brain [the two pathways mapped out in diagram (**a**) are virtually indistinguishable from this angle].

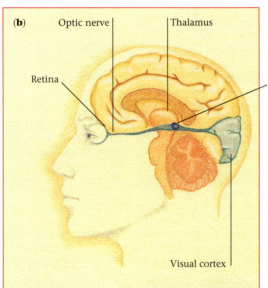

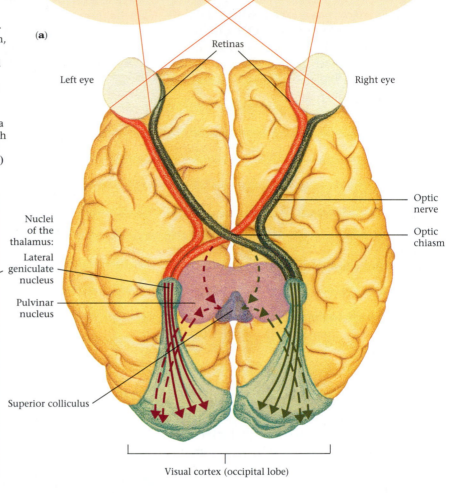

visual pathways are specialized. They engage in *parallel processing,* simultaneously extracting different kinds of information from the same visual input. The main pathway appears to handle information relating to the perception of form, color, brightness, motion, and depth (Livingstone & Hubel, 1988). The second pathway appears to handle the localization of objects in space and the coordination of visual input with other sensory input (Sparks, 1988; Stein & Meredith, 1993). The superior colliculus appears to be a crucial junction in this pathway, where visual, auditory, and tactile information converge and are integrated.

Actually, the assertion that there are two parallel visual pathways is something of an understatement, since the main visual pathway apparently is subdivided into at least two more specialized pathways (Lennie et al., 1990). These subdivisions of the main pathway have been christened the

magnocellular and *parvocellular* channels. The two channels may intermingle a little (Merigan & Maunsell, 1993), but they seem to have separate responsibilities (Schiller, Logothetis, & Charles, 1990). The parvocellular channel, which is funneled through the outer four layers of the LGN, appears to handle the perception of color, form, and texture. The magnocellular pathway, which is funneled through the inner two layers of the LGN, appears to process information regarding motion, depth, and brightness.

Information Processing in the Visual Cortex
Visual input ultimately arrives in the occipital lobe of the cortex. The cells in the visual areas of the cortex communicate with one another extensively in a rich processing network (Gilbert & Wiesel, 1985). Explaining how these cortical cells respond to light once posed a perplexing problem.

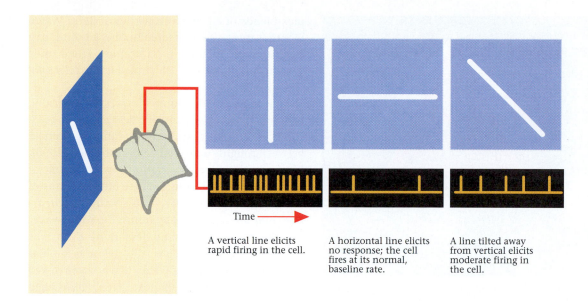

Time →

A vertical line elicits rapid firing in the cell.

A horizontal line elicits no response; the cell fires at its normal, baseline rate.

A line tilted away from vertical elicits moderate firing in the cell.

Researchers investigating the question placed microelectrodes in the visual cortex of animals to record action potentials from individual cells. They would flash spots of light in the retinal receptive fields that the cells were thought to monitor, but there was rarely any response.

According to David Hubel and Torsten Wiesel (1962, 1963), they discovered the solution to this mystery quite by accident. One of the projector slides they used to present a spot to a cat had a crack in it. The spot elicited no response, but when they removed the slide, the crack moved through the cell's receptive field, and the cell fired like crazy in response to the moving dark line. It turns out that cortical cells don't really respond much to little spots—they are much more sensitive to lines, edges, and other more complicated stimuli. Armed with new slides, Hubel and Wiesel embarked on years of painstaking study of the visual cortex (see Figure 4.16). Their work eventually earned them a Nobel prize in 1981.

Hubel and Wiesel (1962, 1979) identified three major types of visual cells in the cortex, which they called simple cells, complex cells, and hypercomplex cells. *Simple cells* are quite specific about which stimuli will make them fire. A simple cell responds best to a line of the correct width, oriented at the correct angle, and located in the correct position in its receptive field. *Complex cells* also care about width and orientation, but they respond to any position in their receptive fields. Some complex cells are most responsive if a line sweeps across their receptive field—but only if it's moving in the "right" direction. *Hypercomplex cells* are cells that are particularly fussy about the length of a stimulus line.

The key point of all this is that the cells in the visual cortex seem to be highly specialized. They have been characterized as *feature detectors*, **neurons that respond selectively to very specific features of more complex stimuli.** Ultimately, most visual stimuli could be represented by combinations of lines such as those registered by these feature detectors. Some theorists believe that feature detectors are registering the basic building blocks of visual perception and that the brain somehow assembles the blocks into a coherent picture of complex stimuli (Maguire, Weisstein, & Klymenko, 1990). Other theorists think that this model is too simple to explain the immense range of human visual capabilities (Sekuler & Blake, 1990).

Viewing the World in Color   3d

So far, we've considered only how the visual system deals with light and dark. Let's journey now into the world of color. On the one hand, you can see perfectly well without seeing in color. Many animals get by with little or no color vision, and no one seemed to suffer back when all photographs, movies, or TV shows were in black and white. On the other hand, color adds not only spectacle but information to human perceptions of the world. Emotionally, color clearly is important to many people, as you well know if you've ever spent a great deal of time deciding on the color of sweater to wear or the color of car to buy.

The Stimulus for Color

As noted earlier, the lights people see are mixtures of different wavelengths. Perceived color is primarily a function of the dominant wavelength in these mixtures. In the visible spectrum, lights with

"One can now begin to grasp the significance of the great number of cells in the visual cortex. Each cell seems to have its own specific duties."

DAVID HUBEL

Figure 4.17
The color solid. The color solid shows how color varies along three perceptual dimensions: brightness (increasing from the bottom to the top of the solid), hue (changing around the solid's perimeter), and saturation (increasing toward the periphery of the solid).

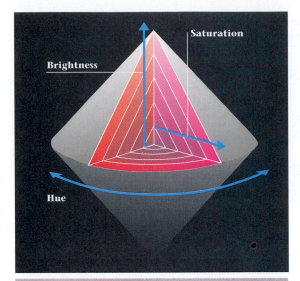

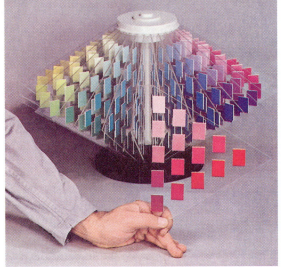

Figure 4.18
Subtractive color mixing. Paints selectively reflect specific wavelengths that give rise to particular colors, as you can see here for blue and yellow, which both also reflect back a little green. When we mix blue and yellow paint, the mixture absorbs all the colors that blue and yellow absorbed individually. The mixture is subtractive because more wavelengths are removed than by each paint alone. The yellow paint in the mixture absorbs the wavelengths associated with blue and the blue paint in the mixture absorbs the wavelengths associated with yellow. The only wavelengths left to be reflected back are some of those associated with green, so the mixture is seen as green.

plex blends of all three properties of light. Wavelength is most closely related to hue, amplitude to brightness, and purity to saturation. These three dimensions of color are illustrated in the *color solid* shown in Figure 4.17.

As a color solid demonstrates systematically, people can perceive many different colors. Indeed, experts estimate that humans can discriminate between roughly a million colors (Boynton, 1990). Most of these diverse variations are the result of mixing a few basic colors. There are two kinds of color mixture: subtractive and additive. ***Subtractive color mixing* works by removing some wavelengths of light, leaving less light than was originally there.** You probably became familiar with subtractive mixing as a child when you mixed yellow and blue paints to make green. Paints yield subtractive mixing because pigments *absorb* most wavelengths, selectively reflecting specific wavelengths that give rise to particular colors (see Figure 4.18). Subtractive color mixing can also be demonstrated by stacking color filters. If you look through a sandwich of yellow and blue cellophane filters, they will block out certain wavelengths. The middle wavelengths that are left will look green.

***Additive color mixing* works by superimposing lights, putting more light in the mixture than exists in any one light by itself.** If you shine red, green, and blue spotlights on a white surface, you'll have an additive mixture. As Figure 4.19 shows, additive and subtractive mixtures of the same colors produce different results.

White light actually includes the entire visible spectrum, as you can demonstrate by allowing white light to pass through a prism (consult Figure 4.6 once again). Accordingly, when all wavelengths are mixed additively, they yield natural white light. Human processes of color perception parallel additive color mixing much more closely

the longest wavelengths appear red, whereas those with the shortest appear violet. Notice the word *appear*. Color is a psychological interpretation. It's not a physical property of light itself.

Although wavelength wields the greatest influence, perception of color depends on com-

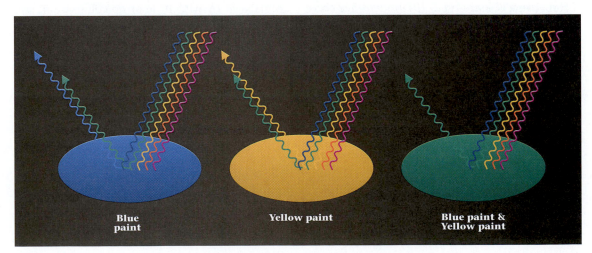

Blue paint   Yellow paint   Blue paint & Yellow paint

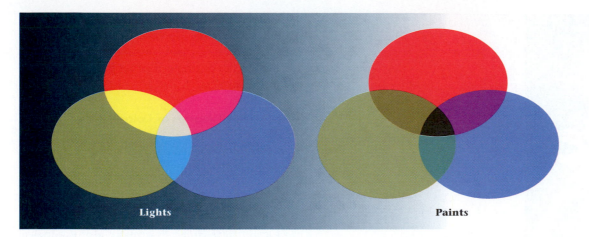

Lights   **Paints**

Figure 4.19
Additive color mixing.
Lights mix additively because all the wavelengths contained in each light reach the eye. If red, blue, and green lights are projected onto a white screen, they produce the colors shown on the left, with white at the intersection of all three lights. If paints of the same three colors were combined in the same way, the subtractive mixture would produce the colors shown on the right, with black at the intersection of all three colors.

than subtractive mixing, as you'll see in the following discussion of theories of color vision.

Trichromatic Theory of Color Vision

The *trichromatic theory* of color vision (*tri* for "three," *chroma* for "color") was first stated by Thomas Young and modified later by Hermann von Helmholtz (1852). **The *trichromatic theory of color vision* holds that the human eye has three types of receptors with differing sensitivities to different light wavelengths.** Helmholtz theorized that the eye contains specialized receptors sensitive to the specific wavelengths associated with red, green, and blue. According to this model, people can see all the colors of the rainbow because the eye does its own "color mixing" by varying the ratio of neural activity among these three types of receptors.

The impetus for the trichromatic theory was the demonstration that a light of any color can be matched by the additive mixture of three *primary colors.* Any three colors that are appropriately spaced out in the visible spectrum can serve as primary colors, although red, green, and blue are usually used. Does it sound implausible that three colors should be adequate for creating all other colors? If so, consider that this is exactly what happens on your color TV screen. Additive mixtures of red, green, and blue fool you into seeing all the colors of a natural scene.

Most of the known facts about color blindness also meshed well with trichromatic theory. **Color blindness encompasses a variety of deficiencies in the ability to distinguish among colors.** Color blindness occurs much more frequently in males than in females. Actually, the term color *blindness* is somewhat misleading, since complete blindness to differences in colors is quite rare. Most people who are color blind are *dichromats;* that is, they make do with only two color channels. There are

three types of dichromats, and each type is insensitive to a different color (red, green, and blue, although the latter is rare) (Gouras, 1991). The three deficiencies seen among dichromats support the notion that there are three channels for color vision, as proposed by trichromatic theory.

Opponent Process Theory of Color Vision

Although trichromatic theory explained some facets of color vision well, it ran aground in other areas. Consider complementary afterimages, for instance. *Complementary colors* **are pairs of colors that produce gray tones when mixed together.** The various pairs of complementary colors can be arranged in a *color circle,* such as the one in Figure 4.20. If you stare at a strong color and then look at a white background, you'll see an *afterimage*—a visual image that persists after a stimulus is removed. The color of the afterimage will be the *complement* of the color you originally stared at. You can demonstrate this effect for yourself by following the instructions in Figure 4.21 (on page 140). Trichromatic theory cannot account for the appearance of complementary afterimages.

Here's another peculiarity to consider. If you ask

Figure 4.20
Complementary colors.
Colors opposite each other on this color circle are complements, or "opposites." Additively, mixing complementary colors produces gray. Opponent process principles help explain this effect as well as the other peculiarities of complementary colors noted in the text.

Figure 4.21
Demonstration of a complementary afterimage. Stare at the dot in the center of the flower for at least 60 seconds, then quickly shift your gaze to the dot in the white rectangle. You should see an afterimage of the flower—but in complementary colors.

Figure 4.22
Three types of cones. Research has identified three types of cones that show varied sensitivity to different wavelengths of light. As the graph shows, these three types of cones correspond only roughly to the red, green, and blue receptors predicted by trichromatic theory, so it is more accurate to refer to them as cones sensitive to short, medium, and long wavelengths.

people to describe colors but restrict them to using three names, they run into difficulty. For example, using only red, green, and blue, they simply don't feel comfortable describing yellow as "reddish green." However, if you let them have just one more name, they usually choose yellow; they can then describe any color quite well (Abramov & Gordon, 1994; Boynton & Gordon, 1965). If colors are reduced to three channels, why are four color names required to describe the full range of possible colors?

In an effort to answer questions such as these, Ewald Hering proposed the *opponent process theory* in 1878. **The *opponent process theory of color vision* holds that color perception depends on receptors that make antagonistic responses to three pairs of colors.** The three pairs of opponent colors posited by Hering were red versus green, yellow versus blue, and black versus white. The antagonistic processes in this theory provide plausible explanations for complementary afterimages and the need for four names (red, green, blue, and

yellow) to describe colors. Opponent process theory also explains some aspects of color blindness. For instance, it can explain why dichromats typically find it hard to distinguish either green from red or yellow from blue.

Reconciling Theories of Color Vision

Advocates of trichromatic theory and opponent process theory argued about the relative merits of their models for almost a century. Most researchers assumed that one theory must be wrong and the other must be right. In recent decades, however, it has become clear that *it takes both theories to explain color vision.* Eventually a physiological basis for both theories was found. Research that earned George Wald a Nobel prize demonstrated that *the eye has three types of cones,* with each type being most sensitive to a different band of wavelengths, as shown in Figure 4.22 (Bowmaker & Dartnall, 1980; Wald, 1964). The three types of cones represent the three different color receptors predicted by trichromatic theory.

Researchers also discovered a biological basis for opponent processes. They found cells in the retina, the LGN, and the visual cortex *that respond in opposite ways to red versus green and blue versus yellow* (DeValois & Jacobs, 1984; Zrenner et al., 1990). For example, there are ganglion cells in the retina that are excited by green and inhibited by red. Other ganglion cells in the retina work in just the opposite way, as predicted in opponent process theory.

In summary, the perception of color appears to involve sequential stages of information processing (Hurvich, 1981). The receptors that do the first stage of processing (the cones) seem to follow the principles outlined in trichromatic theory. In later stages of processing, at least some cells in the retina, the LGN, and the visual cortex seem to follow the principles outlined in opponent process theory (see Figure 4.23). As you can see, vigorous theoretical debate about color vision produced a solution that went beyond the contributions of either theory alone.

Recap of Key Points

- Light varies in terms of wavelength, amplitude, and purity. Light enters the eye through the cornea and pupil and is focused upside down on the retina by the lens. Distant objects appear blurry to nearsighted people and close objects appear blurry to farsighted people. Both problems are due to difficulties in focusing light on the retina precisely.
- The retina is the neural tissue in the eye that ab-

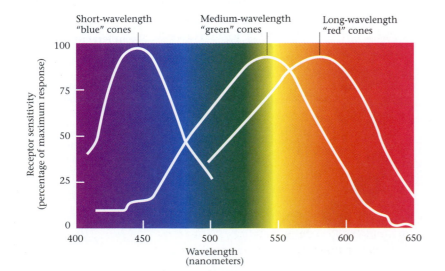

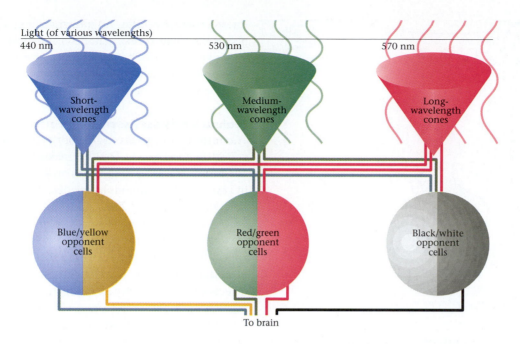

Light (of various wavelengths)

440 nm   530 nm   570 nm

Short-wavelength cones

Medium-wavelength cones

Long-wavelength cones

Blue/yellow opponent cells

Red/green opponent cells

Black/white opponent cells

To brain

Figure 4.23
Explaining color perception. Contemporary theories of color vision include aspects of both the trichromatic and opponent process theories. As predicted by trichromatic theory, there are three types of receptors for color—cones sensitive to short, medium, and long wavelengths. However, these cones are organized into receptive fields that excite or inhibit the firing of higher-level visual cells in the retina, thalamus, and cortex. As predicted by opponent process theory, some of these cells respond in antagonistic ways to blue versus yellow, red versus green, and black versus white when lights of these colors stimulate their receptive fields.

sorbs light, processes images, and sends visual signals to the brain. Rods and cones are the visual receptors found in the retina. Cones, which are concentrated in the fovea, play a key role in daylight vision and color perception. Rods, which have their greatest density just outside the fovea, are critical to night vision and peripheral vision. Dark adaptation and light adaptation both involve changes in the retina's sensitivity to light, allowing the eye to adapt to changes in illumination.

• The retina transforms light into neural impulses that are sent to the brain via the optic nerve. Receptive fields are areas in the retina that affect the firing of visual cells. They vary in shape and size, but center-surround arrangements are common. Lateral antagonism occurs when activity in one cell diminishes signals from nearby cells.

• The optic nerves from the inside half of each eye cross at the optic chiasm and then project to the opposite half of the brain. Hence, input from the left half of the visual field is sent to the right hemisphere, and input from the right half of the visual field is sent to the left hemisphere.

• Two visual pathways send signals to different areas of the primary visual cortex. The main pathway, which is routed through the LGN in the thalamus, appears to handle the perception of form, color, and depth. The second pathway, which is routed through the superior colliculus and then the thalamus, appears to handle the localization of objects in space and the coordination of visual input with other sensory input.

• Nobel prize–winning research by Hubel and Wiesel suggests that the visual cortex contains cells that function as feature detectors. They identified three

types of visual cells in the cortex: simple cells, complex cells, and hypercomplex cells.

• Perceptions of color (hue) are primarily a function of light wavelength, while amplitude affects brightness and purity affects saturation. There are two types of color mixing: additive and subtractive. Human color perception depends on processes that resemble additive color mixing.

• The trichromatic theory holds that people have three types of receptors that are sensitive to wavelengths associated with red, green, and blue. The opponent process theory holds that color perception depends on receptors that make antagonistic responses to red versus green, blue versus yellow, and black versus white. The evidence now suggests that both theories are necessary to account for color vision.

Perceiving Forms, Patterns, and Objects 3e

The drawing in Figure 4.24 (on page 142) is a poster for a circus act involving a trained seal. Take a good look at it. What do you see?

No doubt you see a seal balancing a ball on its nose and a trainer holding a fish and a whip. But suppose you had been told that the drawing is actually a poster for a costume ball. Would you have perceived it differently?

If you focus on the idea of a costume ball (stay with it a minute if you still see the seal and trainer), you will probably see a costumed man and woman in Figure 4.24. She's handing him a hat, and he has a sword in his right hand. This tricky little sketch was made ambiguous quite intentionally. It's a *reversible figure*, a drawing that is compatible with

Figure 4.24
A poster for a trained seal act. Or is it? The picture is an ambiguous figure, which can be interpreted as either of two scenes.

interpret sensory input. An understanding of how people perceive forms, patterns, and objects requires knowledge of how people *organize and interpret* visual input. Several influential approaches to this question emphasize *feature analysis*.

Feature Analysis: Assembling Forms

The information received by your eyes would do you little good if you couldn't recognize objects and forms—ranging from words on a page to mice in your cellar and friends in the distance. This was exactly the fate that befell Dr. P. As you recall, Dr. P could "see" perfectly well. Yet he couldn't make sense out of the world because he was unable to translate what he saw into the recognition of objects and faces. Even people without visual defects can find form perception to be challenging. For example, professors reading essay exams routinely complain about having a hard time recognizing the letter forms that make up their students' handwriting.

According to some theories, perceptions of form and pattern entail *feature analysis* (Lindsay & Norman, 1977; Maguire et al., 1990). **Feature analysis is the process of detecting specific elements in visual input and assembling them into a more complex form.** In other words, you start with the components of a form, such as lines, edges, and corners, and build them into perceptions of squares, triangles, stop signs, bicycles, ice cream cones, and telephones. An application of this model of form perception is diagrammed in Figure 4.25. It shows how, in theory, people might recognize the letter T by registering and assembling the configuration of features that make up this letter.

Feature analysis assumes that form perception

two different interpretations that can shift back and forth.

The point of this demonstration is simply this: *The same visual input can result in radically different perceptions.* No one-to-one correspondence exists between sensory input and what you perceive. *This is a principal reason that people's experience of the world is subjective.* Perception involves much more than passively receiving signals from the outside world. It involves the *interpretation* of sensory input.

In this case, your interpretations result in two different "realities" because your *expectations* have been manipulated. Information given to you about the drawing has created **a *perceptual set*—a readiness to perceive a stimulus in a particular way.** A perceptual set creates a certain slant in how you

Figure 4.25
Feature analysis in form perception. One vigorously debated theory of form perception is that the brain has cells that respond to specific aspects or features of stimuli, such as lines and angles. Neurons functioning as higher-level analyzers then respond to input from these "feature detectors." The more input each analyzer receives, the more active it becomes. Finally, other neurons weigh signals from these analyzers and make a "decision" about the stimulus. In this way perception of a form is arrived at by assembling elements from the bottom up.

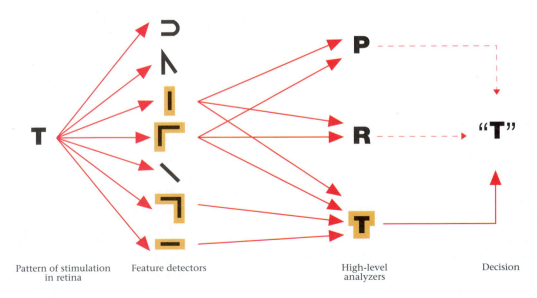

Pattern of stimulation in retina   Feature detectors   High-level analyzers   Decision

involves **bottom-up processing,** a progression from individual elements to the whole (see Figure 4.26). The plausibility of this model was bolstered greatly when Hubel and Wiesel showed that cells in the visual cortex operate as highly specialized feature detectors. Indeed, their findings strongly suggested that at least some aspects of form perception involve feature analysis.

Can feature analysis provide a complete account of how people perceive forms? Probably not. A crucial problem for the theory is that form perception often does not involve bottom-up processing. In fact, there is ample evidence that perceptions of form sometimes involve **top-down processing,** a progression from the whole to the elements (see Figure 4.26). For example, top-down processing was apparent in a study by Johnston and McClelland (1974), who briefly showed subjects arrays of four letters that made up words (example: W O R K) and asked them to identify the letter in a specific position (first, second, and so on) as quickly as possible. When subjects were instructed to focus on the whole stimulus array, they were more successful in identifying the target letters than when they were instructed to focus on the specific position where the target letter would appear. The superiority of the instruction to focus on the whole suggests that people can perceive a word before its individual letters and that top-down processing—working from the whole (the word) to the elements (the letters)—can sometimes be superior to bottom-up processing. It seems unlikely that bottom-up processing can account for the ability to rapidly process words in reading. If readers depended exclusively on bottom-up processing, they would have to analyze the features of each letter to recognize it and then assemble the letters into words. This would be a terribly time-consuming task for each word and would slow down reading speed to a snail's pace.

Subjective contours are another phenomenon traditionally attributed to top-down processing, although that view is changing. **Subjective contours involve the perception of contours where there really are none.** Consider, for instance, the white triangle shown in Figure 4.27. We see the contours of the triangle easily, even though no physical edges or lines are present. It is hard to envision how feature detectors could detect edges that are not really there, so most theorists have argued that bottom-up models of form perception are unlikely to account for subjective contours. Until recently, the prevailing view was that subjective contours depend on viewing stimulus configu-

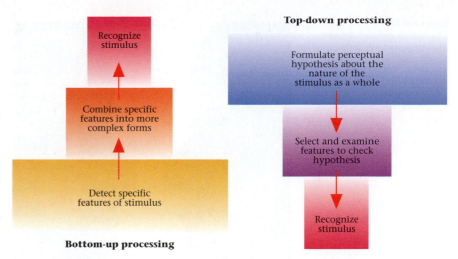

Bottom-up processing

rations as wholes and then filling in the blanks (Rock, 1986). However, in recent years, researchers have demonstrated that feature detectors do respond to the edges in subjective contours (Peterhans & von der Heydt, 1991). At present, several neural theories of subjective contours that emphasize bottom-up processing are under investigation, with promising results (Lesher, 1995).

In sum, it appears that both top-down and bottom-up processing have their niches in form perception. Moreover, the two types of processing are not necessarily incompatible. For example, Anne Treisman (1986) has proposed that the perception of objects involves two stages characterized by different types of processing. In the *preattentive stage,* which requires no conscious effort, the physical features of stimuli are automatically analyzed, using bottom-up processing. The features extracted in the first stage are then combined into recognizable objects in the *focused-attention stage,* which involves conscious effort and top-down processing.

Looking at the Whole Picture: Gestalt Principles

Top-down processing is clearly at work in the principles of form perception described by the Gestalt psychologists. As we saw in Chapter 1, *Gestalt psychology* was an influential school of thought that emerged out of Germany during the first half

Figure 4.26. Bottom-up versus top-down processing. As explained in these diagrams, bottom-up processing progresses from individual elements to whole elements, whereas top-down processing progresses from the whole to the individual elements.

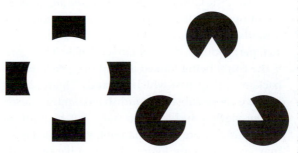

Figure 4.27 Subjective contours. Your perceptions of the triangle on the right and the circle on the left result from subjective contours that are not really there. The effect is so powerful, the triangle and circle appear whiter than the background, which they are not. To demonstrate the illusory nature of these contours for yourself, cover the black circles that mark off the triangle. You'll see that the triangle disappears.

Figure 4.28
The principle of figure and ground. Whether you see two faces or a vase depends on which part of this drawing you see as figure and which as background. Although this reversible drawing allows you to switch back and forth between two ways of organizing your perception, you can't perceive the drawing both ways at once.

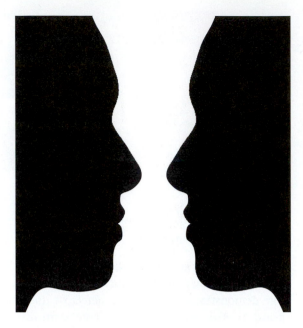

"If you were magically deposited in an unknown city, . . . you would see buildings, people, cars and trees. You would not be aware of detecting colors, edges, movements and distances, and of assembling them into multidimensional wholes. . . . In short, meaningful wholes seem to precede parts and properties, as the Gestalt psychologists emphasized many years ago."

ANNE TREISMAN

of this century. (*Gestalt* is a German word for "form" or "shape.") Gestalt psychologists repeatedly demonstrated that the whole can be greater than the sum of its parts.

A simple example of this principle is the *phi phenomenon,* first described by Max Wertheimer in 1912. **The *phi phenomenon* is the illusion of movement created by presenting visual stimuli in rapid succession.** You encounter examples of the phi phenomenon nearly every day. For example, movies and TV consist of separate still pictures projected rapidly one after the other. You *see* smooth motion, but in reality the "moving" objects merely take slightly different positions in successive frames. Viewed as a whole, a movie has a property (motion) that isn't evident in any of its parts (the individual frames). The Gestalt psychologists formulated a series of principles that describe how the visual system organizes a scene into discrete forms. Let's examine some of these principles.

FIGURE AND GROUND. Take a look at Figure 4.28. Do you see the figure as two silhouetted faces against a white background, or as a white vase against a black background? This reversible figure illustrates the Gestalt principle of *figure and ground.* Dividing visual displays into figure and ground is a fundamental way in which people organize visual perceptions (Baylis & Driver, 1995). The *figure* is the thing being looked at, and the *ground* is the background against which it stands. Figures seem to have more substance and shape, appear closer to the viewer, and seem to stand out in front of the ground. More often than not, your visual field may contain many figures sharing a background.

The following Gestalt principles relate to how these elements are grouped into higher-order figures.

PROXIMITY. Things that are near one another seem to belong together. The black dots in the upper left panel of Figure 4.29a could be grouped into vertical columns or horizontal rows. However, people tend to perceive rows because of the effect of proximity (the dots are closer together horizontally).

SIMILARITY. People also tend to group stimuli that are similar. This principle is apparent in Figure 4.29b, where viewers group elements of similar lightness into the number two.

CONTINUITY. The principle of continuity reflects people's tendency to follow in whatever direction they've been led. Thus, people tend to connect points that result in straight or gently curved lines that create "smooth" paths, as shown in the bottom panel of Figure 4.29c.

SIMPLICITY. The Gestaltists' most general principle was the law of *Pragnanz,* which translates from German as "good form." The idea is that people tend to group elements that combine to form a good figure. This principle is somewhat vague in that it's often difficult to spell out what makes a figure "good" (Biederman, Hilton, & Hummel, 1991). Some theorists maintain that goodness is largely a matter of simplicity, asserting that people tend to organize forms in the simplest way possible (see the middle right panel of Figure 4.29d).

CLOSURE. People often group elements to create a sense of *closure,* or completeness. Thus, you may "complete" figures that actually have gaps in them. This principle is demonstrated in the upper right panel of Figure 4.29e.

COMMON REGION. In recent years Irvin Rock and Stephen Palmer (1990) have suggested some new Gestalt principles. One of these, called *common region,* asserts that elements that share a perceived region tend to be grouped together. Consider the dots in Figure 4.29f. Although they are all similar in size and color, they are grouped in pairs that share a common background.

CONNECTEDNESS. Another new principle suggested by Rock and Palmer (1990) is *connectedness,* which refers to the powerful tendency to perceive any

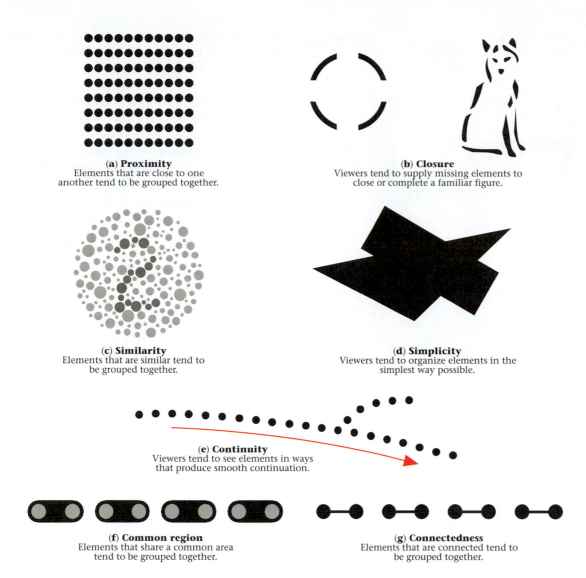

(a) Proximity
Elements that are close to one another tend to be grouped together.

(b) Closure
Viewers tend to supply missing elements to close or complete a familiar figure.

(c) Similarity
Elements that are similar tend to be grouped together.

(d) Simplicity
Viewers tend to organize elements in the simplest way possible.

(e) Continuity
Viewers tend to see elements in ways that produce smooth continuation.

(f) Common region
Elements that share a common area tend to be grouped together.

(g) Connectedness
Elements that are connected tend to be grouped together.

Figure 4.29
Gestalt principles of perceptual organization. Gestalt principles help explain how people subjectively organize perception. **(a) Proximity:** These dots might well be organized in vertical columns rather than horizontal rows, but because of proximity (the dots are closer together horizontally), they tend to be perceived in rows. **(b) Closure:** Even though the figures are incomplete, you fill in the blanks and see a circle and a dog. **(c) Similarity:** Because of similarity of color, you see dots organized into the number 2 instead of a random array. If you did not group similar elements, you wouldn't see the number 2 here. **(d) Simplicity:** You could view this as a complicated 11-sided figure, but given the preference for simplicity, you are more likely to see it as a rectangle and a triangle. **(e) Continuity:** You tend to group these dots in a way that produces a smooth path rather than an abrupt shift in direction. **(f) Common region:** Although all eight dots shown here share a variety of similiarities, they are grouped in pairs that share regions. **(g) Connectedness:** Although all eight dots shown here are similar, they are grouped in pairs that are connected.

uniform, linked region as a single unit. This principle is demonstrated in Figure 4.29g.

Although Gestalt psychology is no longer an active theoretical orientation in modern psychology, its influence is still felt in the study of perception (Banks & Krajicek, 1991). The Gestalt psychologists raised many important questions that still occupy researchers, and they left a legacy of many useful insights about form perception that have stood the test of time.

Formulating Perceptual Hypotheses
The Gestalt principles provide some indications of how people organize visual input. However, scientists are still one step away from understanding how these organized perceptions result in a representation of the real world. Understanding the problem requires distinguishing between two kinds of stimuli: distal and proximal (Hochberg, 1988). *Distal stimuli* are stimuli that lie in the **distance (that is, in the world outside the body).** In vision, these are the objects that you're looking at. They are "distant" in that your eyes don't touch them. What your eyes do "touch" are the images formed by patterns of light falling on your retinas. These images are the *proximal stimuli*, **the stimulus energies that impinge directly on sensory receptors.** The distinction is important, because there are great differences between the objects you perceive and the stimulus energies that represent them.

In visual perception, the proximal stimuli are distorted, two-dimensional versions of their actual, three-dimensional counterparts. For example, consider the distal stimulus of a square such as the one in Figure 4.30 (on page 146). If the square is lying on a desk in front of you, it is actually projecting a trapezoid (the proximal stimulus) on your retinas, because the top of the square is farther from your eyes than the bottom. Obviously, the trapezoid is a distorted representation of the

"The fundamental 'formula' of Gestalt theory might be expressed in this way: There are wholes, the behaviour of which is not determined by that of their individual elements."

MAX WERTHEIMER

Figure 4.30
Distal and proximal stimuli. Proximal stimuli are often distorted, shifting representations of distal stimuli in the real world. If you look directly down at a small, square piece of paper on a desk (**a**), the distal stimulus (the paper) and the proximal stimulus (the image projected on your retina) will both be square. But as you move the paper away on the desktop (**b**) and (**c**), the square distal stimulus projects an increasingly trapezoidal image on your retina, making the proximal stimulus more and more distorted. Nevertheless, you continue to perceive a square.

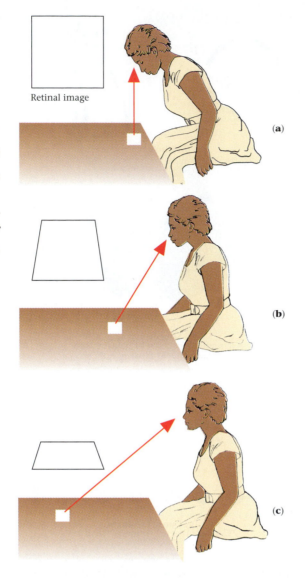

Retinal image

(a)

(b)

(c)

Figure 4.31
A famous reversible figure. What do you see?

square. If what people have to work with is so distorted a picture, how do they get an accurate view of the world out there?

One explanation is that people bridge the gap between distal and proximal stimuli by constantly making and testing *hypotheses* about what's out there in the real world (Gregory, 1973). Thus, **a perceptual hypothesis is an inference about which distal stimuli could be responsible for the proximal stimuli sensed.** In effect, people make educated guesses about what form could be responsible for a pattern of sensory stimulation. The square in Figure 4.30 may project a trapezoidal image on your retinas, but your perceptual system "guesses" correctly that it's a square—and that's what you see.

Let's look at another ambiguous drawing to further demonstrate the process of making a perceptual hypothesis. Figure 4.31 is a famous reversible figure, first published as a cartoon in a humor magazine. Perhaps you see a drawing of a young woman looking back over her right shoulder. Alternatively, you might see an old woman with her chin down on her chest. The ambiguity exists because there isn't enough information to force your perceptual system to accept only one of these hypotheses.

If you can see only one of the women, you may be wondering where the other is. To guide you, Figure 4.32 shows unambiguous drawings of the young woman on the left and of the old woman on the right. Now you should be able to find either woman in Figure 4.31. You just needed some guidance as to how to make the other perceptual hypothesis. Incidentally, studies show that people who are led to *expect* the young woman or the old woman generally see the one they expect (Leeper, 1935). This is another example of how perceptual sets influence what people see.

Psychologists have used a variety of reversible figures to study how people formulate perceptual hypotheses. Another example can be seen in Figure 4.33, which shows the *Necker cube*. The shaded surface can appear as either the front or the rear of the transparent cube. If you look at the cube for a while, your perception will alternate between these possibilities. Later, in the Application on art and illusion, you'll see how M. C. Escher used the Necker cube to create a fascinating piece of art.

The *context* in which something appears often guides people's perceptual hypotheses. To illustrate, take a look at Figure 4.34. What do you see? You probably saw the words "THE CAT." But look again; the middle characters in both words are identical. You identified an "H" in the first word and an "A" in the second because of the surrounding letters, which created an expectation—another example of top-down processing in visual perception. The power of expectations explains why typophocal errors like those in this sentance often pass unoberved (Lachman, 1996).

Perceiving Depth or Distance 3f

More often than not, forms and figures are objects in space. Spatial considerations add a third dimension to visual perception. *Depth perception involves interpretation of visual cues that indicate how near or far away objects are.* To make judgments of distance, people rely on quite a variety of clues, which can be classified into two types: binocular cues and monocular cues (Hochberg, 1988).

Binocular Cues

Because the eyes are set apart, each eye has a slightly different view of the world. *Binocular depth cues are clues about distance based on the differing views of the two eyes.* "Stereo" viewers like the Viewmaster toy you may have had as a child make use of this principle by presenting slightly different flat images of the same scene to each eye. The brain then supplies the "depth," and you perceive a three-dimensional scene.

The principal binocular depth cue is *retinal disparity,* **which refers to the fact that objects within 25 feet project images to slightly different locations on the right and left retinas, so the right and left eyes see slightly different views of the object.** The closer an object gets, the greater the disparity between the images seen by each eye. Thus, retinal disparity increases as objects come closer, providing information about distance. Another binocular cue is *convergence,* **which involves sensing the eyes converging toward each other as they focus on closer objects** (see Figure 4.35).

Monocular Cues

Monocular depth cues are clues about distance based on the image in either eye alone. There are two kinds of monocular cues to depth. One kind is the result of active use of the eye in viewing the world. For example, as an object comes closer, you may sense the accommodation (the change in the curvature of the lens) that must occur for the eye to adjust its focus. Furthermore, if you cover one eye and move your head from side to side, closer objects appear to move more than distant objects. In a similar vein, you may notice when driving along a highway that nearby

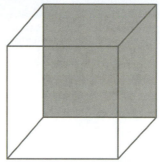

Figure 4.33
The Necker cube. The tinted surface can become either the front or the back of the cube.

objects (such as fence posts along the road) appear to move by more rapidly than objects that are farther away (such as trees in the distance). Thus, you get cues about depth from *motion parallax,* **which involves images of objects at different distances moving across the retina at different rates.**

The other kind of monocular cues are *pictorial depth cues*—**clues about distance that can be given in a flat picture.** There are many pictorial

Figure 4.32
Unambiguous drawings of the reversible figure. These versions of the reversible figure in Figure 4.31 have been redrawn slightly to make the young woman more apparent on the left and the old woman more apparent on the right.

THE CHT

Figure 4.34
Context effects. The context in which a stimulus is seen can affect your perceptual hypotheses.

Figure 4.35
Convergence and depth perception. One binocular depth cue is convergence. The more you have to converge your eyes together to focus on an object, the closer the object must be.

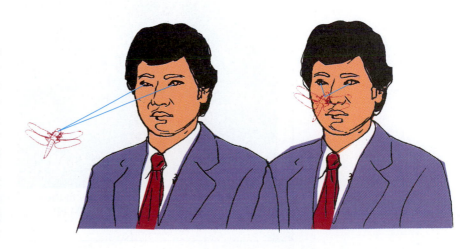

**Figure 4.36
Six pictorial cues to depth.** In most visual experiences, several pictorial cues are present at once. The world rarely looks "flat," even through only one eye. Try looking at the light-and-shadow picture upside down. The change in shadowing reverses what you see.

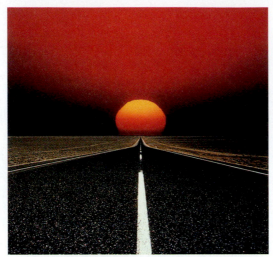

Linear perspective Parallel lines that run away from the viewer seem to get closer together.

Texture gradient A texture is coarser for near areas and finer for more distant ones.

Interposition The shapes of near objects overlap or mask those of more distant ones.

Relative size If separate objects are expected to be of the same size, the larger ones are seen as closer.

Height in plane Near objects are low in the visual field; more distant ones are higher up.

Light and shadow Patterns of light and dark suggest shadows that can create an impression of three-dimensional forms.

cues to depth, which is why some paintings and photographs seem so realistic that you feel you can climb right into them. Six prominent pictorial depth cues are described and illustrated in Figure 4.36. *Linear perspective* is a depth cue reflecting the fact that lines converge in the distance. Because details are too small to see when they are far away, *texture gradients* can provide information about depth. If an object comes between you and another object, it must be closer to you, a cue called *interposition*. *Relative size* is a cue because closer objects appear larger. *Height in plane* reflects the fact that distant objects appear higher in a picture. Finally, the familiar effects of shadowing make *light and shadow* useful in judging distance.

There appear to be some cultural differences in the ability to take advantage of pictorial depth cues in two-dimensional drawings. These differences were first investigated by Hudson (1960, 1967), who presented pictures like that shown in Figure 4.37 to various cultural groups in South Africa. Hudson's approach was based on the assumption that subjects who indicate that the hunter is trying to spear the elephant instead of the antelope don't understand the depth cues

(interposition, relative size, height in plane) in the picture, which place the elephant in the distance. Hudson found that subjects from a rural South African tribe (the Bantu), which had little exposure at that time to pictures and photos, frequently misinterpreted the depth cues in his pictures. Similar difficulties with depth cues in pictures have been documented for other cul-

Figure 4.37
Testing understanding of pictorial depth cues.
In his cross-cultural research, Hudson (1960) asked subjects to indicate whether the hunter is trying to spear the antelope or the elephant. He found cultural disparities in subjects' ability to make effective use of the pictorial depth cues, which place the elephant in the distance and make it an unlikely target.

tural groups that have little experience with two-dimensional representations of three-dimensional space (Berry et al., 1992). Based on this evidence, Deregowski (1989) concluded that the application of pictorial depth cues to pictures is partly an acquired skill that depends on experience. Although this conclusion seems reasonable, most theorists do not accept Deregowski's further assertion that perceptual processes vary to some degree across cultures. Among other things, critics of this idea point out that people from pictureless societies quickly learn how to interpret depth in pictures and that there is little evidence of cultural variability in the perception of depth in *real space* (as opposed to pictures). Hence, most other theorists seem to believe that the basic processes involved in depth perception are probably much the same across cultures (Halpern, 1989a; Hubbard, Baird, & Ajmal, 1989).

Perceiving Geographical Slant

The perception of *geographical slant* involves making judgments about how steep hills and other inclines are in relation to the norm of a flat, horizontal surface. As with depth perception, the perception of geographical slant involves juggling spatial considerations. However, unlike with depth perception, which has a rich tradition of empirical inquiry, the perception of geographical slant has largely been neglected by researchers. Nevertheless, recent work has turned up some thought-provoking findings and raised some interesting questions. We will look at this work in our Featured Study for Chapter 4.

Investigators: Dennis R. Proffitt, Mukul Bhalla, Rich Gossweiler, and Jonathon Midgett (University of Virginia)

Source: Perceiving geographical slant. *Psychonomic Bulletin & Review*, 1995, *2*, 409–428.

Why Hills Look Steeper Than They Are   Featured Study

Accurate perceptions of geographical slant have obvious practical significance for people walking up

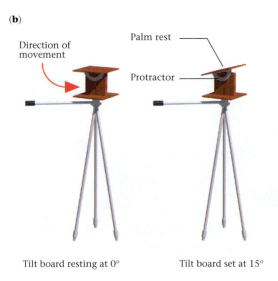

(a)

Cross section of hill

Disk set at 4°
Direction of movement
Disk set at 45°

(b)

Direction of movement
Palm rest
Protractor

Tilt board resting at 0°   Tilt board set at 15°

Figure 4.38 Apparatus used to measure visual and haptic estimates of geographical slant. (a) Visual estimates of pitch were made by adjusting the incline on a disk to match the incline of the hill. **(b)** Haptic estimates of pitch were made by adjusting a tilt board by hand without looking at it. (Adapted from Proffitt et al., 1995)

hills, skiing down mountain slopes, working on pitched roofs, and so forth. Yet anecdotal accounts suggest that people tend to overestimate geographical slant. Thus, Proffitt and his colleagues set out to collect the first systematic data on everyday geographical pitch perception. They ended up conducting a series of five studies. We'll examine the first study in detail and then briefly discuss the follow-up studies.

Method

Subjects. Three hundred students at the University of Virginia agreed to participate in the study when asked by an experimenter stationed near the bottom of various hills around campus. Each participant made estimates for only one hill.

Stimuli. Nine hills on the University of Virginia campus were used as stimuli. The experimenters chose hills with lots of foot traffic, unobstructed views, and wide variation in geographical slant. The inclinations of the nine hills were 2, 4, 5, 6, 10, 21, 31, 33, and 34 degrees. To put these figures in perspective, the authors note that 9 degrees is the steepest incline allowed for roads in Virginia and that a 30-degree hill is about the limit of what most people can walk up (the very steep hills on campus had stairs nearby).

Measures and apparatus. The participants were asked to estimate geographical slant in three ways. They provided a *verbal measure* by estimating the slope of the hill they were viewing in degrees. They provided a *visual measure* by adjusting the incline on the disk shown in Figure 4.38a to match the slope of the hill they were viewing. Finally, they provided a *haptic measure* (one based on touch) by adjusting the tilt board shown in Figure 4.38b to match the slope of the stimulus hill. To keep the latter measure exclusively haptic and not visual, participants were not allowed to look at their hand while they adjusted the tilt board.

Results

The mean slant estimates for all three measures and all nine hills are summarized graphically in Figure 4.39. As you can see, the participants' verbal and visual judgments resulted in large overestimates of all nine hills' geographic slant. For example, participants' verbal estimates for the 5-degree hill in the study averaged 20 degrees. Similarly, their visual estimates for the 10-degree hill averaged 25 degrees. In contrast, the subjects' haptic judgments were much more accurate.

Discussion

Why do hills appear substantially steeper than they are? Why are haptic judgments relatively immune to this peculiar perceptual bias? The authors argue that the data for all three measures make sense from an adaptive point of view. Subjects' verbal and visual estimates reflect their conscious awareness of how challenging hills will be to climb. Overestimates of slant are functional in that they should prevent people from undertaking climbs they are not equipped to handle, and they lead people to pace themselves and conserve energy on the steep hills they do attempt to traverse. Although overestimates of slant may be functional when people make conscious decisions about climbing hills, they would be very dysfunctional if they distorted people's locomotion on hills. If people walking up a 5-degree hill raised their feet to accommodate a 20-degree slope, they would stumble. Accurate tactile perceptions are thus crucial to people's motor responses when they walk up a hill, so it is functional for haptic perceptions to be largely unaffected by the misperception of slant. Thus, learning, or evolution, or some combination has equipped people with perceptual responses that are adaptive.

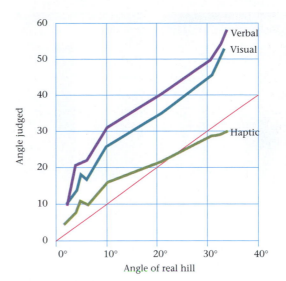

Figure 4.39
Mean slant estimates. The average pitch estimates for all three types of measures are plotted here. The red line shows where accurate estimates would fall. As you can see, verbal and visual measures yielded substantial overestimates, but haptic measures were reasonably accurate. (Adapted from Proffitt et al., 1995)

Comment

The study of sensation and perception is one of the oldest areas of scientific research in psychology. Yet this study shows that there are still fascinating areas of inquiry that remain unexplored. It just takes some creativity and insight to recognize them. This research also illustrates the importance of using more than a single measure of the phenomenon that one is interested in. The investigators chose to assess the dependent variable of slant perception in several ways, leading to a much richer understanding of slant perception than if only one of the three measures had been used. Finally, the highly exaggerated estimates of slant show once again that human perceptions are not simple reflections of reality, although most people tend to assume that they are. The authors note that many of their subjects were "incredulous" during their postexperimental briefings: "To look at a 10-degree hill—typically judged to be about 30 degrees by verbal reports and visual matching—and to be told that it is actually 10 degrees is an astonishing experience for anyone unfamiliar with the facts of geographical slant overestimation" (p. 425).

In their follow-up studies, Proffitt and his colleagues (1995) replicated and extended their original findings. In the second study, they found that verbal and visual overestimates of pitch are even more pronounced when hills are viewed from the top rather than the bottom. They argue that this bias makes functional sense because, as those of us who live in the San Francisco area can testify, steep hills are much harder to descend than ascend. For the third and fourth studies, they created a computer-simulated virtual reality environment, in which they could confront subjects with a wider range of inclines than were readily available out-of-doors and observed the same trends in the misperception of slant. In the fifth study, subjects' fatigue was manipulated by having the participants make slant estimates before or after an exhausting run. Consistent with their adaptive perspective, the investigators found that hills look even steeper when people are tired. Their findings on the influence of fatigue demonstrate once again that perception is a highly subjective process.

Perceptual Constancies in Vision

When a person approaches you from a distance, his or her image on your retinas gradually changes

Figure 4.40
Shape constancy. Notice how the shape of this door changes as it opens, yet viewers perceive the door as having a constant shape. This built-in talent for overriding sensory input creates stability in your perceptual world.

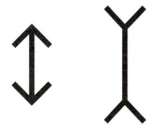

Figure 4.41
The Müller-Lyer illusion. Go ahead, measure them: the two vertical lines are of equal length.

Figure 4.42
Explaining the Müller-Lyer illusion. The figure on the left seems to be closer, since it looks like an outside corner, thrust toward you, whereas the figure on the right looks like an inside corner thrust away from you. Given retinal images of the same length, you assume that the "closer" line is shorter.

in size. Do you perceive that the person is growing right before your eyes? Of course not. Your perceptual system constantly makes allowances for this variation in visual input. The task of the perceptual system is to provide an accurate rendition of distal stimuli based on distorted, ever-changing proximal stimuli. In doing so, it relies in part on perceptual constancies. A *perceptual constancy* is a tendency to experience a stable perception in the face of continually changing sensory input. Among other things, people tend to view objects as having a stable size, shape (see Figure 4.40), brightness, hue, and location in space.

The Power of Misleading Cues: Optical Illusions 3g

In general, perceptual constancies, depth cues, and principles of visual organization (such as the Gestalt laws) help people perceive the world accurately. Sometimes, however, perceptions are based on inappropriate assumptions, and *optical illusions* can result. An *optical illusion* involves an apparently inexplicable discrepancy between the appearance of a visual stimulus and its physical reality.

One famous optical illusion is the *Müller-Lyer* illusion, shown in Figure 4.41. The two vertical lines in this figure are equally long, but they certainly don't look that way. Why not? Several mechanisms probably play a role (Day, 1965; Gregory, 1978). The figure on the left looks like the outside of a building, thrust toward the viewer, while the one on the right looks like an inside corner, thrust away (see Figure 4.42). The vertical

line in the left figure therefore seems closer. If two lines cast equally long retinal images but one seems closer, the closer one is assumed to be shorter. Thus, the Müller-Lyer illusion may be due largely to a combination of size constancy processes and misperception of depth.

The other geometric illusions shown in Figure 4.43 also demonstrate that visual stimuli can be highly deceptive. The *Ponzo illusion,* which is shown at the top of Figure 4.43, appears to result from the same factors at work in the Müller-Lyer illusion (Coren & Girgus, 1978). The upper and lower horizontal lines are the same length, but the upper one appears longer. This illusion probably occurs because the converging lines convey linear perspective, a key depth cue suggesting that the upper line lies farther away. Figure 4.44 shows a drawing by Stanford University psychologist Roger Shepard (1990) that creates a similar illusion. The second monster appears much larger than the first, even though they are really identical in size.

Adelbert Ames designed a striking illusion that makes use of misperception of distance. It's called, appropriately enough, the *Ames room.* It's a specially contrived room built with a trapezoidal rear

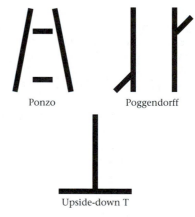

Ponzo   Poggendorff

Upside-down T

Zollner

Figure 4.43
Four geometric illusions. Ponzo: The horizontal lines are the same length. **Poggendorff:** The two diagonal segments lie on the same straight line. **Upside-down T:** The vertical and horizontal lines are the same length. **Zollner:** The long diagonals are all parallel (try covering up some of the short diagonal lines if you don't believe it).

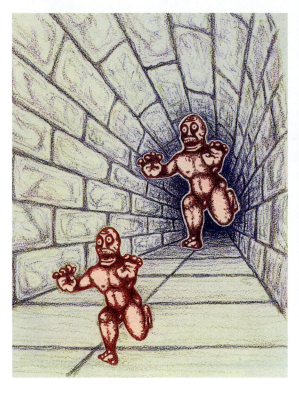

Figure 4.44
A monster of an illusion. The principles underlying the Ponzo illusion also explain the striking illusion seen here, in which two identical monsters appear to be quite different in size. (From Shepard, 1990)

Figure 4.45
The Ames room. The diagram shows the room as it is actually constructed. However, the viewer assumes that the room is rectangular. Because of this reasonable perceptual hypothesis, the normal perceptual adjustments made to preserve size constancy lead to the bizarre perceptions described in the text. For example, naive viewers "conclude" that one boy is much larger than the other, when in fact he is merely closer.

wall and a sloping floor and ceiling. When viewed from the correct point, as in the picture, it looks like an ordinary rectangular room (see Figure 4.45). But in reality, the left corner is much taller and much farther from the viewer than the right corner. Hence, bizarre illusions unfold in the Ames room. People standing in the right corner appear to be giants, while those standing in the left corner appear to be midgets. Even more disconcerting, a person who walks across the room from right to left appears to shrink before your very eyes! The Ames room creates these misperceptions by toying with the perfectly reasonable assumption that the room is vertically and horizontally rectangular.

Impossible figures (see Figure 4.46) create another form of illusion. **Impossible figures are objects that can be represented in two-dimensional pic-**

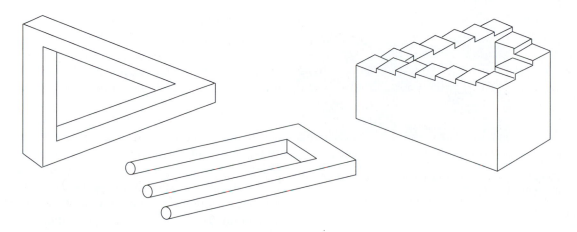

Figure 4.46
Three classic impossible figures. The figures are impossible, yet they clearly exist—on the page. What makes them impossible is that they appear to be three-dimensional representations yet are drawn in a way that frustrates mental attempts to "assemble" their features into possible objects. It's difficult to see the drawings simply as lines lying in a plane—even though this perceptual hypothesis is the only one that resolves the contradiction.

Figure 4.47
Another impossible figure. This impossible figure, drawn by Shepard (1990), seems even more perplexing than the classic impossible figure that it is based on (the one seen in the middle of Figure 4.46).

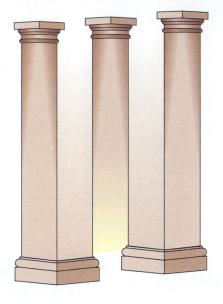

tures but cannot exist in three-dimensional space. These figures may look fine at first glance, but a closer look reveals that they are geometrically inconsistent or impossible. Three widely studied impossible figures are shown in Figure 4.46, and a dramatic new impossible figure drawn by Roger Shepard (1990) can be seen in Figure 4.47. Notice that specific portions of these figures are

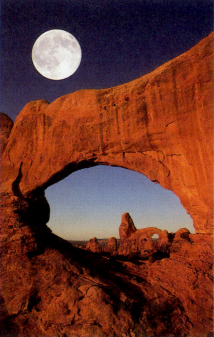

Unlike people in Western nations, the Zulus live in a culture where straight lines and right angles are scarce, if not entirely absent. Thus, they are not affected by such phenomena as the Müller-Lyer illusion nearly as much as people raised in environments that abound with rectangular structures.

A puzzling perceptual illusion common in everyday life is the moon illusion: the moon looks larger when at the horizon than when overhead.

reasonable, but they don't add up to a sensible whole. The parts don't interface properly. The initial illusion that the figures make sense is probably a result of bottom-up processing. You perceive specific features of the figure as acceptable but are baffled as they are built into a whole.

Obviously, illusions such as impossible figures and their real-life relative, the Ames room, involve a conspiracy of cues intended to deceive the viewer. Many visual illusions, however, occur quite naturally. A well-known example is the *moon illusion*. The full moon appears to be much smaller when overhead than when looming over the horizon. As with many of the other illusions we have discussed, the moon illusion appears to be due mainly to size constancy effects coupled with the misperception of distance (Coren & Aks, 1990; Kaufman & Rock, 1962). The moon illusion shows that optical illusions are part of everyday life. Indeed, many people are virtually addicted to an optical illusion called television (an illusion of movement created by a series of still images presented in quick succession).

Cross-cultural studies have uncovered some interesting differences among cultural groups in their propensity to see certain illusions. For example, Segall, Campbell, and Herskovits (1966) found that people from a variety of non-Western cultures are less susceptible to the Müller-Lyer illusion than Western samples. What could account for this difference? The most plausible explanation is that in the West, we live in a "carpentered world" dominated by straight lines, right angles, and rectangular rooms, buildings, and furniture. Thus, our experience prepares us to readily view the Müller-Lyer figures as inside and outside corners of buildings—inferences that help foster the illusion (Segall et al., 1990). In contrast, people in many non-Western cultures, such as the Zulu (see photo at far left) who were tested by Segall and associates (1966), live in a less carpentered world, making them less prone to see the Müller-Lyer figures as building corners. In a similar vein, some investigators have found that cultural groups with little exposure to roads and railroad tracks are less susceptible to the Ponzo illusion than Western groups (Berry et al., 1992). Although there is some debate about the matter (Coren, 1989a; Pollack, 1989), these cultural differences in illusion susceptibility suggest that people's perceptual inferences can be shaped by experience (Segall et al., 1990).

What do optical illusions reveal about visual perception? They drive home the point that people go through life formulating perceptual hypotheses about what lies out there in the real world. The fact that these are only hypotheses becomes especially striking when the hypotheses are wrong, as they are with illusions. Optical illusions also show how contextual factors such as depth cues shape perceptual hypotheses. Finally, like ambiguous figures, illusions clearly demonstrate that human perceptions are not simple reflections of objective reality. Once again, we see that perception of the world is subjective. These insights do not apply to visual perception only. We will encounter these lessons again as we examine other sensory systems, such as hearing, which we turn to next.

Recap of Key Points

• Reversible figures and perceptual sets demonstrate that the same visual input can result in very different perceptions. According to feature analysis theories, people detect specific elements in stimuli and build them into recognizable forms through bottom-up processing.

• However, evidence on word recognition and subjective contours, among other things, suggests that form perception also involves top-down processing, which progresses from the whole to the elements.

• Gestalt psychology emphasized that the whole may be greater than the sum of its parts (features), as illustrated by the Gestalt principles of form perception, including figure-ground, proximity, similarity, continuity, closure, simplicity, common region, and connectedness.

• Other approaches to form perception emphasize that people develop perceptual hypotheses about the distal stimuli that could be responsible for the proximal stimuli that are sensed.

• Depth perception depends primarily on monocular cues, including pictorial cues such as texture gradient, linear perspective, light and shadow, interposition, relative size, and height in plane. People from picture-less societies initially have some difficulty in applying pictorial depth cues to two-dimensional pictures.

• Binocular cues such as retinal disparity and convergence can also contribute to depth perception. Conscious perceptions of geographical slant, as reflected by visual and verbal estimates of pitch, tend to be greatly exaggerated, but haptic (tactile) judgments seem largely immune to this perceptual bias.

• Perceptual constancies in vision help viewers deal with the ever-shifting nature of proximal stimuli. Optical illusions demonstrate that perceptual hypotheses can be inaccurate and that perceptions are not simple reflections of objective reality. Researchers have found some interesting cultural differences in susceptibility to the Müller-Lyer and Ponzo illusions.

OUR SENSE OF HEARING: THE AUDITORY SYSTEM

Stop reading for a moment, close your eyes, and listen carefully. What do you hear?

Chances are, you'll discover that you're immersed in sounds: street noises, a high-pitched laugh from the next room, the hum of a fluorescent lamp, perhaps some background music you put on a while ago but forgot about. As this little demonstration shows, physical stimuli producing sound are present almost constantly, but you're not necessarily aware of these sounds.

Like vision, the auditory (hearing) system provides input about the world "out there," but not until incoming information is processed by the brain. A distal stimulus—a screech of tires, someone laughing, the hum of the refrigerator—produces a proximal stimulus in the form of sound waves reaching the ears. The perceptual system must somehow transform this stimulation into the psychological experience of hearing. We'll begin our discussion of hearing by looking at the stimulus for auditory experience: sound.

The Stimulus: Sound 3h

Sound waves are vibrations of molecules, which means that they must travel through some physical medium, such as air. They move at a fraction of the speed of light. Sound waves are usually generated by vibrating objects, such as a guitar string, a loudspeaker cone, or your vocal cords. However, sound waves can also be generated by forcing air past a chamber (as in a pipe organ), or by suddenly releasing a burst of air (as when you clap).

Like light waves, sound waves are characterized by their *amplitude*, their *wavelength*, and their *purity* (see Figure 4.48 on page 156). The physical properties of amplitude, wavelength, and purity affect mainly the perceived (psychological) qualities of loudness, pitch, and timbre, respectively.

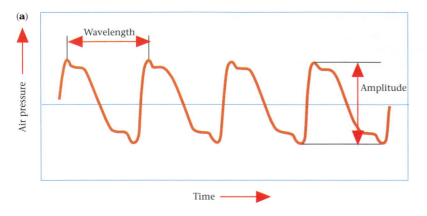

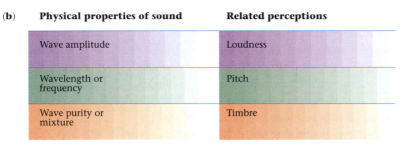

Physical properties of sound	Related perceptions
Wave amplitude	Loudness
Wavelength or frequency	Pitch
Wave purity or mixture	Timbre

**Figure 4.48
Sound, the physical stimulus for hearing.**
(**a**) Like light, sound travels in waves—in this case, waves of air pressure. A smooth curve would represent a pure tone, such as that produced by a tuning fork. Most sounds, however, are complex. For example, the wave shown here is for middle C played on a piano. The sound wave for the same note played on a violin would have the same wavelength (or frequency) as this one, but the "wrinkles" in the wave would be different, corresponding to the differences in timbre between the two sounds. (**b**) The table shows the main relations between objective aspects of sound and subjective perceptions.

However, the physical properties of sound interact in complex ways to produce perceptions of these sound qualities (Hirsh & Watson, 1996).

Human Hearing Capacities   3h

Wavelengths of sound are described in terms of their *frequency,* which is measured in cycles per second, or *hertz (Hz)*. For the most part, higher frequencies are perceived as having higher pitch. That is, if you strike the key for high C on a piano, it will produce higher-frequency sound waves than the key for low C. Although the perception of pitch depends mainly on frequency, the amplitude of the sound waves also influences it.

Just as the visible spectrum is only a portion of the total spectrum of light, so, too, what people can hear is only a portion of the available range of sounds. Humans can hear sounds ranging in frequency from a low of 20 Hz up to a high of about 20,000 Hz. Sounds at either end of this range are harder to hear, and sensitivity to high-frequency tones declines as adults grow older. Other organisms have different capabilities. Low-frequency sounds under 10 Hz are audible to homing pigeons, for example. At the other extreme, bats and porpoises can hear frequencies well above 20,000 Hz.

In general, the greater the amplitude of sound waves, the louder the sound perceived. Whereas frequency is measured in hertz, amplitude is measured in *decibels (dB)*. The relationship between decibels (which measure a physical property of sound) and loudness (a psychological quality) is

complex. A rough rule of thumb is that perceived loudness doubles about every 10 decibels (Stevens, 1955). To make this less abstract, Figure 4.49 shows approximate decibel levels for a wide range of common sounds. Very loud sounds can jeopardize the quality of your hearing. Even brief exposure to sounds over 120 decibels can be painful and may cause damage to your auditory system (Henry, 1984).

As shown in Figure 4.49, the absolute thresholds for the weakest sounds people can hear differ for sounds of various frequencies. The human ear is most sensitive to sounds at frequencies between 2000 and 4000 Hz. That is, these frequencies yield the lowest absolute thresholds. To summarize, amplitude is the principal determinant of loudness, but loudness ultimately depends on an interaction between amplitude and frequency.

People are also sensitive to variations in the purity of sounds. The purest sound is one that has only a single frequency of vibration, such as that produced by a tuning fork. Most everyday sounds are complex mixtures of many frequencies. The purity or complexity of a sound influences how *timbre* is perceived. To understand timbre, think of a note with precisely the same loudness and pitch played on a French horn and then on a violin. The difference you perceive in the sounds is a difference in timbre.

Sensory Processing in the Ear   3h

Like your eyes, your ears channel energy to the neural tissue that receives it. Figure 4.50 (on page 160) shows that the human ear can be divided into three sections: the external ear, the middle ear, and the inner ear. Sound is conducted differently in each section. The external ear depends on the *vibration of air molecules*. The middle ear depends on the *vibration of movable bones*. And the inner ear depends on *waves in a fluid,* which are finally converted into a stream of neural signals sent to the brain (Kiang & Peake, 1988).

The *external ear* consists mainly of the *pinna*, a sound-collecting cone. When you cup your hand behind your ear to try to hear better, you are augmenting that cone. Many animals have large external ears that they can aim directly toward a sound source. However, humans can adjust their aim only crudely, by turning their heads. Sound waves collected by the pinna are funneled along the auditory canal toward the *eardrum,* a taut membrane that vibrates in response.

In the *middle ear,* the vibrations of the eardrum

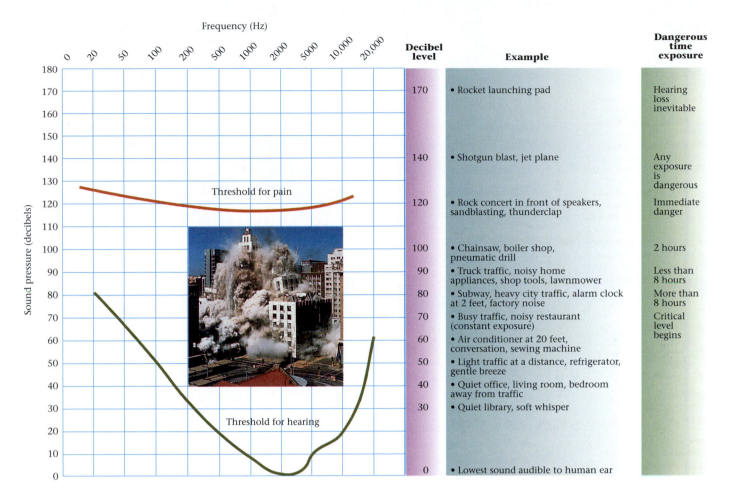

Frequency (Hz)

Decibel level	Example	Dangerous time exposure
170	• Rocket launching pad	Hearing loss inevitable
140	• Shotgun blast, jet plane	Any exposure is dangerous
120	• Rock concert in front of speakers, sandblasting, thunderclap	Immediate danger
100	• Chainsaw, boiler shop, pneumatic drill	2 hours
90	• Truck traffic, noisy home appliances, shop tools, lawnmower	Less than 8 hours
80	• Subway, heavy city traffic, alarm clock at 2 feet, factory noise	More than 8 hours
70	• Busy traffic, noisy restaurant (constant exposure)	Critical level begins
60	• Air conditioner at 20 feet, conversation, sewing machine	
50	• Light traffic at a distance, refrigerator, gentle breeze	
40	• Quiet office, living room, bedroom away from traffic	
30	• Quiet library, soft whisper	
0	• Lowest sound audible to human ear	

are transmitted inward by a mechanical chain made up of the three tiniest bones in your body (the hammer, anvil, and stirrup), known collectively as the *ossicles*. The ossicles form a three-stage lever system that converts relatively large movements with little force into smaller motions with greater force. The ossicles serve to amplify tiny changes in air pressure.

The *inner ear* consists largely of the **cochlea, a fluid-filled, coiled tunnel that contains the receptors for hearing.** The term *cochlea* comes from the Greek word for a spiral-shelled snail, which this chamber resembles (see Figure 4.50). Sound enters the cochlea through the *oval window*, which is vibrated by the ossicles. The ear's neural tissue, analogous to the retina in the eye, lies within the cochlea. This tissue sits on the basilar membrane that divides the cochlea into upper and lower chambers. **The basilar membrane, which runs the length of the spiraled cochlea, holds the auditory receptors.** The auditory receptors are called *hair cells* because of the tiny bundles of hairs that protrude from them. Waves in the fluid of the inner ear stimulate the hair cells. Like the rods and cones in the eye, the hair cells convert this physi-

cal stimulation into neural impulses that are sent to the brain (Dallos, 1981).

Auditory Pathways to the Brain

After leaving the ears, the auditory nerves travel to the lower brainstem, where synapses interconnect in a complex network. Many pathways cross to the other side of the brain, so that input from each ear projects more directly and immediately to the *opposite* side of the brain than to the side the ear is on.

The auditory pathways ascend through the brainstem to the auditory portion of the thalamus. From here, auditory signals are shuttled to the *auditory cortex*, which is located mostly in the temporal lobe of each cerebral hemisphere. Studies suggest that the auditory cortex has specialized cells—similar to the feature detectors found in the visual cortex—that have special sensitivity to certain features of sound (Abeles & Goldstein, 1970).

Much remains to be learned about which physiological structures handle which aspects of auditory information processing. Structures in the brainstem appear critical for locating sounds in space (Aitkin, 1986). Much of the processing of loudness and pitch also appears to occur in lower

Figure 4.49
Sound pressure and auditory experience. Sound pressure, measured in decibels, interacts with frequency to produce different auditory effects. For example, the threshold for human hearing (graphed in green) is a function of both decibel level and frequency. Human hearing is keenest for sounds at a frequency of about 2000–4000 Hz; at other frequencies, higher decibel levels are needed to produce sounds people can detect. On the other hand, the human threshold for pain (graphed in red) is almost purely a function of decibel level. Some common sounds corresponding to various decibel levels are listed to the right, together with the amount of time at which exposure to higher levels becomes dangerous.

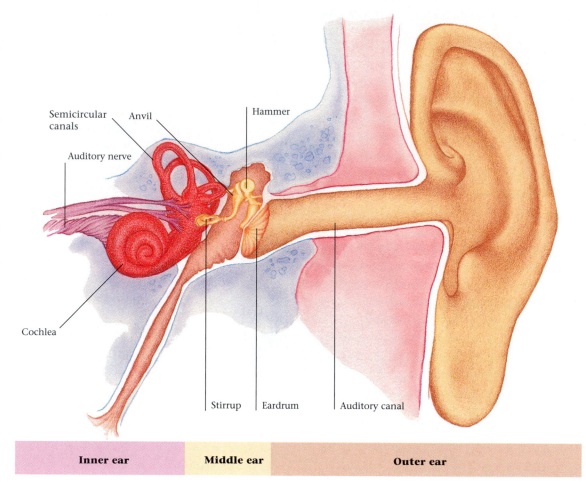

Figure 4.50
The human ear. Converting sound pressure to information processed by the nervous system involves a complex relay of stimuli: Waves of air pressure create vibrations in the eardrum, which in turn cause oscillations in the tiny bones in the inner ear (the hammer, anvil, and stirrup). As they are relayed from one bone to the next, the oscillations are magnified and then transformed into pressure waves moving through a liquid medium in the cochlea. These waves cause the basilar membrane to oscillate, stimulating the hair cells that are the actual auditory receptors (see Figure 4.51).

Semicircular canals

Anvil

Hammer

Auditory nerve

Cochlea

Stirrup | Eardrum | Auditory canal

| Inner ear | Middle ear | Outer ear |

Figure 4.51
The basilar membrane.
The figure shows the cochlea unwound and cut open to reveal the basilar membrane, which is covered with thousands of hair cells (the auditory receptors). Pressure waves in the fluid filling the cochlea cause oscillations to travel in waves down the basilar membrane, stimulating the hair cells to fire. Although the entire membrane vibrates, as predicted by frequency theory, the point along the membrane where the wave peaks depends on the frequency of the sound stimulus, as suggested by place theory.

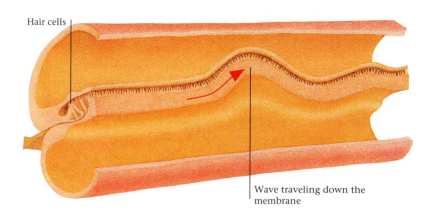

Hair cells

Wave traveling down the membrane

brain centers (Durrant & Lovrinic, 1977). So, what's left for the auditory cortex to handle? Theorists speculate that cortical processing may be critical to the ability to recognize complex patterns (sequences) of sounds—in particular, the patterns that make up human speech.

Auditory Perception: Theories of Hearing

Theories of hearing need to account for how sound waves are physiologically translated into the perceptions of pitch, loudness, and timbre. To date,

most of the theorizing about hearing has focused on the perception of pitch, which is reasonably well understood. Researchers' understanding of loudness and timbre perception is primitive by comparison. Hence, we'll limit our coverage to theories of pitch perception.

Place Theory

There have been two influential theories of pitch perception: *place theory* and *frequency theory*. You'll be able to follow the development of these theories more easily if you can imagine the spiraled cochlea unraveled, so that the basilar membrane becomes a long, thin sheet, lined with about 25,000 individual hair cells (see Figure 4.51). Long ago, Hermann von Helmholtz (1863) proposed that specific sound frequencies vibrate specific portions of the basilar membrane, producing distinct pitches, just as plucking specific strings on a harp produces sounds of varied pitch. This model, called **place theory, holds that perception of pitch corresponds to the vibration of different portions, or places, along the basilar membrane.** Place theory assumes that hair cells at various locations respond independently and that different sets of hair cells are vibrated by different sound frequencies. The brain then detects the frequency of a tone according to which area along the basilar membrane is most active.

Frequency Theory

Other theorists in the 19th century proposed an alternative theory of pitch perception, called frequency theory (Rutherford, 1886). *Frequency theory* **holds that perception of pitch corresponds to the rate, or frequency, at which the entire basilar membrane vibrates.** This theory views the basilar membrane as more like a drumhead than a harp. According to frequency theory, the whole membrane vibrates in unison in response to sounds. However, a particular sound frequency, say 3000 Hz, causes the basilar membrane to vibrate at a corresponding rate of 3000 times per second. The brain detects the frequency of a tone by the rate at which the auditory nerve fibers fire.

Reconciling Place and Frequency Theories

The competition between these two theories is reminiscent of the dispute between the trichromatic and opponent process theories of color vision. Like that argument, the debate between place and frequency theories generated roughly a century of research. Although both theories proved to have some flaws, *both turned out to be valid in part.*

Helmholtz's place theory was basically on the mark except for one detail. The hair cells along the basilar membrane are not independent. They vibrate together, as suggested by frequency theory. The actual pattern of vibration, described in Nobel prize–winning research by Georg von Békésy (1947), is a traveling wave that moves along the basilar membrane. Place theory is correct, however, in that the wave peaks at a particular place, depending on the frequency of the sound wave.

Frequency theory was also found to be flawed when investigators learned that neurons are hard pressed to fire at a maximum rate of about 1000 impulses per second. How, then, can frequency theory account for the translation of 4000 Hz sound waves, which would require 4000 impulses per second? The answer, suggested by Wever and Bray (1937), is that groups of hair cells operate according to the volley principle. **The *volley principle* holds that groups of auditory nerve fibers fire neural impulses in rapid succession, creating volleys of impulses.** These volleys exceed the 1000-per-second limit. Studies suggest that auditory nerves can team up like this to generate volleys of up to 5000 impulses per second (Zwislocki, 1981).

Although the original theories had to be revised, the current thinking is that pitch perception depends on both place and frequency coding of vibrations along the basilar membrane (Goldstein, 1996). Sounds under 1000 Hz appear to be translated into pitch through frequency coding. For sounds between 1000 and 5000 Hz, pitch perception seems to depend on a combination of frequency and place coding. Sounds over 5000 Hz seem to be handled through place coding only. Again we find that theories that were pitted against each other for decades are complementary rather than contradictory.

Auditory Localization: Perceiving Sources of Sound

You're driving down a street when suddenly you hear a siren wailing in the distance. As the wail grows louder, you glance around, cocking your ear to the sound. Where is it coming from? Behind you? In front of you? From one side? This example illustrates a common perceptual task called *auditory localization*—**locating the source of a sound in space.** The process of recognizing where a sound is coming from is analogous to recognizing depth or distance in vision. Both processes involve spatial aspects of sensory input. The fact that human ears are set *apart* contributes to auditory localization, just as the separation of the eyes contributes to depth perception.

Two cues appear critical to auditory localization: the intensity (loudness) and timing of sounds arriving at each ear (Phillips & Brugge, 1985). For example, a sound source to one side of the head produces a greater intensity at the ear nearer to the sound. This is due partly to the loss of sound intensity with distance. Another factor at work is the "shadow," or partial sound barrier, cast by the head itself (see Figure 4.52 on page 162). The intensity difference between the two ears is greatest when the sound source is well to one side. The human perceptual system uses this difference as a clue in localizing sounds. Because the path to the farther ear is longer, a sound takes longer to reach that ear. This reality means that sounds can be localized by comparing the timing of their arrival at each ear. Such comparison of the timing of sounds is remarkably sensitive. People can detect timing differences as small as 1/100,000 of a second (Durlach & Colburn, 1978).

"The psychic activities, by which we arrive at the judgment that a certain object of a certain character exists before us at a certain place, are generally not conscious activities but unconscious ones. . . . It may be permissible to designate the psychic acts of ordinary perception as unconscious inferences.

HERMANN VON HELMHOLTZ

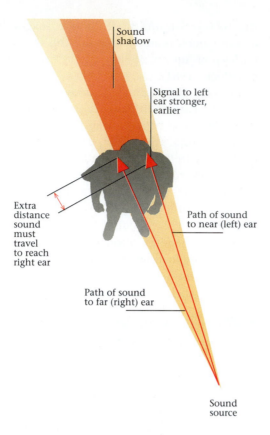

Figure 4.52
Cues in auditory localization. A sound coming from the left reaches the left ear sooner than the right. When the sound reaches the right ear, it is also less intense because it has traveled a greater distance and because it is in the sound shadow produced by the listener's head. These cues are used to localize the sources of sound in space.

Sound shadow

Signal to left ear stronger, earlier

Extra distance sound must travel to reach right ear

Path of sound to near (left) ear

Path of sound to far (right) ear

Sound source

Recap of Key Points

• Sound varies in terms of wavelength (frequency), amplitude, and purity. These properties affect mainly perceptions of pitch, loudness, and timbre, respectively. The human ear is most sensitive to sounds between 2000 and 4000 Hz. Even brief exposure to sounds over 120 decibels can be painful and damaging.

• Sound is transmitted through the external ear via air conduction to the middle ear, where sound waves are translated into the vibration of tiny bones called ossicles. In the inner ear, fluid conduction vibrates hair cells along the basilar membrane in the cochlea. These hair cells are the receptors for hearing. Auditory signals are transmitted through the brainstem and thalamus to the primary auditory cortex in the temporal lobe.

• Place theory proposed that pitch perception depends on where vibrations occur along the basilar membrane. Frequency theory countered with the idea that pitch perception depends on the rate at which the basilar membrane vibrates. Modern evidence suggests that these theories are complementary rather than incompatible.

• Auditory localization involves locating the source of a sound in space. People pinpoint where sounds have come from by comparing interear differences in the intensity and timing of sounds.

OUR CHEMICAL SENSES: TASTE AND SMELL

Psychologists have devoted most of their attention to the visual and auditory systems. Although less is known about the chemical senses, taste and smell also play a critical role in people's experience of the world. Let's take a brief look at what psychologists have learned about **the *gustatory system*—the sensory system for taste**—and its close cousin, **the *olfactory system*—the sensory system for smell**.

Taste: The Gustatory System

True wine lovers go through an elaborate series of steps when they are served a good bottle of wine. Typically, they begin by drinking a little water to cleanse their palate. Then they sniff the cork from the wine bottle, swirl a small amount of the wine around in a glass, and sniff the odor emerging from the glass. Finally, they take a sip of the wine, rolling it around in their mouth for a short time before swallowing it. At last they are ready to confer their approval or disapproval. Is all this activity really a meaningful way to put the wine to a sensitive test? Or is it just a harmless ritual passed on through tradition? You'll find out in this section.

The physical stimuli for the sense of taste are chemical substances that are soluble (dissolvable in water). The gustatory receptors are clusters of taste cells found in the *taste buds* that line the trenches around tiny bumps on the tongue. When these cells absorb chemicals dissolved in saliva, they trigger neural impulses that are routed through the thalamus to the cortex. Interestingly, taste cells have a short life, spanning only about ten days, and they are constantly being replaced (Pfaffmann, 1978). New cells are born at the edge of the taste bud and migrate inward to die at the center.

It's generally (but not universally) agreed that there are four *primary tastes:* sweet, sour, bitter, and salty (Bartoshuk, 1988). Sensitivity to these tastes is distributed somewhat unevenly across the tongue, but the variations in sensitivity are quite small and very complicated (Bartoshuk, 1993; see Figure 4.53). Although most taste cells respond to more than one of the primary tastes, they typically respond best to one. Perceptions of taste quality appear to depend on complex patterns of neural activity initiated by taste receptors (Castelloci, 1986; Pfaffmann, 1974).

"Good and bad are so intimately associated with taste and smell that we have special words for the experiences (e.g., repugnant, foul). The immediacy of the pleasure makes it seem absolute and thus inborn. This turns out to be true for taste but not for smell."

LINDA BARTOSHUK

Some basic taste preferences appear to be innate and to be automatically regulated by physiological mechanisms. In humans, for instance, newborn infants react positively to sweet tastes and negatively to strong concentrations of bitter, salty, or sour tastes (Lipsitt & Behl, 1990). To some extent, these innate taste preferences are flexible, changing to accommodate the body's nutritional needs (Scott, 1990).

Although some basic aspects of taste perception may be innate, taste preferences are largely learned and heavily influenced by social processes (Rozin, 1990). Most parents are aware of this reality and intentionally try—with varied success—to mold their children's taste preferences early in life (Casey & Rozin, 1989). This extensive social influence contributes greatly to the striking ethnic and cultural disparities found in taste preferences (Kittler & Sucher, 1989). Foods that are a source of disgust in Western cultures—such as worms, fish eyes, and blood—may be delicacies in other cultures (see Figure 4.54 on page 164). Indeed, Rozin (1990) asserts that feces may be the only universal source of taste-related disgust in humans. To a large degree, variations in taste preferences depend on what one has been exposed to (Capaldi & VandenBos, 1991). Exposure to various foods varies along ethnic lines because different cultures have different traditions in food preparation, different agricultural resources, different climates to work with, and so forth.

So far, we've been discussing taste, but what we are really interested in is the *perception of flavor.*

Odor contributes greatly to flavor (Bartoshuk, 1991). Although taste and smell are distinct sensory systems, they interact extensively. The ability to identify flavors declines noticeably when odor cues are absent (Mozell et al., 1969). You might have noticed this interaction when you ate a favorite meal while enduring a severe head cold. The food probably tasted bland, because your stuffy nose impaired your sense of smell.

Now that we've explored the dynamics of taste, we can return to our question about the value of

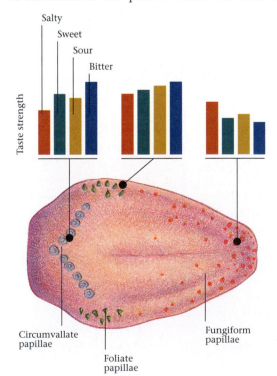

Figure 4.53
The tongue and taste.
Taste buds are clustered around tiny bumps on the tongue called papillae. There are three types of papillae, which are distributed as shown here. The taste buds found in each type of papillae show slightly different sensitivities to the four basic tastes, as mapped out in the graph at the top. Thus, sensitivity to the primary tastes varies across the tongue, but these variations are small and all four primary tastes can be detected wherever there are taste receptors (Source: Adapted from Bartoshuk, 1993).

Figure 4.54
Culture and taste preferences. Taste preferences are largely learned, and they vary dramatically from one society to the next, as these examples demonstrate.

Grubs. For most North Americans, the thought of eating a worm would be totally unthinkable. For the Asmat of New Guinea, however, a favorite delicacy is the plump, white, two-inch larva or beetle grub.

Fish eyes. For some Eskimo children, raw fish eyes are like candy. Here you see a young girl using the Eskimo's all-purpose knife to gouge out the eye of an already-filleted Arctic fish.

Blood. Several tribes in East Africa supplement their diet with fresh blood that is sometimes mixed with milk. They obtain the blood by puncturing a cow's jugular vein with a sharp arrow. The blood-milk drink provides a rich source of protein and iron.

the wine-tasting ritual. This elaborate ritual is indeed an authentic way to put wine to a sensitive test. The aftereffects associated with sensory adaptation make it wise to cleanse one's palate before tasting the wine. Sniffing the cork, and the wine in the glass, is important because odor is a major determinant of flavor. Swirling the wine in the glass helps release the wine's odor. And rolling the wine around in your mouth is especially critical, because it distributes the wine over the full diversity of taste cells. It also forces the wine's odor up into the nasal passages. Thus, each action in this age-old ritual makes a meaningful contribution to the tasting.

Smell: The Olfactory System

Humans are usually characterized as being relatively insensitive to smell. In this regard they are often compared unfavorably to dogs, which are renowned for their ability to track a faint odor over long distances. Are humans really inferior in the sensory domain of smell? Let's examine the facts.

In many ways, the sense of smell is much like the sense of taste. The physical stimuli are chemical substances—volatile ones that can evaporate and be carried in the air. These chemical stimuli are dissolved in fluid—specifically, the mucus in the nose. The receptors for smell are *olfactory cilia*, hairlike structures located in the upper portion of the nasal passages (Cagen & Rhein, 1980) (see Figure 4.55). They resemble taste cells in that they have a short life and are constantly being replaced. The olfactory receptors have axons that synapse directly with cells in the olfactory bulb at the base of the brain. This arrangement is unique. Smell is the only sensory system that is not routed through the thalamus before it projects to the cortex.

Odors cannot be classified as neatly as tastes, since efforts to identify primary odors have proven unsatisfactory. If primary odors exist, there must be a fairly large number of them. Most olfactory receptors respond to a wide range of odors (Sicard & Holley, 1984). Hence, the perception of various

Figure 4.55
The olfactory system. Odor molecules travel through the nasal passages and stimulate olfactory cilia. An enlargement of these hairlike olfactory receptors is shown in the inset. The olfactory nerves transmit neural impulses through the olfactory bulb to the brain.

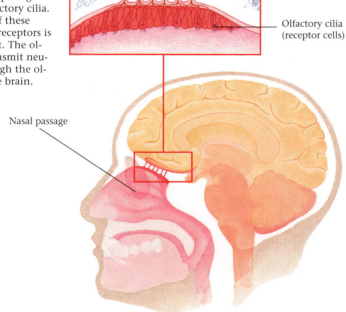

Olfactory bulb
Olfactory nerve
Olfactory cilia (receptor cells)
Nasal passage

odors probably depends on a great many types of receptors that are uniquely responsive to specific chemical structures (Bartoshuk & Beauchamp, 1994). Like the other senses, the sense of smell shows sensory adaptation. The perceived strength of an odor usually fades to less than half its original strength within about 4 minutes (Cain, 1988).

Overall, humans have greater olfactory capacities than widely believed (Cain, 1979). Comparing human olfactory sensitivity to that of dogs is much like comparing human height to that of giraffes, since dogs may possess the keenest sense of smell in the animal kingdom (Marshall & Moulton, 1981). Admittedly, people can't track the faint smell of a timber wolf through a mountain range, but they can track the weak odor of a pizza stand through a crowded street fair. Although there are some species whose sense of smell is superior, human olfaction compares favorably with that of many animals.

Recap of Key Points
• The taste buds are sensitive to four basic tastes: sweet, sour, bitter, and salty. Sensitivity to these tastes is distributed unevenly across the tongue, but the variations are small.
• Taste preferences are largely learned and heavily influenced by one's cultural background. The perception of flavor is influenced greatly by the odor of food.
• Like taste, smell is a chemical sense. Chemical stimuli activate receptors lining the nasal passages, called olfactory cilia. Most of these receptors respond to more than one odor. Human olfactory capabilities are often underestimated.

OUR SENSE OF TOUCH: SENSORY SYSTEMS IN THE SKIN

If there is any sense that people trust almost as much as sight, it is the sense of touch. Yet, like all the senses, touch involves converting the sensation of physical stimuli into a psychological experience—and it can be fooled.

The physical stimuli for touch are mechanical, thermal, and chemical energy that impinge on the skin. These stimuli can produce perceptions of tactile stimulation (the pressure of touch against the skin), warmth, cold, and pain. The human skin is saturated with at least six different types of sensory receptors (E. Gardner, 1975). To some degree, these different types of receptors are specialized for different functions, such as the registration of pressure, hot, cold, and so forth. However, these distinctions are not as clear as researchers had originally expected (Sinclair, 1981).

Feeling Pressure

If you've been to a mosquito-infested picnic lately, you'll appreciate the need to quickly know where tactile stimulation is coming from. The sense of touch is set up to meet this need for tactile localization with admirable precision and efficiency. Cells in the nervous system that respond to touch are sensitive to specific patches of skin. These skin patches, which vary considerably in size, are the functional equivalents of *receptive fields* in vision. Like visual receptive fields, they often involve a center-surround arrangement (see Figure 4.56). Thus, stimuli falling in the center produce the opposite effect of stimuli falling in the surrounding area (Kandel & Jessell, 1991). If a stimulus is applied continuously to a specific spot on the skin, the perception of pressure gradually fades. Hence, sensory adaptation occurs in the perception of touch, as it does in other sensory systems.

The nerve fibers that carry incoming information about tactile stimulation are routed through the spinal cord to the brainstem. There, the fibers from each side of the body cross over mostly to the opposite side of the brain. The tactile pathway then projects through the thalamus and onto the *somatosensory cortex* in the brain's parietal lobe. Some cells in the somatosensory cortex function like the *feature detectors* discovered in vision (Cholewiak & Collins, 1991). They respond to specific features of touch, such as a movement across the skin in a particular direction.

Feeling Hot and Cold

The sensory receptors that register variations in temperature are free nerve endings in the skin. They initiate signals along nerve fibers specific for warmth and cold. When skin temperature is normal, the "warm" and "cold" receptors fire spontaneously, without stimulating any noticeable sensation. If heat is applied, "warm" receptors fire more rapidly and "cold" receptors cease their spontaneous firing (Stevens, 1991). The application of a cold stimulus produces the opposite pattern of neural activity. Signals from the thermal receptors travel through the spinal cord to the brain along a pathway that is shared with pain signals but that

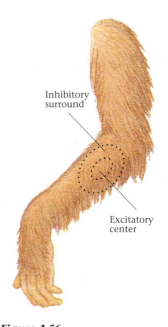

Inhibitory surround

Excitatory center

Figure 4.56
Receptive field for touch.
A receptive field for touch is an area on the skin surface that, when stimulated, affects the firing of a cell that responds to pressure on the skin. Shown here is a center-surround receptive field for a cell in the thalamus of a monkey.

is separate from the pathway for tactile stimulation (Martin & Jessell, 1991).

Feeling Pain

As unpleasant as pain is, the sensation of pain is crucial to survival. Pain is a marvelous warning system. It tells people when they should stop shoveling snow, or it lets them know that they have a pinched nerve that requires treatment. However, chronic pain is a frustrating, demoralizing affliction that affects over 50 million people in American society, at a cost of more than $70 billion annually (Turk, 1994). Thus, there are pressing practical reasons for psychologists' keen interest in the perception of pain.

Pathways to the Brain

The receptors for pain are mostly free nerve endings in the skin. Pain messages are transmitted to the brain via two types of pathways that pass through different areas in the thalamus (Willis, 1985). One is a *fast pathway* that registers localized pain and relays it to the cortex in a fraction of a second. This is the system that hits you with sharp pain when you first cut your finger. The second system uses a *slow pathway* that lags a second or two behind the fast system. This pathway (which also carries information about temperature) conveys the less localized, longer-lasting, aching or burning pain that comes after the initial injury. The slow pathway depends on thin, unmyelinated neurons called *C fibers,* whereas the fast pathway is mediated by thicker, myelinated neurons called *A-delta fibers* (see Figure 4.57).

Puzzles in Pain Perception

As with other perceptions, pain is not an automatic result of certain types of stimulation. The perception of pain can be influenced greatly by expectations, personality, mood, and other factors involving higher mental processes. For instance, in one study researchers manipulated subjects' mood and then asked them to fill out a scale on which they rated their personal pain in 25 body areas (Stalling, 1992). As predicted, subjects in the negative mood condition reported more pain than those in the positive mood condition. The subjective nature of pain is illustrated by placebo effects. As we saw in Chapter 2, many people suffering from pain report relief when given a placebo—an inert "sugar pill" that is presented to them as if it were a painkilling drug (Melzack, 1973).

Further evidence regarding the subjective quality of pain has come from studies that have found ethnic and cultural differences in the pain associated with childbirth (Jordan, 1983) and the experience of chronic pain (Bates, Edwards, & Anderson, 1993). According to Melzack and Wall (1982), culture doesn't affect the process of pain perception so much as the willingness to tolerate certain types of pain, a conclusion echoed by Zatzick and Dimsdale (1990). In any case, cross-cultural research provides support for Beecher's (1956) widely cited conclusion that "the intensity of suffering is largely determined by what the pain means to the patient" (p. 1609).

The psychological element in pain perception becomes clear when something distracts your attention from pain and the hurting temporarily disappears. For example, imagine that you've just hit your thumb with a hammer and it's throbbing with pain. Suddenly, your child cries out that there's a fire in the laundry room. As you race to deal with this emergency, you forget all about the pain in your thumb.

As you can see, then, tissue damage that sends

CONCEPT CHECK 4.4
Comparing Taste, Smell, and Touch

Check your understanding of taste, smell, and touch by comparing these sensory systems on the dimensions listed in the first column below. A few answers are supplied; see whether you can fill in the rest. The answers can be found in Appendix A.

Dimension	Taste	Smell	Touch
Stimulus	_____	Volatile chemicals in air _____	_____
Receptors	_____	_____	Many (at least 6) types _____
Location of receptors	_____	Upper areas of nasal passages _____	_____
Basic elements of perception	Sweet, sour, salty, bitter _____	_____	_____

---

pain impulses on their way to the brain doesn't necessarily result in the experience of pain. Cognitive and emotional processes that unfold in higher brain centers can somehow block pain signals coming from peripheral receptors. Thus, any useful explantion of pain perception must be able to answer a critical question: How does the central nervous system block incoming pain signals?

How Does the CNS Block Incoming Pain Signals?

In an influential effort to answer this question, Ronald Melzack and Patrick Wall (1965) devised the gate-control theory of pain. *Gate-control theory holds that incoming pain sensations must pass through a "gate" in the spinal cord that can be closed, thus blocking ascending pain signals.* The gate in this model is not an anatomical structure but a pattern of neural activity that inhibits incoming pain signals. Melzack and Wall suggested that this imaginary gate can be closed by signals from peripheral receptors or by signals from the brain. They theorized that the latter mechanism can help explain how factors such as attention and expectations can shut off pain signals. As a whole, research suggests that the concept of a gating mechanism for pain has merit (Rollman, 1991). However, relatively little support has been found for the neural circuitry originally hypoth-

esized by Melzack and Wall. Other neural mechanisms, discovered after gate-control theory was proposed, appear to be responsible for blocking the perception of pain.

One of these discoveries was the identification of endorphins. As discussed in Chapter 3, *endorphins* are the body's own natural morphinelike painkillers. Studies suggest that the release of endorphins underlies the pain-relieving effects of placebo drugs (Fields & Levine, 1984). The analgesic effects that can be achieved through the ancient Chinese art of acupuncture may likewise involve endorphins (Murray, 1995). The increased tolerance of pain seen among women during their last two weeks of pregnancy may also be due to increased secretion of endorphins (Gintzler, 1980). Endorphins are widely distributed in the central nervous system. Scientists are still working out the details of how they suppress pain.

The other discovery involved the identification of a descending neural pathway that mediates the suppression of pain (Basbaum & Fields, 1984). This pathway appears to originate in an area of the midbrain called the *periaqueductal gray (PAG)*. Neural activity in this pathway is probably initiated by endorphins acting on PAG neurons, which eventually trigger impulses sent down neural circuits that mostly release serotonin. These circuits synapse in the spinal cord, where they appear to release more

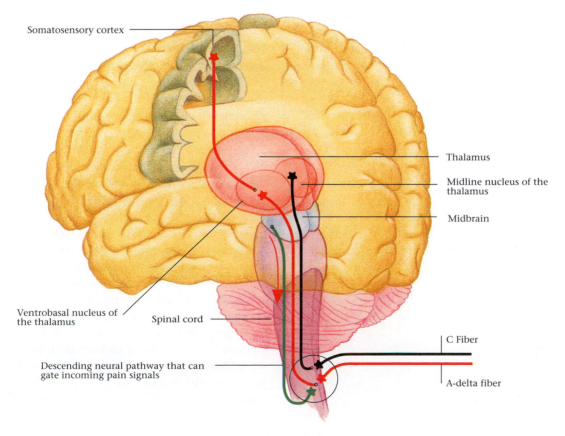

Somatosensory cortex

Thalamus

Midline nucleus of the thalamus

Midbrain

Ventrobasal nucleus of the thalamus

Spinal cord

C Fiber

Descending neural pathway that can gate incoming pain signals

A-delta fiber

Figure 4.57
The two pathways for pain signals. Pain signals are sent from receptors to the brain along the two pathways depicted here. The fast pathway, shown in red, and the slow pathway, shown in black, depend on different types of nerve fibers and are routed through different parts of the thalamus. The gate control mechanism posited by Melzack and Wall (1965) apparently depends on descending signals originating in an area of the midbrain (the pathway shown in green).

endorphins, thus inhibiting the activity of neurons that would normally transmit incoming pain impulses to the brain (see Figure 4.57). The painkilling effects of morphine appear to be at least partly attributable to activity in this descending pathway, as cutting the fibers in this pathway reduces the analgesic effects of morphine (Jessell & Kelly, 1991). In contrast, activation of this pathway by electrical stimulation of the brain can produce an analgesic effect. Clearly, this pathway plays a central role in gating incoming pain signals. The impact of cognitive and emotional factors on pain may be mediated by signals sent down this pathway from higher brain centers.

OUR OTHER SENSES

We have discussed the dynamics of sensation and perception in five sensory domains—vision, hearing, taste, smell, and touch. Since it is widely known that humans have five senses, that should wrap up our coverage, right? Wrong! People have still other sensory systems: the kinesthetic system (which monitors positions of the body) and the vestibular system (sense of balance).

The Kinesthetic System

The *kinesthetic system* monitors the positions of the various parts of the body. To some extent, you know where your limbs are because you commanded the muscles that put them there. Nonetheless, the kinesthetic system allows you to double-check these locations. Where are the receptors for your kinesthetic sense? Some reside in the joints, indicating how much they are bending. Others reside within the muscles, registering their tautness, or extension. Most kinesthetic stimulation is transmitted to the brain along the same pathway as tactile stimulation. However, the two types of information are kept separate (Vierck, 1978).

The Vestibular System

When you're jolting along in a bus, the world outside the bus window doesn't seem to jump about as your head bounces up and down. Yet a movie taken with a camera fastened to the bus would show a bouncing world. How are you and the camera different? Unlike the camera, you are equipped with a *vestibular system*, **which responds to gravity and keeps you informed of your body's location in space.** The vestibular system provides the sense of balance, or equilibrium, compensating for changes in the body's position (Parker, 1980).

The vestibular system shares space in the inner ear with the auditory system. The *semicircular canals* make up the largest part of the vestibular system, which is shown in Figure 4.58. They look like three inner tubes joined at the base. Any rotational motion of the head is uniquely represented by a combination of fluid flows in the semicircular canals (J. Kelly, 1991). These shifts in fluid are detected by hair cells similar to those found along the basilar membrane in the cochlea. Your perceptual system integrates the vestibular input about your body's position with information from other senses. After all, you can see where you are and you know where you've instructed your muscles to take you.

This integration of sensory input raises a point that merits emphasis as we close our tour of the human sensory systems. Although we have discussed the various sensory domains separately, it's important to remember that all the senses send signals to the same brain, where the information is pooled. We have already encountered examples of sensory integration. For example, it's at work when the sight and smell of food influence taste. *Sensory integration is the norm in perceptual experience.* For example, when you sit around a campfire, you *see* it blazing, you *hear* it crackling, you *smell* it burning, and you feel the *touch* of its warmth. If you cook something over it, you may even *taste* it. Thus, perception involves building a unified model of the world out of integrated input from all the senses.

Figure 4.58
The vestibular system.
The semicircular canals in the inner ear (which are shown disproportionately large here) are the sensory organ for balance and head movement. Fluid movements in these canals stimulate neural impulses that travel along the vestibular nerve to the brain.

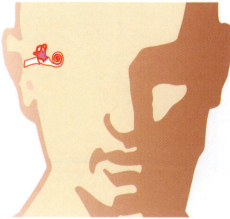

PUTTING IT IN PERSPECTIVE

In this chapter, three of our unifying themes stand out in sharp relief. First, the way in which competing theories of color vision and hearing have been reconciled in recent decades shows how psychology's theoretical diversity can pay dividends. Second, the entire chapter relates to the idea that people's experience of the world is highly subjective. Third, we saw ample evidence of how our behavior is shaped by our cultural heritage. Let's discuss the value of theoretical diversity first.

Contradictory theories about behavior can be disconcerting and frustrating for theorists, researchers, teachers, and students alike. Most of us show a natural human tendency to want to tie things up in a neat, sensible package. As the Gestaltists would have put it, we prefer closure and simplicity.

Yet this chapter provides two dramatic demonstrations of how theoretical diversity can lead to progress in the long run. For decades, the trichromatic and opponent process theories of color vision and the place and frequency theories of pitch perception were viewed as fundamentally incompatible. These competing theories generated and guided the research that now provides a fairly solid understanding of how people perceive color and pitch. As you know, in each case the evidence eventually revealed that the opposing theories were not really incompatible. Both were needed to fully explain the sensory processes that each sought to explain individually. If it hadn't been for these theoretical debates, current understanding of color vision and pitch perception might be far more primitive, as the understanding of timbre still is.

Our coverage of sensation and perception should also have enhanced your appreciation of why human experience of the world is highly subjective. As ambiguous figures and optical illusions clearly show, there is no one-to-one correspondence between sensory input and perceived experience of the world. Perception is an active process in which people organize and interpret the information received by the senses. These interpretations are shaped by a host of factors, including the environmental context and perceptual sets. Small wonder, then, that people often perceive the same event in very different ways.

Finally, this chapter provided numerous examples of how cultural factors can shape behavior—in an area of research where one might expect to find little cultural influence. Most people are not surprised to learn that there are cultural differences in attitudes, values, social behavior, and development. But perception is widely viewed as a basic, universal process that should be invariant across cultures. In most respects it is, as the similarities among cultural groups in perception far outweigh the differences. Nonetheless, we saw cultural variations in depth perception, susceptibility to illusions, taste preferences, and pain tolerance. Thus, even a fundamental, heavily physiological process such as perception can be modified to some degree by one's cultural background.

The following Application demonstrates the subjectivity of perception once again. It focuses on how painters have learned to use the principles of visual perception to achieve a variety of artistic goals.

Recap of Key Points

• Sensory receptors in the skin respond to pressure, temperature, and pain. Tactile localization depends on receptive fields similar to those seen for vision. Some cells in the somatosensory cortex appear to function like feature detectors. There are nerve fibers that respond specifically to warmth and cold.

• Pain signals are sent to the brain along two pathways that are characterized as fast and slow. The perception of pain is highly subjective and may be influenced by mood, attention, and culture. Gate-control theory holds that incoming pain signals can be blocked in the spinal cord. Endorphins and a descending neural pathway appear responsible for the suppression of pain by the central nervous system.

• The kinesthetic system monitors the position of various body parts. Kinesthetic receptors, located in the joints and muscles, send signals to the brain along the same pathway as tactile stimulation. The sense of balance depends primarily on activity in the semicircular canals in the vestibular system.

• This chapter underscored three of our unifying themes: the value of theoretical diversity, the subjective nature of human experience, and the influence of culture on behavior.

APPLICATION: THINKING ABOUT ART AND ILLUSION

Answer the following multiple-choice question:

Artistic works such as paintings:

a render an accurate picture of reality.

b create an illusion of reality.

c provide an interpretation of reality.

d make us think about the nature of reality.

e all of the above.

The answer to this question is (e), "all of the above." Historically, artists have had many and varied purposes, including each of those listed in the question. To realize their goals, they have had to use a number of principles of perception—sometimes quite deliberately, and sometimes not. Let's use the example of painting to explore the role of perceptual principles in art and illusion.

The goal of most early painters was to produce a believable picture of reality. This goal immediately created a problem familiar to most of us who have attempted to draw realistic pictures: the real world is three-dimensional, but a canvas or a sheet of paper is flat. Paradoxically, then, painters who set out to recreate reality have to do so by creating an *illusion* of three-dimensional reality.

Prior to the Renaissance, efforts to create a convincing illusion of reality were awkward by modern standards. Why? Because artists did not understand how to use depth cues. This is apparent in Figure 4.59, a religious scene painted around 1300. The painting clearly lacks a sense of depth. The people seem paper-thin. They have no real position in space.

Many of the principles of geometric perspective that relate to depth perception were discovered during the Renaissance. Figure 4.60 dramatizes the resulting transition in art. It shows a scene depicted by Gentile and Giovanni Bellini, Italian Renaissance painters. It seems much more realistic and lifelike than the painting in Figure 4.59 because it uses a number of pictorial depth cues. Notice how the buildings on the sides converge to make use of linear perspective. Additionally, distant objects are smaller than nearby ones, an application of

Figure 4.59
***Master of the Arrest of Christ* (detail, central part) by S. Francesco, Assisi, Italy (circa 1300).** Notice how the absence of depth cues makes the painting seem flat and unrealistic.

Figure 4.60
A painting by the Italian Renaissance artists Gentile and Giovanni Bellini (circa 1480). In this painting a number of depth cues—including linear perspective, relative size, height in plane, and interposition—enhance the illusion of three-dimensional reality.

Figure 4.61
Claude Monet's *Palazzo da Mula*, Venice (1908). The French Impressionist Monet often used complementary colors to achieve his visual effects.

with separate daubs of pure, bright colors that blurred together to create an alternating perceptual experience. If you view his paintings up close, you see only a shimmering mass of color. When you step back, however, the adjacent colors begin to blend, and forms begin to take shape, as you can see in Figure 4.61. Monet achieved this duality through careful use of color mixing and by working systematically with complementary colors.

Similar methods were used even more precisely and systematically by Georges Seurat, a French artist who used a technique called *Pointillism.* Seurat carefully studied what scientists knew about the composition of color in the 1880s, then applied this knowledge in a calculated, laboratory-like manner. Indeed, critics in his era dubbed him the "little chemist." Seurat constructed his paintings out of tiny dots of pure, intense colors. He used additive color mixing, a departure from the norm in painting, which usually depends on subtractive mixing of pigments. A famous result of Seurat's "scientific" approach to painting was his renowned *Sunday Afternoon on the Island of La Grande Jatte* (see Figure 4.62). As the work of Seurat illustrates, modernist painters were moving away from attempts to recreate the world as it is literally seen.

If 19th-century painters liberated color,

relative size. This painting also uses height in plane, as well as interposition. By taking advantage of pictorial depth cues, an artist can enhance a painting's illusion of reality.

In the centuries since the Renaissance, painters have adopted a number of viewpoints about the portrayal of reality. For instance, the Impressionists of the 19th century did not want to recreate the photographic "reality" of a scene. They set out to interpret a viewer's fleeting perception or *impression* of reality. To accomplish this end, they worked with color in unprecedented ways.

Consider for instance, Claude Monet, a French Impressionist who began to work

Figure 4.62
Georges Seurat's *Sunday Afternoon on the Island of La Grande Jatte* (without artist's border) (1884–1886). Seurat used thousands of tiny dots of color and the principles of color mixing (see detail). The eye and brain combine the points into the colors the viewer actually sees. (The Art Institute of Chicago; Helen Birch Bartlett Memorial Collection, 1926.224)

Figure 4.64
Marcel Duchamp's *Nude Descending a Staircase, No 2* (1912). This painting uses the Gestalt principles of continuity and common fate. (Philadelphia Museum of Art: The Louise and Walter Arensberg Collection)

their successors at the turn of the 20th century liberated form. This was particularly true of the Cubists. Cubism was begun in 1909 by Pablo Picasso, a Spanish artist who went on to experiment with other styles in his prolific career. The Cubists didn't try to *portray* reality so much as to *reassemble* it. They attempted to reduce everything to combinations of geometric forms (lines, circles, triangles, rectangles, and such) laid out in a flat space, lacking depth. In a sense, *they applied the theory of feature analysis to canvas,* as they built their figures out of simple features.

The resulting paintings were decidedly unrealistic, but the painters would leave realistic fragments that provided clues about the subject. Picasso liked to challenge his viewers to decipher the subject of his paintings. Take a look at the painting in Figure 4.63 and see whether you can figure out what Picasso was portraying.

The work in Figure 4.63 is titled *Violin and Grapes.* Note how Gestalt principles of perceptual organization are at work to create these forms. Proximity and similarity serve to bring the grapes together in the bottom

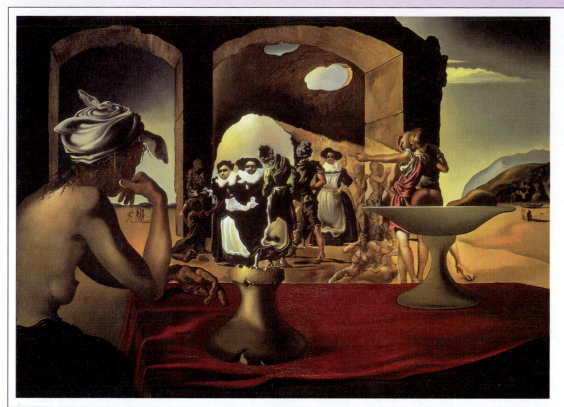

Figure 4.65
Salvador Dali's _Slave Market with the Disappearing Bust of Voltaire_ (1940). This painting playfully includes a reversible figure (two nuns form the bust of Voltaire, a philosopher known for his stringent criticisms of the Catholic church).

right corner. Closure accounts for your being able to see the essence of the violin.

Other Gestalt principles are the key to the effect achieved in the painting in Figure 4.64. This painting, by Marcel Duchamp, a French artist who blended Cubism and a style called Futurism, is titled _Nude Descending a Staircase_. The effect clearly depends on the Gestalt principles of continuity and common fate.

The Surrealists toyed with reality in a different way. Influenced by Sigmund Freud's writings on the unconscious, the Surrealists explored the world of dreams and fantasy. Specific elements in their paintings are often depicted realistically, but the strange juxtaposition of elements yields a disconcerting irrationality reminiscent of dreams. A prominent example of this style is Salvador Dali's _Slave Market with the Disappearing Bust of Voltaire_, shown in Figure 4.65. Notice the reversible figure near the center of the painting. The "bust of Voltaire" is made up of human figures in the distance, standing in front of an arch. Dali often used reversible figures to enhance the ambiguity of his bizarre visions.

Perhaps no one has been more creative in manipulating perceptual ambiguity than M. C. Escher, a modern Dutch artist. Escher's chief goal was to stimulate viewers to think about the nature of reality and the process of visual perception itself. Interestingly, Escher readily acknowledged his debt to psychology as a source of inspiration (Teuber, 1974). He followed the work of the Gestalt psychologists carefully and would even cite specific journal articles that served as the point of departure for his works. For example, the woodcut _Day and Night_ (see Figure 4.66) is largely a manipulation of the figure-ground phenomenon. Escher based it on an article by Molly Harrower (1936) in the _British Journal of Psychology_.

Waterfall, a 1961 lithograph by Escher, is an impossible figure that appears to defy the law of gravity (see Figure 4.67 on the next page). The puzzling problem here is that a level channel of water terminates in a waterfall that "falls" into the _same_ channel two levels "below." This drawing is made up of two impossible triangles. In

Figure 4.66
M. C. Escher's woodcut _Day and Night_ (1938). Notice how figure is gradually transformed into ground and ground into figure.

case you need help seeing them, the waterfall itself forms one side of each triangle.

The Necker cube, a reversible figure mentioned earlier, was the inspiration for Escher's 1958 lithograph *Belvedere*, shown in Figure 4.68. You have to look carefully to realize that this is another impossible figure. Note that the top story runs at a right angle from the first story. Note also how the pillars are twisted around. The pillars that start on one side of the building end up supporting the second story on the other side! Escher's debt to the Necker cube is manifested in several places. Notice, for instance, the drawing of a Necker cube on the floor next to the seated boy (on the lower left).

Like Escher, Victor Vasarely challenged viewers to think about the process of perception. A Hungarian artist, Vasarely pioneered an approach called Kinetic Art because of his interest in creating illusions of motion. Like Georges Seurat, he went about his work with scientific precision. His paintings are based on optical illusions, as squares seem to advance and recede, or spheres seem to inflate and deflate. For example, note how Vasareley used the depth cues of texture gradient and linear perspective to convey the look of great depth in his painting *Tukoer-Ter-Ur*, shown in Figure 4.69.

While Escher and Vasarely challenged viewers to think about perception, Belgian artist René Magritte challenged people to think about the conventions of painting. Many of his works depict paintings on an easel, with the "real" scene continuing unbroken at the edges. The painting in Figure 4.70 is such a picture within a picture. In addition, there are two identical triangles in the painting. One represents a road and the other a nearby tower. Notice how the identical triangles are perceived differently because of the variations in *context*.

Figure 4.67
Escher's lithograph *Waterfall* (1961). Escher's use of depth cues and impossible triangles deceives the brain into seeing water flow uphill.

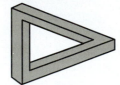

Figure 4.68
Escher's *Belvedere* (1958). This lithograph depicts an impossible figure inspired by the Necker cube. The cube appears in the architecture of the building, in the model held by the boy on the bench, and in the drawing lying at his feet.

Ultimately, Magritte's painting blurs the line between the real world and the illusory world created by the artist, suggesting that there is no line—that everything is an illusion. In this way, Magritte "framed" the ageless, unanswerable question: What is reality?

Recap of Key Points

• The principles of visual perception are often applied to artistic endeavors. Prior to the Renaissance, efforts to create a convincing illusion of three-dimensional reality were awkward because artists did not understand how to use depth cues. After the Renaissance, painters began to routinely use pictorial depth cues to make their scenes more lifelike.

• Nineteenth-century painters, such as the Impressionists, manipulated color in creative, new ways. The Cubists were innovative in manipulating form, as they applied the theory of feature analysis to canvas. The Surrealists toyed with reality, exploring the world of fantasy and dreams.

• Modern artists such as Escher and Vasarely have tried to stimulate viewers to think about the process of perception. Among other things, Escher worked with figure and ground, the Necker cube, and the impossible triangle.

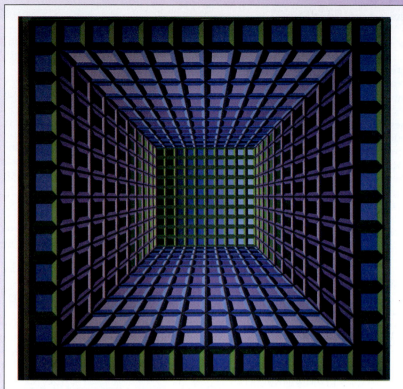

Figure 4.69
Victor Vasarely's *Tukoer-Ter-Ur* (1989). In this painting, Vasarely manipulates texture gradients and linear perspective to create a remarkable illusion of depth.

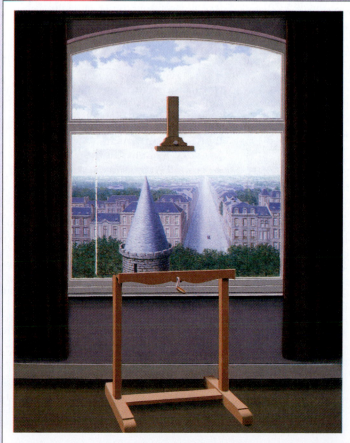

Figure 4.70
René Magritte's *Les Promenades d'Euclide* (1955). Notice how the pair of nearly identical triangles look quite different in different contexts. (The Minneapolis Institute of Arts, The William Hood Dunwoody Fund)

Key Ideas

Psychophysics: Basic Concepts and Issues

◆ Absolute thresholds are not really absolute. Fechner's law asserts that larger and larger increases in stimulus intensity are required to produce just noticeable differences in the magnitude of sensation.

◆ According to signal-detection theory, the detection of sensory inputs is influenced by noise in the system and by decision-making strategies. In recent years, it has become apparent that perception can occur without awareness. Prolonged stimulation may lead to sensory adaptation, which involves a reduction in sensitivity.

Our Sense of Sight: The Visual System

◆ Light varies in terms of wavelength, amplitude, and purity. Light enters the eye through the cornea and pupil and is focused on the retina by the lens.

◆ Rods and cones are the visual receptors found in the retina. Cones play a key role in daylight vision and color perception, and rods are critical to night vision and peripheral vision. Dark adaptation and light adaptation both involve changes in the retina's sensitivity to light.

◆ The retina transforms light into neural impulses that are sent to the brain via the optic nerve. Receptive fields are areas in the retina that affect the firing of visual cells. Two visual pathways to the brain send signals through the thalamus to different areas of the visual cortex. The visual cortex contains cells that appear to function as feature detectors.

◆ Perceptions of color (hue) are primarily a function of light wavelength, while amplitude affects brightness and purity affects saturation. Perceptions of many varied colors depend on processes that resemble additive color mixing. The evidence now suggests that both the trichromatic and opponent process theories are necessary to account for color vision.

◆ According to feature analysis theories, people detect specific elements in stimuli and build them into recognizable forms through bottom-up processing. However, evidence suggests that form perception also involves top-down processing.

◆ Gestalt psychology emphasized that the whole may be greater than the sum of its parts (features), as illustrated by Gestalt principles of form perception. Other approaches to form perception emphasize that people develop perceptual hypotheses about the distal stimuli that could be responsible for the proximal stimuli that are sensed.

◆ Depth perception depends primarily on monocular cues. Binocular cues such as reti-

nal disparity and convergence can also contribute to depth perception. Conscious perceptions of geographical slant tend to be greatly exaggerated, but haptic judgments seem largely immune to this perceptual bias.

◆ Perceptual constancies in vision help viewers deal with the ever-shifting nature of proximal stimuli. Optical illusions demonstrate that perceptual hypotheses can be inaccurate and that perceptions are not simple reflections of objective reality.

Our Sense of Hearing: The Auditory System

◆ Sound varies in terms of wavelength (frequency), amplitude, and purity. These properties affect mainly perceptions of pitch, loudness, and timbre, respectively. Auditory signals are transmitted through the brainstem and thalamus to the primary auditory cortex in the temporal lobe.

◆ Modern evidence suggests that place theory and frequency theory are complementary rather than incompatible explanations of pitch perception. People pinpoint the source of sounds by comparing interear differences in the intensity and timing of sounds.

Our Chemical Senses: Taste and Smell

◆ The taste buds are sensitive to four basic tastes: sweet, sour, bitter, and salty. Sensitivity to these tastes is distributed unevenly across the tongue. Taste preferences are largely learned and are heavily influenced by one's cultural background.

◆ Like taste, smell is a chemical sense. Chemical stimuli activate olfactory receptors lining the nasal passages. Most of these receptors respond to more than one odor.

Our Sense of Touch: Sensory Systems in the Skin

◆ Sensory receptors in the skin respond to pressure, temperature, and pain. There are nerve fibers that respond specifically to warmth and cold. Pain signals are sent to the brain along two pathways that are characterized as fast and slow.

◆ The perception of pain is highly subjective and may be influenced by mood, attention, personality, and culture. Gate-control theory holds that incoming pain signals can be blocked in the spinal cord. Endorphins and a descending neural pathway appear responsible for the suppression of pain by the central nervous system.

Our Other Senses

◆ The kinesthetic system monitors the position of various body parts. The sense of balance depends primarily on activity in the vestibular system.

Putting It in Perspective

◆ This chapter underscored three of our unifying themes: the value of theoretical diversity, the subjective nature of human experience, and the influence of culture on behavior.

Application: Thinking About Art and Illusion

◆ The principles of visual perception are often applied to artistic endeavors. Painters routinely use pictorial depth cues to make their scenes more lifelike. Color mixing, feature analysis, Gestalt principles, reversible figures, and impossible figures have also been used in influential paintings.

Key Terms

Absolute threshold
Additive color mixing
Afterimage
Auditory localization
Basilar membrane
Binocular depth cues
Bottom-up processing
Cochlea
Color blindness
Complementary colors
Cones
Convergence
Dark adaptation
Depth perception
Distal stimuli
Farsightedness
Feature analysis
Feature detectors
Fechner's law
Fovea
Frequency theory
Gate-control theory
Gustatory system
Impossible figures
Just noticeable difference (JND)
Kinesthetic system
Lateral antagonism
Lens
Light adaptation
Monocular depth cues
Motion parallax
Nearsightedness
Olfactory system
Opponent process theory of color vision
Optic chiasm
Optic disk
Optical illusion
Perception

Perceptual constancy
Perceptual hypothesis
Perceptual set
Phi phenomenon
Pictorial depth cues
Place theory
Proximal stimuli
Psychophysics
Pupil
Receptive field of a visual cell
Retina
Retinal disparity
Reversible figure
Rods
Sensation
Sensory adaptation
Signal-detection theory
Subjective contours
Subliminal perception
Subtractive color mixing
Threshold
Top-down processing
Trichromatic theory of color vision
Vestibular system
Volley principle
Weber's law

Key People

Linda Bartoshuk
Gustav Fechner
Hermann von Helmholtz
David Hubel and Torsten Wiesel
Ronald Melzack and Patrick Wall
Anne Treisman
Ernst Weber
Max Wertheimer

Practice Test

1. In psychophysical research, the absolute threshold has been arbitrarily defined as:
   A. the stimulus intensity that can be detected 100% of the time.
   B. the stimulus intensity that can be detected 50% of the time.
   C. the minimum amount of difference in intensity needed to tell two stimuli apart.
   D. a constant proportion of the size of the initial stimulus.

2. A tone-deaf person would probably not be able to tell two musical notes apart unless they were very different. We could say that this person has a relatively large:
   A. just noticeable difference.
   B. relative threshold.
   C. absolute threshold.
   D. detection threshold.

3. In their study of the influence of subliminal perception on attitudes, Krosnick and his colleagues (1992) found:
   A. absolutely no evidence of such influence.
   B. overwhelming evidence that subliminal stimuli can and do influence subjects' attitudes.
   C. that subliminal stimuli may condition positive, but not negative, attitudes.
   D. small but measureable effects in both the positive and negative direction.

4. In farsightedness:
   A. close objects are seen clearly but distant objects appear blurry.
   B. the focus of light from close objects falls behind the retina.
   C. the focus of light from distant objects falls a little short of the retina.
   D. a and b.
   E. a and c.

5. The collection of rod and cone receptors that funnel signals to a particular visual cell in the retina make up that cell's:
   A. blind spot.
   B. optic disk.
   C. opponent process field.
   D. receptive field.

6. Lateral antagonism occurs when:
   A. you turn your head to one side to maximize visual acuity in the dark.
   B. the cones adapt to dark more quickly than the rods.
   C. the cones battle with nearby rods for control of vision.
   D. neural activity in a retinal cell inhibits activity in surrounding cells.

7. Which theory would predict that the American flag would have a green, black, and yellow afterimage?
   A. subtractive color mixing
   B. opponent process theory
   C. additive color mixing
   D. trichromatic theory

8. Treisman (1986) proposes that the preattentive stage of object perception involves _____ processing, and the subsequent focused-attention stage involves _____ processing.
   A. top-down; bottom-up
   B. top-down; top-down
   C. bottom-up; bottom-up
   D. bottom-up; top-down

9. In a painting, train tracks may look as if they go off into the distance because the artist draws the tracks as converging lines, a monocular cue to depth known as:
   A. interposition.
   B. texture gradient.
   C. relative size.
   D. linear perspective.

10. Which of the following statements is true?
    A. There is evidence of cultural variability in the perception of depth both in real, three-dimensional space and in two-dimensional pictures.
    B. There is no evidence of cultural variability in depth perception, either in real space or in two-dimensional pictures.
    C. While there is some evidence of cultural variability in perception of depth in two-dimensional pictures, there is little cultural variability in perception of depth in real space.
    D. While there is some evidence of cultural variability in perception of depth in three-dimensional space, there is little cultural variablity in perception of depth in two-dimensional pictures.

11. The facts that cultural groups with little exposure to roads are less susceptible to the Ponzo illusion and that those with less exposure to buildings are less susceptible to the Müller-Lyer illusion suggest that:
    A. not all cultures test perceptual hypotheses.
    B. people in technologically advanced cultures are more gullible.
    C. optical illusions can be experienced only by cultures that have been exposed to the concept of optical illusions.
    D. perceptual inferences can be shaped by experience.

12. Perception of pitch can best be explained by:
    A. place theory.
    B. frequency theory.
    C. both place theory and frequency theory.
    D. neither theory.

13. In what way(s) is the sense of taste like the sense of smell?
    A. There are four primary stimulus groups for both senses.
    B. Both systems are routed through the thalamus on the way to the cortex.
    C. The physical stimuli for both senses are chemical substances dissolved in fluid.
    D. All of the above.
    E. None of the above.

14. The fact that theories originally seen as being incompatible, such as the trichromatic and opponent process theories of color vision, are now seen as both being necessary to explain sensory processes illustrates:
    A. that psychology evolves in a sociohistorical context.
    B. the subjectivity of experience.
    C. the value of psychology's theoretical diversity.
    D. the nature-nurture controversy.

15. Which school of painting applied the theory of feature analysis to canvas by building figures out of simple features?
    A. Pointillism
    B. Impressionism
    C. Surrealism
    D. Cubism

Answers

1	B	Page 124	6	D	Page 134	11	D	Page 154
2	A	Page 125	7	B	Pages 139–140	12	C	Pages 158–159
3	D	Page 128	8	D	Page 143	13	C	Page 162
4	B	Pages 130–132	9	D	Pages 148–149	14	C	Page 167
5	D	Page 134	10	C	Pages 149–150	15	D	Page 170

5 VARIATIONS IN CONSCIOUSNESS

A young woman sat alone in a room. At tached to her skull were recording electrodes from an EEG machine that monitored the electrical activity in her brain. Connected to the EEG was another device that increased the sound of a tone when the EEG registered a particular pattern of brain waves. As long as the brain-wave pattern persisted, the tone filled the room. When the woman's EEG pattern changed, the room fell silent. As the woman sat quietly, the tone gradually began to sound more frequently. What was happening here?

The young woman was a subject in one of a series of experiments conducted by Joe Kamiya. Kamiya set out to see whether people could learn to control the electrical activity in their brains by altering their mental states (Kamiya, 1969; Nowlis & Kamiya, 1970). The tone provided the subjects with *biofeedback*—information about internal bodily changes that would normally be imperceptible. In the experiment described here, the tone sounded whenever the young woman produced a specific pattern of brain waves called *alpha waves*. Kamiya found that when people are provided with EEG biofeedback, the vast major-ity *can* learn to alter their brain-wave activity to some extent.

In the course of this research, Kamiya also made some other interesting observations. Although subjects could increase alpha activity, they had difficulty explaining *how* they did it. When pressed, subjects would offer explanations, but the explanations tended to be tentative and vague. Their responses were equally hazy when Kamiya asked them to describe *what it felt like* when they were producing alpha-wave activity. They mostly agreed that the alpha state was quite pleasant, but, beyond that, they had great difficulty describing it. When questioned, one subject replied, "You keep asking me to describe this darned alpha state. I can't do it. It has a certain feel about it, sure, but really, it's best left undescribed" (Kamiya, 1969, p. 515).

The difficulty Kamiya's subjects experienced when asked to describe their mental state during alpha activity is hardly unique. Researchers find that people also have difficulty describing the states of consciousness associated with hypnosis, meditation, and drug use. Even everyday mental states can defy description. Can you provide a lucid description of exactly how you feel when you daydream? Ironically, the very thing people are most intimately acquainted with—their conscious experience—eludes their best efforts to describe it. The problem may be that consciousness is the ultimate in subjective experience. Your consciousness can be directly experienced by only one person—you. You cannot merge consciousness with someone else in order to compare notes.

The private, highly subjective nature of consciousness makes it difficult to study empirically. Science requires observation, but researchers cannot directly observe consciousness from the outside. Nonetheless, with a good deal of ingenuity, they have found ways to explore the hidden worlds of consciousness. What they have discovered is the subject of this chapter.

Our review will begin with a few general points about the nature of consciousness. After that, much of the chapter will be a "bedtime story," as we take a long look at sleep and dreams. We'll continue our tour of variations in consciousness by examining hypnosis, meditation, and the effects of mind-altering drugs. Finally, the Application will address a number of practical questions about sleep and dreams.

In biofeedback research, subjects are hooked up to equipment that monitors their brain waves via electrodes attached to the scalp.

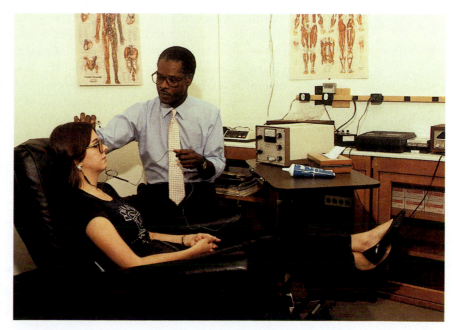

What is consciousness? Definitions vary somewhat, but generally psychologists use the term *consciousness* to refer to one's awareness of internal and external stimuli. Your consciousness includes (1) your awareness of external events ("The professor just asked me a difficult question about medieval history"), (2) your awareness of your internal sensations ("My heart is racing and I'm beginning to sweat"), (3) your awareness of your *self* as the unique being having these experiences ("Why me?"), and (4) your awareness of your thoughts about these experiences ("I'm going to make a fool of myself!"). To put it more concisely, consciousness is personal awareness.

The contents of your consciousness are continually changing. Rarely does consciousness come to a standstill. It moves, it flows, it fluctuates, it wanders. Recognizing this reality, William James (1902) christened this continuous flow the *stream of consciousness*. If you could tape-record your thoughts, you would find an endless flow of ideas that zigzag all over the place. As you will soon learn, even when you sleep your consciousness moves through a series of transitions. To be constantly shifting and changing seems to be part of the essential nature of consciousness.

Variations in Levels of Awareness

While William James emphasized the stream of consciousness, Sigmund Freud (1900) wanted to examine what went on beneath the surface of this stream. As explained in Chapter 1, Freud argued that people's feelings and behavior are influenced by *unconscious* needs, wishes, and conflicts that lie below the surface of conscious awareness. According to Freud, the stream of consciousness has depth. Conscious and unconscious processes are different *levels of awareness*. Thus, Freud was one of the first theorists to recognize that consciousness is not an all-or-none phenomenon.

Since Freud's time, research has shown that people continue to maintain some awareness during sleep and even when they are put under anesthesia for surgery. How do we know? Because some stimuli can still penetrate awareness. For example, people under surgical anesthesia occasionally hear comments made during their surgery, which they later repeat to their surprised surgeons (Bennett, 1993). Admittedly, relatively few surgical patients report recollections of events that occurred while they were anesthetized (Goldmann, 1990). How-

ever, studies using subtle, sensitive measures of recall suggest that memory processes are more active during anesthesia than previously believed (Kihlstrom et al., 1990). Other research indicates that while people are asleep they remain aware of external events to some degree (Badia, 1990; Evans, 1990). For example, in laboratory studies, subjects who are clearly asleep (based on monitoring of physiological indicators) have responded to faint tones by pressing a palm-mounted button (Ogilvie & Wilkinson, 1988). People can also discriminate among different stimuli while asleep. A good example is the new parent who can sleep through a loud thunderstorm or a buzzing alarm clock but who immediately hears the muffled sound of the baby crying down the hall. The parent's selective sensitivity to sounds means that some mental processing must be going on even during sleep.

Indeed, some theorists have recently argued that mental processes during sleep are more similar to waking thought processes than is widely assumed (Kahan & LaBerge, 1994; Moffitt, 1995). For example, when Kahan and LaBerge (1996) had subjects write detailed descriptions of dreaming and waking experiences, they found similar levels of focused attention, public self-consciousness, emotion, and self-reflection (among other things) in the participants' dreaming and waking thoughts. Based on these findings, they argue that mental processes in dreams are surprisingly sophisticated and that dreaming and waking cognition are not fundamentally different.

Consciousness and Brain Activity

Variations in consciousness are intimately related to changes in electrical activity in the brain. Investigators have been exploring this relationship ever since Hans Berger (1929) invented the EEG. **The electroencephalograph (EEG) is a device that monitors the electrical activity of the brain over time by means of recording electrodes attached to the surface of the scalp.** The EEG records and amplifies electrical activity in the outer layer of the brain, the cortex.

Ultimately, the EEG summarizes the rhythm of cortical activity in the brain in terms of line tracings called *brain waves*. These brain-wave tracings vary in *amplitude* (height) and *frequency* (cycles per second, abbreviated *cps*). You can see what brain waves look like if you glance ahead to Figure 5.6.

Human brain-wave activity is usually divided into four principal bands based on the frequency of the brain waves. These bands, named after letters in the Greek alphabet, are *beta* (13–24 cps), *alpha* (8–12 cps), *theta* (4–7 cps), and *delta* (under 4 cps).

Different patterns of EEG activity are associated with different states of consciousness, as is summarized in Table 5.1. For instance, when you are alertly engaged in problem solving, beta waves tend to dominate. When you are relaxed and resting, alpha waves increase. When you slip into deep sleep, delta waves become more prevalent. Although these correlations are far from perfect, changes in brain activity are related to variations in consciousness (Guyton, 1991).

As is often the case with correlations, researchers are faced with a chicken-or-egg puzzle when it comes to the relationship between mental states and the brain's electrical activity. If you become drowsy while you are reading this passage, your brain-wave activity will probably change. But are these changes causing your drowsiness, or is your drowsiness causing the changes in brain-wave activity? Or are the drowsiness and the shifts in brain-wave activity both caused by a *third* factor— perhaps signals coming from a subcortical area in the brain? (See Figure 5.1.) Frankly, no one knows. All that is known for sure is that variations in consciousness are correlated with variations in brain activity.

Measures of brain-wave activity have provided investigators with a method for mapping out the mysterious state of consciousness called sleep. As we will see in the next section, this state turns out to be far more complex and varied than you might expect.

TABLE 5.1 EEG PATTERNS ASSOCIATED WITH STATES OF CONSCIOUSNESS

EEG Pattern	Frequency (cps)	Typical States of Consciousness
Beta (β)	13–24	Normal waking thought, alert problem solving
Alpha (α)	8–12	Deep relaxation, blank mind, meditation
Theta (θ)	4–7	Light sleep
Delta (Δ)	Less than 4	Deep sleep

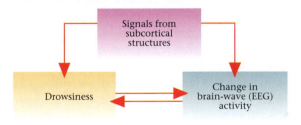

Recap of Key Points

• William James emphasized that consciousness is a continually changing stream of mental activity. Consciousness varies along a continuum of levels of awareness.

• People maintain some degree of awareness during sleep and sometimes while under anesthesia. Some theorists believe that mental processes during sleep are more similar to waking thought processes than had been widely assumed.

• Brain waves vary in amplitude and frequency (cps) and are divided into four bands: beta, alpha, theta, and delta. Variations in consciousness are related to variations in brain activity, as measured by the EEG.

Figure 5.1
The correlation between mental states and electrical activity in the brain. As discussed in Chapter 2, correlations alone do not establish causation. For example, there are strong correlations between drowsiness and a particular pattern of cortical activity, as reflected by EEG brain waves. But does drowsiness cause a change in cortical activity, or do changes in cortical activity cause drowsiness? Or does some third variable account for the changes in both?

BIOLOGICAL RHYTHMS AND SLEEP

Rhythm pervades the world around us. The daily alternation of light and darkness, the annual pattern of the seasons, and the phases of the moon all reflect this rhythmic quality of repeating cycles. Humans and many other animals display biological rhythms that are tied to the passage of time (Schwartz, 1996). *Biological rhythms* are periodic fluctuations in physiological functioning. Birds beginning a winter migration and raccoons going into hibernation show the influence of a yearly cycle. A student trying to fight off sleep while studying late at night shows the influence of a daily cycle of activity and rest. The existence of

these rhythms means that organisms have internal "biological clocks" that somehow monitor the passage of time.

Four time cycles are related to behavior in humans. People's biological rhythms include cycles corresponding roughly to periods of one year, 28 days, 24 hours, and 90 minutes (Aschoff, 1981). The yearly or seasonal cycle has been related to patterns of sexual activity and to the onset of mood disorders such as depression (Nelson, Badura, & Goldman, 1990). The female menstrual cycle appears to be tied to the 28-day lunar month. This cycle has been related to fluctuations in mood, although the data are complex and controversial (Reid, 1991). Males may experience similar but less obvious 28-day cycles that affect their hormonal secretions (Parlee, 1973, 1982). The 90-minute cycle appears related to fluctuations in alertness, daydreaming, and hunger, among other things (Kleitman, 1982; Schulz, 1993). People's yearly, monthly, and 90-minute cycles exert only a modest influence over their mental states. In contrast, daily rhythms exert considerably more influence.

Circadian Rhythms 4a

Circadian rhythms **are the 24-hour biological cycles found in humans and many other species.** In humans, circadian rhythms are particularly influential in the regulation of sleep and wakefulness (Moore, 1990). However, daily cycles also produce rhythmic variations in blood pressure, urine production, hormonal secretions, and other physical functions, some of which are highlighted in Figure 5.2 (Kryger, Roth, & Carskadon, 1994). For instance, body temperature varies rhythmically in a daily cycle, usually peaking in the afternoon and reaching its low point in the depths of the night.

Research indicates that people generally fall asleep as their body temperature begins to drop and awaken as it begins to ascend once again (McGinty, 1993). Researchers have concluded that circadian rhythms can leave individuals physiologically primed to fall asleep most easily at a particular time of day (Richardson, 1993). This optimal time varies from one person to another, depending on their schedules and other factors, but it's interesting to learn that each individual may have an "ideal" time for going to bed.

To study biological clocks, researchers have monitored physiological processes while subjects are cut off from exposure to the cycle of day and night and all other external time cues. For instance, some subjects have spent weeks in a cave or a closed-off room without windows or clocks. Studies of these subjects reveal that circadian rhythms generally persist even when external time cues are eliminated. Interestingly, however, when people are isolated in this way, *they drift toward a 25-hour cycle* (Mistlberger & Rusak, 1994; Welsh, 1993). That is, subjects tend to go to sleep and awaken a little later each day. This trend is charted for one experimental subject in Figure 5.3. Investigators aren't sure why this drift occurs.

Although people's biological clocks continue to function when they're cut off from the light cycle and other time cues, their biological rhythms often become more erratic in these circumstances. This observation and many other findings have led to the conclusion that exposure to light *readjusts* people's biological clocks. The readjustments may be necessary to correct for the tendency to drift toward a 25-hour cycle.

Based on animal studies, researchers have a pretty good idea of how the day-night cycle resets human biological clocks. When exposed to light, some receptors in the retina send direct inputs to a small structure in the hypothalamus, called the *suprachiasmatic nucleus* (SCN) (Schwartz, 1996). The SCN sends signals to the nearby *pineal gland*, whose secretion of the hormone *melatonin* plays a key

Figure 5.2
Examples of circadian rhythms. These graphs show how alertness, core body temperature, and the secretion of growth hormone typically fluctuate in a 24-hour rhythm. Note how alertness tends to diminish with declining body temperature.

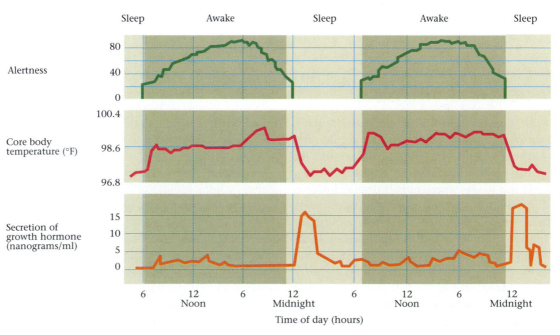

CHAPTER FIVE

role in adjusting biological clocks (Moore, 1995). Circadian rhythms in humans actually appear to be regulated by *several* internal clocks, but the central pacemaker clearly is located in the SCN (Harrington, Rusak, & Mistlberger, 1994).

Ignoring Circadian Rhythms 4a

What happens when you ignore your biological clock and go to sleep at an unusual time? Typically, the quality of your sleep suffers. Getting out of sync with your circadian rhythms also causes *jet lag.* When you fly east or west across several time zones, your biological clock keeps time as usual, even though official clock time changes. You then go to sleep at the "wrong" time and are likely to experience difficulty falling asleep and poor-quality sleep (Moline, 1993). This inferior sleep, which can continue to occur for several days or more, can make you feel fatigued, sluggish, and irritable. People also tend to experience headaches, gastrointestinal distress, and general malaise. If jet lag was simply due to the fatiguing effects of air travel, it would be seen after long flights to the north or south, but it is not seen after flights that do not cross time zones.

People differ in how quickly they can reset their biological clocks to compensate for jet lag, but a rough rule of thumb is that the process takes about a day for each time zone crossed (Colquhoun, 1984; Moline, 1993). However, the speed of readjustment depends on whether one has traveled east or west (see Figure 5.4). Generally, it's easier to fly westward and lengthen your day than it is to fly eastward and shorten it (Graeber, 1994). Why? Perhaps because of the curious tendency to drift toward a 25-hour cycle. Flying westward allows you to follow this natural drift toward lengthening the daily cycle. Flying eastward is more like swimming against a river current.

The findings on jet lag have led researchers to distinguish between two types of alterations in circadian rhythm. When your schedule is altered so that you lengthen your day, you are said to experience a *phase-delay* shift. If you shorten your day, you go through a *phase-advance* shift. The evidence on jet lag suggests that people can accommodate phase-delay changes more easily than phase-advance changes.

Of course, you don't have to hop on a jet to get out of sync with your biological clock. Just going to bed a couple of hours later than usual can affect how you sleep (Czeisler et al., 1980). Rotating work shifts that force people to keep changing their sleep schedule play havoc with biological

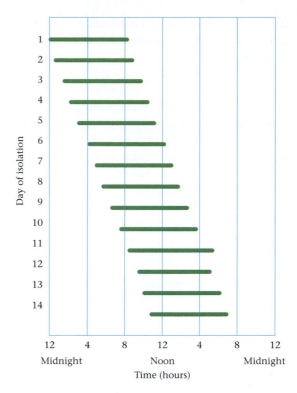

Figure 5.3
Changes in sleep periods of a subject isolated from the day-night cycle. The drift of the sleep periods to the right is characteristic of studies in which subjects are deprived of information about day and night. Subjects typically drift toward a 25-hour "day," retiring later and later with each day spent in isolation. When subjects are reexposed to light-cycle cues, they quickly return to a 24-hour rhythm.

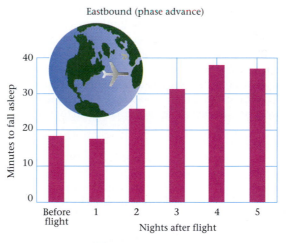

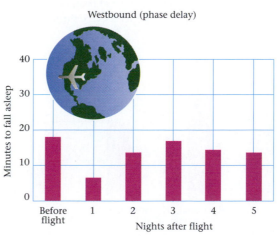

Figure 5.4
Circadian rhythms and jet lag. Jet lag can be assessed in a variety of ways. In a study of people flying between Detroit and London, which requires a 5-hour time shift, Nicholson et al. (1986) looked at the time it took travelers to fall asleep the night before their trip and the next five nights after their flight. As you can see, subjects who flew eastward had increased difficulty falling asleep, whereas subjects who flew westward showed no evidence of jet lag on this measure. The data are consistent with other findings that air travelers generally adjust more slowly after flying east (which shortens their day) than after flying west (which lengthens it). The explanation for this phenomenon may be the natural drift toward a longer daily cycle, which probably makes it easier to extend the biological cycle than to shorten it.

rhythms. Shift rotation is common among nurses, pilots, police officers, and many kinds of industrial workers. Shift rotation tends to be even harder to adjust to than jet lag. As Monk (1994) points out, after flying across several or more time zones, social cues and the light-darkness cycle in your new location *encourage* resynchronization. In contrast, shift workers are typically out of sync with their local light-darkness cycle, and social demands (child care, shopping, household management) *discourage* resynchronization.

Many people who rotate shifts complain bitterly about their sleep problems. Research indicates that their complaints are well founded.

Studies show that workers get less total sleep and poorer quality sleep when they go on rotating shifts (Torsvall et al., 1989). Rotating shifts seem to be especially tough on people over age 50 and those who need more than 9 hours of sleep per "night" (Monk & Folkard, 1985). Shift rotation can also have a negative impact on employees' productivity and accident-proneness at work, the quality of their social relations at home, and their physical and mental health (Johnson et al., 1981; Regestein & Monk, 1991). This point brings us to our Featured Study, in which Charles Czeisler and his colleagues attempted to reduce the problems caused by rotating shifts.

Investigators: Charles A. Czeisler, Martin C. Moore-Ede (Harvard University), and Richard M. Coleman (Stanford University)

Source: Rotating shift work schedules that disrupt sleep are improved by applying circadian principles. *Science,* 1982, *217,* 460–463.

Manipulating Biological Clocks   Featured Study

The purpose of this study was to see whether the negative effects of shift rotation could be reduced by using knowledge acquired in the study of biological rhythms. In effect, the investigators wanted to find out whether workers' biological clocks could be manipulated more effectively. Research on biological rhythms suggested that it would be easier for shift workers to rotate through *phase-delay changes* (progressively later starting times) rather than *phase-advance changes* (progressively earlier starting times). Evidence also suggested that the periods between changes to a new starting time should be as long as feasible. The investigators hypothesized that these alterations in rotation schedules would increase workers' satisfaction, health, and productivity.

Method
Subjects. The subjects were males, ages 19 to 68, who worked at an industrial plant in Utah. Comparisons were made between 85 rotating shift workers and a control group of 68 nonrotating workers who held comparable jobs.

Procedure. The rotating workers had been on a phase-advance schedule, moving successively through

starting times of midnight, 4 P.M., and 8 A.M. The shift changes had been occurring on a weekly basis. The direction of shift rotation was changed to phase delay for all of the rotating workers in the study. Some of these subjects remained on a weekly rotation, while others were moved to a three-week period between shift changes. The dependent variables of workers' satisfaction and health were measured three months after the change of schedules. Worker productivity was assessed nine months after the change.

Results
The changeover to a phase-delay schedule led to improved worker satisfaction in both the one-week and three-week rotation groups. The three-week rotation group, which had been exposed to *two* potentially beneficial alterations in schedule (the change to phase-delay and the change to a longer rotation), reported a larger increase in satisfaction than the one-week group (see Figure 5.5). The three-week group also showed greater improvements in health and work productivity than the one-week group.

Discussion
The results support the hypothesis that the negative effects of shift rotation can be reduced by making workers' schedules more compatible with human circadian rhythms. The findings provide additional evidence that human biological rhythms are important determinants of daytime alertness and efficiency, as well as of sleep quality.

Comment
This study is a nice example of research that is important from both a practical and a theoretical standpoint. It tested basic theories about the advantages of phase-delay as opposed to phase-advance changes in circadian rhythms. At the same time, it gathered information on practical questions about

**Figure 5.5
Schedule changes and worker satisfaction.**
Changing shifts by starting work at progressively later times (phase-delay rotation) instead of progressively earlier times markedly improved workers' satisfaction with their schedules. Improvement was greater for the workers on the 21-day rotation, who had more time to adjust to each change in schedule.

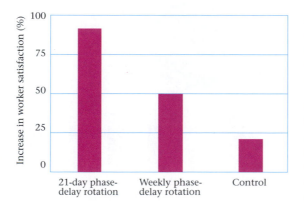

how to design better schedules in the real world of commerce and industry. Thus, it shows how theory and application can be united in a single creative endeavor.

As you can see from our brief review of research in this area, biological rhythms influence behavior more than most people realize. As scientists have come to appreciate this reality, they have begun to look for new ways to help people harness their biological rhythms. A promising line of research has focused on giving people small doses of the pineal gland hormone melatonin, which appears to regulate the human biological clock. Investigators have found that if melatonin is administered in the morning, it can cause phase-delay shifts, and if it is administered in the afternoon or early evening, it can cause phase-advance shifts (Lewy, Ahmed, & Sack, 1995). Preliminary evidence suggests that melatonin can reduce the effects of jet lag and that it can be helpful in treating sleep problems associated with rotating shift work (Arendt, 1994; Folkard, Arendt, & Clark, 1993). Exploratory studies also suggest that melatonin may be effective as a mild sedative that can be useful in the treatment of some forms of insomnia (Zhdanova et al., 1995).

Although these results are encouraging, some words of caution are also in order. In the United States, melatonin is classified as a dietary supplement. Unlike in Canada, Great Britain, and many other countries, it is not a regulated drug. It is sold in health food stores, where it is often touted as a miracle preparation that slows the aging process, enhances sex, and fights cancer and AIDS! There is little or no scientific evidence to support any of these unlikely claims (Arendt, 1996; Bonn, 1996). If people were merely wasting their money, there wouldn't be much cause for concern, but medical experts are worried that health food stores are encouraging people to take excessive doses of what is really an untested drug. The doses used in research on melatonin's sleep-related effects have usually been less than 0.5 milligram; health food stores sell doses ranging up to 5 milligrams—10 times higher than the dose needed to reset one's biological clock (Murphy, 1996). A variety of ill effects have been reported from these preparations, which can raise melatonin levels in the blood to 3,000 times higher than normal. The size of these doses is particularly worrisome, given that there is no research on the health consequences of taking large amounts of melatonin over long periods of time, or on how melatonin interacts with other medications (Bonn, 1996; Hearn, 1995).

Recap of Key Points

• Human biological rhythms include cycles corresponding roughly to one year, 28 days, 24 hours, and 90 minutes. The cycle of sleep and wakefulness is influenced considerably by circadian rhythms.

• When isolated from the light-darkness cycle, people tend to drift toward a 25-hour cycle. Exposure to light may reset biological clocks by affecting the activity of the suprachiasmatic nucleus and the pineal gland, which secretes the hormone melatonin.

• Ignoring your biological clock by going to sleep at an unusual time may have a negative effect on your sleep. Being out of sync with circadian rhythms is one reason for jet lag and for the unpleasant nature of rotating shift work.

• People can accommodate phase-delay changes in their sleep cycle more easily than phase-advance changes. In the Featured Study, investigators successfully applied information on biological rhythms to reduce problems associated with shift rotation.

• Melatonin may have value in efforts to alleviate the effects of jet lag and rotating shift work and it may be an effective sedative for some people, but there is little or no evidence for the other alleged benefits of this hormone.

THE SLEEP AND WAKING CYCLE

Although it is a familiar state of consciousness, sleep is widely misunderstood. Generally, people consider sleep to be a single, uniform state of physical and mental inactivity, during which the brain is "turned off." In reality, sleepers experience quite a bit of physical and mental activity throughout the night. Scientists have learned a great deal about sleep since the 1950s. In this section, we'll discuss some of their insights.

Conducting Sleep Research 4b

The advances in psychology's understanding of sleep are the result of hard work by researchers who have spent countless nighttime hours

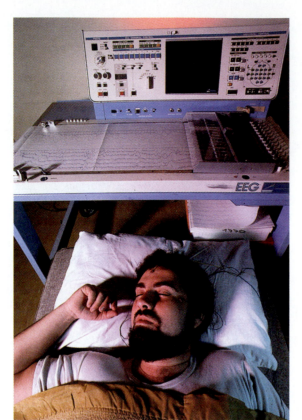

Researchers in a sleep laboratory can observe subjects while using elaborate equipment to record physiological changes during sleep. This kind of research has disclosed that sleep is a complex series of physical and mental states.

watching other people sleep. This work is done in sleep laboratories, where volunteer subjects come to spend the night. Sleep labs have one or more "bedrooms" in which the subjects retire, usually after being hooked up to a variety of physiological recording devices. In addition to an EEG, the other two crucial devices are **an *electromyograph (EMG)*, which records muscular activity and tension, and an *electrooculograph (EOG)*, which records eye movements** (Carskadon & Rechtschaffen, 1994). Typically, other instruments are also used to monitor heart rate, breathing, pulse rate, and body temperature. The researchers observe the sleeping subject through a window (or with a video camera) from an adjacent room, where they also monitor their elaborate physiological recording equipment (see the photo above). For most people, it takes just one night to adapt to the strange bedroom and the recording devices and return to their normal mode of sleeping (Carskadon & Dement, 1994).

Cycling Through the Stages of Sleep 4b

Not only does sleep occur in a context of daily rhythms, but subtler rhythms are evident within the experience of sleep itself. During sleep, people cycle through a series of five stages. Let's take a look at what researchers have learned about the changes that occur during these sleep stages (Anch et al., 1988; Carskadon & Dement, 1994).

Stages 1–4

Although it may only take a few minutes, the onset of sleep is gradual and there is no obvious transition point between wakefulness and sleep (Rechtschaffen, 1994). The length of time it takes people to fall asleep varies considerably. It depends on quite an array of factors, including how long it has been since the person has slept, where the person is in his or her circadian rhythm, the amount of noise or light in the sleep environment, and the person's age, desire to fall asleep, boredom level, recent caffeine or drug intake, and stress level, among other things (Broughton, 1994). In any event, stage 1 is a brief transitional stage of light sleep that usually lasts only a few (1–7) minutes. Breathing and heart rate slow as muscle tension and body temperature decline. The alpha waves that probably dominated EEG activity just before falling asleep give way to lower-frequency EEG activity in which theta waves are prominent (see Figure 5.6). *Hypnic jerks,* those brief muscular contractions that occur as people fall asleep, generally occur during stage 1 drowsiness (Broughton, 1994).

As the sleeper descends through stages 2, 3, and 4 of the cycle, respiration rate, heart rate, muscle tension, and body temperature continue to decline. During stage 2, which typically lasts about 10–25 minutes, brief bursts of higher-frequency brain waves, called *sleep spindles,* appear against a background of mixed EEG activity (refer to Figure 5.6 once again). Gradually, brain waves become higher in amplitude and slower in frequency, as the body moves into a deeper form of sleep, called slow-wave sleep. **Slow-wave sleep (SWS) consists of sleep stages 3 and 4, during which high-amplitude, low-frequency delta waves become prominent in EEG recordings.** Typically individuals reach slow-wave sleep in about a half-hour and stay there for roughly a half-hour. Then the cycle reverses itself and the sleeper gradually moves back upward through the lighter stages. That's when things start to get especially interesting.

REM Sleep

When sleepers reach what should be stage 1 once again, they usually go into the *fifth s*tage of sleep, which is most widely known as *REM sleep.* REM is an abbreviation for *rapid eye movements,* which are prominent during this stage of sleep. In a sleep lab, researchers use an electrooculograph to monitor these lateral (side-to-side) movements that occur beneath the sleeping person's closed eyelids. However, they can be seen with the naked eye if you closely watch someone in the REM stage of sleep (little ripples move back and forth across his or her closed eyelids).

The discovery of periodic rapid eye movements during sleep was made accidentally in the 1950s by Eugene Aserinsky, a graduate student working in Nathaniel Kleitman's lab at the University of Chicago (Aserinsky & Kleitman, 1953; Dement, 1994). The term *REM sleep* was coined by William Dement, another student in Kleitman's lab, who went on to become one of the world's foremost sleep researchers. The REM stage tends to be a "deep" stage of sleep in the conventional sense that it is relatively hard to awaken a person from it (although arousal thresholds vary during REM). The REM stage is also marked by irregular breathing and pulse rate. Muscle tone is extremely relaxed—so much so that bodily movements are minimal and the sleeper is virtually paralyzed. Although REM is a relatively deep stage of sleep, EEG activity is dominated by high-frequency beta waves that resemble those observed when people are alert and awake (see Figure 5.6 again).

This paradox is probably related to the association between REM sleep and dreaming. Soon after the discovery of REM sleep, researchers learned that *this stage of sleep is highly correlated with reports of vivid dreaming.* How do we know that? When researchers have systematically awakened subjects to ask them whether they had been dreaming, most dream reports have come from awakenings during the REM stage. William Dement (1978) compiled the results of eight early studies of this sort, involving nearly 1500 awakenings of subjects. REM awakenings produced dream recall 78% of the time. Awakenings from other stages were accompanied by dream recall only 14% of the time. Although some dreaming occurs in other stages, dreaming is most frequent, vivid, and memorable during REM sleep.

To summarize, **REM sleep is a relatively deep stage of sleep marked by rapid eye movements, high-frequency, low-amplitude brain waves, and vivid dreaming.** It is such a special stage of sleep that the other four stages are often characterized simply as "non-REM sleep." **Non-REM (NREM) sleep consists of sleep stages 1 through 4, which are marked by an absence of rapid eye movements, relatively little dreaming, and varied EEG activity.**

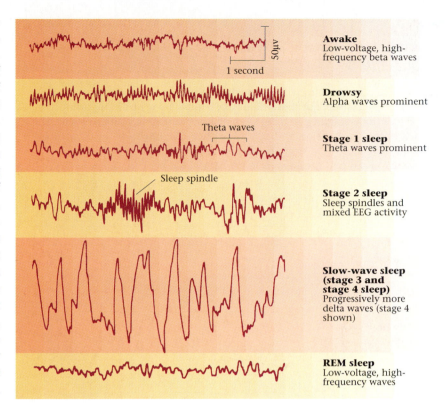

Awake
Low-voltage, high-frequency beta waves

Drowsy
Alpha waves prominent

Theta waves

Stage 1 sleep
Theta waves prominent

Sleep spindle

Stage 2 sleep
Sleep spindles and mixed EEG activity

Slow-wave sleep (stage 3 and stage 4 sleep)
Progressively more delta waves (stage 4 shown)

REM sleep
Low-voltage, high-frequency waves

1 second
50 μV

Figure 5.6
EEG patterns in sleep and wakefulness. Characteristic brain waves vary depending on one's state of consciousness. Generally, as people move from an awake state through deeper stages of sleep, their brain waves decrease in frequency (cycles per second) and increase in amplitude (height). However, brain waves during REM sleep resemble "wide-awake" brain waves.

Repeating the Cycle

During the course of a night, people usually repeat the sleep cycle about four times. Since each cycle runs roughly 90 minutes, this pattern is an example of the 90-minute biological rhythms mentioned earlier. As the night wears on, the cycle changes gradually. The first REM period is relatively short, lasting only a few minutes. Subsequent REM periods get progressively longer, peaking at around 40–60 minutes in length. Additionally, NREM intervals tend to get shorter, and descents into NREM stages usually become more shallow. These trends can be seen in Figure 5.7 (on pages 186–187), which provides an overview of a typical night's sleep cycle.

These trends mean that most slow-wave sleep occurs early in the sleep cycle, gradually giving way to alternating periods of REM sleep and stage 2 sleep. Summing across the entire sleep cycle, young adults typically spend about 60% of their sleep time in light sleep (stages 1 and 2), 20% in slow-wave sleep (stages 3 and 4), and 20% in REM sleep (Mendelson, 1987). Individuals have their unique variations from the typical pattern of sleep, but a particular person's sleep pattern tends to be moderately consistent from night to night. Heredity may influence some aspects of individuals' sleep patterns, such as what time they habitually go to bed, how long they sleep, and whether they nap frequently (Heath et al., 1990). Of course, personal sleep patterns can be disrupted by many things,

CONCEPT CHECK 5.1
Comparing REM and NREM Sleep

A table here could have provided you with a systematic comparison of REM sleep and NREM sleep, but that would have deprived you of the opportunity to check your understanding of these sleep phases by creating your own table. Fill in each of the blanks below with a word or phrase highlighting the differences between REM and NREM sleep with regard to the various characteristics specified. You can find the answers in the back of the book in Appendix A.

Characteristic	REM sleep	NREM sleep
Type of EEG activity	_____	_____
Eye movements	_____	_____
Dreaming	_____	_____
Depth (difficulty in awakening)	_____	_____
Percentage of total sleep (in adults)	_____	_____
Increases or decreases (as percentage of sleep) during childhood	_____	_____
Timing in sleep cycle (dominates early or late)	_____	_____

including stress, depression, and drug use (Borbely, 1986).

Age Trends in Sleep

Age alters the sleep cycle. What we have described so far is the typical pattern for young adults. Children, however, display different patterns (Bliwise, 1994; Roffwarg, Muzio, & Dement, 1966). Newborns will sleep six to eight times in a 24-hour period, often exceeding a total of 16 hours of sleep (see Figure 5.8). Fortunately for parents, during the first several months much of this sleep begins to get consolidated into one particularly long nighttime sleep period (Webb, 1992a). Interestingly, infants spend much more of their sleep time than adults do in the REM stage. In the first few months, REM accounts for about 50% of babies' sleep, as compared to 20% of adults' sleep. During the remainder of the first year, the REM portion of infants' sleep declines to roughly 30%. The REM portion of sleep continues to decrease gradually until it levels off at about 20% during adolescence (see Figure 5.8).

During adulthood, gradual, age-related changes in sleep continue. The proportion of slow-wave sleep declines and the percentage of time spent in stage 1 increases (Bliwise, 1994; Ehlers & Kupfer, 1989). These shifts toward lighter sleep *may*

Figure 5.7
An overview of the cycle of sleep. The white line charts how a typical, healthy, young adult moves through the various stages of sleep during the course of a night. This diagram also shows how dreams and rapid eye movements tend to coincide with REM sleep, whereas posture changes occur in between REM periods (because the body is nearly paralyzed during REM sleep). Notice how the person cycles into REM four times, as descents into NREM sleep get shallower and REM periods get longer. Thus, slow-wave sleep is prominent early in the night, while REM and stage 2 sleep dominate the second half of a night's sleep. Although these patterns are typical, keep in mind that sleep patterns vary from one person to another and that they change with age.

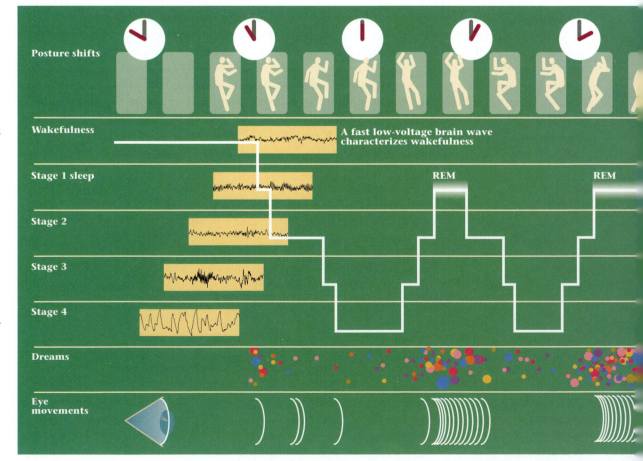

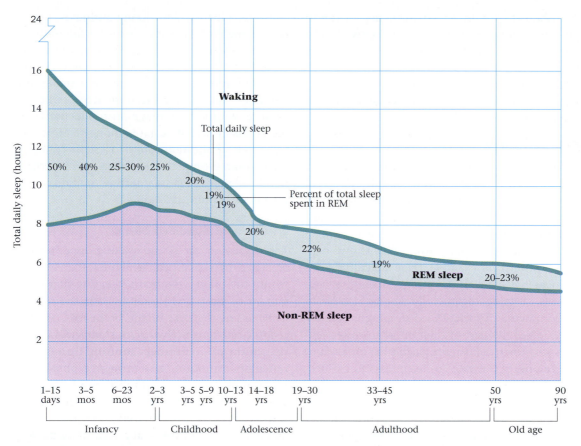

Figure 5.8
Changes in sleep patterns over the life span. Both the total amount of sleep per night and the portion of sleep that is REM sleep change with age. Sleep patterns change most dramatically during infancy, with total sleep time and amount of REM sleep declining sharply in the first two years of life. After a noticeable drop in the average amount of sleep in adolescence, sleep patterns remain relatively stable, although total sleep and slow-wave sleep continue to decline gradually with age. (Adapted from Roffwarg, Muzio, & Dement, 1966; revised by authors since publication)

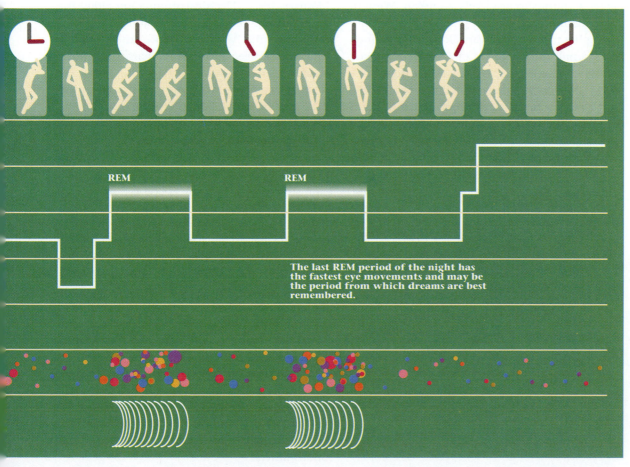

The last REM period of the night has the fastest eye movements and may be the period from which dreams are best remembered.

contribute to the increased frequency of night-time awakenings seen among the elderly. As Figure 5.8 shows, the average amount of total sleep time also declines with advancing age. However, these averages mask important variability, as total sleep *increases* with age in a substantial portion of older people (Webb, 1992a).

Culture and Sleep

Although age clearly affects the nature and structure of sleep itself, the psychological and physiological experience of sleep does not appear to vary systematically across cultures. Cultural disparities in sleep are limited to more peripheral matters, such as sleeping arrangements and napping customs. For example, there are cultural differences in *co-sleeping*, the practice of children and parents sleeping together (McKenna, 1993). In modern Western societies, co-sleeping is actively discouraged. As part of their effort to foster self-reliance, American parents teach their children to sleep alone. In contrast, co-sleeping is more widely accepted in Japanese culture, which emphasizes interdependence and group harmony. Around the world as a whole, co-sleeping is the norm rather than the exception. Strong pressure against co-sleeping appears to be largely an urban, Western phenomenon.

Napping practices also vary along cultural lines. For example, the Temiars of Indonesia depend heavily on daytime naps because their night-time routines (fishing, cooking, watching over the fire) limit their nocturnal sleep to about 4 to 6 hours per night (Stampi, 1989). In many societies, shops close and activities are curtailed in the afternoon to permit people to enjoy a 1- to 2-hour midday nap. These "siesta cultures" are found mostly in tropical regions of the world (Webb & Dinges, 1989). There, this practice is adaptive in that it allows people to avoid working during the hottest part of the day. The siesta is not a fixture in all tropical societies, however. It is infrequent among nomadic groups and those that depend on irregular food supplies. As a rule, the siesta tradition is not found in industrialized societies, where it conflicts with the emphasis on productivity and the philosophy that "time is money." Moreover, when industrialization comes to a siesta culture, it undermines the practice. For instance, modernization in Spain has led to a decline in midday napping there (Kribbs, 1993).

The Neural Bases of Sleep

The rhythm of sleep and waking appears to be regulated by subcortical structures that lie deep within the brain. One brain structure that is important to sleep and wakefulness is the *reticular formation* in the core of the brainstem. **The ascending reticular activating system (ARAS) consists of the afferent fibers running through the reticular formation that influence physiological arousal.** As you can see in Figure 5.9, the ARAS projects diffusely into many areas of the cortex. When these ascending fibers are cut in the brainstem of a cat, the result is continuous sleep (Moruzzi, 1964). Electrical stimulation along the same pathways produces arousal and alertness.

Although the ARAS contributes to the neural regulation of sleep and waking, many other brain structures are also involved (Hobson, 1989). For example, activity in the pons seems to be critical to the generation of REM sleep (Gillin & Shiromani, 1990). Specific areas in the medulla, the thalamus, the hypothalamus, and the limbic system have also been implicated in the control of sleep and waking (see Chapter 3 for the locations of these brain structures). Thus, the ebb and flow of sleep and waking is regulated through activity in a constellation of interacting brain centers.

Efforts to identify the neurotransmitters involved in the regulation of sleep and waking have uncovered similar diffusion of responsibility. Acetylcholine and serotonin appear to be especially important. However, at least three other neurotransmitters—norepinephrine, dopamine, and GABA—influence the course of sleep and arousal, and several other chemicals may play a contributing role (Mendelson, 1987; Jones, 1994). In summary, no single structure in the brain serves as a "sleep center," nor does any one neurotransmitter serve as a "sleep chemical." Instead, sleep depends on the interplay of many neural centers and neurotransmitters.

Figure 5.9
The ascending reticular activating system (ARAS). A number of brain areas and structures interact to regulate sleep and waking. Particularly important is the ARAS (represented by the white arrows), which conveys neural stimulation to many areas of the cortex.

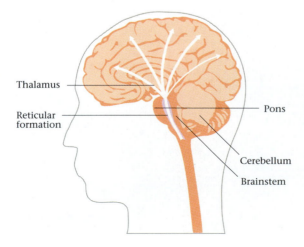

Thalamus

Reticular formation

Pons

Cerebellum

Brainstem

Doing Without: Sleep Deprivation

Scientific research on sleep deprivation presents something of a paradox. On the one hand, research suggests that sleep deprivation is not as detrimental as most people subjectively feel it to be. On the other hand, evidence suggests that sleep deprivation may be a major social problem, undermining efficiency at work and contributing to countless accidents.

Complete Deprivation

What happens when people go completely without sleep for a period of days? As you might expect, complete deprivation of sleep has been related to various negative effects, including weariness, poor concentration, reduced motivation, irritability, and lapses in attention (Johnson, 1982). However, these negative effects tend to be modest, and many researchers have been impressed by how *well* sleep-deprived subjects can perform if they are motivated to do so (Anch et al., 1988). The effects of complete sleep deprivation would probably be more severe except that most people have a hard time going very long without sleep. Most experience great difficulty getting beyond a third or fourth sleepless day.

Partial Deprivation

Partial sleep deprivation, or *sleep restriction,* occurs when people make do with substantially less sleep than normal over a period of time. Partial deprivation occurs far more often in everyday life than complete sleep deprivation. Indeed, many sleep experts believe that much of American society chronically suffers from partial sleep deprivation. It appears that more and more people are trying to squeeze additional waking hours out of their days as they attempt to juggle conflicting work, family, household, and school responsibilities, leading William Dement to comment that "Most Americans no longer know what it feels like to be fully alert" (Toufexis, 1990, p. 79). More research on sleep habits is needed to buttress casual observations about the increased hustle and bustle of American life, but there *are* some empirical data suggesting that people are getting noticeably less sleep (Webb, 1993).

How serious are the effects of partial sleep deprivation? Studies suggest that partial deprivation has an inconsistent impact on performance that depends on the amount of sleep lost and on the nature of the task at hand (Bonnet, 1991; Johnson, 1982). Negative effects are most likely when sub-jects are asked to work on long-lasting, difficult, or uninteresting tasks, or when subjects are asked to restrict their sleep to 5 hours or fewer (Bonnet, 1994).

The most consistent result of sleep deprivation is simply an increase in sleepiness. *However, this increased sleepiness may not be as benign as it sounds.* This drowsiness can impair individuals' capacity for attention, especially when working on monotonous, routine tasks. Evidence indicates that such lapses in attention contribute to a large share of transportation accidents and mishaps in the workplace (Lauber, 1993; Mitler, 1993). Indeed, recent studies suggest that nighttime workers in many industries frequently fall asleep on the job. For example, in one study of train engineers 59% admitted dozing off while on duty (Akerstedt, 1988). Obviously, if a person is running a punch press, driving a bus, or working as an air traffic controller, a momentary lapse in attention could be very, very costly. In recent years, a number of major disasters, such as the nuclear accidents at Three Mile Island and Chernobyl and the running aground of the Exxon *Valdez,* have been blamed in part on lapses in judgment and attention due to sleep deprivation (Mitler, Dinges, & Dement, 1994). Experts have estimated that accidents due to sleepiness cost the U.S. economy over $56 billion annually, lead to the loss of over 52 million work days each year, and result in over 24,000 deaths per year (Coren, 1996).

Selective Deprivation

The unique quality of REM sleep led researchers to look into the effects of a special type of partial sleep deprivation—*selective deprivation.* In a number of laboratory studies, subjects were awakened over

"Sleep deprivation is a major epidemic in our society. . . . Americans spend so much time and energy chasing the American dream, that they don't have much time left for actual dreaming."

WILLIAM DEMENT

A large number of transportation mishaps result from dozing on the job. Truck drivers on long hauls constantly combat the drowsiness that can be brought on by monotonous scenery—and they sometimes lose the battle.

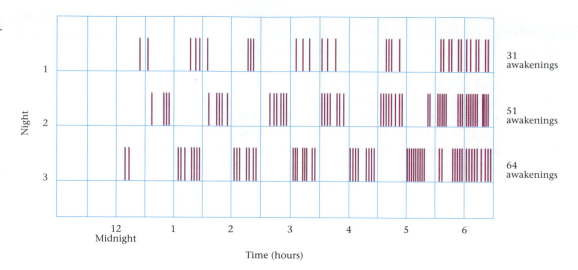

Figure 5.10
The effects of REM deprivation over a period of three nights. The pattern of awakenings illustrates how a REM-deprived subject tends to compensate by repeatedly slipping back into REM sleep. Notice how the awakenings of this subject became more frequent during the course of each night and from night to night. (Based on data from Borbely, 1986)

"When we go to bed at night, we enter an altered state of consciousness that lasts for a number of hours. We cease to see, hear, and feel consciously what occurs around us. The world of sleep and the world of wakefulness are so different that each of us could be said to live in two worlds."

ALEXANDER BORBELY

a period of nights whenever they began to go into the REM stage. These subjects usually got a decent amount of sleep in NREM stages, but they were selectively deprived of REM sleep.

What are the effects of REM deprivation? The evidence indicates that it has little impact on daytime functioning and task performance, but it *does* have some interesting effects on subjects' patterns of sleeping (Ellman et al., 1991; Pearlman, 1982). As the nights go by in REM-deprivation studies, it becomes necessary to awaken the subjects more and more often to deprive them of their REM sleep, because they spontaneously shift into REM more and more frequently. While subjects normally go into REM about four or five times a night, REM-deprived subjects start slipping into REM every time the researchers turn around. In one study, researchers had to awaken a subject 64 times by the third night of REM deprivation, as shown in Figure 5.10 (Borbely, 1986). Furthermore, when a REM-deprivation experiment comes to an end and subjects are allowed to sleep without interruption, they experience a "rebound effect." That is, they spend extra time in REM periods for one to three nights to make up for their REM deprivation.

Similar results have been observed when subjects have been selectively deprived of slow-wave sleep (Klerman, 1993). After seven nights of stage 4 deprivation, subjects experience a rebound effect and spend extra time in stage 4 sleep. Also, as the nights go by, progressively more awakenings are required to prevent stage 4 sleep (Agnew, Webb, & Williams, 1964, 1967). In fact, the need for slow-wave sleep appears to be even more pressing than the need for REM sleep, which may explain why, in a typical night's sleep, people get lots of slow-wave sleep first, and then load up on REM sleep (Borbely, 1994).

What do theorists make of these spontaneous pursuits of REM and slow-wave sleep? They conclude that people must have specific *needs* for REM and slow-wave sleep—and rather strong needs, at that. The realization that humans need these specific types of sleep has contributed to new theorizing about why people sleep, a perplexing question that we turn to next.

Why Do We Sleep?

Theories about why people sleep generally fall into two categories: restorative theories and circadian theories. *Restorative theories* propose that sleep promotes physiological processes that rejuvenate the body each night (Hartmann, 1973; Oswald, 1974). According to this view, the purpose of sleep is to restore energy and other bodily resources depleted by waking activities. *Circadian theories* propose that sleep is an aspect of circadian rhythms regulated by neural mechanisms that are a product of evolution (Enright, 1980; Wever, 1979). According to this view, sleep periods have evolved in humans and other animals because sleep has survival value. For example, sleeping can conserve energy and reduce animals' exposure to predators and other sources of danger.

The demonstration that people need both slow-wave and REM sleep has suggested to some theorists that the restorative and circadian explanations of sleep may *both* be correct. For example, Alexander Borbely (1984, 1994) argues that human sleep is regulated by two interactive processes. Consistent with a circadian theory, sleepiness due to *Process C* fluctuates in a circadian rhythm regulated by a biological clock—see Figure 5.11(a). Consistent with a restorative theory, sleepiness due to *Process S* builds steadily while one remains awake and declines during sleep—see

Figure 5.11(b). According to Borbely, a person's overall need for sleep is the sum of the sleepiness produced by the two processes, as depicted in Figure 5.11(c).

Interestingly, studies show that the time spent in slow-wave sleep depends mainly on how long one has been awake (Process S), while time spent in REM depends mainly on a circadian rhythm (Process C) (Borbely et al., 1989; Knowles et al., 1990). Thus, Borbely's theory suggests that *the need for slow-wave sleep reflects the restorative function of sleep* and that *the need for REM sleep reflects the circadian regulation of sleep.*

The two-process model of sleep regulation provides an intriguing integration of restorative and circadian theories, but Wilse Webb (1988, 1994) argues that it cannot account for the flexibility of sleep patterns—for example, the way workers can adapt to rotating shifts or students can pull all-nighters to cram for exams. To account for this flexibility, Webb suggests a three-process model of sleep regulation that factors *behavioral control* into the picture. Behavioral control consists of actions intended to inhibit sleep (example: drinking coffee) or to facilitate sleep (example: turning off lights). As you can see, theories of sleep regulation are still evolving, and they continue to generate fascinating debate.

Problems in the Night: Sleep Disorders

Not everyone is able to consistently enjoy the luxury of a good night's sleep. In this section we will briefly discuss what is currently known about a variety of sleep disorders.

Insomnia

Insomnia is the most common sleep disorder. **Insomnia refers to chronic problems in getting adequate sleep.** It occurs in three basic patterns: (1) difficulty in falling asleep initially, (2) difficulty in remaining asleep, and (3) persistent early-morning awakening. Insomnia may sound like a minor problem to those who haven't struggled with it, but it can be a very unpleasant malady. Insomniacs have to endure the agony of watching their precious sleep time tick away as they toss and turn in restless frustration.

PREVALENCE. Nearly everyone suffers occasional sleep difficulties because of stress, disruptions of biological rhythms, or other temporary circumstances. Fortunately, these problems clear up spontaneously for most people. However, about 15% of adults report severe or frequent insomnia, and

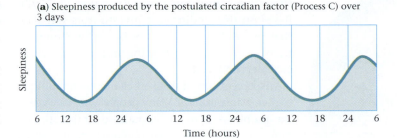

(**a**) Sleepiness produced by the postulated circadian factor (Process C) over 3 days

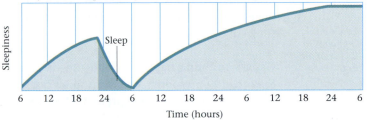

(**b**) Sleepiness produced by the postulated wakefulness factor (Process S) for a subject who sleeps one night and then misses two nights of sleep

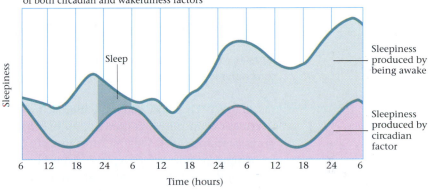

(**c**) The sleepiness experienced by the above subject is the sum of the effects of both circadian and wakefulness factors

another 15% complain of mild or occasional insomnia (Bootzin et al., 1993). The prevalence of insomnia increases noticeably during old age (Mellinger, Balter, & Uhlenhuth, 1985).

Some people may suffer from "pseudoinsomnia," or *sleep state misperception,* which means that they just *think* they are getting an inadequate amount of sleep. When actually monitored in a sleep clinic, about 5% of insomniac patients show sound patterns of sleep (Hauri, 1994). In one well-known case of exaggerated complaining, a British insomniac claimed that he hadn't slept in 10 years! When invited to stay at a sleep clinic for observation, he seemed determined to prove his chronic sleeplessness. However, on the second night he nodded out for 20 minutes. By the fourth night, he could barely keep his eyes open, and soon he was snoring blissfully for hours (Oswald & Adam, 1980). One recent study of pseudoinsomniacs found subtle deficiencies in their sleep (reduced REM and SWS sleep) that might account for their

Figure 5.11
Borbely's two-process theory of sleep. According to Borbely, sleepiness is governed by (**a**) a circadian rhythm (Process C) and by (**b**) how long one has been awake (Process S). (**c**) One's total need for sleep is the sum of the sleepiness produced by the two processes. Slow-wave sleep appears to depend primarily on Process S, whereas REM sleep is mainly a function of Process C.

"The extension of the two-factor model to include a behavioral component points to an additional efficiency of the sleep system. With the inclusion of this component, the model permits sleep a necessary flexibility."

WILSE WEBB

subjective complaints (Salin-Pascual et al., 1992). Based on this finding, the investigators speculate that pseudoinsomniacs may be going through a transitional phase prior to the onset of more clearcut sleep difficulties.

Misperceptions of sleep efficiency are not unique to pseudoinsomniacs. Many people who have genuine problems with insomnia also underestimate how much sleep they get (Reynolds et al., 1991), as do some normal sleepers (Lewis, 1969). The discrepancy between individuals' feelings about how much they sleep and objective reality shows once again that states of consciousness are highly subjective.

CAUSES. Insomnia has many causes (Roehrs, Zorick, & Roth, 1994; Wooten, 1994). In some cases, excessive anxiety and tension prevent relaxation and keep people awake. Insomnia is frequently a side effect of emotional problems, such as depression, or of significant stress, such as pressures at work. Understandably, health problems such as back pain, ulcers, and asthma can lead to insomnia. The use of certain drugs, especially such stimulants as cocaine and amphetamines, may also lead to problems in sleeping.

TREATMENT. The most common approach to the treatment of insomnia is prescription of sedative drugs (sleeping pills). Sedatives are fairly effective in helping people fall asleep more quickly, and they reduce nighttime awakenings and increase total sleep (Mendelson, 1990). Nonetheless, these drugs are probably used to combat insomnia *too* frequently. Sleep experts are virtually unanimous in maintaining that in the past physicians prescribed sleeping pills far too readily. As a result of this criticism, prescriptions for sleeping pills declined significantly during the 1970s and 1980s (Ray & Ksir, 1990). Nonetheless, about 5%–15% of adults still use sleep medication with some regularity (Partinen, 1994).

Sedatives are a poor long-range solution for insomnia for a number of reasons (Mendelson, 1993). For example, there is the danger of overdose, and some people become dependent on sedatives in order to fall asleep. Moreover, with continued use sedatives gradually become less effective, so people need to increase their dose to more dangerous levels, creating a vicious circle of escalating dependency (see Figure 5.12). At higher dose levels, sedatives have carryover effects that can make people drowsy and sluggish the next day. Ironically, most sedatives also interfere with the normal cycle of sleep. Although they promote sleep, they reduce the proportion of time spent in REM and slow-wave sleep (Borbely, 1986). Furthermore, if medication is stopped abruptly, many people experience even worse insomnia than before their treatment was begun—a condition called *rebound insomnia* (Roehrs et al., 1992).

In summary, sedatives do have a place in the treatment of insomnia, but they need to be used cautiously and conservatively. They should be used primarily for short-term treatment of sleep problems. Fortunately, a new generation of sleeping pills that are eliminated from the body "ultra-rapidly" may reduce some of the problems that have been associated with sedatives. These drugs can leave the normal sleep cycle intact while reducing the likelihood of next-day grogginess (Scharf et al., 1991). However, these drugs can cause many of the same problems as traditional sleeping pills if people increase their dosage, which those with sleep problems tend to do (Nicholson, 1994).

Beyond discouraging the use of drugs, it is difficult to generalize about how insomnia should be treated, because its many causes call for different solutions. A number of sleep clinics have been established in recent years to help people who suffer from insomnia and other sleep disorders (Hales, 1987). Work in these clinics has generated some insights about strategies that people can apply on their own when grappling with insomnia. Some of these insights are presented in the Application at the end of this chapter.

Other Sleep Problems

Although insomnia is the most common difficulty associated with sleep, people are plagued by many

Figure 5.12
The vicious circle of dependence on sleeping pills. Because of the body's ability to develop tolerance to drugs, using sedatives routinely to "cure" insomnia can lead to a vicious circle of escalating dependency as larger and larger doses of the sedative are needed to produce the same effect.

other types of sleep problems as well. Let's briefly look at the symptoms, causes, and prevalence of five additional sleep problems, as described by Kryger, Roth, and Dement (1994) and Bootzin et al. (1993).

***Narcolepsy* is a disease marked by sudden and irresistible onsets of sleep during normal waking periods.** A person suffering from narcolepsy goes directly from wakefulness into REM sleep, usually for a short period of time (10–20 minutes). This is a potentially dangerous condition, since some victims fall asleep instantly, even while driving a car or operating machinery. Narcolepsy is infrequent. Its causes are unknown, but some people appear to be genetically predisposed to the disease (Guilleminault, 1989). Stimulant drugs have been used to treat this condition with modest success (Guilleminault, 1994). But as you will see in our upcoming discussion of drugs, stimulants carry many problems of their own.

***Sleep apnea* involves frequent, reflexive gasping for air that awakens a person and disrupts sleep.** Some victims are awakened from their sleep hundreds of times a night. Apnea occurs when a person literally stops breathing for 15 to 60 seconds. This disorder is seen in about 5% of men aged 40 to 60 (Partinen, 1994). As you might expect, sleep apnea often leads to insomnia as a side effect. Severe cases may also cause heart and lung damage. Apnea may be treated with surgery or drug therapy.

***Night terrors* (also called sleep terrors) are abrupt awakenings from NREM sleep accompanied by intense autonomic arousal and feelings of panic.** Night terrors, which can produce remarkable accelerations of heart rate, usually occur during stage 4 sleep early in the night, as shown in Figure 5.13 (Kahn, Fisher, & Edwards, 1991). Victims typically let out a piercing cry, bolt upright, and then stare into space. They usually do not recall a coherent dream, although they may remember a simple, frightening image. The panic normally fades quickly, and a return to sleep is fairly easy. Night terrors occur in adults, but they are especially common in children ages 3 to 8. Night terrors are *not* indicative of an emotional disturbance. Treatment may not be necessary, as night terrors are often a temporary problem.

***Nightmares* are anxiety-arousing dreams that lead to awakening, usually from REM sleep** (see Figure 5.13). Typically, a person who awakens from a nightmare recalls a vivid dream and may find it difficult to get back to sleep. Significant stress in one's life is associated with increased frequency and intensity of nightmares. In adults, there is a correlation between frequent nightmares and neurotic symptoms (Berquier & Ashton, 1992). Although about 10% of adults have occasional nightmares, these frightening episodes are mainly a problem among children. Most youngsters have occasional nightmares, but *persistent* nightmares may reflect an emotional disturbance. If a child's nightmares are frequent and unpleasant, counseling may prove helpful. Otherwise, treatment is unnecessary, as most children outgrow the problem.

***Somnambulism,* or sleepwalking, occurs when a person arises and wanders about while remaining asleep.** Sleepwalking tends to occur during the first 2 hours of sleep, when individuals are in slow-wave sleep. Sleepwalkers may awaken during their journey, or they may return to bed without any recollection of their excursion. The causes of this unusual disorder are unknown, although there does appear to be a genetic predisposition to it (Keefauver & Guilleminault, 1994). Sleepwalking does not appear to be a manifestation of underlying emotional or psychological problems (Mahowald, 1993).

Sleepwalking occurs mostly in children, with a peak incidence around age 11 or 12, but it is occasionally seen in adults. Children usually outgrow the problem, so professional intervention isn't required. However, sleepwalkers *are* prone to accidents. For example, one sleepwalking auto mechanic fell off his second-story porch and fractured his spine, and sleepwalking children have been known to fall down stairs or into swimming pools. Hence, parents may need to take some precautionary measures if the problem persists, such as locking the child in a safety-proofed bedroom. Contrary to popular myth, it is safe to awaken people (gently) from a sleepwalking episode—much safer than letting them wander about.

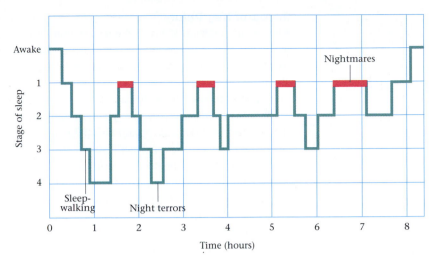

Figure 5.13
Sleep problems and the cycle of sleep. Different sleep problems tend to occur at different points in the sleep cycle. Whereas sleepwalking and night terrors are associated with slow-wave sleep, nightmares are associated with the heightened dream activity of REM sleep.

- Research on sleep is typically done in laboratories where volunteers come to spend the night. Participants are typically hooked up to an EEG, EOG, EMG, and instruments that monitor heart rate, respiration, pulse rate, and body temperature.
- When people fall asleep, they evolve through a series of stages in cycles of approximately 90 minutes. Slow-wave sleep consists of stages 3 and 4, during which delta waves are prominent. During the REM stage, sleepers experience rapid eye movements, brain waves that are characteristic of waking thought, and vivid dreaming. The sleep cycle tends to be repeated about four times a night, as REM sleep gradually becomes more predominant and NREM sleep dwindles.
- The REM portion of sleep declines during childhood, leveling off at around 20% during adolescence. During adulthood, slow-wave sleep declines. Total sleep time decreases for most elderly people, although it increases for some. Culture appears to have little impact on the physiological experience of sleep, but it does influence napping patterns and sleeping arrangements, such as co-sleeping.
- The neural bases of sleep are very complex. Arousal depends on activity in the ascending reticular activating system, but other brain structures also contribute to regulation of the sleep and waking cycle. A variety of neurotransmitters appear to be involved in the modulation of sleep.
- The only consistent effect of sleep deprivation is sleepiness. However, increased sleepiness can be a significant problem that appears to contribute to many transportation accidents and mishaps at work.
- Research on sleep deprivation suggests that people need REM sleep and slow-wave sleep. According to Borbely, slow-wave sleep is regulated by a restorative process, and REM sleep by a circadian process. Webb adds that sleep is also regulated by a third process, which is behavioral control.
- Many people are troubled by sleep disorders. Foremost among these is insomnia, which may affect as much as 30% of the population. Insomnia has a variety of causes. Sleeping pills generally are a poor solution. The optimal treatment for insomnia depends on its apparent cause.
- Narcolepsy is a disease marked by sudden, irresistible onsets of sleep during normal waking periods. Sleep apnea involves frequent gasping for air, which occurs when people stop breathing for up to 60 seconds. Night terrors are abrupt awakenings from NREM sleep accompanied by panic, whereas nightmares are anxiety-arousing dreams that typically awaken one from REM sleep. Somnambulism, or sleepwalking, typically occurs during slow-wave sleep.

THE WORLD OF DREAMS

For the most part, dreams are not taken very seriously in Western societies. Paradoxically, though, Robert Van de Castle (1994) points out that dreams have sometimes changed the world. For example, Van de Castle describes how René Descartes's philosophy of dualism, Frederick Banting's discovery of insulin, Elias Howe's refinement of the sewing machine, Mohandas Gandhi's strategy of nonviolent protest, and Lyndon Johnson's withdrawal from the 1968 presidential race were all inspired by dreams. He also explains how Mary Shelley's *Frankenstein* and Robert Louis Stevenson's *The Strange Case of Dr. Jekyll and Mr. Hyde* emerged out of their dream experiences. In his wide-ranging discussion, Van de Castle also relates how the Surrealist painter Salvador Dali characterized his work as "dream photographs," and how legendary filmmakers Ingmar Bergman, Orson Welles, and Federico Fellini all drew on their dreams in making their films. Thus, Van de Castle concludes that "dreams have had a dramatic influence on almost every important aspect of our culture and history" (p. 10).

Speculation about dreams has a long history, but only in recent years have dreams been subjected to empirical study. In the laboratory, researchers investigate dreaming by awakening subjects from sleep to ask them whether they were dreaming and what they were dreaming about. As you have already learned, this kind of research has uncovered an association between dreaming and REM sleep. Psychologists also learn about dreams by instructing research subjects or therapy patients to try to awaken during the night at home to record their dreams. These kinds of studies have cast some light on when people dream and what they dream about. What remains obscure is *why* people dream.

What Is a Dream?

What exactly is a dream? This question is more complex and controversial than you might guess. The conventional view is that dreams are mental experiences during REM sleep that have a storylike quality, include vivid visual imagery, are often bizarre, and are regarded as perceptually real by the dreamer (Antrobus, 1993). However, theorists have begun to question virtually every aspect of this characterization. Decades of research on the contents of dreams, which we will discuss momentarily, have shown that dreams are not as bizarre as widely assumed (Cartwright, 1994). In recent years, there has been renewed interest in the fact that dreams are not the exclusive property of REM sleep (Pivik, 1991). Moreover, studies that have focused on dream reports from non-REM stages of sleep have found that these dreams appear to be less vivid and storylike than REM dreams (Pivik, 1994). And recent work on reflective awareness in dreams suggests that dreamers realize they are dreaming more often than previously thought (Kahan & LaBerge, 1994). Thus, the concept of dreaming is undergoing some revision in scientific circles.

The Contents of Dreams

What do people dream about? Overall, dreams are not as exciting as advertised. Perhaps dreams are seen as exotic because people are more likely to remember their more bizarre nighttime dramas. After analyzing the contents of more than 10,000 dreams, Calvin Hall (1966) concluded that most dreams are relatively mundane. They tend to unfold in familiar settings with a cast of characters dominated by family, friends, and colleagues.

Certain themes tend to be more common than others in dreams. Table 5.2 lists the most common dreams reported by college students in one study (Griffith, Miyago, & Tago, 1958). If you glance through this list, you will see that people dream quite a bit about sex, aggression, and misfortune. According to Hall, dreams tend to center on classic sources of internal conflict, such as the conflict between taking chances and playing it safe. Hall was struck by how little people dream about public affairs and current events. Typically, dreams are very self-centered; people dream mostly about themselves.

Researchers have found some modest dream-content differences between men and women that seem to reflect conventional gender roles in modern society (Van de Castle, 1993). For example, strangers show up more often in men's dreams, while women are more likely to dream of children. Men's dream reports contain more references to automobiles and weapons, whereas women's reports mention clothing and jewelry more. Men are more likely to dream about acting aggressively; women are more likely to dream about being the

TABLE 5.2 COMMON DREAMS OF COLLEGE STUDENTS AND THE PERCENTAGE HAVING EACH TYPE OF DREAM

Type of Dream	Percentage of Students
Falling	83
Being attacked or pursued	77
Trying repeatedly to do something	71
School, teachers, studying	71
Sexual experiences	66
Arriving too late	64
Eating	62
Being frozen with fright	58
The death of a loved one	57
Being locked up	56
Finding money	56
Swimming	52
Snakes	49
Being inappropriately dressed	46
Being smothered	44
Being nude in public	43
Fire	41
Failing an examination	39
Seeing self as dead	33
Killing someone	26

Source: Griffith, Miyago, and Tago (1958)

target of aggression. In their sexual dreams, men tend to have liaisons with attractive female strangers, whereas women are more likely to dream about sex with their boyfriends and husbands.

Links Between Dreams and Waking Life

Though dreams seem to belong in a world of their own, what people dream about is affected by what is going on in their lives (Kramer, 1994). If you're struggling with financial problems, worried about an upcoming exam, or sexually attracted to a classmate, these themes may very well show up in your dreams. Freud noticed long ago that the contents of waking life tend to spill into dreams; he labeled this spillover the *day residue*. The connection between a person's real world and his or her dream world probably explains why there is some thematic continuity among successive dreams occurring in different REM periods on a given night (Cipolli et al., 1987). It seems likely that the link between the real and dream worlds also accounts for the gender differences in dream content that we just discussed.

On occasion, the content of dreams can also be affected by stimuli experienced while one is dreaming (Arkin & Antrobus, 1991). For example, William Dement sprayed water on one hand of sleeping subjects while they were in the REM stage (Dement & Wolpert, 1958). Subjects who weren't awakened by the water were awakened by the experimenter a short time later and asked what they had been dreaming about. Dement found that 42% of the subjects had incorporated the water into their dreams. They said that they had dreamt that they were in rainfalls, floods, baths, swimming pools, and the like. Some people report that they occasionally experience the same sort of phenomenon at home when the sound of their alarm clock fails to awaken them. The alarm is incorporated into their dream as a loud engine or a siren, for instance. As with day residue, the incorporation of external stimuli into dreams shows that people's dream world is not entirely separate from their real world.

Culture and Dreams

Striking cross-cultural variations occur in beliefs about the nature of dreams and the importance attributed to them. In modern Western society, we typically make a distinction between the "real" world we experience while awake and the "imaginary" world we experience while dreaming. Some people realize that events in the real world can affect their dreams, but few believe that events in

their dreams hold any significance for their waking life. Although a small minority of individuals take their dreams seriously, in Western cultures dreams are largely written off as insignificant, meaningless meanderings of the unconscious (Tart, 1988).

In many non-Western cultures, however, dreams are viewed as important sources of information about oneself, about the future, or about the spiritual world (Kracke, 1991). Although no culture confuses dreams with waking reality, many view events in dreams as another type of reality that may be just as important as, or perhaps even more important than, events experienced while awake. In Australia, for example, "Dreaming is the focal point of traditional aboriginal existence and simultaneously determines their way of life, their culture, and their relationship to the physical and spiritual environment" (Dawson, 1993, p. 1). In some instances, people are even held responsible for their dream actions. Among the New Guinea Arapesh, for example, an erotic dream about someone may be viewed as the equivalent of an adulterous act. In many cultures, dreams are seen as a window into the spiritual world, permitting communication with ancestors or supernatural beings (Bourguignon, 1972). People in some cultures believe that dreams provide information about the future—good or bad omens about upcoming battles, hunts, births, and so forth (Tedlock, 1992).

The tendency to remember one's dreams varies across cultures. In modern Western societies where little significance is attributed to dreams, dream recall tends to be mediocre. Many people remember their dreams only infrequently. In contrast, dream recall tends to be much better in cultures that take dreams seriously. For example, among the Parintintin of Brazil, most people can remember several dreams per night, which they routinely share with others (Kracke, 1992). Similarly, the Senoi of Malaysia gather in groups every morning to discuss and analyze their dreams from the previous night (Domhoff, 1985).

In regard to dream content, both similarities and differences occur across cultures in the types of dreams that people report (Hunt, 1989). Some basic dream themes appear to be nearly universal (dreams of falling, being pursued, having sex). However, the contents of dreams vary some from one culture to another because people in different societies deal with different worlds while awake. For example, in a 1950 study of the Siriono, a hunting-and-gathering people of the Amazon who were almost always hungry and spent most of

Dreaming is the focal point of traditional Aboriginal existence as it is in many other cultures.

their time in a grim search for food, *half* of the reported dreams focused on hunting, gathering, and eating food (D'Andrade, 1961). Shared systems for interpreting the contents of dreams also vary from one society to another. Table 5.3 lists a number of common dream interpretations among the Toraja of Indonesia (Hollan, 1989). Although some of these interpretations (example: standing on mountaintop = becoming a leader) might be common in other societies, some clearly are peculiar to Toraja society (example: buffalo in the rice fields = rats will eat the rice harvest).

Theories of Dreaming

Many theories have been proposed to explain why people dream. Sigmund Freud (1900), who analyzed clients' dreams in therapy, believed that the principal purpose of dreams is *wish fulfillment*. He thought that people fulfill ungratified needs from waking hours through wishful thinking in dreams. For example, someone who is sexually frustrated might have highly erotic dreams, while an unsuccessful person might dream about great accomplishments. Although these examples involve blatant wishful thinking, Freud asserted that the wish-fulfilling quality of many dreams may not be readily apparent because the true meaning of dreams may be disguised.

Other theorists, such as Rosalind Cartwright (1977; Cartwright & Lamberg, 1992), have proposed that dreams provide an opportunity to work through everyday problems. According to her cognitive, *problem-solving view,* there is considerable continuity between waking and sleeping thought. Proponents of this view believe that dreams allow people to engage in creative thinking about problems because dreams are not restrained by logic or realism. Consistent with this view, Cartwright (1991) has found that women going through divorce frequently dream about divorce-related problems and that those who deal overtly with the divorce in their dreams make a better waking adjustment to the divorce than those who do not.

J. Allan Hobson and Robert McCarley argue that dreams are simply the by-product of bursts of activity emanating from subcortical areas in the brain (Hobson, 1988; Hobson & McCarley, 1977; McCarley, 1994). Their *activation-synthesis model* proposes that dreams are side effects of the neural activation that produces "wide awake" brain waves during REM sleep. According to this model, neurons firing periodically in lower brain centers send random signals to the cortex (the seat of complex thought). The cortex supposedly synthesizes (con-

TABLE 5.3 EXAMPLES OF COMMON DREAM INTERPRETATIONS AMONG THE TORAJA OF INDONESIA

"Good" Dreams	Interpretation
Receive gold	Good rice harvest
Carry pig or buffalo meat	Good rice harvest
Act "crazy"	Receive wealth
Objects are thrown at dreamer	Rain will fall
Stand on mountaintop	Become a leader
Steal objects	Receive those objects/become wealthy
Swim in ocean or river	Receive wealth
Jump over or cross water	Become wise/clever
Gored by a buffalo	Buy a buffalo
"Bad" Dreams	Interpretation
Buffalo in the rice fields	Rats will eat rice harvest
Naked	Get sick
Enter a burial cave	Die
Carried off by an ancestor	Die
Objects are stolen/lost/carried away	Lose those objects
House burns or is destroyed	Lose wealth/become poor

Source: Adapted from Hollan (1989)

structs) a dream to make sense out of these signals. The activation-synthesis model does *not* assume that dreams are meaningless. As Hobson (1988, p. 214) puts it, "Dreams are as meaningful as they can be under the adverse working conditions of the brain in REM sleep." However, in contrast to the theories of Freud and Cartwright, this theory obviously downplays the role of emotional factors as determinants of dreams.

These theories, summarized in Figure 5.14 (on page 198), are only three out of a host of theories about the functions of dreams. All of these theories are based more on conjecture than research, and none of them has been tested adequately. In part, this is because the private, subjective nature of dreams makes it difficult to put the theories to an empirical test. Thus, the purpose of dreaming remains a mystery.

We'll encounter more unsolved mysteries in the next two sections of this chapter as we discuss hypnosis and meditation. Whereas sleep and dreams are familiar to everyone, most people have little familiarity with hypnosis and meditation,

"[Dreams are] the royal road to the unconscious."

SIGMUND FREUD

"One function of dreams may be to restore our sense of competence. . . . It is also probable that in times of stress, dreams have more work to do in resolving our problems and are thus more salient and memorable."

ROSALIND CARTWRIGHT

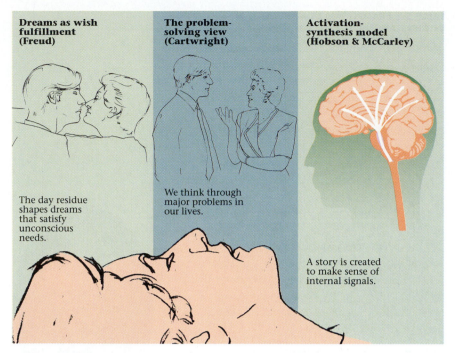

Dreams as wish fulfillment (Freud)

The day residue shapes dreams that satisfy unconscious needs.

The problem-solving view (Cartwright)

We think through major problems in our lives.

Activation-synthesis model (Hobson & McCarley)

A story is created to make sense of internal signals.

Figure 5.14
Three theories of dreaming. Dreams can be explained in a variety of ways. Freud stressed the wish-fulfilling function of dreams. Cartwright emphasizes the problem-solving function of dreams. Hobson and McCarley assert that dreams are merely a by-product of periodic neural activation.

Recap of Key Points
• The conventional view is that dreams are mental experiences during REM sleep that have a storylike quality, include vivid imagery, are often bizarre, and are regarded as real by the dreamer, but theorists have begun to question many aspects of this view.
• Researchers have found modest differences between men and women in dream content that seem to reflect conventional gender roles. The content of one's dreams may be affected by what is going on in one's life and by external stimuli that are experienced during the dream.
• In many non-Western cultures, dreams are viewed as important sources of information. There are dramatic variations across cultures in beliefs about the nature of dreams, dream recall, dream content, and dream interpretation.
• Freud argued that the principal purpose of dreams is wish fulfillment. Cartwright has articulated a problem-solving view, whereas Hobson and McCarley assert that dreams are side effects of the neural activation seen during REM sleep. Ultimately, theories of dreaming remain largely untested.

which both involve deliberate efforts to temporarily alter consciousness.

HYPNOSIS: ALTERED CONSCIOUSNESS OR ROLE PLAYING?

Hypnosis has a long and checkered history. It all began with a flamboyant 18th-century Austrian physician by the name of Franz Anton Mesmer. Working in Paris, Mesmer claimed to cure people of illnesses through an elaborate routine involving a "laying on of hands." Mesmer had some complicated theories about how he had harnessed "animal magnetism." However, we know today that he had simply stumbled onto the power of suggestion. It was rumored that the French government offered him a princely amount of money to disclose how he effected his cures. He refused, probably because he didn't really know. Eventually he was dismissed as a charlatan and run out of town by the local authorities. Although officially discredited, Mesmer inspired followers—practitioners of "mesmerism"—who continued to ply their trade. To this day, our language preserves the memory of Franz Mesmer: When we are under the spell of an event or a story, we are "mesmerized."

Eventually, a Scottish physician, James Braid, became interested in the trancelike state that could be induced by the mesmerists. It was Braid who popularized the term *hypnotism* in 1843, borrowing it from the Greek word for sleep. Braid thought that hypnotism could be used to produce anesthe-

sia for surgeries. However, just as hypnosis was catching on as a general anesthetic, more powerful and reliable chemical anesthetics were discovered, and interest in hypnotism dwindled.

Since then, hypnotism has led a curious dual existence. On the one hand, it has been the subject of numerous scientific studies. Furthermore, it has enjoyed considerable use as a clinical tool by physicians, dentists, and psychologists for over a century (Gibson & Heap, 1991). On the other hand, however, an assortment of entertainers and quacks have continued in the less respectable tradition of mesmerism, using hypnotism for parlor tricks and chicanery. It is little wonder, then, that most people don't know what to make of the whole subject. In this section, we'll work on clearing up some of the confusion surrounding hypnosis.

Hypnotic Induction and Susceptibility

Hypnosis is a systematic procedure that typically produces a heightened state of suggestibility. It may also lead to passive relaxation, narrowed attention, and enhanced fantasy. If only in popular films, virtually everyone has seen a *hypnotic induction* enacted with a swinging pendulum. Actually, there are many techniques for inducing hypnosis (Meyer, 1992). Usually, the hypnotist will suggest to the subject that he or she is relaxing. Repetitively, softly, subjects are told that they are getting tired, drowsy, or sleepy. Often, the hypnotist vividly describes bodily sensations that should be occurring. Subjects are told that their arms are going limp, their feet are getting warm, their eyelids are getting heavy. Gradually, most subjects succumb and become hypnotized.

People differ in how well they respond to hypnotic induction. Ernest and Josephine Hilgard have done extensive research on this variability in *hypnotic susceptibility*. Not everyone can be hypnotized. About 10% of the population doesn't respond well at all. At the other end of the continuum, about 10% of people are exceptionally good hypnotic subjects (Hilgard, 1965). Responsiveness to hypnosis is a stable, measurable trait. It can be estimated pretty effectively with the Stanford Hypnotic Susceptibility Scale (SHSS) or its derivative, the Harvard Group Scale of Hypnotic Susceptibility (Perry, Nadon, & Button, 1992). The distribution of scores on the SHSS is graphed in Figure 5.15.

What makes some people highly susceptible to hypnosis? Variations in hypnotic susceptibility have traditionally been attributed to basic differences between people in personality traits, but decades of research on personality and hypnotizability have actually turned up relatively little (Dixon & Laurence, 1992). The only personality factors that are related to hypnotic susceptibility are the overlapping traits of *absorption* and *imaginativeness*. People who can become deeply absorbed in an intense experience and people with a vivid imagination tend to be more susceptible to hypnosis, but the correlations are rather weak (Kirsch & Council, 1992). The failure to find strong personality predictors of hypnotic susceptibility have led investigators to look for other types of predictors. This research suggests that the trait of hypnotizability depends mainly on subjects' attitudes and expectations about hypnosis (Bertrand, 1989). As you might guess, people with positive attitudes about hypnosis seem to be more cooperative subjects who respond more successfully.

Hypnotic Phenomena

Many interesting effects can be produced through hypnosis. Some of the more prominent ones include:

1. *Anesthesia*. Under the influence of hypnosis, some subjects can withstand treatments that would normally cause considerable pain (Finer, 1980). As a result, some physicians and dentists have used hypnosis as a substitute for anesthetic drugs. Admittedly, drugs are far more reliable pain relievers, making hypnosis something of a scientific curiosity as a solo treatment for acute pain (Gibson & Heap, 1991). Nonetheless, hypnosis can be a surprisingly effective anesthetic for some people.

2. *Sensory distortions and hallucinations*. Hypnotized subjects may be led to experience auditory or visual hallucinations. They may hear sounds or see things that are not there, or fail to hear or see stimuli that are present. In one study, for instance, hypnotized subjects were induced to "see" a cardboard box that blocked their view of a television (Spiegel et al., 1985). Subjects may also have their sensations distorted so that something sweet tastes sour or an unpleasant odor smells fragrant.

3. *Disinhibition*. Generally, it is difficult to get hypnotized subjects to do things that they would normally consider unacceptable. Nonetheless, hypnosis *can* sometimes reduce inhibitions that would normally prevent subjects from acting in ways that they would see as socially undesirable. In experiments, hypnotized subjects have been induced to throw what they believed to be nitric acid into the face of a research assistant. Similarly, stage hypnotists are sometimes successful in getting people to disrobe in public. One lay hypnotist even coaxed a man into robbing a bank (Deyoub, 1984). This disinhibition effect may occur simply because hypnotized people feel that they cannot be held responsible for their actions while they are hypnotized.

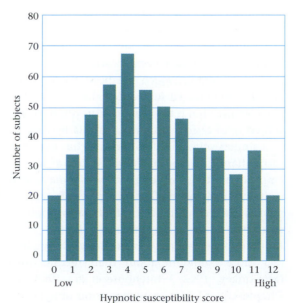

Figure 5.15
Variation in hypnotic susceptibility. This graph shows the distribution of scores of more than 500 subjects on the Stanford Hypnotic Susceptibility Scale. As you can see, responsiveness to hypnotism varies widely, and many people are not very susceptible to hypnotic induction. (Based on data from Hilgard, 1965)

4. *Posthypnotic suggestions and amnesia.* Suggestions made during hypnosis may influence a subject's later behavior (Kihlstrom, 1985). The most common posthypnotic suggestion is the creation of posthypnotic amnesia. That is, subjects are told that they will remember nothing that happened while they were hypnotized. Such subjects usually claim to remember nothing, as ordered.

Theories of Hypnosis

Although a number of theories have been developed to explain hypnosis, it is still not well understood. One popular view is that hypnotic effects occur because subjects are put into a special, altered state of consciousness, called a *hypnotic trance.* Although hypnotized subjects may feel as though they are in an altered state, their patterns of EEG activity cannot be distinguished from their EEG patterns in normal waking states (Dixon & Laurence, 1992; Orne & Dinges, 1989). The failure to find any special physiological changes associated with hypnosis has led some theorists to conclude that hypnosis is a normal state of consciousness that is simply characterized by dramatic role playing.

Hypnosis as Role Playing

Theodore Barber (1979) and Nicholas Spanos (1986; Spanos & Coe, 1992) have been the leading advocates of the view that hypnosis produces a normal mental state in which suggestible people act out the role of a hypnotic subject and behave as they think hypnotized people are supposed to. According to this notion, it is subjects' role expectations that produce hypnotic effects, rather than a special trancelike state of consciousness.

Two lines of evidence support the role-playing view. First, many of the seemingly amazing effects of hypnosis have been duplicated by nonhypnotized subjects or have been shown to be exaggerated. For example, much has been made of the fact that hypnotized subjects can be used as "human planks," but it turns out that nonhypnotized subjects can easily match this feat (Barber, 1986). In a similar vein, anecdotal reports that hypnosis can enhance memory have not stood up well to empirical testing. Although hypnosis may occasionally facilitate recall in some people, experimental studies have tended to find that hypnotized subjects make more memory errors than nonhypnotized subjects, even though they often feel more confident about their recollections (McConkey, 1992; Whitehouse et al., 1988; see Chapters 2 and 7 for more discussion of hypnosis

and memory). These findings suggest that no special state of consciousness is required to explain hypnotic feats.

The second line of evidence involves demonstrations that hypnotized subjects are often acting out a role. For example, Martin Orne (1951) regressed hypnotized subjects back to their sixth birthday and asked them to describe it. They responded with detailed descriptions that appeared to represent great feats of hypnosis-enhanced memory. However, instead of accepting this information at face value, Orne compared it with information that he had obtained from the subjects' parents. It turned out that many of the subjects' memories were inaccurate and invented! Many other studies have also found that age-regressed subjects' recall of the distant past tends to be more fanciful than factual (Perry, Kusel, & Perry, 1988). Thus, the role-playing explanation of hypnosis suggests that situational factors lead some subjects to act out a certain role in a highly cooperative manner.

Hypnosis as an Altered State of Consciousness

Despite the doubts raised by role-playing explanations, many prominent theorists still maintain that hypnotic effects are attributable to a special, altered state of consciousness (Beahrs, 1983; Fromm, 1979, 1992; Hilgard, 1986). These theorists argue that it is doubtful that role playing can explain all hypnotic phenomena. For instance, they assert that even the most cooperative subjects are unlikely to endure surgery without a drug anesthetic just to please their physician and live up to their expected role.

Of late, the most influential explanation of hypnosis as an altered state of awareness has been offered by Ernest Hilgard (1986, 1992). According to Hilgard, hypnosis creates a *dissociation* in consciousness. **Dissociation is a splitting off of mental processes into two separate, simultaneous streams of awareness.** In other words, Hilgard theorizes that hypnosis splits consciousness into two streams. One stream is in communication with the hypnotist and the external world, while the other is a difficult-to-detect "hidden observer." Hilgard believes that many hypnotic effects are a product of this divided consciousness. For instance, he suggests that a hypnotized subject might appear unresponsive to pain because the pain isn't registered in the portion of consciousness that communicates with other people.

One appealing aspect of Hilgard's theory is that *divided consciousness* is a common, normal experi-

"Thousands of books, movies and professional articles have woven the concept of 'hypnotic trance' into the common knowledge. And yet there is almost no scientific support for it."

THEODORE BARBER

ence. For example, people will often drive a car a great distance, responding to traffic signals and other cars, with no recollection of having consciously done so. In such cases, consciousness is clearly divided between driving and the person's thoughts about other matters. Interestingly, this common experience has long been known as *highway hypnosis*. In this condition, there is even an "amnesia" for the component of consciousness that drove the car, similar to posthypnotic amnesia. In summary, Hilgard presents hypnosis as a plausible variation in consciousness that has continuity with everyday experience.

The debate about whether hypnosis involves an altered or normal state of consciousness appears likely to continue for the foreseeable future. As you will see momentarily, a similar debate has dominated the scientific discussion of meditation.

MEDITATION: PURE CONSCIOUSNESS OR RELAXATION?

Recent years have seen growing interest in the ancient discipline of meditation. *Meditation refers to a family of practices that train attention to heighten awareness and bring mental processes under greater voluntary control.* There are many approaches to meditation. In North America, the most widely practiced approaches are those associated with yoga, Zen, and transcendental meditation (TM). All three of these approaches are rooted in Eastern religions (Hinduism, Buddhism, and Taoism). However, meditation has been practiced throughout history as an element of all religious and spiritual traditions, including Judaism and Christianity. Moreover, the practice of meditation can be largely divorced from religious beliefs. In fact, most Americans who meditate have only vague ideas regarding its religious significance. Of interest to psychology is the fact that meditation involves a deliberate effort to alter consciousness.

Most meditative techniques are deceptively simple. For example, in TM a person is supposed to sit in a comfortable position with eyes closed and silently focus attention on a *mantra*. A mantra is a specially assigned Sanskrit word that is personalized to each meditator. This exercise in mental self-discipline is to be practiced twice daily for about 20 minutes. The technique has been described as "diving from the active surface of the mind to its quiet depths" (Bloomfield & Kory, 1976, p. 49). Most proponents of TM believe it involves an altered state of "pure consciousness." Many skeptics counter that meditation is only an effective relaxation technique.

Advocates of TM claim that it can enhance learning, creativity, cognitive development, energy level, work productivity, physical health, mental health, and happiness while reducing tension and anxiety caused by stress and increasing longevity (Alexander et al., 1990; Bloomfield & Kory, 1976).

These are not exactly humble claims. Let's look at the evidence.

Short-Term Effects

What happens when an experienced meditator goes into the meditative state? An intriguing finding in many studies is that alpha waves and theta waves become more prominent in EEG recordings (Fenwick, 1987). Most studies also find that subjects' heart rate, respiration rate, oxygen consumption, and carbon dioxide elimination decline (see Figure 5.16). Many researchers have also observed increases in skin resistance and decreases in blood lactate—physiological indicators associated with relaxation (Davidson, 1976; Dillbeck & Orme-Johnson, 1987; Woolfolk, 1975). Taken together, these changes suggest that meditation leads to a potentially beneficial physiological state characterized by suppression of bodily arousal.

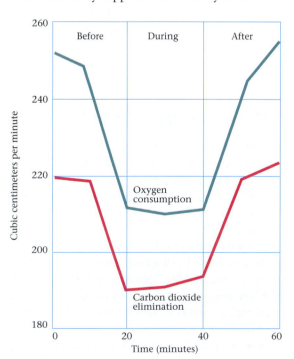

Figure 5.16
The suppression of physiological arousal during transcendental meditation. The physiological changes shown in the graph are evidence of physical relaxation during the meditative state. However, similar changes may also be produced by systematic relaxation procedures. (Based on data from Wallace & Benson, 1972)

However, some researchers argue that a variety of systematic relaxation training procedures can produce similar results (Shapiro, 1984). Hence, debate continues about whether the physiological changes associated with meditation are unique (Holmes, 1987).

Long-Term Effects

The evidence on the long-term effects of meditation is also controversial. Some studies have found that meditation can improve mood, lessen fatigue, and reduce anxiety and drug abuse (Carrington, 1987; Eppley, Abrams, & Shear, 1989; Gelderloos et al., 1991). Studies also suggest that meditation is associated with improved physical health (Orme-Johnson, 1987), superior mental health (Alexander, Rainforth, & Gelderloos, 1991) and even increased longevity among the elderly (Alexander et al., 1989). Some psychologists argue that at least some of these effects may be just as attainable through systematic relaxation or other mental focusing procedures (Shapiro, 1984; Smith, 1975). Critics also wonder whether placebo effects, sampling bias, and other methodological problems may contribute to some of the reported benefits of meditation (Shapiro, 1987).

In summary, it seems safe to conclude that meditation is a potentially worthwhile relaxation strategy. And it's possible that meditation involves more than mere relaxation, as TM advocates insist. Certainly, it is hard to envision mere relaxation providing such a diverse constellation of benefits. At present, however, there is great debate about the notion that meditation produces a unique state of "pure consciousness."

Shapiro (1994) has asserted that it is time for meditation researchers to broaden their horizons and look at other facets of the meditative experience. To date, Western researchers have focused almost exclusively on the value of meditation as a *self-regulation strategy* that may help people deal with stress more effectively. Shapiro argues that researchers should also examine meditation as a *self-exploration strategy* intended to enhance psychological health, and as a *self-liberation strategy* intended to foster spiritual growth. It remains to be seen whether Western psychologists will take up this challenge.

Recap of Key Points

• Hypnosis has had a long and curious history since the era of Mesmerism in the 18th century. Hypnotic susceptibility is a stable trait. It is only weakly correlated with personality, but highly hypnotizable people tend to score somewhat higher than others in absorption and imaginativeness. Hypnosis can produce anesthesia, sensory distortions, disinhibition, and posthypnotic amnesia.

• One approach to hypnosis is to view it as a normal state of consciousness in which subjects assume a hypnotic role. Another approach asserts that hypnosis leads to an altered state in which consciousness is split into two streams of awareness.

• Meditation refers to a family of practices that train attention to heighten awareness and bring mental processes under greater voluntary control. Evidence suggests that meditation leads to a potentially beneficial physiological state characterized by suppression of bodily arousal. However, some experts suggest that the benefits of meditation are not unique to meditation and are a product of any effective relaxation procedure.

ALTERING CONSCIOUSNESS WITH DRUGS

Like hypnosis and meditation, drugs are commonly used in deliberate efforts to alter consciousness. In this section, we focus on the use of drugs for nonmedical purposes, commonly referred to as "drug abuse" or "recreational drug use." Drug abuse reaches into every corner of American society. There were some modest declines in the abuse of a variety of drugs during the 1980s and early 1990s (Cohen et al., 1996; Johnson & Muffler, 1992). Nonetheless, surveys suggest that widespread recreational drug use is here to stay for the foreseeable future.

As with other controversial social problems, recreational drug use often inspires more rhetoric than reason. For instance, a former president of the American Medical Association made headlines when he declared that marijuana "makes a man of 35 sexually like a man of 70." In reality, the research findings do not support this assertion. This influential physician later retracted his statement, admitting that he had made it simply to campaign against marijuana use (Leavitt, 1995). Unfortunately, such scare tactics can backfire by undermining the credibility of drug education efforts.

Recreational drug use involves personal, moral, political, and legal issues that are not matters for science to resolve. However, the more knowledgeable you are about drugs, the more informed your decisions and opinions about them will be. Accordingly, this section describes the types of drugs that are most commonly used for recreational purposes and summarizes their effects on consciousness, behavior, and health.

Principal Abused Drugs and Their Effects

 4c

The drugs that people use recreationally are *psychoactive. Psychoactive drugs* **are chemical substances that modify mental, emotional, or behavioral functioning.** Not all psychoactive drugs produce effects that lead to recreational use. Generally, people prefer drugs that elevate their mood or produce other pleasurable alterations in consciousness.

The principal types of recreational drugs are described in Table 5.4 on page 204. The table lists representative drugs in each of six categories. It also summarizes how the drugs are taken, their medical uses, their effects on consciousness, and their common side effects (based on Julien, 1995; Lowinson, Ruiz, & Millman, 1992). The six categories of psychoactive drugs that we will focus on are narcotics, sedatives, stimulants, hallucinogens, cannabis, and alcohol.

Narcotics, **or** *opiates,* **are drugs derived from opium that are capable of relieving pain.** The main drugs in this category are heroin and morphine, although less potent opiates such as codeine, Demerol, and methadone are also abused. In sufficient dosages these drugs can produce an overwhelming sense of euphoria or well-being. This euphoric effect has a relaxing, "Who cares?" quality that makes the high an attractive escape from reality. Frequent side effects include lethargy, nausea, and impaired mental and motor functioning.

Sedatives **are sleep-inducing drugs that tend to decrease central nervous system (CNS) activation and behavioral activity.** Over the years, the most widely abused sedatives have been the *barbiturates,* which are compounds derived from barbituric acid. People abusing sedatives, or "downers," generally consume larger doses than are prescribed for medical purposes. The desired effect is a euphoria similar to that produced by drinking large amounts of alcohol. Feelings of tension or dejection are replaced by a relaxed, pleasant state of intoxication, accompanied by loosened inhibitions. Prominent side effects include drowsiness and severe impairments in motor coordination and mental functioning.

CONCEPT CHECK 5.2
Relating EEG Activity to Variations in Consciousness

Early in the chapter we emphasized the intimate relationship between brain activity and variations in consciousness. Check your understanding of this relationship by indicating the kind of EEG activity (alpha, beta, theta, or delta) that would probably be dominant in each of the following situations. The answers are in Appendix A.

_____ 1. You are playing a video game.

_____ 2. You are deep in meditation.

_____ 3. You have just fallen asleep.

_____ 4. You are sleepwalking across the lawn.

_____ 5. You are in the midst of a terrible nightmare.

Stimulants **are drugs that tend to increase central nervous system activation and behavioral activity.** Stimulants range from mild, widely available drugs, such as caffeine and nicotine, to stronger, carefully regulated ones, such as cocaine. We will focus on cocaine and amphetamines. Cocaine is a natural substance that comes from the coca shrub. In contrast, amphetamines ("speed") are synthesized in a pharmaceutical laboratory. Cocaine and amphetamines have fairly similar effects, except that cocaine produces a briefer high. Stimulants produce a euphoria very different from that created by narcotics or sedatives. They produce a buoyant, elated, energetic "I can conquer the world!" feeling accompanied by increased alertness. In recent years, cocaine and amphetamines have become available in much more potent (and dangerous) forms than before. "Freebasing" is a chemical treatment used to extract nearly pure cocaine from ordinary street cocaine. "Crack" is the most widely distributed by-product of this process, consisting of chips of pure cocaine that are usually smoked. Amphetamines are increasingly sold as a crystalline powder, called "crank," that may be snorted or injected intravenously. Drug dealers are also beginning to market a smokable form of methamphetamine called "ice." Side effects of stimulants vary with dosage and potency but may include restlessness, anxiety, paranoia, and insomnia.

Hallucinogens **are a diverse group of drugs that have powerful effects on mental and emotional functioning, marked most prominently by distortions in sensory and perceptual**

Drug abusers can come from all walks of life. In particular, prescription psychoactive drugs have potential for abuse.

TABLE 5.4 PSYCHOACTIVE DRUGS: METHODS OF INGESTION, MEDICAL USES, AND EFFECTS

Drugs	Methods of Ingestion	Principal Medical Uses	Desired Effects	Short-Term Side Effects
Narcotics (opiates) Morphine Heroin	Injected, smoked, oral	Pain relief	Euphoria, relaxation, anxiety reduction, pain relief	Lethargy, drowsiness, nausea, impaired coordination, impaired mental functioning, constipation
Sedatives Barbiturates (e.g., Seconal) Nonbarbiturates (e.g., Quaalude)	Oral, injected	Sleeping pill, anticonvulsant	Euphoria, relaxation, anxiety reduction, reduced inhibitions	Lethargy, drowsiness, severely impaired coordination, impaired mental functioning, emotional swings, dejection
Stimulants Amphetamines Cocaine	Oral, sniffed, injected, freebased, smoked	Treatment of hyperactivity and narcolepsy, local anesthetic, (cocaine only)	Elation, excitement, increased alertness, increased energy, reduced fatigue	Increased blood pressure and heart rate, increased talkativeness, restlessness, irritability, insomnia, reduced appetite, increased sweating and urination, anxiety, paranoia, increased aggressiveness, panic
Hallucinogens LSD Mescaline Psilocybin	Oral	None	Increased sensory awareness, euphoria, altered perceptions, hallucinations, insightful experiences	Dilated pupils, nausea, emotional swings, paranoia, jumbled thought processes, impaired judgment, anxiety, panic reaction
Cannabis Marijuana Hashish THC	Smoked, oral	Treatment of glaucoma; other uses under study	Mild euphoria, relaxation, altered perceptions, enhanced awareness	Bloodshot eyes, dry mouth, reduced short-term memory, sluggish motor coordination, sluggish mental functioning, anxiety
Alcohol	Drinking	None	Mild euphoria, relaxation, anxiety reduction, reduced inhibitions	Severely impaired coordination, impaired mental functioning, increased urination, emotional swings, depression, quarrelsomeness, hangover

Note: The principal omission from this table is PCP (phencyclidine hydrochloride), which does not fit neatly into any of the listed categories. PCP has sedative, stimulant, hallucinogenic, and anesthetic effects. Its short-term side effects can be very dangerous. Common side effects include agitation, paranoia, confusion, and severe mental disorientation that has been linked to accidents and suicides.

experience. The principal hallucinogens are LSD, mescaline, and psilocybin. These drugs have similar effects, although they vary in potency. Hallucinogens produce euphoria, increased sensory awareness, and a distorted sense of time. In some users, they lead to profound, dreamlike, "mystical" feelings that are difficult to describe. The latter effect is why they have been used in religious ceremonies for centuries in some cultures. Unfortunately, at the other end of the emotional spectrum hallucinogens can also produce nightmarish feelings of anxiety and paranoia, commonly called a "bad trip." Other side effects include impaired judgment and jumbled thought processes.

Cannabis **is the hemp plant from which marijuana, hashish, and THC are derived.** Marijuana is a mixture of dried leaves, flowers, stems, and seeds taken from the plant. Hashish comes from the plant's resin. Smoking is the usual route of ingestion for both marijuana and hashish. THC,

the active chemical ingredient in cannabis, can be synthesized for research purposes (for example, to give to animals, who can't very well smoke marijuana). When smoked, cannabis has an immediate impact that may last several hours. The desired effects of the drug are a mild, relaxed euphoria and enhanced sensory awareness. Unintended effects may include anxiety, sluggish mental functioning, and impaired memory.

Alcohol **encompasses a variety of beverages containing ethyl alcohol**, such as beers, wines, and distilled spirits. The concentration of ethyl alcohol varies from about 4% in most beers up to 40% in 80-proof liquor, and occasionally more in higher-proof liquors. When people drink heavily, the central effect is a relaxed euphoria that temporarily boosts self-esteem, as problems seem to melt away and inhibitions diminish. Common side effects include severe impairments in mental and motor functioning, mood swings, and quarrelsomeness. Alcohol is the most widely used recreational drug in our society. Because alcohol is legal, many people use it casually without even thinking of it as a drug. Yet experts estimate that the dollar costs (due to absenteeism at work, medical expenses, and so on) of alcohol abuse are nearly double the costs of all other types of drug abuse combined (Segal, 1988).

Factors Influencing Drug Effects

The drug effects summarized in Table 5.4 are the *typical* ones. Drug effects can vary from person to person and even for the same person in different situations. The impact of any drug depends in part on the user's age, mood, motivation, personality, previous experience with the drug, body weight, and physiology. The dose and potency of a drug, the method of administration, and the setting in which a drug is taken also influence its effects (Leavitt, 1995). Our theme of *multifactorial causation* clearly applies to the effects of drugs.

So, too, does our theme emphasizing the *subjectivity of experience*. Expectations are potentially powerful factors that can influence the user's perceptions of a drug's effects. You may recall from our discussion of placebo effects in Chapter 2 that some people who are misled to *think* that they are drinking alcohol show signs of intoxication (Wilson, 1982). If people *expect* a drug to make them feel giddy, serene, or profound, their expectation may contribute to the feelings they experience.

A drug's effects can also change as the person's body develops a tolerance for the chemical as a result of continued use. *Tolerance* **refers to a progressive decrease in a person's responsiveness to a drug.** Tolerance usually leads people to consume larger and larger doses of a drug to attain the effects they desire. Most drugs produce tolerance effects, but some do so more rapidly than others. For example, tolerance to alcohol usually builds slowly, while tolerance to heroin increases much more quickly. Table 5.5 indicates whether various categories of drugs tend to produce tolerance rapidly or gradually.

Mechanisms of Drug Action

Most drugs have effects that reverberate throughout the body. However, psychoactive drugs work primarily by altering neurotransmitter activity in the brain. As we discussed in Chapter 3, neurotransmitters are chemicals that transmit information between neurons at junctions called *synapses*.

The actions of amphetamines illustrate how drugs have selective, multiple effects on neurotransmitter activity. Amphetamines exert their main effects on two of the monoamine neurotransmitters: norepinephrine (NE) and dopamine (DA). Indeed, the name *amphetamines* reflects the kinship between these drugs and the *monoamines*. Amphetamines appear to have two key effects at DA and NE synapses (Cooper, Bloom, & Roth, 1996; King & Ellinwood, 1992), which are summarized in Figure 5.17. First, they increase the release of DA and NE by presynaptic neurons. Second, they interfere with the reuptake of DA and NE from synaptic clefts. These actions serve to increase the levels of

TABLE 5.5 PSYCHOACTIVE DRUGS: TOLERANCE, DEPENDENCE, POTENTIAL FOR FATAL OVERDOSE, AND HEALTH RISKS

Drugs	Tolerance	Risk of Physical Dependence	Risk of Psychological Dependence	Fatal Overdose Potential	Health Risks
Narcotics (opiates)	Rapid	High	High	High	Infectious diseases, accidents, immune suppression
Sedatives	Rapid	High	High	High	Accidents
Stimulants	Rapid	Moderate	High	Moderate to high	Sleep problems, malnutrition, nasal damage, hypertension, respiratory disease, stroke, liver disease, heart attack
Hallucinogens	Gradual	None	Very low	Very low	Accidents
Cannabis	Gradual	None	Low to moderate	Very low	Accidents, lung cancer, respiratory disease, pulmonary disease
Alcohol	Gradual	Moderate	Moderate	Low to high	Accidents, liver disease, malnutrition, brain damage, neurological disorders, heart disease, stroke, hypertension, ulcers, cancer, birth defects

dopamine and norepinephrine at the affected synapses. The key point is that amphetamines selectively influence specific neurotransmitter systems in a variety of ways. Cocaine shares some of these actions (in particular, the interference with reuptake at DA and NE synapses), which is why cocaine and amphetamines produce similar stimulant effects.

The cellular mechanisms underlying stimulant drugs' effects also explain why cocaine and amphetamine highs are often followed by an emotional crash, marked by depression and exhaustion (see Figure 5.18). The slowing of reuptake leaves more neurotransmitter in the affected synapses to stimulate increased activity, but it also gives enzymes that metabolize the neurotransmitter more opportunity to swoop in and inactivate more of the neurotransmitter. Hence, the use of cocaine or amphetamines can eventually lead to a depletion of dopamine and norepinephrine. This depletion appears to be the cause of the emotional crash experienced by many users.

Sedatives appear to exert their key effects at GABA synapses. These effects are complex, but the net result appears to be increased activity in the GABA system (Giannini & Miller, 1989). The mechanisms of action for alcohol are less clear and seem to get more and more complicated as scientists learn more about how alcohol works. Changes in GABA activity are thought to be the main culprit underlying alcohol intoxication, but alcohol also appears to have complex effects on dopamine, serotonin, and other neurotransmitter systems (Tabakoff & Hoffman, 1992). The finding that alcohol and sedatives may converge on many of the same (GABA) synapses probably explains why these drugs are *synergistic*. Drugs are said to be synergistic when their combined effect is greater than the sum of their individual effects. Synergistic effects explain why mixing alcohol and sedatives is so dangerous. The combination of these drugs has caused many fatal overdoses by depressing CNS activity excessively.

The discovery of special receptor sites in the brain for opiate drugs and endogenous opiates (endorphins) has led to new insights about the actions of narcotic drugs, although much remains to be learned (see Chapter 3). These drugs apparently bind to specific subtypes of opiate receptors, and their actions at these receptor sites indirectly elevate dopamine activity (Koob & Bloom, 1988). Neuroscientists' understanding of how LSD works remains relatively primitive, but altered activity at certain types of serotonin receptors may be critical (Ungerleider & Pechnick, 1992). Although scientists have recently found receptors in the brain for THC, the active chemical ingredient in marijuana (Herkenham et al., 1991), the impact of marijuana on neurotransmitter activity remains obscure.

Drug Dependence

People can become either physically or psychologically dependent on a drug. Physical dependence is a common problem with narcotics, sedatives, and alcohol and is an occasional problem with stimulants. **Physical dependence exists when a person must continue to take a drug to avoid withdrawal illness.** The symptoms of withdrawal illness depend on the specific drug. Withdrawal from heroin, barbiturates, and alcohol can produce fever, chills, tremors, convulsions, vomiting, cramps, diarrhea, and severe aches and pains. Withdrawal from stimulants leads to a more subtle syndrome, marked by fatigue, apathy, irritability, depression, and disorientation.

Psychological dependence exists when a person must continue to take a drug to satisfy intense mental and emotional craving for the drug. Psychological dependence is more subtle than physical dependence, but the need it creates can be powerful. Cocaine, for instance, can produce an overwhelming psychological need for continued use. Psychological dependence is possible with all recreational drugs, although it seems rare for hallucinogens.

Both types of dependence are established gradually with repeated use of a drug. Drugs vary in their potential for creating either physical or psychological dependence. Table 5.5 provides estimates of the risk of each kind of dependence for the six categories of recreational drugs covered in our discussion.

Figure 5.17
Amphetamines and neurotransmitters. Like other psychoactive drugs, amphetamines alter neurotransmitter activity at specific synapses. Depicted here are two ways (there may be more) in which amphetamines appear to increase dopamine (DA) activity at DA synapses and norepinephrine (NE) activity at NE synapses.

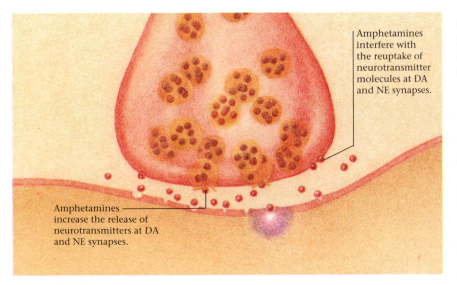

Amphetamines interfere with the reuptake of neurotransmitter molecules at DA and NE synapses.

Amphetamines increase the release of neurotransmitters at DA and NE synapses.

Some theorists have begun to raise doubts about the value of distinguishing between physical and psychological dependence (Koob & Bloom, 1988; Ray & Ksir, 1990). This distinction was originally based on two assumptions. First, it was assumed that there is a physiological basis (tissue changes) for physical dependence but not for psychological dependence. Second, it was assumed that a person who is physically dependent on a drug continues to use it to avoid aversive effects, while a person who is psychologically dependent on a drug continues to use it to experience pleasant effects. Both of these assumptions appear dubious in light of new research. Increased knowledge of how drugs alter synaptic transmission suggests that physiological mechanisms underlie both types of dependence. Evidence also suggests that the motivation to avoid withdrawal may be less important in explaining physical dependence than was previously believed. Thus, the pursuit of pleasant effects may be the critical force underlying both types of dependence. Although the concepts of physical and psychological dependence remain widely used, they are going through a period of transition.

Drugs and Physical Health 4c

The use of some recreational drugs can be damaging to physical health. A study of rats given unlimited access to heroin or cocaine (Bozarth & Wise, 1985) dramatically illustrates this danger. In this study, the rats "earned" drug injections delivered through tubes implanted in their bodies by pressing a lever in an experimental chamber. Even though unlimited food and water were available, rats on cocaine lost an average of 29% of their body weight. Their health deteriorated rapidly, and by the end of the 30-day study 90% of them had died. The health of the rats on heroin deteriorated less rapidly, but 36% of them also died during the study. As is true for many human drug users, serious aversive effects did not deter the rats from continuing their "drug abuse." Many of the rats on cocaine experienced severe seizures. However, they would resume their lever pressing as soon as they stopped writhing from convulsions.

In humans, recreational drug use can affect physical health in a variety of ways. The three principal ways are by triggering an overdose, by producing tissue damage (direct effects), and by causing health-impairing behavior (indirect effects).

Overdose

Any drug can be fatal if a person takes enough of it, but some drugs are much more dangerous than

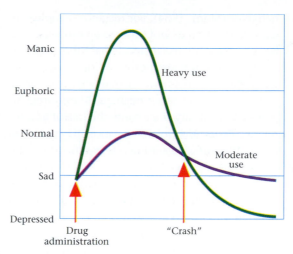

Figure 5.18
The "crash" after use of cocaine or amphetamines. Stimulant drugs induce an emotional high that is often followed by an emotional letdown called a "crash." Larger doses of the drugs tend to precipitate bigger crashes. As your book explains, the crash is attributable to the depletion of certain neurotransmitters.

others. Table 5.5 shows estimates of the risk of accidentally consuming a lethal overdose of each listed drug. Drugs that are CNS depressants—sedatives, narcotics, and alcohol—carry the greatest risk of overdose. It's important to remember that these drugs are synergistic with each other, so many overdoses involve lethal *combinations* of CNS depressants. What happens when a person overdoses on these drugs? The respiratory system usually grinds to a halt, producing coma, brain damage, and death within a brief period.

Fatal overdoses with CNS stimulants usually involve a heart attack, stroke, or cortical seizure. Deaths due to overdoses of stimulant drugs used to be relatively infrequent (Kalant & Kalant, 1979). However, cocaine overdoses have increased sharply as more people have experimented with freebasing, smoking crack, and other more dangerous modes of ingestion (Gold, 1992). Similar increases in amphetamine overdoses seem likely if more potent forms of speed (crank and ice) become widely available.

Direct Effects

In some cases, drugs cause tissue damage directly. For example, snorting cocaine can damage nasal membranes. Cocaine can also alter cardiovascular functioning in ways that increase the risk of heart attack and stroke, and crack smoking is associated with a host of respiratory problems (Kerfoot, Sakoulas, & Hyman, 1996; Morris, 1991). Long-term, excessive alcohol consumption is associated with an elevated risk for a wide range of serious health problems, including liver damage, ulcers, hypertension, stroke, heart disease, neurological disorders, and some types of cancer (D. Goodwin, 1992).

Indirect Effects

The negative effects of drugs on physical health are often indirect results of the drugs' impact on behavior (Blum, 1984). For instance, people using stimulants often do not eat or sleep properly. Sedatives increase the risk of accidental injuries because they severely impair motor coordination. People who abuse downers often trip down stairs, fall off stools, and suffer other mishaps. Many drugs impair driving ability, increasing the risk of automobile accidents. Alcohol, for instance, may contribute to roughly *half* of all automobile fatalities (Coleman, 1993). Intravenous drug users risk contracting infectious diseases that can be spread by unsterilized needles. In recent years, acquired immune deficiency syndrome (AIDS) has been transmitted at an alarming rate through the population of intravenous drug users (Des Jarlais et al., 1992).

The major health risks (other than overdose) of various recreational drugs are listed in the sixth column of Table 5.5. As you can see, alcohol appears to have the most diverse negative effects on physical health. The irony, of course, is that alcohol is the only recreational drug listed that is legal.

Controversies Concerning Marijuana

The possible health risks associated with marijuana use have generated considerable debate in recent years. The preponderance of evidence suggests that heavy use of marijuana *probably* increases the chances for respiratory and pulmonary disease, including lung cancer (Gold, 1989). Reasonably convincing evidence also indicates that marijuana increases the risk of automobile accidents (Leavitt, 1995). These dangers are listed in Table 5.5, but many other widely publicized dangers are omitted because the findings on these other risks remain controversial. Here is a brief overview of the evidence on some of these controversies.

• *Does marijuana cause chromosome breakage?* Findings on this issue are inconsistent, but Cohen (1980) concluded that marijuana does not appear to increase chromosomal breakage. High doses of THC have been shown to cause birth defects in animals, but there is no evidence that marijuana causes birth defects in humans (Blum, 1984). None-

theless, the results of the animal studies are cause for concern, and pregnant women should avoid using marijuana (Roffman & George, 1988).

• *Does marijuana reduce one's immune response?* Cannabis may suppress the body's natural immune response slightly (Nahas, 1976). However, infectious diseases do not appear to be more common among marijuana smokers than among nonsmokers. Hence, marijuana's effect on immune functioning apparently is too small to have any practical importance (Hollister, 1988; Relman, 1982).

• *Does marijuana lead to impotence and sterility in men?* Cannabis appears to produce a small, reversible decline in sperm count among male smokers and may have temporary effects on hormone levels (Bloodworth, 1987). Citing these findings, the popular media have frequently implied that marijuana therefore makes men sterile and impotent. However, the evidence suggests that marijuana has little lasting impact on male smokers' fertility or sexual functioning (Grinspoon & Bakalar, 1992).

Drugs and Psychological Health

There *is* a clear correlation between excessive drug use and poor mental health (Cohen & Weiss, 1996). But does drug abuse *cause* maladjustment? Sorting out cause and effect in this association is difficult. Consider, for example, the findings reported by Shedler and Block (1990). Their subjects were 101 18-year-olds who had participated in a long-running study of cognitive and personality development since they were age 3 (Block & Block, 1980). Shedler and Block found that most of these subjects could be placed in one of three groups, based on their history of drug abuse. They labeled these groups frequent *users* (history of extensive drug use), *experimenters* (occasional use), and *abstainers* (no illicit drug use). Personality assessments indicated that the frequent users were the most maladjusted group.

However, data collected years earlier revealed that the frequent users' maladjustment showed up in early childhood, before they began using drugs, and that their maladjustment was related to poor-quality parenting. These findings suggest that maladjustment may cause drug abuse, rather than vice versa, or that both may be caused by a third variable (ineffective child rearing), as outlined in Figure 5.19. In all likelihood, drugs contribute to the development of psychological disorders through a complex interactive process in which drug abuse and maladjustment feed off of each other.

Figure 5.19
Drug abuse and maladjustment. Many theorists have made the highly plausible assertion that drug abuse causes maladjustment. However, it's also likely that maladjusted people are drawn to recreational drugs, so that maladjustment causes drug abuse. The matter is further complicated by the recent finding by Shedler and Block (1990) that a third variable (ineffective parenting) may make a causal contribution to both drug abuse and maladjustment.

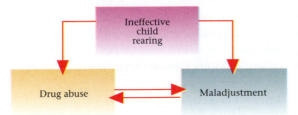

PUTTING IT IN PERSPECTIVE

This chapter highlights four of our unifying themes. First, we can see how psychology evolves in a sociohistorical context. Psychology began as the science of consciousness in the 19th century, but consciousness proved difficult to study empirically. Research on consciousness dwindled after John B. Watson and others redefined psychology as the science of behavior. As recently as 30 years ago, you wouldn't have found a chapter on consciousness in an introductory psychology text. However, in the 1960s, people began to turn inward, showing a new interest in altering consciousness through drug use, meditation, hypnosis, and biofeedback. Psychologists responded to these social trends by beginning to study variations in consciousness in earnest. This renewed interest in consciousness shows how social forces can have an impact on psychology's evolution.

A second theme that predominates in this chapter is the idea that people's experience of the world is highly subjective. We encountered this theme at the start of the chapter when we discussed the difficulty that people have describing their states of consciousness. The subjective nature of consciousness was apparent elsewhere in the chapter, as well. For instance, we found that the alterations of consciousness produced by drugs depend significantly on personal expectations.

Third, we saw once again how culture molds some aspects of behavior. Although the basic physiological process of sleep appears largely invariant from one society to another, culture influences certain aspects of sleep habits and has a dramatic impact on whether people remember their dreams and how they interpret and feel about their dreams. If not for space constraints, we might also have discussed cross-cultural differences in patterns of recreational drug use, which vary considerably from one society to the next.

Finally, the chapter illustrates psychology's theoretical diversity. We discussed conflicting theories about dreams, hypnosis, meditation, and the functions of sleep. For the most part, we did not see these opposing theories converging toward reconciliation, as we did in the areas of sensation and perception. However, it's important to emphasize that rival theories do not always merge neatly into tidy models of behavior. Many theoretical contro-

versies go on indefinitely. This reality does not negate the value of theoretical diversity. While it's always nice to resolve a theoretical debate, the debate itself can advance knowledge by stimulating and guiding empirical research.

Indeed, our upcoming Application demonstrates that theoretical debates need not be resolved in order to advance knowledge. Many theoretical controversies and enduring mysteries remain in the study of sleep and dreams. Nonetheless, researchers have accumulated a great deal of practical information on these topics, which we'll discuss in the next few pages.

Recap of Key Points

• The principal categories of abused drugs are narcotics, sedatives, stimulants, hallucinogens, cannabis, and alcohol. Although it's possible to describe the typical effects of various drugs, the actual effect on any individual depends on a host of factors, including subjective expectations and tolerance to the drug.

• Psychoactive drugs exert their main effects in the brain, where they alter neurotransmitter activity at synaptic sites in a variety of ways. For example, amphetamines increase the release of DA and NE, and like cocaine, they slow reuptake at DA and NE synapses. Sedatives and alcohol appear to exert their key effects at GABA synapses.

• Drugs vary in their potential for psychological and physical dependence. Some theorists have begun to raise doubts about the value of distinguishing between physical and psychological dependence.

• Recreational drug use can prove harmful to health by producing an overdose, by causing tissue damage, or by increasing health-impairing behavior. The chances of accidentally consuming a lethal overdose are greatest for the CNS depressants and cocaine. Direct tissue damage occurs most frequently with alcohol and cocaine.

• The health risks of marijuana have generated debate. There is an association between drug use and poor mental health, but it's hard to tell which causes which.

• Four of our unifying themes were highlighted in this chapter. We saw that psychology evolves in a sociohistorical context, that experience is highly subjective, that culture influences many aspects of behavior, and that psychology is characterized by extensive theoretical diversity.

APPLICATION: ADDRESSING PRACTICAL QUESTIONS ABOUT SLEEP AND DREAMS

Indicate whether the following statements are "true" or "false."

1 Everyone needs 8 hours of sleep a night to maintain sound mental health.

2 Naps rarely have a refreshing effect.

3 Some people never dream.

4 When people cannot recall their dreams, it's because they are trying to repress them.

5 Only an expert in symbolism, such as a psychoanalytic therapist, can interpret the real meaning of dreams.

These assertions were all drawn from the Sleep and Dreams Information Questionnaire (Palladino & Carducci, 1984), which measures practical knowledge about sleep and dreams. Are they true or false? You'll see in this Application.

Common Questions About Sleep

How much sleep do people need? The average amount of daily sleep for young adults is 7.5 hours. However, there is considerable variability in how long people sleep. Based on a synthesis of data from many studies, Webb (1992b) estimates that sleep time is normally distributed (see Appendix B) as shown in Figure 5.20. Thus, sleep needs vary from person to person. Asking how much sleep the average person needs isn't a very useful question, much like asking what shoe size the average person needs. If everyone were given average-size shoes to wear, most people would be very uncomfortable.

Can people learn to get by with less sleep? Some can't, but some can. There are well-documented cases of people who have

learned to live with as little as 3 hours of sleep per night for years (Jones & Oswald, 1968). Thus, the first statement in our series of true-false items is false. If you want to spend less time sleeping, try reducing your sleep time gradually and see how you feel. However, bear in mind the point made earlier in the main body of the chapter—although the effects of sleep deprivation seem pretty benign, lapses of attention due to sleepiness can be quite dangerous if they occur in the wrong place at the wrong time.

Can short naps be refreshing? Some naps are beneficial and some are not. The effectiveness of napping varies from person to person. Also, the benefits of any specific nap depend on the time of day and the amount of sleep one has had recently (Gillberg, 1984). On the negative side, naps are not very *efficient* ways to sleep because you're often just getting into the deeper stages of sleep when your nap time is up. Another potential problem is that overly long naps (more than 2 hours) or naps that occur too close to bedtime can disrupt nighttime sleep (Dinges, 1989).

Nonetheless, many highly productive people (including Thomas Edison, Winston Churchill, and John F. Kennedy) have made effective use of naps. On the positive side, most naps enhance subsequent alertness and reduce sleepiness (Dinges & Broughton, 1989). Evidence also suggests that naps can help offset the effects of frequent nighttime awakenings in older people (Aber & Webb, 1986). In conclusion, naps can be refreshing for most people (so the second statement opening this Application is false), and they can be beneficial in the long run if they don't interfere with nighttime sleep.

How do alcohol and drugs affect sleep? Obviously, stimulants such as cocaine and amphetamines make it difficult to sleep.

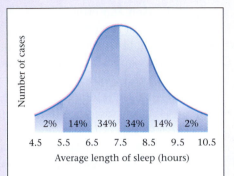

Figure 5.20
Variation in sleep needs. Based on data from a variety of sources, Webb (1992b) estimates that average sleep length among young adults is distributed normally, as shown here. Although most young adults sleep an average of 6.5 to 8.5 hours per night, some people need less and some people need more sleep. (Adapted from Webb, 1992b)

More surprising is the finding that most of the CNS depressants that facilitate sleep (such as alcohol, analgesics, sedatives, and tranquilizers) disrupt the normal sleep cycle. The principal problem is that they reduce the time spent in REM sleep and slow-wave sleep (Gillin, 1994). Unfortunately, these are the sleep stages that appear to be most important to a refreshing night's sleep.

Is there such a thing as sleep learning? Yes, but it won't get you through college. Studies show that cognitive responding to external stimuli can occur during the lighter stages (1 and 2) of sleep (Ogilvie, Wilkinson, & Allison, 1989). This and other lines of evidence suggest that sleep learning is a legitimate possibility (Eich, 1990). However, studies indicate that people have minimal ability to assimilate information of any complexity into long-term memory while asleep (Badia, 1990; Bonnet, 1982). It would be nice if people could learn Spanish by listening to an audiotape while they slept, but the evidence indicates that trying to do so is pointless.

People typically get very upset when they have difficulty falling asleep. Unfortunately, the emotional distress tends to make it even harder for people to get to sleep.

Can people learn to awaken without an alarm clock? Some people who have consistent sleep habits find themselves awakening on their own just before their alarm clock goes off. This phenomenon is fairly common and presumably reflects the influence of circadian rhythms. A smaller number of people claim that they can reliably awaken themselves at predetermined, nonhabitual times. However, when some of these people have been tested carefully in sleep laboratories, their performance has been inconsistent (Zepelin, 1993). Thus, people who claim that they have an internal alarm clock are probably exaggerating its reliability.

What do yawning and snoring have to do with sleep? Yawning is a universal human phenomenon seen in all cultural groups. Contrary to popular belief, yawning is not a response to a buildup of carbon dioxide or a shortage of oxygen. However, as reputed, yawning is strongly correlated with sleepiness. Whether yawning facilitates or impedes sleep, or has no effect, is not yet known (Provine, 1993). The most fascinating and perplexing facet of yawning is that it is contagious—seeing others yawn creates a powerful urge to follow suit. Contagious yawning is not well understood, but it is thought to be a neurologically programmed, reflexive response (Provine, 1989).

Snoring is a common phenomenon that is seen in about 20% of adults (Lugaresi et al., 1994). Snoring increases after age 35 and occurs in men more than women (Kryger, 1993). Many factors, including obesity, colds, allergies, smoking, and some drugs, can contribute to snoring, mainly by forcing people to breathe through their mouths while sleeping. Some people who snore loudly disrupt their own sleep as well as that of their bed partners. It can be very difficult to prevent snoring in some people, whereas other people can reduce their snoring by simply losing weight or sleeping on their side instead of their back (Lugaresi et al., 1994). Snoring may seem like a trivial problem, but it is associated with sleep apnea and cardiovascular disease, and it may have more medical significance than most people realize.

What can be done to avoid sleep problems? There are many ways to improve your chances of getting satisfactory sleep (see Figure 5.21). Most of them involve developing sensible daytime habits that won't interfere with sleep (Catalano, 1990; Coleman, 1986; Hales, 1987; Zarcone, 1994). For example, if you've been having trouble sleeping at night, it's wise to avoid daytime naps, so you're *tired* when bedtime arrives. Some people find that daytime exercise helps them fall asleep more readily at bedtime. Of course, the exercise should be part of a regular regimen that doesn't leave one sore or aching.

It's also a good idea to minimize consumption of stimulants such as caffeine or nicotine. Because coffee and cigarettes aren't prescription drugs, people don't appreciate how much the stimulants they contain can heighten their physical arousal. Many foods (such as chocolate) and beverages (such as cola drinks) contain more caffeine than people realize. Also, bear in mind that ill-advised eating habits can interfere with sleep. Try to avoid going to bed hungry, uncomfortably stuffed, or soon after eating foods that disagree with you.

In addition to these prudent habits, two other preventive measures are worthy of mention. First, try to establish a reasonably regular bedtime. This habit will allow you to take advantage of your circadian rhythm, so you'll be trying to fall asleep when your body is primed to cooperate. Second, create a favorable environment for sleep. This advice belabors what should be obvious, but many people fail to heed it. Make sure you have a good bed that is comfortable for you. Take steps to ensure that your bedroom is quiet enough and that the humidity and temperature are to your liking.

What can be done about insomnia? First, don't panic if you run into a little trouble sleeping. An overreaction to sleep problems can begin a vicious circle of escalating problems, like that depicted in Figure 5.22 (on page 212). If you jump to the conclusion that you are becoming an insomniac, you may approach sleep with anxiety that will aggravate the problem. The harder

1 Keep regular hours.

2 Remember that quality of sleep matters more than quantity.

3 Exercise every day—but not in the evening.

4 Don't smoke.

5 Don't have coffee late in the day.

6 Don't drink alcohol after dinner.

7 Don't nap during the day.

8 Unwind in the evening.

9 Don't go to bed starved or stuffed.

10 Develop a bedtime sleep ritual.

Figure 5.21
Suggestions for better sleep. Dianne Hales, in *How to Sleep Like a Baby* (1987), offers the following advice for people concerned about enhancing the quality of their sleep.

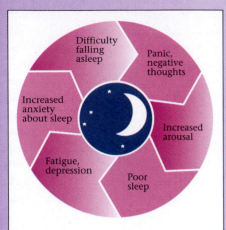

Figure 5.22
The vicious circle of anxiety and sleep difficulty. Anxiety about sleep difficulties leads to poorer sleep, which increases anxiety further, which in turn leads to even greater difficulties in sleeping.

you work at falling asleep, the less success you're likely to have. As noted earlier, temporary sleep problems are common and generally clear up on their own.

One sleep expert, Dianne Hales (1987), lists 101 suggestions for combating insomnia in her book *How to Sleep Like a Baby*. Many involve "boring yourself to sleep" by playing alphabet games, reciting poems, or listening to your clock. Another recommended strategy is to engage in some not-so-engaging activity. For instance, you might try reading your dullest textbook. It could turn out to be a superb sedative.

It's often a good idea to simply launch yourself into a pleasant daydream. This normal presleep process can take your mind off your difficulties. Whatever you think about, try to avoid ruminating about the current stresses and problems in your life. Research has shown that the tendency to ruminate is one of the key factors contributing to insomnia (Kales et al., 1984), as the data in Figure 5.23 show.

Anything that relaxes you—whether it's music, meditation, prayer, or a warm bath—can aid you in falling asleep. Experts have also devised systematic relaxation procedures that can make relaxation efforts more effective. You may want to learn about techniques such as *progressive relaxation* (Jacobson, 1938), *autogenic training* (Schultz & Luthe, 1959), or the *relaxation response* (Benson & Klipper, 1988).

Common Questions About Dreams

Does everyone dream? Yes. Some people just don't *remember* their dreams. However, when these people are brought into a sleep lab and awakened from REM sleep, they report having been dreaming—much to their surprise (Hall & Nordby, 1972). Thus, statement 3 at the start of this Application is false.

Why don't some people remember their dreams? The evaporation of dreams appears to be quite normal. Given the lowered level of awareness during sleep, it's understandable that memory of dreams is mediocre. Dream recall is best when people are awakened during or very soon after a dream (Goodenough, 1991). Most of the time, people who *do* recall dreams upon waking are remembering either their *last* dream from their final REM period or a dream that awakened them earlier in the night. Hobson's (1989) educated guess is that people probably forget 95%–99% of their dreams. This forgetting is natural and is not due to repression, so statement 4 is also false. People who never remember their dreams probably have a sleep pattern that puts too much time between their last REM/dream period and awakening, so even their last dream is forgotten.

Can people improve their recall of dreams? Yes. Most people don't have any significant reason to work at recalling their dreams, so they just let them float away. However, many people have found that they can remember more dreams if they merely place that goal uppermost in their minds as they go to sleep (Goodenough, 1991). Dream recall is also aided by making a point of trying to remember dreams upon first awakening, before opening your eyes or getting out of bed.

Are dreams instantaneous? No. There has long been speculation that dreams flash through consciousness almost instantaneously. According to this notion, complicated plots that would require 20 minutes to think through in waking life could bolt through the dreaming mind in a second or two. However, modern research shows that this isn't the case (Weinstein, Schwartz, & Arkin, 1991). When researchers awaken a subject who has been dreaming (in REM) for 15 minutes and ask the subject to recount the dream, the subject tends to produce approximately 15 minutes' worth of plot.

Do dreams require interpretation? Most theorists would say yes, but interpretation may not be as difficult as generally assumed. People have long believed that dreams are symbolic and that it is necessary to interpret the symbols to understand the meaning of dreams. Freud, for instance, made a distinction between the *manifest content* and the *latent content* of a dream. **The *manifest content* consists of the plot of a dream at a surface level. The *latent content* refers to the hidden or disguised meaning of the events in the plot.** Thus,

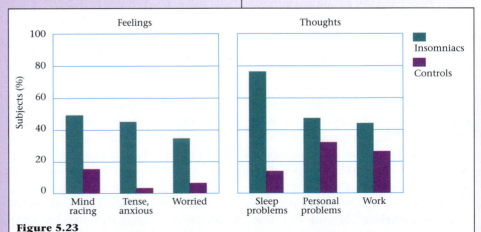

Figure 5.23
Thoughts and emotions associated with insomnia. This graph depicts the percentage of insomniacs and control subjects reporting various presleep feelings and thoughts. Insomniacs' tendency to ruminate about their problems contributes to their sleep difficulties. (Based on data from Kales et al., 1984)

a Freudian therapist might equate such dream events as walking into a tunnel or riding a horse with sexual intercourse.

Freudian theorists assert that dream interpretation is a complicated task requiring considerable knowledge of symbolism. However, many dream theorists argue that symbolism in dreams is less deceptive and mysterious than Freud thought (Faraday, 1974; Foulkes, 1985; Hall, 1979). Calvin Hall makes the point that dreams require some interpretation simply because they are more visual than verbal. That is, pictures need to be translated into ideas. According to Hall, dream symbolism is highly personal and the dreamer may be the person best equipped to decipher a dream (statement 5 is also false). Thus, it is not unreasonable for you to try to interpret your own dreams. Unfortunately, you'll never know whether you're "correct," because there is no definitive way to judge the validity of different dream interpretations.

Can people learn to influence their dreams? Quite possibly, but it is not easy. Researchers in a number of studies have instructed subjects to try to dream about a particular topic. Subjects have been successful often enough to suggest that some dream control is possible. However, there have been many failures as well, suggesting that dream control may be fairly difficult (Tart, 1990).

To date, the most impressive manipulations of dreams with presleep suggestions have been reported by Rosalind Cartwright. When she instructed subjects to dream about a particular personality trait—assertiveness, say—their dreams *were* influenced by the instructions (Cartwright, 1974). Even more intriguing is Cartwright's work with depressed women who were instructed to alter the plots in their dreams. Some of these women were successful in tilting their dream plots toward happier endings. Cartwright believes that these happier endings can carry over to affect waking mood and thus have therapeutic value (Cartwright, 1991; Cartwright & Lamberg, 1992).

What is lucid dreaming? Generally, when people dream, they are not aware that they are dreaming. Occasionally, however, some people experience "lucid" dreams in which they recognize that they are dreaming. Typically, normal dreams become lucid when people puzzle over something bizarre in a dream and recognize that they must be dreaming. **In *lucid dreams* people can think clearly about the circumstances of waking life and the fact that they are dreaming, yet they remain asleep in the midst of a vivid dream.** Perhaps the most intriguing aspect of this dual consciousness is that people can often exert some control over the events unfolding in their lucid dreams (LaBerge, 1990; Tart, 1988).

Reports of lucid dreams have a long history, but the inability of one person to experience another person's dream has always made it difficult to verify the existence of these exotic, paradoxical dreams (LaBerge, 1988). However, Stephen LaBerge reasoned that if lucid dreamers can act deliberately in their dreams, they should be able to make prearranged special eye movements to signal the occurrence of lucid dreams while being carefully monitored with physiological recording devices in a sleep lab. The ability to send such signals while dreaming would provide evidence of some degree of lucidity. This clever utilization of modern sleep monitoring techniques has allowed LaBerge and his colleagues to gather objective evidence that lucid dreaming is a genuine phenomenon that usually occurs during the REM stage (LaBerge et al., 1981).

About one in five people report having lucid dreams more than once a month (Snyder & Gackenbach, 1988). However, with training, some highly motivated people have been fairly successful at learning to have lucid dreams when they want to (Price & Cohen, 1988). The ability of lucid dreamers to communicate with sleep researchers while dreaming may provide new opportunities for investigators to explore the world of dreams (Kahan & LaBerge, 1994).

Could a shocking dream be fatal? According to folklore, if you fall from a height in a dream, you'd better wake up on the plunge downward. Supposedly, if you hit the bottom and die in your dream, the shock to your system will be so great that you will actually die in your sleep. Think about this one for a moment. *If* it were a genuine problem, who would have reported it? You can be sure that no one has ever testified to experiencing a fatal dream. This myth presumably exists because many people do awaken during the downward plunge, thinking that they've averted a close call. A study by Barrett (1988–1989) suggests that dreams of one's own death are relatively infrequent. However, people do have such dreams—and live to tell about them.

Recap of Key Points

• Sleep needs vary greatly, and some people can learn to get by with less sleep. The value of short naps depends on many factors, including one's biological rhythm. Alcohol and many other widely used drugs have a negative effect on sleep.

• Sleep learning is possible, but only in very primitive ways. People's internal alarm clocks are not as reliable as often claimed. Yawning appears to be a neurologically programmed, reflexive response that is associated with sleepiness. Snoring occurs exclusively during sleep and increases after age 35.

• People can do many things to avoid or reduce sleep problems. Mostly, it's a matter of developing good daytime habits that do not interfere with sleep. People troubled by transient insomnia should avoid panic, pursue effective relaxation, and try distracting themselves so they don't work too hard at falling asleep.

• Everyone dreams, but some people don't remember their dreams, probably because of the nature of their sleep cycle. Dream recall can be improved, and some people have even been taught to influence the course of their dreams.

• Freud distinguished between the manifest and latent content of dreams and asserted that dreams require interpretation. Most theorists agree that dreams require some interpretation, but this may not be as complicated as Freud assumed.

• In lucid dreams, people consciously recognize that they are dreaming and exert some control over the events in their dreams. Dreams are not instantaneous, and there's no evidence that they can be fatal.

Key Ideas

On the Nature of Consciousness

◆ Consciousness is the continually changing stream of mental activity. There is some degree of awareness during sleep and sometimes even when patients are under anesthesia. Variations in consciousness are related to brain activity, as measured by the EEG.

Biological Rhythms and Sleep

◆ The cycle of sleep and wakefulness is influenced considerably by circadian rhythms. Exposure to light may reset biological clocks by affecting the activity of the suprachiasmatic nucleus and the pineal gland, which secretes the hormone melatonin.
◆ Being out of sync with circadian rhythms is one reason for jet lag and for the unpleasant nature of rotating shift work. People can accommodate phase-delay changes in their sleep cycle more easily than phase-advance changes.

The Sleep and Waking Cycle

◆ When you fall asleep, you evolve through a series of stages in cycles of approximately 90 minutes. During the REM stage you experience rapid eye movements, brain waves that are characteristic of waking thought, and vivid dreaming. The sleep cycle tends to be repeated about four times in a night, as REM sleep gradually becomes more predominant and NREM sleep dwindles.
◆ The REM portion of sleep declines during childhood, leveling off at around 20% during adolescence. During adulthood, slow-wave sleep declines. Culture appears to have little impact on the physiological experience of sleep, but it does influence sleeping arrangements and napping patterns.
◆ The neural bases of sleep are very complex. The modulation of sleep and arousal depends on a constellation of brain structures and a variety of neurotransmitters.
◆ The only consistent effect of sleep deprivation is sleepiness. However, increased sleepiness can be a significant problem that appears to contribute to many transportation accidents and mishaps at work. Some theorists believe that slow-wave sleep is regulated by a restorative process, and REM sleep by a circadian process.
◆ Many people are troubled by sleep disorders. Foremost among these is insomnia, which has a variety of causes. Other common sleep problems include narcolepsy, sleep apnea, night terrors, nightmares, and somnambulism.

The World of Dreams

◆ The conventional view is that dreams are mental experiences during REM sleep that have a storylike quality, include vivid imagery, are often bizarre, and are regarded as

real by the dreamer, but theorists have begun to question many aspects of this view.
◆ The content of one's dreams may be affected by one's gender, events in one's life, and external stimuli that are experienced during the dream. There are dramatic variations across cultures in dream recall, content, and interpretation. Theories of dreaming remain largely untested, and psychologists do not really know why people dream.

Hypnosis: Altered Consciousness or Role Playing?

◆ Hypnosis has a long and curious history. People vary greatly in their susceptibility to hypnosis. Hypnotic susceptibility is a stable trait. Among other things, hypnosis can produce anesthesia, sensory distortions, disinhibition, and posthypnotic amnesia.
◆ There are two major theoretical approaches to hypnosis that view it either as an altered state of consciousness or as a normal state of consciousness in which subjects assume a hypnotic role.

Meditation: Pure Consciousness or Relaxation?

◆ Meditation has some physiological benefits, but these benefits may not be unique to meditation and may simply be a product of effective relaxation.

Altering Consciousness with Drugs

◆ Most recreational drug use involves an effort to alter consciousness with psychoactive drugs. Psychoactive drugs exert their main effects in the brain, where they alter neurotransmitter activity at synaptic sites in a variety of ways.
◆ Drugs vary in their potential for psychological and physical dependence. Likewise, the dangers to physical health vary depending on the drug. Recreational drug use can prove harmful to health by producing an overdose, by causing tissue damage, or by increasing health-impairing behavior.

Putting It in Perspective

◆ Four of our unifying themes were highlighted in this chapter. We saw that psychology evolves in a sociohistorical context, that experience is highly subjective, that culture influences many aspects of behavior, and that psychology is characterized by extensive theoretical diversity.

Application: Addressing Practical Questions About Sleep and Dreams

◆ Sleep needs vary greatly, and some people can learn to get by with less sleep. The value of short naps depends on many factors. Sleep learning is possible, but only in very primitive ways. People's internal alarm clocks are not as reliable as often claimed.
◆ People can do many things to avoid or re-

duce sleep problems. Mostly, it's a matter of developing good daytime habits that do not interfere with sleep. People troubled by transient insomnia should avoid panic, pursue effective relaxation, and try distracting themselves.
◆ Everyone dreams, but some people cannot remember their dreams, probably because of the nature of their sleep cycle. In lucid dreams, people consciously recognize that they are dreaming and exert some control over the events in their dreams. Most theorists believe that dreams require some interpretation, but this may not be as complicated as once assumed.

Key Terms

Alcohol
Ascending reticular activating system (ARAS)
Biological rhythms
Cannabis
Circadian rhythms
Dissociation
Electroencephalograph (EEG)
Electromyograph (EMG)
Electrooculograph (EOG)
Hallucinogens
Hypnosis
Insomnia
Latent content
Lucid dreams
Manifest content
Meditation
Narcolepsy
Narcotics
Night terrors
Nightmares
Non-REM (NREM) sleep
Opiates
Physical dependence
Psychoactive drugs
Psychological dependence
REM sleep
Sedatives
Sleep apnea
Slow-wave sleep (SWS)
Somnambulism
Stimulants
Tolerance

Key People

Theodore Barber
Alexander Borbely
Rosalind Cartwright
William Dement
Sigmund Freud
Calvin Hall
Ernest Hilgard
J. Alan Hobson
William James
Wilse Webb

Practice Test

1. An EEG would indicate primarily _____ activity while you take this test.
   A. alpha
   B. beta
   C. delta
   D. theta

2. In free-running sleep experiments, subjects have no information regarding the time of day. Under these conditions, subjects tend to:
   A. continue to function on a 24-hour cycle.
   B. experience significant disruptions in their sleep patterns.
   C. drift toward a 25-hour cycle.
   D. have trouble falling asleep.

3. Research conducted by Czeisler and associates found improved worker satisfaction among those workers who:
   A. changed over to a phase-delay schedule.
   B. changed over to a phase-advance schedule.
   C. changed to a shorter rotation.
   D. alternated between a phase-delay schedule and a phase-advance schedule.

4. As the sleep cycle evolves through the night, people tend to:
   A. spend more time in REM sleep and less time in NREM sleep.
   B. spend more time in NREM sleep and less time in REM sleep.
   C. spend a more or less equal amount of time in REM sleep and NREM sleep.
   D. spend more time in stage 4 sleep and less time in REM sleep.

5. Newborn infants spend about _____% of their sleep time dreaming and adults spend about _____ % of their sleep time dreaming.
   A. 20; 50
   B. 50; 20
   C. 20; 20
   D. 50; 50

6. According to Borbely, time spent in _____ sleep depends on how long one has been awake; time spent in _____ sleep depends mainly on a circadian rhythm.
   A. REM; slow-wave
   B. REM; stages 1 and 2
   C. slow-wave; REM
   D. stages 1 and 2; REM

7. Which of the following sleep disorders would be most hazardous to a long-haul truck driver?
   A. sleep apnea
   B. insomnia
   C. narcolepsy
   D. pseudoinsomnia

8. Which of the following is *not* true of cultural influences on dream experiences?
   A. The ability to recall dreams is fairly consistent across cultures.
   B. In some cultures, people are held responsible for their dream actions.
   C. In many cultures, dreams are seen as a window into the spritual world.
   D. People in some cultures believe that dreams provide information about the future.

9. The activation-synthesis theory of dreaming contends that:
   A. dreams are simply the by-product of bursts of activity in the brain.
   B. dreams provide an outlet for energy invested in socially undesirable impulses.
   C. dreams represent the brain's attempt to process information taken in during waking hours.
   D. dreams are an attempt to restore a neurotransmitter balance within the brain.

10. A common driving experience is "highway hypnosis," in which one's consciousness seems to be divided between the driving itself and one's conscious train of thought. This phenomenon is evidence for the idea that hypnosis is:
    A. an exercise in role playing.
    B. a dissociated state of consciousness.
    C. a goal-directed fantasy.
    D. not an altered state of consciousness.

11. Stimulant is to depressant as:
    A. cocaine is to alcohol.
    B. mescaline is to barbiturates.
    C. caffeine is to amphetamines.
    D. alcohol is to barbiturates.

12. Amphetamines work by increasing the levels of _____ in a variety of ways.
    A. GABA and glycine
    B. serotonin and dopamine
    C. acetylcholine
    D. norepinephrine and dopamine

13. Which of the following drugs would be most likely to result in a fatal overdose?
    A. LSD
    B. mescaline
    C. marijuana
    D. barbiturates

14. Which of the following is a true statement about naps?
    A. Daytime naps invariably lead to insomnia.
    B. Daytime naps are invariably refreshing and an efficient way to rest.
    C. Daytime naps are not very efficient ways to sleep, but their effects are variable.
    D. Taking many naps during the day can substitute for a full night's sleep.

15. Peter rarely remembers his dreams. What can we say about Peter?
    A. Peter must be psychologically repressed.
    B. Peter obviously does not dream very much.
    C. Peter's dreams are probably not very memorable.
    D. Peter dreams, but he simply does not remember his dreams.

Answers

1	B	Page 179	6	C	Pages 190–191	11	A	Pages 203–204
2	C	Pages 180–181	7	C	Page 193	12	D	Pages 205–206
3	A	Page 182	8	A	Pages 196–197	13	D	Pages 205, 207
4	A	Page 185	9	A	Pages 197–198	14	C	Page 210
5	B	Pages 186–187	10	B	Page 201	15	D	Page 212

6 LEARNING THROUGH CONDITIONING

You're sitting in the waiting room of your dentist's office. You cringe when you hear the whirring of a dental drill coming from the next room.

• A four-year-old boy pinches his hand in one of his toys and curses loudly. His mother looks up in dismay and says to his father, "Where did he pick up that kind of language?"

• A young girl goes to the front closet, takes out a chain leash for her dog, and jingles the chain loudly. The dog leaps off the couch and comes running, wagging its tail with excitement.

• A seal waddles across the stage, bows ceremoniously, and "doffs his cap" by flipping it into the air and catching it in his mouth. The spectators at the aquatic show clap appreciatively as the trainer tosses the seal a fish as a reward.

• The crowd hushes as an Olympic diver prepares to execute her dive. In a burst of motion she propels herself into the air and glides smoothly through a dazzling corkscrew somersault.

What do all of these scenarios have in common? At first glance, very little. They are a diverse collection of events, some trivial, some impressive. However, they do share one common thread: *They all involve learning*. This may surprise you. When most people think of learning, they envision students reading textbooks or novices working to acquire a specific skill, such as riding a bicycle or skiing. Although these activities do involve learning, they represent only the tip of the iceberg in psychologists' eyes.

Learning **refers to a relatively durable change in behavior or knowledge that is due to experience.** This broad definition means that learning is one of the most fundamental concepts in all of psychology. Learning includes the acquisition of knowledge and skills, but it also shapes personal habits, such as nailbiting; personality traits, such as shyness; emotional responses, such as a fear of storms; and personal preferences, such as a taste for tacos or a distaste for formal clothes. Much of your behavior is the result of learning. If it were possible to strip away your learned responses, little behavior would be left. You would not be able to read this book, find your way home, or cook yourself a hamburger. You would be about as complex and exciting as a turnip.

Although you and I depend on learning, it is *not* an exclusively human process. Most organisms are capable of learning. Even the lowly flatworm can acquire a learned response. As this chapter unfolds, you may be surprised to see that much of the research on learning has been conducted using lower animals as subjects. Why? Mainly because researchers can exert much better experimental control over animal subjects than human subjects. As we saw in Chapter 1, that was one of the reasons that the noted behaviorist John B. Watson advocated the study of animal behavior. For the most part, Watson's plan has worked out well. Decades of research have shown that many principles of learning discovered in animal research apply quite well to humans.

In this chapter, we will focus most of our attention on a specific kind of learning: conditioning. *Conditioning* involves learning associations between events that occur in an organism's environment. In investigating conditioning, psychologists study learning at a very fundamental level. This strategy has paid off with fruitful insights that have laid the foundation for the study of more complex forms of learning, including learning by means of observation. In our chapter Application, you'll see how you can harness the principles of conditioning to improve your self-control.

CLASSICAL CONDITIONING

Do you go weak in the knees at the thought of standing on the roof of a tall building? Does your heart race when you imagine encountering a harmless garter snake? If so, you can understand, at least to some degree, what it's like to have a phobia. *Phobias* **are irrational fears of specific objects or situations.** Mild phobias are commonplace (Eaton, Dryman, & Weissman, 1991). Over the years, students in my classes have described their phobic responses to a diverse array of stimuli, including bridges, elevators, tunnels, heights, dogs, cats, bugs, snakes, professors, doctors, strangers,

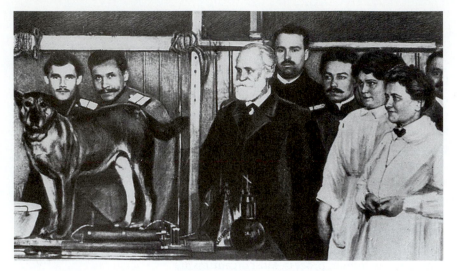

Surrounded by his research staff, the great Russian physiologist Ivan Pavlov (center, white beard) demonstrates his famous classical conditioning experiment with dogs.

"Next time there's a revolution, get up earlier!"

IVAN PAVLOV

thunderstorms, and germs. If you have a phobia, you may have wondered how you managed to acquire such a foolish fear. Chances are, it was through classical conditioning.

Classical conditioning* is a type of learning in which a stimulus acquires the capacity to evoke a response that was originally evoked by another stimulus.** The process was first described in 1903 by Ivan Pavlov, and it is sometimes called ***Pavlovian conditioning in tribute to him. The term *conditioning* comes from Pavlov's determination to discover the "conditions" that produce this kind of learning. The process came to be known as *classical conditioning* to differentiate it from other forms of conditioning that were subsequently described. Over the years, this form of learning also acquired another name: ***respondent conditioning***.

Pavlov's Demonstration: "Psychic Reflexes" 5a

Ivan Pavlov was a prominent Russian physiologist who did Nobel prize–winning research on digestion. Something of a "classic" himself, he was an absent-minded but brilliant professor obsessed with his research. Pavlov apparently was so naive about everyday financial matters that his wife allowed him to carry only a little pocket change. Yet he ran an exceptionally efficient research laboratory in which he was a demanding taskmaster. Legend has it that Pavlov once reprimanded an assistant who arrived late for an experiment because of trying to avoid street fighting in the midst of the Russian Revolution. The assistant defended his tardiness, saying, "But Professor, there's a revolution going on with shooting in the streets!" Pavlov supposedly replied, "What the hell difference does a revolution make when you've work to do in the laboratory? Next time there's a revolution, get up

earlier!" Apparently, dodging bullets wasn't an adequate excuse for delaying the march of scientific progress (Fancher, 1979; Gantt, 1975).

Pavlov was studying the role of saliva in the digestive processes of dogs when he stumbled onto what he called "psychic reflexes" (Pavlov, 1906). Like many great discoveries, Pavlov's was partly accidental, although he had the insight to recognize its significance. His subjects were dogs restrained in harnesses in an experimental chamber (see Figure 6.1). Their saliva was collected by means of a surgically implanted tube in the salivary gland. Pavlov would present meat powder to a dog and then collect the resulting saliva. As his research progressed, he noticed that dogs accustomed to the procedure would start salivating *before* the meat powder was presented. For instance, they would salivate in response to a clicking sound made by the device that was used to present the meat powder.

Intrigued by this unexpected finding, Pavlov decided to investigate further. To clarify what was happening, he paired the presentation of the meat powder with various stimuli that would stand out in the laboratory situation. For instance, in some experiments he used a simple auditory stimulus—the presentation of a tone. After the tone and the meat powder had been presented together a number of times, the tone was presented alone. What happened? The dogs responded by salivating to the sound of the tone alone.

What was so significant about a dog salivating when a tone was presented? The key is that the tone started out as a *neutral* stimulus. That is, it did not originally produce the response of salivation. However, Pavlov managed to change that by pairing the tone with a stimulus (meat powder) that did produce the salivation response. Through this process, the tone acquired the capacity to trigger the response of salivation. What Pavlov had demonstrated was how learned associations—which were viewed as the basic building blocks of the entire learning process—were formed by events in an organism's environment.

Terminology and Procedures 5a

There is a special vocabulary associated with classical conditioning. It often looks intimidating to the uninitiated, but it's really not all that mysterious. The bond Pavlov noted between the meat powder and salivation was a natural, unlearned association. It did not have to be created through conditioning. It is therefore called an *unconditioned* association. Thus, **the *unconditioned stimulus (UCS)* is a stimulus that evokes an uncondi-**

Figure 6.1
Classical conditioning apparatus. An experimental arrangement similar to the one depicted here (taken from Yerkes & Morgulis, 1909) has typically been used in demonstrations of classical conditioning, although Pavlov's original setup (see inset) was quite a bit simpler. The dog is restrained in a harness. A tone is used as the conditioned stimulus (CS), and the presentation of meat powder is used as the unconditioned stimulus (UCS). The tube inserted into the dog's salivary gland allows precise measurement of its salivation response. The pen and rotating drum of paper on the left are used to maintain a continuous record of salivary flow. (Inset) The less elaborate setup that Pavlov originally used to collect saliva on each trial is shown here (Goodwin, 1991).

tioned response without previous conditioning. The *unconditioned response (UCR)* **is an unlearned reaction to an unconditioned stimulus that occurs without previous conditioning.**

In contrast, the link between the tone and salivation was established through conditioning. It is therefore called a *conditioned* association. Thus, **the *conditioned stimulus (CS)* is a previously neutral stimulus that has, through conditioning, acquired the capacity to evoke a conditioned response. The *conditioned response (CR)* is a learned reaction to a conditioned stimulus that occurs because of previous conditioning.** Ironically, the names for the four key elements in classical conditioning (the UCS, UCR, CS, and CR) are the by-product of a poor translation of Pavlov's writing into English. Pavlov actually used the words condition*al* and uncondition*al* to refer to these concepts (Gantt, 1966).

To avoid possible confusion, it is worth noting that the unconditioned response and conditioned response are virtually the same behavior, although there may be subtle differences between them. In Pavlov's initial demonstration, the UCR and CR were both salivation. When evoked by the UCS (meat powder), salivation was an unconditioned response. When evoked by the CS (the tone), salivation was a conditioned response. The procedures involved in classical conditioning are outlined in Figure 6.2 (on page 220).

Pavlov's "psychic reflex" came to be called the *conditioned reflex*. Classically conditioned responses have traditionally been characterized as reflexes and are said to be *elicited* (**drawn forth**) because

most of them are relatively automatic or involuntary. However, research in recent decades has demonstrated that classical conditioning is involved in a wider range of human and animal behavior than previously appreciated, including some types of nonreflexive responding (Turkkan, 1989). Finally, **a *trial* in classical conditioning consists of any presentation of a stimulus or pair of stimuli.** Psychologists are interested in how many trials are required to establish a particular conditioned bond. The number needed to form an association varies considerably. Although classical conditioning generally proceeds gradually, it *can* occur quite rapidly, sometimes in just one pairing of the CS and UCS.

Classical Conditioning in Everyday Life

In laboratory experiments on classical conditioning, researchers have generally worked with extremely simple responses. Besides salivation, frequently studied favorites include eyelid closure, knee jerks, the flexing of various limbs, and fear responses. The study of such simple responses has proven both practical and productive. However, these responses do not even begin to convey the rich diversity of everyday behavior that is regulated by classical conditioning. Let's look at some examples of classical conditioning taken from everyday life.

Conditioned Fear and Anxiety

Classical conditioning often plays a key role in shaping emotional responses such as fear and anxiety. Phobias are a good example of such responses.

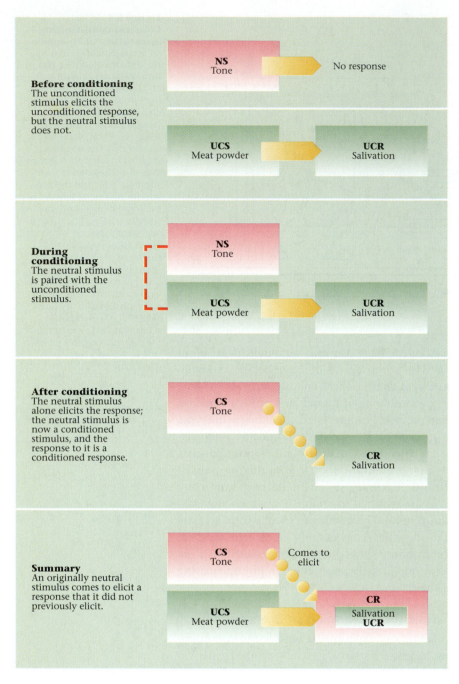

Before conditioning
The unconditioned stimulus elicits the unconditioned response, but the neutral stimulus does not.

NS
Tone → No response

UCS
Meat powder → UCR
Salivation

During conditioning
The neutral stimulus is paired with the unconditioned stimulus.

NS
Tone

UCS
Meat powder → UCR
Salivation

After conditioning
The neutral stimulus alone elicits the response; the neutral stimulus is now a conditioned stimulus, and the response to it is a conditioned response.

CS
Tone → CR
Salivation

Summary
An originally neutral stimulus comes to elicit a response that it did not previously elicit.

CS
Tone → Comes to elicit

UCS
Meat powder → CR
Salivation
UCR

Figure 6.2
The sequence of events in classical conditioning. Moving from top to bottom, this series of diagrams outlines the sequence of events in classical conditioning, using Pavlov's original demonstration as an example. As we encounter other examples of classical conditioning throughout the book, we will see many diagrams like the one in the fourth panel, which summarizes the process.

Figure 6.3
Classical conditioning of a fear response. Many emotional responses that would otherwise be puzzling can be explained by classical conditioning. In the case of one woman's bridge phobia, the fear originally elicited by her father's scare tactics became a conditioned response to the stimulus of bridges.

CS
Bridge

UCS
Father's scare tactics → CR
Fear
UCR

Case studies of patients suffering from phobias suggest that many irrational fears can be traced back to experiences that involve classical conditioning (Merckelbach et al., 1989). It is easy to imagine how such conditioning can occur outside of the laboratory. For example, a student of mine was troubled by a bridge phobia so severe that she couldn't drive on interstate highways because of all the viaducts that had to be crossed. She was able to pinpoint as the source of her phobia something that had happened during her childhood. Whenever her family drove to visit her grandmother, they had to cross a little-used, rickety, dilapidated bridge out in the countryside. Her father, in a misguided attempt at humor, made a major production out of these crossings. He would stop short of the bridge and carry on about the enormous danger. Obviously, he thought the bridge was safe or he wouldn't have driven across it. However, the naive young girl was terrified by her father's scare tactics. Hence, the bridge became a conditioned stimulus eliciting great fear (see Figure 6.3). Unfortunately, the fear spilled over to *all* bridges. Forty years later she was still carrying the burden of this phobia. A number of processes besides conditioning can contribute to the development of phobias (Marks, 1987). Nonetheless, it's clear that classical conditioning is responsible for a great many irrational fears.

Everyday anxiety responses that are less severe than phobias may also be products of classical conditioning. For instance, if you cringe when you hear the sound of a dentist's drill, this response is due to classical conditioning. In this case, the pain you have experienced from dental drilling is the UCS. This pain has been paired with the sound of the drill, which became a CS eliciting your cringe.

If every scare produced a conditioned anxiety or phobia, we would all be emotional wrecks. Fortunately, not every frightening experience leaves a conditioned fear in its wake. As we will discuss, a variety of factors influence whether a conditioned response will be acquired in a particular situation.

Other Conditioned Emotional Responses
Classical conditioning is not limited to producing unpleasant emotions such as fear and anxiety. Many pleasant emotional responses are also acquired through classical conditioning. Consider the following example, described by a 53-year-old woman who wrote a letter to newspaper columnist Bob Greene about the news that a company was bringing back a discontinued product—Beemans gum. She wrote:

That was the year (1949) I met Charlie. I guess first love is always the same. . . . Charlie and I went out a lot. He chewed Beemans gum and he smoked. . . . We would go to all the passion pits—the drive-in movies and the places to park. We did a lot of necking, but we always stopped at a certain point. Charlie wanted to get married when we got out of high school . . . [but] Charlie and I drifted apart. We both ended up getting married to different people.

And the funny thing is . . . for years the combined smell of cigarette smoke and Beemans gum made my knees weak. Those two smells were Charlie to me. When I would smell the Beemans and the cigarette smoke, I could feel the butterflies dancing all over my stomach.

The writer clearly had a unique and long-lasting emotional response to the smell of Beemans gum and cigarettes. The credit for this *pleasant* response goes to classical conditioning (see Figure 6.4).

Advertising campaigns often try to take advantage of classical conditioning. Advertisers routinely pair their products with UCSs that elicit pleasant emotions (Gorn, 1982; Smith & Engel, 1968). The most common strategy is to present a product in association with an attractive person or enjoyable surroundings (see Figure 6.5). Advertisers hope that these pairings will make their products conditioned stimuli that evoke good feelings. For example, Kodak used a child playing with puppies in one of its TV commercials to help associate warm feelings with its film products.

Conditioning and Physiological Responses

Classical conditioning affects not only overt behaviors but physiological processes as well. Consider, for example, your body's immune functioning. When an infectious agent invades your body, your immune system attempts to repel the invasion by producing specialized proteins called *antibodies*. The critical importance of the immune response becomes evident when the immune system is disabled, as occurs with the disease AIDS (acquired immune deficiency syndrome).

Recent advances have revealed that the functioning of the immune system can be influenced by psychological factors, including conditioning. Robert Ader and Nicholas Cohen (1981, 1984, 1993) have shown that classical conditioning procedures can lead to *immunosuppression*—a decrease in the production of antibodies. In a typical study, animals are injected with a drug (the UCS) that *chemically* causes immunosuppression while they are simultaneously given an unusual-tasting liq-

uid to drink (the CS). Days later, after the chemical immunosuppression has ended, some of the animals are reexposed to the CS by giving them the unusual-tasting solution. Measurements of antibody production indicate that animals ex-

Figure 6.4
Classical conditioning and romance. Pleasant emotional responses can be acquired through classical conditioning, as illustrated by one woman's unusual conditioned response to the aroma of Beemans gum and cigarette smoke.

Figure 6.5
Classical conditioning in advertising. Many advertisers attempt to make their products conditioned stimuli that elicit pleasant emotional responses by pairing their products with attractive or popular people or sexual imagery.

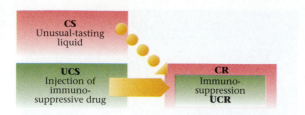

Figure 6.6
Classical conditioning of immunosuppression.
When a neutral stimulus is paired with a drug that chemically causes immunosuppression, it can become a CS that elicits immunosuppression on its own. Thus, even the immune response can be influenced by classical conditioning.

posed to the CS show a reduced immune response (see Figure 6.6).

Immune resistance is only one example of the subtle physiological processes that can be influenced by classical conditioning. Studies suggest that classical conditioning can also elicit *allergic reactions* (MacQueen et al., 1989) and the *release of endorphins* (Fanselow, 1991), the brain's opiatelike painkillers (see Chapters 3 and 4), and that classical conditioning contributes to the growth of drug tolerance (Siegel, 1983, 1989). Thanks in part to findings on the conditioning of physiological processes, experts are reappraising traditional theories of health, pain, and disease to include a larger role for psychological factors.

Basic Processes in Classical Conditioning 5b

Classical conditioning is often portrayed as a mechanical process that inevitably leads to a certain result. This view reflects the reality that most conditioned responses are reflexive and difficult to control. Pavlov's dogs would have been hard pressed to withhold their salivation. Similarly, most people with phobias have great difficulty suppressing their fear. However, this vision of classical conditioning as an "irresistible force" is misleading because it fails to consider the many factors involved in classical conditioning. In this section, we'll look at basic processes in classical conditioning to expand on the rich complexity of this form of learning.

Acquisition: Forming New Responses

We have already discussed *acquisition* without attaching a formal name to the process. **Acquisition refers to the initial stage of learning something.** Pavlov theorized that the acquisition of a conditioned response depends on stimulus *contiguity*, which literally means "touching." **Stimulus contiguity is a temporal (time) association between two events.** Thus, Pavlov thought that the key to classical conditioning is the *pairing* of stimuli in time.

Stimulus contiguity is important, but learning theorists now realize that contiguity alone doesn't automatically produce conditioning. People are

bombarded daily by countless stimuli that could be perceived as being paired, yet only some of these pairings produce classical conditioning. Consider the woman who developed a conditioned emotional reaction to the smell of Beemans gum and cigarettes. Certainly, there were other stimuli that shared contiguity with her boyfriend, Charlie. He smoked, so ashtrays were probably present, but she doesn't get weak in the knees at the sight of an ashtray.

If conditioning does not occur to all the stimuli present in a situation, what determines its occurrence? Evidence suggests that stimuli that are novel, unusual, or especially intense have more potential to become CSs than routine stimuli, probably because they are more likely to stand out among other stimuli (Hearst, 1988).

A number of other factors also influence the acquisition of classically conditioned responses. The timing of the stimulus presentations is especially important (Miller & Barnet, 1993). Many CS-UCS timing arrangements have been investigated. Three such temporal arrangements are diagrammed in Figure 6.7. In *simultaneous conditioning,* the CS and UCS begin and end together. In *short-delayed conditioning,* the CS begins just before the UCS and stops at the same time as the UCS. In *trace conditioning,* the CS begins and ends before the UCS is presented.

Which temporal arrangement works best? The approach that maximizes stimulus contiguity—simultaneous conditioning—is *not* particularly effective in establishing a new conditioned response. Nor is trace conditioning. Short-delayed conditioning is the temporal arrangement that best facilitates the acquisition of most conditioned responses. Ideally the delay between the onset of the CS and UCS should be very brief, about half a second (Heth & Rescorla, 1973; Kamin, 1965). Later in the chapter, we'll see a striking exception to this rule of thumb and some additional factors that influence acquisition.

Extinction: Weakening Conditioned Responses

Fortunately, a newly formed stimulus-response bond does not necessarily last indefinitely. If it did, learning would be inflexible, and organisms would have difficulty adapting to new situations. Instead, the right circumstances produce *extinction,* **the gradual weakening and disappearance of a conditioned response tendency.**

What leads to extinction in classical conditioning? The consistent presentation of the conditioned stimulus *alone,* without the unconditioned stimulus. For example, when Pavlov consistently presented *only* the tone to a previously conditioned dog, the tone gradually lost its capacity to elicit the response of salivation. Such a sequence of events is depicted in the left portion of Figure 6.8, which graphs the amount of salivation by a dog over a series of conditioning trials. Note how the salivation response declines during extinction.

For an example of extinction from outside the laboratory, let's assume that you cringe at the sound of a dentist's drill, which has been paired with pain in the past. You take a job as a dental assistant and you start hearing the drill (the CS) day in and day out without experiencing any pain (the UCS). Your cringing response will gradually diminish and extinguish altogether.

How long does it take to extinguish a conditioned response? That depends on many factors, but particularly the strength of the conditioned bond when extinction begins. Some conditioned responses extinguish quickly, while others are difficult to weaken.

Spontaneous Recovery: Resurrecting Responses

Some conditioned responses display the ultimate in tenacity by "reappearing from the dead" after having been extinguished. Learning theorists use the term *spontaneous recovery* to describe such a resurrection from the graveyard of conditioned associations. **Spontaneous recovery is the reappearance of an extinguished response after a period of nonexposure to the conditioned stimulus.**

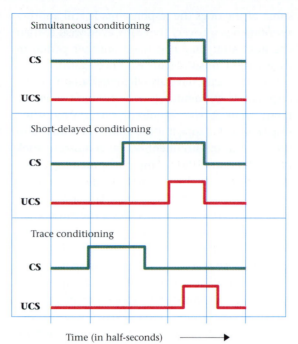

Time (in half-seconds)

Figure 6.7
Temporal relations of stimuli in classical conditioning. The effects of classical conditioning depend in part on the timing of the stimuli. Three ways of pairing the CS and UCS are diagrammed here. The most effective arrangement is short-delayed conditioning, in which the CS begins just before the UCS and stops at the same time as the UCS.

Pavlov (1927) observed this phenomenon in some of his pioneering studies. He fully extinguished a dog's CR of salivation to a tone and then returned the dog to its home cage for a "rest interval" (a period of nonexposure to the CS). On a subsequent day, when the dog was brought back to the experimental chamber for retesting, the tone was sounded and the salivation response reappeared. Although it had returned, the rejuvenated response was weak. The salivation was less than when the response was at its peak strength. If Pavlov consistently presented the CS by itself again, the response reextinguished quickly. However, in

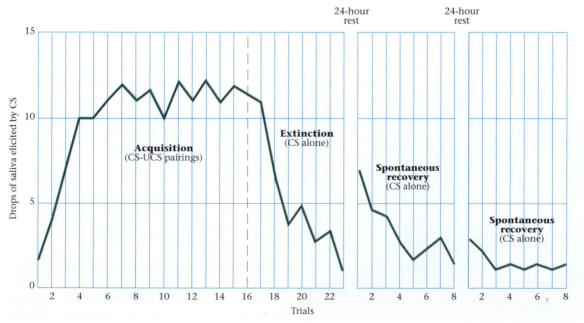

Figure 6.8
Acquisition, extinction, and spontaneous recovery. During acquisition, the strength of the dog's conditioned response (measured by the amount of salivation) increases rapidly and then levels off near its maximum. During extinction, the CR declines erratically until it's extinguished. After a "rest" period in which the dog is not exposed to the CS, a spontaneous recovery occurs, and the CS once again elicits a (weakened) CR. Repeated presentations of the CS alone reextinguish the CR, but after another "rest" interval, a weaker spontaneous recovery occurs.

"Surely this proof of the conditioned origin of a fear response puts us on natural science grounds in our study of emotional behavior."

JOHN B. WATSON

Figure 6.9
The conditioning of Little Albert. The diagram shows how Little Albert's fear response to a white rat was established. Albert's fear response to other white, furry objects illustrates generalization. In the photo, made from a 1919 film, Rosalie Rayner and John B. Watson are shown with Little Albert before he was conditioned to fear the rat.

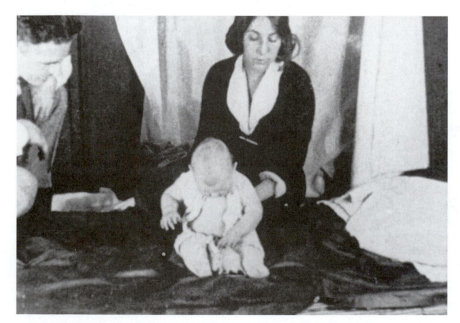

some of the dogs the response made still another spontaneous recovery (typically even weaker than the first) after they had spent another period in their cages (consult Figure 6.8 once again).

Recent studies have also demonstrated that if a response is extinguished in a different environment than it was acquired, the extinguished response will reappear if the animal is returned to the original environment where acquistion took place (Bouton, 1991). This phenomenon, called the *renewal effect,* along with the evidence on spontaneous recovery, suggests that extinction somehow suppresses a conditioned response rather than erasing a learned association. In other words, *extinction does not appear to lead to unlearning* (Bouton, 1994). The theoretical meaning of spontaneous recovery and the renewal effect is complex and the subject of some debate. However, their practical meaning is quite simple. Even if you manage to rid yourself of an unwanted conditioned response (such as cringing when you hear a dental drill), there is an excellent chance that it may make a surprise reappearance later.

Stimulus Generalization and the Case of Little Albert

After conditioning has occurred, organisms often show a tendency to respond not only to the exact CS used but also to other, similar stimuli. For example, Pavlov's dogs might have salivated in response to a different sounding tone, or you might cringe at the sound of a jeweler's as well as a dentist's drill. These are examples of stimulus generalization. *Stimulus generalization* occurs when **an organism that has learned a response to a specific stimulus responds in the same way to new stimuli that are similar to the original stimulus.** Generalization is adaptive given that organisms rarely encounter the exact same stimulus more than once (Thomas, 1992). Stimulus generalization is also commonplace. We have already discussed a real-life example: the woman who acquired a bridge phobia during her childhood because her father scared her whenever they went over a particular old bridge. The original CS for her fear was that specific bridge, but her fear was ultimately *generalized* to all bridges.

John B. Watson, the founder of behaviorism (see Chapter 1), conducted an influential early study of generalization. Watson and a colleague, Rosalie Rayner, examined the generalization of conditioned fear in an 11-month-old boy, known in the annals of psychology as "Little Albert." Like many babies, Albert was initially unafraid of a live white rat. Then Watson and Rayner (1920) paired the presentation of the rat with a loud, startling sound (made by striking a steel bar with a hammer). Albert *did* show fear in response to the loud noise. After seven pairings of the rat and the gong, the rat was established as a CS eliciting a fear response (see Figure 6.9). Five days later, Watson and Rayner exposed the youngster to other stimuli that resembled the rat in being white and furry. They found that Albert's fear response generalized to a variety of stimuli, including a rabbit, a dog, a fur coat, a Santa Claus mask, and Watson's hair.

What happened to Little Albert? Did he grow up with a phobia of Santa Claus? Unfortunately, we have no idea. He was taken from the hospital where Watson and Rayner conducted their study before they got around to extinguishing the conditioned fears that they had created, and he was never heard of again. Watson and Rayner were roundly criticized in later years for failing to ensure that Albert experienced no lasting ill effects. Their failure to do so was fairly typical for their era, but clearly remiss by today's much stricter code of research ethics.

The likelihood and amount of generalization to a new stimulus depends on the similarity between the new stimulus and the original CS (Balsam, 1988). The basic law governing generalization is this: *The more similar new stimuli are to the original CS, the greater the generalization.* This principle can be quantified in graphs called *generalization gradients,* such as the one shown in Figure 6.10. This particular generalization gradient maps out how a dog conditioned to salivate to a tone of 1200 hertz might respond to other tones. As you can see, the strength of the generalization response declines as the similarity between the new stimuli and the original CS decreases.

Stimulus Discrimination

Stimulus discrimination is just the opposite of stimulus generalization. **Stimulus discrimination occurs when an organism that has learned a response to a specific stimulus does *not* respond in the same way to new stimuli that are similar to the original stimulus.** Like generalization, discrimination is adaptive in that an animal's survival may hinge on its being able to distinguish friend from foe, or edible from poisonous food (Thomas, 1992). Organisms can gradually learn to discriminate between an original CS and similar stimuli if they have adequate experience with both. For instance, let's say your pet dog runs around, excitedly wagging its tail, whenever it hears your car pull up in the driveway. Initially it will probably respond to *all* cars that pull into the driveway (stimulus generalization). However, if there is anything distinctive about the sound of your car, your dog may gradually respond with excitement to only your car and not to other cars (stimulus discrimination).

The development of stimulus discrimination usu-

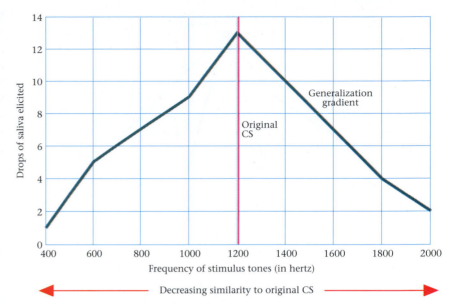

Figure 6.10
A generalization gradient. In a study of stimulus generalization, an organism is typically conditioned to respond to a specific CS, such as a 1200 hertz tone, and then tested with similar stimuli, such as other tones between 400 and 2000 hertz. The graph of the organism's responding is called a *generalization gradient.* The graph normally shows, as depicted here, that generalization declines as the similarity between the new stimuli and the original CS decreases.

CONCEPT CHECK 6.1
Identifying Elements in Classical Conditioning

Check your understanding of classical conditioning by trying to identify the unconditioned stimulus (UCS), unconditioned response (UCR), conditioned stimulus (CS), and conditioned response (CR) in each of the examples below. Fill in the diagram next to each example. You'll find the answers in Appendix A in the back of the book.

1. Sam is 3 years old. One night his parents build a roaring fire in the family room fireplace. The fire spits out a large ember that hits Sam in the arm, giving him a nasty burn that hurts a great deal for several hours. A week later, when Sam's parents light another fire in the fireplace, Sam becomes upset and fearful, crying and running from the room.

2. Melanie is driving to work on a rainy highway when she notices that the brake lights of all the cars just ahead of her have come on. She hits her brakes but watches in horror as her car glides into a four-car pileup. She's badly shaken up in the accident. A month later she's driving in the rain again and notices that she tenses up every time she sees brake lights come on ahead of her.

3. At the age of 24, Max has recently developed an allergy to cats. When he's in the same room with a cat for more than 30 minutes, he starts wheezing. After a few such allergic reactions, he starts wheezing as soon as he sees a cat in a room.

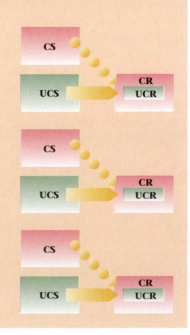

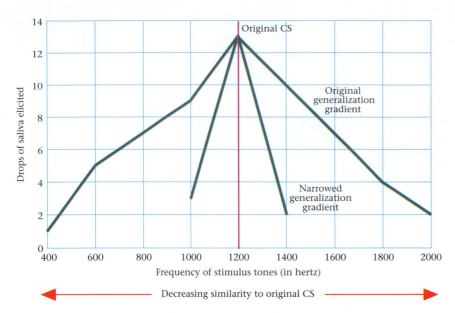

Figure 6.11
Stimulus discrimination and the generalization gradient. Stimulus discrimination is the inverse of stimulus generalization. Hence, as an organism gradually learns to discriminate between a CS and similar stimuli, the generalization gradient that maps out the organism's responding tends to narrow around the original CS.

Figure 6.12
Higher-order conditioning. Higher-order conditioning involves a two-phase process. In the first phase, a neutral stimulus (such as a tone) is paired with an unconditioned stimulus (such as meat powder) until it becomes a conditioned stimulus that elicits the response originally evoked by the UCS (such as salivation). In the second phase, another neutral stimulus (such as a red light) is paired with the previously established CS, so that it also acquires the capacity to elicit the response originally evoked by the UCS.

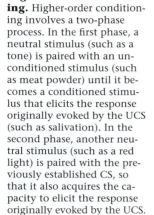

ally requires that the original CS (your car) continues to be paired with the UCS (your arrival) while similar stimuli (the other cars) are not paired with the UCS. As with generalization, a basic law governs discrimination: *The less similar new stimuli are to the original CS, the greater the likelihood (and ease) of discrimination.* Conversely, if a new stimulus is quite similar to the original CS, discrimination will be relatively difficult to learn. What happens to a generalization gradient when an organism learns a discrimination? The generalization gradient gradually narrows around the original CS, which means that the organism is generalizing to a smaller and smaller range of similar stimuli (see Figure 6.11).

Higher-Order Conditioning

Imagine that you were to conduct the following experiment. First, you condition a dog to salivate in response to the sound of a tone by pairing the tone with meat powder. Once the tone is firmly established as a CS, you pair the tone with a new stimulus, let's say a red light, for 15 trials. You then present the red light alone, without the tone. Will the dog salivate in response to the red light?

The answer is "yes." Even though the red light

has never been paired with the meat powder, it will acquire the capacity to elicit salivation by virtue of being paired with the tone (see Figure 6.12). This is a demonstration of *higher-order conditioning,* **in which a conditioned stimulus functions as if it were an unconditioned stimulus.** Higher-order conditioning shows that classical conditioning does not depend on the presence of a genuine, natural UCS. An already established CS will do just fine. In higher-order conditioning, new conditioned responses are built on the foundation of already established conditioned responses. Many human conditioned responses are the product of higher-order conditioning (Rescorla, 1980). The phenomenon of higher-order conditioning greatly extends the reach of classical conditioning.

Recap of Key Points

• Learning refers to a relatively durable change in behavior or knowledge due to experience. Classical conditioning explains how a neutral stimulus can acquire the capacity to elicit a response originally elicited by another stimulus. This kind of conditioning was originally described by Ivan Pavlov, who conditioned dogs to salivate in response to the sound of a tone.

• In classical conditioning, the unconditioned stimulus (UCS) is a stimulus that elicits an unconditioned response without previous conditioning. The unconditioned response (UCR) is an unlearned reaction to an unconditioned stimulus that occurs without previous conditioning. The conditioned stimulus (CS) is a previously neutral stimulus that has acquired the capacity to elicit a conditioned response. The conditioned response (CR) is a learned reaction to a conditioned stimulus.

• Classically conditioned responses are said to be elicited. Many kinds of everyday responses are regulated through classical conditioning, including phobias, anxiety responses, and pleasant emotional responses. Even subtle physiological responses such as immune system functioning respond to classical conditioning.

• Stimulus contiguity plays a key role in the acquisition of new conditioned responses. Short-delayed

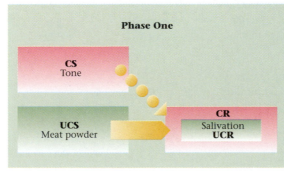

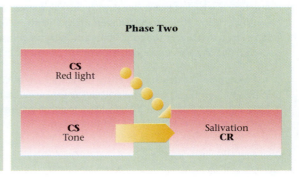

conditioning is the temporal arrangement that works best for acquisition. A conditioned response may be weakened and extinguished entirely when the CS is no longer paired with the UCS. In some cases, spontaneous recovery occurs, and an extinguished response reappears after a period of nonexposure to the CS. Extinction does not appear to involve unlearning.

• Conditioning may generalize to additional stimuli that are similar to the original CS. Watson and Rayner conducted an influential early study of generalization with a subject known as Little Albert, whose fear response to a rat generalized to a variety of other white, furry objects. Generalization gradients reflect the fact that the more similar new stimuli are to the original CS, the greater the likelihood of generalization.

• The opposite of generalization is discrimination, which involves not responding to stimuli that resemble the original CS. When an organism learns a discrimination, the generalization gradient narrows around the original CS. Higher-order conditioning occurs when a CS functions as if it were a UCS, to establish new conditioning.

OPERANT CONDITIONING

Even Pavlov recognized that classical conditioning is not the only form of conditioning. Classical conditioning best explains reflexive responding that is largely controlled by stimuli that *precede* the response. However, humans and other animals make a great many responses that don't fit this description. Consider the response that you are engaging in right now: studying. It is definitely not a reflex (life might be easier if it were). The stimuli that govern it (exams and grades) do not precede it. Instead, your studying is mainly influenced by stimulus events that *follow* the response—specifically, its *consequences*.

In the 1930s, this kind of learning was christened *operant conditioning* by B. F. Skinner. The term was derived from his belief that in this type of responding, an organism "operates" on the environment instead of simply reacting to stimuli. Learning occurs because responses come to be influenced by the outcomes that follow them. Thus, **operant conditioning is a form of learning in which responses come to be controlled by their consequences.** Learning theorists originally distinguished between classical and operant conditioning on the grounds that the former regulated reflexive, involuntary responses, whereas the latter governed voluntary responses. This distinction holds up much of the time, but it is not absolute. Research in recent decades has shown that classical conditioning sometimes contributes to the regulation of voluntary behavior, that operant conditioning can influence involuntary, visceral responses, and that the two types of conditioning jointly and interactively govern some aspects of behavior (Domjan, 1993; Turkkan, 1989).

Thorndike's Law of Effect

Another name for operant conditioning is **instrumental learning**, a term introduced earlier by Ed-

ward L. Thorndike (1913). Thorndike wanted to emphasize that this kind of responding is often *instrumental* in obtaining some desired outcome. His pioneering work provided the foundation for many of Skinner's ideas. Thorndike began studying animal learning around the turn of the century. Setting out to determine whether animals could think, he conducted some classic studies of problem solving in cats. In these studies, a hungry cat was placed in a small cage or "puzzle box" with food available just outside. The cat could escape to obtain the food by performing a specific response, such as pulling a wire or depressing a lever (see Figure 6.13). After each escape, the cat was rewarded with a small amount of food and then returned to the cage for another trial. Thorndike monitored how long it took the cat to get out of the box over a series of trials. If the cat could think, Thorndike reasoned, there would be a sudden drop in the time required to escape when the cat recognized the solution to the problem.

Instead of a sudden drop, Thorndike observed a

Figure 6.13
The learning curve of one of Thorndike's cats. The inset shows one of Thorndike's puzzle boxes. The cat had to perform three separate acts to escape the box, including depressing the pedal on the right. The learning curve shows how the cat's escape time declined gradually over a number of trials.

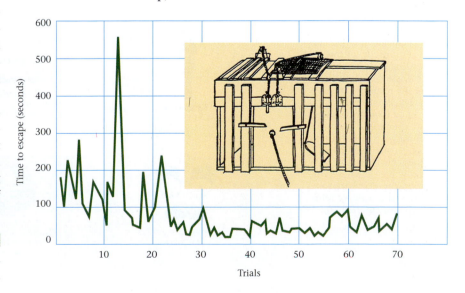

gradual, uneven decline in the time it took cats to escape from his puzzle boxes (see Figure 6.13). The decline in solution time showed that the cats *were* *learning*. But the gradual nature of this decline suggested that this learning did *not* depend on thinking and understanding. Instead, Thorndike attributed this learning to a principle he called the *law of effect*. According to the **law of effect, if a** **response in the presence of a stimulus leads to** **satisfying effects, the association between the** **stimulus and the response is strengthened.** Thorndike viewed instrumental learning as a mechanical process in which successful responses are gradually "stamped in" by their favorable effects. His law of effect became the cornerstone of Skinner's theory, although Skinner used different terminology.

Skinner's Demonstration: It's All a Matter of Consequences 5c

Like Pavlov, Skinner (1953, 1969, 1984) conducted some deceptively simple research that became enormously influential (Lattal, 1992). Ironically, he got off to an inauspicious start. His first book, *The Behavior of Organisms* (1938), sold only 80 copies in its first four years in print. Nonetheless, he went on to become, in the words of historian Albert Gilgen (1982), "without question the most famous American psychologist in the world" (p. 97).

The fundamental principle of operant conditioning is uncommonly simple and was anticipated by Thorndike's law of effect. *Skinner* *demonstrated that organisms tend to repeat those responses that are followed by favorable consequences.* This fundamental principle is embodied in

Skinner's concept of reinforcement. ***Reinforcement*** **occurs when an event following a response increases an organism's tendency to make that response.** In other words, a response is strengthened because it leads to rewarding consequences (see Figure 6.14).

The principle of reinforcement may be simple, but it is immensely powerful. Skinner and his followers have shown that much of everyday behavior is regulated by reinforcement. For example, you put money in a soda vending machine and you get a soft drink back as a result. You go to work because this behavior leads to your receiving paychecks. Perhaps you work extra hard because promotions and raises tend to follow such behavior. You tell jokes, and your friends laugh with you—so you tell some more. The principle of reinforcement clearly governs complex aspects of human behavior. Paradoxically, though, this principle emerged out of Skinner's research on the behavior of rats and pigeons in exceptionally simple situations. Let's look at that research.

Terminology and Procedures 5c

Like Pavlov, Skinner created a prototype experimental procedure that has been repeated (with variations) thousands of times. In this procedure, an animal, typically a rat or a pigeon, is placed in an *operant chamber* that has come to be better known as a "Skinner box." **An *operant chamber*,** **or *Skinner box,* is a small enclosure in which** **an animal can make a specific response that is** **recorded while the consequences of the response are systematically controlled.** In the boxes designed for rats, the main response made

"Operant conditioning shapes behavior as a sculptor shapes a lump of clay."

B. F. SKINNER

Figure 6.14
Reinforcement in operant conditioning. According to Skinner, reinforcement occurs when a response is followed by rewarding consequences and the organism's tendency to make the response increases. The two examples diagrammed here illustrate the basic premise of operant conditioning—that voluntary behavior is controlled by its consequences. These examples involve positive reinforcement (for a comparison of positive and negative reinforcement, see Figure 6.20).

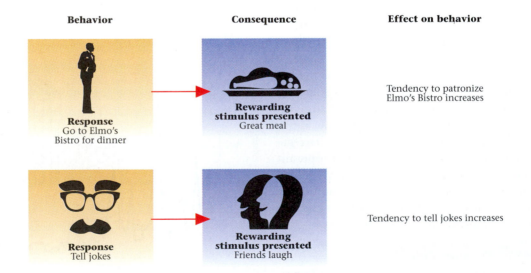

available is pressing a small lever mounted on one side wall (see Figure 6.15). In the boxes made for pigeons, the designated response is pecking a small disk mounted on a side wall. Because operant responses *tend* to be voluntary, they are said to be *emitted* rather than *elicited*. **To *emit* means to send forth.**

The Skinner box permits the experimenter to control the reinforcement contingencies that are in effect for the animal. ***Reinforcement contingencies are the circumstances or rules that determine whether responses lead to the presentation of reinforcers.*** Typically, the experimenter manipulates whether positive consequences occur when the animal makes the designated response. The main positive consequence is usually delivery of a small bit of food into a food cup mounted in the chamber. Because the animals are deprived of food for a while prior to the experimental session, their hunger virtually ensures that the food serves as a reinforcer.

The key dependent variable in most research on operant conditioning is the subjects' *response rate* over time. An animal's rate of lever pressing or disk pecking in the Skinner box is monitored continuously by a device known as a cumulative recorder (see Figure 6.15). **The *cumulative recorder* creates a graphic record of responding and reinforcement in a Skinner box as a function of time.** The recorder works by means of a roll of paper that moves at a steady rate underneath a movable pen. When there is no responding, the pen stays still and draws a straight horizontal line, reflecting the passage of time. Whenever the designated response occurs, however, the pen moves upward a notch. The pen's movements produce a graphic summary of the animal's responding over time. The pen also makes slash marks to record the delivery of each reinforcer.

The results of operant-conditioning studies are usually portrayed in graphs. In these graphs, the horizontal axis is used to mark the passage of time, while the vertical axis is used to plot the accumulation of responses, as shown in Figure 6.16 (on page 230). In interpreting these graphs, the key consideration is the *slope* of the line that represents the record of responding. *A rapid response rate produces a steep slope, whereas a slow response rate produces a shallow slope.* Because the response record is cumulative, the line never goes down. It can only go up as more responses are made or flatten out if the response rate slows to zero. The magnifications shown in Figure 6.16 show how slope and response rate are related.

Figure 6.15
Skinner box and cumulative recorder. (**a**) This diagram highlights some of the key features of an operant chamber, or Skinner box. In this apparatus designed for rats, the response under study is lever pressing. Food pellets, which may serve as reinforcers, are delivered into the food cup on the right. The speaker and light permit manipulations of visual and auditory stimuli, and the electric grid gives the experimenter control over aversive consequences (shock) in the box. (**b**) A cumulative recorder connected to the box keeps a continuous record of responses and reinforcements. Each lever press moves the pen up a step, and each reinforcement is marked with a slash. (**c**) This photo shows the real thing—a rat being conditioned in a Skinner box. Note the food dispenser on the left, which was omitted from the top diagram.

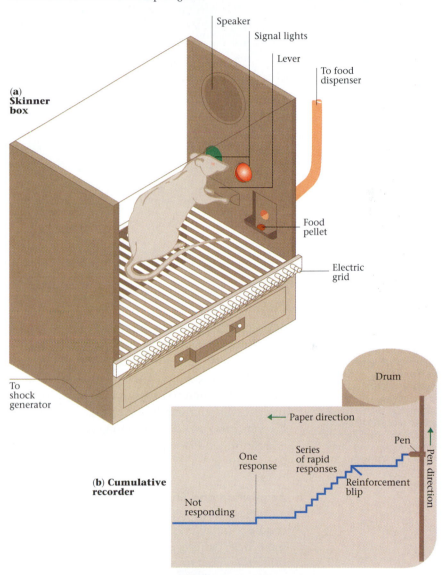

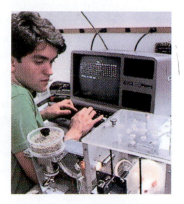

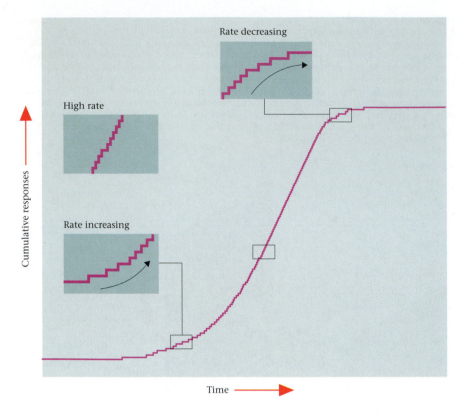

Rate decreasing

High rate

Rate increasing

Cumulative responses

Time

Figure 6.16
A graphic portrayal of operant responding. The results of operant conditioning are often summarized in a graph of cumulative responses over time. The insets magnify small segments of the curve to show how an increasing response rate yields a progressively steeper slope (bottom); a high, steady response rate yields a steep, stable slope (middle); and a decreasing response rate yields a progressively flatter slope (top).

Basic Processes in Operant Conditioning

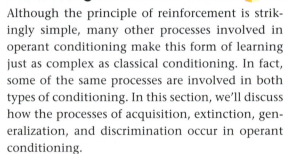

5c

Although the principle of reinforcement is strikingly simple, many other processes involved in operant conditioning make this form of learning just as complex as classical conditioning. In fact, some of the same processes are involved in both types of conditioning. In this section, we'll discuss how the processes of acquisition, extinction, generalization, and discrimination occur in operant conditioning.

Acquisition and Shaping

As in classical conditioning, *acquisition* in operant conditioning refers to the initial stage of learning some new pattern of responding. However, the procedures used to establish a tendency to emit an operant response are different from those used to create the typical conditioned response. Operant responses are usually established through a gradual process called *shaping*: **the reinforcement of closer and closer approximations of a desired response.**

Shaping is necessary when an organism does not, on its own, emit the desired response. For example, when a rat is first placed in a Skinner box, it may not press the lever at all. In this case an experimenter begins shaping by releasing food pellets whenever the rat moves toward the lever. As this response becomes more frequent, the experimenter starts requiring a closer approximation of the desired response, possibly releasing food only when the rat actually touches the lever. As reinforcement increases the rat's tendency to touch the lever, the rat will spontaneously press the lever on occasion, finally providing the experimenter with an opportunity to reinforce the designated response. These reinforcements will gradually increase the rate of lever pressing.

The mechanism of shaping is the key to training animals to perform impressive tricks. When you go to a zoo, circus, or marine park and see bears riding bicycles, monkeys playing the piano, and whales leaping through hoops, you are witnessing the results of shaping. To demonstrate the power of shaping techniques, Skinner once trained some pigeons so that they appeared to play Ping-Pong. They would run about on opposite ends of a Ping-Pong table and peck the ball back and forth. Keller and Marian Breland, a couple of psychologists influenced by Skinner, went into the business of training animals for advertising and entertainment purposes. One of their better known feats was shaping "Priscilla, the Fastidious Pig" to turn on a radio, eat at a kitchen table, put dirty clothes in a hamper, run a vacuum, and then "go shopping" with a shopping cart. Of course, Priscilla picked the sponsor's product off the shelf in her shopping expedition (Breland & Breland, 1961).

Shaping can also be used to mold complex human behavior. For example, *programmed learning* is an application of the shaping principle to educational efforts (Keller, 1968). **Programmed learning is an approach to self-instruction in which information and questions are arranged in a sequence of small steps to permit active responding by the learner.** Questions are set up so that material presented in previous steps makes them easy to answer. This technique may sound foreign to you, but you have probably used it. Many study guides that accompany textbooks use this approach, and most computer-aided instruction also depends on it. Programmed learning provides for rapid and frequent reinforcement of learning efforts by giving the student immediate feedback (the assumption is that correctly answering questions is reinforcing). It involves shaping in that it helps the learner acquire more complex responses through gradual, orderly reinforcement of smaller component responses.

Extinction

In operant conditioning, *extinction* refers to the gradual weakening and disappearance of a response tendency because the response is no longer followed by a reinforcer. Extinction begins in operant conditioning whenever previously available reinforcement is stopped. In laboratory studies with rats, this usually means that the experimenter stops delivering food when the rat presses the lever. When the extinction process is begun, a brief surge often occurs in the rat's responding, followed by a gradual decline in response rate until it approaches zero (see Figure 6.17 on page 232).

The same effects are generally seen in the extinction of human behaviors. Let's say that a child routinely cries at bedtime and that this response is reinforced by attention from mom and dad. If the parents decided to cut off further reinforcement by ignoring the crying, they would be attempting to extinguish this undesirable response. Typically, the child increases its crying behavior for a few days, and then the crying tapers off fairly quickly (Williams, 1959).

A key issue in operant conditioning is how much *resistance to extinction* an organism will display when reinforcement is halted. **Resistance to extinction occurs when an organism continues to make a response after delivery of the reinforcer for it has been terminated.** The greater the resistance to extinction, the longer the responding will continue (see Figure 6.17). Thus, if a researcher

stops giving reinforcement for lever pressing and the response tapers off slowly, the response shows high resistance to extinction. However, if the response tapers off quickly, it shows relatively little resistance to extinction.

Resistance to extinction may sound like a matter of purely theoretical interest, but it's actually quite practical. People often want to strengthen a response in such a way that it will be relatively resistant to extinction. For instance, most parents want to see their child's studying response survive even if the child hits a rocky stretch when studying doesn't lead to reinforcement (good grades).

Shaping—an operant technique in which an organism is rewarded for closer and closer approximations of the desired response—is used in teaching both animals and humans. It is the main means of training animals to perform tricks.

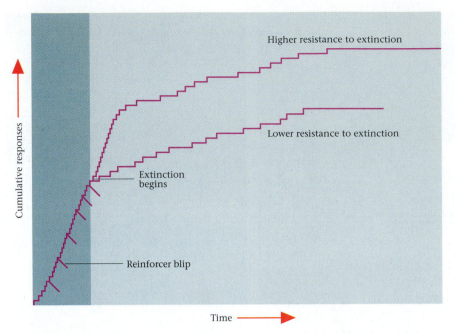

Higher resistance to extinction

Lower resistance to extinction

Extinction begins

Reinforcer blip

Cumulative responses

Time

Figure 6.17
Extinction in operant conditioning. Extinction begins when a response is no longer followed by a reinforcer. Responding persists for a time, but extinction eventually produces a gradual decline in response rate, as can be seen in both graphs of extinction shown here. Responses that are more resistant to extinction taper off more slowly (top graph) than responses that are less resistant to extinction (bottom graph).

This pigeon is learning that pecking the disk pays off only if the disk is lit. The light that signals the availability of the food reinforcer is a discriminative stimulus.

In a similar fashion, a casino wants to see patrons continue to gamble, even if they encounter a lengthy losing streak. Thus, a high degree of resistance to extinction can be desirable in many situations. Resistance to extinction depends on a variety of factors. Chief among them is the *schedule of reinforcement* used during acquisition, a matter that we will discuss a little later in this chapter.

Stimulus Control: Generalization and Discrimination

Operant responding is ultimately controlled by its consequences, as organisms learn response-outcome (R-O) associations (Colwill, 1993). However, stimuli that *precede* a response can also exert considerable influence over operant behavior. When a response is consistently followed by a reinforcer in the presence of a particular stimulus, that stimulus comes to serve as a "signal" indicating that the response is likely to lead to a reinforcer. Once an organism learns the signal, it tends to respond accordingly (Honig & Alsop, 1992). For example, a pigeon's disk pecking may be reinforced only when a small light behind the disk is lit (see the photo below). When the light is out, pecking does not lead to the reward. Pigeons quickly learn to peck the disk only when it is lit. The light that signals the availability of reinforcement is called a discriminative stimulus. *Discriminative stimuli* are cues that influence operant behavior by indicating the probable consequences (reinforcement or nonreinforcement) of a response.

Discriminative stimuli play a key role in the regulation of operant behavior. For example, birds learn that hunting for worms is likely to be reinforced after a rain. Children learn to ask for sweets when their parents are in a good mood. Drivers learn to slow down when the highway is wet. Human social behavior is also regulated extensively by discriminative stimuli. Consider the behavior of asking someone out for a date. Many people emit this response only very cautiously, after receiving many signals (such as eye contact, smiles, encouraging conversational exchanges) that reinforcement (a favorable answer) is fairly likely. In fact, learning to read subtle discriminative stimuli in social interaction is a major part of developing good social skills. Socially unskilled people have difficulty decoding social cues from others (Goldenthal, 1985).

Reactions to a discriminative stimulus are governed by the processes of *stimulus generalization* and *stimulus discrimination*, just like reactions to a CS in classical conditioning. For instance, envision a cat that comes running into the kitchen whenever it hears the sound of a can opener because that sound has become a discriminative stimulus signaling a good chance of its getting fed. If the cat also responded to the sound of a new kitchen appliance (say a blender), this response would represent *generalization*—responding to a new stimulus as if it were the original. *Discrimination* would occur if the cat learned to respond only to the can opener and not to the blender.

As you have learned in this section, the processes of acquisition, extinction, generalization, and discrimination in operant conditioning parallel these same processes in classical conditioning. Table 6.1 compares these processes in the two kinds of conditioning.

Reinforcement: Consequences That Strengthen Responses 5e

Although it is convenient to equate reinforcement with reward and the experience of pleasure, strict behaviorists object to this practice. Why? Because the experience of pleasure is an unobservable event that takes place within an organism. As explained in Chapter 1, most behaviorists believe that scientific assertions must be limited to what can be observed.

In keeping with this orientation, Skinner said that reinforcement occurs whenever an outcome strengthens a response, as measured by an increase in the rate of responding. This definition avoids the issue of what the organism is feeling and focuses on observable events. The central process in reinforcement is the *strengthening of a response tendency.* To know whether an event is reinforcing, researchers must make it contingent on a response and observe whether the rate of this response increases after the supposed reinforcer has been presented.

Thus, reinforcement is defined *after the fact,* in terms of its *effect* on behavior. Something that is clearly reinforcing for an organism at one time may not function as a reinforcer later (Catania, 1992). Food will reinforce lever pressing by a rat only if the rat is hungry. Similarly, something that serves as a reinforcer for one person may not function as a reinforcer for another person. For example, parental approval is a potent reinforcer for most children, but not all.

Delayed Reinforcement

In operant conditioning, a favorable outcome is much more likely to strengthen a response if the outcome follows *immediately.* If a delay occurs between a response and the positive outcome, the response may not be strengthened. Furthermore, studies show that the longer the delay between the designated response and the delivery of the reinforcer, the more slowly conditioning proceeds (Church, 1989; Mazur, 1993).

The relative weakness of a delayed reinforcer is easy to understand in animals because the delay may obscure the connection between the response and the reinforcement. However, a delayed reinforcer is also less effective with *humans* who are well aware of the link between their response and the eventual presentation of the reinforcer. Although people sometimes manage to bridge long delays, they prefer immediate gratification. This is one reason why many people find it difficult to lose weight. The reward for eating is immediate, while the reward for not eating (a trimmer, healthier body) is months away.

Conditioned Reinforcement

Operant theorists make a distinction between unlearned, or primary, reinforcers as opposed to conditioned, or secondary, reinforcers. **Primary reinforcers are events that are inherently reinforcing because they satisfy biological needs.** A given species has a limited number of primary reinforcers because they are closely tied to physiological needs. In humans, primary reinforcers include food, water, warmth, sex, and perhaps affection expressed through hugging and close bodily contact.

Secondary, or conditioned, reinforcers **are events that acquire reinforcing qualities by being associated with primary reinforcers.** The events that function as secondary reinforcers vary among members of a species because they depend on learning.

TABLE 6.1 COMPARISON OF BASIC PROCESSES IN CLASSICAL AND OPERANT CONDITIONING

Process and Definition	Description in Classical Conditioning	Description in Operant Conditioning
Acquisition: The initial stage of learning	CS and UCS are paired, gradually resulting in CR.	Responding gradually increases because of reinforcement, possibly through shaping.
Extinction: The gradual weakening and disappearance of a conditioned response tendency	CS is presented alone until it no longer elicits CR.	Responding gradually slows and stops after reinforcement is terminated.
Stimulus generalization: An organism's responding to stimuli other than the original stimulus used in conditioning	CR is elicited by new stimulus that resembles original CS.	Responding increases in the presence of new stimulus that resembles original discriminative stimulus.
Stimulus discrimination: An organism's lack of response to stimuli that are similar to the original stimulus used in conditioning	CR is not elicited by new stimulus that resembles original CS.	Responding does not increase in the presence of new stimulus that resembles original discriminative stimulus.

Examples of common secondary reinforcers in humans include money, good grades, attention, flattery, praise, and applause. Most of the material things that people work hard to earn are secondary reinforcers. For example, people learn to find stylish clothes, sports cars, fine jewelry, elegant china, and state-of-the-art stereos reinforcing.

Recap of Key Points

• Operant conditioning involves largely voluntary responses that are governed by their consequences. Thorndike paved the way for Skinner's work by investigating instrumental conditioning and describing the law of effect.

• Skinner pioneered the study of operant conditioning, working mainly with rats and pigeons in Skinner boxes. He demonstrated that organisms tend to repeat those responses that are followed by reinforcers. Operant responses are said to be emitted.

• The key dependent variable in operant conditioning is the rate of response over time, which is tracked by a device called a cumulative recorder. When responding over time is shown graphically, steep slopes indicate rapid responding.

• New operant responses can be shaped by gradually reinforcing closer and closer approximations of the desired response. Shaping is the key to training animals to perform impressive tricks. In operant conditioning, extinction occurs when reinforcement for a response is terminated and the rate of that response declines. There are variations in resistance to extinction—that is, how long an organism continues to make a response that is no longer reinforced.

• Operant responses are regulated by discriminative stimuli that are cues for the likelihood of obtaining reinforcers. These stimuli are subject to the same processes of generalization and discrimination that occur in classical conditioning.

• The central process in reinforcement is the strengthening of a response. Something that is reinforcing for an organism at one time may not be reinforcing later. Delayed reinforcement slows the process of conditioning. Primary reinforcers are unlearned; they are closely tied to the satisfaction of physiological needs. In contrast, secondary reinforcers acquire their reinforcing quality through conditioning.

Schedules of Reinforcement 5d

Organisms make innumerable responses that do *not* lead to favorable consequences. It would be nice if people were reinforced every time they took an exam, watched a movie, hit a golf shot, asked for a date, or made a sales call. However, in the real world most responses are reinforced only some of the time. How does this reality affect the potency of reinforcers? To find out, operant psychologists have devoted an enormous amount of attention to how *schedules of reinforcement* influence operant behavior (Ferster & Skinner, 1957; Skinner, 1938, 1953).

A *schedule of reinforcement* **determines which occurrences of a specific response result in the presentation of a reinforcer.** The simplest pattern is continuous reinforcement. *Continuous reinforcement* **occurs when every instance of a designated response is reinforced.** In the laboratory, experimenters often use continuous reinforcement to shape and establish a new response before moving on to more realistic schedules involving intermittent reinforcement. *Intermittent, or partial, reinforcement* **occurs when a designated response is reinforced only some of the time.**

Which do you suppose leads to longer-lasting effects—being reinforced every time you emit a response, or being reinforced only some of the time? Studies show that, given an equal number of reinforcements, *intermittent* reinforcement makes a response more resistant to extinction than continuous reinforcement does (Robbins, 1971; Schwartz & Robbins, 1995). In other words, organisms continue responding longer after removal of reinforcers when a response has been reinforced only *some* of the time.

In fact, schedules of reinforcement that provide only sporadic delivery of reinforcers can yield great resistance to extinction. This explains why behaviors that are reinforced only occasionally can be very durable. Consider a child who persists in throwing temper tantrums on a regular basis. The parents may be proud of the fact that they give in to these temper tantrums (thus reinforcing them) only about one in seven times. They believe that they are working toward eliminating the tantrums, and they may be mystified when the tantrums persist. Parents in this situation usually fail to realize that they are providing steady intermittent reinforcement for the tantrums. This schedule of reinforcement will make the temper tantrums relatively difficult to eliminate.

Reinforcement schedules come in many varieties, but four particular types of intermittent schedules have attracted the most interest. These schedules are described here along with examples drawn from the laboratory and everyday life (see Figure 6.18 for additional examples).

Ratio schedules require the organism to make the designated response a certain number of times to gain each reinforcer. **With a *fixed-ratio (FR) sched-**

ule, the reinforcer is given after a fixed number of nonreinforced responses. *Examples:* (1) A rat is reinforced for every tenth lever press. (2) A salesperson receives a bonus for every fourth set of encyclopedias sold. **With a *variable-ratio (VR) schedule*, the reinforcer is given after a variable number of nonreinforced responses.** The number of nonreinforced responses varies around a predetermined average. *Examples:* (1) A rat is reinforced for every tenth lever press on the average. The exact number of responses required for reinforcement varies from one time to the next. (2) A slot machine in a casino pays off once every six tries on the average. The number of nonwinning responses between payoffs varies greatly from one time to the next.

Interval schedules require a time period to pass between the presentation of reinforcers. **With a *fixed-interval (FI) schedule*, the reinforcer is given for the first response that occurs after a fixed time interval has elapsed.** *Examples:* (1) A rat is reinforced for the first lever press after a 2-minute interval has elapsed and then must wait 2 minutes before being able to earn the next reinforcement. (2) A man washing his clothes periodically checks to see whether each load is finished. The reward (clean clothes) is only available after a fixed time interval (corresponding to how long the washer takes to complete a cycle) has elapsed, and checking responses during the interval is not reinforced. **With a *variable-interval (VI) schedule*, the reinforcer is given for the first response after a variable time interval has elapsed.** The interval length varies around a predetermined average. *Examples:* (1) A rat is reinforced for the first lever press after a 1-minute interval has elapsed, but the following intervals are 3 minutes, 2 minutes, 4 minutes, and so on—with an average length of 2 minutes. (2) A person repeatedly dials a busy phone number (getting through is the reinforcer).

More than 40 years of research has yielded an enormous volume of data on how these schedules of reinforcement are related to patterns of responding (Williams, 1988; Zeiler, 1977). Some of the more prominent findings are summarized in Figure 6.19, which depicts typical response patterns generated by each schedule. For example, with fixed-interval schedules, a pause in responding usually occurs after each reinforcer is delivered, and then responding gradually increases to a rapid rate at the end of the interval. This pattern of behavior yields a "scalloped" response curve. In general, ratio schedules tend to produce more rapid responding than interval schedules. Why? Because

Figure 6.18
Reinforcement schedules in everyday life. Complex human behaviors are regulated by schedules of reinforcement. Piecework in factories is reinforced on a fixed-ratio schedule. Playing roulette is based on variable-ratio reinforcement. Watching the clock at work is rewarded on a fixed-interval basis (the arrival of quitting time is the reinforcer). Surfers waiting for a big wave are rewarded on a variable-interval basis.

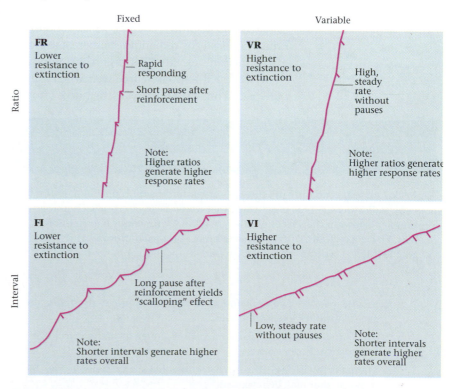

Figure 6.19
Schedules of reinforcement and patterns of response. Each type of reinforcement schedule tends to generate a characteristic pattern of responding. In general, ratio schedules tend to produce more rapid responding than interval schedules (note the steep slopes of the FR and VR curves). In comparison to fixed schedules, variable schedules tend to yield steadier responding (note the smoother lines for the VR and VI schedules on the right) and greater resistance to extinction.

faster responding leads to reinforcement sooner when a ratio schedule is in effect. Variable schedules tend to generate steadier response rates and greater resistance to extinction than their fixed counterparts.

Most of the research on reinforcement schedules was conducted on rats and pigeons in Skinner boxes. However, the available evidence suggests that humans react to schedules of reinforcement in much the same way as lower animals (De Villiers, 1977; Perone, Galizio, & Baron, 1988). For example, when animals are placed on ratio schedules, shifting to a higher ratio (that is, requiring more responses per reinforcement) tends to generate faster responding. People who run factories that pay on a piecework basis (a fixed-ratio schedule) have seen the same reaction in humans. Shifting to a higher ratio (more pieces for the same pay) usually stimulates harder work and greater productivity (although workers often complain).

There are many other parallels between animals' and humans' reactions to different schedules of reinforcement. For instance, with rats and pigeons, variable-ratio schedules yield steady responding and great resistance to extinction. Similar effects are routinely observed among people who gamble. Most gambling is reinforced according to variable-ratio schedules, which tend to produce rapid, steady responding and great resistance to extinction—exactly what casino operators want. The scalloped response curve seen when animals are placed on a fixed-interval schedule is also seen when humans work under this schedule. For example, consider what happens when the exams in a course occur every three weeks (a fixed-interval schedule). There's usually a pause in responding (studying) after each reinforcer (exam), and responding becomes very rapid (cramming) as each interval comes to an end.

In summary, schedules of reinforcement are powerful determinants of patterns of responding. Human behavior is routinely regulated by these schedules, although most people are unaware of their operation.

Positive Reinforcement Versus Negative Reinforcement 5e

According to Skinner, reinforcement can take two forms, which he called *positive reinforcement* and *negative reinforcement*. **Positive reinforcement occurs when a response is strengthened because it is followed by the presentation of a rewarding stimulus.** Thus far, for purposes of simplicity, our examples of reinforcement have involved positive reinforcement. Good grades, tasty meals, paychecks, scholarships, promotions, nice clothes, nifty cars, attention, and flattery are all positive reinforcers.

In contrast, **negative reinforcement occurs when a response is strengthened because it is followed by the removal of an aversive (unpleasant) stimulus.** Don't let the word *negative* confuse you. Negative reinforcement *is* reinforcement. Like all reinforcement it involves a favorable outcome that *strengthens* a response tendency. However, this strengthening takes place because a response leads to the *removal of an aversive stimulus* rather than the arrival of a pleasant stimulus (see Figure 6.20).

In laboratory studies, negative reinforcement is usually accomplished as follows. While a rat is in a Skinner box, a moderate electric shock is delivered to the animal through the floor of the box. When the rat presses the lever, the shock is turned off for a period of time. Thus, lever pressing leads to removal of an aversive stimulus (shock). Although this sequence of events is different from those for positive reinforcement, it reliably strengthens the rat's lever-pressing response.

Everyday human behavior is regulated extensively by negative reinforcement. Consider a handful of examples. You rush home in the winter to get out of the cold. You clean house to get rid of a disgusting mess. You give in to your child's begging to halt the whining. You take medication to get rid of pain or discomfort. You give in to a

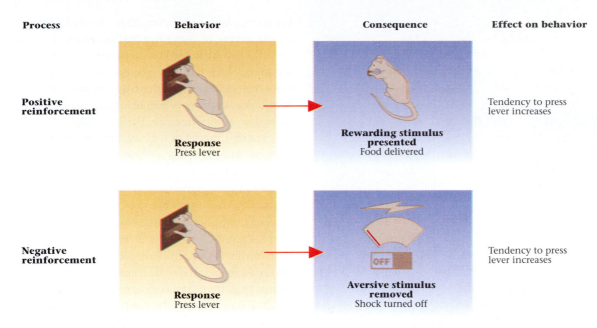

Process	Behavior	Consequence	Effect on behavior

Positive reinforcement

Response Press lever

Rewarding stimulus presented Food delivered

Tendency to press lever increases

Negative reinforcement

Response Press lever

Aversive stimulus removed Shock turned off

Tendency to press lever increases

Figure 6.20
Positive reinforcement versus negative reinforcement. In positive reinforcement, a response leads to the presentation of a rewarding stimulus. In negative reinforcement, a response leads to the removal of an aversive stimulus. Both types of reinforcement involve favorable consequences and both have the same effect on behavior: The organism's tendency to emit the reinforced response is strengthened.

roommate or spouse to bring an unpleasant argument to an end.

Negative Reinforcement and Avoidance Behavior 5f

As you have probably noticed, many people tend to avoid facing awkward situations, difficult challenges, and sticky personal problems. Consistent reliance on avoidance is unfortunate. It's not a healthful or effective coping strategy. How do people learn to rely on such a strategy? In large part, it may be through negative reinforcement.

Escape Learning

The roots of avoidance lie in escape learning. In *escape learning* an organism acquires a response that decreases or ends some aversive stimulation. Psychologists often study escape learning in the laboratory with rats that are conditioned in a *shuttle box*. The shuttle box has two compartments connected by a doorway, which can be opened and closed by the experimenter, as depicted in Figure 6.21(a) on page 238. In a typical study, an animal is placed in one compartment and the shock in the floor of that chamber is turned on, with the doorway open. The animal learns to escape the shock by running to the other compartment. This escape response leads to the removal of an aversive stimulus (shock), so it is strengthened through negative reinforcement. If you were to leave a party where you were getting picked on by peers, you would be engaging in an escape response. Escape learning doesn't necessarily entail leaving the scene of the aversive stimulation. Any behavior that decreases or ends aversive stimula-

tion (for example, turning on the air conditioner to get rid of stifling heat) represents escape learning.

Avoidance Learning

Escape learning often leads to avoidance learning. In *avoidance learning* an organism acquires a response that prevents some aversive stimulation from occurring. In laboratory studies of avoidance learning, the experimenter simply gives the animal a signal that shock is forthcoming. The typical signal is a light that goes on a few seconds prior to the shock. At first the rat runs only when shocked (escape learning). Gradually, however, the animal learns to run to the safe compartment as soon as the light comes on, demonstrating avoidance learning. Similarly, if you were to quit going to parties because of your concern about being picked on by peers, this would represent avoidance learning. Turning on air conditioning *before* a room gets hot would also represent an avoidance response.

Avoidance learning presents an interesting puzzle for learning theorists. Avoidance responses tend to be long-lasting even though the mechanism of continuing reinforcement is obscure. For example, when an animal in a shuttle box learns to avoid shock entirely, it seems to have no opportunity for continued negative reinforcement. After all, the animal can't remove shock that never occurs. In theory, the avoidance response should gradually extinguish, because it is no longer followed by the removal of an aversive stimulus. However, avoidance responses usually remain strong. The best explanation of this paradox appears to be O. Hobart Mowrer's (1947) two-process theory of avoidance.

(a)

Figure 6.21
Escape and avoidance learning. (a) Escape and avoidance learning are often studied with a shuttle box like that shown here. Warning signals, shock, and the animal's ability to flee from one compartment to another can be controlled by the experimenter. (b) According to Mowrer's two-process theory, avoidance begins because classical conditioning creates a conditioned fear that is elicited by the warning signal (panel 1). Avoidance continues because it is maintained by operant conditioning (panel 2). Specifically, the avoidance response is strengthened through negative reinforcement, since it leads to removal of the conditioned fear.

(b) **1. Classical conditioning**

CS Light		
UCS Shock	→	CR Fear UCR

2. Operant conditioning
(negative reinforcement)

Response		Aversive stimulus removed
Run away	→	Conditioned fear reduced

Two-Process Theory of Avoidance

Mowrer's explanation is known as the *two-process theory* because it integrates the processes of classical and operant conditioning. According to this theory, the warning light that goes on in the shuttle box becomes a CS (through classical conditioning) eliciting conditioned fear in the animal. At the same time, the response of fleeing to the other side of the box is operant behavior. In Mowrer's scheme, this response produces negative reinforcement, even after shock is no longer experienced, *because it reduces conditioned fear.* Fear is decidedly unpleasant, and a response that reduces fear should be strengthened through negative reinforcement. In short, two-process theory appears to solve our riddle by asserting that the avoidance response removes an *internal* aversive stimulus—conditioned fear—rather than an external aversive stimulus, such as shock. This idea is diagrammed in Figure 6.21(b).

There are some "holes" in the two-process theory of avoidance. For instance, if it is the reduction of conditioned fear that reinforces avoidance behav-

ior, then avoidance performance should be related to the degree of fear exhibited by animals. However, there is little correlation between an animal's apparent fear and its avoidance performance (Mineka, 1979). Thus, the two-process theory of avoidance learning is still being refined (Bolles & Fanselow, 1980; Hineline, 1981). Nonetheless, it is an excellent model of why avoidance behaviors—such as phobias—are so resistant to extinction (Levis, 1989).

For example, suppose you have a phobia of elevators. According to two-process theory, you acquired your phobia through classical conditioning. At some point in your past, elevators became paired with a frightening stimulus event. Now whenever you need to use an elevator, you experience conditioned fear. If your phobia is severe, you probably take the stairs instead. Taking the stairs is an avoidance response that should lead to consistent negative reinforcement by relieving your conditioned fear.

Thus, phobias are thought to be highly resistant to extinction for two reasons. First, a phobia usually leads to an avoidance response that earns negative reinforcement each time it is made. Second, avoidance behavior prevents any opportunity to extinguish the phobic conditioned response because the person is never exposed to the conditioned stimulus (in this case, riding in an elevator).

Punishment: Consequences That Weaken Responses 5e

Reinforcement is defined in terms of its consequences. It *increases* an organism's tendency to make a certain response. Are there also consequences that *decrease* an organism's tendency to make a particular response? Yes. In Skinner's model of operant behavior, such consequences are called *punishment.*

***Punishment* occurs when an event following a response decreases the tendency to make that response.** In Skinner boxes, the administration of punishment is very simple. When a rat presses the lever or a pigeon pecks the disk, it receives a brief shock. This procedure usually leads to a rapid decline in the animal's response rate. Punishment typically involves presentation of an aversive stimulus (for instance, spanking a child). However, punishment may also involve the removal of a rewarding stimulus (for instance, taking away a child's TV-watching privileges).

The concept of punishment in operant conditioning is confusing to many students on two counts. First, they often confuse it with negative

238   CHAPTER SIX

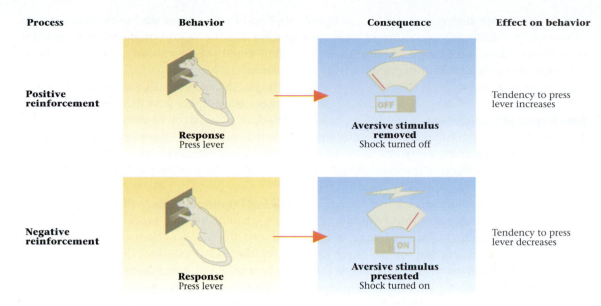

Process	Behavior	Consequence	Effect on behavior

Positive reinforcement

Response — Press lever

Aversive stimulus **removed** — Shock turned off

Tendency to press lever increases

Negative reinforcement

Response — Press lever

Aversive stimulus **presented** — Shock turned on

Tendency to press lever decreases

Figure 6.22

Comparison of negative reinforcement and punishment. Although punishment can occur when a response leads to the removal of a rewarding stimulus, it more typically involves the presentation of an aversive stimulus. Students often confuse punishment with negative reinforcement because they associate both with aversive stimuli. However, as this diagram shows, punishment and negative reinforcement represent opposite procedures that have opposite effects on behavior.

reinforcement, which is entirely different. Negative reinforcement involves the *removal* of an aversive stimulus, thereby *strengthening* a response. Punishment, on the other hand, involves the *presentation* of an aversive stimulus, thereby *weakening* a response. Thus, punishment and negative reinforcement are opposite procedures that yield opposite effects on behavior (see Figure 6.22).

The second source of confusion is that students tend to view punishment in an overly narrow way, equating it with the disciplinary procedures used by parents, teachers, and other authority figures. In the operant model, punishment occurs any time undesirable consequences weaken a response tendency. Defined in this way, the concept of punishment goes far beyond things like parents spanking children and teachers handing out detentions. For example, if you wear a new outfit and your friends promptly make fun of it, your behavior will have been punished and your tendency to emit this response (wear the same clothing) will probably decline. Similarly, if you go to a restaurant and have a horrible meal, your response will have been punished, and your tendency to go to that restaurant will probably decline.

Although he touted the power of reinforcement, Skinner (1938, 1953) argued that punishment is *not* a particularly powerful means of influencing behavior. He based his assertion mainly on studies that manipulated the punishment of lever pressing by rats. Skinner found that the strength of the lever-pressing response recovered quickly once the punishment was halted. He concluded that punishment only *temporarily suppresses* responding rather than producing a genuine, durable weakening of response strength. His research led many

theorists to downplay the effectiveness of punishment for many years.

After decades of research, however, it is now clear that the effects of punishment are just as durable as the effects of reinforcement (Fantino, 1973; Hilgard & Bower, 1981). The reappearance of a response when punishment stops is no different than the disappearance of a response when positive reinforcement stops. After all, the frequency of an operant response is *supposed* to change when the consequences of the response change. Thus, the current assumption is that punishment *can* be just as influential as reinforcement.

Although punishment in operant conditioning encompasses far more than disciplinary acts, it *is*

CONCEPT CHECK 6.3

Recognizing Outcomes in Operant Conditioning

Check your understanding of the various types of consequences that can occur in operant conditioning by indicating whether the examples below involve positive reinforcement (PR), negative reinforcement (NR), punishment (P), or extinction (E). The answers can be found in Appendix A.

_____ 1. Lyle gets a speeding ticket.

_____ 2. Diane's supervisor compliments her on her hard work.

_____ 3. Leon goes to the health club for a rare workout and pushes himself so hard that his entire body aches and he throws up.

_____ 4. Audrey lets her dog out so she won't have to listen to its whimpering.

_____ 5. Richard shoots up heroin to ward off tremors and chills associated with heroin withdrawal.

_____ 6. Edna constantly complains about minor aches and pains to obtain sympathy from colleagues at work. Three co-workers who share an office with her decide to ignore her complaints instead of responding with sympathy.

used frequently for disciplinary purposes. In light of this reality, research on punishment takes on special significance. Let's look at the implications of operant research for the use of punishment as a disciplinary measure.

Side Effects of Punishment

A key problem with punishment is that even when it is effective in weakening a response, it can have unintended side effects (Newsom, Favell, & Rincover, 1983; Van Houten, 1983). One of these side effects is the *general suppression of behavioral activity*. In other words, punishment can suppress many responses besides the punished one. In the laboratory, punished rats may simply freeze up. Similarly, some children who are frequently and severely punished become withdrawn, inhibited, and less active than other children. It is also common for punishment to trigger *strong emotional responses*, including fear, anxiety, anger, and resentment. Strong emotions can temporarily disrupt normal functioning and generate hostility toward the source of the punishment, such as a parent.

Finally, *physical* punishment, which remains common in efforts to discipline children (Straus & Gelles, 1986), often leads to an increase in *aggressive behavior*. Children who are subjected to a lot

Although physical punishment is frequently administered to suppress aggressive behavior, in the long run it actually is associated with an increase in aggressive behavior.

of physical punishment tend to become more aggressive than the average youngster (Parke & Slaby, 1983). You'll see why shortly, when we discuss observational learning.

The truckload of side effects associated with punishment make it less than ideal as a disciplinary procedure. Research on operant conditioning suggests that disciplinary goals can often be accomplished more effectively by *reinforcing desirable behavior* than by *punishing undesirable behavior*.

Making Punishment More Effective

Although punishment is probably overused in disciplinary efforts, it does have a role to play. Fortunately, the undesirable side effects of punishment can be minimized if punishment is handled skillfully. The following guidelines summarize evidence on how to make punishment effective while reducing its side effects (Axelrod & Apsche, 1983; Parke, 1977; Walters & Grusec, 1977).

1. *Apply punishment swiftly.* A delay in delivering punishment—like a delay in delivering reinforcement—undermines its impact. When a parent who is reluctant to punish a child says, "Wait until your father (or mother) gets home . . ." a fundamental mistake in the use of punishment is being made. This problem with delayed punishment also explains the ineffectiveness of punishing a pet hours after it has misbehaved, when the owner finally returns home. For instance, it won't do any good to hit your dog with a newspaper while shoving its face in the feces it previously left on your carpet. This common punishment doesn't teach your dog to stop defecating on your carpet— it teaches the dog to keep its face out of its feces.

2. *Use punishment just severe enough to be effective.* The intensity of punishment is a two-edged sword. Severe punishments usually are more effective in weakening unwanted responses. However, they also increase the likelihood of undesirable side effects. Thus, it's best to use the least severe punishment that seems likely to have some impact.

3. *Make punishment consistent.* Punishment differs markedly from reinforcement when it comes to the effects of consistency. If you want to eliminate a response, you should punish the response every time it occurs. Intermittent schedules of punishment are ineffective in weakening responses. When parents are inconsistent about punishing a particular behavior, they create more confusion than learning.

4. *Explain the punishment.* When children are punished, the reason for their punishment should

be explained as fully as possible, given the constraints of their age. The more that children understand why they are being punished, the more effective the punishment tends to be.

5. *Make an alternative response available and reinforce it.* One shortcoming of punishment is that it only tells a child what *not* to do. Operant responses usually help to obtain some kind of goal. Thus, the response you want to eliminate through punishment probably has a purpose. Reinforcing another response that serves the same purpose usually hastens the weakening of the punished response. For example, many troublesome behaviors emitted by children are primarily attention-seeking devices. Punishment of such responses will be more effective if children are provided with more acceptable ways to gain attention.

6. *Minimize dependence on physical punishment.* Modest physical punishment may be necessary when children are too young to understand a verbal reprimand or the withdrawal of privileges. A light slap on the hand or bottom should suffice. Otherwise, physical punishment should be avoided, because it tends to increase aggressive behavior in children. Also, physical punishment often isn't as effective as most parents assume. Even a vigorous spanking isn't felt by a child an hour later. In contrast, withdrawing valued privileges can give children hours to contemplate the wisdom of changing their ways.

Recap of Key Points

• Schedules of reinforcement influence patterns of operant responding. Continuous reinforcement occurs when every designated response is reinforced. Intermittent schedules of reinforcement include fixed-ratio, variable-ratio, fixed-interval, and variable-interval schedules.

• Intermittent schedules produce greater resistance to extinction than similar continuous schedules. Ratio schedules tend to yield higher rates of response than interval schedules. Shorter intervals and higher ratios are associated with faster responding.

• Responses can be strengthened either through the presentation of positive reinforcers or through the removal of negative reinforcers. Negative reinforcement regulates escape and avoidance learning. Once learned, avoidance responses tend to be long-lasting. The two-process theory provides the best explanation of avoidance behavior and may shed light on why phobias are so difficult to eliminate.

• Punishment involves unfavorable consequences that lead to a decline in response strength. Some of the problems associated with the application of punishment are an increase in aggressive behavior and suppression of behavioral activities.

• Punishment is more effective when it is swift, severe, consistent, explained, and accompanied by an opportunity to earn reinforcement with an alternate response. The removal of positive reinforcers can be used as punishment.

NEW DIRECTIONS IN THE STUDY OF CONDITIONING

As you learned in Chapter 1, science is constantly evolving and changing in response to new research and new thinking. Such change has certainly occurred in the study of conditioning. In this section, we will examine two major changes in thinking about conditioning. First, we'll consider the recent recognition that an organism's biological heritage can limit or channel conditioning. Second, we'll discuss the increased appreciation of the role of cognitive processes in conditioning.

Recognizing Biological Constraints on Conditioning

Learning theorists have traditionally assumed that the fundamental laws of conditioning have great generality—that they apply to a wide range of species. Although no one ever suggested that hamsters could learn physics, until the 1960s most

psychologists assumed that associations could be conditioned between any stimulus an organism could register and any response it could make. However, findings in recent decades have demonstrated that there are limits to the generality of conditioning principles—limits imposed by an organism's biological heritage.

Instinctive Drift:
The Case of the Miserly Raccoons

One biological constraint on learning is instinctive drift. *Instinctive drift* **occurs when an animal's innate response tendencies interfere with conditioning processes.** Instinctive drift was first described by the Brelands, the operant psychologists who went into the business of training animals for commercial purposes (Breland & Breland, 1966). They have described many amusing examples of their "failures" to control behavior through conditioning. For instance, they once were training some raccoons to deposit coins in a piggy bank. They were successful in shaping the raccoons to pick up a coin and put it into a small box, using food as the reinforcer. However, when they gave the raccoons a couple of coins, an unexpected problem arose: the raccoons wouldn't give the coins up! In spite of the reinforcers available for depositing the coins, they would sit and rub the coins together like so many little misers.

What had happened to disrupt the conditioning program? Apparently, associating the coins with food had brought out the raccoons' innate food-washing behavior. Raccoons often rub things together to clean them. The Brelands report that they have run into this sort of instinct-related interference on many occasions with a wide variety of species.

Conditioned Taste Aversion: The "Sauce Béarnaise Syndrome"

A number of years ago, a prominent psychologist, Martin Seligman, dined out with his wife and enjoyed a steak with sauce béarnaise. About 6 hours afterward, he developed a wicked case of stomach flu and endured severe nausea. Subsequently, when he ordered sauce béarnaise, he was chagrined to discover that its aroma alone nearly made him throw up.

Seligman's experience was not unique. Many people develop aversions to food that has been followed by nausea from illness, alcohol intoxication, or food poisoning. However, Seligman was puzzled by what he called his "sauce béarnaise syndrome" (Seligman & Hager, 1972). On the one hand, it appeared to be the straightforward result of classical conditioning. A neutral stimulus (the sauce) had been paired with an unconditioned stimulus (the flu), which caused an unconditioned response (the nausea). Hence, the sauce béarnaise became a conditioned stimulus eliciting nausea (see Figure 6.23).

On the other hand, Seligman recognized that his aversion to béarnaise sauce violated certain basic principles of conditioning. First, the lengthy delay of 6 hours between the CS (the sauce) and

the UCS (the flu) should have prevented conditioning from occurring. In laboratory studies, a delay of more than *30 seconds* between the CS and UCS makes it very difficult to establish a conditioned response, yet this conditioning occurred in just one pairing. Second, why was it that *only* the béarnaise sauce became a CS eliciting nausea? Why not other stimuli that were present in the restaurant? Shouldn't plates, knives, tablecloths, or his wife, for example, also trigger Seligman's nausea?

The riddle of Seligman's sauce béarnaise syndrome was solved by John Garcia (1989) and his colleagues. They conducted a series of studies on *conditioned taste aversion* (Garcia & Koelling, 1966; Garcia, Clarke, & Hankins, 1973; Garcia & Rusiniak, 1980). In these studies, they manipulated the kinds of stimuli preceding the onset of nausea and other noxious experiences in rats, using radiation to artificially induce the nausea (see Figure 6.24). They found that when taste cues were followed by nausea, rats quickly acquired conditioned taste aversions. However, when taste cues were followed by other types of noxious stimuli (such as shock), rats did *not* develop conditioned taste aversions. Furthermore, visual and auditory stimuli followed by nausea also failed to produce conditioned aversions.

In short, Garcia and his co-workers found that taste aversions were conditioned *only* through the pairing of taste stimuli and stimuli inducing nausea. When taste stimuli or nausea-inducing stimuli were paired with other types of stimuli—rather than each other—minimal conditioning occurred (see Figure 6.24). In contrast, the taste-nausea connection was made so readily that conditioned taste aversions could develop in spite of remarkably long CS-UCS delays. These findings contradicted the long-held belief that associations could be created between virtually any stimulus and any response. Garcia found that it was almost impossible to create certain associations, whereas taste-nausea associations (and odor-nausea associations) were almost impossible to prevent.

What is the theoretical significance of this unique readiness to make connections between taste and nausea? Garcia argues that it is a by-product of the evolutionary history of mammals. Animals that consume poisonous foods and survive must learn not to repeat their mistakes. Natural selection will favor organisms that quickly learn what *not* to eat. Thus, evolution may have biologically programmed some organisms to learn certain types of associations more easily than others.

"Taste aversions do not fit comfortably within the present framework of classical or instrumental conditioning: These aversions selectively seek flavors to the exclusion of other stimuli. Interstimulus intervals are a thousandfold too long."

JOHN GARCIA

Figure 6.23 Conditioned taste aversion. Taste aversions can be established through classical conditioning, as in the "sauce béarnaise syndrome." However, as the text explains, taste aversions can be acquired in ways that violate basic principles of classical conditioning.

(a) Garcia and Koelling's (1966) apparatus and procedure
Rats drink saccharin-flavored water out of a tube. Whenever they make contact with the tube, they activate a bright light and noisy buzzer. Some rats also receive an electric shock, whereas other rats are made nauseated by exposure to radiation.

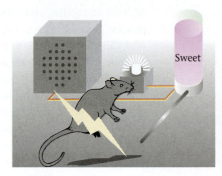
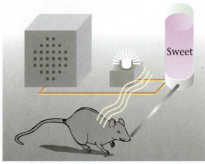

Figure 6.24
Garcia and Koelling's research on conditioned taste aversion. In a landmark series of studies, Garcia and Koelling (1966) demonstrated that some stimulus-response associations are much easier to condition than others. (**a**) Their procedure allowed them to pair a taste stimulus (saccharin-flavored water) with visual and auditory stimuli (a bright light and noisy buzzer), and/or pain-inducing shock or nausea-inducing radiation. (**b**) They found that taste-nausea associations were acquired easily, as were associations between auditory-visual stimuli and pain, whereas other associations were difficult to acquire. As your text discusses, they explained their findings in terms of evolutionary considerations.

(b) Garcia and Koelling's (1966) findings

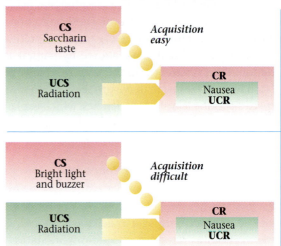
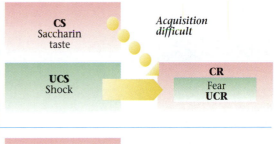

Preparedness and Phobias

Scientists are always looking for explanations that can link a number of observations. In this spirit, Martin Seligman has proposed a concept called *preparedness* to explain his sauce béarnaise syndrome, Garcia's findings, and a variety of other phenomena. *Preparedness* **involves a species-specific predisposition to be conditioned in certain ways and not others.** Seligman believes that preparedness is a biologically programmed result of evolution. Instinctive drift and conditioned taste aversion both appear to involve preparedness. In addition, Seligman (1971) believes that phobic responses in humans are influenced by preparedness.

Although people can acquire phobias of almost anything, certain phobias are vastly more common than others. People tend to develop phobias to snakes, spiders, heights, and darkness relatively easily. However, even after painful experiences with hammers, knives, hot stoves, and electrical outlets, phobic fears of these objects are infrequent. What characteristics do common phobic objects share? Most were once genuine threats to our ancestors. Consequently, a fear response to such objects has survival value for our species. According to Seligman, evolutionary forces gradually programmed humans to acquire fears of these objects easily and rapidly. The concept of preparedness does *not* conflict with previously discussed ideas about the origins of phobias. Seligman still believes that phobic responses may be created through classical conditioning and maintained through operant conditioning (negative reinforcement). The concept of preparedness builds on these ideas to explain why phobic conditioning seems to be *selective*.

Laboratory simulations of phobic conditioning have provided some support for the theory of preparedness (LoLordo & Droungas, 1989; Mineka & Tomarken, 1989). For example, in some studies, slides of common phobic stimuli (snakes, spiders) and stimuli with little phobic potential (flowers, houses) have been paired with shock. Physiological monitoring of the subjects indicates that the common phobic stimuli produce more rapid

People tend to develop phobias to spiders very easily but to hot stoves rarely, even though the latter are just as dangerous. Preparedness theory can explain this paradox.

According to this view, learning is a very general process because the neural substrates of learning and the basic problems confronted by various organisms are much the same across species. For example, it is probably adaptive for virtually any organism to develop the ability to recognize stimuli that signal important events.

However, given that learning can contribute to reproductive success in myriad ways, it makes sense that learning has evolved along different paths in different species (Sherry, 1992). Most animals must learn what is edible and what isn't, how to spot predators quickly, how to attract a mate, and so forth. Any heritable change in learning that makes an organism's performance of these tasks more effective should increase the organism's reproductive success, and hence be favored by natural selection. Thus, differences in the adaptive challenges faced by various species have probably led to some species-specific learning tendencies, which explain how an organism's biological heritage can channel conditioning in certain directions.

Recognizing Cognitive Processes in Conditioning

Pavlov, Skinner, and their followers traditionally viewed conditioning as a mechanical process in which stimulus-response associations are stamped in by experience. Learning theorists asserted that if a flatworm can be conditioned, then conditioning can't depend on higher mental processes. Although this viewpoint did not go entirely unchallenged (for example, Tolman, 1922, 1932), mainstream theories of conditioning did not allocate a major role to cognitive processes. In recent decades, however, research findings have led theorists to shift toward more cognitive explanations of conditioning. Let's review some of these findings and the theories that have resulted.

Blocking

Imagine conducting a seemingly simple study of classical conditioning in rats. In phase one, a tone is paired with shock so that the tone becomes a CS eliciting fear. In phase two, the same tone *and* a light are paired with shock. When the tone and light are presented together (without the shock) this compound stimulus elicits fear. In phase three, only the light is presented to see whether it elicits conditioned fear by itself. What would you predict? The light *has* been paired with shock. According to conventional theories of conditioning, the light should trigger fear. However, this is *not* what Leon Kamin (1968, 1969) found. The light,

conditioning, stronger fear responses, and conditioned fears more resistant to extinction (Hygge & Öhman, 1978; Öhman, Erixon & Lofberg, 1975). These results are consistent with what Seligman would predict. However, other studies have failed to find evidence for preparedness in conditioning, so Seligman's theory remains the source of some debate (McNally, 1987).

An Evolutionary Perspective on Learning

Clearly, several lines of research suggest that there are species-specific biological constraints on conditioning. So, what is the current thinking on the idea that the laws of learning are *universal* across various species? The emerging consensus seems to be that the basic mechanisms of learning are *similar* across species but that these mechanisms have sometimes been modified in the course of evolution as species have adapted to the specialized demands of their environments (Lieberman, 1993).

by itself, was not an effective CS. It evoked either no response at all or else a very weak one.

For some reason, a basic conditioning procedure has failed to bring about conditioning. Why? Research suggests that it is because the light is a *redundant* stimulus that adds no new information (Rescorla & Wagner, 1972; Shanks, 1994). Shock has always been preceded by the tone. The tone is all the rat need pay attention to in order to know when to expect shock. This phenomenon is called *blocking*. **Blocking occurs when a stimulus paired with a UCS fails to become a CS because it is redundant with an established CS.** It is called *blocking* because something is blocking the usual conditioning that should take place when the light and shock are paired.

The significance of blocking is subtle, but immense. It suggests that the rat is not a passive recipient of mechanical conditioning. The animal actively filters out a redundant stimulus, apparently because the stimulus doesn't improve the predictability of the shock. Consider the concepts used to explain blocking: redundancy, information, attention, expectation, and predictability. We're talking about cognitive processes, such as they are, in a rat!

Blocking also has implications for a long-running debate about whether classical conditioning is best conceptualized as stimulus-response (S-R) learning or stimulus-stimulus (S-S) learning. The S-R view asserts that classical conditioning results in the formation of a new association between a stimulus (the CS) and a response (the CR). In contrast, the S-S view assumes that classical conditioning depends on organisms learning to associate a CS with a UCS. According to this notion, classical conditioning leads to a connection between a CS and CR only indirectly, because of the more essential CS-UCS connection (see Figure 6.25). Curiously, although Pavlov favored an S-S interpretation, the S-R view became the dominant model of classical conditioning. However, the findings on blocking and several other lines of recent research suggest that S-S connections are the crucial associations underlying classical conditioning (Domjan, 1993). The contemporary version of the S-S model (which differs from Pavlov's view) posits that classical conditioning results in the formation of an association between the CS and a *mental representation* of the UCS, which, in turn, evokes the conditioned response (see Figure 6.26). As you can see, this new conceptualization of classical conditioning has a strong cognitive flavor.

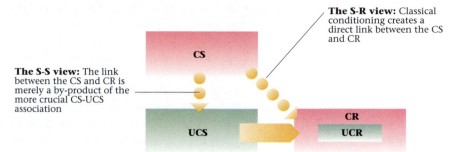

Signal Relations

The cognitive element in conditioning is also prominent in research conducted by Robert Rescorla (1978, 1980; Rescorla & Wagner, 1972). Rescorla asserts that environmental stimuli serve as signals and that some stimuli are better, or more dependable, signals than others. Hence, he has manipulated *signal relations* in classical conditioning—that is, CS-UCS relations that influence whether a CS is a good signal. A "good" signal is one that allows accurate prediction of the UCS.

In essence, Rescorla manipulates the *predictive value* of a conditioned stimulus. How does he do so? He varies the proportion of trials in which the CS and UCS are paired. Consider the following example. A tone and shock are paired 20 times for one group of rats. Otherwise, these rats are never shocked. For these rats the CS (tone) and UCS (shock) are paired in 100% of the experimental trials. Another group of rats also receive 20 pairings of the tone and shock. However, the rates in this group are also exposed to the shock on 20 other trials when the tone does *not* precede it. For this group, the CS and UCS are paired in only 50% of the trials. Thus, the two groups of rats have had an equal number of CS-UCS pairings, but the CS is a better signal or predictor of shock for the 100% CS-UCS group than for the 50% CS-UCS group.

What did Rescorla find when he tested the two groups of rats for conditioned fear? He found that the CS elicits a much stronger response in the 100% CS-UCS group than in the 50% CS-UCS group. Given that the two groups have received an equal number of CS-UCS pairings, this difference

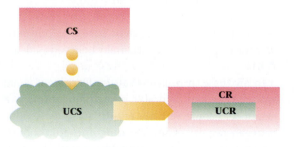

Figure 6.25
S-R versus S-S explanations of classical conditioning. Learning theorists have long debated the question of what is actually learned in classical conditioning. S-R theorists have maintained that conditioning leads to the formation of a new stimulus-response bond (between the CS and CR). S-S theorists have argued that classical conditioning really depends on the formation of an S-S association (between the CS and UCS). According to the S-S view, the connection between the CS and CR is merely an indirect reflection of the more crucial S-S association.

Figure 6.26
Contemporary S-S models of classical conditioning. Although the evidence is mixed, in recent decades the balance of evidence has shifted in favor of S-S explanations of classical conditioning (Domjan, 1993). Most modern S-S models maintain that classical conditioning creates an association between a CS and a mental representation of a UCS, which elicits the conditioned response.

must be due to the greater predictive power of the CS for the 100% group. Numerous studies of signal relations have shown that the predictive value of a CS is an influential factor governing classical conditioning (Rescorla, 1978).

The Rescorla-Wagner (1972) model has dominated the investigation of classical conditioning since the 1970s. Although it has had many failures as well as successes in explaining the various facets of classical conditioning (Miller, Barnet, & Grahame, 1995), it definitely has shifted thinking toward viewing classical conditioning in terms of information processing rather than reflexive responding.

Response-Outcome Relations and Reinforcement

Let's turn to operant behavior for one more example of cognitive processes in conditioning. Imagine that on the night before an important exam you study very hard while repeatedly playing a Bruce Springsteen album. The next morning you earn an A on your exam. Does this result strengthen your tendency to play Springsteen albums before exams? Probably not. Chances are, you will recognize the logical relation between the response of studying hard and the reinforcement of a good grade, and only the response of studying will be strengthened.

However, it's not out of the realm of possibility that you might develop a habit of playing Springsteen before big exams. Skinner (1948) has argued that superstitious behavior can be established through noncontingent reinforcement. ***Noncontingent reinforcement*** **occurs when a response is strengthened by a reinforcer that follows it, even though delivery of the reinforcer was not a result of the response.** There are many anecdotal reports of athletes acquiring superstitious responses (putting on a special pair of socks, eating the same lunch, and so on before a game) through noncontingent reinforcement (Gmelch, 1978). Furthermore, laboratory studies have shown that superstitious responses can be created through noncontingent reinforcement (Ono, 1987). However, the evidence as a whole suggests that noncontingent reinforcement is not as powerful or influential as Skinner originally believed (Killeen, 1981).

In any case, it is clear that reinforcement is *not* automatic when favorable consequences follow a response. People actively reason out the relations between responses and the outcomes that follow. When a response is followed by a desirable out-

"In the last 20 years attention has shifted to the study of Pavlovian conditioning. That shift has been richly rewarded."

ROBERT RESCORLA

come, the response is more likely to be strengthened if the person thinks that the response *caused* the outcome. You might guess that only humans would engage in this causal reasoning. However, evidence suggests that under the right circumstances even pigeons can learn to recognize causal relations between responses and outcomes (Killeen, 1981).

The evidence on blocking, signal relations, and response-outcome relations has provoked psychologists to develop new models of conditioning that have a stronger cognitive flavor than before (Catania, 1979; Rescorla, 1988). These reformulated models view conditioning as a matter of detecting the *contingencies* among environmental events. According to these theories, organisms actively try to figure out what leads to what (the contingencies) in the world around them. Stimuli are viewed as signals that help organisms minimize their aversive experiences and maximize their pleasant experiences. The new, cognitively oriented theories of conditioning are quite a departure from older theories that depicted conditioning as a mindless, mechanical process. We can also see this new emphasis on cognitive processes in our next subject, observational learning.

Recap of Key Points

• Recent decades have brought profound changes in our understanding of conditioning. Instinctive drift occurs when an animal's innate response tendencies interfere with conditioning. Conditioned taste aversions can be readily acquired even when there is a lengthy delay between the CS and UCS. Seligman's concept of preparedness may explain why certain phobias are far more common than others.

• The findings on instinctive drift, conditioned taste aversion, and preparedness have led to the recognition that there are species-specific biological constraints on conditioning. Evolutionary psychologists argue that learning processes vary somewhat across species because learning mechansims have sometimes been modified in the course of evolution.

• Blocking occurs when a stimulus paired with a UCS fails to become a CS because it is redundant with an established CS. Rescorla's work on signal relations showed that the predictive value of a CS is an influential factor governing classical conditioning. When a response is followed by a desirable outcome, the response is more likely to be strengthened if it appears that the response caused the outcome.

• Studies of blocking and signal relations in classical conditioning and response-outcome relations in oper-

Distinguishing Between Classical Conditioning and Operant Conditioning

Check your understanding of the usual differences between classical conditioning and operant conditioning by indicating the type of conditioning process involved in each of the following examples. In the space on the left, place a C if the example involves classical conditioning, an O if it involves operant conditioning, or a B if it involves both. The answers can be found in Appendix A.

_____ 1. Whenever Marcia takes her dog out for a walk, she wears the same old blue windbreaker. Eventually, she notices that her dog becomes excited whenever she puts on this windbreaker.

_____ 2. The Creatures are a successful rock band with three hit albums to their credit. They begin their U.S. tour featuring many new, unreleased songs, all of which draw silence from their concert fans. The same fans cheer wildly when the Creatures play any of their old hits. Gradually, the band reduces the number of new songs it plays and starts playing more of the old standbys.

_____ 3. When Cindy and Mel first fell in love, they listened constantly to the Creatures' hit song "Transatlantic Obsession." Although several years have passed, whenever they hear this song they experience a warm, romantic feeling.

_____ 4. For nearly 20 years Ralph has worked as a machinist in the same factory. His new foreman is never satisfied with his work and criticizes him constantly. After a few weeks of heavy criticism, he experiences anxiety whenever he arrives at work. He starts calling in sick more and more frequently to evade this anxiety.

ant conditioning suggest that cognitive processes play a larger role in conditioning than originally believed. Modern theories hold that conditioning is a matter of detecting the contingencies that govern events.

OBSERVATIONAL LEARNING

Can classical and operant conditioning account for all learning? Absolutely not. Consider how people learn a fairly basic skill such as driving a car. They do not hop naively into an automobile and start emitting random responses until one leads to favorable consequences. On the contrary, most people learning to drive know exactly where to place the key and how to get started. How are these responses acquired? Through *observation*. Most new drivers have years of experience observing others drive, and they put those observations to work. Learning through observation accounts for a great deal of learning in both animals and humans.

Observational learning **occurs when an organism's responding is influenced by the observation of others, who are called models.** This process has been investigated extensively by Albert Bandura (1977, 1986). Bandura does not see observational learning as entirely separate from classical and operant conditioning. Instead, he asserts that it greatly extends the reach of these conditioning processes. Whereas previous conditioning theorists emphasized the organism's direct experi-

ence, Bandura has demonstrated that both classical and operant conditioning can take place vicariously through observational learning.

Essentially, observational learning involves being conditioned indirectly by virtue of observing another's conditioning (see Figure 6.27). To illustrate, suppose you observe a friend behaving assertively with a car salesperson. You see your friend's assertive behavior reinforced by the exceptionally good buy she gets on the car. Your own tendency to behave assertively with salespeople might well be strengthened as a result. Notice that the

Figure 6.27
Observational learning. In observational learning, an observer attends to and stores a mental representation of a model's behavior (example: assertive bargaining) and its consequences (example: a good buy on a car). If the observer sees the modeled response lead to a favorable outcome, the observer's tendency to emit the modeled response will be strengthened.

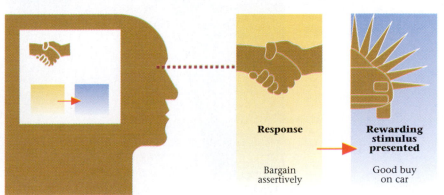

Response

Bargain assertively

Rewarding stimulus presented

Good buy on car

reinforcement is experienced by your friend, not you. The good buy should strengthen your friend's tendency to bargain assertively, but your tendency to do so may also be strengthened indirectly.

Basic Processes

Bandura has identified four key processes that are crucial in observational learning. The first two—attention and retention—highlight the importance of cognition in this type of learning.

• *Attention.* To learn through observation, you must pay attention to another person's behavior and its consequences.

• *Retention.* You may not have occasion to use an observed response for weeks, months, or even years. Hence, you must store a mental representation of what you have witnessed in your memory.

• *Reproduction.* Enacting a modeled response depends on your ability to reproduce the response by converting your stored mental images into overt behavior. This may not be easy for some responses. For example, most people cannot execute a breathtaking windmill dunk after watching Michael Jordan do it in a basketball game.

• *Motivation.* Finally, you are unlikely to reproduce an observed response unless you are motivated to

"Most human behavior is learned by observation through modeling."

ALBERT BANDURA

Through observation, the English titmouse has learned how to break into containers to swipe milk from its human neighbors.

do so. Your motivation depends on whether you encounter a situation in which you believe that the response is likely to pay off for you.

Observational learning has proven especially valuable in explaining complex human behaviors, but animals can also learn through observation. A simple example is the thieving behavior of the English titmouse, a small bird renowned for its early-morning raids on its human neighbors. The titmouse has learned how to open cardboard caps on bottles of milk delivered to the porches of many homes in England. Having opened the bottle, the titmouse skims the cream from the top of the milk. This clever learned behavior has been passed down from one generation of titmouse to the next through observational learning.

Acquisition Versus Performance

Bandura points out that people have many learned responses that they may or may not perform, depending on the situation. Thus, he distinguishes between the *acquisition* of a learned response and the *performance* of that response. He maintains that reinforcement affects which responses are actually performed more than which responses are acquired. People emit thoses responses that they think are likely to be reinforced. For instance, you may study hard for a course in which the professor gives fair exams, because you expect studying to lead to reinforcement in the form of a good grade. In contrast, you may hardly open the text for a course in which the professor gives arbitrary, unpredictable exams, because you do not expect studying to be reinforced. Your performance is different in the two situations because you think the reinforcement contingencies are different. Thus, like Skinner, Bandura asserts that reinforcement is a critical determinant of behavior. However, Bandura maintains that reinforcement influences performance rather than learning per se.

Applications

It is the power of observational learning that makes television such an influential determinant of behavior. Young children are especially impressionable, and extensive evidence indicates that they pick up many responses from viewing models on TV (Huston & Wright, 1982; Liebert & Sprafkin, 1988). Because of this evidence, the amount of aggressive behavior that should be allowed on TV shows is a controversial subject, which brings us to our Featured Study for Chapter 6.

Investigators: Albert Bandura, Dorothea Ross, and Sheila Ross (Stanford University)

Source: Vicarious reinforcement and imitative learning. *Journal of Abnormal & Social Psychology*, 1963b, *67*, 601–607.

This study was designed to explore the influence of observing the consequences of another's behavior on the learning of aggressive behavior in children. In a previous study, the same researchers had shown that children exposed to an aggressive adult model displayed more aggression than children exposed to a similar but nonaggressive model (Bandura, Ross, & Ross, 1961). The first study used live (in-person) adult models who did or did not play very roughly with a five-foot-tall "Bobo doll" while in the same room with the children. A second study by the same research team investigated whether filmed models were as influential as in-person models (Bandura, Ross, & Ross, 1963a). The findings indicated that a TV depiction of an adult model roughing up the Bobo doll led to increased aggression just as exposure to a live model had. In this third study of the series, the investigators used filmed models and manipulated the consequences experienced by the aggressive models. The hypothesis was that children who saw the models rewarded for their aggression would become more aggressive than children who saw the models punished for their aggression.

Method

Subjects. The subjects were 40 girls and 40 boys drawn from a nursery school. The average age for the 80 children was 4 years, 3 months.

Procedure. While at the nursery school, the children were invited (individually) to play in a toy room. On the way to the toy room an adult escort indicated that she needed to stop in her office for a few minutes. The child was told to watch a TV in the office during this brief delay. On the TV, the child was exposed to one of three 5-minute film sequences. In the *aggressive-model-rewarded* condition, Rocky and Johnny are playing and Rocky attacks Johnny, striking him with a baton, throwing a ball at him repeatedly, and dragging him off to a far corner of the room. The final scene shows Rocky having a great time with the toys while helping himself to pop and cookies. In the *aggressive-model-punished* condition, Rocky engages in the same pattern of aggression but the outcome is different. Johnny rises to the challenge and thrashes Rocky, who is shown cowering in a corner in the final scene. In the *nonaggressive-model-control* condition, Rocky and Johnny are simply shown engaged in vigorous play without any aggression. In a fourth condition, the *no-model-control* condition, the child did not watch TV while in the office.

After the brief detour to the adult's office, the children were taken to the toy room, as promised, where they were allowed to play alone with a diverse array of toys that allowed for either aggressive or nonaggressive play. Among the toys were two Bobo dolls that served as convenient targets for aggressive responses. The children's play was observed through a one-way mirror from an adjoining room. The key dependent variable was the number of aggressive acts displayed by the children during the 20-minute play period.

Results

Children in the *aggressive-model-rewarded* condition displayed significantly more total aggression and imitative aggression (specific aggressive acts similar to Rocky's) than children in the *aggressive-model-punished* condition. The amount of imitative aggression exhibited by children in each of the four conditions is summarized in Figure 6.28. A clear elevation of imitative aggression was observed only among the children who saw aggression pay off with reinforcement for the model.

Discussion

The results supported a basic premise of Bandura's theory—that observers are more likely to imitate another's behavior when that behavior leads to positive consequences than when it leads to negative consequences. Of particular interest was the fact that filmed models were shown to influence the likelihood of aggressive behavior in children.

Comment

This classic series of studies by Bandura, Ross, and Ross played a prominent role in the early stages of

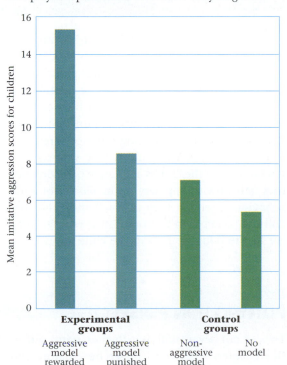

Figure 6.28 Modeling and aggression. Bandura, Ross, and Ross (1963b) found that acts of imitative aggression were most frequent among children exposed to an aggressive model on film whose aggression was rewarded.

the long-running debate about the effects of televised violence. People concerned about media violence noted that aggression on TV shows usually leads to rewards and admiration for heroic TV characters. The findings of this study suggested that youngsters watching aggressive models on TV are likely to learn that aggressive behavior pays off. Critics argued that

Bandura's Bobo doll studies were too artificial to be conclusive. This criticism led to more realistic experiments and correlational studies on the possible link between TV violence and aggressiveness. As a whole, these studies have supported observational learning theory, which suggests that media violence contributes to aggression in the real world (see Chapter 11).

Youngsters acquire a diverse array of responses through observational learning.

Bandura's theory of observational learning has also shed light on many other aspects of behavior. For example, it explains why physical punishment tends to increase aggressive behavior in children, even when it is intended to do just the opposite. Parents who depend on physical punishment often punish a child for hitting other children—by hitting the child. The parents may sincerely intend to reduce the child's aggressive behavior, but they are unwittingly serving as *models* of such behavior. Although they may tell the child that "hitting people won't accomplish anything," they are in the midst of hitting the child in order to accomplish something. Because parents usually accomplish their immediate goal of stopping the child's hitting, the child witnesses the reinforcement of aggressive behavior. In this situation, actions speak louder than words—because of observational learning.

Clearly, observational learning plays an important role in regulating behavior. It represents a third major type of learning that builds on the first two types—classical conditioning and operant conditioning. These three basic types of learning are summarized and compared in a pictorial table on pages 252–253.

PUTTING IT IN PERSPECTIVE

Two of our seven unifying themes stand out in this chapter. First, you can see how nature and nurture interactively govern behavior. Second, looking at psychology in its sociohistorical context, you can see how progress in psychology spills over to affect trends and values in society at large. Let's examine each of these points in more detail.

In regard to nature versus nurture, research on learning clearly demonstrates the enormous power of the environment in shaping behavior. Pavlov's model of classical conditioning shows how experiences can account for everyday fears and other emotional responses. Skinner's model of operant conditioning shows how reinforcement and punishment can mold everything from a child's bedtime whimpering to an adult's restaurant preferences. Indeed, many learning theorists once believed that *all* aspects of behavior could be explained in terms of environmental determinants. In recent decades, however, evidence on instinctive drift, conditioned taste aversion, and preparedness has shown that there are biological constraints on conditioning. Thus, even in explanations of learning—an area once dominated by nurture theories—we see once again that heredity and environment jointly influence behavior.

The history of research on conditioning also shows how progress in psychology can seep into every corner of society. For example, Skinner's ideas on the power of reinforcement and the ineffectiveness of punishment have influenced patterns of discipline in our society. Today's parents and educators appear to depend less on punitive measures than previous generations did. Research on operant conditioning has also affected management styles in the business world, leading to an increased emphasis on positive reinforcement. In the educational arena, the concept of individu-

alized, programmed learning is a spinoff from behavioral research. The fact that the principles of conditioning are routinely applied in homes, businesses, schools, and factories clearly shows that psychology is not an ivory tower endeavor.

In the upcoming Application, you will see how you can apply the principles of conditioning to improve your self-control, as we discuss the technology of behavior modification.

Recap of Key Points

• In observational learning, an organism is conditioned vicariously by watching a model's conditioning. Both classical and operant conditioning can occur through observational learning, which depends on the processes of attention, retention, reproduction, and motivation.

• According to Bandura, reinforcement influences which of several already acquired responses one will perform more than it influences the acquisition of new responses. Observational learning can account for the influence of mass media (such as television) on behavior.

• Our Featured Study was a classic experiment in which Bandura, Ross, and Ross demonstrated that viewing aggressive models on TV could influence aggressiveness in children. The principles of observational learning have also been used to explain why physical punishment increases aggressive behavior.

• Two of our key themes were especially apparent in our coverage of learning and conditioning. One theme involves the interaction of heredity and environment in learning. The other involves the way progress in psychology affects society at large.

THREE TYPES OF LEARNING

Type of learning	Procedure	Diagram	Result

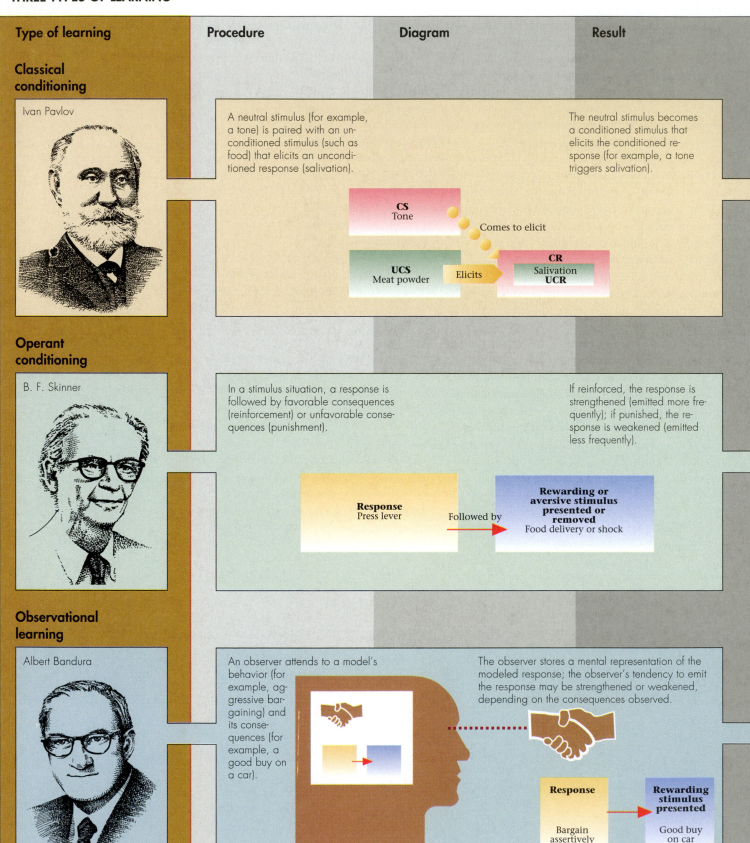

Classical conditioning

Ivan Pavlov

A neutral stimulus (for example, a tone) is paired with an unconditioned stimulus (such as food) that elicits an unconditioned response (salivation).

CS Tone — Comes to elicit

UCS Meat powder — Elicits → **CR** Salivation **UCR**

The neutral stimulus becomes a conditioned stimulus that elicits the conditioned response (for example, a tone triggers salivation).

Operant conditioning

B. F. Skinner

In a stimulus situation, a response is followed by favorable consequences (reinforcement) or unfavorable consequences (punishment).

Response Press lever — Followed by → **Rewarding or aversive stimulus presented or removed** Food delivery or shock

If reinforced, the response is strengthened (emitted more frequently); if punished, the response is weakened (emitted less frequently).

Observational learning

Albert Bandura

An observer attends to a model's behavior (for example, aggressive bargaining) and its consequences (for example, a good buy on a car).

Response Bargain assertively → **Rewarding stimulus presented** Good buy on car

The observer stores a mental representation of the modeled response; the observer's tendency to emit the response may be strengthened or weakened, depending on the consequences observed.

Typical kinds of responses	Examples in animals	Examples in humans

Mostly (but not always) involuntary reflexes and visceral responses

Dogs learn to salivate to the sound of a tone that has been paired with meat powder.

Little Albert learns to fear a white rat and other white, furry objects through classical conditioning

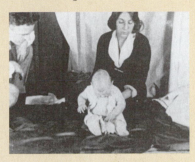

Mostly (but not always) voluntary, spontaneous responses

Circus elephants and other trained animals perform remarkable feats because they have been reinforced for gradually learning closer and closer approximations of responses they do not normally emit.

Casino patrons tend to exhibit high, steady rates of gambling, as most games of chance involve complex variable-ratio schedules of reinforcement.

Mostly voluntary responses, often consisting of novel and complex sequences

An English titmouse learns to break into milk bottles by observing the thievery of other titmice.

A young boy tries to perform a response that he has acquired through observational learning.

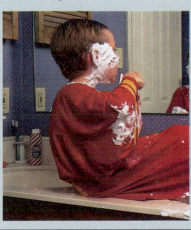

APPLICATION: ACHIEVING SELF-CONTROL THROUGH BEHAVIOR MODIFICATION

Answer the following "yes" or "no."

1 Do you have a hard time passing up food, even when you're not hungry?

2 Do you wish you studied more often?

3 Would you like to cut down on your smoking or drinking?

4 Do you experience diffculty in getting yourself to exercise regularly?

5 Do you wish you had more will power?

If you answered "yes" to any of these questions, you have struggled with the challenge of self-control. This Application discusses how you can use the techniques of behavior modification to improve your self-control. If you stop to think about it, self-control—or rather a lack of it—underlies many of the personal problems that people struggle with in everyday life.

Behavior modification is a systematic approach to changing behavior through the application of the principles of conditioning. Advocates of behavior modification assume that behavior is a product of learning, conditioning, and environmental control. They further assume that *what is learned can be unlearned.* Thus, they set out to "recondition" people to produce more desirable patterns of behavior.

The technology of behavior modification has been applied with great success in schools, businesses, hospitals, factories, child-care facilities, prisons, and mental health centers (Goodall, 1972; Kazdin, 1982; Rachman, 1992). Moreover, behavior modification techniques have proven particularly valuable in efforts to improve self-control. Our discussion will borrow

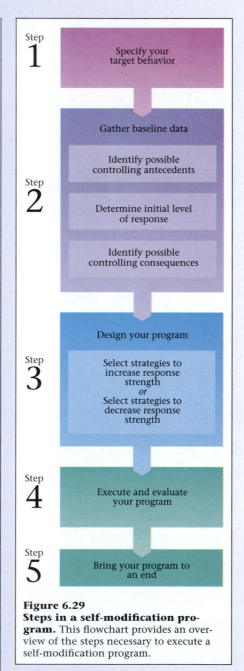

Figure 6.29
Steps in a self-modification program. This flowchart provides an overview of the steps necessary to execute a self-modification program.

liberally from an excellent book on self-modification by David Watson and Roland Tharp (1993). We will discuss five steps in the process of self-modification, which are outlined in Figure 6.29.

Specifying Your Target Behavior

The first step in a self-modification program is to specify the target behavior(s) that you want to change. Behavior modification can only be applied to a clearly defined, overt response, yet many people have difficulty pinpointing the behavior they hope to alter. They tend to describe their problems in terms of unobservable personality *traits* rather than overt *behaviors*. For example, asked what behavior he would like to change, a man might say, "I'm too irritable." That may be true, but it is of little help in designing a self-modification program. To use a behavioral approach, vague statements about traits need to be translated into precise descriptions of specific target behaviors.

To identify target responses, you need to ponder past behavior or closely observe future behavior and list specific *examples* of responses that lead to the trait description. For instance, the man who regards himself as "too irritable" might identify two overly frequent responses, such as arguing with his wife and snapping at his children. These are specific behaviors for which he could design a self-modification program.

Gathering Baseline Data

The second step in behavior modification is to gather baseline data. You need to systematically observe your target behavior for a period of time (usually a week or two) before you work out the details of your program. In gathering your baseline data, you need to monitor three things.

First, you need to determine the initial response level of your target behavior. After all, you can't tell whether your program is working effectively unless you have a baseline for comparison. In most cases, you would simply keep track of how often the target response occurs in a certain time interval. Thus, you might count the daily frequency of snapping at your children, smoking cigarettes, or biting your fingernails. If studying is your target behavior, you will probably monitor hours of study. If you want to modify your eating, you will probably keep track of how many calories you consume. Whatever the unit of measurement, *it is crucial to gather accurate data*. You should keep permanent written records, and it is usually best to portray these records graphically (see Figure 6.30).

Second, you need to monitor the antecedents of your target behavior. *Antecedents are events that typically precede the target response.* Often these events play a major role in evoking your target behavior. For example, if your target is overeating, you might discover that the bulk of your overeating occurs late in the evening while you watch TV. If you can pinpoint this kind of antecedent-response connection, you may be able to design your program to circumvent or break the link.

Third, you need to monitor the typical consequences of your target behavior. Try to identify the reinforcers that are maintaining an undesirable target behavior or the unfavorable outcomes that are suppressing a desirable target behavior. In trying to identify reinforcers, remember that avoidance behavior is usually maintained by negative reinforcement. That is, the payoff for avoidance is usually the removal of something aversive, such as anxiety or a threat to self-esteem. You should also take into account the fact that a response may not be reinforced every time, as most behavior is maintained by intermittent reinforcement.

Designing Your Program

Once you have selected a target behavior and gathered adequate baseline data, it is time to plan your intervention program. Generally speaking, your program will be designed either to increase or to decrease the frequency of a target response.

Increasing Response Strength

Efforts to increase the frequency of a target response depend largely on the use of positive reinforcement. In other words, you reward yourself for behaving properly. Although the basic strategy is quite simple, doing it skillfully involves a number of considerations.

SELECTING A REINFORCER. To use positive reinforcement, you need to find a reward that will be effective for you. Reinforcement is subjective—what is reinforcing for one person may not be reinforcing for another. Figure 6.31 lists questions you can ask yourself to help you determine your personal reinforcers. Be sure to be realistic and choose a reinforcer that is really available to you.

You don't have to come up with spec-

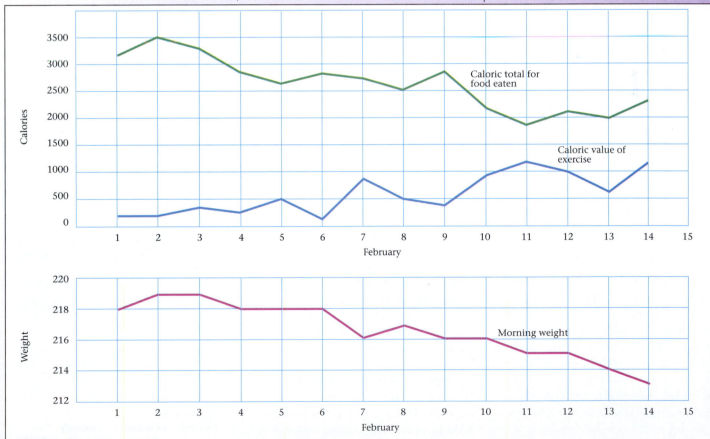

Figure 6.30
Example of record keeping in a self-modification program. Graphic records are ideal for tracking progress in behavior modification efforts. The records shown here illustrate what people would be likely to track in a behavior modification program for weight loss.

What are your reinforcers?

1. What will be the rewards of achieving your goal?
2. What kind of praise do you like to receive, from yourself and others?
3. What kinds of things do you like to have?
4. What are your major interests?
5. What are your hobbies?
6. What people do you like to be with?
7. What do you like to do with those people?
8. What do you do for fun?
9. What do you do to relax?
10. What do you do to get away from it all?
11. What makes you feel good?
12. What would be a nice present to receive?
13. What kinds of things are important to you?
14. What would you buy if you had an extra $20? $50? $100?
15. On what do you spend your money each week?
16. What behaviors do you perform every day? (Don't overlook the obvious or commonplace.)
17. Are there any behaviors you usually perform instead of the target behavior?
18. What would you hate to lose?
19. Of the things you do every day, which would you hate to give up?
20. What are your favorite daydreams and fantasies?
21. What are the most relaxing scenes you can imagine?

Figure 6.31
Selecting a reinforcer. Finding a good reinforcer to use in a behavior modification program can require a lot of thought. The questions listed here can help people identify their personal reinforcers. (From Watson & Tharp, 1989)

tacular new reinforcers that you've never experienced before. *You can use reinforcers that you are already getting.* However, you have to restructure the contingencies so that you get them only if you behave appropriately. For example, if you normally buy two compact discs per week, you might make these purchases contingent on studying a certain number of hours during the week. Making yourself earn rewards that you used to take for granted is often a useful strategy in a self-modification program.

ARRANGING THE CONTINGENCIES. Once you have chosen your reinforcer, you have to set up reinforcement contingencies. These contingencies will describe the exact behavioral goals that must be met and the reinforcement that may then be awarded. For example, in a program to increase exercise, you might make spending $40 on clothes (the reinforcer) contingent on having jogged 15 miles during the week (the target behavior).

Try to set behavioral goals that are both challenging and realistic. You want your goals to be challenging so that they lead to improvement in your behavior. However, setting unrealistically high goals—a common mistake in self-modification—often leads to unnecessary discouragement.

You also need to be concerned about doling out too much reinforcement. If reinforcement is too easy to get, you may become *satiated,* and the reinforcer may lose its motivational power. For example, if you were to reward yourself with virtually all the compact discs you wanted, this reinforcer would lose its incentive value.

One way to avoid the satiation problem is to put yourself on a token economy. A ***token economy* is a system for doling out symbolic reinforcers that are exchanged later for a variety of genuine reinforcers.** Thus, you might develop a point system for exercise behavior, accumulating points that can be spent on compact discs, movies, restaurant meals, and so forth (see Figure 6.32).

SHAPING. In some cases, you may want to reinforce a target response that you are not currently capable of making, such as speaking in front of a large group or jogging 10 miles a day. This situation calls for *shaping,* which is accomplished by reinforcing closer and closer approximations of the desired response. Thus, you might start jogging 2 miles a day and add a half-mile each week until you reach your goal. In shaping your behavior, you should set up a schedule spelling out how and when your target behaviors and reinforcement contingencies should change. Generally, it is a good idea to move forward gradually.

Decreasing Response Strength

Let's turn now to the challenge of reducing the frequency of an undesirable response. You can go about this task in a number of ways. Your principal options include reinforcement, control of antecedents, and punishment.

REINFORCEMENT. Reinforcers can be used in an indirect way to decrease the frequency of a response. This may sound paradoxical, since you have learned that reinforcement strengthens a response. The trick lies in how you define the target behavior. For example, in the case of overeating you might define your target behavior as eating more than 1600 calories a day (an excess response that you want to decrease) or eating less than 1600 calories a day (a deficit response that you want to increase). You can choose the latter definition and reinforce yourself whenever you eat less than 1600 calories in a day. Thus, you can reinforce yourself for *not* emitting a response, or for emitting it less, and thereby decrease a response through reinforcement.

CONTROL OF ANTECEDENTS. A worthwhile strategy for decreasing the occurrence of an undesirable response may be to identify its antecedents and avoid exposure to

Response earning tokens

Response	*Amount*	*Number of Tokens*
Jogging	1/2 mile	4
Jogging	1 mile	8
Jogging	2 miles	16
Tennis	1 hour	4
Tennis	2 hours	8
Sit-ups	25	1
Sit-ups	50	2

Redemption value of tokens

Reinforcer	*Tokens Required*
Purchase one compact disk of your choice	30
Go to movie	50
Go to nice restaurant	100
Take special weekend trip	500

Figure 6.32
Example of a token economy. This token economy was set up to strengthen three types of exercise behavior. The person can exchange tokens for four types of reinforcers.

them. This strategy is especially useful when you are trying to decrease the frequency of a consummatory response, such as smoking or eating. In the case of overeating, for instance, the easiest way to resist temptation is to avoid having to face it. Thus, you might stay away from enticing restaurants, minimize time spent in your kitchen, shop for groceries just after eating (when willpower is higher), and avoid purchasing favorite foods. Control of antecedents can also be helpful in a program to increase studying. The key often lies in *where* you study. You can reduce excessive socializing by studying somewhere devoid of people. Similarly, you can reduce loafing by studying someplace where there is no TV, stereo, or phone to distract you.

PUNISHMENT. The strategy of decreasing unwanted behavior by punishing yourself for that behavior is an obvious option that people tend to overuse. The biggest problem with punishment in a self-modification effort is that it is difficult to follow through and punish yourself. Nonetheless, there may be situations in which your manipulations of reinforcers need to be bolstered by the threat of punishment.

If you're going to use punishment, keep two guidelines in mind. First, do not use punishment alone. Use it in conjunction with positive reinforcement. If you set up a program in which you can earn only negative consequences, you probably won't stick to it. Second, use a relatively mild punishment so that you will actually be able to administer it to yourself. Nurnberger and Zimmerman (1970) developed a creative method of self-punishment. They had subjects write out a check to an organization they hated (for instance, the campaign of a political candidate whom they despised). The check was held by a third party who mailed it if subjects failed to meet their behavioral goals. Such a punishment is relatively harmless, but it can serve as a strong source of motivation.

Executing and Evaluating Your Program

Once you have designed your program, the next step is to put it to work by enforcing the contingencies that you have carefully planned. During this period, you need to continue to accurately record the frequency of your target behavior so you can evaluate your progress. The success of your program depends on your not "cheating." The most common form of cheating is to reward yourself when you have not actually earned it.

You can do two things to increase the likelihood that you will comply with your program. One is to make up a *behavioral contract*—a written agreement outlining a promise to adhere to the contingencies of a behavior modification program. The formality of signing such a contract in front of friends or family seems to make many people take their program more seriously. You can further reduce the likelihood of cheating by having someone other than yourself dole out the reinforcers and punishments.

Behavior modification programs often require some fine-tuning, so don't be surprised if you need to make a few adjustments. Several flaws are especially common in designing self-modification programs. Among those that you should look out for are (1) depending on a weak reinforcer, (2) permitting lengthy delays between appropriate behavior and delivery of reinforcers, and (3) trying to do too much too quickly by setting unrealistic goals. Often, a small revision or two can turn a failing program around and make it a success.

Ending Your Program

Generally, when you design your program you should spell out the conditions under which you will bring it to an end. This involves setting terminal goals such as reaching a certain weight, studying with a certain regularity, or going without cigarettes for a certain length of time. Often, it is a good idea to phase out your program by planning a gradual reduction in the frequency or potency of your reinforcement for appropriate behavior.

Smoking is just one of the many types of behavior that can be controlled with a self-modification program.

If your program is successful, it may fade away without a conscious decision on your part. Often, new, improved patterns of behavior become self-maintaining. Responses such as eating right, exercising regularly, and studying diligently may become habitual. Whether you end your program intentionally or not, you should always be prepared to reinstitute the program if you find yourself slipping back to your old patterns of behavior.

Recap of Key Points

• In behavior modification, the principles of learning are used to change behavior directly. Behavior modification techniques can be used to increase one's self-control. The first step in self-modification involves specifying the overt target behavior to be increased or decreased.

• The second step involves gathering baseline data about the initial rate of the target response and identifying any typical antecedents and consequences associated with the behavior.

• The third step is to design a program. If you are trying to increase the strength of a response, you'll depend on positive reinforcement. The reinforcement contingencies should spell out exactly what you have to do to earn your reinforcer. A number of strategies can be used to decrease the strength of a response, including reinforcement, control of antecedents, and punishment.

• The fourth step involves executing and evaluating your program. Self-modification programs often require some fine-tuning. The final step is to determine how and when you will phase out your program.

Key Ideas

Classical Conditioning

◆ Classical conditioning explains how a neutral stimulus can acquire the capacity to elicit a response originally evoked by another stimulus. This kind of conditioning was originally described by Ivan Pavlov, who conditioned dogs to salivate in response to the sound of a tone.

◆ Many kinds of everyday responses are regulated through classical conditioning, including phobias, anxiety responses, and pleasant emotional responses. Even subtle physiological responses such as immune system functioning respond to classical conditioning.

◆ Stimulus contiguity plays a key role in the acquisition of new conditioned responses. A conditioned response may be weakened and extinguished entirely when the CS is no longer paired with the UCS. In some cases, spontaneous recovery occurs, and an extinguished response reappears after a period of nonexposure to the CS.

◆ Conditioning may generalize to additional stimuli that are similar to the original CS. The opposite of generalization is discrimination, which involves not responding to stimuli that resemble the original CS. Higher-order conditioning occurs when a CS functions as if it were a UCS, to establish new conditioning.

Operant Conditioning

◆ Operant conditioning involves largely voluntary responses that are governed by their consequences. Following the lead of E. L. Thorndike, B. F. Skinner investigated this form of conditioning, working mainly with rats and pigeons in Skinner boxes.

◆ The key dependent variable in operant conditioning is the rate of response over time. When this is shown graphically, steep slopes indicate rapid responding. New operant responses can be shaped by gradually reinforcing closer and closer approximations of the desired response. In operant conditioning, extinction occurs when reinforcement for a response is terminated and the rate of that response declines.

◆ Operant responses are regulated by discriminative stimuli that are cues for the likelihood of obtaining reinforcers. These stimuli are subject to the same processes of generalization and discrimination that occur in classical conditioning.

◆ Delayed reinforcement slows the process of conditioning. Primary reinforcers are unlearned and tied to physiological needs; secondary reinforcers acquire their reinforcing quality through conditioning.

◆ Intermittent schedules of reinforcement produce greater resistance to extinction than similar continuous schedules. Ratio schedules tend to yield higher rates of response than interval schedules. Shorter intervals and higher ratios are associated with faster responding.

◆ Responses can be strengthened through either the presentation of positive reinforcers or the removal of negative reinforcers. Negative reinforcement regulates escape and avoidance learning. The two-process theory provides the best explanation of avoidance behavior and may shed light on why phobias are so difficult to eliminate.

◆ Punishment involves unfavorable consequences that lead to a decline in response strength. Some of the problems associated with the application of punishment are an increase in aggressive behavior and suppression of behavioral activities. Punishment is more effective when it is swift, severe, consistent, and explained.

New Directions in the Study of Conditioning

◆ The findings on instinctive drift, conditioned taste aversion, and preparedness have led to the recognition that there are species-specific biological constraints on conditioning. Evolutionary psychologists argue that learning processes vary somewhat across species because learning mechanisms have sometimes been modified in the course of evolution.

◆ Studies of blocking and signal relations in classical conditioning and response-outcome relations in operant conditioning suggest that cognitive processes play a larger role in conditioning than originally believed.

Observational Learning

◆ In observational learning, an organism is conditioned vicariously by watching a model's conditioning. Both classical and operant conditioning can occur through observational learning, which depends on the processes of attention, retention, reproduction, and motivation.

◆ Observational learning can account for the influence of mass media (such as television) on behavior. Our Featured Study was a classic experiment in which Bandura, Ross, and Ross demonstrated that aggressive models viewed on TV could influence aggressiveness in children.

Putting It in Perspective

◆ Two of our key themes were especially apparent in our coverage of learning and conditioning. One theme involves the interaction of heredity and environment in learning. The other involves the way progress in psychology affects society at large.

Application: Achieving Self-Control Through Behavior Modification

◆ Behavior modification techniques can be used to increase one's self-control. The first step in self-modification involves specifying the overt target behavior to be increased or decreased. The second step involves gathering baseline data.

◆ The third step is to design a program, using procedures such as reinforcement, control of antecedents, and punishment. The fourth step involves executing and evaluating your program. The final step is to determine how and when you will phase out your program.

Key Terms

Acquisition
Antecedents
Avoidance learning
Behavior modification
Behavioral contract
Blocking
Classical conditioning
Conditioned reinforcers
Conditioned response (CR)
Conditioned stimulus (CS)
Continuous reinforcement
Cumulative recorder
Discriminative stimuli
Elicit
Emit
Escape learning
Extinction
Fixed-interval (FI) schedule
Fixed-ratio (FR) schedule
Higher-order conditioning
Instinctive drift
Instrumental learning
Intermittent reinforcement
Law of effect
Learning
Negative reinforcement
Noncontingent reinforcement
Observational learning
Operant chamber
Operant conditioning
Partial reinforcement
Pavlovian conditioning

Phobias
Positive reinforcement
Preparedness
Primary reinforcers
Programmed learning
Punishment
Reinforcement
Reinforcement contingencies
Resistance to extinction
Respondent conditioning
Schedule of reinforcement
Secondary reinforcers
Shaping
Skinner box
Spontaneous recovery
Stimulus contiguity
Stimulus discrimination
Stimulus generalization
Token economy
Trial
Unconditioned response (UCR)
Unconditioned stimulus (UCS)
Variable-interval (VI) schedule
Variable-ratio (VR) schedule

Key People

Albert Bandura
John Garcia
Ivan Pavlov
Robert Rescorla
Martin Seligman
B. F. Skinner
E. L. Thorndike
John B. Watson

Practice Test

1. After repeated pairings of a tone with meat powder, Pavlov found that a dog will salivate when the tone is presented. Salivation to the tone is a(n):
   A. unconditioned stimulus.
   B. unconditioned response.
   C. conditioned stimulus.
   D. conditioned response.

2. Sam's wife always wears the same black nightgown whenever she is "in the mood" for sexual relations. Sam becomes sexually aroused as soon as he sees his wife in the nightgown. For Sam, the nightgown is a(n):
   A. unconditioned stimulus.
   B. unconditioned response.
   C. conditioned stimulus.
   D. conditioned response.

3. Watson and Rayner (1920) conditioned "Little Albert" to fear white rats by banging a hammer on a steel bar as he played with a white rat. Later, it was discovered that Albert feared not only white rats but white stuffed toys and Santa's beard as well. Albert's fear of these other objects can be attributed to:
   A. acquisition.
   B. stimulus generalization.
   C. stimulus discrimination.
   D. an overactive imagination.

4. The phenomenon of higher-order conditioning shows that:
   A. only a genuine, natural UCS can be used to establish a CR.
   B. auditory stimuli are easier to condition than visual stimuli.
   C. visual stimuli are easier to condition than auditory stimuli.
   D. an already established CS can be used in the place of a natural UCS.

5. Which of the following statements is (are) true?
   A. Classical conditioning regulates reflexive, involuntary responses exclusively.
   B. Operant conditioning regulates voluntary responses exclusively.
   C. The distinction between the two types of conditioning is not absolute, with both types jointly and interactively governing some aspects of behavior.
   D. a and b.

6. In a Skinner box, the dependent variable is:
   A. the force with which the lever is pressed or the disk is pecked.
   B. the schedule of reinforcement used.
   C. the rate of responding.
   D. the speed of the cumulative recorder.

7. A primary reinforcer has _____ reinforcing properties; a secondary reinforcer has _____ reinforcing properties.
   A. biological; acquired
   B. conditioned; unconditioned
   C. potent; weak
   D. immediate; delayed

8. The steady, rapid responding of a person playing a slot machine is an example of the pattern of responding typically generated on a _____ schedule.
   A. fixed-ratio
   B. variable-ratio
   C. fixed-interval
   D. variable-interval

9. Positive reinforcement _____ the rate of responding; negative reinforcement _____ the rate of responding.
   A. increases; decreases
   B. decreases; increases
   C. increases; increases
   D. decreases; decreases

10. According to Mowrer, a fear response is acquired due to _____ conditioning; it is maintained due to _____ conditioning.
    A. classical; operant
    B. operant; classical
    C. classical; classical
    D. operant; operant

11. When a stimulus paired with a UCS fails to become a CS because it is redundant with an established CS, this is called:
    A. stimulus discrimination.
    B. sensory preconditioning.
    C. conditioned inhibition.
    D. blocking.

12. According to Rescorla, the strength of a conditioned response depends on:
    A. the number of trials in which the CS and UCS are paired.
    B. the number of trials in which the CS is presented alone.
    C. the percentage of trials in which the CS and UCS are paired.
    D. the percentage of trials in which the UCS is presented alone.

13. Skinner maintained that reinforcement determines the _____ of a response; Bandura maintains that reinforcement determines the _____ of a response.
    A. acquisition; performance
    B. acquisition; acquisition
    C. performance; performance
    D. performance; acquisition

14. The Featured Study by Bandura and his colleagues showed that young children:
    A. who saw models rewarded for their aggression behaved more aggressively than chidren who saw the models punished for their aggression.
    B. will imitate the aggressive behavior of live models but not of filmed models.
    C. will imitate the aggressive behavior of models their own age but not of adult models.
    D. a and b.
    E. a and c.

15. In designing a self-modification program, shaping should be used:
    A. by people who are in poor physical condition.
    B. only when your usual reinforcers are unavailable.
    C. when you want to decrease the frequency of a response.
    D. when you are initially not capable of making the target response.

Answers

1	D	Pages 218–220	6	C	Page 229	11	D	Page 245
2	C	Pages 220–221	7	A	Page 233	12	C	Pages 244–245
3	B	Page 224	8	B	Page 235	13	A	Page 248
4	D	Page 226	9	C	Pages 236–237	14	A	Page 249
5	C	Page 227	10	A	Page 238	15	D	Page 256

7 HUMAN MEMORY

If you live in the United States, you've undoubtedly handled thousands upon thousands of American pennies. Surely, then, you remember what a penny looks like—or do you? Take a look at Figure 7.1. Which drawing corresponds to a real penny? Did you have a hard time selecting the real one? If so, you're not alone. Nickerson and Adams (1979) found that most people can't recognize the real penny in this collection of drawings. And their surprising finding was not a fluke. Undergraduates in England showed even worse memory for British coins (G. Jones, 1990). How can that be? Why do most of us have so poor a memory for an object we see every day?

Let's try another exercise. A definition of a word follows. It's not a particularly common word, but there's a good chance that you're familiar with it. Try to think of the word.

Definition: Favoritism shown or patronage granted by persons in high office to relatives or close friends.

If you can't think of the word, perhaps you can remember what letter of the alphabet it begins with, or what it sounds like. If so, you're experiencing the *tip-of-the-tongue phenomenon,* in which forgotten information feels like it's just out of reach. In this case, the word you may be reaching for is *nepotism.*

You've probably endured the tip-of-the-tongue phenomenon while taking exams. You blank out on a term that you're sure you know. You may feel as if you're on the verge of remembering the term, but you can't quite come up with it. Later, perhaps while you're driving home, the term suddenly comes to you. "Of course," you may say to yourself, "how could I forget that?" That's an interesting question. Clearly, the term was stored in your memory.

As these examples suggest, memory involves more than taking information in and storing it in some mental compartment. In fact, psychologists probing the workings of memory have had to grapple with three enduring questions: (1) How does information get *into* memory? (2) How is information *maintained* in memory? and (3) How is information pulled *back out* of memory? These three questions correspond to the three key processes involved in memory (see Figure 7.2): *encoding* (getting information in), *storage* (maintaining it), and *retrieval* (getting it out).

Figure 7.1
A simple memory test. Nickerson and Adams (1979) presented these 15 versions of an object most people have seen hundreds or thousands of times and asked, "Which one is correct?"

Figure 7.2
Three key processes in memory. Memory depends on three sequential processes: encoding, storage, and retrieval. Some theorists draw an analogy between these processes and elements of information processing by computers.

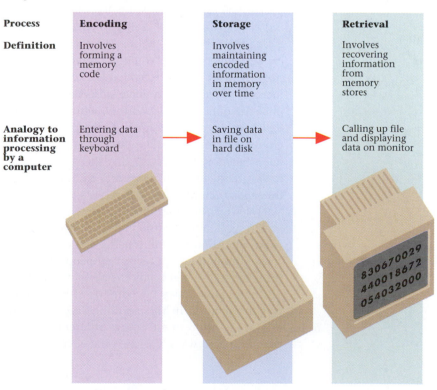

Process	Encoding	Storage	Retrieval
Definition	Involves forming a memory code	Involves maintaining encoded information in memory over time	Involves recovering information from memory stores
Analogy to information processing by a computer	Entering data through keyboard	Saving data in file on hard disk	Calling up file and displaying data on monitor

Encoding involves forming a memory code. For example, when you form a memory code for a word, you might emphasize how it looks, how it sounds, or what it means. Encoding usually requires attention, which is why you may not be able to recall exactly what a penny looks like—most people don't pay much attention to the appearance of a penny. As you'll see throughout this chapter, memory is largely an active process. You're unlikely to remember most things unless you make a conscious effort to do so. *Storage* **involves maintaining encoded information in memory over time.** Psychologists have focused much of their memory research on trying to identify just what factors help or hinder memory storage. But, as the tip-of-the-tongue phenomenon shows, information storage isn't enough to guarantee that you'll remember something. You need to be able to get information out of storage. *Retrieval* **involves recovering information from memory stores.** Research issues concerned with retrieval include the study of how people search memory and why some retrieval strategies are more effective than others.

Most of this chapter is devoted to an examination of memory encoding, storage, and retrieval. As you'll see, these basic processes help explain the ultimate puzzle in the study of memory: why people forget. Just as memory involves more than storage, forgetting involves more than "losing" something from the memory store. Forgetting may be due to deficiencies in any of the three key processes in memory—encoding, storage, or retrieval. After our discussion of forgetting, we will take a brief look at the physiological bases of memory. Finally, we will discuss the theoretical controversy about whether there are separate memory systems for different types of information. The chapter's Application provides some practical advice on how to improve your memory.

ENCODING: GETTING INFORMATION INTO MEMORY

Have you ever been introduced to someone and then realized only 30 seconds into your interaction that you had already "forgotten" his or her name? More often than not, this familiar kind of forgetting is due to a failure to form a memory code for the name. When you're introduced to people, you're often busy sizing them up and thinking about what you're going to say. With your attention diverted in this way, names go in one ear and out the other. You don't remember them because they aren't encoded for storage into memory. Psychologists have observed a similar phenomenon in the laboratory, which has been dubbed the *next-in-line effect*. If subjects in a small group take turns speaking to the group, subsequent memory tests reveal that the subjects tend to not recall much of what was said just before they took their turn (Bond, Pitre, & Van Leeuwen, 1991). Why? Because when subjects are next in line to speak, they are too preoccupied rehearsing to pay attention to what is being said.

Like the problem of forgetting people's names just after you've met them, the next-in-line effect illustrates that active encoding is a crucial process in memory. In this section, we discuss the role of attention in encoding, different types of encoding, and ways to enrich the encoding process.

The Role of Attention

Although we will encounter an exception or two later, you generally need to pay attention to information if you want to remember it. For example, if you sit through a class lecture but pay little attention to it, you're unlikely to remember much of what the professor had to say.

As you meander through life, you're bombarded by an endless array of stimuli. For instance, at this moment you might be sitting in a library somewhere reading this book. Now, when it comes to stimulus input, a library is not exactly Times Square. Yet many stimuli are competing for your attention. Visually, there are the lights above, the printed symbols on this page, books on display nearby, pictures on the wall, and people walking around. In the auditory domain, you might hear the buzz of the lights, the wind whistling through the trees outside, or a conversation a few feet away. Through some of your other senses, you might notice the taste of your chewing gum or the musty smell of old books. Thus, even in the relative quiet of a library, you may be deluged by many stimuli. Indeed, it seems almost miraculous that you ever manage to study! Fortunately, most students *are* able to study under such conditions because they deploy their *attention* in a selective fashion.

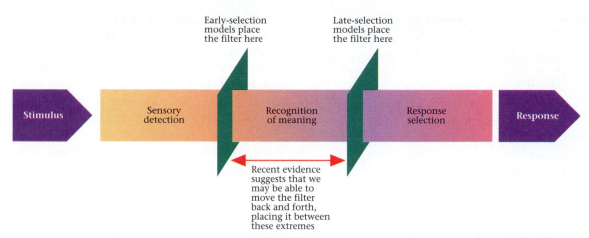

Early-selection models place the filter here

Late-selection models place the filter here

Figure 7.3
Models of selective attention. Early-selection models propose that input is filtered before meaning is processed. Late-selection models hold that filtering occurs after the processing of meaning. There is evidence to support early, late, and intermediate selection, suggesting that the location of the attentional filter may not be fixed.

Stimulus — Sensory detection — Recognition of meaning — Response selection — Response

Recent evidence suggests that we may be able to move the filter back and forth, placing it between these extremes

Attention **involves focusing awareness on a narrowed range of stimuli or events.** Psychologists routinely refer to "selective attention," but the words are really redundant. Attention is selection of input. If you pause to devote a little attention to the matter, you'll realize that selective attention is critical to everyday functioning. If your attention were distributed equally among all stimulus inputs, life would be utter chaos. If you weren't able to filter out most of the potential stimulation around you, you wouldn't be able to read a book, converse with a friend, or even carry on a coherent train of thought.

Attention is usually likened to a *filter* that screens out most potential stimuli while allowing a select few to pass through into conscious awareness. However, a great deal of debate has been devoted to *where* the filter is located in the information-processing system. The key issue in this debate is whether stimuli are screened out *early,* during sensory input, or *late,* after the brain has processed the meaning or significance of the input (see Figure 7.3).

Casual observation suggests the latter. For example, imagine yourself at a crowded party where many conversations are taking place. You're paying attention to one conversation and filtering out the others. However, if someone across the room mentions your name, you will probably notice it, even though you've been ignoring that conversation. If selection is early, how can you register input you've been blocking out? This common phenomenon suggests that attention involves *late* selection, based on the *meaning* of input.

Which view is supported by the weight of scientific evidence—early selection or late selection? Studies have found ample evidence for *both* as well as for intermediate selection (Cowan, 1988; Johnston & Dark, 1986). These findings have led

some theorists to conclude that the location of the attention filter may be flexible rather than fixed (Johnston & Heinz, 1978; Shiffrin, 1988).

Levels of Processing 6a

Attention is critical to the encoding of memories, but not all attention is created equal. You can attend to things in different ways, focusing on different aspects of the stimulus input. According to some theorists, these qualitative differences in *how* people attend to information are the main factors influencing how much they remember. For example, Fergus Craik and Robert Lockhart (1972) argue that different rates of forgetting occur because some methods of encoding create more durable memory codes than others.

Craik and Lockhart propose that incoming information can be processed at different levels. For instance, they maintain that in dealing with verbal information, people engage in three progressively deeper levels of processing: structural, phonemic, and semantic encoding (see Figure 7.4). *Structural encoding* is relatively shallow processing that emphasizes the physical structure of the stimulus. For example, if words are flashed on a screen, structural encoding registers such things as how they were printed (capital, lowercase, and so on) or the length of the words (how many letters). Further analysis may result in *phonemic encoding,* which emphasizes what a word sounds like. Phonemic encoding involves naming or saying (perhaps silently) the words. Finally, *semantic encoding* emphasizes the meaning of verbal input. Semantic encoding involves thinking about the objects and actions the words represent. **Levels-of-processing theory proposes that deeper levels of processing result in longer-lasting memory codes.**

In one experimental test of levels-of-processing theory, Craik and Tulving (1975) compared the

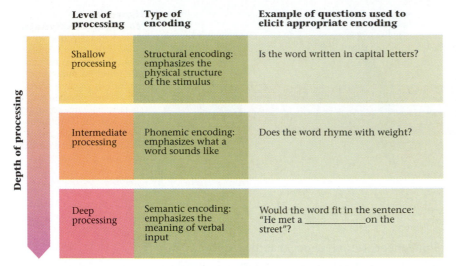

Level of processing	Type of encoding	Example of questions used to elicit appropriate encoding
Shallow processing	Structural encoding: emphasizes the physical structure of the stimulus	Is the word written in capital letters?
Intermediate processing	Phonemic encoding: emphasizes what a word sounds like	Does the word rhyme with weight?
Deep processing	Semantic encoding: emphasizes the meaning of verbal input	Would the word fit in the sentence: "He met a _____ on the street"?

Depth of processing

Figure 7.4
Levels-of-processing theory. According to Craik and Lockhart (1972), structural, phonemic, and semantic encoding—which can be elicited by questions such as those shown on the right—involve progressively deeper levels of processing, which should result in more durable memories.

another? Craik and Lockhart had hoped that the *time required for processing* would prove to be a good indicator of depth. However, Craik and Tulving (1975) found that it's possible to design a task in which structural encoding takes longer than semantic encoding. This finding indicates that processing time is not a reliable index of depth of processing. Thus, the levels in levels-of-processing theory remain vaguely defined.

Enriching Encoding 6a

Structural, phonemic, and semantic encoding do not exhaust the options when it comes to forming memory codes. There are other dimensions to encoding, dimensions that can enrich the encoding process and thereby improve memory.

Elaboration

Semantic encoding can often be enhanced through a process called elaboration. ***Elaboration* is linking a stimulus to other information at the time of encoding.** For example, let's say you read that phobias are often caused by classical conditioning, and you apply this idea to your own fear of spiders. In doing so, you are engaging in elaboration. The additional associations created by elaboration usually help people remember information. Differences in elaboration can help explain why different approaches to semantic processing result in varied amounts of retention (Craik & Tulving, 1975).

Elaboration often consists of thinking of examples that illustrate an idea. The value of examples was demonstrated in a study in which subjects read 32 paragraphs of information about a fictitious African country (Palmere et al., 1983). Each paragraph communicated one main idea, which was followed by no example, 1 example, 2 examples, or 3 examples. The effect of examples on memory was dramatic. As you can see in Figure 7.6, additional examples led to better memory. In this study, the examples were provided to the students, but self-generated examples created through elaboration would probably be even more valuable in enhancing memory.

Visual Imagery

Imagery—the creation of visual images to represent the words to be remembered—can also be used to enrich encoding. Of course, some words are easier to create images for than others. If you were asked to remember the word *juggler*, you could readily form an image of someone juggling

durability of structural, phonemic, and semantic encoding. They directed subjects' attention to particular aspects of briefly presented stimulus words by asking them questions about various characteristics of words (see Figure 7.4). The questions were designed to engage the subjects in different levels of processing. The key hypothesis was that retention of the stimulus words would increase as subjects moved from structural to phonemic to semantic encoding. After responding to 60 words, the subjects received an unexpected test of their memory for the words. As predicted, the subjects' recall was low after structural encoding, notably better after phonemic encoding, and highest after semantic encoding (see Figure 7.5).

The hypothesis that deeper processing leads to enhanced memory has been replicated in many studies (Koriat & Melkman, 1987; Lockhart & Craik, 1990). Nonetheless, the levels-of-processing model is not without its weaknesses. Critics ask, what exactly is a "level" of processing? And how do we determine whether one level is deeper than

Figure 7.5
Retention at three levels of processing. In accordance with levels-of-processing theory, Craik and Tulving (1975) found that structural, phonemic, and semantic encoding led to progressively better retention.

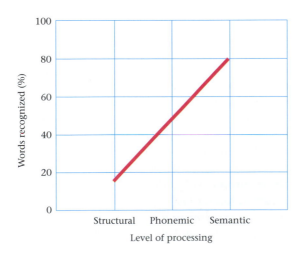

balls. However, if you were asked to remember the word *truth*, you would probably have more difficulty forming a suitable image. The difference is that *juggler* refers to a concrete object, whereas *truth* refers to an abstract concept. Allan Paivio (1969) points out that it is easier to form images of concrete objects than of abstract concepts. He believes that this ease of image formation affects memory.

The beneficial effect of imagery on memory was demonstrated in a study by Paivio, Smythe, and Yuille (1968). They asked subjects to learn a list of 16 pairs of words. They manipulated whether the words were concrete, high-imagery words or abstract, low-imagery words. In terms of imagery potential, the list contained four types of pairings: high-high (*juggler-dress*), high-low (*letter-effort*), low-high (*duty-hotel*), and low-low (*quality-necessity*). Figure 7.7 shows the recall for each type of pairing. The impact of imagery is quite evident. The best recall was of high-high pairings, and the worst recall was of low-low pairings.

According to Paivio (1986), imagery facilitates memory because it provides a second kind of memory code, and two codes are better than one. His **dual-coding theory holds that memory is enhanced by forming semantic and visual codes, since either can lead to recall.** Although some aspects of his theory have been questioned (Marschark & Hunt, 1989), it's clear that the use of mental imagery can enhance memory in many situations (Marschark, 1992).

Self-Referent Encoding

Making material *personally* meaningful can also enrich encoding. For example, if you ride a bus regularly, you've probably heard the driver call out the names of the stops day in and day out for months. Do you remember all of the stops? If you haven't made an effort to memorize them, probably not. But you could probably list those that you've used, or even the ones where your friends get on or off. People's recall of information tends to be slanted in favor of material that is personally relevant (Kahan & Johnson, 1992).

Self-referent encoding **involves deciding how or whether information is personally relevant.** This approach to encoding was compared to structural, phonemic, and semantic encoding in a study by Rogers, Kuiper, and Kirker (1977). Like Craik and Tulving (1975), these researchers manipulated encoding by asking their subjects certain kinds of questions. To induce self-referent encoding, sub-

jects were asked to decide whether adjectives flashed on a screen applied to them personally. The 40 adjectives were terms that could be applied to people, such as *sly, timid,* and *shrewd.* The results showed that self-referent encoding led to improved recall of the adjectives.

The value of self-referent encoding demonstrates once again that encoding plays a critical role in memory. But encoding is only one of the three key processes in memory. We turn next to the process of storage, which for many people is virtually synonymous with memory.

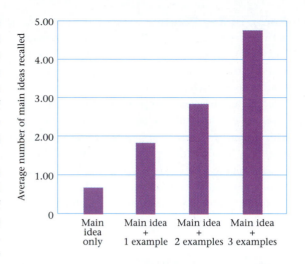

Figure 7.6
Effects of examples on retention of ideas. Palmere et al. (1983) manipulated the number of examples provided to illustrate the main idea of various paragraphs. As the number of examples increased from none to three, so did subjects' retention of the main ideas. (Data from Palmere et al., 1983)

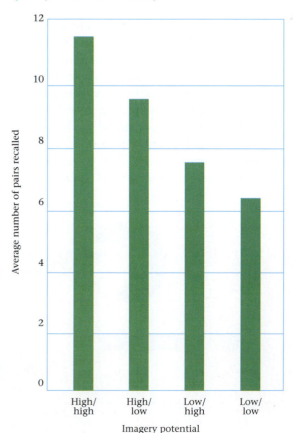

Figure 7.7
The effect of visual imagery on retention. Subjects given pairs of words to remember showed better recall for high-imagery pairings, demonstrating that visual imagery enriches encoding. (Data from Paivio, Smythe, & Yuille, 1968)

• Three key processes contribute to memory: encoding, storage, and retrieval. The next-in-line effect illustrates that active encoding is crucial to memory.

• Attention, which facilitates encoding, is inherently selective and has been compared to a filter. There is evidence of both early and late selection of input. This evidence suggests that people may have some flexibility in where they place their attention filter.

• According to levels-of-processing theory, the kinds of memory codes people create depend on which aspects of a stimulus are emphasized. Structural, phonemic, and semantic encoding emphasize the structure, sound, and meaning of words, respectively.

• Deeper processing results in better recall of information. Structural, phonemic, and semantic encoding represent progressively deeper levels of processing.

• Elaboration enriches encoding by linking a stimulus to other information, such as examples of an idea. The creation of visual images to represent words can enrich encoding. Visual imagery may help by creating two memory codes rather than just one. Encoding that emphasizes personal self-reference may be especially useful in facilitating retention.

STORAGE: MAINTAINING INFORMATION IN MEMORY

Figure 7.8
The Atkinson and Shiffrin model of memory storage. Atkinson and Shiffrin (1971) proposed that memory is made up of three information stores. *Sensory memory* can hold a large amount of information just long enough for a small portion of it to be selected for longer storage. *Short-term memory* has a limited capacity, and unless aided by rehearsal, its storage duration is brief. *Long-term memory* can store an apparently unlimited amount of information for indeterminate periods.

In their efforts to understand memory storage, theorists have historically related it to the technologies of their age (Roediger, 1980). One of the earliest models used to explain memory storage was the wax tablet. Both Aristotle and Plato compared memory to a block of wax that differed in size and hardness for various individuals. Remembering, according to this analogy, was like stamping an impression into the wax. As long as the image remained in the wax, the memory would remain intact.

Current theories of memory reflect the technological advances of the 20th century. Many modern theories draw an analogy between information storage by computers and information storage in human memory. These *information-processing theories* emphasize how information flows through a series of separate memory stores.

The most prominent information-processing model of memory holds that there are three memory stores: a *sensory store*, a *short-term store*, and a *long-term store*. Many psychologists have contributed to this theory, but Richard Atkinson and Richard Shiffrin (1968, 1971) were especially influential. We will use their model, which is diagrammed in Figure 7.8, as a general guide in our discussion of memory storage. According to this model, incoming information must pass through two temporary storage buffers (the sensory and short-term stores) before it can be transferred into long-term storage. Like the wax tablet before it, the information-processing model of memory is a metaphor; the three memory stores are not viewed as anatomical structures in the brain, but rather as functionally distinct types of memory.

Sensory Memory   6b

The *sensory memory* **preserves information in its original sensory form for a brief time, usually only a fraction of a second.** Sensory memory allows the sensation of a visual pattern, sound, or touch to linger for a brief moment after the sensory

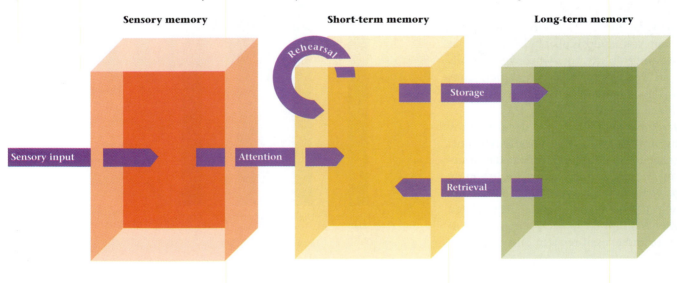

Sensory memory   Short-term memory   Long-term memory

stimulation is over. In the case of vision, people really perceive an *afterimage* rather than the actual stimulus. You can demonstrate the existence of afterimages for yourself by rapidly moving a lighted sparkler in circles in the dark. If you move the sparkler fast enough, you should see a complete circle even though the light source is only a single point (see the adjacent photo). The sensory memory preserves the sensory image long enough for you to perceive a continuous circle rather than separate points of light.

The brief preservation of sensations in sensory memory gives you additional time to try to recognize stimuli. However, you'd better take advantage of sensory storage immediately, because it doesn't last long. This was demonstrated in a classic experiment by George Sperling (1960). His subjects saw three rows of letters flashed on a screen for just ¹/₂₀ of a second. A tone following the exposure signaled which row of letters the subject should report to the experimenter (see Figure 7.9). Subjects were fairly accurate when the signal occurred immediately. However, their accuracy steadily declined as the delay of the tone increased to one second. Why? Because the memory trace in the visual sensory store decays in about ¹/₄ of a second.

Memory traces appear to last a little longer in the auditory domain (Cowan, Lichty, & Grove, 1990), and perhaps in other senses as well. But sensory storage is still fleeting, to say the least. However, the sensory store has a fairly large capac-

Because the image of the sparkler persists briefly in sensory memory, when the sparkler is moved fast enough, the blending of afterimages causes people to see a continuous circle instead of a succession of individual points.

ity. For example, it can register up to 25 visual stimuli and perhaps more. These stimuli consist of raw sensations that need to be analyzed and combined into patterns that make up recognizable letters, words, and so forth. Some of this information processing may occur in sensory memory (Merikle, 1980). However, most of it probably takes place in the short-term memory store, which we consider next.

Short-Term Memory 6b

Short-term memory (STM) **is a limited-capacity store that can maintain unrehearsed information for up to about 20 seconds.** In contrast, information stored in long-term memory may last

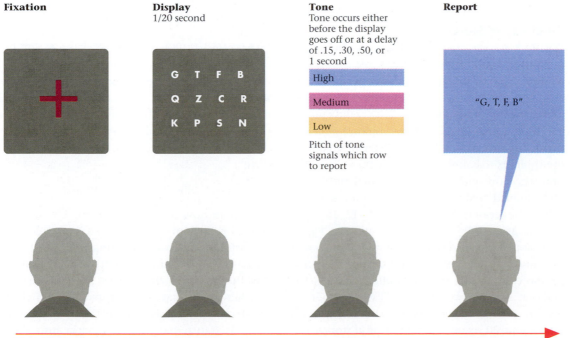

Fixation

Display
1/20 second

G	T	F	B
Q	Z	C	R
K	P	S	N

Tone
Tone occurs either before the display goes off or at a delay of .15, .30, .50, or 1 second

High

Medium

Low

Pitch of tone signals which row to report

Report

"G, T, F, B"

Time (fractions of seconds)

Figure 7.9
Sperling's (1960) study of sensory memory. After the subjects had fixated on the cross, the letters were flashed on the screen just long enough to create a visual afterimage. High, medium, and low tones signaled which row of letters to report. Because subjects had to rely on the afterimage to report the letters, Sperling (1960) was able to measure how rapidly the afterimage decayed by varying the delay between the display and the signal to report.

weeks, months, or years. Actually, you can maintain information in your short-term store for longer than 20 seconds. How? Primarily, by engaging in **rehearsal—the process of repetitively verbalizing or thinking about the information.** You surely have used the rehearsal process on many occasions. For instance, when you get a phone number from the information operator, you probably recite it over and over until you can dial the number. Rehearsal keeps recycling the information through your short-term memory. In theory, this recycling could go on indefinitely, but in reality something eventually distracts you and breaks the rehearsal loop.

People's dependence on recitation to maintain information in short-term memory is apparent from the kinds of mistakes they tend to make when their efforts break down. For example, suppose that you were asked to remember a list of random letters such as

Q P L H S X

presented briefly on a screen. Mistakes on this task usually involve *acoustic confusions,* in which the incorrect answers *sound* like the correct answers (Conrad, 1964; Hanson, 1990). For instance, you might mistakenly convert P to E because they sound alike. Notice, you are far less likely to convert P to R because they *look* alike. Even when information is presented visually, people tend to make acoustic mistakes, because they depend largely on phonemic encoding in short-term memory.

Durability of Storage

Without rehearsal, information in short-term memory quickly *decays* with the passage of time (Cowan, 1995). This rapid decay was demonstrated in a study by Peterson and Peterson (1959). They measured how long undergraduates could remember three consonants if they couldn't rehearse them. To prevent rehearsal, the Petersons required the students to count backward by threes from the time the consonants were presented until they saw a light that signaled the recall test (see Figure 7.10). The recall test occurred 3, 6, 9, 12, 15, or 18 seconds after the subjects began counting. Figure 7.11 plots subjects' recall accuracy as a function of the time elapsed. The results indicate that when people cannot rehearse unfamiliar material, the material is quickly lost from STM. Without rehearsal, the *maximum* duration of STM storage is only about 20 seconds and the *typical* storage duration is even shorter.

"The Magical Number Seven, Plus or Minus Two."

GEORGE MILLER

Capacity of Storage

Short-term memory is also limited in the number of items it can hold. The small capacity of STM was pointed out by George Miller (1956) in a famous paper called "The Magical Number Seven, Plus or Minus Two: Some Limits on Our Capacity for Processing Information." Miller noticed that people could recall only about seven items in tasks that required them to remember unfamiliar material. The common thread in these tasks, Miller argued, was that they required the use of STM.

When short-term memory is filled to capacity, the insertion of new information often *displaces* some of the information currently in STM. For example, if you're memorizing a ten-item list of basic chemical elements, the eighth, ninth, and tenth items in the list will begin to "bump out" earlier items. Similarly, if you're reciting the phone number of a pizza parlor you're about to call when someone asks, "How much is this pizza going to cost?" your retrieval of the cost information into STM may knock part of the phone number out of STM. The limited capacity of STM constrains people's ability to perform tasks in which they need to mentally juggle various pieces of information (Baddeley & Hitch, 1974).

You can increase the capacity of your short-term memory by combining stimuli into larger, possibly higher-order units, called *chunks* (Simon, 1974). **A *chunk* is a group of familiar stimuli stored as a single unit.** You can demonstrate the effect of chunking by asking someone to recall a sequence of 12 letters grouped in the following way:

FB - ITW - AC - IAIB - M

As you read the letters aloud, pause at the hyphens. Your subject will probably attempt to remember each letter separately because there are no obvious groups or chunks. But a string of 12 letters is too long for STM, so errors are likely. Now present the same string of letters to another person, but place the pauses in the following locations:

FBI - TWA - CIA - IBM

The letters now form four familiar chunks that should occupy only four slots in STM, resulting in successful recall (Bower & Springston, 1970).

To successfully chunk the letters I B M, a subject must first recognize these letters as a familiar unit. This familiarity has to be stored somewhere in long-term memory. Hence, in this case information was transferred from long-term into short-term memory. This is not unusual. People routinely

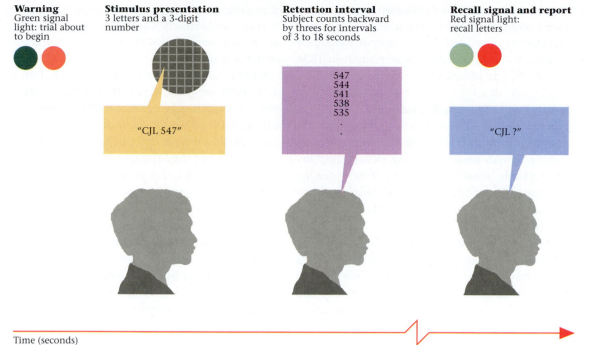

Warning
Green signal light: trial about to begin

Stimulus presentation
3 letters and a 3-digit number

"CJL 547"

Retention interval
Subject counts backward by threes for intervals of 3 to 18 seconds

547
544
541
538
535
.
.

Recall signal and report
Red signal light: recall letters

"CJL ?"

Time (seconds)

Figure 7.10
Peterson and Peterson's (1959) study of short-term memory. After a warning light was flashed, the subjects were given three consonants to remember. The researchers prevented rehearsal by giving the subjects a three-digit number at the same time and telling them to count backward by three from that number until given the signal to recall the letters. By varying the amount of time between stimulus presentation and recall, Peterson and Peterson were able to measure the rate of decay in short-term memory.

draw information out of their long-term memory banks to evaluate and understand information that they are working with in short-term memory.

Short-Term Memory as "Working Memory"

Twenty years of research eventually uncovered a number of problems with the original model of short-term memory (Cowan, 1988; Hilgard & Bower, 1981). Among other things, studies showed that short-term memory is *not* limited to phonemic encoding and that decay and displacement are *not* the only processes responsible for the loss of information from STM. These and other findings suggest that short-term memory involves more than a simple rehearsal buffer, as originally envisioned. To make sense of such findings, Alan Baddeley (1976, 1989, 1992) has proposed a more complex model of short-term memory that characterizes it as "working memory."

According to Baddeley, working memory consists of three components. The first is the *rehearsal loop* that represented all of STM in the original model. This component is at work when you use recitation to temporarily hold on to a phone number. The second component in working memory is a *visuospatial sketchpad* that permits people to temporarily hold and manipulate visual images. This component is at work when you try to mentally rearrange the furniture in your bedroom. The third component is an *executive control system*. It handles the limited amount of information that people can juggle at one time as they engage in reasoning and decision making. This component is at work when you mentally weigh all the pros and cons before deciding whether to buy a particular car.

The two key characteristics that originally defined short-term memory—small capacity and short storage duration—are still present in the concept of working memory. However, Baddeley's model accounts for evidence that STM handles a greater variety of functions and depends on more complicated processes than previously thought.

Long-Term Memory   6b

Long-term memory (LTM) is an unlimited capacity store that can hold information over

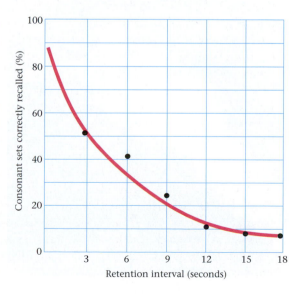

Figure 7.11
The rapid decay of short-term memory. Unaided by rehearsal, subjects' short-term memory for the target consonants declined rapidly. The actual data points (the dots) closely fit the theoretical curve shown here. (Data from Peterson & Peterson, 1959)

lengthy periods of time. Unlike sensory and short-term memory, which decay rapidly, LTM can store information indefinitely. Long-term memories are durable. Some information may remain in LTM across an entire lifetime.

Durability: Is Storage Permanent?

One point of view is that all information stored in long-term memory is stored there *permanently*. According to this view, forgetting occurs only because people sometimes cannot *retrieve* needed information from LTM. To draw an analogy, imagine that memories are stored in LTM like marbles in a barrel. According to this view, none of the marbles ever leak out. When you forget, you just aren't able to dig out the right marble, but it's there—somewhere. An alternative point of view assumes that some memories stored in LTM do vanish forever. According to this view, the barrel is leaky and some of the marbles roll out, never to return.

The notion that LTM storage may be permanent is certainly intriguing. It's based on several lines of research that seem to provide compelling evidence of permanent storage. However, each line of research turns out to be less compelling than it appears at first glance. For example, consider **flashbulb memories, which are unusually vivid and detailed recollections of momentous events.** Many American adults, for instance, can remember exactly where they were, what they were doing, and how they felt when they learned that President John F. Kennedy had been shot. You may have a similar recollection related to the explosion of the *Challenger* spacecraft (see the adja-

cent photo). The vivid detail of people's memories of President Kennedy's assasination over 35 years ago would seen to provide a striking example of permanent storage.

Evidence that appears to support the notion of permanent memory storage also comes from reports of exceptional recall through hypnosis. Hypnotized subjects who have been regressed back to early childhood have described in remarkable detail events that they thought they had forgotten (Spiegel & Spiegel, 1985). These hypnosis-aided recoveries of lost memories suggest that normal forgetfulness is just a matter of poor retrieval.

Finally, there are the studies conducted by Canadian neuroscientist Wilder Penfield. He reported triggering long-lost memories through electrical stimulation of the brain (ESB) during brain surgeries (Penfield & Perot, 1963). As we saw in Chapter 3, patients often remain conscious during brain surgery. When Penfield used ESB to map brain function in patients undergoing surgery for epilepsy, he found that stimulation of the temporal lobe sometimes elicited vivid descriptions of events long past. Patients would describe events that apparently came from their childhood—such as "being in a lumberyard" or "watching Mom make a phone call"—as if they were there once again. Penfield and others inferred that these descriptions were exact playbacks of long-lost memories unearthed by electrical stimulation of the brain.

So, why don't these lines of evidence demonstrate that LTM storage is permanent? Let's look at each. Although flashbulb memories are remarkably durable, studies suggest that they are neither as accurate nor as special as once believed (Neisser & Harsch, 1992). Like other memories, they become less detailed and complete with time (Christianson, 1989; McCloskey, Wible, & Cohen, 1988). Similarly, when hypnosis-aided recollections have been double-checked, they have often turned out to be inaccurate (Orne & Dinges, 1989). That is, hypnotized subjects often make things up and distort recollections to be consistent with their current beliefs. Finally, the "memories" activated by ESB in Penfield's studies often included factual impossibilities and dreamlike elements of fantasy. For instance, the person who recalled being in a lumberyard had never actually been to one. The ESB-induced recollections of Penfield's subjects apparently were hallucinations, dreams, or loose reconstructions of events rather than exact replays of the past (Squire, 1987). Thus, although psychologists can't absolutely rule out the possibility, there is no convincing evidence that all memories

People throughout the United States were watching on television when the *Challenger* space shuttle exploded in the skies over Florida in 1986. For these observers, their experience of the *Challenger* tragedy is likely to be a flashbulb memory—one that will persist in vivid detail.

CHAPTER SEVEN

are stored away permanently (Loftus & Loftus, 1980).

Transferring Information into Long-Term Memory

How is information transferred from short-term memory into long-term memory? According to Atkinson and Shiffrin (1971), information that is being maintained in short-term memory through *rehearsal* is gradually absorbed into long-term memory. Rundus (1971) investigated this hypothesis by asking undergraduates to recall a list of 20 words immediately after they had rehearsed the words aloud. The words were presented slowly, one at a time, so subjects had time to rehearse some of the list before hearing a new word. Rundus kept track of how often each word was rehearsed.

Figure 7.12 shows the probability of recall for each word as a function of its position on Rundus's list. The resultant U-shaped curve, called the *serial-position effect,* is often observed when subjects are tested on their memory of lists. **The *serial-position effect* occurs when subjects show better recall for items at the beginning and end of a list than for items in the middle.** This effect includes two components—a primacy effect and a recency effect—that are often seen in memory research. **A *primacy effect* occurs when items near the beginning of a list are recalled better than other items. A *recency effect* occurs when items near the end of a list are recalled better than other items.**

The mechanisms underlying the serial-position effect are the subject of considerable debate (Greene, 1992). The most widely cited explanation asserts that the seemingly incompatible primacy and recency effects occur together because the short-term and long-term memory stores operate separately. The primacy effect reflects LTM storage. The words at the beginning of the list get

rehearsed more often than the others. Hence, they're more likely to be transferred into LTM than later words. In contrast, the recency effect reflects STM storage. Since the words at the end of the list are the ones most recently presented, they're still available in STM if subjects' recall is tested promptly.

Organization in Long-Term Memory

Consider what your plight would be if your college or local library did not organize its holdings. Imagine searching among hundreds of thousands of randomly shelved books for a specific book on 17th-century Canadian history. Your term paper would probably be long overdue before you found the needed book.

Organization is just as important for long-term memory. Although LTM storage does not appear to be permanent, it undeniably houses a vast

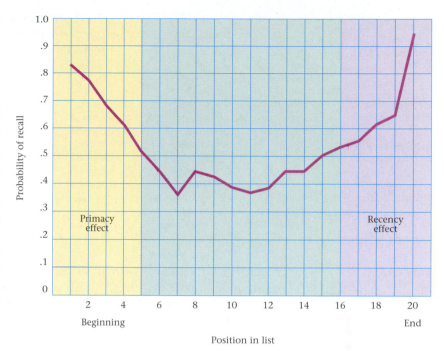

Figure 7.12
The serial-position effect. After hearing a list of items to remember, people reliably recall more of the items from the beginning (primacy effect) and the end (recency effect) of the list than from the middle, producing the characteristic U-shaped curve shown here.

Giraffe	Plumber	Owen	Lettuce
Parsnip	Otto	Parsley	Donkey
Zebra	Noah	Otter	Blacksmith
Radish	Chipmunk	Grocer	Eggplant
Diver	Adam	Badger	Garlic
Broker	Chemist	Camel	Wildcat
Spinach	Turnip	Baboon	Jason
Baker	Simon	Florist	Leopard
Woodchuck	Howard	Rhubarb	Printer
Dancer	Milkman	Melon	Bernard
Weasel	Gerard	Mustard	Carrot
Pumpkin	Panther	Wallace	Sherman
Amos	Oswalk	Dentist	Waiter
Typist	Druggist	Muskrat	Moses
Byron	Reindeer	Mushroom	Cabbage

Figure 7.13
Clustering. The words in this list fall into four categories: animals, men's names, vegetables, and professions. Even when the words are presented in mixed order, people tend to recall them in these groupings. This phenomenon is called clustering. (From Bousfield, 1953)

amount of information. Without at least some organization, that huge supply of information would be virtually useless. Unfortunately, long-term memory stores do not appear to be organized as systematically as a well-run library. Research suggests that LTM is characterized by a hodge-podge of overlapping organizational frameworks. In this section, we'll look at a small sample of these organizational structures.

CLUSTERING AND CONCEPTUAL HIERARCHIES. If you were to memorize the list of 60 words in Figure 7.13, your recall of the list at a later time would demonstrate the existence of organization in long-term memory. Each of the words in this list fits into one of four categories: animals, men's names, vegetables, or professions. Bousfield (1953) showed that subjects recalling this list engage in clustering. *Clustering* is the tendency to remember similar or related items in groups. Even though the words are not presented in organized groups, you would tend to remember them in bunches that belong in the same category.

When possible, information is organized into conceptual hierarchies. A *conceptual hierarchy* is

a multilevel classification system based on common properties among items. A conceptual hierarchy that a person might construct for minerals can be found in Figure 7.14. According to Gordon Bower (1970), organizing information into a conceptual hierarchy can improve recall dramatically.

SEMANTIC NETWORKS. Of course, not all information fits neatly into conceptual hierarchies. Much knowledge seems to be organized into less systematic frameworks, called semantic networks (Collins & Loftus, 1975). A *semantic network* consists of nodes representing concepts, joined together by pathways that link related concepts. A small semantic network is shown in Figure 7.15. The ovals are the nodes, and the words inside the ovals are the interlinked concepts. The lines connecting the nodes are the pathways. A more detailed figure would label the pathways to show how the concepts are related to one another. However, in this instance, the relations should be fairly clear. The length of each pathway represents the degree of association between two concepts. Shorter pathways imply stronger associations.

Semantic networks have proven useful in explaining why thinking about one word (such as *butter*) can make a closely related word (such as *bread*) easier to remember (Meyer & Schvaneveldt, 1976). According to Collins and Loftus (1975), when people think about a word, their thoughts naturally go to related words. These theorists call this process *spreading activation* within a semantic network. They assume that activation spreads out along the pathways of the semantic network surrounding the word. They also theorize that the strength of this activation decreases as it travels outward, much as ripples decrease in size as they radiate outward from a rock tossed into a pond. Consider again the semantic network shown in Figure 7.15. If subjects see the word *red*, words that

Figure 7.14
Conceptual hierarchies and long-term memory. Some types of information can be organized into a multilevel hierarchy of concepts, like the one shown here, which was studied by Bower and others (1969). They found that subjects remember more information when they organize it into a conceptual hierarchy.

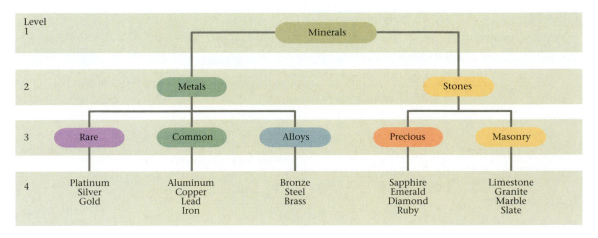

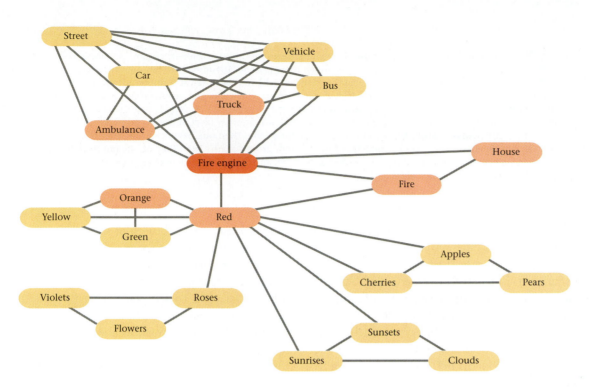

Figure 7.15
A semantic network.
Much of the organization of long-term memory depends on networks of associations among concepts. In this highly simplified depiction of a fragment of a semantic network, the shorter the line linking any two concepts, the stronger the association between them. The coloration of the concept boxes represents activation of the concepts. This is how the network might look just after a person hears the words *fire engine*. (Adapted from Collins & Loftus, 1975)

are closely linked to it (such as *orange*) should be easier to recall than words that have longer links (such as *sunrises*).

SCHEMAS AND SCRIPTS. Imagine that you've just visited Professor Smith's office, which is shown in the adjacent photo. Take a brief look at the photo and then cover it up. Now pretend that you want to describe Professor Smith's office to a friend. Write down what you saw in the office (the picture).

After you finish, compare your description with the picture. Chances are, your description will include elements—filing cabinets, for instance—that were *not* in the office. This common phenomenon demonstrates how *schemas* can influence memory.

A *schema* is an organized cluster of knowledge about a particular object or event abstracted from previous experience with the object or event. For example, college students have schemas for what professors' offices are like. *People are more likely to remember things that are consistent with their schemas than things that are not.* This principle was quite apparent when Brewer and Treyens (1981) tested the recall of 30 subjects who had briefly visited the office shown in the photo. Most subjects recalled the desks and chairs, but few recalled the wine bottle or the picnic basket, which aren't part of a typical office schema. Indeed, the tendency to recall things that are consistent with a schema can lead to memory errors. For instance, nine subjects in the Brewer and Treyens study

falsely recalled that the office contained books. Perhaps you made the same mistake. Information stored in memory is often organized around schemas (Greene, 1992). Thus, recall of objects or events will be influenced by both the actual details observed and the person's schemas for these objects and events.

A *script* is a particular kind of schema. **A *script***

Professor Smith's office is shown in this photo. Follow the instructions in the text to learn how Brewer and Treyens (1981) used it in a study of memory.

Figure 7.16
Figure 7.16
Scripts in long-term memory. Knowing what activity this abstract passage is describing greatly improves recall of the ideas in the passage. Consult the text to learn the activity the passage describes. (From Bransford & Johnson, 1973)

The procedure is actually quite simple. First you arrange things into different groups. Of course, one pile may be sufficient depending on how much there is to do. If you have to go somewhere else due to lack of facilities, that is the next step; otherwise you are pretty well set. It is important not to overdo things. That is, it is better to do too few things at once than too many. In the short run this may not seem important, but complications can easily arise. A mistake can be expensive as well. At first the whole procedure will seem complicated. Soon, however, it will become just another facet of life. It is difficult to foresee any end to the necessity for this task in the immediate future, but then one never can tell. After the procedure is completed, one arranges the materials into different groups again. Then they can be put into their appropriate places. Eventually they will be used once more, and the whole cycle will then have to be repeated. However, that is part of life.

Figure 7.17
An updated overview of memory storage. This diagram builds on the Atkinson and Shiffrin model (see Figure 7.8) to summarize our coverage of memory storage. The model shown here depicts short-term memory as a multicomponent working memory, differentiates between maintenance and elaborative rehearsal, and lists some of the organizational frameworks used in long-term memory. Also consult Concept Check 7.1 to compare the encoding, storage capacity, and storage duration of the three memory stores.

organizes **what people know about common activities.** People have scripts for many activities, such as getting up in the morning or going to a restaurant (Rumelhart & Norman, 1988; Schank & Abelson, 1977). A script resembles an outline of a play. It specifies the standard roles, objects, sequences of events, and results of some activity. For example, going to a restaurant involves fairly standard roles (customer, chef, waiter), objects (tables, plates, menus), sequences of events (looking at the menu, ordering the food, eating, paying the bill), and results (hunger is satisfied). People show considerable agreement on the scripts for many common activities, such as attending a lecture, going grocery shopping, or visiting a doctor (Bower, Black, & Turner, 1979).

Stop for a moment and read the story in Figure 7.16. It describes a familiar activity, but the ideas are presented so abstractly that the activity is difficult to recognize. People who read the passage without being told what it's about show poor recall of the ideas in the story (Bransford & Johnson, 1973). In contrast, people who are told that the passage is about washing clothes recall over twice as much information. Now that you know what the story is about, you can use your script for washing clothes to organize the passage's abstract ideas.

In summary, memory storage is a complex matter, involving several memory stores and a host of organizational devices. To help you make sense of all this information, Figure 7.17 provides an overview of memory storage. It summarizes how we have elaborated on, and sometimes amended, the model of three memory stores introduced at the beginning of this section. It closes out our discussion of memory storage, as we now turn to the process of retrieval.

Recap of Key Points
• Information-processing theories of memory assert that people have three kinds of memory stores: a sensory memory, a short-term memory, and a long-term memory. The sensory store preserves information in its original form, sometimes for only a fraction of a second.
• Short-term memory largely depends on phonemic encoding and has a limited capacity of about seven chunks of information. STM can maintain unrehearsed information for up to about 20 seconds.
• Short-term memory is working memory, and it appears to involve more than a simple rehearsal loop. According to Baddely, working memory also includes

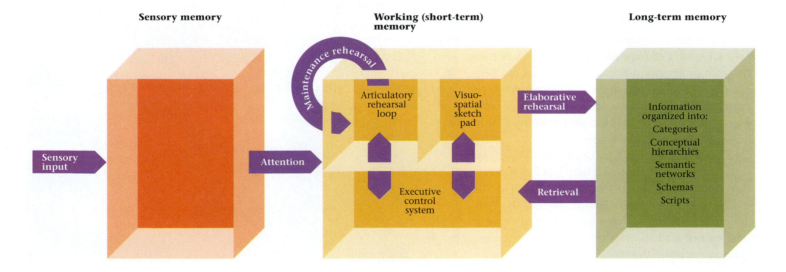

- a visuospatial sketchpad and an executive control system.
- Long-term memory is an unlimited capacity store that may hold information indefinitely. Flashbulb memories, reports of exceptional recall through hypnosis, and Penfield's ESB research suggest that LTM storage may be permanent, but the evidence is not convincing.
- Information is transferred from STM to LTM primarily through rehearsal. The serial-position effect includes two components: a primacy effect that has been attributed to LTM storage, and a recency effect that has been attributed to STM storage.

- Information in long-term memory can be organized in simple clusters or multilevel classification systems called conceptual hierarchies. Semantic networks consist of concepts joined by pathways. A spreading activation model proposes that activation spreads along the paths of a network to activate closely associated words.
- A schema is an organized cluster of knowledge about a particular object or sequence of events. A particular kind of schema, called a script, specifies what people know about common activities. People are more likely to remember things that are consistent with their schemas and scripts.

RETRIEVAL: GETTING INFORMATION OUT OF MEMORY

Entering information into long-term memory is a worthy goal, but an insufficient one if you can't get the information back out again when you need it. Fortunately, recall often occurs without much effort, but occasionally a planned search of LTM is necessary. For instance, imagine that you were asked to recall the names of all 50 states in the United States. You would probably conduct your memory search systematically, recalling states in alphabetical order or by geographical location. Although this example is rather trivial, retrieval is a complex process, as you'll see in this section.

Using Cues to Aid Retrieval

At the beginning of this chapter we discussed the *tip-of-the-tongue phenomenon*—the temporary **inability to remember something you know, accompanied by a feeling that it's just out of reach.** The tip-of-the-tongue phenomenon is a common experience that is typically triggered by a name that one can't quite recall. Most people experience this temporary frustration about about once a week, although its occurrence increases with age (A. Brown, 1991). The tip-of-the-tongue phenomenon clearly is due to a failure in retrieval. Fortunately, memories can often be jogged with *retrieval cues*—stimuli that help gain access to memories. This was apparent when Roger Brown and David McNeill (1966) studied the tip-of-the-tongue phenomenon. They gave subjects definitions of obscure words and asked them to think of the words. Our example at the beginning of the chapter (the definition for *nepotism*) was taken from their study. Brown and McNeill found that subjects groping for obscure words were cor-

rect in guessing the first letter of the missing word 57% of the time. This figure far exceeds chance and shows that partial recollections are often headed in the right direction.

Thus, when partial recollections give you clues about the sound or first letter of a word on the tip of your tongue, it pays to follow up on these clues (Read & Bruce, 1982). Retrieval cues appear to aid memory efforts in a variety of ways. In some cases they may allow narrowing of the search. In other instances they may trigger a series of associations that lead to the missing word. In other words, a cue may lead you into the maze of associations surrounding the forgotten information.

Reinstating the Context of an Event

Let's test your memory: What did you have for breakfast two days ago? If you can't immediately answer, you might begin by imagining yourself sitting at the breakfast table. Trying to recall an event by putting yourself back in the context in which it occurred involves working with *context cues* to aid retrieval.

Context cues often facilitate the retrieval of information (Smith, 1988). Most people have experienced the effects of context cues on many occasions. For instance, when people return after a number of years to a place where they used to live, they typically are flooded with long-forgotten memories. Or consider how often you have gone from one room to another to get something (scissors, perhaps), only to discover that you can't remember what you were after. However, when you return to the first room (the original context), you suddenly recall what it was ("Of course, the scissors!"). These examples illustrate the potentially powerful effects of context cues on memory.

The technique of reinstating the context of an event has been used in legal investigations to enhance eyewitness recall. The eyewitness may be encouraged to retrieve information about a crime by replaying the sequence of events. The value of reinstating the context of an event may account for how hypnosis occasionally stimulates eyewitness recall (Meyer, 1992). The hypnotist usually attempts to reinstate the context of the event by telling the witness to imagine being at the scene of the crime once again. Unfortunately, as we discussed in Chapters 2 and 5, hypnosis seems to increase subjects' tendencies to report incorrect information (Orne & Dinges, 1989). Concerns about the accuracy of hypnosis-aided recall have led courts to be very cautious about allowing hypnosis-aided recollections as admissible testimony.

Associating Mood and Retrieval

So, we know that reinstating the context of an event can often aid recall. Would it also be helpful to recreate the *mood* one was in when the original event took place? Research on *mood-dependent memory* suggests that the answer is "sometimes." **Mood-dependent memory (also called *state-dependent memory*) is improved recall that is attributed to being in the same emotional state during encoding and subsequent retrieval.** Mood-dependent memory has been observed in a number of studies (Guenther, 1988). Consider, for instance, a study by Gordon Bower (1981). He manipulated subjects' mood state to be happy or sad while they learned a list of words and while they attempted to recall the words later. If the initial learning occurred during a happy state, recall was better in a happy state. Similarly, subjects who memorized the list in a sad mood recalled more when they were in a sad mood at the time of retrieval. Mood-dependent memory has also been seen when emotional states have been manipulated through the administration of drugs (Eich, 1980). Theorists speculate that mood-dependent memory may occur because mood states can serve as effective retrieval cues.

Although many studies have found mood-dependent memory effects, many have *not* (Blaney, 1986; Bower & Mayer, 1991). Investigators are trying to sort out the conditions under which mood-dependent memory is most likely to occur (Riskind, 1991). After reviewing the relevant research, Eich (1995) concludes that mood-dependent memory is more likely when people are trying

to recall internal mental processes rather than external events, and when experimenters' manipulations of subjects' moods create strong, stable emotional states.

In recent years, increasing attention has been devoted to *mood-congruence effects*, another phenomenon involving mood and memory. **A mood-congruence effect occurs when memory is better for information that is consistent with one's ongoing mood.** Thus, when people are in a happy mood, they tend to recall pleasant information more than unpleasant information. Similarly, people who are in a sad or depressed mood tend to recall unpleasant information more than pleasant information. Mood-congruence memory effects appear to be more reliable than mood-dependent effects (Blaney, 1986; Ellis & Ashbrook, 1991).

Reconstructing Memories

When you retrieve information from long-term memory, you're not able to pull up a "mental videotape" that provides an exact replay of the past. To some extent, your memories are sketchy *reconstructions* of the past that may be distorted and may include details that did not actually occur (Roediger, Wheeler, & Rajaram, 1993). The reconstructive nature of memory was first highlighted many years ago by Sir Frederic Bartlett, a prominent English psychologist. Bartlett (1932) had his subjects read the tale called "The War of the Ghosts," which is reproduced in Figure 7.18. Subjects read the story twice and waited 15 minutes. Then they were asked to write down the tale as best they could recall it.

What did Bartlett find? As you might expect, subjects condensed the story, leaving out boring details. Of greater interest was Bartlett's discovery that subjects inevitably *changed* the tale to some extent. The canoe became a boat or the two young men were hunting beavers instead of seals. Subjects often introduced entirely *new elements* and twists. For instance, in one case, the death at the end was attributed to fever and the character was described as "foaming at the mouth" (instead of "something black came out of his mouth"). Bartlett concluded that the distortions in recall occurred because subjects reconstructed the tale to fit with their established schemas.

Current schema theories also emphasize the reconstructive nature of memory (Brewer & Nakamura, 1984). These theories propose that part of what people recall about an event is the details of that particular event and part is a reconstruction of the event based on their schemas. (Re-

"It is in the nature of the mind to forget and in the nature of man to worry over his forgetfulness."

GORDON BOWER

"One reason most of us, as jurors, place so much faith in eyewitness testimony is that we are unaware of how many factors influence its accuracy."

ELIZABETH LOFTUS

THE WAR OF THE GHOSTS

One night two young men from Egulac went down to the river to hunt seals, and while they were there it became foggy and calm. Then they heard war cries, and they thought: "Maybe this is a war party." They escaped to the shore, and hid behind a log. Now canoes came up, and they heard the noise of paddles, and saw one canoe coming up to them. There were five men in the canoe, and they said:
"What do you think? We wish to take you along. We are going up the river to make war on the people."
One of the young men said: "I have no arrows."
"Arrows are in the canoe," they said.
"I will not go along. I might be killed. My relatives do not know where I have gone. But you," he said, turning to the other, "may go with them."
So one of the young men went, but the other returned home.
And the warriors went up to the river to a town on the other side of Kalama. The people came down to the water, and they began to fight, and many were killed. But presently the young man heard one of the warriors say: "Quick, let us go home: that Indian has been hit." Now he thought: "Oh, they are ghosts." He did not feel sick, but they said he had been shot.
So the canoes went back to Egulac and the young man went ashore to his house, and made a fire. And he told everybody and said: "Behold I accompanied the ghosts, and we went to fight. Many of our fellows were killed, and many of those who attacked us were killed. They said I was hit, and I did not feel sick."
He told it all, and then he became quiet. When the sun rose he fell down. Something black came out of his mouth. His face became contorted. The people jumped up and cried.
He was dead.

member your visit to Professor Smith's office?) According to this view, general, schematic knowledge becomes more influential in determining recall as the details of an event blur with the passage of time.

Research by Elizabeth Loftus (1979, 1992) and others on the *misinformation effect* has shown that reconstructive distortions show up frequently in eyewitness testimony. Studies of the misinformation effect include three stages. In the first stage, subjects view an event. In the second stage, they are exposed to information about this event, some of which is misleading. In the third stage, their recall of the original event is tested to see if the postevent misinformation altered their memory of the original event. For example, in one study Loftus and Palmer (1974) showed subjects a videotape of an automobile accident. Subjects were then "grilled" as if they were providing eyewitness testimony, and biasing information was introduced. Some subjects were asked, "How fast were the cars going when they *hit* each other?" Other subjects were asked, "How fast were the cars going when they *smashed into* each other?" A week later, subjects' recall of the accident was tested and they were asked whether they remembered seeing any broken glass in the accident (there was none). Subjects who had earlier been asked about the cars *smashing into* each other were more likely to "recall" broken glass. Why would they add this detail to their reconstructions of the accident? Probably because broken glass is consistent with their schema for cars *smashing* together (see Figure 7.19).

Although postevent misinformation does not inevitably introduce errors into recollections of events,

the misinformation effect has been replicated in numerous studies by Loftus and other researchers (Lindsay, 1993). However, there is considerable debate about the mechanisms underlying the effect (Ceci & Bruck, 1993). Loftus (1979) has argued for an "overwriting" explanation in which the new misinformation destroys and replaces the original memory of the event (much like saving a new version of a file on a computer). An alternative explanation is that the new misinformation interferes with the retrieval of the original memory (Bekerian & Bowers, 1983). Other theorists argue that subjects can access both the original memory and the altered memory, but they have difficulty distinguishing which one was the original (Lindsay & Johnson, 1989). This explanation attributes the misinformation effect to difficulties in *source monitoring,* the memory process that we consider next.

Figure 7.19
The effect of leading questions on eyewitness recall. Subjects who were asked leading questions in which cars were described as *hitting* or *smashing* each other were prone to recall the same accident differently one week later, demonstrating the reconstructive nature of memory.

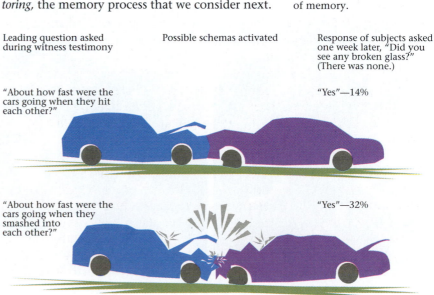

Leading question asked during witness testimony | Possible schemas activated | Response of subjects asked one week later, "Did you see any broken glass?" (There was none.)

"About how fast were the cars going when they hit each other?"

"Yes"—14%

"About how fast were the cars going when they smashed into each other?"

"Yes"—32%

"Our long-term goal is to develop ways of determining which aspects of mental experience create one's sense of a personal past and one's conviction (accurate or not) that memories, knowledge, beliefs, attitudes, and feelings are tied to reality in a veridical fashion."

MARCIA K. JOHNSON

In recent years, rock star Billy Joel and movie star Eddie Murphy have both endured highly publicized lawsuits accusing them of plagiarism. We can only speculate, but perhaps these incidents involved cryptomnesia—inadvertent plagiarism that occurs when people come up with an idea that they think is original, when they really were exposed to it earlier. Cryptomnesia may often occur because of source-monitoring errors in retrieval.

Source Monitoring

Marcia Johnson and her colleagues maintain that *source monitoring*—**the process of making attributions about the origins of memories**—is a crucial facet of memory retrieval that contributes to many of the mistakes that people make in reconstructing their experiences (Johnson, 1996; Johnson, Hashtroudi, & Lindsay, 1993; Lindsay & Johnson, 1991). According to Johnson, memories are not tagged with labels that specify their sources. Hence, when people pull up specific memory records, they have to make decisions *at the time of retrieval* about where the memories came from (example: "Did I read that in the *New York Times* or *Rolling Stone*?"). Much of the time, these decisions are so easy and automatic, people make them without being consciously aware of the source-monitoring process. In other instances, however, they may consciously struggle to pinpoint the source of a memory. **A *source-monitoring error* occurs when a memory derived from one source is misattributed to another source.** For example, you might attribute something that your roomate said to your psychology professor, or something you heard on *Oprah* to your psychology textbook.

Source-monitoring errors appear to be commonplace and may shed light on many interesting memory phenomena. For instance, in studies of eyewitness suggestibility, some subjects have gone so far as to insist that they "remember" seeing something that was only verbally suggested to them. Most theories have a hard time explaining how people can have memories of events that they never actually saw or experienced, but this paradox doesn't seem all that perplexing when it is explained as a source-monitoring error. The source-monitoring approach can also make sense of *cryptomnesia*—inadvertent plagiarism that occurs when people come up with an idea that they think is original, when they were actually exposed to it earlier. Source-monitoring errors also appear to underlie the common tendency for people to mix up fictional information from novels and movies with factual information from news reports and personal experiences. For example, a veteran of the Vietnam war might unwittingly describe a scene from the movie *Apocalypse Now* as a personal experience from his war days.

Marcia Johnson's source-monitoring theory has built and expanded on an earlier concept that she called *reality monitoring,* which she now views as a subtype of source monitoring. **Reality monitoring refers to the process of deciding whether memories are based on external sources (one's perceptions of actual events) or internal sources (one's thoughts and imaginations).** People engage in reality monitoring when they reflect on whether something actually happened or they only thought about it happening. This dilemma may sound like an odd problem that would arise only infrequently, but it isn't. People routinely ponder questions like: "Did I pack the umbrella or only think about packing it?" "Did I take my morning pill or only intend to do so?" "Did I turn off the stove, or did I imagine doing it?" Studies indicate that people focus on several types of clues in making their reality-monitoring decisions (Johnson & Raye, 1981; Johnson, Kahan, & Raye, 1984). When memories are rich in sensory information (you can recall the feel of shoving the umbrella into your suitcase) or contextual information (you can clearly see yourself in the hallway packing your umbrella), or when memories can be retrieved with little effort, one is more likely to infer that the event really happened. In contrast, one is more likely to infer that an event did not actually occur when memories of it lack sensory or contextual details or are difficult to retrieve.

Recap of Key Points

• The tip-of-the-tongue phenomenon shows that recall is often guided by partial information about a word. Reinstating the context of an event can facilitate recall. This factor may account for cases in which hypnosis appears to aid recall of previously forgotten information. However, hypnosis seems to increase people's tendency to report incorrect information.

- Mood-dependent memory is improved recall attributed to being in the same mood during encoding and retrieval. Mood congruence effects occur when memory is better for information that is consistent with one's current mood. Mood-congruence effects are more reliable than mood-dependent effects.

- Memories are not exact replicas of past experiences. As Bartlett showed many years ago, memory is partially reconstructive. Research on the misinformation effect shows that information learned after an event can alter one's memory of it.

- Source monitoring is the process of making attributions about the origins of memories. Source-monitoring errors appear to be common and may explain why people sometimes "recall" something that was only suggested to them or something they only imagined. Reality monitoring involves deciding whether memories are based on perceptions of actual events or just thinking about the events.

FORGETTING: WHEN MEMORY LAPSES

Why do people forget information—even information they would like to remember? Many theorists believe that there isn't one simple answer to this question. They point to the complex, multifaceted nature of memory and assert that forgetting can be caused by deficiencies in encoding, storage, retrieval, or some combination of these processes.

How Quickly We Forget: Ebbinghaus's Forgetting Curve

The first person to conduct scientific studies of forgetting was Hermann Ebbinghaus. He published a series of insightful memory studies way back in 1885. Ebbinghaus studied only one subject—himself. To give himself lots of new material to memorize, he invented *nonsense syllables*—consonant-vowel-consonant arrangements that do not correspond to words (such as BAF, XOF, VIR, and MEQ). He wanted to work with meaningless materials that would be uncontaminated by his previous learning.

Ebbinghaus was a remarkably dedicated researcher. For instance, in one study he went through over 14,000 practice repetitions, as he tirelessly memorized 420 lists of nonsense syllables (Slamecka, 1985). He tested his memory of these lists after various time intervals. Figure 7.20 shows what he found. This diagram, called a *forgetting curve,* graphs retention and forgetting over time. Ebbinghaus's forgetting curve shows a precipitous drop in retention during the first few hours after the nonsense syllables were memorized. He forgot more than 60% of the syllables in less than 9 hours! Thus, he concluded that most forgetting occurs very rapidly after learning something.

That's a depressing conclusion. What is the point of memorizing information if you're going to for-get it all right away? Fortunately, subsequent research showed that Ebbinghaus's forgetting curve was unusually steep (Postman, 1985). Forgetting isn't usually as swift or as extensive as Ebbinghaus thought. One problem was that he was working with such meaningless material. When subjects memorize more meaningful material, such as prose or poetry, forgetting curves aren't nearly as steep. Studies of how well people recall their high school classmates suggest that forgetting curves for autobiographical information are even shallower (Bahrick, Bahrick, & Wittlinger, 1975). Also, different methods of measuring forgetting yield varied estimates of how quickly people forget. This variation underscores the importance of the methods used to measure forgetting, the matter we turn to next.

Measures of Forgetting

To study forgetting empirically, psychologists need to be able to measure it precisely. Measures of

"Left to itself every mental content gradually loses its capacity for being revived. . . . Facts crammed at examination time soon vanish."

HERMANN EBBINGHAUS

Figure 7.20
Ebbinghaus's forgetting curve for nonsense syllables. From his experiments on himself, Ebbinghaus concluded that forgetting is extremely rapid immediately after the original learning and then levels off. However, subsequent research has suggested that this forgetting curve is unusually steep. (Data from Ebbinghaus, 1885)

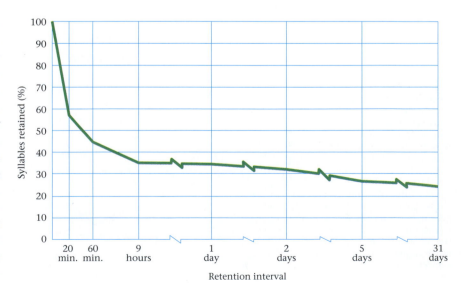

forgetting inevitably measure retention as well. **Retention refers to the proportion of material retained (remembered).** In studies of forgetting, the results may be reported in terms of the amount forgotten or the amount retained. In these studies, the *retention interval* is the length of time between the presentation of materials to be remembered and the measurement of forgetting. The three principal methods used to measure forgetting are recall, recognition, and relearning (Lockhart, 1992).

Who is the current U.S. secretary of state? What movie won the Academy Award for best picture last year? These questions involve recall measures of retention. **A *recall* measure of retention requires subjects to reproduce information on their own without any cues.** If you were to take a recall test on a list of 25 words you had memorized, you would simply be told to write down on a blank sheet of paper as many of the words as you could remember.

In contrast, in a recognition test you might be shown a list of 100 words and asked to choose the 25 words that you had memorized. **A *recognition* measure of retention requires subjects to select previously learned information from an array of options.** Subjects not only have cues to work with, they have the answers right in front of them. In educational testing, essay questions and fill-in-the-blanks questions are recall measures of retention. Multiple-choice, true-false, and matching questions are recognition measures.

If you're like most students, you probably prefer multiple-choice tests over essay tests. This preference is understandable, because evidence shows that recognition measures tend to yield higher scores than recall measures of memory for the same information (Greene, 1992). This reality was demonstrated many years ago by Luh (1922), who measured subjects' retention of nonsense syllables with both a recognition test and a recall test. As Figure 7.21 shows, subjects' performance on the recognition measure was far superior to their performance on the recall measure. There are two ways of looking at this disparity between recall and recognition tests. One view is that recognition tests are especially *sensitive* measures of retention. The other view is that recognition tests are excessively *easy* measures of retention.

Actually, there is no guarantee that a recognition test will be easier than a recall test. This tends to be the case, but the difficulty of a recognition test can vary greatly, depending on the number, similarity, and plausibility of the options provided as possible answers. To illustrate, see whether you know the answer to the following multiple-choice question:

The capital of Washington is:
  a. Seattle
  b. Spokane
  c. Tacoma
  d. Olympia

Most students who aren't from Washington find this a fairly difficult question. The answer is Olympia. Now take a look at the next question:

The capital of Washington is:
  a. London
  b. New York
  c. Tokyo
  d. Olympia

Virtually anyone can answer this question because the incorrect options are readily dismissed. Although this illustration is a bit extreme, it shows that two recognition measures of the same information can be dramatically different in difficulty.

The third method of measuring forgetting is relearning. **A *relearning* measure of retention requires a subject to memorize information a second time to determine how much time or effort is saved by having learned it before.** To use this method, a researcher measures how much time (or how many practice trials) a subject needs to memorize something. At a later date, the subject is asked to relearn the information. The researcher measures how much more quickly the material is memorized the second time. Subjects' *savings scores* provide an estimate of their retention. For example, if it takes you 20 minutes to memorize a list the first time and only 5 minutes to memorize it a week later, you've saved 15 minutes. Your savings score of 75% ($^{15}/_{20} = {}^3/_4 =$ 75%) suggests that you have retained 75% and forgotten the remaining 25% of the informa-

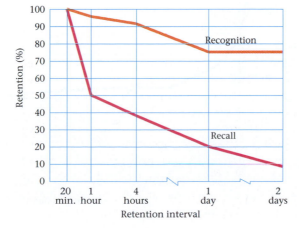

Figure 7.21
Recognition versus recall in the measurement of retention. Luh (1922) had subjects memorize lists of nonsense syllables and then measured their retention with either a recognition test or a recall test at various intervals up to two days. As you can see, the forgetting curve for the recall test was quite steep, whereas the recognition test yielded much higher estimates of subjects' retention.

CHAPTER SEVEN

tion. Relearning measures can detect retention that is overlooked by recognition tests (Nelson, 1978).

Why We Forget

Measuring forgetting is only the first step in the long journey toward explaining why forgetting occurs. In this section, we explore the possible causes of forgetting, looking at factors that may affect encoding, storage, and retrieval processes.

Ineffective Encoding

A great deal of forgetting may only *appear* to be forgetting. The information in question may never have been inserted into memory in the first place. Since you can't really forget something you never learned, this phenomenon is sometimes called *pseudoforgetting*. We opened the chapter with an example of pseudoforgetting. People usually assume that they know what a penny looks like, but most have actually failed to encode this information. Pseudoforgetting is usually due to *lack of attention*.

Even when memory codes *are* formed for new information, subsequent forgetting may be due to *ineffective* encoding. The research on levels of processing shows that some approaches to encoding lead to more forgetting than others (Craik & Tulving, 1975). For example, if you're distracted while you read your textbooks, you may be doing little more than saying the words to yourself. This is *phonemic encoding,* which is inferior to *semantic encoding* for retention of verbal material. When you can't remember the information that you've read, your forgetting may be due to ineffective encoding.

Decay

Instead of focusing on encoding, decay theory attributes forgetting to the impermanence of memory storage. **Decay theory proposes that forgetting occurs because memory traces fade with time.** The implicit assumption is that decay occurs in the physiological mechanisms responsible for memories. According to decay theory, the mere passage of time produces forgetting. This notion meshes nicely with commonsense views of forgetting.

As we saw earlier, decay *does* contribute to the loss of information from the sensory and short-term memory stores. However, the critical task for theories of forgetting is to explain the loss of information from long-term memory. Researchers have *not* been able to demonstrate that decay causes LTM forgetting (Slamecka, 1992).

If decay theory is correct, the principal cause of forgetting should be the passage of time. In studies of long-term memory, however, researchers have found that time passage is not as influential as what happens during the time interval. This was first shown in a clever experiment by Jenkins and Dallenbach (1924). Their subjects memorized a list of nonsense syllables and were tested for recall after 1, 2, 4, or 8 hours. The catch was that half the subjects slept during the retention interval and the other half went about their normal waking activities. According to decay theory, since the same amount of time had elapsed for both groups, they should have exhibited an equal amount of forgetting. However, as you can see in Figure 7.22, the subjects who remained awake forgot more than those who slept.

Why did the subjects who remained awake forget more? Their greater forgetting was blamed on interference from the competing information that they had to process while awake. Many subsequent studies have shown that forgetting depends not on the amount of time that has passed since learning but on the amount, complexity, and type of information that subjects have had to assimilate during the retention interval. The negative impact of competing information on retention is called *interference*.

Interference

Interference theory **proposes that people forget information because of competition from other material.** Although demonstrations of decay in long-term memory have remained elusive, hundreds of studies have shown that interference influences forgetting (Bjork, 1992; Postman, 1971). In the experiment just discussed, Jenkins and Dallenbach (1924) manipulated the amount of interference by having subjects sleep or remain awake during the retention interval.

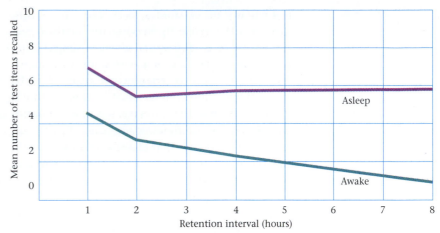

Figure 7.22
Interference and retention. By sending some of their subjects off to bed after learning a list of nonsense syllables while allowing others to engage in their normal waking activities, Jenkins and Dallenbach (1924) demonstrated that much of forgetting is attributable to interference. The subjects who slept forgot the least.

In many other studies, researchers have controlled interference by varying the *similarity* between the original material given to subjects (the test material) and the material studied in the intervening period. Interference is assumed to be greatest when intervening material is most similar to the test material. Decreasing the similarity should reduce interference and cause less forgetting. This is exactly what McGeoch and McDonald (1931) found in an influential study. They had subjects memorize test material that consisted of a list of two-syllable adjectives. They varied the similarity of intervening learning by having subjects then memorize one of five lists. In order of decreasing similarity to the test material, they were synonyms of the test words, antonyms of the test words, unrelated adjectives, nonsense syllables, and numbers. Later, subjects' recall of the test material was measured. Figure 7.23 shows that as the similarity of the intervening material decreased, the amount of forgetting also decreased—because of reduced interference.

There are two kinds of interference: *retroactive* interference and *proactive* interference. **Retroactive interference occurs when new information impairs the retention of previously learned information.** Retroactive interference occurs between the original learning and the retest on that learning, during the retention interval. For example, the interference manipulated by McGeoch and McDonald (1931) was retroactive interference. In contrast, **proactive interference occurs when previously learned information interferes with the retention of new information.** Proactive interfer-

ence is rooted in learning that comes *before* exposure to the test material.

To illustrate the distinction between retroactive and proactive interference, imagine that you have to memorize a great deal of information for an economics test tomorrow. If you memorize the information on economics and then study psychology, the interference from the psychology study will be retroactive interference. However, if you study psychology first and then economics, the interference from the psychology study will be proactive interference (see Figure 7.24). The evidence indicates that both types of interference can have powerful effects on how much you forget. They may exert their effects by disrupting *retrieval* (Tulving & Psotka, 1971), which we turn to next.

Retrieval Failure

People often remember things that they were unable to recall at an earlier time. This may be obvious only during struggles with the tip-of-the-tongue phenomenon, but it happens frequently. In fact, a great deal of forgetting may be due to breakdowns in the process of retrieval.

Why does an effort to retrieve something fail on one occasion and succeed on another? That's a tough question. One theory is that retrieval failures may be more likely when there is a mismatch between retrieval cues and the encoding of the information you're searching for. According to Tulving and Thomson (1973), a good retrieval cue is consistent with the original encoding of the information to be recalled. If the sound of a word—its phonemic quality—was emphasized during encoding, an effective retrieval cue should emphasize the sound of the word. If the meaning of the word was emphasized during encoding, semantic cues should be best.

A general statement of the principle at work here was formulated by Tulving and Thomson (1973). **The *encoding specificity principle* states that the value of a retrieval cue depends on how well it corresponds to the memory code.** This principle provides one explanation for the inconsistent success of retrieval efforts.

Another line of research also indicates that memory is influenced by the "fit" between the processing during encoding and retrieval. **Transfer-appropriate processing occurs when the initial processing of information is similar to the type of processing required by the subsequent measure of retention.** For example, Morris, Bransford, and Franks (1977) gave subjects a list of words and a task that required either semantic or

Figure 7.23
Effects of interference.
According to interference theory, more interference from competing information should produce more forgetting. McGeoch and McDonald (1931) controlled the amount of interference with a learning task by varying the similarity of an intervening task. The results were consistent with interference theory. The amount of interference is greatest at the left of the graph, as is the amount of forgetting. As interference decreases (moving to the right on the graph), retention improves.

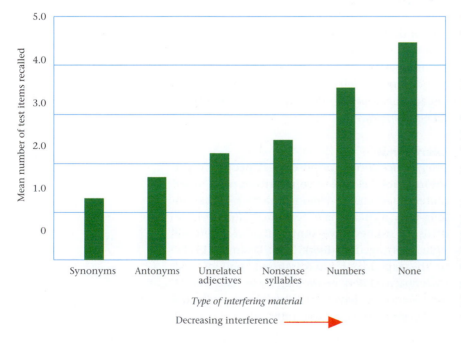

Type of interfering material

Decreasing interference ➡️

CHAPTER SEVEN

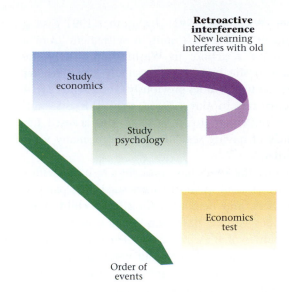

Retroactive interference
New learning interferes with old

Proactive interference
Old learning interferes with new

Figure 7.24
Retroactive and proactive interference. Retroactive interference occurs when learning produces a "backward" effect, reducing recall of previously learned material. Proactive interference occurs when learning produces a "forward" effect, reducing recall of subsequently learned material.

phonemic processing. Retention was measured with recognition tests that emphasized either the meaning or the sound of the words. Semantic processing yielded higher retention when the testing emphasized semantic factors, while phonemic processing yielded higher retention when the testing emphasized phonemic factors. Thus, retrieval failures are more likely when there is a poor fit between the processing done during encoding and the processing invoked by the measure of retention (Roediger, 1992).

Motivated Forgetting

Many years ago, Sigmund Freud (1901) came up with an entirely different explanation for retrieval failures. As we noted in Chapter 1, Freud asserted that people often keep embarrassing, unpleasant, or painful memories buried in their unconscious. For example, a person who was deeply wounded by perceived slights at a childhood birthday party might suppress all recollection of that party. In his therapeutic work with patients, Freud recovered many such buried memories. He theorized that the memories were there all along, but their retrieval was blocked by unconscious avoidance tendencies.

The tendency to forget things one doesn't want to think about is called *motivated forgetting,* or to use Freud's terminology, *repression.* In Freudian theory, **repression refers to keeping distressing thoughts and feelings buried in the unconscious** (see Chapter 12). Psychologists have not been able to unambiguously demonstrate the operation of repression in controlled laboratory experiments (Holmes, 1990). Nonetheless, a number of experiments *suggest* that people don't remember anxi-

ety-laden material as readily as emotionally neutral material, just as Freud proposed (Guenther, 1988). Thus, when you forget unpleasant things such as a dental appointment, a promise to help a friend move, or a term paper deadline, motivated forgetting may be at work.

The Repressed Memories Controversy

Although the concept of repression has been around for a century, interest in this phenomenon has surged in recent years, thanks to a spate of prominent reports involving the return of long-lost memories of sexual abuse and other traumas during childhood. For example, in 1990 a highly publicized story of repressed memory unfolded in a courtroom in Redwood City, California, where George Franklin was tried for a local murder that had occurred over 20 years earlier (Morain, 1991). The victim was Susan Nason, an 8-year-old girl who had been beaten to death in 1969. The murder remained unsolved for two decades until Franklin's own daughter, Eileen, a childhood friend of the victim, came forward to describe a previously repressed memory of how she had seen her father commit the murder. Eileen's memory of this traumatic incident began to resurface in 1989, when her 5-year-old daughter looked at her in a way that reminded her of how Susan had looked just prior to the murder. With the help of her therapist, Eileen gradually reconstructed a detailed memory of how her father had raped Susan and then used a rock to bludgeon the little girl to death. Along the way, Eileen also recovered long-repressed memories of how her father had beaten and sexually abused her for years. Unusual though it may have been, Eileen's testimony apparently

Check your understanding of why people forget by identifying the probable causes of forgetting in each of the following scenarios. You will find the answers in Appendix A.

____ 1. Ellen can't recall the reasons for the Webster-Ashburton Treaty because she was daydreaming when it was discussed in history class.

____ 2. Arnold hates his job at Taco Heaven and is always forgetting when he is scheduled to work.

____ 3. Ray's new assistant in the shipping department is named John Cocker. Ray keeps calling him Joe, mixing him up with the rock singer Joe Cocker.

____ 4. Tania studied history on Sunday morning and sociology on Sunday evening. It's Monday, and she's struggling with her history test because she keeps mixing up prominent historians with influential sociologists.

was convincing, as it led to a remarkable verdict. With little else to go on after 20 years, the jury still convicted Eileen's father of murder—on the basis of her repressed memories alone. The conviction stood up for six years before it was overturned in a 1996 ruling that released George Franklin from prison. Plans for a retrial were subsequently dropped after Eileen Franklin's sister testified that Eileen's repressed memory was recovered through hypnosis, which made her recollection inadmissible in California courts (Garcia & Wykes, 1996).

The Franklin case is only one of many recent stories involving repressed memories. The media have been flooded with reports of people—including some celebrities—who have recovered long-lost recollections of sexual abuse. For example, in 1991 TV star Roseanne suddenly recalled years of abuse by her parents, and a former Miss America remembered being sexually assaulted by her fa-

Tom Rutherford (shown here with his wife, Joyce) received a $1 million settlement in a suit against a church therapist and a Springfield, Missouri, church in a false memory case. The Rutherford's daughter, Beth, had "recalled" under the church counselor's guidance, childhood memories of having been raped repeatedly by her minister father, gotten pregnant, and undergone a painful coat-hanger abortion. Her father lost his job and was ostracized. After he later revealed he'd had a vasectomy when Beth was age 4, and a physical exam revealed that at age 23 she was still a virgin, the memories were shown to be false.

ther (Wielawski, 1991). In another 1991 case, a woman won a $1.4 million settlement from a church-run school in Washington, where she claimed she had been repeatedly raped by her teacher two decades previously (Toufexis, 1991). A similar case in Akron, Ohio, resulted in a $5 million settlement for a woman who accused her uncle of having sexually abused her many years earlier.

Thus, the 1990s have brought a rash of lawsuits in which adult plaintiffs have sued their parents, teachers, and neighbors for alleged child abuse decades earlier, based on previously repressed memories of these travesties. For the most part, these parents, teachers, and neighbors have denied the allegations. Many of them have seemed genuinely befuddled by the accusations, which have torn some previously happy families apart. In an effort to make sense of the charges, some accused parents have argued that their children's recollections are false memories created inadvertently by well-intentioned therapists through the power of suggestion. Recovered recollections of sexual abuse have become so common, an advocacy and support group has been formed for people who feel that they have been victimized by "false memory syndrome." Thousands of families have sought help from the False Memory Syndrome Foundation.

The controversy surrounding repressed memories raises some interesting questions: How authentic or accurate are recovered recollections of previously repressed memories of childhood sexual abuse? If some of these memories are not accurate, where did they come from? Could many of these recollections be attributable to people's suggestibility—as accused parents, teachers, and neighbors often claim? The crux of the problem is that child abuse usually takes place behind closed doors; in the absence of corroborative evidence, there is no way to reliably distinguish genuine recovered memories from false ones. A handful of repressed memories have been substantiated by independent witnesses or belated admissions of guilt from the accused. But in the vast majority of cases, the allegations of abuse have been vehemently denied, and independent corroboration has not been available.

What do psychologists and psychiatrists have to say about the authenticity of repressed memories? They are sharply divided on the issue. Many, especially clinicians involved in the treatment of psychological disorders, largely accept repressed memories at face value (Briere & Conte, 1993;

A Case History of False Memory Syndrome

Suffering from a prolonged bout of depression and desperate for help, Melody Gavigan, 39, a computer specialist from Long Beach, California, checked herself into a local psychiatric hospital. As Gavigan recalls the experience, her problems were just beginning. During five weeks of treatment there, a family and marriage counselor repeatedly suggested that her depression stemmed from incest during her childhood. While at first Gavigan had no recollection of any abuse, the therapist kept prodding. "I was so distressed and needed help so desperately, I latched on to what he was offering me," she says. "I accepted his answers."

When asked for details, she wrote page after page of what she believed were emerging repressed memories. She told about running into the yard after being raped in the bathroom. She incorporated into another lurid rape scene an actual girlhood incident, in which she had dislocated a shoulder. She went on to recall being molested by her father when she was only a year old—as her diapers were being changed— and sodomized by him at five. Following what she says was the therapist's advice, Gavigan confronted her father with her accusations, severed her relationship with him, moved away, and formed an incest survivors' group.

But she remained uneasy. Signing up for a college psychology course, she examined her newfound memories more carefully and concluded that they were false. Now Gavigan has begged her father's forgiveness and filed a lawsuit against the psychiatric hospital for the pain that she and her family suffered.

Herman, 1992; Terr, 1994). They assert that it is common for patients to bury traumatic incidents in their unconscious. Citing new evidence that sexual abuse in childhood is far more widespread than most people realize, they argue that most repressed memories of abuse are probably genuine. They attribute the recent upsurge in reports of repressed memories to therapists' and clients' increased sensitivity to an issue that people used to be reluctant to discuss.

In contrast, many other psychologists have expressed skepticism about the recent flood of repressed memories (Lindsay & Poole, 1995; Loftus, 1993; Tavris, 1993). These psychologists do not argue that people are lying about their repressed memories. Rather, they maintain that some suggestible people wrestling with emotional problems have been convinced by persuasive therapists that their emotional problems must be the result of abuse that occurred years before. Critics blame a minority of therapists who presumably have good intentions but who operate under the dubious assumption that virtually all psychological problems are attributable to childhood sexual abuse. Using hypnosis, dream interpretation, and leading questions, they supposedly prod and probe patients until they inadvertently create the memories of abuse that they are searching for.

Psychologists who doubt the authenticity of repressed memories support their analysis by pointing to discredited cases of recovered memories. For example, with the help of a church counselor, one woman recovered memories of how her minister father had repeatedly raped her, got her pregnant, and then aborted the pregnancy with a coat-hanger, but subsequent evidence revealed that the woman was still a virgin and that her father had had a vasectomy years before (Testa, 1996). The skeptics also point to published case histories that clearly involved suggestive questioning and to cases in which patients have recanted repressed memories of sexual abuse after realizing that these memories were implanted by their therapists (see Figure 7.25). Those who question the accuracy of repressed memories also point to research on the misinformation effect, source monitoring, and other studies that demonstrate the relative ease of creating "memories" of events that never happened. As an example of this type of research, we'll take a detailed look at a recent laboratory experiment in which hypnosis was used to create false memories.

Figure 7.25
A case of recovered memories recanted. Revelations of repressed memories of sexual abuse are viewed with skepticism in some quarters. One reason is that some people who have recovered previously repressed recollections of child abuse have subsequently realized that their "memories" were the product of suggestion. A number of case histories, such as the one summarized here (from Jaroff, 1993), have demonstrated that therapists who relentlessly search for memories of child abuse in their patients sometimes instill the memories they are seeking.

Creating False Memories Through Hypnosis   Featured Study

In studies of *hypnotic pseudomemory*, subjects are given false information about an event while hypnotized and are subsequently tested for their recall of this event in a nonhypnotized state to see whether any false memories are reported. Hypnotic pseudomemory was first demonstrated by Laurence and Perry (1983), who successfully implanted memories of being awakened by loud noises in the middle of a

Investigators: Peter W. Sheehan, Vanessa Green, and Patricia Truesdale (University of Queensland, Australia)

Source: Influence of rapport on hypnotically induced pseudomemory. *Journal of Abnormal Psychology*, 1992, *101*, 690–700.

specific night in 13 of their 27 subjects. Follow-up studies showed that it is easier to create hypnotic pseudomemories in subjects who are high in hypnotic susceptibility and in situations where falsely suggested events are not readily verifiable. The study by Sheehan, Green, and Truesdale extended this line of research by examining the importance of hypnotic rapport. The investigators hypothesized that pseudomemory responses would be more frequent when there was good hypnotist-subject rapport and less frequent when rapport was reduced.

Method

Subjects and design. Scales measuring hypnotic susceptibility were administered to over 800 undergraduate psychology students. Eighty-eight students who scored very high in hypnotic susceptibility and 88 students who scored very low in hypnotic susceptibility were selected to serve as subjects. Three independent variables were manipulated: subjects' hypnotic susceptibility (high versus low), subjects' mental state when false information was introduced (hypnotized versus nonhypnotized), and the level of rapport between the experimenter/hypnotist and the subject (present versus reduced).

Materials and procedure. The subjects were told that the study was concerned with how people rated their emotional arousal after viewing certain events or after being hypnotized. The subjects then viewed a 43-second videotape of a bank robbery and subsequently answered some questions and made some ratings regarding the robbery. Half the subjects were then told that they would be hypnotized and regressed back to when they observed the video to enhance their recall of the robbery. In reality, the experimenters' intent was to introduce three pieces of false information about the robbery while the subjects were hypnotized. The false information consisted of suggestions (1) that the robber had entered from the bank's right door when he had really entered from the left door, (2) that the robber had worn a mask when he really did not, and (3) that the robber had sworn a lot when no swear words were actually spoken. Nonhypnotized subjects were exposed to the same suggestions in a slightly different context. The rapport between the experimenter/hypnotist and subjects was manipulated by reducing normal rapport for half of the subjects. In the reduced rapport condition, the experimenter displayed visible irritation with the subjects and criticized them for

not cooperating. In the final stage of the experiment, the subjects were tested for their recall of the robbery events depicted in the videotape. The key dependent variable was the number of pseudomemories reported (whether subjects mentioned the robber entering from the right, wearing a mask, or swearing a lot), which could vary from 0 to 3.

Results

A significant pseudomemory effect was seen only among hypnotized subjects who were highly susceptible to hypnosis. Furthermore, as predicted, these subjects reported more pseudomemories when they had experienced rapport with the hypnotist and fewer pseudomemories when rapport was reduced.

Discussion

Building on previous studies, this experiment demonstrated once again that it is not all that difficult to implant false memories in some subjects, especially those who are high in hypnotic susceptibility. Based on this experiment and two companion studies described in the same article, the authors conclude that hypnotist-subject rapport is another factor that influences the likelihood of creating hypnotic pseudomemories.

Comment

This study by Sheehan and his colleagues is relevant to a number of issues revolving around hypnosis and memory. Like many other studies (such as the Featured Study in Chapter 2), it raises doubts about the wisdom of using hypnosis to enhance eyewitness recall. More germane to our current topic, it adds to the body of studies that show how subtle suggestions made to hypnotized patients might be converted into "memories" of things they never saw. The trivial memory distortions created in this experiment may seem a far cry from the vivid, detailed recollections of previously forgotten sexual abuse that have generated the repressed memories controversy. But these hypnotic pseudomemories were created in normal, healthy subjects, in a matter of minutes, with little effort. Skeptics who doubt the authenticity of repressed memories argue that it is easy to imagine how relentless suggestions from persuasive therapists over the course of months of hypnotherapy could create much more elaborate false memories in vulnerable, confused patients struggling to understand profound personal problems.

The debate about repressed memories of sexual abuse has grown increasingly bitter and emotionally charged (Loftus & Ketcham, 1994; Pope, 1996). Those who are skeptical about repressed memories argue that thousands of innocent families are being ripped apart by unquestioned acceptance of recovered memories of sexual abuse. The other camp raises an equally disturbing concern that the recent skepticism about repressed memories will turn the clock back to a time when women and children were reluctant to report abuse because they were often ignored, ridiculed, or made to feel guilty. Unfortunately, the repressed memories controversy isn't likely to be settled soon, given that there is no way to definitively evaluate the authenticity of most recovered recollections of child abuse. Scientists can only nibble away at the issue by conducting studies on the misinformation effect, hypnotic pseudomemory, therapeutic practices, and so forth, that shed light on specific pieces of the puzzle.

Recap of Key Points

• Ebbinghaus's early studies of nonsense syllables suggested that people forget very rapidly. Subsequent research showed that Ebbinghaus's forgetting curve was exceptionally steep.

• Forgetting can be measured by asking people to recall, recognize, or relearn information. Different methods of measuring retention often produce different estimates of forgetting. Recognition measures tend to yield higher estimates of retention than recall measures.

• Some forgetting, including pseudoforgetting, is due to ineffective encoding of information. Decay theory proposes that forgetting occurs spontaneously with the passage of time. It has proven difficult to show that decay occurs in long-term memory.

• Interference theory proposes that people forget information because of competition from other material. Proactive interference occurs when new learning interferes with old information. Retroactive interference occurs when previous learning interferes with new learning.

• Forgetting may also be a matter of retrieval failure. According to the encoding specificity principle, the effectiveness of a retrieval cue depends on how well it corrresponds to the memory code that represents the stored item. Research also suggests that retrieval failures are more likely when there is a poor fit between the processing done during encoding and the processing required by the measure of retention.

• Repression involves the motivated forgetting of painful or unpleasant memories. Recent years have seen a surge of reports of repressed memories of sexual abuse in childhood. The authenticity of these repressed memories is the subject of controversy because empirical studies have demonstrated that it is not all that difficult to create false memories.

• In the Featured Study, Sheehan and associates demonstrated that false memories can be created through hypnosis, especially with highly hypnotizable subjects who have rapport with the hypnotist.

IN SEARCH OF THE MEMORY TRACE: THE PHYSIOLOGY OF MEMORY

For decades, neuroscientists have ventured forth in search of the physiological basis for memory. On several occasions scientists have been excited by new leads, only to be led down blind alleys. For example, as we noted earlier, Wilder Penfield's work with electrical stimulation of the brain during surgery suggested that the cortex houses exact tape recordings of past experiences (Penfield & Perot, 1963). At the time, scientists believed that this was a major advance. Ultimately, it was not.

Similarly, James McConnell rocked the world of science when he reported that he had chemically transferred a specific memory from one flatworm to another. McConnell (1962) created a conditioned reflex (contraction in response to light) in flatworms and then transferred RNA (a basic molecular constituent of all living cells) from trained worms to untrained worms. The untrained worms showed evidence of "remembering" the conditioned reflex. McConnell boldly speculated that in the future, chemists might be able to formulate pills containing the information for Physics 201 or History 101! Unfortunately, the RNA transfer studies proved difficult to replicate (Gaito, 1976). Today, 30 years after McConnell's "breakthrough," we are still a long way from breaking the chemical code for memory.

Investigators continue to explore a variety of leads about the physiological basis for memory. In light of past failures, these lines of research should probably be viewed with guarded optimism, but we'll look at some of the more promising approaches. You may want to consult Chapter 3 if you need to refresh your memory about the physiological processes and structures discussed in this section.

The Biochemistry of Memory 6c

One line of research suggests that memory formation results in *alterations in synaptic transmission* at specific sites. According to this view, specific memories depend on biochemical changes that occur at specific synapses. Like McConnell, Eric Kandel and his colleagues have studied conditioned reflexes in a simple organism—a sea slug. They have shown that specific forms of learning in the sea slug result in an increase or decrease in the release of neurotransmitters by

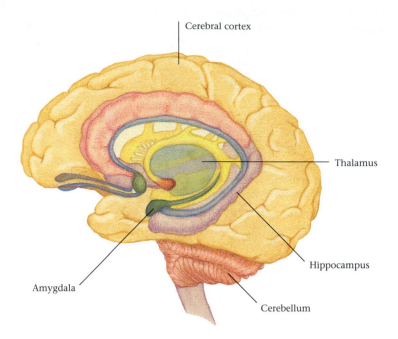

Cerebral cortex

Thalamus

Hippocampus

Cerebellum

Amygdala

Figure 7.26
The anatomy of memory.
All the brain structures identified here have been implicated in efforts to discover the anatomical structures involved in memory. Although researchers have made some exciting discoveries, the physiological bases of memory are extremely complex and are not yet well understood.

presynaptic neurons (Kandel & Schwartz, 1982; Kennedy, Hawkins, & Kandel, 1992). Working with sea snails, Daniel Alkon (1989) has found that classical conditioning alters chemical processes in the cell membranes of specific postsynaptic neurons. Kandel and Alkon believe that durable changes in synaptic transmission may be the neural building blocks of more complex memories as well. Of course, critics point out that it's risky to generalize from marine mollusks to humans.

Manipulations that alter hormone levels shortly after an organism has learned a new response can affect memory storage in a variety of animals. These hormonal changes can either facilitate or impair memory, depending on the specific hormone and the amount of change (McGaugh, 1992). James McGaugh (1990) theorizes that hormones influence memory storage by modulating activity at opiate receptor sites and norepinephrine and GABA synapses in the brain. Other animal studies suggest that adequate protein synthesis is necessary for the formation of memories (Rose, 1992; Rosenzweig et al., 1992). For example, the administration of drugs that interfere with protein synthesis impairs long-term memory storage in rats.

Autopsies of people who suffered from *Alzheimer's disease* provide additional clues about the biochemistry of memory. Alzheimer's disease, which produces severe memory impairment and other cognitve deficits in a significant minority of people over age 65, appears to be due, in part, to inadequate synthesis of the neurotransmitter *ace-*

tylcholine (Albert & Moss, 1992). As you can see, the biochemical bases of memory are complex, to say the least.

The Neural Circuitry of Memory 6c

Richard F. Thompson (1989, 1992) and his colleagues have shown that specific memories may depend on *localized neural circuits* in the brain. In other words, memories may create unique, reusable pathways in the brain along which signals flow. Thompson has traced the pathway that accounts for a rabbit's memory of a conditioned eyeblink response. The key link in this circuit is a microscopic spot in the *cerebellum*, a structure in the hindbrain (see Figure 7.26). When this spot is destroyed, the conditioned stimulus no longer elicits the eyeblink response, even though the unconditioned stimulus still does. This finding does *not* mean that the cerebellum is the key to all memory. Thompson theorizes that other memories probably create entirely different pathways in other areas of the brain. The key implication of Thompson's work is that it may be possible to map out specific neural circuits that correspond to specific memories.

Evidence on *long-term potentiation* also supports the idea that memory traces consist of specific neural circuits. **Long-term potentiation (LTP) is a long-lasting increase in neural excitability at synapses along a specific neural pathway.** Thus far, researchers have produced LTP artificially by sending a burst of high-frequency electrical stimulation along a neural pathway (Racine & deJonge, 1988). Many theorists suspect that natural events produce the same sort of potentiated neural circuit when a memory is formed (Martinez & Derrick, 1996; Morris, 1992).

In some cases, memory formation may alter the anatomy of the brain by stimulating neural growth (Rosenzweig, 1996). For instance, new branches in the dendritic trees of certain neurons are found in rats that learn to run a series of mazes (Greenough, 1985). As you may recall from Chapter 3, dendritic trees are specialized to receive signals from other neurons. Hence, increased dendritic branching probably leads to the formation of additional synapses and the creation of new neural pathways. These new neural circuits may reflect the storage of learned information.

The Anatomy of Memory 6c

Cases of *organic amnesia*—extensive memory loss due to head injury—are another source of clues about the physiological bases of memory (Mayes,

1992). There are two basic types of amnesia: retrograde and anterograde (see Figure 7.27). **In *retrograde amnesia* a person loses memories for events that occurred prior to the onset of amnesia.** For example, a 25-year-old gymnast who sustains a head trauma might find the prior three years, or seven years, or perhaps her entire lifetime erased. **In *anterograde amnesia* a person loses memories for events that occur after the onset of amnesia.** For instance, after her accident, the injured gymnast might suffer impaired ability to remember people she meets, where she has parked her car, and so on.

Because victims' current memory functioning is impaired, cases of anterograde amnesia have been especially rich sources of information about the brain and memory. One well-known case, that of a man referred to as H. M., has been followed by Brenda Milner and her colleagues since 1953 (Corkin, 1984; Milner, Corkin, & Teuber, 1968; Scoville & Milner, 1957). H. M. had surgery to relieve debilitating epileptic seizures. Unfortunately, the surgery inadvertently wiped out most of his ability to form long-term memories. H. M.'s short-term memory is fine, but he has no recollection of anything that has happened since 1953 (other than about the most recent 20 seconds of his life). He doesn't recognize the doctors treating him, he can't remember routes to and from places, and he doesn't know his age. He can't remember what he did yesterday, let alone what he has done for the last 35 to 40 years. He doesn't even recognize a current photo of himself, as aging has changed his appearance considerably.

H. M.'s memory losses have been attributed to the removal of his *hippocampus,* a structure in the *limbic system* (see Figure 7.26). Damage to the hippocampus has also been found in other cases of anterograde amnesia (Shimamura, 1992). However, it appears that amnesia can also be caused by damage to other nearby areas, specifically the *amygdala* and certain nuclei in the *thalamus* (Markowitsch & Pritzel, 1985; Mishkin, Malamut, & Backevalier, 1984).

Do these findings mean that memories are housed in the hippocampus and adjacent areas? Probably not. The hippocampus and amygdala appear to play a key role in the *consolidation* of memories (McGaugh, 1989). **Consolidation is a hypothetical process involving the gradual conversion of information into durable memory codes stored in long-term memory.** The current thinking is that memories are consolidated in subcortical structures in the limbic system but that

they are stored in various areas of the cortex. Which areas? Memories are probably stored in the same cortical areas that were originally involved in processing the sensory input that led to the memories (Mishkin & Appenzeller, 1987; Squire, Knowlton, & Musen, 1993). For instance, memories of visual information may be stored in areas of the visual cortex.

In summary, a host of biochemical processes, neural circuits, and anatomical structures have been implicated as playing a role in memory. Does all this sound confusing? It should, because it is. The bottom line is that neuroscientists are still assembling the pieces of the puzzle that will explain the physiological basis of memory. Although they have identified many of the puzzle pieces, they're not sure how the pieces fit together. Their difficulty is probably due to the complex, multifaceted nature of memory. Looking for the physiological basis for memory is only slightly less daunting than looking for the physiological basis for thought itself.

Recap of Key Points

- Memory traces may reflect alterations in neurotransmitter release at specific locations. Manipulations of hormone levels and protein synthesis can affect memory. Various lines of research also suggest that norepinephrine, acetylcholine, and GABA may be involved in the biochemical coding of memory.
- Thompson's research suggests that memory traces may consist of localized neural circuits. Memories may also depend on long-term potentiation, which is a durable increase in neural excitability at synapses along a specific neural pathway. Memory formation may also stimulate neural growth.
- In retrograde amnesia, a person loses memory for events prior to the amnesia. In anterograde amnesia, a person shows memory deficits for events subsequent to the onset of the amnesia. Research on amnesia has implicated the hippocampus and amygdala as brain structures involved in the consolidation of memories.

Retrograde amnesia

Memory loss

Onset of amnesia

Memory loss

Anterograde amnesia

Figure 7.27
Retrograde versus anterograde amnesia. In retrograde amnesia, patients lose their memory for events that occurred during some period prior to the onset of their amnesia. In anterograde amnesia, patients exhibit memory deficits for events that occur subsequent to the onset of their amnesia.

"Some effects of temporal lobe lesions in man are hard to reconcile with any unitary-process theory of memory."

BRENDA MILNER

ARE THERE MULTIPLE MEMORY SYSTEMS?

Some theorists believe that evidence on the physiology of memory is confusing because investigators are unwittingly probing into several distinct memory systems that have different physiological bases. A number of research findings inspired this view, foremost among them being the discovery of *implicit memory*. Let's look at this perplexing phenomenon.

Implicit Versus Explicit Memory

As noted earlier, patients with anterograde amnesia often appear to have virtually no ability to form long-term memories. If they're shown a list of words and subsequently given a test of retention, their performance is miserable. However, different findings emerge when "sneaky" techniques are used to measure their memory indirectly. For instance, they might be asked to work on a word recognition task that is not presented as a measure of retention. In this task, they are shown fragments of words (example: _ss_ss__ for assassin) and are asked to complete the fragments with the first appropriate word that comes to mind. The series of word fragments includes ones that correspond to words on a list they saw earlier. In this situation, the amnesiac subjects respond with words that were on the list just as frequently as normal subjects who also saw the initial list (Schacter, Chiu, & Ochsner, 1993). Thus, the amnesiacs *do* remember words from the list. However, when asked, they don't even remember having been shown the list.

The demonstration of long-term retention in amnesiacs who previously appeared to have no long-term memory shocked memory experts when it was first reported by Warrington and Weiskrantz (1970). However, this surprising finding has been replicated in many subsequent studies. This phenomenon has come to be known as implicit memory. **Implicit memory is apparent when retention is exhibited on a task that does not require intentional remembering.** Implicit memory is contrasted with *explicit memory*, **which involves intentional recollection of previous experiences.**

Is implicit memory peculiar to people suffering from amnesia? No. When normal subjects are exposed to material and their retention of it is measured indirectly, they, too, show implicit memory (Schacter, 1987, 1989). To draw a parallel with everyday life, implicit memory is simply incidental, unintentional remembering (Mandler, 1989).

People frequently remember things that they didn't deliberately store in memory. For example, you might recall the color of a jacket that your professor wore yesterday. Likewise, people remember things without deliberate retrieval efforts. For instance, you might be telling someone about a restaurant, which somehow reminds you of an unrelated story about a mutual friend.

Research has uncovered many interesting differences between implicit and explicit memory (Roediger, 1990; Tulving & Schacter, 1990). Explicit memory is conscious, is accessed directly, and can be best assessed with recall or recognition measures of retention. Implicit memory is unconscious, must be accessed indirectly, and can be best assessed with variations on relearning (savings) measures of retention. Implicit memory is largely unaffected by amnesia, age, the administration of certain drugs (such as alcohol), the length of the retention interval, and manipulations of interference. In contrast, explicit memory is affected very much by all these factors.

Some theorists think these differences are found because implicit and explicit memory rely on *different cognitive processes* in encoding and retrieval (Graf & Gallie, 1992; Jacoby, 1988; Roediger, 1990). However, many other theorists argue that the differences exist because implicit and explicit memory are handled by *independent memory systems* (Schacter, 1992, 1994; Squire, 1994). These independent systems are referred to as declarative and procedural memory.

Declarative Versus Procedural Memory 6c

Many theorists have suggested that people have separate memory systems for different kinds of information (see Figure 7.28). The most basic division of memory into distinct systems contrasts *declarative memory* with *nondeclarative* or *procedural memory* (Winograd, 1975). **The *declarative memory system* handles factual information.** It contains recollections of words, definitions, names, dates, faces, events, concepts, and ideas. **The *nondeclarative* or *procedural memory system* houses memory for actions, skills, and operations.** It contains memories of how to execute such actions as riding a bike, typing, and tying one's shoes. To illustrate the distinction, if you know the rules of tennis (the number of games in a set, scoring, and such), this factual information is stored in declarative memory. If you remember how to hit a serve

"Memory systems constitute the major subdivisions of the overall organization of the memory complex. . . . An operating component of a system consists of a neural substrate and its behavioral or cognitive correlates."

ENDEL TULVING

and swing through a backhand, these perceptual-motor skills are stored in procedural memory.

Some theorists believe that an association exists between implicit memory and the procedural memory system (Squire et al., 1993). Why? Because memory for skills is largely unconscious. People execute perceptual-motor tasks such as playing the piano or typing with little conscious awareness of what they're doing. In fact, performance on such tasks often deteriorates if people think too much about what they're doing. Another parallel with implicit memory is that the memory for skills (such as typing and bike riding) doesn't decline much over long retention intervals. Thus, the procedural memory system may handle implicit remembering, while the declarative memory system handles explicit remembering.

The notion that declarative and procedural memories are separate is supported by certain patterns of memory loss seen in amnesiacs. In many cases, declarative memory is severely impaired while procedural memory is left largely intact (Squire, 1987). For example, H. M., the victim of amnesia discussed earlier, can learn and remember new motor skills, even though he can't remember what he currently looks like. The sparing of procedural memory in amnesia could explain why implicit remembering is largely unaffected.

Procedural memory is considered a relatively primitive type of memory. It can be observed even in lower animals. Among the "operations" thought to be stored in procedural memory are automatic glandular and muscular reflexes governed by classical conditioning. Declarative memory involves more complex mental processes that are seen only in higher organisms.

There is considerable debate about whether procedural and declarative memory are independent systems with separate neural bases. At present, the evidence is complex and often contradictory (Hintzman, 1990).

Semantic Versus Episodic Memory

Endel Tulving (1986, 1993) has further subdivided declarative memory into episodic and semantic memory (see Figure 7.28). Both contain factual information, but episodic memory contains *personal facts* and semantic memory contains *general facts*. The **episodic memory system is made up of chronological, or temporally dated, recollections of personal experiences.** Episodic memory is a record of things you've done, seen, and heard. It includes information about *when* you did these things, saw them, or heard them. It contains recol-

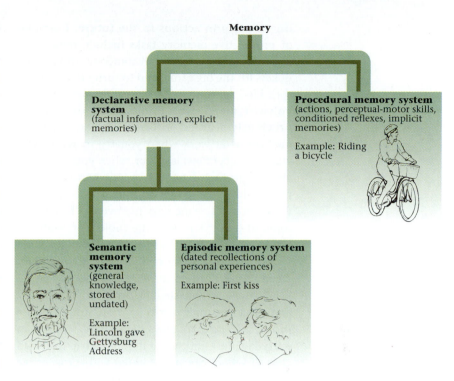

lections about being in a ninth-grade play, visiting the Grand Canyon, attending a Depeche Mode concert, or going to a movie last weekend.

The *semantic memory system* **contains general knowledge that is not tied to the time when the information was learned.** Semantic memory contains information such as Christmas is December 25th, dogs have four legs, and Phoenix is located in Arizona. You probably don't remember when you learned these facts. Information like this is usually stored undated. The distinction between episodic and semantic memory can be better appreciated by drawing an analogy to books: Episodic memory is like an autobiography, while semantic memory is like an encyclopedia.

The memory deficits seen in some cases of amnesia suggest that episodic and semantic memory are separate systems. For instance, some amnesiacs forget most personal facts, while their recall of general facts is largely unaffected (Wood, Ebert, & Kinsbourne, 1982). However, debate continues about whether episodic and semantic memory represent physiologically separate systems (Neely, 1989; Squire et al., 1993).

Prospective Versus Retrospective Memory

A 1984 paper with a clever title, "Remembering to Do Things: A Forgotten Topic" (Harris, 1984), introduced yet another distinction between types of memory: *prospective memory* versus *retrospective memory*. **Prospective memory** involves remember-

Figure 7.28
Theories of independent memory systems. There is some evidence that different types of information are stored in separate memory systems, which may have distinct physiological bases. The diagram shown here, which blends the ideas of several theorists, is an adaptation of Larry Squire's (1987) scheme. Endel Tulving (1985, 1987), another highly influential theorist in this area, makes similar distinctions but would diagram the relations among systems differently. Tulving's theory proposes a "nested" organization, in which episodic memory is part of semantic memory, which is part of procedural memory. Note also that implicit and explicit memory are not memory systems. They are observed behavioral phenomena that appear to be handled by different hypothetical memory systems (the procedural and declarative memory systems), which cannot be observed directly.

ing to perform actions in the future. Examples of prospective memory tasks include remembering to walk the dog, to call someone, to grab the tickets for the big game, and to turn off your lawn sprinkler. In contrast, *retrospective memory* **involves remembering events from the past or previously learned information.** Retrospective memory is at work when you try to recall who won the Super Bowl last year, when you reminisce about your high school days, or when you try to recall what your professor said in a lecture last week. Prospective memory has been a "forgotten" topic in that it has been the subject of relatively little study. But that has begun to change, as research on prospective memory has increased in recent years (Einstein & McDaniel, 1996).

Researchers interested in prospective memory argue that the topic merits far more study because prospective memory plays such a pervasive role in everyday life. Think about it—a brief trip to attend class at school can be saturated with prospective memory tasks. You may need to remember to pack your notebook, take your umbrella, turn off your coffee pot, and grab your car keys before you even get out the door. People seem to vary tremendously in their ability to successfully carry out prospective memory tasks (Searleman, 1996). Individuals who appear deficient in prospective memory are often characterized as "absent-minded."

Much remains to be learned about the factors that influence prospective memory. *Habitual tasks,* such as remembering to pick up your mail, appear to be easier to remember than *infrequent tasks,* such as remembering to stop your mail delivery for an upcoming vacation (Searleman, 1996). Another key factor appears to be whether a prospective memory task is tied to some sort of cue. *Event-based tasks* involve future actions that should be triggered by a specific cue. For example, remembering to give a message to a friend is cued by seeing the friend, or remembering to take medication with one's meal is cued by the meal. *Time-based tasks* require that an action be performed at a certain time or after a certain length of time has elapsed. For example, you might want to start your video recorder at a specific time to tape an interesting show, or you might need to remember to turn off the oven after an hour of baking. Evidence suggests that the cues available in event-based prospective memory tasks make these tasks easier to remember than time-based tasks (Einstein & McDaniel, 1996).

Are prospective memory and retrospective memory independent cognitive systems with different neural bases? Perhaps, but it is much too early to tell. Suggestive of independence, some studies have indicated that there may be little positive correlation between performance on prospective and retrospective memory tasks (Searleman, 1996). And some research suggests that areas

---

CONCEPT CHECK 7.3
Recognizing Various Types of Memory

Check your understanding of the various types of memory discussed in this chapter by matching the definitions below with the following: (a) declarative memory, (b) episodic memory, (c) explicit memory, (d) implicit memory, (e) long-term memory, (f) procedural memory, (g) prospective memory, (h) retrospective memory, (i) semantic memory, (j) sensory memory, (k) short-term memory. The answers can be found in Appendix A.

_____ 1. Memory for factual information.

_____ 2. An unlimited capacity store that can hold information over lengthy periods of time.

_____ 3. The preservation of information in its original sensory form for a brief time, usually only a fraction of a second.

_____ 4. Type of memory apparent when retention is exhibited on a task that does not require intentional remembering.

_____ 5. Chronological, or temporally dated, recollections of personal experiences.

_____ 6. The repository of memories for actions, skills, and operations.

_____ 7. General knowledge that is not tied to the time when the information was learned.

_____ 8. Remembering to perform future actions.

_____ 9. A limited-capacity store that can maintain unrehearsed information for about 20 seconds.

in the frontal lobe of the brain may be critical to prospective memory (Cockburn, 1995). But far more evidence is needed before scientists can conclude that prospective memory and retrospective memory are separate systems. This issue promises to be a fertile area of future research.

PUTTING IT IN PERSPECTIVE

One of our integrative themes—the idea that people's experience of the world is subjective—stood head and shoulders above the rest in this chapter. Let's briefly review how the study of memory has illuminated this idea.

First, our discussion of attention as inherently selective should have shed light on why people's experience of the world is subjective. To a great degree, what you see in the world around you depends on where you focus your attention. This is one of the main reasons that two people can be exposed to the "same" events and walk away with entirely different perceptions. For instance, imagine that you and a friend were to meet a prominent politician at a fund-raiser. The two of you might come away with different impressions of the person because you attended to the meaning of what was said while your friend paid attention to the politician's body language.

Second, the reconstructive nature of memory should further explain people's tendency to view the world with a subjective slant. When you observe an event, you don't store an exact copy of the event in your memory. Instead, you store a rough, "bare bones" approximation of the event that may be reshaped as time goes by. With the passage of time, people tend to put more and more of a personal, subjective imprint on memories.

Finally, people sometimes forget those things that they don't want to remember. This propensity for motivated forgetting introduces yet another source of personal bias into people's views of the past. In short, a host of natural human tendencies in cognitive processing conspire to make each individual's experience of the world highly subjective.

Another of our unifying themes also surfaced in this chapter. The multifaceted nature of memory demonstrated once again that behavior is governed by multiple causes. For instance, your memory of a specific event may be influenced by the following factors:

- The amount of attention you devote to the event.
- The level at which you process the incoming information.
- Whether you enrich your encoding with some form of elaboration.
- Whether you have an opportunity to transfer the information into long-term memory.
- How you organize the information.
- How you search through your memory store.
- The extent to which you use schemas to reconstruct the event.
- The amount of interference you experience.

Given the multifaceted nature of memory, it should come as no surprise that there are many ways to improve memory. We discuss a variety of strategies in our Application section.

Recap of Key Points
• Implicit memory involves unintentional remembering, whereas explicit memory involves intentional recall. Implicit memory is unconscious, must be accessed indirectly, and is largely unaffected by amnesia, age, drugs, and the length of the retention interval. Differences between implicit and explicit memory suggest that people may have several separate memory systems.
• Declarative memory is memory for facts, while procedural memory is memory for actions and skills. Theorists suspect that the declarative memory system handles explicit memory, whereas the procedural memory system handles implicit memory.
• Declarative memory can be subdivided into episodic memory, for personal facts, and semantic memory, for general facts. Theorists have also distinguished between retrospective memory (remembering past events) and prospective memory (remembering to do things in the future).
• Our discussion of attention and memory enhances our understanding of why our experience of the world is highly subjective. Work in this area also shows that behavior is governed by multiple causes.

APPLICATION: **IMPROVING EVERYDAY MEMORY**

Answer the following "true" or "false."

1 Memory strategies were recently invented by psychologists.

2 Imagery can be used to remember concrete words only.

3 Overlearning of information leads to poor retention.

4 Outlining what you read is not likely to affect retention.

5 Massing practice in one long study session is better than distributing practice across several shorter sessions.

Mnemonic devices **are methods used to increase the recall of information.** They have a long history, so the first statement is false. In fact, one of the mnemonic devices covered in this Application—the method of loci—was described in Greece as early as 86–82 B.C. (Yates, 1966). Actually, mnemonic devices were much more important in ancient times than they are today. In ancient Greece and Rome, for instance, paper and pencils were not readily available for people to write down things they needed to remember, so they had to depend heavily on mnemonic devices.

Are mnemonic devices the key to improving one's everyday memory? No. Mnemonic devices clearly can be helpful in some situations (Wilding & Valentine, 1996), but they are not a panacea. They can be hard to use and hard to apply to many everyday situations. Most books and training programs designed to improve memory probably overemphasize mnemonic techniques (Searleman & Herrmann, 1994). Although less exotic strategies such as increasing rehearsal,

engaging in deeper processing, and organizing material are more crucial to everyday memory, we will discuss some popular mnemonics as we proceed through this Application. Along the way, you'll learn that all of our opening true-false statements are false.

Engage in Adequate Rehearsal

Practice makes perfect, or so you've heard. In reality, practice is not likely to guarantee perfection, but it usually leads to improved retention. Studies show that retention improves with increased rehearsal (Greene, 1992). This improvement occurs because rehearsal can help transfer information into long-term memory.

Continued rehearsal may also improve your *understanding* of assigned material. This payoff was apparent in a study that examined the effects of repetition (Bromage & Mayer, 1986). Undergraduate subjects listened to an audiotaped lecture on photography from one to three times. Information in the lecture was classified into three levels of importance. As Figure 7.29 shows, increased repetition led to increased recall for information at all three levels of importance. However, repetition had its greatest impact on the retention of the *most important* information, yielding enhanced understanding of the lecture. Thus, as you go over information again and again, your increased familiarity with the material may permit you to focus selectively on the most important points.

It even pays to overlearn material (Driskell, Willis, & Copper, 1992). *Overlearning* **refers to continued rehearsal of material after you first appear to have mastered it.** In one study, after subjects had mastered a list of nouns (they recited the list without error), Krueger (1929) required them to continue rehearsing for

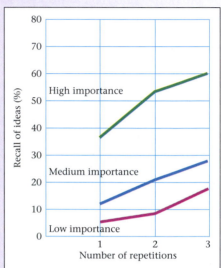

Figure 7.29
Effects of repetition on understanding. In the Bromage and Mayer (1986) study, repetition facilitated retention, as in other studies, but they found that repetition most aided the recall of high-importance ideas.

50% or 100% more trials. Measuring retention at intervals up to 28 days, Krueger found that greater overlearning was related to better recall of the list. The practical implication of this finding is simple: You should not quit rehearsing material just because you appear to have mastered it.

Schedule Distributed Practice

Let's assume that you need to study 9 hours for an exam. Should you "cram" all your studying into one 9-hour period (massed practice)? Or is it better to distribute your study among, say, three 3-hour periods on successive days (distributed practice)? The evidence indicates that retention tends to be greater after distributed practice than after massed practice (Glenberg, 1992; Payne & Wenger, 1996). For instance, Underwood (1970) studied children (ages 9 to 14) who practiced a list of words four times, either in one long session or in four separate sessions. He found that distributed practice led to better recall than a similar amount of massed practice (see Figure 7.30). The superiority of distributed practice suggests that cramming is an ill-advised approach to studying for exams.

Minimize Interference

Because interference is a major cause of forgetting, you'll probably want to think about how you can minimize it. This issue is especially important for students, because memorizing information for one course can interfere with the retention of information for another course. It may help to allocate study for specific courses to separate days. Thorndyke and Hayes-Roth (1979) found that similar material produced less interference when it was learned on different days. Thus, the day before an exam in a course, you should study for that course only—if possible. If demands in other courses make that plan impossible, you should study the test material last.

Of course, studying for other classes is not the only source of interference in a student's life. Other normal waking activities also produce interference. Therefore, it's a good idea to conduct one last, thorough review of material as close to exam time as possible (Anderson, 1980). This strategy will help you reduce memory loss

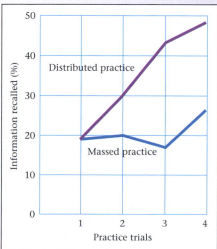

Figure 7.30
Effects of massed versus distributed practice on retention. Children in the Underwood (1970) study showed better recall of information when practice sessions were distributed over time as opposed to being massed together in one session.

due to interference from intervening activities.

Engage in Deep Processing

Research on levels of processing suggests that how *often* you go over material is less critical than the *depth* of processing that you engage in (Craik & Tulving, 1975). Thus, if you expect to remember what you read, you have to wrestle fully with its meaning. Many students could probably benefit if they spent less time on rote repetition and devoted more effort to actually paying attention to and analyzing the meaning of their reading assignments. In particular, it is useful to make material *personally* meaningful. When you read your textbooks, try to relate information to your own life and experience. For example, when you read about classical conditioning, try to think of responses that you display that are attributable to classical conditioning.

Emphasize Transfer-Appropriate Processing

It's also useful to keep the concept of *transfer-appropriate processing* in mind. A study comparing fact-oriented processing and problem-oriented processing of the same information found that problem-oriented processing was more helpful when testing required students to solve problems (Adams et al., 1988). Thus, students should tailor their study methods to the type of test they will be given. For instance, if a test will be made up of problems to solve, the best way to prepare is to practice solving problems like those that will be on the test.

Organize Information

Retention tends to be greater when information is well organized. The value of organization has been apparent in studies of people who exhibit remarkable memory capability. For example, Ericsson and Polson (1988) have studied a waiter, known as J. C., who can remember up to 20 complicated dinner orders without taking notes. They found that control subjects tried to memorize dinner requests in the

order in which the requests were presented, whereas J. C. organized information by dinner element (salad dressings, vegetables, and so on). J. C. also used acronyms to remember orders within a dinner element. For instance, he used the word *boot* to remember salad dressing orders for blue cheese, oil and vinegar, oil and vinegar, and Thousand Island.

Gordon Bower (1970) has shown that hierarchical organization is particularly helpful when it is applicable. Thus, it may be a good idea to *outline* reading assignments for school. Consistent with this reasoning, there is some empirical evidence that outlining material from textbooks can enhance retention of the material (McDaniel, Waddill, & Shakesby, 1996).

Enrich Encoding with Verbal Mnemonics

When you memorize abstract information, it helps to make the information personally meaningful, but it's not always easy to do so. For instance, when you study chemistry you may have a hard time relating to polymers at a personal level. Thus, many mnemonic devices—such as acrostics, acronyms, and narrative methods—are designed to make abstract material more meaningful.

Acrostics and Acronyms

Acrostics are phrases (or poems) in which the first letter of each word (or line) functions as a cue to help you recall information to be remembered. For instance, you may remember the order of musical notes with the saying "Every good boy does fine" (or "deserves favor"). A slight variation on acrostics is the *acronym*—a word formed out of the first letters of a series of words. Students memorizing the order of colors in the light spectrum often store the name "Roy G. Biv" to remember red, orange, yellow, green, blue, indigo, and violet. Notice that this acronym takes advantage of the principle of chunking.

Narrative Methods

Another useful way to remember a list of words is to create a story that includes the words in the appropriate order. The narrative both increases the meaningfulness of the words and links them in a specific order. Examples of this technique can be seen in Figure 7.31. Bower and Clark (1969) found that this procedure greatly enhanced subjects' recall of lists of unrelated words (as shown in Figure 7.31).

Why—and how—would you use the narrative method? Let's assume that you always manage to forget to put one item in

Word lists	Stories
Bird Costume Mailbox Head River Nurse Theater Wax Eyelid Furnace	A man dressed in a *Bird Costume* and wearing a *Mailbox* on his *Head* was seen leaping into the *River*. A *Nurse* ran out of a nearby *Theater* and applied *Wax* to his *Eyelids,* but her efforts were in vain. He died and was tossed into the *Furnace*.
Rustler Penthouse Mountain Sloth Tavern Fuzz Gland Antler Pencil Vitamin	A *Rustler* lived in a *Penthouse* on top of a *Mountain*. His specialty was the three-toed *Sloth*. He would take his captive animals to a *Tavern* where he would remove *Fuzz* from their *Glands*. Unfortunately, all this exposure to sloth fuzz caused him to grow *Antlers*. So he gave up his profession and went to work in a *Pencil* factory. As a precaution he also took a lot of *Vitamin* E.

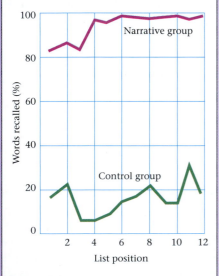

Figure 7.31
Narrative methods of remembering. Bower and Clark (1969) presented subjects with 12 lists of words. Subjects in the "narrative group" were asked to recall the words by constructing a story out of them (like the stories shown here). Subjects in the control group were given no special instructions. Recoding the material in story form dramatically improved recall, as the graph clearly shows.

your gym bag on your way to the pool. Short of pasting a list on the inside of the bag, how can you remember everything you need? You could make up a story like the following that includes the items you need:

The wind and rain in COMBINATION *nearly* LOCKed *out the rescue efforts.* CAP, *the flying ace,* TOWELed *the soap from his eyes, pulled his* GOGGLES *from his* SUIT *pocket, and* COMBed *the* BRUSH *for survivors.*

Rhymes

Another verbal mnemonic that people often rely on is rhyming. You've probably repeated, "I before E except after C . . ." thousands of times. Perhaps you also remember the number of days in each month with the old standby, "Thirty days hath September . . ." Rhyming something to remember it is an old and useful trick.

Enrich Encoding with Visual Mnemonics 6a

Memory can be enhanced by the use of visual imagery. As you may recall, Allan Paivio (1986) believes that visual images create a second memory code and that two codes are better than one for enhancing recall. Many popular mnemonic devices depend on visual imagery, including the link method, method of loci, and keyword method.

Link Method

The *link method* involves forming a mental image of items to be remembered in a way that links them together. For instance, suppose you need to remember some items to pick up at the drugstore: a news magazine, shaving cream, film, and pens. To remember these items, you might visualize a public figure on the magazine cover shaving with a pen while being photographed. There is some evidence that the more bizarre you make your image, the more helpful it is likely to be (McDaniel & Einstein, 1986).

Method of Loci

The *method of loci* involves taking an imaginary walk along a familiar path

where images of items to be remembered are associated with certain locations. The first step is to commit to memory a series of loci, or places along a path. Usually these loci are specific locations in your home or neighborhood. Then envision each thing you want to remember in one of these locations. Try to form distinctive, vivid images. When you need to remember the items, imagine yourself walking along the path. The various loci on your path should serve as cues for the retrieval of the images that you formed (see Figure 7.32). The method of loci assures that items are remembered in their correct order because the order is determined by the sequence of locations along the pathway.

Keyword Method

Visual images are also useful when you need to form an association between a pair of items, such as a person's name and face or a foreign word and its English translation. However, there is a potential problem that you may recall from our earlier discussion of visual imagery. It's difficult to generate images to represent abstract words (Paivio, 1969). A way to avoid this problem is to employ **the *keyword method*, in which you associate a concrete word with an abstract word and generate an image to represent the concrete word.**

A practical use of this method is to help you remember the names of people you meet (Morris, Jones, & Hampson, 1978). Just associate a concrete word with the name and then form an image of the associated word. The associated word, which is the *keyword,* should sound like the name that's being learned. For example, you might use *Garden* as a keyword for *Gordon*. And *debtor man* might be a good keyword for Detterman, if you form an image of Mr. Detterman dressed in ragged clothes. The keyword method can also be helpful in learning the words of a foreign language (Atkinson & Raugh, 1975; Gruneberg, Sykes, & Gillett, 1994). For example, imagine that you're having difficulty remembering that *boulangerie* is French for *bakery*. To remember this French word you might use the keyword *boo-lingerie* and picture a ghost hanging in lingerie in your favorite bakery.

Figure 7.32
The method of loci. In this example from Bower (1970), a person about to go shopping pairs items to remember with familiar places (loci) arranged in a natural sequence: (1) hot dogs/driveway; (2) cat food/garage interior; (3) tomatoes/front door; (4) bananas/coat closet shelf; (5) whiskey/kitchen sink. The shopper then uses imagery to associate the items on the shopping list with the loci, as shown in the drawing: (1) giant hot dog rolls down a driveway; (2) a cat noisily devours cat food in the garage; (3) ripe tomatoes are splattered on the front door; (4) bunches of bananas are hung from the closet shelf; (5) the contents of a bottle of whiskey gurgle down the kitchen sink. As the last panel shows, the shopper recalls the items by mentally touring the loci associated with them.

Levin and Levin (1990) trained students to apply the keyword method to unfamiliar terms in a plant classification system. They coupled this approach with the link method, which was used to group terms that belonged together in categories. The researchers found that these methods enhanced students' memory of the classification system (see Figure 7.33).

Recap of Key Points
• Mnemonic devices are methods used to increase the recall of information. Rehearsal, even when it involves overlearning, facilitates retention. Distributed practice tends to be more efficient than massed practice.
• It is wise to plan study sessions so as to minimize interference. Processing during rehearsal should be deep and appropriate for the method of testing. Evidence also suggests that organization enhances retention, so outlining texts may be valuable.
• Meaningfulness can be enhanced through the use of verbal mnemonics such as acrostics, acronyms, and narrative methods. The link method, the method of loci, and the keyword method are mnemonic devices that depend on the value of visual imagery.

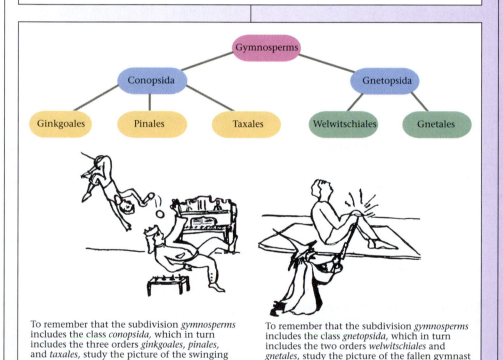

To remember that the subdivision *gymnosperms* includes the class *conopsida*, which in turn includes the three orders *ginkgoales*, *pinales*, and *taxales*, study the picture of the swinging gymnast with the ice cream cone in his hand. The ice cream is about to splat in the face of the king who is leaping from the bench of his royal piano after sitting on some tacks.

To remember that the subdivision *gymnosperms* includes the class *gnetopsida*, which in turn includes the two orders *welwitschiales* and *gnetales*, study the picture of the fallen gymnast holding his sore knee tops. He is being treated (or tricked!) by a witch doctor who is sticking a very long needle into his injured knee.

Figure 7.33
Combining the keyword and link methods to aid recall. Levin and Levin (1990) set out to help students memorize a difficult plant classification system (a portion of the system is shown in the top part of the figure). They taught students to use a technique called pictorial mnemonomy, which essentially combines the keyword and link methods. Students were trained to generate keywords for the abstract terms in the hierarchy and to form images that linked the keywords that corresponded to portions of the classification system (two examples are shown in the bottom part of the figure). This creative use of visual imagery enhanced students' recall of the plant classification system.

Key Ideas

Encoding: Getting Information into Memory

◆ The multifaceted process of memory begins with encoding. Attention, which facilitates encoding, is inherently selective and has been compared to a filter. There is evidence of both early and late selection of input.

◆ According to levels-of-processing theory, the kinds of memory codes people create depend on which aspects of a stimulus are emphasized; deeper processing results in better recall of information. Structural, phonemic, and semantic encoding represent progressively deeper and more effective levels of processing.

◆ Elaboration enriches encoding by linking a stimulus to other information. Visual imagery may work in much the same way, creating two memory codes rather than just one. Encoding that emphasizes personal self-reference may be especially useful in facilitating retention.

Storage: Maintaining Information in Memory

◆ The sensory memory store preserves information in its original form, sometimes for only a fraction of a second. Short-term memory has a limited capacity (capable of holding about seven chunks of information) and can maintain unrehearsed information for up to about 20 seconds. Short-term memory is working memory, and it appears to involve more than a simple rehearsal loop.

◆ Long-term memory is an unlimited capacity store that may hold information indefinitely. Several lines of evidence suggest that LTM storage may be permanent, but the evidence is not convincing. Information is transferred from STM to LTM primarily through rehearsal.

◆ Information in LTM can be organized in simple clusters, conceptual hierarchies, or semantic networks, which consist of concepts joined together by pathways. A schema is an organized cluster of knowledge about a particular object or sequence of events. A particular kind of schema, called a script, specifies what people know about common activities.

Retrieval: Getting Information out of Memory

◆ Reinstating the context of an event can facilitate recall. This factor may account for cases in which hypnosis appears to aid recall. Mood congruence effects are a more reliable phenomenon than mood-dependent memory.

◆ Memories are not exact replicas of past experiences. Memory is partially reconstructive. Research on the misinformation effect shows that information learned after an event can alter one's memory of it. Source-monitoring errors appear to be common and may explain why people sometimes "recall" something that was only suggested to them or something they only imagined.

Forgetting: When Memory Lapses

◆ Ebbinghaus's early studies of nonsense syllables suggested that people forget very rapidly. Subsequent research showed that Ebbinghaus's forgetting curve was exceptionally steep. Forgetting can be measured by asking people to recall, recognize, or relearn information.

◆ Some forgetting, including pseudo-forgetting, is due to ineffective encoding of information. Decay theory proposes that forgetting occurs spontaneously with the passage of time. It has proven difficult to show that decay occurs in long-term memory. Interference theory proposes that people forget information because of competition from other material.

◆ Repression involves the motivated forgetting of painful or unpleasant memories. Recent years have seen a surge of reports of repressed memories of sexual abuse in childhood. The authenticity of these repressed memories is the subject of controversy because empirical studies have demonstrated that it is not all that difficult to create false memories.

In Search of the Memory Trace: The Physiology of Memory

◆ Memory traces may reflect alterations in neurotransmitter release at specific locations. Hormones, norepinephrine, acetylcholine, and protein synthesis may be involved in the biochemical coding of memory. Memory traces may also consist of localized neural circuits that undergo long-term potentiation. Research on amnesia has implicated the hippocampus and amygdala as brain structures involved in the consolidation of memories.

Are There Multiple Memory Systems?

◆ Differences between implicit and explicit memory suggest that people may have several separate memory systems. Declarative memory is memory for facts, while procedural memory is memory for actions and skills. Declarative memory can be subdivided into episodic memory, for personal facts, and semantic memory, for general facts. Theorists have also distinguished between retrospective and prospective memory.

Putting It in Perspective

◆ Our discussion of attention and memory enhances people's understanding of why our experience of the world is highly subjective. Work in this area also shows that behavior is governed by multiple causes.

Application: Improving Everyday Memory

◆ Rehearsal, even when it involves overlearning, facilitates retention. Distributed practice tends to be more efficient than massed practice. It is wise to plan study sessions so as to minimize interference. Processing during rehearsal should be deep and appropriate for the method of testing.

◆ Meaningfulness can be enhanced through the use of verbal mnemonics such as acrostics, acronyms, and narrative methods. The link method, the method of loci, and the keyword method are mnemonic devices that depend on the value of visual imagery.

Key Terms

Anterograde amnesia
Attention
Chunk
Clustering
Conceptual hierarchy
Consolidation
Decay theory
Declarative memory system
Dual-coding theory
Elaboration
Encoding
Encoding specificity principle
Episodic memory system
Explicit memory
Flashbulb memories
Forgetting curve
Implicit memory
Interference theory
Keyword method
Levels-of-processing theory
Link method
Long-term memory (LTM)
Long-term potentiation (LTP)
Method of loci
Mnemonic devices
Mood-congruence effect
Mood-dependent memory
Nondeclarative memory system
Nonsense syllables
Overlearning
Primacy effect
Proactive interference
Procedural memory system
Prospective memory
Reality monitoring
Recall
Recency effect
Recognition
Rehearsal
Relearning
Repression
Retention
Retrieval
Retroactive interference
Retrograde amnesia
Retrospective memory
Schema
Script
Self-referent encoding
Semantic memory system
Semantic network
Sensory memory
Serial-position effect
Short-term memory (STM)
Source monitoring
Source-monitoring error
State-dependent memory
Storage
Tip-of-the-tongue phenomenon
Transfer-appropriate processing

Key People

Richard Atkinson and Richard Shiffrin
Gordon Bower
Fergus Craik and Robert Lockhart
Hermann Ebbinghaus
Marcia Johnson
Elizabeth Loftus
George Miller
Brenda Milner
Endel Tulving

Practice Test

1. Getting information into memory is called _____; getting information out of memory is called _____.
   A. storage; retrieval
   B. encoding; storage
   C. encoding; retrieval
   D. storage; encoding

2. The word *big* is flashed on a screen. A mental picture of the word *big* represents a _____ code; the definition "large in size" represents a _____ code; "sounds like pig" represents a _____ code.
   A. structural; phonemic; semantic
   B. phonemic; semantic; structural
   C. structural; semantic; phonemic
   D. phonemic; structural; semantic

3. The capacity of short-term memory is:
   A. about 50,000 words.
   B. unlimited.
   C. about 25 stimuli.
   D. about 7 "chunks" of information.

4. Which statement best represents current evidence on the durability of long-term storage?
   A. All forgetting involves breakdowns in retrieval.
   B. LTM is like a barrel of marbles in which none of the marbles ever leak out.
   C. There is no convincing evidence that all one's memories are stored away permanently.
   D. All long-term memories gradually decay at a constant rate.

5. Dorothy memorized her shopping list. When she got to the store, however, she found she had forgotten many of the items from the middle of the list. This is an example of:
   A. inappropriate encoding.
   B. retrograde amnesia.
   C. proactive interference.
   D. the serial-position effect.

6. An organized cluster of knowledge about a particular object or sequence of events is called a:
   A. semantic network.
   B. conceptual hierarchy.
   C. schema.
   D. retrieval cue.

7. The tip-of-the-tongue phenomenon:
   A. is a temporary inability to remember something you know, accompanied by a feeling that it's just out of reach.
   B. is clearly due to a failure in retrieval.
   C. reflects a permanent loss of information from LTM.
   D. is both a and b.

8. Under which of the following conditions is an individual most likely to infer that a remembered event actually occurred?
   A. Memory lacks sensory details.
   B. Memory lacks contextual details.
   C. Memory is easily retrieved.
   D. Similar events occurred in a dream.

9. If decay theory is correct:
   A. information can never be permanently lost from long-term memory.
   B. forgetting is simply a case of retrieval failure.
   C. the principal cause of forgetting should be the passage of time.
   D. all of the above.

10. Implications from studies of hypnotic pseudomemory include all but which of the following?
    A. Women generally report more pseudomemories than men.
    B. It is not very difficult to implant false memories in some subjects.
    C. Rapport between hypnotist and subject generally leads to an increase in the occurrence of pseudomemories.
    D. Subjects who are highly susceptible to hypnosis are most likely to experience hypnotic pseudomemories.

11. Many amnesiacs demonstrate _____ memory, even though their _____ memory is extremely impaired.
    A. declarative; procedural
    B. conscious; unconscious
    C. implicit; explicit
    D. semantic; episodic

12. Your memory of how to brush your teeth is contained in your _____ memory.
    A. declarative
    B. procedural
    C. structural
    D. episodic

13. Your knowledge that birds fly, that the sun rises in the east, and that 2 + 2 = 4 is contained in your _____ memory.
    A. structural
    B. procedural
    C. implicit
    D. semantic

14. Overlearning:
    A. refers to continued rehearsal of material after the point of apparent mastery.
    B. promotes improved recall.
    C. should not be done, since it leads to increased interference.
    D. both a and b.

15. The method of loci involves:
    A. taking an imaginary walk along a familiar path where you have associated images of items you want to remember with certain locations.
    B. forming a mental image of items to be remembered in a way that links them together.
    C. creating a phrase in which the first letter of each word functions as a cue to help you recall more abstract words that begin with the same letter.
    D. creating a story that includes each of the words to be remembered in the appropriate order.

Answers

1	C Page 261	6	C Page 273	11	C Page 290		
2	C Pages 263–264	7	D Page 275	12	B Pages 290–291		
3	D Page 268	8	C Page 278	13	D Page 291		
4	C Pages 270–271	9	C Page 281	14	D Page 294		
5	D Pages 270–271	10	A Page 286	15	A Page 296		

8 LANGUAGE AND THOUGHT

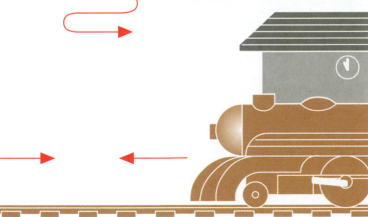

"Dr. Watson—Mr. Sherlock Holmes," said Stamford, introducing us.

"How are you?" he said, cordially, gripping my hand with a strength for which I should hardly have given him credit. "You have been in Afghanistan, I perceive."

"How on earth did you know that?" I asked, in astonishment. (From A Study in Scarlet *by Arthur Conan Doyle)*

If you've ever read any Sherlock Holmes stories, you know that the great detective continually astonished his stalwart companion, Dr. Watson, with his extraordinary deductions. Obviously, Holmes could not arrive at his conclusions without a chain of reasoning. Yet to him even an elaborate reasoning process was a simple, everyday act. Consider his feat of knowing at once, upon first meeting Watson, that the doctor had been in Afghanistan. When asked, Holmes explained his reasoning as follows:

"I knew you came from Afghanistan. From long habit the train of thought ran so swiftly through my mind that I arrived at the conclusion without being conscious of the intermediate steps. There were such steps, however. The train of reasoning ran: "Here is a gentleman of a medical type, but with the air of a military man. Clearly an army doctor, then. He has just come from the tropics, for his face is dark, and that is not the natural tint of his skin, for his wrists are fair. He has undergone hardship and sickness, as his haggard face says clearly. His left arm

has been injured. He holds it in a stiff and unnatural manner. Where in the tropics could an English army doctor have seen much hardship and got his arm wounded? Clearly in Afghanistan.' The whole train of thought did not occupy a second."

Admittedly, Sherlock Holmes's deductive feats are fictional. But even to read about them appreciatively—let alone imagine them, as Sir Arthur Conan Doyle did—is a remarkably complex mental act. Our everyday thought processes seem ordinary to us only because we take them for granted, just as Holmes saw nothing extraordinary in what to him was a simple deduction.

In reality, everyone is a Sherlock Holmes, continually performing magical feats of thought. Even elementary perception—for instance, watching a football game or a ballet—involves elaborate cognitive processes. People must sort through distorted, constantly shifting perceptual inputs and deduce what they see out there in the real world. Imagine, then, the complexity of thought required to read a book, fix an automobile, or balance a checkbook.

Of course, all this is not to say that human thought processes are flawless or unequaled. You probably own a $10 calculator that can run circles around you when it comes to computing square roots. As we'll see, some of the most interesting research in this chapter focuses on ways in which people's thinking can be limited, simplistic, or outright illogical.

THE COGNITIVE REVOLUTION IN PSYCHOLOGY

As we have noted before, *cognition* **refers to the mental processes involved in acquiring knowledge.** In other words, cognition involves thinking. When psychology first emerged as an independent science in the 19th century, it focused on the mind. Mental processes were explored through *introspection*—analysis of one's own conscious experience (see Chapter 1). Unfortunately, early psychologists' study of mental processes ran aground, as the method of introspection yielded unreliable results. Psychology's empirical approach depends on observation, and private mental events proved difficult to observe. Further-

more, during the first half of the 20th century, the study of cognition was actively discouraged by the theoretical dominance of behaviorism. Herbert Simon, a pioneer of cognitive psychology, recalls that "you couldn't use a word like *mind* in a psychology journal—you'd get your mouth washed out with soap" (Holden, 1986, p. 55).

Although it wasn't fully recognized until a decade later, the 1950s brought a "cognitive revolution" in psychology (Baars, 1986). Renegade theorists, such as Herbert Simon, began to argue that behaviorists' exclusive focus on overt responses was doomed to yield an incomplete understand-

"You couldn't use a word like mind *in a psychology journal—you'd get your mouth washed out with soap."*

HERBERT SIMON

ing of human functioning. More important, creative new research led to exciting progress in the study of cognitive processes. For example, Gardner (1985) notes that three major advances were reported at a watershed 1956 conference—in just one day! First, Herbert Simon and Allen Newell described the first computer program to successfully simulate human problem solving. Second, Noam Chomsky outlined a new model that changed the way psychologists studied language. Third, George Miller delivered the legendary paper that we discussed in Chapter 7, arguing that the capacity of short-term memory is seven (plus or minus two) items. Since then, cognitive science has grown into a robust, interdisciplinary enterprise (H. Simon, 1992).

Why did the 1950s bring great progress in the empirical study of cognition, when earlier efforts had largely failed? Because modern researchers replaced the highly subjective method of introspection with more objective methods (Bower & Clapper, 1989). For example, modern psycholo-gists manipulate aspects of cognitive tasks and then make observations of the subjects' reaction time, accuracy, and errors—variables that can be measured objectively. Or they ask subjects to think out loud during problem solving while researchers record the subjects' thoughts. Or they monitor physiological indicators of mental processes, such as electrical recordings of evoked potentials in brain cells. Since the 1950s, psychologists have also used computers to simulate human information processing.

You saw some of these research methods in the previous chapter, where we discussed the topic that cognitive psychologists have studied the most—memory. You'll see more of them in this chapter, as we examine language use and development, problem solving, and decision making. We'll begin with an exploration of language. If you were to ask people, "What characteristic most distinguishes humans from other living creatures?" a great many would reply, "Language." Would they be right? Let's find out.

LANGUAGE: TURNING THOUGHTS INTO WORDS

Consider the following conversation:

> TEACHER: *What want you?*
> STUDENT: *Eat more apple.*
> TEACHER: *Who want eat more apple?*
> STUDENT: *Me Nim eat more apple.*
> TEACHER: *What color apple?*
> STUDENT: *Apple red.*
> TEACHER: *Want you more eat?*
> STUDENT: *Banana, raisin.*

The sophistication of this exchange might not impress you—until you learn that the "student" is a 2½-year-old chimpanzee named Nim Chimpsky. (Yes, the chimp was named after Noam Chomsky, the prominent linguist who has argued that language is unique to humans.) The conversation sounds odd in part because it was conducted in sign language. Herbert Terrace (1986) taught Nim to use sign language while raising the chimp like a human child in a human family.

If you look again at the conversation, you can see that Nim's responses are appropriate and apparently intelligent. Does this mean that language is not uniquely human? This question provides the point of departure for our discussion of *psycholinguistics*—**the study of the psychological mechanisms underlying the use of language.**

Communicating with Chimpanzees

Suppose you wanted to discover whether you could teach language to an animal. It's a good bet you'd pick an animal like the chimpanzee, an intelligent primate widely regarded as humans' closest cousin. But how would you go about teaching language to a chimp?

In early studies, researchers tried to teach chimps to *speak*. These efforts were not very fruitful. For instance, after six years of patient hard work, Hayes and Hayes (1951) managed to train a chimp named Viki to say a grand total of three words ("mama," "papa," and "cup"). Investigators concluded that chimps simply didn't have the appropriate vocal apparatus to acquire human speech.

But is speech the only way to use language? Of course not. At this moment you're reading a written expression of language. Like speech, writing may not be a realistic form of communication for chimps, but what about other nonoral expressions of language? Once researchers working with apes shifted away from using speech as the vehicle for teaching language, some interesting things began to happen. David Premack (1971), for example, used small plastic symbols of various colors and shapes as substitutes for written words. He taught a chimp named Sarah to arrange these arbitrary symbols on a magnetic board to communicate simple messages (see Figure 8.1).

Other researchers tried training chimps to use a nonoral human language: American Sign Language (ASL). ASL is a complex language of hand gestures and facial expressions used by thousands of deaf people in the United States. The first effort of this sort was begun by Allen and Beatrice Gardner (1969), who worked with a chimp named Washoe. The Gardners approached the task as if Washoe were a deaf child. They signed to her regularly, rewarded her imitations, and taught her complex signs by physically moving her hands through the required motions. In four years, Washoe acquired a sign vocabulary of roughly 160 words! She learned to combine these words into simple sentences, such as "Washoe sorry," "Gimme flower," and "More fruit." The Gardners concluded that Washoe's language development was roughly equivalent to that of a 3-year-old human.

Although psychologists can communicate with chimpanzees through sign language, there are doubts as to whether the chimps are genuinely acquiring language. For example, Herbert Terrace (1986) initially believed that his research showed that Nim could create sentences. However, he began to reconsider after carefully examining videotapes of Nim's "conversations." Nim's constructions were far less original than those of a young child. More critically, the chimp showed little progress toward mastering the *rules* of language. Many of Nim's constructions simply repeated the

Figure 8.1
Four symbols used in the Premack (1971) study. Because animals lack the vocal apparatus needed to produce human speech, psychologists have tried a number of devices to give animals the means of producing or manipulating words. After experimenting with a joystick like that used in computer games, Premack settled on distinctive plastic shapes as Sarah's word equivalents.

constructions made by caretakers. Terrace concluded that Nim's sentences were the products of imitation and operant conditioning, rather than spontaneous generations based on the rules of language.

After watching films of the Gardners' training efforts, he drew the same conclusion about Washoe. Terrace believes that Washoe, Nim, and other chimps have simply learned to make certain responses to earn reinforcement, much as pigeons can learn to peck a disk for a food reward. Nonetheless, Terrace has argued that research on communicating with chimps should continue in order to determine how much progress apes can make. The Featured Study for this chapter describes how Sue Savage-Rumbaugh and her colleagues trained a bright young chimp to communicate at a more advanced level than other chimpanzees that have been studied.

Can Chimps Learn Language?   Featured Study

The purpose of this study was to provide a developmental account of how a chimpanzee acquired the ability to communicate with his caretakers by touching geometric symbols on a keyboard. Each symbol represents a word. This "language" is called *Yerkish,* in honor of Robert Yerkes, an eminent psychologist who conducted pioneering research on animal behavior during the first half of this century. The chimp, named Kanzi, was born at the Yerkes Primate Research Center in Atlanta and remained with his mother until he was 2½ years old.

Kanzi's mother was trained to communicate with her caretakers by using the keyboard. Kanzi was permitted to attend his mother's training sessions, in which she showed moderate progress, but his interest in the keyboard was sporadic. Following separation from his mother, Kanzi's attitude toward the key-

board showed an unexpected change. He appeared to search for specific symbols, and his behavior suggested that he had learned that particular symbols referred to particular items. In a relatively short time, Kanzi's progress in communicating through Yerkish far outstripped his mother's accomplishments. This report summarizes Kanzi's language development from 2½ to 4 years of age.

Method
Subject. The subject was a male pygmy chimpanzee. The *Pan paniscus* species has not been studied much for its ability to acquire language, although evidence suggests that pygmy chimpanzees may be more intelligent than other apes.
Procedure. Researchers kept a complete record of all of Kanzi's "utterances" over a 17-month period begin-

Investigators: Sue Savage-Rumbaugh, Kelly McDonald, Rose A. Sevcik, William D. Hopkins, and Elizabeth Rupert (Yerkes Regional Primate Research Center, Emory University and the Language Research Center, Georgia State University)

Source: Spontaneous symbol acquisition and communication use by pygmy chimpanzees (*Pan paniscus*). *Journal of Experimental Psychology: General*, 1986, *115*, 211–235.

Kanzi, a pygmy chimpanzee, learned to communicate with his caretakers via computer-controlled symbol boards. He acquired this skill by watching his mother and caretakers using the boards—an example of observational learning. (Top) Kanzi uses his computer-monitored keyboard with Sue Savage-Rumbaugh. (Bottom) Kanzi selects a symbol from his computer-monitored keyboard.

ning when he was $2\frac{1}{2}$ years old. The symbols were automatically recorded by a computer-monitored keyboard when the chimp was indoors. When outdoors, Kanzi pointed to the symbols on a thin "pointing board" (see the photos above). These utterances were recorded by hand and entered into the computer later. During all daily activities with Kanzi (playing, eating, resting, traveling in the woods, and so forth), the caretakers used the graphic symbols to communicate with each other and with Kanzi.

Results

Kanzi made rapid progress in his ability to communicate with symbols. At the end of the 17-month study, he had acquired 50 words and had used them in 800 different combinations. The symbols primarily described foods, actions (such as chase,

groom, grab), and locations (trailer, treehouse, refrigerator). Kanzi's ability to combine symbols occurred very early, although he did not use this skill often. A large portion of Kanzi's symbol combinations were spontaneous. That is, they were not elicited by Kanzi's teachers. In contrast to Nim, whose constructions almost always involved Nim's receiving something, Kanzi produced constructions in which he was either the actor or the recipient of an action. To do this, Kanzi had to use word order to distinguish between statements such as "Person chase Kanzi" and "Kanzi chase Person."

Discussion

This study provides stronger support than previous research for the hypothesis that chimps may be able to follow rules of language in generating spontaneous sentences. To specify whether he wanted to chase or be chased, Kanzi had to differentiate between symbol combinations in a way that seems to involve the use of grammatical rules. The study also describes the first instance in which a chimp used symbols without specific training. Kanzi first acquired the use of symbols through observing his mother's responses at the keyboard.

Comment

Kanzi's accomplishments are impressive. Nonetheless, theorists still wonder whether chimps such as Kanzi are really using symbols in the same way that humans use words. In essence, the critics chorus, "But is it really language?" To shed more light on this controversy, let's examine the properties and structure of language. Then we'll reconsider this intriguing question.

What Is Language?

A *language* consists of symbols that convey meaning, plus rules for combining those symbols, that can be used to generate an infinite variety of messages. Language systems include a number of critical properties (Ratner & Gleason, 1993).

First, language is *symbolic*. People use spoken sounds and written words to represent objects, actions, events, and ideas. The word *lamp*, for instance, refers to a class of objects that have certain properties. The symbolic nature of language greatly expands what people can communicate about. Symbols allow one to refer to objects that may be in another place and to events that happened at another time (for example, a lamp broken at work yesterday). Language symbols are flexible in that a variety of somewhat different objects may be called by the same name (consider the diversity of lamps, for example).

Second, language is *semantic,* or meaningful. The symbols used in a language are arbitrary in that no built-in relationship exists between the look or sound of words and the objects they stand for. Take, for instance, the writing object that you may have in your hand right now. It's represented by the word *pen* in English, *stylo* in French, and *pluma* in Spanish. Although these words are arbitrary (others could have been chosen), they have *shared meanings* for people who speak English, French, and Spanish.

Third, language is *generative*. A limited number of symbols can be combined in an infinite variety of ways to *generate* an endless array of novel messages. Everyone has some "stock sayings," but every day you create sentences that you have never spoken before. You also comprehend many sentences that you have never encountered before (like this one).

Fourth, language is *structured*. Although people can generate an infinite variety of sentences, these sentences must be structured in a limited number of ways. There are rules that govern the arrangement of words into phrases and sentences. Some arrangements are acceptable and some are not. For example, you might say, "The swimmer jumped into the pool," but you would never recombine the same words to say, "Pool the into the jumped swimmer." The structure of language allows people to be inventive with words and still understand each other. Let's take a closer look at the structural properties of language.

The Structure of Language

Human languages have a hierarchical structure (Ratner & Gleason, 1993). As Figure 8.2 on page 306 shows, basic sounds are combined into units with meaning, which are combined into words. Words are combined into phrases, which are combined into sentences.

Phonemes

At the base of the language hierarchy are *phonemes, the basic units of sound in a spoken language.* Considering that an unabridged English dictionary contains more than 450,000 words, you might imagine that there must be a huge number of phonemes. In fact, linguists estimate that humans are capable of producing only about 100 such basic sounds. Moreover, no one language uses all of these phonemes. Different languages use different groups of about 20 to 80 phonemes.

For all its rich vocabulary, the English language is composed of about 40 to 45 phonemes, corresponding roughly to the 26 letters of the alphabet plus several variations. Some representative English phonemes are listed in Table 8.1 on page 306. A letter in the alphabet is represented by more than one phoneme if it has more than one pronunciation. For example, the letter *a* is pronounced differently in the words *father, had, call,* and *take.* Each of these pronunciations is represented by a

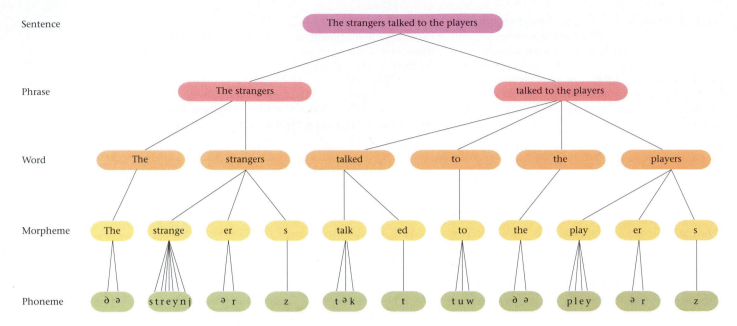

Sentence	The strangers talked to the players
Phrase	The strangers	talked to the players
Word	The	strangers	talked	to	the	players
Morpheme	The	strange	er	s	talk	ed	to	the	play	er	s
Phoneme	ð ə	s t r e y n j	ə r	z	t ə k	t	t u w	ð ə	p l e y	ə r	z

Figure 8.2
An analysis of a simple English sentence. As this example shows, verbal language has a hierarchical structure. At the base of the hierarchy are the *phonemes,* which are units of vocal sound that do not, in themselves, have meaning. The smallest units of meaning in a language are *morphemes,* which include not only root words but such meaning-carrying units as the past tense suffix *ed* and the plural *s.* Complex rules of syntax govern how the words constructed from morphemes may be combined into phrases, and phrases into meaningful statements, or sentences.

different phoneme. In addition, some phonemes are represented by combinations of letters, such as *ch* and *th.* From this handful of basic sounds, speakers can generate all the words in the English language—and invent new ones besides.

Morphemes
***Morphemes* are the smallest units of meaning in a language.** There are approximately 50,000 English morphemes, which include root words as

TABLE 8.1 EXAMPLES OF SOME ENGLISH LANGUAGE PHONEMES

Symbol	Examples
p	**p**at, a**pp**le
b	**b**at, am**b**le
d	**d**ip, love**d**
g	**g**uard, o**g**re
f	**f**at, **ph**ilosophy
s	**s**ap, pa**ss**, pea**c**e
z	**z**ip, pad**s**, **x**ylophone
y	**y**ou, ba**y**, f**eu**d
w	**w**itch, q**u**een
l	**l**eaf, pa**l**ace
ē	b**ee**t, b**ea**t, bel**ie**ve
e	**a**te, b**ai**t, **ei**ght
i	b**i**t, **i**njury
u	b**oo**t, tw**o**, thr**ough**
U	p**u**t, f**oo**t, c**ou**ld
oy	b**oy**, d**oi**ly
ay	b**i**te, s**igh**t, **i**sland
š	**sh**oe, mu**sh**, deduc**ti**on

Source: Adapted from Moates and Schumacher (1980)

well as prefixes and suffixes. Many words, such as *fire, guard,* and *friend,* consist of a single morpheme. Many others represent combinations of morphemes. For example, the word *unfriendly* consists of three morphemes: the root word *friend,* the prefix *un,* and the suffix *ly.* Each of the morphemes contributes to the meaning of the entire word. The suffix changes the noun *friend* into the adjective *friendly,* and the prefix produces an adjective (*unfriendly*) with the opposite meaning.

Syntax
Of course, most utterances consist of more than a single word. As we've already noted, people don't combine words randomly. ***Syntax* is a system of rules that specify how words can be arranged into phrases and sentences.** A simple rule of syntax is that declarative sentences (sentences that make a statement) must have both a *subject* (what the speaker is talking about) and a *predicate* (a statement about the subject). Thus, "The sound of cars is annoying" is a sentence. However, "The sound of cars" is not a sentence, because it lacks a predicate.

Rules of syntax underlie all language use, even though you may not be aware of them. Thus, although they may not be able to verbalize the rule, virtually all English speakers know that an *article* (such as *the*) comes before the word it modifies. For example, you would never say *swimmer the* instead of *the swimmer.* How people learn the complicated rules of syntax is one of the major puzzles investigated by psycholinguists.

Having reviewed the properties and structure of language, what can we conclude about the ape language controversy? Have chimpanzees such as Sarah, Washoe, Nim, and Kanzi genuinely begun to acquire language? Let's take another look.

Another Look at the Ape Language Controversy

We noted that language is characterized by four key properties: it's symbolic, semantic, generative, and structured. The communication abilities of the trained chimps clearly meet the first two criteria. Chimps have learned to use symbols to convey meaningful messages. Evidence regarding the third criterion has been ambiguous. Chimps have generated many new combinations of symbols, but doubts have been raised about the spontaneity and originality of their language constructions. Until recently, evidence regarding the fourth criterion has been negative. There was little reason to believe that chimps followed rules of syntax to create structured arrangements of words. Researchers who called the chimps' word combinations "sentences" were using the concept very loosely.

Thus, the findings of Sue Savage-Rumbaugh and her colleagues in our Featured Study may be a dramatic breakthrough. Kanzi's word combinations appear to be more spontaneous and novel than those used by other chimps. His apparent mastery of rules of syntax is an unprecedented accomplishment. Moreover, in subsequent work since the 1986 study, Kanzi's younger sister, Mulika, who was born when he was 3, has duplicated many of his accomplishments, and Kanzi has continued to make progress. He has spontaneously acquired some understanding of spoken English, invented his own rules of grammar, and learned to respond to increasingly complex commands (Greenfield & Savage-Rumbaugh, 1991; Savage-Rumbaugh et al., 1992). One can argue that Kanzi's symbolic communication includes all the basic properties of a rudimentary language.

Although more research is needed, it seems that language may not be unique to humans. In fact, recent studies have reported some success in language training with other nonhuman species besides apes. For example, researchers have taught language-like communication to dolphins (Herman, Morrel-Samuels, & Pack, 1990), sea lions (Schusterman & Gisiner, 1988), and an African gray parrot (Pepperberg, 1990).

Language in Evolutionary Context

Even if language is not unique to humans, they do appear to be exceptionally well suited for learning language. There's little comparison between hu-

All parrots are known for their ability to mimic human speech. This African gray parrot named Alex, however, is special in that he seems to know what words actually mean. Here he is getting ready to answer the question, "What is red and triangular?"

man linguistic abilities and those of apes or other animals. As remarkable as the language studies with apes are, they should make us marvel even more at the fluency, flexibility, and complexity of human language. A normal human toddler quickly surpasses even the most successfully trained chimps. In mastering language, children outstrip chimps the way jet airplanes outrace horse-drawn buggies.

Why are humans so well-suited for learning language? Steven Pinker (1994) argues that humans' special talent for language is a species-specific trait that is the product of natural selection. According to Pinker, language is a valuable means of communication that has enormous adaptive value. As Pinker and Bloom (1992) point out, "There is an obvious advantage in being able to acquire information about the world secondhand . . . one can avoid having to duplicate the possibly time-consuming and dangerous trial-and-error process that won that knowledge" (p. 460). It does not take much imagination to envision how more effective communication among our ancient ancestors could have aided hunting, gathering, fighting, mating, and the avoidance of poisons, predators, and other dangers.

Although the adaptive value of language seems obvious, some scholars take issue with the assertion that human language is the product of evolution. For example, David Premack (1985) has expressed skepticism that small differences in language skill would influence reproductive fitness in primitive societies where all one had to communicate about was the location of the closest mastadon herd. In an effort to refute this argument, Pinker and Bloom (1992) point out that very small adaptive disparities are sufficient to fuel evolutionary change. For example, they cite an estimate that a 1% difference in mortality rates among overlapping Neanderthal and human populations could have led to the extinction of Neanderthals in just 30 generations. They also note that a trait variation that produces on average just 1% more offspring than its alternative genetic expression would increase in prevalence from 0.1% to 99.9% of the population in 4000 generations. Four thousand generations may seem like an eternity, but in the context of evolution, it is a modest amount of time.

Whether or not evolution gets credit, language in humans develops remarkably rapidly. By the time most children enter school, they already have a vocabulary of thousands of words. How does this remarkable development of language happen? What stages do children go through in progressing from babbling to sophisticated speech? The next section takes up these questions.

Milestones in Language Development

Learning to use language requires learning a number of skills that become important at different points in a child's development (Siegler, 1986). We'll examine this developmental sequence by looking first at how children learn to pronounce words, then at their use of single words, and finally at their ability to combine words to form sentences (see Table 8.2).

Moving Toward Producing Words

Three-month-old infants display a surprising language-related talent: They can distinguish phonemes from all the world's languages, including phonemes that they do not hear in their environment. In contrast, adults cannot readily discriminate phonemes that are not used in their native language. Actually, neither can 1-year-old children, as this curious ability gradually disappears between 4 months and 12 months of age (Werker & Desjardins, 1995). The exact mechanisms responsible for this transition are not understood, but it is clear that long before infants utter their first words, they are making remarkable progess in learning the sound structure of their native language.

During the first 6 months of life, a baby's vocalizations are dominated by crying, cooing, and laughter, which have limited value as a means of communication. Soon, infants are *babbling*, producing a wide variety of sounds that correspond to phonemes and, eventually, many consonant-vowel combinations. Babbling becomes more complex and increasingly resembles the language spoken by parents and others in the child's environment (Boysson-Bardies & Vihman, 1991). These trends probably reflect ongoing neural development and the maturation of the infant's vocal apparatus (Sachs, 1985), as well as exposure to parents' and others' use of language. Babbling lasts until around 18 months, continuing even after children utter their first words.

At around 10 to 13 months of age, most children begin to utter sounds that correspond to words. Most infants' first words are similar in phonetic form and meaning—even in different languages (Gleason & Ratner, 1993). The initial words resemble the syllables that infants most often babble spontaneously and typically refer to people

TABLE 8.2 OVERVIEW OF TYPICAL LANGUAGE DEVELOPMENT

Age	General Characteristics
Months	
1–5	*Reflexive communication:* Vocalizes randomly, coos, laughs, cries, engages in vocal play, discriminates language from nonlanguage sounds
6–18	*Babbling:* Verbalizes in response to speech of others; responses increasingly approximate human speech patterns
10–13	*First words:* Uses words typically to refer to objects
12–18	*One-word sentence stage:* Vocabulary grows slowly; uses nouns primarily; overextensions begin
18–24	*Vocabulary spurt:* Fast-mapping facilitates rapid acquisition of new words
Years	
2	*Two-word sentence stage:* Uses telegraphic speech; uses more pronouns and verbs
2.5	*Three-word sentence stage:* Modifies speech to take listener into account; overregularizations begin
3	Uses complete simple active sentence structure; uses sentences to tell stories that are understood by others; uses plurals
3.5	*Expanded grammatical forms:* Expresses concepts with words; uses four-word sentences
4	Uses imaginary speech; uses five-word sentences
5	*Well-developed and complex syntax:* Uses more complex syntax. Uses more complex forms to tell stories
6	Displays metalinguistic awareness

Note: Children often show individual differences in the exact ages at which they display the various developmental achievements outlined here.

and things in the child's environment. For example, words such as *dada, mama,* and *papa* are names for parents in many languages because they consist of sounds that are easy to produce.

Using Words

After children utter their first words, their vocabulary grows slowly for the next few months (Barrett, 1989). Toddlers typically can say between 3 and 50 words by 18 months. However, their *receptive vocabulary* is larger than their *productive vocabulary*. That is, they can comprehend more words spoken by others than they can actually produce to express themselves (Pease & Gleason, 1985). Thus, toddlers can *understand* 50 words months before they can *say* 50 words. Toddlers' early words tend to refer most often to *objects* and secondarily to familiar *actions* (Gentner, 1982; Nelson, Hampson, & Shaw, 1993).

Youngsters' vocabularies soon begin to grow at a dizzying pace, as a *vocabulary spurt* often begins at around 18 months (Goldfield & Reznick, 1990; see Figure 8.3). By the age of 6, the average child has a vocabulary of approximately 10,000 words, which builds to an astonishing 40,000 words by age 10 (Anglin, 1993). In building these impressive vocabularies, some 2-year-olds learn as many as 20 new words every week. *Fast mapping* appears to be the key to this rapid growth of vocabulary (Dollaghan, 1985; Taylor & Gelman, 1989). **Fast mapping is the process by which children map a word onto an underlying concept after only one exposure to the word.** Thus, children often add words like *ball, dog,* and *cookie* to their vocabularies after their first encounter with objects that illustrate these concepts.

Of course, these efforts to learn new words are not flawless. Toddlers often make errors, such as overextensions (G. Miller, 1991). **An *overextension* occurs when a child incorrectly uses a word to describe a wider set of objects or actions than it is meant to.** For example, a child might use the word *ball* for anything round—oranges, apples, even the moon. Overextensions are far from random and typically make sense given children's limited vocabularies. They usually appear in children's speech between ages 1 and 2½. Specific overextensions typically last up to several months (Clark, 1983). These mistakes show that toddlers are actively trying to learn the rules of language—albeit with mixed success. Overextensions sometimes lead parents and others to provide corrective information, so overextensions may help children learn new words and concepts.

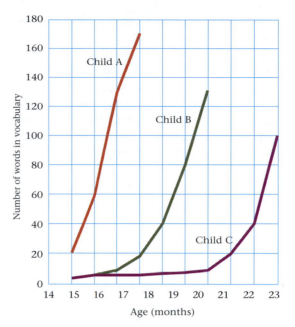

Figure 8.3
The vocabulary spurt.
Children typically acquire their first ten words very slowly, but they soon go through a vocabulary spurt—a period during which they rapidly acquire many new words. The vocabulary spurt usually begins at around 18 months, but children vary, as these graphs of three toddlers' vocabulary growth show. (Adapted from Goldfield & Reznick, 1990)

While toddlers increase their ability to communicate as they learn new words, they remain unable to express themselves in sentences. They appear to compensate for this limitation by using a single word to represent the meaning of several words. **Holophrases are single-word utterances that appear to function like sentences.** Some theorists doubt the idea that these one-word utterances represent primitive sentences (Dore, 1985). However, children do appear to be intentionally selective in choosing words that convey their needs (Barrett, 1982). For example, a child who wants a banana will say *banana* rather than *want* because *banana* is the more informative term. After all, there are many things a child could want, but relatively few reasons why a child would be interested in a banana.

Combining Words

Children typically begin to combine words into sentences between 18 and 24 months of age. Early sentences in English are characterized as "telegraphic" because they resemble telegrams (Reich, 1986). **Telegraphic speech consists mainly of content words; articles, prepositions, and other less critical words are omitted.** Thus, a child might say, "Give doll"

Although researchers have made some remarkable advances in teaching apes language, the language development of a typical human toddler quickly surpasses that of even the most successfully trained chimps.

rather than "Please give me the doll." Although not unique to the English language, telegraphic speech is not cross-culturally universal, as once thought (de Villiers & de Villiers, 1992).

Researchers sometimes track language development by keeping tabs on subjects' *mean length of utterance (MLU)—the average length of young-sters' spoken statements (measured in morphemes)*. After children begin to combine words, their vocal expressions gradually become longer, as Figure 8.4 shows (Riley, 1987).

By the end of their third year, most children can express complex ideas such as plurals or the past tense. However, their efforts to learn language continue to generate revealing mistakes. *Over-regularization occurs when grammatical rules are incorrectly generalized to irregular cases where they do not apply*. For example, children will say things like, "The girl goed home" or "I hitted the ball." Cross-cultural research suggests that these overregularizations occur in many languages (Slobin, 1985). Most theorists believe that overregularizations demonstrate that children are working actively to master the *rules* of language (Marcus, 1996). Children don't learn the fine points of grammar and usage in a single leap but gradually acquire them in small steps.

Refining Language Skills

Youngsters make their largest strides in language development in their first four to five years. However, they continue to refine their language skills during their school-age years. They generate longer and more complicated sentences as they receive formal training in written language. Overregular-

izations decline as they are taught subtle exceptions to grammatical rules.

As their language skills develop, school-age children begin to appreciate ambiguities in language. They can, for instance, recognize two possible meanings in sentences such as "Visiting relatives can be bothersome." This interest in ambiguities indicates that they're developing *metalinguistic awareness—the ability to reflect on the use of language*. As metalinguistic awareness grows, children begin to "play" with language, coming up with puns and jokes. They begin to make more frequent and sophisticated use of metaphors, such as "We were packed in the room like sardines" (Gentner, 1988). They also learn to recognize the hidden meanings often found in everyday discourse (Capelli, Nakagawa, & Madden, 1990). For example, a grouchy 8-year-old may appreciate an older sister's real meaning when she sarcastically remarks, "My, aren't *we* in a good mood today."

In the final analysis, what's most striking about children's language development is how swiftly it occurs. Bright college students receiving systematic training often struggle to learn a foreign language, yet even toddlers with below-average intelligence acquire a decent mastery of their native tongue in a mere 30 months or so with little formal instruction. How do they do it? Theorists have proposed several explanations of language acquisition. We examine these theories next.

Theories of Language Acquisition

Since the 1950s, there has been a great debate about the key processes involved in language acquisition. As with arguments in other areas of psychology that we have seen previously, this one centers on the *nature versus nurture* issue. The debate was stimulated by the influential behaviorist B. F. Skinner (1957), who argued that environmental factors govern language development. His provocative analysis brought a rejoinder from Noam Chomsky (1959), who emphasized biological determinism. Let's examine their views and subsequent theories that stake out a middle ground.

Behaviorist Theories

The behaviorist approach to language was first outlined by Skinner in his book *Verbal Behavior* (1957). He argued that children learn language the same way they learn everything else: through imitation, reinforcement, and other established principles of conditioning. According to Skinner, vocalizations that are not reinforced gradually decline in frequency. The remaining vocalizations

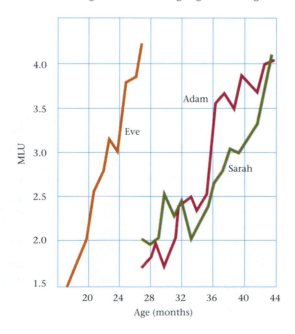

Figure 8.4
Age and mean length of utterance. These graphs depict the age-related increase in mean length of utterance (MLU) for three children studied by Brown (1973). As you can see, MLU increases rapidly among 2- and 3-year-old children.

are shaped with reinforcers until they are correct. Behaviorists assert that by controlling reinforcement, parents encourage their children to learn the correct meaning and pronunciation of words (Staats & Staats, 1963). For example, as children grow older, parents may insist on closer and closer approximations of the word *water* before supplying the requested drink.

Behavioral theorists also use the principles of imitation and reinforcement to explain how children learn syntax. According to the behaviorists' view, children learn how to construct sentences by imitating the sentences of adults and older children. If children's imitative statements are understood, parents are able to answer their questions or respond to their requests, thus reinforcing their verbal behavior. Learning theory asserts that parents shape children's syntax by translating understandable but ungrammatical statements into correct grammatical form.

Nativist Theories

Skinner's explanation of language acquisition soon inspired a critique and rival explanation from Noam Chomsky (1959, 1965). Chomsky pointed out that there are an infinite number of sentences in a language. It's therefore unreasonable to expect that children learn language by imitation. For example, in English, we add *ed* to the end of a verb to construct past tense. Children routinely overregularize this rule, producing incorrect verbs such as *goed, eated,* and *thinked*. Mistakes such as these are inconsistent with Skinner's emphasis on imitation, because most adult speakers don't use ungrammatical words like *goed*. Children can't imitate things they don't hear.

Critics have also challenged the behaviorist position that children learn to construct correct sentences through reinforcement. An influential study by Brown and Hanlon (1970) indicated that parents typically respond to meaning and factual accuracy in their youngsters' speech rather than to grammar. Thus, a mother curling her daughter's hair probably won't correct the ungrammatical statement "Her curl my hair," because it is factually accurate. In other words, parents may not engage in much of the language shaping that is critical to the behavioral explanation of language development (Maratsos, 1983; Pinker, 1990).

An alternative theory favored by Chomsky and others is that humans have an inborn or "native" propensity to develop language (Chomsky, 1975, 1986; Crain, 1991; McNeill, 1970). In this sense, *native* is a variation on the word nature as it's used

in the nature versus nurture debate. *Nativist theory* proposes that humans are equipped with a **language acquisition device (LAD)—an innate mechanism or process that facilitates the learning of language.** According to this view, humans learn language for the same reason that birds learn to fly—because they're biologically equipped for it. The exact nature of the LAD has not been spelled out in nativist theories. It presumably consists of brain structures and neural wiring that leave humans well prepared to discriminate among phonemes, to fast-map morphemes, to acquire rules of syntax, and so on.

Why does Chomsky believe that children have an innate capacity for learning language? One reason is that nearly all children seem to acquire language quickly and effortlessly. How could they develop so complex a skill in such a short time unless they have a built-in capacity for it? Another reason is that language development tends to unfold at roughly the same pace for most children, even though children obviously vary in intellectual capacity and are reared in diverse home environments. This finding suggests that language development is determined by biological maturation more than personal experience. The nativists also cite evidence that the early course of language development appears to be pretty similar across quite a variety of cultures (Slobin, 1985, 1992). They interpret this to mean that children all over the world are guided by the same innate capabilities.

According to Chomsky, children learn *the rules of language,* not specific verbal responses, as Skinner had proposed. For instance, Chomsky has studied how the acquisition of *transformational rules*

"Even at low levels of intelligence, at pathological levels, we find a command of language that is totally unattainable by an ape."

NOAM CHOMSKY

contributes to the mastery of syntax. These rules allow people to translate back and forth between the *deep* and *surface* structure of sentences (see Figure 8.5). **The *deep structure* of a sentence consists of its underlying meaning. The *surface structure* of a sentence consists of the word arrangement used to express this meaning (what people actually say).** Transformational rules account for the ability to derive the same meaning from different sentence constructions. As an illustration, consider the following two sentences:

The boy hit the ball.
The ball was hit by the boy.

The surface structure of these sentences is different. However, both sentences convey the same idea, because people readily transform them into the same deep structure. Chomsky believes that the language acquisition device explains why children acquire complex transformational rules with surprising swiftness.

Interactionist Theories

Like Skinner, Chomsky has his critics. His nativist theory has been attacked on a number of grounds. Some critics assert that Chomsky's "language acquisition device" isn't much of an explanation. They ask: What exactly is a language acquisition device? How does the LAD work? What are the neural mechanisms involved? They argue that the LAD concept is terribly vague.

Other critics question whether the rapidity of early language development is as exceptional as nativists assume. They assert that it isn't fair to compare the rapid progress of toddlers, who are immersed in their native language, against the struggles of students, who may devote only 10 to 15 hours per week to their foreign language course. It is more appropriate to compare youngsters and adults who are learning the same second language after having moved to a new country. Although some studies find that children have an advantage in this situation (Johnson & Newport, 1989), many other studies suggest that adults can learn a second language about as readily as young children (Snow, 1993). Nativist theories have also been undermined by recent evidence that parents *do* provide their children with subtle corrective feedback about grammar (Bohannon, MacWhinney, & Snow, 1990; Bohannon & Stanowicz, 1988).

The problems apparent in Skinner's and Chomsky's explanations of language development have led some psychologists to outline *interactionist theories* of language acquisition. These theories assert that biology and experience *both* make important contributions to the development of language.

Interactionist theories come in two basic varieties. *Cognitive theories* assert that language development is simply an important aspect of more general cognitive development (Meltzoff & Gopnik, 1989; Piaget, 1983). Hence, language acquisition is tied to children's progress in thinking—which depends on both maturation and experience. According to this view, when children begin to add *ed* to verbs to express past tense, it's because they understand the *idea* of the past. *Social communication theorists* emphasize the functional value of interpersonal communication and the social context in which language evolves (Bohannon & Warren-Leubecker, 1989; Farrar, 1990). They argue that language development is modulated to some extent by interaction with mature language users and the feedback they provide.

Like the nativists, interactionists believe that the human organism is biologically well equipped for learning language. They also agree that much of this learning involves the acquisition of rules. However, they stress that these realities do *not* mean that language development is automatic or that environment is irrelevant. Like the behaviorists, they believe that verbal exchanges with parents and others play a critical role in molding language skills. "According to this view, children are not little grammarians, motivated to decode the syntax of the language around them through the operation of their LAD, but social beings who

Figure 8.5
Chomsky's concepts of deep and surface structure. The deep structure of a sentence consists of its abstract meaning. The surface structure consists of the actual word arrangements that express this meaning. The same idea (deep structure) can be expressed in a variety of ways (surface structure) through the use of transformational rules.

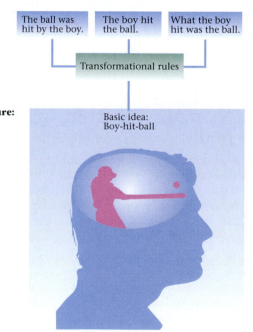

Surface structure: The actual sequence of words used to express a thought

The ball was hit by the boy.   The boy hit the ball.   What the boy hit was the ball.

Transformational rules

Deep structure: The basic thought or meaning expressed in a sentence

Basic idea: Boy-hit-ball

acquire language in the service of their needs to communicate with others" (Ratner & Gleason, 1993, p. 337). Thus, interactionist theories maintain that both an innate predisposition and a supportive environment contribute to language development.

Culture, Language, and Thought

Another long-running controversy in the study of language concerns the relations between culture, language, and thought. Obviously, people from different cultures generally speak different languages. But does your training in English lead you to think about certain things differently than someone who was raised to speak Chinese or French? In other words, does a cultural group's language determine their thought? Or does thought determine language?

Benjamin Lee Whorf (1956) has been the most prominent advocate of **linguistic relativity, the hypothesis that one's language determines the nature of one's thought.** Whorf speculated that different languages lead people to view the world differently. His classic example compared English and Eskimo views of snow. He asserted that the English language has just one word for snow, whereas the Eskimo language has many words that distinguish among falling snow, wet snow, and so on. Because of this language gap, Whorf argued that Eskimos perceive snow differently than English-speaking people do. However, Whorf's conclusion about these perceptual differences was based on casual observation rather than systematic cross-cultural comparisons of perceptual processes. Moreover, critics subsequently noted that advocates of the linguistic relativity hypothesis had carelessly overestimated the number of Eskimo words for snow, while conveniently ignoring the variety of English words that refer to snow, such as slush and blizzard (Martin, 1986; Pullum, 1991).

Nonetheless, Whorf's hypothesis has been the subject of spirited debate. In one of the better-designed experimental tests of this hypothesis, Eleanor Rosch (1973) compared the color perceptions of English-speaking people with those of the Dani, an agricultural people who live in New Guinea. The Dani were chosen because their language includes relatively few *basic color terms* (widely used words for widely agreed on colors). In fact, the Dani have terms for only two basic colors (bright and dark). In contrast, the English language includes eleven basic color terms. Previous research had shown that English speakers learn arbitrary, nonsense names for these eleven basic colors more easily than for nonbasic colors. If language determines thought, this advantage in learning new names for the eleven basic colors should *not* be seen among the Dani, since they don't think in terms of these colors. However, the Dani also found it easier to learn nonsense names for the eleven basic colors. Thus, Rosch concluded that the Dani think about color much as English speakers do, even though their language treats color differently. Rosch's findings clearly contradict Whorf's hypothesis.

Is there any evidence that is consistent with the linguistic relativity hypothesis? Yes. Bloom's (1981) research on *counterfactual thinking* suggests that language may shape thought. *Counterfactual assertions* are propositions that begin with a premise that is implied to be false. For example, the statement "If I knew French, I could read the works of Voltaire" implies that the speaker does *not* know French. The English language easily accommodates such "If only" hypotheticals, but the Chinese language is ill-equipped to handle them. Thus, a Chinese speaker would express the same idea in a factual rather than hypothetical manner ("I don't know French, so I can't read the works of Voltaire"). Bloom investigated the repercussions of this linguistic disparity by comparing Chinese and American college students' ability to understand counterfactual assertions. He found that the Chinese students made many more errors in interpreting counterfactual statements. Hence, he concluded that the Chinese and English languages foster somewhat different types of thinking.

Does the language you speak determine how you think? Yes, says Benjamin Lee Whorf, who uses the classic example of the Eskimo language, which has numerous words for snow, thus making Eskimos perceive snow differently from English speakers.

Additional evidence for linguistic relativity comes from research on people who are fluent in two languages. Some studies suggest that bilingual individuals think about things somewhat differently in one language as opposed to the other. For example, in forming impressions of people, Chinese-English bilinguals have some social schemas for characterizing people that work in English but not Chinese, and vice versa (Hoffman, Lau, & Johnson, 1986).

So, what is the status of the linguistic relativity hypothesis? The preponderance of evidence provides little support for the original, strong version of the hypothesis—that a given language makes certain ways of thinking obligatory or impossible (Berry et al., 1992; Eysenck, 1984). However, a weaker version of the linguistic relativity hypothesis—that a given language makes certain ways of thinking easier or more difficult—may be tenable in light of the evidence on counterfactual thinking and bilingual speakers.

In everyday life, many people clearly recognize that language may slant thought along certain lines. This possibility is the basis for concern about sexist language. Women who object to being called "girls," "chicks," and "babes" believe that these terms influence the way people think about women. Concerns about words such as "mankind," "manpower," "policeman," "chairman," and "foreman" are also based on the belief that these words constrain the way people think about women's roles in modern society. In a similar vein, car dealers who sell "preowned cars," airlines that outline precautions for "water landings," and politicians who refer to tax increases as "revenue enhancement initiatives" are manipulating language to influence thought. We'll see additional examples of how language can sway thinking in our later discussion of decision making, but first we turn to the subject of problem solving.

Recap of Key Points

• During the first half of the 20th century, the study of cognition was largely suppressed by the theoretical dominance of behaviorism. However, the 1950s brought a cognitive revolution in psychology, as Simon, Chomsky, Miller, and many others reported major advances in the study of mental processes.

• Psychologists' interest in language acquisition has been extended to include the study of whether chimpanzees can learn a language. Chimpanzees can learn signs or symbols to represent words and can combine them to communicate with their caretakers.

• However, some theorists doubt whether chimps generate sentences and really learn rules of language. Our Featured Study, which followed the language development of a chimp named Kanzi, was relevant to this issue. Sue Savage-Rumbaugh and her colleagues concluded that Kanzi was capable of generating spontaneous sentences that followed rules relating to the ordering of words.

• Languages are symbolic, semantic, generative, and structured. Human languages are structured hierarchically. At the bottom of the hierarchy are the basic sound units, called phonemes. At the next level are morphemes, the smallest units of meaning.

• Words are morphemes or are formed of morphemes. Words are combined into phrases and sentences according to the rules of syntax. Humans' remarkable ability to learn language is probably a product of natural selection.

• Long before they utter their first words, infants are making progress in mastering the sound structure of their native language. The initial vocalizations by infants are similar across languages, but beginning when the child is about 6 months of age, the sounds begin to resemble the surrounding language.

• Children typically utter their first words around their first birthday. Vocabulary growth is slow at first, but a vocabulary spurt often begins at around 18 months. Early words are often overextended to refer to objects that look similar to the correctly named object.

• Single words, called holophrases, are also used to express the meaning of several words. Children begin to combine words by the end of their second year. Their early sentences are telegraphic, in that they omit many nonessential words. Over the next several years, children gradually learn the complexities of syntax.

• According to Skinner and other behaviorists, children acquire a language through imitation and reinforcement. Chomsky argued that imitation cannot explain the fact that children routinely say things they have never heard.

• Nativist theories assert that humans have an innate capacity to learn language rules. Today, theorists are moving toward interactionist perspectives, which emphasize the role of both biology and experience.

• The theory of linguistic relativity asserts that language determines thought, thus suggesting that people from different cultures may think about the world somewhat differently. To date, the balance of evidence suggests that thought determines language more than vice versa, and that cognitive processes are largely invariant across cultures. However, a weak version of the linguistic relativity hypothesis, which simply proposes that one's language makes certain ways of thinking easier or more difficult, may be tenable.

PROBLEM SOLVING: IN SEARCH OF SOLUTIONS

Look at the two problems below. Can you solve them?

In the Thompson family there are five brothers, and each brother has one sister. If you count Mrs. Thompson, how many females are there in the Thompson family?

Fifteen percent of the people in Topeka have unlisted telephone numbers. You select 200 names at random from the Topeka phone book. How many of these people can be expected to have unlisted phone numbers?

These problems, borrowed from Sternberg (1986, p. 214), are exceptionally simple, but many people fail to solve them. The answer to the first problem is two. The only females in the family are Mrs. Thompson and her one daughter, who is a sister to each of her brothers. The answer to the second problem is none. You won't find any people with unlisted phone numbers in the phone book.

Why do many people fail to solve these simple problems? You'll learn why in a moment, when we discuss barriers to effective problem solving. But first, let's examine a scheme for classifying problems into a few basic types.

Types of Problems 6d

Problem solving refers to active efforts to discover what must be done to achieve a goal that is not readily attainable. Obviously, if a goal is readily attainable, there isn't a problem. But in problem-solving situations, one must go beyond the information given to overcome obstacles and reach a goal. Jim Greeno (1978) has proposed that problems can be categorized into three basic classes:

1. *Problems of inducing structure* require people to discover the relations among numbers, words, symbols, or ideas. The *series completion problems* and the *analogy problems* in Figure 8.6 on page 316 are examples of problems of inducing structure.

2. *Problems of arrangement* require people to arrange the parts of a problem in a way that satisfies some criterion. The parts can usually be arranged in many ways, but only one or a few of the arrangements form a solution. The *string problem* and the *anagrams* in Figure 8.6 fit in this category. Arrangement problems are often solved with a burst of insight. **Insight is the sudden discovery of the correct solution following incorrect attempts based primarily on trial and error.**

3. *Problems of transformation* require people to carry out a sequence of transformations in order to reach a specific goal. The *hobbits and orcs problem* and the *water jar problem* in Figure 8.6 are examples of transformation problems. Transformation problems can be challenging. Even though you know exactly what the goal is, it's often not obvious how the goal can be achieved.

Greeno's list is not an exhaustive scheme for classifying problems, but it provides a useful system for understanding some of the variety seen in everyday problems.

Well-Defined Versus Ill-Defined Problems

Problems vary in their clarity (Simon, 1973). The six classic problems shown in Figure 8.6 are all **well-defined problems—problems in which the initial state, the goal state, and the constraints are clearly specified.** Well-defined problems can be difficult, but patience and hard work usually yield progress and there is little ambiguity about what represents a solution. **In ill-defined problems, one or more elements among the initial state, the goal state, and the constraints are incompletely or unclearly specified.** In other words, ill-defined problems are riddled with uncertainty. In particular, there is often ambiguity about what represents the best solution. Thus, if your problem is to build a better mousetrap, write a poem for your creative writing class, design an improved curriculum, or come up with a creative advertising campaign, you'll have to wrestle with an ill-defined problem. The concepts of well-defined and ill-defined problems should be viewed as endpoints on a continuum, rather than an either-or distinction (Voss & Post, 1988). Laboratory studies of problem solving have tended to focus on relatively well-defined problems, but in the real world most problems are ill-defined to some degree (Holyoak, 1990). Fortunately, though, many of the strategies that are useful in dealing with well-defined problems are also relevant to ill-defined problems.

Barriers to Effective Problem Solving 6d

On the basis of their studies of problem solving, psychologists have identified a number of barriers that frequently impede subjects' efforts to arrive at solutions. Common obstacles to effective problem

A. Analogy
What word completes the analogy?
Merchant : Sell : : Customer : _____
Lawyer : Client : : Doctor : _____

B. String problem
Two strings hang from the ceiling but are too far apart to allow a person to hold one and walk to the other. On the table are a book of matches, a screwdriver, and a few pieces of cotton. How could the strings be tied together?

C. Hobbits and orcs problem
Three hobbits and three orcs arrive at a river bank, and they all wish to cross onto the other side. Fortunately, there is a boat, but unfortunately, the boat can hold only two creatures at one time. Also, there is another problem. Orcs are vicious creatures, and whenever there are more orcs than hobbits on one side of the river, the orcs will immediately attack the hobbits and eat them up. Consequently, you should be certain that you never leave more orcs than hobbits on either river bank. How should the problem be solved? It must be added that the orcs, though vicious, can be trusted to bring the boat back! (From Matlin, 1989, p. 319)

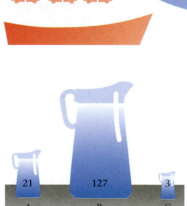

D. Water jar problem
Suppose that you have a 21-cup jar, a 127-cup jar, and a 3-cup jar. Drawing and discarding as much water as you like, you need to measure out exactly 100 cups of water. How can this be done?

E. Anagram
Rearrange the letters in each row to make an English word.
RWAET
KEROJ

F. Series completion
What number or letter completes each series?
1 2 8 3 4 6 5 6 _____
A B M C D M _____

Figure 8.6
Six standard problems used in studies of problem solving. Try solving the problems and identifying which class each belongs to before reading further. The problems can be classified as follows. The *analogy problems* and *series completion problems* are problems of inducing structure. The solutions for the analogy problems are *Buy* and *Patient*. The solutions for the series completion problems are *4* and *E*. The *string problem* and the *anagram problems* are problems of arrangement. To solve the string problem, attach the screwdriver to one string and set it swinging as a pendulum. Hold the other string and catch the swinging screwdriver. Then you need only untie the screwdriver and tie the strings together. The solutions for the anagram problems are *WATER* and *JOKER*. The *hobbits and orcs problem* and the *water jar problem* are problems of transformation. The solutions for these problems are outlined in Figures 8.7 and 8.8.

solving include a focus on irrelevant information, functional fixedness, mental set, and the imposition of unnecessary constraints.

Irrelevant Information

We began our discussion of problem solving with two simple problems that people routinely fail to solve (see page 315). The catch is that these problems contain *irrelevant information* that leads people astray. In the first problem, the number of brothers is irrelevant in determining the number of females in the Thompson family. In the second problem, subjects tend to focus on the figures of 15% and 200 names. But this numerical information is irrelevant, since all the names came out of the phone book.

Sternberg (1986) points out that people often incorrectly assume that all the numerical information in a problem is necessary to solve it. They therefore try to figure out how to use quantitative information before they even consider whether it's relevant. Effective problem solving requires that you attempt to figure out what information is relevant and what is irrelevant before proceeding.

Functional Fixedness

Another common barrier to successful problem solving, identified by Gestalt psychologists, is *functional fixedness—the tendency to perceive an item only in terms of its most common use.* Functional fixedness has been seen in the difficulties that people have with the string problem (Maier, 1931). Solving this problem requires finding a novel use for one of the objects: the screwdriver. Subjects tend to think of the screwdriver in terms of its usual functions—turning screws and perhaps prying things open. They have a hard time viewing the screwdriver as a weight. Their rigid way of thinking about the screwdriver illustrates functional fixedness.

Mental Set

Rigid thinking is also at work when a mental set interferes with effective problem solving. A *mental set exists when people persist in using problem-solving strategies that have worked in the past.* The effects of mental set were seen in a classic study by Gestalt psychologist Abraham Luchins (1942). He asked subjects to work a series of water jar problems, like the one introduced earlier. Six such problems are outlined in Figure 8.9, which shows the capacities of the three jars and the amounts of water to be measured out. Try solving these problems.

Were you able to develop a formula for solving these problems? The first four all require the same strategy, which was described in Figure 8.8. You have to fill jar B, draw off the amount that jar A holds once, and draw off the amount that jar C holds twice. Thus, the formula for your solution is B – A – 2C. Although there is an obvious and much simpler solution (A – C) for the fifth problem (see Figure 8.13 on page 320), Luchins found that most subjects stuck with the more cumbersome strategy that they had used in problems 1–4. Moreover, most subjects couldn't solve the sixth problem in the allotted time, because they kept trying to use their proven strategy, which does *not* work for this problem. The subjects' reliance on their "tried and true" strategy is an illustration of mental set in problem solving. This tendency to let one's thinking get into a rut is a common barrier to successful problem solving.

Unnecessary Constraints

Effective problem solving requires specifying all the constraints governing a problem *without assuming any constraints that don't exist.* An example

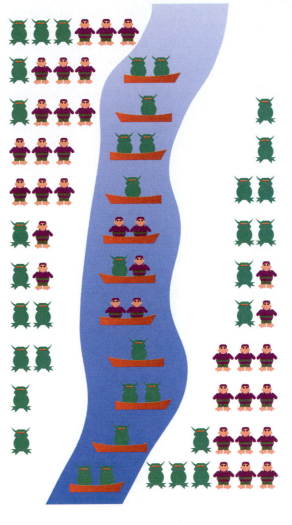

Figure 8.7
Solution to the hobbits and orcs problem. This problem is difficult because it is necessary to temporarily work "away" from the goal, which frustrates a straightforward means/ends approach.

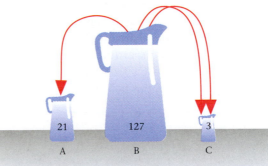

Figure 8.8
The method for solving the water jar problem. The formula is B – A – 2C.

Problem	Capacity of empty jars			Desired amount of water
	A	B	C	
1	14	163	25	99
2	18	43	10	5
3	9	42	6	21
4	20	59	4	31
5	23	49	3	20
6	28	76	3	25

Figure 8.9
Additional water jar problems. Using jars A, B, and C, with the capacities indicated in each row, figure out how to measure out the desired amount of water specified on the far right. (Based on Luchins, 1942)

of a problem in which people place an unnecessary constraint on the solution is shown in Figure 8.10 (Adams, 1980). Without lifting your pencil from the paper, try to draw four straight lines that will cross through all nine dots. Most people will not draw lines outside the imaginary boundary that surrounds the dots. Notice that this constraint is not part of the problem statement. It's imposed only by the problem solver. Correct solutions, two of which are shown in Figure 8.14 on page 320, extend outside the imaginary boundary. People often make assumptions that impose unnecessary constraints on problem-solving efforts.

Approaches to Problem Solving

In their classic treatise on problem solving, Allen Newell and Herbert Simon (1972) use a spatial metaphor to describe the process of problem solving. They use the term **problem space to refer to the set of possible pathways to a solution considered by the problem solver.** Thus, they see problem solving as a search in space. The problem solver's task is to find a solution path among the potential pathways that could lead from the problem's initial state to its goal state. The problem space metaphor highlights the fact that people must choose from among a variety of conceivable pathways or strategies in attempting to solve problems. In this section, we'll examine some general strategies.

Algorithms and Heuristics

Trial and error is a common approach to solving problems. **Trial and error involves trying possible solutions and discarding those that are in error until one works.** Trial and error is often applied haphazardly, but people sometimes try to be systematic. **An *algorithm* is a methodical, step-by-step procedure for trying all possible alternatives in searching for a solution to a problem.** For instance, to solve the anagram IHCRA, you could write out all the possible arrangements of these letters until you eventually reached an answer (CHAIR). If an algorithm is available for a problem, it guarantees that one can eventually find a solution.

Algorithms can be effective when there are relatively few possible solutions to be tried out. However, algorithms do not exist for many problems, and they can become impractical when the problem space is large. Consider, for instance, the problem shown in Figure 8.11. The challenge is to move just two matches to create a pattern containing four equal squares. Sure, you could follow an algorithm in moving pairs of matches about. But you'd better allocate plenty of time to this effort, as there are over 60,000 possible rearrangements to check out (see Figure 8.15 on page 320 for the solution).

Because algorithms are inefficient, people often use shortcuts called *heuristics* in problem solving. **A *heuristic* is a guiding principle or "rule of thumb" used in solving problems or making decisions.** Heuristics are often useful because they selectively narrow the problem space, but they don't guarantee success. Helpful heuristics in problem solving include using means/ends analysis, forming subgoals, working backward, searching for analogies, and changing the representation of a problem.

Means/Ends Analysis

Transformation problems often benefit from a heuristic known as means/ends analysis, which has been studied extensively by Newell and Simon (1972). **Means/ends analysis involves identifying differences that exist between the current state and the goal state and making changes that will reduce these differences.**

Although means/ends analysis is a useful strategy, it doesn't always lead to optimal progress in problem solving. Consider the hobbits and orcs problem, which requires transporting everyone across the river. Means/ends analysis suggests that it is a good idea to take as many passengers as possible across the river on each trip and bring as few as possible back. Thus, most people keep sending the boat back with just one passenger in it. To solve this problem, however, at one point it's necessary to send two passengers back. This is a difficult move for most people because it seems to go against

Figure 8.10
The nine-dot problem.
Without lifting your pencil from the paper, draw no more than four lines that will cross through all nine dots.

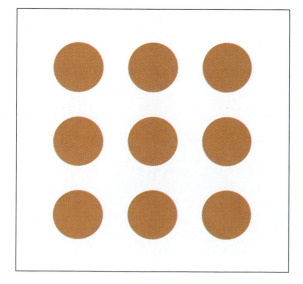

the goal (Thomas, 1974). In general, problems become difficult whenever people have to make moves that violate the means/ends strategy (Atwood & Polson, 1976).

Forming Subgoals

Means/ends analysis often leads people to tackle problems by formulating *subgoals,* intermediate steps toward a solution. When you reach a subgoal, you've solved part of the problem. Some problems have fairly obvious subgoals, and research has shown that people take advantage of them. For instance, in analogy problems, the first subgoal usually is to figure out the possible relations between the first two parts of the analogy. In a study by Simon and Reed (1976), subjects working on complex problems were given subgoals that weren't obvious. Providing subgoals helped the subjects solve the problems much more quickly.

The wisdom of formulating subgoals can be seen in the *tower of Hanoi problem,* depicted in Figure 8.12. The terminal goal for this problem is to move all three rings on peg A to peg C, while abiding by two restrictions: only the top ring on a peg can be moved, and a ring must never be placed above a smaller ring. See whether you can solve the problem before continuing.

Dividing this problem into subgoals facilitates a solution (Kotovsky, Hayes, & Simon, 1985). If you think in terms of subgoals, your first task is to get ring 3 to the bottom of peg C. Breaking this task into sub-subgoals, subjects can figure out that they should move ring 1 to peg C, ring 2 to peg B, and ring 1 from peg C to peg B. These maneuvers allow you to place ring 3 at the bottom of peg C, thus meeting your first subgoal. Your next subgoal—getting ring 2 over to peg C—can be accomplished in just two steps: move ring 1 to peg A and ring 2 to peg C. It should then be obvious how to achieve your final subgoal—getting ring 1 over to peg C.

Working Backward

Try to work the *lily pond problem* described below:

The water lilies on the surface of a small pond double in area every 24 hours. From the time the first water lily appears until the pond is completely covered takes 60 days. On what day is half of the pond covered with lilies?

If you're working on a problem that has a well-specified end point, you may find the solution more readily if you begin at the end and work backward. This strategy is the key to solving the lily pond problem. If the entire pond is covered on the 60th day, and the area covered doubles every

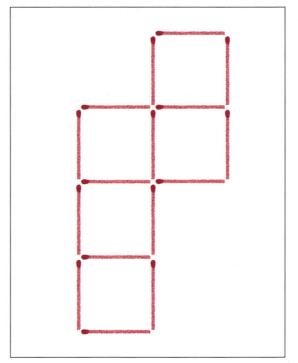

Figure 8.11
The matchstick problem.
Move two matches to form four equal squares.

day, how much is covered on the 59th day? One-half of the pond will be covered, and that happens to be the exact point you were trying to reach. The lily pond problem is remarkably simple when you work backward. In contrast, if you move forward from the starting point, you wrestle with questions about the area of the pond and the size of the lilies, and you find the problem riddled with ambiguities.

The potential advantages of working backward can also be seen in the following problem:

Try to arrange four 7s to make the number 56. You can add, subtract, multiply, and divide, and you can use parentheses to group 7s, but you must use all four 7s.

This problem is difficult because there are so many ways of combining the 7s. It's easier to solve if you work backward from the number 56. There are relatively few ways of breaking up 56, such as 28×2, 14×4, and 7×8. The advantage of 7×8 is

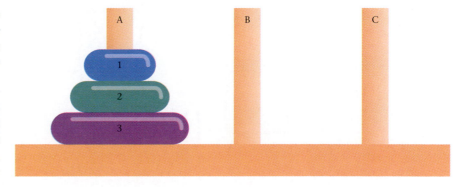

Figure 8.12
The tower of Hanoi problem. Your mission is to move the rings from peg A to peg C. You can move only the top ring on a peg and can't place a larger ring above a smaller one. The solution is explained in the text.

Figure 8.13

Figure 8.13
Solutions to the additional water jar problems. The solution for problems 1–4 is the same (B – A – 2C) as the solution shown in Figure 8.8. This method will work for problem 5, but there also is a simpler solution (A – C), which is the only solution for problem 6. Many subjects exhibit a mental set on these problems, as they fail to notice the simpler solution for problem 5.

Problem 5

| 23 | 49 | 3 |
| A | B | C |

Problem 6

| 28 | 76 | 3 |
| A | B | C |

Figure 8.14
Two solutions to the nine-dot problem. The key to solving the problem is to recognize that nothing in the problem statement forbids going outside the imaginary boundary surrounding the dots.

that it uses one of the 7s, leaving you to combine the three remaining 7s to make the number 8. Do you see the solution now? You can express 8 as 7 + 1, using up another 7. All that's left is to use two 7s to express the number 1. Since $7/7 = 1$, the answer to the problem is $(7/7 + 7) \times 7$. Working backward is a good strategy when you can see that you have many options available at the beginning of a problem but will have relatively few options

available near the end. It's also worth considering when you stop making progress by working forward.

Searching for Analogies

Searching for analogies is another of the major heuristics for solving problems. If you can spot an analogy between problems, you may be able to use the solution to a previous problem to solve a current one. Of course, using this strategy depends on recognizing the similarity between two problems, which may itself be a challenging problem. People often are unable to recognize that two problems are similar, but once informed of the similarity, they do reasonably well in making use of the analogous solution (Gick & Holyoak, 1980; Reed, Ernst, & Banerji, 1974). Try applying this strategy to the following two problems:

A teacher had 23 pupils in his class. All but 7 of them went on a museum trip and thus were away for the day. How many students remained in class that day?

Susan gets in her car in Boston and drives toward New York City, averaging 50 miles per hour. Twenty minutes later, Ellen gets in her car in New York City and starts driving toward Boston, averaging 60 miles per hour. Both women take the same route, which extends a total of 220 miles between the two cities. Which car is nearer to Boston when they meet?

Figure 8.15
Solution to the matchstick problem. The key to solving this problem is to "open up" the figure, something many subjects are reluctant to do because they impose unnecessary constraints on the problem.

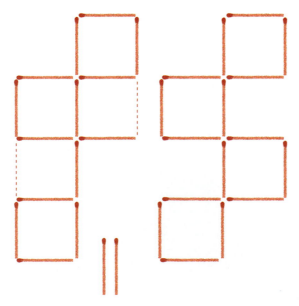

These problems, taken from Sternberg (1986, pp. 213 and 215), resemble the ones that opened our discussion of problem solving. Each has an obvious solution that's hidden in irrelevant quantitative information. If you recognized this similarity, you probably solved the problems easily. If not, take another look now that you know what the analogy is. Neither problem requires any calculation whatsoever. The answer to the first problem is 7. As for the second problem, when the two cars meet they're in the same place. Obviously, they have to be the same distance from Boston.

Changing the Representation of the Problem

Whether you solve a problem often hinges on how you envision it—your *representation of the problem*. Many problems can be represented in a variety of ways, such as verbally, mathematically, or spatially. You might represent a problem with a list, a table, an equation, a graph, a matrix of facts or numbers, a hierarchical tree diagram, or a sequential flowchart (Halpern, 1996). Recent studies have shown that diagrams can faciliate reasoning on some types of problems by making it easier to find crucial information and by making alternative possibilities more salient (Bauer Johnson-Laird, 1993). There isn't one ideal way to represent problems. The best representation will depend on the nature of the problem. But when you fail to make progress with your initial representation, changing your representation is often a good strategy. As an illustration, see whether you can solve the *bird and train problem* (from Bransford & Stein, 1993, p. 11):

Two train stations are 50 miles apart. At 1 P.M. on Sunday a train pulls out from each of the stations and the trains start toward each other. Just as the trains pull out from the stations, a hawk flies into the air in front of the first train and flies ahead to the front of the second train. When the hawk reaches the second train, it turns around and flies toward the first train. The hawk continues in this way until the trains meet. Assume that both trains travel at the speed of 25 miles per hour and the hawk flies at a constant speed of 100 miles per hour. How many miles will the hawk have flown when the trains meet?

This problem asks about the *distance* the bird will fly, so people tend to represent the problem spatially, as shown in Figure 8.16. Represented this way, the problem can be solved, but the steps are tedious and difficult. But consider another angle. The problem asks how far the bird will fly in the time it takes the trains to meet. Since we know how fast the bird flies, all we really need to know is how much *time* it takes for the trains to meet. Changing the representation of the problem from a question of *distance* to a question of *time* makes for an easier solution, as follows: The train stations are 50 miles apart. Since the trains are traveling toward each other at the same speed, they will meet midway and each will have traveled 25 miles. The trains are moving at 25 miles per hour. Hence, the time it takes them to meet 25 miles from each station is one hour. Since the bird flies at 100 miles per hour, it will fly 100 miles in the hour it takes the trains to meet.

Let's consider one more problem in which

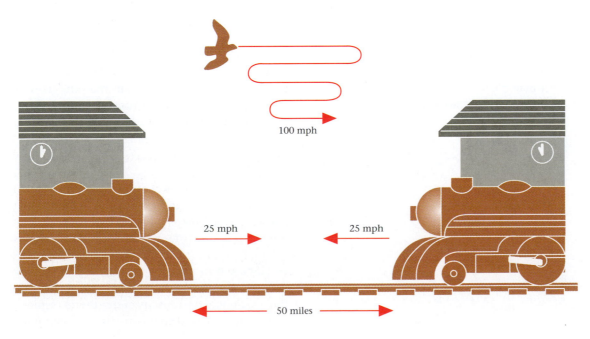

**Figure 8.16
Representing the bird and train problem.** The typical inclination is to envision this problem spatially, as shown here. However, this representation makes the problem much more difficult than it really is.

100 mph

25 mph

25 mph

50 miles

representation plays a crucial role. See whether you can solve the *Buddhist monk problem:*

At sunrise, a Buddhist monk sets out to climb a tall mountain. He follows a narrow path that winds around the mountain and up to a temple. He stops frequently to rest and climbs at varying speeds, arriving around sunset. After staying a few days, he begins his return journey. As before, he starts at sunrise, rests often, walks at varying speeds, and arrives around sunset. Prove that there must be a spot along the path that the monk will pass on both trips at precisely the same time of day.

Why should there be such a spot? The monk's walking speed varies. Shouldn't it all be a matter of coincidence if he reaches a spot at the same time each day? Moreover, if there is such a spot, how would you prove it? Subjects who represent this problem in terms of verbal, mathematical, or spatial information struggle. Subjects who work with a graphic representation fare much better. The best way to represent the problem is to envision the monk (or two different monks) ascending and descending the mountain at the same time. The two monks must meet at some point. If you construct a graph (see Figure 8.17) you can vary the speed of the monk's descent in endless ways, but you can see that there's always a place where they meet. The location of this place and the time of day can vary, but there will always be a crossing point where the monk(s) is (are) in the same place at the same time.

The problems described thus far have consisted primarily of *domain-free problems*—puzzles in which you could search for a solution without having special knowledge or expertise. In contrast, games such as chess and problems encountered in the classroom require knowledge in a particular subject domain. When this is the case, you need both subject-matter knowledge and strategies to become proficient (Glaser, 1984). Let's discuss some of the principles involved in acquiring expertise to solve *domain-specific problems.*

Expertise and Problem Solving

Recent years have seen increased interest in ***expertise*—consistently superior performance on a specified set of tasks or problems.** Psychologists have studied expertise in many skills, starting with chess and medical diagnosis, and moving on to computer programming, physics, bridge, dance, music, and various sports (Ericsson & Lehmann, 1996). The research in this area consistently demonstrates that *expertise is domain-specific.* That is, people who are characterized as experts excel at problem solving in a particular field where they have training, but not in other fields (Glaser & Chi, 1988). Thus, a brilliant physicist's expertise is normally limited to physics, and an advertising wizard's expertise is usually limited to advertising. As one would expect, when experts are compared to *novices* (people with little experience in a specific domain), the experts are found to be faster and more accurate in solving problems in their fields (VanLehn, 1989). But the interesting question is: Why? Recent studies have provided some thought-provoking answers.

Enhanced Working Memory

One way to investigate expertise is to look closely at how experts and novices solve problems and to determine how the two groups differ. One of the classic studies on expertise was conducted by a Dutch psychologist, Adriaan de Groot, during the 1940s and was later published in his book *Thought and Choice in Chess* (1965). In one study, de Groot compared experts' and novices' ability to recall pieces on a chessboard as it might appear 20 moves into a game (see the photos on page 323). The subjects had 5 seconds to view the board before the pieces were removed. Then the subjects were asked to place the pieces back on the board to reproduce what they had just seen. The master players exhibited far better memory, correctly placing about 90% of the pieces, compared to only 40% for the weaker players.

Why did the master chess players have such an advantage? Researchers eventually concluded that master players' better memory was the result of their organizing the chess pieces into chunks (Chase & Simon, 1973; Gobet & Simon, 1996). As we discussed in Chapter 7, a *chunk* is a familiar stimulus grouping that is stored as a single unit, thus expanding the capacity of short-term memory. Studies also showed that expertise in electronics,

Figure 8.17
Solution to the Buddhist monk problem. If you represent this problem graphically and think in terms of two monks, it is readily apparent that the monk does pass a single spot at the same time each day.

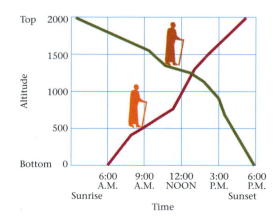

Check your understanding of problem solving by answering some questions about the following problem. Begin by trying to solve the problem.

The candle problem. Using the objects shown—candles, a box of matches, string, and some tacks—figure out how you could mount a candle on a wall so that it could be used as a light.

Work on the problem for a while, then turn to page 324 to see the solution. After you've seen the solution, respond to the following questions. The answers are in Appendix A.

1. If it didn't occur to you that the matchbox could be converted from a container to a platform, this illustrates _____ _____.

2. While working on the problem, if you thought to yourself, "How can I create a platform attached to the wall?" you used the heuristic of _____ _____.

3. If it occurred to you suddenly that the matchbox could be used as a platform, this realization would be an example of _____.

4. If you had a hunch that there might be some similarity between this problem and the string problem in Figure 8.6 (the similarity is the novel use of an object), your hunch would illustrate the heuristic of _____ _____.

5. In terms of Greeno's three types of problems, the candle problem is a(n) _____ problem.

Asked to reproduce these chessboard configurations after seeing them for only a few seconds, chess masters would outperform ordinary players by a wide margin—but only for the configuration shown at the top. For the one on the bottom, masters do no better than weaker players, even though the number of pieces is the same. The reason? The configuration at the bottom is impossible under the rules of chess and thus lacks the familiar patterns that the master has stored in memory as "chunks."

radiology, and computer programming depend in part on organizing information into larger and larger meaningful chunks (Greeno & Simon, 1988).

Expert performance in a variety of domains appears to depend on superior utilization of working memory (Ericsson & Charness, 1994). This observation has led Ericsson and Kintsch (1995) to conclude that experts use a variety of strategies to enhance the functioning of their working memory. Thus, chunking may be only one of several ways in which experts expand the capacity and efficiency of working memory. Enhanced working memory presumably allows experts to juggle more information in their area of expertise with greater agility than others.

Metacognition

Metacognition involves thinking about one's thinking. Experts appear to harness metacognition more effectively than others by engaging in more planning and evaluation in their problem-solving efforts. For instance, experts plan more than novices in solving complex physics problems (Larkin & Reif, 1979). Effective planning also contributes

to skill in bridge (Charness, 1989) and to excellence in solving financial problems (Hershey et al., 1990). Experts are also better than novices at monitoring the progress of their problem solving (VanLehn, 1989). They pay more attention to their progress, and they are more likely than novices to recognize when they are making an error. Hence, they are more flexible about shifting away from an unproductive strategy. They are also superior to novices in judging the difficulty level of a problem. Thanks to astute evaluation of their progress, experts tend to allocate their time more effectively than novices.

Recognition of Analogies

As people acquire expertise in an area, they get better at recognizing that problems may have similar solutions even when the problems involve very different situations. In contrast, novices often fail to detect important analogies (Novick, 1988; Reed,

The solution to the candle problem in Concept Check 8.2.

The Embedded Figures Test. Can you find the simple design on the left within the more complex design on the right? Respondents are asked to solve a series of problems like this one on the Embedded Figures Test, which measures field dependence–independence. The more adept subjects are at spotting the embedded figures, the more field independent they are assumed to be. (From Witkin et al., 1977)

Dempster, & Ettinger, 1985). To study subjects' recognition of analogous problems, Chi, Glaser, and Rees (1982) asked eight novices and eight experts to sort 24 physics problems into categories. Novices tended to categorize problems on the basis of superficial features. For instance, they would place inclined-plane problems in one category and spring problems in another category. Experts tended to categorize problems on the basis of the physics principles relevant to solving the problems. This finding reflects a general trend: *With the growth of expertise, people tend to shift their attention from surface aspects of problems to their deeper structures* (Hardiman, Dufresne, & Mestre, 1989). Thus, expertise often includes an enhanced ability to recognize that different problems have analogous solutions. The recognition of these analogies depends in part on how people represent problems (Kotovsky & Fallside, 1989; Kotovsky & Simon, 1990).

Deliberate Practice

An old joke asks, "How do you get to Carnegie Hall?" The punchline is "Practice, practice, practice." The recent empirical evidence supports this commonsense view. Ericsson and Charness (1994) maintain that, above all else, *expert performance depends on extensive training and practice.* They note that the level of performance attained by outstanding musicians and athletes can be predicted by the nature of their practice regimen. These researchers downplay the importance of innate talent and assert that expert performance is attained only after ten or more years of intense practice on a nearly daily basis. They bolster this point by noting that most elite performers start practice at a relatively young age. Although Ericsson and Charness may be a little too hasty in dismiss-

ing the importance of innate talent (Gardner, 1995), they marshal a tremendous body of research that is a convincing testament to the critical importance of practice and hard work.

Culture, Cognitive Style, and Problem Solving

Given that acquired expertise influences problem solving, shouldn't the varied experiences of people from different cultures lead to cross-cultural variations in problem solving? Yes, researchers have found cultural differences in the cognitive style that people exhibit in solving problems.

Back in the 1940s, Herman Witkin was intrigued by the observation that some airplane pilots would fly into a cloud bank upright but exit it upside down without realizing that they had turned over. Witkin's efforts to explain this aviation problem led to the discovery of an interesting dimension of cognitive style (Witkin, 1950; Witkin et al., 1962). *Field dependence–independence* **refers to individuals' tendency to rely primarily on external versus internal frames of reference when orienting themselves in space.** People who are *field dependent* rely on external frames of reference and tend to accept the physical environment as a given instead of trying to analyze or restructure it. People who are *field independent* rely on internal frames of reference and tend to analyze and try to restructure the physical environment rather than accepting it as is. In solving problems, field-dependent people tend to focus on the total context of a problem instead of zeroing in on specific aspects or breaking it into component parts. In contrast, field-independent people are more likely to focus on specific features of a problem and to reorganize the component parts. A person's field dependence–independence can be measured with the Embedded Figures Test, which requires subjects to identify simple designs from within more complex ones (see Figure 8.18).

Research has shown that field dependence–independence is related to diverse aspects of cognitive, emotional, and social functioning (Witkin & Goodenough, 1981). Each style has its strengths and weaknesses, but in many types of problem solving, field independence seems more advantageous. For example, studies have shown that field-independent subjects outperform field-dependent subjects on a variety of classic laboratory problems, including the string problem, matchstick problem, candle problem, and water jar problem (Witkin et al., 1962). Based on these and other findings, Witkin and his colleagues suggest that

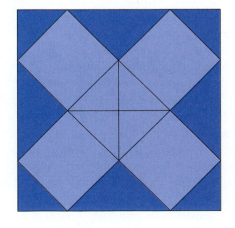

field-independent subjects are better than field-dependent subjects in handling problems of arrangement, problems typically solved with a burst of insight, problems that depend on overcoming functional fixedness, and problems that require one to discard a mental set. Field-independent subjects' superiority on these types of problems has been attributed to their tendency to work at restructuring situations, their propensity to analyze and rearrange the elements of a problem, and their ability to overcome the context in which problems are presented.

An extensive body of research suggests that some cultures encourage a field-dependent cognitive style, whereas others foster a field-independent style (Berry, 1990; Witkin & Berry, 1975). The educational practices in modern Western societies seem to nourish field independence. A field-independent style is also more likely to be predominant in nomadic societies that depend on hunting and gathering for subsistence and in societies with lenient child-rearing practices that encourage personal autonomy. In contrast, a field-dependent style is found more in sedentary agricultural societies and in societies that stress strict child-rearing practices and conformity. According to John Berry (1976), the predominant cognitive style in a society depends in large part on the culture's ecological demands—that is, the types of skills that are necessary to survive or flourish in the culture. For example, in cultures that depend on hunting and gathering for subsistence, the need to extract information from the surrounding field to locate game and food makes a field-independent style more adaptive. Consistent with this analysis, the Eskimo hunters of the Arctic wastelands and the Aboriginal hunters of the desert wastelands in Australia, who both need to extract information from particularly difficult environments, are among the most field-independent peoples of the world (Goodenough, 1986).

Problems are not the only kind of cognitive challenge that people grapple with on a regular basis. Life also seems to constantly demand decisions. As you might expect, cognitive psychologists have shown great interest in the process of decision making, which is our next subject.

Recap of Key Points

• In studying problem solving, psychologists have differentiated among several types of problems. In problems that require inducing structure, the problem solver must discover the relations among the parts of

a problem. Transformation problems require that the problem solver carry out a sequence of transformations (moves) in order to reach a specific goal. Arrangement problems require the problem solver to arrange the parts in a way that satisfies a general goal.

• Problems vary in the degree to which they are well defined. In the real world most problems are ill-defined to some degree. Common barriers to problem solving include functional fixedness, mental set, getting bogged down in irrelevant information, and placing unnecessary constraints on one's solutions.

• A variety of strategies, or heuristics, are used for solving problems. Means/ends analysis requires reducing the differences between the current problem state and the goal state. When people form subgoals, they try breaking the problem into several parts.

• Sometimes it is useful to start at the goal state and work backward toward the initial state. Other general strategies include searching for analogies between new problems and old problems, and changing the representation of problems.

• The solution of many kinds of problems requires acquiring both subject-matter knowledge and general strategies. Experts are better than novices at solving problems in their domain of expertise because they have more organized chunks of knowledge in memory and because they make better use of working memory.

• Experts' metacognition is also superior, as they are better than novices at planning and evaluation. Experts also tend to be better at identifying useful analogies between problems. Ultimately, expertise appears to be the product of extensive training and intense practice.

• Because of varied ecological demands, some cultures

Cultural factors appear to influence whether people become field dependent or field independent. For example, because of their demanding environment, the Aboriginal hunters of the desert wastelands of Australia are among the most field-independent people in the world.

encourage a field-dependent cognitive style, whereas others foster more field independence. People who are field independent tend to analyze and restructure problems more than those who are field dependent.

• Field-independent subjects tend to have an advantage over field-dependent subjects on insight problems and problems that require one to overcome functional fixedness or mental set.

DECISION MAKING: CHOICES AND CHANCES

Decisions, decisions. Life is full of them. You decided to read this book today. Earlier today you decided when to get up, whether to eat breakfast, and if so, what to eat. Usually you make routine decisions like these with little effort. But on occasion you need to make important decisions that require more thought. Big decisions—such as selecting a car, a home, or a job—tend to be difficult. The alternatives usually have a number of attributes that need to be weighed. For instance, in choosing among several cars, you may want to compare their costs, roominess, fuel economy, handling, acceleration, stylishness, reliability, safety features, and warranties.

Decision making **involves evaluating alternatives and making choices among them.** Most people try to be systematic and rational in their decision making. However, the work that earned Herbert Simon the 1978 Nobel Prize in economics showed that people don't always live up to these goals. Before Simon's work, most traditional theories in economics assumed that people made rational choices to maximize their economic gains. Simon (1957) noted that people have a limited ability to process and evaluate information on numerous facets of possible alternatives. He demonstrated that people tend to use simple strategies in decision making that focus on only a few facets of the available options. According to Simon's theory of *bounded rationality*, people use sensible decision strategies, given their cognitive limitations, but these limitations often result in "irrational" decisions that are less than optimal.

Spurred by Simon's analysis, psychologists have devoted several decades to the study of how cognitive biases distort people's decision making. The results of this research have sometimes been disturbing, leading some theorists to conclude that "normal adult human subjects do a singularly bad job at the business of reasoning, even when they are calm, clearheaded, and under no pressure to perform quickly" (Stich, 1990, pp. 173–174). Researchers' focus on *biases and mistakes* in making decisions may seem a little peculiar, but as Kahne-man (1991) has pointed out, the study of people's misguided decisions has illuminated the process of decision making, just as the study of illusions and forgetting has enhanced our understanding of visual perception and memory, respectively.

Making Choices: Selecting an Alternative

Many decisions involve choices about *preferences,* which can be made using a variety of strategies (Hogarth, 1987). For instance, imagine that Boris has found two reasonably attractive apartments and is trying to decide between them. How should he go about selecting between his alternatives? Let's look at some strategies Boris might use in trying to make his decision.

If Boris wanted to use an *additive strategy,* he would list the attributes that influence his decision. Then he would rate the desirability of each apartment on each attribute. For example, let's say that Boris wants to consider four attributes: rent, noise level, distance to campus, and cleanliness. He might make ratings from –3 (a very negative impression) to +3 (a very positive impression), like those shown in Table 8.3. Finally, he would add up the ratings for each alternative and select the one with the highest total. Given the ratings in Table 8.3, Boris should select apartment B.

To make an additive strategy more useful, you can *weight* attributes differently, based on their importance (Goldstein, 1990). For example, if Boris considers distance to campus to be twice as important as the other considerations, he could multiply his ratings of this attribute by 2. The distance rating would then be +6 for apartment A and –2 for apartment B, and apartment A would become the preferred choice. Of course, Boris could further refine his strategy by making more elaborate weightings of various attributes.

Additive strategies are examples of compensatory models in decision making. **Compensatory decision models allow attractive attributes to compensate for unattractive attributes.** For example, even though small cars are not as safe in collisions as large cars, you might allow their attractive attributes (lower cost, better gas mileage) to compensate for their lower safety ratings.

In deciding on preferences, people often use a relatively simple strategy called *elimination by aspects,* in which choices are made by gradually eliminating less attractive alternatives (Slovic, 1990; Tversky, 1972). In this strategy alternatives are eliminated by evaluating them on each attribute or aspect in turn. Whenever any alternative fails to satisfy some minimum criterion for an attribute, it is eliminated from further consideration. Elimination by aspects is an example of a noncompensatory decision scheme. **Noncompensatory decision models do not allow some attributes to compensate for others.** In such models, a single bad rating can eliminate an alternative.

To illustrate, suppose Juanita is looking for a new car. She may begin by eliminating all cars that cost over $14,000. Then she may eliminate cars that don't average at least 20 miles per gallon of gas. By continuing to reject choices that don't satisfy some minimum criterion on selected attributes, she can gradually eliminate alternatives until only a single car remains.

The final choice in elimination by aspects depends on the order in which attributes are evaluated. For example, if cost was the last attribute Juanita evaluated, she could have previously eliminated all cars that cost under $14,000! If she has only $14,000 to spend, her decision-making strategy would not have brought her very far. Thus, when using elimination by aspects, it's best to evaluate attributes in the order of their importance.

Both the additive and the elimination-by-aspects strategies have advantages, but which strategy do people actually tend to use? To determine how people select a decision strategy, John Payne (1976) gave subjects information about apartments and asked them to select one. The information about each attribute of each apartment was typed on a card, as shown in Figure 8.19. The cards were placed on the table face down so a subject had to turn a card over to see its value. This setup allowed Payne to determine subjects' decision strategies by watching the order in which they turned over the cards. Payne also told subjects to think aloud as they did the task, so he could monitor their thoughts. The task included many variations in which people had to choose from 2, 6, or 12 apartments while weighing 4, 8, or 12 attributes.

When the decision task involved few apartments and attributes, people used mainly a compensatory model, such as an additive strategy. However,

TABLE 8.3 APPLICATION OF THE ADDITIVE MODEL TO CHOOSING AN APARTMENT

Attribute	Apartment	
	A	B
Rent	+1	+2
Noise level	−2	+3
Distance to campus	+3	−1
Cleanliness	+2	+2
Total	**+4**	**+6**

as more options and factors were added, making the decision task more difficult, people shifted to a noncompensatory model, such as elimination by aspects. Thus, subjects adapt their decision strategies to the demands of the task. When they have many alternatives and their choices become complex and difficult, they tend to deal with the information overload by shifting toward simpler, noncompensatory strategies (Payne, Bettman, & Johnson, 1992).

Difficulties in choosing between alternatives can also lead people to delay their decisions. Tversky and Shafir (1992) note that "the experience of conflict is the price one pays for the freedom to choose" (p. 358). They argue that when alternatives are not dramatically different in attractiveness, people struggle with conflict and often defer decisions, taking additional time to look for a new car, apartment, or whatever. The research of Tversky and Shafir (1992) suggests that these delayed decisions are common even when the available alternatives are quite satisfactory. As an everyday illustration of this phenomenon, they describe a friend who had decided to buy an expensive encyclopedia for his children. Much to his chagrin, when he visited a bookstore to make his purchase he discovered that there were two appealing encyclopedias available. Although both encyclopedias

**Figure 8.19
Examples of cards used in the Payne (1976) study of decision making.** Face down, the cards read "Noise level," "Cleanliness," and so on; to discover their value, the subjects had to turn the cards face up. The procedure used in this study is an excellent example of the ways in which psychologists try to make cognitive processes observable and thus open to scientific investigation.

were acceptable, he found it difficult to choose between the two, and as a result he bought neither.

Delaying a decision allows one to ponder the matter further, to seek additional information, and perhaps even to discover new alternatives. But do these delays and the additional reflection that they allow actually lead to better decisions? Perhaps not. Some recent studies suggest that it is possible for people to "think too much" about a decision (Wilson & Schooler, 1991). Why should extra reflection impair decision making? One possible reason is that additional deliberation may lead people to compare their alternatives on more attributes, which are progressively less critical, thus cluttering the picture with more and more information that is less and less important.

Taking Chances: Risky Decision Making

Suppose you have the chance to play a dice game in which you might win some money. You must decide whether it would be to your advantage to play. You're going to roll a fair die. If the number 6 appears, you win $5. If one of the other five numbers appears, you win nothing. It costs you $1 every time you play. Should you participate?

This problem calls for a type of decision making that is somewhat different from making choices about preferences. In selecting alternatives that reflect preferences, people generally weigh known outcomes (apartment A will require a long commute to campus, car B will get 30 miles per gallon, and so forth). In contrast, *risky decision making* **involves making choices under conditions of uncertainty.** Uncertainty exists when people don't know what will happen. At best, they know the probability that a particular event will occur.

Factors Weighed in Risky Decisions

One way to decide whether to play the dice game would be to figure out the *expected value* of participation in the game. To do so, you would need to calculate the average amount of money you could expect to win or lose each time you play. The value of a win is $4 ($5 minus the $1 entry fee). The value of a loss is –$1. To calculate expected value, you also need to know the probability of a win or loss. Since a die has six faces, the probability of a win is 1 out of 6, and the probability of a loss is 5 out of 6. Thus, on five out of every six trials, you lose $1. On one out of six, you win $4. The game is beginning to sound unattractive, isn't it? We can figure out the precise expected value as follows:

"People treat their own cases as if they were unique, rather than part of a huge lottery. You hear this silly argument that 'The odds don't apply to me.' Why should God, or whoever runs this lottery, give you special treatment?"

AMOS TVERSKY

Expected value =

$$(\tfrac{1}{6} \times 4) + (\tfrac{5}{6} \times -1) = \tfrac{4}{6} + (-\tfrac{5}{6}) = -\tfrac{1}{6}$$

The expected value of this game is –⅙ of a dollar, which means that you lose an average of about 17 cents per turn. Now that you know the expected value, surely you won't agree to play. Or will you?

If we want to understand why people make the decisions they do, the concept of expected value is not enough. People frequently behave in ways that are inconsistent with expected value (Slovic, Lichtenstein, & Fischhoff, 1988). Any time the expected value is negative, a gambler should expect to lose money. Yet a great many people gamble at racetracks and casinos and buy lottery tickets. Although they realize that the odds are against them, they continue to gamble. Even people who don't gamble buy homeowner's insurance, which has a negative expected value. After all, when you buy insurance, your expectation (and hope!) is that you will lose money on the deal.

To explain decisions that violate expected value, some theories replace the objective value of an outcome with its *subjective utility* (Fischhoff, 1988). Subjective utility represents what an outcome is personally worth to an individual. For example, buying a few lottery tickets may allow you to dream about becoming wealthy. Buying insurance may give you a sense of security. Subjective utilities like these vary from one person to another. If we know an individual's subjective utilities, we can better understand that person's risky decision making.

Another way to improve our understanding of risky decision making is to consider individuals' estimates of the *subjective probability* of events (Shafer & Tversky, 1988). If people don't know actual probabilities, they must rely on their personal estimates of probabilities. Subjective probabilities introduce another bit of illogic into decision making.

Heuristics in Judging Probabilities

- What are your chances of passing your next psychology test if you study only 3 hours?
- How likely is a major downturn in the stock market during the upcoming year?
- What are the odds of your getting into graduate school in the field of your choice?

These questions ask you to make probability estimates. Amos Tversky and Daniel Kahneman (1974, 1982) have conducted extensive research on the *heuristics,* or mental shortcuts, that people use in grappling with probabilities. Sometimes these heuristics yield reasonable estimates, but often they do not.

Availability is one such heuristic. **The *availability heuristic* involves basing the estimated probability of an event on the ease with which relevant instances come to mind.** For example, you may estimate the divorce rate by recalling the number of divorces among your friends' parents. Recalling specific instances of an event is a reasonable strategy to use in estimating the event's probability. However, if instances occur frequently but you have difficulty retrieving them from memory, your estimate will be biased. For instance, it's easier to think of words that begin with a certain letter than words that contain that letter at some other position. Hence, people should tend to respond that there are more words starting with the letter *K* than words having a *K* in the third position. To test this hypothesis, Tversky and Kahneman (1973) selected five consonants (*K, L, N, R, V*) that occur more frequently in the third position of a word than in the first. Subjects were asked whether each of the letters appears more often in the first or third position. Most of the subjects erroneously believed that all five letters were much more frequent in the first than in the third position, confirming the hypothesis.

Representativeness is another guide in estimating probabilities identified by Kahneman and Tversky (1982). **The *representativeness heuristic* involves basing the estimated probability of an event on how similar it is to the typical prototype of that event.** To illustrate, imagine that you flip a coin six times and keep track of how often the result is heads (H) or tails (T). Which of the following sequences is more likely?

1. T T T T T T
2. H T T H T H

People generally believe that the second sequence is more likely. After all, coin tossing is a random affair, and the second sequence looks much more representative of a random process than the first. In reality, the probability of each exact *sequence* is precisely the same (½ × ½ × ½ × ½ × ½ × ½ = ¹⁄₆₄). We'll see more examples of how the representativeness heuristic works in our upcoming Application on pitfalls in decision making.

The Framing of Questions
Another consideration in making decisions involving risks is the *framing of questions* (Tversky &

Kahneman, 1988, 1991). ***Framing* refers to how decision issues are posed or how choices are structured.** People often allow a decision to be shaped by the language or context in which it's presented, rather than explore it from different perspectives. Consider the following scenario, which is adapted from Kahneman and Tversky (1984, p. 343):

Imagine that the U.S. is preparing for the outbreak of a dangerous disease, which is expected to kill 600 people. Two alternative programs to combat the disease have been proposed. Assume that the exact scientific estimates of the consequences of the programs are as follows.
  • If Program A is adopted, 200 people will be saved.
  • If Program B is adopted, there is a one-third probability that all 600 people will be saved and a two-thirds probability that no people will be saved.

Kahneman and Tversky found that 72% of their subjects chose the "sure thing" (Program A) over the "risky gamble" (Program B). However, they obtained different results when the alternatives were reframed as follows:

  • If Program C is adopted, 400 people will die.
  • If Program D is adopted, there is a one-third probability that nobody will die and a two-thirds probability that all 600 people will die.

Although framed differently, Programs A and B represent exactly the same probability situation as Programs C and D (see Figure 8.20 on page 330). In spite of this equivalence, 78% of the subjects chose Program D. Thus, subjects chose the sure thing when the decision was framed in terms of lives saved, but they went with the risky gamble when the decision was framed in terms of lives lost. Additional experiments have shown that these results reflect a general trend in thinking about decisions. *When seeking to obtain gains, people tend to avoid risky options. However, when seeking to cut their losses, people are much more likely to take risks.*

Obviously, sound decision making should yield consistent decisions that are not altered dramatically by superficial changes in how options are presented, so framing effects once again highlight the foibles of human decision making. Fortunately, however, there are some limiting conditions that reduce the likelihood of framing effects (Miller & Fagley, 1991). Interestingly, in light of our previous discussion of thinking too much about decisions, framing effects are less likely when subjects are asked to provide rationales for their choices.

"The human mind suppresses uncertainty. We're not only convinced that we know more about our politics, our businesses, and our spouses than we really do, but also that what we don't know must be unimportant."

DANIEL KAHNEMAN

Figure 8.20
The framing of questions. This chart shows that Programs A and C involve an identical probability situation, as do Programs B and D. When choices are framed in terms of possible gains, people prefer the safer plan. However, when choices are framed in terms of losses, people are more willing to take a gamble.

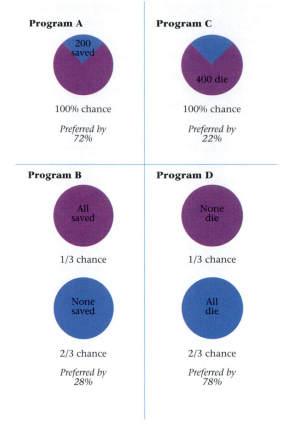

Thus, in some instances, additional reflection can lead to more rather than less sophisticated decision making.

Nonetheless, framing effects have been found in many studies, which have examined everything from gambling behavior (Elliott & Archibald, 1989), to product preferences (Neale & Northcraft, 1986), to decisions about genetic risks (Huys, Evers-Kiebooms, & d'Ydewalle, 1990). Clearly, framing is a factor in many of the choices people face in everyday life. For instance, some oil companies charge gas station patrons an extra nickel or so per gallon when they pay with a credit card. This fee clearly is a credit surcharge that results in a small financial loss. However, the oil companies never explicitly label it as a surcharge. Instead, they assert that they offer a discount for cash. Thus, they frame the decision as a choice between the normal price or an opportunity for a gain. They understand that it's easier for customers to foresake a gain than it is to absorb a loss.

The Spectre of Regret

Yet another factor at work in decision making is the need to avoid regret about making a bad decision. Let's say you just inherited a few thousand dollars. You need to decide whether to salt it away in a safe certificate of deposit that will guarantee a return of 6% or to make an investment in a start-up company that could result in a big payoff or the loss of all the money. Once the outcome is known (the start-up company succeeds or fails), you will surely contemplate "what might have been." If you made the wrong decision, you will experience great regret. According to Larrick (1993), many decisions can be understood in terms of the need to avoid the unpleasant psychological consequences that result from a poor decision. People vary in their vulnerability to feeling regret. Those who are particularly vulnerable to regret tend to make safer decisions that reduce the likelihood of experiencing regret (Josephs et al., 1992). Who is especially vulnerable to regret? Researchers have just begun to investigate this question, but a key determinant appears to be self-esteem. People with low self-esteem are more susceptible to threats to their self-image. In contrast, people with high self-esteem tend to be more sanguine about mistakes in decision making.

In summary, the evidence on decision making suggests that people try to follow systematic and logical strategies, but they often aren't as rational as they could be—even when they think they are.

PUTTING IT IN PERSPECTIVE

Four of our unifying themes have been especially prominent in this chapter. The first is the continuing question about the relative influences of heredity and environment. The controversy about how children acquire language skills replays the nature versus nurture debate. The behaviorist theory, that children learn language through imitation and reinforcement, emphasizes the importance of the environment. The nativist theory, that children come equipped with an innate language acquisition device, argues for the importance of biology. The debate is far from settled, but the accumulating evidence suggests that both theories may contain a kernel of truth. It appears that language development depends on both nature and nurture, as more recent interactionist theories of language acquisition have proposed.

The second pertinent theme is the empirical

nature of psychology. For many decades, psychologists paid little attention to cognitive processes, because most of them assumed that thinking is too private to be studied scientifically. During the 1950s and 1960s, however, psychologists began to devise creative new ways to measure mental processes. These innovations fueled the cognitive revolution that put the *psyche* (the mind) back in psychology. Thus, once again, we see how empirical methods are the lifeblood of the scientific enterprise.

Third, the study of cognitive processes shows how there are both similarities and differences across cultures in behavior. On the one hand, we saw that language development unfolds in much the same way in widely disparate cultures and that thought processes are largely invariant in spite of sharp differences in cultures' linguistic heritage. On the other hand, we learned that there are cultural variations in cognitive style that reflect the ecological demands of one's environment. And, although the evidence does not support the strong version of the linguistic relativity hypothesis, we saw that a culture's language may make certain ways of thinking easier or more difficult. Thus, cognitive processes are moderated—albeit to a limited degree—by cultural factors.

The fourth theme is the subjective nature of human experience. We have seen that decision making is a highly subjective process. Indeed, reframed in new language, choices that are objectively identical can subjectively seem very different. The subjectivity of decision processes will continue to be prominent in the upcoming Application, which discusses common pitfalls in decision making.

Recap of Key Points

• Decision making is another example of the cognitive processes studied by psychologists. An additive decision model is used when people make decisions by rating the attributes of each alternative and selecting the alternative that has the highest sum of ratings.

• When elimination by aspects is used, people gradually eliminate alternatives if their attributes fail to satisfy some minimum criterion. To some extent, people adapt their decision-making strategy to the situation, moving toward simpler, noncompensatory strategies when choices become complex.

• Difficulties in choosing between alternatives can cause conflict and lead people to delay decisions, even when the available alternatives are quite satisfactory. Some studies suggest that it may be possible for

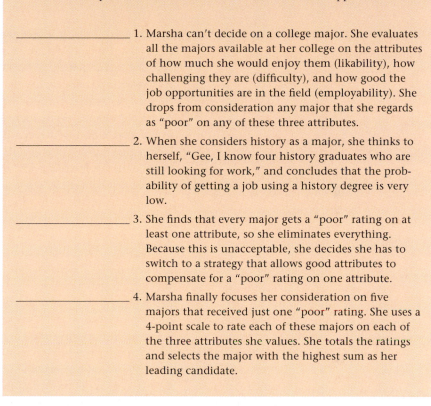

CONCEPT CHECK 8.3
Recognizing Heuristics in Decision Making

Check your understanding of heuristics in decision making by trying to identify the heuristics used in the following example. Each numbered element in the anecdote below illustrates a problem-solving heuristic. Write the relevant heuristic in the space on the left. You can find the answers in Appendix A.

_____ 1. Marsha can't decide on a college major. She evaluates all the majors available at her college on the attributes of how much she would enjoy them (likability), how challenging they are (difficulty), and how good the job opportunities are in the field (employability). She drops from consideration any major that she regards as "poor" on any of these three attributes.

_____ 2. When she considers history as a major, she thinks to herself, "Gee, I know four history graduates who are still looking for work," and concludes that the probability of getting a job using a history degree is very low.

_____ 3. She finds that every major gets a "poor" rating on at least one attribute, so she eliminates everything. Because this is unacceptable, she decides she has to switch to a strategy that allows good attributes to compensate for a "poor" rating on one attribute.

_____ 4. Marsha finally focuses her consideration on five majors that received just one "poor" rating. She uses a 4-point scale to rate each of these majors on each of the three attributes she values. She totals the ratings and selects the major with the highest sum as her leading candidate.

people to think too much about decisions, perhaps because additional deliberation clouds the picture with more and more information that is less and less important.

• Models of how people make risky decisions focus on the expected value or subjective utility of various outcomes and the objective or subjective probability that these outcomes will occur.

• People use the representativeness and availability heuristics in estimating probabilities. Decisions can be influenced by how they are framed and the desire to avoid regret about making a bad decision.

• Four of our unifying themes surfaced in the chapter. Our discussion of language acquisition revealed once again that all aspects of behavior are shaped by both nature and nurture. The recent progress in the study of cognitive processes showed how science depends on empirical methods.

• Research on decision making illustrated the importance of subjective perceptions. We also saw that cognitive processes are moderated—to a limited degree— by cultural factors.

APPLICATION: UNDERSTANDING PITFALLS IN REASONING ABOUT DECISIONS

Consider the following scenario:

Laura is in a casino watching people play roulette. The 38 slots in the roulette wheel include 18 black numbers, 18 red numbers, and 2 green numbers. Hence, on any one spin, the probability of red or black is slightly less than 50-50 (.474 to be exact). Although Laura hasn't been betting, she has been following the pattern of results in the game very carefully. The ball has landed in red seven times in a row. Laura concludes that black is long overdue and she jumps into the game, betting heavily on black.

Has Laura made a good bet? Do you agree with Laura's reasoning? Or do you think that Laura misunderstands the laws of probability? You'll find out momentarily, as we discuss how people reason their way to decisions—and how their reasoning can go awry.

The pioneering work of Amos Tversky and Daniel Kahneman (1974, 1982) has led to an explosion of research on risky decision making. In their efforts to identify the heuristics that people use in decision making, investigators have stumbled onto quite a few misconceptions, oversights, and illusions. It turns out that people deviate in predictable ways from optimal decision strategies—with alarming regularity. As a whole, many decisions are not as rational or as systematic as people believe they are. Fortunately, there is evidence that increased awareness of common shortcomings in reasoning about decisions can lead to improved decision making (Agnoli & Krantz, 1989; Fischhoff, 1982; Keren, 1990). With this goal in mind, let's look at some common pitfalls in decision making.

The Gambler's Fallacy

As you may have guessed by now, Laura's reasoning in our opening scenario is flawed. A great many people tend to believe that Laura has made a good bet (Tversky & Kahneman, 1982). However, they're wrong. Laura's behavior illustrates **the *gambler's fallacy*—the belief that the odds of a chance event increase if the event hasn't occurred recently.** People believe that the laws of probability should yield fair results and that a random process must be self-correcting. These aren't bad assumptions in the long run. However, they don't apply to individual, independent events.

The roulette wheel does not remember its recent results and make adjustments for them. Each spin of the wheel is an independent event. The probability of black on each spin remains at .474, even if red comes up 100 times in a row! The gambler's fallacy reflects the pervasive influence of the *representativeness heuristic*. In betting on black, Laura is predicting that future results will be more representative of a random process. This logic can be used to estimate the probability of black across a *string of spins*. But it doesn't apply to a *specific spin* of the roulette wheel.

Ignoring Base Rates and the Laws of Probability

Steve is very shy and withdrawn, invariably helpful, but with little interest in people or in the world of reality. A meek and tidy soul, he has a need for order and structure and a passion for detail. Do you think Steve is a salesperson or a librarian? (Adapted from Tversky & Kahneman, 1974, p. 1124)

Using the *representativeness heuristic*, subjects tend to guess that Steve is a librarian because he resembles their prototype of a librarian (Tversky & Kahneman, 1982). In reality, this is not a very wise guess, because it *ignores the base rates* of librarians and salespeople in the population. Virtually everyone knows that salespeople outnumber librarians by a wide margin (roughly 75 to 1 in the United States). This fact makes it much more likely that Steve is in sales. But in estimating probabilities, people often ignore information on base rates.

Obviously, people do not always neglect base rate information (Bar-Hillel, 1990). However, people are particularly bad about applying base rates to themselves. For instance, Weinstein (1984) found that people underestimated the risks of their own health-impairing habits while viewing others' risks much more accurately. Thus, smokers were realistic in estimating the degree to which smoking increases someone else's risk of heart attack but underestimated the risk for themselves. Similarly, people starting new companies ignore the high failure rate for new businesses, and burglars underestimate the likelihood that they will end up in jail. Thus, in risky decision making, people often think that they can beat the odds. As Amos Tversky puts it, "People treat their own cases as if they were unique, rather than part of a huge lottery. You hear this silly argument that 'The odds don't apply to me.' Why should God, or whoever runs this lottery, give you special treatment?" (McKean, 1985, p. 27).

The Conjunction Fallacy

Imagine that you're going to meet a man who is an articulate, ambitious, power-hungry wheeler-dealer. Do you think it's more likely that he's a college teacher or a college teacher who's also a politician?

People tend to guess that the man is a "college teacher who's a politician" because the description fits with the typical

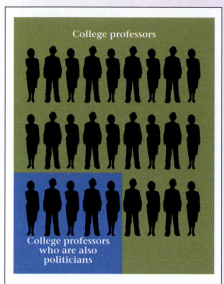

Figure 8.21
The conjunction fallacy. People routinely fall victim to the conjunction fallacy, but as this diagram makes obvious, the probability of being in a subcategory (college teachers who are politicians) cannot be higher than the probability of being in the broader category (college teachers). As this case illustrates, it often helps to represent a problem in a diagram.

prototype of politicians. But stop and think for a moment. The broader category of college teachers completely includes the smaller subcategory of college teachers who are politicians (see Figure 8.21). The probability of being in the subcategory cannot be higher than the probability of being in the broader category. It's a logical impossibility!

Tversky and Kahneman (1983) call this error the *conjunction fallacy*. **The *conjunction fallacy* occurs when people estimate that the odds of two uncertain events happening together are greater than the odds of either event happening alone.** The conjunction fallacy has been observed in a number of studies and has generally been attributed to the powerful influence of the representativeness heuristic (Birnbaum, Anderson, & Hynan, 1990), although other factors may also contribute (Gavanski & Roskos-Ewoldsen, 1991).

The Law of Small Numbers

*Envision a small urn filled with a mixture of red and green beads. You know that two-thirds of the beads are one color and one-*third *are the other color. However, you don't know whether red or green predominates. A blindfolded person reaches into the urn and comes up with 3 red beads and 1 green bead. These beads are put back in the urn and a second person scoops up 14 red beads and 10 green beads. Both samplings suggest that red beads outnumber green beads in the urn. But which sample provides better evidence? (Adapted from McKean, 1985, p. 25)*

Many subjects report that the first sampling is more convincing, because of the greater preponderance of red over green. What are the actual odds that each sampling accurately reflects the dominant color in the urn? The odds for the first sampling are 4 to 1. These aren't bad odds, but the odds that the second sampling is accurate are much higher—16 to 1. Why? Because the second sample is substantially larger than the first. The likelihood of misleading results is much greater in a small sample than a large one. For example, in flipping a fair coin, the odds of getting all heads in a sample of 5 coin flips dwarfs the odds of getting all heads in a sample of 100 coin flips.

Most people appreciate the value of a large sample as an abstract principle, but they don't fully understand that results based on small samples are more variable and more likely to be a fluke (Well, Pollatsek, & Boyce, 1990). Hence, they frequently assume that results based on small samples are representative of the population. Tversky and Kahneman (1971) call this the *belief in the law of small numbers*. This misplaced faith in small numbers explains why people are often willing to draw general conclusions based on a few individual cases.

Overestimating the Improbable

Various causes of death are paired up below. In each pairing, which is the more likely cause of death?

Cause of Death	Rate	Cause of Death	Rate
Asthma	920	Tornadoes	44
Syphilis	200	Botulism	1
Tuberculosis	1,800	Floods	100
Suicide	12,000	Homicide	9,200

TABLE 8.4 ACTUAL MORTALITY RATES FOR SELECTED CAUSES OF DEATH

Note: Mortality rates are per 1 billion people and are based on U.S. statistics. Source: Halpern (1996)

Asthma or tornadoes?
Syphilis or botulism (food poisoning)?
Tuberculosis or floods?
Suicide or murder?

Table 8.4 shows the actual mortality rates for each of the causes of death just listed. As you can see, the first choice in each pair is the more common cause of death. If you guessed wrong for several pairings, don't feel bad. Like many other people, you may be a victim of the tendency to *overestimate the improbable*. People tend to greatly overestimate the likelihood of dramatic, vivid—but infrequent—events that receive heavy media coverage. Thus, the number of fatalities due to tornadoes, floods, food poisonings, and murders is usually overestimated (Slovic, Fischhoff, & Lichtenstein, 1982). Fatalities due to asthma and other common diseases, which receive less media coverage, tend to be underestimated. For instance, a majority of subjects estimate that tornadoes kill more people than asthma, even though asthma fatalities outnumber tornado fatalities by a ratio of over 20 to 1. This tendency to exaggerate the improbable reflects the operation of the *availability heuristic*. Instances of floods, tornadoes, and such are readily available in memory because people are exposed to a great deal of publicity about such events.

Confirmation Bias and Belief Perseverance

Imagine a young physician examining a sick patient. The patient is complaining of a high fever and a sore throat. The physician must decide on a diagnosis from among a

The *availability heuristic* can be dramatized by juxtaposing the unrelated phenomena of floods and tuberculosis. Many people are killed by floods, but far more die from TB. However, since the news media report flood fatalities with frequency and rarely focus on deaths by TB, people tend to give a higher probability rating to risk from the weather element than to the disease.

myriad possible diseases. The physician thinks that it may be the flu. She asks the patient if he feels "achey all over." The answer is "yes." The physician asks if the symptoms began a few days ago. Again, the response is "yes." The physician concludes that the patient has the flu. (Adapted from Halpern, 1984, pp. 215–216)

Do you see any flaws in the physician's reasoning? Has she probed into the causes of the patient's malady effectively? No, she has asked about symptoms that would be consistent with her preliminary diagnosis, but she has not inquired about symptoms that could rule it out. Her questioning of the patient illustrates *confirmation bias*—**the tendency to seek information that supports one's decisions and beliefs while ignoring disconfirming information.** This bias is common in medical diagnosis and other forms of decision making (Green, 1990; Klayman & Ha, 1987). There's nothing wrong with searching for confirming evidence to support one's decisions. However, people should also seek

disconfirming evidence—which they often neglect to do.

Confirmation bias contributes to another, related problem called *belief perseverance*—**the tendency to hang onto beliefs in the face of contradictory evidence** (Gorman, 1989). It is difficult to dislodge an idea after having embraced it. To investigate this phenomenon, researchers have given subjects evidence to establish a belief (example: high risk takers make better firefighters) and later exposed the subjects to information discrediting the idea. These studies have shown that the disconfirming evidence tends to fall on deaf ears (Ross & Anderson, 1982). Thus, once people arrive at a decision, they are prone to accept supportive evidence at face value while subjecting contradictory evidence to tough, skeptical scrutiny.

The Overconfidence Effect

Make high and low estimates of the total U.S. Defense Department budget in 1986.

Choose estimates far enough apart to be 98% confident that the actual figure lies between them. In other words, you should feel that there is only a 2% chance that the correct figure is lower than your low estimate or higher than your high estimate. Write your estimates in the spaces provided, before reading further.

High estimate:_____
Low estimate:_____

When working on problems like this one, people reason their way to their best estimate and then create a confidence interval around it. For instance, let's say that you arrived at $200 billion as your best estimate of the defense budget. You would then expand a range around that estimate—say $150 billion to $250 billion—that you're sure will contain the correct figure. The answer in this case is $286 billion. If the answer falls outside your estimated range, you are not unusual. In making this type of estimate, people consistently tend to make their confidence intervals too narrow (Lichtenstein, Fischhoff, & Phillips, 1982). For example, subjects' 98% confidence intervals should include the correct answer 98% of the time, but they actually do so only about 60% of the time.

The crux of the problem is that people tend to put too much faith in their estimates, beliefs, and decisions, even when they should know better, a principle called the *overconfidence effect* (Gigerenzer, Hoffrage, & Kleinbölting, 1991). This effect is seen even when people make probability predictions about themselves. For instance, in one study (Vallone et al., 1990), college students were asked to make predictions about personal matters for the upcoming fall quarter and the entire academic year. Their predictions concerned such things as whether they would drop any courses, whether they would vote in an upcoming election, or whether they would break up with their boyfriend or girlfriend. The subjects were also asked to rate their confidence in each of their predictions, from 50% confidence to 100% confidence (the predictions were either-or propositions, making 50% a chance level of accuracy and the lowest possible level of confidence). The accuracy of the subjects' predictions was assessed at the end of the year. The analyses of thousands of predictions revealed that the students were more confident than accurate. Moreover, the more confident subjects were about their predictions, the more likely it was that they were *over*confident (see Figure 8.22).

The overconfidence effect is also seen among experts in many walks of life (Fischhoff, 1988). Studies have shown that physicians, weather forecasters, military leaders, gamblers, investors, and scientists tend to be overconfident about their predictions. As Daniel Kahneman puts it, "The human mind suppresses uncertainty. We're not only convinced that we know more about our politics, our businesses, and our spouses than we really do, but also that what we don't know must be unimportant" (McKean, 1985, p. 27). Thus, in making major decisions, it usually pays to gather as much information as possible and to move forward cautiously.

Recap of Key Points

• The heuristics that people use in decision making lead to various flaws in reasoning. For instance, the use of the representative-

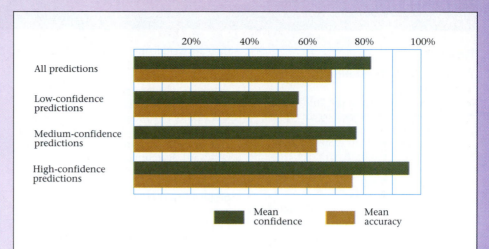

Figure 8.22
Results of the Vallone et al. (1990) study. The subjects in this study (sample 1) made 3776 predictions about personal matters. Their mean confidence level for all these predictions was 82.3%, but their mean accuracy was only 68.2%. When the predictions were divided into low-, medium-, and high-confidence predictions, an interesting pattern emerged. As subjects' confidence level went up, the gap between their confidence and their accuracy increased. This finding suggests that the more confident you are about a personal projection, the more likely it is that you are overconfident.

ness heuristic contributes to the gambler's fallacy, ignoring base rates, the conjunction fallacy, and faith in small numbers.
• The availability heuristic underlies the tendency to overestimate the improbable. People tend to cling to their beliefs in spite of contradictory evidence, in part because they exhibit confirmation bias—the ten-

dency to only seek information that supports one's view.
• People generally fail to appreciate these shortcomings, which leads to the overconfidence effect. Evidence suggests that the more confident you feel about a prediction, the more likely it is that you are overconfident.

Key Ideas

The Cognitive Revolution in Psychology

◆ During the first half of the 20th century, the study of cognition was largely suppressed by the theoretical dominance of behaviorism. However, the 1950s brought a cognitive revolution in psychology.

Language: Turning Thoughts into Words

◆ Chimpanzees can learn signs or symbols to represent words and can combine them to communicate with their caretakers. However, some theorists doubt whether chimps really learn rules of language. In the Featured Study, Sue Savage-Rumbaugh and her colleagues demonstrated that Kanzi was capable of generating spontaneous sentences that followed rules relating to the ordering of words.

◆ Languages are symbolic, semantic, generative, and structured. Human languages are structured hierarchically. Humans' remarkable ability to learn language is probably a product of natural selection.

◆ Long before they utter their first words, infants are making progress in mastering the sound structure of their native language. Children typically utter their first words around their first birthday. Vocabulary growth is slow at first, but a vocabulary spurt often begins at around 18 months.

◆ Early words are often overextended to refer to objects that look similar to the correctly named object. Single words, called holophrases, are also used to express the meaning of several words. Children begin to combine words by the end of their second year. Their early sentences are telegraphic.

◆ According to Skinner and other behaviorists, children acquire a language through imitation and reinforcement. Nativist theories assert that humans have an innate capacity to learn language rules. Today, theorists are moving toward interactionist perspectives, which emphasize the role of both biology and experience.

◆ The theory of linguistic relativity asserts that language determines thought, thus suggesting that people from different cultures may think about the world somewhat differently. To date, the balance of evidence suggests that thought determines language more than vice versa and that cognitive processes are largely invariant across cultures.

Problem Solving: In Search of Solutions

◆ Psychologists have differentiated among several types of problems, including problems of inducing structure, problems of transformation, and problems of arangement. Problems vary in the degree to which

they are well defined. Common barriers to problem solving include functional fixedness, mental set, getting bogged down in irrelevant information, and placing unnecessary constraints on one's solutions.

◆ A variety of strategies, or heuristics, are used for solving problems, including means/ends analysis, forming subgoals, working backward, searching for analogies, and changing the representation of a problem.

◆ Experts are better than novices at solving problems in their domain of expertise because they make better use of working memory, planning, and evaluation. Experts also tend to be better at identifying useful analogies between problems. Ultimately, expertise appears to be the product of extensive training and intense practice.

◆ Because of varied ecological demands, some cultures encourage a field-dependent cognitive style, whereas others foster more field independence. People who are field independent tend to analyze and restructure problems more than those who are field dependent.

Decision Making: Choices and Chances

◆ An additive model is used when people make decisions by rating the attributes of each alternative and selecting the alternative that has the highest sum of ratings. When elimination by aspects is used, people gradually eliminate alternatives if their attributes fail to satisfy some minimum criterion. Some studies suggest that it may be possible for people to think too much about decisions.

◆ Models of how people make risky decisions focus on the expected value or subjective utility of various outcomes and the objective or subjective probability that these outcomes will occur. People use the representativeness and availability heuristics in estimating probabilities. Decisions can be influenced by how they are framed and the desire to avoid regret about making a bad decision.

Putting It in Perspective

◆ Four of our unifying themes surfaced in the chapter. Our discussion of language acquisition revealed once again that all aspects of behavior are shaped by both nature and nurture. The recent progress in the study of cognitive processes showed how science depends on empirical methods. Research on decision making illustrated the importance of subjective perceptions. We also saw that cognitive processes are moderated—to a limited degree—by cultural factors.

Application: Understanding Pitfalls in Reasoning About Decisions

◆ The heuristics that people use in decision making lead to various flaws in reasoning.

For instance, the use of the representativeness heuristic contributes to the gambler's fallacy, ignoring base rates, the conjunction fallacy, and faith in small numbers. The availability heuristic underlies the tendency to overestimate the improbable.

◆ People tend to cling to their beliefs in spite of contradictory evidence, in part because they exhibit confirmation bias—the tendency to only seek information that supports one's view. People generally fail to appreciate these shortcomings, which leads to the overconfidence effect.

Key Terms

Algorithm
Availability heuristic
Belief perseverance
Cognition
Compensatory decision models
Confirmation bias
Conjunction fallacy
Decision making
Deep structure
Expertise
Fast mapping
Field dependence–independence
Framing
Functional fixedness
Gambler's fallacy
Heuristic
Holophrases
Ill-defined problems
Insight
Language
Language acquisition device (LAD)
Linguistic relativity
Mean length of utterance (MLU)
Means/ends analysis
Mental set
Metacognition

Metalinguistic awareness
Morphemes
Noncompensatory decision models
Overextension
Overregularization
Phonemes
Problem solving
Problem space
Psycholinguistics
Representativeness heuristic
Risky decision making
Surface structure
Syntax
Telegraphic speech
Trial and error
Well-defined problems

Key People

Noam Chomsky
Daniel Kahneman
Sue Savage-Rumbaugh
Herbert Simon
B. F. Skinner
Amos Tversky

Practice Test

1. The results of the Featured Study by Savage-Rumbaugh et al. (1986) provide support for the hypothesis that:
   A. chimps may be able to use rules of language to produce spontaneous sentences.
   B. with special training, chimps can learn an oral language.
   C. chimps that have appeared to use language have simply learned to make certain responses to earn reinforcement.
   D. chimps can learn words, but cannot combine them into sentences.

2. Which statement best summarizes the current status of the ape language controversy?
   A. Chimps can acquire the use of symbols, but cannot combine them into phrases or sentences.
   B. Chimps are as well suited for learning and using language as humans.
   C. Chimps are incapable even of learning the symbols of a language.
   D. Language may not be a uniquely human capacity, but the linguistic capacities of humans are far superior.

3. The 2-year-old child who refers to every four-legged animal as "doggie" is making which of the following errors?
   A. underextension
   B. overextension
   C. overregularization
   D. underregularization

4. Chomsky proposed that children learn a language:
   A. because they possess an innate language acquisition device.
   B. through imitation, reinforcement, and shaping.
   C. as the quality of their thought improves with age.
   D. because they need to in order to get their increasingly complex needs met.

5. The linguistic relativity hypothesis is the notion that:
   A. one's language determines the nature of one's thought.
   B. one's thought determines the nature of one's language.
   C. language and thought are separate and independent processes.
   D. language and thought interact, with each influencing the other.

6. Arrangement problems are generally solved _____; transformation problems are generally solved _____.
   A. suddenly; gradually
   B. suddenly; suddenly
   C. gradually; suddenly
   D. gradually; gradually

7. Problems that require a common object to be used in an unusual way may be difficult to solve because of:
   A. mental set.
   B. irrelevant information.
   C. unnecessary constraints.
   D. functional fixedness.

8. A heuristic is:
   A. a flash of insight.
   B. a guiding principle or "rule of thumb" used in problem solving.
   C. a methodical procedure for trying all possible solutions to a problem.
   D. a way of making a compensatory decision.

9. In solving problems, people who are field dependent:
   A. rely on external frames of reference.
   B. tend to accept the physical environment as a given.
   C. tend to focus on specific features of a problem.
   D. all of the above.
   E. a and b

10. The field-independent style is predominant in:
    A. Western societies.
    B. sedentary agricultural societies.
    C. societies that stress strict child-rearing practices.
    D. all of the above.

11. _____ decision models allow attractive attributes to compensate for unattractive attributes; _____ decision models do not allow some attributes to compensate for others.
    A. Compensatory; noncompensatory
    B. Noncompensatory; additive
    C. Noncompensatory; compensatory
    D. Compensatory; nonadditive

12. When you estimate the probability of an event by judging the ease with which relevant instances come to mind, you are relying on:
    A. an additive decision-making model.
    B. the representativeness heuristic.
    C. the availability heuristic.
    D. a noncompensatory model.

13. Which of the following statements is (are) true?
    A. People often allow a decision to be framed by the language or context in which it is presented.
    B. When the probability of an outcome is stated in terms of success, people tend to reject that alternative.
    C. When the probability of an outcome is stated in terms of failure, people tend to accept that alternative.
    D. All of the above.

14. The belief that the probability of heads is higher after a long string of tails:
    A. is rational and accurate.
    B. is an example of the "gambler's fallacy."
    C. reflects the influence of the representativeness heuristic.
    D. b and c.

15. The more confident you are about your predictions of upcoming events in your life:
    A. the less likely it is that your predictions are accurate.
    B. the less likely it is that your predictions are overconfident.
    C. the more likely it is that your predictions are overconfident.
    D. a and b.

Answers

1	A	Pages 304–305	6	A	Page 315	11	A	Pages 326–327
2	D	Page 307	7	D	Page 317	12	C	Page 329
3	B	Page 309	8	B	Page 318	13	A	Pages 329–330
4	A	Page 311	9	E	Page 324	14	D	Page 332
5	A	Page 313	10	A	Page 325	15	C	Pages 334–335

9 INTELLIGENCE AND PSYCHOLOGICAL TESTING

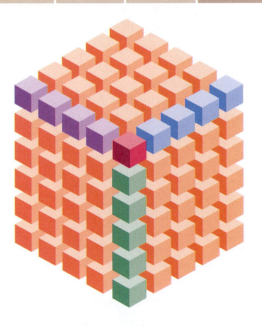

Have you ever thought about the role that psychological testing has played in your life? In all likelihood, your years in grade school and high school were punctuated with a variety of intelligence tests, achievement tests, creativity tests, aptitude tests, and occupational interest tests. In the lower grades, you were probably given standardized achievement tests once or twice a year. For instance, you may have taken the Iowa Tests of Basic Skills, which measured your progress in reading, language, vocabulary, mathematics, and study skills. Perhaps you still have vivid memories of the serious atmosphere in the classroom, the very formal instructions ("Do not break the seal on this test until your examiner tells you to do so"), and the heavy pressure to work fast (I can still see Sister Dominic marching back and forth with her intense gaze riveted on her stopwatch).

Where you're sitting at this very moment may have been influenced by your performance on standardized tests. That is, the college you chose to attend may have hinged on your SAT or ACT scores. Moreover, your interactions with standardized tests may be far from finished. Even at this point in your life, you may be selecting your courses to gear up for the Graduate Record Exam (GRE), the Law School Admission Test (LSAT), the Medical College Admission Test (MCAT), or certification tests in fields such as accounting or nursing. After graduation, when you go job hunting, you may find that prospective employers expect you to take still more batteries of psychological tests as they attempt to assess your personality, your motivation, and your talents.

The vast enterprise of modern testing evolved from psychologists' pioneering efforts to measure *general intelligence*. The first useful intelligence tests, which were created soon after the turn of the century, left a great many "descendants." Today, there are over 2600 published psychological tests that measure a diverse array of mental abilities and other behavioral traits (Katz & Slomka, 1990). Indeed, psychological testing has become a big business that annually generates millions of dollars of revenues.

Clearly, American society has embraced psychological testing (Hanson, 1993). Each year in the United States alone, people take *hundreds of millions* of intelligence and achievement tests (Medina & Neill, 1990). Scholarships, degrees, jobs, and self-concepts are on the line as Americans attempt to hurdle a seemingly endless succession of tests. Because your life is so strongly affected by how you perform on psychological tests, it pays to be aware of their strengths and limitations. In this chapter we'll explore many questions about testing, including the following:

• How did psychological testing become so prevalent in modern society?
• How do psychologists judge the validity of their tests?
• What exactly do intelligence tests measure?
• Is intelligence inherited? If so, to what extent?
• How do psychological tests measure creativity?

We'll begin by introducing some basic concepts in psychological testing. Then we'll explore the history of intelligence tests, because they provided the model for subsequent psychological tests. Next we'll address practical questions about how intelligence tests work. After examining the nature versus nurture debate as it relates to intelligence, we'll explore some new directions in the study of intelligence. In the Application, we'll discuss efforts to measure and understand another type of mental ability: creativity.

Most children become familiar with standardized psychological tests—intelligence, achievement, and aptitude tests—in school settings.

A *psychological test* is a standardized measure of a sample of a person's behavior. Psychological tests are measurement instruments. They're used to measure the *individual differences* that exist among people in abilities, aptitudes, interests, and aspects of personality.

Your responses to a psychological test represent a *sample* of your behavior. The word *sample* should alert you to one of the key limitations of psychological tests: A particular behavior sample may not be representative of your characteristic behavior. Everyone has bad days. A stomachache, a fight with a friend, a problem with your car—all might affect your responses to a particular test on a particular day.

This sampling problem is not unique to psychological testing. It's an unavoidable problem for any measurement technique that relies on sampling. For example, a physician taking your blood pressure might get an unrepresentative reading. Likewise, a football scout clocking a prospect's 40-yard sprint time might get a misleading figure. Because of the limitations of the sampling process, test scores should always be interpreted *cautiously.* Many psychological tests are precise measurement devices. However, because of the ever-present sampling problem, test results should *not* be viewed as the final word on one's personality and abilities.

Principal Types of Tests 7a

Psychological tests are used extensively in research, but most of them were developed to serve a practical purpose outside of the laboratory. Most tests can be placed in one of two broad categories: mental ability tests and personality tests.

Mental Ability Tests

Psychological testing originated with efforts to measure general mental ability. Today, tests of mental abilities remain the most common kind of psychological test. This broad class of tests includes three principal subcategories: intelligence tests, aptitude tests, and achievement tests.

Intelligence tests measure general mental ability. They're intended to assess intellectual potential rather than previous learning or accumulated knowledge. *Aptitude tests* are also designed to measure potential more than knowledge, but they break mental ability into separate components. Thus, **aptitude tests assess specific types of mental abilities.** For example, the Differential Aptitude

Tests assess verbal reasoning, numerical ability, abstract reasoning, perceptual speed and accuracy, mechanical reasoning, space relations, spelling, and language usage (see Figure 9.1). Like aptitude tests, *achievement tests* have a specific focus, but they're supposed to measure previous learning instead of potential. Thus, **achievement tests gauge a person's mastery and knowledge of various subjects** (such as reading, English, or history).

Personality Tests

If you had to describe yourself in a few words, what words would you use? Are you introverted? Independent? Ambitious? Enterprising? Conventional? Assertive? Domineering? Words such as these refer to personality traits. These *traits* can be assessed systematically with over 500 personality tests. *Personality tests* measure various aspects of personality, including motives, interests, values, and attitudes. Many psychologists prefer to call these tests personality *scales* because, unlike tests of mental abilities, the questions do not have right and wrong answers. We'll look at the different types of personality scales in our upcoming chapter on personality (Chapter 12).

Standardization and Norms 7b

Both personality scales and tests of mental abilities are *standardized* measures of behavior. **Standardization refers to the uniform procedures used in the administration and scoring of a test.** All subjects get the same instructions, the same questions, and the same time limits, so that their scores can be compared meaningfully. This means, for instance, that a person taking the Differential Aptitude Tests (DAT) in 1975 in San Diego, and another taking the DAT in 1985 in Atlanta, and another taking it in 1995 in Peoria all confront exactly the same test-taking task.

The standardization of a test's scoring system includes the development of test norms. **Test norms provide information about where a score on a psychological test ranks in relation to other scores on that test.** Why are test norms needed? Because in psychological testing, everything is relative. Psychological tests tell you how you score *relative to other people.* They tell you, for instance, that you are average in creativity or slightly above average in clerical ability. These interpretations are derived from the test norms that help you understand what your test score means.

Verbal reasoning

Choose the correct pair of words to fill the blanks. The first word of the pair goes in the blank space at the beginning of the sentence; the second word of the pair goes in the blank at the end of the sentence.

_____ is to fin as bird is to _____

A water–feather **C** fish–wing
B shark–nest **D** flipper–fly
E fish–sky

The correct answer is **C**.

Numerical reasoning

Choose the correct answer for the problem.

$$\begin{array}{r} 18 \\ 10 \\ +17 \\ \hline \end{array}$$

A 13
B 11
C 7
D 6
E none of these

The correct answer is **E**.

Abstract reasoning

The four "problem figures" make a series. Find the one among the "answer figures" that would be next in the series.

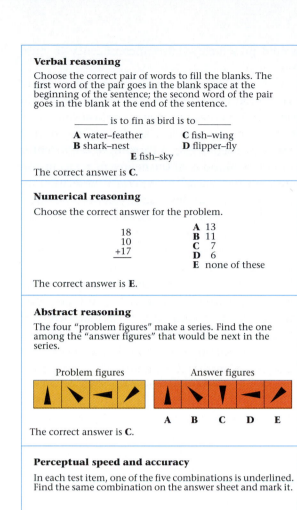

Problem figures   Answer figures

A B C D E

The correct answer is **C**.

Perceptual speed and accuracy

In each test item, one of the five combinations is underlined. Find the same combination on the answer sheet and mark it.

Test items | Sample of answer sheet

1. XY Xy XX <u>YX</u> Yy
2. 6g <u>6G</u> G6 Gg g6
3. <u>nm</u> mn mm nn nv

1 Xy Yy YX XX XY
2 g6 Gg 6g G6 6G
3 nn mn nv nm mm

Mechanical reasoning

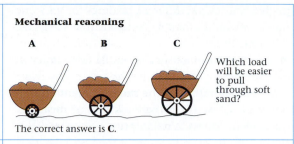

A   B   C

Which load will be easier to pull through soft sand?

The correct answer is **C**.

Space relations

Which one of the following figures could be made by folding the pattern at the left? The pattern always shows the outside of the figure.

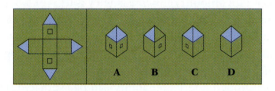

A B C D

The correct answer is **C**.

Spelling

Decide which word is not spelled correctly.

A numeral
B interest
C desloyal
D salary

The correct answer is **C**.

Language usage

Decide which of the lettered parts of the sentence contains an error and mark the corresponding letter on the answer sheet. If there is no error, mark *No Error*.

Jane and Tom / is going / to the office / this morning.
A   **B**   **C**   **D**

The correct answer is **B**.

Usually, test norms allow you to convert your "raw score" on a test into a *percentile*. A *percentile score* indicates the percentage of people who score at or below the score one has obtained. For example, imagine that you take a 40-item assertiveness scale and obtain a raw score of 26. In other words, you indicate a preference for the assertive option on 26 of the questions. Your score of 26 has little meaning until you consult the test norms and find out that it places you at the 82nd percentile. This normative information would indicate that you appear to be as or more assertive than 82% of the sample of people who provided the basis for the test norms.

The sample of people that the norms are based on is called a test's *standardization group*. Ideally, test norms are based on a large sample of people who were carefully selected to be representative of the broader population. For example, the norms for most intelligence tests are based on samples of 2000–6000 people whose demographic characteristics closely match the overall demographics of the United States (Woodcock, 1994). Although intelligence tests have been standardized pretty carefully, the representativeness of standardization groups for other types of tests varies considerably from one test to another.

Reliability 7b

Any kind of measuring device, whether it's a tire gauge, a stopwatch, or a psychological test, should be reasonably consistent. That is, repeated measurements should yield reasonably similar results. Psychologists call this quality *reliability*. To better appreciate the importance of reliability, think about how you would react if a tire pressure gauge were to give you several different readings for the same tire. You would probably conclude that the gauge is broken and toss it into the trash. Consistency in measurement obviously is essential to accuracy in measurement.

***Reliability* refers to the measurement consistency of a test (or of other kinds of measurement techniques).** A reliable test is one that yields similar results on repetition of the test. Like most other types of measuring devices, psychological tests are not perfectly reliable. That is, they usually don't yield exactly the same scores when repeated. A certain amount of inconsistency is unavoidable, because human behavior is variable. For example, if you take the Beck Depression Inventory on two different occasions, you're not likely to respond to all 21 items in the same way both times.

Although a test's reliability can be estimated in several ways, the most widely used approach is to check test-retest reliability. ***Test-retest reliability* is estimated by comparing subjects' scores on two administrations of a test.** If we wanted to check the test-retest reliability of a newly developed test of assertiveness, we would ask a group of subjects to take the test on two occasions, probably a few weeks apart (see Figure 9.2). The underlying assumption is that assertiveness is a fairly stable aspect of personality that won't change in a matter of a few weeks. Thus, changes in subjects' scores across the two administrations of the test

would presumably reflect inconsistency in measurement.

Reliability estimates require the computation of correlation coefficients, which we introduced in Chapter 2. Correlation plays a critical role in research on testing, so let's reexamine the concept briefly (see Figure 9.3). **A *correlation coefficient* is a numerical index of the degree of relationship between two variables.** A *positive* correlation indicates that two variables covary in the *same* direction. Thus, high scores on variable X are associated with high scores on variable Y, and low scores on X tend to go with low scores on Y. A *negative* correlation indicates that two variables covary in the *opposite* direction. Hence, high scores on X are associated with low scores on Y, and high scores on Y go with low scores on X. The actual coefficient of correlation can vary between 0 and +1.00. The closer a correlation comes to either +1.00 or –1.00 (that is, the farther it is from 0), the stronger the association between the two variables.

In estimating test-retest reliability, the two variables that must be correlated are the two sets of scores from the two administrations of the test. If people get fairly similar scores on the two administrations of our hypothetical assertiveness test, this consistency yields a substantial positive correlation. The magnitude of the correlation gives us a precise indication of the test's consistency. The closer the correlation comes to +1.00, the more reliable the test is.

There are no absolute guidelines about acceptable levels of reliability. What's acceptable depends to some extent on the nature and purpose of the test (Reynolds, 1994). The reliability estimates for most psychological tests are above .70. Many exceed .90. The higher the reliability coefficient, the more consistent the test is. As reliability goes down, concern about measurement error increases.

Validity ⟨7b⟩

Even if a test is quite reliable, we still need to be concerned about its validity. ***Validity* refers to the ability of a test to measure what it was designed to measure.** If we develop a new test of assertiveness, we have to provide some evidence that it really measures assertiveness. Increasingly, the term *validity* is also used to refer to the accuracy or usefulness of the *inferences* or *decisons* based on a test (Moss, 1994). This broader conception of validity highlights the fact that a specific test might be valid for one purpose, such as placing students

Figure 9.2
Test-retest reliability.
Subjects' scores on the first administration of an assertiveness test are represented on the left, and their scores on a second administration of the same test a few weeks later are shown on the right. If subjects obtain similar scores on both administrations, as in the top graph, the test measures assertiveness consistently and has high reliability. If they get very different scores on the second administration, as in the bottom graph, the test has low reliability.

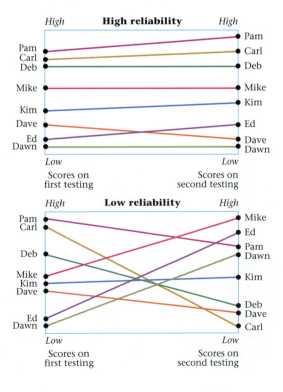

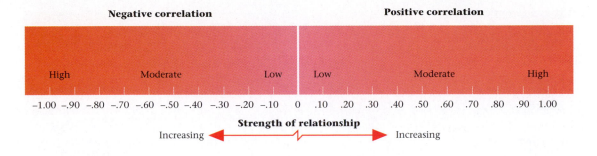

Figure 9.3
Correlation and reliability. As explained in Chapter 2, a positive correlation means that two variables covary in the *same* direction; a negative correlation means that two variables covary in the *opposite* direction. The closer the correlation coefficient gets to either −1.00 or +1.00, the stronger the relationship. At a minimum, reliability estimates for psychological tests must be moderately high positive correlations.

in school, and invalid for another purpose, such as making employment decisions for a particular occupation. Validity can be estimated in several ways, depending on the nature and purpose of a test (Golden, Sawicki, & Franzen, 1990).

Content Validity

Achievement tests and educational tests such as classroom exams should have adequate content validity. **Content validity refers to the degree to which the content of a test is representative of the domain it's supposed to cover.** Imagine a poorly prepared physics exam that includes questions on material that were not covered in class or in assigned reading. The professor has compromised the content validity of the exam. Content validity is evaluated with logic more than with statistics.

Criterion-Related Validity

Psychological tests are often used to make predictions about specific aspects of individuals' behavior. They are used to predict performance in college, job capability, and suitability for training programs, as just a few examples. Criterion-related validity is a central concern in such cases. **Criterion-related validity is estimated by correlating subjects' scores on a test with their scores on an independent criterion (another measure) of the trait assessed by the test.**

For example, let's say you developed a test to measure aptitude for becoming an airplane pilot. You could check its validity by correlating subjects' scores on your aptitude test with subsequent ratings of their performance in their pilot training (see Figure 9.4). The performance ratings would be the independent criterion of pilot aptitude. If your test has reasonable validity, people who score high on the test should tend to earn high performance ratings during training, and low scorers should tend to get low ratings. In other words, there ought to be a reasonably strong positive correlation between the test and the criterion measure.

Such a correlation would help validate your test's predictive ability.

Construct Validity

Many psychological tests attempt to measure abstract personal qualities, such as creativity, intelligence, extraversion, or independence. No obvious criterion measures exist for these abstract qualities, which are called *hypothetical constructs*. In measuring abstract qualities, psychologists are concerned about **construct validity—the extent to which there is evidence that a test measures a particular hypothetical construct.**

The process of demonstrating construct validity can be complicated. It usually requires a series of studies that examine the correlations between the test and various measures *related* to the trait in question. A thorough demonstration of construct validity requires looking at the relations between a test and many related measures. For example, some

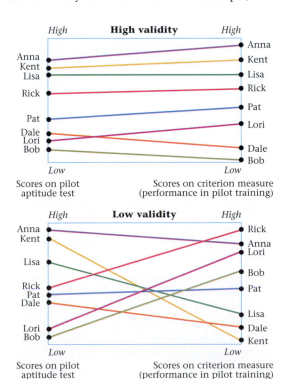

Figure 9.4
Criterion-related validity. To evaluate the criterion-related validity of a pilot aptitude test, a psychologist would correlate subjects' test scores with a criterion measure of their aptitude, such as ratings of their performance in a pilot training program. Test validity is high if scores on the two measures are highly correlated. If little or no relationship exists between the two sets of scores, validity is low, which means that the aptitude test does not measure what it is supposed to measure.

Figure 9.5
Construct validity.
Psychologists evaluate a scale's construct validity by studying how scores on the scale correlate with a variety of variables. For example, some of the evidence on the construct validity of the Expression Scale from the Psychological Screening Inventory is summarized here. This scale is supposed to measure the personality trait of *extraversion*. As you can see on the left side of this network of correlations, the scale correlates negatively with measures of social introversion, social discomfort, and neuroticism, just as one would expect if the scale is really tapping extraversion. On the right, you can see that the scale is correlated positively with measures of sociability and self-acceptance and another index of extraversion, as one would anticipate. At the bottom, you can see how the scale correlates with several traits that should be unrelated to extraversion: responsibility, intelligence, and tolerance. These correlations are close to zero, as they should be. Thus, the network of correlations depicted here supports the idea that the Expression Scale measures extraversion.

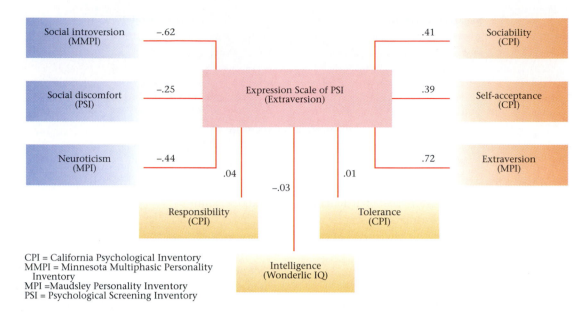

CPI = California Psychological Inventory
MMPI = Minnesota Multiphasic Personality Inventory
MPI = Maudsley Personality Inventory
PSI = Psychological Screening Inventory

of the evidence on the construct validity of a measure of extraversion (the Expression scale from the Psychological Screening Inventory) is summarized in Figure 9.5. This network of correlation coefficients shows that the Expression scale correlates negatively, positively, or not at all, with various measures, much as one would expect if the scale is really assessing extraversion. Ultimately, it's the overall pattern of correlations that provides convincing (or unconvincing) evidence of a test's construct validity.

The complexities involved in demonstrating construct validity will be apparent in our upcom-

ing discussion of intelligence testing. The ongoing debate about the construct validity of intelligence tests is one of the oldest debates in psychology. We'll look first at the origins of intelligence tests. This historical review will help you appreciate the current controversies about intelligence testing.

Recap of Key Points
• Psychological tests are standardized measures of behavior—usually mental abilities or aspects of personality. Test scores are interpreted by consulting test norms to find out what represents a high or low score.

CONCEPT CHECK 9.1
Recognizing Basic Concepts in Testing

Check your understanding of basic concepts in psychological testing by answering the questions below. Select your responses from the following concepts. The answers are in Appendix A.

Test norms   Criterion-related validity
Test-retest reliability   Construct validity
Content validity

1. At the request of the HiTechnoLand computer store chain, Professor Charlz develops a test to measure aptitude for selling computers. Two hundred applicants for sales jobs at HiTechnoLand stores are asked to take the test on two occasions, a few weeks apart. A correlation of +.82 is found between applicants' scores on the two administrations of the test. Thus, the test appears to possess reasonable

_____.

2. All 200 of these applicants are hired and put to work selling computers. After six months Professor Charlz correlates the new workers' aptitude test scores with the dollar value of the computers that each sold during the first six months on the job. This correlation turns out to be –.21. This finding suggests that the test may lack _____.

3. Back at the university, Professor Charlz is teaching a course in theories of personality. He decides to use the same midterm exam that he gave last year, even though the exam includes questions about theorists that he did not cover or assign reading on this year. There are reasons to doubt the _____ of Professor Charlz's midterm exam.

- As measuring devices, psychological tests should produce consistent results, a quality called reliability. Test-retest reliability is estimated by comparing subjects' scores on two administrations of a test. The result should be a fairly high positive correlation.
- Validity refers to the degree to which there is evidence that a test measures what it was designed to measure. Content validity is crucial on classroom tests. Criterion-related validity is critical when tests are used to predict performance. Construct validity is critical when a test is designed to measure a hypothetical construct.

THE EVOLUTION OF INTELLIGENCE TESTING

Psychological tests play a prominent role in our society, but this wasn't always so. The first psychological tests were invented only a little over a hundred years ago. Since then, the reliance on psychological tests has grown gradually. In this section, we discuss the pioneers who launched psychological testing with their efforts to measure general intelligence.

Galton's Studies of Hereditary Genius

It all began with the work of a British scholar, Sir Francis Galton, in the later part of the 19th century. Galton was a precocious child who was reading before he was age 3 and reciting Shakespeare at age 6. Although he never held an academic appointment, he made notable contributions to the fields of meteorology, photography, geography, sociology, genetics, statistics, education, and psychology (Jensen, 1994a). Galton counted the eminent naturalist Charles Darwin among his cousins. Thus, it was natural that he took an interest in how intellectual genius seems to run in families. Galton studied family trees and found that success and eminence appeared consistently in some families over generations. For the most part, these families were much like Galton's family. They were well-bred, upper-class families with access to superior schooling and to social connections that pave the way to success. Yet Galton discounted the advantages of such an upbringing. In his book *Hereditary Genius*, Galton (1869) concluded that success runs in families because great intelligence is passed from generation to generation through genetic inheritance.

Influenced by Darwin's evolutionary perspective, Galton viewed intelligence as the crucial feature of humans' fitness, which had been shaped over the course of thousands of centuries by natural selection. Galton's conviction about the importance and genetic basis of intelligence were so strong that he advocated eugenic programs. *Eugenics* **refers to efforts to control reproduction to gradually improve the hereditary characteristics in a population.** Galton wanted to encourage intellectually superior people to mate together to improve the quality of the human race. He envisioned a "golden book of natural nobility" that would list Britain's brightest young marital candidates. More disturbingly, Galton wanted to discourage (or prevent) people of lesser intelligence from having children. Fortunately, Galton never saw his dream realized. However, his ideas show that the concept of intelligence has had controversial social and political implications from the very beginning.

To show that intelligence is governed by heredity, Galton needed an objective measure of intelligence. His approach to this problem was guided by the theoretical views of his day. Thus, he assumed that the contents of the mind are built out of elementary *sensations,* and he hypothesized that exceptionally bright people should exhibit exceptional sensory acuity. Working from this premise, he tried to assess innate mental ability by measuring simple sensory processes. Among other things, he measured sensitivity to high-pitched sounds, color perception, and reaction time (the speed of one's response to a stimulus). These efforts met with little success. Research eventually showed that the sensory processes he measured were largely unrelated to other criteria of mental ability that an intelligence test ought to predict (such as success in school or professional life).

In pursuing this line of investigation, Galton coined the phrase *nature versus nurture* to refer to the heredity-environment issue (Hilgard, 1989). Along the way, he also invented the concepts of *correlation* and *percentile test scores.* Although Galton's mental tests were a failure, his work created an interest in the measurement of mental ability, setting the stage for a subsequent breakthrough by Alfred Binet, a prominent French psychologist.

Binet's Breakthrough 🌀 7c

Like Galton, Alfred Binet was a person of independent wealth who was free to study whatever he

"Imagine a Utopia . . . in which a system of competitive examinations . . . had been so developed as to embrace every important quality of mind and body, and where a considerable sum was allotted to the endowment of such marriages as promised to yield children who would grow into eminent servants of the State."

Sir Francis Galton

"The intelligence of anyone is susceptible of development. With practice, enthusiasm, and especially with method one can succeed in increasing one's attention, memory, judgment, and in becoming literally more intelligent than one was before."

ALFRED BINET

happened to find intriguing. Fortunately for psychology, after he earned his law degree and a doctorate in natural science, his interest turned to mental testing. In 1904, after some lobbying by Binet, the minister of public instruction in France asked Binet to devise a test to identify mentally subnormal children (Matarazzo, 1994). The commission was motivated by admirable goals. It wanted to single out youngsters in need of special training. It also wanted to avoid complete reliance on teachers' evaluations, which might often be subjective and biased.

In response to this need, Binet and a colleague, Theodore Simon, published a creative, new test of general mental ability in 1905 and a much-improved revision in 1908. They had the insight to load their test with items that required abstract reasoning, rather than the sensory skills measured by Galton and his followers. Their scale was a success because it was inexpensive, easy to administer, objective, and capable of predicting children's performance in school fairly well (Siegler, 1992). Thanks to these qualities, its use spread across Europe and America.

The Binet-Simon scale expressed a child's score in terms of "mental level" or "mental age." A child's *mental age* **indicated that he or she displayed the mental ability typical of a child of that chronological (actual) age.** Thus, a child with a mental age of 6 performed like the average 6-year-old on the test. Of course, if the child's chronological age was 10, this wasn't a good sign. When youngsters were found to have a mental age substantially lower than their actual age, it was inferred that they were low in intelligence. For example, if the test indicated that a 12-year-old child had a mental age of 7, the child was considered to be subnormal.

Binet realized that his scale was a somewhat crude initial effort at measuring mental ability. He revised it again in 1911. Unfortunately, his revising came to an abrupt end with his death in 1911. However, other psychologists continued to build on Binet's work. Lewis Terman and David

Wechsler picked up the torch for the testing movement.

Terman and the Stanford-Binet 7c

In America, Binet's test was initially put into use by Henry Goddard (1908). He translated the test into English with virtually no changes in content. However, Lewis Terman and his colleagues at Stanford University soon went to work on a major expansion and revision of the test. Their work led to the 1916 publication of the Stanford-Binet Intelligence Scale (Terman, 1916). Although this revision was quite loyal to Binet's original conceptions, it incorporated a new scoring scheme based on the "intelligence quotient" suggested by William Stern (1914). **An *intelligence quotient (IQ)* is a child's mental age divided by chronological age, multiplied by 100.** As you can see below, IQ scores originally involved actual quotients:

$$IQ = \frac{\text{Mental age}}{\text{Chronological age}} \times 100$$

The ratio of mental age to chronological age made it possible to compare children of different ages. In Binet's system, such comparisons were awkward. It was not clear, for example, whether a 12-year-old with a mental age of 9 was more or less intelligent than a 9-year-old with a mental age of 6, although both showed the same 3-year lag in mental development. The IQ ratio placed all children (regardless of age) on the same scale, which was centered at 100 if their mental age corresponded to their chronological age. Thus, in our examples, the 12-year-old would receive an IQ score of 75, while the 9-year-old would obtain an IQ score of 67 (see Table 9.1 for the calculations).

Terman's technical and theoretical contributions to psychological testing were modest, but he made an articulate case for the potential educational benefits of testing and became the key force behind American schools' widespread adoption of IQ tests (Chapman, 1988). As a result of his efforts, the Stanford-Binet quickly became the world's fore-

"It is the method of tests that has brought psychology down from the clouds and made it useful to men; that has transformed the 'science of trivialities' into the 'science of human engineering.'"

LEWIS TERMAN

TABLE 9.1 CALCULATING THE INTELLIGENCE QUOTIENT

Measure	Child 1	Child 2	Child 3	Child 4
Mental age (MA)	6 years	6 years	9 years	12 years
Chronological age (CA)	6 years	9 years	12 years	9 years
$IQ = \frac{MA}{CA} \times 100$	$\frac{6}{6} \times 100 = 100$	$\frac{6}{9} \times 100 = 67$	$\frac{9}{12} \times 100 = 75$	$\frac{12}{9} \times 100 = 133$

CHAPTER NINE

most intelligence test and the standard of comparison for virtually all intelligence tests that followed (Gregory, 1996). When new IQ tests were developed in subsequent years, their validity was often demonstrated by showing that they correlated strongly with the Stanford-Binet. Although many new IQ tests geared to specific populations, age groups, and purposes have been developed, the apparent variety is somewhat misleading. Most of the tests remain loyal to the conception of intelligence originally formulated by Binet and Terman. Since its publication in 1916, the Stanford-Binet has been updated periodically (in 1937, 1960, 1973, and 1986). Although it's about 80 years old, the Stanford-Binet is still one of the world's most widely used psychological tests.

Wechsler's Innovations 7c

While Terman was busy testing schoolchildren, David Wechsler was hard at work with a different clientele. As chief psychologist at New York's massive Bellevue Hospital, Wechsler was charged with overseeing the psychological assessment of thousands of adult patients. He found the Stanford-Binet somewhat unsatisfactory for this purpose. Although Terman had added items to extend the test's use to adults, it had always been designed with children in mind.

Thus, Wechsler set out to improve on the measurement of intelligence in *adults*. In 1939 he published the first high-quality IQ test designed specifically for adults, which came to be known as the Wechsler Adult Intelligence Scale (WAIS) (Wechsler, 1955, 1981). Judging from the success that his test enjoyed, Wechsler had filled an important need. Ironically, Wechsler (1949, 1967, 1991) eventually devised downward extensions of his scale for children.

The Wechsler scales were characterized by at least two major innovations (Prifitera, 1994). First, Wechsler made his scales less dependent on subjects' verbal ability than the Stanford-Binet. He included many items that required nonverbal reasoning. To highlight the distinction between verbal and nonverbal ability, he formalized the computation of separate scores for verbal IQ, performance (nonverbal) IQ, and full-scale (total) IQ. The Wechsler tests are also divided into 11 smaller subtests that determine the verbal and performance IQ scores.

Second, Wechsler discarded the intelligence quotient in favor of a new scoring scheme based on the *normal distribution*. This scoring system has since been adopted by most other IQ tests, including the Stanford-Binet. Although the term *intelligence quotient* lingers on in our vocabulary, scores on intelligence tests are no longer based on an actual quotient. We'll take a close look at the modern scoring system for IQ tests a little later.

Intelligence Testing Today

Today, psychologists and educators have many IQ tests available for their use. Basically, these tests fall into two categories: *individual tests* and *group tests*. Individual IQ tests are administered only by psychologists who have special training for this purpose. A psychologist works face to face with a single examinee at a time. The Stanford-Binet and the Wechsler scales are both individual IQ tests.

The problem with individual IQ tests is that they're expensive and time-consuming to administer. Therefore, researchers have developed a number of IQ tests that can be administered to large groups of people at once. Because of their cost-effectiveness, group tests such as the Otis-Lennon School Ability Test and the Lorge-Thorndike Intelligence Test enjoy wide usage at all educational levels (Vane & Motta, 1990). Indeed, if you've taken an IQ test, chances are that it was a group test. As you'll see in the next section, many school districts routinely administer group IQ tests.

"The subtests [of the WAIS] are different measures of intelligence, not measures of different kinds of intelligence."

DAVID WECHSLER

Recap of Key Points

• The first crude efforts to devise intelligence tests were made by Sir Francis Galton, who wanted to show that intelligence is inherited. Galton is also known for inventing correlation, and percentile test scores and for campaigning for eugenics programs.

• Modern intelligence testing began with the work of Alfred Binet, a French psychologist who published the first useful intelligence test in 1904. Binet's scale measured a child's mental age.

• Lewis Terman revised the original Binet scale to produce the Stanford-Binet in 1916. It introduced the intelligence quotient and became the standard of comparison for subsequent intelligence tests.

• David Wechsler devised an improved measure of intelligence for adults and a series of IQ tests that reduced the emphasis on verbal ability. He also introduced a new scoring system based on the normal distribution.

• Today, there are many individual and group intelligence tests. An individual IQ test is administered to a single examinee by a psychologist who has special training for this purpose. Group IQ tests can be administered to many people simultaneously.

BASIC QUESTIONS ABOUT INTELLIGENCE TESTING

Misconceptions abound when it comes to intelligence tests. In this section we'll use a question-and-answer format to explain the basic principles underlying intelligence testing.

Why Are People Given Intelligence Tests?

Most IQ testing is conducted by school districts, which are largely free to formulate their own unique testing programs. There is little federal or state policy regarding ideal patterns of testing. Some districts administer group IQ tests to all students at regular intervals. Others administer individual IQ tests only on an occasional basis, as needed. Boehm (1985) lists three major functions of IQ testing in educational settings:

1. *Screening and diagnosis*. Children who are troubled by learning problems in school are most likely to be helped if their problems can be diagnosed early and accurately. IQ tests usually play a key role in these diagnostic efforts. The tests can be useful in distinguishing mental retardation from specific learning disabilities.

2. *Selection and placement*. Many districts use IQ scores to sort students into appropriate programs and courses. For instance, IQ tests usually play a key role in identifying "gifted" children, who are then funneled into special programs. IQ tests may also be used by districts that group all students according to their academic ability. Evidence regarding the value of this "tracking" is inconclu-

sive, but many school administrators believe that it facilitates more effective teaching.

3. *Evaluation and research*. The highly standardized nature of IQ tests also makes them useful in the evaluation of educational programs. The well-known Head Start program, for instance, was evaluated in part by examining changes in participants' IQ scores.

Psychologists also use IQ tests in clinical diagnosis (Matarazzo & Herman, 1985). Clinicians use individual IQ tests to measure general ability and to assess strengths, weaknesses, and peculiarities in a client's cognitive functioning. Individual IQ tests can also be used to help differentiate between organic brain damage and other kinds of mental disorders.

Are IQ Tests Widely Used in Other Cultures?

In other Western cultures with European roots, the answer to this questions is yes. In most non-Western cultures, the answer is only very little. IQ testing has a long history and continues to be a major enterprise in many Western countries, such as Britain, France, Norway, Canada, and Australia (Irvine & Berry, 1988). However, efforts to export IQ tests to non-Western societies have met with mixed results. The tests have been well received in some non-Western cultures, such as Japan, where the Binet-Simon scales were introduced as early as 1908 (Iwawaki & Vernon, 1988), but they have been met with indifference or resistance in other cultures, such as China and India (Chan & Vernon, 1988; Sinha, 1983).

The bottom line is that Western IQ tests do not translate well into the language and cognitive frameworks of many non-Western cultures (Berry, 1994). Using an intelligence test with a cultural group other than the one for which it was originally designed can be problematic. The entire process of test administration, with its emphasis on rapid information processing, decisive responding, and the notion that ability can be quantified, is foreign to some cultures. Moreover, different cultures have different conceptions of what intelligence is and value different mental skills (Das, 1994; Segall et al., 1990). In a landmark treatise on culture and cognition, Cole and his colleagues (1971) concluded that "people will be good at doing things that are important to them and that

The familiar IQ test, so important in our society, is viewed as having little relevance in many non-Western societies. This reality illustrates the fact that the ingredients of intelligence are culture-specific. In other words, different cultures value different mental skills.

they have occasion to do often" (p. xi). *In other words, the ingredients of intelligence are culture-specific.* Even when a non-Western culture is largely in agreement with Western views about the ingredients of intelligent behavior, it can be difficult to construct equivalent tests that measure these ingredients with equal reliability and validity in both cultural contexts.

What Kinds of Questions Are on Intelligence Tests?

The nature of the questions found on IQ tests varies somewhat from test to test. These variations depend on whether the test is intended for children or adults (or both) and whether the test is designed for individuals or groups. Overall, the questions are fairly diverse in format. The Wechsler scales, with their numerous subtests, provide a representative example of the kinds of items that appear on most IQ tests. As you can see in Figure 9.6, the items in the Wechsler subtests require subjects to furnish information, recognize vocabulary, and demonstrate basic memory. Generally speaking, examinees are required to manipulate words, numbers, and images through abstract reasoning.

Figure 9.6
Subtests on the Wechsler Adult Intelligence Scale (WAIS). The WAIS is subdivided into a series of tests that yield separate verbal and performance (nonverbal) IQ scores. Sample test items that closely resemble those on the WAIS are shown on the right.

Wechsler Adult Intelligence Scale (WAIS)

Test	Description	Example
Verbal scale		
Information	Taps general range of information	On what continent is France?
Comprehension	Tests understanding of social conventions and ability to evaluate past experience	Why are children required to go to school?
Arithmetic	Tests arithmetic reasoning through verbal problems	How many hours will it take to drive 150 miles at 50 miles per hour?
Similarities	Asks in what way certain objects or concepts are similar; measures abstract thinking	How are a calculator and a typewriter alike?
Digit span	Tests attention and rote memory by orally presenting series of digits to be repeated forward or backward	Repeat the following numbers backward: 2 4 3 5 1 8 6
Vocabulary	Tests ability to define increasingly difficult words	What does audacity mean?
Performance scale		
Digit symbol	Tests speed of learning through timed coding tasks in which numbers must be associated with marks of various shapes	Shown: 1 2 3 4 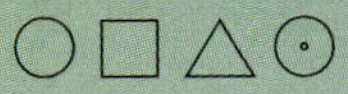 Fill in: 1 4 3 2
Picture completion	Tests visual alertness and visual memory through presentation of an incompletely drawn figure; the missing part must be discovered and named	Tell me what is missing: 
Block design	Tests ability to perceive and analyze patterns by presenting designs that must be copied with blocks	Assemble blocks to match this design: 
Picture arrangement	Tests understanding of social situations through a series of comic-strip-type pictures that must be arranged in the right sequence to tell a story	Put the pictures in the right order:  1 2 3
Object assembly	Tests ability to deal with part/whole relationships by presenting puzzle pieces that must be assembled to form a complete object	Assemble the pieces into a complete object: 

What Do Modern IQ Scores Mean?

As we've discussed, scores on intelligence tests once represented a ratio of mental age to chronological age. However, this system has given way to one based on the normal distribution and the standard deviation (see Chapter 2). **The *normal distribution* is a symmetric, bell-shaped curve that represents the pattern in which many characteristics are dispersed in the population.** When a trait is normally distributed, most cases fall near the center of the distribution (an average score) and the number of cases gradually declines as one moves away from the center in either direction (see Figure 9.7).

The normal distribution was first discovered by 18th-century astronomers. They found that their measurement errors were distributed in a predictable way that resembled a bell-shaped curve. Since then, research has shown that many human traits, ranging from height to running speed to spatial ability, also follow a normal distribution. Psychologists eventually recognized that intelligence scores also fall into a normal distribution. This insight permitted David Wechsler to devise a more sophisticated scoring system for his tests that has been adopted by virtually all subsequent IQ tests. In this system, raw scores are translated into *deviation IQ scores that locate subjects precisely within the normal distribution, using the standard deviation as the unit of measurement.*

For most IQ tests, the mean of the distribution is set at 100 and the standard deviation (SD) is set at 15. These choices were made to provide continuity with the original IQ ratio (mental age to chronological age) that was centered at 100. In this system, which is depicted in Figure 9.7, a score of 115 means that a person scored exactly one SD (15 points) above the mean. A score of 85 means that a person scored one SD below the mean. A score of 100 means that a person showed average performance. You don't really need to know how to work with standard deviations to understand this system (but if you're interested, consult Appendix B). *The key point is that modern IQ scores indicate exactly where you fall in the normal distribution of intelligence.* Thus, a score of 120 does not indicate that you answered 120 questions correctly. Nor does it mean that you have

Figure 9.7
The normal distribution. Many characteristics are distributed in a pattern represented by this bell-shaped curve. The horizontal axis shows how far above or below the mean a score is (measured in plus or minus standard deviations). The vertical axis is used to graph the number of cases obtaining each score. In a normal distribution, the cases are distributed in a fixed pattern. For instance, 68.26% of the cases fall between +1 and −1 standard deviation. Modern IQ scores indicate where a person's measured intelligence falls in the normal distribution. On most IQ tests, the mean is set at an IQ of 100 and the standard deviation at 15. Thus, an IQ of 130 means that a person scored 2 standard deviations above the mean. Any deviation IQ score can be converted into a percentile score, which indicates the percentage of cases obtaining a lower score. The mental classifications at the bottom of the figure are descriptive labels that roughly correspond to ranges of IQ scores.

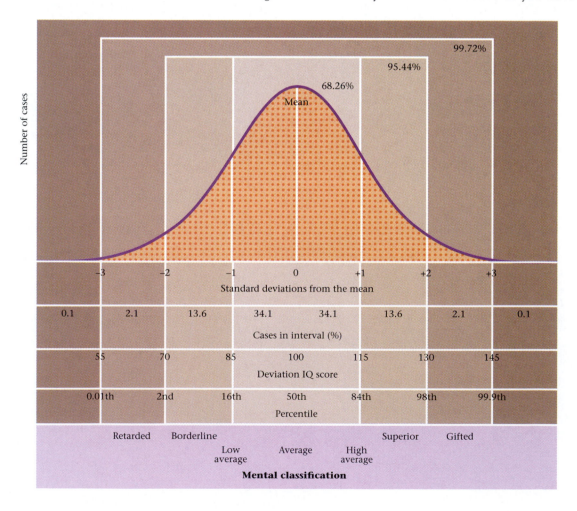

120 "units" of intelligence. A deviation IQ score places you at a specific point in the normal distribution of intelligence.

IQ scores are always based on how people perform in comparison to the test norms for their own age group. Thus, 5-year-olds are compared to other 5-year-olds and 12-year-olds to 12-year-olds. Everyone is lumped together in adulthood after age 15 to 18, depending on the test. Thus, an IQ score is always indicative of individuals' *relative standing* in their own age group. Hence, IQ scores don't routinely increase as children grow older. Obviously, most children become more intelligent with age. However, their IQ scores remain constant unless their relative standing in their age group changes.

Deviation IQ scores can be converted into percentile scores (see Figure 9.7). In fact, a major advantage of this scoring system is that a specific score on a specific test always translates into exactly the same percentile score, regardless of the person's age group. The old system of IQ ratio scores lacked this consistency.

Do Intelligence Tests Measure Potential or Knowledge?

Intelligence tests are intended to measure intellectual potential. They do so by presenting novel questions that require test takers to think on their feet, rather than questions that simply tap factual knowledge. However, because people's backgrounds differ, it's not easy to devise items that are completely unaffected by differences in knowledge. Test developers try to circumvent this problem by requiring subjects to *apply* relatively *common* knowledge. Nevertheless, IQ tests unavoidably contain items that are influenced by the test taker's previous learning. *Hence, IQ tests measure a blend of potential and knowledge.* Test developers try to tilt the balance toward the assessment of potential as much as possible, but factual knowledge clearly has an impact on intelligence test scores (Glaser, 1991; Zigler & Seitz, 1982).

Do Intelligence Tests Have Adequate Reliability?

Do IQ tests produce consistent results when people are retested? Yes. Most IQ tests report commendable reliability estimates. The correlations often range into the .90s. In comparison to most other types of psychological tests, IQ tests are exceptionally reliable. However, like other tests, they *sample* behavior, and a specific testing may yield an unrepresentative score.

Variations in examinees' motivation to take an IQ test or in their anxiety about the test can sometimes produce misleading scores (Spielberger & Sydeman, 1994; Zimmerman & Woo-Sam, 1984). The most common problem is that low motivation or high anxiety may drag a person's score down on a particular occasion. For instance, a fourth-grader who is made to feel that the test is terribly important may get jittery and be unable to concentrate. The same child might score much higher on a subsequent testing by another examiner who creates a more comfortable atmosphere. Although the reliability of IQ tests is excellent, caution is always in order in interpreting test scores. IQ scores should be viewed as estimates that are accurate within plus or minus 5 points about two-thirds of the time.

Do Intelligence Tests Have Adequate Validity?

Do intelligence tests measure what they're supposed to measure? Yes, but this answer has to be qualified very carefully. IQ tests are valid measures of the kind of intelligence that's necessary to do well in academic work. But if the purpose is to assess intelligence in a broader sense, the validity of IQ tests is questionable.

As you may recall, intelligence tests were originally designed with a relatively limited purpose in mind: to predict school performance. This has continued to be the principal purpose of IQ testing. Efforts to document the validity of IQ tests have usually concentrated on their relationship to grades in school. Typically, positive correlations in the .50s are found between IQ scores and school grades (Kline, 1991). Even higher correlations (between .60 and .80) are found between IQ scores and the number of years of school that people complete (Ceci, 1991).

These correlations are about as high as one could expect, given that many factors besides a person's intelligence are likely to affect grades and school progress. For example, school grades may be influenced by a student's motivation, diligence, or personality, not to mention teachers' subjective biases. Thus, IQ tests are reasonably valid indexes of school-related intellectual ability, or academic intelligence.

However, over the years people have mistakenly come to believe that IQ tests measure mental ability in a truly general sense. In reality, IQ tests have always focused on the abstract reasoning and verbal fluency that are essential to academic success. The tests do not tap social competence, practical problem solving, creativity, mechanical ingenuity, or artistic talent.

When Robert Sternberg and his colleagues (1981) asked people to list examples of intelligent behavior, they found that the examples fell into three categories: (1) *verbal intelligence,* (2) *practical intelligence,* and (3) *social intelligence* (see Figure 9.8). Thus, people generally recognize three basic types of intelligence. For the most part, IQ tests assess only the first of these three types. Although IQ tests are billed as measures of *general* mental ability, they actually focus somewhat narrowly on a specific type of intelligence: academic/verbal intelligence. Hence, IQ tests are not valid indicators of intelligence in a truly general sense.

Are IQ Scores Stable over Time?

You've probably heard of hopeful parents who have their 2- or 3-year-old preschoolers tested to see whether they're exceptionally bright. These parents would have been better off saving the money spent on preschool testing, as IQ scores are relatively unstable during the preschool years and are not good predictors of scores in adolescence and adulthood. As children grow older, their IQ scores eventually stabilize (Brody, 1992; Hayslip, 1994). By age 7 or 8, IQ tests are reasonably accurate, but far from perfect, predictors of adult IQ (see Figure 9.9). Although IQ scores tend to stabilize after early childhood, they are *not* set in concrete. Substantial changes are seen in some people.

Do Intelligence Tests Predict Vocational Success?

Vocational success is a vague, value-laden concept that's difficult to quantify. Nonetheless, researchers have attacked this question by examining correlations between IQ scores and specific indicators of vocational success, such as the prestige of subjects' occupations or ratings of subjects' job performance. On the positive side of the ledger, it's clear that IQ is related to occupational attainment. People who score high on IQ tests are more likely than those who score low to end up in high-status jobs (Austin & Hanisch, 1990; Herrnstein & Murray, 1994; Ree & Earles, 1992). Because IQ tests measure school ability fairly well and school performance is important in reaching certain occupations, this link between IQ scores and job status makes sense. Of course, the correlations between IQ and occupational attainment are moderate, and there are plenty of exceptions to the general trend. Some people plow through the educational system with bulldog determination and hard work, in spite of limited ability as measured by IQ tests. Such people may go on to prestigious jobs, while people who are brighter (according to their test results), but less motivated, settle for lower-status jobs.

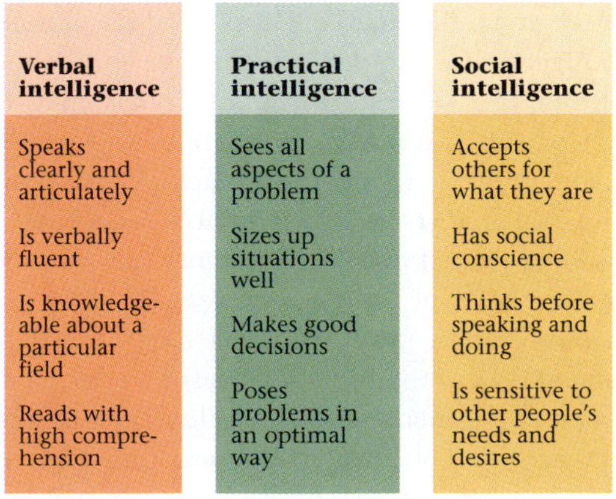

On the negative side of the ledger, IQ scores are mediocre predictors of performance within a particular occupation (Ghiselli, 1966, 1973; Sternberg & Wagner, 1993). For example, in summarizing data for 446 occupations, Jensen (1993a) reported a median correlation of .27 between general intelligence and job performance. Thus, knowing the IQ scores of 100 freshly graduated attorneys will not be much help in predicting which graduates will go on to become the best lawyers. Why not? In part, the problem is statistical. The range of IQ scores among the attorneys will be restricted, with most scores probably falling between 115 and 135. In other words, most of the attorneys will be bunched together with fairly similar scores. Without much variation in the predictor variable (here, IQ scores), you don't have much to work with in making predictions—about vocational success or anything else. Consider an analogy: Could you predict basketball ability based on height if all your subjects were between 6 feet and 6 feet 2 inches tall? Other considerations may also undermine IQ tests' prediction of occupational success. For instance, after a person graduates from school, practical and social intelligence (which are not assessed by IQ tests) may become more important determinants of success than academic/verbal intelligence (Sternberg & Wagner, 1993).

Doubts about the ability of IQ tests to predict job performance have led to controversy over the use of IQ tests in employee selection. Over the

Figure 9.8
Laypersons' conceptions of intelligence. Robert Sternberg and his colleagues (1981) asked subjects to list examples of behaviors characteristic of intelligence. The examples tended to sort into three groups that represent the three types of intelligence recognized by the average person: verbal intelligence, practical intelligence, and social intelligence.

Verbal intelligence	Practical intelligence	Social intelligence
Speaks clearly and articulately	Sees all aspects of a problem	Accepts others for what they are
Is verbally fluent	Sizes up situations well	Has social conscience
Is knowledgeable about a particular field	Makes good decisions	Thinks before speaking and doing
Reads with high comprehension	Poses problems in an optimal way	Is sensitive to other people's needs and desires

years, many companies have used intelligence tests in deciding whom to hire or promote. However, there's lively debate about whether IQ tests are sufficiently valid indicators of job potential in most occupational areas (Barrett & Depinet, 1991; Hunter & Hunter, 1984; McClelland, 1973, 1993). Moreover, the use of intelligence testing in making employment decisions has been challenged on legal grounds. Because of these challenges, the practice has declined dramatically (Gatewood & Perloff, 1990).

Essentially, court rulings and laws now require that tests used in employment selection measure specific abilities that are clearly related to job performance (Schmidt, Ones, & Hunter, 1992). Companies are increasingly turning to personality tests to select employees who are conscientious, calm under pressure, persistent, reliable, and so forth (Hogan, Hogan, & Roberts, 1996). Psychologists are also trying to develop tests of practical intelligence to aid employers in their hiring decisions (Sternberg et al., 1995). Thus, psychological tests that measure abilities relevant to specific jobs continue to be valuable tools in selecting employees (Landy, Shankster, & Kohler, 1994); however, IQ tests may not be particularly well suited for this purpose. Some critics feel that IQ tests have also been misused in selecting children for special education programs. We'll discuss this issue in the next section, where we focus on mental retardation and giftedness.

Recap of Key Points

- IQ tests are mostly administered in schools, but patterns of use vary greatly from one school district to another. Intelligence tests are useful in screening for learning problems, in student placement and research, and in clinical assessment.
- Intelligence testing is largely a Western enterprise and IQ tests are not widely used in most non-Western cultures. One reason is that different cultures have different conceptions of intelligence.
- Intelligence tests contain a diverse mixture of questions. In the modern scoring system, deviation IQ scores indicate where people fall in the normal distribution of intelligence for their age group. On most tests, the mean is set at 100 and the standard deviation is set at 15.
- Although they are intended to measure potential for learning, IQ tests inevitably assess a blend of potential and knowledge. IQ tests are exceptionally reliable, with reliability coefficients typically ranging into the .90s.
- IQ tests are reasonably valid measures of academic intelligence in that they predict school grades and the number of years of school that people complete. However, they do not tap social or practical intelligence, and they do not measure intelligence in a truly general sense.
- IQ scores become fairly stable during the grade-school years. IQ scores are correlated with occupational attainment. Nonetheless, they do not predict performance within an occupation very well. There is little evidence for their validity in selecting employees.

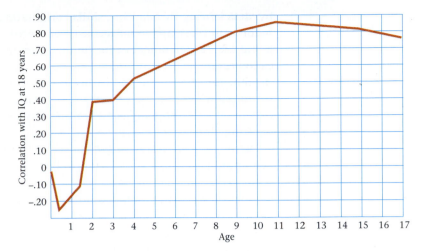

Figure 9.9
The gradual stabilization of IQ scores. This graph plots out the correlations between IQ scores obtained during childhood and subsequent adult IQ, measured at age 18. As you can see, preschool IQ scores are not very good predictors of adult IQ. However, IQ scores stabilize during the school years, and by age 9 the scores correlate in the .80s with adult IQ. (Adapted from Bayley, 1949)

EXTREMES OF INTELLIGENCE

What are the cutoff scores for extremes in intelligence that lead children to be designated as retarded or gifted? On the low end, IQ scores roughly two standard deviations or more below the mean are regarded as subnormal. On the high end, children who score more than two or three standard deviations above the mean are regarded as gifted. However, designations of mental retardation and giftedness should not be based exclusively on IQ test results. Let's look more closely at the concepts of mental retardation and intellectual giftedness.

Mental Retardation

According to the American Association on Mental Retardation (AAMR), *mental retardation* refers to **subaverage general mental ability accompanied** by deficiencies in adaptive skills, originating before age 18. Adaptive skills consist of everyday living skills in ten domains, including communication (example: writing a letter), self-care (dressing oneself), home living (preparing meals), social interaction (coping with others' demands), community use (shopping), and health/safety (recognizing illness).

There are two noteworthy aspects to this definition. First, the IQ criterion of subnormality is arbitrary. In the most recent release of its manual on mental retardation, the AAMR (1992) set a flexible cutoff line, which is a score of 70 to 75 or below. This cutoff line could be drawn elsewhere. Indeed, the AAMR used to draw the line exactly at 70. The recent shift toward 75 is controversial in that the higher cutoff could double the number of people classified as retarded (from roughly 2.5% to 5% of the population). Many experts doubt the wisdom of this change, given the stigma associated with retardation and the fact that services for the mentally retarded are already strained. Second, the requirement of deficits in everyday living skills is included because experts feel that retardation should not be determined solely on the basis of individuals' test ability (Bunch, 1994). This requirement acknowledges that "school learning" is not the only important kind of learning.

Levels of Retardation

Mental retardation has traditionally been classified into four levels characterized as mild, moderate, severe, or profound. Table 9.2 lists the IQ range for each level, the percentage of retarded people falling into each category, and the typical behavioral characteristics of individuals at each level.

This table shows that the vast majority of retarded people are *mildly* retarded. Only about 5%

of retarded people exhibit the profound or severe mental deficiency that most people envision when they think of retardation. Mildly retarded individuals are not readily distinguishable from the rest of the population. The mental deficiency of children in the mildly retarded category often is not noticed until they have been in school a few years. Thus, the belief that most retarded people are dramatically different from everyone else is largely untrue.

Although everyday living skills should be weighed in diagnoses of retardation, IQ scores and school performance remain the dominant considerations. Some theorists maintain that many youngsters in the mildly retarded category are "6-hour retarded children" (Koegel & Edgerton, 1984). What they mean is that many youngsters are only "retarded" for the 6 hours of the school day. Outside of school, many are considered normal. Furthermore, many of these children manage to shed the label of retardation when they reach adulthood and leave the educational system (Jacobson & Mulick, 1992; Landesman & Ramey, 1989). Most of them become self-supporting and are integrated into the community. Their neighbors and co-workers usually are unaware of their history of academic difficulties.

Origins of Retardation

Many organic conditions can cause mental retardation. For example, *Down syndrome* is a condition marked by distinctive physical characteristics (such as slanted eyes, stubby limbs, and thin hair) that is associated with mild to severe retardation. Most children exhibiting this syndrome carry an extra chromosome. *Phenylketonuria* is a metabolic disorder (due to an inherited enzyme deficiency) that can lead to retardation if it is not caught and

TABLE 9.2 CHARACTERISTICS OF THE MENTALLY RETARDED

Category of Retardation	Percentage of Retarded Population	Education Possible	Life Adaptation Possible
Mild 50–70 IQ	85%	Sixth grade (maximum) by late teens; special education helpful	Can be self-supporting in nearly normal fashion if environment is stable and supportive; may need help with stress
Moderate 35–50 IQ	10%	Second to fourth grade by late teens; special education necessary	Can be semi-independent in sheltered environment; needs help with even mild stress
Severe 20–35 IQ	3–4%	Limited speech, toilet habits, and so forth with systematic training	Can help contribute to self-support under total supervision
Profound below 20 IQ	1–2%	Little or no speech; not toilet-trained; relatively unresponsive to training	Requires total care

Note: Percentages from Szymanski and Crocker (1989)

treated in infancy. In *hydrocephaly,* an excessive accumulation of cerebrospinal fluid in the skull destroys brain tissue and causes retardation. Although over 350 such organic syndromes are known to cause retardation (Belmont, 1994), diagnosticians are able to pin down an organic cause for retardation in less than 25% of cases (Scott & Carran, 1987). However, this percentage appears to be increasing as scientists unravel more of the genetic bases for various kinds of disorders (Hodapp, 1994).

The cases of unknown origin tend to involve milder forms of retardation. A number of theories attempt to identify the factors that underlie retardation in the absence of a known organic pathology. The *biological hypothesis* proposes that mild retardation is caused by subtle physiological defects that are difficult to detect. The *environmental hypothesis* suggests that mild retardation is caused by a variety of unfavorable environmental factors. Consistent with this hypothesis, the vast majority of mildly retarded children come from impoverished homes characterized by marital instability, poor nutrition, and parental neglect.

Some theorists are critical of the concept of retardation and locate its "causes" in the educational system (Braginsky & Braginsky, 1974; Mercer, 1973). They argue that in the absence of clear organic pathology, mental retardation is nothing but a convenient label pinned on youngsters who do not perform well in school. In support of this position, they emphasize that (1) the IQ cutoff for retardation is arbitrary, (2) most mildly retarded people are indistinguishable from normals, and (3) most mildly retarded people shed this label once they leave school. According to this view, most "retarded" children are not fundamentally different from "normal" children. Theorists who subscribe to this view claim that many schools and teachers use the diagnosis of retardation to shunt slow learners into special education programs where they will be someone else's problem.

Programs for the Retarded

Programs for the mentally retarded are remarkably diversified (Jacobson & Schwartz, 1991). Children suffering from profound retardation obviously require different services than those who are only mildly retarded. In recent years, program design has been guided by the *normalization principle,* which stresses the dignity of retarded people and their right to live in the least restrictive environment possible (Jacobson, 1991; Szymanski & Crocker, 1989). Normalization emphasizes the value of making treatment facilities resemble, as much as possible, the conditions of everyday life in normal society. Thus, the use of large, regimented residential care facilities that offer little privacy or responsibility is declining. They are being replaced by smaller facilities that are better integrated into local communities. In the schools, normalization has led to *mainstreaming*—the practice of keeping retarded children in regular classes as much as possible. To date, evidence on the benefits of mainstreaming is equivocal (Gottlieb, Alter, & Gottlieb, 1991). The goal of normalization is to make it easier for retarded people to be absorbed into the mainstream of society.

Giftedness

Like mental retardation, giftedness is widely misunderstood. In part, this is because television and movies inaccurately portray gifted children as social misfits and "nerds."

Identifying Gifted Children

Some curious discrepancies exist between policy and practice in how gifted children are identified. According to federal law in the United States, designations of giftedness should be based on superior potential in any of six areas: general intelligence, specific aptitudes (in math, for example), creativity, leadership, performing arts, or athletics (Gallagher & Courtright, 1986). Furthermore, experts consistently assert that schools should not rely too heavily on IQ tests to identify gifted children (Tannenbaum, 1986; Wallach, 1985).

In practice, however, efforts to identify gifted children focus almost exclusively on IQ scores and rarely consider qualities such as creativity, leadership, or special talent (Horowitz, 1994). Most school districts consider children who fall in the upper 2%–3% of the IQ distribution to be gifted. Thus, the minimum IQ score for gifted programs usually falls somewhere between 130 and 145.

Personal Qualities of the Gifted

Gifted children have long been stereotyped as weak, sickly, socially inept "bookworms" who are often emotionally troubled. The empirical evidence largely contradicts this view. The best evidence comes from a major longitudinal study of gifted children begun by Lewis Terman in 1921 (Terman, 1925; Terman & Oden, 1959). Other investigators have continued to study this group through the

Ten-year-old Alexandra Nechita is an accomplished painter whose works bring up to $50,000 from collectors and have been featured in a coffeetable book. She began painting on canvas at age 6, and her first shows were at age 7.

present (Cronbach, 1992; Vaillant & Vaillant, 1990). This project represents psychology's longest-running study.

Terman's original subject pool consisted of around 1500 youngsters who had an average IQ of 150. In comparison to normal subjects, Terman's gifted children were found to be above average in height, weight, strength, physical health, emotional adjustment, mental health, and social maturity. As a group, Terman's subjects continued to exhibit better-than-average physical health, emotional stability, and social satisfaction throughout their adult years. Other studies have also found that samples of gifted children are either average or above average in social and emotional development (Janos & Robinson, 1985).

Terman's gifted children grew up to be very successful by conventional standards. By midlife they had produced 92 books, 235 patents, and nearly 2200 scientific articles. Although Terman's gifted children accomplished a great deal, no one

in the group achieved recognition for genius-level contributions. In retrospect, this finding may not be surprising. The concept of giftedness is applied to two very different groups. One consists of high-IQ children who are the cream of the crop in school. The other consists of eminent adults who make enduring contributions in their fields. According to Siegler and Kotovsky (1986), a sizable gap exists between these two groups. The accomplishments of the latter group involve a much higher level of giftedness. Joseph Renzulli (1986) theorizes that this rarer form of giftedness depends on the intersection of three factors: high intelligence, high creativity, and high motivation (see Figure 9.10). He emphasizes that high intelligence alone does not usually foster genuine greatness. Hence, parents of children selected for gifted school programs should have realistic expectations. Their children are not likely to be geniuses.

Recap of Key Points

• IQ scores below 70–75 are usually diagnostic of mental retardation, but these diagnoses should not be based solely on test results, as adaptive behavior should also be evaluated carefully. Four levels of retardation have been distinguished. The vast majority of retarded people are mildly retarded. Most mildly retarded children grow up to be self-supporting adults.

• Although over 350 biological conditions can cause retardation, biological causes can be pinpointed in only a minority of cases. According to the biological hypothesis, cases of unknown origin are mostly caused by subtle, undetected physiological defects.

• The environmental hypothesis suggests that cases of unknown origin are mostly caused by unfavorable environmental factors, such as poverty, neglect, and poor nutrition. Programs for the retarded emphasize the normalization principle, which often leads to mainstreaming.

• Children who obtain IQ scores above 130 may be viewed as gifted, but cutoffs for accelerated programs vary, and schools rely too much on IQ scores. Research by Terman showed that gifted children tend to be socially mature and well adjusted and that they mostly go on to be very successful in life.

• Genius-level contributions are rare because they depend on a combination of high intelligence, creativity, and motivation.

Figure 9.10
A three-ring conception of giftedness. According to Renzulli (1986), high intelligence is only one of three requirements for true giftedness. He proposes that a combination of exceptional ability, creativity, and motivation leads some people to make enduring contributions in their fields.

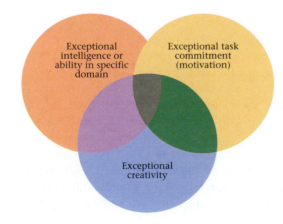

HEREDITY AND ENVIRONMENT AS DETERMINANTS OF INTELLIGENCE

Most early pioneers of intelligence testing, such as Sir Francis Galton, Lewis Terman, Henry Goddard, and Robert Yerkes, maintained that intelligence is inherited (Cravens, 1992). Small wonder, then, that this view lingers on among many people. Gradually, however, it has become clear that both heredity and environment influence intelligence (Locurto, 1991; Plomin, 1990; Scarr, 1989). Does this mean that the nature versus nurture debate has been settled with respect to intelligence? Absolutely not. Theorists and researchers continue to argue vigorously about which is more important, in part because the issue has such far-reaching sociopolitical implications.

Theorists who believe that intelligence is largely inherited downplay the value of special educational programs for underprivileged groups (Jensen, 1980). They assert that a child's intelligence cannot be increased noticeably, because a child's genetic destiny cannot be altered. Other theorists take issue with this point, asserting that inherited characteristics are not necessarily unchangeable (Angoff, 1988; Scarr, 1981). Environmental theorists also argue that the genetic view has been used to rationalize unjust inequities in some groups' access to education and training. For example, Lewontin, Rose, and Kamin (1984) assert that "the IQ test in practice has been used in both the United States and England to shunt vast numbers of working-class and minority children into inferior and dead-end educational tracks" (p. 87). Thus, environmental theorists tend to maintain that even more funds should be allocated for remedial education programs, improved schooling in lower-class neighborhoods, and college financial aid for the underprivileged. Because the debate over the role of heredity in intelligence has direct relevance to important social issues and political decisions, we'll take a detailed look at this complex controversy.

Evidence for Hereditary Influence 7d

Galton's observation that intelligence runs in families was quite accurate. However, *family studies* can determine only whether genetic influence on a trait is *plausible*, not whether it is certain. Family members share not just genes, but similar environments. If high intelligence (or low intelligence) appears in a family over several generations, this consistency could reflect the influence of either shared genes or shared environment. Because of this problem, researchers must turn to *twin studies* and *adoption studies* to obtain more definitive evidence on whether heredity affects intelligence.

Twin Studies

The best evidence regarding the role of genetic factors in intelligence comes from studies that compare identical and fraternal twins. The rationale for twin studies is that both identical and fraternal twins normally develop under similar environmental conditions. However, identical twins share more genetic kinship than fraternal twins. Hence, if pairs of identical twins are more similar in intelligence than pairs of fraternal twins, it's presumably because of their greater genetic similarity. (See Chapter 3 for a more detailed explanation of the logic underlying twin studies.)

What are the findings of twin studies regarding intelligence? McGue and colleagues (1993) discuss the results of over 100 studies of intellectual similarity for various kinds of kinship relations and child-rearing arrangements. The key data from their review are highlighted in Figure 9.11 on page 358. This figure plots the average correlation observed for various types of relationships. As you can see, the average correlation reported for identical twins (.86) is very high, indicating that identical twins tend to be quite similar in intelligence. The average correlation for fraternal twins (.60) is significantly lower. This correlation indicates that fraternal twins also tend to be similar in intelligence, but noticeably less so than identical twins. These results support the notion that IQ is inherited to a considerable degree.

Of course, critics have tried to poke holes in this line of reasoning. They argue that identical twins are more alike in IQ because parents and others treat them more similarly than they treat fraternal twins. This environmental explanation of the findings has some merit. After all, identical twins are always the same sex, and gender influences how a child is raised. However, this explanation seems unlikely in light of the evidence on identical twins reared apart because of family breakups or adoption (Bouchard et al., 1990). *Although reared in different environments*, these identical twins still display greater similarity in IQ (average correlation: .72) than fraternal twins reared together (average correlation: .60). Moreover, the gap in IQ

Figure 9.11
Studies of IQ similarity.
The graph shows the mean correlations of IQ scores for people of various types of relationships, as obtained in studies of IQ similarity. Higher correlations indicate greater similarity. The results show that greater genetic similarity is associated with greater similarity in IQ, suggesting that intelligence is partly inherited (compare, for example, the correlations for identical and fraternal twins). However, the results also show that living together is associated with greater IQ similarity, suggesting that intelligence is partly governed by environment (compare, for example, the scores of siblings reared together and reared apart). (Data from McGue et al., 1993)

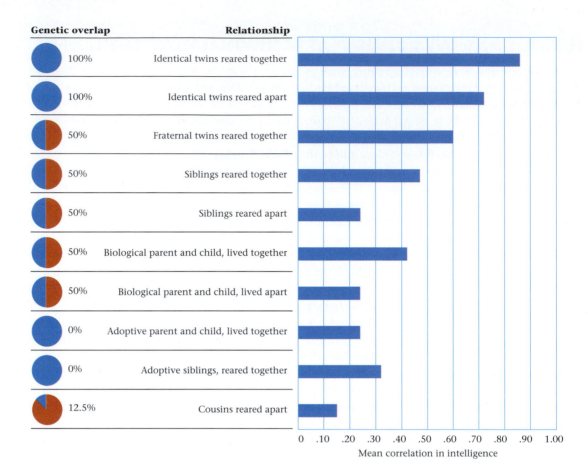

Genetic overlap	Relationship
100%	Identical twins reared together
100%	Identical twins reared apart
50%	Fraternal twins reared together
50%	Siblings reared together
50%	Siblings reared apart
50%	Biological parent and child, lived together
50%	Biological parent and child, lived apart
0%	Adoptive parent and child, lived together
0%	Adoptive siblings, reared together
12.5%	Cousins reared apart

0   .10   .20   .30   .40   .50   .60   .70   .80   .90   1.00
Mean correlation in intelligence

"No one should expect a child who is innately dull to gain a scholarship to a grammar school, or one whose inborn ability is merely average to win first-class honors at Oxford or Cambridge."

CYRIL BURT

similarity between identical twins reared apart and fraternal twins reared together appears to widen in middle and late adulthood, suggesting paradoxically that the influence of heredity increases with age (Pedersen et al., 1992).

The Burt Affair and Its Aftermath

One of the best-known studies of intelligence in identical twins reared apart has been the subject of enormous controversy and has been largely discredited. It appears that Sir Cyril Burt (1955), one of England's most prominent psychologists, either fabricated much of his data or kept such sloppy records that his data are scientifically worthless. This episode is worth examining because it highlights the sociopolitical implications of the IQ debate.

Burt was a great admirer of Sir Francis Galton, and like Galton, he believed that intelligence is largely inherited. He also believed that intelligence could be measured precisely with mental tests. Burt's views were influential in shaping an educational system in Britain that emphasized standardized testing and that tended to exclude underprivileged youngsters from higher education opportunities. As one official British document

put it, most children should be educated to be "efficient members of the class to which they belong" (Green, 1992, p. 329). When many critics began questioning the assumptions underlying this educational system, Burt mustered evidence to support the policy he believed in. He eventually published data on over 50 pairs of identical twins reared apart, reporting a correlation of .86 for the twins' scores on group IQ tests. These results provided strong support for the idea that intelligence is largely inherited (Burt's data are not included in Figure 9.11).

However, around the time of Burt's death, Leon Kamin and Arthur Jensen noted some peculiarities in Burt's data and began to question their authenticity. Leslie Hearnshaw, an expert in the history of psychology who was writing a biography of Burt, was given full access to Burt's private papers and records to clear up the matter. In this biography, Hearnshaw (1979) concluded that at least some of Burt's twin data were fabricated. Hearnshaw's conclusion left Burt's reputation in posthumous ruins for a decade. However, in recent years, two other biographies of Burt have arrived at different conclusions. In two independent examinations of the Burt affair, Robert

Joynson (1989) and Ronald Fletcher (1991) argue that Hearnshaw did a "hatchet job" on Burt and that the peculiarities in Burt's data were the product of sloppy record keeping rather than intentional fraud. Which view is accurate? At this point, with Burt long deceased and most of his records destroyed, it may not be possible to settle the matter decisively (Green, 1992; Scarr, 1994b). However, even Burt's admirers have reluctantly acknowledged that his twin data cannot be trusted.

How could faked or ineptly collected data go undetected by the scientific community for almost two decades? The main reason was that Burt's data were fairly similar to what was actually found in other studies (Scarr, 1994). The IQ correlations that he reported for identical twins reared apart were only slightly higher than those reported by other researchers. Fraudulent or misleading findings are usually detected when they cannot be replicated, but Burt's findings were "replicated." Hence, there was little reason for suspicion.

The Burt story shows why even the world's most eminent scientists cannot be exempted from the critical scrutiny of their peers. More than anything else, however, the Burt affair illustrates how difficult it can be to maintain objectivity about issues that have profound social and political ramifications. Although we can't be sure, it appears that Burt may have risked his distinguished reputation to bolster the hereditarian view of intelligence. On the other hand, Burt's admirers argue that his detractors maliciously destroyed his reputation to bolster the environmental view of intelligence (Jensen, 1992). Either way, it's clear that scientists are not always as objective or detached as they would like to be.

Adoption Studies

Research on adopted children also provides evidence about the effects of heredity (and of environment, as we shall see). If adopted children resemble their biological parents in intelligence even though they were not reared by these parents, this finding supports the genetic hypothesis. The relevant studies indicate that there is indeed more than chance similarity between adopted children and their biological parents (Turkheimer, 1991; refer again to Figure 9.11).

Heritability Estimates

Various experts have sifted through mountains of correlational evidence to estimate the *heritability* of intelligence. A *heritability ratio* is an estimate of the proportion of trait variability in a population that is determined by variations in genetic inheritance. Heritability can be estimated for any trait. For example, the heritability of height is estimated to be around 90% (Plomin, 1994). Heritability can be estimated in a variety of ways that appear logically and mathematically defensible (Loehlin, 1994; Schonemann, 1994). Given the variety of methods available and the strong views that experts bring to the IQ debate, it should come as no surprise that heritability estimates for intelligence vary considerably (see Figure 9.12).

At the high end, a few theorists, such as Arthur Jensen (1980), maintain that the heritability of IQ is about 80%. That is, they believe that only about 20% of the variation in intelligence is attributable to environmental factors. Most studies suggest that the heritability of IQ is between 50% and 70% (Bouchard et al., 1990; Loehlin, 1989). The consensus estimate of experts hovers around 60% (Snyderman & Rothman, 1987).

Even the estimates at the low end suggest that heredity has a substantial impact on intelligence. However, it's important to understand that heritability estimates have certain limitations (Erdle, 1990; Rutter, Silberg, & Simonoff, 1993). First, a heritability estimate is a *group statistic* based on studies of trait variability within a specific group. A heritability estimate cannot be applied meaningfully to *individuals*. In other words, even if the heritability of intelligence truly is 80%, this does not mean that each individual's intelligence is 80% inherited. Second, the heritability of a specific trait may vary from one group to another depending on a variety of factors. For instance, in a group with a given gene pool, heritability will increase if there's a shift toward rearing group members in more similar circumstances. Why? Because the extent of environmental differences will be reduced. To date, heritability estimates for intelligence have been based largely on research with

Figure 9.12
The concept of heritability. A heritability ratio is an estimate of the portion of variation in a trait determined by heredity—with the remainder presumably determined by environment—as these pie charts illustrate. Typical heritability estimates for intelligence range between a high of 70% and a low of 50%, although some estimates (such as Jensen's) have fallen outside this range. Bear in mind that heritability ratios are *estimates* and have certain limitations that are discussed in the text.

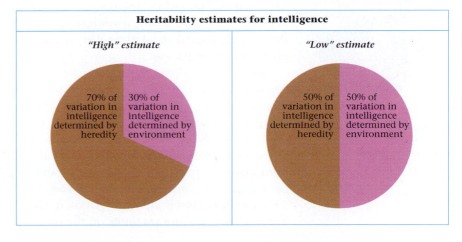

Heritability estimates for intelligence

"High" estimate

70% of variation in intelligence determined by heredity

30% of variation in intelligence determined by environment

"Low" estimate

50% of variation in intelligence determined by heredity

50% of variation in intelligence determined by environment

white, middle-class subjects. Hence, they should be applied only to such groups.

Evidence for Environmental Influence

Heredity unquestionably influences intelligence, but a great deal of evidence indicates that upbringing also affects mental ability. We'll examine three lines of research—concerning adoption, environmental deprivation or enrichment, and home environment—that show how life experiences shape intelligence.

Adoption Studies

Research with adopted children provides useful evidence about the impact of experience as well as heredity (Locurto, 1990; Plomin & DeFries, 1980). Many of the correlations in Figure 9.11 reflect the influence of the environment. For example, adopted children show some resemblance to their foster parents in IQ. This similarity is usually attributed to the fact that their foster parents shape their environment. Adoption studies also indicate that siblings reared together are more similar in IQ than siblings reared apart. This is true even for identical twins who have the same genetic endowment. Moreover, entirely unrelated children who are raised in the same home also show a significant resemblance in IQ. All of these findings indicate that environment influences intelligence.

Environmental Deprivation and Enrichment

If environment affects intelligence, children who are raised in substandard circumstances should experience a gradual decline in IQ as they grow older (since other children will be progressing more rapidly). This *cumulative deprivation hypothesis* was tested decades ago. Researchers studied children consigned to understaffed orphanages and children raised in the poverty and isolation of the back hills of Appalachia (Sherman & Key, 1932; Stoddard, 1943). Generally, investigators *did* find that environmental deprivation led to the predicted erosion in IQ scores.

Conversely, children who are removed from a deprived environment and placed in circumstances more conducive to learning should benefit from their environmental enrichment. Their IQ scores should gradually increase. This hypothesis has been tested by studying children who have been moved from disadvantaged homes into middle- and upper-class adoptive homes (Scarr & Weinberg, 1977, 1983; Schiff & Lewontin, 1986; Skodak & Skeels, 1947). Although there are limits on the improve-

ments seen, the IQs of these children tend to increase noticeably (typically 10–12 points). These findings also show that environment influences IQ.

Home-Environment Studies

In recent years researchers have examined the influence of environment on intelligence in yet another way. This new approach involves going into intact homes (mother and father living together with their children) to make an elaborate, systematic assessment of the quality of the intellectual environment there. If environment shapes intelligence, these assessments of home environments should correlate with youngsters' IQ scores, which they do (Okagaki, 1994).

What kind of home environment nurtures the development of intelligence? Many factors appear to be involved (Bradley, 1989; Bradley & Caldwell, 1980; Hanson, 1975). It helps if parents run an orderly household *and* encourage exploration, experimentation, and independence. In the ideal home, parents are warm, affectionate, and highly involved with their children. They provide a diverse array of age-appropriate toys, as well as more formal learning materials (such as books). The parents speak articulately and are interested in intellectual pursuits (and therefore serve as role models for these behaviors). When children reach school age, parents encourage them to work hard in school and reward them when they make progress. Throughout childhood, the parents emphasize achievement motivation and provide tangible assistance with schoolwork.

The Interaction of Heredity and Environment

Clearly, heredity and environment both influence intelligence to a significant degree. Indeed, many theorists now assert that the question of which is more important ought to take a back seat to the question of *how they interact* to govern IQ.

The current thinking is that heredity may set certain limits on intelligence and that environmental factors determine where individuals fall within these limits (Scarr & Carter-Saltzman, 1982; Weinberg, 1989). According to this idea, genetic makeup places an upper limit on a person's IQ that can't be exceeded even when environment is ideal. Heredity is also thought to place a lower limit on an individual's IQ, although extreme circumstances (for example, being locked in an attic until age 10) could drag a person's IQ beneath this boundary. Theorists use the term ***reaction range*** to refer to these genetically determined limits

"My research has been aimed at asking in what kind of environments genetic differences shine through and when do they remain hidden."

SANDRA SCARR

on IQ (or other traits). Sandra Scarr, a prominent theorist who emphasizes the reaction-range concept, explains it as follows:

Each person has a range of potential in development. For example, a person with "medium-tall" genes for height who grows up in a poor environment may be shorter than average. In a good nutritional environment, the person would grow up taller than average. But no matter how well-fed, someone with "short" genes will never be taller than average. It works the same way with shyness, intelligence, and almost any other aspect of personality and behavior. (Quoted in Hall, 1987, p. 18)

According to the reaction-range model, children reared in high-quality environments that promote the development of intelligence should score near the top of their potential IQ range (see Figure 9.13). Children reared under less ideal circumstances should score lower in their reaction range. The reaction range for most people is *estimated* to be around 20–25 points on the IQ scale (Weinberg, 1989).

The concept of a reaction range can explain why high-IQ children sometimes come from poor environments. It can also explain why low-IQ children sometimes come from very good environments. Moreover, it can explain these apparent paradoxes without discounting the role that environment undeniably plays. But how can the genetic boundaries on a person's intelligence be measured? That's the problem with the reaction-range concept. There is no readily apparent way to measure the range, which makes it difficult to test the reaction-range model empirically. The impossibility of measuring individuals' genetically determined intellectual potential also makes it difficult to resolve the debate about the causes of ethnic differences in IQ

scores. We'll try to sort through this complex issue in the next section.

Cultural Differences in IQ Scores

The age-old nature versus nurture debate lies at the core of the current controversy about ethnic differences in average IQ. Although the full range of IQ scores is seen in all ethnic groups, the average IQ for many of the larger minority groups in the United States (such as African Americans, Native Americans, and Hispanics) is somewhat lower than the average for whites. The disparity ranges from 3 to 15 points, depending on the group tested and the IQ scale used (Coleman et al., 1966; Perlman & Kaufman, 1990; Suzuki & Vraniak, 1994). There is little argument about the existence of these group differences, variously referred to as racial, ethnic, or cultural differences in intelligence. The controversy concerns *why* the differences are found. A vigorous debate continues as to whether cultural differences in intelligence are due to the influence of heredity or of environment.

Heritability as an Explanation

In 1969 Arthur Jensen sparked a heated war of words by arguing that cultural differences in IQ are largely due to heredity. The cornerstone for Jensen's argument was his analysis suggesting that the heritability of intelligence is about 80%. Essentially, he asserted that (1) intelligence is largely genetic in origin, and (2) therefore, genetic factors are "strongly implicated" as the cause of ethnic differences in intelligence. Jensen's article triggered outrage, bitter criticism, and even death threats, as well as a flurry of research that shed additional light on the determinants of intelligence.

"Despite more than half a century of repeated efforts by psychologists to improve the intelligence of children, particularly those in the lower quarter of the IQ distribution relative to those in the upper half of the distribution, strong evidence is still lacking as to whether or not it can be done."

ARTHUR JENSEN

Figure 9.13
Reaction range. The concept of reaction range posits that heredity sets limits on one's intellectual potential (represented by the horizontal bars), while the quality of one's environment influences where one scores within this range (represented by the dots on the bars). People raised in enriched environments should score near the top of their reaction range, whereas people raised in poor-quality environments should score near the bottom of their range. Genetic limits on IQ can be inferred only indirectly, so theorists aren't sure whether reaction ranges are narrow (like Ted's) or wide (like Chris's). The concept of reaction range can explain how two people with similar genetic potential can be quite different in intelligence (compare Tom and Jack) and how two people reared in environments of similar quality can score quite differently (compare Alice and Jack).

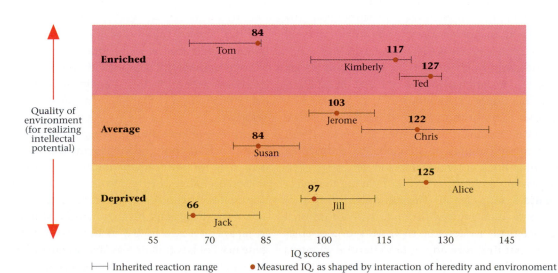

Quality of environment (for realizing intellectal potential)

Enriched — Tom 84, Kimberly 117, Ted 127

Average — Jerome 103, Chris 122, Susan 84

Deprived — Alice 125, Jill 97, Jack 66

IQ scores — 55 70 85 100 115 130 145

⊢—⊣ Inherited reaction range   ● Measured IQ, as shaped by interaction of heredity and environment

In their 1994 best-seller, Herrnstein and Murray added fuel to the fire of the race-intelligence controversy.

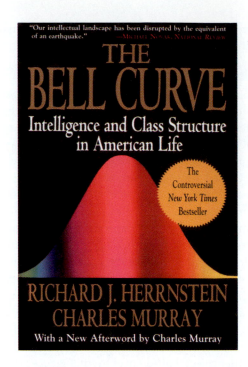

"Our intellectual landscape has been disrupted by the equivalent of an earthquake." —MICHAEL NOVAK, NATIONAL REVIEW

THE BELL CURVE

Intelligence and Class Structure in American Life

The Controversial New York Times Bestseller

RICHARD J. HERRNSTEIN
CHARLES MURRAY

With a New Afterword by Charles Murray

Twenty-five years later, Richard Herrnstein and Charles Murray (1994) reignited the same controversy with the publication of their widely discussed book *The Bell Curve.* Their main thesis is that in recent decades intellectual ability, which they believe is largely inherited, has become the primary determinant of individuals' success in life. They go on to argue that ethnic and cultural differences in average intelligence are substantial and not easily reduced and that these differences have profound and disturbing implications. Perhaps having learned from Jensen's nightmarish experiences, they try to tiptoe around the incendiary issue of whether ethnic differences in average IQ are due to heredity. But their discussions of "dysgenic pressures" in ethnic groups clearly imply that these disparities are at least partly genetic in origin. Moreover, the implicit message throughout the book is that disadvantaged groups cannot avoid their fate because it is their genetic destiny.

The central idea of *The Bell Curve,* that we are evolving toward a meritocracy based on intellect, may have merit. Nonetheless, it is curious that neither of the authors has ever published a single scientific article on intelligence (Dorfman, 1995). By choosing to present their data exclusively in a popular book intended for the general reader, Herrnstein and Murray avoided having their data analyses subjected to the critical scrutiny that scientific data must withstand. It is not unusual for scientists to describe their work in a popular book, but this normally occurs after the scientists have published many technical articles on a topic, which they then attempt to summarize for the layperson. Herrnstein and Murray did not have any work of their own on intelligence to summarize.

In any event, heritability explanations for ethnic differences in IQ have a variety of flaws and weaknesses (Dorfman, 1995; Lewontin, 1976; Mackenzie, 1984; Sternberg, 1995). For example, a heritability estimate applies only to the specific group on which the estimate is based. Heritability estimates for intelligence have been based on studies dominated by white subjects (Brody, 1992). Hence, there is doubt about the validity of applying this estimate to other cultural groups.

Moreover, even if one accepts the assumption that the heritability of IQ is very high, it does not follow logically that differences in group averages must be due largely to heredity. Leon Kamin has presented a compelling analogy that highlights the logical fallacy in this reasoning (see Figure 9.14):

We fill a white sack and a black sack with a mixture of different genetic varieties of corn seed. We make certain that the proportions of each variety of seed are identical in each sack. We then plant the seed from the white sack in fertile Field A, while that from the black sack is planted in barren Field B. We will observe that within Field A, as within Field B, there is considerable variation in the height of individual corn plants. This variation will be due largely to genetic factors (seed differences). We will also observe, however, that the average height of plants in Field A is greater than that in Field B. That difference will be entirely due to environmental factors (the soil). The same is true of IQs: differences in the average IQ of various human populations could be entirely due to environmental differences, even if within each population all variation were due to genetic differences! (Eysenck & Kamin, 1981, p. 97)

Kamin's analogy shows that even if the heritability of intelligence is high, group differences in average IQ *could* still be caused entirely (or in part) by environmental factors, a reality acknowledged by Arthur Jensen (1994b) and the authors of *The Bell Curve.*

Further evidence on how group differences in a heritable trait could be environmental in origin comes from recent observations of dramatic generational changes in the average height of Japanese males. Angoff (1988) notes that between 1946 and 1982, the average height of young adult males in Japan increased by 3.3 inches. Obviously, the gene pool of a population as large as Japan's could not have changed overnight (in evolutionary terms, one or two generations is more like a fraction a second). Instead, this increased stature has been attributed to environmental factors (mostly nutritional changes). Thus, although height is a highly heritable trait (surely more so than intelligence), we see that group differences (between generations) in average height can be environmental in origin.

The available evidence certainly does not allow us to rule out the possibility that ethnic and cultural disparities in average intelligence are partly genetic in origin. And the hypothesis should not be dismissed without study simply because many people find it offensive or distateful. However, there are several alternative explanations for the culture gap in intelligence that seem more plausible. Let's look at them.

Socioeconomic Disadvantage as an Explanation

Some theorists have approached the issue by trying to show that socioeconomic disadvantages are the main cause of ethnic differences in average IQ. Many social scientists argue that minority students' IQ scores are depressed because these children tend to grow up in deprived environments that create a disadvantage—both in school and on IQ tests. Obviously, living circumstances vary greatly within ethnic groups, but there is no question that, on the average, whites and minorities tend to be raised in very different circumstances. Most minority groups have endured a long history of economic discrimination and are greatly overrepresented in the lower social classes. A lower-class upbringing tends to carry a number of disadvantages that work against the development of a youngster's full intellectual potential (Blau, 1981). In comparison to the middle and upper classes, lower-class children are more likely to come from large families and from single-parent homes, factors that may often limit the parental attention they receive. Lower-class children also tend to be exposed to fewer books, to have fewer learning supplies, to have less privacy for concentrated study, and to get less parental assistance in learning. Typically, they also have poorer role models for language development, experience less pressure to work hard on intellectual pursuits, and attend poorer-quality schools that are underfunded and understaffed (Wolf, 1965). Many of these children grow up in crime-, drug-, and gang-infested neighborhoods where it is far more important to develop street intelligence than school intelligence. Some theorists also argue that children in the

Between-group differences (cause: the soils in which the plants were grown)

Barren field
Within-group differences (cause: genetic variations in the seeds)

Fertile field
Within-group differences (cause: genetic variations in the seeds)

Figure 9.14
Genetics and between-group differences on a trait. Kamin's analogy (see text) shows how between-group differences on a trait (the height of corn plants) could be due to environment, even if the trait is largely inherited. The same reasoning presumably applies to the trait of human intelligence.

lower classes are more likely to suffer from malnutrition or to be exposed to environmental toxins (Brody, 1992). Either of these circumstances could interfere with youngsters' intellectual development.

In light of these disadvantages, it's not surprising that children from higher classes tend to get higher IQ scores (Bouchard & Segal, 1985; White, 1982). The average IQ in the lowest social classes runs about 20–30 points lower than the average IQ in the highest social classes (Locurto, 1991). This is true even if race is factored out of the picture by studying whites exclusively. Admittedly, there is room for argument about the direction of the causal relationships underlying this association between social class and intelligence (Turkheimer, 1994). Nonetheless, given the overrepresentation of minorities in the lower classes, many researchers argue that ethnic differences in intelligence are really social class differences in disguise.

Stereotype Vulnerability as an Explanation

Socioeconomic disadvantages clearly are a major factor in various minority groups' poor performance on IQ and other standardized tests, but some theorists maintain that other factors and processes are also at work. For example, Claude Steele (1992), a social psychologist at Stanford University, has argued that derogatory stereotypes of stigmatized groups' intellectual capabilities create unique feelings of vulnerability in the educational arena. These feelings can undermine group members' performance on tests, as well as other measures of academic achievement.

Steele points out that demeaning stereotypes of stigmatized groups are widely disseminated, creating a subtle climate of prejudice, even in the absence of overt discrimination. He further notes that members of minority groups are keenly aware of any negative stereotypes that exist regarding their intellect. Hence, when a black or Hispanic American does poorly on a test, he or she must confront a disturbing possibility: *that others will attribute the failure to racial inferiority*. Steele maintains that females face the same problem when they venture into academic domains where stereotypes suggest that they are inferior to males, such as mathematics, engineering, and the physical sciences. That is, *they worry about people blaming their failures on their sex*. According to Steele, minorities and women in male-dominated fields are in a no-win situation. When they do well and contradict stereotypes, people tend to view their success with suspicion, but when they do poorly, people readily view their failure as vindication of the stereotypes.

Steele maintains that stigmatized groups' apprehension about "confirming" people's negative stereotypes can contribute to academic under-

achievement in at least two ways. First, it can undermine their emotional investment in academic work. As Steele notes, "Doing well in school requires a belief that school achievement can be a promising basis of self-esteem, and that belief needs constant reaffirmation even for advantaged students" (1992, p. 72). When this belief is relentlessly undercut instead of frequently reaffirmed, students tend to "disidentify" with school and write off academic pursuits as a source of self-worth. Their academic motivation declines and their performance suffers as a result. Second, standardized tests such as IQ tests may be especially anxiety arousing for members of stigmatized groups because the importance attributed to the tests makes one's stereotype vulnerability particularly salient. This anxiety may impair students' test performance by temporarily disrupting their cognitive functioning. We'll look at how Steele tested his theory in our Featured Study.

Investigators: Claude M. Steele (Stanford University) and Joshua Aronson (University of Texas, Austin)

Source: Stereotype threat and the intellectual performance of African Americans. *Journal of Personality and Social Psychology*, 1995, 69, 797–811.

"I believe that in significant part the crisis in black Americans' education stems from the power of this vulnerability to undercut identification with schooling."

CLAUDE STEELE

Racial Stereotypes and Test Performance — Featured Study

In this article, Steele and Aronson report on a series of four studies that tested various aspects of Steele's theory about the ramifications of stereotype vulnerability. We will examine their first study in some detail and then discuss the remaining studies more briefly. The purpose of the first study was to test the hypothesis that raising the threat of stereotype vulnerability would have a negative impact on African American students' performance on a mental ability test.

Method

Subjects. The participants were 114 black and white undergraduates attending Stanford University who were recruited through campus advertisements. As expected, given Stanford's highly selective admissions, both groups of students were well above average in academic ability, as evidenced by their mean scores on the verbal subtest of the Scholastic Assessment Test (SAT). The study compared black and white students with high and roughly equal ability and preparation (based on their SAT scores) to rule out cultural disadvantage as a factor.

Procedure. The participants were asked to take a challenging, 30-minute test of verbal ability composed of items from the verbal subtest of the Graduate Record Exam (GRE). In one condition, the issue of stereotype vulnerability was not made salient, as the test was presented to subjects as a device to permit the researchers to analyze participants' problem-solving

strategies. In another condition, the specter of stereotype vulnerability was raised, as the test was presented as an excellent index of one's general verbal ability. The principal dependent variable was subjects' performance on the verbal test.

Results

When the black students' stereotype vulnerability was not made salient, the performance of the black and white students did not differ, as you can see in Figure 9.15. However, when the same test was presented in a way that increased blacks' stereotype vulnerability, the black students scored significantly lower than their white counterparts (see Figure 9.15).

Discussion

Based on their initial study, the authors inferred that stereotype vulnerability does appear to impair minority group members' test performance. They went on to replicate their finding in a second study of 40 black and white female students. In a third study, they demonstrated that their manipulations of stereotype vulnerability were indeed activating thoughts about negative stereotypes, ability-related self-doubts, and performance apprehension in their African American participants. Their fourth study showed that stereotype vulnerability can be activated even when a test is not explicitly presented as an index of one's ability. Looking at their research as a whole, Steele and Aronson conclude that stereotype vulnerability "is an underappreciated source of classic deficits in standardized test performance (e.g., IQ) suffered by blacks and other stereotype-threatened groups" (p. 810).

Comment

More evidence is clearly needed on the effects of stereotype vulnerability, but Steele's theory promises to clear up some of the confusion surrounding the controversial issue of racial disparities in IQ scores. It seems likely that socioeconomic disadvantage makes a substantial contribution to cultural differences in average IQ, but various lines of evidence suggest that this factor cannot account for the culture gap by itself (Neisser et al., 1996). For years, many theorists have argued that test bias accounts for the rest of the culture gap, but as we will discuss momentarily, recent research suggests otherwise. Thus, Steele's groundbreaking research gives scientists an entirely new explanatory tool for understanding the vexing cultural disparities in average IQ.

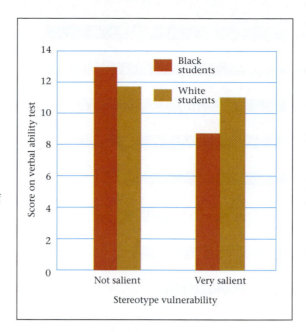

Figure 9.15
Stereotype vulnerability and test performance. Steele and Aronson (1995) compared the performance of black and white students of equal ability on a 30-item verbal ability test constructed from difficult GRE questions. When the black students' stereotype vulnerability was not salient, their performance did not differ from that of the white students; but when the specter of stereotype vulnerability was raised, the black students performed significantly worse than the white students.

Cultural Bias on IQ Tests as an Explanation

Some critics of IQ tests have argued that cultural differences in IQ scores are partly due to a cultural bias built into IQ tests. They argue that because IQ tests are constructed by white, middle-class psychologists, they naturally draw on experience and knowledge typical of white, middle-class lifestyles and use language and vocabulary that reflect the white, middle-class origins of their developers (Helms, 1992).

According to Jane Mercer (1975), when IQ tests are given to minorities, they measure *both mental ability and assimilation into the mainstream culture.* She assessed the degree to which Mexican American and African American children came from homes that were assimilated into the dominant Anglo-American culture. She found that the IQ scores of these ethnic children were correlated with the "Anglicization" of their home backgrounds.

Other lines of research also suggest that IQ tests are slanted in favor of white, middle-class students, at the expense of lower-class ethnic minorities (Bernal, 1984; Cole, 1981; Hilliard, 1984; Williams et al., 1980). Hence, most testing experts assert that minority students' IQ scores should be interpreted with extra caution (Puente, 1990). However, the balance of evidence suggests that the cultural slant on IQ tests is modest. The charges of bias stimulated a great deal of research on the issue in the 1970s and 1980s. *As a whole, the accumulated evidence suggests that cultural bias produces only weak and inconsistent effects on the IQ scores of minority examinees* (R. Kaplan, 1985; Oakland & Parmelee, 1985; Reynolds, 1995). Thus, cultural bias on IQ tests appears to be less of a problem than the cultural disadvantage associated with a lower-class upbringing.

Taken as a whole, the various alternative explanations for cultural and ethnic disparities in average IQ provide serious challenges to genetic explanations, which appear weak at best—and suspiciously racist at worst. Unfortunately, since the earliest days of IQ testing some people have used IQ tests to further elitist goals. The current controversy about ethnic differences in IQ is just another replay of a record that has been heard before. For instance, beginning in 1913, Henry Goddard tested a great many immigrants to the United States at Ellis Island in New York. Goddard reported that the vast majority of Italian, Hungarian, and Jewish immigrants tested out as *feeble-minded* (Kamin, 1974). As you can see, claims about ethnic deficits in intelligence are nothing new—only the victims have changed.

There is, however, one new twist to the debate about cultural differences in intelligence. A handful of recent studies have suggested that some ethnic minority groups—those of Asian American descent—score slightly *above average* on IQ tests (Lynn, 1987, 1991, 1995; Vernon, 1982). Admittedly, the comparative data on Asian Americans' IQ performance are still sparse and are largely based on just two of the many Asian American nationalities (Chinese and Japanese subjects), so a

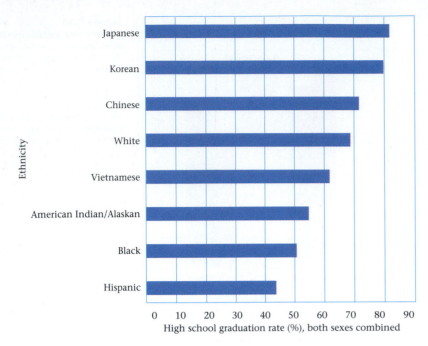

Figure 9.16
Asian Americans' academic success. On various measures of educational success, such as the high school graduation rates shown here, the performance of Asian American students tends to exceed that of other ethnic groups in the United States. More research is needed on the matter, but most theorists believe that cultural factors are responsible for Asian Americans' academic prowess. (Data from Sue & Okazaki, 1990)

great deal of additional research is needed (Suzuki & Gutkin, 1994). But the IQ data are consistent with the much more extensive data available on Asian Americans' school performance. These data clearly show that most Asian American groups tend to earn higher grade point averages and to have higher graduation rates than those of other ethnic groups, including whites (Sue & Okazaki, 1990; see Figure 9.16).

The outstanding intellectual and educational attainments of Asian Americans constitute a perplexing phenomenon in search of an explanation. The tentative explanations proposed thus far focus primarily on how Asian cultural values may encourage and nurture educational achievement. Investigators theorize that in comparison to most other groups, Asian families place greater emphasis on the value of education, put their children under more pressure to succeed in school, instill more respect for elders such as teachers, and exert more control over their children's study habits. Sue and Okazaki (1990) also speculate that Asian Americans have come to view education as their most realistic route to upward mobility, as racial discrimination has limited their opportunities for advancement through noneducational routes (such as entertainment, politics, and sports).

Evidence on most of these hypotheses is lacking, but one recent study of black, white, Hispanic, and Asian American students did find that Asian American students (1) are more likely to report that their parents have high standards for school performance, (2) are more prone to attribute academic success to hard work, (3) spend

about twice as much time on homework as other students, and (4) are more likely to belong to a peer group that emphasizes academic success (Steinberg, Dornbusch, & Brown, 1992). A great deal of additional study is needed to pin down the reasons for Asian Americans' academic prowess. One investigator (Lynn, 1987, 1991) has proposed a highly speculative genetic theory, but most researchers are confident that cultural factors are responsible for Asian Americans' educational success.

The debate about ethnic and racial differences in intelligence illustrates how IQ tests have often become entangled in thorny social conflicts. This is unfortunate, because it brings politics to the testing enterprise. Intelligence testing has many legitimate and valuable uses. However, the controversy associated with intelligence tests has undermined their value, leading to some of the new trends that we discuss in the next section.

Recap of Key Points

• The debate about the influence of heredity and environment on intelligence has important sociopolitical implications, as illustrated by the saga of Cyril Burt, who may have risked his reputation to further the hereditarian view.

• Twin studies show that identical twins, even when raised apart, are more similar in IQ than fraternal twins, suggesting that intelligence is inherited. Adoption studies reveal that people resemble their parents in intelligence, even when not raised by them. Estimates of the heritability of intelligence mostly range from 50% to 70%, but heritability ratios have certain limitations.

• Many lines of evidence, including adoption studies, studies of environmental deprivation and enrichment, and home environment studies, indicate that environment is also an important determinant of intelligence. The concept of reaction range posits that heredity places limits on one's intellectual potential while the environment determines where one falls within these limits.

• Arthur Jensen sparked great controversy by arguing that cultural differences in average IQ are largely due to heredity. Although the authors of *The Bell Curve* tried to sidestep the issue, their book ignited the same controversy.

• Genetic explanations for cultural differences in IQ have been challenged on a variety of grounds. Even if the heritability of IQ is great, group differences in intelligence may not be due to heredity. Moreover, ethnicity varies with social class, so socioeconomic

Understanding Correlational Evidence on the Heredity-Environment Question

Check your understanding of how correlational findings relate to the nature versus nurture issue by indicating how you would interpret the meaning of each "piece" of evidence described below. The figures inside the parentheses are the mean IQ correlations observed for the relationships described (based on McGue et al., 1993), which are shown in Figure 9.11. In the spaces on the left, enter the letter H if the findings suggest that intelligence is shaped by heredity, enter the letter E if the findings suggest that intelligence is shaped by the environment, and enter the letter B if the findings suggest that intelligence is shaped by both (or either) heredity and environment. The answers can be found in Appendix A.

_____ 1. Identical twins reared apart are more similar (.72) than fraternal twins reared together (.60).

_____ 2. Identical twins reared together are more similar (.86) than identical twins reared apart (.72).

_____ 3. Siblings reared together are more similar (.47) than siblings reared apart (.24).

_____ 4. Biological parents and the children they rear are more similar (.42) than unrelated persons who are reared apart (no correlation if sampled randomly).

_____ 5. Adopted children show similarity to their biological parents (.24) and to their adoptive parents (.24).

---

disadvantage may account for low IQ scores among minority students.

• Claude Steele has collected some thought-provoking data suggesting that stereotype vulnerability contributes to the culture gap in average IQ. Cultural bias on IQ tests may also contribute a little to ethnic differences in IQ, but it does not appear to be a crucial factor. Asian American students' comparative success in the educational arena appears to be due to cultural factors.

NEW DIRECTIONS IN THE ASSESSMENT AND STUDY OF INTELLIGENCE

Intelligence testing has been through a period of turmoil, and changes are on the horizon. In fact, many changes have occurred already. Let's discuss some of the major new trends and projections for the future.

Reducing Reliance on IQ Tests

In 1982 a task force assembled by the National Academy of Sciences recommended a reduced emphasis on standardized tests in the United States. Today, a reduction in reliance on IQ tests is clearly under way. Many school districts are shifting from IQ tests to achievement and aptitude tests. The problem is not so much that IQ tests are flawed—experts generally agree that they are reasonably sound measurement instruments (Snyderman & Rothman, 1987). However, these experts also agree that intelligence tests are terribly misunderstood by the general public. IQ scores are typically viewed as "magical" numbers that capture the essence of individuals' ability (Weinberg, 1989). Far too many people erroneously believe that IQ tests measure an innate, fixed mental capacity that is truly general in scope and of the utmost significance for success in life. Some authorities (Reschly, 1981; Turnbull, 1979) have argued that the concept of IQ is so bound up in myth that it has outlived its usefulness. They suggest that the term IQ should be done away with and that intelligence scales should be relabeled as tests of academic ability. Movement in this direction is apparent, as most group intelligence tests have deleted the word *intelligence* from their names (Fremer, 1994). The trend has even spilled over to aptitude testing. For example, in 1993 the Educational Testing Service changed the name of the Scholastic Aptitude Test to the Scholastic Assessment Test because of concern that the term *aptitude* incorrectly implied that the test measures innate intelligence (Jordan, 1993).

Increasing Emphasis on Specific Abilities

As the emphasis on measurement of *general* mental ability decreases, many scholars are advocating more assessment of *specific* mental abilities (Carroll & Horn, 1981; Das, 1992; Gardner, 1983, 1993). Intelligence testing grew out of a particular theoretical climate in the first few decades of this cen-

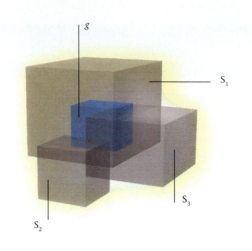

Figure 9.17
Spearman's *g*. In his analysis of the structure of intellect, Charles Spearman found that *specific* mental talents (S₁, S₂, S₃, and so on) were highly intercorrelated. Thus, he concluded that all cognitive abilities share a common core, which he labeled *g* for general mental ability.

Figure 9.18
Guilford's model of mental abilities. In contrast to Spearman (see Figure 9.17), J. P. Guilford concluded that intelligence is made up of many separate abilities. According to his analysis, we may have as many as 150 distinct mental abilities that can be characterized in terms of the operations, contents, and products of intellectual activity.

tury. At that time, Charles Spearman's (1904, 1923) ideas about the structure of intellect were dominant. Spearman developed an advanced statistical procedure called factor analysis. In **factor analysis, correlations among many variables are analyzed to identify closely related clusters of variables.** If a number of variables correlate highly with one another, the assumption is that a single factor is influencing all of them. Factor analysis attempts to identify these hidden factors.

Spearman used factor analysis to examine the correlations among tests of many specific mental abilities. He concluded that all cognitive abilities share an important core factor, which he labeled *g* for general mental ability. Spearman recognized that people also have "special" abilities (such as numerical reasoning or memory). However, he

thought that individuals' ability in these specific areas is largely determined by their general mental ability (see Figure 9.17). Thus, test developers came to see *g* as the Holy Grail in their quest to measure mental ability. Since then, intelligence tests have usually been designed to tap as much of *g* as possible.

A very different view of the structure of intellect began to emerge in the 1940s. Using a somewhat different approach to factor analysis, L. L. Thurstone (1938, 1955) concluded that intelligence involves multiple abilities. Thurstone argued that Spearman and his followers placed far too much emphasis on *g*. In contrast, Thurstone found that he could carve intelligence into seven distinct factors called *primary mental abilities:* word fluency, verbal comprehension, spatial ability, perceptual speed, numerical ability, inductive reasoning, and memory. Following in this tradition, J. P. Guilford (1959, 1985) upped the ante. His theory divided intelligence into *150* separate abilities—and did away with *g* entirely (see Figure 9.18). Thurstone's and Guilford's theories attracted favorable attention, but their ideas had relatively little effect on the day-to-day enterprise of intelligence testing (Horn, 1979).

However, another approach to carving up intelligence *has* had some impact. This approach was originally proposed by Raymond Cattell (1963) and was further developed by John Horn (1985). They suggest that *g* should be divided into *fluid intelligence* and *crystallized intelligence*. **Fluid intelligence involves reasoning ability, memory capacity, and speed of information processing.** *Crystallized intelligence* **involves ability to apply acquired knowledge and skills in problem solving.** Cattell originally assumed that fluid intelligence is largely determined by biological factors, and crystallized intelligence by education and experience. However, not all theorists who use the fluid-crystallized distinction assume that fluid intelligence has a stronger biological basis (Lohman, 1989).

The distinction between fluid and crystallized intelligence is central to the hierarchical model of intelligence that guided the most recent revision of the Stanford-Binet IQ test (Thorndike, Hagen, & Sattler, 1986). For the first 70 years of its existence, the Stanford-Binet yielded just one score, which was widely viewed as the ultimate index of general intelligence. However, the Stanford-Binet was broken into subtests for the first time in its long history in the 1986 revision. As Figure 9.19 shows, the modern Stanford-Binet includes 15 subtests. This major change in the structure of the Stanford-

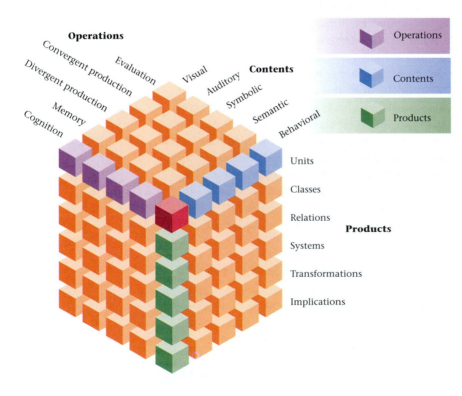

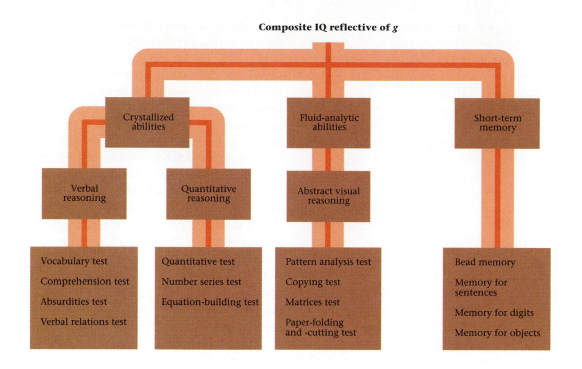

Composite IQ reflective of *g*

| Crystallized abilities | | Fluid-analytic abilities | Short-term memory |

| Verbal reasoning | Quantitative reasoning | Abstract visual reasoning | |

Vocabulary test	Quantitative test	Pattern analysis test	Bead memory
Comprehension test	Number series test	Copying test	Memory for sentences
Absurdities test	Equation-building test	Matrices test	Memory for digits
Verbal relations test		Paper-folding and -cutting test	Memory for objects

Figure 9.19
The organization of the modern Stanford-Binet. The most recent version of the classic Stanford-Binet Intelligence Test is based on the hierarchical model of intelligence diagrammed here (Thorndike, Hagen, & Sattler, 1986). The modern Stanford-Binet yields a composite score that presumably reflects *g*, four second-order scores for broad types of mental ability (verbal reasoning, quantitative reasoning, abstract/visual reasoning, and short-term memory), and scores on 15 subtests that measure specific mental abilities.

Binet seems to reflect a general trend toward devising tests of mental ability that assess specific abilities. Many theorists believe that assessments of specific abilities may provide more useful information than assessments of general mental ability.

Exploring Biological Indexes of Intelligence

Although specific abilities are increasingly emphasized in the world of education, in the world of research some investigators continue to stalk *g* with single-minded determination. In particular, biologically oriented theorists, such as Arthur Jensen (1987, 1993b) and Hans Eysenck (1988, 1989), are attempting to find raw physiological indicators of general intelligence. Their search for a "culture-free" measure of intelligence has led them to focus on sensory processes, much as Sir Francis Galton did over a hundred years ago. Armed with much more sophisticated equipment, they hope to succeed where Galton failed.

Jensen's (1982, 1987) studies of mental speed are representative of this line of inquiry. In his studies, Jensen measures *reaction time* (RT), using a panel of paired buttons and lights. On each trial, the subject rests a hand on a "home button." When one of the lights is activated, the subject is supposed to push the button for that light as quickly as possible. The time between the onset of the stimulus light and the release of the home button is the subject's reaction time. RT is typically averaged over a number of trials involving varied numbers of lights. Modest correlations (.20s to .30s) have been found between faster RTs and higher scores on conventional IQ tests.

Jensen's findings suggest an association between raw mental speed and intelligence, as Galton originally suggested. This correlation is theoretically interesting and, in retrospect, not all that surprising. Many conventional IQ tests have imposed demanding time limits on examinees, working under the assumption that "fast is smart."

However, the correlation between RT and IQ appears to be too weak to give RT any practical value as an index of intelligence. Critics also argue that there is no basis for equating RT with *g* and that RT is not a pure measure of neural processing (Lohman, 1989). They assert that RTs are affected by subjects' prior practice, their motivation, and their strategy for dealing with the trade-off between speed and accuracy (Carroll, 1987; Longstreth, 1984). Although a variety of investigators continue to search for useful measures of raw mental speed (Deary & Stough, 1996; Vernon & Mori, 1992), research on cognitive processes in intelligent behavior suggests that speed is *not* the critical factor in intelligence (Sternberg, 1985). We turn to some of this cognitive research next.

Investigating Cognitive Processes in Intelligent Behavior

As noted in Chapters 1 and 8, psychologists are increasingly taking a cognitive perspective in their efforts to study many topics. For over a century,

"To understand intelligent behavior, we need to move beyond the fairly restrictive tasks that have been used both in experimental laboratories and in psychometric tests of intelligence."

ROBERT STERNBERG

Figure 9.20
Sternberg's triarchic theory of intelligence. Sternberg's model of intelligence consists of three parts: the contextual subtheory, the experiential subtheory, and the componential subtheory. Much of Sternberg's research has been devoted to the componential subtheory, as he has attempted to identify the cognitive processes that contribute to intelligence. He believes that these processes fall into three groups: metacomponents, performance components, and knowledge-acquisition components.

the investigation of intelligence has been approached primarily from a *testing perspective*. This perspective emphasizes measuring the *amount* of intelligence people have and figuring out why some have more than others. In contrast, the *cognitive perspective* focuses on how people *use* their intelligence. The interest is in process rather than amount. In particular, cognitive psychologists focus on the information-processing strategies that underlie intelligence. This new perspective is generating intriguing insights that are changing the way psychologists think about intelligence.

The application of the cognitive perspective to intelligence has been spearheaded by Robert Sternberg (1984, 1988b, 1991). His *triarchic theory of human intelligence* consists of three parts: the contextual, experiential, and componential subtheories, which are outlined in Figure 9.20. In his *contextual subtheory,* Sternberg argues that intelligence is a culturally defined concept. He asserts that different manifestations of intelligent behavior are valued in different contexts. For example, the verbal skills emphasized in North American culture may take a backseat to hunting skills in another culture.

In his *experiential subtheory,* Sternberg explores the relationships between experience and intelligence. He emphasizes two factors as the hallmarks of intelligent behavior. The first is the ability to deal effectively with novelty—new tasks, demands, and situations. The second factor is the ability to learn how to handle familiar tasks automatically and effortlessly.

Sternberg's *componential subtheory* proposes that intelligent thought depends on three sets of mental processes: metacomponents, performance components, and knowledge-acquisition components. He calls *metacomponents* "executive" processes because they give directions to the other two kinds of components. They are high-level processes used in planning how to attack a problem. Metacomponents include processes such as defining the nature of a problem, selecting the steps needed to solve a problem, allocating resources (attention) to problems, and monitoring solutions to problems. According to Sternberg, "metacomponents decide what to do, *performance components* actually do it." For purposes of illustration, consider an analogy problem: lawyer is to client as doctor is to _____. Some of the processes involved in solving this problem include *encoding* the concepts in the problem, *inferring* the relationship between lawyer and client, and *applying* the inferred relation to a new domain, arriving at the answer of "patient." *Knowledge-acquisition components* are the processes involved in learning and storing information. The strategies that you may use to help memorize things exemplify the processes that fall in this category.

Investigations of cognitive processes in intelligent behavior have interesting implications for intelligence testing. Cognitive research has shown that more-intelligent subjects spend more time figuring out how to best represent problems and planning how to solve them than less-intelligent subjects do. Thus, Sternberg (1985) concludes that metacomponents are crucial to intelligent behavior. Furthermore, because planning takes time, Sternberg argues that traditional IQ tests place too much emphasis on speed. He also argues that IQ tests are too narrow in terms of what they attempt to measure, which is a theme echoed by others.

Expanding the Concept of Intelligence

In recent years, many theorists have concluded that the focus of traditional IQ tests is too narrow (Ceci & Liker, 1986; Frederiksen, 1986). These theorists argue that to assess intelligence in a truly general sense, tests should sample from a broader range of tasks. This view has been articulated particularly well by Howard Gardner (Gardner, 1983, 1993; Gardner & Hatch, 1989).

According to Gardner, IQ tests have generally emphasized verbal and mathematical skills, to the exclusion of other important skills. He suggests the existence of a number of relatively autonomous *human intelligences,* which are listed in

Contextual subtheory
Specifies the behaviors considered intelligent in a particular culture

Metacomponents
Control, monitor, and evaluate cognitive processing

Experiential subtheory
Specifies how experiences affect intelligence and how intelligence affects a person's experiences

Componential subtheory
Specifies the cognitive processes that underlie all intelligent behavior

Performance components
Execute strategies assembled by metacomponents

Knowledge-acquisition components
Encode, combine, and compare information

TABLE 9.3 GARDNER'S SEVEN INTELLIGENCES

Intelligence	End-States	Core Components
Logical-mathematical	Scientist Mathematician	Sensitivity to, and capacity to discern, logical or numerical patterns; ability to handle long chains of reasoning
Linguistic	Poet Journalist	Sensitivity to the sounds, rhythms, and meanings of words; sensitivity to the different functions of language
Musical	Composer Violinist	Abilities to produce and appreciate rhythm, pitch, and timbre; appreciation of the forms of musical expressiveness
Spatial	Navigator Sculptor	Capacities to perceive the visual-spatial world accurately and to perform transformations on one's initial perceptions
Bodily-kinesthetic	Dancer Athlete	Abilities to control one's body movements and to handle objects skillfully
Interpersonal	Therapist Salesperson	Capacities to discern and respond appropriately to the moods, temperaments, motivations, and desires of other people
Intrapersonal	Person with detailed, accurate self-knowledge	Access to one's own feelings and the ability to discriminate among them and draw upon them to guide behavior; knowledge of one's own strengths, weaknesses, desires, and intelligences

Source: Gardner and Hatch (1989)

Table 9.3 (Gardner & Hatch, 1989). To build his list of separate intelligences, Gardner reviewed the evidence on cognitive capacities in normal individuals, people suffering from brain damage, and special populations, such as prodigies and idiot savants. He concluded that humans exhibit seven intelligences: logical-mathematical, linguistic, musical, spatial, bodily-kinesthetic, interpersonal, and intrapersonal. These intelligences obviously include a variety of talents that are not assessed by conventional IQ tests.

Gardner is currently investigating whether these intelligences are largely independent, as his theory asserts. He has devised scales to measure each form of intelligence to examine interrelations among them. Subjects who score more than one standard deviation above the mean on a scale are said to have a "strength" in that area. Subjects who score more than one standard deviation below the mean on a scale are said to have a "weakness" in that area. If subjects were to show strength in most areas or weakness in most areas, this result would support the idea that g is the key to intelligence. For the most part, however, Gardner has found that people tend to display a mixture of strong, intermediate, and weak abilities. A great deal of additional research is needed to evaluate Gardner's ambitious and refreshing theory of intelligence.

PUTTING IT IN PERSPECTIVE

As you probably noticed, three of our integrative themes surfaced in this chapter. Our discussions illustrated that cultural factors shape behavior, that psychology evolves in a sociohistorical context, and that heredity and environment jointly influence behavior.

Pervasive psychological testing is largely a Western phenomenon. Most non-Western cultures depend far less than we do on standardized tests. Indeed, the entire enterprise of testing is downright foreign to many cultures. The concept of general intelligence also has a special, Western flavor to it. Many non-Western cultures have very different ideas about the nature of intelligence.

Within Western societies, the observed ethnic differences in average intelligence also illustrate the importance of cultural factors, as these disparities appear to be due in large part to cultural disadvantage and other culture-related considerations. Thus, we see once again that if we hope to achive a sound understanding of behavior, we need to appreciate the cultural contexts in which behavior unfolds.

Human intelligence is shaped by a complex interaction of hereditary and environmental factors. We've drawn a similar conclusion before in other chapters where we examined other aspects of behavior. However, this chapter should have en-

Recognizing Theories of Intelligence

Check your understanding of various theories on the nature of intelligence by matching the names of their originators with the brief descriptions of the theories' main themes that appear below. Choose from the following theorists: (a) Sir Francis Galton, (b) Howard Gardner, (c) Arthur Jensen, (d) Sandra Scarr, and (e) Robert Sternberg. The answers are in Appendix A.

_____ 1. This theorist posited seven human intelligences: logical-mathematical, linguistic, musical, spatial, bodily-kinesthetic, interpersonal, and intrapersonal.

_____ 2. On the basis of his study of eminence and success in families, he concluded that intelligence is inherited.

_____ 3. This theorist stated that the heritability of intelligence is about 80% and that IQ differences between ethnic groups are mainly due to genetics.

_____ 4. This theorist stated that heredity sets certain limits on intelligence and that environmental factors determine where one falls within those limits.

_____ 5. His theory of intelligence is divided into three parts: the contextual, experiential, and componential subtheories.

hanced your appreciation of this idea in at least two ways. First, we examined more of the details of how scientists arrive at the conclusion that heredity and environment jointly shape behavior. Thus, you saw how psychologists have conducted family studies, twin studies, adoption studies, environmental enrichment studies, environmental deprivation studies, and home environment studies in their efforts to document the influence of genetics and experience on intelligence.

Second, we encountered dramatic illustrations of the immense importance attached to the nature versus nurture debate. There is reason to believe that Cyril Burt was willing to risk scandal by faking research results to influence this critical debate. When Leon Kamin first questioned the authenticity of Burt's findings, he was bitterly attacked by Burt's admirers. Arthur Jensen has also been the target of savage criticism. After his controversial 1969 article, he was widely characterized as a racist. When he gave speeches, he was often greeted by protestors carrying signs, such as "Kill Jensen" and "Jensen Must Perish." As you can see, the debate about the inheritance of intelligence inspires passionate feelings in many people. In part, this is because the debate has far-reaching social and political implications, which brings us to another prominent theme in the chapter.

There may be no other area in psychology where the connections between psychology and society at large are so obvious. Prevailing social attitudes have always exerted some influence on testing practices and the interpretation of test results. In the first half of the 20th century, a strong current of racial and class prejudice was apparent in the United States and Britain. This prejudice supported the idea that IQ tests measured innate ability and that "undesirable" groups scored poorly because of their genetic inferiority. Although these beliefs did not go unchallenged within psychology, their widespread acceptance in the field reflected the social values of the time.

Research and theory in psychology leave their mark on society as well. The ebb and flow of the nature versus nurture debate has often spilled over to affect governmental social policies. For example, Burt's views on the inheritance of intelligence clearly influenced the evolution of the British educational system. More generally, the development of mental ability tests has had an enormous impact on educational systems in North America and Europe.

It's ironic that IQ tests have sometimes been associated with social prejudice. When used properly, intelligence tests provide relatively objective measures of mental ability that are less prone to bias than the subjective judgments of teachers or employers.

Today, psychological tests serve many diverse purposes. In the upcoming Application, we focus on creativity tests and on the nature of creative thinking and creative people.

Recap of Key Points

• In the future, schools and society may place less emphasis on intelligence tests because of widespread misconceptions about them. There will probably be greater emphasis on the measurement of specific mental abilities and less emphasis on tapping Spearman's *g*.

• The distinction between fluid and crystallized intelligence is the basis for the most recent revision of the Stanford-Binet IQ test. Although biological indexes of intelligence are being explored, they seem to have little practical utility.

• Research on intelligence increasingly uses a cognitive perspective, which emphasizes the need to understand how people use their intelligence. Many modern theorists, such as Robert Sternberg and Howard Gardner, argue that the concept of intelligence should be expanded to encompass a greater variety of skills.

• Three of our integrative themes stood out in the chapter. Our discussions of intelligence showed how heredity and environment interact to shape behavior, how psychology evolves in a sociohistorical context, and how one has to consider cultural contexts to fully understand behavior.

APPLICATION: MEASURING AND UNDERSTANDING CREATIVITY

Answer the following "true" or "false."

1 Creative ideas often come out of nowhere.

2 Creativity usually occurs in a burst of insight.

3 Creativity depends on inspiration far more than on perspiration.

4 Creativity and intelligence are unrelated.

Intelligence is not the only type of mental ability that psychologists have studied. They have devised tests to explore a variety of mental abilities. Among these, creativity is certainly one of the most interesting. In this Application, we'll discuss psychologists' efforts to measure and understand creativity. As we progress, you'll learn that all the above statements are false.

People tend to view creativity as an essential trait for artists, musicians, and writers, but it is important in *many* walks of life. Consider, for instance, the dilemma that the well-known attorney Vincent Bugliosi found himself in during a murder trial (as related by Bransford & Stein, 1993). As the prosecuting attorney, Bugliosi was handicapped because there were no eyewitnesses to the murder. He had built a solid case against the defendant, but it rested entirely on circumstantial evidence. Near the end of the trial, the defense lawyer made a penetrating argument that seemed to undermine the prosecution's case. The defense attorney argued that circumstantial evidence is like a chain, and that a chain is only as strong as its weakest link. He then proceeded to show that there were several weak links in the circumstantial chain constructed by Bugliosi.

If you were the prosecuting attorney, how would you counter this argument? Bugliosi realized that there *were* weak links in his case, but he did not want to lose the case to a clever analogy. He needed his own analogy—one that would make the evidence appear stronger. What was his solution? He argued that circumstantial evidence is like a *rope* rather than a chain. A rope is made up of a number of independent strands. Bugliosi pointed out that a few strands can break without affecting the overall strength of the rope very much. He acknowledged that his case included some weak strands, but he asserted that they were not fatal the way that weak links in a chain would be. His rebuttal must have been convincing, because he won the case. Faced with a difficult problem, Bugliosi came up with a creative solution. But what is it that made his strategy creative? To answer this question, we have to examine the nature of creativity.

The Nature of Creativity

What makes thought creative? **Creativity involves the generation of ideas that are original, novel, and useful.** Creative thinking is fresh, innovative, and inventive. But novelty by itself is not enough. In addition to being unusual, creative thinking must be adaptive. It must be appropriate to the situation and problem. Bugliosi's rope analogy, for example, was an adaptive response to a tough situation. Bugliosi could have compared circumstantial evidence to a basset hound or a windshield wiper. These analogies certainly would have been novel, but they wouldn't have solved his problem.

Does Creativity Occur in a Burst of Insight?

It is widely believed that creativity usually involves sudden flashes of insight and great leaps of imagination. Robert Weisberg (1986) calls this belief the "aha! myth." Undeniably, creative bursts of insight do occur (Feldman, 1988). However, the evidence suggests that major creative achievements generally are logical extensions of existing ideas, involving long, hard work and many small, faltering steps forward (Weisberg, 1988, 1993). Creative ideas do not come out of nowhere. Creative ideas come from a deep well of experience and training in a specific area, whether it's music, painting, business, or science. As Snow (1986) puts it, "Creativity is not a light bulb in the mind, as most cartoons depict it. It is an accomplishment born of intensive study, long reflection, persistence, and interest" (p. 1033).

Does Creativity Depend on Unconscious Thought Processes?

Some fascinating reports have attributed creative breakthroughs to unconscious thought processes (Ghiselin, 1952). For example, creative giants such as Mozart, Dostoyevsky, and Coleridge reported that dazzling insights came to them while sleeping or daydreaming. These stories have led some theorists to conclude that creativity depends on the unconscious, which is not constrained by normal logic and rationality (Kris, 1952).

As a whole, however, reports of unconscious breakthroughs are few and of dubious accuracy. In at least some cases, it appears that artists have fabricated stories of unconscious breakthroughs to attract publicity, to confound rivals, or to enhance the legend of their genius (Weisberg, 1993). Most cognitive psychologists have concluded that creativity emerges out of normal problem-solving efforts that depend on conscious thought processes (Hayes, 1989; Simon, 1988) and that creativity can be learned or enhanced, at least to some degree (Ford & Harris, 1992).

Does Creativity Depend on Divergent Thinking?

According to many theorists, the key to creativity lies in *divergent thinking*—thinking "that goes off in different directions," as J. P. Guilford (1959) put it. In his model of mental abilities (see Figure 9.18 on page 368), Guilford distinguished between convergent thinking and divergent thinking. **In *convergent thinking* one tries to narrow down a list of alternatives to converge on a single correct answer.** For example, when you take a multiple-choice exam, you try to eliminate incorrect options until you hit on the correct response. Most training in school encourages convergent thinking. **In *divergent thinking* one tries to expand the range of alternatives by generating many possible solutions.** Imagine that you work for an advertising agency. To come up with as many slogans as possible for a client's product, you must use divergent thinking. Some of your slogans may be clear losers, and eventually you will have to engage in convergent thinking to pick the best, but coming up with the range of new possibilities depends on divergent thinking.

Thirty years of research on divergent thinking has yielded mixed results. As a whole, the evidence suggests that divergent thinking contributes to creativity, but it clearly does not represent the *essence* of creativity, as originally proposed (Barron & Harrington, 1981; Brown, 1989). In retrospect, it was probably unrealistic to expect creativity to depend on a single cognitive skill. According to Sternberg (1988a), the cognitive processes that underlie creativity are multifaceted.

Measuring Creativity

Although its nature may be elusive, creativity clearly is important in today's world. Creative masterpieces in the arts and literature enrich human existence. Creative insights in the sciences illuminate people's understanding of the world. Creative inventions fuel technological progress. Thus, it is understandable that psychologists have been interested in measuring creativity with psychological tests.

How Do Psychological Tests Measure Creativity?

A diverse array of psychological tests have been devised to measure individuals' creativity (Cooper, 1991). Usually, the items on creativity tests give respondents a specific starting point and then require them to generate as many possibilities as they can in a short period of time. Typical items on a creativity test might include the following: (1) List as many uses as you can for a newspaper. (2) Think of as many fluids that burn as you can. (3) Imagine that people no longer need sleep and think of as many consequences as you can. Subjects' scores on these tests depend on the *number* of alternatives they generate and on the *originality* and *usefulness* of the alternatives.

One of the more widely used creativity tests is the Remote Associates Test (RAT) developed by Sarnoff and Martha Mednick (1967). This test is based on the assumption that creative people see unusual relationships and make nonobvious connections between ideas. Items on the test require subjects to figure out the obscure links (the remote associations) among three words by coming up with a fourth word that is related to the three stimulus words. Examples of items similar to those found on the RAT are shown in Figure 9.21.

How Well Do Tests Predict Creative Productivity?

In general, studies indicate that creativity tests are mediocre predictors of creative achievement in the real world (Hocevar & Bachelor, 1989). Why? One reason is that these tests measure creativity in the abstract, as a *general trait*. However, the accumulation of evidence suggests that *creativity is specific to particular domains* (Amabile, 1983, 1990; Brown, 1989). Despite some rare exceptions, creative people usually excel in a single field, in which they typically have considerable training and expertise. A remarkably innovative physicist might have no potential to be a creative poet or an inventive advertising executive. Measuring this person's creativ- ity outside of physics may be meaningless. Thus, creativity tests may have limited value because they measure creativity out of context.

Why Is Creative Achievement So Difficult to Predict?

Even if better tests of creativity were devised, predicting creative achievement would probably still prove difficult. Why? Because creative achievement depends on many factors besides creativity. Creative productivity over the course of an individual's career will depend on his or her motivation, personality, and intelligence, as well as situational factors, including training, mentoring, and good fortune (Amabile, 1983).

Research by Benjamin Bloom (1985) and his colleagues on the development of talent highlights the importance of training and hard work. Investigators put together richly detailed case histories for 120 exceptionally successful people from six fields, including concert pianists and sculptors. In all fields, they found that great success depended on high-quality training. The accomplished pianists and sculptors had moved through a succession of outstanding teachers and mentors during their formative years. The study also found that creative success was attributable to dogged determination. Consider the following remarks, which were typical of those interviewed: "What I got at [school] was the absolute determination to be an artist no matter what"; "I had to pursue it—I had to push"; "You have to have discipline and . . . total belief in what you're doing" (Sloane & Sosniak, 1985, pp. 135–136).

Correlates of Creativity

What are creative people like? Are they brighter, or more open minded, or less well adjusted than average? A great deal of research has been conducted on the correlates of creativity.

Is There a Creative Personality?

Creative people exhibit the full range of personality traits, but investigators *have* found modest correlations between certain personality characteristics and creativity (Barron & Harrington, 1981; Ochse, 1990). At the core of this set of personality characteristics are the related traits of independence, autonomy, self-confidence, and nonconformity. Creative people tend to think for themselves and are less easily influenced by the opinions of others than the average person is. Creative people also tend to be more tolerant of complexity, contradiction, and ambiguity than others. They don't feel compelled to simplify everything, and they're not as troubled by uncertainty as many people are. Sternberg and Lubart (1992) also suggest that creative people are willing to grow and change, willing to take risks, and willing to work at overcoming obstacles.

Are Creativity and Intelligence Related?

Are creative people exceptionally smart? Conceptually, creativity and intelligence represent different types of mental ability. Thus, it's not surprising that creativity and intelligence are only weakly related (Horn, 1976; Wallach & Kogan, 1965). They're not entirely unrelated, however (Haensly & Reynolds, 1989), as creativity in most fields requires a minimum level of intelligence. Hence, most highly creative people are probably above average in intelligence (Ochse, 1990).

Is There a Connection Between Creativity and Mental Illness?

There may be a connection between truly exceptional creativity and mental illness. The list of creative geniuses who suffered from psychological disorders is endless (Prentky, 1989). Kafka, Hemingway, Rembrandt, Van Gogh, Chopin, Tchaikovsky, Descartes, and Newton are but a few examples. Of course, a statistical association cannot be demonstrated by citing a handful of examples.

In this case, however, some statistical data are available. And these data *do* suggest a correlation between creative genius and maladjustment—in particular, mood disorders such as depression. When Jami-

son (1988) studied 47 British writers and artists who had achieved certain major honors, she found that 38% of her sample had been treated for mood disorders. Similarly, Andreasen (1987) found that 24 of 30 writers (80%) who had been invited as visiting faculty to the prestigious Iowa Writers Workshop had suffered a mood disorder at some point in their lives. These figures are far above the base rate (roughly 8%) for mood disorders in the general population. Subsequent studies have also found an association between creativity and mood disorders, as well as other kinds of psychological disorders (Ludwig, 1994, 1995; Schildkraut, Hirshfeld, & Murphy, 1994). Thus, accumulating empirical data tentatively suggest that there may be a correlation between major creative achievement and vulnerability to mood disorders. According to Prentky (1989), creativity and maladjustment probably are *not* causally related. Instead, he speculates that certain cognitive styles may both foster creativity and predispose people to psychological disorders. Another, more mundane possibility is that creative individuals' elevated pathology may simply reflect all the difficulty and frustration they experience as they struggle to get their ideas or works noticed or accepted (Csikszentmihalyi, 1994).

Instructions: For each set of three words, try to think of a fourth word that is related to all three words. For example, the words ROUGH, RESISTANCE, and BEER suggest the word DRAFT because of the phrases ROUGH DRAFT, DRAFT RESISTENCE, and DRAFT BEER.

1.	CHARMING	STUDENT	VALIANT
2.	FOOD	CATCHER	HOT
3.	HEARTED	FEET	BITTER
4.	DARK	SHOT	SUN
5.	CANADIAN	GOLF	SANDWICH
6.	TUG	GRAVY	SHOW
7.	ATTORNEY	SELF	SPENDING
8.	MAGIC	PITCH	POWER
9.	ARM	COAL	PEACH
10.	TYPE	GHOST	STORY

Figure 9.21
Remote associates as an index of creativity. One of the more widely used creativity tests is the Remote Associates Test (RAT) developed by Sarnoff and Martha Mednick (1967). The items shown here (from Matlin, 1989) are similar to those on the RAT. See whether you can identify the remote associations between the three stimulus words by coming up with a fourth word that is related to all three. The answers can be found in Figure 9.22.

Recap of Key Points

- Creativity involves the generation of original, novel, and useful ideas. Creativity does not usually involve sudden insight and it does not depend on unconscious thought processes. Divergent thinking contributes to creativity, but does not represent its essence.

- Creativity tests are mediocre predictors of creative productivity in the real world. One problem is that creativity is specific to particular domains of expertise. Another problem is that creative achievement depends on a host of factors besides one's creativity.

- Creativity is only weakly related to personality. The association between creativity and intelligence is also modest, although creativity probably requires above-average intelligence. Recent evidence suggests that creative geniuses may exhibit heightened vulnerability to mood disorders.

1. PRINCE	6. BOAT
2. DOG	7. DEFENSE
3. COLD	8. BLACK
4. GLASSES	9. PIT
5. CLUB	10. WRITER

Figure 9.22
Answers to the remote associates items.

Key Ideas

Key Concepts in Psychological Testing

◆ Psychological tests are standardized measures of behavior—usually mental abilities or aspects of personality. Test scores are interpreted by consulting test norms to find out what represents a high or low score. Psychological tests should produce consistent results, a quality called reliability.

◆ Validity refers to the degree to which there is evidence that a test measures what it was designed to measure. Content validity is crucial on classroom tests. Criterion-related validity is critical when tests are used to predict performance. Construct validity is critical when a test is designed to measure a hypothetical construct.

The Evolution of Intelligence Testing

◆ The first crude efforts to devise intelligence tests were made by Sir Francis Galton, who wanted to show that intelligence is inherited. Modern intelligence testing began with the work of Alfred Binet, who devised a scale to measure a child's mental age.

◆ Lewis Terman revised the original Binet scale to produce the Stanford-Binet in 1916. It introduced the intelligence quotient and became the standard of comparison for subsequent tests. David Wechsler devised an improved measure of intelligence for adults and a new scoring system based on the normal distribution.

Basic Questions About Intelligence Testing

◆ Intelligence tests are useful in screening for learning problems, in student placement and research, and in clinical assessment. Intelligence testing is largely a Western enterprise; IQ tests are not widely used in most non-Western cultures.

◆ In the modern scoring system, deviation IQ scores indicate where people fall in the normal distribution of intelligence for their age group. Although they are intended to measure potential for learning, IQ tests inevitably assess a blend of potential and knowledge.

◆ IQ tests are exceptionally reliable. They are reasonably valid measures of academic intelligence, but they do not tap social or practical intelligence. IQ scores become fairly stable during the grade-school years. IQ scores are correlated with occupational attainment. Nonetheless, they do not predict performance within an occupation very well.

Extremes of Intelligence

◆ IQ scores below 70–75 are usually diagnostic of mental retardation, but these diagnoses should not be based solely on test re-

sults. Four levels of retardation have been distinguished. Most mildly retarded children grow up to be self-supporting adults. Although many biological conditions can cause retardation, biological causes can be pinpointed in only a small minority of cases.

◆ Children who obtain IQ scores above 130 may be viewed as gifted, but cutoffs for accelerated programs vary. Research by Terman showed that gifted children tend to be socially mature and well adjusted.

Heredity and Environment as Determinants of Intelligence

◆ Twin studies show that identical twins are more similar in IQ than fraternal twins, suggesting that intelligence is inherited, at least in part. Estimates of the heritability of intelligence mostly range from 50% to 70%, but heritability ratios have certain limitations.

◆ Many lines of evidence indicate that environment is also an important determinant of intelligence. The concept of reaction range posits that heredity places limits on one's intellectual potential while the environment determines where one falls within these limits.

◆ Genetic explanations for cultural differences in IQ have been challenged on a variety of grounds. Even if the heritability of IQ is great, group differences in intelligence may not be due to heredity. Moreover, ethnicity varies with social class, so socioeconomic disadvantage may account for low IQ scores among minority students. Stereotype vulnerability and cultural bias on IQ tests may also contribute to ethnic differences in average IQ.

New Directions in the Assessment and Study of Intelligence

◆ In the future, there will probably be greater emphasis on the measurement of specific mental abilities and less emphasis on tapping Spearman's g. The distinction between fluid and crystallized intelligence is the basis for the most recent revision of the Stanford-Binet IQ test.

◆ Although biological indexes of intelligence are being explored, they seem to have little practical utility. Research on intelligence increasingly employs a cognitive perspective, which emphasizes the need to understand how people use their intelligence. Many modern theorists argue that the concept of intelligence should be expanded to encompass a greater variety of skills.

Putting It in Perspective

◆ Three of our integrative themes stood out in the chapter. Our discussions of intelligence showed how heredity and environment interact to shape behavior, how psy-

chology evolves in a sociohistorical context, and how one has to consider cultural contexts to fully understand behavior.

Application: Measuring and Understanding Creativity

◆ Creativity involves the generation of original, novel, and useful ideas. Creativity does not usually involve sudden insight, and it consists of more than divergent thinking. Creativity tests are mediocre predictors of creative productivity in the real world.

◆ Creativity is only weakly related to intelligence and personality. Recent evidence suggests that creative geniuses may exhibit heightened vulnerability to mood disorders.

Key Terms

Achievement tests
Aptitude tests
Construct validity
Content validity
Convergent thinking
Correlation
  coefficient
Creativity
Criterion-related
  validity
Crystallized
  intelligence
Deviation IQ scores
Divergent thinking
Eugenics
Factor analysis
Fluid intelligence
Heritability ratio
Intelligence quotient
  (IQ)
Intelligence tests
Mental age
Mental retardation

Normal distribution
Percentile score
Personality tests
Psychological test
Reaction range
Reliability
Standardization
Test norms
Test-retest reliability
Validity

Key People

Alfred Binet
Sir Cyril Burt
Sir Francis Galton
Howard Gardner
Arthur Jensen
Sandra Scarr
Claude Steele
Robert Sternberg
Lewis Terman
David Wechsler

Practice Test

1. Which of the following does not belong with the others?
   A. aptitude tests
   B. personality tests
   C. intelligence tests
   D. achievement tests

2. If you score at the 75th percentile on a standardized test, this means that:
   A. 75% of those who took the test scored better than you did.
   B. 25% of those who took the test scored less than you did.
   C. 75% of those who took the test scored less than you did.
   D. you answered 75% of the questions correctly.

3. If a test has good test-retest reliability:
   A. there is a strong correlation between items on the test.
   B. it accurately measures what it says it measures.
   C. it can be used to predict future performance.
   D. the test yields similar scores if taken at two different times.

4. Which of the following is a true statement regarding Francis Galton?
   A. He advocated the control of reproduction to gradually improve the intellectual abilities of the human race.
   B. He advocated the development of special programs to tap the intellectual potential of the culturally disadvantaged.
   C. He developed tests that identified those children who were unable to profit from a normal education.
   D. He took the position that intelligence is more a matter of environment than heredity.

5. On most modern IQ tests, a score of 115 would be:
   A. about normal.
   B. about 15% higher than the average of one's agemates.
   C. an indication of genius.
   D. one standard deviation above the mean.

6. IQ tests have proven to be good predictors of:
   A. social intelligence.
   B. practical problem-solving intelligence.
   C. school performance.
   D. all of the above.

7. Mr. and Mrs. Proudparent are beaming because little Newton, at the tender age of 3, is a genius according to the preschool intelligence test he took. What sort of advice do they need to hear?
   A. As children, geniuses tend to be very temperamental.
   B. Preschool IQ scores tend to be poor predictors of later IQ.
   C. They shouldn't make a fuss about Newton's exceptional abilities because it could lead to excessive egotism on his part.
   D. They should put more faith in this score than in IQ scores obtained later, since accumulating experience as one gets older makes measuring intelligence increasingly unreliable.

8. Which of the following is a true statement about mental retardation?
   A. Most retarded people are unable to live normal lives due to their mental deficiencies.
   B. With special tutoring, a mentally retarded person can attain average intelligence.
   C. The majority of mentally retarded people are not readily distinguished from the rest of the supposedly normal population.
   D. Diagnoses of mental retardation are based exclusively on IQ scores.

9. Most school districts consider children who _____ to be gifted.
   A. have IQ scores above 115
   B. score in the upper 2%–3% of the IQ distribution
   C. have parents in professional careers
   D. demonstrate high levels of leadership and creativity

10. In which of the following cases would you expect to find the greatest similarity in IQ?
    A. between fraternal twins
    B. between identical twins
    C. between non-twin siblings
    D. between parent and child

11. Evidence indicating that upbringing affects one's mental ability is provided by which of the following findings?
    A. that identical twins are more similar in IQ than fraternal twins
    B. that there is more than a chance similarity between adopted children and their biological parents
    C. that siblings reared together are more similar in IQ than siblings reared apart
    D. that identical twins reared apart are more similar in IQ than siblings reared together

12. Which of the following is a likely consequence of stereotype vulnerability for members of minority groups?
    A. Academic motivation declines.
    B. Academic performance often suffers.
    C. Standardized tests may be especially anxiety arousing.
    D. All of the above are likely consequences.

13. Which of the following is a current trend in the assessment of intelligence?
    A. less reliance on achievement and aptitude tests in schools
    B. more reliance on IQ tests in schools
    C. more emphasis on general ability rather than specific abilities
    D. more emphasis on specific abilities rather than general ability

14. When you try to narrow down a list of alternatives to arrive at a single correct answer, you engage in:
    A. convergent thinking.
    B. divergent thinking.
    C. creativity.
    D. insight.

15. Nora has a blind date with Nick who, she's been told, is considered a true genius by the faculty in the art department. Now she's having second thoughts, because she's always heard that geniuses are a little off their rocker. Does she have reason to be concerned?
    A. Yes. It's been well documented that the stress of creative achievement often leads to schizophrenic symptoms.
    B. No. Extensive research on creativity and psychological disorders shows no evidence for any connection.
    C. Perhaps. There is evidence of a correlation between major creative achievement and vulnerability to mood disorders.
    D. Of course not. The stereotype of the genius who's mentally ill is purely a product of the jealousy of untalented people.

Answers

1	B	Page 340	6	C	Pages 351–352	11	C	Pages 358–360
2	C	Page 341	7	B	Pages 352–353	12	D	Pages 363–365
3	D	Page 342	8	C	Page 354	13	D	Pages 367–368
4	A	Page 345	9	B	Page 355	14	A	Page 374
5	D	Page 350	10	B	Pages 357–359	15	C	Page 375

10
MOTIVATION AND EMOTION

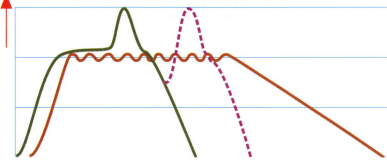

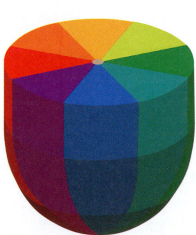

In September 1983, for the first time in 132 years the United States lost the America's Cup, the foremost trophy in the sport of sailing. An Australian team with a superior new boat design won the Cup. The Australians were understandably ecstatic. In contrast, the U.S. team was devastated by its abrupt and unexpected defeat. Dennis Conner, the team's skipper, wept openly in despair after the last race.

Within months, however, Conner had begun a relentless campaign to recapture the America's Cup in the next race in 1987. Working 365 days a year, he secured an unprecedented $15 million in financial backing. He investigated hundreds of new boat designs, supervised the building of four boats, assembled and trained a crackerjack crew, and sailed in hundreds of races to prepare. Describing his frantic pace, Conner's wife said, "He never relaxes, and we never go on vacations. Hell to Dennis would be a day on the beach." Conner's crew would certainly agree with his wife. Working 12 to 15 hours a day, six or seven days a week, they were pushed through a grueling training regimen for 17 months. Training thousands of miles from their homes, most of them saw their wives or girlfriends only once during this time.

In 1987 the long hours of hard work and sacrifice paid off. Conner and his crew trounced their opponents and recaptured the America's Cup. The jubilation of victory was readily apparent when Conner accepted the trophy. So, did Connor finally relax after the vindication of his 1987 victory? No, he continued his frenetic work pace in the hopes of successfully defending the America's Cup. In 1992 and 1995, however, he once again experienced the bitter taste of defeat.

The saga of Dennis Conner and his crew is packed with motivational riddles. What motivated these men to dedicate their lives to the pursuit of a yachting trophy? Money? No, the well-educated crew members were paid a mere $75 per week during their brutal, monastic months of training. Fame? For Conner perhaps, but the other crew members knew that their names wouldn't become household words. A deep-rooted love of sailing? Maybe for some of them, but Conner noted, "I don't like to sail. I like to compete." That was the key theme for most of the crew. More than anything else, they seemed to be propelled by the excitement of competition and the thrill of victory. As Conner put it, "The bottom line is, people like to win."

Conner's story is also filled with strong emotions. When he lost the America's Cup in 1983, he experienced tremendous dejection and disappointment. When he won the Cup back in 1987, he experienced enormous joy and happiness. His tale illustrates the intimate relation between motivation and emotion—the topics we'll examine in this chapter.

We'll begin by discussing theoretical perspectives on motivation. Then we'll take a close look at a handful of selected motives that have been studied extensively, including hunger, sex, affiliation, and achievement. To close, we'll analyze the elements of emotion and examine theories that attempt to explain the experience of emotion. In the Application we'll expand on the dynamics of human sexual behavior, addressing practical issues.

The saga of Dennis Conner and his crew is packed with motivational riddles and intense emotions.

MOTIVATIONAL THEORIES AND CONCEPTS

Why did many of Dennis Conner's crew members give up good jobs to join his quest for the America's Cup? Why did the renowned artist Vincent Van Gogh cut off his ear? Why did Greta Garbo suddenly retire from making movies at the peak of her highly acclaimed movie career? Why did you decide to attend college? Why did you start reading this chapter today? In asking these questions, we're looking for the motives underlying the actions.

Motives are the needs, wants, interests, and desires that propel people in certain directions. In short, **motivation** involves goal-directed behavior.

There are a number of theoretical approaches to motivation. These theories differ most basically in whether they emphasize the innate, biological basis of motivation or the learned, social basis of motivation. Let's look at some motivational theories and the concepts they employ.

The Evolutionary View

Psychologists who take an evolutionary perspective assert that human motives and those of other species are the products of evolution, just as anatomical characteristics are. They argue that natural selection favors behaviors that maximize reproductive success—that is, passing on genes to the next generation. Thus, they explain motives such as affiliation, achievement, dominance, aggression, and sex drive in terms of their adaptive value. If a species is intensely competitive, they say, it's because competitiveness gives a survival advantage, so that proportionately more competitive genes are passed on to the next generation.

In recent decades, theorists have broadened Darwin's original concept of reproductive fitness to better explain altruistic behavior. Traditional evolutionary theory has had difficulty explaining self-sacrifice. If organisms try to maximize their reproductive success, why would a soldier throw himself on a hand grenade to protect a comrade? And why does a blackbird risk death to signal the approach of a hawk to others in the flock? In 1964, W. D. Hamilton proposed the theory of *inclusive fitness* to explain this apparent paradox. According to Hamilton, an organism may contribute to passing on its genes by sacrificing itself to save others that share the same genes. Altruistic behavior that evolves as members of a species protect their own offspring, for example, can be extended to other, more distantly related members of the species. Thus, inclusive fitness is the sum of an individual's own reproductive success, plus the effects the individual has on the reproductive success of others. The concept of inclusive fitness suggests that the probability of altruistic behavior

decreases as the degree of relatedness between a helper and potential recipient declines, a prediction that was supported in a recent study (Burnstein, Crandall, & Kitayama, 1994).

Evolutionary analyses of motivation are based on the premise that motives can best be understood in terms of the adaptive problems they have solved over the course of many generations. Consider, for instance, the *affiliation motive,* or need for belongingness, which we will discuss later in this chapter. The potential survival and reproductive benefits of affiliation are diverse. They include sharing of food, help with offspring, collaboration in hunting or defense, opportunities for sexual interaction, and so forth (Baumeister & Leary, 1995). David Buss (1995) points out that it is not by accident that achievement, power, and intimacy are among the most heavily studied social motives, as the satisfaction of each of these motives is likely to influence one's reproductive success.

Evolutionary theorists have come up with intriguing hypotheses related to a host of topics, including hunger, territoriality, aggression, and cooperation, but their analyses of mating patterns have drawn the most attention (see Figure 10.1). For example, Robert Trivers's (1972) *parental investment theory* asserts that a species' mating patterns depend on what each sex has to invest, in the way of time, energy, and survival risk, to maximize the transmission of its genes to the next generation. In many mammalian species, males have to invest little beyond the act of copulation, so their reproductive potential is maximized by mating with as many females as possible. In contrast, females typically have to invest weeks or months of effort to carry and nourish offspring, thereby limiting the number of offspring they can

Figure 10.1
Evolutionary hypotheses about mating behavior.
Evolutionary psychologists have proposed quite a variety of hypotheses about gender differences in mating behavior, such as those outlined here, which attempt to explain why males tend to have more sexual partners and why males tend to be more upset by sexual infidelity, whereas females tend to be more distressed by emotional infidelity.

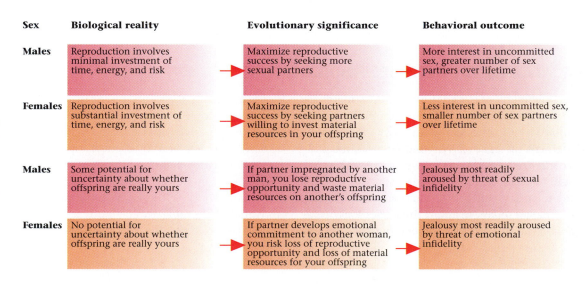

Sex	Biological reality	Evolutionary significance	Behavioral outcome
Males	Reproduction involves minimal investment of time, energy, and risk	Maximize reproductive success by seeking more sexual partners	More interest in uncommitted sex, greater number of sex partners over lifetime
Females	Reproduction involves substantial investment of time, energy, and risk	Maximize reproductive success by seeking partners willing to invest material resources in your offspring	Less interest in uncommitted sex, smaller number of sex partners over lifetime
Males	Some potential for uncertainty about whether offspring are really yours	If partner impregnated by another man, you lose reproductive opportunity and waste material resources on another's offspring	Jealousy most readily aroused by threat of sexual infidelity
Females	No potential for uncertainty about whether offspring are really yours	If partner develops emotional commitment to another woman, you risk loss of reproductive opportunity and loss of material resources for your offspring	Jealousy most readily aroused by threat of emotional infidelity

CHAPTER TEN

produce in a breeding season, regardless of how many males they mate with. Hence, females have no incentive for mating with many males. In mammalian species, females typically can optimize their reproductive potential by being selective in mating. Among humans, this selectivity supposedly entails seeking partners who have more material resources that can be invested in feeding and caring for offspring. Thus, Trivers uses evolutionary concepts to explain why males in many species mate with a greater variety of partners than females do.

In a similar vein, evolutionary psychologists predict that among humans, males and females should differ in the events that most readily activate jealousy (Buss, 1996). Because males always have to worry about paternity (whether their children are really theirs), *sexual infidelity* by partners is hypothesized to be particularly threatening to their reproductive success. In contrast, females are always certain that their offspring are theirs, but they supposedly have to worry more about losing a male partner's material resouces, which depend on his emotional commitment. Hence, males' *emotional infidelity* is hypothesized to be particularly threatening to females (see Figure 10.1). In a test of these hypotheses, Buss and his colleagues (1992) found that sexual infidelity elicited the greatest jealousy in men, whereas emotional infidelity triggered the greatest jealousy in women (see Figure 10.2). A recent cross-cultural study replicated these results in the United States, Germany, and the Netherlands (Buunk et al., 1996). Although there are other plausible explanations for these results (DeSteno & Salovey, 1996; Harris & Christenfeld, 1996), the findings mesh especially well with evolutionary models of mating behavior.

The application of evolutionary concepts to human motivation has generated some debate (Ruse, 1987; Kenrick & Simpson, 1997). Some critics argue that evolutionary analyses overestimate the influence of biology on human behavior while ignoring the importance of environmental and cultural factors. In light of this criticism, it is ironic that some of the most interesting cross-cultural research in recent years has been guided by an evolutionary perspective. Cross-cultural research provides rich opportunities for testing evolutionary hypotheses, which assume that cultural variations in behavior occur because different cultures have had to adapt to different environmental demands. Although some evolutionary theorists do seem to subscribe to a naive brand of genetic determinism, the argument that evolutionary theo-

ries ignore culture and environment is clearly not accurate.

Another line of criticism suggests that evolutionary theory can be used to assert that the status quo in society is the inevitable outcome of natural selection (Gould, 1993; Lewontin, Rose, & Kamin, 1984). For example, if males have dominant status over females, one might argue that evolutionary forces must have favored this arrangement. Historically, evolutionary theory *has* often been used to justify existing social arrangements and customs (Caporael & Brewer, 1991; Rapoport, 1991). However, this is a political issue that has no bearing on the theory's scientific validity or utility. Of interest to us, though, is the way in which the debate about the scientific merits of evolutionary theory has become intertwined with debate about the political implications of the theory. This controversy demonstrates once again that psychological theories can have far-reaching social and political ramifications and that psychology evolves in a sociohistorical context.

Drive Theories

Many theories view motivational forces in terms of *drives*. The drive concept appears in a diverse array of theories that otherwise have little in common, such as psychoanalytic (Freud, 1915) and behaviorist formulations (Hull, 1943). This approach to understanding motivation was explored most fully by Clark Hull in the 1940s and 1950s.

Hull's concept of drive was derived from Walter Cannon's (1932) observation that organisms seek to maintain **homeostasis, a state of physiological equilibrium or stability.** The body maintains homeostasis in various ways. For example, human body temperature normally fluctuates around 98.6

"Evolutionary psychologists develop hypotheses about the psychological mechanisms that have evolved in humans to solve particular adaptive problems that humans have faced under ancestral conditions."

DAVID BUSS

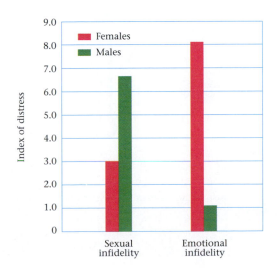

Figure 10.2
The gender gap in jealousy. Buss et al. (1992) asked subjects to vividly imagine scenarios involving either sexual or emotional infidelity by their partner. Subjects' distress while imagining these scenarios was assessed by monitoring various indexes of emotional and physiological arousal. As these results show, sexual infidelity generated the most distress in males, whereas emotional infidelity elicited the most arousal in females.

degrees Fahrenheit (see Figure 10.3). If your body temperature rises or drops noticeably, automatic responses occur: If your temperature goes up, you'll perspire; if your temperature goes down, you'll shiver. These reactions are designed to move your temperature back toward 98.6 degrees. Thus, your body reacts to many disturbances in physiological stability by trying to restore equilibrium.

Drive theories apply the concept of homeostasis to behavior. A *drive* is an **internal state of tension that motivates an organism to engage in activities that should reduce this tension.** These unpleasant states of tension are viewed as disruptions of the preferred equilibrium. According to drive theories, when individuals experience a drive, they're motivated to pursue actions that will lead to *drive reduction.* The hunger motive provides a simple example of drive theory in action. If you go without food for a while, you begin to experience some discomfort. This internal tension (the drive) motivates you to obtain food. Eating reduces the drive and restores physiological equilibrium. Most drive theories assume that people begin life with a small set of unlearned, biological drives and that they gradually develop a larger, more diverse set of acquired drives through learning and socialization.

Drive theories have been very influential, and the drive concept continues to be widely used in modern psychology. *However, drive theories cannot explain all motivation.* Homeostasis appears irrelevant to some human motives, such as a "thirst for knowledge." Also, motivation may exist without drive arousal. This point is easy to illustrate. Think of all the times that you've eaten when you weren't the least bit hungry. You're driving or walking home from class, amply filled by a solid lunch, when an ice cream parlor beckons seductively. You stop in and have a couple of scoops of your favorite flavor. Not only are you motivated to eat in the absence of internal tension, you may cause yourself some internal tension—from overeating. Because drive theories assume that people always try to reduce internal tension, they can't explain this behavior very well. Incentive theories, which represent a different approach to motivation, can account for this behavior more readily.

Incentive Theories

Incentive theories propose that external stimuli regulate motivational states (Bolles, 1975; McClelland, 1975; Skinner, 1953). **An *incentive* is an external goal that has the capacity to motivate behavior.** Ice cream, a juicy steak, a monetary prize, approval from friends, an A on an exam, and a promotion at work are all incentives. Some of these incentives may reduce drives, but others may not.

Drive and incentive models of motivation are often contrasted as *push versus pull* theories. Drive theories emphasize how *internal* states of tension *push* people in certain directions. Incentive theories emphasize how *external* stimuli *pull* people in certain directions. According to drive theories, the source of motivation lies *within* the organism. According to incentive theories, the source of motivation lies *outside* the organism, in the environment. This means that incentive models don't operate according to the principle of homeostasis, which hinges on internal changes in the organism. Thus, in comparison to drive theories, incentive theories emphasize environmental factors and downplay the biological bases of human motivation.

As you're painfully aware, people can't always obtain the goals they desire, such as good grades or choice promotions. *Expectancy-value models* of motivation are incentive theories that take this reality into account (Atkinson & Birch, 1978). Ac-

Figure 10.3
Temperature regulation as an example of homeostasis. The regulation of body temperature provides a simple example of how organisms often seek to maintain homeostasis, or a state of physiological equilibrium. When your temperature moves out of an acceptable range, automatic bodily reactions (such as sweating or shivering) occur that help restore equilibrium. Of course, these automatic reactions may not be sufficient by themselves, so you may have to take other actions (such as turning a furnace up or down) to bring your body temperature back into its comfort zone.

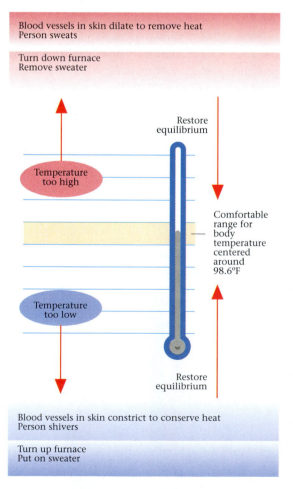

Blood vessels in skin dilate to remove heat
Person sweats

Turn down furnace
Remove sweater

Restore equilibrium

Temperature too high

Comfortable range for body temperature centered around 98.6°F

Temperature too low

Restore equilibrium

Blood vessels in skin constrict to conserve heat
Person shivers

Turn up furnace
Put on sweater

CHAPTER TEN

cording to expectancy-value models, one's motivation to pursue a particular course of action will depend on two factors: (1) *expectancy* about one's chances of attaining the incentive and (2) the *value* of the desired incentive.

Thus, your motivation to pursue a promotion at work will depend on your estimate of the likelihood that you can snare the promotion (expectancy) and on how appealing the promotion is to you (value). In a similar fashion, your motivation to buy lottery tickets will depend on the size of the prize and on your belief about your chances of winning. State-run lotteries clearly recognize this reality. To lure people into playing these lotteries, officials make incentive value high by offering games with huge financial prizes (but with very low odds of winning). They also elevate the expectancy of winning by offering games in which there are many daily winners (of small prizes).

The Range and Diversity of Human Motives

Motivational theorists of all persuasions agree on one point: Humans display an enormous diversity of motives. Most theories distinguish between *biological motives* that originate in bodily needs, such as hunger, and *social motives* that originate in social experiences, such as the need for achievement.

People have a limited number of biological needs. According to K. B. Madsen (1968, 1973), most theories identify 10 to 15 such needs, some of which are listed on the left side of Figure 10.4. As you can see, most biological motives reflect needs that are essential to survival, such as the needs for food, water, and maintenance of body temperature within an acceptable range.

People all share the same biological needs, but their social needs vary depending on their experiences. For example, some people acquire a need for orderliness, and some don't. Although people have a limited number of biological needs, they can acquire an unlimited number of social needs through learning and socialization. Some examples of social motives—from an influential list compiled by Henry Murray (1938)—are shown on the right side of Figure 10.4. He theorized that most people have needs for achievement, autonomy, affiliation, dominance, exhibition, and order, among other things. Of course, the strength of these needs varies from person to person, depending on personal history.

Although the distinction between biological and social needs is not absolute, this dichotomy allows us to impose some organization on the diverse motives seen in human behavior. We turn next to a theory that provides a more elaborate scheme for organizing human motives.

Arranging Needs in a Hierarchy: Maslow's Theory 10c

Abraham Maslow (1962, 1970), a prominent humanistic theorist, proposed a sweeping overview of human motivation. His theory strikes a unique balance between biological and social needs and integrates many of the motivational concepts that we've discussed.

Maslow's theory assumes that people have many needs that compete for expression. At this very moment, your need for sleep may be pitted against your need for achievement, as you work to earn a good grade in your psychology class. Of course, not all needs are created equal. Maslow proposed that human motives are organized hierarchically.

Examples of Biological Needs in Humans
Hunger motive
Thirst motive
Sex motive
Temperature motive (need for appropriate body temperature)
Excretory motive (need to eliminate bodily wastes)
Sleep and rest motive
Activity motive (need for optimal level of stimulation and arousal)
Aggression motive

Examples of Social Needs in Humans
Achievement motive (need to excel)
Affiliation motive (need for social bonds)
Autonomy motive (need for independence)
Nurturance motive (need to nourish and protect others)
Dominance motive (need to influence or control others)
Exhibition motive (need to make an impression on others)
Order motive (need for orderliness, tidiness, organization)
Play motive (need for fun, relaxation, amusement)

Figure 10.4
The diversity of human motives. People are motivated by a wide range of needs, which can be divided into two broad classes: biological motives and social motives. The list on the left (adapted from Madsen, 1973) shows some important biological needs in humans. The list on the right (adapted from Murray, 1938) provides examples of prominent social needs in humans.

"What a man can be, he must be."

ABRAHAM MASLOW

His *hierarchy of needs* **is a systematic arrangement of needs according to priority, which assumes that basic needs must be met before less basic needs are aroused.** Maslow believed that human nature dictates the order of the various levels of needs.

This hierarchical arrangement is usually portrayed as a pyramid (see Figure 10.5). The needs at the bottom of the pyramid are the most basic. They are fundamental physiological needs that are essential to survival, such as the needs for food, water, a stable body temperature, and so on. They must be satisfied fairly well before the individual can become concerned about needs at higher levels in the hierarchy. When a person manages to satisfy a level of needs reasonably well (complete satisfaction is not necessary), *this satisfaction activates needs at the next level.*

The second tier in Maslow's pyramid is made up of safety and security needs. These needs reflect concern about *long-term* survival. When safety and security needs are met adequately, needs for love and belongingness become more prominent. When these needs are gratified, esteem needs are activated. People then become more concerned about their achievements and the recognition, respect, and status that they earn.

Consistent with his humanistic perspective, Maslow theorized that people have growth needs that emerge out of the human striving for *personal growth*—that is, evolution toward a higher state of being (see Chapter 1). The growth needs—such as the needs for knowledge, understanding, and aesthetic beauty—are found in the uppermost reaches of Maslow's hierarchy. Foremost among them is the *need for self-actualization,* **which is the need to fulfill one's potential.** It is the highest need in Maslow's motivational hierarchy. Maslow summarized this concept with a very simple statement: "What a man *can* be, he *must* be." According to Maslow, people will be frustrated if they are unable to fully use their talents or pursue their true interests. For example, if you have musical talent but must work as an accountant, or if you have scholarly interests but must work as a sales clerk, your need for self-actualization will be frustrated.

Maslow's theory has been influential in some quarters. For example, it has been popular in the world of business, where it has guided many efforts to enhance employees' productivity and job satisfaction (Aamodt, 1991). However, growth needs such as self-actualization have proven difficult to measure and study. Thus, Maslow's theory rests on a thin foundation of research (Geller, 1982). Moreover, some of this research has raised doubts about basic assumptions in the theory (Neher, 1991). Individuals' needs are not always prioritized in the order proposed by Maslow. For example, some people put a higher priority on meeting their esteem needs than their love and belongingness needs, which ordinarily are more basic. And unmet lower needs do not completely preclude the activation of higher needs. Chronic hunger may not prevent someone from yearning for love and affection, and homelessness may not destroy a person's need for respect.

**Figure 10.5
Maslow's hierarchy
of needs.** According to Maslow, human needs are arranged in a hierarchy, and people must satisfy their basic needs before they can satisfy higher needs. In the diagram, higher levels in the pyramid represent progressively less basic needs. Individuals progress upward in the hierarchy when lower needs are satisfied reasonably well, but they may regress back to lower levels if basic needs are no longer satisfied.

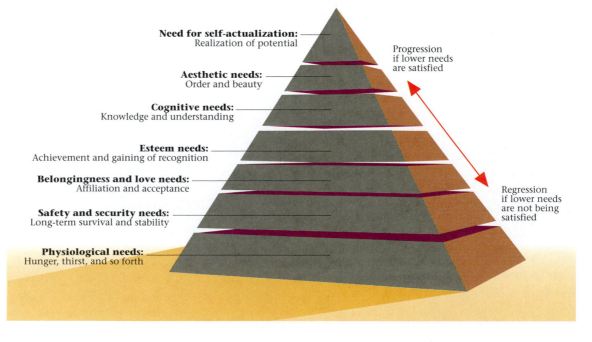

Need for self-actualization:
Realization of potential

Aesthetic needs:
Order and beauty

Cognitive needs:
Knowledge and understanding

Esteem needs:
Achievement and gaining of recognition

Belongingness and love needs:
Affiliation and acceptance

Safety and security needs:
Long-term survival and stability

Physiological needs:
Hunger, thirst, and so forth

Progression
if lower needs
are satisfied

Regression
if lower needs
are not being
satisfied

CHAPTER TEN

Thus, Maslow's theory has its strengths and its weaknesses—just as all the other motivational theories do. No one theory has come to dominate the investigation of motivation in contemporary psychology. Perhaps it's unrealistic to expect a single theory to explain the great variety of motives that inspire goal-directed behavior. In any case, in the remainder of this chapter you'll see the influence of all the motivational theories that we've discussed.

Our next task is to take a closer look at selected motives. To a large degree, our choices reflect the motives psychologists have studied the most. Given the range and diversity of human motives, we can only examine a handful in depth. So we'll draw two examples each from the two broad classes of human needs (biological and social). We'll focus on hunger and sexual motivation to show how researchers have dissected biological needs. Then we'll examine affiliation and achievement to illustrate how psychologists have analyzed social motives. As we explore these four motives, we'll be moving upward through Maslow's hierarchy. Thus, you'll see the influence of physiological factors gradually declining, giving way to social and environmental factors.

Recap of Key Points

• Motivation involves goal-oriented behavior. Some motivational theories emphasize the biological roots of motives; others emphasize the social roots.

• Evolutionary theorists explain motives in terms of their adaptive value. For example, parental investment theory asserts that mating patterns depend on what each sex has to invest in procreation.

• Evolutionary theory can explain why males tend to have more sexual partners than females and why males are more prone to sexual jealousy. However, evolutionary analyses are controversial.

• Drive theories apply a homeostatic model to motivation. They assume that organisms seek to reduce unpleasant states of tension called drives. In contrast,

incentive theories emphasize how external goals energize behavior.

• Madsen's list of biological needs and Murray's list of social needs illustrate that a diverse array of motives govern human behavior.

• Maslow's hierarchy of needs assumes that basic needs must be satisfied reasonably well before higher needs are activated. His model integrates biological and social needs. According to Maslow, people's growth needs include the need to realize their full potential, a motive called the need for self-actualization.

CONCEPT CHECK 10.1
Applying Motivational Concepts

Check your understanding of the motivational concepts that we've discussed by analyzing the examples of motivated behavior described here. Indicate which theoretical approach seems to provide the best explanation for the behavior and which level of needs in Maslow's hierarchy has been activated. The answers are in Appendix A.

Scenario	Relevant theory	Level of needs
1. You're alone in a strange city, and you feel lonely. You yearn for someone to talk to. You go for a walk along the waterfront, hoping to meet someone.	_____	_____
2. You're working two hours overtime every night. You don't like staying late, but your company really needs to get the work done and you can't pass up the substantial bonus (triple pay) they're offering.	_____	_____
3. You become fascinated by modern architecture, so you go get a bunch of books out of the library because you want to understand the thinking behind postmodernism.	_____	_____
4. You're among the nation's poor, and you can't put adequate food on the table for your family. You give your children all of the food available for dinner, telling them you don't feel hungry, when you're really starving.	_____	_____

THE MOTIVATION OF HUNGER AND EATING

Why do people eat? Because they're hungry. What makes them hungry? A lack of food. Any grade-school child can explain these basic facts. So hunger is a simple motivational system, right? Wrong! Hunger is deceptive. It only looks simple. Actu-

ally, it's a terribly puzzling and complex motivational system. Despite extensive studies of hunger, scientists are still struggling to understand the factors that regulate eating behavior. Let's examine a few of these factors.

You have probably had embarrassing occasions when your stomach growled loudly at an inopportune moment. Someone may have commented, "You must be starving!" Most people equate a rumbling stomach with hunger, and, in fact, the first scientific theories of hunger were based on this simple equation. In an elaborate 1912 study, Walter Cannon and A. L. Washburn verified what most people have noticed based on casual observation: There is an association between stomach contractions and the experience of hunger.

Based on this correlation, Cannon theorized that stomach contractions *cause* hunger. However, as we've seen before, correlation is no assurance of causation, and his theory was eventually discredited. Stomach contractions often accompany hunger, but they don't cause it. How do we know? Because later research showed that people continue to experience hunger even after their stomach has been removed out of medical necessity (Wangensteen & Carlson, 1931). If hunger can occur without a stomach, then stomach contractions can't be the cause of hunger. This realization led to more elaborate theories of hunger that focus on (1) the role of the brain, (2) blood sugar level, and (3) hormones.

Brain Regulation

Research with laboratory animals eventually suggested that the experience of hunger is controlled in the brain—specifically, in the hypothalamus. As we have noted before, the *hypothalamus* is a tiny structure involved in the regulation of a variety of biological needs related to survival. Researchers have typically investigated the role of the hypothalamus in behavior by subjecting animals to *electrical stimulation of the brain (ESB)*. They implant an electrode in the hypothalamus and then pass various currents through the electrode to either destroy (lesion) or activate the area of the brain at the base of the electrode (see Chapter 3).

A great many animal studies have shown that the activation and destruction of two areas in the hypothalamus are associated with changes in eating (see Figure 10.6). Investigators have found that when they activate the *lateral hypothalamus* (LH) through ESB, animals promptly begin to eat, even if they're already full. The animals stop eating when the electrical stimulation of the LH is halted. In contrast, when researchers destroy the LH, animals typically ignore available food and frequently starve (Anand & Brobeck, 1951; Teitelbaum & Epstein, 1962). The opposite pattern is seen when researchers stimulate or lesion the *ventromedial nucleus of the hypothalamus* (VMH) (Brobeck, Tepperman, & Long, 1943; Wyrwicka & Dobrzecka, 1960). Activation of the VMH curtails eating behavior, whereas destroying the VMH leads to extensive overeating and obesity. Indeed, it is not unusual for animals with VMH lesions to balloon up to three times their original weight.

Given these results, investigators originally concluded that activation of the lateral hypothalamus *starts* the experience of hunger and that activation of the ventromedial hypothalamus *stops* the experience of hunger. They weren't entirely sure what normally leads to the activation of these dual centers in the absence of artificial electrical stimulation, but they concluded that the LH and VMH are the brain's on-off switches that control hunger (Stellar, 1954).

Doubts about this dual-centers model of hunger soon surfaced, however. Researchers noticed that hypothalamic stimulation and lesioning lead to some peculiarities in the eating behavior of experimental animals. For example, rats with VMH lesions usually engage in massive overeating. However, they're *lazy*, and if they're forced to work for their food (by pressing a lever), they end up eating less than normal (Graff & Stellar, 1962). They also are *picky* and reject food that doesn't taste good (Ferguson & Keesey, 1975). Critics argued that if the animals were really hungry, they wouldn't be so lazy or picky. Another line of research suggested that most of the effects of LH lesions on eating were due, not to the destruction of the lateral hypothalamus, but to the *disruption of dopamine circuits* that pass through the lateral hypothalamus (Winn, Tarbuck, & Dunnett, 1984; Winn, 1995).

The dual-centers model has been further complicated by recent research on how neurotransmitters contribute to the brain's regulation of hunger and eating. Sarah Leibowitz and her colleagues have found that increased levels of norepinephrine are associated with increased carbohydrate intake in laboratory animals and that serotonin activity is associated with the inhibition of carbohydrate consumption (Leibowitz et al., 1985; 1989). Another neurotransmitter, galanin, appears to stimulate fat intake (Tempel, Leibowitz, & Leibowitz, 1988). Moreover, the evidence suggests that these neurochemical changes related to

Lesioning the ventromedial nucleus of the hypothalamus in rats can lead to such overeating that they triple their weight.

eating mainly unfold in a third area of the hypothalamus—the *paraventricular nucleus*. Other researchers have found that yet another transmitter—neuropeptide Y—has an even stronger impact on eating. The infusion of neuropeptide Y into various sites in the hypothalamus can trigger ravenous eating, and repeated injections lead to rapid weight gain and obesity (Stanley et al., 1986). The impact of neuropeptide Y is greatest when it is injected into yet another area of the hypothalamus—the *perifornical hypothalamus*—where it may moderate activity in neural pathways releasing dopamine (Gillard, Dang, & Stanley, 1993).

These findings have muddied the waters quite a bit, to say the least. The once popular notion that the lateral and ventromedial hypothalamus are on-off centers for hunger has been discarded as much too simplistic. Contemporary theories of hunger focus more on *neural circuits,* rather than on *anatomical centers* in the brain. Accumulating evidence suggests that the hypothalamus contains a confluence of interacting systems that regulate eating by monitoring a diverse array of physiological processes. Let's look at some other physiological processes that appear to provide input to these systems.

Blood Glucose Regulation

Much of the food taken into the body is converted into *glucose,* which circulates in the blood. *Glucose* **is a simple sugar that is an important source of energy.** Manipulations that decrease blood glucose level can increase hunger. Manipulations that increase glucose level can make people feel satiated (full). Based on these findings, Jean Mayer (1955, 1968) proposed that hunger is regulated by the rise and fall of blood glucose levels.

Glucostatic theory proposed that fluctuations in blood glucose level are monitored in the brain by **glucostats—neurons sensitive to glucose in the surrounding fluid.** Glucostats located in the hypothalamus were thought to control the experience of hunger. In its simplest form, glucostatic theory quickly ran into a major complication. People who are diabetic typically have high levels of glucose in their blood (which should make them feel full), but they still feel hungry much of the time. Mayer accounted for this fact by reasoning that it's not the *level of glucose* in the blood that is monitored by glucostats but rather *cells' uptake of glucose* from the blood. Thus, diabetics' frequent hunger makes sense because their disease involves a deficiency in extracting glucose from

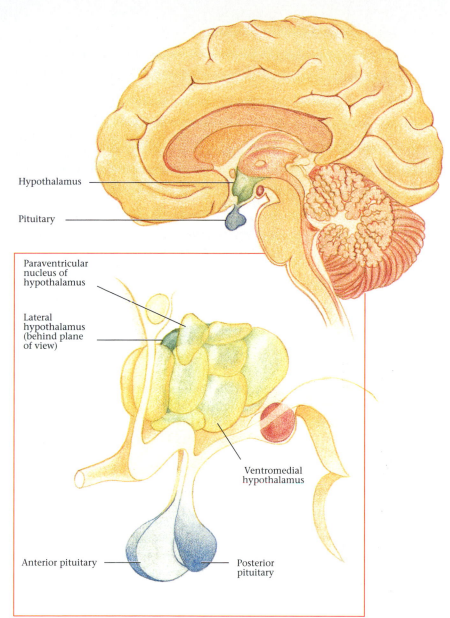

the blood. Associations between blood glucose utilization and hunger have been found (Thompson & Campbell, 1977). It appears likely that hunger is regulated, in part, through glucostatic mechanisms, but the location of the glucostats and the exact nature of glucostatic regulation remain obscure (Logue, 1991).

Hormonal Regulation

Insulin **is a hormone secreted by the pancreas.** It must be present for cells to extract glucose from the blood. Indeed, an inadequate supply of insulin is what causes diabetes. Many diabetics are unable to use the glucose in their blood unless they are given insulin injections. In nondiabetic individuals, insulin injections stimulate hunger. Normal secretion of insulin by the pancreas is also associated with increased hunger (Rodin et al., 1985)

Figure 10.6
The hypothalamus. This small structure at the base of the forebrain plays a role in regulating a variety of human biological needs, including hunger. The detailed blowup on the left shows that the hypothalamus is made up of a variety of discrete areas. Scientists used to believe that the lateral and ventromedial areas were the brain's start and stop centers for eating. However, more recent research suggests that the paraventricular nucleus and perhaps other areas in the hypothalamus are more crucial to the regulation of hunger.

These findings suggest that insulin secretions contribute to the experience of hunger, perhaps in conjunction with glucose fluctuations. Actually, insulin may not be the only hormone involved in hunger regulation. A hormone called cholecystokinin (CCK) is apparently secreted when food enters the digestive system. Investigators suspect that CCK plays a role in the experience of satiety that brings eating to a halt (McHugh & Moran, 1985; Smith & Gibbs, 1992).

Environmental Factors in the Regulation of Hunger 8a

Hunger clearly is a biological need, but eating is not regulated by biological factors alone. Studies show that social and environmental factors govern eating to a considerable extent. Three key environmental factors are (1) learned preferences and habits, (2) food-related cues, and (3) stress.

Learned Preferences and Habits

Are you fond of eating calves' brains? How about eels or snakes? Could I interest you in a grasshopper or some dog meat? Probably not, but these are delicacies in some regions of the world. Arctic Eskimos like to eat maggots! You probably prefer chicken, apples, eggs, lettuce, potato chips, pizza, cornflakes, or ice cream. These preferences are acquired through learning. People from different cultures display very different patterns of food consumption (Kittler & Sucher, 1989). If you doubt this, just visit a grocery store in an ethnic neighborhood (not your own, of course). As Paul Rozin (1996) points out, immigrant groups "seem to retain their ethnic identity through food long after they have become assimilated in most other ways" (p. 20).

The fact that culture influences food preferences is evident in these photos. Eel on a stick is popular in Burma, while dog is served at restaurants in China.

Humans do have some innate taste preferences of a general sort (for sweet over sour, for instance). But learning wields a great deal of influence over *what* people prefer to eat (Birch, 1987). Taste preferences are partly a function of learned associations formed through classical conditioning. For example, youngsters can be conditioned to prefer flavors paired with high caloric intake or pleasant social interactions (Logue, 1991). Of course, as we learned in Chapter 6, taste aversions can also be acquired through conditioning when foods are followed by nausea (Bernstein & Meachum, 1990).

Eating habits are also shaped by obervational learning (see Chapter 6). To a large degree, food preferences are a matter of exposure (Rozin, 1990). People generally prefer familiar foods. But geographical, cultural, religious, and ethnic factors limit people's exposure to various foods. Young children are more likely to taste an unfamiliar food if an adult tries it first. Repeated exposures to a new food usually lead to increased liking. However, as many parents have learned the hard way, forcing a child to eat a specific food can backfire; coercion tends to have a negative effect on a youngster's preference for the mandated food (Birch, 1990). Individuals' reactions to foods are also shaped by the reactions of others around them, such as parents, siblings, and peers. For instance, if you're trying squid for the first time, you're more likely to have a favorable reaction if a companion savors a bite with delight, as opposed to spitting it out in disgust.

Learned habits and social considerations also influence *how much* people eat. For instance, most people tend to consume more food when they are with others than when alone (de Castro & Brewer, 1992). The influence of habit is apparent when artificial sugar is substituted for real sugar in subjects' diets *without their knowledge*. Because of this substitution, they get far fewer calories, which should lead to increased eating to compensate for the caloric loss. But most people don't increase their food intake for at least six days (Bellisle, 1979). They continue to eat in their usual way—out of habit. Even the feeling of satiation experienced after eating may be caused by learning (Birch, 1990). When people eat, the absorption of nutrients into the body takes a while. Usually, they stop eating before physiological mechanisms could signal the end of hunger. Why? Probably because certain eating experiences have consistently been associated with eventual satiation, so feeling full becomes a conditioned response to these food stimuli. Thus, people learn that three (or four, or five . . .) pieces of pizza will result in satiation.

Food-Related Cues

Hunger can also be influenced by exposure to environmental cues that have been associated with eating (Birch et al., 1989). You have no doubt had your hunger aroused by television commercials for delicious-looking food or by seductive odors coming from the kitchen. These experiences illustrate how food-related cues can trigger hunger. Stanley Schachter (1971) conducted numerous studies on how external cues affect hunger. In one study, Schachter and Gross (1968) manipulated the apparent time by altering the clock in a room so that it ran fast or slow. The subjects had been asked to remove their watches, so they were misled about the time of day. When offered crackers, obese subjects ate nearly twice as many when they thought (erroneously) that it was late rather than early in the afternoon. Nonobese subjects, on the other hand, ate fewer crackers when they thought it was late—because they didn't want to spoil their appetite for dinner. Thus, the control of time cues affected eating in both groups, but with opposite results.

In other studies Schachter manipulated external cues such as how tasty and appealing food appeared, how obvious its availability was, and how much effort was required to eat it. All of these external cues were found to influence eating behavior to some extent (Schachter & Rodin, 1974). Thus, it's clear that hunger and eating are governed in part by a variety of food-related cues.

Stress, Arousal, and Eating

When I have an exceptionally stressful day, I often head for the refrigerator, a grocery store, or a restaurant—usually in pursuit of something chocolate. In other words, I sometimes deal with life's hassles by stuffing myself with my favorite foods. My response is not particularly unusual. Studies have shown that stress leads to increased eating in a substantial portion of people (Greeno & Wing, 1994). Some studies suggest that stress-induced eating may be more common in women than men (Grunberg & Straub, 1992) and more likely among chronic dieters (Polivy, Herman, & McFarlane, 1994). Actually, it may be stress-induced *arousal* rather than stress itself that stimulates eating. Stressful events often lead to physiological arousal (see Chapter 13), and several lines of evidence suggest a link between heightened arousal and

overeating (Striegel-Moore & Rodin, 1986). Thus, stress is another environmental factor that can influence hunger, although it's not clear whether the effects are direct or indirect.

Eating and Weight: The Roots of Obesity

We just saw that hunger is regulated by a complex interaction of biological and psychological factors. The same kinds of complexities emerge when investigators explore the roots of *obesity,* **the condition of being overweight.** The criteria of obesity vary considerably. Typically, people are assumed to be overweight if their weight exceeds their ideal body weight by 15% to 20%.

Although American culture seems obsessed with slimness, more and more people are struggling with the problem of obesity. Recent surveys of adults in the United States suggest that 31% of men and 24% of women are overweight (Brownell & Rodin, 1994). If obesity merely frustrated people's vanity, there would be little cause for concern. Unfortunately, obesity is a significant health problem that elevates one's mortality risk (see Figure 10.7). Overweight people are more vulnerable than others to cardiovascular diseases, diabetes, hypertension, respiratory problems, digestive diseases, stroke, arthritis, and back problems (Bray, 1992; Kissebah, Freedman, & Peiris, 1989). Cognizant of these problems, many people attempt to lose weight. At any given time, about 24% of men and 40% of women are dieting (Brownell & Rodin, 1994). Although concerns have been raised that dieting carries its own risks, the evidence clearly indicates that weight loss efforts involving moderate changes in eating and exercise are more beneficial than harmful to people's health (French & Jeffery, 1994).

Figure 10.7
Obesity and mortality.
This graph shows the increased mortality risks for men who are either 20% or 40% above average weight for their age and height. Clearly, obesity is a significant health risk. (Data from VanItallie, 1979)

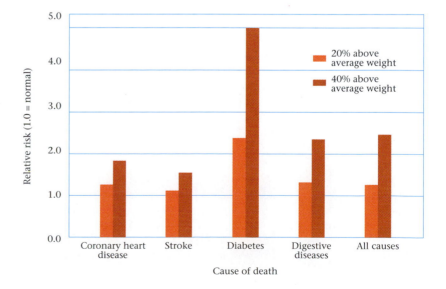

"People's metabolic machinery is constituted in such a way that the fatter they are, the fatter they are primed to become."

JUDITH RODIN

**Figure 10.8
The heritability of weight.** Body mass index is a measure of weight that controls for variations in height. Twin studies reveal that identical twins are much more similar in body mass index than fraternal twins, suggesting that genetic factors account for much of the variation among people in the propensity to become overweight. (Data from Stunkard et al., 1990)

Sensitivity to External Cues

Stanley Schachter (1971) advanced the hypothesis that obese people are extrasensitive to external cues that affect hunger and are relatively insensitive to internal physiological signals. According to this notion, fat people pay little attention to messages from their bodies but respond readily to environmental cues such as the availability of food, the attractiveness of food, and the time of day. Schachter argued that obese people eat excessively because they can't ignore food-related cues that trigger eating. Such people may walk into a shopping mall intending to eat nothing, just to shop in a few stores. But they end up eating because their hunger is aroused by the sight and aroma of cinnamon rolls, hot dogs, and tacos.

Although Schachter's theory has received some support, studies have also led to some modifications in the theory. Judith Rodin's (1978, 1981) research has blurred Schachter's key distinction between the internal and external determinants of hunger. She has demonstrated that the sight, smell, and sound of a grilling steak (external determinants) can elicit insulin secretions (internal determinants) that lead to increased hunger. She has also found that food-related stimuli produce the greatest insulin responses in people who tend to respond to food-related cues by eating. Rodin's findings raise the possibility that people who are responsive to external food cues may really be responding to internal signals (insulin secretion). Their problem may be that they secrete insulin too readily in response to food-related cues.

After reviewing the accumulated evidence, Rodin (1981) has argued that the link between sensitivity to external cues and obesity is weaker than Schachter believed. Many obese people are not exceptionally responsive to food-related stimuli. Indeed, obese people do not overeat as much as is widely assumed (Rodin, Schank, & Striegel-Moore, 1989). Moreover, many people who are highly responsive to food cues and eat a great deal still remain slender. Thus, Rodin asserts that obesity must depend on factors besides sensitivity to external food cues. She theorizes that responsiveness to external cues contributes to obesity, but only in conjunction with genetic and other factors, such as those we are about to discuss.

Genetic Predispositions

You may know some people who can eat constantly without gaining weight. You may also know less fortunate people who get chubby eating far less. Differences in physiological makeup must be the cause of this paradox. Research suggests that these differences may have a genetic basis.

In one influential adoption study, adults raised by foster parents were compared to their biological and foster parents in regard to weight (Stunkard et al., 1986). The investigators found that the adoptees resembled their biological parents in weight, but not their adoptive parents. In a subsequent twin study, Stunkard, Harris, Pederson, and McClearn (1990) found that identical twins reared apart were far more similar in weight than fraternal twins reared together (see Figure 10.8). Based on a study of over 4000 twins, Allison et al. (1994) estimate that genetic factors account for 61% of the variation in weight among men and 73% among women (see Chapter 9 for a discussion of the logic underlying twin studies and heritability estimates). Thus, weight seems to be influenced by genetic makeup. This finding suggests that some people may inherit a vulnerability to obesity.

The Concept of Set Point

People who lose weight on a diet have a rather strong (and depressing) tendency to gain back the weight they lose. The reverse is also true: People who have to work to put weight on often have trouble keeping it on. These observations suggest that each person's body may have a *set point*, a **natural point of stability in body weight.** Theorists who subscribe to this view believe that obesity is usually the result of an elevated set point (Keesey & Powley, 1975, 1986; Nisbett, 1972).

According to set-point theory, the body monitors levels of fat stores to keep them fairly stable. When fat stores slip below a crucial set point, the body supposedly begins to compensate for this change. This compensation process apparently leads to increased hunger and decreased metabolism. The location and nature of the cells that monitor fat stores are unknown. Some proponents

Correlation of body weight mass index

Relationship	Genetic relatedness
Identical twin	100%
Fraternal twin	50%

Reared together
Reared apart

of this theory believe that the hypothalamus is involved (Keesey, 1986).

What determines a person's set point? Advocates of set-point theory note that when people gain or lose weight, these shifts do *not* lead to an increase or decrease in the *number* of fat cells. Instead, fat cells increase or decrease in average *size* (Hirsch et al., 1989). Although the number of fat cells in the body can be increased at any age (through persistent overeating), the count typically stabilizes in early childhood (Knittle et al., 1981). This curious stability suggests that the number of fat cells has something to do with one's set point.

Can a person's set point be changed? The evidence on this issue is not very encouraging. Studies suggest that long-term excessive eating can gradually increase one's set point, but decreasing it seems to be very difficult (Keesey, 1986). This finding does *not* mean that all obese people are doomed to remain obese forever. However, it does suggest that most overweight people must be prepared to make *permanent* changes in their eating and exercise habits if they expect to keep their weight down (Keesey, 1988).

Dietary Restraint

Some investigators have proposed that vacillations in *dietary restraint* contribute to obesity (Heatherton et al., 1988; Herman & Polivy, 1984, 1988). According to this theory, chronic dieters are *restrained eaters*—people who consciously work overtime to control their eating impulses and who feel guilty when they fail. To lose weight, restrained eaters go hungry much of the time, but they are constantly thinking about food. However, when their cognitive control is disrupted, they become *disinhibited* and eat to excess. The crux of the problem is that restrained eaters assume "Either I am on a diet, or I am out of control." A variety of events, such as drinking alcohol or experiencing emotional distress, can disrupt restrained eaters' control. But for many, the most common source of disinhibition is simply the perception that they have cheated on their diet. "I've already blown it," they think to themselves after perhaps just one high-calorie appetizer, "so I might as well enjoy as much as I want." They then proceed to consume a large meal or to go on an eating binge for the remainder of the day.

Paradoxically, then, dietary restraint is thought to lead to frequent overeating and thus contribute to obesity. Research on the theory of dietary restraint is mixed. There is ample evidence to support the disinhibition hypothesis—the idea that restrained eaters often overeat after disruptions of self-control (Ruderman, 1986). And there is evidence that restrained eaters experience greater weight fluctuations than unrestrained eaters, as the theory would predict (Heatherton, Polivy, & Herman, 1991). However, some studies suggest that vacillations in dietary restraint may be just as common among people of normal weight as among obese people (Rodin et al., 1989). Thus, there is plenty of room for argument about whether dietary restraint is a key factor contributing to the development of obesity.

Many people who aren't obese also struggle to maintain a weight that they consider ideal. Their

---

CONCEPT CHECK 10.2

Understanding Factors in the Regulation of Hunger

Check your understanding of the effects of the various factors that influence hunger by indicating whether hunger would tend to increase or decrease in each of the situations described below. Indicate your choice by marking an I (increase), a D (decrease), or a ? (can't be determined without more information) next to each situation. You'll find the answers in Appendix A at the back of the book.

_____ 1. The ventromedial nucleus of a rat's brain is destroyed by lesioning.

_____ 2. The glucose level in Marlene's bloodstream decreases.

_____ 3. Norman, who is not diabetic, receives an injection of insulin.

_____ 4. You're offered an exotic, strange-looking food from another culture and told that everyone in that culture loves it.

_____ 5. Your watch has broken, but the clock on the wall says it's an hour past your usual dinnertime.

_____ 6. Elton has been going crazy all day. It seems like everything's happening at once, and he feels totally stressed out. Finally he's been able to break away for a few minutes so he can catch a bite to eat.

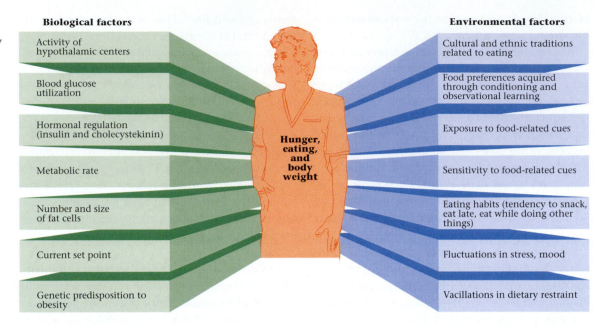

Figure 10.9
The factors influencing hunger, eating, and body weight. Multifactorial causation is readily apparent in the regulation of hunger, eating, and weight, which are shaped by a complex array of interacting biological and environmental factors.

Biological factors

- Activity of hypothalamic centers
- Blood glucose utilization
- Hormonal regulation (insulin and cholecystekinin)
- Metabolic rate
- Number and size of fat cells
- Current set point
- Genetic predisposition to obesity

Hunger, eating, and body weight

Environmental factors

- Cultural and ethnic traditions related to eating
- Food preferences acquired through conditioning and observational learning
- Exposure to food-related cues
- Sensitivity to food-related cues
- Eating habits (tendency to snack, eat late, eat while doing other things)
- Fluctuations in stress, mood
- Vacillations in dietary restraint

hunger and weight are governed by the same factors that influence hunger and weight in the obese. These factors, which are summarized in Figure 10.9, include activity in hypothalamic centers, blood glucose fluctuations, insulin secretion, metabolic rate, fat cell distribution, body weight set point, acquired food preferences, learned eating habits, exposure and sensitivity to food cues, stress, and more. As you can see then, hunger is a basic motive, but it's not a simple one. Neither is sex, the biological motive that we'll consider next.

Recap of Key Points

- Eating is regulated by a complex interaction of biological and environmental factors. In the brain, the lateral and ventromedial areas of the hypothalamus were once viewed as on-off centers for the control of hunger, but their exact role is now unclear.
- Recent research suggests that the paraventricular and perifornical areas in the hypothalamus may be more important to the regulation of hunger. Neural circuits releasing norepinephrine, dopamine, galanin, and neuropeptide Y may influence hunger.
- Fluctuations in blood glucose also seem to play a role in hunger, but the exact location of the

"glucostats" and their mode of functioning are yet to be determined. Hormonal regulation of hunger depends primarily on insulin secretions.
- Learning processes, such as classical conditioning and observational learning, exert a great deal of influence over both what people eat and how much they eat. Cultural traditions also shape food preferences. Food-related cues in the environment and stress-induced arousal can stimulate eating.
- Surveys suggest that 31% of men and 24% of women in the United States are overweight. Obesity is a serious health problem. Schachter hypothesized that obesity develops mainly in people who are overly sensitive to external cues that trigger eating. However, Rodin showed that oversensitivity to external cues is only one factor among many determinants of obesity.
- Evidence indicates that there is a genetic predisposition to obesity. Weight problems can also be caused by an elevated set point for body weight. According to set-point theory, the body monitors fat stores to keep them fairly stable.
- Restrained eaters work hard to control their eating and feel guilty when they fail. Vacillations in dietary restraint resulting in disinhibition may contribute to obesity in some people.

SEXUAL MOTIVATION AND BEHAVIOR

How does sex resemble food? Sometimes it seems that people are obsessed with both. People joke and gossip about sex constantly. Magazines, novels, movies, and television shows are saturated with sexual activity and innuendo. The advertising industry uses sex to sell everything from mouthwash to designer jeans to automobiles. This intense interest in sex reflects the importance of sexual motivation. In this portion of the chapter, we'll examine the factors that influence sexual desire and sexual orientation, and we'll describe the physiology of the human sexual response. In the Application, we'll return to the topic of sexuality and discuss some of the factors that promote rewarding sexual relationships.

Determinants of Sexual Desire

Sex is essential for the survival of a species, but it's not essential to an *individual's* survival. Sexual motivation is not driven by deprivation to the extent that hunger is—you can live out a long life without sex, but without food your life will be very short. Like hunger, sexual desire is influenced by a complicated network of biological and social factors.

Hormonal Regulation

Hormones secreted by the *gonads*—the ovaries in females and the testes in males—can influence sexual motivation. **Estrogens are the principal class of gonadal hormones in females. *Androgens* are the principal class of gonadal hormones in males.** Actually, both classes of hormones are produced in both sexes, but the relative balance is much different. The hypothalamus and the pituitary gland regulate these hormonal secretions.

The influence of hormones on sexual desire can be seen quite vividly in the animal kingdom (Feder, 1984). In many species, females are sexually receptive only just prior to ovulation, coinciding with an elevation in circulating levels of gonadal hormones. Hormones also influence sexual desire in males. For instance, if a male rat's testes are removed, the lack of a key androgen (testosterone) results in a lack of sexual interest. Testosterone injections can revive sexual desire in such castrated animals. Thus, it's clear that gonadal hormones regulate the sex drive in many animals.

Moving up the phylogenetic scale from rats to primates, hormones exert less and less influence over sexual behavior (Chambers & Phoenix, 1987). However, several lines of evidence suggest that they do contribute to the modulation of sexual desire in humans. For example, males who develop an endocrine disorder called *hypogonadism* during adulthood exhibit abnormally low levels of androgens and reduced sexual motivation, which can be revived by hormone replacement therapy (Davidson & Rosen, 1992; Zini et al., 1990). Experiments with male sex offenders suggest that drugs that drastically lower testosterone

levels can be used to reduce sexual interest, although they certainly do not preclude further sexual assaults (Bradford & Pawlak, 1993). Curiously, *androgen* levels seem related to sexual motivation in *both* sexes. High levels of testosterone in female and male subjects correlate with higher rates of sexual activity (Bancroft et al., 1991; Knussmann, Christiansen, & Couwenbergs, 1986). In contrast, *estrogen* levels among women do *not* correlate well with sexual interest (Myers et al, 1990). There may be a modest association between females' sex drive and their ovulation/menstruation cycles, but its hormonal basis is yet to be determined (Harvey, 1987; Stanislaw & Rice, 1988).

The correlations between hormone levels and sexual activity in humans are interesting, but most of the evidence comes from abnormal syndromes or extreme manipulations of hormone levels. At present, there is little reason to believe that normal hormonal swings have much impact on sexual desire in humans.

Pheromones

The female gypsy moth can lure males for sexual liaisons from up to 2 miles away (Hopson, 1979). How does she do it? She secretes a powerful pheromone. **A *pheromone* is a chemical secreted by one animal that affects the behavior of another.** These chemical messengers are usually detected through the sense of smell. They influence various aspects of behavior in lower animals, including sexuality.

Do pheromones influence human behavior? Possibly, but not in the way that many popular articles have suggested. Some popular magazines imply that humans secrete pheromones that incite compelling sexual desire. Some "adult" magazines even advertise pheromone substances that supposedly serve as sexual stimulants. At present, however, there is no convincing evidence that pheromones exert any impact on sex drive in humans or other higher primates such as monkeys (Quadagno, 1987).

Nonetheless, human pheromones *may* cause a very interesting phenomenon. When women live together (in a sorority, for example), their menstrual cycles gradually tend to become more synchronized (McClintock, 1971). This ovulatory synchronization also occurs among some animals (such as mice) when they are housed together, and it has been linked to pheromones (Bronson & Whitten, 1968).

In a clever study, Russell, Switz, and Thompson (1980) showed that pheromones may be responsible for ovulatory synchronization in humans. They collected samples of underarm sweat from women and dissolved these samples in alcohol. A second set of women regularly rubbed these sweat-and-alcohol preparations on their lips. A control group used alcohol-only preparations. The ovulatory cycles of the women who received the sweat preparations began to synchronize with the cycles of the women who donated the sweat. Thus, humans may indeed respond to pheromones, but the response isn't necessarily related to sex drive.

Pheromones are the substances most recently touted for their aphrodisiac value. But fascination with *aphrodisiacs*—**substances thought to increase sexual desire**—dates back to prehistoric times. Today, most people realize that supposed aphrodisiacs ranging from oysters to vitamin E have no real impact on sex drive. At present, no known substances can *reliably* increase sexual desire through any direct physical mechanism.

Attraction to a Partner

Although people habitually use the term *sex drive,* human sexual motivation seems to operate in accordance with an incentive model more than a drive model. Thus, key considerations are the availability of a potential partner and attraction to that partner. Humans are not unique in this regard. Many organisms respond to the external stimulus of an available partner.

In fact, a *new* partner can revive dwindling sexual interest in many animals. This phenomenon has a curious name, *the Coolidge effect,* which derives from the following story. President Calvin Coolidge and his wife were touring a farm. Mrs. Coolidge was informed that a rooster on the farm often copulated 20 or more times in a day. "Tell *that* to Mr. Coolidge," she supposedly said. When informed of the rooster's feat, the president asked if it was always with the same hen. He was told that the rooster enjoyed a different hen each time. "Tell that to Mrs. Coolidge," was his reply.

Today, no one is sure whether the story is true, but the Coolidge effect refers to the preference for variety in sexual partners that is seen in males of many species, including rats, bulls, and monkeys (Bermant & Davidson, 1974). Citing Trivers's parental investment theory, evolutionary theorists argue that this mating pattern occurs because males maximize their reproductive success by having sex with as many females as possible. Is there any evidence that the Coolidge effect also occurs in humans? Well, if college students' preferences are a valid guide, the answer would appear to be yes. Buss and Schmitt (1993) found that college men indicate that they would ideally like to have 18 sex partners across their lives, whereas college women report that they would prefer only 4 or 5 partners. Surveys inquiring about adults' actual sexual histories also indicate that men engage in premarital and extramarital sex with a larger number of partners than women do, on the average (Janus & Janus, 1993).

Many species of animals are *selective* in their attraction to sexual partners. In particular, females often choose to mate only with the largest, most colorful, or most dominant of the available candidates. Most humans are selective, too. Human selectivity is influenced greatly by learning. This reality explains why people differ substantially in what they find physically attractive (Patzer, 1985). Of course, humans further complicate sexual attraction by considering a host of factors besides physical beauty. Sexual interest may be influenced by a potential partner's personality, competence, and values, not to mention one's affection for the person (Symons, 1979).

A number of studies suggest that gender differences exist in the factors that typically motivate human sexual activity. In comparison to women, men appear to be motivated more by the desire for physical gratification. In contrast, women are more likely to be motivated by their desire to express love and emotional commitment (Carroll, Volk, & Hyde, 1985). In one study of college students, Whitley (1988) asked subjects, "What was your most important reason for having sexual intercourse on the most recent occasion?" Lust and pleasure motives were cited by 51% of the men but only 9% of the women. Love and emotional reasons were cited by 51% of the women but only 24% of the men. Similar gender differences have been found in a community survey that looked at a broader sample of subjects than just college students (Leigh, 1989). Although some theorists speculate that these disparities exist because males and females are socialized to have different attitudes about sex (Carroll et al., 1985), evolutionary theorists argue that the differences are consistent with parental investment theory. Our Featured Study, a large-scale, cross-cultural investigation of mating preferences, has also yielded evidence consistent with evolutionary theories of sexual motivation.

Investigator: David M. Buss (University of Michigan)

Source: Sex differences in human mate preferences: Evolutionary hypotheses tested in 37 cultures. *Behavioral and Brain Sciences,* 1989, *12,* 1–49.

According to evolutionary theories, human females enhance their chances of passing on their genes not by seeking larger or stronger partners (as in the animal kingdom), but by seeking male partners that possess or are likely to acquire more material resources that can be invested in children. Thus, evolutionary theorists assert that women emphasize education, income, status, ambition, and industriousness in potential partners. Men, on the other hand, are assumed to maximize their reproductive outlook by seeking female partners with good breeding potential. Thus, men are thought to look for youth, attractiveness, good health, and other characteristics presumed to be associated with higher fertility. If these evolutionary analyses of sexual motivation are on the mark, gender differences in mating preferences should transcend culture.

Method

To test this hypothesis, David Buss coordinated the efforts of 50 scientists from around the world, who collected data on what people want in a mate. They surveyed more than 10,000 people from 37 cultures distributed across six continents and five islands. Subjects responded to two questionnaires, which asked them to rate the importance of 32 characteristics in potential mates.

Results

The findings revealed that males and females exhibit both similarities and differences in mating preferences. Many characteristics, such as kindness, emotional stability, dependability, and a pleasant disposition, were rated very highly by both sexes. However, a few crucial differences between males' and females' priorities were found, and these differences were universal across cultures. As a group, women placed a higher value than men on potential partners' status, ambition, and financial prospects (see Figure 10.10). These priorities were not limited to industrialized or capitalist countries; they were apparent in third-world cultures, socialist countries, and all varieties of economic systems. In contrast, men consistently showed more interest than women in potential partners' youthfulness and physical attractiveness (see Figure 10.11).

Cross-cultural variations in mate preferences were relatively modest. The most prominent variation was in the emphasis placed on chastity—a partner's lack of previous sexual intercourse. Chastity was highly valued in some societies but viewed with indifference in others. Some cross-cultural variability was also seen in the emphasis placed on partners' housekeeping skills and religious commitment.

Discussion

According to Buss, social scientists have traditionally assumed that mating preferences are shaped by learning and that they vary considerably from culture to culture. His findings suggest that culture matters, but only in a limited way. He also concludes that his data provide striking support for evolutionary theories of sexual motivation. As predicted, women emphasized males' prospects for acquisition of material resources, whereas men emphasized females' reproductive capacity.

Comment

Buss's fascinating data are consistent with evolutionary theories of sexual motivation, but, as is often the case with tests of evolutionary hypotheses, one can posit alternative explanations for the findings. For example, women's emphasis on males' material resources could be a by-product of economic forces

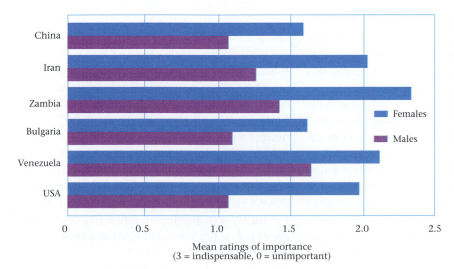

**Figure 10.10
Gender and potential mates' financial prospects.** Consistent with evolutionary theory, Buss (1989) found that females place more emphasis on potential partners' financial prospects than do males. Moreover, he found that this trend transcended culture. The specific results for 6 of the 37 cultures studied by Buss are shown here.

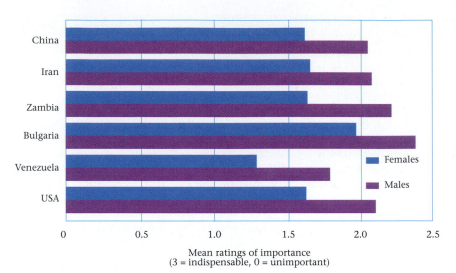

Figure 10.11
Gender and potential mates' physical attractiveness. Consistent with evolutionary theory, Buss (1989) found that all over the world, males place more emphasis on potential partners' good looks than do females. The specific results for 6 of the 37 cultures studied by Buss are shown here.

rather than the result of biological imperatives (Wallen, 1989). Women may have learned to value males' economic clout because their own economic potential has been severely limited in virtually all cultures by a long history of discrimination.

Nonetheless, this study exemplifies the rich potential of psychology's new commitment to cross-cultural research (see Chapter 1). Interestingly, though, Buss (1994) notes that his data "were

extraordinarily difficult to obtain." Authorities in some countries tried to sabotage the study, while others banned it completely. These nightmares and the logistical difficulties inherent in gathering data from 37 disparate cultures illustrate the extra-challenging nature of cross-cultural research. Of course, sexual behavior is a particularly sensitive topic of study, as we'll see throughout this section.

Erotic Materials

A potential partner is not the only external stimulus that can awaken sexual interest. Erotic reading material, photographs, and films can stimulate sexual desire. The intensity of sexual arousal generally increases as the depictions of sexual activity become more explicit (Miller, Byrne, & Fisher, 1980). Of course, people don't all respond favorably to sexually explicit media (Fisher et al., 1988).

Women are more likely than men to report that they dislike erotic materials (Mosher & MacIan, 1994). However, when physiological responses to erotic stimuli are measured in laboratory studies, men and women usually show similar responsiveness (Rubinsky et al., 1987). How can this paradox be explained? It may be a comment on the nature of the pornography industry. Erotic materials generally are scripted to appeal to males and often portray women in degrading roles that elicit negative reactions from female viewers (Dworkin, 1981). In formal studies, however, researchers often present less sexist material to their subjects (unless they are specifically exploring the effects of sexist erotica).

How much impact does erotic material have on actual sexual behavior? The empirical data on this hotly debated question are inconsistent and open

to varied interpretations. The balance of evidence suggests that exposure to erotic material elevates the likelihood of overt sexual activity for a few hours immediately after the exposure (Donnerstein, Linz, & Penrod, 1987). This relatively modest effect may explain why attempts to find a correlation between the availability of erotica and sex crime rates have yielded contradictory results. Some studies find an association (Court, 1984), but many do not (Kutchinsky, 1985). For example, although little pornography is available in India, the prevalence of rape is relatively high. Japan, however, has a low incidence of rape in spite of widely available pornography (Pratap, 1990). Of course, even if a correlation were found consistently, it would not demonstrate that erotic materials cause sex crimes.

Although erotic materials don't appear to incite overpowering sexual urges, they may alter *attitudes* in ways that eventually influence sexual behavior. Zillmann and Bryant (1984) found that male and female undergraduates exposed to a large dose of pornography (three or six films per week for six weeks) developed more liberal attitudes about sexual practices. For example, they came to view premarital and extramarital sex as more acceptable. Another study by Zillmann and Bryant

CHAPTER TEN

(1988) suggests that viewing sexually explicit films may make some people dissatisfied with their own sexual interactions. In comparison to control subjects, the subjects exposed to a steady diet of pornography reported less satisfaction with their partners' physical appearance, sexual curiosity, and sexual performance. Thus, pornography may create unrealistic expectations about sexual relations.

Research on *aggressive pornography* has raised concerns about its effects (Check & Guloien, 1989). Aggressive pornography typically depicts violence against women. Many films show women who gradually give in to and enjoy rape and other sexually degrading acts after some initial resistance. Some studies indicate that this type of material increases male subjects' aggressive behavior toward women, at least in the context of the research laboratory (Malamuth & Donnerstein, 1982; Zillmann & Weaver, 1989). In the typical study, male subjects work on a laboratory task and are led to believe (falsely) that they are delivering electric shocks to other subjects. In this situation, their aggression toward females tends to be elevated after exposure to aggressive pornography. Exposure to aggressive pornography may also make sexual coercion seem less offensive and desensitize males to the horror of sexual violence (Mullin & Linz, 1995). In particular, it helps perpetuate the myth that women enjoy being raped and ravaged (Linz, 1989; Malamuth, 1984). Although concern has been focused primarily on the effects of explicit, X-rated pornography, a great deal of sexual violence can be found in mainstream, R-rated films (Palys, 1986). These films can also affect males' attitudes about sexual coercion and violence, and they are viewed by far more people.

The effects of aggressive pornography are especially worrisome in light of new evidence about rape. Although it is difficult to obtain accurate information about the prevalence of rape (some experts believe that 90% of all rapes are never reported), the incidence of rape appears to be growing (Kilpatrick, Edmunds, & Seymour, 1992). Estimates suggest that as many as one-quarter of young women in the United States may be victims of rape or attempted rape (Koss, 1993; Parrot & Bechhofer, 1991). Only a minority of reported rapes are committed by strangers (see Figure 10.12). Particularly common is *date rape,* which occurs when a woman is forced to have sex in the context of dating. Research suggests that date rape is a serious problem on college campuses. In one survey of students at 32 colleges, 1 in 7 women reported that they had been victimized by date rape

or an attempted date rape (Koss, Gidycz, & Wisniewski, 1987). Moreover, 1 in 12 men admitted either to having forced a date into sex or to having tried to do so. However, *none* of these men identified himself as a rapist. There surely are other factors at work, but many theorists *suspect* that aggressive pornography has contributed to this failure to see sexual coercion for what it is.

The Mystery of Sexual Orientation

Although the factors that modulate sexual desire are reasonably well understood, the determinants of *sexual orientation* are more obscure. ***Sexual orientation* refers to a person's preference for emotional and sexual relationships with individuals of the same sex, the other sex, or either sex. *Heterosexuals* seek emotional-sexual relationships with members of the other sex, *bisexuals* with members of either sex, and *homosexuals* with members of the same sex.** In recent years, the terms *gay* and *straight* have become widely used to refer to homosexuals and heterosexuals, respectively. Although *gay* can refer to homosexuals of either sex, most homosexual women prefer to call themselves *lesbians*.

People tend to view heterosexuality and homosexuality as an all-or-none distinction. However, in a large-scale survey of sexual behavior, Alfred Kinsey and his colleagues (1948, 1953) discovered that many people who define themselves as heterosexuals have had homosexual experiences—and vice versa. Thus, Kinsey and others have concluded that it is more accurate to view heterosexuality and homosexuality as end points on a continuum. Indeed, Kinsey devised a seven-point scale, shown in Figure 10.13 on page 398, that can be used to characterize individuals' sexual orientation.

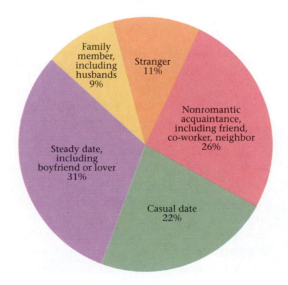

Figure 10.12
Rape victim-offender relationships. Based on a national survey of 3187 college women, Mary Koss and her colleagues (1988) identified a sample of 468 women who indicated that they had been a victim of rape and who provided information on their relationship to the offender. Contrary to the prevailing stereotype, only a small minority (11%) of these women were raped by a stranger. (Data based on Koss et al., 1988)

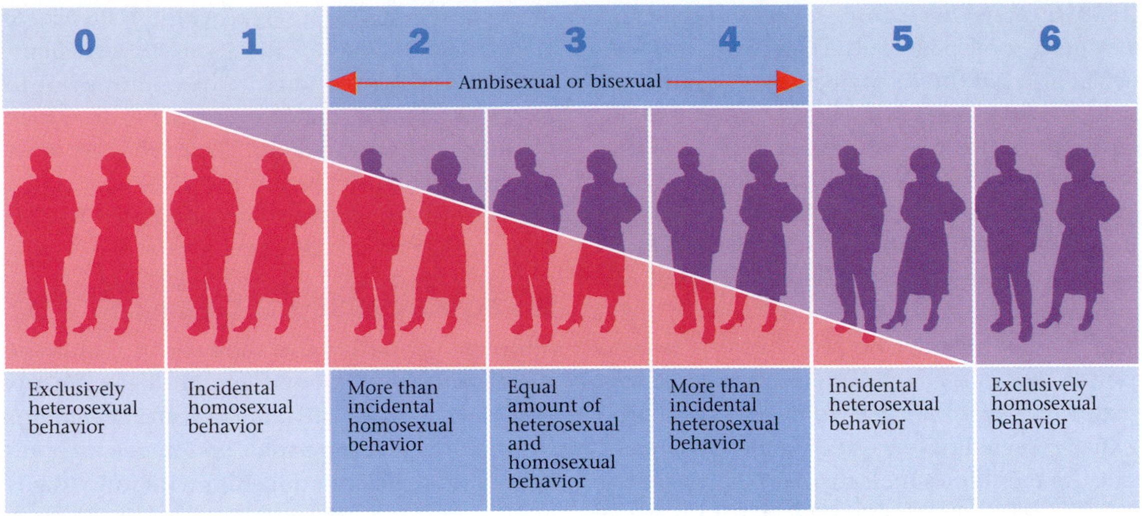

Figure 10.13
Homosexuality and heterosexuality as endpoints on a continuum.
Sex researchers view heterosexuality and homosexuality as falling on a continuum rather than make an all-or-none distinction. Kinsey and his associates (1948, 1953) created this seven-point scale (from 0 to 6) to describe people's sexual orientation. They used the term *ambisexual* to describe those who fall in the middle of the scale, but such people are commonly called *bisexual* today.

In spite of fascinating, groundbreaking research in recent years, the determinants of sexual orientation remain obscure. Like so many other issues in psychology, the debate about the roots of homosexuality centers around the relative importance of nature versus nurture.

How are people distributed on this scale? No one knows for sure. Prejudicial attitudes about homosexuality make it hard to get candid information from people. Estimates of the incidence of homosexuality vary widely—from 4% to 17% (Gonsiorek & Weinrich, 1991). A frequently cited estimate of the number of people who are homosexual is 10%. If homosexuals and bisexuals are lumped together, recent studies *suggest* that this figure is reasonably accurate for males but an overestimate for females (Ellis & Ames, 1987; Janus & Janus, 1993).

Environmental Theories

Over the years, many environmental theories have been floated to explain the origins of homosexuality, but when tested empirically, these theories have garnered remarkably little support. For example, psychoanalytic and behavioral theorists, who usually agree on very little, both proposed environmental explanations for the development of homosexuality. The Freudian theorists argued that a male is likely to become gay when raised by a weak, detached, ineffectual father who is a poor heterosexual role model and an overprotective, close-binding mother, with whom the boy identifies. Behavioral theorists argued that homosexuality is a learned preference acquired when same-sex stimuli have been paired with sexual arousal, perhaps through chance seductions by adult homosexuals. Extensive research on homosexuals' upbringing and childhood experiences have failed to support either of these theories (Bell, Weinberg, & Hammersmith, 1981).

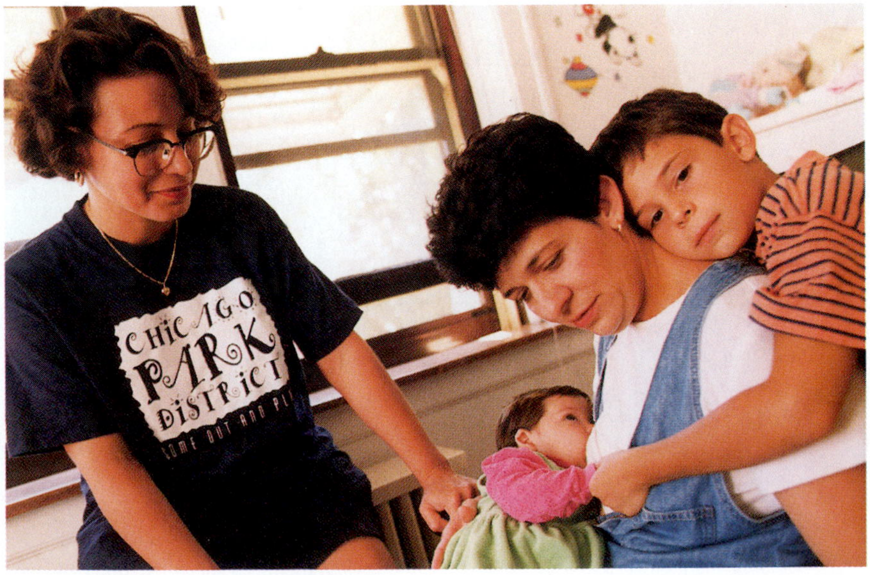

However, efforts to research homosexuals' personal histories have yielded a number of interesting insights. Extremely feminine behavior in young boys or masculine behavior in young girls does predict the subsequent development of homosexuality (Bailey & Zucker, 1995). For example, 75%–90% of highly feminine young boys become gay (Blanchard et al., 1995). Consistent with this finding, most gay men and women report that they can trace their homosexual leanings back to their early childhood, even before they understood what sex was really about (Garnets & Kimmel, 1991). Most also report that because of negative parental and societal attitudes about homosexuality, they initially struggled to deny their sexual orientation. Hence, they felt that their homosexuality was not a matter of choice and not something that they could readily change (Breedlove, 1994). These findings obviously suggest that the roots of homosexuality are more biological than environmental.

Biological Theories

Nonetheless, initial efforts to find a biological basis for homosexuality met with little success. Most theorists originally assumed that hormonal differences between heterosexuals and homosexuals must underlie a person's sexual orientation (Doerr et al., 1976; Dorner, 1988). However, studies comparing circulating hormone levels in gays and straights found only small, inconsistent differences that could not be linked to sexual orientation in any convincing way (Garnets & Kimmel, 1991; Gladue, 1988).

Thus, like environmental theorists, biological theorists were stymied for quite a while in their efforts to explain the roots of homosexuality. However, that picture has changed dramatically in recent years. As Brian Gladue (1994) puts it, "a remarkable set of findings from the past decade strongly suggests the influence of fundamental biological processes in the development of homosexuality" (p. 150). One example is a study by Bailey and Pillard (1991), whose subjects were gay men who had either a twin brother or an adopted brother. They found that 52% of the subjects' identical twins were gay, that 22% of their fraternal twins were gay, and that 11% of their adoptive brothers were gay. A companion study (Bailey et al., 1993) of lesbians has yielded a similar pattern of results (see Figure 10.14). Given that identical twins share more genetic overlap than fraternal twins, who share more genes than unrelated adoptive siblings, these results suggest that there is a genetic predisposition to homosexuality (see Chapter 3 for an explanation of the logic underlying twin and adoption studies). A similar conclusion emerged from another recent study that used genetic mapping techniques. In this study, Hamer and associates (1993) linked male homosexuality to genetic material on the X chromosome.

In another line of research, LeVay (1991, 1993) has reported anatomical differences between gay and straight men in a region of the brain thought to influence sexual behavior. He focused on a tiny cluster of neurons in the anterior hypothalamus that is known to be larger in men than women. Because the structure is too small to be measured effectively in the living brain, it is studied posthumously. LeVay compared the autopsied brains of 19 homosexual and 16 heterosexual men and found that the targeted structure tended to be about half as large in the gay men. Other investigators, using similar techniques, have found evidence that another area in the hypothalamus (the suprachiasmatic nucleus) is larger and more elongated in gay men than straight men (Swaab, Gooren, & Hofman, 1992). Interestingly, the elongated shape found in gay males is normally characteristic of females. LeVay stresses that the findings on brain structure should be interpreted with caution, as most of the subjects had died of AIDS, which clearly can wreak havoc in the brain. Although the data on disparities in brain structure are preliminary, they point to a biological basis for sexual orientation.

Many theorists suspect that disparities between heterosexuals and homosexuals in brain structure may reflect the organizing effects of prenatal hormones on neurological development. Several lines of research suggest that hormonal secretions during critical periods of prenatal development may shape sexual development, organize the brain in a lasting manner, and influence subsequent sexual orientation (Berenbaum & Snyder, 1995). For example, researchers have found elevated rates of homosexuality among women exposed prenatally to a synthetic hormone (DES) that was formerly used to reduce the risk of miscarriage (by their mothers) and among women who have an adrenal disorder that results in abnormally high androgen levels during prenatal development (Breedlove, 1994; Meyer-Bahlburg et al., 1995).

Despite the recent breakthroughs, much remains to be learned about the determinants of sexual orientation. The pathways to homosexuality appear to be somewhat different for males as opposed to females (Gladue, 1994). Indeed, homosexuality may be highly heterogenous in origin and there may be quite a variety of pathways for each sex. The fact that identical twins of gay subjects turn out to be gay only about half the time suggests that the genetic predisposition to homosexuality is not overpowering. Environmental influences of some kind probably contribute to the development

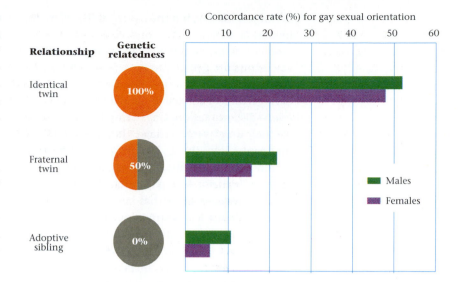

Figure 10.14
Genetics and sexual orientation. A *concordance rate* indicates the percentage of twin pairs or other pairs of relatives that exhibit the same characteristic. If relatives who share more genetic relatedness show higher concordance rates than relatives who share less genetic overlap, this evidence suggests a genetic predisposition to the characteristic. Recent studies of both gay men and lesbian women have found higher concordance rates among identical twins than fraternal twins, who, in turn, exhibit more concordance than adoptive siblings. These findings are consistent with the hypothesis that genetic factors influence sexual orientation. (Data from Bailey & Pillard, 1991; Bailey et al., 1993)

of homosexuality, but the nature of these environmental factors remains a mystery.

Once again, though, we can see that the nature versus nurture debate can have far-reaching social and political implications. Homosexuals have long been victims of extensive—and in many instances *legal*—discrimination. Gays cannot legally formalize their unions in marriage, they are not allowed to openly join the U.S. military, and they are barred from some jobs (for example, many school districts will not hire gay teachers). However, if research were to show that being gay is largely a matter of biological destiny, much like being black or female or short, many of the arguments against equal rights for gays would disintegrate. Why ban gays from teaching, for instance, if their sexual preference cannot "rub off" on their students? Although I would argue that discrimination against gays should be brought to an end either way, many individuals' opinions about gay rights may be swayed by the outcome of the nature-nurture debate on the roots of homosexuality.

The Human Sexual Response

Assuming people are motivated to engage in sexual activity, exactly what happens to them physically? This may sound like a simple question. But scientists really knew very little about the physiology of the human sexual response before William Masters and Virginia Johnson did groundbreaking research in the 1960s. Although our society seems obsessed with sex, until relatively recently it did *not* encourage scientists to study sex. At first Masters and Johnson even had difficulty finding journals that were willing to publish their studies.

Masters and Johnson used physiological recording devices to monitor the bodily changes of volunteers engaging in sexual activities. They even equipped an artificial penile device with a camera to study physiological reactions inside the vagina! Their observations and interviews with their subjects yielded a detailed description of the human sexual response and won them widespread acclaim.

Masters and Johnson (1966, 1970) divide the sexual response cycle into four stages: excitement, plateau, orgasm, and resolution. Figure 10.15 shows how the intensity of sexual arousal changes as women and men progress through these stages. Let's take a closer look at these phases in the human sexual response.

Excitement Phase

During the initial phase of excitement, the level of physical arousal usually escalates rapidly. In both sexes, muscle tension, respiration rate, heart rate, and blood pressure increase quickly. **Vasocongestion—engorgement of blood vessels**—produces penile erection and swollen testes in males. In females, vasocongestion leads to a swelling and hardening of the clitoris, expansion of the vaginal lips, and vaginal lubrication.

Plateau Phase

During the plateau phase, physiological arousal usually continues to build, but at a much slower pace. In women, further vasocongestion produces a tightening of the vaginal entrance, as the clitoris withdraws under the clitoral hood. Many men secrete a bit of fluid at the tip of the penis. This is not ejaculate, but it may contain sperm. When foreplay is lengthy, it's normal for arousal to fluctuate in both sexes. This fluctuation is more apparent in men; erections may increase and decrease noticeably. In women, this fluctuation may be reflected in changes in vaginal lubrication.

Orgasm Phase

Orgasm **occurs when sexual arousal reaches its peak intensity and is discharged in a series of muscular contractions that pulsate through the pelvic area.** Heart rate, respiration rate, and blood pressure increase sharply during this exceedingly pleasant spasmodic response. In males, orgasm is accompanied by ejaculation of the seminal fluid. The subjective experience of orgasm is very similar

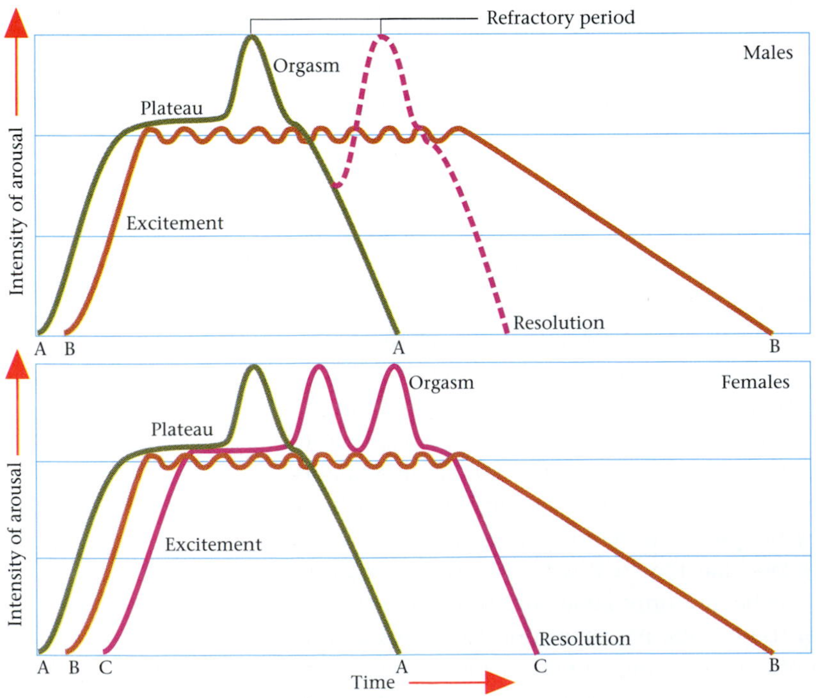

Figure 10.15
The human sexual response cycle. There are similarities and differences between men and women in patterns of sexual arousal. Pattern A, which culminates in orgasm and resolution, is the most typical sequence for both sexes. Pattern B, which involves sexual arousal without orgasm followed by a slow resolution, is also seen in both sexes but is more common among women. Pattern C, which involves multiple orgasms, is seen almost exclusively in women, as men go through a refractory period before they are capable of another orgasm. (Based on Masters & Johnson, 1966)

CHAPTER TEN

for men and women. When subjects provide written descriptions of what their orgasms feel like (without using specific words for genitals), even psychologists and physicians can't tell which came from women and which came from men (Vance & Wagner, 1976; Wiest, 1977).

However, there *are* some interesting gender differences in the orgasm phase of the sexual response cycle. On the one hand, women are more likely than men to be *multiorgasmic*. A woman is said to be multiorgasmic if she experiences more than one climax in a very brief time period (pattern C in Figure 10.15). On the other hand, women are more likely than men to engage in intercourse without experiencing an orgasm (pattern B). Attitudes and sexual practices may have more to do with this difference than physiological processes.

Resolution Phase

During the resolution phase, the physiological changes produced by sexual arousal subside. If orgasm has not occurred, the reduction in sexual tension may be relatively slow and sometimes unpleasant. After orgasm, men experience a *refractory period*, a time following orgasm during which males are largely unresponsive to further stimulation. The length of the refractory period varies from a few minutes to a few hours and increases with age.

Masters and Johnson's exploration of the human sexual response led to major insights into the nature and causes of sexual problems. Ironically, although Masters and Johnson broke new ground in studying the *physiology* of sexual arousal, their research demonstrated that sexual problems are typically caused by *psychological* factors, as we'll discuss further in the chapter Application. Their conclusion shows once again that human sexuality involves a fascinating blend of biological and social processes. We turn next to a related motive—affiliation—that is more social in origin.

Recap of Key Points

• Hormones exert considerable influence over sexual motivation in many animals. Androgen levels appear to be related to sexual motivation in both sexes. Although some interesting correlations exist between hormonal fluctuations and sexual activity in humans, we are not sure whether normal hormonal swings have much impact on human sexual desire.

• In a similar manner, pheromones appear to be important determinants of sexual desire in lower animals but of limited relevance to humans, although they may underline ovulatory synchronization.

• Attraction to a potential partner is a critical determinant of sexual interest in humans. Consistent with evolutionary theory, males tend to have more sexual partners and more interest in uncommitted sex than females.

• The Featured Study by Buss demonstrated that there are gender differences in mating preferences that largely transcend cultural boundaries. Males emphasize potential partners' youthfulness and attractiveness, whereas females emphasize potential partners' status and financial prospects.

• People respond to a variety of erotic materials, which may elevate sexual desire for only a few hours but may have an enduring impact on attitudes about sex. Aggressive pornography may make sexual coercion seem less offensive and may contribute to date rape.

• Modern theorists view heterosexuality and homosexuality not as an all-or-none distinction, but as endpoints on a continuum. Although most gays can trace their homosexual leanings back to early childhood, research has not supported Freudian or behavioral theories of sexual orientation.

• Recent studies suggest that there is a genetic predisposition to homosexuality and that some subtle disparities in brain structure may be associated with homosexuality. Idiosyncrasies in prenatal hormonal secretions may also contribute to the development of homosexuality, but much remains to be learned.

• The human sexual response cycle can be divided into four stages: excitement, plateau, orgasm, and resolution. The subjective experience of orgasm is fairly similar for both sexes. Intercourse leads to orgasm in women less consistently than in men, but women are much more likely to be multiorgasmic. Men experience a refractory period after an orgasm.

"The conviction has grown that the most effective treatment of sexual incompatibility involves the technique of working with both members of the family unit."

WILLIAM MASTERS AND VIRGINIA JOHNSON

AFFILIATION: IN SEARCH OF BELONGINGNESS

How would you like to spend the rest of your life alone on a pleasant but deserted island? Most people would find this to be a terrible fate. Why?

Because the fundamental human need to be with others would be thwarted. Some animals (bears, tigers, and bald eagles, for example) don't mind going it alone. Humans, however, react very badly to prolonged periods of social isolation. Humans are social animals and have to have meaningful contact with others.

The *affiliation motive* is the need to associate with others and maintain social bonds. Affiliation encompasses one's needs for companionship, friendship, and love. People need more than mere interpersonal contact, they need enduring social bonds that are marked by mutual concern for one another. Abraham Maslow (1970) called this motive the *need for belongingness.* He viewed it as a very basic motive, placing it at the third level in his hierarchy of needs.

In a recent theoretical overview of research on affiliation, Roy Baumeister and Mark Leary (1995) argued that it has a strong evolutionary basis, as social bonds offer a host of survival and reproductive benefits. They noted that by coalescing together, our ancestors could share food, provide better care for their offspring, engage in more effective hunting or gathering, enhance their defense against predators, diffuse risks, and provide more opportunities for mating. Small wonder, then, that humans seem to form bonds readily and go to great lengths to preserve their interpersonal attachments. In discussing the significance of affiliation, Baumeister and Leary described evidence that the quality of people's personal relationships is a major determinant of their happiness. They also discussed the strong link between affiliation issues and negative emotions—how the threat of rejection triggers anxiety, how concern about losing a partner evokes jealousy, and how loneliness is associated with depression. In sum, Baumeister and Leary made an eloquent case for the pervasive importance of affiliation, asserting that "much of what human beings do is done in the service of belongingness" (p. 498).

Although virtually everyone exhibits the need for belongingness, some people have stronger affiliation needs than others. Much of the research on affiliation has looked into these individual differences. In this research, investigators usually measure subjects' need for affiliation with some variant of Henry Murray's Thematic Apperception Test (Morgan & Murray, 1935; Murray, 1943). Psychologists need a way to measure the strength of social motives such as affiliation, and the Thematic Apperception Test (TAT) has proven useful for this purpose (McClelland, Koestner, & Weinberger, 1992). The TAT is a *projective test,* a test that requires subjects to respond to vague, ambiguous stimuli in ways that may reveal personal motives and traits (see Chapter 12). The stimulus materials for the TAT are pictures of people in ambiguous scenes open to interpretation. Examples include a man working at a desk and a woman seated in a chair staring off into space. Subjects are asked to write or tell stories about what's happening in the scenes and what the characters are feeling. The themes of these stories are then scored to measure the strength of various needs. Figure 10.16 shows examples of stories dominated by affiliation and achievement themes.

How do people who score high in the need for affiliation differ from those who score low? First, *they devote more time to interpersonal activities.* For example, they join more social groups such as clubs and church organizations (Smart, 1965). They make more phone calls and visits to friends (McClelland & Winter, 1969), and they tend to devote more time to conversation and letter writing than others do (McAdams & Constantian, 1983). Second, *people with strong affiliation needs worry more about acceptance than those with a low affiliation drive* (Koestner & McClelland, 1992). For

Figure 10.16
Measuring motives with the Thematic Apperception Test (TAT). Subjects taking the TAT tell or write stories about what is happening in a scene, such as this one showing a man at work. The two stories shown here illustrate strong affiliation motivation and strong achievement motivation. The italicized parts of the stories are thematic ideas that would be identified by a TAT scorer.

Affiliation arousal
George is an engineer who is working late. He is *worried that his wife will be annoyed* with him for neglecting her. She has been *objecting* that he cares more about his work than his wife and family. He seems *unable to satisfy* both his boss and his wife, but he *loves her* very much and will do his best to *finish up* fast and get home to her.

Achievement arousal
George is an engineer who *wants to win* a competition in which the man with the *most practicable drawing* will be awarded the contract to build a bridge. He is taking a moment to think *how happy he will be* if he wins. He has been *baffled by how to make such a long span strong,* but he remembers to *specify a new steel alloy* of great strength, submits his entry, but does not win, and is *very unhappy.*

example, they experience greater anxiety when they're being evaluated socially by peers. They also go out of their way to avoid being argumentative in groups, because they fear rejection.

ACHIEVEMENT: IN SEARCH OF EXCELLENCE

At the beginning of this chapter, we discussed Dennis Conner's lengthy, laborious, and tenacious pursuit of the America's Cup. He and his crew made great sacrifices and worked countless hours to achieve their goal. What motivates people to push themselves so hard? In all likelihood, it's a strong need for achievement. The *achievement motive* is the need to master difficult challenges, to outperform others, and to meet high standards of excellence. Above all else, the need for achievement involves the desire to excel—especially in competition with others. In Maslow's hierarchy of needs, achievement is found at the fourth level, among the esteem needs.

David McClelland and his colleagues (McClelland et al., 1953; McClelland, 1985) have been studying the achievement motive for about 40 years. McClelland believes that achievement motivation is of the utmost importance. He has estimated the average achievement motivation for *entire societies* by using TAT-like scoring procedures to assess the themes in representative examples of literature from those societies (rather than individuals' stories). These estimates of entire societies' need for achievement at specific times correlate with progress and productivity in those societies (Winter, 1992). For example, estimates of changes in achievement motivation in ancient Greece relate closely to the rise and fall of Greek civilization (McClelland, 1961). Also, estimates of achievement need in the United States have fluctuated in tandem with inventive activity as measured by the U.S. Patent Index (deCharms & Moeller, 1962). This remarkable correspondence between achievement motivation and patent activity is graphed in Figure 10.17.

McClelland sees the need for achievement as the spark that ignites economic growth, scientific progress, inspirational leadership, and masterpieces in the creative arts. It's difficult to argue with his assertion about the immense importance of achievement motivation. Consider how much poorer our culture would be if people such as Charles Darwin, Thomas Edison, Ernest Hemingway, Pablo Picasso, Marie Curie, Abraham Lincoln, Susan B. Anthony, Winston Churchill, and

Martin Luther King hadn't had a fire burning in their hearts.

Individual Differences in the Need for Achievement 8b

You've no doubt heard the stories of Lincoln as a young boy, reading through the night by firelight. Find a biography of any high achiever, and you'll probably find a similar drive—throughout the person's life. The need for achievement is a fairly stable aspect of personality. Hence, research in this area has focused mostly on individual differences in achievement motivation. Subjects' need for achievement can be measured effectively with the Thematic Apperception Test (C. Smith, 1992; Spangler, 1992).

The research on individual differences in achievement motivation has yielded interesting findings on the characteristics of people who score high in the need for achievement. They tend to work harder and more persistently on tasks than people low in the need for achievement (Brown, 1974). They also are more future-oriented than others and more likely to delay gratification in order to pursue long-term goals (Mischel, 1961; Raynor & Entin, 1982). In terms of careers, they typically go into competitive, entrepreneurial occupations that provide them with an opportunity to excel (McClelland, 1987). Apparently, their persistence and hard

"People with a high need for achievement are not gamblers; they are challenged to win by personal effort, not by luck."

DAVID MCCLELLAND

Figure 10.17 Achievement need and inventive activity. Applying TAT-like scoring techniques to popular American literature, deCharms and Moeller (1962) concluded that Americans' need for achievement began to decline around 1890. They also found some correspondence between achievement motivation and inventive activity, as measured by the U.S. Patent Index, suggesting that a culture's need for achievement may affect its productivity.

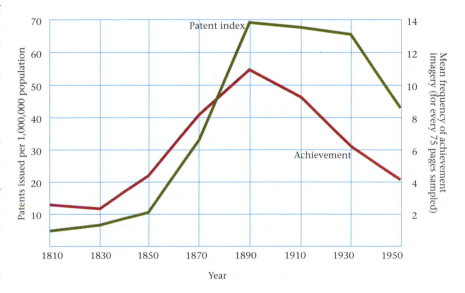

Most people attribute Michael Jordan's success in basketball to his remarkable ability, which is undeniably important. But the contribution of his extremely high need for achievement should not be underestimated. Jordan's competitive zeal is legendary, and he is widely regarded as on of the hardest working athletes in professional sports.

work often pay off. High achievement motivation correlates positively with measures of career success and with upward social mobility among lower-class men (Crockett, 1962; McClelland & Boyatzis, 1982).

Do people high in achievement need always tackle the biggest challenges available? Not necessarily. A curious finding has emerged in laboratory studies in which subjects have been asked to choose how difficult a task they want to work on. Subjects high in the need for achievement tend to select tasks of intermediate difficulty (McClelland & Koestner, 1992). For instance, in one study, where subjects playing a ring-tossing game were allowed to stand as close to or far away from the target peg as they wanted, high achievers tended to prefer a moderate degree of challenge (Atkinson & Litwin, 1960). Research on the situational determinants of achievement behavior has suggested a reason why.

Situational Determinants of Achievement Behavior 8b

Your achievement drive is not the only determinant of how hard you work. Situational factors can also influence achievement strivings. John Atkinson (1974, 1981, 1992) has elaborated extensively on McClelland's original theory of achievement motivation and has identified some important situational determinants of achievement behavior. Atkinson theorizes that the tendency to pursue achievement in a particular situation depends on the following factors:

• The strength of one's *motivation* to *achieve success*. This is viewed as a stable aspect of personality.
• One's estimate of the *probability of success* for the task at hand. This varies from task to task.
• The *incentive value of success*. This depends on the tangible and intangible rewards for success on the specific task.

The latter two variables are situational determinants of achievement behavior. That is, they vary from one situation to another. According to Atkinson, the pursuit of achievement increases as the probability and incentive value of success go up.

Let's apply Atkinson's model to a simple example. According to his theory, your tendency to pursue a good grade in calculus should depend on your general motivation to achieve success, your estimate of the probability of getting a good grade in the class, and the value you place on getting a good grade in calculus. Thus, given a certain motivation to achieve success, you will pursue a good grade in calculus less vigorously if your professor gives impossible exams (thus lowering your expectancy of success) or if a good grade in calculus is not required for your major (lowering the incentive value of success).

The joint influence of these situational factors may explain why high achievers prefer tasks of intermediate difficulty. Atkinson notes that the probability of success and the incentive value of success on tasks are interdependent to some degree. As tasks get easier, success becomes less satisfying. As tasks get harder, success becomes more satisfying, but its likelihood obviously declines. When the probability and incentive value of success are weighed together, moderately challenging tasks seem to offer the best overall value in terms of maximizing one's sense of accomplishment.

Factoring in the Fear of Failure 8b

According to Atkinson, a person's fear of failure must also be considered to understand achievement behavior (Atkinson & Birch, 1978). He maintains that people vary in their *motivation to avoid failure*. This motive is considered a stable aspect of personality. Together with situational factors such as the probability of failure and the negative value placed on failure, it influences achievement strivings. Figure 10.18 diagrams the factors in Atkinson's model that are thought to govern achievement behavior.

As with the motive to achieve success, the motive to avoid failure can stimulate achievement. For example, you might work very hard and very persistently in calculus primarily because you couldn't tolerate the shame associated with failure. In other words, you might work more to avoid a bad grade than to earn a good grade.

Fear is one of the most fundamental emotions. Thus, the relationship between achievement behavior and *fear* of failure illustrates how motiva-

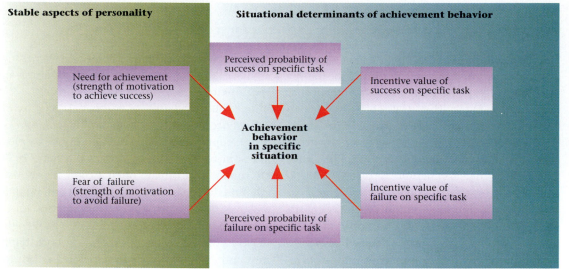

Figure 10.18
Determinants of achievement behavior. According to John Atkinson, a person's pursuit of achievement in a particular situation depends on several factors. Some of these factors, such as need for achievement or fear of failure, are relatively stable motives that are part of the person's personality. Many other factors, such as the likelihood and value of success or failure, vary from one situation to another, depending on the circumstances.

Labels in figure:
Stable aspects of personality
Situational determinants of achievement behavior
Need for achievement (strength of motivation to achieve success)
Perceived probability of success on specific task
Incentive value of success on specific task
Achievement behavior in specific situation
Fear of failure (strength of motivation to avoid failure)
Perceived probability of failure on specific task
Incentive value of failure on specific task

tion and emotion are often intertwined. On the one hand, *emotion can cause motivation*. For example, *anger* about your work schedule may motivate you to look for a new job. *Jealousy* of an ex-girlfriend may motivate you to ask out her roommate. On the other hand, *motivation can cause emotion*. For example, your motivation to win a photography contest may lead to great *anxiety* during the judging and either great *joy* if you win or great *gloom* if you don't. Although motivation and emotion are closely related, they're *not* the same thing. We'll analyze the nature of emotion in the next section.

Recap of Key Points

• Affiliation encompasses various needs for social bonds. Individual differences in the need for affiliation are usually measured with the TAT. People who are relatively high in the need for affiliation tend to devote more time to interpersonal activities and worry more about acceptance than others do.

• Achievement involves the need to excel, especially in competition with others. The need for achievement is usually measured with the TAT. People who are relatively high in the need for achievement work harder and more persistently than others. They delay gratification well and pursue competitive careers.

• Situational factors also influence achievement behavior. The pursuit of achievement tends to increase when the probability of success and the incentive value of success are high. However, the pursuit of achievement can be inhibited by a fear of failure.

CONCEPT CHECK 10.3
Understanding the Determinants of Achievement Behavior

According to John Atkinson, one's pursuit of achievement in a particular situation depends on several factors. Check your understanding of these factors by identifying each of the following vignettes as an example of one of the following six determinants of achievement behavior: (a) need for achievement; (b) perceived probability of success; (c) incentive value of success; (d) fear of failure; (e) perceived probability of failure; (f) incentive value of failure. The answers can be found in Appendix A.

_____ 1. Donna has just received a B in biology. Her reaction is typical of the way she responds to many situations involving achievement: "I didn't get an A, it's true, but at least I didn't flunk; that's what I was really worried about."

_____ 2. Belinda is nervously awaiting the start of the finals of the 200-meter dash in the last meet of her high school career. "I've gotta win this race! This is the most important race of my life!"

_____ 3. Corey grins as he considers the easy time he's going to have this semester. "I won't need to study much for this course. This teacher never flunks anyone."

_____ 4. Diana's just as hard-charging as ever. She's gotten the highest grade on every test throughout the semester, yet she's still up all night studying for the final. "I know I've got an A in the bag, but I want to be the best student Dr. McClelland's ever had!"

The most profound and important experiences in life are saturated with emotion. Think of the joy that people feel at weddings, the *grief* they feel at funerals, the *ecstasy* they feel when they fall in love. Emotions also color everyday experiences. For instance, you might experience *anger* when a professor treats you rudely, *dismay* when you learn that your car needs expensive repairs, and *happiness* when you see that you aced your economics exam. In some respects, emotions lie at the core of mental health. The two most common complaints that lead people to seek psychotherapy are *depression* and *anxiety*. Clearly, emotions play a pervasive role in people's lives. Reflecting this reality, modern psychologists have increased their research on emotion in recent decades (Davidson & Cacioppo, 1992).

But exactly what is an emotion? Everyone has plenty of personal experience with emotion, but it's an elusive concept to define. Emotion includes cognitive, physiological, and behavioral components, which are summarized in the following definition: **Emotion involves (1) a subjective conscious experience (the cognitive component) accompanied by (2) bodily arousal (the physiological component) and by (3) characteristic overt expressions (the behavioral component).** That's a pretty complex definition. Let's take a closer look at each of these three components of emotion.

The Cognitive Component: Subjective Feelings 8c

Over 550 words in the English language refer to emotions (Averill, 1980). Ironically, however, people often have difficulty describing their emotions to others (Zajonc, 1980). Emotion is a highly personal, subjective experience. In studying the cognitive component of emotions, psychologists generally rely on subjects' verbal reports of what they're experiencing. Their reports indicate that emotions are potentially intense internal feelings that sometimes seem to have a life of their own. Although a considerable degree of control is possible, people can't click their emotions on and off like a bedroom light. Many people have to struggle to control their emotions (Ellis, 1985; see the Chapter 13 Application).

People's cognitive appraisals of events in their lives are key determinants of the emotions they experience (Lazarus, 1991). A specific event, such as giving a speech, may be highly threatening and thus anxiety arousing for one person but a "ho-hum," routine matter for another. The conscious experience of emotion includes an *evaluative* aspect. People characterize their emotions as pleasant or unpleasant (Lang, 1995; Schlosberg, 1954). Of course, individuals often experience "mixed emotions" that include both pleasant and unpleasant qualities (Harris, 1993). For example, an executive just given a promotion with challenging new responsibilities may experience both happiness and anxiety. A young man who has just lost his virginity may experience a mixture of apprehension, guilt, and delight.

The Physiological Component: Autonomic Arousal 8c

Imagine your reaction as your car spins out of control on an icy highway. Your fear is accompanied by a variety of physiological changes. Your heart rate and breathing accelerate. Your blood pressure surges, and your pupils dilate. The hairs on your skin stand erect, giving you "goose bumps," and you start to perspire. Although the physical reactions may not always be as obvious as in this scenario, *emotions are accompanied by visceral arousal* (Cacioppo et al., 1993). Surely you've experienced a "knot in your stomach" or a "lump in your throat"—thanks to anxiety.

The physiological arousal associated with emotion occurs mainly through the actions of the *autonomic nervous system,* which regulates the activity of glands, smooth muscles, and blood vessels (see Figure 10.19). As you may recall from Chapter 3, the autonomic nervous system is responsible for the highly emotional *fight-or-flight response,* which is largely modulated by the release of adrenal *hormones* that radiate throughout the body. Hormonal changes clearly play a crucial role in emotional responses to stress and may contribute to many other emotions as well (Baum, Grunberg, & Singer, 1992).

The autonomic responses that accompany emotions are ultimately controlled in the brain. The hypothalamus, amygdala, and adjacent structures in the *limbic system* have long been viewed as the seat of emotions in the brain (Izard & Saxton, 1988; MacLean, 1993). Recent evidence suggests tha the *amygdala* (see Figure 10.20) plays a particu-

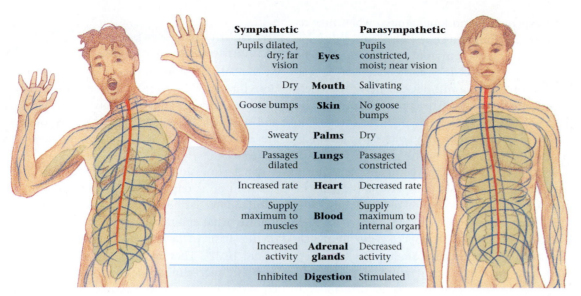

Sympathetic		Parasympathetic
Pupils dilated, dry; far vision	**Eyes**	Pupils constricted, moist; near vision
Dry	**Mouth**	Salivating
Goose bumps	**Skin**	No goose bumps
Sweaty	**Palms**	Dry
Passages dilated	**Lungs**	Passages constricted
Increased rate	**Heart**	Decreased rate
Supply maximum to muscles	**Blood**	Supply maximum to internal organ
Increased activity	**Adrenal glands**	Decreased activity
Inhibited	**Digestion**	Stimulated

Figure 10.19
Emotion and autonomic arousal. The autonomic nervous system (ANS) is composed of the nerves that connect to the heart, blood vessels, smooth muscles, and glands (consult Figure 3.10 for a more detailed view). The ANS is divided into the *sympathetic system,* which mobilizes bodily resources in response to stress, and the *parasympathetic system,* which conserves bodily resources. Emotions are frequently accompanied by sympathetic ANS activation, which leads to goose bumps, sweaty palms, and the other physical responses listed on the left side of the diagram.

larly central role in the modulation of emotion (LeDoux, 1993). Although researchers have mostly focused on subcortical structures in their efforts to unravel the neural bases of emotion, the cognitive appraisals of events that are crucial to emotion depend on higher mental processes that unfold in the cerebral cortex. Thus, emotions appear to be instigated and regulated by activity in a constellation of interacting brain centers and systems (LeDoux, 1986, 1992).

Of course, activity in any area of the brain depends on *neurotransmitters*—the chemicals that carry signals from one neuron to another throughout the central nervous system. Efforts to identify the neurotransmitters crucial to the experience of emotion have only begun recently. Relatively little is known, although several lines of evidence suggest that dopamine circuits may play a major role in pleasant emotions (White & Milner, 1992), while norepinephrine circuits contribute to the modulation of arousal (Panksepp, 1993). A host of neuropeptide transmitters, including endorphins, also appear to activate and inhibit specific emotions (Panksepp, 1993).

One prominent part of emotional arousal is **the galvanic skin response (GSR), an increase in the electrical conductivity of the skin that occurs when sweat glands increase their activity.** GSR is a convenient and sensitive index of autonomic arousal that has been used as a measure of emotion in many laboratory studies.

The connection between emotion and autonomic arousal provides the basis for the *polygraph,* or *lie detector,* a device that records autonomic fluctuations while a subject is questioned. A polygraph can't actually detect lies. It's really an emotion detector. It monitors key indicators of autonomic arousal, typically heart rate, respiration rate, and GSR. The assumption is that when subjects lie, they experience emotion (presumably anxiety) that produces noticeable changes in these physiological indicators (see Figure 10.21 on page 408). The polygraph examiner asks a subject a number of nonthreatening questions to establish the subject's baseline on these autonomic indicators. Then the examiner asks the critical questions (for example, "Where were you on the night of the burglary?") and observes whether the subject's autonomic arousal changes.

The polygraph is a potentially useful tool that can help police check out leads and alibis. However, its capacity to assess truthfulness is *far* from perfect (Lykken, 1981; Saxe, 1994). Part of the problem is that people who are telling the truth

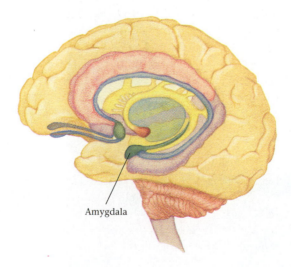

Figure 10.20
The amygdala. Emotions are controlled by a constellation of interacting brain systems, but the amygdala appears to play a particularly crucial role.

Amygdala

may experience emotional arousal when they respond to incriminating questions. Thus, polygraph tests often lead to accusations against people who are actually innocent. Another problem is that some people can lie without experiencing anxiety or autonomic arousal. The crux of the problem, as Leonard Saxe (1994) notes, is that "there is no evidence of a unique physiological reaction to deceit" (p. 71).

A study by Benjamin Kleinmuntz and Julian Szucko (1984) suggests that polygraph exams are inaccurate about one-fourth to one-third of the time. They arranged for lie detector tests for theft suspects, including 50 suspects who ultimately confessed their guilt and 50 suspects who were ultimately proven innocent by others' confessions. Their results indicated that the lie detector tests would have led to guilty verdicts for about one-third of the suspects who were proven innocent. Furthermore, about one-fourth of the suspects who later confessed would have been judged innocent based on their lie detector results. As a general rule, polygraph examiners do a better job of identifying guilty suspects than ruling out innocent ones (Honts & Perry, 1992).

Because of their high error rates, polygraph results cannot be submitted as evidence in most types of courtrooms. In spite of the courts' conservativism, many companies have required prospective and current employees to take lie detector tests to weed out thieves. In 1988, however, the U.S. Congress passed a law curtailing this practice. The passage of this law was stimulated in part by research results such as those seen in the Kleinmuntz and Szucko study.

Figure 10.21
Emotion and the polygraph. A lie detector measures the autonomic arousal that most people experience when they tell a lie. After using nonthreatening questions to establish a baseline, a polygraph examiner looks for signs of arousal (such as the sharp change in GSR shown here) on incriminating questions. Unfortunately, the polygraph is not a very dependable index of whether people are lying.

The Behavioral Component: Nonverbal Expressiveness

 8c

At the behavioral level, people reveal their emotions through characteristic overt expressions such as smiles, frowns, furrowed brows, clenched fists, and slumped shoulders. In other words, *emotions are expressed in "body language," or nonverbal behavior.*

Facial expressions reveal a variety of basic emotions. In an extensive research project, Paul Ekman and Wallace Friesen have asked subjects to identify what emotion a person was experiencing on the basis of facial cues in photographs (see Figure 10.22). They have found that subjects are generally successful in identifying six fundamental emotions: happiness, sadness, anger, fear, surprise, and disgust (Ekman & Friesen, 1975, 1984). There is also evidence, although it is open to more debate, that four other emotions (contempt, shame, guilt, and interest) can be reliably distinguished based on facial expressions (Ekman, 1992). Our ability to decipher the emotional significance of facial expressions is no small accomplishment in that Ekman (1980) estimates that the human facial muscles can create over 7000 different expressions.

Some theorists believe that muscular feedback from one's own facial expressions contributes to one's conscious experience of emotions (Izard, 1971, 1990; Tomkins, 1980, 1991). Proponents of the *facial-feedback hypothesis* assert that facial muscles send signals to the brain and that these signals help the brain recognize the emotion that one is experiencing. According to this view, smiles,

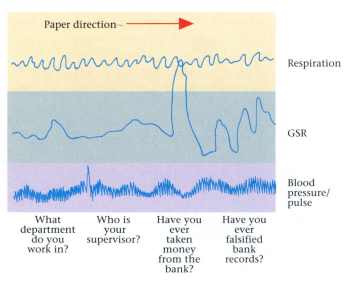

Paper direction—

Respiration

GSR

Blood pressure/ pulse

| What department do you work in? | Who is your supervisor? | Have you ever taken money from the bank? | Have you ever falsified bank records? |

frowns, and furrowed brows help create the subjective experience of various emotions. Consistent with this idea, studies show that if subjects are instructed to contract their facial muscles to mimic facial expressions associated with certain emotions, they tend to report that they actually experience these emotions (Laird, 1984; Levenson, 1992).

The facial expressions that go with various emotions may be largely innate (Eibl-Ebesfeldt, 1975). People who have been blind since birth smile and frown much like everyone else, even though they've never seen a smile or frown (Charlesworth & Kreutzer, 1973). The idea that facial expressions of emotion might be biologically built in has led to extensive cross-cultural research on the dynamics of emotion. Let's look at what investigators have learned about culture and the elements of emotional experience.

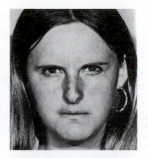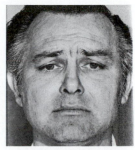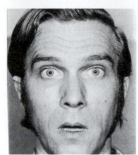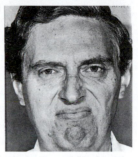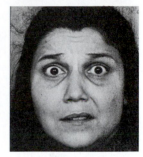

Culture and the Elements of Emotion

Are emotions innate reactions that are universal across cultures? Or are they socially learned reactions that are culturally variable? The voluminous research on this lingering question has not yielded a simple answer. Investigators have found both remarkable similarities and dramatic differences between cultures in the experience of emotion.

Cross-Cultural Similarities in Emotional Experience

After demonstrating that Western subjects could discern specific emotions from facial expressions, Ekman and Friesen (1975) took their facial-cue photographs on the road to other societies to see whether nonverbal expressions of emotion transcend cultural boundaries. Testing subjects in Argentina, Spain, Japan, and other countries, they

found considerable cross-cultural agreement in the identification of happiness, sadness, anger, fear, surprise, and disgust based on facial expressions (see Figure 10.23). Still, Ekman and Friesen wondered whether this agreement might be the result of learning rather than biology, given that people in different cultures often share considerable exposure to Western mass media (magazines, newspapers, television, and so forth), which provide many visual depictions of people's emotional reactions. To rule out this possibility, they took their photos to a remote area in New Guinea and showed them to a group of natives (the Fore) who had had virtually no contact with Western culture. Even the people from this preliterate culture did a fair job of identifying the emotions portrayed in the pictures (see the data in the bottom row of Figure 10.23). Subsequent comparisons of

Figure 10.22
Recognizing emotions from facial expressions. Ekman and Friesen (1975, 1984) have used photographs such as these to study people's ability to distinguish emotions based on facial expressions. Their data indicate that people generally can identify the six fundamental emotions portrayed in these photos: happiness, anger, sadness, surprise, disgust, and fear. Can you identify the emotions expressed in each photo?

	Fear	Disgust	Happiness	Anger

Country	\multicolumn{4}{c}{Agreement in judging photos (%)}			
United States	85	92	97	67
Brazil	67	97	95	90
Chile	68	92	95	94
Argentina	54	92	98	90
Japan	66	90	100	90
New Guinea	54	44	82	50

Figure 10.23
Cross-cultural comparisons of people's ability to recognize emotions from facial expressions. Ekman and Friesen (1975) found that people in highly disparate cultures showed fair agreement on the emotions portrayed in these photos. This consensus across cultures suggests that facial expressions of emotions may have a biological basis.

many other societies have also shown considerable cross-cultural congruence in the judgment of facial expressions (Ekman, 1992, 1993; Izard, 1991). Although some theorists disagree (Russell, 1994, 1995), there is reasonably convincing evidence that people in widely disparate cultures express their emotions and interpret those expressions in much the same way (Ekman, 1994; Izard, 1994).

Cross-cultural similarities have also been found in the cognitive and physiological elements of emotional experience (Scherer & Wallbott, 1994). For example, in making cognitive appraisals of events that might elicit emotional reactions, people from different cultures generally think along the same lines (Mauro, Sato, & Tucker, 1992; Mesquita & Frijda, 1992). That is, they evaluate situations along the same dimensions (pleasant versus unpleasant, expected versus unexpected, fair versus unfair, and so on). Understandably, then, the types of events that trigger specific emotions are fairly similar across cultures (Scherer et al., 1988). Around the globe, achievements lead to joy, injustices lead to anger, and risky situations lead to fear. Finally, as one might expect, the physiological arousal that accompanies emotion also appears to be largely invariant across cultures (Wallbott & Scherer, 1988). Thus, researchers have found a great deal of cross-cultural continuity and uniformity in the cognitive, physiological, and behavioral (expressive) elements of emotional experience.

Cross-Cultural Differences in Emotional Experience

The cross-cultural similarities in emotional experience are impressive, but researchers have also found many cultural disparities in how people think about and express their emotions. Foremost among these disparities are the fascinating variations in how cultures categorize emotions. Some basic categories of emotion that are universally understood in Western cultures appear to go unrecognized—or at least unnamed—in some non-Western cultures. James Russell (1991) has compiled numerous examples of English words for emotions that have no equivalent in other languages. For example, Tahitians have no word that corresponds to *sadness*. Many non-Western groups, including the Yoruba of Nigeria, the Kaluli of New Guinea, and the Chinese, lack a word for *depression*. The concept of *anxiety* seems to go unrecognized among Eskimos and the Yoruba, and the Quichua of Ecuador lack a word for *remorse*.

Russell (1991) also notes that the English language lacks words for certain emotions that are viewed as basic emotions in other cultures. For example, we do not have an equivalent of the German word *Schadenfreude,* which refers to pleasure derived from another's displeasure. The English language also lacks an equivalent for the Japanese concept of *itoshii* (longing for an absent loved one). After reviewing the extensive evidence on the issue, Russell concludes that "people of different cultures and speaking different languages categorize the emotions somewhat differently" (p. 444).

A similar conclusion can be drawn about nonverbal expressions of emotion. Although the natural facial expressions associated with basic emotions appear to be pancultural, people can and do learn to control and modify these expressions. ***Display rules* are norms that regulate the appropriate expression of emotions.** They prescribe when, how, and to whom people can show various emotions. These norms vary from one culture to another (Ekman, 1992). The Ifaluk, for instance, severely restrict expressions of happiness because they believe that this emotion often leads people to neglect their duties (Lutz, 1987). Japanese culture emphasizes the suppression of negative emotions in public. More so than in other cultures, the Japanese are socialized to mask emotions such as anger, sadness, and disgust with stoic facial expressions or polite smiling. Thus, nonverbal expressions of emotions vary somewhat across cultures because of culture-specific display rules.

Recap of Key Points

- Emotion is made up of cognitive, physiological, and behavioral components. The cognitive component involves subjective feelings that have an evaluative aspect.
- The physiological component of emotion, which may be coordinated by the amygdala in the brain, is dominated by autonomic arousal. This arousal is the basis for the lie detector, which is really an emotion detector. Polygraphs are not all that accurate in assessing individuals' veracity.
- At the behavioral level, emotions are expressed through body language, with facial expressions being particularly prominent. Ekman and Friesen have found considerable cross-cultural agreement in the identification of emotions based on facial expressions.
- Cross-cultural similarities have also been found in the cognitive and physiological components of emotion. However, there are some striking cultural variations in how people categorize and display their emotions.

THEORIES OF EMOTION

How do psychologists explain the experience of emotion? A variety of theories and conflicting models exist. Some have been vigorously debated for over a century. As we describe these theories, you'll recognize a familiar bone of contention. Like theories of motivation, theories of emotion differ in their emphasis on the innate biological basis of emotion versus the social, environmental basis.

James-Lange Theory 8d

As we noted in Chapter 1, William James was a prominent early theorist who urged psychologists to explore the functions of consciousness. James (1884) developed a theory of emotion over 100 years ago that remains influential today. At about the same time, he and Carl Lange (1885) independently proposed that *the conscious experience of emotion results from one's perception of autonomic arousal*. Their theory stood common sense on its head. Everyday logic suggests that when you stumble onto a rattlesnake in the woods, the conscious experience of fear leads to visceral arousal (the fight-or-flight response). The James-Lange

theory of emotion asserts the opposite: that the perception of visceral arousal leads to the conscious experience of fear (see Figure 10.24). In other words, while you might assume that your pulse is racing because you're fearful, James and Lange argued that you're fearful because your pulse is racing.

The James-Lange theory emphasizes the physiological determinants of emotion. According to this view, *different patterns of autonomic activation lead to the experience of different emotions*. Hence, people supposedly distinguish emotions such as fear, joy, and anger on the basis of the exact configuration of physical reactions they experience.

Cannon-Bard Theory 8d

Walter Cannon (1927) found the James-Lange theory unconvincing. Cannon, who developed the concepts of homeostasis and the fight-or-flight response, pointed out that physiological arousal may occur without the experience of emotion (if one exercises vigorously, for instance). He also argued that visceral changes are too slow to precede

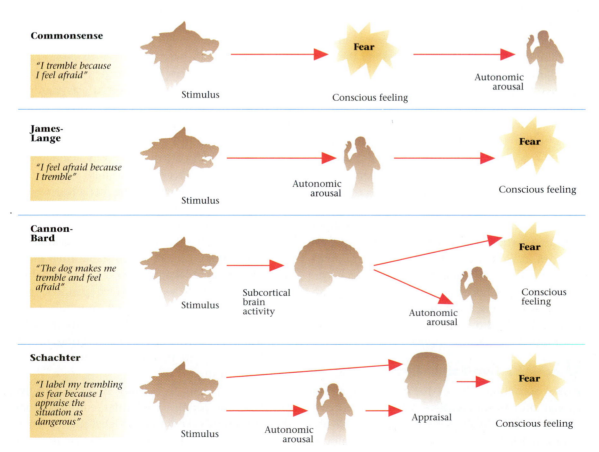

Commonsense

"I tremble because I feel afraid"

Stimulus → Fear → Autonomic arousal

Conscious feeling

James-Lange

"I feel afraid because I tremble"

Stimulus → Autonomic arousal → Fear

Conscious feeling

Cannon-Bard

"The dog makes me tremble and feel afraid"

Stimulus → Subcortical brain activity → Fear / Autonomic arousal

Conscious feeling

Schachter

"I label my trembling as fear because I appraise the situation as dangerous"

Stimulus → Autonomic arousal → Appraisal → Fear

Conscious feeling

**Figure 10.24
Theories of emotion.**
Three influential theories of emotion are contrasted with one another and with the commonsense view. The James-Lange theory was the first to suggest that feelings of arousal cause emotion, rather than vice versa. Schachter built on this idea by adding a second factor—interpretation (appraisal and labeling) of arousal.

In their naturalistic study of the two-factor theory of emotion, Dutton and Aron (1974) manipulated emotional arousal by arranging for males to encounter a female confederate on this precarious-looking bridge.

"Cognitive factors play a major role in determining how a subject interprets his bodily feelings."

STANLEY SCHACHTER

the conscious experience of emotion. Finally, he argued that people experiencing very different emotions, such as fear, joy, and anger, exhibit almost identical patterns of autonomic arousal.

Thus, Cannon espoused a different explanation of emotion. Later, Philip Bard (1934) elaborated on it. The resulting Cannon-Bard theory argues that emotion occurs when the *thalamus* sends signals *simultaneously* to the cortex (creating the conscious experience of emotion) and to the autonomic nervous system (creating visceral arousal). The Cannon-Bard model is compared to the James-Lange model in Figure 10.24. Cannon and Bard were off the mark a bit in pinpointing the thalamus as the neural center for emotion. However, many modern theorists agree with the Cannon-Bard view that emotions originate in subcortical brain structures (Buck, 1984; Izard, 1984; Tomkins, 1980).

Ultimately, the key issue in the debate between the James-Lange and Cannon-Bard views turned out to be whether different emotions are associated with different patterns of autonomic arousal. The research findings mostly supported the Cannon-Bard point of view for several decades. Investigators found that different emotions are *not* reliably associated with different patterns of autonomic activation (Strongman, 1978). However, more recent studies have detected some subtle differences in the patterns of visceral arousal that accompany basic emotions such as happiness, sadness, anger, and fear (Ekman, Levenson, & Friesen, 1983; Levenson, 1992).

The debate continues, because many psychologists doubt whether people can actually *distinguish* between these slightly different patterns of physiological activation (Zillmann, 1983). Humans are not particularly adept at recognizing their autonomic fluctuations. Thus, there must be some other explanation for how people differentiate various emotions.

Schachter's Two-Factor Theory 8d

Stanley Schachter believes that people look at situational cues to differentiate between alternative emotions. According to Schachter (1964; Schachter & Singer, 1962, 1979), the experience of emotion

depends on two factors: (1) autonomic arousal and (2) cognitive interpretation of that arousal. Schachter proposes that when you experience visceral arousal, you search your environment for an explanation (see Figure 10.24). If you're stuck in a traffic jam, you'll probably label your arousal as anger. If you're taking an important exam, you'll probably label it as anxiety. If you're celebrating your birthday, you'll probably label it as happiness.

Schachter agrees with the James-Lange view that emotion is inferred from arousal. However, he also agrees with the Cannon-Bard position that different emotions yield indistinguishable patterns of arousal. He reconciles these views by arguing that people look to external rather than internal cues to differentiate and label their specific emotions. In essence, Schachter suggests that people think along the following lines: "If I'm aroused and you're obnoxious, I must be angry."

The two-factor theory of emotion has been tested in numerous studies that have produced mixed results. Some aspects of the model have been supported and some have not (Reisenzein, 1983). A naturalistic study of interpersonal attraction by Dutton and Aron (1974) provides a particularly clever example of research that supported the two-factor theory. They arranged for young men crossing a footbridge in a park to encounter a young woman who asked them to stop briefly to fill out a questionnaire. The woman offered to explain the research at some future time and gave the men her phone number. Autonomic arousal was manipulated by enacting this scenario on two very different bridges. One was a long suspension bridge that swayed precariously 230 feet above a river (see the above photo). The other bridge was a solid, safe structure a mere 10 feet above a small stream. The experimenters reasoned that the men crossing the shaky, frightening bridge would be experiencing emotional arousal and that some of them might attribute that arousal to the woman rather than to the bridge. If so, they might mislabel their emotion as lust rather than fear and infer that they were attracted to the woman. The dependent variable was how many of the men later called the woman to pursue a date. As predicted, more of the men who met the woman on the precarious bridge called her for a date than did those who met her on the safe bridge.

The Dutton and Aron study supports the hypothesis that people often infer emotion from their physiological arousal and label that emotion in accordance with their cognitive explanation for it. The fact that the explanation may be inaccurate sheds light on why people frequently seem confused about their own emotions.

Although the two-factor theory has received support, studies have revealed some limitations as well (Leventhal & Tomarken, 1986). Situations can't mold emotions in just any way at any time. In searching to explain arousal, subjects don't limit themselves to the immediate situation. They may consider memories of past events (Sinclair et al., 1994). And contrary to Schacter's proposal, unexplained arousal is not experienced as a neutral state until situational cues signal a pleasant or unpleasant emotion. Rather, unexplained arousal is generally experienced as a negative state (Zimbardo, LaBerge, & Butler, 1993). Thus, emotions are not as pliable as the two-factor theory initially suggested.

Evolutionary Theories of Emotion 8d

As the limitations of the two-factor theory were exposed, theorists began returning to ideas espoused by Charles Darwin over a century ago. Darwin (1872) believed that emotions developed because of their adaptive value. Fear, for instance, would help an organism avoid danger and thus would aid in survival. Hence, Darwin viewed human emotions as a product of evolution. This premise serves as the foundation for several prominent theories of emotion developed independently by S. S. Tomkins (1980, 1991), Carroll Izard (1984, 1991), and Robert Plutchik (1984, 1993).

These *evolutionary theories* consider emotions to be largely innate reactions to certain stimuli. As such, emotions should be immediately recognizable under most conditions without much thought. After all, primitive animals that are incapable of complex thought seem to have little difficulty in recognizing their emotions. Evolutionary theorists believe that emotion evolved before thought. They assert that thought plays a relatively small role in emotion, although they admit that learning and cognition may have some influence on human emotions. Evolutionary theories generally assume that emotions originate in subcortical brain structures (such as the hypothalamus and most of the limbic system) that evolved before the higher brain areas (in the cortex) associated with complex thought.

Evolutionary theories also assume that evolution has equipped humans with a small number of innate emotions with proven adaptive value. Hence, the principal question that evolutionary theories of emotion wrestle with is, Wh*at are the*

fundamental emotions? Figure 10.25 summarizes the conclusions of the leading theorists in this area. As you can see, Tomkins, Izard, and Plutchik have not come up with identical lists, but there is considerable agreement. All three conclude that people exhibit eight to ten primary emotions. Moreover, six of these emotions appear on all three lists: fear, anger, joy, disgust, interest, and surprise.

Of course, people experience more than just eight to ten emotions. How do evolutionary theories account for this variety? They propose that the many emotions that people experience are produced by (1) blends of primary emotions and (2) variations in intensity. For example, Robert Plutchik (1980, 1993) has devised an elegant model of how primary emotions such as fear and surprise may blend into secondary emotions such as awe. Plutchik's model also posits that various emotions, such as apprehension, fear, and terror, involve one primary emotion experienced at different levels of intensity (see Figure 10.26).

Silvan Tomkins	Carroll Izard	Robert Plutchik
Fear	Fear	Fear
Anger	Anger	Anger
Enjoyment	Joy	Joy
Disgust	Disgust	Disgust
Interest	Interest	Anticipation
Surprise	Surprise	Surprise
Contempt	Contempt	
Shame	Shame	
	Sadness	Sadness
Distress		
	Guilt	
		Acceptance

Figure 10.25
Primary emotions. Evolutionary theories of emotion attempt to identify primary emotions. Three leading theorists—Silvan Tomkins, Carroll Izard, and Robert Plutchik—have compiled different lists of primary emotions, but this chart shows great overlap among the basic emotions identified by these theorists. (Based on Mandler, 1984)

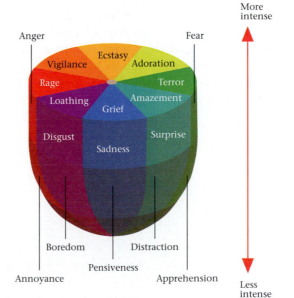

Figure 10.26
Emotional intensity in Plutchik's model. According to Plutchik, diversity in human emotion is a product of variations in emotional intensity, as well as a blending of primary emotions. Each vertical slice in the diagram is a primary emotion that can be subdivided into emotional expressions of varied intensity, ranging from most intense (top) to least intense (bottom).

PUTTING IT IN PERSPECTIVE

Five of our organizing themes were particularly prominent in this chapter: the influence of cultural contexts, the dense connections between psychology and society at large, psychology's theoretical diversity, the interplay of heredity and environment, and the multiple causes of behavior.

Our discussion of motivation and emotion demonstrated once again that there are both similarities and differences across cultures in behavior. The neural, biochemical, genetic, and hormonal processes underlying hunger and eating, for instance, are universal. But cultural factors influence what people prefer to eat, how much they eat, and whether they worry about dieting. In a similar vein, researchers have found a great deal of cross-cultural congruence in the cognitive, physiological, and expressive elements of emotional experience, but they have also found cultural variations in how people think about and express their emotions. Thus, as we have seen in previous chapters, psychological processes are characterized by both cultural variance and invariance.

Our discussion of the controversies surrounding evolutionary theory, aggressive pornography, and the determinants of sexual orientation show once again that psychology is not an ivory tower enterprise. It evolves in a sociohistorical context that helps to shape the debates in the field, and these debates often have far-reaching social and political ramifications for society at large.

We began the chapter with a discussion of various theoretical perspectives on motivation and ended with a review of different theories of emotion. Obviously, this area of inquiry is marked by great theoretical diversity, and there has been little movement toward reconciling the contradictory theories. Why are there so many conflicting theories of motivation and emotion? In this case, theoretical diversity appears to exist because motivation and emotion are such broad areas of study. It's probably unrealistic to expect one theory to apply equally well to such diverse phenomena.

The age-old nature versus nurture question was at the center of many of the theoretical debates in the chapter. We repeatedly saw that biological and social factors jointly govern behavior. For example, we learned that eating behavior, sexual desire, and the experience of emotion all depend on complicated interactions between biological and environmental determinants. Indeed, complicated interactions permeated the entire chapter, demonstrating that if we want to fully understand behavior, we have to take multiple causes into account.

In the upcoming Application, the complexity of human sexuality will be apparent once again, as we focus on issues that relate to sexual satisfaction. We'll look at advances in the understanding of sexual problems and their treatment, to extract some practical suggestions about enhancing sexual relationships.

Recap of Key Points

• The James-Lange theory asserts that emotion results from one's perception of autonomic arousal. The Cannon-Bard theory counters with the proposal that emotions originate in subcortical areas of the brain.

• According to Schachter's two-factor theory, people infer emotion from arousal and then label it in accordance with their cognitive explanation for the arousal. Evolutionary theories of emotion maintain that emotions are innate reactions that require little cognitive interpretation.

• Our look at motivation and emotion showed once again that psychology is characterized by theoretical diversity, that biology and environment shape behavior interactively, that behavior is governed by multiple causes, that psychological processes are characterized by both cultural variance and invariance, and that psychology evolves in a sociohistorical context.

APPLICATION: **UNDERSTANDING HUMAN SEXUALITY**

Answer the following "true" or "false."

1 Sexual problems are highly resistant to treatment.

2 Sexual problems belong to couples more than to individuals.

3 It's not a good idea for partners to openly discuss sex, because this creates unhealthy pressures.

4 Sexual fantasies about people other than one's partner are normal.

The answers for these questions are (1) false, (2) true, (3) false, and (4) true. If you answered several of the questions incorrectly, you have misconceptions about sexuality that may at some point affect your sexual relations. If so, you're not unusual. Although modern society seems obsessed with sex, misconceptions about sexuality are commonplace. In this Application, we'll take a practical look at sex—a very important motive that generates some of people's most powerful emotions.

Sexual intercourse is really a pretty simple activity. Most animals execute the act with a minimum of difficulty. However, humans manage to make sexual relations terribly complicated, and many people suffer from sexual problems. Fortunately, recent advances in psychology's understanding of sexual functioning have yielded many useful ideas on how to improve sexual relationships.

In the interests of simplicity, my advice is directed to heterosexual couples, although much of it is probably applicable to gay and lesbian readers, as well. Obviously, many readers may be involved in a sexual relationship at present, but if not, I'll assume that some-

day they will be. I'll also assume that readers' sexual partnerships will be (or are) based on a sincere bond of affection. Clinical interviews and surveys suggest that affection is very important to rewarding sexual relations.

Key Factors in Rewarding Sexual Relationships

Let's begin with some general points about some of the factors that promote rewarding sexual relationships (based on Barbach, 1982; Crooks & Baur, 1996; Hyde & DeLamater, 1997; Reinisch, 1990).

1. A surprising number of people are ignorant about the realities of sexual functioning. So, the first step in promoting sexual satisfaction is to acquire accurate information about sex. The shelves of most bookstores are bulging with popular books on sex, but many of them are loaded with inaccuracies. The best source of information is probably a college textbook on human sexuality. Enrolling in a course on sexuality is also a good idea. More and more colleges are offering such courses today.

2. The sexual value systems that people acquire incidentally during childhood are likely to affect them as adults. Negative values may be derived from the "conspiracy of silence" that surrounds the topic of sex in many homes. Unfortunately, sexual problems can be caused by a negative sexual value system in which sex is associated with immorality and depravity. The guilt feelings caused by this orientation can interfere with sexual functioning. Given this possibility, experts on sexuality often encourage adults to examine the sources and implications of their sexual values.

3. As children, people often learn that

they shouldn't talk about sex. Many people carry this attitude into adulthood and have great difficulty discussing sex, even with their partner. Good communication is extremely important in a sexual relationship. Figure 10.27 lists common problems in sexual relations reported by a sample of 100 couples (Frank, Anderson, & Rubenstein, 1978). Many of the problems reported by the couples—such as choosing an inconvenient time, too little foreplay, and too little tenderness after sex—are largely the result of poor communication. People can't expect their partners to be mind readers. Couples have to share their thoughts and feelings to promote mutual satisfaction.

4. The mind is the ultimate erogenous zone, and fantasizing about sexual encounters is commonplace for both sexes (Cado & Leitenberg, 1990; Jones & Barlow, 1990). Although Freudian theory originally saw sexual fantasy as an unhealthy by-product of sexual frustration and immaturity, the modern view is that *not* having sexual fantasies is a sign of pathology (Leitenberg & Henning, 1995). Research suggests that fantasies can help people of both sexes enhance their sexual excitement (Davidson, 1985). This research also reveals that it's not abnormal to fantasize about people other than one's lover or about sexual activities that one wouldn't actually engage in (Sue, 1979).

Understanding Sexual Dysfunction

Many people struggle with *sexual dysfunctions—impairments in sexual functioning that cause subjective distress.* One study of patients coming to a family practice center for medical treatment found that 75% had sexual problems of some kind (Schein et al., 1988). This estimate may be a little high for the population as a whole, as some of these sexual problems may have been spinoffs of the patients' medical problems. Nonetheless, it is clear that sexual problems are more common than many people appreciate. Figure 10.28 shows the percentage of subjects in another study reporting the principal kinds of dysfunctions that we'll discuss (Frank et al., 1978). These data suggest that roughly half of all couples are troubled to some degree by sexual problems.

Traditionally, people have assumed that a sexual problem lies in *one partner*. Although it's convenient to refer to a man's erectile difficulties or a woman's orgasmic difficulties, research indicates that most sexual problems emerge out of partners' unique ways of relating to each other. Masters and Johnson argue convincingly that *sexual problems belong to couples rather than to individuals*.

In this section, we'll examine the symptoms and causes of the three most common sexual dysfunctions: erectile difficulties, premature ejaculation, and orgasmic difficulties (based on Levay, Weissberg, & Woods, 1981; Masters & Johnson, 1980). In the next section, we'll discuss possible ways to overcome these problems.

Erectile difficulties occur when a man is persistently unable to achieve or maintain an erection adequate for inter-course. *Impotence* is the traditional name for this problem. However, sex researchers prefer to avoid this term because of its demeaning connotation.

The most common cause of erectile difficulties is anxiety about sexual performance. What leads to this troublesome anxiety? The cause can range from a man's doubts about his virility to conflict about the morality of his sexual desires. Anxiety about sexual performance can also be caused by an overreaction to a previous incident in which a man could not achieve sexual arousal. Many temporary conditions, such as fatigue, worry about work, an argument with one's partner, a depressed mood, or too much alcohol, can also cause transient erectile difficulties.

Recent research suggests that physiological factors (other than those produced by anxiety) may also contribute to erectile difficulties. A host of common diseases (such as diabetes) can produce erectile problems as a side effect, as can quite a variety of medications. Many experts now estimate that organic factors may contribute to erectile dysfunction in as many as one quarter of cases.

Premature ejaculation occurs when sexual relations are impaired because a man consistently reaches orgasm too quickly. What is "too quickly"? Any time requirement is hopelessly arbitrary. The subjective feelings of the partners are the critical consideration. If either partner feels that ejaculation is persistently too soon for sexual gratification, there's a problem.

What causes premature ejaculation? Some men simply don't exert much effort to prolong intercourse. Most of these men don't view their ejaculations as premature, but their partners often feel quite differently. Among men who *are* concerned about their partners' satisfaction, problems may occur because their early sexual experiences emphasized the desirability of a rapid climax. Furtive sex in the backseat of a car, quick efforts at masturbation, and experiences with prostitutes are situations in which men typically attempt to achieve orgasm very quickly. A pattern of rapid ejaculation may be entrenched by these formative experiences.

Orgasmic difficulties occur when people experience sexual arousal but have persistent problems in achieving orgasm. When this problem occurs in men, it's often called *retarded ejaculation*. The traditional name for this problem in women, *frigidity*, is no longer used because of its derogatory implications. Since the problem is more common among women, we limit this discussion to females.

Negative attitudes about sex are the primary cause of orgasmic difficulties among women. A woman who has been taught that sex is dirty and depraved will be likely to approach sex with shame and guilt. These negative attitudes can inhibit expression of her sexuality and thus impair orgasmic responsiveness. A lack of authentic affection for her partner, fear of pregnancy, or excessive concern about achieving orgasm may also contribute to orgasmic difficulties.

Coping with Specific Problems

With the advent of modern sex therapy, sexual problems no longer have to be chronic sources of shame and frustration. *Sex therapy* is the professional treatment of sexual dysfunctions. With professional assistance, most sexual difficulties can be resolved effectively (Arentewicz & Schmidt, 1983). Masters and Johnson have reported high success rates for their treat-

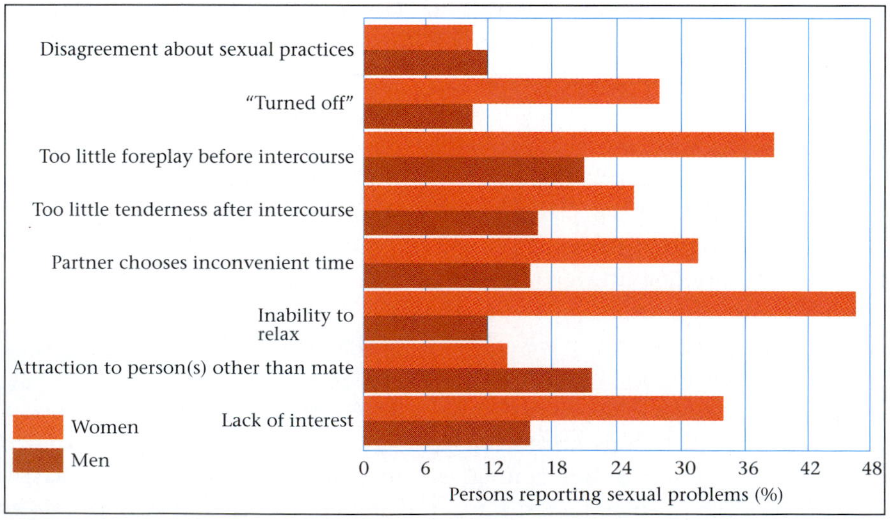

Figure 10.27
Common problems in sexual relations. The figure shows the percentages of men and women in a sample of 100 couples reporting various kinds of sexual problems. (Data based on Frank, Anderson, & Rubenstein, 1978)

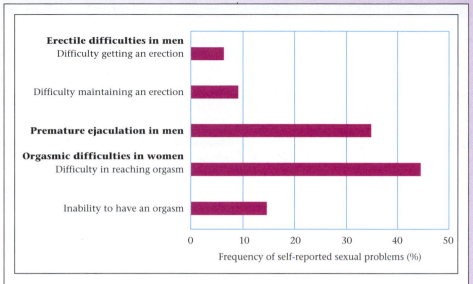

Figure 10.28
Sexual dysfunctions in normal couples. This graph shows the prevalence of various sexual dysfunctions in a sample of 100 "normal" couples, 80 percent of whom reported having happy or satisfying marriages. These data indicate that the most common dysfunctions are premature ejaculation in men and orgasmic difficulties in women. (Data based on Frank, Anderson, & Rubenstein, 1978)

ments of specific problems, which are shown in Table 10.1. Some critics argue that the cure rates reported by Masters and Johnson are overly optimistic in comparison with those of other investigators (Zilbergeld & Evans, 1980). Nonetheless, there is clear consensus that sexual dysfunctions can be conquered with encouraging regularity.

Of course, sex therapy isn't for everyone. It can be expensive and time-consuming. In some areas, it's difficult to find. However, many people can benefit from ideas drawn from the professional practice of sex therapy (Hartman & Fithian, 1974; H. Kaplan, 1979, 1983; Masters & Johnson, 1980). In this section, we'll briefly discuss a few of the experts' recommendations for dealing with erectile difficulties, premature ejaculation, and orgasmic difficulties.

The key to overcoming psychologically based erectile difficulties is to decrease the man's performance anxiety. It's a good idea for a couple to openly discuss the problem so that the woman can be reassured that it's not due to a lack of affection for her. Obviously, it's crucial for her to be emotionally supportive.

Masters and Johnson use a procedure called sensate focus in the treatment of erectile difficulties and other dysfunctions. *Sensate focus is an exercise in which partners take turns pleasuring each other with guided verbal feedback, while certain kinds of stimulation are temporarily forbidden.* One partner stimulates the other, who simply lies back and enjoys it, while giving instructions and feedback about what feels good. Initially, the partners are not allowed to touch each other's genitals or to attempt intercourse. This prohibition should free the man from feeling a pressure to perform. Over a number of

TABLE 10.1 Success Rates in the Treatment of Sexual Dysfunctions		
Dysfunction	Number of cases	Success rate
Erectile difficulties	552	77%
Premature ejaculation	432	96%
Orgasmic difficulties	730	75%

Source: Data from Masters and Johnson (1970); Kolodny, Masters, and Johnson (1979)

sessions, the couple gradually include genital stimulation in their sensate focus, but intercourse is still banned. With the pressure to perform removed, a man may experience arousals that begin to restore his confidence in his sexual response.

Men troubled by premature ejaculation range from those who climax almost instantly to those who can't last as long as their partner would like. In the latter case, simply slowing down the tempo of intercourse may help. The problem of instant ejaculation is more challenging to remedy. Sex therapists rely primarily on certain sensate focus exercises in which the man is repeatedly brought to the verge of orgasm. These sensate focus exercises can help him gradually improve control over his ejaculation response.

Orgasmic difficulties among women are often due to negative attitudes about sex. Thus, a restructuring of values often is the key to dealing with problems in achieving orgasm. Sensate focus exercises can also help a woman to better get in touch with her sexual response and preferences. In sensate focus, the guided verbal feedback that she gives her partner can improve his appreciation of her erotic preferences.

Recap of Key Points

• Rewarding sexual relationships are more likely when partners have genuine affection for each other, sound knowledge about sexual functioning, favorable attitudes toward sex, and good communication. It is also helpful to enjoy sexual fantasy.

• Sexual dysfunctions involve impairments in sexual functioning. Erectile difficulties are primarily due to anxiety about performance. Premature ejaculation is frequently due to formative sexual experiences that emphasized rapid climax.

• Negative attitudes about sex are the most common cause of orgasmic difficulties. A variety of suggestions were discussed for coping with specific sexual problems. Sensate focus exercises can be helpful in many instances.

Key Ideas

Motivational Theories and Concepts

◆ Some motivational theories emphasize the biological roots of motives; others emphasize the social roots. Evolutionary theories, which are controversial, explain motives in terms of their adaptive value.

◆ Drive theories apply a homeostatic model to motivation. They assume that organisms seek to reduce unpleasant states of tension called drives. In contrast, incentive theories emphasize how external goals energize behavior.

◆ Maslow's hierarchy of needs assumes that basic needs must be satisfied reasonably well before higher needs are activated. According to Maslow, people's growth needs include the need for self-actualization.

The Motivation of Hunger and Eating

◆ Eating is regulated by a complex interaction of biological and environmental factors. In the brain, the lateral and ventromedial areas of the hypothalamus appear to be involved in the control of hunger, but their exact role is unclear. Recent research suggests that the paraventricular and perifornical areas in the hypothalamus may be more important.

◆ Fluctuations in blood glucose also seem to play a role, but the exact location of the "glucostats" and their mode of functioning are yet to be determined. Hormonal regulation of hunger depends primarily on insulin secretions.

◆ Learning processes, such as classical conditioning and observational learning, influence both what people eat and how much they eat. Cultural traditions also shape food preferences. Food-related cues in the environment and stress-induced arousal can stimulate eating.

◆ Oversensitivity to external cues may contribute to obesity. Evidence indicates that there is a genetic predisposition to obesity. Weight problems can also be caused by an elevated set point for body weight and vacillations in dietary restraint.

Sexual Motivation and Behavior

◆ Scientists are not sure whether normal hormonal swings have much impact on human sexual desire. Pheromones appear to be important determinants of sexual desire in lower animals but of limited relevance to humans.

◆ Attraction to a potential partner is a critical determinant of sexual interest in humans. The Featured Study by Buss demonstrated that there are gender differences in mating preferences that largely transcend cultural boundaries. People respond to a variety of erotic materials, which may influence sexual behavior primarily by altering attitudes.

◆ The determinants of sexual orientation are not well understood. Recent studies suggest that there may be a genetic predisposition to homosexuality and that idiosyncrasies in prenatal hormonal secretions may contribute, but much remains to be learned. The human sexual response cycle can be divided into four stages: excitement, plateau, orgasm, and resolution.

Affiliation: In Search of Belongingness

◆ Individual differences in the need for affiliation are usually measured with the TAT. People who are relatively high in the need for affiliation tend to devote more time to interpersonal activities and worry more about acceptance than others do.

Achievement: In Search of Excellence

◆ People who are relatively high in the need for achievement work harder and more persistently than others. The pursuit of achievement tends to increase when the probability of success and the incentive value of success are high.

The Elements of Emotional Experience

◆ Emotion is made up of cognitive, physiological, and behavioral components. The cognitive component involves subjective feelings that have an evaluative aspect. The physiological component is dominated by autonomic arousal. At the behavioral level, emotions are expressed through body language, with facial expressions being particularly prominent.

◆ Ekman and Friesen have found considerable cross-cultural agreement in the identification of emotions based on facial expressions. Cross-cultural similarities have also been found in the cognitive and physiological components of emotion. However, there are some striking cultural variations in how people categorize and display their emotions.

Theories of Emotion

◆ The James-Lange theory asserts that emotion results from one's perception of autonomic arousal. The Cannon-Bard theory counters with the proposal that emotions originate in subcortical areas of the brain. According to Schachter's two-factor theory, people infer emotion from arousal and then label it in accordance with their cognitive explanation for the arousal. Evolutionary theories of emotion maintain that emotions are innate reactions that require little cognitive interpretation.

Putting It in Perspective

◆ Our look at motivation and emotion showed once again that psychology is characterized by theoretical diversity, that biol-ogy and environment shape behavior interactively, that behavior is governed by multiple causes, that psychological processes are characterized by both cultural variance and invariance, and that psychology evolves in a sociohistorical context.

Application: Understanding Human Sexuality

◆ Rewarding sexual relationships are more likely when partners have genuine affection for each other, sound knowledge about sexual functioning, favorable attitudes toward sex, and good communication. It is also helpful to enjoy sexual fantasy.

◆ Sexual dysfunctions involve impairments in sexual functioning, including erectile difficulties, premature ejaculation, and orgasmic difficulties. Couples have a variety of options for coping with specific sexual problems.

Key Terms

Achievement motive
Affiliation motive
Androgens
Aphrodisiacs
Bisexuals
Display rules
Drive
Emotion
Erectile difficulties
Estrogens
Galvanic skin response (GSR)
Glucose
Glucostats
Heterosexuals
Hierarchy of needs
Homeostasis
Homosexuals
Incentive
Insulin
Lie detector
Motivation
Need for self-actualization
Obesity
Orgasm

Orgasmic difficulties
Pheromone
Polygraph
Premature ejaculation
Refractory period
Sensate focus
Set point
Sex therapy
Sexual dysfunctions
Sexual orientation
Vasocongestion

Key People

John Atkinson
Walter Cannon
Paul Ekman and Wallace Friesen
William James
Abraham Maslow
William Masters and Virginia Johnson
David McClelland
Henry Murray
Judith Rodin
Stanley Schachter

Practice Test

1. In drive theories, the source of motivation lies _____ the organism; in incentive theories, the source of motivation lies _____ the organism.
   A. inside; outside
   B. inside; inside
   C. outside; inside
   D. outside; outside

2. According to expectancy-value models, your motivation to ask a particular person for a date depends on:
   A. your expectancy about the likelihood that the person will say "yes."
   B. the person's attractiveness (to you).
   C. both a and b.
   D. neither a nor b.

3. As individuals move to higher levels in Maslow's hierarchy, their needs become _____ biological and _____ social in origin.
   A. more; less
   B. more; more
   C. less; more
   D. less; less

4. Results of the early studies of hypothalamic manipulations in animals implied that the lateral hypothalamus may be a _____ center, and the ventromedial nucleus of the hypothalamus may be a _____ center.
   A. "start sleeping"; "stop sleeping"
   B. "start eating"; "stop eating"
   C. "stop eating"; "start eating"
   D. "start copulating"; "stop copulating"

5. Which of the following is the most common source of disinhibition for restrained eaters?
   A. emotional distress
   B. the fear of becoming too thin
   C. drinking alcohol in large quantities
   D. the perception that they have cheated on their diet

6. For men, sexual activity is more likely to be motivated by desire for _____; for women, it's more likely to be motivated by desire for _____.
   A. physical gratification; expression of love and emotional commitment
   B. expression of love and emotional commitment; physical gratification
   C. neither a nor b; there is no evidence for gender differences in this area
   D. a is true, except in the case of homosexuals

7. Some recent studies suggest that exposure to aggressive pornography:
   A. may increase males' aggressive behavior toward women.
   B. may perpetuate the myth that women enjoy being raped.
   C. both a and b.
   D. neither a nor b.

8. In research on affiliation, individual differences in affiliation are usually measured:
   A. by observing subjects' actual social behavior.
   B. by asking subjects about their affiliation needs.
   C. with the Thematic Apperception Test.
   D. with the Minnesota Multiphasic Personality Inventory.

9. Which of the following determinants of achievement behavior is (are) situational?
   A. the strength of one's motivation to achieve success
   B. one's estimate of the probability of success on the task at hand
   C. the incentive value of success on the task at hand
   D. both b and c

10. A polygraph (lie detector) works by:
    A. monitoring physiological indices of autonomic arousal.
    B. directly assessing the truthfulness of a person's statements.
    C. monitoring the person's facial expressions.
    D. all of the above.

11. Which of the following statements about cross-cultural comparisons of emotional experience is *not* true?
    A. The types of events that trigger specific emotions are fairly similar across cultures.
    B. The physiological reactions that accompany emotions tend to be similar across cultures.
    C. People of different cultures tend to categorize the emotions somewhat differently.
    D. All of the above statements are true.

12. According to the James-Lange theory of emotion:
    A. the experience of emotion depends on autonomic arousal and on one's cognitive interpretation of that arousal.
    B. different patterns of autonomic activation lead to the experience of different emotions.
    C. emotion occurs when the thalamus sends signals simultaneously to the cortex and to the autonomic nervous system.
    D. emotions develop because of their adaptive value.

13. Which theory of emotion implies that people can change their emotions simply by changing the way they label their arousal?
    A. the James-Lange theory
    B. the Cannon-Bard theory
    C. Schachter's two-factor theory
    D. opponent-process theory

14. The fact that eating behavior, sexual desire, and the experience of emotion all depend on interactions between biological and environmental determinants lends evidence to which of your text's organizing themes?
    A. psychology's theoretical diversity
    B. psychology's empiricism
    C. people's experience of the world is subjective
    D. the joint influence of heredity and environment

15. Which of the following statements is (are) true?
    A. Sexual problems are very resistant to treatment.
    B. Partners usually agree about how often they should have sexual relations.
    C. Sexual fantasies about people other than one's partner are normal.
    D. all of the above

Answers

1	A	Page 382	6	A	Page 394	11	D	Page 410
2	C	Page 383	7	C	Page 397	12	B	Page 411
3	C	Page 384	8	C	Page 402	13	C	Page 412
4	B	Page 386	9	D	Page 404	14	D	Page 414
5	D	Page 391	10	A	Page 407	15	C	Page 415

11

HUMAN DEVELOPMENT ACROSS THE LIFE SPAN

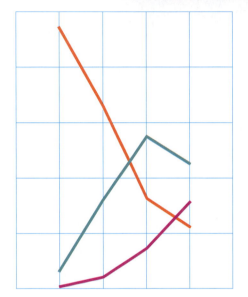

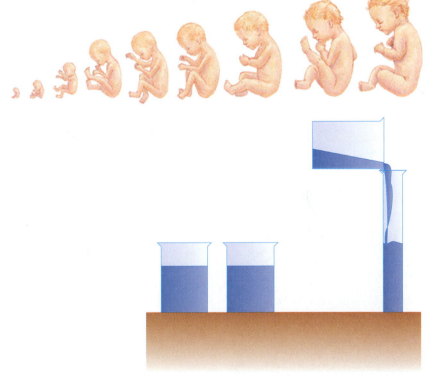

Archie Leach grew up in a lower-middle-class British home saturated with frustration and unhappiness. Archie's mother was obsessed with money and felt that her husband never earned enough. When Archie wanted anything, she constantly harped on the fact that money didn't "grow on trees." As a youngster, Archie was a frail, sad-eyed boy. He was often sullen and wrapped up in himself. His parents were miserable with each other, and his mother suffered from depression. When Archie was 10, his father had his mother committed to a mental hospital. Archie was bewildered by his mother's disappearance. His father gave him only a vague explanation, saying that she had gone away for a "rest." Archie, who didn't learn the truth for more than 20 years, thought that his mother had abandoned him. Understandably, he was deeply hurt and felt betrayed.

As a young man, Archie tried to break into theater in New York. However, at the age of 25, "Archie Leach possessed a low opinion of himself as an actor . . . Archie was still the confused, troubled boy from Bristol, who through his work sought but did not find the affection he had never received from his parents" (Harris, 1987, p. 42). He was a shy, moody young man who was especially awkward with the opposite sex. One acquaintance remarked, "He was literally tongue-tied around women."

In spite of these humble beginnings, Archie Leach eventually enjoyed great success in the world of entertainment. Blessed with classic good looks, he began to cultivate the image of an elegant man-about-town. "He looked graceless at first, but he knew that to succeed he had to become someone else, and he was not to be put off" (Wansell, 1983, p. 50).

Archie moved to Los Angeles and started working in films. He made remarkable progress in his effort to transform himself into a sophisticated ladies' man. He earned leading roles in better and better films and went on to star in 72 movies spanning four decades, using the stage name Cary Grant. He became a matinee idol, involved in romances with some of the world's most beautiful and desirable women. As one of his biographers put it, by the end of his career Cary Grant had come to personify such adjectives as "dapper, debonair, charming, jaunty, ageless, dashing, blithe, witty, [and] stylish" (Harris, 1987, p. 4).

Archie Leach's evolution into Cary Grant is a developmental story marked by both continuity and transition.

Archie Leach's transformation into Cary Grant was a stunning triumph, but many remnants of Archie's past were apparent beneath the surface of Cary Grant's public persona. Having felt betrayed by his mother when she mysteriously disappeared, he had lifelong difficulties trusting women. This lack of trust and the moody self-absorption that he had shown as a child contributed greatly to his four failed marriages. Although he could be glib and charming, he continued to feel strained in social encounters, and he spent much of his time in seclusion. In spite of his acclaimed brilliance as a movie star, he remained terribly insecure. He was never able to shake his mother's obsessive concern about money. Indeed, his miserliness was legendary. He amassed a fortune estimated to be worth $40 million, but he "saved the string from parcels and the tinsel from the Christmas tree, cut the buttons off the shirts he was about to discard in order to save them for future use, [and] marked the wine bottle to make sure that none was drunk while he was not there" (Wansell, 1983, p. 233).

What does Cary Grant have to do with developmental psychology? His story provides an interesting illustration of the two themes that permeate the study of human development: *transition* and *continuity*. In investigating human development, psychologists try to shed light on how people arrive at their various destinations in life. They focus on how people evolve through transitions over time. In looking at these transitions, developmental psychologists inevitably find continuity with the past. This continuity may be the most fascinating element in the story of Cary Grant's personal development. The metamorphosis of shy, awkward little Archie Leach into urbane, debonair Cary Grant was a more radical transformation than most people go through. Nonetheless, the threads of continuity connecting Archie's childhood to the development of Cary Grant's adult personality were quite obvious.

Development is the sequence of age-related changes that occur as a person progresses from conception to death. It is a reasonably orderly, cumulative process that includes both the biological and behavioral changes that take place as people grow older. An infant's newfound ability to grasp objects, a child's gradual mastery of grammar, an adolescent's spurt in physical growth, a young adult's increasing commitment to a vocation, and an elderly person's struggle with reduced hearing sensitivity all represent development. These transitions are predictable changes that are related to age.

Traditionally, psychologists have been most in-terested in development during childhood. Our coverage reflects this emphasis. However, as Cary Grant's story illustrates, development is a lifelong process. We'll divide the life span into four broad periods: (1) the prenatal period, between conception and birth, (2) childhood, (3) adolescence, and (4) adulthood. We'll examine aspects of development that are especially dynamic during each period. Let's begin by looking at events that occur before birth, during prenatal development.

PROGRESS BEFORE BIRTH: PRENATAL DEVELOPMENT

Development begins with conception. Conception occurs when fertilization creates a *zygote*, a **one-celled organism formed by the union of a sperm and an egg.** All of the other cells in your body developed from this single cell. Each of your cells contains enduring messages from your parents carried on the *chromosomes* that lie within its nucleus. Each chromosome houses many *genes*, the functional units in hereditary transmission. Genes carry the details of your hereditary blueprints, which are revealed gradually throughout life (see Chapter 3 for more information on genetic transmission).

The *prenatal period* extends from conception to birth, usually encompassing nine months of pregnancy. A great deal of important development occurs before birth. In fact, development during the prenatal period is remarkably rapid. If you were an average-sized newborn and your physical growth had continued during the first year of your life at a prenatal pace, by your first birthday you would have weighed 200 pounds! Fortunately, you didn't grow at that rate—and no human does—because in the final weeks before birth the frenzied pace of prenatal development tapers off dramatically. In this section, we'll examine the usual course of prenatal development and discuss how environmental events can leave their mark on development even before birth exposes the newborn to the outside world.

The Course of Prenatal Development 9a

The prenatal period is divided into three phases: (1) the germinal stage (the first two weeks), (2) the embryonic stage (two weeks to two months), and (3) the fetal stage (two months to birth). Some key developments in these phases are outlined here.

Germinal Stage

The *germinal stage* is the first phase of prenatal development, encompassing the first two weeks after conception. This brief stage begins when a zygote is created through fertilization. Within 36 hours, rapid cell division begins, and the zygote becomes a microscopic mass of multiplying cells. This mass of cells slowly migrates along the mother's fallopian tube to the uterine cavity. On about the seventh day, the cell mass begins to implant itself in the uterine wall. This process takes about a week and is far from automatic. Many zygotes are rejected at this point. As many as one in five pregnancies end with the woman never being aware that conception has occurred (Wilcox et al., 1988).

During the implantation process, the placenta begins to form. **The *placenta* is a structure that allows oxygen and nutrients to pass into the fetus from the mother's bloodstream and bodily wastes to pass out to the mother.** This critical exchange takes place across thin membranes that block the passage of blood cells, keeping the fetal and maternal bloodstreams separate.

Embryonic Stage

The *embryonic stage* is the second stage of prenatal development, lasting from two weeks until the end of the second month. During this stage, most of the vital organs and bodily systems begin to form in the developing organism, which is now called an *embryo*. Structures such as the heart, spine, and brain emerge gradually as cell division becomes more specialized. Although the embryo is typically only about an inch long at the end of this stage, it's already beginning to look human. Arms, legs, hands, feet, fingers, toes, eyes, and ears are already discernible.

The embryonic stage is a period of great vulner-

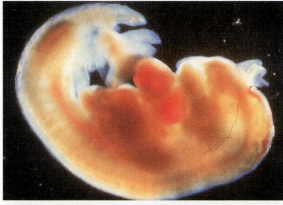

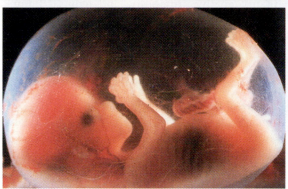

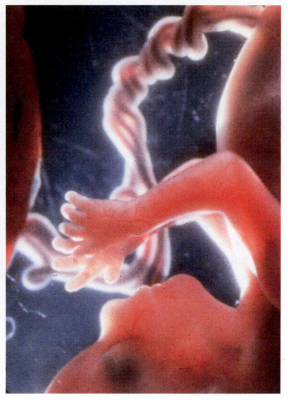

Prenatal development is remarkably rapid. (Top left) This 30-day-old embryo is just 6 millimeters in length. (Bottom left) At 14 weeks, the fetus is approximately 2 inches long. Note the well-developed fingers. The fetus can already move its legs, feet, hands, and head and displays a variety of basic reflexes. (Right) After 4 months of prenatal development, facial features are beginning to emerge.

ability because virtually all the basic physiological structures are being formed. If anything interferes with normal development during the embryonic phase, the effects can be devastating. Most miscarriages occur during this period (Simpson, 1991). Most major structural birth defects are also due to problems that occur during the embryonic stage (Mortensen, Sever, & Oakley, 1991).

Fetal Stage

The *fetal stage* is the third stage of prenatal development, lasting from two months through birth. Some highlights of fetal development are summarized in Figure 11.1. The first two months of the fetal stage bring rapid bodily growth, as muscles and bones begin to form (Moore & Persaud, 1993). The developing organism, now called a *fetus,* becomes capable of physical movements as skeletal structures harden. Organs formed in the embryonic stage continue to grow and gradually begin to function. Sex organs start to develop during the third month.

During the final three months of the prenatal period, brain cells multiply at a brisk pace. A layer

Figure 11.1
Overview of fetal development. This chart outlines some of the highlights of development during the fetal stage.

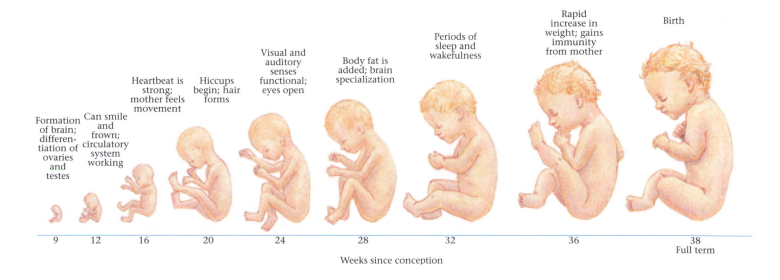

Formation of brain; differentiation of ovaries and testes

Can smile and frown; circulatory system working

Heartbeat is strong; mother feels movement

Hiccups begin; hair forms

Visual and auditory senses functional; eyes open

Body fat is added; brain specialization

Periods of sleep and wakefulness

Rapid increase in weight; gains immunity from mother

Birth

9   12   16   20   24   28   32   36   38
Full term

Weeks since conception

of fat is deposited under the skin to provide insulation, and the respiratory and digestive systems mature. All of these changes ready the fetus for life outside the cozy, supportive environment of its mother's womb. Sometime between 22 weeks and 26 weeks the fetus reaches the *age of viability—* **the age at which a baby can survive in the event of a premature birth.** The probability of survival is still pretty slim at 22 or 23 weeks, but it climbs steadily over the next month to an 85% survival rate at 26 to 28 weeks (Main & Main, 1991).

Environmental Factors and Prenatal Development

Although the fetus develops in the protective buffer of the womb, events in the external environment can affect it indirectly through the mother. Because the developing organism and its mother are linked through the placenta, a mother's eating habits, drug use, and physical health, among other things, can affect prenatal development. Figure 11.2 shows the periods of prenatal development during which various structures are most vulnerable to damage.

Maternal Nutrition

The developing fetus needs a variety of essential nutrients. Thus, it's not surprising that severe maternal malnutrition increases the risk of birth complications and neurological deficits for the newborn

(Rosenblith, 1992). The effects of severe malnutrition are a major problem in underdeveloped nations where food shortages are common. The impact of moderate malnutrition, which is more common in modern societies, is more difficult to gauge, in part because maternal malnutrition is often confounded with other risk factors associated with poverty, such as drug abuse and limited access to health care (Worthington-Roberts & Klerman, 1990). Nonetheless, some studies *have* found a correlation between moderate maternal dietary deficits during the prenatal period and infants' apathy, irritability, and reduced immunity to infectious diseases (Chandra, 1991; Zeskind & Ramey, 1981). These studies suggest that it's important for pregnant women to have nutritionally balanced diets.

Maternal Drug Use

A major source of concern about fetal and infant well-being is the mother's consumption of drugs, including such widely used substances as tobacco and alcohol, as well as prescription and recreational drugs. Unfortunately, most drugs consumed by a pregnant woman can pass through the membranes of the placenta.

Virtually all "recreational" drugs (see Chapter 5) can be harmful, with sedatives, narcotics, and cocaine being particularly dangerous. Babies of heroin users are born addicted to narcotics and have an increased risk of early death due to prematurity, birth defects, respiratory difficulties, and problems associated with their addiction (Finnegan & Kandall, 1992). Cocaine use during pregnancy is associated with a host of serious birth defects, including heart abnormalities and brain seizures (Chasnoff et al., 1989; Lester et al., 1991). Problems can also be caused by a great variety of drugs prescribed for legitimate medical reasons, and even some over-the-counter drugs (Niebyl, 1991). The impact of drugs on the embryo or fetus varies greatly depending on the drug, the dose, and the phase of prenatal development.

Alcohol consumption during pregnancy may also carry risks. It has long been clear that *heavy* drinking by a mother can be hazardous to a fetus. *Fetal alcohol syndrome* **is a collection of congenital (inborn) problems associated with excessive alcohol use during pregnancy.** Typical problems include microcephaly (a small head), heart defects, irritability, hyperactivity, and retarded mental and motor development (Julien, 1995). Previously, the available evidence suggested that it was safe

Figure 11.2
Periods of vulnerability in prenatal development. Generally, structures are most susceptible to damage when they are undergoing rapid development. The darker regions of the bars indicate the most sensitive periods for various organs and structures, while the lighter regions indicate periods of continued, but lessened, vulnerability. As a whole, sensitivity is greatest in the embryonic stage, but some structures remain vulnerable throughout prenatal development.

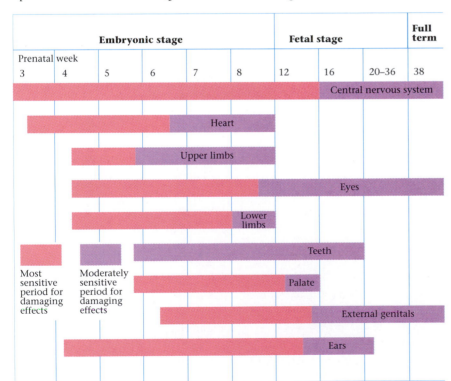

for women to drink in moderation during pregnancy. However, more recent studies indicate that even normal social drinking *may* be harmful to the fetus. For example, slight deficits in IQ, reaction time, motor skills, and attention span and increased impusiveness have been found in children born to women who consumed about three drinks a day during pregnancy (Barr et al., 1990; Hunt et al., 1995; Streissguth et al., 1989).

Tobacco use during pregnancy may also be hazardous to prenatal development. Smoking produces a number of subtle physiological changes in the mother that appear to reduce the flow of oxygen and nutrients to the fetus. Pregnant women who smoke have an increased risk for miscarriage, stillbirth, prematurity, and other birth complications (Niswander, 1982; Wen et al., 1990). Maternal smoking may also increase a child's risk for sudden infant death syndrome (Haglund & Cnattingius, 1990), slower than average cognitive development (Sexton, Fox, & Hebel, 1990), and attention deficit disorder (Milberger et al., 1996).

Maternal Illness

The fetus is largely defenseless against infections because its immune system matures relatively late in the prenatal period. The placenta screens out quite a number of infectious agents, but not all. Thus, many maternal illnesses can interfere with prenatal development. Diseases such as rubella (German measles), syphilis, cholera, smallpox, mumps, and even severe cases of the flu can be hazardous to the fetus (Isada & Grossman, 1991; Nesbitt & Abdul-Karim, 1982). The nature of any damage depends, in part, on when the mother contracts the illness.

Genital herpes and acquired immune deficiency syndrome (AIDS) are two very deadly diseases that pregnant women can also transmit to their offspring. Genital herpes is typically transmitted during the birth process itself when newborns come into contact with their mothers' genital lesions (Hanshaw, Dudgeon, & Marshall, 1985). Herpes can cause microcephaly, paralysis, deafness, blindness, and brain damage in infants and is fatal for many newborns (Rosenblith, 1992). The transmission of AIDS may also occur during birth, when newborns are exposed to their mothers' blood cells (Mott, Fazekas, & James, 1985). About 30% of pregnant women who carry the virus for AIDS pass the disease on to their babies (Valleroy, Harris, & Way, 1990). AIDS tends to progress rapidly in infants, and few survive for more than a year.

Premature births and infant deaths are much more common in the United States than most people realize. Shown here is the author's son, born prematurely in September 1992, receiving postnatal treatment in a hospital intensive care unit. Although prematurity is associated with a variety of developmental problems, T. J., like a great many premature infants, has matured into a robust, healthy child (see page 309 for a picture of him at age 15 months).

Prenatal Health Care

Many of the prenatal dangers that we have discussed are preventable if pregnant women receive adequate care and guidance from health professionals. Good quality medical care that begins early in pregnancy is associated with reduced prematurity and higher survival rates for infants (Malloy, Kao, & Lee, 1992). Because of poverty and a lack of health insurance, however, many pregnant women in the United States receive little or no prenatal medical care. This problem is particularly acute among racial minorities, especially African Americans (Edelman, 1987). Other factors surely contribute, but the lack of readily available health care for low-income groups is thought to be the main cause of the surprisingly high infant mortality in the United States. In spite of its relative affluence and its leadership in medical technology, the United States ranks an embarrassing 21st in the world in the prevention of infant mortality (see Figure 11.3 on page 426). Experts on child development from psychology, medicine, and many other fields have argued that the U.S. government sorely needs to increase its funding of prenatal health care for low-income groups (Gibbs, 1990). Given the high cost of intensive care for prematurely born infants, this investment would almost surely save money in the long run (see Figure 11.4 on page 426). Unfortunately, in recent years, federal spending on children's programs has *declined* rather than increased.

Science has a long way to go before it uncovers all the factors that shape development before birth. For example, the prenatal effects of fluctuations in maternal emotions are not well understood. Nonetheless, it's clear that critical developments unfold quickly during the prenatal period. In the

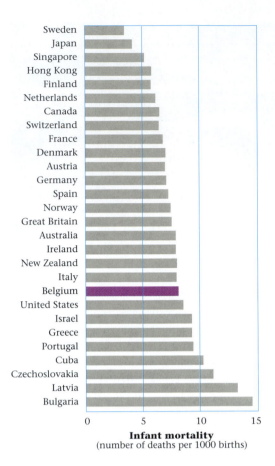

Figure 11.3
Cross-cultural comparisons of infant mortality.
Infant mortality is the death rate per 1000 births during the first year of life. Although the United States takes pride in its modern, sophisticated medical system, it ranks only 21st in the prevention of infant mortality. One of the main factors underlying this poor showing appears to be low-income mothers' limited access to medical care during pregnancy.

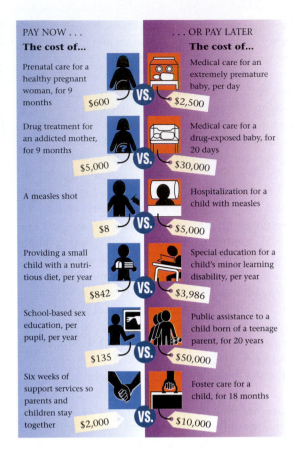

Figure 11.4
The high cost of not investing in preventive care for children. This *Time* magazine graphic shows why it would be financially prudent to spend more public funds on preventive health care measures for young children. As you can see, the cost of providing medical care to pregnant women who cannot afford it is a pittance in comparison to the cost that government agencies often absorb later when a child is born prematurely. Infants born six to eight weeks early often spend a month or more in an intensive care unit, at a cost of $75,000 to $100,000.

next section, you'll learn that development continues at a fast pace during the early years of childhood.

Recap of Key Points

• Prenatal development proceeds through the germinal, embryonic, and fetal stages as the zygote is differentiated into a human organism. The embryonic stage is a period of great vulnerability, as most physiological structures are being formed.

• Maternal malnutrition during the prenatal period has been linked to birth complications and other subsequent problems. Maternal drug use can be very dangerous, although the risks depend on the drug used, the dose, and phase of prenatal development.

• A variety of maternal illnesses can interfere with prenatal development. Many problems can be avoided if expectant mothers have access to good health care.

THE WONDROUS YEARS OF CHILDHOOD

A certain magic is associated with childhood. Young children have an extraordinary ability to captivate adults' attention, especially their parents'. Legions of parents apologize repeatedly to friends and strangers alike as they talk on and on about the cute things their kids do. Most wondrous of all are the rapid and momentous developmental changes of the childhood years. Helpless infants become curious toddlers almost overnight. Before parents can catch their breath, these toddlers are schoolchildren engaged in spirited play with young friends. Then, suddenly, they're insecure adolescents, worrying about dates, part-time jobs, cars, and college. The whirlwind transitions of childhood often seem miraculous.

Of course, the transformations that occur in childhood only *seem* magical. In reality, they reflect an orderly, predictable, gradual progression. In this section you'll see what psychologists have learned about this progression. We'll examine various aspects of development that are especially dynamic during childhood. Language development, which is very rapid during early childhood, is omitted from this section because we covered it in the chapter on language and thought (see Chapter 8). Let's begin by looking at perceptual abilities.

Experiencing the World: Perceptual Development

Like other aspects of development, perceptual development reflects the influence of both nature and nurture (M. Bornstein, 1992). Studies of infants' perception have focused heavily on vision, as is the case with studies of adults' perception. Ironically, the newborn child's visual capability appears to be mediocre compared to its hearing skills.

Visual Acuity and Depth Perception

Newborn children see blurred images because of poor visual acuity. Their visual acuity is estimated to be only about 20/660, as opposed to the ideal of 20/20 (Courage & Adams, 1990). Part of the problem is that the eye muscles that control visual accommodation (adjustment of the curvature of the lens) are still developing. Hence, in the first few months of life, infants aren't able to focus on objects very well (Banks, 1980).

Infants are far from blind, however. Even newborn babies can perceive color (Adams, 1989). From birth infants attend to moving stimuli, and they can track a moving object at close range at about age two months—albeit with rather jerky eye movements (Aslin, 1987). At around three months of age, most infants begin to recognize a photograph of their mother's face (Barerra & Maurer, 1981). Visual accommodation improves considerably between one and three months and is similar to adults' accommodation at about six months (Aslin & Smith, 1988). Visual acuity gradually improves to about 20/100 by six months and approaches 20/20 at around age 2 (Courage & Adams, 1990).

Infants' ability to perceive depth has been examined extensively in research with an apparatus called a visual cliff. **The *visual cliff* is a glass platform that extends over a several-foot drop-off (the cliff)** (see the photo below). If a child crawls across the shallow or "top" side of the apparatus but refuses to crawl onto the glass over the drop-off to the deep side, researchers conclude that the child can perceive depth. Eleanor Gibson and Richard Walk (1960) found that babies start balking at crawling "over the edge" at around six months of age. This finding suggested that most infants are capable of depth perception around the middle of their first year. Subsequent research showed that depth perception is not the only factor governing infants' behavior on the visual cliff. Studies indicate that infants need about 6–8 weeks of crawling experience before they develop a fear of venturing out over the cliff (Bertenthal, Campos, & Kermoian, 1994).

Experiments with younger children who can't yet crawl *suggest* that depth perception may be present long before six months of age. To test for depth perception in younger infants, researchers set them down on each side of the visual cliff surface and monitor their heart rate to see whether it varies. Surprisingly, heart rate in two-month-old children decreases when they're on the deep side. This suggests, with some ambiguity, that they can perceive the difference between the two sides but are not yet afraid of the drop-off (Bertenthal &

The visual cliff apparatus shown here is used to investigate the development of depth perception.

Campos, 1990). Thus, there is evidence that some primitive depth perception may exist by two months of age.

Hearing and Other Senses

Although not fully developed, newborns' hearing is more advanced than their vision. In fact, even before birth the fetus shows responsiveness to a variety of auditory stimuli (Fifer & Moon, 1988). Immediately after birth, newborns show some ability to tell where sounds are coming from, a process called *auditory localization* (Aslin, 1987). This was first demonstrated by Michael Wertheimer (1961), an enterprising psychologist who started performing experiments on his newborn daughter as soon as he entered the delivery room after her birth. He used a clicker device to make noises from different locations in the delivery room. He noted that his daughter consistently turned her head in the direction of the noise. Subsequent research has demonstrated that infants' localization of sounds is much less precise than that of adults, but their precision increases steadily through the first year and a half (Hillier, Hewitt, & Morrongiello, 1992; Morrongiello, 1988). Babies can distinguish their mother's voice within the first week of life (Spence & DeCasper, 1987). This fact probably explains why infants are comforted by their mother's presence even before they can recognize her face.

Early development in the other senses has not been studied as extensively as vision and hearing. However, it's clear that newborns can taste the differences among sweet, sour, and bitter substances (Lipsitt & Behl, 1990). By four months they show an affinity for salty tastes (Beauchamp, Cowart, & Moran, 1986). Infants' sense of smell allows them to learn to recognize familiar odors within the first two weeks (Makin & Porter, 1989),

and they're sensitive to even relatively light touches (Stack & Muir, 1992). Thus, basic capabilities seem to develop reasonably early in the senses of taste, smell, and touch. Overall, the perceptual abilities of very young infants are advanced in comparison to their motor abilities, which we'll consider next.

Exploring the World: Motor Development

One of the earliest topics studied by developmental psychologists was motor development. *Motor development* refers to the progression of muscular coordination required for physical activities. Basic motor skills include grasping and reaching for objects, manipulating objects, sitting up, crawling, walking, running, and so forth.

Basic Principles

A number of principles are apparent in motor development. One is the *cephalocaudal trend—the head-to-foot direction of motor development.* Children tend to gain control over the upper part of their bodies before the lower part. You've seen this trend in action if you've seen an infant learn to crawl. Infants gradually shift from using their arms for propelling themselves to using their legs. The *proximodistal trend is the center-outward direction of motor development.* Children gain control over their torso before their extremities. Thus, infants initially reach for things by twisting their entire body, but gradually they learn to extend just their arms.

Early motor development depends in part on physical growth, which is very rapid during infancy and is apparently more uneven than previously appreciated. Infants typically grow to quadruple their birth weight during the first year, while height increases by 75%. Until recently, it was assumed that this physical growth involved a gradual, steady process that yielded smooth, continuous growth curves like the one for height shown in Figure 11.5. But this conclusion was based on studies that measured children's height and weight every few months and averaged the results across many children—a method that seems to have led to deceptively smooth growth curves. A much more irregular pattern of growth was noted in a recent study in which investigators measured infants' height (from birth to 21 months) as frequently as *daily* and plotted *individual* growth curves. Lampl, Veldhuis, and Johnson (1992) found that lengthy periods of no growth were punctuated by sudden bursts of growth. Infants routinely went two to four weeks, and sometimes even 60

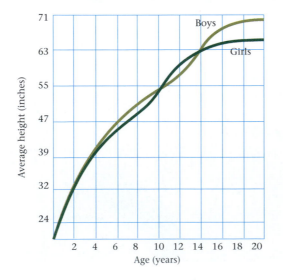

Figure 11.5
A classic growth curve for height. The traditional methods used to plot growth curves for height and other physical attributes (averaging across many children who are measured every few months) ensure that the curves look deceptively smooth, like the one shown here (from Malina, 1975). These results imply that physical growth unfolds at a relatively constant pace. However, recent research (Lampl et al., 1992) discussed in the text suggests that physical growth actually lurches forward unevenly in brief bursts.

days, with no growth and then grew as much as a half-inch in just one day. These remarkable growth spurts tended to be accompanied by restlessness and irritability. More research is needed to determine whether this pattern of episodic growth continues beyond infancy, but parents who sometimes feel that their children are changing overnight may not be imagining it!

Early progress in motor skills has traditionally been attributed almost entirely to the process of maturation. *Maturation* **is development that reflects the gradual unfolding of one's genetic blueprint.** It is a product of genetically programmed physical changes that come with age—as opposed to experience and learning. However, recent research that has taken a closer look at the *process* of motor deveopment suggests that infants are active agents rather than passive organisms waiting for their brain and limbs to mature (Thelen, 1995). According to the new view, the driving force behind motor development is infants' ongoing exploration of their world and their need to master specific tasks (such as grasping a larger toy or looking out a window). Progress in motor development is attributed to infants' experimentation and their learning and remembering the consequences of their activities. Although modern researchers acknowledge that maturation facilitates motor development, they argue that its contribution has been overestimated.

Understanding Developmental Norms

Parents often pay close attention to early motor development, comparing their child's progress with developmental norms. *Developmental norms* **indicate the average age at which individuals display various behaviors and abilities.** For example, the generalizations that "average children" say their first word at about 12 months and start combining words into sentences at around 24 months are developmental norms. Developmental norms are useful benchmarks as long as parents don't expect their children to progress exactly at the pace specified in the norms.

Some parents get unnecessarily alarmed when their children fall behind developmental norms. What these parents overlook is that developmental norms are group *averages*. Variations from the average are entirely normal. This normal variation stands out in Figure 11.6, which shows norms for many basic motor skills. The left side, interior mark, and right side of the bars in the diagram indicate the ages at which 25%, 50%, and 90% of youngsters can demonstrate each motor skill.

Figure 11.6
Landmarks in motor development. The left edge, interior mark, and right edge of each bar indicate the age at which 25%, 50%, and 90% of infants have mastered each motor skill shown. Developmental norms typically report only the median age of mastery (the interior mark), which can be misleading in light of the variability in age of mastery apparent in this chart.

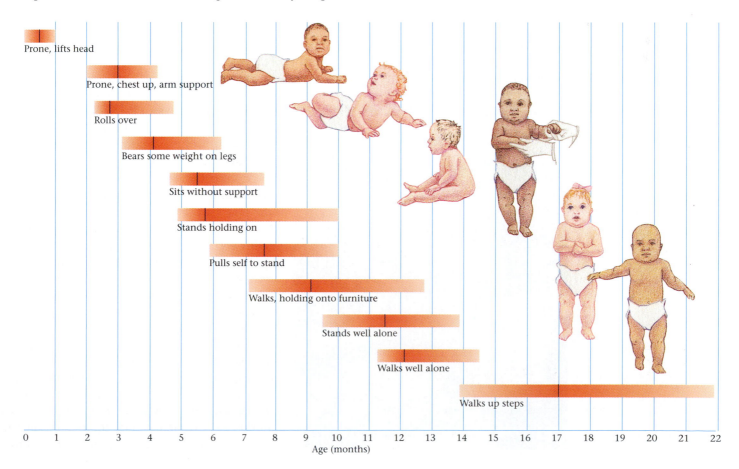

Typically, information on developmental norms includes only the median age of attainment indicated by the interior (50%) mark in each bar. This exclusive focus on average progress fails to convey the immense variability seen in youngsters' development. As Figure 11.6 shows, a substantial portion of normal, healthy children often don't achieve a particular milestone until long after the average time cited in norms.

Cultural Variations and Their Significance

Cross-cultural research has highlighted the dynamic interplay between experience and maturation in motor development. Relatively rapid motor development has been observed in some cultures that provide special practice in basic motor skills. For example, soon after birth the Kipsigis people of Kenya begin active efforts to train their infants to sit up, stand, and walk. Thanks to this training, Kipsigis children achieve these developmental milestones (but not others) about a month earlier than babies in the United States (Super, 1976). West Indian children in Jamaica also exhibit advanced motor development that has been linked to a special regimen of motor exercises practiced in early infancy (Hopkins & Westra, 1988, 1990). In contrast, relatively slow motor development has been found in some cultures that discourage motor exploration. For example, among the Ache, a nomadic people living in the rain forests of Paraguay, safety concerns dictate that children under three rarely venture more than three feet from their mothers, who carry them virtually everywhere. As a result of these constraints, Ache children are

delayed in acquiring a variety of motor skills and typically begin walking about a year later than other children (Kaplan & Dove, 1987).

Cultural variations in the emergence of basic motor skills demonstrate that environmental factors can accelerate or slow early motor development. Nonetheless, the similarities across cultures in the sequence and timing of early motor development outweigh the differences. This reality suggests that *early* motor development depends to a considerable extent on maturation. *Later* motor development is another matter, however. As children in any culture grow older, they acquire more specialized motor skills, some of which may be unique to their culture. Maturation becomes less influential and experience becomes more critical. Obviously, maturation by itself will never lead to the development of ballet or football skills, for example, without exposure to appropriate training.

Easy and Difficult Babies: Differences in Temperament

Infants show considerable variability in temperament. *Temperament* **refers to characteristic mood, activity level, and emotional reactivity.** From the very beginning, some babies seem animated and cheerful while others seem sluggish and ornery. Infants show consistent differences in emotional tone, tempo of activity, and sensitivity to environmental stimuli very early in life (Stifter & Fox, 1990; Worobey & Blajda, 1989).

Alexander Thomas and Stella Chess have conducted a major *longitudinal* study of the development of temperament (Thomas & Chess, 1977, 1989; Thomas, Chess, & Birch, 1970). **In a** *longitudinal design* **investigators observe one group of subjects repeatedly over a period of time.** This approach to the study of development is often contrasted with the cross-sectional approach (the logic of both approaches is diagrammed in Figure 11.7). **In a** *cross-sectional design* **investigators compare groups of subjects of differing age at a single point in time.** For example, in a cross-sectional study an investigator tracing the growth of children's vocabulary might compare 50 six-year-olds, 50 eight-year-olds, and 50 ten-year-olds. In contrast, an investigator using the longitudinal method would assemble one group of 50 six-year-olds and measure their vocabulary at age six, again at age eight, and once more at age ten.

Each method has its advantages. Cross-sectional studies can be completed more quickly, easily, and cheaply than longitudinal studies, which often

Tribes across the world use a variety of methods to foster rapid development of motor abilities in their children. The Kung San of the Kalahari, Botswana, teach their young to dance quite early, using poles to develop the kinesthetic sense of balance.

extend over many years. But longitudinal studies tend to be more sensitive to developmental changes (Nunnally, 1982).

To some extent, the choice of a research design to investigate development depends on what the investigators want to learn about. Thomas and Chess wanted to learn about the long-term stability of children's temperaments. Given this goal, they needed to follow the same children in a longitudinal study to assess their temperamental stability over time. They began their study in 1956 with a group of 141 middle-class children. In 1961 they added a second group of 95 children of working-class parents. They have tracked the development of most of these subjects into adolescence and adulthood.

Thomas and Chess found that "temperamental individuality is well established by the time the infant is two to three months old" (Thomas & Chess, 1977, p. 153). They identified three basic styles of temperament that were apparent in most of the children. About 40% of the youngsters were *easy children* who tended to be happy, regular in sleep and eating, adaptable, and not readily upset. Another 15% were *slow-to-warm-up children* who tended to be less cheery, less regular in their sleep and eating, and slower in adapting to change. These children were wary of new experiences, and their emotional reactivity was moderate. *Difficult children* constituted 10% of the group. They tended to be glum, erratic in sleep and eating, resistant to change, and relatively irritable. The remaining 35% of the children showed mixtures of these three temperaments.

A child's temperament at three months was a fair predictor of the child's temperament at age ten. Infants categorized as "difficult" developed more emotional problems requiring counseling than other children did. Although basic changes in temperament were seen in some children, Thomas and Chess concluded that temperament is generally stable over time.

Some critics have expressed concern because Thomas and Chess's data were based on parents' highly subjective ratings of their children's temperament (Mebert, 1991). But other investigators, who have used a variety of methods to assess infant temperament, have also found it to be fairly stable (Kochanska & Radke-Yarrow, 1992; Pedlow et al., 1993; Ruff et al., 1990). One prominent example is the work of Jerome Kagan and his colleagues, who have relied on direct observations of children in their studies of temperament (Kagan & Snidman, 1991; Kagan, Snidman, & Arcus, 1992).

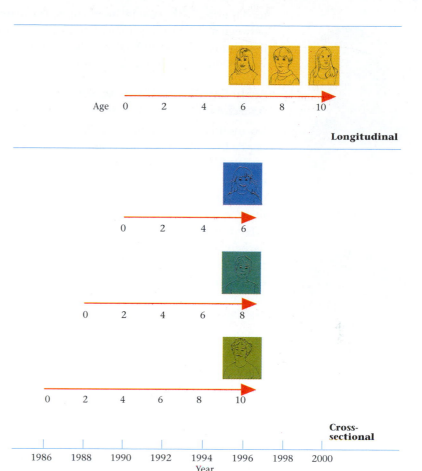

They have found that about 15%–20% of infants display an *inhibited temperament* characterized by shyness, timidity, and wariness of unfamiliar people, objects, and events. At the other end of the spectrum, about 25%–30% of infants exhibit an *uninhibited temperament*. These children are less restrained, approaching unfamiliar people, objects, and events with little trepidation. Evidence indicates that these temperamental styles are reasonably stable into middle childhood. Moreover, a recent twin study suggests that these temperamental styles are mainly determined by one's genetic inheritance (Robinson et al., 1992).

Additional studies examining other aspects of temperament have also found that heredity wields considerable influence over temperament (Braungart et al., 1992; Saudino & Eaton, 1991). Nonetheless, even though temperamental characteristics appear to be largely inborn, studies have demonstrated that environmental factors *can* influence a child's temperament (Belsky, Fish, & Isabella, 1991; Rothbart & Ahadi, 1994). According to Thomas and Chess, parents' reactions to their children may promote either stability or change in temperament, depending on how a child's emotional

Figure 11.7
Longitudinal versus cross-sectional research. In a longitudinal study of development between ages 6 and 10, the same children would be observed at 6, again at 8, and again at 10. In a cross-sectional study of the same age span, a group of 6-year-olds, a group of 8-year-olds, and a group of 10-year-olds would be compared simultaneously. Note that data collection could be completed immediately in the cross-sectional study, whereas the longitudinal study would require 4 years to complete.

tone meshes with parental preferences. The match between a child's temperament and a parent's expectations can also influence early emotional development, which is our next subject.

Early Emotional Development: Attachment

Do mothers and infants forge lasting emotional bonds in the first few hours after birth? Do early emotional bonds affect later development? These are just some of the questions investigated by psychologists interested in attachment. **Attachment refers to the close, emotional bonds of affection that develop between infants and their caregivers.** Researchers have shown a keen interest in how infant-mother attachments are formed early in life. Children eventually form attachments to many people, including their fathers, siblings, grandparents, and others. However, a child's first important attachment usually occurs with his or her mother because in most cultures she is the principal caregiver in the early months of life (Lamb, 1987).

Contrary to popular belief, infants' attachment to their mothers is *not* instantaneous. Initially, babies show little in the way of a special prefer-

"Important theoretical and practical questions in this realm of interest can be resolved by the use of monkeys."

HARRY AND MARGARET HARLOW

Even if fed by a wire surrogate mother, the Harlows' infant monkeys cuddled up with a terry cloth surrogate that provided contact comfort. When threatened by a frightening toy, the monkeys sought security from their terry cloth mothers.

ence for their mothers. They can be handed over to strangers such as babysitters with relatively little difficulty. This situation typically changes at around 6 to 8 months of age, when infants begin to show a preference for their mother's company and often protest when separated from her (Lamb, Ketterlinus, & Fracasso, 1992). This is the first manifestation of *separation anxiety*—**emotional distress seen in many infants when they are separated from people with whom they have formed an attachment.** Separation anxiety, which may occur with fathers and other familiar caregivers as well as the mother, typically peaks at around 14 to 18 months and then begins to decline.

Theories of Attachment

Why do children gradually develop a special attachment to their mothers? This question sounds simple enough, but it has been the subject of a lively theoretical dialogue. Behaviorists have argued that the infant-mother attachment develops because mothers are associated with the powerful, reinforcing event of being fed. Thus, the mother becomes a conditioned reinforcer. This reinforcement theory of attachment came into question as a result of Harry and Margaret Harlow's famous studies of attachment in infant rhesus monkeys (Harlow & Harlow, 1962).

The Harlows removed monkeys from their mothers at birth and raised them in the laboratory with two types of artificial "substitute mothers." One type of artificial mother was made of terry cloth and could provide "contact comfort" (see the adjacent photo). The other type of artificial mother was made of wire. Half of the monkeys were fed from a bottle attached to a wire mother and the other half were fed by a cloth mother. The young monkeys' attachment to their substitute mothers was tested by introducing a frightening stimulus, such as a strange toy. If reinforcement through feeding were the key to attachment, the frightened monkeys should have scampered off to the mother that had fed them. This was not the case. The young monkeys scrambled for their cloth mothers, even if they were *not* fed by them.

The Harlows' work made a simple reinforcement explanation of attachment unrealistic for animals, let alone for more complex human beings. Attention then turned to an alternative explanation of attachment proposed by John Bowlby (1969, 1973, 1980; Ainsworth & Bowlby, 1991). Influenced by psychoanalytic and evolutionary theories, Bowlby argued that there must be a biological basis for attachment. According to his view,

CHAPTER ELEVEN

infants are biologically programmed to emit behavior (smiling, cooing, clinging, and so on) that triggers an affectionate, protective response from adults. Bowlby also asserted that adults are programmed by evolutionary forces to be captivated by this behavior and to respond with warmth and love. Bowlby's theory has guided much of the research on attachment over the last several decades, including Mary Ainsworth's influential work on patterns of attachment (Bretherton, 1991, 1992).

Patterns of Attachment

Research by Ainsworth and her colleagues (Ainsworth, 1979; Ainsworth et al., 1978) suggests that attachment emerges out of a complex interplay between infant and mother. Studies reveal that mothers who are sensitive and responsive to their children's needs tend to evoke stronger attachments than mothers who are relatively insensitive or inconsistent in their responding (Cox et al., 1992; Isabella & Belsky, 1991; van den Boom, 1994). However, infants are not passive bystanders as this process unfolds. They are active participants who influence the process with their crying, smiling, fussing, and babbling. Difficult infants who are prone to distress, spit up most of their food, make bathing a major battle, refuse to go to sleep, and rarely smile may sometimes slow the process of attachment in the mother by undermining her responsiveness (Mangelsdorf et al., 1990).

Infant-mother attachments vary in quality. Ainsworth and her colleagues (1978) found that these attachments follow three patterns (see Figure 11.8). Fortunately, most infants develop a *secure attachment*. They play and explore comfortably with their mother present, become visibly upset when she leaves, and are quickly calmed by her return. However, some children display a pattern called *anxious-ambivalent attachment*. They appear anxious even when their mothers are near and protest excessively when she leaves, but they are not particularly comforted when she returns. Children in the third category seek little contact with their mothers and often are not distressed when she leaves, a condition labeled *avoidant attachment*. The type of attachment that emerges between an infant and mother may depend in part on the infant's temperament (Izard et al., 1991; Vaughn et al., 1992). Insecure (ambivalent or avoidant) attachments probably occur more often with temperamentally difficult infants who are fussy, fretful, glum, and socially unresponsive. In fact, one recent study that compared the influence of maternal sensitivity and infant temperament on attachment quality concluded that infant temperament was more important (Seifer et al., 1996).

Effects of Secure Attachment

Clearly, some children have stronger attachments to their mothers than other children do. And infants who are securely attached to their mothers tend to exhibit secure attachments with their fathers, as well (Fox, Kimmerly, & Schafer, 1991). Evidence suggests that the quality of these attachment relationships can have important conse-

"Where familial security is lacking, the individual is handicapped by the lack of what might be called a secure base from which to work."

MARY SALTER AINSWORTH

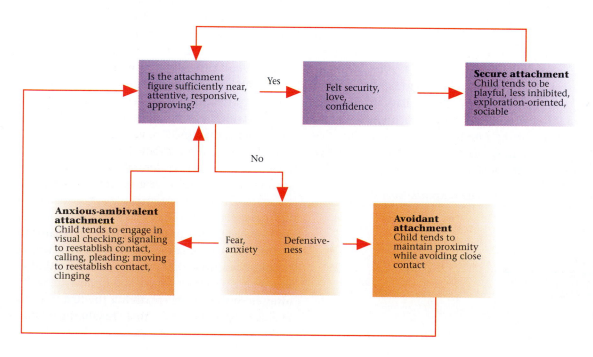

Figure 11.8
Overview of the attachment process. The unfolding of attachment depends on the interaction between a mother (or other caregiver) and an infant. Research by Mary Ainsworth and others suggests that attachment relations fall into three categories—secure, avoidant, and anxious-ambivalent—which depend on how sensitive and responsive caregivers are to their children's needs. The feedback loops shown in the diagram reflect the fact that babies are not passive bystanders in the attachment drama; their reactions to caregivers can affect the caregivers' behavior. Consult Chapter 16 for a discussion of how patterns of attachment in infancy may affect people's romantic relationships in adulthood. (Adapted from Shaver & Hazan, 1994)

quences for children. Infants with a relatively secure attachment tend to become resilient, competent toddlers with high self-esteem (Goldsmith & Harman, 1994). In their preschool years, they display more persistence, curiosity, self-reliance, and leadership and have better peer relations (Lamb et al., 1992; Turner, 1991). At age 11 they have better social skills and more close friends than youngsters who lacked a secure attachment during infancy (Elicker, Englund, & Sroufe, 1992). Recent studies have also found a relationship between secure attachment and more advanced cognitive development during childhood and adolescence (Jacobsen, Edelstein, & Hofmann, 1994).

Bonding at Birth, Day Care, and Attachment

Does a strong attachment relationship depend on infant-mother "bonding" during the first few hours after birth? Some theorists think so. For instance, Klaus, Kennell, and Klaus (1995) have suggested that extensive skin-to-skin contact between a newborn and its mother immediately after birth can promote more effective attachment later. This practice is intuitively appealing and can be a highly pleasurable "magic moment" for both infants and mothers. However, the data on its effects are unimpressive. Even short-term benefits have proven difficult to demonstrate. And there is no convincing evidence that this practice leads to healthier attachment relationships in the long run (Bretherton, 1992; Eyer, 1992; Rosenblith, 1992).

As for day care, its impact on attachment is the subject of heated debate. The crucial question is whether daily infant-mother separations might disrupt the attachment process. The issue is an important one, given that 53% of mothers with an infant under the age of one work outside the home. Research by Jay Belsky (1988, 1990b, 1992) suggests that babies who receive nonmaternal care for more than 20 hours per week have an increased risk of developing insecure attachments to their mothers. Belsky's findings have raised many eyebrows, but they need to be put in perspective. First, the data suggest that the proportion of day-

care infants who exhibit insecure attachments is only slightly higher than the norm in American society and even lower than the norm in some other societies (Lamb, Sternberg, & Prodromidis, 1992). Second, many studies have found that maternal employment is *not* harmful to children (Demo, 1992), and some studies have even found that day care can have beneficial effects on youngsters' intellectual and social development (Andersson, 1992; Caldwell, 1993). Third, the effects of day care appear to depend on the quality of the care provided. Negative effects seem minimal and may even be outweighed by positive effects when children are cared for in spacious, well-equipped, adequately staffed facilities that provide lots of individual attention and carefully planned activities (Howes, Phillips, & Whitebook, 1992; Scarr et al., 1993). Unfortunately, the United States has not invested as heavily in the provision of high-quality day care as many other industrialized nations (Kamerman, 1993; Zigler & Gilman, 1993).

Culture and Attachment

Separation anxiety emerges in children at about 6–8 months and peaks at about 14–18 months in cultures around the world (Grossman & Grossman, 1990). This finding suggests that attachment is a universal feature of human development. However, studies have found some interesting cultural variations in the proportion of infants who fall into the three attachment categories described by Ainsworth. Working with white, middle-class subjects in the United States, Ainsworth and colleagues (1978) found that 67% of infants displayed a secure attachment, 21% an anxious-ambivalent attachment, and 12% an avoidant attachment. As Table 11.1 shows, studies in Germany and Japan have yielded very different figures. Avoidant attachments were far more common in the German sample but were nonexistent in the Japanese sample, which yielded more anxious-ambivalent attachments than the U.S. sample.

Researchers have attributed these disparities in attachment patterns to cultural variations in child-rearing practices. More so than American parents, German parents intentionally try to encourage independence rather than clinging dependence at an early age, thus producing more avoidant attachments (Grossman et al., 1985). In contrast, Japanese parents do not attempt to foster a similar kind of early independence, and infants are rarely away from their mothers during the first year, so avoidant attachments are rare (Takahashi, 1990).

TABLE 11.1 PATTERNS OF ATTACHMENT (%) FROM THREE CULTURAL SAMPLES

Country (study)	Avoidant	Secure	Anxious-Ambivalent
USA (Ainsworth et al., 1978)	21	67	12
Germany (Grossman et al., 1981)	52	35	13
Japan (Takahashi, 1986)	0	68	32

Source: Adapted from Cole (1992)

Recap of Key Points

• Visual acuity improves throughout the first year. Research with the visual cliff suggests that depth perception is clearly established by six months of age and perhaps earlier. In comparison, hearing is more advanced during the early months of life.

• Motor development follows cephalocaudal (head-to-foot) and proximodistal (center-outward) trends and depends in part on physical growth, which appears to be more uneven than previously appreciated.

• Early motor development depends on both maturation and learning. Developmental norms for motor skills and other types of development are only group averages, and parents should not be alarmed if their children's progress does not match these norms exactly. Cultural variations in the pacing of motor development demonstrate the importance of learning.

• Cross-sectional and longitudinal studies are both well suited to developmental research. Cross-sectional studies are quicker, easier, and less expensive to conduct. Longitudinal studies are more sensitive to developmental changes.

• Temperamental differences among children are apparent during the first few months of life. Thomas and Chess found that most infants could be classified as easy, slow-to-warm-up, or difficult children. These differences in temperament are fairly stable and probably have a genetic basis. Children's temperaments can have far-reaching effects because of the reactions they tend to elicit from parents.

• Infants' attachments to their caregivers develop gradually. Separation anxiety usually appears around six to eight months of age. Reinforcement explanations of attachment appear inadequate in light of the Harlows' research with infant monkeys. They showed that the monkeys' attachment to artificial mothers was based on contact comfort rather than feeding.

• Bowlby's theory that attachment is biologically programmed has been influential. Research shows that attachment emerges out of an interplay between infant and mother.

• Infant-mother attachments fall into three categories: secure, anxious-ambivalent, and avoidant. A secure attachment fosters self-esteem, persistence, curiosity, and self-reliance, among other desirable traits.

• Bonding during the first few hours after birth does not appear to be crucial to secure attachment. The effects of day care on attachment are a source of concern, but the evidence is hotly debated. Cultural variations in child rearing can affect the patterns of attachment seen in a society.

Becoming Unique: Personality Development

How do individuals develop their unique constellations of personality traits over time? Many theories have addressed this question. The first major theory of personality development was put together by Sigmund Freud back around the turn of the century. As we'll discuss in Chapter 12, he claimed that the basic foundation of an individual's personality is firmly laid down by age 5. Half a century later, Erik Erikson (1963) proposed a sweeping revision of Freud's theory that has proven very influential. Like Freud, Erikson concluded that events in early childhood leave a permanent stamp on adult personality. However, unlike Freud, Erikson theorized that personality continues to evolve over the entire life span.

Building on Freud's earlier work, Erikson devised a stage theory of personality development. As you'll see in reading this chapter, many theories describe development in terms of stages. A *stage* is a developmental period during which characteristic patterns of behavior are exhibited and certain capacities become established. Stage theories assume that (1) individuals must progress through specified stages in a particular order because each stage builds on the previous stage, (2) progress through these stages is strongly related to age, and (3) development is marked by major discontinuities that usher in dramatic transitions in behavior (see Figure 11.9).

"Human personality in principle develops according to steps predetermined in the growing person's readiness to be driven toward, to be aware of, and to interact with a widening social radius."

ERIK ERIKSON

Erikson's Stage Theory

Erikson partitioned the life span into eight stages, each of which brings a *psychosocial crisis* involving transitions in important social relationships. According to Erikson, personality is shaped by how individuals deal with these psychosocial crises. Each crisis involves a struggle between two opposing tendencies, such as trust versus mistrust or initiative versus guilt, both of which are experienced by the person. Erikson described the stages in terms of these antagonistic tendencies, which

Figure 11.9
Stage theories of development. Some theories view development as a relatively continuous process, albeit not as smooth and perfectly linear as depicted on the left. In contrast, stage theories assume that development is marked by major discontinuities (as shown on the right) that bring fundamental, qualitative changes in capabilities or characteristic behavior.

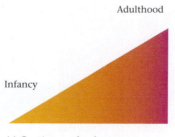

(a) Continuous development

(a) Discontinuous development

represent personality traits that people display in varying degrees over the remainder of their lives. Although the names for Erikson's stages suggest either-or outcomes, he viewed each stage as a tug of war that determined the subsequent *balance* between opposing polarities in personality. Erikson's theory is also based on the **epigenetic principle—the idea that the parts give rise to the whole.** In other words, each stage has its own special time of ascendancy and adds its own unique contribution to personality. All eight stages in Erikson's theory are charted in Figure 11.10. We describe the first four childhood stages here and discuss the remaining stages in the upcoming sections on adolescence and adulthood.

TRUST VERSUS MISTRUST. Erikson's first stage encompasses the first year of life, when an infant has to depend completely on adults to take care of its basic needs for such necessities as food, a warm blanket, and changed diapers. If an infant's basic biological needs are adequately met by its caregivers and sound attachments are formed, the child should develop an optimistic, trusting attitude toward the world. However, if the infant's basic needs are taken care of poorly, a more distrusting, pessimistic personality may result.

AUTONOMY VERSUS SHAME AND DOUBT. Erikson's second stage unfolds during the second year of life, when parents begin toilet training and other efforts to regulate the child's behavior. The child must begin to take some personal responsibility for feeding, dressing, and bathing. If all goes well, he or she acquires a sense of self-sufficiency. But, if parents are never satisfied with the child's efforts and there are constant parent-child conflicts, the

child may develop a sense of personal shame and self-doubt.

INITIATIVE VERSUS GUILT. In Erikson's third stage, lasting roughly from ages 3 to 6, the challenge facing children is to strive for a certain degree of independence from their parents. Children experiment and take initiatives that may sometimes conflict with their parents' rules. Overcontrolling parents may begin to instill feelings of guilt, and self-esteem may suffer. Parents need to support their children's emerging independence while maintaining appropriate controls. In the ideal situation, children will retain their sense of initiative while learning to respect the rights and privileges of other family members.

INDUSTRY VERSUS INFERIORITY. In the fourth stage (age 6 through puberty), the challenge of learning to function socially is extended beyond the family to the broader social realm of the neighborhood and school. Children who are able to function effectively in this less nurturant social sphere where productivity is highly valued should develop a sense of competence.

Evaluating Erikson's Theory

The strength of Erikson's theory is that it accounts for both continuity and transition in personality development. It accounts for transition by showing how new challenges in social relations stimulate personality development throughout life. It accounts for continuity by drawing connections between early childhood experiences and aspects of adult personality.

On the negative side, it's an "idealized" description of "typical" developmental patterns. Thus,

Figure 11.10
Erikson's stage theory.
Erikson's theory of personality development posits that people evolve through eight stages over the life span. Each stage is marked by a *psychosocial crisis* that involves confronting a fundamental question, such as "Who am I and where am I going?" The stages are described in terms of alternative traits that are potential outcomes from the crises. Development is enhanced when a crisis is resolved in favor of the healthier alternative (which is listed first for each stage).

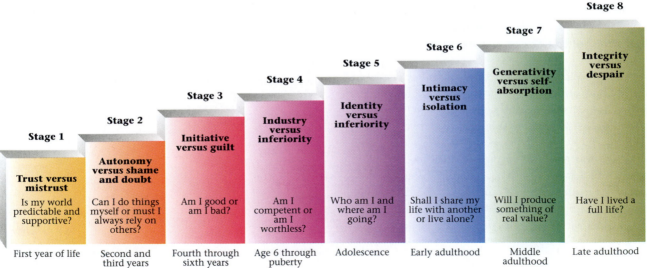

it's not well suited for explaining the enormous personality differences that exist among people. Inadequate explanation of individual differences is a common problem with stage theories of development. This shortcoming surfaces again in the next section, where we'll examine Jean Piaget's stage theory of cognitive development.

The Growth of Thought: Cognitive Development

 9c

Four-year-old Susan was asked where she got her name. She answered, "My mommy named me." "What if your mother had called you Jack?" "Then I'd be a boy."... Susan also claimed that if the name of the sun were changed and it was called the moon, "then it would be dark in the daytime."

A three-year-old girl, with a gleam in her eye, approached a plant. Her mother cautioned her not to touch it. "Why not?" "Because you might hurt it." "No, I won't, 'cause it can't cry." (Ault, 1977, p. 3)

These are just a few examples of how young children's thinking differs from that of adults. They illustrate why people speak of the freshness of seeing the world through children's eyes. Children have a different view, and not just because they are less informed (or shorter) than you or I. Children's thought processes are fundamentally different from ours.

Cognitive development **refers to age-related transitions in modes of thinking, including reasoning, remembering, and problem solving.** The investigation of cognitive development has been dominated in recent decades by the theory of Jean Piaget (1929, 1952, 1983). Piaget was a Swiss scholar who studied children's thinking from the 1920s until his death in 1980. Most of our discussion of cognitive development is devoted to Piaget's theory and the research it generated, although we'll also delve into information-processing approaches to cognitive development.

Overview of Piaget's Stage Theory

Jean Piaget was an interdisciplinary scholar whose own cognitive development was exceptionally rapid. In his early 20s, after he had earned a doctorate in natural science and published a novel, Piaget's interest turned to psychology. He met Theodore Simon, who had collaborated with Alfred Binet in devising the first useful intelligence tests. Working in Simon's Paris laboratory, Piaget administered intelligence tests to many children to develop better test norms. In doing this testing, Piaget discovered that he was intrigued by the

reasoning underlying the children's *wrong* answers. He decided that measuring children's intelligence was less interesting than studying how children *use* their intelligence. In 1921 he moved to Geneva, where he spent the rest of his life studying cognitive development. Many of his ideas were based on insights gleaned from careful observations of his own three children during their infancy.

Like Erikson's theory, Piaget's model is a *stage theory* of development. Piaget proposed that youngsters progress through four major stages of cognitive development, which are characterized by fundamentally different thought processes: (1) the *sensorimotor period* (birth to age 2), (2) the *preoperational period* (ages 2 to 7), (3) the *concrete operational period* (ages 7 to 11), and (4) the *formal operational period* (age 11 onward). Figure 11.11 provides an overview of each of these periods. Piaget regarded his age norms as approximations and acknowledged that transitional ages may vary, but he was convinced that all children progress through the stages of cognitive development in the same order.

Noting that children actively explore the world around them, Piaget asserted that interaction with the environment and maturation gradually alter the way children think. According to Piaget, children progress in their thinking through the complementary processes of assimilation and accommodation. *Assimilation* **involves interpreting new experiences in terms of existing mental structures without changing them.** A child may, for instance, have an idea of how Velcro operates from putting on and taking off a bib. Presented with shoes that have Velcro fasteners, that child is likely to pick up the new task (fastening the shoes) quite easily.

Accommodation **involves changing existing mental structures to explain new experiences.**

"It is virtually impossible to draw a clear line between innate and acquired behavior patterns."

JEAN PIAGET

Figure 11.11
Piaget's stage theory. Piaget's theory of cognitive development identifies four stages marked by fundamentally different modes of thinking through which youngsters evolve. The approximate age norms and some key characteristics of thought at each stage are summarized here.

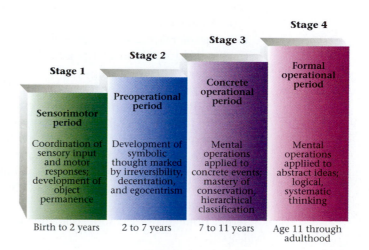

Stage 1 — **Sensorimotor period** — Coordination of sensory input and motor responses; development of object permanence — Birth to 2 years

Stage 2 — **Preoperational period** — Development of symbolic thought marked by irreversibility, decentration, and egocentrism — 2 to 7 years

Stage 3 — **Concrete operational period** — Mental operations applied to concrete events; mastery of conservation, hierarchical classification — 7 to 11 years

Stage 4 — **Formal operational period** — Mental operations applied to abstract ideas; logical, systematic thinking — Age 11 through adulthood

Jean Piaget (in beret) devised his theory of cognitive development by observing children and questioning them.

Accommodation and assimilation often occur interactively. For instance, children accustomed to popping the caps off soda bottles with a bottle opener may try to use the opener in this way the first time they encounter a twist-off cap. When this strategy (of assimilation) fails to yield results, the children may try other approaches in a trial-and-error fashion. When the solution (twisting the cap) is discovered, their mental structures for handling soda bottles may be altered. If so, these alterations in mental structures involve accommodation. With the companion processes of assimilation and accommodation in mind, let's turn now to the four stages in Piaget's theory.

Sensorimotor Period

One of Piaget's foremost contributions was to greatly enhance the understanding of mental development in the earliest months of life. The first stage in his theory is the *sensorimotor period,* which lasts from birth to about age two. Piaget called this stage *sensorimotor* because infants are developing the ability to coordinate their sensory input with their motor actions.

The major development during the sensorimotor stage is the gradual appearance of symbolic thought. At the beginning of this stage, a child's behavior is dominated by innate reflexes. But by the end of the stage, the child can use mental symbols to represent objects (for example, a mental image of a favorite toy). The key to this transition is the acquisition of the concept of object permanence.

Object permanence develops when a child recognizes that objects continue to exist even when they are no longer visible. Although you surely take the permanence of objects for granted, infants aren't aware of this permanence at first. If you show a 3-month-old child an eye-catching toy and then cover the toy with a pillow, the child will not attempt to search for the toy. Piaget inferred from this observation that the child does not understand that the toy continues to exist under the pillow. The notion of object permanence does not dawn on children overnight. The first signs of this insight usually appear between 4 and 8 months of age, when children will often pursue an object that is *partially* covered in their presence. Progress is gradual, and children typically don't master the concept of object permanence until they're about 18 months old.

The significance of object permanence is immense. Once children realize that disappearing objects continue to exist, they begin to use mental images to represent the absent objects. This is the primitive beginning of symbolic thought, which will gradually expand the boundaries of their thinking.

Preoperational Period

During the *preoperational period,* which extends roughly from age 2 to age 7, children gradually improve in their use of mental images. Although progress in symbolic thought continues, Piaget emphasized the *shortcomings* in preoperational thought.

Consider a simple problem that Piaget presented to youngsters. He would take two identical beakers and fill each with the same amount of water. After a child had agreed that the two beakers contained the same amount of water, he would pour the water from one of the beakers into a much taller and thinner beaker (see Figure 11.12). He would then ask the child whether the two differently shaped beakers still contained the same amount of water. Confronted with a problem like this, children in the preoperational period generally said no. They typically focused on the higher water line in the taller beaker and insisted that there was more water in the slender beaker. They had not yet mastered the principle of conservation. **Conservation is Piaget's term for the awareness that physical quantities remain constant in spite of changes in their shape or appearance.** Why are preoperational children unable to solve conservation problems? According to Piaget, their inability to understand conservation is due to some basic flaws in preoperational thinking. These flaws include centration, irreversibility, and egocentrism.

CENTRATION. *Centration* **is the tendency to focus on just one feature of a problem, neglecting other important aspects.** When working on the conservation problem with water, preoperational children tend to concentrate on the height of the water while ignoring the width. They have difficulty focusing on several aspects of a problem at once.

IRREVERSIBILITY. *Irreversibility* **is the inability to envision reversing an action.** Preoperational children can't mentally "undo" something. For instance, in grappling with the conservation of water, they don't think about what would happen if the water were poured back from the narrow beaker into the original beaker.

EGOCENTRISM. *Egocentrism* **in thinking is characterized by a limited ability to share another person's viewpoint.** Indeed, Piaget felt that preoperational children fail to appreciate that there are points of view other than their own. For instance, if you ask a preoperational girl whether her sister has a sister, she'll probably say no if they are the only two girls in the family. She's unable to view sisterhood from her sister's perspective (this also shows irreversibility). A notable feature of egocentrism is *animism*—**the belief that all things are living,** just like oneself. Thus, youngsters attribute lifelike, human qualities to inanimate objects, asking questions such as, "When does the ocean stop to rest?" or "Why does the wind get so mad?"

As you can see, Piaget emphasized the weaknesses apparent in preoperational thought. Indeed, that is why he called this stage *pre*operational. The ability to perform *operations*—internal transformations, manipulations, and reorganizations of mental structures—emerges in the next stage.

Concrete Operational Period

The development of mental operations marks the beginning of the *concrete operational period,* which usually lasts from about age 7 to age 11. Piaget called this stage *concrete* operations because children can perform operations only on images of tangible objects and actual events.

Among the operations that children master during this stage are reversibility and decentration. *Reversibility* permits a child to mentally undo an action. *Decentration* allows the child to focus on more than one feature of a problem simultaneously. The newfound ability to coordinate several aspects of a problem helps the child appreciate that there are several ways to look at things. This ability in turn leads to a decline in egocentrism.

As children master concrete operations, they

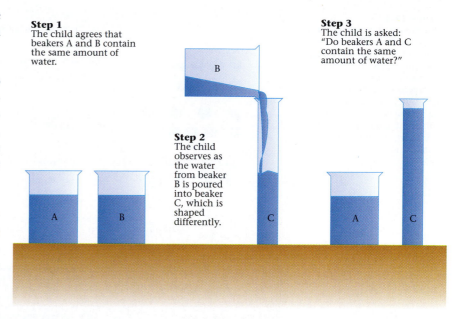

Step 1
The child agrees that beakers A and B contain the same amount of water.

Step 2
The child observes as the water from beaker B is poured into beaker C, which is shaped differently.

Step 3
The child is asked: "Do beakers A and C contain the same amount of water?"

develop a variety of new problem-solving capacities. Let's examine another problem studied by Piaget. Give a preoperational child seven carnations and three daisies. Tell the child the names for the two types of flowers and ask the child to sort them into carnations and daisies. That should be no problem. Now ask the child whether there are more carnations or more daisies. Most children will correctly respond that there are more carnations. Now ask the child whether there are more carnations or more flowers. At this point, most preoperational children will stumble and respond incorrectly that there are more carnations than flowers. Generally, preoperational children can't handle *hierarchical classification* problems that require them to focus simultaneously on two levels of classification. However, the child who has advanced to concrete operations is not as limited by centration and can work successfully with hierarchical classification.

Children in the concrete operational period are also able to grasp the principle of conservation as it applies to liquid, mass, number, volume, area, and length (see Figure 11.13 on page 340). Children master some conservation problems (conservation of number, for instance) earlier than others (such as volume). This difference in mastery may be due in part to differences in the complexity of the concepts involved. However, this piecemeal progress also illustrates the *gradual* nature of cognitive development. Children in the concrete operational period also begin to appreciate the logic of relations. Unlike preoperational children, they can understand that if Sue is younger than Sara

Figure 11.12
Piaget's conservation task. After watching the transformation shown, a preoperational child will usually answer that the taller beaker contains more water. In contrast, the child in the concrete operations period tends to respond correctly, recognizing that the amount of water in beaker C remains the same as the amount in beaker A.

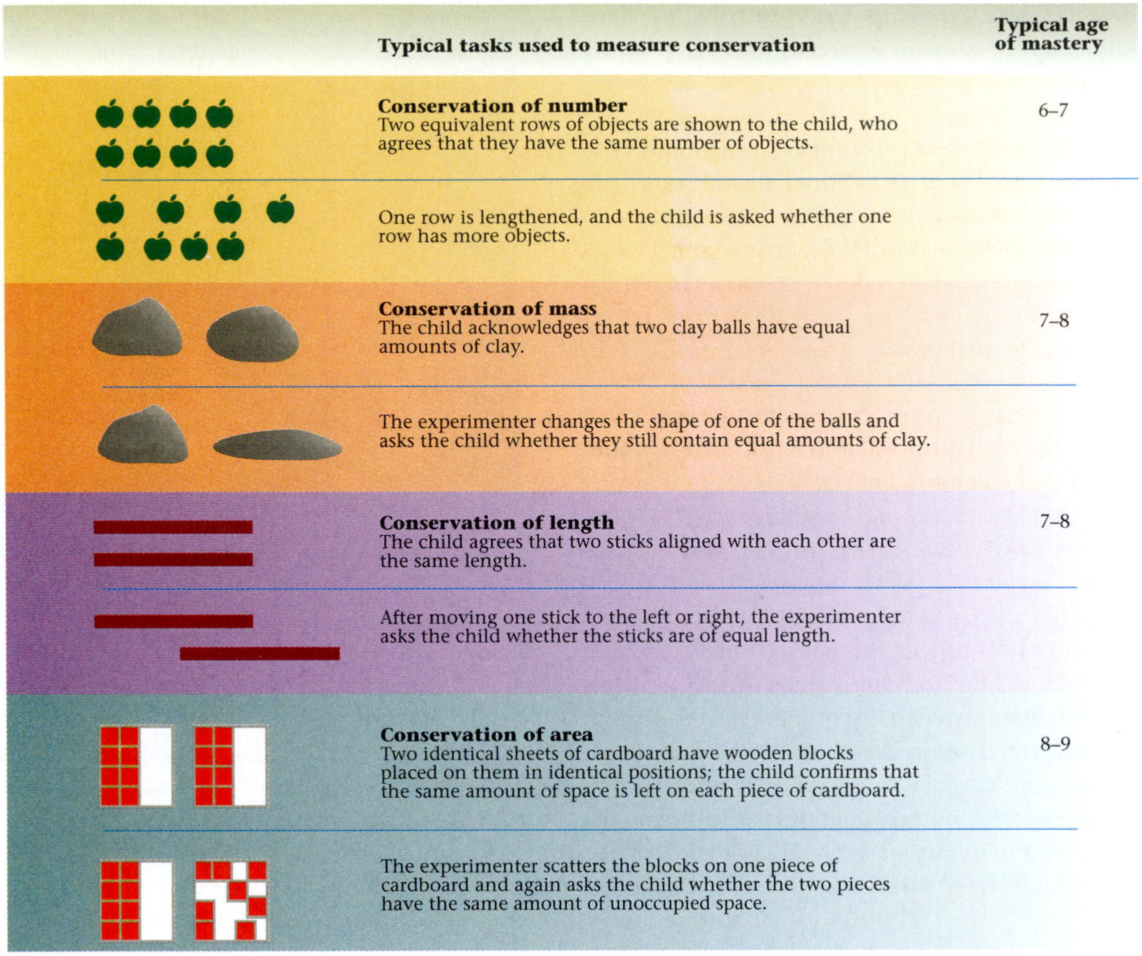

Figure 11.13

The gradual mastery of conservation. Children master Piaget's conservation problem during the concrete operations period, but their mastery is gradual. As outlined here, children usually master the conservation of number at age 6 or 7, but they may not understand the conservation of area until age 8 or 9.

Typical tasks used to measure conservation	Typical age of mastery
Conservation of number Two equivalent rows of objects are shown to the child, who agrees that they have the same number of objects.	6–7
One row is lengthened, and the child is asked whether one row has more objects.	
Conservation of mass The child acknowledges that two clay balls have equal amounts of clay.	7–8
The experimenter changes the shape of one of the balls and asks the child whether they still contain equal amounts of clay.	
Conservation of length The child agrees that two sticks aligned with each other are the same length.	7–8
After moving one stick to the left or right, the experimenter asks the child whether the sticks are of equal length.	
Conservation of area Two identical sheets of cardboard have wooden blocks placed on them in identical positions; the child confirms that the same amount of space is left on each piece of cardboard.	8–9
The experimenter scatters the blocks on one piece of cardboard and again asks the child whether the two pieces have the same amount of unoccupied space.	

and Sara is younger than Sandy, then Sue is younger than Sandy.

Formal Operational Period

The final stage in Piaget's theory is the *formal operational period,* which typically begins at around 11 years of age. In this stage, children begin to apply their operations to *abstract* concepts in addition to concrete objects. Indeed, during this stage, youngsters come to *enjoy* the heady contemplation of abstract concepts. Many adolescents spend hours mulling over hypothetical possibilities related to abstractions such as justice, love, and free will.

According to Piaget, youngsters graduate to relatively adult modes of thinking in the formal operations stage. He did *not* mean to suggest that no further cognitive development occurs once children reach this stage. However, he believed that after children achieve formal operations, further developments in thinking are changes in *degree* rather than fundamental changes in the *nature* of thinking.

Adolescents in the formal operational period become more *systematic* in their problem-solving efforts. Children in earlier developmental stages tend to attack problems quickly, with a trial-and-error approach. In contrast, children who have achieved formal operations are more likely to think things through. They envision possible courses of action and try to use logic to reason out the likely consequences of each possible solution before they act. Thus, thought processes in the formal operational period can be characterized as abstract, systematic, logical, and reflective.

Evaluating Piaget's Theory

Jean Piaget made a landmark contribution to psychology's understanding of children. He founded the field of cognitive development and fostered a new view of children that saw them as active agents constructing their own worlds (Fischer & Hencke, 1996; Flavell, 1996). His theory "has no rival in developmental psychology in scope and depth" (Beilin, 1992, p. 191). Above all else, Piaget sought answers to new questions. As he acknowledged in a 1970 interview, "It's just that no adult ever had the idea of asking children about conservation. It was so obvious that if you change the shape of an object, the quantity will be conserved. Why ask a child? The novelty lay in asking the question" (Hall, 1987, p. 56). Piaget's theory has proven to be extremely useful in guiding an enormous volume of empirical research that continues through today (Miller, 1993). Broadly speaking, this research has supported a great many of Piaget's central propositions (Siegler, 1991). In such a far-reaching theory, however, there are bound to be some weak spots. Let's briefly examine some criticisms of Piaget's theory:

1. In some areas, Piaget may have underestimated young children's cognitive development. Some researchers have found evidence that children begin to develop object permanence earlier than Piaget thought (Baillargeon, 1987, 1994). Others have marshaled evidence that preoperational children exhibit less egocentrism and animism than Piaget believed (Newcombe & Huttenlocher, 1992). Studies also suggest that children show some conservation and some aspects of formal operational thought earlier than Piaget's findings suggested (Flavell, 1985).

2. Piaget's model suffers from problems that plague most stage theories. Like Erikson, Piaget had little to say about individual differences in development (Siegler, 1994). Also, people often simultaneously display patterns of thinking that are characteristic of several different stages. For instance, even well-educated adults who have clearly achieved formal operations often show decidedly egocentric thought. This "mixing" of stages calls into question the value of organizing development in terms of stages (Flavell, 1992; Miller, 1993).

3. Piaget believed that his theory described universal processes that should lead children everywhere to progress through uniform stages of thinking at roughly the same ages. Subsequent research has shown that he was partly right but that he underestimated the influence of cultural factors on cognitive development. Piaget was right in that the *sequence* of stages that he outlined has turned out to be largely invariant across cultures (Segall et al., 1990). However, the *timetable* that children follow in passing through these stages varies considerably across cultures (Dasen, 1994; Rogoff, 1990).

As with any theory, Piaget's is not flawless. However, without Piaget's theory to guide research, many crucial questions about cognitive development might not have been confronted until decades later (if at all). Thus, in his review of Piaget's career and contributions, Harry Beilin (1992) as-

serts that "assessing the impact of Piaget on developmental psychology is like assessing the impact of Shakespeare on English literature or Aristotle on philosophy—impossible. The impact is too monumental to embrace and too omnipresent to detect" (p. 191).

Progress in Information Processing

Piaget's ideas continue to be influential, but in recent years an information-processing perspective has been used more and more frequently in the study of cognitive development (Klahr, 1992). We discussed information-processing models of cognition in Chapters 7 and 8. As you may recall, *information-processing theories* draw an analogy between the mind and the computer. They focus on how people receive, encode, store, organize, retrieve, and use information. The information-processing perspective has proven especially fruitful in illuminating developmental changes in attention, memory, and processing speed.

ATTENTION. Attention involves focusing awareness on a narrowed range of stimuli. Preschool children have very short attention spans and are easily distracted. Their ability to sustain attention improves between ages 1 and 4, but most 4-year-olds still have a hard time focusing on a task for very long (Ruff & Lawson, 1990). As school-age children grow older, their attention spans lengthen and they acquire more conscious control over what they pay attention to (Schiff & Knopf, 1985).

CONCEPT CHECK 11.1
Recognizing Piaget's Stages

Check your understanding of Piaget's theory by indicating the stage of cognitive development illustrated by each of the examples below. For each scenario, fill in the letter for the appropriate stage in the space on the left. The answers are in Appendix A.

a. Sensorimotor period   c. Concrete operational period
b. Preoperational period   d. Formal operational period

_____ 1. Upon seeing a glass lying on its side, Sammy says, "Look, the glass is tired. It's taking a nap."

_____ 2. Maria is told that a farmer has 9 cows and 6 horses. The teacher asks: "Does the farmer have more cows or more animals?" She answers, "more animals."

_____ 3. Alice is playing in the living room with a small red ball. The ball rolls under the sofa. She stares for a moment at the place where the ball vanished and then turns her attention to a toy truck sitting in front of her.

Throughout childhood, progress also occurs in youngsters' ability to focus their attention *selectively*. Between the ages of 7 and 13, children are still improving in their ability to filter out irrelevant input (Miller & Weiss, 1981). For example, they gradually become more adept at focusing on a story being read to them while ignoring the noise in the background and other activity in the room.

MEMORY. When adults are asked to recall their earliest memories, their oldest recollections typically date back to age 3, and it is very rare for anyone to remember a specific incident that occurred before they were 2 (Nelson, 1993). This finding does *not* mean that infants have no capacity for memory. When tested carefully using nonverbal methods, even 3-month-old infants exhibit long-term memories that last days, weeks, and in some cases even a few months (Rovee-Collier, 1993). For reasons that are not well understood, however, these early memories simply don't endure into adulthood.

After children develop language skills, their memory ability improves gradually throughout childhood. Much of this improvement appears to be attributable to the fact that older children acquire deliberate strategies that enhance their storage and retrieval of information. What are these strategies? The first to appear is *rehearsal*, which involves repetitively verbalizing or thinking about material. If instructed to do so, children can start using rehearsal at around age 5 (McGilly & Siegler, 1989). Most children routinely depend on rehearsal by about age 8 (Lovett & Flavell, 1990). Around the age of 9, children begin to depend more on *organization* to improve their recall (Hasselhorn, 1992). At first, this simply involves grouping things into categories based on similarities. *Elaboration*, which involves building additional associations onto information to be recalled, tends to show up only after age 11 (Schneider & Pressley, 1989). Thus, an accumulation of new strategies accounts for much of children's improvement in active memorization. However, increased speed in information processing, which we will discuss next, also contributes to more effective use of memory (Fry & Hale, 1996).

PROCESSING SPEED. As one might expect, children's speed in processing information increases as they grow older. When subjects are asked to perform various mental tasks as quickly as possible, average processing time declines steadily with age, especially between middle childhood and early adolescence (Hale, 1990; Kail, 1988). Interestingly, the rate of improvement is similar across a wide variety of tasks. Robert Kail (1991) reviewed 72 studies that reported age comparisons in processing speed on a diverse array of cognitive tasks. When he mapped out age-related declines in processing time on specific tasks, the graphs for various tasks showed a remarkable resemblance (see Figure 11.14). These similarities presumably reflect developmental change in some very general component of information processing, but the exact nature of this component remains to be determined.

The information-processing perspective on cognitive development has added to psychology's understanding of how children progress in their thinking. Moreover, the application of this approach in relation to cognitive development has barely begun, so its greatest contributions probably lie in the future. However, the influence of Piaget's much older theory will be felt in the next section, which examines moral development.

The Development of Moral Reasoning

In Europe, a woman was near death from cancer. One drug might save her, a form of radium that a druggist in the same town had recently discovered. The druggist was charging $2,000, ten times what the drug cost him to make. The sick woman's husband, Heinz, went to everyone he knew to borrow the money, but he could only get together about half of what it cost. He told the druggist that his wife was dying and asked him to sell it cheaper or let him pay later. But the druggist said, "No." The husband got desperate and broke into the man's store to steal the drug for his wife. Should the husband have done that? Why? (Kohlberg, 1969, p. 379)

What's your answer to Heinz's dilemma? Would you have answered the same way three years ago? In the fifth grade? Can you guess what you might have said at age 6?

By presenting similar dilemmas to subjects and studying their responses, Lawrence Kohlberg (1976, 1984; Colby & Kohlberg, 1987) devised a model of how moral reasoning develops. What is morality? That's a complicated question that philosophers have debated for centuries. For our purposes, it will suffice to say that *morality* involves the ability to discern right from wrong and to behave accordingly.

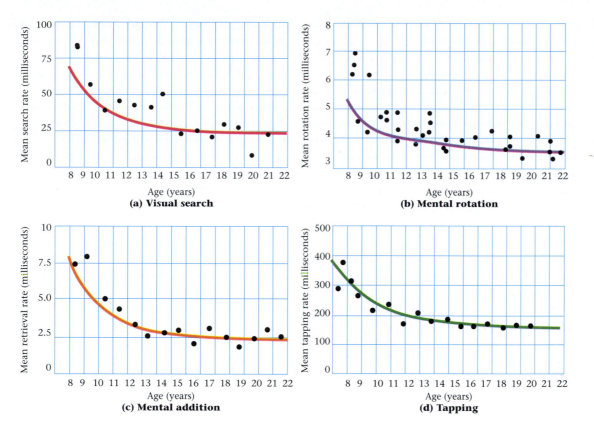

(a) Visual search

Age (years)

Mean search rate (milliseconds)

(b) Mental rotation

Age (years)

Mean rotation rate (milliseconds)

(c) Mental addition

Age (years)

Mean retrieval rate (milliseconds)

(d) Tapping

Age (years)

Mean tapping rate (milliseconds)

Figure 11.14
The relationship between age and information-processing speed during childhood and adolescence. When age-related decreases in information-processing time are mapped out between the ages of 8 and 22, the curves for various cognitive tasks, such as the four shown here, tend to be remarkably similar. This similarity suggests that some very general aspect of information processing changes with age. (Data from Kail, 1988, 1991)

Kohlberg's Stage Theory

Kohlberg's model is the most influential of a number of competing theories that attempt to explain how youngsters develop a sense of right and wrong. His work was derived from much earlier work by Jean Piaget (1932). Piaget theorized that moral development is determined by cognitive development. By this he meant that the way individuals think out moral issues depends on their level of cognitive development. This assumption provided the springboard for Kohlberg's research.

Kohlberg's theory focuses on moral *reasoning* rather than overt *behavior*. This point is best illustrated by describing Kohlberg's method of investigation. He presented his subjects with thorny moral questions such as Heinz's dilemma. He then asked them what the actor in the dilemma should do, and more important, why. It was the *why* that interested Kohlberg. He examined the nature and progression of subjects' moral reasoning.

The result of this work is the stage theory of moral reasoning outlined in Figure 11.15. Kohlberg found that individuals progress through a series of

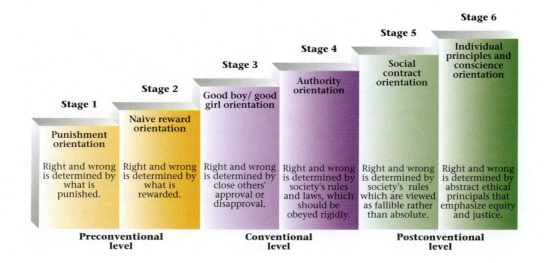

Stage 1
Punishment orientation
Right and wrong is determined by what is punished.

Stage 2
Naive reward orientation
Right and wrong is determined by what is rewarded.

Stage 3
Good boy/ good girl orientation
Right and wrong is determined by close others' approval or disapproval.

Stage 4
Authority orientation
Right and wrong is determined by society's rules and laws, which should be obeyed rigidly.

Stage 5
Social contract orientation
Right and wrong is determined by society's rules which are viewed as fallible rather than absolute.

Stage 6
Individual principles and conscience orientation
Right and wrong is determined by abstract ethical principals that emphasize equity and justice.

Preconventional level

Conventional level

Postconventional level

Figure 11.15
Kohlberg's stage theory.
Kohlberg's model posits three levels of moral reasoning, each of which can be divided into two stages. This chart summarizes how individuals think about right and wrong at each stage.

three levels of moral development, each of which can be broken into two sublevels, yielding a total of six stages. Each stage represents a different approach to thinking about right and wrong.

Younger children at the *preconventional level* think in terms of external authority. Acts are wrong because they are punished, or right because they lead to positive consequences. Older children who have reached the *conventional level* of moral reasoning see rules as necessary for maintaining social order. They therefore accept these rules as their own. They "internalize" these rules not to avoid punishment but to be virtuous and win approval from others. Moral thinking at this stage is relatively inflexible. Rules are viewed as absolute guidelines that should be enforced rigidly.

During adolescence, some youngsters move on to the *postconventional level,* which involves working out a personal code of ethics. Acceptance of rules is less rigid, and moral thinking shows some flexibility. Subjects at the postconventional level allow for the possibility that someone might not comply with some of society's rules if they conflict with personal ethics. For example, subjects at this level might applaud a newspaper reporter who goes to jail rather than reveal a source of information who was promised anonymity.

Evaluating Kohlberg's Theory

How has Kohlberg's theory fared in research? The central ideas have received reasonable support. Progress in moral reasoning is indeed closely tied to cognitive development (Rest & Thoma, 1985; Walker, 1988). Studies also show that youngsters generally do progress through Kohlberg's stages of moral reasoning in the order that he proposed (Colby & Kohlberg, 1984; Walker, 1989). Furthermore, relations between age and level of moral reasoning are in the predicted directions (Rest, 1986; Walker, 1989). Representative age trends are shown in Figure 11.16. As children get older, stage 1 and stage 2 reasoning declines, while stage 3 and stage 4 reasoning increases. However, there is great variation in the age at which people reach specific stages. Furthermore, only a small percentage of people ever reach stage 6.

Like all influential theorists, Kohlberg has his critics. They have raised the following issues:

1. It's not unusual to find that a person shows signs of several adjacent levels of moral reasoning at a particular point in development (Walker & Taylor, 1991). As we noted in the critique of Piaget, this mixing of stages is a problem for virtually all stage theories.

2. Researchers have focused too heavily on how people reason about the specific dilemmas devised by Kohlberg. As Wark and Krebs (1996) put it, "It is somewhat disconcerting to consider how much we have learned about people's judgments about Heinz and his dilemma, and how little we have learned about real-life moral judgment" (pp. 220–221).

3. Sizable cultural disparities have been found in people's progress through Kohlberg's stages. When subjects from small, technologically unsophisticated village societies are tested, they rarely show reasoning beyond stage 3 in Kohlberg's scheme (Snarey & Keljo, 1991). The concerns about social justice that are paramount in Kohlberg's analysis of morality are not necessarily emphasized in other societies (J. Miller, 1991; Walker & Moran, 1991). Evidence is mounting that Kohlberg's dilemmas may not be valid indicators of moral development in some cultures. Some critics believe that the value judgments built into Kohlberg's theory reflect a liberal, individualistic ideology characteristic of modern Western nations that is much more culture-specific than Kohlberg appreciated (Shweder, Mahapatra, & Miller, 1990).

4. Carol Gilligan (1982) has argued that Kohlberg's theory is biased against females. According to Gilligan, Kohlberg equates morality with justice, a view that reflects males' typical socialization. She maintains that females are socialized to equate morality with caring for others and self-sacrifice. Hence, she has hypothesized that

"Children are almost as likely to reject moral reasoning beneath their level as to fail to assimilate reasoning too far above their level."

LAWRENCE KOHLBERG

Figure 11.16
Age and moral reasoning. The percentages of different types of moral judgments made by subjects at various ages are graphed here (based on Kohlberg, 1963, 1969). As predicted, preconventional reasoning declines as children mature, conventional reasoning increases during middle childhood, and postconventional reasoning begins to emerge during adolescence. But at each age, children display a mixture of various levels of moral reasoning.

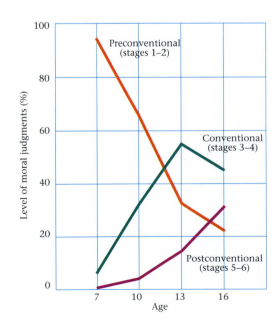

Kohlberg's approach may underestimate the moral development of female subjects. Her assertion that Kohlberg's measurement techniques shortchange females has *not* been supported by subsequent research, which has failed to find significant gender differences in age-related progress through Kohlberg's stages (Thoma, 1986; Walker, 1991). However, there is some evidence that females are more likely than males to interpret moral dilemmas in terms of caring rather than justice (Donenberg & Hoffman, 1988; Gilligan, Hamner, & Lyons, 1990). Thus, Kohlberg's theory may capture the essence of moral development in males better than in females.

Moral reasoning is just one of several areas of development in which there is some debate about differences between males and females. You'll see another example in the next section, which is concerned with selected aspects of social development. Our Application will further explore the nature and meaning of gender differences in development and behavior.

Interacting with Others: Social Development

Psychologists have studied many aspects of social development. In sampling from this domain, we'll look at two kinds of social behavior that have been the focus of much research: altruism and aggression. *Altruism* **is selfless concern for the welfare of others that leads to sharing, cooperation, and helping behavior.** *Aggression* **is any behavior that is intended to hurt someone, either physically or verbally** (through insults, for instance). These two very different kinds of interpersonal behavior tend to show opposite developmental trends.

Age Trends in Altruism and Aggression

Altruism begins to emerge in children as they approach age 2 and tends to increase as children grow older, at least through the grade-school years (Zahn-Waxler & Smith, 1992). Interestingly, there's a modest positive correlation between a child's altruism and his or her level of moral reasoning. Children who exhibit more sophisticated moral reasoning tend to be more helpful and concerned about others than children who display lower levels of moral reasoning (Eisenberg et al., 1991).

In contrast, aggression generally declines with age, although this generalization has to be qualified carefully, because aggression changes in form as children grow older. Younger children display more *instrumental aggression,* which is intended to achieve some goal such as retrieving a toy. Older children display more *hostile aggression,* which is intended solely to hurt another (McCabe & Lipscomb, 1988).

CONCEPT CHECK 11.2
Analyzing Moral Reasoning

Check your understanding of Kohlberg's theory of moral development by analyzing hypothetical responses to the following moral dilemma.

A midwest biologist has conducted numerous studies demonstrating that simple organisms such as worms and paramecia can learn through conditioning. It occurs to her that perhaps she could condition fertilized human ova to provide a dramatic demonstration that abortions destroy adaptable, living human organisms. This possibility appeals to her, as she is ardently opposed to abortion. However, there is no way to conduct the necessary research on human ova without sacrificing the lives of potential human beings. She desperately wants to conduct the research, but obviously, the sacrifice of human ova is fundamentally incompatible with her belief in the sanctity of human life. What should she do? Why? [Submitted by a student (age 13) to Professor Barbara Banas at Monroe Community College]

In the spaces on the left of each numbered response indicate the level of moral reasoning shown, choosing from the following: (a) preconventional level, (b) conventional level, or (c) postconventional level. The answers are in Appendix A.

_____ 1. She should do the research. Although it's wrong to kill, there's a greater good that can be realized through the research.

_____ 2. She shouldn't do the research because people will think that she's a hypocrite and condemn her.

_____ 3. She should do the research because she may become rich and famous as a result.

With increasing age, aggression also tends to become less physical and more verbal.

In spite of these age trends, huge differences occur in altruism and aggression among children of the same age. Some children are much more altruistic or more aggressive than others. Among grade-school children, for instance, a small minority (10%–15%) of highly aggressive children account for the vast majority of aggressive acts (Perry, Kusel, & Perry, 1988). Moreover, this early aggression is predictive of subsequent problems with aggression in adolescence and adulthood (Loeber & Hay, 1997). Furthermore, there is ample evidence of gender differences in aggression. From age 3 onward, boys tend to be noticeably more aggressive than girls (Hyde, 1986; Legault & Strayer, 1990).

The Roots of Altruism and Aggression

Among other things, altruism and aggression both appear to be influenced by (1) genetic predisposition, (2) parental modeling and reinforcement, and (3) portrayals of role models in the mass media.

A child's genetic makeup may create a predisposition toward either altruistic or aggressive behavior. In one *twin study* (see Chapter 3) that focused on both traits, identical twins were found to be much more similar to each other than fraternal twins were on measures of altruism and aggression (Rushton et al., 1986). This finding suggests that heredity influences individual differences in altruism and aggression. How can heredity mold interpersonal behavior? Investigators aren't sure, but inherited differences in *temperament* could be the bridge between genes and social behavior (Bates, 1987). Aspects of temperament, such as character-istic mood, activity level, and emotional reactivity, may foster a predisposition toward helpful or hurtful behavior.

Parents can have a great impact on their children's tendencies to be altruistic or aggressive. Parents who model cooperative and helpful behavior in their interactions with others and who praise and reward youngsters' altruistic acts promote altruism in their children (Eisenberg, 1992; Zahn-Waxler & Smith, 1992). Similarly, parents who are belligerent with others, use physical punishment and coercion to discipline their children, and permit or sometimes even reinforce their children's acts of aggression tend to raise more aggressive offspring (Dishion, 1990; Eron, 1982; Patterson, DeBaryshe, & Ramsey, 1989). In regard to both altruism and aggression, the evidence clearly indicates that what parents *do* is more influential than what they *say*. It doesn't do much good for parents to preach the value of altruism if they then refuse to help a neighbor who needs a ride or a relative who needs a babysitter.

Altruism and aggression are also influenced by a child's exposure to role models in the mass media, especially television (Huston & Wright, 1982). Children spend an average of about 2 to 4 hours per day watching television, with viewing time increasing up through early adolescence (see Figure 11.17). On the positive side, televised portrayals of altruistic behavior have been shown to increase helpfulness and cooperation in children (Hearold, 1986; Liebert & Sprafkin, 1988). Unfortunately, the power of television works both ways, and most children are fed far more aggression than altruism in their video diet.

The National Television Violence Study, a large-scale study of the content of network and cable television shows conducted in 1994–1995, revealed that 57% of programs contain violence. It has been estimated that the typical child has vicariously witnessed 8,000 murders and 100,000 other acts of violence on TV by the time the child finishes grade school (Huston et al., 1992). Moreover, much of this violence is portrayed in an unrealistic, antiseptic fashion that is believed to desensitize viewers to the horrible realities of violent behavior. A large body of studies suggests that this extensive exposure to media violence contributes to the development of aggressiveness in some children (Friedrich-Cofer & Huston, 1986). This important issue, which has been the subject of a great deal of research, brings us to our Featured Study for this chapter.

Figure 11.17
Developmental patterns in children's television viewing. As children grow up, they spend more and more time watching TV until about age 11 or 12, when viewing time begins to decline slightly. Thus, the typical child watches TV about 20–25 hours per week. Small wonder, then, that TV influences children's behavior. (Adapted from Liebert & Sprafkin, 1988)

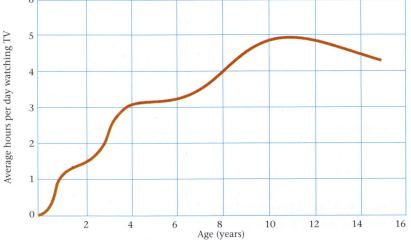

Investigators: Leonard D. Eron, L. Rowell Huesmann, Patrick Brice, Paulette Fischer, and Rebecca Mermelstein (University of Illinois at Chicago)

Source: Age trends in the development of aggression, sex typing, and related television habits. *Developmental Psychology*, 1983, *19*(1), 71–77.

Earlier research by Leonard Eron and his colleagues found an association between the amount of violence in a third-grader's television diet and the child's aggressiveness both in the third grade and ten years later at the age of 19 (Eron, 1963; Eron et al., 1972; Lefkowitz et al., 1977). The connection between television violence and aggression was found to be much stronger for males than for females. This study was designed to expand on the earlier research in two ways. First, given that the link between television violence and aggression was already apparent in the third grade, the research team decided to focus on even younger children, beginning in the first grade. Second, given the substantial changes in gender roles in American society since the original research began in 1960, the investigators wanted to take another look at possible gender differences.

Method

Subjects and design. The subjects were 758 grade-school children drawn primarily from the public schools in a socially diversified suburb of Chicago. An "overlapping" longitudinal design was used over a period of three years. Thus, the researchers followed one set of children from the first through the third grade and simultaneously followed another set of children from the third through the fifth grade.

Measures. The two key measures focused on the children's television viewing habits and their level of aggressiveness. The children were asked to indicate (in age-appropriate booklets on colored paper) how often they watched any of 80 television shows that were popular among children. The amount of violence in each of these 80 shows was rated independently by graduate students. The violence ratings for each child's eight favorite shows were added to produce an index of exposure to media violence for each young subject. The children's aggressiveness was measured by obtaining peer ratings from the young-sters' classmates. Every child in each grade-school class that was studied rated the aggressiveness of every other child in the class (on age-appropriate forms that inquired about ten specific types of aggressive acts). The classmates' pooled ratings provided the index of each subject's aggressiveness.

Results

As is usually the case when subjects are followed longitudinally, the number of subjects declined over time as some children left the school system. Although the sample shrank to 505 children, the loss of subjects created few problems in interpreting the results because the loss was spread evenly across both sexes and all grades. Positive correlations were found between the measures of exposure to media violence and peer-rated aggressiveness in all five grades. The correlations were small (median = .23), but all were statistically significant. In contrast to earlier results, the correlations between television violence and aggressiveness were significant for both boys and girls. Indeed, the correlations were a little stronger for the girls.

Discussion

The results replicate previous findings linking media violence to aggressive behavior in children. The results also suggest that this link may be forged at a very young age, even in the first grade. The roughly similar correlations found for girls and boys suggest that both sexes may be equally subject to the influence of media violence. This is a new finding that may be due to shifting gender roles or to the emergence of aggressive female role models on television, which were rare in the 1960s when the original research was begun.

Comment

This study was featured because it focused on an important social issue in a realistic way. Most studies of media violence have been laboratory experiments that sacrifice realism for the power of experimental control and the ability to draw conclusions about cause and effect (Freedman, 1984). Such experiments are extremely important, but their dependent measures of aggression (such as pressing a button labeled "hurt" or hitting an inflated plastic doll) have often been criticized as unrealistic. In contrast, this

The effect of television violence on children has been the subject of heated debate since the advent of TV. In the 1960s, research by Leonard Eron and his colleagues suggested that TV violence had more impact on boys than on girls. The Featured Study was designed, in part, to see whether similar gender differences would be found in the 1980s.

study looked at real-world viewing habits and actual everyday aggression—in all their complexity.

Of course, this was a correlational study, and we always have to be cautious in drawing causal conclusions based on correlational data. Theorists have pointed out that a number of possible causal relationships could account for the correlation between high exposure to media violence and high aggressiveness (see Figure 11.18). One possibility is that exposure to media violence causes higher aggressiveness. Another

Figure 11.18
The correlation between exposure to media violence and aggression. The more violence children watch on TV, the more aggressive they tend to be, but this correlation could reflect a variety of underlying causal relationships. Although watching violent shows might increase aggressiveness, it is also possible that aggressive children are drawn to violent shows. Or perhaps a third variable (such as a genetic predisposition to aggressiveness) causes both high exposure to media violence and high aggressiveness.

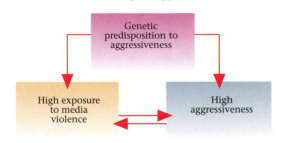

Genetic predisposition to aggressiveness

High exposure to media violence

High aggressiveness

very realistic possibility is that high aggressiveness causes an increased interest in violent television shows (Bushman, 1995). Alternatively, a third variable, such as a genetic predisposition to aggressiveness, could cause both elevated aggressiveness and increased interest in media violence. The plausibility of this interpretation was bolstered by recent evidence that genetic factors influence the amount of television that children watch (Plomin et al., 1990).

Standing alone, our Featured Study would not allow us to conclude that exposure to television violence causes an increase in aggressive tendencies. However, the study does not stand alone. It's part of a vast body of research on media violence and aggression that includes a wealth of experimental studies. Taken as a whole, this research provides convincing evidence that media violence makes a modest but real contribution to causing aggressive behavior in American society (Hearold, 1986; Liebert & Sprafkin, 1988).

In summary, a multiplicity of factors shape the development of altruism and aggression (Parke & Slaby, 1983; Zahn-Waxler & Smith, 1992). In this section, we highlighted the roles of heredity, parental models, and television. However, the development of altruism and aggression may also be influenced by cultural ideals and youngsters' physique, moral education, and peer group relations.

CONCEPT CHECK 11.3
Recognizing Links Between Areas of Development

Check your understanding of interrelations among various aspects of development by identifying the connections between areas of development as shown in the figure below.

Development in one area often influences development in another area. In fact, there are intimate relations between all areas of development. The diagram below identifies a few links mentioned in our discussion of the childhood years.

In the space provided, describe the possible influences indicated by the arrows. To illustrate the nature of the task, the answer for (d) is provided. The remaining answers can be found in Appendix A.

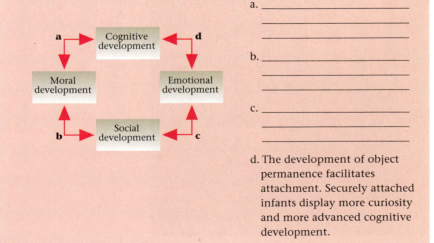

a. _____
_____
_____

b. _____
_____
_____

c. _____
_____
_____

d. The development of object permanence facilitates attachment. Securely attached infants display more curiosity and more advanced cognitive development.

Recap of Key Points

• A stage is a developmental period during which characteristic patterns of behavior are exhibited. Stage theories assume that individuals must progress through a series of specified stages in a particular order, that progress through these stages is related to age, and that development is marked by major discontinuities.

• Erik Erikson's theory of personality development proposes that individuals evolve through eight stages over the life span. In each stage the person wrestles with two opposing tendencies evoked by that stage's psychosocial crisis. Successful progress through the four childhood stages should yield a trustful, autonomous person with a sense of initiative and industry.

• According to Piaget's theory of cognitive development, the key advance during the sensorimotor period is the child's gradual recognition of the permanence of objects. The preoperational period is marked by certain deficiencies in thinking—notably, centration, irreversibility, and egocentrism.

• During the concrete operations period, children develop the ability to perform operations on mental representations, making them capable of conservation and hierarchical classification. The stage of formal operations ushers in more abstract, systematic, and logical thought.

• Piaget may have underestimated some aspects of children's cognitive development and his theory, like other stage theories, does not explain individual differences very well. Nonetheless, his work has greatly improved psychology's understanding of cognitive development.

• The other major approach to the study of cognitive development is rooted in information-processing models. The information-processing perspective has proven especially useful in explaining progress in attention and memory ability.

• According to Kohlberg, moral reasoning progresses through six stages that are related to age and determined by cognitive development. Age-related progress in moral reasoning has been found in research, although there is a great deal of overlap between adjacent stages.

• Altruism and aggression, two important aspects of social behavior, tend to increase and decrease, respectively, with age. The development of altruism and aggression is affected by genetic inheritance, parental training, and role models in the mass media. Our Featured Study showed how exposure to television violence correlates with peer-rated aggression, even in very young children.

THE TRANSITION OF ADOLESCENCE

Adolescence is a transitional period between childhood and adulthood. Its age boundaries are not exact, but in our society adolescence begins at around age 13 and ends at about age 22. Although most societies have at least a brief period of adolescence, it is *not* universal across cultures (Schlegel & Barry, 1991; Whiting, Burbank, & Ratner, 1986). In some cultures, young people move directly from childhood to adulthood. A protracted period of adolescence is seen primarily in industrialized nations. In these societies, rapid technological progress has made lengthy education, and therefore prolonged economic dependence, the norm. Thus, in our own culture junior high school, high school, and college students often have a "marginal" status. They are capable of reproduction and so are physiologically mature. Yet they have not achieved the emotional and economic independence from their parents that are the hallmarks of adulthood. Let's begin our discussion of adolescent development with its most visible aspect: the physical changes that transform the body of a child into that of an adult.

Puberty and the Growth Spurt

Recall for a moment your junior high school days. Didn't it seem that your body grew so fast about this time that your clothes just couldn't "keep up"? This phase of rapid growth in height and weight is called the *adolescent growth spurt*. Brought on by hormonal changes, it typically starts about 11 years of age in girls and about two years later in boys (Malina, 1990). (Technically, this spurt should be called the *pre*adolescent growth spurt because it actually occurs *prior* to puberty, which is generally recognized as the beginning of adolescence.)

The term **pubescence** is used to describe the **two-year span preceding puberty during which the changes leading to physical and sexual maturity take place.** In addition to growing taller and heavier during pubescence, children begin to develop the physical features that characterize adults of their respective sexes. These features are termed *secondary sex characteristics*—**physical features that distinguish one sex from the other but that are not essential for reproduction.** For example, males go through a voice change, develop facial hair, and experience greater skeletal and muscle growth in the upper torso, leading to broader shoulders (see Figure 11.19 on page 450). Females experience breast growth and a widening of the pelvic bones plus increased fat deposits in this area, resulting in wider hips (Litt & Vaughan, 1992).

Note, however, that the capacity to reproduce is not attained in pubescence. This comes later. **Puberty is the stage during which sexual functions reach maturity, which marks the beginning of adolescence.** It is during puberty that the *primary sex characteristics*—**the structures necessary for reproduction**—develop fully. In the male, these include the testes, penis, and related internal structures. Primary sex characteristics in the female include the ovaries, vagina, uterus, and other internal structures.

In females, the onset of puberty is typically signaled by *menarche*—**the first occurrence of menstruation.** American girls typically reach menarche at about age 12$\frac{1}{2}$, with further sexual maturation continuing until approximately 16. Most American boys begin to produce sperm by age 14, with complete sexual maturation occurring around 18 (Brooks-Gunn & Reiter, 1990; Tanner, 1978). Interestingly, there have been *generational* changes in the timing of puberty. Today's adolescents begin puberty at a younger age, and complete it more rapidly, than did their counterparts in earlier

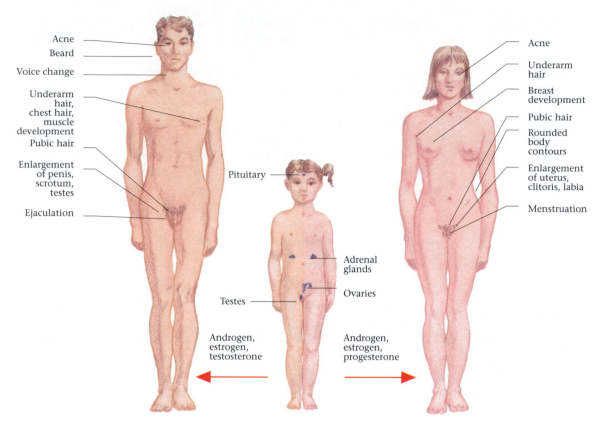

Figure 11.19
Physical development at puberty. Hormonal changes during puberty lead not only to a growth spurt but also to the development of secondary sex characteristics. The pituitary gland sends signals to the adrenal glands and gonads (ovaries and testes), which secrete hormones responsible for various physical changes that differentiate males and females.

Acne
Beard
Voice change
Underarm hair, chest hair, muscle development
Pubic hair
Enlargement of penis, scrotum, testes
Ejaculation

Pituitary

Acne
Underarm hair
Breast development
Pubic hair
Rounded body contours
Enlargement of uterus, clitoris, labia
Menstruation

Adrenal glands
Ovaries
Testes

Androgen, estrogen, testosterone

Androgen, estrogen, progesterone

generations. This trend apparently reflects improvements in nutrition and medical care (Brooks-Gunn, 1991).

Although variation in the onset of pubescence and puberty is normal, adolescents who mature unusually early or unusually late often feel uneasy about it. Girls who mature early and boys who mature late seem to feel especially awkward and self-conscious about their looks (Siegel, 1982). Early maturation can enhance an adolescent's popularity with peers, but mature appearance can also bring pressures and temptations that a youngster may not be ready for. In both males and females, early maturation is associated with less self-control and emotional stability, greater use of alcohol and drugs, and more trouble with the law (Duncan et al., 1985; Stattin & Magnusson, 1990; Sussman et al., 1985). Among females, early maturation is also correlated with poorer school performance, earlier experience of intercourse, more unwanted pregnancies, and greater risk for eating problems and disorders (Graber et al., 1994; Stattin & Magnusson, 1990). Thus, one might speculate that early maturation often thrusts both sexes (but especially females) toward the adult world too soon.

Time of Turmoil?

Back around the turn of the century, G. Stanley Hall (1904), one of psychology's great pioneers

(see Chapter 1), proposed that the adolescent years are characterized by convulsive instability and disturbing inner turmoil. Hall attributed this turmoil to adolescents' erratic physical changes and resultant confusion about self-image. Over the decades, a host of theorists have agreed with Hall's characterization of adolescence as a stormy period.

Statistics on *adolescent suicide* would seem to support the idea that adolescence is a time marked by turmoil, but the figures can be interpreted in various ways. On the one hand, suicide rates among adolescents have risen alarmingly in recent decades (see Figure 11.20a). On the other hand, even with this steep increase, suicide rates for adolescents are about the same as or lower than those for older age groups (see Figure 11.20b).

Actually, the suicide crisis among teenagers involves *attempted* suicide more than *completed* suicide. It's estimated that when all age groups are lumped together, suicide attempts outnumber actual suicidal deaths by a ratio of about 8 to 1 (Cross & Hirschfeld, 1986). However, this ratio of attempted to completed suicides is much higher for adolescents than for any other age group. Studies suggest that the ratio among adolescents may be anywhere from 50:1 to 200:1 (Garland & Zigler, 1993). According to David Curran (1987), suicide attempts by adolescents tend to be a "communicative gesture designed to elicit caring" (p. 12). Put

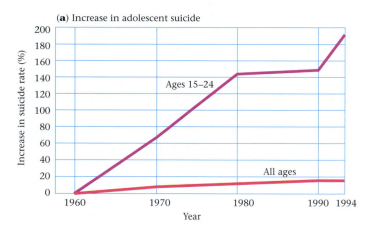

(a) Increase in adolescent suicide

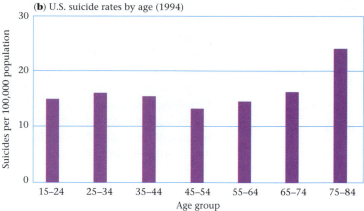

(b) U.S. suicide rates by age (1994)

another way, they are desperate cries for attention, help, and support.

What drives an adolescent to such a dramatic but dangerous gesture? Research suggests that the "typical" suicidal adolescent has a long history of stress and personal problems extending from childhood (Jacobs, 1971; de Wilde et al., 1992). Unfortunately, for some teenagers these problems—conflicts with parents, difficulties in school, loneliness, and so on—escalate during adolescence. As their efforts to cope with these problems fail, many teenagers rebel against parental and school authority, withdraw from social relations, and make dramatic gestures such as running away from home. These actions often lead to progressive social isolation. When the individual is socially isolated, a pressing problem with great emotional impact may precipitate an attempted suicide. The precipitating problem—a poor grade in school, not being allowed to go somewhere or to buy something special—may appear trivial to an objective observer. But the seemingly trivial problem may serve as the final thread in a tapestry of frustration and distress.

Returning to our original question, does the weight of evidence support the idea that adolescence is usually a period of turmoil and turbulence? Overall, the consensus of the experts appears to be that it is not (Petersen, 1988). The increase in adolescent suicide is a disturbing social tragedy that requires attention from parents, schools, and the helping professions (see the Chapter 14 Application for a discussion of suicide prevention). But even with the recent increases in suicidal behavior, only a small minority of adolescents attempt suicide (Meehan et al., 1992).

What about the remainder of the adolescent population? Research reveals that adolescents do experience more stress and more negative emotions than younger children do (Larson & Asmussen, 1991; Larson & Ham, 1993). And adolescence does bring a modest increase in parent-child conflict (Paikoff & Brooks-Gunn, 1991; Smetana et al., 1991). However, parent-adolescent relations are not as difficult or contentious as advertised (Galambos, 1992). On the whole, the evidence indicates that most teenagers navigate through adolescence without any more turmoil than one is likely to encounter in other periods of life (Hauser & Bowlds, 1990; Offer et al., 1988). Based on her extensive studies of adolescents, Anne Petersen (1987) concludes, "The adolescent's journey toward adulthood is inherently marked by change and upheaval, but need not be fraught with chaos or deep pain" (p. 34).

Although turbulence and turmoil are not *universal* features of adolescence, challenging adaptations *do* have to be made during this period. In particular, most adolescents struggle to some extent in their effort to achieve a sound sense of identity.

The Search for Identity 9b

Erik Erikson was especially interested in personality development during adolescence, which is the fifth of the eight major life stages he described. The psychosocial crisis during this stage pits *identity* against *confusion*. According to Erikson (1968), the premiere challenge of adolescence is the struggle to form a clear sense of identity. This struggle involves working out a stable concept of oneself as a unique individual and embracing an ideology or system of values that provides a sense of direction. In Erikson's view, adolescents grapple with questions such as "Who am I, and where am I going in life?"

Erikson recognized that the process of identity formation begins before adolescence and often

Figure 11.20
Adolescent suicide. (a) In recent decades, the suicide rate for adolescents and young adults (15–24 years old) has increased far more than the suicide rate for the population as a whole. **(b)** Nonetheless, suicide rates for this youthful age group remain about the same or lower than suicide rates for older age groups. (Data from *Monthly Vital Statistics Report*, October 23, 1995)

extends beyond it, as his own life illustrates (Coles, 1970; Roazen, 1976). Erikson's mother, who was Jewish, was abandoned by her Danish father before Erik's birth in 1902 in Germany. Within a few years, his mother married a Jewish doctor and the two of them raised Erik in the Jewish faith as Erik Homburger. Erik was viewed as a Jew by his schoolmates, but he was viewed as a gentile at his temple because of his decidedly Scandinavian appearance. Thus, Erikson struggled with identity confusion early in life.

During adolescence Erikson began to resist family pressures to study medicine. Instead, he wandered about Europe until he was 25, trying to "find himself" as an artist. His interest in psychoanalysis was sparked by an introduction to Sigmund Freud's youngest daughter, Anna, a pioneer of child psychoanalysis. After his psychoanalytic training, he moved to the United States. When he became a naturalized citizen in 1939, he changed his surname from Homburger to Erikson. Clearly, Erikson was struggling with the question of "Who am I?" well into adulthood. Small wonder, then, that he focused a great deal of attention on identity formation.

Although the struggle for a sense of identity is a lifelong process (Waterman & Archer, 1990), it does tend to be especially intense during adolescence. Adolescents' increased concern about identity is probably due to the conjunction of several significant transitions (Lloyd, 1985). First, rapid physical changes stimulate thought about self-image during adolescence. Second, changes in cognitive processes (in Piaget's terminology, the arrival of formal operations) promote personal introspection. Third, decisions about vocational direction require self-contemplation.

Adolescents deal with identity formation in a variety of ways. According to James Marcia (1966, 1980), the presence or absence of *crisis* and *commitment* can combine in various ways to produce four different *identity statuses* (see Figure 11.21). These are not stages that people pass through, but orientations that may occur at a particular time. An individual may get locked into one of these patterns or go through several at various times. Marcia's four identity statuses are as follows:

• *Foreclosure* is a premature commitment to visions, values, and roles prescribed by one's parents. This path allows a person to circumvent much of the "struggle" for an identity. However, it may backfire and cause problems later.

• A *moratorium* involves delaying commitment for a while to experiment with alternative ideologies and careers. Such experimentation can be valuable. Unfortunately, some people remain indefinitely in what should be a temporary phase.

• *Identity diffusion* is a state of rudderless apathy. Some people simply refuse to confront the challenge of charting a life course and committing to an ideology. Although this stance allows them to evade the struggle, the lack of direction can become problematic.

• *Identity achievement* involves arriving at a sense of self and direction after some consideration of alternative possibilities. Commitments have the strength of some conviction, although they're not absolutely irrevocable.

Erikson, Marcia, and many other theorists believe that adequate identity formation is a cornerstone of sound psychological health. Identity confusion can interfere with important developmental transitions that should unfold during the adult years, as you'll see in the next section, which takes a look at developmental trends during adulthood.

Recap of Key Points

• The growth spurt at puberty is a prominent event involving the development of reproductive maturity and secondary sex characteristics. Early or late maturation during adolescence affects youngsters' self-concept.

• Adolescent suicide rates have climbed dramatically in recent decades, and *attempted* suicides have increased even more. Nonetheless, various lines of research suggest that adolescence is no more tumultuous than other periods of life.

• According to Erikson, the key challenge of adolescence is to make some progress toward a sense of identity. Marcia identified four patterns of identity formation: foreclosure, moratorium, identity diffusion, and identity achievement.

Figure 11.21
Marcia's four identity statuses. According to Marcia (1980), the occurrence of an identity crisis and the development of personal commitments can combine into four possible identity statuses, as shown in this diagram.

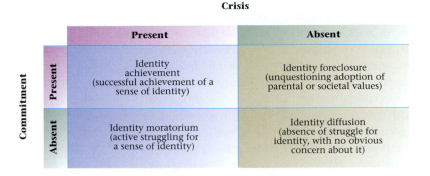

Crisis

		Present	Absent
Commitment	**Present**	Identity achievement (successful achievement of a sense of identity)	Identity foreclosure (unquestioning adoption of parental or societal values)
	Absent	Identity moratorium (active struggling for a sense of identity)	Identity diffusion (absence of struggle for identity, with no obvious concern about it)

THE EXPANSE OF ADULTHOOD

As people progress through adulthood, they periodically ask themselves, "How am I doing for my age?" In pondering this question, they are likely to be influenced by their social clocks. **A *social clock* is a person's notion of a developmental schedule that specifies what he or she should have accomplished by certain points in life.** For example, if you feel that you should be married by the time you're 30, that belief creates a marker on your social clock. Social clocks are personalized to some degree but are very much a product of one's culture. Social clocks may influence the stressfulness of various life changes. Important transitions that come too early or too late according to one's social clock produce more stress than transitions that occur "on time" (Chiriboga, 1987). In particular, it appears that lagging behind one's personal schedule in regard to certain achievements produces frustration and reduced self-esteem (Helson, Mitchell, & Moane, 1984). Thus, many people pay great heed to their social clocks as they proceed through adulthood. With this thought in mind, let's look at some of the major developmental transitions in adult life.

Personality Development 9b

In recent years, research on adult personality development has been dominated by one key question: How stable is personality over the life span? We'll look at this issue, the question of the midlife crisis, and Erikson's view of adulthood in our discussion of personality development in the adult years.

The Question of Stability

At midlife, Jerry Rubin went from being an outraged, radical political activist to being a subdued, conventional Wall Street businessman. His transformation illustrates that major personality changes sometimes occur during adulthood. But how common are such changes? Is a grouchy 20-year-old going to be a grouchy 40-year-old and a grouchy 65-year-old? Or can the grouchy young adult become a mellow senior citizen?

After tracking subjects through adulthood, many researchers have been impressed by the amount of change observed. Roger Gould (1975) studied two samples of men and women and concluded that "the evolution of a personality continues through the fifth decade of life." In a study following women from their college years through their 40s, Helson and Moane (1987) found that "personality does

change from youth to middle age in consistent and often predictable ways." After tracking development between the ages of 20 and 42, Whitbourne and her colleagues (1992) found "consistent patterns of personality change."

In contrast, many other researchers have been struck by the stability and durability they have found in personality. The general conclusion that emerged from several longitudinal studies using objective assessments of personality traits was that personality tends to be quite stable over periods of 20 to 40 years (Block, 1981; Caspi & Herbener, 1990; Costa & McCrae, 1994). These studies found that personality in early adulthood was an excellent predictor of personality right through to late adulthood.

In sum, researchers assessing the stability of personality in adulthood have reached very different conclusions (Kogan, 1990). How can these contradictory conclusions be reconciled? This appears to be one of those debates in which researchers are eyeing the same findings—but from different perspectives. Hence, some conclude that the glass is half full, whereas others conclude that it's half empty. In his discussion of this controversy, Lawrence Pervin (1994) concludes that personality is characterized by *both* stability and change. It appears that some personality traits (such as emotional stability, extraversion, and assertiveness) tend to remain stable, while others (such as masculinity and femininity) tend to change systematically as people grow older (Conley, 1985; Helson & Stewart, 1994).

The Question of the Midlife Crisis

There has also been a spirited debate about whether most people go through a *midlife crisis*. The two most influential studies of adult development in the 1970s (Gould, 1978; Levinson et al., 1978) both concluded that a midlife crisis is a normal transition experienced by a majority of people. However, since these landmark studies, a host of subsequent studies have failed to detect an increase in emotional turbulence at midlife (Baruch, 1984; Eisler & Ragsdale, 1992; Roberts & Newton, 1987). How can we explain this discrepancy? Levinson and Gould both studied samples that were less than ideal. Levinson's was unusually small, and Gould's was not very representative. Moreover, both researchers depended primarily on interview and case study methods to gather their data. As we noted in Chapter 2, when knitting together impressionistic case studies, it is easy for investigators to see what they expect to see. Given that the midlife crisis has long been part of developmental folklore, Levinson and Gould may have been prone to interpret their case study data in this light (McCrae & Costa, 1984). In any case, investigators relying on more objective measures of emotional stability have found signs of midlife crises in only a tiny minority (2%–5%) of subjects (Chiriboga, 1989; McCrae & Costa, 1990). Thus, it's clear that the fabled midlife crisis is not universal, and it probably isn't even typical.

Erikson's View of Adulthood

Insofar as personality changes during the adult years, Erik Erikson's (1963) theory offers some clues about the nature of changes people can expect. In his eight-stage model of development over the life span, Erikson divided adulthood into three stages (see again Figure 11.10).

INTIMACY VERSUS ISOLATION. In early adulthood, the key concern is whether one can develop the capacity to share intimacy with others. Successful resolution of the challenges in this stage should promote empathy and openness, rather than shrewdness and manipulativeness.

GENERATIVITY VERSUS SELF-ABSORPTION. In middle adulthood, the key challenge is to acquire a genuine concern for the welfare of future generations, which results in providing unselfish guidance to younger people. Self-absorption is characterized by self-indulgent concerns with meeting one's own needs and desires.

INTEGRITY VERSUS DESPAIR. During the retirement years, the challenge is to avoid the tendency to dwell on the mistakes of the past and on one's imminent death. People need to find meaning and satisfaction in their lives, rather than wallow in bitterness and resentment.

Empirical research on the adult stages in Erikson's theory has been sparse, but a recent study that examined personality development during the adult years provided support for some of Erikson's key ideas. Data collected by Susan Whitbourne and her colleagues (1992) suggest that personality development proceeds in an orderly sequence of stages and that favorable resolutions of psychosocial crises in earlier stages lead to more favorable outcomes in later stages.

Transitions in Family Life

Many of the important transitions in adulthood involve changes in family responsibilities and relationships. Predictable patterns of development can be seen in families, just as they can in individuals (Carter & McGoldrick, 1988). **The *family life cycle* is a sequence of stages that families tend to progress through.** However, in contemporary American society, shifting social trends are distorting the traditional family life cycle (Birchler, 1992). In the eyes of most people, the typical American family consists of a husband and wife who have never been married to anyone else, rearing two or more children, with the man serving as the principal breadwinner and the woman filling the homemaker role. This configuration was never as dominant as widely assumed, and today it is estimated that only about 7% of American families match this idealized image (Demo, 1992). The increasing prevalence of people remaining single, cohabitating, getting divorced, being single parents, having stepfamilies, voluntarily remaining childless, having children out of wedlock, and of wives and mothers working has conspired to make the traditional nuclear family a deceptive mirage that does not reflect the diversity of family life in America.

Diversity aside, everyone emerges from families, and most people go on to form their own families. However, the transitional period during which young adults are "between families" until they form a new family is being prolonged by more and more individuals. The percentage of young adults who are postponing marriage until their late twenties or early thirties has risen dramatically (Sporakowski, 1988). This trend is probably the result of a number of factors. Chief among them are the availability of new career options for women, increased educational requirements in the world of work, and increased emphasis on personal autonomy. Remaining single is a much more acceptable option today than it was a few decades ago (Stein, 1989). The classic stereotype of single people as being lonely, frustrated, and unchosen is gradually evaporating (Shostak, 1987). Nonetheless, over 90% of adults eventually marry.

Adjusting to Marriage

The newly married couple usually settle into their roles as husband and wife gradually. Difficulties with this transition are more likely when spouses come into a marriage with different expectations about marital roles (Kitson & Sussman, 1982; Lye

& Biblarz, 1993). Unfortunately, substantial differences in role expectations seem particularly likely in this era of transition in gender roles. For instance, males differ from females in their view of what equality in marriage means. When the subjects in one survey (Machung, 1989) were asked to define an egalitarian marriage, half the men could not. The other half defined it in purely psychological terms, saying a marriage is "equal" if it is based on mutual understanding and trust. The women were considerably more concrete and task oriented. They defined marital equality in terms of an equal sharing of chores and responsibilities. However, the evidence indicates that such equality is atypical. As Figure 11.22 shows, wives are still doing the bulk of the housework in America, even when they are employed outside the home (Berardo, Shehan, & Leslie, 1987; Blair & Johnson, 1992). Obviously, women's and men's marital role expectations often are at odds.

In general, however, the first few years of married life tend to be characterized by great happiness—the proverbial "marital bliss." Numerous studies have measured spouses' overall satisfaction in different stages of the family life cycle and found a U-shaped relationship like that shown in Figure 11.23 (Belsky, 1990a; Glenn, 1990). This U shape reflects the fact that satisfaction tends to be greatest at the beginning and end of the family life cycle, with a noticeable decline in the middle. The conventional explanation for this pattern is that the burdens of child rearing undermine couples' satisfaction, which gradually climbs back up again as children grow up and these burdens ease.

The prechildren phase of the family life cycle used to be rather short for most newly married couples. Traditionally, couples just *assumed* that they would proceed to have children. However, in recent years more couples have found themselves struggling to decide *whether* to have children. Often, this decision occurs after numerous postponements, when the couple finally acknowledges that "the right time" is never going to arrive (Crane, 1985). People who choose to remain childless cite factors such as the financial burdens of having children, the loss of educational or career opportunities, reduced leisure time, and worry about the responsibilities associated with child rearing (Bram, 1985; Seccombe, 1991).

Adjusting to Parenthood

Although an increasing number of people are choosing to remain childless, the vast majority of married couples continue to plan on having children (Roosa, 1988). Despite the challenges involved in rearing children, most parents report little regret about their choice and rate parenthood as a very positive experience (Demo, 1992; Goetting, 1986). Nonetheless, the arrival of the first child represents a *major* transition. The disruption of old routines can create a full-fledged crisis. The

Figure 11.22
Who does the housework? Berardo, Shehan, and Leslie (1987) studied the proportion of housework done by husbands, wives, and other family members. As these pie charts show, wives continue to do a highly disproportionate share of the housework, even if they are employed.

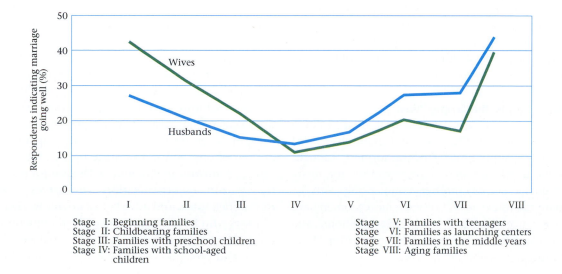

Stage   I: Beginning families
Stage II: Childbearing families
Stage III: Families with preschool children
Stage IV: Families with school-aged children

Stage   V: Families with teenagers
Stage VI: Families as launching centers
Stage VII: Families in the middle years
Stage VIII: Aging families

Figure 11.23
Marital satisfaction across the family life cycle. This graph depicts the percentage of husbands and wives who said their marriage was going well "all the time" at various stages of the family life cycle. Rollins and Feldman (1970) broke the family life cycle into eight stages. The U-shaped relationship shown here has been found in other studies as well, although its relevance is limited to families that have children in the traditional childbearing years.

new mother, already physically exhausted by the birth process, is particularly prone to postpartum stress (Hock et al., 1995). Wives are especially vulnerable when they have to shoulder the major burden of infant care (Kalmuss, Davidson, & Cushman, 1992).

Crisis during the transition to first parenthood is far from universal, however (Ruble et al., 1988). Couples who have high levels of intimacy, closeness, and commitment tend to experience a smoother transition to parenthood (Lewis, Owen, & Cox, 1988). Interestingly, older males who father their first child relatively late tend to experience a smoother transition than younger men (Cooney et al., 1993). The key to making this transition less stressful may be to have *realistic expectations* about parental responsibilities (Kalmuss et al., 1992). Studies find that stress is greatest in new parents who have overestimated the benefits and underestimated the costs of their new role.

As children grow up, parental influence over them tends to decline, and the early years of parenting—that once seemed so difficult—are often recalled with fondness. When youngsters reach adolescence and seek to establish their own identities, gradual realignments occur in parent-child relationships. Parent-adolescent relations generally are not as bitter or contentious as widely assumed, but conflicts are common (Silverberg, Tennenbaum, & Jacob, 1992). The conflicts tend to involve everyday matters (chores and appearance) more than substantive issues (sex and drugs) (Barber, 1994). When conflict does occur, mothers often are more adversely affected by it than fathers (Steinberg & Silverberg, 1987). This may be because women's self-esteem tends to be more closely tied to the quality of their family relationships. Ironically, although recent studies have shown that adolescence is not as turbulent or difficult for youngsters as once believed, their parents *are* stressed out. Parents overwhelmingly rate adolescence as the most difficult stage of child rearing (Gecas & Seff, 1990).

Adjusting to the Empty Nest

When parents have launched all their children into the adult world, they find themselves faced with an "empty nest." This was formerly thought to be a difficult period of transition for many parents, especially mothers familiar only with the maternal role. Today, however, more women have experience with other roles outside the home, and most look forward to their "liberation" from child-rearing responsibilities (Reinke et al., 1985). Hence,

the empty nest transition appears to have little lasting negative impact (Birchler, 1992).

The postparental period often provides couples with new freedom to devote attention to each other. Many couples take advantage of this opportunity by traveling or developing new leisure interests. And as offspring strike out on their own, couples' marital satisfaction tends to start climbing to higher levels once again (Brubaker, 1990). It tends to remain fairly high until one of the spouses (usually the husband) dies.

Transitions in Work

When adults meet for the first time, their initial "How do you do?" is often followed by "What do you do for a living?" Work clearly occupies an important place in most adults' lives. People who are satisfied with their jobs tend to exhibit better mental and physical health than those who are not (Holt, 1982; Warr, 1987).

Typical Patterns of Career Development

The most influential theory of vocational development is that outlined by Donald Super (1957, 1985, 1988). He breaks the vocational life cycle into five major stages and a variety of substages (see Table 11.2). We'll use Super's model to sketch an overview of vocational development while borrowing insights from other theorists (Campbell & Heffernan, 1983; Ginzberg, 1972; Jordaan, 1974; Schein, 1978).

The *exploration stage* typically lasts into the mid-20s, when most young adults attempt to achieve full entry into the world of work. This stage usually involves finishing any remaining schooling and securing the crucial first job. Many people in this phase are still only tentatively committed to their chosen occupational area. If their first experiences are not rewarding, they may shift to another area, where they will continue the process of exploration.

However, if their initial experiences are gratifying, people may commit to an occupational area and move on to the *establishment stage*. With few exceptions, future job moves will take place *within* this occupational area. Many people, particularly those in the professions, are guided and supported in their efforts during this stage by an older co-worker. A *mentor* **is someone with a senior position within an organization who serves as a role model, tutor, and adviser to a novice worker.** Workers who have a mentor benefit in numerous ways. They may acquire technical, managerial, social, and problem-solving skills. They may also

TABLE 11.2 STAGES OF VOCATIONAL DEVELOPMENT

Stage	Approximate Ages	Key Events and Transitions
Growth stage	**0–14**	**A period of general physical and mental growth**
Prevocational substage	0–3	No interest in or concern with vocations
Fantasy substage	4–10	Fantasy is basis for vocational thinking
Interest substage	11–12	Vocational thought is based on individual's likes and dislikes
Capacity substage	13–14	Ability becomes the basis for vocational thought
Exploration stage	**15–24**	**General exploration of work**
Tentative substage	15–17	Needs, interests, capacities, values, and opportunities become bases for tentative occupational decisions
Transition substage	18–21	Reality increasingly becomes a basis for vocational thought and action
Trial substage	22–24	First trial job is entered after the individual has made an initial vocational commitment
Establishment stage	**25–44**	**The individual seeks to enter a permanent occupation**
Trial substage	25–30	A period of some occupational change due to unsatisfactory choices
Stabilization substage	31–44	A period of stable work in a given occupational field
Maintenance stage	**45–65**	**Continuation in one's chosen occupation**
Decline stage	**65+**	**Adaptation to leaving work force**
Deceleration substage	65–70	Period of declining vocational activity
Retirement substage	71+	A cessation of vocational activity

Source: Adapted from Zaccaria (1970)

develop increased self-confidence and greater understanding of the workings of their organization (Burke, 1984).

As the years go by, opportunities for further career advancement and occupational mobility generally decline. Around their mid-40s, many people cross into the *maintenance stage*. In this stage, they worry more about retaining their achieved status than improving it. With decreased emphasis on career advancement, many people shift energy and attention away from work concerns in favor of family concerns or leisure activities.

In the *decline stage* people have to prepare to leave the workplace as retirement looms near. Individuals approach retirement with highly varied attitudes (Atchley, 1982, 1991). Many are filled with apprehension, unsure about how they will occupy themselves and worried about their financial survival. Nonetheless, many studies have shown that retirement has no adverse effect on overall health or life satisfaction (Smith, Patterson, & Grant, 1992). Although retirement may lead to decreased income, it can also increase time available for travel, hobbies, household tasks, and friends (George, Fillenbaum, & Palmore, 1984).

Women's Career Development

Although women's participation in the workforce has increased dramatically in recent decades (see Figure 11.24), most of the research on vocational development has focused on *men's* careers. Until the mid-1970s, it was simply taken for granted that the theories and concepts used to explain men's career development would apply equally well to women. However, evidence suggests that patterns of vocational development are different for women than for men (Katz & Feroz, 1992; Schneer & Reitman, 1994). For example, a study of career progress among men and women (Larwood & Gattiker, 1984) uncovered some interesting gender differences. For the male subjects, it was possible to trace a clear, consistent path that led to

Figure 11.24
Women in the workforce. The percentage of women (over age 16) who work outside the home has been rising steadily throughout this century. (Data from U.S. Bureau of Labor Statistics, 1991)

AN OVERVIEW OF HUMAN DEVELOPMENT

Stage of development	Infancy (birth–2)	

Physical and sensorimotor development

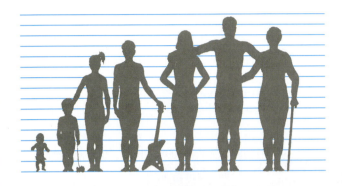

Rapid brain growth; 75% of adult brain weight is attained by age 2.

Ability to localize sounds is apparent at birth; ability to recognize parent's voice within first week.

Rapid improvement occurs in visual acuity; depth perception is clearly present by 6 months, perhaps earlier.

Landmarks in motor development: infants sit without support around 6 months, walk around 12–14 months, run freely around 2 years.

Major stage theories	Piaget	Sensorimotor	
	Kohlberg	Premoral	
	Erikson	Trust vs. distrust	Autonomy vs. shame
	Freud (see Chapter 12)	Oral	Anal

Cognitive development

Object permanence gradually develops; by age 2, infants capable of symbolic thought.

Infant shows orienting response (pupils dilate, head turns) and attention to new stimulus, habituation (reduced orienting response) to repeated stimulus.

Babbling increasingly resembles spoken language.

First word is used around age 1; holophrases (one-word "sentences") are used around 18 months; frequent overextensions (words applied too broadly) occur.

Social and personality development

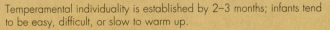

Temperamental individuality is established by 2–3 months; infants tend to be easy, difficult, or slow to warm up.

Attachment to caregiver(s) is usually evident around 6–8 months; secure attachment facilitates exploration.

"Stranger anxiety" often appears around 6–7 months; separation anxiety peaks around 14–18 months.

Information compiled by Barbara Hansen Lemme, College of DuPage

Early childhood
(2–6)

Connections among neurons continue to increase in density.

Visual acuity reaches 20/20.

Bladder and bowel control is established.

Hand preference is usually solidified by 3–4 years; coordination improves; children learn to dress themselves.

Middle childhood
(6–12)

In girls, growth spurt begins around age 10½, bringing dramatic increases in height and weight.

Level of pituitary activity and sex hormones increases.

In girls, puberty begins around age 12; menstruation starts.

Girls' secondary sexual characteristics (such as breast development and widening hips) begin to emerge.

Preoperational	Concrete operational
Preconventional	Conventional
Initiative vs. guilt	Industry vs. inferiority
Phallic	Latency

Thought is marked by egocentrism (limited ability to view world from another's perspective).

Thought is marked by centration (inability to focus on more than one aspect of a problem at a time) and irreversibility (inability to mentally undo an action).

Telegraphic speech (omitting nonessential words) appears at 2–3 years; syntax is well developed by age 5; vocabulary increases dramatically.

Short-term memory capacity increases from two items at age 2 to five items around age 6–7; attention span improves.

Conservation (understanding that physical qualities can remain constant in spite of transformations in shape) is gradually mastered.

Child develops decentration (ability to focus on more than one feature of a problem at a time) and reversibility (ability to mentally undo an action).

Metalingustic awareness (ability to reflect on use of language) leads to play with language, use of puns, riddles, metaphors.

Long-term memory improves with increasing use of encoding strategies of rehearsal and organization.

Child realizes that gender does not change and begins to learn gender roles and form gender identity; social behavior is influenced by observational learning, resulting in imitation.

Child progresses from parallel (side-by-side, noninteractive) play to cooperative play.

Social world is extended beyond family; first friendships are formed.

Child experiences great increase in social skills, improved understanding of others' feelings; social world is dominated by same-sex peer relationships.

Role-taking skills emerge; fantasy is basis for thoughts about vocations and jobs.

Altruism tends to increase, aggression tends to decrease; aggression tends to become verbal rather than physical, hostile more than instrumental.

Adolescence
(12–20)

In boys, growth spurt begins around age 12½, bringing dramatic increases in height and weight.

Level of pituitary activity and hormones increases.

Boys' secondary sexual characteristics (such as voice change and growth of facial hair) begin to emerge.

In boys, puberty begins around age 14; boys become capable of ejaculation.

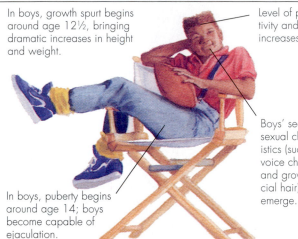

Formal operational

Postconventional (if attained)

Identity vs. confusion

Genital

Deductive reasoning improves; problem solving becomes more systematic, with alternative possibilities considered before solution is selected.

Thought becomes more abstract and reflective; individual develops ability to mentally manipulate abstract concepts as well as concrete objects.

Individual engages in idealistic contemplation of hypotheticals, "what could be."

Long-term memory continues to improve as elaboration is added to encoding strategies.

Person experiences increased interactions with opposite-sex peers; dating begins.

Attention is devoted to identify formation, questions such as "Who am I?" and "What do I want out of life?"

Realistic considerations about abilities and training requirements become more influential in thoughts about vocations and jobs.

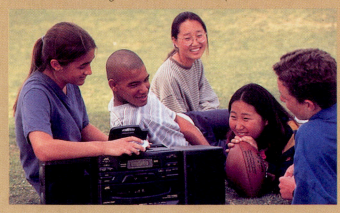

Young adulthood
(20–40)

Reaction time and muscular strength peak in early to mid-20s.

External signs of aging begin to show in 30s; skin loses elasticity; hair is thinner, more likely to be gray.

Maximum functioning of all body systems, including senses, attained; slow decline begins in 20s.

Lowered metabolic rate contributes to increased body fat relative to muscle; gain in weight is common.

Intimacy vs. isolation

Intellectual abilities and speed of information processing are stable.

Greater emphasis is on application, rather than acquisition, of knowledge.

There is some evidence of a trend toward dialectical thought (ideas stimulate opposing ideas), leading to more contemplation of contradictions, pros and cons.

Energies are focused on intimate relationships, learning to live with marriage partner, starting a family, managing a home.

Trial period is given for occupational choices, followed by stabilization of vocational commitment; emphasis is on self-reliance, becoming one's own person.

For many, close relationship develops with mentor (older person who serves as role model, advisor, and teacher).

Middle adulthood
(40–65)

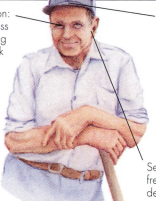

Changes occur in vision: increased farsightedness and difficulty recovering from glare; slower dark adaptation.

Number of active brain cells declines, but significance of this neural loss is unclear.

In women, menopause occurs around age 50; in both sexes, sexual activity declines, although capacity for arousal changes only slightly.

Sensitivity to high-frequency sounds decreases especially in males after age 55.

Generativity vs. self-absorption

There is some evidence for a trend toward improved judgment or "wisdom" based on accumulation of life experiences.

Effectiveness of retrieval from long-term memory begins slow decline, usually not noticeable until after age 55.

Individual experiences gradual decline in speed of learning, problem solving, and information processing.

In spite of decreased speed in cognitive processes, intellectual productivity and problem-solving skills usually remain stable.

Midlife transition around age 40 leads to reflection, increased awareness of mortality, and passage of time but ususually is not a personal crisis.

"Sandwich generation" is caught between needs of aging parents and children reaching adulthood.

Career development peaks; there is some tendency to shift energy from career concerns to family concerns.

Late adulthood
(65 and older)

Height decreases slightly because of changes in vertebral column; decline in weight also common.

Sensitivity of vision, hearing, and taste noticeably decreases.

Chronic diseases, especially heart disease, cancer, and stroke, increase.

Rate of aging is highly individualized.

Integrity vs. despair

Individual experiences gradual decline in cognitive speed and effectiveness of working memory.

Intellectual productivity depends on factors such as health and lifestyle; many people in 60s and 70s remain quite productive.

Decision making tends to become more cautious.

Fluid intelligence often declines, but crystallized intelligence remains stable or increases.

Physical changes associated with aging require adjustments that affect life satisfaction.

Marital satisfaction often increases, but eventually death of spouse presents coping challenge.

Living arrangements are a significant determinant of satisfaction, as 60%–90% of time is spent at home.

vocational success. Among the women, however, success was much less predictable and was characterized as nearly "random."

Why was there no pattern for women? Vocational development among women may be less predictable because women are more likely than men to experience career interruptions, leaving the workforce temporarily to concentrate on child rearing or family crises (Phillips & Imhoff, 1997). Additionally, many women continue to subjugate their career goals to their husbands' goals (Unger & Crawford, 1992). Women are also less likely than men to enjoy the benefits of mentoring (Ragins & Cotton, 1991). Finally, although women have made great inroads in many sectors of the workplace, they still face discrimination. Because of sex bias in hiring and promotion practices, women continue to be overrepresented in low-status, "pink ghetto" jobs (secretary, waitress, day-care aide). Moreover, when men and women work in comparable jobs, the average woman earns only 72 cents for every dollar earned by the average man (Ries & Stone, 1992). Sex discrimination remains an issue when it comes to advancing to top management positions (Melamed, 1995). Fewer than 2% of the corporate officers of Fortune 500 companies are female (Morrison & Von Glinow, 1990). There appears to be a "glass ceiling" that prevents most women from advancing beyond middle management positions.

Aging and Physical Changes

People obviously experience many physical changes as they progress through adulthood. In both sexes, hair tends to thin out and become gray, and many males confront receding hairlines and baldness. To the dismay of many, the proportion of body fat tends to increase with age. Overall, weight tends to increase in most adults through the mid-50s, when a gradual decline may begin. These changes have little functional significance, but in our youth-oriented society, they often lead people to view themselves as less attractive.

The number of active neurons in the brain declines during adulthood. The rate of neuronal loss is hard to measure and appears to vary in different parts of the brain (Duara, London, & Rapoport, 1985). Although this gradual loss of brain cells sounds alarming, it is a normal part of the aging process. Its functional significance is the subject of some debate, but it doesn't appear to contribute to any of the age-related dementias. A **dementia is an abnormal condition marked by multiple cog-**nitive deficits that include memory impairment. Dementia can be caused by quite a variety of diseases, such as Alzheimer's disease, Parkinson's disease, and AIDS, to name just a few. Because some of these diseases are more prevalent in older adults, dementia is seen in about 15% of people over age 65 (Elias, Elias, & Elias, 1990). However, it is important to emphasize that dementia and "senility" are not part of the normal aging process. As Cavanaugh (1993) notes, "The term *senility* has no valid medical or psychological meaning, and its continued use simply perpetuates the myth that drastic mental decline is a product of normal aging" (p. 85).

In the sensory domain, the key developmental changes occur in vision and hearing. The proportion of people with 20/20 visual acuity declines with age. Farsightedness, difficulty adapting to darkness, and poor recovery from glare are common among older people (Fozard, 1990; Kline & Schieber, 1985). Hearing sensitivity begins declining gradually in early adulthood. Noticeable hearing losses requiring corrective treatment are apparent in about three-quarters of people over the age of 75 (Olsho, Harkins, & Lenhardt, 1985). These sensory losses could be problematic, but in modern society they can usually be compensated for with eyeglasses and hearing aids.

Age-related changes also occur in hormonal functioning during adulthood. Among women, these changes lead to *menopause*. This ending of menstrual periods, accompanied by a loss of fertility, typically occurs around age 50. Not long ago, menopause was thought to be almost universally accompanied by severe emotional strain. However, it is now clear that women's reactions to menopause vary greatly, depending on their expectations (Matthews, 1992). Most women experience little psychological distress (McKinlay, McKinlay, & Brambilla, 1987). Although people sometimes talk about "male menopause," men don't really go through an equivalent experience. Middle-aged males experience hormonal changes, but they're very gradual.

Aging and Cognitive Changes

The evidence indicates that general intelligence is fairly stable throughout most of adulthood, with a small decline in *average* test scores often seen after age 60 (Hertzog & Schaie, 1988; Schaie, 1990, 1994). However, this seemingly simple assertion masks many complexities and needs to be qualified carefully. First, group averages can be deceptive in that mean scores can be dragged down by a small minority of people who show a decline. For example, when Schaie (1990) calculated the percentage of people who maintain stable performance on various abilities (see Figure 11.25), he found that about 80% showed no decline by age 60, and that about two-thirds were still stable through age 81. Second, even when age-related decreases in intellectual performance are found, they tend to be small in all but a few individuals (Salthouse, 1991). Third, some forms of intelligence are more vulnerable to aging than others. As we noted in Chapter 9, many theorists distinguish between *fluid intelligence,* which refers to basic information-processing skills, and *crystallized intelligence,* which refers to the application of accumulated knowledge. Research suggests that fluid intelligence is much more likely to decline with age, whereas crystallized intelligence tends to remain stable (Horn & Hofer, 1992).

What about memory? Numerous studies report decreases in older adults' memory capabilities (Baltes & Kliegl, 1992; Hultsch & Dixon, 1990). However, most of these studies have asked subjects to memorize simple lists of words or paired associations. Older subjects often find these artificial laboratory tasks meaningless and uninteresting. Investigators have only recently begun to study age-related changes in memory for more realistic content. There *do* seem to be some modest decreases in memory for prose, television shows, conversations, past activities, and personal plans (Kausler, 1985), but the memory losses associated with aging are moderate and are *not* universal (Shimamura et al., 1995). According to Salthouse (1994) an age-related decline in the capacity of *working memory* (see Chapter 7) underlies older adults' poorer performance on memory tasks. He attributes most of the decline in working memory to age-related decreases in the raw speed of mental processing.

In the cognitive domain, aging does seem to take its toll on *speed* first. Many studies indicate that speed in learning, solving problems, and processing information tends to decline with age

(Drachman, 1986; Salthouse & Babcock, 1991). Although additional data are needed, some evidence suggests that the erosion of processing speed may be a gradual, lengthy trend commencing in middle adulthood. The general nature of this trend (across differing tasks) suggests that it may be due to age-related changes in neurological functioning (Cerella, 1990; Myerson et al., 1990). Alternatively, it could reflect increased cautiousness among older adults (Reese & Rodeheaver, 1985). Although mental speed declines with age, problem-solving ability remains largely unimpaired if older people are given adequate time to compensate for their reduced speed.

It should be emphasized that many people remain capable of great intellectual accomplishments well into their later years (Simonton, 1990). This reality was verified in a study of scholarly, scientific, and artistic productivity that examined lifelong patterns of work among 738 men who lived at least through the age of 79. Dennis (1966) found that the 40s decade was the most productive in most professions. However, productivity was remarkably stable through the 60s and even the 70s in many areas.

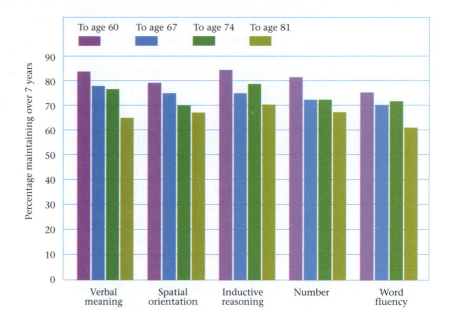

Figure 11.25
Age and the stability of primary mental abilities. In his longitudinal study of cognitive performance begun in 1956, Schaie (1983, 1993) has repeatedly assessed the five basic mental abilites listed along the bottom of this chart. The data graphed here show the percentage of subjects who maintained stable levels of performance on each ability through various ages up to age 81. As you can see, even through the age of 81, the majority of subjects show no significant decline on most abilities. (From Schaie, 1990)

PUTTING IT IN PERSPECTIVE

Many of our seven integrative themes surfaced to some degree in our coverage of human development. We saw theoretical diversity in the discussions of attachment, cognitive development, and personality development. We saw that psychology evolves in a sociohistorical context, investigating complex, real-world issues—such as the controversies over the effects of day care and televised violence. We encountered multifactorial causation of behavior in the development of temperament, attachment, altruism, and aggression, among other things. We saw cultural invariance and cultural diversity in our examination of attachment, motor development, cognitive development, and moral development.

But above all else, we saw how heredity and environment jointly mold behavior. We've encountered the dual influence of heredity and environment before, but this theme is rich in complexity, and each chapter draws out different aspects and implications. Our discussion of development amplified the point that genetics and experience work *interactively* to shape behavior. What does it mean to say that heredity and environment interact? To put it metaphorically, it means that they're entangled in the dance of development from the very beginning. In the language of science, an interaction means that the effects of one variable depend on the effects of another. In other words, heredity and environment do not operate independently. Children with "difficult" temperaments will elicit different reactions from different parents, depending on the parents' personalities and expectations. Likewise, a particular pair of parents will affect different children in different ways, depending on the inborn characteristics of the children. An interplay, or feedback loop, exists between biological and environmental factors. For instance, a temperamentally difficult child may elicit negative reactions from parents, which serve to make the child more difficult, which evokes more negative reactions. If this child develops into an ornery 11-year-old, which do we blame—genetics or experience? Clearly, this outcome is due to the reciprocal effects of both.

All aspects of development are shaped jointly by heredity and experience. We often estimate their relative weight or influence, as if we could cleanly divide behavior into genetic and environmental components. Although we can't really carve up behavior that neatly, such comparisons can be of great theoretical interest, as you'll see in our upcoming Application, which discusses the nature and origins of gender differences in behavior.

Recap of Key Points

- During adulthood, personality is marked by both stability and change. Doubts have surfaced about whether a midlife crisis is a normal developmental transition. Adults who move successfully through the three stages of adulthood posited by Erikson should develop intimacy, generativity, and integrity.

- Although shifting social trends are disrupting the traditional family life cycle, many landmarks in adult development involve transitions in family relationships. Difficulty adjusting to marriage is more likely when spouses have different role expectations. Marital satisfaction tends to be highest at the beginning and end of the family life cycle.

- Unrealistic expectations make the adjustment to parenthood more stressful. Parent-adolescent relations are not as contentious as widely assumed. For most parents, the empty nest transition no longer appears to be as stressful as it once was.

- Vocational development tends to proceed through stages of exploration, establishment, maintenance, and decline. Patterns of vocational development are less predictable in females than males.

- During adulthood, age-related physical transitions include changes in appearance, neuron losses, sensory losses (especially in vision and hearing), and hormonal changes. Menopause is not as problematic as widely suggested.

- In the cognitive domain, general intelligence is fairly stable, with a small decline in average test scores seen after the age of 60. Fluid intelligence is more likely to decline with age than crystallized intelligence.

- Many studies have found decreases in older adults' memory capabilities, but the losses are moderate and variable. Mental speed declines in late adulthood. Nonetheless, many people remain very productive well into old age.

- Many of our seven integrative themes stood out in this chapter. But above all else, our discussion of development showed how heredity and environment interactively shape behavior.

APPLICATION: **UNDERSTANDING GENDER DIFFERENCES**

Answer the following "true" or "false."

1 Females are more socially oriented than males.

2 Males outperform females on most spatial tasks.

3 Females are more irrational than males.

4 Males are less sensitive to nonverbal cues than females.

5 Females are more emotional than males.

Are there genuine behavioral differences between the sexes similar to those mentioned above? If so, why do these differences exist? How do they develop? These are the complex and controversial questions that we'll explore in this Application.

Before proceeding further, we need to clarify how some key terms are used, as terminology in this area of research has been evolving and remains a source of confusion (Deaux, 1993; Unger & Crawford, 1993). *Sex* **refers to the biologically based categories of female and male.** In contrast, *gender* **refers to culturally constructed distinctions between femininity and masculinity.** Individuals are *born* female or male. However, they *become* feminine or masculine through complex developmental processes that take years to unfold.

The statements at the beginning of this Application reflect popular gender stereotypes in our society. *Gender stereotypes* **are widely held beliefs about females' and males' abilities, personality traits, and social behavior.** Table 11.3 lists some characteristics that are part of the masculine and feminine stereotypes in North American society. The table shows something you may have already noticed on your own. The male stereotype is much more flattering, suggesting that men have virtually cornered the market on competence and rationality. After all, everyone knows that females are more dependent, emotional, irrational, submissive, and talkative than males. Right? Or is that not the case? Let's look at the research.

How Do the Sexes Differ in Behavior?

Gender differences **are actual disparities between the sexes in typical behavior or average ability.** Mountains of research, literally thousands of studies, exist on gender differences. It's difficult to sort through this huge body of research, but fortunately, many review articles on gender differences have been published in recent years. As noted in Chapter 2, *review articles* summarize and reconcile the findings of a large number of studies on a specific issue. Reviews that use meta-analysis have been particularly valuable. *Meta-analysis* **combines the statistical results of many studies of the same question, yielding an estimate of the size and consistency of a variable's effects.**

What does this research show? Are the stereotypes of males and females accurate? Well, the findings are a mixed bag. The research indicates that genuine behavioral differences *do* exist between the sexes and that people's stereotypes are not entirely inaccurate (Eagly, 1995; Swim, 1994). But the differences are fewer in number, smaller in size, and far more complex than stereotypes suggest. As you'll see, only two of the differences mentioned in our opening true-false questions (the even-numbered items) have been largely supported by the research.

Cognitive Abilities

In the cognitive domain, it appears that there are three genuine gender differences. First, on the average, females tend to exhibit slightly better *verbal skills* than males. Females tend to start speaking a little earlier, and they have larger vocabularies and better reading

TABLE 11.3 ELEMENTS OF TRADITIONAL GENDER STEROTYPES

Masculine	Feminine
Active	Aware of others' feelings
Adventurous	Considerate
Aggressive	Creative
Ambitious	Cries easily
Competitive	Devotes self to others
Dominant	Emotional
Independent	Enjoys art and music
Leadership qualities	Excitable in a crisis
Likes math and science	Expresses tender feelings
Makes decisions easily	Feelings hurt
Mechanical aptitude	Gentle
Not easily influenced	Home oriented
Outspoken	Kind
Persistent	Likes children
Self-confident	Neat
Skilled in business	Needs approval
Stands up under pressure	Tactful
Takes a stand	Understanding

Source: Adapted from Ruble (1983)

scores during the grade-school years (Halpern, 1992). In particular, females seem stronger on tasks that require rapid access to semantic and other information in long-term memory (Halpern, 1997). Second, starting during high school, males show a slight advantage on tests of *mathematical ability*. When all students are compared, males' advantage is fairly small (Feingold, 1988a; Hyde, Fennema, & Lamon, 1990). However, at the high end of the ability distribution, the gender gap is larger, as far more males than females are found to be mathematically precocious. For instance, when gifted seventh- and eighth-graders take the Math subtest of the SAT, boys outnumber girls 17 to 1 in the group scoring over 700 (Benbow, 1988). Third, starting in the grade-school years, males tend to score higher than females on various measures of *visual-spatial ability* (Voyer, Voyer, & Bryden, 1995). The size of these gender differences varies from moderate to small depending on the exact nature of the spatial task. Males appear to be strongest on tasks that require visual transformations in working memory (Halpern, 1997).

Social Behavior and Personality

In regard to social behavior and personality, research findings support some additional gender differences that are reasonably well documented. First, studies indicate that males tend to be more *aggressive* than females, both verbally and physically (Hyde, 1986; Knight, Fabes, & Higgins, 1996). This disparity shows up early in childhood. Its continuation into adulthood is supported by the fact that men account for a grossly disproportionate number of the violent crimes in our society (Kenrick, 1987). Second, there are gender differences in *nonverbal communication*. The evidence indicates that females are more sensitive than males to subtle nonverbal cues (Hall, 1990). Females also smile and gaze at others more than males do (Hall & Halberstadt, 1986). Third, two separate reviews conclude that gender differences occur in *influenceability* (Becker, 1986; Eagly & Carli, 1981). That is, females appear to be slightly more susceptible to

persuasion and conforming to group pressure than males are. Fourth, males are more sexually active than females in a variety of ways, and they have more permissive attitudes about casual, premarital, and extramarital sex (Oliver & Hyde, 1993). In regard to personality, males score higher on assertiveness scales, whereas females score higher on measures of anxiety, trust, and tender-mindedness (empathy and nurturance) (Feingold, 1994).

Some Qualifications

Although there are some genuine gender differences in behavior, bear in mind that these are *group* differences that indicate nothing about individuals. Essentially, research results compare the "average man" with the "average woman." However, you are—and every individual is—unique. The average female and male are ultimately figments of our imagination. Furthermore, most of the genuine group differences noted are relatively modest in magnitude. Figure 11.26 shows how scores on a trait, perhaps verbal ability, might be distributed for men and women. Although the group averages are detectably different, you can see the great variability within each group (sex) and the huge overlap between the two group distributions.

To summarize, the actual behavioral differences between males and females are fewer and smaller than popular stereotypes suggest. Many supposed gender differences have turned out to be more mythical than real (Tavris, 1992). Nonetheless, there are some genuine gender differences that require explanation, which is the matter we'll attend to next.

Biological Origins of Gender Differences

What accounts for the development of the gender differences that do exist? To what degree are they the product of learning or of biology? This question is yet another manifestation of the nature versus nurture issue. Investigations of the biological origins of gender differences have centered on the evolutionary bases of behavior, hormones, and brain organization.

Evolutionary Explanations

Evolutionary psychologists argue that gender differences in behavior reflect different natural selection pressures operating on the sexes over the course of human history. Evolutionary analyses usually begin by arguing that gender differences in behavior transcend culture because cultural invariance suggests that biological factors are at work (Kenrick & Trost, 1993). Although research has turned up some fascinating exceptions, the better-documented gender differences in cognitive abilities, aggression, and sexual behavior do appear to be pancultural (Beller & Gafni, 1996; Halpern, 1997).

According to evolutionary psychologists, these differences are found around the world because males and females have confronted different adaptive demands. For example, as we discussed in Chapter 10, males supposedly are more sexually active and permissive because they invest less than females in the process of procreation and can maximize their reproductive success by seeking many sexual partners (Buss, 1996). The gender gap in aggression is also explained in terms of reproductive fitness. Because females are more selective about mating than males, males have to engage in more competition for sexual partners than females do. Greater aggressiveness is thought to be adaptive for males in this competition for sexual access because it should foster social dominance over other males and facilitate the acquisition of the material resources emphasized by females when they evaluate potential partners (Kenrick & Trost, 1997). Evolutionary theorists assert that gender differences in spatial ability reflect the division of labor in ancestral hunting and gathering societies in which males typically handled the hunting and females the gathering. Males' superiority on most spatial tasks has been attributed to the adaptive demands of hunting (Eals & Silverman, 1994).

Evolutionary analyses of gender differences are interesting, but controversial. On the one hand, it seems eminently plausible that evolutionary forces could have led to some divergence between males and females in typical behavior. On the other

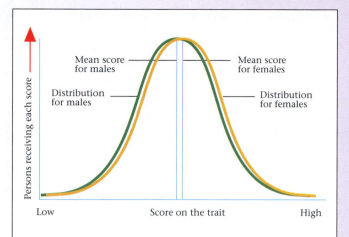

Figure 11.26
The nature of gender differences. Gender differences are group differences that indicate little about individuals because of the great overlap between the groups. For a given trait, one sex may score higher on the average, but far more variation occurs within each sex than between the sexes.

Labels on figure:
Persons receiving each score

Mean score for males
Distribution for males

Mean score for females
Distribution for females

Low — Score on the trait — High

hand, evolutionary hypotheses are highly speculative and difficult to test empirically (Fausto-Sterling, 1992; Halpern, 1997). For example, it is quite a leap to infer that modern paper-and-pencil tests of spatial ability assess a talent that would have made high scorers superior hunters millions of years ago. But the crux of the problem is that evolutionary analyses can be used to explain almost anything. For example, if the situation regarding spatial ability were reversed—if females scored higher than males—evolutionary theorists might attribute females' superiority to the adaptive demands of gathering food, weaving baskets, and making clothes—and it would be difficult to prove otherwise.

The Role of Hormones

Hormones play a key role in sexual differentiation during prenatal development. Biological sex is determined by the sex chromosomes: An XX pairing produces a female and an XY pairing produces a male. However, both male and female embryos are essentially the same until about 8 to 12 weeks after conception, when male and female gonads (sex glands) begin to produce different hormonal secretions. The high level of androgens (the principal class of male hormones) in males and the low level

of androgens in females lead to the differentiation of male and female genital organs.

The critical role of prenatal hormones in sexual differentiation becomes apparent when something interferes with normal prenatal hormonal secretions. There are about a half-dozen endocrine disorders that can cause overproduction or underproduction of specific gonadal hormones during prenatal development. Scientists have also studied children born to mothers who were given an androgenlike drug to prevent miscarriage. The general trend in this research is that females exposed prenatally to abnormally high levels of androgens exhibit more male-typical behavior than other females and that males exposed prenatally to abnormally low levels of androgens exhibit more female-typical behavior than other males (Collaer & Hines, 1995). For example, girls with *congenital adrenal hyperplasia* tend to show "tomboyish" interests in vigorous outdoor activities and in "male" toys and have elevated scores on measures of aggressiveness and spatial ability.

These findings suggest that prenatal hormones contribute to the shaping of gender differences in humans. But there are a few problems with this evidence (Basow, 1992; Fausto-Sterling, 1992). First, the evidence is more voluminous and the findings much stronger for females than for males. Second, it's always dangerous to draw conclusions about the general population based on small samples of people who have abnormal conditions. Third, most of the endocrine disorders studied have multiple effects (besides altering hormone levels) that create a variety of sometimes worrisome confounds in the research. Fourth, most of the research is necessarily correla-

tional, and it is always risky to draw causal conclusions based on correlational data.

A handful of more recent studies have reported associations between circulating levels of male and female hormones and measures of specific traits, such as aggressiveness (Inoff-Germain et al., 1988) and spatial ability (Kimura & Hampson, 1994). For example, testosterone given to normal aging men to enhance their sexual functioning also increases their performance on visual-spatial tests (Janowsky, Oviatt, & Orwoll, 1994). Looking at the evidence as a whole, it *does* seems likely that hormones contribute to gender differences in behavior. However, the findings in this line of research have been equivocal and inconsistent, and a great deal remains to be learned.

Disparities in Brain Organization

Interpretive problems have also cropped up in efforts to link gender differences to specialization of the cerebral hemispheres in the brain. As you may recall from Chapter 3, in most people the left hemisphere is more actively involved in verbal processing, whereas the right hemisphere is more active in visual-spatial processing (Sperry, 1982; Springer & Deutsch, 1993). After these findings surfaced, theorists began to wonder whether this division of labor in the brain might be related to gender differences in verbal and spatial skills. Consequently, they began looking for sex-related disparities in brain organization.

Some thought-provoking findings *have* been reported. For instance, some studies have found that *males tend to exhibit more cerebral specialization than females* (Bryden, 1988; Hines, 1990). In other words, there's a trend for males to depend more heavily than females do on the left hemisphere in verbal processing and more heavily on the right in spatial processing. Differences between males and females have also been found in the size of the corpus callosum, the band of fibers that connects the two hemispheres of the brain (Steinmetz et al., 1995). Some studies suggest that *females tend to have a larger corpus callosum*, which might allow for better interhemispheric transfer of information, which in turn might underlie the more bilateral organization of females' brains (Innocenti, 1994). Thus, some theorists have concluded that differences between the sexes in brain organization are responsible for gender differences in verbal and spatial ability (Geschwind & Galaburda, 1987; Kimura & Hampson, 1993).

This idea is intriguing, but psychologists have a long way to go before they can explain gender differences in terms of right brain/left brain specialization. Studies have not been consistent in finding that males have stronger cerebral lateralization than females (Halpern, 1992; Kinsbourne, 1980), and the finding of a larger corpus callosum in females has proven controversial (Bleier, 1988; Byne & Parsons, 1993). Moreover, it seems peculiar that strong lateralization would produce an advantage for males on one kind of task (spatial) and a disadvantage on another kind of task (verbal). Thus, the theory linking cerebral specialization to gender differences in mental abilities remains highly speculative.

In summary, researchers have made some intriguing progress in their efforts to document the biological roots of gender differences in behavior. However, the idea that "anatomy is destiny" has proven difficult to demonstrate. Many theorists remain convinced that gender differences are largely shaped by experience. Let's examine their evidence.

Environmental Origins of Gender Differences

Socialization is the acquisition of the norms and behaviors expected of people in a particular society. It includes all the efforts made by a society to ensure that its members learn to behave in a manner that's considered appropriate. The socialization process has traditionally included efforts to train children about gender roles. *Gender roles are expectations about what is appropriate behavior for each sex.* Investigators have identified three key processes involved in the socialization of gender roles: operant conditioning, observational learning, and self-socialization. First we'll examine these processes. Then we'll look at the principal sources of gender-role socialization: families, schools, and the media.

Operant Conditioning

In part, gender roles are shaped by the power of reward and punishment—the key processes in *operant conditioning* (see Chapter 6). Parents, teachers, peers, and others often reinforce (usually with tacit approval) "gender-appropriate" behavior and respond negatively to "gender-inappropriate" behavior (Fagot & Hagan, 1991; Fagot, Leinbach, & O'Boyle, 1992). If you're a man, you might recall getting hurt as a young boy and being told that "men don't cry." If you succeeded in inhibiting your crying, you may have earned an approving smile or even something tangible like an ice cream cone. The reinforcement probably strengthened your tendency to "act like a man" and suppress emotional displays. If you're a woman, chances are your crying wasn't discouraged as gender-inappropriate. Studies suggest that fathers may encourage and reward gender-appropriate behavior in their youngsters more than mothers do and that boys experience more pressure to behave in gender-appropriate ways than girls do (Lytton & Romney, 1991). Thus, a 10-year-old boy who enjoys playing with dollhouses is particularly likely to elicit disapproval from his parents, especially his father.

Observational Learning

As a young girl, did you imitate the behavior of your mother, your aunts, and your older sisters? As a young boy, did you imitate your father and other male role models? Such behaviors reflect *observational learning,* in which behavior is shaped by the observation of others' behavior and its consequences (see Chapter 6). In everyday language, observational learning results in *imitation.*

Children imitate both males and females, but most children tend to imitate same-sex role models more than opposite-sex role models (Bussey & Bandura, 1984; Perry & Bussey, 1979). Thus, imitation often leads young girls to play with dolls, dollhouses, and toy stoves. Young boys are more likely to tinker with toy trucks, miniature gas stations, or tool kits. Parents and other adults are not the only role models who contribute to the process of observational learning; same-sex peers may be even more influential than adults (Maccoby, 1990).

Self-Socialization

Children themselves are active agents in their own gender-role socialization. Several *cognitive theories* of gender-role development emphasize self-socialization (Bem, 1985; Cross & Markus, 1993; Martin & Halverson, 1987). Self-socialization entails three steps. First, children learn to classify themselves as male or female and to recognize their sex as a permanent quality (around ages 5 or 6). Second, this self-categorization motivates them to value those characteristics and behaviors associated with their sex. Third, they strive to bring their behavior in line with what is considered gender-appropriate in their culture. In other words, children get involved in their own socialization, working diligently to discover the rules that are supposed to govern their behavior. After gender stereotypes are internalized, they probably continue to influence behavior throughout life. Most people strive to behave in ways that are consistent with their own and others' expectations, and those expectations color what people see (Geis, 1993).

Sources of Gender-Role Socialization

There are three *main* sources of influence in gender-role socialization: families, schools, and the media. Of course, we are now in an era of transition in gender roles, so the generalizations that follow may say more about how you were socialized than about how children will be socialized in the future. We'll discuss this transition after describing the traditional picture.

FAMILIES. A great deal of gender-role socialization takes place in the home. A recent review of research (Lytton & Romney, 1991) suggests that parents don't treat girls and boys as differently as one might expect, but there *are* disparities (Lott & Maluso, 1993; Turner & Gervai, 1995). For example, fathers engage in more "rough-housing" play with their sons than with their daughters, even in infancy (Culp, Cook, & Housley, 1983). As children grow, boys and girls are encouraged to play with different types of toys (Etaugh & Liss, 1992). Not surprisingly, substantial gender differences are found in toy preferences. Generally, boys have less leeway to play with "feminine" toys than girls do with "masculine" toys.

When children are old enough to help with household chores, the assignments tend to depend on sex (McHale et al., 1990). For example, girls wash dishes and boys mow the lawn. Likewise, the leisure activities that children are encouraged to engage in vary by sex. Johnny plays in Little League and Mary practices the piano. Given these patterns, it's not surprising that parents' traditional or nontraditional attitudes about gender roles have been shown to influence the gender roles acquired by their children (Weisner & Wilson-Mitchell, 1990). Older siblings may also influence youngsters' gender-role socialization (Wagner, Schubert, & Schubert, 1993).

SCHOOLS. Schools and teachers clearly contribute to the socialization of gender roles. The books that children use in learning to read can influence their ideas about what is suitable behavior for males and females (Schau & Scott, 1984). Traditionally, males have been more likely to be portrayed as clever, heroic, and adventurous in these books, while females have been more likely to be shown doing domestic chores. The depiction of stereotypical gender roles in textbooks has declined considerably since the 1970s, but researchers still find subtle differences in how males and females tend to be portrayed (Kortenhaus & Demarest, 1993; Noddings, 1992; Purcell & Stewart, 1990).

Preschool and grade-school teachers frequently reward sex-appropriate behavior in their pupils (Fagot et al., 1985). Interestingly, teachers tend to pay greater attention to males, helping them, praising them, and scolding them more than females (Sadker & Sadker, 1985). As youngsters progress through the school system, they are often channeled in career directions considered appropriate for their sex (Read, 1991). For example, males have been more likely to be encouraged to study mathematics and to work toward becoming engineers or doctors. Females have often been encouraged to take classes in home economics and to work toward becoming nurses or homemakers.

MEDIA. Television is another source of gender-role socialization (Luecke-Aleksa et al., 1995). Television shows have traditionally depicted men and women in highly stereotypic ways (Signorielli, 1989). Women are often portrayed as submissive, passive, and emotional. Men are more likely to be portrayed as independent, assertive, and competent. Another form of gender bias in television is its inordinate emphasis on physical attractiveness in women. Men on television may or may not be good-looking, but the vast majority of women are young, attractive, and sexy (Davis, 1990). TV commercials are especially likely to portray men and women in stereotypical ways (Bretl & Cantor, 1988); women are routinely shown worrying about trivial matters such as a ring around their husband's shirt collar or the shine of their dishes. Music videos frequently portray women as sex objects, and these portrayals appear to influence viewers' attitudes about sexual conduct (Hansen & Hansen, 1988).

One study strikingly demonstrates just how influential television can be. Many children's shows on public/educational television strive to promote nontraditional gender roles. Repetti (1984) found that children who watch a great deal of educational television tend to be less traditional in their views of gender roles than other children are. Of course, print media can also contribute to gender-role socialization. For example, "women's magazines" tend to encourage female readers to worry about their appearance and to strive to please men (Peirce, 1990). Thus, it appears that media content influences the gender roles acquired by youngsters.

Gender Roles in Transition

Gender roles are in a period of transition in our society. Many women and men are rebelling against traditional role expectations based on sex. Many parents are trying to raise their children with fewer preconceived notions about how males and females "ought" to behave. Some social critics view this as a healthy trend because they believe that traditional roles have been too narrow and restrictive for both sexes (Bem, 1985; Goldberg, 1983). Such theorists argue that conventional sex roles lock people into rigid straitjackets that prevent them from realizing their full potential. Other social critics (Davidson, 1988; Gilder, 1986) believe that changes in gender roles may harm intimate relationships between men and women and hurt the quality of family life. Thus, vigorous debate continues about the effects of evolving gender roles, illustrating once again that psychological issues and research often have profound social and political implications in our modern world.

Recap of Key Points

• *Sex* refers to the biological reality of being male or female, whereas *gender* refers to distinctions between being masculine or feminine. Gender differences in behavior are fewer in number and smaller in magnitude than gender stereotypes suggest.

• In the cognitive domain, research reviews suggest that there are genuine gender differences in verbal ability, mathematical ability, and spatial ability. In regard to social behavior and personality, differences have been found in aggression, nonverbal communication, influenceability, sexual behavior, assertiveness, anxiety, trust, and tender-mindedness.

• Evolutionary theorists maintain that gender differences transcend culture because males and females have confronted different adaptive demands over the course of human history. Extensive evidence suggests that prenatal hormones contribute to human gender differences, but the research is marred by interpretive problems. Research linking gender differences to cerebral specialization is intriguing, but much remains to be learned.

• A vast research literature shows that gender differences are shaped by socialization processes. Operant conditioning, observational learning, and self-socialization contribute to the development of gender differences. Families, schools, and the media are among the main sources of gender-role socialization.

Key Ideas

Progress Before Birth: Prenatal Development

◆ Prenatal development proceeds through the germinal, embryonic, and fetal stages as the zygote is differentiated into a human organism. During this period, development may be affected by maternal malnutrition, maternal drug use, and some maternal illnesses. Many problems can be avoided if expectant mothers have access to good health care.

The Wondrous Years of Childhood

◆ Visual acuity improves throughout the first year. In comparison, hearing is more advanced during the early months of life. Motor development follows cephalocaudal and proximodistal trends.

◆ Early motor development depends on both maturation and learning. Developmental norms for motor skills and other types of development are only group averages, and parents should not be alarmed if their children's progress does not match these norms exactly.

◆ Temperamental differences among children are apparent during the first few months of life. These differences in temperament are fairly stable and may have far-reaching effects because of the reactions they tend to elicit from parents.

◆ Infants' attachments to their mothers develop gradually. Reinforcement explanations of attachment appear inadequate in light of the Harlows' research with infant monkeys. Bowlby's theory that attachment is biologically programmed has been influential.

◆ Research shows that attachment emerges out of an interplay between infant and mother. Infant-mother attachments fall into three categories: secure, anxious-ambivalent, and avoidant. Bonding during the first few hours after birth does not appear to be crucial to secure attachment. The effects of day care on attachment are a source of concern, but the evidence is hotly debated. Cultural variations in child rearing can affect the patterns of attachment seen in a society.

◆ Erik Erikson's theory of personality development proposes that individuals evolve through eight stages over the life span. In each stage the person wrestles with changes (crises) in social relationships.

◆ According to Piaget's theory of cognitive development, the key advance during the sensorimotor period is the child's gradual recognition of the permanence of objects. The preoperational period is marked by certain deficiencies in thinking—notably, centration, irreversibility, and egocentrism.

◆ During the concrete operations period, children develop the ability to perform operations on mental representations, making them capable of conservation and hierarchical classification. The stage of formal operations ushers in more abstract, systematic, and logical thought.

◆ The other major approach to the study of cognitive development is rooted in information-processing models. The information-processing perspective has proven especially useful in explaining progress in attention and memory ability.

◆ According to Kohlberg, moral reasoning progresses through three levels that are related to age and determined by cognitive development. Age-related progress in moral reasoning has been found in research, although there is a great deal of overlap between adjacent stages.

◆ Altruism and aggression, two important aspects of social behavior, tend to increase and decrease, respectively, with age. Our Featured Study showed how exposure to television violence correlates with peer-rated aggression, even in very young children.

The Transition of Adolescence

◆ The growth spurt at puberty is a prominent event involving the development of reproductive maturity and secondary sex characteristics. Adolescence appears no more tumultuous than other periods of life, in spite of the recent surge in attempted suicide by adolescents.

◆ According to Erikson, the key challenge of adolescence is to make some progress toward a sense of identity. Marcia identified four patterns of identity formation.

The Expanse of Adulthood

◆ During adulthood, personality is marked by both stability and change. Doubts have surfaced about whether a midlife crisis is a normal developmental transition. Many landmarks in adult development involve transitions in family relationships, including adjusting to marriage, parenthood, and the empty nest.

◆ Vocational development tends to proceed through stages of exploration, establishment, maintenance, and decline. Patterns of vocational development are less predictable in females than males.

◆ During adulthood, age-related physical transitions include changes in appearance, neuron losses, sensory losses, and hormonal changes. In the cognitive domain, mental speed declines, but many people remain very productive well into old age.

Putting It in Perspective

◆ Many of our seven integrative themes stood out in this chapter. But above all else, our discussion of development showed how heredity and environment interactively shape behavior.

Application: Understanding Gender Differences

◆ Gender differences in behavior are fewer in number and smaller in magnitude than gender stereotypes suggest. Research reviews suggest that there are genuine (albeit small) gender differences in verbal ability, mathematical ability, spatial ability, aggression, nonverbal communication, influenceability, sexual behavior, and several personality traits.

◆ Evolutionary theorists believe that gender differences reflect the influence of natural selection. Some research *does* link gender differences in humans to hormones and brain organization, but the research is marred by interpretive problems. Operant conditioning, observational learning, and self-socialization contribute to the development of gender differences.

Key Terms

Accommodation
Age of viability
Aggression
Altruism
Animism
Assimilation
Attachment
Centration
Cephalocaudal trend
Cognitive development
Conservation
Cross-sectional design
Dementia
Development
Developmental norms
Egocentrism
Embryonic stage
Epigenetic principle
Family life cycle
Fetal alcohol syndrome
Fetal stage
Gender
Gender differences
Gender roles
Gender stereotypes
Germinal stage
Irreversibility
Longitudinal design
Maturation
Menarche
Mentor
Meta-analysis
Motor development
Object permanence
Placenta
Prenatal period
Primary sex characteristics
Proximodistal trend
Puberty
Pubescence
Secondary sex characteristics
Separation anxiety
Sex
Social clock
Socialization
Stage
Temperament
Visual cliff
Zygote

Key People

Mary Ainsworth
John Bowlby
Erik Erikson
Harry and Margaret Harlow
Lawrence Kohlberg
Jean Piaget
Alexander Thomas and Stella Chess

Practice Test

1. The stage of prenatal development during which the developing organism is most vulnerable to injury is the:
   A. zygotic stage.
   B. germinal stage.
   C. fetal stage.
   D. embryonic stage.

2. The cephalocaudal trend in the motor development of children can be described simply as a:
   A. head-to-foot direction.
   B. center-outward direction.
   C. foot-to-head direction.
   D. body-appendages direction.

3. Developmental norms:
   A. can be used to make extremely precise predictions about the age at which an individual child will reach various developmental milestones.
   B. indicate the maximum age at which a child can reach a particular developmental milestone and still be considered "normal."
   C. indicate the average age at which individuals reach various developmental milestones.
   D. involve both a and b.

4. When the development of the same subjects is studied over a period of time, the study is called a:
   A. cross-sectional study.
   B. life history study.
   C. longitudinal study.
   D. sequential study.

5. Support would have been provided for the behavioral notion that the infant-caregiver attachment is simply a result of conditioning if Harlow's monkeys had favored:
   A. the substitute monkey mother that provided milk.
   B. the cloth-covered monkey mother whether it provided milk or not.
   C. neither of the two substitute monkey mothers.
   D. the two substitute monkey mothers equally.

6. During the second year of life, toddlers begin to take some personal responsibility for feeding, dressing, and bathing themselves in an attempt to establish what Erikson calls a sense of:
   A. superiority.
   B. industry.
   C. generativity.
   D. autonomy.

7. Five-year-old David watches as you pour water from a short, wide glass into a tall, narrow one. He says there is now more water than before. This response demonstrates that:
   A. David understands the concept of conservation.
   B. David does not understand the concept of conservation.
   C. David's cognitive development is "behind" for his age.
   D. b and c.

8. Which of the following is *not* one of the criticisms of Piaget's theory of cognitive development?
   A. Piaget may have underestimated the cognitive skills of children in some areas.
   B. Piaget may have underestimated the influence of cultural factors on cognitive development.
   C. The theory does not clearly address the issue of individual differences in development.
   D. Evidence for the theory is based on children's answers to questions.

9. If a child's primary reason for not drawing pictures on the living room wall with crayons is to avoid the punishment that would inevitably follow this behavior, she would be said to be at which level of moral development?
   A. conventional
   B. postconventional
   C. preconventional
   D. unconventional

10. The Featured Study on the effects of exposure to media violence found that:
    A. the link between media violence and aggressiveness may be forged at a very young age.
    B. the link between media violence and aggressiveness is significantly stronger for girls than for boys.
    C. media violence plays the most significant causal role in aggressiveness in children.
    D. all of the above.

11. Girls who mature _____ and boys who mature _____ feel especially uneasy about puberty and self-conscious about their looks.
    A. early; early
    B. early; late
    C. late; early
    D. late; late

12. Sixteen-year-old Foster wants to spend a few years experimenting with different lifestyles and careers before he settles on who and what he wants to be. Foster is in the adolescent phase called:
    A. moratorium.
    B. foreclosure.
    C. identity achievement.
    D. identity diffusion.

13. Bernardo, a newlywed, believes a marriage is "equal" if it's based on mutual understanding and trust. His new wife, Leslie, says an equal marriage means husband and wife sharing chores and responsibilities. Which of the following is true about the views of these two?
    A. Bernardo's views are typical for men; Leslie's are not typical for women.
    B. Leslie's views are typical for women; Bernardo's are not typical for men.
    C. Both have views that are typical for their gender.
    D. Neither has views that are typical for their gender.

14. Which of the following is *not* a way in which men's and women's career development differ?
    A. For women, there is not a clear path leading to success.
    B. Women are more likely to experience career interruptions.
    C. Many women subordinate their career goals to their husbands'.
    D. Because they typically occupy subordinate positions, women are more likely than men to have mentors.

15. Males have been found to differ slightly from females in three well-documented areas of mental abilities. Which of the following is *not* one of these?
    A. verbal ability
    B. mathematical ability
    C. intelligence
    D. visual-spatial abilities

Answers

1	D	Pages 422–424	6	D	Page 436	11	B Page 450
2	A	Page 428	7	B	Pages 438–439	12	A Page 452
3	C	Pages 429–430	8	D	Page 441	13	C Page 455
4	C	Page 430	9	C	Page 444	14	D Page 462
5	A	Page 432	10	A	Page 447	15	C Page 466

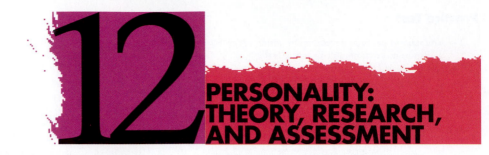

12 PERSONALITY: THEORY, RESEARCH, AND ASSESSMENT

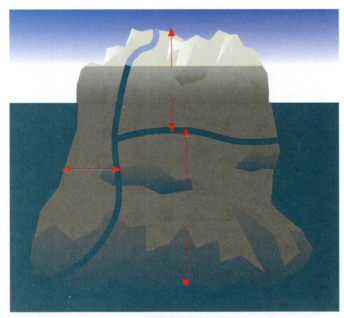

I have a close friend who has to be one of the world's great optimists. A few years ago, he was riding an all-terrain vehicle in a California desert and flipped it into the air. The vehicle landed on him, shattering one of his legs. Two days later, he called me long-distance (from the hospital) to tell me about the accident. Still in great pain from extensive surgery, and facing more operations, not to mention a year or two on crutches, he was joking about it. He was in his usual—make that unalterable—cheerful, lighthearted mood. Most of us, of course, would have been rather dejected and gloomy under such circumstances. Consider another example. A few years ago, I went with the same friend to see the Chicago Cubs play a doubleheader. For most Cubs fans such as ourselves, the baseball that day was boring and depressing. In the first game, the Cubs were shut out, losing 1 to 0. In game two, after eight innings, they still hadn't scored a run and were getting trounced, 9 to 0, when I said, "Let's get out of here. This is disgusting." He turned to me in genuine surprise, saying, "What? Leave? We're gonna rally!"

My friend's optimism is a key facet of his *personality*. In fact, it dominates his behavior to such an extent that Gordon Allport, an influential personality theorist, would call it a *cardinal trait*. In this chapter, we'll explore the mystery of personality. What exactly is personality? How does it develop over time? For instance, how does someone like my friend get to be so upbeat and optimistic? Is personality largely biological in origin, or is experience critical? What makes for a healthy personality?

Traditionally, the study of personality has been dominated by "grand theories," broad in scope, attempting to explain a great many facets of behavior. Our discussion will reflect this emphasis, as we'll devote most of our time to the sweeping theories of Freud, Jung, Skinner, Rogers, and several others.

However, in recent decades the study of personality has shifted toward narrower research programs that examine specific aspects of personality (Singer & Kolligian, 1987). The last section of the chapter will reflect this trend, as we review several contemporary empirical approaches to personality. In the chapter Application, we'll discuss how psychological tests are used to measure various aspects of personality.

THE NATURE OF PERSONALITY

Personality is a complex hypothetical construct that has been defined in a variety of ways. Let's take a closer look at the concepts of personality and personality traits.

Defining Personality: Consistency and Distinctiveness

What does it mean to say that my friend has an optimistic personality? This assertion indicates that he has a fairly *consistent tendency* to behave in a cheerful, hopeful, enthusiastic way, looking at the bright side of things, across a wide variety of situations. Although no one is entirely consistent in behavior, this quality of *consistency across situations* lies at the core of the concept of personality.

Distinctiveness is also central to the concept of personality. Personality is used to explain why not everyone acts the same in similar situations. If you were stuck in an elevator with three people, each might react differently. One might crack jokes to relieve the tension. Another might make ominous predictions that "we'll never get out of here." The third might calmly think about how to escape. These varied reactions to the same situation occur because each person has a different personality. Each person has traits that are seen in other people, but each individual has his or her own distinctive *set* of personality traits.

In summary, the concept of personality is used to explain (1) the stability in a person's behavior over time and across situations (consistency) and (2) the behavioral differences among people reacting to the same situation (distinctiveness). We can combine these ideas into the following definition: ***Personality* refers to an individual's unique constellation of consistent behavioral traits.** Let's look more closely at the concept of *traits*.

Personality Traits: Dispositions and Dimensions

Everyone makes remarks like "Jan is very *conscientious*." Or you might assert that "Bill is too *timid* to succeed in that job." These descriptive statements refer to personality traits. **A *personality trait* is a durable disposition to behave in a particular way in a variety of situations.** Adjectives such as *honest, dependable, moody, impulsive, suspicious, anxious, excitable, domineering*, and *friendly* describe dispositions that represent personality traits.

Most approaches to personality assume that some traits are more basic than others. According to this notion, a small number of fundamental traits determine other, more superficial traits. For example, a person's tendency to be impulsive, restless, irritable, boisterous, and impatient might all be derived from a more basic tendency to be excitable.

Gordon Allport (1937, 1961) was one of the first theorists to make systematic distinctions among traits in terms of their importance. After sifting through an unabridged dictionary, Allport identified over 4500 personality traits. To impose some order on this chaos, he distinguished three levels of traits. **A *cardinal trait* is a dominant trait that characterizes nearly all of a person's behavior.** The influence of a cardinal trait is overwhelming. Mother Teresa's altruism, Machiavelli's manipulativeness, and William F. Buckley's arrogance would be examples of cardinal traits. According to Allport, cardinal traits are rare. Only a small minority of people display them.

In Allport's model, **central traits are prominent, general dispositions found in anyone.** They're the basic building blocks of personality. Central traits are influential, but they don't rule behavior in the way that cardinal traits do. How many central traits does a person usually have? Allport's research led him to conclude that most people have only five to ten central traits.

At the bottom of Allport's hierarchy are secondary traits. **Secondary traits are dispositions that surface in some situations but not others.** For example, a person might be passive in most circumstances but highly aggressive in dealing with subordinates at work. This occasional aggressiveness would be a secondary trait.

Following Allport's lead, a number of psychologists have taken on the challenge of identifying the basic traits that form the core of personality. For example, Raymond Cattell (1950, 1966, 1990) has used the statistical procedure of *factor analysis* to reduce Allport's list of traits to just 16 basic dimensions of personality. As you may recall from Chapter 9, **in *factor analysis*, correlations among many variables are analyzed to identify closely related clusters of variables.** If the measurements of a number of variables (in this case, personality traits) correlate highly with one another, the assumption is that a single factor is influencing all of them. Factor analysis is used to identify these hidden factors. In factor analyses of personality traits, these hidden factors are viewed as very basic, higher-order traits that determine less basic, more specific traits. Based on his factor analytic work, Cattell concluded that an individual's personality can be described completely by measuring just 16 traits. The 16 crucial traits are listed in Figure 12.20, which can be found in the chapter Application, where we discuss a personality test that Cattell designed to assess these traits.

Robert McCrae and Paul Costa (1985, 1987) have used factor analysis to arrive at an even simpler, *five-factor model of personality* (see Figure 12.1). McCrae and Costa maintain that most personality traits are derived from just five higher-order traits that have come to be known as the "Big Five": extraversion, neuroticism, openness to experience, agreeableness, and conscientiousness. Let's take a closer look at these traits:

1. *Extraversion.* People who score high in extraversion are characterized as outgoing, sociable, upbeat, friendly, assertive, and gregarious. Referred to as *positive emotionality* in some trait models (Church, 1994), extraversion has been studied extensively in research for many decades.

2. *Neuroticism.* People who score high in neuroticism tend to be anxious, hostile, self-conscious, insecure, and vulnerable. Like extraversion, this trait has been the subject of thousands of studies. In some trait models it is called *negative emotionality* (Church, 1994).

3. *Openness to experience.* Openness is associated with curiosity, flexibility, vivid fantasy, imaginativeness, artistic sensitivity, and unconventional attitudes. McCrae (1996) maintains that its importance has been underestimated. Citing evidence that openness fosters liberalism, he argues that this trait is the key determinant of people's political attitudes and ideology.

4. *Agreeableness.* Those who score high in agreeableness tend to be sympathetic, trusting, cooperative, modest, and straightforward. People who score at the opposite end of this personality dimension are characterized as suspicious, antagonistic, and aggressive.

5. *Conscientiousness.* Conscientious people tend to be diligent, disciplined, well-organized, punctual, and dependable. Referred to as *constraint* in some trait models, conscientiousness is associated

with higher self-esteem and productivity (Costa, McCrae & Dye, 1991).

Like Cattell, McCrae and Costa maintain that personality can be described adequately by measuring the basic traits that they've identified. Their bold claim has been supported in many studies by other researchers, and the five-factor model has become the dominant conception of personality structure in contemporary psychology (Goldberg, 1993; John, 1990: Ozer & Reise, 1994). However, some theorists have been critical of the model (McAdams, 1992; Tellegen, 1993). For example, Jack Block (1995) has questioned the generality of the model. He points out that the higher-order traits that emerge in factor analyses depend to some extent on the exact mix of the much larger set of specific traits that are measured in the first place. Thus, he asserts that the five-factor model is more arbitrary than widely appreciated. Other critics of the five-factor model maintain that more than five traits are necessary to account for most of the variation seen in human personality (Benet & Waller, 1995; Cattell, 1990; Wiggins, 1992). Ironically, other theorists have argued for three- or four-factor models of personality (Church & Burke, 1994; Eysenck, 1992).

The debate about how many dimensions are necessary to describe personality is likely to continue for many years to come. As you'll see throughout the chapter, the study of personality is an area in psychology that has a long history of "dueling theories." We'll divide these diverse personality theories into four broad groups that share certain assumptions, emphases, and interests: (1) psychodynamic perspectives, (2) behavioral perspectives, (3) humanistic perspectives, and (4) biological perspectives. We'll begin our discussion of personal-

ity theories by examining the life and work of Sigmund Freud.

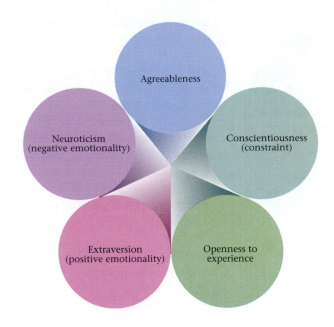

Figure 12.1
The five-factor model of personality. Trait models attempt to analyze personality into its basic dimensions. McCrae and Costa (1985, 1987) maintain that personality can be described adequately with the five higher-order traits identified here.

Recap of Key Points

• The concept of personality explains the consistency in people's behavior over time and across situations while also explaining their distinctiveness. Allport distinguished among three levels of traits: cardinal traits, central traits, and secondary traits.

• Factor analysis can be used to identify higher-order traits from which specific traits are derived. There is considerable debate as to how many trait dimensions are necessary to account for the variation in personality.

• Nonetheless, the five-factor model has become the dominant conception of personality structure. The "Big Five" personality traits are extraversion, neuroticism, openness to experience, agreeableness, and conscientiousness.

PSYCHODYNAMIC PERSPECTIVES

Psychodynamic theories **include all the diverse theories descended from the work of Sigmund Freud, which focus on unconscious mental forces.** Freud inspired many brilliant scholars who followed in his intellectual footsteps. Some of these followers simply refined and updated Freud's theory. Others veered off in new directions and established independent, albeit related, schools of thought. Today, the psychodynamic umbrella covers a large collection of loosely related theories

that we can only sample from in this text. In this chapter, we'll examine the ideas of Sigmund Freud in some detail. Then we'll take a briefer look at the psychodynamic theories of Carl Jung and Alfred Adler.

Freud's Psychoanalytic Theory 10a

Born in 1856, Sigmund Freud grew up in a middle-class Jewish home in Vienna, Austria. He showed an early interest in intellectual pursuits and became

"No one who, like me, conjures up the most evil of those half-tamed demons that inhabit the human beast, and seeks to wrestle with them, can expect to come through the struggle unscathed."

SIGMUND FREUD

Freud's psychoanalytic theory was based on decades of clinical work. He treated a great many patients in the consulting room pictured here. The room contains numerous artifacts from other cultures—and the original psychoanalytic couch.

an intense, hardworking young man, driven to achieve fame. He experienced his share of inner turmoil and engaged in regular self-analysis for over 40 years. Freud lived in a Victorian era, marked by sexual repression. His life was also affected by the first great World War, which devastated Europe, and by the growing anti-Semitism of the times. We'll see that the sexual repression and aggressive hostilities that Freud witnessed left their mark on his view of human nature.

Freud was a physician specializing in neurology when he began his medical practice in Vienna toward the end of the 19th century. Like other neurologists in his era, he often treated people troubled by nervous problems such as irrational fears, obsessions, and anxieties. Eventually he devoted himself to the treatment of mental disorders using an innovative procedure he had developed, called *psychoanalysis,* that required lengthy verbal interactions with patients during which Freud probed deeply into their lives.

Freud's (1901, 1924, 1940) *psychoanalytic theory* grew out of his decades of interactions with his clients in psychoanalysis. Psychoanalytic theory attempts to explain personality, motivation, and psychological disorders by focusing on the influence of early childhood experiences, on unconscious motives and conflicts, and on the methods people use to cope with their sexual and aggressive urges.

Most of Freud's contemporaries were uncomfortable with his theory for at least three reasons. First, in arguing that people's behavior is governed by unconscious factors of which they are

unaware, Freud made the disconcerting suggestion that individuals are not masters of their own minds. Second, in claiming that adult personalities are shaped by childhood experiences and other factors beyond one's control, he suggested that people are not masters of their own destinies. Third, by emphasizing the great importance of how people cope with their sexual urges, he offended those who held the conservative, Victorian values of his time.

Thus, Freud endured a great deal of criticism, condemnation, and outright ridicule, even after his work began to attract more favorable attention. Consider the following recollection from one of Freud's friends: "In those days when one mentioned Freud's name everyone would begin to laugh, as if someone had told a joke. Freud was the queer fellow who wrote a book about dreams . . . He was the man who saw sex in everything. It was considered bad taste to bring up Freud's name in the presence of ladies" (Donn, 1988, p. 57). Let's examine the ideas that generated so much controversy.

Structure of Personality

Freud divided personality structure into three components: the id, the ego, and the superego (see Figure 12.2). He saw a person's behavior as the outcome of interactions among these three components.

The *id* is the primitive, instinctive component of personality that operates according to the pleasure principle. Freud referred to the id as the reservoir of psychic energy. By this he meant that the id houses the raw biological urges (to eat, sleep, defecate, copulate, and so on) that energize human behavior. The id operates according to the *pleasure principle,* **which demands immediate gratification of its urges.** The id engages in *primary-process thinking,* which is primitive, illogical, irrational, and fantasy oriented.

The *ego* is the decision-making component of personality that operates according to the reality principle. The ego mediates between the id, with its forceful desires for immediate satisfaction, and the external social world, with its expectations and norms regarding suitable behavior. The ego considers social realities—society's norms, etiquette, rules, and customs—in deciding how to behave. The ego is guided by the *reality principle,* **which seeks to delay gratification of the id's urges until appropriate outlets and situations can be found.** In short, to stay out of trouble, the

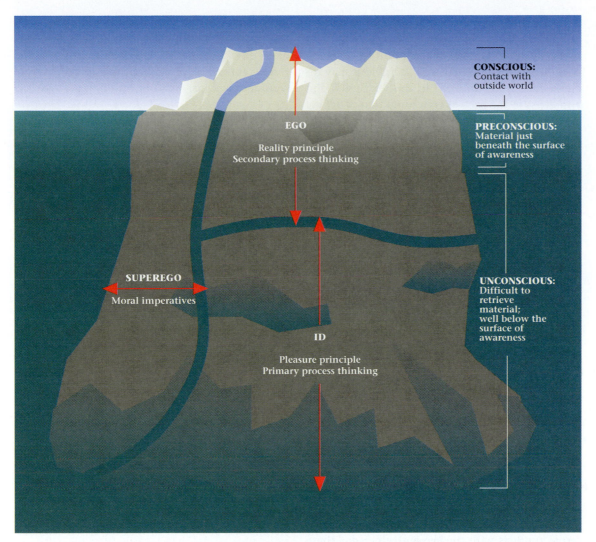

EGO

Reality principle
Secondary process thinking

SUPEREGO

Moral imperatives

ID

Pleasure principle
Primary process thinking

CONSCIOUS:
Contact with
outside world

PRECONSCIOUS:
Material just
beneath the surface
of awareness

UNCONSCIOUS:
Difficult to
retrieve
material;
well below the
surface of
awareness

Figure 12.2
Freud's model of person-ality structure. Freud theorized that people have three levels of awareness: the conscious, the preconscious, and the unconscious. The enormous size of the unconscious is often dramatized by comparing it to the portion of an iceberg that lies beneath the water's surface. Freud also divided personality structure into three components—id, ego, and superego—which operate according to different principles and exhibit different modes of thinking. In Freud's model, the id is entirely unconscious, but the ego and superego operate at all three levels of awareness.

ego often works to tame the unbridled desires of the id.

In the long run, the ego wants to maximize gratification, just as the id does. However, the ego engages in *secondary-process thinking,* which is relatively rational, realistic, and oriented toward problem solving. Thus, the ego strives to avoid negative consequences from society and its representatives (for example, punishment by parents or teachers) by behaving "properly." It also attempts to achieve long-range goals that sometimes require putting off gratification.

While the ego concerns itself with practical realities, the *superego* **is the moral component of personality that incorporates social standards about what represents right and wrong.** Throughout their lives, but especially during childhood, people receive training about what constitutes good and bad behavior. Many social norms regarding morality are eventually internalized. The superego emerges out of the ego at around 3 to 5 years of

age. In some people, the superego can become irrationally demanding in its striving for moral perfection. Such people are plagued by excessive feelings of guilt.

According to Freud, the id, ego, and superego are distributed differently across three levels of awareness, which we'll describe next.

Levels of Awareness

Perhaps Freud's most enduring insight was his recognition of how unconscious forces can influence behavior. He inferred the existence of the unconscious from a variety of observations that he made with his patients. For example, he noticed that "slips of the tongue" often revealed a person's true feelings. He also realized that his patients' dreams often expressed hidden desires. Most important, through psychoanalysis he often helped patients to discover feelings and conflicts of which they had previously been unaware.

Freud contrasted the unconscious with the

conscious and preconscious, creating three levels of awareness. **The _conscious_ consists of whatever one is aware of at a particular point in time.** For example, at this moment your conscious may include the train of thought in this text and a dim awareness in the back of your mind that your eyes are getting tired and you're beginning to get hungry. **The _preconscious_ contains material just beneath the surface of awareness that can easily be retrieved.** Examples might include your middle name, what you had for supper last night, or an argument you had with a friend yesterday. **The _unconscious_ contains thoughts, memories, and desires that are well below the surface of conscious awareness but that nonetheless exert great influence on behavior.** Examples of material that might be found in your unconscious include a forgotten trauma from childhood, hidden feelings of hostility toward a parent, and repressed sexual desires.

Freud's conception of the mind is often compared to an iceberg that has most of its mass hidden beneath the water's surface (see Figure 12.2). He believed that the unconscious (the mass below the surface) is much larger than the conscious or preconscious. As you can see in Figure 12.2, he proposed that the ego and superego operate at all three levels of awareness. In contrast, the id is entirely unconscious, expressing its urges at a conscious level through the ego. Of course, the id's desires for immediate satisfaction often trigger internal conflicts with the ego and superego. These conflicts play a key role in Freud's theory.

Conflict and the Tyranny of Sex and Aggression

Freud assumed that behavior is the outcome of an ongoing series of internal conflicts. He saw internal battles between the id, ego, and superego as routine. Why? Because the id wants to gratify its urges immediately, but the norms of civilized society frequently dictate otherwise. For example, your id might feel an urge to clobber a co-worker who constantly irritates you. However, society frowns on such behavior, so your ego would try to hold this urge in check. Hence, you would find yourself in conflict. You may be experiencing conflict at this very moment. In Freudian terms, your id may be secretly urging you to abandon reading this chapter so that you can fix a snack and watch some television. Your ego may be weighing this appealing option against your society-induced need to excel in school.

Freud believed that people's lives are dominated by conflict. He asserted that individuals career from one conflict to another. The following scenario provides a concrete illustration of how the three components of personality interact to create constant conflicts:

Imagine lurching across your bed to shut off your alarm clock as it rings obnoxiously. It's 7 A.M. and time to get up for your history class. However, your id (operating according to the pleasure principle) urges you to return to the immediate gratification of additional sleep. Your ego (operating according to the reality principle) points out that you really must go to class since you haven't been able to decipher the textbook on your own. Your id (in its typical unrealistic fashion) smugly assures you that you will get the A grade that you need and suggests lying back to dream about how impressed your roommates will be. Just as you're relaxing, your superego jumps into the fray. It tries to make you feel guilty about all the money your parents paid in tuition for the class that you're about to skip. You haven't even gotten out of bed yet, but there's already a pitched battle in your psyche.

Let's say your ego wins the battle. You pull yourself out of bed and head for class. On the way, you pass a donut shop and your id clamors for cinnamon rolls. Your ego reminds you that you're supposed to be on a diet. Your id wins this time. After you've attended your history lecture, your ego reminds you that you need to do some library research for a paper in philosophy. However, your id insists on returning to your apartment to watch some sitcom reruns. As you reenter your apartment, you're overwhelmed by how messy it is. It's your roommates' mess, and your id suggests that you tell them off. As you're about to lash out, however, your ego convinces you that diplomacy will be more effective. Three sitcoms later you find that you're in a debate with yourself about whether to go to the gym to work out or to the student union to watch MTV. It's only midafternoon—and already you've been through a series of internal conflicts.

Freud believed that conflicts centering on sexual and aggressive impulses are especially likely to have far-reaching consequences. Why did he emphasize sex and aggression? Two reasons were prominent in his thinking. First, he thought that sex and aggression are subject to more complex and ambiguous social controls than other basic motives. The norms governing sexual and aggressive behavior are subtle, and people often get inconsistent messages about what's appropriate. Thus, Freud believed that these two drives are the source of much confusion. Second, he noted that the sexual and aggressive drives are thwarted more regularly than other basic biological urges. Think about it: If you get hungry or thirsty, you can simply head for a nearby vending machine or a drinking fountain. But if a department store clerk infuriates you, you aren't likely to reach across the counter and slug him or her. Likewise, when you see a person who inspires lustful urges, you don't normally walk up and propose a tryst in a nearby broom closet. There's nothing comparable to vending machines or drinking fountains for the satisfaction of sexual and aggressive urges. Freud ascribed great importance to these needs because social norms dictate that they be routinely frustrated.

Anxiety and Defense Mechanisms

Most internal conflicts are trivial and are quickly resolved one way or the other. Occasionally, however, a conflict will linger for days, months, or even years, creating internal tension. More often than not, such prolonged and troublesome conflicts involve sexual and aggressive impulses that society wants to tame. These conflicts are often played out entirely in the unconscious. Although you may not be aware of these unconscious battles, they can produce *anxiety* that slips to the surface of conscious awareness. The anxiety can be attributed to your ego worrying about (1) the id getting out of control and doing something terrible that leads to severe negative consequences or (2) the superego getting out of control and making you feel guilty about a real or imagined transgression.

The arousal of anxiety is a crucial event in Freud's theory of personality functioning (see Figure 12.3). Anxiety is distressing, so people try to rid themselves of this unpleasant emotion any way they can. This effort to ward off anxiety often involves the use of defense mechanisms. *Defense mechanisms* **are largely unconscious reactions that protect a person from unpleasant emotions such as anxiety and guilt.** Typically, they're mental maneuvers that work through self-deception. Consider *rationalization,* **which is creating false but plausible excuses to justify unacceptable behavior.** For example, after cheating someone in a business transaction, you might reduce your guilt by rationalizing that "everyone does it."

According to Freud, the most basic defense mechanism is repression, which is frequently used in conjunction with other defenses. *Repression* **is keeping distressing thoughts and feelings buried in the unconscious.** People tend to repress desires that make them feel guilty, conflicts that make them anxious, and memories that are painful. Repression has been called "motivated forgetting." If you forget a dental appointment or the

name of someone you don't like, repression may be at work.

Self-deception can also be seen in projection and displacement. *Projection* **is attributing one's own thoughts, feelings, or motives to another.** Usually, the thoughts one projects onto others are thoughts that would make one feel guilty. For example, if lusting for a co-worker makes you feel guilty, you might attribute any latent sexual tension between the two of you to the *other person's* desire to seduce you. *Displacement* **is diverting emotional feelings (usually anger) from their original source to a substitute target.** If your boss gives you a hard time at work and you come home and slam the door, kick the dog, and scream at your spouse, you're displacing your anger onto irrelevant targets. Unfortunately, social constraints often force people to hold back their anger, and they end up lashing out at the people they love most.

Other prominent defense mechanisms include reaction formation, regression, and identification. *Reaction formation* **is behaving in a way that's exactly the opposite of one's true feelings.** Guilt about sexual desires often leads to reaction formation. For example, Freud theorized that many males who ridicule homosexuals are defending against their own latent homosexual impulses. As far-fetched as this idea may sound, it was supported in a recent study of homophobic men (Adams, Wright, & Lohr, 1996). The telltale sign of reaction formation is the exaggerated quality of the opposite behavior. *Regression* **is a reversion to immature patterns of behavior.** When anxious about their self-worth, some adults respond with childish boasting and bragging (as opposed to subtle efforts to impress others). For example, a fired executive having difficulty finding a new job might start making ridiculous statements about his incomparable talents and achievements. Such bragging is regressive when it's marked by massive exaggerations that virtually anyone can see through. *Identification* **is bolstering self-esteem by forming an imaginary or real alliance with some person or group.** Youngsters often shore up precarious feelings of self-worth by identifying with

Figure 12.3
Freud's model of personality dynamics. According to Freud, unconscious conflicts between the id, ego, and superego sometimes lead to anxiety. This discomfort may lead to the use of defense mechanisms, which may temporarily relieve anxiety.

Intrapsychic conflict (between id, ego, and superego) → Anxiety → Reliance on defense mechanisms

TABLE 12.1 DEFENSE MECHANISMS, WITH EXAMPLES

Defense Mechanism	Definition	Example
Repression	Keeping distressing thoughts and feelings buried in the unconscious	A traumatized soldier has no recollection of the details of a close brush with death.
Projection	Attributing one's own thoughts, feelings, or motives to another	A woman who dislikes her boss thinks she likes her boss but feels that the boss doesn't like her.
Displacement	Diverting emotional feelings (usually anger) from their original source to a substitute target	After parental scolding, a young girl takes her anger out on her little brother.
Reaction formation	Behaving in a way that is exactly the opposite of one's true feelings	A parent who unconsciously resents a child spoils the child with outlandish gifts.
Regression	A reversion to immature patterns of behavior	An adult has a temper tantrum when he doesn't get his way.
Rationalization	Creating false but plausible excuses to justify unacceptable behavior	A student watches TV instead of studying, saying that "additional study wouldn't do any good anyway."
Identification	Bolstering self-esteem by forming an imaginary or real alliance with some person or group	An insecure young man joins a fraternity to boost his self-esteem.

Note: See Table 13.2 for additional examples of defense mechanisms.

rock stars, movie stars, or famous athletes. Adults may join exclusive country clubs or civic organizations as a means of identification.

Additional examples of the defense mechanisms we've described can be found in Table 12.1. If you see defensive maneuvers that you've used, you

shouldn't be surprised. According to Freud, everyone uses defense mechanisms to some extent. They become problematic only when people depend on them excessively. The seeds for psychological disorders are sown only when defenses lead to wholesale distortion of reality.

A great variety of theorists have made extensive additions to Freud's original list of defenses (Vaillant, 1992). We'll examine some of these additional defense mechanisms in the next chapter, when we discuss the role of defenses in coping with stress. For now, however, let's turn our attention to Freud's ideas about the development of personality.

Development: Psychosexual Stages

Freud believed that "the child is father to the man." In fact, he made the rather startling assertion that the basic foundation of an individual's personality has been laid down by the tender age of 5. To shed light on these crucial early years, Freud formulated a stage theory of development. He emphasized how young children deal with their immature but powerful sexual urges (he used the term *sexual* in a general way to refer to many urges for physical pleasure). According to Freud, these sexual urges shift in focus as children progress from one stage of development to another. Indeed, the names for the stages (oral, anal, genital, and so on) are based on where children are focus-

---

CONCEPT CHECK 12.1
Identifying Defense Mechanisms

Check your understanding of defense mechanisms by identifying specific defenses in the story below. Each example of a defense mechanism is underlined, with a number beneath it. Write in the defense at work in each case in the numbered spaces after the story. The answers are in Appendix A.

My girlfriend recently broke up with me after we had dated seriously for several years. At first, I cried a great deal and <u>locked myself in my room, where I pouted endlessly.</u> [1] I was sure that my former girlfriend felt as miserable as I did. <u>I told several friends that she was probably lonely and depressed.</u> [2] Later, I decided that I hated her. <u>I was happy about the breakup and talked about how much I was going to enjoy my newfound freedom.</u> [3] I went to parties and socialized a great deal and just forgot about her. It's funny—<u>at one point I couldn't even remember her phone number!</u> [4] Then I started pining for her again. But eventually I began to look at the situation more objectively. I realized that she had many faults and that <u>we were bound to break up sooner or later, so I was better off without her.</u> [5]

1._____   4._____

2._____   5._____

3._____

TABLE 12.2 FREUD'S STAGES OF PSYCHOSEXUAL DEVELOPMENT

Stage	Approximate Ages	Erotic Focus	Key Tasks and Experiences
Oral	0–1	Mouth (sucking, biting)	Weaning (from breast or bottle)
Anal	2–3	Anus (expelling or retaining feces)	Toilet training
Phallic	4–5	Genitals (masturbating)	Identifying with adult role models; coping with Oedipal crisis
Latency	6–12	None (sexually repressed)	Expanding social contacts
Genital	Puberty onward	Genitals (being sexually intimate)	Establishing intimate relationships; contributing to society through working

ing their erotic energy during that period. Thus, **psychosexual stages** are **developmental periods with a characteristic sexual focus that leave their mark on adult personality.**

Freud theorized that each psychosexual stage has its own, unique developmental challenges or tasks (see Table 12.2). The way these challenges are handled supposedly shapes personality. The notion of *fixation* plays an important role in this process. **Fixation is a failure to move forward from one stage to another as expected.** Essentially, the child's development stalls for a while. Fixation can be caused by *excessive gratification* of needs at a particular stage or by *excessive frustration* of those needs. Either way, fixations left over from childhood affect adult personality. Generally, fixation leads to an overemphasis on the psychosexual needs prominent during the fixated stage. Freud described a series of five psychosexual stages. Let's examine some of the highlights in this sequence.

ORAL STAGE. This stage encompasses the first year of life. During this period, the main source of erotic stimulation is the mouth (in biting, sucking, chewing, and so on). In Freud's view, the handling of the child's feeding experiences is crucial to subsequent development. He attributed considerable importance to the manner in which the child is weaned from the breast or the bottle. According to Freud, fixation at the oral stage could form the basis for obsessive eating or smoking later in life (among many other things).

ANAL STAGE. In their second year, children get their erotic pleasure from their bowel movements, through either the expulsion or retention of feces. The crucial event at this time is toilet training, which represents society's first systematic effort to regulate the child's biological urges. Severely pu-

nitive toilet training leads to a variety of possible outcomes. For example, excessive punishment might produce a latent feeling of hostility toward the "trainer," usually the mother. This hostility might generalize to women as a class. Another possibility is that heavy reliance on punitive measures could lead to an association between genital concerns and the anxiety that the punishment arouses. This genital anxiety derived from severe toilet training could evolve into anxiety about sexual activities later in life.

PHALLIC STAGE. Around age 4, the genitals become the focus for the child's erotic energy, largely through self-stimulation. During this pivotal stage, the *Oedipal complex* emerges. That is, little boys develop an erotically tinged preference for their mother. They also feel hostility toward their father, whom they view as a competitor for mom's affection. Similarly, little girls develop a special attachment to their father. Around the same time, they learn that little boys have very different genitals, and supposedly they develop *penis envy*. According to Freud, young girls feel hostile toward their mother because they blame her for their anatomical "deficiency."

To summarize, **in the *Oedipal complex* children manifest erotically tinged desires for their opposite-sex parent, accompanied by feelings of hostility toward their same-sex parent.** The name for this syndrome was taken from a tragic myth from ancient Greece. In this story, Oedipus was separated from his parents at birth. Not knowing the identity of his real parents, when he grew up he

Early childhood experiences such as toilet training (a parental attempt to regulate a child's biological urges) can influence an individual's personality, with consequences lasting throughout adulthood.

inadvertently killed his father and married his mother.

According to Freud, the way parents and children deal with the sexual and aggressive conflicts inherent in the Oedipal complex is of paramount importance. The child has to resolve the Oedipal dilemma by purging the sexual longings for the opposite-sex parent and by crushing the hostility felt toward the same-sex parent. In Freud's view, healthy psychosexual development hinges on the resolution of the Oedipal conflict. Why? Because continued hostility toward the same-sex parent may prevent the child from identifying adequately with that parent. Freudian theory predicts that without such identification, sex typing, conscience, and many other aspects of the child's development won't progress as they should.

LATENCY AND GENITAL STAGES. From around age 6 through puberty, the child's sexuality is largely suppressed—it becomes *latent*. Important events during this *latency stage* center on expanding social contacts beyond the immediate family. With puberty, the child progresses into the *genital stage*. Sexual urges reappear and focus on the genitals once again. At this point, sexual energy is normally channeled toward peers of the other sex, rather than toward oneself as in the phallic stage.

In arguing that the early years shape personality, Freud did not mean that personality development comes to an abrupt halt in middle childhood. However, he did believe that the foundation for adult personality has been solidly entrenched by this time. He maintained that future developments are rooted in early, formative experiences and that significant conflicts in later years are replays of crises from childhood.

In fact, Freud believed that unconscious sexual conflicts rooted in childhood experiences cause most personality disturbances. His steadfast belief in the psychosexual origins of psychological disorders eventually led to bitter theoretical disputes with two of his most brilliant colleagues: Carl Jung and Alfred Adler. Jung and Adler both argued that Freud overemphasized sexuality. Freud rejected their ideas, and the other two theorists felt compelled to go their own way, developing their own theories of personality.

Jung's Analytical Psychology

Carl Jung was born to middle-class Swiss parents in 1875. The son of a Protestant pastor, he was a deeply introverted, lonely child, but an excellent student. Jung had earned his medical degree and was an established young psychiatrist in Zurich when he began to write to Freud in 1906. When the two men had their first meeting, they were so taken by each other's insights, they talked nonstop for 13 hours! They exchanged 359 letters before their friendship and theoretical alliance were torn apart. Their relationship was ruptured irreparably in 1913 by a variety of theoretical disagreements.

Jung called his new approach *analytical psychology* to differentiate it from Freud's psychoanalytic theory. Jung's analytical psychology eventually attracted many followers. Perhaps because of his conflicts with Freud, Jung claimed to deplore the way schools of thought often become dogmatic, discouraging new ideas. Although many theorists came to characterize themselves as "Jungians," Jung himself often remarked, "I am not a Jungian" and said, "I do not want anybody to be a Jungian. I want people above all to be themselves" (van der Post, 1975).

Like Freud, Jung (1921, 1933) emphasized the unconscious determinants of personality. However, he proposed that the unconscious consists of two layers. The first layer, called the *personal unconscious,* is essentially the same as Freud's version of the unconscious. **The *personal unconscious* houses material that is not within one's conscious awareness because it has been repressed or forgotten.** In addition, Jung theorized the existence of a deeper layer he called the collective unconscious. **The *collective unconscious* is a storehouse of latent memory traces inherited from people's ancestral past.** According to Jung, each person shares the collective unconscious with the entire human race (see Figure 12.4). It contains the "whole spiritual heritage of mankind's evolution, born anew in the brain structure of every individual" (Jung, quoted in Campbell, 1971, p. 45).

Jung called these ancestral memories *archetypes*. They are not memories of actual, personal experiences. Instead, *archetypes* are emotionally charged images and thought forms that have universal meaning. These archetypal images and ideas show up frequently in dreams and are often manifested in a culture's use of symbols in art, literature, and religion. According to Jung, symbols from very different cultures often show striking similarities because they emerge from archetypes that are shared by the whole human race. For instance, Jung found numerous cultures in which the *mandala*, or "magic circle," has served

"I am not a Jungian . . . I do not want anybody to be a Jungian. I want people above all to be themselves."

CARL JUNG

Figure 12.4
Jung's vision of the collective unconscious. Much like Freud, Jung theorized that each person has conscious and unconscious levels of awareness. However, he also proposed that the entire human race shares a collective unconscious, which exists in the deepest reaches of everyone's awareness. He saw the collective unconscious as a store-house of hidden ancestral memories, called archetypes. Jung believed that important cultural symbols emerge from these universal arche-types. Thus, he argued that remarkable resemblances among symbols from disparate cultures (such as the mandalas shown here) are evidence of the existence of the collective unconscious.

Mandalas from various cultures

Russia

Navajo Indians

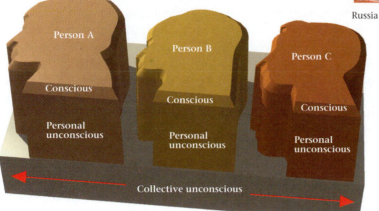

Tibet

as a symbol of the unified wholeness of the self (see Figure 12.4). Jung felt that an understanding of archetypal symbols helped him make sense of his patients' dreams. This was of great concern to him, as he thought that dreams contain important messages from the unconscious. Like Freud, he depended extensively on dream analysis in his treatment of patients.

Jung's unusual ideas about the collective uncon-scious had little impact on the mainstream of thinking in psychology. Their influence was felt more in other fields, such as anthropology, phi-losophy, art, and religious studies. However, many of Jung's other ideas *have* been incorporated into the mainstream of psychology. For instance, Jung was the first to describe the introverted (inner-directed) and extraverted (outer-directed) person-ality types. **Introverts tend to be preoccupied with the internal world of their own thoughts, feelings, and experiences.** Like Jung himself, they generally are contemplative and aloof. In contrast, **extraverts tend to be interested in the external world of people and things.** They're more likely to be outgoing, talkative, and friendly, instead of reclusive.

Adler's Individual Psychology

Like Freud, Alfred Adler grew up in Vienna in a middle-class Jewish home. He was a sickly child who struggled to overcome rickets and an almost fatal case of pneumonia. At home, he was over-shadowed by an exceptionally bright and success-ful older brother. Nonetheless, he went on to earn his medical degree, and he practiced ophthalmol-ogy and general medicine before his interest turned to psychiatry. He was a charter member of Freud's inner circle—the Vienna Psychoanalytic Society. However, he soon began to develop his own theory of personality, perhaps because he didn't want to be dominated once again by an "older brother" (Freud). His theorizing was denounced by Freud in 1911, and Adler was forced to resign from the Psychoanalytic Society. He took 9 of its 23 mem-bers with him to form his own organization. Adler's new approach to personality was christened *indi-vidual psychology*.

Like Jung, Adler (1917, 1927) argued that Freud had gone overboard in centering his theory on sexual conflicts. According to Adler, the foremost source of human motivation is a striving for

"The goal of the human soul is conquest, perfection, security, superiority."

ALFRED ADLER

superiority. In his view, this striving does not necessarily translate into the pursuit of dominance or high status. Adler saw **striving for superiority as a universal drive to adapt, improve oneself, and master life's challenges.** He noted that young children understandably feel weak and helpless in comparison with more competent older children and adults. These early inferiority feelings supposedly motivate them to acquire new skills and develop new talents. Thus, Adler maintained that striving for superiority is the prime goal of life, rather than physical gratification (as suggested by Freud).

Adler asserted that everyone has to work to overcome some feelings of inferiority—a process he called compensation. **Compensation involves efforts to overcome imagined or real inferiorities by developing one's abilities.** Adler believed that compensation is entirely normal. However, in some people inferiority feelings can become excessive, resulting in what is widely known today as an *inferiority complex*—exaggerated feelings of weakness and inadequacy. Adler thought that either parental pampering or parental neglect could cause an inferiority complex. Thus, he agreed with Freud on the importance of early childhood experiences, although he focused on different aspects of parent-child relations.

Adler explained personality disturbances by noting that excessive inferiority feelings can pervert the normal process of striving for superiority. He asserted that some people engage in *overcompensation* to conceal, even from themselves, their feelings of inferiority. Instead of working to master life's challenges, people with an inferiority complex work to achieve status, gain power over others, and acquire the trappings of success (fancy clothes, impressive cars, or whatever looks important to them). They tend to flaunt their success in an effort to cover up their underlying inferiority complex. However, the problem is that such people engage in unconscious self-deception, worrying more about *appearances* than *reality*.

Adler's theory stressed the social context of personality development. For instance, it was Adler who first focused attention on the possible importance of *birth order* as a factor governing personality. He noted that only children, firstborns, second children, and subsequent children enter different home environments that are likely to affect their personality. Thus, he hypothesized that children without siblings are often spoiled by excessive attention from parents, that firstborns often are problem children because they become upset when they're "dethroned" by a second child, and that second-born children tend to be competitive because they have to struggle to catch up with an older sibling. Adler's hypotheses stimulated hundreds of studies on the effects of birth order. This research has proved very interesting, although birth order effects have turned out to be weaker and less consistent than Adler expected (Ernst & Angst, 1983; Falbo & Polit, 1986).

Evaluating Psychodynamic Perspectives

The psychodynamic approach has provided a number of far-reaching, truly "grand" theories of personality. These theories yielded some bold new insights when they were first presented. Although one might argue about exact details of interpretation, psychodynamic theory and research have demonstrated that (1) unconscious forces can influence behavior, (2) internal conflict often plays a key role in generating psychological distress, and (3) early childhood experiences can influence adult personality (Kihlstrom, 1990; Westen, 1990). Many widely used concepts in psychology emerged out of psychodynamic theories, including the unconscious, defense mechanisms, introversion-extraversion, and the inferiority complex.

In addition to being praised, psychodynamic formulations have also been criticized on several grounds, including the following (Eysenck, 1990b; Fine, 1990; Macmillan, 1991):

1. *Poor testability.* Scientific investigations require testable hypotheses. Psychodynamic ideas have often been too vague and conjectural to permit a clear scientific test. For instance, how would you prove or disprove the assertion that the id is entirely unconscious?

2. *Inadequate evidence.* The empirical evidence on psychodynamic theories has often been characterized as "inadequate." For example, the evidence regarding Jung's collective unconscious is limited, speculative, and logically flawed (Neher, 1996). Psychodynamic theories depend too heavily on clinical case studies in which it's much too

Adler's theory has been used to analyze the tragic life of the legendary actress Marilyn Monroe (Ansbacher, 1970). During her childhood, Monroe suffered from parental neglect that left her with acute feelings of inferiority and a lack of social interest. Her inferiority feelings led her to overcompensate by flaunting her beauty, marrying celebrities (Joe DiMaggio and Arthur Miller), keeping film crews waiting for hours, and seeking the adoration of her fans.

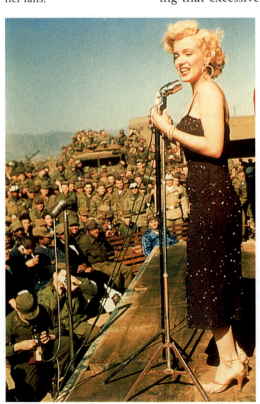

easy for clinicians to see what they expect to see. Recent reexaminations of Freud's own clinical work suggest that he frequently distorted his patients' case histories to make them mesh with his theory (Esterson, 1993; Sulloway, 1991). Another problem is that the subjects observed in clinical situations are not particularly representative of the population at large. Insofar as researchers have accumulated evidence on psychodynamic theories, the evidence has provided only modest support for the central hypotheses (Fisher & Greenberg, 1985, 1996).

3. *Sexism*. Many critics have argued that psychodynamic theories are characterized by a sexist bias against women. Freud believed that females' penis envy made them feel inferior to men. He also thought that females tended to develop weaker superegos and to be more prone to neurosis than men. The sex bias in modern psychodynamic theories has been reduced considerably. Nonetheless, the psychodynamic approach has generally provided a rather male-centered point of view (Chehrazi, 1986; Chodorow, 1978).

It's easy to ridicule Freud for concepts such as penis envy, and it's easy to point to Freudian ideas that have turned out to be wrong. However, you have to remember that Freud, Jung, and Adler began to fashion their theories about a century ago. It's not entirely fair to compare these theories to other models that are only a decade or two old. That's like asking the Wright brothers to race the Concorde. Freud and his colleagues deserve great credit for breaking new ground with their speculations about psychodynamics. In psychology as a whole, no other school has been as influential, with the exception of behaviorism, which we turn to next.

Recap of Key Points

• Psychodynamic approaches include all the theories derived from Freud's insights. Freud described personality structure in terms of three components—the id, ego, and superego—which are routinely involved in an ongoing series of internal conflicts.

• Freud described three levels of awareness: the conscious, the preconscious, and the unconscious. His theory emphasized the importance of unconscious processes.

• Freud theorized that conflicts centering on sex and aggression are especially likely to lead to significant anxiety. According to Freud, anxiety and other unpleasant emotions such as guilt are often warded off with defense mechanisms. Defenses such as repression, rationalization, projection, displacement, reaction formation, regression, and identification work primarily through self-deception.

• Freud believed that the first five years of life are extremely influential in shaping adult personality. He described a series of five psychosexual stages of development: oral, anal, phallic, latency, and genital.

• Certain experiences during these stages—such as weaning during the oral stage and toilet training during the anal stage—can have lasting effects on adult personality. Resolution of the Oedipal complex, which emerges during the phallic stage, is thought to be particularly critical to healthy development.

• Jung's most innovative concept was the collective unconscious, a storehouse of latent memory traces inherited from people's ancestral past. Archetypes are emotionally charged images that have universal meaning. Jung also provided the first description of introversion and extraversion.

• Adler's individual psychology emphasizes how people strive for superiority to compensate for their feelings of inferiority. He explained personality disturbances in terms of overcompensation and inferiority complexes. His theory alerted researchers to the possible influence of birth order on personality.

• Overall, psychodynamic theories have produced many ground-breaking insights about the unconscious, the role of internal conflict, and the importance of early childhood experiences in personality development. However, psychodynamic theories have been criticized for their poor testability, their inadequate base of empirical evidence, and their male-centered views.

BEHAVIORAL PERSPECTIVES

Behaviorism is a theoretical orientation based on the premise that scientific psychology should study only observable behavior. As we saw in Chapter 1, behaviorism has been a major school of thought in psychology since 1913, when John B. Watson began campaigning for the behavioral point of view. Research in the behavioral tradition has focused largely on learning. For many decades behaviorists devoted relatively little attention to the study of personality. However, their interest in personality began to pick up after John Dollard and Neal Miller (1950) attempted to translate

"The practice of looking inside the organism for an explanation of behavior has tended to obscure the variables which are immediately available for a scientific analysis. These variables lie outside the organism, in its immediate environment and in its environmental history. . . . The objection to inner states is not that they do not exist, but that they are not relevant."

B. F. SKINNER

Figure 12.5
A behavioral view of personality. Staunch behaviorists devote little attention to the structure of personality because it is unobservable, but they implicitly view personality as an individual's collection of response tendencies. A possible hierarchy of response tendencies for a specific stimulus situation is shown here.

selected Freudian ideas into behavioral terminology. Dollard and Miller showed that behavioral concepts could provide enlightening insights about the complicated subject of personality.

In this section, we'll examine three behavioral views of personality, as we discuss the ideas of B. F. Skinner, Albert Bandura, and Walter Mischel. For the most part, you'll see that behaviorists explain personality the same way they explain everything else—in terms of learning.

Skinner's Ideas Applied to Personality 10b

As we noted in Chapters 1 and 6, modern behaviorism's most prominent theorist has been B. F. Skinner, an American psychologist who lived from 1904 to 1990. After earning his doctorate in 1931, Skinner spent most of his career at Harvard University. There he achieved renown for his research on learning in lower organisms, mostly rats and pigeons. Skinner's (1953, 1957) principles of *operant conditioning* were never meant to be a theory of personality. However, his ideas have affected thinking in all areas of psychology and have been applied to the explanation of personality. Here we'll examine Skinner's views as they relate to personality structure and development.

Personality Structure: A View from the Outside

Skinner made no provision for internal personality structures similar to Freud's id, ego, and superego because such structures can't be observed. Following in the tradition of Watson's radical behaviorism, Skinner showed little interest in what goes on "inside" people. He argued that it's useless

to speculate about private, unobservable cognitive processes. Instead, he focused on how the external environment molds overt behavior. Indeed, he argued for a strong brand of *determinism,* asserting that behavior is fully determined by environmental stimuli. He claimed that free will is but an illusion, saying, "There is no place in the scientific position for a self as a true originator or initiator of action" (Skinner, 1974, p. 225).

How can Skinner's theory explain the consistency that can be seen in individuals' behavior? According to his view, people show some consistent patterns of behavior because they have some stable *response tendencies* that they have acquired through experience. These response tendencies may change in the future, as a result of new experience, but they're enduring enough to create a certain degree of consistency in a person's behavior. Implicitly, then, Skinner viewed an individual's personality as a *collection of response tendencies that are tied to various stimulus situations*. A specific situation may be associated with a number of response tendencies that vary in strength, depending on past conditioning (see Figure 12.5).

Personality Development as a Product of Conditioning

Skinner's theory accounts for personality development by explaining how various response tendencies are acquired through learning. He believed that most human responses are shaped by the type of conditioning that he described: operant conditioning. As we discussed in Chapter 6, Skinner maintained that environmental consequences—reinforcement, punishment, and extinction—determine people's patterns of responding. On the one hand, when responses are followed by favorable consequences (reinforcement), they are strengthened. For example, if your joking at a party pays off with favorable attention, your tendency to joke at parties will increase (see Figure 12.6). On the other hand, when responses lead to negative consequences (punishment), they are weakened. Thus, if your impulsive decisions always backfire, your tendency to be impulsive will decline.

Because response tendencies are constantly being strengthened or weakened by new experiences, Skinner's theory views personality development as a continuous, lifelong journey. Unlike Freud and many other theorists, Skinner saw no reason to break the developmental process into stages. Nor did he attribute special importance to early childhood experiences.

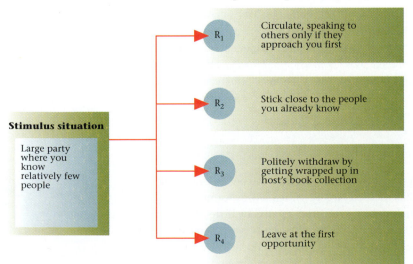

Operant response tendencies

Stimulus situation

Large party where you know relatively few people

R₁ — Circulate, speaking to others only if they approach you first

R₂ — Stick close to the people you already know

R₃ — Politely withdraw by getting wrapped up in host's book collection

R₄ — Leave at the first opportunity

Skinner believed that conditioning in humans operates much the same as in the rats and pigeons that he studied in his laboratory. Hence, he assumed that conditioning strengthens and weakens response tendencies "mechanically"—that is, without the person's conscious participation. Thus, Skinner was able to explain consistencies in behavior (personality) without being concerned about individuals' cognitive processes.

Skinner's ideas continue to be highly influential, but his mechanical, deterministic, noncognitive view of personality has not gone unchallenged by other behaviorists. In recent decades, several theorists have developed somewhat different behavioral models with a more cognitive emphasis.

Bandura's Social Learning Theory 10b

Albert Bandura is a modern theorist who has helped reshape the theoretical landscape of behaviorism. Bandura grew up in Canada and earned his doctorate in psychology at the University of Iowa. He has spent his entire academic career at Stanford University, where he has conducted influential research on behavior therapy and the determinants of aggression.

Cognitive Processes and Reciprocal Determinism

Bandura is one of several behaviorists who have added a cognitive flavor to behaviorism since the 1960s. Bandura (1977), Walter Mischel (1973), and Julian Rotter (1982) take issue with Skinner's "pure" behaviorism. They point out that humans obviously are conscious, thinking, feeling beings. Moreover, these theorists argue that in neglecting cognitive processes, Skinner ignored the most distinctive and important feature of human behavior. Bandura and like-minded theorists call their modified brand of behaviorism *social learning theory* or *social cognitive theory*.

Bandura (1982, 1986) agrees with the fundamental thrust of behaviorism in that he believes that personality is largely shaped through learning. However, he contends that conditioning is not a mechanical process in which people are passive participants. Instead, he maintains that people actively seek out and process information about their environment to maximize favorable outcomes. As Bandura (1995) puts it, "A major function of thought is to enable people to predict events and to develop ways to control those that affect their lives" (p. 6).

Comparing his theory to Skinner's highly deter-

Figure 12.6
Personality development and operant conditioning. According to Skinner, people's characteristic response tendencies are shaped by reinforcers and other consequences that follow behavior. Thus, if your joking at a party leads to attention and compliments, your tendency to be witty and humorous will be strengthened.

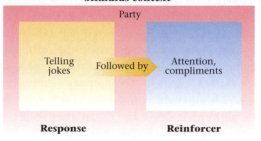

ministic view, Bandura advocates a position that he calls *reciprocal determinism*. According to this notion, the environment does determine behavior (as Skinner would argue). However, behavior also determines the environment (in other words, people can act to alter their environment). Moreover, personal factors (cognitive structures such as beliefs and expectancies) determine and are determined by both behavior and the environment (see Figure 12.7). Thus, **reciprocal determinism is the idea that internal mental events, external environmental events, and overt behavior all influence each other.** According to Bandura, humans are neither masters of their own destiny nor hapless victims buffeted about by the environment. Instead, the truth lies somewhere between these two extremes.

Observational Learning

Bandura's foremost theoretical contribution has been his description of observational learning,

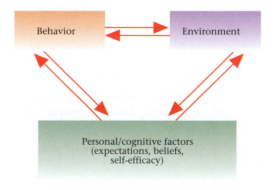

Figure 12.7
Bandura's reciprocal determinism. Bandura rejects Skinner's highly deterministic view that freedom is an illusion and argues that internal mental events, external environmental contingencies, and overt behavior all influence one another.

which we introduced in Chapter 6. *Observational learning* **occurs when an organism's responding is influenced by the observation of others, who are called models.** According to Bandura, both classical and operant conditioning can occur vicariously when one person observes another's conditioning. For example, if you watched your sister get burned by a bounced check upon selling her old stereo, this could strengthen your tendency to be suspicious of others. Although your sister would be the one actually experiencing the negative consequences, they might also influence you—through observational learning.

Bandura maintains that people's characteristic patterns of behavior are shaped by the *models* that they're exposed to. He isn't referring to the fashion models who dominate the mass media—although they do qualify. In observational learning, **a *model* is a person whose behavior is observed by another.** At one time or another, everyone serves as a model for others. Bandura's key point is that many response tendencies are the product of imitation. The effort of some individuals to emulate fashion models is just a special instance of a general phenomenon.

As social learning theory has been refined, it has become apparent that some models are more influential than others (Bandura, 1986). Both children and adults tend to imitate people they like or respect more than people they don't. People are also especially prone to imitate the behavior of people whom they consider attractive or powerful (such as rock stars). In addition, imitation is more likely when people see similarity between models and themselves. Thus, children tend to imitate same-sex role models somewhat more than opposite-sex models. Finally, people are more likely to copy a model if they observe that the model's behavior leads to positive outcomes.

According to social learning theory, models have a great impact on personality development. Children learn to be assertive, conscientious, self-sufficient, dependable, easygoing, and so forth by observing others behaving in these ways. Parents, teachers, relatives, siblings, and peers serve as models for young children. Bandura and his colleagues have done extensive research showing how models influence the development of aggressiveness, sex roles, and moral standards in children (Bandura, 1973; Bussey & Bandura, 1984; Mischel & Mischel, 1976). Their research on modeling and aggression has been particularly influential. In one classic study, Bandura, Ross, and Ross (1963b) showed how the observation of filmed characters who model aggression can contribute to children's learning of aggressive behavior (see the Featured Study for Chapter 6).

Self-Efficacy

Bandura discusses how a variety of personal factors (aspects of personality) govern behavior. In recent years, the factor he has emphasized most is self-efficacy (Bandura, 1990, 1993, 1995). *Self-efficacy* **refers to one's belief about one's ability to perform behaviors that should lead to expected outcomes.** When self-efficacy is high, individuals feel confident that they can execute the responses necessary to earn reinforcers. When self-efficacy is low, individuals worry that the necessary responses may be beyond their abilities. Perceptions of self-efficacy are subjective and specific to certain kinds of tasks. For instance, you might feel extremely confident about your ability to handle difficult social situations but doubtful about your ability to handle academic challenges.

Perceptions of self-efficacy can influence which challenges people tackle and how well they perform. Studies have found that feelings of greater self-efficacy are associated with greater success in giving up smoking and following an exercise regimen (Schwarzer & Fuchs, 1995); greater persistence and effort in academic pursuits and higher levels of academic performance (Zimmerman, 1995); enhanced performance in athletic competition (Bandura, 1990); and consideration of a broader range of occupations in making career choices (Bores-Rangel et al., 1990), for example.

What are the developmental antecedents of high self-efficacy? Schneewind (1995) asserts that parents can foster self-efficacy by providing a stimulating environment and by being responsive to their children's behavior. An emphasis on warm support for children, early independence training, and nonpunitive disciplinary techniques is also helpful. In contrast, parents who are authoritarian, intrusive, overprotective, or neglectful are likely to undermine self-efficacy in their offspring.

With its heavy emphasis on learning, Bandura's theory is firmly grounded in the tradition of behaviorism. However, its cognitive element allows it to account for aspects of human behavior that Skinner's theory can't explain. A similar brand of cognitive-oriented behaviorism is apparent in the theorizing of Walter Mischel, whose ideas we'll examine next.

"Most human behavior is learned by observation through modeling."

ALBERT BANDURA

Mischel and the Person-Situation Controversy

Walter Mischel was born in Vienna, not far from Freud's home. His family immigrated to the United States in 1939, when he was 9. After earning his doctorate in psychology, he spent many years on the faculty at Stanford, as a colleague of Bandura's. He has since moved to Columbia University.

Like Bandura, Mischel (1973, 1984) is an advocate of social learning theory. Mischel's chief contribution to personality theory has been to focus attention on the extent to which situational factors govern behavior. This contribution has embroiled him in a fundamental controversy about the consistency of human behavior across varying situations.

According to social learning theory, people make responses that they think will lead to reinforcement in the situation at hand. They try to gauge the reinforcement contingencies and adjust their behavior to the circumstances. Thus, if you believe that hard work in your job will pay off by leading to raises and promotions, you'll probably be diligent and industrious. But if you think that hard work in your job is unlikely to be rewarded, you may act lazy and irresponsible.

Social learning theory predicts that people will often behave differently in different situations. Mischel (1968, 1973) reviewed decades of research and concluded that, indeed, people exhibit far less consistency across situations than had been widely assumed. For example, studies show that a person who is honest in one situation may be dishonest in another. Someone who wouldn't dream of being dishonest in a business deal might engage in wholesale cheating in filling out tax returns. Similarly, some people are quite shy in one situation and outgoing in another. In light of these realities, Mischel maintains that behavior is characterized by more *situational specificity* than consistency.

Mischel's position has generated great controversy because it strikes at the heart of the concept of personality itself. As we discussed at the beginning of the chapter, the concept of personality is used to explain consistency in people's behavior over time and situations. If there isn't much consistency, there isn't much need for the concept of personality.

Mischel's views have attracted many critics who have sought to defend the value of the personality concept. For instance, Epstein (1980, 1986) argued that the methods used in much of the research reviewed by Mischel led to an underestimate of cross-situational consistency. Block (1981) and McCrae and Costa (1990) marshaled data indicating that personality traits are reasonably stable over periods of many years. Critics also noted that it is unreasonable to expect complete cross-situational consistency, because specific traits are more easily expressed in some situations than others (Kenrick & Funder, 1991). For example, a person's fun-loving, humorous qualities aren't likely to be apparent at a funeral where everyone is expected to be somber. Thus, Mischel's provocative theories have sparked a robust debate about the relative importance of the *person* as opposed to the *situation* in determining behavior.

This debate has led to a growing recognition that *both* the person and the situation are important determinants of behavior (Shoda, Mischel, & Wright, 1994). Social learning theorists assert that people do exhibit consistency in their behavior, but this consistency is tied to specific situations. For example, Person A may be consistently aggressive—*when subjected to teasing or provocation by peers*. Hence, to understand and predict a person's behavior one has to try to figure out the salient psychological features of situations that evoke certain responses. Thus, Mischel's work has increased the attention paid to the situational determinants of behavior and how they interact with personality variables (Kenrick & Funder, 1988).

Evaluating Behavioral Perspectives

Behavioral theories are firmly rooted in extensive empirical research rather than clinical intuition. Skinner's ideas have shed light on how environmental consequences and conditioning mold people's characteristic behavior. Bandura's social learning theory has expanded the horizons of behaviorism and increased its relevance to the study of personality. Mischel deserves credit for increasing psychology's awareness of how situational factors shape behavior. Of course, each theoretical approach has its shortcomings, and the behavioral approach is no exception. Major lines of criticism include the following (Liebert & Spiegler, 1990; Maddi, 1989):

1. *Overdependence on animal research.* Many principles in behavioral theories have been discovered through research on animals. Some critics argue that behaviorists have depended too much on animal research and that they have indiscrimi-

"It seems remarkable how each of us generally manages to reconcile his seemingly diverse behavior into one self-consistent whole."

WALTER MISCHEL

nately generalized from animal behavior to human behavior.

2. *Dehumanizing nature of radical behaviorism.* Skinner and other radical behaviorists have been criticized heavily for denying the existence of free will and the importance of cognitive processes. The critics argue that the radical behaviorist viewpoint strips human behavior of its most uniquely human elements and that it therefore cannot provide an accurate model of human functioning.

3. *Fragmentation of personality.* Behaviorists have also been criticized for providing a fragmented view of personality. The behavioral approach carves personality up into stimulus-response associations. There are no unifying structural concepts (such as Freud's ego) that tie these pieces together. Humanistic theorists, whom we shall cover next, have been particularly vocal in criticizing this piecemeal analysis of personality.

Recap of Key Points

• Behavioral theories explain how personality is shaped through learning. Skinner had little interest in unobservable cognitive processes and embraced a strong determinism.

• Skinner's followers view personality as a collection of response tendencies tied to specific stimulus situations. They assume that personality development is a lifelong process in which response tendencies are shaped and reshaped by learning, especially operant conditioning.

• Social learning theory focuses on how cognitive factors such as expectancies regulate learned behavior. Bandura's concept of observational learning accounts for the acquisition of responses from models. High self-efficacy has been related to successful health regimens, academic success, athletic performance, and occupational choice.

• Mischel has questioned the degree to which people display cross-situational consistency in behavior. Mischel's arguments have increased psychologists' awareness of the situational determinants of behavior.

• Behavioral approaches to personality are based on rigorous research. They have provided ample insights into how environmental factors and learning mold personalities. The behaviorists have been criticized for their overdependence on animal research, their fragmented analysis of personality, and radical behaviorism's dehumanizing view of human nature.

HUMANISTIC PERSPECTIVES

Humanistic theory emerged in the 1950s as something of a backlash against the behavioral and psychodynamic theories that we have just discussed (DeCarvalho, 1991). The principal charge hurled at these two models was that they are dehumanizing. Freudian theory was criticized for its belief that behavior is dominated by primitive, animalistic drives. Behaviorism was criticized for its preoccupation with animal research and for its mechanistic, fragmented view of personality. Critics argued that both schools of thought are too deterministic and that both fail to recognize the unique qualities of human behavior.

Many of these critics blended into a loose alliance that came to be known as humanism, because of its exclusive focus on human behavior. *Humanism* **is a theoretical orientation that emphasizes the unique qualities of humans, especially their freedom and their potential for personal growth.** Humanistic psychologists don't believe that animal research can reveal anything of any significance about the human condition. In contrast to most psychodynamic and behavioral

theorists, humanistic theorists take an optimistic view of human nature. They assume that (1) people can rise above their primitive animal heritage and control their biological urges, and (2) people are largely conscious and rational beings who are not dominated by unconscious, irrational needs and conflicts.

Humanistic theorists also maintain that a person's subjective view of the world is more important than objective reality. According to this notion, if you think that you're homely or bright or sociable, this belief will influence your behavior more than the realities of how homely, bright, or sociable you actually are. Therefore, the humanists embrace the *phenomenological approach,* **which assumes that one has to appreciate individuals' personal, subjective experiences to truly understand their behavior.** As Carl Rogers put it, "The best vantage point for understanding behavior is from the internal frame of reference of the individual himself" (1951, p. 494). Let's look at Rogers's ideas.

"I have little sympathy with the rather prevalent concept that man is basically irrational, and that his impulses, if not controlled, will lead to destruction of others and self. Man's behavior is exquisitely rational, moving with subtle and ordered complexity toward the goals his organism is endeavoring to achieve."

CARL ROGERS

Carl Rogers (1951, 1961, 1980) was one of the founders of the human potential movement. This movement emphasizes self-realization through sensitivity training, encounter groups, and other exercises intended to foster personal growth. Rogers grew up in a religious, upper-middle-class home in the suburbs of Chicago. He was a bright student, but he had to rebel against his parents' wishes in order to pursue his graduate study in psychology. While he was working at the University of Chicago in the 1940s, Rogers devised a major new approach to psychotherapy. Like Freud, Rogers based his personality theory on his extensive therapeutic interactions with many clients. Because of its emphasis on a person's subjective point of view, Rogers's approach is called a *person-centered theory*.

The Self

Rogers viewed personality structure in terms of just one construct. He called this construct the *self,* although it's more widely known today as the *self-concept*. A *self-concept* **is a collection of beliefs about one's own nature, unique qualities, and typical behavior.** Your self-concept is your own mental picture of yourself. It's a collection of self-perceptions. For example, a self-concept might include beliefs such as "I'm easygoing" or "I'm sly and crafty" or "I'm pretty" or "I'm hardworking." According to Rogers, individuals are aware of their self-concept. It's not buried in their unconscious.

Rogers stressed the subjective nature of the self-concept. Your self-concept may not be entirely consistent with your experiences. Most people tend to distort their experiences to some extent to promote a relatively favorable self-concept. For example, you may believe that you're quite bright, but your grade transcript might suggest otherwise. Rogers called the gap between self-concept and reality incongruence. *Incongruence* **is the degree of disparity between one's self-concept and one's actual experience.** In contrast, if a person's self-concept is reasonably accurate, it's said to be *congruent* with reality (see Figure 12.8). Everyone experiences *some* incongruence. The crucial issue is how much. As we'll see, Rogers maintained that too much incongruence undermines one's psychological well-being.

Development of the Self

In terms of personality development, Rogers was concerned with how childhood experiences pro-

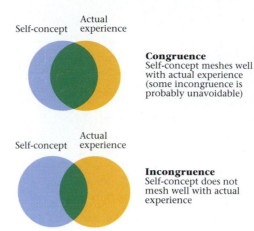

Congruence
Self-concept meshes well with actual experience (some incongruence is probably unavoidable)

Incongruence
Self-concept does not mesh well with actual experience

Figure 12.8
Rogers's view of personality structure. In Rogers's model, the self-concept is the only important structural construct. However, Rogers acknowledged that one's self-concept may not be consistent with the realities of one's actual experience—a condition called incongruence.

mote congruence or incongruence between one's self-concept and one's experience. According to Rogers, people have a strong need for affection, love, and acceptance from others. Early in life, parents provide most of this affection. Rogers maintained that some parents make their affection *conditional*. That is, it depends on the child's behaving well and living up to expectations. When parental love seems conditional, children often block out of their self-concept those experiences that make them feel unworthy of love. They do so because they're worried about parental acceptance, which appears precarious. At the other end of the spectrum, some parents make their affection *unconditional*. Their children have less need to block out unworthy experiences because they've been assured that they're worthy of affection, no matter what they do.

Hence, Rogers believed that unconditional love from parents fosters congruence and that conditional love fosters incongruence. He further theorized that if individuals grow up believing that affection from others is highly conditional, they will go on to distort more and more of their experiences in order to feel worthy of acceptance from a wider and wider array of people (see Figure 12.9).

A person's self-concept evolves throughout childhood and adolescence. As individuals' self-concept gradually stabilizes, they begin to feel comfortable with it and are usually loyal to it. This loyalty produces two effects. First, the self-concept becomes a "self-fulfilling prophecy" in that the person tends to behave in ways that are consistent with it. If you see yourself as an even-tempered, reflective person, you'll consciously work at behaving in these ways. If you happen to behave impulsively, you'll probably feel some discomfort because you're "acting out of character." Second, people become resistant to information that con-

Figure 12.9
Rogers's view of personality development and dynamics. Rogers's theory of development posits that conditional love leads to a need to distort experiences, which fosters an incongruent self-concept. Incongruence makes one prone to recurrent anxiety, which triggers defensive behavior, which fuels more incongruence.

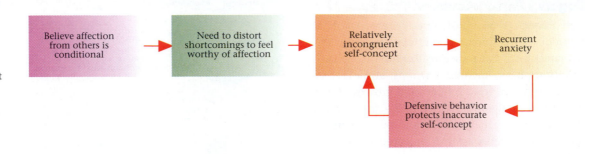

Believe affection from others is conditional → Need to distort shortcomings to feel worthy of affection → Relatively incongruent self-concept → Recurrent anxiety

Defensive behavior protects inaccurate self-concept

"It is as if Freud supplied to us the sick half of psychology and we must now fill it out with the healthy half."

ABRAHAM MASLOW

tradicts their self-concept. Contradictory information threatens their comfortable equilibrium. If your experiences begin to suggest that you're not as even-tempered as you thought, you'll probably try to find ways to dismiss this evidence.

Anxiety and Defense

According to Rogers, experiences that threaten people's personal views of themselves are the principal cause of troublesome anxiety. The more inaccurate your self-concept is, the more likely you are to have experiences that clash with your self-perceptions. Thus, people with highly incongruent self-concepts are especially likely to be plagued by recurrent anxiety (see Figure 12.9).

To ward off this anxiety, individuals often behave defensively in an effort to reinterpret their experience so that it appears consistent with their self-concept. Thus, they ignore, deny, and twist reality to protect and perpetuate their self-concept. Consider a young woman who, like most people, considers herself a "nice person." Let's suppose that in reality she is rather conceited and selfish. She gets feedback from both boyfriends and girlfriends that she is a "self-centered, snotty brat." How might she react in order to protect her self-concept? She might ignore or block out those occasions when she behaves selfishly. She might attribute her girlfriends' negative comments to their jealousy of her good looks. Perhaps she would blame her boyfriends' negative remarks on their disappointment because she won't get more serious with them. Meanwhile, she might start doing some kind of charity work to show everyone (including herself) that she really is a nice person. As you can see, people will sometimes go to great lengths to defend their self-concept.

Maslow's Theory of Self-Actualization

 10c

Abraham Maslow, who grew up in Brooklyn, described his childhood as "unhappy, lonely, [and] isolated." To follow through on his interest in psychology, he had to resist parental pressures to go into law. Maslow spent much of his career at Brandeis University, where he created an influential theory of motivation and provided crucial leadership for the fledgling humanistic movement.

Like Rogers, Maslow (1968, 1970) argued that psychology should take an optimistic view of human nature instead of dwelling on the causes of disorders. "To oversimplify the matter somewhat," he said, "it's as if Freud supplied to us the sick half of psychology and we must now fill it out with the healthy half" (1968, p. 5). Maslow's key contribution to personality theory was his description of the *self-actualizing person* as an example of the healthy personality. As you may recall from Chapter 10, Maslow proposed that humans are driven by a **need for self-actualization, which is the need to fulfill one's potential.** Thus, Maslow agreed with Rogers that people have an innate drive toward fulfillment and personal growth. Moreover, he believed that this fulfillment is crucial to psychological health, saying, "A musician must make music, an artist must paint, a poet must write, if he is to be ultimately at peace with himself. What a man can be, he *must* be" (1970, p. 46).

Working from this premise, Maslow set out to discover the nature of the healthy personality. He tried to identify people of exceptional mental health, so that he could investigate their characteristics. In one case, he used psychological tests and interviews to sort out the healthiest 1% of a sizable population of college students. He also studied admired historical figures (such as Thomas Jefferson and William James) and personal acquaintances characterized by superior adjustment. Over a period of years, he accumulated his case histories and gradually sketched, in broad strokes, a picture of ideal psychological health.

According to Maslow, *self-actualizing persons* **are people with exceptionally healthy person-**

alities, marked by continued personal growth. Maslow identified various traits characteristic of self-actualizing people. Many of these traits are listed in Figure 12.10. In brief, Maslow found that self-actualizers are accurately tuned in to reality and that they're at peace with themselves. He found that they're open and spontaneous and that they retain a fresh appreciation of the world around them. Socially, they're sensitive to others' needs and enjoy rewarding interpersonal relations. However, they're not dependent on others for approval or uncomfortable with solitude. They thrive on their work, and they enjoy their sense of humor. Maslow also noted that they have "peak experiences" (profound emotional highs) more often than others. Finally, he found that they strike a nice balance between many polarities in personality. For instance, they can be both childlike and mature, both rational and intuitive, both conforming and rebellious.

Evaluating Humanistic Perspectives

The humanists added a refreshing new perspective to the study of personality. Their argument that a person's subjective views may be more important than objective reality has proven compelling. As we noted earlier, even behavioral theorists have begun to take into account subjective personal factors such as beliefs and expectancies. The humanistic approach also deserves credit for making the self-concept an important construct in psychology. Today, theorists of many persuasions use the self-concept in their analyses of personality. Finally, the humanists have often been applauded for focusing attention on the issue of what constitutes a healthy personality.

Of course, there's a negative side to the balance sheet as well. Critics have identified some weaknesses in the humanistic approach to personality, including the following (Burger, 1993):

1. *Poor testability*. Like psychodynamic theorists, the humanists have been criticized for generating hypotheses that are difficult to put to a scientific test. Humanistic concepts such as personal growth and self-actualization are difficult to define and measure.

2. *Unrealistic view of human nature*. Critics also charge that the humanists have been unrealistic in their assumptions about human nature and their descriptions of the healthy personality. For instance, Maslow's self-actualizing people sound nearly *perfect*. In reality, Maslow had a hard time finding such people. When he searched among

the living, the results were so disappointing that he turned to the study of historical figures. Thus, humanistic portraits of psychological health are perhaps a bit too optimistic.

3. *Inadequate evidence*. For the most part, humanistic psychologists haven't been particularly research oriented. Although Rogers and Maslow both conducted and encouraged empirical research, many of their followers have been scornful of efforts to quantify human experience to test

---

Characteristics of self-actualizing people

- Clear, efficient perception of reality and comfortable relations with it
- Spontaneity, simplicity, and naturalness
- Problem centering (having something outside themselves they "must" do as a mission)
- Detachment and need for privacy
- Autonomy, independence of culture and environment
- Continued freshness of appreciation
- Mystical and peak experiences

- Feelings of kinship and identification with the human race
- Strong friendships, but limited in number
- Democratic character structure
- Ethical discrimination between good and evil
- Philosophical, unhostile sense of humor
- Balance between polarities in personality

Figure 12.10
Maslow's view of the healthy personality. Humanistic theorists emphasize psychological health instead of maladjustment. Maslow's description of characteristics of self-actualizing people evokes a picture of the healthy personality.

CONCEPT CHECK 12.2
Recognizing Key Concepts in Personality Theories

Check your understanding of psychodynamic, behavioral, and humanistic personality theories by identifying key concepts from these theories in the scenarios below. The answers can be found in Appendix A.

1. Thirteen-year-old Sarah watches a TV show in which the leading female character manipulates her boyfriend by acting helpless and purposely losing a tennis match against him. The female lead repeatedly expresses her slogan, "Never let them [men] know you can take care of yourself." Sarah becomes more passive and less competitive around boys her own age.

   Concept: _____

2. Marilyn has a secure, enjoyable, reasonably well-paid job as a tenured English professor at a state university. Her friends are dumbfounded when she announces that she's going to resign and give it all up to try writing a novel. She tries to explain, "I need a new challenge, a new mountain to climb. I've had this lid on my writing talents for years, and I've got to break free. It's something I have to try. I won't be happy until I do."

   Concept: _____

3. Johnny, who is 4, seems to be emotionally distant from and inattentive to his father. He complains whenever he's left with his dad. In contrast, he often cuddles up in bed with his mother and tries very hard to please her by behaving properly.

   Concept: _____

hypotheses. Humanistic theories are based primarily on clinical observation. More experimental research is needed to catch up with the theorizing in the humanistic camp. This is precisely the opposite of the situation that we'll encounter in the next section, on biological perspectives, where more theorizing is needed to catch up with the burgeoning research.

Recap of Key Points

• Humanistic theories are phenomenological and take an optimistic view of people's conscious, rational ability to chart their own courses of action. Rogers focused on the self-concept as the critical aspect of personality. Incongruence is the degree of disparity between one's self-concept and actual experience.

• Rogers maintained that unconditional love fosters congruence, whereas conditional love fosters incongruence. Incongruence makes one vulnerable to recurrent anxiety, which tends to trigger defensive behavior that protects one's inaccurate self-concept.

• Maslow theorized that psychological health depends on fulfilling one's need for self-actualization, which is the need to realize one's human potential. His work led to the description of self-actualizing persons as idealized examples of psychological health.

• Humanistic theories deserve credit for highlighting the importance of subjective views of oneself and for confronting the question of what makes for a healthy personality. Humanistic theories lack a firm base of research, are difficult to put to an empirical test, and may be overly optimistic about human nature.

BIOLOGICAL PERSPECTIVES

Like many identical twins reared apart, Jim Lewis and Jim Springer found they had been leading eerily similar lives. Separated four weeks after birth in 1940, the Jim twins grew up 45 miles apart in Ohio and were reunited in 1979. Eventually, they discovered that both drove the same model blue Chevrolet, chain-smoked Salems, chewed their fingernails and owned dogs named Toy. Each had spent a good deal of time vacationing at the same three-block strip of beach in Florida. More important, when tested for such personality traits as flexibility, self-control, and sociability, the twins responded almost exactly alike. (Leo, 1987, p. 63)

So began a *Time* magazine summary of a major twin study conducted at the University of Minnesota Center for Twin and Adoption Research. Since 1979 the investigators at this center have been

Is personality largely inherited? The story of these identical twins would certainly suggest so. Although they were reared apart from 4 weeks after their birth, Jim Lewis (left) and Jim Springer (right) exhibit remarkable correspondence in personality. Some of the similarities in their lives—such as the benches built around trees in their yards—seem uncanny.

studying the personality resemblance of identical twins reared apart. Thanks in part to publicity like the *Time* article, they have managed to locate and complete testing on over 40 rare pairs of identical twins separated early in life.

Not all the twin pairs have been as similar as Jim Lewis and Jim Springer, but many of the parallels have been uncanny (Lykken et al., 1992). One pair of previously separated female twins both arrived at the Minneapolis airport wearing seven rings on their fingers. One had a son named Richard Andrew and the other had a son named Andrew Richard! Still another pair of separated twin sisters shared the same phobia of bodies of water, and they dealt with it in the same peculiar way—backing into the ocean. In their research on separated identical twins the Minnesota team also encountered a pair who were habitual gigglers, a pair who were gunsmith hobbyists, a pair who obsessively counted things, a pair who had been married five times, and a pair who both captained their volunteer fire department.

Could personality be largely inherited? These anecdotal reports of striking resemblances between identical twins reared apart certainly raise this possibility. As you'll see, this idea is not entirely new. In this section we'll discuss early biological theories of personality, review Hans Eysenck's modern theory, and look at recent behavioral genetics research on the heritability of personality.

Early Theories of Physique and Personality
 10d

In the first half of this century, Ernst Kretschmer (1921) and William Sheldon (1940) independently proposed theories that linked personality to physique on the grounds that both are governed by genetic endowment. Sheldon (1942) conducted elaborate research in which he rated male subjects' bodies along three dimensions. *Endomorphy* referred to the degree to which a person's body was fat, round, and soft. *Ectomorphy* referred to a thin, flat, frail body type. *Mesomorphy* referred to a hard, strong, muscular body type. Sheldon also rated the same subjects on 50 personality dimensions. He found high correlations between the three body types and the clusters of personality traits summarized in Figure 12.11.

Sheldon's findings initially appeared to provide impressive support for his theory. However, his research was marred by a fatal flaw: Sheldon had made the ratings of both physique and personality himself. In retrospect, there's little doubt that he

Endomorphic
Sociable, relaxed, affectionate, even-tempered

Mesomorphic
Energetic, competitive, aggressive, bold

Ectomorphic
Inhibited, apprehensive, intellectual, introverted, self-conscious

Figure 12.11 Sheldon's biological theory. Sheldon asserted that endomorphy, mesomorphy, and ectomorphy were associated with the personality traits listed here. His theory has not been supported by subsequent research.

fell prey to experimenter bias. In making the personality ratings, he was influenced by subjects' readily apparent physiques, and he saw what he expected to see. His findings were not replicated in subsequent studies by other researchers. Ultimately, the idea that physique and personality go hand in hand was abandoned in favor of more sophisticated biological theories of personality. Let's look at one such theory, devised by Hans Eysenck.

Eysenck's Theory

Hans Eysenck was born in Germany but fled to London during the era of Nazi rule. He went on to become one of Britain's most prominent psychologists. Eysenck is drawn to controversy like a moth to a flame. He has been embroiled in two of psychology's most heated debates—on the heritability of intelligence (see Chapter 9) and on the effectiveness of psychotherapy (see Chapter 15).

Eysenck (1967, 1982, 1991) views personality structure as a hierarchy of traits, in which many superficial traits are derived from a smaller number of more basic traits, which are derived from a handful of fundamental higher-order traits, as shown in Figure 12.12. He has used factor analysis to identify three higher-order traits. *Extraversion* involves being sociable, assertive, active, and lively. *Neuroticism* involves being anxious, tense, moody, and low in self-esteem. *Psychoticism* involves being egocentric, impulsive, cold, and antisocial.

According to Eysenck, "Personality is determined to a large extent by a person's genes" (1967, p. 20). How is heredity linked to personality in Eysenck's model? In part, through conditioning concepts borrowed from behavioral theory. Eysenck theorizes that some people can be conditioned more readily than others because of differences in their physiological functioning. These variations in "conditionability" are assumed to influence the personality traits that people acquire through conditioning processes.

Eysenck has shown a special interest in explaining variations in *extraversion-introversion*, the trait

"Personality is determined to a large extent by a person's genes."

HANS EYSENCK

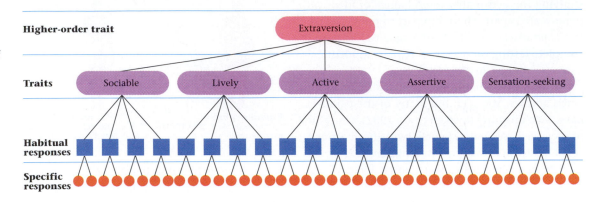

Figure 12.12
Eysenck's model of personality structure. Eysenck described personality structure as a hierarchy of traits. In this scheme, a few higher-order traits, such as extraversion, determine a host of lower-order traits, which determine a person's habitual responses.

Figure 12.13
Twin studies of personality. Loehlin (1992) has summarized the results of twin studies that have examined the Big Five personality traits. The N under each trait indicates the number of twin studies that have examined that trait. The chart plots the average correlations obtained for identical and fraternal twins in these studies. As you can see, identical twins have shown greater resemblance in personality than fraternal twins have, suggesting that personality is partly inherited.

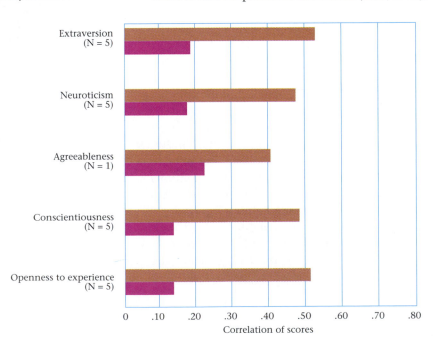

dimension first described years earlier by Carl Jung. He has proposed that introverts tend to have higher levels of physiological arousal than extraverts. This higher arousal purportedly motivates them to avoid social situations that will further elevate their arousal and makes them more easily conditioned than extraverts. According to Eysenck, people who condition easily acquire more conditioned inhibitions than others. These inhibitions, coupled with their relatively high arousal, make them more bashful, tentative, and uneasy in social situations. This social discomfort leads them to turn inward. Hence, they become introverted.

Is there any research to support Eysenck's explanation of the origins of introversion? Yes, but the evidence is rather inconsistent. Many studies *have* found that introverts tend to exhibit higher levels of arousal than extraverts (Bullock & Gilliland, 1993; Wilson, 1990), but many studies have also failed to find the predicted differences (Gale, 1983).

Even Eysenck (1990a) acknowledges that the evidence on his theory is mixed and that the concept of physiological arousal has turned out to be much more multifaceted and difficult to measure than he originally anticipated. It will be interesting to see whether more consistent results are obtained in the future, as investigators improve and refine their methods for measuring physiological arousal.

Behavioral Genetics and Personality 10d

Recent research in behavioral genetics has provided impressive support for the idea that personality is partly inherited (Plomin, Chipuer, & Loehlin, 1990; Rose, 1995). For instance, Figure 12.13 shows the mean correlations observed for identical and fraternal twins in studies of the Big Five personality traits summarized by Loehlin (1992). Higher correlations are indicative of greater similarity on a trait. On all five traits, identical twins have been found to be much more similar than fraternal twins. Based on these and many other data, Loehlin (1992) concludes that genetic factors exert considerable influence over personality.

As we noted in our discussion of the heritability of intelligence in Chapter 9, some skeptics wonder whether identical twins might exhibit more trait similarity than fraternal twins because they're treated more alike. In other words, they wonder whether environmental factors (rather than heredity) could be responsible for identical twins' greater similarity in many traits. This nagging question can be answered only by studying identical twins reared apart, which is why the twin study at the University of Minnesota is so important. The Minnesota researchers began to search for twins reared apart in 1979, offering to fly such twin pairs to Minneapolis for days of extensive interviews and psychological testing. Our Featured Study reports some of the results from this project.

Investigators: Auke Tellegen, David T. Lykken, Thomas J. Bouchard, Jr., Kimberly J. Wilcox, Nancy L. Segal, and Stephen Rich (University of Minnesota)

Source: Personality similarity in twins reared apart and together. *Journal of Personality and Social Psychology,* 1988, *54,* 1031–1039.

The investigators set out to assess the personality correspondence of identical and fraternal twins, some of whom were reared together and some of whom were reared apart. A few other studies have been conducted of personality in identical twins reared apart. However, no previous study had managed to use the same personality test to compare all four possible groups (identical reared together, identical reared apart, fraternal reared together, and fraternal reared apart).

Method

Sample. The subjects included 217 pairs of identical twins reared together and 114 pairs of fraternal twins reared together. These twins were studied as part of an ongoing project between 1970 and 1984. They were compared to 44 pairs of identical twins reared apart and 27 pairs of fraternal twins reared apart, who were studied as part of an additional project begun in 1979. Because twins are sometimes misclassified as identical or fraternal by appearance, the investigators double-checked their subjects' type of twinship with highly accurate blood tests and fingerprint comparisons.

The age of separation for the twins reared apart ranged from birth to 4½ years. Most were separated quite early in life, as the typical (median) age of separation was 2½ months. The twins reared apart remained separated for a median period of almost 34 years.

Measures. All subjects responded to the Multidimensional Personality Questionnaire developed by Tellegen. It is a 300-item personality scale that measures 11 personality traits and 3 higher-order dimensions of personality. The higher-order dimensions, identified through factor analysis, are (1) *positive emotionality* (similar to extraversion in the five-factor model), (2) *negative emotionality* (similar to neuroticism in the five-factor model), and (3) *constraint* (similar to conscientiousness in the five-factor model).

The investigators computed correlations to determine how similar the various types of twin sets were to each other with regard to each of the personality dimensions. The investigators also used sophisticated statistical modeling procedures to estimate the proportion of variability in each trait governed by (1) heredity, (2) shared family environment, and (3) unique aspects of experience.

Results

The correlations for all four types of twin sets with regard to the three basic dimensions of personality are shown in Figure 12.14. These correlations reveal that identical twins reared together are more similar on all

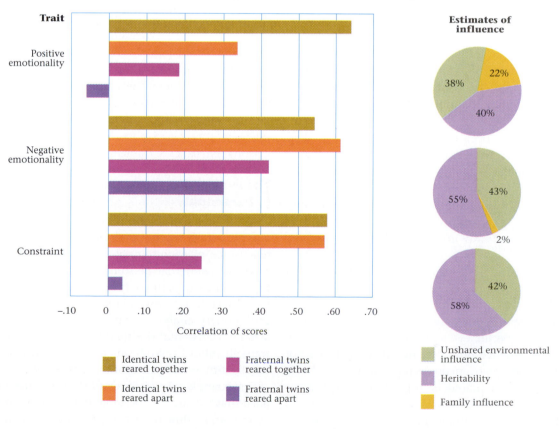

Figure 12.14
Personality resemblance in the Tellegen et al. (1988) study. On all three basic personality traits examined in this study, identical twins were more similar than fraternal twins—even if the identical twins were reared apart. These correlational data yielded relatively high estimates of heritability, which are shown on the right. Evidence of environmental influence on personality was also apparent in the data, but the investigators were surprised to find that the impact of family environment appeared negligible on two out of three personality traits.

three traits than fraternal twins reared together. More telling, though, are the results for the identical twins reared apart. On all three traits, identical twins reared apart are still more similar to each other than fraternal twins reared together.

Figure 12.14 also shows the proportion of variation in each trait allocated to heredity, family environment, and unique experience, as determined by the statistical modeling procedures. The genetic components, which are heritability estimates, range from 40% to 58%. A noticeable effect for family environment was found only for the positive emotionality trait, where the family component was estimated to be 22%. The remaining variance for the three traits, ranging from 38% to 43%, was attributed to the effect of unique experiences. Some of this "leftover" variance was also due to measurement error (the less-than-perfect reliability of any psychological test).

Discussion

The investigators maintain that their results support the hypothesis that genetic blueprints shape the contours of personality. They estimate that the heritability of personality, as a whole, is roughly 50% and that some traits may be influenced more by heredity than others. Stepping back to view the study's results as a whole, they conclude that "personality differences are more influenced by genetic diversity than they are by environmental diversity."

Comment

As this research project progressed during the 1980s, the popular press reported on many highly publicized incidents of eerie resemblances between the separated identical twins in the study. These reports often suggested that personality is all in the genes. However, bizarre similarities observed in a few individuals have little value as scientific evidence. Uncanny parallels can occur between entirely unrelated people. Moreover, it's easy to focus on a few unusual parallels and forget about dozens of dissimilarities. So, psychologists around the world eagerly awaited the actual findings of the study, which would measure the impact of heredity and environment with scientific precision.

The precise, quantitative data lived up to the expectations created by the anecdotal reports, yielding some of the best evidence to date that personality is molded by heredity. However, it should be noted that debate continues over the *degree* to which personality is shaped by heredity. Estimates regarding the heritability of personality from other lines of research have generally been somewhat lower than those seen in our Featured Study—typically in the neighborhood of 20% to 40% (Loehlin, 1992; Plomin, Chipuer, & Loehlin, 1990). Furthermore, a subsequent study of twins from the Minnesota sample that measured their personality with a different test—the Minnesota Multiphasic Personality Inventory (see the Application)—yielded an average heritability estimate of .44 (DiLalla et al., 1996).

Research on the heritability of personality has inadvertently turned up an interesting finding that was apparent in our Featured Study. A number of recent studies have found that shared family environment has surprisingly little impact on personality (Plomin & Daniels, 1987; Hoffman, 1991). Furthermore, when unrelated children reared together have been compared in adoption studies, researchers have found little or no personality resemblance. For many years, social scientists have assumed that the environment shared by children growing up together leads to some personality resemblance among them. However, recent findings seriously undermine this widespread belief.

These findings have led Robert Plomin (1990) to ask, "Why are children in the same family so different from one another?" Researchers have only just begun to explore this perplexing question. Plomin speculates that children in the same family experience home environments that are not nearly as homogeneous as previously assumed. He notes that children in the same home may be treated quite differently, as a child's gender and birth order can influence parents' approaches to

child rearing. Temperamental differences between children may also evoke differences in styles of parenting. And parents' approaches to child rearing may change over time as the parents grow older, so that different siblings end up being raised in different ways. Focusing on how environmental factors vary *within* families represents a promising new way to explore the determinants of personality (Baker & Daniels, 1990).

The Evolutionary Approach to Personality

In the realm of biological perspectives on personality, the most recent development has been the emergence of evolutionary theory. Evolutionary theorists assert that personality has a biological basis because natural selection has favored certain traits over the course of human history. Thus, evolutionary analyses focus on how various personality traits—and the ability to recognize these traits in others—may have contributed to reproductive fitness in ancestral human populations.

For example, David Buss (1991, 1995) has argued that the Big Five personality traits stand out as important dimensions of personality across a

Check your understanding of the implications of the personality theories we've discussed by indicating which theorist is likely to have made the statements below. The answers are in Appendix A.

Choose from the
following theorists:

Alfred Adler

Albert Bandura

Hans Eysenck

Sigmund Freud

Abraham Maslow

Walter Mischel

Quotes

_____ 1. "If you deliberately plan to be less than you are capable of being, then I warn you that you'll be deeply unhappy for the rest of your life."

_____ 2. "I feel that the major, most fundamental dimensions of personality are likely to be those on which [there is] strong genetic determination of individual differences."

_____ 3. "People are in general not candid over sexual matters . . . they wear a heavy overcoat woven of a tissue of lies, as though the weather were bad in the world of sexuality."

variety of cultures because those traits have had significant adaptive implications. Buss points out that humans historically have depended heavily on groups, which afford protection from predators or enemies, opportunities for sharing food, and a diverse array of other benefits. In the context of these group interactions, people have had to make difficult but crucial judgments about the characteristics of others, asking such questions as: Who will make a good member of my coalition? Who can I depend on when in need? Who will share their resources? Thus, Buss argues, "those individuals able to accurately discern and act upon these individual differences likely enjoyed a considerable reproductive advantage" (p. 22). According to Buss, the Big Five emerge as fundamental dimensions of personality because humans have evolved special sensitivity to variations in the ability to bond with others (extraversion), the willingness to cooperate and collaborate (agreeableness), the tendency to be reliable and ethical (conscientiousness), the capacity to be an innovative problem solver (openness to experience), and the ability to handle stress (low neuroticism). In a nutshell, the Big Five supposedly reflect the most salient features of ancestral humanities' adaptive landscape.

Although evolutionary theorists have some interesting ideas about why certain dimensions of personality are particularly important, they have had little to say on the foremost issue in the study of personality: What are the origins of individual differences in personality? The central concern of personality research has been to explain why people are different—why some people are extra-

verted and others are introverted, why some are trusting and others suspicious, and so forth. Buss (1995) acknowledges that evolutionary psychologists have not confronted this issue and that it may be "problematic."

Evaluating Biological Perspectives

Although early theories linking physique to personality were much too simple, subsequent researchers have compiled convincing evidence that biological factors help shape personality. Nonetheless, we must take note of some weaknesses in biological approaches to personality:

1. As we discussed in Chapter 9, heritability estimates suffer from some conceptual problems. Critics of heritability studies, such as McGuire and Haviland (1985), have characterized heritability ratios as "notoriously biased and inaccurate" (p. 1435). Although their language is a bit strong, heritability ratios should be regarded as ballpark estimates that will vary depending on sampling procedures and other considerations.

2. The results of efforts to carve behavior into genetic and environmental components are ultimately artificial. The effects of nature and nurture are twisted together in complicated interactions that can't be separated cleanly (Brody & Crowley, 1995; Scarr, 1992). For example, a genetically influenced trait, such as a young child's surly, sour temperament, might evoke a particular style of parenting. In essence then, the child's genes have molded his or her environment. People's genetic inheritance also appears to influence the types of experiences that they prefer. For example, a child

"In sum, the five factors of personality, in this account, represent important dimensions of the social terrain that humans were selected to attend to and act upon."

DAVID BUSS

with a genetic propensity toward aggressiveness may be drawn to violent TV shows. Thus, genetic and environmental influences on personality are not entirely independent because the environmental circumstances that people are exposed to may be shaped in part by their genes.

3. At present there's no comprehensive biological theory of personality. Eysenck's model doesn't provide a systematic overview of how biological factors govern personality development (and was never intended to). In regard to personality, evolutionary theory is even more limited in scope. Additional theoretical work is needed to catch up with recent empirical findings on the biological basis for personality.

Recap of Key Points

• Sheldon theorized that physique determines personality, but his theory has been discredited. Contempo-rary biological theories stress the genetic origins of personality.

• Eysenck views personality structure as a hierarchy of traits. He believes that heredity influences individual differences in physiological functioning that affect how easily people acquire conditioned responses.

• Twin studies of the Big Five personality traits find that identical twins are more similar in personality than fraternal twins, thus suggesting that personality is partly inherited. Our Featured Study on the personality resemblance of twins reared apart yielded relatively high estimates for the heritability of personality, ranging from 40% to 58%.

• Recent research in behavioral genetics has suggested that shared family environment has surprisingly little impact on personality. The biological approach has been criticized because of methodological problems with heritability ratios and because it offers no systematic model of how physiology shapes personality.

CONTEMPORARY EMPIRICAL APPROACHES TO PERSONALITY

So far, our coverage has been devoted to grand, panoramic theories of personality. In this section we'll examine some contemporary empirical approaches that are narrower in scope, tending to focus on specific traits. In modern personality research programs, investigators attempt to describe and measure an important personality trait, shed light on its development, and ascertain its relationship to other traits and behaviors.

Psychologists have studied many widely discussed traits, such as independence, shyness, impulsiveness, optimism, introversion, and self-esteem. However, personality researchers take pride in their ability to discover subtler traits that are not readily apparent to everyone. Hence, they've focused much of their attention on personality traits that the average person probably doesn't think about. To get a sense of this kind of research, we'll take a look at three such traits in this section: (1) locus of control, (2) sensation seeking, and (3) self-monitoring.

Locus of Control: Life as a Pawn

Locus of control is a personality dimension first described by Julian Rotter (1966, 1975, 1990), a prominent social learning theorist. *Locus of control is a generalized expectancy about the degree to which individuals control their outcomes.* Individuals with an *external locus of control*

believe that their successes and failures are governed by external factors such as fate, luck, and chance. "Externals" feel that their outcomes are largely beyond their control—that they're pawns of fate. In contrast, individuals with an *internal locus of control* believe that their successes and failures are determined by their actions and abilities (internal, or personal, factors). "Internals" consequently feel that they have more influence over their outcomes than people with an external locus of control.

Of course, locus of control is not an either-or proposition. Like any other dimension of personality, it should be thought of as occurring on a continuum. Some people are very external, some are very internal, but most people fall somewhere in between.

Which is healthier—an internal or an external locus of control? Studies indicate that people with an external locus of control develop more symptoms of psychological disorders than people characterized by an internal locus of control (Ormel & Schaufeli, 1991). A meta-analysis of 91 studies estimated a correlation of .31 between externality and feelings of depression (Benassi, Sweeney, & Dufour, 1988). In light of this link to depression, it is not surprising that externality correlates with the number of suicidal thoughts reported by college students (Burger, 1984). Why is externality associated with poor adjustment? We can only speculate that people tend to feel better about their life when they believe that they can exert some control over their outcomes.

Research also indicates that internality is related to higher academic achievement (Findley & Cooper, 1983). Youngsters with an internal locus of control get somewhat better grades than youngsters characterized by an external locus of control. Why? Probably because internals work harder than externals. If you think that your grades are a matter of luck, you're not likely to work very hard. Furthermore, an external locus of control allows people to readily make excuses for poor performance (Basgall & Snyder, 1988). Externals can protect their self-esteem by blaming lousy grades or failures in other areas on bad luck.

After a few decades of research, it's becoming clear that a person's locus of control may not be quite as generalized as originally thought. Some people display an internal locus of control regarding events in one domain of life while displaying an external locus of control regarding events in another domain. For instance, a person might feel powerless (external) about influencing the political process but feel very responsible (internal) for more personal events. In light of this finding, some researchers are studying locus of control as it relates to specific domains of behavior.

The domain attracting the most attention is personal health. Health-related locus of control appears to affect how people deal with the threat of illness (Marshall, 1991; Wallston & Wallston, 1981). Internals are more likely than externals to seek information about possible health problems. Internals also have a greater tendency to take preventive steps to maintain their health, such as giving up smoking, starting an exercise program, or getting regular medical checkups.

Sensation Seeking: Life in the Fast Lane

Perhaps you have friends who prefer "life in the fast lane." If so, they're probably high in the personality trait of sensaton seeking. **Sensation seeking is a generalized preference for high or low levels of sensory stimulation.** People who are high in sensation seeking prefer a high level of stimulation. They're always looking for new and exhilarating experiences. People who are low in sensation seeking prefer more modest levels of stimulation. They tend to choose tranquillity over excitement. Sensation seeking was first described by Marvin Zuckerman (1971, 1979), a biologically oriented theorist influenced by Hans Eysenck's views. Zuckerman (1990, 1991) believes that there is a strong genetic predisposition to high or low sensation seeking.

Sensation-seeking tendencies are measured by Zuckerman's (1979) Sensation Seeking Scale (see Figure 12.15). Sensation seeking is distributed along a continuum, and many people fall in the middle. Factor analyses indicate that the personality trait of sensation seeking consists of four related components. When compared to low sensation seekers, those high in sensation seeking display the following four sets of characteristics (Zuckerman, 1979; Zuckerman, Buchsbaum, & Murphy, 1980):

• *Thrill and adventure seeking.* They're more willing to engage in activities that may involve a physical risk. Thus, they're more likely to go mountain climbing, skydiving, surfing, and scuba diving.

• *Experience seeking.* They're more willing to volunteer for unusual experiments or activities that they may know little about. They tend to relish extensive travel, provocative art, wild parties, and unusual friends.

• *Disinhibition.* High sensation seekers are relatively uninhibited. Hence, they are prone to engage in heavy drinking, recreational drug use, gambling, and sexual experimentation.

• *Susceptibility to boredom.* High sensation seekers' chief foe is monotony. They have a low tolerance for routine and repetition, and they quickly and easily become bored.

Compatibility in sensation seeking may influence the progress of romantic relationships. Schroth (1991) found that the more dissimilar partners were in sensation seeking, the less satisfied with their relationship they tended to be. According to Zuckerman, incompatibility in sensation seeking places strain on intimate relationships. He theorizes that persons very high and very low in sensation seeking may have difficulty understanding and relating to each other, not to mention finding mutually enjoyable activities.

How do high sensation seekers stack up in terms of adjustment and mental health? On the positive side of the ledger, high sensation seekers are relatively tolerant of stress. They find many types of potentially stressful events to be less threatening and anxiety arousing than others (Franken, Gibson, & Rowland, 1992). On the negative side of the ledger, high sensation seekers are more likely than others to have difficulty in school, to exhibit poor

**Figure 12.15
A brief scale to assess
sensation seeking.** Follow
the instructions for this scale
to obtain a rough estimate
of your own sensation-seeking
tendencies.

Measuring sensation seeking

Answer "true" or "false" to each of the items listed below by circling "T" or "F." A "true" means that the item expresses your preference most of the time. A "false" means that you do not agree that the item is generally true for you. After completing the test, score your responses according to the instructions that follow the test items.

T F   1.   I would really enjoy skydiving.
T F   2.   I can imagine myself driving a sports car in a race and loving it.
T F   3.   My life is very secure and comfortable—the way I like it.
T F   4.   I usually like emotionally expressive or artistic people, even if they are sort of wild.
T F   5.   I like the idea of seeing many of the same warm, supportive faces in my everyday life.
T F   6.   I like doing adventurous things and would have enjoyed being a pioneer in the early days of this
                country.
T F   7.   A good photograph should express peacefulness creatively.
T F   8.   The most important thing in living is fully experiencing all emotions.
T F   9.   I like creature comforts when I go on a trip or vacation.
T F   10.   Doing the same things each day really gets to me.
T F   11.   I love snuggling in front of a fire on a wintry day.
T F   12.   I would like to try several types of drugs as long as they didn't harm me permanently.
T F   13.   Drinking and being rowdy really appeals to me on the weekend.
T F   14.   Rational people try to avoid dangerous situations.
T F   15.   I prefer Figure A to Figure B.

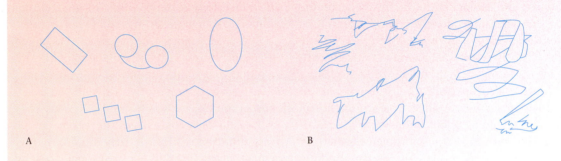

A   B

Give yourself 1 point for answering "true" to the following items: 1, 2, 4, 6, 8, 10, 12, and 13. Also give yourself 1 point for answering "false" to the following items: 3, 5, 7, 9, 11, 14, and 15. Add up your points, and compare your total to the following norms: 11–15, high sensation seeker; 6–10, moderate sensation seeker; 1–5, low sensation seeker. Bear in mind that this is a shortened version of the Sensation Seeking Scale and that it provides only a rough approximation of your status on this personality trait.

health habits, and to engage in ill-advised, risky behavior (Horvath & Zuckerman, 1993; Zuckerman, 1979, 1990). High sensation seeking is also associated with problem drinking, recreational drug use, delinquency, and criminal behavior (Newcomb & McGee, 1991; Stacy, Newcomb, & Bentler, 1993). Thus, high sensation seeking may be more maladaptive than adaptive.

Self-Monitoring: Life as Theater

The trait of self-monitoring, originally unearthed by Mark Snyder, has been under investigation since the mid-1970s. *Self-monitoring* **refers to the degree to which people attend to and control the impression they make on others in social interactions.** According to Snyder (1979, 1987), people vary in their awareness of how they're being perceived by others. People who are high in self-monitoring are very sensitive to how their self-presentation is going over. They seek information about how they're expected to behave in a situation, and, when necessary, they shrewdly adjust their behavior to create the right impression. For high self-monitors, "All the world's a stage."

Being tuned in to how others view you is one thing, but high self-monitors also show a gift for creating the right impression. They tend to be skilled at adjusting their self-presentations to produce desired audience responses (Larkin, 1988). In other words, they are good actors. They control their emotions well and can feign emotions when necessary. They deliberately regulate nonverbal signals (for instance, facial expressions and gestures) that are fairly spontaneous in most people. People who are high in self-monitoring tend to invest a lot of effort in "reading" and remembering others' self-presentations (Lassiter, Stone, & Weigold, 1988). Ironically, they are good at spotting deceptive impression management *in other people*. For instance, they can tell when others are trying to butter them up. Like sensation seeking, self-monitoring appears to be determined in part by people's genetic makeup (Gangestad & Simpson, 1993; Gangestad & Snyder, 1985).

Some interesting correlations have been found between self-monitoring and patterns of dating and sexual activity (Jones, 1993; Snyder & Simpson, 1984; Snyder, Simpson, & Gangestad, 1986). In comparison to low self-monitors, high self-monitors date a greater variety of partners (see Figure 12.16), choose their dates on the basis of external appearances more than attitudes and values, have sex with more partners, and change partners more quickly when new opportunities arise. When they do stay in one relationship for a while, it's less likely to grow steadily in intimacy than when low self-monitors stay in a single relationship. Thus, people high in self-monitoring may make genuine emotional commitments less readily than those who are low in self-monitoring.

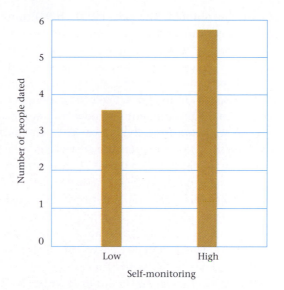

Figure 12.16
Self-monitoring and dating. Snyder and Simpson (1984) found that college students who were high in self-monitoring had dated more people in the preceding 12 months than had students low in self-monitoring. Apparently, high self-monitors commit themselves to romantic relationships less readily than low self-monitors do.

CULTURE AND PERSONALITY

Are there connections between culture and personality? The investigation of this question dates back to the 1940s and 1950s, when researchers set out to describe various cultures' *modal personality* (Kardiner & Linton, 1945) or *national character* (Kluckhohn & Murray, 1948). These investigations, which were largely guided by Freud's psychoanalytic theory, met with relatively little success (Bruner, 1974). Part of the problem may have been the rather culture-bound, Eurocentric nature of Freudian theory, but the crux of the problem was that it was unrealistic to expect to find a single, dominant personality type in each culture (Draguns, 1979). As we have seen repeatedly, given the realities of multifactorial causation, behavior is never that simple. In retrospect, the research on modal personality overestimated the impact of cultural contexts and the uniformity of people within societies.

Studies of the links between culture and personality dwindled after the disappointments of the 1940s and 1950s. However, in recent years, psychology's new interest in cultural factors has led to a renaissance of culture-personality research. This research has sought to determine whether Western personality constructs are relevant to other cultures and whether there are cultural differences in the prevalence of specific personality traits. Like cross-cultural research in other areas of psychology, these studies have found evidence of both continuity and variability across cultures.

For the most part, continuity has been apparent in cross-cultural comparisons of the *trait structure* of personality. When English language personality scales have been translated and administered in other cultures, the predicted dimensions of personality have emerged from the factor analyses. For example, when scales that tap the Big Five personality traits have been administered and subjected to factor analysis in other cultures, the usual five traits have typically emerged (Katigbak, Church, & Akamine, 1996; Paunonen et al., 1992; Stumpf, 1993). Far more data are needed before theorists are ready to conclude that the basic structure of personality is pancultural, but the cross-cultural similarities observed thus far are impressive.

In contrast, when researchers have compared cultural groups on specific aspects of personality, some intriguing disparities have surfaced. For example, cultural variations have been found in *locus of control* and *self-monitoring*. Generally, studies find that samples from Western cultures have a more internal locus of control than samples from Asian cultures. Studies also suggest that people from industrialized nations tend to be more internal than those from developing nations (Berry et al., 1992). Only a few cross-cultural studies of self-monitoring have been conducted, but these studies indicate that subjects from the United States and Australia score higher in self-monitoring than subjects from Taiwan, Japan, Hong Kong, and Korea (Gudykunst et al., 1989; Gudykunst, Yang, & Nishida, 1987).

Perhaps the most interesting recent work on culture and personality has been that of Hazel

"Most of what psychologists currently know about human nature is based on one particular view—the so-called Western view of the individual as an independent, self-contained, autonomous entity."

HAZEL MARKUS AND
SHINOBU KITAYAMA

Markus and Shinobu Kitayama (1991, 1994) comparing American and Asian conceptions of the self. According to Markus and Kitayama, American parents teach their children to be self-reliant, to feel good about themselves, and to view themselves as special individuals. Children are encouraged to excel in competitive endeavors and to strive to stand out from the crowd. They are told that "the squeaky wheel gets the grease" and that "you have to stand up for yourself." Thus, Markus and Kitayama argue that *American culture fosters an independent view of the self.* American youngsters learn to define themselves in terms of their personal attributes, abilities, accomplishments, and possessions. Their unique strengths and achievements become the basis for their sense of self-worth. Hence, they are prone to exaggerate their uniqueness and to overestimate their abilities.

Most of us take this individualistic mentality for granted. Indeed, Markus and Kitayama maintain that "most of what psychologists currently know about human nature is based on one particular view—the so-called Western view of the individual as an independent, self-contained, autonomous entity" (1991, p. 224). However, they marshal convincing evidence that this view is *not* universal. They argue that in Asian cultures such as Japan and China, socialization practices foster a more *interdependent view of the self,* which emphasizes the fundamental connectedness of people to each other (see Figure 12.17). In these cultures, parents teach their children that they can rely on family and friends, that they should be modest about their personal accomplishments so they don't diminish others' achievements, and that they should view themselves as part of a larger social matrix. Children are encouraged to fit in with others and to avoid standing out from the crowd. A popular

Culture can shape personality. Children in Asiatic cultures, for example, grow up with a value system that allows them to view themselves as interconnected parts of larger social units. Hence, they tend to avoid positioning themselves so that they stand out from others.

adage in Japan reminds children that "the nail that stands out gets pounded down." Hence, Markus and Kitayama assert that Asian youngsters typically learn to define themselves in terms of the groups they belong to. Their harmonious relations with others and their pride in group achievements become the basis for their sense of self-worth. Because their self-esteem does not hinge so much on personal strengths, they have little need to exaggerate their uniqueness or their abilities. Consistent with this analysis, Markus and Kitayama report that Asian subjects tend to view themselves as more similar to their peers than American subjects do and that they consistently downplay their personal achievements more than Americans do.

Markus and Kitayama speculate that the interdependent view of self may also be the norm in many African and Latin American cultures, but more comparative data are needed to evaluate this possibility. In any case, the cultural variations in

Figure 12.17
Culture and conceptions of self. According to Markus and Kitayama (1991), Western cultures foster an independent view of the self as a unique individual who is separate from others, as diagrammed on the left. In contrast, Asian cultures encourage an interdependent view of the self as part of an interconnected social matrix, as diagrammed on the right. The interdependent view leads people to define themselves in terms of their social relationships (for instance, as someone's daughter, employee, colleague, or neighbor).

Independent self-system

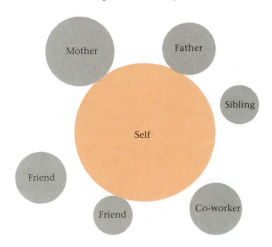

Interdependent self-system

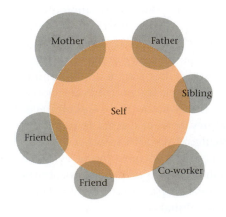

conceptions of self that they have uncovered are fascinating and will surely be the subject of much future research. Their findings demonstrate once again that we cannot assume that Western models of psychological processes will apply equally well in other cultures.

PUTTING IT IN PERSPECTIVE

The preceding discussion of culture and personality obviously highlighted the text's theme that people's behavior is influenced by their cultural heritage. This chapter has also been ideally suited for embellishing two other unifying themes: psychology's theoretical diversity and the idea that psychology evolves in a sociohistorical context.

No other area of psychology is characterized by as much theoretical diversity as the study of personality, where there are literally dozens of insightful theories. Some of this diversity exists because different theories attempt to explain different facets of behavior. However, much of this theoretical diversity reflects genuine disagreements on basic questions about personality. These disagreements are apparent on the next two pages, where you'll find an illustrated comparative overview of the ideas of Freud, Skinner, Rogers, and Eysenck, as representatives of the psychodynamic, behavioral, humanistic, and biological approaches to personality.

In previous chapters we've often seen movement toward reconciling contradictory theories. Has there been any such movement in the area of personality theory? Yes, but only a little. Eysenck has blended many behavioral concepts into his biological model. The humanistic perspective has left a mark on some of the more recent psychodynamic theories (for example, Kohut, 1971). Moreover, the emergence of social learning theory within the behavioral school of thought, with its focus on cognitive processes, has expanded the common ground shared by behaviorism and other theoretical approaches. Although these trends are interesting, the four major theoretical perspectives continue to provide four very different vantage points from which to examine the mysteries of personality.

The study of personality also highlights the sociohistorical context in which psychology evolves. Personality theories have left many marks on modern culture; we can mention only a handful as illustrations. The theories of Freud, Adler, and Skinner have had an enormous impact on child-rearing practices. The ideas of Freud and Jung have found their way into literature (influ-encing the portrayal of fictional characters) and the visual arts. For example, Freud's theory helped inspire surrealism's interest in the world of dreams (see Figure 12.18). Social learning theory has become embroiled in the public policy debate about whether media violence should be controlled, because of its effects on viewers' aggressive behavior. Maslow's hierarchy of needs and Skinner's affirmation of the value of positive reinforcement have given rise to new approaches to management in the world of business and industry.

Figure 12.18
Freud and surrealism. The theories of Freud and Jung had considerable influence on the arts. For instance, their ideas about the unconscious guided the surrealists' explorations of the irrational world of dreams. Salvador Dali's 1936 painting *Soft Construction with Boiled Beans: Premonition of Civil War* is a bizarre image that symbolizes how a society can tear itself apart. Freud once commented, "I was tempted to consider the surrealists, which apparently have chosen me for their patron saint, as a bunch of complete nuts . . . [but] the young Spaniard [Dali], with the magnificent eyes of a fanatic and his undeniable technical mastery, has caused me to reconsider" (quoted in Gerard, 1968). (Philadelphia Museum of Art: The Louise and Walter Arensberg Collection)

FOUR VIEWS OF PERSONALITY

Theorist and orientation	Source of data and observations	Key motivational forces
A psychodynamic view Sigmund Freud 	Case studies from clinical practice of psychoanalysis 	Sex and aggression; need to reduce tension resulting from internal conflicts
A behavioral view B. F. Skinner 	Laboratory experiments, primarily with animals 	Pursuit of primary (unlearned) and secondary (learned) reinforcers; priorities depend on personal history
A humanistic view Carl Rogers 	Case studies from clinical practice of client-centered therapy 	Actualizing tendency (motive to develop capacities, and experience personal growth) and self-actualizing tendency (motive to maintain self-concept and behave in ways that are consistent with self-concept)
A biological view Hans Eysenck 	Twin, family, and adoption studies of heritability; factor analysis studies of personality structure 	No specific motivational forces singled out.

Model of personality structure

Three interacting components (id, ego, superego) operating at three levels of consciousness

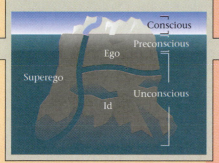

Collections of response tendencies tied to specific stimulus situations

Operant response tendencies

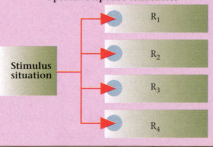

Self-concept, which may or may not mesh well with actual experience

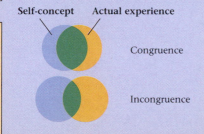

Hierarchy of traits, with specific traits derived from more fundamental, general traits

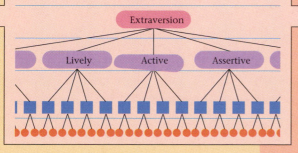

View of personality development

Emphasis on fixation or progress through psychosexual stages; experiences in early childhood (such as toilet training) can leave lasting mark on adult personality

Personality evolves gradually over the life span (not in stages); responses (such as extraverted joking) followed by reinforcement (such as appreciative laughter) become more frequent

Children who receive unconditional love have less need to be defensive; they develop more accurate, congruent self-concept; conditional love fosters incongruence

Emphasis on unfolding of genetic blueprint with maturation; inherited predispositions interact with learning experiences

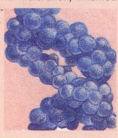

Roots of disorders

Unconscious fixations and unresolved conflicts from childhood, usually centering on sex and aggression

Maladaptive behavior due to faulty learning; the "symptom" *is* the problem, not a sign of underlying disease

Incongruence between self and actual experience (inaccurate self-concept); overdependence on others for approval and sense of worth

Genetic vulnerability activated in part by environmental factors

Sociohistorical forces also leave their imprint on psychology. This chapter provided many examples of how personal experiences, prevailing attitudes, and historical events have contributed to the evolution of ideas in psychology. For example, Freud's pessimistic view of human nature and his emphasis on the dark forces of aggression were shaped to some extent by his exposure to the hostilities of World War I and prevailing anti-Semitic sentiments. Freud's emphasis on sexuality was surely influenced by the Victorian climate of sexual repression that existed in his youth. Adler's views also reflected the social context in which he grew up. His interest in inferiority feelings and compensation appear to have sprung from his own sickly childhood and the difficulties he had to overcome. Likewise, it's reasonable to speculate that Jung's childhood loneliness and introversion may have sparked his interest in the introversion-extraversion dimension of personality. In a similar vein, we saw that both Rogers and Maslow had to resist parental pressures in order to pursue their career interests. Their emphasis on the need to achieve personal fulfillment may have originated in these experiences.

Progress in the study of personality has also been influenced by developments in other areas of psychology. For instance, the enterprise of psychological testing originally emerged out of efforts to measure general intelligence. Eventually, however, the principles of psychological testing were applied to the challenge of measuring personality. In the upcoming Application we discuss the logic and limitations of personality tests.

Recap of Key Points

• Modern personality research programs have tended to focus on specific personality traits. One such trait is locus of control, which is the degree to which people feel that they influence their outcomes. An internal locus of control is associated with better adjustment and higher academic achievement.

• Sensation seeking is a trait describing the degree to which people seek high or low levels of sensory stimulation. High sensation seekers are willing to take risks, are open to new experiences, and are susceptible to boredom.

• Self-monitoring is the degree to which people attend to and control the impressions they make on others. High self-monitors are skilled at impression management, but make genuine emotional commitments less readily than others.

• Although far more research is needed, some studies suggest that the basic trait structure of personality may be much the same across cultures. However, notable differences have been found when researchers have compared cultural groups on measures of specific personality traits, such as locus of control and self-monitoring.

• Markus and Kitayama assert that American culture fosters an independent conception of self, whereas Asian cultures foster an interdependent view of the self.

• The study of personality illustrates how psychology is characterized by great theoretical diversity. There has been relatively little movement toward reconciling contradictory theories of personality. The study of personality also demonstrates how ideas in psychology are shaped by sociohistorical forces and how cultural factors influence psychological processes.

APPLICATION: **UNDERSTANDING PERSONALITY ASSESSMENT**

Answer the following "true" or "false."

1 Responses to personality tests are subject to unconscious distortion.

2 The results of personality tests are often misunderstood.

3 Personality test scores should be interpreted with caution.

4 Personality tests serve many important functions.

If you answered "true" to all four questions, you earned a perfect score. Yes, personality tests are subject to distortion. Admittedly, test results are often misunderstood, and they should be interpreted cautiously. In spite of these problems, however, psychological tests can be quite useful.

Everyone engages in efforts to size up his or her own personality as well as that of others. When you think to yourself that "Mary Ann is shrewd and poised," or when you remark to a friend that "Howard is timid and submissive," you're making personality assessments. In a sense, then, personality assessment is an ongoing part of daily life. Given the popular interest in personality assessment, it's not surprising that psychologists have devised formal measures of personality.

The Uses of Personality Scales

Why are psychological tests used to measure personality? They have a variety of purposes. Benjamin Kleinmuntz (1985) lists four principal uses of personality tests:

1. Personality tests are used extensively by mental health professionals in the *clini-cal diagnosis* of psychological disorders. Although diagnoses are not made on the basis of test results alone, personality scales can be helpful in arriving at diagnostic decisions.

2. Personality measurement may be done for the purpose of *counseling* individuals about a variety of normal, everyday problems. Counselors often use personality scales to help people chart career plans and make vocational decisions.

3. Formal personality assessment often plays a key role in *personnel selection* in business, industry, government, and the military services. This use of personality testing has become controversial in recent years. Nonetheless, many organizations continue to use personality scales to assess applicants' suitability for various jobs.

4. Personality scales are frequently used in *psychological research.* Empirical studies on a great variety of issues require precise measurement of some aspect of personality. For instance, let's say you want to investigate whether introversion is related to a certain style of child rearing. Your task is simplified greatly if you have a personality test that measures introversion.

Personality tests can be divided into two broad categories: *self-report inventories* and *projective tests*. In this Application, we'll discuss some representative tests from both categories and discuss their strengths and weaknesses.

Self-Report Inventories

Self-report inventories **are personality tests that ask individuals to answer a series of questions about their characteristic behavior.** The logic underlying this approach is very simple: Who knows you better? Who has known you longer? Who has more access to your private feelings?

Some self-report inventories, such as the Sensation Seeking Scale and the Self-Monitoring Scale, are designed to measure one specific personality trait. Others can be used to measure many dimensions of personality simultaneously. Single-trait scales are used primarily in research. In clinical, counseling, and personnel work, psychologists rely more on multitrait inventories. We'll discuss three examples of multitrait scales: the MMPI, the 16PF, and the NEO Personality Inventory.

The MMPI

The most widely used multitrait scale is the Minnesota Multiphasic Personality Inventory (MMPI). This test was developed in the 1940s (Hathaway & McKinley, 1943) but has recently undergone a major revision and modernization. The authors of MMPI-2 set out to maintain the original character of the scale while replacing obsolete items, eliminating sexist language, and updating the test norms (Graham, 1990).

The MMPI was originally designed to aid clinicians in the diagnosis of psychological disorders. Consequently, it measures mostly aspects of personality that, when manifested to an extreme degree, are thought to be symptoms of disorders. Examples include traits such as paranoia, depression, and hysteria.

The MMPI is a rather lengthy test. The revised version consists of 567 statements to which the subject answers "true," "false," or "cannot say." The MMPI yields scores on the 14 subscales described in Table 12.3. Four of the subscales are *validity scales* that provide indications about whether a subject has been careless or deceptive in taking the test. The remaining 10 are *clinical scales* that measure various aspects of personality.

Are the MMPI clinical scales valid? That is, do they measure what they were

TABLE 12.3 PERSONALITY CHARACTERISTICS ASSOCIATED WITH HIGH MMPI SCORES

Scale	Characteristics Associated with Higher Scores
Validity scale	
Cannot say (?)	May increase evasiveness.
Lie scale (L)	Indicates a tendency to present oneself in an overly favorable or highly virtuous light.
Infrequency scale (F)	Items on this scale are endorsed very infrequently by most people. Suggests carelessness, confusion, or "faking illness."
Subtle defensiveness (K)	Measures defensiveness of a subtle nature.
Clinical scale	
Hypochondriasis (Hs)	Indicates person is preoccupied with self, complaining, hostile, and presenting numerous physical problems that tend to be chronic.
Depression (D)	Indicates person is moody, shy, despondent, pessimistic, and distressed; one of the most frequently elevated scales in clinical patients.
Hysteria (Hy)	Indicates person tends to rely on neurotic defenses such as denial and repression to deal with stress and tends to be dependent, naive, outgoing, infantile, and narcissistic.
Psychopathic deviation (Pd)	May indicate rebelliousness, impulsiveness, hedonism, antisocial behavior, difficulty in marital or family relationships, and trouble with the law or authority in general.
Masculinity/femininity (MF)	Indicates departure from traditional gender roles. High-scoring men are described as sensitive, aesthetic, passive, or feminine. They may show conflicts over sexual identity and low heterosexual drive. Because the direction of scoring is reversed, high-scoring women are seen as masculine, rough, aggressive, self-confident, unemotional, and insensitive.
Paranoia (Pa)	Often indicates person is suspicious, aloof, shrewd, guarded, worrisome, and overly sensitive and likely to project or externalize blame.
Psychasthenia (Pt)	Indicates person is tense, anxious, ruminative, preoccupied, obsessional, phobic, rigid, and frequently self-condemning and feeling inferior and inadequate.
Schizophrenia (Sc)	Often indicates person is withdrawn, shy, unusual, or strange and has peculiar thoughts or ideas, poor reality contact, and perhaps delusions and hallucinations.
Hypomania (Ma)	Indicates person is social, outgoing, impulsive, overly energetic, optimistic, and in some cases amoral, flighty, grandiose, and impulsive.
Social introversion (Sie)	Indicates person is introverted, shy, withdrawn, socially reserved, submissive, overcontrolled, lethargic, conventional, tense, inflexible, and guilt-prone.

Source: Adapted from Keller, Butcher, and Slutske (1990)

designed to measure? The validity of the MMPI has been investigated in hundreds of studies (Butcher & Keller, 1984). Originally, it was assumed that the 10 clinical subscales would provide direct indexes of specific types of disorders. In other words, a high score on the depression scale would be indicative of depression, a high score on the paranoia scale would be indicative of a paranoid disorder, and so forth. However, research revealed that the relations between MMPI scores and various types of pathology are much more complex than anticipated. People with most types of disorders show elevated scores on *several* MMPI subscales. This means that certain score *profiles* are indicative of specific disor-

ders (see Figure 12.19). Thus, the interpretation of the MMPI is quite complicated and critics have expressed concerns about various flaws in the test that were not addressed by the recent revision (Helmes & Reddon, 1993; Kline, 1992). Nonetheless, the MMPI can be a helpful diagnostic tool for the clinician. The fact that the inventory has been translated into more than 115 languages is a testimonial to its usefulness (Butcher, 1990).

The 16PF and NEO Personality Inventory

Raymond Cattell (1957, 1965) set out to identify and measure the *basic dimensions* of the *normal* personality. He started with

a previously compiled list of 4504 personality traits. This massive list was reduced to 171 traits by weeding out terms that were virtually synonymous. Cattell then used factor analysis to identify clusters of closely related traits and the factors underlying them. Eventually, he reduced the list of 171 traits to 16 *source traits*. The Sixteen Personality Factor (16PF) Questionnaire is a 187-item scale that assesses these 16 basic dimensions of personality (Cattell, Eber, & Tatsuoka, 1970), which are listed in Figure 12.20.

As we noted in the main body of the chapter, some theorists believe that only five trait dimensions are required to provide a full description of personality. This

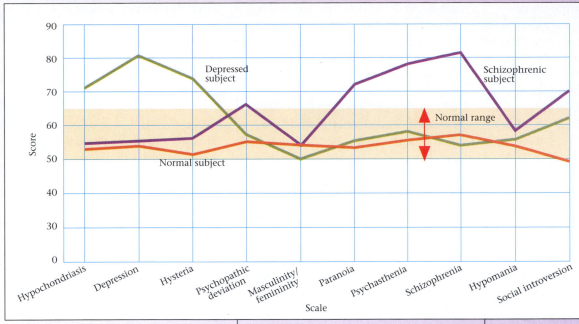

Figure 12.19
MMPI profiles. Scores on the 10 clinical scales of the MMPI are often plotted as shown here to create a profile for a client. The normal range for scores on each subscale is 50 to 65. People with disorders frequently exhibit elevated scores on several clinical scales rather than just one.

view has led to the creation of a relatively new test—the NEO Personality Inventory. Developed by Paul Costa and Robert McCrae (1985, 1992), the NEO Inventory is designed to measure the Big Five traits: neuroticism, extraversion, openness to experience, agreeableness, and conscientiousness. In spite of its short life span, the NEO is already widely used in research and clinical work. Some testing experts, such as Joseph Mattarazzo (1992), believe that the NEO represents the wave of the future in personality assessment.

Strengths and Weaknesses of Self-Report Inventories

To appreciate the strengths of self-report inventories, consider how else you might inquire about an individual's personality. For instance, if you want to know how assertive someone is, why not just ask the person? Why administer an elaborate 50-item personality inventory that measures assertiveness? The advantage of the personality inventory is that it can provide a more objective and more precise estimate, one that is better grounded in extensive comparative data. Take a moment to consider: How assertive are you? You probably have some vague idea, but to accurately gauge your assertiveness you would need a great deal of comparative information about others' assertiveness, which you lack.

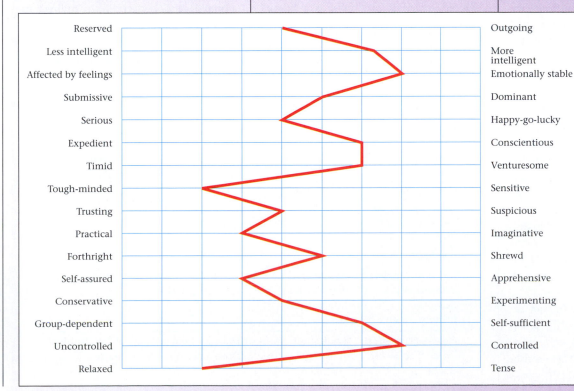

Figure 12.20
The Sixteen Personality Factor Questionnaire (16PF). Unlike the MMPI, Cattell's 16PF is designed to assess normal aspects of personality. The pairs of traits listed across from each other in the figure define the 16 factors measured by this self-report inventory. The profile shown is the average profile seen among a group of airline pilots who took the test.

In contrast, a self-report inventory inquires about your typical behavior in a variety of circumstances requiring assertiveness and generates an exact comparison with the typical behavior reported by many other respondents for the same circumstances.

Although self-report inventories are much more thorough and precise than casual observations, they are only as accurate as the information that respondents provide. They are susceptible to several sources of error (Kline, 1995; Paulhus, 1991; Shedler, Mayman, & Manis, 1993), including the following:

1. *Deliberate deception.* Some self-report inventories include many questions whose purpose is easy to figure out. This problem makes it possible for some respondents to intentionally fake particular personality traits.

2. *Social desirability bias.* Without realizing it, some people consistently respond to questions in ways that make them look good. The social desirability bias isn't a matter of deception so much as wishful thinking.

3. *Response sets.* A response set is a systematic tendency to respond to test items in a particular way that is unrelated to the content of the items. For instance, some people, called "yea-sayers," tend to agree with virtually every statement on a test. Other people, called "nay-sayers," tend to disagree with nearly every statement.

Test developers have devised a number of strategies to reduce the impact of deliberate deception, social desirability bias, and response sets (Berry, Wetter, & Baer, 1995; Jackson, 1973). For instance, it's possible to insert a "lie scale" into a test to assess the likelihood that a respondent is engaging in deception. The MMPI has a lie scale made up of 15 items that ask the subject to acknowledge minor faults that virtually everyone has. Subjects who report themselves to be nearly faultless on these questions are probably being deceptive.

The best way to reduce the impact of social desirability bias is to identify items that are sensitive to this bias and drop them from the test. Problems with response sets can be reduced by systematically vary-

ing the way in which test items are worded. The key is to balance the items so that responses of agreement and disagreement are equally likely to be indicative of the trait being measured.

Projective tests, which all take a rather indirect approach to the assessment of personality, are used extensively in clinical work. *Projective tests* **ask subjects to respond to vague, ambiguous stimuli in ways that may reveal the subjects' needs, feelings, and personality traits** (see Table 12.4 for examples). The Rorschach test, for instance, consists of a series of ten inkblots. Respondents are asked to describe what they see in the blots (see the photo on page 513). In the Thematic Apperception Test (TAT), a series of pictures of simple scenes are presented to subjects, who are asked to tell stories about what is happening in the scenes and what the characters are feeling. For instance, one TAT card shows a young boy contemplating a violin resting on a table in front of him (see Figure 12.21 for another example).

The Projective Hypothesis

The "projective hypothesis" is that ambiguous materials can serve as a blank screen onto which people project their characteristic concerns, conflicts, and desires (Frank, 1939). Thus, a competitive person who is shown the TAT card of the boy at the table with the violin might concoct a story about how the boy is contemplating an upcoming musical competition at which he hopes to excel. The same card shown to a person high in impulsiveness might elicit a story about how the boy is planning to sneak out the door to go dirtbike riding with friends.

The scoring and interpretation of projective tests is very complicated. Rorschach responses may be analyzed in terms of content, originality, the feature of the inkblot that determined the response, and the amount of the inkblot used, among other criteria. In fact, five different systems exist for scoring the Rorschach (Edberg, 1990). TAT stories are examined in terms of heroes, needs, themes, and outcomes.

Strengths and Weaknesses of Projective Tests

Proponents of projective tests assert that the tests have two unique strengths. First, they are not transparent to subjects. That is, the subject doesn't know how the test provides information to the tester. Hence, it's difficult for people to engage in intentional deception. Second, the indirect ap-

TABLE 12.4 REPRESENTATIVE PROJECTIVE TESTS

Test	Stimuli Presented	Response Request
Rorschach test (Rorschach, 1942)	10 cards, each with a bilaterally symmetric inkblot	"Tell me what this might be."
Thematic Apperception Test (TAT) (Murray, 1943)	10 to 12 (out of 30 available) cards depicting simple scenes	"Tell me a story about each picture. Tell me what is happening, what the characters are thinking and feeling . . ."
Menninger Word Association Test (Rapaport, Gill, & Schafer, 1968)	60 nouns	"Tell me the first word that comes to mind."
Rotter Incomplete Sentence Blank (Rotter & Rafferty, 1950)	40 sentence stems such as "My greatest fear is . . ."	"Finish the sentence in writing as rapidly as possible."
Draw-a-Person Test (Machover, 1949)	Blank sheet of paper	"Draw a whole person." (When finished: "Draw a person of the other sex.")

Subjects are shown a series of 10 inkblots from the Rorschach test and are asked to describe the forms that they see in these ambiguous stimuli. Evidence on the reliability and validity of the Rorschach is controversial.

proach used in these tests may make them especially sensitive to unconscious, latent features of personality.

Unfortunately, there is inadequate evidence for the reliability (consistency) and validity of projective measures. In particular, doubts have been raised about the research evidence on the Rorschach test (Wood, Nezworski, & Stejskal, 1996). In spite of these problems, projective tests continue to be widely used by clinicians (Piotrowski, Sherry, & Keller, 1985). In fact, about 30 years ago, a reviewer characterized the critics of projective tests as "doubting statisticians" and the users of projective tests as "enthusiastic clinicians" (Adcock, 1965), and little has changed since then.

The continued popularity of projective techniques suggests that they are effective in eliciting information that is valuable to many clinicians. Although the subjectivity of the projective tests raises serious concerns about their use in clinical diagnosis, some projective measures have shown adequate reliability and validity for research purposes when users agree on a systematic scoring procedure (Parker, 1983). For instance, as we discussed in Chapter 10, adaptations of the Thematic Apperception Test have yielded reliable measurements of the need for achievement, and the test has been invaluable in research on motivation (Spangler, 1992).

Although the problems associated with self-report inventories and projective tests can't be eliminated entirely, these measurement strategies have proven useful in personality assessment. In light of the potential for distortion, however, the results of personality tests should be interpreted with caution. Of course, as we saw in Chap-

ter 9, prudence is *always* in order when interpreting psychological test results of any kind.

Recap of Key Points
• Personality assessment is useful in clinical diagnosis, counseling, personnel selection, and research. Personality scales can be divided into self-report inventories and projective tests.
• Self-report measures ask subjects to describe themselves. The MMPI is a widely used inventory that measures pathological aspects of personality. The 16PF assesses 16 dimensions of the normal personality. The NEO personality inventory measures the Big Five personality traits.
• Self-report inventories are vulnerable to certain sources of error, including deception, the social desirability bias, and response sets.
• Projective tests, such as the Rorschach and TAT, assume that subjects' responses to ambiguous stimuli reveal something about their personality. While the projective hypothesis seems plausible, projective tests' reliability and validity are disturbingly low.

Figure 12.21
The Thematic Apperception Test (TAT). In taking the TAT, a respondent is asked to tell stories about scenes such as this one. The themes apparent in each story can be scored to provide insight about the respondent's personality.

Key Ideas

The Nature of Personality

◆ The concept of personality explains the consistency in people's behavior over time and situations while also explaining their distinctiveness. There is considerable debate as to how many trait dimensions are necessary to account for the variation in personality, but the Big Five model has become the dominant conception of personality structure.

Psychodynamic Perspectives

◆ Freud's psychoanalytic theory emphasizes the importance of the unconscious. Freud described personality structure in terms of three components—the id, ego, and superego—which are routinely involved in an ongoing series of internal conflicts.

◆ Freud theorized that conflicts centering on sex and aggression are especially likely to lead to significant anxiety. According to Freud, anxiety and other unpleasant emotions such as guilt are often warded off with defense mechanisms.

◆ Freud described a series of five psychosexual stages of development: oral, anal, phallic, latency, and genital. Certain experiences during these stages can have lasting effects on adult personality.

◆ Jung's most innovative and controversial concept was the collective unconscious. Adler's individual psychology emphasizes how people strive for superiority to compensate for their feelings of inferiority.

◆ Overall, psychodynamic theories have produced many ground-breaking insights about the unconscious, the role of internal conflict, and the importance of early childhood experiences in personality development. However, psychodynamic theories have been criticized for their poor testability, their inadequate base of empirical evidence, and their male-centered views.

Behavioral Perspectives

◆ Behavioral theories view personality as a collection of response tendencies tied to specific stimulus situations. They assume that personality development is a lifelong process in which response tendencies are shaped and reshaped by learning, especially operant conditioning.

◆ Social learning theory focuses on how cognitive factors such as expectancies and self-efficacy regulate learned behavior. Bandura's concept of observational learning accounts for the acquisition of responses from models. Mischel has questioned the degree to which people display cross-situational consistency in behavior.

◆ Behavioral approaches to personality are based on rigorous research. They have provided ample insights into how environmen-

tal factors and learning mold personalities. The behaviorists have been criticized for their overdependence on animal research, their fragmented analysis of personality, and radical behaviorism's dehumanizing view of human nature.

Humanistic Perspectives

◆ Humanistic theories are phenomenological and take an optimistic view of human potential. Rogers focused on the self-concept as the critical aspect of personality. He maintained that anxiety is attributable to incongruence between one's self-concept and reality. Maslow theorized that psychological health depends on fulfilling one's need for self-actualization.

◆ Humanistic theories deserve credit for highlighting the importance of subjective views of oneself and for confronting the question of what makes for a healthy personality. Humanistic theories lack a firm base of research, are difficult to put to an empirical test, and may be overly optimistic about human nature.

Biological Perspectives

◆ Contemporary biological theories stress the genetic origins of personality. Eysenck suggests that heredity influences individual differences in physiological functioning that affect how easily people acquire conditioned responses. Our Featured Study on the personality resemblance of twins reared apart provides impressive evidence that genetic factors shape personality.

◆ Recent research in behavioral genetics has suggested that shared family environment has surprisingly little impact on personality. Evolutionary theorists argue that the major dimensions of personality reflect humans' adaptive landscape. The biological approach has been criticized because of methodological problems with heritability ratios and because it offers no systematic model of how physiology shapes personality.

Contemporary Empirical Approaches to Personality

◆ Modern personality research programs have tended to focus on specific personality traits. One such trait is locus of control, which is the degree to which people feel that they influence their outcomes. Sensation seeking is a trait describing the degree to which people seek high or low levels of sensory stimulation. Self-monitoring is the degree to which people attend to and control the impressions they make on others.

Culture and Personality

◆ Some studies suggest that the basic trait structure of personality may be much the same across cultures. However, notable differences have been found when researchers

have compared cultural groups' conceptions of self.

Putting It in Perspective

◆ The study of personality illustrates how psychology is characterized by great theoretical diversity. It also demonstrates how ideas in psychology are shaped by sociohistorical forces and how cultural factors influence psychological processes.

Application: Understanding Personality Assessment

◆ Personality assessment is useful in clinical diagnosis, counseling, personnel selection, and research. Self-report measures ask subjects to describe themselves. Self-report inventories are vulnerable to certain sources of error, including deception, the social desirability bias, and response sets.

◆ Projective tests assume that subjects' responses to ambiguous stimuli reveal something about their personality. While the projective hypothesis seems plausible, projective tests' reliability and validity are disturbingly low.

Key Terms

Archetypes
Behaviorism
Cardinal trait
Central traits
Collective
    unconscious
Compensation
Conscious
Defense mechanisms
Displacement
Ego
Extraverts
Factor analysis
Fixation
Humanism
Id
Identification
Incongruence
Introverts
Locus of control
Model
Need for self-
    actualization
Observational
    learning
Oedipal complex
Personal
    unconscious
Personality
Personality trait
Phenomenological
    approach
Pleasure principle
Preconscious
Projection
Projective tests

Psychodynamic
    theories
Psychosexual stages
Rationalization
Reaction formation
Reality principle
Reciprocal
    determinism
Regression
Repression
Secondary traits
Self-actualizing
    persons
Self-concept
Self-efficacy
Self-monitoring
Self-report inventories
Sensation seeking
Striving for superiority
Superego
Unconscious

Key People

Alfred Adler
Gordon Allport
Albert Bandura
Raymond Cattell
Hans Eysenck
Sigmund Freud
Carl Jung
Abraham Maslow
Walter Mischel
Carl Rogers
B. F. Skinner

Practice Test

1. Harvey Hedonist has devoted his life to the search for physical pleasure and immediate need gratification. Freud would say that Harvey is dominated by:
   A. his ego.
   B. his superego.
   C. his id.
   D. Bacchus.

2. Furious at her boss for what she considers to be unjust criticism, Clara turns around and takes out her anger on her subordinates. Clara may be using the defense mechanism of:
   A. displacement.
   B. reaction formation.
   C. identification.
   D. replacement.

3. Freud believed that most personality disturbances are due to:
   A. the failure of parents to reinforce healthy behavior.
   B. a poor self-concept resulting from excessive parental demands.
   C. unconscious and unresolved sexual conflicts rooted in childhood experiences.
   D. the exposure of children to unhealthy role models.

4. According to Alfred Adler, the prime motivating force in a person's life is:
   A. physical gratification.
   B. existential anxiety.
   C. striving for superiority.
   D. the need for power.

5. Which of the following learning mechanisms does B. F. Skinner see as being the major means by which behavior is learned?
   A. classical conditioning
   B. operant conditioning
   C. observational learning
   D. insight learning

6. Always having been a good student, Irving is confident that he will do well in his psychology course. According to Bandura's social learning theory, Irving would be said to have:
   A. strong feelings of self-efficacy.
   B. a sense of superiority.
   C. strong feelings of self-esteem.
   D. strong defense mechanisms.

7. Which of the following approaches to personality is least deterministic?
   A. the humanistic approach
   B. the psychoanalytic approach
   C. the social learning approach
   D. the behavioral approach

8. Which of the following did Carl Rogers believe fosters a congruent self-concept?
   A. conditional love
   B. appropriate role models
   C. immediate-need gratification
   D. unconditional love

9. The strongest support for the theory that personality is heavily influenced by genetics is provided by strong personality similarity between:
   A. identical twins reared together.
   B. identical twins reared apart.
   C. fraternal twins reared together.
   D. nontwins reared together.

10. Which of the following is the best way to regard heritability estimates?
   A. as reliable but not necessarily valid estimates
   B. as ballpark estimates of the influence of genetics
   C. as accurate estimates of the influence of genetics
   D. as relatively useless estimates of the influence of genetics

11. An external locus of control has been found to correlate with:
   A. a healthy sense of self.
   B. feelings of anxiety and depression.
   C. a sense of self-efficacy.
   D. higher achievement.

12. If given a choice between staying home to read a good book and spending the day at an amusement park, Meg is likely to stay home. Marvin Zuckerman would say that Meg is probably:
   A. a low self-monitor.
   B. someone with a more internal locus of control.
   C. relatively low in sensation seeking.
   D. psychologically repressed.

13. In which of the following cultures is an independent view of the self most likely to be the norm?
   A. China
   B. Japan
   C. Africa
   D. America

14. Which of the following is *not* a shortcoming of self-report personality inventories?
   A. The accuracy of the results is a function of the honesty of the respondent.
   B. Respondents may attempt to answer in a way that makes them look good.
   C. There is sometimes a problem with "yea-sayers" or "nay-sayers."
   D. They are objective measures that are easy to administer and score.

15. Which of the following is a projective test?
   A. the Rorschach Inkblot Test
   B. the Minnesota Multiphasic Personality Inventory
   C. Cattell's 16 Personality Factor Questionnaire
   D. the NEO Personality Inventory

Answers

1	C	Pages 476–477	6	A	Page 488	11	B	Pages 500–501
2	A	Page 479	7	A	Pages 489–490	12	C	Page 501
3	C	Page 482	8	D	Page 491	13	D	Page 504
4	C	Pages 483–484	9	B	Page 496	14	D	Page 512
5	B	Page 486	10	B	Page 498	15	A	Pages 512–513

13

STRESS, COPING, AND HEALTH

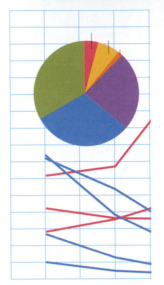

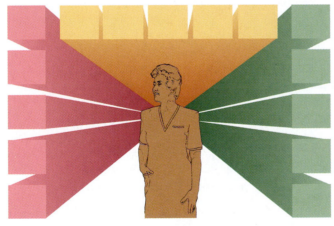

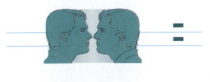

516

You're in your car headed home from school with a classmate. Traffic is barely moving. A radio report indicates that the traffic jam is only going to get worse. You groan audibly as you fiddle impatiently with the radio dial. Another driver nearly takes your fender off trying to cut into your lane. Your pulse quickens as you shout insults at the person, who can't even hear you. You think about the term paper that you have to work on tonight. Your stomach knots up as you recall all the crumpled drafts you tossed into the wastebasket last night. If you don't finish that paper soon, you won't be able to find any time to study for your math test, not to mention your biology quiz. Suddenly, you remember that you promised the person you're dating that the two of you would get together tonight. There's no way. Another fight looms on the horizon. Your classmate asks how you feel about the tuition increase that the college announced yesterday. You've been trying not to think about it. You're already in debt up to your ears. Your parents are bugging you about changing schools, but you don't want to leave your friends. Your heartbeat quickens as you contemplate the debate you're sure to have with your parents. You feel wired with tension as you realize that the stress in your life never seems to let up.

Many circumstances can create stress. It comes in all sorts of packages: big and small, pretty and ugly, simple and complex. All too often, the package comes as a surprise. In this chapter we'll try to sort out these packages. We'll discuss the nature of stress, how people cope with stress, and the potential effects of stress. Among other things, we'll discuss the following questions:

• Why is the same event stressful for one person but not another?
• Is change of any kind inherently stressful?
• How do people typically cope with stress?
• How does stress affect psychological and physical health?

Our examination of the relationship between stress and physical illness will lead us into a broader discussion of the psychology of health. The way people in health professions think about physical illness has changed considerably in the past 10 to 20 years. The traditional view of physical illness as a purely biological phenomenon has given way to

a biopsychosocial model of illness (Smilkstein, 1990). **The *biopsychosocial model* holds that physical illness is caused by a complex interaction of biological, psychological, and sociocultural factors.** This model does not suggest that biological factors are unimportant. It simply asserts that these factors operate in a psychosocial context that is also influential.

What has led to this shift in thinking? In part, it's a result of changing patterns of illness. Prior to the 20th century, the principal threats to health were *contagious diseases* caused by infectious agents—diseases such as smallpox, typhoid fever, diphtheria, yellow fever, malaria, cholera, tuberculosis, and polio. Today, none of these diseases is among the leading killers in the United States. They were tamed by improvements in nutrition, public hygiene, sanitation, and medical treatment (Grob, 1983). Unfortunately, the void left by contagious diseases has been filled all too quickly by *chronic diseases* that develop gradually, such as heart disease, cancer, and stroke (see Figure 13.1 on page 518). Psychosocial factors, such as stress, health habits, and lifestyle, play a large role in the development of these chronic diseases.

The growing recognition that psychological factors influence physical health has led to the emergence of a new specialty area within psychology. ***Health psychology* is concerned with how psychosocial factors relate to the promotion and maintenance of health and with the causation, prevention, and treatment of illness.** In the second half of this chapter, we'll explore this new domain of health psychology, tackling such questions as:

• How do patterns of behavior contribute to heart disease?
• How strong is the association between stress and physical illness?
• Why do people continue to pursue health-impairing lifestyles when they know that they're endangering their health?
• Why do people delay needed medical treatment and ignore the advice of their doctors?

In our chapter Application, we'll focus on strategies for improving stress management. However, you can't manage stress very effectively if you can't recognize it, so let's take an in-depth look at the nature of stress.

Figure 13.1
Changing patterns of illness. Trends in the death rates for various diseases during the 20th century reveal that contagious diseases (shown in blue) have declined as a threat to health. However, the death rates for stress-related chronic diseases (shown in red) have remained quite high. The pie chart (inset) shows the results of these trends: three chronic diseases (heart disease, cancer, and stroke) account for 62.4% of all deaths.

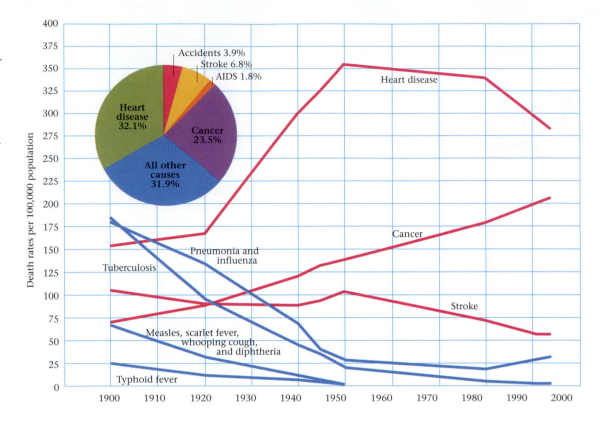

THE NATURE OF STRESS

The word *stress* has been used in different ways by different theorists. We'll define **stress as any circumstances that threaten or are perceived to threaten one's well-being and that thereby tax one's coping abilities.** The threat may be to immediate physical safety, long-range security, self-esteem, reputation, peace of mind, or many other things that one values. This is a complex concept, so let's explore a little further.

Stress as an Everyday Event

The word *stress* tends to spark images of overwhelming, traumatic crises. People may think of tornadoes, hurricanes, floods, and earthquakes. Undeniably, major disasters of this sort are extremely stressful events (Rubonis & Bickman, 1991; Weisaeth, 1993). However, these unusual events are only a small part of what stress is. Many everyday events, such as waiting in line, having car trouble, shopping for Christmas presents, misplacing your checkbook, and staring at bills you can't pay, are also stressful. In recent years, researchers have found that everyday problems and the minor nuisances of life are also important forms of stress (Kohn, Lafreniere, & Gurevich, 1991). Of course, major and minor stressors are not entirely inde-

pendent. A major stressful event, such as going through a divorce, can trigger a cascade of minor stressors, such as looking for an attorney, moving, taking on new household responsibilities, and so forth (Pillow, Zautra, & Sandler, 1996).

You might guess that minor stresses would produce minor effects, but that isn't necessarily true. Research indicates that routine hassles may have significant harmful effects on mental and physical health (Delongis, Folkman, & Lazarus, 1988).

Why would minor hassles be related to mental health? The answer isn't entirely clear yet, but it may be because of the *cumulative* nature of stress (Seta, Seta, & Wang, 1991). Stress adds up. Routine stresses at home, at school, and at work might be fairly benign individually, but collectively they could create great strain. Everyday hassles are common, frequent stressors that may pile up until they eventually overwhelm you.

Appraisal: Stress Lies in the Eye of the Beholder

The experience of feeling stressed depends on what events one notices and how one chooses to appraise or interpret them. Events that are stressful for one person may be routine for another. For example, many people find flying in an airplane somewhat stressful, but frequent fliers may not be bothered at all. Some people enjoy the excitement of going out on a date with someone new; others find the uncertainty terrifying.

In discussing appraisals of stress, Lazarus and Folkman (1984) distinguish between primary and secondary appraisal. *Primary appraisal* **is an initial evaluation of whether an event is (1) irrelevant to you, (2) relevant but not threatening, or (3) stressful.** When you view an event as stressful, you're likely to make a *secondary appraisal,* **which is an evaluation of your coping resources and options for dealing with the stress.** Thus, your primary appraisal would determine whether you see an upcoming job interview as stressful. Your secondary appraisal would determine how stressful this interview appears in light of your ability to deal with it.

Often, people aren't very objective in their appraisals of potentially stressful events. A study of hospitalized patients awaiting surgery showed only a slight correlation between the objective seriousness of a person's upcoming surgery and the amount of fear experienced by the patient (Janis, 1958). Clearly, some people are more prone than others to feel threatened by life's difficulties. A number of studies have shown that anxious, neurotic people report more stress than others (Brett et al., 1990), as do people who are relatively unhappy (Seidlitz & Diener, 1993). Thus, stress lies in the eye (actually, the mind) of the beholder. People's appraisals of stressful events are highly subjective.

Of course, appraisals of potentially stressful events are also influenced by various aspects of the events themselves. Two factors that stand out are (1) the controllability of the events and (2) the predictability of the events. *In general, events are more stressful when they are uncontrollable and unpredictable* (Folkman, 1984; Matthews et al., 1989). However, the effects of controllability and predictability are complex and the evidence is inconsistent (Arthur, 1986; Burger, 1989). Apparently, some people would rather not have the increased responsibility—to take charge and cope—that comes with the potential for control. And there are situations in which people prefer not to know about stress in advance. For instance, when understudy actors or rookie athletes are pressed into service as last-minute substitutes for more experienced performers, many comment, "It was better that way. I didn't have time to dwell on it and get nervous."

"We developed the Hassle Scale because we think scales that measure major events miss the point. They don't tell us anything about what goes on day in and day out, hour after hour, in a person's life. The constant, minor irritants may be much more important than the large, landmark changes."

RICHARD LAZARUS

MAJOR TYPES OF STRESS

An enormous variety of events can be stressful for one person or another. Although they're not entirely independent, the four principal types of stress are (1) frustration, (2) conflict, (3) change, and (4) pressure. As you read about each of these, you'll surely recognize four very familiar adversaries.

Frustration

I had a wonderful relationship with a married man for three months. One day when we planned to spend the entire day together, he called and said he wouldn't be meeting me. Someone had mentioned me to his wife, and he said that to keep his marriage together he would have to stop seeing me. I cried all morning. The grief was like losing someone through death. I still hurt, and I wonder if I'll ever get over him.

This scenario illustrates frustration. As psychologists use the term, *frustration* **occurs in any situation in which the pursuit of some goal is thwarted.** In essence, you experience frustration when you want something and you can't have it. Everyone has to deal with frustration virtually every day. Traffic jams, for instance, are a routine source of frustration that can affect mood and blood pressure (Schaeffer et al., 1988). Fortunately, most frustrations are brief and insignificant. You may be quite upset when you go to a repair shop to pick up your ailing stereo and find that it hasn't been fixed as promised. However, a week later you'll probably have your stereo back, and the frustration will be forgotten.

Of course, some frustrations can be sources of significant stress. Failures and losses are two common kinds of frustration that are often highly stressful. Everyone fails in at least some of his or her endeavors. Some people make failure almost inevitable by setting unrealistically high goals for themselves. For example, many business executives tend to forget that for every newly appointed vice president in the business world, there are dozens of middle-level executives who don't get promoted. Losses can be especially frustrating because people are deprived of something that they're accustomed to having. For example, few things are more frustrating than losing a dearly loved boyfriend, girlfriend, spouse, or parent.

Conflict

Should I or shouldn't I? I became engaged at Christmas. My fiance surprised me with a ring. I knew if I refused the ring he would be terribly hurt and our relationship would suffer. However, I don't really know whether or not I want to marry him. On the other hand, I don't want to lose him either.

Like frustration, conflict is an unavoidable feature of everyday life. The perplexing question "Should I or shouldn't I?" comes up countless times in everyone's life. *Conflict* **occurs when two or more incompatible motivations or behavioral impulses compete for expression.** As we discussed in Chapter 12, Sigmund Freud proposed nearly a century ago that internal conflicts generate considerable psychological distress. This link between conflict and distress was measured with new precision in recent studies by Laura King and Robert Emmons (1990, 1991). They used an elaborate questionnaire to assess the overall amount of internal conflict experienced by subjects. They found that higher levels of conflict were associated with higher levels of anxiety, depression, and physical symptoms.

Conflicts come in three types, which were originally described by Kurt Lewin (1935) and investigated extensively by Neal Miller (1944, 1959). These three basic types of conflict—approach-approach, avoidance-avoidance, and approach-avoidance—are diagrammed in Figure 13.2.

In an *approach-approach conflict* **a choice must be made between two attractive goals.** The problem, of course, is that you can choose just one of the two goals. For example: You have a free afternoon; should you play tennis or racquetball? You're out for a meal; do you want the pizza or the spaghetti? You can't afford both—should you buy the blue sweater or the gray jacket?

Among the three kinds of conflict, the approach-approach type tends to be the least stressful. People don't usually stagger out of restaurants exhausted by the stress of choosing which of several appealing entrees to eat. Approach-approach conflicts typically have a reasonably happy ending, whichever way you decide to go. Nonetheless, approach-approach conflicts over important issues may sometimes be troublesome. If you're torn between two appealing college majors or two attractive boyfriends, you may find the decision-making process quite stressful, since whichever alternative is not chosen represents a loss of sorts.

In an *avoidance-avoidance conflict* **a choice must be made between two unattractive goals.** Forced to choose between two repelling alternatives, you are, as they say, "caught between a rock and a hard place." For example, should you continue to collect unemployment checks, or should you take that degrading job at the car wash? Or suppose you have painful backaches. Should you submit to surgery that you dread, or should you continue to live with the back pain? Obviously, avoidance-avoidance conflicts are most unpleasant and highly stressful.

In an *approach-avoidance conflict* **a choice must be made about whether to pursue a single goal that has both attractive and unattractive aspects.** For instance, imagine that you're offered a career promotion that will mean a large increase in pay, but you'll have to move to a city that you hate. Approach-avoidance conflicts are common and can be quite stressful. Any time you have to take a risk to pursue some desirable outcome, you're likely to find yourself in an approach-avoidance conflict. Should you risk rejection by asking out a person that you are attracted to? Should you risk your savings by investing in a new business that could fail?

Approach-avoidance conflicts often produce *vacillation.* That is, you go back and forth, beset by indecision. You decide to go ahead, then you de-

Figure 13.2
Types of conflict. Psychologists have identified three basic types of conflict. In approach-approach and avoidance-avoidance conflicts, a person is torn between two goals. In an approach-avoidance conflict, there is only one goal under consideration, but it has both positive and negative aspects.

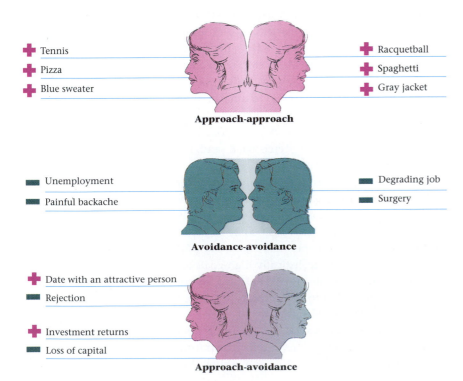

Tennis
Pizza
Blue sweater

Racquetball
Spaghetti
Gray jacket

Approach-approach

Unemployment
Painful backache

Degrading job
Surgery

Avoidance-avoidance

Date with an attractive person
Rejection

Investment returns
Loss of capital

Approach-avoidance

cide not to, and then you decide to go ahead again. Humans are not unique in this respect. Many years ago, Neal Miller (1944) observed the same vacillation in his ground-breaking research with rats. He created approach-avoidance conflicts in hungry rats by alternately feeding and shocking them at one end of a runway apparatus. Eventually, these rats tended to hover near the center of the runway, alternately approaching and retreating from the goal box at the end of the alley.

In a series of studies of approach-avoidance conflict, Miller (1959) plotted how an organism's tendency to approach a goal (the approach gradient in Figure 13.3) and to retreat from a goal (the avoidance gradient in Figure 13.3) both increase as the organism nears the goal. He found that avoidance motivation increases more rapidly than approach motivation (as reflected by the avoidance gradient's steeper slope in Figure 13.3). As a result of his analysis, Miller concluded that *in trying to resolve an approach-avoidance conflict, one should focus more on decreasing avoidance motivation than on increasing approach motivation.*

How would this insight apply to a complex human dilemma? Imagine that you're counseling a friend who is vacillating over whether to ask someone out on a date. Miller would say that you should downplay the negative aspects of possible rejection (thus lowering the avoidance gradient) rather than dwell on how much fun the date could be (thus raising the approach gradient).

Change

After my divorce, I lived alone for four years. Six months ago I married a wonderful woman who has two children from her previous marriage. My biggest stress is suddenly having to adapt to living with three people instead of by myself. I was pretty set in my ways. I had certain routines. Now everything is chaos. I love my wife and I'm fond of the kids. They're not really doing anything wrong. But my house and my life just aren't the same, and I'm having trouble dealing with it all.

It has been proposed that life changes, such as a change in marital status, represent a key type of stress. **Life changes** are any noticeable alterations in one's living circumstances that require readjustment. As we discussed in Chapter 2, Thomas Holmes, Richard Rahe, and their colleagues set out to explore the relations between stressful life events and physical illness (Holmes & Rahe, 1967; Rahe & Arthur, 1978). Theorizing that stress might make people more vulnerable to illness, they interviewed thousands of tuberculosis patients to find out what

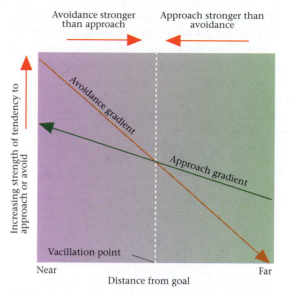

Figure 13.3
Vacillation in approach-avoidance conflict. According to Miller, as you near a goal that has positive and negative features, avoidance motivation tends to increase faster than approach motivation, sending you into retreat. However, if you retreat far enough, you'll eventually reach a point where approach motivation is stronger than avoidance motivation, and you may decide to go ahead once again. The ebb and flow of this process leads to vacillation.

kinds of events had preceded the onset of their disease. Surprisingly, the most frequently cited events were not uniformly negative. There were plenty of aversive events, as expected. But there were also many seemingly positive events, such as getting married, having a baby, or getting promoted.

Why would positive events, such as moving to a nicer home, produce stress? According to Holmes and Rahe, it's because they produce *change.* In their view, changes in personal relationships, changes at work, changes in finances, and so forth can be stressful even when the changes are welcomed.

Based on this analysis, Holmes and Rahe (1967) developed the Social Readjustment Rating Scale

CONCEPT CHECK 13.1
Identifying Types of Conflict

Check your understanding of the three basic types of conflict by identifying the type experienced in each of the following examples. The answers are in Appendix A.

Examples

_____ 1. John can't decide whether to take a demeaning job in a car wash or to go on welfare.

_____ 2. Mary wants to apply to a highly selective law school, but she hates to risk the possibility of rejection.

_____ 3. Ellen has been shopping for a new car and is torn between a nifty little sports car and a classy sedan, both of which she really likes.

Types of conflict

a. approach-approach

b. avoidance-avoidance

c. approach-avoidance

(SRRS) to measure life change as a form of stress. The scale assigns numerical values to 43 major life events. These values are supposed to reflect the magnitude of the readjustment required by each change (see Table 13.1). In using the scale, respondents are asked to indicate how often they experienced any of these 43 events during a certain time period (typically, the past year). The numbers associated with each event checked are then added. This total is an index of the amount of change-related stress the person has recently experienced.

The SRRS and similar scales based on it have been used in thousands of studies by researchers all over the world. Overall, these studies have shown that people with higher scores on the SRRS tend to be more vulnerable to many kinds of physical illness and to many types of psychological problems as well (Creed, 1993; Derogatis & Coons, 1993: Gruen, 1993). These results have attracted a great deal of attention, and the SRRS has been reprinted in many popular newspapers and magazines. The attendant publicity has led to the widespread conclusion that life change is inherently stressful.

However, many experts have criticized this research, citing problems with the methods used (Rabkin, 1993; Raphael, Cloitre, & Dohrenwend, 1991) and problems in interpreting the findings (Brett et al., 1990; Watson & Pennebaker, 1989). At this point, it's a key interpretive issue that concerns us. Many critics have argued that the SRRS does not measure *change* exclusively. The main problem is that the list of life changes on the SRRS is dominated by events that are clearly negative or undesirable (death of a spouse, being fired from a job, and so on). These negative events probably generate great frustration. Although there are some positive events on the scale, it could be that frustration (generated by negative events), rather than change, creates most of the stress assessed by the scale.

To investigate this possibility, researchers began to take into account the desirability and undesirability of subjects' life changes. Subjects were asked to indicate the desirability of the events that they checked off on the SRRS and similar scales. The findings in these studies clearly indicated that life change is not the crucial dimension measured by the SRRS. Although positive events *can* be stressful for some people (Brown & McGill, 1989), negative life events cause most of the stress tapped by the SRRS (Smith, 1993; Turner & Wheaton, 1995).

In conclusion, the SRRS assesses a wide range of stressful experiences, not just life change. At present, there's little reason to believe that change is *inherently or inevitably* stressful. Undoubtedly, some life changes may be quite challenging, but others may be quite benign.

TABLE 13.1 SOCIAL READJUSTMENT RATING SCALE

Life Event	Mean Value
Death of a spouse	100
Divorce	73
Marital separation	65
Jail term	63
Death of a close family member	63
Personal injury or illness	53
Marriage	50
Fired at work	47
Marital reconciliation	45
Retirement	45
Change in health of family member	44
Pregnancy	40
Sex difficulties	39
Gain of a new family member	39
Business readjustment	39
Change in financial state	38
Death of a close friend	37
Change to a different line of work	36
Change in number of arguments with spouse	35
Mortgage or loan for major purchase (home, etc.)	31
Foreclosure of mortgage or loan	30
Change in responsibilities at work	29
Son or daughter leaving home	29
Trouble with in-laws	29
Outstanding personal achievement	28
Wife begins or stops work	26
Begin or end school	26
Change in living conditions	25
Revision of personal habits	24
Trouble with boss	23
Change in work hours or conditions	20
Change in residence	20
Change in school	20
Change in recreation	19
Change in church activities	19
Change in social activities	18
Mortgage or loan for lesser purchase (car, TV, etc.)	17
Change in sleeping habits	16
Change in number of family get-togethers	15
Change in eating habits	15
Vacation	13
Christmas	12
Minor violations of the law	11

Pressure

My father questioned me at dinner about some things I didn't want to talk about. I know he doesn't want to hear my answers, at least not the truth. My father told me when I was little that I was his favorite because I was "pretty near perfect." I've spent my life trying to keep up that image, even though it's obviously not true. Recently, he has begun to realize this, and it's made our relationship very strained and painful.

At one time or another, most people have remarked that they're "under pressure." What does this mean? **Pressure involves expectations or demands that one behave in a certain way.** You are under pressure to *perform* when you're expected to execute tasks and responsibilities quickly, efficiently, and successfully. For example, salespeople are usually under pressure to move merchandise. Professors at research institutions are often under pressure to publish in prestigious journals. Stand-up comedians are under intense pressure to make people laugh. Pressures to *conform* to others' expectations are also common in our lives. People in the business world are expected to dress in certain ways. Suburban homeowners are expected to keep their lawns well manicured. Teenagers are expected to adhere to their parents' values and rules.

Although widely discussed by the general public, the concept of pressure has received scant attention from researchers. Specific aspects of pressure, such as work overload, have been examined in studies of work stress (Holt, 1993), but until recently no attempt had been made to investigate pressure as a general form of stress. However, in the 1980s researchers began to explore the effects of pressure.

For instance, an effort was made to devise a scale to measure pressure as a form of life stress. The result was a 48-item self-report measure called the Pressure Inventory. It assesses self-imposed pressure, pressure from work and school, and pressure from family relations, peer relations, and intimate relations. In research with this scale, a strong relationship has been found between pressure and a variety of psychological symptoms and problems (Weiten, 1988b). In fact, pressure has turned out to be more strongly related to measures of mental health than the SRRS and other established measures of stress are (see Figure 13.4).

In another line of research, Roy Baumeister (1984; Baumeister & Steinhilber, 1984) has investigated how the pressure to perform affects performance of skilled tasks. As we will discuss later, Baumeister's research indicates that pressure often has a negative effect on task performance. To put it more bluntly, many people "choke" under pressure. These two lines of research suggest that pres-

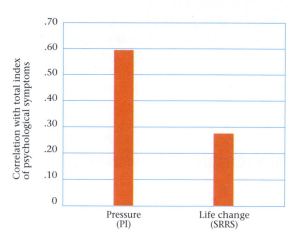

Figure 13.4
Pressure and psychological symptoms. A comparison of pressure and life change as sources of stress suggests that pressure may be more strongly related to mental health than change is. In one study, Weiten (1988b) found a correlation of .59 between scores on the Pressure Inventory (PI) and symptoms of psychological distress. In the same sample, the correlation between SRRS scores and psychological symptoms was only .28.

sure may be an important form of stress that merits more attention from stress theorists.

Recap of Key Points

• Stress involves circumstances and experiences that are perceived as threatening. Stress is a common, everyday event, and even seemingly minor stressors or hassles can be problematic.

• To a large degree, stress is very subjective and lies in the eye of the beholder. Stressful events are *usually* viewed as less threatening when they are controllable and predictable.

• Major types of stress include frustration, conflict, change, and pressure. Frustration occurs when an obstacle prevents one from attaining some goal.

CONCEPT CHECK 13.2
Recognizing Sources of Stress

Check your understanding of the major sources of stress by indicating which type or types of stress are at work in each of the examples below. Bear in mind that the four basic types of stress are not mutually exclusive. There's some potential for overlap, so that a specific experience might include both change and pressure, for instance. The answers are in Appendix A.

Examples

_____ 1. Marie is late for an appointment but is stuck in line at the bank.

_____ 2. Maureen decides that she won't be satisfied unless she gets straight A's this year.

_____ 3. Melvin has just graduated from business school and has taken an exciting new job.

_____ 4. Morris has just been fired from his job and needs to find another.

Types of stress

a. frustration

b. conflict

c. change

d. pressure

- There are three principal types of conflict: approach-approach, avoidance-avoidance, and approach-avoidance. The third type is especially stressful. Vacillation is a common response to approach-avoidance conflict.
- A large number of studies with the SRRS suggest that change is stressful. Although this may be true, it is now clear that the SRRS is a measure of general stress rather than just change-related stress. Two kinds of pressure (to perform and conform) also appear to be stressful.

RESPONDING TO STRESS

People's response to stress is complex and multidimensional. Stress affects the individual at several levels. Consider again the chapter's opening scenario, in which you're driving home in heavy traffic and thinking about overdue papers, tuition increases, and parental pressures. Let's look at some of the reactions that were mentioned. When you groan in reaction to the traffic report, you're experiencing an *emotional response* to stress, in this case annoyance and anger. When your pulse quickens and your stomach knots up, you're exhibiting *physiological responses* to stress. When you shout insults at another driver, your verbal aggression is a *behavioral response* to the stress at hand. Thus, we can analyze a person's reactions to stress at three levels: (1) emotional responses, (2) physiological responses, and (3) behavioral responses. Figure 13.5, which diagrams these three levels of response, provides an overview of the stress process.

Emotional Responses

When people are under stress, they often react emotionally. More often than not, stress tends to elicit unpleasant emotions rather than pleasurable ones (Lazarus, 1993). The link between stress and emotion was apparent in a study of 96 women who filled out daily diaries about the stresses and moods that they experienced over a 28-day period (Caspi, Bolger, & Eckenrode, 1987). The investiga-

tors found that daily fluctuations in stress correlated with daily fluctuations in mood. As stress increased, mood tended to become more negative. As the researchers put it, "Some days everything seems to go wrong, and by day's end, minor difficulties find their outlet in rotten moods" (p. 184). Other studies that have tracked stress and mood on a daily basis have also found intimate relationships between the two (Affleck et al., 1994; Repetti, 1993).

Emotions Commonly Elicited

There are no simple one-to-one connections between certain types of stressful events and particular emotions, but researchers *have* begun to uncover some strong links between specific *cognitive reactions to stress (appraisals)*, and specific emotions (Smith & Lazarus, 1993). For example, self-blame tends to lead to guilt, helplessness to sadness, and so forth. Although many emotions can be evoked by stressful events, some are certainly more likely than others. Common emotional responses to stress include the following (Lazarus, 1993; Woolfolk & Richardson, 1978):

- *Annoyance, anger, and rage.* Stress frequently produces feelings of anger ranging in intensity from mild annoyance to uncontrollable rage. Frustration is particularly likely to generate anger.

Figure 13.5
Overview of the stress process. A potentially stressful event, such as a major exam, elicits a subjective appraisal of how threatening the event is. If the event is viewed with alarm, the stress may trigger emotional, psychological, and behavioral reactions, as people's response to stress is multidimensional.

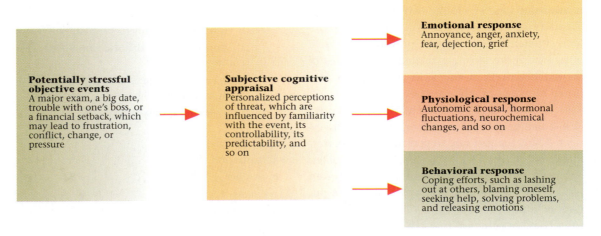

Potentially stressful objective events
A major exam, a big date, trouble with one's boss, or a financial setback, which may lead to frustration, conflict, change, or pressure

Subjective cognitive appraisal
Personalized perceptions of threat, which are influenced by familiarity with the event, its controllability, its predictability, and so on

Emotional response
Annoyance, anger, anxiety, fear, dejection, grief

Physiological response
Autonomic arousal, hormonal fluctuations, neurochemical changes, and so on

Behavioral response
Coping efforts, such as lashing out at others, blaming oneself, seeking help, solving problems, and releasing emotions

• *Apprehension, anxiety, and fear.* Stress probably evokes anxiety and fear more often than any other emotions. As we saw in Chapter 12, Freudian theory has long recognized the link between conflict and anxiety. However, anxiety can also be elicited by the pressure to perform, the threat of impending frustration, or the uncertainty associated with change.

• *Dejection, sadness, and grief.* Sometimes stress—especially frustration—simply brings you down. Routine setbacks, such as traffic tickets and poor grades, often produce feelings of dejection. More profound setbacks, such as deaths and divorces, typically leave one grief-stricken.

Of course, the above list is not exhaustive. In his insightful analyses of stress-emotion relations, Richard Lazarus (1991, 1993) mentions five other emotions that often figure prominently in reactions to stress: guilt, shame, envy, jealousy, and disgust.

Effects of Emotional Arousal

Emotional reponses are a natural and normal part of life. Even unpleasant emotions serve important purposes. Like physical pain, painful emotions can serve as warnings that one needs to take action. However, strong emotional arousal can also interfere with efforts to cope with stress. For example, there's evidence that high emotional arousal can interfere with attention and memory retrieval and impair judgment and decision making (Janis, 1993; Mandler, 1993).

Although emotional arousal may hurt coping efforts, this isn't *necessarily* the case. The *inverted-U hypothesis* predicts that task performance should improve with increased emotional arousal—up to

a point, after which further increases in arousal become disruptive and performance deteriorates (Anderson, 1990; Mandler, 1993). This idea is referred to as the inverted-U hypothesis because when performance is plotted as a function of arousal, the resulting graphs approximate an upside-down U (see Figure 13.6). In these graphs, the level of arousal at which performance peaks is characterized as the *optimal level of arousal* for a task.

This optimal level of arousal appears to depend in part on the complexity of the task at hand. The conventional wisdom is that *as a task becomes more complex, the optimal level of arousal (for peak performance) tends to decrease*. This relationship is depicted in Figure 13.6. As you can see, a fairly high level of arousal should be optimal on simple tasks (such as driving 8 hours to help a friend in a crisis). However, performance should peak at a lower level of arousal on complex tasks (such as making a major decision in which you have to weigh many factors).

The research evidence on the inverted-U hypothesis is inconsistent and subject to varied interpretations (Neiss, 1988, 1990). Hence, it may be risky to generalize this principle to the complexities of everyday coping efforts. Nonetheless, the inverted-U hypothesis provides a plausible model of how emotional arousal could have either beneficial or disruptive effects on coping, depending on the nature of the stressful demands.

Physiological Responses 8c

As we just discussed, stress frequently elicits strong emotional responses. Now we'll look at the important physiological changes that often accompany these responses.

Figure 13.6
Arousal and performance. Graphs of the relationship between emotional arousal and task performance tend to resemble an inverted U, as increased arousal is associated with improved performance up to a point, after which higher arousal leads to poorer performance. The optimal level of arousal for a task depends on the complexity of the task. On complex tasks, a relatively low level of arousal tends to be optimal. On simple tasks, however, performance may peak at a much higher level of arousal.

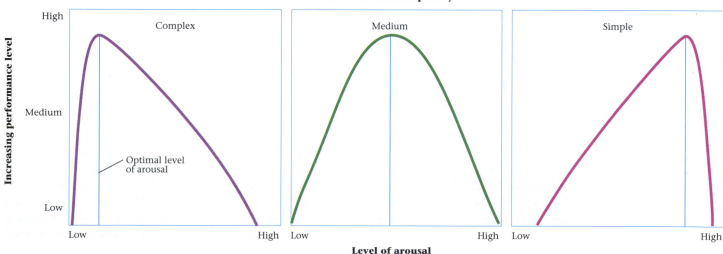

Level of task complexity

Level of arousal

The Fight-or-Flight Response

Walter Cannon (1932) was one of the first theorists to describe the fight-or-flight response. **The fight-or-flight response is a physiological reaction to threat in which the autonomic nervous system mobilizes the organism for attacking (fight) or fleeing (flight) an enemy.** As you may recall from Chapter 3, the autonomic nervous system (ANS) controls blood vessels, smooth muscles, and glands. The fight-or-flight response is mediated by the *sympathetic* division of the ANS. In one experiment, Cannon studied the fight-or-flight response in cats by confronting them with dogs. Among other things, he noticed an immediate acceleration in their breathing and heart rate and a reduction in their digestive processes.

The physiological arousal associated with the fight-or-flight response is also seen in humans. In a sense, this automatic reaction is a "leftover" from humanity's evolutionary past. It's clearly an adaptive response in the animal kingdom, where the threat of predators often requires a swift response of fighting or fleeing. But among humans, the fight-or-flight response appears less adaptive. Most human stresses can't be handled simply through fight or flight. Work pressures, marital problems, and financial difficulties require far more complex responses. Moreover, people's stresses often continue for lengthy periods of time, so that their fight-or-flight response leaves them in a state of enduring physiological arousal. Concern about the effects of prolonged physical arousal was first voiced by Hans Selye, a Canadian scientist who conducted extensive research on stress. Let's look at his ideas.

The General Adaptation Syndrome

The concept of stress was identified and named by Hans Selye (1936, 1956, 1982). Selye was born in Vienna but spent his entire professional career at McGill University in Montreal. Beginning in the 1930s, Selye exposed laboratory animals to a diverse array of both physical and psychological stressors (heat, cold, pain, mild shock, restraint, and so on). The patterns of physiological arousal seen in the animals were largely the same, regardless of the type of stress. Thus, Selye concluded that stress reactions are *nonspecific*. In other words, he maintained that the reactions do not vary according to the specific type of stress encountered. Initially, Selye wasn't sure what to call this nonspecific response to a variety of noxious agents. In the 1940s he decided to call it *stress*, and the word has been part of our vocabulary ever since.

Selye (1956, 1974) formulated an influential theory of stress reactions called the general adaptation syndrome. **The *general adaptation syndrome* is a model of the body's stress response, consisting of three stages: alarm, resistance, and exhaustion.** In the first stage of the general adaptation syndrome, an *alarm reaction* occurs when an organism first recognizes the existence of a threat. Physiological arousal occurs as the body musters its resources to combat the challenge. Selye's alarm reaction is essentially the fight-or-flight response originally described by Cannon.

However, Selye took his investigation of stress a few steps further by exposing laboratory animals to *prolonged* stress, similar to the chronic stress often endured by humans. As stress continues, the organism may progress to the second phase of the general adaptation syndrome, the *stage of resistance*. During this phase, physiological changes stabilize as coping efforts get under way. Typically, physiological arousal continues to be higher than normal, although it may level off somewhat as the organism becomes accustomed to the threat.

If the stress continues over a substantial period of time, the organism may enter the third stage, the *stage of exhaustion*. According to Selye, the body's resources for fighting stress are limited. If the stress can't be overcome, the body's resources may be depleted, and physiological arousal will decrease. Eventually, the organism may collapse from exhaustion. During this phase, the organism's resistance declines, as shown in Figure 13.7. This reduced resistance may lead to what Selye called "diseases of adaptation."

Selye's theory and research forged a link between stress and physical illness. He demonstrated that physiological arousal that begins by being adaptive can lead to diseases if prolonged. His belief that stress reactions are nonspecific has been questioned (Mason, 1975). Nonetheless, his model provided guidance for a generation of researchers who worked out the details of how stress reverberates throughout the body. Let's look at some of those details.

Brain-Body Pathways

Even in cases of moderate stress, you may notice that your heart has started beating faster, you've begun to breathe harder, and you're perspiring more than usual. How does all this (and much more) happen? It appears that there are two major pathways along which the brain sends signals to the endocrine system in response to stress (Asterita, 1985; Koranyi, 1989). As we noted in Chapter 3,

"There are two main types of human beings: 'racehorses,' who thrive on stress and are only happy with a vigorous, fast-paced lifestyle; and 'turtles,' who in order to be happy require peace, quiet, and a generally tranquil environment."

HANS SELYE

the *endocrine system* consists of glands located at various sites in the body that secrete chemicals called hormones. The hypothalamus is the brain structure that appears to initiate action along these two pathways.

The first pathway (see Figure 13.8) is routed through the autonomic nervous system. In response to stress, your hypothalamus activates the sympathetic division of the ANS. A key part of this activation involves stimulating the central part of the adrenal glands (the adrenal medulla) to release large amounts of *catecholamines* into the bloodstream. These hormones radiate throughout your body, producing the physiological changes seen in the fight-or-flight response. The net result of catecholamine elevation is that your body is mobilized for action. Heart rate and blood flow increase, and more blood is pumped to your brain and muscles. Respiration and oxygen consumption speed up, which facilitates alertness. Digestive processes are inhibited to conserve your energy. The pupils of your eyes dilate, increasing visual sensitivity.

The second pathway involves more direct communication between the brain and the endocrine system (see Figure 13.8). The hypothalamus sends

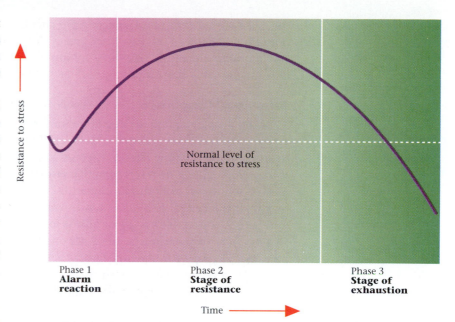

signals to the so-called master gland of the endocrine system, the pituitary gland. In turn, the pituitary secretes a hormone (ACTH) that stimulates the outer part of the adrenal glands (the adrenal cortex) to release another important set of hormones—*corticosteroids*. These hormones stimulate

Figure 13.7
The general adaptation syndrome. According to Selye, the physiological response to stress can be broken into three phases. During the first phase, the body mobilizes its resources for resistance after a brief initial shock. In the second phase, resistance levels off and eventually begins to decline. If the third phase of the general adaptation syndrome is reached, resistance is depleted, leading to health problems and exhaustion.

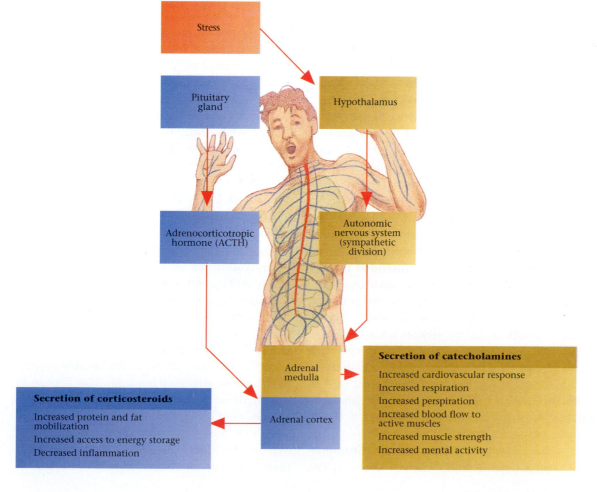

Figure 13.8
Brain-body pathways in stress. In times of stress, the brain sends signals along two pathways. The pathway through the autonomic nervous system controls the release of catecholamine hormones that help mobilize the body for action. The pathway through the pituitary gland and the endocrine system controls the release of corticosteroid hormones that increase energy and ward off tissue inflammation.

the release of more fats and proteins into circulation, thus helping to increase your energy. They also mobilize chemicals that help inhibit tissue inflammation in case of injury.

Behavioral Responses

Although people respond to stress at several levels, it's clear that behavior is the crucial dimension of their reactions. Most behavioral responses to stress involve coping. *Coping* **refers to active efforts to master, reduce, or tolerate the demands created by stress.** Notice that this definition is neutral as to whether coping efforts are healthful or maladaptive. The popular use of the term often implies that coping is inherently healthful. When people say that someone "coped with her problems," the implication is that she handled them effectively.

In reality, however, coping responses may be adaptive or maladaptive (Moos & Schaefer, 1993). For example, if you were flunking a history course at midterm, you might cope with this stress by (1) increasing your study efforts, (2) seeking help from a tutor, (3) blaming your professor, or (4) giving up on the class without really trying. Clearly, the first two of these coping responses would be more adaptive than the last two.

People cope with stress in many ways, but most individuals exhibit certain styles of coping that are fairly consistent across situations (Endler & Parker, 1990; Haan, 1993). Given the immense variety in coping strategies, we can only highlight some of the more common patterns. In this section we'll focus most of our attention on styles of coping that tend to be less than ideal. We'll discuss a variety of more healthful coping strategies in the chapter Application on stress management.

Striking Out at Others

People often respond to stressful events by striking out at others with aggressive behavior. *Aggression* **is any behavior that is intended to hurt someone, either physically or verbally.** Many years ago, a team of psychologists (Dollard et al., 1939) proposed the *frustration-aggression hypothesis,* which held that aggression is always caused by frustration. Decades of research have supported this idea of a causal link between frustration and aggression (Berkowitz, 1989). However, this research has also shown that there isn't an inevitable, one-to-one correspondence between frustration and aggression.

In discussing qualifications to the frustration-aggression hypothesis, Leonard Berkowitz (1969,

1989) has concluded that (1) frustration does not *necessarily* lead to aggression, (2) many situational factors influence whether frustration will lead to aggression, (3) the likelihood of aggression increases with the amount of negative emotions aroused, and (4) frustration may produce responses other than aggression (for example, apathy). Although these are important qualifications, it's clear that frustration often does lead to aggression.

Frequently people lash out aggressively at others who had nothing to do with their frustration, apparently because they can't vent their anger at the real source. For example, you'll probably suppress your anger rather than lash out verbally at your boss or at a police officer who's giving you a speeding ticket. Twenty minutes later, however, you might be verbally brutal to a colleague at work or to a gas station attendant. As we discussed in Chapter 12, this diversion of anger to a substitute target was noticed long ago by Sigmund Freud, who called it *displacement.*

Freud theorized that behaving aggressively could get pent-up emotion out of one's system and thus be adaptive. He coined the term *catharsis* **to refer to this release of emotional tension.** There *is* some experimental evidence to support Freud's theory of catharsis (Hokanson & Burgess, 1962). However, the balance of evidence indicates that aggressive behavior does *not* reliably lead to catharsis (Tavris, 1989). As Carol Tavris notes, "Aggressive catharses are almost impossible to find in continuing relationships because parents, children, spouses, and bosses usually feel obliged to aggress back at you" (1982, p. 131). Thus, the interpersonal conflicts that often emerge from aggressive behavior may increase rather than relieve stress. For example, if you pick a fight with your spouse after a terrible day at work, you may create new stress for yourself.

Giving Up

When confronted with stress, people sometimes simply give up and withdraw from the battle. This response of apathy and inaction tends to be associated with the emotional reactions of sadness and dejection. As you might guess, giving up is not a highly regarded method of coping.

Martin Seligman (1974, 1983) has developed a model of this giving-up syndrome that appears to shed light on its causes. In Seligman's research, animals were subjected to electric shocks that they couldn't escape. The animals were then given an opportunity to learn a response that would allow them to escape the shock. However, many of the animals became so apathetic and listless that they didn't even try to learn the escape response. When researchers made similar manipulations with *human* subjects using inescapable noise (rather than shock), they observed parallel results (Hiroto & Seligman, 1975). Seligman called this syndrome learned helplessness. ***Learned helplessness* is passive behavior produced by exposure to unavoidable aversive events.**

Seligman originally considered learned helplessness to be a product of conditioning. However, research with human subjects has led Seligman and his colleagues to revise their theory. The current model proposes that a person's *cognitive interpretation* of aversive events determines whether he or she develops learned helplessness (Abramson, Seligman, & Teasdale, 1978; Seligman, 1990). Specifically, helplessness seems to occur when people believe that events are beyond their control. This belief is particularly likely to emerge when they attribute setbacks to personal inadequacies instead of situational factors (see the discussion of attributional style and depression in Chapter 14).

Indulging Oneself

Stress sometimes leads to self-indulgence. When troubled by stress, many people engage in excessive consummatory behavior—unwise patterns of eating, drinking, smoking, using drugs, spending money, and so forth. As I mentioned in Chapter 10, when I have an exceptionally stressful day, I often head for the refrigerator, the grocery store, or a restaurant in pursuit of something chocolate. I have a friend who copes with stress by making a beeline for the nearest shopping mall to indulge in a spending spree.

It appears that my friend and I are not so unusual in our excessive consummatory behavior. It makes sense that when things are going poorly in one area of their lives, people may try to compensate by pursuing substitute forms of satisfaction. When this happens, consummatory responses probably rank high among the substitutes. They're relatively easy to execute, and they tend to be pleasurable. Thus, it's not surprising that studies have linked stress to increases in eating (Grunberg & Straub, 1992), smoking (Cohen & Lichtenstein, 1990), and consumption of alcohol and drugs (Peyser, 1993).

Defensive Coping

Many people exhibit consistent styles of defensive coping in response to stress (Vaillant, 1994). We noted in the previous chapter that Sigmund Freud originally developed the concept of the defense mechanism. Though rooted in the psychoanalytic tradition, this concept has gained widespread acceptance from psychologists of most persuasions. Building on Freud's initial insights, modern psychologists have broadened the scope of the concept and added to Freud's list of defense mechanisms.

***Defense mechanisms* are largely unconscious reactions that protect a person from unpleasant emotions such as anxiety and guilt.** Many specific defense mechanisms have been identified. For example, Laughlin (1979) lists 49 different defenses. We described 7 common defense mechanisms in our discussion of Freud's theory in the previous chapter. Table 13.2 introduces another 5 defenses that people use with some regularity. Although widely discussed in the popular press, defense mechanisms are often misunderstood. To clear up some of the misconceptions, we'll use a question/answer format to elaborate on the nature of defense mechanisms.

What exactly do defense mechanisms defend against? Above all else, defense mechanisms shield the individual from the emotional discomfort that's so often elicited by stress. Their main purpose is to ward off unwelcome emotions or to reduce their intensity. Foremost among the emotions guarded against is *anxiety*. Defenses are also used to suppress dangerous feelings of *anger* so that they don't explode into acts of aggression. *Guilt* and *dejection* are two other emotions that people often try to evade through defensive maneuvers.

How do they work? Through *self-deception*. Defense mechanisms accomplish their goals by distorting reality so that it doesn't appear so threat-

"*Learned helplessness is the giving-up reaction, the quitting response that follows from the belief that whatever you do doesn't matter.*"

MARTIN SELIGMAN

One way people react to stress is by overdoing consummatory behavior, such as eating or drinking.

TABLE 13.2 COMMON DEFENSE MECHANISMS

Mechanism	Description	Example
Denial of reality	Protecting oneself from unpleasant reality by refusing to perceive or face it	A smoker concludes that the evidence linking cigarette use to health problems is scientifically worthless.
Fantasy	Gratifying frustrated desires by imaginary achievements	A socially inept and inhibited young man imagines himself chosen by a group of women to provide them with sexual satisfaction
Intellectualization (isolation)	Cutting off emotion from hurtful situations or separating incompatible attitudes so that they appear unrelated	A prisoner on death row awaiting execution resists appeal on his behalf and coldly insists that the letter of the law be followed.
Undoing	Atoning for or trying to magically dispel unacceptable desires or acts	A teenager who feels guilty about masturbation ritually touches door knobs a prescribed number of times following each occurrence of the act.
Overcompensation	Covering up felt weaknesses by emphasizing some desirable characteristic, or making up for frustration in one area by overgratification in another	A dangerously overweight woman goes on eating binges when she feels neglected by her husband.

Note: See Table 12.1 for another list of defense mechanisms.

ening. For example, suppose you're not doing well in school and you're in danger of flunking out. Initially you might use *denial* to block awareness of the possibility that you could flunk. This defense might temporarily fend off feelings of anxiety. If it becomes difficult to deny the obvious, you could resort to *fantasy*. You might daydream about how you'll salvage adequate grades by getting spectacular scores on the upcoming final exams, when the objective fact is that you're hopelessly behind in your studies. Thus, defense mechanisms work their magic by bending reality in self-serving ways.

Are they conscious or unconscious? Both. Freud originally assumed that defenses operate entirely at an unconscious level. However, the concept of the defense mechanism has been broadened by other theorists to include maneuvers that people may be aware of. Thus, defense mechanisms may operate at varying levels of awareness, although they're largely unconscious.

Are they normal? Definitely. Everyone uses defense mechanisms on a fairly regular basis. They're entirely normal patterns of coping. The notion that only neurotic people use defense mechanisms is inaccurate.

Are they healthy? This is a much more complicated question. More often than not, the answer is "no." Generally, defensive coping is less than op-

timal for a number of reasons. First, defensive coping is an avoidance strategy, and avoidance rarely provides a genuine solution to problems. Holahan and Moos (1985, 1990) found that people who exhibit high resistance to stress use avoidance strategies less than people who are frequently troubled by stress. Second, a repressive coping style has been related to poor health, in part because repression often leads people to delay facing up to their problems (Weinberger, 1990). For example, if you were to block out obvious warning signs of cancer or diabetes and fail to obtain needed medical care, your defensive behavior could be fatal. Third, defenses such as denial and fantasy represent wishful thinking, which is likely to accomplish little. In fact, in a study of how students coped with the stress of taking the Medical College Admissions Test (MCAT), Bolger (1990) found that students who engaged in a lot of wishful thinking experienced greater increases in anxiety than other students as the test approached.

Although, defensive behavior tends to be relatively unhealthful, some defenses are healthier than others and defense mechanisms can sometimes be adaptive (Erickson, Feldman, & Steiner, 1996; Vaillant, 1994). For example, *overcompensation* for athletic failures could lead you to work extra hard in the classroom. Creative use of *fantasy* is sometimes the key to dealing effectively with a temporary period of frustration, such as a stint in the military service or a period of recovery in the hospital.

Shelley Taylor and Jonathon Brown (1988, 1994) have reviewed several lines of evidence suggesting that "positive illusions" may be adaptive for mental health and well-being. First, they note that "normal" people tend to have overly favorable self-images. In contrast, depressed subjects exhibit less favorable—but more realistic—self concepts. Second, normal subjects overestimate the degree to which they control chance events. In comparison, depressed subjects are less prone to this illusion of control. Third, normal individuals are more likely than depressed subjects to display unrealistic optimism in making projections about the future.

Colvin and Block (1994) have expressed considerable skepticism about the idea that illusions are adaptive. They make an eloquent case for the traditional view that accuracy and realism are healthy. Part of the problem in sorting out the evidence on this complex issue is that both ends of the correlational equation are difficult to measure. What exactly is an illusion? It is not easy to precisely determine whether a subject's self-concept is overly favorable. In a similar vein, mental health and well-being are difficult to quantify.

Thus, it is hard to make sweeping generalizations about the adaptive value of self-deception.

Some personal illusions may help some people deal with some of life's difficulties. But Taylor and Brown would be the first to stress that they are talking about modest illusions, not wholesale distortions of reality. Roy Baumeister (1989) theorizes that it's all a matter of degree and that there is an "optimal margin of illusion." According to Baumeister, extreme distortions of reality are maladaptive, but small illusions are often beneficial.

Constructive Coping

Our discussion thus far has focused on coping strategies that usually are less than ideal. Of course, people also exhibit many healthful strategies for dealing with stress. We'll use the term *constructive coping* to refer to relatively healthful efforts that people make to deal with stressful events. No strategy of coping can *guarantee* a successful outcome. Even the healthiest coping responses may turn out to be ineffective in some circumstances. Thus, the concept of constructive coping is simply meant to connote a healthful, positive approach, without promising success.

Constructive coping does *not* appear to depend particularly on one's intelligence—at least not the abstract, "academic" intelligence measured by conventional IQ tests (Epstein, 1990). To investigate this matter Epstein and Meier (1989) devised an elaborate scale to assess the degree to which people

"Rather than perceiving themselves, the world, and the future accurately, most people regard themselves, their circumstances, and the future as considerably more positive than is objectively likely. . . . These illusions are not merely characteristic of human thought; they appear actually to be adaptive, promoting rather than undermining good mental health."

SHELLEY TAYLOR

engage in constructive coping and thinking. They found constructive thinking to be favorably related to mental and physical health and to measures of "success" in work, love, and social relationships. However, subjects' IQ scores were only weakly related to their constructive coping scores and largely unrelated to the measures of success in work, love, and social relationships.

What makes certain coping strategies constructive? Frankly, it's a gray area in which psychologists' opinions vary to some extent. Nonetheless, a consensus about the nature of constructive coping has emerged from the sizable literature on stress management. Key themes in this literature include the following:

1. Constructive coping involves confronting problems directly. It is task relevant and action oriented. It entails a conscious effort to rationally evaluate your options so that you can try to solve your problems.

2. Constructive coping is based on reasonably realistic appraisals of your stress and coping resources. A little self-deception may sometimes be adaptive, but excessive self-deception and highly unrealistic negative thinking are not.

3. Constructive coping involves learning to recognize, and in some cases inhibit, potentially disruptive emotional reactions to stress.

4. Constructive coping includes making efforts to ensure that your body is not especially vulnerable to the possibly damaging effects of stress.

The principles just described provide a rather general and abstract picture of constructive coping. We'll look at patterns of constructive coping in more detail in the Application, which discusses various stress management strategies that people can use.

Thus far, we've probed the nature of stress and described how people typically respond to stress. We turn next to the possible outcomes of struggles with stress. We'll look first at the effects of stress on psychological functioning, and then we'll consider how stress affects physical health.

Recap of Key Points

• Stress often triggers emotional reactions. These reactions typically include anger, fear, and sadness.

• Emotional arousal may interfere with coping. According to the inverted-U hypothesis, task performance improves with increased arousal up to a point and then declines. The optimal level of arousal on a task depends on the complexity of the task.

• Physiological arousal in response to stress was originally called the fight-or-flight response by Cannon. This automatic response has limited adaptive value in our modern world.

• Selye's general adaptation syndrome describes three stages in physiological reactions to stress: alarm, resistance, and exhaustion. Diseases of adaptation may appear during the stage of exhaustion.

• There are two major pathways along which the brain sends signals to the endocrine system in response to stress. The first pathway, routed through the autonomic nervous system, releases a class of hormones called catecholamines into the bloodstream. The second pathway, routed through the pituitary gland, releases a class of hormones called corticosteroids.

• The behavioral response to stress takes the form of coping. Popular use of the term *coping* implies that it is inherently healthful, but in reality some coping responses are less than optimal.

• One of the not-so-healthful coping responses is striking out at others with acts of aggression, which is typically a response to frustration. Giving up and self-indulgence are coping patterns that tend to be of limited value. Seligman explains giving up in terms of learned helplessness.

• Defensive coping is quite common. Defense mechanisms protect against emotional distress through self-deception. Defensive behavior may sometimes be adaptive.

• Several lines of evidence suggest that positive illusions may be healthful, but there is some debate about the matter. It is probably a matter of degree. Small illusions may be beneficial, but extreme distortions of reality are usually maladaptive.

• Ultimately, the adaptive value of any coping strategy depends on the situation. Relatively healthful coping tactics are called constructive coping.

THE EFFECTS OF STRESS ON PSYCHOLOGICAL FUNCTIONING

People struggle with many stresses every day. Most stresses come and go without leaving any enduring imprint. However, when stress is severe or when many stressful demands pile up, one's psychological functioning may be affected.

Research on the effects of stress has focused

mainly on negative outcomes, so our coverage is slanted in that direction. However, it's important to emphasize that stress is not inherently bad. You would probably suffocate from boredom if you lived a stress-free existence. Stress makes life challenging and interesting. Moreover, it can have beneficial effects. Stress can force people to develop new skills, learn new insights, and acquire new personal strengths (Holahan & Moos, 1990). Along the way, though, stress can be harrowing, sometimes leading to impairments in performance, to burnout, and to other problems.

Impaired Task Performance

Frequently, stress takes its toll on the ability to perform effectively on a task at hand. For instance, Roy Baumeister's work shows how pressure can interfere with performance. Baumeister's (1984) theory assumes that pressure to perform often makes people self-conscious and that this elevated self-consciousness disrupts their attention.

Baumeister (1984) found support for his theory in a series of laboratory experiments in which he manipulated the pressure to perform well on a simple perceptual-motor task. Even more impressive, his theory was supported in a study of the past performance of professional sports teams in championship contests (Baumeister & Steinhilber, 1984). According to Baumeister, when a championship series such as baseball's World Series goes to the final, decisive game, the home team is under greater pressure than the visiting team. Why?

Because players desperately want to succeed in front of their hometown fans. Conventional wisdom suggests that home teams have the advantage in sports. But Baumeister and Steinhilber (1984) analyzed past championships in professional baseball (from 1924 to 1982) and basketball (from 1967 to 1982) and found that the winning percentage for home teams was significantly lower in final games than in early games in both sports (see Figure 13.9).

More recently, Schlenker et al. (1995) have pointed out that home team championship chokes have been infrequent in professional baseball and basketball since the Baumeister and Steinhilber (1984) study, and they question the reliability of the phenomenon. In reply, Baumeister (1995) argues that a modest home choking effect is still apparent even when the data from 1983 to 1993 are included. He also speculates that changes in the nature of American professional sports may have made modern athletes less susceptible to choking under pressure. The bottom line, in my estimation, is that looking for a choking effect in professional sports always represented an inordinately difficult test of the hypothesis that pressure impairs performance. In professional sports championships, both teams are under incredible pressure and the disparity between the home and visiting team may not amount to much. Moreover, gifted professional athletes are probably less likely to choke under pressure than virtually any other sample one might assemble. Laboratory

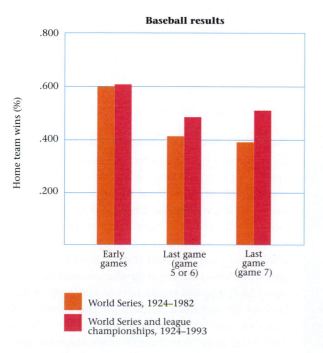

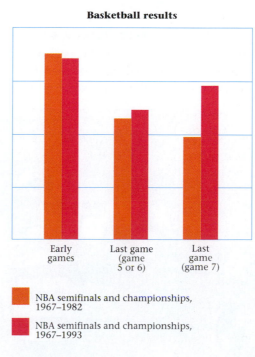

Figure 13.9
Choking under pressure? The results graphed in orange were reported in Baumeister and Steinhilber's (1984) study, which summarized World Series and NBA championship contests in each sport's modern era up through 1982. The results graphed in red include more recent years in both sports and the league championships in baseball, as compiled by Schlenker et al. (1995). The earlier study suggested that when it comes to the last game, the home team frequently chokes under pressure. With more recent results added in, the choking effect is much less pronounced, although home teams still fare more poorly in final games than in earlier games.

research on "normal" subjects is much more pertinent to the issue, and it suggests that choking under pressure is fairly common (Baumeister, 1995).

Burnout

Burnout is an overused buzzword that has different meanings for different people. Nonetheless, Ayala Pines and her colleagues (Pines & Aronson, 1988; Pines, Aronson, & Kafry, 1981) have described burnout in a systematic way that has facilitated scientific study of the syndrome. According to their theory, **burnout involves physical, mental, and emotional exhaustion that is attributable to long-term involvement in emotionally demanding situations.** The physical exhaustion includes chronic fatigue, weakness, and low energy. The mental exhaustion is manifested in highly negative attitudes toward oneself, one's work, and life in general. The emotional exhaustion includes feeling hopeless, helpless, and trapped.

What causes burnout? After years of studying the phenomenon, Pines (1993) concludes that "the cause of burnout lies in our need to believe that our lives are meaningful and that the things we do are useful, important, even heroic" (p. 391). When events undermine this belief, burnout is the result. According to Pines and her colleagues (1981), burnout "usually does not occur as the result of one or two traumatic events but sneaks up through a general erosion of the spirit" (p. 3). For the most part, burnout is brought on gradually by heavy, chronic work-related stress.

Posttraumatic Stress Disorders

The effects of stress are not necessarily apparent right away. A time lag may occur between the stressful event and the appearance of its effects.

Posttraumatic stress disorders were first recognized in Vietnam veterans. Research eventually showed that delayed stress reactions can be caused by a variety of highly stressful events other than combat. The bombing of the federal building in Oklahoma City traumatized relatives and witnesses well after the event.

The *posttraumatic stress disorder* (PTSD) involves disturbed behavior that is attributed to a major stressful event but that emerges after the stress is over. Posttraumatic stress disorders were first seen in large numbers during the 1970s in veterans of the Vietnam war. Among Vietnam veterans, posttraumatic disorders typically began to surface anywhere from 9 to 60 months after their discharge from military service. There were, of course, immediate stress reactions among the soldiers as well—but these were expected. The delayed reactions were something of a surprise, and they continue to be a problem for many former soldiers today. Studies suggest that nearly a half-million Vietnam veterans still suffer from posttraumatic stress disorder (Schlenger et al., 1992).

Because of media attention, posttraumatic stress disorders are widely associated with the experiences of Vietnam veterans, but they have also been seen in response to other cases of severe stress. A study by Helzer, Robins, and McEvoy (1987) suggests that posttraumatic stress disorders have been experienced by roughly 5 out of 1000 men and 13 out of 1000 women in the general population.

What types of stress besides combat are severe enough to produce posttraumatic disorders? Among females, the most common cause found by Helzer and his colleagues was a physical attack, such as a rape. Other causes among women included seeing someone die (or seriously hurt), experiencing a close brush with death, being in a serious accident, and discovering a spouse's affair. Among men, all the posttraumatic disorders were attributable to combat experiences or to seeing someone die. Studies show that PTSD is also common in the wake of major disasters, such as floods, fires, hurricanes, earthquakes, and so forth (Green, 1991; Koopman, Classen, & Spiegel, 1994).

Psychological Problems and Disorders

Posttraumatic stress disorders are caused by a single episode of extreme stress. Of greater relevance to most people are the effects of chronic, prolonged everyday stress. On the basis of clinical impressions, psychologists have long suspected that chronic stress contributes to many types of psychological problems and mental disorders. Since the late 1960s, advances in the measurement of stress have allowed researchers to verify these suspicions in empirical studies. In the domain of common psychological problems, studies indicate that stress may contribute to poor academic performance (Lloyd et al., 1980), insomnia (Hartmann,

CHAPTER THIRTEEN

1985), nightmares (Cernovsky, 1989), sexual difficulties (Malatesta & Adams, 1984), alcohol abuse (Jennison, 1992), drug abuse (Lester, Nebel, & Baum, 1994), and unhappiness (Heady & Wearing, 1989).

Above and beyond these everyday problems, research reveals that stress often plays a role in the onset of full-fledged psychological disorders, including depression (Gruen, 1993), schizophrenia (Spring, 1989), anxiety disorders (Lester et al., 1994), and eating disorders (Strober, 1989). We'll discuss these relations between stress and mental disorders in detail in Chapter 14.

Of course, stress is only one of many factors that may contribute to psychological disorders. Nonetheless, it's sobering to realize that stress can have a dramatic impact on one's mental health. It's every bit as sobering to realize that stress can have a dramatic impact on one's physical health. We briefly mentioned the link between stress and physical illness before, but we now turn our attention to a systematic review of the evidence on the relationship between stress and physical health.

Recap of Key Points

• Research on the effects of stress has concentrated on negative outcomes, although positive effects may occur. Baumeister's work on choking under pressure suggests that pressure can interfere with task performance, even by well-trained athletes.

• Burnout involves chronic exhaustion as a result of stress. Posttraumatic stress disorders are disturbances that surface in the aftermath of a major stressful event.

• Stress can contribute to a host of common problems, such as poor academic performance, insomnia, and sexual difficulties. Stress has also been related to the development of various psychological disorders, including depression, schizophrenia, anxiety disorders, and eating disorders.

THE EFFECTS OF STRESS ON PHYSICAL HEALTH

The assertion that stress can contribute to physical diseases is not entirely new. Evidence that stress can cause physical illness began to accumulate back in the 1930s and 1940s. By the 1950s, the concept of psychosomatic disease was widely accepted. *Psychosomatic diseases* are physical ailments with a genuine organic basis that are caused in part by psychological factors, especially emotional distress. The underlying assumption is that stress-induced autonomic arousal plays a key role in the development of psychosomatic diseases. Please note that psychosomatic diseases are *genuine* physical ailments. The term is sometimes misused to refer to ailments that are all in one's head, an entirely different phenomenon, which we'll discuss in Chapter 14.

Common psychosomatic diseases include hypertension, ulcers, asthma, skin disorders such as eczema and hives, and migraine and tension headaches (Kaplan, 1989). These diseases do not *necessarily* have a strong psychological component in every affected individual. There's a genetic predisposition to many psychosomatic diseases, and in some people these diseases are largely physiological in origin (Weiner & Fawzy, 1989). More often than not, however, psychological factors contribute to psychosomatic diseases. When they do, stress is one of the chief culprits (Creed, 1993).

Prior to the 1970s, it was thought that stress contributed to the development of only a few physical diseases (the psychosomatic diseases). However, in the 1970s researchers began to uncover new links between stress and a great variety of diseases previously believed to be purely physiological in origin. Although there's room for debate on some specific diseases, it is thought that stress *may* be related to the onset and course of heart disease, stroke, tuberculosis, arthritis, diabetes, leukemia, cancer, various types of infectious disease, and the common cold (Elliott, 1989; Elliott & Eisdorfer, 1982). In this section we'll look at the evidence on the apparent link between stress and physical illness, beginning with heart disease, which is far and away the leading cause of death in North America.

Type A Behavior and Heart Disease

Heart disease accounts for nearly 40% of the deaths in the United States every year. *Coronary* heart disease involves a reduction in blood flow in the coronary arteries, which supply the heart with blood. This type of heart disease accounts for about 90% of heart-related deaths.

Atherosclerosis is the principal cause of coronary heart disease. *Atherosclerosis* is a condition characterized by a gradual narrowing of the coronary arteries. A buildup of fatty deposits and other debris on the inner walls of the arteries is the usual cause of this narrowing. Atherosclerosis progresses slowly over a period of years. However, when a narrowed coronary artery is blocked completely (by a blood clot, for instance), the abrupt interruption of blood flow can produce a heart attack.

In the 1960s and 1970s a pair of cardiologists, Meyer Friedman and Ray Rosenman (1974), were investigating the causes of coronary heart disease. Originally, Friedman and Rosenman were interested in the usual factors thought to produce a high risk of heart attack: smoking, obesity, physical inactivity, and so forth. Although they found that these factors were relevant, they eventually recognized that a piece of the puzzle was missing. Many people who smoked constantly, got little exercise, and were severely overweight avoided the ravages of heart disease. At the same time, other people who seemed to be in much better shape in regard to these risk factors experienced the misfortune of a heart attack.

Gradually, Friedman and Rosenman unraveled the riddle. What was their explanation for these perplexing findings? Personality and stress! Specifically, they found a connection between coronary risk and a syndrome they called the *Type A personality*, which involves self-imposed stress and intense reactions to stress.

Elements of Type A Behavior

Friedman and Rosenman divided people into two basic types—Type A and Type B—who exhibit differing characteristics (Rosenman, 1993). **The *Type A personality* includes three elements: (1) a strong competitive orientation, (2) impatience and time urgency, and (3) anger and hostility.** Type A's are ambitious, hard-driving perfectionists who are exceedingly time-conscious. They routinely try to do several things at once. Thus, a Type A person may watch TV, talk on the phone, work on a report, and eat dinner all at the same time. Type A's are so impatient that they frequently finish others' sentences for them! They fidget frantically over the briefest delays. Often they are highly competitive, achievement-oriented workaholics who drive themselves with many deadlines. They speak rapidly and emphatically. They are cynical about life and hostile toward others. They are easily irritated and are quick to anger. In contrast, **the *Type B personality* is marked by relatively relaxed, patient, easygoing, amicable behavior.** Type B's are less hurried, less competitive, and less easily angered than Type A's. The strength of one's Type A tendencies can be measured with either structured interviews or questionnaires. The checklist in Figure 13.10 lists some questions that are representative of those used in measurements of Type A behavior.

Which aspects of Type A behavior are most strongly related to increased coronary risk? Are competitiveness, time urgency, and hostility equally important? These are questions of current interest in research on the Type A syndrome. Based on recent studies, many researchers believe that hostility may be more important for coronary risk than other elements of the Type A personality (Adams, 1994; Burg, 1995; Miller et al., 1996). In particular, investigators have been impressed by the apparent relationship between *cynical hostility* and coronary disease, hypertension, and early mortality. People high in cynical hostility are moody, suspicious, resentful, and distrusting. They are quick to anger and to criticize others. When they get upset, they tend to show relatively strong physiological reactions. In comparison to others, they exhibit elevated heart rate and blood pressure reactivity (Smith & Brown, 1991) and elevated

Figure 13.10
The Type A personality. The ten questions shown here highlight some of the behavioral traits associated with the Type A personality.

Measuring Type A behavior

You can use the checklist below to *estimate* the likelihood of your being a Type A personality. However, the checklist should be regarded as providing only a rough estimate, because Friedman and Rosenman (1974) emphasize that how you answer certain questions in their interview is often more significant than the answers themselves. Nonetheless, if you answer "yes" to a majority of the items below, you may want to consider reading their book, *Type A Behavior and Your Heart.*

_____ 1. Do you find it difficult to restrain yourself from hurrying others' speech (finishing their sentences for them?)

_____ 2. Do you often try to do more than one thing at a time (such as eat and read simultaneously)?

_____ 3. Do you often feel guilty if you use extra time to relax?

_____ 4. Do you tend to get involved in a great number of projects at once?

_____ 5. Do you find yourself racing through yellow lights when you drive?

_____ 6. Do you need to win in order to derive enjoyment from games and sports?

_____ 7. Do you generally move, walk, and eat rapidly?

_____ 8. Do you agree to take on too many responsibilities?

_____ 9. Do you detest waiting in lines?

_____ 10. Do you have an intense desire to better your position in life and impress others?

secretions of stress hormones (Pope & Smith, 1991). More research is needed and the evidence is far from conclusive (Rosenman, 1991), but cynical hostility may prove to be the most toxic element of the Type A syndrome.

Evaluating the Risk

How strong is the link between Type A personality and coronary risk? Based on preliminary data, Friedman and his associates originally estimated that Type A's are *six* times more prone to heart attack than Type B's. At the other extreme, some studies have failed to find an association between Type A behavior and coronary risk (Ragland & Brand, 1988; Shekelle et al., 1985). What can we make of these inconsistent findings? Miller and his associates (1991) have demonstrated convincingly that most of the studies that have not found a link between Type A behavior and coronary disease have been characterized by one or more of several methodological limitations (chief among them being poor sample selection). Nonetheless, the mixed findings suggest that the relationship between Type A behavior and coronary risk is more modest than originally believed. Taken as a whole, the data suggest that the increased coronary risk for Type A's is perhaps double that for Type B's (Lyness, 1993; Weaver & Rodnick, 1986). The modest nature of this relationship probably means that Type A behavior increases coronary risk for only a portion of the population.

Explaining the Connection

Why is Type A behavior associated with coronary risk? Research on the Type A syndrome has uncovered a number of possible explanations (see Figure 13.11).

First, Type A individuals appear to exhibit greater physiological reactivity than Type B's (Lyness, 1993; Smith & Brown, 1991). The frequent ups and downs in heart rate and blood pressure may create wear and tear in their cardiovascular systems.

Second, Type A's probably create more stress for themselves than others do. For example, their competitiveness may lead them to put themselves under a lot of pressure, and their hostility may provoke many arguments and conflicts with others. Consistent with this line of thinking, Smith and colleagues (1988) found that subjects high in hostility reported more hassles, more negative life events, more marital conflict, and more work-related stress than subjects who were lower in hostility.

Third, thanks to their antagonistic ways of relating to others, Type A personalities tend to have less social support than other people do (Smith & Christensen, 1992). As we'll discuss shortly, research suggests that social support is an important coping resource that promotes health and buffers the effects of stress.

Fourth, perhaps because of their cynicism and their tendency to push themselves to work hard, Type A's tend to exhibit health habits that may contribute to the development of cardiovascular disease. For example, in comparison to others, they drink more alcohol, get less exercise, and ignore symptoms of fatigue more often (Houston & Vavak, 1991; Leiker & Hailey, 1988).

In sum, there are a variety of plausible explanations for the connection between the Type A syndrome and heart disease. With all these mechanisms at work, it's not surprising that Type A behavior is associated with increased coronary risk. What's surprising is that the association isn't even stronger.

Stress and Other Diseases

The development of questionnaires to measure life stress has allowed researchers to look for correlations between stress and a variety of diseases. These researchers have uncovered many connections between stress and illness. For example, Thomason and colleagues (1992) found an

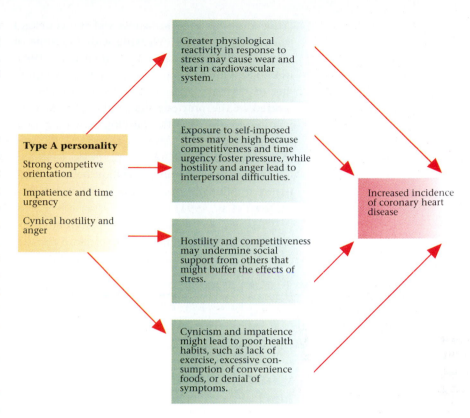

Figure 13.11 Mechanisms that may link Type A personality to heart disease. Explanations for the apparent link between Type A behavior and heart disease are many and varied. Four widely discussed possibilities are summarized in the middle column of this diagram.

association between life stress and the course of rheumatoid arthritis. Working with a sample of female students, Williams and Deffenbacher (1983) found that life stress was correlated with the number of vaginal (yeast) infections the women reported in the previous year. Other studies have connected stress to the development of genital herpes (VanderPlate, Aral, & Magder, 1988) and periodontal disease (Green et al., 1986). Researchers have also found an association between high stress and flareups of inflammatory bowel disease (Garrett et al., 1991).

These are just a handful of representative examples of studies relating stress to physical diseases. Table 13.3 provides a longer list of health problems that have been linked to stress. Many of these stress-illness connections are based on tentative or inconsistent findings, but the sheer length and diversity of the list is remarkable. Why should stress increase the risk for so many kinds of illness? A partial answer may lie in immunal functioning.

Stress and Immunal Functioning

The apparent link between stress and many types of illness raises the possibility that stress may undermine immunal functioning. **The *immune response* is the body's defensive reaction to invasion by bacteria, viral agents, or other foreign substances.** The immune response works to protect the body from many forms of disease. Immunal reactions are multifaceted, but they depend heavily on actions initiated by specialized white blood cells, called *lymphocytes*.

A wealth of studies indicate that experimentally induced stress can impair immunal functioning *in animals* (Ader & Cohen, 1984, 1993). Stressors such as crowding, shock, and restraint reduce various aspects of lymphocyte reactivity in laboratory animals.

Studies by Janice Kiecolt-Glaser and her colleagues have also related stress to suppressed immunal activity *in humans*. In one study, medical students provided researchers with blood samples so that their immunal response could be assessed (Kiecolt-Glaser et al., 1984). The students provided the baseline sample a month before final exams and contributed the "high-stress" sample on the first day of their finals. The subjects also responded to the SRRS as a measure of recent stress. Reduced levels of immune activity were found during the extremely stressful finals week. Reduced immunal activity was also correlated with higher scores on the SRRS.

Other studies have found evidence of reduced immunal activity among people who scored relatively high on a stress scale measuring daily hassles (Levy et al., 1989), among recently divorced or separated men (Kiecolt-Glaser et al., 1988), and among people struggling with the stress of loneliness (Glaser et al., 1985). Thus, scientists are beginning to assemble some impressive evidence that stress can temporarily suppress human immunal functioning, which may make people more vulnerable to infections. This possibility brings us to our Featured Study, which broke new ground exploring the possible link between stress and infectious disease.

TABLE 13.3 HEALTH PROBLEMS THAT MAY BE LINKED TO STRESS

Health Problem	Representative Evidence
Common cold	Stone et al. (1992)
Ulcers	Ellard et al. (1990)
Asthma	Plutchik et al. (1978)
Headaches	Featherstone & Beitman (1984)
Menstrual discomfort	Siegel, Johnson, & Sarason (1979)
Vaginal infections	Williams & Deffenbacher (1983)
Genital herpes	VanderPlate, Aral, & Magder (1988)
Skin disorders	Fava et al. (1989)
Rheumatoid arthritis	Thomason et al. (1992)
Chronic back pain	Craufurd, Creed, & Jayson (1990)
Female reproductive problems	Fries, Nillius, & Petersson (1974)
Diabetes	Gonder-Frederick et al. (1990)
Complications of pregnancy	Pagel et al. (1990)
Hernias	Rahe & Holmes (1965)
Glaucoma	Cohen & Hajioff (1972)
Hyperthyroidism	H. Weiner (1978)
Hemophilia	Buxton et al. (1981)
Tuberculosis	Wolf & Goodell (1968)
Leukemia	Greene & Swisher (1969)
Stroke	Harmsen et al. (1990)
Appendicitis	Creed (1989)
Multiple sclerosis	Grant et al. (1989)
Periodontal disease	Green et al. (1986)
Hypertension	Egan et al. (1983)
Cancer	Cooper (1984)
Coronary heart disease	Rosengren, Tibblin & Wilhelmsen (1991)
Inflammatory bowel disease	Garrett et al. (1991)

Investigators: Sheldon Cohen (Carnegie-Mellon University), David A. J. Tyrrell (Medical Research Council, Salisbury, England), and Andrew P. Smith (University of Wales College of Cardiff)

Source: Negative life events, perceived stress, negative affect, and susceptibility to the common cold. *Journal of Personality and Social Psychology,* 1993, *64,* 131–140.

Researchers have consistently found an association between stress and suppressed immune functioning, but as Sheldon Cohen and his colleagues note, "It is unclear whether the immune changes related to stress in these studies are of the type or magnitude that would influence susceptibility to infection" (p. 131). The handful of studies that have linked stress to actual infections have been plagued by a number of methodological shortcomings (Cohen & Williamson, 1991). For instance, these studies have usually failed to control for variations in subjects' personality, health habits, exposure to infected friends and family, and preexisting antibodies to the virus used. Hence, Cohen, Tyrrell, and Smith set out to conduct a more carefully controlled study of whether stress elevates vulnerability to infectious disease.

Method

Subjects and procedure. The subjects were 154 men and 266 women who volunteered to participate in trials at the Medical Research Council's Common Cold Unit in Salisbury, England, where they were given free accommodations and quarantined for nine days. The volunteers' ages ranged from 18 to 54 (mean = 34). During their first two days on the unit, the subjects were given medical exams to verify that they were in good health and were administered a series of questionnaires to assess their recent stress, aspects of their personality, and various health habits. They were then given—with their informed consent—nasal drops that contained either a respiratory virus or a harmless saline solution. A double-blind procedure was used so that neither the subjects nor the investigators knew who received the virus. The subjects were subsequently followed for six days to see whether they developed a viral infection (based on cultures of their nasal secretions) or cold symptoms (based on daily temperature readings for fever and clinical examinations for sore throat, nasal stuffiness, and so on).

Measurement instruments. Subjects provided information about their recent stress by filling out a major life events scale similar to the SRRS, a measure of their subjective, perceived stress, and an assessment of their emotional tone during the previous week. These scales were examined individually and combined into an overall stress index. The subjects also reponded to personality scales that measured their self-esteem, self-efficacy, and extraversion. Their health practices were assessed with questionnaires that inquired about their exercise, dietary, sleep, and alcohol consumption habits.

Results

Participants were divided into high-stress and low-stress subjects based on whether they scored above or below the median on each of the stress scales. When the entire sample was analyzed, high-stress subjects were somewhat more likely than low-stress subjects to develop a viral infection and to manifest cold symptoms. However, the results revealed that being housed with a person who became infected (and thus infectious) partly obscured the effects of stress on colds, because these subjects were reexposed to the virus (from their roommate's sneezing, coughing, and so on). Hence, the most telling comparisons were the analyses of cold rates in the subsample of subjects who did not have an infectious roommate, which are shown in Figure 13.12. In these comparisons, on all the stress measures high-stress subjects were more likely to develop colds than low-stress subjects. The associations between high stress and an increased incidence of colds were still significant even after the investigators controlled statistically for variations in subjects' personality and health practices.

Discussion

The authors assert that their control procedures eliminated a variety of possible alternative explanations for the apparent link between stress and vulnerability to infection. Hence they conclude that their study demonstrates "what up to now has been somewhat speculative, that psychological stress is associated with increased susceptibility to biologically verified infectious disease processes" (p. 139).

Comment

As you can see in Figure 13.12, the differences between the high-stress and low-stress subjects in the incidence of colds were not particularly large, but as we will discuss momentarily, these results are consistent with other research suggesting that the association between stress and illness is modest in strength. What makes this study outstanding is the enormous effort that the researchers went through to

Figure 13.12
Stress and vulnerability to the common cold.
After exposing subjects to a respiratory virus, Cohen, Tyrrell, and Smith (1993) compared low-stress and high-stress subjects to see if the latter were more susceptible to colds. The data shown here are for subjects who did *not* have an infected roommate. As you can see, all four measures of stress were predictive of the incidence of colds, with high-stress subjects consistently developing more colds.

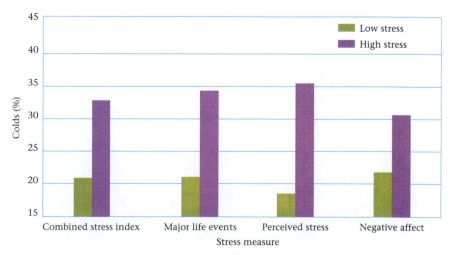

control for possible confounding variables. The quarantine conditions, which were highly unusual, obviously reduced the likelihood that subjects would develop colds from other sources besides the virus tested. The monitoring of infections and colds with reliable biological measures (daily temperature readings, nasal cultures, and so on) circumvented the possibility that high-stress subjects might simply report more subjective symptoms of illness than low-stress subjects. By statistically controlling for subjects' health practices, the investigators eliminated the possibility that the stress-illness association might be

due to stress increasing unhealthy habits (smoking, drinking, and so on) that could undermine immunal resistance. The investigators neutralized other possible confounds by using a double-blind procedure and by controlling for various demographic variables, preexisting antibodies, and personality differences. Given the enormous multiplicity of factors that influence behavior, one can never control for every possible confound and conduct "the perfect study." However, this study illustrates the great lengths that researchers go to in the hopes of coming close.

Sizing Up the Link Between Stress and Illness

A wealth of evidence shows that stress is related to physical health, and converging lines of evidence suggest that stress contributes to the *causation* of illness. But we have to put this intriguing finding in perspective. Virtually all of the relevant research is correlational, so it can't demonstrate *conclusively* that stress causes illness (see Figure 13.13). Subjects' elevated levels of stress and illness could both be due to a third variable, perhaps some aspect of personality. For instance, some evidence suggests that neuroticism may make people overly prone to interpret events as stressful and overly prone to interpret unpleasant sensations as symptoms of illness, thus inflating the correlation between stress and illness (Brett et al., 1990; Watson & Pennebaker, 1989).

Moreover, critics note that many of the studies have used methods that might have increased the apparent association between stress and illness (Schroeder & Costa, 1984). For example, researchers often have subjects make after-the-fact reports of how much stress and illness they endured during the previous year or two. If some subjects have a

tendency to recall more stress than others and to recall more illness than others, the difference in subjects' memories would artificially increase the correlation between stress and illness. Although more and more studies (such as our Featured Study) are controlling for these kinds of problems, the vast majority have not.

In spite of methodological problems favoring inflated correlations, the research in this area consistently indicates that the *strength* of the relationship between stress and health is modest. The correlations typically fall in the .20s and .30s. Clearly, stress is not an irresistible force that produces inevitable effects on health. Actually, this should come as no surprise, as stress is but one factor operating in a complex network of biopsychosocial determinants of health. Other key factors include one's genetic endowment, exposure to infectious agents and environmental toxins, nutrition, exercise, alcohol and drug use, smoking, use of medical care, and cooperation with medical advice. Furthermore, some people handle stress better than others, which is the matter we turn to next.

Recap of Key Points

• Stress appears to play a role in many types of illnesses, not just psychosomatic diseases. The Type A personality has been implicated as a contributing cause of coronary heart disease. The Type A personality involves three elements: competitiveness, time urgency, and hostility. Cynical hostility may be the most toxic element of the Type A syndrome.

• The increased coronary risk for Type A's is perhaps double that for Type B's. At least four mechanisms have been hypothesized to contribute to the association between Type A personality and heart disease.

• Researchers have found associations between stress and the onset of a great variety of specific diseases, although the evidence on many is highly tentative.

Figure 13.13
The stress-illness correlation. One or more aspects of personality, physiology, or memory could play the role of a postulated third variable in the relationship between high stress and high incidence of illness. For example, neuroticism may lead some subjects to view more events as stressful and to remember more illness, thus inflating the apparent correlation between stress and illness.

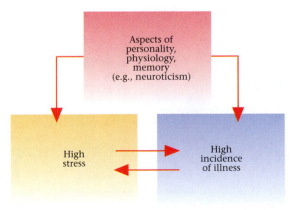

Stress may play a role in a host of diseases because it can temporarily suppress the effectiveness of the immune system. The Featured Study provided a well-controlled demonstration of how stress may increase susceptibility to the common cold.

• Although there's little doubt that stress can contribute to the development of physical illness, the link between stress and illness is modest. Stress is only one factor in a complex network of biopsychosocial variables that shape health.

FACTORS MODERATING THE IMPACT OF STRESS

Some people seem to be able to withstand the ravages of stress better than others. Why? Because a number of *moderator variables* can lessen the impact of stress on physical and mental health. We'll look at four key moderator variables—social support, hardiness, optimism, and autonomic reactivity—to shed light on individual differences in how well people tolerate stress.

Social Support

Friends may be good for your health! This startling conclusion emerges from studies on social support as a moderator of stress. **Social support refers to various types of aid and succor provided by members of one's social networks.** In one study, Jemmott and Magloire (1988) examined the effect of social support on immunal functioning in a group of students going through the stress of final exams. They found that students who reported stronger social support had higher levels of an antibody that plays a key role in warding off respiratory infections. Positive correlations between high social support and greater immunal functioning were also seen in another study, which focused on spouses of cancer patients (Baron et al., 1990).

Many other studies have found evidence that social support is favorably related to physical health (Uchino, Cacioppo, & Kiecolt-Glaser, 1996; Vogt et al., 1992). Indeed, in a major review of the relevant research, House, Landis, and Umberson (1988) argue that the evidence linking social support to health is roughly as strong as the evidence linking smoking to cancer. Social support seems to be good medicine for the mind as well as the body, as most studies find an association between social support and mental health (Sarason, Pierce, & Sarason, 1994). The mechanisms underlying the connection between social support and wellness are the subject of considerable debate (Hobfoll & Vaux, 1993). It appears that social support serves as a protective buffer for people during times of high stress, reducing the negative impact of stressful events. Furthermore, social support has its own positive effects on health, which may be apparent even when one isn't under great stress (Cohen & Syme, 1985).

The power of social support is such that even pets may provide social bonds that buffer the effects of stress. For instance, Siegel (1990) found that elderly pet owners required less medical care than comparable subjects who did not own pets. In another study, women exposed to brief stress showed less physiological reaction when in the company of their pets (Allen et al., 1991).

Of course, social *bonds* are not equivalent to social *support*. Indeed, some people in one's social circles may be a source of more *stress* than *support* (Rook, 1990; Vinokur & van Ryn, 1993). Friends and family can put one under pressure, make one feel guilty, break promises, and so forth.

Hardiness

Another line of research indicates that a syndrome called *hardiness* may moderate the impact of stressful events. Suzanne Kobasa Ouellette reasoned that if stress affects some people less than others, then some people must be *hardier* than others. Hence, she set out to ascertain what factors might be the key to these differences in hardiness.

Kobasa (1979) used a modified version of the Holmes and Rahe (1967) stress scale (SRRS) to measure the amount of stress experienced by a group of executives. As in most other studies, she found a modest correlation between stress and the incidence of physical illness. However, she carried her investigation one step further than previous studies. She compared the high-stress executives who exhibited the expected high incidence of illness against the high-stress executives who stayed healthy. She administered a battery of psychological tests and found that the hardier executives "were more committed, felt more in control, and had bigger appetites for challenge" (Kobasa, 1984, p. 70). These traits have also shown up in many other studies of hardiness (Ouellette, 1993).

Thus, **hardiness is a syndrome marked by**

"The basic notion throughout the research has been that persons' general orientations toward life or characteristic interests and motivations would influence how any given stressful life event was interpreted and dealt with and, thereby, the event's ultimate impact on the physiological and biological organism."

SUZANNE OUELLETTE (FORMERLY KOBASA)

commitment, challenge, and control that is purportedly associated with strong stress resistance. Hardiness may reduce the effects of stress by altering stress appraisals (Florian, Mikulincer, & Taubman, 1995). Hardy subjects tend to appraise potentially stressful events as less threatening and less undesirable than others do (Rhodewalt & Zone, 1989). However, there are some doubts about the relevance of the hardiness syndrome to women and there is active debate about the key elements of hardiness (Funk, 1992; Wiebe, 1991).

Optimism and Conscientiousness

Defining *optimism* **as a general tendency to expect good outcomes,** Michael Scheier and Charles Carver (1985) found a correlation between optimism and relatively good physical health in a sample of college students. In another study that focused on surgical patients, optimism was found to be associated with a faster recovery and a quicker return to normal activities after coronary artery bypass surgery (Scheier et al., 1989). Research suggests that optimists cope with stress in more adaptive ways than pessimists (Aspinwall & Taylor, 1992; Scheier & Carver, 1992). Optimists are more likely to engage in action-oriented, problem-focused coping. They are more willing than pessimists to seek social support, and they are more likely to emphasize the positive in their appraisals of stressful events. In comparison, pessimists are more likely to deal with stress by giving up or engaging in denial.

In a related line of research, Christopher Peterson and Martin Seligman have studied how people explain bad events (personal setbacks, mishaps, disappointments, and such). They identified a *pessimistic explanatory style* in which some people tend to blame setbacks on their personal shortcomings. In a retrospective study of men who graduated from Harvard back in the 1940s, they found an association between this pessimistic explanatory style and relatively poor health (Peterson, Seligman, & Vaillant, 1988). In their attempt to explain this association, they speculate that pessimism leads to passive coping efforts and poor health care practices. A subsequent study also found an association between pessimism and suppressed immune function (Kamen-Siegel et al., 1991).

Optimism versus pessimism is not the only dimension of personality that has been examined as a possible moderator of physical health. Howard Friedman and his colleagues have found evidence that *conscientiousness,* one of the Big Five personality traits discussed in Chapter 12, may have an impact on physical health. Friedman et al. (1993) related personality measures to longevity in the sample of gifted children first studied by Lewis Terman (see Chapter 9), which has been followed closely by researchers since 1921. Data were available on six personality traits, which were measured when the subjects were children. The one trait that predicted greater longevity was conscientiousness. Friedman et al. (1993) reasoned, logically enough, that conscientiousness may simply have fostered better health habits, but a follow-up study (Friedman et al., 1995) found little evidence that this was the case. Hence, the investigators have now turned their attention to how conscientiousness may have affected subjects' coping or stress tolerance.

Autonomic Reactivity

In light of the physiological response that people often make to stress, it makes sense that physical makeup might influence stress tolerance. According to this line of thinking, those individuals who have a relatively placid autonomic nervous system should be less affected by stress than those who are equipped with a highly reactive ANS. Thus far, most of the research on autonomic reactivity has focused on autonomically regulated cardiovascular (heart rate and blood pressure) reactivity in response to stress.

Subjects who are exposed to stressful tasks in laboratory settings show fairly consistent personal differences in cardiovascular reactivity over time and across a variety of tasks (Sherwood, 1993; Manuck et al., 1993). There may be a genetic basis for these differences in cardiovascular reactivity (Smith et al., 1987), which can be seen even in children (Matthews, Woodall, & Stoney, 1990). However, the research thus far has largely focused on reactions to simple, short-term stressors in the laboratory (challenging mental tasks) that are relatively pale imitations of real-life stress. Hence, more research is needed on reactions to chronic, ongoing stress and stress emanating from social interactions (Lassner, Matthews, & Stoney, 1994; Kelsey, 1993). Nonetheless, the preponderance of evidence suggests that certain patterns of cardiovascular reactivity *probably* make some people more vulnerable than others to stress-related heart disease (Blascovich & Katkin, 1993).

Individual differences among people in social support, hardiness, optimism, conscientiousness, and physiological makeup explain why stress doesn't have the same impact on everyone. Differences in lifestyle may play an even larger role in determining health. We'll examine some critical aspects of lifestyle in the next section.

Recap of Key Points
• There are individual differences in how much stress people can tolerate without experiencing ill effects. Social support is a key moderator of the relationship between stress and illness, although social relationships are *not* equivalent to social support.

• The factors associated with hardiness—commitment, challenge, and control—may increase stress tolerance. Optimism may lead to more effective coping with stress, whereas pessimism has been related to passive coping and poor health practices.

• A recent study of Terman's sample of gifted children suggests that conscientiousness is associated with greater longevity. Physiological factors, such as cardiovascular reactivity, may also influence stress tolerance.

HEALTH-IMPAIRING BEHAVIOR

Some people seem determined to dig an early grave for themselves. They do precisely those things that are bad for their health. For example, some people drink heavily even though they know that they're damaging their liver. Others eat all the wrong foods even though they know that they're increasing their risk of a second heart attack. Behavior that's downright *self-destructive* is surprisingly common. In this section we'll discuss how health is affected by smoking, nutrition, exercise, and drug use, and we'll look at behavioral factors in AIDS. We'll also discuss *why* people develop health-impairing lifestyles.

Smoking

The smoking of tobacco is widespread in our culture, with current consumption running around 2800 cigarettes a year per adult in the United States (Fiore, 1992). The percentage of people who smoke has declined noticeably since the mid-1960s. Nonetheless, about 28% of adult men and 24% of adult women in the United States continue to smoke regularly.

The evidence clearly shows that smokers face a much greater risk of premature death than nonsmokers (Jarvik & Schneider, 1992; U.S. Department of Health and Human Services, 1989, 1990). For example, a 25-year-old male who smokes two packs a day has an estimated life expectancy *8.3 years shorter* than that of a similar nonsmoker (Schlaadt & Shannon, 1994). The overall risk is positively related to the number of cigarettes smoked and their tar and nicotine content. Cigar and pipe smoking are also associated with elevated health risks, although they are less hazardous than cigarette smoking. Jarvik and Schneider (1992) put the health costs of smoking in perspective by noting that smoking accounts for roughly 60 times as many deaths per year as cocaine and heroin use combined.

Why are mortality rates higher for smokers? Smoking increases the likelihood of developing a surprisingly large range of diseases. Lung cancer and heart disease are the two types of illness that kill the largest number of smokers (Fielding, 1985). However, smokers also have an elevated risk for oral, bladder, and kidney cancer, as well as cancer of the larynx, esophagus, and pancreas (Newcomb & Carbone, 1992); arteriosclerosis, hypertension, stroke, and other cardiovascular diseases (McBride, 1992); and bronchitis, emphysema, and other pulmonary diseases (Sherman, 1992).

The increased prevalence of diseases among smokers may not be due to their smoking alone. Some studies suggest that smokers are more likely than nonsmokers to exhibit a *variety* of health-impairing habits (Castro et al., 1989). For example, they may tend to consume more alcohol, more coffee, and more unhealthful foods than nonsmokers, while exercising less as well.

The dangers of smoking are not limited to smokers themselves. Family members and co-workers who spend a lot of time around smokers are exposed to secondhand smoke, which can increase their risk for a variety of illnesses, especially lung cancer (Byrd, 1992). One report estimates that "passive smoking" is the third leading cause of preventable deaths in the United States (Glantz & Parmley, 1991). Young children with asthma are particularly vulnerable to the effects of passive smoking (Shephard, 1989).

Studies show that if people can give up smoking, their health risks decline reasonably quickly (Samet, 1992). Five years after people stop smoking,

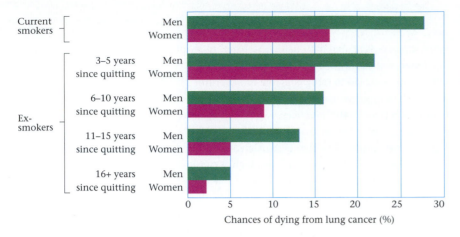

their health risk is already noticeably lower than that of people who continue to smoke (see Figure 13.14). Evidence suggests that most smokers would like to quit but are reluctant to give up a major source of pleasure, and they worry about craving cigarettes, gaining weight, and becoming tense and irritable (Grunberg, Bowen, & Winders, 1986; Orleans et al., 1991).

Unfortunately, it's difficult to give up cigarettes. People who enroll in formal smoking cessation programs aren't any more successful than people who try to quit on their own (Cohen et al., 1989). Long-term success rates are in the vicinity of only 25%, and some studies report even lower figures. For example, in one study of self-quitters, after six months only 3% had maintained complete abstinence from smoking (Hughes et al., 1992). As Figure 13.15 shows, relapse rates for quitting smoking are often as bad as those seen in efforts to give up heroin or alcohol (Hunt & Matarazzo, 1982). Nonetheless, the fact that there are nearly 40 million ex-smokers in the United States indicates that it is possible to quit smoking successfully. Interestingly, many people fail several or more times before they eventually succeed. Evidence suggests that the readiness to give up smoking builds gradually as people cycle through periods of abstinence and relapse (Biener & Abrams, 1991; Prochaska, 1994).

Poor Nutritional Habits

Evidence is accumulating that patterns of nutrition influence susceptibility to a variety of diseases and health problems. In addition to the problems associated with obesity, which we discussed in Chapter 10, other possible connections between eating patterns and health include the following:

1. Heavy consumption of foods that elevate serum cholesterol level (eggs, cheeses, butter, shellfish, sausage, and the like) appears to increase the risk of heart disease (Muldoon, Manuck, & Matthews, 1990). Eating habits are only one of several factors that influence serum cholesterol level, but they do make an important contribution. Unfortunately, recent studies have turned up disturbing—and baffling—evidence that lower cholesterol levels are associated with increases in depression, suicide, and accidents (Kaplan, Manuck, & Shumaker, 1992).

2. High salt intake is thought to be a contributing factor to the development of hypertension (Kaplan, 1986), although there is still some debate about its exact role.

3. High caffeine consumption may elevate one's risk for hypertension (France & Ditto, 1988) and for coronary disease (LaCroix et al., 1986). However, the findings are inconsistent, and one large-scale study of over 45,000 subjects found no association between caffeine consumption and cardiovascular risk (Grobbee et al., 1990).

4. High-fat diets have been implicated as possible contributors to some forms of cancer, especially cancers of the colon, prostate, and breast (S. Levy, 1985). Some studies also suggest that high-fiber diets may reduce one's risk for colon and rectal cancer (Rosen, Nystrom, & Wall, 1988), but the evidence is far from conclusive.

5. Vulnerability to osteoporosis, an abnormal loss of bone mass observed most commonly in postmenopausal women, appears to be elevated by a lifelong pattern of inadequate calcium intake (Fahey & Gallagher-Allred, 1990).

6. Nutritional patterns play a role in the course and management of a host of diseases, among them gallstones, kidney stones, gout, peptic ulcers, and rheumatoid arthritis (Werbach, 1988). Eating habits may also contribute to the causation of some of these diseases, although the evience is less compelling on this point.

Figure 13.14
Quitting smoking and cancer risk. Research indicates that various types of health risks asociated with smoking decline gradually after people give up tobacco. The data shown here, from the U.S. Surgeon General's report on smoking, illustrate this trend for lung cancer. (Data from U.S. Department of Health and Human Services, 1990)

Figure 13.15
Relapse in efforts to quit smoking. It is quite difficult to give up smoking. As the graph shows, the relapse rates for returning to smoking within a year are similar to those for returning to alcohol and heroin use. (Data from Hunt & Matarazzo, 1982)

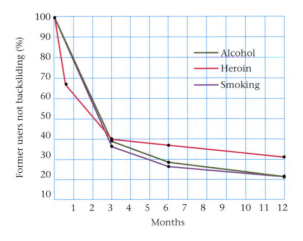

CHAPTER THIRTEEN

Of course, nutritional habits interact with other factors—genetics, exercise, environment, and so on—to determine whether one develops a particular disease. Nonetheless, the examples just described indicate that eating habits *can* influence one's physical health.

Unfortunately, nutritional deficiencies are more widespread in the United States than most people realize. One recent study found that 70% of men and 80% of women consumed a diet deficient in at least one of 15 essential nutrients (Murphy et al., 1992). For the most part, these deficiencies are not due to low income or inability to afford appropriate foods. Instead, most malnutrition in America is attributable to lack of knowledge about nutrition and lack of effort to ensure good nutrition (Quillin, 1987).

Lack of Exercise

There is considerable evidence linking lack of exercise to poor health. Research indicates that regular exercise is associated with increased longevity (Paffenbarger, Hyde, & Wing, 1990). Why would exercise help people live longer? Because physical fitness promotes a diverse array of specific benefits. For one thing, an appropriate exercise program can enhance cardiovascular fitness and thereby reduce susceptibility to deadly cardiovascular problems (Froelicher, 1990; Hagberg, 1990). Second, fitness may indirectly reduce one's risk for a variety of obesity-related health problems, such as diabetes and respiratory difficulties (Bray, 1990). Third, recent studies suggest that physical fitness is also associated with a decreased risk for colon cancer in men and for breast and reproductive cancer in women (Blair et al., 1992; Calabrese, 1990). The apparent link between exercise and reduced cancer risk has been a pleasant surprise for scientists, who are now scrambling to figure out the physiological mechanisms underlying this association. Fourth, exercise can serve as a buffer that reduces the potentially damaging physical effects of stress (J. Brown, 1991). This buffering effect may occur because people high in fitness show less physiological reactivity to stress than those who are less fit.

Alcohol and Drug Use 4c

Recreational drug use is another common health-impairing habit. The risks associated with the use of various drugs were discussed in detail in Chapter 5. Unlike smoking, poor eating habits, and inactivity, drugs can kill directly and immediately when they are taken in an overdose or when they

impair the user enough to cause an accident. In the long run, various recreational drugs may also elevate one's risk for infectious diseases; respiratory, pulmonary, and cardiovascular diseases; liver disease; gastrointestinal problems; cancer; neurological disorders; and pregnancy complications (see Chapter 5). Ironically, the greatest physical damage in the population as a whole is caused by alcohol, the one recreational drug that's legal (Blum, 1984).

Behavior and AIDS

At present, some of the most problematic links between behavior and health may be those related to AIDS. AIDS stands for *Acquired immune deficiency syndrome,* **a disorder in which the immune system is gradually weakened and eventually disabled by the human immunodeficiency virus (HIV).** Being infected with the HIV virus is *not* equivalent to having AIDS. AIDS is the final stage of the HIV infection process, typically manifested about ten years after the original infection (Bartlett, 1993; Brettle & Leen, 1991). With the onset of AIDS, one is left virtually defenseless against a host of opportunistic infectious agents. AIDS inflicts its harm indirectly by opening the door to other diseases. The symptoms of AIDS vary widely depending on the specific constellation of diseases that one develops. Ultimately, AIDS is a fatal disorder and there is no cure on the horizon. Unfortunately, the worldwide prevalence of this deadly disease continues to increase at an alarming rate.

Until recently, the average length of survival for people after the onset of the AIDS syndrome was about 18 to 24 months (Libman, 1992). Encouraging new advances in the treatment of AIDS with drugs called *protease inhibitors* hold out promise for substantially longer survival, but these drugs have been rushed into service and their long-term efficacy remains unknown (Deeks et al., 1997; Cohen, 1997). Spurred by findings linking stress to immune function, researchers have begun to explore whether stress might speed up the progression of AIDS. Some studies have found a very modest association between stress and the course of AIDS, but others have not (Kessler et al., 1991). Taken as a whole, the present evidence suggests that stress is *not* a key factor modulating how rapidly AIDS progresses (Kalichman, 1995).

Transmission

The HIV virus is transmitted through person-to-person contact involving the exchange of bodily fluids, primarily semen and blood. The two principal modes of transmission in the United States have been sexual contact and the sharing of needles by intravenous (IV) drug users. In the United States, sexual transmission has occurred primarily among gay and bisexual men, but in the world as a whole, infection through heterosexual relations is much more common (Mann, Tarantola, & Netter, 1992; see Figure 13.16). In heterosexual relations, male-to-female transmission is more prevalent than female-to-male transmission (Ickovics & Rodin, 1992). The HIV virus can be found in the tears and saliva of infected individuals, but the concentrations are low and there is no evidence that the infection can be spread through casual contact. Even most forms of noncasual contact, including kissing, hugging, and sharing food with infected individuals appear safe (Kalichman, 1995).

Misconceptions

Misconceptions about AIDS are widespread. Ironically, the people who hold these misconceptions fall into two polarized camps. On the one hand, a great many people have unrealistic fears that AIDS can be readily transmitted through casual contact with infected individuals. These people worry unnecessarily about contracting AIDS from a handshake, a sneeze, or an eating utensil. They tend to be paranoid about interacting with homosexuals, thus fueling discrimination against gays in regard to housing, employment, and so forth. Some people also believe that it is dangerous to donate blood, when in fact blood donors are at no risk whatsoever.

On the other hand, many young heterosexuals who are sexually active with a variety of partners foolishly downplay their risk for HIV, naively as-

suming that they are safe as long as they avoid IV drug use and sexual relations with gay or bisexual men (Friedman & Goodman, 1992). They greatly underestimate the probability that their sexual partners previously may have used IV drugs or had unprotected sex with an infected individual. Also, because AIDS is usually accompanied by discernible symptoms, many young people believe that prospective sexual partners who carry the HIV virus will exhibit telltale signs of illness. However, as we have already noted, having AIDS and being infected with HIV are not the same thing, and HIV carriers often remain healthy and symptom-free for many years after they are infected. In sum, many myths about AIDS persist, in spite of extensive efforts to educate the public about this complex and controversial disease. Figure 13.17 contains a short quiz to test your knowledge of the facts about AIDS.

Prevention

The behavioral changes that minimize the risk of developing AIDS are fairly straightforward, although making the changes is often much easier said than done. In all groups, the more sexual partners a person has, the higher the risk that one will be exposed to the HIV virus. Thus, people can reduce their risk by having sexual contacts with fewer partners and by using condoms to control the exchange of semen. It is also important to curtail certain sexual practices (in particular, anal sex) that increase the probability of semen/blood mixing. Intravenous drug users could greatly reduce their risk by abandoning their drug use, but this is unlikely, since most are physically dependent on the drugs. Alternatively, they need to improve the sterilization of their needles and avoid sharing syringes with other users.

Efforts to alter high-risk behaviors that contribute to the spread of AIDS have met with considerable success in the gay male community, although there is still room for much more improvement (Fisher & Fisher, 1992). Unfortunately, there has been relatively little progress among IV drug users (Friedman, de Jong, & Des Jarlais, 1988). Experts are also disappointed because the evidence suggests that heterosexuals have not modified their sexual practices much in response to the threat of AIDS (Catania et al., 1992).

How Does Health-Impairing Behavior Develop?

It may seem puzzling that people behave in self-destructive ways. How does this happen? Several

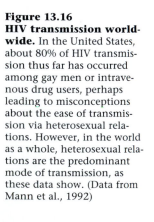

Figure 13.16
HIV transmission worldwide. In the United States, about 80% of HIV transmission thus far has occurred among gay men or intravenous drug users, perhaps leading to misconceptions about the ease of transmission via heterosexual relations. However, in the world as a whole, heterosexual relations are the predominant mode of transmission, as these data show. (Data from Mann et al., 1992)

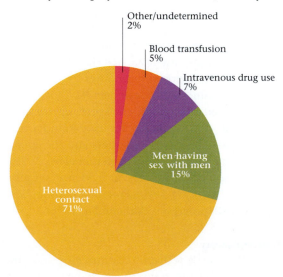

Other/undetermined 2%

Blood transfusion 5%

Intravenous drug use 7%

Men having sex with men 15%

Heterosexual contact 71%

factors are involved. First, many health-impairing habits creep up on people slowly. For instance, drug use may grow imperceptibly over years, or exercise habits may decline ever so gradually. Second, many health-impairing habits involve activities that are quite pleasant at the time. Actions such as eating favorite foods, smoking cigarettes, or getting "high" are potent reinforcing events. Third, the risks associated with most health-impairing habits are chronic diseases such as cancer that usually lie 10, 20, or 30 years down the road. It's relatively easy to ignore risks that lie in the distant future.

Finally, people have a curious tendency to underestimate the risks that accompany their own health-impairing behaviors while viewing the risks associated with others' self-destructive behaviors much more accurately (van der Velde, van der Pligt, & Hooykaas, 1994; Weinstein & Klein, 1995, 1996). Many people are well aware of the dangers associated with certain habits, but when it's time to apply this information to themselves, they often discount it. They figure, for instance, that smoking will lead to cancer or a heart attack *in someone else*.

So far, we've seen that physical health may be affected by stress and by aspects of lifestyle. Next, we'll look at the importance of how people react to physical symptoms, health problems, and health care efforts.

Recap of Key Points

• People frequently display health-impairing lifestyles. Smokers have much higher mortality rates than nonsmokers because they are more vulnerable to a host of diseases. Health risks decline reasonably quickly for people who give up smoking, but quitting is very difficult and relapse rates are high.

• Poor nutritional habits have been linked to heart disease, hypertension, and cancer, among other things. Lack of exercise elevates one's risk for cardiovascular diseases. Alcohol and drug use carry the immediate risk of overdose and elevate the long-term risk of many diseases.

• Aspects of behavior influence one's risk of AIDS, which is transmitted through person-to-person con-

tact involving the exchange of bodily fluids, primarily semen and blood. Misconceptions about AIDS are common, and the people who hold these misconceptions tend to fall into polarized camps, either overestimating or underestimating their risk of infection.

• Health-impairing habits tend to develop gradually and often involve pleasant activities. The risks may be easy to ignore because they lie in the distant future and because people tend to underestimate risks that apply to them personally.

AIDS Risk Knowledge Test

Answer the following "true" or "false."

T F   **1.** The AIDS virus cannot be spread through kissing.

T F   **2.** A person can get the AIDS virus by sharing kitchens and bathrooms with someone who has AIDS.

T F   **3.** Men can give the AIDS virus to women.

T F   **4.** The AIDS virus attacks the body's ability to fight off diseases.

T F   **5.** You can get the AIDS virus by someone sneezing, like a cold or the flu.

T F   **6.** You can get AIDS by touching a person with AIDS.

T F   **7.** Women can give the AIDS virus to men.

T F   **8.** A person who got the AIDS virus from shooting up drugs cannot give the virus to someone by having sex.

T F   **9.** A pregnant woman can give the AIDS virus to her unborn baby.

T F   **10.** Most types of birth control also protect against getting the AIDS virus.

T F   **11.** The AIDS virus cannot be spread through kissing.

T F   **12.** AIDS can be caused by inheriting a bad gene.

T F   **13.** Condoms make intercourse completely safe.

T F   **14.** Oral sex is safe if partners "do not swallow."

T F   **15.** A person must have many different sexual partners to be at risk for AIDS.

T F   **16.** It is more important to take precautions against AIDS in large cities than in small cities.

T F   **17.** A positive result on the AIDS virus antibody test often occurs for people who do not even have the virus.

T F   **18.** Only receptive (passive) anal intercourse transmits the AIDS virus.

T F   **19.** Donating blood carries no AIDS risk for the donor.

T F   **20.** Most people who have the AIDS virus look quite ill.

Answers: 1. T 2. F 3. T 4. T 5. F 6. F 7. T 8. F 9. T 10. F 11. T 12. F 13. F 14. F 15. F 16. F 17. F 18. F 19. F 20. F

Figure 13.17
A quiz on knowledge of AIDS. Because misconceptions about AIDS abound, it may be wise to take this brief quiz to test your knowledge of AIDS. (Adapted from Kalichman, 1995)

REACTIONS TO ILLNESS

Some people respond to physical symptoms and illnesses by ignoring warning signs of developing diseases, while others engage in active coping ef-

forts to conquer their diseases. Let's examine the decision to seek medical treatment, the sick role, and compliance with medical advice.

The Decision to Seek Treatment

Have you ever experienced nausea, diarrhea, stiffness, headaches, cramps, chest pains, or sinus problems? Of course you have; we all experience some of these problems periodically. However, whether we view these sensations as *symptoms* is a matter of individual interpretation. When two persons experience the same unpleasant sensations, one may shrug them off as a nuisance while the other may rush to a physician. Studies suggest that people who are relatively high in anxiety and low in self-esteem tend to report more symptoms of illness than others (Pennebaker, 1982). Those who are extremely attentive to bodily sensations and health concerns also report more symptoms than the average person (Barsky, 1988).

Variations in the perceived seriousness and disruptiveness of symptoms help explain the differences among people in their readiness to seek medical treatment (Cameron, Leventhal, & Leventhal, 1993). The biggest problem in regard to treatment seeking is the tendency of many people to delay the pursuit of needed professional consultation. Delays can be critical because early diagnosis and quick intervention may facilitate more effective treatment of many health problems. Unfortunately, procrastination is the norm even when people are faced with a medical emergency, such as a heart attack. Why do people dawdle in the midst of a crisis? Robin DiMatteo (1991), a leading expert on patient behavior, mentions a number of reasons, noting that people delay because they often (a) misinterpret and downplay the significance of their symptoms, (b) fret about looking silly if the problem turns out to be nothing, (c) worry about "bothering" their physician, (d) are reluctant to disrupt their plans (to go out to dinner, see a movie, and so forth), and (e) waste time on trivial matters (such as taking a shower, gathering personal items, or packing clothes) before going to a hospital emergency room.

The Sick Role

Although many people tend to delay medical consultations, some people are positively eager to seek care. These people have learned that there are potential benefits to adopting the "sick role" (Lubkin, 1990; Parsons, 1979). For instance, fewer demands are placed on sick people, who often can selectively decide which demands to ignore. Sick people may also find themselves to be the center of attention from friends and relatives. This increase in attention from others can be highly rewarding, especially to those who have received little attention previously. Moreover, much of this attention is favorable, in that the sick person is showered with affection, concern, and sympathy.

Thus, some people grow to *like* the sick role, although they may not be aware of this feeling. Such people readily seek professional care, but they also tend to behave in subtle ways that prolong their illness (Kinsman, Dirks, & Jones, 1982). For example, they may only pretend to go along with medical advice, a common problem that we'll discuss next.

Adherence to Medical Advice

Many patients fail to adhere to the instructions they receive from physicians and other health care professionals. Such nonadherence is not limited to people who have come to like the sick role, and it's a major problem in our medical care system. The evidence suggests that noncompliance with medical advice may occur 30% to 60% of the time (Kaplan & Simon, 1990).

This point is not intended to suggest that you should passively accept all professional advice from medical personnel. However, when you have doubts about a prescribed treatment, you should speak up and ask questions. Passive resistance can backfire. For instance, if a physician sees no improvement in a patient who falsely insists that he has been taking his medicine, the physician may abandon an accurate diagnosis in favor of an inaccurate one. The inaccurate diagnosis could lead to inappropriate treatments that might be harmful to the patient.

Why don't people comply with the advice that they've sought out from highly regarded health care professionals? Physicians tend to attribute noncompliance to patients' personality traits, but research indicates that other factors are more important. Three considerations are especially prominent (DiMatteo & Friedman, 1982; Evans & Haynes, 1990):

1. Frequently, noncompliance is due to a failure by the patient to understand the instructions as given. Highly trained professionals often forget that what seems obvious and simple to them may be obscure and complicated to many of their patients.

2. Another key factor is how aversive or difficult the instructions are. If the prescribed regimen is unpleasant, compliance will tend to decrease. And the more that following instructions interferes with routine behavior, the less probable it is that the patient will cooperate successfully.

"A person will not carry out a health behavior if significant barriers stand in the way, or if the steps interfere with favorite or necessary activities."

ROBIN DiMATTEO

3. If a patient has a negative attitude toward a physician, the probability of noncompliance will increase. When patients are unhappy with their interactions with the doctor, they're more likely to ignore the medical advice provided.

In response to the noncompliance problem, some health psychologists are exploring ways to increase patients' adherence to medical advice. They've found that the communication process between the practitioner and the patient is of critical importance. Courtesy, encouragement, reassurance, taking time to answer questions, and decreased reliance on medical jargon can improve compliance (DiNicola & DiMatteo, 1984; Hall, Roter, & Katz, 1988). Thus, there's a new emphasis in medicine on enhancing health care professionals' communication skills.

PUTTING IT IN PERSPECTIVE

Which of our themes were prominent in this chapter? As you probably noticed, our discussion of stress and health illustrated multifactorial causation and the subjectivity of experience.

The way in which multiple factors influence behavior was apparent in our discussion of the stress process. If you glance back at Figure 13.5, you'll see a complicated array of variables that are involved in the experience of stress.

Our discussion of the psychology of health provided an even more complex illustration of multifactorial causation. As we noted in Chapter 1, people are likely to think simplistically, in terms of single causes. In recent years, the highly publicized research linking stress to health has led many people to point automatically to stress as an explanation for illness. In reality, stress has only a modest impact on physical health. Stress can increase the risk for illness, but health is governed by a dense network of factors. Important factors include inherited vulnerabilities, physiological reactivity, exposure to infectious agents, health-impairing habits, reactions to symptoms, treatment-seeking behavior, compliance with medical advice, hardiness, and social support. In other words, stress is but one actor on a crowded stage. This should be apparent in Figure 13.18, which shows the multitude of biopsychosocial factors that jointly influence physical health. It illustrates multifactorial causation in all its complexity.

The subjectivity of experience was demonstrated by the frequently repeated point that stress lies in the eye of the beholder. The same promotion at work may be stressful for one person and invigorating for another. One person's pressure is another's challenge. When it comes to stress, objective reality is not nearly as important as subjective perceptions. More than anything else, the impact of stressful events seems to depend on how people view them. The critical importance of individual stress appraisals will continue to be apparent in our Application on coping and stress management. Many stress-management strategies depend on altering one's appraisals of events.

Recap of Key Points

• Ignoring physical symptoms may result in the delay of medical treatment. At the other extreme, a minority of people learn to like the sick role because it earns them attention and allows them to avoid stress.
• Noncompliance with medical advice is a major problem. The likelihood of noncompliance is greater when instructions are difficult to understand, when recommendations are difficult to follow, and when patients are unhappy with their doctor.
• Two of our integrative themes were prominent in this chapter. First, we saw that behavior and health are influenced by multiple causes. Second, we saw that experience is highly subjective, as stress lies in the eye of the beholder.

Figure 13.18
Biopsychosocial factors in health. Physical health can be influenced by a remarkably diverse set of variables, including biological, psychological, and social factors. The host of factors that affect health provide an excellent example of multifactorial causation.

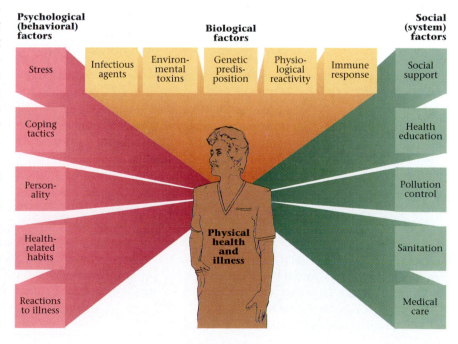

Psychological (behavioral) factors: Stress, Coping tactics, Personality, Health-related habits, Reactions to illness

Biological factors: Infectious agents, Environmental toxins, Genetic predisposition, Physiological reactivity, Immune response

Social (system) factors: Social support, Health education, Pollution control, Sanitation, Medical care

Physical health and illness

APPLICATION: IMPROVING COPING AND STRESS MANAGEMENT

Answer the following "true" or "false."

1 The key to managing stress is to avoid or circumvent it.

2 It's best to suppress emotional reactions to stress.

3 Laughing at one's problems is immature.

4 Leaning on others in times of stress is an ill-advised coping strategy.

Courses and books on stress management have multiplied at a furious pace in the last decade. They summarize experts' advice on how to cope with stress more effectively. How do these experts feel about the four statements above? As you'll see in this Application, most would agree that all four are false.

The key to managing stress does *not* lie in avoiding it. Stress is an inevitable element in the fabric of modern life. As Hans Selye noted, "contrary to public opinion, we must not—and indeed can't—avoid stress" (1973, p. 693). Although researchers have tended to focus on the negative effects of stress, studies have shown that stress can lead to personal growth and self-improvement (Holahan & Moos, 1990). Thus, most stress-management programs encourage people to confront stress rather than sidestep it. This requires training people to engage in action-oriented, rational, reality-based *constructive coping*.

People cope with stress in a variety of ways. This variety was apparent in a study by Carver, Scheier, and Weintraub (1989). They found that they could sort their subjects' coping tactics into 14 categories, which are listed in Table 13.4. Carver and his colleagues correlated subjects' reliance on each coping strategy with various per-

sonality measures, such as their self-esteem and anxiety. The researchers found that some coping patterns (active coping, planning, positive reinterpretation) were associated with relatively high self-esteem and low anxiety (see Table 13.4). Thus, as we noted earlier, some coping tactics are more healthful than others. In this Application, we'll examine a variety of constructive coping tactics, beginning with Albert Ellis's ideas about changing one's appraisals of stressful events.

Reappraisal: Ellis's Rational Thinking

Albert Ellis (1977, 1985) is a prominent theorist who believes that people can short-circuit their emotional reactions to stress by altering their appraisals of stressful

TABLE 13.4 TYPES OF COPING STRATEGIES

Coping Strategy	Example	Correlation with Self-Esteem	Correlation with Anxiety
Active coping	I take additional action to try to get rid of the problem.	.27*	−.25*
Planning	I try to come up with a strategy about what to do.	.22*	−.15*
Suppression of competing activities	I put aside other activities in order to concentrate on this.	.07	−.10
Restraint coping	I force myself to wait for the right time to do something.	−.03	−.19*
Seeking social support for instrumental reasons	I ask people who have had similar experiences what they did.	.12	.01
Seeking social support for emotional reasons	I talk to someone about how I feel.	.06	.14
Positive reinterpretation and growth	I look for something good in what is happening.	.16*	−.25*
Acceptance	I learn to live with it.	.12	−.15
Turning to religion	I seek God's help.	−.06	.11
Focus on and venting of emotions	I get upset and let my emotions out.	−.01	.36*
Denial	I refuse to believe that it has happened.	−.28*	.35*
Behavioral disengagement	I give up the attempt to get what I want.	−.31*	.37*
Mental disengagement	I turn to work or other substitute activities to take my mind off things.	−.08	.21*
Alcohol-drug disengagement	I drink alcohol or take drugs in order to think about it less.	−.11	.11

*Statistically significant.

events. Ellis's insights about stress appraisal are the foundation for a widely used system of therapy that he devised. *Rational-emotive therapy* is an approach that focuses on altering clients' patterns of irrational thinking to reduce maladaptive emotions and behavior.

Ellis maintains that *you feel the way you think*. He argues that problematic emotional reactions are caused by negative self-talk, which he calls catastrophic thinking. *Catastrophic thinking* involves unrealistically negative appraisals of stress that exaggerate the magnitude of one's problems. Ellis uses a simple A-B-C sequence to explain his ideas (see Figure 13.19):

A: *Activating event*. The A in Ellis's system stands for the activating event that produces the stress. The activating event may be any potentially stressful transaction. Examples might include an automobile accident, the cancellation of a date, a delay while waiting in line at the bank, or a failure to get a promotion you were expecting.

B: *Belief system*. B stands for your belief about the event, or your appraisal of the stress. According to Ellis, people often view minor setbacks as disasters. Thus, they engage in catastrophic thinking: "How awful this is. I can't stand it! Things never turn out fair for me. I'll never get promoted." C: *Consequence*. C stands for the consequences of your negative thinking. When your appraisals of stressful events are overly negative, the consequence tends to be emotional distress. Thus, people feel angry, anxious, panic stricken, or dejected.

Ellis asserts that most people don't understand the importance of phase B in this three-stage sequence. They unwittingly believe that the activating event (A) causes the consequent emotional turmoil (C). However, Ellis maintains that A does *not* cause C. It only appears to do so. Instead, Ellis asserts, B causes C. One's emotional distress is actually caused by one's catastrophic thinking.

According to Ellis, it's commonplace for people to turn inconvenience into disaster and to make mountains out of molehills. Ellis theorizes that unrealistic appraisals of stress are derived from irrational assumptions that people hold. He maintains that if you scrutinize your catastrophic thinking, you'll find that your reasoning is based on a logically indefensible premise, such as "I must have approval from everyone" or "I must perform well in all endeavors." These faulty assumptions, which people often hold unconsciously, generate catastrophic thinking and emotional turmoil.

How can you reduce your unrealistic appraisals of stress? To accomplish this, Ellis asserts that you must learn (1) how to detect catastrophic thinking and (2) how to dispute the irrational assumptions that cause it. Detection involves acquiring the ability to spot unrealistic pessimism and wild exaggeration in your thinking. Examine your self-talk closely. Ask yourself why you're getting upset. Force yourself to verbalize your concerns, silently or out loud. Look for key words that often show up in catastrophic thinking, such as *should*, *ought*, *never*, and *must*.

Disputing your irrational assumptions requires subjecting your reasoning process to scrutiny. Try to root out the assumptions from which you derive your conclusions. Once the underlying premises are unearthed, their irrationality may be obvious. If your assumptions seem reasonable, ask yourself whether your conclusions follow logically. Try to replace your catastrophic thinking with more rational analyses. These strategies should help you redefine stressful situations in ways that are less threatening. Strangely enough, another way to make stressful situations less threatening is to turn to humor.

Humor as a Stress Reducer

A few years ago, the Chicago area experienced its worst flooding in about a century. Thousands of people saw their homes wrecked when two rivers spilled over their banks. As the waters receded, the flood victims returning to their homes were subjected to the inevitable TV interviews. A remarkable number of victims, surrounded by the ruins of their homes, *joked* about their misfortune. When the going gets tough, it may pay to laugh about it. In a study of coping styles, McCrae (1984) found that 40% of his subjects used humor to deal with stress.

While some psychologists have long suspected that humor might be a worthwhile coping response, evidence to that effect has emerged only in recent years (Lefcourt et al., 1995; Nezu, Nezu, &

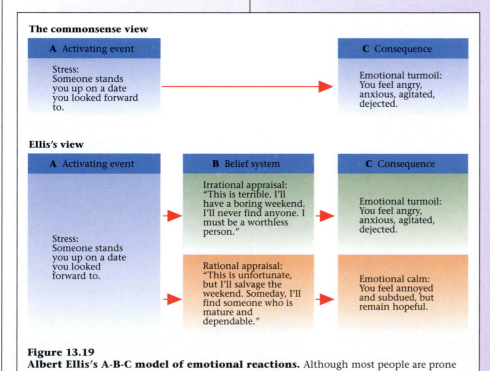

Figure 13.19
Albert Ellis's A-B-C model of emotional reactions. Although most people are prone to attribute their negative emotional reactions directly to events, Ellis argues that people *feel* the way they *think*.

Blissett, 1988). In analyzing the stress-reducing effects of humor, Dixon (1980) noted that finding a humorous aspect in a stressful situation redefines the situation in a less threatening way. Dixon also pointed out that laughter can serve to discharge pent-up emotions. These dual functions of humor may make joking about life's difficulties a particularly useful coping strategy.

Releasing Pent-Up Emotions

Try as you might to redefine situations as less stressful, you no doubt still go through times when you feel wired with stress-induced tension. When this happens, there's merit in the commonsense notion that you should try to release the emotions welling up inside. Why? Because the physiological arousal that accompanies emotions can become problematic. For example, research suggests that people who inhibit the expression of anger and other emotions are somewhat more likely than other people to have elevated blood pressure (Jorgensen et al., 1996).

A recent study looked at the repercussions of "psychological inhibition" in gay men who conceal their homosexual identity (Cole et al., 1996). Many gay individuals inhibit the public expression of their homosexuality to avoid stigmatization, discrimination, and even physical assault. Although hiding one's gay identity may be a sensible impression management strategy, it entails vigilant inhibition of one's true feelings. To investigate the possible effects of this inhibition, Cole et al. (1996) tracked the incidence of cancer, pneumonia, bronchitis, sinusitis, and tuberculosis in a sample of 222 HIV-negative gay and bisexual men over a period of five years. As you can see in Figure 13.20, they found that the overall incidence of these diseases was higher among the men who concealed their homosexual identity. The investigators speculate that psychological inhibition is somehow detrimental to health.

If inhibition is bad, perhaps expression is good. Although there's no guarantee of it, you can sometimes reduce your physiological arousal by *expressing* your emotions. The key, of course, is to express your

emotions in a mature and socially acceptable manner. This is particularly important when the emotion is anger.

Evidence is accumulating that verbalization, or "talking it out," can be valuable in dealing with stress (Clark, 1993). James Pennebaker (1990) and his colleagues have shown that talking or writing about traumatic events can have beneficial effects. For example, in one study of college students, half of the subjects were asked to write essays about their difficulties in adjusting to college. The other half wrote three essays about superficial topics. The subjects who wrote about their personal problems enjoyed better health in the following months than the other subjects did (Pennebaker, Colder, & Sharp, 1990). So, if you can find a good listener, you may be able to discharge problematic emotions by letting your secret fears, misgivings, and suspicions spill out in a candid conversation.

Learning to Relax

Relaxation is a valuable stress-management technique that can soothe emotional turmoil and suppress problematic physiological arousal (Lehrer & Woolfolk, 1984, 1993). One study even suggests that relaxation training may improve the effectiveness of the immune response (Kiecolt-Glaser et al., 1985).

The value of relaxation became apparent to Herbert Benson (1975; Benson & Klipper, 1988) as a result of his research on meditation. Benson, a Harvard Medical School cardiologist, believes that relaxation is the key to the beneficial effects of meditation. According to Benson, the elaborate religious rituals and beliefs associated with meditation are irrelevant to its effects. After "demystifying" meditation, Benson set out to devise a simple, nonreligious procedure that could provide similar benefits. He calls his procedure the *relaxation response*. Although there are several other worthwhile approaches to relaxation

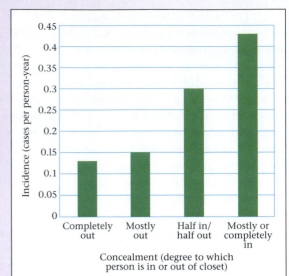

Figure 13.20
Elevated health risk among gay men who conceal their homosexual identity. In a sample of gay and bisexual men, Cole et al. (1996) found that the more the men concealed their homosexual identity, the more likely they were to experience various diseases. The investigators speculate that the elevated incidence of disease may reflect the costs of inhibiting one's true feelings.

training, we'll examine Benson's procedure, as its simplicity makes it especially useful. From his study of a variety of relaxation techniques, Benson concluded that four factors promote effective relaxation:

1. *A quiet environment.* It's easiest to induce the relaxation response in a distraction-free environment. After you become experienced with the relaxation response, you may be able to practice it in a crowded subway. Initially, however, you should practice it in a quiet, calm place.

2. *A mental device.* To shift attention inward and keep it there, you need to focus your attention on a constant stimulus, such as a sound or word recited repetitively.

3. *A passive attitude.* It's important not to get upset when your attention strays to distracting thoughts. You must realize that such distractions are inevitable. Whenever your mind wanders from your attentional focus, *calmly* redirect attention to your mental device.

4. *A comfortable position.* Reasonable body comfort is essential to avoid a major source of potential distraction. Simply sitting up straight generally works well. Lying down is too conducive to sleep.

Benson's simple relaxation procedure is described in Figure 13.21. For full benefit, it should be practiced daily.

Minimizing Physiological Vulnerability

Your body is intimately involved in your response to stress, and the wear and tear of stress can be injurious to your health. To combat this potential problem, it helps to keep your body in relatively sound shape. It's a good idea to consume a nutritionally balanced diet, get adequate sleep, and engage in at least a moderate amount of exercise. It's also a good idea to learn how to control overeating and the use of tobacco, alcohol, and other drugs. Doing these things will not make you immune to the ravages of stress. However, failure to do them may increase your vulnerability to stress-related diseases. We've discussed sleep patterns, drug use, and eating habits in other chapters, so the coverage here will focus exclusively on exercise.

The potential benefits of regular exercise are substantial. Fortunately, evidence indicates that you don't have to be a dedicated athlete to benefit from exercise (Blair et al., 1989). Even a moderate amount of exercise—such as taking a brisk, half-hour walk each day—can reduce your risk of disease (see Figure 13.22).

Successful participation in an exercise program can also lead to improvements in your mood and ability to deal with stress. For example, King, Taylor, and Haskell (1993) found that an exercise regimen led to a decline in depression and anxiety in a study of older adults who also benefited from reductions in perceived stress.

Embarking on an exercise program is difficult for many people. Exercise is time-consuming, and if you're out of shape, your initial attempts may be discouraging. To avoid these problems, it's wise to do the following (Greenberg, 1990):

1. Select an activity that you find enjoyable.
2. Increase your participation gradually.
3. Exercise regularly without overdoing it.
4. Reinforce yourself for your efforts.

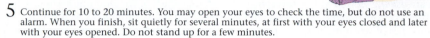
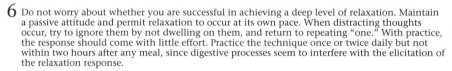

1 Sit quietly in a comfortable position.

2 Close your eyes.

3 Deeply relax all your muscles, beginning at your feet and progressing up to your face. Keep them relaxed.

4 Breathe through your nose. Become aware of your breathing. As you breathe out, say the word "one" silently to yourself. For example, breath in . . . out, "one"; in . . . out, "one"; and so forth. Breathe easily and naturally.

5 Continue for 10 to 20 minutes. You may open your eyes to check the time, but do not use an alarm. When you finish, sit quietly for several minutes, at first with your eyes closed and later with your eyes opened. Do not stand up for a few minutes.

6 Do not worry about whether you are successful in achieving a deep level of relaxation. Maintain a passive attitude and permit relaxation to occur at its own pace. When distracting thoughts occur, try to ignore them by not dwelling on them, and return to repeating "one." With practice, the response should come with little effort. Practice the technique once or twice daily but not within two hours after any meal, since digestive processes seem to interfere with the elicitation of the relaxation response.

Figure 13.21
Benson's relaxation procedure. According to Benson, his simple relaxation procedure can yield benefits similar to meditation. To experience these benefits, you should practice the procedure daily. (From Benson, 1975)

If you choose a competitive sport (such as tennis), try to avoid falling into the competition trap. If you become obsessed with winning, you'll put yourself under pressure and *add* to the stress in your life.

Recap of Key Points

• Action-oriented, realistic, constructive coping can be helpful in managing the stress of daily life. Ellis emphasizes the importance of reappraising stressful events to detect and dispute catastrophic thinking. According to Ellis, emotional distress is often due to irrational assumptions that underlie one's thinking.

• Humor may be useful in efforts to redefine stressful situations. In some cases, it may pay to release pent-up emotions. Talking it out may help. A study of gay men who concealed their homosexual identity suggests that inhibition of one's true feelings may be unhealthy.

• Relaxation techniques, such as Benson's relaxation response, can reduce the wear and tear of stress. Physical vulnerability may also be reduced by getting adequate sleep, consuming a nutritionally sound diet, and controlling overeating and drug use.

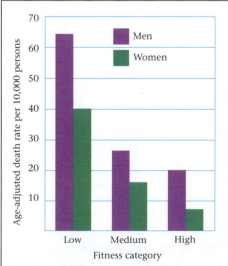

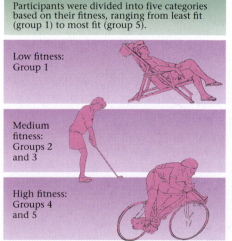

Participants were divided into five categories based on their fitness, ranging from least fit (group 1) to most fit (group 5).

Low fitness: Group 1

Medium fitness: Groups 2 and 3

High fitness: Groups 4 and 5

Figure 13.22
Physical fitness and mortality. Blair and colleagues (1989) studied death rates among men and women who exhibited low, medium, or high fitness. As you can see, fitness was associated with lower mortality rates in both sexes.

Key Ideas

The Nature of Stress

◆ Stress is a common, everyday event, and even seemingly minor stressors or hassles can be problematic. To a large degree, stress lies in the eye of the beholder. Stressful events are *usually* viewed as less threatening when they are controllable and predictable.

◆ Major types of stress include frustration, conflict, change, and pressure. Frustration occurs when an obstacle prevents one from attaining some goal. There are three principal types of conflict: approach-approach, avoidance-avoidance, and approach-avoidance.

◆ A large number of studies with the SRRS suggest that change is stressful. Although this may be true, it is now clear that the SRRS is a measure of general stress rather than just change-related stress. Two kinds of pressure (to perform and conform) also appear to be stressful.

Responding to Stress

◆ Emotional reactions to stress typically include anger, fear, and sadness. Emotional arousal may interfere with coping. The optimal level of arousal on a task depends on the complexity of the task.

◆ Physiological arousal in response to stress was originally called the fight-or-flight response by Cannon. Selye's general adaptation syndrome describes three stages in physiological reactions to stress: alarm, resistance, and exhaustion.

◆ There are two major pathways along which the brain sends signals to the endocrine system in response to stress. Actions along these paths release two sets of hormones, catecholamines and corticosteroids, into the bloodstream.

◆ Some coping responses are less than optimal. One of these is striking out at others with acts of aggression. Giving up and indulging oneself are other coping patterns that tend to be of limited value. Defense mechanisms protect against emotional distress through self-deception. Illusions may sometimes be adaptive.

The Effects of Stress on Psychological Functioning

◆ Common negative effects of stress in terms of psychological functioning include impaired task performance, burnout, post-traumatic stress disorders, and other psychological problems and disorders.

The Effects of Stress on Physical Health

◆ The Type A personality has been implicated as a contributing cause of coronary heart disease. The Type A personality involves three elements: competitiveness, time urgency, and hostility. Cynical hostility may be the most toxic element of the Type A syndrome.

◆ Stress may play a role in a host of diseases because it can temporarily suppress the effectiveness of the immune system. The Featured Study provided a well-controlled demonstration of how stress may increase susceptibility to the common cold.

◆ Although there's little doubt that stress can contribute to the development of physical illness, the link between stress and illness is modest.

Factors Moderating the Impact of Stress

◆ Social support is a key moderator of the relationship between stress and illness. The factors associated with hardiness—commitment, challenge, and control—may increase stress tolerance. Optimism and conscientiousness may lead to more effective coping with stress. Physiological factors, such as cardiovascular reactivity, may also influence stress tolerance.

Health-Impairing Behavior

◆ People display many forms of health-impairing behavior. Smokers have much higher mortality rates than nonsmokers because they are more vulnerable to a host of diseases.

◆ Poor nutritional habits have been linked to heart disease, hypertension, and cancer, among other things. Lack of exercise elevates one's risk for cardiovascular diseases. Alcohol and drug use carry the immediate risk of overdose and elevate the long-term risk of many diseases.

◆ Aspects of behavior also influence one's risk of AIDS. Misconceptions about AIDS are common, and the people who hold these misconceptions tend to fall into polarized camps, either overestimating or underestimating their risk of infection. Health-impairing habits tend to develop gradually and often involve pleasant activities.

Reactions to Illness

◆ Ignoring physical symptoms may result in the delay of needed medical treatment. At the other extreme, a minority of people learn to like the sick role because it earns them attention and allows them to avoid stress. Noncompliance with medical advice is a major problem.

Putting It in Perspective

◆ Two of our integrative themes were prominent in this chapter. First, we saw that behavior and health are influenced by multiple causes. Second, we saw that experience is highly subjective, as stress lies in the eye of the beholder.

Application: Improving Coping and Stress Management

◆ Action-oriented, realistic, constructive coping can be helpful in managing the stress of daily life. Ellis emphasizes the importance of reappraising stressful events to detect and dispute catastrophic thinking. Humor may be useful in efforts to redefine stressful situations.

◆ In some cases, it may pay to release pent-up emotions by expressing them. Talking it out may help. Relaxation techniques, such as Benson's relaxation response, can reduce the wear and tear of stress. Regular exercise can lead to improved physical and mental health.

Key Terms

Acquired immune deficiency syndrome (AIDS)
Aggression
Approach-approach conflict
Approach-avoidance conflict
Avoidance-avoidance conflict
Biopsychosocial model
Burnout
Catastrophic thinking
Catharsis
Conflict
Constructive coping
Coping
Defense mechanisms
Fight-or-flight response
Frustration
General adaptation syndrome
Hardiness
Health psychology
Immune response
Learned helplessness
Life changes
Optimism
Posttraumatic stress disorder (PTSD)
Pressure
Primary appraisal
Psychosomatic diseases
Rational-emotive therapy
Secondary appraisal
Social support
Stress
Type A personality
Type B personality

Key People

Walter Cannon
Robin DiMatteo
Albert Ellis
Meyer Friedman and Ray Rosenman
Thomas Holmes and Richard Rahe
Richard Lazarus
Neal Miller
Suzanne Ouellette (formerly Kobasa)
Michael Scheier and Charles Carver
Hans Selye
Shelley Taylor

Practice Test

1. It is the weekend before a major psychology exam on Monday, and Janine suddenly realizes she must have left her psychology textbook in the classroom on Friday. After her initial panic, she decides that there is no real problem because she has already read the material and has an outline from which she can study. According to Lazarus and Folkman, Janine has just made:
   A. a polysubjective appraisal of stress.
   B. a primary appraisal of stress.
   C. a secondary appraisal of stress.
   D. a rational-emotive appraisal of stress.

2. The four principal sources of stress are:
   A. frustration, conflict, pressure, and anxiety.
   B. frustration, anger, pressure, and change.
   C. anger, anxiety, depression, and annoyance.
   D. frustration, conflict, pressure, and change.

3. When your boss tells you that a complicated report that you have not yet begun to write must be on her desk by this afternoon, you may experience:
   A. burnout.
   B. pressure.
   C. a double bind.
   D. catharsis.

4. You want very badly to ask someone for a date, but you are afraid to risk rejection. You are experiencing:
   A. an approach-avoidance conflict.
   B. an avoidance-avoidance conflict.
   C. frustration.
   D. self-imposed pressure.

5. Research suggests that a high level of arousal may be most optimal for the performance of a task when:
   A. the task is complex.
   B. the task is simple.
   C. the rewards are high.
   D. an audience is present.

6. The alarm stage of Hans Selye's general adaptation syndrome is essentially the same as:
   A. the fight-or-flight response.
   B. constructive coping.
   C. catharsis.
   D. secondary appraisal.

7. The brain structure responsible for initiating action along the two major pathways through which the brain sends signals to the endocrine system is the:
   A. hypothalamus.
   B. thalamus.
   C. corpus callosum.
   D. medulla.

8. You have been doing poorly in your psychology class and you are in danger of flunking. Which of the following qualifies as a defense mechanism in response to this situation?
   A. You seek the aid of a tutor.
   B. You decide to withdraw from the class and take it another time.
   C. You deny the reality that you are hopelessly behind in the class, convinced that you will somehow ace the final without seeking help.
   D. You consult with the instructor to see what you can do to pass the class.

9. Physical, mental, and emotional exhaustion attributable to long-term involvement in emotionally demanding situations can be referred to as:
   A. learned helplessness.
   B. burnout.
   C. fallout.
   D. posttraumatic stress disorder.

10. Which element of the Type A personality seems to be most strongly related to increased coronary risk?
    A. time-consciousness
    B. perfectionism
    C. ambitiousness
    D. cynical hostility

11. Possible explanations for the association of Type A behavior with coronary risk include:
    A. the greater physiological reactivity of Type A individuals compared to Type B's.
    B. Type A individuals' tendency to create more stress for themselves than others.
    C. the fact that Type A individuals tend to have less social support than others.
    D. all of the above.

12. Research has found that optimists are more likely than pessimists to:
    A. take their time in confronting problems.
    B. identify the negatives before they identify the positives.
    C. engage in action-oriented, problem-solving coping.
    D. seek social support only after they have exhausted all individual efforts to deal with the problem.

13. Which of the following has *not* been found to be a mode of transmission for the HIV virus?
    A. sexual contact among homosexual men
    B. the sharing of needles by intravenous drug users
    C. heterosexual contact
    D. sharing food

14. The fact that health is governed by a dense network of factors is an illustration of the theme of:
    A. psychology in a sociohistorical context.
    B. the phenomenology of experience.
    C. multifactorial causation.
    D. empiricism.

15. The three phases in Albert Ellis's explanation of emotional reactions are:
    A. alarm, resistance, exhaustion.
    B. id, ego, superego.
    C. activating event, belief system, consequence.
    D. antecedent conditions, behavior, consequence.

Answers

1	C Page 519	6	A Page 526	11	D Page 537
2	D Page 519	7	A Page 527	12	C Page 542
3	B Page 523	8	C Pages 529–530	13	D Page 546
4	A Page 520	9	B Page 534	14	C Page 549
5	B Page 525	10	D Page 536	15	C Page 551

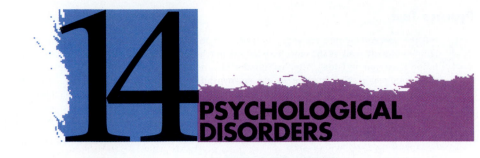

14 PSYCHOLOGICAL DISORDERS

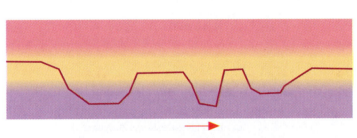

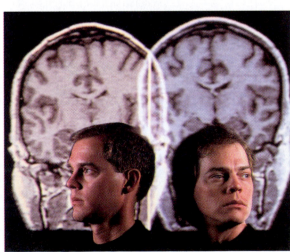

"The government of the United States was overthrown more than a year ago! I'm the president of the United States of America and Bob Dylan is vice president!" So said Ed, the author of a prominent book on journalism, who was speaking to a college journalism class, as a guest lecturer. Ed also informed the class that he had killed both John and Robert Kennedy, as well as Charles de Gaulle, the former president of France. He went on to tell the class that all rock music songs were written about him, that he was the greatest karate expert in the universe, and that he had been fighting "space wars" for 2000 years. The students in the class were mystified by Ed's bizarre, disjointed "lecture," but they assumed that he was putting on a show that would eventually lead to a sensible conclusion. However, their perplexed but expectant calm was shattered when Ed pulled a hatchet from the props he had brought with him and hurled the hatchet at the class! Fortunately, he didn't hit anyone, as the hatchet sailed over the students' heads. At that point, the professor for the class realized that Ed's irrational behavior was not a pretense. The professor evacuated the class quickly while Ed continued to rant and rave about his presidential administration, space wars, vampires, his romances with female rock stars, and his personal harem of 38 "chicks." (Adapted from Pearce, 1974)

Clearly, Ed's behavior was abnormal. Even he recognized that when he agreed later to be admitted to a mental hospital, signing himself in as the "President of the United States of America." What causes such abnormal behavior? Does Ed have a mental illness, or does he just behave strangely? What is the basis for judging behavior as normal versus abnormal? Are people who have psychological disorders dangerous? How common are such disorders? Can they be cured? These are just a few of the questions that we will address in this chapter as we discuss psychological disorders and their complex causes.

ABNORMAL BEHAVIOR: MYTHS, REALITIES, AND CONTROVERSIES

Misconceptions about abnormal behavior are common. Hence, we need to clear up some preliminary issues before we describe the various types of disorders. In this section, we will discuss (1) the medical model of abnormal behavior, (2) the criteria of abnormal behavior, (3) stereotypes regarding psychological disorders, (4) the classification of psychological disorders, and (5) how common such disorders are.

The Medical Model Applied to Abnormal Behavior

In Ed's case, there's no question that his behavior was abnormal. But does it make sense to view his unusual and irrational behavior as an illness? This is a controversial question. **The *medical model* proposes that it is useful to think of abnormal behavior as a disease.** This point of view is the basis for many of the terms used to refer to abnormal behavior, including mental *illness*, psychological *disorder*, and psycho*pathology* (*pathology* refers to manifestations of disease). The medical model gradually became the dominant way of thinking about abnormal behavior during the 18th and 19th centuries, and its influence remains strong today.

The medical model clearly represented progress over earlier models of abnormal behavior. Prior to the 18th century, most conceptions of abnormal behavior were based on superstition. People who behaved strangely were thought to be possessed by demons, to be witches in league with the devil, or to be victims of God's punishment. Their disorders were "treated" with chants, rituals, exorcisms, and such. If the people's behavior was seen as threatening, they were candidates for chains, dungeons, torture, and death (see Figure 14.1).

The rise of the medical model brought improvements in the treatment of those who exhibited abnormal behavior. As victims of an illness, they were viewed with more sympathy and less hatred and fear. Although living conditions in early asylums were often deplorable, gradual progress was made toward more humane care of the mentally ill. It took time, but ineffectual approaches to treatment eventually gave way to scientific investigation of the causes and cures of psychological disorders.

Figure 14.1

Historical conceptions of mental illness. In the Middle Ages people who behaved strangely were sometimes thought to be in league with the devil. The top drawing depicts some of the cruel methods used to extract confessions from suspected witches and warlocks. Some psychological disorders were also thought to be caused by demonic possession. The bottom illustration is a detail from Di Benvenuto's *St. Catherine Exorcising Possessed Woman.* (Denver Art Museum Collection)

"Minds can be 'sick' only in the sense that jokes are 'sick' or economies are 'sick.'"

THOMAS SZASZ

Problems with the Medical Model

In recent decades, critics have suggested that the medical model may have outlived its usefulness. A particularly vocal critic has been Thomas Szasz (1974, 1990). He asserts that "strictly speaking, disease or illness can affect only the body; hence there can be no mental illness. . . . Minds can be 'sick' only in the sense that jokes are 'sick' or economies are 'sick'" (1974, p. 267). He further argues that abnormal behavior usually involves a deviation from social norms rather than an illness. He contends that such deviations are "problems in living" rather than medical problems. According to Szasz, the medical model's disease analogy converts moral and social questions about what is acceptable behavior into medical questions. Under the guise of "healing the sick," this conversion allegedly allows modern society to lock up deviant people and to enforce its norms of conformity.

Some critics are also troubled because medical diagnoses of abnormal behavior pin potentially derogatory labels on people (Becker, 1973; Rothblum, Solomon, & Albee, 1986). Being labeled as psychotic, schizophrenic, or mentally ill carries a social stigma that can be difficult to shake. Even after a full recovery, someone who has been labeled mentally ill may have difficulty finding a place to live, getting a job, or making friends. Deep-seated prejudice against people who have been labeled mentally ill is commonplace.

The medical model has also been criticized because it suggests that people with behavioral problems should adopt the passive role of medical patient (Korchin, 1976). In this passive role, mental patients are implicitly encouraged to wait for their therapists to do the work to effect a cure. Such passiveness can be problematic even when an illness is purely physical. In psychological disorders, this passiveness can seriously undermine the likelihood of improvement in the person's condition.

Putting the Medical Model in Perspective

So, what position should we take on the medical model? In this chapter, we will assume an intermediate position, neither accepting nor discarding the model entirely. There certainly are significant problems with the medical model, and the issues raised by its critics deserve serious attention. However, in its defense, the medical model *has* stimulated scientific research on abnormal behavior. Moreover, some of the problems that are blamed on the disease analogy are not unique to this conception of abnormality. For example, people who displayed strange, irrational behavior were labeled and stigmatized long before the medical model came along.

Hence, we'll take the position that the disease analogy can be useful, as long as we remember that it is *only* an analogy. Medical concepts such as *diagnosis, etiology,* and *prognosis* have proven useful in the treatment and study of abnormality. **Diagnosis involves distinguishing one illness from another. Etiology refers to the apparent causation and developmental history of an illness. A prognosis is a forecast about the probable course of an illness.** These medically based concepts have widely shared meanings that permit clinicians, researchers, and the public to communicate more effectively in their discussions of abnormal behavior.

Criteria of Abnormal Behavior

If your next-door neighbor scrubs his front porch twice every day and spends virtually all his time cleaning and recleaning his house, is he normal? If your sister-in-law goes to one physician after another seeking treatment for ailments that appear imaginary, is she psychologically healthy? How are we to judge what's normal and what's abnormal? More important, who's to do the judging?

These are complex questions. In a sense, *all* people make judgments about normality in that they all express opinions about others' (and perhaps their own) mental health. Of course, formal diagnoses of psychological disorders are made by mental health professionals. In making these diagnoses, clinicians rely on an overlapping hodgepodge of criteria, which reflect the lack of scientific consensus on how to define the concept of mental disorder (Wakefield, 1992). Three criteria are most frequently used in judgments of abnormality:

1. *Deviance.* As Szasz has pointed out, people are often said to have a disorder because their behavior deviates from what their society considers acceptable. What constitutes normality varies somewhat from one culture to another, but all cultures have such norms. When people ignore these standards and expectations, they may be labeled mentally ill. Consider transvestites, for instance. **Transvestism is a sexual disorder in which a man achieves sexual arousal by dressing in women's clothing.** This behavior is regarded as disordered because a man who wears a dress, brassiere, and nylons is deviating from our culture's norms. The example of transvestism illustrates the arbitrary nature of cultural standards regarding normality, as in our society it is normal for women to dress in men's clothing, but not vice versa. Thus, the same overt behavior (cross-sex dressing) is acceptable for women and deviant for men.

2. *Maladaptive behavior.* In many cases, people are judged to have a psychological disorder because their everyday adaptive behavior is impaired. This is the key criterion in the diagnosis of substance use (drug) disorders. In and of itself, alcohol and drug use is not terribly unusual or deviant. However, when the use of cocaine, for instance, begins to interfere with a person's social or occupational functioning, a substance use disorder exists. In such cases, it is the maladaptive quality of the behavior that makes it disordered.

3. *Personal distress.* Frequently, the diagnosis of a psychological disorder is based on an individual's

report of great personal distress. This is usually the criterion met by people who are troubled by depression or anxiety disorders. Depressed people, for instance, may or may not exhibit deviant or maladaptive behavior. Such people are usually

Behavior that is deviant in one culture or context may be quite normal in another. In the drag subculture, transvestism is considered the norm, but it would be considered deviant in, say, the corporate culture of a company headquarters.

CONCEPT CHECK 14.1
Applying the Criteria of Abnormal Behavior

Check your understanding of the criteria of abnormal behavior by identifying the criteria met by each of the examples below and checking them off in the table provided. Remember, a specific behavior may meet more than one criterion. The answers are in Appendix A.

Behavioral examples

1. Alan's performance at work has suffered because he has been drinking alcohol to excess. Several co-workers have suggested that he seek help for his problem, but he thinks that they're getting alarmed over nothing. "I just enjoy a good time once in a while," he says.

2. Monica has gone away to college and feels lonely, sad, and dejected. Her grades are fine, and she gets along okay with the other students in the dormitory, but inside she's choked with gloom, hopelessness, and despair.

3. Walter believes that he's Napoleon reborn. He believes that he is destined to lead the U.S. military forces into a great battle to recover California from space aliens.

4. Phyllis panics with anxiety whenever she leaves her home. Her problem escalated gradually until she was absent from work so often that she was fired. She hasn't been out of her house in nine months and is deeply troubled by her problem.

Criteria met by each example

	Maladaptive behavior	Deviance	Personal distress
1. Alan	_____	_____	_____
2. Monica	_____	_____	_____
3. Walter	_____	_____	_____
4. Phyllis	_____	_____	_____

labeled as having a disorder when they describe their subjective pain and suffering to friends, relatives, and mental health professionals.

Although two or three criteria may apply in a particular case, people are often viewed as disordered when only one criterion is met.

Normality and Abnormality as a Continuum

Antonyms such as normal versus abnormal and mental health versus mental illness imply that people can be divided neatly into two distinct groups: those who are normal and those who are not. In reality, it is often difficult to draw a line that clearly separates normality from abnormality. On occasion, everyone experiences personal distress. Everybody acts in deviant ways once in a while. And everyone displays some maladaptive behavior. People are judged to have psychological disorders only when their behavior becomes *extremely* deviant, maladaptive, or distressing. Thus, normality and abnormality exist on a continuum. It's a matter of degree, not an either-or proposition (see Figure 14.2).

The Cultural Bounds of Normality

As we will discuss later, the major categories of psychological disorders transcend culture, and researchers have found considerable continuity across cultures in regard to what is considered normal or abnormal (Butcher, Narikiyo, & Vitousek, 1993). Nonetheless, judgments of abnormality are influenced to some extent by cultural norms and values (Lewis-Fernandez & Kleinman, 1994). Behavior that is considered deviant or maladaptive in one society may be quite acceptable in another. For example, in modern Western society people who "hear voices" are assumed to be irrational and are routinely placed in mental hospitals. However, in some cultures hearing voices is commonplace and hardly merits a raised eyebrow.

Cultural norms regarding acceptable behavior can also change over time. For example, consider how views of homosexuality have changed in our society. Homosexuality used to be listed as a sexual disorder in the American Psychiatric Association's diagnostic system. However, in 1973 a committee appointed by the association voted to delete homosexuality from the official list of psychological disorders. This action occurred for several reasons (Rothblum, Solomon, & Albee, 1986). First, attitudes toward homosexuality in our society had become more accepting. Second, gay rights activists campaigned vigorously for the change. Third, research showed that gays and heterosexuals do not differ overall on measures of psychological health. As you might guess, this change stimulated a great deal of debate.

Gays are not the only group that has tried to influence the psychiatric diagnostic system. For example, in recent years women's groups have lobbied against adding a new diagnosis originally called *masochistic personality disorder* and subsequently renamed *self-defeating personality disorder*. They campaigned against this diagnostic category because they believed it would be used to blame battered women for their partners' violence against them (Caplan, 1995; Tavris, 1995). Concerned groups have also campaigned against the inclusion of a new diagnosis called *premenstrual dysphoric disorder,* on the grounds that it has sexist overtones (Parlee, 1992).

The key point is that diagnoses of psychological disorders involve *value judgments* about what represents normal or abnormal behavior. The criteria of mental illness are not nearly as value-free as the criteria of physical illness. In evaluating physical diseases, people can usually agree that a weak heart or a bad kidney is pathological, regardless of their personal values. However, judgments about mental illness reflect prevailing cultural values, social trends, and political forces, as well as scientific knowledge (Kirk & Kutchins, 1992).

Stereotypes of Psychological Disorders

We've seen that mental illnesses are not diseases in a strict sense and that judgments of mental health are not value-free. However, still other myths about abnormal behavior need to be exposed as such. Let's examine three stereotypes about psychological disorders that are largely inaccurate:

1. *Psychological disorders are incurable.* Admittedly, there are mentally ill people for whom treat-

Figure 14.2
Normality and abnormality as a continuum.
There isn't a sharp boundary between normal and abnormal behavior. Behavior is normal or abnormal in degree, depending on the extent to which one's behavior is deviant, personally distressing, or maladaptive.

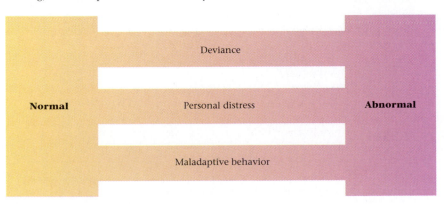

Normal
Deviance
Personal distress
Abnormal
Maladaptive behavior

ment is largely a failure. However, they are greatly outnumbered by people who *do* get better, either spontaneously or through formal treatment (Lambert & Bergin, 1992). The vast majority of people who are diagnosed as mentally ill eventually improve and lead normal, productive lives. Even the most severe psychological disorders can be treated successfully.

2. *People with psychological disorders are often violent and dangerous.* There appears to be only a modest association between mental illness and violence-prone tendencies (Monahan, 1992). This stereotype exists because incidents of violence involving the mentally ill tend to command media attention. For example, our opening case history, which described Ed's breakdown and the incident with the hatchet, was written up in a national news magazine. People such as John Hinckley, Jr.,

whose mental illness led him to attempt an assassination of President Ronald Reagan (and wounding of press secretary James Brady), receive extensive publicity. However, these individuals are not representative of the large number of people who have struggled with psychological disorders.

3. *People with psychological disorders behave in bizarre ways and are very different from normal people.* This is true only in a small minority of cases, usually involving relatively severe disorders. As noted earlier, the line between normal and abnormal behavior can be difficult to draw. At first glance, people with psychological disorders usually are indistinguishable from those without disorders. This brings us to our Featured Study for the chapter, which shows that even mental health professionals may have difficulty distinguishing normality from abnormality.

Distinguishing Between Normality and Abnormality   **Featured Study**

Investigator: David L. Rosenhan (Stanford University)

Source: On being sane in insane places. *Science*, 1973, *179*, 250–258.

Voicing doubts about the validity of psychiatric diagnosis, David Rosenhan set out to demonstrate that "notions of normality and abnormality may not be quite as accurate as people believe they are" (p. 250). To test his thesis, he arranged for a number of normal people to seek admission to mental hospitals. He wanted to see how long it would take for the hospital staffs to recognize the normality of the "pseudopatients."

Method

Eight people with no history of psychiatric problems sought admission to a diverse collection of mental hospitals located in five states. The pseudopatients arrived at the hospitals complaining of one false symptom—hearing voices. Except for this single symptom, they acted as they normally would and gave accurate information when interviewed about their personal history and current mental status. The pseudopatients were instructed to stop simulating the symptom and behave in their usual manner if they were admitted to the hospital. Rosenhan wanted to find out what percentage of the pseudopatients would be admitted and how long they would be kept hospitalized.

Results

The pseudopatients were admitted to the mental hospital in every instance. In all, Rosenhan's confederates were admitted to 12 different hospitals (some did it twice). The length of their hospitalization ranged from 7 to 52 days. The average stay was 19 days. In all but one case, the admitting diagnosis was schizophrenia, which is a severe disorder. After the study was completed, the pseudopatients'

hospital charts were obtained. The records indicated that they were discharged with a diagnosis of *schizophrenia—in remission.* (The phrase *in remission* indicates that a disorder is currently abated or under control.) In a sense, this means that the normality of the pseudopatients was unrecognized even when they were released after ample opportunity for observation by the staff.

Interestingly, the other patients in the hospitals recognized the normality of the pseudopatients more frequently than did the professional staff of psychiatrists, psychologists, nurses, and attendants. Many patients came forward and said something like, "You're not crazy. You're a journalist or a professor checking up on the hospital." In part, this happened because the pseudopatients openly took notes on their experiences in the hospital. Their note taking was not hidden from the hospital staff, but the examination of the patients' charts (after the study) revealed that the staff viewed the note taking as a *symptom* of the pseudopatients' mental disorder.

Discussion

The results support the assertion that it's often difficult to distinguish normality from abnormality. The pseudopatients' notes about life on the psychiatric wards offer a clue as to why. They were impressed by the largely "normal" quality of the real patients' behavior. They concluded that people with genuine mental illness act normally most of the time and act in a deviant manner only a small fraction of the time. The pseudopatients' notes also revealed that the hospital staff spent surprisingly little time interacting with patients. Most of the time they were segregated from the patients in a glassed-off enclosure known as

"How many people, one wonders, are sane but not recognized as such in our psychiatric institutions?"

DAVID ROSENHAN

One of the findings of the Rosenhan study was that hospital staff spent minimal time interacting with patients, preferring to stay in an enclosure from which they could view their charges. Rosenhan surmised that this lack of contact contributed to the staff's continued perception of the pseudopatients as being "abnormal."

"the cage." This lack of interaction presumably contributed to the staff's failure to detect that the pseudopatients were normal. The study also showed that psychiatric labels can influence perceptions of patients' behavior. Once the pseudopatients were labeled as schizophrenic, even innocuous behavior such as taking notes was viewed as a sign of pathology.

Comment

Rosenhan's study provoked a great deal of controversy. In defense of the hospitals' admission of the pseudopatients, Robert Spitzer (1975) argued that it would have been inhumane to turn away people who came to a psychiatric facility complaining of hearing voices. That's undeniably true. Spitzer also asserted that the symptom of hearing voices made schizophrenia the most probable diagnosis for the pseudopatients. That's also true. However, it overlooks the fact that the hospital staff did not have to make an immediate diagnosis. With most of the symptoms of schizophrenia absent, the hospital staff could have deferred the diagnosis pending further observation and the collection of additional information. If they had been more deliberate, some staff members might have detected the normality of the pseudopatients.

Rosenhan's study showed that our mental health system has a powerful bias toward seeing pathology in anyone who walks in the door. This slant toward seeing mental illness is not entirely unreasonable. After all, people don't go to mental hospitals because they're feeling terrific. However, this bias may need to be tempered. People often go to physicians with reports of physical symptoms and end up being assured that they're not really sick. In our mental health system, the slant toward seeing pathology should not be so powerful that it precludes a similar result.

Some critics of the medical model argued that Rosenhan's work demonstrated that the entire diagnostic system for mental disorders lacked validity. A more reasonable conclusion would be that Rosenhan showed that mental illness can be feigned easily. In any case, the diagnostic system for mental illness survived the controversy evoked by the Rosenhan study. Let's look at how this system has evolved into its current form.

Psychodiagnosis: The Classification of Disorders

Obviously, we cannot lump all psychological disorders together without giving up all hope of understanding them better. A sound taxonomy of mental disorders can facilitate empirical research and enhance communication among scientists and clinicians (Adams & Cassidy, 1993). Hence, a great deal of effort has been invested in devising an elaborate system for classifying psychological disorders.

Guidelines for psychodiagnosis were vague and informal prior to 1952 when the American Psychiatric Association unveiled its *Diagnostic and Statistical Manual of Mental Disorders* (Grob, 1991). Known as DSM-I, this classification scheme described about 100 disorders. Revisions intended to improve the system were incorporated into the second edition (DSM-II) published in 1968, but the diagnostic guidelines were still pretty sketchy, and there was widespread dissatisfaction with the lack of consistency in psychiatric diagnosis (Wilson, 1993). All too often, several clinicians evaluating the same patient would arrive at different diagnoses. Thus, the revisions of the next two editions, DSM-III (1980) and DSM-III-R (1987), sought, first and foremost, to improve the consistency of psychodiagnosis. To achieve this end, diagnostic guidelines were made more explicit, concrete, and detailed (see Figure 14.3). These revisions *did* lead to substantial increases in diagnostic consistency for many disorders, although there is still considerable room for improvement (Garfield, 1993). The current edition, DSM-IV, was introduced in 1994. More than ever before, the architects of the most recent DSM worked to base their revision on empirical research, as opposed to

A. Excessive anxiety and worry (apprehensive expectation), occurring more days than not for at least six months, about a number of events or activities (such as work or school performance).

B. The person finds it difficult to control the worry.

C. The anxiety and worry are associated with at least three of the following six symptoms (with at least some symptoms present for more days than not for the past six months):
(1) restlessness or feeling keyed up or on edge
(2) being easily fatigued
(3) difficulty concentrating or mind going blank
(4) irritability
(5) muscle tension
(6) sleep disturbance (difficulty falling or staying asleep, or restless unsatisfying sleep)

D. The focus of the anxiety and worry is not confined to features of an Axis I disorder, e.g., the anxiety or worry is not about having a panic attack (as in panic disorder), being embarrassed in public (as in social phobia), being contaminated (as in obsessive-compulsive disorder), being away from home or close relatives (as in separation anxiety disorder), gaining weight (as in anorexia nervosa), or having a serious illness (as in hypochondriasis), and is not part of posttraumatic stress disorder.

E. The anxiety, worry, or physical symptoms cause clinically significant distress or impairment in social, occupational, or other important areas of functioning.

F. Not due to the direct effects of a substance (e.g., drugs of abuse, medication) or a general medical condition (e.g., hyperthyroidism), and does not occur exclusively during a mood disorder, psychotic disorder, or a pervasive developmental disorder.

Figure 14.3
Example of the diagnostic criteria in the DSM diagnostic system. This list of the conditions to be met for a diagnosis of generalized anxiety disorder shows the degree of detail in modern diagnostic criteria. (Adapted with permission from the *Diagnostic and Statistical Manual of Mental Disorders,* 4th ed. Copyright 1994 American Psychiatric Association.)

the consensus of experts (Widiger et al., 1991). Each revision of the DSM system has expanded the list of disorders covered. The current version (DSM-IV) describes about three times as many types of psychological disorders as DSM-I.

The Multiaxial System

The publication of DSM-III in 1980 introduced a new multiaxial system of classification, which asks for judgments about individuals on five separate dimensions, or "axes." Figure 14.4 (on page 564) provides an overview of the entire system and the five axes. The diagnoses of disorders are made on Axes I and II. Clinicians record any major disorders that are apparent on Axis I (Clinical Syndromes). They use Axis II (Personality Disorders) to list milder, long-running personality disturbances, which often coexist with Axis I syndromes. People may receive diagnoses on both axes.

The remaining axes are used to record supplemental information. A patient's physical disorders are listed on Axis III (General Medical Conditions). On Axis IV (Psychosocial and Environmental Problems), the clinician makes notations regarding the types of stress experienced by the individual in the past year. On Axis V (Global Assessment of Functioning), estimates are made of the individual's current level of adaptive functioning (in social and occupational behavior, viewed as a whole), and of the individual's highest level of functioning in the past year. Figure 14.5 shows an example of a multiaxial evaluation. Most theorists agree

that the multiaxial system is a step in the right direction because it recognizes the importance of information besides a traditional diagnostic label.

Controversies Surrounding the DSM

Since the publication of the third edition in 1980, the DSM system has become the dominant classification scheme for mental disorders around the world (Maser, Kaelber, & Weise, 1991; Williams, 1994). Nonetheless, the DSM system has garnered its share of criticism. First, some critics argue that the heavy focus on improving the consistency of psychodiagnosis has drawn attention away from an equally basic issue—the *validity* of the diagnostic categories (Carson, 1991). Precise, detailed descriptions of disorders are of little value unless the descriptions mesh well with the constellations of problems that people actually experience. For example, as we will discuss shortly, some theorists have questioned whether *hypochondria* is a discrete, independent disorder or merely a general symptom of psychological distress associated with a variety of disorders (Iezzi & Adams, 1993). More research is needed on these kinds of validity issues.

Second, because decisions about how to revise the DSM system are made by committees, some critics maintain that the rhetorical skills of committee members have often been more influential than the weight of empirical evidence on an issue (Kirk & Kutchins, 1992). For instance, concerns have been raised about new diagnoses being added to the system simply because of the eloquence and

Figure 14.4
Overview of the DSM diagnostic system.
Published by the American Psychiatric Association, the *Diagnostic and Statistical Manual of Mental Disorders* is the formal classification system used in the diagnosis of psychological disorders. It is a *multiaxial* system, which means that information is recorded on the five axes described here. (Adapted with permission from the *Diagnostic and Statistical Manual of Mental Disorders,* 4th ed. Copyright 1994 American Psychiatric Association.)

Axis I
Clinical Syndromes

1. *Disorders usually first diagnosed in infancy, childhood, or adolescence*
This category includes disorders that arise before adolescence, such as attention deficit disorders, autism, mental retardation, enuresis, and stuttering.

2. *Organic mental disorders*
These disorders are temporary or permanent dysfunctions of brain tissue caused by diseases or chemicals. Examples are delirium, dementia, and amnesia.

3. *Substance-related disorders*
This category refers to the *maladaptive* use of drugs and alcohol. Mere consumption and recreational use of such substances are not disorders. This category requires an abnormal pattern of use, as with alcohol abuse and cocaine dependence.

4. *Schizophrenia and other psychotic disorders*
The schizophrenias are characterized by psychotic symptoms (for example, grossly disorganized behavior, delusions, and hallucinations) and by over 6 months of behavioral deterioration. This category also includes delusional disorder and schizoaffective disorder.

5. *Mood disorders*
The cardinal feature is emotional disturbance. Patients may, or may not, have psychotic symptoms. These disorders include major depression, bipolar disorder, dysthymic disorder, and cyclothymic disorder.

6. *Anxiety disorders*
These disorders are characterized by physiological signs of anxiety (for example, palpitations) and subjective feelings of tension, apprehension, or fear. Anxiety may be acute and focused (panic disorder) or continual and diffuse (generalized anxiety disorder).

7. *Somatoform disorders*
These disorders are dominated by somatic symptoms that resemble physical illnesses. These symptoms cannot be accounted for by organic damage. There *must* also be strong evidence that these symptoms are produced by psychological factors or conflicts. This category includes somatization and conversion disorders and hypochondriasis.

8. *Dissociative disorders*
These disorders all feature a sudden, temporary alteration or dysfunction of memory, consciousness, identity, and behavior, as in dissociative amnesia and multiple personality.

9. *Sexual and gender-identity disorders*
There are three basic types of disorders in this category: gender identity disorders (discomfort with identity as male or female), paraphilias (preference for unusual acts to achieve sexual arousal), and sexual dysfunctions (impairments in sexual functioning).

Axis II
Personality Disorders

These disorders are patterns of personality traits that are longstanding, maladaptive, and inflexible and involve impaired functioning or subjective distress. Examples include borderline, schizoid, and antisocial personality disorders.

Axis III
General Medical Conditions

Physical disorders or conditions are recorded on this axis. Examples include diabetes, arthritis, and hemophilia.

Axis IV
Psychosocial and Environmental Problems

Axis IV is for reporting psychosocial and environmental problems that may affect the diagnosis, treatment, and prognosis of mental disorders (Axis I and II). A psychosocial or environmental problem may be a negative life event, an environmental difficulty or deficiency, a familial or other interpersonal stress, an inadequacy of social support or personal resources, or another problem that describes the context in which a person's difficulties have developed.

Axis V
Global Assessment of Functioning (GAF) Scale

Code	Symptoms
100	Superior functioning in a wide range of activities
90	Absent or minimal symptoms, good functioning in all areas
80	Symptoms transient and expectable reactions to psychosocial stressors
70	Some mild symptoms or some difficulty in social, occupational, or school functioning, but generally functioning pretty well
60	Moderate symptoms or difficulty in social, occupational, or school functioning
50	Serious symptoms or impairment in social, occupational, or school functioning
40	Some impairment in reality testing or communication or major impairment in family relations, judgment, thinking, or mood
30	Behavior considerably influenced by delusions or hallucinations, serious impairment in communication or judgment, or inability to function in almost all areas
20	Some danger of hurting self or others, occasional failure to maintain minimal personal hygiene, or gross impairment in communication
10	Persistent danger of severely hurting self or others
1	

persuasiveness of a few advocates on a committee, in the absence of adequate research (Tavris, 1995). The influence of expert opinion has also been blamed for the opposite problem—the retention of traditional diagnostic categories that perhaps should have been discarded based on available empirical evidence (Carson, 1991).

Third, recent editions of the DSM sparked controversy by adding everyday problems that are not traditionally thought of as mental illnesses to the diagnostic system. For example, the DSM system includes a *developmental coordination disorder* (basically, extreme clumsiness in children), a *nicotine dependence disorder* (distress derived from quitting smoking), and a *pathological gambling disorder* (difficulty controlling one's gambling). Critics argue that this approach "medicalizes" everyday problems and casts the shadow of pathology on normal behavior (Kirk & Kutchins, 1992). In part, everyday problems were added to the diagnostic system so that more people could bill their insurance companies for professional treatment of the conditions (Garfield, 1986). Many health insurance policies permit reimbursement only for the treatment of disorders on the official (DSM) list. There's merit in making it easier for more people to seek needed professional help. Nonetheless, the pros and cons of including everyday problems in DSM are complicated.

Shifting definitions of normality and abnormality inevitably affect estimates regarding the number of people who suffer from psychological disorders. The changes made in DSM-III stimulated a flurry of research on the prevalence of specific mental disorders that has continued through the present. Let's examine some of this research.

The Prevalence of Psychological Disorders

How common are psychological disorders? What percentage of the population is afflicted with mental illness? Is it 10%? Perhaps 25%? Could the figure range as high as 40% or 50%?

Such estimates fall in the domain of *epidemiology*—**the study of the distribution of mental or physical disorders in a population.** In epidemiology, *prevalence* **refers to the percentage of a population that exhibits a disorder during a specified time period.** In the case of mental disorders, the most interesting data are the estimates of *lifetime prevalence*, the percentage of people who endure a specific disorder at any time in their lives.

A DSM multiaxial evaluation (patient: 49-year-old male)	
Axis I	Major depressive disorder Cocaine abuse
Axis II	Borderline personality disorder (provisional, rule out dependent personality disorder)
Axis III	Hypertension
Axis IV	Psychosocial stressors: recent divorce, permitted to see his children only infrequently, job is in jeopardy
Axis V	Current global assessment of functioning (GAF): 46

Figure 14.5
Example of a multiaxial evaluation. A multiaxial evaluation for a depressed man with a cocaine problem might look like this.

Estimates of lifetime prevalence suggest that psychological disorders are more common than most people realize. Prior to the advent of DSM-III, studies suggested that about *one-fifth* of the population exhibited clear signs of mental illness (Neugebauer, Dohrenwend, & Dohrenwend, 1980). However, the older studies did not assess drug-related disorders very effectively, because these disorders were vaguely described in DSM-I and DSM-II. More recent studies, using the explicit criteria for substance use disorders in recent editions of the DSM system, have found psychological disorders in roughly *one-third* of the population! This increase in mental illness is more apparent than real, as it is mostly attributable to more effective tabulation of drug-related disorders. As Figure 14.6 shows, the most common disorders are

Figure 14.6
Prevalence of common psychological disorders in the United States. The estimated percentage of people who have, at any time in their life, suffered from one of four types of psychological disorders or from a disorder of any kind (top bar) is shown here. (Based on combined data from several chapters in Robins & Regier, 1991)

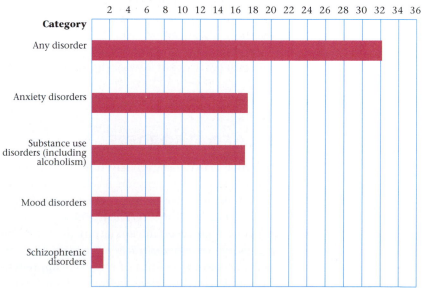

(1) anxiety disorders, (2) substance (alcohol and drugs) use disorders, and (3) mood disorders (Regier & Kaelber, 1995; Robins, Locke, & Regier, 1991).

The raw numbers are even more dramatic than the prevalence rates in Figure 14.6. Estimates based on these prevalence rates suggest that the United States contains nearly 4 million people who will be troubled at some time in their lives by schizophrenic disorders. Roughly 20 million people will experience mood disorders (mostly depression). And over 40 million will wrestle with substance use disorders or anxiety disorders. If you're thinking that these estimates add up to more than one-third of the population, you're right. It's because some people have more than one disorder. About half of the people who have experienced a psychological disorder qualify for a second diagnosis (Kessler, 1995). In any case, it's clear that psychological disorders are widespread. When psychologists note that mental illness can strike anyone, they mean it quite literally.

We are now ready to start examining the specific types of psychological disorders. Obviously, we cannot cover all of the disorders listed in DSM-IV. However, we will introduce most of the major categories of disorders to give you an overview of the many forms abnormal behavior takes. In discussing each set of disorders, we will begin with brief descriptions of the specific syndromes or subtypes that fall in the category. Then we'll focus on the *etiology* of the disorders in that category. Although many paths can lead to specific disorders, some are more common than others. We'll highlight some of the common paths to enhance your understanding of the roots of abnormal behavior.

Recap of Key Points
• The medical model assumes that it is useful to view abnormal behavior as a disease. This view has been criticized on the grounds that it turns ethical questions about deviance into medical questions.

• Critics also argue that the medical model stigmatizes those labeled mentally ill and encourages the adoption of a passive patient role. Although there are serious problems with the medical model, the concept is useful if one remembers that it is only an analogy.

• Three criteria are used in deciding whether people suffer from psychological disorders: deviance, personal distress, and maladaptive behavior. Often it is difficult to clearly draw a line between normality and abnormality. Judgments about normality and abnormality are influenced to some extent by cultural norms.

• Contrary to popular stereotypes, people with psychological disorders are not particularly bizarre or dangerous. Psychological disorders are not a manifestation of personal weakness, and even the most severe disorders are potentially curable.

• Research by David Rosenhan, described in our Featured Study, showed that pseudopatients were routinely admitted to mental hospitals, which were unable to detect the patients' normalcy. His study showed that the distinction between normality and abnormality is not clear-cut.

• DSM-IV is the official psychodiagnostic classification system in the United States. This system describes over 200 disorders and asks for information about patients on five axes, or dimensions.

• Controversies about DSM illustrate that judgments about psychological disorders are not value-free and that they are influenced by social trends and political realities.

• It is difficult to obtain good data on the prevalence of psychological disorders. Nonetheless, it is clear that they are more common than widely believed, affecting roughly one-third of the population. According to recent studies, the most common syndromes are substance use disorders, anxiety disorders, and mood disorders.

ANXIETY DISORDERS

Everyone experiences anxiety from time to time. It is a natural and common reaction to many of life's difficulties. For some people, however, anxiety becomes a chronic problem. These people experience high levels of anxiety with disturbing regularity. **Anxiety disorders are a class of disorders marked by feelings of excessive apprehension and anxiety.** There are four principal types of anxiety disorders: generalized anxiety disorders, phobic disorders, obsessive-compulsive disorders, and panic disorders. These disorders are not mutually exclusive, as many people who develop one anxiety syndrome often suffer from another at some point in their lives (Massion, Warshaw, & Keller, 1993). People with anxiety disorders also exhibit elevated rates of depression (Clark, Beck, & Beck, 1994). Studies suggest that anxiety disorders are quite common, occurring in roughly 17% of the population (Robins & Regier, 1991). Most of these cases are generalized anxiety disorders or phobic disorders (Blazer et al., 1991; Eaton, Dryman, & Weissman, 1991).

Generalized Anxiety Disorder

The *generalized anxiety disorder* is marked by a chronic, high level of anxiety that is not tied to any specific threat. This anxiety is sometimes called "free-floating anxiety" because it is nonspecific. People with this disorder worry constantly about yesterday's mistakes and tomorrow's problems. In particular, they worry about minor matters related to family, finances, work, and personal illness (Sanderson & Barlow, 1990). They often dread decisions and brood over them endlessly. Their anxiety is commonly accompanied by physical symptoms, such as trembling, muscle tension, diarrhea, dizziness, faintness, sweating, and heart palpitations.

Phobic Disorder

In a phobic disorder, an individual's troublesome anxiety has a specific focus. A *phobic disorder* is marked by a persistent and irrational fear of an object or situation that presents no realistic danger. Although mild phobias are extremely common, people are said to have a phobic disorder only when their fears seriously interfere with their everyday behavior. The following case provides an example of a phobic disorder:

Hilda is 32 years of age and has a rather unusual fear. She is terrified of snow. She cannot go outside in the snow. She cannot even stand to see snow or hear about it on the weather report. Her phobia severely constricts her day-to-day behavior. Probing in therapy revealed that her phobia was caused by a traumatic experience at age 11. Playing at a ski lodge, she was buried briefly by a small avalanche of snow. She had no recollection of this experience until it was recovered in therapy. (Adapted from Laughlin, 1967, p. 227)

As Hilda's unusual snow phobia illustrates, people can develop phobic responses to virtually anything. Nonetheless, certain types of phobias are relatively common, as the data in Figure 14.7 show. Particularly common are acrophobia (fear of heights), claustrophobia (fear of small, enclosed places), brontophobia (fear of storms), hydrophobia (fear of water), and various animal and insect phobias (Eaton et al., 1991). People troubled by phobias typically realize that their fears are irrational, but they still are unable to calm themselves when confronted by a phobic object.

Panic Disorder and Agoraphobia

A *panic disorder* is characterized by recurrent attacks of overwhelming anxiety that usually occur suddenly and unexpectedly. These paralyzing attacks are accompanied by physical symptoms of anxiety. After a number of anxiety attacks, victims often become apprehensive, wondering when their next panic will occur. Their concern about exhibiting panic in public may escalate to the point where they are afraid to leave home. This creates a condition called agoraphobia, which is a common complication of panic disorders.

Agoraphobia is a fear of going out to public places (its literal meaning is "fear of the marketplace or open places"). Because of this fear, some people become prisoners confined to their homes, although many will venture out if accompanied by a trusted companion (Hollander, Simeon, & Gorman, 1994). As its name suggests, agoraphobia has traditionally been viewed as a phobic disorder.

Figure 14.7
Common phobias. The most frequently reported phobias in a large-scale survey of mental health (Eaton, Dryman, & Weissman, 1991) are listed here. The percentages reflect the portion of respondents who reported each type of phobia. Although the data show that phobias are quite common, people are said to have full-fledged phobic *disorders* only when their phobias seriously interfere with their activities. Overall, about 40% of the subjects who reported each fear qualified as having a phobic disorder.

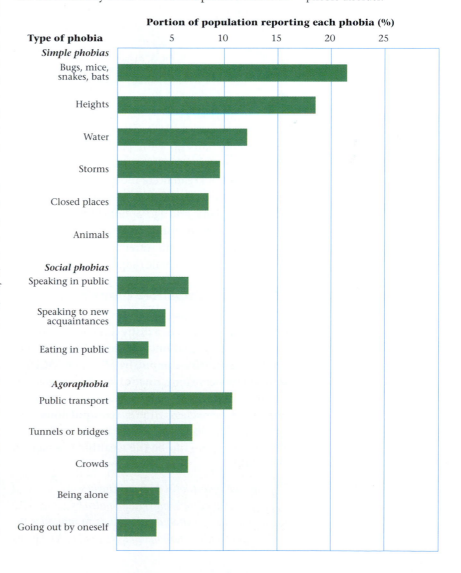

As a young man (shown in the photo), Howard Hughes was a handsome, dashing daredevil pilot and movie producer who appeared to be reasonably well adjusted. However, as the years went by, his behavior gradually became more and more mal-adaptive, as obsessions and compulsions came to dominate his life. In his later years (shown in the drawing), he spent most of his time in darkened rooms, naked, unkempt, and dirty, following bizarre rituals to alleviate his anxieties. (The drawing was done by an NBC artist and was based on descriptions from men who had seen Hughes.)

methodically cleaning a single telephone. He once wrote a three-page memo instructing assistants on exactly how to open cans of fruit for him. The following is just a small portion of the instructions that Hughes provided for a driver who delivered films to his bungalow. "Get out of the car on the traffic side. Do not at any time be on the side of the car between the car and the curb. . . . Carry only one can of film at a time. Step over the gutter opposite the place where the sidewalk dead-ends into the curb from a point as far out into the center of the road as possible. Do not ever walk on the grass at all, also do not step into the gutter at all. Walk to the bungalow keeping as near to the center of the sidewalk as possible." (Adapted from Barlett & Steele, 1979, pp. 227–237)*

The typical age of onset for OCD is early adulthood (Sturgis, 1993). Obsessions often center on inflicting harm on others, personal failures, suicide, or sexual acts. People troubled by obsessions may feel that they have lost control of their mind. Compulsions usually involve stereotyped rituals that temporarily relieve anxiety. Common examples include constant handwashing, repetitive cleaning of things that are already clean, and endless rechecking of locks, faucets, and such (Foa & Kozak, 1995). Unusual rituals intended to bring good luck are also a common form of compulsive behavior.

Although many of us can be compulsive at times, full-fledged obsessive-compulsive disorders occur in roughly 2%–4% of the population (Karno & Golding, 1991). The frequency of obsessive-compulsive disorder seems to be increasing, but this trend may simply reflect changes in clinicians' diagnostic tendencies. Recent years have seen increased research on OCD and advances in its treatment that may have made clinicians more sensitive to the syndrome (Stoll, Tohen, & Baldessarini, 1992). Most victims of OCD exhibit both obsessions and compulsions, but some experience only one or the other (Marks, 1987).

However, recent studies suggest that agoraphobia shares more kinship with panic disorders than phobic disorders (Turner et al., 1986). Nonetheless, agoraphobia can occur independently of panic disorder, and some theorists question the wisdom of lumping panic and agoraphobia together in the DSM classification system (Noyes, 1988). The vast majority of people who suffer from panic disorder or agoraphobia are female (Rapee & Barlow, 1993).

Obsessive-Compulsive Disorder 11a

Obsessions are *thoughts* that repeatedly intrude on one's consciousness in a distressing way. Compulsions are *actions* that one feels forced to carry out. Thus, an **obsessive-compulsive disorder (OCD) is marked by persistent, uncontrollable intrusions of unwanted thoughts (obsessions) and urges to engage in senseless rituals (compulsions).** To illustrate, let's examine the bizarre behavior of a man once reputed to be the wealthiest person in the world:

The famous industrialist Howard Hughes was obsessed with the possibility of being contaminated by germs. This led him to devise extraordinary rituals to minimize the possibility of such contamination. He would spend hours

Etiology of Anxiety Disorders 11a

Like most psychological disorders, anxiety disorders develop out of complicated interactions among a variety of biological and psychological factors.

Biological Factors

In studies that assess the impact of heredity on psychological disorders, investigators look at *concordance rates*. **A *concordance rate* indicates the percentage of twin pairs or other pairs of relatives that exhibit the same disorder.** If relatives who share more genetic similarity show higher concordance rates than relatives who share less genetic overlap, this finding supports the genetic hypothesis. *Twin studies,* which compare identical and fraternal twins (see Chapter 3), suggest that there may be a weak genetic predisposition to anxiety disorders (see Figure 14.8; Kendler et al., 1992; Pauls et al., 1995). These findings are consistent with the idea that inherited differences in temperament might make some people more vulnerable than others to anxiety disorders. As we noted in Chapter 11, Kagan and his colleagues (1992) have found that about 15%–20% of infants display an *inhibited temperament,* characterized by shyness, timidity, and wariness, which appears to have a strong genetic basis. Recent research suggests that this temperament is a risk factor for the development of anxiety disorders (Rosenbaum et al., 1992).

Another line of research suggests that *anxiety sensitivity* may make people vulnerable to anxiety disorders (Fowles, 1993; Reiss, 1991). According to this notion, some people are very sensitive to the internal physiological symptoms of anxiety and are prone to overreact with fear when they experience these symptoms. Anxiety sensitivity may fuel an inflationary spiral in which anxiety breeds more anxiety, which eventually spins out of control in the form of an anxiety disorder.

Recent evidence suggests that a link may exist between anxiety disorders and neurochemical activity in the brain. As you learned in Chapter 3, *neurotransmitters* are chemicals that carry signals from one neuron to another. Therapeutic drugs (such as Valium) that reduce excessive anxiety appear to alter neurotransmitter activity at GABA synapses. This finding and other lines of evidence suggest that disturbances in the neural circuits using GABA may play a role in some types of anxiety disorders (Lloyd, Fletcher, & Minchin, 1992). Abnormalities in other neural circuits using serotonin have recently been implicated in panic and obsessive-compulsive disorders (Stein & Uhde, 1995). Thus, scientists are beginning to unravel the neurochemical bases for anxiety disorders.

Conditioning and Learning

Many anxiety responses may be *acquired through classical conditioning and maintained through operant conditioning* (see Chapter 6). According to Mowrer (1947), an originally neutral stimulus (the snow in Hilda's case, for instance) may be paired with a frightening event (the avalanche) so that it becomes a conditioned stimulus eliciting anxiety (see Figure 14.9). Once a fear is acquired through classical conditioning, the person may start avoiding the anxiety-producing stimulus. The avoidance response is negatively reinforced because it is followed by a reduction in anxiety. This process involves operant conditioning (see Figure 14.9). Thus, separate conditioning processes may create and then sustain specific anxiety responses (Levis, 1989). Consistent with this view, one recent study of people suffering from two types of social phobia found that 44% of the subjects could identify a traumatic conditioning experience that probably contributed to their anxiety disorder (Stemberger et al., 1995).

The tendency to develop phobias of certain types of objects and situations may be explained by Martin Seligman's (1971) concept of *preparedness.* Like many theorists, Seligman believes that classical conditioning creates most phobic responses. *However, he suggests that people are biologically prepared by their evolutionary history to acquire some fears much more easily than others.* His theory would explain why people develop phobias of ancient sources of threat (such as snakes and spiders) much more readily than modern sources of threat (such as electrical outlets or hot irons). Some laboratory

Concordance rate (%)
(lifetime risk)

Relationship	Genetic relatedness
Identical twins	100%
Fraternal twins	50%

Figure 14.8
Twin studies of anxiety disorders. The concordance rate for anxiety disorders in identical twins is higher than that for fraternal twins, who share less genetic overlap. These results suggest that there is a genetic predisposition to anxiety disorders. (Data based on Noyes et al., 1987; Slater & Shields, 1969; Torgersen, 1979, 1983)

(a) Classical conditioning: Acquisition of phobic fear

(b) Operant conditioning: Maintaining of phobic fear
(negative reinforcement)

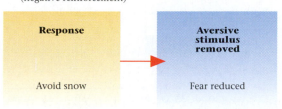

Figure 14.9
Conditioning as an explanation for phobias. (**a**) Many phobias appear to be acquired through classical conditioning when a neutral stimulus is paired with an anxiety-arousing stimulus. (**b**) Once acquired, a phobia may be maintained through operant conditioning. Avoidance of the phobic stimulus reduces anxiety, resulting in negative reinforcement.

studies of conditioned fears have yielded evidence consistent with Seligman's theory. For example, Cook and Mineka (1989) found that monkeys acquired conditioned fears of stimuli that they should be prepared to fear, such as snakes, with relative ease in comparison to other stimuli, such as flowers. As a whole, however, research has provided only modest support for the role of preparedness in the acquisition of phobias (McNally, 1987; Öhman & Soares, 1993).

There are a number of problems with conditioning models of phobias (Rachman, 1990). For instance, many people with phobias cannot recall or identify a traumatic conditioning experience that led to their phobia. Conversely, many people endure extremely traumatic experiences that should create a phobia but do not. To provide better explanations for these complexities, conditioning models of anxiety disorders are currently being revised to include a larger role for cognitive factors (much like conditioning theories in general, as we noted in Chapter 6).

One of these revisions is an increased emphasis on how observational learning can lead to the development of conditioned fears. *Observational learning* occurs when a new response is acquired through watching the behavior of another (consult Chapters 6 and 12). Laboratory studies have shown that conditioned fears can be created in animals through observational learning (Mineka & Cook, 1986). Case studies suggest that anxiety responses are often acquired indirectly in humans as well (Rachman, 1990). In particular, parents frequently pass on their anxieties to their children. Thus, if a father hides in a closet every time there's a thunderstorm, his children may acquire their father's fear of storms.

Cognitive Factors

Cognitive theorists maintain that certain styles of thinking make some people particularly vulnerable to anxiety disorders. According to these theorists, some people are more likely to suffer from problems with anxiety because they tend to (a) misinterpret harmless situations as threatening, (b) focus excessive attention on perceived threats, and (c) selectively recall information that seems threatening (Beck, 1988; McNally, 1990, 1994). In one intriguing test of the cognitive view, anxious and nonanxious subjects were asked to read 32 sentences that could be interpreted in either a threatening or a nonthreatening manner (Eysenck et al., 1991). For instance, one such sentence was "The doctor examined little Emma's growth," which could mean that the doctor checked her height or the growth of a tumor. As Figure 14.10 shows, the anxious subjects interpreted the sentences in a threatening way more often than the nonanxious subjects did. Thus, consistent with our theme that human experience is highly subjective, the cognitive view holds that some people are prone to anxiety disorders because they see threat in every corner of their lives.

Personality

Certain personality traits appear to be related to the likelihood of developing anxiety disorders. Foremost among them is *neuroticism,* one of the Big Five traits described in Chapter 12. People who score high in neuroticism tend to be self-conscious, nervous, jittery, insecure, guilt-prone, and gloomy. Neuroticism is correlated with an elevated prevalance of anxiety disorders and a poorer prognosis for recovery (Clark, Watson, & Mineka, 1994). The mechanisms underlying this association are the subject of debate. One possibility is that the correlation between neuroticism and anxiety disorders may reflect the operation of a third variable—a genetic predisposition to both (Carey & DiLalla, 1994). This explanation appears plausible given the evidence for a genetic component in both neuroticism and anxiety disorders, but more research is needed to rule out other explanations.

Stress

Finally, recent studies have supported the long-held suspicion that anxiety disorders are stress related. For instance, Blazer, Hughes, and George (1987) found an association between stress and the development of generalized anxiety disorders. Men who experienced high stress were 8.5 times more likely to develop these disorders than men under low stress. In another study, Faravelli and Pallanti (1989) found that patients with panic disorder had experienced a dramatic increase in stress

Figure 14.10
Cognitive factors in anxiety disorders.
Eysenck and his colleagues (1991) compared how subjects with anxiety problems and nonanxious subjects tended to interpret sentences that could be viewed as threatening or nonthreatening. Consistent with cognitive models of anxiety disorders, anxious subjects were more likely to interpret the sentences in a threatening light.

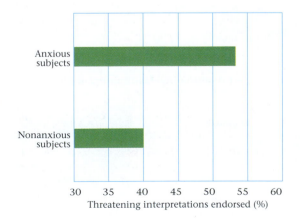

CHAPTER FOURTEEN

in the month prior to the onset of their disorder (see Figure 14.11). Thus, there is reason to believe that high stress often helps to precipitate the onset of anxiety disorders.

Recap of Key Points

• The anxiety disorders include generalized anxiety disorder, phobic disorder, panic disorder, and obsessive-compulsive disorder. Many people who develop one anxiety disorder also suffer from another.

• Twin studies suggest that there is a weak genetic predispostion to anxiety disorders. These disorders may be more likely in people who have an inhibited temperament or in those who are especially sensitive to the physiological symptoms of anxiety.

• Abnormalities in neurotransmitter activity at GABA synapses or serotonin synapses may also play a role in anxiety disorders.

• Many anxiety responses, especially phobias, may be caused by classical conditioning and maintained by operant conditioning. Parents who model anxiety may promote these disorders through observational learning.

• Cognitive theorists maintain that certain styles of thinking—especially a tendency to overinterpret harmless situations as threatening—make some people vulnerable to anxiety disorders. Stress and the personality trait of neuroticism may also predispose people to anxiety disorders.

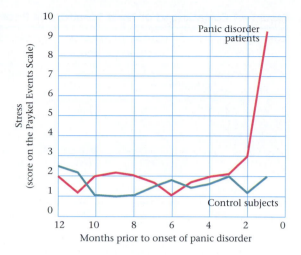

Figure 14.11
Stress and panic disorder. Faravelli and Pallanti (1989) assessed the amount of stress experienced during the 12 months before the onset of panic disorder in a group of 64 patients with this disorder and in a control group drawn from hospital employees and their friends. As you can see, there was a dramatic increase in stress in the month prior to the onset of the patients' panic disorders. These data suggest that stress may contribute to the development of panic disorders.

SOMATOFORM DISORDERS

Chances are, you have met people who always seem to be complaining about aches, pains, and physical maladies of doubtful authenticity. You may have thought to yourself, "It's all in his head," and concluded that the person exhibited a "psychosomatic" condition. However, as we discussed in Chapter 13, the term *psychosomatic* is widely misused. *Psychosomatic diseases* **are genuine physical ailments caused in part by psychological factors, especially emotional distress.** These diseases, which include maladies such as ulcers, asthma, and high blood pressure, have a genuine organic basis and are not imagined ailments. They are recorded on the DSM axis for physical problems (Axis III). When physical illness appears *entirely* psychological in origin, we are dealing with somatoform disorders, which are recorded on Axis I. *Somatoform disorders* **are physical ailments that have no authentic organic basis and that are due to psychological factors.** Although their symptoms are more imaginary than real, victims of somatoform disorders are *not* simply faking illness. Deliberate feigning of illness for personal gain is another matter altogether, called *malingering*.

People with somatoform disorders typically seek treatment from physicians practicing neurology, internal medicine, or family medicine, instead of from psychologists or psychiatrists. Making accurate diagnoses of somatoform disorders can be difficult, because the causes of physical ailments are sometimes hard to identify. In some cases, somatoform disorders are misdiagnosed when a genuine organic cause for a person's physical symptoms goes undetected in spite of extensive medical examinations and tests (Rubin, Zorumski, & Guze, 1986).

We will discuss three specific types of somatoform disorders: somatization disorders, conversion disorders, and hypochondriasis (see Table 14.1). Diagnostic difficulties make it hard to obtain sound data on the prevalence of somatoform disorders. Hypochondriasis seems to be fairly common, but somatization and conversion disorders appear to be relatively infrequent (Barsky, 1989).

Somatization Disorder

Individuals with somatization disorders are often said to "cling to ill health." A *somatization disorder* **is marked by a history of diverse physical complaints that appear to be psychological in origin.** Somatization disorders occur mostly in women (Martin & Yutzy, 1994). Victims report an endless succession of minor physical ailments. They

TABLE 14.1 COMPARISONS OF THREE SOMATOFORM DISORDERS WITH PSYCHOSOMATIC DISEASES

Condition	Physical Complaints	Organic Basis	Psychological Basis	Typical Symptom Pattern	Typical Examples
Psychosomatic diseases	Yes	Yes	Yes*	Varied stress-related diseases	Ulcers, high blood pressure
Somatization disorders	Yes	No	Yes	History of minor symptoms in many organ systems	Vague complaints of back pain, chest pain, dizziness
Conversion disorders	Yes	No	Yes	Major loss of function in a single organ system	Hysterical paralysis, glove anesthesia
Hypochondriasis	Yes	No	Yes	Preoccupation with health concerns	Unwarranted fear of infection

*The psychological component in diseases that are usually psychosomatic may be minimal in some cases.

usually have a long and complicated history of medical treatment from many doctors. The distinguishing feature of this disorder is the diversity of the victims' physical complaints. Over the years, they report a mixed bag of cardiovascular, gastrointestinal, pulmonary, neurological, and genitourinary symptoms. The unlikely nature of such a smorgasbord of symptoms occurring together often alerts a physician to the possible psychological basis for the patient's problems.

Conversion Disorder

Conversion disorder **is characterized by a significant loss of physical function (with no apparent organic basis), usually in a single organ system.** Common symptoms include partial or complete loss of vision, partial or complete loss of hearing, partial paralysis, severe laryngitis or mutism, and loss of feeling or function in limbs, such as that seen in the following case:

Mildred was a rancher's daughter who lost the use of both of her legs during adolescence. Mildred was at home alone one afternoon when a male relative attempted to assault her. She screamed for help, and her legs gave way as she slipped to the floor. She was found on the floor a few minutes later when her mother returned home. She could not get up, so she was carried to her bed. Her legs buckled when she made subsequent attempts to walk on her own. Due to her illness, she was waited on hand and foot by her family and friends. Neighbors brought her homemade things to eat or to wear. She became the center of attention in the household. (Adapted from Cameron, 1963, pp. 312–313)

People with conversion disorders are usually troubled by more severe ailments than people with somatization disorders. In some cases of conversion disorder, there are telltale clues about the psycho-logical origins of the illness because the patient's symptoms are not consistent with medical knowledge about their apparent disease. For instance, the loss of feeling in one hand that is seen in "glove anesthesia" is inconsistent with the known facts of neurological organization (see Figure 14.12).

Hypochondriasis

Hypochondriacs constantly monitor their physical condition, looking for signs of illness. Any tiny alteration from their physical norm leads them to conclude that they have contracted a disease. *Hypochondriasis* **(more widely known as hypochondria) is characterized by excessive preoccupation with health concerns and incessant worry about developing physical illnesses.** The following case illustrates the nature of hypochondria:

Jeff is a middle-aged man who works as a clerk in a drug store. He spends long hours describing his health problems to anyone who will listen. Jeff is an avid reader of popular magazine articles on medicine. He can tell you all about the latest medical discoveries. He takes all sorts of pills and vitamins to ward off possible illnesses. He's the first to try every new product on the market. Jeff is constantly afflicted by new symptoms of illness. His most recent problems were poor digestion and a heartbeat that he thought was irregular. He frequently goes to physicians who can find nothing wrong with him physically. They tell him that he is healthy. He thinks they use "backward techniques." He suspects that his illness is too rare to be diagnosed successfully. (Adapted from Suinn, 1984, p. 236)

When hypochondriacs are assured by their physician that they do not have any real illness, they often are skeptical and disbelieving. As in Jeff's case, they frequently assume that the physician must be incompetent, and they go shopping for another doctor. Hypochondriacs don't subjectively suffer from physical distress as much as they *overinterpret* every conceivable sign of illness. Hypochondria frequently appears alongside other psychological disorders, especially anxiety disorders and depression (Simon & VonKorff, 1991). For example, Howard Hughes's obsessive-compulsive disorder was coupled with profound hypochondria. Indeed, hypochondria coexists with other disorders so often, some theorists have raised doubts about whether it should be viewed as a separate diagnostic category (Iezzi & Adams, 1993).

Etiology of Somatoform Disorders

Inherited aspects of physiological functioning, such as a highly reactive autonomic nervous system, may predispose some people to somatoform disorders (Weiner, 1992). However, available evidence suggests that these disorders are largely a function of personality and learning. Let's look at personality factors first.

Personality Factors

People with certain types of personality traits seem to be particularly likely to develop somatoform disorders. The prime candidates appear to be people with *histrionic* personality characteristics (Nemiah, 1985; Slavney, 1990). The histrionic personality tends to be self-centered, suggestible, excitable, highly emotional, and overly dramatic. Such people thrive on the attention that they get when they become ill. The personality trait of *neuroticism* also seems to elevate individuals' susceptibility to somatoform disorders (Kirmayer, Robbins, & Paris, 1994).

Cognitive Factors

In recent years, theorists have devoted increased attention to how cognitive peculiarities might contribute to somatoform disorders. For example, Barsky, Wyshak, and Klerman (1990) assert that some people focus excessive attention on their internal physiological processes and amplify normal bodily sensations into symptoms of distress, which lead them to pursue unnecessary medical treatment. Recent evidence also suggests that people with somatoform disorders tend to have a faulty standard of good health, equating health with a complete absence of symptoms and discomfort, which is unrealistic (Barsky et al., 1993).

The Sick Role

As we discussed in Chapter 13, some people grow fond of the role associated with being sick (Lubkin,

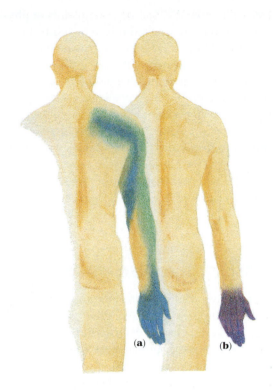

Figure 14.12
Glove anesthesia. In conversion disorders, the physical complaints are sometimes inconsistent with the known facts of physiology. For instance, given the patterns of nerve distribution in the arm shown in (**a**), it is impossible that a loss of feeling in the hand exclusively, as shown in (**b**), has a physical cause, indicating that the patient's problem is psychological in origin.

CONCEPT CHECK 14.2
Distinguishing Anxiety and Somatoform Disorders

Check your understanding of the nature of anxiety and somatoform disorders by making preliminary diagnoses for the cases described below. Read each case summary and write your tentative diagnosis in the space provided. The answers are in Appendix A.

1. Morris religiously follows an exact schedule every day. His showering and grooming ritual takes two hours. He follows the same path in walking to his classes every day, and he always sits in the same seat in each class. He can't study until his apartment is arranged perfectly. Although he tries not to, he thinks constantly about flunking out of school. Both his grades and his social life are suffering from his rigid routines.

   Preliminary diagnosis: _____

2. Jane has been unemployed for the last eight years because of poor health. She has suffered through a bizarre series of illnesses of mysterious origin. Troubles with devastating headaches were followed by months of chronic back pain. Then she developed respiratory problems, frequently gasping for breath. Her current problem is stomach pain. Physicians have been unable to find any physical basis for her maladies.

   Preliminary diagnosis: _____

3. Nathan owns a small restaurant that's in deep financial trouble. He dreads facing the possibility that his restaurant will fail. One day, he suddenly loses all feeling in his right arm and the ability to control the arm. He's hospitalized for his condition, but physicians can't find any organic cause for his arm trouble.

   Preliminary diagnosis: _____

1990; Pilowsky, 1978). Their complaints of physical symptoms may be reinforced by indirect benefits derived from their illness. What are the benefits commonly associated with physical illness? One payoff is that becoming ill is a superb way to avoid having to confront life's challenges. Many people with somatoform disorders are avoiding facing up to marital problems, career frustrations, family responsibilities, and the like. After all, when you're sick, others cannot place great demands on you. Another benefit is that physical problems can provide a convenient excuse when people fail, or worry about failing, in endeavors that are critical to their self-esteem (Organista & Miranda, 1991).

Attention from others is another payoff that may reinforce complaints of physical illness. When people become ill, they command the attention of family, friends, co-workers, neighbors, and doctors. The sympathy that illness often brings may strengthen the person's tendency to feel ill. This clearly occurred in Mildred's case of conversion disorder. Her illness paid handsome dividends in terms of attention, consolation, and kindhearted assistance from others.

DISSOCIATIVE DISORDERS

Dissociative disorders are among the more unusual syndromes that we will discuss. *Dissociative disorders* **are a class of disorders in which people lose contact with portions of their consciousness or memory, resulting in disruptions in their sense of identity.** We'll describe three dissociative syndromes—dissociative amnesia, dissociative fugue, and multiple-personality disorder—all of which are relatively uncommon.

Dissociative Amnesia and Fugue

Dissociative amnesia and fugue are overlapping disorders characterized by serious memory deficits. *Dissociative amnesia* **is a sudden loss of memory for important personal information that is too extensive to be due to normal forgetting.** Memory losses may occur for a single traumatic event (such as an automobile accident or home fire) or for an extended period of time surrounding the event. **In** *dissociative fugue*, **people lose their memory for their entire lives along with their sense of personal identity.** These people forget their name, their family, where they live, and where they work! In spite of this wholesale forgetting, they remember matters unrelated to their identity, such as how to drive a car and how to do math.

Multiple-Personality Disorder

Multiple-personality disorder (MPD) **involves the coexistence in one person of two or more largely complete, and usually very different, personalities.** The formal name for this disorder was changed to *dissociative identity disorder* in the recent revision of the DSM system, but it remains more widely known by its traditional name. In multiple-personality disorders, the divergences in behavior go far beyond those that people normally display in adapting to different roles in life. People with multiple personalities feel that they have more than one identity. Each personality has his or her own name, memories, traits, and physical mannerisms. Although rare, this "Dr. Jekyll and Mr. Hyde" syndrome is frequently portrayed in novels, movies, and television shows. In popular media portrayals, the syndrome is often mistakenly called *schizophrenia*. As you will see later, schizophrenic disorders are entirely different.

In a multiple-personality disorder, the original, or "host" personality, often is unaware of the alternate personalities. In contrast, the alternate personalities usually are aware of the original one and have varying amounts of awareness of each other. The alternate personalities commonly display traits that are quite foreign to the original personality. For instance, a shy, inhibited person might develop a flamboyant, extraverted alternate personality. Transitions between personalities often occur suddenly.

During the 1980s, there was a dramatic increase in the diagnosis of multiple-personality disorders (Ross et al., 1991). Some theorists believe that these disorders used to be underdiagnosed—that is, they often went undetected (Saxe et al., 1993). However, it appears more likely that a handful of clinicians have begun overdiagnosing the condition (Frankel, 1990; Thigpen & Cleckley, 1984). Consistent with this view, a survey of all the psychiatrists in Switzerland found that 90% of them had never seen a case of MPD, whereas three of the psychiatrists had each seen more than 20 MPD patients (Modestin, 1992). The data from this study suggest that 6 psychiatrists (out of 655 surveyed) accounted for two-thirds of the MPD diagnoses in Switzerland.

Etiology of Dissociative Disorders

Psychogenic amnesia and fugue are usually attributed to excessive stress. However, relatively little is known about why this extreme reaction to stress occurs in a tiny minority of people but not in the vast majority who are subjected to similar stress. Some theorists speculate that certain personality traits—fantasy-proneness and a tendency to become intensely absorbed in personal experiences—may make some people more susceptible to dissociative disorders, but adequate evidence is lacking on this line of thought (Kihlstrom, Glisky, & Angiulo, 1994).

The causes of multiple-personality disorders are particularly obscure. Some skeptical theorists, such as Nicholas Spanos (1994, 1996) believe that people with multiple personalities are engaging in intentional role playing to use mental illness as a face-saving excuse for their personal failings. He also argues that a small minority of therapists help create MPD in their patients by subtly encouraging the emergence of alternate personalities. According to Spanos, multiple-personality disorder is a creation of modern North American culture, much as demonic possession was a creation of early Christianity. To bolster his argument, he discusses how MPD patients' symptom presentations seem to have been influenced by popular media. For example, the typical MPD patient used to report having two or three personalities, but since the publication of *Sybil* (Schreiber, 1973) and other books describing patients with many personalities, the average number of alternate personalities has climbed to about 15. In a similar vein, there has been a dramatic upsurge in the number of MPD patients reporting that they were victims of ritual satanic abuse during childhood that dates back to the publication of *Michelle Remembers* (Smith & Pazder, 1980), a book about an MPD patient who purportedly was tortured by a satanic cult.

In spite of these troubling concerns, many clinicians are convinced that multiple-personality disorder is an authentic disorder (Gleaves, 1996; Kihlstrom, Tataryn, & Hoyt, 1993). They argue that there is no incentive for either patients or therapists to manufacture cases of MPD, which are often greeted with skepticism and outright hostility. They maintain that most cases of MPD are rooted in severe emotional trauma that occurred during childhood. A substantial majority of people with multiple-personality disorder report a history of disturbed home life, beatings and rejection from parents, and sexual abuse (Ross et al., 1990; Spiegel, 1994). In the final analysis, however, very little is known about the causes of multiple-personality disorder, which remains a controversial diagnosis.

Recap of Key Points

• Somatoform disorders are physical ailments that have no authentic organic basis. They are different from psychosomatic diseases, which are genuine physical ailments caused in part by psychological factors.

• Somatoform disorders include somatization disorder, conversion disorder, and hypochondriasis. These disorders often emerge in people with highly suggestible, histrionic personalities and in people who focus excess attention on their internal physiological processes. Somatoform disorders may be a learned avoidance strategy reinforced by attention and sympathy.

• Dissociative disorders include dissociative amnesia, fugue, and multiple-personality disorder (dissociative identity disorder). These disorders are uncommon and their causes are not well understood.

• Some theorists believe that people with multiple-personality disorder are engaging in intentional role playing to use an exotic mental illness as a face-saving excuse for their personal failings. Multiple-personality disorders may be rooted in emotional trauma that occurred during childhood.

MOOD DISORDERS

What did Abraham Lincoln, Marilyn Monroe, Ernest Hemingway, Winston Churchill, Janis Joplin, and Leo Tolstoy have in common? Yes, they all achieved great prominence, albeit in different ways at different times. But, more pertinent to our interest, they all suffered from severe mood disorders. Although mood disorders can be terribly debilitating, people with mood disorders may still achieve greatness, because such disorders tend to be *episodic*. In other words, mood disturbances often come and go, interspersed among periods of normality. These episodes of disturbance can vary greatly in length, but they typically last several months (Coryell & Winokur, 1992).

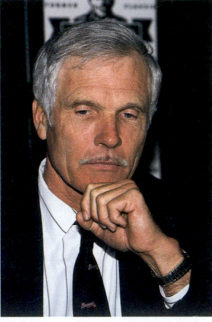

Patty Duke and Ted Turner are two well-known figures who have struggled with mood disorders.

There are two basic types of mood disorders: unipolar and bipolar (see Figure 14.13). People with *unipolar disorders* experience emotional extremes at just one end of the mood continuum, as they are troubled only by *depression*. People with *bipolar disorders* experience emotional extremes at both ends of the mood continuum, going through periods of both *depression and mania* (excitement and elation). Bipolar disorders tend to result in more episodes of emotional disturbance than unipolar disorders (Winokur et al., 1993). The mood swings in bipolar disorders can be patterned in many ways.

Recent studies suggest that periods of emotional disturbance may follow a seasonal pattern in some people (Oren & Rosenthal, 1992). **In a *seasonal affective disorder (SAD)* an individual's periods of depression or mania tend to occur repeatedly at about the same time each year.** The most common seasonal pattern is recurrent depression in winter (Wehr & Rosenthal, 1989). Researchers suspect that seasonal patterns in mood disorders are tied to seasonal variations in biological rhythms (Lewy et al., 1989). Whether SAD represents a distinct category of disorder is an interesting question that is the focus of current research (Allen et al., 1993).

Depressive Disorder 11b

The line between normal dejection and unhappiness and abnormal depression can be difficult to draw (Grove & Andreasen, 1992). Ultimately, it

Of course, everybody has ups and downs in terms of mood. Life would be dull indeed if people's emotional tone were constant. Everyone experiences depression occasionally. Likewise, everyone has days that he or she sails through on an emotional high. Such emotional fluctuations are natural, but some people are subject to extreme and sustained distortions of mood. *Mood disorders* **are a class of disorders marked by emotional disturbances of varied kinds that may spill over to disrupt physical, perceptual, social, and thought processes.**

Figure 14.13
Episodic patterns in mood disorders. Time-limited episodes of emotional disturbance come and go unpredictably in mood disorders. People with unipolar disorders suffer from bouts of depression only, whereas people with bipolar disorders experience both manic and depressive episodes. The time between episodes of disturbance varies greatly with the individual and the type of disorder.

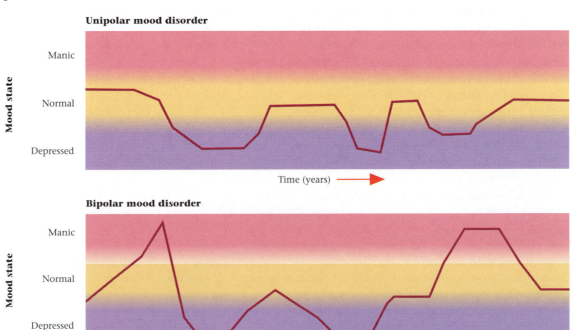

requires a subjective judgment. Crucial considerations in this judgment include the duration of the depression and its disruptive effects. When a depression significantly impairs everyday adaptive behavior for more than a few weeks, there is reason for concern.

In *depressive disorders* **people show persistent feelings of sadness and despair and a loss of interest in previous sources of pleasure.** People are given this diagnosis if they have had two or more episodes of major depression. Negative emotions form the heart of the depressive syndrome, but many other symptoms may also appear. The most common symptoms of depressive disorders are summarized and compared with the symptoms of mania in Table 14.2. Depressed people often give up activities that they used to find enjoyable. For example, a depressed person might quit going bowling or might give up a favorite hobby like photography. Reduced appetite and insomnia are common. People with depression often lack energy. They tend to move sluggishly and talk slowly. Anxiety, irritability, and brooding are commonly observed. Self-esteem tends to sink as the depressed person begins to feel worthless. Depression plunges people into feelings of hopelessness, dejection, and boundless guilt. To make matters worse, people who suffer from depression often exhibit other disorders as well. Coexisting anxiety disorders and substance use disorders are particularly frequent (Rohde, Lewinsohn, & Seeley, 1991).

The severity of depressive disorders varies considerably. When people display relatively mild symptoms of depression, they're given a diagnosis of *dysthymic disorder,* **which consists of chronic depression that is insufficient in severity to merit diagnosis of a major depressive episode.** The onset of unipolar disorder can occur at any point in the life span and is *not* strongly related to age (Lewinsohn et al., 1986).

How common are depressive disorders? Very common. Research suggests that about 7% of the population endure a depressive disorder at some time (Weissman et al., 1991). However, this figure may underestimate the amount of depression likely to be seen in future years, as there is evidence that the prevalence of depression is higher in more recent age cohorts (Lewinsohn et al., 1993). In particular, age cohorts born since World War II appear to be increasingly at risk for depression (Smith & Weissman, 1992). The factors underlying this rise in depression are not readily apparent, and researchers are scrambling to collect data that

might shed light on this unanticipated trend. Researchers are also hard at work trying to figure out why the prevalence of depression is about twice as high in women as it is in men (Nolen-Hoeksema & Girgus, 1994; Wolk & Weissman, 1995).

Bipolar Disorder 11b

Bipolar disorders **(formerly known as manic-depressive disorders) are marked by the experience of both depressed and manic periods.** One or more manic episodes is sufficient to qualify for this diagnosis. The symptoms seen in manic periods generally are the opposite of those seen in depression (see Table 14.2 for a comparison). In a manic episode, a person's mood becomes elevated to the point of euphoria. Self-esteem skyrockets as the person bubbles over with optimism, energy, and extravagant plans. He or she becomes hyperactive and may go for days without sleep. The individual talks rapidly and shifts topics wildly, as his or her mind races at breakneck speed. Judgment is often impaired. Some people in manic periods gamble impulsively, spend money frantically, or become sexually reckless. Like depressive disorders, bipolar disorders vary considerably in severity. People are given a diagnosis of *cyclothymic disorder* **when they exhibit chronic but relatively mild symptoms of bipolar disturbance.**

You may be thinking that the euphoria in manic episodes sounds appealing. If so, you are not entirely wrong. In their milder forms, manic states can seem attractive. The increases in energy, self-esteem, and optimism can be deceptively seductive. Because of the increase in energy, many bipolar patients report temporary surges of productivity and creativity (Goodwin & Jamison, 1990).

TABLE 14.2 COMPARISONS OF COMMON SYMPTOMS IN MANIC AND DEPRESSIVE EPISODES

Characteristics	Manic Episode	Depressive Episode
Emotional	Elated, euphoric, very sociable, impatient at any hindrance	Gloomy, hopeless, socially withdrawn, irritable
Cognitive	Characterized by racing thoughts, flight of ideas, desire for action, and impulsive behavior; talkative, self-confident; experiencing delusions of grandeur	Characterized by slowness of thought processes, obsessive worrying, inability to make decisions, negative self-image, self-blame, and delusions of guilt and disease
Motor	Hyperactive, tireless, requiring less sleep than usual, showing increased sex drive and fluctuating appetite	Less active, tired, experiencing difficulty in sleeping, showing decreased sex drive and decreased appetite

Source: Sarason and Sarason (1987)

Although manic episodes may have some positive aspects, bipolar disorders ultimately prove to be troublesome for most victims. Manic periods often have a paradoxical negative undercurrent of uneasiness and irritability (Rehm & Tyndall, 1993). Moreover, mild manic episodes usually escalate to higher levels that become scary and disturbing. Impaired judgment leads many victims to do things that they greatly regret later, as you'll see in the following case history:

Robert, a dentist, awoke one morning with the idea that he was the most gifted dental surgeon in his tristate area. He decided that he should try to provide services to as many people as possible, so that more people could benefit from his talents. Thus, he decided to remodel his two-chair dental office, installing 20 booths so that he could simultaneously attend to 20 patients. That same day he drew up plans for this arrangement, telephoned a number of remodelers, and invited bids for the work. Later that day, impatient to get rolling on his remodeling, he rolled up his sleeves, got himself a sledgehammer, and began to knock down the walls in his office. Annoyed when that didn't go so well, he smashed his dental tools, washbasins and X-ray equipment. Later, Robert's wife became concerned about his behavior and summoned two of her adult daughters for assistance. The daughters responded quickly, arriving at the family home with their husbands. In the ensuing discussion, Robert—after bragging about his sexual prowess—made advances toward his daughters. He had to be subdued by their husbands. (Adapted from Kleinmuntz, 1980, p. 309)

Although not rare, bipolar disorders are much less common than unipolar disorders. Bipolar disorders affect a little under 1% of the population (Smith & Weissman, 1992). Unlike depressive disorders, bipolar disorders are seen equally often in males and females (Tohen & Goodwin, 1995). As Figure 14.14 shows, the onset of bipolar disorders is age related, with the peak of vulnerability occurring between the ages of 20 and 29 (Goodwin & Jamison, 1990).

Etiology of Mood Disorders 11b

Quite a bit is known about the etiology of mood disorders, although the puzzle certainly hasn't been assembled completely. There appear to be a number of routes into these disorders, involving intricate interactions between psychological and biological factors.

Genetic Vulnerability

The evidence strongly suggests that genetic factors influence the likelihood of developing major depression or a bipolar disorder (Rieder, Kaufmann, & Knowles, 1994). *Twin studies* have found a huge disparity between identical and fraternal twins in concordance rates for mood disorders. The concordance rate for identical twins is much higher (see Figure 14.15). This evidence suggests that heredity can create a *predisposition* to mood disorders. Environmental factors probably determine whether this predisposition is converted into an actual disorder. The influence of genetic factors appears to be slightly stronger for bipolar disorders than for unipolar disorders (Nurnberger & Gershon, 1992).

Molecular geneticists are currently using gene mapping techniques (see Chapter 3) to try to pinpoint the specific genes that shape vulnerability to mood disorders. Some exciting findings that appeared to be major breakthroughs have been reported in journal articles and widely heralded in the popular press, but these findings have not stood the test of replication (De Bruyn et al., 1994; Gershon & Nurnberger, 1995). Although genetic mapping technology holds great promise, scientists do *not* appear to be on the verge of unraveling the genetic code for mood disorders.

Neurochemical Factors

Heredity may influence susceptibility to mood disorders by creating a predisposition toward certain types of neurochemical abnormalities in the brain. Correlations have been found between mood disorders and the activity of three neurotransmitters in the brain: norepinephrine, serotonin, and acetylcholine—although evidence on acetylcholine is modest (Delgado et al., 1992). Originally, abnormalities at norepinephrine (NE) synapses were believed to be most critical (see Figure 14.16). Depression was thought to be due to decreased

Figure 14.14
Age of onset for bipolar mood disorder. The onset of bipolar disorder typically occurs in adolescence or early adulthood. The data graphed here, which were combined from 10 studies, show the distribution of age of onset for 1304 bipolar patients. As you can see, bipolar disorder emerges most frequently during the 20s decade. (Data from Goodwin & Jamison, 1990)

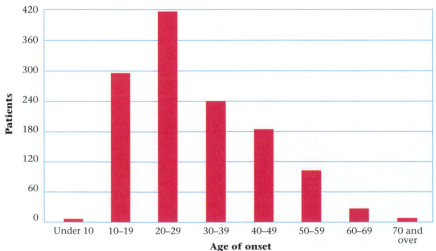

secretion of NE and mania to increased release of NE. Further research eventually demonstrated that alterations in the *release* of norepinephrine were not as important as changes in the sensitivity of the synaptic *receptors* that NE binds to (Schildkraut, Green, & Mooney, 1985). Although researchers still think that disturbances in neural circuits using norepinephrine contribute to mood disorders, the preponderance of recent evidence suggests that aberrations in serotonin circuits may be more important (Delgado et al., 1992). Actually, biochemical models of mood disorders that focus on a single neurotransmitter system are now regarded as too simple to provide a full explanation for these disorders. Investigators now believe that mood disorders are caused by intricate, interactive imbalances among the three implicated neurotransmitters and perhaps other brain chemicals (Thase & Howland, 1995).

Although the details remain elusive, there is little doubt that at least some mood disorders have a neurochemical basis. A variety of drug therapies are fairly effective in the treatment of severe mood disorders. Most of these drugs are known to affect the availability (in the brain) of the neurotransmitters that have been related to mood disorders (Nathan et al., 1995). This unlikely coincidence bolsters the plausibility of the idea that neurochemical changes produce mood disturbances.

If alterations in neurotransmitter activity are the basis for many mood disorders, what causes the alterations in neurotransmitter activity? These changes probably depend on people's reactions to environmental events. Thus, a number of psychological factors have been implicated in the etiology of mood disorders. We'll examine evidence on the role of cognitive factors next.

Cognitive Factors

A variety of theories emphasize how cognitive factors contribute to depressive disorders. We will discuss Aaron Beck's (1976, 1987) influential cognitive theory of depression in Chapter 15, where his approach to therapy is described. In this section, we'll examine Martin Seligman's *learned helplessness model* of depression and its most recent descendant, *hopelessness theory*. Based largely on animal research, Seligman (1974) proposed that depression is caused by learned helplessness—passive "giving up" behavior produced by exposure to unavoidable aversive events (see Chapter 13). He originally considered learned helplessness to be a product of conditioning but eventually revised his theory, giving it a cognitive slant. The

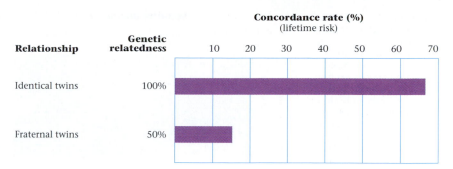

reformulated theory of learned helplessness postulated that the roots of depression sometimes lie in people's patterns of *attribution* (Abramson, Seligman, & Teasdale, 1978). **Attributions are inferences that people draw about the causes of events, others' behavior, and their own behavior.** People routinely make attributions because they want to *understand* their personal fates and the events that take place around them. For example, if your boss criticizes your work, you will probably ask yourself why. Was your work really that sloppy? Was your boss just in a grouchy mood? Was the criticism a manipulative effort to motivate you to work harder? Each of these potential explanations is an attribution.

Attributions can be analyzed along a number of

Figure 14.15
Twin studies of mood disorders. The concordance rate for mood disorders in identical twins is much higher than that for fraternal twins, who share less genetic overlap. These results suggest that there must be a genetic predisposition to mood disorders. The disparity in concordance between the two types of twins is greater for mood disorders than for either anxiety disorders (see Figure 14.8) or schizophrenic disorders (see Figure 14.20), which suggests that genetic factors may be particularly important in mood disorders. (Data from Gershon, Berrettini, & Goldin, 1989)

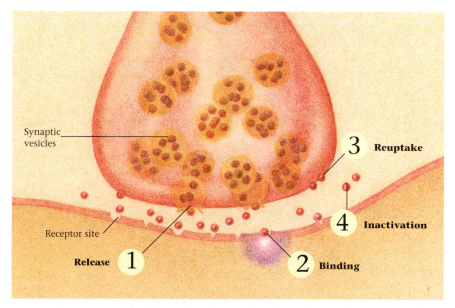

Figure 14.16
Hypotheses about the neurochemical bases for depression. Until recently, neurochemical models of depression centered on the hypothesis that depression is associated with lowered levels of activation at norepinephrine (NE) synapses. Originally, it was assumed that the reduction in NE activity was due to decreased release of NE (1), but studies eventually suggested that alterations in the sensitivity of NE receptors (2) also played a role. The hypothesis linking low NE levels to depression is supported by evidence that two major classes of antidepressant drugs increase NE levels. Tricyclic antidepressants appear to inhibit reuptake (3), leaving more NE in the synapse, while MAO inhibitors seem to slow the inactivation of NE (4). Although all these findings remain relevant to the understanding of the neurochemical bases of depression, recent studies suggest that complex imbalances in *several* neurotransmitter systems may contribute to depression and that abnormalities in serotonin circuits may be particularly critical.

Figure 14.17
Attributional style and depression. Possible attributions for poor performance on a standardized math exam are shown here. Note how the explanations in each cell vary in terms of whether causes are seen as internal or external, stable or unstable, and specific or global. People who consistently explain their failures, problems, and setbacks with internal, stable, and global attributions are particularly vulnerable to depression (the deeper the color in the cell, the more depressing the attribution tends to be).

Stability dimension

	Unstable cause (temporary)		Stable cause (permanent)	
Internal cause	Specific	Global	Specific	Global
	"I lost my concentration on the math test."	"I was exhausted the day I took the test."	"I'm lousy when it comes to math."	"I'm stupid. I'll never make it in college."
External cause	Specific	Global	Specific	Global
	"The heat distracted me during the math test."	"Those testing rooms are always uncomfortable."	"The math sections of standardized tests just aren't realistic."	"Standardized tests are too hard; they're not realistic."

Internal-external dimension

dimensions. Three important dimensions are illustrated in Figure 14.17. The most prominent dimension is the degree to which people attribute events to *internal, personal factors versus external, situational factors*. For instance, if you performed poorly on a standardized mathematics test, you might attribute your poor showing to your lack of intelligence (an internal attribution) or to the horrible heat and humidity in the exam room (an external attribution).

Another key dimension is the degree to which people attribute events to factors that are *stable or unstable over time*. Thus, you might blame your poor test performance on exhaustion (an internal but unstable factor that could change next time) or on your low intelligence (an internal but stable factor). Attributions can also have *global versus specific implications*. Thus, you might attribute your low test score to your lack of intelligence (which has general, global implications) or to your poor math ability (the implications are specific to math). Figure 14.17 provides additional examples of attributions that might be made for poor test performance.

Figure 14.18
Interpreting the correlation between negative thinking and depression. Cognitive theories of depression assert that consistent patterns of negative thinking cause depression. Although these theories are highly plausible, depression could cause negative thoughts, or both could be caused by a third factor, such as neurochemical changes in the brain.

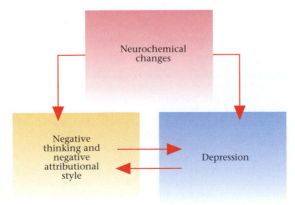

The learned helplessness model of depression focuses on the *attributional style* that people display, especially when they are trying to explain failures, setbacks, and other negative events. Studies show that *people who consistently tend to make internal, stable, and global attributions are more prone to depression* than people who exhibit the opposite attributional styles (Robins, 1988; Sweeney, Anderson, & Bailey, 1986). Why? Because in making internal, stable, and global attributions, people blame their setbacks on personal inadequacies (internal), which they see as unchangeable (stable), and draw far-reaching (global) conclusions about their lack of worth as a human being. In other words, they draw depressing conclusions about themselves.

Hopelessness theory builds on these insights by postulating a sense of hopelessness as the key mediating variable or "final pathway" leading to a specific subtype of depression and by incorporating additional factors that may interact with attributional style to foster this sense of hopelessness (Abramson, Metalsky, & Alloy, 1989; Metalsky et al., 1993). According to hopelessness theory, attributional style is just one of several or more factors—along with high stress, low self-esteem, and so forth—that may contribute to hopelessness, and thus depression. Although hopelessness theory casts a wider net than the learned helplessness model to provide a more complete explanation of depressive disorder, it continues to emphasize the importance of people's cognitive interpretations of the events in their lives.

In sum, the helplessness and hopelessness models of depression maintain that negative thinking is what leads to depression in many people. The principal problem with cognitive theories is their difficulty in separating cause from effect (Barnett & Gotlib, 1988). Does negative thinking cause depression? Or does depression cause negative thinking? Could both be caused by a third variable, such as neurochemical changes (see Figure 14.18)? Evidence can be mustered to support all three of these possibilities, suggesting that negative thinking, depression, and neurochemical alterations may feed off one another as depression deepens.

In accord with this line of thinking, Susan Nolen-Hoeksema (1990, 1991) has found that depressed people who ruminate about their depression remain depressed longer than those who try to distract themselves. People who respond to depression with rumination repetitively focus their attention on their depressing feelings, thinking constantly about how sad, lethargic, and unmotivated they are. According to Nolen-Hoeksema, excessive rumination tends to extend and amplify individuals' episodes of depression. She believes that women are more likely to ruminate than men and that this disparity may be the primary reason why depression is more prevalent in women.

Interpersonal Roots

Behavioral approaches to understanding depression emphasize how inadequate social skills put people on the road to depressive disorders (see Figure 14.19; Lewinsohn & Gotlib, 1995; Segrin & Abramson, 1994). According to this notion, depression-prone people lack the social finesse needed to acquire many important kinds of reinforcers, such as good friends, top jobs, and desirable spouses. This paucity of reinforcers could understandably lead to negative emotions and depression. Consistent with this theory, researchers have found correlations between poor social skills and depression (Dykman et al., 1991).

Another interpersonal factor is that depressed people tend to be depressing (Joiner, 1994). Individuals suffering from depression often are irritable and pessimistic. They complain a lot and they aren't particularly enjoyable companions. As a consequence, depressed people tend to court rejection from those around them (Coyne, Burchill, & Stiles, 1990). Depressed people thus have fewer sources of social support than nondepressed people. Social rejection and lack of support may in turn aggravate and deepen a person's depression (Segrin & Dillard, 1992). To compound these problems, recent evidence indicates that depressed people may gravitate to partners who view them unfavorably and hence reinforce their negative views of themselves (Giesler, Josephs, & Swann, 1996).

Precipitating Stress

Mood disorders sometimes appear mysteriously in people who are leading benign, nonstressful lives. For this reason, experts used to believe that mood disorders are not influenced much by stress. However, recent advances in the measurement of personal stress have altered this picture. The evidence available today suggests the existence of a moderately strong link between stress and the onset of mood disorders (Johnson & Roberts, 1995; Kendler et al., 1995). Stress also appears to affect how people with mood disorders respond to treatment and whether they experience a relapse of their disorder (Monroe et al., 1996).

Of course, many people endure great stress with-

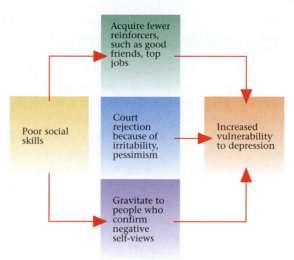

Figure 14.19
Interpersonal factors in depression. Behavioral theories about the etiology of depression emphasize how inadequate social skills may contribute to the development of the disorder.

out getting depressed. The impact of stress varies, in part, because people vary in their degree of *vulnerability* to mood disorders (Monroe & Simons, 1991). Similar interactions between stress and vulnerability probably influence the development of many kinds of disorders, including those that are next on our agenda—the schizophrenic disorders.

Recap of Key Points
• The principal mood disorders are depressive disorder, dysthymic disorder, bipolar disorder, and cyclothymic disorder. Mood disorders are episodic, and seasonal patterns have been observed in some patients.
• Depressive disorders are marked by profound sadness, slowed thought processes, low self-esteem, and loss of interest in previous sources of pleasure. Unipolar depressions are more common than bipolar disorders, and they appear to be increasing in prevalence.
• Bipolar disorders are marked by the experience of both depressed and manic episodes. Manic episodes are characterized by inflated self-esteem, high energy, grandiose plans, and racing thoughts.
• Evidence indicates that people vary in their genetic vulnerability to the severe mood disorders. These disorders are accompanied by changes in neurochemical activity in the brain. Abnormalities at norepinephrine and serotonin synapses appear particularly critical.
• Cognitive models posit that negative thinking contributes to depression. An attributional style emphasizing internal, stable, and global attributions has been implicated, as has a tendency to ruminate about one's problems.
• Interpersonal inadequacies may contribute to depressive disorders. Poor social skills may lead to a paucity of life's reinforcers and frequent rejection. The development of mood disorders is also affected by personal stress.

SCHIZOPHRENIC DISORDERS

Literally, *schizophrenia* means "split mind." However, when Eugen Bleuler coined the term in 1911 he was referring to the fragmentation of thought processes seen in the disorder—not to a "split personality." Unfortunately, writers in the popular media often assume that the split-mind notion, and thus schizophrenia, refers to the rare syndrome in which a person manifests two or more personalities. As you have already learned, this syndrome is actually called *multiple-personality disorder*. Schizophrenia is a much more common, and altogether different, type of disorder.

Schizophrenic disorders are a class of disorders marked by disturbances in thought that spill over to affect perceptual, social, and emotional processes. People with schizophrenic disorders often display some of the same symptoms seen in people with severe mood disorders, and the two groups of disorders may not be entirely distinct (Taylor, 1992). However, disturbed *thought* lies at the core of schizophrenic disorders, whereas disturbed *emotion* lies at the core of mood disorders.

How common is schizophrenia? Prevalence estimates suggest that about 1%–1.5% of the population may suffer from schizophrenic disorders (Keith, Regier, & Rae, 1991). That may not sound like much, but it means that in the United States alone there may be 4 million people troubled by schizophrenic disturbances.

General Symptoms 11c

There are a number of distinct schizophrenic syndromes, but they share some general characteristics that we will examine before looking at the subtypes. Many of these characteristics are apparent in the following case history (adapted from Sheehan, 1982).

Sylvia was first diagnosed as schizophrenic at age 15. She has been in and out of many types of psychiatric facilities since then. She has never been able to hold a job for any length of time. During severe flare-ups of her disorder, her personal hygiene deteriorates. She rarely washes, she wears clothes that neither fit nor match, she smears makeup on heavily but randomly, and she slops food all over herself. Sylvia occasionally hears voices talking to her. She tends to be argumentative, aggressive, and emotionally volatile. Over the years, she has been involved in innumerable

fights with fellow patients, psychiatric staff members, and strangers. Her thoughts can be highly irrational, as is apparent from the following quote, which was recorded while she was a patient in a psychiatric facility called Creedmoor:

"Mick Jagger wants to marry me. If I have Mick Jagger, I don't have to covet Geraldo Rivera. Mick Jagger is St. Nicholas and the Maharishi is Santa Claus. I want to form a gospel rock group called the Thorn Oil, but Geraldo wants me to be the music critic on Eyewitness News, so what can I do? Got to listen to my boyfriend. Teddy Kennedy cured me of my ugliness. I'm pregnant with the son of God. I'm going to marry David Berkowitz and get it over with. Creedmoor is the headquarters of the American Nazi Party. They're eating the patients here. Archie Bunker wants me to play his niece on his TV show. I work for Epic Records. I'm Joan of Arc. I'm Florence Nightingale. The door between the ward and the porch is the dividing line between New York and California. Divorce isn't a piece of paper, it's a feeling. Forget about Zip Codes. I need shock treatments. The body is run by electricity. My wiring is all faulty. A fly is a teenage wasp. I'm marrying an accountant. I'm in the Pentecostal Church, but I'm considering switching my loyalty to the Charismatic Church." (Sheehan, 1982, pp. 104–105)

Sylvia's case clearly shows that schizophrenic thinking can be bizarre and that schizophrenia can be a severe and debilitating disorder. Although no single symptom is inevitably present, the following symptoms are commonly seen in schizophrenia (Grebb & Cancro, 1989).

Irrational Thought

Disturbed, irrational thought processes are the central feature of schizophrenic disorders. Various kinds of delusions are common. **Delusions are false beliefs that are maintained even though they clearly are out of touch with reality.** For example, one patient's delusion that he is a tiger (with a deformed body) has persisted for 15 years (Kulick, Pope, & Keck, 1990). More typically, affected persons believe that their private thoughts are being broadcast to other people or that thoughts are being injected into their mind against their will (Maher & Spitzer, 1993). In *delusions of grandeur*, people maintain that they are famous or important. Sylvia expressed an endless array of grandiose delusions, such as thinking that Mick Jagger wanted to marry her, that she had dictated the hobbit stories to J. R. R. Tolkien, and that she was going to win the Nobel prize for medicine.

In addition to delusions, the schizophrenic person's train of thought deteriorates. Thinking becomes chaotic rather than logical and linear. There is a "loosening of associations," as people shift topics in disjointed ways. The quotation from Sylvia illustrates this symptom dramatically. The entire quote involves a wild flight of ideas, but at one point (beginning with the sentence "Creedmoor is the headquarters . . .") she rattles off ten consecutive sentences that have no apparent connection to each other.

Deterioration of Adaptive Behavior

Schizophrenia usually involves a noticeable deterioration in the quality of the person's routine functioning in work, social relations, and personal care. Friends will often make remarks such as "Hal just isn't himself anymore." This deterioration is readily apparent in Sylvia's inability to get along with others or to function in the work world. It's also apparent in her neglect of personal hygiene.

Distorted Perception

A variety of perceptual distortions may occur with schizophrenia, the most common being auditory hallucinations. **Hallucinations are sensory perceptions that occur in the absence of a real, external stimulus or are gross distortions of perceptual input.** Schizophrenics frequently report that they hear voices of nonexistent or absent people talking to them. Sylvia, for instance, said she heard messages from Paul McCartney. These voices often provide an insulting, running commentary on the person's behavior ("You're an idiot for shaking his hand"). They may be argumentative ("You don't need a bath"), and they may issue commands ("Prepare your home for visitors from outer space").

Disturbed Emotion

Normal emotional tone can be disrupted in schizophrenia in a variety of ways. Although it may not be an accurate indicator of their underlying emotional experience (Kring et al., 1993), some victims show little emotional responsiveness, a symptom referred to as "blunted or flat affect." Others show inappropriate emotional responses that don't jell with the situation or with what they are saying. For instance, a schizophrenic patient might cry over a Smurfs cartoon and then laugh about a news story describing a child's tragic death.

People with schizophrenia may also become emotionally volatile. This pattern was displayed by Sylvia, who often overreacted emotionally in erratic, unpredictable ways.

Other Features

People with schizophrenic disorders may display a variety of other, less central symptoms. Many exhibit *social withdrawal,* interacting with others only reluctantly. Some experience a *disturbed sense of self* or individuality. Also common is *poverty of speech,* which involves hesitant, uncommunicative verbal interactions. Sometimes, *abnormal motor behavior* is observed. A patient may rock back and forth constantly or become immobilized for a long time.

Subtypes 11c

Four subtypes of schizophrenic disorders are recognized, including a category for people who don't fit neatly into any of the first three categories. The major symptoms of each subtype are as follows (Black & Andreasen, 1994).

Paranoid Type

As its name implies, **paranoid schizophrenia is dominated by delusions of persecution, along with delusions of grandeur.** In this common form of schizophrenia, people come to believe that they have many enemies who want to harass and oppress them. They may become suspicious of friends and relatives or they may attribute the persecution to mysterious, unknown persons. They are convinced that they are being watched and manipulated in malicious ways. To make sense of this persecution, they often develop delusions of grandeur. They believe that they must be enormously important people, frequently seeing themselves as great inventors or as great religious or political leaders. For example, in the case described at the beginning of the chapter, Ed's belief that he was president of the United States was a delusion of grandeur.

Catatonic Type

Catatonic schizophrenia **is marked by striking motor disturbances, ranging from muscular rigidity to random motor activity.** Some patients go into an extreme form of withdrawal known as a catatonic stupor. They may remain virtually motionless and seem oblivious to the environment around them for long periods of time. Others go into a state of catatonic excitement. They become hyperactive and incoherent. Some alternate between these dramatic extremes. The catatonic subtype is not particularly common, and its prevalence seems to be declining.

Disorganized Type

In *disorganized schizophrenia,* **a particularly severe deterioration of adaptive behavior is seen.** Prominent symptoms include emotional indifference, frequent incoherence, and virtually complete social withdrawal. Aimless babbling and giggling are common. Delusions often center on bodily functions ("My brain is melting out my ears").

Undifferentiated Type

People who are clearly schizophrenic but who cannot be placed into any of the three previous categories are said to have *undifferentiated schizophrenia,* **which is marked by idiosyncratic mixtures of schizophrenic symptoms.** The undifferentiated subtype is fairly common.

Positive Versus Negative Symptoms

Many theorists have raised doubts about the value of dividing schizophrenic disorders into the four subtypes just described (Nicholson & Neufeld, 1993). Critics note that the catatonic subtype is disappearing and that undifferentiated cases aren't so much a subtype as a hodgepodge of "leftovers." Critics also point out that there aren't meaningful differences between the subtypes in etiology, prognosis, or response to treatment. The absence of such differences casts doubt on the value of the current classification scheme.

Because of problems such as these, Nancy Andreasen (1990) and others (Carpenter, 1992; McGlashan & Fenton, 1992) have proposed an alternative approach to subtyping. This new scheme divides schizophrenic disorders into just two categories based on the predominance of negative versus positive symptoms. *Negative symptoms* involve behavioral deficits, such as flattened emotions, social withdrawal, apathy, impaired attention, and poverty of speech. *Positive symptoms* involve behavioral excesses or peculiarities, such as hallucinations, delusions, bizarre behavior, and wild flights of ideas. Andreasen believes that researchers will find consistent differences between these two subtypes in etiology, prognosis, and response to treatment.

Some progress along these lines has been made. For example, negative symptoms appear to be associated with a relatively poor prognosis and less

"Schizophrenia disfigures the emotional and cognitive faculties of its victims, and sometimes nearly destroys them."

NANCY ANDREASEN

responsiveness to drug treatment, but the findings have been rather weak and inconsistent (Carpenter, 1991; Fenton & McGlashan, 1994). It is hard to say whether the proposed subdivision based on positive versus negative symptoms will prove useful. The distinction is intriguing, but theorists are already arguing about which schizophrenic symptoms are positive and which are negative. Moreover, most patients display a *mixture* of positive and negative symptoms (Carson & Sanislow, 1993).

Course and Outcome

Schizophrenic disorders usually emerge during adolescence or early adulthood and only infrequently after age 45 (Murphy & Helzer, 1986). The emergence of schizophrenia may be sudden or gradual. Once it clearly emerges, the course of schizophrenia is variable (Ciompi, 1980; Marengo et al., 1991), but patients tend to fall into three broad groups. Some patients, presumably those with milder disorders, are treated successfully and enjoy a full recovery. Other patients experience a partial recovery so that they can return to their normal life. However, they have frequent relapses and are in and out of treatment facilities for much of the remainder of their lives. Finally, a third group of patients endure chronic illness that sometimes results in permanent hospitalization. Overall, about half of schizophrenic patients experience a significant recovery (Hegarty et al., 1994). For unknown reasons, gender is associated with the course and outcome of schizophrenia. The differences are modest, but in comparison to females, males tend to have an earlier onset of the disease, more hospitalizations, and higher relapse rates (Szymanski et al., 1995).

A number of factors are related to the likelihood of recovery from schizophrenic disorders (Lehmann & Cancro, 1985). A patient has a relatively *favorable prognosis* when (1) the onset of the disorder has been sudden rather than gradual, (2) the onset has occurred at a later age, (3) the patient's social and work adjustment were relatively good prior to the onset of the disorder, and (4) the patient has a relatively healthy, supportive family situation to return to. All of these predictors are related to the etiology of schizophrenic illness, which is the matter we turn to next.

Etiology of Schizophrenia

You can probably identify, at least to some extent, with people who suffer from mood disorders, somatoform disorders, and anxiety disorders. You can probably imagine events that could unfold that might leave you struggling with depression, grappling with anxiety, or worrying about your physical health. But what could possibly have led Ed to believe that he had been fighting space wars and vampires? What could account for Sylvia's thinking that she was Joan of Arc or that she had dictated the hobbit novels to Tolkien? As mystifying as these delusions may seem, you'll see that the etiology of schizophrenic disorders is not all that different from the etiology of other psychological disorders. We'll begin our discussion by examining the matter of genetic vulnerability.

Genetic Vulnerability

Evidence is plentiful that hereditary factors play a role in the development of schizophrenic disorders (Byerley & Coon, 1995). For instance, in twin studies, concordance rates average around 48% for identical twins, in comparison to about 17% for fraternal twins (Gottesman, 1991). Studies also indicate that a child born to two schizophrenic parents has about a 46% probability of developing a schizophrenic disorder (as compared to the probability in the general population of about 1%). These and other findings that demonstrate the genetic roots of schizophrenia are summarized in Figure 14.20. Overall, the picture is similar to that seen for mood disorders. Several converging lines of evidence indicate that some people inherit a polygenically transmitted *vulnerability* to schizophrenia (Fowles, 1992). As with mood disorders, efforts to pinpoint the specific genes responsible for this vulnerability through *genetic mapping* techniques have yielded some interesting leads (Kendler et al., 1996) but no clear, definitive findings, although researchers remain optimistic (Crowe, 1994).

Neurochemical Factors

Like mood disorders, schizophrenic disorders appear to be accompanied by changes in the activity of one or more neurotransmitters in the brain (Knable et al., 1995). Excess *dopamine* activity has been implicated as a possible cause of schizophrenia because most of the drugs that are useful in the treatment of schizophrenia are known to dampen dopamine activity in the brain (Marder & Van Putten, 1995). However, the evidence linking schizophrenia to high dopamine levels is riddled with inconsistencies, complexities, and interpretive problems (Carson & Sanislow, 1993). Perhaps some of these inconsistencies will be resolved by a new theory that links schizophrenia to abnormally high dopamine activity in subcortical areas of the brain, coupled with abnormally low dopamine activity

in the prefrontal cortex (Davis et al., 1991). Another new line of thought on the neurochemistry of schizophrenia emphasizes that neurotransmitter systems are not entirely independent. Researchers are currently exploring how interactions between the dopamine and serotonin neurotransmitter systems may contribute to schizophrenia (Kapur & Remington, 1996). Thus, investigators are gradually making progress in their search for the neurochemical bases of schizophrenia.

Structural Abnormalities in the Brain

Various studies have suggested that schizophrenic individuals have difficulty in focusing their attention (Dawson et al., 1993). Some theorists believe that many bizarre aspects of schizophrenic behavior may be due mainly to an inability to filter out unimportant stimuli (Judd et al., 1992). This lack of selectivity supposedly leaves victims of the disorder flooded with overwhelming, confusing sensory input.

These problems with attention and basic information processing suggest that schizophrenic disorders may be caused by neurological defects (Perry & Braff, 1994). Until recently, this theory was based more on speculation than on actual research. However, new advances in brain imaging technology are beginning to yield some intriguing data. Research with CT scans and MRI scans (see Chapter 3) suggests that there is an association between enlarged brain ventricles (the hollow, fluid-filled cavities in the brain) and chronic schizophrenic disturbance (Raz, 1993; Suddath et al., 1990). The significance of enlarged ventricles in the brain is hotly debated, however. Enlarged ventricles are not unique to schizophrenia—they are a sign of many kinds of brain pathology. The current thinking seems to be that this brain abnormality

Figure 14.20
Genetic vulnerability to schizophrenic disorders. Relatives of schizophrenic patients have an elevated risk for schizophrenia. This risk is greater among closer relatives. Although environment also plays a role in the etiology of schizophrenia, the concordance rates shown here suggest that there must be a genetic vulnerability to the disorder. These concordance estimates are based on pooled data from 40 studies conducted between 1920 and 1987. (Data from Gottesman, 1991)

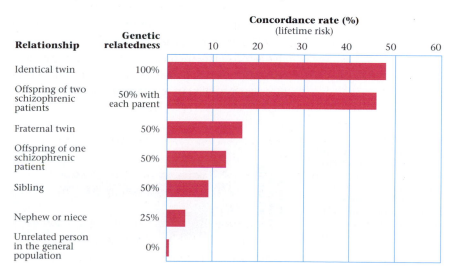

Figure 14.21
**Communication devi-
ance and schizophrenia.**
Communication deviance
probably fosters vulnerability
to schizophrenia by undermining a youngster's reality
contact and by encouraging
withdrawal.

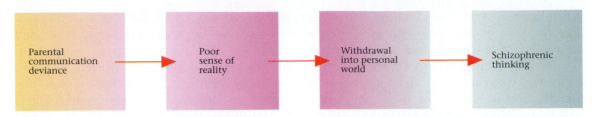

probably is an effect rather than a cause of schizophrenia (Flaum et al., 1995). Researchers are currently more intrigued by the finding that the
thalamus is smaller and shows less metabolic activity in schizophrenic patients, as compared to normal control subjects (Buchsbaum et al., 1996).
Given the crucial role of the thalamus as the brain's
relay center (see Chapter 3), these previously undetected abnormalities could have great functional
significance.

Communication Deviance

Over the years, hundreds of investigators have
tried to relate patterns of family interaction to the
development of schizophrenia. Popular theories
have come and gone as empirical evidence has
overturned once plausible hypotheses (Goldstein,
1988). Vigorous research and debate in this area
continue today. The current emphasis is on families' communication patterns and their expression
of emotions.

Various theorists assert that vulnerability to
schizophrenia is increased by exposure to defective interpersonal communication during childhood. Studies have found a relationship between
schizophrenia and *communication deviance*
(Goldstein, 1987; Singer, Wynne, & Toohey, 1978).
Communication deviance on the part of parents
and family members includes unintelligible speech,
stories with no endings, heavy use of unusual
words, extensive contradictions, and poor attention to children's communication efforts. The evidence suggests that schizophrenia is more likely to
develop when youngsters grow up in homes
characterized by such vague, muddled, fragmented
communication. Researchers speculate that communication deviance gradually undermines a

child's sense of reality and encourages youngsters
to withdraw into their own private world, setting
the stage for schizophrenic thinking later in life
(see Figure 14.21).

Expressed Emotion

Studies of expressed emotion have primarily focused on how this element of family dynamics
influences the *course* of schizophrenic illness, after
the onset of the disorder (Leff & Vaughn, 1985).
Expressed emotion (EE) is the degree to which a
relative of a schizophrenic patient displays highly
critical or emotionally overinvolved attitudes toward the patient. Audiotaped interviews of relatives' communication are carefully evaluated for
critical comments, resentment toward the patient,
and excessive emotional involvement (overprotective, overconcerned attitudes).

Studies show that a family's expressed emotion
is a good predictor of the course of a schizophrenic
patient's illness (Kavanaugh, 1992). After release
from a hospital, schizophrenic patients who return to a family high in expressed emotion show
relapse rates three or four times that of patients
who return to a family low in expressed emotion
(see Figure 14.22; Parker & Hadzi-Pavlovic, 1990).
However, Rosenfarb et al. (1995) caution against
placing all the blame on the families high in expressed emotion. They found that patients returning to high-EE homes exhibited more odd and
disruptive behavior than patients returning to low-
EE homes. Thus, the more critical, negative attitudes experienced by patients in high-EE homes
may be caused in part by their own behavior.

Precipitating Stress

Most theories of schizophrenia assume that stress
plays a key role in triggering schizophrenic disorders (Fowles, 1992; Zubin, 1986). According to
this notion, various biological and psychological
factors influence individuals' *vulnerability* to schizophrenia. High stress may then serve to precipitate
a schizophrenic disorder in someone who is vulnerable. A recent study indicates that high stress
can also trigger relapses in schizophrenic patients
who have made progress toward recovery (Ventura
et al., 1989).

**Figure 14.22
Expressed emotion and
relapse rates in schizo-
phrenia.** Schizophrenic patients who return to a home
that is high in expressed
emotion have higher relapse
rates than those who return
to a home low in expressed
emotion. (Data adapted from
Leff & Vaughn, 1981)

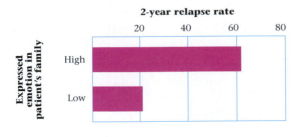

Schizophrenia is the last of the major, Axis I diagnostic categories that we will consider. We'll complete our overview of various types of abnormal behavior with a brief look at the personality disorders. These disorders are recorded on Axis II in the DSM classification system.

Recap of Key Points

• Schizophrenic disorders are characterized by deterioration of adaptive behavior, irrational thought, delusions, distorted perception, hallucinations, and disturbed mood.

• Schizophrenic disorders are classified as paranoid, catatonic, disorganized, or undifferentiated. A new classification scheme based on the predominance of positive versus negative symptoms is under study.

• Schizophrenic disorders usually emerge during adolescence or young adulthood. A patients' prognosis is better if the disorder emerges suddenly at a later age.

• Research has linked schizophrenia to a genetic vulnerability and changes in neurotransmitter activity at dopamine and perhaps serotonin synapses. Structural abnormalities in the brain, such as enlarged ventricles, are associated with schizophrenia, but their causal significance is debated.

• Precipitating stress and unhealthy family dynamics, including communication deviance and a negative emotional climate (high expressed emotion), may also contribute to the development of schizophrenia.

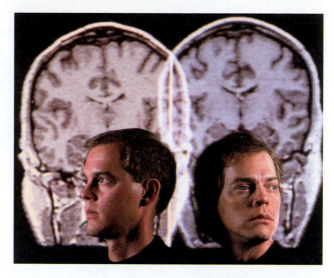

The MRI scans in the background were taken from the identical twins in the foreground, only one of whom suffers from schizophrenia. The scan on the right, obtained from the schizophrenic twin, shows enlarged ventricles (the dark spaces in the scan), which are the hollow, fluid-filled cavities in the brain.

CONCEPT CHECK 14.3
Distinguishing Schizophrenic and Mood Disorders

Check your understanding of the nature of schizophrenic and mood disorders by making preliminary diagnoses for the cases described below. Read each case summary and write your tentative diagnosis in the space provided. The answers are in Appendix A.

1. Max hasn't slept in four days. He's determined to write the "great American novel" before his class reunion, which is a few months away. He expounds eloquently on his novel to anyone who will listen, talking at such a rapid pace that no one can get a word in edgewise. He feels like he's wired with energy and is supremely confident about the novel, even though he's only written 10 to 20 pages. Last week, he charged $8000 worth of new computer software, which is supposed to help him write his book.

   Preliminary diagnosis: _____

2. Maurice maintains that he invented the atomic bomb, even though he was born after its invention. He says he invented it to punish homosexuals, Nazis, and short people. It's short people that he's really afraid of. He's sure that all the short people on TV are talking about him. He thinks that short people are conspiring to make him look like a Republican. Maurice frequently gets in arguments with people and is emotionally volatile. His grooming is poor, but he says it's okay because he's the secretary of state.

   Preliminary diagnosis: _____

3. Margaret has hardly gotten out of bed for weeks, although she's troubled by insomnia. She doesn't feel like eating and has absolutely no energy. She feels dejected, discouraged, spiritless, and apathetic. Friends stop by to try to cheer her up, but she tells them not to waste their time on "pond scum."

   Preliminary diagnosis: _____

PERSONALITY DISORDERS

We have seen repeatedly that it is often difficult to draw that imaginary line between healthy and disordered behavior. This is especially true in the case of personality disorders, which are relatively mild disturbances in comparison to most of the Axis I disorders. **Personality disorders are a class of disorders marked by extreme, inflexible personality traits that cause subjective distress or**

OVERVIEW OF THREE CATEGORIES OF PSYCHOLOGICAL DISORDERS

Axis I category	Subtypes	Prevalence/well-known victim

Anxiety disorders

Edward Munch's *The Scream* expresses overwhelming feelings of anxiety.

Generalized anxiety disorder: Chronic, high level of anxiety not tied to any specific threat

Phobic disorder: Persistent, irrational fear of object situation that presents no real danger

Panic disorder: Recurrent attacks of overwhelming anxiety that occur suddenly and unexpectedly

Obsessive-compulsive disorder: Persistent, uncontrollable intrusions of unwanted thoughts and urges to engage in senseless rituals

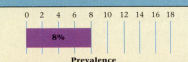

Prevalence — 17%

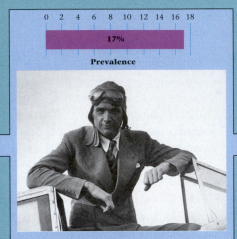

The famous industrialist Howard Hughes suffered from obsessive-compulsive disorder.

Mood disorders

Vincent van Gogh's *Portrait of Dr. Gachet* captures the profound dejection experienced in depressive disorders.

Depressive disorder: Two or more major depressive episodes marked by feelings of sadness, worthlessness, despair

Dysthymic disorder: Chronic depressed mood, but symptoms insufficient to merit diagnosis of major depressive episode

Bipolar disorder: One or more manic episodes marked by inflated self-esteem, grandiosity, and elevated mood and energy, usually accompanied by major depressive episodes

Cyclothymic disorder: Chronic manic and depressed moods, but symptoms insufficient to merit diagnosis of bipolar disorder

Prevalence — 8%

Actress Patty Duke suffers from bipolar disorder.

Schizophrenic disorders

The perceptual distortions seen in schizophrenia probably contributed to the bizarre imagery apparent in this portrait of a cat painted by Louis Wain.

Paranoid schizophrenia: Delusions of persecution and delusions of grandeur; frequent auditory hallucinations

Catatonic schizophrenia: Motor disturbances ranging from immobility to excessive, purposeless activity

Disorganized schizophrenia: Flat or inappropriate emotions; disorganized speech and adaptive behavior

Undifferentiated schizophrenia: Idiosyncratic mixtures of schizophrenic symptoms that cannot be placed into above three categories

Prevalence — 1%

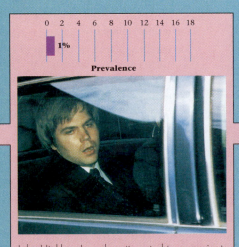

John Hinkley, Jr., who attempted to assassinate President Reagan, suffers from schizophrenia.

Etiology: Biological factors

Genetic vulnerability: Twin studies and other evidence suggest a mild genetic predisposition to anxiety disorders.

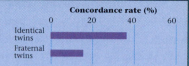

Concordance rate (%)

Anxiety sensitivity: Oversensitivity to physical symptoms of anxiety may lead to overreactions to feelings of anxiety, so anxiety breeds more anxiety.

Inhibited temperament: Inherited temperament marked by shyness, timidity, and wariness may be a risk factor.

Neurochemical bases: Disturbances in neural circuits releasing GABA may contribute to some disorders; abnormalities at serotonin synapses have been implicated in panic and obsessive-compulsive disorders.

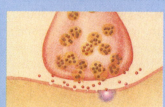

Genetic vulnerability: Twin studies and other evidence suggest a genetic predisposition to mood disorders.

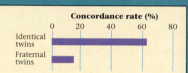

Concordance rate (%)

Neurochemical bases: Disturbances in neural circuits releasing norepinephrine may contribute to some mood disorders; abnormalities at serotonin synapses have also been implicated as a factor in depression.

Sleep disturbances: Disruption of biological rhythms and sleep patterns may lead to neurochemical changes that contribute to mood disorders.

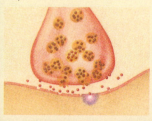

Genetic vulnerability: Twin studies and other evidence suggest a mild genetic predisposition to schizophrenic disorders.

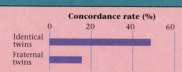

Concordance rate (%)

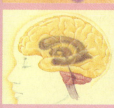

Neurochemical bases: Overactivity in neural circuits releasing dopamine is associated with schizophrenia; this overactivity may be modulated by abnormalities in serotonin circuits.

Structural abnormalities in brain: Enlarged brain ventricles are associated with schizophrenia, but they may be an effect rather than a cause of the disorder; new evidence suggests that the thalamus is smaller and shows less metabolic activity in schizophrenic patients.

Etiology: Psychological factors

Learning: Many anxiety responses may be acquired through classical conditioning or observational learning; phobic responses may be maintained by operant reinforcement.

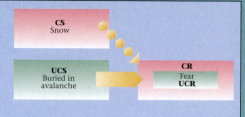

Personality: Neuroticism is correlated with an elevated prevalence of anxiety disorders.

Stress: High stress may help to precipitate the onset of anxiety disorders.

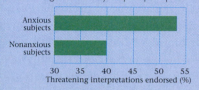

Threatening interpretations endorsed (%)

Cognition: People who misinterpret harmless situations as threatening and who focus excessive attention on perceived threats are more vulnerable to anxiety disorders.

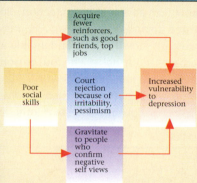

Interpersonal roots: Behavioral theories emphasize how inadequate social skills can result in a paucity of reinforcers and other effects that make people vulnerable to depression.

Stress: High stress can act as precipitating factor that triggers depression or bipolar disorder.

Cognition: Internal, stable, and global attributions for setbacks can contribute to the development of depression; rumination may extend and amplify depression.

Expressed emotion: A family's expressed emotion is a good predictor of the course of a schizophrenic patient's illness.

Stress: High stress can precipitate schizophrenic disorder in people who are vulnerable to schizophrenia.

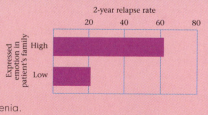

2-year relapse rate

Communication deviance: Muddled, fragmented communication in family can undermine child's sense of reality and foster withdrawal and schizophrenic thinking.

impaired social and occupational functioning. Essentially, people with these disorders display certain personality traits to an excessive degree and in rigid ways that undermine their adjustment. Personality disorders usually emerge during late childhood or adolescence and often continue throughout adulthood. It is difficult to estimate the prevalence of these subtle disorders, but it is clear that they are common (Lyons, 1995).

DSM-IV lists ten personality disorders. These disorders are described briefly in Table 14.3. If you examine this table, you will find a diverse collection of maladaptive personality syndromes. You may also notice that some personality disorders essentially are mild versions of more severe Axis I disorders. Some of these disorders are more common in men and some in women, as the figures in the far right column of the table indicate.

The ten personality disorders are grouped into three related clusters, as shown in Table 14.3. The three disorders in the *anxious-fearful cluster* are marked by maladaptive efforts to control anxiety and fear about social rejection. People with the three disorders in the *odd-eccentric cluster* are distrustful, socially aloof, and unable to connect with others emotionally. The four personality disorders in the *dramatic-impulsive cluster* have less in common with each other than those grouped in the first two clusters. The histrionic and narcissistic personalities share a flair for overdramatizing everything. Impulsiveness is the common ground shared by the borderline and antisocial personality disorders.

Diagnostic Problems

Many critics have argued that the personality disorders overlap too much with Axis I disorders and with each other (Livesley et al., 1994; Oldham et al., 1995). The extent of this problem was documented in a study by Leslie Morey (1988). Morey reviewed the cases of 291 patients who had received a specific personality disorder diagnosis to see how many could have met the criteria for any of the other personality disorders. Morey found massive overlap among the diagnoses. For example, among patients with a diagnosis of histrionic personality disorder, 56% also qualified for a borderline disorder, 54% for a narcissistic disorder, 32% for an avoidant disorder, 30% for a dependent disorder, and 29% for a paranoid disorder. Clearly, there are fundamental problems with Axis II as a classification system, and revisions are sorely needed (Widiger, 1993). The overlap among the personality disorders makes it virtually impossible to achieve consistent diagnoses.

In light of these problems, a variety of theorists have questioned the wisdom of the current *categorical approach* to describing personality disor-

TABLE 14.3 PERSONALITY DISORDERS

Cluster	Disorder	Description	% male
Anxious/fearful	Avoidant personality disorder	Excessively sensitive to potential rejection, humiliation, or shame; socially withdrawn in spite of desire for acceptance from others	50
	Dependent personality disorder	Excessively lacking in self-reliance and self-esteem; passively allowing others to make all decisions; constantly subordinating own needs to others' needs	31
	Obsessive-compulsive personality disorder	Preoccupied with organization, rules, schedules, lists, trivial details; extremely conventional, serious, and formal; unable to express warm emotions	50
Odd/eccentric	Schizoid personality disorder	Defective in capacity for forming social relationships; showing absence of warm, tender feelings for others	78
	Schizotypal personality disorder	Showing social deficits and oddities of thinking, perception, and communication that resemble schizophrenia	55
	Paranoid personality disorder	Showing pervasive and unwarranted suspiciousness and mistrust of people; overly sensitive; prone to jealousy	67
Dramatic/impulsive	Histrionic personality disorder	Overly dramatic; tending to exaggerated expressions of emotion; egocentric, seeking attention	15
	Narcissistic personality disorder	Grandiosely self-important; preoccupied with success fantasies; expecting special treatment; lacking interpersonal empathy	70
	Borderline personality disorder	Unstable in self-image, mood, and interpersonal relationships; impulsive and unpredictable	38
	Antisocial personality disorder	Chronically violating the rights of others; failing to accept social norms, to form attachments to others, or to sustain consistent work behavior; exploitive and reckless	82

Source: Adapted from Millon (1981)

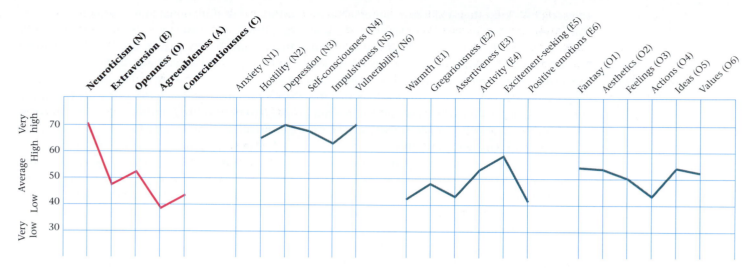

ders, which assumes (incorrectly, they argue) that people can reliably be placed in discontinuous (nonoverlapping) diagnostic categories (Trull & McCrae, 1994; Widiger & Frances, 1994). These theorists argue instead for a *dimensional approach,* which would describe personality disorders in terms of how people score on a limited number of continuous personality dimensions (see Figure 14.23). The dimensional approach assumes that personality disorders involve maladaptive variants of normal personality traits (Widiger & Costa, 1994). Although there is considerable evidence to support this assumption, the practical logistics of using a dimensional approach to describe personality disorders are formidable. Agreement would have to be reached about which personality dimensions should be assessed and how they should be measured. Many advocates of the dimensional approach argue that the system should be built around the five-factor model that has dominated recent research on personality traits (Clark & Livesley, 1994; McCrae, 1994), but other alternatives have also been proposed (Benjamin, 1993; Siever & Davis, 1991). Concerns have also been raised about the clinical utility of replacing prototypical descriptions of personality disorders with intricate personality profiles (Millon, 1994). For example, will it really enhance clinicians' understanding of obsessive-compulsive personality disorder to describe it as a syndrome marked by high scores on the traits of neuroticism and conscientiousness and low scores on the traits of agreeableness and openness to experience? Would these trait scores really capture the essence of the obsessive-compulsive syndrome? There is spirited debate about this matter.

The controversies over how to define various personality disorders have clearly hindered research on their etiology, prognosis, and treatment. The only personality disorder that has a long history of extensive research is the antisocial personality disorder, which we examine next.

Antisocial Personality Disorder

The antisocial personality disorder has a misleading name. The antisocial designation does *not* mean that people with this disorder shun social interaction. In fact, rather than shrinking from social interaction, many are sociable, friendly, and superficially charming. People with this disorder are *antisocial* in that they choose to *reject widely accepted social norms* regarding moral principles and behavior.

Description

People with antisocial personalities chronically violate the rights of others. They often use their social charm to cultivate others' liking or loyalty for purposes of exploitation. **The *antisocial personality disorder* is marked by impulsive, callous, manipulative, aggressive, and irresponsible behavior that reflects a failure to accept social norms.** Since they haven't accepted the social norms they violate, people with antisocial personalities rarely feel guilty about their transgressions. Essentially, they lack an adequate conscience. The antisocial personality disorder occurs much more frequently among males than females. Studies suggest that it is a moderately common disorder, seen in roughly 2%–4% of the population (Robins, Tipp, & Przybeck, 1991).

Many people with antisocial personalities get involved in illegal activities. Hare (1983) estimates that about 40% of convicted felons in prisons meet the criteria for an antisocial personality disorder. However, many people with antisocial

Figure 14.23
Example of a dimensional approach to borderline personality disorder. Advocates of a dimensional approach to personality disorders would describe these disorders in terms of how patients score on certain basic personality dimensions, such as the Big Five traits assessed by the NEO Personality Inventory (shown on the far left, with selected subtraits shown to the right). The personality profile shown here charts the mean scores for a group of 64 females diagnosed with borderline personality disorder (Sanderson & Clarkin, 1994). Similar personality profiles have been developed for other personality disorders, but some critics have expressed doubts about whether these profiles will really improve the diagnosis of personality disorders.

personalities keep their exploitive, amoral behavior channeled within the boundaries of the law. Such people may even enjoy high status in our society (Sutker & Allain, 1983). In other words, the concept of the antisocial personality disorder can apply to cut-throat business executives, scheming politicians, unprincipled lawyers, and money-hungry evangelists, as well as to con artists, drug dealers, thugs, burglars, and petty thieves.

People with antisocial personalities exhibit quite a variety of maladaptive traits (Hare, 1993; Harpur, Hart, & Hare, 1994). Among other things, they rarely experience genuine affection for others. However, they may be skilled at faking affection so they can exploit people. Sexually, they are predatory and promiscuous. They also tend to be irresponsible and impulsive. They can tolerate little frustration, and they pursue immediate gratification. These characteristics make them unreliable employees, unfaithful spouses, inattentive parents, and undependable friends. Many people with antisocial personalities have a checkered history of divorce, child abuse, and job instability.

Etiology

Many theorists believe that biological factors contribute to the development of antisocial personality disorders. Twin and adoption studies suggest a genetic predisposition toward these disorders (Gottesman & Goldsmith, 1994; Sutker, Bugg, & West, 1993). Eysenck (1982) has noted that people with antisocial personalities lack the inhibitions that most of us have about violating moral standards. Their lack of inhibitions prompted Eysenck to theorize that such people might inherit relatively sluggish autonomic nervous systems, leading to slow acquisition of inhibitions through classical conditioning. Eysenck's ideas have been supported in some empirical studies, but the findings are inconsistent (Brantley & Sutker, 1984; Raine, Venables, & Williams, 1990). As a whole, the evidence suggests that biological factors may create a genuine but weak predisposition toward antisocial behavior.

Efforts to relate psychological factors to antisocial behavior have emphasized inadequate socialization in dysfunctional family systems (Sutker et al., 1993). It's easy to envision how antisocial traits could be fostered in homes where parents make haphazard or halfhearted efforts to socialize their children to be respectful, truthful, responsible, unselfish, and so forth. Consistent with this idea, studies find that individuals with antisocial personalities tend to come from homes where discipline is erratic, ineffective, or physically abusive (Luntz & Widom, 1994). Such people are also more likely to emerge from homes where one or both parents exhibit antisocial traits. These parents presumably model exploitive, amoral behavior, which their children acquire through observational learning.

Investigating the roots of antisocial personality disorders has proven difficult because people with these disorders generally don't voluntarily seek help from our mental health system. They feel little guilt and don't usually see anything wrong with themselves. Their antisocial traits may become apparent only when they run afoul of the law and are ordered into treatment by the courts. Such court-ordered treatment is only one example of the many interfaces between our mental health system and our legal system. We'll explore some of these interfaces in the next section, which focuses on abnormal behavior and the law.

Recap of Key Points

• There are ten personality disorders that represent mild forms of disturbance allocated to Axis II in DSM. Personality disorders can be grouped into three clusters: anxious-fearful, odd-eccentric, and dramatic-impulsive.

• Specific personality disorders are poorly defined and there is excessive overlap among them, creating diagnostic problems. Some theorists believe that these problems could be reduced by replacing the current categorical approach to personality disorders with a dimensional approach.

• The antisocial personality disorder involves manipulative, impulsive, exploitive, aggressive behavior. Research on the etiology of this disorder has implicated genetic vulnerability, autonomic reactivity, inadequate socialization, and observational learning.

PSYCHOLOGICAL DISORDERS AND THE LAW

Societies use laws to enforce their norms of conformity. Given this function, the law in our society has something to say about many issues related to abnormal behavior. In this section we examine the concepts of insanity, competency, and involuntary commitment.

Insanity

Insanity is *not* a diagnosis; it's a legal concept. **Insanity is a legal status indicating that a person cannot be held responsible for his or her actions because of mental illness.** Why is this an issue in the courtroom? Because criminal acts must be intentional. The law reasons that people who are "out of their mind" may not be able to appreciate the significance of what they're doing. The insanity defense is used in criminal trials by defendants who admit that they committed the crime but claim that they lacked intent.

No simple relationship exists between specific diagnoses of mental disorders and court findings of insanity. Most people with diagnosed psychological disorders would *not* qualify as insane. The people most likely to qualify are those troubled by severe disturbances that display delusional behavior. The courts apply various rules in making judgments about a defendant's sanity, depending on the jurisdiction. According to one widely used rule, called the *M'naghten rule, insanity exists when a mental disorder makes a person unable to distinguish right from wrong.* As you can imagine, evaluating insanity as defined in the M'naghten rule can be difficult for judges and jurors, not to mention the psychologists and psychiatrists who are called into court as expert witnesses.

Although highly publicized and controversial, the insanity defense is actually used less frequently and less successfully than widely believed (Phillips, Wolf, & Coons, 1988). One study found that the general public estimates that the insanity defense is used in 37% of felony cases, when in fact it is used in less than 1% (Silver, Cirincione, & Steadman, 1994). Another study of over 60,000 indictments in Baltimore found that only 190 defendants (0.31%) pleaded insanity, and of these, only 8 were successful (Janofsky et al., 1996).

Competency

Competency (or fitness in some states) refers to a defendant's capacity to stand trial. To be competent, defendants must be able to understand the nature and purpose of the legal proceedings and be able to assist their attorney. If they're not able, they're declared incompetent and can't be brought to trial unless they become competent once again.

What's the difference between insanity and incompetence? Insanity refers to a defendant's mental state *at the time of the alleged crime.* Competency refers to a defendant's mental state *at the time of the trial.* Given the potential for delay in our legal system, the crime and the trial may take place many months or even years apart. Insanity can't even become an issue unless a defendant is competent to stand trial. Far more people are found to be incompetent than insane. As with insanity, no simple relationship exists between specific diagnoses and being declared incompetent (Nicholson & Kugler, 1991).

What happens to defendants who are declared incompetent or insane? Essentially, they're turned over to the mental health system for treatment. However, this simple statement masks immense variability in the handling of their cases. What happens to a defendant depends on the nature of the offense, the rules applied in the specific jurisdiction, the nature of the mental disorder, the likelihood of recovery and a return to competence, and a host of other factors.

Involuntary Commitment

The issues of insanity and competency surface only in *criminal* proceedings. Far more people are affected by *civil* proceedings relating to involuntary commitment. **In *involuntary commitment* people are hospitalized in psychiatric facilities against their will.** What are the grounds for such a dramatic action? They vary some from state to state. Generally, people are subject to involuntary commitment when mental health professionals and legal authorities believe that a mental disorder makes them (1) dangerous to themselves (usually suicidal), (2) dangerous to others (potentially violent), or (3) in need of treatment (applied in cases of severe disorientation). In emergency situations psychologists and psychiatrists can authorize *temporary* commitment, usually for 24 to 72

In his trial for murdering two people in an anti-abortion protest, John Salvi's attorneys attempted to mount an insanity defense, which was unsuccessful. Evidence shows that insanity pleas are successful far less often than most people believe.

hours. Orders for long-term involuntary commitment are usually set up for renewable six-month periods and can be issued by a court only after a formal hearing. Mental health professionals provide extensive input in these hearings, but the courts make the final decisions.

Most involuntary commitments occur because people appear to be *dangerous* to themselves or others. There's a problem, however, in that it's difficult to predict dangerousness. Studies suggest that clinicians' short-term predictions about which patients are likely to become violent are only moderately accurate and that their long-term predictions of violent behavior are largely inaccurate (Apperson, Mulvey, & Lidz, 1993; Faust & Ziskin, 1988; McNiel & Binder, 1995). This inaccuracy in predicting dangerousness is unfortunate, because involuntary commitment involves the *detention* of people for what they *might* do in the future. Such detention goes against the grain of the American legal principle that people are *innocent until proven guilty*. The inherent difficulty in predicting dangerousness makes involuntary commitment a complex and controversial issue.

CULTURE AND PATHOLOGY

The legal rules governing insanity, competency, and involuntary commitment obviously are culture-specific. And we noted earlier that judgments of normality and abnormality are influenced by cultural norms and values. In light of these realities, would it be reasonable to infer that psychological disorders are culturally variable phenomena? Many social scientists have concluded that the answer to this question is yes. Embracing a *relativistic view* of psychological disorders, they have argued that the criteria of mental illness vary greatly across cultures and that there are no universal standards of normality and abnormality (Lewis-Fernandez & Kleinman, 1994; Marsella, 1979). According to the relativists, the DSM diagnostic system reflects an ethnocentric, Western, white, urban, middle- and upper-class cultural orientation that has limited relevance in other cultural contexts.

Not everyone agrees with this conclusion, however. Many social scientists subscribe to a *pancultural view* of psychological disorders, arguing that the criteria of mental illness are much the same around the world and that basic standards of normality and abnormality are universal across cultures (Frances et al., 1991; Murphy, 1976). Theorists who accept the pancultural view of psychopathology typically maintain that Western diagnostic concepts have validity and utility in other cultural contexts.

The debate about culture and pathology basically boils down to three specific issues: (1) Are the psychological disorders seen in Western societies found throughout the world? (2) Are the symptom patterns of mental disorders invariant across cultures? (3) Are the prevalence rates for mental illness much the same from one society to the next?

Let's briefly examine the evidence on each of these questions and then reconsider the relativistic and pancultural views of psychological disorders.

Are Equivalent Disorders Found Around the World?

Most investigators agree that the principal categories of serious psychological disturbance—schizophrenia, depression, and bipolar illness—are identifiable in all cultures (Butcher, Narikiyo, & Vitousek, 1993). Most behaviors that are regarded as clearly abnormal in Western culture are also viewed as abnormal in other cultures. People who are delusional, hallucinatory, disoriented, or incoherent are thought to be disturbed in all societies, although there are cultural disparities in exactly what is considered delusional or hallucinatory.

Cultural variations are more apparent in the recognition of less severe forms of psychological disturbance (Tseng et al., 1986). Additional research is needed, but relatively mild types of pathology that do not disrupt behavior in obvious ways appear to go unrecognized in many societies. Thus, syndromes such as generalized anxiety disorder, hypochondria, and narcissistic personality disorder, which are firmly established as important diagnostic categories in the DSM, are viewed in some cultures as "run of the mill" difficulties and peculiarities rather than as full-fledged disorders.

Finally, researchers have discovered a small number of *culture-bound disorders* that further illustrate the diversity of abnormal behavior around the world (Simons & Hughes, 1993). **Culture-bound disorders are abnormal syndromes found only in a few cultural groups.** For example, *koro,* an obsessive fear that one's penis will withdraw into one's abdomen, is seen only among Chinese males in Malaya and several other regions of southern Asia. *Windigo,* which involves an intense craving for human flesh and fear that one will turn into a cannibal, is seen only among Algonquin Indian cultures. *Anorexia nervosa,* which involves an intense fear of becoming fat, a loss of appetite, and refusal to eat adequately, is seen only in affluent Western cultures.

Are Symptom Patterns Culturally Invariant?

Do the major types of psychological disorders manifest themselves in the same way around the world? For the most part, yes. The constellations of symptoms associated with schizophrenia, depression, and bipolar illness are largely the same across widely disparate societies (Draguns, 1980, 1990). However, cultural variations in symptom patterns are also seen. For example, delusions are a common symptom of schizophrenia in all cultures, but the specific delusions that people report are tied to their cultural heritage (Brislin, 1993). In technologically advanced societies, schizophrenic patients report that thoughts are being inserted into their minds through transmissions from electric lines, satellites, or microwave ovens. Victims of schizophrenia in less technological societies experience the same phenomenon but blame sorcerers or demons. Of the major disorders, symptom patterns are probably most variable for depression. For example, profound feelings of guilt and self-deprecation lie at the core of depression in Western cultures but are far less central to depression in many other societies. In non-Western cultures, depression tends to be expressed in terms of somatic symptoms, such as complaints of fatigue, headaches, and backaches, more than psychological symptoms, such as dejection and low self-esteem (Jenkins, Kleinman, & Good, 1991). These differences presumably occur because people learn to express symptoms of psychological distress in ways that are acceptable in their culture.

Are Prevalence Rates Similar Across Cultures?

The prevalence estimates for schizophrenia and bipolar disorder, which both hover around 1%, appear to be roughly comparable across diverse cultures (Butcher et al., 1993; Smith & Weissman, 1992). This cross-cultural similarity may be attributable to the strong biological component in these disorders or to the fact that they are severe disturbances that are more readily distinguished from normal behavior than milder disorders are. The prevalence rates for most other diagnostic categories vary considerably across cultures (Escobar, 1993). This variability is probably due to a combination of factors. First, there are methodological problems in obtaining comparable samples from different cultures. Second, diagnostic practices vary across cultures. Even for a universally recognized disorder, such as depression, different societies will use different cutoffs in drawing the line between normality and abnormality. Third, the environmental factors at work in specific cultures—the predominant attitudes, values, family dynamics, and sources of stress—probably foster some disorders more readily than others.

So, what can we conclude about the validity of the relativistic versus pancultural views of psychological disorders? Both views appear to have some merit. As we have seen in other areas of research, psychopathology is characterized by both cultural variance and invariance. Investigators have identified some universal standards of normality and abnormality and found considerable similarity across cultures in the syndromes that are regarded as pathological, their patterns of symptoms, and in their prevalence. However, researchers have also discovered many cultural variations in the recognition, definition, symptomatology, and prevalence of various psychological disorders. Given this extensive variability, the relativists' concerns about the ethnocentric nature of the DSM diagnostic system seem well founded.

PUTTING IT IN PERSPECTIVE

Our examination of abnormal behavior and its roots has highlighted four of our organizing themes: multifactorial causation, the interplay of heredity and environment, the sociohistorical context in which psychology evolves, and the influence of culture on psychological phenomena.

We can safely assert that every disorder described in this chapter has multiple causes. The development of mental disorders involves an interplay among a variety of psychological, biological, and social factors. For instance, a host of variables have been implicated in the etiology of schizophrenic disorders, including genetic predisposition, neurochemical changes, brain abnormalities, attention deficits, social deficits, coping skills, communication problems, family emotional atmosphere, styles of child rearing, life stress, social support, and society's response to the emergence of the disorder. Moreover, these variables interact in complex ways.

We also saw that most psychological disorders depend on an interaction of genetics and experience. This interaction shows up most clearly in the *stress-vulnerability models* for mood disorders and schizophrenic disorders. *Vulnerability* to these disorders seems to depend primarily on heredity, although experience contributes. Stress is largely a function of environment, although physiological factors may influence people's stress reactions. According to stress-vulnerability theories, disorders emerge when high vulnerability intersects with high stress. A high biological vulnerability may not be converted into a disorder if a person's stress is low. Similarly, high stress may not lead to a disorder if vulnerability is low. Thus, the impact of heredity depends on the environment, and the effect of environment depends on heredity.

This chapter also demonstrated that psychology evolves in a sociohistorical context. We saw that the formal definitions of normality and abnormality codified in the DSM system are not shaped exclusively by scientific research. For instance, because of changing social values and lobbying by a special-interest group, homosexuality is no longer classified as pathological, while some relatively minor problems in living are officially regarded as pathological to accommodate our insurance system. Currently, authorities are carefully reconsidering the legal definition of insanity because many people were outraged when John Hinckley, Jr. was found not guilty by reason of insanity after attempting to shoot then-President Ronald Reagan. These points are not raised to belittle the enormous contributions that science has made to our understanding of mental disorders. Modern conceptions of normality and abnormality are largely shaped by empirical research, but social trends, economic necessities, and political realities also play a role.

Finally, our discussion of psychological disorders showed once again that psychological phenomena are shaped to some degree by cultural parameters. Although some standards of normality and abnormality transcend cultural boundaries, cultural norms influence many aspects of psychopathology.

Indeed, a certain cultural orientation is implicit in our upcoming Application on suicide. Our culture views suicide as a cowardly, abnormal act to be prevented whenever possible. In contrast, there are other cultures in which suicide is considered to be an acceptable and even courageous act under certain circumstances. We'll take the traditional view in our culture and focus on suicide prevention.

Recap of Key Points

• Insanity is a legal concept applied to people who cannot be held responsible for their actions because of mental illness. The insanity defense is used less frequently and less successfully than widely believed.

• Competency refers to a defendant's capacity to understand legal proceedings at the time of a trial. When people appear to be dangerous to themselves or others, courts may rule that they are subject to involuntary commitment in a hosptial.

• The principal categories of psychological disturbance are identifiable in all cultures. But milder disorders may go unrecognized in some societies, and culture-bound disorders further illustrate the diversity of abnormal behavior around the world.

• The symptoms associated with specific disorders are largely the same across different cultures. The prevalence rates for schizophrenia and bipolar disorder are roughly similar around the world, but substantial cultural variations are seen in the prevalence of many other disorders.

• This chapter highlighted four of the text's unifying themes, showing that behavior is governed by multiple causes, that heredity and environment jointly influence mental disorders, that psychology evolves in a sociohistorical context, and that pathology is characterized by both cultural variance and invariance.

APPLICATION: **UNDERSTANDING AND PREVENTING SUICIDE**

Answer the following "true" or "false."

1 People who talk about suicide don't actually commit suicide.

2 Suicides usually take place with little or no warning.

3 People who attempt suicide are fully intent on dying.

4 People who are suicidal remain so forever.

These four statements are all false. They are myths about suicide that we will dispose of momentarily. First, however, let's discuss the magnitude of this tragic problem.

Prevalence of Suicide

There are about 250,000 suicide attempts in the United States each year. Roughly one in eight of these attempts is "successful." This makes suicide the eighth leading cause of death in the United States. Worse yet, official statistics may underestimate the scope of the problem. Many suicides are disguised as accidents, either by the suicidal person or by survivors who try to cover up afterward. Thus, experts estimate that there may be ten times more suicides than officially reported (Hirschfeld & Davidson, 1988).

Who Commits Suicide?

Anyone can commit suicide. No segment of society is immune. Nonetheless, some groups are at higher risk than others (Buda & Tsuang, 1990; Cross & Hirschfeld, 1986). For instance, the prevalence of suicide varies according to *marital status* (see Figure 14.24). Married people commit suicide less frequently than divorced, bereaved, or single people. In regard to *occupational status*, suicide rates are particularly high among people who are unemployed and among prestigious and pressured professionals, such as doctors and lawyers.

Sex and *age* have complex relations to suicide rates. On the one hand, women *attempt* suicide more often than men. On the other hand, men are more likely to actually kill themselves in an attempt, so they *complete* more suicides than women. In regard to age, suicide attempts peak between ages 24 and 44, but completed suicides are most frequent after age 55. However, age trends are different for men and women, as you can see in Figure 14.25, which graphs suicide rates by sex and age group.

Unfortunately, suicide rates have tripled among adolescents and young adults in the last several decades (Brent & Kolko, 1990). *College students* are at higher risk than their noncollege peers. Academic

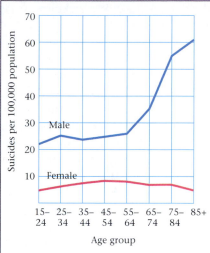

Figure 14.25
Suicide rates in the United States, by age and sex. At all ages, more men than women commit suicide. The age patterns for the two sexes are also noticeably different: Whereas the rate of male suicides peaks in the retirement years, the rate of female suicides peaks in middle adulthood. (Data from *Statistical Abstract of the United States*, 1990)

pressures and setbacks do *not* appear to be the principal cause of this elevated suicide rate among collegians. Interpersonal problems and loneliness seem to be more important.

Suicide is *not* limited to people with severe mental illness. However, elevated suicide rates are found for most categories of psychological disorders (Black & Winokur, 1990), and retrospective evaluations of people who attempt suicide indicate that about 90% experienced some type of mental illness around the time of their suicide (Beautrais et al., 1996). Suicide rates are highest for people with mood disorders (see Figure 14.26), alcohol and drug disorders, and schizophrenic disorders (Conwell et al., 1996; Fenton et al., 1997). Although the correlations between demographic factors and suicide rates are interesting, demographic factors have

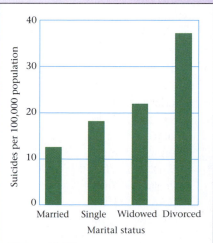

Figure 14.24
Marital status and suicide rates. As these data show, marital status is correlated with the likelihood of suicide. The suicide rate for singles is about 50% higher than for married individuals, and the rate for divorced people is about three times higher. (Adapted from McIntosh, 1991)

little practical value in predicting suicide at the individual level (Garland & Zigler, 1993).

Myths About Suicide

We opened this application with four false statements about suicide. Let's examine these myths as they have been discussed by various suicide experts (Fremouw, de Perczel, & Ellis, 1990; Rickgarn, 1994; Shneidman, 1985).

Myth 1: People who talk about suicide don't actually commit suicide. Undoubtedly, there are many people who threaten suicide without ever going through with it. Nonetheless, there is no group at higher risk for suicide than those who openly discuss the possibility. Many people who kill themselves have a history of earlier threats that they did not carry out.

Myth 2: Suicide usually takes place with little or no warning. It is estimated that eight out of ten suicide attempts are preceded by some kind of warning. These warnings may range from clear threats to vague statements. For example, at dinner with friends the night before he committed suicide, one prominent attorney cut up his American Express card, saying, "I'm not going to need this anymore." The prob-

ability of an actual suicide attempt is greatest when a threat is clear, when it includes a detailed plan, and when the plan involves a relatively deadly method.

Myth 3: People who attempt suicide are fully intent on dying. It appears that only about 3%–5% of those who attempt suicide definitely want to die. About 30% of the people who make an attempt seem ambivalent. They arrange things so that their fate is largely a matter of chance. The remaining two-thirds of suicide attempts are made by people who appear to have no interest in dying! They only want to send out a dramatic distress signal. Thus, they arrange their suicide so that a rescue is quite likely. These variations in intent probably explain why only about one-eighth of suicide attempts end in death.

Myth 4: People who are suicidal remain so forever. Many people who become suicidal do so for a limited period of time. If they manage to ride through their crisis period, thoughts of suicide may disappear entirely. Apparently, time heals many wounds—if it is given the opportunity.

Preventing Suicide

There is no simple and dependable way to prevent someone from going ahead with a

threatened suicide. One expert on suicide (Wekstein, 1979) makes the point that "perhaps nobody really knows *exactly* what to do when dealing with an imminent suicide" (p. 129). However, we will review some general advice that may be useful if you ever have to help someone through a suicidal crisis (Fremouw et al., 1990; Rosenthal, 1988; Shneidman, Farberow, & Litman, 1970).

1. *Take suicidal talk seriously.* When people talk about suicide in vague generalities, it's easy to dismiss it as "idle talk" and let it go. However, people who talk about suicide are a high-risk group, and their veiled threats should not be ignored. According to Rosenthal (1988), the first step in suicide prevention is to directly ask such people if they're contemplating suicide.

2. *Provide empathy and social support.* It's important to show the suicidal person that you care. People often contemplate suicide because they see the world around them as indifferent and uncaring. Hence, you must demonstrate to the suicidal person that you are genuinely concerned. Even if you are thrust into a situation where you barely know the suicidal person, you need to provide empathy. Suicide threats are often a last-ditch cry for help. It is therefore imperative that you offer to help.

3. *Identify and clarify the crucial problem.* The suicidal person is often terribly confused and feels lost in a sea of frustration and problems. It is a good idea to try to help sort through this confusion. Encourage the person to try to identify the crucial problem. Once it is isolated, it may not seem quite so overwhelming. You could also point out that the person's confusion is clouding his or her ability to rationally judge the seriousness of the problem.

4. *Suggest alternative courses of action.* People thinking about suicide often see it as the only solution to their problems. This is obviously an irrational view. Try to chip away at this premise by offering other possible solutions for the problem that has been identified as crucial. Suicidal people often are too distraught and disoriented to do this on their own.

5. *Capitalize on any doubts.* For most people, life is not easy to give up. They are

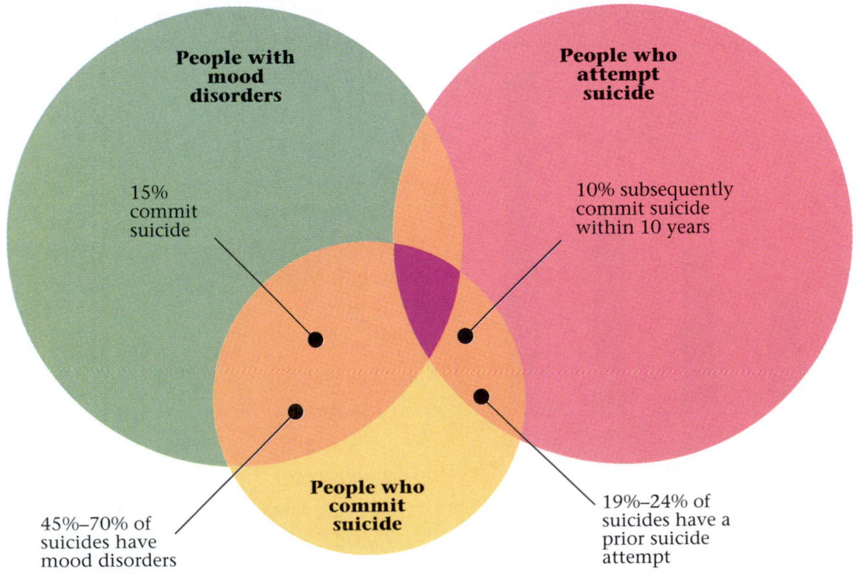

People with mood disorders

People who attempt suicide

15% commit suicide

10% subsequently commit suicide within 10 years

45%–70% of suicides have mood disorders

People who commit suicide

19%–24% of suicides have a prior suicide attempt

Figure 14.26
The relationship between suicide and mood disorders. Two groups with elevated risk of suicide are people with mood disorders and people who have made previous suicide attempts. Between them, these groups account for a high percentage of suicides. (Adapted from Avery & Winokur, 1978)

Celebrities who have been so troubled as to take their own lives include grunge rocker Kurt Colbain, writer Sylvia Plath (*The Bell Jar*), and Vincent Foster, a prominent member of President Clinton's staff.

Most mental health professionals have at least some experience in dealing with suicidal crises. Many cities have suicide prevention centers with 24-hour hotlines. These centers are staffed with people who have been specially trained to deal with suicidal problems. It is important to try to get a suicidal person to seek professional assistance. Just because you talk a person out of attempting a threatened suicide does not mean that the crisis is over. The contemplation of suicide indicates that a person is experiencing great distress. Given this reality, professional intervention is crucial.

Recap of Key Points

• Suicide attempts result in death about one-eighth of the time, and suicide is the eighth leading cause of death in the United States. Suicide rates are correlated with age, sex, and marital status, among other things.

• People with psychological disorders, especially mood disorders, show elevated suicide rates. Suicidal people usually provide warnings, often are not intent on dying, and may not remain suicidal if they survive their crisis.

• Suicidal talk should be taken seriously. Efforts at suicide prevention emphasize empathy, clarification of the person's problems, and professional assistance.

racked by doubts about the wisdom of their decision. Many people will voice their unique reasons for doubting whether they should take the suicidal path. Zero in on these doubts. They may be your best argu-

ments for life over death. For instance, if a person expresses concern about how her or his suicide will affect family members, capitalize on this source of doubt.

6. *Encourage professional consultation.*

Key Ideas

Abnormal Behavior: Myths, Realities, and Controversies

◆ The medical model assumes that it is useful to view abnormal behavior as a disease. This view has been criticized on the grounds that it turns ethical questions about deviance into medical questions.

◆ Three criteria are used in deciding whether people suffer from psychological disorders: deviance, personal distress, and maladaptive behavior. People with psychological disorders are not particularly bizarre or dangerous, and even the most severe disorders are potentially curable. Research by David Rosenhan, described in our Featured Study, showed that the distinction between normality and abnormality is not clear-cut.

◆ DSM-IV is the official psychodiagnostic classification system in the United States. This system describes over 200 disorders and asks for information about patients on five axes, or dimensions.

◆ It is difficult to obtain good data on the prevalence of psychological disorders. Nonetheless, it is clear that they are more common than widely believed, affecting roughly one-third of the population.

Anxiety Disorders

◆ The anxiety disorders include generalized anxiety disorder, phobic disorder, panic disorder, and obsessive-compulsive disorder. Heredity, oversensitivity to the physiological symptoms of anxiety, and abnormalities in GABA or serotonin activity may contribute to these disorders.

◆ Many anxiety responses, especially phobias, may be caused by classical conditioning and maintained by operant conditioning. Cognitive theorists maintain that a tendency to overinterpret harmless situations as threatening may make some people vulnerable to anxiety disorders. Stress and neuroticism may also predispose people to anxiety disorders.

Somatoform Disorders

◆ Somatoform disorders include somatization disorder, conversion disorder, and hypochondriasis. These disorders often emerge in people with highly histrionic personalities and in people who focus excess attention on their internal physiological processes. Somatoform disorders may be a learned avoidance strategy reinforced by attention and sympathy.

Dissociative Disorders

◆ Dissociative disorders include dissociative amnesia and fugue and multiple personality (dissociative identity disorder). These disorders are uncommon and their causes are not well understood.

Mood Disorders

◆ The principal mood disorders are depressive disorder and bipolar disorder. Mood disorders are episodic, and seasonal patterns have been observed in some patients.

◆ Evidence indicates that people vary in their genetic vulnerability to the severe mood disorders. These disorders are accompanied by changes in neurochemical activity in the brain. Cognitive models posit that negative thinking contributes to depression. Depression is often rooted in interpersonal inadequacies and sometimes is stress related.

Schizophrenic Disorders

◆ Schizophrenic disorders are characterized by deterioration of adaptive behavior, irrational thought, distorted perception, and disturbed mood. Schizophrenic disorders are classified as paranoid, catatonic, disorganized, or undifferentiated.

◆ Research has linked schizophrenia to a genetic vulnerability, changes in neurotransmitter activity, and structural abnormalities in the brain. Precipitating stress and unhealthy family dynamics, including communication deviance and high expressed emotion, may also contribute to the development of schizophrenia.

Personality Disorders

◆ Ten personality disorders that represent mild forms of disturbance are allocated to Axis II in DSM. Personality disorders can be grouped into three clusters: anxious-fearful, odd-eccentric, and dramatic-impulsive.

◆ The antisocial personality disorder involves manipulative, impulsive, exploitive, aggressive behavior. Research on the etiology of this disorder has implicated genetic vulnerability, autonomic reactivity, inadequate socialization, and observational learning.

Psychological Disorders and the Law

◆ Insanity is a legal concept applied to people who cannot be held responsible for their actions because of mental illness. Competency refers to a defendant's capacity to understand legal proceedings at the time of a trial. When people appear to be dangerous to themselves or others, courts may rule that they are subject to involuntary commitment in a hosptial.

Culture and Pathology

◆ The principal categories of psychological disturbance are identifiable in all cultures. But milder disorders may go unrecognized in some societies. The symptoms associated with specific disorders are largely the same across different cultures, but the prevalence rates of many disorders vary considerably.

Putting It in Perspective

◆ This chapter highlighted four of our unifying themes, showing that behavior is governed by multiple causes, that heredity and environment jointly influence mental disorders, that psychology evolves in a sociohistorical context, and that pathology is characterized by both cultural variance and invariance.

Application: Understanding and Preventing Suicide

◆ Suicide attempts result in death about one-eighth of the time, and suicide is the eighth leading cause of death in the United States. Suicidal people usually provide warnings, often are not intent on dying, and may not remain suicidal if they survive their crisis. Efforts at suicide prevention emphasize empathy, clarification of the person's problems, and professional assistance.

Key Terms

Agoraphobia
Antisocial personality disorder
Anxiety disorders
Attributions
Bipolar disorders
Catatonic schizophrenia
Competency
Concordance rate
Conversion disorder
Culture-bound disorders
Cyclothymic disorder
Delusions
Depressive disorders
Diagnosis
Disorganized schizophrenia
Dissociative amnesia
Dissociative disorders
Dissociative fugue
Dissociative identity disorder
Dysthymic disorder
Epidemiology
Etiology
Generalized anxiety disorder
Hallucinations
Hypochondriasis
Insanity
Involuntary commitment
Medical model
Mood disorders
Multiple-personality disorder
Obsessive-compulsive disorder (OCD)
Panic disorder
Paranoid schizophrenia
Personality disorders
Phobic disorder
Prevalence
Prognosis
Psychosomatic diseases
Schizophrenic disorders
Seasonal affective disorder (SAD)
Somatization disorder
Somatoform disorders
Transvestism
Undifferentiated schizophrenia

Key People

Nancy Andreasen
David Rosenhan
Martin Seligman
Thomas Szasz

Practice Test

1. According to Thomas Szasz, abnormal behavior usually involves:
   A. behavior that is statistically unusual.
   B. behavior that deviates from social norms.
   C. a disease of the mind.
   D. biological imbalance.

2. Although Sue always feels a high level of dread, worry, and anxiety, she still manages to meet her daily responsibilities. Sue's behavior:
   A. should not be considered abnormal, since her adaptive functioning is not impaired.
   B. should not be considered abnormal, since everyone sometimes experiences worry and anxiety.
   C. can still be considered abnormal, since she feels great personal distress.
   D. a and b.

3. The fact that people acquire phobias of ancient sources of threat (such as snakes) much more readily than modern sources of threat (such as electrical outlets) can best be explained by:
   A. classical conditioning.
   B. operant conditioning.
   C. observational learning.
   D. preparedness.

4. Which of the following statements about multiple-personality disorder is (are) true?
   A. The original personality is always aware of the alternate personalities.
   B. The alternate personalities are usually unaware of the original personality.
   C. The personalities are typically all quite similar to one another.
   D. During the 1980s, there was a dramatic increase in the diagnosis of multiple-personality disorder.
   E. None of the above.

5. People with unipolar disorders experience _____; people with bipolar disorders experience _____.
   A. alternating periods of depression and mania; mania only
   B. depression only; alternating periods of depression and mania
   C. mania only; alternating periods of depression and mania
   D. alternating periods of depression and mania; depression and mania simultaneously

6. A concordance rate indicates:
   A. the percentage of twin pairs or other close relatives that exhibit the same disorder.
   B. the percentage of people with a given disorder that are currently receiving treatment.
   C. the prevalence of a given disorder in the general population.
   D. the rate of cure for a given disorder.

7. People who consistently tend to make _____ attributions for negative events are more prone to depression.
   A. internal, specific, unstable
   B. internal, global, stable
   C. external, specific, unstable
   D. external, global, stable

8. Mary believes that while she sleeps at night, space creatures are attacking her and invading her uterus, where they will multiply until they are ready to take over the world. Mary was chosen for this task, she believes, because she is the only one with the power to help the space creatures succeed. Mary would most likely be diagnosed as _____ schizophrenic.
   A. paranoid
   B. catatonic
   C. disorganized
   D. undifferentiated

9. As an alternative to the current classification scheme, it has been proposed that schizophrenic disorders be divided into just two categories based on:
   A. whether the prognosis is favorable or unfavorable.
   B. whether the disorder is mild or severe.
   C. the predominance of thought disturbances versus emotional disturbances.
   D. the predominance of negative versus positive symptoms.

10. Most of the drugs that are useful in the treatment of schizophrenia are known to dampen _____ activity in the brain, suggesting that disruptions in the activity of this neurotransmitter may contribute to the development of the disorder.
    A. norepinephrine
    B. serotonin
    C. acetylcholine
    D. dopamine

11. The main problem with the current classification scheme for personality disorders is that:
    A. it falsely implies that nearly everyone has at least one personality disorder.
    B. the criteria for diagnosis are so detailed and specific that even extremely disturbed people fail to meet them.
    C. the categories often overlap, making diagnosis unreliable.
    D. it contains too few categories to be useful.

12. The diagnosis of antisocial personality disorder would apply to an individual who:
    A. withdraws from social interaction due to an intense fear of rejection or criticism.
    B. withdraws from social interaction due to a lack of interest in interpersonal intimacy.
    C. is emotionally cold, suspicious of everyone, and overly concerned about being slighted by others.
    D. is callous, impulsive, and manipulative.

13. Involuntary commitment to a psychiatric facility:
    A. can occur only after a mentally ill individual has been convicted of a violent crime.
    B. usually occurs because people appear to be a danger to themselves or others.
    C. no longer occurs under modern civil law.
    D. will be a lifelong commitment, even if the individual is no longer mentally ill.

14. Those who embrace a relativistic view of psychological disorders would agree that:
    A. the criteria of mental illness vary greatly across cultures.
    B. there are universal standards of normality and abnormality.
    C. Western diagnostic concepts have validity and utility in other cultural contexts.
    D. b and c.

15. Which of the following statements is (are) true?
    A. People who threaten to commit suicide are almost always bluffing.
    B. Suicides usually take place with little or no warning.
    C. People who are suicidal remain so forever.
    D. None of the above.

Answers

1	B	Page 558	6	A	Pages 576, 578	11	C	Page 590
2	C	Pages 559–560	7	B	Page 580	12	D	Pages 591–592
3	D	Pages 569–570	8	A	Pages 583–584	13	B	Page 593
4	D	Page 574	9	D	Page 584	14	A	Page 594
5	B	Page 576	10	D	Page 585	15	D	Page 598

15 PSYCHOTHERAPY

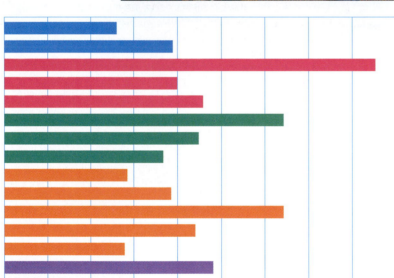

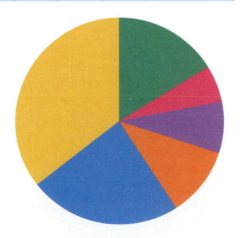

What do you picture when you hear the term *psychotherapy*? If you're like most people, you probably envision a troubled patient lying on a couch in a book-lined office, with the therapist asking penetrating questions and providing sage advice. Typically, people believe that psychotherapy is only for those who are "sick" and that therapists have special powers that allow them to "see through" their clients. It is also widely believed that successful therapy requires years of deep probing into a client's innermost secrets. Many people further assume that therapists routinely tell their patients how to lead their lives. Like most stereotypes, this picture of psychotherapy is a mixture of fact and fiction, as you'll see in the upcoming pages.

In this chapter, we'll take a down-to-earth look at the complex process of psychotherapy. We'll start by discussing some general questions about the provision of therapy, including:

• Who seeks therapy?
• Why is it that many people who need therapy don't receive it?
• What kinds of professionals provide therapy?
• What are the differences between psychiatrists and psychologists?
• How many different types of therapy are there?

After we've considered these general issues, we'll examine some of the more widely used approaches to psychotherapy, analyzing their goals, techniques, and effectiveness. In the Application at the end of the chapter, we focus on practical issues involved in finding and choosing a therapist, in case you ever have to advise someone about seeking psychotherapy.

THE ELEMENTS OF PSYCHOTHERAPY: TREATMENTS, CLIENTS, AND THERAPISTS

Sigmund Freud is widely credited with launching modern psychotherapy. Ironically, the landmark case that inspired Freud was actually treated by one of his colleagues, Josef Breuer. Around 1880, Breuer began to treat a young woman named Anna O (a pseudonym). Anna exhibited a variety of physical maladies, including headaches, coughing, and a loss of feeling and movement in her right arm. Much to his surprise, Breuer discovered that Anna's physical symptoms cleared up when he encouraged her to talk about emotionally charged experiences from her past.

When Breuer and Freud discussed the case, they speculated that talking things through had enabled Anna to drain off bottled up emotions that had caused her symptoms. Breuer found the intense emotional exchange in this treatment not to his liking, so he didn't follow through on his discovery. However, Freud applied Breuer's insight to other patients, and his successes led him to develop a systematic treatment procedure, which he called *psychoanalysis*. Anna O called her treatment "the talking cure." However, as you'll see, psychotherapy isn't always curative, and many modern therapies place little emphasis on talking.

Freud's breakthrough ushered in a century of progress for psychotherapy. Psychoanalysis spawned many offspring as Freud's followers developed their own systems of treatment. Since then, approaches to psychotherapy have steadily grown more numerous, more diverse, and more effective. Today, people can choose from a bewildering array of therapies.

In psychotherapy, a person with psychological problems enlists the help of a professional (the therapist) in dealing with those problems. Insight therapies can be conducted with groups as well as individuals.

Treatments: How Many Types Are There?

In their efforts to help people, psychotherapists use many treatment methods. Included among them are discussion, advice, emotional support, persuasion, conditioning procedures, relaxation training, role playing, drug therapy, biofeedback, and group therapy. Some therapists also use a variety of "unconventional" procedures, such as rebirthing, poetry therapy, and primal therapy. No one knows exactly how many distinct types of psychotherapy there are. One expert (Kazdin, 1994) estimates that there may be over 400 approaches to treatment. Fortunately, we can impose some order on this chaos. As varied as therapists' procedures are, approaches to treatment can be classified into three major categories:

1. *Insight therapies*. Insight therapy is "talk therapy" in the tradition of Freud's psychoanalysis. This is probably the approach to treatment that you envision when you think of psychotherapy. In insight therapies, clients engage in complex, often lengthy verbal interactions with their therapists. The goal in these discussions is to pursue increased insight regarding the nature of the client's difficulties and to sort through possible solutions. Insight therapy can be conducted with an individual or with a group. Broadly speaking, family therapy and marital therapy fall in this category.

2. *Behavior therapies*. Behavior therapies are based on the principles of learning, which were introduced in Chapter 6. Instead of emphasizing personal insights, behavior therapists make direct efforts to alter problematic responses (phobias, for instance) and maladaptive habits (drug use, for instance). Behavior therapists work on changing clients' overt behaviors. They use different procedures for different kinds of problems. Most of their procedures involve classical conditioning, operant conditioning, or observational learning.

3. *Biomedical therapies*. Biomedical approaches to therapy involve interventions into a person's biological functioning. The most widely used procedures are drug therapy and electroconvulsive (shock) therapy. As the name bio*medical* therapies suggests, these treaments have traditionally been provided only by physicians with a medical degree (usually psychiatrists). This situation may change, however, as psychologists have begun to campaign for prescription privileges (DeLeon & Wiggins, 1996; Pachman, 1996). They have made some progress toward this goal, even though many psychologists have argued against pursuing the right to prescribe medication (DeNelsky, 1996; Hayes & Heiby, 1996).

Later in this chapter we will examine approaches to therapy that fall into each of these three categories. Although we'll find different methods in each category, the three major treatment classes are not entirely incompatible. For example, a client might be seen in insight therapy while also receiving medication.

Clients: Who Seeks Therapy?

In the therapeutic triad (therapists, treatments, clients), the greatest diversity of all is seen among the clients. They bring to therapy the full range of human problems: anxiety, depression, unsatisfactory interpersonal relations, troublesome habits, poor self-control, low self-esteem, marital conflicts, self-doubt, a sense of emptiness, and feelings of personal stagnation. Therapy is sought by people who feel troubled, but the nature and severity of that trouble varies greatly from one person to another. The two most common presenting problems are excessive anxiety and depression (Narrow et al., 1993).

A client in treatment does *not* necessarily have an identifiable psychological disorder. Some people seek professional help for everyday problems (career decisions, for instance) or vague feelings of discontent (Strupp, 1996). Thus, therapy includes efforts to foster clients' personal growth, as well as professional interventions for mental disorders.

People vary considerably in their willingness to seek psychotherapy. As you can see in Figure 15.1, women are more likely than men to receive therapy. Treatment is also more likely when people have medical insurance and when they have more education (Olfson & Pincus, 1996). *Unfortunately, it appears that many people who need therapy don't receive it* (Pekarik, 1993). As Figure 15.2 shows for specific types of disorders, only a portion of the people who need treatment receive it (Regier et al., 1993). People who could benefit from therapy do not seek it for a variety of reasons. Some are unaware of its availability, and some believe that it is always expensive. The biggest roadblock is that many people equate being in therapy with admitting personal weakness.

A small portion of clients are essentially forced into psychotherapy. In most cases, this coercion involves gentle pressure from a spouse, a parent, a

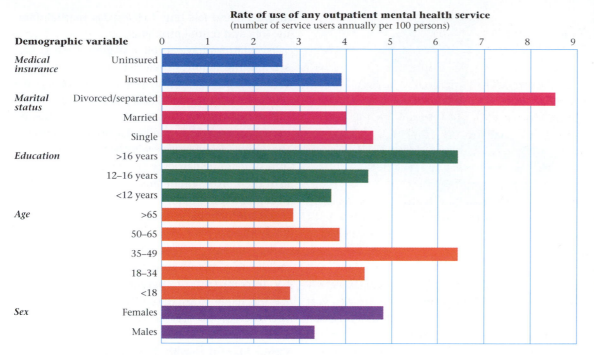

Rate of use of any outpatient mental health service
(number of service users annually per 100 persons)

Figure 15.1
Therapy utilization rates. Olfson and Pincus (1996) gathered data on the use of nonhospital outpatient mental health services in the United States in relation to various demographic variables. As you can see, people are more likely to enter therapy if they have medical insurance than if they do not. In regard to marital status, utilization rates are particularly high among those who are divorced or separated. The use of therapy is greater among those who have more education and, in terms of age, utilization peaks in the 35–49 age bracket. Finally, females are more like to pursue therapy than males.

friend, or an employer. Sometimes, however, people are ordered into treatment by the courts, as in cases of involuntary commitment to a mental hospital.

Therapists: Who Provides Professional Treatment?

People troubled by personal problems often solicit help from their friends, relatives, clergy, and primary care physicians. These sources of assistance may provide excellent advice, but their counsel does not qualify as therapy. Psychotherapy refers to *professional* treatment by someone with special training. However, a common source of confusion about psychotherapy is the variety of "helping professions" available to offer assistance (Murstein & Fontaine, 1993). Psychology and psychiatry are the principal professions involved in the provision of psychotherapy, delivering the lion's share of mental health care (see Figure 15.3). However, therapy is also provided by psychiatric social workers, psychiatric nurses, and counselors. Let's look at the various mental health professions.

Psychologists

Two types of psychologists may provide therapy, although the distinction between them is more theoretical than real. ***Clinical psychologists*** and ***counseling psychologists*** specialize in the diagnosis and treatment of psychological disorders and everyday behavioral problems. In theory, clinical psychologists' training emphasizes the

treatment of full-fledged disorders. In contrast, counseling psychologists' training is supposed to be slanted toward the treatment of everyday adjustment problems in normal people. In practice, however, there is great overlap between clinical and counseling psychologists in training, skills, and the clientele that they serve, so that they are virtually interchangeable.

Both types of psychologists must earn a doctoral degree (Ph.D., Psy.D., or Ed.D.). A doctorate in psychology requires about five to seven years of training beyond a bachelor's degree. The process of gaining admission to a Ph.D. program in clinical psychology is highly competitive (about as difficult as getting into medical school). Psycholo-

Figure 15.2
The likelihood of treatment among people with various disorders. Not everyone who has a psychological disorder receives professional treatment. This graph shows the percentage of people with specific disorders who obtained mental health treatment during a one-year period. Note that for most types of disorders, only a minority of afflicted people receive treatment. (Data based on Regier et al., 1993)

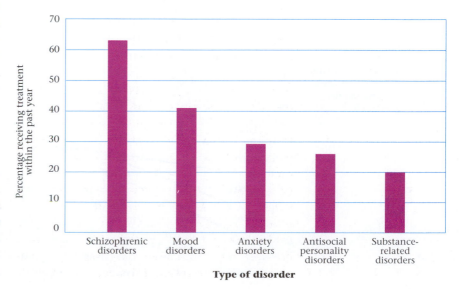

Figure 15.3
**Who people see for
therapy.** Based on a na-
tional survey, Olfson and
Pincus (1994) estimated that
in 1987 Americans made
79.5 million outpatient psychotherapy visits. Information on the therapist's
profession was missing for
11% of these visits. The pie
chart shows how the remaining visits were distributed
among psychologists, psy-
chiatrists, other mental
health professionals (social
workers, counselors, and
such) and general medical
professionals (typically physicians specializing in family
practice, internal medicine,
or pediatrics). As you can
see, psychologists and psychiatrists account for about
62% of outpatient treatment.

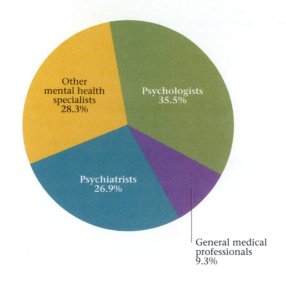

gists receive most of their training on university campuses, although they serve a one- to two-year internship in a clinical setting, such as a hospital.

In providing therapy, psychologists use either insight or behavioral approaches. In comparison to psychiatrists, they are more likely to use behavioral techniques and less likely to use psychoanalytic methods. Clinical and counseling psychologists do psychological testing as well as psychotherapy, and many also conduct research.

Psychiatrists

Psychiatrists are physicians who specialize in the diagnosis and treatment of psychological disorders. Many psychiatrists also treat everyday behavioral problems. However, in comparison to psychologists, psychiatrists devote more time to relatively severe disorders (schizophrenia, mood

disorders) and less time to everyday marital, fam-ily, job, and school problems.

Psychiatrists have an M.D. degree. Their gradu-ate training requires four years of coursework in medical school and a four-year apprenticeship in a residency at a hospital. Their psychotherapy train-ing occurs during their residency, since the re-quired coursework in medical school is essentially the same for everyone, whether they are going into surgery, pediatrics, or psychiatry.

In their provision of therapy, psychiatrists tend to emphasize biomedical treatments that the other, nonmedical helping professions cannot provide (drug therapy, for instance). Psychiatrists use a variety of insight therapies, but psychoanalysis and its descendants remain dominant in psychia-try. In comparison to psychologists, psychiatrists are less likely to use group therapies or behavior therapies.

Other Mental Health Professionals

Several other mental health professions also pro-vide psychotherapy services, and some of these professions are growing even more rapidly than clinical psychology and psychiatry (see Figure 15.4). In hospitals and other institutions, *clinical social workers* and *psychiatric nurses* often work as part of a treatment team with a psychologist or psychia-trist. Psychiatric nurses, who may have a bachelor's or master's degree in their field, play a large role in hospital inpatient treatment. Clinical social work-ers generally have a master's degree and typically work with patients and their families to ease the patient's integration back into the community. Although social workers have traditionally worked in hospitals and social service agencies, many also provide a wide range of therapeutic services as independent practitioners.

Many kinds of *counselors* also provide therapeu-tic services. Counselors are usually found working in schools, colleges, and assorted human service agencies (youth centers, geriatric centers, family planning centers, and so forth). Counselors typi-cally have a master's degree. They often specialize in particular types of problems, such as vocational counseling, marital counseling, rehabilitation counseling, and drug counseling.

Although there are clear differences among the helping professions in education and training, their roles in the treatment process overlap consider-ably. In this chapter, we will refer to psychologists or psychiatrists as needed, but otherwise we'll use the terms *clinician, therapist,* and *mental health*

Figure 15.4
**Recent growth in the
mental health profes-
sions.** Mounting demands
for clinical services have led
to rapid growth in the mental health professions. This
growth has been particularly
rapid in clinical social work
and marriage and family
counseling. (Data from
Phares, 1992)

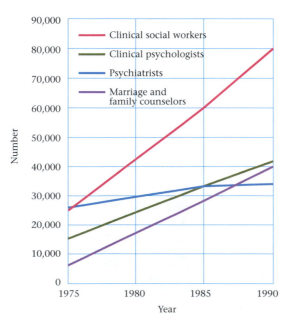

professional to refer to psychotherapists of all kinds, regardless of their professional degree.

Now that we have discussed the basic elements in psychotherapy, we can examine specific approaches to treatment in terms of their goals, procedures, and effectiveness. We'll begin with a few, representative insight therapies.

Recap of Key Points

• Approaches to treatment are diverse, but they can be grouped into three categories: insight therapies, behavior therapies, and biomedical therapies.

• Clients bring a wide variety of problems to therapy and do not necessarily have a disorder. People vary in their willingness to seek treatment, and many people who need therapy do not receive it.

• Therapists come from a variety of professional backgrounds. Clinical and counseling psychologists, psychiatrists, clinical social workers, psychiatric nurses, and counselors are the principal providers of therapeutic services.

• Each of these professions shows different preferences for approaches to treatment. Psychologists typically practice insight or behavior therapy. Psychiatrists tend to depend on psychoanalytic approaches to insight therapy and on biomedical therapies.

INSIGHT THERAPIES

There are many schools of thought about how to do insight therapy. Therapists with various theoretical orientations use different methods to pursue different kinds of insights. However, what these varied approaches have in common is that **insight therapies involve verbal interactions intended to enhance clients' self-knowledge and thus promote healthful changes in personality and behavior.**

Although there may be hundreds of insight therapies, the leading eight or ten approaches appear to account for the lion's share of treatment. In this section, we'll delve into psychoanalysis, related psychodynamic approaches, client-centered therapy, and cognitive therapy. We'll also discuss how insight therapy can be done with groups as well as individuals.

Psychoanalysis 11d

After the case of Anna O, Sigmund Freud worked as a psychotherapist for almost 50 years in Vienna. Through a painstaking process of trial and error, he developed innovative techniques for the treatment of psychological disorders and distress. His system of *psychoanalysis* came to dominate psychiatry for many decades. Although the dominance of psychoanalysis has eroded in recent years (Reiser, 1989), a diverse collection of psychoanalytic approaches to therapy continue to evolve and to remain influential today (Eagle & Wolitzky, 1992).

Psychoanalysis **is an insight therapy that emphasizes the recovery of unconscious conflicts, motives, and defenses through techniques such as free association and transference.** To appreciate the logic of psychoanalysis, we have to look at Freud's thinking about the roots of mental disorders. Freud mostly treated anxiety-dominated disturbances, such as phobic, panic, obsessive-compulsive, and conversion disorders, that were then called *neuroses*.

Freud believed that neurotic problems are caused by unconscious conflicts left over from early childhood. As explained in Chapter 12, he thought that these inner conflicts involved battles among the id, ego, and superego, usually over sexual and aggressive impulses. He theorized that people depend on defense mechanisms to avoid confronting these conflicts, which remain hidden in the depths of the unconscious. However, he noted that defensive maneuvers often lead to self-defeating behavior. Furthermore, he asserted that defenses tend to be only partially successful in alleviating anxiety, guilt, and other distressing emotions. With this model in mind, let's take a look at the therapeutic procedures used in psychoanalysis.

Probing the Unconscious

Given Freud's assumptions, we can see that the logic of psychoanalysis is quite simple. The analyst attempts to probe the murky depths of the unconscious to discover the unresolved conflicts causing the client's neurotic behavior. In a sense, the analyst functions as a "psychological detective." In this effort to explore the unconscious, the therapist relies on two techniques: free association and dream analysis.

In *free association* **clients spontaneously express**

"The news that reaches your consciousness is incomplete and often not to be relied on."

SIGMUND FREUD

their thoughts and feelings exactly as they occur, with as little censorship as possible. Clients
lie on a couch so they will be better able to let
their mind drift freely. In free associating, clients
expound on anything that comes to mind, regardless of how trivial, silly, or embarrassing it might
be. Gradually, most clients begin to let everything
pour out without conscious censorship. The analyst
studies these free associations for clues about what is
going on in the client's unconscious.

In *dream analysis* the therapist interprets the
symbolic meaning of the client's dreams. For
Freud, dreams were the "royal road to the unconscious," the most direct means of access to patients' innermost conflicts, wishes, and impulses.
Clients are encouraged and trained to remember
their dreams, which they describe in therapy. The
therapist then analyzes the symbolism in these
dreams to interpret their meaning.

To better illustrate these matters, let's look at an
actual case treated through psychoanalysis (adapted
from Greenson, 1967, pp. 40–41). Mr. N was
troubled by an unsatisfactory marriage. He claimed
to love his wife, but he preferred sexual relations
with prostitutes. Mr. N reported that his parents
also endured lifelong marital difficulties. His childhood conflicts about their relationship appeared
to be related to his problems. Both dream analysis
and free association can be seen in the following
description of a session in Mr. N's treatment:

*Mr. N reported a fragment of a dream. All that he could
remember is that he was waiting for a red traffic light to
change when he felt that someone had bumped into him
from behind. . . . The associations led to Mr. N's love of
cars, especially sports cars. He loved the sensation, in
particular, of whizzing by those fat, old expensive cars. . . .
His father always hinted that he had been a great athlete,
but he never substantiated it. . . . Mr. N doubted whether
his father could really perform. His father would flirt with
a waitress in a cafe or make sexual remarks about women
passing by, but he seemed to be showing off. If he were
really sexual, he wouldn't resort to that.*

As is characteristic of free association, Mr. N's
train of thought meandered about with little direction. Nonetheless, clues about his unconscious
conflicts are apparent. What did Mr. N's therapist
extract from this session? The therapist saw sexual
overtones in the dream fragment, where Mr. N
was bumped from behind. The therapist also inferred that Mr. N had a competitive orientation
toward his father, based on the free association
about whizzing by fat, old expensive cars. As you
can see, analysts must *interpret* their clients' dreams

and free associations. This is a critical process
throughout psychoanalysis.

Interpretation

Interpretation **refers to the therapist's attempts
to explain the inner significance of the client's
thoughts, feelings, memories, and behaviors.**
Contrary to popular belief, analysts do not interpret everything, and they generally don't try to
dazzle clients with startling revelations. Instead,
analysts move forward inch by inch, offering interpretations that should be just out of the client's
own reach. Mr. N's therapist eventually offered
the following interpretations to his client:

*I said to Mr. N near the end of the hour that I felt he was
struggling with his feelings about his father's sexual life.
He seemed to be saying that his father was sexually not a
very potent man. . . . He also recalls that he once found a
packet of condoms under his father's pillow when he was
an adolescent and he thought, "My father must be going to
prostitutes." I then intervened and pointed out that the
condoms under his father's pillow seemed to indicate more
obviously that his father used the condoms with his mother,
who slept in the same bed. However, Mr. N wanted to
believe his wish-fulfilling fantasy: mother doesn't want
sex with father and father is not very potent. The patient
was silent and the hour ended.*

As you may have already guessed, the therapist
concluded that Mr. N's difficulties were rooted in
an Oedipal complex (see Chapter 12). He had
unresolved sexual feelings toward his mother and
hostile feelings about his father. These unconscious conflicts, rooted in Mr. N's childhood, were
distorting his intimate relations as an adult.

Resistance

How would you expect Mr. N to respond to the
therapist's suggestion that he was in competition
with his father for the sexual attention of his
mother? Obviously, most clients would have great
difficulty accepting such an interpretation. Freud
fully expected clients to display some resistance to
therapeutic efforts. *Resistance* **refers to largely
unconscious defensive maneuvers intended to
hinder the progress of therapy.** Why would clients try to resist the helping process? Because they
don't want to face up to the painful, disturbing
conflicts that they have buried in their unconscious. Although they have sought help, they are
reluctant to confront their real problems.

Resistance can take many forms. Clients may
show up late for their sessions, may merely pretend to engage in free association, or may express

hostility toward their therapist. For instance, Mr. N's therapist noted that after the session just described, "The next day he [Mr. N] began by telling me that he was furious with me . . ." Analysts use a variety of strategies to deal with their clients' resistance. Often, a key consideration is the handling of transference, which we consider next.

Transference

Transference **occurs when clients unconsciously start relating to their therapist in ways that mimic critical relationships in their lives.** Thus, a client might start relating to a therapist as if the therapist were an overprotective mother, a rejecting brother, or a passive spouse. In a sense, the client *transfers* conflicting feelings about important people onto the therapist. For instance, in his treatment, Mr. N transferred some of the competitive hostility he felt toward his father onto his analyst.

Psychoanalysts often encourage transference so that clients can reenact relations with crucial people in the context of therapy. These reenactments can help bring repressed feelings and conflicts to the surface, allowing the client to work through them. The therapist's handling of transference is complicated and difficult, because transference may arouse confusing, highly charged emotions in the client.

Undergoing psychoanalysis is not easy. It can be a slow, painful process of self-examination that routinely requires three to five years of hard work. Ultimately, if resistance and transference can be handled effectively, the therapist's interpretations should lead the client to profound insights. For instance, Mr. N eventually admitted, "The old boy is probably right, it does tickle me to imagine that my mother preferred me and I could beat out my father. Later, I wondered whether this had something to do with my own screwed-up sex life with my wife." According to Freud, once clients recognize the unconscious sources of conflicts, they can resolve these conflicts and discard their neurotic defenses.

Modern Psychodynamic Therapies

Though still available, classical psychoanalysis as done by Freud is not widely practiced anymore. Freud's psychoanalytic method was geared to a particular kind of clientele that he was seeing in Vienna many years ago. As his followers fanned out across Europe and America, many found it necessary to adapt psychoanalysis to different cultures, changing times, and new kinds of patients. Thus, many variations on Freud's original approach

to psychoanalysis have developed over the years. These descendants of psychoanalysis are collectively known as *psychodynamic approaches* to therapy.

Some of these adaptations, such as those made by Carl Jung (1917) and Alfred Adler (1927), were sweeping revisions based on fundamental differences in theory. Other variations, such as those devised by Melanie Klein (1948) and Heinz Kohut (1971), made more subtle changes in theory. Still other revisions (Alexander, 1954; Stekel, 1950) simply involved efforts to modernize and streamline psychoanalytic techniques, rather than theory. Hence, today we have a rich diversity of psychodynamic approaches to therapy. Although these many variations are beyond the scope of our review, a few key trends seen in modern psychodynamic therapies are summarized in Table 15.1.

Client-Centered Therapy 11d

You may have heard of people going into therapy to "find themselves" or to "get in touch with their real feelings." These now-popular phrases emerged out of the human potential movement, which was stimulated in part by Carl Rogers's work (Rogers, 1951, 1986). Using a humanistic perspective, Rogers devised client-centered therapy (also known as person-centered therapy) in the 1940s and 1950s.

Client-centered therapy **is an insight therapy that emphasizes providing a supportive emotional climate for clients, who play a major role in determining the pace and direction of their therapy.** You may wonder why the troubled,

TABLE 15.1 SOME DIFFERENCES BETWEEN CLASSICAL AND MODERN PSYCHOANALYSIS

Classical Psychoanalysis	*Modern Psychoanalysis*
Frequency of treatment is usually four to five times a week.	Frequency of treatment is typically one to two times per week.
Patient is treated "on the couch."	Patient is typically seen "face to face."
Treatment goals emphasize character reconstruction.	Treatment emphasizes problem resolution, enhanced adaptation, and support of ego functions with limited character change.
Approach emphasized the neutrality and nonintrusion of the analyst.	Therapist assumes an active and directive stance.
Technique emphasizes free association, uncovering, interpretation, and analysis of the transference and resistance.	A wide range of interventions are used, including interpretative, supportive, and educative techniques. Transference is typically kept less intense.

Source: Adapted from Baker (1985)

Note: Baker divides contemporary psychodynamic therapies into three subgroups. "Modern psychoanalysis," profiled in the right column, refers to the group that has remained most loyal to Freud's ideas while modifying clinical techniques.

untrained client is put in charge of the pace and direction of the therapy. Rogers (1961) provides a compelling justification:

It is the client who knows what hurts, what directions to go, what problems are crucial, what experiences have been deeply buried. It began to occur to me that unless I had a need to demonstrate my own cleverness and learning, I would do better to rely upon the client for the direction of movement in the process. (pp. 11–12)

Rogers's theory about the principal causes of neurotic anxieties is quite different from the Freudian explanation. As discussed in Chapter 12, Rogers maintains that most personal distress is due to inconsistency, or "incongruence," between a person's self-concept and reality. According to his theory, incongruence makes people feel threatened by realistic feedback about themselves from others. For example, if you inaccurately viewed yourself as a hard-working, dependable person, you would feel threatened by contradictory feedback from friends or co-workers. According to Rogers, anxiety about such feedback often leads to reliance on defense mechanisms, to distortions of reality, and to stifled personal growth. Excessive incongruence is thought to be rooted in clients' overdependence on others for approval and acceptance.

Given Rogers's theory, client-centered therapists stalk insights that are quite different from the repressed conflicts that psychoanalysts go after. Client-centered therapists help clients to realize that they do not have to worry constantly about pleasing others and winning acceptance. They encourage clients to respect their own feelings and values. They help people restructure their self-concept to correspond better to reality. Ultimately, they try to foster self-acceptance and personal growth.

Therapeutic Climate

According to Rogers, the *process* of therapy is not as important as the emotional *climate* in which the therapy takes place. He believes that it is critical for the therapist to provide a warm, supportive, accepting climate. This creates a safe environment in which clients can confront their shortcomings without feeling threatened. The lack of threat should reduce clients' defensive tendencies and thus help them open up. To create this atmosphere of emotional support, client-centered therapists must provide three conditions:

1. *Genuineness.* The therapist must be genuine with the client, communicating honestly and spon-

taneously. The therapist should not be phony or defensive.

2. *Unconditional positive regard.* The therapist must also show complete, nonjudgmental acceptance of the client as a person. The therapist should provide warmth and caring for the client, with no strings attached. This does not mean that the therapist must approve of everything that the client says or does. A therapist can disapprove of a particular behavior while continuing to value the client as a human being.

3. *Empathy.* Finally, the therapist must provide accurate empathy for the client. This means that the therapist must understand the client's world from the client's point of view. Furthermore, the therapist must be articulate enough to communicate this understanding to the client.

Rogers firmly believed that a supportive emotional climate is the critical force promoting healthy changes in therapy. In recent years, however, some client-centered therapists have begun to place more emphasis on the therapeutic process (Rice & Greenberg, 1992).

Therapeutic Process

In client-centered therapy, the client and therapist work together as equals. The therapist provides relatively little guidance and keeps interpretation and advice to a minimum. So, just what does the client-centered therapist do, besides creating a supportive climate? Primarily, the therapist provides feedback to help clients sort out their feelings. The therapist's key task is *clarification.* Client-centered therapists try to function like a human mirror, reflecting statements back to their clients, but with enhanced clarity. They help clients become more aware of their true feelings by highlighting themes that may be obscure in the clients' rambling discourse. The reflective nature of client-centered therapy can be seen in the following exchange between a client and therapist:

CLIENT: *I really feel bad today . . . just terrible.*

THERAPIST: *You're feeling pretty bad.*

CLIENT: *Yeah, I'm angry and that's made me feel bad, especially when I can't do anything about it. I just have to live with it and shut up.*

THERAPIST: *You're very angry and feel like there's nothing you can safely do with your feelings.*

CLIENT: *Uh-huh. I mean . . . if I yell at my wife she gets hurt. If I don't say anything to her I feel tense.*

"To my mind, empathy is in itself a healing agent."

CARL ROGERS

THERAPIST: *You're between a rock and a hard place—no matter what you do, you'll wind up feeling bad.*

CLIENT: *I mean she chews ice all day and all night. I feel stupid saying this. It's petty, I know. But when I sit there and try to concentrate I hear all these slurping and crunching noises. I can't stand it . . . and I yell. She feels hurt—I feel bad—like I shouldn't have said anything.*

THERAPIST: *So when you finally say something you feel bad afterward.*

CLIENT: *Yeah, I can't say anything to her without getting mad and saying more than I should. And then I cause more trouble than it's worth.* (Duke & Nowicki, 1979, p. 565)

By working with clients to clarify their feelings, client-centered therapists hope to gradually build toward more far-reaching insights. In particular, they try to help clients better understand their interpersonal relationships and become more comfortable with their genuine selves. Obviously, these are ambitious goals. Client-centered therapy resembles psychoanalysis in that both seek to achieve a major reconstruction of a client's personality. We'll see more limited and specific goals in cognitive therapy, which we consider next.

Cognitive Therapy

In Chapter 13, we saw that people's cognitive interpretations of events make all the difference in the world in how well they handle stress. In Chapter 14, we learned that cognitive factors play a key role in the development of depressive disorders. Citing the importance of findings such as these, two former psychoanalysts—Aaron Beck (1976, 1987) and Albert Ellis (1973, 1989)—independently devised cognitive-oriented therapies that became highly influential (Arnkoff & Glass, 1992). Since we covered the main ideas underlying Ellis's *rational-emotive therapy* in our discussion of coping strategies (see the Application for Chapter 13), we'll focus on Beck's system of *cognitive therapy* here. **Cognitive therapy is an insight therapy that emphasizes recognizing and changing negative thoughts and maladaptive beliefs.**

In recent years cognitive therapy has been applied fruitfully to a wide range of disorders (Beck, 1991; Hollon & Beck, 1994), but it was originally devised as a treatment for depression. According to cognitive therapists, depression is caused by "errors" in thinking (see Table 15.2). They assert that depression-prone people tend to (1) blame their setbacks on personal inadequacies without considering circumstantial explanations, (2) focus

selectively on negative events while ignoring positive events, (3) make unduly pessimistic projections about the future, and (4) draw negative conclusions about their worth as a person based on insignificant events. For instance, imagine that you got a low grade on a minor quiz in a class. If you made the kinds of errors in thinking just described, you might blame the grade on your woeful stupidity, dismiss comments from a classmate that it was an unfair test, gloomily predict that you will surely flunk the course, and conclude that you are not genuine college material.

Goals and Techniques

The goal of cognitive therapy is to change the way clients think. To begin, clients are taught to detect their automatic negative thoughts. These are self-defeating statements that people are prone to make when analyzing problems. Examples might include "I'm just not smart enough," "No one really likes me," or "It's all my fault." Clients are then trained to subject these automatic thoughts to reality testing. The therapist helps them see how unrealistically negative the thoughts are.

The therapist's goal is not to promote unwarranted optimism but rather to help the client to use more reasonable standards of evaluation. For example, a cognitive therapist might point out that a client's failure to get a desired promotion at work may be attributable to many factors and that this setback doesn't mean that the client is

"Most people are barely aware of the automatic thoughts which precede unpleasant feelings or automatic inhibitions."

AARON BECK

TABLE 15.2 COGNITIVE ERRORS THAT PROMOTE DEPRESSION, ACCORDING TO BECK'S COGNITIVE THEORY

Cognitive Error	Description
Overgeneralizing	If it is true in one case, it applies to any case that is even slightly similar.
Selective abstraction	The only events that matter are failures, deprivation, and so on. I should measure myself by errors, weaknesses, etc.
Excessive responsibility (assuming personal causality)	I am responsible for all bad things, failures, and so on.
Assuming temporal causality (predicting without sufficient evidence)	If it has been true in the past, then it is always going to be true.
Self-references	I am the center of everyone's attention, especially when it comes to bad performances or personal attributes.
"Catastrophizing"	Always think of the worst. It is most likely to happen to you.
Dichotomous thinking	Everything is either one extreme or another (black or white: good or bad).

Source: Beck (1976)

incompetent. Gradually, the therapist digs deeper, looking for the unrealistic assumptions that underlie clients' constant negative thinking. These, too, have to be changed.

Unlike client-centered therapists, cognitive therapists are actively involved in determining the pace and direction of treatment. They usually talk extensively in the therapy sessions. They may argue openly with clients as they try to persuade them to alter their patterns of thinking. The assertive nature of cognitive therapy is apparent in the following exchange between a patient and a therapist:

THERAPIST: *What has your marriage been like?*

PATIENT: *It has been miserable from the very beginning . . . Raymond has always been unfaithful . . . I have hardly seen him in the past five years.*

THERAPIST: *You say that you can't be happy without Raymond . . . Have you found yourself happy when you are with Raymond?*

PATIENT: *No, we fight all the time and I feel worse.*

THERAPIST: *Then why do you feel that Raymond is essential for your living?*

PATIENT: *I guess it's because without Raymond I am nothing.*

THERAPIST: *Would you please repeat that?*

PATIENT: *Without Raymond I am nothing.*

THERAPIST: *What do you think of that idea?*

PATIENT: *. . . Well, now that I think about it, I guess it's not completely true.*

THERAPIST: *You said you are "nothing" without Raymond. Before you met Raymond, did you feel you were "nothing"?*

PATIENT: *No, I felt I was somebody.*

THERAPIST: *Are you saying then that it's possible to be something without Raymond?*

PATIENT: *I guess that's true. I can be something without Raymond.*

THERAPIST: *If you were somebody before you knew Raymond, why do you need him to be somebody now?*

PATIENT: *(puzzled) Hmmm . . . Well, I just don't think that I can find anybody else like him.*

THERAPIST: *Did you have male friends before you knew Raymond?*

PATIENT: *I was pretty popular then.*

THERAPIST: *If I understand you correctly then, you were*

able to fall in love before with other men and other men have fallen in love with you.

PATIENT: *Uh huh.*

THERAPIST: *Why do you think you will be unpopular without Raymond now?*

PATIENT: *Because I will not be able to attract any other man.*

THERAPIST: *Have any men shown an interest in you since you have been married?*

PATIENT: *A lot of men have made passes at me but I ignore them.*

THERAPIST: *If you were free of the marriage, do you think that men might be interested in you—knowing that you were available?*

PATIENT: *I guess that maybe they would be.*
(Beck et al., 1979, pp. 217–219)

Kinship with Behavior Therapy

Cognitive therapy borrows heavily from behavioral approaches to treatment, which we will discuss shortly. Specifically, cognitive therapists often use "homework assignments" that focus on changing clients' overt behaviors. Clients may be instructed to engage in overt responses on their own, outside of the clinician's office. For example, one shy, insecure young man in cognitive therapy was told to go to a singles bar and engage three different women in conversations for up to five minutes each (Rush, 1984). He was instructed to record his thoughts before and after each of the conversations. This assignment elicited various maladaptive patterns of thought that gave the young man and his therapist plenty to talk about in subsequent sessions. As this example illustrates, cognitive therapy is a creative blend of "talk therapy" and behavior therapy, although it is primarily an insight therapy.

Cognitive therapy was originally designed as a treatment for individuals. However, it has recently been adapted for use with groups (Covi & Primakoff, 1988). Most insight therapies can be conducted on either an individual or a group basis (Kaplan & Sadock, 1993), so let's take a look at the dynamics of group therapy.

Group Therapy

Although it dates back to the early part of the 20th century, group therapy came of age during World War II and its aftermath in the 1950s (Rosenbaum, Lakin, & Roback, 1992). During this period, the expanding demand for therapeutic services forced clinicians to use group techniques (Scheidlinger, 1993). *Group therapy* is the simultaneous treatment of several or more clients in a group. Most major insight therapies have been adapted for use with groups. In fact, the ideas underlying Rogers's client-centered therapy spawned the much-publicized encounter group movement. Although group therapy can be conducted in a variety of ways, we can provide a general overview of the process as it usually unfolds (see Vinogradov & Yalom, 1988; Yalom, 1995).

Participants' Roles

A therapy group typically consists of 4 to 15 people, with 8 participants regarded as an ideal number. The therapist usually screens the participants, excluding persons who seem likely to be disruptive. Some theorists maintain that judicious selection of participants is crucial to effective group treatment (Salvendy, 1993). There is some debate about whether or not it is best to have a homogeneous group, made up of people who are similar in age, sex, and psychological problem. Practical necessities usually dictate that groups are at least somewhat diversified.

In group therapy, participants essentially function as therapists for one another. Group members describe their problems, trade viewpoints, share experiences, and discuss coping strategies. Most important, they provide acceptance and emotional support for each other. In this supportive atmosphere, group members work at peeling away the social masks that cover their insecurities. Once their problems are exposed, members work at correcting them. As members come to value one another's opinions, they work hard to display healthy changes to win the group's approval.

In group treatment, the therapist's responsibilities include selecting participants, setting goals for the group, initiating and maintaining the therapeutic process, and protecting clients from harm (Weiner, 1993). The therapist often plays a relatively subtle role in group therapy, staying in the background and focusing mainly on promoting group cohesiveness. The therapist models supportive behaviors for the participants and tries to promote a healthy climate. He or she always retains a special status, but the therapist and clients are on much more equal footing in group therapy than in individual therapy. The leader in group therapy expresses emotions, shares feelings, and copes with challenges from group members. In other words, group therapists participate in the group's exchanges and bare their own souls.

Advantages of the Group Experience

Group therapies obviously save time and money, which can be critical in understaffed mental hospitals and other institutional settings. Therapists in private practice usually charge less for group than individual therapy, making therapy affordable for more people. However, group therapy is *not* just a less costly substitute for individual therapy. For many types of patients and problems, group therapy can be just as effective as individual treatment (Piper, 1993). Moreover, group therapy has unique strengths of its own (Yalom, 1995). For example, in group therapy, participants often come to realize that their misery is not unique. They are reassured to learn that many other people have similar or even worse problems. Another advantage is that group therapy provides an opportunity

Group treatments have proven particularly helpful when members share similar problems, such as alcoholism, overeating, or having been sexually abused as a child.

for participants to work on their social skills in a safe environment. Yet another advantage is that certain types of problems and clients respond especially well to the social support that group therapy can provide.

Whether insight therapies are conducted on a group basis or an individual basis, clients usually invest considerable time, effort, and money. Are these therapies worth the investment? Let's examine the evidence on their effectiveness.

Evaluating Insight Therapies

In 1952 Hans Eysenck shocked mental health professionals by reporting that there was no sound evidence that insight therapy actually helped people. What was the basis for this startling claim? Eysenck reviewed numerous studies of therapeutic outcome for clients suffering from what were then called neurotic disorders (mostly anxiety, somatoform, and mild depressive disorders in contemporary terminology). He found that about two-thirds of the clients recovered. A two-thirds recovery rate sounds reasonable, except that Eysenck found the same recovery rate among *untreated* neurotics. As we noted in Chapter 14, psychological disorders sometimes clear up on their own. A *spontaneous remission* is a recovery from a disorder that occurs without formal treatment. His estimate of the spontaneous remission rate for neurotic disorders led Eysenck to conclude that the therapeutic effects of insight therapy are small or nonexistent.

In the ensuing years, critics pounced on Eysenck's article looking for flaws (Jacobson & Christensen, 1996). They found a variety of shortcomings in his data. For instance, Eysenck used different time frames in comparing the recovery rates of treated and untreated individuals. The two-thirds recovery rate in the untreated groups was based on a *two-year* time period, whereas the two-thirds recovery rate for the treated groups occurred in a *two-month* time frame (Strupp & Howard, 1992). Moreover, the treated and untreated groups were not matched in terms of the severity of their disorders, their attitudes and expectations about therapy and recovery, or any other relevant variables that might influence therapeutic outcomes. Eysenck also made many arbitrary judgments about "recoveries" that were consistently unfavorable to the treated groups. After reexamining Eysenck's data, Bergin (1971) argued that the data really suggested that the spontaneous remission rate for neurotic problems was in the vicinity of 30% to 40%. Although Eysenck's conclusions were unduly pessimistic, he made an important contribution to the mental health field by sparking debate and research on the effectiveness of insight therapy.

Evaluating the effectiveness of any approach to psychotherapy is a complicated matter (Garfield, 1992; Howard et al., 1996). This is especially true for insight therapies. If you were to undergo insight therapy, how would you judge its effectiveness? By how you felt? By looking at your behavior? By asking your therapist? By consulting your friends and family? What would you be looking for? Various schools of thought pursue entirely different goals. Thus, measures of therapeutic outcome tend to be subjective, with little consensus about the best way to assess therapeutic progress (Lambert & Hill, 1994). Moreover, people enter therapy with diverse problems of varied severity, so the efficacy of treatment can only be evaluated meaningfully for specific clinical problems (Goldfried, Greenberg, & Marmar, 1990).

A key problem is that both therapists and clients are biased strongly in the direction of evaluating therapy favorably (Rachman & Wilson, 1980). Why? Therapists want to see improvement because it reflects on their professional competence. Obviously, they hope to see clients getting better as a result of their work. Clients are slanted toward a favorable evaluation because they want to justify their effort, their heartache, their expense, and their time.

In spite of these difficulties, hundreds of therapy outcome studies have been conducted since Eysenck prodded researchers into action. These studies have examined a broad range of specific clinical problems and used diverse methods to assess therapeutic outcomes, including scores on psychological tests and ratings by family members, as well as therapists' and clients' ratings. Although Eysenck (1993) remains skeptical, these studies consistently indicate that insight therapy *is* superior to no treatment or to placebo treatment and that the effects of therapy are reasonably durable (Barlow, 1996; Lambert & Bergin, 1994; Lipsey & Wilson, 1993). In one recent, widely discussed study that focused on patients' self-reports, the vast majority of the respondents subjectively felt that they had derived considerable benefit from their therapy (Seligman, 1995).

Admittedly, this outcome research does not indicate that insight therapy leads to miraculous results. The superiority of therapy over no treatment is usually characterized as modest. Moreover, when professional therapy is compared to paraprofessional interventions (mostly peer self-help groups), the differences in efficacy are often negligible (Christensen & Jacobson, 1994; Lambert & Bergin, 1994). Nonetheless, many studies suggest that insight therapies can be cost-effective interventions (Gabbard et al., 1997).

Recap of Key Points

• Insight therapies involve verbal interactions intended to enhance self-knowledge. Freudian approaches to therapy assume that neuroses originate from unresolved conflicts lurking in the unconscious. Therefore, in psychoanalysis free association and dream analysis are used to explore the unconscious.

• When an analyst's probing hits sensitive areas, resistance can be expected. The transference relationship may be used to overcome this resistance so that the client can handle interpretations that lead to insight.

• Classical psychoanalysis is not widely practiced anymore, but Freud's legacy lives on in a rich diversity of modern psychodynamic therapies.

• Rogers's client-centered therapy assumes that neurotic anxieties are derived from incongruence between a person's self-concept and reality. Accordingly, the client-centered therapist tries to provide a supportive climate in which clients can restructure their self-concept.

• Rogers asserts that a supportive climate requires genuineness, unconditonal positive regard, and empathy. The process of client-centered therapy emphasizes clarification of the client's feelings and self-acceptance.

• Beck's cognitive therapy concentrates on changing the way clients think about events in their lives. Cognitive therapists reeducate clients to detect and challenge automatic negative thoughts that cause depression and anxiety. Cognitive therapists also use behavioral techniques in efforts to alter clients' overt behaviors.

• Most theoretical approaches to insight therapy have been adapted for use with groups. Group therapists usually play a subtle role, staying in the background and working to promote group cohesiveness.

• Participants in group therapy essentially act as therapists for one another, exchanging insights and emotional support. Group therapy has unique advantages in comparison to individual therapy.

• Eysenck's work in the 1950s raised doubts about the effectiveness of insight therapy and stimulated research on its efficacy. Evaluating the effectiveness of any approach to therapy is complex and difficult, as it is hard for both therapists and clients to be objective. Nonetheless, the weight of modern evidence suggests that insight therapies are superior to no treatment or to placebo treatment.

BEHAVIOR THERAPIES

Behavior therapy is different from insight therapy in that behavior therapists make no attempt to help clients achieve grand insights about themselves. Why not? Because behavior therapists believe that such insights aren't necessary to produce constructive change. For example, consider a client troubled by compulsive gambling. The behavior therapist doesn't care whether this behavior is rooted in unconscious conflicts or parental rejection. What the client needs is to get rid of the maladaptive behavior. Consequently, the therapist simply designs a program to eliminate the compulsive gambling. Actually, behavior therapists may work with clients to attain some limited insights about how situational factors evoke troublesome behaviors (Franks & Barbrack, 1983). This information can be helpful in designing a behavior therapy program.

The crux of the difference between insight therapy and behavior therapy is this: Insight therapists treat pathological symptoms as signs of an underlying problem, whereas behavior therapists

think that the symptoms *are* the problem. Thus, **behavior therapies involve the application of learning principles to direct efforts to change clients' maladaptive behaviors.**

Behaviorism has been an influential school of thought in psychology since the 1920s. Nevertheless, behaviorists devoted little attention to clinical issues until the 1950s, when behavior therapy emerged out of three independent lines of research fostered by B. F. Skinner and his colleagues (Skinner, Solomon, & Lindsley, 1953) in the United States, Hans Eysenck (1959) and his colleagues in Britain, and Joseph Wolpe (1958) and his colleagues in South Africa (Glass & Arnkoff, 1992). Since then, there has been an explosion of interest in behavioral approaches to psychotherapy.

General Principles 11e

Behavior therapies are based on certain assumptions (Agras & Berkowitz, 1988). *First, it is assumed that behavior is a product of learning.* No matter how self-defeating or pathological a client's behavior

"Neurotic anxiety is nothing but a conditioned response."

JOSEPH WOLPE

might be, the behaviorist believes that it is the result of past learning and conditioning. *Second, it is assumed that what has been learned can be unlearned.* The same learning principles that explain how the maladaptive behavior was acquired can be used to get rid of it. Thus, behavior therapists attempt to change clients' behavior by applying the principles of classical conditioning, operant conditioning, and observational learning.

Behavior therapies are close cousins of the self-modification procedures described in the Chapter 6 Application. Both use the same principles of learning to alter behavior directly. In discussing *self-modification*, we examined some relatively simple procedures that people can apply to themselves to improve everyday self-control. In our discussion of *behavior therapy*, we will examine more complex procedures used by mental health professionals in the treatment of more severe problems.

Like self-modification, behavior therapy requires that clients' vague complaints ("My life is filled with frustration") be translated into concrete behavioral goals ("I need to learn assertive responses for dealing with colleagues"). Once the troublesome behaviors have been targeted, the therapist can design a program to alter these behaviors. The nature of the therapeutic program will depend on the types of problems identified. Specific procedures are designed for specific types of problems, as you'll see in our discussion of systematic desensitization.

Systematic Desensitization 11e

Devised by Joseph Wolpe (1958), systematic desensitization revolutionized psychotherapy by giving therapists their first useful alternative to traditional "talk therapy" (Fishman & Franks, 1992). *Systematic desensitization* **is a behavior therapy used to reduce phobic clients' anxiety responses through counterconditioning.** The treatment assumes that most anxiety responses are acquired through classical conditioning (as we discussed in Chapter 14). According to this model, a harmless stimulus (for instance, a bridge) may be paired with a fear-arousing event (lightning striking it), so that it becomes a conditioned stimulus eliciting anxiety. The goal of systematic desensitization is to weaken the association between the conditioned stimulus (the bridge) and the conditioned response (anxiety). Systematic desensitization involves three steps.

First, the therapist helps the client build an anxiety hierarchy. The hierarchy is a list of anxiety-arousing stimuli related to the specific source of anxiety, such as flying, academic tests, or snakes. The client ranks the stimuli from the least anxiety arousing to the most anxiety arousing. This ordered list of stimuli is the *anxiety hierarchy*. An example of an anxiety hierarchy for one woman's fear of heights is shown in Figure 15.5.

The second step involves training the client in deep muscle relaxation. This second phase may begin during early sessions while the therapist and cli-

Figure 15.5
Example of an anxiety hierarchy. Systematic desensitization requires the construction of an anxiety hierarchy like the one shown here, which was developed for a woman who had a fear of heights but wanted to go hiking in the mountains.

An anxiety hierarchy for systematic desensitization	
Degree of fear	
5	I'm standing on the balcony of the top floor of an apartment tower.
10	I'm standing on a stepladder in the kitchen to change a light bulb.
15	I'm walking on a ridge. The edge is hidden by shrubs and treetops.
20	I'm sitting on the slope of a mountain, looking out over the horizon.
25	I'm crossing a bridge 6 feet above a creek. The bridge consists of an 18-inch-wide board with a handrail on one side.
30	I'm riding a ski lift 8 feet above the ground.
35	I'm crossing a shallow, wide creek on an 18-inch-wide board, 3 feet above water level.
40	I'm climbing a ladder outside the house to reach a second-story window.
45	I'm pulling myself up a 30-degree wet, slippery slope on a steel cable.
50	I'm scrambling up a rock, 8 feet high.
55	I'm walking 10 feet on a resilient, 18-inch-wide board, which spans an 8-foot-deep gulch.
60	I'm walking on a wide plateau, 2 feet from the edge of a cliff.
65	I'm skiing an intermediate hill. The snow is packed.
70	I'm walking over a railway trestle.
75	I'm walking on the side of an embankment. The path slopes to the outside.
80	I'm riding a chair lift 15 feet above the ground.
85	I'm walking up a long, steep slope.
90	I'm walking up (or down) a 15-degree slope on a 3-foot-wide trail. On one side of the trail the terrain drops down sharply; on the other side is a steep upward slope.
95	I'm walking on a 3-foot-wide ridge. The slopes on both sides are long and more than 25 degrees steep.
100	I'm walking on a 3-foot-wide ridge. The trail slopes on one side. The drop on either side of the trail is more than 25 degrees.

ent are still constructing the anxiety hierarchy. Various therapists use different relaxation training procedures. Whatever procedures are used, the client must learn to engage in deep, thorough relaxation on command from the therapist.

In the third step, the client tries to work through the hierarchy, learning to remain relaxed while imagining each stimulus. Starting with the least anxiety-arousing stimulus, the client imagines the situation as vividly as possible while relaxing. If the client experiences strong anxiety, he or she drops the imaginary scene and concentrates on relaxation. The client keeps repeating this process until he or she can imagine a scene with little or no anxiety. Once a particular scene is conquered, the client moves on to the next stimulus situation in the anxiety hierarchy. Gradually, over a number of therapy sessions, the client progresses through the hierarchy, unlearning troublesome anxiety responses.

As clients conquer *imagined* phobic stimuli, they may be encouraged to confront the *real* stimuli. Although desensitization to imagined stimuli *can* be effective by itself, contemporary behavior therapists usually follow it up with direct exposures to the real anxiety-arousing stimuli (Emmelkamp & Scholing, 1990). Indeed, behavioral interventions emphasizing direct exposures to anxiety-arousing situations have become behavior therapists' treatment of choice for phobic and other anxiety disorders (Goldfried et al., 1990). Usually, these real-life confrontations prove harmless and individuals' anxiety responses decline.

According to Wolpe (1958, 1990), the principle at work in systematic desensitization is simple. Anxiety and relaxation are incompatible responses. The trick is to recondition people so that the conditioned stimulus elicits relaxation instead of anxiety. This is *counterconditioning*—an attempt to reverse the process of classical conditioning by associating the crucial stimulus with a new conditioned response. Although Wolpe's explanation of how systematic desensitization works has been questioned, the technique's effectiveness in eliminating specific anxieties has been well documented (Spiegler & Guevremont, 1993; G. T. Wilson, 1990).

Aversion Therapy 11e

Aversion therapy is far and away the most controversial of the behavior therapies. It's not something that you would sign up for unless you were pretty desperate. Psychologists usually suggest it only as a treatment of last resort, after other interventions have failed. What's so terrible about aver-

sion therapy? The client has to endure decidedly unpleasant stimuli, such as shocks or drug-induced nausea.

Aversion therapy **is a behavior therapy in which an aversive stimulus is paired with a stimulus that elicits an undesirable response.** For example, alcoholics have had an *emetic drug* (one that causes nausea and vomiting) paired with their favorite drinks during therapy sessions (Nathan, 1993). By pairing the drug with alcohol, the therapist hopes to create a conditioned aversion to alcohol (see Figure 15.6).

Aversion therapy takes advantage of the automatic nature of responses produced through classical conditioning. Admittedly, alcoholics treated with aversion therapy know that they won't be given an emetic outside of their therapy sessions. However, their reflex response to the stimulus of alcohol may be changed so they respond to it with nausea and distaste (remember the "sauce béarnaise syndrome" described in Chapter 6?). Obviously, this response should make it much easier to resist the urge to drink.

Troublesome behaviors eliminated successfully with aversion therapy have included drug abuse, sexual deviance, gambling, shoplifting, stuttering, cigarette smoking, and overeating (Sandler, 1975;

Figure 15.6
Aversion therapy. Aversion therapy uses classical conditioning to create an aversion to a stimulus that has elicited problematic behavior. For example, in the treatment of drinking problems, alcohol may be paired with a nausea-inducing drug to create an aversion to drinking.

Wolpe, 1990). Typically, aversion therapy is only one element in a larger treatment program. Of course, this procedure should be used only with willing clients when other options have failed (Rimm & Cunningham, 1985).

Social Skills Training

Many psychological problems grow out of interpersonal difficulties. Behavior therapists point out that people are not born with social finesse—they acquire social skills through learning. Unfortunately, some people have not learned how to be friendly, how to make conversation, how to express anger appropriately, and so forth. Social ineptitude can contribute to anxiety, feelings of inferiority, and various kinds of disorders. In light of these findings, therapists are increasingly using social skills training in efforts to improve clients' social abilities (Liberman, Mueser, & DeRisi, 1989). This approach to therapy has yielded promising results in the treatment of depression, shyness, social anxiety, and even schizophrenia (Becker, 1990; Penn & Mueser, 1996; Wixted, Bellack, & Hersen, 1990).

Social skills training **is a behavior therapy designed to improve interpersonal skills that emphasizes modeling, behavioral rehearsal, and shaping.** This type of behavior therapy can be conducted with individual clients or in groups. Social skills training depends on the principles of operant conditioning and observational learning.

With *modeling*, the client is encouraged to watch socially skilled friends and colleagues in order to acquire appropriate responses (eye contact, active listening, and so on) through observation. In *behavioral rehearsal*, the client tries to practice social techniques in structured role-playing exercises. The therapist provides corrective feedback and uses approval to reinforce progress. Eventually, of course, clients try their newly acquired skills in real-world interactions. Usually, they are given specific homework assignments. *Shaping* is used in that clients are gradually asked to handle more complicated and delicate social situations. For example, a nonassertive client may begin by working on making requests of friends. Only much later will he be asked to tackle standing up to his boss at work.

Biofeedback

Biofeedback is another widely used therapy that has emerged from the behavioral tradition. **In *biofeedback* a bodily function (such as heart rate) is monitored, and information about the func-**
tion is fed back to the person to facilitate improved control of the physiological process. Armed with precise information about internal bodily functions, people are able to exert far more control over some of them than was previously thought possible.

To see how biofeedback works, let's look at *electromyograph (EMG)* feedback intended to enhance relaxation. An EMG is a device used to measure skeletal-muscular tension in the body. In a typical training session, a client is hooked up to an EMG and its recordings are transformed into an auditory signal. Usually, the signal is a tone that increases and decreases in volume. The therapist explains to the client that changes in the tone will reflect changes in his or her level of muscular tension. The client is instructed to raise or lower the tone.

Although people often have difficulty describing how they do it, most can learn to exert better control over their level of muscular tension. Essentially, EMG feedback helps them improve their ability to engage in deep muscle relaxation. Promising results have been obtained with EMG feedback in the treatment of anxiety (Öst, 1990), tension and migraine headaches (Blanchard, 1994), and high blood pressure (Olson & Kroon, 1987).

In some respects, biofeedback is a *biological* intervention and it could be classified as a biomedical therapy. However, it is usually grouped with the behavior therapies because its use is not limited to physicians and because the strategy emerged out of behavioral research. Studies have revealed that biofeedback can help people exert some control over brain-wave activity, skin temperature, blood pressure, heart rate, and muscle tension (Adler & Adler, 1984). Early proponents of biofeedback may have gotten carried away in making overly extravagant claims about its benefits. Nonetheless, this unique intervention appears to have potential for treating many stress-related problems.

Evaluating Behavior Therapies

Behavior therapists have historically placed more emphasis on the importance of measuring therapeutic outcomes than insight therapists have. Hence, there is ample evidence attesting to the effectiveness of behavior therapy (Liberman & Bedell, 1989; Rachman & Wilson, 1980). How does the effectiveness of behavior therapy compare to that of insight therapy? In direct comparisons, the differences are usually small. However, these modest differences tend to favor behavioral approaches for certain types of disorders (Lambert & Bergin,

1992). Of course, behavior therapies are not well suited to the treatment of some types of problems (vague feelings of discontent, for instance). Furthermore, it's misleading to make global statements about the effectiveness of behavior therapies, because they include many procedures designed for different purposes. For example, the value of systematic desensitization for phobias has no bearing on the value of aversion therapy for sexual deviance.

For our purposes, it is sufficient to note that there is favorable evidence on the efficacy of most of the widely used behavioral interventions. Behavior therapies can make important contributions to the treatment of phobias, obsessive-compulsive disorders, sexual dysfunction, schizophrenia, drug-related problems, eating disorders, psychosomatic disorders, hyperactivity, autism, and mental retardation (Emmelkamp, 1994; Liberman & Bedell, 1989).

Many of these problems would not be amenable to treatment with the biomedical therapies, which we consider next. To some extent, the three major approaches to treatment have different strengths. Let's see where the strengths of the biomedical therapies lie.

Recap of Key Points

• Behavior therapies use the principles of learning in direct efforts to change specific aspects of behavior. Wolpe's systematic desensitization, a treatment for phobias, involves the construction of an anxiety hierarchy, relaxation training, and step-by-step movement through the hierarchy, pairing relaxation with each phobic stimulus.

• In aversion therapy, a stimulus associated with an unwanted response is paired with an unpleasant stimulus in an effort to eliminate the maladaptive response. Social skills training can improve clients' interpersonal skills through shaping, modeling, and behavioral rehearsal.

• Biofeedback involves providing information about bodily functions to a person so that he or she can attempt to exert some control over those physiological processes. There is ample evidence that behavior therapies are effective in the treatment of a wide variety of disorders.

BIOMEDICAL THERAPIES

In the 1950s, a French surgeon looking for a drug that would reduce patients' autonomic response to surgical stress noticed that chlorpromazine produced a mild sedation. Based on this observation, Delay and Deniker (1952) decided to give chlorpromazine to hospitalized schizophrenic patients. They wanted to see whether the drug would have calming effects. Their experiment was a dramatic success. Chlorpromazine became the first effective antipsychotic drug, and a revolution in psychiatry was begun. Hundreds of thousands of severely disturbed patients who had appeared doomed to spend the remainder of their lives in mental hospitals were gradually sent home, thanks to the therapeutic effects of antipsychotic drugs. Today, biomedical therapies such as drug treatment lie at the core of psychiatric practice.

Biomedical therapies are physiological interventions intended to reduce symptoms associated with psychological disorders. These therapies assume that psychological disorders are caused, at least in part, by biological malfunctions. As we discussed in the previous chapter, this assumption clearly has merit for many disorders, especially the more severe ones. We will discuss two biomedical approaches to psychotherapy: drug therapy and electroconvulsive (shock) therapy.

Treatment with Drugs 11e

Psychopharmacotherapy involves the treatment of mental disorders with medication. We will refer to this kind of treatment more simply as *drug therapy*. Therapeutic drugs for psychological problems fall into three major groups: (1) antianxiety

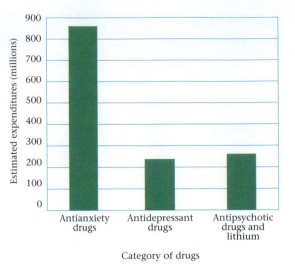

Figure 15.7
Expenditures on drugs used in the treatment of psychological problems and disorders. Hundreds of millions of dollars are spent on psychopharmaco-therapy in the United States each year. Of the three categories of therapeutic drugs, the antianxiety drugs are the most frequently prescribed, as these data on outpatient expenditures reflect. (Data based on Zorc et al., 1991)

drugs, (2) antipsychotic drugs, and (3) antidepressant drugs. Another important drug that does not fit neatly into any of these categories is lithium, which is used in the treatment of bipolar mood disorders. Of these drugs, the antianxiety agents are the most widely prescribed (see Figure 15.7). Surprisingly, only about 17% of the prescriptions for drugs used in the treatment of psychological problems are written by psychiatrists (Beardsley et al., 1988). The vast majority of these prescriptions are written by primary care physicians.

Antianxiety Drugs

Most of us know someone who pops pills to relieve anxiety. The drugs involved in this common coping strategy are *antianxiety drugs,* **which relieve tension, apprehension, and nervousness.**

TABLE 15.3 SIDE EFFECTS OF XANAX AND VALIUM

Side Effects	Patients Experiencing Side Effects (%)	
	Xanax	Valium
Drowsiness	36.0	49.4
Lightheadedness	18.6	24.0
Dry mouth	14.9	13.0
Depression	11.9	17.0
Nausea, vomiting	9.3	10.0
Constipation	9.3	11.3
Insomnia	9.0	6.7
Confusion	9.3	14.1
Diarrhea	8.5	10.5
Tachycardia, palpitations	8.1	7.2
Nasal congestion	8.1	7.2
Blurred vision	7.0	9.1

Source: Evans (1981)

The most popular of these drugs are Valium and Xanax. These are the trade names (the proprietary names that pharmaceutical companies use in marketing drugs) for diazepam and alprazolam, respectively.

Valium, Xanax, and other drugs in the *benzodiazepine* family are often called *tranquilizers.* These drugs exert their effects almost immediately, and they can be fairly effective in alleviating feelings of anxiety (Ballenger, 1995). However, their effects are measured in hours, so their impact is relatively short-lived. Antianxiety drugs are routinely prescribed for people with anxiety disorders, but they are also given to millions of people who simply suffer from chronic nervous tension. In the mid-1970s, pharmacists in the United States were filling nearly *100 million* prescriptions each year for Valium and similar antianxiety drugs. Many critics characterized this level of use as excessive (Lickey & Gordon, 1991).

All the drugs used to treat psychological problems have potentially troublesome side effects that show up in some patients but not others. The antianxiety drugs are no exception. The most common side effects of Valium and Xanax are listed in Table 15.3. Some of these side effects—such as drowsiness, depression, nausea, and confusion—present serious problems for some patients. There is also some potential for abuse, drug dependence, and overdoses with these drugs (Taylor, 1995). Another drawback is that patients who have been on antianxiety drugs for a while often experience withdrawal symptoms when their drug treatment is stopped (Lader, 1990). These problems led to a moderate decline in the prescription of Valium and similar drugs in the 1980s.

Currently, clinicians and researchers are experimenting with a newer antianxiety drug called Buspar (buspirone) that does not belong to the benzodiazepine family. It appears to have little potential for abuse or dependence (Cole & Yonkers, 1995). Unlike Valium, Buspar is slow acting, exerting its effects in one to three weeks, but with fewer sedative side effects (Norman & Burrows, 1990).

Antipsychotic Drugs

Antipsychotic drugs are used primarily in the treatment of schizophrenia. They are also given to people with severe mood disorders who become delusional. The trade names (and generic names) of some prominent drugs in this category are Thorazine (chlorpromazine), Mellaril (thioridazine), and Haldol (haloperidol). *Antipsychotic* **drugs are used to gradually reduce psychotic** symptoms, including hyperactivity, mental confusion, hallucinations, and delusions. These drugs appear to decrease activity at dopamine synapses, although the exact relationship between their neurochemical effects and their clinical effects remains obscure (Marder & Van Putten, 1995).

Studies suggest that about 70%–90% of psychotic patients respond favorably (albeit in varied degrees) to antipsychotic medication (Buckley & Meltzer, 1995). When antipsychotic drugs are effective, they work their magic gradually, as shown in Figure 15.8. Patients usually begin to respond within two days to a week. Further improvement may occur for several months. Many schizophrenic patients are placed on antipsychotics indefinitely because these drugs can reduce the likelihood of a relapse into an active schizophrenic episode.

Antipsychotic drugs undeniably make a huge contribution to the treatment of severe mental disorders, but they are not without problems. They have many unpleasant side effects (Lader & Herrington, 1990). Drowsiness, constipation, and cotton mouth are common. The drugs may also produce effects that resemble the symptoms of Parkinson's disease, including muscle tremors, muscular rigidity, and impaired motor coordination. After being released from a hospital, many schizophrenic patients, supposedly placed on antipsychotics indefinitely, discontinue their drug regimen because of the disagreeable side effects. Unfortunately, relapse into another schizophrenic episode occurs in about two-thirds of patients after they stop taking antipsychotic medication (Marder & Van Putten, 1995).

In addition to minor side effects, antipsychotics may cause a more severe and lasting problem called *tardive dyskinesia*. **Tardive dyskinesia is a neurological disorder marked by involuntary writhing and ticlike movements of the mouth, tongue, face, hands, or feet.** Once this debilitating syndrome is established, there is no cure, although spontaneous remission is possible (Gardos et al., 1994). There has been a heated debate about how often this serious side effect occurs as a result of antipsychotic drug therapy (Brown & Funk, 1986). The evidence suggests that it occurs in fewer than 20% of patients who take antipsychotics over a prolonged period (Khot & Wyatt, 1991). As the prevalence of this problem has come to be recognized, many experts have urged psychiatrists to be more conservative about prescribing antipsychotic drugs on a long-term basis, but reliance on antipsychotics has remained stable because of the lack of effective alternatives (Cohen & McCubbin, 1990).

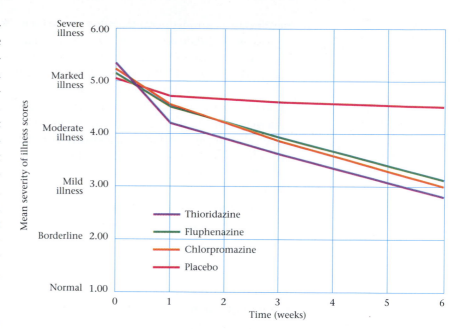

A new antipsychotic drug called Clozaril (clozapine) was introduced in 1990. Its mechanisms of action are not well understood, but it appears to exert its effects at certain subtypes of dopamine receptors and serotonin receptors (Owens & Risch, 1995). Although it's not risk-free, it seems to produce fewer side effects than traditional antipsychotics. Clozaril appears to be effective with the full range of schizophrenic patients (Breier et al., 1994). However, its main claim to fame is that it helps a significant portion of the patients who do not respond to traditional antipsychotics and the patients who have severe problems with the side effects of older antipsychotics (Carpenter et al., 1995). Unfortunately, the cost of Clozaril therapy is extremely expensive, running about $5000 per year for each patient (Jann, Jenike, & Lieberman, 1994).

Antidepressant Drugs

As their name suggests, *antidepressant drugs* **gradually elevate mood and help bring people out of a depression.** Until recently, there were two principal classes of antidepressants: *tricyclics* (such as Elavil) and *MAO inhibitors* (such as Nardil). These two sets of drugs affect neurochemical activity in different ways and tend to work with different patients. Overall, they are beneficial for about 80% of depressed patients (Potter, Manji, & Rudorfer, 1995). The tricyclics have fewer problematic side effects than the MAO inhibitors (Charney et al., 1995). Like antipsychotic drugs, antidepressants exert their effects gradually over a period of weeks.

Psychiatrists are currently enthusiastic about a

Figure 15.8
The time course of antipsychotic drug effects. Antipsychotic drugs reduce psychotic symptoms gradually, over a span of weeks, as graphed here. In contrast, patients given placebo pills show little improvement. (Data from Cole, Goldberg, & Davis, 1966; Davis, 1985)

newer class of antidepressants, called *selective serotonin reuptake inhibitors,* which slow the reuptake process at serotonin synapses. The drugs in this class, which include Prozac (fluoxetine), Paxil (paroxetine), and Zoloft (sertraline), seem to yield rapid therapeutic gains in the treatment of depression (Jann et al., 1994). Prozac also appears to have value in the treatment of obsessive-compulsive disorders (Hollander & Wong, 1995). However, Prozac is not a "miracle drug," as suggested by some popular magazines. Like all drugs for psychological disorders, Prozac has side effects and risks that must be carefully weighed against its benefits (Tollefson, 1995).

Lithium

Lithium **is a chemical used to control mood swings in patients with bipolar mood disorders.** Lithium can help to prevent *future* episodes of both mania and depression in patients with bipolar illness (Bowden, 1995). Lithium can also be used in efforts to bring patients with bipolar illness out of *current* manic or depressive episodes. However, antipsychotics and antidepressants are more frequently used for these purposes. On the negative side of the ledger, lithium does have some dangerous side effects if its use isn't managed skillfully (Lenox & Manji, 1995). Lithium levels in the patient's blood must be monitored carefully because high concentrations can be highly toxic and even fatal. Kidney and thyroid gland complications are the major problems associated with lithium therapy (Post, 1989).

Evaluating Drug Therapies

Drug therapies can produce clear therapeutic gains for many kinds of patients. What's especially impressive is that they can be effective with disorders that otherwise defy therapeutic endeavors. Nonetheless, drug therapies are controversial. Critics of drug therapy have raised a number of issues, including the following (Breggin, 1990, 1991; Cohen & McCubbin, 1990; Lickey & Gordon, 1991). First, some critics argue that drug therapies often produce superficial curative effects. For example, Valium does not really solve problems with anxiety; it merely provides temporary relief from an unpleasant symptom. Moreover, this temporary relief may lull patients into complacency about their problem and prevent them from working toward a more lasting solution. Second, critics charge that many drugs are overprescribed and many patients overmedicated. According to these critics, a number of physicians routinely hand out prescriptions without giving adequate consideration to more complicated and difficult interventions. This problem is compounded by the fact that drugs calm patients and make it easier for hospital staff to run their wards. Thus, critics argue that there is a tendency in some institutions to overmedicate patients to minimize disruptive behavior. Third, some critics, especially Peter Breggin (1990, 1991), charge that the damaging side effects of therapeutic drugs are underestimated by psychiatrists and that these side effects are often worse than the illnesses that the drugs are supposed to cure. Citing problems such as tardive dyskinesia, lithium toxicity, addiction to antianxiety agents, and so forth, these critics argue that the risks of therapeutic drugs aren't worth the benefits.

In their relatively even-handed evaluation of psychiatric drugs, Lickey and Gordon (1991) acknowledge that the issues raised by the critics of drug therapy are legitimate sources of concern, but after reviewing the evidence they defend the value of therapeutic drugs. They argue that drug therapies were never touted as *cures* and that "the relief of symptoms is a genuine benefit that must not be dismissed as trivial" (p. 358). They agree that some drugs are overprescribed and that most drugs have potentially serious side effects, but they conclude that overall, the benefits of drug therapy far exceed any harm done.

Obviously, drug therapies have stirred up some debate. However, this controversy pales in comparison to the furious debates inspired by electroconvulsive (shock) therapy (ECT). ECT is so controversial that the residents of Berkeley, California, voted in 1982 to outlaw ECT in their city. However, in subsequent lawsuits, the courts ruled that scientific questions cannot be settled through a vote, and they overturned the law. What makes ECT so controversial? You'll see in the next section.

Electroconvulsive Therapy (ECT)

In the 1930s, a Hungarian psychiatrist named Ladislas von Meduna speculated that epilepsy and schizophrenia could not coexist in the same body. On the basis of this observation, which turned out to be inaccurate, von Meduna theorized that it might be useful to induce epileptic-like seizures in schizophrenic patients. Initially, a drug was used to trigger these seizures. However, by 1938 a pair of Italian psychiatrists (Cerletti & Bini, 1938) demonstrated that it was safer to elicit the seizures with electric shock. Thus, modern electroconvulsive therapy was born.

Electroconvulsive therapy (ECT) is a biomedical treatment in which electric shock is used to produce a cortical seizure accompanied by convulsions. In ECT, electrodes are attached to the skull over the temporal lobes of the brain (see photo). A light anesthesia is induced, and the patient is given a variety of drugs to minimize the likelihood of complications, such as spinal fractures. An electric current is then applied either to the right side or to both sides of the brain for about a second. Unilateral shock delivered to the right hemisphere is the preferred method of treatment today (Abrams, 1993). The current triggers a brief (about 30 seconds) convulsive seizure, during which the patient usually loses consciousness. The patient normally awakens in an hour or two and manifests some confusion, disorientation, and nausea, which usually clear up in a matter of hours. People typically receive between 6 and 20 treatments as inpatients at a hospital (Fink, 1992).

The clinical use of ECT peaked in the 1940s and 1950s, before effective drug therapies were widely available. ECT has long been controversial, and its use did decline in the 1960s and 1970s. Nonetheless, there has been a recent resurgence in the use of ECT, and it is *not* a rare form of therapy. Estimates suggest that about 100,000 people receive ECT treatments yearly in the United States (Hermann et al., 1995). Some critics argue that ECT is overused because it is a lucrative procedure that boosts psychiatrists' income while consuming relatively little of their time in comparison to insight therapy (Frank, 1990).

Controversy about ECT is also fueled by patients' reports that the treatment is painful, dehumanizing, and terrifying. Additional concerns have been raised by allegations that staff members at some hospitals have used the threat of ECT to keep patients in line (Breggin, 1979). Although improvements in the administration of ECT have made it less disagreeable than it once was, many patients continue to report that they find the treatment extremely aversive (Breggin, 1991).

Effectiveness of ECT

The evidence on the therapeutic efficacy of ECT is open to varied interpretations. Proponents of ECT maintain that it is a remarkably effective treatment (Abrams, 1992; Fink, 1992; Swartz, 1993). However, opponents of ECT argue that it is no more effective than a placebo (Breggin, 1991; Friedberg, 1976). Reported improvement rates for ECT treatment range from negligible to very high (Small, Small, & Milstein, 1986). The findings on

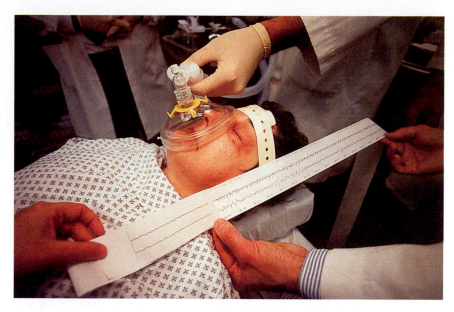

This patient has just received electroconvulsive therapy (ECT). In ECT an electric shock is used to elicit a brief cortical seizure. The shock is delivered through electrodes attached to the patient's skull.

relapse rates after treatment are also inconsistent (Frank, 1990; Weiner, 1984).

In light of these problems, conclusions about the value of ECT must be tentative. Although ECT was once considered appropriate for a wide range of disorders, in recent decades it has primarily been recommended for the treatment of depression. Accumulating evidence suggests that it may also have value for manic patients (Mukherjee, Sackeim, & Schnur, 1994). Overall, there does seem to be enough favorable evidence to justify *conservative* use of ECT in treating severe mood disorders in patients who have not responded to medication (Rudorfer & Goodwin, 1993; Weiner & Coffey, 1988).

Curiously, to the extent that ECT may be effective, no one is sure why. The discarded theories about how ECT works could fill several books. Until recently, it was widely accepted that the occurrence of a cortical seizure was critical to the treatment. However, this once firm conclusion is now being questioned by some theorists (Sackeim, 1988). Today, many ECT advocates theorize that the treatment must affect neurotransmitter activity in the brain. However, the evidence supporting this view is fragmentary, inconsistent, and inconclusive (Abrams, 1992; Kapur & Mann, 1993). ECT opponents have a radically different, albeit equally unproven, explanation for why ECT might appear to be effective: They maintain that some patients find ECT so utterly terrifying that they muster all their will power to climb out of their depression to avoid further ECT treatments.

The debate about whether ECT works, and how it works, does *not* make ECT unique among approaches to psychotherapy. Controversies exist

CONCEPT CHECK 15.4
Understanding Biomedical Therapies

Check your understanding of biomedical therapies by matching each treatment with its chief use. The answers are in Appendix A.

Treatment

_____ 1. Antianxiety drugs

_____ 2. Antipsychotic drugs

_____ 3. Antidepressant drugs

_____ 4. Lithium

_____ 5. Electroconvulsive therapy (ECT)

Chief purpose

a. To reduce psychotic symptoms

b. To bring a major depression to an end

c. To suppress tension, nervousness, and apprehension

d. To prevent future episodes of mania or depression in bipolar disorders

regarding the effectiveness of many psychotherapies. However, this controversy is especially problematic because ECT may carry substantial risks.

Risks Associated with ECT

Even ECT proponents acknowledge that memory losses, impaired attention, and other cognitive deficits are common short-term side effects of electroconvulsive therapy (Sobin et al., 1995). However, ECT proponents assert that these deficits are mild and usually disappear within six months (Calev et al., 1993). In contrast, ECT critics maintain that these cognitive losses are significant and often permanent (Breggin, 1991; Frank, 1990). The physiological bases of these cognitive deficits are not well understood, but the evidence indicates that ECT does not cause any structural damage in the brain (Devanand et al., 1994).

So, what can be concluded about ECT and cog-nitive deficits? The truth probably lies somewhere in between the positions staked out by the proponents and opponents of ECT. In a relatively dispassionate review of the ECT controversy, Small and associates (1986) asserted that "there is little doubt that ECT produces both short- and long-term intellectual impairment." However, they concluded that this impairment isn't inevitable and that it isn't permanent in the vast majority of cases. Nonetheless, given the concerns about the risks of ECT and the doubts about its efficacy, it appears that the use of ECT will remain controversial for some time to come.

Recap of Key Points

• Biomedical therapies are physiological interventions for psychological problems. A great variety of disorders are treated with drugs. Antianxiety drugs, such as Valium and Xanax, are used to relieve excessive apprehension.

• Antipsychotic drugs are used primarily in the treatment of schizophrenia. Antidepressants are used to bring people out of episodes of depression. Bipolar mood disorders are mainly treated with lithium.

• Drug therapies can be quite effective, but they have their drawbacks. All of the drugs produce problematic side effects, and some of these side effects (such as tardive dyskinesia) can be troublesome. Some critics maintain that drugs' curative effects are superficial and that some drugs are overprescribed.

• Electroconvulsive therapy (ECT) is used to trigger a cortical seizure that is believed to have therapeutic value for mood disorders, especially depression. There is contradictory evidence about the effectiveness of ECT.

• Overall, the evidence seems sufficient to justify conservative use of ECT, although its mechanism of action remains mysterious and there are some concerns about cognitive side effects.

BLENDING APPROACHES TO THERAPY

In this chapter we have reviewed many approaches to therapy. However, there is no law that a client must be treated with just one approach. Often, a clinician will use several techniques in working with a client. For example, a depressed person might receive cognitive therapy (an insight therapy), social skills training (a behavior therapy), and antidepressant medication (a biomedical therapy). Multiple approaches are particularly likely when a treatment *team* provides therapy.

Studies suggest that combining approaches to treatment has merit (Frank, 1991; Klerman et al., 1994). One representative study compared the value of cognitive-behavior therapy alone, drug therapy alone, and a combination of cognitive-behavior therapy and drug therapy for patients with generalized anxiety disorder (Power et al., 1990). As you can see in Figure 15.9, the greatest improvement was found in the group treated with both approaches to therapy. Thus, there is much to be said for combining approaches to treatment.

The value of multiple approaches may explain why a significant trend seems to have crept into the field of psychotherapy: a movement away from strong loyalty to individual schools of thought and a corresponding move toward integrating various approaches to therapy (Arkowitz, 1992; Norcross & Goldfried, 1992). Most clinicians used to depend exclusively on one system of therapy while rejecting the utility of all others. This era of fragmentation may be drawing to a close. In recent surveys of psychologists' theoretical orientations, researchers have been surprised to find that the greatest proportion of respondents describe themselves as *eclectic* in approach (Garfield & Bergin, 1994) (see Figure 15.10).

Eclecticism in the practice of therapy involves drawing ideas from two or more systems of therapy, instead of committing to just one system. Therapists can be eclectic in a number of ways (Arkowitz, 1992). Two common approaches are theoretical integration and technical eclecticism. In *theoretical integration,* two or more systems of therapy are combined or blended to take advantage of the strengths of each. Paul Wachtel's (1977, 1991) efforts to blend psychodynamic and behavioral therapies is a prominent example. *Technical eclecticism* involves borrowing ideas, insights, and techniques from a variety of sources while tailoring one's intervention strategy to the unique needs of each client. Advocates of technical eclecticism, such as Arnold Lazarus (1976, 1989), maintain that therapists should ask themselves, "What is the best approach for this specific client, problem, and situation?" and then adjust their strategy accordingly.

Increasing eclecticism is only one of several recent trends in the field of psychotherapy. Many other changes have also occurred in the delivery of mental health services. We'll examine some of

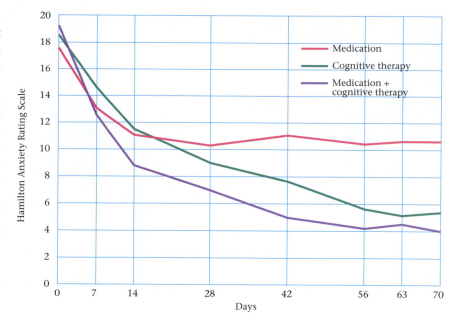

Figure 15.9
The value of combining approaches to treatment. Working with patients suffering from generalized anxiety disorder, Power and colleagues (1990) compared the efficacy of medication, cognitive therapy, and a combination of medication and cognitive therapy. Each approach led to reduced anxiety, but the most effective treatment was the combination of medication and cognitive therapy.

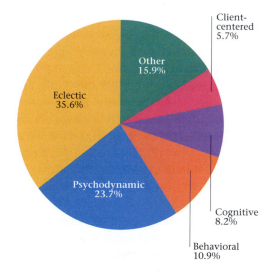

Figure 15.10
The leading approaches to therapy among psychologists. The pooled data from a survey of 415 clinical and counseling psychologists (Smith, 1982) and another survey of 479 clinical psychologists (Norcross & Prochaska, 1982) indicate that the most widely used approaches to therapy are (in order) eclectic, psychodynamic, behavioral, cognitive, and client-centered.

these changes in the next two sections, which discuss efforts to respond to increasing cultural diversity in America and shifting patterns of institutional care for mental disorders.

CULTURE AND THERAPY

Modern psychotherapy emerged during the second half of the 19th century in Europe and America, spawned in part by a cultural milieu that viewed the self as an independent, reflective, rational being, capable of self-improvement (Cushman, 1992). Psychological disorders were assumed to have natural causes like physical diseases and to be amenable to medical treatments

Cultural barriers have emerged in the psychotherapy process. A number of minority groups in the United States shy away from using professional services in this field. Those who do try it also tend to quickly terminate treatment more often than white Americans.

frustrating interactions with American bureaucracies and are distrustful of large, intimidating, foreign institutions, such as hospitals and community mental health centers.

2. *Language barriers.* Effective communication is crucial to the provision of psychotherapy, yet most hospitals and mental health agencies are not adequately staffed with therapists who speak the languages used by minority groups in their service areas. The resulting communication problems make it awkward and difficult for many minority group members to explain their problems and to obtain the type of help that they need.

3. *Access barriers.* Many minority groups suffer from elevated rates of joblessness and poverty. In our society, people who are unemployed or employed in economically marginal jobs typically do not have health insurance. Their lack of health insurance severely restricts their options in pursuing treatment for psychological problems.

4. *Institutional barriers.* When all is said and done, Stanley Sue and Nolan Zane (1987) argue that the "single most important explanation for the problems in service delivery involves the inability of therapists to provide culturally responsive forms of treatment" (p. 37). The vast majority of therapists have been trained almost exclusively in the treatment of white, middle-class Americans and are not familiar with the cultural backgrounds and unique characteristics of various ethnic groups. This culture gap often leads to misunderstandings and ill-advised treatment strategies (Hughes, 1993). Unfortunately, there is a grievous shortage of ethnic therapists to meet the needs of various ethnic groups (Mays & Albee, 1992).

derived from scientific research. But the individualized, medicalized institution of modern psychotherapy reflects Western cultural values that are far from universal (Dana, 1993). In many nonindustrialized societies, psychological disorders are attributed to supernatural forces (possession, withcraft, angry gods, and so forth), and victims seek help from priests, shamans, and folk healers, rather than doctors (Wittkower & Warnes, 1984). Thus, efforts to export Western psychotherapies to non-Western cultures have met with mixed success. Indeed, the highly culture-bound origins of modern therapies have raised questions about their applicability to ethnic minorities *within* Western culture.

Research on how cultural factors influence the process and outcome of psychotherapy has burgeoned in recent years, motivated in part by the need to improve mental health services for ethnic minority groups in American society. The data are ambiguous for a couple of ethnic groups, but studies suggest that American minority groups generally underutilize therapeutic services (Mays & Albee, 1992). Why? A variety of barriers appear to contribute to this problem, including the following (Cheung, 1991; Mays & Albee, 1992; Sue, Zane, & Young, 1994).

1. *Cultural barriers.* In times of psychological distress, some cultural groups are reluctant to turn to formal, professional sources of assistance. Given their socialization, they prefer to rely on informal assistance from family members, the clergy, respected elders, herbalists, acupuncturists, and so forth, who share their cultural heritage. Many members of minority groups have a history of

What can be done to improve mental health services for American minority groups? Researchers in this area have offered a variety of suggestions (Homma-True et al., 1993; Pedersen, 1994; Sue & Zane, 1987; Yamamoto et al., 1993). Discussions of possible solutions usually begin with the need to recruit and train more ethnic minority therapists. Studies show that ethnic minorities are more likely to go to mental health facilities that are staffed by a higher proportion of people who share their ethnic background (Sue et al., 1994). Furthermore, clients' satisfaction with therapy tends to be greater when they are treated by therapists from their own culture. Therapists can also be given special training to work more effectively with people from different cultural backgrounds. For example, Wade and Bernstein (1991) found that a cultural sensitivity training program for white therapists working with an African American clientele resulted in improved client satisfaction. Finally, most authorities urge further investigation of how traditional approaches to therapy can be modified and tailored to be more compatible with specific cultural groups' attitudes, values, norms, and traditions.

Recap of Key Points
• Combinations of insight, behavioral, and biomedical therapies are often used fruitfully in the treatment of psychological disorders. Many modern therapists are eclectic, using specific ideas, techniques, and strategies gleaned from a number of theoretical approaches.

• The highly culture-bound origins of Western therapies have raised doubts about their applicability to other cultures and even to ethnic groups in Western society. Because of cultural, language, and access barriers, therapeutic services are underutilized by ethnic minorities in America.

• However, the crux of the problem is the failure of institutions to provide culturally sensitive and responsive forms of treatment for ethnic minorities. More culturally responsive approaches to treatment will require more minority therapists, special training for therapists, and additional investigation of how traditional therapies can be tailored to be more compatible with specific ethnic groups' cultural heritage.

INSTITUTIONAL TREATMENT IN TRANSITION

Traditionally, much of the treatment of mental illness has been carried out in institutional settings, primarily in mental hospitals. **A *mental hospital* is a medical institution specializing in providing inpatient care for psychological disorders.** In the United States, a national network of state-funded mental hospitals started to emerge in the 1840s through the efforts of Dorothea Dix and other reformers (see Figure 15.11). Prior to these reforms, the mentally ill who were poor were housed in jails and poorhouses or were left to wander the countryside. Dix was horrified by this lack of care. She lobbied tirelessly to raise funds for public mental hospitals. Thanks to the movement that she began, nearly 300 public mental hospitals were established in the United States between 1845 and 1945. The people who built these hospitals believed that they would provide humane and effective treatment for those suffering from psychological disorders.

Today, mental hospitals continue to play an important role in the delivery of mental health

Figure 15.11
Dorothea Dix and the advent of mental hospitals in America. During the 19th century, Dorothea Dix (inset) campaigned tirelessly to obtain funds for building mental hospitals. Many of these hospitals, such as the New York State Lunatic Asylum, were extremely large facilities. Although public mental hospitals improved the care of the mentally ill, they had a variety of shortcomings, which eventually prompted the deinstitutionalization movement.

services. However, since World War II, institutional care for mental illness has undergone a series of major transitions—and the dust hasn't settled yet. Let's look at how institutional care has evolved in recent decades.

Disenchantment with Mental Hospitals

By the 1950s, it had become apparent that public mental hospitals were not fulfilling their goals very well (Mechanic, 1980). Experts began to realize that hospitalization often *contributed* to the development of pathology instead of curing it.

What were the causes of these unexpected negative effects? Part of the problem was that the facilities were usually underfunded. In 1960, for instance, state mental hospitals made do with only one-sixth as much money per patient as general hospitals treating the same disorders (Bloom, 1984). The lack of adequate funding meant that the facilities were overcrowded and understaffed. Hospital personnel were undertrained and overworked, making them hard-pressed to deliver minimal custodial care. Despite gallant efforts at treatment, the demoralizing conditions made most public mental hospitals decidedly nontherapeutic. Although there certainly were *some* high-quality mental hospitals, most public facilities had degenerated into huge custodial warehouses (Scull, 1990).

As psychiatric hospitals were scrutinized closely, doubts were raised about the wisdom of hospitalization, even if adequate funding could be found (Korchin, 1976). Critics noted that hospitals placed people into a passive patient role, leading many to stop taking responsibility for their lives. Many patients adapted to this paternalistic care and became fearful of leaving the hospital. Their ability to manage their lives outside of an institutional setting declined rather than improved.

These problems were aggravated by the fact that state mental hospitals served large geographic regions but were rarely placed near major population centers. Hence, most patients were uprooted from their community. Institutionalized 50, 100, or 300 miles from their homes, they lost contact with their families, friends, and employers. This deprived the patients of needed social support and made their potential return to the community more difficult. Thus, critics concluded that there were fundamental flaws in our system of mental hospitals.

The Community Mental Health Movement

Disenchantment with the public mental hospital system inspired the community mental health movement that emerged in the 1960s (Scull, 1990). The community mental health movement emphasizes (1) local, community-based care, (2) reduced dependence on hospitalization, and (3) the prevention of psychological disorders. The community mental health movement jumped into prominence in 1963 when John F. Kennedy became the first American president ever to address the nation on the subject of mental health. Kennedy enthusiastically endorsed the community mental health philosophy. He outlined a major plan to eventually build about 1500 community mental health centers that would operate according to this philosophy. Thus, in 1963 much of the responsibility for the treatment of psychological disorders was turned over to an entirely new kind of institution.

What do community mental health centers do? **Community mental health centers are facilities that provide comprehensive mental health care for their local communities.** Their key services usually include the following: (1) short-term, local inpatient care, (2) extensive outpatient therapy, (3) crisis intervention services, and (4) community education about mental health.

Community mental health centers supplement mental hospitals with decentralized and more accessible services. They were never intended to replace mental hospitals, although they have had an effect on patterns of hospitalization.

Deinstitutionalization

Mental hospitals continue to care for many people troubled by chronic mental illness, but their role in patient care has diminished. Since the 1960s, a policy of deinstitutionalization has been followed by the American mental health care establishment. **Deinstitutionalization refers to transferring the treatment of mental illness from inpatient institutions to community-based facilities that emphasize outpatient care.** This shift in responsibility was made possible by two developments: (1) the emergence of effective drug therapies for severe disorders and (2) the deployment of community mental health centers to coordinate local care (Wyatt, 1985).

The exodus of patients from mental hospitals has been dramatic. In 1955 about *one-half* of the hospital beds in the United States were occupied by psychiatric patients. During the 1980s that figure declined to less than one-fourth (Kiesler, 1993). The average inpatient population in state and county mental hospitals has dropped from a peak of around 550,000 in the mid-1950s to around 90,000 today, as shown in Figure 15.12(a). The average length of hospitalization has also declined. In Veterans Administration hospitals, for example, the average length of stay for psychotic patients peaked at 672 days in 1958. The average length of stay in these facilities fell to 92 days by 1980. Thus, as intended, deinstitutionalization has led to more outpatient and less inpatient care of psychological disorders.

These trends do *not* mean that hospitalization for mental illness has become a thing of the past. A great many people are still hospitalized, but there's been a shift toward placing them in local general hospitals instead of distant psychiatric hospitals (Kiesler, 1992), as Figure 15.12(b) shows. Today, traditional mental hospitals (both public and private) account for only 41% of psychiatric inpatient admissions, as you can see in Figure 15.12(c). The patients admitted to general hospitals stay for a relatively brief time. The median stay is about 12 days. In keeping with the philosophy of deinstitutionalization, these facilities try to get patients stabilized and back into the community as swiftly as possible. Thus, hospitalization is still a frequent intervention, but long-term institutionalization is far less common today than it once was.

Evaluating Deinstitutionalization

How has deinstitutionalization worked out? It gets mixed reviews. On the positive side, many people have benefited by avoiding disruptive and unnecessary hospitalization. There's ample evidence that alternatives to hospitalization can be both more effective and less costly than inpatient care (Kiesler, 1982, 1992; Sledge et al., 1996). Moreover, many authorities maintain that treatment *inside* mental hospitals has improved because of deinstitutionalization. This improvement would have been virtually impossible if the patient population hadn't been brought down to a more manageable size.

Unfortunately, some unanticipated problems have arisen (Grob, 1994; A. Johnson, 1990; Scull, 1990). Many patients suffering from chronic psychological disorders had nowhere to go when they were released. They had no families, friends, or homes to return to. Many had no work skills and

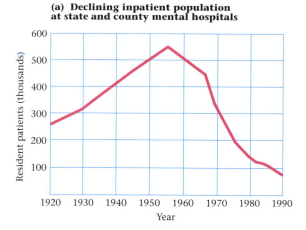

(a) Declining inpatient population at state and county mental hospitals

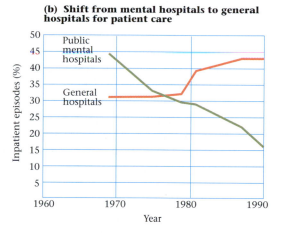

(b) Shift from mental hospitals to general hospitals for patient care

Figure 15.12
Trends in the institutional treatment of mental illness. (**a**) The inpatient population in public mental hospitals has declined dramatically since the late 1950s, as a result of deinstitutionalization and the use of drug therapy. (**b**) When inpatient care is required today, traditional public mental hospitals provide less of it than in the past. (**c**) Today, general hospitals and private mental hospitals handle about two-thirds of inpatient care episodes. (**d**) The extent of the revolving door problem is apparent from these figures on the percentage of inpatient admissions that are readmissions at various types of facilities. (Data from Manderscheid & Sonnenschein, 1992)

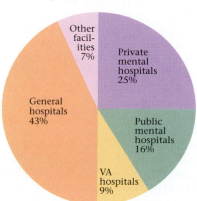

(c) Distribution of inpatient care episodes (1990)

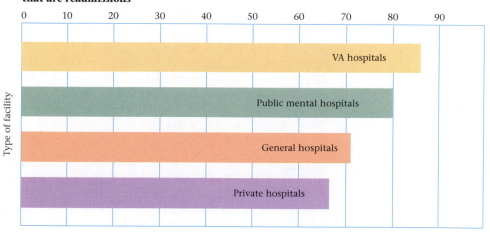

(d) Percentage of psychiatric inpatient admissions that are readmissions

were poorly prepared to live on their own. These people were supposed to be absorbed by "halfway houses," sheltered workshops, and other types of intermediate care facilities. Unfortunately, many communities were never able to fund and build the planned facilities. Meanwhile, the increased burden on community mental health centers left them strapped to provide needed services. This problem worsened in the 1980s, as federal funds for community mental health centers were reduced.

To some extent, patients were released into communities that weren't prepared to handle them. Thus, deinstitutionalization left two major problems in its wake: a "revolving door" population of people who flow in and out of psychiatric facilities, and a sizable population of homeless mentally ill people.

Mental Illness, the Revolving Door, and Homelessness

Although the proportion of hospital days attributable to mental illness has dwindled, admission rates for psychiatric hospitalization have actually climbed. What has happened? Deinstitutionalization and drug therapy have created a revolving door through which many mentally ill people pass again and again and again (Geller, 1992).

Most of the people caught in the mental health system's revolving door suffer from chronic, severe disorders (usually schizophrenia) that frequently require hospitalization (Haywood et al., 1995). However, they respond well to drug therapies in the hospital. Once they're stabilized through drug therapy, they no longer qualify for expensive hospital treatment according to the new standards created by deinstitutionalization. Thus, they're sent back out the door, into communities that often aren't prepared to provide adequate outpatient care. Because they lack appropriate care and support, their condition deteriorates and they soon require readmission to a hospital, where the cycle begins once again. Studies reveal that 50% of the patients released from public mental hospitals are readmitted within one year (Kiesling, 1983). Over two-thirds of all psychiatric inpatient admissions involve rehospitalizing a former patient, as Figure 15.12(d) shows.

Deinstitutionalization has also been blamed for the growing population of homeless people. Although it's difficult to collect statistics on the homeless, many urban areas have seen sharp increases in the number of people living in the streets and various types of temporary shelters since the 1980s (Foscarinis, 1991). The escalating number of homeless women and children has been particularly noticeable (Milburn & D'Ercole, 1991). The popular media routinely equate homelessness with mental illness, and it is widely assumed that deinstitutionalization is largely responsible for the rapid growth of homelessness in America. However, the empirical evidence suggests that the relations between deinstitutionalization, homelessness, and mental illness are more complicated than most people realize. The first step in sorting out these relations is to investigate the prevalence of psychological disorders among the homeless, which brings us to our Featured Study.

Investigators: Ellen L. Bassuk, Lenore Rubin, and Alison Lauriat (Harvard University)

Source: Is homelessness a mental health problem? *American Journal of Psychiatry*, 1984, *141*(12), 1546–1550.

From Back Wards to Back Alleys? — Featured Study

A great deal of debate has revolved around the extent of mental illness among the homeless. Before the 1970s, the urban homeless population was made up mostly of males living in "skid row" areas. Many were alcoholic, but their principal problem was their marginal job skills. Since the advent of deinstitutionalization, this pattern seems to have changed. However, this assertion has often been based on casual observation and anecdotal evidence. This study attempted to collect systematic data on the mental health of the homeless.

Method

A one-day census of all the people using shelters for the homeless in the Boston area was conducted in February 1983. Local authorities collected demographic data on the "guests" using the 27 shelters serving the Boston area at the time. Based on these demographic data, the research team carefully selected a single shelter facility as the most representative of the lot. On one night in April 1983, nine experienced mental health professionals interviewed all the guests at this shelter to assess their mental health. The median age of the 78 subjects was 34. Most (83%) were male, and about two-thirds were at least high school graduates.

Results

The interviewers found psychological disorders in the vast majority of the subjects at the shelter that night. Major psychotic disorders (mostly schizophrenia) were found in 40% of the guests. Another 29% were chronic alcoholics. Most of the subjects with severe psychotic disorders were not receiving any form of therapy, even though most clearly could have benefited from treatment. The investigators noted, "Many of the schizophrenic guests were so disorganized that they were unable to phrase even a few sentences coherently; their stories were disjointed, rambling, unreal, at times grandiose, and almost always difficult to follow" (p. 1547).

The social isolation of the subjects was remarkable. Of those using the facility, 74% reported no existing family relationships, 73% indicated that they had no friends to lean on, and 40% said they had no ongoing social relations with anyone. The handful of healthy individuals in the shelter were either children accompanying their parents or adults who had just arrived in Boston looking for work.

Discussion

The authors conclude that there is a great deal of mental illness among the homeless. They acknowledge, however, that their evidence did not clearly link this problem to deinstitutionalization. Only 28% of the shelter guests had ever been hospitalized for psychiatric reasons. Thus, most were not castaways from the mental health system. However, most of the subjects were young, and many had reached adulthood after deinstitutionalization changed patterns of hospitalization. Bassuk and her colleagues speculate that before the era of deinstitutionalization, many more of the guests would have been hospitalized. They conclude that "shelters have become 'open asylums' to replace the institutions of several decades ago" (p. 1549).

Comment

Many additional studies of homelessness and mental illness have been conducted since this groundbreaking investigation. These studies have consistently found elevated rates of mental illness among the homeless, although the prevalence rates for specific disorders have varied from one study to the next. Taken as a whole, the evidence suggests that roughly one-third of the homeless suffer from severe mental illness (schizophrenic and mood disorders), that another one-third or so are struggling with alcohol and drug problems, and that 10% to 20% are

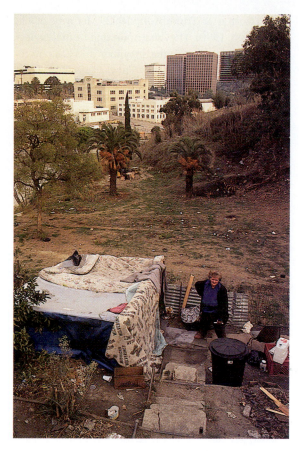

Casual observation suggests that homelessness among the mentally ill has increased in recent years. This Featured Study provides empirical documentation that homelessness and mental illness frequently go together.

troubled by both mental illness and substance abuse (Drake, Osher, & Wallach, 1991; Fischer & Breakey, 1991).

The results of this research are disheartening. Before Dorothea Dix's 19th-century crusade, the mentally ill were left to fend for themselves. The findings on mental illness among the homeless suggest that society is moving backward toward a similar state of affairs. Actually, the people living in the streets and shelters may be only the tip of the iceberg. Many other people with mental disorders live in decrepit flophouses. Thus, deinstitutionalization has apparently moved some disordered people from the back wards of our mental hospitals to the back alleys of our slums.

Deinstitutionalization probably has contributed to the growth of homelessness, as Bassuk and her colleagues argue, but many experts in this area maintain that it is misleading to blame the problem of homelessness chiefly on deinstitutionalization (Kanter, 1989; Kiesler, 1991). They note, for instance, that although mental illness is common among the homeless, studies suggest that only about 5%–7% of the homeless population require psychiatric hospitalization (Dennis et al., 1991). They also point out that the causal processes underlying the correlation between homelessness and

mental illness are probably bidirectional (Goodman, Saxe, & Harvey, 1991).

Those who criticize the tendency to equate homelessness with mental illness worry that this equation diverts attention from the real causes of the homelessness crisis (Kiesler, 1991). They marshal evidence to show that the sharp increase in the homeless population is due to a variety economic, social, and political trends, including increased unemployment and poverty, decreased supprt for welfare and subsidized housing programs, the loss of much low-income housing to urban renewal, and so forth (Cohen & Thompson, 1992; McCarty et al., 1991; Rossi, 1990). They maintain that homelessness is primarily an economic problem and that it requires economic solutions. They argue that most homeless people need housing and jobs more than they need mental health care.

The issue is a complex one, however, and other theorists disagree. For example, although Baum and Burnes (1993) acknowledge that economic and social trends have contributed to increased homelessness, they assert that that today's homeless are a deeply troubled population, beset by high rates of mental illness, substance dependence, and disabling physical conditions. They maintain that that it would foolish to chart our governmental policy on homelessness working under the assumption that this population merely needs economic assistance.

In light of the revolving door problem and homelessness among the mentally ill, what can we conclude about deinstitutionalization? It ap-pears to be a worthwhile idea that has been poorly executed. Overall, the policy has probably been a benefit to countless people with milder disorders but a cruel trick on many others with severe, chronic disorders. Ultimately, it's clear that our society is not providing adequate care for a sizable segment of the mentally ill population (Isaac & Armat, 1990; Torrey, 1996). That's not a new development. Inadequate care for mental illness has always been the norm. Societies always struggle with the problem of what to do with the mentally ill and how to pay for their care (English & McCarrick, 1989).

What's the solution? Virtually no one advocates returning to the era of custodial warehouses. Many *do* advocate increasing the quality and availability of intermediate care facilities and programs (Drake et al., 1991; McCarty et al., 1991). Only time will tell whether American society will be willing to make the financial commitment to follow through on this recommendation.

PUTTING IT IN PERSPECTIVE

In our discussion of psychotherapy, one of our unifying themes—the value of theoretical diversity—was particularly prominent, and one other theme—the importance of culture—surfaced briefly. Let's discuss the latter theme first. The approaches to psychotherapy described in this chapter are products of modern, white, middle-class, Western culture. Some of these therapies have proven useful in some other cultures, but many have turned out to be irrelevant or counter-productive when used with different cultural groups, including ethnic minorities in Western society. Thus, we have seen once again that cultural factors influence psychological processes and that Western psychology cannot assume that its theories and practices have universal applicability.

As for theoretical diversity, its value can be illustrated with a rhetorical question: Can you imagine what the state of modern psychotherapy would be if everyone in psychology and psychiatry had simply accepted Freud's theories about the nature and treatment of psychological disorders? If not for theoretical diversity, psychotherapy might still be in the dark ages. Psychoanalysis can be a useful method of therapy, but it would be a tragic state of affairs if it were the *only* treatment available to people experiencing psychological distress. Multi-tudes of people have benefited from alternative approaches to treatment, such as client-centered therapy, cognitive therapy, behavior therapies, and biomedical therapies. These alternatives emerged out of tension between psychoanalytic theory and the four other major theoretical perspectives identified in Chapter 1: the humanistic perspective (which generated client-centered therapy), the behavioral perspective (behavior therapies), the physiological perspective (biomedical therapies), and the cognitive perspective (cognitive therapy).

We've seen throughout this text that human existence is complex and highly varied. People have diverse problems, rooted in varied origins, that call for the pursuit of different therapeutic goals. Thus, it's fortunate that people can choose from a diverse array of approaches to psychotherapy. Table 15.4 summarizes and compares the approaches that we've discussed in this chapter. The table shows that the major types of psychotherapy overlap relatively little. Each type has its own vision of the nature of human discontent and the ideal remedy.

Of course, diversity can be confusing. The range and variety of available treatments in modern psychotherapy leaves many people puzzled about their options. Thus, in our Application we'll sort

TABLE 15.4 COMPARISON OF MAJOR APPROACHES TO PSYCHOTHERAPY

Type of Psychotherapy	Primary Founders	Origin of Disorder	Therapeutic Goals	Therapeutic Techniques
Psychoanalysis	Freud	Unconscious conflicts resulting from fixations in earlier development	Insights regarding unconscious conflicts and motives; personality reconstruction	Free association, dream analysis, interpretation, catharsis, transference
Client-centered therapy	Rogers	Incongruence between self-concept and actual experience; dependence on acceptance from others	Congruence between self-concept and experience; acceptance of genuine self; self-determination; personal growth	Genuineness, empathy, unconditional positive regard, clarification, reflecting back to client
Cognitive therapy	Beck Ellis	Irrational assumptions and negative, self-defeating thinking about events related to self	Detection of negative thinking; substitution of more realistic thinking	Thought stopping, recording automatic thoughts, refuting negative thinking, reattribution, homework assignments
Behavior therapy	Wolpe Bandura	Maladaptive patterns of behavior acquired through learning	Elimination of symptomatic, maladaptive behaviors; acquisition of more adaptive responses	Classical and operant conditioning, reinforcement, punishment, extinction, shaping, aversion conditioning, systematic desensitization, social skills training, biofeedback
Biomedical therapies		Physiological malfunction, primarily abnormal neurotransmitter activity	Elimination of symptoms; prevention of relapse	Antipsychotic, antianxiety, and antidepressant drugs; lithium; electroconvulsive therapy (ECT)

through the practical issues involved in selecting a therapist.

Recap of Key Points

• Institutional treatment of mental illness has changed a great deal in the last 40 years. Disenchantment with the negative effects of mental hospitals led to the advent of more localized community mental health centers and a policy of deinstitutionalization. Long-term hospitalization for mental disorders is largely a thing of the past.

• Unfortunately, deinstitutionalization has left some unanticipated problems in its wake. Adequate outpatient facilities and care have not been provided for the mentally ill, resulting in the revolving door problem. Our Featured Study suggested that mental disorders are commonplace among the homeless.

• Although deinstitutionalization may have made a contribution to the growth of homelessness in America, many theorists argue that homelessness is primarily an economic problem. Other theorists disagree, arguing that the homeless need more than just economic assistance.

• Our discussion of psychotherapy highlighted the value of theoretical diversity. Conflicting theoretical orientations have generated varied approaches to treatment. Variety in treatment options allows clients to look for interventions suited to their unique needs. Our coverage of therapy also showed once again that cultural factors shape psychological processes.

APPLICATION: **LOOKING FOR A THERAPIST**

Answer the following "true" or "false."

1 Psychotherapy is an art as well as a science.

2 Psychotherapy can be harmful or damaging to a client.

3 Psychotherapy does not have to be expensive.

4 It is a good idea to shop around when choosing a therapist.

5 The type of professional degree that a therapist holds is relatively unimportant.

All of these statements are true. Do any of them surprise you? If so, you're in good company. Many people know relatively little about the practicalities of selecting a therapist.

The task of finding an appropriate therapist is no less complex than shopping for any other major service. Should you see a psychologist or psychiatrist? Should you opt for individual therapy or group therapy? Should you see a client-centered therapist or a behavior therapist? The unfortunate part of this complexity is that people seeking psychotherapy often feel overwhelmed by personal problems. The last thing they need is to be confronted by yet another complex problem.

Nonetheless, the importance of finding a good therapist cannot be overestimated. Therapy can sometimes have harmful rather than helpful effects. We have already discussed how drug therapies and ECT can sometimes be damaging, but problems are not limited to these interventions. Talking about your problems with a therapist may sound pretty harmless, but studies indicate that insight therapies can also backfire (Lambert & Bergin, 1994;

Searching for a proper therapist from the bewildering array available is serious business. It is essential to locate a practitioner who is skilled and who is right for your needs.

McGlashan et al., 1990). Although a great many talented therapists are available, psychotherapy, like any other profession, has incompetent practitioners as well. Therefore, you should shop for a skilled therapist, just as you would for a good attorney or a good mechanic.

In this application, we'll go over some information that should be helpful if you ever have to look for a therapist for yourself or for a friend or family member (based on Amada, 1985; Bruckner-Gordon, Gangi, & Wallman, 1988; Ehrenberg & Ehrenberg, 1986; Pittman, 1994).

When Should You Seek Professional Treatment?

There is no simple answer to this question. Obviously, people *consider* the possibility of professional treatment when they are psychologically distressed. However, they have other options besides psychotherapy.

There is much to be said for seeking advice from family, friends, the clergy, and so forth. Insights about personal problems do not belong exclusively to people with professional degrees.

So, when should you turn to professionals for help? You should begin to think seriously about therapy when (1) you have no one to lean on, (2) the people you lean on indicate that they're getting tired of it, (3) you feel helpless and overwhelmed, or (4) your life is seriously disrupted by your problems. Of course, you do not have to be falling apart to justify therapy. You may want to seek professional advice simply because you want to get more out of life.

Where Do You Find Therapeutic Services?

Psychotherapy can be found in a variety of settings. Contrary to general belief, most therapists are not in private practice. Many work in institutional settings such as community mental health centers, hospitals, and human service agencies. The principal sources of therapeutic services are described in Table 15.5. The exact configuration of therapeutic services available will vary from one community to another. To find out what your community has to offer, it is a good idea to consult your friends, your local phone book, or your local community mental health center.

Is the Therapist's Profession Important?

Psychotherapists may be trained in psychology, psychiatry, social work, counseling, psychiatric nursing, or marriage and family therapy. Researchers have *not* found any reliable associations between therapists' professional background and therapeutic efficacy (Beutler, Machado, & Neufeldt, 1994), probably because many talented therapists can be found in all of these professions. Thus, the kind of degree that a therapist holds doesn't need to be a crucial consideration in your selection process. At the present time, it *is* true that only a psychiatrist can prescribe drugs for disorders that merit drug therapy. However, critics argue that many psychiatrists are too quick to use drugs to solve problems (Breggin, 1991). In any case, other types of therapists can refer you to a psychiatrist if they think that drug therapy would be helpful. If you have a health insurance policy that covers psychotherapy, you may want to check to see whether it carries any restrictions about the therapist's profession.

Is the Therapist's Sex Important?

This depends on your attitude. If *you* feel that the therapist's sex is important, then for you it is. The therapeutic relationship must be characterized by trust and rapport. Feeling uncomfortable with a therapist of one sex or the other could inhibit the therapeutic process. Hence, you should feel free to look for a male or female therapist if you prefer to do so. This point is probably most relevant to female clients whose troubles may be related to the extensive sexism in our society (A. Kaplan,

TABLE 15.5 PRINCIPAL SOURCES OF THERAPEUTIC SERVICES

Source	Comments
Private practitioners	Self-employed therapists are listed in the Yellow Pages under their professional category, such as psychologists or psychiatrists. Private practitioners tend to be relatively expensive, but they also tend to be highly experienced therapists.
Community mental health centers	Community mental health centers have salaried psychologists, psychiatrists, and social workers on staff. The centers provide a variety of services and often have staff available on weekends and at night to deal with emergencies.
Hospitals	Several kinds of hospitals provide therapeutic services. There are both public and private mental hospitals that specialize in the care of people with psychological disorders. Many general hospitals have a psychiatric ward, and those that do not usually have psychiatrists and psychologists on staff and on call. Although hospitals tend to concentrate on inpatient treatment, many provide outpatient therapy as well.
Human service agencies	Various social service agencies employ therapists to provide short-term counseling. Depending on your community, you may find agencies that deal with family problems, juvenile problems, drug problems, and so forth.
Schools and workplaces	Most high schools and colleges have counseling centers where students can get help with personal problems. Similarly, some large businesses offer in-house counseling to their employees.

1985). It is entirely reasonable for women to seek a therapist with a feminist perspective if that would make them feel more comfortable.

Speaking of sex, you should be aware that sexual exploitation is an occasional problem in the context of therapy. Studies indicate that a small minority of therapists take advantage of their clients sexually (Pope, Keith-Spiegel, & Tabachnick, 1986). These incidents almost always involve a male therapist making advances to a female client. The available evidence indicates that these sexual liaisons are usually harmful to clients (Williams, 1992). There are absolutely no situations in which therapist-client sexual relations are an ethical therapeutic practice. If a therapist makes sexual advances, a client should terminate treatment.

Is Therapy Always Expensive?

Psychotherapy does not have to be prohibitively expensive. Private practitioners tend to be the most expensive, charging between $25 and $100 per (50-minute)

hour. These fees may seem high, but they are in line with those of similar professionals, such as dentists and attorneys. Community mental health centers and social service agencies are usually supported by tax dollars. Hence, they can charge lower fees than most therapists in private practice. Many of these organizations use a sliding scale, so that clients are charged according to how much they can afford to pay. Thus, most communities have inexpensive opportunities for psychotherapy. Moreover, many health insurance plans provide at least partial reimbursement for the cost of psychotherapy.

Is the Therapist's Theoretical Approach Important?

Logically, you might expect that the diverse approaches to therapy vary in effectiveness. For the most part, this is *not* what researchers find, however. After reviewing many studies of therapeutic efficacy, Jerome Frank (1961) and Lester Luborsky and his colleagues (1975) both quote the dodo bird who has just judged a race in

Alice in Wonderland: "*Everybody* has won, and *all* must have prizes." Improvement rates for various theoretical orientations usually come out pretty close in most studies (Lambert & Bergin, 1994). In their landmark review of outcome studies, Smith and Glass (1977) estimated the effectiveness of many major approaches to therapy. As Figure 15.13 shows, the estimates cluster together closely.

However, these findings are a little misleading, as these estimates of overall effectiveness have been averaged across many types of patients and many types of problems. Most experts seem to think that *for certain types of problems, some approaches to therapy are more effective than others*. For example, Martin Seligman (1995) asserts that panic disorders respond best to cognitive therapy, that specific phobias are most amenable to treatment with systematic desensitization, and that obsessive-compulsive disorders are best treated with behavior therapy or medication. Thus, for a specific type of problem, a therapist's theoretical approach *may* make a difference.

It is also important to point out that the finding that different approaches to therapy are roughly equal in overall effi-

cacy does not mean that all *therapists* are created equal. Some therapists unquestionably are more effective than others. However, these variations in effectiveness appear to depend on individual therapists' personal skills rather than on their theoretical orientation (Beutler et al., 1994). Good, bad, and mediocre therapists are found within each school of thought.

The key point is that effective therapy requires skill and creativity. Arnold Lazarus, who devised multimodal therapy, emphasizes that therapists "straddle the fence between science and art." Therapy is scientific in that interventions are based on extensive theory and empirical research (Forsyth & Strong, 1986). Ultimately, though, each client is a unique human being, and the therapist has to creatively fashion a treatment program that will help that individual.

What Should You Look for in a Prospective Therapist?

Some clients are timid about asking prospective therapists questions about their training, approach, fees, and so forth. However, these are reasonable questions, and

the vast majority of therapists will be most accommodating in providing answers. Usually, you can ask your preliminary questions over the phone. If things seem promising, you may decide to make an appointment for an interview (you probably will have to pay for the interview). In this interview, the therapist will gather more information to determine the likelihood of helping you, given the therapist's training and approach to treatment. At the same time, you should be making a similar judgment about whether *you* believe the therapist can help you with your problems.

What should you look for? First, you should look for personal warmth and sincere concern. Try to judge whether you will be able to talk to this person in a candid, nondefensive way. Second, look for empathy and understanding. Is the person capable of appreciating your point of view? Third, look for self-confidence. Self-assured therapists will communicate a sense of competence without trying to intimidate you with jargon or boasting needlessly about what they can do for you. When all is said and done, you should *like* your therapist. Otherwise, it will be difficult to establish the needed rapport.

What If There Isn't Any Progress?

If you feel that your therapy isn't going anywhere, you should probably discuss these feelings with your therapist. Don't be surprised, however, if the therapist suggests that it may be your own fault. Freud's concept of resistance has some validity. Some clients *do* have difficulty facing up to their problems. Thus, if your therapy isn't progressing, you may need to *consider* whether your resistance may be slowing progress. This self-examination isn't easy, as you are not an unbiased observer. Some common signs of resistance identified by Ehrenberg and Ehrenberg (1986) are listed in Figure 15.14.

Given the very real possibility that poor progress may be due to resistance, you should not be too quick to leave therapy when dissatisfied. However, it *is* possible that your therapist isn't sufficiently skilled or that the two of you are incompatible.

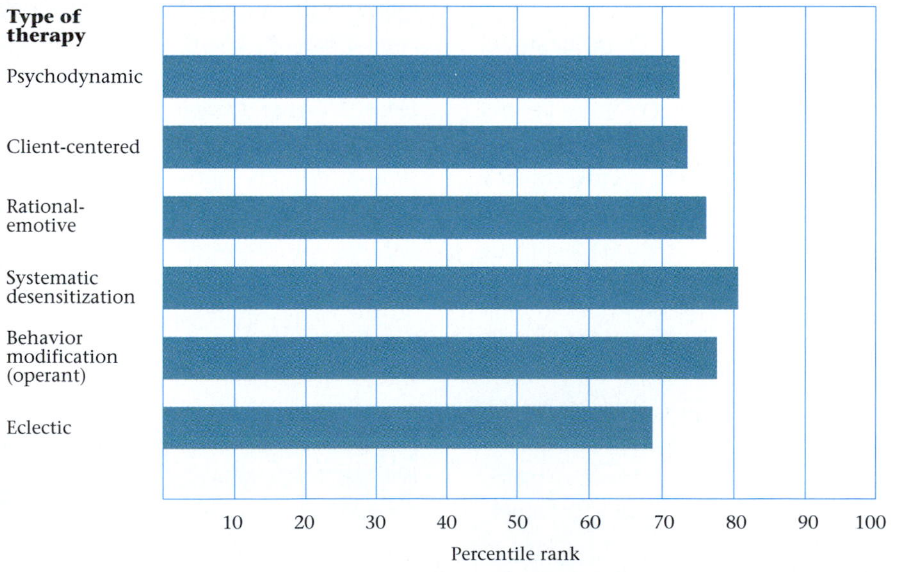

Figure 15.13
Estimates of the effectiveness of various approaches to psychotherapy. Smith and Glass (1977) reviewed nearly 400 studies in which clients who were treated with a specific type of therapy were compared with a control group made up of individuals with similar problems who went untreated. The bars indicate the percentile rank (on outcome measures) attained by the average client treated with each type of therapy when compared to control subjects. The higher the percentile, the more effective the therapy was. As you can see, the various approaches were fairly similar in their overall effectiveness.

Thus, after careful and deliberate consideration, you should feel free to terminate your therapy.

What Is Therapy Like?

It is important to have realistic expectations about therapy, or you may be unnecessarily disappointed. Some people expect miracles. They expect to turn their life around quickly with little effort. Others expect their therapist to run their lives for them. These are unrealistic expectations.

Therapy usually is a slow process. Your problems are not likely to melt away quickly. Moreover, therapy is hard work, and your therapist is only a facilitator. Ultimately, *you* have to confront the challenge of changing your behavior, your feelings, or your personality. This process may not be pleasant. You may have to face up to some painful truths about yourself. As Ehrenberg and Ehrenberg (1986) point out, "Psychotherapy takes time, effort, and courage."

Recap of Key Points

- Many practical considerations are relevant to the task of seeking professional treatment. Therapeutic services are available in many settings, and such services do not have to be expensive.
- Excellent therapists and mediocre therapists can be found in all of the mental health professions. Thus, therapists' personal skills are more important than their professional degree.
- The various theoretical approaches to therapy appear to be fairly similar in overall effectiveness. However, for certain types of problems, some approaches are probably more effective than others, and all therapists are not created equal.
- In selecting a therapist, warmth, empathy, confidence, and likability are desirable traits, and it is reasonable to insist on a therapist of one sex or the other.

Signs of resistance in therapy
If you're dissatisfied with your progress in therapy, resistance may be the problem when:
1   You have nothing specific or concrete to complain about.
2   Your attitude about therapy changes suddenly just as you reach the truly sensitive issues.
3   You've had the same problem with other therapists in the past.
4   Your conflicts with the therapist resemble those that you have with other people.
5   You start hiding things from your therapist.

Figure 15.14
Signs of resistance. Resistance in therapy may be subtle, but Ehrenberg and Ehrenberg (1986) have identified some telltale signs to look for.

- If progress is slow, your own resistance may be the problem. Therapy requires time, hard work, and the courage to confront your problems.

Key Ideas

The Elements of Psychotherapy: Treatments, Clients, and Therapists

◆ Approaches to treatment are diverse, but they can be grouped into three categories: insight therapies, behavior therapies, and biomedical therapies.

◆ Therapists come from a variety of professional backgrounds. Clinical and counseling psychologists, psychiatrists, clinical social workers, psychiatric nurses, and counselors are the principal providers of therapeutic services.

Insight Therapies

◆ Insight therapies involve verbal interactions intended to enhance self-knowledge. In psychoanalysis, free association and dream analysis are used to explore the unconscious. When an analyst's probing hits sensitive areas, resistance can be expected.

◆ The transference relationship may be used to overcome this resistance so that the client can handle interpretations that lead to insight. Classical psychoanalysis is not widely practiced anymore, but Freud's legacy lives on in a rich diversity of modern psychodynamic therapies.

◆ The client-centered therapist tries to provide a supportive climate in which clients can restructure their self-concept. The process of therapy emphasizes clarification of the client's feelings and self-acceptance.

◆ Beck's cognitive therapy concentrates on changing the way clients think about events in their lives. Cognitive therapists reeducate clients to detect and challenge automatic negative thoughts that cause depression and anxiety.

◆ Most theoretical approaches to insight therapy have been adapted for use with groups. Group therapy has unique advantages in comparison to individual therapy.

◆ Evaluating the effectiveness of any approach to therapy is complex and difficult, as it is hard for both therapists and clients to be objective. Nonetheless, the weight of the evidence suggests that insight therapies are superior to no treatment or placebo treatment.

Behavior Therapies

◆ Behavior therapies use the principles of learning in direct efforts to change specific aspects of behavior. Wolpe's systematic desensitization is a counterconditioning treatment for phobias. In aversion therapy, a stimulus associated with an unwanted response is paired with an unpleasant stimulus in an effort to eliminate the maladaptive response.

◆ Social skills training can improve clients' interpersonal skills through shaping, modeling, and behavioral rehearsal. Biofeedback involves providing information about bodily functions to a person so that he or she can attempt to exert some control over those physiological processes. There is ample evidence that behavior therapies are effective in the treatment of a wide variety of disorders.

Biomedical Therapies

◆ Biomedical therapies are physiological interventions for psychological problems. Antianxiety drugs are used to relieve excessive apprehension. Antipsychotic drugs are used primarily in the treatment of schizophrenia. Antidepressants are used to bring people out of episodes of depression. Bipolar mood disorders are treated with lithium.

◆ Drug therapies can be quite effective, but they have their drawbacks. All of the drugs produce problematic side effects, and some of these side effects can be troublesome.

◆ Electroconvulsive therapy (ECT) is used to trigger a cortical seizure that is believed to have therapeutic value for mood disorders, especially depression. There is contradictory evidence about the effectiveness and risks of ECT.

Blending Approaches to Therapy

◆ Combinations of insight, behavioral, and biomedical therapies are often used fruitfully in the treatment of psychological disorders. Many modern therapists are eclectic, using specific ideas, techniques, and strategies gleaned from a number of theoretical approaches.

Culture and Therapy

◆ The highly culture-bound origins of Western therapies have raised doubts about their applicability to other cultures and even to ethnic groups in Western society. Because of cultural, language, and access barriers, therapeutic services are underutilized by ethnic minorities in America. However, the crux of the problem is the failure of institutions to provide culturally sensitive and responsive forms of treatment for ethnic minorities.

Institutional Treatment in Transition

◆ Disenchantment with the negative effects of mental hospitals led to the advent of more localized community mental health centers and a policy of deinstitutionalization. Long-term hospitalization for mental disorders is largely a thing of the past.

◆ Unfortunately, deinstitutionalization has left some unanticipated problems in its wake, such as the revolving door problem. Our Featured Study suggested that mental disorders are commonplace among the homeless.

Putting It in Perspective

◆ Our discussion of psychotherapy highlighted the value of theoretical diversity. Conflicting theoretical orientations have generated varied approaches to treatment. Our coverage of therapy also showed once again that cultural factors shape psychological processes.

Application: Looking for a Therapist

◆ Therapeutic services are available in many settings, and such services do not have to be expensive. Excellent therapists and mediocre therapists can be found in all of the mental health professions, using the full range of therapeutic approaches.

◆ In selecting a therapist, warmth, empathy, confidence, and likability are desirable traits, and it is reasonable to insist on a therapist of one sex or the other. If progress is slow, your own resistance may be the problem.

Key Terms

Antianxiety drugs
Antidepressant drugs
Antipsychotic drugs
Aversion therapy
Behavior therapies
Biofeedback
Biomedical therapies
Client-centered therapy
Clinical psychologists
Cognitive therapy
Community mental health centers
Counseling psychologists
Deinstitutionalization
Dream analysis
Electroconvulsive therapy (ECT)
Free association
Group therapy
Insight therapies
Interpretation
Lithium
Mental hospital
Psychiatrists
Psychoanalysis
Psychopharmacotherapy
Resistance
Social skills training
Spontaneous remission
Systematic desensitization
Tardive dyskinesia
Transference

Key People

Aaron Beck
Hans Eysenck
Sigmund Freud
Carl Rogers
Joseph Wolpe

Practice Test

1. The goal of behavior therapy is to:
   A. identify the early childhood unconscious conflicts that are the source of the client's symptoms.
   B. change the client's thought patterns so that negative emotions can be controlled.
   C. alter the frequency of specific problematic responses by using conditioning techniques.
   D. alter the client's brain chemistry by prescribing specific drugs.

2. After undergoing psychoanalysis for several months, Karen has suddenly started "forgetting" to attend her therapy sessions. Karen's behavior is most likely a form of:
   A. resistance.
   B. transference.
   C. insight.
   D. catharsis.

3. Because Suzanne has an unconscious sexual attraction to her father, she behaves seductively toward her therapist. Suzanne's behavior is most likely a form of:
   A. resistance.
   B. transference.
   C. misinterpretation.
   D. an unconscious defense mechanism.

4. The key task of the client-centered therapist is:
   A. interpretation of the client's thoughts, feelings, memories, and behaviors.
   B. clarification of the client's feelings.
   C. confrontation of the client's irrational thoughts.
   D. modification of the client's problematic behaviors.

5. A therapist openly challenges a client's statement that she is a failure as a woman because her boyfriend left her, insisting that she justify it with evidence. Which type of therapy is probably being used?
   A. psychodynamic therapy
   B. client-centered therapy
   C. behavior therapy
   D. cognitive therapy

6. Based on a review of numerous studies of therapeutic outcome, Eysenck (1952) concluded that the recovery rate for neurotics treated with:
   A. insight therapy was about the same as the spontaneous remission rate for neurotic disorders.
   B. insight therapy was significantly higher than the spontaneous remission rate for neurotic disorders.
   C. group therapy was significantly higher than the recovery rate for neurotics treated with individual therapy.
   D. individual therapy was significantly higher than the recovery rate for neurotics treated with group therapy.

7. Systematic desensitization is particularly effective for the treatment of _____ disorders.
   A. generalized anxiety
   B. panic
   C. obsessive-compulsive
   D. phobic

8. Linda's therapist has her practice active listening skills in structured role-playing exercises. Later, Linda is gradually asked to practice these skills with family members, friends, and finally, her boss. Linda is undergoing:
   A. systematic desensitization.
   B. biofeedback.
   C. a token economy.
   D. social skills training.

9. After being released from a hospital, many schizophrenic patients stop taking their antipsychotic medication because:
   A. their mental impairment causes them to forget.
   B. of the unpleasant side effects.
   C. most schizophrenics don't believe they are ill.
   D. all of the above.

10. A recently developed drug, Prozac, appears to have value for _____ disorders.
    A. depressive
    B. schizophrenic
    C. obsessive-compulsive
    D. both a and c

11. Modern psychotherapy:
    A. was spawned by a cultural milieu that viewed the self as an independent, rational being.
    B. embraces universal cultural values.
    C. has been successfully exported to many non-Western cultures.
    D. both b and c.

12. The community mental health movement emphasizes:
    A. segregation of the mentally ill from the general population.
    B. increased dependence on long-term inpatient care.
    C. the prevention of psychological disorders.
    D. all of the above.

13. Many people repeatedly go in and out of mental hospitals. Typically, such people are released because _____; they are eventually readmitted because _____.
    A. they have been stabilized through drug therapy; their condition deteriorates once again due to inadequate outpatient care
    B. they run out of funds to pay for hospitalization; they once again can afford it
    C. they have been cured of their disorder; they develop another disorder
    D. they no longer want to be hospitalized; they voluntarily recommit themselves

14. The type of professional training a therapist has:
    A. is the most important indicator of his or her competence.
    B. should be the major consideration in choosing a therapist.
    C. is not all that important, since talented therapists can be found in all of the mental health professions.
    D. a and b.

15. Variations in the effectiveness of therapists depends primarily on:
    A. their personal skills and creativity.
    B. differences in their theoretical orientation.
    C. both a and b.
    D. neither a nor b.

Answers

1	C	Page 604	6	A	Page 614	11	A	Page 625
2	A	Page 608	7	D	Page 616	12	C	Page 628
3	B	Page 609	8	D	Page 618	13	A	Page 630
4	B	Page 610	9	B	Page 621	14	C	Page 635
5	D	Pages 611–612	10	D	Page 622	15	A	Page 636

16 SOCIAL BEHAVIOR

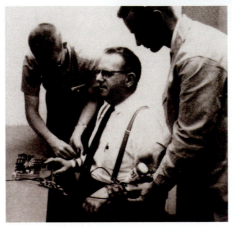

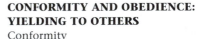

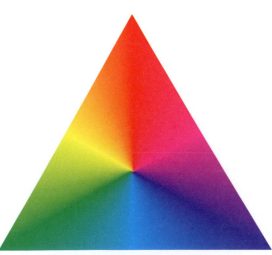

When Muffy, "the quintessential yuppie," met Jake, "the ultimate working-class stiff," her friends got very nervous.

Muffy is a 28-year-old stockbroker and a self-described "snob" with a group of about ten close women friends. Snobs all. They're graduates of fancy business schools. All consultants, investment bankers, and CPAs. All "cute, bright, fun to be with, and really intelligent," according to Muffy. They're all committed to their high-powered careers, but they all expect to marry someday, too.

Unfortunately, most of them don't date much. In fact, they spend a good deal of time "lamenting the dearth of 'good men.'" Well, lucky Muffy actually met one of those "good men." Jake is a salesman. He comes from a working-class neighborhood. His clothes come from Sears.

He wasn't like the usual men Muffy dated. He treats Muffy the way she's always dreamed of being treated. He listens; he cares; he remembers. "He makes me feel safe and more cherished than any man I've ever known," she says.

So she decided to bring him to a little party of about 30 of her closest friends. . . .

Perhaps it was only Jake's nerves that caused him to commit some truly unforgivable faux pas that night. His sins were legion. Where do we start? First of all, he asked for a beer when everyone else was drinking white wine. He wore a worn turtleneck while everyone else had just removed the Polo tags from their clothing. He smoked. . . .

"The next day at least half of the people who had been at the party called to give me their impressions. They all said that they felt they just had to let me know that they thought Jake 'lacked polish' or 'seemed loud' or 'might not be a suitable match,'" Muffy says.

Now, you may think that Muffy's friends are simply very sensitive, demanding people. But you'd be wrong. Actually, they've been quite accepting of some of the other men that Muffy has brought to their little parties. Winston, for example, was a great favorite.

"He got drunk, ignored me, and asked for other women's phone numbers right in front of me. But he was six-foot-four, the classic preppie, with blond hair, horn-rimmed glasses, and Ralph Lauren clothes."

So now Muffy is confused. "Jake is the first guy I've been out with in a long time that I've really liked. I was excited about him and my friends knew that. I was surprised by their reaction. I'll admit there's some validity to all their comments, but it's hard to express how violent it was. It made me think about what these women really want in a man. Whatever they say, what they really want is someone they can take to a business dinner. They want someone who comes with a tux. Like a Ken doll."

Muffy may have come to a crossroads in her young life. It's clear that there's no way she can bring Jake among her friends for a while.

"I don't want their reaction to muddy my feelings until I get them sorted out," she says.

The preceding account is a real story, taken from a book about contemporary intimate relationships titled *Tales from the Front* (Kavesh & Lavin, 1988, pp. 118–121). Muffy is on the horns of a difficult dilemma. Romantic relationships are important to most people, but so are friendships, and Muffy may have to choose between the two. Muffy's story illustrates the significance of social relations in people's lives. It also foreshadows each of the topics that we'll cover in this chapter, as we look at behavior in its social context.

Social psychology is the branch of psychology concerned with the way individuals' thoughts, feelings, and behaviors are influenced by others. Our coverage of social psychology will focus on six broad topics, and an Application on prejudice will integrate ideas introduced in the main body of the chapter. Let's return to Muffy's story to get a glimpse of the various facets of social behavior that we'll examine in the coming pages:

• *Person perception.* The crux of Muffy's problem is that Jake didn't make a very good impression on her friends, primarily because her friends have preconceived views of "working-class stiffs." To what extent do people's expectations color their impressions of others? Can a bad first impression be overcome?

• *Attribution processes.* Muffy is struggling to understand her friends' rejection of Jake. When she implies that Jake's rejection is due to their snotty elitism, she's engaging in attribution, making an inference about the causes of her friends' behavior. How do people use attributions to explain social behavior? What kinds of bias are apparent in people's attributional tendencies?

• *Interpersonal attraction.* Jake and Muffy are different in many important ways—is it true that opposites attract? Why does Jake's lack of similarity to Muffy's friends lead to such disdain?

• *Attitudes.* Muffy's girlfriends have negative attitudes about working-class men. How are attitudes formed? What leads to attitude change? How do attitudes affect people's behavior?

• *Conformity and obedience.* Muffy's friends discourage her from dating Jake, putting her under pressure to conform to their values. What factors influence conformity? Can people be coaxed into doing things that contradict their values?

• *Behavior in groups.* Muffy belongs to a tight-knit group of friends who think along similar lines. Do people behave differently when they are in groups as opposed to when they are alone? Why do people in groups often think alike?

Social psychologists study how people are affected by the actual, imagined, or implied presence of others. Their interest is not limited to individuals' interactions with others, as people can engage in social behavior even when they're alone. For instance, if you were driving by yourself on a deserted highway and tossed your trash out your car window, your littering would be a social action. It would defy social norms, reflect your socialization and attitudes, and have repercussions (albeit, small) for other people in your society. Social psychologists often study individual behavior in a social context. This interest in understanding individual behavior should be readily apparent in our first section, on person perception.

PERSON PERCEPTION: FORMING IMPRESSIONS OF OTHERS

Can you remember the first meeting of your introductory psychology class? What kind of impression did your professor make on you that day? Did your instructor appear to be confident? Easygoing? Pompous? Open-minded? Cynical? Friendly? Were your first impressions supported or undermined by subsequent observations? When you interact with people, you're constantly engaged in *person perception,* **the process of forming impressions of others.** People show considerable ingenuity in piecing together clues about others' characteristics. However, impressions are often inaccurate because of the many biases and fallacies that occur in person perception. In this section we consider some of the factors that influence, and often distort, people's perceptions of others.

Effects of Physical Appearance

"You shouldn't judge a book by its cover." "Beauty is only skin deep." People know better than to let physical attractiveness determine their perceptions of others' personal qualities. Or do they? Studies have shown that judgments of others' personality are often swayed by their appearance, especially their physical attractiveness. People tend to ascribe desirable personality characteristics to those who are good looking, seeing them as more sociable, friendly, poised, warm, and well adjusted than those who are less attractive (Dion, 1986; Eagly et al., 1991). In reality, research findings suggest that there is little correlation between attractiveness and personality traits (Feingold, 1992). Why do we inaccurately assume that a connection exists between good looks and personality? According to Alan Feingold (1992), one key factor is

that extremely attractive people are scarce in the real world but vastly overrepresented in the entertainment media, so that "the impressions we form of good-looking people are shaped primarily by Hollywood and Madison Avenue" (p. 333). In movies and TV shows, the stars "are not only inordinately attractive, but they also ooze charm and sensuality."

Physical attractiveness influences perceptions of competence less than perceptions of personality, but people nevertheless tend to view good-looking individuals as more intelligent and successful than their less attractive counterparts (Eagly et al., 1991). For example, in a study of male employees in two large accounting firms, Ross and Ferris (1981) found that physical attractiveness was positively related to evaluations of the employees' performance and their salary increases. Good looks seem to have relatively little impact on perceptions of honesty and integrity (Eagly et al., 1991). However, there is a tendency to view people with *baby-faced features*—such as large eyes, smooth skin, and a rounded chin—as more honest and trustworthy (Zebrowitz, Voinescu, & Collins, 1996). Baby-faced individuals are also seen as relatively warm, submissive, helpless, and naive (Zebrowitz, 1996).

Observers are also quick to draw inferences about people based on how they move, talk, and gesture—that is, their style of nonverbal expressiveness (Ambady & Rosenthal, 1992). For example, research suggests that people with a "youthful" gait, characterized by bouncy rhythm, swaying hips, and swinging arms, are viewed as happier and more powerful than people who exhibit a stiffer, "older" gait (Montepare & Zebrowitz-McArthur, 1988).

Cognitive Schemas

Even though every individual is unique, people tend to categorize one another. For instance, in our opening story, Muffy is characterized as "the quintessential yuppie." In another story in *Tales from the Front,* a man describes his date as a "BUP"—a "boring, uptight prude." Such labels reflect the use of cognitive schemas in person perception.

As we discussed in the chapter on memory (Chapter 7), *schemas* are cognitive structures that guide information processing. People have schemas for everything from inanimate objects (bicycles, apartments) to human activities (eating lunch, going to a gas station). Individuals use schemas to organize the world around them—including their social world. **Social schemas are organized clusters of ideas about categories of social events and people.** People have social schemas for events such as dates, picnics, committee meetings, and family reunions, as well as for certain categories of people, such as "dumb jocks," "social climbers," "frat rats," and "wimps" (see Figure 16.1).

Individuals depend on social schemas because the schemas help them to efficiently process and store the wealth of information that they take in about others in their interactions. When a schema is activated, it's likely to influence one's perceptions of a person (Fiske & Taylor, 1991). For example, in our opening story, Muffy's friends apparently categorized Jake as a "working-class stiff." The activation of this schema probably increased their tendency to notice behaviors that fit their schema for working-class stiffs, such as beer drinking and smoking, while overlooking his kindness and other good points.

Stereotypes

Some of the schemas that individuals apply to people, such as "BUP," are unique products of their personal experiences, while other schemas, such as "yuppie," may be part of their shared cultural background. *Stereotypes* are special types of schemas that fall into the latter category (Anderson & Klatzky, 1987). **Stereotypes are widely held beliefs that people have certain characteristics because of their membership in a particular group.**

The most common stereotypes in our society are those based on sex and on membership in ethnic or occupational groups. Preconceived notions that Jews are mercenary, that blacks have rhythm, that Germans are methodical, and that Italians are pas-

sionate are examples of common *ethnic stereotypes*. People who subscribe to traditional *gender stereotypes* tend to assume that women are emotional, submissive, illogical, and passive, while men are unemotional, dominant, logical, and aggressive. *Occupational stereotypes* suggest that lawyers are manipulative, accountants are conforming, artists are moody, and so forth.

Stereotyping is a normal cognitive process that saves on the time and effort required to get a handle on people individually (Macrae, Milne, & Bodenhausen, 1994). Stereotypes save energy by simplifying our social world. However, this conservation of energy often comes at some cost in terms of accuracy. Stereotypes frequently are broad overgeneralizations that ignore the diversity within social groups and foster inaccurate perceptions of people (Stephan, 1989). Obviously, not all Jews, males, and lawyers behave alike. Most people who subscribe to stereotypes realize that not all members of a group are identical. For instance, they may admit that some Jews aren't mercenary, some

In general, people have a bias toward viewing good-looking men and women as bright, competent, and talented. However, people sometimes downplay the talent of successful women who happen to be attractive, attributing their success to their good looks instead of to their competence.

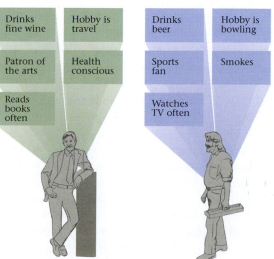

Sophisticated professional   **Working-class stiff**

Figure 16.1
Examples of social schemas. Everyone has social schemas for various "types" of people, such as sophisticated professionals or working-class stiffs. Social schemas are clusters of beliefs that guide information processing.

men aren't competitive, and some lawyers aren't manipulative. However, they may still tend to assume that Jews, males, and lawyers are *more likely* than others to have these characteristics. Even if stereotypes mean only that people think in terms of slanted *probabilities,* their expectations may lead them to misperceive individuals with whom they interact. As we've noted in previous chapters, perception is subjective, and people often see what they expect to see.

Subjectivity in Person Perception

Stereotypes and other schemas create biases in person perception that frequently lead to confirmation of people's expectations about others. If there's any ambiguity in someone's behavior, people are likely to interpret what they see in a way that's consistent with their expectations (E. Jones, 1990). Thus, after dealing with a pushy female customer, a salesman who holds traditional gender stereotypes might characterize the woman as "emotional." In contrast, he might characterize a pushy male who exhibits exactly the same behavior as "aggressive."

People not only see what they expect to see, they also tend to overestimate how often they see it (Hamilton & Sherman, 1989; Johnson & Mullen, 1994). *Illusory correlation* **occurs when people estimate that they have encountered more confirmations of an association between social traits than they have actually seen.** Statements like "I've never met an honest lawyer" illustrate this effect.

Memory processes can contribute to confirmatory biases in person perception in a variety of ways. Often, individuals selectively recall facts that fit with the schemas they apply to people (Fiske & Taylor, 1991). Evidence for such a tendency was found in a study by Cohen (1981). In this experiment, subjects watched a videotape of a woman, described as either a waitress or a librarian, who engaged in a variety of activities, including listening to classical music, drinking beer, and watching TV. When asked to recall what the woman did during the filmed sequence, subjects tended to remember activities consistent with their stereotypes of waitresses and librarians. For instance, subjects who thought the woman was a waitress tended to recall her beer drinking, while subjects who thought she was a librarian tended to recall her listening to classical music.

Another source of subjectivity in person perception is that people exhibit an *egocentric slant* in making social judgments (Dunning & Hayes, 1996).

Variations in person perception arise in part because people tend to use their own behavior as the standard of comparison when evaluating others. For example, Dunning and Cohen (1992) asked students to evaluate the athleticism of a person who spent about three hours a week playing basketball. Subjects who engaged in several hours a week of athletic activity themselves rated the person as less athletic than subjects who reported little or no athletic activity. Obviously, if several people use different standards (based on their own behavior) in evaluating the same individual, they are likely to draw very different, perhaps idiosyncratic, conclusions.

An Evolutionary Perspective on Bias in Person Perception

Why is the process of person perception riddled with bias? Evolutionary psychologists argue that many of the biases seen in social perception were adaptive in humans' ancestral environment (Krebs & Denton, 1997). For example, they argue that person perception is swayed by physical attractiveness because attractiveness was associated with reproductive potential in women, and with health, vigor, and the accumulation of material resources in men. What about baby-faced features? Evolutionary theorists assert that the tendency to view babies as helpless creatures requiring nurture would be highly adaptive and has probably been preprogammed in humans by natural selection (Springer & Berry, 1997). The tendency to view baby-faced adults as naive, submissive, and honest may simply be a spillover effect from humans' evolutionary heritage.

Evolutionary theorists attribute the human tendency to automatically categorize others to our distant ancestors' need to quickly separate friend from foe. They assert that humans are programmed by evolution to immediately classify people as members of an *ingroup*—**a group that one belongs to and identifies with,** or as members of an *outgroup*—**a group that one does not belong to or identify with.** This crucial categorization is thought to structure subsequent perceptions. As Krebs and Denton (1997) put it, "It is as though the act of classifying others as ingroup or outgroup members activates two quite different brain circuits" (p. 27). Ingroup members tend to be viewed in a favorable light, whereas outgroup members tend to be viewed in terms of various negative stereotypes. According to Krebs and Denton, these negative stereotypes ("They are inferior; they are all alike; they will exploit us") move outgroups out of our domain of empathy, so we feel justified in not liking them or discriminating against them.

Thus, evolutionary psychologists ascribe much of the bias in person perception to cognitive mechanisms that have been shaped by natural selection. Their speculation is thought provoking, but empirical work is needed to test their hypotheses.

Recap of Key Points

• People's perceptions of others can be distorted by a variety of factors, including physical appearance. People tend to attribute desirable characteristics, such as intelligence, competence, warmth, and friendliness, to those who are good looking.

• Baby-faced people are viewed as honest. Perceptions of people are also influenced by their style of nonverbal expressiveness.

• People use social schemas to categorize others into types. Stereotypes are widely held social schemas that lead people to expect that others will have certain characteristics because of their membership in a specific group.

• Gender, ethnic, and occupational stereotypes are common. In interacting with others, stereotypes may lead people to see what they expect to see and to overestimate how often they see it. Another source of subjectivity in person perception is the egocentric slant that people bring to their judgments.

• Evolutionary psychologists argue that many biases in person perception were adaptive in humans' ancestral past. The human tendency to automatically categorize others may reflect the primitive need to quickly separate friend from foe.

ATTRIBUTION PROCESSES: EXPLAINING BEHAVIOR

It's Friday evening and you're sitting around at home feeling bored. You call a few friends to see whether they'd like to go out. They all say that they'd love to go, but they have other commitments and they can't. Their commitments sound vague, and you feel that their reasons for not going out with you are rather flimsy. How do you explain these rejections? Do your friends really have commitments? Are they worn out by school and work? Are they just lazy and apathetic about going out? When they said that they'd love to go, were they being sincere? Or do they find you boring? Could they be right? Are you boring? These questions illustrate a process that people engage in routinely: the explanation of behavior. *Attributions* play a key role in these explanatory efforts, and they have significant effects on social relations.

Attributions: What? Why? When?

 12a

Although we discussed attributions briefly in Chapter 14, let's review what they are, elaborate on why people make them, and discuss when people are likely to engage in attributional thinking.

What are attributions? **Attributions are inferences that people draw about the causes of events, others' behavior, and their own behavior.** If you conclude that a friend turned down your invitation because she's overworked, you've made an attribution about the cause of her behavior (and, implicitly, rejected other possible expla-

nations). If you conclude that you're stuck at home with nothing to do because you failed to plan ahead, you've made an attribution about the cause of an event (being stuck at home). If you conclude that you failed to plan ahead because you're a procrastinator, you've made an attribution about the cause of your own behavior.

Why do people make attributions? Individuals make attributions mainly because they have a strong need to understand their experiences. They want to make sense out of their own behavior, others' actions, and the events in their lives.

When do people make attributions? People don't attempt to explain everything that happens around them. You're not likely to mull over why a friend said "Hi" this morning, or why a colleague took the elevator to get to the 20th floor of the building you work in. However, if your friend *did not* say "Hi," or if your colleague *walked* up 20 flights of stairs instead of taking the elevator, you might wonder why. A variety of factors influence whether people are stimulated to engage in attributional thinking (Hilton, Fein, & Miller, 1993; E. Jones, 1990; Weiner, 1985). Generally, people are more likely to make attributions (1) when unusual events grab their attention, (2) when events have personal consequences for them, (3) when others behave in unexpected ways, and (4) when they are suspicious about the motives underlying someone's behavior.

Having looked at the what, why, and when of attribution, we'll devote the remainder of our dis-

"Often the momentary situation which, at least in part, determines the behavior of a person is disregarded and the behavior is taken as a manifestation of personal characteristics."

FRITZ HEIDER

Figure 16.2
Kelley's covariation model of attribution. According to Kelley (1967, 1973), people consider three factors in making attributions: consensus, consistency, and distinctiveness. Each of these factors can vary along a continuum, yielding a complex "Rubik's cube" for attributional thinking.

cussion in this section to *how* people explain the causes of behavior. Specifically, we'll examine theoretical models that identify the key dimensions of attributions and look at various sources of bias in attributional thinking.

Internal Versus External Attributions

Fritz Heider (1958) was the first to describe how people make attributions. He asserted that people tend to locate the cause of behavior either *within a person,* attributing it to personal factors, or *outside a person,* attributing it to environmental factors.

Elaborating on Heider's insight, various theorists have agreed that explanations of behavior and events can be categorized as internal or external attributions (Jones & Davis, 1965; Kelley, 1967; Weiner, 1974). **Internal attributions ascribe the causes of behavior to personal dispositions, traits, abilities, and feelings. External attributions ascribe the causes of behavior to situational demands and environmental constraints.** For example, if a friend's business fails, you might attribute it to your friend's lack of business acumen (an internal, personal factor) or to negative trends in the nation's economic climate (an external, situational explanation). Parents who find out that their teenage son has just banged up the car may blame it on his carelessness (a personal disposition) or on slippery road conditions (a situational factor).

Internal and external attributions can have a tremendous impact on everyday interpersonal interactions. Blaming a friend's business failure on poor business acumen as opposed to a poor economy will have a great impact on how you view your friend—not to mention on whether you'll lend him or her money in the future. Likewise, if parents attribute their son's automobile accident to slippery road conditions, they're likely to deal with the event very differently than if they attribute it to his carelessness.

Given the importance of personal versus situational attributions, the next question should be obvious: What leads people to make an internal or external attribution? Let's examine a theory that attempts to address this question.

Kelley's Covariation Model

Harold H. Kelley (1967, 1973) has devised a theory that identifies some of the important factors that people consider in making internal or external attributions. Kelley's *covariation model* is based on the assumption that people attribute behavior to factors that are present when the behavior takes place and absent when it does not. According to Kelley, when people attempt to infer the causes of an actor's behavior, they usually consider three types of information: consistency, distinctiveness, and consensus (see Figure 16.2). Let's look at how a professor might weigh each of these factors in figuring out why a hypothetical student (let's call him Bruce) is frequently argumentative in class.

Consistency refers to whether an actor's behavior in a situation is the same over time (across occasions). In our hypothetical case, the professor would ask, "Is Bruce always argumentative in my class meetings?"

Distinctiveness refers to whether a person's behavior is unique to the specific entity that is the target of the person's actions. Thus, the professor might ask, "Is Bruce argumentative only with me, or is he argumentative with all his professors?"

Consensus refers to whether other people in the same situation tend to respond like the actor. Thus, the professor might think, "Are Bruce's classmates also argumentative?"

According to Kelley, low consistency favors an external attribution, but high consistency is compatible with either an internal or an external attribution. Highly consistent behavior is likely to lead to external attributions when distinctiveness and consensus are high and to internal attributions when distinctiveness and consensus are low (see Figure 16.3).

Studies have supported many specific predictions of Kelley's model, but research has revealed that people generally are not as deliberate, thoughtful, and logical as the model assumes (Fiske &

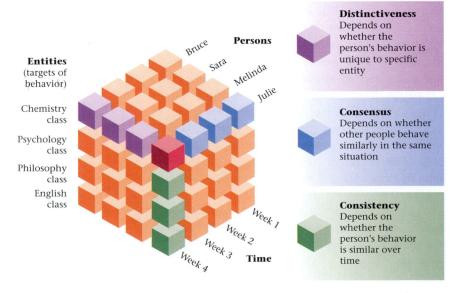

Entities
(targets of behavior)

Chemistry class

Psychology class

Philosophy class

English class

Persons — Bruce, Sara, Melinda, Julie

Time — Week 1, Week 2, Week 3, Week 4

Distinctiveness
Depends on whether the person's behavior is unique to specific entity

Consensus
Depends on whether other people behave similarly in the same situation

Consistency
Depends on whether the person's behavior is similar over time

Taylor, 1991). Attributions often involve simplistic mental shortcuts, and they can be distorted by a variety of illogical biases.

Attributions for Success and Failure

Some psychologists have sought to discover additional dimensions of attributional thinking besides the internal-external dimension. After studying the attributions that people make in explaining success and failure, Bernard Weiner and his colleagues concluded that people often focus on the *stability* of the causes underlying behavior (Weiner, 1974; Weiner et al., 1972). According to Weiner, the stable-unstable dimension in attribution cuts across the internal-external dimension, creating four types of attributions for success and failure, as shown in Figure 16.4.

Let's apply Weiner's model to a concrete event. Imagine that you're contemplating why you failed to get a job that you wanted. You might attribute your setback to internal factors that are stable (lack of ability) or unstable (inadequate effort to put together an eye-catching résumé). Or you might attribute your setback to external factors that are stable (too much outstanding competition) or unstable (bad luck). If you got the job, the explanations you might offer for your success would fall into the same four categories: internal-stable (your excellent ability), internal-unstable (your hard work to assemble a superb résumé), external-stable (lack of topflight competition), and external-unstable (good luck).

Weiner (1980, 1986) eventually added a third dimension—the *controllability* of events—to his model. Other theorists have built on Weiner's foundation in various ways. As we discussed in Chapter 14, attributional theories of depression focus on the internal-external and stability dimensions and on whether people's attributions have *global* (far-reaching) or *specific* implications about their personal qualities. Studies suggest that internal, stable, and global attributions for personal setbacks can help foster feelings of depression (Nolen-Hoeksema, Girgus, & Seligman, 1992; Peterson, Maier, & Seligman, 1993). The correlations between attributional style and feelings of depression are modest (Anderson et al., 1994), but they show that attributions can have important implications for how people see themselves—as well as others. However, attributions are not entirely logical and objective. We turn next to the matter of biases in attribution processes.

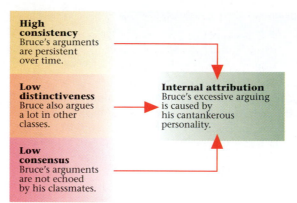

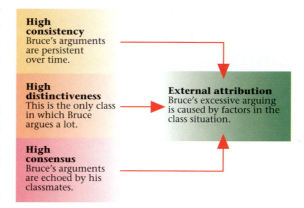

Bias in Attribution

Attributions are only inferences. Your attributions may not be the correct explanations for events. Paradoxical as it may seem, people often arrive at inaccurate explanations even when they contemplate the causes of *their own behavior*. Attributions ultimately represent *guesswork* about the causes of events, and these guesses tend to be slanted in certain directions. Let's look at the principal biases seen in attribution.

Actor-Observer Bias

Your view of your own behavior can be quite different from the view of someone else observing

Figure 16.3
Examples of attributional thinking. In Kelley's model, high consistency, low distinctiveness, and low consensus should lead to an internal attribution, whereas high consistency, high distinctiveness, and high consensus should lead to an external attribution. These principles are applied here to the example in the text about Bruce's arguing in class.

Figure 16.4
Attributions for success and failure. Weiner's model assumes that people's explanations for success and failure emphasize internal versus external causes and stable versus unstable causes. Examples of causal factors that fit into each of the four cells in Weiner's model are shown in the diagram.

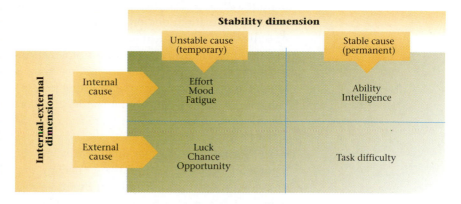

Check your understanding of attribution processes by analyzing possible explanations for an athletic team's success. Imagine that the women's track team at your school has just won a regional championship that qualifies it for the national tournament. Around the campus, you hear people attribute the team's success to a variety of factors. Examine the attributions shown below and place each of them in one of the cells of Weiner's model of attribution (just record the letter inside the cell). The answers are in Appendix A.

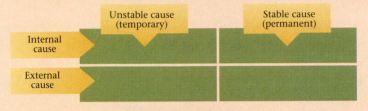

a. "They won only because the best two athletes on Central State's team were out with injuries—talk about good fortune!"

b. "They won because they have some of the best talent in the country."

c. "Anybody could win this region; the competition is far below average in comparison to the rest of the country."

d. "They won because they put in a great deal of last-minute effort and practice, and they were incredibly fired up for the regional tourney after last year's near miss."

you. When an actor and an observer draw inferences about the causes of the actor's behavior, they often make different attributions. A common form of bias seen in observers is the *fundamental attribution error*, **which refers to observers' bias in favor of internal attributions in explaining others' behavior** (Ross, 1977). Of course, in many instances, an internal attribution may not be an "error" (Harvey, Town, & Yarkin, 1981). However, observers have a curious tendency to overestimate the likelihood that an actor's behavior reflects personal qualities rather than situational factors. Why? One reason is that situational pressures may not be readily apparent to an observer. As Gilbert and Malone (1995, p. 25) put it, "When one tries to point to a situation, one often stabs empty air." Another reason is that attributing others' behavior to their dispositions is a relatively simple, effortless process that borders on automatic (Trope & Liberman, 1993). In contrast, explaining people's behavior in terms of situational factors is a more complex process that requires more thought and effort (Krull & Erickson, 1995).

To illustrate the gap that often exists between actors' and observers' attributions, imagine that you're visiting your bank and you fly into a rage over a mistake made on your account. Observers

who witness your rage are likely to make an internal attribution and infer that you are surly, temperamental, and quarrelsome. They may be right, but if asked, you'd probably attribute your rage to the frustrating situation. Perhaps you're normally a calm, easygoing person, but today you've been in line for 20 minutes, you just straightened out a similar error by the same bank last week, and you're being treated rudely by the teller. Observers often are unaware of historical and situational considerations such as these, so they tend to make internal attributions for another's behavior (White & Younger, 1988).

In contrast, the circumstances that have influenced an actor's behavior tend to be more salient to the actor. Hence, actors are more likely than observers to locate the cause of their behavior in the situation. In general, then, *actors favor external attributions for their behavior, while observers are more likely to explain the same behavior with internal attributions* (Jones & Nisbett, 1971; Watson, 1982).

Defensive Attribution

In attempting to explain the calamities and setbacks that befall other people, an observer's tendency to make internal attributions may become even stronger than normal. Let's say that a friend gets mugged and severely beaten. You may attribute the mugging to your friend's carelessness or stupidity ("He should have known better than to be in that neighborhood at that time") rather than to bad luck. Why? Because if you attribute your friend's misfortune to bad luck, you have to face the ugly reality that it could just as easily happen to you. To avoid disturbing thoughts such as these, people often attribute mishaps to victims' negligence (Salminen, 1992; Thornton, 1984, 1992).

Defensive attribution **is a tendency to blame victims for their misfortune, so that one feels less likely to be victimized in a similar way.** Blaming victims for their calamities also helps people maintain their belief that they live in a just world, where they're unlikely to experience similar troubles (Lerner & Miller, 1978). The bias toward making defensive attributions is not all that strong (Burger, 1981), but the phenomenon can have unfortunate consequences. Blaming victims for their setbacks causes them to be seen in a negative light, and undesirable traits are unfairly attributed to them. Thus, it is assumed that burglary victims must be careless, that people who get fired must be incompetent, that poor people must be lazy, that rape victims must be seductive ("She probably asked for it"), and so on. As you can see, defensive attribution can lead to unwarranted derogation of victims of misfortune.

Self-Serving Bias

The self-serving bias in attribution comes into play when people attempt to explain success and failure. This bias may either strengthen or weaken one's normal attributional tendencies, depending on whether one is trying to explain positive or negative outcomes (Bradley, 1978; Brown & Rogers, 1991). **The *self-serving bias* is the tendency to attribute one's successes to personal factors and one's failures to situational factors.** Interestingly, this bias grows stronger as time passes after an event, so that people tend to take progressively more credit for their successes and less responsibility for their failures (Burger, 1986).

In explaining *failure*, the usual actor-observer biases are apparent. Actors tend to make external attributions, blaming their failures on unfavorable situational factors, while observers attribute the same failures to the actors' personal shortcomings. Thus, if you fail an exam, you may place the blame on the poorly constructed test items, lousy teaching, distractions in the hallway, or a bad week at work (all external attributions). However, an observer is more likely to attribute your failure to your lack of ability or lack of study (both internal attributions).

In explaining *success,* the usual actor-observer differences are reversed to some degree. Thus, if you get a high exam score, you'll probably make an internal attribution and point to your ability or your hard work (Forsyth & McMillan, 1981). In contrast, an observer may be more likely to infer that the test was easy or that you were lucky (external attributions). Although actors like to take credit for their successes, this tendency is diminished when people realize that their audience knows better (Schlenker, Weigold, & Hallam, 1990). Interestingly, when a person's contribution to a success is too obvious to be missed, he or she may act modest and publicly attribute the success to good luck or other situational factors.

Culture and Attributional Tendencies

Do the patterns of attribution observed in subjects from Western societies transcend culture? More research is needed, but the preliminary evidence suggests not. Some interesting cultural disparities have emerged in research on attribution processes.

According to Harry Triandis (1989, 1994), cultural differences in *individualism* versus *collectivism*

CONCEPT CHECK 16.2
Recognizing Bias in Social Cognition

Check your understanding of bias in social cognition by identifying various types of errors that are common in person perception and attribution. Imagine that you're a nonvoting student member of a college committee at Southwest State University that is hiring a new political science professor. As you listen to the committee's discussion, you hear examples of (a) the illusory correlation effect, (b) stereotyping, (c) the fundamental attribution error, and (d) defensive attribution. Indicate which of these is at work in the excerpts from committee members' deliberations below. The answers are in Appendix A.

_____ 1. "I absolutely won't consider the fellow who arrived 30 minutes late for his interview. Anybody who can't make a job interview on time is either irresponsible or hopelessly disorganized. I don't care what he says about the airline messing up his reservations."

_____ 2. "You know, I was very, very impressed with the young female applicant, and I would love to hire her, but every time we add a young woman to the faculty in liberal arts, she gets pregnant within the first year." The committee chairperson, who has heard this line from this professor before replies, "You always say that, so I finally did a systematic check of what's happened in the past. Of the last 14 women hired in liberal arts, only one has become pregnant within a year."

_____ 3. "The first one I want to rule out is the guy who's been practicing law for the last ten years. Although he has an excellent background in political science, I just don't trust lawyers. They're all ambitious, power-hungry, manipulative cutthroats. He'll be a divisive force in the department."

_____ 4. "I say we forget about the two candidates who lost their faculty slots in the massive financial crisis at Western Polytechnic last year. I know it sounds cruel, but they brought it on themselves with their fiscal irresponsibility over at Western. Thank goodness we'll never let anything like that happen around here. As far as I'm concerned, if these guys couldn't see that crisis coming, they must be pretty dense."

The winning Olympic diving champions from mainland China, a collectivist society, probably possess a far different attributional bias about their success than that which would be held by their Western colleagues, who are influenced by a culture centered on individualism.

how one's actions will affect other group members. Child-rearing patterns in collectivist cultures emphasize the importance of obedience, reliability, and proper behavior, whereas individualistic cultures emphasize the development of independence, self-esteem, and self-reliance.

A variety of factors influence whether societies cherish individualism as opposed to collectivism. Among other things, increases in a culture's affluence, education, urbanization, and social mobility tend to foster more individualism (Triandis, 1994). Many contemporary societies are in transition, but generally speaking, North American and Western European cultures tend to be individualistic, whereas Asian, African, and Latin American cultures tend to be higher in collectivism (Hofstede, 1980, 1983) (see Figure 16.5).

How does individualism versus collectivism relate to patterns of attribution? The evidence suggests that collectivist cultures may promote different attributional biases than individualistic cultures. For example, people from collectivist societies may be less prone to the *fundamental attribution error* than those from individualistic societies. In Western culture, people are viewed as autonomous individuals who are responsible for their actions. Endorsing beliefs such as "You can do anything you put your mind to" or "You have no one to blame but yourself," Westerners typically explain behavior in terms of people's personality traits and unique abilities. In contrast, collectivists, who value interdependence and obedience, are more likely to assume that one's behavior reflects adherence to group norms. Consistent with this analysis, researchers have found that American subjects explain others' behavior in terms of internal attributions more than Hindu subjects

influence attributional tendencies as well as other aspects of social behavior. ***Individualism*** involves **putting personal goals ahead of group goals and defining one's identity in terms of personal attributes rather than group memberships.** In contrast, ***collectivism*** involves **putting group goals ahead of personal goals and defining one's identity in terms of the groups one belongs to** (such as one's family, tribe, work group, social class, caste, and so on). In comparison to individualistic cultures, collectivist cultures place a higher priority on shared values and resources, cooperation, mutual interdependence, and concern for

Figure 16.5
Individualism versus collectivism around the world. Hofstede (1980, 1983) used survey data from over 100,000 employees of a large, multinational corporation to estimate the emphasis on individualism versus collectivism in 50 nations and 3 "regions," for which he combined data for adjacent countries. Data were not available for much of what used to be the Communist bloc or for much of Africa, but his large, diverse international sample remains unequaled to date. As you can see, Hofstede's estimates suggest that North American and Western European nations tend to be relatively individualistic, whereas more collectivism is found in Asian, African, and Latin American countries.

Hofstede's (1983) rankings of national cultures' individualism

1. United States	19. Israel	37. Hong Kong
2. Australia	20. Spain	38. Chile
3. Great Britain	21. India	40. Singapore
4. Canada	22. Argentina	40. Thailand
4. Netherlands	22. Japan	40. West Africa region
6. New Zealand	24. Iran	42. El Salvador
7. Italy	25. Jamaica	43. Taiwan
8. Belgium	26. Arab region	44. South Korea
9. Denmark	26. Brazil	45. Peru
10. France	28. Turkey	46. Costa Rica
11. Sweden	29. Uraguay	47. Indonesia
12. Ireland	30. Greece	47. Pakistan
13. Norway	31. Philippines	49. Columbia
14. Switzerland	32. Mexico	50. Venezuela
15. West Germany	34. East Africa region	51. Panama
16. South Africa	34. Portugal	52. Ecuador
17. Finland	34. Yugoslavia	53. Guatemala
18. Austria	36. Malaysia	

(Miller, 1984) or Japanese subjects do (Weisz, Rothbaum, & Blackburn, 1984).

Although the *self-serving bias* has been documented in a variety of cultures (Fletcher & Ward, 1988), it may be particularly prevalent in individualistic, Western societies, where an emphasis on competition and high self-esteem motivates people to try to impress others, as well as themselves. In contrast, Japanese subjects exhibit a *self-effacing bias* in explaining success (Kashima & Triandis, 1986; Markus & Kitayama, 1991). They tend to attribute their successes to help they receive from others or to the ease of the task, while downplaying the importance of their ability; they attribute their failures mainly to lack of effort. Studies have also failed to find the usual self-serving bias in Nepalese subjects (Smith & Bond, 1994). In a similar vein, Lee and Seligman (1997) found that a Chinese sample exhibited a much weaker self-serving bias than a similar sample of white Americans. A great deal of additional research is needed before any broad conclusions can be drawn, but collectivism may put a different spin on attributional bias.

Attributions are an important aspect of social behavior. For example, in recent years researchers have learned that certain patterns of attribution can play a key role in either the growth or the deterioration of intimate relationships (Fincham & Bradbury, 1993). In the next section, we'll look at a variety of other factors that influence the development of close relationships.

Recap of Key Points

- Attributions are inferences about the causes of events and behavior. Individuals make attributions to understand their social world, especially when behavior is unusual, is unexpected, or has personal consequences.
- Attributions can be classified as internal or external. Internal attributions ascribe behavior to personal dispositions and traits, whereas external attributions locate the cause of behavior in the environment.
- Kelley's model of attribution suggests that internal attributions are more likely when one's behavior is consistent, not distinctive to an entity, and low in consensus value. Weiner's model proposes that attributions for success and failure should be analyzed in terms of the stability of causes, as well as along the internal-external dimension.
- Actors and observers often make different attributions for the same event or behavior. Observers favor internal attributions to explain another's behavior (the fundamental attribution error), while actors favor external attributions to explain their own behavior.
- In defensive attribution, people unfairly blame victims for their misfortune (with internal attributions) to reduce their own feelings of vulnerability. The self-serving bias is the tendency to attribute one's good outcomes to personal factors and one's bad outcomes to situational factors.
- Cultures vary in their emphasis on individualism as opposed to collectivism, and these differences appear to influence attributional tendencies. The fundamental attribution error and the self-serving bias in attribution may be by-products of Western cultures' individualism.

CLOSE RELATIONSHIPS: LIKING AND LOVING

"I just don't know what she sees in him. She could do so much better for herself. I suppose he's a nice guy, but they're just not right for each other." Can't you imagine Muffy's friends making these comments in discussing her relationship with Jake? You've probably heard similar remarks on many occasions. These comments illustrate people's interest in analyzing the dynamics of attraction. **Interpersonal attraction** refers to positive feelings toward another. Social psychologists use this term broadly to encompass a variety of experiences, including liking, friendship, admiration, lust, and love. In this section, we'll analyze key factors that influence attraction and examine several theoretical perspectives on the mystery of love.

Key Factors in Attraction

Many factors influence who is attracted to whom. Here we'll discuss factors that promote the development of liking, friendship, and love. Although these are different types of attraction, the interpersonal dynamics at work in each are surprisingly similar. Each is influenced by proximity, physical attractiveness, similarity, and reciprocity.

Proximity Effects

It would be difficult for you to develop a friendship with someone you never met. It happens occasionally (among pen pals or users of on-line computer services, for instance), but attraction usually depends on people being in the same place at the same time, making proximity a major factor in attraction. *Proximity* **refers to geographic, residential, and other forms of spatial closeness** (classroom seating, office arrangements, and so forth). Generally, people become acquainted with, and attracted to, people who live, work, shop, and play nearby. The importance of spatial factors in living arrangements was apparent in a classic study of friendship patterns among married graduate students living in university housing projects (Festinger, Schachter, & Back, 1950). The closer people's doors were, the more likely they were to become friends.

Proximity effects may seem self-evident, but it's sobering to realize that your friendships and love interests are shaped by arbitrary office desk arrangements, dormitory floor assignments, and traffic patterns in apartment complexes. In spite of the increasing geographic mobility in modern society, people still tend to marry someone who grew up nearby (Ineichen, 1979).

Physical Attractiveness

Although people often say that "beauty is only skin deep," the empirical evidence suggests that most people don't really believe that homily. The importance of physical attractiveness was demonstrated in a recent study of college students in which unacquainted men and women were sent off on a "get-acquainted" date (Sprecher & Duck, 1994). The investigators were mainly interested in how communication might affect the process of

According to the matching hypothesis, males and females who are similar in physical attractiveness are likely to be drawn together. This type of matching may also influence the formation of friendships.

attraction, but to put this factor in context they also measured subjects' perceptions of their date's physical attractiveness and similarity to themselves. They found that the quality of communication during the date did have some effect on females' interest in friendship, but the key determinant of romantic attraction for both sexes was the physical attractiveness of the other person. Many other studies have demonstrated the singular prominence of physical attractiveness in the initial stage of dating and have shown that it continues to influence the course of commitment as dating relationships evolve (Hendrick & Hendrick, 1992; Patzer, 1985). In the realm of romance, being physically attractive appears to be more important for females than males (Feingold, 1990).

Although people prefer physically attractive partners in romantic relationships, they may consider their own level of attractiveness in pursuing dates. **The *matching hypothesis* proposes that males and females of approximately equal physical attractiveness are likely to select each other as partners.** The matching hypothesis is supported by evidence that married couples tend to be very similar in level of physical attractiveness (Feingold, 1988b). However, there's some debate about whether people match up by their own choice (Aron, 1988; Kalick & Hamilton, 1986). Some theorists believe that people mostly pursue high attractiveness in partners and that their matching is the result of social forces beyond their control, such as rejection by more attractive others.

Most of the studies of physical beauty and attraction have focused on dating relationships, and only a few have looked at friendship formation. However, the studies of friendship suggest that people prefer attractiveness in their opposite-sex friends as well as their dates (Lyman, Hatlelid, & Macurdy, 1981). Researchers have also found evidence for matching effects in same-sex friendships (McKillip & Riedel, 1983). Interestingly, this same-sex matching appears to occur among male friends but not among female friends (Feingold, 1988b).

Similarity Effects

Is it true that "birds of a feather flock together," or do "opposites attract"? Research provides far more support for the former than the latter. Married and dating couples tend to be similar in age, race, religion, social class, personality, education, intelligence, physical attractiveness, and attitudes (Brehm, 1992; Hendrick & Hendrick, 1992). In married couples, personality similarity appears to be associated with greater marital happiness (Caspi

& Herbener, 1990). Similarity is also seen among friends. For instance, adolescent friends are more similar than nonfriends in educational goals and performance, political and religious activities, illicit drug use, and self-concept (Deutsch et al., 1991; Kandel, 1978). Adult friends also tend to be relatively similar in terms of income, education, occupational status, ethnicity, and religion (Blieszner & Adams, 1992).

The most obvious explanation for these correlations is that similarity causes attraction. Laboratory experiments on *attitude similarity,* conducted by Donn Byrne and his colleagues, suggest that similarity does cause liking (Byrne, 1971; Byrne, Clore, & Smeaton, 1986). In these studies, subjects who have previously provided information on their own attitudes are led to believe that they'll be meeting a stranger. They're given information about the stranger's views that has been manipulated to show various degrees of similarity to their own views. As attitude similarity increases, subjects' ratings of the likability of the stranger increase. This evidence supports the notion that similarity promotes attraction, but it's also consistent with a somewhat different explanation proposed by Rosenbaum (1986).

Rosenbaum has marshaled evidence suggesting that similarity effects occur in attraction not because similarity fosters liking but because *dissimilarity* leads to *dislike* of others. In one study of his "repulsion hypothesis," Rosenbaum found that Democrats did not rate other Democrats (similar others) higher than controls as much as they rated Republicans (dissimilar others) lower than controls. Rosenbaum acknowledges that similarity sometimes causes liking, but he maintains that *dissimilarity causes disdain* more frequently. Thus, there is reason to believe that liking is influenced by *both* similarity and dissimilarity in attitudes (Smeaton, Byrne, & Murnen, 1989; Tan & Singh, 1995).

Reciprocity Effects

In his book *How to Win Friends and Influence People,* Dale Carnegie (1936) suggested that people can gain others' liking by showering them with praise and flattery. However, we've all heard that "flattery will get you nowhere." Which advice is right? The evidence suggests that flattery will get you somewhere, with some people, some of the time.

In interpersonal attraction, **reciprocity** involves **liking those who show that they like you.** In general, research indicates that we tend to like those who show that they like us and that we tend to see others as liking us more if we like them.

Thus, it appears that liking breeds liking and loving promotes loving (Byrne & Murnen, 1988).

A recent study suggests that in romantic relationships this reciprocity effect even extends to partners "idealizing" each other. Murray, Holmes, and Griffin (1996a) asked 180 married or dating couples to rate themselves, their partner, and their ideal partner on a variety of traits and to rate their satisfaction with their relationship. Common sense would suggest that an accurate view of one's partner would be the best foundation for a stable, satisfying intimate relationship, but this is not what the investigators found. Instead, they discovered that most people viewed their partners more favorably than the partners viewed themselves. Individuals' perceptions of their romantic partners seemed to reflect their ideals for a partner more than reality. Moreover, the data showed that people were happier in their relationship when they idealized their partners and when their partners idealized them. A follow-up study found that relationships were more likely to persist—even in the face of conflicts and doubts—when partners idealized one another (Murray, Holmes, & Griffin, 1996b). These results mesh well with the finding, discussed in Chapter 13, that small positive illusions may be good for people's mental and physical well-being. Apparently, they are good for healthy romantic relationships as well.

Perspectives on the Mystery of Love 12b

People have always been interested in love and romance, but the scientific study of love has a short history that, for all practical purposes, dates back only to the 1970s. Love has proven to be an elusive subject of study. It's difficult to define, difficult to measure, and frequently difficult to understand. Nonetheless, psychologists have begun to make some progress in their study of love. Let's look at their theories and research.

Passionate and Companionate Love

Two early pioneers in research on love were Elaine Hatfield (formerly Walster) and Ellen Berscheid (Berscheid, 1988; Berscheid & Walster, 1978; Hatfield, 1988; Hatfield & Rapson, 1993; Walster & Berscheid, 1974). They have proposed that romantic relationships are characterized by two kinds of love: passionate love and companionate love. *Passionate love* **is a complete absorption in another that includes tender sexual feelings and the agony and ecstasy of intense emotion.** *Companionate love* **is warm, trusting, tolerant affec-**

"The emotion of romantic love seems to be distressingly fragile. As a 16th-century sage poignantly observed, 'the history of a love affair is the drama of its fight against time.'"

ELLEN BERSCHEID

"Passionate love is like any other form of excitement. By its very nature, excitement involves a continuous interplay between elation and despair, thrills and terror."

ELAINE HATFIELD

tion for another whose life is deeply intertwined with one's own. Passionate and companionate love *may* coexist, but they don't necessarily go hand in hand.

Although they're rigorous researchers who have made major contributions to the scientific study of love, Berscheid and Hatfield have also been willing to offer down-to-earth, practical insights about the nature of love. For instance, they've identified some common myths about love that can foster disappointment in romantic relationships (Berscheid & Walster, 1978):

Myth 1: When you fall in love, you'll know it. People often spend a great deal of time agonizing over whether they're really in love or only experiencing infatuation. When people consult others about their doubts, they're commonly told, "If it were true love, you'd know it." This assertion, which amounts to replying, "You must not be in love," just isn't true. Berscheid and Hatfield review extensive evidence that confusion about a romantic relationship is not the least bit unusual and that it does *not* mean that one isn't really in love.

Myth 2: Love is a purely positive experience. Our society's idealized views of love often suggest that it should be a purely enjoyable experience. In reality, pain, anger, and ambivalent feelings are common in love relationships, and it's unrealistic to expect love to be entirely pleasant. People often are more critical and less tolerant of lovers than they are of friends. The intense nature of passionate love means that love is capable of taking one to emotional peaks in *either* direction.

Myth 3: True love lasts forever. Love may last forever, but you certainly can't count on it. Some people perpetuate this myth in an interesting way. If their love relationship disintegrates, they conclude that it was never genuine love, only infatuation or comfortable compatibility. Hatfield and Berscheid theorize that passionate love peaks early in a relationship and then declines rapidly, while companionate love is more likely to continue to grow. Robert Sternberg has built on this idea in some detail, so let's turn to his research.

A Triangular View of Love

The distinction between passionate and companionate love has been further refined by Robert Sternberg (1988a), who suggests that love has three facets rather than just two. He subdivides companionate love into intimacy and commitment. *Intimacy* **refers to warmth, closeness, and sharing in a relationship.** *Commitment* **is an intent to maintain a relationship in spite of the difficulties and costs that may arise.** Thus, the three elements in Sternberg's triangular view of love are *passion, intimacy,* and *commitment.* Sternberg has described eight types of relationships that can result from the presence or absence of the three components of love (see Figure 16.6). When all three components are present, *consummate love* is said to exist.

Sternberg has mapped out the probable relations between the passage of time and the three components of love, as shown in Figure 16.7. Like Hatfield and Berscheid, he suspects that passion reaches its zenith in the early phases of love and then erodes. He believes that intimacy and commitment increase with time, although at different rates. Sternberg's relatively new model hasn't generated much research yet. However, one study of dating couples found that measures of their level of commitment and intimacy were among the best predictors of whether their relationships continued (Hendrick, Hendrick, & Adler, 1988). In another study that used factor analysis to sort out the conceptual structure of love, Aron and Westbay (1996) ended up dividing love into the same three components proposed by Sternberg: passion, intimacy, and commitment.

Love as Attachment

In another ground-breaking analysis of love, Cindy Hazan and Phillip Shaver (1987) have looked not at the components of love but at similarities between love and attachment relationships in infancy. We noted in Chapter 11 that infant-caretaker bonding, or *attachment,* emerges in the first year of

Figure 16.6 Sternberg's triangular theory of love. According to Robert Sternberg (1988a), love includes three components: intimacy, passion, and commitment. These components are portrayed here as points on a triangle. The absence of all three components is called nonlove, which is not shown in the diagram. The other possible combinations of these three components yield the seven types of relationships mapped out here.

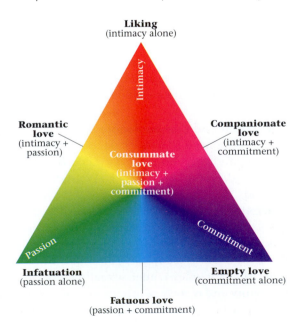

Liking
(intimacy alone)

Intimacy

Romantic love
(intimacy + passion)

Companionate love
(intimacy + commitment)

Consummate love
(intimacy + passion + commitment)

Passion

Commitment

Infatuation
(passion alone)

Empty love
(commitment alone)

Fatuous love
(passion + commitment)

life. Early attachments vary in quality, and infants tend to fall into three groups, which depend in part on parents' caregiving styles (Ainsworth et al., 1978). Most infants develop a *secure attachment*. However, some are very anxious when separated from their caretaker, a syndrome called *anxious-ambivalent attachment*. A third group of infants, characterized by *avoidant attachment,* never bond very well with their caretaker (see Figure 16.8).

According to Hazan and Shaver, romantic love is an attachment process, and people's intimate relationships in adulthood follow the same form as their attachments in infancy. According to their theory, a person who had an anxious-ambivalent attachment in infancy will tend to have romantic relations marked by anxiety and ambivalence in adulthood. In other words, people relive their early bonding with their parents in their adult relationships.

Hazan and Shaver's (1987) initial survey study provided striking support for their theory. They found that adults' love relationships could be sorted into groups that paralleled the three patterns of attachment seen in infants. *Secure adults* (56% of the subjects) found it relatively easy to get close to others, described their love relations as trusting, rarely worried about being abandoned, and reported the fewest divorces. *Anxious-ambivalent adults* (20% of the subjects) reported a preoccupation with love accompanied by expectations of

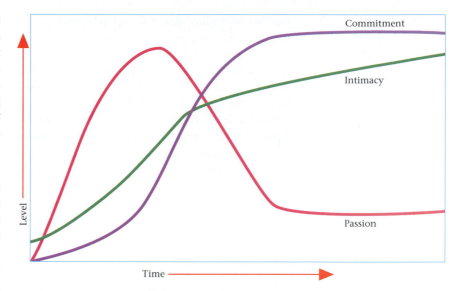

rejection and described their love relations as volatile and marked by jealousy. *Avoidant adults* (24% of the subjects) found it difficult to get close to others and described their love relations as lacking intimacy and trust. Consistent with their theory, Hazan and Shaver (1987) found that the percentage of adults falling into each category was roughly the same as the percentage of infants in each comparable category. Also, subjects' recollections of their childhood relations with their parents were consistent with the idea that people relive their infant attachment experiences in adulthood.

Understandably, Hazan and Shaver's theory has attracted considerable interest and has generated a

Figure 16.7
Sternberg's view of love over time. In his triangular theory of love, Sternberg theorizes that passion peaks early in a relationship, whereas intimacy and commitment continue to build gradually.

Parents' caregiving style	Infant attachment	Adult attachment style
Warm/responsive She/he was generally warm and responsive; she/he was good at knowing when to be supportive and when to let me operate on my own; our relationship was almost always comfortable, and I have no major reservations or complaints about it.	**Secure attachment** An infant-caregiver bond in which the child welcomes contact with a close companion and uses this person as a secure base from which to explore the environment.	**Secure** I find it relatively easy to get close to others and am comfortable depending on them and having them depend on me. I don't often worry about being abandoned or about someone getting too close to me.
Cold/rejecting She/he was fairly cold and distant, or rejecting, not very responsive; I wasn't her/his highest priority, her/his concerns were often elsewhere; it's possible that she/he would just as soon not have had me.	**Avoidant attachment** An insecure infant-caregiver bond, characterized by little separation protest and a tendency of the child to avoid or ignore the caregiver.	**Avoidant** I am somewhat uncomfortable being close to others; I find it difficult to trust them, difficult to allow myself to depend on them. I am nervous when anyone gets too close, and often love partners want me to be more intimate than I feel comfortable being.
Ambivalent/inconsistent She/he was noticeably inconsistent in her/his reactions to me, sometimes warm and sometimes not; she/he had her/his own agenda, which sometimes got in the way of her/his receptiveness and responsiveness to my needs; she/he definitely loved me but didn't always show it in the best way.	**Anxious/ambivalent attachment** An insecure infant-caregiver bond, characterized by strong separation protest and a tendency of the child to resist contact initiated by the caregiver, particularly after a separation.	**Anxious/ambivalent** I find that others are reluctant to get as close as I would like. I often worry that my partner doesn't really love me or won't want to stay with me. I want to merge completely with another person, and this desire sometimes scares people away.

Figure 16.8
Infant attachment and romantic relationships. According to Hazan and Shaver (1987), people's romantic relationships in adulthood are similar in form to their attachment patterns in infancy, which are determined in part by parental caregiving styles. The theorized relations between parental styles, attachment patterns, and intimate relations are outlined here. (Data for parental caregiving styles and adult attachment styles based on Hazan and Shaver, 1986, 1987; infant attachment patterns adapted from Shaffer, 1985)

number of studies within a relatively short period of time. For example, research has shown that securely attached individuals have more committed, satisfying, interdependent, well-adjusted, and longer-lasting relationships compared to people with either anxious-ambivalent or avoidant attachment styles (Collins & Read, 1990; Feeney & Noller, 1990; Simpson, 1990). Moreover, studies have shown that people with different attachment styles are predisposed to think, feel, and behave differently in their relationships (Collins, 1996). For example, anxious-ambivalent people find conflict with a partner more stressful than others and feel more negative about their relationship after dealing with a conflict (Simpson, Rholes, & Phillips, 1996). Avoidant individuals tend to engage in more casual sex than others because this strategy allows them to get physically close to others without incurring the vulnerability of genuine intimacy (Brennan & Shaver, 1995). How do people with various attachment styles tend to pair up? More data are needed to answer this interesting question, but preliminary evidence suggests that avoidant and anxious-ambivalent people are not drawn to their mirror images. In an analysis of 240 couples, Kirkpatrick and Davis (1994) did not find *any* pairings between two avoidant people or two anxious-ambivalent people.

Studies have also suggested that attachment patterns may have far-reaching repercussions that extend into many aspects of people's lives besides their romantic relationships. For instance, researchers have found correlations between attachment styles and job satisfaction, gender roles, religious beliefs, patterns of self-disclosure, vulnerability to drinking problems, and attitudes about work (Shaver & Hazan, 1993, 1994). Thus, Hazan and Shaver's innovative ideas about the long-term effects of infant attachment experiences have triggered an avalanche of thought-provoking research.

Culture and Close Relationships

Relatively little cross-cultural research has been conducted on the dynamics of close relationships. The limited evidence suggests that there are both similarities and differences between cultures in romantic relationships. For the most part, similarities have been seen when research has focused on what people look for in prospective mates. As we discussed in Chapter 10, David Buss (1989, 1994) has collected data on mate preferences in 37 divergent cultures and found that people all over the world value mutual attraction, kindness, intelligence, emotional stability, dependability, and

good health. Buss also found that gender differences in mating priorities were nearly universal, with males placing more emphasis on physical attractiveness and females putting a higher priority on social status and financial resources. Preliminary evidence also suggests that people's standards of physical attractiveness may largely transcend culture (Cunningham, Druen, & Barbee, 1997).

Cultures vary, however, in their emphasis on love—especially passionate love—as a prerequisite for marriage. Love as the basis for marriage is an 18th-century invention of Western culture (Stone, 1977). As Hatfield and Rapson (1993) note, "Marriage-for-love represents an ultimate expression of individualism" (p. 2). In contrast, marriages arranged by families and other go-betweens remain common in cultures high in collectivism, including India (Gupta, 1992), Japan (Iwao, 1993), and China (Xiaghe & Whyte, 1990). This practice is declining in some societies as a result of Westernization, but in collectivist societies people contemplating marriage still tend to think in terms of "What will my parents and other people say?" rather than "What does my heart say?" (Triandis, 1994). Studies show that attitudes about love in collectivist societies reflect these cultural priorities. For example, in comparison to Western subjects, subjects from Japan, India, and South Africa report that they value romantic love less (Furnham, 1984; Simmons, von Kolke, & Shimizu, 1986).

People from Western societies are often dumbfounded by collectivist cultures' deemphasis on love and their penchant for arranged marriages. Most of us assume that our modern conception of love as the basis for marriage must result in better marital relationships than collectivist cultures' "antiquated" beliefs and practices. However, a variety of researchers have noted that there is little empirical support for this ethnocentric view (Dion & Dion, 1991; Triandis, 1994). They cite, for example, a study of couples in India, which found that love tended to grow over the years in arranged marriages, whereas it tended to decline among couples who married for love (Gupta & Singh, 1982). Some theorists have conjectured that Western cultures' increased emphasis on passionate love might be linked to their rapidly escalating divorce rates (Simpson, Campbell, & Berscheid, 1986). The dearth of cross-cultural research on love means that we can only speculate on these matters. But smug assumptions about the superiority of Western ways look awfully shaky given those extremely high divorce rates.

An Evolutionary Perspective on Attraction

As we discussed in Chapter 10, evolutionary psychologists assert that humans' mating preferences have been shaped by natural selection. Consistent with the notion that humans unconsciously seek to maximize their reproductive success, evidence indicates that men generally are more interested than women in seeking youthfulness and physical attractiveness in their mates because these traits should be associated with higher fertility. On the other hand, research shows that women place a greater premium on prospective mates' ambition, industriousness, social status, financial potential, and willingness to invest their material resources in children (Buss, 1996).

Does the gender gap in mating priorities influence the tactics people actually use in pursuing romantic relationships? Research suggests that the answer is yes. Buss (1988) asked 208 newlywed individuals to describe the things they did when they first met their spouse, and during the remainder of their courtship, to make themselves more appealing to their partner. He found that men were more likely than women to emphasize their material resources by doing such things as flashing lots of money, buying nice gifts, showing off expensive possessions, and bragging about their importance at work (see Figure 16.9). In contrast, women were more likely than men to work at enhancing their appearance by dieting, wearing stylish clothes, trying new hairstyles, and getting a tan.

A recent study by Schmitt and Buss (1996) suggests that people adjust their tactics of attraction depending on whether they are pursuing a short-term or long-term relationship, in ways that make sense from an evolutionary perspective. For example, in the context of short-term relationships, men are thought to face the adaptive problem of finding sexually accessible women. In this context, the tactics of attraction that are rated most effective for women are those that signal sexual availability (such as flirting or dressing seductively) or that raise doubts about the availability of a rival (such as claiming she's just a tease). In contrast, in the context of long-term relationships, men supposedly face the adaptive problem of maintaining exclusive sexual access to be certain of the paternity of any children. In this context, the tactics of attraction that are rated most effective for women are those that signal sexual exclusivity (such as rejecting sexual overtures from other men) or that raise doubts about a rival's fidelity (such as saying she's promiscuous). Schmitt and Buss (1996) found evidence that men are likely to make similar adjustments in their tactics of attraction. In the context of short-term relationships, tactics that involve giving resources immediately are rated as most effective, whereas for long-term relationships, tactics that show potential for accumulating material resources or that raise doubts about a rival's resource potential are assumed to be optimal. Thus, evolutionary psychologists analyze romantic relationships in terms of the adaptive problems they have presented over the course of human history.

Recap of Key Points

• People tend to like and love others who live in proximity and who are physically attractive. The matching hypothesis asserts that people who are similar in physical attractiveness are more likely to be drawn together than those who are not.

• Byrne's research suggests that similarity causes attraction, although it may also be true that dissimilarity causes dislike. Reciprocity involves liking those who show that they like you. In romantic relation-

Tactics of attraction	Mean frequency (N = 102)	Mean frequency (N = 106)
Tactics used significantly more by males	Men	Women
Display resources	0.67	0.44
Brag about resources	0.73	0.60
Display sophistication	1.18	0.88
Display strength	0.96	0.44
Display athleticism	1.18	0.94
Show off	0.70	0.47
Tactics used significantly more by females	Men	Women
Wear makeup	0.02	1.63
Keep clean and groomed	2.27	2.44
Alter appearance—general	0.39	1.27
Wear stylish clothes	1.22	2.00
Act coy	0.54	0.73
Wear jewelry	0.25	2.21
Wear sexy clothes	0.68	0.91
Tactics for which no significant sex differences were found	Men	Women
Act provocative	0.77	0.90
Flirt	2.13	2.09
Keep hair groomed	2.20	2.31
Increase social exposure	0.89	0.90
Act nice	1.77	1.86
Display humor	2.42	2.28
Act promiscuous	0.30	0.21
Act submissive	1.24	1.11
Dissemble (feign agreement)	1.26	1.09
Touch	2.26	2.16

Figure 16.9
Similarities and differences between the sexes in tactics of attraction. Buss (1988) asked newlywed subjects to rate how often they had used 23 tactics of attraction to make themselves more appealing to their partner. The tactics used by one sex significantly more often than the other are listed in the first two sections of the figure. Although there were significant differences between the sexes, there were also many similarities. The 11 tactics used most frequently by each sex (those above the median) are highlighted, showing considerable overlap between males and females in the tactics they use most. (Note: Higher means in the data reflect higher frequency of use, but the numbers do not indicate frequency per day or week.)

ships, reciprocity often extends to idealizing one's partner.

• Berscheid and Hatfield have identified some popular myths about love, such as (1) when you fall in love, you'll know it; (2) love is purely a positive experience; and (3) true love lasts forever. Sternberg builds on their distinction between passionate and companionate love by dividing the latter into intimacy and commitment.

• Hazan and Shaver's theory suggests that love relationships in adulthood mimic attachment patterns in infancy. People tend to be secure, avoidant, or anxious-ambivalent in their romantic relationships. Those who are secure tend to have more committed, satisfying relationships.

• The characteristics that people seek in prospective mates are much the same around the world. The gender differences in mating preferences seen in Western societies also appear to transcend culture. However, cultures vary considerably in their emphasis on passionate love as a prerequisite for marriage.

• Consistent with evolutionary theory, men tend to seek youthfulness and attractiveness in their mates, whereas women emphasize prospective mates' financial potential and willingness to invest material resources in children. These preferences are reflected in people's courtship tactics, which vary depending on whether they are seeking short-term or long-term relationships.

ATTITUDES: MAKING SOCIAL JUDGMENTS

In our chapter-opening story, Muffy's friends exhibited decidedly negative attitudes about working-class men. Their example reveals a basic feature of attitudes: they're evaluative. They involve making social judgments. Social psychology's interest in attitudes has a much longer history than its interest in attraction. Indeed, in its early days social psychology was defined as the study of attitudes. In this section we'll discuss the nature of attitudes, efforts to change attitudes through persuasion, and theories about the process of attitude change.

What are attitudes? William McGuire (1985) provides a succinct definition in *The Handbook of Social Psychology*: **Attitudes** **locate objects of thought on dimensions of judgment.** "Objects of thought" may include social issues (capital punishment or gun control, for example), groups (liberals, farmers), institutions (the Lutheran church, the Supreme Court), consumer products (yogurt, computers), and people (the president, your next-door neighbor). "Dimensions of judgment" refer to the various ways in which people might make favorable or unfavorable evaluations of the objects of their thoughts. Although attitudes are social judgments, they're not exclusively cognitive. Attitudes are complex mixtures of cognitive, emotional, and behavioral components.

Components of Attitudes

Social psychologists have traditionally viewed attitudes as being made up of three components (Rajecki, 1990), although alternative models of attitudes are gaining influence (Tesser & Shaffer, 1990). We can see concrete examples of the three components of an attitude if we look at what one of my former teachers meant years ago when he told me that I had an "attitude problem."

The *cognitive component* of an attitude is made up of the *beliefs* that people hold about the object of an attitude. I believed that my teacher was boring, incompetent, and uninterested in his students—you can imagine why he characterized my attitude as a "problem." The *affective component* of an attitude consists of the *emotional feelings* stimulated by an attitude object. At the time, my feelings for my teacher ranged from active dislike to contempt, with some occasional sympathy mixed in. The *behavioral component* of an attitude consists of *predispositions* to act in certain ways toward an attitude object. In the case of my attitude problem, my behavioral tendencies included ignoring lectures, talking in class, and not turning in assignments (see Figure 16.10 for another example of an attitude divided into its components).

Of course, people exhibit positive as well as negative attitudes. For instance, I had many teachers whom I viewed as bright, dedicated individuals (cognitive component), who elicited feelings of liking and admiration (affective component), and who inspired rapt attention and hard work (behavioral component). Although attitudes include predispositions toward certain behaviors, the relations between attitudes and behavior can get complicated, as you'll see.

Attitudes and Behavior

In the early 1930s, when prejudice against Asians was common in the United States, Richard LaPiere journeyed across the country with a Chinese couple. He was more than a little surprised when they weren't turned away from any of the restaurants they visited in their travels—184 restaurants in all. About six months after his trip, LaPiere surveyed the same restaurants and asked whether they would serve Chinese customers. Roughly half of the restaurants replied to the survey, and over 90% of them indicated that they would *not* seat Chinese patrons. Thus, LaPiere (1934) found that people who voice prejudicial attitudes may not behave in discriminatory ways. Since then, theorists have often asked: Why don't attitudes predict behavior better?

Admittedly, LaPiere's study had a fundamental flaw that you may already have detected. The person who seated LaPiere and his Chinese friends may not have been the same person who responded to the mail survey sent later. Nonetheless, numerous follow-up studies, using more sophisticated methods, have shown that attitudes are mediocre predictors of people's behavior (McGuire, 1985). That's not to say that they are irrelevant or meaningless. Kraus (1995) reviewed 88 attitude-behavior studies and found that the average correlation between attitudes and behavior was .38. That figure is high enough to justify Eagly's (1992) conclusion that researchers have identified "many conditions under which attitudes are substantial predictors of behavior" (p. 697). But on the whole, social psychologists have been surprised by how often a favorable attitude toward a candidate or product does not translate into a vote or a purchase.

Why aren't attitude-behavior relations more consistent? Because a host of variables influence the connection between attitudes and behavior, including the strength or certainty of the attitudes measured, their stability, their accessibility in memory, and their relevance to the behavior in question (Krauss, 1995; Rajecki, 1990). One major factor contributing to inconsistency is that people often discuss the cognitive and affective components of their attitudes (beliefs and feelings) in a *general* way that isn't likely to predict *specific* behaviors (Ajzen & Fishbein, 1980; Perloff, 1993). Although you may express favorable beliefs and feelings about protecting civil liberties (a very general concept), you may not be willing to give $25 to the American Civil Liberties Union (a very specific action). Maybe you're a tightwad and your favorable feelings, although genuine, never translate into financial contributions. Or maybe you have negative feelings toward the ACLU for unrelated reasons.

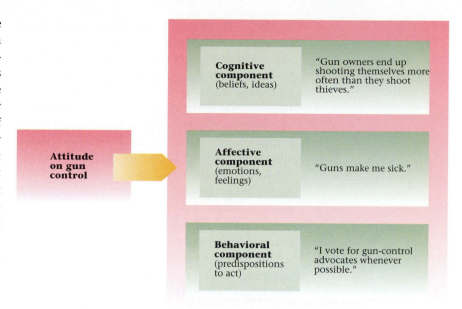

Another reason for the inconsistent relations between attitudes and behavior is that the behavioral component in an attitude consists only of *predispositions* toward certain actions. Whether you follow through on these predispositions depends on situational constraints—especially your subjective perceptions of how people expect you to behave. Thus, Icek Ajzen (1985, 1991) maintains that attitudes interact with situational norms to shape people's intentions, which then determine their behavior. Although you may be strongly opposed to marijuana use, you may not say anything when friends start passing a joint around at a party because you don't want to turn the party into an argument. However, in another situation governed by different norms, such as a class discussion, you may speak out forcefully against marijuana use. If so, you may be trying to change others' attitudes, the process we'll discuss next.

Trying to Change Attitudes: Factors in Persuasion

The fact that attitudes aren't always good predictors of a person's behavior doesn't stop others from trying to change those attitudes. Indeed, every day you're bombarded by efforts to alter your attitudes. To illustrate, let's trace the events of an imaginary morning. You may not even be out of bed before you start hearing radio advertisements intended to influence your attitudes about specific mouthwashes, computers, athletic shoes, and telephone companies. When you unfurl your newspaper, you find not only more ads but quotes from government officials and special interest groups, carefully crafted to shape your opinions.

Figure 16.10
The components of attitudes. Attitudes can be broken into cognitive, affective, and behavioral components, as illustrated here for a hypothetical person's attitude about gun control.

When you arrive at school, you encounter a group passing out leaflets that urge you to repent your sins and join them in worship. In class, your economics professor champions the wisdom of free markets in international trade. At lunch, the person you've been dating argues about the merits of an "open relationship." Your discussion is interrupted by someone who wants both of you to sign a petition. "Doesn't it ever let up?" you wonder. When it comes to persuasion, the answer is "no." As Anthony Pratkanis and Elliot Aronson (1992) put it, we live in the "age of propaganda." In light of this reality, let's examine some of the factors that determine whether persuasion works.

The process of persuasion includes four basic elements: source, receiver, message, and channel (see Figure 16.11). **The *source* is the person who sends a communication, and the *receiver* is the person to whom the message is sent.** Thus, if you watch a presidential news conference on TV, the president is the source, and you and millions of other viewers are the receivers. **The *message* is the information transmitted by the source, and the *channel* is the medium through which the message is sent.** Although the research on communication channels is interesting, we'll confine our discussion to source, message, and receiver variables, which are most applicable to persuasion.

Source Factors

Occasional exceptions to the general rule are seen, but persuasion tends to be more successful when the source has high *credibility* (O'Keefe, 1990). What gives a person credibility? Either expertise or trustworthiness. People try to convey their *expertise* by mentioning their degrees, their training, and their experience or by showing an impressive grasp of the issue at hand (Hass, 1981).

Expertise is a plus, but *trustworthiness* is even more important (McGinnies & Ward, 1980). If you were told that your state needs to reduce corporate taxes to stimulate its economy, would you be more

likely to believe it from the president of a huge corporation in your state or from an economics professor from out of state? Probably the latter. Trustworthiness is undermined when a source, such as the corporation president, appears to have something to gain. In contrast, trustworthiness is enhanced when people appear to argue against their own interests (Hunt, Smith, & Kernan, 1985). This effect explains why salespeople often make remarks like, "Frankly, my snowblower isn't the best. They have a better brand down the street. Of course, you'll have to spend quite a bit more . . ."

Likability also increases the effectiveness of a persuasive source (Roskos-Ewoldsen & Fazio, 1992), and some of the factors at work in attraction therefore have an impact on persuasion. Thus, the favorable effect of *physical attractiveness* on likability can make persuasion more effective. For instance, when Chaiken (1979) asked students to obtain signatures for a petition, he found that the more attractive students were more successful. We also respond better to sources who share *similarity* with us in ways that are relevant to the issue at hand (Mackie, Worth, & Asuncion, 1990).

The importance of source variables can be seen in advertising. Many companies spend a fortune to obtain an ideal spokesperson, such as Bill Cosby, who combines trustworthiness, expertise (a doctorate in education), and likability. Companies quickly abandon spokespersons when their likability declines.

Message Factors

If you were going to give a speech to a local community group advocating a reduction in state taxes on corporations, you'd probably wrestle with a number of questions about how to structure your message. Should you look at both sides of the issue, or should you present just your side? should you use all of the arguments at your disposal, or should you concentrate on the stronger arguments? Should you deliver a low-key, logical speech? Or

Figure 16.11
Overview of the persuasion process. The process of persuasion essentially boils down to *who* (the source) communicates *what* (the message) *by what means* (the channel) *to whom* (the receiver). Thus, there are four sets of variables that influence the process of persuasion: source, message, channel, and receiver factors. The diagram lists some of the more important factors in each category (including some that are not discussed in the text due to space limitations). (Adapted from Lippa, 1994)

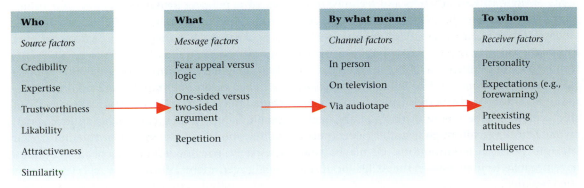

Who	What	By what means	To whom
Source factors	*Message factors*	*Channel factors*	*Receiver factors*
Credibility	Fear appeal versus logic	In person	Personality
Expertise	One-sided versus two-sided argument	On television	Expectations (e.g., forewarning)
Trustworthiness		Via audiotape	Preexisting attitudes
Likability	Repetition		Intelligence
Attractiveness			
Similarity			

should you try to strike fear into the hearts of your listeners? These questions are concerned with message factors in persuasion.

Let's assume that you're aware that there are two sides to the taxation issue. On the one hand, you're convinced that lower corporate taxes will bring new companies to your state and stimulate economic growth. On the other hand, you realize that reduced tax revenues may hurt the quality of education and roads in your state (but you think the benefits will outweigh the costs). Should you present a *one-sided argument* that ignores the possible problems for education and road quality? Or should you present a *two-sided argument* that acknowledges concern about education and road quality and then downplays the probable magnitude of these problems? In general, two-sided arguments seem to be more effective (O'Keefe, 1990). Just mentioning that there are two sides to an issue can increase your credibility with an audience (Jones & Brehm, 1970).

In presenting your side, should you use every argument you can think of, or should you focus on the stronger points? A recent study suggests that it is wise to concentrate on your stong arguments (Friedrich et al., 1996). The investigators exposed students to a variety of weak and strong arguments advocating a new senior comprehensive exam at their school. They found that adding strong arguments paid off, but adding weak arguments hurt rather than helped (see Figure 16.12). It appears that weak arguments may actually raise doubts rather than add to your case.

On the other hand, raw repetition of a message does seem to be an effective strategy. The validity effect refers to the finding that simply repeating a statement causes it to be perceived as more valid or true. It doesn't matter whether the statement is true, false, or clearly just an opinion; if you repeat something often enough, some people come to believe it (Boehm, 1994).

Persuasive messages frequently attempt to arouse fear. Opponents of nuclear power scare us with visions of meltdowns. Antismoking campaigns emphasize the threat of cancer, and deodorant ads highlight the risk of embarrassment. You could follow their lead and argue that if corporate taxes aren't reduced, your state will be headed toward economic ruin and massive unemployment. *Do appeals to fear work?* Yes—if they are successful in arousing fear. Research reveals that many messages intended to induce fear fail to do so. However, studies involving a wide range of issues (nuclear policy, auto safety, dental hygiene, and

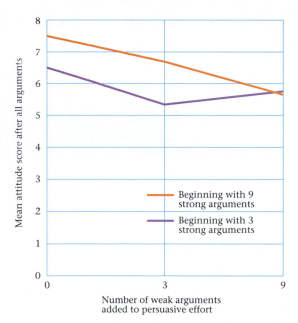

Figure 16.12
The effect of adding weak arguments to one's case. Friedrich et al. (1996) exposed students to various arguments in favor of requiring a new comprehensive exam for seniors at their school. This graph shows the effects of adding 0, 3, or 9 weak arguments to 3 or 9 strong arguments. As you can see, in this instance, adding weak arguments generally had a negative effect on overall persuasion.

so on) have shown that messages that are effective in arousing fear tend to increase persuasion (Perloff, 1993). According to Rogers (1983), fear appeals are most likely to work when your listeners view the dire consequences that you describe as exceedingly unpleasant, fairly probable if they don't take your advice, and avoidable if they do.

Receiver Factors

What about the receiver of the persuasive message? Are some people easier to persuade than others? Undoubtedly, but the traits that account for these differences interact with other considerations in complicated ways. Transient factors, such as the forewarning a receiver gets about a persuasive effort and the receiver's initial position on an issue, generally seem to be more influential than the receiver's personality or intelligence.

An old saying suggests that "to be forewarned is to be forearmed." The value of *forewarning* applies to targets of persuasive efforts (Petty & Cacioppo, 1979; Pfau et al., 1990). When you shop for a new TV, you *expect* salespeople to work at persuading you, and to some extent this forewarning reduces the impact of their arguments.

A receiver's resistance to persuasion will depend in part on the nature of the attitude or belief that the source is trying to change. Obviously, resistance is greater when you have to advocate a position that is incompatible with the receiver's existing attitudes or beliefs. In general, people display a *disconfirmation bias* in evaluating arguments (Edwards & Smith, 1996). Arguments that are in conflict with one's prior attitudes are scrutinized longer and subjected to more skeptical analysis

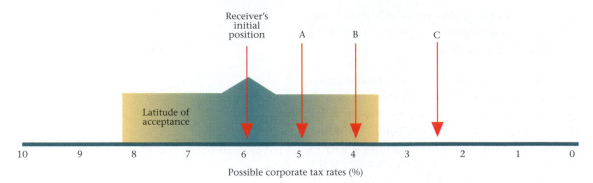

Figure 16.13
Latitude of acceptance and attitude change. In relation to the receiver's initial stance on what the corporate tax rate should be, positions A and B both fall within the receiver's latitude of acceptance, but position B should produce a larger attitude shift. Position C is outside the receiver's latitude of acceptance and should fall on deaf ears.

than are arguments that are consistent with one's prior beliefs. Studies also show that attitudes that are personally important to an individual are particularly hard to change (Zuwerink & Devine, 1996). In a similar vein, a deeply entrenched attitude that one is committed to is relatively difficult to alter (Pomerantz, Chaiken, & Tordesillas, 1995).

The effect of a persuasive effort also depends on the size of the discrepancy between a *receiver's initial position* on an issue and the position advocated by the source. Persuasion tends to work best when there's a moderate discrepancy between the two positions. Why? According to *social judgment theory*, people are usually willing to consider alternative views on an issue if the views aren't too different from their own (Sherif & Hovland, 1961; Upshaw, 1969). **A *latitude of acceptance* is a range** of potentially acceptable positions on an issue, centered on one's initial attitude position. Persuasive messages that fall outside a receiver's latitude of acceptance usually fall on deaf ears. When a message falls within a receiver's latitude of acceptance, successful persuasion is much more likely (Rajecki, 1990). Moreover, within the latitude of acceptance, a larger discrepancy between the receiver's initial position and the position advocated should produce greater attitude change than a smaller discrepancy does (see Figure 16.13).

Our review of source, message, and receiver variables has shown that attempting to change attitudes through persuasion involves a complex interplay of factors—and we haven't even looked beneath the surface yet. How do people acquire

---

CONCEPT CHECK 16.3
Understanding Attitudes and Persuasion

Check your understanding of the components of attitudes and the elements of persuasion by analyzing hypothetical political strategies. Imagine you're working on a political campaign and you're invited to join the candidate's inner circle in strategy sessions, as staff members prepare the candidate for upcoming campaign stops. During the meetings, you hear various strategies discussed. For each strategy below, indicate which component of voters' attitudes (cognitive, affective, or behavioral) is being targeted for change, and indicate which element in persuasion (source, message, or receiver factors) is being manipulated. The answers are in Appendix A.

1. "You need to convince this crowd that your program for regulating nursing homes is sound. Whatever you do, don't acknowledge the two weaknesses in the program that we've been playing down. I don't care if you're asked point blank. Just slide by the question and keep harping on the program's advantages." _____ _____

2. "You haven't been smiling enough lately, especially when the TV cameras are rolling. Remember, you can have the best ideas in the world, but if you don't seem likable, you're not gonna get elected. By the way, I think I've lined up some photo opportunities that should help us create an image of sincerity and compassion." _____ _____

3. "This crowd is already behind you. You don't have to alter their opinions on any issue. Get right to work convincing them to contribute to the campaign. I want them lining up to give money." _____ _____

attitudes in the first place? What dynamic processes within people produce attitude change? We turn to these theoretical issues next.

Theories of Attitude Formation and Change

Many theories have been proposed to explain the mechanisms at work in attitude change, whether or not it occurs in response to persuasion. We'll look at five theoretical perspectives: learning theory, balance theory, dissonance theory, self-perception theory, and the elaboration likelihood model.

Learning Theory

We've seen repeatedly that *learning theory* can help explain a wide range of phenomena, from conditioned fears to the acquisition of sex roles to the development of personality traits. Now we can add attitude formation and change to our list.

The affective, or emotional, component in an attitude can be created through *classical conditioning,* just as other emotional responses can (Chaiken, Wood, & Eagly, 1996). As we discussed in Chapter 6, advertisers routinely try to take advantage of classical conditioning by pairing their products with stimuli that elicit pleasant emotional responses, such as extremely attractive models, highly likable spokespersons, and cherished events (the Olympics, for instance). This conditioning process is diagrammed in Figure 16.14.

Operant conditioning may come into play when you openly express an attitude, such as "I believe that husbands should do more housework." Some people may endorse your view, while others may jump down your throat. Agreement from other people generally functions as a reinforcer, strengthening your tendency to express a specific attitude (Insko, 1965). Disagreement often functions as a form of punishment, which may gradually weaken your commitment to your viewpoint.

Another person's attitudes may rub off on you through *observational learning* (Oskamp, 1991). If you hear your uncle say, "Republicans are nothing but puppets of big business," and your mother heartily agrees, your exposure to your uncle's attitude and your mother's reinforcement of your uncle may influence your attitude toward the Republican party. Studies show that parents and their children tend to have similar political attitudes (Sears, 1975). Observational learning presumably accounts for much of this similarity. The opinions of teachers, coaches, co-workers, talk-show hosts,

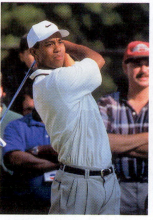

CS
Products
(e.g., autos, foods)

UCS
Likable
celebrity

CR
Pleasant emotional
response
UCR

Figure 16.14
Classical conditioning of attitudes in advertising. Advertisers routinely pair their products with likable celebrities in the hope that their products will come to elicit pleasant emotional responses.

rock stars, and so forth are also likely to sway people's attitudes through observational learning.

Dissonance Theory

Leon Festinger's *dissonance theory* assumes that inconsistency among attitudes propels people in the direction of attitude change. Dissonance theory burst into prominence in 1959 when Festinger and J. Merrill Carlsmith published a famous study of counterattitudinal behavior. Let's look at their findings and at how dissonance theory explains them.

Festinger and Carlsmith (1959) had male college students come to a laboratory, where they worked on excruciatingly dull tasks, such as turning pegs repeatedly. When a subject's hour was over, the experimenter confided that some participants' motivation was being manipulated by telling them that the task was interesting and enjoyable before they started it. Then, after a moment's hesitation, the experimenter asked if the subject could help him out of a jam. His usual helper was delayed and he needed someone to testify to the next "subject" (really an accomplice) that the experimental task was interesting. He offered to pay the subject if he would tell the person in the adjoining waiting room that the task was enjoyable and involving.

This entire scenario was enacted to coax subjects into doing something that was inconsistent with their true feelings—that is, to engage in *counterattitudinal behavior.* Some subjects received a token payment of $1 for their effort, while others received a more substantial payment of $20 (an

"Cognitive dissonance is a motivating state of affairs. Just as hunger impels a person to eat, so does dissonance impel a person to change his opinions or his behavior."

LEON FESTINGER

amount equivalent to about $60 today, in light of inflation). Later, a second experimenter inquired about the subjects' true feelings regarding the dull experimental task. Figure 16.15 summarizes the design of the Festinger and Carlsmith study.

Who do you think rated the task more favorably—the subjects who were paid $1 or those who were paid $20? Both common sense and learning theory would predict that the subjects who received the greater reward ($20) should come to like the task more. In reality, however, the subjects who were paid $1 exhibited more favorable attitude change—just as Festinger and Carlsmith had predicted. Why? Dissonance theory provides an explanation.

According to Festinger (1957), *cognitive dissonance* **exists when related cognitions are inconsistent—that is, when they contradict each other.** Festinger's model assumes that dissonance is possible only when cognitions are relevant to each other, as unrelated cognitions ("I am hardworking" and "Fire engines are red") can't contradict each other. However, when cognitions are related, they may be consonant ("I am hardworking" and "I'm staying overtime to get an important job done") or dissonant ("I am hardworking" and "I'm playing hooky from work"). When it exists, cognitive dissonance is supposed to create an unpleasant state of tension that motivates people to reduce their dissonance—usually by altering their cognitions.

In the study by Festinger and Carlsmith, the subjects' contradictory cognitions were "The task is boring" and "I told someone the task was enjoyable." The subjects who were paid $20 for lying had an obvious reason for behaving inconsistently with their true attitudes, so these subjects experienced little dissonance. In contrast, the subjects paid $1 had no readily apparent justification for their lie and experienced high dissonance. To reduce it, they tended to persuade themselves that the task was more enjoyable than they had originally thought. Thus, dissonance theory sheds light on why people sometimes come to believe their own lies.

Cognitive dissonance is also at work when people turn attitudinal somersaults to justify efforts that haven't panned out, a syndrome called *effort justification.* Aronson and Mills (1959) studied effort justification by putting college women through a "severe initiation" before they could qualify to participate in what promised to be an interesting discussion of sexuality. In the initiation, the women had to read obscene passages out loud to a male experimenter. After all that, the highly touted discussion of sexuality turned out to be a boring, taped lecture on reproduction in lower animals. Subjects in the severe initiation condition experienced highly dissonant cognitions ("I went through a lot to get here" and "This discussion is terrible"). How did they reduce their dissonance? Apparently by changing their attitude about the discussion, since they rated it more favorably than subjects in two control conditions. Effort justification may be at work in many facets of everyday life. For example, people who wait in line for an hour or more to get into an exclusive restaurant often praise the restaurant afterward even if they have been served a mediocre meal.

Dissonance theory has been tested in hundreds of studies with mixed, but largely favorable, results. The dynamics of dissonance appear to underlie many attitude changes, including shifts in complex and socially significant attitudes, such as prejudice (Aronson, 1980; Leippe & Eisenstadt, 1994). Research has supported Festinger's claim that dissonance involves genuine psychological discomfort and even physiological arousal (Croyle & Cooper, 1983; Elliot & Devine, 1994).

However, dissonance effects are not among the most reliable phenomena in social psychology, perhaps because there are variations among people in the need for cognitive consistency (Cialdini, Trost, & Newsom, 1995). Moreover, even when people exhibit a clear preference for consistency, it's difficult to predict when dissonance will occur.

Figure 16.15
Design of the Festinger and Carlsmith (1959) study. The sequence of events in this landmark study of counterattitudinal behavior and attitude change is outlined here. The diagram omits a third condition (no dissonance), in which subjects were not induced to lie. The results in the nondissonance condition were similar to those found in the low-dissonance condition.

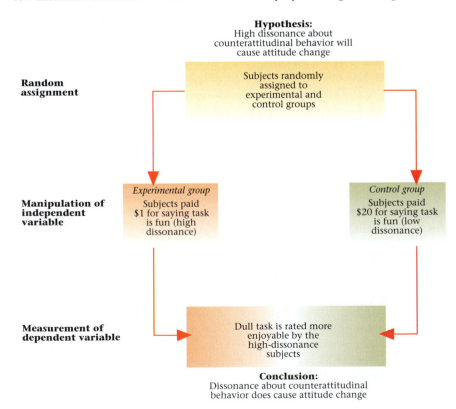

If I learn that my favorite novelist is a child abuser, does this arouse dissonance? For me it does, because I expect a great novelist to be compassionate. For other people it might not, depending on their vision of a great novelist. To some extent, inconsistency between cognitions lies in the eye of the beholder. Thus, researchers continue to debate the factors that determine whether cognitive dissonance will occur (Cooper & Fazio, 1984; Steele, 1988; Thibodeau & Aronson, 1992).

Self-Perception Theory

After taking a close look at studies of counter-attitudinal behavior, Daryl Bem (1967) concluded that self-perception, rather than dissonance, explains why people sometimes come to believe their own lies. According to Bem's *self-perception theory,* people often *infer* their attitudes from their behavior. Thus, Bem argued that in the study by Festinger and Carlsmith (1959), the subjects paid $1 probably thought to themselves, "A dollar isn't enough money to get me to lie, so I must have found the task enjoyable."

This thinking isn't much different from what dissonance theory would predict. Both theories suggest that people often think, "If I said it, it must be true." But the two theories propose that similar patterns of thought unfold for entirely different reasons. According to dissonance theory, subjects think along these lines because they're struggling to reduce tension caused by inconsistency among their cognitions. According to self-perception theory, subjects are engaged in normal attributional efforts to better understand their own behavior. Bem originally believed that most findings explained by dissonance were really due to self-perception. However, studies eventually showed that self-perception is at work primarily when subjects do not have well-defined attitudes regarding the issue at hand (Chaiken & Baldwin, 1981).

Although self-perception theory did not replace dissonance theory, Bem's work shed new light on the relationship between attitudes and behavior. Conventional wisdom assumes that people's atti-

tudes determine their behavior. Thus, a person might say, "I don't like plays [attitude]. Therefore, I don't go to them [behavior]." However, Bem suggested that causation sometimes flows in the opposite direction: Observing one's own behavior leads to conclusions about what one's attitudes must be (see Figure 16.16). For example, a person might say, "Gee, I don't go to any plays. I guess I don't like them." Research on attribution eventually showed that efforts to explain one's own behavior *are* commonplace and that people often *do* infer their attitudes from their behavior.

Elaboration Likelihood Model

A more recent theory of attitude change proposed by Richard Petty and John Cacioppo (1986) asserts that there are two basic "routes" to persuasion. The *central route* is taken when people carefully ponder the content and logic of persuasive messages. The *peripheral route* is taken when persuasion depends on nonmessage factors, such as the attractiveness and credibility of the source, or on conditioned emotional responses (see Figure 16.17). For example, a politician who campaigns by delivering carefully researched speeches that thoughtfully analyze complex issues is following the central route to persuasion. In contrast, a politician who depends on marching bands, flag waving, celebrity endorsements, and emotional slogans is following the peripheral route.

Both routes can lead to persuasion. However, according to the *elaboration likelihood model,* the durability of attitude change depends on the extent to which people elaborate on (think about)

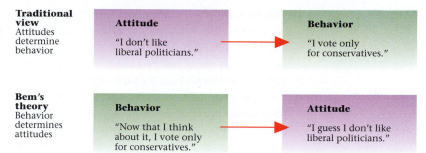

Figure 16.16
Bem's self-perception theory. The traditional view is that attitudes determine behavior. However, Bem proposed that behavior often determines (or causes people to draw inferences about) their attitudes.

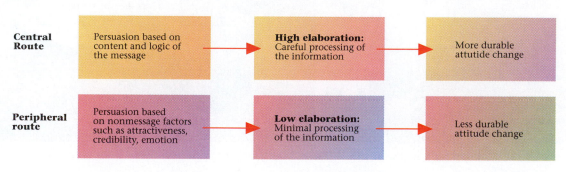

Figure 16.17
The elaboration likelihood model. According to the elaboration likelihood model (Petty & Cacioppo, 1986), the central route to persuasion leads to more enduring attitude change than the peripheral route to persuasion.

the contents of persuasive communications. Studies suggest that the central route to persuasion leads to more enduring attitude change than the peripheral route (Chaiken, 1987; Tesser & Shaffer, 1990). Research also suggests that attitudes changed through central processes predict behavior better than attitudes changed through peripheral processes (Petty, Cacioppo, & Schumann, 1983).

The elaboration likelihood model adds another complication to the complex relations between attitudes and behavior. We'll see more complications in the next section, which is concerned with related aspects of social influence—conformity and obedience.

Recap of Key Points

• Attitudes are made up of cognitive, affective, and behavioral components. Attitudes and behavior aren't as consistent as one might assume, in part because people expect very general attitudes to predict very specific behaviors and in part because attitudes only create predispositions to behave in certain ways.

• A source of persuasion who is credible, expert, trustworthy, likable, and physically attractive tends to be relatively effective in stimulating attitude change.

• Although there are some situational limitations, two-sided arguments and fear arousal are effective elements in persuasive messages. However, adding weak arguments to one's case may hurt more than help.

• Persuasion is undermined when a receiver is forewarned, when the sender advocates a position that is incompatible with the receiver's existing attitudes, or when a receiver's initial position is very discrepant from the position advocated.

• Attitudes may be shaped through classical conditioning, operant conditioning, and observational learning. Festinger's dissonance theory asserts that inconsistent attitudes cause tension and that people alter their attitudes to reduce cognitive dissonance.

• Dissonance theory has been used to explain attitude change following counterattitudinal behavior and efforts that haven't panned out. Some of these phenomena can be explained by self-perception theory, which posits that people may infer their attitudes from their behavior.

• The elaboration likelihood model of persuasion holds that the central route to persuasion tends to yield longer-lasting attitude change than the peripheral route.

CONFORMITY AND OBEDIENCE: YIELDING TO OTHERS

The mass suicide in Jonestown in the late 1970s was a shocking example of obedience to an authority figure. History repeated itself in 1997 when 39 members of the Heaven's Gate cult took their lives at a mansion in Rancho Santa Fe, California.

I'll never forget the night of the Jonestown massacre in Guyana, when Jim Jones ordered his People's Temple followers to commit mass suicide by drinking cyanide-laced Kool-Aid. I was at a small party watching *Saturday Night Live* when the show was interrupted to report the tragedy in Guyana. This dreadful example of blind obedience to authority seemed so implausible that people at the party assumed that it was one of the comedy show's fake news bulletins, just another cynical joke about religion from *Saturday Night Live*! It wasn't until sometime later, when a second news bulletin was

broadcast, that we began to realize that we were dealing with reality.

As the Jonestown massacre demonstrates, the power of social influence can be astonishing. When the full story of Jonestown was assembled weeks later, it became apparent that a small minority of Jones's followers had refused to cooperate (a few escaped, a few were shot), but most went along with their orders and took their own lives. How can we explain such extraordinary obedience? Was it due to the unique character of the people of Jonestown? Probably not. Both anecdotal and empirical evidence suggest that in the right circumstances most people can be coaxed, pressured, or coerced into doing virtually anything. In this section, we'll analyze the dynamics of social influence at work in conformity and obedience.

Conformity

If you keep a well-manicured lawn, are you exhibiting conformity? According to social psychologists, it depends on whether your behavior is the result of group pressure. *Conformity* occurs when **people yield to real or imagined social pressure.** For example, if you maintain a well-groomed lawn only to avoid complaints from your neighbors, you're conforming to social pressure. However, if you maintain a nice lawn because you genuinely prefer a nice lawn, that's *not* conformity.

Asch's Studies

In the 1950s, Solomon Asch (1951, 1955, 1956) devised a clever procedure that reduced ambiguity about whether subjects were conforming, allowing him to investigate the variables that govern conformity. Let's re-create one of Asch's (1955) classic experiments. The subjects are male undergraduates recruited for a study of visual perception. A group of seven subjects are shown a large card with a vertical line on it and then are asked to indicate which of three lines on a second card matches the original "standard line" in length (see Figure 16.18). All seven subjects are given a turn at the task, and they announce their choice to the group. The subject in the sixth chair doesn't know it, but everyone else in the group is an accomplice of the experimenter, and they're about to make him wonder whether he has taken leave of his senses.

The accomplices give accurate responses on the first two trials. On the third trial, line number 2 clearly is the correct response, but the first five "subjects" all say that line number 3 matches the standard line. The genuine subject is bewildered

and can't believe his ears. Over the course of the next 15 trials, the accomplices all give the same incorrect response on 11 of them. How does the real subject respond? The line judgments are easy and unambiguous. So, if the subject consistently agrees with the accomplices, he isn't making honest mistakes—he's conforming.

Averaging across all 50 subjects, Asch (1955) found that the young men conformed on 37% of the trials. The subjects varied considerably in their tendency to conform, however. Of the 50 subjects, 13 never caved in to the group, while 14 conformed on more than half the trials.

In subsequent studies, Asch (1956) found that *group size* and *group unanimity* are key determinants of conformity. To examine the impact of group size, Asch repeated his procedure with groups that included from 1 to 15 accomplices. Little conformity was seen when a subject was pitted against just one person, but conformity increased rapidly as group size went from 2 to 4, and then leveled off (see Figure 16.19). Thus, Asch reasoned that as groups grow larger, conformity increases—up to a point, a conclusion that has been echoed by other researchers (Tanford & Penrod, 1984).

However, group size made little difference if just one accomplice "broke" with the others, wrecking their unanimous agreement. The presence of another dissenter lowered conformity to about one-quarter of its peak, even when the dissenter made *inaccurate* judgments that happened to conflict with the majority view. Apparently, the subjects just needed to hear someone else question the accuracy of the group's perplexing responses. The importance of unanimity in fostering conformity has been replicated in subsequent research (Nemeth & Chiles, 1988).

What additional factors influence the likelihood

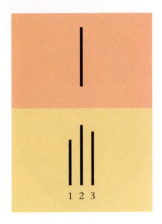

Figure 16.18
Stimuli used in Asch's conformity studies. Subjects were asked to match a standard line (top) with one of three other lines displayed on another card (bottom). The task was easy—until experimental accomplices started responding with obviously incorrect answers, creating a situation in which Asch evaluated subjects' conformity.

Figure 16.19
Conformity and group size. This graph shows the percentage of trials on which subjects conformed as a function of group size in Asch's research. Asch found that conformity became more frequent as group size increased up to about four, and then conformity leveled off. (Data from Asch, 1955)

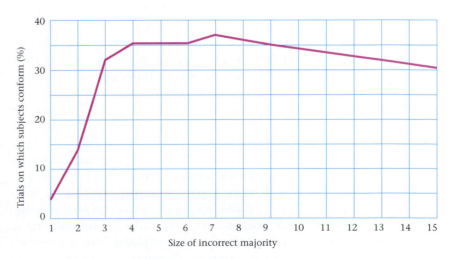

"That we have found the tendency to conformity in our society so strong that reasonably intelligent and well-meaning young people are willing to call white black is a matter of concern."

SOLOMON ASCH

of conformity? Among other things, people are more likely to conform when they are in ambiguous situations or when they have reasons to doubt their own judgments (Campbell, Tesser, & Fairey, 1986). Interestingly, if the situation is ambiguous, increasing the importance of the judgment—that is, the incentives for being accurate—only serves to heighten participants' tendency to conform (Baron, Vandello, & Brunsman, 1996). In other words, when the pressure is on, people tend to follow the leader. In this regard, research also shows that people tend to follow the lead of high-status individuals more than low-status individuals (Driskell & Mullen, 1990). Another major consideration is whether pressure comes from members of an *ingroup* or an *outgroup*. As a general rule, pressure from ingroup members tends to produce more conformity than pressure from outgroup members (Abrams et al., 1990).

Compliance

At first, Asch wasn't sure whether the conforming subjects in his studies were changing their beliefs in response to social pressure or were just pretending to change them. When subjects were interviewed later, many reported that they had begun to doubt their eyesight and that they thought "the majority must be right." These interviews suggested that the subjects had actually changed their beliefs. However, critics asserted that the subjects may have been trying to rationalize their conformity after the fact. A study that included a condition in which subjects made their responses anonymously, instead of publicly, settled the question. Conformity declined dramatically when subjects recorded their responses privately, suggesting that subjects in the Asch studies were not really changing their beliefs (Deutsch & Gerard, 1955).

Based on this finding, theorists concluded that Asch's experiments evoked a particular type of conformity called compliance. *Compliance* **occurs when people yield to social pressure in their public behavior, even though their private beliefs have not changed.** In the Asch studies, compliance resulted from subtle, implied pressure, but it usually occurs in response to explicit rules, requests, and commands. For example, if you agree to wear formal clothes to a fancy restaurant that requires formal attire, even though you despise such rules, you're displaying compliance. Similarly, if you reluctantly follow a supervisor's suggestions at work, even though you think they're lousy ideas, you're complying with a superior's wishes. This type of compliance with an authority

figure's directions is commonplace, as we'll see in our next section.

Obedience

Obedience **is a form of compliance that occurs when people follow direct commands, usually from someone in a position of authority.** To a surprising extent, when an authority figure says, "Jump!" many people simply ask, "How high?" Consider the following anecdote. A number of years ago, the area I lived in experienced a severe flood that required the mobilization of the National Guard and various emergency services. At the height of the crisis, a young man arrived at the scene of the flood, announced that he was from an obscure state agency that no one had ever heard of, and proceeded to take control of the emergency. City work crews, the fire department, local police, municipal officials, and the National Guard followed his orders with dispatch for several days, evacuating entire neighborhoods—until an official thought to check and found out that the man was just someone who had walked in off the street. The imposter, who had had small armies at his beck and call for several days, had no training in emergency services, just a history of unemployment and psychological problems.

After news of the hoax spread, people criticized red-faced local officials for their compliance with the imposter's orders. However, many of the critics probably would have cooperated in much the same way if they had been in the officials' shoes. For most people, willingness to obey someone in authority is the rule, not the exception.

Milgram's Studies

Stanley Milgram wanted to study this tendency to obey authority figures. Like many other people after World War II, he was troubled by how readily the citizens of Germany had followed the orders of dictator Adolf Hitler, even when the orders required morally repugnant actions, such as the slaughter of millions of Jews. Milgram, who had worked with Solomon Asch, set out to design a standard laboratory procedure for the study of obedience, much like Asch's procedure for studying conformity. The clever experiment that Milgram devised became one of the most famous and controversial studies in the annals of psychology. It has been hailed as a "monumental contribution" to science and condemned as "dangerous, dehumanizing, and unethical research" (Ross, 1988). Because of its importance, it's our Featured Study for this chapter.

Investigator: Stanley Milgram (Yale University)

Source: Behavioral study of obedience. *Journal of Abnormal and Social Psychology*, 1963, *67*, 371–378.

"I was just following orders." That was the essence of Adolf Eichmann's defense when he was tried for his war crimes, which included masterminding the Nazis' attempted extermination of European Jews. Milgram wanted to determine the extent to which people are willing to follow authorities' orders. In particular, he wanted to identify the factors that lead people to follow commands that violate their ethics, such as commands to harm an innocent stranger.

Method

The subjects were a diverse collection of 40 men from the local community, recruited through advertisements to participate in a study at Yale University. When a subject arrived at the lab, he met the experimenter and another subject, a likable, 47-year-old accountant, who was actually an accomplice of the experimenter. The "subjects" were told that the study would concern the effects of punishment on learning. They drew slips of paper from a hat to get their assignments, but the drawing was fixed so that the real subject always became the "teacher" and the accomplice the "learner."

The subject then watched as the learner was strapped into an electrified chair through which a shock could be delivered to the learner whenever he made a mistake on the task (left photo in Figure 16.20). The subject was told that the shocks would be painful but would not cause tissue damage, and he was then taken to an adjoining room that housed the shock generator that he would control in his role as the teacher. This elaborate apparatus (right photo in Figure 16.20) had 30 switches designed to administer shocks varying from 15 to 450 volts, with labels ranging from "Slight shock" to "Danger: severe shock" and "XXX." Although the apparatus looked and sounded realistic, it was a fake, and the learner was never shocked.

As the "learning experiment" proceeded, the accomplice made many mistakes that necessitated shocks from the teacher, who was instructed to increase the shock level after each wrong answer. At "300 volts," the learner began to pound on the wall between the two rooms in protest and soon stopped responding to the teacher's questions. At this point, subjects ordinarily turned to the experimenter for guidance. The experimenter, a 31-year-old male in a gray lab coat, firmly indicated that no response was the same as a wrong answer and that the teacher should continue to give stronger and stronger shocks to the now silent learner. If the subject expressed unwillingness to continue, the experimenter responded sternly with one of four prearranged prods, such as, "It is absolutely essential that you continue."

When a subject refused to obey the experimenter, the session came to an end. The dependent variable was the maximum shock the subject was willing to administer before refusing to cooperate. After each session, the true purpose of the study was explained to the subject, who was reassured that the shock was fake and the learner was unharmed.

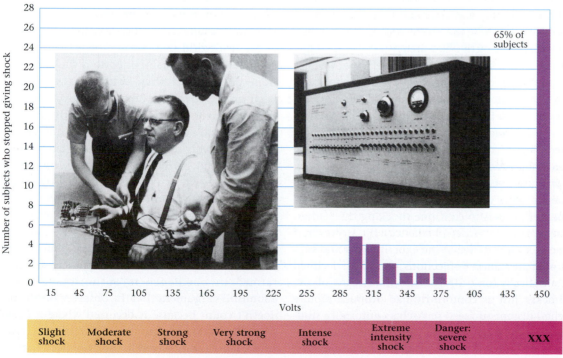

Figure 16.20
Milgram's experiment on obedience. The photo on the left shows the "learner" being connected to the shock generator during one of Milgram's experimental sessions. The photo on the right shows the fake shock generator used in the study. The surprising results of the Milgram (1963) study are summarized in the bar graph. Although subjects frequently protested, the vast majority (65%) delivered the entire series of shocks to the learner. (Photos copyright 1965 by Stanley Milgram. From the film *Obedience,* distributed by The Pennsylvania State University.)

Results

No subjects stopped cooperating before the learner reached the point of pounding on the wall, but 5 quit at that point. As the graph in Figure 16.20 shows, only 14 out of 40 subjects defied the experimenter before the full series of shocks was completed. Thus, 26 of the 40 subjects (65%) administered all 30 levels of shock. Although they tended to obey the experimenter, many subjects voiced and displayed considerable distress about harming the learner. The horrified subjects groaned, bit their lips, stuttered, trembled, and broke into a sweat, but continued administering the shocks.

Discussion

Based on these results, Milgram concluded that obedience to authority is even more common than he or others had anticipated. Before the study was conducted, Milgram had described it to 40 psychiatrists and had asked them to predict how much shock subjects would be willing to administer to their innocent victims. Most of the psychiatrists had predicted that fewer than 1% of the subjects would continue to the end of the series of shocks!

In interpreting his results, Milgram argued that strong pressure from an authority figure can make decent people do terribly indecent things to others. Applying this insight to Nazi war crimes and other travesties, Milgram asserted that some sinister actions may not be due to actors' evil character so much as to situational pressures that can lead normal people to engage in acts of treachery and violence. Thus, he arrived at the disturbing conclusion that given the right circumstances, anyone might obey orders to inflict harm on innocent strangers.

Comment

In itself, obedience is not necessarily bad or wrong. Social groups of any size depend on a reasonable amount of obedience to function smoothly. Life would be chaotic if orders from police, parents, physicians, bosses, generals, and presidents were routinely ignored. However, Milgram's study suggests that many people are overly willing to submit to the orders of someone in command.

If you're like most people, you're probably confident that you wouldn't follow an experimenter's demands to inflict harm on a helpless victim. But the empirical findings indicate that you're probably wrong. After many replications, the results are deplorable, but clear: Most people can be coerced into engaging in actions that violate their morals and values. This finding is disheartening, but it sharpens our understanding of moral atrocities, such as the Nazi persecutions of Jews and the mass suicide at Jonestown.

After his initial demonstration, Milgram (1974) tried about 20 variations on his experimental procedure, looking for factors that influence subjects' obedience. In one variation, Milgram moved the study away from Yale's campus to see if the prestige of the university was contributing to the subjects' obedience. When the study was run in a seedy office building by the "Research Associates of Bridgeport," only a small decrease in obedience was observed (48% of the subjects gave all the shocks).

In another version of the study, Milgram borrowed a trick from Asch's conformity experiments and set up teams of three teachers that included two more accomplices. When they drew lots, the real subject was always selected to run the shock apparatus in consultation with his fellow teachers. When both accomplices accepted the experimenter's orders to continue shocking the learner, the pressure increased obedience a bit. However, if the accomplices defied the experimenter and supported the subject's objections, obedience declined dramatically (only 10% of the subjects gave all the shocks), just as conformity had dropped rapidly when dissent surfaced in Asch's conformity studies. Dissent from another "teacher" turned out to be one of the few variations that reduced subjects' obedience appreciably. As a whole, Milgram was surprised at how high subjects' obedience remained as he changed various aspects of his experiment.

The Ensuing Controversy

Milgram's study evoked a controversy that continues through today. Some critics argued that Milgram's results couldn't be generalized to apply to the real world (Baumrind, 1964; Orne & Holland, 1968). They maintained that subjects went along only because they knew it was an experiment and "everything must be okay." Or they argued that subjects who agree to participate in a scientific study *expect to obey* orders from an experimenter. Milgram (1964, 1968) replied by arguing that if subjects had thought "everything must be okay," they wouldn't have experienced the enormous distress that they clearly showed.

As for the idea that research subjects expect to follow an experimenter's commands, Milgram pointed out that so do real-world soldiers and bureaucrats who are accused of villainous acts performed in obedience to authority. "I reject Baumrind's argument that the observed obedience doesn't count because it occurred where it is appropriate," said Milgram (1964). "That is precisely why it *does* count." Overall, the evidence supports the generalizability of Milgram's results, which

"The essence of obedience is that a person comes to view himself as the instrument for carrying out another person's wishes, and he therefore no longer regards himself as responsible for his actions."

STANLEY MILGRAM

were consistently replicated for many years, in diverse settings, with a variety of subjects and procedural variations (Miller, 1986).

Critics also questioned the ethics of Milgram's procedure (Baumrind, 1964; Kelman, 1967). They noted that without prior consent, subjects were exposed to extensive deception that could undermine their trust in people and to severe stress that could leave emotional scars. Moreover, most subjects also had to confront the disturbing fact that they caved in to the experimenter's commands to inflict harm on an innocent victim.

Milgram's defenders argued that the brief distress experienced by his subjects was a small price to pay for the insights that emerged from his obedience studies. Looking back, however, many psychologists seem to share the critics' concerns about the ethical implications of Milgram's work. His procedure is questionable by contemporary standards of research ethics, and no replications of his obedience study have been conducted in the United States since the mid-1970s (Blass, 1991)—a bizarre epitaph for what may be psychology's best-known experiment.

Cultural Variations in Conformity and Obedience

Are conformity and obedience unique to American culture? By no means. The Asch and Milgram experiments have been repeated in many societies, where they have yielded results roughly similar to those seen in the United States. Thus, the phenomena of conformity and obedience seem to transcend culture.

The replications of Milgram's obedience study have largely been limited to industrialized nations similar to the United States. Comparisons of the results of these studies must be made with caution because the composition of the samples and the experimental procedures have varied somewhat. But many of the studies have reported even higher obedience rates than those seen in Milgram's American samples. For example, obedience rates over 80% have been reported for samples from Italy, Germany, Austria, Spain, and Holland (Smith & Bond, 1994). Thus, the surprisingly high level of obedience observed by Milgram does not appear to be peculiar to the United States.

The Asch experiment has been repeated in a more diverse range of societies than the Milgram experiment. Like many other cultural differences in social behavior, variations in conformity appear to be related to the degree of *individualism versus collectivism* seen in a society. Various theo-

rists have argued that collectivistic cultures, which emphasize respect for group norms, cooperation, and harmony, probably encourage more conformity than individualistic cultures, with their emphasis on independence and assertiveness (Schwartz, 1990). As Matsumoto (1994, p. 162) puts it, "To conform in American culture is to be weak or deficient somehow. But this is not true in other cultures. Many cultures foster more collective, group-oriented values, and concepts of conformity, obedience, and compliance enjoy much higher status."

Consistent with this analysis, a recent review of 133 conformity studies drawn from 17 countries found higher levels of conformity in collectivistic cultures than in individualistic cultures (Bond & Smith, 1996). Interestingly, the same review uncovered a decline in the amount of conformity seen in U.S. studies since the 1950s, which may reflect cultural change in North America.

Our discussion of conformity and obedience foreshadows our last major topic in this chapter, behavior in groups. Social pressure, for instance, is often at work in group interactions, and being part of a group can have a dramatic impact on an individual's behavior (as it did in the Asch studies). Our review of behavior in groups will begin with a look at the nature of groups.

Recap of Key Points

• Conformity involves yielding to social pressure. Asch found that subjects often conform to the group, even when the group reports inaccurate judgments on a simple line-judging task.

• Conformity becomes more likely as group size increases, up to a group size of four, and then levels off. If a small group isn't unanimous, conformity declines rapidly.

• In Milgram's landmark study of obedience to authority, adult men drawn from the community showed a remarkable tendency, in spite of their misgivings, to follow orders to shock an innocent stranger. Milgram concluded that situational pressures can make decent people do indecent things.

• Critics asserted that Milgram's results were not generalizable to the real world and that his methods were unethical. The generalizability of Milgram's findings has stood the test of time, but his work also helped to stimulate stricter ethical standards for research.

• The Asch and Milgram experiments have been replicated in many cultures. These replications have uncovered modest cultural variations in the propensity to conform or to obey an authority figure.

Social psychologists study groups as well as individuals, but exactly what is a group? Are all the divorced fathers living in Baltimore a group? Are three strangers moving skyward in an elevator a group? What if the elevator gets stuck? How about four students from your psychology class who study together regularly? A jury deciding a trial? The Boston Celtics? The U.S. Congress? Some of these collections of people are groups and others aren't. Let's examine the concept of a group to find out which of these collections qualify.

In social psychologists' eyes, **a *group* consists of two or more individuals who interact and are interdependent.** The divorced fathers in Baltimore aren't likely to qualify on either count. Strangers sharing an elevator might interact briefly, but they're not interdependent. However, if the elevator got stuck and they had to deal with an emergency together, they could suddenly become a group. Your psychology classmates who study together are a group, as they interact and depend on each other to achieve shared goals. So do the members of a jury, a sports team such as the Celtics, and a large organization such as the U.S. Congress.

Groups vary in many ways. Obviously, a study group, the Celtics, and Congress are very different in terms of size, purpose, formality, longevity, similarity of members, and diversity of activities. Can anything meaningful be said about groups if they're so diverse? Yes. In spite of their immense variability, groups share certain features that affect their functioning. Among other things, most groups have *roles* that allocate special responsibilities to some members, *norms* about suitable behavior, a *communication structure* that reflects who talks to whom, and a *power structure* that determines which members wield the most influence (Forsyth, 1990).

Thus, when people join together in a group, they create a social organism with unique characteristics and dynamics that can take on a life of its own. One of social psychology's enduring insights is that in a given situation you may behave quite differently when you're in a group than when you're alone. To illustrate this point, let's look at some interesting research on helping behavior.

Behavior Alone and in Groups: The Case of the Bystander Effect

Imagine that you have a precarious medical condition and that you must go through life worrying about whether someone will leap forward to provide help if the need ever arises. Wouldn't you feel more secure when around larger groups? After all, there's "safety in numbers." Logically, as group size increases, the probability of having a "good Samaritan" on the scene increases. Or does it?

We've seen before that human behavior isn't necessarily logical. When it comes to helping behavior, many studies have uncovered an apparent paradox called the ***bystander effect:* People are less likely to provide needed help when they are in groups than when they are alone.**

Evidence that your probability of getting help *declines* as group size increases was first described by John Darley and Bibb Latané (1968), who were conducting research on the determinants of altruism. As noted in Chapter 11, *altruism* is selfless concern for the welfare of others that leads to helping behavior. In the Darley and Latané study, students in individual cubicles connected by an intercom participated in discussion groups of three sizes. (The separate cubicles allowed the researchers to examine each individual's behavior in a group context, a technique that minimizes con-

Groups of all kinds have to work productively and arrive at collective decisions. The social dynamics of these processes are complicated, and a variety of factors can undermine productivity or effective decision making.

founded variables in individual-group comparisons.) Early in the discussion, a student who was an experimental accomplice hesitantly mentioned that he was prone to seizures. Later in the discussion, the same accomplice feigned a severe seizure and cried out for help. Although a majority of subjects sought assistance for the student, Figure 16.21 shows that the tendency to seek help *declined* with increasing group size.

Similar trends have been seen in many other experiments, in which over 6000 subjects have had opportunities to respond to apparent emergencies, including fires, asthma attacks, faintings, crashes, and flat tires, as well as less pressing needs to answer a door or to pick up objects dropped by a stranger (Latané & Nida, 1981). Many of the experiments have been highly realistic studies conducted in subways, stores, and shopping malls, and many have compared individuals against groups in face-to-face interaction. Pooling the results of this research, Latané and Nida (1981) estimated that subjects who were alone provided help 75% of the time, whereas subjects in the presence of others provided help only 53% of the time. They concluded that the only significant limiting condition on the bystander effect is that it is less likely to occur when the need for help is not ambiguous.

What accounts for the bystander effect? A number of factors may be at work. Bystander effects are most likely in ambiguous situations because people look around to see whether others think there's an emergency. If everyone hesitates, their inaction suggests that there's no real need for help. The *diffusion of responsibility* that occurs in a group is also important. If you're by yourself when you encounter someone in need of help, the responsibility to provide help rests squarely on your shoulders. However, if other people are present, the responsibility is divided among you, and you may all say to yourselves, "Someone else will help." A reduced sense of responsibility may contribute to other aspects of behavior in groups, as we'll see in the next section.

Group Productivity and Social Loafing

Have you ever driven through a road construction project—at a snail's pace, of course—and become irritated because so many workers seem to be just standing around? Maybe the irony of the posted sign "Your tax dollars at work" made you imagine that they were all dawdling. And then again, perhaps not. Individuals' productivity often *does* decline in larger groups (Latané, Williams, & Harkins,

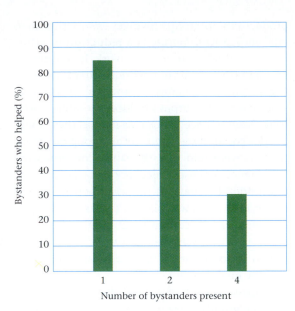

Figure 16.21
The bystander effect. As the number of apparent bystanders increased, the percentage of subjects who sought help for a victim of a (feigned) seizure declined. (Data from Darley & Latané, 1968)

1979). This reality is unfortunate, as many important tasks can only be accomplished in groups. Group productivity is crucial to committees, sports teams, firefighting crews, sororities, study groups, symphonies, and work teams of all kinds, from the morning crew in a little diner to the board of directors of a Fortune 500 company.

Two factors appear to contribute to reduced individual productivity in larger groups. One factor is *reduced efficiency* resulting from the *loss of coordination* among workers' efforts. As you put more people on a yearbook staff, for instance, you'll probably create more and more duplication of effort and increase how often group members end up working at cross purposes.

The second factor contributing to low

productivity in groups involves *effort* rather than efficiency. *Social loafing* is a reduction in effort by individuals when they work in groups as compared to when they work by themselves. To investigate social loafing, Latané et al. (1979) measured the sound output produced by subjects who were asked to cheer or clap as loud as they could. So they couldn't see or hear other group members, subjects were told that the study concerned the importance of sensory feedback and were asked to don blindfolds and put on headphones through which loud noise was played. This maneuver permitted a simple deception: Subjects were *led to believe* that they were working alone or in a group of two or six, when in fact *individual* output was actually measured.

When subjects *thought* that they were working in larger groups, their individual output declined. Since lack of coordination could not affect individual output, the subjects' decreased sound production had to be due to reduced effort. Latané and his colleagues also had the same subjects clap and shout in genuine groups of two and six and found an additional decrease in production that was attributed to loss of coordination. Figure 16.22 shows how social loafing and loss of coordination combined to reduce productivity as group size increased.

The social-loafing effect has been replicated in numerous studies in which subjects have worked on a variety of tasks, including cheering, pumping air, swimming in a relay race, solving mazes, evaluating editorials, and brainstorming for new ideas (Karau & Williams, 1995; Shepperd, 1993). According to Latané (1981), the bystander effect and social loafing share a common cause: diffusion of responsibility in groups. As group size increases,

the responsibility for getting a job done is divided among more people, and many group members ease up because their individual contribution is less recognizable. Thus, social loafing occurs in situations where individuals can "hide in the crowd." Consistent with this line of thinking, research shows that social loafing is more likely (a) in larger groups, (b) on tasks where individual output is hard to evaluate, and (c) in situations where group members expect their co-workers to perform well and "carry them" (Karau & Williams, 1993).

Social loafing is not inevitable. In some circumstances people may increase their effort when they work as part of a group. For instance, if a task is important and a person is worried about co-workers being unwilling, unable, or too unreliable to contribute their fair share, the person may work harder to make up for other group members' inadequacies, a phenomenon called *social compensation* (Williams & Karau, 1991).

Cultural factors may also influence the likelihood of social loafing. Studies with subjects from Japan, China, and Taiwan suggest that social loafing may be less prevalent in collectivistic cultures, which place a high priority on meeting group goals and contributing to ones' ingroups (Karau & Williams, 1996; Matsumoto, 1994).

Decision Making in Groups

Productivity is not the only issue that commonly concerns groups. When people join together in groups, they often have to make decisions about what the group will do and how it will use its resources. Whether it's your study group deciding what type of pizza to order, a jury deciding on a verdict, or Congress deciding on whether to pass a bill, groups make decisions.

Evaluating decision making is often more complicated than evaluating productivity. In many cases, the "right" decision may not be readily apparent. Who can say whether your study group ordered the right pizza or whether Congress passed the right bills? Nonetheless, social psychologists have discovered some interesting tendencies in group decision making. We'll take a brief look at *group polarization* and then discuss *groupthink* in some detail.

Group Polarization

Who leans toward more cautious decisions: individuals or groups? Common sense suggests that groups will work out compromises that cancel out members' extreme views. Hence, the collective wis-

Figure 16.22
The effect of loss of coordination and social loafing on group productivity. The amount of sound produced per person declined noticeably when people worked in actual groups of two or six (orange line). This decrease in productivity reflects both loss of coordination and social loafing. Sound per person also declined when subjects merely thought they were working in groups of two or six (purple line). This smaller decrease in productivity is due to social loafing. (Data from Latané, Williams, & Harkins, 1979)

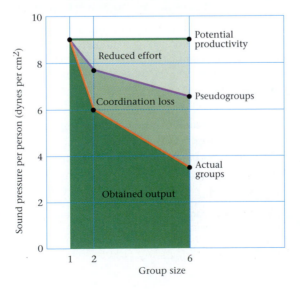

dom of the group should yield relatively conservative choices. Is common sense correct? To investigate this question, Stoner (1961) asked individual subjects to give their recommendations on tough decisions and then asked the same subjects to engage in group discussion to arrive at joint recommendations. When Stoner compared individuals' average recommendation against their group decision generated through discussion, he found that groups arrived at *riskier* decisions than individuals did. Stoner's finding was replicated in other studies (Pruitt, 1971), and the phenomenon acquired the name *risky shift*.

However, investigators eventually determined that groups can shift either way, toward risk or caution, depending on which way the group is leaning to begin with (Myers & Lamm, 1976). A shift toward a more extreme position, an effect called *polarization,* is often the result of group discussion. Thus, **group polarization occurs when group discussion strengthens a group's dominant point of view and produces a shift toward a more extreme decision in that direction** (see Figure 16.23). Group polarization does *not* involve widening the gap between factions in a group, as its name might suggest. In fact, group polarization can contribute to consensus in a group, as we'll see in our upcoming discussion of groupthink.

Group polarization is more likely when groups wrestle with important issues rather than trivial matters (Kerr, 1992). Why does group polarization occur? One reason is that group discussion often exposes group members to persuasive arguments that they had not thought about previously (Stasser, 1992). Another reason is that when people discover that their views are shared by others, they tend to express even stronger views because they want to be liked by their ingroups (Hogg, Turner, & Davidson, 1990).

Groupthink

In contrast to group polarization, which is a normal process in group dynamics, groupthink is more like a "disease" that can infect decision making in groups. *Groupthink* **occurs when members of a cohesive group emphasize concurrence at the expense of critical thinking in arriving at a decision.** As you might imagine, groupthink doesn't produce very effective decision making. Indeed, groupthink often leads to major blunders that may look incomprehensible after the fact. Irving Janis (1972) first described groupthink in his effort to explain how President John F. Kennedy and his advisers could have miscalculated so badly

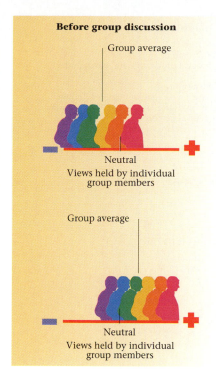
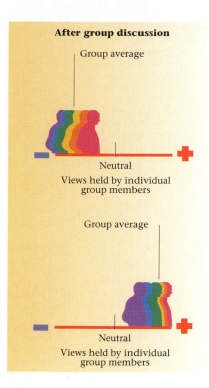

Before group discussion | **After group discussion**

Group average

Neutral
Views held by individual
group members

Group average

Neutral
Views held by individual
group members

**Figure 16.23
Group polarization.** Two examples of group polarization are diagrammed here. In the first example (top) a group starts out mildly opposed to an idea, but after discussion sentiment against the idea is stronger. In the second example (bottom), a group starts out with a favorable disposition toward an idea, and this disposition is strengthened by group discussion.

in deciding to invade Cuba at the Bay of Pigs in 1961. The attempted invasion failed miserably and, in retrospect, seemed remarkably ill-conceived.

Applying his many years of research and theory on group dynamics to the Bay of Pigs fiasco, Janis developed a model of groupthink, which is summarized in Figure 16.24. When groups get caught up in groupthink, members suspend their critical judgment and the group starts censoring dissent as the pressure to conform increases. Soon, everyone begins to think alike. Moreover, "mind guards" try to shield the group from information that contradicts the group's view.

If the group's view is challenged from outside, victims of groupthink tend to think in simplistic "us versus them" terms. Members begin to overestimate the ingroup's unanimity, and they begin to view the outgroup as the enemy. Groupthink also promotes incomplete gathering of information. The group's search for information is biased in favor of facts and opinions that support their decision.

What causes groupthink? According to Janis, a key precondition is high group cohesiveness. *Group cohesiveness* **refers to the strength of the liking relationships linking group members to each other and to the group itself.** Members of cohesive groups are close-knit, are committed, have "team spirit," and are very loyal to the group. Cohesiveness itself isn't bad. It can facilitate group productivity (Mullen & Copper, 1994) and help groups achieve great things. But

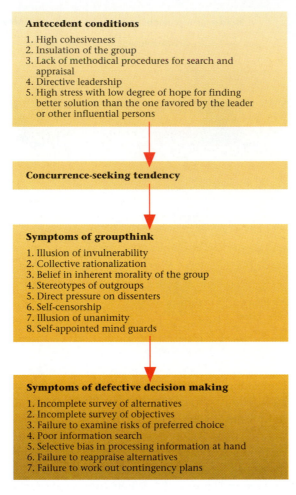

Figure 16.24
Overview of Janis's model of groupthink.
The antecedent conditions, symptoms, and resultant effects of groupthink postulated by Janis (1972) are outlined here. His model of groupthink has been very influential, but practical difficulties have limited research on the theory. (Adapted from Janis & Mann, 1977)

Antecedent conditions

1. High cohesiveness
2. Insulation of the group
3. Lack of methodical procedures for search and appraisal
4. Directive leadership
5. High stress with low degree of hope for finding better solution than the one favored by the leader or other influential persons

Concurrence-seeking tendency

Symptoms of groupthink

1. Illusion of invulnerability
2. Collective rationalization
3. Belief in inherent morality of the group
4. Stereotypes of outgroups
5. Direct pressure on dissenters
6. Self-censorship
7. Illusion of unanimity
8. Self-appointed mind guards

Symptoms of defective decision making

1. Incomplete survey of alternatives
2. Incomplete survey of objectives
3. Failure to examine risks of preferred choice
4. Poor information search
5. Selective bias in processing information at hand
6. Failure to reappraise alternatives
7. Failure to work out contingency plans

Janis maintains that the danger of groupthink is greater when groups are highly cohesive. Groupthink is also more likely when a group works in relative isolation, when the group's power structure is dominated by a strong, direc-tive leader, and when the group is under stress to make a major decision (see Figure 16.24). Under these conditions, group discussions can easily lead to group polarization, strengthening the group's dominant view.

Only a handful of experiments have been conducted to test Janis's theory, because the antecedent conditions thought to foster groupthink—such as high decision stress, strong group cohesiveness, and dominating leadership—are difficult to create effectively in laboratory settings (Aldag & Fuller, 1993). Although one recent experimental study by Turner and her associates (1992) found support for certain aspects of Janis's theory, the evidence on groupthink consists almost entirely of retrospective case studies of major decision-making fiascos. In analyzing these cases Janis and other investigators may have tended to see what they expected to see. A recent reexamination of the cases studied by Janis raised doubts about whether high cohesiveness and decision stress are crucial antecedents of groupthink (Tetlock et al., 1992). Critics have argued that in some circumstances high cohesiveness may *reduce* groupthink by making members confident that they will not be punished for dissent. Janis's model has also been criticized on the grounds that it omits a variety of factors that may influence the likelihood of groupthink, such as group norms and task characteristics (Aldag & Fuller, 1993). In sum, Janis's model of groupthink should probably be characterized as an innovative, sophisticated, intuitively appealing theory that needs to be subjected to much more empirical study.

PUTTING IT IN PERSPECTIVE

Our discussion of social psychology has provided a final embellishment on three of our seven unifying themes. One of these is the value of psychology's commitment to empiricism—that is, its reliance on systematic observation through research to arrive at conclusions. The second theme that stands out is the importance of cultural factors in shaping behavior, and the third is the extent to which people's experience of the world is highly subjective. Let's consider the virtues of empiricism first.

It's easy to question the need to do scientific research on social behavior, because studies in social psychology often seem to verify common sense. While most people wouldn't presume to devise their own theory of color vision, question the significance of REM sleep, or quibble about the principal causes of schizophrenia, everyone has beliefs about the nature of love, how to persuade others, the limits of obedience, and people's willingness to help in times of need. Thus, when studies demonstrate that credibility enhances persuasion, or that good looks facilitate attraction, it's tempting to conclude that social psychologists go to great lengths to document the obvious, and some critics say, "Why bother?"

You saw why in this chapter. Research in social psychology has repeatedly shown that the predictions of logic and common sense are often wrong. Consider just a few examples. Even psychiatric experts failed to predict the remarkable obedience to authority uncovered in Milgram's research. The bystander effect in helping behavior violates cold-blooded mathematical logic. Research on counter-attitudinal behavior has shown that (under the right conditions) the smaller the reward people are given for doing something, the more they like doing it. Dissonance research has also shown that after a severe initiation, the bigger the letdown, the more favorable people's feelings are. These principles defy common sense.

Thus, research on social behavior provides dramatic illustrations of why psychologists put their faith in empiricism. The moral of social psychology's story is this: Although scientific research often supports ideas based on common sense and logic, we can't count on this result. If psychologists want to achieve sound understanding of the principles governing behavior, they have to put their ideas to an empirical test.

Our coverage of social psychology also demonstrated once again that, cross-culturally, behavior is characterized by both variance and invariance. As one might expect, social behavior seems particularly sensitive to the influence of cultural factors, such as the emphasis on individualism or collectivism in a society. Thus, we saw substantial cultural differences in patterns of attribution, the role of love in mating relationships, attitudes about conformity, the tendency to obey authority figures, and the likelihood of social loafing. Although basic social phenomena such as stereotyping, attraction, obedience, and conformity probably occur all over the world, cross-cultural studies of social behavior show that research findings based on American samples may not generalize precisely to other cultures.

Research in social psychology is also uniquely well suited for making the point that people's view of the world is highly personal and subjective. In this chapter we saw how physical appearance can color perception of a person's ability or personality, how social schemas can lead people to see what they expect to see in their interactions with others, how pressure to conform can make people begin to doubt their senses, and how groupthink can lead group members down a perilous path of shared illusions.

The subjectivity of social perception will surface once again in our chapter Application. It focuses on a practical problem that social psychologists have shown great interest in—prejudice.

Recap of Key Points

- People who help someone in need when they are alone are less likely to provide help when a group is present. This phenomenon, called the bystander effect, occurs primarily because a group creates diffusion of responsibility.
- Individuals' productivity often declines in larger groups because of loss of coordination and because of social loafing. Social loafing seems to be due mostly to diffusion of responsibility and may be less prevalent in collectivist cultures.
- Group polarization occurs when discussion leads a group to shift toward a more extreme decision in the direction the group was already leaning. In groupthink, a cohesive group suspends critical judgment in a misguided effort to promote agreement in decision making.
- Social psychology illustrates the value of empiricism because research in this area often proves that common sense is wrong. Cross-cultural research on social behavior illustrates that findings based on American samples may not generalize precisely to other cultures. Additionally, several lines of research on social perception demonstrate that people's experience of the world is highly subjective.

APPLICATION:
UNDERSTANDING PREJUDICE

Answer the following "true" or "false."

1 Prejudice and discrimination amount to the same thing.

2 Stereotypes are always negative or unflattering.

3 Ethnic and racial groups are the only widespread targets of prejudice in modern society.

4 People see members of their own ingroup as being more alike than the members of outgroups.

Prejudice is a major social problem. It harms victims' self-concepts, suppresses human potential, creates tension and strife between groups, and even instigates wars. The first step toward reducing prejudice is to understand its roots. Hence, in this Application, we'll use concepts and prin-

ciples from each of the chapter's six sections to achieve a better understanding of why prejudice is so common. Along the way, you'll learn the answers to the true-false questions above.

Prejudice and discrimination are closely related concepts, and the terms have become nearly interchangeable in popular use. Social scientists, however, prefer to define their terms precisely, so let's clarify which is which. *Prejudice* **is a negative attitude held toward members of a group.** Like other attitudes, prejudice includes three components (see Figure 16.25): beliefs ("Indians are mostly alcoholics"), emotions ("I despise Jews"), and behavioral dispositions ("I wouldn't hire a Mexican"). Racial prejudice receives the lion's share of publicity, but prejudice is *not* limited to ethnic groups. Women, homosexuals, the aged, the handicapped, and the mentally ill are also targets of widespread prejudice. Thus, many people hold

prejudicial attitudes toward one group or another, and many have been victims of prejudice.

Prejudice may lead to *discrimination,* **which involves behaving differently, usually unfairly, toward the members of a group.** Prejudice and discrimination tend to go hand in hand, but as LaPiere's (1934) pioneering study of discrimination in restaurant seating showed, attitudes and behavior do not necessarily correspond (see Figure 16.26). In our discussion, we'll concentrate primarily on the attitude of prejudice. Let's begin by looking at processes in person perception that promote prejudice.

Stereotyping and Subjectivity in Person Perception 12d

Perhaps no factor plays a larger role in prejudice than *stereotypes.* That's not to say that stereotypes are inevitably negative. Although it's an overgeneralization, it's hardly insulting to assert that Americans are ambitious or that the Japanese are industrious. Unfortunately, many people *do* subscribe to derogatory stereotypes of various ethnic groups. Although studies suggest that negative racial stereotypes have diminished over the last 50 years, they're not a thing of the past (Devine & Elliot, 1995; Dovidio & Gaertner, 1991; Smith, 1991). According to a variety of investigators, modern racism has merely become more subtle (Ponterotto & Pedersen, 1993). Many people carefully avoid overt expressions of prejudicial attitudes but covertly continue to harbor negative views of racial minorities. These people endorse racial equality as an abstract principle but often oppose concrete programs intended to promote equality, on the grounds that discrimination is no longer a problem. Recent studies suggest that modern sexism has

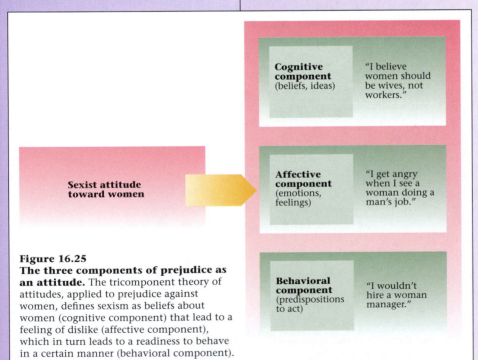

Figure 16.25
The three components of prejudice as an attitude. The tricomponent theory of attitudes, applied to prejudice against women, defines sexism as beliefs about women (cognitive component) that lead to a feeling of dislike (affective component), which in turn leads to a readiness to behave in a certain manner (behavioral component).

Sexist attitude toward women

Cognitive component (beliefs, ideas)
"I believe women should be wives, not workers."

Affective component (emotions, feelings)
"I get angry when I see a woman doing a man's job."

Behavioral component (predispositions to act)
"I wouldn't hire a woman manager."

Figure 16.26
Relationship between prejudice and discrimination. As these examples show, prejudice can exist without discrimination and discrimination without prejudice. In the green cells, there is a disparity between attitude and behavior.

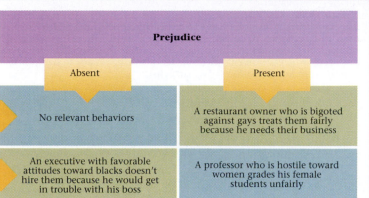

		Prejudice	
		Absent	Present
Discrimination	Absent	No relevant behaviors	A restaurant owner who is bigoted against gays treats them fairly because he needs their business
	Present	An executive with favorable attitudes toward blacks doesn't hire them because he would get in trouble with his boss	A professor who is hostile toward women grades his female students unfairly

become subtle in much the same way as racism (Swim et al., 1995).

Research shows that stereotypes are insidious in that they can even infiltrate the thinking of people who are genuinely low in prejudice (Monteith, 1993). According to Devine (1989), prejudicial stereotypes are highly accessible cognitive schemas that are often activated automatically, even

Besides racial minorities, others that have been stereotyped and discriminated against include the physically challenged, who have organized themselves into a political force demanding rights.

in people who truly renounce prejudice. Thus, a man who rejects prejudice against homosexuals may still feel uncomfortable sitting next to a gay male on a bus, even though he regards his reaction as inappropriate. Studies also show that people are particularly likely to think in terms of derogatory stereotypes when they are in a negative mood (Esses & Zanna, 1995).

Moreover, stereotypes are highly resistant to change. When people encounter members of a group that they view with prejudice who deviate from the stereotype of that group, they often discount this evidence by assuming that the atypical group members constitute a distinct subtype of that group, such as wealthy African Americans or conservative homosexuals (Devine & Baker, 1991; Kunda & Oleson, 1995). Consigning deviants to a subtype that is viewed as unrepresentative of the group allows people to preserve their stereotype of the group.

Stereotypes also persist because the *subjectivity* of person perception makes it likely that people will see what they expect to see when they actually come into contact with groups that they view with prejudice (Stephan, 1989). For example, Duncan (1976) had white subjects watch and evaluate interaction on a TV monitor that was supposedly live (actually it was a

videotape), and varied the race of a person who gets into an argument and gives another person a slight shove. The shove was coded as "violent behavior" by 73% of the subjects when the actor was black but by only 13% of the subjects when the actor was white. As we've noted before, people's perceptions are highly subjective. Because of stereotypes, even "violence" may lie in the eye of the beholder.

Memory biases are also tilted in favor of confirming people's prejudices. For example, if a man believes that "women are not cut out for leadership roles," he may dwell with delight on his female supervisor's mistakes and quickly forget about her achievements. Thus, the *illusory correlation effect* can contribute to the maintenance of prejudicial stereotypes (Hamilton & Sherman, 1989). Obviously, actual interaction can do only so much to counteract stereotypes, since gender stereotypes remain common even though men and women interact extensively.

Biases in Attribution 12d

Attribution processes can also help perpetuate stereotypes and prejudice. Research taking its cue from Weiner's (1980) model of attribution has shown that people often make *biased attributions for success and failure*. For example, men and women don't get equal credit for their successes (Deaux, 1984; Swim & Sanna, 1996). Observers often discount a woman's success by attributing it to good luck, sheer effort, or the ease of the task (except on traditional feminine tasks). In comparison, a man's success is more likely to be attrib-

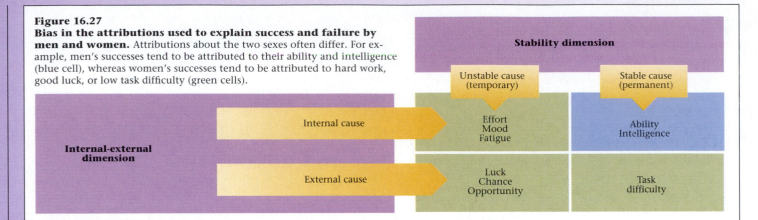

Figure 16.27
Bias in the attributions used to explain success and failure by men and women. Attributions about the two sexes often differ. For example, men's successes tend to be attributed to their ability and intelligence (blue cell), whereas women's successes tend to be attributed to hard work, good luck, or low task difficulty (green cells).

Stability dimension

	Unstable cause (temporary)	Stable cause (permanent)
Internal cause	Effort Mood Fatigue	Ability Intelligence
External cause	Luck Chance Opportunity	Task difficulty

Internal-external dimension

uted to his outstanding ability (see Figure 16.27). These biased patterns of attribution help sustain the stereotype that men are more competent than women. Similar patterns of bias have been seen in attributional explanations of ethnic minorities' successes and failures (Jackson, Sullivan, & Hodge, 1993; Kluegel, 1990). Generally, when minorities experience stereotype-inconsistent success, it is discounted by attributing it to external factors or to unstable, internal causes.

Recall that the *fundamental attribution error* is a bias toward explaining events by pointing to the personal characteristics of the actors as causes (internal attributions). Research suggests that people are particularly likely to make this error when evaluating targets of prejudice (Hewstone, 1990; Pettigrew, 1979). Thus, when people take note of ethnic neighborhoods dominated by crime and poverty, the personal qualities of the residents are blamed for these problems, while other explanations emphasizing situational factors (job discrimination, poor police service, and so on) are downplayed or ignored. The old saying "They should be able to pull themselves up by their bootstraps" is a blanket dismissal of how situational factors may make it especially difficult for minorities to achieve upward mobility.

Defensive attribution, which involves unjustly blaming victims of misfortune for their adversity, can also contribute to prejudice. A prominent example in recent years has been the assertion by some people that homosexuals brought the AIDS crisis on themselves and so deserve their fate (Anderson, 1992). By blaming AIDS on gays' alleged character flaws, heterosexuals may be unknowingly seeking to reassure themselves that they're immune to a similar fate.

Proximity and Similarity Effects in Attraction

The dynamics of interpersonal attraction may foster prejudice and discrimination in at least two ways. First, *proximity effects* help perpetuate ethnic prejudice wherever segregated patterns of housing and schooling limit opportunities for meaningful interracial contact. Insofar as people tend to become friends with those who live near them and go to school with them, they aren't likely to become friends with minorities who are excluded from their neighborhoods, schools, and country clubs. Given the right circumstances, increased intergroup contact can lead to reduced prejudice (Gaertner et al., 1990; Pettigrew, 1997).

Second, the contribution of *similarity effects* to prejudice may be considerable if Rosenbaum's (1986) "repulsion hypothesis" is correct. A recent study did find evidence that dissimilarity can cause disdain (Pilkington & Lydon, 1997). This tendency probably promotes prejudice against many groups, including minorities, homosexuals, the handicapped, and the aged.

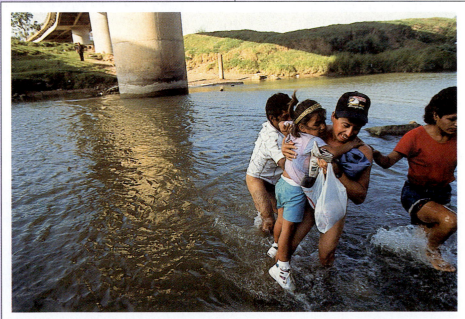

The serious social problem of racial prejudice victimizes virtually all nonwhite groups, such as these Mexican immigrants crossing the Mexico–United States border. The predisposition to divide the world into ingroups and outgroups is readily apparent in the widespread tendency to blame many social ills on illegal immigrants.

Forming and Preserving Prejudicial Attitudes 12d

If prejudice is an attitude, where does it come from? Many prejudices appear to be handed down as a legacy from parents (Ponterotto & Pedersen, 1993). Prejudicial attitudes can be found in children as young as ages 4 to 7 (Aboud, 1987). This transmission of prejudice across generations presumably depends to some extent on *observational learning*. For example, if a young boy hears his father ridicule homosexuals, his exposure to his father's attitude is likely to affect his attitude about gays. If the young boy then goes to school and makes disparaging remarks about gays that are reinforced by approval from peers, his prejudice will be strengthened through *operant conditioning*. Consistent with this analysis, one recent study found that college students' opinions on racial issues were swayed by overhearing others voice racist or antiracist sentiments (Blanchard, Lilly, & Vaughn, 1991). Thus, social norms that condone expressions of prejudice help to sustain prejudicial attitudes.

Another problem is that when people meet individuals who behave in ways that conform to their prejudicial expectations, they are all too willing to generalize from the individual to the group. For example, a recent study showed that encountering a single black person who performs a negative or stereotypical action can reaffirm whites' stereotypes of blacks (Henderson-King & Nisbett, 1996). The investigators attribute the inordinately large influence of a single person to a common pitfall in reasoning—*belief in the law of small numbers* (see the Application in Chapter 8).

Dividing the World into Ingroups and Outgroups 12d

As noted in the main body of the chapter, when people join together in groups, they sometimes divide the social world into "us versus them," or *ingroups versus outgroups*. These social dichotomies promote ***ethnocentrism**—a tendency to view one's own group as superior to others and as the standard for judging the worth of foreign ways.*

As you might anticipate, people tend to evaluate outgroup members less favorably than ingroup members (Meindl & Lerner, 1984; Wilder, 1981). The more strongly one identifies with an ingroup, the more prejudiced one tends to be toward competing outgroups (Crocker & Luhtanen, 1990). People also tend to think simplistically about outgroups. They tend to see diversity among the members of their ingroup but to overestimate the homogeneity of the outgroup (Judd & Park, 1988; Ostrom & Sedikides, 1992). At a simple, concrete level, the essense of this process is captured by the statement "They all look alike." Indeed, studies have found that blacks and whites do have more difficulty distinguishing the faces of outgroup members (Anthony, Copper, & Mullen, 1992). The illusion of homogeneity in the outgroup makes it easier to sustain stereotypic beliefs about its members (Judd, Ryan, & Park, 1991). This point disposes of our last unanswered question from the list that opened the Application. Just in case you missed one of the answers, they all were false.

Our discussion has shown that a plethora of processes conspire to create and maintain personal prejudices against a diverse array of outgroups. Most of the factors at work reflect normal, routine processes in social behavior. Thus, it is understandable that most people—whether privileged or underprivileged, minority members or majority members—probably harbor some prejudicial attitudes. Our analysis of the causes of prejudice may have permitted you to identify prejudices of your own or their sources. Perhaps it's wishful thinking on my part, but an enhanced awareness of your personal prejudices may help you to become a little more tolerant of the endless diversity seen in human behavior. If so, that alone would mean that my efforts in writing this book have been amply rewarded.

Recap of Key Points

• Prejudice is supported by selectivity and memory biases in person perception and stereotyping. Stereotypes are highly resistant to change.

• Attributional biases, such as the tendency to assume that others' behavior reflects their dispositions, can contribute to prejudice. The tendency to attribute others' failures to personal factors and the tendency to derogate victims can also foster prejudice.

• Proximity and similarity effects in attraction contribute to prejudice by reducing the potential for intergroup contact. Negative attitudes about groups are often acquired through observational learning and strengthened through operant conditioning.

• The tendency to favor one's ingroups promotes ethnocentrism. The propensity to see outgroups as homogenous serves to strengthen prejudice.

Key Ideas

Person Perception: Forming Impressions of Others

◆ People tend to attribute desirable characteristics, such as intelligence, competence, warmth, and friendliness, to those who are good looking. Perceptions of people are also influenced by their style of nonverbal expressiveness.

◆ Stereotypes are widely held social schemas that lead people to expect that others will have certain characteristics because of their membership in a specific group. In interacting with others, stereotypes may lead people to see what they expect to see and to overestimate how often they see it.

Attribution Processes: Explaining Behavior

◆ Individuals make attributions to understand their social world. Internal attributions ascribe behavior to personal dispositions and traits, whereas external attributions locate the cause of behavior in the environment.

◆ Kelley's model of attribution suggests that internal attributions are more likely when one's behavior is consistent, not distinctive to an entity, and low in consensus value. Weiner's model proposes that attributions for success and failure should be analyzed in terms of the stability of causes, as well as along the internal-external dimension.

◆ Observers favor internal attributions to explain another's behavior (the fundamental attribution error), while actors favor external attributions to explain their own behavior. Other attributional biases include defensive attribution and the self-serving bias.

◆ Cultures vary in their emphasis on individualism as opposed to collectivism, and these differences appear to influence attributional tendencies.

Close Relationships: Liking and Loving

◆ People tend to like and love others who live in close proximity, who are similar, who reciprocate expressions of affection, and who are physically attractive.

◆ Berscheid and Hatfield have identified some popular myths about love. Sternberg builds on their distinction between passionate and companionate love by dividing the latter into intimacy and commitment. Hazan and Shaver's theory suggests that love relationships in adulthood mimic attachment patterns in infancy.

◆ The characteristics that people seek in prospective mates are much the same around the world. However, cultures vary considerably in their emphasis on passionate love as a prerequisite for marriage.

◆ Consistent with evolutionary theory, gender differences in mating preferences appear to transcend culture and to influence the tactics that people use in efforts to attract others.

Attitudes: Making Social Judgments

◆ Attitudes are made up of cognitive, affective, and behavioral components. Attitudes and behavior aren't as consistent as one might assume, in part because people expect very general attitudes to predict very specific behaviors.

◆ A source of persuasion who is credible, expert, trustworthy, likable, and physically attractive tends to be relatively effective. Two-sided arguments and fear arousal are effective elements in persuasive messages. Persuasion is undermined when a receiver is forewarned or when a receiver's initial position is very discrepant from the position advocated.

◆ Attitudes may be shaped through classical conditioning, operant conditioning, and observational learning. Festinger's dissonance theory asserts that inconsistent attitudes cause tension and that people alter their attitudes to reduce cognitive dissonance.

◆ Self-perception theory posits that people may infer their attitudes from their behavior. The elaboration likelihood model of persuasion holds that the central route to persuasion tends to yield longer-lasting attitude change than the peripheral route.

Conformity and Obedience: Yielding to Others

◆ Asch found that conformity becomes more likely as group size increases, up to a group size of four, and then levels off. If a small group isn't unanimous, conformity declines rapidly.

◆ In Milgram's study of obedience, subjects showed a remarkable tendency to follow orders to shock an innocent stranger. Milgram concluded that situational pressures can make decent people do indecent things.

◆ The generalizability of Milgram's findings has stood the test of time, but his work also helped to stimulate stricter ethical standards for research.

◆ The Asch and Milgram experiments have been replicated in many cultures. These replications have uncovered modest cultural variations in the propensity to conform or to obey an authority figure.

Behavior in Groups: Joining with Others

◆ The bystander effect occurs primarily because a group creates diffusion of responsibility. Individuals' productivity often declines in larger groups because of loss of coordination and because of social loafing.

◆ Group polarization occurs when discussion leads a group to shift toward a more extreme decision in the direction the group was already leaning. In groupthink, a cohesive group suspends critical judgment in a misguided effort to promote agreement in decision making.

Putting It in Perspective

◆ Our study of social psychology illustrated the value of empiricism, the cultural limits of research based on American samples, and the subjectivity of perception.

Application: Understanding Prejudice

◆ Prejudice is supported by subjectivity and memory biases in person perception and stereotyping. Attributional biases can also foster prejudice.

◆ Proximity and similarity effects and learning can contribute to prejudice. The tendency to favor one's ingroups and to see outgroups as homogenous also serve to strengthen prejudice.

Key Terms

Attitudes
Attributions
Bystander effect
Channel
Cognitive dissonance
Collectivism
Commitment
Companionate love
Compliance
Conformity
Defensive attribution
Discrimination
Ethnocentrism
External attributions
Fundamental
  attribution error
Group
Group cohesiveness
Group polarization
Groupthink
Illusory correlation
Individualism
Ingratiation
Ingroup
Internal attributions
Interpersonal
  attraction
Intimacy
Latitude of
  acceptance

Matching hypothesis
Message
Obedience
Outgroup
Passionate love
Person perception
Prejudice
Proximity
Receiver
Reciprocity
Self-serving bias
Social loafing
Social psychology
Social schemas
Source
Stereotypes

Key People

Solomon Asch
Ellen Berscheid
Leon Festinger
Elaine Hatfield
Fritz Heider
Irving Janis
Harold Kelley
Stanley Milgram
Bernard Weiner

Practice Test

1. Stereotypes:
   A. are special types of schemas that are part of people's shared cultural background.
   B. are widely held beliefs that people have certain characteristics because of their membership in a particular group.
   C. are equivalent to prejudice.
   D. both a and b.

2. Event 1: Your spouse kissed you good-bye this morning as usual.
   Event 2: Your spouse failed to kiss you good-bye this morning, an unusual event. Which of the following statements is true?
   A. Event 1 is more likely to stimulate attributional thinking.
   B. Event 2 is more likely to stimulate attributional thinking.
   C. Both events are equally likely to stimulate attributional thinking.
   D. Neither event will stimulate any attributional thinking.

3. According to Kelley, a behavior is most likely to be attributed to personal factors under conditions of:
   A. high consistency, high distinctiveness, and high consensus.
   B. high consistency, low distinctiveness, and low consensus.
   C. low consistency, high distinctiveness, and high consensus.
   D. low consistency, low distinctiveness, and high consensus.

4. Bob explains his failing grade on a term paper by saying that he really didn't work very hard at it. According to Weiner's model, Bob is making an _____ attribution about his failure.
   A. internal-stable
   B. internal-unstable
   C. external-stable
   D. external-unstable

5. Bruce was seriously injured in a car accident. If you make a defensive attribution, you will attribute Bruce's accident to _____, because _____.
   A. his poor driving ability; you know from experience he is a bad driver
   B. his poor driving ability; you can then reassure yourself a similar fate won't happen to you
   C. bad luck; Bruce himself will probably explain his accident this way
   D. bad luck; you know it could just as easily have happened to you

6. Actors tend to attribute their own successes to _____ factors; observers tend to attribute actors' successes to _____ factors.
   A. situational; personal
   B. situational; situational
   C. personal; personal
   D. personal; situational

7. According to Hazan and Shaver (1987):
   A. romantic relationships in adulthood follow the same form as attachment relationships in infancy.
   B. those who had ambivalent attachments in infancy are doomed never to fall in love as adults.
   C. those who had avoidant attachments in infancy often overcompensate by becoming excessively intimate in their adult love relationships.
   D. all of the above.

8. Cross-cultural similarities are most likely to be found in which of the following areas?
   A. what people look for in prospective mates
   B. the overall value of romantic love
   C. passionate love as a prerequisite for marriage
   D. the tradition of prearranged marriages

9. Persuasion tends to work best when there is _____ discrepancy between a receiver's initial position on an issue and the position advocated by the source.
   A. an extreme
   B. a moderate
   C. little
   D. no

10. Cognitive dissonance theory predicts that after people engage in counterattitudinal behavior, they will:
    A. convince themselves they really didn't perform the behavior.
    B. change their attitude to make it more consistent with their behavior.
    C. change their attitude to make it less consistent with their behavior.
    D. do nothing.

11. "I always choose romance novels rather than biographies. I guess I must like romance novels better." This thought process illustrates the premise of _____ theory.
    A. cognitive dissonance
    B. learning
    C. social loafing
    D. self-perception

12. The results of Milgram's (1963) study imply that:
    A. in the real world, most people will refuse to follow orders to inflict harm on a stranger.
    B. many people will obey an authority figure even if innocent people get hurt.
    C. most people are willing to give obviously wrong answers when ordered to do so.
    D. most people stick to their own judgment, even when group members unanimously disagree.

13. According to Latané (1981), social loafing is due to:
    A. social norms that stress the importance of positive interactions among group members.
    B. duplication of effort among group members.
    C. diffusion of responsibility in groups.
    D. a bias toward making internal attributions about the behavior of others.

14. Groupthink occurs when members of a cohesive group:
    A. are initially unanimous about an issue.
    B. stress the importance of caution in group decision making.
    C. emphasize concurrence at the expense of critical thinking in arriving at a decision.
    D. shift toward a less extreme position after group discussion.

15. Discrimination:
    A. refers to a negative attitude toward members of a group.
    B. refers to unfair behavior toward the members of a group.
    C. is the same thing as prejudice.
    D. all of the above.

Answers

1	D	Page 643	6	D	Pages 648–649	11	D	Page 665
2	B	Page 645	7	A	Page 655	12	B	Page 670
3	B	Pages 646–647	8	A	Page 656	13	C	Page 674
4	B	Page 647	9	B	Page 662	14	C	Page 675
5	B	Page 648	10	B	Page 664	15	B	Page 678

APPENDIX A
ANSWERS TO CONCEPT CHECKS

Chapter 1

Concept Check 1.1

1. c. John B. Watson (1930, p. 103) dismissing the importance of genetic inheritance while arguing that traits are shaped entirely by experience.

2. a. Wilhelm Wundt (1904 revision of an earlier text, p. v) campaigning for a new, independent science of psychology.

3. b. William James (1890) commenting negatively on the structuralists' efforts to break consciousness into its elements and his view of consciousness as a continuously flowing stream.

Concept Check 1.2

1. b. B. F. Skinner (1971, p. 17) explaining why he believes that freedom is an illusion.

2. a. Sigmund Freud (1905, pp. 77–78) arguing that it is possible to probe into the unconscious depths of the mind.

3. c. Carl Rogers (1961, p. 27) commenting on others' assertion that he had an overly optimistic (Pollyannaish) view of human potential and discussing humans' basic drive toward personal growth.

Concept Check 1.3

a. 2. Psychology is theoretically diverse.

b. 6. Heredity and environment jointly influence behavior.

c. 4. Behavior is determined by multiple causes.

d. 7. Our experience of the world is highly subjective.

Chapter 2

Concept Check 2.1

1. IV: Film violence (present versus absent)

   DV: Heart rate and blood pressure (there are two DVs)

2. IV: Courtesy training (training versus no training)

   DV: Number of customer complaints

3. IV: Stimulus complexity (high versus low) and stimulus contrast (high versus low) (there are two IVs)

   DV: Length of time spent staring at the stimuli

4. IV: Group size (large versus small)

   DV: Conformity

Concept Check 2.2

1. d. Survey. You would distribute a survey to obtain information on subjects' social class, education, and attitudes about nuclear disarmament.

2. c. Case study. Using a case study approach, you could interview people with anxiety disorders, interview their parents, and examine their school records to look for similarities in childhood experiences. As a second choice, you might have people with anxiety disorders fill out a survey about their childhood experiences.

3. b. Naturalistic observation. To answer this question properly, you would want to observe baboons in their natural environment, without interference.

4. a. Experiment. To demonstrate a causal relationship, you would have to conduct an experiment. You would manipulate the presence or absence of food-related cues in controlled circumstances where subjects had an opportunity to eat some food, and monitor the amount eaten.

Concept Check 2.3

1. b and e. The other three conclusions all equate correlation with causation.

2. a. Negative. As age increases, more people tend to have visual problems and acuity tends to decrease.

   b. Positive. Studies show that highly educated people tend to earn higher incomes and that people with less education tend to earn lower incomes.

   c. Negative. As shyness increases, the size of one's friendship network should decrease. However, research suggests that this inverse association may be weaker than widely believed.

Concept Check 2.4

Methodological flaw	Study 1	Study 2
Sampling bias	✓	✓
Placebo effects	✓	
Confounding of variables	✓	
Distortions in self-report data		✓
Experimenter bias	✓	

Explanations for Study 1. Sensory deprivation is an unusual kind of experience that may intrigue certain potential subjects, who may be more adventurous or more willing to take risks than the population at large. Using the first 80 students who sign up for this study may not yield a sample that is representative of the population. Assigning the first 40 subjects who sign up to the experimental group may confound these extraneous variables with the treatment (students who sign up most quickly may be the most adventurous). In announcing that he will be examining the *detrimental* effects of sensory deprivation, the experimenter has created expectations in the subjects. These expectations could lead to placebo effects. The experimenter has also revealed that he has a bias about the outcome of the study. Since he supervises the treatments, he knows which subjects are in the experimental and control groups, thus aggravating potential problems with experimenter bias. For example, he might unintentionally give the control group subjects better instructions on how to do the pursuit-rotor task and thereby slant the study in favor of finding support for his hypothesis.

Explanations for Study 2. Sampling bias is a problem because the researcher has sampled only subjects from a low-income, inner-city neighborhood. A sample obtained in this way is not likely to be representative of the population at large. People are sensitive about the issue of racial prejudice, so distortions in self-report data are also likely. Many subjects may be swayed by social desirability bias and rate themselves as less prejudiced than they really are.

Chapter 3

Concept Check 3.1

1. E **2.** D **3.** A **4.** C **5.** B

Concept Check 3.2

1. e. GABA.

2. b. and c. Serotonin and norepinephrine.

3. c. Norepinephrine.

4. f. Endorphins.

5. d. Dopamine.

6. a. Acetylcholine.

Concept Check 3.3

1. Left hemisphere damage, probably to Wernicke's area.

2. Deficit in dopamine synthesis in an area of the midbrain.

3. Deficit in acetylcholine synthesis and damage to the hippocampus.

4. Disturbance in dopamine activity, possibly associated with enlarged ventricles in the brain.

Please note that neuropsychological assessment is not as simple as this introductory exercise may suggest. There are many possible causes of most disorders, and we discussed only a handful of leading causes for each.

Concept Check 3.4

1. Closer relatives; more distant relatives.

2. Identical twins; fraternal twins.

3. Biological parents; adoptive parents.

4. Genetic overlap or closeness; trait similarity.

Chapter 4

Concept Check 4.1

1.

Dimension	Rods	Cones
Physical shape	Elongated	Stubby
Number in the retina	125 million	6.4 million
Area of the retina in which they are dominant receptor	Periphery	Center/fovea
Critical to color vision	No	Yes
Critical to peripheral vision	Yes	No
Sensitivity to dim light	Strong	Weak
Speed of dark adaptation	Slow	Rapid

2. Consider the responses of two ganglion cells in the retina whose firing is affected by light falling in center-surround receptive fields, like those drawn onto the grid in the lower right corner. An identical amount of light falls in the center of each receptive field. However, more light is falling in the surround of the receptive field on the left. Hence, the cell for this receptive field responds at a lower level than its neighbor because of greater inhibition by the surround (thanks to lateral antagonism). This reduced responding translates into the dark spots that you see. Why don't you see a dark spot at the intersection you are staring at? Because when you stare directly at a point, the image falls on the fovea, where receptive fields are much

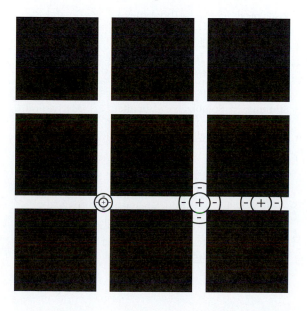

smaller, like the one drawn in the lower left corner. This receptive field does not produce a reduced response because an equal amount of light is falling in the center and the surround.

Concept Check 4.2

✓ **1.** Interposition. The arches in front cut off part of the corridor behind them.

✓ **2.** Height in plane. The back of the corridor is higher on the horizontal plane than the front of the corridor is.

✓ **3.** Texture gradient. The more distant portions of the hallway are painted in less detail than the closer portions are.

✓ **4.** Relative size. The arches in the distance are smaller than those in the foreground.

✓ **5.** Light and shadow. Light shining in from the crossing corridor (it's coming from the left) contrasts with shadow elsewhere.

✓ **6.** Linear perspective. The lines of the corridor converge in the distance.

Concept Check 4.3

	Dimension	Vision	Hearing
1.	Stimulus	Light waves	Sound waves
2.	Elements of stimulus and related perceptions	Wavelength/hue Amplitude/ brightness Purity/saturation	Frequency/pitch Amplitude/ loudness Purity/timbre
3.	Receptors	Rods and cones	Hair cells
4.	Location of receptors	Retina	Basilar membrane
5.	Main location of processing in brain	Occipital lobe, visual cortex	Temporal lobe, auditory cortex
6.	Spatial aspect of perception	Depth perception	Auditory localization
7.	Typical Weber fraction	1/60 (brightness)	1/10 (loudness)

Concept Check 4.4

Dimension	Taste	Smell	Touch
Stimulus	Soluble chemicals in saliva	Volatile chemicals in air	Mechanical, thermal, and chemical energy due to external contact
Receptors	Clusters of taste cells	Olfactory cilia (hairlike structures)	Many (at least 6) types
Location of receptors	Taste buds on tongue	Upper area of nasal passages	Skin
Basic elements of perception	Sweet, sour, salty, bitter	No satisfactory classification scheme	Pressure, hot, cold, pain

Chapter 5

Concept Check 5.1

Characteristic	REM sleep	NREM sleep
Type of EEG activity	"Wide awake" brain waves, mostly beta	Varied, lots of delta waves
Eye movements	Rapid, lateral	Slow or absent
Dreaming	Frequent, vivid	Less frequent
Depth (difficulty in awakening)	Varied, generally difficult to awaken	Varied, generally easier to awaken
Percentage of total sleep (in adults)	About 20%	About 80%
Increases or decreases (as percentage of sleep) during childhood	Percent decreases	Percent increases
Timing in sleep (dominates early or late)	Dominates late in cycle	Dominates early in cycle

Concept Check 5.2

1. Beta. Video games require alert information processing, which is associated with beta waves.

2. Alpha. Meditation involves relaxation, which is associated with alpha waves, and studies show increased alpha in meditators.

3. Theta. In stage 1 sleep, theta waves tend to be prevalent.

4. Delta. Sleepwalking usually occurs in deep NREM sleep, which is dominated by delta activity.

5. Beta. Nightmares are dreams, so you're probably in REM sleep, which paradoxically produces "wide awake" beta waves.

Chapter 6

Concept Check 6.1

1. CS: Fire in fireplace
   UCS: Pain from burn   CR/UCR: Fear

2. CS: Brake lights in rain
   UCS: Car accident   CR/UCR: Tensing up

3. CS: Sight of cat
   UCS: Cat dander   CR/UCR: Wheezing

Concept Check 6.2

1. FR. Each sale is a response and every third response earns reinforcement.

2. VI. A varied amount of time elapses before the response of doing yard work can earn reinforcement.

3. VR. Reinforcement occurs after a varied number of unreinforced casts (time is irrelevant; the more casts Martha makes, the more reinforcers she will receive).

4. CR. The designated response (reading a book) is reinforced (with a gold star) each and every time.

5. FI. A fixed time interval (three years) has to elapse before Skip can earn a salary increase (the reinforcer).

Concept Check 6.3

1. Punishment.

2. Positive reinforcement.

3. Punishment.

4. Negative reinforcement (for Audrey); the dog is positively reinforced for its whining.

5. Negative reinforcement.

6. Extinction. When Edna's co-workers start to ignore her complaints, they are trying to extinguish the behavior (which had been positively reinforced when it won sympathy).

Concept Check 6.4

1. Classical conditioning. Marcia's blue windbreaker is a CS eliciting excitement in her dog.

2. Operant conditioning. Playing new songs leads to negative consequences (punishment), which weaken the tendency to play new songs. Playing old songs leads to positive reinforcement, which gradually strengthens the tendency to play old songs.

3. Classical conditioning. The song was paired with the passion of new love so that it became a CS eliciting emotional, romantic feelings.

4. Both. Ralph's workplace is paired with criticism so that his workplace becomes a CS eliciting anxiety. Calling in sick is operant behavior that is strengthened through negative reinforcement (because it reduces anxiety).

Chapter 7

Concept Check 7.1

Feature	Sensory memory	Short-term memory	Long-term memory
Encoding format	Copy of input	Largely phonemic	Largely semantic
Storage capacity	Large	Small (7 ± 2 chunks)	No known limit
Storage duration	¼ to 2 seconds	Up to 20 seconds	Minutes to years

Concept Check 7.2

1. Ineffective encoding due to lack of attention.

2. Retrieval failure due to motivated forgetting.

3. Proactive interference (previous learning of Joe Cocker's name interferes with new learning).

4. Retroactive interference (new learning of sociology interferes with older learning of history).

Concept Check 7.3

1. a. Declarative memory.

2. e. Long-term memory.

3. j. Sensory memory.

4. d. Implicit memory.

5. b. Episodic memory.

6. f. Procedural memory.

7. i. Semantic memory.

8. c. Prospective memory.

9. k. Short-term memory.

Chapter 8

Concept Check 8.1

1. 1. Holophrase in which the word is overextended to refer to a similar object.

2. 4. Words are combined into a sentence, but the rule for past tense is overgeneralized.

3. 3. Telegraphic sentence.

4. 5. Words are combined into a sentence, and past tense is used correctly.

5. 2. Holophrase without overextension.

Concept Check 8.2

1. Functional fixedness.

2. Forming subgoals.

3. Insight.

4. Searching for analogies.

5. Arrangement problem.

Concept Check 8.3

1. Elimination by aspects.

2. Availability heuristic.

3. Shift to compensatory model.

4. Additive model.

Chapter 9

Concept Check 9.1

1. Test-retest reliability.

2. Criterion-related validity.

3. Content validity.

Concept Check 9.2

1. H. Given that the identical twins were reared apart, their greater similarity in comparison to fraternals reared together can only be due to heredity. This comparison is probably the most important piece of evidence supporting the genetic determination of IQ.

2. E. We tend to associate identical twins with evidence supporting heredity, but in this comparison genetic similarity is held constant since both sets of twins are identical. The only logical explanation for the greater similarity in identicals reared together is the effect of their being reared together (environment).

3. E. This comparison is similar to the previous one. Genetic similarity is held constant and a shared environment produces greater similarity than being reared apart.

4. B. This is nothing more than a quantification of Galton's original observation that intelligence runs in families. Since families share both genes and environment, either or both could be responsible for the observed correlation.

5. B. The similarity of adopted children to their biological parents can only be due to shared genes, and the similarity of adopted children to their foster parents can only be due to shared environment, so these correlations show the influence of both heredity and environment.

Concept Check 9.3

1. b. Gardner.

2. a. Galton.

3. c. Jensen.

4. d. Scarr.

5. e. Sternberg.

Chapter 10

Concept Check 10.1

	Relevant theory	Level of needs
1.	Drive theory (a deficit creates internal tension)	Love and belongingness needs
2.	Incentive theory (you're motivated by the triple bonus)	Safety and security needs
3.	Maslow's theory (interests reflect higher growth needs)	Cognitive and aesthetic needs
4.	Evolutionary theory (self-sacrifice to promote welfare of close kin)	Physiological needs

Concept Check 10.2

1. I. Early studies indicated that the VMH was a "stop eating" center, since artificially stimulating it curtails eating in rats while lesioning leads to overeating. Subsequent research indicates that the situation is somewhat more complicated; the VMH is not simply a "stop eating" center.

2. I. According to Mayer (1955, 1968), hunger increases when the amount of glucose in the blood decreases. Glucostats in the brain apparently monitor the uptake of glucose by cells in the body.

3. I. Insulin, a hormone produced by the pancreas, must be present for cells to extract glucose from the blood. If insulin is increased, more glucose is extracted, glucostats respond to the increase, and one experiences increased hunger.

4. D. Food preferences are learned; we tend to like what we are accustomed to eating. So no matter how delicious someone from another culture thinks some exotic delicacy is, you're not likely to be eager to eat it.

5. ? Schachter and Gross (1968) found that obese people tend to snack when external cues indicate that it's dinnertime, while nonobese people tend not to, so they won't spoil their dinner.

6. I. Stress leads to increased eating in many people, although it could be stress-induced *arousal* that leads to eating, rather than stress itself.

Concept Check 10.3

1. d. Fear of failure.

2. c. Incentive value of success.

3. e. Perceived probability of failure.

4. a. Need for achievement.

Chapter 11

Concept Check 11.1

1. b. Animism is characteristic of the preoperational period.

2. c. Mastery of hierarchical classification occurs during the concrete operational period.

3. a. Lack of object permanence is characteristic of the sensorimotor period.

Concept Check 11.2

1. c. Commitment to personal ethics is characteristic of postconventional reasoning.

2. b. Concern about approval of others is characteristic of conventional reasoning.

3. a. Emphasis on positive or negative consequences is characteristic of preconventional reasoning.

Concept Check 11.3

a. Moral reasoning changes as cognitive development progresses.

b. Youngsters who are in higher stages of moral development tend to display more altruistic social behavior.

c. Securely attached infants show more leadership and tend to have better social skills.

Chapter 12

Concept Check 12.1

1. Regression.

2. Projection.

3. Reaction formation.

4. Repression.

5. Rationalization.

Concept Check 12.2

1. Bandura's observational learning. Sarah imitates a role model from television.

2. Maslow's need for self-actualization. Marilyn is striving to realize her fullest potential.

3. Freud's Oedipal complex. Johnny shows preference for his opposite-sex parent and emotional distance from his same-sex parent.

Concept Check 12.3

1. Maslow (1971, p. 36) commenting on the need for self-actualization.

2. Eysenck (1977, pp. 407–408) commenting on the biological roots of personality.

3. Freud (in Malcolm, 1980) commenting on the repression of sexuality.

Chapter 13

Concept Check 13.1

1. b. A choice between two unattractive options.

2. c. Weighing the positive and negative aspects of a single goal.

3. a. A choice between two attractive options.

Concept Check 13.2

1. a. Frustration due to delay.

2. d. Pressure to perform.

3. c. Change associated with leaving school and taking a new job.

4. a. Frustration due to loss of job.

   c. Change in life circumstances.

   d. Pressure to perform (in quickly obtaining new job).

Concept Check 13.3

1. Denial of reality.

2. Undoing.

3. Fantasy.

4. Overcompensation.

5. Intellectualization.

Chapter 14

Concept Check 14.1

	Deviance	Maladaptive behavior	Personal distress
1. Alan	_____	✓	_____
2. Monica	_____	_____	✓
3. Walter	✓	_____	_____
4. Phyllis	✓	✓	✓

Concept Check 14.2

1. Obsessive-compulsive disorder (key symptoms: frequent rituals, ruminations about school).

2. Somatization disorder (key symptoms: history of physical complaints involving many different organ systems).

3. Conversion disorder (key symptoms: loss of function in single organ system).

Concept Check 14.3

1. Bipolar disorder, manic episode (key symptoms: extravagant plans, hyperactivity, reckless spending).

2. Paranoid schizophrenia (key symptoms: delusions of persecution and grandeur, along with deterioration of adaptive behavior).

3. Major depression (key symptoms: feelings of despair, low self-esteem, lack of energy).

Chapter 15

Concept Check 15.1

1. c   **2.** a   **3.** b

Concept Check 15.2

1. d   **2.** b   **3.** a   **4.** c

Concept Check 15.3

1. a. Systematic desensitization.

2. c. Aversion therapy.

3. b. Social skills training.

Concept Check 15.4

1. c **2.** a **3.** b **4.** d **5.** b

Chapter 16

Concept Check 16.1

	Unstable	Stable
Internal	d	b
External	a	c

Concept Check 16.2

1. c. Fundamental attribution error (assuming that arriving late reflects personal qualities).

2. a. Illusory correlation effect (overestimating how often one has seen confirmations of the assertion that young, female professors get pregnant soon after being hired).

3. b. Stereotyping (assuming that all lawyers have certain traits).

4. d. Defensive attribution (derogating the victims of misfortune to minimize the apparent likelihood of a similar mishap).

Concept Check 16.3

1. *Target:* Cognitive component of attitudes (beliefs about program for regulating nursing homes).

Persuasion: Message factor (advice to use one-sided instead of two-sided arguments).

2. *Target:* Affective component of attitudes (feelings about candidate).

Persuasion: Source factor (advice on appearing likable, sincere, and compassionate).

3. *Target:* Behavioral component of attitudes (making contributions).

Persuasion: Receiver factor (considering audience's initial position regarding the candidate).

Concept Check 16.4

1. False. **2.** True. **3.** False. **4.** False.
5. True. **6.** False.

APPENDIX B
STATISTICAL METHODS

Empiricism depends on observation; precise observation depends on measurement; and measurement requires numbers. Thus, scientists routinely analyze numerical data to arrive at their conclusions. Over 2000 empirical studies are cited in this text, and all but a few of the simplest ones required a statistical analysis. *Statistics* **is the use of mathematics to organize, summarize, and interpret numerical data.** We discussed statistics briefly in Chapter 2, but in this Appendix we take a closer look.

To illustrate statistics in action, let's assume that we want to test a hypothesis that has generated quite an argument in your psychology class. The hypothesis is that college students who watch a great deal of television aren't as bright as those who watch TV infrequently. For the fun of it, your class decides to conduct a correlational study of itself, collecting survey and psychological test data. Your classmates all agree to respond to a short survey on their TV viewing habits. Because everyone at your school has had to take the Scholastic Aptitude Test (SAT), the class decides to use scores on the SAT verbal subtest as an index of how bright students are. All of them agree to allow the records office at the college to furnish their SAT scores to the professor, who replaces each student's name with a subject number (to protect students' right to privacy). Let's see how we could use statistics to analyze the data collected in our pilot study (a small, preliminary investigation).

Graphing Data

After collecting our data, our next step is to organize the data to get a quick overview of our numerical results. Let's assume that there are 20 students in your class, and when they estimate how many hours they spend per day watching TV, the results are as follows:

3	2	0	3	1
3	4	0	5	1
2	3	4	5	2
4	5	3	4	6

One of the simpler things that we can do to organize data is to create a *frequency distribution*—**an orderly arrangement of scores indicating the frequency of each score or group of scores.** Figure B.1(a) shows a frequency distribution for our data on TV viewing. The column on the left lists the possible scores (estimated hours of TV viewing) in order, and the column on the right lists the number of subjects with each score. Graphs can provide an even better overview of the data. One approach is to portray the data in a *histogram*, **which is a bar graph that presents data from a frequency distribution.** Such a histogram, summarizing our TV viewing data, is presented in Figure B.1(b).

Another widely used method of portraying data graphically is the *frequency polygon*—**a line figure used to present data from a frequency distribu-**

Figure B.1
Graphing data. (a) Our raw data are tallied into a frequency distribution. **(b)** The same data are portrayed in a bar graph called a histogram. **(c)** A frequency polygon is plotted over the histogram. **(d)** The resultant frequency polygon is shown by itself.

Score	Tallies	Frequency
6	I	1
5	III	3
4	IIII	4
3	IIIII	5
2	III	3
1	II	2
0	II	2

(a) Frequency distribution

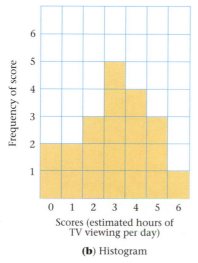

(b) Histogram

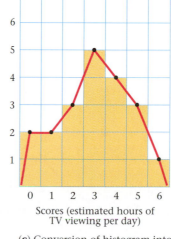

(c) Conversion of histogram into frequency polygon

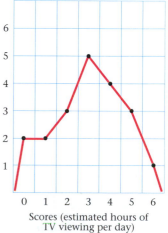

(d) Frequency polygon

Figure B.2
Measures of central tendency. The mean, median, and mode usually converge, as in this case—unless a distribution is skewed, as shown in Figure B.3.

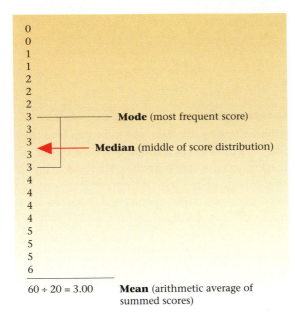

0
0
1
1
2
2
2
3 ——— **Mode** (most frequent score)
3
3
3 ◄— **Median** (middle of score distribution)
3
3
4
4
4
4
5
5
5
6

60 ÷ 20 = 3.00   **Mean** (arithmetic average of summed scores)

instance, in this case we might compare the average amount of TV watching in our sample against national estimates, to determine whether our subjects appear to be representative of the population. The three measures of central tendency, the median, the mean, and the mode, give us indications regarding the typical score in a data set. As explained in Chapter 2, **the** *median* **is the score that falls in the center of a distribution, the** *mean* **is the arithmetic average of the scores,** and **the** *mode* **is the score that occurs most frequently.**

All three measures of central tendency are calculated for our TV viewing data in Figure B.2. As you can see, in this set of data, the mean, median, and mode all turn out to be the same score, which is 3. Although our example in Chapter 2 emphasized that the mean, median, and mode can yield different estimates of central tendency, the correspondence among them seen in our TV viewing data is quite common. Lack of agreement usually occurs when a few extreme scores pull the mean away from the center of the distribution, as shown in Figure B.3. The curves plotted in Figure B.3 are simply "smoothed out" frequency polygons based on data from many subjects. They show that when a distribution is symmetric, the measures of central tendency fall together, but this is not true in skewed or unbalanced distributions.

Figure B.3(b) shows a *negatively skewed distribution,* **in which most scores pile up at the high end of the scale** (the negative skew refers to the direction in which the curve's "tail" points). A *positively skewed distribution,* **in which scores pile up at the low end of the scale,** is shown in Figure B.3(c). In both types of skewed distributions, a few extreme scores at one end pull the mean, and to a lesser degree the median, away from the mode. In these situations, the mean may

tion. Figures B.1(c) and B.1(d) show how our TV viewing data can be converted from a histogram to a frequency polygon. In both the bar graph and the line figure, the horizontal axis lists the possible scores and the vertical axis is used to indicate the frequency of each score. This use of the axes is nearly universal for frequency polygons, although sometimes it is reversed in histograms (the vertical axis lists possible scores, so the bars become horizontal).

Our graphs improve on the jumbled collection of scores that we started with, but *descriptive statistics,* **which are used to organize and summarize data,** provide some additional advantages. Let's see what the three measures of central tendency tell us about our data.

Measuring Central Tendency

In examining a set of data, it's routine to ask "What is a typical score in the distribution?" For

Figure B.3
Measures of central tendency in skewed distributions. In a symmetrical distribution (**a**), the three measures of central tendency converge. However, in a negatively skewed distribution (**b**) or in a positively skewed distribution (**c**), the mean, median, and mode are pulled apart as shown here. Typically, in these situations the median provides the best index of central tendency.

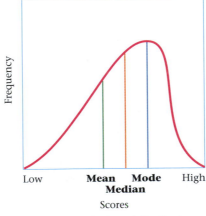

(a) Symmetrical distribution

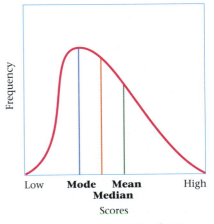

(b) Negatively skewed distribution   **(c)** Positively skewed distribution

be misleading and the median usually provides the best index of central tendency.

In any case, the measures of central tendency for our TV viewing data are reassuring, since they all agree and they fall reasonably close to national estimates regarding how much young adults watch TV (Huston & Wright, 1982). Given the small size of our group, this agreement with national norms doesn't *prove* that our sample is representative of the population, but at least there's no obvious reason to believe that they're unrepresentative.

Measuring Variability

Of course, everyone in our sample did not report identical TV viewing habits. Virtually all data sets are characterized by some variability. *Variability* **refers to how much the scores tend to vary or depart from the mean score.** For example, the distribution of golf scores for a mediocre, erratic golfer would be characterized by high variability, while scores for an equally mediocre but consistent golfer would show less variability.

The *standard deviation* **is an index of the amount of variability in a set of data.** It reflects the dispersion of scores in a distribution. This principle is portrayed graphically in Figure B.4, where the two distributions of golf scores have the same mean but the upper one has less variability because the scores are "bunched up" in the center (for the consistent golfer). The distribution in Figure B.4(b) is characterized by more variability, as the erratic golfer's scores are more spread out. This distribution will yield a higher standard deviation than the distribution in Figure B.4(a).

The formula for calculating the standard deviation is shown in Figure B.5, where d stands for each score's deviation from the mean and Σ stands for summation. A step-by-step application of this formula to our TV viewing data, shown in Figure B.5, reveals that the standard deviation for our TV viewing data is 1.64. The standard deviation has a variety of uses. One of these uses will surface in the next section, where we discuss the normal distribution.

The Normal Distribution

The hypothesis in our study is that brighter students watch less TV than relatively dull students. To test this hypothesis, we're going to correlate TV viewing with SAT scores. But to make effective use of the SAT data, we need to understand what SAT scores mean, which brings us to the normal distribution.

The *normal distribution* **is a a symmetric, bell-**

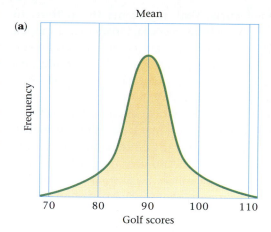

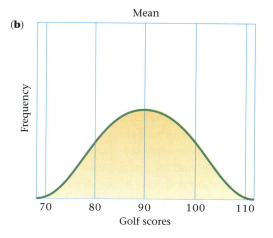

Figure B.4
The standard deviation and dispersion of data. Although both these distributions of golf scores have the same mean, their standard deviations will be different. In **(a)** the scores are bunched together and there is less variability than in **(b)**, yielding a lower standard deviation for the data in distribution **(a)**.

TV viewing score (X)	Deviation from mean (d)	Deviation squared (d²)
0	−3	9
0	−3	9
1	−2	4
1	−2	4
2	−1	1
2	−1	1
2	−1	1
3	0	0
3	0	0
3	0	0
3	0	0
3	0	0
4	+1	1
4	+1	1
4	+1	1
4	+1	1
5	+2	4
5	+2	4
5	+2	4
6	+3	9

$N = 20$

$\Sigma X = 60$ $\Sigma d^2 = 54$

$$\text{Mean} = \frac{\Sigma X}{N} = \frac{60}{20} = 3.0$$

$$\text{Standard deviation} = \sqrt{\frac{\Sigma d^2}{N}} = \sqrt{\frac{54}{20}}$$

$$= \sqrt{2.70} = 1.64$$

Figure B.5
Steps in calculating the standard deviation.
(1) Add the scores (ΣX) and divide by the number of scores (N) to calculate the mean (which comes out to 3.0 in this case). (2) Calculate each score's deviation from the mean by subtracting the mean from each score (the results are shown in the second column). (3) Square these deviations from the mean and total the results to obtain (Σd^2) as shown in the third column. (4) Insert the numbers for N and Σd^2 into the formula for the standard deviation and compute the results.

shaped curve that represents the pattern in which many human characteristics are dispersed in the population. A great many physical qualities (for example, height, nose length, and running speed) and psychological traits (intelligence, spatial reasoning ability, introversion) are distributed in a manner that closely resembles this bell-shaped curve. When a trait is normally distributed, most scores fall near the center of the distribution (the mean) and the number of scores gradually declines as one moves away from the center in either direction. The normal distribution is *not* a law of nature. It's a mathematical function, or theoretical curve, that approximates the way nature seems to operate.

The normal distribution is the bedrock of the scoring system for most psychological tests, including the SAT. As we discuss in Chapter 9, psychological tests are *relative measures*; they assess how people score on a trait in comparison to other people. The normal distribution gives us a precise way to measure how people stack up in comparison to each other. The scores under the normal curve are dispersed in a fixed pattern, with the standard deviation serving as the unit of measurement, as shown in Figure B.6. About 68% of the scores in the distribution fall within plus or mi-

nus 1 standard deviation of the mean, while 95% of the scores fall within plus or minus 2 standard deviations of the mean. Given this fixed pattern, if you know the mean and standard deviation of a normally distributed trait, you can tell where any score falls in the distribution for the trait.

Although you may not have realized it, you probably have taken many tests in which the scoring system is based on the normal distribution. On the SAT, for instance, raw scores (the number of items correct on each subtest) are converted into standard scores that indicate where you fall in the normal distribution for the trait measured. In this conversion, the mean is set arbitrarily at 500 and the standard deviation at 100, as shown in Figure B.7. Therefore, a score of 400 on the SAT verbal subtest means that you scored 1 standard deviation below the mean, while an SAT score of 600 indicates that you scored 1 standard deviation above the mean. Thus, SAT scores tell you how many standard deviations above or below the mean your score was. This system also provides the metric for IQ scales and many other types of psychological tests (see Chapter 9).

Test scores that place examinees in the normal distribution can always be converted to percentile scores, which are a little easier to interpret. A

Figure B.6
The normal distribution. Many characteristics are distributed in a pattern represented by this bell-shaped curve (each dot represents a case). The horizontal axis shows how far above or below the mean a score is (measured in plus or minus standard deviations). The vertical axis shows the number of cases obtaining each score. In a normal distribution, most cases fall near the center of the distribution, so that 68.26% of the cases fall within plus or minus 1 standard deviation of the mean. The number of cases gradually declines as one moves away from the mean in either direction, so that only 13.59% of the cases fall between 1 and 2 standard deviations above or below the mean, and even fewer cases (2.14%) fall between 2 and 3 standard deviations above or below the mean.

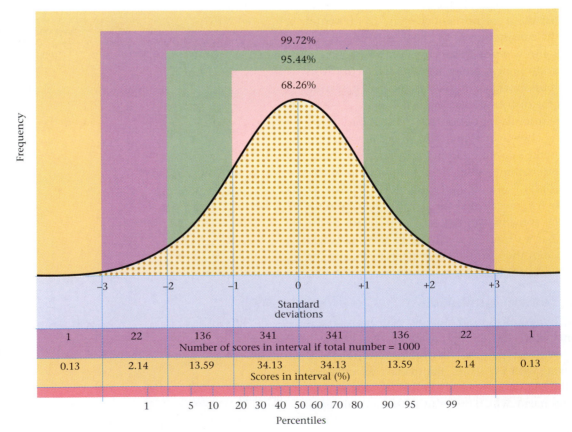

percentile score indicates the percentage of people who score at or below the score you obtained. For example, if you score at the 60th percentile, 60% of the people who take the test score the same or below you, while the remaining 40% score above you. There are tables available that permit us to convert any standard deviation placement in a normal distribution into a precise percentile score. Figure B.6 gives some percentile conversions for the normal curve.

Of course, not all distributions are normal. As we saw in Figure B.3, some distributions are skewed in one direction or the other. As an example, consider what would happen if a classroom exam were much too easy or much too hard. If the test were too easy, scores would be bunched up at the high end of the scale, as in Figure B.3(b). If the test were too hard, scores would be bunched up at the low end, as in Figure B.3(c).

Measuring Correlation

To determine whether TV viewing is related to SAT scores, we have to compute a *correlation coefficient*—a numerical index of the degree of relationship that exists between two variables. As discussed in Chapter 2, a *positive* correlation means that there is a *direct* relationship between two variables—say *X* and *Y*. This means that high scores on variable *X* are associated with high scores on variable *Y* and that low scores on *X* are associated with low scores on *Y*. A *negative* correlation indicates that there is an *inverse* relationship between two variables. This means that people who score high on variable *X* tend to score low on variable *Y*, whereas those who score low on *X* tend to score

high on *Y*. In our study, we hypothesized that as TV viewing increases, SAT scores will decrease, so we should expect a negative correlation between TV viewing and SAT scores.

The *magnitude* of a correlation coefficient indicates the *strength* of the association between two variables. This coefficient can vary between 0 and ±1.00. The coefficient is usually represented by the letter *r* (for example, *r* = .45). A coefficient near 0 tells us that there is no relationship between two variables. A coefficient of +1.00 or –1.00 indicates that there is a perfect, one-to-one correspondence between two variables. A perfect correlation is found only rarely when working with real data. The closer the coefficient is to either –1.00 or +1.00, the stronger the relationship is.

The direction and strength of correlations can be illustrated graphically in scatter diagrams (see Figure B.8). A *scatter diagram* is a graph in which paired *X* and *Y* scores for each subject are plot-

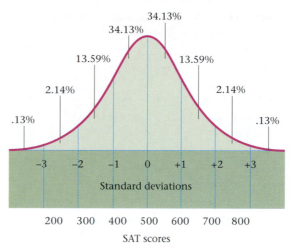

Figure B.7
The normal distribution and SAT scores. The normal distribution is the basis for the scoring system on many standardized tests. For example, on the Scholastic Aptitude Test (SAT), the mean is set at 500 and the standard deviation at 100. Hence, an SAT score tells you how many standard deviations above or below the mean you scored. For example, a score of 700 means you scored 2 standard deviations above the mean.

Figure B.8
Scatter diagrams of positive and negative correlations. Scatter diagrams plot paired *X* and *Y* scores as single points. Score plots slanted in the opposite direction result from positive (top row) as opposed to negative (bottom row) correlations. Moving across both rows (to the right), you can see that progressively weaker correlations result in more and more scattered plots of data points.

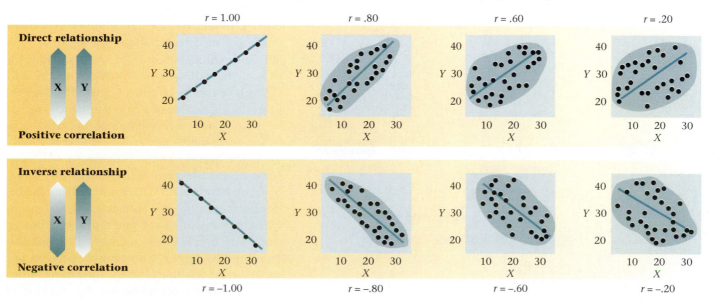

Figure B.9
Scatter diagram of the correlation between TV viewing and SAT scores. Our hypothetical data relating TV viewing to SAT scores are plotted in this scatter diagram. Compare it to the scatter diagrams seen in Figure B.8 and see whether you can estimate the correlation between TV viewing and SAT scores in our data (see the text for the answer).

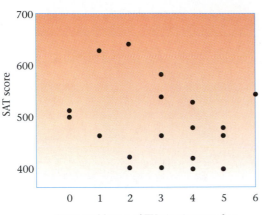

Estimated hours of TV viewing per day

Figure B.10
Computing a correlation coefficient. The calculations required to compute the Pearson product-moment coefficient of correlation are shown here. The formula looks intimidating, but it's just a matter of filling in the figures taken from the sums of the columns shown above the formula.

ted as single points. Figure B.8 shows scatter diagrams for positive correlations in the upper half and for negative correlations in the bottom half. A perfect positive correlation and a perfect negative correlation are shown on the far left. When a correlation is perfect, the data points in the scatter diagram fall exactly in a straight line. However, positive and negative correlations yield lines slanted in the opposite direction because the lines map out opposite types of associations. Moving to the right in Figure B.8, you can see what happens when the magnitude of a correlation decreases.

The data points scatter farther and farther from the straight line that would represent a perfect relationship.

What about our data relating TV viewing to SAT scores? Figure B.9 shows a scatter diagram of these data. Having just learned about scatter diagrams, perhaps you can estimate the magnitude of the correlation between TV viewing and SAT scores. The scatter diagram of our data looks a lot like the one seen in the bottom right corner of Figure B.8, suggesting that the correlation will be in the vicinity of –.20.

The formula for computing the most widely used measure of correlation—the Pearson product-moment correlation—is shown in Figure B.10, along with the calculations for our data on TV viewing and SAT scores. The data yield a correlation of $r = -.24$. This coefficient of correlation reveals that we have found a weak inverse association between TV viewing and performance on the SAT. Among our subjects, as TV viewing increases, SAT scores decrease, but the trend isn't very strong. We can get a better idea of how strong this correlation is by examining its predictive power.

Correlation and Prediction

As the magnitude of a correlation increases (gets closer to either –1.00 or +1.00), our ability to predict one variable based on knowledge of the other variable steadily increases. This relationship between the magnitude of a correlation and predictability can be quantified precisely. All we have to do is square the correlation coefficient (multiply it by itself) and this gives us the *coefficient of determination*, **the percentage of variation in one variable that can be predicted based on the other variable.** Thus, a correlation of .70 yields a coefficient of determination of .49 (.70 × .70 = .49), indicating that variable X can account for 49% of the variation in variable Y. Figure B.11 shows how the coefficient of determination goes up as the magnitude of a correlation increases.

Unfortunately, a correlation of .24 doesn't give us much predictive power. We can account only for a little over 6% of the variation in variable Y. So, if we tried to predict individuals' SAT scores based on how much TV they watched, our predictions wouldn't be very accurate. Although a low correlation doesn't have much practical, predictive utility, it may still have theoretical value. Just knowing that there is a relationship between two variables can be theoretically interesting. However, we haven't yet addressed the question of whether our observed correlation is strong enough

Subject number	TV viewing score (X)	X²	SAT score (Y)	Y²	XY
1	0	0	500	250,000	0
2	0	0	515	265,225	0
3	1	1	450	202,500	450
4	1	1	650	422,500	650
5	2	4	400	160,000	800
6	2	4	675	455,625	1350
7	2	4	425	180,625	850
8	3	9	400	160,000	1200
9	3	9	450	202,500	1350
10	3	9	500	250,000	1500
11	3	9	550	302,500	1650
12	3	9	600	360,000	1800
13	4	16	400	160,000	1600
14	4	16	425	180,625	1700
15	4	16	475	225,625	1900
16	4	16	525	275,625	2100
17	5	25	400	160,000	2000
18	5	25	450	202,500	2250
19	5	25	475	225,625	2375
20	6	36	550	302,500	3300
$N = 20$	$\Sigma X = 60$	$\Sigma X^2 = 234$	$\Sigma Y = 9815$	$\Sigma Y^2 = 4,943,975$	$\Sigma XY = 28,825$

Formula for Pearson product-moment correlation coefficient

$$r = \frac{(N)\Sigma XY - (\Sigma X)(\Sigma Y)}{\sqrt{[(N)\Sigma X^2 - (\Sigma X)^2][(N)\Sigma Y^2 - (\Sigma Y)^2]}}$$

$$= \frac{(20)(28,825) - (60)(9815)}{\sqrt{[(20)(234) - (60)^2][(20)(4,943,975) - (9815)^2]}}$$

$$= \frac{-12,400}{\sqrt{[1080][2,545,275]}}$$

$$= -.237$$

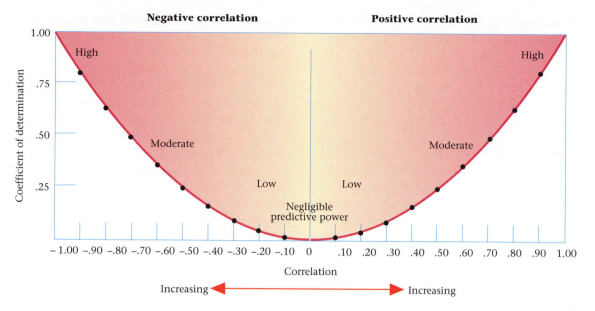

Negative correlation   Positive correlation

Figure B.11
Correlation and the coefficient of determination.
The coefficient of determination is an index of a correlation's predictive power. As you can see, whether positive or negative, stronger correlations yield greater predictive power.

Correlation

Increasing ◄──────► Increasing

Hypothesis Testing

to support our hypothesis that there is a relationship between TV viewing and SAT scores. To make this judgment, we have to turn to inferential statistics and the process of hypothesis testing.

Inferential statistics go beyond the mere description of data. *Inferential statistics* **are used to interpret data and draw conclusions.** They permit researchers to decide whether their data support their hypotheses.

In Chapter 2, we showed how inferential statistics can be used to evaluate the results of an experiment; the same process can be applied to correlational data. In our study of TV viewing we hypothesized that we would find an inverse relationship between amount of TV watched and SAT scores. Sure enough, that's what we found. However, we have to ask ourselves a critical question: Is this observed correlation large enough to support our hypothesis, or might a correlation of this size have occurred by chance?

We have to ask a similar question nearly every time we conduct a study. Why? Because we are working only with a sample. In research, we observe a limited *sample* (in this case, 20 subjects) to draw conclusions about a much larger *population* (college students in general). There's always a possibility that if we drew a different sample from the population, the results might be different. Perhaps our results are unique to our sample and not generalizable to the larger population. If we were able to collect data on the entire population, we would not have to wrestle with this problem, but our dependence on a sample necessitates the use of inferential statistics to precisely evaluate the like-

lihood that our results are due to chance factors in sampling. Thus, inferential statistics are the key to making the inferential leap from the sample to the population (see Figure B.12).

Although it may seem backward, in hypothesis testing we formally test the *null* hypothesis. As applied to correlational data, the ***null hypothesis*** **is the assumption that there is no true relationship between the variables observed.** In our study, the null hypothesis is that there is no genuine association between TV viewing and SAT scores. We want to determine whether our results will permit us to *reject* the null hypothesis and thus conclude that our *research hypothesis* (that there *is* a relationship between the variables) has been supported. Why do we test directly the null hypothesis instead of the research hypothesis? Because our probability calculations depend on

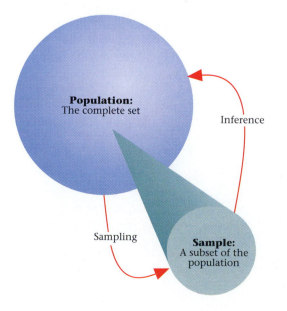

Population:
The complete set

Inference

Sampling

Sample:
A subset of the population

assumptions tied to the null hypothesis. Specifically, we compute the probability of obtaining the results that we have observed if the null hypthesis is indeed true. The calculation of this probability hinges on a number of factors. A key factor is the amount of variability in the data, which is why the standard deviation is an important statistic.

Statistical Significance

When we reject the null hypothesis, we conclude that we have found *statistically significant* results. *Statistical significance* **is said to exist when the probability that the observed findings are due to chance is very low, usually less than 5 chances in 100.** This means that if the null hypothesis is correct and we conduct our study 100 times, drawing a new sample from the population each time, we will get results such as those observed only 5 times out of 100. If our calculations allow us to reject the null hypothesis, we conclude that our results support our research hypothesis. Thus, statistically significant results typically are findings that *support* a research hypothesis.

The requirement that there be less than 5 chances in 100 that research results are due to chance is the *minimum* requirement for statistical significance. When this requirement is met, we say the results are significant at the .05 level. If researchers calculate that there is less than 1 chance in 100 that their results are due to chance factors in sampling, the results are significant at the .01 level. If there is less than a 1 in 1000 chance that findings are attributable to sampling error, the results are significant at the .001 level. Thus, there are several *levels* of significance that you may see cited in scientific articles.

Because we are only dealing in matters of probability, there is always the possibility that our decision to accept or reject the null hypothesis is wrong. The various significance levels indicate the probability of erroneously rejecting the null hypothesis (and inaccurately accepting the research hypothesis). At the .05 level of significance, there are 5 chances in 100 that we have made a mistake when we conclude that our results support our hypothesis, and at the .01 level of significance the chance of an erroneous conclusion is 1 in 100. Although researchers hold the probability of this type of error quite low, the probability is never zero. This is one of the reasons that competently executed studies of the same question can yield contradictory findings. The differences may be due to chance variations in sampling that can't be prevented.

What do we find when we evaluate our data linking TV viewing to students' SAT scores? The calculations indicate that, given our sample size and the variability in our data, the probability of obtaining a correlation of −.24 by chance is greater than 20%. That's not a high probability, but it's *not* low enough to reject the null hypothesis. Thus, our findings are not strong enough to allow us to conclude that we have supported our hypothesis.

Statistics and Empiricism

In summary, conclusions based on empirical research are a matter of probability, and there's always a possibility that the conclusions are wrong. However, two major strengths of the empirical approach are its precision and its intolerance of error. Scientists can give you precise estimates of the likelihood that their conclusions are wrong, and because they're intolerant of error, they hold this probability extremely low. It's their reliance on statistics that allows them to accomplish these goals.

APPENDIX C
INDUSTRIAL/ORGANIZATIONAL PSYCHOLOGY

BY FRANK LANDY

The Pennsylvania State University

Throughout this book we have seen many examples of how psychology has been applied to practical problems in a wide variety of settings. But we have yet to discuss in earnest one setting that has received a great deal of attention from the earliest beginnings of psychology—the work setting. *Industrial and organizational (I/O) psychology* **is the branch of psychology concerned with the application of psychological principles in the workplace.** There are approximately 5000 members of the Society for Industrial and Organizational Psychology (SIOP), which is the major professional organization for I/O psychologists. In this appendix, we will describe the history of I/O psychology and then delve into its three main areas. But first we need a clearer picture of what I/O psychology encompasses.

Overview of I/O Psychology

Industrial and organizational psychology differs from other psychology subfields in the settings where it is practiced, in its content, and in its approach.

Settings

In one sense, I/O psychology is defined more clearly by *where* it happens than by *what* I/O psychologists actually do. I/O psychology is practiced in work settings, just as school psychology is practiced in educational settings. But even though the context in which research and application are carried out may be unique, I/O psychology makes use of the findings of many other branches of psychology. Thus, principles of human motivation are relevant to the study of productivity and safety behavior, theories of attitude formation help in understanding the job satisfaction of workers, aspects of psychophysiology are relevant to a consideration of job stress, clinical theories of adjustment are applicable to the emotional consequences of job loss, and theories of intelligence are used to develop tests that might assist in hiring or promotion decisions. In fact, a good deal of the work of the I/O psychologist involves adapting or extending the basic principles of other specialty areas of psychology to the work setting.

With respect to *how* I/O psychologists practice their profession, they use most of the same techniques as their colleagues in other areas, such as life span or social psychology. Like other psychologists, the I/O psychologist may do research in a laboratory or in a field setting (at the work site, for instance). I/O psychologists use the same basic experimental designs and statistical tests as other behavioral researchers, depend just as heavily on earlier research for theoretical guidance, and publish the results of their research in scholarly journals.

Content

More than anything else, the *content* of I/O psychology helps set it apart from other branches of psychology. As Figure C.1 shows, the I/O psychologist has three primary areas of interest: (1) personnel psychology, (2) organizational psychology, and (3) human factors, or human engineering, psychology. Although we will consider each of these areas in detail shortly, it might be helpful to briefly describe them here.

Personnel psychology **deals with determining whether people have the knowledge, skills, abilities, and personality necessary to perform various types of work effectively.** This subarea of I/O psychology is concerned with the broad topic of employment testing as well as with such related topics as job training and performance evaluation. Personnel psychologists see the job or work environment as the "given" and the population of

Figure C.1
Subfields of industrial/organizational psychology. The domain of I/O psychology can be divided into three specialized areas of interest.

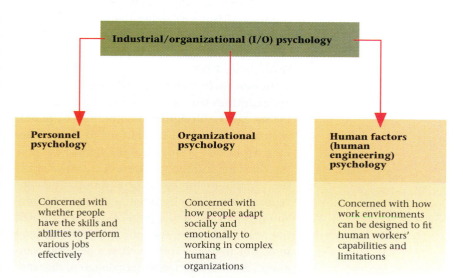

Industrial/organizational (I/O) psychology

Personnel psychology

Concerned with whether people have the skills and abilities to perform various jobs effectively

Organizational psychology

Concerned with how people adapt socially and emotionally to working in complex human organizations

Human factors (human engineering) psychology

Concerned with how work environments can be designed to fit human workers' capabilities and limitations

The simple act of replacing a typewriter with a personal computer can have ramifications in many aspects of an employee's work besides interaction with the physical equipment. A systems approach helps explain the various repercussions of such changes.

individuals who might be workers as the variable factor. Their goal is to find the workers who have the right attributes to fit the demands of the job.

Organizational psychology **is concerned with how people adapt emotionally and socially to working in complex human organizations.** It focuses on work motivation, job satisfaction, leadership, organizational climate, teamwork, and related topics. From this perspective, the concern of the I/O psychologist is to understand the factors that contribute to the right emotional "fit" between people and their work. For example, one of the pioneers of applied psychology, Hugo Münsterberg (1913), dealt with the problem of boredom on the factory floor by having kittens play there with balls of yarn, thus providing an interesting diversion for the workers. The modern I/O psychologist concentrates on making the job itself more interesting (in the jargon of the field, "enriching" the job) rather than getting workers to forget how boring the work actually is (Hackman & Oldham, 1975; Herzberg, Mausner, & Snyderman, 1959).

Human factors (human engineering) psychology **examines the way in which work environments can be designed or modified to match the capabilities and limitations of human beings.** From this perspective, the human being is the constant and the job or work environment is the variable in the behavior equation. The concept of the work environment is used very broadly and includes the actual physical setting in which the work takes place, the tools and resources used in conducting the work (such as a personal computer), and the arrangement or design of the work tasks (including such things as the scheduling of

work hours). Thus, the challenge to the human factors psychologist is to design or redesign a work environment so that it best fits the capabilities and allows for the limitations of the humans who will inhabit it.

A Systems Approach

The division of I/O psychology into three facets is somewhat misleading because it implies that these areas operate independently. In practice, this is seldom true. In fact, the actual work, the people who do the work, and the work environment define a larger entity that might be labeled the "socio-technical system." Changes made in one part of the system usually affect other parts of the system.

Changing the design of a task so that it is more complex (a human factors activity) may have a substantial impact on the satisfaction that a worker derives from that task (an organizational topic) and who might do best at that task (a personnel psychology topic). As an example, consider the simple act of replacing a secretary's typewriter with a personal computer. On the surface, this might be seen as a "human factor" change, since it is a modification of the tools of the job. But the new technology also changes other aspects of the work. The secretary may no longer need to go to the filing cabinet to insert or retrieve documents, as files can now be accessed electronically without moving from a desk. As a result, the secretary may become more isolated and lose opportunities for social interaction with other workers. In addition, the introduction of the computer changes the skill and ability mix necessary for success on the job. Unless the worker is capable of interacting effectively with the hardware and software of the computer system, he or she is likely to experience performance problems (and accompanying feelings of frustration). In addition to these changes, the performance of the worker might be more closely monitored. Keystrokes can be counted and an average per minute calculated, errors can be detected, and other measures of performance can be collected and used to reward or punish the worker. Finally, supervisors might interact with employees by sending messages through a computerized electronic mail system rather than by talking directly with them, losing a personal element. In short, replacing a typewriter with a personal computer is much more complex than it seems on the surface.

The fact that the three areas of I/O psychology are not mutually exclusive is both a burden and an opportunity for I/O psychologists. The burden lies in being sensitive to the impact that making a change in one part of this sociotechnical system has on other parts of the system. The opportunity lies in having several options for dealing with real-world problems. For example, if an organization is having a problem with accidents or productivity, an I/O psychologist might suggest redesigning the work environment to be safer or more efficient. Alternatively, the psychologist might design a motivational program to encourage workers to engage in safer or more productive work. Finally, the psychologist might suggest changing the methods used to select or train workers. Any or all of these methods might be effective in reducing accidents or improving productivity.

A Brief History

Although psychology as a science was born in the late 19th century, various specialty areas, including I/O psychology, came along somewhat later. The first Ph.D. granted in I/O psychology was in 1915, more than 30 years after the first Ph.D. in experimental psychology. It was presented to Lilian Gilbreth by Brown University. In this section, we will examine the development of I/O psychology from a historical perspective.

Personnel Psychology

Personnel psychology was the first of the three I/O subfields to appear. This development, which occurred around 1900, was the result of several forces, the foremost being psychology's emerging interest in measuring and recording individual differences. Sir Francis Galton (1869) had started the trend before the turn of the century, when he related skull measurements to personality traits (see Chapter 9). Subsequently, pioneers such as James McKeen Cattell, Alfred Binet, and Henry Goddard began to develop tests to measure individuals' sensory capacities and intelligence.

It was a short step to take these new tests into industrial settings to identify employees or applicants best suited to the work at hand (DuBois, 1970). As a result, personnel psychology, particularly testing, was an early defining characteristic of I/O psychology. One of the earliest figures in the development of testing techniques in industry was Hugo Münsterberg, a student of Wundt hired in 1892 by William James to direct the psychological laboratories at Harvard (Hale, 1980). By 1908 Münsterberg had established a significant role for psychological testing in industrial settings, and by 1913 he had written the first scientific textbook on I/O psychology. In short order, he trained several students who further deepened and broadened this testing activity. World War I provided an opportunity, on a massive scale, to apply ability testing to a national need, as intelligence tests were adapted for use in placing military recruits into specialized assignments (Yerkes, 1921). The respectability acquired by psychological testing from this wartime application carried over into industry following the war, and modern personnel psychology emerged. By 1932 there were dozens of texts describing the goals and methods of personnel psychology (such as Burtt, 1929; Viteles, 1932). Similar pressures for mass testing exerted by World War II further enhanced the importance of personnel testing, which retains a prominent role in I/O psychology today.

Organizational Psychology

Until 1930, analyses of workers' motivation and satisfaction were limited to economic and ability issues. The generally accepted position was that workers would be happy and productive in direct proportion to their pay. In addition, it was believed that people would be frustrated in jobs for which they were overqualified or underqualified (Fryer, 1931; Münsterberg, 1913).

The dominant theory of the period was that of Frederick W. Taylor (1911), variously known as "scientific management" or "Taylorism." Taylor believed that one need only identify the most efficient way to physically carry out a piece of work (lay a brick, shovel coal), pick a worker capable of the work and willing to follow orders without question, and pay that worker in proportion to production rate. Taylor was an industrial engineer by training and saw issues in simple cost-benefit terms. Taylor's views were quite popular with management (although detested and resisted vigorously by the labor movement) and fit well with the factory system and assembly-line production methods of his era. His methods were adopted not only in the United States but also in countries as diverse as Sweden, Japan, Germany, and the Soviet Union.

The Taylorists' views were eventually undermined by some influential experiments conducted at a Western Electric facility near Chicago in 1930. This work was described by Elton Mayo, an Australian psychologist working in the management school of Harvard University (Roethlisberger & Dickson, 1939). The research team discovered that employees' attitudes toward their supervisors and their company had substantial effects on productivity—effects that seemed to be independent of pay level or other working conditions, such as lighting or rest breaks. This was a revolutionary discovery because it implied that attitudes have direct effects on behavior. Previously, managers had believed that only physical or "real" stimuli, such as heat, light, and pay, affect behavior. The quality of Mayo's experiments and the accuracy of his conclusions have been called into question over the years (e.g., Landsberger, 1958; Landy, 1988). Nevertheless, at the time the results appeared, they caused an earthquake in the world of business management. A new paradigm was introduced to replace scientific management, and the human relations movement was launched. This movement proposed that many factors beyond pay level contribute to the satisfaction and productivity of workers and that these factors can be identified in the attitudes that workers hold toward various aspects of their work. The implication was that supervisors should be more sensitive to the feelings of workers as a way of improving productivity. The human relations movement gave birth to 60 years of interest in job satisfaction, an interest that remains high today.

Human Factors Psychology

Research and application of human factors psychology was narrow prior to World War II. It consisted of applying industrial engineering principles to manufacturing jobs to eliminate waste. The central practitioners were Frederick W. Taylor (1911) and the Gilbreths, Frank and Lilian (1917), and the system that was applied was "scientific management," an approach that had little enthusiasm for human abilities and emotions. Instead, the concentration was on paying high wages for "efficient" work behavior. In that sense, it was perfectly in line with the emerging school of behaviorism being promoted by John B. Watson (see Chapters 1 and 6).

World War II changed all that. Airplanes, ships, submarines, and weapons had undergone a radical transformation since World War I, resulting in greater attention to developing technical systems that could be used effectively by humans. Of particular concern was the fact that far more accidents involving aircraft occurred than had been anticipated. "Human error," rather than equipment failure, seemed to play the major role in most of these accidents. Out of a need to understand the best and safest combination of human and machine was born modern human factors psychology. Much of the complex equipment used today, particularly in high-technology arenas such as aviation, nuclear power, and computers, shows the influence of the human factors specialist.

Taylor's scientific management approach was popular with early 20th-century industrialists, who applied it to the factory system.

APPENDIX C

In the next three sections of this appendix, we will consider each of the facets of I/O psychology in greater detail. In the final section, we will reconsider how these three facets are bound tightly together in a sociotechnical system.

Personnel Psychology

The fundamental challenge for the personnel psychologist is to match the attributes of workers with the demands of jobs. Workers' attributes include their knowledge, skills, personality, and motivation. In an ideal world, there is a job for everyone, and the problem is trying to decide which person gets which job. One approach to solving this problem would be to distinguish among people in terms of their attributes in deciding who to put in which job. Thus, the spokesperson's job would be filled by the person who is the best communicator, the detective's job by the person with the best reasoning ability, and the dentist's role by the individual with the best eye-hand coordination. Although these are overly simple examples, they provide a feel for what the task of the personnel psychologist is.

Of course, most organizations do not have unlimited positions that would permit them to place everyone who applies in the job that is best suited for his or her ability mix. In addition, sometimes the employer cannot find exactly the right person to meet the demands of a job. In other words, no one who applies has the necessary abilities. In the first instance—more applicants than jobs—the personnel psychologist might develop a specific test battery that will identify the best applicants for a job and reject the rest. In the second instance—no candidates with the necessary abilities—the personnel psychologist might develop training programs to provide candidates with those skills. In this situation, since the organization cannot hire the individual with the right skills, the solution is to hire those capable of *developing* those skills or abilities through a training program.

Job Analysis

Thus far, we have been discussing predictors of job success—skills, abilities, personal characteristics—as if job success itself were easy to define and measure. But this is not necessarily true. Consider the job of teacher or sales representative. Psychologists may have some vague notion that teaching success is defined by student accomplishment, or that sales success is defined by dollar volume, but from a behavioral standpoint, they still have

Human factors analysis plays an important role in the design of complex high-tech equipment, such as airplane control panels, to help reduce the risk of accidents.

little idea of *what exactly* they are trying to predict with their tests.

To remedy this problem, the personnel psychologist often engages in a process known as job analysis. *Job analysis* **is a method for breaking a job into its constituent parts.** It is a way to identify the most important parts of the job description—the requirements that are of primary interest to the employer. To use the job of firefighter as an example, it is true that firefighters clean equipment, give tours of firehouses to schoolchildren, and cook meals for each other during their work shifts. But these are not the *central* or defining tasks of the firefighter. The central tasks are putting out fires, saving lives, and saving property.

A job analysis is a way of separating the peripheral aspects of a job from the central aspects. Once this task has been accomplished, the next step is determining the knowledge, skills, abilities, or other personal characteristics necessary for successful completion of those tasks. When these key attributes have been identified, an appropriate test can be selected.

Test Selection and Administration

In Chapter 9 you learned that *psychological tests* are standardized measures of individuals' mental abilities and personality traits. Psychological tests are used extensively in personnel psychology. They

What would be the best way to evaluate the job performance of an employee such as a firefighter? Personnel psychologists develop methods for such performance evaluations.

Performance Evaluation

In the jargon of personnel psychology, *performance evaluation* consists of efforts to assess the quality of employees' work. The specific aspects of job performance that are assessed should be guided by the job analysis. If the job analysis indicates that two or three aspects of behavior on the job are crucial, they are the ones that should be measured. A key rule of performance evaluation is that workers should be assessed on important rather than trivial job aspects.

Many procedures might be used to evaluate the performance of an employee. Someone could simply observe the person in the performance of the required duties. The problem with this method is that the observer may not know enough about the technical aspects of the work to recognize when a task is being performed well. Another problem is that it might take a good deal of time before there is an opportunity to observe the aspects of behavior on the job that are actually important.

Alternatively, someone could count the objective products of a person's job performance (for example, the number of fires extinguished or lives saved by a firefighter). The problem with this technique is that some jobs don't have an objective product that can be associated with a particular person. The "objective" products of many if not most jobs depend on the efforts of several people, not just one.

As a result of these and other problems, the most common form of performance evaluation is the supervisory rating (Landy & Farr, 1980, 1983). In this approach, the supervisor is asked to consider the behavior of the employee in certain critical areas and to assign a numerical rating that represents how well or poorly the employee performs in these areas. Typically, the rating scale consists of a series of statements that can be used to describe the employee's performance. Associated with these statements are numbers that convey the supervisor's judgment about the performance in question. Figure C.2 provides an example of a rating scale that could be used in the performance evaluation of firefighters.

Rating scales have both advantages and disadvantages. One advantage is that the basic information comes from those who presumably know the employee's performance best. In providing their ratings, supervisors can synthesize information based on observations made over a long period of time, perhaps six months or a year. One disadvantage is that these ratings can be influenced by irrelevant factors. For example, just as some teach-

permit employers to estimate how much ability applicants have without waiting to see whether the people succeed or fail on the job. Another advantage of *standardized* tests is that they permit comparisons among applicants who take the test at different times, because the test items and administration procedures are identical. This is particularly important when many people are competing for the same job.

Personnel psychologists can consult a number of resources in identifying psychological tests appropriate for particular employment decisions. First, the scientific literature describes research on various types of jobs, the abilities they require, and the tests that assess these abilities. Next, several basic reference sources, such as the *Mental Measurement Yearbook* (Conoley & Impara, 1995), describe a broad variety of tests for various purposes. Finally, it is possible to develop a new test to predict performance in a specific job.

Once a suitable test has been found, the next step is to administer it to candidates and decide which of them has the greatest probability of being successful on the job. In most instances, the prediction is that the higher the test score, the greater the likelihood of job success. Of course, this approach is based on the assumption that the employment test is reliable and valid (see Chapter 9). That is, the test must be a reasonably consistent measuring device, and there must be evidence that it really measures what it was designed to measure. In the last several years, personality testing has seen renewed interest. In part, this is the result of the popularity of the Big Five theory of personality (see Chapter 12).

ers are hard graders and others are lenient, some supervisors are tough raters and others are much easier. Thus, Mary may be rated as an excellent employee and Charles may be rated as a poor employee not because their behaviors differ but because Mary has an easy supervisor and Charles has a tough one. Another common influence is simply how much the supervisor likes the subordinate. If their personal relationship is a good one, the ratings may be higher than the worker's performance really merits. Fortunately, supervisors can be trained to avoid rating errors (McIntyre, Smith, & Hassett, 1984), and rating scales can be developed in ways that eliminate many of the pitfalls of the rating process.

Test Validity

At some point, it is important for the personnel psychologist to verify that the tests developed to identify the best job candidates are successful in doing so. Using a test to hire people is analogous to testing a hypothesis in research (see Chapter 2). In this case, the hypothesis is that people who score better on the test will perform better on the job than those who score poorly on the test. If reliable performance measures are available, a statistical analysis can be used to test this hypothesis precisely. Such an analysis involves computing the correlation between test scores and performance scores (such as supervisory ratings). If the result is *a strong positive correlation* (see Appendix B), this finding supports the "hypothesis" that underlies using the test. This process of demonstrating that a test is a reasonably accurate predictor of job performance is known as *validation*. Many other approaches can be used to demonstrate the validity of a test besides this correlational method, but all have the same goal—demonstrating that those who score better on the test will do better on the job.

Equal Employment Opportunity and Testing

Because tests often play an important role in deciding who will be hired or promoted, they have been the subject of close scrutiny by federal agencies, public interest groups, and applicants themselves. The Equal Employment Opportunity Commission is responsible for assuring that tests are fair to all applicants, regardless of race, religion, gender, or age. Recently, through the Americans with Disabilities Act, this employment protection has been extended to cover disabled applicants and workers as well.

This rather simple goal has led to a complex tangle of legal, administrative, and philosophical

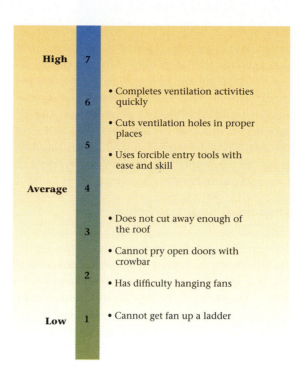

Figure C.2
Rating scales used in performance evaluation. Supervisors' ratings are often used to evaluate employees' job performance. To reduce the subjectivity of these ratings, I/O psychologists often design behaviorally anchored rating scales, in which numerical ratings are tied to unambiguous descriptions of relevant job behaviors. The scale shown here is used to evaluate one aspect of the firefighters' work. (Adapted from Landy, 1989)

disputes—a tangle that has resulted not just from the need to demonstrate that a test is "fair" to all applicants but also from an attempt to correct inequities in past hiring practices. In the past, this correction has often involved a requirement that hiring decisions conform to a certain numerical goal until an imbalance (such as too few women in a workforce) has been eliminated. Thus, the notion of "hiring quotas" was introduced. Although hiring goals or quotas were made illegal by the Civil Rights Act of 1991, the desire to hire a particular portion of minority or female applicants to make up for their absence in the current workforce may clash with the decision that would be made on the basis of test scores alone. This situation has created a good deal of debate among representatives of the federal government, employers, and personnel psychologists.

Much of this debate has centered on the validity of tests used in hiring decisions. The debate often occurs in the context of legal suits brought against employers by unsuccessful applicants, who typically claim that the tests used have an "adverse impact" on minority or female applicants. As a result, the federal courts have become heavily involved in the evaluation of the technical merits of tests and have issued rulings regarding what can and cannot be done in making hiring decisions. It is unlikely that the basic debate will change in the next decade. Many unsuccessful job applicants will continue to believe that the tests used are unfair. Many employers and personnel psychologists will continue to believe that the tests are valid and that their use is warranted. In addition, many politicians will continue to use the issue to their advantage. The modern personnel psychologist needs to cut through the ideological and political smoke and continue to develop and administer good tests. I/O psychologists can be activists in this area because they are capable of distinguishing between fair and unfair employment tests. By applying what they know, they can help applicants, employers, and society as a whole.

Organizational Psychology

Most people do not work alone. They work with colleagues, subordinates, and supervisors, often on project teams. As we saw earlier, organizational psychology is concerned with the human relations aspects of work. Organizational psychologists are interested in how organizational factors influence workers' social and emotional functioning. In this section, we'll discuss two topics that have been of special interest to organizational psychologists: work motivation and job satisfaction.

Work Motivation

Why do some people spend their free time in athletic activities while others choose to read books or go to concerts? Why do some people approach tasks enthusiastically while others are more passive or uninterested? Over the years, many theories have been proposed to account for these differences in motivation. In Chapter 10 we saw that theorists such as Henry Murray, Abraham Maslow, and David McClelland analyzed the nature of motivation in very different ways.

As you might expect, employers and I/O psychologists have a particular interest in motivational principles as they apply in the work setting. Why do some employees accept the goals of the organization and their supervisor while other employees reject those goals? Why do some employees work hard while others appear lazy and uncooperative? The answers to these questions might make the difference between survival and failure for businesses. Let's examine two theories that have special relevance for an understanding of work motivation: equity theory and expectancy theory.

EQUITY THEORY. The concept of *homeostasis* assumes that organisms attempt to maintain a state of equilibrium or balance (see Chapter 10). This balance may be either physiological or psychological. In the work setting, a balance is sought between the worker's inputs and outcomes. In essence, *equity theory* proposes that individuals compare what they are investing in the work (skills, abilities, experience, effort, loyalty) with the rewards they are receiving for that investment (money, opportunities for promotion, praise). If the perceived rewards match the perceived inputs, a condition of balance (or equity) results, and the individual continues to expend the necessary amount of energy to keep the system in balance. However, if a worker perceives that a job's rewards do not match the inputs required (a condition of inequity), he or she will seek changes to bring the system back into balance (Adams, 1965).

In the most common circumstance of inequity or imbalance, workers believe that inputs exceed rewards. In this situation, they presumably seek to decrease their inputs (usually by reducing effort) or increase their outcomes (typically by asking for a raise). The mechanics of this theory are outlined in Figure C.3. The most recent forms of equity theory propose that the individual not only assesses his or her *own* inputs and outcomes but compares them to the inputs and outcomes of other relevant people, such as co-workers, neighbors, and so forth (Goodman, 1974).

It follows from equity theory that *excess* rewards also have implications for motivation. In this circumstance, the theory suggests that the individual will actually *increase* inputs (strive for higher productivity or a higher-quality performance) or decrease outcomes (by rejecting pay increases or deferring credit to co-workers). This part of the theory does not seem to square with the experience of most people. Few workers feel that they are *over*rewarded.

Nevertheless, equity theory does have important implications for the more common *under*-rewarded situation. From a practical standpoint, the critical issue is making sure that employees have realistic expectations of outcomes and that

Figure C.3
Equity theory as a model of work motivation. According to equity theory, when workers feel underpaid or overpaid, they adjust the pace or quality of their work to restore equity as outlined here. However, evidence suggests that equity theory is more applicable to the condition of underpayment than overpayment. (Adapted from Mowday, 1979)

	Underpayment	Overpayment
Hourly payment (fixed amount per hour)	Subjects underpaid by the hour will produce less or poorer-quality output than equitably paid subjects.	Subjects overpaid by the hour will produce more or higher-quality output than equitably paid subjects.
Piece-rate payment (fixed amount per piece)	Subjects underpaid by piece rate will produce a larger number of low-quality units than will equitably paid subjects.	Subjects overpaid by piece rate will produce fewer units of higher quality than equitably paid subjects.

rewards match efforts. In the expanded form of equity theory, which posits that people evaluate the inputs and outcomes of others, workers have additional strategies for bringing the system into balance. A worker could, for example, attempt to increase the inputs of co-workers while holding their outcomes constant. The worker could do so by urging them to work harder or by complaining to the boss that they are not doing their fair share of the work. Although equity theory can become quite complex, with many variables to consider, it has proven useful in understanding some aspects of motivation in the workplace.

EXPECTANCY THEORY. A quite different approach to work motivation can be found in *expectancy theory,* which proposes that individuals choose to expend energy in a particular direction (work hard or not work hard) based on their answers to two key questions (Porter & Lawler, 1968): (1) Is the reward offered for effort one that they value? and (2) Will the supervisor actually provide the promised reward if the requested level of effort is expended?

For example, suppose you work for a computer software company as a sales representative. Your supervisor promises that if you sell a lot of software, you will receive the designation of "employee of the month." This reward may hold little appeal for you. You may prefer more tangible outcomes in the form of cash bonuses, commissions, or other monetary incentives. In this situation, the offered reward has little value and you may be less likely to expend energy in the way the company expects. Suppose your supervisor promises that if you reach a certain level of sales, you will get a large cash bonus. However, you may have been burned by this supervisor in the past when you achieved sales goals and the supervisor back-pedaled, claiming that you had misunderstood the agreement. In this instance, even though the reward is attractive, the probability of actually receiving it would be low. As a result, you would be unlikely to expend the effort requested.

This theory of motivation gets its name from the idea that workers' *expectations* about rewards influence their efforts (Peak, 1955; Rotter, 1955). The theory proposes that unless both a valuable reward and a reasonable expectation for receiving that reward exist, a worker will expend little effort. The practical implications of expectancy theory are that employers should offer employees rewards that they value and that employers should be careful to follow through on promises to employees.

Although equity theory and expectancy theory are different in important respects, they share one distinct similarity: Both emphasize cognitive factors. Each proposes that people plan, evaluate, and consciously modify their courses of action. This is a clear trend in contemporary theories of work motivation, which assume that cognition is central to motivated behavior.

Job Satisfaction

Closely associated with work motivation is job satisfaction. Recently, the term "quality of working life" has been used as a synonym for job satisfaction. Presumably, people want to gain satisfaction from their work and to avoid dissatisfaction. What factors lead to job satisfaction and what are its consequences? There has been more research on these topics than almost any others in I/O psychology. Thousands of research studies have led to the basic finding that the primary sources of job satisfaction are interesting and challenging work, pleasant co-workers, adequate pay and other financial benefits, opportunities for advancement, effective and supportive supervisors, and acceptable company policies. In contrast, job dissatisfaction results from the absence of these characteristics. Many of us have had what we called "boring" jobs. This is the other side of the satisfaction coin. For a fascinating glimpse at the most "demotivating" and "unsatisfying" jobs that one might have, read the entertaining and illuminating books of Barbara Garson (1988, 1994).

Most organizations take the emotional temperature of their employees by administering questionnaires on a regular basis. These questionnaires typically ask workers to rate their levels of satisfaction on each of the basic factors just listed. Organizations go to the trouble of gathering this information because they believe that job satisfaction is related to employee absenteeism, turnover, and productivity. For instance, most managers believe that dissatisfied employees are likely to take excessive sick leave or to seek employment elsewhere. There is good reason to believe that such a relationship exists (Brayfield & Crockett, 1955; Herzberg et al., 1959; Mobley, Horner, & Hollingsworth, 1978). Because absenteeism and turnover are costly, employers try to reduce them by increasing job satisfaction. Most managers also believe that job satisfaction leads to increased productivity. That assumption is more questionable. Several decades of research have failed to demonstrate that satisfaction causes productivity. Some research, however, does indicate that *productivity causes satisfaction* (Locke, 1976). In other words, it appears that workers who are able to accomplish work goals and overcome work-related challenges are happier than those who do not have such experiences.

What are the implications of the research findings on job satisfaction? First, if a company wants a stable workforce, it should try to minimize employee dissatisfaction with key job factors (pay, opportunities for advancement, and so on). The concerned employer can make necessary adjustments based on the analysis of work-related attitude questionnaires distributed on a regular basis. In addition, an employer that wants high productivity and happy employees should ensure that they have the necessary resources (equipment and technical support) and should solve any problems that arise on the job. In short, the employer's job is to remove obstacles to success.

There are, of course, other reasons for fostering job satisfaction beyond boosting productivity and reducing absenteeism. There is no reason that people should not derive happiness from their work, just as there is no reason that they should not derive happiness from other activities. Conversely, evidence suggests that dissatisfying and stressful work environments can lead to physical and psychological damage (Karasek & Theorell, 1990; Landy, Quick, & Kasl, 1994). Any environment in which people spend half or more of their waking hours is bound to have the potential for affecting psychological well-being. Organizational psychologists look for ways to make the effects more positive. As an example, stressful work environments are those with high levels of uncertainty and conflict, and low levels of control. I/O psychologists would address this stress by developing worker feedback and communication systems to reduce uncertainty and increase information flow, by introducing team building to reduce conflict, and by developing systems for worker input into decision making to foster some feeling of control.

Human Factors Psychology

If you have ever fiddled with the controls on a stove trying to figure out which knob affects which burner, you have experienced a human factors problem. Similarly, whenever you get into an unfamiliar rental car and begin to search for the controls for the lights and the windshield wipers, you are once again dealing with a human factors issue. In fact, human factors psychology has been referred to facetiously as "knobs and dials" psychology (Carter, 1978) because early in its development the field concentrated on devising the most effective ways of displaying information (the best design for dials) and the most effective way of taking actions (the best design for knobs). This research dealt with the best placement of knobs and dials, the arrangement associated with the fewest performance errors, and so forth. Human factors specialists were also referred to as human engineering psychologists, because they designed environments and equipment to match the capabilities and limitations of human operators. Both human attributes and engineering principles were taken into account.

Human factors specialists seek to understand the human-machine relationship in various environments. Although such psychologists might be involved in designing home environments, health care environments, educational environments, and consumer products, we will concentrate on the application of human factors principles to the work environment. The basic challenge in human engineering efforts is depicted in Figure C.4.

As you can see, there are several components to the human-machine system. An important component is information in the environment. That information is displayed to the human being through devices such as dials, meters, computer screens, and printouts. In your car, the gas gauge is a display that provides important information, as are the speedometer, the odometer, and the oil and temperature lights. The fact that you must interpret and possibly use this information creates a design challenge. How can this information be *best* displayed? Systems specialists refer to this "confrontation" of the individual and the information as an "interface" problem and strive to make the interface as effective as possible. As Figure C.4 illustrates, the individual must interpret the information in the display and choose a course of action (or inaction) based on that information. This creates a second interface, between the individual and the device that modifies or has an influence on the system.

Let's take the simple example of a machine operator adjusting the speed of a machine. The actual speed of the machine is presented in a digital read-out on the face of the machine. This is the *display* part of the system. If the speed is too fast or too slow, it can be adjusted with a series of keyboard buttons on the machine console. This is the *control* part of the system. Thus, the operator looks

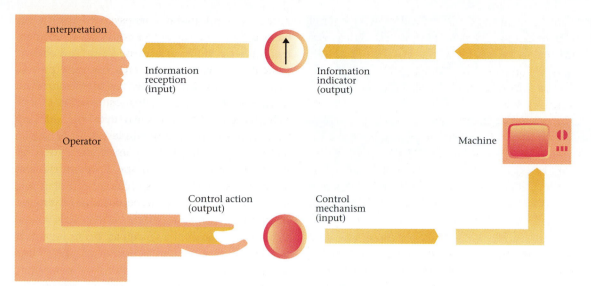

Figure C.4
The challenge of human engineering. The communication between people and machines can be viewed as an information flow loop that connects their respective inputs and outputs. Human factors psychologists attempt to make person-machine interfaces as effective as possible.

Interpretation

Information reception (input)

Information indicator (output)

Operator

Machine

Control action (output)

Control mechanism (input)

at the digital display for information, keys in a series of commands that speed up or slow down the machine, and then reexamines the display to make sure that the target speed has been achieved. If the speed is still too fast or too slow or if the adjustment has been too extreme, the operator keys in new and more refined information and keeps checking the digital display until the desired speed has been achieved. This is a description of a simple combination of human, display, and control. A less elegant but equally relevant example is the system that includes the driver of an automobile, the speedometer, and the gas pedal. When the driver notices that the needle on the speedometer has gone over the speed limit, he or she exerts less pressure on the gas pedal and the speed indicator drops.

Most of the early human factors research was geared toward achieving satisfactory interfaces between human and display and human and control. For example, it was discovered that many of the airplane accidents that occurred in World War II were caused by either faulty displays or faulty controls. Faulty displays included dials that were placed outside of the pilot's line of vision or that presented information in a way that was difficult to interpret. Many of the control problems came from confusion of one control with another. For example, the knobs that activated the flaps were identical in shape to those that activated the landing gear. As a result, many pilots who meant to retract the landing gear shortly after takeoff actually engaged the flaps, causing a crash. The solution to this problem turned out to be relatively simple. Each knob was given a distinctive shape that conveyed its particular function. Thus, the knob that controlled the landing gear

was shaped like a wheel, whereas the knob that controlled flaps was actually shaped like a flap. Meanwhile, dials were arranged more centrally so that they were easier to see and were given a standard location in all planes.

Similar principles of human engineering are applied today in many areas of technology. As an example, the design of control rooms for nuclear power plants has been influenced greatly by human factors psychology. Consider the control panel in Figure C.5 (on page 710). Just drawing lines and borders and providing labels for clusters of controls and displays helps make the information-processing task easier and reduces the probability of error.

Human factors specialists follow a number of principles in designing equipment and environments. One central principle is *response stereotypy,* which is people's tendency to expect that a control will work in a particular way. Most people believe that when they want to open a door, they should turn the knob clockwise or push the handle down. When they have to turn the doorknob counter-clockwise or pull the handle up, they become confused and less efficient. Therefore, one of the most basic design principles is to see how people will carry out an action when left to themselves. If they show a clear preference (or response stereotype), the operator actions should be designed to take advantage of that preference. If people show no clear preference, other principles of design can be used. But engineers should be careful about designing a system that directly contradicts the natural tendencies or expectations of the users of that system.

Human factors specialists face many other challenges in today's work environment. One such

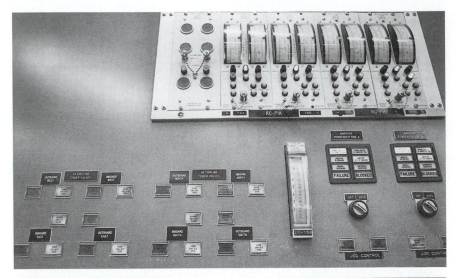

Figure C.5
Improving visual displays in the work environment. Visual displays can often be enhanced to help workers find information more quickly. The top photo shows a section of a display panel from a nuclear power plant control room before it was redesigned. The bottom picture shows how this display panel was modified to make it easier for operators to locate needed information quickly.

challenge is robotics at the work site. Specialists must design controls for these robots to be compatible with the response tendencies of those who will command or operate them. Similarly, human engineers need to determine the best interface for remote computer-controlled devices used by operators in nuclear power plants, chemical plants, and similar facilities who cannot "see" what they are doing.

Another challenge for human factors specialists is the reduction of work-related stress. Some work designs can lead to greater stress than others (Karasek & Theorell, 1990). For example, a computer in the workplace can be a blessing or a curse. If the computer is fast and failure-free, it can be a real enhancement. But if it is slow in responding or difficult to control through software, it can create frustrations. Similarly, a system in which either too much or too little information is presented to the operator can create stress leading to both health-related problems and performance errors. No one wants to be a passenger in a plane

flown by a pilot under stress or to live in the vicinity of a nuclear power plant where the control room operators are stressed out. The guiding principle in work design is to prevent the demands of a job from exceeding the resources or capacities of the person who holds that job.

With the great advances in technology and hardware in the workplace in the last decade, human factors engineering has become more closely allied with cognitive psychology. Today, the goal is less the design of accessible knobs and dials and more the design of effective information systems. In addition, human factors specialists have begun to consider related areas, such as the arrangement of work shift schedules (Costa et al., 1989) and mental models of the work to be performed (Brehmer, 1987).

A Systems Approach to Industrial Safety: Putting It All Together

Industrial safety can serve as an example of the interrelation among personnel psychology, organizational psychology, and human factors psychology. Consider the problem of excessive accidents in using a punch press machine at a metal fabricating plant. How could accidents be reduced? Working from a personnel psychology perspective, one approach to the problem would be to determine whether particular individuals seem to have more accidents than others. If that is the case, experts could examine the basic abilities of these people and institute either a training or a selection program to reduce the accident rate.

An organizational psychologist might approach the problem by assuming that workers are receiving conflicting motivational signals. For example, it might be that the operators ridicule each other for being too cautious. In this case, the employer might provide cash incentives for safe behavior or might show workers how high the accident rate is when precautions are not taken.

Alternatively, it might be just as effective to work from a human factors perspective and place an "interlock" system on the machine that would prevent an operator from taking actions that might lead to an accident. Thus, if people are losing too many fingers in the punch press, the machine could be redesigned so that the press functions only when each hand is pressing a different button. If either button is not depressed, the punch will not operate. These systems are now part of most such machines. Of course, the safest system could probably be developed by using all three approaches rather than just one.

GLOSSARY

A

Absolute refractory period The minimum length of time after an action potential during which another action potential cannot begin.

Absolute threshold The minimum amount of stimulation that an organism can detect for a specific type of sensory input.

Accommodation Changing existing mental structures to explain new experiences.

Achievement motive The need to master difficult challenges, to outperform others, and to meet high standards of excellence.

Achievement tests Tests that gauge a person's mastery and knowledge of various subjects.

Acquired immune deficiency syndrome (AIDS) A disorder in which the immune system is gradually weakened and eventually disabled by the human immunodeficiency virus (HIV).

Acquisition The formation of a new conditioned response tendency.

Action potential A brief change in a neuron's electrical charge.

Additive color mixing Formation of colors by superimposing lights, putting more light in the mixture than exists in any one light by itself.

Adoption studies Research studies that assess hereditary influence by examining the resemblance between adopted children and both their biological and their adoptive parents.

Afferent nerve fibers Axons that carry information inward to the central nervous system from the periphery of the body.

Affiliation motive The need to associate with others and maintain social bonds.

Afterimage A visual image that persists after a stimulus is removed.

Age of viability The age at which a baby can survive in the event of a premature birth.

Aggression Any behavior that is intended to hurt someone, either physically or verbally.

Agonist A chemical that mimics the action of a neurotransmitter.

Agoraphobia A fear of going out to public places.

Alcohol A variety of beverages containing ethyl alcohol.

Algorithm A methodical, step-by-step procedure for trying all possible alternatives in searching for a solution to a problem.

Altruism Selfless concern for the welfare of others that leads to helping behavior.

Amnesia A significant memory loss that is too extensive to be due to normal forgetting. See also *Anterograde amnesia, Psychogenic amnesia, Retrograde amnesia.*

Androgens The principal class of gonadal hormones in males.

Animism The belief that all things are living.

Antagonist A chemical that opposes the action of a neurotransmitter.

Antecedents In behavior modification, events that typically precede the target response.

Anterograde amnesia Loss of memories for events that occur after a head injury.

Antianxiety drugs Medications that relieve tension, apprehension, and nervousness.

Antidepressant drugs Medications that gradually elevate mood and help bring people out of a depression.

Antipsychotic drugs Medications used to gradually reduce psychotic symptoms, including hyperactivity, mental confusion, hallucinations, and delusions.

Antisocial personality disorder A type of personality disorder marked by impulsive, callous, manipulative, aggressive, and irresponsible behavior that reflects a failure to accept social norms.

Anxiety disorders A class of disorders marked by feelings of excessive apprehension and anxiety.

Aphrodisiacs Substances thought to increase sexual desire.

Applied psychology The branch of psychology concerned with everyday, practical problems.

Approach-approach conflict A conflict situation in which a choice must be made between two attractive goals.

Approach-avoidance conflict A conflict situation in which a choice must be made about whether to pursue a single goal that has both attractive and unattractive aspects.

Aptitude tests Psychological tests used to assess talent for specific types of mental ability.

Archetypes According to Jung, emotionally charged images and thought forms that have universal meaning.

Ascending reticular activating system (ARAS) The afferent fibers running through the reticular formation that influence physiological arousal.

Assimilation According to Piaget, interpreting new experiences in terms of existing mental structures, without changing them.

Attachment A close, emotional bond of affection between infants and their caregivers.

Attention Focusing awareness on a narrowed range of stimuli or events.

Attitudes Orientations that locate objects of thought on dimensions of judgment.

Attributions Inferences that people draw about the causes of events, others' behavior, and their own behavior.

Auditory localization Locating the source of a sound in space.

Autonomic nervous system (ANS) The system of nerves that connect to the heart, blood vessels, smooth muscles, and glands.

Availability heuristic Basing the estimated probability of an event on the ease with which relevant instances come to mind.

Aversion therapy A behavior therapy in which an aversive stimulus is paired with a stimulus that elicits an undesirable response.

Avoidance-avoidance conflict A conflict situation in which a choice must be made between two unattractive goals.

Avoidance learning Learning that has occurred when an organism engages in a response that prevents aversive stimulation from occurring.

Axon A long, thin fiber that transmits signals away from the neuron cell body to other neurons, or to muscles or glands.

B

Basilar membrane A structure that runs the length of the cochlea in the inner ear and holds the auditory receptors, called hair cells.

Behavior Any overt (observable) response or activity by an organism.

Behavior modification A systematic approach to changing behavior through the application of the principles of conditioning.

Behavior therapies Application of the principles of learning to direct efforts to change clients' maladaptive behaviors.

Behavioral contract A written agreement outlining a promise to adhere to the contingencies of a behavior modification program.

Behavioral genetics An interdisciplinary field that studies the influence of genetic factors on behavioral traits.

Behaviorism A theoretical orientation based on the premise that scientific psychology should study only observable behavior.

Belief perseverance The tendency to hang onto beliefs in the face of contradictory evidence.

Binocular depth cues Clues about distance based on the differing views of the two eyes.

Biofeedback A therapy method in which a bodily function (such as heart rate) is monitored and information about it is fed back to a person to facilitate improved control of the physiological process.

Biological rhythms Periodic fluctuations in physiological functioning.

Biomedical therapies Physiological interventions intended to reduce symptoms associated with psychological disorders.

Biopsychosocial model A model of illness that holds that physical illness is caused by a complex interaction of biological, psychological, and sociocultural factors.

Bipolar disorders (formerly known as manic-depressive disorders) Mood disorders marked by the experience of both depressed and manic periods.

Bisexuals Persons who seek emotional-sexual relationships with members of either sex.

Blocking In classical conditioning, a phenomenon that occurs when a stimulus paired with a UCS fails to become a CS because it is redundant with an established CS.

Blood-brain barrier A semipermeable membrane–like mechanism that stops some chemicals from passing between the bloodstream and the brain.

Bottom-up processing In form perception, progression from individual elements to the whole.

Burnout Physical, mental, and emotional exhaustion that is attributable to work-related stress.

Bystander effect A paradoxical social phenomenon in which people are less likely to provide needed help when they are in groups than when they are alone.

C

Cannabis The hemp plant from which marijuana, hashish, and THC are derived.

Cardinal trait A dominant trait that characterizes nearly all of a person's behavior.

Case study An in-depth investigation of an individual subject.

Catastrophic thinking Unrealistically pessimistic appraisals of stress that exaggerate the magnitude of one's problems.

Catatonic schizophrenia A type of schizophrenia marked by striking motor disturbances, ranging from muscular rigidity to random motor activity.

Catharsis The release of emotional tension.

Central nervous system (CNS) The brain and the spinal cord.

Central traits Prominent, general dispositions found in anyone.

Centration The tendency to focus on just one feature of a problem, neglecting other important aspects.

Cephalocaudal trend The head-to-foot direction of motor development.

Cerebral cortex The convoluted outer layer of the cerebrum.

Cerebral hemispheres The right and left halves of the cerebrum.

Cerebral laterality The degree to which the left or right hemisphere controls various cognitive and behavioral functions.

Cerebrospinal fluid (CSF) A solution that fills the hollow cavities (ventricles) of the brain and circulates around the brain and spinal cord.

Channel The medium through which a message is sent.

Chromosomes Threadlike strands of DNA (deoxyribonucleic acid) molecules that carry genetic information.

Chunk A group of familiar stimuli stored as a single unit.

Circadian rhythms The 24-hour biological cycles found in humans and many other species.

Classical conditioning A type of learning in which a neutral stimulus acquires the ability to evoke a response that was originally evoked by another stimulus.

Client-centered therapy An insight therapy that emphasizes providing a supportive emotional climate for clients, who play a major role in determining the pace and direction of their therapy.

Clinical psychologists Psychologists who specialize in the diagnosis and treatment of psychological disorders and everyday behavioral problems.

Clinical psychology The branch of psychology concerned with the diagnosis and treatment of psychological problems and disorders.

Clustering The tendency to remember similar or related items in groups.

Cochlea The fluid-filled, coiled tunnel in the inner ear that contains the receptors for hearing.

Coefficient of determination The percentage of variation in one variable that can be predicted based on the other variable.

Cognition The mental processes involved in acquiring knowledge.

Cognitive development Transitions in youngsters' patterns of thinking, including reasoning, remembering, and problem solving.

Cognitive dissonance A psychological state that exists when related cognitions are inconsistent.

Cognitive therapy An insight therapy that emphasizes recognizing and changing negative thoughts and maladaptive beliefs.

Collective unconscious According to Jung, a storehouse of latent memory traces inherited from people's ancestral past.

Collectivism Putting group goals ahead of personal goals and defining one's identity in terms of the groups one belongs to.

Color blindness Deficiency in the ability to distinguish among colors.

Commitment An intent to maintain a relationship in spite of the difficulties and costs that may arise.

Community mental health centers Facilities that provide comprehensive mental health care for their local communities.

Companionate love Warm, trusting, tolerant affection for another whose life is deeply intertwined with one's own.

Compensation According to Adler, efforts to overcome imagined or real inferiorities by developing one's abilities.

Compensatory decision models In decision making, strategies that allow attractive attributes to compensate for unattractive attributes.

Competency (or fitness in some states) A defendant's capacity to stand trial.

Complementary colors Pairs of colors that produce gray tones when added together.

Compliance A type of conformity that occurs when people yield to social pressure in their public behavior, even though their private beliefs have not changed.

Conceptual hierarchy A multilevel classification system based on common properties among items.

Concordance rate The percentage of twin pairs or other pairs of relatives that exhibit the same disorder.

Conditioned reinforcers. See *Secondary reinforcers.*

Conditioned response (CR) A learned reaction to a conditioned stimulus that occurs because of previous conditioning.

Conditioned stimulus (CS) A previously neutral stimulus that has, through conditioning, acquired the capacity to evoke a conditioned response.

Cones Specialized visual receptors that play a key role in daylight vision and color vision.

Confirmation bias The tendency to seek information that supports one's decisions and beliefs while ignoring disconfirming information.

Conflict A state that occurs when two or more incompatible motivations or behavioral impulses compete for expression.

Conformity The tendency for people to yield to real or imagined social pressure.

Confounding of variables A condition that exists whenever two variables are linked together in a way that makes it difficult to sort out their independent effects.

Conjunction fallacy An error that occurs when people estimate that the odds of two uncertain events happening together are greater than the odds of either event happening alone.

Conscious Whatever one is aware of at a particular point in time.

Conservation Piaget's term for the awareness that physical quantities remain constant in spite of changes in their shape or appearance.

Consolidation A hypothetical process involving the gradual conversion of information into durable memory codes stored in long-term memory.

Construct validity The extent to which there is evidence that a test measures a particular hypothetical construct.

Constructive coping Relatively healthful efforts that people make to deal with stressful events.

Content validity The degree to which the content of a test is representative of the domain it's supposed to cover.

Continuous reinforcement Reinforcing every instance of a designated response.

Control group Subjects in a study who do not receive the special treatment given to the experimental group.

Convergence A cue to depth that involves sensing the eyes converging toward each other as they focus on closer objects.

Convergent thinking Narrowing down a list of alternatives to converge on a single correct answer.

Conversion disorder A somatoform disorder characterized by a significant loss of physical function (with no apparent organic basis), usually in a single organ system.

Coping Active efforts to master, reduce, or tolerate the demands created by stress.

Corpus callosum The structure that connects the two cerebral hemispheres.

Correlation The extent to which two variables are related to each other.

Correlation coefficient A numerical index of the degree of relationship between two variables.

Counseling psychologists Psychologists who specialize in the treatment of everyday adjustment problems.

Creativity The generation of ideas that are original, novel, and useful.

Criterion-related validity Test validity that is estimated by correlating subjects' scores on a test with their scores on an independent criterion (another measure) of the trait assessed by the test.

Cross-sectional design A research design in which investigators compare groups of subjects of differing age who are observed at a single point in time.

Crystallized intelligence One's ability to apply acquired skills and knowledge in problem solving.

Culture The widely shared customs, beliefs, values, norms, institutions, and other products of a community that are transmitted socially across generations.

Culture-bound disorders Abnormal syndromes found only in a few cultural groups.

Cumulative recorder A graphic record of reinforcement and responding in a Skinner box as a function of time.

Cyclothymic disorder Exhibiting chronic but relatively mild symptoms of bipolar disturbance.

D

Dark adaptation The process in which the eyes become more sensitive to light in low illumination.

Data collection techniques Procedures for making empirical observations and measurements.

Decay theory The idea that forgetting occurs because memory traces fade with time.

Decision making The process of evaluating alternatives and making choices among them.

Declarative memory system Memory for factual information.

Deep structure The underlying meaning of a sentence.

Defense mechanisms Largely unconscious reactions that protect a person from unpleasant emotions such as anxiety and guilt.

Defensive attribution The tendency to blame victims for their misfortune, so that one feels less likely to be victimized in a similar way.

Deinstitutionalization Transferring the treatment of mental illness from inpatient institutions to community-based facilities that emphasize outpatient care.

Delusions False beliefs that are maintained even though they are clearly out of touch with reality.

Dementia An abnormal condition marked by multiple cognitive defects that include memory impairment.

Dendrites Branchlike parts of a neuron that are specialized to receive information.

Dependent variable In an experiment, the variable that is thought to be affected by the manipulation of the independent variable.

Depressive disorders Mood disorders characterized by persistent feelings of sadness and despair and a loss of interest in previous sources of pleasure.

Depth perception Interpretation of visual cues that indicate how near or far away objects are.

Descriptive statistics Statistics that are used to organize and summarize data.

Development The sequence of age-related changes that occur as a person progresses from conception to death.

Developmental norms The average age at which individuals display various behaviors and abilities.

Deviation IQ scores Scores that locate subjects precisely within the normal distribution, using the standard deviation as the unit of measurement.

Diagnosis Distinguishing one illness from another.

Discrimination Behaving differently, usually unfairly, toward the members of a group.

Discriminative stimuli Cues that influence operant behavior by indicating the probable consequences (reinforcement or nonreinforcement) of a response.

Disorganized schizophrenia A type of schizophrenia in which particularly severe deterioration of adaptive behavior is seen.

Displacement Diverting emotional feelings (usually anger) from their original source to a substitute target.

Display rules Cultural norms that regulate the appropriate expressions of emotions.

Dissociation A splitting off of mental processes into two separate, simultaneous streams of awareness.

Dissociative amnesia A sudden loss of memory for important personal information that is too extensive to be due to normal forgetting.

Dissociative disorders A class of disorders in which people lose contact with portions of their consciousness or memory, resulting in disruptions in their sense of identity.

Dissociative fugue A disorder in which people lose their memory for their entire lives along with their sense of personal identity.

Dissociative identity disorder. See *Multiple-personality disorder.*

Distal stimuli Stimuli that lie in the distance (that is, in the world outside the body).

Divergent thinking Trying to expand the range of alternatives by generating many possible solutions.

Dominant gene A gene that is expressed when paired genes are heterozygous (different).

Double-blind procedure A research strategy in which neither subjects nor experimenters know which subjects are in the experimental or control groups.

Dream analysis A psychoanalytic technique in which the therapist interprets the symbolic meaning of the client's dreams.

Drive An internal state of tension that motivates an organism to engage in activities that should reduce this tension.

Dual-coding theory Paivio's theory that memory is enhanced by forming semantic and visual codes, since either can lead to recall.

Dualism The idea that the mind and body are fundamentally distinct entities.

Dysthymic disorder A chronic depression that is insufficient in severity to merit diagnosis of a major depressive episode.

E

Efferent nerve fibers Axons that carry information outward from the central nervous system to the periphery of the body.

Ego According to Freud, the decision-making component of personality that operates according to the reality principle.

Egocentrism A limited ability to share another person's viewpoint.

Elaboration Linking a stimulus to other information at the time of encoding.

Electrical stimulation of the brain (ESB) Sending a weak electric current into a brain structure to stimulate (activate) it.

Electroconvulsive therapy (ECT) A biomedical treatment in which electric shock is used to produce a cortical seizure accompanied by convulsions.

Electroencephalograph (EEG) A device that monitors the electrical activity of the brain over time by means of recording electrodes attached to the surface of the scalp.

Electromyograph (EMG) A device that records muscular activity and tension.

Electrooculograph (EOG) A device that records eye movements.

Elicit To draw out or bring forth.

Embryonic stage The second stage of prenatal development, lasting from two weeks until the end of the second month.

Emit To send forth.

Emotion A subjective conscious experience (the cognitive component) accompanied by bodily arousal (the physiological component) and by characteristic overt expressions (the behavioral component).

Empiricism The premise that knowledge should be acquired through observation.

Encoding Forming a memory code.

Encoding specificity principle The idea that the value of a retrieval cue depends on how well it corresponds to the memory code.

Endocrine system A group of glands that secrete chemicals into the bloodstream that help control bodily functioning.

Endorphins The entire family of internally produced chemicals that resemble opiates in structure and effects.

Epidemiology The study of the distribution of mental or physical disorders in a population.

Epigenetic principle The idea that in the course of development the parts give rise to the whole.

Episodic memory system Chronological, or temporally dated, recollections of personal experiences.

Erectile difficulties A sexual dysfunction that occurs when a man is persistently unable to achieve or maintain an erection adequate for intercourse.

Escape learning A type of learning in which an organism acquires a response that decreases or ends some aversive stimulation.

Estrogens The principal class of gonadal hormones in females.

Ethnocentrism The tendency to view one's own group as superior to others and as the standard for judging the worth of foreign ways.

Etiology The apparent causation and developmental history of an illness.

Eugenics Efforts to control reproduction to gradually improve hereditary characteristics in a population.

Evolutionary psychology Theoretical perspective that examines behavioral processes in terms of their adaptive value for a species over the course of many generations.

Excitatory PSP An electric potential that increases the likelihood that a postsynaptic neuron will fire action potentials.

Experiment A research method in which the investigator manipulates a variable under carefully controlled conditions and observes whether any changes occur in a second variable as a result.

Experimental group The subjects in a study who receive some special treatment in regard to the independent variable.

Experimenter bias A phenomenon that occurs when a researcher's expectations or preferences about the outcome of a study influence the results obtained.

Expertise Consistently superior performance on a specified set of tasks or problems.

Explicit memory Intentional recollection of previous experiences.

External attributions Ascribing the causes of behavior to situational demands and environmental constraints.

Extinction The gradual weakening and disappearance of a conditioned response tendency.

Extraneous variables Any variables other than the independent variable that seem likely to influence the dependent variable in a specific study.

Extraverts People who tend to be interested in the external world of people and things.

F

Factor analysis Statistical analysis of correlations among many variables to identify closely related clusters of variables.

Family life cycle A sequence of stages that families tend to progress through.

Family studies Scientific studies in which researchers assess hereditary influence by examining blood relatives to see how much they resemble each other on a specific trait.

Farsightedness A visual deficiency in which distant objects are seen clearly but close objects appear blurry.

Fast mapping The process by which children map a word onto an underlying concept after only one exposure to the word.

Feature analysis The process of detecting specific elements in visual input and assembling them into a more complex form.

Feature detectors Neurons that respond selectively to very specific features of more complex stimuli.

Fechner's law A psychophysical law stating that larger and larger increases in stimulus intensity are required to produce perceptible increments in the magnitude of sensation.

Fetal alcohol syndrome A collection of congenital (inborn) problems associated with excessive alcohol use during pregnancy.

Fetal stage The third stage of prenatal development, lasting from two months through birth.

Field dependence-independence Individuals' tendency to rely primarily on external versus internal frames of reference when orienting themselves in space.

Fight-or-flight response A physiological reaction to threat in which the autonomic nervous system mobilizes the organism for attacking (fight) or fleeing (flight) an enemy.

Fixation According to Freud, failure to move forward from one psychosexual stage to another as expected.

Fixed-interval (FI) schedule A reinforcement schedule in which the reinforcer is given for the first response that occurs after a fixed time interval has elapsed.

Fixed-ratio (FR) schedule A reinforcement schedule in which the reinforcer is given after a fixed number of nonreinforced responses.

Flashbulb memories Unusually vivid and detailed recollections of momentous events.

Fluid intelligence One's reasoning ability, memory capacity, and speed of information processing.

Forebrain The largest and most complicated region of the brain, encompassing a variety of structures, including the thalamus, hypothalamus, limbic system, and cerebrum.

Forgetting curve A graph showing retention and forgetting over time.

Fovea A tiny spot in the center of the retina that contains only cones; visual acuity is greatest at this spot.

Framing How issues are posed or how choices are structured.

Fraternal twins Twins that result when two eggs are fertilized simultaneously by different sperm cells, forming two separate zygotes. Also called *Dizygotic twins*.

Free association A psychoanalytic technique in which clients spontaneously express their thoughts and feelings exactly as they occur, with as little censorship as possible.

Frequency distribution An orderly arrangement of scores indicating the frequency of each score or group of scores.

Frequency polygon A line figure used to present data from a frequency distribution.

Frequency theory The theory that perception of pitch corresponds to the rate, or frequency, at which the entire basilar membrane vibrates.

Frustration The feeling that people experience in any situation in which their pursuit of some goal is thwarted.

Functional fixedness The tendency to perceive an item only in terms of its most common use.

Functionalism A school of psychology based on the belief that psychology should investigate the function or purpose of consciousness, rather than its structure.

Fundamental attribution error Observers' bias in favor of internal attributions in explaining others' behavior.

G

Galvanic skin response (GSR) An increase in the electrical conductivity of the skin that occurs when sweat glands increase their activity.

Gambler's fallacy The belief that the odds of a chance event increase if the event hasn't occurred recently.

Gate-control theory The idea that incoming pain sensations must pass through a "gate" in the spinal cord that can be closed, thus blocking pain signals.

Gender Culturally constructed distinctions between masculinity and femininity.

Gender differences Actual disparities between the sexes in typical behavior or average ability.

Gender roles Expectations about what is appropriate behavior for each sex.

Gender stereotypes Widely held beliefs about males' and females' abilities, personality traits, and behavior.

General adaptation syndrome Selye's model of the body's stress response, consisting of three stages: alarm, resistance, and exhaustion.

Generalized anxiety disorder A psychological disorder marked by a chronic, high level of anxiety that is not tied to any specific threat.

Genes DNA segments that serve as the key functional units in hereditary transmission.

Genetic mapping The process of determining the location and chemical sequence of specific genes on specific chromosomes.

Genotype A person's genetic makeup.

Germinal stage The first phase of prenatal development, encompassing the first two weeks after conception.

Gestalt psychology A theoretical orientation based on the idea that the whole is greater than the sum of its parts.

Glia Cells found throughout the nervous system that provide structural support and insulation for neurons.

Glucose A simple sugar that is an important source of energy.

Glucostats Neurons sensitive to glucose in the surrounding fluid.

Group Two or more individuals who interact and are interdependent.

Group cohesiveness The strength of the liking relationships linking group members to each other and to the group itself.

Group polarization A phenomenon that occurs when group discussion strengthens a group's dominant point of view and produces a shift toward a more extreme decision in that direction.

Group therapy The simultaneous treatment of several or more clients in a group.

Groupthink A process in which members of a cohesive group emphasize concurrence at the expense of critical thinking in arriving at a decision.

Gustatory system The sensory system for taste.

H

Hallucinations Sensory perceptions that occur in the absence of a real, external stimulus, or gross distortions of perceptual input.

Hallucinogens A diverse group of drugs that have powerful effects on mental and emotional functioning, marked most prominently by distortions in sensory and perceptual experience.

Handedness A preference for using one's right or left hand in most activities.

Hardiness A personality syndrome that is marked by commitment, challenge, and control and that is purportedly associated with strong stress resistance.

Health psychology The subfield of psychology concerned with how psychosocial factors relate to the promotion and maintenance of health and with the causation, prevention, and treatment of illness.

Heritability ratio An estimate of the proportion of trait variability in a population that is determined by variations in genetic inheritance.

Heterosexuals Persons who seek emotional-sexual relationships with members of the other sex.

Heterozygous condition The situation that occurs when two genes in a specific pair are different.

Heuristic A strategy, guiding principle, or rule of thumb used in solving problems or making decisions.

Hierarchy of needs Maslow's systematic arrangement of needs according to priority, which assumes that basic needs must be met before less basic needs are aroused.

Higher-order conditioning A type of conditioning in which a conditioned stimulus functions as if it were an unconditioned stimulus.

Hindbrain The part of the brain that includes the cerebellum and two structures found in the lower part of the brainstem: the medulla and the pons.

Histogram A bar graph that presents data from a frequency distribution.

Holophrases Children's single-word utterances that appear to function like sentences.

Homeostasis A state of physiological equilibrium or stability.

Homosexuals Persons who seek emotional-sexual relationships with members of the same sex.

Homozygous condition The situation that occurs when two genes in a specific pair are the same.

Hormones The chemical substances released by the endocrine glands.

Human factors (human engineering) psychology A subarea of industrial/organizational psychology that examines the ways in which work environments can be designed or modified to match the characteristics of human beings.

Humanism A theoretical orientation that emphasizes the unique qualities of humans, especially their freedom and their potential for personal growth.

Hypnosis A systematic procedure that typically produces a heightened state of suggestibility.

Hypochondriasis A somatoform disorder characterized by excessive preoccupation with health concerns and incessant worry about developing physical illnesses.

Hypothalamus A structure found near the base of the forebrain that is involved in the regulation of basic biological needs.

Hypothesis A tentative statement about the relationship between two or more variables.

I

Id According to Freud, the primitive, instinctive component of personality that operates according to the pleasure principle.

Identical twins Twins that emerge from one zygote that splits for unknown reasons. Also called *Monozygotic twins.*

Identification Bolstering self-esteem by forming an imaginary or real alliance with some person or group.

Ill-defined problems Problems in which one or more elements among the initial state, the goal state, and the constraints are incompletely or unclearly specified.

Illusory correlation A misperception that occurs when people estimate that they have encountered more confirmations of an association between social traits than they have actually seen.

Immune response The body's defensive reaction to invasion by bacteria, viral agents, or other foreign substances.

Implicit memory Type of memory apparent when retention is exhibited on a task that does not require intentional remembering.

Impossible figures Objects that can be represented in two-dimensional pictures but cannot exist in three-dimensional space.

Incentive An external goal that has the capacity to motivate behavior.

Incongruence The degree of disparity between one's self-concept and one's actual experience.

Independent variable In an experiment, a condition or event that an experimenter varies in order to see its impact on another variable.

Individualism Putting personal goals ahead of group goals and defining one's identity in terms of personal attributes rather than group memberships.

Industrial and organizational (I/O) psychology The branch of psychology concerned with the application of psychological principles to the workplace.

Inferential statistics Statistics that are used to interpret data and draw conclusions.

Ingratiation A conscious effort to cultivate others' liking by complimenting them, agreeing with them, and doing them favors.

Ingroup The group that people belong to and identify with.

Inhibitory PSP An electric potential that decreases the likelihood that a postsynaptic neuron will fire action potentials.

Insanity A legal status indicating that a person cannot be held responsible for his or her actions because of mental illness.

Insight In problem solving, the sudden discovery of the correct solution following incorrect attempts based primarily on trial and error.

Insight therapies Psychotherapy methods characterized by verbal interactions intended to enhance clients' self-knowledge and thus promote healthful changes in personality and behavior.

Insomnia Chronic problems in getting adequate sleep.

Instinctive drift The tendency for an animal's innate responses to interfere with conditioning processes.

Instrumental learning. See *Operant conditioning.*

Insulin A hormone secreted by the pancreas that helps cells extract glucose from the blood.

Intelligence quotient (IQ) A child's mental age divided by chronological age, multiplied by 100.

Intelligence tests Psychological tests that measure general mental ability.

Interference theory The idea that people forget information because of competition from other material.

Intermittent reinforcement A reinforcement schedule in which a designated response is reinforced only some of the time.

Internal attributions Ascribing the causes of behavior to personal dispositions, traits, abilities, and feelings.

Interneurons Neurons that communicate only with other neurons.

Interpersonal attraction Positive feelings toward another.

Interpretation In psychoanalysis, the therapist's attempts to explain the inner significance of the client's thoughts, feelings, memories, and behaviors.

Intimacy Warmth, closeness, and sharing in a relationship.

Introspection Careful, systematic observation of one's own conscious experience.

Introverts People who tend to be preoccupied with the internal world of their own thoughts, feelings, and experiences.

Involuntary commitment A civil proceeding in which people are hospitalized in psychiatric facilities against their will.

Irreversibility The inability to envision reversing an action.

J

Job analysis Breaking a job into its constituent parts.

Journal A periodical that publishes technical and scholarly material, usually in a narrowly defined area of inquiry.

Just noticeable difference (JND) The smallest difference in the amount of stimulation that a specific sense can detect.

K

Keyword method A mnemonic technique in which one associates a concrete word with an abstract word and generates an image to represent the concrete word.

Kinesthetic system The sensory system that monitors the positions of the various parts of one's body.

L

Language A set of symbols that convey meaning, and rules for combining those symbols, that can be used to generate an infinite variety of messages.

Language acquisition device (LAD) An innate mechanism or process that facilitates the learning of language.

Latent content According to Freud, the hidden or disguised meaning of the events in a dream.

Lateral antagonism Neural activity in a cell that opposes activity in surrounding cells.

Latitude of acceptance A range of potentially acceptable positions on an issue centered on one's initial attitude position.

Law of effect The principle that if a response in the presence of a stimulus leads to satisfying effects, the association between the stimulus and the response is strengthened.

Learned helplessness Passive behavior produced by exposure to unavoidable aversive events.

Learning A relatively durable change in behavior or knowledge that is due to experience.

Lens The transparent eye structure that focuses the light rays falling on the retina.

Lesioning Destroying a piece of the brain.

Levels-of-processing theory The theory holding that deeper levels of mental processing result in longer-lasting memory codes.

Lie detector. See *Polygraph.*

Life changes Any noticeable alterations in one's living circumstances that require readjustment.

Light adaptation The process whereby the eyes become less sensitive to light in high illumination.

Limbic system A densely connected network of structures roughly located along the border between the cerebral cortex and deeper subcortical areas.

Linguistic relativity The theory that one's language determines the nature of one's thought.

Link method Forming a mental image of items to be remembered in a way that links them together.

Lithium A chemical used to control mood swings in patients with bipolar mood disorders.

Locus of control A generalized expectancy about the degree to which individuals control their outcomes.

Long-term memory (LTM) An unlimited capacity store that can hold information over lengthy periods of time.

Long-term potentiation (LTP) A long-lasting increase in neural excitability in synapses along a specific neural pathway.

Longitudinal design A research design in which investigators observe one group of subjects repeatedly over a period of time.

Lucid dreams Dreams in which people can think clearly about the circumstances of waking life and the fact that they are dreaming, yet they remain asleep in the midst of a vivid dream.

M

Manifest content According to Freud, the plot of a dream at a surface level.

Matching hypothesis The idea that males and females of approximately equal physical attractiveness are likely to select each other as partners.

Maturation Development that reflects the gradual unfolding of one's genetic blueprint.

Mean The arithmetic average of the scores in a distribution.

Mean length of utterance (MLU) The average length of children's spoken statements (measured in phonemes).

Means/ends analysis In problem solving, identifying differences that exist between the current state and the goal state, and making changes that will reduce these differences.

Median The score that falls exactly in the center of a distribution of scores.

Medical model The view that it is useful to think of abnormal behavior as a disease.

Meditation A family of mental exercises in which a conscious attempt is made to focus attention in a nonanalytical way.

Menarche The first occurrence of menstruation.

Mental age In intelligence testing, a score that indicates that a child displays the mental ability typical of a child of that chronological (actual) age.

Mental hospital A medical institution specializing in providing inpatient care for psychological disorders.

Mental retardation Subnormal general mental ability accompanied by deficiencies in everyday living skills originating prior to age 18.

Mental set Persisting in using problem-solving strategies that have worked in the past.

Mentor Someone with a senior position within an organization who serves as a role model, tutor, or adviser to a novice worker.

Message The information transmitted by a source.

Meta-analysis Combining the statistical results of many studies of the same question, yielding an estimate of the size and consistency of a variable's effects.

Metacognition Thinking about one's thinking.

Metalinguistic awareness The ability to reflect on the use of language.

Method of loci A mnemonic device that involves taking an imaginary walk along a familiar path where images of items to be remembered are associated with certain locations.

Midbrain The segment of the brain stem that lies between the hindbrain and the forebrain.

Mnemonic devices Strategies for enhancing memory.

Mode The score that occurs most frequently in a distribution.

Model A person whose behavior is observed by another.

Monocular depth cues Clues about distance based on the image from either eye alone.

Mood-congruence effect A phenomenon that occurs when memory is better for information that is consistent with one's ongoing mood.

Mood-dependent memory See *State-dependent memory.*

Mood disorders A class of disorders marked by emotional disturbances of varied kinds that may spill over to disrupt physical, perceptual, social, and thought processes.

Morphemes The smallest units of meaning in a language.

Motion parallax Cue to depth that involves images of objects at different distances moving across the retina at different rates.

Motivated forgetting Purposeful suppression of memories.

Motivation Goal-directed behavior.

Motor development The progression of muscular coordination required for physical activities.

Motor neurons Neurons that carry messages from the nervous system to the muscles that actually move the body.

Multiple-personality disorder A type of dissociative disorder characterized by the coexistence in one person of two or more largely complete, and usually very different, personalities.

Myelin sheath Insulating material, derived from glial cells, that encases some axons of neurons.

N

Narcolepsy A disease marked by sudden and irresistible onsets of sleep during normal waking periods.

Narcotics (opiates) Drugs derived from opium that are capable of relieving pain.

Natural selection Principle stating that characteristics that provide a survival advantage are more likely to be passed on to subsequent generations and thus come to be "selected" over time.

Naturalistic observation A descriptive research method in which the researcher engages in careful, usually prolonged, observation of behavior without intervening directly with the subjects.

Nearsightedness A visual deficiency in which close objects are seen clearly but distant objects appear blurry.

Need for self-actualization The need to fulfill one's potential.

Negative reinforcement The strengthening of a response because it is followed by the removal of an aversive (unpleasant) stimulus.

Negatively skewed distribution A distribution in which most scores pile up at the high end of the scale.

Nerves Bundles of neuron fibers (axons) that are routed together in the peripheral nervous system.

Neuromodulators Chemicals that increase or decrease (modulate) the activity of specific neurotransmitters.

Neurons Individual cells in the nervous system that receive, integrate, and transmit information.

Neurotransmitters Chemicals that transmit information from one neuron to another.

Night terrors Abrupt awakenings from NREM sleep accompanied by intense autonomic arousal and feelings of panic.

Nightmares Anxiety-arousing dreams that lead to awakening, usually from REM sleep.

Non-REM (NREM) sleep Sleep stages 1 through 4, which are marked by an absence of rapid eye movements, relatively little dreaming, and varied EEG activity.

Noncompensatory decision models Decision-making models that do not allow some attributes to compensate for others.

Noncontingent reinforcement The strengthening of a response by a reinforcer that follows it, even though delivery of the reinforcer was not a result of the response.

Nondeclarative memory system Memory for actions, skills, and operations.

Nonsense syllables Consonant-vowel-consonant arrangements that do not correspond to words.

Normal distribution A symmetric, bell-shaped curve that represents the pattern in which many characteristics are dispersed in the population.

Null hypothesis In inferential statistics, the assumption that there is no true relationship between the variables being observed.

O

Obedience A form of compliance that occurs when people follow direct commands, usually from someone in a position of authority.

Obesity The condition of being overweight.

Object permanence Recognizing that objects continue to exist even when they are no longer visible.

Observational learning A type of learning that occurs when an organism's responding is influenced by the observation of others, who are called models.

Obsessive-compulsive disorder (OCD) A type of anxiety disorder marked by persistent, uncontrollable intrusions of unwanted thoughts (obsessions) and urges to engage in senseless rituals (compulsions).

Oedipal complex According to Freud, children's manifestation of erotically tinged desires for their opposite-sex parent, accompanied by feelings of hostility toward their same-sex parent.

Olfactory system The sensory system for smell.

Operant chamber See *Skinner box.*

Operant conditioning A form of learning in which voluntary responses come to be controlled by their consequences.

Operational definition A definition that describes the actions or operations that will be made to measure or control a variable.

Opiates. See *Narcotics.*

Opponent process theory The theory that color perception depends on receptors that make antagonistic responses to three pairs of colors.

Optic chiasm The point at which the optic nerves from the inside half of each eye cross over and then project to the opposite half of the brain.

Optic disk A hole in the retina where the optic nerve fibers exit the eye.

Optical illusion An apparently inexplicable discrepancy between the appearance of a visual stimulus and its physical reality.

Optimism A general tendency to expect good outcomes.

Organizational psychology A subarea of industrial/organizational psychology concerned with how people adapt emotionally and socially to working in complex human organizations.

Orgasm The release of sexual tension that occurs when arousal reaches its peak intensity and is discharged in a series of muscular contractions that pulsate through the pelvic area.

Orgasmic difficulties Sexual dysfunctions that occur when people experience sexual arousal but have persistent problems in achieving orgasm.

Outgroup People who are not part of the ingroup.

Overextensions Using a word incorrectly to describe a wider set of objects or actions than it is meant to.

Overlearning Continued rehearsal of material after one first appears to have mastered it.

Overregularization In children, incorrect generalization of grammatical rules to irregular cases where they do not apply.

P

Panic disorder A type of anxiety disorder characterized by recurrent attacks of overwhelming anxiety that usually occur suddenly and unexpectedly.

Paranoid schizophrenia A type of schizophrenia that is dominated by delusions of persecution along with delusions of grandeur.

Parasympathetic division The branch of the autonomic nervous system that generally conserves bodily resources.

Partial reinforcement. See *Intermittent reinforcement.*

Pariticipants See *Subjects.*

Passionate love A complete absorption in another that includes tender sexual feelings and the agony and ecstasy of intense emotion.

Pavlovian conditioning. See *Classical conditioning.*

Percentile score A figure that indicates the percentage of people who score below the score one has obtained.

Perception The selection, organization, and interpretation of sensory input.

Perceptual asymmetries Left-right imbalances between the cerebral hemispheres in the speed of visual or auditory processing.

Perceptual constancy A tendency to experience a stable perception in the face of continually changing sensory input.

Perceptual hypothesis An inference about which distal stimuli could be responsible for the proximal stimuli sensed.

Perceptual set A readiness to perceive a stimulus in a particular way.

Performance evaluation Efforts to assess the quality of employees' work.

Peripheral nervous system All those nerves that lie outside the brain and spinal cord.

Person perception The process of forming impressions of others.

Personal unconscious According to Jung, the level of awareness that houses material that is not within one's conscious awareness because it has been repressed or forgotten.

Personality An individual's unique constellation of consistent behavioral traits.

Personality disorders A class of psychological disorders marked by extreme, inflexible personality traits that cause subjective distress or impaired social and occupational functioning.

Personality tests Psychological tests that measure various aspects of personality, including motives, interests, values, and attitudes.

Personality trait A durable disposition to behave in a particular way in a variety of situations.

Personnel psychology A subarea of industrial/organizational psychology that deals with determining whether people have the knowledge, skills, and abilities to perform various types of work effectively.

Phenomenological approach The assumption that one must appreciate individuals' personal, subjective experiences to truly understand their behavior.

Phenotype The ways in which a person's genotype is manifested in observable characteristics.

Pheromone A chemical secreted by one animal that affects the behavior of another.

Phi phenomenon The illusion of movement created by presenting visual stimuli in rapid succession.

Phobias Irrational fears of specific objects or situations.

Phobic disorder A type of anxiety disorder marked by a persistent and irrational fear of an object or situation that presents no realistic danger.

Phonemes The smallest units of sound in a spoken language.

Physical dependence The condition that exists when a person must continue to take a drug to avoid withdrawal illness.

Pictorial depth cues Clues about distance that can be given in a flat picture.

Pituitary gland The "master gland" of the endocrine system; it releases a great variety of hormones that fan out through the body, stimulating actions in the other endocrine glands.

Place theory The idea that perception of pitch corresponds to the vibration of different portions, or places, along the basilar membrane.

Placebo effects The fact that subjects' expectations can lead them to experience some change even though they receive an empty, fake, or ineffectual treatment.

Placenta A structure that allows oxygen and nutrients to pass into the fetus from the mother's bloodstream and bodily wastes to pass out to the mother.

Pleasure principle According to Freud, the principle upon which the id operates, demanding immediate gratification of its urges.

Polygenic traits Characteristics that are influenced by more than one pair of genes.

Polygraph A device that records autonomic fluctuations while a subject is questioned, in an effort to determine whether the subject is telling the truth.

Population The larger collection of animals or people from which a sample is drawn and that researchers want to generalize about.

Positive reinforcement Reinforcement that occurs when a response is strengthened because it is followed by the presentation of a rewarding stimulus.

Positively skewed distribution A distribution in which scores pile up at the low end of the scale.

Postsynaptic potential (PSP) A voltage change at the receptor site on a postsynaptic cell membrane.

Posttraumatic stress disorder Disturbed behavior that is attributed to a major stressful event but that emerges after the stress is over.

Preconscious According to Freud, the level of awareness that contains material just beneath the surface of conscious awareness that can easily be retrieved.

Prejudice A negative attitude held toward members of a group.

Premature ejaculation Impairment of sexual relations because the man consistently reaches orgasm too quickly.

Prenatal period The period from conception to birth, usually encompassing nine months of pregnancy.

Preparedness A species-specific predisposition to be conditioned in certain ways and not others.

Pressure Expectations or demands that one behave in a certain way.

Prevalence The percentage of a population that exhibits a disorder during a specified time period.

Primacy effect The fact that items at the beginning of a list are recalled better than other items on the list.

Primary appraisal An initial evaluation of whether an event is (1) irrelevant to oneself, (2) relevant, but not threatening, or (3) stressful.

Primary reinforcers Events that are inherently reinforcing because they satisfy biological needs.

Primary sex characteristics The sexual structures necessary for reproduction.

Proactive interference A memory problem that occurs when previously learned information interferes with the retention of new information.

Problem solving Active efforts to discover what must be done to achieve a goal that is not readily available.

Problem space The set of possible pathways to a solution considered by the problem solver.

Procedural memory system The repository of memories for actions, skills, and operations.

Prognosis A forecast about the probable course of an illness.

Programmed learning An approach to self-instruction in which information and questions are arranged in a sequence of small steps to permit active responding by the learner.

Projection Attributing one's own thoughts, feelings, or motives to another.

Projective tests Psychological tests that ask subjects to respond to vague, ambiguous stimuli in ways that may reveal the subjects' needs, feelings, and personality traits.

Prospective memory The ability to remember to perform actions in the future.

Proximal stimuli The stimulus energies that impinge directly on sensory receptors.

Proximity Geographic, residential, and other forms of spatial closeness.

Proximodistal trend The center-outward direction of motor development.

Psychiatrists Physicians who specialize in the diagnosis and treatment of psychological disorders.

Psychiatry A branch of medicine concerned with the diagnosis and treatment of psychological problems and disorders.

Psychoactive drugs Chemical substances that modify mental, emotional, or behavioral functioning.

Psychoanalysis An insight therapy that emphasizes the recovery of unconscious conflicts, motives, and defenses through techniques such as free association and transference.

Psychoanalytic theory A theory developed by Freud that attempts to explain personality, motivation, and mental disorders by focusing on unconscious determinants of behavior.

Psychodynamic theories All the diverse theories descended from the work of Sigmund Freud that focus on unconscious mental forces.

Psychogenic amnesia A sudden loss of memory for important personal information that is too extensive to be due to normal forgetting.

Psycholinguistics The study of the psychological mechanisms underlying the use of language.

Psychological dependence The condition that exists when a person must continue to take a drug in order to satisfy intense mental and emotional craving for the drug.

Psychological test A standardized measure of a sample of a person's behavior.

Psychology The science that studies behavior and the physiological and cognitive processes that underlie it, and the profession that applies the accumulated knowledge of this science to practical problems.

Psychopharmacotherapy The treatment of mental disorders with medication.

Psychophysics The study of how physical stimuli are translated into psychological experience.

Psychosexual stages According to Freud, developmental periods with a characteristic sexual focus that leave their mark on adult personality.

Psychosomatic diseases Physical ailments with a genuine organic basis that are caused in part by psychological factors, especially emotional distress.

Puberty The period of early adolescence marked by rapid physical growth and the development of sexual (reproductive) maturity.

Pubescence The two-year span preceding puberty during which the changes leading to physical and sexual maturity take place.

Punishment An event that follows a response that weakens or suppresses the tendency to make that response.

Pupil The opening in the center of the iris that helps regulate the amount of light passing into the rear chamber of the eye.

R

Random assignment The constitution of groups in a study such that all subjects have an equal chance of being assigned to any group or condition.

Rational-emotive therapy An approach to therapy that focuses on altering clients' patterns of irrational thinking to reduce maladaptive emotions and behavior.

Rationalization Creating false but plausible excuses to justify unacceptable behavior.

Reaction formation Behaving in a way that's exactly the opposite of one's true feelings.

Reaction range Genetically determined limits on IQ or other traits.

Reality monitoring The process of deciding whether memories are based on external sources (our perceptions of actual events) or internal sources (our thoughts and imaginations).

Reality principle According to Freud, the principle on which the ego operates, which seeks to delay gratification of the id's urges until appropriate outlets and situations can be found.

Recall measure of retention A memory test that requires subjects to reproduce information on their own without any cues.

Receiver The person to whom a message is sent.

Recency effect A memory problem that occurs when items near the end of a list are recalled better than other items on the list.

Receptive field of a visual cell The retinal area that, when stimulated, affects the firing of that cell.

Recessive gene A gene whose influence is masked when paired genes are different (heterozygous).

Reciprocal determinism The assumption that internal mental events, external environmental events, and overt behavior all influence each other.

Reciprocity Liking those who show that they like you.

Recognition measure of retention A memory test that requires subjects to select previously learned information from an array of options.

Reference group A particular group of people used as a standard in social comparisons.

Refractory period A time following orgasm during which males are largely unresponsive to further stimulation.

Regression A reversion to immature patterns of behavior.

Rehearsal The process of repetitively verbalizing or thinking about information to be stored in memory.

Reinforcement An event following a response that strengthens the tendency to make that response.

Reinforcement contingencies The circumstances or rules that determine whether responses lead to the presentation of reinforcers.

Relearning measure of retention A memory test that requires a subject to memorize information a second time to determine how much time or effort is saved by having learned it before.

Reliability The measurement consistency of a test (or of other kinds of measurement techniques).

REM sleep A deep stage of sleep marked by rapid eye movements, high-frequency brain waves, and dreaming.

Replication The repetition of a study to see whether the earlier results are duplicated.

Representativeness heuristic Basing the estimated probability of an event on how similar it is to the typical prototype of that event.

Repression Keeping distressing thoughts and feelings buried in the unconscious.

Research methods Differing approaches to the manipulation and control of variables in empirical studies.

Resistance Largely unconscious defensive maneuvers a client uses to hinder the progress of therapy.

Resistance to extinction In operant conditioning, the phenomenon that occurs when an organism continues to make a response after delivery of the reinforcer for it has been terminated.

Response set A tendency to respond to questions in a particular way that is unrelated to the content of the questions.

Respondent conditioning. See *Classical conditioning*.

Resting potential The stable, negative charge of a neuron when it is inactive.

Retention The proportion of material retained (remembered).

Retina The neural tissue lining the inside back surface of the eye; it absorbs light, processes images, and sends visual information to the brain.

Retinal disparity A cue to the depth based on the fact that objects within 25 feet project images to slightly different locations on the left and right retinas, so the right and left eyes see slightly different views of the object.

Retrieval Recovering information from memory stores.

Retroactive interference A memory problem that occurs when new information impairs the retention of previously learned information.

Retrograde amnesia Loss of memories for events that occurred prior to a head injury.

Retrospective memory The ability to remember events from the past or previously learned information.

Reversible figure A drawing that is compatible with two different interpretations that can shift back and forth.

Risky decision making Making choices under conditions of uncertainty.

Rods Specialized visual receptors that play a key role in night vision and peripheral vision.

S

Sample The collection of subjects selected for observation in an empirical study.

Sampling bias A problem that occurs when a sample is not representative of the population from which it is drawn.

Scatter diagram A graph in which paired X and Y scores for each subject are plotted as single points.

Schedule of reinforcement A specific presentation of reinforcers over time.

Schema An organized cluster of knowledge about a particular object or sequence of events.

Schizophrenic disorders A class of psychological disorders marked by disturbances in thought that spill over to affect perceptual, social, and emotional processes.

Script A type of schema that organizes what people know about common activities.

Seasonal affective disorder (SAD) A mood disorder in which the individual's periods of depression or mania tend to occur repeatedly at about the same time each year.

Secondary appraisal An evaluation of one's coping resources and options for dealing with a stressful event.

Secondary (conditioned) reinforcers Stimulus events that acquire reinforcing qualities by being associated with primary reinforcers.

Secondary sex characteristics Physical features that are associated with gender but that are not directly involved in reproduction.

Secondary traits Personality traits that surface in some situations, but not others.

Sedatives Sleep-inducing drugs that tend to decrease central nervous system activation and behavioral activity.

Self-actualizing persons People with exceptionally healthy personalities, marked by continued personal growth.

Self-concept A collection of beliefs about one's own nature, unique qualities, and typical behavior.

Self-efficacy One's belief about one's ability to perform behaviors that should lead to expected outcomes.

Self-esteem A person's overall assessment of her or his personal adequacy or worth.

Self-monitoring The degree to which people attend to and control the impression they make on others in social interactions.

Self-referent encoding Deciding how or whether information is personally relevant.

Self-report inventories Personality tests that ask individuals to answer a series of questions about their characteristic behavior.

Self-serving bias The tendency to attribute one's successes to personal factors and one's failures to situational factors.

Semantic memory system General knowledge that is not tied to the time when the information was learned.

Semantic network Concepts joined together by links that show how the concepts are related.

Sensate focus A sex therapy exercise in which partners take turns pleasuring each other with guided verbal feedback, while certain kinds of stimulation are temporarily forbidden.

Sensation The stimulation of sense organs.

Sensation seeking A generalized preference for high or low levels of sensory stimulation.

Sensory adaptation A gradual decline in sensitivity to prolonged stimulation.

Sensory memory The preservation of information in its original sensory form for a brief time, usually only a fraction of a second.

Sensory neurons Neurons that receive information from outside the nervous system.

Separation anxiety Emotional distress seen in many infants when they are separated from people with whom they have formed an attachment.

Serial-position effect In memory tests, the fact that subjects show better recall for items at the beginning and end of a list than for items in the middle.

Set point A natural point of stability in body weight.

Sex The biologically based categories of male and female.

Sex therapy The professional treatment of sexual dysfunctions.

Sexual dysfunctions Impairments in sexual functioning that cause subjective distress.

Sexual orientation A person's preference for emotional and sexual relationships with individuals of the same sex, the other sex, or either sex.

Shaping The reinforcement of closer and closer approximations of a desired response.

Short-term memory (STM) A limited-capacity store that can maintain unrehearsed information for about 20 to 30 seconds.

Signal-detection theory A psychophysiological theory proposing that the detection of stimuli involves decision processes as well as sensory processes, which are influenced by a variety of factors besides the physical intensity of a stimulus.

Skinner box A small enclosure in which an animal can make a specific response that is systematically recorded while the consequences of the response are controlled.

Sleep apnea A sleep disorder characterized by frequent reflexive gasping for air that awakens a person and disrupts sleep.

Slow-wave sleep (SWS) Sleep stages 3 and 4, during which low-frequency delta waves become prominent in EEG recordings.

Social clock A person's notion of a developmental schedule that specifies what he or she should have accomplished by certain points in life.

Social comparison theory The idea that people compare themselves with others to understand and evaluate their own behavior.

Social desirability bias A tendency to give socially approved answers to questions about oneself.

Social loafing A reduction in effort by individuals when they work in groups as compared to when they work by themselves.

Social psychology The branch of psychology concerned with the way individuals' thoughts, feelings, and behaviors are influenced by others.

Social schemas Organized clusters of ideas about categories of social events and people.

Social skills training A behavior therapy designed to improve interpersonal skills that emphasizes shaping, modeling, and behavioral rehearsal.

Social support Various types of aid and succor provided by members of one's social networks.

Socialization The acquisition of the norms, roles, and behaviors expected of people in a particular society.

Soma The cell body of a neuron; it contains the nucleus and much of the chemical machinery common to most cells.

Somatic nervous system The system of nerves that connect to voluntary skeletal muscles and to sensory receptors.

Somatization disorder A type of somatoform disorder marked by a history of diverse physical complaints that appear to be psychological in origin.

Somatoform disorders A class of psychological disorders involving physical ailments with no authentic organic basis that are due to psychological factors.

Somnambulism (sleepwalking) Arising and wandering about while remaining asleep.

Source The person who sends a communication.

Source monitoring The process of making attributions about the origins of memories.

Source-monitoring error An error that occurs when a memory derived from one source is misattributed to another source.

Spatial summation Creation of an excitatory postsynaptic potential when several or more PSPs occur simultaneously at different receptor sites.

Split-brain surgery A procedure in which the bundle of fibers that connects the cerebral hemispheres (the corpus callosum) is cut to reduce the severity of epileptic seizures.

Spontaneous recovery In classical conditioning, the reappearance of an extinguished response after a period of nonexposure to the conditioned stimulus.

Spontaneous remission Recovery from a disorder without formal treatment.

SQ3R A study system designed to promote effective reading by means of five steps: survey, question, read, recite, and review.

Stage A developmental period during which characteristic patterns of behavior are exhibited and certain capacities become established.

Standard deviation An index of the amount of variability in a set of data.

Standardization The uniform procedures used in the administration and scoring of a test.

State-dependent memory Improved recall that is attributed to being in the same emotional state during encoding and subsequent retrieval.

Statistical significance The condition that exists when the probability that the observed findings are due to chance is very low.

Statistics The use of mathematics to organize, summarize, and interpret numerical data. See also *Descriptive statistics, Inferential statistics.*

Stereotaxic instrument A device used to implant electrodes at precise locations in the brain.

Stereotypes Widely held beliefs that people have certain characteristics because of their membership in a particular group.

Stimulants Drugs that tend to increase central nervous system activation and behavioral activity.

Stimulus Any detectable input from the environment.

Stimulus contiguity A temporal (time) association between two events.

Stimulus discrimination The phenomenon that occurs when an organism that has learned a response to a specific stimulus does not respond in the same way to stimuli that are similar to the original stimulus.

Stimulus generalization The phenomenon that occurs when an organism that has learned a response to a specific stimulus responds in the same way to new stimuli that are similar to the original stimulus.

Storage Maintaining encoded information in memory over time.

Stress Any circumstances that threaten or are perceived to threaten one's well-being and that thereby tax one's coping abilities.

Striving for superiority According to Adler, the universal drive to adapt, improve oneself, and master life's challenges.

Structuralism A school of psychology based on the notion that the task of psychology is to analyze consciousness into its basic elements and to investigate how these elements are related.

Subjective contours The perception of contours where there really are none.

Subjects The persons or animals whose behavior is systematically observed in a study.

Subliminal perception The registration of sensory input without conscious awareness.

Subtractive color mixing Formation of colors by removing some wavelengths of light, leaving less light than was originally there.

Superego According to Freud, the moral component of personality that incorporates social standards about what represents right and wrong.

Surface structure The word arrangement used to express the underlying meaning of a sentence.

Survey A descriptive research method in which researchers use questionnaires or interviews to gather information about specific aspects of subjects' behavior.

Sympathetic division The branch of the autonomic nervous system that mobilizes the body's resources for emergencies.

Synapse A junction where information is transmitted from one neuron to the next.

Synaptic cleft A microscopic gap between the terminal button of a neuron and the cell membrane of another neuron.

Syntax A system of rules that specify how words can be combined into phrases and sentences.

Systematic desensitization A behavior therapy used to reduce clients' anxiety responses through counterconditioning.

T

Tactile system The sensory system for touch.

Tardive dyskinesia A neurological disorder marked by chronic tremors and involuntary spastic movements.

Telegraphic speech Speech that consists mainly of content words; articles, prepositions, and other less critical words are omitted.

Temperament An individual's characteristic mood, activity level, and emotional reactivity.

Temporal summation Creation of an excitatory postsynaptic potential when several or more PSPs follow one another in rapid succession at a receptor site.

Terminal buttons Small knobs at the end of axons that secrete chemicals called neurotransmitters.

Test norms Standards that provide information about where a score on a psychological test ranks in relation to other scores on that test.

Test-retest reliability A type of reliability estimated by comparing subjects' scores on two administrations of a test.

Testwiseness The ability to use the characteristics and format of a cognitive test to maximize one's score.

Thalamus A structure in the forebrain through which all sensory information (except smell) must pass to get to the cerebral cortex.

Theory A system of interrelated ideas that is used to explain a set of observations.

Threshold A dividing point between energy levels that do and do not have a detectable effect.

Tip-of-the-tongue phenomenon A temporary inability to remember something accompanied by a feeling that it's just out of reach.

Token economy A system for doling out symbolic reinforcers that are exchanged later for a variety of genuine reinforcers.

Tolerance A progressive decrease in a person's responsiveness to a drug.

Top-down processing In form perception, a progression from the whole to the elements.

Transfer-appropriate processing The situation that occurs when the initial processing of information is similar to the type of processing required by the subsequent measures of attention.

Transference In therapy, the phenomenon that occurs when clients start relating to their therapists in ways that mimic critical relationships in their lives.

Transvestism A sexual disorder in which a man achieves sexual arousal by dressing in women's clothing.

Trial In classical conditioning, any presentation of a stimulus or pair of stimuli.

Trial and error Trying possible solutions sequentially and discarding those that are in error until one works.

Trichromatic theory of color vision The theory that the human eye has three types of receptors with differing sensitivities to different wavelengths.

Twin studies A research design in which hereditary influence is assessed by comparing the resemblance of identical twins and fraternal twins with respect to a trait.

Type A personality Personality characterized by (1) a strong competitive orientation, (2) impatience and time urgency, and (3) anger and hostility.

Type B personality Personality characterized by relatively relaxed, patient, easygoing, amicable behavior.

U

Unconditioned response (UCR) An unlearned reaction to an unconditioned stimulus that occurs without previous conditioning.

Unconditioned stimulus (UCS) A stimulus that evokes an unconditioned response without previous conditioning.

Unconscious According to Freud, thoughts, memories, and desires that are well below the surface of conscious awareness but that nonetheless exert great influence on behavior.

Undifferentiated schizophrenia A type of schizophrenia marked by idiosyncratic mixtures of schizophrenic symptoms.

V

Validity The ability of a test to measure what it was designed to measure.

Variability The extent to which the scores in a data set tend to vary from each other and from the mean.

Variable-interval (VI) schedule A reinforcement schedule in which the reinforcer is given for the first response after a variable time interval has elapsed.

Variable-ratio (VR) schedule A reinforcement schedule in which the reinforcer is given after a variable number of nonreinforced responses.

Variables Any measurable conditions, events, characteristics, or behaviors that are controlled or observed in a study.

Vasocongestion Engorgement of blood vessels.

Vestibular system The sensory system that responds to gravity and keeps people informed of their body's location in space.

Visual cliff A glass platform that extends over a several-foot drop-off (the cliff), used in studying depth perception in infants.

Volley principle The theory holding that groups of auditory nerve fibers fire neural impulses in rapid succession, creating volleys of impulses.

W

Weber's law The theory stating that the size of a just noticeable difference is a constant proportion of the size of the initial stimulus.

Well-defined problems Problems in which the initial state, the goal state, and the constraints are clearly specified.

Z

Zygote A one-celled organism formed by the union of a sperm and an egg.

REFERENCES

Aamodt, M. G. (1991). *Applied industrial/organizational psychology.* Belmont, CA: Wadsworth.

Abeles, M., & Goldstein, M. H. (1970). Functional architecture in cat primary auditory cortex: Columnar organization and organization according to depth. *Journal of Neurophysiology, 33,* 172–187.

Aber, R., & Webb, W. B. (1986). Effects of a limited nap on night sleep in older subjects. *Psychology and Aging, 1,* 300–302.

Aboud, F. E. (1987). The development of ethnic self-identification and attitudes. In J. S. Phinney & M. J. Rotheram (Eds.), *Children's ethnic socialization: Pluralism and development.* Newbury Park, CA: Sage.

Abramov, I., & Gordon, J. (1994). Color appearance: On seeing red—or yellow, or green, or blue. *Annual Review of Psychology, 45,* 451–485.

Abrams, D., Wetherell, M., Cochrane, S., Hogg, M. A., & Turner, J. C. (1990). Knowing what to think by knowing who you are: Self-categorization and the nature of norm formation, conformity and group polarization. *British Journal of Social Psychology, 29,* 97–119.

Abrams, R. (1992). *Electroconvulsive therapy.* New York: Oxford University Press.

Abrams, R. (1993). ECT technique: Electrode placement, stimulus type, and treatment frequency. In C. E. Coffey (Ed.), *The clinical science of electroconvulsive therapy.* Washington, DC: American Psychiatric Press.

Abramson, L. Y., Metalsky, G. I., & Alloy, L. B. (1989). Hopelessness depression: A theory-based subtype of depression. *Psychological Review, 96,* 358–372.

Abramson, L. Y., Seligman, M. E. P., & Teasdale, J. (1978). Learned helplessness in humans: Critique and reformulation. *Journal of Abnormal Psychology, 87,* 32–48.

Adams, H. E., & Cassidy, J. F. (1993). The classification of abnormal behavior: An overview. In P. B. Sutker & H. E. Adams (Eds.), *Comprehensive handbook of psychopathology* (2nd ed.). New York: Plenum.

Adams, H. E., Wright, L. W., Jr., & Lohr, B. A. (1996). Is homophobia associated with homosexual arousal? *Journal of Abnormal Psychology, 105,* 440–445.

Adams, J. L. (1980). *Conceptual blockbusting.* San Francisco: W. H. Freeman.

Adams, J. S. (1965). Inequity in social exchange. In L. Berkowitz (Ed.), *Advances in experimental social psychology* (Vol. 2). New York: Academic Press.

Adams, L. T., Kasserman, J. E., Yearwood, A. A., Perfetto, G. A., Bransford, J. D., & Franks, J. J. (1988). Memory access: The effects of fact-oriented versus problem-oriented acquisition. *Memory & Cognition, 16,* 167–175.

Adams, R. D., & Victor, M. (1993). *Principles of neurology* (5th ed.). New York: McGraw-Hill.

Adams, R. J. (1989). Newborns' discrimination among mid- and long-wavelength stimuli. *Journal of Experimental Child Psychology, 47,* 130–141.

Adams, S. H. (1994). Role of hostility in women's health during midlife: A longitudinal study. *Health Psychology, 13,* 488–495.

Adcock, C. J. (1965). Thematic Apperception Test. In O. K. Buros (Ed.), *Sixth Mental Measurements Yearbook.* Highland Park, NY: Gryphon Press.

Ader, R., & Cohen, N. (1981). Conditioned immunopharmacologic responses. In R. Ader (Ed.), *Psychoneuroimmunology.* New York: Academic Press.

Ader, R., & Cohen, N. (1984). Behavior and the immune system. In W. D. Gentry (Ed.), *Handbook of behavioral medicine.* New York: Guilford Press.

Ader, R., & Cohen, N. (1993). Psychoneuroimmunology: Conditioning and stress. *Annual Review of Psychology, 44,* 53–85.

Adler, A. (1917). *Study of organ inferiority and its psychical compensation.* New York: Nervous and Mental Diseases Publishing Co.

Adler, A. (1927). *Practice and theory of individual psychology.* New York: Harcourt, Brace & World.

Adler, A. (1964). *Superiority and social interest: A collection of later writings* (Edited by H. L. Ansbacher & R. Ansbacher). New York: Viking Press.

Adler, C. S., & Adler, S. M. (1984). Biofeedback. In T. B. Karasu (Ed.), *The psychiatric therapies.* Washington, DC: American Psychiatric Association.

Affleck, G., Tennen, H., Urrows, S., & Higgins, P. (1994). Person and contextual features of daily stress reactivity: Individual differences in relations of undesirable daily events with mood disturbance and chronic pain intensity. *Journal of Personality and Social Psychology, 66*(2), 329–340.

Agnew, H. W., Webb, W. B., & Williams, R. L. (1964). The effects of stage 4 sleep deprivation. *Electroencephalography and Clinical Neurophysiology, 17,* 68–70.

Agnew, H. W., Webb, W. B., & Williams R. L. (1967). Comparison of stage 4 and 1-REM sleep deprivation. *Perceptual and Motor Skills, 24,* 851–858.

Agnoli, F., & Krantz, D. H. (1989). Suppressing natural heuristics by formal instruction: The case of the conjunction fallacy. *Cognitive Psychology, 21,* 515–550.

Agras, W. S., & Berkowitz, R. (1988). Behavior therapy. In J. A. Talbott, R. E. Hales, & S. C. Yudofsky (Eds.), *The American Psychiatric Press textbook of psychiatry.* Washington, DC: American Psychiatric Press.

Ainsworth, M. D. S. (1979). Attachment as related to mother-infant interaction. In J. S. Rosenblatt, R. A. Hinde, C. Beer, & M. Busnel (Eds.), *Advances in the study of behavior* (Vol. 9). New York: Academic Press.

Ainsworth, M. D. S., Blehar, M. C., Waters, E., & Wall, S. (1978). *Patterns of attachment: A psychological study of the strange situation.* Hillsdale, NJ: Erlbaum.

Ainsworth, M. D. S., & Bowlby, J. (1991). An ethological approach to personality development. *American Psychologist, 46,* 333–341.

Aitkin, L. (1986). *The auditory midbrain.* Clifton, NJ: Humana Press.

Ajzen, I. (1985). From intentions to actions: A theory of planned behavior. In J. Kuhl & J. Beckman (Eds.), *Action-control: From cognition to behavior.* Heidelberg: Springer.

Ajzen, I. (1991). The theory of planned behavior. *Organizational Behavior and Human Decision Processes, 50,* 179–211.

Ajzen, I., & Fishbein, M. (1980). *Understanding attitudes and predicting behavior.* Englewood Cliffs, NJ: Prentice-Hall.

Akerstedt, T. (1988). Sleepiness as a consequence of shift work. *Sleep, 11,* 17–34.

Albert, M. S. (1992). Alzheimer's disease: Cognitive aspects. In L. R. Squire (Ed.), *Encyclopedia of learning and memory.* New York: Macmillan.

Albert, M. S., & Moss, M. B. (1992). The assessment of memory disorders in patients with Alzheimer's disease. In L. R. Squire & N. Butters (Eds.), *Neuropsychology of memory* (2nd ed.). New York: Guilford Press.

Albert, R. D. (1988). The place of culture in modern psychology. In P. Bronstein & K. Quina (Eds.), *Teaching a psychology of people: Resources for gender and sociocultural awareness.* Washington, DC: American Psychological Association.

Aldag, R. J., & Fuller, S. R. (1993). Beyond fiasco: A reappraisal of the groupthink phenomenon and a new model of group decision processes. *Psychological Bulletin, 113,* 533–552.

Alexander, C. N., Chandler, H. M., Langer, E. J., Newman, R. I., & Davies J. L. (1989). Transcendental meditation, mindfulness, and longevity: An experimental study with the elderly. *Journal of Personality and Social Psychology, 57,* 950–964.

Alexander, C. N., Davies, J. L., Dixon, C. A., Dillbeck, M. C., Druker, S. M., Oetzel, R. M., Muehlman, J. M., & Orme-Johnson, D. W. (1990). Growth of higher states of consciousness: The Vedic psychology of human development. In C. N. Alexander & E. J. Langer (Eds.), *Higher stages of human development: Perspectives on adult growth.* New York: Oxford University Press.

Alexander, C. N., Rainforth, M. V., & Gelderloos, P. (1991). Transcendental Meditation, self actualization, and psychological health: A conceptual overview and statistical meta-analysis. *Journal of Social Behavior and Personality, 6*(5), 189–247.

Alexander, F. (1954). Psychoanalysis and psychotherapy. *Journal of the American Psychoanalytic Association, 2,* 722–733.

Alkon, D. L. (1989). Memory storage and neural systems. *Scientific American, 261,* 42–50.

Allen, J. M., Lam, R. W., Remick, R. A., & Sadovnick, A. D. (1993). Depressive symptoms and family history in seasonal and nonseasonal mood disorders. *American Journal of Psychiatry, 150,* 443–448.

Allen, K. M., Blascovich, J., Tomaka, J., & Kelsey, R. M. (1991). Presence of human friends and pet dogs as moderators of autonomic responses to stress in women. *Journal of Personality and Social Psychology, 61,* 582–589.

Allen, W. R. (1981). Moms, dads and boys: Race and sex differences in the socialization of male children. In L. E. Gary (Ed.), *Black men.* Beverly Hills, CA: Sage.

Allison, D. B., Heshka, S., Neale, M. C., Lykken, D. T., & Heymsfield, S. B. (1994). A genetic analysis of relative weight among 4,020 twin pairs, with an emphasis on sex effects. *Health Psychology, 13,* 362–365.

Allport, G. W. (1937). *Personality: A psychological interpretation.* New York: Holt.

Allport, G. W. (1961). *Pattern and growth in personality*. New York: Holt, Rinehart & Winston.

Altman, I. (1990). Centripetal and centrifugal trends in psychology. In L. Brickman & H. Ellis (Eds.), *Preparing psychologists for the 21st century: Proceedings of the National Conference on Graduate Education in Psychology*. Hillsdale, NJ: Erlbaum.

Amabile, T. M. (1983). *The social psychology of creativity*. New York: Springer-Verlag.

Amabile, T. M. (1990). Within you, without you: The social psychology of creativity, and beyond. In M. A. Runco & R. S. Albert (Eds.), *Theories of creativity*. Newbury Park, CA: Sage.

Amada, G. (1985). *A guide to psychotherapy*. Lanham, MD: Madison Books.

Ambady, N., & Rosenthal, R. (1993). Half a minute: Predicting teacher evaluations from thin slices of nonverbal behavior and physical attractiveness. *Journal of Personality and Social Psychology, 64*, 431–441.

American Association on Mental Retardation. (1992). *Mental retardation: Definition, classification, and systems of supports*. Washington, DC: Author.

American Psychiatric Association. (1952). *Diagnostic and statistical manual of mental disorders*. Washington, DC: Author.

American Psychiatric Association. (1968). *Diagnostic and statistical manual of mental disorders* (2nd ed.). Washington, DC: Author.

American Psychiatric Association. (1980). *Diagnostic and statistical manual of mental disorders* (3rd ed.). Washington, DC: Author.

American Psychiatric Association. (1987). *Diagnostic and statistical manual of mental disorders* (3rd ed., rev.). Washington, DC: Author.

American Psychiatric Association. (1993). *DSM-IV draft criteria*. Washington, DC: Author.

American Psychiatric Association. (1994). *Diagnostic and statistical manual of mental disorders* (4th ed.). Washington, DC: Author.

American Psychological Association. (1984). *Behavioral research with animals*. Washington, DC: Author.

American Psychological Association. (1992). Ethical principles of psychologists and code of conduct. *American Psychologist, 47*, 1597–1611.

American Psychological Association. (1993). *Profile of all APA members: 1993*. Washington, DC: Author.

Anand, B. K., & Brobeck, J. R. (1951). Hypothalamic control of food intake in rats and cats. *Yale Journal of Biology and Medicine, 24*, 123–140.

Anch, A. M., Browman, C. P., Mitler, M. M., & Walsh, J. K. (1988). *Sleep: A scientific perspective*. Englewood Cliffs, NJ: Prentice Hall.

Anderson, B. F. (1980). *The complete thinker*. Englewood Cliffs, NJ: Prentice-Hall.

Anderson, C. A., Miller, R. S., Riger, A. L., Dill, J. C., & Sedikides, C. (1994). Behavioral and characterological attributional styles as predictors of depression and loneliness: Review, refinement, and test. *Journal of Personality and Social Psychology, 66*, 549–558.

Anderson, K. J. (1990). Arousal and the inverted-U hypothesis: A critique of Neiss's "reconceptualizing arousal." *Psychological Bulletin, 107*, 96–100.

Anderson, S. M., & Klatzky, R. L. (1987). Traits and social stereotypes: Levels of categorization in person perception. *Journal of Personality and Social Psychology, 53*, 235–246.

Anderson, V. N. (1992). For whom is this world just? Sexual orientation and AIDS. *Journal of Applied Social Psychology, 22*(3), 248–259.

Andersson, B. E. (1992). Effects of day-care on cognitive and socioemotional competence of thirteen-year-old Swedish schoolchildren. *Child Development, 63*, 20–36.

Andreasen, N. C. (1987). Creativity and mental illness: Prevalence rates in writers and their first-degree relatives. *American Journal of Psychiatry, 144*, 1288–1292.

Andreasen, N. C. (1988). Brain imaging: Applications in psychiatry. *Science, 239*, 1381–1388.

Andreasen, N. C. (1990). Positive and negative symptoms: Historical and conceptual aspects. In N. C. Andreasen (Ed.), *Modern problems of pharmacopsychiatry: Positive and negative symptoms and syndromes*. Basel: Karger.

Anglin, J. M. (1993). Vocabulary development: A morphological analysis. *Monographs of the Society for Research in Child Development, 58*.

Angoff, W. H. (1988). The nature-nurture debate, aptitudes, and group differences. *American Psychologist, 43*(9), 713–720.

Annett, M. (1972). The distribution of manual asymmetry. *British Journal of Psychology, 63*, 343–358.

Annett, M. (1985). *Left, right, hand and brain: The right shift theory*. Hillsdale, NJ: Erlbaum.

Ansbacher, H. (1970, February). Alfred Adler, individual psychology. *Psychology Today*, pp. 42–44, 66.

Anthony, T., Copper, C., & Mullen, B. (1992). Cross-racial facial identification: A social cognitive integration. *Personality and Social Psychology Bulletin, 18*, 296–301.

Antill, J. K. (1987). Parents' beliefs and values about sex roles, sex differences, and sexuality: Their sources and implications. In P. Shaver & C. Hendrick (Eds.), *Sex and gender*. Newbury Park, CA: Sage.

Antrobus, J. (1993). Characteristics of dreams. In M. A. Carskadon (Ed.), *Encyclopedia of sleep and dreaming*. New York: Macmillan.

Apperson, L. J., Mulvey, E. P., & Lidz, C. W. (1993). Short-term clinical prediction of assaultive behavior: Artifacts of research methods. *American Journal of Psychiatry, 150*, 1374–1379.

Arendt, J. (1994). Clinical perspectives for melatonin and its agonists. *Biological Psychiatry, 35*, 1–2.

Arendt, J. (1996). Melatonin: Claims made in the popular media are mostly nonsense. *British Medical Journal, 312*, 1242–1243.

Arentewicz, G., & Schmidt, G. (Eds.). (1983). *The treatment of sexual disorders*. New York: Basic Books.

Arkin, A. M., & Antrobus, J. S. (1991). The effects of external stimuli applied prior to and during sleep on sleep experience. In S. J. Ellman & J. S. Antrobus (Eds.), *The mind in sleep: Psychology and psychophysiology* (2nd ed.). New York: Wiley.

Arkowitz, H. (1992). Integrative theories of therapy. In D. K. Freedheim (Ed.), *History of psychotherapy: A century of change*. Washington, DC: American Psychological Association.

Arnkoff, D. B., & Glass, C. R. (1992). Cognitive therapy and psychotherapy. In D. K. Freedheim (Ed.), *History of psychotherapy: A century of change*. Washington, DC: American Psychological Association.

Aron, A. (1988). The matching hypothesis reconsidered again: Comment on Kalick and Hamilton. *Journal of Personality and Social Psychology, 54*, 441–446.

Aron, A., & Westbay, L. (1996). Dimensions of the prototype of love. *Journal of Personality and Social Psychology, 70*, 535–551.

Aronson, E. (1980). Large commitments for small rewards. In L. Festinger (Ed.), *Retrospections on social psychology*. New York: Oxford University Press.

Aronson, E., Brewer, M., & Carlsmith, J. M. (1985). Experimentation in social psychology. In G. Lindzey & E. Aronson (Eds.), *Handbook of social psychology* (3rd ed., Vol. 1). New York: Random House.

Aronson, E., & Mills, J. (1959). The effect of severity of initiation on liking for a group. *Journal of Abnormal and Social Psychology, 59*, 177–181.

Arthur, A. Z. (1986). Stress of predictable and unpredictable shock. *Psychological Bulletin, 100*, 379–383.

Asch, S. E. (1951). Effects of group pressure on the modification and distortion of judgments. In H. Guetzkow (Ed.), *Groups, leadership and men*. Pittsburgh: Carnegie Press.

Asch, S. E. (1955). Opinions and social pressures. *Scientific American, 193*(5), 31–35.

Asch, S. E. (1956). Studies of independence and conformity: A minority of one against a unanimous majority. *Psychological Monographs, 70*(9, Whole No. 416).

Aschoff, J. (1981). *Handbook of behavioral neurobiology: Vol. 4. Biological rhythms*. New York: Plenum.

Aserinsky, E., & Kleitman, N. (1953). Regularly occurring periods of eye mobility and concomitant phenomena during sleep. *Science, 118*, 273–274.

Ash, M. G. (1985). Gestalt psychology: Origins in Germany and reception in the United States. In C. E. Buxton (Ed.), *Points of view in the modern history of psychology*. Orlando: Academic Press.

Aslin, R. N. (1987). Visual and auditory development in infancy. In J. D. Osofsky (Ed.), *Handbook of infant development* (2nd ed.). New York: Wiley.

Aslin, R. N., & Smith, L. B. (1988). Perceptual development. *Annual Review of Psychology, 39*, 435–473.

Aspinwall, L. G., & Taylor, S. E. (1992). Modeling cognitive adaptation: A longitudinal investigation of the impact of individual differences and coping on college adjustment and performance. *Journal of Personality and Social Psychology, 63*, 989–1003.

Asterita, M. F. (1985). *The physiology of stress*. New York: Human Sciences Press.

Atchley, R. C. (1982). The process of retirement: Comparing women and men. In M. Szinovacz (Ed.), *Women's retirement*. Beverly Hills, CA: Sage.

Atchley, R. C. (1991). *Social forces and aging*. Belmont, CA: Wadsworth.

Atkinson, J. W. (1974). The mainsprings of achievement-oriented activity. In J. W. Atkinson & J. O. Raynor (Eds.), *Motivation and achievement*. New York: Wiley.

Atkinson, J. W. (1981). Studying personality in the context of an advanced motivational psychology. *American Psychologist, 36*, 117–128.

Atkinson, J. W. (1992). Motivational determinants of thematic apperception. In C. P. Smith (Ed.), *Motivation and personality: Handbook of thematic content analysis*. New York: Cambridge University Press.

Atkinson, J. W., & Birch, D. (1978). *Introduction to motivation*. New York: Van Nostrand.

Atkinson, J. W., & Litwin, G. H. (1960). Achievement motive and test anxiety conceived as motive to approach success and to avoid failure.

Journal of Abnormal and Social Psychology, 60, 52–63.

Atkinson, R. C., & Raugh, M. R. (1975). An application of the mnemonic keyword method to the acquisition of a Russian vocabulary. *Journal of Experimental Psychology: Human Learning and Memory, 104,* 126–133.

Atkinson, R. C., & Shiffrin, R. M. (1968). Human memory: A proposed system and its control processes. In K. W. Spence & J. T. Spence (Eds.), *The psychology of learning and motivation* (Vol. 2). New York: Academic Press.

Atkinson, R. C., & Shiffrin, R. M. (1971). The control of short-term memory. *Scientific American, 225,* 82–90.

Atwood, M. E., & Polson, P. G. (1976). A process model for water jar problems. *Cognitive Psychology, 8,* 191–216.

Ault, R. L. (1977). *Children's cognitive development.* New York: Oxford University Press.

Austin, J. T., & Hanisch, K. A. (1990). Occupational attainment as a function of abilities and interests: A longitudinal analysis using Project TALENT data. *Journal of Applied Psychology, 75,* 77–86.

Averill, J. A. (1980). A constructivist view of emotion. In R. Plutchik & H. Kellerman (Eds.), *Emotion: Theory, research, and experience: Vol. 1. Theories of emotion.* New York: Academic Press.

Avery, D., & Winokur, G. (1978). Suicide, attempted suicide, and relapse rates in depression. *Archives of General Psychiatry, 35,* 749–753.

Axelrod, S., & Apsche, J. (1983). *The effects of punishment on human behavior.* New York: Academic Press.

Baars, B. J. (1986). *The cognitive revolution in psychology.* New York: Guilford Press.

Baddeley, A. D. (1976). *The psychology of memory.* New York: Basic Books.

Baddeley, A. D. (1989). The uses of working memory. In P. R. Soloman, G. R. Goethals, C. M. Kelley, & B. R. Stephens (Eds.), *Memory: Interdisciplinary approaches.* New York: Springer-Verlag.

Baddeley, A. D. (1992). Working memory. *Science, 255,* 556–559.

Baddeley, A. D., & Hitch, G. (1974). Working memory. In G. H. Bower (Ed.), *The psychology of learning and motivation* (Vol. 8). New York: Academic Press.

Badia, P. (1990). Memories in sleep: Old and new. In R. R. Bootzin, J. F. Kihlstrom, & D. L. Schacter (Eds.), *Sleep and cognition.* Washington, DC: American Psychological Association.

Bahrick, H. P., Bahrick, P. C., & Wittlinger, R. P. (1975). Fifty years of memories of names and faces: A cross-sectional approach. *Journal of Experimental Psychology: General, 104,* 54–75.

Bailey, J. M., & Pillard, R. C. (1991). A genetic study of male homosexual orientation. *Archives of General Psychology, 48,* 1089–1097.

Bailey, J. M., Pillard, R. C., Neale, M. C. I., & Agyei, Y. (1993). Heritable factors influence sexual orientation in women. *Archives of General Psychiatry, 50,* 217–223.

Bailey, J. M., & Zucker, K. J. (1995). Childhood sex-typed behavior and sexual orientation: A conceptual analysis and quantitative review. *Developmental Psychology, 31,* 43–55.

Baillargeon, R. (1987). Object permanence in 3.5- and 4.5-month-old infants. *Developmental Psychology, 23,* 655–664.

Baillargeon, R. (1994). How do infants learn about the physical world? *Current Directions in Psychological Science, 3,* 133–140.

Bakan, P. (1971, August). The eyes have it. *Psychology Today,* pp. 64–69.

Bakan, P. (1990). Nonright-handedness and the continuum of reproductive casualty. In S. Coren (Ed.), *Left-handedness: Behavioral implications and anomalies.* Amsterdam: North-Holland.

Baker, E. L. (1985). Psychoanalysis and psychoanalytic therapy. In S. J. Lynn & J. P. Garske (Eds.), *Contemporary psychotherapies: Models and methods.* Columbus, OH: Charles E. Merrill.

Baker, L. A., & Daniels, D. (1990). Nonshared environmental influences and personality differences in adult twins. *Journal of Personality and Social Psychology, 58,* 103–110.

Baker, S. W. (1980). Psychosexual differentiation in the human. *Biology of Reproduction, 22,* 61–72.

Ballenger, J. C. (1995). Benzodiazepines. In A. F. Schatzberg & C. B. Nemeroff (Eds.), *The American Psychiatric Press textbook of psychopharmacology.* Washington, DC: American Psychiatric Press.

Balsam, P. D. (1988). Selection, representation, and equivalence of controlling stimuli. In R. C. Atkinson, R. J. Herrnstein, G. Lindzey, & R. D. Luce (Eds.), *Stevens' handbook of experimental psychology.* New York: Wiley.

Baltes, P. B., & Kliegl, R. (1992). Further testing of limits of cognitive plasticity: Negative age differences in a mnemonic skill are robust. *Developmental Psychology, 28,* 121–125.

Bancroft, J., Sherwin, B., Alexander, G., Davidson, D., & Walker, A. (1991). Oral contraceptives, androgens, and the sexuality of young women: II. The role of androgens. *Archives of Sexual Behavior, 20,* 121–135.

Bandura, A. (1973). *Aggression: A social learning analysis.* Englewood Cliffs, NJ: Prentice-Hall.

Bandura, A. (1977). *Social learning theory.* Englewood Cliffs, NJ: Prentice-Hall.

Bandura, A. (1982). The psychology of chance encounters and life paths. *American Psychologist, 37,* 747–755.

Bandura, A. (1986). *Social foundations of thought and action: A social-cognitive theory.* Englewood Cliffs, NJ: Prentice-Hall.

Bandura, A. (1990). Perceived self-efficacy in the exercise of personal agency. *Journal of Applied Sport Psychology, 2*(2), 128–163.

Bandura, A. (1993). Perceived self-efficacy in cognitive development and functioning. *Educational Psychologist, 28*(2), 117–148.

Bandura, A. (1995). Exercise of personal and collective efficacy in changing societies. In A. Bandura (Ed.), *Self-efficacy in changing societies.* New York: Cambridge University Press.

Bandura, A., Ross, D., & Ross, S. A. (1961). Transmission of aggression through imitation of aggressive models. *Journal of Abnormal and Social Psychology, 63,* 575–582.

Bandura, A., Ross, D., & Ross, S. A. (1963a). Imitation of film-mediated aggressive models. *Journal of Abnormal and Social Psychology, 66,* 3–11.

Bandura, A., Ross, D., & Ross, S. A. (1963b). Vicarious reinforcement and imitative learning. *Journal of Abnormal and Social Psychology, 67*(6), 601–607.

Banks, M. S. (1980). The development of visual accommodation during early infancy. *Child Development, 51,* 646–666.

Banks, W. P., & Krajicek, D. (1991). Perception. *Annual Review of Psychology, 42,* 305–331.

Barbach, L. G. (1982). *For each other: Sharing sexual intimacy.* New York: Doubleday.

Barber, B. K. (1994). Cultural, family, and personal contexts of parent-adolescent conflict. *Journal of Marriage and the Family, 56,* 375–386.

Barber, T. X. (1979). Suggested ("hypnotic") behavior: The trance paradigm versus an alternative paradigm. In E. Fromm & R. E. Shor (Eds.), *Hypnosis: Developments in research and new perspectives.* New York: Aldine.

Barber, T. X. (1986). Realities of stage hypnosis. In B. Zilbergeld, M. G. Edelstien, & D. L. Araoz (Eds.), *Hypnosis: Questions and answers.* New York: Norton.

Bard, P. (1934). On emotional experience after decortication with some remarks on theoretical views. *Psychological Review, 41,* 309–329.

Barerra, M. E., & Maurer, D. (1981). Recognition of mother's photographed face by the three-month-old infant. *Child Development, 52,* 714–716.

Bar-Hillel, M. (1990). Back to base-rates. In R. M. Hogarth (Ed.), *Insights in decision making: A tribute to Hillel J. Einhorn.* Chicago: University of Chicago Press.

Barinaga, M. (1989). Manic depression gene put in limbo. *Science, 246,* 886–887.

Barlett, D. L., & Steele, J. B. (1979). *Empire: The life, legend and madness of Howard Hughes.* New York: Norton.

Barlow, D. H. (1996). Health care policy, psychotherapy research, and the future of psychotherapy. *American Psychologist, 50,* 1050–1058.

Barnett, P. A., & Gotlib, I. H. (1988). Psychosocial functioning and depression: Distinguishing among antecedents, concomitants, and consequences. *Psychological Bulletin, 104,* 97–126.

Baron, R. S., Cutrona, C. E., Hicklin, D., Russell, D. W., & Lubaroff, D. M. (1990). Social support and immune function among spouses of cancer patients. *Journal of Personality and Social Psychology, 59,* 344–352.

Baron, R. S., Vandello, J. A., & Brunsman, B. (1996). The forgotten variable in conformity research: Impact of task importance on social influence. *Journal of Personality and Social Psychology, 71,* 915–927.

Barr, H. M., Streissguth, A. P., Darby, B. L., & Sampson, P. D. (1990). Prenatal exposure to alcohol, caffeine, tobacco, and aspirin: Effects on fine and gross motor performance in 4-year-old children. *Developmental Psychology, 26,* 339–348.

Barrett, D. (1988–1989). Dreams of death. *Omega, 19*(2), 95–101.

Barrett, G. V., & Depinet, R. L. (1991). A reconsideration of testing for competence rather than intelligence. *American Psychologist, 46,* 1012–1024.

Barrett, M. D. (1982). The holophrastic hypothesis: Conceptual and empirical issues. *Cognition, 11,* 47–76.

Barrett, M. D. (1989). Early language development. In A. Slater & G. Bremner (Eds.), *Infant development.* London: Erlbaum.

Barron, F., & Harrington, D. M. (1981). Creativity, intelligence and personality. *Annual Review of Psychology, 32,* 439–476.

Barsky, A. J. (1988). The paradox of health. *New England Journal of Medicine, 318,* 414–418.

Barsky, A. J. (1989). Somatoform disorders. In H. I. Kaplan & B. J. Sadock (Eds.), *Comprehensive textbook of psychiatry/V.* Baltimore: Williams & Wilkins.

Barsky, A. J., Coeytaux, R. R., Sarnie, M. K., & Cleary, P. D. (1993). Hypochondriacal patients' beliefs about good health. *American Journal of Psychiatry, 150,* 1085–1090.

Barsky, A. J., Wyshak, G., & Klerman, G. L. (1990). The Somatosensory Amplification Scale and its relationship to hypochondriasis. *Journal of Psychiatry Research, 24,* 323–334.

Bartlett, F. C. (1932). *Remembering: A study in experimental and social psychology.* New York: Macmillan.

Bartlett, J. G. (1993). *The Johns Hopkins Hospital guide to medical care of patients with HIV infection* (3rd ed.). Baltimore, MD: Williams & Wilkins.

Bartoshuk, L. M. (1988). Taste. In R. C. Atkinson, R. J. Herrnstein, G. Lindzey, & R. D. Luce (Eds.), *Stevens' handbook of experimental psychology: Perception and motivation* (Vol. 1). New York: Wiley.

Bartoshuk, L. M. (1990). Distinctions between taste and smell relevant to the role of experience. In E. D. Capaldi & T. L. Powley (Eds.), *Taste, experience, and feeding.* Washington, DC: American Psychological Association.

Bartoshuk, L. M. (1991). Taste, smell and pleasure. In R. C. Bolles (Ed.), *The hedonics of taste.* Hillsdale, NJ: Erlbaum.

Bartoshuk, L. M. (1993a). Genetic and pathological taste variation: What can we learn from animal models and human disease? In D. Chadwick, J. Marsh, & J. Goode (Eds.), *The molecular basis of smell and taste transduction.* New York: Wiley.

Bartoshuk, L. M. (1993b). The biological basis of food perception and acceptance. *Food Quality and Preference, 4,* 21–32.

Bartoshuk, L. M., & Beauchamp, G. K. (1994). Chemical senses. *Annual Review of Psychology, 45,* 419–449.

Baruch, G. K. (1984). The psychological well-being of women in the middle years. In G. K. Baruch & J. Brooks-Gunn (Eds.), *Women in midlife.* New York: Plenum.

Basbaum, A. I., & Fields, H. L. (1984). Endogenous pain control systems: Brainstem spinal pathways and endorphin circuitry. *Annual Review of Neuroscience, 7,* 309–338.

Basgall, J. A., & Snyder, C. R. (1988). Excuses in waiting: External locus of control and reactions to success-failure feedback. *Journal of Personality and Social Psychology, 54,* 656–662.

Basow, S. A. (1992). *Gender: Stereotypes and roles.* Pacific Grove, CA: Brooks/Cole.

Bassuk, E. L., Rubin, L., & Lauriat, A. (1984). Is homelessness a mental health problem? *American Journal of Psychiatry, 141,* 1546–1550.

Bates, J. E. (1987). Temperament in infancy. In J. D. Osofsky (Ed.), *Handbook of infant development* (2nd ed.). New York: Wiley.

Bates, M. S., Edwards, W. T., & Anderson, K. O. (1993). Ethnocultural influences on variation in chronic pain perception. *Pain, 52*(1), 101–112.

Bauer, M. I., & Johnson-Laird, P. N. (1993). How diagrams can improve reasoning. *Psychological Science, 4,* 372–378.

Baum, A. S., & Burnes, D. W. (1993). *A nation in denial: The truth about homelessness.* Boulder, CO: Westview Press.

Baum, A., Grunberg, N. E., & Singer, J. E. (1992). Biochemical measurements in the study of emotion. *Psychological Science, 3,* 56–60.

Baumeister, R. F. (1984). Choking under pressure: Self-consciousness and paradoxical effects of incentives on skillful performance. *Journal of Personality and Social Psychology, 46,* 610–620.

Baumeister, R. F. (1989). The optimal margin of illusion. *Journal of Social and Clinical Psychology, 8,* 176–189.

Baumeister, R. F. (1995). Disputing the effects of championship pressures and home audiences. *Journal of Personality and Social Psychology, 68,* 644–648.

Baumeister, R. F., & Steinhilber, A. (1984). Paradoxical effects of supportive audiences on performance under pressure: The home field disadvantage in sports championships. *Journal of Personality and Social Psychology, 47,* 85–93.

Baumeister, R. J., & Leary, M. R. (1995). The need to belong: Desire for interpersonal attachments as a fundamental human motivation. *Psychological Bulletin, 117,* 497–529.

Baumrind, D. (1964). Some thoughts on the ethics of reading Milgram's "Behavioral study of obedience." *American Psychologist, 19,* 421–423.

Baumrind, D. (1985). Research using intentional deception: Ethical issues revisited. *American Psychologist, 40,* 165–174.

Bayley, N. (1949). Consistency and variability in the growth of intelligence from birth to eighteen years. *Journal of Genetic Psychology, 75,* 165–196.

Baylis, G. C., & Driver, J. (1995). One-sided edge assignment in vision: 1. Figure-ground segmentation and attention to objects. *Current Directions in Psychological Science, 4,* 140–146.

Beahrs, J. O. (1983). Co-consciousness: A common denominator in hypnosis, multiple personality and normalcy. *American Journal of Clinical Hypnosis, 26*(2), 100–113.

Beaman, A. L. (1991). An empirical comparison of meta-analytic and traditional reviews. *Personality and Social Psychology Bulletin, 17,* 252–257.

Beardsley, R. S., Gardocki, G. J., Larson, D. B., & Hidalgo, J. (1988). Prescribing of psychotropic medication by primary care physicians and psychiatrists. *Archives of General Psychiatry, 45,* 1117–1119.

Beauchamp, G. K., Cowart, B. J., & Moran, M. (1986). Developmental changes in salt acceptability in human infants. *Developmental Psychobiology, 19,* 17–25.

Beautrais, A. L., Joyce, P. R., Mulder, R. T., Fergusson, D. M., Deavoll, B. J., & Nightingale, S. K. (1996). Prevalence and comorbidity of mental disorders in persons making serious suicide attempts: A case-control study. *American Journal of Psychiatry, 153,* 1009–1014.

Beck, A. T. (1976). *Cognitive therapy and the emotional disorders.* New York: International Universities Press.

Beck, A. T. (1987). Cognitive therapy. In J. K. Zeig (Ed.), *The evolution of psychotherapy.* New York: Brunner/Mazel.

Beck, A. T. (1988). Cognitive approaches to panic disorder: Theory and therapy. In S. Rachman & J. Maser (Eds.), *Panic: Psychological perspectives.* Hillsdale, NJ: Erlbaum.

Beck, A. T. (1991). Cognitive therapy: A 30-year retrospective. *American Psychologist, 46,* 368–375.

Beck, A. T., Rush, A. J., Shaw, B. F., & Emery, G. (1979). *Cognitive therapy of depression.* New York: Guilford Press.

Becker, B. J. (1986). Influence again: An examination of reviews and studies of gender differences in social influence. In J. S. Hyde & M. C. Linn (Eds.), *The psychology of gender: Advances through meta-analysis.* Baltimore: Johns Hopkins University Press.

Becker, H. S. (1973). *Outsiders: Studies in the sociology of deviance.* New York: Free Press.

Becker, R. E. (1990). Social skills training. In A. S. Bellack & M. Hersen (Eds.), *Handbook of comparative treatments for adult disorders.* New York: Wiley.

Beecher, H. K. (1956). Relationship of significance of wound to pain experience. *Journal of the American Medical Association, 161,* 1609–1613.

Beilin, H. (1992). Piaget's enduring contribution to developmental psychology. *Developmental Psychology, 28,* 191–204.

Bekerian, D. A., & Bowers, J. M. (1983). Eyewitness testimony: Were we misled? *Journal of Experimental Psychology: Learning, Memory, and Cognition, 1,* 139–145.

Békésy, G. von. (1947). The variation of phase along the basilar membrane with sinusoidal vibrations. *Journal of the Acoustical Society of America, 19,* 452–460.

Bell, A. P., Weinberg, M. S., & Hammersmith, S. K. (1981). *Sexual preference: Its development in men and women.* Bloomington: Indiana University Press.

Beller, M., & Gafni, N. (1996). The 1991 international assessment of educational progress in mathematics and sciences: The gender differences perspective. *Journal of Educational Psychology, 88,* 365–377.

Bellisle, F. (1979). Human feeding behavior. *Neuroscience and Biobehavioral Reviews, 3,* 163–169.

Belmont, J. M. (1994). Organic mental retardation. In R. J. Sternberg (Ed.), *Encyclopedia of human intelligence.* New York: Macmillan.

Belsky, J. (1985). Exploring differences in marital change across the transition to parenthood: The role of violated expectations. *Journal of Marriage and the Family, 47,* 1037–1044.

Belsky, J. (1988). The "effects" of infant day care reconsidered. *Early Childhood Research Quarterly, 3,* 235–272.

Belsky, J. (1990a). Children and marriage. In F. D. Fincham & T. N. Bradbury (Eds.), *The psychology of marriage: Basic issues and applications.* New York: Guilford Press.

Belsky, J. (1990b). Infant day care, child development, and family policy. *Society, 27*(5), 10–12.

Belsky, J. (1992). Consequences of child care for children's development: A deconstructionist view. In A. Booth (Ed.), *Child care in the 1990s.* Hillsdale, NJ: Erlbaum.

Belsky, J., Fish, M., & Isabella, R. (1991). Continuity and discontinuity in infant negative and infant positive emotionality: Family antecedents and attachment consequences. *Developmental Psychology, 27,* 421–431.

Bem, D. J. (1967). Self-perception: An alternative interpretation of cognitive dissonance phenomena. *Psychological Review, 74,* 183–200.

Bem, S. L. (1985). Androgyny and gender schema theory: A conceptual and empirical integration. In T. B. Sonderegger (Ed.), *Nebraska symposium on motivation, 1984: Psychology and gender* (Vol. 32). Lincoln: University of Nebraska Press.

Benassi, V. A., Sweeney, P. D., & Dufour, C. L. (1988). Is there a relationship between locus of control orientation and depression? *Journal of Abnormal Psychology, 97,* 357–367.

Benbow, C. P. (1988). Sex differences in mathematical reasoning ability in intellectually talented preadolescents: Their nature, effects, and possible causes. *Behavioral and Brain Sciences, 11,* 169–232.

Benet, V., & Waller, N. G. (1995). The big seven factor model of personality description: Evidence for its cross-cultural generality in a Spanish sample. *Journal of Personality and Social Psychology, 69,* 701–718.

Benjamin, L. (1993). *Interpersonal diagnosis and treatment of personality disorders: A structural approach.* New York: Guilford Press.

Benjamin, L. T., Jr., Cavell, T. A., &

Shallenberger, W. R, III. (1984). Staying with initial answers on objective tests: Is it a myth? *Teaching of Psychology, 11,* 133–141.

Benjamin, L. T., Jr., Durkin, M., Link, M., Vestal, M., & Acord, J. (1992). Wundt's American doctoral students. *American Psychologist, 47,* 123–131.

Bennett, H. L. (1993). The mind during surgery: The uncertain effects of anesthesia. *Advances, 9*(1), 5–16.

Benson, H. (1975). *The relaxation response.* New York: Morrow.

Benson, H., & Klipper, M. Z. (1988). *The relaxation response.* New York: Avon.

Berardo, D. H., Shehan, C. L., & Leslie, G. R. (1987). A residue of tradition: Jobs, careers, and spouses' time in housework. *Journal of Marriage and the Family, 49,* 381–390.

Berenbaum, S. A., & Snyder, E. (1995). Early hormonal influences on childhood sex-typed activity and playmate preferences: Implications for the development of sexual orientation. *Developmental Psychology, 31,* 31–42.

Berger, H. (1929). Über das elektrenkephalogramm des menschen. *Archiv für Psychiatrie und Nervenkrankheiten, 99,* 555–574.

Bergin, A. E. (1971). The evaluation of therapeutic outcomes. In A. E. Bergin & S. L. Garfield (Eds.), *Handbook of psychotherapy and behavior change: An empirical analysis.* New York: Wiley.

Berkowitz, L. (1969). The frustration-aggression hypothesis revisited. In L. Berkowitz (Ed.), *Roots of aggression: A re-examination of the frustration-aggression hypothesis.* New York: Atherton.

Berkowitz, L. (1989). Frustration-aggression hypothesis: Examination and reformulation. *Psychological Bulletin, 106,* 59–73.

Bermant, G., & Davidson, J. M. (1974). *Biological bases of sexual behavior.* New York: Harper & Row.

Bernal, E. M. (1984). Bias in mental testing: Evidence for an alternative to the heredity-environment controversy. In C. R. Reynolds & R. T. Brown (Eds.), *Perspectives on bias in mental testing.* New York: Plenum.

Bernstein, I. L., & Meachum, C. L. (1990). Food aversion learning: Its impact on appetite. In E. D. Capaldi & T. L. Powley (Eds.), *Taste, experience, and feeding.* Washington, DC: American Psychological Association.

Berquier, A., & Ashton, R. (1992). Characteristics of the frequent nightmare sufferer. *Journal of Abnormal Psychology, 101,* 246–250.

Berry, D. T. R., Wetter, M. W., & Baer, R. A. (1995). Assessment of malingering. In J. N. Butcher (Ed.), *Clinical personality assessment: Practical Approaches.* New York: Oxford University Press.

Berry, J. W. (1976). *Human ecology and cognitive style: Comparative studies in cultural and psychological adaptation.* New York: Sage/Halsted.

Berry, J. W. (1990). Cultural variations in cognitive style. In S. P. Wapner (Ed.), *Bio-psycho-social factors in cognitive style.* Hillsdale, NJ: Erlbaum.

Berry, J. W. (1994). Cross-cultural variations in intelligence. In R. J. Sternberg (Ed.), *Encyclopedia of human intelligence.* New York: Macmillan.

Berry, J. W., Poortinga, Y., Segall, M., & Dasen, P. (1992). *Cross-cultural psychology.* New York: Cambridge University Press.

Berscheid, E. (1988). Some comments on love's anatomy: Or, whatever happened to old-fashioned lust. In R. J. Sternberg & M. L. Barnes (Eds.), *The psychology of love.* New Haven, CT: Yale University Press.

Berscheid, E., & Walster, E. (1978). *Interpersonal attraction.* Reading, MA: Addison-Wesley.

Bertenthal, B. I., & Campos, J. J. (1990). A systems approach to the organizing effects of self-produced locomotion during infancy. In C. Rovee-Collier (Ed.), *Advances in infancy research* (Vol. 6). Norwood, NJ: Ablex.

Bertenthal, B., Campos, J. J., & Kermoian, R. (1994). An epigenetic perspective on the development of self-produced locomotion and its consequences. *Current Directions in Psychological Science, 3,* 140–145.

Bertrand, L. D. (1989). The assessment and modification of hypnotic susceptibility. In N. P. Spanos & J. F. Chaves (Eds.), *Hypnosis: The cognitive-behavioral perspective.* Buffalo, NY: Prometheus.

Best, D. L., & Ornstein, P. A. (1986). Children's generation and communication on mnemonic organizational strategies. *Developmental Psychology, 22,* 845–853.

Betancourt, H., & Lopez, S. R. (1993). The study of culture, ethnicity, and race in American psychology. *American Psychologist, 48,* 629–637.

Beutler, L. E., Machado, P. P. P., & Neufeldt, S. A. (1994). Therapist variables. In A. E. Bergin & S. L. Garfield (Eds.), *Handbook of psychotherapy and behavior change* (4th ed.). New York: Wiley.

Biederman, I., Hilton, H. J., & Hummel, J. E. (1991). Pattern goodness and pattern recognition. In G. R. Lockhead & J. R. Pomerantz (Eds.), *The perception of structure.* Washington, DC: American Psychological Association.

Biener, L., & Abrams, D. B. (1991). The contemplation ladder: Validation of a measure of readiness to consider smoking cessation. *Health Psychology, 10,* 360–365.

Binet, A. (1911). Nouvelle recherches sur la mesure du niveau intellectuel chez les enfants d'école. *L'Année Psychologique, 17,* 145–201.

Binet, A., & Simon, T. (1905). Méthodes nouvelles pour le diagnostic du niveau intellectuel des anormaux. *L'Année Psychologique, 11,* 191–244.

Binet, A., & Simon, T. (1908). Le développement de l'intelligence chez les enfants. *L'Année Psychologique, 14,* 1–94.

Birch, L. L. (1987). The acquisition of food acceptance patterns in children. In R. A. Boakes, D. A. Popplewell, & M. J. Burton (Eds.), *Eating habits: Food, physiology and learned behaviour.* New York: Wiley.

Birch, L. L. (1990). The control of food intake by young children: The role of learning. In E. D. Capaldi & T. L. Powley (Eds.), *Taste, experience, and feeding.* Washington, DC: American Psychological Association.

Birch, L. L., McPhee, L., Sullivan, S., & Johnson, S. (1989). Conditioned meal initiation in young children. *Appetite, 13,* 105–113.

Birchler, G. R. (1992). Marriage. In V. B. Van Hasselt & M. Hersen (Eds.), *Handbook of social development: A lifespan perspective.* New York: Plenum.

Birnbaum, M. H., Anderson, C. J., & Hynan, L. G. (1990). Theories of bias in probability judgement. In J. P. Caverni, J. M. Fabre, & M. Gonzalez (Eds.), *Cognitive biases.* Amsterdam: North-Holland.

Bjork, R. A. (1992). Interference and forgetting. In L. R. Squire (Ed.), *Encyclopedia of learning and memory.* New York: Macmillan.

Black, D. W., & Andreasen, N. C. (1994). Schizophrenia, schizophreniform disorder, and delusional (paranoid) disorder. In R. E. Hales, S. C. Yudofsky, & J. A. Talbott (Eds.), *The American Psychiatric Press textbook of psychiatry* (2nd ed.). Washington, DC: American Psychiatric Press.

Black, D. W., & Winokur, G. (1990). Suicide and psychiatric diagnosis. In S. J. Blumenthal & D. J. Kupfer (Eds.), *Suicide over the life cycle: Risk factors, assessment, and treatment of suicidal patients.* Washington, DC: American Psychiatric Press.

Blair, S. L., & Johnson, M. P. (1992). Wives' perceptions of the fairness of the division of household labor: The intersection of housework and ideology. *Journal of Marriage and the Family, 54,* 570–581.

Blair, S. N., Kohl, H. W., Gordon, N. F., & Paffenbarger, R. S. (1992). How much physical activity is good for health? In G. S. Omenn, J. E. Fielding, & L. B. Lave (Eds.), *Annual review of public health* (Vol. 13). Palo Alto, CA: Annual Reviews.

Blair, S. N., Kohl, H. W., Paffenbarger, R. S., Clark, D. G., Cooper, K. H., & Gibbons, L. W. (1989). Physical fitness and all-cause mortality: A prospective study of healthy men and women. *Journal of the American Medical Association, 262,* 2395–2401.

Blakeslee, T. R. (1980). *The right brain.* Garden City, NY: Doubleday/Anchor.

Blanchard, E. B. (1994). Behavioral medicine and health psychology. In A. E. Bergin & S. L. Garfield (Eds.), *Handbook of psychotherapy and behavior change* (4th ed.). New York: Wiley.

Blanchard, F. A., Lilly, T., & Vaughn, L. A. (1991). Reducing the expression of racial prejudice. *Psychological Science, 2,* 101–105.

Blanchard, R., Zucker, K. J., Bradley, S. J., & Hume, C. S. (1995). Birth order and siblings sex ratio in homosexual male adolescents and probably prehomosexual feminine boys. *Developmental Psychology, 31,* 22–30.

Blaney, P. H. (1986). Affect and memory: A review. *Psychological Bulletin, 99,* 229–246.

Blascovich, J., & Katkin, E. S. (1993). Cardiovascular reactivity to psychological stress and disease: Conclusions. In J. Blascovich & E. S. Katkin (Eds.), *Cardiovascular reactivity to psychological stress and disease.* Washington, DC: American Psychological Association.

Blass, T. (1991). Understanding behavior in the Milgram obedience experiment: The role of personality, situations, and their interactions. *Journal of Personality and Social Psychology, 60,* 398–413.

Blau, Z. S. (1981). *Black children/white children: Competence, socialization and social structure.* New York: Free Press.

Blazer, D. G., Hughes, D., & George, L. K. (1987). Stressful life events and the onset of generalized anxiety syndrome. *American Journal of Psychiatry, 144,* 1178–1183.

Blazer, D. G., Hughes, D., George, L. K., Swartz, M., & Boyer, R. (1991). Generalized anxiety disorder. In L. N. Robins & D. A. Regier (Eds.), *Psychiatric disorders in America: The epidemiologic catchment area study.* New York: Free Press.

Bleier, R. (1988). A decade of feminist critiques in the natural sciences. *Signs: Journal of Women in Culture and Society, 14,* 186–195.

Bleuler, E. (1911). *Dementia praecox or the group F schizophrenias.* New York: International Universities Press.

Blieszner, R., & Adams, R. G. (1992). *Adult friendship.* Newbury Park, CA: Sage.

Bliwise, D. L. (1994). Normal aging. In M. H. Kryger, T. Roth, & W. C. Dement (Eds.), *Principles and practice of sleep medicine* (2nd ed.). Philadelphia: Saunders.

Block, J. (1981). Some enduring and consequential structures of personality. In A. I. Rabins, J. Aronoff, A. Barclay & R. Zucker (Eds.), *Further explorations in personality*. New York: Wiley.

Block, J. (1995). A contrarian view of the five-factor approach to personality description. *Psychological Bulletin, 117*, 187–215.

Block, J. H., & Block, J. (1980). The role of ego-control and ego-resiliency in the organization of behavior. In W. A. Collins (Ed.), *Minnesota symposia on child psychology* (Vol. 13). Hillsdale, NJ: Erlbaum.

Bloodworth, R. C. (1987). Major problems associated with marijuana abuse. *Psychiatric Medicine, 3*(3), 173–184.

Bloom, A. H. (1981). *The linguistic shaping of thought: A study of the impact of language on thinking in China and the West*. Hillsdale, NJ: Erlbaum.

Bloom, B. L. (1984). *Community mental health: A general introduction*. Pacific Grove, CA: Brooks/Cole.

Bloom, B. S. (Ed.). (1985). *Developing talent in young people*. New York: Ballantine.

Bloomfield, H. H., & Kory, R. B. (1976). *Happiness: The TM program, psychiatry, and enlightenment*. New York: Simon & Schuster.

Blum, K. (1984). *Handbook of abusable drugs*. New York: Gardner Press.

Boehm, A. E. (1985). Educational applications of intelligence testing. In B. B. Wolman (Ed.), *Handbook of intelligence: Theories, measurements, and applications*. New York: Wiley.

Boehm, L. E. (1994). The validity effect: A search for mediating variables. *Personality and Social Psychology Bulletin, 20*, 285–293.

Bogen, J. E. (1969). The other side of the brain II: An appositional mind. *Bulletin of the Los Angeles Neurological Society, 34*, 135–162.

Bogen, J. E. (1985). The dual brain: Some historical and methodological aspects. In D. F. Benson & E. Zaidel (Eds.), *The dual brain: Hemispheric specialization in humans*. New York: Guilford Press.

Bogen, J. E. (1990). Partial hemispheric independence with the neocommissures intact. In C. Trevarthen (Ed.), *Brain circuits and functions of the mind. Essays in honor of Roger W. Sperry*. Cambridge, MA: Cambridge University Press.

Bohannon, J. N., III, MacWhinney, B., & Snow, C. (1990). No negative evidence revisited: Beyond learnability or who has to prove what to whom. *Developmental Psychology, 26*, 221–226.

Bohannon, J. N., III, & Stanowicz, L. (1988). The issue of negative evidence: Adult responses to children's language errors. *Developmental Psychology, 24*, 684–689.

Bohannon, J. N., III, & Warren-Leubecker, A. (1989). Theoretical approaches to language acquisition. In J. Berko Gleason (Ed.), *The development of language*. Columbus, OH: Merrill.

Bolger, N. (1990). Coping as a personality process: A prospective study. *Journal of Personality and Social Psychology, 59*, 525–537.

Bolles, R. C. (1975). *Theory of motivation*. New York: Harper & Row.

Bolles, R. C., & Fanselow, M. S. (1980). A perceptual-defensive-recuperative model of fear and pain. *Behavioral and Brain Sciences, 3*, 291–323.

Bond, C. F., Jr., Pitre, U., & Van Leeuwen, M. D. (1991). Encoding operations and the next-in-line effect. *Personality and Social Psychology Bulletin, 17*, 435–441.

Bond, R., & Smith, P. B. (1996). Culture and conformity: A meta-analysis of studies using Asch's line judgment task. *Psychological Bulletin, 119*, 111–137.

Bonn, D. (1996). Melatonin's multifarious marvels: Miracle or myth? *Lancet, 347*, 184.

Bonnet, M. H. (1982). Performance during sleep. In W. B. Webb (Ed.), *Biological rhythms, sleep and performance*. New York: Wiley.

Bonnet, M. H. (1991). Sleep deprivation. In M. Kryger, T. Roth, & W. C. Dement (Eds.), *Principles and practice of sleep medicine* (2nd ed.). Philadelphia: Saunders.

Bonnet, M. H. (1994). Sleep deprivation. In M. H. Kryger, T. Roth, & W. C. Dement (Eds.), *Principles and practice of sleep medicine* (2nd ed.). Philadelphia: Saunders.

Bootzin, R. R., Manber, R., Perlis, M. L., Salvio, M. A., & Wyatt, J. K. (1993). Sleep disorders. In P. B. Sutker & H. E. Adams (Eds.), *Comprehensive handbook of psychopathology* (2nd ed.). New York: Plenum.

Borbely, A. A. (1984). Sleep regulation: Outline of a model and its implications for depression. In A. A. Borbely & J. L. Valatx (Eds.), *Sleep mechanisms*. Berlin: Springer-Verlag.

Borbely, A. A. (1986). *Secrets of sleep*. New York: Basic Books.

Borbely, A. A. (1994). Sleep homeostasis and models of sleep regulation. In M. H. Kryger, T. Roth, & W. C. Dement (Eds.), *Principles and practice of sleep medicine* (2nd ed.). Philadelphia: Saunders.

Borbely, A. A., Achermann, P., Trachsel, L., & Tobler, I. (1989). Sleep initiation and initial sleep intensity: Interactions of homeostatic and circadian mechanisms. *Journal of Biological Rhythms, 4*(2), 149–160.

Bores-Rangel, E., Church, A. T., Szendre, D., & Reeves, C. (1990). Self-efficacy in relation to occupational consideration and academic performance in high school equivalency students. *Journal of Counseling Psychology, 37*, 407–418.

Boring, E. G. (1966). A note on the origin of the word psychology. *Journal of the History of the Behavioral Sciences, 2*, 167.

Bornstein, M. H. (1992). Perception across the lifespan. In M. H. Bornstein & M. E. Lamb (Eds.), *Developmental psychology: An advanced textbook* (3rd ed.). Hillsdale, NJ: Erlbaum.

Bornstein, R. F. (1989). Subliminal techniques as propaganda tools: Review and critique. *Journal of Mind and Behavior, 10*, 231–262.

Bornstein, R. F. (1992). Subliminal mere exposure effects. In R. F. Bornstein & T. S. Pittman (Eds.), *Perception without awareness: Cognitive, clinical, and social perspectives*. New York: Guilford Press.

Bouchard, T. J., Jr., Lykken, D. T., McGue, M., Segal, N. L., & Tellegen, A. (1990). Sources of human psychological differences: The Minnesota study of twins reared apart. *Science, 250*, 223–228.

Bouchard, T. J., Jr., & Segal, N. L. (1985). Environment and IQ. In B. B. Wolman (Ed.), *Handbook of intelligence: Theories, measurements and applications*. New York: Wiley.

Bourguignon, E. (1972). Dreams and altered states of consciousness in anthropological research. In F. L. K. Hsu (Ed.), *Psychological anthropology* (2nd ed.). Cambridge, MA: Schenkman.

Bousfield, W. A. (1953). The occurrence of clustering in the recall of randomly arranged associates. *Journal of General Psychology, 49*, 229–240.

Bouton, M. E. (1991). Context and retrieval in extinction and in other examples of interference in simple associative learning. In L. Dachowski & C. F. Flaherty (Eds.), *Current topics in animal learning: Brain, emotion, and cognition*. Hillsdale, NJ: Erlbaum.

Bouton, M. E. (1994). Context, ambiguity, and classical conditioning. *Current Directions in Psychological Science, 3*, 49–53.

Bowden, C. L. (1995). Treatment of bipolar disorder. In A. F. Schatzberg & C. B. Nemeroff (Eds.), *The American Psychiatric Press textbook of psychopharmacology*. Washington, DC: American Psychiatric Press.

Bower, G. H. (1970). Organizational factors in memory. *Cognitive Psychology, 1*, 18–46.

Bower, G. H. (1981). Mood and memory. *American Psychologist, 36*, 129–148.

Bower, G. H., Black, J. B., & Turner, T. J. (1979). Scripts in memory for text. *Cognitive Psychology, 11*, 177–220.

Bower, G. H., & Clapper, J. P. (1989). Experimental methods in cognitive science. In M. I. Posner (Ed.), *Foundations of cognitive science*. Cambridge, MA: MIT Press.

Bower, G. H., & Clark, M. C. (1969). Narrative stories as mediators of serial learning. *Psychonomic Science, 14*, 181–182.

Bower, G. H., Clark, M. C., Lesgold, A. M., & Winzenz, D. (1969). Hierarchical retrieval schemes in recall of categorized word lists. *Journal of Verbal Learning and Verbal Behavior, 8*, 323–343.

Bower, G. H., & Mayer, J. D. (1991). In search of mood-dependent retrieval. In D. Kuiken (Ed.), *Mood and memory*. Newbury Park, CA: Sage.

Bower, G. H., & Springston, F. (1970). Pauses as recoding points in letter series. *Journal of Experimental Psychology, 83*, 421–430.

Bowlby, J. (1969). *Attachment and loss: Vol. 1. Attachment*. New York: Basic Books.

Bowlby, J. (1973). *Attachment and loss: Vol. 2. Separation, anxiety and anger*. New York: Basic Books.

Bowlby, J. (1980). *Attachment and loss: Vol. 3. Sadness and depression*. New York: Basic Books.

Bowmaker, J. K., & Dartnall, H. J. A. (1980). Visual pigments of rods and cones in a human retina. *Journal of Physiology, 298*, 501–511.

Boynton, R. M. (1990). Human color perception. In K. N. Leibovic (Ed.), *Science of vision*. New York: Springer-Verlag.

Boynton, R. M., & Gordon, J. (1965). Bezold-Brucke hue shift measured by color naming technique. *Journal of the Optical Society of America, 55*, 78–86.

Bozarth, M. A., & Wise, R. A. (1985). Toxicity associated with long-term intravenous heroin and cocaine self-administration in the rat. *Journal of the American Medical Association, 254*(1), 81–83.

Bradford, J., & Pawlak, A. (1993). Effects of cyproterone acetate on sexual arousal patterns of pedophiles. *Archives of Sexual Behavior, 22*, 629–641.

Bradley, G. W. (1978). Self-serving biases in the attribution process: A re-examination of the fact or fiction question. *Journal of Personality and Social Psychology, 35*, 56–71.

Bradley, R. H. (1989). The use of the HOME inventory in longitudinal studies of child development. In M. H. Bornstein & N. A. Krasnegor (Eds.), *Stability and continuity in mental development: Behavioral and biological perspectives*. Hillsdale, NJ: Erlbaum.

Bradley, R. H., & Caldwell, B. M. (1980). The relation of home environment, cognitive competence and IQ among males and females. *Child Development, 51*, 1140–1148.

Bradshaw, J. L. (1981). In two minds. *Behavioral and Brain Sciences, 4*, 101–102.

Bradshaw, J. L. (1989). *Hemispheric specialization and psychological function*. New York: Wiley.

Braginsky, B. M., & Braginsky, D. D. (1974, March). The mentally retarded: Society's Hansels and Gretels. *Psychology Today*, pp. 18, 20–21, 24, 26, 28–30.

Braginsky, D. D. (1985). Psychology: Handmaiden to society. In S. Koch & D. E. Leary (Eds.), *A century of psychology as science*. New York: McGraw-Hill.

Bram, S. (1985). Childlessness revisited: A longitudinal study of voluntarily childless couples, delayed parents, and parents. *Lifestyles: A Journal of Changing Patterns, 8*(1), 46–66.

Bransford, J. D., & Johnson, M. K. (1973). Considerations of some problems of comprehension. In W. G. Chase (Ed.), *Visual information processing*. New York: Academic Press.

Bransford, J. D., & Stein, B. S. (1993). *The IDEAL problem solver*. New York: W. H. Freeman.

Brantley, P. J., & Sutker, P. B. (1984). Antisocial behavior disorders. In H. E. Adams & P. B. Sutker (Eds.), *Comprehensive handbook of psychopathology*. New York: Plenum.

Braungart, J. M., Plomin, R., DeFries, J. C., & Fulker, D. W. (1992). Genetic influence on tester-related infant temperament as assessed by Bayley's Infant Behavior Record: Nonadoptive and adoptive siblings and twins. *Developmental Psychology, 28*, 40–47.

Bray, G. A. (1990). Exercise and obesity. In C. Bouchard, R. J. Shephard, T. Stephens, J. R. Sutton, & B. D. McPherson (Eds.), *Exercise, fitness and health: A consensus of current knowledge*. Champaign, IL: Human Kinetics Books.

Bray, G. A. (1992). Pathophysiology of obesity. *American Journal of Clinical Nutrition, 55*, 488S–494S.

Brayfield, A. H., & Crockett, W. H. (1955). Employee attitudes and employee performance. *Psychological Bulletin, 52*, 396–424.

Breedlove, S. M. (1992). Sexual differentiation of the brain and behavior. In J. B. Becker, S. M. Breedlove, & D. Crews (Eds.), *Behavioral endocrinology*. Cambridge, MA: MIT Press.

Breedlove, S. M. (1994). Sexual differentiation of the human nervous system. *Annual Review of Psychology, 45*, 389–418.

Breggin, P. R. (1979). *Electroshock: Its brain disabling effects*. New York: Springer.

Breggin, P. R. (1990). Brain damage, dementia and persistent cognitive dysfunction associated with neuroleptic drugs: Evidence, etiology, implications. *The Journal of Mind and Behavior, 11*(3/4), 425–464.

Breggin, P. R. (1991). *Toxic psychiatry*. New York: St. Martin's Press.

Brehm, S. S. (1992). *Intimate relationships* (2nd ed.). New York: McGraw-Hill.

Brehmer, B. (1987). Models of diagnostic judgments. In J. Rasmussen, K. Duncan, & J. Lepat (Eds.), *New technology and human error*. Chichester, England: Wiley.

Breier, A., Buchanan, R. W., Kirkpatrick, B., Davis, O. R., Irish, D., Summerfelt, A., & Carpenter, W. T. (1994). Effects of clozapine on positive and negative symptoms in outpatients with schizophrenia. *American Journal of Psychiatry, 151*, 20–26.

Breland, K., & Breland, M. (1961). The misbe-

havior of organisms. *American Psychologist, 16*, 681–684.

Breland, K., & Breland, M. (1966). *Animal behavior*. New York: Macmillan.

Brennan, K. A., & Shaver, P. R. (1995). Dimensions of adult attachment, affect regulation, and romantic relationship functioning. *Personality and Social Psychology Bulletin, 21*, 267–283.

Brent, D. A., & Kolko, D. J. (1990). The assessment and treatment of children and adolescents at risk for suicide. In S. J. Blumenthal & D. J. Kupfer (Eds.), *Suicide over the life cycle: Risk factors, assessment, and treatment of suicidal patients*. Washington, DC: American Psychiatric Press.

Breslau, N., Kilbey, M. M., & Andreski, P. (1991). Nicotine dependence, major depression, and anxiety in young adults. *Archives of General Psychiatry, 48*, 1069–1074.

Breslau, N., Kilbey, M. M., & Andreski, P. (1993). Nicotine dependence and major depression: New evidence from a prospective investigation. *Archives of General Psychiatry, 50*, 31–35.

Bretherton, I. (1991). The roots and growing points of attachment theory. In C. M. Parkes, J. Stevenson-Hinde, & P. Marris (Eds.), *Attachment across the life cycle*. New York: Routledge & Kegan Paul.

Bretherton, I. (1992). Attachment and bonding. In V. B. Van Hasselt & M. Hersen (Eds.), *Handbook of social development: A lifespan perspective*. New York: Plenum.

Bretl, D. J., & Cantor, J. (1988). The portrayal of men and women in U.S. television commercials: A recent content analysis and trend over 15 years. *Sex Roles, 18*, 595–609.

Brett, J. F., Brief, A. P., Burke, M. J., George, J. M., & Webster, J. (1990). Negative affectivity and the reporting of stressful life events. *Health Psychology, 9*, 57–68.

Brettle, R. P., & Leen, L. S. (1991). The natural history of HIV and AIDS in women. *AIDS, 5*, 1283–1292.

Brewer, C. L. (1991). Perspectives on John B. Watson. In G. A. Kimble, M. Wertheimer, & C. White (Eds.), *Portraits of pioneers in psychology*. Hillsdale, NJ: Erlbaum.

Brewer, W. F., & Nakamura, G. V. (1984). The nature and function of schemas. In R. S. Wyer & T. K. Sroll (Eds.), *Handbook of social cognition*. Hillsdale, NJ: Erlbaum.

Brewer, W. F., & Treyens, J. C. (1981). Role of schemata in memory for places. *Cognitive Psychology, 13*, 207–230.

Briere, J., & Conte, J. R. (1993). Self-reported amnesia for abuse in adults molested as children. *Journal of Traumatic Stress, 6*(1), 21–31.

Briggs, S. R. (1989). The optimal level of measurement for personality constructs. In D. M. Buss & N. Cantor (Eds.), *Personality psychology: Recent trends and emerging directions*. New York: Springer.

Bringmann, W. G., & Balk, M. M. (1992). Another look at Wilhelm Wundt's publication record. *History of Psychology Newsletter, 24*(3/4), 50–66.

Brislin, R. (1993). *Understanding culture's influence on behavior*. Fort Worth: Harcourt Brace College Publishers.

Brobeck, J. R., Tepperman, T., & Long, C. N. (1943). Experimental hypothalamic hyperphagia in the albino rat. *Yale Journal of Biology and Medicine, 15*, 831–853.

Brody, N. (1992). *Intelligence*. San Diego: Academic Press.

Brody, N., & Crowley, M. J. (1995). Environmental (and genetic) influences on personality and intelligence. In D. H. Saklofske & M. Zeidner (Eds.), *International handbook of personality and intelligence*. New York: Plenum Press.

Bromage, B. K., & Mayer, R. E. (1986). Quantitative and qualitative effects of repetition on learning from technical text. *Journal of Educational Psychology, 78*, 271–278.

Bronson, F. H., & Whitten, W. (1968). Estrus accelerating pheromone of mice: Assay, androgen-dependency, and presence in bladder urine. *Journal of Reproduction and Fertility, 15*, 131–134.

Bronstein, P., & Quina, K. (1988). Perspectives on gender balance and cultural diversity in the teaching of psychology. In P. Bronstein & K. Quina (Eds.), *Teaching a psychology of people: Resources for gender and sociocultural awareness*. Washington, DC: American Psychological Association.

Brooks-Gunn, J. (1991). Maturational timing variations in adolescent girls, antecedents of. In R. M. Lerner, A. C. Petersen, & J. Brooks-Gunn (Eds.), *Encyclopedia of adolescence*. New York: Garland.

Brooks-Gunn, J., & Reiter, E. O. (1990). The role of pubertal process. In S. S. Feldman & G. R. Elliot (Eds.), *At the threshold: The developing adolescent*. Cambridge, MA: Harvard University Press.

Broughton, R. (1994). Important underemphasized aspects of sleep onset. In R. D. Ogilvie & J. R. Harsh (Eds.), *Sleep onset: Normal and abnormal processes*. Washington, DC: American Psychological Association.

Brown, A. S. (1991). A review of the tip-of-the-tongue experience. *Psychological Bulletin, 109*, 204–223.

Brown, J. D. (1991). Staying fit and staying well: Physical fitness as a moderator of life stress. *Journal of Personality and Social Psychology, 60*, 555–561.

Brown, J. D., & McGill, K. L. (1989). The cost of good fortune: When positive life events produce negative health consequences. *Journal of Personality and Social Psychology, 57*, 1103–1110.

Brown, J. D., & Rogers, R. J. (1991). Self-serving attributions: The role of physiological arousal. *Personality and Social Psychology Bulletin, 17*, 501–506.

Brown, M. (1974). Some determinants of persistence and initiation of achievement-related activities. In J. W. Atkinson & J. O. Raynor (Eds.), *Motivation and achievement*. Washington, DC: Halsted.

Brown, P., & Funk, S. C. (1986). Tardive dyskinesia: Barriers to the professional recognition of an iatrogenic disease. *Journal of Health and Social Behavior, 27*, 116–132.

Brown, R. (1973). *A first language: The early stages*. Cambridge: Harvard University Press.

Brown, R., & Hanlon, C. (1970). Derivational complexity and order of acquisition. In J. R. Hayes (Ed.), *Cognition and the development of language*. New York: Wiley.

Brown, R., & McNeill, D. (1966). The "tip-of-the-tongue" phenomenon. *Journal of Verbal Learning and Verbal Behavior, 5*(4), 325–337.

Brown, R. T. (1989). Creativity: What are we to measure? In J. A. Glover, R. R. Ronning, & C. R. Reynolds (Eds.), *Handbook of creativity*. New York: Plenum.

Brownell, H. H., & Gardner, H. (1981). Hemisphere specialization: Definitions not incantations. *Behavioral and Brain Sciences, 4*, 64–65.

Brownell, K. D., & Rodin, J. (1994). The dieting maelstrom. *American Psychologist, 49*, 781–791.

Brubaker, T. (1990). Families in later life: A burgeoning research area. *Journal of Marriage and the Family, 52,* 959–982.

Bruce, R. L. (1980). Biological psychology. In J. Radford & D. Rose (Eds.), *The teaching of psychology: Method, content and context.* New York: Wiley.

Bruckner-Gordon, F., Gangi, B. K., & Wallman, G. U. (1988). *Making therapy work: Your guide to choosing, using, and ending therapy.* New York: Harper & Row.

Bruder, G. E. (1995). Cerebral laterality and psychopathology: Perceptual and event-related potential asymmetries in affective and schizophrenic disorders. In R. J. Davidson & K. Hugdahl (Eds.), *Brain asymmetry.* Cambridge, MA: MIT Press.

Bruner, J. S. (1968). *Processes of cognitive growth: Infancy.* Worcester, MA: Clark University Press with Barre Publishers.

Bruner, J. S. (1974). Concluding comments and summary of conference. In J. L. M. Dawson & W. J. Lonner (Eds.), *Readings in cross-cultural psychology.* Hong Kong: University of Hong Kong Press.

Bryden, M. P. (1982). *Laterality: Functional asymmetry in the intact brain.* New York: Academic Press.

Bryden, M. P. (1988). An overview of the dichotic listening procedure and its relation to cerebral organization. In K. Hugdahl (Ed.), *Handbook of dichotic listening.* Chichester, England: Wiley.

Bryden, M. P. (1993). Perhaps not so sinister. *Contemporary Psychology, 38,* 71–72.

Bryson, S. E. (1990). Autism and anomalous handedness. In S. Coren (Ed.), *Left-handedness: Behavioral implications and anomalies.* Amsterdam: North-Holland.

Buchsbaum, M. S., Someya, T., Teng, C. Y., Abel, L., Chin, S., Najafi, A., Haier, R. J., Wu, J., & Bunney, W. E., Jr. (1996). PET and MRI of the thalamus in never-medicated patients with schizophrenia. *American Journal of Psychiatry, 153,* 191–199.

Buck, R. (1984). *The communication of emotion.* New York: Guilford Press.

Buckley, P. F., & Meltzer, H. Y. (1995). Treatment of schizophrenia. In A. F. Schatzberg & C. B. Nemeroff (Eds.), *The American Psychiatric Press textbook of psychopharmacology.* Washington, DC: American Psychiatric Press.

Buda, M., & Tsuang, M. T. (1990). The epidemiology of suicide: Implications for clinical practice. In S. J. Blumenthal & D. J. Kupfer (Eds.), *Suicide over the life cycle: Risk factors, assessment, and treatment of suicidal patients.* Washington, DC: American Psychiatric Press.

Buhler, C., & Allen, M. (1972). *Introduction to humanistic psychology.* Pacific Grove, CA: Brooks/Cole.

Bullock, W. A., & Gilliland, K. (1993). Eysenck's arousal theory of introversion-extraversion: A converging measures investigation. *Journal of Personality and Social Psychology, 64,* 113–123.

Bunch, B. (1994). Mainstreaming. In R. J. Sternberg (Ed.), *Encyclopedia of human intelligence.* New York: Macmillan.

Burg, M. W. (1995). Anger, hostility, and coronary heart disease: A review. *Mind/Body Medicine, 1,* 159–172.

Burger, J. M. (1981). Motivational biases in the attribution of responsibility for an accident: A meta-analysis of the defensive-attribution hypothesis. *Psychological Bulletin, 90,* 496–512.

Burger, J. M. (1984). Desire for control, locus of control, and proneness to depression. *Journal of Personality, 52,* 71–89.

Burger, J. M. (1986). Temporal effects on attributions: Actor and observer differences. *Social Cognition, 4,* 377–387.

Burger, J. M. (1989). Negative reactions to increases in perceived personal control. *Journal of Personality and Social Psychology, 56,* 246–256.

Burger, J. M. (1993). *Personality.* Pacific Grove, CA: Brooks/Cole.

Burke, R. J. (1984). Mentors in organizations. *Group and Organization Studies, 9,* 353–372.

Burnstein, E., Crandall, C., & Kitayama, S. (1994). Some neo-Darwinian decision rules for altruism: Weighing cues for inclusive fitness as a function of the biological importance of the decision. *Personality and Social Psychology, 67,* 773–789.

Burt, C. (1955). The evidence for the concept of intelligence. *British Journal of Educational Psychology, 25,* 158–177.

Burtt, H. E. (1929). *Psychology and industrial efficiency.* New York: Appleton.

Bushman, B. J. (1995). Moderating role of trait aggressiveness in the effects of violent media on aggression. *Journal of Personality and Social Psychology, 69,* 950–960.

Buss, D. M. (1988). The evolution of human intrasexual competition: Tactics of mate attraction. *Journal of Personality and Social Psychology, 54,* 616–628.

Buss, D. M. (1989). Sex differences in human mate preferences: Evolutionary hypotheses tested in 37 cultures. *Behavioral and Brain Sciences, 12,* 1–49.

Buss, D. M. (1991). Evolutionary personality psychology. *Annual Review of Psychology, 42,* 459–491.

Buss, D. M. (1994). Mate preferences in 37 cultures. In W. J. Lonner & R. S. Malpass (Eds.), *Psychology and culture.* Boston: Allyn & Bacon.

Buss, D. M. (1995). Evolutionary psychology: A new paradigm for psychological science. *Psychological Inquiry, 6,* 1–30.

Buss, D. M. (1996). The evolutionary psychology of human social strategies. In E. T. Higgins & A. W. Kruglanski (Eds.), *Social psychology: Handbook of basic principles.* New York: Guilford Press.

Buss, D. M., Larsen, R. J., Westen, D., & Semmelroth, J. (1992). Sex differences in jealousy: Evolution, physiology, and psychology. *Psychological Science, 3,* 251–255.

Buss, D. M., & Schmitt, D. P. (1993). Sexual strategies theory: A contextual evolutionary analysis of human mating. *Psychological Review, 100,* 204–232.

Bussey, K., & Bandura, A. (1984). Influence of gender constancy and social power on sex-linked modeling. *Journal of Personality and Social Psychology, 47,* 1292–1302.

Butcher, J. N. (1990). *The MMPI-2 in psychological treatment.* New York: Oxford University Press.

Butcher, J. N., & Keller, L. S. (1984). Objective personality assessment. In G. Goldstein & M. Hersen (Eds.), *Handbook of psychological assessment.* New York: Pergamon Press.

Butcher, J. N., Narikiyo, T., & Vitousek, K. B. (1993). Understanding abnormal behavior in cultural context. In P. B. Sutker & H. E. Adams (Eds.), *Comprehensive handbook of psychopathology.* New York: Plenum Press.

Buunk, B. P., Angleitner, A., Oubaid, V., & Buss, D. M. (1996). Sex differences in jealousy in evolutionary and cultural perspective: Test from the Netherlands, Germany, and the United States. *Psychological Science, 7,* 359–363.

Buxton, C. E. (1985). American functionalism. In C. E. Buxton (Ed.), *Points of view in the modern history of psychology.* Orlando: Academic Press.

Buxton, M. N., Arkey, Y., Lagos, J., Deposito, F., Lowenthal, F., & Simring, S. (1981). Stress and platelet aggregation in hemophiliac children and their family members. *Research Communications in Psychology, Psychiatry and Behavior, 6*(1), 21–48.

Byerley, W., & Coon, H. (1995). Strategies to identify genes for schizophrenia. In J. M. Oldham & M. B. Riba (Eds.), *Review of Psychiatry* (Vol. 14). Washington, DC: American Psychiatric Press.

Byne, W., & Parsons, B. (1993). Human sexual orientation: The biological theories reappraised. *Archives of General Psychiatry, 50,* 228–239.

Byrd, J. C. (1992). Environmental tobacco smoke: Medical and legal issues. *Medical Clinics of North America, 76,* 377–398.

Byrne, D. (1971). *The attraction paradigm.* New York: Academic Press.

Byrne, D., Clore, G. L., & Smeaton, G. (1986). The attraction hypothesis: Do similar attitudes affect anything? *Journal of Personality and Social Psychology, 51,* 1167–1170.

Byrne, D., & Murnen, S. K. (1988). Maintaining loving relationships. In R. J. Sternberg & M. L. Barnes (Eds.), *The psychology of love.* New Haven, CT: Yale University Press.

Cacioppo, J. T., Klein, D. J., Berntson, G. G., & Hatfield, E. (1993). The psychophysiology of emotions. In M. Lewis & J. M. Haviland (Eds.), *Handbook of emotions.* New York: Guilford Press.

Cado, S., & Leitenberg, H. (1990). Guilt reactions to sexual fantasies during intercourse. *Archives of Sexual Behavior, 19,* 49–63.

Cagen, R. H., & Rhein, L. D. (1980). Biochemical basis of recognition of taste and olfactory stimuli. In H. van der Starre (Ed.), *Olfaction and taste* (Vol. 7). London: IRL Press.

Cain, W. S. (1979). To know with the nose: Keys to odor identification. *Science, 203,* 467–470.

Cain, W. S. (1988). Olfaction. In R. C. Atkinson, R. J. Herrnstein, G. Lindzey, & R. D. Luce (Eds.), *Stevens' handbook of experimental psychology: Perception and motivation* (Vol. 1). New York: Wiley.

Calabrese, L. H. (1990). Exercise, immunity, cancer, and infection. In C. Bouchard, R. J. Shephard, T. Stephens, J. R. Sutton, & B. D. McPherson (Eds.), *Exercise, fitness, and health: A consensus of knowledge.* Champaign, IL: Human Kinetics Books.

Caldwell, B. M. (1993). Impact of day care on the child. *Pediatrics, 91,* 225–228.

Calev, A., Phil, D., Pass, H. L., Shapira, B., Fink, M., Tubi, N., & Lerer, B. (1993). ECT and memory. In C. E. Coffey (Ed.), *The clinical science of electroconvulsive therapy.* Washington, DC: American Psychiatric Press.

Caligor, L., & May, R. (1968). *Dreams and symbols: Man's unconscious language.* New York: Basic Books.

Cameron, L., Leventhal, E. A., & Leventhal, H. (1993). Symptom representations and affect as determinants of care seeking in a community-dwelling, adult sample population. *Health Psychology, 12,* 171–179.

Cameron, N. (1963). *Personality development and psychopathology.* Boston: Houghton Mifflin.

Campbell, J. (1971). *Hero with a thousand faces.* New York: Harcourt Brace Jovanovich.

Campbell, J. D., Tesser, A., & Fairey, P. J. (1986). Conformity and attention to stimulus: Some temporal and contextual dynamics. *Journal of Personality and Social Psychology, 51,* 315–324.

Campbell, R. E., & Heffernan, J. M. (1983). Adult vocational behavior. In W. B. Walsh & S. H. Osipow (Eds.), *Handbook of vocational psychology: Vol. 1. Foundations.* Hillsdale, NJ: Erlbaum.

Cannon, W. B. (1927). The James-Lange theory of emotions: A critical examination and an alternate theory. *American Journal of Psychology, 39,* 106–124.

Cannon, W. B. (1929). *Bodily changes in pain, hunger, fear and rage.* New York: Appleton.

Cannon, W. B. (1932). *The wisdom of the body.* New York: Norton.

Cannon, W. B., & Washburn, A. L. (1912). An explanation of hunger. *American Journal of Physiology, 29,* 444–454.

Capaldi, E. D., & VandenBos, G. R. (1991). Taste, food exposure, and eating behavior. *Hospital and Community Psychiatry, 42*(8), 787–789.

Capelli, C. A., Nakagawa, N., & Madden, C. M. (1990). How children understand sarcasm: The role of context and intonation. *Child Development, 61,* 1824–1841.

Caplan, P. (1995). *They say you're crazy.* Reading, MA: Addison-Wesley.

Caporael, L. R., & Brewer, M. B. (1991). The quest for human nature: Social and scientific issues in evolutionary psychology. *Journal of Social Issues, 47,* 1–9.

Caporael, L. R., & Brewer, M. B. (1995). Hierarchical evolutionary theory: There is an alternative, and it's not creationism. *Psychological Inquiry, 6,* 31–34.

Carey, G., & DiLalla, D. L. (1994). Personality and psychopathology: Genetic perspectives. *Journal of Abnormal Psychology, 103,* 32–43.

Carnegie, D. (1936). *How to win friends and influence people.* New York: Simon & Schuster.

Carpenter, W. T. (1991). Psychopathology and common sense: Where we went wrong with negative symptoms. *Biological Psychiatry, 29,* 735–737.

Carpenter, W. T. (1992). The negative symptom challenge. *Archives of General Psychiatry, 49,* 236–237.

Carpenter, W. T., Conley, R. R., Buchanan, R. W., Breier, A., & Tamminga, C. A. (1995). Patient response and resource management: Another view of clozapine treatment of schizophrenia. *American Journal of Psychiatry, 152,* 827–832.

Carrington, P. (1987). Managing meditation in clinical practice. In M. A. West (Ed.), *The psychology of meditation.* Oxford: Clarendon Press.

Carroll, J. B. (1987). Jensen's mental chronometry: Some comments and questions. In S. Modgil & C. Modgil (Eds.), *Arthur Jensen: Consensus and controversy.* New York: Falmer Press.

Carroll, J. B., & Horn, J. L. (1981). On the scientific basis of ability testing. *American Psychologist, 36,* 1012–1020.

Carroll, J. L., Volk, K. D., & Hyde, J. S. (1985). Differences between males and females in motives for engaging in sexual intercourse. *Archives of Sexual Behavior, 14*(2), 131–139.

Carskadon, M. A., & Dement, W. C. (1994). Normal human sleep: An overview. In M. H. Kryger, T. Roth, & W. C. Dement (Eds.), *Principles and practice of sleep medicine* (2nd ed.). Philadelphia: Saunders.

Carskadon, M. A., & Rechtschaffen, A. (1994). Monitoring and staging human sleep. In M. H. Kryger, T. Roth, & W. C. Dement (Eds.), *Principles and practice of sleep medicine* (2nd ed.). Philadelphia: Saunders.

Carson, R. C. (1991). Dilemmas in the pathway

of the DSM-IV. *Journal of Abnormal Psychology, 100,* 302–307.

Carson, R. C., & Sanislow, C. A., III. (1993). The schizophrenias. In P. B. Sutker & H. E. Adams (Eds.), *Comprehensive handbook of psychopathology* (2nd ed.). New York: Plenum.

Carter, E. A., & McGoldrick, M. (1988). Overview: The changing family life cycle—A framework for family therapy. In E. A. Carter & M. McGoldrick (Eds.), *The changing family cycle: A framework for family therapy* (2nd ed.). New York: Gardner Press.

Carter, R. (1978). Knobology underwater. *Human Factors, 20,* 641–647.

Cartwright, R. D. (1974). The influence of a conscious wish on dreams: A methodological study of dream meaning and function. *Journal of Abnormal Psychology, 83,* 387–393.

Cartwright, R. D. (1977). *Night life: Explorations in dreaming.* Englewood Cliffs, NJ: Prentice-Hall.

Cartwright, R. D. (1991). Dreams that work: The relation of dream incorporation to adaptation to stressful events. *Dreaming, 1,* 3–9.

Cartwright, R. D. (1994). Dreams and their meaning. In M. H. Kryger, T. Roth, & W. C. Dement (Eds.), *Principles and practice of sleep medicine* (2nd ed.). Philadelphia: Saunders.

Cartwright, R. D., & Lamberg, L. (1992). *Crisis dreaming.* New York: HarperCollins.

Carver, C. S., Scheier, M. F., & Weintraub, J. K. (1989). Assessing coping strategies: A theoretically based approach. *Journal of Personality and Social Psychology, 56,* 267–283.

Casey, R., & Rozin, P. (1989). Changing children's food preferences: Parent opinions. *Appetite, 12,* 171–182.

Caspi, A., Bolger, N., & Eckenrode, J. (1987). Linking person and context in the daily stress process. *Journal of Personality and Social Psychology, 52,* 184–195.

Caspi, A., & Harbener, E. S. (1990). Continuity and change: Assortative marriage and the consistency of personality in adulthood. *Journal of Personality and Social Psychology, 58*(2), 250–258.

Castelloci, V. F. (1986). The chemical senses: Taste and smell. In E. R. Kandel & J. H. Schwartz (Eds.), *Principles of neural science.* New York: Elsevier.

Castro, K. G., Newcomb, M. D., McCreary, C., & Baezconde-Garbanati, L. (1989). Cigarette smokers do more than just smoke cigarettes. *Health Psychology, 8,* 107–129.

Catalano, E. M. (1990). *Getting to sleep.* Oakland, CA: New Harbinger.

Catania, A. C. (1979). *Learning.* Englewood Cliffs, NJ: Prentice-Hall.

Catania, A. C. (1992). Reinforcement. In L. R. Squire (Ed.), *Encyclopedia of learning and memory.* New York: Macmillan.

Catania, J. A., Coates, T. J., Stall, R., Turner, H., Peterson, J., Hearst, N., Dolcini, M. M., Hudes, E., Gagnon, J., Wiley, J., & Groves, R. (1992). Prevalence of AIDS-related risk factors and condom use in the United States. *Science, 258,* 1101–1106.

Cattell, J. M. (1890). Mental tests and measurements. *Mind, 15,* 373–381.

Cattell, R. B. (1950). *Personality: A systematic, theoretical and factual study.* New York: McGraw-Hill.

Cattell, R. B. (1957). *Personality and motivation: Structure and measurement.* New York: Harcourt, Brace & World.

Cattell, R. B. (1963). Theory of fluid and crystal-

lized intelligence: A critical experiment. *Journal of Educational Psychology, 54,* 1–22.

Cattell, R. B. (1965). *The scientific analysis of personality.* Baltimore: Penguin.

Cattell, R. B. (1966). *The scientific analysis of personality.* Chicago: Aldine.

Cattell, R. B. (1990). Advances in Cattellian personality theory. In L. A. Pervin (Ed.), *Handbook of personality: Theory and research.* New York: Guilford Press.

Cattell, R. B., Eber, H. W., & Tatsuoka, M. M. (1970). *Handbook of the Sixteen Personality Factor Questionnaire (16PF).* Champaign, IL: Institute for Personality and Ability Testing.

Cavanaugh, J. C. (1993). *Adult development and aging* (2nd ed.). Pacific Grove, CA: Brooks/Cole.

Ceci, S. J. (1991). How much does schooling influence general intelligence and its cognitive components? A reassessment of the evidence. *Developmental Psychology, 27,* 703–722.

Ceci, S. J., & Bruck, M. (1993). Suggestibility of the child witness: A historical review and synthesis. *Psychological Bulletin, 113,* 403–439.

Ceci, S. J., & Liker, J. (1986). Academic and nonacademic intelligence: An experimental separation. In R. J. Sternberg & R. K. Wagner (Eds.), *Practical intelligence: Nature and origins of competence in the everyday world.* Cambridge: Cambridge University Press.

Cerella, J. (1990). Aging and information-processing rate. In J. E. Birren & K. W. Schaie (Eds.), *Handbook of the psychology of aging* (3rd ed.). San Diego: Academic Press.

Cerletti, U., & Bini, L. (1938). Un nuevo metodo di shockterapie "L'elettro-shock". *Boll. Acad. Med. Roma, 64,* 136–138.

Cernovsky, Z. Z. (1989). Life stress measures and reported frequency of sleep disorders. In T. W. Miller (Ed.), *Stressful life events.* Madison, CT: International Universities Press.

Chadorow, N. (1978). *The reproduction of mothering.* Berkeley: University of California Press.

Chaiken, S. (1979). Communicator's physical attractiveness and persuasion. *Journal of Personality and Social Psychology, 37,* 1387–1397.

Chaiken, S. (1987). The heuristic model of persuasion. In M. P. Zanna, J. M. Olson, & C. P. Herman (Eds.), *Social influence: The Ontario symposium* (Vol. 5). Hillsdale, NJ: Erlbaum.

Chaiken, S., & Baldwin, M. W. (1981). Affective-cognitive consistency and the effect of salient behavioral information on the self-perception of attitudes. *Journal of Personality and Social Psychology, 41,* 1–12.

Chaiken, S., Wood, W., & Eagly, A. H. (1996). Principles of persuasion. In E. T. Higgins & A. W. Kruglanski (Eds.), *Social psychology: Handbook of basic principles.* New York: Guilford Press.

Chambers, K. C., & Phoenix, C. H. (1987). Differences among ovariectomized female rhesus macaques in the display of sexual behavior without and with estradiol treatment. *Behavioral Neuroscience, 101,* 303–308.

Chan, J. W. C., & Vernon, P. E. (1988). Individual differences among the peoples of China. In S. H. Irvine & J. W. Berry (Eds.), *Human abilities in cultural context.* New York: Cambridge University Press.

Chandra, R. K. (1991). Interactions between early nutrition and the immune system. In *Ciba Foundation Symposium No. 156.* Chichester, England: Wiley.

Chapman, P. D. (1988). *Schools as sorters: Lewis M. Terman, applied psychology, and the intelligence* *testing movement*. New York: New York University Press.

Charlesworth, W. R., & Kreutzer, M. A. (1973). Facial expression of infants and children. In P. Ekman (Ed.), *Darwin and facial expression*. New York: Academic Press.

Charness, N. (1989). Expertise in chess and bridge. In D. Klahr & K. Kotovsky (Eds.), *Complex information processing: The impact of Herbert A. Simon*. Hillsdale, NJ: Erlbaum.

Charney, D. S., Miller, H. L., Licinio, J., & Salomon, R. (1995). Treatment of depression. In A. F. Schatzberg & C. B. Nemeroff (Eds.), *The American Psychiatric Press textbook of psychopharmacology*. Washington, DC: American Psychiatric Press.

Chase, W. G., & Simon, H. A. (1973). Perception in chess. *Cognitive Psychology, 4,* 55–81.

Chasnoff, I. J., Griffith, D. R., MacGregor, S., Dirkes, K., & Burns, K. A. (1989). Temporal patterns of cocaine use in pregnancy: Perinatal outcome. *Journal of the American Medical Association, 261,* 1741–1744.

Check, J. V. P., & Guloien, T. H. (1989). Reported proclivity for coercive sex following repeated exposure to sexually violent pornography, nonviolent dehumanizing pornography, and erotica. In D. Zillmann & J. Bryant (Eds.), *Pornography: Research advances and policy considerations*. Hillsdale, NJ: Erlbaum.

Chehrazi, S. (1986). Female psychology. *Journal of the American Psychoanalytic Association, 34,* 111–162.

Cheung, F. (1991). The use of mental health services by ethnic minorities. In H. F. Myers, P. Wohlford, L. P. Guzman, & R. Echemendia (Eds.), *Ethnic minority perspectives on clinical training and services in psychology*. Washington, DC: American Psychological Association.

Chi, M. T. H., Glaser, R., & Rees, E. (1982). Expertise in problem solving. In R. J. Sternberg (Ed.), *Advances in the psychology of human intelligence* (Vol. 1). Hillsdale, NJ: Erlbaum.

Chiriboga, D. A. (1987). Personality in later life. In P. Silverman (Ed.), *The elderly as modern pioneers*. Bloomington: Indiana University Press.

Chiriboga, D. A. (1989). Mental health at the midpoint: Crisis, challenge, or relief? In S. Hunter & M. Sundel (Eds.), *Mid life myths: Issues, findings, and practice implications*. Newbury Park, CA: Sage.

Chodorow, N. (1978). *The reproduction of mothering*. Berkeley: University of California Press.

Cholewiak, R., & Collins, A. (1991). Sensory and physiological bases of touch. In M. A. Heller & W. Schiff (Eds.), *The psychology of touch*. Hillsdale, NJ: Erlbaum.

Chomsky, N. (1957). *Syntactic structures*. The Hague: Mouton.

Chomsky, N. (1959). A review of B. F. Skinner's "Verbal Behavior." *Language, 35,* 26–58.

Chomsky, N. (1965). *Aspects of theory of syntax*. Cambridge, MA: MIT Press.

Chomsky, N. (1975). *Reflections on language*. New York: Pantheon.

Chomsky, N. (1986). *Knowledge of language: Its nature, origins, and use*. New York: Praeger.

Christensen, A., & Jacobson, N. S. (1994). Who (or what) can do psychotherapy: The status and challenge of nonprofessional therapies. *Psychological Science, 5,* 8–14.

Christensen, L. (1988). Deception in psychological research: When is its use justified? *Personality and Social Psychology Bulletin, 14,* 664–675.

Christianson, S. (1989). Flashbulb memories: Special, but not so special. *Memory & Cognition, 17,* 435–443.

Chumlea, W. C. (1982). Physical growth in adolescence. In B. B. Wolman (Ed.), *Handbook of developmental psychology*. Englewood Cliffs, NJ: Prentice-Hall.

Church, A. T. (1994). Relating to Tellegen and five-factor models of personality structure. *Journal of Personality and Social Psychology, 67,* 898–909.

Church, A. T., & Burke, P. J. (1994). Exploratory and confirmatory tests of the Big Five and Tellegen's three- and four-dimensional models. *Journal of Personality and Social Psychology, 66,* 93–114.

Church, R. M. (1989). Theories of timing behavior. In S. P. Klein & R. R. Mowrer (Eds.), *Contemporary learning theories: Instrumental conditioning theory and the impact of biological constraints on learning*. Hillsdale, NJ: Erlbaum.

Cialdini, R. B., Trost, M. R., & Newsom, J. T. (1995). Preference for consistency: The development of a valid measure and the discovery of surprising behavioral implications. *Journal of Personality and Social Psychology, 69,* 318–328.

Ciompi, L. (1980). Catamnestic long-term study on the course of life and aging in schizophrenics. *Schizophrenia Bulletin, 6,* 607–618.

Cipolli, C., Baroncini, P., Fagioli, I., & Fumai, A. (1987). The thematic continuity of mental sleep experience in the same night. *Sleep, 10*(5), 473–479.

Clark, D. A., Beck, A. T., & Beck, J. S. (1994). Symptom differences in major depression, dysthymia, panic disorder, and generalized anxiety disorder. *American Journal of Psychiatry, 151,* 205–209.

Clark, E. V. (1983). Meanings and concepts. In J. H. Flavell & E. M. Markman (Eds.), *Handbook of child psychology* (Vol. 3). New York: Wiley.

Clark, L. A., & Livesley, W. J. (1994). Two approaches to identifying the dimensions of personality disorder: Convergence on the five-factor model. In P. T. Costa, Jr., & T. A. Widiger (Eds.), *Personality disorders and the five-factor model of personality*. Washington, DC: American Psychological Association.

Clark, L. A., Watson, D., & Mineka, S. (1994). Temperament, personality, and the mood and anxiety disorders. *Journal of Abnormal Psychology, 103,* 103–116.

Clark, L. F. (1993). Stress and the cognitive-conversational benefits of social interaction. *Journal of Social and Clinical Psychology, 12,* 25–55.

Cockburn, J. (1995). Task interruption in prospective memory: A frontal lobe function? *Cortex, 31,* 87–97.

Cohen, C. E. (1981). Person categories and social perception: Testing some boundaries of the processing effects of prior knowledge. *Journal of Personality and Social Psychology, 40,* 441–452.

Cohen, C. I., & Thompson, K. S. (1992). Homeless mentally ill or mentally ill homeless? *American Journal of Psychiatry, 149,* 816–823.

Cohen, D., & McCubbin, M. (1990). The political economy of tardive dyskinesia: Asymmetries in power and responsibility. *The Journal of Mind and Behavior, 11*(3/4), 465–488.

Cohen, G., Fleming, N. F., Glatter, K. A., Haghigi, D. B., Halberstadt, J., McHugh, K. B., & Woolf, A. (1996). Epidemiology of substance use. In L. S. Friedman, N. F. Fleming, D. H. Rob-

erts, & S. E. Hyman (Eds.), *Source book of substance abuse and addiction*. Baltimore: Williams & Wilkins.

Cohen, J. (1997). Advances painted in shades of gray at a D.C. conference. *Science, 275,* 615–616.

Cohen, S. (1980). *The substance abuse problem*. New York: Haworth Press.

Cohen, S., & Hajioff, J. (1972). Life events and the onset of acute closed-angle glaucoma. *Journal of Psychosomatic Research, 16,* 335–341.

Cohen, S., & Lichtenstein, E. (1990). Perceived stress, quitting smoking, and smoking relapse. *Health Psychology, 9,* 466–478.

Cohen, S., Lichtenstein, E., Prochaska, J. O., Rossi, J. S., Gritz, E. R., Carr, C. R., Orleans, C. T., Schoenbach, V. J., Biener, L., Abrams, D., DiClemente, C., Curry, S., Marlatt, G. A., Cummings, K. M., Emont, S. L., Giovino, A., & Ossip-Klien, D. (1989). Debunking myths about self-quitting: Evidence from 10 prospective studies of persons who attempt to quit smoking by themselves. *American Psychologist, 44,* 1355–1365.

Cohen, S., & Syme, S. L. (Eds.). (1985). *Social support and health*. New York: Academic Press.

Cohen, S., Tyrrell, D. A. J., & Smith, A. P. (1993). Negative life events, perceived stress, negative affect, and susceptibility to the common cold. *Journal of Personality and Social Psychology, 64,* 131–140.

Cohen, S. T., & Weiss, R. (1996). Substance abuse and mental illness. In L. S. Friedman, N. F. Fleming, D. H. Roberts, & S. E. Hyman (Eds.), *Source book of substance abuse and addiction*. Baltimore: Williams & Wilkins.

Cohen, S., & Williamson, G. M. (1991). Stress and infectious disease in humans. *Psychological Bulletin, 109*(1), 5–24.

Colby, A., & Kohlberg, L. (1984). Invariant sequence and internal consistency in moral judgment stages. In W. M. Kurtines & J. L. Gewirtz (Eds.), *Morality, moral behavior, and moral development*. New York: Wiley.

Colby, A., & Kohlberg, L. (1987). *The measurement of moral judgment* (Vols. 1–2). New York: Cambridge University Press.

Colby, A., Kohlberg, L., Gibbs, J., & Lieberman, M. (1983). A longitudinal study of moral development. *Monographs of the Society for Research in Child Development, 48*(1 & 2, Serial No. 200).

Cole, J. O., Goldberg, S. C., & Davis, J. M. (1966). Drugs in the treatment of psychosis. In P. Solomon (Ed.), *Psychiatric drugs*. New York: Grune & Stratton.

Cole, J. O., & Yonkers, K. A. (1995). Nonbenzodiazepine anxiolytics. In A. F. Schatzberg & C. B. Nemeroff (Eds.), *The American Psychiatric Press textbook of psychopharmacology*. Washington, DC: American Psychiatric Press.

Cole, M. (1992). Culture in development. In M. H. Bornstein & M. E. Lamb (Eds.), *Developmental psychology: An advanced textbook* (3rd ed.). Hillsdale, NJ: Erlbaum.

Cole, M., Gay, J., Glick, J. A., Sharp, D. W. (1971). *The cultural context of learning and thinking: An exploration in experimental anthropology*. New York: Basic Books.

Cole, N. S. (1981). Bias in testing. *American Psychologist, 36,* 1067–1077.

Cole, S. W., Kemeny, M. E., Taylor, S. E., & Visscher, B. R. (1996). Elevated physical health risk among gay men who conceal their homosexual identity. *Health Psychology, 15,* 243–251.

Coleman, J. S., Campbell, E. O., Hobson, C. J., McPartland, J., Moody, A. M., Weinfeld, F. D., & York, R. L. (1966). *Equality of educational op-*

portunity. Washington, DC: U.S. Government Printing Office.

Coleman, P. (1993). Overview of substance abuse. *Primary Care, 20*(1), 1–18.

Coleman, R. M. (1986). *Wide awake at 3:00 a.m.* New York: W. H. Freeman.

Coles, R. (1970). *Erik H. Erikson: The growth of his work.* Boston: Little, Brown.

Collaer, M. L., & Hines, M. (1995). Human behavioral sex differences: A role for gonadal hormones during early development? *Psychological Bulletin, 118*, 55–107.

Collins, A. M., & Loftus, E. F. (1975). A spreading activation theory of semantic processing. *Psychological Review, 82*, 407–428.

Collins, N. L. (1996). Working models of attachment: Implications for explanation, emotion, and behavior. *Journal of Personality and Social Psychology, 71*, 810–832.

Collins, N. L., & Read, S. J. (1990). Adult attachment, working models, and relationship quality in dating couples. *Journal of Personality and Social Psychology, 58*, 644–663.

Colquhoun, W. P. (1984). Effects of personality on body temperature and mental efficiency following transmeridian flight. *Aviation, Space & Environmental Medicine, 55*(6), 493–496.

Colvin, S. R., & Block, J. (1994). Do positive illusions foster mental health? An examination of the Taylor and Brown formulation. *Psychological Bulletin, 116*, 3–20.

Colwill, R. M. (1993). An associative analysis of instrumental learning. *Current Directions in Psychological Science, 2*(4), 111–116.

Conley, J. J. (1985). Longitudinal stability of personality traits: A multitrait-multimethod-multioccasion analysis. *Journal of Personality and Social Psychology, 49*, 1266–1282.

Conoley, J. C., & Impara, J. C. (1995). *The twelfth mental measurements yearbook.* Lincoln, NE: Brus Institute of Mental Measurements.

Conrad, R. (1964). Acoustic confusions in immediate memory. *British Journal of Psychology, 55*, 75–84.

Conwell, Y., Duberstein, P. R., Cox, C., Herrmann, J. H., Forbes, N. T., & Caine, E. D. (1996). Relationships of age and axis I diagnoses in victims of completed suicide: A psychological autopsy study. *American Journal of Psychiatry, 153*, 1001–1008.

Cook, M., & Mineka, S. (1989). Observational conditioning of fear to fear-relevant versus fear-irrelevant stimuli in rhesus monkeys. *Journal of Abnormal Psychology, 98*, 448–459.

Cooney, T. M., Pedersen, F. A., Indelicato, S., & Palkovitz, R. (1993). Timing of fatherhood: Is "on-time" optimal? *Journal of Marriage and the Family, 55*, 205–215.

Cooper, C. L. (1984). The social-psychological precursors to cancer. *Journal of Human Stress, 10*(1), 4–11.

Cooper, E. (1991). A critique of six measures for assessing creativity. *Journal of Creative Behavior, 25*(3), 194–204.

Cooper, H. M. (1990). Meta-analysis and the integrative research review. *Review of Personality and Social Psychology, 11*, 142–163.

Cooper, H. M., & Lemke, K. M. (1991). On the role of meta-analysis in personality and social psychology. *Personality and Social Psychology Bulletin, 17*, 245–251.

Cooper, J., & Fazio, R. H. (1984). A new look at dissonance theory. In L. Berkowitz (Ed.), *Advances in experimental social psychology* (Vol. 17). New York: Academic Press.

Cooper, J. R., Bloom, F. E., & Roth, R. H. (1996). *The biochemical basis of neuropharmacology.* New York: Oxford University Press.

Corballis, M. C. (1980). Laterality and myth. *American Psychologist, 35*, 284–295.

Corballis, M. C. (1991). *The lopsided ape.* New York: Oxford University Press.

Coren, S. (1989a). Cross-cultural studies of visual illusions: The physiological confound. *Behavioral and Brain Sciences, 12*(1), 76–77.

Coren, S. (1989b). Left-handedness and accident-related injury risk. *American Journal of Public Health, 79*, 1–2.

Coren, S. (1992). *The left-hander syndrome: The causes and consequences of left-handedness.* New York: Free Press.

Coren, S. (1996). *Sleep thieves: An eye-opening exploration into the science and mysteries of sleep.* New York: Free Press.

Coren, S., & Aks, D. J. (1990). Moon illusion in pictures: A multimechanism approach. *Journal of Experimental Psychology: Human Perception and Performance, 16*, 365–380.

Coren, S., & Girgus, J. S. (1978). *Seeing is deceiving: The psychology of visual illusions.* Hillsdale, NJ: Erlbaum.

Coren, S., & Halpern, D. F. (1991). Left-handedness: A marker for decreased survival fitness. *Psychological Bulletin, 109*, 90–106.

Coren, S., & Porac, C. (1977). Fifty centuries of right-handedness: The historical record. *Science, 198*, 631–632.

Corkin, S. (1984). Lasting consequences of bilateral medial temporal lobectomy: Clinical course and experimental findings in H. M. *Seminars in Neurology, 4*, 249–259.

Coryell, W., & Winokur, G. (1992). Course and outcome. In E. S. Paykel (Ed.), *Handbook of affective disorders* (2nd ed.). New York: Guilford Press.

Costa, G., Cesana, G., Katsuaka, K., & Wedderburn, A. (1989). *Shiftwork: Health, sleep and performance.* Frankfurt, Germany: Peter Lang.

Costa, P. T., Jr., & McCrae, R. (1985). *NEO Personality Inventory.* Odessa, FL: Psychological Assessment Resources.

Costa, P. T., Jr., & McCrae, R. (1992). *Revised NEO Personality Inventory: NEO PI and NEO Five-Factor Inventory* (Professional Manual). Odessa, FL: Psychological Assessment Resources.

Costa, P. T., Jr., & McCrae, R. R. (1994). Set like plaster? Evidence for the stability of adult personality. In T. F. Heatherton & J. L. Weinberger (Eds.), *Can personality change?* Washington, DC: American Psychological Association.

Costa, P. T., Jr., McCrae, R. R., & Dye, D. A. (1991). Facet scales for agreeableness and conscientiousness: A revision of the NEO Personality Inventory. *Personality and Individual Differences, 12*, 887–898.

Cote, L., & Crutcher, M. D. (1991). The basal ganglia. In E. R. Kandel, J. H. Schwartz, & T. M. Jessell (Eds.), *Principles of neural science* (3rd ed.). New York: Elsevier.

Courage, M. L., & Adams, R. J. (1990). Visual acuity assessment from birth to three years using the acuity card procedures: Cross-sectional and longitudinal samples. *Optometry and Vision Science, 67*, 713–718.

Court, J. H. (1984). Sex and violence: A ripple effect. In N. Malamuth & E. Donnerstein (Eds.), *Pornography and sexual aggression.* Orlando, FL: Academic Press.

Covi, L., & Primakoff, L. (1988). Cognitive group therapy. In A. J. Frances & R. E. Hales (Eds.), *Review of psychiatry: Volume 7.* Washington, DC: American Psychiatric Press.

Cowan, N. (1988). Evolving conceptions of memory storage, selective attention, and their mutual constraints within the human information-processing system. *Psychological Bulletin, 104*, 163–191.

Cowan, N. (1995). *Attention and memory: An integrated framework.* New York: Oxford University Press.

Cowan, N., Lichty, W., & Grove, T. R. (1990). Properties of memory for unattended spoken syllables. *Journal of Experimental Psychology: Learning, Memory, & Cognition, 16*, 258–269.

Cox, M. J., Owen, M. T., Henderson, V. K., & Margand, N. A. (1992). Prediction of infant-father and infant-mother attachment. *Developmental Psychology, 28*, 474–483.

Coyne, J. C., Burchill, S. A. L., & Stiles, W. B. (1990). An interactional perspective on depression. In C. R. Snyder &. D. R. Forsyth (Eds.), *Handbook of social and clinical psychology: The health perspective.* New York: Pergamon Press.

Craik. F. I. M., & Lockhart, R. S. (1972). Levels of processing: A framework for memory research. *Journal of Verbal Learning and Verbal Behavior, 11*, 671–684.

Craik, F. I. M., & Tulving, E. (1975). Depth of processing and the retention of words in episodic memory. *Journal of Experimental Psychology: General, 104*, 268–294.

Crain, S. (1991). Language acquisition in the absence of experience. *Behavioral and Brain Sciences, 14*, 597–650.

Crane, P. T. (1985). Voluntary childlessness: Some notes on the decision making process. In D. B. Gutknecht & E. W. Butler (Eds.), *Family, self, and society: Emerging issues, alternatives, and interventions* (2nd ed.). New York: UPA.

Craufurd, D. I. O., Creed, F., & Jayson, M. D. (1990). Life events and psychological disturbance in patients with low-back pain. *Spine, 15*, 490–494.

Cravens, H. (1992). A scientific project locked in time: The Terman Genetic Studies of Genius, 1920s–1950s. *American Psychologist, 47*, 183–189.

Crawford, H. J., & Gruzelier, J. H. (1992). A midstream view of the neuropsychophysiology of hypnosis: Recent research and future directions. In E. Fromm & M. R. Nash (Eds.), *Contemporary hypnosis research.* New York: Guilford Press.

Creed, F. (1989). Appendectomy. In G. W. Brown & T. O. Harris (Eds.), *Life events and illness.* New York: Guilford Press.

Creed, F. (1993). Stress and psychosomatic disorders. In L. Goldberger & S. Breznitz (Eds.), *Handbook of stress: Theoretical and clinical aspects* (2nd ed.). New York: Free Press.

Creed, T. L. (1987). Subliminal deception: Pseudoscience on the college lecture circuit. *The Skeptical Inquirer, 11*, 358–366.

Crocker, J., & Luhtanen, R. (1990). Collective self-esteem and ingroup bias. *Journal of Personality and Social Psychology, 58*, 60–67.

Crockett, H. (1962). The achievement motive and differential occupational mobility in the United States. *American Sociological Review, 27*, 191–204.

Cronbach, L. J. (1992). *Acceleration among the Terman males: Correlates in midlife and after.* Paper presented at the Symposium in Honor of Julian Stanley, San Francisco.

Crooks, R., & Baur, K. (1996). *Our sexuality*. Pacific Grove, CA: Brooks/Cole.

Cross, C. K., & Hirschfeld, R. M. A. (1986). Epidemiology of disorders in adulthood: Suicide. In G. L. Klerman, M. M. Weissman, P. S. Appelbaum, & L. H. Roth (Eds.), *Psychiatry: Vol. 5. Social, epidemiologic, and legal psychiatry*. New York: Basic Books.

Cross, S. E., & Markus, H. R. (1993). Gender in thought, belief, and action: A cognitive approach. In A. E. Beall & R. J. Sternberg (Eds.), *The psychology of gender*. New York: Guilford Press.

Crowe, R. (1983). Antisocial personality disorder. In R. Tarter (Ed.), *The child at psychiatric risk*. New York: Oxford University Press.

Crowe, R. R. (1994). Molecular genetic research in schizophrenia. In N. C. Andreasen (Ed.), *Schizophrenia: From mind to molecule*. Washington, DC: American Psychiatric Press.

Croyle, R. T., & Cooper, J. (1983). Dissonance arousal: Physiological evidence. *Journal of Personality and Social Psychology, 45,* 782–791.

Csikszentmihalyi, M. (1994). Creativity. In R. J. Sternberg (Ed.), *Encyclopedia of human intelligence*. New York: Macmillan.

Culp, R. E., Cook, A. S., & Housley, P. C. (1983). A comparison of observed and reported adult-infant interactions: Effects of perceived sex. *Sex Roles, 9,* 475–479.

Cunningham, M. R., Druen, P. B., & Barbee, A. P. (1997). Angels, mentors, and friends: Trade-offs among evolutionary, social, and individual variables in physical appearance. In J. A. Simpson, & D. T. Kenrick (Eds.), *Evolutionary social psychology*. Mahwah, NJ: Erlbaum.

Cunningham, S. (1985, June). Animals stolen, facility damaged in lab break-in. *APA Monitor*, pp. 1–2.

Curran, D. K. (1987). *Adolescent suicidal behavior*. Washington: Hemisphere.

Cushman, P. (1992). Psychotherapy to 1992: A historically situated interpretation. In D. K. Freedheim (Ed.), *History of psychotherapy: A century of change*. Washington, DC: American Psychological Association.

Czeisler, C. A., Moore-Ede, M. C., & Coleman, R. M. (1982). Rotating shift work schedules that disrupt sleep are improved by applying circadian principles. *Science, 217,* 460–463.

Czeisler, C. A., Weitzman, E. D., Moore-Ede, M. C., Zimmerman, J. C., & Knauer, R. S. (1980). Human sleep: Its duration and organization depend on its circadian phase. *Science, 210,* 1264–1267.

D'Andrade, R. G. (1961). Anthropological studies of dreams. In F. Hsu (Ed.), *Psychological anthropology: Approaches to culture and personality*. Homewood, IL: Dorsey Press.

Dallos, P. (1981). Cochlear physiology. *Annual Review of Psychology, 32,* 153–190.

Damon, W. (1988). *The moral child*. New York: Free Press.

Dana, R. H. (1993). *Multicultural assessment perspectives for professional psychology*. Boston: Allyn & Bacon.

Danziger, K. (1990). *Constructing the subject: Historical origins of psychological research*. Cambridge, England: Cambridge University Press.

Darley, J. M., & Latané, B. (1968). Bystander intervention in emergencies: Diffusion of responsibility. *Journal of Personality and Social Psychology, 8,* 377–383.

Darwin, C. (1859). *On the origin of species*. London: Murray.

Darwin, C. (1871). *Descent of man*. London: Murray.

Darwin, C. (1872). *The expression of emotions in man and animals*. New York: Philosophical Library.

Das, J. P. (1992). Beyond a unidimensional scale of merit. *Intelligence, 16*(2), 137–149.

Das, J. P. (1994). Eastern views of intelligence. In R. J. Sternberg (Ed.), *Encyclopedia of human intelligence*. New York: Macmillan.

Dasen, P. R. (1994). Culture and cognitive development from a Piagetian perspective. In W. J. Lonner & R. Malpass (Eds.), *Psychology and culture*. Boston: Allyn & Bacon.

Davidson, J. (1976). Physiology of meditation and mystical states of consciousness. *Perspectives in Biology and Medicine, 19,* 345–380.

Davidson, J. (1985). The utilization of sexual fantasies by sexually experienced university students. *Journal of American College Health, 34*(1), 24–32.

Davidson, J., & Rosen, R. (1992). Hormonal determinants of erectile function. In R. Rosen, & S. Leiblum (Eds.), *Erectile disorders: Assessment and treatment*. New York: Guilford Press.

Davidson, N. (1988). *The failure of feminism*. Buffalo: Promethus.

Davidson, R. J., & Cacioppo, J. T. (1992). New developments in the scientific study of emotion: An introduction to the special section. *Psychological Science, 3,* 21–22.

Davis, D. M. (1990). Portrayals of women in prime-time network television: Some demographic characteristics. *Sex Roles, 23,* 325–332.

Davis, H. P., & Squire, L. R. (1984). Protein synthesis and memory: A review. *Psychological Bulletin, 96,* 518–559.

Davis, J. M. (1985). Antipsychotic drugs. In H. I. Kaplan & B. J. Sadock (Eds.), *Comprehensive textbook of psychiatry/IV*. Baltimore: Williams & Wilkins.

Davis, K. L., Kahn, R. S., Ko, G., & Davidson, M. (1991). Dopamine in schizophrenia: A review and reconceptualization. *American Journal of Psychiatry, 148,* 1474–1486.

Dawson, M. E., Hazlett, E. A., Filion, D. L., Neuchterlein, K. H., & Schell, A. M. (1993). Attention and schizophrenia: Impaired modulation of the startle reflex. *Journal of Abnormal Psychology, 102,* 633–641.

Dawson, W. A. (1993). Aboriginal dreaming. In M. A. Carskadon (Ed.), *Encyclopedia of sleep and dreaming*. New York: Macmillan.

Day, R. H. (1965). Inappropriate constancy explanation of spatial distortions. *Nature, 207,* 891–893.

Deary, I. J., & Stough, C. (1996). Intelligence and inspection time. *American Psychologist, 51,* 599–608.

Deaux, K. (1984). From individual differences to social categories: Analysis of a decade's research on gender. *American Psychologist, 39,* 105–116.

Deaux, K. (1993). Commentary: Sorry, wrong number—A reply to Gentile's call. *Psychological Science, 4,* 125–126.

De Boysson-Bardies, B., & Vihman, M. (1991). Adaptation to language: Evidence from babbling and early words in four languages. *Language, 61,* 297–319.

De Bruyn, A., Mendelbaum, K., Sandkuijl, L. A., Delvenne, V., Hirsch, D., Staner, L., Mendlewicz, J., & Van Broeckhoven, C. (1994). Nonlinkage of bipolar illness to tyrosine hydroxylase, tyrosinase, and D2 and D4 dopamine receptor genes on chromosome 11. *American Journal of Psychiatry, 151,* 102–106.

DeCarvalho, R. J. (1991). *The founders of humanistic psychology*. New York: Praeger.

de Castro, J. M., & Brewer, E. M. (1992). The amount eaten in meals by humans is a power function of the number of people present. *Physiology and Behavior, 51,* 121–125.

deCharms, R., & Moeller, G. H. (1962). Values expressed in American children's readers: 1800–1950. *Journal of Abnormal and Social Psychology, 64,* 136–142.

Deeks, S. G. (1997). HIV-1 protease inhibitors: A review for clinicians. *The Journal of the American Medical Association, 277,* 145–149.

Deeks, S. G., Smith, M., Holodniy, M., & Kahn, J. O. (1997). HIV-1 protease inhibitors: A review for clinicians. *Journal of the Amercian Medical Association, 277,* 145–154.

de Groot, A. D. (1965). *Thought and choice in chess*. The Hague: Mouton.

Delay, J., & Deniker, P. (1952). *Trente-huit cas de psychoses traitees par la cure prolongee et continue de 4560 RP*. Paris: Masson et Cie.

DeLeon, P. H., & Wiggins, J. G., Jr. (1996). Prescription privileges for psychologists. *American Psychologist, 51,* 225–229.

Delgado, J. M. R. (1969). *Physical control of the mind*. New York: Harper & Row.

Delgado, P. L., Price, L. H., Heninger, G. R., & Charney, D. S. (1992). Neurochemistry. In E. S. Paykel (Ed.), *Handbook of affective disorders* (2nd ed.). New York: Guilford Press.

DeLongis, A., Folkman, S., & Lazarus, R. S. (1988). The impact of daily stress on health and mood: Psychological and social resources as mediators. *Journal of Personality and Social Psychology, 54,* 486–495.

Delprato, D. J., & Midgley, B. D. (1992). Some fundamentals of B. F. Skinner's behaviorism. *American Psychologist, 47,* 1507–1520.

DeMaio, T. J. (1984). Social desirability and survey measurement: A review. In C. F. Turner & E. Martin (Eds.), *Surveying subjective phenomena* (Vol. 2). New York: Russell Sage Foundation.

Dement, W. C. (1978). *Some must watch while some must sleep*. New York: Norton.

Dement, W. C. (1994). History of sleep physiology and medicine. In M. H. Kryger, T. Roth, & W. C. Dement (Eds.), *Principles and practice of sleep medicine* (2nd ed.). Philadelphia: Saunders.

Dement, W. C., & Wolpert, E. (1958). The relation of eye movements, bodily motility, and external stimuli to dream content. *Journal of Experimental Psychology, 53,* 543–553.

Demo, D. H. (1992). Parent-child relations: Assessing recent changes. *Journal of Marriage and the Family, 54,* 104–117.

DeNelsky, G. Y. (1996). The case against prescription privileges for psychologists. *American Psychologist, 51,* 207–212.

Dennis, D. L., Buckner, J. C., Lipton, F. R., & Levine, I. S. (1991). A decade of research and services for homeless mentally ill persons: Where do we stand? *American Psychologist, 46,* 1129–1138.

Dennis, W. (1966). Age and creative productivity. *Journal of Gerontology, 21*(1), 1–8.

Deregowski, J. B. (1989). Real space and represented space: Cross-cultural perspectives. *Behavioral and Brain Sciences, 12,* 51–119.

Derogatis, L. R., & Coons, H. L. (1993). Self-report measures of stress. In L. Goldberger & S.

Breznitz (Eds.), *Handbook of stress: Theoretical and clinical aspects* (2nd ed.). New York: Free Press.

Des Jarlais, D. C., Friedman, S. R., Woods, J., & Milliken, J. (1992). HIV infection among intravenous drug users: Epidemiology and emerging public health perspectives. In J. H. Lowinson, P. Ruiz, & R. B. Millman (Eds.), *Substance abuse: A comprehensive textbook* (2nd ed.). Baltimore: Williams & Wilkins.

DeSteno, D. A., & Salovey, P. (1996). Evolutionary origins of sex differences in jealousy? Questioning the "fitness" of the model. *Psychological Science, 7,* 367–372.

Deutsch, F. M., Sullivan, L., Sage, C., & Basile, N. (1991). The relations among talking, liking, and similarity between friends. *Personality and Social Psychology Bulletin, 17,* 406–411.

Deutsch, M., & Gerard, H. B. (1955). A study of normative and informational social influences upon individual judgment. *Journal of Abnormal and Social Psychology, 51,* 629–636.

DeValois, R. L., & Jacobs, G. H. (1984). Neural mechanisms of color vision. In I. Darian-Smith (Ed.), *The nervous system* (Vol. 3). Baltimore: Williams & Wilkins.

Devanand, D. P., Dwork, A. J., Hutchinson, E. R., Bolwig, T. G., & Sackeim, H. A. (1994). Does ECT alter brain structure? *American Journal of Psychiatry, 151,* 957–970.

De Villiers, P. (1977). Choice in concurrent schedules and a quantitative formulation of the law of effect. In W. K. Honig & J. E. R. Staddon (Eds.), *Handbook of operant behavior.* Englewood Cliffs, NJ: Prentice-Hall.

de Villiers, P. A., & de Villiers, J. G. (1992). Language development. In M. H. Bornstein & M. E. Lamb (Eds.), *Developmental psychology: An advanced textbook* (3rd ed.). Hillsdale, NJ: Erlbaum.

de Wilde, E. J., Kienhorst, I. C. W. M., Diekstra, R. F. W., & Wolters, W. H. G. (1992). The relationship between adolescent suicidal behavior and life events in childhood and adolescence. *American Journal of Psychiatry, 149,* 45–51.

Devine, P. G. (1989). Stereotypes and prejudice: Their automatic and controlled components. *Journal of Personality and Social Psychology, 56,* 5–18.

Devine, P. G., & Baker, S. M. (1991). Measurements of racial stereotypes subtyping. *Personality and Social Psychology Bulletin, 17,* 44–50.

Devine, P. G., & Elliot, A. J. (1995). Are racial stereotypes really fading? The Princeton trilogy revisited. *Personality and Social Psychology Bulletin, 21,* 1139–1150.

Deyoub, P. L. (1984). Hypnotic stimulation of antisocial behavior: A case report. *International Journal of Clinical and Experimental Hypnosis, 32*(3), 301–306.

Diamond, A., & Goldman-Rakic, P. S. (1989). Comparison of human infants and rhesus monkeys on Piaget's AB task: Evidence for dependence on dorsolateral prefrontal cortex. *Experimental Brain Research, 74,* 24–40.

DiLalla, D. L., Carey, G., Gottesman, I. I., & Bouchard, T. J., Jr. (1996). Heritability of MMPI personality indicators of psychopathology. *Journal of Abnormal Psychology, 105,* 491–499.

Dillbeck, M. C., & Orme-Johnson, D. W. (1987). Physiological differences between transcendental meditation and rest. *American Psychologist, 42,* 879–881.

DiMatteo, M. R. (1991). *The psychology of health, illness, and medical care: An individual perspective.* Pacific Grove, CA: Brooks/Cole.

DiMatteo, M. R., & Friedman, H. S. (1982). *Social psychology and medicine.* Cambridge, MA: Oelgeschlager, Gunn & Hain.

Dinges, D. F. (1989). Napping patterns and effects in human adults. In D. F. Dinges & R. J. Broughton (Eds.), *Sleep and alertness: Chronobiological, behavioral, and medical aspects of napping.* New York: Raven.

Dinges, D. F., & Broughton, R. J. (1989). The significance of napping: A synthesis. In D. F. Dinges & R. J. Broughton (Eds.), *Sleep and alertness: Chronobiological, behavioral, and medical aspects of napping.* New York: Raven.

DiNicola, D. D., & DiMatteo, M. R. (1984). Practitioners, patients, and compliance with medical regimens: A social psychological perspective. In A. Baum, S. E. Taylor, & J. E. Singer (Eds.), *Handbook of psychology and health: Vol. 4. Social psychological aspects of health.* Hillsdale, NJ: Erlbaum.

Dinsmoor, J. A. (1992). Setting the record straight: The social views of B. F. Skinner. *American Psychologist, 47,* 1454–1463.

Dion, K. K. (1986). Stereotyping based on physical attractiveness: Issues and conceptual perspectives. In C. P. Herman, M. P. Zanna, & E. T. Higgins (Eds.), *Appearance, stigma and social behavior: The Ontario symposium on personality and social psychology* (Vol. 3). Hillsdale, NJ: Erlbaum.

Dion, K. K., & Dion, K. L. (1991). Psychological individualism and romantic love. *Journal of Social Behavior and Personality, 6,* 17–33.

Dishion, T. J. (1990). The family ecology of boys' peer relations in middle childhood. *Child Development, 61,* 874–892.

Dixon, M., & Laurence, J. R. (1992). Two hundred years of hypnosis research: Questions resolved? Questions unanswered! In E. Fromm & M. R. Nash (Eds.), *Contemporary hypnosis research.* New York: Guilford Press.

Dixon, N. F. (1980). Humor: A cognitive alternative to stress? In I. G. Sarason & C. D. Spielberger (Eds.), *Stress and anxiety* (Vol. 7). Washington, DC: Hemisphere.

Doerr, P., Pirke, K. M., Kockott, G., & Dittmor, F. (1976). Further studies on sex hormones in male homosexuals. *Archives of General Psychiatry, 33,* 611–614.

Dollaghan, C. (1985). Child meets word: "Fast mapping" in pre-school children. *Journal of Speech and Hearing Research, 28,* 449–454.

Dollard, J., Doob, L. W., Miller, N. E., Mowrer, O. H., & Sears, R. R. (1939). *Frustration and aggression.* New Haven, CT: Yale University Press.

Dollard, J., & Miller, N. E. (1950). *Personality and psychotherapy: An analysis in terms of learning, thinking and culture.* New York: McGraw-Hill.

Domhoff, G. W. (1985). *The mystique of dreams: A search for Utopia through Senoi dream therapy.* Berkeley: University of California Press.

Domjan, M. (1993). *The principles of learning and behavior.* Pacific Grove, CA: Brooks/Cole.

Domjan, M., & Purdy, J. E. (1995). Animal research in psychology: More than meets the eye of the general psychology student. *American Psychologist, 50,* 496–503.

Donenberg, G. R., & Hoffman, L. W. (1988). Gender differences in moral development. *Sex Roles, 18,* 701–717.

Donlon, T. F. (Ed.). (1984). *The college board technical handbook for the Scholastic Aptitude Test and achievement tests.* New York: College Entrance Examination Board.

Donn, L. (1988). *Freud and Jung: Years of friendship, years of loss.* New York: Scribner's.

Donnerstein, E. (1980). Aggressive erotica and violence against women. *Journal of Personality and Social Psychology, 39,* 269–277.

Donnerstein, E., Linz, D., & Penrod, S. (1987). *The question of pornography: Research findings and policy implications.* New York: Free Press.

Dore, J. (1985). Holophrases revisited: Their logical development from dialog. In M. D. Barrett (Ed.), *Children's single-word speech.* Chichester, England: Wiley.

Dorfman, D. D. (1995). Soft science with a neoconservative agenda. *Contemporary Psychology, 40,* 418–421.

Dorner, G. (1988). Neuroendocrine response to estrogen and brain differentiation. *Archives of Sexual Behavior, 17*(1), 57–75.

Dovidio, J. F., & Gaertner, S. L. (1991). Changes in the expression of racial prejudice. In H. J. Knopke, R. J. Norrell, & R. W. Rogers (Eds.), *Opening doors: Perspectives in race relations in contemporary America.* Tuscaloosa: University of Alabama Press.

Drachman, D. A. (1986). Memory and cognitive function in normal aging. *Developmental Neuropsychology, 2,* 277–285.

Draguns, J. G. (1979). Culture and personality. In A. J. Marsella, R. G. Tharp, & T. J. Ciborowski (Eds.), *Perspectives on cross-cultural psychology.* New York: Academic Press.

Draguns, J. G. (1980). Psychological disorders of clinical severity. In H. C. Triandis & J. Draguns (Eds.), *Handbook of cross-cultural psychology* (Vol. 6). Boston: Allyn & Bacon.

Draguns, J. G. (1990). Applications of cross-cultural psychology in the field of mental health. In R. Brislin (Ed.), *Applied cross-cultural psychology.* Newbury Park, CA: Sage.

Drake, R. E., Osher, F. C., & Wallach, M. A. (1991). Homelessness and dual diagnosis. *American Psychologist, 46,* 1149–1158.

Driskell, J. E., & Mullen, B. (1990). Status, expectations, and behavior: A meta-analytic review and test of the theory. *Personality and Social Psychology Bulletin, 16,* 541–553.

Driskell, J. E., Willis, R. P., & Copper, C. (1992). Effect of overlearning on retention. *Journal of Applied Psychology, 77*(5), 615–622.

Duara, R. London, E. D., & Rapoport, S. I. (1985). Changes in structure and energy metabolism of the aging brain. In C. E. Finch & E. L. Schneider (Eds.), *Handbook of the biology of aging.* (2nd ed.). New York: Van Nostrand Reinhold.

DuBois, P. (1970). *A history of psychological testing.* Boston: Allyn & Bacon.

Duke, M., & Nowicki, S., Jr. (1979). *Abnormal psychology: Perspectives on being different.* Pacific Grove, CA: Brooks/Cole.

Duncan, B. L. (1976). Differential social perception and attribution of intergroup violence: Testing the lower limits of stereotyping of blacks. *Journal of Personality and Social Psychology, 34,* 590–598.

Duncan, P. D., Ritter, P. L., Dornbusch, S. M., Gross, R. T., & Carlsmith, J. M. (1985). The effects of pubertal timing on body image, school behavior, and deviance. *Youth and Adolescence, 14,* 227–235.

Dunning, D., & Cohen, G. L. (1992). Egocentric definitions of traits and abilities in social judgment. *Journal of Personality and Social Psychology, 63,* 341–355.

Dunning, D., & Hayes, A. F. (1996). Evidence for egocentric comparison in social judgment. *Journal of Personality and Social Psychology, 71,* 213–229.

Durlach, N. I., & Colburn, H. S. (1978). Binaural phenomenon. In E. C. Carterette & M. P. Friedman (Eds.), *Handbook of perception* (Vol. 4). New York: Academic Press.

Durrant, J., & Lovrinic, J. (1977). *Bases of hearing science.* Baltimore: Williams & Wilkins.

Dutton, D., & Aron, A. (1974). Some evidence for heightened sexual attraction under conditions of high anxiety. *Journal of Personality and Social Psychology, 30,* 510–517.

Dworkin, A. (1981). *Pornography: Men possessing women.* New York: Putnam.

Dykman, B. M., Horowitz, L. M., Abramson, L. Y., & Usher, M. (1991). Schematic and situational determinants of depressed and nondepressed students' interpretation feedback. *Journal of Abnormal Psychology, 100,* 45–55.

Eagle, M. N., & Wolitzky, D. L. (1992). Psychoanalytic theories of psychotherapy. In D. K. Freedheim (Ed.), *History of psychotherapy: A century of change.* Washington, DC: American Psychological Association.

Eagly, A. H. (1992). Uneven progress: Social psychology and the study of attitudes. *Journal of Personality and Social Psychology, 63,* 693–710.

Eagly, A. H. (1995). The science and politics of comparing women and men. *American Psychologist, 50,* 145–158.

Eagly, A. H., Ashmore, R. D., Makhijani, M. G., & Longo, L. C. (1991). What is beautiful is good, but . . .: A meta-analytic review of research on the physical attractiveness stereotype. *Psychological Bulletin, 110,* 109–128.

Eagly, A. H., & Carli, L. L. (1981). Sex of researchers and sex-typed communications as determinants of sex differences in influenceability: A meta-analysis of social influence studies. *Psychological Bulletin, 90,* 1–20.

Eals, M., & Silverman, I. (1994). The hunter-gatherer theory of spatial sex differences: Proximate factors mediating the female advantage in recall of object arrays. *Ethology and Sociobiology, 15,* 95–115.

Eaton, W. W., Dryman, A., & Weissman, M. M. (1991). Panic and phobia. In L. N. Robins & D. A. Regier (Eds.), *Psychiatric disorders in America: The epidemiologic catchment area study.* New York: Free Press.

Ebbinghaus, H. (1885/1964). *Memory: A contribution to experimental psychology* (H. A. Ruger & E. R. Bussemius, Trans.). New York: Dover. (Original work published 1885)

Eccles, J. E. (1965). The synapse. *Scientific American, 212,* 56–66.

Edberg, P. (1990). Rorschach assessment. In A. Goldstein & M. Hersen (Eds.), *Handbook of psychological assessment.* New York: Pergamon Press.

Edelman, M. W. (1987). *Families in peril.* Cambridge, MA: Harvard University Press.

Edwards, B. (1989). *Drawing on the right side of the brain.* Los Angeles: J. P. Tarcher.

Edwards, K., & Smith, E. E. (1996). A disconfirmation bias in the evaluation of arguments. *Journal of Personality an Social Psychology, 71,* 5–24.

Efron, R. (1990). *The decline and fall of hemispheric specialization.* Hillsdale, NJ: Erlbaum.

Egan, J. P. (1975). *Signal detection theory and ROC-analysis.* New York: Academic Press.

Egan, K. J., Kogan, H. N., Garber, A., & Jarrett, M. (1983). The impact of psychological distress on the control of hypertension. *Journal of Human Stress, 9*(4), 4–10.

Ehlers, D. L., & Kupfer, D. J. (1989). Effects of age on delta and REM sleep parameters. *Electroencephalography & Clinical Neurophysiology, 72*(2), 118–125.

Ehrenberg, O., & Ehrenberg, M. (1986). *The psychotherapy maze.* Northvale, NJ: Aronson.

Eibl-Eibesfeldt, I. (1975). *Ethology: The biology of behavior.* New York: Holt, Rinehart & Winston.

Eibl-Eibesfeldt, I. (1979). *The biology of peace and war.* London: Thames and Hudson.

Eich, E. (1980). The cue-dependent nature of state-dependent retrieval. *Memory & Cognition, 8,* 157–173.

Eich, E. (1990). Learning during sleep. In R. R. Bootzin, J. F. Kihlstrom, & D. L. Schacter (Eds.), *Sleep and cognition.* Washington, DC: American Psychological Association.

Eich, E. (1995). Searching for mood dependent memory. *Psychological Science, 6,* 67–75.

Einstein, G. O., & McDaniel, M. A. (1996). Remembering to do things: Remembering a forgotten topic. In D. J. Herrmann, C. McEvoy, C. Hertzog, P. Hertel, & M. K. Johnson (Eds.), *Basic and applied memory research: Practical applications* (Vol. 2). Mahwah, NJ: Erlbaum.

Einstein, G. O., Morris, J., & Smith, S. (1985). Note-taking, individual differences, and memory for lecture information. *Journal of Educational Psychology, 77*(5), 522–532.

Eisenberg, N. (1992). *The caring child.* Cambridge, MA: Harvard University Press.

Eisenberg, N., Miller, P. A., Shell, R., McNalley, S., & Shea, C. (1991). Prosocial development in adolescence: A longitudinal study. *Developmental Psychology, 27,* 849–857.

Eisler, R. M., & Ragsdale, K. (1992). Masculine gender role and midlife transition in men. In V. B. Van Hasselt & M. Hersen (Eds.), *Handbook of social development: A lifespan perspective.* New York: Plenum.

Ekman, P. (1980). *The face of man.* New York: Garland Publishing.

Ekman, P. (1992). Facial expressions of emotion: New findings, new questions. *Psychological Science, 3,* 34–38.

Ekman, P. (1993). Facial expression and emotion. *American Psychologist, 48,* 384–392.

Ekman, P. (1994). Strong evidence for universals in facial expressions: A reply to Russell's mistaken critique. *Psychological Bulletin, 115,* 268–287.

Ekman, P., & Friesen, W. V. (1975). *Unmasking the face.* Englewood Cliffs, NJ: Prentice-Hall.

Ekman, P., & Friesen, W. V. (1984). *Unmasking the face.* Palo Alto: Consulting Psychologists Press.

Ekman, P., Levenson, R. W., & Friesen, W. V. (1983). Autonomic nervous system activity distinguishes among emotions. *Science, 221,* 1208–1210.

Elbert, T., Pantev, C., Wienbruch, C., Rockstroh, B., & Taub, E. (1995). Increased cortical representation of the fingers of the left hand in string players. *Science, 270,* 305–307.

Elias, M. F., Elias, J. W., & Elias, P. K. (1990). Biological and health influences on behavior. In J. E. Birren & K. W. Schaie (Eds.), *Handbook of the psychology of aging.* San Diego: Academic Press.

Elicker, J., Englund, M., & Sroufe, L. A. (1992). Predicting peer competence and peer relationships in childhood from early parent-child relationships. In R. D. Parke & G. W. Ladd (Eds.), *Family-peer relationships: Modes of linkage.* Hillsdale, NJ: Erlbaum.

Ellard, K., Beaurepaire, J., Jones, M., Piper, D., & Tennant, C. (1990). Acute chronic stress in duodenal ulcer disease. *Gastroenterology, 99,* 1628–1632.

Elliot, A. J., & Devine, P. G. (1994). On the motivational nature of cognitive dissonance: Dissonance as psychological discomfort. *Journal of Personality and Social Psychology, 67,* 382–394.

Elliott, C. S., & Archibald, R. B. (1989). Subjective framing and attitudes toward risk. *Journal of Economic Psychology, 10,* 321–328.

Elliott, E. (1989). Stress and illness. In S. Cheren (Ed.), *Psychosomatic medicine: Theory, physiology, and practice* (Vol. 1). Madison, CT: International Universities Press.

Elliott, G. R., & Eisdorfer, C. (Eds.). (1982). *Stress and human health: Analysis and implications of research.* New York: Springer.

Ellis, A. (1973). *Humanistic psychotherapy: The rational-emotive approach.* New York: Julian Press.

Ellis, A. (1977). *Reason and emotion in psychotherapy.* Seacaucus, NJ: Lyle Stuart.

Ellis, A. (1985). *How to live with and without anger.* New York: Citadel Press.

Ellis, A. (1989). Rational-emotive therapy. In R. J. Corsini & D. Wedding (Eds.), *Current Psychotherapies.* Itasca, IL: F. E. Peacock.

Ellis, H. C., & Ashbrook, P. W. (1991). The "state" of mood and memory research: A selective review. In D. Kuiken (Ed.), *Mood and memory: Theory, research, and applications.* Newbury Park, CA: Sage.

Ellis, L., & Ames, M. A. (1987). Neurohormonal functioning and sexual orientation: A theory of homosexuality-heterosexuality. *Psychological Bulletin, 101,* 233–258.

Ellman, S. J., Spielman, A. J., Luck, D., Steiner, S. S., & Halperin, R. (1991). REM deprivation: A review. In S. J. Ellman & J. S. Antrobus (Eds.), *The mind in sleep: Psychology and psychophysiology* (2nd ed.). New York: Wiley.

Emmelkamp, P. M. G. (1994). Behavior therapy with adults. In A. E. Bergin & S. L. Garfield (Eds.), *Handbook of psychotherapy and behavior change* (4th ed.). New York: Wiley.

Emmelkamp, P. M. G., & Scholing, A. (1990). Behavioral treatment for simple and social phobias. In R. Noyes, Jr., M. Roth, & G. D. Burrows (Eds.), *Handbook of anxiety: The treatment of anxiety* (Vol. 4). Amsterdam: Elsevier.

Endler, N. S., & Parker, J. D. A. (1990). Multidimensional assessment of coping: A critical evaluation. *Journal of Personality and Social Psychology, 58,* 844–854.

Engen, T. (1971). Psychophysics: 1. Discrimination and detection. In F. W. Kling & L. A. Riggs (Eds.), *Experimental Psychology* (3rd ed., Vol. 1). New York: Holt, Rinehart & Winston.

English, J. T., & McCarrick, R. G. (1989). The economics of psychiatry. In H. I. Kaplan & B. J. Sadock (Eds.), *Comprehensive textbook of psychiatry/V* (Vol. 2). Baltimore: Williams & Wilkins.

Enright, J. T. (1980). *The timing of sleep and wakefulness.* New York: Springer.

Eppley, K., Abrams, A., & Shear, J. (1989). The differential effects of relaxation techniques on trait anxiety: A meta-analysis. *Journal of Clinical Psychology, 45*(6), 957–974.

Epstein, S. P. (1980). The stability of confusion: A reply to Mischel and Peake. *Psychological Review, 90,* 179–184.

Epstein, S. P. (1982). Conflict and stress. In L. Goldberger & S. Breznitz (Eds.), *Handbook of stress: Theoretical and clinical aspects.* New York: Free Press.

Epstein, S. P. (1986). Does aggregation produce

spuriously high estimates of behavior stability? *Journal of Personality and Social Psychology, 50,* 1199–1210.

Epstein, S. P. (1990). Cognitive-experiential self-theory. In L. A. Pervin (Ed.), *Handbook of personality: Theory and research.* New York: Guilford Press.

Epstein, S. P., & Meier, P. (1989). Constructive thinking: A broad coping variable with specific components. *Journal of Personality and Social Psychology, 57,* 332–350.

Erdberg, P. (1990). Rorschach assessment. In G. Goldstein & M. Hersen (Eds.), *Handbook of psychological assessment* (2nd ed.). New York: Pergamon Press.

Erdle, S. (1990). Limitations of the heritability coefficient as an index of genetic and environmental influences on human behavior. *American Psychologist, 45,* 553–554.

Erickson, S. J., Feldman, S. S., & Steiner, H. (1996). Defense mechanisms and adjustments in normal adolescents. *American Journal of Psychiatry, 153,* 826–828.

Ericsson, K. A., & Charness, N. (1994). Expert performance: Its structure and acquisition. *American Psychologist, 49,* 725–747.

Ericsson, K. A., & Kintsch, W. (1995). Long-term working memory. *Psychological Review, 102,* 211–245.

Ericsson, K. A., & Lehmann, A. C. (1996). Expert and exceptional performance: Evidence of maximal adaptation to task constraints. *Annual Review of Psychology, 47,* 273–305.

Ericsson, K. A., & Polson, P. G. (1988). An experimental analysis of the mechanisms of a memory skill. *Journal of Experimental Psychology: Learning, Memory and Congnition, 14,* 305–316.

Erikson, E. (1963). *Childhood and society.* New York: Norton.

Erikson, E. (1968). *Identity: Youth and crisis.* New York: Norton.

Ernst, C., & Angst, J. (1983). Birth order: Its influence on personality. *Behavioral and Brain Sciences, 10*(1), 55.

Eron, L. D. (1963). Relationship of TV viewing habits and aggressive behavior in children. *Journal of Abnormal and Social Psychology, 67,* 193–196.

Eron, L. D. (1982). Parent-child interaction, television violence, and aggression of children. *American Psychologist, 37,* 197–211.

Eron, L. D., Huesmann, L. R., Brice, P., Fischer, P., & Mermelstein, R. (1983). Age trends in the development of aggression, sex-typing, and related television habits. *Developmental Psychology, 19,* 71–77.

Eron, L. D., Huesmann, L. R., Lefkowitz, M. M., & Walder, L. O. (1972). Does television violence cause aggression? *American Psychologist, 27,* 253–263.

Escobar, J. I. (1993). Psychiatric epidemiology. In A. C. Gaw (Ed.), *Culture, ethnicity, and mental illness.* Washington, DC: American Psychiatric Press.

Esses, V. M., & Zanna, M. P. (1995). Mood and the expression of ethnic stereotypes. *Journal of Personality and Social Psychology, 69,* 1052–1068.

Esterson, A. (1993). *Seductive mirage: An exploration of the work of Sigmund Freud.* Chicago: Open Court.

Etaugh, C., & Liss, M. B. (1992). Home, school, and playroom: Training grounds for adult gender roles. *Sex Roles, 26,* 129–147.

Evans, C. E., & Haynes, R. B. (1990). Patient compliance. In R. E. Rakel (Ed.), *Textbook of family practice.* Philadelphia: Saunders.

Evans, F. J. (1990). Behavioral responses during sleep. In R. R. Bootzin, J. F. Kihlstrom, & D. L. Schacter (Eds.), *Sleep and cognition.* Washington, DC: American Psychological Association.

Evans, R. L. (1981). New drug evaluations: Alprazolam. *Drug Intelligence and Clinical Pharmacy, 15,* 633–637.

Eyer, D. E. (1992). *Scientific fictions and realities.* New Haven, CT: Yale University Press.

Eysenck, H. J. (1952). The effects of psychotherapy: An evaluation. *Journal of Consulting Psychology, 16,* 319–324.

Eysenck, H. J. (1959). Learning theory and behaviour therapy. *Journal of Mental Science, 195,* 61–75.

Eysenck, H. J. (1967). *The biological basis of personality.* Springfield, IL: Charles C Thomas.

Eysenck, H. J. (1977). *Crime and personality.* London: Routledge & Kegan Paul.

Eysenck, H. J. (1981). Is intelligence inherited? In H. J. Eysenck versus L. Kamin, *The intelligence controversy.* New York: Wiley.

Eysenck, H. J. (1982). *Personality, genetics and behavior: Selected papers.* New York: Praeger.

Eysenck, H. J. (1988). The concept of "intelligence": Useful or useless? *Intelligence, 12*(1), 1–16.

Eysenck, H. J. (1989). Discrimination reaction time and "*g*": A reply to Humphreys. *Intelligence, 13*(4), 325–326.

Eysenck, H. J. (1990a). Biological dimensions of personality. In L. A. Pervin (Ed.), *Handbook of personality: Theory and research.* New York: Guilford Press.

Eysenck, H. J. (1990b). *Decline and fall of the Freudian empire.* Washington, DC: Scott-Townsend.

Eysenck, H. J. (1991). Dimensions of personality: 16, 5, or 3?—Criteria for a taxonomic paradigm. *Personality and Individual Differences, 12,* 773–790.

Eysenck, H. J. (1992). Four ways five factors are not basic. *Personality and Individual Differences, 13,* 667–673.

Eysenck, H. J. (1993). Forty years on: The outcome problem in psychotherapy revisted. In T. R. Giles (Ed.), *Handbook of effective psychotherapy.* New York: Plenum Press.

Eysenck, H. J., & Eysenck, S. B. G. (1983). Recent advances in the cross-cultural study of personality. In J. N. Butcher & C. S. Spielberger (Eds.), *Advances in personality assessment* (Vol. 2). Hillsdale, NJ: Erlbaum.

Eysenck, H. J., & Kamin, L. (1981). *The intelligence controversy.* New York: Wiley.

Eysenck, M. W. (1984). *A handbook of cognitive psychology.* Hillsdale, NJ: Erlbaum.

Eysenck, M. W., Mogg, K., May, J., Richards, A., & Mathews, A. (1991). Bias in interpretation of ambiguous sentences related to threat in anxiety. *Journal of Abnormal Psychology, 100,* 144–150.

Fagley, N. S. (1987). Positional response bias in multiple-choice tests of learning: Its relation to testwiseness and guessing strategy. *Journal of Educational Psychology, 79,* 95–97.

Fagot, B. I., & Hagan, R. (1991). Observations of parent reactions to sex-stereotyped behaviors: Age and sex effects. *Child Development, 62,* 617–628.

Fagot, B. I., Hagan, R., Leinbach, M. D., & Kronsberg, S. (1985). Differential reactions to assertive and communicative acts of toddler boys and girls. *Child Development, 56,* 1499–1505.

Fagot, B. I., Leinbach, M. D., & O'Boyle, C. (1992). Gender labeling, gender stereotyping, and parenting behaviors. *Developmental Psychology, 28,* 225–230.

Fahey, P. J., & Gallagher-Allred, C. (1990). Nutrition. In R. E. Rakel (Ed.), *Textbook of family practice* (4th ed.). Philadelphia: Saunders.

Falbo, T., & Polit, D. F. (1986). Quantitative review of the only child literature: Research evidence and theory development. *Psychological Bulletin, 100,* 176–189.

Fancher, R. E. (1979). *Pioneers of psychology.* New York: Norton.

Fancher, R. E. (1985). *The intelligence men: Makers of the IQ controversy.* New York: Norton.

Fanselow, M. S. (1991). Analgesia as a response to aversive Pavlovian conditioned stimuli: Cognitive and emotional mediators. In M. R. Denny (Ed.), *Fear, avoidance and phobias.* Hillsdale, NJ: Erlbaum.

Fantino, E. (1973). Aversive control. In J. A. Nevin (Ed.), *The study of behavior: Learning, motivation, emotion and instinct.* Glenview, IL: Scott, Foresman.

Faraday, A. (1974). *The dream game.* New York: Harper & Row.

Faravelli, C., & Pallanti, S. (1989). Recent life events and panic disorders. *American Journal of Psychiatry, 146,* 622–626.

Farrar, M. J. (1990). Discourse and the acquisition of grammatical morphemes. *Journal of Child Language, 17,* 607–624.

Faust, D., & Ziskin, J. (1988). The expert witness in psychology and psychiatry. *Science, 241,* 31–35.

Fausto-Sterling, A. (1992). *Myths of gender.* New York: Basic Books.

Fava, G. A., Perini, G. I., Santonastaso, P., & Fornasa, C. V. (1989). Life events and psychological distress in dermatologic disorders: Psoriasis, chronic urticaria, and fungal infections. In T. W. Miller (Ed.), *Stressful life events.* Madison, CT: International Universities Press.

Featherstone, H. J., & Beitman, B. D. (1984). Marital migraine: A refractory daily headache. *Psychosomatics, 25*(1), 30–38.

Fechner, G. T. (1860). *Elemente der psychophysik* (Vol. 1). Leipzig: Breitkopf & Harterl.

Feder, H. H. (1984). Hormones and sexual behavior. *Annual Review of Psychology, 35,* 165–200.

Feeney, D. M. (1987). Human rights and animal welfare. *American Psychologist, 42,* 593–599.

Feeney, J. A., & Noller, P. (1990). Attachment style as a predictor of adult romantic relationships. *Journal of Personality and Social Psychology, 58,* 281–291.

Feingold, A. (1988a). Cognitive gender differences are disappearing. *American Psychologist, 43,* 95–103.

Feingold, A. (1988b). Matching for attractiveness in romantic partners and same-sex friends: A meta-analysis and theoretical critique. *Psychological Bulletin, 104,* 226–235.

Feingold, A. (1990). Gender differences in effects of physical attractiveness on romantic attraction: A comparison across five research paradigms. *Journal of Personality and Social Psychology, 59,* 981–993.

Feingold, A. (1992). Good-looking people are not what we think. *Psychological Bulletin, 111,* 304–341.

Feingold, A. (1994). Gender differences in personality: A meta-analysis. *Psychological Bulletin, 116*, 429–456.

Feldman, D. H. (1988). Creativity: Dreams, insights, and transformations. In R. J. Sternberg (Ed.), *The nature of creativity: Contemporary psychological perspectives*. Cambridge: Cambridge University Press.

Fenton, W. S., & McGlashan, T. H. (1994). Antecedents, symptom progression, and long-term outcome of the deficit syndrome in schizophrenia. *American Journal of Psychiatry, 151*, 351–356.

Fenton, W. S., McGlashan, T. H., Victor, B. J., & Blyler, C. R. (1997). Symptoms, subtype, and suicidality in patients with schizophrenia spectrum disorders. *American Journal of Psychiatry, 154*, 199–204.

Fenwick, P. (1987). Meditation and the EEG. In M. A. West (Ed.), *The psychology of meditation*. Oxford: Clarendon Press.

Ferguson, N. B. L., & Keesey, R. E. (1975). Effect of a quinine-adulterated diet upon body-weight maintenance in male rats with ventromedial hypothalamic lesions. *Journal of Comparative and Physiological Psychology, 89*, 478–488.

Ferster, C. S., & Skinner, B. F. (1957). *Schedules of reinforcement*. New York: Appleton- Century-Crofts.

Festinger, L. (1957). *A theory of cognitive dissonance*. Stanford, CA: Stanford University Press.

Festinger, L., & Carlsmith, J. M. (1959). Cognitive consequences of forced compliance. *Journal of Abnormal and Social Psychology, 58*, 203–210.

Festinger, L., Schachter, S., & Back, K. (1950). *Social pressures in informal groups: A study of human factors in housing*. New York: Harper.

Fielding, J. E. (1985). Smoking: Health effects and control. *New England Journal of Medicine, 313*, 491–498, 555–561.

Fields, H. L., & Levine, J. D. (1984). Placebo analgesia: A role for endorphins. *Trends in Neuroscience, 7*, 271–273.

Fifer, W. P., & Moon, C. (1988). Auditory experience in the fetus. In W. P. Smotherman & S. R. Robinson (Eds.), *Behavior of the fetus*. Caldwell, NJ: Telford.

Fincham, F. D., & Bradbury, T. N. (1993). Marital satisfaction, depression, and attributions: A longitudinal analysis. *Journal of Personality and Social Psychology, 63*, 442–452.

Findley, M. J., & Cooper, H. M. (1983). Locus of control and academic achievement: A literature review. *Journal of Personality and Social Psychology, 44*, 419–427.

Fine, R. (1990). *The history of psychoanalysis*. New York: Continuum.

Finer, B. (1980). Hypnosis and anaesthesia. In G. D. Burrows & L. Dennerstein (Eds.), *Handbook of hypnosis and psychosomatic medicine*. Amsterdam: Elsevier/North Holland Biomedical Press.

Fink, M. (1992). Electroconvulsive therapy. In E. S. Paykel (Ed.), *Handbook of affective disorders* (2nd ed.). New York: Guilford Press.

Finnegan, L. P., & Kandall, S. R. (1992). Maternal and neonatal effects of alcohol and drugs. In J. H. Lowinson, P. Ruiz, & R. B. Millman (Eds.), *Substance abuse: A comprehensive textbook*. Baltimore: Williams & Wilkins.

Fiore, M. C. (1992). Trends in cigarette smoking in the United States: The epidemiology of tobacco use. *Medical Clinics of North America, 76*, 289–303.

Fischer, K. W., & Hencke, R. W. (1996). Infants' construction of actions in context: Piaget's con-

tribution to research on early development. *Psychological Science, 7*, 204–210.

Fischer, P. J., & Breakey, W. R. (1991). The epidemiology of alcohol, drug, and mental disorders among homeless persons. *American Psychologist, 46*, 1115–1128.

Fischhoff, B. (1982). Debiasing. In D. Kahneman, P. Slovic, & A. Tversky (Eds.), *Judgment under uncertainty: Heuristics and biases*. Cambridge: Cambridge University Press.

Fischhoff, B. (1988). Judgment and decision making. In R. J. Sternberg & E. E. Smith (Eds.), *The psychology of human thought*. Cambridge: Cambridge University Press.

Fisher, J. D., & Fisher, W. A. (1992). Changing AIDS-risk behavior. *Psychological Bulletin, 111*, 455–474.

Fisher, S., & Greenberg, R. P. (1985). *The scientific credibility of Freud's theories and therapy*. New York: Columbia University Press.

Fisher, S., & Greenberg, R. P. (1996). *Freud scientifically reappraised: Testing the theories and therapy*. New York: Wiley.

Fisher, W. A., Byrne, D., White, L. A., & Kelley, K. (1988). Erotophobia-erotophilia as a dimension of personality. *Journal of Sex Research, 25*(1), 123–151.

Fishman, D. B., & Franks, C. M. (1992). Evolution and differentiation within behavior therapy: A theoretical epistemological review. In D. K. Freedheim (Ed.), *History of psychotherapy: A century of change*. Washington, DC: American Psychological Association.

Fiske, S. T., & Taylor, S. E. (1991). *Social cognition*. New York: McGraw-Hill.

Flaum, M., Swayze, V. W., O'Leary, D. S., Yuh, W. T. C., Ehrhardt, J. C., Arndt, S. V., & Andreasen, N. C. (1995). Effects of diagnosis, laterality, and gender on brain morphology in schizophrenia. *American Journal of Psychiatry, 152*, 704–714.

Flavell, J. H. (1985). *Cognitive development*. Englewood Cliffs, NJ: Prentice-Hall.

Flavell, J. H. (1992). Cognitive development: Past, present, and future. *Developmental Psychology, 28*, 998–1005.

Flavell, J. H. (1996). Piaget's Legacy. *Psychological Science, 7*, 200–203.

Fletcher, G. J. O., & Ward, C. (1988). Attribution theory and processes: A cross-cultural perspective. In M. H. Bond (Ed.), *The cross-cultural challenge to social psychology*. Newbury Park, CA: Sage.

Fletcher, R. (1991). *Cyril Burt, still lively after all these years*. New Brunswick, NJ: Transaction.

Flor-Henry, P. (1990). Sinistrality and psychopathology. In S. Coren (Ed.), *Left-handedness: Behavioral implications and anomalies*. Amsterdam: North-Holland.

Florian, V., Mikulincer, M., & Taubman, O. (1995). Does hardiness contribute to mental health during a stressful real-life situation? The roles of appraisal and coping. *Journal of Personality and Social Psychology, 68*, 687–695.

Foa, E. B., & Kozak, M. J. (1995). DSM-IV field trial: Obsessive-compulsive disorder. *American Journal of Psychiatry, 152*, 90–96.

Folkard, S., Arendt, J., & Clark, M. (1993). Can melatonin improve shift workers' tolerance of the night shift? Some preliminary findings. *Chronobiology International, 10*, 315–320.

Folkman, S. (1984). Personal control and stress and coping processes: A theoretical analysis. *Jour-*

nal of Personality and Social Psychology, 46, 839–852.

Ford, D. Y., & Harris, J. J. (1992). The elusive definition of creativity. *Journal of Creative Behavior, 26*(3), 186–198.

Forsyth, D. R. (1990). *An introduction to group dynamics*. Pacific Grove, CA: Brooks/Cole.

Forsyth, D. R., & McMillan, J. H. (1981). Attributions, affect, and expectations: A test of Weiner's three-dimensional model. *Journal of Educational Psychology, 73*, 393–403.

Forsyth, D. R., & Strong, S. R. (1986). The scientific study of counseling and psychotherapy: A unificationist view. *American Psychologist, 41*, 113–119.

Foscarinis, M. (1991). The politics of homelessness: A call to action. *American Psychologist, 46*, 1232–1238.

Foulkes, D. (1985). *Dreaming: A cognitive-psychological analysis*. Hillsdale, NJ: Erlbaum.

Fowler, R. D. (1986, May). Howard Hughes: A psychological autopsy. *Psychology Today*, pp. 22–33.

Fowler, R. D. (1990). Report of the chief executive officer: A year of recovery. *American Psychologist, 45*, 803–806.

Fowles, D. C. (1992). Schizophrenia: Diathesis-stress revisited. *Annual Review of Psychology, 43*, 303–336.

Fowles, D. C. (1993). A motivational theory of psychopathology. In W. Spaulding (Ed.), *Nebraska Symposium on Motivation: Integrated views of motivation, cognition and emotion* (Vol. 41). Lincoln: University of Nebraska Press.

Fox, L. H., & Washington, J. (1985). Programs for the gifted and talented: Past, present, and future. In F. D. Horowitz & M. O'Brien (Eds.), *The gifted and talented: Developmental perspectives*. Washington, DC: American Psychological Association.

Fox, N. A., Kimmerly, N. L., & Schafer, W. D. (1991). Attachment to mother/attachment to father: A meta-analysis. *Child Development, 62*, 210–225.

Fozard, J. L. (1990). Vision and hearing in aging. In J. E. Birren & K.W. Schaie (Eds.), *Handbook of the psychology of aging* (3rd ed.). San Diego: Academic Press.

France, C., & Ditto, B. (1988). Caffeine effects on several indices of cardiovascular activity at rest and during stress. *Journal of Behavioral Medicine, 11*, 473–482.

Frances, A. J., First, M. B., Widiger, T. A., Miele, G. M., Tilly, S. M., Davis, W. W., & Pincus, H. A. (1991). An A to Z guide to DSM-IV conundrums. *Journal of Abnormal Psychology, 100*, 407–412.

Frank, E. (1991). Interpersonal psychotherapy as a maintenance treatment for patients with recurrent depression. *Psychotherapy, 28*, 259–266.

Frank, E., Anderson, C., & Rubinstein, D. (1978). Frequency of sexual dysfunction in "normal" couples. *New England Journal of Medicine, 299*, 111–115.

Frank, J. D. (1961). *Persuasion and healing*. Baltimore: Johns Hopkins University Press.

Frank, L. K. (1939). Projective methods for the study of personality. *Journal of Psychology, 8*, 343–389.

Frank, L. R. (1990). Electroshock: Death, brain damage, memory loss, and brainwashing. *The Journal of Mind and Behavior, 11*(3/4), 489–512.

Frankel, F. H. (1990). Hypnotizability and dissociation. *American Journal of Psychiatry, 147,* 823–829.

Franken, R. E., Gibson, K. J., & Rowland, G. L. (1992). Sensation seeking and the tendency to view the world as threatening. *Personality and Individual Differences, 13*(1), 31–38.

Franks, C. M., & Barbrack, C. R. (1983). Behavior therapy with adults: An integrative perspective. In M. Hersen, A. E. Kazdin, & A. S. Bellack (Eds.), *The clinical psychology handbook.* New York: Pergamon Press.

Frederiksen, N. (1986). Toward a broader conception of human intelligence. In R. J. Sternberg & R. K. Wagner (Eds.), *Practical intelligence: Nature and origins of competence in the everyday world.* Cambridge: Cambridge University Press.

Freedman, J. L. (1984). Effect of television violence on aggressiveness. *Psychological Bulletin, 96,* 227–246.

Fremer, J. (1994). Group tests. In R. J. Sternberg (Ed.), *Encyclopedia of human intelligence.* New York: Macmillan.

Fremouw, W. J., de Perczel, M., & Ellis, T. E. (1990). *Suicide risk: Assessment and response guidelines.* New York: Pergamon Press.

French, S. A., & Jeffery, R. W. (1994). Consequences of dieting to lose weight: Effects on physical and mental health. *Health Psychology, 13,* 195–212.

Freud, S. (1900/1953). *The interpretation of dreams.* In J. Strachey (Ed.), *The standard edition of the complete psychological works of Sigmund Freud* (Vols. 4 and 5). London: Hogarth.

Freud, S. (1901/1960). *The psychopathology of everyday life.* In J. Strachey (Ed.), *The standard edition of the complete psychological works of Sigmund Freud* (Vol. 6). London: Hogarth.

Freud, S. (1905/1953). *Fragment of an analysis of a case of hysteria.* In J. Strachey (Ed.), *The standard edition of the complete psychological works of Sigmund Freud* (Vol. 7). London: Hogarth.

Freud, S. (1915/1959). Instincts and their vicissitudes. In E. Jones (Ed.), *The collected papers of Sigmund Freud* (Vol. 4). New York: Basic Books.

Freud, S. (1920). *A general introduction to psychoanalysis.* New York: Boni & Liveright.

Freud, S. (1924). *A general introduction to psychoanalysis.* New York: Boni & Liveright.

Freud, S. (1933/1964). *New introductory lectures on psychoanalysis.* In J. Strachey (Ed.), *The standard edition of the complete psychological works of Sigmund Freud* (Vol. 22). London: Hogarth.

Freud, S. (1940). An outline of psychoanalysis. *International Journal of Psychoanalysis, 21,* 27–84.

Friedberg, J. (1976). *Shock treatment is not good for your brain.* San Francisco: Glide Publications.

Friedman, H. S., Tucker, J. S., Schwartz, J. E., Martin, L. R., Tomlinson-Keasey, C., Wingard, D. L., & Criqui, M. H. (1995). Childhood conscientiousness and longevity: Health behaviors and cause of death. *Journal of Personality and Social Psychology, 68,* 696–703.

Friedman, H. S., Tucker, J. S., Tomlinson-Keasey, C., Schwartz, J. E., Wingard, D. L., & Criqui, M. H. (1993). Does childhood personality predict longevity? *Journal of Personality and Social Psychology, 65,* 176–185.

Friedman, L. S., & Goodman, E. (1992). Adolescents at risk for HIV infection. *Primary Care, 19*(1), 171–190.

Friedman, M., & Rosenman, R. F. (1974). *Type A behavior and your heart.* New York: Knopf.

Friedman, S. R., de Jong, W. M., & Des Jarlais, D. C. (1988). Problems and dynamics of organiz-

ing intravenous drug users for AIDS prevention. *Health Education Research, 3,* 49–57.

Friedrich, J., Fetherstonhaugh, D., Casey, S., & Gallagher, D. (1996). Argument integration and attitude change: Suppression effects in the integration of one-sided arguments that vary in persuasiveness. *Personality and Social Psychology Bulletin, 22,* 179–191.

Friedrich-Cofer, L., & Huston, A. C. (1986). Television violence and aggression: The debate continues. *Psychological Bulletin, 100,* 364–371.

Fries, H., Nillius, J., & Petersson, F. (1974). Epidemiology of secondary amenorrhea. *American Journal of Obstetrics and Gynecology, 118,* 473–479.

Froelicher, V. F. (1990). Exercise, fitness, and coronary heart disease. In C. Bouchard, R. J. Shephard, T. Stephens, J. R. Sutton, & B. D. McPherson (Eds.), *Exercise, fitness, and health: A consensus of current knowledge.* Champaign, IL: Human Kinetics Books.

Fromm, E. (1979). The nature of hypnosis and other altered states of consciousness: An ego-psychological theory. In E. Fromm & R. E. Shor (Eds.), *Hypnosis: Developments in research and new perspectives.* New York: Aldine.

Fromm E. (1992). An ego-psychological theory of hypnosis. In E. Fromm & M. R. Nash (Eds.), *Contemporary hypnosis research.* New York: Guilford Press.

Frumkes, T. E. (1990). Classical and modern psychophysical studies of dark and light adaptation and their relationship to underlying retinal function. In K. N. Leibovic (Ed.), *Science of vision.* New York: Springer-Verlag.

Fry, A. F., & Hale, S. (1996). Processing speed, working memory, and fluid intelligence: Evidence for a developmental cascade. *Psychological Science, 7,* 237–241.

Fryer, D. (1931). *The measurement of interests in relation to human adjustment.* New York: Henry Holt and Company.

Funder, D. C., & Colvin, C. R. (1991). Explorations in behavioral consistency: Properties of persons, situations, and behaviors. *Journal of Personality and Social Psychology, 60,* 773–794.

Funk, S. C. (1992). Hardiness: A review of theory and research. *Health Psychology, 11*(5), 335–345.

Furnham, A. (1984). Value systems and anomie in three cultures. *International Journal of Psychology, 19,* 565–579.

Furnham, A. (1986). Response bias, social desirability, and dissimulation. *Personality and Individual Differences, 7,* 385–400.

Furumoto, L. (1980). Mary Whiton Calkins (1863–1930). *Psychology of Women Quarterly, 5,* 55–68.

Furumoto, L., & Scarborough, E. (1986). Placing women in the history of psychology: The first American women psychologists. *American Psychologist, 41,* 35–42.

Gabbard, G. O., Lazar, S. G., Hornberger, J., & Spiegel, D. (1997). The economic impact of psychotherapy: A review. *American Journal of Psychiatry, 154,* 147–155.

Gaertner, S. L., Mann, J. A., Dovidio, J. F., Murrell, A. J., & Pomare, M. (1990). How does cooperation reduce intergroup bias? *Journal of Personality and Social Psychology, 59,* 692–704.

Gaito, J. (1976). Molecular psychobiology of memory: Its appearance, contributions, and decline. *Physiological Psychology, 4,* 476–484.

Galambos, N. L. (1992). Parent-adolescent rela-

tions. *Current Directions in Psychological Science, 1*(5), 146–149.

Galanter, E. (1962). Contemporary psychophysics. In R. Brown (Ed.), *New directions in psychology.* New York: Holt, Rinehart & Winston.

Gale, A. (1983). Electroencephalographic studies of extraversion-introversion: A case study in the psychophysiology of individual differences. *Personality and Individual Differences, 4,* 371–380.

Galin, D. (1974). Implications for psychiatry of left and right cerebral specialization: A neuropsychological context for unconscious processes. *Archives of General Psychiatry, 31,* 572–583.

Gallagher, J. J., & Courtright, R. D. (1986). The educational definition of giftedness and its policy implications. In R. J. Sternberg & J. E. Davidson (Eds.), *Conceptions of giftedness.* Cambridge: Cambridge University Press.

Galton, F. (1869). *Hereditary genius: An inquiry into its laws and consequences.* New York: Appleton.

Gangestad, S. W., & Simpson, J. A. (1993). Development of a scale measuring genetic variation related to expressive control. *Journal of Personality, 61*(2), 133–158.

Gangestad, S. W., & Snyder, M. (1985). On the nature of self-monitoring: An examination of latent causal structure. In P. Shaver (Ed.), *Review of personality and social psychology* (Vol. 6). Beverly Hills, CA: Sage.

Gantt, W. H. (1966). Conditional or conditioned, reflex or response? *Conditioned Reflex, 1,* 69–74.

Gantt, W. H. (1975, April 25). Unpublished lecture, Ohio State University. Cited in D. Hothersall, (1984), *History of psychology.* New York: Random House.

Garcia, E., & Wykes, S. L. (1996, July 4). Franklin free. *San Jose Mercury News,* 1B.

Garcia, J. (1989). Food for Tolman: Cognition and cathexis in concert. In T. Archer & L. G. Nilsson (Eds.), *Aversion, avoidance, and anxiety: Perspectives on aversively motivated behavior.* Hillsdale, NJ: Erlbaum.

Garcia, J., Clarke, J. C., & Hankins, W. G. (1973). Natural responses to scheduled rewards. In P. P. G. Bateson & P. Klopfer (Eds.), *Perspectives in ethology.* New York: Plenum.

Garcia, J., & Koelling, R. A. (1966). Learning with prolonged delay of reinforcement. *Psychonomic Science, 5,* 121–122.

Garcia, J., & Rusiniak, K. W. (1980). What the nose learns from the mouth. In D. Muller-Schwarze & R. M. Silverstein (Eds.), *Chemical signals.* New York: Plenum.

Gardner, E. (1975). *Fundamentals of neurology.* Philadelphia: Saunders.

Gardner, H. (1975, August 9). Brain damage: Window on the mind. *Saturday Review,* pp. 26–29.

Gardner, H. (1983). *Frames of mind: The theory of multiple intelligences.* New York: Basic Books.

Gardner, H. (1985). *The mind's new science: A history of the cognitive revolution.* New York: Basic Books.

Gardner, H. (1993). *Multiple intelligences: The theory in practice.* New York: Basic Books.

Gardner, H. (1995). Why would anyone become an expert? *American Psychologist, 50,* 802–803.

Gardner, H., & Hatch, T. (1989). Multiple intelligences go to school: Educational implications of the theory of multiple intelligences. *Educational Researcher, 18*(8), 4–10.

Gardner, R. A., & Gardner, B. T. (1969). Teaching sign language to a chimpanzee. *Science, 165,* 664–672.

Gardos, G., Casey, D. E., Cole, J. O., Perenyi, A., Kocsis, E., Arato, M., Samson, J. A., & Conley, C. (1994). Ten-year outcome of tardive dyskinesia. *American Journal of Psychiatry, 151,* 836–841.

Garfield, S. L. (1986). Problems in diagnostic classification. In T. Millon & G. L. Klerman (Eds.), *Contemporary directions in psychopathology: Toward the DSM-IV.* New York: Guilford Press.

Garfield, S. L. (1992). Major issues in psychotherapy research. In D. K. Freedheim (Ed.), *History of psychotherapy: A century of change.* Washington, DC: American Psychological Association.

Garfield, S. L. (1993). Methodological problems in clinical diagnosis. In P. B. Sutker & H. E. Adams (Eds.), *Comprehensive handbook of psychopathology* (2nd ed.). New York: Plenum.

Garfield, S. L., & Bergin, A. E. (1994). Introduction and historical overview. In A. E. Bergin & S. L. Garfield (Eds.), *Handbook of psychotherapy and behavior change* (4th ed.). New York: Wiley.

Garland, A. F., & Zigler, E. (1993). Adolescent suicide prevention: Current research and social policy implications. *American Psychologist, 48*(2), 169–182.

Garnets, L., & Kimmel, D. (1991). Lesbian and gay male dimensions in the psychological study of human diversity. In J. D. Goodchilds (Ed.), *Psychological perspectives on human diversity in America.* Washington, DC: American Psychological Association.

Garrett, V. D., Brantley, P. J., Jones, G. N., & McKnight, G. T. (1991). The relation between daily stress and Crohn's disease. *Journal of Behavioral Medicine, 14*(1), 87–96.

Garson, B. (1988). *The electronic sweatshop.* New York: Simon & Schuster.

Garson, B. (1994). *All the livelong day.* New York: Penguin.

Garvey, C. R. (1929). List of American psychology laboratories. *Psychological Bulletin, 26,* 652–660.

Gatewood, R., & Perloff, R. (1990). Testing and industrial application. In G. Goldstein & M. Hersen (Eds.), *Handbook of psychological assessment.* New York: Pergamon Press.

Gavanski, I., & Roskos-Ewoldsen, D. R. (1991). Representativeness and conjoint probability. *Journal of Personality and Social Psychology, 61,* 181–194.

Gazzaniga, M. S. (1970). *The bisected brain.* New York: Appleton-Century-Crofts.

Gazzaniga, M. S., Bogen, J. E., & Sperry, R. W. (1965). Observations on visual perception after disconnexion of the cerebral hemispheres in man. *Brain, 88,* 221–236.

Gecas, V., & Seff, M. A. (1990). Families and adolescents: A review of the 1980s. *Journal of Marriage and the Family, 52,* 941–958.

Geis, F. L. (1993). Self-fulfilling prophecies: A social psychological view of gender. In A. E. Beall & R. J. Sternberg (Eds.), *The psychology of gender.* New York: Guilford Press.

Geldard, F. A. (1962). *Fundamentals of psychology.* New York: Wiley.

Gelderloos, P., Walton, K. G., Orme-Johnson, D. W., & Alexander, C. N. (1991). Effectiveness of the Transcendental Meditation program in preventing and treating substance misuse: A review. *The International Journal of Addictions, 26*(3), 293–325.

Geller, J. L. (1992). A historical perspective on the role of state hospitals viewed from the era of the "revolving door." *American Journal of Psychiatry, 149,* 1526–1533.

Geller, L. (1982). The failure of self-actualization theory: A critique of Carl Rogers and Abraham Maslow. *Journal of Humanistic Psychology, 22,* 56–73.

Gentner, D. (1982). Why nouns are learned before verbs: Linguistic relativity versus natural partitioning. In S. A. Kuczaj, II (Ed.), *Language development: Vol. 2. Language, thought, and culture.* Hillsdale, NJ: Erlbaum.

Gentner, D. (1988). Metaphor as structure mapping: The relational shift. *Child Development, 59,* 47–59.

George, L. K., Fillenbaum, G. G., & Palmore, E. (1984). Sex differences in the antecedents and consequences of retirement. *Journal of Gerontology, 39,* 364–371.

George, M. S., Terence A. K., Parekh, P. I., Horwitz, B., Herscovitch, P., & Post, R. M. (1995). Brain activity during transient sadness and happiness in healthy women. *American Journal of Psychiatry, 152,* 341–351.

Gerard, M. (Ed.). (1968). *Dali.* Paris: Draeger.

Gergen, K. J., Gulerce, A., Lock, A., & Misra, G. (1996). Psychological science in cultural context. *American Psychologist, 51,* 496–503.

Gershon, E. S., Berrettini, W. H., & Goldin, L. R. (1989). Mood disorders: Genetic aspects. In H. I. Kaplan & B. J. Sadock (Eds.), *Comprehensive textbook of psychiatry/V.* Baltimore: Williams & Wilkins.

Gershon, E. S., & Nurnberger, J. I., Jr. (1995). Bipolar illness. In J. M. Oldham & M. B. Riba (Eds.), *Review of psychiatry* (Vol. 14). Washington, DC: American Psychiatric Press.

Geschwind, N., & Galaburda, A. M. (1987). *Cerebral lateralization: Biological mechanisms, associations, and pathology.* Cambridge, MA: MIT Press.

Ghez, C. (1991). The cerebellum. In E. R. Kandel, J. H. Schwartz, & T. M. Jessell (Eds.), *Principles of neural science* (3rd ed.). New York: Elsevier.

Ghiselin, B. (Ed.). (1952). *The creative process.* New York: Mentor.

Ghiselli, E. E. (1966). *The validity of occupational aptitude tests.* New York: Wiley.

Ghiselli, E. E. (1973). The validity of aptitude tests in personnel selection. *Personnel Psychology, 26,* 461–477.

Giannini, A. J., & Miller, N. S. (1989). Drug abuse: A biopsychiatric model. *American Family Practice, 40*(5), 173–182.

Gibbs, N. (1990, October 8). Shameful bequests to the next generation. *Time,* pp. 42–48.

Gibson, E. J., & Walk, R. D. (1960). The "visual cliff." *Scientific American, 202,* 64–71.

Gibson, H. B., & Heap, M. (1991). *Hypnosis in therapy.* Hillsdale, NJ: Erlbaum.

Gick, M. L., & Holyoak, K. (1980). Analogical problem solving. *Cognitive Psychology, 12,* 306–355.

Giesler, R. B., Josephs, R. A., & Swann, W. B., Jr. (1996). Self-verification in clinical depression: The desire for negative evaluation. *Journal of Abnormal Psychology, 105,* 358–368.

Gigerenzer, G., Hoffrage, U., & Kleinbölting, H. (1991). Probabilistic mental models: A Brunswikian theory of confidence. *Psychological Review, 98,* 506–528.

Gilbert, C. D., & Wiesel, T. N. (1985). Intrinsic connectivity and receptive field properties in visual cortex. *Vision Research, 25,* 365–374.

Gilbert, D. T., & Malone, P. S. (1995). The correspondence bias. *Psychological Bulletin, 117,* 21–38.

Gilbreth, F. B., & Gilbreth L. M. (1917). *Applied motion study.* New York: Sturgis & Walton Company.

Gilder, G. (1986). *Men and marriage.* New York: Pelican.

Gilgen, A. R. (1982). *American psychology since World War II: A profile of the discipline.* Westport, CT: Greenwood Press.

Gillard, E. R., Dang, D. Q., & Stanley, B. G. (1993). Evidence that neuropeptide Y and dopamine in the perifornical hypothalamus interact antagonistically in the control of food intake. *Brain Research, 628,* 128–136.

Gillberg, M. (1984). The effects of two alternative timings of a one-hour nap on early morning performance. *Biological Psychology, 19*(1), 45–54.

Gilligan, C. (1982). *In a different voice: Psychological theory and women's development.* Cambridge, MA: Harvard University Press.

Gilligan, C., Hamner, T., & Lyons, N. (1990). *Making connections.* Cambridge: Harvard University Press.

Gillin, J. C. (1994). Sleep and psychoactive drugs of abuse and dependence. In M. H. Kryger, T. Roth, & W. C. Dement (Eds.), *Principles and practice of sleep medicine* (2nd ed.). Philadelphia: Saunders.

Gillin, J. C., & Shiromani, P. (1990). Cholinergic mechanisms in sleep: Basic and clinical applications. In J. Montplaisir & R. Godbout (Eds.), *Sleep and biological rhythms: Basic mechanisms and applications to psychiatry.* New York: Oxford University Press.

Ginsburg, H. J., & Miller, S. M. (1982). Sex differences in children's risk-taking behavior. *Child Development, 53,* 426–428.

Gintzler, A. R. (1980). Endorphin-mediated increases in pain threshold during pregnancy. *Science, 210,* 193–195.

Ginzberg, E. (1972). Toward a theory of occupational choice: A restatement. *Vocational Guidance Quarterly, 20,* 169–176.

Gladue, B. A. (1988). Hormones in relationship to homosexual/bisexual/heterosexual gender orientation. In J. M. A. Sitesen (Ed.), *Handbook of sexology: The pharmacology and endocrinology of sexual function* (Vol. 6). Amsterdam: Elsevier.

Gladue, B. A. (1994). The biopsychology of sexual orientation. *Current Directions in Psychological Science, 3,* 150–154.

Glantz, S. A., & Parmley, W. W. (1991). Passive smoking and heart disease: Epidemiology, physiology, and biochemistry. *Circulation, 83*(1), 1–12.

Glaser, R. (1984). Education and thinking: The role of knowledge. *American Psychologist, 39,* 93–104.

Glaser, R. (1991). Intelligence as an expression of acquired knowledge. In H. A. H. Rowe (Ed.), *Intelligence: Reconceptualization and measurement.* Hillsdale, NJ: Erlbaum.

Glaser, R., & Chi, M. T. H. (1988). Overview. In M. T. H. Chi, R. Glaser, & M. J. Farr (Eds.), *The nature of expertise.* Hillsdale, NJ: Erlbaum.

Glaser, R., Kiecolt-Glaser, J. K., Speicher, C. E., & Holliday, J. E. (1985). Stress, loneliness, and changes in herpes virus latency. *Journal of Behavioral Medicine, 8,* 249–260.

Glass, C. R., & Arnkoff, D. B. (1992). Behavior therapy. In D. K. Freedheim (Ed.), *History of psychotherapy: A century of change.* Washington, DC: American Psychological Association.

Gleason, J. B., & Ratner, N. B. (1993). Language development in children. In J. B. Gleason & N. B.

Ratner (Eds.), *Psycholinguistics*. Fort Worth: Harcourt Brace Jovanovich.

Gleaves, D. H. (1996). The sociocognitive model of dissociative disorder: A reexamination of the evidence. *Psychological Bulletin, 120,* 42–59.

Glenberg, A. M. (1992). Distributed practice effects. In L. R. Squire (Ed.), *Encyclopedia of learning and memory.* New York: Macmillan.

Glenn, N. D. (1990). Quantitative research on marital quality in the 1980s: A critical review. *Journal of Marriage and the Family, 52,* 818–831.

Gmelch, G. (1978, August). Baseball magic. *Human Nature,* pp. 32–39.

Gobet, F., & Simon, H. A. (1996). Recall of rapidly presented random chess positions is a function of skill. *Psychonomic Bulletin & Review, 3,* 159–163.

Goddard, H. H. (1908). The Binet and Simon tests of intellectual capacity. *The Training School, 5,* 3–9.

Goddard, H. H. (1917). Mental tests and the immigrant. *Journal of Delinquency, 2,* 243–277.

Goetting, A. (1986). Parental satisfaction: A review of research. *Journal of Family Issues, 7*(1), 83–109.

Gold, M. S. (1989). *Marijuana.* New York: Plenum.

Gold, M. S. (1992). Cocaine (and crack): Clinical aspects. In J. H. Lowinson, P. Ruiz, & R. B. Millman (Eds.), *Substance abuse: A comprehensive textbook* (2nd ed.). Baltimore: Williams & Wilkins.

Goldberg, H. (1983). *The new male-female relationship.* New York: Morrow.

Goldberg, L. R. (1993). The structure of phenotypic personality traits. *American Psychologist, 48,* 26–34.

Golden, C. J., Sawicki, R. F., & Franzen, M. D. (1990). Test construction. In G. Goldstein & M. Hersen (Eds.), *Handbook of psychological assessment.* New York: Pergamon Press.

Goldenberg, H. (1983). *Contemporary clinical psychology.* Pacific Grove, CA: Brooks/Cole.

Goldenthal, P. (1985). Posing and judging facial expressions of emotion: The effects of social skills. *Journal of Social and Clinical Psychology, 3,* 325–338.

Goldfield, B. A., & Reznick, J. S. (1990). Early lexical acquisition: Rate, content, and the vocabulary spurt. *Journal of Child Language, 17,* 171–183.

Goldfried, M. R., Greenberg, L. S., & Marmar, C. (1990). Individual psychotherapy: Process and outcome. *Annual Review of Psychology, 41,* 659–688.

Goldman, J., & Coté, L. (1991). Aging of the brain: Dementia of the Alzheimer's type. In E. R. Kandel, J. H. Schwartz, & T. M. Jessell (Eds.), *Principles of neural science* (3rd ed.). New York: Elsevier.

Goldman-Rakic, P. S. (1995). Toward a circuit model of working memory and the guidance of voluntary motor action. In J. C. Houk, J. L. Davis, & D. G. Beiser (Eds.), *Models of information processing in the basal ganglia: Computational neuroscience.* Cambridge, MA: MIT Press.

Goldmann, L. (1990). Cognitive processing and general anesthesia. In R. R. Bootzin, J. F. Kihlstrom, & D. L. Schacter (Eds.), *Sleep and cognition.* Washington, DC: American Psychological Association.

Goldsmith, H. H., & Harman, C. (1994). Temperament and attachment; individuals and relationships. *Current Directions in Psychological Science, 3,* 53–57.

Goldstein, E. B. (1989). *Sensation and perception.* Belmont, CA: Wadsworth.

Goldstein, E. B. (1996). *Sensation and perception* (4th ed.). Pacific Grove, CA: Brooks/Cole.

Goldstein, M. J. (1987). Family interaction patterns that antedate the onset of schizophrenia and related disorders: A further analysis of data from a longitudinal prospective study. In K. Hahlweg & M. J. Goldstein (Eds.), *Understanding major mental disorder: The contribution of family interaction research.* New York: Family Process Press.

Goldstein, M. J. (1988). The family and psychopathology. *Annual Review of Psychology, 39,* 283–299.

Goldstein, W. M. (1990). Judgments of relative importance in decision making: Global vs. local interpretations of subjective weight. *Organizational Behavior and Human Decision Processes, 47,* 313–336.

Gonder-Frederick, L. A., Carter, W. R., Cox, D. J., & Clarke, W. L. (1990). Environmental stress and blood glucose change in insulin-dependent diabetes mellitus. *Health Psychology, 9,* 503–515.

Gonsiorek, J. C., & Weinrich, J. D. (1991). The definition and scope of sexual orientation. In J. C. Gonsiorek & J. D. Weinrich (Eds.), *Homosexuality: Research implications for public policy.* Newbury Park, CA: Sage.

Goodall, K. (1972, November). Field report: Shapers at work. *Psychology Today,* pp. 53–63, 132–138.

Goodenough, D. R. (1986). History of the field dependence construct. In M. Bertini, L. Pizzamiglio, & S. Wapner (Eds.), *Field dependence in psychological theory, research, and application.* Hillsdale, NJ: Erlbaum.

Goodenough, D. R. (1991). Dream recall: History and current status of the field. In S. J. Ellman & J. S. Antrobus (Eds.), *The mind in sleep: Psychology and psychophysiology* (2nd ed.). New York: Wiley.

Goodman, L., Saxe, L., & Harvey, M. (1991). Homelessness as psychological trauma. *American Psychologist, 46,* 1219–1225.

Goodman, P. S. (1974). An examination of referents used in the evaluation of pay. *Organizational Behavior and Human Performance, 12,* 170–195.

Goodwin, C. J. (1991). Misportraying Pavlov's apparatus. *American Journal of Psychology, 104*(1), 135–141.

Goodwin, D. W. (1992). Alcohol: Clinical aspects. In J. H. Lowinson, P. Ruiz, & R. B. Millman (Eds.), *Substance abuse: A comprehensive textbook* (2nd ed.). Baltimore: Williams & Wilkins.

Goodwin, F. K., & Jamison, K. R. (1990). *Manic-depressive illness.* New York: Oxford University Press.

Goodwin, G. M. (1992). Tricyclic and newer antidepressants. In E. S. Paykel (Ed.), *Handbook of affective disorders.* New York: Guilford Press.

Gordon, H. W. (1990). The neurobiological basis of hemisphericity. In C. Trevarthen (Ed.), *Brain circuits and functions of the mind. Essays in honor of Roger W. Sperry.* Cambridge, MA: Cambridge University Press.

Gordon, P. (1990). Learnability and feedback. *Developmental Psychology, 26,* 217–220.

Gorman, M. E. (1989). Error, falsification and scientific inference: An experimental investigation. *Quarterly Journal of Experimental Psychology, 41*(2-A), 385–412.

Gorn, G. J. (1982). The effects of music in advertising on choice behavior: A classical conditioning approach. *Journal of Marketing, 46,* 94–101.

Gottesman, I. I. (1991). *Schizophrenia genesis: The origins of madness.* New York: W. H. Freeman.

Gottesman, I. I. (1993). Origins of schizophrenia: Past as prologue. In R. Plomin & G. E. McClearn (Eds.), *Nature, nurture and psychology.* Washington, DC: American Psychological Association.

Gottesman, I. I., & Goldsmith, H. H. (1994). Developmental psychopathology of antisocial behavior: Inserting genes into its ontogenesis and epigenesis. In C.A. Nelson (Ed.), *Threats to optimal development: Integrating biological, psychological, and social risk factors.* Hillsdale, NJ: Erlbaum.

Gottlieb, J., Alter, M., & Gottlieb, B. W. (1991). Mainstreaming mentally retarded children. In J. L. Matson & J. A. Mulick (Eds.), *Handbook of mental retardation.* New York: Pergamon Press.

Gould, R. L. (1975, February). Adult life stages: Growth toward self-tolerance. *Psychology Today,* pp. 74–78.

Gould, R. L. (1978). *Transformations: Growth and change in adult life.* New York: Simon & Schuster.

Gould, S. J. (1993). The sexual politics of classification. *Natural History, 20*–29.

Gouras, P. (1991). Color vision. In E. R. Kandel, J. H. Schwartz, & T. M. Jessell (Eds.), *Principles of neural science* (3rd ed.). New York: Elsevier.

Graber, J. A., Brooks-Gunn, J., Paikoff, R. L., & Warren, M. P. (1994). Prediction of eating problems: An 8-year study of adolescent girls. *Developmental Psychology, 30,* 823–834.

Graeber, R. C. (1994). Jet lag and sleep disruption. In M. H. Kryger, T. Roth, & W. C. Dement (Eds.), *Principles and practice of sleep medicine* (2nd ed.). Philadelphia: Saunders.

Graf, P., & Gallie, K. A. (1992). A transfer-appropriate processing account for memory and amnesia. In L. R. Squire & N. Butters (Eds.), *Neuropsychology of memory* (2nd ed.). New York: Guilford Press.

Graff, H., & Stellar, E. (1962). Hyperphagia, obesity and finickiness. *Journal of Comparative and Physiological Psychology, 55,* 418–424.

Graham, J. R. (1990). *MMPI-2: Assessing personality and psychopathology.* New York: Oxford University Press.

Grant, I., McDonald, W. I., Patterson, T., & Trimble, M. R. (1989). Multiple sclerosis. In G. W. Brown & T. O. Harris (Eds.), *Life events and illness.* New York: Guilford Press.

Graziano, W. G. (1995). Evolutionary psychology: Old music, but now on CDs? *Psychological Inquiry, 6,* 41–44.

Grebb, J. A., & Cancro, R. (1989). Schizophrenia: Clinical features. In H. I. Kaplan & B. J. Sadock (Eds.), *Comprehensive textbook of psychiatry/V.* Baltimore: Williams & Wilkins.

Green, B. F. (1992). Expose or smear? The Burt affair. *Psychological Science, 3,* 328–331.

Green, B. L. (1991). Evaluating the effects of disasters. *Psychological Assessment, 3,* 538–546.

Green, D. W. (1990). Confirmation bias, problem-solving and cognitive models. In J. P. Caverni, J. M. Fabre, & M. Gonzalez (Eds.), *Cognitive biases.* Amsterdam: North-Holland.

Green., L. W., Tryon W. W., Marks, B., & Huryn, J. (1986). Periodontal disease as a function of life events stress. *Journal of Human Stress, 12*(1), 32–36.

Greenberg, J. S. (1990). *Comprehensive stress management*. Dubuque, IA: William C. Brown.

Greene, R. L. (1992). *Human memory: Paradigms and paradoxes*. Hillsdale, NJ: Erlbaum.

Greene, W. A., & Swisher, S. N. (1969). Psychological and somatic variables associated with the development and course of monozygotic twins discordant for leukemia. *Annals of the New York Academy of Sciences, 164,* 394–408.

Greenfield, P. M., & Savage-Rumbaugh, E. S. (1991). Imitation, grammatical development, and the invention of protogrammar by an ape. In N. A. Krasnegor, D. M. Rumbaugh, R. L. Schiefelbusch, & M. Studdert-Kennedy (Eds.), *Biological and behavioral determinants of language development*. Hillsdale, NJ: Erlbaum.

Greeno, C. G., & Wing, R. R. (1994). Stress-induced eating. *Psychological Bulletin, 115,* 444–464.

Greeno, J. G. (1978). Nature of problem solving abilities. In W. K. Estes (Ed.), *Handbook of learning and cognitive processes* (Vol. 5). Hillsdale, NJ: Erlbaum.

Greeno, J. G., & Simon, H. A. (1988). Problem solving and reasoning. In R. C. Atkinson, R. J. Herrnstein, G. Lindzey, & R. D. Luce (Eds.), *Stevens' handbook of experimental psychology* (Vol. 2). New York: Wiley.

Greenough, W. T. (1985). The possible role of experience-dependent synaptogenesis, or synapses on demand in the memory process. In N. M. Weinberger, J. L. McGaugh, & G. Lynch (Eds.), *Memory systems of the brain*. New York: Guilford Press.

Greenough, W. T. (1991). The animal rights assertions: A researcher's perspective. *Psychological Science Agenda, 4*(3), 10–12.

Greenson, R. R. (1967). *The technique and practice of psychoanalysis* (Vol. 1). New York: International Universities Press.

Greenwald, A. G. (1992). New look 3: Unconscious cognition reclaimed. *American Psychologist, 47,* 766–779.

Greenwald, A. G., Spangenberg, E. R., Pratkanis, A. R., & Eskenazi, J. (1991). Double-blind tests of subliminal self-help audiotapes. *Psychological Science, 2,* 119–122.

Gregory, R. J. (1996). *Psychological testing: History, principles, and applications* (2nd ed.). Boston: Allyn & Bacon.

Gregory, R. L. (1973). *Eye and brain*. New York: McGraw-Hill.

Gregory, R. L. (1978). *Eye and brain* (2nd ed.). New York: McGraw-Hill.

Griffith, R. M., Miyago, M., & Tago, A. (1958). The universality of typical dreams: Japanese vs. Americans. *American Anthropologist, 60,* 1173–1179.

Grinspoon, L., & Bakalar, J. B. (1992). Marihuana. In J. H. Lowinson, P. Ruiz, & R. B. Millman (Eds.), *Substance abuse: A comprehensive textbook* (2nd ed.). Baltimore: Williams & Wilkins.

Grob, G. N. (1983). Disease and environment in American history. In D. Mechanic (Ed.), *Handbook of health, health care, and the health professions*. New York: Free Press.

Grob, G. N. (1991). Origins of DSM-I: A study in appearance and reality. *American Journal of Psychiatry, 148,* 421–431.

Grob, G. N. (1994). *The mad among us: A history of the care of America's mentally ill*. New York: Free Press.

Grobbee, D. E., Rimm, E. B., Giovannucci, E., Colditz, G., Stampfer, M., & Willett, W. (1990). Coffee, caffeine, and cardiovascular disease in men. *New England Journal of Medicine, 323,* 1026–1032.

Grossman, S. P., Dacey, D., Halaris, A. E., Collier, T., & Routtenberg, A. (1978). Aphagia and adipsia after preferential desruction of nerve cell bodies in hypothalamus. *Science, 202,* 537–539.

Grossmann, K., Grossmann, K. E., Spangler, S., Suess, G., & Unzner, L. (1985). Maternal sensitivity and newborn orientation responses as related to quality of attachment in northern Germany. In I. Bretherton & E. Waters (Eds.), Growing points of attachment theory. *Monographs of the Society for Research for Child Development, 50,* (1–2, Serial No. 209).

Grossmann, K. E., & Grossmann, K. (1990). The wider concept of attachment in cross-cultural research. *Human Development, 33,* 31–47.

Grossmann, K. E., Grossmann, K., Huber, F., & Wartner, U. (1981). Children's behavior towards their mothers at 12 months and their fathers at 18 months in Ainsworth's Strange Situation. *International Journal of Behavioral Development, 4,* 157–181.

Grove, W. M., & Andreasen, N. C. (1992). Concepts, diagnosis and classification. In E. S. Paykel (Ed.), *Handbook of affective disorders* (2nd ed.). New York: Guilford Press.

Gruen, R. J. (1993). Stress and depression: Toward the development of integrative models. In L. Goldberger & S. Breznitz (Eds.), *Handbook of stress: Theoretical and clinical aspects*. New York: Free Press.

Grunberg, N. E., Bowen, D. J., & Winders, S. E. (1986). Effects of nicotine on body weight and food consumption in female rats. *Psychopharmacology, 90,* 101–105.

Grunberg, N. E., & Straub, R. O. (1992). The role of gender and taste class in the effects of stress on eating. *Health Psychology, 11,* 97–100.

Gruneberg, M. M., Sykes, R. N., & Gillett, E. (1994). The facilitating effects of mnemonic strategies on two learning disabled adults. *Neuropsychological Rehabilitation, 4,* 241–254.

Gudykunst, W. B., Gao, G., Nishida, T., Bond, M. H., Leung, K., Wang, G., & Barraclough, R. A. (1989). A cross-cultural comparison of self-monitoring. *Communication Research Reports, 6*(1), 7–12.

Gudykunst, W. B., Yang, S., & Nishida, T. (1987). Cultural differences in self-consciousness and self-monitoring. *Communication Research, 14*(1), 7–34.

Guenther, K. (1988). Mood and memory. In G. M. Davies & D. M. Thomson (Eds.), *Memory in context: Context in memory*. New York: Wiley.

Guilford, J. P. (1939). *General psychology*. Princeton, NJ: Van Nostrand Reinhold.

Guilford, J. P. (1959). Three faces of intellect. *American Psychologist, 14,* 469–479.

Guilford, J. P. (1985). The structure-of-intellect model. In B. B. Wolman (Ed.), *Handbook of intelligence: Theories, measurements and applications*. New York: Wiley.

Guilleminault, C. (1989). Narcolepsy syndrome. In M. H. Kryger, T. Roth, & W. C. Dement (Eds.), *Principles and practice of sleep medicine*. Philadelphia: Saunders.

Guilleminault, C. (1994). Narcolepsy syndrome. In M. H. Kryger, T. Roth, & W. C. Dement (Eds.), *Principles and practice of sleep medicine* (2nd ed.). Philadelphia: Saunders.

Gupta, G. R. (1992). Love, arranged marriage, and the Indian social structure. In J. J. Macionis & N. V. Benokraitis (Eds.), *Seeing ourselves: Classic, contemporary and cross-cultural reading in sociology*. Englewood Cliffs, NJ: Prentice-Hall.

Gupta, U., & Singh, P. (1982). Exploratory study of love and liking type of marriages. *Indian Journal of Applied Psychology, 19,* 92–97.

Guyton, A. C. (1991). *Textbook of medical physiology*. Philadelphia: Saunders.

Haan, N. (1989). Personality at midlife. In S. Hunter & M. Sundel (Eds.), *Mid life myths: Issues, findings, and practice*. Newbury Park, CA: Sage.

Haan, N. (1993). The assessment of coping, defense, and stress. In L. Goldberger & S. Breznitz (Eds.), *Handbook of stress: Theoretical and clinical aspects* (2nd ed.). New York: Free Press.

Hackman, J. R., & Oldham, G. R. (1975). Development of the job diagnostic survey. *Journal of Applied Psychology, 60,* 159–170.

Haensly, P. A., & Reynolds, C. R. (1989). Creativity and intelligence. In J. A. Glover, R. R. Ronning, & C. R. Reynolds (Eds.), *Handbook of creativity*. New York: Plenum.

Hagberg, J. M. (1990). Exercise, fitness, and hypertension. In C. Bouchard, R. J. Shephard, T. Stephens, J. R. Sutton, & B. D. McPherson (Eds.), *Exercise, fitness, and health: A consensus of current knowledge*. Champaign, IL: Human Kinetics Books.

Haglund, B., & Cnattingius, S. (1990). Cigarette smoking as a risk factor for sudden infant death syndrome: A population-based study. *American Journal of Public Health, 80,* 29–32.

Hale, M. (1980). *Human science and social order*. Philadelphia, PA: Temple University Press.

Hale, S. (1990). A global developmental trend in cognitive processing speed in children. *Child Development, 61,* 653–663.

Hales, D. (1987). *How to sleep like a baby*. New York: Ballantine.

Hall, C. S. (1966). *The meaning of dreams*. New York: McGraw-Hill.

Hall, C. S. (1979). The meaning of dreams. In D. Goleman & R. J. Davidson (Eds.), *Consciousness: Brain, states of awareness, and mysticism*. New York: Harper & Row.

Hall, C. S., & Nordby, V. J. (1972). *The individual and his dreams*. New York: Mentor.

Hall, E. (1987). *Growing and changing: What the experts say*. New York: Random House.

Hall, G. S. (1904). *Adolescence*. New York: Appleton.

Hall, J. A. (1990). *Nonverbal sex differences: Communication accuracy and expressive style* (2nd ed.). Baltimore: Johns Hopkins University Press.

Hall, J. A., & Halberstadt, A. G. (1986). Smiling and gazing. In J. S. Hyde & M. C. Linn (Eds.), *The psychology of gender: Advances through meta-analysis*. Baltimore: Johns Hopkins University Press.

Hall, J. A., Roter, D. L., & Katz, N. R. (1988). Meta-analysis of correlates of provider behavior in medical encounters. *Medical Care, 26,* 1–19.

Halpern, D. F. (1984). *Thought and knowledge: An introduction to critical thinking*. Hillsdale, NJ: Erlbaum.

Halpern, D. F. (1989a). Things and pictures of things: Are perceptual processes invariant across cultures? *Behavioral and Brain Sciences, 12*(1), 84–85.

Halpern, D. F. (1989b). *Thought and knowledge: An introduction to critical thinking* (2nd ed.). Hillsdale, NJ: Erlbaum.

Halpern, D. F. (1992). *Sex differences in cognitive abilities*. Hillsdale, NJ: Erlbaum.

Halpern, D. F. (1996). *Thought and knowledge: An introduction to critical thinking*. Mahwah, NJ: Erlbaum.

Halpern, D. F. (1997). Sex differences in intelligence and their implications for education. *American Psychologist, 52*, in press.

Halpern, D. F., & Coren, S. (1988). Do right-handers live longer? *Nature, 333*, 213.

Hamer, D. H., Hu, S., Magnuson, V. L., Hu, N., & Pattatucci, A. M. L. (1993). A linkage between DNA markers on the X chromosome and male sexual orientation. *Science, 261*, 321–327.

Hamilton, D. L., & Sherman, S. J. (1989). Illusory correlations: Implications for stereotype theory and research. In D. Bar-Tal, C. F. Graumann, A. W. Kruglanski, & W. Stroebe (Eds.), *Stereotyping and prejudice: Changing conceptions*. New York: Springer-Verlag.

Hamilton, W. D. (1964). The evolution of social behavior. *Journal of Theoretical Biology, 7*, 1–52.

Hansen, C. H., & Hansen, R. D. (1988). How rock music videos can change what is seen when boy meets girl: Priming stereotypic appraisal of social interactions. *Sex Roles, 19*, 287–316.

Hanshaw, J. B., Dudgeon, J. A., & Marshall, W. C. (1985). *Viral diseases of the fetus and newborn*. Philadelphia: Saunders.

Hanson, F. A. (1993). *Testing testing: Social consequences of the examined life*. Berkeley: University of California Press.

Hanson, R. A. (1975). Consistency and stability of home environmental measures related to IQ. *Child Development, 46*, 470–480.

Hanson. V. L. (1990). Recall of order information by deaf signers: Phonetic coding in temporal order of recall. *Memory & Cognition, 18*, 604–610.

Hardiman, P. T., Dufresne, R., & Mestre, J. P. (1989). The relation between problem categorization and problem solving among experts and novices. *Memory & Cognition, 17*, 627–638.

Hare, R. D. (1983). Diagnosis of antisocial personality disorder in criminals. *American Journal of Psychiatry, 140*, 887–890.

Hare, R. D. (1993). *Without conscience: The disturbing world of the psychopaths among us*. New York: Pocket Books.

Harlow, H. F., & Harlow, M. (1962). Social deprivation in monkeys. *Scientific American, 207*(5), 136–146.

Harmsen, P., Rosengren, A., Tsipogianni, A., & Wilhelmsen, L. (1990). Risk factors for stroke in middle-aged men in Goteborg, Sweden. *Stroke, 21*, 23–29.

Harpur, T. J., Hart, S. D., & Hare, R. D. (1994). Personality of the psychopath. In P. T. Costa, Jr., & T. A. Widiger (Eds.), *Personality disorders and the five-factor model of personality*. Washington, DC: American Psychological Association.

Harriman, L. C. (1986). Marital adjustment as related to personal and marital changes accompanying parenthood. *Family Relations, 35*, 233–239.

Harrington, M. E., Rusak, B., & Mistlberger, R. E. (1994). Anatomy and physiology of the mammalian circadian system. In M. H. Kryger, T. Roth, & W. C. Dement (Eds.), *Principles and practice of sleep medicine* (2nd ed.). Philadelphia: Saunders.

Harris, C. R., & Christenfeld, N. (1996). Gender, jealously, and reason. *Psychological Science, 7*, 364–366.

Harris, J. E. (1984). Remembering to do things: A forgotten topic. In J. E. Harris & P. E. Morris (Eds.), *Everyday memory, actions, and absent-mindedness*. New York: Academic Press.

Harris, L. J. (1990). Cultural influences on handedness: Historical and contemporary theory and evidence. In S. Coren (Ed.), *Left-handedness: Behavioral implications and anomalies*. Amsterdam: North-Holland.

Harris, L. J. (1993). Do left handers die sooner than right handers? Commentary on Coren and Halpern's (1991) "Left-handedness: A marker for decreased survival fitness." *Psychological Bulletin, 114*, 203–234.

Harris, P. L. (1993). Understanding emotion. In M. Lewis & J. M. Haviland (Eds.), *Handbook of emotion*. New York: Guilford Press.

Harris, W. G. (1987). *Cary Grant: A touch of elegance*. New York: Doubleday.

Harrower, M. R. (1936). Some factors determining figure-ground articulation. *British Journal of Psychology, 26*(4), 407–424.

Harte, J. L., Eifert, G. H., & Smith, R. (1995). The effects of running and meditation on beta-endorphin, corticotropin-releasing hormone and cortisol in plasma, and on mood. *Biological Psychology, 40*, 251–265.

Hartline, H. K., & Ratliff, F. (1957). Inhibitory interaction of receptor units in the eye of Limulus. *Journal of General Physiology, 40*, 357–376.

Hartman, W. E., & Fithian, M. A. (1974). *Treatment of sexual dysfunction: A bio-psycho-social approach*. New York: Aronson.

Hartmann, E. (1973). *The functions of sleep*. New Haven, CT: Yale University Press.

Hartmann, E. (1985). Sleep disorders. In H. I. Kaplan & B. J. Sadock (Eds.), *Comprehensive textbook of psychiatry/IV*. Baltimore: Williams & Wilkins.

Harvey, J. H., Town, J. P., & Yarkin, K. L. (1981). How fundamental is "the fundamental attribution error"? *Journal of Personality and Social Psychology, 40*, 346–349.

Harvey, S. M. (1987). Female sexual behavior: Fluctuations during the menstrual cycle. *Journal of Psychosomatic Research, 31*(1), 101–110.

Hass, R. G. (1981). Effects of source characteristics on cognitive responses and persuasion. In R. E. Petty, T. M. Ostrom, & T. C. Brock (Eds.), *Cognitive responses in persuasion*. Hillsdale, NJ: Erlbaum.

Hasselhorn, M. (1992). Task dependency and the role of category typicality and metamemory in the development of an organizational strategy. *Child Development, 63*, 202–214.

Hastorf, A., & Cantril, H. (1954). They saw a game: A case study. *Journal of Abnormal and Social Psychology, 49*, 129–134.

Hatfield, E. (1988). Passionate and companionate love. In R. J. Sternberg & M. L. Barnes (Eds.), *The psychology of love*. New Haven, CT: Yale University Press.

Hatfield, E., & Rapson, R. L. (1993). *Love, sex, and intimacy: Their psychology, biology, and history*. New York: HarperCollins.

Hathaway, S. R., & McKinley, J. C. (1943). *Manual for the Minnesota Multiphasic Personality Inventory*. New York: Psychological Corporation.

Hauri, P. (1994). Primary insomnia. In M. H. Kryger, T. Roth, & W. C. Dement (Eds.), *Principles and practice of sleep medicine* (2nd ed.). Philadelphia: Saunders.

Hauser, S. T., & Bowlds, M. K. (1990). Stress, coping, and adaptation. In S. S. Feldman & G. R. Feldman (Eds.), *At the threshold: The developing adolescent*. Cambridge, MA: Harvard University Press.

Hawkes, C. H. (1992). Endorphins: The basis of pleasure? *Journal of Neurology, Neurosurgery & Psychiatry, 55*, 247–250.

Hawton, K., Cole, D., O'Grady, J., & Osborn, M. (1982). Motivational aspects of deliberate self-positioning in adolescents. *British Journal of Psychiatry, 141*, 286–290.

Hayes, J. R. (1989). Cognitive processes in creativity. In J. A. Glover, R. R. Ronning, & C. R. Reynolds (Eds.), *Handbook of creativity*. New York: Plenum.

Hayes, K. J., & Hayes, C. (1951). The intellectual development of a home-raised chimpanzee. *Proceedings of the American Philosophical Society, 95*, 105–109.

Hayes, S. C., & Heiby, E. (1996). Psychology's drug problem: Do we need a fix or should we just say no? *American Psychologist, 51*, 198–206.

Hayslip, B., Jr. (1994). Stability of intelligence. In R. J. Sternberg (Ed.), *Encyclopedia of human intelligence*. New York: Macmillan.

Haywood, T. W., Kravitz, H. M., Grossman, L. S., Cavanaugh, J. L., Jr., Davis, J. M., & Lewis, D. A. (1995). Predicting the "revolving door" phenomenon among patients with schizophrenic, schizoaffective, and affective disorders. *American Journal of Psychiatry, 152*, 861–956.

Hazan, C., & Shaver, P. (1986). *Parental caregiving style questionnaire*. Unpublished questionnaire.

Hazan, C., & Shaver, P. (1987). Romantic love conceptualized as an attachment process. *Journal of Personality and Social Psychology, 52*, 511–524.

Hazelrigg, P. J., Cooper, H., & Strathman, A. J. (1991). Personality moderators of the experimenter expectancy effect: A reexamination of five hypotheses. *Personality and Social Psychology Bulletin, 17*, 569–579.

Heady, B., & Wearing, A. (1989). Personality, life events, and subjective well-being: Toward a dynamic equilibrium model. *Journal of Personality and Social Psychology, 57*, 731–739.

Hearn, W. (1995, Nov. 6). Melatonin caution: Latest magic bullet may not hit target. *American Medical News, 28*, 30.

Hearnshaw, L. S. (1979). *Cyril Burt: Psychologist*. Ithaca, NY: Cornell University Press.

Hearold, S. (1986). A synthesis of 1,043 effects of television on social behavior. In G. Comstock (Ed.), *Public communications and behavior* (Vol. 1). New York: Academic Press.

Hearst, E. (1979). One hundred years: Themes and perspectives. In E. Hearst (Ed.), *The first century of experimental psychology*. Hillsdale, NJ: Erlbaum.

Hearst, E. (1988). Fundamentals of learning and conditioning. In R. C. Atkinson, R. J. Herrnstein, G. Lindzey, & R. D. Luce (Eds.), *Stevens' handbook of experimental psychology*. New York: Wiley.

Heath, A. C., Kendler, K. S., Eaves, L. J., & Martin, N. (1990). Evidence for genetic influences on sleep disturbance and sleep patterns in twins. *Sleep, 13*, 318–335.

Heath, R. G. (Ed.). (1964). *The role of pleasure in behavior*. New York: Harper & Row.

Heatherton, T. F., Herman, C. P., Polivy, J., King, G. A., & McGree, S. T. (1988). The (mis)measurement of restraint: An analysis of conceptual and psychometric issues. *Journal of Abnormal Psychology, 97*, 19–28.

Heatherton, T. F., Polivy, J., & Herman, C. P. (1991). Restraint, weight loss, and variability of body weight. *Journal of Abnormal Psychology, 100,* 78–83.

Hegarty, J. D., Balderssarini, R. J., Tohen, M., Waternaux, C., & Oepen, G. (1994). One hundred years of schizophrenia: A meta-analysis of the outcome literature. *American Journal of Psychiatry, 151,* 1409–1416.

Heider, F. (1958). *The psychology of interpersonal relations.* New York: Wiley.

Hellige, J. B. (1990). Hemispheric asymmetry. *Annual Review of Psychology, 41,* 55–80.

Hellige, J. B. (1993). Unity of thought and action: Varieties of interaction between left and right cerebral hemispheres. *Current Directions in Psychological Science, 2*(1), 21–25.

Helmes, E., & Reddon, J. R. (1993). A perspective on developments in assessing psychopathology: A critical review of the MMPI and MMPI-2. *Psychological Bulletin, 113,* 453–471.

Helmholtz, H. von. (1852). On the theory of compound colors. *Philosophical Magazine, 4,* 519–534.

Helmholtz, H. von. (1863). *On the sensations of tone as a physiological basis for the theory of music* (A. J. Ellis, Trans.). New York: Dover.

Helms, J. E. (1992). Why is there no study of cultural equivalence in standard cognitive ability testing? *American Psychologist, 47,* 1083–1101.

Helson, R., & Moane, G. (1987). Personality change in women from college to midlife. *Journal of Personality and Social Psychology, 53,* 176–186.

Helson, R., Mitchell, V., & Moane, G. (1984). Personality and patterns of adherence and non-adherence to the social clock. *Journal of Personality and Social Psychology, 46,* 1079–1096.

Helson, R., & Stewart, A. (1994). Personality change in adulthood. In T. F. Heatherton & J. L. Weinberger (Eds.), *Can personality change?* Washington, DC: American Psychological Association.

Helzer, J. E., Robins, L. N., & McEvoy, L. (1987). Post-traumatic stress disorder in the general population: Findings of the epidemiologic catchment area survey. *The New England Journal of Medicine, 317*(26), 1630–1634.

Henderson-King, E. I., & Nisbett, R. E. (1996). Anti-black prejudice as a function of exposure to the negative behavior of a single black person. *Journal of Personality and Social Psychology, 71,* 654–664.

Hendrick, S. S., & Hendrick, C. (1992). *Liking, loving, and relating* (2nd ed.). Pacific Grove, CA: Brooks/Cole.

Hendrick, S. S., Hendrick, C., & Adler, N. L. (1988). Romantic relationships: Love, satisfaction, and staying together. *Journal of Personality and Social Psychology, 54,* 980–988.

Henry, K. R. (1984). Cochlear damage resulting from exposure to four different octave bands of noise at three different ages. *Behavioral Neuroscience, 1,* 107–117.

Hering, E. (1878). *Zür lehre vom lichtsinne.* Vienna: Gerold.

Herkenham, M., Lynn, A. B., deCosta, B. R., & Richfield, E. K. (1991). Neuronal localization of cannabinoid receptors in the basal ganglia of the rat. *Brain Research, 547,* 267–274.

Herman, C. P., & Polivy, J. (1984). A boundary model for the regulation of eating. In A. B. Stunkard & E. Stellar (Eds.), *Eating and its disorders.* New York: Raven.

Herman, C. P., & Polivy, J. (1988). Studies of eating in normal dieters. In B. T. Walsh (Ed.), *Eating behavior in eating disorders.* Washington, DC: American Psychiatric Press.

Herman, J. H. (1993). Color in dreams. In M. A. Carskadon (Ed.), *Encyclopedia of sleep and dreaming.* New York: Macmillan.

Herman, J. L. (1992). *Trauma and recovery.* New York: Basic Books.

Herman, L. M., Morrel-Samuels, P., & Pack, A. A. (1990). Bottlenosed dolphin and human recognition of veridical and degraded video displays of an artificial gestural language. *Journal of Experimental Psychology: General, 119,* 215–230.

Hermann, R. C., Dorwart, R. A., Hoover, C. W., & Brody, J. (1995). Variation in ECT use in the United States. *American Journal of Psychiatry, 152,* 869–875.

Herrnstein, R. J., & Murray, C. (1994). *The bell curve: Intelligence and class structure in American life.* New York: Free Press.

Hershey, D. A., Walsh, D. A., Read, S. J., & Chulef, A. S. (1990). The effects of expertise on financial problem solving: Evidence for goal-directed, problem-solving scripts. *Organizational Behavior and Human Decision Processes, 46,* 77–101.

Hertzog, C., & Schaie, K. W. (1988). Stability and changes in adult intelligence: 2. Simultaneous analysis of longitudinal means and covariance structures. *Psychology and Aging, 3,* 122–130.

Herzberg, F., Mausner, B., & Snyderman, B. (1959). *The motivation to work.* New York: Wiley.

Heth, C. D., & Rescorla, R. A. (1973). Simultaneous and backward fear conditioning in the rat. *Journal of Comparative and Physiological Psychology, 82,* 434–443.

Hettich, P. I. (1992). *Learning skills for college and career.* Pacific Grove, CA: Brooks/Cole.

Hewstone, M. (1990). The "ultimate attribution error"? A review of the literature on intergroup causal attribution. *European Journal of Social Psychology, 20,* 311–335.

Hilgard, E. R. (1965). *Hypnotic susceptibility.* New York: Harcourt, Brace & World.

Hilgard, E. R. (1986). *Divided consciousness: Multiple controls in human thought and action.* New York: Wiley.

Hilgard, E. R. (1987). *Psychology in America: A historical survey.* San Diego: Harcourt Brace Jovanovich.

Hilgard, E. R. (1989). The early years of intelligence measurement. In R. L. Linn (Ed.), *Intelligence: Measurement, theory, and public policy.* Urbana: University of Illinois Press.

Hilgard, E. R. (1992). Dissociation and theories of hypnosis. In E. Fromm & M. R. Nash (Eds.), *Contemporary hypnosis research.* New York: Guilford Press.

Hilgard, E. R., & Bower, G.H. (1981). *Theories of learning.* Englewood Cliffs, NJ: Prentice- Hall.

Hilliard, A. G., III. (1984). IQ testing as the emperor's new clothes: A critique of Jensen's *Bias in Mental Testing.* In C. R. Reynolds & R. T. Brown (Eds.), *Perspectives on bias in mental testing.* New York: Plenum.

Hillier, L., Hewitt, K. L., & Morrongiello, B. A. (1992). Infants' perception of illusions in sound localization: Reaching to sounds in the dark. *Journal of Experimental Child Psychology, 53,* 159–179.

Hillner, K. P. (1984). *History and systems of modern psychology: A conceptual approach.* New York: Gardner Press.

Hilton, J. L., Fein, S., & Miller, D. T. (1993). Suspicion and dispositional inference. *Personality and Social Psychology Bulletin, 19,* 501–512.

Hineline, P. N. (1981). The several roles of stimuli in negative reinforcement. In P. Harzem & M. D. Zeiler (Eds.), *Predictability, correlation and continuity.* Chichester, England: Wiley.

Hines, M. (1990). Gonadal hormones and human cognitive development. In J. Balthazart (Ed.), *Hormones, brain and behavior in vertebrates: 1. Sexual differentiation, neuroanatomical aspects, neurotransmitters and neuropeptides.* Basel: Karger.

Hintzman, D. L. (1990). Human learning and memory: Connections and dissociations. *Annual Review of Psychology, 41,* 109–139.

Hiroto, D. S., & Seligman, M. E. P. (1975). Generality of learned helplessness in man. *Journal of Personality and Social Psychology, 31,* 311–327.

Hirsch, J., Fried, S. K., Edens, N. K., & Leibel, R. L. (1989). The fat cell. *Medical Clinics of North America, 73,* 83–96.

Hirschfeld, R. M. A., & Davidson, L. (1988). Risk factors for suicide. In A. J. Frances & R. E. Hales (Eds.), *Review of psychiatry* (Vol. 7). Washington, DC: American Psychiatric Press.

Hirsh, I. J., & Watson, C. S. (1996). Auditory psychophysics and perception. *Annual Review of Psychology, 47,* 461–484.

Hobfoll, S. E., & Vaux, A. (1993). Social support: Resources and context. In L. Goldberger & S. Breznitz (Eds.), *Handbook of stress: Theoretical and clinical aspects* (2nd ed.). New York: Free Press.

Hobson, J. A. (1988). *The dreaming brain.* New York: Basic Books.

Hobson, J. A. (1989). *Sleep.* New York: Scientific American Library.

Hobson, J. A., & McCarley, R. W. (1977). The brain as a dream state generator: An activation-synthesis hypothesis of the dream process. *American Journal of Psychiatry, 134,* 1335–1348.

Hocevar, D., & Bachelor, P. (1989). A taxonomy and critique of measurements used in the study of creativity. In J. A. Glover, R. R. Ronning, & C. R. Reynolds (Eds.), *Handbook of creativity.* New York: Plenum.

Hochberg, J. (1988). Visual perception. In R. C. Atkinson, R. J. Herrnstein, G. Lindzey, & R. D. Luce (Eds.), *Stevens' handbook of experimental psychology* (2nd ed., Vol. 1). New York: Wiley.

Hock, E., Schirtzinger, M. B., Lutz, W. J., & Widaman, K. (1995). Maternal depressive symptomatology over the transition to parenthood: Assessing the influence of marital satisfaction and marital sex role traditionalism. *Journal of Family Psychology, 9,* 79–88.

Hodapp, R. M. (1994). Cultural-familial mental retardation. In R. J. Sternberg (Ed.), *Encyclopedia of human intelligence.* New York: Macmillan.

Hodgkin, A. L., & Huxley, A. F. (1952). Currents carried by sodium and potassium ions through the membrane of the giant axon of Loligo. *Journal of Physiology, 116,* 449–472.

Hoffman, C., Lau, I., & Johnson, D. R. (1986). The linguistic relativity of person cognition: An English-Chinese comparison. *Journal of Personality and Social Psychology, 51,* 1097–1105.

Hoffman, L. W. (1991). The influence of the family environment on personality: Accounting for sibling differences. *Psychological Bulletin, 110,* 187–203.

Hofstede, G. (1980). *Culture's consequences: International differences in work-related values.* Beverly Hills, CA: Sage.

Hofstede, G. (1983). Dimensions of national cultures in fifty countries and three regions. In J. Deregowski, S. Dzuirawiec, & R. Annis (Eds.),

Explications in cross-cultural psychology. Lisse: Swets and Zeitlinger.

Hogan, R., Hogan, J., & Roberts, B. W. (1996). Personality measurement and employment decisions. *American Psychologist, 51,* 469–477.

Hogarth, R. M. (1987). *Judgement and choice.* New York: Wiley.

Hogg, M. A., Turner, J. C., & Davidson, B. (1990). Polarized norms and social frames of reference: A test of the self-categorization theory of group polarization. *Basic and Applied Social Psychology, 11,* 77–100.

Hokanson, J. E., & Burgess, M. (1962). The effects of three types of aggression on vascular processes. *Journal of Abnormal and Social Psychology, 65,* 446–449.

Holahan, C. J., & Moos, R. H. (1985). Life stress and health: Personality, coping, and family support in stress resistance. *Journal of Personality and Social Psychology, 49,* 739–747.

Holahan, C. J., & Moos, R. H. (1990). Life stressors, resistance factors, and improved psychological functioning: An extension of the stress resistance paradigm. *Journal of Personality and Social Psychology, 58,* 909–917.

Holden, C. (1986, October). The rational optimist. *Psychology Today,* pp. 55–60.

Hollan, D. (1989). The personal use of dream beliefs in the Toraja Highlands. *Ethos, 17,* 166–186.

Hollander, E., Simeon, D., & Gorman, J. M. (1994). Anxiety disorders. In R. E. Hales, S. C. Yudofsky, & J. A. Talbott (Eds.), *The American Psychiatric Press textbook of psychiatry* (2nd ed.). Washington, DC: American Psychiatric Press.

Hollander, E., & Wong, C. (1995). Development in the treatment of obsessive-compulsive disorder. *Primary Psychiatry, 2,* 28–33.

Hollands, C. (1989). Trivial and questionable research on animals. In G. Langley (Ed.), *Animal experimentation: The consensus changes.* New York: Chapman & Hall.

Hollingworth, L. S. (1914). *Functional periodicity: An experimental study of the mental and motor abilities of women during menstruation.* New York: Teachers College, Columbia University.

Hollingworth, L. S. (1916). Sex differences in mental tests. *Psychological Bulletin, 13,* 377–383.

Hollister, L. E. (1988). Marijuana and immunity. *Journal of Psychoactive Drugs, 20,* 3–7.

Hollon, S. D., & Beck, A. T. (1994). Cognitive and cognitive-behavioral therapies. In A. E. Bergin & S. L. Garfield (Eds.), *Handbook of psychotherapy and behavior change* (4th ed.). New York: Wiley.

Holmes, D. S. (1987). The influence of meditation versus rest on physiological arousal: A second examination. In M. A. West (Ed.), *The psychology of meditation.* Oxford: Clarendon Press.

Holmes, D. S. (1990). The evidence for repression: An examination of sixty years of research. In J. Singer (Ed.), *Repression and dissociation: Implications for personality, theory, psychopathology, and health.* Chicago: University of Chicago Press.

Holmes, T. H., & Rahe, R. H. (1967). The Social Readjustment Rating Scale. *Journal of Psychosomatic Research, 11,* 213–218.

Holt, R. R. (1982). Occupational stress. In L. Goldberger & S. Breznitz (Eds.), *Handbook of stress: Theoretical and clinical aspects.* New York: Free Press.

Holt, R. R. (1993). Occupational stress. In L. Goldberger & S. Breznitz (Eds.), *Handbook of stress: Theoretical and clinical aspects* (2nd ed.). New York: Free Press.

Holyoak, K. J. (1990). Problem solving. In D. N. Osherson & E. E. Smith (Eds.), *Thinking: An invitation to cognitive science* (Vol. 3). Cambridge, MA: MIT Press.

Homma-True, R., Greene, B., Lopez, S. R., & Trimble, J. E. (1993). Ethnocultural diversity in clinical psychology. *The Clinical Psychologist, 46*(2), 50–63.

Honig, W. K., & Alsop, B. (1992). Operant behavior. In L. R. Squire (Ed.), *Encyclopedia of learning and memory.* New York: Macmillan.

Honts, C. R., & Perry, M. V. (1992). Polygraph admissibility: Changes and challenges. *Law and Human Behavior, 16,* 357–379.

Hooper, J., & Teresi, D. (1986). *The 3-pound universe—The brain.* New York: Laurel.

Hopkins, B., & Westra, T. (1988). Maternal handling and motor development: An intracultural study. *Genetic, Social and General Psychology Monographs, 14,* 377–420.

Hopkins, B., & Westra, T. (1990). Motor development, maternal expectations, and the role of handling. *Infant Behavior and Development, 13,* 117–122.

Hopson, J. L. (1988, July/August). A pleasurable chemistry. *Psychology Today,* pp. 29–30, 32–33.

Hopson, J. S. (1979). *Scent signals: The silent language of sex.* New York: Morrow.

Horn, J. L. (1976). Human abilities: A review of research and theory in the early 1970s. *Annual Review of Psychology, 27,* 437–485.

Horn, J. L. (1979). Trends in the measurement of intelligence. In R. J. Sternberg & D. K. Detterman (Eds.), *Human intelligence: Perspectives on its theory and measurement.* Norwood, NJ: Ablex.

Horn, J. L. (1985). Remodeling old models of intelligence. In B. B. Wolman (Ed.), *Handbook of intelligence.* New York: Wiley.

Horn, J. L., & Hofer, S. M. (1992). Major abilities and development in the adult period. In R. J. Sternberg & C. A. Berg (Eds.), *Intellectual development.* Cambridge: Cambridge University Press.

Hornstein, G. A. (1992). The return of the repressed: Psychology's problematic relations with psychoanalysis, 1909–1960. *American Psychologist, 47,* 254–263.

Horowitz, F. D. (1992). John B. Watson's legacy: Learning and environment. *Developmental Psychology, 28,* 360–367.

Horowitz, F. D. (1994). Giftedness. In R. J. Sternberg (Ed.), *Encyclopedia of human intelligence.* New York: Macmillan.

Horowitz, F. D., & O'Brien, M. (1986). Gifted and talented children: State of knowledge and directions for research. *American Psychologist, 41,* 1147–1152.

Horvath, P., & Zuckerman, M. (1993). Sensation seeking, risk appraisal, and risky behavior. *Personality and Individual Differences, 14*(1), 41–52.

Hothersall, D. (1984). *History of psychology.* New York: Random House.

House, J. S., Landis, K. R., & Umberson, D. (1988). Social relationships and health. *Science, 241,* 540–545.

Houston, B. K., & Vavak, C. R. (1991). Hostility: Developmental factors, psychosocial correlates, and health behaviors. *Health Psychology, 10,* 9–17.

Howard, A., Pion, G. M., Gottfredson, G. D., Flattau, P. E., Oskamp, S., Pfafflin, S. M., Bray, D. W., & Burstein, A. G. (1986). The changing face of American psychology: A report from the committee on employment and human resources. *American Psychologist, 41,* 1311–1327.

Howard, K. I., Moras, K., Brill, P. L., Martinovich, Z., & Lutz, W. (1996). Evaluation of psychotherapy: Efficacy, effectiveness, and patient progress. *American Psychologist, 51,* 1059–1064.

Howes, C., Phillips, D. A., & Whitebook, M. (1992). Thresholds of quality: Implications for the social development of children in center-based child care. *Child Development, 63,* 449–460.

Hubbard, T. L., Baird, J. C., & Ajmal, A. (1989). Different skills or different knowledge? *Behavioral and Brain Sciences, 12*(1), 86–87.

Hubel, D. H. (1979, September). The brain. *Scientific American,* pp. 38–47.

Hubel, D. H., & Wiesel, T. N. (1962). Receptive fields, binocular interaction and functional architecture in the cat's visual cortex. *Journal of Physiology, 160,* 106–154.

Hubel, D. H., & Wiesel, T. N. (1963). Receptive fields of cells in striate cortex of very young visually inexperienced kittens. *Journal of Neurophysiology, 26,* 994–1002.

Hubel, D. H., & Wiesel, T. N. (1979). Brain mechanisms of vision. In Scientific American (Eds.), *The brain.* San Franciso: W. H. Freeman.

Hudson, W. (1960). Pictorial depth perception in sub-cultural groups in Africa. *Journal of Social Psychology, 52,* 183–208.

Hudson, W. (1967). The study of the problem of pictorial perception among unacculturated groups. *International Journal of Psychology, 2,* 89–107.

Hugdahl, K. (1995). Classical conditioning and implicit learning: The right hemisphere hypothesis. In R. J. Davidson & K. Hugdahl (Eds.), *Brain asymmetry.* Cambridge, MA: MIT Press.

Hughes, C. C. (1993). Culture in clinical psychiatry. In A. C. Gaw (Ed.), *Culture, ethnicity, and mental illness.* Washington, DC: American Psychiatric Press.

Hughes, J. R., Gulliver, S. B., Fenwick, J. W., Valliere, W. A., Cruser, K., Pepper, S., Shea, P., Solomon, L. J., & Flynn, B. S. (1992). Smoking cessation among self-quitters. *Health Psychology, 11,* 331–334.

Hughes, J., Smith, T. W., Kosterlitz, H. W., Fothergill, L. A., Morgan, B. A., & Morris, H. R. (1975). Identification of two related pentapeptides from the brain with the potent opiate agonist activity. *Nature, 258,* 577–579.

Hull, C. L. (1943). *Principles of behavior.* New York: Appleton.

Hultsch, D. F., & Dixon, R. A. (1990). Learning and memory in aging. In J. E. Birren & K. W. Schaie (Eds.), *Handbook of the psychology of aging* (3rd ed.). San Diego: Academic Press.

Humphreys, M. S., Bain, J. D., & Pike, R. (1989). Different ways to cue a coherent memory system: A theory for episodic, semantic, and procedural tasks. *Psychological Review, 96,* 208–233.

Hunt, E., Streissguth, A. P., Kerr, B., & Olsen, H. C. (1995). Mothers' alcohol consumption during pregnancy: Effects on spatial-visual reasoning in 14-year-old children. *Psychological Science, 6,* 339–342.

Hunt, H. (1989). *The multiplicity of dreams: Memory, imagination and consciousness.* New Haven, CT: Yale University Press.

Hunt, J. M., Smith, M. F., & Kernan, J. B. (1985). The effects of expectancy disconfirmation and argument strength on message processing level: An application to personal selling. In E. C.

Hirschman & M. B. Holbrook (Eds.), *Advances in consumer research* (Vol. 12). Provo, UT: Association for Consumer Research.

Hunt, W. A., & Matarazzo, J. D. (1982). Changing smoking behavior: A critique. In R. J. Gatchel, A. Baum, & J. E. Singer (Eds.), *Handbook of psychology and health: Vol. 1. Clinical psychology and behavioral medicine, overlapping disciplines*. Hillsdale, NJ: Erlbaum.

Hunter, J. E., & Hunter, R. F. (1984). Validity and utility of alternative predictors of job performance. *Psychological Bulletin, 96*, 72–98.

Hurvich, L. M. (1981). *Color vision*. Sunderland, MA: Sinnauer Associates.

Huston, A. C., Donnerstein, E., Fairchild, H., Feshbach, N. D., Katz, P. A., Murray, J. P., Rubinstein, E. A., Wilcox, B. L., & Zuckerman, D. (1992). *Big world, small screen: The role of television in American society*. Lincoln: University of Nebraska Press.

Huston, A. C., & Wright, J. C. (1982). Effects of communications media on children. In C. B. Kopp & J. B. Krakow (Eds.), *The child: Development in a social context*. Reading, MA: Addison-Wesley.

Huys, J., Evers-Kiebooms, G., & d'Ydewalle, G. (1990). Framing biases in genetic risk perception. In J. P. Caverni, J. M. Fabre, & M. Gonzalez (Eds.), *Cognitive biases*. Amsterdam: North-Holland.

Hyde, J. S. (1986). Gender differences in aggression. In J. S. Hyde & M. C. Linn (Eds.), *The psychology of gender differences: Advances through meta-analysis*. Baltimore: Johns Hopkins University Press.

Hyde, J. S., & DeLamater, J. (1997). *Understanding human sexuality*. New York: McGraw-Hill.

Hyde, J. S., Fennema, E., & Lamon, S. J. (1990). Gender differences in mathematics performance: A meta-analysis. *Psychological Bulletin, 107*, 139–155.

Hyde, J. S., & Linn, M. C. (Eds.). (1986). *The psychology of gender: Advances through meta-analysis*. Baltimore: Johns Hopkins University Press.

Hyde, J. S., & Linn, M. C. (1988). Gender differences in verbal ability: A meta-analysis. *Psychological Bulletin, 104*, 53–69.

Washington, DC: American Psychiatric Press.

Hygge, S., & Öhman, A. (1978). Modeling processes in the acquisition of fear: Vicarious electrodermal conditioning to fear-relevant stimuli. *Journal of Personality and Social Psychology, 36*, 271–279.

Iaccino, J. F. (1993). *Left brain-right brain differences: Inquiries, evidence, and new approaches*. Hillsdale, NJ: Erlbaum.

Ickovics, J. R., & Rodin, J. (1992). Women and AIDS in the United States: Epidemiology, natural history, and mediating mechanisms. *Health Psychology, 11*, 1–16.

Iezzi, A., & Adams, H. E. (1993). Somatoform and factitious disorders. In P. B. Sutker & H. E. Adams (Eds.), *Comprehensive handbook of psychopathology* (2nd ed.). New York: Plenum.

Ineichen, B. (1979). The social geography of marriage. In M. Cook & G. Wilson (Eds.), *Love and attraction*. New York: Pergamon.

Innocenti, G. M. (1994). Some new trends in the study of the corpus callosum. *Behavioral and Brain Research, 64*, 1–8.

Inoff-Germain, G., Arnold, G. S., Nottelman, E. D., Susman, E. J., Cutler, G. B., Jr., & Chrousos, G. P. (1988). Relations between hormone levels and observational measures of ag-

gressive behavior of young adolescents in family interactions. *Developmental Psychology, 24*, 129–139.

Insko, C. A. (1965). Verbal reinforcement of attitudes. *Journal of Personality and Social Psychology, 2*, 621–623.

Irvine, S. H., & Berry, J. W. (1988). *Human abilities in cultural context*. New York: Cambridge University Press.

Isaac, R. J., & Armat, V. C. (1990). *Madness in the streets: How psychiatry and the law abandoned the mentally ill*. New York: Free Press.

Isabella, R. A., & Belsky, J. (1991). Interactional synchrony and the origins of infant-mother attachment: A replication study. *Child Development, 62*, 373–384.

Isada, N. B., & Grossman, J. H., III. (1991). Perinatal infections. In S. G. Gabbe, J. R. Niebyl, & J. L. Simpson (Eds.), *Obstetrics: Normal and problem pregnancies*. New York: Churchill Livingstone.

Iwao, S. (1993). *The Japanese woman: Traditional image and changing reality*. New York: Free Press.

Iwawaki, S., & Vernon, P. E. (1988). Japanese abilities and achievements. In S. H. Irvine & J. W. Berry (Eds.), *Human abilities in cultural context*. New York: Cambridge University Press.

Izard, C. E. (1971). *The face of emotion*. New York: Appleton-Century-Crofts.

Izard, C. E. (1984). Emotion-cognition relationships and human development. In C. E. Izard, J. Kagan, & R. B. Zajonc (Eds.), *Emotions, cognition and behavior*. Cambridge, England: Cambridge University Press.

Izard, C. E. (1990). Facial expressions and the regulation of emotions. *Journal of Personality and Social Psychology, 58*, 487–498.

Izard, C. E. (1991). *The psychology of emotions*. New York: Plenum.

Izard, C. E. (1994). Innate and universal facial expressions: Evidence from developmental and cross-cultural research. *Psychological Bulletin, 115*, 288–299.

Izard, C. E., Haynes, O. M., Chisholm, G., & Baak, K. (1991). Emotional determinants of infant-mother attachment. *Child Development, 62*, 906–917.

Izard, C. E., & Saxton, P. M. (1988). Emotions. In R. C. Atkinson, R. J. Herrnstein, G. Lindzey, & R. D. Luce (Eds.), *Stevens' handbook of experimental psychology* (Vol. 1). New York: Wiley.

Jackson, D. N. (1973). Structured personality assessment. In B. B. Wolman (Ed.), *Handbook of general psychology*. Englewood Cliffs, NJ: Prentice-Hall.

Jackson, L. A., Sullivan, L. A., & Hodge, C. N. (1993). Stereotype effects on attributions, predictions, and evaluations: No two social judgments are quite alike. *Journal of Personality and Social Psychology, 65*, 69–84.

Jacobs, J. (1971). *Adolescent suicide*. New York: Wiley Interscience.

Jacobsen, T., Edelstein, W., & Hofmann, V. (1994). A longitudinal study of the relation between representations of attachment in childhood and cognitive functioning in childhood and adolescence. *Developmental Psychology, 30*, 112–124.

Jacobson, E. (1938). *Progressive relaxation*. Chicago: University of Chicago Press.

Jacobson, J. W. (1991). Administrative and policy dimensions of developmental disabilities services. In J. L. Matson & J. A. Mulick (Eds.), *Handbook of mental retardation*. New York: Pergamon Press.

Jacobson, J. W., & Mulick, J. A. (1992). A new definition of mental retardation or a new definition of practice? *Psychology in Mental Retardation and Developmental Disabilities, 18*, 9–14.

Jacobson, J. W., & Schwartz, A. A. (1991). Evaluating living situations of people with developmental disabilities. In J. L. Matson & J. A. Mulick (Eds.), *Handbook of mental retardation*. New York: Pergamon Press.

Jacobson, N. S., & Christensen, A. (1996). Studying the effectiveness of psychotherapy: How well can clinical trials do the job? *American Psychologist, 51*, 1031–1039.

Jacobson, T., Wolfgang, E., & Hofmann, V. (1994). A longitudinal study of the relation between representations of attachment in childhood and cognitive functioning in childhood and adolescence. *Developmental Psychology, 30*, 112–124.

Jacoby, L. L. (1988). Memory observed and memory unobserved. In U. Neisser & E. Winograd (Eds.), *Remembering reconsidered: Ecological and traditional approaches to the study of memory*. Cambridge: Cambridge University Press.

Jacoby, L. L., & Whitehouse, K. (1989). An illusion of memory: False recognition influenced by unconscious perception. *Journal of Experimental Psychology: General, 118*, 126–135.

James, W. (1884). What is emotion. *Mind, 19*, 188–205.

James, W. (1890). *The principles of psychology*. New York: Holt.

James, W. (1902). *The varieties of religious experience*. New York: Modern Library.

Jamison, K. R. (1988). Manic-depressive illness and accomplishment: Creativity, leadership, and social class. In F. K. Goodwin & K. R. Jamison (Eds.), *Manic-depressive illness*. Oxford, England: Oxford University Press.

Jamison, K. R., Gerner, R. H., Hammen, C., & Padesky, C. (1980). Clouds and silver linings: Positive experiences associated with the primary affective disorders. *American Journal of Psychiatry, 137*, 198–202.

Jangid, R. K., Vyas, J. N., & Shukla, T. R. (1988). The effect of the Transcendental Meditation Programme on normal individuals. *Journal of Personality & Clinical Studies, 4*(1), 145–149.

Janis, I. L. (1958). *Psychological stress*. New York: Wiley.

Janis, I. L. (1972). *Victims of groupthink*. Boston: Houghton Mifflin.

Janis, I. L. (1993). Decision making under stress. In L. Goldberger & S. Breznitz (Eds.), *Handbook of stress: Theoretical and clinical aspects* (2nd ed.). New York: Free Press.

Janis, I. L., & Mann, L. (1977). *Decision making: A psychological analysis of conflict, choice, and commitment*. New York: Free Press.

Jann, M. W., Jenike, M. A., & Lieberman, J. A. (1994). The new psychopharmaceuticals. *Patient Care, 28*(2), 47–61.

Janofsky, J. S., Dunn, M. H., Roskes, E. J., Briskin, J. K., & Rudolph, M. S. L. (1996). Insanity defense pleas in Baltimore city: An analysis of outcome. *American Journal of Psychiatry, 153*, 1464–1468.

Janos, P. M., & Robinson, N. M. (1985). Psychosocial development in intellectually gifted children. In F. D. Horowitz & M. O'Brien (Eds.), *The gifted and talented: Developmental perspectives*. Washington, DC: American Psychological Association.

Janowsky, J. S., Oviatt, S. K., & Orwoll, E. S.

(1994). Testosterone influences spatial cognition in older men. *Behavioral Neuroscience, 108,* 325–332.

Janus, S. S., & Janus, C. L. (1993). *The Janus report on sexual behavior.* New York: Wiley.

Jaroff, L. (1993, November 29). Lies of the mind. *Time,* pp. 52–59.

Jarvik, M. E., & Schneider, N. G. (1992). Nicotine. In J. H. Lowinson, P. Ruiz, & R. B. Millman (Eds.), *Substance abuse: A comprehensive textbook* (2nd ed.). Baltimore: Williams & Wilkins.

Jemmott, J. B., III, & Magloire, K. (1988). Academic stress, social support, and secretory immunoglobin A. *Journal of Personality and Social Psychology, 55,* 803–810.

Jenkins, J. G., & Dallenbach, K. M. (1924). Oblivescence during sleep and waking. *American Journal of Psychology, 35,* 605–612.

Jenkins, J. H., Kleinman, A., & Good, B. J. (1991). Cross-cultural studies of depression. In J. Becker & A. Kleinman (Eds.), *Psychosocial aspects of depression.* Hillsdale, NJ: Erlbaum.

Jennison, K. M. (1992). The impact of stressful life events and social support on drinking among older adults: A general population survey. *International Journal of Aging and Human Development, 35,* 99–123.

Jensen, A. R. (1969). How much can we boost IQ and scholastic achievement? *Harvard Educational Review, 39,* 1–23.

Jensen, A. R. (1980). *Bias in mental testing.* New York: Free Press.

Jensen, A. R. (1982). Reaction time and psychometric g. In H. J. Eysenck (Ed.), *A model for intelligence.* Springer-Verlag.

Jensen, A. R. (1987). Process differences and individual difference in some cognitive tasks. *Intelligence, 11,* 107–136.

Jensen, A. R. (1992). The Cyril Burt scandal, research taboos, and the media. *The General Psychologist, 28*(3), 16–21.

Jensen, A. R. (1993a). Test validity: g versus "tacit knowledge." *Current Directions in Psychological Science, 2*(1), 9–10.

Jensen, A. R. (1993b). Why is reaction time correlated with psychometric g? *Current Directions in Psychological Science, 2*(2), 53–56.

Jensen, A. R. (1994a). Francis Galton. In R. J. Sternberg (Ed.), *Encyclopedia of human intelligence.* New York: Macmillan.

Jensen, A. R. (1994b). Race and IQ scores. In R. J. Sternberg (Ed.), *Encyclopedia of human intelligence.* New York: Macmillan.

Jessell, T. M., & Kelly, D. D. (1991). Pain and analgesia. In E. R. Kandel, J. H. Schwartz, & T. M. Jessell (Eds.), *Principles of neural science* (3rd ed.). New York: Elsevier.

John, O. P. (1990). The "big five" factor taxonomy: Dimensions of personality in the natural language and in questionnaires. In L. A. Pervin (Ed.), *Handbook of personality: Theory and research.* New York: Guilford Press.

Johnson, A. B. (1990). *Out of bedlam: The truth about deinstitutionalization.* New York: Basic Books.

Johnson, B. D., & Muffler, J. (1992). Sociocultural aspects of drug use and abuse in the 1990s. In J. H. Lowinson, P. Ruiz, & R. B. Millman (Eds.), *Substance abuse: A comprehensive textbook* (2nd ed.). Baltimore: Williams & Wilkins.

Johnson, C., & Mullen, B. (1994). Evidence for the accessibility of paired distinctiveness in distinctiveness-based illusory correlation in stereotyping. *Personality and Social Psychology Bulletin, 20,* 65–70.

Johnson, D. (1990). Animal rights and human lives: Time for scientists to right the balance. *Psychological Science, 1,* 213–214.

Johnson, J. S., & Newport, E. L. (1989). Critical period effects in second language learning: The influence of maturational state on the acquisition of English as a second language. *Cognitive Psychology, 21,* 60–99.

Johnson, L. C. (1982). Sleep deprivation and performance. In W. B. Webb (Ed.), *Biological rhythms, sleep and performance.* New York: Wiley.

Johnson, L. C., Tepas, D. I., Colquhoun, W. P., & Colligan, M. J. (1981). *Biological rhythms, sleep and shift work.* New York: Spectrum.

Johnson, M. K. (1996). Fact, fantasy, and public policy. In D. J. Herrmann, C. McEvoy, C. Hertzog, P. Hertel, & M. K. Johnson (Eds.), *Basic and applied memory research: Theory in context* (Vol. 1). Mahwah, NJ: Erlbaum.

Johnson, M. K., Hashtroudi, S., & Lindsay, D. S. (1993). Source monitoring. *Psychological Bulletin, 114,* 3–28.

Johnson, M. K., Kahan, T. L., & Raye, C. L. (1984). Dreams and reality monitoring. *Journal of Experimental Psychology: General, 113,* 329–344.

Johnson, M. K., & Raye, C. L. (1981). Reality monitoring. *Psychological Review, 88,* 67–85.

Johnson, S. L., & Roberts, J. E. (1995). Life events and bipolar disorder: Implications from biological theories. *Psychological Bulletin, 117,* 434–449.

Johnston, J. C., & McClelland, J. L. (1974). Perception of letters in words: Seek not and ye shall find. *Science, 184,* 1192–1194.

Johnston, W. A., & Dark, V. J. (1986). Selective attention. *Annual Review of Psychology, 37,* 43–75.

Johnston, W. A., & Heinz, S. P. (1978). Flexibility and capacity demands of attention. *Journal of Experimental Psychology: General, 107,* 420–435.

Joiner, T. E. (1994). Contagious depression: Existence, specificity to depressed symptoms, and the role of reassurance seeking. *Journal of Personality and Social Psychology, 67,* 287–296.

Jones, B. E. (1994). Basic mechanisms of sleep-wake states. In M. H. Kryger, T. Roth, & W. C. Dement (Eds.), *Principles and practice of sleep medicine* (2nd ed.). Philadelphia: Saunders.

Jones, E. E. (1990). *Interpersonal perception.* New York: W. H. Freeman.

Jones, E. E., & Davis, K. E. (1965). From acts to dispositions: The attribution process in person perception. In L. Berkowitz (Ed.), *Advances in experimental social psychology* (Vol. 2). New York: Academic Press.

Jones, E. E., & Nisbett, R. E. (1971). The actor and the observer: Divergent perceptions of the causes of behavior. In E. E. Jones, D. E. Kanouse, H. H. Kelley, R. E. Nisbett, S. Valins, & B. Weiner (Eds.), *Attribution: Perceiving the causes of behavior.* Morristown, NJ: General Learning Press.

Jones, G. V. (1990). Misremembering a common object: When left is not right. *Memory & Cognition, 18*(2), 174–182.

Jones, J. C., & Barlow, D. H. (1990). Self-reported frequency of sexual urges, fantasies, and masturbatory fantasies in heterosexual males and females. *Archives of Sexual Behavior, 19,* 269–279.

Jones, J. S., & Oswald, I. (1968). Two cases of healthy insomnia. *Electroencephalography and Clinical Neurophysiology, 24,* 378–380.

Jones, M. (1993). Influence of self-monitoring on dating motivations. *Journal of Research in Personality, 27*(2), 197–206.

Jones, N. A., & Fox, N. A. (1992). Electroencephalogram asymmetry during emotionally evocative films and its relation to positive and negative affectivity. *Brain and Cognition, 20*(2), 280–299.

Jones, R. A., & Brehm, J. W. (1970). Persuasiveness of one- and two-sided communications as a function of awareness there are two sides. *Journal of Experimental Social Psychology, 6,* 47–56.

Jordaan, J. P. (1974). Life stages as organizing modes of career development. In E. L. Herr (Ed.), *Vocational guidance and human development.* Boston: Houghton Mifflin.

Jordan, B. (1983). *Birth in four cultures.* Quebec, Canada: Eden Press.

Jordan, M. (1993, March 27). SAT changes name, but it won't score 1,600 with critics. *Washington Post,* p. A7.

Jorgensen, R. S., Johnson, B. T., Kolodziej, M. E., & Schreer, G. E. (1996). Elevated blood pressure and personality: A meta-analytic review. *Psychological Bulletin, 120,* 293–320.

Joseph, R. (1992). *The right brain and the unconscious.* New York: Plenum.

Joseph, R. (1996). *Neuropsychiatry, neuropsychology, and clinical neuroscience. Emotion, evolution, cognition, language, memory, brain damage, and abnormal behavior* (2nd ed.). Baltimore: Williams & Wilkins.

Josephs, R. A., Larrick, R. P., Steele, C. M., & Nisbett, R. E. (1992). Protecting the self from the negative consequences of risky decisions. *Journal of Personality and Social Psychology, 62,* 26–37.

Jourard, S. M., & Landsman, T. (1980). *Healthy personality: An approach from the viewpoint of humanistic psychology.* New York: Macmillan.

Joynson, R. B. (1989). *The Burt affair.* London: Routledge.

Judd, C. M., & Park, B. (1988). Out-group homogeneity: Judgments of variability at the individual and group levels. *Journal of Personality and Social Psychology, 54,* 778–788.

Judd, C. M., Ryan, C. S., & Park, B. (1991). Accuracy in the judgment of in-group and out-group variability. *Journal of Personality and Social Psychology, 61,* 366–379.

Judd, L. L., McAdams, L. A., Budnick, B., & Braff, D. L. (1992). Sensory gating effects in schizophrenia: New results. *American Journal of Psychiatry, 149,* 488–493.

Julien, R. M. (1995). *A primer of drug action.* New York: W. H. Freeman.

Jung, C. G. (1917/1953). On the psychology of the unconscious. In H. Read, M. Fordham, & G. Adler (Eds.), *Collected works of C. G. Jung* (Vol. 7). Princeton, NJ: Princeton University Press.

Jung, C. G. (1921/1960). *Psychological types.* In H. Read, M. Fordham, & G. Adler (Eds.), *Collected works of C. G. Jung* (Vol. 6). Princeton, NJ: Princeton University Press.

Jung, C. G. (1933). *Modern man in search of a soul.* New York: Harcourt, Brace & World.

Kagan, J., & Snidman, N. (1991). Temperamental factors in human development. *American Psychologist, 46,* 856–862.

Kagan, J., Snidman, N., & Arcus, D. M. (1992). Initial reactions to unfamiliarity. *Current Directions in Psychological Science, 1*(6), 171–174.

Kahan, T. L., & Johnson, M. K. (1992). Self-effects in memory for person information. *Social Cognition, 10*(1), 30–50.

Kahan, T. L., & LaBerge, S. (1994). Lucid dreaming as metacognition: Implications for cognitive science. *Consciousness and Cognition, 3,* 246–264.

Kahan, T. L., & LaBerge, S. (1996). Cognition

and metacognition in dreaming and waking: Comparisons of first- and third-person ratings. *Dreaming, 6*, 235–249.

Kahn, E., Fisher, C., & Edwards, A. (1991). Night terrors and anxiety dreams. In S. J. Ellman & J. S. Antrobus (Eds.), *The mind in sleep: Psychology and psychophysiology* (2nd ed.). New York: Wiley.

Kahneman, D. (1991). Judgment and decision making: A personal view. *Psychological Science, 2*, 142–145.

Kahneman, D., & Tversky, A. (1982). Subjective probability: A judgment of representativeness. In D. Kahneman, P. Slovic, & A. Tversky (Eds.), *Judgment under uncertainty: Heuristics and biases.* Cambridge: Cambridge University Press.

Kahneman, D., & Tversky, A. (1984). Choices, values, and frames. *American Psychologist, 39*, 341–350.

Kail, R. (1988). Developmental functions for speeds of cognitive processes. *Journal of Experimental Child Psychology, 45*, 339–364.

Kail, R. (1991). Developmental change in speed of processing during childhood and adolescence. *Psychological Bulletin, 109*, 490–501.

Kail, R., & Hagen, J. W. (1982). Memory in childhood. In B. B. Wolman (Ed.), *Handbook of developmental psychology.* Englewood Cliffs, NJ: Prentice-Hall.

Kalant, H., & Kalant, O. J. (1979). Death in amphetamine users: Causes and rates. In D. E. Smith (Ed.), *Amphetamine use, misuse and abuse.* Boston: G. K. Hall.

Kalat, J. W. (1993). *Introduction to psychology.* Pacific Grove, CA: Brooks/Cole.

Kales, A., & Kales, J. D. (1984). *Evaluation and treatment of insomnia.* New York: Oxford University Press.

Kales, J. D., Kales, A., Bixler, E. O., Soldatos, C. R., Cadieux, R. J., Kashurba, G. J., & Vela-Bueno, A. (1984). Biopsychobehavioral correlates of insomnia: V. Clinical characteristics and behavioral correlates. *American Journal of Psychiatry, 141*, 1371–1376.

Kalichman, S. C. (1995). *Understanding AIDS: A guide for mental health professionals.* Washington, DC: American Psychological Association.

Kalick, S. M., & Hamilton, T. E., III. (1986). The matching hypothesis reexamined. *Journal of Personality and Social Psychology, 51*, 673–682.

Kalmuss, D., Davidson, A., & Cushman, L. (1992). Parenting expectations, experiences, and adjustment to parenthood: A test of the violated expectations framework. *Journal of Marriage and the Family, 52*, 516–526.

Kamen-Siegel, L., Rodin, J., Seligman, M. E. P., & Dwyer, J. (1991). Explanatory style and cell-mediated immunity in elderly men and women. *Health Psychology, 10*, 229–235.

Kamerman, S. B. (1993). International perspectives on child care policies and programs. *Pediatrics, 91*, 248–252.

Kamin, L. J. (1965). Temporal and intensity characteristics of the conditioned stimulus. In W. F. Prokasy (Ed.), *Classical conditioning.* New York: Appleton-Century-Crofts.

Kamin, L. J. (1968). "Attention-like" processes in classical conditioning. In M. R. Jones (Ed.), *Miami symposium on the prediction of behavior: Aversive stimulation.* Miami: University of Miami Press.

Kamin, L. J. (1969). Predictability, surprise, attention and conditioning. In B. A. Campbell & R. M. Church (Eds.), *Punishment and aversive behavior.* New York: Appleton-Century-Crofts.

Kamin, L. J. (1974). *The science and politics of IQ.* Hillsdale, NJ: Erlbaum.

Kamin, L. J. (1981). Some historical facts about IQ testing. In H. J. Eysenck versus L. Kamin, *The intelligence controversy.* New York: Wiley.

Kamiya, J. (1969). Operant control of the EEG rhythm and some of its reported effects on consciousness. In C. T. Tart (Ed.), *Altered states of consciousness.* New York: Wiley.

Kandel, D. B. (1978). Similarity in real-life adolescent friendship pairs. *Journal of Personality and Social Psychology, 36*, 306–312.

Kandel, E. R. (1991a). Disorders of thought: Schizophrenia. In E. R. Kandel, J. H. Schwartz, & T. M. Jessell (Eds.), *Principles of neural science* (3rd ed.). New York: Elsevier.

Kandel, E. R. (1991b). Nerve cells and behavior. In E. R. Kandel, J. H. Schwartz, & T. M. Jessell (Eds.), *Principles of neural science* (3rd ed.). New York: Elsevier.

Kandel, E. R., & Jessell, T. M. (1991). Touch. In E. R. Kandel, J. H. Schwartz, & T. M. Jessell (Eds.), *Principles of neural science* (3rd ed.). New York: Elsevier.

Kandel, E. R., & Schwartz, J. H. (1982). Molecular biology of learning: Modification of transmitter release. *Science, 218*, 433–442.

Kandel, E. R., & Schwartz, J. H. (1991). Directly gated transmission at central synapses. In E. R. Kandel, J. H. Schwartz, & T. M. Jessell (Eds.), *Principles of neural science* (3rd ed.). New York: Elsevier.

Kanter, A. S. (1989). Homeless but not helpless: Legal issues in the care of homeless people with mental illness. *Journal of Social Issues, 45*(3), 91–104.

Kaplan, A. G. (1985). Female or male therapists for women patients: New formulations. *Psychiatry, 48*, 111–121.

Kaplan, H., & Dove, H. (1987). Infant development among the Ache of Eastern Paraguay. *Developmental Psychology, 23*, 190–198.

Kaplan, H. I. (1985). History of psychosomatic medicine. In H. I. Kaplan & B. J. Sadock (Eds.), *Comprehensive textbook of psychiatry/IV.* Baltimore: Williams & Wilkins.

Kaplan, H. I. (1989). History of psychosomatic medicine. In H. I. Kaplan & B. J. Sadock (Eds.), *Comprehensive textbook of psychiatry/V.* Baltimore: Williams & Wilkins.

Kaplan, H. I., & Sadock, B. J. (Eds.). (1993). *Comprehensive group psychotherapy.* Baltimore: Williams & Wilkins.

Kaplan, H. S. (1979). *Disorders of sexual desire and other new concepts and techniques in sex therapy.* New York: Simon & Schuster.

Kaplan, H. S. (1983). *The evaluation of sexual disorders: Psychological and medical aspects.* New York: Brunner/Mazel.

Kaplan, N. M. (1986). Dietary aspects of the treatment of hypertension. In L. Breslow, J. E. Fielding, & L. B. Lave (Eds.), *Annual review of public health* (Vol. 7). Palo Alto, CA: Annual Reviews.

Kaplan, R. M., Manuck, S. B., & Shumaker, S. (1992). Does lowering cholesterol cause increases in depression, suicide, and accidents? In H. S. Freidman (Ed.), *Hostility coping and health.* Washington, DC: American Psychological Association.

Kaplan, R. M. (1985). The controversy related to the use of psychological tests. In B. B. Wolman (Ed.), *Handbook of intelligence: Theories, measurements, and applications.* New York: Wiley.

Kaplan, R. M., & Simon, H. J. (1990). Compliance in medical care: Reconsideration of self-predictions. *Annals of Behavioral Medicine, 12*, 66–71.

Kapur, S., & Mann, J. J. (1993). Antidepressant action and the neurobiologic effects of ECT: Human studies. In C. E. Coffey (Ed.), *The clinical science of electroconvulsive therapy.* Washington, DC: American Psychiatric Press.

Kapur, S., & Remington, G. (1996). Serotonin-dopamine interaction and its relevance to schizophrenia. *American Journal of Psychiatry, 153*, 466–476.

Karasek, R., & Theorell, T. (1990). *Healthy Work.* New York: Basic Books.

Karau, S. J., & Williams, K. D. (1993). Social loafing: A meta-analytic review and theoretical integration. *Journal of Personality and Social Psychology, 65*, 681–706.

Karau, S. J., & Williams, K. D. (1995). Social loafing: Research findings, implications, and future directions. *Current Directions in Psychological Science, 4*, 134–140.

Kardiner, A., & Linton, R. (1945). *The individual and his society.* New York: Columbia University Press.

Karno, M., & Golding, J. M. (1991). Obsessive compulsive disorder. In L. N. Robins & D. A. Regier (Eds.), *Psychiatric disorders in America: The epidemiologic catchment area study.* New York: Free Press.

Kashima, Y., & Triandis, H. C. (1986). The self-serving bias in attributions as a coping strategy: A cross-cultural study. *Journal of Cross-Cultural Psychology, 17*, 83–98.

Katigbak, M. S., Church, A. T., & Akamine, T. X. (1996). Cross-cultural generalizability of personality dimensions: Relating indigenous and imported dimensions in two cultures. *Journal of Personality and Social Psychology, 70*, 99–114.

Katz, L. J., & Feroz, R. (1992). Work. In V. B. Van Hasselt & M. Hersen (Eds.), *Handbook of social development: A lifespan perspective.* New York: Plenum.

Katz, L. J., & Slomka, G. T. (1990). Achievement testing. In G. Goldstein & M. Hersen (Eds.), *Handbook of psychological assessment.* New York: Pergamon Press.

Kaufman, L., & Rock, I. (1962). The moon illusion I. *Science, 136*, 953–961.

Kausler, D. H. (1985). Episodic memory: Memorizing performance. In N. Charness (Ed.), *Aging and human performance.* Chichester, England: Wiley.

Kavanagh, D. J. (1992). Recent developments in expressed emotion in schizophrenia. *British Journal of Psychiatry, 160*, 601–620.

Kavesh, L., & Lavin, C. (1988). *Tales from the front.* New York: Doubleday.

Kazdin, A. E. (1982). History of behavior modification. In A. S. Bellack, M. Hersen, & A. E. Kazdin (Eds.), *International handbook of behavior modification and behavior therapy.* New York: Plenum.

Kazdin, A. E. (1994). Methodology, design, and evaluation in psychotherapy research. In A. E. Bergin & S. L. Garfield (Eds.), *Handbook of psychotherapy and behavior change* (4th ed.). New York: Wiley.

Keefauver, S. P., & Guilleminault, C. (1994). Sleep terrors and sleepwalking. In M. H. Kryger, T. Roth, & W. C. Dement (Eds.), *Principles and practice of sleep medicine* (2nd ed.). Philadelphia: Saunders.

Keesey, R. E. (1986). A set-point theory of obesity. In K. D. Brownell & J. P. Foreyt (Eds.), *Handbook of eating disorders: Physiology, psychology, and treatment of obesity, anorexia, and bulimia*. New York: Basic Books.

Keesey, R. E. (1988). The body-weight set point. *Postgraduate Medicine, 83,* 114–127.

Keesey, R. E., & Powley, T. L. (1975). Hypothalamic regulation of body weight. *American Scientist, 63,* 558–565.

Keesey, R. E., & Powley, T. L. (1986). The regulation of body weight. *Annual Review of Psychology, 37,* 109–133.

Keith, S. J., Regier, D. A., & Rae, D. S. (1991). Schizophrenic disorders. In L. N. Robins & D. A. Regier (Eds.), *Psychiatric disorders in America: The epidemiologic catchment area study*. New York: Free Press.

Keller, F. S. (1968). Goodbye teacher . . . . *Journal of Applied Behavior Analysis, 1,* 79–89.

Keller, L. S., Butcher, J. N., & Slutske, W. S. (1990). Objective personality assessment. In G. Goldstein & M. Hersen (Eds.), *Handbook of psychological assessment*. New York: Pergamon Press.

Kelley, H. H. (1950). The warm-cold variable in first impressions of persons. *Journal of Personality, 18,* 431–439.

Kelley, H. H. (1967). Attributional theory in social psychology. *Nebraska Symposium on Motivation, 15,* 192–241.

Kelley, H. H. (1973). The processes of causal attribution. *American Psychologist, 28,* 107–128.

Kelly, D. D. (1991). Sleep and dreaming. In E. R. Kandel, J. H. Schwartz, & T. M. Jessell (Eds.), *Principles of neural science* (3rd ed.). New York: Elsevier.

Kelly, J. P. (1991). The sense of balance. In E. R. Kandel, J. H. Schwartz, & T. M. Jessell (Eds.), *Principles of neural science* (3rd ed.). New York: Elsevier.

Kelman, H. C. (1967). Human use of human subjects: The problem of deception in social psychological experiments. *Psychological Bulletin, 67,* 1–11.

Kelman, H. C. (1982). Ethical issues in different social science methods. In T. L. Beauchamp, R. R. Faden, R. J. Wallace, Jr., & L. Walters (Eds.), *Ethical issues in social science research*. Baltimore: Johns Hopkins University Press.

Kelsey, R. M. (1993). Habituation of cardiovascular reactivity to psychological stress: Evidence and implications. In J. Blascovich & E. S. Katkin (Eds.), *Cardiovascular reactivity to psychological stress and disease*. Washington, DC: American Psychological Association.

Kendler, K. S., Kessler, R. C., Walters, E. E., MacLean, C., Neale, M. C., Heath, A. C., & Eaves, L. J. (1995). Stressful life events, genetic liability, and onset of an episode of major depression in women. *American Journal of Psychiatry, 152,* 833–842.

Kendler, K. S., MacLean, C. J., O'Neill, A., Burke, J., Murphy, B., Duke, F., Shinkwin, R., Easter, S. M., Webb, B. T., Zhang, J., Walsh, D., & Straub, R. E. (1996). Evidence for a schizophrenia vulnerability locus on chromosome 8p in the Irish study of high-density schizophrenia families. *American Journal of Psychiatry, 153,* 1534–1540.

Kendler, K. S., Neale, M. C., Kessler, R. C., Heath, A. C., & Eaves, L. J. (1992). Generalized anxiety disorder in women: A population-based twin study. *Archives of General Psychiatry, 49,* 267–272.

Kennedy, T. E., Hawkins, R. D., & Kandel, E. R. (1992). Molecular interrelationships between

short- and long-term memory. In L. R. Squire & N. Butters (Eds.), *Neuropsychology of Memory* (2nd ed.). New York: Wiley.

Kenrick, D. T. (1987). Gender, genes, and the social environment. In P. C. Shaver & C. Hendrick (Eds.), *Review of Personality and Social Psychology* (Vol. 8). Beverly Hills, CA: Sage.

Kenrick, D. T. (1995). Evolutionary theory versus the confederacy of dunces. *Psychological Inquiry, 6,* 56–62.

Kenrick, D. T., & Funder, D. C. (1988). Profiting from controversy: Lessons from the person-situation debate. *American Psychologist, 43,* 23–34.

Kenrick, D. T., & Funder, D. C. (1991). The person-situation debate: Do personality traits really exist? In N. J. Derlega, B. A. Winstead, & W. H. Jones (Eds.), *Personality: Contemporary theory and research*. Chicago: Nelson-Hall.

Kenrick, D. T., & Keefe, R. C. (1992). Age preferences in mates reflect sex differences in human reproductive strategies. *Behavioral and Brain Sciences, 15,* 75–133.

Kenrick, D. T., & Simpson, J. A. (1997). Why social psychology and evolutionary psychology need one another. In J. A. Simpson & D. T. Kenrick (Eds.), *Evolutionary social psychology*. Mahwah, NJ: Erlbaum.

Kenrick, D. T., & Stringfield, D. (1980). Personality traits and the eye of the beholder: Crossing some traditional philosophical boundaries in the search for consistency in all of the people. *Psychological Review, 87,* 88–104.

Kenrick, D. T., & Trost, M. R. (1993). The evolutionary perspective. In A. E. Beall & R. J. Sternberg (Eds.), *The psychology of gender*. New York: Guilford Press.

Kenshalo, D. R. (1970). Psychophysical studies of temperature sensitivity. In W. D. Neff (Ed.), *Contributions to Sensory Physiology* (Vol. 4). New York: Academic Press.

Keren, G. (1990). Cognitive aids and debiasing methods: Can cognitive pills cure cognitive ills? In J. P. Caverni, J. M. Fabre, & M. Gonzalez (Eds.), *Cognitive biases*. Amsterdam: North-Holland.

Kerfoot, P., Sakoulas, G., & Hyman, S. E. (1996). Cocaine. In L. S. Friedman, N. F. Fleming, D. H. Roberts, & S. E. Hyman (Eds.), *Source book of substance abuse and addiction*. Baltimore: Williams & Wilkins.

Kerr, N. L. (1992). Issue importance and group decision making. In S. Worchel, W. Wood, & J. A. Simpson (Eds.), *Group process and productivity*. Newbury Park, CA: Sage.

Kessler, R. C. (1995). Epidemiology of psychiatric comorbidity. In M. T. Tsuang, M. Tohen, & G. E. P. Zahner (Eds.), *Textbook in psychiatric epidemiology*. New York: Wiley.

Kessler, R. C., Foster, C., Joseph, J., Ostrow, D., Wortman, C., Phair, J., & Chmiel, J. (1991). Stressful life events and symptom onset in HIV infection. *American Journal of Psychiatry, 148,* 733–738.

Key, W. B. (1973). *Subliminal seduction*. Englewood Cliffs, NJ: Prentice-Hall.

Key, W. B. (1976). *Media sexploitation*. Englewood Cliffs, NJ: Prentice-Hall.

Key, W. B. (1980). *The clam-plate orgy and other subliminal techniques for manipulating your behavior*. Englewood Cliffs, NJ: Prentice-Hall.

Khot, V., & Wyatt, R. J. (1991). Not all that moves is tardive dyskinesia. *American Journal of Psychiatry, 148,* 661–666.

Kiang, N. Y. S., & Peake, W. T. (1988). Physics

and physiology of hearing. In R. C. Atkinson, R. J. Herrnstein, G. Lindzey, & R. D. Luce (Eds.), *Stevens' handbook of experimental psychology* (2nd ed., Vol. 1). New York: Wiley.

Kiecolt-Glaser, J. K., Garner, W., Speicher, C., Penn, G. M., Holliday, J., & Glaser, R. (1984). Psychosocial modifiers of immunocompetence in medical students. *Psychosomatic Medicine, 46*(1), 7–14.

Kiecolt-Glaser, J. K., Glaser, R., Williger, D., Stout, J., Messick, G., Sheppard, S., Ricker, D., Romisher, S. C., Briner, W., Bonnell, G., & Donnerberg, R. (1985). Psychosocial enhancement of immunocompetence in a geriatric population. *Health Psychology, 4,* 25–42.

Kiecolt-Glaser, J. K., Kennedy, S., Malkoff, S., Fisher, L., Speicher, C. E., & Glaser, R. (1988). Marital discord and immunity in males. *Psychosomatic Medicine, 50,* 213–229.

Kiesler, C. A. (1982). Public and professional myths about mental hospitalization. *American Psychologist, 37,* 1232–1339.

Kiesler, C. A. (1991). Homelessness and public policy priorities. *American Psychologist, 46,* 1245–1252.

Kiesler, C. A. (1992). U.S. mental health policy: Doomed to fail. *American Psychologist, 47,* 1077–1082.

Kiesler, C. A. (1993). Mental health policy and mental hospitalization. *Current Directions in Psychological Science, 2*(3), 93–95.

Kiesling, R. (1983). Critique of Kiesler articles. *American Psychologist, 38,* 1127–1128.

Kihlstrom, J. F. (1985). Hypnosis. *Annual Review of Psychology, 36,* 385–418.

Kihlstrom, J. F. (1990). The psychological unconscious. In L. A. Pervin (Ed.), *Handbook of personality: Theory and research*. New York: Guilford Press.

Kihlstrom, J. F., Barnhardt, T. M., & Tataryn, D. J. (1992). Implicit perception. In R. F. Bornstein & T. S. Pittman (Eds.), *Perception without awareness: Cognitive, clinical, and social perspectives*. New York: Guilford Press.

Kihlstrom, J. F., Glisky, M. L., & Angiulo, M. J. (1994). Dissociative tendencies and dissociative disorders. *Journal of Abnormal Psychology, 103,* 117–124.

Kihlstrom, J. F., Schacter, D. L., Cork, R. C., Hurt, C. A., & Behr, S. E. (1990). Implicit and explicit memory following surgical anesthesia. *Psychological Science, 1,* 303–306.

Kihlstrom, J. F., Tataryn, D. J., & Hoyt, I. P. (1993). Dissociative disorders. In P. B. Sutker & H. E. Adams (Eds.), *Comprehensive handbook of psychopathology* (2nd ed.). New York: Plenum.

Killeen, P. R. (1981). Learning as causal inference. In M. L. Commons & J. A. Nevin (Eds.), *Quantitative analyses of behavior: Vol. 1. Discriminative properties of reinforcement schedules*. Cambridge, MA: Ballinger.

Kilpatrick, D. G., Edmunds, C. N., & Seymour, A. (1992). *Rape in America*. Arlington, VA: National Victim Center.

Kimura, D. (1967). Functional asymmetry of the brain in dichotic listening. *Cortex, 3,* 163–178.

Kimura, D. (1973). The asymmetry of the human brain. *Scientific American, 228,* 70–78.

Kimura, D., & Hampson, E. (1993). Neural and hormonal mechanisms mediating sex differences in cognition. In P. A. Vernon (Ed.), *Biological approaches to the study of human intelligence*. Norwood, NJ: Ablex.

Kimura, D., & Hampson, E. (1994). Cognitive

pattern in men and women is influenced by fluctuations in sex hormones. *Psychological Science, 3,* 57–61.

King, A. C., Taylor, C. B., & Haskell, W. L. (1993). Effects of differing intensities and formats of 12 months of exercise training on psychological outcomes in older adults. *Health Psychology, 12,* 292–300.

King, G. R., & Ellinwood, E. H. (1992). Amphetamines and other stimulants. In J. H. Lowinson, P. Ruiz, & R. B. Millman (Eds.), *Substance abuse: A comprehensive textbook* (2nd ed.). Baltimore: Williams & Wilkins.

King, L. A., & Emmons, R. A. (1990). Conflict over emotional expression: Psychological and physical correlates. *Journal of Personality and Social Psychology, 58,* 864–877.

King, L. A., & Emmons, R. A. (1991). Psychological, physical, and interpersonal correlates of emotional expressiveness, conflict and control. *European Journal of Personality, 5,* 131–150.

Kinsbourne, M. (1980). If sex differences in brain lateralization exist, they have yet to be discovered. *Behavioral and Brain Sciences, 3,* 241–242.

Kinsbourne, M. (1982). Hemispheric specialization and the growth of human understanding. *American Psychologist, 37,* 411–420.

Kinsey, A. C., Pomeroy, W. B., & Martin, C. E. (1948). *Sexual behavior in the human male.* Philadelphia: Saunders.

Kinsey, A. C., Pomeroy, W. B., Martin, C. E., & Gebhard, P. H. (1953). *Sexual behavior in the human female.* Philadelphia: Saunders.

Kinsman, R. A., Dirks, J. F., & Jones, N. F. (1982). Psychomaintenance of chronic physical illness: Clinical assessment of personal styles affecting medical management. In T. Millon, C. Green, & R. Meagher (Eds.), *Handbook of clinical health psychology.* New York: Plenum.

Kirk, S. A., & Kutchins, H. (1992). *The selling of DSM: The rhetoric of science in psychiatry.* New York: Aldine de Gruyter.

Kirkpatrick, L. A., & Davis, K. E. (1994). Attachment style, gender, and relationship stability: A longitudinal study. *Journal of Personality and Social Psychology, 66,* 502–512.

Kirmayer, L. J., Robbins, J. M., & Paris, J. (1994). Somatoform disorders: Personality and the social matrix of somatic distress. *Journal of Abnormal Psychology, 103,* 125–136.

Kirsch, I., & Council, J. R. (1992). Situational and personality correlates of hypnotic responsiveness. In E. Fromm & M. R. Nash (Eds.), *Contemporary hypnosis research.* New York: Guilford Press.

Kissebah, A. H., Freedman, D. S., & Peiris, A. N. (1989). High risks of obesity. *Medical Clinics of North America, 73,* 111–138.

Kitson, G. C., & Sussman, M. B. (1982). Marital complaints, demographic characteristics, and symptoms of mental distress in divorce. *Journal of Marriage and the Family, 44,* 87–101.

Kittler, P. G., & Sucher, K. (1989). *Food and culture in America: A nutrition handbook.* New York: Van Nostrand Reinhold.

Klahr, D. (1992). Information-processing approaches to cognitive development. In M. H. Bornstein & M. E. Lamb (Eds.), *Developmental psychology: An advanced textbook* (3rd ed.). Hillsdale, NJ: Erlbaum.

Klaus, P. H., Kennel, J. H., & Klaus, M. H. (1995). *Bonding: Building the foundations of secure attachment & independence.* Reading, MA: Addison-Wesley.

Klayman, J., & Ha, Y-W. (1987). Confirmation, disconfirmation, and information in hypothesis testing. *Psychological Review, 94,* 211–228.

Klein, M. (1948). *Contributions to psychoanalysis.* London: Hogarth.

Kleinmuntz, B. (1980). *Essentials of abnormal psychology.* San Francisco: Harper & Row.

Kleinmuntz, B. (1985). *Personality and psychological assessment.* Malabar, FL: Robert E. Krieger.

Kleinmuntz, B., & Szucko, J. J. (1984). Lie detection in ancient and modern times: A call for contemporary scientific study. *American Psychologist, 39,* 766–776.

Kleitman, N. (1982). Basic rest-activity cycle—22 years later. *Sleep, 5,* 311–317.

Klerman, E. B. (1993). Deprivation, selective: NREM sleep. In M. A. Carskadon (Ed.), *Encyclopedia of sleep and dreaming.* New York: Macmillan.

Klerman, G. L. (1990). Treatment of recurrent unipolar major depressive disorder. *Archives of General Psychiatry, 47,* 1158–1162.

Klerman, G. L., & Weissman, M. M. (1986). The interpersonal approach to understanding depression. In T. Millon & G. L. Klerman (Eds.), *Contemporary directions in psychopathology: Toward the DSM-IV.* New York: Guilford Press.

Klerman, G. L., Weissman, M. M., Markowitz, J. C., Glick, I., Wilner, P. J., Mason, B., & Shear, M. K. (1994). Medication and psychotherapy. In A. E. Bergin & S. L. Garfield (Eds.), *Handbook of psychotherapy and behavior change* (4th ed.). New York: Wiley.

Kline, D. W., & Schieber, F. (1985). Vision and aging. In J. E. Birren & K. W. Schaie (Eds.), *Handbook of the psychology of aging* (2nd ed.). New York: Van Nostrand Reinhold.

Kline, P. (1991). *Intelligence: The psychometric view.* New York: Routledge, Chapman, & Hall.

Kline, P. (1992). *The handbook of psychological testing.* London: Routledge.

Kline, P. (1995). A critical review of the measurement of personality and intelligence. In D. H. Saklofske & M. Zeidner (Eds.), *International handbook of personality and intelligence.* New York: Plenum Press.

Kluckhohn, C., & Murray, H. A. (1948). *Personality in nature, society and culture.* New York: Knopf.

Kluegel, J. R. (1990). Trends in whites' explanations of the black-white gap in socioeconomic status. *American Sociological Review, 55,* 512–525.

Knable, M. B., Kleinman, J. E., & Weinberger, D. R. (1995). Neurobiology of schizophrenia. In A. F. Schatzberg & C. B. Nemeroff (Eds.), *The American Psychiatric Press textbook of psychopharmacology.* Washington, DC: American Psychiatric Press.

Knesper, D. J., & Pagnucco, D. J. (1987). Estimated distribution of effort by providers of mental health services to U.S. adults in 1982 and 1983. *American Journal of Psychiatry, 144,* 883–888.

Knight, G. P., Fabes, R. A., & Higgins, D. A. (1996). Concerns about drawing causal inference from meta-analysis: An example in the study of gender differences in aggression. *Psychological Bulletin, 119,* 410–421.

Knittle, J. L., Merritt, R. J., Dixon-Shanies, D., Ginsberg-Fellner, F., Timmers, K. I., & Katz, D. P. (1981). Childhood obesity. In R. M. Suskind (Ed.), *Textbook of pediatric nutrition.* New York: Raven.

Knowles, J. B., Coulter, M., Wahnon, S., Reitz, W., & MacLean, A. W. (1990). Variation in process S: Effects on sleep continuity and architecture. *Sleep, 13*(2), 97–107.

Knussman, R., Christiansen, K., & Couwenbergs, C. (1986). Relations between sex hormone levels and sexual behavior in men. *Archives of Sexual Behavior, 15*(5), 429–445.

Kobasa, S. C. (1979). Stressful life events, personality, and health: An inquiry into hardiness. *Journal of Personality and Social Psychology, 37,* 1–11.

Kobasa, S. O. (1984, September). How much stress can you survive? *American Health,* pp. 64–77.

Kochanska, G., & Radke-Yarrow, M. (1992). Inhibition in toddlerhood and the dynamics of the child's interaction with an unfamiliar peer at age five. *Child Development, 63,* 325–335.

Koegel, P., & Edgerton, R. B. (1984). Black "six-hour retarded children" as young adults. In R. B. Edgerton (Ed.), *Lives in process: Mildly retarded adults in a large city.* Washington DC: American Association on Mental Deficiency.

Koester, J. (1991). Voltage-grated ion channels and the generation of the action potential. In E. R. Kandel, J. H. Schwartz, & T. M. Jessell (Eds.), *Principles of neural science* (3rd ed.). New York: Elsevier.

Koestner, R., & McClelland, D. C. (1992). The affiliation motive. In C. P. Smith (Ed.), *Motivation and personality: Handbook of thematic content analysis.* New York: Cambridge University Press.

Kogan, N. (1990). Personality and aging. In J. E. Birren & K. W. Schaie (Eds.), *Handbook of the psychology of aging.* San Diego: Academic Press.

Kohlberg, L. (1963). The development of children's orientations toward a moral order: I. Sequence in the development of moral thought. *Vita Humana, 6,* 11–33.

Kohlberg, L. (1964). Development of moral character and moral ideology. In L. W. Hoffman & M. L. Hoffman (Eds.), *Review of child development research* (Vol. 1). New York: Russell Sage Foundation.

Kohlberg, L. (1969). Stage and sequence: The cognitive-developmental approach to socialization. In D. A. Goslin (Ed.), *Handbook of socialization theory and research.* Chicago: Rand McNally.

Kohlberg, L. (1976). Moral stages and moralization: Cognitive-developmental approach. In T. Lickona (Ed.), *Moral development and behavior: Theory, research and social issues.* New York: Holt, Rinehart & Winston.

Kohlberg, L. (1981). *Essays on moral development* (Vol. 1). New York: Harper & Row.

Kohlberg, L. (1984). *Essays on moral development: Vol. 2. The psychology of moral development.* San Francisco: Harper & Row.

Kohn, P. M., Lafreniere, K., & Gurevich, M. (1991). Hassles, health, and personality. *Journal of Personality and Social Psychology, 61,* 478–482.

Kohut, H. (1971). *Analysis of the self.* New York: International Universities Press.

Kolb, B., & Whishaw, I. Q. (1990). *Fundamentals of human neuropsychology.* New York: W. H. Freeman.

Kolodny, R. C., Masters, W. H., & Johnson, V. E. (1979). *Textbook of sexual medicine.* Boston: Little, Brown.

Koob, G. F., & Bloom, F. E. (1988). Cellular and molecular mechanisms of drug dependence. *Science, 242,* 715–723.

Koopman, C., Classen, C., & Spiegel, D. (1994). Predictors of posttraumatic stress symptoms among survivors of the Oakland/Berkeley, Calif., firestorm. *American Journal of Psychiatry, 151*, 888–894.

Koranyi, E. K. (1989). Physiology of stress reviewed. In S. Cheren (Ed.), *Psychosomatic medicine: Theory, physiology, and practice* (Vol. 1). Madison, CT: International Universities Press.

Korchin, S. J. (1976). *Modern clinical psychology: Principles of intervention in the clinic and community*. New York: Basic Books.

Koriat, A., & Melkman, R. (1987). Depth of processing and memory organization. *Psychological Research, 49*, 183–188.

Kortenhaus, C. M., & Demarest, J. (1993). Gender role stereotyping in children's literature: An update. *Sex Roles, 3*, 219–232.

Koss, M. P. (1993). Rape: Scope, impact, interventions, and public policy responses. *American Psychologist, 48*, 1062–1069.

Koss, M. P., Gidycz, C. A., & Wisniewski, N. (1988). The scope of rape: Incidence and prevalence of sexual aggression and victimization in a national sample of higher education students. *Journal of Consulting and Clinical Psychology, 55*, 162–170.

Kotovsky, K., & Fallside, D. (1989). Representation and transfer in problem solving. In D. Klahr & K. Kotovsky (Eds.), *Complex information processing: The impact of Herbert Simon*. Hillsdale, NJ: Erlbaum.

Kotovsky, K., & Simon, H. A. (1990). What makes some problems really hard: Explorations in the problem space of difficulty. *Cognitive Psychology, 22*, 143–183.

Kotovsky, K., Hayes, J. R., & Simon, H. A. (1985). Why are some problems hard? Evidence from Tower of Hanoi. *Cognitive Psychology, 17*, 248–294.

Kracke, W. (1991). Myths in dreams, thought in images: An Amazonian contribution to the psychoanalytic theory of primary process. In B. Tedlock (Ed.), *Dreaming: Anthropological and psychological interpretations*. Santa Fe, NM: School of American Research Press.

Kracke, W. (1992). Languages of dreaming: Anthropological approaches to the study of dreaming in other cultures. In J. Gackenback & A. Sheik (Eds.), *Dream images: A call to mental arms*. Amityville, NY: Baywood.

Kramer, M. (1994). The scientific study of dreaming. In M. H. Kryger, T. Roth, & W. C. Dement (Eds.), *Principles and practice of sleep medicine* (2nd ed.). Philadelphia: Saunders.

Kraus, S. J. (1995). Attitudes and the prediction of behavior: A meta-analysis of the empirical literature. *Personality and Social Psychology Bulletin, 21*, 58–75.

Kravitz, D. A., & Martin, B. (1986). Ringelmann rediscovered: The original article. *Journal of Personality and Social Psychology, 50*, 936–941.

Krebs, D. (1987). The challenge of altruism in biology and psychology. In C. Crawford, M. Smith, & D. Krebs (Eds.), *Sociobiology and psychology: Ideas, issues and applications*. Hillsdale, NJ: Erlbaum.

Krebs, D. L., & Denton, K. (1997). Social illusions and self-deception: The evolution of biases in person perception. In J. A. Simpson & D. T. Kenrick (Eds.), *Evolutionary social psychology*. Mahwah, NJ: Erlbaum.

Kretschmer, E. (1921). *Physique and character*. New York: Harcourt.

Kribbs, N. B. (1993). Siesta. In M. A. Carskadon (Ed.), *Encyclopedia of sleep and dreaming*. New York: Macmillan.

Kring, A. M., Kerr, S. L., Smith, D. A., & Neale, J. M. (1993). Flat affect in schizophrenia does not reflect diminished subjective experience of emotion. *Journal of Abnormal Psychology, 102*(4), 507–517.

Kripke, D. F., Simons, R. N., Garfunkel, L., & Hammond, C. (1979). Short and long sleep and sleeping pills: Is increased mortality associated? *Archives of General Psychiatry, 36*, 103–116.

Kris, E. (1952). *Psychoanalytic explorations in art*. New York: International Universities Press.

Krosnick, J. A., Betz, A. L., Jussim, L. J., & Lynn, A. R. (1992). Subliminal conditioning of attitudes. *Personality and Social Psychology Bulletin, 18*, 152–162.

Krueger, L. E. (1989). Reconciling Fechner and Stevens: Toward a unified psychophysical law. *Behavioral and Brain Sciences, 12*, 251–320.

Krueger, W. C. F. (1929). The effect of overlearning on retention. *Journal of Experimental Psychology, 12*, 71–78.

Krull, D. S., & Erickson, D. J. (1995). Inferential hopscotch: How people draw social inferences from behavior. *Current Directions in Psychological Science, 4*, 35–38.

Kryger, M. H. (1993). Snoring. In M. A. Carskadon (Ed.), *Encyclopedia of sleep and dreaming*. New York: Macmillan.

Kryger, M. H., Roth, T., & Carskadon, M. (1994). Circadian rhythms in humans: An overview. In M. H. Kryger, T. Roth, & W. C. Dement (Eds.), *Principles and practice of sleep medicine* (2nd ed.). Philadelphia: Saunders.

Kryger, M. H., Roth, T., & Dement, W. C. (1994). *Principles and practice of sleep medicine* (2nd ed.). Philadelphia: Saunders.

Kulick, A. R., Pope, H. G., & Keck, P. E. (1990). Lycanthropy and self-identification. *Journal of Nervous & Mental Disease, 178*(2), 134–137.

Kunda, Z., & Oleson, K. C. (1995). Maintaining stereotypes in the face of disconfirmation: Constructing grounds for subtyping deviants. *Journal of Personality and Social Psychology, 68*, 565–579.

Kupfermann, I. (1991). Hypothalamus and the limbic system: Motivation. In E. R. Kandel, J. H. Schwartz, & T. M. Jessell (Eds.), *Principles of neural science* (3rd ed.). New York: Elsevier.

Kutchinsky, B. (1985). Pornography and its effects in Denmark and the United States. *Comparative Social Research, 8*, 281–300.

LaBerge, S. (1988). Lucid dreaming in western literature. In J. Gackenbach & S. LaBerge (Eds.), *Conscious mind, sleeping brain: Perspectives on lucid dreaming*. New York: Plenum.

LaBerge, S. (1990). Lucid dreaming: Psychophysiological studies of consciousness during REM sleep. In R. R. Bootzin, J. F. Kihlstrom, & D. L. Schacter (Eds.), *Sleep and cognition*. Washington, DC: American Psychological Association.

LaBerge, S., Nagel, L., Dement, W. C., & Zarcone, V., Jr. (1981). Lucid dreaming verified by volitional communication during REM sleep. *Perceptual and Motor Skills, 52*, 727–732.

La Cerra, P., & Kurzban, R. (1995). The structure of scientific revolutions and the nature of the adapted mind. *Psychological Inquiry, 6*, 62–65.

Lachman, S. J. (1996). Processes in perception: Psychological transformations of highly structured stimulus material. *Perceptual and Motor Skills, 83*, 411–418.

LaCroix, A. Z., Mead, L. A., Liang, K. Y., Thomas, C. B., & Pearson, T. A. (1986). Coffee consumption and the incidence of coronary heart disease. *New England Journal of Medicine, 315*, 977–982.

Lader, M. H. (1990). Benzodiazepine withdrawal. In R. Noyes, Jr., M. Roth, & G. D. Burrows (Eds.), *Handbook of anxiety: The treatment of anxiety* (Vol. 4). Amsterdam: Elsevier.

Lader, M. H., & Herrington, R. (1990). *Biological treatments in psychiatry*. Oxford: Oxford University Press.

Laird, J. D. (1984). The real role of facial response in the experience of emotion: A reply to Tourangeau and Ellsworth, and others. *Journal of Personality and Social Psychology, 47*, 909–917.

Lakein, A. (1973). *How to get control of your time and your life*. New York: Peter H. Wyden.

Lamb, M. E. (1982). Parent-infant interaction, attachment and socioemotional development in infancy. In R. N. Emde & R. J. Harmon (Eds.), *The development of attachment and affiliative systems*. New York: Plenum.

Lamb, M. E. (Ed.). (1987). *The father's role: Cross-cultural perspectives*. Hillsdale, NJ: Erlbaum.

Lamb, M. E., Ketterlinus, R. D., & Fracasso, M. P. (1992). Parent-child relationships. In M. H. Bornstein & M. E. Lamb (Eds.), *Developmental psychology: An advanced textbook* (3rd ed.). Hillsdale, NJ: Erlbaum.

Lamb, M. E., Sternberg, K. J., & Prodromidis, M. (1992). Nonmaternal care and the security of infant-mother attachment: A reanalysis of the data. *Infant Behavior and Development, 15*, 71–83.

Lambert, M. J., & Bergin, A. E. (1992). Achievements and limitations of psychotherapy research. In D. K. Freedheim (Ed.), *History of psychotherapy: A century of change*. Washington, DC: American Psychological Association.

Lambert, M. J., & Bergin, A. E. (1994). The effectiveness of psychotherapy. In A. E. Bergin & S. L. Garfield (Eds.), *Handbook of psychotherapy and behavior change* (4th ed.). New York: Wiley.

Lambert, M. J., & Hill, C. E. (1994). Assessing psychotherapy outcomes and processes. In A. E. Bergin & S. L. Garfield (Eds.), *Handbook of psychotherapy and behavior change* (4th ed.). New York: Wiley.

Lampl, M., Veldhuis, J. D., & Johnson, M. L. (1992). Saltation and stasis: A model of human growth. *Science, 258*, 801–803.

Landesman, S., & Ramey, C. (1989). Developmental psychology and mental retardation: Integrating scientific principles with treatment practices. *American Psychologist, 44*, 409–415.

Landsberger, H. A. (1958). *Hawthorne revisited: Management and the worker, its critics and developments in human relations in industry*. Ithaca: New York State School of Industrial and Labor Relations.

Landy, D., & Sigall, H. (1974). Beauty is talent: Task evaluation as a function of the performer's physical attractiveness. *Journal of Personality and Social Psychology, 29*, 299–304.

Landy, F. J. (1988). The early years of I/O: "Dr. Mayo." *The Industrial and Organizational Psychologist, 25*, 53–55.

Landy, F. J. (1989). *Psychology of work behavior*. Pacific Grove, CA: Brooks/Cole.

Landy, F. J., & Bittner, K. (1991). The early history of job satisfaction. In C. J. Cranny (Ed.), *Job satisfaction: Advances in theory and research*. Lexington, MA: Lexington Books.

Landy, F. J., & Farr, J. L. (1980). Performance rating. *Psychological Bulletin, 87*, 72–107.

Landy, F. J., & Farr, J. L. (1983). *The measure-*

ment of work performance: Methods, theory, and applications. New York: Academic Press.

Landy, F. J., Quick, J. C., & Kasl, S. (1994). Work, stress, and well being. *International Journal of Stress Management, 1*, 33–73.

Landy, F. J., Shankster, L. J., & Kohler, S. S. (1994). Personnel selection and placement. *Annual Review of Psychology, 45*, 261–296.

Lang, P. J. (1995). The emotion probe: Studies of motivation and attention. *American Psychologist, 50*, 372–385.

Lange, C. (1885). One leuds beveegelser. In K. Dunlap (Ed.), *The emotions.* Baltimore: Williams & Wilkins.

LaPiere, R. T. (1934). Attitude and actions. *Social Forces, 13*, 230–237.

Larkin, J. A. (1988). Are good teachers perceived as high self-monitors? *Personality and Social Psychology Bulletin, 13*, 64–72.

Larkin, J. H., & Reif, F. (1979). Understanding and teaching problem solving in physics. *European Journal of Science Education, 1*, 191–203.

Larrick, R. P. (1993). Motivational factors in decision theories: The role of self-protection. *Psychological Bulletin, 113*, 440–450.

Larson, R., & Asmussen, L. (1991). Anger, worry, and hurt in early adolescence: An enlarging world of negative emotions. In M. E. Colten & S. Gore (Eds.), *Adolescent stress: Causes and consequences.* New York: Aldine de Gruyter.

Larson, R., & Ham, M. (1993). Stress and "storm and stress" in early adolescence: The relationship of negative events with dysphoric affect. *Developmental Psychology, 29*(1), 130–140.

LaRue, A., & Jarvik, L. F. (1982). Old age and biobehavioral changes. In B. B. Wolman (Ed.), *Handbook of developmental psychology.* Englewood Cliffs, NJ: Prentice-Hall.

Larwood, L., & Gattiker, U. (1984, August). *A comparison of the career paths used by successful men and women.* Paper presented at the meeting of the American Psychological Association, Toronto, Ontario.

Lassiter, G. D., Stone, J. I., & Weigold, M. F. (1988). Effect of leading questions on the self-monitoring correlation. *Personality and Social Psychology Bulletin, 13*, 537–545.

Lassner, J. B., Matthews, K. A., & Stoney, C. M. (1994). Are cardiovascular reactors to asocial stress also reactors to social stress? *Journal of Personality and Social Psychology, 66*, 69–77.

Latané, B. (1981). The psychology of social impact. *American Psychologist, 36*, 343–356.

Latané, B., & Nida, S. A. (1981). Ten years of research on group size and helping. *Psychological Bulletin, 89*, 308–324.

Latané, B., Williams, K., & Harkins, S. (1979). Many hands make light the work: The causes and consequences of social loafing. *Journal of Personality and Social Psychology, 37*, 822–832.

Lattal, K. A. (1992). B. F. Skinner and psychology [Introduction to the Special Issue]. *American Psychologist, 27*, 1269–1272.

Lau, R. R. (1988). Beliefs about control and health behavior. In D. Gochman (Ed.), *Health behavior: Emerging research perspectives.* New York: Plenum.

Lauber, J. K. (1993). Public safety in transportation. In M. A. Carskadon (Ed.), *Encyclopedia of sleep and dreaming.* New York: Macmillan.

Laughlin, H. (1967). *The neuroses.* Washington, DC: Butterworth.

Laughlin, H. (1979). *The ego and its defenses.* New York: Aronson.

Laurence, J. R., & Perry, C. (1983). Hypnotically created memory among highly hypnotizable subjects. *Science, 222*, 523–524.

Lazarus, A. A. (1976). *Multimodal behavior therapy.* New York: Springer.

Lazarus, A. A. (1989). Multimodal therapy. In R. J. Corsini & D. Wedding (Eds.), *Current Psychotherapies.* Itasca, IL: F. E. Peacock.

Lazarus, A. A., & Wilson, G. T. (1976). Behavior modification: Clinical and experimental perspectives. In B. B. Wolman (Ed.), *The therapist's handbook: Treatment methods of mental disorders.* New York: Van Nostrand Reinhold.

Lazarus, R. S. (1991). *Emotion and adaptation.* New York: Oxford University Press.

Lazarus, R. S. (1993). Why we should think of stress as a subset of emotion. In L. Goldberger & S. Breznitz (Eds.), *Handbook of stress: Theoretical and clinical aspects* (2nd ed.). New York: Free Press.

Lazarus, R. S., & Folkman, S. (1984). *Stress, appraisal and coping.* New York: Springer.

Le Boeuf, M. (1980). *Imagineering.* New York: McGraw-Hill.

Leahey, T. H. (1987). *A history of psychology: Main currents in psychological thought* (2nd ed.). Englewood Cliffs, NJ: Prentice-Hall.

Leahey, T. H. (1992). The mythical revolutions of American psychology. *American Psychologist, 47*, 308–318.

Leavitt, F. (1995). *Drugs and behavior* (3rd ed.). Thousand Oaks, CA: Sage Publications.

LeBoeuf, M. (1980, February). Managing time means managing yourself. *Business Horizons, 41*–46.

LeDoux, J. E. (1986). The neurobiology of emotion. In J. E. LeDoux & W. Hirst (Eds.), *Mind and brain: Dialogues in cognitive neuroscience.* Cambridge, England: Cambridge University Press.

LeDoux, J. E. (1992). Systems and synapses of emotional memory. In L. R. Squire, N. M. Weinberger, G. Lynch, & J. L. McGuagh (Eds.), *Memory: Organization and locus of change.* New York: Oxford University Press.

LeDoux, J. E. (1993). Emotional networks in the brain. In M. Lewis & J. M. Haviland (Eds.), *Handbook of emotions.* New York: Guilford Press.

Lee, Y. T., & Seligman, M. E. P. (1997). Are Americans more optimistic than the Chinese? *Personality and Social Psychology Bulletin, 23*, 32–40.

Leeper, R. W. (1935). A study of a neglected portion of the field of learning: The development of sensory organization. *Journal of Genetic Psychology, 46*, 41–75.

Lefcourt, H. M., Davidson, K., Shepherd, R., Phillips, M., Prkachin, K., & Mills, D. (1995). Perspective-taking humor: Accounting for stress moderation. *Journal of Social and Clinical Psychology, 14*, 373–391.

Leff, J., & Vaughn, C. (1981). The role of maintenance therapy and relatives' expressed emotion in relapse of schizophrenia: A two-year follow-up. *British Journal of Psychiatry, 139*, 102–104.

Leff, J., & Vaughn, C. (1985). *Expressed emotion in families.* New York: Guilford Press.

Lefkowitz, M. M., Eron, L. D., Walder, L. O., & Huesmann, L. R. (1977). *Growing up to be violent.* New York: Pergamon Press.

Legault, F., & Strayer, F. F. (1990). The emergence of sex-segregation in preschool peer groups. In F. F. Strayer (Ed.), *Social interaction and behavioral development during early childhood.* Montreal: La Maison D'Ethologie de Montreal.

Lehmann, H. E., & Cancro, R. (1985). Schizophrenia: Clinical features. In H. I. Kaplan & B. J. Sadock (Eds.), *Comprehensive textbook of psychiatry/IV.* Baltimore: Williams & Wilkins.

Lehrer, P. M., & Woolfolk, R. L. (1984). Are stress reduction techniques interchangeable, or do they have specific effects? A review of the comparative empirical literature. In R. L. Woolfolk & P. M. Lehrer (Eds.), *Principles and practice of stress management.* New York: Guilford Press.

Leibovic, K. N. (1990). Vertebrate photoreceptors. In K. N. Leibovic (Ed.), *Science of vision.* New York: Springer-Verlag.

Leibowitz, S. F., Weiss, G. F., Walsh, U. A., & Viswanath, D. (1989). Medial hypothalamic serotonin: Role in circadian patterns of feeding and macronutrient selection. *Brain Research, 503*, 132–140.

Leibowitz, S. F., Weiss, G. F., Yee, F., & Tretter, J. B. (1985). Noradrenergic innervation of the paraventricular nucleus: Specific role in control of carbohydrate ingestions. *Brain Research Bulletin, 14*, 561–567.

Leigh, B. C. (1989). Reasons for having and avoiding sex: Gender, sexual orientation, and relationship to sexual behavior. *The Journal of Sex Research, 26*(2), 299–309.

Leiker, M., & Hailey, B. J. (1988). A link between hostility and disease: Poor health habits. *Behavioral Medicine, 14*, 129–133.

Leippe, M. R., & Eisenstadt, D. (1994). Generalization of dissonance reduction: Decreasing prejudice through induced compliance. *Journal of Personality and Social Psychology, 67*, 395–413.

Leitenberg, H., & Henning, K. (1995). Sexual fantasy. *Psychological Bulletin, 117*, 469–496.

Lennie, P., Trevarthen, C., Van Essen, D., & Wassle, H. (1990). Parallel processing of visual information. In L. Spillmann & J. S. Werner (Eds.), *Visual perception: The neurophysiological foundations.* San Diego: Academic Press.

Lenox, R. H., & Manji, H. K. (1995). Lithium. In A. F. Schatzberg & C. B. Nemeroff (Eds.), *The American Psychiatric Press textbook of psychopharmacology.* Washington, DC: American Psychiatric Press.

Leo, J. (1987, January). Exploring the traits of twins. *Time*, p. 63.

Lerner, M. J., & Miller, D. T. (1978). Just world research and the attribution process: Looking back and ahead. *Psychological Bulletin, 85*, 1030–1051.

Lesher, G. W. (1995). Illusory contours: Toward a neurally based perceptual theory. *Psychonomic Bulletin & Review, 2*, 279–321.

Lester, B. M., Corwin, M. J., Sepkoski, C., Seifer, R., Peucker, M., McLaughlin, S., & Golub, H. L. (1991). Neurobehavioral syndromes in cocaine-exposed newborn infants. *Child Development, 62*, 694–705.

Lester, N., Nebel, L. E., & Baum, A. (1994). Psychophysiological and behavioral measurement of stress: Applications to mental health. In W. R. Avison & I. H. Gotlib (Eds.), *Stress and mental health: Contemporary issues and prospects for the future.* New York: Plenum Press.

Levay, A. N., Weissberg, J. H., & Woods, S. M. (1981). Intrapsychic factors in sexual dysfunctions. In H. I. Lief (Ed.), *Sexual problems in medical practice.* Chicago: American Medical Association.

LeVay, S. (1991). A difference in hypothalamic structure between heterosexual and homosexual men. *Science, 253*, 1034–1037.

LeVay, S. (1993). *The sexual brain.* Cambridge, MA: MIT Press.

Levenson, R. W. (1992). Autonomic nervous system differences among emotions. *Psychological Science, 3*, 23–27.

Leventhal, H., & Tomarken, A. J. (1986). Emotion: Today's problems. *Annual Review of Psychology, 37*, 565–610.

Levin, M. E., & Levin, J. R. (1990). Scientific mnemonomies: Methods for maximizing more than memory. *American Educational Research Journal, 27*(2), 301–321.

Levin, S., Yurgelun-Todd, D., & Craft, S. (1989). Contributions of clinical neuropsychology to the study of schizophrenia. *Journal of Abnormal Psychology, 98*, 341–356.

Levine, J. D., Fields, H. L., & Basbaum, A. I. (1993). Peptides and the primary afferent nociceptor. *Journal of Neuroscience, 13*, 2273–2286.

Levine, M. W., & Shefner, J. M. (1991). *Fundamentals of sensation and perception.* Pacific Grove, CA: Brooks/Cole.

Levinson, D. J., with Darrow, C. M., Klein, E. G., Levinson, M. H., & McKee, B. (1978). *The seasons of a man's life.* New York: Knopf.

Levis, D. J. (1989). The case for a return to a two-factor theory of avoidance: The failure of non-fear interpretations. In S. B. Klein & R. R. Bowrer (Eds.), *Contemporary learning theories: Pavlovian conditioning and the status of traditional learning theory.* Hillsdale NJ: Erlbaum.

Levy, J. (1985, May). Right brain, left brain: Fact or fiction. *Psychology Today,* pp. 38–44.

Levy, J., & Nagylaki, T. (1972). A model for the genetics of handedness. *Genetics, 72*, 117–128.

Levy, J., Trevarthen, C., & Sperry, R. W. (1972). Perception of bilateral chimeric figures following hemispheric disconnection. *Brain, 95*, 61–78.

Levy, S. M. (1985). *Behavior and cancer.* San Francisco: Jossey-Bass.

Levy, S. M., Herberman, R. B., Simons, A., Whiteside, T., Lee, J., McDonald, R., & Beadle, M. (1989). Persistently low natural killer cell activity in normal adults: Immunological, hormonal and mood correlates. *Natural Immune Cell Growth Regulation, 8*, 173–186.

Lewicki, P., Hill, T., & Czyzewska, M. (1992). Nonconscious acquisition of information. *American Psychologist, 47*, 796–801.

Lewin, K. (1935). *A dynamic theory of personality.* New York: McGraw-Hill.

Lewinsohn, P. M., Duncan, E. M., Stanton, A. K., & Hautzinger, M. (1986). Age at first onset for nonbipolar depression. *Journal of Abnormal Psychology, 95*, 378–383.

Lewinsohn, P. M., & Gotlib, I. H. (1995). Behavioral theory and treatment of depression. In E. E. Beckham & W. R. Leber (Eds.), *Handbook of depression* (2nd ed.). New York: Guilford Press.

Lewinsohn, P. M., Rohde, P., Seeley, J. R., & Fischer, S. A. (1993). Age-cohort changes in the lifetime occurrence of depression and other mental disorders. *Journal of Abnormal Psychology, 102*, 110–120.

Lewis, D. O., Pincus, J. H., Feldman, M., Jackson, L., & Bard, B. (1986). Psychiatric, neurological, and psychoeducational characteristics of 15 death row inmates in the United States. *American Journal of Psychiatry, 143*, 838–845.

Lewis, J. M., Owen, M. T., & Cox, M. J. (1988). The transition to parenthood: III. Incorporation of the child into the family. *Family Process, 27*, 411–421.

Lewis, M., & Feiring, C. (1989). Infant, mother, and mother-infant interaction behavior and sub-sequent attachment. *Child Development, 60*, 831–837.

Lewis, S. A. (1969). Subjective estimates of sleep: An EEG evaluation. *British Journal of Psychology, 60*, 203–208.

Lewis-Fernandez, R., & Kleinman, A. (1994). Culture, personality, and psychology. *Journal of Abnormal Psychology, 103*, 67–71.

Lewontin, R. C. (1976). Race and intelligence. In N. J. Block & G. Dworkin (Eds.), *The IQ controversy: Critical readings.* New York: Pantheon.

Lewontin, R. C., Rose, S., & Kamin, L. (1984). *Not in our genes: Biology, ideology and human nature.* New York: Pantheon.

Lewy, A. J., Ahmed, S., & Sack, R. L. (1995). Phase shifting the human circadian clock using melatonin. *Behavioral Brain Research, 73*, 131–134.

Lewy, A. J., Sack, R. L., Singer, C. M., White, D. M., & Hoban, T. M. (1989). Winter depression and the phase-shift hypothesis for bright light's therapeutic effects: History, theory and experimental evidence. In N. E. Rosenthal & M. C. Blehar (Eds.), *Seasonal affective disorders and phototherapy.* New York: Guilford Press.

Liberman, R. P., & Bedell, J. R. (1989). Behavior therapy. In H. I. Kaplan & B. J. Sadock (Eds.), *Comprehensive textbook of psychiatry/V.* Baltimore: Williams & Wilkins.

Liberman, R. P., Mueser, K. T., & DeRisi, W. J. (1989). *Social skills training for psychiatric patients.* New York: Pergamon Press.

Libman, H. (1992). Pathogenesis, natural history, and classification of HIV infection. *Primary Care, 19*(1), 1–17.

Lichtenstein, S., Fischhoff, B., & Phillips, L. D. (1982). Calibration of probabilities: The state of the art to 1980. In D. Kahneman, P. Slovic, & A. Tversky (Eds.), *Judgment under uncertainty: Heuristics and biases.* Cambridge: Cambridge University Press.

Lickey, M. E., & Gordon, B. (1991). *Medicine and mental illness: The use of drugs in psychiatry.* New York: W. H. Freeman.

Lieberman, D. A. (1993). *Learning: Behavior and cognition* (2nd ed.). Pacific Grove, CA: Brooks/Cole.

Lieberman, M. A. (1993). Self-help groups. In H. I. Kaplan & B. J. Sadock (Eds.), *Comprehensive group psychotherapy.* Baltimore: Williams & Wilkins.

Liebert, R. M., & Spiegler, M. D. (1990). *Personality: Strategies and issues.* Pacific Grove, CA: Brooks/Cole.

Liebert, R. M., & Sprafkin, J. (1988). *The early window: Effects of television on children and youth.* Oxford, England: Pergamon Press.

Lindgren, H. C. (1969). *The psychology of college success: A dynamic approach.* New York: Wiley.

Lindsay, D. S. (1993). Eyewitness suggestibility. *Current Directions in Psychological Science, 2*(3), 86–89.

Lindsay, D. S., & Johnson, M. K. (1989). The eyewitness suggestibility effects and memory for source. *Memory & Cognition, 17*, 349–358.

Lindsay, D. S., & Johnson, M. K. (1991). Recognition memory and source monitoring. *Bulletin of the Psychonomic Society, 29*, 203–205.

Lindsay, D. S., & Poole, D. A. (1995). Remembering childhood sexual abuse in therapy: Psychotherapists' self-reported beliefs, practices, and experiences. *Journal of Psychiatry & Law,* 461–476.

Lindsay, P. H., & Norman, D. A. (1977). *Human information processing.* New York: Academic Press.

Linn, M. C., & Petersen, A. C. (1986). A meta-analysis of gender differences in spatial ability: Implications for mathematics and science achievement. In J. S. Hyde & M. C. Linn (Eds.), *The psychology of gender: Advances through meta-analysis.* Baltimore: Johns Hopkins University Press.

Linz, D. (1989). Exposure to sexually explicit materials and attitudes toward rape: A comparison study results. *Journal of Sex Research, 26*, 50–84.

Lippa, R. A. (1994). *Introduction to social psychology.* Pacific Grove, CA: Brooks/Cole.

Lipsey, M. W., & Wilson, D. B. (1993). The efficacy of psychological, educational, and behavioral treatment: Confirmation from meta-analysis. *American Psychologist, 48*, 1181–1209.

Lipsitt, L. P., & Behl, G. (1990). Taste-mediated differences in the sucking behavior of human newborns. In E. D. Capaldi & T. L. Powley (Eds.), *Taste, experience, and feeding.* Washington, DC: American Psychological Association.

Litt, I. F., & Vaughan, V. C., III. (1992). Adolescence. In R. E. Behrman (Ed.), *Nelson textbook of pediatrics.* Philadelphia: Saunders.

Livesley, W. J., Schroeder, M. L., Jackson, D. N., & Jang, K. L. (1994). Categorical distinctions in the study of personality disorder: Implications for classification. *Journal of Abnormal Psychology, 103*, 6–17.

Livingstone, M., & Hubel, D. (1988). Segregation of form, color, movement, and depth: Anatomy, physiology, and perception. *Science, 240*, 740–749.

Lloyd, C., Alexander, A. A., Rice, D. G., & Greenfield, N. S. (1980). Life events as predictors of academic performance. *Journal of Human Stress, 6*(3), 15–26.

Lloyd, G. K., Fletcher, A., & Minchin, M. C. W. (1992). GABA agonists as potential anxiolytics. In G. D. Burrows, S. M. Roth, & R. Noyes, Jr. (Eds.), *Handbook of anxiety* (Vol. 5). Oxford: Elsevier.

Lloyd, M. A. (1985). *Adolescence.* New York: HarperCollins.

Locke, D. C. (1992). *Increasing multicultural understanding: A comprehensive model.* Newbury Park, CA: Sage.

Locke, E. A. (1976). The nature and causes of job satisfaction. In M. D. Dunnette (Ed.), *The handbook of industrial and organizational psychology.* Chicago: Rand McNally.

Lockhart, R. S. (1992). Measurement of memory. In L. R. Squire (Ed.), *Encyclopedia of learning and memory.* New York: Macmillan.

Lockhart, R. S., & Craik, F. I. (1990). Levels of processing: A retrospective commentary on a framework for memory research. *Canadian Journal of Psychology, 44*(1), 87–112.

Locurto, C. (1990). The malleability of IQ as judged from adoption studies. *Intelligence, 14*, 275–292.

Locurto, C. (1991). *Sense and nonsense about IQ: The case for uniqueness.* New York: Praeger.

Loeber, R., & Hay, D. (1997). Key issues in the development of aggression and violence from childhood to early adulthood. *Annual Review of Psychology, 48*, 371–410.

Loehlin, J. C. (1989). Partitioning environmental and genetic contributions to behavioral development. *American Psychologist, 44*, 1285–1292.

Loehlin, J. C. (1992). *Genes and environment in personality development*. Newbury Park, CA: Sage.

Loehlin, J. C. (1994). Behavior genetics. In R. J. Sternberg (Ed.), *Encyclopedia of human intelligence*. New York: Macmillan.

Loftus, E. F. (1979). *Eyewitness testimony*. Cambridge, MA: Harvard University Press.

Loftus, E. F. (1992). When a lie becomes memory's truth: Memory distortion after exposure to misinformation. *Current Directions in Psychological Science, 1*, 121–123.

Loftus, E. F. (1993). The reality of repressed memories. *American Psychologist, 48*, 518–537.

Loftus, E. F., & Ketcham, K. (1994). *The myth of repressed memory: False memories and allegations of sexual abuse*. New York: St. Martin's Press.

Loftus, E. F., & Klinger, M. R. (1992). Is the unconscious smart or dumb? *American Psychologist, 47*, 761–765.

Loftus, E. F., & Loftus, G. R. (1980). On the permanence of stored information in the human brain. *American Psychologist, 35*, 409–420.

Loftus, E. F., & Palmer, J. C. (1974). Reconstruction of automobile destruction: An example of the interaction between language and memory. *Journal of Verbal Learning and Verbal Behavior, 13*, 585–589.

Logue, A. W. (1991). *The psychology of eating and drinking* (2nd ed.). New York: W. H. Freeman.

Lohman, D. F. (1989). Human intelligence: An introduction to advances in theory and research. *Review of Educational Research, 59*(4), 333–373.

LoLordo, V. M., & Droungas, A. (1989). Selective associations and adaptive specializations: Taste aversions and phobias. In S. B. Klein & R. R. Mower (Eds.), *Contemporary learning theories: Instrumental conditioning theory and the impact of biological constraints on learning*. Hillsdale, NJ: Erlbaum.

London, W. P. (1990). Left-handedness and alcoholism. In S. Coren (Ed.), *Left-handedness: Behavioral implications and anomalies*. Amsterdam: North-Holland.

Longman, D. G., & Atkinson, R. H. (1991). *College learning and study skills*. St. Paul, MN: West.

Longstreth, L. E. (1984). Jensen's reaction-time investigations of intelligence: A critique. *Intelligence, 8*, 139–160.

Lott, B., & Maluso, D. (1993). The social learning of gender. In A. E. Beall & R. J. Sternberg (Eds.), *The psychology of gender*. New York: Guilford Press.

Lovett, S. B., & Flavell, J. H. (1990). Understanding and remembering: Children's knowledge about the differential effects of strategy and task variables on comprehension and memorization. *Child Development, 61*, 1842–1858.

Lowinson, J. H., Ruiz, P., & Millman, R. B. (1992). *Substance abuse: A comprehensive textbook*. Baltimore: Williams & Wilkins.

Lubkin, I. M. (1990). Illness roles. In I. M. Lubkin (Ed.), *Chronic illness: Impact and interventions* (2nd ed.). Boston: Jones and Bartlett.

Luborsky, L., Singer, B., & Luborsky, L. (1975). Comparative studies of psychotherapies: Is it true that everyone has won and all must have prizes? *Archives of General Psychiatry, 32*, 995–1008.

Luchins, A. S. (1942). Mechanization in problem solving. *Psychological Monographs, 54*(6, Whole No. 248).

Ludwig, A. M. (1994). Mental illness and creative activity in female writers. *American Journal of Psychiatry, 151*, 1650–1656.

Ludwig, A. M. (1995). *The price of greatness: Resolving the creativity and madness controversy*. New York: Guilford Press.

Luecke-Aleksa, D., Anderson, D. R., Collins, P. A., & Schmitt, K. L. (1995). Gender constancy and television viewing. *Developmental Psychology, 31*, 773–780.

Lugaresi, E., Cirignotta, F., Montagna, P., & Sforza, E. (1994). Snoring: Pathogenic, clinical, and therapeutic aspects. In M. H. Kryger, T. Roth, & W. C. Dement (Eds.), *Principles and practice of sleep medicine* (2nd ed.). Philadelphia: Saunders.

Luh, C. W. (1922). The conditions of retention. *Psychological Monographs, 31*.

Luntz, B. K., & Widom, C. S. (1994). Antisocial personality disorder in abused and neglected children grown up. *Journal of Psychiatry, 151*, 670–674.

Lutz, C. (1987). Goals, events and understanding in Ifaluk emotion theory. In N. Quinn & D. Holland (Eds.), *Cultural models in language and thought*. Cambridge, England: Cambridge University Press.

Lye, D. N., & Biblarz, T. J. (1993). The effects of attitudes toward family life and gender roles on marital satisfaction. *Journal of Family Issues, 14*, 157–188.

Lykken, D. T. (1981). *A tremor in the blood: Uses and abuses of the lie detector*. New York: McGraw-Hill.

Lykken, D. T., McGue, M., Tellegen, A., & Bouchard, T. J., Jr. (1992). Emergenesis: Genetic traits that may not run in families. *American Psychologist, 47*, 1565–1577.

Lyman, B., Hatlelid, D., & Macurdy, C. (1981). Stimulus-person cues in first-impression attraction. *Perceptual and Motor Skills, 52*, 59–66.

Lyness, S. A. (1993). Predictors of differences between Type A and Type B individuals in heart rate and blood pressure reactivity. *Psychological Bulletin, 114*, 266–295.

Lynn, R. (1987). The intelligence of the mongoloids: A psychometric, evolutionary and neurological theory. *Personality and Individual Differences, 8*, 813–844.

Lynn, R. (1991). Educational achievements of Asian Americans. *American Psychologist, 46*(8), 875–876.

Lynn, R. (1995). Cross-cultural differences in intelligence and personality. In D. H. Saklofske & M. Zeidner (Eds.), *International handbook of personality and intelligence*. New York: Plenum Press.

Lyons, M. J. (1995). Epidemiology of personality disorders. In M. T. Tsuang, M. Tohen, & G. E. P. Zahner (Eds.), *Textbook in psychiatric epidemiology*. New York: Wiley.

Lytton, H., & Romney, D. M. (1991). Parents' differential socialization of boys and girls: A meta-analysis. *Psychological Bulletin, 109*, 267–296.

Maccoby, E. E. (1990). Gender and relationships: A developmental account. *American Psychologist, 45*, 513–520.

Maccoby, E. E., & Jacklin, C. N. (1974). *The psychology of sex differences*. Stanford, CA: Stanford University Press.

MacDonald, J., Twardon, E. M., & Shaffer, H. J. (1996). Alcohol. In L. S. Friedman, N. F. Fleming, D. H. Roberts, & S. E. Hyman (Eds.), *Source book of substance abuse and addiction*. Baltimore: Williams & Wilkins.

Machover, K. (1949). *Personality projection in the drawing of the human figure*. Springfield, IL: Charles C Thomas.

Machung, A. (1989). Talking career, thinking job: Gender differences in career and family expectations of Berkeley seniors. *Family Studies, 15*, 35–58.

Mackenzie, B. (1984). Explaining race differences in IQ: The logic, the methodology, and the evidence. *American Psychologist, 39*, 1214–1233.

Mackie, D. M., Worth, L. T., & Asuncion, A. G. (1990). Processing of persuasive in-group messages. *Journal of Personality and Social Psychology, 58*, 812–822.

MacLean, P. D. (1954). Studies on limbic system ("vioscel brain") and their bearing on psychosomatic problems. In E. D. Wittkower & R. A. Cleghorn (Eds.), *Recent developments in psychosomatic medicine*. Philadelphia: Lippincott.

MacLean, P. D. (1993). Cerebral evolution of emotion. In M. Lewis & J. M. Haviland (Eds.), *Handbook of emotions*. New York: Guilford Press.

Macmillan, M. (1991). *Freud evaluated: The completed arc*. Amsterdam: North-Holland.

MacQueen, G., Marshall, J., Perdue, M., Siegel, S., & Bienenstock, J. (1989). Pavlovian conditioning of rat mucosal mast cells to secrete rat mast cell protease II. *Science, 243*, 83–86.

Macrae, C. N., Milne, A. B., & Bodenhausen, G. V. (1994). Stereotypes as energy-saving devices: A peek inside the cognitive toolbox. *Journal of Personality and Social Psychology, 66*, 37–47.

Maddi, S. R. (1989). *Personality theories: A comparative analysis*. Chicago, IL: Dorsey Press.

Madsen, K. B. (1968). *Theories of motivation*. Copenhagen: Munksgaard.

Madsen, K. B. (1973). Theories of motivation. In B. B. Wolman (Ed.), *Handbook of general psychology*. Englewood Cliffs, NJ: Prentice-Hall.

Maguire, W., Weisstein, N., & Klymenko, V. (1990). From visual structure to perceptual function. In K. N. Leibovic (Ed.), *Science of vision*. New York: Springer-Verlag.

Maher, B. A., & Spitzer, M. (1993). Delusions. In P. B. Sutker & H. E. Adams (Eds.), *Comprehensive handbook of psychopathology* (2nd ed.). New York: Plenum.

Mahowald, M. W. (1993). Sleepwalking. In M. A. Carskadon (Ed.), *Encyclopedia of sleep and dreaming*. New York: Macmillan.

Maier, N. R. F. (1931). Reasoning and learning. *Psychological Review, 38*, 332–346.

Main, D. M., & Main, E. K. (1991). Preterm birth. In S. G. Gabbe, J. R. Niebyl, & J. L. Simpson (Eds.), *Obstetrics: Normal and problem pregnancies*. New York: Churchill Livingstone.

Makin, J. W., & Porter, R. H. (1989). Attractiveness of lactating females' breast odors to neonates. *Child Development, 60*, 803–810.

Malamuth, N. M. (1984). Violence against women: Cultural and individual cases. In N. M. Malamuth & E. Donnerstein (Eds.), *Pornography and sexual aggression*. New York: Academic Press.

Malamuth, N. M., & Donnerstein, E. (1982). The effects of aggressive-pornographic mass media stimuli. In L. Berkowitz (Ed.), *Advances in experimental social psychology* (Vol. 15). New York: Academic Press.

Malatesta, V. J., & Adams, H. E. (1984). The sexual dysfunctions. In H. E. Adams & P. B. Sutker (Eds.), *Comprehensive handbook of psychopathology*. New York: Plenum.

Malcolm, J. (1980: Pt. 1, Nov. 24; Pt. 2, Dec. 1). The impossible profession. *The New Yorker*, pp. 55–133, 54–152.

Malina, R. M. (1975). *Growth and development: The first twenty years in man*. Minneapolis: Burgess Publishing.

Malina, R. M. (1990). Physical growth and performance during the transitional years (9–16). In R. Montemayor, G. R. Adams, & T. P. Gullotta (Eds.), *From childhood to adolescence: A transitional period?* Newbury Park, CA: Sage.

Malloy, M. H., Kao, T., & Lee, Y. J. (1992). Analyzing the effect of prenatal care on pregnancy outcome: A conditional approach. *American Journal of Public Health, 82,* 448–453.

Manderscheid, R. W., & Sonnenschein, M. A. (1992). *Mental health, United States, 1992.* Washington, DC: U.S. Department of Health and Human Services.

Mandler, G. (1984). *Mind and body.* New York: Norton.

Mandler, G. (1989). Memory: Conscious and unconscious. In P. R. Soloman, G. R. Goethals, C. M. Kelley, & B. R. Stephens (Eds.), *Memory: Interdisciplinary approaches.* New York: Springer-Verlag.

Mandler, G. (1993). Thought, memory, and learning: Effects of emotional stress. In L. Goldberger & S. Breznitz (Eds.), *Handbook of stress: Theoretical and clinical aspects* (2nd ed.). New York: Free Press.

Mangelsdorf, S., Gunnar, M., Kestenbaum, R., Lang, S., & Andreas, D. (1990). Infant proneness-to-distress temperament, maternal personality, and mother-infant attachment: Associations and goodness of fit. *Child Development, 61,* 830–831.

Mann, J., Tarantola, D. J. M., & Netter, T. W. (1992). *A global report: AIDS in the world.* New York: Oxford University Press.

Manuck, S. B., Kamarck, T. W., Kasprowicz, A. S., & Waldstein, S. R. (1993). Stability and patterning of behaviorally evoked cardiovascular reactivity. In J. Blascovich & E. S. Katkin (Eds.), *Cardiovascular reactivity to psychological stress and disease.* Washington, DC: American Psychological Association.

Maratsos, M. (1983). Some current issues in the study of the acquisition of grammar. In J. H. Flavell & E. M. Markman (Eds.), *Handbook of child psychology* (Vol. 3). New York: Wiley.

Marcel, A. (1983). Conscious and unconscious perception: Experiments on visual masking and word recognition. *Cognitive Psychology, 15,* 197–237.

Marcia, J. E. (1966). Development and validation of ego identity status. *Journal of Personality and Social Psychology, 3,* 551–558.

Marcia, J. E. (1980). Identity in adolescence. In J. Adelson (Ed.), *Handbook of adolescent psychology.* New York: Wiley.

Marcus, G. F. (1996). Why do children say "breaked"? *Current Directions in Psychological Science, 5,* 81–85.

Marder, S. R., & Van Putten, T. (1995). Antipsychotic medications. In A. F. Schatzberg & C. B. Nemeroff (Eds.), *The American Psychiatric Press textbook of psychopharmacology.* Washington, DC: American Psychiatric Press.

Marengo, J., Harrow, M., Sands, J., & Galloway, C. (1991). European versus U. S. data on the course of schizophrenia. *American Journal of Psychiatry, 148,* 606–611.

Mark, V. (1996). Conflicting communicative behavior in a split-brain patient: Support for dual consciousness. In S. R. Hameroff, A. W. Kaszniak, & A. C. Scott (Eds.), *Toward a science of consciousness. The first Tucson discussions and debates.* Cambridge, MA: MIT Press.

Markowitsch, H. J., & Pritzel, M. (1985). The neuropathology of amnesia. *Progress in Neurobiology, 25,* 189–287.

Marks, I. M. (1987). *Fears, phobias, and rituals: Panic, anxiety, and their disorders.* New York: Oxford University Press.

Markus, H. R., & Kitayama, S. (1991). Culture and the self: Implications for cognition, emotion, and motivation. *Psychological Review, 98,* 224–253.

Markus, H. R., & Kitayama, S. (1994). The cultural construction of self and emotion: Implications for social behavior. In S. Kitayama & H. R. Markus (Eds.), *Emotions and culture: Empirical studies of mutual influence.* Washington, DC: American Psychological Association.

Marschark, M. (1992). Coding processes: Imagery. In L. R. Squire (Ed.), *Encyclopedia of learning and memory.* New York: Macmillan.

Marschark, M., & Hunt, R. R. (1989). A reexamination of the role of imagery in learning and memory. *Journal of Experimental Psychology: Learning, Memory, and Cognition, 15,* 710–720.

Marsella, A. J. (1979). Cross-cultural studies of mental disorders. In A. J. Marsella, R. Tharp, & T. Ciborowski (Eds.), *Perspectives in cross-cultural psychology.* New York: Academic Press.

Marshall, D. A., & Moulton, D. G. (1981). Olfactory sensitivity to x-ionone in humans and dogs. *Chemical Senses, 6,* 53–61.

Marshall, G. N. (1991). A multidimensional analysis of internal health locus of control beliefs: Separating the wheat from the chaff? *Journal of Personality and Social Psychology, 61,* 483–491.

Martin, C. L., & Halverson, C. F., Jr. (1987). The role of cognition in sex role acquisition. In D. B. Carter (Ed.), *Current conceptions of sex roles and sex typing: Theory and research.* New York: Praeger.

Martin, J. H. (1991). The collective electrical behavior of cortical neurons: The electroencephalogram and the mechanisms of epilepsy. In E. R. Kandel, J. H. Schwartz, & T. M. Jessell (Eds.), *Principles of neural science* (3rd ed.). New York: Elsevier.

Martin, J. H., Brust, J. C. M., & Hilal, S. (1991). Imaging the living brain. In E. R. Kandel, J. H. Schwartz, & T. M. Jessell (Eds.), *Principles of neural science.* (3rd ed.). New York: Elsevier.

Martin, J. H., & Jessell, T. M. (1991). Anatomy of the somatic sensory system. In E. R. Kandel, J. H. Schwartz, & T. M. Jessell (Eds.), *Principles of neural science.* (3rd ed.). New York: Elsevier.

Martin, L. (1986). "Eskimo words for snow": A case study in the genesis and decay of an anthropological example. *American Psychologist, 88,* 418–423.

Martin, R. L., & Yutzy, S. H. (1994). Somatoform disorders. In R. E. Hales, S. C. Yudofsky, & J. A. Talbott (Eds.), *The American Psychiatric Press textbook of psychiatry* (2nd ed.). Washington, DC: American Psychiatric Press.

Martinez, J. L., & Derrick, B. E. (1996). Long–term potentiation and learning. *Annual Review of Psychology, 47,* 173–203.

Maser, J. D., Kaelber, C., & Weise, R. E. (1991). International use and attitudes toward DSM-III and DSM-III-R: Growing consensus in psychiatric classification. *Journal of Abnormal Psychology, 100,* 271–279.

Maslach, C. (1979). Negative emotional biasing of unexplained arousal. *Journal of Personality and Social Psychology, 37,* 953–969.

Maslow, A. H. (1954). *Motivation and personality.* New York: Harper & Row.

Maslow, A. H. (1962). *Toward a psychology of being.* Princeton, NJ: Van Nostrand.

Maslow, A. H. (1968). *Toward a psychology of being.* New York: Van Nostrand.

Maslow, A. H. (1970). *Motivation and personality.* New York: Harper & Row.

Maslow, A. H. (1971). *Farther reaches of human nature.* New York: Viking Penguin.

Mason, J. W. (1975). A historical view of the stress field, Part II. *Journal of Human Stress, 1,* 22–36.

Massion, A. O., Warshaw, M. G., & Keller, M. B. (1993). Quality of life and psychiatric morbidity in panic disorder and generalized anxiety disorder. *American Journal of Psychiatry, 150,* 600–607.

Masters, R. D. (1995). Mechanism and function in evolutionary psychology: Emotion, cognitive neuroscience, and personality. *Psychological Inquiry, 6,* 65–68.

Masters, W. H., & Johnson, V. E. (1966). *Human sexual response.* Boston: Little, Brown.

Masters, W. H., & Johnson, V. E. (1970). *Human sexual inadequacy.* Boston: Little, Brown.

Masters, W. H., & Johnson, V. E. (1979). *Homosexuality in perspective.* Boston: Little, Brown.

Masters, W. H., & Johnson, V. E. (1980). *Human sexual inadequacy* (2nd ed.). New York: Bantam Books.

Matarazzo, J. D. (1992). Psychological testing and assessment in the 21st century. *American Psychologist, 47,* 1007–1018.

Matarazzo, J. D. (1994). Alfred Binet. In R. J. Sternberg (Ed.), *Encyclopedia of human intelligence.* New York: Macmillan.

Matarazzo, J. D., & Herman, D. O. (1985). Clinical uses of the WAIS-R: Base rates of differences between VIQ and PIQ in the WAIS-R standardization sample. In B. B. Wolman (Ed.), *Handbook of intelligence: Theories, measurements, and applications.* New York: Wiley.

Matlin, M. W. (1989). *Cognition.* New York: Holt, Rinehart & Winston.

Matsumoto, D. (1994). *People: Psychology from a cultural perspective.* Pacific Grove, CA: Brooks/Cole.

Matthews, K. A. (1992). Myths and realities of the menopause. *Psychosomatic Medicine, 54*(1), 1–9.

Matthews, K. A., Scheier, M. F., Brunson, B. I., & Carducci, B. (1989). Why do unpredictable events lead to reports of physical symptoms? In T. W. Miller (Ed.), *Stressful life events.* Madison, CT: International Universities Press.

Matthews, K. A., Woodall, K. L., & Stoney, C. M. (1990). Changes in and stability of cardiovascular responses to behavioral stress. *Child Development, 61,* 1134–1144.

Mauro, R., Sato, K., & Tucker, J. (1992). The role of appraisal in human emotions: A cross-cultural study. *Journal of Personality and Social Psychology, 62,* 301–317.

Mayer, J. (1955). Regulation of energy intake and the body weight: The glucostatic theory and the lipostatic hypothesis. *Annals of the New York Academy of Science, 63,* 15–43.

Mayer, J. (1968). *Overweight: Causes and control.* Englewood Cliffs, NJ: Prentice-Hall.

Mayes, A. R. (1992). What are the functional deficits that underlie amnesia? In L. R. Squire & N. Butters (Eds.), *Neuropsychology of memory* (2nd ed.). New York: Guilford Press.

Mays, V. M., & Albee, G. W. (1992). Psychotherapy and ethnic minorities. In D. K. Freedheim (Ed.), *History of psychotherapy: A century of change.* Washington, DC: American Psychological Association.

Mays, V. M., Rubin, J., Sabourin, M., & Walker, L. (1996). Moving toward a global psychology: Changing theories and practice to meet the needs of a changing world. *American Psychologist, 51,* 485–487.

Mazur, J. E. (1993). Predicting the strength of a conditioned reinforcer: Effects of delay and uncertainty. *Current Directions in Psychological Science, 2*(3), 70–74.

McAdams, D. P. (1992). The five-factor model in personality: A critical appraisal. *Journal of Personality, 60,* 329–361.

McAdams, D. P., & Constantian, C. A. (1983). Intimacy and affiliation motives in daily living: An experience sampling analysis. *Journal of Personality and Social Psychology, 45,* 851–861.

McBride, P. E. (1992). The health consequences of smoking: Cardiovascular diseases. *Medical Clinics of North America, 76,* 333–353.

McCabe, A., & Lipscomb, T. J. (1988). Sex differences in children's verbal aggression. *Merrill-Palmer Quarterly, 34,* 389–401.

McCarley, R. W. (1994). Dreams and the biology of sleep. In M. H. Kryger, T. Roth, & W. C. Dement (Eds.), *Principles and practice of sleep medicine* (2nd ed.). Philadelphia: Saunders.

McCarty, D., Argeriou, M., Huebner, R. B., & Lubran, B. (1991). Alcoholism, drug abuse, and the homeless. *American Psychologist, 46,* 1139–1148.

McClearn, G. E., Plomin, R., Gora-Maslak, G., & Crabbe, J. C. (1991). The gene chase in behavioral science. *Psychological Science, 2,* 222–229.

McClelland, D. C. (1961). *The achieving society.* Princeton, NJ: Van Nostrand.

McClelland, D. C. (1965). Achievement and entrepreneurship: A longitudinal study. *Journal of Personality and Social Psychology, 1,* 389–392.

McClelland, D. C. (1973). Testing for competence rather than for "intelligence." *American Psychologist, 28,* 1–14.

McClelland, D. C. (1975). *Power: The inner experience.* New York: Irvington.

McClelland, D. C. (1985). How motives, skills and values determine what people do. *American Psychologist, 40,* 812–825.

McClelland, D. C. (1987). Characteristics of successful entrepreneurs. *Journal of Creative Behavior, 3,* 219–233.

McClelland, D. C. (1993). Intelligence is not the best predictor of job performance. *Current Directions in Psychological Science, 2*(1), 5–6.

McClelland, D. C., Atkinson, J. W., Clark, R. A., & Lowell, E. L. (1953). *The achievement motive.* New York: Appleton-Century-Crofts.

McClelland, D. C., & Boyatzis, R. E. (1982). The leadership motive pattern and long-term success in management. *Journal of Applied Psychology, 67,* 737–743.

McClelland, D. C., & Koestner, R. (1992). The achievement motive. In C. P. Smith (Ed.), *Motivation and personality: Handbook of thematic content analysis.* New York: Cambridge University Press.

McClelland, D. C., Koestner, R., & Weinberger, J. (1992). How do self-attributed and implicit motives differ? In C. P. Smith (Ed.), *Motivation and personality: Handbook of thematic content analysis.* New York: Cambridge University Press.

McClelland, D. C., & Winter, D. G. (1969). *Motivating economic achievement.* New York: Free Press.

McClintock, M. K. (1971). Menstrual synchrony and suppression. *Nature, 299,* 244–245.

McCloskey, M., Wible, C. G., & Cohen, N. J. (1988). Is there a special flashbulb-memory mechanism? *Journal of Experimental Psychology: General, 117,* 171–181.

McConkey, K. M. (1992). The effects of hypnotic procedures on remembering: The experimental findings and their implications for forensic hypnosis. In E. Fromm & M. R. Nash (Eds.), *Contemporary hypnosis research.* New York: Guilford Press.

McConnell, J. V. (1962). Memory transfer through cannibalism in planarians. *Journal of Neuropsychiatry, 3*(Suppl. 1), 542–548.

McConnell, J. V., Cutler, R. L., & McNeil, E. B. (1958). Subliminal stimulation: An overview. *American Psychologist, 13,* 229–242.

McCrae, R. R. (1984). Situational determinants of coping responses: Loss, threat and challenge. *Journal of Personality and Social Psychology, 46,* 919–928.

McCrae, R. R. (1994). A reformulation of Axis II: Personality and personality-related problems. In P. T. Costa, Jr., & T. A. Widiger (Eds.), *Personality disorders and the five-factor model of personality.* Washington, DC: American Psychological Association.

McCrae, R. R. (1996). Social consequences of experimental openness. *Psychological Bulletin, 120,* 323–337.

McCrae, R. R., & Costa, P. T., Jr. (1984). *Emerging lives, enduring dispositions: Personality in adulthood.* Boston: Little, Brown.

McCrae, R. R., & Costa, P. T., Jr. (1985). Updating Norman's "adequate taxonomy": Intelligence and personality dimensions in natural language and in questionnaires. *Journal of Personality and Social Psychology, 49,* 710–721.

McCrae, R. R., & Costa, P. T., Jr. (1987). Validation of the five-factor model of personality across instruments and observers. *Journal of Personality and Social Psychology, 52,* 81–90.

McCrae, R. R., & Costa, P. T., Jr. (1990). *Personality in adulthood.* New York: Guilford Press.

McDaniel, M. A., & Einstein, G. O. (1986). Bizarre imagery as an effective memory aid: The importance of distinctiveness. *Journal of Experimental Psychology: Learning, Memory & Cognition, 12,* 54–65.

McDaniel, M. A., Waddill, P. J., & Shakesby, P. S. (1996). Study strategies, interest, and learning from text: The application of material appropriate processing. In D. J. Herrmann, C. McEvoy, C. Hertzog, P. Hertel, & M. K. Johnson (Eds.), *Basic and applied memory research: Theory in context* (Vol. 1). Mahwah, NJ: Erlbaum.

McGaugh, J. L. (1989). Modulation of memory storage processes. In P. R. Soloman, G. R. Goethals, C. M. Kelley, & B. R. Stephens (Eds.), *Memory: Interdisciplinary approaches.* New York: Springer-Verlag.

McGaugh, J. L. (1990). Significance and remembrance: The role of neuromodulatory systems. *Psychological Science, 1,* 15–25.

McGaugh, J. L. (1992). Hormones and memory. In L. R. Squire (Ed.), *Encyclopedia of learning and memory.* New York: Macmillan.

McGeoch, J. A., & McDonald, W. T. (1931). Meaningful relation and retroactive inhibition. *American Journal of Psychology, 43,* 579–588.

McGilly, K., & Siegler, R. S. (1989). How children choose among serial recall strategies. *Child Development, 60,* 172–182.

McGinnies, E., & Ward, C. D. (1980). Better liked than right: Trustworthiness and expertise as factors in credibility. *Personality and Social Psychology Bulletin, 6,* 467–472.

McGinty, D. (1993). Thermoregulation. In M. A. Carskadon (Ed.), *Encyclopedia of sleep and dreaming.* New York: Macmillan .

McGinty, D., & Szymusiak, D. (1988). Neuronal unit activity patterns in behaving animals: Brainstem and limbic system. *Annual Review of Psychology, 39,* 135–168.

McGlashan, T. H., & Fenton, W. S. (1992). The positive-negative distinction in schizophrenia: Review of natural history validators. *Archives of General Psychiatry, 49,* 63–72.

McGlashan, T. H., Mohr, D. C., Beutler, L. E., Engle, D., Shoham-Salomon, V., Bergan, J., Kaszniak, A. W., & Yost, E. B. (1990). Identification of patients at risk for nonresponse and negative outcome in psychotherapy. *Journal of Consulting and Clinical Psychology, 58,* 622–628.

McGue, M., Bouchard, T. J., Jr., Iacono, W. G., & Lykken, D. T. (1993). Behavioral genetics of cognitive ability: A life-span perspective. In R. Plomin & G. E. McClearn (Eds.), *Nature, nurture and psychology.* Washington, DC: American Psychological Association.

McGuire, T. R., & Haviland, J. M. (1985). Further considerations for behavior-genetic analysis of humans. *Journal of Personality and Social Psychology, 49,* 1434–1436.

McGuire, W. J. (1985). Attitudes and attitude change. In G. Lindzey & E. Aronson (Eds.), *Handbook of social psychology* (Vol. 2). New York: Random House.

McHale, S. M., Bartko, W. T., Crouter, A. C., & Perry-Jenkins, M. (1990). Children's housework and psychosocial functioning: The mediating effects of parents' sex-role behaviors and attitudes. *Child Development, 61,* 1413–1426.

McHugh, P. R., & Moran, T. H. (1985). The stomach: A conception of its dynamic role in satiety. *Progress in Psychobiology and Physiological Psychology,* pp. 197–232.

McIntosh, J. L. (1991). Epidemiology of suicide in the U.S. In A. A. Leenaars (Ed.), *Life span perspectives of suicide.* New York: Plenum.

McIntyre, R. M., Smith, D. E., & Hassett, C. E. (1984). Accuracy of performance ratings as affected by rater training and perceived purpose of rating. *Journal of Applied Psychology, 69*(1), 147–156.

McKean, K. (1985, June). Decisions, decisions. *Discover,* pp. 22–31.

McKenna, J. J. (1993). Co-sleeping. In M. A. Carskadon (Ed.), *Encyclopedia of sleep and dreaming.* New York: Macmillan.

McKillip, J., & Riedel, S. L. (1983). External validity of matching on physical attractiveness for same and opposite sex couples. *Journal of Applied Social Psychology, 13,* 328–337.

McKinlay, J. B., McKinlay, S. M., & Brambilla, D. (1987). The relative contributions of endocrine changes and social circumstances to depression in mid-aged women. *Journal of Health and Social Behavior, 28*(4), 345–363.

McNally, R. J. (1987). Preparedness and phobias: A review. *Psychological Bulletin, 101,* 283–303.

McNally, R. J. (1990). Psychological approaches to panic disorder: A review. *Psychological Bulletin, 108,* 403–419.

McNally, R. J. (1994). Cognitive bias in panic disorder. *Current Directions in Psychological Science, 3,* 129–132.

McNeil, D. E., & Binder, R. L. (1995). Correlates of accuracy in the assessment of psychiatric inpatients' risk of violence. *American Journal of Psychiatry, 152,* 901–906.

McNeill, D. (1970). *The acquisition of language: The study of developmental psycholinguistics*. New York: Harper & Row.

Mebert, C. J. (1991). Dimensions of subjectivity in parents' ratings of infant temperament. *Child Development, 62*, 352–361.

Mechanic, D. (1980). *Mental health and social policy*. Englewood Cliffs, NJ: Prentice-Hall.

Medina, N. J., & Neill, D. M. (1990). *Fallout from the testing explosion: How 100 million standardized exams undermine equity and excellence in America's public schools* (3rd ed.). Cambridge, MA: Fair Test.

Mednick, S. A., & Mednick, M. T. (1967). *Examiner's manual, Remote Associates Test*. Boston, MA: Houghton Mifflin.

Meehan, P. J., Lamb, J. A., Saltzman, L. E., & O'Carroll, P. W. (1992). Attempted suicide among young adults: Progress toward a meaningful estimate of prevalence. *American Journal of Psychiatry, 149*, 41–44.

Meindl, J. R., & Lerner, M. J. (1984). Exacerbation of extreme responses to an out-group. *Journal of Personality and Social Psychology, 47*, 71–84.

Melamed, T. (1995). Barriers to women's career success: Human capital, career choices, structural determinants, or simply sex discrimination. *Applied Psychology, 44*, 295–314.

Mellinger, G. D., Balter, M. B., & Uhlenhuth, E. H. (1985). Insomnia and its treatment: Prevalence and correlations. *Archives of General Psychiatry, 42*, 225–232.

Meltzoff, A. N., & Gopnik, A. (1989). On linking nonverbal imitation, representation, and language learning in the first two years of life. In G. E. Speidel & K. E. Nelson (Eds.), *The many faces of imitation in language learning*. New York: Springer-Verlag.

Melzack, R. (1973). *The puzzle of pain*. New York: Basic Books.

Melzack, R., & Wall, P. D. (1965). Pain mechanisms: A new theory. *Science, 150*, 971–979.

Melzack, R., & Wall, P. D. (1982). *The challenge of pain*. New York: Basic Books.

Mendelson, W. B. (1987). *Human sleep: Research and clinical care*. New York: Plenum.

Mendelson, W. B. (1990). Insomnia: The patient and the pill. In R. R. Bootzin, J. F. Kihlstrom, & D. L. Schacter (Eds.), *Sleep and cognition*. Washington, DC: American Psychological Association.

Mendelson, W. B. (1993). Sleeping pills. In M. A. Carskadon (Ed.), *Encyclopedia of sleep and dreaming*. New York: Macmillan.

Mentzer, R. L. (1982). Response biases in multiple-choice test item files. *Educational and Psychological Measurement, 42*, 437–448.

Mercer, J. R. (1973). *Labeling the mentally retarded*. Berkeley: University of California Press.

Mercer, J. R. (1975). Sociocultural factors in educational labeling. In M. J. Begab & S. A. Richardson (Eds.), *The mentally retarded and society: A social science perspective*. Baltimore: University Park Press.

Merckelbach, H., De Ruiter, C., Van Den Hout, M. A., & Hoekstra, R. (1989). Conditioning experiences and phobias. *Behavior Research and Therapy, 27*(6), 657–662.

Merigan, W. H., & Maunsell, J. H. (1993). How parallel are the primate visual pathways? *Annual Review of Neuroscience, 16*, 36–403.

Merikle, P. M. (1980). Selection from visual persistence by perceptual groups and category membership. *Journal of Experimental Psychology: General, 109*, 279–295.

Mesquita, B., & Frijda, N. H. (1992). Cultural variations in emotions: A review. *Psychological Bulletin, 112*, 179–204.

Metalsky, G. I., Joiner, T. E., Jr., Hardin, T. S., & Abramson, L. Y. (1993). Depressive reactions to failure in a naturalistic setting: A test of the hopelessness and self-esteem theories of depression. *Journal of Abnormal Psychology, 102*, 101–109.

Meyer, D. E., & Schvaneveldt, R. W. (1976). Meaning, memory structure, and mental processes. *Science, 192*, 27–33.

Meyer, R. G. (1992). *Practical clinical hypnosis: Techniques and applications*. New York: Lexington Books.

Meyer-Bahlburg, H. F. L., Ehrhardt, A. A., Rosen, L. R., Gruen, R. S., Veridiano, N. P., Vann, F. H., & Neuwalder, H. F. (1995). Prenatal estrogens and the development of homosexual orientation. *Developmental Psychology, 31*, 12–21.

Middlebrooks, J. C., & Knudsen, E. I. (1984). A neural code for auditory space in the cat's superior colliculus. *The Journal of Neuroscience, 4*, 2621–2634.

Milberger, S., Biederman, J., Faraone, S. V., Chen, L., & Jones, J. (1996). Is maternal smoking during pregnancy a risk factor for attention deficit hyperactivity disorder in children? *American Journal of Psychiatry, 153*, 1138–1142.

Milburn, N., & D'Ercole, A. (1991). Homeless women: Moving toward a comprehensive model. *American Psychologist, 46*, 1161–1169.

Milgram, S. (1963). Behavioral study of obedience. *Journal of Abnormal and Social Psychology, 67*, 371–378.

Milgram, S. (1964). Issues in the study of obedience. *American Psychologist, 19*, 848–852.

Milgram, S. (1968). Reply to the critics. *International Journal of Psychiatry, 6*, 294–295.

Milgram, S. (1974). *Obedience to authority*. New York: Harper & Row.

Miller, A. G. (1986). *The obedience experiments: A case study of controversy in social science*. New York: Praeger.

Miller, C. T., Byrne, D., & Fisher, J. D. (1980). Order effects on sexual and affective responses to erotic stimuli by males and females. *Journal of Sex Research, 16*, 131–147.

Miller, G. A. (1956). The magical number seven, plus or minus two: Some limits on our capacity for processing information. *Psychological Review, 63*, 81–97.

Miller, G. A. (1991). *The science of words*. New York: Scientific American Library.

Miller, J. G. (1984). Culture and the development of everyday social explanation. *Journal of Personality and Social Psychology, 46*, 961–978.

Miller, J. G. (1991). A cultural perspective on the morality of beneficence and interpersonal responsibility. In S. Ting-Toomey & F. Korzenny (Eds.), *International and intercultural communication annual* (Vol. 15). Newbury Park, CA: Sage.

Miller, N. E. (1941). The frustration-aggression hypothesis. *Psychological Review, 48*, 337–342.

Miller, N. E. (1944). Experimental studies of conflict. In J. M. Hunt (Ed.), *Personality and the behavior disorders* (Vol. 1). New York: Ronald.

Miller, N. E. (1959). Liberalization of basic S-R concepts: Extension to conflict behavior, motivation, and social learning. In S. Koch (Ed.), *Psychology: A study of a science* (Vol. 2). New York: McGraw-Hill.

Miller, N. E. (1985). The value of behavioral research on animals. *American Psychologist, 40*, 423–440.

Miller, P. H. (1993). *Theories of developmental psychology*. New York: Freeman.

Miller, P. H., & Weiss, M. G. (1981). Children's attention allocation, understanding of attention, and performance on the incidental learning task. *Child Development, 52*, 1183–1190.

Miller, P. M., & Fagley, N. S. (1991). The effects of framing, problem variations, and providing rationale on choice. *Personality and Social Psychology Bulletin, 17*(5), 517–522.

Miller, R. R., & Barnet, R. C. (1993). The role of time in elementary associations. *Current Directions in Psychological Science, 2*(4), 106–111.

Miller, R. R., Barnet, R. C., & Grahame, N. J. (1995). Assessment of the Rescorla-Wagner model. *Psychological Bulletin, 117*, 363–386.

Miller, T. Q., Smith, T. W., Turner, C. W., Guijarro, M. L., & Hallet, A. J. (1996). A meta-analytic review of research on hostility and physical health. *Psychological Bulletin, 119*, 322–348.

Miller, T. Q., Turner, C. W., Tindale, R. S., Posavac, E. J., & Dugoni, B. L. (1991). Reasons for the trend toward null findings in research on Type A behavior. *Psychological Bulletin, 110*, 469–485.

Millman, J., Bishop, C. H., & Ebel, R. (1965). An analysis of test-wiseness. *Educational and Psychological Measurement, 25*, 707–726.

Millon, T. (1981). *Disorders of personality: DSM-III, axis II*. New York: Wiley.

Millon, T. (1994). Personality disorders: Conceptual distinctions and classification issues. In P. T. Costa, Jr., & T. A. Widger (Eds.), *Personality disorders and the five-factor model of personality*. Washington, DC: American Psychological Association.

Millstone, E. (1989). Methods and practices of animal experimentation. In G. Langley (Ed.), *Animal experimentation: The consensus changes*. New York: Chapman & Hall.

Milner, B., Corkin, S., & Teuber, H. (1968). Further analysis of the hippocampal amnesic syndrome: 14-year follow-up study of H. M. *Neuropsychologia, 6*, 215–234.

Mineka, S. (1979). The role of fear in theories of avoidance learning, flooding and extinction. *Psychological Bulletin, 86*, 985–1010.

Mineka, S., & Cook, M. (1986). Immunization against the observational conditioning of snake fear in rhesus monkeys. *Journal of Abnormal Psychology, 95*, 307–318.

Mineka, S., & Tomarken, A. J. (1989). The role of cognitive biases in the origins and maintenance of fear and anxiety disorders. In T. Archer & L. G. Nilsson (Eds.), *Aversion, avoidance, and anxiety: Perspectives on aversively motivated behavior*. Hillsdale, NJ: Erlbaum.

Mingay, D. J. (1987). The effects of hypnosis on eyewitness memory: Reconciling forensic claims and research findings. *Applied Psychology: An International Review, 36*, 163–183.

Mischel, W. (1961). Delay of gratification, need for achievement, and acquiescence in another culture. *Journal of Abnormal and Social Psychology, 62*, 543–552.

Mischel, W. (1968). *Personality and assessment*. New York: Wiley.

Mischel, W. (1973). Toward a cognitive social learning conceptualization of personality. *Psychological Review, 80*, 252–283.

Mischel, W. (1984). Convergences and challenges in the search for consistency. *American Psychologist, 39*, 351–364.

Mischel, W. (1990). Personality dispositions revisited and revised: A view after three decades. In

L. A. Pervin (Ed.), *Handbook of personality: Theory and research*. New York: Guilford Press.

Mischel, W., & Mischel, H. N. (1976). A cognitive social learning approach to morality and self-regulation. In T. Lickona (Ed.), *Moral development and behavior: Theory, research and social issues*. New York: Holt, Rinehart & Winston.

Mishkin, M., & Appenzeller, T. (1987). The anatomy of memory. *Scientific American, 256*, 80–89.

Mishkin, M., Malamut, B., & Backevalier, J. (1984). Memories and habits: Two neural systems. In G. Lynch, J. L. McGaugh, & N. M. Weinberger (Eds.), *The neurobiology of learning and memory*. New York: Guilford Press.

Mistlberger, R. E., & Rusak, B. (1994). Circadian rhythms in mammals: Formal properties and environmental influences. In M. H. Kryger, T. Roth, & W. C. Dement (Eds.), *Principles and practice of sleep medicine* (2nd ed.). Philadelphia: Saunders.

Mitler, M. M. (1993). Public safety in the workplace. In M. A. Carskadon (Ed.), *Encyclopedia of sleep and dreaming*. New York: Macmillan.

Mitler, M. M., Dinges, D. F., & Dement, W. C. (1994). Sleep medicine, public policy, and public health. In M. H. Kryger, T. Roth, & W. C. Dement (Eds.), *Principles and practice of sleep medicine* (2nd ed.). Philadelphia: Saunders.

Moates, D. R., & Schumacher, G. M. (1980). *An introduction to cognitive psychology*. Belmont, CA: Wadsworth.

Mobley, W. H., Horner, S. O., & Hollingsworth, A. T. (1978). An evaluation of precursors of hospital employee turnover. *Journal of Applied Psychology, 63*, 408–414.

Modestin, J. (1992). Multiple personality disorder in Switzerland. *American Journal of Psychiatry, 149*, 88–92.

Moffitt, A. (1995). Dreaming: Functions and meaning. *Impuls, 3*, 18–31.

Moghaddam, F. M., Taylor, D. M., & Wright, S. C. (1993). *Social psychology in cross-cultural perspective*. New York: W. H. Freeman.

Moline, M. L. (1993). Jet lag. In M. A. Carskadon (Ed.), *Encyclopedia of sleep and dreaming*. New York: Macmillan.

Monahan, J. (1992). Mental disorder and violent behavior: Perceptions and evidence. *American Psychologist, 47*, 511–521.

Monk, T. H., & Folkard, S. (1985). Individual differences in shiftwork adjustment. In S. Folkard & T. H. Monk (Eds.), *Hours of work—Temporal factors in work scheduling*. New York: Wiley.

Monk, T. H. (1994). Shift work. In M. H. Kryger, T. Roth, & W. C. Dement (Eds.), *Principles and practice of sleep medicine* (2nd ed.). Philadelphia: Saunders.

Monroe, S. M., & Simons, A. D. (1991). Diathesis-stress theories in the context of life stress research: Implications for the depressive disorders. *Psychological Bulletin, 110*, 406–425.

Monroe, S. M., Roberts, J. E., Kupfer, D. J., & Frank, E. (1996). Life stress and treatment course of recurrent depression: II. Postrecovery associations with attrition, symptom course, and recurrence over 3 years. *Journal of Abnormal Psychology, 105*, 313–328.

Monteith, M. J. (1993). Self-regulation of prejudiced responses: Implications for progress in prejudice-reduction efforts. *Journal of Personality and Social Psychology, 65*, 469–478.

Montemayor, R. (1986). Family variation in parent-adolescent storm and stress. *Journal of Adolescent Research, 1*, 15–31.

Montepare, J. M., & Zebrowitz-McArthur, L. (1988). Impressions of people created by age-related qualities of their gaits. *Journal of Personality and Social Psychology, 55*, 547–556.

Moore, K. L., & Persaud, T. V. N. (1993). *Before we are born*. Philadelphia: Saunders.

Moore, R. Y. (1990). The circadian system and sleep-wake behavior. In J. Montplaisir & R. Godbout (Eds.), *Sleep and biological rhythms: Basic mechanisms and applications to psychiatry*. New York: Oxford University Press.

Moore, R. Y. (1995). Neural control of the pineal gland. *Behavioral Brain Research, 73*, 125–130.

Moore-Ede, M. C., Sulzman, F. M., & Fuller, C. A. (1982). *The clocks that time us*. Cambridge, MA: Harvard University Press.

Moos, R. H., & Schaefer, J. A. (1993). Coping resources and processes: Current concepts and measures. In L. Goldberger & S. Breznitz (Eds.), *Handbook of stress: Theoretical and clinical aspects* (2nd ed.). New York: Free Press.

Morain, D. (1991, January 30). Man sentenced to life term for 1969 murder of girl. *Los Angeles Times*, p. 3.

Morey, L. C. (1988). Personality disorders in DSM-III and DSM-III-R: Convergence, coverage, and internal consistency. *American Journal of Psychiatry, 145*, 573–577.

Morgan, C. D., & Murray, H. A. (1935). A method for investigating fantasies: The Thematic Apperception Test. *Archives of Neurology and Psychiatry, 34*, 289–306.

Morris, C. D., Bransford, J. D., & Franks, J. J. (1977). Levels of processing versus transfer appropriate processing. *Journal of Verbal Learning and Verbal Behavior, 16*, 519–533.

Morris, D. C. (1991, September). Cocaine heart disease. *Hospital Practice*, pp. 81–90.

Morris, P. E., Jones, S., & Hampson, P. (1978). An imagery mnemonic for the learning of people's names. *British Journal of Psychology, 69*, 335–336.

Morris, R. G. M. (1992). Long-term potentiation: Behavioral role. In L. R. Squire (Ed.), *Encyclopedia of learning and memory*. New York: Macmillan.

Morrison, A. M., & Von Glinow, M. A. (1990). Women and minorities in management. *American Psychologist, 45*, 200–208.

Morrongiello, B. A. (1988). Infants' localization of sounds in the horizontal plane: Estimates of minimum audible angle. *Developmental Psychology, 24*, 8–13.

Mortensen, M. E., Sever, L. E., & Oakley, G. P., Jr. (1991). Teratology and the epidemiology of birth defects. In S. G. Gabbe, J. R. Niebyl, & J. L. Simpson (Eds.), *Obstetrics: Normal and problem pregnancies*. New York: Churchill Livingstone.

Moruzzi, G. (1964). Reticular influences on the EEG. *Electroencephalography and Clinical Neurophysiology, 16*, 2–17.

Mosher, D., & Maclan, P. (1994). College men and women respond to X-rated videos intended for male or female audiences: Gender and sexual scripts. *Journal of Sex Research, 31*, 99–113.

Moss, P. (1994). Validity. In R. J. Sternberg (Ed.), *Encyclopedia of human intelligence*. New York: Macmillan.

Mott, S. R., Fazekas, N. F., & James, S. R. (1985). *Nursing care of children and families: A holistic approach*. Reading, MA: Addison-Wesley.

Mowday, R. T. (1979). Equity theory predictions of behavior in organizations. In R. M. Steers & L. W. Porter (Eds.), *Motivation and work behavior* (2nd ed.). New York: McGraw-Hill.

Mowrer, O. H. (1947). On the dual nature of learning: A reinterpretation of "conditioning" and "problem-solving." *Harvard Educational Review, 17*, 102–150.

Mozell, M. M., Smith, B. P., Smith P. E., Sullivan, R. L., & Swender, P. (1969). Nasal chemoreception in flavor identification. *Archives of Otolaryngology, 90*, 367–373.

Mukherjee, S., Sackeim, H. A., & Schnur, D. B. (1994). Electroconvulsive therapy of acute manic episodes: A review of 50 years' experience. *American Journal of Psychiatry, 151*, 169–176.

Muldoon, M. F., Manuck, S. B., & Matthews, K. A. (1990). Effects of cholesterol lowering on mortality: A quantitative review of primary prevention trials. *British Medical Journal, 301*, 309–314.

Mullen, B., & Copper, C. (1994). The relation between group cohesiveness and performance: An integration. *Psychological Bulletin, 115*, 210–227.

Mullin, C. R., & Linz, D. (1995). Desensitization and resensitization to violence against women: Effects of exposure to sexually violent films on judgments of domestic violence victims. *Journal of Personality and Social Psychology, 69*, 449–459.

Mumford, M. D., & Gustafson, S. B. (1988). Creativity syndrome: Integration, application, and innovation. *Psychological Bulletin, 103*, 27–43.

Münsterberg, H. (1908). *On the witness stand*. New York: Doubleday.

Münsterberg, H. (1913). *Psychology and industrial efficiency*. Boston, MA: Houghton Mifflin.

Murphy, C. (1996, Aug. 20). Researchers urge skepticism on melatonin at NIH-sponsored meeting, scientists say claims for hormone are largely unfounded. *Washington Post*, Z07.

Murphy, J. M. (1976). Psychiatric labeling in cross-cultural perspective. *Science, 191*, 1019–1028.

Murphy, J. M., & Helzer, J. E. (1986). Epidemiology of schizophrenia in adulthood. In G. L. Klerman, M. M. Weissman, P. S. Appelbaum, & L. H. Roth (Eds.), *Psychiatry: Social, epidemiologic, and legal psychiatry* (Vol. 5). New York: Basic Books.

Murphy, S. P., Rose, D., Hudes, M., & Viteri, F. E. (1992). Demographic and economic factors associated with dietary quality for adults in the 1987–88 nationwide food consumption theory. *Journal of the American Dietetic Association, 92*, 1352–1357.

Murray, H. A. (1938). *Explorations in personality*. New York: Oxford University Press.

Murray, H. A. (1943). *Thematic Apperception Test—Manual*. Cambridge, MA: Harvard University Press.

Murray, J. B. (1995). Evidence for acupuncture's analgesic effectiveness and proposals for the physiological mechanisms involved. *Journal of Psychology, 129*, 443–461.

Murray, S. L., Holmes, J. G., & Griffin, D. W. (1996a). The benefits of positive illusions: Idealization and the construction of satisfaction in close relationships. *Journal of Personality and Social Psychology, 70*, 79–98.

Murray, S. L., Holmes, J. G., & Griffin, D. W. (1996b). The self-fulfilling nature of positive illusions in romantic relationships: Love is not blind, but prescient. *Journal of Personality and Social Psychology, 71*, 1155–1180.

Murstein, B. I., & Fontaine, P. A. (1993). The public's knowledge about psychologists and other mental health professionals. *American Psychologist, 48*, 839–845.

Myers, D. G., & Lamm, H. (1976). The group polarization phenomenon. *Psychological Bulletin, 83*, 602–627.

Myers, L., Dixen, J., Morrissette, D., Carmichael, M., & Davidson, J. (1990). Effects of estrogen, androgen, and progestin on sexual psychophysiology and behavior in postmenopausal women. *Journal of Clinical Endocrinology and Metabolism, 70*, 1124–1131.

Myerson, J., Hale, S., Wagstaff, D., Poon, L. W., & Smith, G. A. (1990). The information-loss model: A mathematical theory of age-related cognitive slowing. *Psychological Review, 97*, 475–487.

Nahas, G. G. (1976). *Marijuana: Chemistry, biochemistry and cellular effects*. New York: Springer.

Narrow, W. E., Regier, D. A., Rae, D. S., Manderscheid, R. W., & Locke, B. Z. (1993). Use of services by persons with mental and addictive disorders: Findings from the National Institute of Mental Health Epidemiologic Catchment Area Program. *Archives of General Psychiatry, 50*, 95–107.

Nathan, K. I., Musselman, D. L., Schatzberg A. F., & Nemeroff, C. B. (1995). Biology of mood disorders. In A. F. Schatzberg & C. B. Nemeroff (Eds.), *The American Psychiatric Press textbook of psychopharmacology*. Washington, DC: American Psychiatric Press.

Nathan, P. E. (1993). Alcoholism: Psychopathology, etiology, and treatment. In P. B. Sutker & H. E. Adams (Eds.), *Comprehensive handbook of psychopathology*. New York: Plenum Press.

Neale, M. A., & Northcraft, G. B. (1986). Experts, amateurs, and refrigerators: Comparing expert and amateur negotiators in a novel task. *Organizational Behavior and Human Decision Processes, 38*, 305–317.

Neely, J. H. (1989). Experimental dissociations and the episodic/semantic memory distinction. In H. L. Roediger, III, & F. I. M. Craik (Eds.), *Varieties of memory and consciousness*. Hillsdale, NJ: Erlbaum.

Neher, A. (1991). Maslow's theory of motivation: A critique. *Journal of Humanistic Psychology, 31*, 89–112.

Neher, A. (1996). Jung's theory of archetypes: A critique. *Journal of Humanistic Psychology, 36*, 61–91.

Neiss, R. (1988). Reconceptualizing arousal: Psychobiological states in motor performance. *Psychological Bulletin, 103*, 345–366.

Neiss, R. (1990). Ending arousal's reign of error: A reply to Anderson. *Psychological Bulletin, 107*, 101–105.

Neisser, U. (1967). *Cognitive psychology*. New York: Appleton-Century-Crofts.

Neisser, U., Boodoo, G., Bouchard, T. J., Jr., Boykin, A. W., Brody, N., Ceci, S. J., Halpern, D. F., Loehlin, J. C., Perloff, R., Sternberg, R. J., & Urbina, S. (1996). Intelligence: Knowns and unknowns. *American Psychologist, 51*, 77–101.

Neisser, U., & Harsch, N. (1992). Phantom flashbulbs: False recollections of hearing the news about *Challenger*. In E. Winograd & U. Neisser (Eds.), *Affect and accuracy in recall: Studies of "flashbulb" memories*. New York: Cambridge University Press.

Nelson, K. (1993). The psychological and social origins of autobiographical memory. *Psychological Science, 4*, 7–14.

Nelson, K., Hampson, J., & Shaw, L. K. (1993). Nouns in early lexicons: Evidence, explanations and implications. *Journal of Child Language, 20*, 61–84.

Nelson, R. J., Badura, L. L., & Goldman, B. D.

(1990). Mechanisms of seasonal cycles of behavior. *Annual Review of Psychology, 41*, 81–108.

Nelson, T. O. (1978). Detecting small amounts of information in memory: Savings for nonrecognized items. *Journal of Experimental Psychology: Human Learning and Memory, 4*, 453–468.

Nemeth, C., & Chiles, C. (1988). Modelling courage: The role dissent in fostering independence. *European Journal of Social Psychology, 18*, 275–280.

Nemiah, J. C. (1985). Somatoform disorders. In H. I. Kaplan & B. J. Sadock (Eds.), *Comprehensive textbook of psychiatry/IV*. Baltimore: Williams & Wilkins.

Nesbitt, R. E. L., Jr., & Abdul-Karim, R. W. (1982). Coincidental disorders complicating pregnancy. In D. N. Danforth (Ed.), *Obstetrics and gynecology*. Philadelphia: Harper & Row.

Neugebauer, R., Dohrenwend, B. P., & Dohrenwend, B. S. (1980). Formulation of hypotheses about the true prevalence of functional psychiatric disorders among adults in the United States. In B. P. Dohrenwend, B. S. Dohrenwend, M. S. Gould, B. Link, R. Neugebauer, & R. Wunsch-Hitzig (Eds.), *Mental illness in the United States: Epidemiological estimates*. New York: Praeger.

Newcomb, M. D., & McGee, L. (1991). Influence of sensation seeking on general deviance and specific problem behaviors from adolescence to young adulthood. *Journal of Personality and Social Psychology, 61*, 614–628.

Newcomb, P. A., & Carbone, P. P. (1992). The health consequences of smoking: Cancer. *Medical Clinics of North America, 76*, 305–331.

Newcombe, N., & Huttenlocher, J. (1992). Children's early ability to solve perspective-taking problems. *Developmental Psychology, 28*, 635–643.

Newell, A., Shaw, J. C., & Simon, H. A. (1958). Elements of a theory of human problem solving. *Psychological Review, 65*, 151–166.

Newell, A., & Simon, H. A. (1972). *Human problem solving*. Englewood Cliffs, NJ: Prentice-Hall.

Newsom, C., Favell, J. E., & Rincover, A. (1983). Side effects of punishment. In S. Axelrod & J. Apsche (Eds.), *The effects of punishment on human behavior*. New York: Academic Press.

Nezu, A. M., Nezu, C. M., & Blissett, S. E. (1988). Sense of humor as a moderator of the relation between stressful events and psychological distress: A prospective analysis. *Journal of Personality and Social Psychology, 54*, 520–525.

Nicholson, A. N. (1994). Hypnotics: Clinical pharmacology and therapeutics. In M. H. Kryger, T. Roth, & W. C. Dement (Eds.), *Principles and practice of sleep medicine* (2nd ed.). Philadelphia: Saunders.

Nicholson, A. N., Pascoe, P. A., Spencer, M. B., Stone, B. M., Roehis, T., & Roth, T. (1986). Sleep after transmeridian flights. *Lancet, 2*, 1205–1208.

Nicholson, I. R., & Neufeld, R. W. J. (1993). Classification of the schizophrenias according to symptomatology: A two-factor model. *Journal of Abnormal Psychology, 102*, 259–270.

Nicholson, R. A., & Kugler, K. E. (1991). Competent and incompetent criminal defendants: A quantitative review of comparative research. *Psychological Bulletin, 109*, 355–370.

Nickerson, R. S., & Adams, M. J. (1979). Long-term memory for a common object. *Cognitive Psychology, 11*, 287–307.

Niebyl, J. R. (1991). Drugs in pregnancy and lactation. In S. G. Gabbe, J. R. Niebyl, & J. L.

Simpson (Eds.), *Obstetrics: Normal and problem pregnancies*. New York: Churchill Livingstone.

Niedenthal, P. M. (1990). Implicit perception of affective information. *Journal of Experimental Social Psychology, 26*, 505–527.

Nisbett, R. E. (1972). Hunger, obesity, and the ventromedial hypothalamus. *Psychological Review, 79*, 433–453.

Niswander, K. R. (1982). Prenatal care. In R. C. Benson (Ed.), *Current obstetric and gynecologic diagnosis and treatment*. Los Altos, CA: Lange Medical Publications.

Noddings, N. (1992). Gender and the curriculum. In P. W. Jackson (Ed.), *Handbook of research on curriculum*. New York: Macmillan.

Nolen-Hoeksema, S. (1990). *Sex differences in depression*. Stanford, CA: Stanford University Press.

Nolen-Hoeksema, S. (1991). Responses to depression and their effects on the duration of depressive episodes. *Journal of Abnormal Psychology, 100*, 569–582.

Nolen-Hoeksema, S., & Girgus, J. S. (1994). The emergence of gender differences in depression during adolescence. *Psychological Bulletin, 115*, 424–443.

Nolen-Hoeksema, S., Girgus, J. S., & Seligman, M. E. P. (1992). Predictors and consequences of childhood depressive symptoms: A 5-year longitudinal study. *Journal of Abnormal Psychology, 101*, 405–422.

Norcross, J. C., & Goldfried, M. R. (Eds.). (1992). *Handbook of psychotherapy integration*. New York: Basic Books.

Norcross, J. C., & Prochaska, J. O. (1982). National survey of clinical psychologists: Affiliations and orientations. *Clinical Psychologist, 35*(3), 1, 4–6.

Norman, T. R., & Burrows, G. D. (1990). Buspirone for the treatment of generalized anxiety disorder. In R. Noyes, Jr., M. Roth, & G. D. Burrows (Eds.), *Handbook of anxiety: The treatment of anxiety* (Vol. 4). Amsterdam: Elsevier.

Novick, L. R. (1988). Analogical transfer, problem similarity, and expertise. *Journal of Experimental Psychology: Learning, Memory, and Cognition, 14*, 510–520.

Nowlis, D. P., & Kamiya, J. (1970). The control of electroencephalographic alpha rhythms through auditory feedback and the associated mental activity. *Psychophysiology, 6*, 476–484.

Noyes, R., Clarkson, C., Crowe, R. R., Yates, W. R., & McChesney, C. M. (1987). A family study of generalized anxiety disorder. *American Journal of Psychiatry, 144*, 1019–1024.

Noyes, R., Jr. (1988). Revision of the DSM-III classification of anxiety disorders. In R. Noyes, Jr., M. Roth & G. D. Burrows (Eds.), *Handbook of anxiety: Classification, etiological factors and associated disturbances* (Vol. 2). Amsterdam: Elsevier.

Nunnally, J. C. (1982). The study of human change: Measurement, research strategies, and methods of analysis. In B. B. Wolman (Ed.), *Handbook of developmental psychology*. Englewood Cliffs, NJ: Prentice-Hall.

Nurnberger, J. I., & Zimmerman, J. (1970). Applied analysis of human behavior: An alternative to conventional motivational inferences and unconscious determination in therapeutic programming. *Behavior Therapy, 1*, 59–69.

Nurnberger, J. I., Jr., & Gershon, E. S. (1992). Genetics. In E. S. Paykel (Ed.), *Handbook of affective disorders* (2nd ed.). New York: Guilford Press.

Oakland, T., & Parmelee, R. (1985). Mental measurement of minority-group children. In B. B.

Wolman (Ed.), *Handbook of intelligence: Theories, measurements, and applications.* New York: Wiley.

Ochse, R. (1990). *Before the gates of excellence: The determinants of creative genius.* Cambridge, England: Cambridge University Press.

Offer, D., Ostrov, E., Howard, K. I., & Atkinson, R. (1988). *The teenage world: Adolescents' self-image in ten countries.* New York: Plenum.

Ogilvie, R. D., & Wilkinson, R. T. (1988). Behavioral versus EEG-based monitoring of all-night sleep/wake patterns. *Sleep, 11*(2), 139–155.

Ogilvie, R. D., Wilkinson, R.T., & Allison, S. (1989). The detection of sleep onset: Behavioral, physiological, and subjective convergence. *Sleep, 12*(5), 458–474.

Öhman, A. (1979). Fear relevance, autonomic conditioning, and phobias: A laboratory model. In P. O. Sjoden & S. Bates (Eds.), *Trends in behavior therapy.* New York: Academic Press.

Öhman, A., Erixon, G., & Lofberg, I. (1975). Phobias and preparedness: Phobic versus neutral pictures as conditional stimuli for human autonomic responses. *Journal of Abnormal Psychology, 84,* 41–45.

Öhman, A., & Soares, J. J. F. (1993). On the automatic nature of phobic fear: Conditioned electrodermal responses to masked fear-relevant stimuli. *Journal of Abnormal Psychology, 102,* 121–132.

Okagaki, L. (1994). Socialization of intelligence. In R. J. Sternberg (Ed.), *Encyclopedia of human intelligence.* New York: Macmillan.

O'Keefe, D. J. (1990). *Persuasion: Theory and research.* Newbury Park, CA: Sage.

Oldham, J. M., Skodol, A. E., Kellman, H. D., Hyler, S. E., Doidge, N., Rosnick, L., & Gallaher, P. E. (1995). Comorbidity of axis I and axis II disorders. *American Journal of Psychiatry, 152,* 571–578.

Olds, J. (1956). Pleasure centers in the brain. *Scientific American, 193,* 105–116.

Olds, J., & Milner, P. (1954). Positive reinforcement produced by electrical stimulation of the septal area and other regions of the rat brain. *Journal of Comparative and Physiological Psychology, 47,* 419–427.

Olds, M. E., & Fobes, J. L. (1981). The central basis of motivation: Intracranial self-stimulation studies. *Annual Review of Psychology, 32,* 523–574.

O'Leary, K. D., Kent, R. N., & Kanowitz, J. (1975). Shaping data collection congruent with experimental hypotheses. *Journal of Applied Behavior Analysis, 8,* 43–51.

Olfson, M., & Pincus, H. A. (1994). Outpatient psychotherapy in the United States, I: Volume, costs, and user characteristics. *American Journal of Psychiatry, 151,* 1281–1288.

Olfson, M., & Pincus, H. A. (1996). Outpatient mental health care in nonhospital settings: Distribution of patients across provider groups. *American Journal of Psychiatry, 153,* 1353–1356.

Oliver, M. B., & Hyde, J. S. (1993). Gender differences in sexuality: A meta-analysis. *Psychological Bulletin, 114,* 29–51.

Oliver, M. B., & Shibley, J. H. (1993). Gender differences in sexuality: A meta-analysis. *Psychological Bulletin, 114,* 29–51.

Olsho, L. W., Harkins, S. W., & Lenhardt, M. L. (1985). Aging and the auditory system. In J. E. Birren & K. W. Schaie (Eds.), *Handbook of the psychology of aging* (2nd ed.). New York: Van Nostrand Reinhold.

Olson, R. P., & Kroon, J. S. (1987). Biobehavioral treatment of essential hypertension. In M. S.

Schwartz (Ed.), *Biofeedback: A practitioner's guide.* New York: Guilford Press.

Ono, K. (1987). Superstitious behavior in humans. *Journal of the Experimental Analysis of Behavior, 47,* 261–271.

Oren, D. A., & Rosenthal, N. E. (1992). Seasonal affective disorders. In E. S. Paykel (Ed.), *Handbook of affective disorders* (2nd ed.). New York: Guilford Press.

Organista, P. B., & Miranda, J. (1991). Psychosomatic symptoms in medical outpatients: An investigation of self-handicapping theory. *Health Psychology, 10,* 427–431.

Orleans, C. T., Rimer, B. K., Cristinzio, S., Keintz, M. K., & Fleisher, L. (1991). A national survey of older smokers: Treatment needs of a growing population. *Health Psychology, 10,* 343–351.

Orme-Johnson, D. W. (1987). Transcendental meditation and reduced health care utilization. *Psychosomatic Medicine, 49,* 493–507.

Ormel, J., & Schaufeli, W. B. (1991). Stability and change in psychological distress and their relationship with self-esteem and locus of control: A dynamic equilibrium model. *Journal of Personality and Social Psychology, 60,* 288–299.

Orne, M. T. (1951). The mechanisms of hypnotic age regression: An experimental study. *Journal of Abnormal and Social Psychology, 46,* 213–225.

Orne, M. T., & Dinges, D. F. (1989). Hypnosis. In H. I. Kaplan & B. J. Sadock (Eds.), *Comprehensive textbook of psychiatry/V* (Vol. 2). Baltimore: Williams & Wilkins.

Orne, M. T., & Holland, C. C. (1968). On the ecological validity of laboratory deceptions. *International Journal of Psychiatry, 6,* 282–293.

Ornstein, R. E. (1977). *The psychology of consciousness.* New York: Harcourt Brace Jovanovich.

Oskamp, S. (1991). *Attitudes and opinions.* Englewood Cliffs, NJ: Prentice Hall.

Öst, L. (1987). Age of onset in different phobias. *Journal of Abnormal Psychology, 96,* 223–229.

Öst, L. (1990). Relaxation training and biofeedback for the treatment of anxiety. In R. Noyes, Jr., M. Roth, & G. D. Burrows (Eds.), *Handbook of anxiety: The treatment of anxiety* (Vol. 4). Amsterdam: Elsevier.

Ostrom, T. M., & Sedikides, C. (1992). Outgroup homogeneity effects in natural and minimal groups. *Psychological Bulletin, 112,* 536–552.

Oswald, I. (1974). *Sleep.* Middlesex, NY: Penguin.

Oswald, I., & Adam, K. (1980). The man who had not slept for ten years. *British Medical Journal, 281,* 1684–1685.

Ouellette, S. C. (1993). Inquiries into hardiness. In L. Goldberger & S. Breznitz (Eds.), *Handbook of stress: Theoretical and clinical aspects* (2nd ed.). New York: Free Press.

Owens, M. J., & Risch, S. C. (1995). Atypical antipsychotics. In A. F. Schatzberg & C. B. Nemeroff (Eds.), *The American Psychiatric Press textbook of psychopharmacology.* Washington, DC: American Psychiatric Press.

Ozer, D. J., & Reise, S. P. (1994). Personality assessment. *Annual Review of Psychology, 45,* 357–388.

Pachman, J. S. (1996). The dawn of a revolution in mental health. *American Psychologist, 51,* 213–215.

Paffenbarger, R. S., Hyde, R. T., & Wing, A. L. (1990). Physical activity and physical fitness as determinants of health and longevity. In C.

Bouchard, R. J. Shephard, T. Stephens, J. R. Sutton, & B. D. McPherson (Eds.), *Exercise, fitness, and health: A consenses of current knowledge.* Champaign, IL: Human Kinetics Books.

Pagel, M. D., Erdly, W. W., & Becker, J. (1987). Social networks: We get by with (and in spite of) a little help from our friends. *Journal of Personality and Social Psychology, 53,* 793–804.

Pagel, M. D., Smilkstein, G., Regen, H., & Montano, D. (1990). Psychosocial influences on new-born outcomes: A controlled prospective study. *Social Science Medicine, 30,* 597–604.

Paikoff, R. L., & Brooks-Gunn, J. (1991). Do parent-child relationships change during puberty? *Psychological Bulletin, 110,* 47–66.

Paivio, A. (1969). Mental imagery in associative learning and memory. *Psychological Review, 76,* 241–263.

Paivio, A. (1986). *Mental representations: A dual coding approach.* New York: Oxford University Press.

Paivio, A., Smythe, P. E., & Yuille, J. C. (1968). Imagery versus meaningfulness of nouns in paired-associate learning. *Canadian Journal of Psychology, 22,* 427–441.

Palladino, J. J., & Carducci, B. J. (1984). Students' knowledge of sleep and dreams. *Teaching of Psychology, 11,* 189–191.

Palmere, M., Benton, S. L., Glover, J. A., & Ronning, R. (1983). Elaboration and recall of main ideas in prose. *Journal of Educational Psychology, 75,* 898–907.

Palys, T. S. (1986). Testing the common wisdom: The social content of video pornography. *Canadian Psychology, 27,* 22–35.

Panksepp, J. (1986). The neurochemistry of behavior. *Annual Review of Psychology, 37,* 77–107.

Panksepp, J. (1993). Neurochemical control of moods and emotions: Amino acids to neuropeptides. In M. Lewis & J. M. Haviland (Eds.), *Handbook of emotions.* New York: Guilford Press.

Parke, R. D. (1977). Some effects of punishment on children's behavior—revisited. In E. M. Hetherington & R. D. Parke (Eds.), *Contemporary readings in child psychology.* New York: McGraw-Hill.

Parke, R. D., & Slaby, R. G. (1983). The development of aggression. In E. M. Hetherington (Ed.), *Handbook of child psychology: Socialization, personality, and social development* (Vol. 4). New York: Wiley.

Parker, D. E. (1980). The vestibular apparatus. *Scientific American, 243*(5), 118–135.

Parker, G., & Hadzi-Pavlovic, D. (1990). Expressed emotion as a predictor of schizophrenic relapse: An analysis of aggregated data. *Psychological Medicine, 20,* 961–965.

Parker, K. (1983). A meta-analysis of the reliability and validity of the Rorschach. *Journal of Personality Assessment, 42,* 227–231.

Parks, T. E. (1984). Illusory figures: A (mostly) atheoretical review. *Psychological Bulletin, 95,* 282–300.

Parlee, M. B. (1973). The premenstrual syndrome. *Psychological Bulletin, 80,* 454–465.

Parlee, M. B. (1982). Changes in moods and activation levels during the menstrual cycle in experimentally naive subjects. *Psychology of Women Quarterly, 7,* 119–131.

Parlee, M. B. (1992). On PMS and psychiatric abnormality. *Feminism and Psychology, 2*(1), 105–108.

Parrot, A., & Bechhofer, L. (1991). *Acquaintance rape: The hidden crime.* New York: Wiley.

Parsons, T. (1979). Definitions of health and illness in light of the American values and social structure. In E. G. Jaco (Ed.), *Patients, physicians and illness: A sourcebook in behavioral science and health*. New York: Free Press.

Partinen, M. (1994). Epidemiology of sleep disorders. In M. H. Kryger, T. Roth, & W. C. Dement (Eds.), *Principles and practice of sleep medicine* (2nd ed.). Philadelphia: Saunders.

Patterson, G. R., DeBaryshe, B. D., & Ramsey, E. (1989). A developmental perspective on antisocial behavior. *American Psychologist, 44,* 329–335.

Patzer, G. L. (1985). *The physical attractiveness phenomena*. New York: Plenum.

Pauk, W. (1990). *How to study in college*. Boston: Houghton Mifflin.

Paul, S. M., Crawley, J. N., & Skolnick, P. (1986). The neurobiology of anxiety: The role of the GABA/benzodiazepine receptor complex. In P. A. Berger & H. K. H. Brodie (Eds.), *American handbook of psychiatry: Biological psychiatry* (2nd ed., Vol. 8). New York: Basic Books.

Paulhus, D. L. (1989). Socially desirable responding: Some new solutions to old problems. In D. M. Buss & N. Cantor (Eds.), *Personality psychology: Recent trends and emerging directions*. New York: Springer-Verlag.

Paulhus, D. L. (1991). Measurement and control of response bias. In J. P. Robinson, P. Shaver, & L. S. Wrightsman (Eds.), *Measures of personality and social psychological attitudes*. San Diego: Academic Press.

Pauls, D. L., Alsobrook, J. P. I., Goodman, W., Rasmussen, S., & Leckman, J. F. (1995). A family study of obsessive-compulsive disorder. *American Journal of Psychiatry, 152,* 76–84.

Paunonen, S. V., Jackson, D. N., Trzebinski, J., & Forsterling, F. (1992). Personality structure across cultures: A multimethod evaluation. *Journal of Personality and Social Psychology, 62,* 447–456.

Pavlov, I. P. (1906). The scientific investigation of psychical faculties or processes in the higher animals. *Science, 24,* 613–619.

Pavlov, I. P. (1927). *Conditioned reflexes* (G. V. Anrep, Trans.). London: Oxford University Press.

Payne, D. G., & Wenger, M. J. (1996). Practice effects in memory: Data, theory, and unanswered questions. In D. J. Herrmann, C. McEvoy, C. Hertzog, P. Hertel, & M. K. Johnson (Eds.), *Basic and applied memory research: Practical applications* (Vol. 2). Mahwah, NJ: Erlbaum.

Payne, J. W. (1976). Task complexity and contingent processing in decision making: An information search and protocol analysis. *Organizational Behavior and Human Performance, 16,* 366–387.

Payne, J. W., Bettman, J. R., & Johnson, E. J. (1992). Behavioral decision research: A constructive processing perspective. *Annual Review of Psychology, 43,* 87–131.

Peak, H. (1955). Attitude and motivation. In M. R. Jones (Ed.), *Nebraska symposium on motivation*. Lincoln: University of Nebraska Press.

Pearce, L. (1974). Duck! It's the new journalism. *New Times, 2*(10), 40–41.

Pearlman, C. A. (1982). Sleep structure variation and performance. In W. B. Webb (Ed.), *Biological rhythms, sleep and performance*. New York: Wiley.

Pease, D., & Gleason, J. B. (1985). Gaining meaning: Semantic development. In J. B. Gleason (Ed.), *The development of language*. Columbus: Charles E. Merrill.

Pedersen, N. L., Plomin, R., Nesselroade, J. R., & McClearn, G. E. (1992). A quantitative genetic analysis of cognitive abilities during the second half of the life span. *Psychological Science, 3,* 346–353.

Pedersen, P. (1994). A culture-centered approach to counseling. In W. J. Lonner & R. Malpass (Eds.), *Psychology and culture*. Boston: Allyn & Bacon.

Pedlow, R., Sanson, A., Prior, M., & Oberklaid, F. (1993). Stability of maternally reported temperament from infancy to 8 years. *Developmental Psychology, 29,* 998–1007.

Peirce, K. (1990). A feminist theoretical perspective on the socialization of teen-age girls through *Seventeen* magazine. *Sex Roles, 23,* 491–500.

Pekarik, G. (1993). Beyond effectiveness: Uses of consumer-oriented criteria in defining treatment success. In T. R. Giles (Ed.), *Handbook of effective psychotherapy*. New York: Plenum Press.

Penfield, W., & Perot, P. (1963). The brain's record of auditory and visual experience. *Brain, 86,* 595–696.

Penn, D. L., & Mueser, K. T. (1996). Research update on the psychosocial treatment of schizophrenia. *American Journal of Psychiatry, 153,* 607–617.

Pennebaker, J. W. (1982). *The psychology of physical symptoms*. New York: Springer-Verlag.

Pennebaker, J. W. (1990). *Opening up: The healing power of confiding in others*. New York: Morrow.

Pennebaker, J. W., Colder, M., & Sharp, L. K. (1990). Accelerating the coping process. *Journal of Personality and Social Psychology, 58,* 528–537.

Pennebaker, J. W., Kiecolt-Glaser, J. K., & Glaser, R. (1988). Disclosure of traumas and immune function: Health implications for psychotherapy. *Journal of Consulting and Clinical Psychology, 56,* 239–245.

Pepperberg, I. M. (1990). Cognition in an African gray parrot (*Psittacus erithacus*): Further evidence for comprehension of categories and labels. *Journal of Comparative Psychology, 104,* 41–52.

Perlman, M. D., & Kaufman, A. S. (1990). Assessment of child intelligence. In G. Goldstein & M. Hersen (Eds.), *Handbook of psychological assessment*. New York: Pergamon Press.

Perloff, R. M. (1993). *The dynamics of persuasion*. Hillsdale, NJ: Erlbaum.

Perone, M., Galizio, M., & Baron, A. (1988). The relevance of animal-based principles in the laboratory study of human operant conditioning. In G. Davey & C. Cullen (Eds.), *Human operant conditioning and behavior modification*. New York: Wiley.

Perris, C. (1992). Bipolar-unipolar distinction. In E. S. Paykel (Ed.), *Handbook of affective disorders*. New York: Guilford Press.

Perry, C., Nadon, R., & Button, J. (1992). The measurement of hypnotic ability. In E. Fromm & M. R. Nash (Eds.), *Contemporary hypnosis research*. New York: Guilford Press.

Perry, D. G., & Bussey, K. (1979). The social learning theory of sex differences: Imitation is alive and well. *Journal of Personality and Social Psychology, 37,* 1699–1712.

Perry, D. G., Kusel, S. J., & Perry, L. C. (1988). Victims of peer aggression. *Developmental Psychology, 24,* 807–814.

Perry, W., & Braff, D. L. (1994). Information-processing deficits and thought disorder in schizophrenia. *American Journal of Psychiatry, 151,* 363–367.

Pert, C. B., & Snyder, S. H. (1973). Opiate receptor: Demonstration in the nervous tissue. *Science, 179,* 1011–1014.

Pervin, L. A. (1994). Personality stability, personality change, and the question of process. In T. F. Heatherton & J. L. Weinberger (Eds.), *Can personality change?* Washington, DC: American Psychological Association.

Peterhans, E., & Von Der Heydt, R. (1991). Elements of form perception in monkey prestriate cortex. In A. Gorea, Y. Fregnac, Z. Kapoula, & J. Findlay (Eds.), *Representations of vision—Trends and tacit assumptions in vision research*. Cambridge, MA: Cambridge University Press.

Peters, M. (1995). Handedness and its relations to other indices of cerebral lateralization. In R. J. Davidson, & K. Hugdahl (Eds.), *Brain asymmetry*. Cambridge, MA: MIT Press.

Petersen, A. C. (1987, September). Those gangly years. *Psychology Today,* pp. 28–34.

Petersen, A. C. (1988). Adolescent development. *Annual Review of Psychology, 39,* 583–607.

Peterson, C., Maier, S. F., & Seligman, M. E. P. (1993). *Learned helplessness: A theory for the age of personal control*. New York: Oxford University Press.

Peterson, C., Seligman, M. E. P., & Vaillant, G. E. (1988). Pessimistic explanatory style is a risk factor for physical illness: A thirty-five-year longitudinal study. *Journal of Personality and Social Psychology, 55,* 23–27.

Peterson, L. R., & Peterson, M. J. (1959). Short-term retention of individual verbal items. *Journal of Experimental Psychology, 58,* 193–198.

Pettigrew, T. F. (1979). The ultimate attribution error: Extending Allport's analysis of prejudice. *Personality and Social Psychology Bulletin, 5,* 461–476.

Pettigrew, T. F. (1997). Generalized intergroup contact effects on prejudice. *Personality and Social Psychology Bulletin, 23,* 173–185.

Petty, R. E., & Cacioppo, J. T. (1979). Effects of forewarning of persuasive intent and involvement on cognitive responses and persuasion. *Personality and Social Psychology Bulletin, 5,* 173–176.

Petty, R. E., & Cacioppo, J. T. (1986). *Communication and persuasion: Central and peripheral routes to attitude change*. New York: Springer-Verlag.

Petty, R. E., Cacioppo, J. T., & Schumann, D. (1983). Central and peripheral routes to advertising effectiveness: The moderating role of involvement. *Journal of Consumer Research, 10,* 134–148.

Peyser, H. S. (1993). Stress, ethyl alcohol, and alcoholism. In L. Goldberger & S. Breznitz (Eds.), *Handbook of stress: Theoretical and clinical aspects* (2nd ed.). New York: Free Press.

Pfaffmann, C. (1951). Taste and smell. In S. S. Stevens (Ed.), *Handbook of experimental psychology*. New York: Wiley.

Pfaffmann, C. (1974). Specificity of the sweet receptors of the squirrel monkey. *Chemical Senses and Flavor, 1,* 61–67.

Pfaffmann, C. (1978). The vertebrate phylogeny, neural code, and integrative process of taste. In C. Carterette & M. P. Friedman (Eds.), *Handbook of perception* (Vol. 6A). New York: Academic Press.

Pfau, M., Kenski, H. C., Nitz, M., & Sorenson, J. (1990). Efficacy of inoculation strategies in promoting resistance to political attack messages: Application to direct mail. *Communication Monographs, 57,* 25–43.

Phares, E. J. (1992). *Clinical psychology: Concepts,*

methods, & profession. Pacific Grove, CA: Brooks/Cole.

Phillips, D. P., & Brugge, J. F. (1985). Progress in neurophysiology of sound localization. *Annual Review of Psychology, 36*, 245–274.

Phillips, M. R., Wolf, A. S., & Coons, D. J. (1988). Psychiatry and the criminal justice system: Testing the myths. *American Journal of Psychiatry, 145*, 605–610.

Phillips, R. G., & LeDoux, J. E. (1992). Differential contribution of amygdala and hippocampus to cued and contextual fear conditioning. *Behavioral Neuroscience, 106*, 274–285.

Phillips, S. D., & Imhoff, A. R. (1997). Women and career development: A decade of research. *Annual Review of Psychology, 48*, 31–59.

Piaget, J. (1929). *The child's conception of the world*. New York: Harcourt, Brace.

Piaget, J. (1932). *The moral judgment of the child*. Glencoe, IL: Free Press.

Piaget, J. (1952). *The origins of intelligence in children*. New York: International Universities Press.

Piaget, J. (1954). *The construction of reality in the child*. New York: Basic Books.

Piaget, J. (1983). Piaget's theory. In P. H. Mussen (Ed.), *Handbook of child psychology* (Vol. 1). New York: Wiley.

Pilkington, N. W., & Lydon, J. E. (1997). The relative effect of attitude similarity and attitude dissimilarity on interpersonal attraction: Investigating the moderating roles of prejudice and group membership. *Personality and Social Psychology Bulletin, 23*, 107–122.

Pillow, D. R., Zautra, A. J., & Sandler, I. (1996). Major life events and minor stressors: Identifying mediational links in the stress process. *Journal of Personality and Social Psychology, 70*, 381–394.

Pilowsky, I. (1978). A general classification of abnormal illness behaviors. *British Journal of Psychology, 51*, 131–137.

Pines, A. M. (1993). Burnout. In L. Goldberger & S. Breznitz (Eds.), *Handbook of stress: Theoretical and clinical aspects* (2nd ed.). New York: Free Press.

Pines, A. M., & Aronson, E. (1988). *Career burnout: Causes and cures*. New York: Free Press.

Pines, A. M., Aronson, E., & Kafry, D. (1981). *Burnout: From tedium to personal growth*. New York: Free Press.

Pinker, S. (1990). Language acquisition. In D. N. Osherson & H. Lasnik (Eds.), *Language: An invitation to cognitive science* (Vol. 1). Cambridge, MA: MIT Press.

Pinker, S. (1994). *Language is to us as flying is to geese*. New York: Morrow.

Pinker, S., & Bloom, P. (1992). Natural language and natural selection. In J. H. Barkow, L. Cosmides, & J. Tooby (Eds.), *The adapted mind: Evolutionary psychology and the generation of culture*. New York: Oxford University Press.

Piotrowski, C., Sherry, D., & Keller, J. W. (1985). Psychodiagnostic test usage: A survey of the Society for Personality Assessment. *Journal of Personality Assessment, 49*(2), 115–119.

Pipe, M. (1990). Mental retardation and left-handedness: Evidence and theories. In S. Coren (Ed.), *Left-handedness: Behavioral implications and anomalies*. Amsterdam: North-Holland.

Piper, W. E. (1993). Group psychotherapy research. In H. I. Kaplan & B. J. Sadock (Eds.), *Comprehensive group psychotherapy*. Baltimore: Williams & Wilkins.

Pittman, F., III. (1994, January/Febuary). A

buyer's guide to psychotherapy. *Psychology Today*, pp. 50–53, 74–81.

Pivik, R. T. (1991). Tonic states and phasic events in relation to sleep mentation. In S. J. Ellman & J. S. Antrobus (Eds.), *The mind in sleep: Psychology and psychophysiology* (2nd ed.). New York: Wiley.

Pivik, R. T. (1994). The psychophysiology of dreams. In M. H. Kryger, T. Roth, & W. C. Dement (Eds.), *Principles and practice of sleep medicine* (2nd ed.). Philadelphia: Saunders.

Plomin, R. (1990). *Nature and nurture: An introduction to human behavioral genetics*. Pacific Grove, CA: Brooks/Cole.

Plomin, R. (1993). Nature and nurture: Perspective and prospective. In R. Plomin & G. E. McClearn (Eds.), *Nature, nurture and psychology*. Washington, DC: American Psychological Association.

Plomin, R. (1994). Nature, nurture, and development. In R. J. Sternberg (Ed.), *Encyclopedia of human intelligence*. New York: Macmillan.

Plomin, R., Chipuer, H. M., & Loehlin, J. C. (1990). Behavioral genetics and personality. In L. A. Pervin (Ed.), *Handbook of personality: Theory and research*. New York: Guilford Press.

Plomin, R., Corley, R., DeFries, J. C., & Fulker, D. W. (1990). Individual differences in television viewing in early childhood: Nature as well as nurture. *Psychological Science, 1*, 371–377.

Plomin, R., & Daniels, D. (1987). Why are children in the same family so different from each other? *Behavioral and Brain Sciences, 10*, 1–16.

Plomin, R., & DeFries, J. C. (1980). Genetics and intelligence: Recent data. *Intelligence, 4*, 15–24.

Plomin, R., & Rende, R. (1991). Human behavioral genetics. *Annual Review of Psychology, 42*, 161–190.

Plous, S. (1991). An attitude survey of animal rights activists. *Psychological Science, 2*, 194–196.

Plutchik, R. (1980, February). A language for the emotions. *Psychology Today*, pp. 68–78.

Plutchik, R. (1984). Emotions: A general psychoevolutionary theory. In K. R. Scherer & P. Ekman (Eds.), *Approaches to emotion*. Hillsdale, NJ: Erlbaum.

Plutchik, R. (1993). Emotions and their vicissitudes: Emotions and psychopathology. In M. Lewis & J. M. Haviland (Eds.), *Handbook of emotions*. New York: Guilford Press.

Plutchik, R., Williams, M. H., Jerrett, I., Karasu, T. B., & Kane, C. (1978). Emotions, personality, and life stresses in asthma. *Journal of Psychosomatic Research, 22*, 425–431.

Polivy, J., Herman, C. P., & McFarlane, T. (1994). Effects of anxiety on eating: Does palatability moderate distress–induced overeating in dieters? *Journal of Abnormal Psychology, 103*, 505–510.

Pollack, R. H. (1989). Pictures, maybe; illusions, no. *Behavioral and Brain Sciences, 12*(1), 92–93.

Pomerantz, E. M., Chaiken, S., & Tordesillas, R. S. (1995). Attitude strength and resistance processes. *Journal of Personality and Social Psychology, 69*, 408–419.

Ponterotto, J. G., & Pedersen, P. B. (1993). *Preventing prejudice: A guide for counselors and educators*. Newbury Park, CA: Sage.

Pope, K. S. (1996). Memory, abuse, and science: Questioning claims about the false memory syndrome epidemic. *American Psychologist, 51*, 957–974.

Pope, K. S., Keith-Spiegel, P., & Tabachnick, B. G. (1986). Sexual attraction to clients. *American Psychologist, 41*, 147–158.

Pope, M. K., & Smith, T. W. (1991). Cortisol

excretion in high and low cynically hostile men. *Psychosomatic Medicine, 53*(4), 386–392.

Porac, C., & Coren, S. (1981). *Lateral preferences and human behavior*. New York: Springer-Verlag.

Porter, L. W., & Lawler, E. E. (1968). *Managerial attitudes and performance*. Homewood, IL: Dorsey Press.

Posner, M. I., & Raichle, M. E. (1994). *Images of mind*. New York: Scientific American Library.

Post, R. M. (1989). Mood disorders: Somatic treatment. In H. I. Kaplan & B. J. Sadock (Eds.), *Comprehensive textbook of psychiatry/V* (Vol. 2). Baltimore: Williams & Wilkins.

Postman, L. (1971). Transfer, interference and forgetting. In J. W. Kling & L. A. Riggs (Eds.), *Experimental psychology* (3rd ed.). New York: Holt, Rinehart & Winston.

Postman, L. (1985). Human learning and memory. In G. A. Kimble & K. Schlesinger (Eds.), *Topics in the history of psychology*. Hillsdale, NJ: Erlbaum.

Potter, W. Z., Manji, H. K., & Rudorfer, M. V. (1995). Tricyclics and tetracyclics. In A. F. Schatzberg & C. B. Nemeroff (Eds.), *The American Psychiatric Press textbook of psychopharmacology*. Washington, DC: American Psychiatric Press.

Power, K. G., Simpson, R., Swanson, V., & Wallace, L. (1990). A controlled comparison of cognitive-behavioral therapy, diazepam, and placebo, alone and in combination, for the treatment of generalized anxiety disorder. *Journal of Anxiety Disorders, 4*, 267–292.

Pratap, A. (1990, August 13). Romance and a little rape. *Time*, p. 69.

Pratkanis, A. R., & Aronson, E. (1992). *Age of propaganda: The everyday use and abuse of persuasion*. New York: W. H. Freeman.

Premack, D. (1971). Language in the chimpanzee? *Science, 172*, 808–822.

Premack, D. (1985). "Gavagai!" or the future history of the animal language controversy. *Cognition, 19*, 207–296.

Prentky, R. (1989). Creativity and psychopathology: Gamboling at the seat of madness. In J. A. Glover, R. R. Ronning, & C. R. Reynolds (Eds.), *Handbook of creativity*. New York: Plenum.

Pribram, K. H. (1981). Emotions. In S. B. Filskov & T. J. Boll (Eds.), *Handbook of clinical neuropsychology*. New York: Wiley.

Price, D. L., Walker, L. C., Martin, L. J., Borchelt, D. R., Wong, P. C., & Sisodia, S. S. (1995). Biology of Alzheimer's disease and animal models. In A. F. Schatzberg & C. B. Nemeroff (Eds.), *The American Psychiatric Press textbook of psychopharmacology*. Washington, DC: American Psychiatric Press.

Price, R. F., & Cohen, D. B. (1988). Lucid dream induction: An empirical evaluation. In J. Gackenbach & S. LaBerge (Eds.), *Conscious mind, sleeping brain: Perspectives on lucid dreaming*. New York: Plenum.

Prifitera, A. (1994). Wechsler scales of intelligence. In R. J. Sternberg (Ed.), *Encyclopedia of human intelligence*. New York: Macmillan.

Prince, G. (1978). Putting the other half to work. *Training: The Magazine of Human Resources Development, 15*, 57–61.

Prochaska, J. O. (1994). Strong and weak principles for progressing from precontemplation to action on the basis of twelve problem behaviors. *Health Psychology, 13*, 47–51.

Proffitt, D. R., Bhalla, M., Gossweiler, R., & Midgett, J. (1995). Perceiving geographical slant. *Psychonomic Bulletin & Review, 2*, 409–428.

Provine, R. R. (1989). Faces as releasers of contagious yawning: An approach to face detection using normal human subjects. *Bulletin of the Psychonomic Society, 27*, 211–214.

Provine, R. R. (1993). Yawning. In M. A. Carskadon (Ed.), *Encyclopedia of sleep and dreaming*. New York: Macmillan.

Pruitt, D. G. (1971). Choice shifts in group discussion: An introductory review. *Journal of Personality and Social Psychology, 20*, 339–360.

Pucetti, R. (1981). The case for mental duality: Evidence from split brain data and other considerations. *Behavioral and Brain Sciences, 4*, 93–123.

Puente, A. E. (1990). Psychological assessment of minority group members. In G. Goldstein & M. Hersen (Eds.), *Handbook of psychological assessment*. New York: Pergamon Press.

Pugh, E. N., Jr. (1988). Vision: Physics and retinal physiology. In R. C. Atkinson, R. J. Herrnstein, G. Lindzey, & R. D. Luce (Eds.), *Stevens' handbook of experimental psychology* (Vol. 1). New York: Wiley.

Pullum, G. K. (1991). *The Great Eskimo vocabulary hoax*. Chicago: University of Chicago Press.

Purcell, P., & Stewart, L. (1990). Dick and Jane in 1989. *Sex Roles, 22*, 177–185.

Quadagno, D. M. (1987). Pheromones and human sexuality. *Medical Aspects of Human Sexuality, 21*(11), 149–154.

Quillin, P. (1987). *Healing nutrients*. New York: Random House.

Rabkin, J. G. (1993). Stress and psychiatric disorders. In L. Goldberger & S. Breznitz (Eds.), *Handbook of stress: Theoretical and clinical aspects* (2nd ed.). New York: Free Press.

Rachman, S. J. (1990). *Fear and courage*. New York: W. H. Freeman.

Rachman, S. J. (1992). Behavior therapy. In L. R. Squire (Ed.), *Encyclopedia of learning and memory*. New York: Macmillan.

Rachman, S. J., & Wilson, G. T. (1980). *The effects of psychological therapy*. New York: Pergamon Press.

Racine, R. J., & deJonge, M. (1988). Short-term and long-term potentiation in projection pathways and local circuits. In P. W. Landfield & S. A. Deadwyler (Eds.), *Long-term potentiation: From biophysics to behavior*. New York: Liss.

Ragins, B. R., & Cotton, J. L. (1991). Easier said than done: Gender differences in perceived barriers to gaining a mentor. *Academy of Management Journal, 34*, 939–951.

Ragland, D. R., & Brand, R. J. (1988). Type A behavior and mortality from coronary heart disease. *The New England Journal of Medicine, 318*(2), 65–69.

Rahe, R. H., & Arthur, R. H. (1978). Life change and illness studies. *Journal of Human Stress, 4*(1), 3–15.

Rahe, R. H., & Holmes, T. H. (1965). Social, psychologic, and psychophysiologic aspects of inguinal hernia. *Journal of Psychosomatic Research, 8*, 487–491.

Raichle, M. E. (1994). Images of the mind: Studies with modern imaging techniques. *Annual Review of Psychology, 45*, 333–356.

Raine, A., Venables, P. H., & Williams, M. (1990). Relationships between central and autonomic measures of arousal at age 15 years and criminality at age 24 years. *Archives of General Psychiatry, 47*, 1003–1007.

Rajecki, D. W. (1990). *Attitudes*. Sunderland, MA: Sinnaver Associates.

Rapaport, D., Gill, M., & Schafer, R. (1968). *Diagnostic psychological testing*. New York: International Universities Press.

Rapaport, K., & Burkhart, B. R. (1984). Personality and attitudinal characteristics of sexually coercive college males. *Journal of Abnormal Psychology, 93*, 216–221.

Rapee, R. M., & Barlow, D. H. (1993). Generalized anxiety disorder, panic disorder, and the phobias. In P. B. Sutker & H. E. Adams (Eds.), *Comprehensive handbook of psychopathology* (2nd ed.). New York: Plenum.

Raphael, K. G., Cloitre, M., & Dohrenwend, B. P. (1991). Problems of recall and misclassification with checklist methods of measuring stressful life events. *Health Psychology, 10*, 62–74.

Rapoport, A. (1991). Ideological commitments in evolutionary theories. *Journal of Social Issues, 47*, 83–99.

Rasmussen, T., & Milner, B. (1977). The role of early left brain injury in determining lateralization of cerebral speech functions. *Annals of the New York Academy of Sciences, 299*, 355–369.

Ratner, N. B., & Gleason, J. B. (1993). An introduction to psycholinguistics: What do language users know? In J. B. Gleason & N. B. Ratner (Eds.), *Psycholinguistics*. Fort Worth: Harcourt Brace Jovanovich.

Ray, O., & Ksir, C. (1990). *Drugs, society & human behavior*. St. Louis: Times Mirror/Mosby.

Raynor, J. O., & Entin, E. E. (1982). Future orientation and achievement motivation. In J. O. Raynor & E. E. Entin (Eds.), *Motivation, career striving, and aging*. New York: Hemisphere.

Raz, S. (1993). Structural cerebral pathology in schizophrenia: Regional or diffuse? *Journal of Abnormal Psychology, 102*, 445–452.

Read, C. R. (1991). Achievement and career choices: Comparisons of males and females. *Roeper Review, 13*, 188–193.

Read, J. D., & Bruce, D. (1982). Longitudinal tracking of difficult memory retrievals. *Cognitive Psychology, 14*, 280–300.

Rechtschaffen, A. (1994). Sleep onset: Conceptual issues. In R. D. Ogilvie & J. R. Harsh (Eds.), *Sleep onset: Normal and abnormal processes*. Washington, DC: American Psychological Association.

Ree, M. J., & Earles, J. A. (1992). Intelligence is the best predictor of job performance. *Current Directions in Psychological Science, 1*, 86–89.

Reed, J. G., & Baxter P. M. (1992). *Library use: A handbook for psychology*. Washington, DC: American Psychological Association.

Reed, S. K., Dempster, A., & Ettinger, M. (1985). Usefulness of analogous solutions for solving algebra word problems. *Journal of Experimental Psychology: Learning, Memory and Cognition, 11*, 106–125.

Reed, S. K., Ernst, G. W., & Banerji, R. (1974). The role of analogy in transfer between similar problem states. *Cognitive Psychology, 6*, 436–450.

Reese, H. W., & Rodeheaver, D. (1985). Problem solving and complex decision making. In J. E. Birren & K. W. Schaie (Eds.), *Handbook of the psychology of aging* (2nd ed.). New York: Van Nostrand Reinhold.

Regan, T. (1989). Ill-gotten gains. In G. Langley (Ed.), *Animal experimentation: The consensus changes*. New York: Chapman & Hall.

Regestein, Q. R., & Monk, T. H. (1991). Is the poor sleep of shift workers a disorder? *American Journal of Psychiatry, 148*, 1487–1493.

Regier, D. A., & Kaelber, C. T. (1995). The Epidemiologic Catchment Area (ECA) program: Studying the prevalence and incidence of psychopathology. In M. T. Tsuang, M. Tohen, & G. E. P. Zahner (Eds.), *Textbook in psychiatric epidemiology*. New York: Wiley.

Regier, D. A., Narrow, W. E., Rae, D. S., Manderscheid, R. W., Locke, B. Z., & Goodwin, F. K. (1993). The de facto US Mental and Addictive Disorders Service System: Epidemiologic Catchment Area prospective 1-year prevalence rates of disorders in services. *Archives of General Psychiatry, 50*, 85–94.

Rehm, L. P., & Tyndall, C. I. (1993). Mood disorders: Unipolar and bipolar. In P. B. Sutker & H. E. Adams (Eds.), *Comprehensive handbook of psychopathology* (2nd ed.). New York: Plenum.

Reich, P. A. (1986). *Language development*. Englewood Cliffs, NJ: Prentice-Hall.

Reid, R. L. (1991). Premenstrual syndrome. *The New England Journal of Medicine, 324*(17), 1208–1210.

Reinisch, J. M. (1990). *The Kinsey Institute new report on sex: What you must know to be sexually literate*. New York: St. Martin's Press.

Reinke, B. J., Ellicott, A. M., Harris, R. L., & Hancock, E. (1985). Timing of psychosocial changes in women's lives. *Human Development, 28*, 259–280.

Reisenzein, R. (1983). The Schachter theory of emotion: Two decades later. *Psychological Bulletin, 94*, 239–264.

Reiser, M. F. (1989). The future of psychoanalysis in academic psychiatry: Plain talk. *Psychoanalytic Quarterly, 58*(2), 185–209.

Reiss, S. (1991). Expectancy model of fear, anxiety and panic. *Clinical Psychology Review, 11*, 141–154.

Relman, A. (1982). Marijuana and health. *New England Journal of Medicine, 306*(10), 603–604.

Renzulli, J. S. (1986). The three-ring conception of giftedness: A developmental model for creative productivity. In R. J. Sternberg & J. E. Davidson (Eds.), *Conceptions of giftedness*. Cambridge: Cambridge University Press.

Repetti, R. L. (1984). Determinants of children's sex-stereotyping: Parental sex-role traits and television viewing. *Personality and Social Psychology Bulletin, 10*, 457–468.

Repetti, R. L. (1993). Short-term effects of occupational stressors on daily mood and health complaints. *Health Psychology, 12*, 125–131.

Reschly, D. (1981). Psychological testing in educational classification and placement. *American Psychologist, 36*, 1094–1102.

Rescorla, R. A. (1978). Some implications of a cognitive perspective on Pavlovian conditioning. In S. H. Hulse, H. Fowler, & W. K. Honig (Eds.), *Cognitive processes in animal behavior*. Hillsdale, NJ: Erlbaum.

Rescorla, R. A. (1980). *Pavlovian second-order conditioning*. Hillsdale, NJ: Erlbaum.

Rescorla, R. A. (1987). A Pavlovian analysis of goal-directed behavior. *American Psychologist, 42*, 119–129.

Rescorla, R. A. (1988). Pavlovian conditioning: It's not what you think it is. *American Psychologist, 43*, 151–160.

Rescorla, R. A., & Solomon, R. L. (1967). Two-process learning theory: Relationships between Pavlovian conditioning and instrumental learning. *Psychological Review, 74*, 151–182.

Rescorla, R. A., & Wagner, A. R. (1972). A theory of Pavlovian conditioning: Variations in the effectiveness of reinforcement and nonreinforcement. In A. H. Black & W. F. Prokasky

(Eds.), *Classical conditioning: II. Current research and theory*. New York: Appleton-Century-Crofts.

Rest, J. R. (1983). Morality. In P. H. Mussen (Ed.), *Handbook of child psychology* (4th ed., Vol. 3). New York: Wiley.

Rest, J. R. (1986). *Moral development: Advances in research and theory*. New York: Praeger.

Rest, J. R., & Thoma, S. J. (1985). Relation of moral judgment development to formal education. *Developmental Psychology, 21,* 709–714.

Reynolds, C. F., III, Kupfer, D. J., Buysse, D. J., Coble, P. A., & Yeager, A. (1991). Subtyping DSM-III-R primary insomnia: A literature review by the DSM-IV work group on sleep disorders. *American Journal of Psychiatry, 148,* 432–438.

Reynolds, C. R. (1994). Reliability. In R. J. Sternberg (Ed.), *Encyclopedia of human intelligence*. New York: Macmillan.

Reynolds, C. R. (1995). Test bias and the assessment of intelligence and personality. In D. H. Saklofske & M. Zeidner (Eds.), *International handbook of personality and intelligence*. New York: Plenum Press.

Rhodewalt, F., & Zone, J. B. (1989). Appraisal of life change, depression, and illness in hardy and nonhardy women. *Journal of Personality and Social Psychology, 56,* 81–88.

Rice, L. N., & Greenberg, L. S. (1992). Humanistic approaches to psychotherapy. In D. K. Freedheim (Ed.), *History of psychotherapy: A century of change*. Washington, DC: American Psychological Association.

Richardson, G. S. (1993). Circadian rhythms. In M. A. Carskadon (Ed.), *Encyclopedia of sleep and dreaming*. New York: Macmillan.

Richardson, J. G., & Simpson, C. H. (1982). Children, gender and social structure: An analysis of the contents of letters to Santa Claus. *Child Development, 53,* 429–436.

Rickgarn, R. L. V. (1994). *Perspectives on college student suicide*. Amityville, NY: Baywood Publishing.

Rieder, R. O., Kaufmann, C. A., & Knowles, J. A. (1994). Genetics. In R. E. Hales, S. C. Yudofsky, & J. A. Talbott (Eds.), *The American Psychiatric Press textbook of psychiatry* (2nd ed.). Washington, DC: American Psychiatric Press.

Ries, P., & Stone, A. J. (1992). *The American woman 1992–93: A status report*. New York: Norton.

Riley, L. R. (1987). *Psychology of language development: A primer*. Toronto: C. J. Hogrefe.

Rimm, D. C., & Cunningham, H. M. (1985). Behavior therapies. In S. J. Lynn & J. P. Garske (Eds.), *Contemporary psychotherapies: Models and methods*. Columbus, OH: Charles E. Merrill.

Riskind, J. H. (1991). The mediating mechanisms in mood and memory: A cognitive-priming formulation. In D. Kuiken (Ed.), *Mood and memory: Theory, research, and applications*. Newbury Park, CA: Sage.

Roazen, P. (1976). *Erik H. Erikson: The power and limits of a vision*. New York: Free Press.

Robbins, D. (1971). Partial reinforcement: A selective review of the alleyway literature since 1960. *Psychological Bulletin, 76,* 415–431.

Roberts, P., & Newton, P. M. (1987). Levinsonian studies of women's adult development. *Psychology and Aging, 2,* 154–163.

Robins, C. J. (1988). Attributions and depression: Why is the literature so inconsistent? *Journal of Personality and Social Psychology, 54,* 880–889.

Robins, L. N., & Regier, D. A. (Eds.). (1991).

Psychiatric disorders in America: The epidemiologic catchment area study. New York: Free Press.

Robins, L. N., Helzer, J. E., Weissman, M. M., Orvaschel, H., Gruenberg, E., Burke, J. D., Jr., & Regier, D. A. (1984). Lifetime prevalence of specific psychiatric disorders in three sites. *Archives of General Psychiatry, 41,* 949–958.

Robins, L. N., Locke, B. Z., & Regier, D. A. (1991). An overview of psychiatric disorders in America. In L. N. Robins & D. A. Regier (Eds.), *Psychiatric disorders in America: The epidemiologic catchment area study*. New York: Free Press.

Robins, L. N., Tipp, J., & Przybeck, T. (1991). Antisocial personality. In L. N. Robins & D. A. Regier (Eds.), *Psychiatric disorders in America: The epidemiologic catchment area study*. New York: Free Press.

Robinson, F. P. (1970). *Effective study* (4th ed.). New York: Harper & Row.

Robinson, J. L., Kagan, J., Reznick, J. S., & Corley, R. (1992). The heritability of inhibited and uninhibited behavior: A twin study. *Developmental Psychology, 28,* 1030–1037.

Rock, I. (1986). The description and analysis of object and event perception. In K. R. Boff, L. Kaufman, & J. P. Thomas (Eds.), *Handbook of perception and human performance* (Vol. 2). New York: Wiley.

Rock, I., & Palmer, S. (1990). The legacy of Gestalt psychology. *Scientific American,* 84–90.

Rodin, J. (1978). Has the distinction between internal versus external control of feeding outlived its usefulness? In G. A. Bray (Ed.), *Recent advances in obesity research* (Vol. 2). London: Newman.

Rodin, J. (1981). Current status of the internal-external hypothesis for obesity: What went wrong? *American Psychologist, 36,* 361–372.

Rodin, J., Schank, D., & Striegel-Moore, R. H. (1989). Psychological features of obesity. *Medical Clinics of North America, 73,* 47–66.

Rodin, J., Wack, J., Ferrannini, E., & Defronzo, R. A. (1985). Effect of insulin and glucose on feeding behavior. *Metabolism, 34,* 826–831.

Roediger, H. L., III. (1980). Memory metaphors in cognitive psychology. *Memory & Cognition, 8,* 231–246.

Roediger, H. L., III. (1990). Implicit memory: Retention without remembering. *American Psychologist, 45,* 1043–1056.

Roediger, H. L., III. (1992). Retrieval processes in memory. In L. R. Squire (Ed.), *Encyclopedia of learning and memory*. New York: Macmillan.

Roediger, H. L., Wheeler, M. A., & Rajaram, S. (1993). Remembering, knowing, and reconstructing the past. In D. L. Medin (Ed.), *The psychology of learning and motivation: Advances in research and theory*. San Diego, CA: Academic Press.

Roehrs, T. A., Merlotti, L., Zorick, F., & Roth, T. (1992). Rebound insomnia in normals and patients with insomnia after abrupt and tapered discontinuation. *Psychopharmacology, 108*(1–2), 67–71.

Roehrs, T. A, Zorick, F., & Roth, T. (1994). Transient and short-term insomnia. In M. H. Kryger, T. Roth, & W. C. Dement (Eds.), *Principles and practice of sleep medicine* (2nd ed.). Philadelphia: Saunders.

Roethlisberger, F. J., & Dickson, W. J. (1939). *Management and the worker*. Cambridge, MA: Harvard University Press.

Roffman, R. A., & George, W. H. (1988). Cannabis abuse. In D. M. Donovan & G. A. Marlatt

(Eds.), *Assessment of addictive behaviors*. New York: Guilford Press.

Roffwarg, H. P., Muzio, J. N., & Dement, W. C. (1966). Ontogenetic development of the human sleep-dream cycle. *Science, 152,* 604–619.

Rogers, C. R. (1951). *Client-centered therapy: Its current practice, implications, and theory*. Boston: Houghton Mifflin.

Rogers, C. R. (1961). *On becoming a person: A therapist's view of psychotherapy*. Boston: Houghton Mifflin.

Rogers, C. R. (1980). *A way of being*. Boston: Houghton Mifflin.

Rogers, C. R. (1986). Client-centered therapy. In I. L. Kutash & A. Wolf (Eds.), *Psychotherapist's casebook*. San Francisco: Jossey-Bass.

Rogers, R. W. (1983). Cognitive and physiological processes in fear appeals and attitude change: A revised theory of protection motivation. In J. Cacioppo & R. Petty (Eds.), *Social psychophysiology*. New York: Guilford Press.

Rogers, T. B., Kuiper, N. A., & Kirker, W. S. (1977). Self-reference and the encoding of personal information. *Journal of Personality and Social Psychology, 35,* 677–688.

Rogoff, B. (1990). *Apprenticeship in thinking*. New York: Oxford University Press.

Rohde, P., Lewinsohn, P. M., & Seeley, J. R. (1991). Comorbidity of unipolar depression: II. Comorbidity with other mental disorders in adolescents and adults. *Journal of Abnormal Psychology, 100,* 214–222.

Role, L. W., & Kelly, J. P. (1991). The brain stem: Cranial nerve nuclei and the monoaminergic systems. In E. R. Kandel, J. H. Schwartz, & T. M. Jessell (Eds.), *Principles of neural science* (3rd ed.). New York: Elsevier.

Rollins, B., & Feldman, H. (1970). Marital satisfaction over the family life cycle. *Journal of Marriage and the Family, 32,* 20–28.

Rollman, G. B. (1991). Pain responsiveness. In M. A. Heller & W. Schiff (Eds.), *The psychology of touch*. Hillsdale, NJ: Erlbaum.

Rook, K. S. (1990). Parallels in the study of social support and social strain. *Journal of Social and Clinical Psychology, 9,* 118–132.

Roosa, M. W. (1988). The effect of age in the transition to parenthood: Are delayed childbearers a unique group? *Family Relations, 37,* 322–327.

Rorschach, H. (1942). *Psychodiagnostics: A diagnostic test based on perception*. Berne: Huber.

Rosch, E. H. (1973). Natural categories. *Cognitive Psychology, 4,* 328–350.

Rose, R. J. (1995). Genes and human behavior. *Annual Review of Psychology, 46,* 625–654.

Rose, S. P. R. (1992). Protein synthesis in long-term memory in vertebrates. In L. R. Squire (Ed.), *Encyclopedia of learning and memory*. New York: Macmillan.

Rosen, M., Nystrom, L., & Wall, S. (1988). Diet and cancer mortality in the counties of Sweden. *American Journal of Epidemiology, 127,* 42–49.

Rosenbaum, J. F., Biederman, J., Bolduc, E. A., Hirschfeld, D. R., Faraone, S. V., & Kagan, J. (1992). Comorbidity of parental anxiety disorders as risk for childhood-onset anxiety in inhibited children. *American Journal of Psychiatry, 149,* 475–481.

Rosenbaum, M., Lakin, M., & Roback, H. B. (1992). Psychotherapy in groups. In D. K. Freedheim (Ed.), *History of psychotherapy: A century of change*. Washington, DC: American Psychological Association.

Rosenbaum, M. E. (1986). The repulsion hypothesis: On the nondevelopment of relationships. *Journal of Personality and Social Psychology, 51*, 1156–1166.

Rosenblith, J. F. (1992). *In the beginning: Development from conception to age two.* Newbury Park, CA: Sage.

Rosenfarb, I. S., Goldstein, M. J., Mintz, J., & Nuechterlein, K. H. (1995). Expressed emotion and subclinical psychopathology observable within the transactions between schizophrenic patients and their family members. *Journal of Abnormal Psychology, 104*, 259–267.

Rosengren, A., Tibblin, G., & Wilhelmsen, L. (1991). Self-perceived psychological stress and incidence of coronary artery disease in middle-aged men. *American Journal of Cardiology, 68*, 1171–1175.

Rosenhan, D. L. (1973). On being sane in insane places. *Science, 179*, 250–258.

Rosenman, R. H. (1991). Type A behavior pattern and coronary heart disease: The hostility factor? *Stress Medicine, 7*(4), 245–253.

Rosenman, R. H. (1993). Relationships of the Type A behavior pattern with coronary heart disease. In L. Goldberger & S. Breznitz (Eds.), *Handbook of stress: Theoretical and clinical aspects* (2nd ed.). New York: Free Press.

Rosenstein, D., & Oster, H. (1988). Differential facial responses to four basic tastes in newborns. *Child Development, 59*, 1555–1568.

Rosenthal, H. (1988). *Not with my life I don't: Preventing your suicide and that of others.* Muncie, IN: Accelerated Development.

Rosenthal, R. (1976). *Experimenter effects in behavioral research.* New York: Halsted.

Rosenthal, R. (1994). Interpersonal expectancy effects: A 30-year perspective. *Current Directions in Psychological Science, 3*, 176–179.

Rosenthal, R., & Fode, K. L. (1963). Three experiments in experimenter bias. *Psychological Reports, 12*, 491–511.

Rosenzweig, M. R. (1996). Aspects of the search for neural mechanisms of memory. *Annual Review of Psychology, 47*, 1–32.

Rosenzweig, M. R., Bennett, E. L., Martinez, J. L., Colombo, P. J., Lee, D. W., & Serrano, P. A. (1992). Studying stages of memory formation with chicks. In L. R. Squire & N. Butters (Eds.), *Neuropsychology of memory* (2nd ed.). New York: Guilford Press.

Rosenzweig, S. (1985). Freud and experimental psychology: The emergence of idiodynamics. In S. Koch & D. E. Leary (Eds.), *A century of psychology as a science.* New York: McGraw-Hill.

Roskos-Ewoldsen, D. R., & Fazio, R. H. (1992). The accessibility of source likability as a determinant of persuasion. *Personality and Social Psychology Bulletin, 18*, 19–25.

Ross, B. (1991). William James: Spoiled child of American psychology. In G. A. Kimble, M. Wertheimer, & C. White (Eds.), *Portraits of pioneers in psychology.* Hillsdale, NJ: Erlbaum.

Ross, C. A., Anderson, G., Fleisher, W. P., & Norton, G. R. (1991). The frequency of multiple personality disorder among psychiatric inpatients. *American Journal of Psychiatry, 148*, 1717–1720.

Ross, C. A., Miller, S. D., Reagor, P., Bjornson, L., Fraser, G. A., & Anderson, G. (1990). Structured interview data on 102 cases of multiple personality disorder from four centers. *American Journal of Psychiatry, 147*, 596–601.

Ross, J., & Ferris, K. R. (1981). Interpersonal attraction and organizational outcome: A field experiment. *Administrative Science Quarterly, 26*, 617–632.

Ross, L. D. (1977). The intuitive psychologist and his shortcomings: Distortions in the attribution process. In L. Berkowitz (Ed.), *Advances in experimental social psychology* (Vol. 10). New York: Academic Press.

Ross, L. D. (1988). The obedience experiments: A case study of controversy. *Contemporary Psychology, 33*, 101–104.

Ross, L. D., & Anderson, C. A. (1982). Shortcomings in the attribution process: On the origins and maintenance of erroneous social assessments. In D. Kahneman, P. Slovic, & A. Tversky (Eds.), *Judgement under uncertainty: Heuristics and biases.* Cambridge: Cambridge University Press.

Rossi, P. H. (1990). The old homeless and the new homelessness in historical perspective. *American Psychologist, 45*(8), 954–959.

Rothbart, M. K., & Ahadi, S. A. (1994). Temperament and the development of personality. *Journal of Abnormal Psychology, 103*, 55–66.

Rothblum, E. D., Solomon, L. J., & Albee, G. W. (1986). A sociopolitical perspective of DSM-III. In T. Millon & G. L. Klerman (Eds.), *Contemporary directions in psychopathology: Toward the DSM-IV.* New York: Guilford Press.

Rotter, J. B. (1955). The role of psychological situations in determining the direction of human behavior. In M. R. Jones (Ed.), *Nebraska symposium on motivation.* Lincoln: University of Nebraska Press.

Rotter, J. B. (1966). Generalized expectancies for internal versus external control of reinforcement. *Psychological Monographs, 80*(Whole No. 609).

Rotter, J. B. (1975). Some problems and misconceptions related to the construct of internal versus external control of reinforcement. *Journal of Consulting and Clinical Psychology, 43*, 56–67.

Rotter, J. B. (1982). *The development and application of social learning theory.* New York: Praeger.

Rotter, J. B. (1990). Internal versus external control of reinforcement: A case history of a variable. *American Psychologist, 45*, 489–493.

Rotter, J. B., & Rafferty, J. E. (1950). *Manual: The Rotter incomplete sentence blank.* New York: Psychological Corporation.

Rovee-Collier, C. (1993). The capacity for long-term memory in infancy. *New Directions in Psychological Science, 2*(4), 130–135.

Roy, A. (1989). Suicide. In H. I. Kaplan & B. J. Sadock (Eds.), *Comprehensive textbook of psychiatry/V.* Baltimore: Williams & Wilkins.

Rozin, P. (1990). The importance of social factors in understanding the acquisition of food habits. In E. D. Capaldi & T. L. Powley (Eds.), *Taste, experience, and feeding.* Washington, DC: American Psychological Association.

Rozin, P. (1996). Towards a psychology of food and eating: From motivation to module to model to marker, morality, meaning, and metaphor. *Current Directions in Psychological Science, 5*, 18–24.

Rubin, E. H., Zorumski, C. F., & Guze, S. B. (1986). Somatoform disorders. In T. Millon & G. L. Klerman (Eds.), *Contemporary directions in psychopathology: Toward the DSM-IV.* New York: Guilford Press.

Rubinsky, H., Eckerman, D., Rubinsky, E., & Hoover, C. (1987). Early-phase physiological response patterns to psychosexual stimuli: Comparisons of male and female patterns. *Archives of Sexual Behavior, 16*, 45–55.

Ruble, D. N., Fleming, A. S., Hackel, L. S., &

Stangor, C. (1988). Changes in the marital relationship during the transition to first time motherhood: Effects of violated expectations concerning division of household labor. *Journal of Personality and Social Psychology, 55*, 78–87.

Ruble, T. L. (1983). Sex stereotypes: Issues of change in the 70s. *Sex Roles, 9*, 397–402.

Rubonis, A. V., & Bickman, L. (1991). Psychological impairment in the wake of disaster: The disaster-psychopathology relationship. *Psychological Bulletin, 109*, 384–399.

Ruderman, A. J. (1986). Dietary restraint: A theoretical and empirical review. *Psychological Bulletin, 99*, 247–262.

Rudorfer, M. V., & Goodwin, F. K. (1993). Introduction. In C. E. Coffey (Ed.), *The clinical science of electroconvulsive therapy.* Washington, DC: American Psychiatric Press.

Ruff, H. A., & Lawson, K. R. (1990). Development of sustained, focused attention in young children during free play. *Developmental Psychology, 26*, 85–93.

Ruff, H. A., Lawson, K. R., Parrinello, R., & Weissberg, R. (1990). Long-term stability of individual differences in sustained attention in the early years. *Child Development, 61*, 60–75.

Rumelhart, D., & Norman, D. (1988). Representation in memory. In R. C. Atkinson, R. J. Herrnstein, G. Lindzey, & R. D. Luce (Eds.), *Stevens' handbook of experimental psychology* (Vol. 2). New York: Wiley.

Rundus, D. (1971). Analysis of rehearsal processes in free recall. *Journal of Experimental Psychology, 89*, 63–77.

Ruse, M. (1987). Sociobiology and knowledge: Is evolutionary epistemology a viable option? In C. Crawford, M. Smith, & D. Krebs (Eds.), *Sociobiology and psychology: Ideas, issues and applications.* Hillsdale, NJ: Erlbaum.

Rush, A. J. (1984). Cognitive therapy. In T. B. Karasu (Ed.), *The psychiatric therapies.* Washington, DC: American Psychiatric Press.

Rushton, J. P., Fulker, D. W., Neale, M. C., Nias, D. K. B., & Eysenck, H. J. (1986). Altruism and aggression: The heritability of individual differences. *Journal of Personality and Social Psychology, 50*, 1192–1198.

Russell, J. A. (1991). Culture and the categorization of emotions. *Psychological Bulletin, 110*, 426–450.

Russell, J. A. (1994). Is there universal recognition of emotion from facial expression? A review of the cross-cultural studies. *Psychological Bulletin, 115*, 102–141.

Russell, J. A. (1995). Facial expressions of emotion: What lies beyond minimal universality? *Psychological Bulletin, 118*, 379–391.

Russell, M. J., Switz, G. M., & Thompson, K. (1980). Olfactory influences on the human menstrual cycle. *Pharmacology, Biochemistry and Behavior, 13*, 737–738.

Russo, N. F., & Denmark, F. L. (1987). Contributions of women to psychology. *Annual Review of Psychology, 38*, 279–298.

Rutherford, W. (1886). A new theory of hearing. *Journal of Anatomy and Physiology, 21*, 166–168.

Rutter, M., Silberg, J., & Simonoff, E. (1993). Whither behavioral genetics?—A developmental psychopathological perspective. In R. Plomin & G. E. McClearn (Eds.), *Nature, nurture and psychology.* Washington, DC: American Psychological Association.

Sachs, J. (1985). Prelinguistic development. In

J. B. Gleason (Ed.), *The development of language.* Columbus: Charles E. Merrill.

Sackeim, H. A. (1988). Mechanisms of action of electroconvulsive therapy. In A. J. Frances & R. E. Hales (Eds.), *Annual review of psychiatry* (Vol. 7). Washington, DC: American Psychiatric Press.

Sacks, O. (1987). *The man who mistook his wife for a hat.* New York: Harper & Row.

Sadker, M., & Sadker, D. (1985, March). Sexism in the schoolroom of the '80s. *Psychology Today,* pp. 54–57.

Salin-Pascual, R. J., Roehrs, T. A., Merlotti, L. A., Zorick, F., & Roth., T. (1992). Long-term study of the sleep of insomnia patients with sleep state misperception and other insomnia patients. *American Journal of Psychiatry, 149,* 904–908.

Salminen, S. (1992). Defensive attribution hypothesis and serious occupational accidents. *Psychological Reports, 70,* 1195–1199.

Salthouse, T. A. (1991). Mediation of adult age differences in cognition by reductions in working memory and speed of processing. *Psychological Science, 2,* 179–183.

Salthouse, T. A. (1994). The nature of the influence of speed on adult age differences in cognition. *Developmental Psychology, 30,* 240–259.

Salthouse, T. A., & Babcock, R. L. (1991). Decomposing adult age differences in working memory. *Developmental Psychology, 27,* 763–776.

Salvendy, J. T. (1993). Selection and preparation of patients and organization of the group. In H. I. Kaplan & B. J. Sadock (Eds.), *Comprehensive group psychotherapy.* Baltimore: Williams & Wilkins.

Samelson, F. (1981). Struggle for scientific authority: The reception of Watson's behaviorism, 1913–1920. *Journal of the History of the Behavioral Sciences, 17,* 399–425.

Samet, J. M. (1992). The health benefits of smoking cessation. *Medical Clinics of North America, 76,* 399–414.

Samples, R. E. (1975, February). Are you teaching only one side of the brain? *Learning: The Magazine for Creative Teaching,* pp. 25–28.

Sanders, G. S., & Simmons, W. L. (1983). Use of hypnosis to enhance eyewitness accuracy: Does it work? *Journal of Applied Psychology, 68*(1), 70–77.

Sanderson, C., & Clarkin, J. F. (1994). Use of the NEO-PI personality dimensions in differential treatment planning. In P. T. Costa, Jr., & T. A. Widiger (Eds.), *Personality disorders and the five-factor model of personality.* Washington, DC: American Psychological Association.

Sanderson, W. C., & Barlow, D. H. (1990). A description of patients diagnosed with DSM-III-R generalized anxiety disorder. *Journal of Nervous and Mental Disease, 178,* 588–591.

Sandler, J. (1975). Aversion methods. In F. H. Kanfer & A. P. Goldstein (Eds.), *Helping people change: A textbook of methods.* New York: Pergamon Press.

Sapolsky, R. M. (1992). Neuroendocrinology and the stress-response. In J. B. Becker, S. M. Breedlove, & D. Crews (Eds.), *Behavioral Endocrinology.* Cambridge, MA: MIT Press.

Sarason, I. G., Pierce, G. R., & Sarason, B. R. (1994). General and specific perceptions of social support. In W. R. Avison & I. H. Gotlib (Eds.), *Stress and mental health: Contemporary issues and prospects for the future.* New York: Plenum Press.

Sarason, I. G., & Sarason, B. G. (1987). *Abnormal psychology: The problem of maladaptive behavior.* Englewood Cliffs, NJ: Prentice-Hall.

Sarnacki, R. E. (1979). An examination of testwiseness in the cognitive domain. *Review of Educational Research, 49,* 252–279.

Sato, M. (1973). Gustatory receptor mechanism in mammals. *Advances in Biophysics, 4,* 103–152.

Saudino, K. J., & Eaton, W. O. (1991). Infant temperament and genetics: An objective twin study of motor activity level. *Child Development, 62,* 1167–1174.

Sauter, S., Hurrell, J. J., & Cooper, C. L. (1988). *Job control and worker health.* New York: Wiley.

Savage-Rumbaugh, S., McDonald, K., Sevcik, R. A., Hopkins, W. D., & Rupert, E. (1986). Spontaneous symbol acquisition and communication use by pygmy chimpanzees (*Pan paniscus*). *Journal of Experimental Psychology: General, 115,* 211–235.

Savage-Rumbaugh, S., Sevcik, R. A., Brakke, K. E., & Rumbaugh, D. M. (1992). Symbols: Their communicative use, communication, and combination by bonobos (*Pan paniscus*). In L. P. Lipsitt & C. Rovee-Collier (Eds.), *Advances in infancy research* (Vol. 7). Norwood, NJ: Ablex.

Saxe, G. N., van der Kolk, B. A., Berkowitz, R., Chinman, G., Hall, K., Lieberg, G., & Schwartz, J. (1993). Dissociative disorders in psychiatric inpatients. *American Journal of Psychiatry, 150,* 1037–1042.

Saxe, L. (1994). Detection of deception: Polygraph and integrity tests. *Current Directions in Psychological Science, 3,* 69–73.

Scarr, S. (1981). Genetics and the development of intelligence. In S. Scarr (Ed.), *Race, social class, and individual differences in IQ.* Hillsdale, NJ: Erlbaum.

Scarr, S. (1989). Protecting general intelligence: Constructs and consequences for interventions. In R. L. Linn (Ed.), *Intelligence: Measurement, theory, and public policy.* Urbana: University of Illinois Press.

Scarr, S. (1992). Developmental theories for the 1990s: Development and individual differences. *Child Development, 63,* 1–19.

Scarr, S. (1994a). Culture-fair and culture-free tests. In R. J. Sternberg (Ed.), *Encyclopedia of human intelligence.* New York: Macmillan.

Scarr, S. (1994b). Cyril L. Burt. In R. J. Sternberg (Ed.), *Encyclopedia of human intelligence.* New York: Macmillan.

Scarr, S., & Carter-Saltzman, L. (1979). Twin method: Defense of a critical assumption. *Behavior Genetics, 9,* 527–542.

Scarr, S., & Carter-Saltzman, L. (1982). Genetics and intelligence. In R. J. Sternberg (Ed.), *Handbook of human intelligence.* Cambridge, MA: Cambridge University Press.

Scarr, S., & Weinberg, R. A. (1976). IQ test performance of black children adopted by white families. *American Psychologist, 31,* 726–739.

Scarr, S., & Weinberg, R. A. (1977). Intellectual similarities within families of both adopted and biological children. *Intelligence, 32,* 170–190.

Scarr, S., & Weinberg, R. A. (1983). The Minnesota adoption studies: Genetic differences and malleability. *Child Development, 54,* 260–267.

Scarr, S., Phillips, D., McCartney, K., & Abbott-Shim, M. (1993). Quality of child care as an aspect of family and child care policy in the United States. *Pediatrics, 91,* 182–188.

Schachter, S. (1959). *The psychology of affiliation.* Stanford, CA: Stanford University Press.

Schachter, S. (1964). The interaction of cognitive and physiological determinants of emotional state. In L. Berkowitz (Ed.), *Advances in experimental social psychology* (Vol. 1). New York: Academic Press.

Schachter, S. (1971). *Emotion, obesity and crime.* New York: Academic Press.

Schachter, S., & Gross, L. (1968). Manipulated time and eating behavior. *Journal of Personality and Social Psychology, 10,* 98–106.

Schachter, S., & Rodin, J. (1974). *Obese humans and rats.* Hillsdale, NJ: Erlbaum.

Schachter, S., & Singer, J. E. (1962). Cognitive, social and physiological determinants of emotional state. *Psychological Review, 69,* 379–399.

Schachter, S., & Singer, J. E. (1979). Comments on the Maslach and Marshall-Zimbardo experiments. *Journal of Personality and Social Psychology, 37,* 989–995.

Schacter, D. L. (1987). Implicit memory: History and current status. *Journal of Experimental Psychology: Learning, Memory and Cognition, 14,* 501–518.

Schacter, D. L. (1989). On the relation between memory and consciousness: Dissociable interactions and conscious experience. In H. L. Roediger, III, & F. I. M. Craik (Eds.), *Varieties of memory and consciousness.* Hillsdale, NJ: Erlbaum.

Schacter, D. L. (1992). Understanding implicit memory: A cognitive neuroscience approach. *American Psychologist, 47,* 559–569.

Schacter, D. L. (1994). Priming and multiple memory systems: Perceptual mechanisms of implicit memory. In D. L. Schacter & E. Tulving (Eds.), *Memory systems.* Cambridge, MA: MIT Press.

Schacter, D. L., Chui, C. Y. P., & Ochsner, K. N. (1993). Implicit memory: A selective review. *Annual Review of Neuroscience, 16,* 159–182.

Schaeffer, M., Street, S., Singer, J., & Baum, A. (1988). Effects of control on the stress reactions of commuters. *Journal of Applied Social Psychology, 18,* 944–957.

Schaie, K. W. (1983). The Seattle longitudinal study: A twenty-one year exploration of psychometric intelligence in adulthood. In K. W. Schaie (Ed.), *Longitudinal studies of adult psychological development.* New York: Guilford Press.

Schaie, K. W. (1990). Intellectual development in adulthood. In J. E. Birren & K. W. Schaie (Eds.), *Handbook of the psychology of aging* (3rd ed.). San Diego: Academic Press.

Schaie, K. W. (1993). The Seattle longitudinal studies of adult intelligence. *Current Directions, 2,* 171–175.

Schaie, K. W. (1994). The course of adult intellectual development. *American Psychologist, 49,* 304–313.

Schank, R., & Abelson, R. (1977). *Scripts, plans, goals, and understanding.* Hillsdale, NJ: Erlbaum.

Scharf, M. B., Mayleben, D. W., Kaffeman, M., Kvall, R., & Ochs, R. (1991). Dose response effects of zolpidem in normal geriatric subjects. *Journal of Clinical Psychiatry, 52,* 77–83.

Schau, C. G., & Scott, K. P. (1984). Impact of gender characteristics of instructional materials: An integration of the research literature. *Journal of Educational Psychology, 76,* 183–193.

Scheflin, A. W. (1994). Forensic hypnosis: Unanswered questions. *Australian Journal of Clinical & Experimental Hypnosis, 22,* 25–37.

Scheidlinger, S. (1993). History of group psychotherapy. In H. I. Kaplan & B. J. Sadock (Eds.), *Comprehensive group psychotherapy.* Baltimore: Williams & Wilkins.

Scheier, M. F., & Carver, C. S. (1985). Optimism, coping and health: Assessment and implications of generalized expectancies. *Health Psychology, 4,* 219–247.

Scheier, M. F., & Carver, C. S. (1992). Effects of optimism on psychological and physical well-being: Theoretical overview and empirical update. *Cognitive Theory and Research, 16*(2), 201–228.

Scheier, M. F., Matthews, K. A., Owens, J. F., Magovern, G. J., Sr., Lefebvre, R. C., Abbott, R. A., & Carver, C. S. (1989). Dispositional optimism and recovery from coronary artery bypass surgery: The beneficial effects on physical and psychological well-being. *Journal of Personality and Social Psychology, 57,* 1024–1040.

Scheier, M. F., Weintraub, J. K., & Carver, C. S. (1986). Coping with stress: Divergent strategies of optimists and pessimists. *Journal of Personality and Social Psychology, 51,* 1257–1264.

Schein, E. H. (1978). *Career dynamics: Matching individual and organizational needs.* Reading, MA: Addison-Wesley.

Schein, M., Zyranski, S. J., Levine, S., & Medalie, J. H. (1988). The frequency of sexual problems among family practice patients. *Family Practice Research Journal, 7*(3), 122–134.

Scherer, K. R., & Wallbott, H. G. (1994). Evidence for universality and cultural variation of differential emotion response patterning. *Journal of Personality and Social Psychology, 66,* 310–328.

Scherer, K. R., Wallbott, H. G., Matsumoto, D., & Kudoh, T. (1988). Emotional experience in cultural context: A comparison between Europe, Japan, and the United States. In K. R. Scherer (Ed.), *Facets of emotions.* Hillsdale, NJ: Erlbaum.

Schiff, A. R., & Knopf, I. J. (1985). The effect of task demands on attention allocation in children of different ages. *Child Development, 56,* 621–630.

Schiff, M., & Lewontin, R. (1986). *Education and class: The irrelevance of IQ genetic studies.* Oxford: Clarendon Press.

Schildkraut, J. J., Green, A. I., Mooney, J. J. (1985). Affective disorders: Biochemical aspects. In H. I. Kaplan & B. J. Sadock (Eds.), *Comprehensive textbook of psychiatry/IV.* Baltimore: Williams & Wilkins.

Schildkraut, J. J., Hirshfeld, A. J., & Murphy, J. M. (1994). Mind and mood in modern art, II: Depressive disorders, spirituality, and early deaths in the abstract expressionist artists of the New York School. *American Journal of Psychiatry, 151,* 482–488.

Schiller, P. H., Logothetis, N. K., & Charles, E. R. (1990). Functions of the colour-opponent and broad-band channels of the visual systems. *Nature, 343,* 68–70.

Schlaadt, R. G., & Shannon, P. T. (1994). *Drugs: Use, misuse, and abuse* (4th ed.). Englewood Cliffs, NJ: Prentice-Hall.

Schlegel, A., & Barry, H., III. (1991). *Adolescence: An anthropological inquiry.* New York: Free Press.

Schlenger, W. E., Kulka, R. A., Fairbank, J. A., Hough, R. L., Jordan, B. K., Marmar, C. R., & Weiss, D. S. (1992). The prevalence of post-traumatic stress disorder in the Vietnam generation: A multimethod, multisource assessment of psychiatric disorder. *Journal of Traumatic Stress, 5*(3), 333–363.

Schlenker, B. R. (1980). *Impression management: The self-concept, social identity, and interpersonal relations.* Pacific Grove, CA: Brooks/Cole.

Schlenker, B. R., Phillips, S. T., Boniecki, K. A., & Schlenker, D. R. (1995). Championship pressures: Choking or triumphing in one's own terri-

tory? *Journal of Personality and Social Psychology, 68,* 632–643.

Schlenker, B. R., Weigold, M. F., & Hallam, J. R. (1990). Self-serving attributions in social context: Effects of self-esteem and social pressure. *Journal of Personality and Social Psychology, 58,* 855–863.

Schlosberg, H. (1954). Three dimensions of emotion. *Psychological Review, 61,* 81–88.

Schmidt, F. L. (1992). What do data really mean? Research findings, meta-analysis, and cumulative knowledge in psychology. *American Psychologist, 47,* 1173–1181.

Schmidt, F. L., Ones, D. S., & Hunter, J. E. (1992). Personnel selection. *Annual Review of Psychology, 43,* 627–670.

Schmitt, D. P., & Buss, D. M. (1996). Strategic self-promotion and competitor derogation: Sex and context effects on the perceived effectiveness of mate attraction tactics. *Journal of Personality and Social Psychology, 70,* 1185–1204.

Schneer, J. A., & Reitman, F. (1994). The importance of gender in mid-career: A longitudinal study of MBAs. *Journal of Organizational Behavior Management, 15,* 199–207.

Schneewind, K. A. (1995). Impact of family processes on control beliefs. In A. Bandura (Ed.), *Self-efficacy in changing societies.* New York: Cambridge University Press.

Schneider, W., & Pressley, M. (1989). *Memory development between 2 and 20.* New York: Springer-Verlag.

Schonemann, P. H. (1994). Heritability. In R. J. Sternberg (Ed.), *Encyclopedia of human intelligence.* New York: Macmillan.

Schreiber, F. R. (1973). *Sybil.* New York: Warner.

Schroeder, D. H., & Costa, P. T., Jr. (1984). Influence of life events stress on physical illness: Substantive effects or methodological flaws? *Journal of Personality and Social Psychology, 46,* 853–863.

Schroth, M. L. (1991). Dyadic adjustment and sensation seeking compatibility. *Personality and Individual Differences, 12*(5), 467–471.

Schultz, J. H., & Luthe, W. (1959). *Autogenic training.* New York: Grune & Stratton.

Schulz, H. (1993). Ultradian rhythms. In M. A. Carskadon (Ed.), *Encyclopedia of sleep and dreaming.* New York: Macmillan.

Schuman, H., & Kalton, G. (1985). Survey methods. In G. Lindzey & E. Aronson (Eds.), *Handbook of social psychology* (3rd ed.). New York: Random House.

Schusterman, R. J., & Gisiner, R. (1988). Artificial language comprehension in dolphins and sea lions: The essential cognitive skills. *Psychological Record, 38,* 311–348.

Schwartz, B., & Robbins, S. J. (1995). *Psychology of learning and behavior* (4th ed.). New York: Norton.

Schwartz, G. E. (1974, April). The facts on transcendental meditation, part II: TM relaxes some people and makes them feel better. *Psychology Today,* pp. 39–44.

Schwartz, S. H. (1990). Individualism-collectivism: Critique and proposed refinements. *Journal of Cross-Cultural Psychology, 21,* 139–157.

Schwartz, W. J. (1996). Internal timekeeping. *Science & Medicine, 3,* 44–53.

Schwarzer, R., & Fuchs, R. (1995). Changing risk behaviors and adopting health behaviors: The role of self-efficacy beliefs. In A. Bandura (Ed.), *Self-efficacy in changing societies.* New York: Cambridge University Press.

Scott, K. G., & Carran, D. T. (1987). The epidemiology and prevention of mental retardation. *American Psychologist, 42,* 801–804.

Scott, T. R. (1990). The effect of physiological need on taste. In E. D. Capaldi & T. L. Powley (Eds.), *Taste, experience, and feeding.* Washington, DC: American Psychological Association.

Scoville, W. B., & Milner, B. (1957). Loss of recent memory after bilateral hippocampal lesions. *Journal of Neurology, Neurosurgery & Psychiatry, 20,* 11–21.

Scull, A. (1990). Deinstitutionalization: Cycles of despair. *The Journal of Mind and Behavior, 11*(3/4), 301–312.

Searleman, A. (1996). Personality variables and prospective memory performance. In D. J. Herrmann, C. McEvoy, C. Hertzog, P. Hertel, & M. K. Johnson (Eds.), *Basic and applied memory research: Practical applications* (Vol. 2). Mahwah, NJ: Erlbaum.

Searleman, A., & Fugagli, A. K. (1987). Suspected autoimmune disorders and left-handedness: Evidence from individuals with diabetes, Crohn's disease and ulcerative colitis. *Neuropsychologia, 25,* 267–374.

Searleman, A., & Herrmann, D. (1994). *Memory from a broader perspective.* New York: McGraw-Hill.

Sears, D. O. (1975). Political socialization. In F. I. Greenstein & N. W. Polsby (Eds.), *Handbook of political science* (Vol. 2). Reading, MA: Addison-Wesley.

Sears, R. (1977). Sources of life satisfaction of the Terman gifted men. *American Psychologist, 32,* 119–128.

Sears, D. O. (1986). College sophomores in the laboratory: Influences of a narrow database on social psychology's view of human nature. *Journal of Personality and Social Psychology, 51,* 515–530.

Seccombe, K. (1991). Assessing the costs and benefits of children: Gender comparisons among childfree husbands and wives. *Journal of Marriage and the Family, 53,* 191–202.

Segal, B. (1988). *Drugs and behavior.* New York: Gardner Press.

Segall, M. H., Campbell, D. T., Herskovits, M. J. (1966). *The influence of culture on visual perception.* Indianapolis: Bobbs-Merrill.

Segall, M. H., Dasen, P. R., Berry, J. W., & Poortinga, Y. H. (1990). *Human behavior in global perspective: An introduction to cross-cultural psychology.* New York: Pergamon Press.

Segrin, C., & Abramson, L. Y. (1994). Negative reactions to depressive behaviors: A communication theories analysis. *Journal of Abnormal Psychology, 103,* 655–668.

Segrin, C., & Dillard, J. P. (1992). The interactional theory of depression: A meta-analysis of the research literature. *Journal of Social and Clinical Psychology, 11,* 43–70.

Seidlitz, L., & Diener, E. (1993). Memory for positive versus negative life events: Theories for the differences between happy and unhappy persons. *Journal of Personality and Social Psychology, 64,* 654–664.

Seifer, R., Schiller, M., Sameroff, A. J., Resnick, S., & Riordan, K. (1996). Attachment, maternal sensitivity, and infant temperament during the first year of life. *Developmental Psychology, 32,* 12–25.

Sekuler, R., & Blake, R. (1990). *Perception.* New York: McGraw-Hill.

Seligman, M. E. P. (1971). Phobias and preparedness. *Behavior Therapy, 2,* 307–321.

Seligman, M. E. P. (1974). Depression and learned helplessness. In R. J. Friedman & M. M. Katz (Eds.), *The psychology of depression: Contemporary theory and research.* New York: Wiley.

Seligman, M. E. P. (1983). Learned helplessness. In E. Levitt, B. Rubin, & J. Brooks (Eds.), *Depression: Concepts, controversies and some new facts.* Hillsdale, NJ: Erlbaum.

Seligman, M. E. P. (1990). *Learned optimism.* New York: Pocket Books.

Seligman, M. E. P. (1995). The effectiveness of psychotherapy. *American Psychologist, 50,* 965–974.

Seligman, M. E. P., & Hager, J. L. (1972, August). Biological boundaries of learning (The sauce béarnaise syndrome). *Psychology Today,* pp. 59–61, 84–87.

Seligman, M. E. P., & Johnston, J. C. (1973). A cognitive theory of avoidance learning. In F. J. McGuigan & D. B. Lumsden (Eds.), *Contemporary approaches to conditioning and learning.* Washington: V. H. Winston.

Selye, H. (1936). A syndrome produced by diverse nocuous agents. *Nature, 138,* 32.

Selye, H. (1956). *The stress of life.* New York: McGraw-Hill.

Selye, H. (1973). The evolution of the stress concept. *American Scientist, 61*(6), 672–699.

Selye, H. (1974). *Stress without distress.* New York: Lippincott.

Selye, H. (1982). History and present status of the stress concept. In L. Goldberger & S. Breznitz (Eds.), *Handbook of stress: Theoretical and clinical aspects.* New York: Free Press.

Seta, J. J., Seta, C. E., & Wang, M. A. (1991). Feelings of negativity and stress: An averaging-summation analysis of impressions of negative life experiences. *Personality and Social Psychology Bulletin, 17,* 376–384.

Sexton, M., Fox, N. L., & Hebel, J. R. (1990). Prenatal exposure to tobacco: II. Effects on cognitive functioning at age three. *International Journal of Epidemiology, 19,* 72–77.

Shafer, G., & Tversky, A. (1988). Languages and designs for probability judgement. In D. E. Bell, H. Raiffa, & A. Tversky (Eds.), *Decision making: Descriptive, normative, and prescriptive interactions.* New York: Cambridge University Press.

Shaffer, D. R. (1985). *Developmental psychology: Theory, research, and applications.* Pacific Grove, CA: Brooks/Cole.

Shaffer, D. R. (1989). *Developmental psychology: Childhood and adolescence.* Pacific Grove, CA: Brooks/Cole.

Shanks, D. R. (1994). Human associative learning. In N. J. Mackintosh (Ed.), *Animal learning and cognition.* San Diego, CA: Academic Press.

Shapiro, D. H., Jr. (1984). Overview: Clinical and physiological comparison of meditation with other self-control strategies. In D. H. Shapiro, Jr., & R. N. Walsh (Eds.), *Meditation: Classic and contemporary perspectives.* New York: Aldine.

Shapiro, D. H., Jr. (1987). Implications of psychotherapy research for the study of meditation. In M. A. West (Ed.), *The psychology of meditation.* Oxford: Clarendon Press.

Shapiro, D. H., Jr. (1994). Examining the content and context of meditation: A challenge for psychology in the areas of stress management, psychotherapy, and religion/values. *Journal of Humanistic Psychology, 84,* 101–185.

Shapiro, S., Skinner, E. A., Kessler, L. G., Von Korff, M., German, P. S., Tischler, G. L., Leaf, P. J., Benham, L., Cottler, L., & Regier, D. A. (1984). Utilization of health and mental health services. *Archives of General Psychiatry, 41,* 971–978.

Sharpe, D., Adair, J. G., & Roese, N. J. (1992). Twenty years of deception research: A decline in subjects' trust? *Personality and Social Psychology Bulletin, 18,* 585–590.

Shaver P. R., & Hazan, C. (1993). Adult attachment: Theory and research. In W. Jones & D. Perlman (Eds.), *Advances in personal relationships* (Vol. 4). London: Jessica Kingsley.

Shaver, P. R., & Hazan, C. (1994). Attachment. In A. L. Weber & J. H. Harvey (Eds.), *Perspectives on close relationships.* Boston: Allyn & Bacon.

Shedler, J., & Block, J. (1990). Adolescent drug use and psychological health: A longitudinal inquiry. *American Psychologist, 45,* 612–630.

Shedler, J., Mayman, M., & Manis, M. (1993). The illusion of mental health. *American Psychologist, 48,* 1117–1131.

Sheehan, P. W., Green, V., & Truesdale, P. (1992). Influence of rapport on hypnotically induced pseudomemory. *Journal of Abnormal Psychology, 101,* 690–700.

Sheehan, S. (1982). *Is there no place on earth for me?* Boston: Houghton Mifflin.

Shekelle, R. B., Hulley, S. B., Neaton, J. D., Billings, J. H., Borhani, N. O., Gerace, T. A., Jacobs, D. R., Lasser, N. L., Mittlemark, M. B., & Stamler, J. (1985). The MRFIT behavior pattern study: II. Type A behavior and incidence of coronary heart disease. *American Journal of Epidemiology, 122,* 559–570.

Sheldon, W. H. (with S. S. Stevens & W. B. Tucker). (1940). *The varieties of human physique: An introduction to constitutional psychology.* New York: Harper.

Sheldon, W. H. (with the collaboration of S. S. Stevens). (1942). *The varieties of temperament: A psychology of constitutional differences.* New York: Harper.

Shepard, R. N. (1990). *Mind sights.* New York: W. H. Freeman.

Shephard, R. J. (1989). Passive smoking: Attitudes, health, and performance. In T. Ney & A. Gale (Eds.), *Smoking and human behavior.* Chichester, England: Wiley.

Shepherd, G. M. (1988). *Neurobiology.* New York: Oxford University Press.

Shepperd, J. A. (1993). Productivity loss in performance groups: A motivation analysis. *Psychological Bulletin, 113,* 67–81.

Sherif, M., & Hovland, C. I. (1961). *Social judgment: Assimilation and contrast effects in communication and attitude change.* New Haven, CT: Yale University Press.

Sherman, C. B. (1992). The health consequences of cigarette smoking: Pulmonary diseases. *Medical Clinics of North America, 76,* 355–375.

Sherman, M., & Key, C. B. (1932). The intelligence of isolated mountain children. *Child Development, 3,* 279–290.

Sherry, D. F. (1992). Evolution and learning. In L. R. Squire (Ed.), *Encyclopedia of learning and memory.* New York: Macmillan.

Sherwood, A. (1993). Use of impedance cardiography in cardiovascular reactivity research. In J. Blascovich & E. S. Katkin (Eds.), *Cardiovascular reactivity to psychological stress and disease.* Washington, DC: American Psychological Association.

Shiffrin, R. M. (1988). Attention. In R. C. Atkinson, R. J. Herrnstein, G. Lindzey, & R. D. Luce (Eds.), *Stevens' handbook of experimental psychology* (Vol. 2). New York: Wiley.

Shimamura, A. P. (1992). Amnesia, organic. In L. R. Squire (Ed.), *Encyclopedia of learning and memory.* New York: Macmillan.

Shimamura, A. P., Berry, J. M., Mangels, J. A., Rusting, C. L., & Jurica, P. J. (1995). Memory and cognitive abilities in university professors: Evidence for successful aging. *Psychological Science, 6,* 271–277.

Shneidman, E. S. (1985). *At the point of no return.* New York: Wiley.

Shneidman, E. S., Farberow, N. L., & Litman, R. E. (Eds.). (1970). *The psychology of suicide.* New York: Science House.

Shoda, Y., Mischel, W., & Wright, J. C. (1994). Intraindividual stability in the organization and patterning of behavior: Incorporating psychological situations into the idiographic analysis of personality. *Journal of Personality and Social Psychology, 67,* 674–687.

Shostak, A. (1987). Singlehood. In M. B. Sussman & S. K. Steinmetz (Eds.), *Handbook of marriage and the family.* New York: Plenum.

Shweder, R. A., Mahapatra, M., & Miller, J. G. (1990). Culture and moral development. In J. W. Stigler, R. A. Shweder, & G. Herdt (Eds.), *Cultural psychology.* New York: Cambridge University Press.

Shweder, R. A., & Sullivan, M. A. (1993). Cultural psychology: Who needs it? *Annual Review of Psychology, 44,* 497–523.

Sicard, G., & Holley, A. (1984). Receptor cell responses to odorants: Similarities and differences among odorants. *Brain Research, 292,* 283–296.

Siegel, J. M. (1990). Stressful life events and use of physician services among the elderly. *Journal of Personality and Social Psychology, 58,* 1081–1086.

Siegel, J. M., Johnson, J. H., & Sarason, I. G. (1979). Life changes and menstrual discomfort. *Journal of Human Stress, 5,* 41–46.

Siegel, O. (1982). Personality development in adolescence. In B. B. Wolman, (Ed.), *Handbook of developmental psychology.* Englewood Cliffs, NJ: Prentice-Hall.

Siegel, S. (1983). Classical conditioning, drug tolerance, and drug dependence. In Y. Israel, F. B. Glaser, H. Kalant, R. E. Popham, W. Schmidt, & R. G. Smart (Eds.), *Research advances in alcohol and drug problems* (Vol. 7). New York: Plenum.

Siegel, S. (1989). Pharmacological conditioning and drug effects. In A. J. Goudie & M. W. Emmett-Oglesby (Eds.), *Psychoactive drugs: Tolerance and sensitization.* Clifton, NJ: Humana Press.

Siegel, S., Hinson, R. E., Krank, M. D., & McCully, J. (1982). Heroin "overdose" death: Contribution of drug-associated environmental cues. *Science, 216,* 436–437.

Siegler, R. S. (1986). *Children's thinking.* Englewood Cliffs, NJ: Prentice-Hall.

Siegler, R. S. (1991). *Children's thinking* (2nd ed.). Englewood Cliffs, NJ: Prentice-Hall.

Siegler, R. S. (1992). The other Alfred Binet. *Developmental Psychology, 28,* 179–190.

Siegler, R. S. (1994). Cognitive variability: A key to understanding cognitive development. *Current Directions in Psychological Science, 3*(1), 1–5.

Siegler, R. S., & Kotovsky, K. (1986). Two levels of giftedness: Shall ever the twain meet? In R. J. Sternberg & J. E. Davidson (Eds.), *Conceptions of giftedness.* Cambridge: Cambridge University Press.

Siever, L. J., & Davis, K. L. (1991). A psychobiological perspective on the personality disorders. *American Journal of Psychiatry, 148,* 1647–1658.

Sigelman, C. K., & Shaffer, D. R. (1991). *Life-*

span human development. Pacific Grove, CA: Brooks/Cole.

Signorielli, N. (1989). Television and conceptions about sex roles: Maintaining conventionality and the status quo. *Sex Roles, 21,* 341–360.

Silver, E., Cirincion, C., & Steadman, H. J. (1994). Demythologizing inaccurate perceptions of the insanity defense. *Law & Human Behavior, 18,* 63–70.

Silverberg, S. B., Tennenbaum, D. L., & Jacob, T. (1992). Adolescence and family interaction. In V. B. Van Hasselt & M. Hersen (Eds.), *Handbook of social development: A lifespan perspective*. New York: Plenum.

Silverman, I., & Eals, M. (1992). Sex differences in spatial ability: Evolutionary theory and data. In J. Barkow, L. Cosmides, & J. Tooby (Eds.), *The adapted mind*. New York: Oxford University Press.

Simmons, C. H., von Kolke, A., & Shimizu, H. (1986). Attitudes toward romantic love among American, German, and Japanese students. *Journal of Social Psychology, 126,* 327–336.

Simon, E. J. (1992). Opiates: Neurobiology. In J. H. Lowinson, P. Ruiz, & R. B. Millman (Eds.), *Substance abuse: A comprehensive textbook* (2nd ed.). Baltimore: Williams & Wilkins.

Simon, F., Arendt, J., & Clark, M. (1993). Can melatonin improve shift workers' tolerance of the night shift? Some preliminary findings. *Chronobiology International, 10,* 315–320.

Simon, G. E., & VonKorff, M. (1991). Somatization and psychiatric disorder in the NIMH epidemiologic catchment area study. *American Journal of Psychiatry, 148,* 1494–1500.

Simon, H. A. (1957). *Models of man.* New York: Wiley.

Simon, H. A. (1973). The structure of ill-structured problems. *Artificial Intelligence, 4,* 181–201.

Simon, H. A. (1974). How big is a chunk? *Science, 183,* 482–488.

Simon, H. A. (1988). Creativity and motivation: A response to Csikszentmihalyi. *New Ideas in Psychology, 6*(2), 177–181.

Simon, H. A. (1992). Alternative representations for cognition: Search and reasoning. In H. L. Pick, Jr., P. Van Den Broek, & D. C. Knill (Eds.), *Cognition: Conceptual and methodological issues*. Washington, DC: American Psychological Association.

Simon, H. A., & Gilmartin, K. (1973). A simulation of memory for chess positions. *Cognitive Psychology, 5,* 29–46.

Simon, H. A., & Reed, S. K. (1976). Modeling strategy shifts in a problem-solving task. *Cognitive Psychology, 8,* 86–97.

Simons, R. C., & Hughes, C. C. (1993). Culture-bound syndromes. In A. C. Gaw (Ed.), *Culture, ethnicity, and mental illness*. Washington, DC: American Psychiatric Press.

Simonton, D. K. (1990). Creativity and wisdom in aging. In J. E. Birren & K. W. Schaie (Eds.), *Handbook of the psychology of aging*. San Diego: Academic Press.

Simpson, J. A. (1990). Influence of attachment styles on romantic relationships. *Journal of Personality and Social Psychology, 59,* 971–980.

Simpson, J. A., Campbell, B., & Berscheid, E. (1986). The association between romantic love and marriage: Kephart (1967) twice revisited. *Personality and Social Psychology Bulletin, 12,* 363–372.

Simpson, J. A., Rholes, W. S., & Phillips, D. (1996). Conflict in close relationships: An attachment perspective. *Journal of Personality and Social Psychology, 71,* 899–914.

Simpson, J. L. (1991). Fetal wastage. In S. G. Gabbe, J. R. Niebyl, & J. L. Simpson (Eds.), *Obstetrics: Normal and problem pregnancies*. New York: Churchill Livingstone.

Sinclair, D. (1981). *Mechanisms of cutaneous stimulation*. Oxford, England: Oxford University Press.

Sinclair, R. C., Hoffman, C., Mark, M. M., Martin, L. L., & Pickering, T. L. (1994). Construct accessibility and the misattribution of arousal: Schachter and Singer revisited. *Psychological Science, 5,* 15–19.

Singer, J. L., & Kolligian, J., Jr. (1987). Personality: Developments in the study of private experience. *Annual Review of Psychology, 38,* 533–574.

Singer, M. T., Wynne, L. C., & Toohey, M. L. (1978). Communication disorders and the families of schizophrenics. In L. C. Wynne, R. L. Cromwell, & S. Matthysse (Eds.), *The nature of schizophrenia: New approaches to research and treatment*. New York: Wiley Medical.

Sinha, D. (1983). Human assessment in the Indian context. In S. H. Irvine & J. W. Berry (Eds.), *Human assessment and cultural factors*. New York: Plenum.

Skinner, B. F. (1938). *The behavior of organisms.* New York: Appleton-Century-Crofts.

Skinner, B. F. (1948). Superstition in the pigeon. *Journal of Experimental Psychology, 38,* 168–172.

Skinner, B. F. (1953). *Science and human behavior.* New York: Macmillan.

Skinner, B. F. (1957). *Verbal behavior.* New York: Appleton-Century-Crofts.

Skinner, B. F. (1967). Autobiography. In E. G. Boring & G. Lindzey (Eds.), *A history of psychology in autobiography* (Vol. 5). New York: Appleton-Century-Crofts.

Skinner, B. F. (1969). *Contingencies of reinforcement.* New York: Appleton-Century-Crofts.

Skinner, B. F. (1971). *Beyond freedom and dignity.* New York: Knopf.

Skinner, B. F. (1974). *About behaviorism.* New York: Knopf.

Skinner, B. F. (1984). Selection by consequences. *Behavioral and Brain Sciences, 7*(4), 477–510.

Skinner, B. F., Solomon, H. C., & Lindsley, O. R. (1953). *Studies in behavior therapy: Status report I.* Waltham, MA: Unpublished report, Metropolitan State Hospital.

Skodak, M., & Skeels, H. M. (1947). A follow-up study of one hundred adopted children in Iowa. *American Psychologist, 2,* 278.

Slamecka, N. J. (1985). Ebbinghaus: Some associations. *Journal of Experimental Psychology: Learning, Memory and Cognition, 11,* 414–435.

Slamecka, N. J. (1992). Forgetting. In L. R. Squire (Ed.), *Encyclopedia of learning and memory*. New York: Macmillan.

Slater, E., & Shields, J. (1969). Genetical aspects of anxiety. In M. H. Lader (Ed.), *Studies of anxiety*. Ashford, England: Headley Brothers.

Slaughter, M. (1990). The vertebrate retina. In K. N. Leibovic (Ed.), *Science of vision*. New York: Springer-Verlag.

Slavney, P. R. (1990). *Perspectives on hysteria.* Baltimore: Johns Hopkins University Press.

Sledge, W. H., Tebes, J., Rakfeldt, J., Davidson, L., Lyons, L., & Druss, B. (1996). Day hospital/crisis respite care versus inpatient care, part I: Clinical outcomes. *American Journal of Psychiatry, 153,* 1065–1073.

Sloane, K. D., & Sosniak, L. A. (1985). The development of accomplished sculptors. In B. S. Bloom (Ed.), *Developing talent in young people*. New York: Ballantine.

Slobin, D. I. (1985). *A cross linguistic study of language acquisition.* Hillsdale, NJ: Erlbaum.

Slobin, D. I. (1992). *The crosslinguistic study of language acquisition.* Hillsdale, NJ: Erlbaum.

Slovic, P. (1990). Choice. In D. N. Osherson & E. E. Smith (Eds.), *Thinking: An invitation to cognitive science* (Vol. 3). Cambridge, MA: MIT Press.

Slovic, P., Fischhoff, B., & Lichtenstein, S. (1982). Facts versus fears: Understanding perceived risk. In D. Kahneman, P. Slovic, & A. Tversky (Eds.), *Judgment under uncertainty: Heuristics and biases*. Cambridge, England: Cambridge University Press.

Slovic, P., Lichtenstein, S., & Fischhoff, B. (1988). Decision making. In R. C. Atkinson, R. J. Herrnstein, G. Lindzey, & R. D. Luce (Eds.), *Stevens' handbook of experimental psychology* (Vol. 2). New York: Wiley.

Small, I. F., Small, J. G., & Milstein, V. (1986). Electroconvulsive therapy. In P. A. Berger & H. K. H. Brodie (Eds.), *American handbook of psychiatry: Biological psychiatry* (2nd ed., Vol. 8). New York: Basic Books.

Smart, R. (1965). Social-group membership, leadership and birth order. *Journal of Social Psychology, 67,* 221–225.

Smeaton, G., Byrne, D., & Murnen, S. K. (1989). The repulsion hypothesis revisited: Similarity irrelevance or dissimilarity bias. *Journal of Personality and Social Psychology, 56,* 54–59.

Smetana, J. G., Yau, J., Restrepo, A., & Braeges, J. L. (1991). Conflict and adaptation in adolescence: Adolescent-parent conflict. In M. E. Colten & S. Gore (Eds.), *Adolescent stress: Causes and consequences*. New York: Aldine de Gruyter.

Smilkstein, G. (1990). Psychosocial influences on health. In R. E. Rakel (Ed.), *Textbook of family practice*. Philadelphia: Saunders.

Smith, A. L., & Weissman, M. M. (1992). Epidemiology. In E. S. Paykel (Ed.), *Handbook of affective disorders* (2nd ed.). New York: Guilford Press.

Smith, C. A., & Lazarus, R. S. (1993). Appraisal components, core relational themes, and the emotions. *Cognition and Emotion, 7,* 233–269.

Smith, C. P. (1983). Ethical issues: Research on deception, informed consent, and debriefing. In L. Wheeler & P. Shaver (Eds.), *Review of personality and social psychology* (Vol. 4). Beverly Hill, CA: Sage.

Smith, C. P. (1992). Reliability issues. In C. P. Smith (Ed.), *Motivation and personality: Handbook of thematic content analysis*. New York: Cambridge University Press.

Smith, D. (1982). Trends in counseling and psychotherapy. *American Psychologist, 37,* 802–809.

Smith, G. H., & Engel, R. (1968). Influence of a female model on perceived characteristics of an automobile. *Proceedings of the 76th Annual Convention of the American Psychological Association, 3,* 681–682.

Smith, G. P., & Gibbs, J. (1992). The development and proof of the cholecystokinin hypothesis of satiety. In C. T. Dourish, S. J. Cooper, S. D. Iversen, & L. L. Iversen (Eds.), *Multiple cholecystokinin receptors in the CNS*. Oxford, England: Oxford University Press.

Smith, J. C. (1975). Meditation and psychotherapy: A review of the literature. *Psychological Bulletin, 32,* 553–564.

Smith, J. C. (1993). *Understanding stress and coping.* New York: Macmillan.

Smith, L. W., Patterson, T. L., & Grant, I. (1992). Work, retirement, and activity: Coping challenges for the elderly. In V. B. Van Hasselt & M. Hersen (Eds.), *Handbook of social development: A lifespan perspective*. New York: Plenum.

Smith, M., & Pazder, L. (1980). *Michelle remembers*. New York: Pocket Books.

Smith, M. L., & Glass, G. V. (1977). Meta-analysis of psychotherapy outcome studies. *American Psychologist, 32*, 752–760.

Smith, P. B., & Bond, M. H. (1994). *Social psychology across cultures: Analysis and perspectives*. Boston: Allyn & Bacon.

Smith, S. (1988). Environmental context-dependent memory. In G. M. Davies & D. M. Thomson (Eds.), *Memory in context: Context in memory*. New York: Wiley.

Smith, T. W. (1991). *Ethnic images. GSS Topical Report No. 19*. Chicago: National Opinion Research Center.

Smith, T. W., & Brown, P. C. (1991). Cynical hostility, attempts to exert social control, and cardiovascular reactivity in married couples. *Journal of Behavioral Medicine, 14*(6), 581–592.

Smith, T. W., & Christensen, A. J. (1992). Hostility, health, and social contexts. In H. S. Friedman (Ed.), *Hostility coping and health*. Washington, DC: American Psychological Association.

Smith, T. W., Pope, M. K., Sanders, J. D., Allred, K. D., & O'Keefe, J. L. (1988). Cynical hostility at home and work: Psychosocial vulnerability across domains. *Journal of Research in Personality, 22*, 525–548.

Smith, T. W., Turner, C. W., Ford, M. H., Hunt, S. C., Barlow, G. K., Stults, B. M., & Williams, R. R. (1987). Blood pressure reactivity in adult male twins. *Health Psychology, 6*, 209–220.

Smuts, B. B. (1992). Male aggression against women: An evolutionary perspective. *Human Nature, 3*, 1–44.

Snarey, J. R., & Keljo, K. (1991). In a gemeinschaft voice: The cross-cultural expansion of moral development theory. In W. M. Kurtines & J. L. Gewirtz (Eds.), *Handbook of moral behavior and development* (Vol. 1). Hillsdale, NJ: Erlbaum.

Snow, C. E. (1993). Bilingualism and second language acquisition. In J. B. Gleason & N. B. Ratner (Eds.), *Psycholinguistics*. Fort Worth: Harcourt Brace Jovanovich.

Snow, R. E. (1986). Individual differences in the design of educational programs. *American Psychologist, 41*, 1029–1039.

Snyder, A. (1989). *Relationship excellence: Right brain relationship skills for left brain personalities*. Seattle: Gresham Publishing.

Snyder, M. (1979). Self-monitoring processes. In L. Berkowitz (Ed.), *Advances in experimental social psychology* (Vol. 12). New York: Academic Press.

Snyder, M. (1987). *Public appearances/Private realities: The psychology of self-monitoring*. New York: W. H. Freeman.

Snyder, M., & Simpson, J. A. (1984). Self-monitoring and dating relationships. *Journal of Personality and Social Psychology, 47*, 1281–1291.

Snyder, M., Simpson, J. A., & Gangestad, S. (1986). Personality and sexual relations. *Journal of Personality and Social Psychology, 51*, 181–190.

Snyder, S. H. (1980). Brain peptides as neurotransmitters. *Science, 209*, 976–983.

Snyder, S. H. (1986). *Drugs and the brain*. New York: Scientific American Books.

Snyder, T., & Gackenbach, J. (1988). Individual differences associated with lucid dreaming. In J. Gackenbach & S. LaBerge (Eds.), *Conscious mind, sleeping brain: Perspectives on lucid dreaming*. New York: Plenum.

Snyderman, M., & Rothman, S. (1987). Survey of expert opinion on intelligence and aptitude testing. *American Psychologist, 42*, 137–144.

Sobin, C., Sackeim, H. A., Prudic, J., Devanand, D. P., Moody, B. J., & McElhiney, M. C. (1995). Predictors of retrograde amnesia following ECT. *American Journal of Psychiatry, 152*, 995–1001.

Sommer, B. (1987). *Not another diet book: A right-brain program for successful weight management*. Alameda, CA: Hunter House.

Sotiriou, P. E. (1993). *Integrating college study skills: Reasoning in reading, listening and writing*. Belmont, CA: Wadsworth.

Spangler, W. D. (1992). Validity of questionnaire and TAT measures of need for achievement: Two meta-analyses. *Psychological Bulletin, 112*, 140–154.

Spanos, N. P. (1986). Hypnotic behavior: A social-psychological interpretation of amnesia, analgesia, and "trance logic." *Behavioral & Brain Sciences, 9*(3), 449–467.

Spanos, N. P. (1994). Multiple identity enactments and multiple personality disorder: A sociocognitive perspective. *Psychological Bulletin, 116*, 143–165.

Spanos, N. P. (1996). *Multiple identities and false memories*. Washington, DC: American Psychological Association.

Spanos, N. P., & Coe, W. C. (1992). A social-psychological approach to hypnosis. In E. Fromm & M. R. Nash (Eds.), *Contemporary hypnosis research*. New York: Guilford Press.

Spanos, N. P., Weekes, J. R., & Bertrand, L. D. (1985). Multiple personality: A social psychological perspective. *Journal of Abnormal Psychology, 94*, 362–376.

Sparks, D. L. (1988). Neural cartography: Sensory and motor maps in the superior colliculus. *Brain, Behavior and Evolution, 31*, 49–56.

Spearman, C. (1904). "General intelligence" objectively determined and measured. *American Journal of Psychology, 15*, 201–293.

Spearman, C. (1923). *The nature of "intelligence" and the principles of cognition*. London: Macmillan.

Spence, M. J., & DeCasper, A. J. (1987). Prenatal experience with low-frequency maternal-voice sound influence neonatal perception of maternal voice samples. *Infant Behavior and Development, 10*, 133–142.

Spencer, S. J., & Steele, C. M. (1992). *The effects of stereotype vulnerability on women's math performance*. Paper presented at the American Psychological Association convention, Washington, DC.

Sperling, G. (1960). The information available in brief visual presentations. *Psychological Monographs, 74*(11, Whole No. 498).

Sperry, R. W. (1982). Some effects of disconnecting the cerebral hemispheres. *Science, 217*, 1223–1226, 1250.

Spiegel, D. (1994). Dissociative disorders. In R. E. Hales, S. C. Yudofsky, & J. A. Talbott (Eds.), *The American Psychiatric Press textbook of psychiatry* (2nd ed.). Washington, DC: American Psychiatric Press.

Spiegel, D., Cutcomb, S., Ren, C., & Pribram, K. (1985). Hypnotic hallucination alters evoked potentials. *Journal of Abnormal Psychology, 94*, 249–255.

Spiegel, D., & Spiegel, H. (1985). Hypnosis. In H. I. Kaplan & B. J. Sadock (Eds.), *Comprehensive textbook of psychiatry/IV*. Baltimore: Williams & Wilkins.

Spiegler, M. D., & Guevremont, D. C. (1993). *Contemporary behavior therapy*. Pacific Grove, CA: Brooks/Cole.

Spielberger, C. D. (1990). Report of the treasurer: 1989: The 1980s: A roller coaster decade for APA finances. *American Psychologist, 45*, 807–812.

Spielberger, C. D., & Sydeman, S. J. (1994). Anxiety. In R. J. Sternberg (Ed.), *Encyclopedia of human intelligence*. New York: Macmillan.

Spielman, A., & Herrera, C. (1991). Sleep disorders. In S. J. Ellman & J. S. Antrobus (Eds.), *The mind in sleep: Psychology and psychophysiology* (2nd ed.). New York: Wiley.

Spitzer, R. L. (1975). On pseudoscience in science, logic in remission and psychiatric diagnosis: A critique of Rosenhan's "On being sane in insane places." *Journal of Abnormal Psychology, 84*, 442–452.

Sporakowski, M. J. (1988). A therapist's views on the consequences of change for the contemporary family. *Family Relations, 37*, 373–378.

Sprecher, S., & Duck, S. (1994). Sweet talk: The importance of perceived communication for romantic and friendship attraction experienced during a get-acquainted date. *Personality and Social Psychology Bulletin, 20*, 391–400.

Spring, B. (1989). Stress and schizophrenia: Some definitional issues. In T. W. Miller (Ed.), *Stressful life events*. Madison, CT: International Universities Press.

Springer, K., & Berry, D. S. (1997). Rethinking the role of evolution in the ecological model of social perception. In J. A. Simpson & D. T. Kenrick (Eds.), *Evolutionary psychology*. Mahwah, NJ: Erlbaum.

Springer, S. P., & Deutsch, G. (1989). *Left brain, right brain* (3rd ed.). New York: W. H. Freeman.

Springer, S. P., & Deutsch, G. (1993). *Left brain, right brain* (4th ed.). New York: W. H. Freeman.

Squire, L. R. (1987). *Memory and brain*. New York: Oxford University Press.

Squire, L. R. (1994). Declarative and nondeclarative memory: Multiple brain systems supporting learning and memory. In D. L. Schacter & E. Tulving (Eds.), *Memory systems*. Cambridge, MA: MIT Press.

Squire, L. R., Knowlton, B., & Musen, G. (1993). The structure and organization of memory. *Annual Review of Psychology, 44*, 453–495.

Staats, A. W., & Staats, C. K. (1963). *Complex human behavior*. New York: Holt, Rinehart & Winston.

Stack, D. M., & Muir, D. W. (1992). Adult tactile stimulation during face-to-face interactions modulates five-month-olds' affect and attention. *Child Development, 63*, 1509–1525.

Stacy, A. W., Newcomb, M. D., & Bentler, P. M. (1993). Cognitive motivations and sensation seeking as long-term predictors of drinking problems. *Journal of Social and Clinical Psychology, 12*, 1–24.

Stalling, R. B. (1992). Mood and pain: The influence of positive and negative affect on reported body aches. *Journal of Social Behavior and Personality, 7*(2), 323–334.

Stampi, C. (1989). Ultrashort sleep/wake patterns and sustained performance. In D. F. Dinges & R. J. Broughton (Eds.), *Sleep and alertness: Chronobiological, behavioral, and medical aspects of napping*. New York: Raven.

Stanislaw, H., & Rice, F. J. (1988). Correlation between sexual desire and menstrual cycle characteristics. *Archives of Sexual Behavior, 17*(6), 499–508.

Stanley, B. G., Kyrkouli, S. E., Lampert, S., & Leibowitz, S. F. (1986). Neuropeptide Y chronically injected into the hypothalamus: A powerful neurochemical inducer of hyperphagia and obesity. *Peptides, 7*, 1189–1192.

Stasser, G. (1991). Pooling of unshared information during group discussion. In S. Worchel, W. Wood, & J. Simpson (Eds.), *Group process and productivity*. Beverly Hills, CA: Sage.

Stattin, H., & Magnusson, D. (1990). *Pubertal maturation in female development*. Hillsdale, NJ: Erlbaum.

Steele, C. M. (1988). The psychology of self-affirmation: Sustaining the integrity of the self. In L. Berkowitz (Ed.), *Advances in experimental social psychology* (Vol. 21). New York: Academic Press.

Steele, C. M. (1992, April). Race and the schooling of black Americans. *The Atlantic Monthly*, pp. 68–78.

Steele, C. M., & Aronson, J. (1992). *Effects of stereotype vulnerability on black Americans' test performance*. Unpublished manuscript in preparation.

Steele, C. M., & Aronson, J. (1995). Stereotype threat and the intellectual test performance of African Americans. *Journal of Personality and Social Psychology, 69*, 797–811.

Stein, B. E., & Meredith, M. A. (1993). *Vision, touch, and audition: Making sense of it all*. Cambridge, MA: MIT Press.

Stein, M. B., & Uhde, T. W. (1995). Biology of anxiety disorders. In A. F. Schatzberg & C. B. Nemeroff (Eds.), *The American Psychiatric Press textbook of psychopharmacology*. Washington, DC: American Psychiatric Press.

Stein, P. J. (1989). The diverse world of single adults. In J. M. Henslin (Ed.), *Marriage and family in a changing society* (3rd ed.). New York: Free Press.

Steinberg, L., & Silverberg, S. B. (1987). Influences on marital satisfaction during the middle stages of the family life cycle. *Journal of Marriage and the Family, 49*, 751–760.

Steinberg, L., Dornbusch, S. M., & Brown, B. B. (1992). Ethnic differences in adolescent achievement. *American Psychologist, 47*, 723–729.

Steinmetz, H., Staiger, J. F., Schluag, G., Huang, Y., & Jancke, L. (1995). Corpus callosum and brain volume in women and men. *Neuroreport, 6*, 1002–1004.

Stekel, W. (1950). *Techniques of analytical psychotherapy*. New York: Liveright.

Stellar, E. (1954). The physiology of motivation. *Psychological Review, 61*, 5–22.

Stemberger, R. T., Turner, S. M., Beidel, D. C., & Calhoun, K. S. (1995). Social phobia: An analysis of possible developmental factors. *Journal of Abnormal Psychology, 104*, 526–531.

Stephan, W. G. (1989). A cognitive approach to stereotyping. In D. Bar-Tal, C. F. Graumann, A. W. Kruglanski, & W. Stroebe (Eds.), *Stereotyping and prejudice: Changing conceptions*. New York: Springer-Verlag.

Steriade, M., Ropert, N., Kitsikis, A., & Oakson, G. (1980). Ascending activating neuronal networks in midbrain reticular core and related rostral systems. In S. A. Hobson & A. M. Brazier (Eds.), *The reticular formation revisited: Specifying function for a nonspecific system*. New York: Raven.

Stern, W. (1914). *The psychological method of testing intelligence*. Baltimore: Warwick & York.

Sternberg, R. J. (1984). Toward a triarchic theory of intelligence. *Behavioral and Brain Sciences, 7*, 269–315.

Sternberg, R. J. (1985). *Beyond IQ: A triarchic theory of human intelligence*. New York: Cambridge University Press.

Sternberg, R. J. (1986). *Intelligence applied: Understanding and increasing your intellectual skills*. New York: Harcourt Brace Jovanovich.

Sternberg, R. J. (1988a). A three-facet model of creativity. In R. J. Sternberg (Ed.), *The nature of creativity: Contemporary psychological perspectives*. Cambridge, England: Cambridge University Press.

Sternberg, R. J. (1988b). *The triarchic mind: A new theory of human intelligence*. New York: Viking Press.

Sternberg, R. J. (1988c). Triangulating love. In R. J. Sternberg & M. L. Barnes (Eds.), *The psychology of love*. New Haven, CT: Yale University Press.

Sternberg, R. J. (1991). Theory-based testing of intellectual abilities: Rationale for the triarchic abilities test. In H. A. H. Rowe (Ed.), *Intelligence: Reconceptualization and measurement*. Hillsdale, NJ: Erlbaum.

Sternberg, R. J. (1995). For whom the bell curve tolls: A review of *The Bell Curve*. *Psychological Science, 6*, 257–261.

Sternberg, R. J., & Lubart, T. I. (1992). Buy low and sell high: An investment approach to creativity. *Current Directions in Psychological Science, 1*(1), 1–5.

Sternberg, R. J., & Wagner, R. K. (1993). The g-ocentric view of intelligence and job performance is wrong. *Current Directions in Psychological Science, 2*(1), 1–5.

Sternberg, R. J., Conway, B. E., Ketron, J. L., & Bernstein, M. (1981). People's conceptions of intelligence. *Journal of Personality and Social Psychology, 41*, 37–55.

Sternberg, R. J., Wagner, R. K., Williams, W. M., & Horvath, J. A. (1995). Testing common sense. *American Psychologist, 50*, 912–927.

Stevens, J. C. (1991). Thermal sensibility. In M. A. Heller & W. Schiff (Eds.), *The psychology of touch*. Hillsdale, NJ: Erlbaum.

Stevens, S. S. (1955). The measurement of loudness. *Journal of the Acoustical Society of America, 27*, 815–819.

Stevens, S. S. (1957). On the psychophysical law. *Psychological Review, 64*, 153–181.

Stevens, S. S. (1975). *Psychophysics: Introduction to its perceptual, neural, and social prospects*. New York: Wiley.

Stevenson, J. M. (1988). Suicide. In J. A. Talbott, R. E. Hales, & S. C. Yudofsky (Eds.), *The American Psychiatric Press textbook of psychiatry*. Washington, DC: American Psychiatric Press.

Stich, S. P. (1990). Rationality. In D. N. Osherson & E. E. Smith (Eds.), *Thinking: An invitation to cognitive science* (Vol. 3). Cambridge, MA: MIT Press.

Stifter, C. A., & Fox, N. A. (1990). Infant reactivity: Physiological correlates of newborn and 5-month temperament. *Developmental Psychology, 26*, 582–588.

Stoddard, G. (1943). *The meaning of intelligence*. New York: Macmillan.

Stoll, A. L., Tohen, M., & Baldessarini, R. J. (1992). Increasing frequency of the diagnosis of obsessive-compulsive disorder. *American Journal of Psychiatry, 149*, 638–640.

Stone, A. A., Bovbjerg, D. H., Neale, J. M., Napoli, A., Valdimarsdottir, H., Cox, D., Hayden, F. G., & Gwaltney, J. M. (1992). Development of the common cold symptoms following experimental rhinovirus infection is related to prior stressful events. *Behavioral Medicine, 18*, 115–120.

Stone, L. (1977). *The family, sex and marriage in England 1500–1800*. New York: Harper & Row.

Stoner, J. A. F. (1961). *A comparison of individual and group decisions involving risk*. Unpublished master's thesis, Massachusetts Institute of Technology.

Straus, M. A., & Gelles, R. J. (1986). Societal change and change in family violence from 1975 to 1985 as revealed in two national surveys. *Journal of Marriage and the Family, 48*, 465–479.

Streissguth, A. P., Barr, H. M., Sampson, P. D., Darby, B. L., & Martin, D. C. (1989). IQ at age 4 in relation to maternal alcohol use and smoking during pregnancy. *Developmental Psychology, 25*, 3–11.

Striegel-Moore, R., & Rodin, J. (1986). The influence of psychological variables in obesity. In K. D. Brownell & J. P. Foreyt (Eds.), *Handbook of eating disorders: Physiology, psychology, and treatment of obesity, anorexia and bulimia*. New York: Basic Books.

Strober, M. (1989). Stressful life events associated with bulimia in anorexia nervosa: Empirical findings and theoretical speculations. In T. W. Miller (Ed.), *Stressful life events*. Madison, CT: International Universities Press.

Strongman, K. T. (1978). *The psychology of emotion*. New York: Wiley.

Strupp, H. H. (1996). The tripartite model and the *Consumer Reports* study. *American Psychologist, 51*, 1017–1024.

Strupp, H. H., & Howard, K. I. (1992). A brief history of psychotherapy research. In D. K. Freedheim (Ed.), *History of psychotherapy: A century of change*. Washington, DC: American Psychological Association.

Stumpf, H. (1993). The factor structure of the Personality Research Form: A cross-national evaluation. *Journal of Personality, 61*, 27–48.

Stunkard, A. J., Harris, J. R., Pederson, N. L., & McClearn, G. E. (1990). The body-mass index of twins who have been reared apart. *New England Journal of Medicine, 322*, 1483–1487.

Stunkard, A. J., Sorensen, T., Hanis, C., Teasdale, T. W., Chakraborty, R., Schull, W. J., & Schulsinger, F. (1986). An adoption study of human obesity. *New England Journal of Medicine, 314*, 193–198.

Sturgis, E. T. (1993). Obsessive-compulsive disorders. In P. B. Sutker & H. E. Adams (Eds.), *Comprehensive handbook of psychopathology* (2nd ed.). New York: Plenum.

Suddath, R. L., Christison, G. W., Torrey, E. F., Casanova, M. F., & Weinberger, D. R. (1990). Anatomical abnormalities in the brains of monozygotic twins discordant for schizophrenia. *The New England Journal of Medicine, 322*(12), 789–794.

Sue, D. (1979). Erotic fantasies of college students during coitus. *Journal of Sex Research, 15*, 299–305.

Sue, S. (1991). Ethnicity and culture in psychological research and practice. In J. D. Goodchilds (Ed.), *Psychological perspectives on human diversity in America*. Washington, DC: American Psychological Association.

Sue, S., & Okazaki, S. (1990). Asian-American educational achievements: A phenomenon in search of an explanation. *American Psychologist, 45*, 913–920.

Sue, S., & Zane, N. (1987). The role of culture

and cultural techniques in psychotherapy: A critique and reformulation. *American Psychologist, 42,* 37–45.

Sue, S., Zane, N., & Young, K. (1994). Research on psychotherapy with culturally diverse populations. In A. E. Bergin & S. L. Garfield (Eds.), *Handbook of psychotherapy and behavior change* (4th ed.). New York: Wiley.

Suinn, R. M. (1984). *Fundamentals of abnormal psychology.* Chicago: Nelson-Hall.

Sulloway, F. J. (1991). Reassessing Freud's case histories: The social construction of psychoanalysis. *ISIS, 82,* 245–275.

Suls, J., & Marco, C. A. (1990). Relationship between JAS- and FTAS-Type A behavior and Non-CHD illness: A prospective study controlling for negative affectivity. *Health Psychology, 9,* 479–492.

Super, C. M. (1976). Environmental effects on motor development: A case of African infant precocity. *Developmental Medicine and Child Neurology, 18,* 561–567.

Super, D. E. (1957). *The psychology of careers.* New York: Harper & Row.

Super, D. E. (1985). Career and life development. In D. Brown & L. Brooks (Eds.), *Career choice and development.* San Francisco: Jossey-Bass.

Super, D. E. (1988). Vocational adjustment: Implementing a self-concept. *The Career Development Quarterly, 36,* 351–357.

Sussman, E. J., Nottlemann, E. D., Inhoff-Germain, G. E., Dorn, L. D., Cutler, G. B., Jr., Loriaux, D. L., & Chrousos, G. P. (1985). The relation of development and social-emotional behavior in young adolescents. *Journal of Youth and Adolescence, 14,* 245–264.

Sutker, P. B., & Allain, A. N. (1983). Behavior and personality assessment in men labeled adaptive sociopaths. *Journal of Behavioral Assessment, 5,* 65–79.

Sutker, P. B., Bugg, F., & West, J. A. (1993). Antisocial personality disorder. In P. B. Sutker & H. E. Adams (Eds.), *Comprehensive handbook of psychopathology* (2nd ed.). New York: Plenum.

Suzuki, L. A., & Gutkin, T. B. (1994). Asian Americans. In R. J. Sternberg (Ed.), *Encyclopedia of human intelligence.* New York: Macmillan.

Suzuki, L. A., & Vraniak, D. A. (1994). Ethnicity, race, and measured intelligence. In R. J. Sternberg (Ed.), *Encyclopedia of human intelligence.* New York: Macmillan.

Swaab, D. F., Gooren, L. J. G., & Hofman, M. A. (1992). The human hypothalamus in relation to gender and sexual orientation. *Progress in Brain Research, 93,* 205–219.

Swartz, C. M. (1993). Clinical and laboratory predictors of ECT response. In C. E. Coffey (Ed.), *The clinical science of electroconvulsive therapy.* Washington, DC: American Psychiatric Press.

Sweeney, P. D., Anderson, K., & Bailey, S. (1986). Attributional style in depression: A meta-analytic review. *Journal of Personality and Social Psychology, 50,* 974–991.

Swets, J. A., Tanner, W. P., & Birdsall, T. G. (1961). Decision processes in perception. *Psychological Review, 68,* 301–340.

Swim, J. K. (1994). Perceived versus meta-analytic effect sizes: An assessment of the accuracy of gender stereotypes. *Journal of Personality and Social Psychology, 66,* 21–36.

Swim, J. K., Aikin, K. J., Hall, W. S., & Hunter, B. A. (1995). Sexism and racism: Old-fashioned and modern prejudices. *Journal of Personality and Social Psychology, 68,* 199–214.

Swim, J. K., & Sanna, L. J. (1996). He's skilled, she's lucky: A meta-analysis of observers' attributions for women's and men's successes and failures. *Personality and Social Psychology Bulletin, 22,* 507–519.

Symons, D. (1979). *The evolution of human sexuality.* New York: Oxford University Press.

Szasz, T. (1974). *The myth of mental illness.* New York: Harper & Row.

Szasz, T. (1990). Law and psychiatry: The problems that will not go away. *The Journal of Mind and Behavior, 11(3/4),* 557–564.

Szymanski, L. S., & Crocker, A.C. (1989). Mental retardation. In H. I. Kaplan & B. J. Sadock (Eds.), *Comprehensive textbook of psychiatry/V.* Baltimore: Williams & Wilkins.

Szymanski, S., Lieberman, J. A., Alvir, J. M., Mayerhoff, D., Loebel, A., Geisler, S., Chakos, M., Koreen, A., Jody, D., Kane, J., Woerner, M., & Cooper, T. (1995). Gender differences in onset of illness, treatment response, course, and biologic indexes in first-episode schizophrenic patients. *American Journal of Psychiatry, 152,* 698–703.

Tabakoff, B., & Hoffman, P. L. (1992). Alcohol: Neurobiology. In J. H. Lowinson, P. Ruiz, & R. B. Millman (Eds.), *Substance abuse: A comprehensive textbook* (2nd ed.). Baltimore: Williams & Wilkins.

Takahashi, K. (1986). Examining the Strange Situation procedure with Japanese mothers and 12-month-old infants. *Developmental Psychology, 19,* 184–191.

Takahashi, K. (1990). Are the key assumptions of the "Strange Situation" procedure universal? *Human Development, 33,* 23–30.

Tan, D. T. Y., & Singh, R. (1995). Attitudes and attraction: A developmental study of the similarity-attraction and dissimilarity-repulsion hypotheses. *Personality and Social Psychology Bulletin, 21,* 975–986.

Tanford, S., & Penrod, S. (1984). Social influence model: A formal integration of research on majority and minority influence processes. *Psychological Bulletin, 95,* 189–225.

Tannenbaum, A. J. (1986). Giftedness: A psychosocial approach. In R. J. Sternberg & J. E. Davidson (Eds.), *Conceptions of giftedness.* Cambridge, England: Cambridge University Press.

Tanner, J. M. (1978). *Fetus into man: Physical growth from conception to maturity.* Cambridge, MA: Harvard University Press.

Tart, C. T. (1988). From spontaneous event to lucidity: A review of attempts to consciously control nocturnal dreaming. In J. Gackenbach & S. LaBerge (Eds.), *Conscious mind, sleeping brain: Perspectives on lucid dreaming.* New York: Plenum.

Tart, C. T. (1990). Toward the experimental control of dreaming: A review of the literature. In C. T. Tart (Ed.), *Altered states of consciousness* (3rd ed.). San Francisco: Harper.

Tavris, C. (1982). *Anger: the misunderstood emotion.* New York: Simon & Schuster.

Tavris, C. (1989). *Anger: The misunderstood emotion* (2nd ed.). New York: Simon & Schuster.

Tavris, C. (1992). *The mismeasure of woman.* New York: Simon & Schuster.

Tavris, C. (1993, Jan. 3). Beware the incest-survivor machine. *New York Times Book Review,* p. 1+.

Tavris, C. (1995). Diagnosis and the DSM: The illusion of science in psychiatry. *The General Psychologist, 31,* 72–76.

Taylor, C. B. (1995). Treatment of anxiety disorders. In A. F. Schatzberg & C. B. Nemeroff (Eds.), *The American Psychiatric Press textbook of psychopharmacology.* Washington, DC: American Psychiatric Press.

Taylor, F. W. (1911). *The principles of scientific management.* New York: Harper & Row.

Taylor, M., & Gelman, S. A. (1989). Incorporating new words into the lexicon: Preliminary evidence for language hierarchies in two-year-old children. *Child Development, 60,* 625–636.

Taylor, M. A. (1992). Are schizophrenia and affective disorder related? A selective literature review. *American Journal of Psychiatry, 149,* 22–32.

Taylor, S. E., & Brown, J. D. (1988). Illusion and well-being: A social psychological perspective on mental health. *Psychological Bulletin, 103,* 193–210.

Taylor, S. E., & Brown, J. D. (1994). Positive illusions and well-being revisited: Separating fact from fiction. *Psychological Bulletin, 116,* 21–27.

Tedlock, B. (1992). Zuni and Quiche dream sharing and interpreting. In B. Tedlock (Ed.), *Dreaming: Anthropological and psychological interpretations.* Santa Fe, NM: School of American Research Press.

Teitelbaum, P., & Epstein, A. (1962). The lateral hypothalamic syndrome: Recovery of feeding and drinking after lateral hypothalamic lesions. *Psychological Review, 69,* 74–90.

Tellegen, A. (1993). Folk concepts and psychological concepts of personality disorder. *Psychological Inquiry, 4,* 122–130.

Tellegen, A., Lykken, D. T., Bouchard, T. J., Jr., Wilcox, K. J., Segal, N. L., & Rich, S. (1988). Personality similarity in twins reared apart and together. *Journal of Personality and Social Psychology, 54,* 1031–1039.

Tempel, D. L., Leibowitz, K. J., & Leibowitz, S. F. (1988). Effects of PVN galanin on macronutrient selection. *Peptides, 9,* 309–314.

Terman, L. M. (1916). *The measurement of intelligence.* Boston: Houghton-Mifflin.

Terman, L. M. (1922). The great conspiracy. *New Republic, 33,* 116–120.

Terman, L. M. (1925). *Genetic studies of genius: Vol. 1. Mental and physical traits of a thousand gifted children.* Stanford, CA: Stanford University Press.

Terman, L. M., Baldwin, B. T., & Bronson, E. (1925). *Genetic studies of genius: I. Mental and physical traits of a thousand gifted children.* Stanford, CA: Stanford University Press.

Terman, L. M., & Merrill, M. A. (1937). *Measuring intelligence.* Boston: Houghton Mifflin.

Terman, L. M., & Merrill, M. A. (1960). *Stanford-Binet intelligence scale.* Boston: Houghton Mifflin.

Terman, L. M., & Merrill, M. A. (1973). *Stanford-Binet intelligence scale: 1972 norms edition.* Boston: Houghton-Mifflin.

Terman, L. M., & Oden, M. H. (1959). *Genetic studies of genius: Vol. 5. The gifted group at mid-life.* Stanford, CA: Stanford University Press.

Terr, L. (1994). *Unchained memories.* New York: Basic Books.

Terrace, H. S. (1986). *Nim: A chimpanzee who learned sign language.* New York: Columbia University Press.

Tesser, A., & Shaffer, D. R. (1990). Attitudes and attitude change. *Annual Review of Psychology, 41,* 479–523.

Tessier-Lavigne, M. (1991). Phototransduction and information processing in the retina. In E. R. Kandel, J. H. Schwartz, & T. M. Jessell (Eds.), *Principles of neural science* (3rd ed.). New York: Elsevier.

Testa, K. (1996). Church to pay $1 million in

false-memory case. *San Jose Mercury News*, 8A.

Tetlock, P. E., Peterson, R. S., McGuire, C., Chang, S., & Feld, P. (1992). Assessing political group dynamics: A test of the groupthink model. *Journal of Personality and Social Psychology, 63,* 403–425.

Teuber, M. (1974). Sources of ambiguity in the prints of Maurits C. Escher. *Scientific American, 231,* 90–104.

Teyler, T. J., & DiScenna, P. (1984). Long-term potentiation as a candidate mnemonic device. *Brain Research Reviews, 7,* 15–28.

Thase, M. E., & Howland, R. H. (1995). Biological processes in depression: An updated review and integration. In E. E. Beckham & W. R. Leber (Eds.), *Handbook of depression* (2nd ed.). New York: Guilford Press.

Thelen, E. (1995). Motor development: A new synthesis. *American Psychologist, 50, 79*–95.

Thibodeau, R., & Aronson, E. (1992). Taking a closer look: Reasserting the role of the self-concept in dissonance theory. *Personality and Social Psychology Bulletin, 18,* 591–602.

Thigpen, C. H., & Cleckley, H. M. (1984). On the incidence of multiple personality disorder: A brief communication. *International Journal of Clinical and Experimental Hypnosis, 32,* 63–66.

Thoma, S. J. (1986). Estimating gender differences in the comprehension and preference of moral issues. *Developmental Review, 6,* 165–180.

Thomas, A., & Chess, S. (1977). *Temperament and development.* New York: Brunner/Mazel.

Thomas, A., & Chess, S. (1989). Temperament and personality. In G. A. Kohnstamm, J. E. Bates, & M. K. Rothbart (Eds.), *Temperament in childhood.* New York: Wiley.

Thomas, A., Chess, S., & Birch, H. G. (1970). The origin of personality. *Scientific American, 223*(2), 102–109.

Thomas, D. R. (1992). Discrimination and generalization. In L. R. Squire (Ed.), *Encyclopedia of learning and memory.* New York: Macmillan.

Thomas, J. C. (1974). An analysis of behavior in the hobbits-orcs problem. *Cognitive Psychology, 6,* 257–269.

Thomason, B. T., Brantkey, P. J., Jones, G. N., Dyer, H. R., & Morris, J. L. (1992). The relation between stress and disease activity in rheumatoid arthritis. *Journal of Behavioral Medicine, 15,* 215–220.

Thompson, A. P. (1983). Extramarital sex: A review of the research literature. *Journal of Sex Research, 19*(1), 1–22.

Thompson, D. A., & Campbell, R. G. (1977). Hunger in humans induced by 2-deoxy-D-glucose: Glucoprivic control of taste preference and food intake. *Science, 198,* 1065–1068.

Thompson, R. F. (1989). A model system approach to memory. In P. R. Solomon, G. R. Goethals, C. M. Kelley, & B. R. Stephens (Eds.), *Memory: Interdisciplinary approaches.* New York: Springer-Verlag.

Thompson, R. F. (1992). Memory. *Current Opinion in Neurobiology, 2,* 203–208.

Thorndike, E. L. (1913). *Educational psychology: The psychology of learning* (Vol. 2). New York: Teachers College.

Thorndike, R. L., Hagen, E. P., & Sattler, J. M. (1986). *The Stanford-Binet intelligence scale: Fourth edition technical manual.* Chicago: Riverside Publishing Company.

Thorndyke, P. W., & Hayes-Roth, B. (1979). The use of schemata in the acquisition and transfer of knowledge. *Cognitive Psychology, 11,* 83–106.

Thornton, B. (1984). Defensive attribution of responsibility: Evidence for an arousal-based motivational bias. *Journal of Personality and Social Psychology, 46,* 721–734.

Thornton, B. (1992). Repression and its mediating influence on the defensive attribution of responsibility. *Journal of Research in Personality, 26,* 44–57.

Thurstone, L. L. (1938). *Primary mental abilities* (Psychometric Monographs No. 1). Chicago: University of Chicago Press.

Thurstone, L. L. (1955). *The differential growth of mental abilities* (Psychometric Laboratory Rep. No. 14). Chapel Hill: University of North Carolina.

Todd, J. T., & Morris, E. K. (1992). Case histories in the great power of steady misrepresentation. *American Psychologist, 47,* 1441–1453.

Tohen, M., & Goodwin, F. K. (1995). Epidemiology of bipolar disorder. In M. T. Tsuang, M. Tohen, & G. E. P. Zahner (Eds.), *Textbook in psychiatric epidemiology.* New York: Wiley.

Tollefson, G. (1995). Selective serotonin reuptake inhibitors. In A. F. Schatzberg & C. B. Nemeroff (Eds.), *The American Psychiatric Press textbook of psychopharmacology.* Washington, DC: American Psychiatric Press.

Tolman, E. C. (1922). A new formula for behaviorism. *Psychological Review, 29,* 44–53.

Tolman, E. C. (1932). *Purposive behavior in animals and men.* New York: Appleton-Century-Crofts.

Tomkins, S. S. (1980). Affect as amplification: Some modifications in theory. In R. Plutchik & H. Kellerman (Eds.), *Emotion: Theory, research and experience* (Vol. 1). New York: Academic Press.

Tomkins, S. S. (1991). *Affect, imagery, consciousness: 3. Anger and fear.* New York: Springer-Verlag.

Tooby, J., & Cosmides, L. (1989). Evolutionary psychology and the generation of culture: Part 1. Theoretical considerations. *Ethology and Sociobiology, 10,* 29–49.

Tooby, J., & Cosmides, L. (1990). On the universality of human nature and the uniqueness of the individual: The role of genetics and adaptation. *Journal of Personality, 58,* 17–68.

Torgersen, S. (1979). The nature and origin of common phobic fears. *British Journal of Psychiatry, 119,* 343–351.

Torgersen, S. (1983). Genetic factors in anxiety disorders. *Archives of General Psychiatry, 40,* 1085–1089.

Torrey, E. F. (1996). *Out of the shadows.* New York: Wiley.

Torsvall, L., Akerstedt, T., Gillander, K., & Knutsson, A. (1989). Sleep on the night shift: 24-hour EEG monitoring of spontaneous sleep/walk behavior. *Psychophysiology, 26*(3), 352–358.

Toufexis, A. (1990, December 17). Drowsy America. *Time,* pp. 78–85.

Toufexis, A. (1991, October 28). When can memories be trusted? *Time,* pp. 86–88.

Treisman, A. M. (1986). Features and objects in visual processing. *Scientific American, 255,* 114–125.

Triandis, H. C. (1989). Self and social behavior in differing cultural contexts. *Psychological Review, 96,* 269–289.

Triandis, H. C. (1994). *Culture and social behavior.* New York: McGraw-Hill.

Trivers, R. L. (1972). Parental investment and sexual selection. In B. Campbell (Ed.), *Sexual selection and the descent of man.* Chicago: Aldine.

Trope, Y., & Liberman, A. (1993). The use of trait conceptions to identify other people's behavior and to draw inferences about their personalities. *Personality and Social Psychology Bulletin, 19,* 553–562.

Trull, T. J., & McCrae, R. R. (1994). A five-factor perspective on personality disorder research. In P. T. Costa, Jr., & T. A. Widiger (Eds.), *Personality disorders and the five-factor model of personality.* Washington, DC: American Psychological Association.

Tseng, W. S., Di, X., Ebata, K., Hsu, J., & Yuhua, C. (1986). Diagnostic pattern for neuroses in China, Japan, and the United States. *American Journal of Psychiatry, 43,* 1010–1014.

Tulving, E. (1985). How many memory systems are there? *American Psychologist, 40,* 385–398.

Tulving, E. (1986). What kind of a hypothesis is the distinction between episodic and semantic memory? *Journal of Experimental Psychology: Learning, Memory and Cognition, 12,* 307–311.

Tulving, E. (1987). Multiple memory systems and consciousness. *Human Neurobiology, 6*(2), 67–80.

Tulving, E. (1993). What is episodic memory? *Current Directions in Psychological Science, 2*(3), 67–70.

Tulving, E., & Psotka, J. (1971). Retroactive inhibition in free recall: Inaccessability of information available in the memory store. *Journal of Experimental Psychology, 87,* 1–8.

Tulving, E., & Schacter, D. L. (1990). Priming and human memory systems. *Science, 247,* 301–306.

Tulving, E., & Thomson, D. M. (1973). Encoding specificity and retrieval processes in episodic memory. *Psychological Review, 80,* 352–373.

Turk, D. C. (1994). Perspectives on chronic pain: The role of psychological factors. *Current Directions in Psychological Science, 3,* 45–48.

Turkheimer, E. (1991). Individual and group differences in adoption studies of IQ. *Psychological Bulletin, 110,* 392–405.

Turkheimer, E. (1994). Socioeconomic status and intelligence. In R. J. Sternberg (Ed.), *Encyclopedia of human intelligence.* New York: Macmillan.

Turkkan, J. S. (1989). Classical conditioning: The new hegemony. *Behavioral and Brain Sciences, 12,* 121–179.

Turnbull, W. W. (1979). Intelligence testing in the year 2000. In R. J. Sternberg & D. K. Detterman (Eds.), *Human intelligence: Perspectives on its theory and measurement.* Norwood, NJ: Ablex.

Turner, J. R., & Wheaton, B. (1995). Checklist measurement of stressful life events. In S. Cohen, R. C. Kessler, & L. U. Gordon (Eds.), *Measuring stress: A guide for health and social scientists.* New York: Oxford University Press.

Turner, M. E., Pratkanis, A. R., Probasco, P., & Leve, C. (1992). Threat, cohesion, and group effectiveness: Testing a social identity maintenance perspective on groupthink. *Journal of Personality and Social Psychology, 63,* 781–796.

Turner, P. J. (1991). Relations between attachment, gender, and behavior with peers in preschool. *Child Development, 62,* 1475–1488.

Turner, P. J., & Gervai, J. (1995). A multidimensional study of gender typing in preschool children and their parents: Personality, attitudes, preferences, behavior, and cultural differences. *Developmental Psychology, 31,* 759–772.

Turner, S. M., McCann, B. S., Beidel, D. C., & Mezzich, J. E. (1986). DSM-III classification of the anxiety disorders: A psychometric study. *Journal of Abnormal Psychology, 95,* 168–172.

Tversky, A. (1972). Elimination by aspects: A theory of choice. *Psychological Review, 79,* 281–299.

Tversky, A., & Kahneman, D. (1971). Belief in the law of small numbers. *Psychological Bulletin, 76,* 105–110.

Tversky, A., & Kahneman, D. (1973). Availability: A heuristic for judging frequency and probability. *Cognitive Psychology, 5,* 207–232.

Tversky, A., & Kahneman, D. (1974). Judgments under uncertainty: Heuristics and biases. *Science, 185,* 1124–1131.

Tversky, A., & Kahneman, D. (1982). Judgment under uncertainty: Heuristics and biases. In D. Kahneman, P. Slovic, & A. Tversky (Eds.), *Judgment under uncertainty: Heuristics and biases.* New York: Cambridge University Press.

Tversky, A., & Kahneman, D. (1983). Extensional versus intuitive reasoning: The conjunction fallacy in probability judgment. *Psychological Review, 90,* 283–315.

Tversky, A., & Kahneman, D. (1988). Rational choice and the framing of decisions. In D. E. Bell, H. Raiffa, & A. Tversky (Eds.), *Decision making: Descriptive, normative, and prescriptive interactions.* New York: Cambridge University Press.

Tversky, A., & Kahneman, D. (1991). Loss aversion in riskless choice: A reference-dependent model. *Quarterly Journal of Economics, 106*(4), 1039–1061.

Tversky, A., & Shafir, E. (1992). Choice under conflict: The dynamics of deferred decision. *Psychological Science, 3,* 358–361.

Uchino, B. N., Cacioppo, J. T., & Kiecolt-Glaser, J. K. (1996). The relationship between social support and physiological processes: A review with emphasis on underlying mechanisms and implications for health. *Psychological Bulletin, 119,* 488–531.

Ulrich, R. E. (1991). Animal rights, animal wrongs and the question of balance. *Psychological Science, 2,* 197–201.

Underwood, B. J. (1961). Ten years of massed practice on distributed practice. *Psychological Review, 68,* 229–247.

Underwood, B. J. (1970). A breakdown of the total-time law in free-recall learning. *Journal of Verbal Learning and Verbal Behavior, 9,* 573–580.

Unger, R. K., & Crawford, M. (1992). *Women and gender: A feminist psychology.* New York: McGraw-Hill.

Unger, R. K., & Crawford, M. (1993). Commentary: Sex and gender—The troubled relationship between terms and concepts. *Psychological Science, 4,* 122–124.

Ungerleider, J. T., & Pechnick, R. (1992). Hallucinogens. In J. H. Lowinson, P. Ruiz, & R. B. Millman (Eds.), *Substance abuse: A comprehensive textbook* (2nd ed.). Baltimore: Williams & Wilkins.

Upshaw, H. S. (1969). The personal reference scale: An approach to social judgment. In L. Berkowitz (Ed.), *Advances in experimental social psychology* (Vol. 4). New York: Academic Press.

U.S. Department of Health and Human Services. (1989). *Reducing the health consequences of smoking: 25 years of progress.* Rockville, MD: U.S. Government Printing Office.

U.S. Department of Health and Human Services. (1990). *The health benefits of smoking cessation: A report of the surgeon general.* Washington, DC: U.S. Government Printing Office.

Vaillant, G. E. (1992). *Ego mechanisms of defense:*

A guide for clinicians and researchers. Washington, DC: American Psychiatric Press.

Vaillant, G. E. (1994). Ego mechanisms of defense and personality psychopathology. *Journal of Abnormal Psychology, 103,* 44–50.

Vaillant, G. E., & Vaillant, C. O. (1990). Determinants and consequences of creativity in a cohort of gifted women. *Psychology of Women Quarterly, 14,* 607–616.

Valenstein, E. S. (1973). *Brain control.* New York: Wiley.

Valleroy, L. A., Harris, J. R., & Way, P. O. (1990). The impact of HIV infection on child survival in the developing world. *AIDS, 4,* 667–672.

Vallone, R. P., Griffin, D. W., Lin, S., & Ross, L. (1990). Overconfident prediction of future actions and outcomes by self and others. *Journal of Personality and Social Psychology, 58,* 582–592.

Vance, E. B., & Wagner, N. N. (1976). Written descriptions of orgasm: A study of sex differences. *Archives of Sexual Behavior, 5,* 87–98.

Van de Castle, R. L. (1993). Content of dreams. In M. A. Carskadon (Ed.), *Encyclopedia of sleep and dreaming.* New York: Macmillan.

Van de Castle, R. L. (1994). *Our dreaming mind.* New York: Ballantine Books.

Vandenberg, S. G., & Vogler, G. P. (1985). Genetic determinants of intelligence. In B. B. Wolman (Ed.), *Handbook of intelligence: Theories, measurements, and applications.* New York: Wiley.

van den Boom, D. C. (1994). The influence of temperament and mothering on attachment and exploration: An experimental manipulation of sensitive responsiveness among lower-class mothers and irritable infants. *Child Development, 65,* 1457–1477.

VanderPlate, C., Aral, S. O., & Magder, L. (1988). The relationship among genital herpes simplex virus, stress, and social support. *Health Psychology, 7,* 159–168.

van der Post, L. (1975). *Jung and the story of our time.* New York: Vintage Books.

van der Velde, F. W., van der Pligt, J., & Hooykaas, C. (1994). Perceiving AIDS-related risk: Accuracy as a function of differences in actual risk. *Health Psychology, 13,* 25–33.

Vane, J. R., & Motta, R. W. (1990). Group intelligence tests. In G. Goldstein & M. Hersen (Eds.), *Handbook of psychological assessment.* New York: Pergamon Press.

Van Houten, R. (1983). Punishment: From the animal laboratory to the applied setting. In S. Axelrod & J. Apsche (Eds.), *The effects of punishment on human behavior.* New York: Academic Press.

VanItallie, T. B. (1979). Obesity: Adverse effects on health and longevity. *American Journal of Clinical Nutrition, 32,* 2727.

VanLehn, K. (1989). Problem solving and cognitive skill acquisition. In M. I. Posner (Ed.), *Foundations of cognitive science.* Cambridge, MA: MIT Press.

Vaughn, B. E., Hinde-Stevenson, J., Waters, E., Kotsaftis, A., Lefever, G. B., Shouldice, A., Trudel, M., & Belsky, J. (1992). Attachment security and temperament in infancy and early childhood: Some conceptual clarifications. *Developmental Psychology, 28,* 463–473.

Ventura, J., Nuechterlein, K. H., Lukoff, D., & Hardesty, J. P. (1989). A prospective study of stressful life events and schizophrenic relapse. *Journal of Abnormal Psychology, 98,* 407–411.

Vernon, P. A., & Mori, M. (1992). Intelligence,

reaction times, and peripheral nerve conduction velocity. *Intelligence, 16,* 273–288.

Vernon, P. E. (1982). *The abilities and achievements of Orientals in North America.* New York: Academic Press.

Vierck, C. (1978). Somatosensory system. In R. B. Masterson (Ed.), *Handbook of sensory neurobiology.* New York: Plenum.

Vinogradov, S., & Yalom, I. D. (1988). Group therapy. In J. A. Talbott, R. E. Hales, & S. C. Yudofsky (Eds.), *The American Psychiatric Press textbook of psychiatry.* Washington, DC: American Psychiatric Press.

Vinokur, A. D., & van Ryn, M. (1993). Social support and undermining in close relationships: Their independent effects on the mental health of unemployed persons. *Journal of Personality and Social Psychology, 65,* 350–359.

Viteles, M. (1932). *Industrial psychology.* New York: Norton.

Vogt, T., Mullooly, J., Ernst, D., Pope, C., & Hollis, J. (1992). Social networks as predictors of ischemic heart disease, cancer, stroke and hypertension: Incidence, survival and mortality. *Journal of Clinical Epidemiology, 45,* 659–666.

Vokey, J. R., & Read, J. D. (1985). Subliminal messages: Between the devil and the media. *American Psychologist, 40,* 1231–1239.

Voss, J. F., & Post, T. A. (1988). On the solving of ill-structured problems. In M. T. H. Chi, R. Glaser, & M. J. Farr (Eds.), *The nature of expertise.* Hillsdale, NJ: Erlbaum.

Voyer, D., Voyer, S., & Bryden, M. P. (1995). Magnitude of sex differences in spatial abilities: A meta-analysis and consideration of critical variables. *Psychological Bulletin, 117,* 250–270.

Wachtel, P. L. (1977). *Psychoanalysis and behavior therapy: Toward an integration.* New York: Basic Books.

Wachtel, P. L. (1991). From eclectism to synthesis: Toward a more seamless psychotherapeutic integration. *Journal of Psychotherapy Integration, 1,* 43–54.

Wade, P., & Bernstein, B. (1991). Culture sensitivity training and counselor's race: Effects on Black female client's perceptions and attrition. *Journal of Counseling Psychology, 38,* 9–15.

Wagner, M. E., Schubert, H. J. P., & Schubert, D. S. P. (1993). Sex-of-sibling effects: Part 1. Gender role, intelligence, achievement, and creativity. In H. W. Reese (Ed.), *Advances in child development and behavior* (Vol. 24). San Diego: Academic Press.

Wakefield, J. C. (1992). The concept of mental disorder: On the boundary between biological facts and social values. *American Psychologist, 47,* 373–388.

Wald, G. (1964). The receptors of human color vision. *Science, 145,* 1007–1017.

Walker, L. J. (1988). The development of moral reasoning. In R. Vasta (Ed.), *Annals of child development* (Vol. 5). Greenwich, CT: JAI Press.

Walker, L. J. (1989). A longitudinal study of moral reasoning. *Child Development, 60,* 157–166.

Walker, L. J. (1991). Sex differences in moral reasoning. In W. M. Kurtines & J. L. Gewirtz (Eds.), *Handbook of moral behavior and development* (Vol. 2). Hillsdale, NJ: Erlbaum.

Walker, L. J., & Moran, T. J. (1991). Moral reasoning in a Communist Chinese society. *Journal of Moral Education, 20,* 139–155.

Walker, L. J., & Taylor, J. H. (1991). Strange transitions in moral reasoning: A longitudinal study of developmental processes. *Developmental Psychology, 27,* 330–337.

Wallace, R. K., & Benson, H. (1972). The physiology of meditation. *Scientific American, 226,* 84–90.

Wallach, M. A. (1985). Creativity testing and giftedness. In F. D. Horowitz & M. O'Brien (Eds.), *The gifted and talented: Developmental perspectives.* Washington, DC: American Psychological Association.

Wallach, M. A., & Kogan, N. (1965). *Modes of thinking in young children.* New York: Holt, Rinehart & Winston.

Wallbott, H. G., & Scherer, K. R. (1988). How universal and specific is emotional experience? Evidence from 27 countries. In K. R. Scherer (Ed.), *Facets of emotions.* Hillsdale, NJ: Erlbaum.

Wallen, K. (1989). Mate selection: Economics and affection. *Behavioral and Brain Sciences, 12,* 37–38.

Wallston, K. A., & Wallston, B. S. (1981). Health locus of control scales. In H. M. Lefcourt (Ed.), *Research with the locus of control construct* (Vol. 1). New York: Academic Press.

Walraven, J., Enroth-Cugell, C., Hood, D. C., MacLeod, D. I. A., & Schnapf, J. L. (1990). The control of visual sensitivity: Receptoral and postreceptoral processes. In L. Spillmann & J. S. Werner (Eds.), *Visual perception: The neurophysiological foundations.* San Diego: Academic Press.

Walster, E., & Berscheid, E. (1974). A little bit about love: A minor essay on a major topic. In T. L. Huston (Ed.), *Foundations of interpersonal attraction.* New York: Academic Press.

Walter, T., & Siebert, A. (1990). *Student success: How to succeed in college and still have time for your friends.* Fort Worth: Holt, Rinehart & Winston.

Walters, C. C., & Grusec, J. E. (1977). *Punishment.* San Francisco: W. H. Freeman.

Wangensteen, O. H., & Carlson, A. J. (1931). Hunger sensation after total gastrectomy. *Proceedings of the Society for Experimental Biology, 28,* 545–547.

Wansell, G. (1983). *Haunted idol: The story of the real Cary Grant.* New York: Ballantine.

Wark, G. R., & Krebs, D. L. (1996). Gender and dilemma differences in real-life moral judgment. *Developmental Psychology, 32,* 220–230.

Warner, R. (1989). Deinstitutionalization: How did we get where we are? *Journal of Social Issues, 45*(3), 17–30.

Warr, P. B. (1987). *Work, unemployment, and mental health.* Oxford: Clarendon Press.

Warrington, E. K., & Weiskrantz, L. (1970). Amnesic syndrome: Consolidation or retrieval? *Nature, 228,* 629–630.

Warwick, D. P. (1975, February). Social scientists ought to stop lying. *Psychology Today,* pp. 38, 40, 105–106.

Washburn, M. F. (1908). *The animal mind.* New York: MacMillan.

Waterman, A., & Archer, S. (1990). A life-span perspective on identity formation: Development in form, function, and process. In P. B. Baltes, D. L. Featherman, & R. M. Lerner (Eds.), *Life-span development and behavior* (Vol. 10). Hillsdale, NJ: Erlbaum.

Watson, D. (1982). The actor and the observer: How are their perceptions of causality divergent? *Psychological Bulletin, 92,* 682–700.

Watson, D. L., & Tharp, R. G. (1989). *Self-directed behavior: Self-modification for personal adjustment* (5th ed.). Pacific Grove, CA: Brooks/Cole.

Watson, D. L., & Tharp, R. G. (1993). *Self-directed behavior: Self-modification for personal adjustment* (6th ed.). Pacific Grove, CA: Brooks/Cole.

Watson, D., & Pennebaker, J. W. (1989). Health complaints, stress, and distress: Exploring the central role of negative affectivity. *Psychological Review, 96,* 234–254.

Watson, J. B. (1913). Psychology as the behaviorist views it. *Psychological Review, 20,* 158–177.

Watson, J. B. (1919). *Psychology from the standpoint of a behaviorist.* Philadelphia: Lippincott.

Watson, J. B. (1924). *Behaviorism.* New York: Norton.

Watson, J. B. (1930). *Behaviorism.* New York: Norton.

Watson, J. B., & Rayner, R. (1920). Conditioned emotional reactions. *Journal of Experimental Psychology, 3,* 1–14.

Weaver, R. C., & Rodnick, J. E. (1986). Type-A behavior: Clinical significance, evaluation, and management. *Journal of Family Practice, 23*(3), 255–261.

Webb, W. B. (1988). An objective behavioral model of sleep. *Sleep, 11,* 488–496.

Webb, W. B. (1992a). Developmental aspects and a behavioral model of human sleep. In C. Stampi (Ed.), *Why we nap: Evolution, chronobiology, and functions of polyphasic and ultrashort sleep.* Boston: Birkhaeuser.

Webb, W. B. (1992b). *Sleep: The gentle tyrant.* Bolton, MA: Anker.

Webb, W. B. (1993). Individual differences. In M. A. Carskadon (Ed.), *Encyclopedia of sleep and dreaming.* New York: Macmillan.

Webb, W. B. (1994). Prediction of sleep onset. In R. D. Ogilvie & J. R. Harsh (Eds.), *Sleep onset: Normal and abnormal processes.* Washington, DC: American Psychological Association.

Webb, W. B., & Dinges, D. F. (1989). Cultural perspectives on napping and the siesta. In D. F. Dinges & R. J. Broughton (Eds.), *Sleep and alertness: Chronobiological, behavioral, and medical aspects of napping.* New York: Raven.

Wechsler, D. (1939). *The measurement of adult intelligence.* Baltimore: Williams & Wilkins.

Wechsler, D. (1949). *Wechsler intelligence scale for children.* New York: Psychological Corporation.

Wechsler, D. (1955). *Manual, Wechsler adult intelligence scale.* New York: Psychological Corporation.

Wechsler, D. (1967). *Manual for the Wechsler preschool and primary scale of intelligence.* New York: Psychological Corporation.

Wechsler, D. (1981). *Manual for the Wechsler adult intelligence scale-revised.* New York: Psychological Corporation.

Wechsler, D. (1991). *WISC-III manual.* San Antonio, TX: Psychological Corporation.

Wehr, T. A., & Rosenthal, N. E. (1989). Seasonality and affective illness. *American Journal of Psychiatry, 146,* 829–839.

Weinberg, R. A. (1989). Intelligence and IQ: Landmark issues and great debates. *American Psychologist, 44,* 98–104.

Weinberger, D. A. (1990). The construct validity of the repressive coping style. In J. L. Singer (Ed.), *Repression and dissociation.* Chicago: University of Chicago Press.

Weinberger, D. R., Wagner, R. J., & Wyatt, R. L. (1983). Neuropathological studies of schizophrenia: A selective review. *Schizophrenia Bulletin, 9,* 198–212.

Weinberger, J. (1992). Validating and demystifying subliminal psychodynamic activation. In R. F. Bornstein & T. S. Pittman (Eds.), *Perception without awareness: Cognitive, clinical, and social perspectives.* New York: Guilford Press.

Weiner, B. (1980). *Human motivation.* New York: Holt, Rinehart & Winston.

Weiner, B. (1985). "Spontaneous" causal thinking. *Psychological Bulletin, 97,* 74–84.

Weiner, B. (1986). *An attributional theory of motivation and emotion.* New York: Springer-Verlag.

Weiner, B. (Ed.). (1974). *Achievement motivation and attribution theory.* Morristown, NJ: General Learning Press.

Weiner, B., Frieze, I., Kukla, A., Reed, L., Rest, S., & Rosenbaum, R. M. (1972). Perceiving the causes of success and failure. In E. E. Jones, D. E. Kanouse, H. H. Kelley, R. E. Nisbett, S. Valins, & B. Weiner (Eds.), *Perceiving the causes of behavior.* Morristown, NJ: General Learning Press.

Weiner, H. (1978). Emotional factors. In S. C. Werner & S. H. Ingbar (Eds.), *The thyroid.* New York: Harper & Row.

Weiner, H. (1992). *Perturbing the organism: The biology of stressful experience.* Chicago: University of Chicago Press.

Weiner, H., & Fawzy, F. I. (1989). An integrative model of health, disease, and illness. In S. Cheren (Ed.), *Psychosomatic medicine: Theory, physiology, and practice* (Vol. 1). Madison, CT: International Universities Press.

Weiner, M. F. (1993). Role of the leader in group psychotherapy. In H. I. Kaplan & B. J. Sadock (Eds.), *Comprehensive group psychotherapy.* Baltimore: Williams & Wilkins.

Weiner, R. D. (1984). Does electroconvulsive therapy cause brain damage? *Behavioral and Brain Sciences, 7,* 1–22.

Weiner, R. D., & Coffey, C. E. (1988). Indications for use of electroconvulsive therapy. In A. J. Frances & R. E. Hales (Eds.), *Review of psychiatry* (Vol. 7). Washington, DC: American Psychiatric Press.

Weinstein, L. N., Schwartz, D. G., & Arkin, A. M. (1991). Qualitative aspects of sleep mentation. In S. J. Ellman & J. S. Antrobus (Eds.), *The mind in sleep: Psychology and psychophysiology* (2nd ed.). New York: Wiley.

Weinstein, N. D. (1984). Why it won't happen to me: Perceptions of risk factors and susceptibility. *Health Psychology, 3,* 431–458.

Weinstein, N. D., & Klein, W. M. (1995). Resistance of personal risk perceptions to debiasing interventions. *Health Psychology, 14,* 132–140.

Weinstein, N. D., & Klein, W. M. (1996). Unrealistic optimism: Present and future. *Journal of Social and Clinical Psychology, 15,* 1–8.

Weisaeth, L. (1993). Disasters: Psychological and psychiatric aspects. In L. Goldberger & S. Breznitz (Eds.), *Handbook of stress: Theoretical and clinical aspects* (2nd ed.). New York: Free Press.

Weisberg, R. W. (1986). *Creativity: Genius and other myths.* New York: W. H. Freeman.

Weisberg, R. W. (1988). Problem solving and creativity. In R. J. Sternberg (Ed.), *The nature of creativity: Contemporary psychological perspectives.* Cambridge, England: Cambridge University Press.

Weisberg, R. W. (1993). *Creativity: Beyond the myth of genius.* New York: W. H. Freeman.

Weisner, T. S., & Wilson-Mitchell, J. E. (1990). Nonconventional family life-styles and sex typing in six-year-olds. *Child Development, 61,* 1915–1933.

Weissman, M. M., Bruce, M. L., Leaf, P. J.,

Florio, L. P., & Holzer, C., III. (1991). Affective disorders. In L. N. Robins & D. A. Regier (Eds.), *Psychiatric disorders in America: The epidemiologic catchment area study*. New York: Free Press.

Weisz, J. R., Rothbaum, F. M., & Blackburn, T. C. (1984). Standing out and standing in: The psychology of control in America and Japan. *American Psychologist, 39*, 955–969.

Weiten, W. (1984). Violation of selected item-construction principles in educational measurement. *Journal of Experimental Education, 51*, 46–50.

Weiten, W. (1986). *Psychology applied to modern life: Adjustment in the 80s*. Pacific Grove, CA: Brooks/Cole.

Weiten W. (1988a). Objective features of introductory psychology textbooks as related to professors' impressions. *Teaching of Psychology, 15*, 10–16.

Weiten, W. (1988b). Pressure as a form of stress and its relationship to psychological symptomatology. *Journal of Social and Clinical Psychology, 6*(1), 127–139.

Weiten, W., & Diamond, S. S. (1979). A critical review of the jury-simulation paradigm: The case of defendant characteristics. *Law and Human Behavior, 3*, 71–93.

Weiten, W., Guadagno, R. E., & Beck, C. A. (1996). Students' perceptions of textbook pedagogical aids. *Teaching of Psychology, 23*, 105–107.

Weiten, W., & Wight, R. D. (1992). Portraits of a discipline: An examination of introductory psychology textbooks in America. In A. E. Puente, J. R. Matthews, & C. L. Brewer (Eds.), *Teaching psychology in America: A history*. Washington, DC: American Psychological Association.

Wekstein, L. (1979). *Handbook of suicidology*. New York: Brunner/Mazel.

Well, A. D., Pollatsek, A., & Boyce, S. J. (1990). Understanding the effects of sample size on the variability of the mean. *Organizational Behavior and Human Decision Processes, 47*, 289–312.

Wells, C. G. (1991). *Right-brain sex: How to reach the heights of sensual pleasure by releasing the erotic power of your mind*. New York: Avon.

Welsh, D. K. (1993). Timing of sleep and wakefulness. In M. A. Carskadon (Ed.), *Encyclopedia of sleep and dreaming*. New York: Macmillan.

Wen, S. W., Goldenberg, R. L., Cutter, G. R., Hoffman, H. J., Cliver, S. P., Davis, R. O., & DuBard, M. B. (1990). Smoking, maternal age, fetal growth, and gestational age at delivery. *American Journal of Obstetrics and Gynecology, 162*, 53–58.

Werbach, M. R. (1988). *Nutritional influences on illness: A sourcebook of clinical research*. Tarzana, CA: Third Line Press.

Werker, J. F., & Desjardins, R. N. (1995). Listening to speech in the 1st year of life: Experiential influences on phoneme perception. *Current Directions in Psychological Science, 4*, 76–81.

Wertheimer, M. (1912). Experimentelle studien über das sehen von bewegung. *Zeitschrift für Psychologie, 60*, 312–378.

Wertheimer, M. (1961). Psychomotor coordination of auditory and visual space at birth. *Science, 134*, 1692.

Westen, D. (1990). Psychoanalytic approaches to personality. In L. A. Pervin (Ed.), *Handbook of personality: Theory and research*. New York: Guilford Press.

Wever, E. G., & Bray, C. W. (1937). The perception of low tones and the resonance-volley theory. *Journal of Psychology, 3*, 101–114.

Wever, R. A. (1979). *The circadian system of man: Results of experiments under temporal isolation*. New York: Springer-Verlag.

Whitbourne, S. K., Zuschlag, M. K., Elliot, L. B., & Waterman, A. S. (1992). Psychosocial development in adulthood: A 22-year sequential study. *Journal of Personality and Social Psychology, 63*, 260–271.

White, K. R. (1982). The relation between socioeconomic status and academic achievement. *Psychological Bulletin, 91*, 461–481.

White, N. M., & Milner, P. M. (1992). The psychobiology of reinforcers. *Annual Review of Psychology, 43*, 443–472.

White, P. A., & Younger, D. P. (1988). Differences in the ascription of transient internal states to self and other. *Journal of Experimental Psychology, 24*, 292–309.

Whitehouse, W. G., & Dinges, D. F., Orne, E. C., & Orne, M. T. (1988). Hypnotic hyperamnesia: Enhanced memory accessibility or report bias? *Journal of Abnormal Psychology, 97*, 298–295.

Whiting, J. W. M., Burbank, V. K., & Ratner, M. S. (1986). The duration of maidenhood. In J. B. Lancaster & B. A. Hamburg (Eds.), *School age pregnancy and parenthood*. Hawthorne, NY: Aldine de Gruyter.

Whitley, B. E., Jr. (1988). *College students' reasons for sexual intercourse: A sex role perspective*. Paper presented at the 96th Annual Meeting of the American Psychological Association, Atlanta.

Whorf, B. L. (1956). Science and linguistics. In J. B. Carroll (Ed.), *Language, thought and reality: Selected writings of Benjamin Lee Whorf*. Cambridge, MA: MIT Press.

Widiger, T. A. (1993). The DSM-III-R categorical personality disorder diagnoses: A critique and an alternative. *Psychological Inquiry, 4*, 75–90.

Widiger, T. A., & Costa, P. T., Jr. (1994). Personality and personality disorders. *Journal of Abnormal Psychology, 103*, 78–91.

Widiger, T. A., & Frances, A. J. (1994). Toward a dimensional model for the personality disorders. In P. T. Costa, Jr., & T. A. Widiger (Eds.), *Personality disorders and the five-factor model of personality*. Washington, DC: American Psychological Association.

Widiger, T. A., Frances, A. J., Pincus, H. A., Davis, W. W., & First, M. B. (1991). Toward an empirical classification for the DSM-IV. *Journal of Abnormal Psychology, 100*, 280–288.

Wiebe, D. J. (1991). Hardiness and stress moderation: A test of proposed mechanisms. *Journal of Personality and Social Psychology, 60*, 89–99.

Wielawski, I. (1991, October 3). Unlocking the secrets of memory. *Los Angeles Times*, p. 1.

Wiest, W. (1977). Semantic differential profiles of orgasm and other experiences among men and women. *Sex Roles, 3*, 399–403.

Wiggins, J. S. (1992). Have model, will travel. *Journal of Personality, 60*, 527–532.

Wilcox, A. J., Weinberg, C. R., O'Connor, J. F., Baurd, D. D., Schlatterer, J. P., Canfield, R. E., Armstrong, E. G., & Nisula, B. C. (1988). Incidence of early loss of pregnancy. *New England Journal of Medicine, 319*, 189–194.

Wilder, D. A. (1981). Perceiving persons as a group: Categorization and intergroup relations. In D. L. Hamilton (Ed.), *Cognitive processing in stereotyping and intergroup behavior*. Hillsdale, NJ: Erlbaum.

Wilding, J., & Valentine, E. (1996). Memory expertise. In D. J. Herrmann, C. McEvoy, C. Hertzog, P. Hertel, & M. K. Johnson (Eds.), *Basic and applied memory research: Theory in context* (Vol. 1). Mahwah, NJ: Erlbaum.

Williams, B. A. (1988). Reinforcement, choice, and response strength. In R. C. Atkinson, R. J. Herrnstein, G. Lindzey, & R. D. Luce (Eds.), *Stevens' handbook of experimental psychology*. New York: Wiley.

Williams, C. D. (1959). The elimination of tantrum behavior by extinction procedures. *Journal of Abnormal and Social Psychology, 59*, 269.

Williams, J. B. W. (1994). Psychiatric classification. In R. E. Hales, S. C. Yudofsky, & J. A. Talbott (Eds.), *The American Psychiatric Press textbook of psychiatry* (2nd ed.). Washington, DC: American Psychiatric Press.

Williams, K. D., & Karau, S. J. (1991). Social loafing and social comparison: The effects of expectations of co-worker performance. *Journal of Personality and Social Psychology, 61*, 570–581.

Williams, L. V. (1986). *Teaching for the two-sided mind: A guide to right brain–left brain education*. New York: Simon & Schuster.

Williams, M. H. (1992). Exploitation and inference: Mapping the damage from therapist-patient sexual involvement. *American Psychologist, 47*, 412–421.

Williams, N. A., & Deffenbacher, J. L. (1983). Life stress and chronic yeast infections. *Journal of Human Stress, 9*(1), 26–31.

Williams, R., & Stockmyer, J. (1987). *Unleashing the right side of the brain: The LARC creativity program*. New York: Viking Penguin.

Williams, R. L., Dotson, W., Dow, P., & Williams, W. S. (1980). The war against testing: A current status report. *Journal of Negro Education, 49*, 263–273.

Williams, R. W., & Herrup, K. (1988). The control of neuron number. *Annual Review of Neuroscience, 11*, 423–453.

Willis, W. D. (1985). *The pain system. The neural basis of nociceptive transmission in the mammalian nervous system*. Basel: Karger.

Wilson, E. O. (1975, October 12). Human decency is animal. *New York Times Magazine*, pp. 38–50.

Wilson, G. (1990). Personality, time of day and arousal. *Personality and Individual Differences, 11*, 153–168.

Wilson, G. T. (1982). Alcohol and anxiety: Recent evidence on the tension reduction theory of alcohol use and abuse. In K. R. Blankstein & J. Polivy (Eds.), *Self-control and self-modification of emotional behavior*. New York: Plenum.

Wilson, G. T. (1990). Clinical issues and strategies in the practice of behavior therapy. In C. M. Franks, G. T. Wilson, P. C. Kendall, & J. P. Foreyt (Eds.), *Review of behavior therapy* (Vol. 12). New York: Guilford Press.

Wilson, M. (1993). DSM-III and the transformation of American psychiatry: A history. *American Journal of Psychiatry, 150*, 399–410.

Wilson, R. S. (1986). Continuity and change in cognitive ability profile. *Behavior Genetics, 16*, 45–60.

Wilson, T. D., & Schooler, J. W. (1991). Thinking too much: Introspection can reduce the quality of preferences and decisions. *Journal of Personality and Social Psychology, 60*, 181–192.

Wingerson, L. (1990). *Mapping our genes: The genome project and the future of medicine*. New York: Penguin.

Winn, P. (1995). The lateral hypothalmus and motivated behavior: An old syndrome reassessed and a new perspective gained. *Current Directions in Psychological Science, 4*, 182–187.

Winn, P., Tarbuck, A., & Dunnett, S. B. (1984). Ibotenic acid lesions of the lateral hypothalamus: Comparison with the electrolytic lesion syndrome. *Neuroscience, 12,* 225–240.

Winograd, T. (1975). Frame representations and the declarative-procedural controversy. In D. Bobrow & A. Collins (Eds.), *Representation and understanding: Studies in cognitive science.* New York: Academic Press.

Winokur, G., Coryell, W., Endicott, J., & Akiskal, H. (1993). Further distinctions between manic-depressive illness (bipolar disorder) and primary depressive disorder (unipolar depression). *American Journal of Psychiatry, 150,* 1176–1181.

Winter, D. G. (1992). Content analysis of archival materials, personal documents, and everyday verbal productions. In C. P. Smith (Ed.), *Motivation and personality: Handbook of thematic content analysis.* New York: Cambridge University Press.

Wise, R. (1995). D-sub-1- and D-sub-2-type contributions to psychomotor sensitization and reward: Implications for pharmacological treatment strategies. *Clinical Neuropharmacology, 18,* S74–S83.

Wise, R. A., & Bozarth, M. A. (1987). A psychomotor stimulant theory of addiction. *Psychological Review, 94,* 469–92.

Wise, R. A., & Rompre, P. P. (1989). Brain dopamine and reward. *Annual Review of Psychology, 40,* 191–225.

Witkin, H. A. (1950). Individual differences in ease of perception of embedded figures. *Journal of Personality, 19,* 1–15.

Witkin, H. A., & Berry, J. W. (1975). Psychological differentiation in cross-cultural perspective. *Journal of Cross-Cultural Psychology, 6,* 4–87.

Witkin, H. A., & Goodenough, D. (1981). *Cognitive styles: Essence and origins.* New York: International Universities Press.

Witkin, H. A., Dyk, R. B., Paterson, H. F., Goodenough, D. R., & Karp, S. (1962). *Psychological differentiation.* New York: Wiley.

Witkin, H. A., Moore, C. A., Goodenough, D. R., & Cox, P. W. (1977). Field-dependent and field-independent cognitive styles and their educational implications. *Review of Educational Research,* 1–64.

Wittkower, E. D., & Warnes, H. (1984). Cultural aspects of psychotherapy. In J. E. Mezzich & C. E. Berganza (Eds.), *Culture and psychopathology.* New York: Columbia University Press.

Wixted, J. T., Bellack, A. S., & Hersen, M. (1990). Behavior therapy. In A. S. Bellack & M. Hersen (Eds.), *Handbook of comparative treatments for adult disorders.* New York: Wiley.

Wolf, R. M. (1965). The measurement of environments. In C. W. Harris (Ed.), *Proceedings of the 1964 invited conference on testing problems.* Princeton, NJ: Educational Testing Service.

Wolf, S., & Goodell, H. (1968). *Stress and disease.* Springfield, IL: Charles C Thomas.

Wolk, S. I., & Weissman, M. M. (1995). Women and depression. In J. M. Oldham & M. B. Riba (Eds.), *Review of psychiatry* (Vol. 14). Washington, DC: American Psychiatric Press.

Wolpe, J. (1958). *Psychotherapy by reciprocal inhibition.* Stanford, CA: Stanford University Press.

Wolpe, J. (1987). The promotion of scientific therapy: A long voyage. In J. K. Zeig (Ed.), *The evolution of psychotherapy.* New York: Brunner/Mazel.

Wolpe, J. (1990). *The practice of behavior therapy.* Elmsford, NY: Pergamon Press.

Wonder, J. (1992). *Whole brain thinking: Working both sides of the brain to achieve peak job performance.* New York: Morrow.

Wood, F., Ebert, V., & Kinsbourne, M. (1982). The episodic-semantic memory distinction in memory and amnesia: Clinical and experimental observations. In L. Cermak (Ed.), *Human memory and amnesia.* Hillsdale, NJ: Erlbaum.

Wood, J. M., Nezworski, M. T., & Stejskal, W. J. (1996). The comprehensive system for the Rorschach: A critical examination. *Psychological Science, 7,* 3–10.

Woodcock, R. W. (1994). Norms. In R. J. Sternberg (Ed.), *Encyclopedia of human intelligence.* New York: Macmillan.

Woolfolk, R. L. (1975). Psychophysiological correlates of meditation. *Archives of General Psychiatry, 32,* 1326–1333.

Woolfolk, R. L., & Richardson, F. C. (1978). *Stress, sanity and survival.* New York: Sovereign/Monarch.

Woolsey, C. N. (1981). *Cortical sensory organization.* Clifton, NJ: Humana Press.

Wooten, V. (1994). Medical causes of insomnia. In M. H. Kryger, T. Roth, & W. C. Dement (Eds.), *Principles and practice of sleep medicine* (2nd ed.). Philadelphia: Saunders.

Worobey, J., & Blajda, V. M. (1989). Temperament ratings at 2 weeks, 2 months, and 1 year: Differential stability of activity and emotionality. *Developmental Psychology, 25,* 257–263.

Worthington-Roberts, B. S., & Klerman, L. V. (1990). Maternal nutrition. In I. R. Merkatz & J. E. Thompson (Eds.), *New perspectives on prenatal care.* New York: Elsevier.

Wundt, W. (1874/1904). *Principles of physiological psychology.* Leipzig: Engelmann.

Wyatt, R. J. (1985). Science and psychiatry. In H. I. Kaplan & B. J. Sadock (Eds.), *Comprehensive textbook of psychiatry/IV.* Baltimore: Williams & Wilkins.

Wyler, A. R., Masuda, M., & Holmes, T. H. (1968). The seriousness of illness rating scale. *Journal of Psychosomatic Research, 11,* 363–374.

Wyler, A. R., Masuda, M., & Holmes, T. H. (1971). Magnitude of life events and seriousness of illness. *Psychosomatic Medicine, 33*(2), 115–122.

Wyrwicka, W., & Dobrzecka, C. (1960). Relationship between feeding and satiation centers of the hypothalamus. *Science, 132,* 805–806.

Xiaghe, X., & Whyte, M. K. (1990). Love matches and arranged marriages: A Chinese replication. *Journal of Marriage and the Family, 52,* 709–722.

Yalom, I. D. (1995). *The theory and practice of group psychotherapy* (4th ed.). New York: Basic Books.

Yamamoto, J., Silva, J. A., Justice, L. R., Chang, C. Y., & Leong, G. B. (1993). Cross-cultural psychotherapy. In A. C. Gaw (Ed.), *Culture, ethnicity, and mental illness.* Washington, DC: American Psychiatric Press.

Yates, F. A. (1966). *The art of memory.* London: Routledge & Kegan Paul.

Yerkes, R. M. (1921). *Memories of the National Academy of Sciences: Psychological examining in the United States Army* (Vol. 15). Washington, DC: U.S. Government Printing Office.

Yerkes, R. M., & Morgulis, S. (1909). The method of Pavlov in animal psychology. *Psychological Bulletin, 6,* 257–273.

Young, T. (1802). On the theory of light and colours. *Philosophical Transactions of the Royal Society of London, 92,* 12–48.

Zaccaria, J. (1970). *Theories of occupational choice and vocational development.* Boston: Houghton Mifflin.

Zahn-Waxler, C., & Smith, K. D. (1992). The development of prosocial behavior. In V. B. Van Hasselt & M. Hersen (Eds.), *Handbook of social development: A lifespan perspective.* New York: Plenum.

Zajonc, R. B. (1980). Feeling and thinking: Preferences need no inferences. *American Psychologist, 35,* 151–175.

Zarcone, V. P., Jr. (1994). Sleep hygiene. In M. H. Kryger, T. Roth, & W. C. Dement (Eds.), *Principles and practice of sleep medicine* (2nd ed.). Philadelphia: Saunders.

Zatzick, D. F., & Dimsdale, J. E. (1990). Cultural variations in response to painful stimuli. *Psychosomatic Medicine, 52*(5), 544–557.

Zebrowitz, L. A. (1996). *Reading faces.* Boulder, CO: Westview Press.

Zebrowitz, L. A., Voinescu, L., & Collins, M. A. (1996). "Wide-eyed" and "crooked-face": Determinants of perceived and real honesty across the life span. *Personality and Social Psychology Bulletin, 22,* 1258–1269.

Zechmeister, E. B., & Nyberg, S. E. (1982). *Human memory: An introduction to research and theory.* Pacific Grove, CA: Brooks/Cole.

Zeiler, M. (1977). Schedules of reinforcement: The controlling variables. In W. K. Honig & J. E. R. Staddon (Eds.), *Handbook of operant behavior.* Englewood Cliffs, NJ: Prentice-Hall.

Zenhausen, R. (1978). Imagery, cerebral dominance and style of thinking: A unified field model. *Bulletin of the Psychonomic Society, 12,* 381–384.

Zepelin, H. (1993). Internal alarm clock. In M. A. Carskadon (Ed.), *Encyclopedia of sleep and dreaming.* New York: Macmillan.

Zeskind, P. S., & Ramey, C. T. (1981). Preventing intellectual and interactional sequelae of fetal malnutrition: A longitudinal, transactional and synergistic approach to development. *Child Development, 52,* 213–218.

Zhdanova, I. V., Wurtman, R. J., Lynch, H. J., Ives, J. R., Dollins, A. B., Morabito, C., Matheson, J. K., & Schomer, D. L. (1995). Sleep-inducing effects of low doses of melatonin ingested in the evening. *Clinical Pharmacology and Therapeutics, 57,* 552–558.

Zigler, E. F., & Gilman, E. (1993). Day care in America: What is needed? *Pediatrics, 91,* 175–178.

Zigler, E. F., & Seitz, V. (1982). Social policy and intelligence. In R. J. Sternberg (Ed.), *Handbook of human intelligence.* Cambridge, MA: Cambridge University Press.

Zilbergeld, B., & Evans, M. (1980, August). The inadequacy of Masters and Johnson. *Psychology Today,* pp. 28–34, 37–43.

Zillmann, D. (1983). Transfer of excitation in emotional behavior. In J. T. Cacioppo & R. Petty (Eds.), *Social psychophysiology: A sourcebook.* New York: Guilford Press.

Zillmann, D., & Bryant, J. (1984). Effects of massive exposure to pornography. In N. M. Malamuth & E. Donnerstein (Eds.), *Pornography and sexual aggression.* New York: Academic Press.

Zillmann, D., & Bryant, J. (1988). Pornography's impact on sexual satisfaction. *Journal of Applied Social Psychology, 18,* 438–453.

Zillmann, D., & Weaver, J. B. (1989). Pornography and men's sexual callousness toward women. In D. Zillmann & J. Bryant (Eds.), *Pornography: Research advances and policy considerations.* Hillsdale, NJ: Erlbaum.

Zimbardo, P. G., LaBerge, S., & Butler, L. D. (1993). Psychological consequences of unexplained arousal: A posthypnotic suggestion paradigm. *Journal of Abnormal Psychology, 102,* 466–473.

Zimmerman, B. J. (1995). Self-efficacy and educational development. In A. Bandura (Ed.), *Self-efficacy in changing societies.* New York: Cambridge University Press.

Zimmerman, I. L., & Woo-Sam, J. M. (1984). Intellectual assessment of children. In G. Goldstein & M. Hersen (Eds.), *Handbook of psychological assessment.* New York: Pergamon Press.

Zini, D., Carani, C., Baldini, A., Ghizzani, A., & Marrama, P. (1990). Sexual behavior of men with isolated hypogonadotropic hypogonadism or prepubertal anterior panhypopituitarism. *Hormones and Behavior, 24,* 174–185.

Zola-Morgan, S. M., & Squire, L. R. (1990). The primate hippocampal formation: Evidence for a time-limited role in memory formation. *Science, 250,* 288–289.

Zorc, J. J., Larson, D. B., Lyons, J. S., & Beardsley, R. S. (1991). Expenditures for psychotropic medications in the United States in 1985. *American Journal of Psychiatry, 148,* 644–647.

Zorumski, C. F., & Isenberg, K. E. (1991). Insights into the structure and function of GABA-benzodiazepine receptors: Ion channels and psychiatry. *American Journal of Psychiatry, 148,* 162–173.

Zrenner, E., Abramov, I., Akita, M., Cowey, A., Livingstone, M., & Valberg, A. (1990). Color perception: Retina to cortex. In L. Spillman & J. S. Werner (Eds.), *Visual perception: The neurophysiological foundations.* San Diego: Academic Press.

Zubin, J. (1986). Implications of the vulnerability model for DSM-IV with special reference to schizophrenia. In T. Millon & G. L. Klerman (Eds.), *Contemporary directions in psychopathology: Toward the DSM-IV.* New York: Guilford Press.

Zuckerman, M. (1971). Dimensions of sensation seeking. *Journal of Consulting and Clinical Psychology, 36,* 45–52.

Zuckerman, M. (1979). *Sensation seeking: Beyond the optimal level of arousal.* Hillsdale, NJ: Erlbaum.

Zuckerman, M. (1990). The psychophysiology of sensation seeking. *Journal of Personality, 58*(1), 313–345.

Zuckerman, M. (1991). *Psychobiology of personality.* New York: Cambridge University Press.

Zuckerman, M., Buchsbaum, M. S., & Murphy, D. L. (1980). Sensation seeking and its biological correlates. *Psychological Bulletin, 88,* 187–214.

Zuwerink, J. R., & Devine, P. G. (1996). Attitude importance and resistance to persuasion: It's not just the thought that counts. *Journal of Personality and Social Psychology, 70,* 931–944.

Zwislocki, J. J. (1981). Sound analysis in the ear: A history of discoveries. *American Scientist, 69,* 184–192.

NAME INDEX

SUBJECT INDEX

heritability of, 359, 361–362
stability of, 352, 353
Sternberg's triarchic theory of, 370
twin studies of, 112, 113
types of, 352, 370–371
intelligence quotient (IQ), 346
intelligence tests (testing), 13, 339, 345–353
cultural bias in, 365
defined, 340
functions of, 348, 351
history of, 345–347
new directions in, 367–371
in other cultures, 348–349
reduced reliance on, 367
reliability of, 351
vocational success and, 352–353
validity of, 351–352
interactionist theories, 312–313
interference, 281–282, 283
minimizing, 295
interference theory, 281
intermittent reinforcement, 234
internal attributions, 646, 647
interneurons, 74
interpersonal attraction, 641, 651–657
culture and, 656
evolutionary perspective on, 657
key factors in, 651–653
sexual, 394
tactics of, 657
interposition, 148, 149, 169
interpretation
of dreams, 212–213
in psychoanalysis, 608
of sensory input, 142
of situations as threats, 570
interval schedules, 235, 236
interviews, 41
intimacy, 654
versus isolation, 454
intravenous drug users, 208, 546
introspection, 4, 301
introversion, 495–496
introverts, 483
inverted-U hypothesis, 525
involuntary commitment, 593-594
ions, 75, 76, 77
Iowa Tests of Basic Skills, 339
IQ. See intelligence; intelligence quotient
IQ scores, meaning of, 350–351
iris, 130, 131
irrational thinking, 551, 582–583
irreversibility, 439

J

Jahn, Helmut, 100
James-Lange theory, 411
Japan
attachment patterns in, 434
attribution style in, 651
emotional expression in, 410
height in, 362–363
sleep patterns in, 188
view of self in, 504
Japanese Americans, 25

jealousy, 381
jet lag, 181
Jim twins, 494
job analysis, 703–704
job satisfaction, 707–708
job status, IQ and, 352
job success, test scores and, 352–353, 704
Joel, Billy, 278
Johns Hopkins University, 3
Jonestown massacre, 666
journal articles, finding, 66–69
journals, 41, 66
juries, decision making in, 48
just noticeable difference (JND), 125, 126

K

Kanzi, 303–304, 307
Kennedy, John F., 628, 675
keyword method, 296, 297
kinesthesis, 166
Weber fraction for, 125
Kinetic Art, 172
Kipsigis people, 430
koro, 594–595
Kung San, 430

L

labeling, stigmatization and, 558
laboratories, early psychology, 3, 4
language, 302–314
acquisition of, 308–313
brain areas for, 97, 99
culture and, 313–314
defined, 305
in evolutionary context, 307–308
properties of, 305–306, 307
structure of, 305–307
thought and, 313–314
language acquisition device (LAD), 311, 312
language development, 308–313
language learning
in animals, 302–305, 307
in humans, 308–310
theories of, 310–313
latency period, 481, 482
latent content, 212
lateral antagonism, 134–135
lateral geniculate nucleus (LGN), 135, 136
lateral hypothalamus (LH), 386
latitude of acceptance, 662
law of effect, 227–228
law of small numbers, 333, 681
Leach, Archie, 421
learned helplessness, 529, 579–580
learning
of anxiety disorders, 569–570
of attitudes, 663
defined, 217
of food preferences, 388
personality development and, 486–489
lectures, getting more from, 31–32
left-handedness, 104–106, 118
lens, 130, 131
Les Promenades d'Euclide (Magritte), 173

lesbians, 397
lesioning, of brain, 89
levels-of-processing theory, 263–264, 295
Library Use: A Handbook for Psychology (Reed & Baxter), 66
lie detector, 407–408
lie scales, 512
life changes, 453
disease and, 40, 41, 521–522
life expectancy, 543
light, as stimulus for vision, 129, 130, 133
light adaptation, 133
light and shadow, as depth cue, 148, 149
likeability, 660
limbic system, 94–97, 289, 406–407
linear perspective, 148, 149, 168
linguistic relativity, 313–314
link method, 296, 297
literature searches, computerlized, 68, 69
lithium, 622
Little Albert, 224
localization, of sounds, 159–160, 428
locus of control, 500–501, 503
long-term memory (LTM), 266, 269–274
durability of, 270–271
organization of information in, 271–274
transfer of information into, 271
long-term potentiation (LTP), 288
longevity, handedness and, 105–106
longitudinal design, 430, 431
longitudinal study
of gifted cohort, 355–356
of temperament, 430–432
loss, 519
loudness, 155–156, 157–158
love, 653–656
as attachment, 654–656
components of, 654
culture and, 656
over time, 654, 655
as reason for marriage, 394
unconditional, 491
LSD, 82, 204, 206
lucid dreaming, 213
lung cancer, 543
lympocytes, 538

M

machines, human interaction with, 708–710
"Magical Number Seven, Plus or Minus Two, The" (Miller), 268
magnetic resonance imaging (MRI) scans, 90, 91, 92
magnitude estimation, 126
magnocellular channel, 136
Magritte, René, 172–173
mainstreaming, 355
maladaptive behavior, 559, 560

maladjustment
creativity and, 375
drug abuse and, 208
Malaysia, 196
males. See gender
malingering, 571
malnutrition, 424, 545
mandalas, 482–483
mania, 576, 577–578
manic-depressive disorders, 577–578
manifest content, 212
mantra, 201
MAO inhibitors, 579, 621
marijuana, 204, 205
controversies concerning, 208
marital satisfaction, 454, 456
marital status, suicide and, 597
marriage, 454–455, 656
See also mating patterns
masochistic personality disorder, 560
massed practice, 294–295
Master of the Arrest of Christ (Francesco), 168
matching hypothesis, 652
maternal nutrition, 424
mathematical ability, 466
mating patterns, evolutionary approach to, 380–381, 394, 656, 657
maturation, 429
language development and, 311
sexual, 449–450
mean, 53, 692
mean length of utterance (MLU), 310
meaning, memory and, 295
means/ends analysis, 318–319
measurement, as goal of scientific enterprise, 37–38
media
aggression and, 446, 447–448
sex-role socialization by, 469
violence in, 250, 447–448
medial forebrain bundle, 96
median, 53, 692
medical advice, nonadherence to, 548–549
medical model, 557–558
medical treatment, seeking, 548
medicine, psychology and, 39
meditation, 59, 201–202, 552
medulla, 92, 93
melatonin, 180, 183
Mellaril, 620
memory
aging and, 463
in children, 442
declarative versus procedural, 290–291
emotions and, 276
encoding stage of, 262–265
hypnosis and, 46–47, 200, 270, 276
implicit versus explicit, 290
improving, 294–297
key processes in, 261, 262
mood-dependent, 276

memory *(continued)*
    neurotransmitters and, 81
    physiology of, 287–289
    prospective versus
        retrospective, 291–292
    reconstructive nature of, 276–
        277
    repressed, 283–285
    semantic versus episodic, 291
    stereotypes and, 644
    storage in, 266–274
    working, 269, 274
    See also forgetting; long-term
        memory; short-term
        memory
memory systems, 290–293
menarche, 449
meninges, 87
Menninger Word Association Test,
    512
menopause, 462
menstrual cycle, 179–180, 393–394
menstruation, 449
Mental Measurement Yearbook, 704
mental abilities, primary, 368
mental ability tests, 340
    See also intelligence tests
mental age, 346
mental health professionals, 605–
    606
mental health services, 626, 634–
    637
    use of, 604, 605
mental hospitals, 561–562, 627–
    629
mental illness. *See* psychological
    disorders
mental processes. *See* cognition;
    problem solving; thinking
mental retardation, 353–355
mental set, 317
mentor, 456
mescaline, 204
mesmerism, 198
mesomorphy, 495
message, persuasive, 660–661
meta-analysis, 58, 66, 465
metacognition, 323
metalinguistic awareness, 310
method of loci, 296, 297
Mexican Americans, 26, 365
Michelle Remembers (Smith &
    Padzer), 575
microelectrodes, 75, 76
midbrain, 92, 93, 94
Middle Ages, 558
middle ear, 156-157, 158
midlife crisis, 453–454
Minnesota Multiphasic Personality
    Inventory (MMPI), 509–510,
    512
minority groups, 25-26, 678–679
    hiring of, 705
    IQ scores of, 361–366
    psychotherapy and, 626
    stereotypes of, 643–644
    See also culture
miscarriage, 423
misinformation effect, 277
MMPI, 509–510, 512

M'naghten rule, 593
mnemonic devices, 294, 295–296
mode, 53, 692
models (modeling), 247–250, 446,
    488, 618
    See also observational learning
molecular genetics, 113
Monet, Claude, 169
monkeys, attachment in, 432
monoamines, 82–83, 205
monocular depth cues, 147–149
monozygotic twins. *See* identical
    twins
Monroe, Marilyn, 484
mood
    pain perception and, 164
    stress and, 524
mood-congruence effect, 276
mood-dependent memory, 276
mood disorders, 575–581
    creativity and, 375
    drug treatment for, 620–622
    etiology of, 578–581, 589
    overview of, 588–589
    prevalence of, 565, 566, 588
    suicide and, 597–598
moon illusion, 154
moral development, 442–445
morality, superego and, 477
morphemes, 306
morphine, 83–84, 166, 203
mortality
    handedness and, 105–106
    infant, 425, 426
    obesity and, 389
    physical fitness and, 553
    smoking and, 543
mothers
    attachment to infants by, 432–
        433
    bonding with infants by, 434
    empty nest of, 456
    prenatal health care of, 425
    relations with adolescent
        children, 456
    See also parents
motion, illusion of, 8, 144
motion parallax, 147
motivated forgetting, 283, 479
motivation
    Adler on, 483–484
    defined, 379
    emotion and, 405
    in observational learning, 248
    sexual, 393–397
    theories of, 379–385
    work, 702, 706–707
motives, 380
    biological, 383, 385–401
    diversity of, 383
    Maslow's hierarchy of, 383–384
    social, 383, 401–405
motor cortex, 97–98
motor development, 428–440
motor neurons, 74
movements, brain control of, 97–
    98
movies, 144
MRI (magnetic resonance imaging)
    scans, 90, 91, 92

Mulika, 307
Müller-Lyer illusion, 152, 154
multiaxial system, 563, 564, 565
multifactorial causation, 24
    of drug effects, 205
    of eating behavior, 392
    of memory abilities, 293
    of physical illness, 549
    of psychological disorders, 114,
        595-596
multiple-choice exams, 33, 280
multiple-personality disorder, 574–
    575
multiple sclerosis, 74
Murphy, Eddie, 278
mutations, 108
myelin sheath, 74, 75, 77

N

napping, 188, 210
narcolepsy, 193
narcotics, 203, 204, 205
narrative methods, mnemonic,
    295–296
National Television Violence
    Study, 446
Native Americans, 25
nativist theories, 311–312
natural selection, 4, 15, 244, 307,
    345, 380, 466, 498, 657
naturalistic observation, 49, 52
nature versus nurture, 6, 27
    coining of term, 345
    in gender differences, 466
    in homosexuality, 400
    in intelligence, 357–366, 371–
        372
    in language development, 310–
        313, 330
    in learning, 251
    See also environment; heredity
Navratilova, Martina, 104
NE. *See* norepinephrine
nearsightedness, 130, 132
Nechita, Alexandra, 356
Necker cube, 146, 172
need for self-actualization, 384,
    492
needs, hierarchy of, 383–384
negative correlation, 54, 342, 343,
    695
negative emotionality, 474
negative reinforcement, 236–238,
    255
    versus punishment, 239
negative self-talk, 551
negative thinking, 580, 611
negatively skewed distribution,
    692
NEO Personality Inventory, 511,
    591
nerves, 86, 87
nervous system
    aging and, 462
    cells in, 74
    communication in, 73–84
    endocrine system and, 107–108
    organization of, 85–88
neural impulse, 75–77
neuromodulators, 80, 84

neurons
    basic structure of, 74–75
    communication between, 77–
        79
    decline with age, 462
    motor, 74
    number of, 85–86
    resting potential in, 75
    sensory, 74
    in visual cortex, 137
neuropeptide Y, 386
neuropeptides, 84
neuroscientists, 88
neuroses, 607
neuroticism, 474, 495, 540, 570,
    573
neurotransmitters, 77–79
    anxiety disorders and, 569
    drug use and, 205–206
    eating behavior and, 386–387
    emotions and, 407
    hormones as, 107
    memory and, 287–288
    in mood disorders, 82, 578–579
    schizophrenia and, 82, 83, 585
    sleep and, 188
    types of, 80–84
neutral stimulus, 218, 220
New Guinea, 162, 196, 313, 409
newborns
    perception in, 427
    sleep patterns in, 186, 187
next-in-line effect, 262
nicotine, 81–82, 211
night terrors, 193
night vision, 132
nightmares, 193
Nim Chimpsky, 302
nodes of Ranvier, 74, 75
noise, in signal detection, 126–127
noncompensatory decision
    models, 327
noncontingent reinforcement, 246
non-REM (NREM) sleep, 185, 186,
    187
nonsense syllables, 279
nonverbal communication, 408,
    410
    gender differences in, 466
nonverbal expressiveness, 642
norepinephrine (NE), 81, 82, 107,
    205, 206, 386
    emotions and, 407
    in mood disorders, 578–579
normal distribution, 347, 350,
    693–694
normality
    criteria of, 559–560, 561–562
    culture and, 560
normalization principle, 355
norms
    developmental, 429–430
    group, 672
    social, 681
note taking, 31–32
Novocaine, 77
Nude Descending a Staircase
    (Duchamp), 170, 171
null hypothesis, 697, 698

nutrition
    health and, 544–545
    maternal, 424
nutritional deficiencies, 545

O

obedience, 642, 668–671
obesity, 389–391
object permanence, 438, 441
objectivity, in experiments, 60
observation, as research method,
    41, 49, 52
observational learning, 247–250,
    252–253
    of aggression, 249–250, 447–
        448, 488
    of attitudes, 663, 681
    basic processes in, 248–249
    of fears, 570
    food preferences and, 388
    of gender roles, 468
    personality development and,
        487–488
obsessions, 568
obsessive-compulsive disorder,
    568, 569, 636
occipital lobe, 97, 136
occupation, 456
    IQ and, 352
    See also career success
occupational stereotypes, 643
octopus, 73
odors, 161, 162–163
Oedipal complex, 481–482
Oklahoma City bombing, 534
olfactory cilia, 162
olfactory system, 160, 162–163
openness to experience, 474
operant chamber, 228–229
operant conditioning, 227–241
    of attitudes, 663, 681
    basic processes in, 230–233
    defined, 227
    of gender roles, 468
    of phobias, 569
    overview of, 252–253
    for self-control programs, 254–
        257
    terminology of, 228–229
operational definition, 40
opiates, 203, 204, 205
opponent process theory, 139–140,
    141
optic chiasm, 135, 136
optic disk, 131–132
optic nerve, 131, 134, 135
optical illusions, 152–155
optimal level of arousal, 525
optimism, 542
oral stage, 481
organizational psychology, 699,
    700, 702, 706–708
orgasm, 400
orgasmic difficulties, 416, 417
orgasmic phase, of sexual response
    cycle, 400–401
ossicles, 157, 158
osteoporosis, 544
outgroups, 644, 668, 681
oval window, 157
overcompensation, 484, 530

overconfidence effect, 334–335
overdose, drug, 205, 206, 207
overeating, 390, 391
overestimating the improbable,
    333
overextension, 309
overlearning, 294
overregularization, 310, 311
ovulatory synchronization, 393–
    394

P

pain
    endorphins and, 83–84
    perception of, 164–166
    Weber fraction for, 125
Palazzo da Mula (Monet), 169
pancreas, 107, 387
panic disorder, 567, 570–571, 636
parallel processing, 136
paranoid schizophrenia, 583
parasympathetic division, 86, 407,
    526
paraventricular nucleus, 386
parent-adolescent relations, 456
parental investment theory, 380,
    394
parenthood, 455–456
parents (parenthood), 455–456
    influence on child's
        intelligence, 360
    punishing of children by, 240–
        241
    relation with adolescent
        children, 451
    role in gender-role
        socialization, 468–469
    as role models, 446
    See also home environment
parietal lobe, 97
Parkinsonism, 82, 94
paroxetine, 622
parrots, 307
participants, in research, 40
parvocellular channel, 136
passionate love, 653–654
Pavlov's experiment, 218, 219
Pavlovian conditioning. See
    classical conditioning
Paxil, 622
PCP (phencyclidine
    hydrochloride), 204
peak experiences, 493
Pearson product-moment
    correlation, 696
penis, 400
penis envy, 481
pennies, 261
percentile score, 341, 351, 694–695
perception, 123–124
    auditory, 155–160
    of color, 137–140, 141
    cultural differences in, 149–151
    depth, 147–152
    distorted, 583
    of forms and patterns, 141–147
    olfactory, 162–163
    subjectivity of, 27, 142, 167
    subliminal, 127–128
    of taste, 160–162
    visual, 129–136

perceptual asymmetries, 102–103,
    118
perceptual constancies, 151–152
perceptual development, 427–428
perceptual hypotheses, 145–147,
    155
performance, acquisition versus,
    248
performance anxiety, 416, 417
performance evaluation, 704–705
periaqueductal gray (PAG), 165
perifornical hypothalamus, 387
peripheral nervous system, 86–87
person-centered theory, 491–492
person perception, 641, 642–645,
    678–679
person-situation controversy, 489
personal distress, 559–560
personal unconscious, 482, 483
personality
    assessment of, 509–513
    basic traits of, 473–475
    behavioral perspective on, 485–
        490, 506–507
    biological perspectives on, 494–
        500, 506–507
    consistency in, 489
    creativity and, 374–375
    culture and, 503–505
    defined, 473
    EEG patterns and, 89
    evolutionary perspective on,
        498–499
    gender differences in, 466
    genetic factors in, 495, 496–498
    humanistic perspectives on,
        490–494, 506–507
    multiple, 574–575
    nature of, 473–474
    physical attractiveness and, 642
    physique and, 495
    as product of conditioning,
        486–487
    psychodynamic perspective on,
        475–485, 506–507
    social learning and, 487–488
    somatoform disorders and, 573
    stability of, 453
    theories of, 506–507
    twin studies of, 496–498
    Type A, 536–537
    Type B, 536
personality development, 434–436,
    453–454, 458–461, 480–482,
    486–487, 507
personality disorders, 560, 564,
    587, 590–592
    classification of, 590
    dimensional approach to, 591
    etiology of, 592
    prevalence of, 591
personality psychology, 20, 21
personality structure, 507
    behavioral view of, 486
    psychodynamic view of, 476–
        477
personality testing, 340, 344, 509–
    513

personality traits, 473–475
    anxiety disorders and, 570
    Big Five, 503, 511, 474–475,
        496, 498–499
    hierarchy of, 495, 496
    natural selection of, 498–499
    stability of, 489
    twin studies of, 112, 113
personnel psychology, 509, 699–
    700, 701, 703–706
persuasion, factors in, 659–662
pessimistic explanatory style, 542
PET (positron emission
    tomography) scans, 90, 91
phallic stage, 481–482
phase-advance shift, 181, 182
phase-delay shift, 181, 182
phenomenological approach, 490
phenotype, 110
phenylketonuria, 354
pheromones, 393–394
phi phenomenon, 8, 144
philosophy, 2
phobias, 217–218, 219–220, 238
    conditioning of, 569–570
    preparedness and, 243–244
    systematic desensitization for,
        616–617
    treatment for, 636
    types of, 567
phobic disorder, 567, 569
phonemes, 305–306, 308
phonemic encoding, 263, 264,
    281, 282–283
phrases, 306
physical appearance, 642–643
physical attractiveness, 396–397,
    642–643, 644, 652
    of message source, 660
    as portrayed in media, 469
physical changes, aging and, 462
physical dependence, on drugs,
    205, 206–207
physical development, 458–461
    in adolescents, 449–450
    in infants, 428–430
physical fitness, 553
physical illness
    benefits of, 574
    biopsychosocial model of, 517,
        549
    life changes and, 521–522
    reactions to, 547–549
    seeking treatment for, 548
    stress and, 535–543
    See also disease
physiological arousal, 82, 87, 201,
    406–407, 411, 412, 526–528
physiological psychology, 20, 21
physiological recordings, 41, 184,
    407–408
physiological responses,
    conditioning and, 221–222
physiology, 2
Picasso, Pablo, 170
pictorial depth cues, 147–149
    in paintings, 168–169
pineal gland, 180
pinna, 156, 158
pitch, 155, 156

pitch perception, theories of, 158–159
pituitary gland, 93, 107, 527
place theory, 158–159
placebo, 59
placebo effects, 59–60, 128, 164
placenta, 422, 424
plagiarism, 278
plateau phase, of sexual response cycle, 400
Plath, Sylvia, 599
pleasure centers, in brain, 95–96
pleasure principle, 476, 477
Poggendorff illusion, 152
Pointillism, 169
polygenic traits, 110, 113–114
polygraph, 407–408
pons, 92, 93, 188
Ponzo illusion, 152, 153, 154
population, 58, 59, 697
pornography, 396–397
positive correlation, 54, 342, 343, 695
positive emotionality, 474
positive illusions, 531
positive reinforcement, 236, 237
positively skewed distribution, 692
positron emission tomography (PET) scans, 90, 91
postconventional level, 444
posthypnotic suggestion, 200
postsynaptic potentials (PSPs), 78–80
posttraumatic stress disorders, 534
potassium ions, 76
practice, expertise and, 324
Pragnanz, 144
preconscious, 477, 478
preconventional level, 444
predictability, 519
prediction
    confidence and, 334–335
    correlation and, 55, 696–697
    as goal of scientific enterprise, 38
preferences, taste, 161, 162
prefrontal cortex, 98
pregnancy, 422, 424–425
prejudice, 363, 658–659, 678–681
premature birth, 425
premature ejaculation, 416, 417
premenstrual dysphoric disorder, 560
prenatal development, 422–426
    environmental influences on, 424–425
prenatal health care, 425, 426
preoperational period, 437, 438–439, 441
preparedness, 243–244, 569–570
pressure (social), 522–523
    choking under, 533
pressure (tactile), 163
    Weber fraction for, 125
Pressure Inventory, 523
prevalence of psychological disorders, 565–566, 588
    cultural variations in, 595
primacy effect, 271
primary appraisal, 519

primary auditory cortex, 97
primary colors, 139
primary motor cortex, 97–98
primary-process thinking, 476
primary reinforcers, 233
primary sex characteristics, 449
primary somatosensory cortex, 97
primary visual cortex, 97, 135–136
Principles of Psychology (James), 4
prism, 130, 138
proactive interference, 282, 283
probabilities, judging, 328–329, 332
probability, 698
    subjective, 328
problem solving, 315–325, 532
    approaches to, 318–322
    barriers to, 315–318
    in childhood, 440
    culture and, 324–325
    defined, 315
    expertise and, 322–324
problem-solving view, of dreaming, 197, 198
problem space, 318
problems
    representation of, 321–322
    types of, 315, 316
    well-defined versus ill-defined, 315
procedural memory system, 290–291
procrastination, 548
productivity, group, 673–674
prognosis, 558
programmed learning, 230
projection, 479, 480
projective hypothesis, 512
projective tests, 402, 512–513
prospective memory, 291–292
protease inhibitors, 545
proximal stimuli, 145–146, 155
proximity, as Gestalt principle, 144, 145, 170
proximity effects, in interpersonal attraction, 651–652, 680
proximodistal trend, 428
Prozac, 622
pseudoforgetting, 281
pseudomemory, hypnotic, 285
pseudopatients, 561–562
psilocybin, 204
psyche, 2
psychiatric hospitals, 628
psychiatric nurses, 606
psychiatrists, 606, 635
psychiatry, 21
PsychINFO, 68, 69
psychoactive drugs, 203–208
    dependence on, 205, 206–207
    effects of, 205
    physical health and, 207–208
    psychological health and, 208
psychoanalysis, 8, 476, 603, 607–609, 633, 636
    modern, 609
    procedures in, 607-609
psychoanalytic theory, 9, 11, 475–482
    of homosexuality, 398
psychodiagnosis, 562–565

psychodynamic approaches
    to personality, 475–485, 506–507
    to therapy, 607–609, 636
psycholinguists, 302
Psychological Abstracts, 66, 67–68
Psychological Screening Inventory, 344
psychological dependence, on drugs, 205, 206–207
psychological disorders, 566–592
    classification of, 562–565
    creativity and, 375
    culture and, 594–595
    in homeless, 630–632
    law and, 592–594
    prevalence of, 565–566, 588
    recovery rates for, 614
    stress and, 534–535
    treatment for, 603–632
psychological tests (testing), 339, 340, 374
    by employers, 704–706
    key concepts in, 340–344
    reliability of, 341–342, 351
    as research method, 41
    standardization of, 340–341
    types of, 340
    validity of, 342–344, 351–352
psychologists, 605–606
    settings for, 20
    types of, 21
psychology
    appeal of, 1
    applied, 12–13
    as college major, 17
    defined, 17
    empirical nature of, 22–23, 114–115
    ethics in, 61–64
    history of, 2–17, 18–19
    origins of term, 2
    overemphasis on Western culture in, 14
    professionalization of, 12–13
    relation to other sciences, 39
    research areas in, 20–21
    schools of thought in, 4–12
    as science, 39
    settings for doing, 20
    specialties in, 21
    women in, 5
psychometrics, 20, 21
psychopharmcotherapy, 619–622
psychophysical scaling, 125
psychophysics, 124–129
psychosexual stages, 480–482
psychosocial crises, 435–436, 451, 454
psychosomatic diseases, 535, 571, 572
psychotherapists. *See* therapists
psychotherapy, 604
    availability of, 634–635
    behavioral approaches to, 615–619
    biomedical approaches to, 619–624
    combining approaches to, 624–625

costs of, 635
culture and, 625–627
effectiveness of, 614, 618–619, 636
elements of, 603–607
ethics in, 635
insight approaches to, 607–615
psychoticism, 495
puberty, 108, 449–450
pubescence, 449
publishing, of scientific findings, 41
Puerto Rican Americans, 26
punctuality, cultural differences in, 26
punishment, 238–341
    guidelines for, 240–241
    of oneself, 257
    personality development and, 486
    physical, 240, 241, 250
    side effects of, 240
pupil, 130–131
purity
    of light, 129
    of sound waves, 155, 156

Q

questionnaires, 41, 50, 51
questions
    framing of, 329–330
    on IQ tests, 349
quitting smoking, 544

R

raccoons, 242
racial stereotypes, 363–365, 678–679
racism, 678
random assignment, 45
rape, 396, 397, 534
ratio schedules, 234–236
rational-emotive therapy, 550–551, 611, 636
rationalization, 479, 480
reaction formation, 479, 480
reaction range, 360–361
reaction time, 369
reading, improving, 30–31
reality monitoring, 278
reality principle, 476–477
reasoning. *See* decision making; problem solving
recall, 265, 280
    See also retention
receiver, of persuasive messages, 661–662
recency effect, 271
receptive field
    tactile, 163
    of a visual cell, 134, 137
receptor sites, in synapses, 78, 79, 81, 82, 83, 84, 206, 579
receptors
    auditory, 157, 158
    gustatory, 160, 161
    olfactory, 162
    tactile, 163–164
    visual, 132, 140
recessive gene, 109, 110
reciprocal determinism, 487

reciprocity effects, 653
recognition measure of retention, 280
recovery rates, for psychological disorders, 614
recreational drug use, 202
    See also psychoactive drugs
reflexes, 219
    conditioned, 287–288
refractory period, 401
regression, 479, 480
regret, in decision making, 330
rehearsal, 268, 269, 271, 294, 442
    behavioral, 618
reinforcement, 230, 233–234
    of attachment behavior, 432
    conditioned, 233–234
    defined, 228
    extinction and, 231
    in language development, 311
    negative 236–238, 239, 255
    noncontingent, 246
    in observational learning, 248
    personality development and, 486
    positive versus negative, 236–237
    schedules of, 234–236
    for self-control programs, 255–256
    timing of, 233
reinforcement contingencies, 229
relationships, close, 651–657
relative size, 148, 149, 169
relaxation
    meditation and, 201, 202
    systematic, 212
relaxation response, 552, 553
relaxation training, 617, 618
relearning measure of retention, 280, 290
reliability, of tests, 341–342, 351
REM sleep, 184–185, 186, 187, 188
    deprivation of, 190
    dreams and, 185, 195
    need for, 191
"Remembering to Do Things" (Harris), 291
Remote Associates Test, 374, 375
repetition, in persuasive messages, 661
replication, of research, 57–58
representative sample, 58, 59
representativeness heuristic, 329, 332, 333
repressed memories controversy, 283–285
repression, 283, 479, 480
research
    in behavior genetics, 110–114
    deception in, 62–63
    ethics in, 671
    evaluating, 57–61
    pitfalls in, 58–61
    use of animals in, 63–64
research areas, in psychology, 20–21
research laboratories, early, 3, 4
research methods, 40, 42, 52
    descriptive/correlational, 48–51
    experimental, 42–48

resistance
    to extinction, 231
    to persuasion, 661
    in psychoanalysis, 608–609, 636–637
resolution phase, of sexual response cycle, 401
respondent conditioning. *See* classical conditioning
response. *See* conditioned response; unconditioned response
response-outcome (R-O) associations, 232, 246
response rate
    reinforcement schedules and, 235–236
    in Skinner box, 229, 230
response set, 60, 512
response stereotypy, 709
response tendencies, 233, 486, 487
responsibility, diffusion of, 673, 674
resting potential, 75
restorative theories, of sleep, 190
retarded ejaculation, 416
retention
    defined, 280
    improving, 294–297
    interference and, 281–282
    level of processing and, 264
    in observational learning, 248
retention interval, 280, 281
reticular formation, 93, 188
retina, 129, 130, 131–135, 140
retinal disparity, 147
retirement, 457
retrieval, memory, 262, 275–278
retrieval cues, 275, 282
retrieval failure, 282–283
retroactive interference, 282, 283
retrograde amnesia, 289
retrospective memory, 291–292
reuptake, 78, 79, 205–206
reversibility, 439
reversible figures, 141–142, 146, 147, 171
review articles, 66
rhymes, 296
rhythms, biological, 179–183
risk taking, in children, 49
risky decision making, 328–330, 332–335
risky shift, 675
RNA transfer, 287
robotics, 709–710
rods, 131, 132–133
role expectations, 455
role models, 446, 468, 488
role playing, hypnosis as, 200
roles, in groups, 672
romantic love, 654, 655
Rorschach test, 512, 513
Rotter Incomplete Sentence Blank, 512
Rubin, Jerry, 453
rumination, 580
runner's high, 84
Rutherford, Tom, 284

S

safety and security needs, 384
salt intake, 544
Salvi, John, 593
sample, 58, 59, 697
sampling, 340
sampling bias, 58, 59
Sarah, 303
saturation, of colors, 129, 130
sauce béarnaise syndrome, 242
savings scores, 280
scatter diagrams, 695–696
Schachter's two-factor theory, 412–413
schedules of reinforcement, 234–236
schemas, 273–274, 276–277, 643
schizophrenic disorders, 582–587
    brain abnormalities and, 92, 585–586
    communication deviance and, 586
    culture and, 595
    drug treatment for, 620–621
    etiology of, 114, 584–587, 589
    expressed emotion and, 586
    family studies of, 110, 111
    genetic vulnerability to, 114
    neurochemical factors in, 82, 83, 585
    onset of, 584
    overview of, 588–589
    positive versus negative symptoms of, 584
    prevalence of, 565, 566, 582, 588
    prognosis for, 584
    stress and, 586
    subtypes of, 583–584
    symptoms of, 582–583
school performance
    of Asian Americans, 366
    IQ scores and, 351, 352
schools
    IQ testing in, 348
    socialization in, 469
scientific approach
    advantages of, 41–42
    goals of, 37–38
    steps in, 39–41
scientific management, 702, 703
scientific method, 6, 22
scripts, 273–274
sea slug, 287
seasonal affective disorder (SAD), 576
secondary appraisal, 519
secondary-process thinking, 477
secondary reinforcers, 233–234
secondary sex characteristics, 108, 449, 450
secondary traits, 474
secure attachment, 433–434, 655–656
sedatives, 192, 203, 204, 205, 206
selective attention, 263
selective breeding, 110
selective serotonin reuptake inhibitors, 622
self, independent versus interdependent view of, 504

self-actualization, 384, 492–493
self-concept, 11, 531
    Rogers on, 491–492
self-control, behavior modification programs for, 254–257
self-deception, 479, 529–531
self-defeating personality disorder, 560
self-destructive behavior, 543–547
self-effacing bias, 651
self-efficacy, 488
self-esteem, 504
    coping and, 550
    decision making and, 330
self-help tapes, 128
self-indulgence, 529
self-monitoring, 502–503
self-perception theory, 665
self-referent encoding, 265
self-report data, 50
    distortions in, 60
self-report inventories, 509–512
self-serving bias, 649, 651
self-socialization, 468
self-stimulation centers, in brain, 95–96
self-talk, 551
semantic encoding, 263, 264, 281, 282–283
semantic memory system, 291
semantic networks, 272–273
semicircular canals, 166
senility, 462
Senoi, 196
sensate focus, 417
sensation, 123–124
    absolute thresholds for, 124–125
    brain centers for, 97
    magnitude of, 125–126
    psychophysics of, 124–129
    See also specific senses
sensation seeking, 501–502
Sensation-Seeking Scale, 501, 502
sensorimotor period, 437, 438
sensory adaptation, 128–129, 163
sensory memory, 266–267, 274
sensory neurons, 74
sensory receptors, for touch, 163
sentences, 306, 309–310
separation anxiety, 432, 434
septum, 94
serial-position effect, 271
Serious Illness Rating Scale (SIRS), 40
serotonin, 81, 82, 386, 622
    anxiety disorders and, 569
    mood disorders and, 578, 579
    LSD and, 206
    pain perception and, 165
    sleep and, 188
sertraline, 622
set point, 390–391
Seurat, Georges, 169
sex, 465
sex cells, 108
sex chromosomes, 467
sex crimes, 396
sex drive, 393
    Freud's conception of, 478–479
sex therapy, 416–417

synapses, 75, 77–80, 205, 579
  actions of neurotransmitters at, 80–84
  memory and, 287–288
synaptic cleft, 77–78
synaptic vesicles, 77–79
synergism, drug, 206, 207
syntax, 306
systematic desensitization, 616–617, 636
systems approach, to industrial/organizational psychology, 700–701

T

Tales from the Front (Kavesh & Lavin), 641
Tan, Amy, 101
tardive dyskinesia, 621
task performance
  arousal and, 525
  stress and, 533–534
taste, 160–162
  absolute threshold for, 125
  in infants, 428
taste aversion, 242, 243
taste buds, 160, 161
taste preferences, 161, 162, 388
taxonomy, of psychological disorders, 562
Taylorism, 702, 703
Teaching for the Two-Sided Mind (Williams), 117
technical eclecticism, 625
technology, in workplace, 708–710
teenagers. *See* adolescence
telegraphic speech, 309–310
television
  aggression and, 249–250, 446, 447–448
  as illusion, 154
  sex-role socialization by, 469
Temiars, 188
temper tantrums, 234
temperament
  genetic basis of, 446
  in infants, 430–432
temperature
  body, 180, 381–382
  perception of, 163–164
temporal lobe, 97, 157
temporal summation, 79–80
terminal buttons, 75, 77–79
test norms, 340–341
test performance, racial stereotypes and, 364–365
test-retest reliability, 342
test-taking strategies, 32–33
testosterone, 393, 467
testwiseness, 32
textbooks, gender stereotypes in, 469
texture gradient, 148, 149
thalamus, 93, 94, 135, 164, 165, 289, 586
THC, 204
Thematic Apperception Test (TAT), 402, 403, 512, 513

theoretical diversity, 23, 167
  in approaches to psychotherapy, 632
  in motivation and emotion, 414
  in personality, 505
theoretical integration, 625
theory, defined, 23, 38
theory construction, 38
therapist(s)
  in behavior therapies, 616–618
  in client-centered therapy, 609–611
  in cognitive therapy, 611–612
  false memory syndrome and, 285
  finding, 634
  in group therapy, 613
  in psychoanalysis, 607–609
  types of, 605–606, 635
therapy. *See* psychotherapy
thermal receptors, 163
theta waves, 184, 201
thinking (thought), 301
  abstract, 440
  of children, 437
  creative, 373–374
  culture and, 313–314
  divergent versus convergent, 374
  irrational, 551
  language and, 313–314
  negative, 580, 611
  schizophrenic, 582–583
  See also cognitive development; decision making; problem solving
Thorazine, 620
thought
Thought and Choice in Chess (de Groot), 322
threshold, 124
thyroid gland, 107
timbre, 155, 156
time management, 29, 31
timing, in classical conditioning, 222, 223
tip-of-the-tongue phenomenon, 261, 275
toilet training, 436, 481
token economy, 256
tolerance, drug, 205, 222
tongue, 160, 161
top-down processing, 143
Toraja, 197
touch, 163–166
  absolute threshold for, 125
  brain and, 97
tower of Hanoi problem, 319
trance, hypnotic, 200
tranquilizers, 620
transcendental meditation (TM), 201
transfer-appropriate processing, 282, 295
transference, 609
transformational rules, 311–312
transvestism, 559
trial, experimental, 219
trial and error, 318
trichromatic theory, 139, 141

tricyclics, 579, 621
trust versus mistrust, 436
trustworthiness, 660
Tukoer-Ter-Ur (Vasarely), 172, 173
Turner, Ted, 576
twin studies, 111–112, 113
  of altruism/aggression, 446
  of anxiety disorders, 569
  of intelligence, 357–358
  of mood disorders, 578, 579
  of personality, 494–495, 496, 497–498
  of schizophrenia, 585
twins, weight similarity in, 390
two-factor theory, of emotion, 412–413
two-process theory, of avoidance behavior, 238
Type A personality, 536–537
Type B personality, 536

U

ultraviolet spectrum, 129
unconditional positive regard, 610
unconditioned response (UCR), 219, 220, 222, 224
unconditioned stimulus (UCS), 218–219, 220, 221, 222, 223, 224, 226, 245–246
unconscious, 178, 477–478, 479, 530
  collective, 482, 483
  creativity and, 373
  Freud on, 8–9
  personal, 482, 483
  probing of, 607–608
understanding, as goal of scientific enterprise, 38
undifferentiated schizophrenia, 584
undoing, 530
uninhibited temperament, 431
unipolar disorders, 576
University of Leipzig, 3
University of Minnesota Center for Twin and Adoption Research, 494–495, 496, 497–498
Unleashing the Right Side of the Brain (Williams & Stockmyer), 117
U.S. Patent Index, 403

V

vacillation, 520–521
validity
  of DSM categories, 563
  of tests, 342–344, 351–352, 705
Valium, 83, 620
values, sexual, 415
van Gogh, Vincent, 149
variability, in a set of data, 53–54, 693
variable-interval (VI) schedules, 235, 236
variable-ratio (VR) schedules, 235, 236
variables
  confounding of, 45
  correlations between, 54–56

in experiments, 43, 45, 46, 47
  extraneous, 44–45, 59
  multiple, 45–46, 47
Vasarely, Victor, 172, 173
vasocongestion, 400
ventricles, of brain, 87, 92, 585
ventromedial nucleus of the hypothalamus (VHS), 386
Verbal Behavior (Skinner), 310
verbal skills, gender differences in, 58, 466
verifiability, 6
vestibular system, 166
Veterans Administration, 13
viability, age of, 424
victim, blaming, 648
Vietnam veterans, 534
violence
  media, 250, 447–448
  mental illness and, 561
  on television, 446
  against women, 397
Violin and Grapes (Picasso), 170
vision
  absolute threshold for, 125
  aging and, 462
  basic processes in, 129–131
  color, 137–140, 141
  constancies in, 151–152
  in split-brain patients, 101–102
  Weber fraction for, 125
visual acuity, 132
  in infants, 427
visual agnosia, 123
visual cliff, 427
visual cortex, 97
  information processing in, 136–137
visual fields, 101, 102, 136
visual imagery, 264–265, 296–297
visual pathways, in brain, 135–136
visual-spatial tasks, 466
  hemispheric specialization in, 103
visual system, 129–155
vocabulary, development of, 309
vocalizations, of infants, 308, 310–311
vocational life cycle, 456–457
vocational success. *See* career success
volley principle, 159
vulnerability
  genetic, 114
  to mood disorders, 581
  to schizophrenia, 585
  stress and, 586, 596

W

Washoe, 303
water jar problem, 316, 317, 320
Waterfall (Escher), 171, 172
wavelength
  of light waves, 129, 130, 137–138, 140
  of sound waves, 155, 156
Weber fraction, 125
Weber's law, 125
Wechsler Adult Intelligence Scale (WAIS), 347, 349

well-defined problems, 315
Wernicke's area, 99
Western Electric, 702
white blood cells, 538
windigo, 595
wine tasting, 160, 162
wish fulfillment, dreams as, 197, 198
wishful thinking, defense mechanisms as, 530
witches, 558

withdrawal illness, 206
women
    career development of, 457, 462
    empty nest and, 456
    in history of psychology, 5
    pornography and, 396–397
    role of, 15
    violence against, 397
words, 306
    children's learning of, 308–310

work, 456–457
work motivation, 702, 706–707
work shifts, 181–182
workaholics, 536
workers, psychology of, 699–710
working backward, 319–320
working memory, 269, 274
    aging and, 463
    problem solving and, 322–323
World War I, 12–13, 701
World War II, 13, 23, 703

X
X rays, of brain, 90, 91
Xanax, 620

Y
yawning, 211

Z
Zollner illusion, 152
Zoloft, 622
Zulus, 154
zygote, 108, 422

CREDITS

This page constitutes an extension of the copyright page. We have made every effort to trace the ownership of all copyrighted material and to secure permission from copyright holders. In the event of any questions arising as to the use of any material, we will be pleased to make the necessary corrections in future printings. Thanks are due to the following authors, publishers, and agents for permission to use the material indicated.

Photo Credits

Contents

xxi: (middle) Courtesy of the Clark University Archives; (bottom) David M. Goody/Tom Stack & Associates; **xxii:** From "Use of Hypnosis to Enhance Eye-Witness Accuracy: Does It Work?" G. S. Sanders & W. L. Simmons, State University of New York at Albany, 1983, courtesy of Glenn S. Sanders; **xxvi:** © Goldberg/Monkmeyer Press Photo; **xxvii:** AP/Wide World Photos; **xxviii:** (top) Author's collection; (middle) Craig McClain; **xxix:** © Jon Alcorn/Zuma; **xxx:** © Lizzie Himmel; **xxxiv:** © Joe McNally/Matrix; **xxxv:** © Michael Newman/Photo Edit; **xxxvi:** Photo copyright 1965 by Stanley Milgram. From the film *Obedience,* distributed by The Pennsylvania State University. Reprinted by permission of Alexandra Milgram.

Visual Guide

xliv: (top screen, left) © Enrico Ferorelli; (top screen right) Corbis-Bettmann; (bottom screen) Courtesy of Clark University; **xlv:** From *Mind Sights,* by Roger N. Shepard. Copyright © 1990 by Roger N. Shepard. Reprinted with permisson of W. H. Freeman andCompany; **xlvi:** (top screen) Marcus Raichle, MD, Washington University School of Medicine, St. Louis, Missouri.

Chapter 1

l: (top) David M. Goody/Tom Stack & Associates; (bottom) Courtesy of the Clark University Archives; **2:** (left) Jodi Cobb/National Geographic Image Collection; (right) Joel Sartore/National Geographic Image Collection; **4:** Archives of the History of American Psychology, University of Akron, Akron, Ohio; **5:** Archives of the History of American Psychology, University of Akron, Akron, Ohio; **8:** David M. Goody/Tom Stack & Associates; **10:** Courtesy of the Clark University Archives; **11:** Copyright 1971 Time Inc. Reprinted by permission; **13** (top) Archives of the History of American Psychology University of Akron, Akron, Ohio; (bottom) Corbis-Bettmann; **18:** (telephone) Culver Pictures, Inc.; (Wundt lab) Archives of the History of American Psychology, University of Akron, Akron, Ohio; (Clark Conference) Compliments of Clark University, Worcester, Massachusetts; (Queen Victoria) Stock Montage, Inc.; (Wright brothers) Stock Montage, Inc.; (early auto) Culver Pictures, Inc.; (lightbulb) Culver Pictures, Inc.; (Pavlov lab) Corbis-Bettmann; (WWI intelligence test) Corbis-Bettmann; (Washburn) Courtesy of the Archives of the History of

American Psychology, University of Akron, Akron, Ohio; (Hollingworth) Courtesy of the Archives of the History of American Psychology, University of Akron, Akron, Ohio; (suffragetts) Culver Pictures, Inc.; **19:** (Pearl Harbor) Culver Pictures, Inc.; (shuttle launch) NASA; (group therapy) © Karen Pruess from *Life Time: A New Image of Aging,* published by Unity Press, Santa Cruz, California, 1978; (brain) Luminair Multimedia; (atomic bomb) Culver Pictures, Inc.; (Vietnam) AP/Wide World Photos; (Maccoby) Stanford University News Service; (Clark Conference) UPI/Corbis-Bettmann; (Erikson) AP/Wide World Photos; (1950s TV) Culver Pictures, Inc.; **25:** (top left) Myrleen Ferguson/PhotoEdit; (top right) Bob Daemmrich/The Image Works; (bottom left) © Mark Burnett/Stock, Boston; (bottom right) Elizabeth Crews/The Image Works; **26:** (left) © Robert Brenner/PhotoEdit; (right) Bob Daemmrich/Stock, Boston; **27:** Preferred Stock and Gazelle Technologies.

Chapter 2

36, 46: From "Use of Hypnosis to Enhance Eye-Witness Accuracy: Does It Work?" G. S. Sanders & W. L. Simmons, State University of New York at Albany, 1983, courtesy of Glenn S. Sanders; **49:** Courtesy of Harvey Ginsburg, Ph.D., Southwest Texas State University; **58:** Philippe Plailly/Photo Researchers, Inc.; **59:** © Alan Oddie/Photo Edit; **60:** Courtesy of Robert Rosenthal; **62:** © Charles Gupton/Stock, Boston; **63:** (top) Yale University; (bottom) Paul Conklin/Uniphoto; **67:** Craig McClain.

Chapter 3

74: Science Source/Photo Researchers, Inc.; **82:** © Dan McCoy/Rainbow; **83:** © 1991 Analisa Kraft; **89:** Anderson PhotoImages; EEG read-out from "Current Concepts: The Sleep Disorders," by P. Hauri, 1982, The Upjohn Company, Kalamazoo, Michigan. Reprinted by permission. **91:** (top left) © Alvis Upitis/The Image Bank; (top right) © Dan McCoy/Rainbow; (bottom left) Marcus Raichle, MD, Washington University School of Medicine, St. Louis, Missouri; (bottom right) © Dan McCoy/Rainbow; **93:** © Manfred Kage/Peter Arnold, Inc.; **96:** Anderson PhotoImages; **100:** (left) Charles Bennett-AP/Wide World Photos; (right) © F. Capri/Saga/Archive Photos; **101:** Courtesy of Roger Sperry; **103:** Courtesy of Doreen Kimura; **104:** Corbis-UPI/Bettmann Newsphotos; **106:** (top) Courtesy of the University of British Columbia; (bottom) Courtesy of California State University, San Bernardino; **111:** (left) Courtesy of Donruss, Inc.; (right) Reproduced with the permission of and copyright 1991 by The Upper Deck Co.; **114:** The Pennsylvania State University Center for Development and Health Genetics.

Chapter 4

123: Carl Vanderschuit/Photo Bank, Inc.; **124:** Archives of the History of American Psychology, University of Akron, Akron, Ohio; **127:** Wilson Bryan Key/Mediaprobe, Inc.; **132:** Craig McClain; **137:** Ira Wyman/Sygma; **138:** Cour-

tesy BASF; **144:** Courtesy of Anne Treisman; **145:** Archives of the History of American Psychology, University of Akron, Akron, Ohio; **148:** (top left) © Peter Turner/The Image Bank; (top right, middle left, bottom left) Catherine Murphy; (middle right) © 1988 Bill Pogue; (bottom right) U.S. Department of Energy; **149:** van Gogh, Vincent, *Hospital Corridor* at Saint Remy (1889), gouche and watercolor, 124 1/8 × 18 5/8 inches (61.3 × 47.3 cm), collection, The Museum of Modern Art, New York, Abby Aldrich Rockefeller Bequest. Photograph © 1996 The Museum of Modern Art; **152:** Craig McClain ; **153:** Luminair Multimedia; **154:** (left) © Linda Bartlett/Science Source/Photo Researchers, Inc.; (right) © N. R. Rowan/The Image Works; **157:** © Lawrence Hughes/The Image Bank; **159:** Stock Montage, Inc.; **161:** Courtesy of the Yale School of Medicine; **162:** (left) © Malcolm S. Kirk; (middle) Guy Mary-Rousseliere/Catholic Mission, Northwest, Canada; (right) © Danielle Pelligrini/Science Source/Photo Researchers, Inc.; **168:** (top) *Maestro della Cattura di Cristo, Cattura di Cristo, parte centrale,* Assisi, S. Francisco, Scala/Art Resource, New York; (bottom) *Brera Predica di S. Marco Pinaocteca,* by Gentile and Giovanni Belini in Egitto Scala/Art Resource, New York; **169:** (top) Monet, Claude, *Palazzo da Mula,* Venice, 1908. Photo by Richard Carafelli, Chester Dale Collection, © Board of Trustees, National Gallery of Art; (bottom) Georges Seurat, French, 1859–1891, *Sunday Afternoon on the Island of La Grande Jatte,* oil on canvas, 1884–1886, 207.6 × 308 cm, Helen Birch Bartlett Memorial Collection, 1926.224, © 1990 The Art Institute of Chicago, all rights reserved; **170:** (top) Pablo Picasso, *Violin and Grapes (Céret and Sorgues)* (spring–early fall 1912), oil on canvas, 20 × 24 inches (50.6 × 61 cm), collection, The Museum of Modern Art, New York, Mrs. David M. Levy Bequest, Copyright ARS, N.Y./SPADEM, 1912; (bottom) Duchamp, Marcel, 1912; *Nude Descending a Staircase, No. 2,* oil on canvas, 58" × 35". Philadelphia Museum of Art: Louise and Walter Arensburg Collection, # '50-134-69. Reproduced by permission; **171:** (top) Dali, Salvador, *The Slave Market with Disappearing Bust of Voltaire* (1940), oil on canvas, 18 1/4 × 25 3/8 inches. Collection of The Salvador Dali Museum, St. Petersburg, Florida. Copyright © 1997 The Salvador Dali Museum, Inc. © DeMart Pro Arte/ARS N.Y., 1940; (bottom) Courtesy of Haags Gemeentemuseum, © 1988 M. C. Escher, Cordon Art, Baarn; **172:** Courtesy of Haags Gemeentemuseum, © 1988 M. C. Escher, Cordon Art, Baarn; **173:** (top) Vasarely, Victor, *Tukoer-Ter-Ur,* 1989 Private Collection, Monaco. Erich Lessing/Art Resource, N.Y. Copyright © Artist Rights Society, N.Y.; (bottom) Magritte, René, *Les Promenades d'Euclide,* The Minneapolis Institute of Arts, The William Hood Dunwoody Fund. Copyright C. Herscovic/ARS N.Y., 1955.

Chapter 5

177: Gene Sladek; **184:** © Richard Nowitz; **189:** (top) Courtesy of William Dement; (bottom) © Robert E. Daemmrich/Tony Stone Images; **190:**

Courtesy of Alexander Borbely; **192:** Division of News and Public Affairs, University of Florida; **196:** © Penny Tweedle/Woodfin Camp & Associates; **197:** (top) National Library of Medicine; (bottom) Rush Presbyterian St. Luke's Medical Center; **200:** Biomedical Research Foundation; **201:** Courtesy of Ernest R. Hilgard; **203:** © Dennis MacDonald/Photo Edit; **211:** © Topham/The Image Works.

Chapter 6

216: © Goldberg/Monkmeyer Press Photo; **218:** (top) Corbis-Bettmann; (bottom) Sovfoto/Eastfoto; **221:** (top) Craig McClain; (bottom) © Pictor/Uniphoto; **224:** Archives of the History of American Psychology, University of Akron, Akron, Ohio; **228:** Courtesy of B. F. Skinner; **229:** Richard Wood/The Picture Cube; **231:** (top left) Courtesy of Animal Behavior Enterprises, Inc.; (top right) © Gerald Davis/Colorific!; (bottom) © Elena Rooraid/Photo Edit; **232:** Hank Morgan/Rainbow; **235:** (top left) © Jeff Greenberg/Photo Edit; (top right) © Alain Keler/Sygma; (bottom left): © David Woods/The Stock Market; (bottom right) © Rick Doyle/Uniphoto; **240:** © Spencer Grant/Monkmeyer Press Photo; **242:** Courtesy of John Garcia; **244:** (top) © Runk/Schoenberger/Grant Heilman, Inc.; (bottom) Tom McCarthy/SKA; **246:** University of Pennsylvania; **248:** (top) Courtesy of Albert Bandura; (bottom) J. Markham/Bruce Coleman, Inc.; **250:** Chip Henderson/Tony Stone Images; **253:** (top left) Corbis-Bettmann; (top right) Archives of the History of American Psychology, University of Akron, Akron, Ohio; (middle left) © Elena Rooraid/Photo Edit; (middle right) © Alain Keler/Sygma; (bottom left) © J. Markham/Bruce Coleman, Inc.; (bottom right) © Chip Henderson/Tony Stone Images; **257:** © Goldberg/Monkmeyer Press Photo.

Chapter 7

260: AP/Wide World Photos; **267:** Marshall Cavendish Picture Library; **268:** Courtesy of George Miller; **270:** AP/Wide World Photos; **273:** Courtesy of W. F. Brewer, from Brewer, W. F., & Treyens, J. C. (1981). "Role of schemata in memory of places," *Cognitive Psychology, 13,* 207–230. **276:** (top) Courtesy of Gordon Bower; (bottom) University of Washington News and Information Office; **278:** (top) Denise Applewhite/Communications Department, Princeton University; (bottom left) Corbis-UPI/Bettmann Newsphotos; (bottom right) Corbis-UPI/Bettmann Newsphotos; **279:** Welcome Institute for the History of Medicine, London; **284:** Andy Lavalley-AP/Wide World Photos; **289:** Montreal Neurological Institute; **290:** Courtesy of Endel Tulving.

Chapter 8

300: (top) Author's collection; (middle) Craig McClain; **301:** Carnegie-Mellon University; **304:** Language Research Center, Georgia State University; **307:** Michael Goldman, *Time* Magazine, © Time, Inc.; **309:** Author's collection; **311:** Donna Coveney/MIT News Office; **313:** © B & C Alexander/Photo Researchers, Inc.; **323–324:** Craig McClain; **325:** Australian Tourist Council/PhotoEdit; **328:** Stanford University News and Publication Service; **329:** Courtesy of Daniel Kahneman; **334:** © Shannon Stapleton/Sygma.

Chapter 9

338: © Jon Alcorn/Zuma; **339:** © Daemmrich/The Image Works; **345:** Welcome Institute for the History of Medicine, London; **346:** (top) Corbis-Bettmann; (bottom) Archives of the History of American Psychology, University of Akron, Akron, Ohio; **347:** Archives of the History of American Psychology, University of Akron, Akron, Ohio; **348:** © Jason Laure/The Image Works; **356:** © Jon Alcorn/Zuma; **358:** National Library of Medicine; **360:** Courtesy of Sandra Scarr; **361:** Courtesy of Arthur R. Jensen; **362:** Cover of *The Bell Curve: Intelligence and Class Structure in American Life,* by R. J. Herrnstein and C. Murray, 1994, The Free Press, New York; **364:** Department of Psychology, Stanford University; **370:** Michael Marsland/Yale University.

Chapter 10

378: © Lizzie Himmel; **379:** (top) Corbis-UPI/Bettmann Newsphotos; (bottom) Guy Gurney/*Sports Illustrated*; **381:** Courtesy of David M. Buss; **384:** Courtesy of Abraham Maslow; **386:** Courtesy of Neal Miller, Yale University; **388:** (left) © Mimi Forsyth/Monkmeyer Press Photo; (right) © Michele Burgess/Stock, Boston; **390:** Courtesy of Judith Rodin; **398:** © Lizzie Himmel; **401:** Corbis-UPI/Bettmann Newsphotos; **403:** Courtesy of David C. McClelland; **404:** © Scott Cunningham/NBA/Allsport; **408:** © Michael Abramson/Woodfin Camp & Associates; **409:** From *Unmasking the Face,* © 1975 by Paul Ekman, photographs courtesy of Paul Ekman; **412:** (top) Courtesy of Donald D. Dutton, Department of Psychology, University of British Columbia; (bottom) © Bill Apple, courtesy of Stanley Schachter.

Chapter 11

421: The Kobal Collection; **423:** (top left) © Petit Format/Science Source/Photo Researchers, Inc.; (bottom left) © Petit Format/Guigoz SS/Photo Researchers, Inc.; (right) © Petit Format/Nestle/Science Source/Photo Researchers, Inc.; **425:** Author's collection; **427:** © Enrico Ferorelli; **430:** Korner/AnthroPhoto; **432:** (top) Courtesy of University of Wisconsin Primate Laboratory; (bottom) © Martin Rogers/Stock, Boston; **433:** Erik Hesse; **435:** AP/Wide World Photos; **437, 438:** © Yves de Braine/Black Star; **444:** Courtesy of Harvard University News Office; **447:** © Dan Habib/Impact Visuals; **458:** © Dorothy Littlell Greco/Stock, Boston; **459:** (left) © Myrleen Cate/Tony Stone Images; (right) © Bob Daemmrich/The Image Works; **460:** (left) © David Young-Wolff/Photo Edit; (right) © Lori Adamski Peek/Tony Stone Images; **461:** (left) © B. Bachman/The Image Works; (right) © Don Smetzer/Tony Stone Worldwide.

Chapter 12

476: (top) National Library of Medicine; (bottom) AP/Wide World Photos; **481:** © Pascal Quittemelle/Stock, Boston; **482:** Culver Pictures, Inc.; **483:** (top) From *C. G. Jung Bild Und Wort,* © Walter-Verlag AG, Olten, Switzerland, 1977; (bottom) Culver Pictures, Inc.; **484:** Corbis-Bettmann; **486:** Courtesy of B. F. Skinner; **487:** © Bruce Ayres/Tony Stone Images; **488:** Courtesy of Professor Albert Bandura; **489:** University photographer Joe Pineiro, Columbia University; **490:** Courtesy of Center for Studies of the Person; **492:** Courtesy of Abraham Maslow;

494: © Michael Nichols/Magnum Photos; **495:** Mark Gerson, FPIPP, London, courtesy of Hans Eysenck; **499:** Courtesy of David M. Buss; **504:** (top left) Photo and Campus Services, University of Michigan; (middle left) Courtesy of Shinobu Kitayama; (right) © Lawrence Migdale/Tony Stone Images; **505:** Salvador Dali, *Soft Construction with Boiled Beans: Premonition of Civil War.* Photo by Graydon Wood, 1995, Philadelphia Museum of Art: The Louise and Walter Arensberg Collection. © DeMart Pro Arte/ARS N.Y., 1936; **506:** (top to bottom) AP/Wide World Photos; © Richard Wood/The Picture Cube; © Richard T. Nowitz/Photo Researchers, Inc.; © Tony Freemann/Photo Edit; **507:** (top to bottom) © Pascal Quittemelle/Stock, Boston; © Bruce Ayres/Tony Stone Images; © Lawrence Migdale/Tony Stone Images; **513:** (top) © Mimi Forsyth/Monkmeyer Press Photo; (bottom) Reprinted by permission of the publishers from Henry A. Murray, Thematic Apperception, Cambridge, Mass., Harvard University Press, Copyright © 1943 by The President and Fellows of Harvard College, © 1971 by Henry A. Murray.

Chapter 13

519: Courtesy of Richard Lazarus; **526:** © Yousuf Karsh/Woodfin Camp & Associates; **529:** (top) Courtesy of Martin E. P. Seligman; (bottom) © Mark Richards/Photo Edit; **531:** Courtesy of Shelley Taylor; **534:** © J. Pat Carter/Gamma Liaison Network; **541:** Photo by Conte, courtesy of Suzanne Ouellette (formerly Kobasa); **548:** Steve Walag, University of California, Riverside.

Chapter 14

556: © Joe McNally/Matrix; **558:** (top) Culver Pictures, Inc.; (middle) Di Benvenuto, *St. Catherine Exorcising Possessed Woman.* Denver Art Museum Collection; (bottom) Courtesy of Thomas Szasz; **559:** © Bill Bachman/Photo Researchers, Inc.; **561:** Stanford University News Service; **562:** Tom McCarthy; **568:** (top) Corbis-Bettmann; (bottom) AP/Wide World Photos; **576:** (left) AP/Wide World Photos; (right) © Rick Maiman/Sygma; **584:** Courtesy of Nancy Andreasen; **587:** © Joe McNally/Matrix; **588:** (left, top to bottom) Munch, Edvard, *The Scream.* National Gallery, Oslo, Norway/Art Resource/New York; Vincent van Gogh, *Vincent: Portrait of Dr. Gachet.* Musee d'Orsay, Paris. Erich Lessing/Art Resource, NY; Derek Bayes, *Life* Magazine, © Time, Inc.; (right, top to bottom) Corbis-Bettmann; AP/Wide World Photos; © Trippett/Sipa Press; **593:** © Sygma; **599:** (left) © Jay Blakesberg/Sgyma; (top right) UPI/Corbis-Bettmann; (bottom right) The White House/Gamma-Liaison Network.

Chapter 15

602: © Michael Newman/Photo Edit; **603:** © Ann Chwatsky; **607:** National Library of Medicine; **610:** Courtesy of Center for Studies of the Person; **611:** Courtesy of Aaron Beck; **613:** © Richard Nowitz/Photo Researchers, Inc.; **616:** Courtesy of Joseph Wolpe; **623:** © Joe McNally/Matrix; **626:** © Michael Newman/Photo Edit; **627:** (top) Detail of painting in Harrisburg State Hospital, photo by Ken Smith/LLR Collection; (bottom) Culver Pictures, Inc.; **631:** © A. Ramey/Stock, Boston; **634:** Tom McCarthy.

Chapter 16

640: Photo copyright 1965 by Stanley Milgram. From the film *Obedience*, distributed by The Pennsylvania State University. Reprinted by permission of Alexandra Milgram.; **643:** © Michael Newman/Photo Edit; **646:** University of Kansas; **650:** © Dave Black; **652:** © Bob Torrez/Tony Stone Images; **653:** Courtesy of Ellen Berscheid; **654:** Courtesy of Elaine Hatfield; **663:** (top photos, left to right) © Roger Sandler/Gamma-Liaison Network; © Brad Markel/Gamma Liaison Network; © Jonathan Exley/Gamma-Liaison Network; (bottom): Photo by Karen Zabulon, © 1982, courtesy of New School for Social Research, by permission of Trudy Festinger; **666:** (left) Corbis-UPI/Bettmann; (right) © *Orange County Register*/Saba Press Photos; **668:** Courtesy of Solomon Asch; **669:** Photos copyright 1965 by Stanley Milgram. From the film *Obedience*, distributed by The Pennsylvania State University. Reprinted by permission of Alexandra Milgram; **670:** Photo by Eric Kroll, courtesy of Alexandra Milgram; **672:** © Michael Newman/Photo Edit; **679:** © Amy C. Etra/Photo Edit; **680:** Joel Sartore/National Geographic Image Collection.

Appendix C

700: © Daemmrich/The Image Works; **701:** Culver Pictures, Inc.; **702:** © Mike Surowiak/Tony Stone Images; **703:** © Grant Haller/Leo de Wys; **710:** Courtesy of General Public Utility.

Figure Credits

Chapter 1

Figure 1.4: Adapted from data from the American Psychological Association by permission.

Figure 1.9: From *Increasing Multicultural Understanding: A Comprehensive Model*, by Don C. Locke, 1992, pp. 15–16, 18, 22, 25–26, 51, 53–54, 56, 68–69, 72, 74, 89–93, 139–140, 153–143. Copyright © 1992 by Sage Publications, Inc. Reprinted by permission of Sage Publications, Inc..

Figure 1.10: Description from "The Warm-Cold Variable in Frist Impressions of Persons," by H. H. Kelley, 1950. *Journal of Personality, 8,* 431–439. Copyright © 1950 by the Ecological Society of America. Reprinted by permission.

Figure 1.12: From questionnaire "Managing Time Means Managing Yourself," by LeBoeuf, 1980, p. 45. *Business Horizons Magazine,* February, 1980. Copyright by the Foundation for the School of Business at Indiana University. Used by permission.

Figure 1.13: Adapted from "The Psychology of College Success: A Dynamic Approach" by H.C. Lindgren, 1969. John Wiley & Sons. Copyright © 1969 by Henry Clay Lindgren. Adapted by permission of H.C. Lindgren.

Figure 1.14 and 1.15: Adapted from "Staying with Initial Answers on Objective Tests: Is It a Myth?" by L. T. Benjamin, Jr., T. A. Cavell, & W. R. Shallenberger III, 1984, *Teaching of Psychology, 11* (3), 133–141. Copyright © 1984 Lawrence Erlbaum Associates, Inc. Adapted by permission of the author.

Chapter 2

Figure 2.9: From *The Psychotic Patient: Medication and Psychotherapy*, by David Greenfeld, M.D. The Free Press, 1985. Copyright © 1985 by David Greenfeld. Reprinted by permission of the author.

Table 2.2: Adapted from "Personality and Attitudinal Characteristics of Sexually Coercive College Males," by D. Rapaport and B. R. Burkhart, 1984. *Journal of Abnomal Psychology, 93* (2), 216–221. Copyright © 1984 by the American Psychological Association. Adapted by permission of the author.

Figure 2.18: Adapted from *Library Use: A Handbook for Psychology* (2nd ed.), by J. G. Reed & P. M. Baxter, p. 50, 1992. Copyright © 1992 by the American Psychological Association. Adapted by permission of the author.

Figure 2.19: This material is reprinted with permission of the American Psychological Association, publisher of Psychological Abstracts and the PsycINFO Database (Copyright © 1967–1997 by the American Psychological Association), and may not be reproduced without its prior permission.

Figure 2.20: From Volume 82, 1995. This material is reprinted with permission of the American Psychological Association, publisher of Psychological Abstracts and the PsycINFO Database (Copyright © 1967–1997 by the American Psychological Association), and may not be reproduced without its prior permission.

Chapter 3

Figure 3.26: From *The Lefthander Syndrome: The Causes and Consequences of Left Handedness*, by Stanley Coren, p. 50. The Free Press, a division of Macmillan. Copyright © 1992 by Stanley Coren. Reprinted by permission of Stanley Coren.

Figure 3.27: From "Left-Handedness: A Marker for Decreased Survival Fitness," by S. Coren and D. F. Halpern, 1991. *Psychological Bulletin, 109,* 90–106. Copyright © 1991 by the American Psychological Association. Reprinted by permission of the author.

Figure 3.33: Based on *Schizophrenia Genesis: The Origins of Madness*, by I. I. Gottesman, 1991. Copyright © 1991 W. H. Freeman Company.

Figure 3.34: Adapted from *Introduction to Psychology* (4th ed.), by James W. Kalat, 1996, p. 78. Brooks/Cole Publishing Company.

Figure 3.35: Based on data from "Behavioral Genetics of Cognitive Ability: A Life-Span Perspective," by M. McGue, T. J. Bouchard, W. G. Iacono, & D. T. Lykken, 1993. In R. Plomin & G. E. McClearn (Eds.), *Nature, Nurture and Psychology*. Copyright © 1993 by the American Psychological Association.

Figure 3.36: Cartoon courtesy of Roy Doty.

Figure 3.37: Reprinted by permission of Jeremy P. Tarcher, Inc., a division of The Putnam Publishing Group from *Drawing on the Right Side of the Brain*, by Betty Edwards. Copyright © 1989 Betty Edwards.

Figure 3.38 and 3.39: Data from "The Asymmetry of the Human Brain," by D. Kimura, 1973, *Scientific American, 228,* 70–78.

Chapter 4

Table 4.1: From "Contemporary Psychophysics," by E. Galanter, 1962, in *New Directions in Psychology*, R. Brown (Ed.). Holt, Rinehart & Winston. © 1962 Eugene Galanter. Reprinted by permission.

Table 4.2: Table from *Fundamentals of Psychology*, by F. A. Geldard, 1962. Copyright © 1962 by John Wiley & Sons, Inc. Reprinted by permission of John Wiley & Sons, Inc.

Figure 4.6: Based on Figure 4.6 in *Introduction to Psychology*, by James Kalat. Copyright © 1986 Wadsworth, Inc.

Figure 4.22: Based on data from "Human Color Vision and Color Blindness," by G. Wald and P. K. Brown, 1965, *Symposium Cold Spring Harbor Laboratory of Quantitaitve Biology, 30,* 345–359 (p. 351). Copyright © 1965. Reprinted by permission of the author.

Figure 4.37: Adapted by permission from an illustration by Ilil Arbel on page 83 of "Pictorial Perception and Culture," by Jan B. Deregowski in *Scientific American, 227* (5) November 1972. Copyright © 1972 by Scientific American, Inc. All rights reserved.

Figure 4.38: From "Perceiving Geographical Slant," by D. R. Proffitt, M. Bhalla, R. Gossweiler, & J. Midgett, 1995. *Psychonomic Bulletin & Review, 214,* 409–428. Copyright © 1995 by Psychonomic Society Publications. Reprinted by permission.

Figure 4.39: From "Perceiving Geographical Slant," by D. R. Proffitt, M. Bhalla, R. Gossweiler, & J. Midgett, 1995. *Psychonomic Bulletin & Review, 214,* 409–428. Copyright © 1995 by Psychonomic Society Publications. Reprinted by permission.

Figure 4.44: From *Mind Sights,* by Roger N. Shepard. Copyright © 1990 by Roger N. Shepard. Reprinted with permission of W. H. Freeman and Company.

Figure 4.47: Redrawn from *Mind Rights,* by R. Shepard, 1990, p. 144. Copyright © 1990 by W. H. Freeman. Redrawn by permission of the publisher.

Figure 4.49: Table 5-3, adapted from *Introduction to Psychology* (9th ed.), by Rita L. Atkinson, Richard C. Atkinson, Edward F. Smith, & Ernest R. Hilgard, copyright © 1987 by Harcourt Brace & Company. Reprinted by permission of the publisher.

Figure 4.53: Adapted from "Genetic and Pathological Taste Variation: What Can We Learn from Animal Models and Human Disease?" by L. M. Bartoshuk, 1993. In D. Chadwick, J. Marsh, & J. Goode (Eds.), *The Molecular Basis of Smell and Taste Transaction*, pp. 251–267. Copyright © 1993 by John Wiley & Sons, Inc. Reprinted by permission of John Wiley & Sons, Inc.

Chapter 5

Figure 5.2: Adapted from *Wide Awake at 3:00 AM by Choice or by Chance*, by Richard M. Coleman. Copyright © 1986 by Richard M. Coleman. Reprinted with permission of W. H. Freeman and Company. All rights reserved.

Figure 5.5: Adapted from "Rotating Shift Work Schedules That Disrupt Sleep Are Improved by Applying Circadian Principles," by C. A. Czeisler, M. C. Moore-Ede, & R. M. Coleman, 1982. *Science, 217,* 460–463. Copyright © 1982 by the American Association for the Advancement of Science. Adapted by permission of the author.

Figure 5.6: Figure from "Current Concepts: The Sleep Disorders," by P. Hauri, 1982, The Upjohn

Company, Kalamazoo, Michigan. Reprinted by permission.

Figure 5.8: Figure adapted from an updated revision of a figure in "Ontogenetic Development of Human Sleep Dream Cycle," by H. P. Roffwarg, J. N. Muzio, & W. C. Dement, 1966. *Science, 152,* 604–609. Copyright © 1966 by the American Association for the Advancement of Science. Adapted and revised by permission of the author.

Figure 5.10: Figure from *Secrets of Sleep,* by Alexander Borbely, English Translation. Copyright © 1986 by Basic Books, Inc. © 1984 Deutsche Verlags-Anstalt GmbH, Stuttgart. Reprinted by permission of Basic Books, Inc., a division of HarperCollins Publishers.

Figure 5.11: From Pinel, John, *Bio Psychology,* p. 380. Copyright © 1997 by Allyn and Bacon. Reprinted by permission.

Table 5.2: Figure from "The University of Typical Dreams: Japanese vs. Americans," by R. M. Griffith, O. Miyago, & A. Tago, 1958. *American Anthropologist, 60,* 1173–1179. Copyright ©1958 by the American Anthropological Association. Reproduced by permission of the American Anthropological Association from *American Anthropologist 60:6,* pt. 1, December 1958. Not for further reproduction.

Table 5.3: Adapted from "The Personal Use of Dream Beliefs in the Toraja Highlands," by D. Hollan, 1989. *Ethos, 17,* 166–186. Copyright © 1989 by the American Anthropological Association. Reproduced by permission of the American Anthropological Association from *Ethos 17:2,* June 1989. Not for further reproduction.

Figure 5.15: From Figure 4-6, adapted from *Hypnotic Susceptibility,* by Ernest R. Hilgard, 1965. Harcourt Brace Jovanovich. Copyright © 1965 by Ernest R. Hilgard. Reprinted by permission of Ernest R. Hilgard.

Figure 5.16: (Redrawn from illustration on p. 86 by Lorelle A. Raboni of *Scientific American, 226,* 85–90, Feb. 1972). From "The Physiology of Meditation," by R. K. Wallace and H. Benson. Copyright © 1972 by Scientific American, Inc.

Figure 5.20: Adapted from *Sleep, the Gentle Tyrant* (2nd ed.), by Wilse B. Webb, 1992. Copyright © 1992 by Anker Publishing Co., Bolton, MA. Adapted by permission.

Figure 5.21: Adapted from "Ten Commandments for Better Sleep" in *How to Sleep Like a Baby, Wake Up Refreshed and Get More Out of Life,* by Dianne Hales. Copyright © 1987 by Ballantine Books. Reprinted by permission.

Figure 5.23: Based on data from *Evaluation and Treatment of Insomnia,* by A. Kales and J. D. Kales, p. 95, 1984. Copyright © 1984 by Oxford University Press. Reprinted by permission.

Chapter 6

Figure 6.1: Adapted from "The Method of Pavlov in Animal Psychology," by R. M. Yerkes & S. Morgulis, 1909. *Psychological Bulletin, 6,* 257–273. American Psychological Association.

Figure 6.28: Based on data from "Imitation of Film-Mediated Aggressive Models," by A. Bandura, D. Ross, & S. A. Ross, 1963. *Journal of Abnormal and Social Psychology, 66,* 3–11. Copyright © 1963 by the American Psychological Association.

Figure 6.31: Adapted from *Self-Directed Behavior: Self-Modification for Personal Adjustment,* by D. L. Watson & R. G. Tharp, 1989. Copyright © 1989 by Wadsworth, Inc. Adapted by permission of Brooks/Cole Publishing Company.

Chapter 7

Figure 7.1: From "Long-Term Memory for a Common Object," by R. S. Nickerson & M. J. Adams, 1979. *Cognitive Psychology, 11,* 287–307. Copyright © 1979 by Academic Press, Inc. Reprinted by permission.

Figure 7.11: From "Short-Term Retention of Individual Verbal Items," by L. R. Peterson & M. J. Peterson, 1959. *Journal of Experimental Psychology, 58,* 193–198. Copyright © 1959 by the American Psychological Association. Reprinted by permission.

Figure 7.12: Adapted from "Analysis of Rehearsal Processes in Free Recall," by D. Rundus, 1971. *Journal of Experimental Psychology, 89,* 63–77. Copyright © 1971 by the American Psychological Association. Adapted by permission of the author.

Figure 7.13: Adapted from "The Occurrence of Clustering in the Recall of Randomly Arranged Associates," by W. A. Bousfield, 1953. *Journal of General Psychology, 49,* 229–240. Reprinted with permission of the Helen Dwight Reid Education Foundation. Published by Heldref Publications, 1319 Eighteenth St. N.W., Washington, D.C. 20036-1802. Copyright © 1953.

Figure 7.14: Adapted from "Organizational Factors in Memory," by G. Bower, 1970. *Cognitive Psychology, 1*(1), 18–46. Copyright © 1970 by Academic Press, Inc. Reprinted by permission.

Figure 7.15: Adapted from "A Spreading Activation Theory of Semantic Processing," by A. M. Collins & E. F. Loftus, 1975. *Psychological Review, 82,* 407–428. Copyright © 1975 by the American Psychological Association. Adapted by permission.

Figure 7.16: From "Considerations of Some Problems of Comprehension," by J. D. Bransford & M. K. Johnson. In W. B. Chase (Ed.), *Visual Information Processing,* p. 400. Copyright © 1973 by Academic Press, Inc. Reprinted by permission.

Figure 7.18: Excerpt from *Remembering: A Study in Experimental and Social Psychology,* by F. C. Bartlett, p. 65, 1932, Cambridge University Press. Copyright © 1932. Reprinted with the permission of Cambridge University Press.

Figure 7.19: Adapted from "Reconstruction of Automobile Destruction: An Example of Interaction Between Language and Memory," by E. Loftus and J. C. Palmer, 1974. *Journal of Verbal Learning and Verbal Behavior, 13,* 585–589. Copyright © 1974 Academic Press, Inc. Adapted by permission.

Figure 7.25: From "Lies of the Mind," by Leon Jaroff, 1993, *Time* Magazine, November 29, 1993, p. 52. Copyright © 1993 Time Inc. Reprinted by permission.

Figure 7.29: Data from "Quantitative and Qualitative Effects of Repetition on Learning from Technical Text," by B. K. Bromage and R. E. Mayer, 1986. *Journal of Educational Psychology, 78*(4), 271–278. Copyright © 1986 by the American Psychological Association. Adapted by permission.

Figure 7.30: Adapted from "A Breakdown of the Total-Time Law in Free-Recall Learning," by B. J. Underwood, 1970. *Journal of Verbal Learning and Verbal Behavior, 9,* 573–580. Copyright © 1970 by Academic Press, Inc. Adapted by permission.

Figure 7.31: Adapted from "Narrative Stories as Mediators of Serial Learning," by G. H. Bower & M. C. Clark, 1969. *Psychonomic Science, 14,* 181–182. Copyright © 1969 by the Psychonomic Society. Adapted by permisson of the Psychonomic Society.

Figure 7.32: From "Analysis of a Mnemonic Device," by G. H. Bower, 1970, American Scientist, 58, Sept–Oct., 496–499. Copyright © 1970 by Scientific Research Society. Reprinted by permission.

Figure 7.33: Adapted from "Scientific Mnemonomies: Methods for Maximizing More than Memory," by M. E. Levin & J. R. Levin, 1990. *American Educational Research Journal, 27*(2), 301–321. Copyright © 1990 by American Educational Research Association. Adapted by permission.

Chapter 8

Figure 8.2: Figure from *Child Development: A Topical Approach,* by A. Clarke-Stewart, S. Friedman, & J. Koch, p. 417, 1985. Copyright © 1985 by John Wiley & Sons, Inc. Reprinted by permission of John Wiley & Sons, Inc.

Table 8.1: From *An Introduction to Cognitive Psychology,* by D. R. Moates & G. M. Schumacher. Copyright © 1980 by Wadsworth, Inc. Reprinted by permission.

Figure 8.3: Adapted from "Early Lexical Acquisition: Rate, Content, and the Vocabulary Spurt," by B. A. Goldfield & J. S. Resnick, 1990. *Journal of Child Language, 17,* 171–183. Copyright © 1990 by Cambridge University Press. Adapted by permission.

Figure 8.4: Adapted and reprinted by permission of the publisher from *First Language: The Early Stages,* by R. Brown, p. 55. Cambridge, Mass.: Harvard University Press, Copyright © 1973 by the President and Fellows of Harvard College.

Figure 8.9: Based on "Mechanization in Problem Solving," by A. S. Luchins, 1942, *Psychological Monographs, 54* (Whole No. 248).

Figure 8.10: Adapted from *Conceptional Blockbusting: A Guide to Better Ideas,* by James L. Adams, pp. 17–18. Copyright © 1980 by James L. Adams. Reprinted by permison of W. H. Freeman & Co., Publishers.

Figure 8.11: From *Basic Psychology* (3rd ed.), by Howard H. Kendler, 1974, pp. 403, 404. Copyright © 1974 The Benjamin-Cummings Publishing Co. Adapted by permission of Howard H. Kendler.

Figure 8.13: Based on "Mechanization in Problem Solving," by A. S. Luchins, 1942, *Psychological Monographs, 54* (Whole No. 248).

Figure 8.14: Adapted from *Conceptional Blockbusting: A Guide to Better Ideas,* by James L. Adams, pp. 17–18. Copyright © 1980 by James L. Adams. Reprinted by permison of W. H. Freeman & Co., Publishers.

Figure 8.15: From *Basic Psychology* (3rd ed.), by Howard H. Kendler, pp. 403–404, 1974. Copyright © 1974 The Benjamin-Cummings Publishing Co. Adapted by permission of Howard H. Kendler.

Figure 8.18: From "Field-Dependent and Field-Independent Cognitive Styles and Their Educational Implications," by H. A. Witkin, C. A. Moore, D. Goodenough, & P. W. Cox, 1977. *Review of Educational Research,* Winter 1977, pp. 1–164. Copyright © 1977 by the American Educational Research Association, Washington, D.C. Reprinted by permission of the publisher.

Figure 8.19: Figure from "Task Complexity and Contigent Processing in Decision Making: An Information Search and Protocol Analysis," by J. W. Payne, 1976. *Organizational Behavior and Human Performance, 16,* 366–387. Copyright © 1976 by Academic Press, Inc. Reprinted by permission.

Figure 8.20: Adapted from *Introduction to Psychology* (2nd ed.), by James W. Kalat, p. 343. Copyright © 1990 by Wadsworth, Inc. Adapted by permission.

Chapter 9

Figure 9.1: Sample items from *Differential Aptitude Tests* (5th ed.). Copyright © 1990 by The Psychological Corporation. Reproduced by permission. All rights reserved.

Figure 9.8: Adapted from "People's Conceptions of Intelligence," by R. J. Sternberg, B. E. Conway, J. L. Keton, & M. Bernstein, 1981. *Journal of Personality and Social Psychology, 41*(1), p. 45. Copyright © 1981 by the American Psychological Association. Adapted by permission of the author.

Figure 9.9: From "Consistency and Variability in the Growth of Intelligence from Birth to Eighteen Years," by N. Bayley, 1949. *Journal of Genetic Psychology, 75,* 165–196. Reprinted by permission of the Helen Dwight Reid Educational Foundation. Published by Heldref Publications, 1319 Eighteenth Street, N.W., Washington, D.C. Copyright © 1949.

Table 9.2: Adapted from *Psychology: The Personal Science,* by John C. Ruch, 1984, p. 457. Copyright © 1984 by Wadsworth, Inc. Reprinted by permission. [Additional data from Szymanskit & Crocker, 1989.]

Figure 9.10: Adapted from "The Three-Ring Conception of Giftedness: A Developmental Model for Creative Productivity," by J. S. Renzulli. In R.J. Sternberg & J. E. Davidson (Eds.), *Conceptions of Giftedness,* pp. 53–92. Copyright © 1986 Cambridge University Press. Adapted by permission.

Figure 9.11: Adapted from "Familial Studies of Intelligence: A Review," by T. J. Bouchard & M. McGue, 1981. *Science, 212,* 1055–1059. Copyright © 1981 by the American Association for the Advancement of Science. Adapted by permission. Additional data from McGue, et al., 1993.

Figure 9.15: Data from "Stereotype Threat and the Intellectual Test Performance of African Americans," by C. M. Steele & J. Aronson, 1995, *Journal of Personality and Social Psychology, 69,* 797-811. Copyright © 1995 by the American Psychological Association.

Figure 9.16: Based on data in "Asian-American Educational Achievements: A Phenomenon in Search of an Explanation," by S. Sue & S. Okazaki, 1990. *American Psychologist, 42,* 37–45.

Copyright © 1990 by the American Psychological Association.

Figure 9.19: Reprinted with permission of The Riverside Publishing Co. from *Stanford-Binet Intelligence Scale Guide for Administering and Scoring* (4th ed.), by R. L. Thorndike, E. P. Hagen, & J. M. Sattler. The Riverside Publishing Co., 8420 W. Bryn Mawr Avenue, Chicago, IL 60631. Copyright © 1986.

Figure 9.20: Adapted from *Beyond IQ: A Triarchic Theory of Human Intelligence,* by Robert J. Sternberg, 1985. Copyright © 1985 Cambridge University Press. Adapted by permision.

Table 9.3: Adapted from "Multiple Intelligences Go to School: Educational Implications of the Theory of Multiple Intelligences," by H. Gardner & T. Hatch, 1989. *Educational Researcher, 18*(8), 4–10. Copyright © 1989 by the American Educational Research Association. Adapted by permission of the publisher.

Figure 9.21 and 9.22: From *Examiner's Manual, Remote Associates Test,* by Sarnoff and Martha Mednick, 1967. Houghton Mifflin Co., Copyright © 1967. Reprinted by permission of Sarnoff Mednick.

Chapter 10

Figure 10.6: Adapted from *The Human Central Nervous System: A Synopsis and Atlas,* by R. Nieuwenhuys, 1988, Springer-Verlag.

Figure 10.7: Adapted from "Obsesity: Adverse Effects on Health and Longevity," by T. B. VanItallie, 1979. *American Journal of Clinical Nutrition, 32,* 2727. Copyright © 1979 American Journal of Clinical Nutrition, American Society for Clinical Nutrition. Adapted by permission.

Figure 10.8: Data from "The Body-Mass Index of Twins Who Have Been Reared Apart," by A. J. Stunkard, J. R. Harris, N. L. Pederson, & G. E. McClearn, 1990. *New England Journal of Medicine, 322,* 1483–1487.

Figure 10.10 and 10.11: Data from "Sex Differences in Human Mate Preferences: Evolutionary Hypotheses Tested in 37 Cultures," by D. M. Buss, 1989. *Behavioral and Brain Sciences, 12,* 1–49.

Figure 10.15: *Based on Human Sexual Response,* by W. H. Masters & V. E. Johnson, 1966. Copyright (1966) Little, Brown and Company.

Figure 10.16: Descriptions reprinted by permission of Dr. David McClelland.

Figure 10.17: Based on data from "Values Expressed in American Children's Readers: 1800–1900," by R. de Charms & G. H. Moeller, 1962. *Journal of Abnormal and Social Psychology, 64,* 136–142. Copyright © 1962 by the American Psychological Association. Reprinted by permission.

Figure 10.23: From *Unmasking the Face,* © 1975 by Paul Ekman, photographs courtesy of Paul Ekman.

Figure 10.26: Based on art in "A Language for Emotions," by R. Plutchik, 1980. *Psychology Today, 13*(9), 68–78. Reprinted with permission from *Psychology Today* Magazine. Copyright © 1980 (Sussex Publishers, Inc.).

Figures 10.27, 10.28: Abstracted from information appearing in "Frequency of Sexual Dysfunction in 'Normal' Couples," by E. Frank, C. Anderson, & D. Rubenstein, 1978. *The New England Journal of Medicine, 299,* 111–115. Copy-

right © 1978 by The New England Journal of Medicine. Adapted by permission.

Table 10.1: Based on *Homosexuality in Perspectives,* by W. H. Masters and V. E. Johnson, 1979. Copyright © 1979 by Little, Brown and Company.

Chapter 11

Figure 11.2: Figure adapted from Moore, K. L.: *The Developing Human: Clinically Oriented Embryology* (4th ed.). Philadelphia, W.B. Saunders Co., 1988. Reprinted by permission.

Figure 11.4: From a chart by Steve Hart in *Time* Magazine, October 8, 1990, p. 45. Copyright © 1990 by Time Inc. Reproduced by permission.

Figure 11.5: From *Growth and Development: The First Twenty Years in Man,* by R. M. Malina, 1975, p. 19., Burgess Publishing Company. Copyright © 1975 by Burgess International Group, Edina, MN. Reprinted by permission.

Figure 11.8: Adapted from "Attachment," by P. R. Shaver & C. Hazan. In A. Weber & J. H. Harvey (Eds.), *Perspectives on Close Relationships.* Copyright © 1994 by Allyn and Bacon. Reprinted by permission.

Figure 11.14: Parts a–c from "Developmental Functions for Speeds of Cognitive Processes," by R. Kail, 1988. *Journal of Experimental Child Psychology, 45,* 361. Copyright © 1988 by Academic Press. Reprinted by permission .

Figure 11.14: Part d from "Processing Time Declines Exponentially During Childhood and Adolescence," by R. Kail, 1991. *Developmental Psychology, 27,* 265. Copyright © 1991 by the American Psychological Association. Reprinted by permission of the author.

Figure 11.16: Adapted from "The Development of Children's Orientations Toward a Moral Order: I: Sequence in the Development of Moral Thought," by L. Kohlberg, 1963. *Vita Humana, 6,* 11–33. Copyright © 1963 by S. Karger AG, Basel. Reprinted by permission.

Figure 11.17: From Liebert, Robert M., & Sprafkin, Joyce, *The Early Window: Effects of Television on Children and Youth* (3rd ed.), p. 5. Copyright © 1988 by Allyn and Bacon. Reprinted by permission.

Figure 11.21: Adapted from "Identity in Adolescence," by J. E. Marcia, 1980. In J. Adelson (Ed.), *Handbook of Adolescent Psychology,* pp. 159–210. Copyright © 1980 by John Wiley & Sons, Inc. Adapted by permission of John Wiley & Sons, Inc.

Figure 11.22: Adapted from "A Residue of Tradition: Jobs, Careers and Spouses' Time in Housework," by Donna H. Berardo, Constance L. Shehan, & Gerald R. Leslie, 1987. *Journal of Marriage and Family, 49* (May 1987), 381–90. Copyright © 1987 by the National Council on Family Relations, 3989 Central Ave., N.E., Suite 550, Minneapolis, MN 55421. Reprinted by permission.

Figure 11.23: Based on "Marital Satisfaction Over the Family Cycle," by Boyd C. Rollins & Harold Feldman, 1970. *Journal of Marriage and Family, 32* (February 1970), p. 25. Copyright © 1975 by the National Council on Family Relations, 3989 Central Ave., N.E., Suite 550, Minneapolis, MN 55421. Reprinted by permission.

Table 11.2: Adapted from *Theories of Occupational Choice and Vocational Development,* by J.

Zaccharia, pp. 51–52. Copyright © 1970 by Time Share Corporation, New Hampshire.

Figure 11.25: From "Intellectual Development in Adulthood," by K. W. Schaie, 1990. In J. E. Birren and K. W. Schaie (Eds.), *Handbook of the Psychology of Aging* (3rd ed.), pp. 291–309. Reprinted by permission of Academic Press, Inc.

Table 11.3: Adapted from "Sex Stereotypes: Issues of Change in the 70s," by T. L. Ruble, 1983. *Sex Roles, 9,* 397–402. Copyright © 1983 Plenum Publishing Company. Adapted by permission.

Chapter 12

Figure 12.10: Adapted from *Personality: Theory, Research and Application,* by C. R. Potkay & B. P. Allen, p. 246. Brooks/Cole Publishing Company. Copyright © 1986 by C. R. Potkay and Bem Allen. Adapted by permission of the author.

Figure 12.12: From H. J. Eysenck, *The Biological Basis of Personality,* p. 36, 1976. Courtesy of Charles C Thomas, Publisher, Springfield, Illinois. Reprinted by permission.

Figure 12.14: Adapted from "Personality Similarity in Twins Reared Apart and Together," by A. Tellegen, D. T. Lykken, T. J. Bouchard, Jr., K. J. Wilcox, N. L. Segal, & S. Rich, 1988. *Journal of Personality and Social Psychology, 54*(6), 1031–1039. Copyright © 1988 by the American Psychological Association. Adapted by permission of the author.

Figure 12.15: Reprinted by permission from page 101 of *Adjustment and Competence: Concepts and Applications,* by A. F. Grasha & D. S. Kirschenbaum. Copyright © 1986 by West Publishing Company. All rights reserved.

Figure 12.17: Adapted from "Culture and the Self: Implications for Cognition, Emotion, and Motivation," by H. R. Markus & S. Kitayama, 1991. *Psychological Review, 98,* 224–253. Copyright © 1991 by the American Psychological Association. Adapted by permission.

Table 12.3: Adapted and reprinted with permission from L. S. Keller, J. N. Butcher, & W. S. Slutske, "Objective Personality Assessment," 1990. In G. Goldstein and M. Hersen (Eds.), *Handbook of Psychological Assessment,* pp. 345–386. Copyright © 1990 Pergamon Press, Ltd.

Figure 12.20: From R. B. Cattrell in *Psychology Today* (July) 1973, 40–46. Reprinted by permission from *Psychology Today Magazine.* Copyright © 1973 (Sussex Publishers, Inc.).

Chapter 13

Table 13.1: Reprinted with permission from *Journal of Psychosomatic Research, 11,* 213–218, by T.H. Holmes and R. Rahe in "The Social Readjustment Rating Scale," 1967, Elsevier Science Publishing Co., Inc.

Figure 13.7: Adapted from *The Stress of Life,* by Hans Selye, p. 121, 1956. Copyright © 1956 by McGraw-Hill Publishing Company. Adapted by permission.

Table 13.2: Adapted from *Abnormal Psychology and Modern Life* (8th Ed.), by R. C. Carson, J. N. Butcher, & J. C. Coleman, pp. 64–65, 1988. Copyright © 1988 by Scott, Foresman and Company. Adapted by permission of the publisher.

Figure 13.9: Based on "Paradoxical Effects of Supportive Audiences on Performance Under Pressure: The Home Field Disadvantages in Sports Championships," by R. F. Baumeister & A. Steinhilber, 1984. *Journal of Personality and Social Psychology, 47*(1), 85-95. Copyright © 1984 by the American Psychological Association. Reprinted by permission. Added data from "Championship Pressures: Choking or Triumphing in One's Own Territory?" by B. R. Schlenker, et al., *Journal of Personality and Social Psychology, 68,* 632–643.

Figure 13.12: From "Negative Life Events, Perceived Stress, Negative Affect, and Susceptibility to the Common Cold," by S. Cohen, D. A. J. Tyrrell, & A. P. Smith, 1993. *Journal of Personality and Social Psychology, 64,* 131–140. Copyright © 1993 by the American Psychological Association. Reprinted by permission of the author.

Figure 13.15: Adapted from "Associative Learning, Habit and Health Behavior," by W. A. Hunt, J. D. Matarazzo, S. M. Weiss, & W. D. Gentry, 1979. *Journal of Behavioral Medicine, 2*(2), 113. Copyright © 1979 by the Plenum Publishing Company. Adapted by permission. Additional data from Hunt & Matarazzo, 1982.

Figure 13.16: Data from "A Global Report: AIDS in the World," by J. Mann, D. J. M. Tarantola, & T. W. Netter, 1992. Oxford University Press.

Figure 13.17: Adapted from *Understanding AIDS: A Guide for Mental Health Professionals,* by S. C. Kalichman, 1995. American Psychological Association. Reprinted by permission of the author.

Table 13.4: From "Assessing Coping Strategies: A Theoretically Based Approach," by C. S. Carver, M. F. Scheier, & J. K. Weintraub, 1989. *Journal of Personality and Social Psychology, 56*(2), 267–283. Copyright © 1989 by the American Psychological Association. Reprinted by permission of the author.

Figure 13.20: Data from "Elevated Physical Health Risk Among Gay Men Who Conceal Their Homosexual Identity," by S. W. Cole, M. E. Taylor, B. R. Visscher, 1996, *Health Psychology, 15,* 243–251.

Figure 13.21: Text adapted from *The Relaxation Response,* pp. 14–15, by Herbert Benson & Miriam Z. Klipper. Copyright © 1975 by William Morrow & Company, Inc. By permission of William Morrow & Co., Inc.

Figure 13.22: Based on data from "Physical Fitness and All-Cause Mortality," by S. N. Blair, W. H. Kohl, R. S. Paffenbarger, D. G. Clark, K. H. Cooper, & L. W. Gibbons, 1989. *Journal of American Medical Association, 262,* 2395–2401. Copyright © 1989 American Medical Association. Reprinted by permission.

Chapter 14

Figure 14.3: Adapted with permission from the *Diagnostic and Statistical Manual of Mental Disorders,* third edition, revised (1987) and from *DSM-IV Draft Criteria,* 1994. Copyright © 1987 and 1994 American Psychiatric Association.

Figure 14.4: Adapted with permission from the *Diagnostic and Statistical Manual of Mental Disorders,* 4th edition, revised. Copyright © 1994 American Psychiatric Association.

Figure 14.6: Based on data from L. N. Robins & D. A. Regier (Eds.), in *Psychiatric Disorders in America: The Epidemiologic Catchment Area Study,* 1991. Copyright © 1991 The Free Press, a division of Macmillan.

Figure 14.7: Adapted from "Panic and Phobia," by W. W. Eaton, A. Dryman, & M. M. Weissman. Adapted and reprinted with the permission of The Free Press, an imprint of Simon & Schuster, from *Psychiatric Disorders in America: The Epidemiologic Catchmen Area Study,* edited by Lee N. Robins & Darrel A. Regier. Copyright © 1991 by Lee N. Robins and Darrel A. Regier.

Figure 14.10: From "Bias in Interpretation of Ambiguous Sentences Related to Threat in Anxiety," by M. W. Eysenck, K. Mogg, J. May, A. Richards, & A. Mathews, 1991. *Journal of Abnormal Psychology, 100,* 144–150. Copyright © 1991 by the American Psychological Association. Reprinted by permission of the author.

Figure 14.11: Adapted from "Recent Life Events and Panic Disorders," by C. Faravelli & S. Pallanti, 1989. *American Journal of Psychiatry, 146,* 622–626. Copyright © 1989 by the American Psychiatric Association. Adapted by permission.

Table 14.2: Sarason/Sarason, *Abnormal Psychology: The Problem of Maladaptive Behavior* (5th ed.), © 1987, p. 283. Reprinted by permission of Prentice-Hall, Inc., Englewood Cliffs, NJ.

Figure 14.14: From *Manic-Depressive Illness,* by Frederick K. Goodwin & Kay R. Jamison, p. 132. Copyright © 1990 by Oxford University Press., Inc. Reprinted by permission.

Figure 14.15: Based on data from "Mood Disorders: Genetic Aspects," by E. S. Gershon, W. H. Berrettini, & L. R. Goldin. In H. I. Kaplan & B. J. Sadock (Eds.), *Comprehensive Textbook of Psychiatry.* Copyright © 1989 by Williams & Wilkins.

Figure 14.20: Adapted from "Clues to the Genetics and Neurobiology of Schizophrenia," by S. E. Nicol & I. I. Gottesman, 1983. *American Scientist, 71,* 398–404. Copyright © 1983 by Sigma Xi. Additional data from *Schizophrenia Genesis: The Origins of Madness,* by I. I. Gottesman, 1991. Copyright © 1991 by W. H. Freeman.

Figure 14.22: Data adapted from "The Role of Maintenance Therapy and Relatives' Expression Emotion in Relapse of Schizophrenia: A Two-Year Follow-Up," by J. Leff & C. Vaughn, 1981. *British Journal of Psychiatry, 138,* 102–104.

Figure 14.23: Adapted from "Use of the NEO-PI Personality Dimensions in Differential Treatment Planning," by C. Sanderson & J. F. Clarkin, 1994. In *Personality Disorders and the Five-Model of Personality,* by P. T. Costa and T. Widiger, 1994, p. 233. Copyright © 1994 by the American Psychological Association. Adapted by permission of the author.

Figure 14.24: Adapted from "Epidemiology of Suicide in the U.S.," by J. L. McIntosh, 1991. In A. A. Leenaars (Ed.), *Life Span Perspectives of Suicide,* p. 64. Copyright © 1991 by Plenum Publishing. Adapted by permission.

Figure 14.26: Adapted from "Suicide, Attempted Suicide and Relapse Rates in Depression," by D. Avery & G. Winokur, June 1978. *Archives of General Psychiatry, 35,* 749–753. Copyright © 1978 by the American Medical Association. Adapted by permission.

Chapter 15

Figure 15.1: Data from "Outpatient Mental Health Care in Nonhospital Settings: Distribution of Patients Across Provider Groups," by M.

TO THE OWNER OF THIS BOOK:

I hope that I've been able to make this book likable. I'd like to learn your reactions to using this textbook. Only through your comments and the comments of others can I hope to improve the next edition of *Psychology: Themes and Variations, 4th edition*:

School: _____

Your instructor's name: _____

1. What did you like most about *Psychology: Themes and Variations*?_____

_____

2. What did you like least about the book? _____

_____

3. Were all the chapters assigned for you to read?   Yes _____   No _____

   If not, which ones were omitted? _____

4. Did you use the Concept Checks?   Yes _____   No _____

   Were they helpful?   Yes _____   No _____

_____

5. How interesting and informative were the Application sections? _____

_____

6. How helpful were the themes in fostering an understanding of basic insights about psychology?_____

_____

7. Was the Psyk.trek CD-ROM assigned to you, or did you purchase it separately? What did you find most/least helpful about using this CD?

_____

_____

_____

8. In the space below (or in a separate letter) please let me know what other comments about the book you'd like to make. (For example, did you like the Integrated Running Glossary? The Practice Tests?). I'd be delighted to hear from you!

_____

_____

_____

_____

_____

Optional:

Your name: _____ Date: _____

May Brooks/Cole quote you, either in promotion for *Psychology: Themes and Variations, 4th edition,* or in future publishing ventures?

Yes: _____ No: _____

Sincerely,

Wayne Weiten

- -

FOLD HERE

| | | | |

BUSINESS REPLY MAIL

FIRST CLASS PERMIT NO. 358 PACIFIC GROVE, CA

POSTAGE WILL BE PAID BY ADDRESSEE

ATT: *Wayne Weiten* _____

Brooks/Cole Publishing Company
511 Forest Lodge Road
Pacific Grove, California 93950-9968

- -

FOLD HERE